	1376 Death of Black Prince. Chaucer on mission to Ca...
Monk's tragedies Anelida	1377 *February 17, April 30:* Chaucer on missions in Fr... treaty and marriage of Richard. *June 22:* deat... accession of his grandson, Richard II, age 10. Government controlled by Gaunt.
House of Fame Boece Boethian balades Palamon and Arcite	1378 *January 16–March 9:* Chaucer in France concerning marriage of Richard to French king's daughter Marie. *April 18:* daily pitcher of wine replaced by annuity of 20 marks. *May 28–September 19:* Chaucer in Lombardy to treat with Barnabo Visconti (Gower given Chaucer's power of attorney). 1380 *May 1:* Chaucer released from suit for "raptus" of Cecily Champain. (?) Birth of Lewis Chaucer. 1381 Peasants' Revolt. *June 19:* deed of Geoffrey Chaucer, son of John Chaucer, vintner of London, quitclaiming his father's house.
Troylus and Criseyde Legend of Good Women	1382 Richard II marries Anne of Bohemia. 1383 Chaucer obtains first loan against his annuity. 1385 *October 12:* Chaucer appointed justice of the peace in Kent. Political struggle between Gaunt and his brother, Thomas of Woodstock. *September:* death of Joan of Kent. 1386 Justice of peace reaffirmed. *February 19:* Philippa admitted to fraternity of Lincoln Cathedral. *August:* Chaucer elected member of Parliament from Kent. *October 5:* Aldgate house rented to Richard Forester. *October 15:* Scrope-Grosvenor trial. *December 4:* Adam Yardley appointed controller of customs.
Canterbury Prologue early Tales (Knight, Part VII)	1387 *June 18:* last payment of annuity of Philippa Chaucer.
Fabliaux (Miller, Reeve)	1388 *May 1:* Chaucer surrenders his royal annuities to John Scalby of Lincolnshire. 1389 King Richard assumes power. Chaucer appointed clerk of the King's works (more than £30 a year).
Marriage group (Wife of Bath, Friar, Summoner, Merchant, Clerk, Franklin) Astrolabe Equatorie	1390 Commissions to repair St. George's Chapel, Windsor; to oversee repairs on the lower Thames sewers and conduits; to build bleachers for jousts at Smithfield, etc. The three robberies. Chaucer appointed subforester of North Petherton, Somerset. 1391 *June 17:* another clerk of the works appointed. 1393 Chaucer granted a gift of £10 from Richard for services rendered "in this year now present." 1394 Death of Queen Anne. Chaucer granted a new annuity of £20.
	1395 Richard marries Isabella of France. Thomas Chaucer marries heiress Maud Burghersh.
Balades to Scogan, Bukton	1396 John of Gaunt marries Katherine Swynford. 1398 Chaucer borrows against his annuity; action for debt against Chaucer; letters of protection from the King. 1399 Deposition of Richard II. Election of Henry IV. Death of John of Gaunt. *October 13:* on his coronation day, Henry doubles Chaucer's annuity. *December 24:* Chaucer signs 53-year lease for tenement in the garden of the Lady Chapel, Westminster Abbey.
	1400 *September 29:* last record of Chaucer: quittance given by him for a tun of wine received. *October 25:* date of Chaucer's death on tombstone in Westminster Abbey (erected in 1556).

The Complete
Poetry
and Prose of
Geoffrey
Chaucer

The Portrait of Chaucer in Hoccleve's *Regement of Princes,* MS. Harl. 4866, fol. 88. The British Library, London

Second Edition

The Complete Poetry and Prose of Geoffrey Chaucer

Edited by

John H. Fisher

John C. Hodges Professor
University of Tennessee

Holt, Rinehart and Winston, Inc.

New York   Chicago   San Francisco   Philadelphia
Montreal   Toronto   London   Sydney   Tokyo

Publisher	Charlyce Jones Owen
Special Projects Editor	Pamela C. Forcey
Senior Production Manager	Nancy J. Myers
Design Supervisor	Gloria I. Gentile
Book and Cover Design	Arthur D. Ritter
Page Makeup	Neil W. Kelley

Library of Congress Cataloging-in-Publication Data

Chaucer, Geoffrey, d. 1400.
   [Works. 1989]
   The complete poetry and prose of Geoffrey Chaucer /
edited by John H. Fisher. — 2nd ed.
     p. cm.
   Bibliography: p.
   Includes index.
   I. Fisher, John H.   II. Title.
PR1851.F5   1989
821′.1—dc19   88–29400
                CIP

ISBN 0-03-028612-3

Printed in the United States of America

9 0 1 2 3 032 9 8 7 6 5 4 3 2 1

Holt, Rinehart and Winston, Inc.
The Dryden Press
Saunders College Publishing

TO JANE
My Lady Sovereyne

Preface to the Second Edition

This edition continues to be addressed to the student reader. It is intended to make Chaucer's texts accessible with a minimum of scholarly interference. The headnotes have been rewritten to reflect scholarship and criticism to 1988, and the bibliography has been revised to include important books and articles through 1987.

The texts and notes remain as they were in the first edition. Each has been drawn from an authoritative manuscript and glossed and annotated so that each page can be read without reference to other parts of the book. The critical, biographical, and linguistic essays are grouped at the end so as not to impede the approach to the text. A glossary of frequent forms is included at the end of the book. The lighter punctuation of the text is intended to free Chaucer's brisk idiom from the trammels of the comma and semicolon. The variants printed along with the explanatory notes at the foot of each page have been selected to display scribal *usus scribendi* rather than for textual criticism. The exhaustive collations, analyses of textual problems, and summaries of scholarship in the volumes of the *Variorum Chaucer*, as they appear, will become the basis for scholarly discussion. In the meanwhile, the textual and explanatory notes of the 1987 *Riverside Chaucer* provide fuller information for purposes of research.

This edition offers Chaucer's complete

works. *Romaunt of the Rose* has been included even though little of this Middle English version can have been by Chaucer because Chaucer tells us that he translated this important work and because of the close parallels between the language of translation and the language of Chaucer's poems. The *Equatorie of the Planets* has been included because of the probability that it is Chaucer's work and because of the way it complements the *Treatise on the Astrolabe*. Because of the uncertain chronology, the works have been arranged in logical rather than chronological order. *Canterbury Tales* and *Troylus and Criseyde* are what most readers will want to turn to first. The minor poems follow in quasi-chronological order. The short poems are grouped by theme and genre. The *Canterbury Tales* are presented in the Ellesmere order for reasons given in the introductory essays. The ten groupings have been called "parts" rather than "fragments" to reflect our growing awareness of the organic unity of the *Canterbury* collection.

● ● ●

The scholars and friends who helped with the original edition must be acknowledged again: Donald Howard, Robert Raymo, Beryl Rowland, Donald Sands, James Wimsatt, Francis Utley, Derek Brewer, Judith Fisher, John Braymer, Meta Braymer, Dorothy Lewis, Martha Gill, and Elizabeth Carroll, and Pamela Forcey, Arthur Ritter, and Kenney Withers of Holt, Rinehart and Winston. Holt, Rinehart and Winston and the Hodges Better English Fund of the University of Tennessee provided funds for acquisition of microfilms and travel to study the manuscripts. The Huntington, Morgan, Bodleian, and Cambridge University Libraries kindly gave permission to publish texts and illustrations from their manuscripts, as indicated in the notes on the illustrations. J.D. Price and the Cambridge University Press gave permission for the text in this edition to be based on Dr. Price's edition of The *Equatorie of the Planetis* (Cambridge University Press, 1955). A.E. Gunther and the Oxford University Press gave permission for the reproduction of of the first twenty-two figures in R.T. Gunther, *Chaucer and Messahala on the Astrolabe* (Oxford University Press, 1929). Mark Allen and James Wimsett have looked over and made suggestions about the revised headnotes and bibliography. James Kelly of the University of Tennessee Publications Service has edited our discs for the desktop publishing through which the new material has replaced that of the earlier versions. And as always, Jane Law Fisher has been a collaborator in all stages of the operation.

J.H.F.
Knoxville, Tennessee
June, 1988

Contents

Canterbury Tales 1

Short Poems 667

List of Plates

List of Abbreviations and a Putative Chronology of the Works

BD	*Book of the Duchess*, 1369		TC	*Troylus and Criseyde*, between 1382 and 1385
Romaunt	*Romaunt of the Rose*, before 1370			
RR	*Roman de la Rose* (French version)		LGW	*Legend of Good Women*, 1385 or 1386
PF	*Parliament of Fowls*, 1377		CT	*Canterbury Tales*, begun in 1386
HF	*House of Fame*, 1380 or 1381		Astrolabe	*Treatise on the Astrolabe*, 1391
Boece	between 1381 and 1385		Equatorie	*Equatorie of the Planets*, 1392

Gen Pro	General Prologue		PardT	Pardoner's Tale
KT	Knight's Tale		PhysT	Physician's Tale
MilT	Miller's Tale		ShipT	Shipman's Tale
RvT	Reeve's Tale		PrioressT	Prioress's Tale
CkT	Cook's Tale		*Thopas*	*Tale of Sir Thopas*
MLT	Man of Law's Tale		*Mel*	*Tale of Melibee*
WBT	Wife of Bath's Tale		MkT	Monk's Tale
WBP	Wife of Bath's Prologue		NPT	Nun's Priest's Tale
FrT	Friar's Tale		2ndNT	Second Nun's Tale
SumT	Summoner's Tale		CYT	Canon's Yeoman's Tale
ClT	Clerk's Tale		MancT	Manciple's Tale
MerchT	Merchant's Tale		ParsT	Parson's Tale
SqT	Squire's Tale		Ret	Chaucer's Retraction
FrankT	Franklin's Tale			

Designations for Parts of the Canterbury Tales

Ellesmere	Chaucer Society		Ellesmere	Chaucer Society
I	A		VI	C
II	B¹		VII	B²*
III	D		VIII	G
IV	E		IX	H
V	F		X	I

* B² is numbered continuously from B¹, beginning with 1190 and ending with 4652. To find the Chaucer Society number, add 1190 to the Ellesmere number in Part VII; to find the Ellesmere number, subtract 1190 from the Chaucer Society number in B². The other parts are numbered similarly in the two systems.

The Complete
Poetry
and Prose of
Geoffrey
Chaucer

Canterbury Tales

INTRODUCTION

Canterbury Tales

HE FRAME OF the *Canterbury Tales* employs the archetypal fiction of a journey. This journey, however, is a pilgrimage, and the participants pilgrims, which at once suggests the possibilities of literal and metaphoric levels of meaning. The narrative is so convincing that John M. Manly, *Some New Light on Chaucer* (1926), tried to identify the pilgrims with people Chaucer knew in the London of his day, and F. J. Furnivall, *A Temporary Preface* (1868), tried to work out the details of the pilgrimage. Was it to Canterbury and back or only one way? Where did the pilgrims spend the nights? Which tales should be assigned to mornings and which to afternoons? And Charles Owen has continued this inquiry in *Pilgrimage and Storytelling* (1977).

But the more closely one reads, the more evident it becomes that the details of the journey are neither clear nor complete. We see the plan being scaled down as the work progresses. In the General Prologue, the Host proposes that each pilgrim tell four tales (I.792-94). By the Squire's Epilogue, halfway through the collection, it has become "A tale or two" (V.698). And in the final Prologue, the Host says to the Parson, "every man save thou hath told his tale" (X.25). Even this is not true, of course, for not every pilgrim has told a tale. Furthermore, what we have is not in final form. The Cook's and Squire's Tales and the *Tale of Sir Thopas* break off incomplete. The Man of Law says that he will tell a tale in prose and goes on immediately to tell one in rhymed stanzas. The Man of Law's and Nun's Priest's Tales are followed in many manuscripts by epilogues that connect with nothing. The Physician's, Shipman's, and Second Nun's Tales have no prologues. The Shipman refers to himself as a "wyf" whose "sely housbonde . . . moot us clothe" (VII.3-12). The Second Nun calls herself as an "unworthy sone of Eve" (VIII.62). The Merchant refers to "thise fooles that been seculeer" (IV.1251) as though he were a religious.

Within the frame of the *Canterbury Tales* there are ten parts that appear in different orders in different manuscripts. Most scholars believe that Chaucer never achieved a final order for the parts, and that the various orders are all scribal. In this edition, we adopt the order of the Ellesmere manuscript although it has problems. Five of the parts contain references to towns along the Canterbury Way. In Part I, the Prologue begins in Southwark (I.20), and the Host refers to Deptford, just five miles out of Southwark (I.3906). In Part III, the Summoner speaks of Sittingbourne *forty* miles from London (III.847). In Part VII, the Host refers to Rochester, only

thirty miles from London (VII.1926). In Part VIII, the Canon and his Yeoman catch up with the party at Boughton in the Blean forest, just four miles from Canterbury (VIII.556). And the Manciple's Tale begins three miles on, at Harbledown, still in the Blean forest (IX.2). The apparent error in the Ellesmere order led early editors to place Part VII after Part II, in what was called the Chaucer Society order (see p.xiii in the front matter above), but this raises its own problems. The Ellesmere order is aesthetically quite satisfactory. Its evolution has been discussed by Charles Owen (above) and by N. F. Blake, *The Textual Tradition of the Canterbury Tales* (1985).

Clearly the *Canterbury Tales* as it has come down to us is not a final realization of whatever plan Chaucer may have been working toward. Whatever completeness we sense in the collection derives largely from the brilliant opening of the General Prologue, with its images of springtime, germination, and commencement, and the almost equally effective Prologue to the Parson's Tale, with its images of sunset, death, and completion. We need not deplore the fact that what comes between is not logically or technically "finished." Those critics like Ralph Baldwin, *The Unity of the Canterbury Tales* (1955), who view the achievement of the work as metaphoric rather than realistic, see the collection framed, like the life of man, between Creation and Doomsday, and the uncertain structure of what happens in between as representative of the associative method of the medieval miniaturist or tapestry weaver which can show in the same picture Jesus both as an infant and sitting in majesty or William the Conqueror both crossing the English Channel and fighting at Hastings.

Pilgrimages (quests) are so familiar in literature and life that there seems little point in asking where Chaucer got his idea. Parallels for both the frame and individual tales are presented in W. F. Bryan and G. Dempster, *Sources and Analogues of Chaucer's Canterbury Tales* (1940). But the originality of Chaucer's treatment is stressed by Christian Zacher, *Curiosity and Pilgrimage: The Literature of Discovery in Fourteenth-Century England* (1976), and Donald Howard, *Writers and Pilgrims: Medieval Pilgrimage Narratives and Their Posterity* (1980).

However, the purpose of the pilgrimage frame is not its picaresque adventures but the opportunity it provided for experiments with style. Whatever unity Chaucer's collection has is more rhetorical than conceptual. From his earliest pieces, Chaucer shows an interest in experimenting with different "voices" and "styles." Like other medieval writers, he viewed style as a function of social class. Charles Muscatine, *Chaucer and the French Tradition* (1957), discussed the difference between his "courtly" and "bourgeois" styles. The most original feature of Chaucer's plan—for which there was no precedent in earlier frame stories, and which has not been successfully duplicated since—was to bring together a collection of participants from different classes and to have them tell stories whose full effectiveness depends on the differences in their subjects and their styles. The dramatic interchanges between the pilgrims themselves enhance the stylistic contrasts between their tales. The "marriage group" (see the introduction to Part III, p. 104) is the high point of this reciprocal structure, which produces an effect quite beyond that of any individual tale in isolation. It is this orchestration of tellers and tales that creates the sense of unity in the *Canterbury Tales*.

One interesting way to look at the Canterbury collection is as a study in genres, as the author himself suggested in the Miller's Prologue (I.3179-80). Chaucer the craftsman devised a frame in which many kinds of medieval narrative could find a natural ambience. The *romances* are the Knight's and Franklin's Tales, the Wife of Bath's Tale (with a special twist), and the *Tale of Sir Thopas* (in which the genre is burlesqued). The *fabliaux* are the Miller's, Reeve's, Summoner's, Friar's, and Merchant's Tales, and presumably the Cook's, if it had been completed. The *pious tales* are the Man of Law's, Clerk's, Prioress's, Physician's, and Second Nun's, and presumably the Monk's. The *exempla* are the Pardoner's, Nun's Priest's, Manciple's, and (for lack of a better place to put it) the Canon's Yeoman's Tales. The Friar's, Summoner's, and Canon's Yeoman's Tales could also be classified as "muck raking" tales, exposés of the corruption of a trade or profession, like Upton Sinclair's or Ida Tarbell's in modern times. Recent critics have organized the tales in other social and moral patterns. But merely to rearrange them in this fashion shows the effect of their context in the Canterbury collection. The dramatic interplay of characters and styles is the principal achievement of Chaucer's work.

The movement of criticism from drama of action to drama of style is in keeping with recent movements of interest from surface structure to deep structure. The surface structure of the *Canterbury Tales* was fully developed by R. M. Lumiansky, *Of Sondry Folk: The Dramatic Principle of the Canterbury Tales* (1955). The deep structure of the collection has been stressed by Ralph Baldwin (above), Donald Howard, *The Idea of the Canterbury Tales* (1976), and other recent studies. Dramatic unity as a critical principle has been challenged by Robert Jordan, *Chaucer and the Shape of Creation: The Aesthetic Possibilities of Inorganic Structure* (1967), and C. David Benson, *Chaucer's Drama of Styles: Poetic Variety and Contrast in the Canterbury Tales* (1986).

Plate 1. The opening of the Knight's Tale, *Canterbury Tales*, Ellesmere MS., fol. 10ʳ. The Huntington Library, San Marino, California

INTRODUCTION

Canterbury Tales, Part I

HERE IS NO QUESTION about the position of Part I of the *Canterbury Tales*, since it begins with the General Prologue. As with other great works of art, the effectiveness of the Prologue is not as simple as it seems. It comes not only from the inevitable phrasing—the gift of a master poet—but also from the subtle organization of material to produce a unified impression. No society exists without a sense of organization. Principles differ, but some ideals have greater value than others, and there are always leaders and followers. Chaucer's scale of values is the traditional Hellenic-Christian "chain of being," extending from inanimate matter through vegetable, animal, and man, up to God. Chaucer slants our thinking subliminally towards this hierarchy by the order in which he presents the ideas in the first eighteen lines of the Prologue: April showers vitalize the earth; flowers and tender leaves signalize the rebirth of vegetable life; mating birds express the life urge in animals; people longing to go on pilgrimages reveal the divine aspirations that distinguish humanity. The "estates" in medieval society were similarly viewed as a hierachical chain, with religion usually at the top. Chaucer's decision to begin his list of pilgrims with the highest ranking secular group

establishes an initial tension with the spirituality of the pilgrimage frame.

As with the ordering of materials, tradition enriched the individual portraits in the General Prologue. The verbal icons, emblems, and images through which Chaucer compressed so much meaning into his seemingly artless sketches grew out of a long tradition of personification in the sermons and penitentials, which had its roots in the moralizing "characters" of Theophrastus and other classical satirists that has been treated by Benjamin Boyce, *The Theophrastan Character in England* (1947). Preachers had developed a popular tradition of personifying both the estates and the vices and virtues. What gives universality to Chaucer's Knight is an underlying conception of "knighthood"; to the Monk, of "monkhood"; to the Wife of Bath of "wifehood." In some pilgrims we can also see traditional attributes of "pride," "avarice," "lechery," and so on. While Muriel Bowden, *A Commentary on the General Prologue* (2nd ed., 1967), expands on J. M. Manly's treatment of the individualizing characteristics of the pilgrims, Jill Mann, *Chaucer and Medieval Estates Satire* (1973), elucidates their typicality.

In addition to being a self-contained commentary on what William Blake called "the lineaments of universal human life," the General Prologue introduces two motifs that help to organize the collection. The first is the literary persona of Chaucer the Pilgrim, whose voice glosses the poetry with ironic comments that warn us not to take any character or situation at face value. The second is the personage of the Host and the game he proposes. The Host becomes the elected leader of the pilgrims. (The Knight continues as the natural leader and bails the Host out when he gets into trouble, as at the end of the Pardoner's Tale, VI.960.) The Host combines the functions of conductor and chorus in the unfolding drama. The story-telling contest he proposes knits the collection into a composition.

The Knight's Tale is the stylistic yardstick against which all the following links and tales are to be measured. Chivalry and courtly love provide the motives for action in an idealized society. Like all courtly love, the love of Palamon and Arcite is both ennobling and destructive. Its destructive aspect reflects the classical tradition in which love was regarded as madness, resulting, like the love of Paris and Helen, not only in personal suffering but in social turmoil. The ennobling aspect was invented by medieval Europe, where—along with religion—romantic love was cultivated as a way to improve the manners and morals of a warrior class whose main business was fighting and killing. The love of Palamon and Arcite is a study of how love first disrupts their behavior and then, under the guidance of Theseus, educates and matures them.

An important aspect of this ennoblement of love was the Boethian world view. Boethius' *Consolation of Philosophy* was attractive to both rulers and lovers because both tried to control events in this temporal world only to discover how often outcomes are determined by chance rather than by justice. Chaucer's two pieces dealing most seriously with chivalric love, the Knight's Tale and *Troylus and Criseyde*, are also the two most influenced by Boethian philosophy (see the Introduction to *Boece*, p. 815 below). In this ethic, the misfortunes of the world are exercises through which the noble spirit achieves serenity. Heroic death is nearly as satisfactory a conclusion as success. Perhaps more so. Certainly the death of Arcite is treated more elaborately than the wedding of Palamon and Emelye.

Chaucer's Knight's Tale is an adaptation in 2,250 lines of Boccaccio's 10,000-line epic on the adventures of Theseus, *Il Teseide.* While preserving Theseus as the model of the just ruler, Chaucer omitted most of the material dealing with his exploits and focused on the love story, which he remodeled into an example of sensibility and decorum well appreciated by the "gentils" in the Miller's Prologue.

Part I exemplifies the social interpretations of style as adumbrated by the thirteenth-century English rhetorician John of Garland, who adapted the Ciceronian conceptions of the *high*, *middle*, and *low* styles to the three classes of society, *courtly*, *civic*, and *rustic*. The Knight's Tale represents the high style; the Miller's, the middle style; and the Reeve's, the low style. The last two are "fabliaux"—medieval humorous tales, usually bawdy, about middle- and low-class characters and situations. One of their principal devices is burlesquing the values and behavior of the courtly system. At almost every point, the Miller's and Reeve's Tales are burlesques of courtly decorum. In the Miller's Tale, the credulity of the old carpenter contrasts with the nobility of Theseus; the lasciviousness of Nicholas and the silliness of Absolon with the refined suffering of Palamon and Arcite; the sensuality of Alisoun with the docile restraint of Emelye. The hot colter episode in the Miller's Tale and the fight between Aleyn and the miller in the Reeve's Tale are ridiculous parallels with the tournament at the end of the Knight's Tale.

Instead of the Athenian court or civic Oxford, the Reeve's Tale is set in the rustic fens of Trumpington. Instead of serving for love, or even planning a seduction, the two clerks simply stumble into their sexual adventure, which reveals no sentiment beyond animal urgency. Unlike Palamon and Arcite who are courtly knights, or Nicholas and Absolon who are city slickers, John and Aleyn are country boys whose lack of sophistication is marked by their northern idiom—the first use of dialect for characterization in English literature.

The Cook's Tale takes a further step down the scale of loves, from courtly sentiment to calculated seduction to animal enjoyment to the unwholesome prostitution of a "wyf that heeld for contenance / A shoppe, and swyved for hir sustenaunce" (I.4421). Chaucer had been willing to explore the social and stylistic implications of the first three levels. He seems unwilling to do more than allude to the last. It is impossible to tell whether he had more of a plot in mind, but it does not matter. The Cook's Tale is effective as it stands. Chaucer in his first four tales has managed to establish clear-cut hierarchies of classes, values, and styles. The patterned variety of the Canterbury tales is beginning to emerge.

C. S. Lewis, *The Allegory of Love* (1936), expounds the traditional view of courtly love, while H. A. Kelly, *Love and Marriage in the Age of Chaucer* (1975), presents a more skeptical view. Jeffrey Helterman, "The Dehumanizing Metaphor of The Knight's Tale" *ELH* (1971), discusses the bestial subtext. Analogues to the fabliaux are found in L. D. Benson and T. M. Andersson, *The Literary Context of Chaucer's Fabliaux* (1971). Janette Richardson, *Blameth Nat Me: A Study of the Imagery in Chaucer's Fabliaux* (1970) shows how the ironic imagery testifies to Chaucer's artistry.

Canterbury Tales

PART I

GENERAL PROLOGUE

Here bigynneth the Book of the Tales of Caunterbury.

Whan that Aprill with his shoures soote
The droghte of March hath perced to the roote,
And bathed every veyne in swich licour
Of which vertu engendred is the flour;
Whan Zephirus eek with his sweete breeth   5
Inspired hath in every holt and heeth

The tendre croppes, and the yonge sonne
Hath in the Ram his halfe cours yronne,
And smale foweles maken melodye,
That slepen al the nyght with open eye—   10
So priketh hem nature in hir corages—
Thanne longen folk to goon on pilgrimages,

Text based on the Ellesmere MS (E), with variants from Hengwrt (Hg), and other MSS; see "The Text of This Edition," p. 966.

1 April, accent on the first syllable. Note that the first two measures of the poem begin with accented beats. **his,** its; *it* did not have a separate possessive until the 17th century. **shoures soote,** gentle showers. The unmutated form of *swete, swote* or *soote* was generally used to translate Lat. *suavis; swete* was used to translate *dulcis.* **2 droghte of March,** dryness of March. Early spring is a relatively dry season in southern England. **3 veyne,** veins in the plants. **swich licour,** such liquid. **4 vertu,** potency, from Lat. *virtus.* **5 Zephirus,** the west wind; in classical mythology husband of Flora, goddess of flowers, and father of Carpus, god of fruit. **eek,** also. **6 Inspired . . . holt and heeth,** breathed into, woodland and plain. **7 croppes,** new foliage. **yonge sonne,** just beginning its annual journey after the vernal equinox. In Chaucer's time the English legal year began on 25 March. **8 Hath in the Ram his halfe cours yronne,** the zodiacal house of Aries (the Ram) in Chaucer's time extended from 12 March to 11 April. Halfway through this would place the date ca. 27 March—but see MLT II.5 below. Hence, it has been concluded that Chaucer meant "has completed the half of the Ram's course [that occurs in April—the other half having occurred in March]," i.e., was entering the house of Taurus which began 12 April. If 18 April in MLT refers to the second day of the pilgrimage, the first day would be 17 April. Skeat argued that 17 April 1387, the week after Easter, was the most probable date. *halfe:* E&c *half;* some MSS read *half his.* **11 corages,** hearts.

And palmeres for to seken straunge strondes
To ferne halwes, kowthe in sondry londes;
And specially from every shires ende 15
Of Engelond to Caunterbury they wende
The hooly blisful martir for to seke
That hem hath holpen whan that they were
    seeke.
    Bifil that in that seson on a day
In Southwerk at the Tabard as I lay 20
Redy to wenden on my pilgrymage
To Caunterbury with ful devout corage,
At nyght was come into that hostelrye
Wel nyne and twenty in a compaignye
Of sondry folk, by aventure yfalle 25
In felaweship, and pilgrimes were they alle,
That toward Caunterbury wolden ryde.
The chambres and the stables weren wyde,
And wel we weren esed atte beste.
And shortly, whan the sonne was to reste, 30
So hadde I spoken with hem everichon
That I was of hir felaweship anon,
And made forward erly for to ryse,
To take oure wey ther as I yow devyse.
    But nathelees, whil I have tyme and space, 35
Er that I ferther in this tale pace,
Me thynketh it acordaunt to resoun
To telle yow al the condicioun
Of ech of hem, so as it semed me,
And whiche they weren, and of what degree, 40

And eek in what array that they were inne,
And at a knyght than wol I first bigynne.

    A KNYGHT ther was, and that a worthy
        man,
That fro the tyme that he first bigan
To riden out, he loved chivalrie, 45
Trouthe and honour, fredom and curteisie.
Ful worthy was he in his lordes werre,
And therto hadde he riden, no man ferre,
As wel in cristendom as in hethenesse,
And evere honoured for his worthynesse. 50
    At Alisaundre he was whan it was wonne.
Ful ofte tyme he hadde the bord bigonne
Aboven alle nacions in Pruce.
In Lettow hadde he reysed and in Ruce,
No Cristen man so ofte of his degree. 55
In Gernade at the seege eek hadde he be
Of Algezir, and riden in Belmarye.
At Lyeys was he and at Satalye,
Whan they were wonne, and in the Grete See
At many a noble armee hadde he be. 60
At mortal batailles hadde he been fiftene,
And foughten for oure feith at Tramyssene
In lystes thries, and ay slayn his foo.
This ilke worthy knyght hadde been also
Somtyme with the lord of Palatye 65
Agayn another hethen in Turkye,
And everemoore he hadde a sovereyn prys.

13 **palmeres,** professional pilgrims whose emblem was a palm frond. **strondes,** lands. **14 ferne halwes, kowthe,** faraway saints (or shrines), known. **sondry,** various. **17 blisful martir,** blessed St. Thomas à Becket, martyred in Canterbury Cathedral in 1170. **18 holpen . . . seeke,** helped, sick. **20 Southwerk,** the borough south of London Bridge. **Tabard,** inn identified by a sign shaped like a smock. **24 Wel nyne and twenty,** evidently Chaucer intended thirty storytellers (including himself), but the number cannot be made to fit the text. **25 aventure,** chance. **28 wyde,** spacious. **29 esed atte beste,** accommodated in the best manner. **30 shortly,** to be brief about it. **32 anon,** immediately. **33 made forward,** (we) made an agreement. **34 devyse,** (will) relate. **36 pace,** pass (go). **38 condicioun,** circumstances. **40 whiche . . . degree,** what, status (rank). **45 chivalrie,** the ethical code of chivalry, also feats of arms. **46 Trouthe . . . fredom,** integrity, generosity. **47 lordes werre,** feudal lord's war. **48 ferre,** further. **49 hethenesse,** heathen lands. **51 Alisaundre,** Alexandria, captured 1365. The Knight's campaigns range from 1344 to 1386—unlikely for one man; all are against pagans at war with Christian Europe. **52 bord bigonne,** sat in the place of honor at banquets. **53 nacions in Pruce,** the Knights of the Teutonic Order, fighting in Prussia against the invaders from Central Asia, were organized by nationality, like the students in medieval universities. **54 Lettow . . . Ruce,** Lithuania and Russia, areas of warfare for the Teutonic Order, **reysed,** campaigned. **56, 57, 62 Gernade,** Granada. **Algezir,** a city in Granada, captured in 1344. **Belmarye, Tramyssene,** Moorish kingdoms in North Africa. All of these names are associated with the struggles of the Christians against the Moors in Spain and North Africa throughout the 14th century. **58 Lyeys . . . Satalye,** Saracen cities in Asia Minor, won in 1361 and 1367. These two and the capture of Alexandria (l. 51 above) were campaigns of Pierre de Lusignan, Christian King of Cyprus. **59 Grete See,** Mediterranean. **60 armee,** armed invasion. Hg&c *aryve,* evidently an error. **62–63 foughten . . . In lystes,** single combat by champions to decide the outcome of a battle. **65 Palatye,** another city in Asia Minor, in 1365 bound by treaty to Cyprus. **67 sovereyn prys,** high reputation.

And though that he were worthy, he was wys,
And of his port as meeke as is a mayde.
He nevere yet no vileynye ne sayde   70
In al his lyf unto no maner wight.
He was a verray, parfit, gentil knyght.
But for to tellen yow of his array,
His hors weren goode, but he was nat gay.
Of fustian he wered a gypoun   75
Al bismotered with his habergeoun,
For he was late ycome from his viage,
And wente for to doon his pilgrymage.

    With hym ther was his sone, a yong
      SQUIER,
A lovyere and a lusty bacheler,   80
With lokkes crulle as they were leyd in presse.
Of twenty yeer of age he was, I gesse.
Of his stature he was of evene lengthe,
And wonderly delyvere, and of greet strengthe.
And he hadde been somtyme in chyvachie   85
In Flaundres, in Artoys, and Pycardie,
And born hym weel, as of so litel space,
In hope to stonden in his lady grace.
Embrouded was he, as it were a meede
Al ful of fresshe floures, whyte and reede.   90
Syngynge he was or floytynge al the day.
He was as fressh as is the monthe of May.
Short was his gowne, with sleves longe and
    wyde.

Wel koude he sitte on hors and faire ryde.
He koude songes make and wel endite,   95
Juste and eek daunce, and weel purtreye and
    write.
So hoote he lovede that by nyghtertale
He slepte namoore than dooth a nyghtyngale.
Curteis he was, lowely, and servysable,
And carf biforn his fader at the table.   100

    A YEMAN hadde he and servantz namo
At that tyme, for hym liste ride so,
And he was clad in cote and hood of grene.
A sheef of pecok arwes, bright and kene,
Under his belt he bar ful thriftily—   105
Wel koude he dresse his takel yemanly;
His arwes drouped noght with fetheres lowe—
And in his hand he baar a myghty bowe.
A not-heed hadde he, with a broun visage.
Of wodecraft wel koude he al the usage.   110
Upon his arm he baar a gay bracer,
And by his syde a swerd and a bokeler,
And on that oother syde a gay daggere
Harneised wel and sharp as point of spere;
A Cristophre on his brest of silver sheene.   115
An horn he bar, the bawdryk was of grene;
A forster was he, soothly, as I gesse.

    Ther was also a Nonne, a PRIORESSE,
That of hir smylyng was ful symple and coy;

---

68 **worthy . . . wys,** "fortitudo et sapientia" were the most valued qualities of the hero from classical times onward. 69 **port . . . meeke as is a mayde,** behavior; in *Republic* II, Plato wrote, "where shall we find [in a soldier] at once a meek and magnanimous temperament?" 71 **wight,** person. 72 **verray, parfit, gentil,** true, perfect, courteous. 74 **hors . . . gay,** horses, gaily dressed. 75 **fustian . . . gypoun,** coarse cloth tunic. 76 **bismotered . . . habergeoun,** soiled by his coat of mail. 77 **late . . . viage,** recently, journey. 80 **lovyere,** lover, southern, perhaps deprecatory, dialect form. **bacheler,** bachelors in arms aspired to be knights as bachelors of arts to be masters. 81 **crulle . . . presse,** curly as if they had been artificially dressed. 83 **evene lengthe,** average, i.e., not odd. 84 **delyvere,** agile. 85 **chyvachie,** cavalry action. 86 **Flaundres, Artoys, Pycardie,** in 1383 the English engaged in a "crusade" in Flanders and neighboring districts in support of Urban VI of Rome against the French supporters of Clement VII of Avignon. This was merely another episode in the 100 Years War. 88 **lady,** lady's. 89 **Embrouded . . . meede,** embroidered, meadow. 91 **floytynge,** fluting (or whistling). 93 **Short was his gowne,** etc., very fashionable dress; see Chaucer Society woodcut, p. 188. 95 **make . . . endite,** compose the music, compose the lyric. 96 **purtreye,** draw, the Squire possessed all the genteel accomplishments. 99 **lowely,** humble. 100 **carf,** carved, another gentlemanly accomplishment. 101 **hadde he,** i.e., the Knight. 102 **hym liste,** he chose. 103 **grene,** Lincoln green was the traditional color of foresters' clothes. 104 **pecok arwes,** like the Squire and several of the subsequent pilgrims, the Yeoman is decked out in his fiesta finery for the pilgrimage. 108 **myghty bowe,** longbowmen had proved to be England's most effective weapon against French chivalry in the 100 Years War. 109 **not-heed,** closely cut hair; cf. the long curls of the Squire, and the Cavaliers and Roundheads of 1642. 111 **gay bracer,** ornamented leather wrist-guard. 112 **bokeler,** small shield. 114 **Harneised wel,** with a good sheath and belt. 115 **A Cristophre,** a Christopher medal; St. Christopher is the patron saint of travelers. 116 **bawdryk,** baldric. 119 **coy,** reserved (Lat. *quietus*), or affecting reserve (see *LGW* 1548).

Hire gretteste ooth was but by Seint Loy.   120
And she was cleped madame Eglentyne.
Ful weel she soong the service dyvyne,
Entuned in hir nose ful semely,
And Frenssh she spak ful faire and fetisly,
After the scole of Stratford atte Bowe,   125
For Frenssh of Parys was to hire unknowe.
At mete wel ytaught was she with-alle:
She leet no morsel from hir lippes falle,
Ne wette hir fyngres in hir sauce depe.
Wel koude she carie a morsel and wel kepe   130
That no drope ne fille upon hire brest.
In curteisie was set ful muchel hir lest.
Hir over-lippe wyped she so clene
That in hir coppe ther was no ferthyng sene
Of grece, whan she dronken hadde hir draughte.
Ful semely after hir mete she raughte.   136
And sikerly she was of greet desport,
And ful plesaunt, and amyable of port,
And peyned hire to countrefete cheere
Of court, and to been estatlich of manere,   140
And to ben holden digne of reverence.
But, for to speken of hire conscience,
She was so charitable and so pitous
She wolde wepe, if that she saugh a mous
Kaught in a trappe, if it were deed or bledde.   145

Of smale houndes hadde she that she fedde
With rosted flessh, or milk and wastel-breed.
But soore wepte she if oon of hem were deed,
Or if men smoot it with a yerde smerte—
And al was conscience and tendre herte.   150
Ful semyly hir wympul pynched was,
Hir nose tretys, hir eyen greye as glas,
Hir mouth ful smal, and therto softe and reed.
But sikerly she hadde a fair forheed;
It was almoost a spanne brood, I trowe,   155
For, hardily, she was nat undergrowe.
Ful fetys was hir cloke, as I was war.
Of smal coral aboute hire arm she bar
A peire of bedes, gauded al with grene,   159
And theron heng a brooch of gold ful sheene
On which ther was first write a crowned A,
And after *Amor vincit omnia.*

Another NONNE with hir hadde she,
That was hir chapeleyne, and preestes thre.

A MONK ther was, a fair for the maistrie,   165
An outridere, that lovede venerie,
A manly man, to been an abbot able.
Ful many a deyntee hors hadde he in stable.
And whan he rood, men myghte his brydel heere

---

120 Seint Loy, St. Eligius, a particularly handsome, genteel French saint of the 6th century. **121 Eglentyne,** a typical romance heroine's name, but there was a Madam Argentyn in St. Leonard's nunnery near Stratford-at-Bow (just outside of London) which Chaucer had visited as a youth. She was not prioress. **123 Entuned in hir nose,** authorities point out that this is the correct way to sing Gregorian chant. **124 fetisly,** elegantly. **125 scole of Stratford atte Bowe,** i.e., she spoke provincial (Anglo-Norman) French. **127 mete,** dining; the description of the Prioress' table manners resembles some of the Duenna's satirical comments on women in *RR* 13,374ff. (Dunn-Robbins 62.86ff.). **132 curteisie . . . lest,** elegant manners, pleasure. **134 coppe . . . ferthyng,** cup, spot the size of a farthing (dime). **136 semely . . . raughte,** politely, reached. **137 sikerly . . . desport,** certainly, geniality. **138 port,** bearing. **139 countrefete cheere,** imitate the behavior. **141 digne,** worthy. **145 Kaught in a trappe,** this was, by way of contrast, a period of such hardship for poor human beings that it had led to the Peasants' Revolt (1381). **146 houndes,** church law forbade nuns to have dogs. **147 wastel-breed,** white bread, made with bolted flour (Fr. *gâteau*). At this time peasants ate black bread, and meat only on the rarest occasions. **148 oon:** E&c *any.* **149 men smoot,** the Germanic impersonal used for the passive. **yerde smerte,** yardstick smartly. **151 semyly . . . wympul,** correctly, nun's headdress. **152 tretys,** well-shaped (aristocratic); the description—up to the forehead—is that of a romance heroine. **greye,** blue(?)—a favorite color for medieval aristocratic eyes, male or female. **154 fair forheed,** a high forehead was admired. There is some evidence that for nuns it should have not been so exposed; and coupled with the next two lines it suggests fleshiness. **156 hardily,** certainly. **nat undergrowe,** in medieval England, where food was scarce, fatness connoted wealth (see the Monk and Friar). **157 fetys . . . war,** elegant, aware. **158–59 smal coral . . . peire of bedes,** set (peire) of small coral beads, a rosary. **gauded,** divided by green beads; e.g., the modern rosary known as Our Lady's Psalter consists of fifteen decades of beads commemorating the 150 Psalms. **162** *Amor vincit* &c, Virgil, *Eclog* x.69 and proverbial. **164 chapeleyne,** an official in a nunnery, secretary and assistant to the prioress. **preestes thre,** this brings the number of pilgrims in the Prologue to thirty-two, and only one priest appears later (*CT* VII.2809). Perhaps it should read *and the prest is thre,* or else Chaucer left the line incomplete and someone filled in the phrase for rhyme (it appears in all MSS). **165 maistrie,** better than all others (Fr. *pour la maistrie,* a medical term meaning "of special efficacy"). **166 outridere,** an official who rode about overseeing the monastery's farms and manors (see *CT* VII.61 below). **venerie,** hunting (*double entendre* on venery, "sexual pleasure"?). **168 deyntee,** superior (Lat. *dignitatem*); on pride in horses see *CT* x.433.

Gynglen in a whistlynge wynd als cleere 170
And eek as loude as dooth the chapel belle
Ther as this lord was kepere of the celle.
The reule of Seint Maure or of Seint Beneit,
By cause that it was old and somdel streit,
This ilke Monk leet olde thynges pace, 175
And heeld after the newe world the space.
He yaf nat of that text a pulled hen
That seith that hunters been nat hooly men,
Ne that a monk, whan he is recchelees,
Is likned til a fissh that is waterlees— 180
This is to seyn, a monk out of his cloystre.
But thilke text heeld he nat worth an oystre.
And I seyde his opinioun was good.
What, sholde he studie and make hymselven
   wood,
Upon a book in cloystre alwey to poure, 185
Or swynken with his handes, and laboure,
As Austyn bit? How shal the world be served?
Lat Austyn have his swynk to hym reserved!
Therfore he was a prikasour aright.
Grehoundes he hadde as swift as fowel in flight.
Of prikyng and of huntyng for the hare 191
Was al his lust; for no cost wolde he spare.
I seigh his sleves ypurfiled at the hond
With grys, and that the fyneste of a lond.
And, for to festne his hood under his chyn, 195

He hadde of gold ywroght a ful curious pyn,
A love-knotte in the gretter ende ther was.
His heed was balled, that shoon as any glas,
And eek his face, as he hadde been enoynt.
He was a lord ful fat and in good poynt; 200
His eyen stepe and rollynge in his heed,
That stemed as a forneys of a leed;
His bootes souple; his hors in greet estaat.
Now certeinly he was a fair prelaat.
He nas nat pale as a forpyned goost. 205
A fat swan loved he best of any roost.
His palfrey was as broun as is a berye.

A FRERE ther was, a wantowne and a merye,
A lymytour, a ful solempne man.
In alle the ordres foure is noon that kan 210
So muchel of daliaunce and fair langage.
He hadde maad ful many a mariage
Of yonge wommen at his owene cost.
Unto his ordre he was a noble post.
Ful wel biloved and famulier was he 215
With frankeleyns over al in his contree,
And eek with worthy wommen of the toun,
For he hadde power of confessioun,
As seyde hymself, moore than a curat,
For of his ordre he was licenciat. 220
Ful swetely herde he confessioun,

170 **Gynglen,** small bells were fashionable harness decorations; the flowers "Canterbury bells" take their name from clusters of small bells often worn by pilgrims' horses. 172 **celle,** a dependent priory (to whose supervision the Monk, it is implied, devoted little time). 173 **Seint Maure . . . Seint Beneit,** St. Benedict, founder of the Benedictine order in 529 at Monte Cassino, Italy, and author of the most famous monastic rule; St. Maurus, according to legend a pupil of St. Benedict, introduced the Benedictine Rule into France c.550. 174 **streit,** strict. 175 **ilke . . . pace,** same, pass. 176 **space,** course. 177 **pulled,** plucked. 178 **hunters . . . hooly,** Nimrod, Gen. 10:9, or St. Jerome on Ps. 90, but a medieval commonplace. 179 **recchelees,** reckless, disobedient. 180 **fissh . . . waterlees,** *Vitae Patrum,* *PL* 73.858, but another commonplace. 184 **What . . . wood,** why, crazy. 186 **swynken,** work. 187 **Austyn . . . bit,** St. Augustine commands. In *De Opere Monachorum, PL* 40.547, St. Augustine instructed monks to avoid idleness through regular manual labor, but this is another commonplace of monastic rules. 188 *his swynk:* E&c *his owene swynk.* 189, 191–92 **prikasour . . . pryking . . . hare . . . lust,** hard riding, tracking, rabbit, pleasure; but all of these terms could have sexual *double entendre* (see *CT*1.4231, and Gower, *Mirour de l'omme,* 21053). 193 **ypurfiled,** fur-trimmed. 194 **grys,** fine gray fur. 196 **curious,** intricate. 199 **enoynt,** anointed (with oil). 200 **in good poynt,** stout (Fr. *embonpoint*). 201 **stepe,** bright, flashing. 202 **stemed . . . a leed,** glowed like the fire under a pot (ancient utensils were made of lead or lead alloys). 203 **greet estaat,** fine condition. 205 **forpyned,** distressed. 207 **palfrey,** riding horse. 208 **wantowne,** lively; but many of the terms describing the Friar have sexual *double entendre:* here "morally lax." 209 **lymytour,** a friar who paid a fee for an exclusive territory in which to beg (see ll. 252bc below). **solempne,** important. 210 **ordres foure,** Dominican, Franciscan, Carmelite, Augustinian. **kan,** knows. 211 **daliaunce,** blandishment. 212 **maad . . . mariage,** presumably because the women had been his mistresses. 214 **post,** support. 215 *Ful:* E&c *And.* 216–17 **frankeleyns . . . wommen,** the mendicant orders had originally been founded to minister to the poor; see ll. 240–50 below. *And eek:* E&c *eek* om. 218–20 **confessioun . . . licenciat,** one of the principal tensions of the church in the Middle Ages was the conflicting authority of the friars and parish priests to hear confession and grant absolution for sins. The fact that pardoners could also provide forgiveness for sins further confused the situation. **curat,** the assistant priest who did the work in a parish, often in the absence of the vicar (see l. 509 below).

And plesaunt was his absolucioun—
He was an esy man to yeve penaunce
Ther as he wiste to have a good pitaunce.
For unto a poure ordre for to yive   225
Is signe that a man is wel yshryve,
For if he yaf, he dorste make avaunt,
He wiste that a man was repentaunt;
For many a man so hard is of his herte,
He may nat wepe, althogh hym soore
    smerte.   230
Therfore in stede of wepynge and preyeres
Men moote yeve silver to the poure freres.
His typet was ay farsed ful of knyves
And pynnes for to yeven faire wyves.
And certeinly he hadde a murye note: 235
Wel koude he synge and pleyen on a rote;
Of yeddynges he baar outrely the pris.
His nekke whit was as the flour delys;
Therto he strong was as a champioun.
He knew the tavernes wel in every toun,   240
And everich hostiler and tappestere
Bet than a lazar or a beggestere,
For unto swich a worthy man as he
Acorded nat, as by his facultee,
To have with sike lazars aqueyntaunce.   245
It is nat honeste, it may nat avaunce,
For to deelen with no swich poraille,
But al with riche and selleres of vitaille.
And over al ther as profit sholde arise
Curteis he was and lowely of servyse.   250
Ther nas no man nowher so vertuous.
He was the beste beggere in his hous,

And yaf a certeyn ferme for the graunt—   252ᵇ
Noon of his bretheren cam ther in his
    haunt—   252ᶜ
For thogh a wydwe hadde noght a sho,
So plesaunt was his "In principio,"
Yet wolde he have a ferthyng er he wente.   255
His purchas was wel bettre than his rente.
And rage he koude, as it were right a whelpe.
In love-dayes ther koude he muchel helpe,
For ther he was nat lyk a cloysterer
With a thredbare cope, as is a poure scoler, 260
But he was lyk a maister or a pope.
Of double worstede was his semycope,
That rounded as a belle out of the presse.
Somwhat he lipsed for his wantownesse
To make his Englissh sweete upon his
    tonge.   265
And in his harpyng, whan that he hadde
    songe,
His eyen twynkled in his heed aryght,
As doon the sterres in the frosty nyght.
This worthy lymytour was cleped Huberd.

A MARCHANT was ther with a forked
    berd,   270
In mottelee, and hye on horse he sat,
Upon his heed a Flaundryssh bevere hat,
His bootes clasped faire and fetisly.
His resons he spak ful solempnely,
Sownynge alwey th'encrees of his wynnyng.   275
He wolde the see were kept for any
    thyng   276

---

224 pitaunce, gift. **226 yshryve,** shriven, absolved. **227 avaunt,** boast. **233 typet . . . farsed,** hood, stuffed; as the mendicant orders degenerate, the friars took on functions of peddlers, quack doctors, etc. **234** *faire:* E&c *yonge*. **236 rote,** fiddle. **237 yeddynges . . . pris,** ballads, prize. **238, 264 nekke whit . . . lipsed,** a white neck and lisping were regarded as indications of sensuality. **flour delys,** lily. **239 champioun,** champion brawler. **240** *every:* E&c *al the.* **241 hostiler . . . tappestere,** innkeeper, barmaid (the "-stere" is the OE feminine suffix). **242 lazar . . . beggestere,** leper (or merely sick person), beggarmaid. **244 Acorded nat . . . facultee,** it was not suitable, ability. **247 deelen . . . poraille,** deal, poor trash. **248 vitaille,** food. **250 lowely,** humbly. **252b ferme,** rent; see "lymytour" l. 209 above. Lines 252b and c are omitted in E&c. Chaucer may have marked them for excision. **252c haunt,** territory. **253 sho,** shoe. **254 In principio,** The fourteen opening verses of the Gospel of St. John were the friars' habitual salutation, used as a sort of magic incantation. **256 purchas,** income. **257 rage . . . whelpe,** usually interpreted "romp like a puppy," but equally possibly "be nasty as a dog" to anyone who did not make a donation. **258 love-dayes,** days set apart for settlement of differences by arbitration, in which the clergy often acted as arbiters. Eventually the "day" came to denote simply the practice of conciliation rather than legal proceeding. **259 cloysterer,** recluse. **260 cope,** cloak. **263 presse,** bell mold. **268 frosty nyght,** see the Monk's eyes above. Dante associated sins of passion with heat, sins of malice with cold. **269 Huberd,** not a common name in the 14th century, but in Roman de Renart the kite is named Hubert. **270 forked berd,** high fashion for the time. **271 mottelee,** cloth of mixed color. **hye on horse,** i.e., in order to be imposing. **272 Flaundryssh bevere hat,** beaverskin hat made in Flanders. **273 fetisly,** elegantly. **274 resons,** opinions. **275 Sownynge . . . wynnyng,** implying, profit. **276 wolde . . . kept for any thyng,** wanted, protected at any cost.

Bitwixe Middelburgh and Orewelle.
Wel koude he in eschaunge sheeldes selle.
This worthy man ful wel his wit bisette—
Ther wiste no wight that he was in dette,   280
So estatly was he of his governaunce
With his bargaynes and with his chevyssaunce.
For sothe he was a worthy man withalle,
But, sooth to seyn, I noot how men hym calle.

A CLERK ther was of Oxenford also   285
That unto logyk hadde longe ygo.
As leene was his hors as is a rake,
And he nas nat right fat, I undertake,
But looked holwe, and therto sobrely.
Ful thredbare was his overeste courtepy,   290
For he hadde geten hym yet no benefice,
Ne was so worldly for to have office.
For hym was levere have at his beddes heed
Twenty bookes, clad in blak or reed,
Of Aristotle and his philosophie,   295
Than robes riche, or fithele, or gay sautrie.
But al be that he was a philosophre,
Yet hadde he but litel gold in cofre.
But al that he myghte of his freendes hente,
On bookes and on lernynge he it spente,   300
And bisily gan for the soules preye
Of hem that yaf hym wherwith to scoleye.

Of studie took he moost cure and moost heede.
Noght o word spak he moore than was neede,
And that was seyd in forme and reverence,   305
And short and quyk and ful of hy sentence.
Sownynge in moral vertu was his speche,
And gladly wolde he lerne and gladly teche.

A SERGEANT OF THE LAWE, war
    and wys,
That often hadde been at the Parvys,   310
Ther was also, ful riche of excellence.
Discreet he was and of greet reverence—
He semed swich, his wordes weren so wise.
Justice he was ful often in assise,
By patente and by pleyn commissioun.   315
For his science and for his heigh renoun,
Of fees and robes hadde he many oon.
So greet a purchasour was nowher noon:
Al was fee symple to hym in effect,
His purchasyng myghte nat been infect.   320
Nowher so bisy a man as he ther nas,
And yet he semed bisier than he was.
In termes hadde he caas and doomes alle
That from the tyme of Kyng William were yfalle.
Therto he koude endite and make a thyng,   325
Ther koude no wight pynche at his writyng;
And every statut koude he pleyn by rote.

277 Middelburgh and Orewelle, Middleburgh, Dutch port licensed (stapled) to import English wool 1384–88 (which helps date the composition of the General Prologue); Orwell, the river by Ipswich, one of the English staple ports. **278 eschaunge sheeldes selle,** make money exchanging currencies; "sheeldes" were French gold *florins d'escu.* **279 bisette,** employed. **281 estatly . . . governaunce,** dignified, management. **282 chevyssaunce,** buying and selling on credit for interest. **284 noot how,** don't know what. **285 clerk,** student (all university students then were ostensibly studying for the clergy). **286 logyk,** the top of the bachelor of arts "trivium" (grammar, rhetoric, logic), before proceeding to the master of arts "quadrivium" (arithmetic, geometry, astronomy, music). Perhaps mild humor is intended. **290 overeste courtepy,** overcoat. **291 benefice,** ecclesiastical appointment. **292 office,** secular appointment as clerk in government or for a rich lord. **294 Twenty bookes,** a single large codex, handwritten on enough vellum to make, for example, fifty pairs of shoes, might be worth as much as one-sixth the price of a town house. **296 fithele . . . sautrie,** fiddle, psaltery (harp). **297–98 philosophre . . . gold,** *double entendre* on philosophers as alchemists, whose chief preoccupation was thought to be trying to turn base metals to gold, often with the help of the "philosopher's stone." **299 hente,** get; in a period of patronage, most students in the university were aided by wealthy patrons. **302 scoleye,** study, attend school. **303 cure,** attention. **305 in forme and reverence,** formally and respectfully. **306 sentence,** implication. **307 Sownynge,** resounding, reflecting. **309 Sergeant of the Lawe,** one of about twenty justices especially appointed by the king to act as judges and barons of the exchequer. **war,** wary. **310 Parvys,** paradise, the court in front of a church; in this instance, the porch of St. Paul's Cathedral where lawyers met their clients. **314 Justice . . . assise,** judge, country court. **315 patente . . . pleyn commissioun,** royal warrant, full commission. **316 science . . . renoun,** knowledge, reputation. **317 robes,** payment was frequently in the form of clothing, jewelry, etc. **318 purchasour,** this was the period in which skillful operators were beginning to be able to purchase feudally entailed properties. **319 fee symple,** owned outright, without legal restrictions. **320 infect,** invalidated. **323 In termes . . . caas . . . doomes,** in negotiating, cases, decisions (i.e., the precedents of common law). **324 William,** William the Conqueror. **325 endite and make a thyng,** compose and draw up a legal document. **326 wight pynche,** person protest; again possibly *double entendre,* since there was a contemporary sergeant of the law named Thomas Pynchbek. **327 koude he pleyn by rote,** knew he fully by heart.

He rood but hoomly in a medlee cote,
Girt with a ceint of silk, with barres smale—
Of his array telle I no lenger tale.   330

   A FRANKELEYN was in his compaignye.
Whit was his berd as is the dayesye;
Of his complexioun he was sangwyn.
Wel loved he by the morwe a sop in wyn.
To lyven in delit was evere his wone,   335
For he was Epicurus owene sone,
That heeld opinioun that pleyn delit
Was verray felicitee parfit.
An housholdere, and that a greet, was he;
Seint Julian he was in his contree.   340
His breed, his ale, was alweys after oon.
A bettre envyned man was nowher noon.
Withoute bake mete was nevere his hous,
Of fissh and flessh, and that so plenteuous,
It snewed in his hous of mete and drynke,   345
Of alle deyntees that men koude thynke.
After the sondry sesons of the yeer,
So chaunged he his mete and his soper.
Ful many a fat partrich hadde he in muwe,
And many a breem and many a luce in stuwe.
Wo was his cook but if his sauce were   351
Poynaunt and sharp, and redy al his geere.
His table dormant in his halle alway
Stood redy covered al the longe day.
At sessiouns ther was he lord and sire.   355
Ful ofte tyme he was knyght of the shire.

An anlaas and a gipser al of silk
Heeng at his girdel, whit as morne milk.
A shirreve hadde he been, and a contour.
Was nowher swich a worthy vavasour.   360

   An HABERDASSHERE and a
     CARPENTER,
A WEBBE, a DYERE, and a TAPYCER,
And they were clothed alle in o lyveree
Of a solempne and a greet fraternitee.
Ful fressh and newe hir geere apiked was: 365
Hir knyves were chaped noght with bras
But al with silver; wroght ful clene and weel
Hire girdles and hir pouches everydeel.
Wel semed ech of hem a fair burgeys
To sitten in a yeldehalle on a deys.   370
Everich, for the wisdowm that he kan,
Was shaply for to been an alderman.
For catel hadde they ynogh and rente,
And eek hir wyves wolde it wel assente;
And elles certeyn were they to blame.   375
It is ful fair to been ycleped "madame,"
And goon to vigilies al bifore,
And have a mantel roialliche ybore.

   A COOK they hadde with hem for the nones
To boille the chiknes with the marybones,   380
And poudre-marchant tart and galyngale.
Wel koude he knowe a draughte of Londoun
   ale.

---

328 hoomly . . . medlee, informally, cloth of mixed color. **329 ceint . . . barres,** belt, metal ornaments. **331 Frankeleyn,** a wealthy landowner. **332** *berd:* E *heed.* **333 sangwyn,** the four medieval temperaments (humors) were choleric, phlegmatic, melancholic, and sanguine, the last being characterized by excess of blood and a ruddy complexion. **334 morwe . . . sop in wyn,** morning, bread soaked in wine. **335 delit . . . wone,** sensual pleasure, habit. **336 Epicurus,** the popular view equates Epicureanism with hedonism. **337–38 pleyn delit . . . verray felicitee,** total pleasure, true bliss. **340 Seint Julian,** patron saint of hospitality. **341 after oon,** uniformly good. **342 envyned,** provided with wine. **347–48 sesons . . . chaunged,** menu in accordance with the seasons, such as hot or cold, feast day or fast day. **349 muwe,** coop. **350 breem . . . luce in stuwe,** bream, pike in fish pond. **352 Poynaunt,** piquant. **353 dormant,** laid out; trestle tables were ordinarily removed between meals. **355 sessiouns . . . lord and sire,** at county courts the lord of the manor presided. **356 knyght of the shire,** representative to parliament. **357 anlaas . . . gipser,** dagger, purse. **359 A shirreve . . . a contour,** a sheriff, a tax collector. E&c second *a* om. **360 vavasour,** holder of land by subinfeudation. **361–62 Haberdasshere . . . Webbe . . . Tapycer,** dealer in men's clothes and sewing notions, weaver, tapestry weaver. **363–64 o lyveree . . . fraternitee,** same uniform; the guildsmen belonged to a liveried parish fraternity having both religious and social functions, perhaps the Guild of St. Fabian and St. Sebastian of St. Botolph's Church in Aldersgate Ward, which was a center of the cloth trade. **365 apiked,** furbished. **366 chaped,** mounted. **369–70 burgeys . . . yeldehalle . . . deys,** prosperous citizen, guildhall, platform. **371 kan,** knew. **372 shaply . . . alderman,** suitable, elected official. **373 catel . . . rente,** chattels (property), income. Only prosperous people could afford the entertaining and other expenses attendant upon civic office. **377 vigilies,** services before guild festivals at which aldermen's wives would enjoy precedence. **379 nones,** occasion. **380 marybones,** marrowbones. **381 poudre-marchant tart . . . galyngale,** tart spice, sweet spice. **382 knowe . . . Londoun ale,** recognize; London ale was particularly good.

He koude rooste and sethe and broille and
   frye,
Maken mortreux, and wel bake a pye.
But greet harm was it, as it thoughte me,   385
That on his shyne a mormal hadde he.
For blankmanger, that made he with the beste.

   A SHIPMAN was ther, wonynge fer by
   weste.
For aught I woot, he was of Dertemouthe.
He rood upon a rouncy, as he kouthe,   390
In a gowne of faldyng to the knee.
A daggere hangynge on a laas hadde he
Aboute his nekke, under his arm adoun.
The hoote somer hadde maad his hewe al broun.
And certeinly he was a good felawe.   395
Ful many a draughte of wyn had he ydrawe
Fro Burdeux-ward, whil that the chapman
   sleepe.
Of nyce conscience took he no keepe.
If that he faught, and hadde the hyer hond,
By water he sente hem hoom to every lond.   400
But of his craft to rekene wel his tydes,
His stremes, and his daungers hym bisides,
His herberwe, and his moone, his lodemenage,
Ther nas noon swich from Hulle to Cartage.
Hardy he was and wys to undertake.   405
With many a tempest hadde his berd been shake.
He knew alle the havenes, as they were,
Fro Gootlond to the cape of Fynystere,
And every cryke in Britaigne and in Spayne.
His barge ycleped was the Maudelayne.   410

With us ther was a DOCTOUR OF PHISIK;
In al this world ne was ther noon hym lik,
To speke of phisik and of surgerye,
For he was grounded in astronomye.
He kepte his pacient a ful greet deel   415
In houres by his magyk natureel.
Wel koude he fortunen the ascendent
Of his ymages for his pacient.
He knew the cause of everich maladye,   419
Were it of hoot, or coold, or moyste, or drye,
And where engendred, and of what humour.
He was a verray, parfit praktisour.
The cause yknowe, and of his harm the roote,
Anon he yaf the sike man his boote.
Ful redy hadde he his apothecaries   425
To sende hym drogges and his letuaries,
For ech of hem made oother for to wynne—
Hir frendshipe nas nat newe to bigynne.
Wel knew he the olde Esculapius,
And Deyscorides, and eek Rufus,   430
Olde Ypocras, Haly, and Galyen,
Serapion, Razis, and Avycen,
Averrois, Damascien, and Constantyn,
Bernard, and Gatesden, and Gilbertyn.
Of his diete mesurable was he,   435
For it was of no superfluitee,
But of greet norissyng and digestible.
His studie was but litel on the Bible.
In sangwyn and in pers he clad was al,
Lyned with taffata and with sendal,   440
And yet he was but esy of dispence.
He kepte that he wan in pestilence,

---

383 sethe, boil. *broille:* E&c *boille.* **384 mortreux,** stews. **386 mormal,** a pustulous sore. **387 blankmanger,** a white pudding of milk, rice, and condiments. **388 wonynge,** living. **389 Dertemouthe,** a port in Devonshire notorious for smugglers and pirates. **390 rouncy . . . kouthe,** a pack horse; he rode like a sailor. **391 faldyng,** coarse wool. **392 laas,** lace, strap. **396 *ydrawe:*** E&c *drawe.* **397 Burdeux-ward . . . chapman,** coming from Bordeaux, merchant. **398 nyce . . . keepe,** scrupulous, heed. **399 hyer hond,** victory. **400 By water,** he threw his victims overboard. **401 craft to rekene,** skill to calculate. **402 stremes,** currents. **403 herberwe . . . moone . . . lodemenage,** anchorage, moon (most legitimate seamen navigate during the day by the sun), piloting. **404 Hulle . . . Cartage,** Hull in northern England, Carthage in North Africa or Cartagena in Spain. **408 Gootlond . . . Fynystere,** Gotland in the Baltic, "land's end" in Spain. **409 cryke . . . Britaigne,** creek (smuggler's haven), Brittany. **410 Maudelayne,** Peter Risshenden was in 1391 recorded as the master of a ship named the Maudeleyne out of Darmouth. **414 astronomye,** astrology; the effects of medicines and treatments (natural magic) were thought to depend upon a person's horoscope. **416 houres,** the favorable hours of the horoscope. **417–18 ascendent . . . ymages,** presumably astrological representations related to the patient's horoscope. **420 hoot . . . coold** &c, the four humors. **422 verray, parfit,** true, perfect. **424 boote,** remedy. **426 letuaries,** electuaries (drugs in syrups). **427 wynne,** profit. **429ff. Esculapius,** Dioscorides, Rufus, Hippocrates, Galen, famous Greek physicians. **Serapion,** Hali (Ali Ben el-Abbas), Rhazes, Avicenna, Averroes, Persian and Arabic physicians. **Damascien,** Constantinus Africanus, early Christian physicians. **Bernard** Gordon, John Gaddesden, Gilbertus Anglicus, famous British physicians. Gaddesden was an instructor at Merton College and court physician. *Rufus:* E *Risus,* and various readings in other MSS. **435 mesurable,** moderate. **439 sangwyn . . . pers,** red, blue. **440 taffata . . . sendal,** varieties of silk. **441 esy of dispence,** moderate of expenditure. **442 wan, pestilence,** acquired, plague.

For gold in phisik is a cordial;
Therefore he lovede gold in special.

A good WIF was ther OF biside BATHE,   445
But she was somdel deef, and that was scathe.
Of clooth makyng she hadde swich an haunt,
She passed hem of Ypres and of Gaunt.
In al the parisshe wif ne was ther noon
That to the offrynge bifore hire sholde goon;   450
And if ther dide, certeyn so wrooth was she
That she was out of alle charitee.
Hir coverchiefs ful fyne weren of ground.
I dorste swere they weyeden ten pound
That on a Sonday weren upon hir heed.   455
Hir hosen weren of fyn scarlet reed,
Ful streite yteyd, and shoes ful moyste and
        newe.
Boold was hir face, and fair, and reed of hewe.
She was a worthy womman al hir lyve.
Housbondes at chirche dore she hadde fyve,   460
Withouten oother compaignye in youthe—
But therof nedeth nat to speke as nowthe.
And thries hadde she been at Jerusalem.
She hadde passed many a straunge strem.
At Rome she hadde been, and at Boloigne,   465
In Galice at Seint-Jame, and at Coloigne.
She koude muchel of wandrynge by the weye.
Gat-tothed was she, soothly for to seye.
Upon an amblere esily she sat,
Ywympled wel, and on hir heed an hat   470
As brood as is a bokeler or a targe,
A foot-mantel aboute hir hipes large,
And on hir feet a paire of spores sharpe.

In felaweshipe wel koude she laughe and carpe.
Of remedies of love she knew per chaunce,   475
For she koude of that art the olde daunce.

A good man was ther of religioun,
And was a poure PERSOUN of a toun,
But riche he was of hooly thoght and werk.
He was also a lerned man, a clerk,   480
That Cristes gospel trewely wolde preche.
His parisshens devoutly wolde he teche.
Benygne he was, and wonder diligent,
And in adversitee ful pacient,
And swich he was preved ofte sithes.   485
Ful looth were hym to cursen for his tithes,
But rather wolde he yeven, out of doute,
Unto his poure parisshens aboute
Of his offryng and eek of his substaunce.
He koude in litel thyng have suffisaunce.   490
Wyd was his parisshe and houses fer asonder,
But he ne lefte nat, for reyn ne thonder,
In siknesse nor in meschief to visite
The ferreste in his parisshe, muche and lite,
Upon his feet, and in his hand a staf.   495
This noble ensample to his sheep he yaf,
That first he wroghte, and afterward he taughte.
Out of the gospel he tho wordes caughte,
And this figure he added eek therto,
That if gold ruste, what shal iren do?   500
For if a preest be foul, on whom we truste,
No wonder is a lewed man to ruste.
And shame it is, if a preest take keep,
A shiten shepherde and a clene sheep.
Wel oghte a preest ensample for to yive,   505

---

443 **gold** &c, *double entendre: aurum potibile* was a certified medieval medicine. 445 **biside Bathe,** St. Michael's *juxta Bathon* was a parish just north of Bath given over to weaving. 446 **scathe,** unfortunate. 447 **haunt,** skill. 448 **passed . . . Ypres . . . Gaunt,** surpassed; perhaps humorous since the west of England weavers were known to be inferior to those of the Low Countries (Ypres and Ghent are both in modern Belgium). 450 **offrynge bifore,** precedence in church was evidently important, see l. 377 above and *Parson's Tale, CT,* x.407. 453 **coverchiefs . . . ground,** kerchiefs, texture. 454 **ten pound,** again humorous exaggeration. 456 **hosen,** tight, laced leggings. 457 **streite,** straitly (closely). 460 **chirche door,** the marriage was performed at the door, after which the couple entered the church for mass. 461 **Withouten,** without counting. 463ff. **Jerusalem** &c, Rome, Boulogne (France), St. James of Compostella in Galicia (Spain), Cologne (Germany). 467 **koude,** knew. 468 **Gat-tothed,** gap-toothed, by physiognomists supposed to indicate a bold, lascivious nature. Some MSS have *Gap-tothed.* 469 **amblere,** easy-gaited saddle horse. 470 **Ywympled,** swathed in a headdress that covered all but the face. 471 **bokeler . . . targe,** terms for shields. 472 **foot-mantel,** a protective outer skirt. 474 **carpe,** joke. 475 **remedies,** one of Ovid's erotic books is the *Remedia Amoris.* 478 **Persoun,** Parson. 482 **parisshens,** parishioners. 485 **swich . . . sithes,** such, times. 486 **cursen . . . tithes,** excommunicate, one tenth of one's income owed to the church. 489 **offryng . . . substaunce,** voluntary offering to the priest, income from property belonging to the church. 490 **suffisaunce,** sufficiency. 494 **ferreste . . . muche and lite,** farthest, great and small. 495 **staf,** emblem of the good shepherd. 497 **wroghte,** performed. 502 **lewed,** ignorant. 503 **keep,** heed. 504 **shiten,** befouled with excrement.

By his clennesse, how that his sheep sholde lyve.
He sette nat his benefice to hyre
And leet his sheep encombred in the myre
And ran to Londoun unto Seinte Poules
To seken hym a chaunterie for soules,   510
Or with a bretherhed to been withholde,
But dwelte at hoom, and kepte wel his folde
So that the wolf ne made it nat myscarie.
He was a shepherde and noght a mercenarie.
And though he hooly were and vertuous,   515
He was nat to synful men despitous,
Ne of his speche daungerous ne digne,
But in his techyng discreet and benygne.
To drawen folk to hevene by fairnesse,
By good ensample, this was his bisynesse.   520
But it were any persone obstinat,
What so he were, of heigh or lough estat,
Hym wolde he snybben sharply for the nonys.
A bettre preest I trowe that nowher noon ys.
He waited after no pompe and reverence   525
Ne maked hym a spiced conscience,
But Cristes loore and his apostles twelve
He taughte, but first he folwed it hymselve.

With hym ther was a PLOWMAN, was his
    brother,
That hadde ylad of dong ful many a fother.   530
A trewe swynkere and a good was he,
Lyvynge in pees and parfit charitee.
God loved he best with al his hoole herte
At alle tymes, thogh him gamed or smerte,
And thanne his neighebore right as hymselve.

He wolde thresshe, and therto dyke and delve,
For Cristes sake, for every poure wight,   537
Withouten hire, if it lay in his myght.
His tithes payde he ful faire and wel,
Bothe of his propre swynk and his catel.   540
In a tabard he rood upon a mere.

    Ther was also a REVE, and a MILLERE,
A SOMNOUR, and a PARDONER also,
A MAUNCIPLE, and myself—ther were namo.

    The MILLERE was a stout carl for the nones;
Ful byg he was of brawn, and eek of bones.   546
That proved wel, for over al ther he cam,
At wrastlynge he wolde have alwey the ram.
He was short-sholdred, brood, a thikke knarre;
Ther was no dore that he nolde heve of harre,
Or breke it at a rennyng with his heed.   551
His berd as any sowe or fox was reed,
And therto brood, as though it were a spade.
Upon the cop right of his nose he hade
A werte, and theron stood a toft of herys   555
Reed as the brustles of a sowes erys.
His nosethirles blake were and wyde.
A swerd and bokeler bar he by his syde.
His mouth as greet was as a greet forneys.
He was a janglere and a goliardeys,   560
And that was moost of synne and harlotries.
Wel koude he stelen corn and tollen thries.
And yet he hadde a thombe of gold, pardee.
A whit cote and a blew hood wered he.   564
A baggepipe wel koude he blowe and sowne,

507ff. **hyre . . . ran to Londoun,** hire someone to care for his parish and himself take another job in London (see l. 219 above). **510 chaunterie,** cathedral chapel endowed for a priest to say daily masses for the souls of the endowers. **511 bretherhed . . . withholde,** guild, to be supported. **512** *dwelte, kepte:* E *dweleth, kepeth.* **516 despitous,** contemptuous. Some MSS *men nat.* **517 daungerous ne digne,** disdainful nor haughty. **521 But it,** but if any person. **523 snybben . . . nonys,** scold, promptly (without hesitation). **525 waited after,** expected. *waited:* E *waiteth.* **526 spiced,** overfastidious, affected. **530 fother,** cart load. **531 swynkere,** laborer. **534 gamed or smerte,** pleasant or unpleasant. **535 neighebore,** medieval Christian doctrine was summed up in Matthew 22:37–39: "Thou shalt love the Lord thy God with all thy heart, and with all thy soul, and with all thy mind. This is the first and great commandment. And the second is like unto it, Thou shalt love thy neighbour as thyself." **536 dyke and delve,** ditch and dig. **537 wight,** person. **540 propre swynk . . . catel,** own labor, property. **541 tabard,** workingman's smock. For whatever it may signify, this was also the name of the Southwark inn at which Chaucer's Canterbury pilgrimage begins. **mere,** a gentle mount traditionally ridden by priests and women. **545 carl,** Danish form of churl, fellow. This description should be compared with that in RvT, *CT* I.3925ff. **548 ram,** a prize at country contests. **549 knarre,** knot (as in wood). **550 dore . . . of harre,** door off its hinges. **551 rennyng,** running (at), butting—such heaving and butting were evidently the Miller's ideas of sport. **554 cop,** ridge. **557 nosethirles,** nostrils. **558 bokeler,** shield. **559 forneys,** furnace; medieval representations of the gaping mouth of hell come to mind. **560 janglere . . . goliardeys,** windbag, teller of dirty stories. By Chaucer's day *goliard* meant a vagabond cleric with a reputation like that of any casual traveling man. **562 tollen thries,** take his toll or percentage thrice. **563 thombe of gold,** *double entendre,* a thumb skilled in testing grain and flour, but there was also a proverb, "An honest miller has a golden thumb," meaning there is no such thing as an honest miller.

And therwithal he broghte us out of towne.

A gentil MAUNCIPLE was ther of a temple,
Of which achatours myghte take exemple
For to be wise in byynge of vitaille.
For wheither that he payde or took by taille,
Algate he wayted so in his achaat   571
That he was ay biforn and in good staat.
Now is nat that of God a ful fair grace
That swich a lewed mannes wit shal pace
The wisdom of an heep of lerned men?   575
Of maistres hadde he mo than thries ten
That weren of lawe expert and curious,
Of which ther were a duszeyne in that hous
Worthy to been stywardes of rente and lond
Of any lord that is in Engelond,   580
To maken hym lyve by his propre good
In honour dettelees, but if he were wood,
Or lyve as scarsly as hym list desire;
And able for to helpen al a shire
In any caas that myghte falle or happe—   585
And yet this Manciple sette hir aller cappe.

The REVE was a sclendre colerik man.
His berd was shave as ny as ever he kan.
His heer was by his erys ful round yshorn.
His top was dokked lyk a preest biforn.   590
Ful longe were his legges and ful lene,
Ylyk a staf: ther was no calf ysene.
Wel koude he kepe a gerner and a bynne.
Ther was noon auditour koude on him wynne.

Wel wiste he by the droghte and by the reyn   595
The yeldynge of his seed and of his greyn.
His lordes sheep, his neet, his dayerye,
His swyn, his hors, his stoor, and his pultrye
Was hoolly in this Reves governynge,
And by his covenant yaf the rekenynge,   600
Syn that his lord was twenty yeer of age.
Ther koude no man brynge hym in arrerage.
Ther nas baillif, ne hierde, nor oother hyne
That he ne knew his sleighte and his covyne;
They were adrad of hym as of the deeth.   605
His wonyng was ful faire upon an heeth;
With grene trees shadwed was his place.
He koude bettre than his lord purchace;
Ful riche he was astored pryvely.
His lord wel koude he plesen subtilly,   610
To yeve and lene hym of his owene good,
And have a thank, and yet a cote and hood.
In youthe he hadde lerned a good myster,
He was a wel good wrighte, a carpenter.
This Reve sat upon a ful good stot,   615
That was al pomely grey and highte Scot.
A long surcote of pers upon he hade,
And by his syde he baar a rusty blade.
Of Northfolk was this Reve of which I telle,
Biside a toun men clepen Baldeswelle.   620
Tukked he was as is a frere aboute,
And evere he rood the hyndreste of oure route.

A SOMONOUR was ther with us in that
   place

567 **Maunciple . . . temple,** business agent for a college, in this case for one of the Inns of Court, two of which occupied buildings confiscated when the order of Knights Templars was suppressed in 1312. Chaucer may have attended such an institution and observed such a clever servant. 568 **achatours,** purchasers. 570 **taille,** talley, i.e., on credit. 571 **wayted . . . achaat,** attended, buying. 574 **swich a lewed . . . pace,** such an unlearned, surpass. 577 **curious,** cunning. 579 **stywardes . . . rente,** stewards (managers), income. 581 **lyve by . . . good,** live within his own means. 582 **wood,** crazy. 583 **scarsly,** economically. 585 **caas . . . falle or happe,** situation, befall or happen. 586 **sette hir aller cappe,** deceived them all. 587 **Reve,** reeve, manager of a farm. **colerik,** of bilious humor, peevish. 588 **shave,** being shaved in a full-bearded age was unnatural, sinister. In illustrations, Satan is never bearded *vs.* the full-bearded Lord. 590 **dokked,** cut short, see the Yeoman, l. 109 above. 593 **kepe a gerner,** protect a granary. 594 **auditour,** the lord's accountant who audited the Reeve's receipts and expenditures. 597 **neet,** cattle. 598 **stoor,** livestock. 600 **covenant,** contract. 603 **baillif, hierde, hyne,** farm boss, herdsman, farm laborer. 604 **sleighte . . . covyne,** trick, dishonesty. E&c *ne* om. 606 **wonyng,** home. 608 **bettre . . . purchace,** had more money with which to buy. 609 **astored,** wealth in Chaucer's time would be reckoned more in food and equipment stored away than in money in the bank. 611 **lene,** lend. 612 **cote and hood,** payment was frequently in clothing, see l. 317 above. E&c *yet a gowne.* 613 **myster,** mystery, craft. 615 **stot,** farm horse. 616 **pomely . . . highte,** dappled, was called. 617 **surcote of pers,** blue overcoat. 619–20 **Northfolk . . . Baldeswelle,** Chaucer was indirectly concerned with the management of some of the Norfolk estates of the young Earl of Pembroke (although not this one). Perhaps he had had dealings there with someone like this reeve. 622 **hyndreste . . . route,** last in our company; since the Miller evidently rode at the head of the procession (l. 566 above), it appears that Chaucer was already preparing for their quarrel. 623 **Somonour,** a process-server for the ecclesiastical courts, which were charged with regulating morals and domestic life, and were, by Chaucer's time, in very low repute.

That hadde a fyr-reed cherubynnes face,

For sawcefleem he was, with eyen narwe.   625

As hoot he was and lecherous as a sparwe,

With scalled browes blake and piled berd.

Of his visage children were aferd.

Ther nas quyksilver, lytarge, ne brymstoon,

Boras, ceruce, ne oille of tartre noon,   630

Ne oynement that wolde clense and byte,

That hym myghte helpen of his whelkes white,

Nor of the knobbes sittynge on his chekes.

Wel loved he garleek, oynons, and eek lekes,

And for to drynken strong wyn, reed as
  blood.   635

Thanne wolde he speke and crie as he were
  wood,

And whan that he wel dronken hadde the wyn,

Thanne wolde he speke no word but Latyn.

A fewe termes hadde he, two or thre,

That he had lerned out of som decree—   640

No wonder is, he herde it al the day,

And eek ye knowen wel how that a jay

Kan clepen "Watte" as wel as kan the pope.

But whoso koude in oother thyng hym grope,

Thanne hadde he spent al his philosophie.   645

Ay "Questio quid iuris" wolde he crie.

He was a gentil harlot and a kynde;

A bettre felawe sholde men noght fynde.

He wolde suffre for a quart of wyn

A good felawe to have his concubyn   650

A twelf-monthe, and excuse hym atte fulle.

Ful prively a fynch eek koude he pulle.

And if he foond owher a good felawe,

He wolde techen hym to have noon awe

In swich caas of the ercedekenes curs,   655

But if a mannes soule were in his purs,

For in his purs he sholde ypunysshed be.

"Purs is the ercedekenes helle," seyde he.

But wel I woot he lyed right in dede.

Of cursyng oghte ech gilty man him drede,   660

For curs wol slee right as assoillyng savith,

And also war hym of a *Significavit.*

In daunger hadde he at his owene gise

The yonge girles of the diocise,

And knew hir conseil, and was al hir reed.   665

A gerland hadde he set upon his heed

As greet as it were for an alestake.

A bokeleer hadde he maad hym of a cake.

    With hym ther rood a gentil PARDONER

Of Rouncivale, his freend and his compeer,   670

That streight was comen fro the court of Rome.

Ful loude he soong "Com hider, love, to me!"

This Somonour bar to hym a stif burdoun.

Was nevere trompe of half so greet a soun.

This Pardoner hadde heer as yelow as wex,   675

But smothe it heeng as dooth a strike of flex.

By ounces henge his lokkes that he hadde,

And therwith he his shuldres overspradde,

But thynne it lay, by colpons oon and oon.

But hood, for jolitee, wered he noon,   680

624–25 fyr-reed ... sawcefleem ... narwe, suffering from a skin disease which caused facial swelling and narrowing of the eyes. **626 hoot,** hot, lascivious. **627 scalled ... piled,** scabby, bald in spots. **629–30 quyksilver, lytarge, brymstoon, Boras, ceruce, oille of tartre,** mercury, white lead, sulfur, borax, again white lead, cream of tartar. **632 whelkes,** pustules. **634 garleek** &c, foods thought in the Middle Ages to inflame sexual desire and cause skin disease. The Israelites hungered after these pungent Egyptian foods in contrast to manna, Numbers 11:5. **636 wood,** demented. **637–38** Lines omitted in Hg&c. **643 clepen "Watte,"** say "Wat" (Walter). **644 grope,** test. **646 Questio quid iuris,** "The question is, what point of law applies?" A familiar tag in legal proceedings. **647 harlot,** rascal. **652 fynch ... pulle,** perhaps *double entendre,* pluck a bird (blackmail), but with sexual or even homosexual overtones. **653 owher ... good felawe,** anywhere, boon companion. **655 ercedekenes curs,** archdeacon's excommunication; the archdeacon presided over ecclesiastical courts, whose punishments were supposed to be penance and excommunication rather than prison and execution. **656 But if,** unless. **660 him drede:** E&c *him* om. **661 assoillyng,** absolution. **662 war ... Significavit,** beware, "Be it known" (the opening of a writ of excommunication). **663 daunger ... gise,** power, pleasure. **664 girles,** *double entendre,* the word could still mean simply young person (of either sex), but it was beginning to be restricted to young females, and Chaucer so uses it at I.3769. **665 reed,** counselor. **667 greet ... alestake,** the sign of a tavern was a horizontal stake projecting into the street, adorned by a wreath or bush. **668 bokeleer ... cake,** shield, round loaf. **669–70 Pardoner of Rouncivale ... compeer,** Pardoners were employed by religious and charitable institutions (like the dependent house of the Spanish order of Our Lady of Roncevaux which maintained a hospital at Charing Cross, just outside of London) to sell indulgences, or commutations of penances imposed for sins. By the 14th century sale of indulgences was a major source of revenue for all branches of the Church and very serious abuses had arisen. The Sumnour should have been the one protecting people against these abuses. **672 "Com hider ...,"** line from a popular love song. **673 stif burdoun,** strong bass. **676–77 strike of flex ... ounces,** hank of flax, small bits. **679 colpons oon,** strands one. **680 jolitee,** pleasure, affectation.

For it was trussed up in his walet.
Hym thoughte he rood al of the newe jet;
Dischevelee, save his cappe, he rood al bare.
Swiche glarynge eyen hadde he as an hare.
A vernycle hadde he sowed upon his cappe.   685
His walet lay biforn hym in his lappe,
Bretful of pardoun, comen from Rome al
    hoot.
A voys he hadde as smal as hath a goot.
No berd hadde he, ne nevere sholde have.
As smothe it was as it were late shave.   690
I trowe he were a geldyng or a mare.
But of his craft, fro Berwyk into Ware,
Ne was ther swich another pardoner.
For in his male he hadde a pilwe-beer,
Which that he seyde was Oure Lady veyl.   695
He seyde he hadde a gobet of the seyl
That Seint Peter hadde, whan that he wente
Upon the see, til Jhesu Crist hym hente.
He hadde a croys of latoun ful of stones,
And in a glas he hadde pigges bones.   700
But with thise relikes, whan that he fond
A poure person dwellynge upon lond,
Upon a day he gat hym moore moneye
Than that the person gat in monthes tweye.
And thus, with feyned flaterye and japes,   705
He made the person and the peple his apes.
But trewely to tellen atte laste,
He was in chirche a noble ecclesiaste.
Wel koude he rede a lessoun or a storie,
But alderbest he song an offertorie,   710
For wel he wiste, whan that song was songe,
He moste preche and wel affile his tonge

To wynne silver, as he ful wel koude;
Therefore he song the murierly and loude.

    Now have I toold you shortly, in a clause,   715
Th'estaat, th'array, the nombre, and eek the
    cause
Why that assembled was this compaignye
In Southwerk at this gentil hostelrye
That highte the Tabard, faste by the Belle.
But now is tyme to yow for to telle   720
How that we baren us that ilke nyght,
Whan we were in that hostelrie alyght.
And after wol I telle of oure viage
And al the remenaunt of oure pilgrimage.
But first I pray yow, of youre curteisye,   725
That ye n'arette it nat my vileynye,
Thogh that I pleynly speke in this mateere,
To telle yow hir wordes and hir cheere,
Ne thogh I speke hir wordes proprely.
For this ye knowen al so wel as I,   730
Whoso shal telle a tale after a man,
He moot reherce as ny as evere he kan
Everich a word, if it be in his charge,
Al speke he never so rudeliche and large,
Or ellis he moot telle his tale untrewe,   735
Or feyne thyng, or fynde wordes newe.
He may nat spare, althogh he were his brother;
He moot as wel seye o word as another.
Crist spak hymself ful brode in hooly writ,
And wel ye woot no vileynye is it.   740
Eek Plato seith, whoso kan hym rede,
The wordes moote be cosyn to the dede.
Also I prey yow to foryeve it me,

---

682 newe jet, new fashion. **683 Dischevelee . . . bare,** with hair loose, bareheaded; until recently going bareheaded in public had been considered immodest. **684 Swiche glarynge,** such staring. **685 vernycle,** a small veronica. St. Veronica was reputed to have lent Jesus her kerchief to wipe his face when he was carrying the cross to Calvary. When he returned it to her, his features were miraculously imprinted on it. Copies of this "vera icon" (true likeness) were sold in Rome as pilgrims' mementos. **686 E&c** *lay* om. **687 Bretful of pardoun,** brimful; here as elsewhere (see "relikes and pardoun," *CT* vi.920), "pardoun" is plural. **691 geldyng,** the signs lead to the conclusion that the Pardoner was impotent. His impotence intimates the impotence of his pardons as the Sumnour's disease intimates the corruption of the ecclesiastical courts. **692 Berwyk . . . Ware,** Berwick-on-Tweed, south of Edinburgh, Ware, north of London—i.e., from one end of England to the other. **694 pilwe-beer,** pillowcase. **696 gobet,** big piece. **698 hente,** grasped, when he tried to walk on the water, Matthew 14:31. **699 latoun . . . stones,** fake gold (copper alloy), set with fake jewels. **700–701 bones . . . relikes,** fake religious relics. **702 upon lond,** in the country. **705 feyned . . . japes,** pretended, tricks. **706 apes,** made monkeys of them. **710 alderbest,** best of all. **711 wiste,** knew. **712 affile,** file, sharpen. **719 Belle,** no inn named the Bell has been identified near the Southwark Tabard. This was the name of one of the licensed houses of prostitution in Southwark in the 16th century, and perhaps in the 14th. **721 baren . . . ilke,** conducted, same. **726 arette . . . vileynye,** attribute, vulgarity. **728 cheere,** attitude(s). **729 proprely,** exactly. **733 charge,** power. **734 large,** broadly, indecorously. **736 feyne,** pretend. **737 he were,** the protagonist of the tale. **738 o word,** one word. **740 woot,** know. **741 Plato,** *Timaeus* 29, but Chaucer took it from Boethius, cf. III pr.12, 1. 207 in his translation.

Al have I nat set folk in hir degree
Heere in this tale, as that they sholde stonde. 745
My wit is short, ye may wel understonde.

   Greet chiere made oure Hoost us everichon,
And to the soper sette he us anon.
He served us with vitaille at the beste. 749
Strong was the wyn, and wel to drynke us leste.
A semely man oure HOOSTE was withalle
For to been a marchal in an halle.
A large man he was with eyen stepe—
A fairer burgeys was ther noon in Chepe—
Boold of his speche, and wys, and wel ytaught,
And of manhod hym lakked right naught. 756
Eek therto he was right a myrie man,
And after soper pleyen he bigan,
And spak of myrthe amonges othere thynges,
Whan that we hadde maad our rekenynges, 760
And seyde thus: "Now, lordynges, trewely,
Ye been to me right welcome, hertely;
For by my trouthe, if that I shal nat lye,
I saugh nat this yeer so myrie a compaignye
Atones in this herberwe as is now. 765
Fayn wolde I doon yow myrthe, wiste I how.
And of a myrthe I am right now bythoght,
To doon yow ese, and it shal coste noght.

   "Ye goon to Caunterbury—God yow speede!
The blisful martir quite yow youre meede! 770
And wel I woot, as ye goon by the weye,
Ye shapen yow to talen and to pleye.
For trewely, confort ne myrthe is noon
To ride by the weye doumb as a stoon.
And therfore wol I maken yow disport, 775
As I seyde erst, and doon yow som confort.
And if yow liketh alle by oon assent
For to stonden at my juggement,
And for to werken as I shal yow seye,
To-morwe, whan ye riden by the weye, 780

Now, by my fader soule that is deed,
But ye be myrie, I wol yeve yow myn heed!
Hoold up youre hondes, withouten moore
   speche."
   Oure conseil was nat longe for to seche. 784
Us thoughte it was noght worth to make it wys,
And graunted hym withouten moore avys,
And bad him seye his voirdit as hym leste.

   "Lordynges," quod he, "now herkneth for
   the beste,
But taak it nought, I prey yow, in desdeyn.
This is the poynt, to speken short and pleyn, 790
That ech of yow, to shorte with oure weye,
In this viage shal telle tales tweye
To Caunterbury-ward, I mene it so,
And homward he shal tellen othere two,
Of aventures that whilom han bifalle. 795
And which of yow that bereth hym best of alle,
That is to seyn, that telleth in this caas
Tales of best sentence and moost solaas,
Shal have a soper at oure aller cost
Heere in this place, sittynge by this post, 800
Whan that we come agayn fro Caunterbury.
And for to make yow the moore mury,
I wol myselven goodly with yow ryde,
Right at myn owene cost, and be youre gyde.
And whoso wole my juggement withseye 805
Shal paye al that we spenden by the weye.
And if ye vouchesauf that it be so,
Tel me anon withouten wordes mo,
And I wol erly shape me therfore."

   This thyng was graunted, and oure othes
   swore 810
With ful glad herte, and preyden hym also
That he wolde vouchesauf for to do so,
And that he wolde been oure governour,
And of our tales juge and reportour,

---

744 nat set, in a court poem, the author might be expected to observe precedence in the order of the tales. **751 semely,** appropriate, impressive. *Hooste:* final e lacking here and elsewhere in MSS but meter always calls for disyllabic pronunciation. **752 marchal,** marshall, major-domo. **753 stepe,** bright, prominent. **754 burgeys . . . Chepe,** citizen, Cheapside, the main business street of London. **758 pleyen,** to be sociable. **760 maad our rekenynges,** paid our bills. **765 Atones . . . herberwe,** at one time, hostel. **766 Fayn . . . wiste,** gladly, if I knew. **767 myrthe,** an entertainment. **770 quite . . . meede,** repay, reward. **771 woot,** know. **772 talen . . . pleye,** tell tales, enjoy yourselves. **775 disport,** diversion. **778 stonden . . . juggement,** accept my direction or idea. **784 conseil . . . seche,** deliberation, seek. **785 make it wys,** make an issue of it. **786 avys,** deliberation. **787 voirdit . . . leste,** verdict (idea), desired. **791 shorte with,** make shorter. **795 whilom,** once upon a time. **796 bereth hym,** conducts himself. **798 sentence . . . solaas,** wisdom, delight. **799 at oure aller cost,** at the expense of all of us. **803** *goodly:* some MSS *gladly.* **805 withseye,** contradict. **807 vouchesauf,** agree. **809 shape,** prepare. **814 reportour,** accountant.

And sette a soper at a certeyn pris,   815
And we wol reuled been at his devys
In heigh and lough. And thus by oon assent
We been acorded to his juggement.
And therupon the wyn was fet anon.
We dronken, and to reste wente echon   820
Withouten any lenger taryynge.
Amorwe, whan that day gan for to sprynge,
Up roos oure Hoost, and was oure aller cok,
And gadrede us togidre alle in a flok,
And forth we riden a litel moore than paas 825
Unto the wateryng of Seint Thomas.

And there oure Hoost bigan his hors areste
And seyde, "Lordynges, herkneth, if yow leste.
Ye woot youre foreward, and it yow recorde.
If even-song and morwe-song accorde,   830
Lat se now who shal telle the firste tale.
As evere mote I drynke wyn or ale,
Whoso be rebel to my juggement
Shal paye for al that by the wey is spent.   834
Now draweth cut, er that we ferrer twynne;
He which that hath the shorteste shal bigynne.
Sire Knyght," quod he, "my mayster and my
    lord,

Now draweth cut, for that is myn accord.
Cometh neer," quod he, "my lady Prioresse.
And ye, sire Clerk, lat be youre shamefastnesse,
Ne studieth noght; ley hond to, every man!"
     Anon to drawen every wight bigan,   842
And shortly for to tellen as it was,
Were it by aventure, or sort, or cas,
The sothe is this, the cut fil to the Knyght,   845
Of which ful blithe and glad was every
    wyght,
And telle he moste his tale, as was resoun,
By foreward and by composicioun,
As ye han herd. What nedeth wordes mo?
And whan this goode man saugh that it
    was so,
As he that wys was and obedient   851
To kepe his foreward by his free assent,
He seyde, "Syn I shal bigynne the game,
What, welcome be the cut, a Goddes name!
Now lat us ryde, and herkneth what I seye." 855
And with that word we ryden forth oure
    weye,
And he bigan with right a myrie cheere
His tale anon, and seyde in this manere.

---

816 devys, will. **817 heigh and lough,** in all respects. **822** *gan for:* other MSS *bigan.* **823 aller,** of all. **825 litel . . . paas,** leisurely, at little more than a footpace. **826 wateryng of Seint Thomas,** a place for watering horses about a mile and a half on from the Tabard. **829 foreward,** agreement. **835 draweth cut . . . ferrer,** draw straws, farther. **841 studieth,** don't daydream. **842 wight,** person. **844 aventure, sort, cas,** all mean "by chance." **845 sothe,** truth. **847 resoun,** reasonable. **848 foreward . . . composicioun,** agreement, arrangement.

KNIGHT'S TALE

Heere bigynneth the Knyghtes Tale.

Iamque domos patrias Scithice post aspera gentis Prelia laurigero &c.

Whilom, as olde stories tellen us,
Ther was a duc that highte Theseus. 860
Of Atthenes he was lord and governour,
And in his tyme swich a conquerour,
That gretter was ther noon under the sonne.
Ful many a riche contree hadde he wonne,
What with his wysdom and his chivalrie; 865
He conquered al the regne of Femenye,
That whilom was ycleped Scithia,
And wedded the queene Ypolita,
And broghte hire hoom with hym in his
  contree
With muchel glorie and greet solempnytee, 870
And eek hir yonge suster Emelye.
And thus with victorie and with melodye
Lete I this noble duc to Atthenes ryde,
And al his hoost in armes hym bisyde.

And certes, if it nere to long to heere, 875
I wolde yow have toold fully the manere
How wonnen was the regne of Femenye
By Theseus and by his chivalrye,
And of the grete bataille for the nones
Bitwixen Atthenes and Amazones, 880
And how asseged was Ypolita,
The faire, hardy queene of Scithia,
And of the feste that was at hir weddynge,
And of the tempest at hir hoom-comynge—
But al that thyng I moot as now forbere. 885
I have, God woot, a large feeld to ere,
And wayke been the oxen in my plough.
The remenant of the tale is long ynough.
I wol nat letten eek noon of this route.
Lat every felawe telle his tale aboute, 890
And lat se now who shal the soper wynne;

Iamque domos, this line and a half from Statius, *Thebaid* 12. 519–20, is found also as a motto in *Anelida and Arcite* (short poem no. 2), l. 22 and note, which appears to have been a trial run on some of the KT material. **860–61 duc . . . highte . . . Atthenes,** duke, called. Medieval people looked upon Athens as the fountainhead of secular social and political theory. Theseus in this tale is a "mirror for princes." The opening details are a summary of the summary in Boccaccio's *Teseida* of Statius' *Thebaid.* **865 wysdom . . . chivalrie,** "sapientia et fortitudo," see the Knight, Gen Pro 68. **866 regne of Femenye,** country of the Amazons. This place name (from Lat. *femina,* woman) was evidently invented by Chaucer. *Tes.* makes Teseo's war against the Amazons a "purgation" of their "sin" of feminism. **867 whilom . . . ycleped Scithia,** formerly called Scythia (region north of the Black Sea). **868 Ypolita,** Hippolyta, queen of the Amazons. **871 *yonge:* E *faire.* In *Tes.*,** Teseo sees the beauty of Emilia and plans to wed her to his kinsman Acate, who dies before the wedding can take place. **876 *yow have toold:*** in other MSS *have toold yow; yow* may have been missing from the exemplar. **878 chivalrye,** knights. **879 for the nones,** a line filler, i.e., on that occasion. **881 asseged,** besieged. **884 tempest,** the detail of the tempest is added by Chaucer, possibly in reference to a storm that occurred just as Queen Anne arrived in England for her wedding to Richard II. **885 moot,** must. **886 woot . . . ere,** knows, plow. **887 wayke,** weak. **889 letten eek . . . route,** hinder also, company.

And ther I lefte, I wol ayeyn bigynne.
This duc, of whom I make mencioun,
Whan he was come almoost unto the toun,
In al his wele and in his mooste pride, 895
He was war, as he caste his eye aside,
Where that ther kneled in the heighe weye
A compaignye of ladyes, tweye and tweye,
Ech after oother, clad in clothes blake.
But swich a cry and swich a wo they make 900
That in this world nys creature lyvynge
That herde swich another waymentynge,
And of this cry they nolde nevere stenten
Til they the reynes of his brydel henten.
"What folk been ye, that at myn hom-
    comynge 905
Perturben so my feste with criynge?"
Quod Theseus. "Have ye so greet envye
Of myn honour, that thus compleyne and crye?
Or who hath yow mysboden or offended?
And telleth me if it may been amended, 910
And why that ye been clothed thus in blak."
The eldeste lady of hem alle spak,
Whan she hadde swowned with a deedly cheere,
That it was routhe for to seen and heere,
And seyde: "Lord, to whom Fortune hath yeven
Victorie, and as a conqueror to lyven, 916
Nat greveth us youre glorie and youre honour,
But we biseken mercy and socour.
Have mercy on oure wo and oure distresse!
Som drope of pitee, thurgh thy gentillesse, 920
Upon us wrecched wommen lat thou falle.
For, certes, lord, ther is noon of us alle,
That she ne hath been a duchesse or a queene.
Now be we caytyves, as it is wel seene,
Thanked be Fortune and hire false wheel, 925
That noon estaat assureth to be weel.
And certes, lord, to abyden youre presence,

Heere in this temple of the goddesse Clemence
We han ben waitynge al this fourtenyght.
Now help us, lord, sith it is in thy myght. 930
"I, wrecche, which that wepe and wayle thus,
Was whilom wyf to Kyng Cappaneus,
That starf at Thebes—cursed be that day!
And alle we that been in this array
And maken al this lamentacioun, 935
We losten alle oure housbondes at that toun,
Whil that the seege theraboute lay.
And yet now the olde Creon, weylaway,
That lord is now of Thebes the citee,
Fulfild of ire and of iniquitee, 940
He, for despit and for his tirannye,
To do the dede bodyes vileynye
Of alle oure lordes whiche that been yslawe,
He hath alle the bodyes on an heep ydrawe,
And wol nat suffren hem, by noon assent, 945
Neither to been yburyed nor ybrent,
But maketh houndes ete hem in despit."
And with that word, withouten moore respit,
They fillen gruf and criden pitously, 949
"Have on us wrecched wommen som mercy,
And lat oure sorwe synken in thyn herte."
This gentil duc doun from his courser sterte
With herte pitous, whan he herde hem speke.
Hym thoughte that his herte wolde breke
Whan he saugh hem so pitous and so maat, 955
That whilom weren of so greet estaat,
And in his armes he hem alle up hente,
And hem conforteth in ful good entente,
And swoor his ooth, as he was trewe knyght,
He wolde doon so ferforthly his myght 960
Upon the tiraunt Creon hem to wreke,
That al the peple of Grece sholde speke
How Creon was of Theseus yserved
As he that hadde his deeth ful wel deserved.

---

895 **wele**, prosperity. 896 **war ... caste his eye**, aware, looked around. 897 E *heighe* om; different metrical adjustments in other MSS. 902 **waymentynge**, lamenting. 903 **nolde ... stenten**, would not stop. 904 **henten**, seized. 906 **Perturben**, disturb. 909 **mysboden**, injured. 913 **deedly cheere**, deathly expression. 914 **routhe**, pity. 915 *And seyde:* Hg&c *She seyde.* 918 **biseken**, beseech. 920 **gentillesse**, nobility. 924 **caytyves**, miserable wretches. 925 **Fortune ... wheel**, the wheel of the goddess Fortuna, described in *Boece* II, pr.2. 926 **weel**, prosperous. 927 **abyden**, to wait for. 928 **Clemence**, Pity; this goddess is in *Tes.* and *Theb.* 931 *wayle:* E *crie.* 932 **whilom ... Cappaneus**, formerly; Cappaneus was one of the seven who besieged Thebes in the original legend. 933 **starf**, died. 938 **olde Creon**, a fixed epithet in *Roman de Thèbes*, "Creon li Vieuz"; Creon, who became ruler of Thebes after the conclusion of the war with the seven, was the medieval "type" of a tyrant. **weylaway**, alas. 941 **despit**, spite. 942 **vileynye**, disgrace. 943 **yslawe**, slain. E&c *slawe.* 946 **ybrent**, burned. 948 **respit**, delay. 949 **gruf**, groveling. 952 **courser**, in *Tes.* Teseo, Ipolita, and Emilia ride in a chariot. 955 **maat**, overcome, as in "checkmate." 957 **hente**, took. 960 **ferforthly**, to whatever extent. 961 **wreke**, avenge.

justice

And right anoon, withouten moore abood,
His baner he desplayeth, and forth rood   966
To Thebes-ward, and al his hoost biside.
No neer Atthenes wolde he go ne ride,
Ne take his ese fully half a day,
But onward on his wey that nyght he lay,   970
And sente anon Ypolita the queene,
And Emelye, hir yonge suster sheene,
Unto the toun of Atthenes to dwelle,
And forth he rit; ther is namoore to telle.

The rede statue of Mars, with spere and
        targe,
So shyneth in his white baner large,   976
That alle the feeldes glyteren up and doun,
And by his baner born is his penoun
Of gold ful riche, in which ther was ybete   979
The Mynotaur, which that he slough in Crete.

Thus rit this duc, thus rit this conquerour,
And in his hoost of chivalrie the flour,
Til that he cam to Thebes and alighte
Faire in a feeld, ther as he thoughte to fighte.
But shortly for to speken of this thyng,   985
With Creon, which that was of Thebes kyng,
He faught, and slough hym manly as a knyght
In pleyn bataille, and putte the folk to flyght.
And by assaut he wan the citee after,
And rente adoun bothe wall and sparre and
        rafter.   990
And to the ladyes he restored agayn
The bones of hir housbondes that were slayn,
To doon obsequies, as was tho the gyse.
But it were al to longe for to devyse
The grete clamour and the waymentynge   995
That the ladyes made at the brennynge

Of the bodies, and the grete honour
That Theseus, the noble conquerour,
Dooth to the ladyes, whan they from hym
        wente;
But shortly for to telle is myn entente.   1000

Whan that this worthy duc, this Theseus,
Hath Creon slayn, and wonne Thebes thus,
Stille in that feeld he took al nyght his reste,
And dide with al the contree as hym leste.

To ransake in the taas of bodyes dede,   1005
Hem for to strepe of harneys and of wede,
The pilours diden bisynesse and cure
After the bataille and disconfiture.
And so bifel that in the taas they founde,
Thurgh-girt with many a grevous blody
        wounde,   1010
Two yonge knyghtes liggynge by and by,
Bothe in oon armes, wroght ful richely,
Of whiche two Arcita highte that oon,
And that oother knyght highte Palamon.
Nat fully quyke, ne fully dede they were.   1015
But by hir cote-armures and by hir gere
The heraudes knewe hem best in special
As they that weren of the blood roial
Of Thebes, and of sustren two yborn.
Out of the taas the pilours han hem torn,   1020
And han hem caried softe unto the tente
Of Theseus, and he ful soone hem sente
To Atthenes, to dwellen in prisoun
Perpetuelly—he nolde no raunsoun.   1024

And whan this worthy duc hath thus ydon,
He took his hoost, and hoom he rood anon
With laurer crowned as a conquerour.
And ther he lyveth in joye and in honour

---

965 abood, delay. **966 desplayeth,** unfurling of flags was a sign that troops were going into battle. **968 neer . . . go,** nearer, walk. **971 anon,** immediately. **972 sheene,** bright (pretty). **974 rit,** rides. **975 targe,** shield. **977 feeldes glyteren,** the banner and pennant lighted up the landscape (but Skeat suggests that "feeldes" is here the heraldic term for the background upon which arms are blazoned). **979–80 ybete . . . Mynotaur,** embroidered; the Minotaur commemorated Theseus' adventure in the Labyrinth. **984 Faire,** in a fair (appropriate) field. **987–88 manly . . . pleyn bataille,** man to man, fair battle. **990 rente adoun . . . sparre,** tore down, beam. **992** *housbondes:* Hg&c *freendes.* **993 gyse,** custom. **994 devyse,** recount. **1000 shortly,** briefly (an example of rhetorical *occupatio*). **1004 hym leste,** pleased him. **1005 taas,** heaps. **1006 strepe . . . harneys . . . wede,** strip, armor, clothes. **1007 pilours . . . cure,** pillagers, care. **1010 Thurgh-girt,** pierced through. **1011 liggynge by and by,** lying side by side. **1012 oon armes, wroght,** identical armor, fashioned. **1013 highte,** was called. **1015 quyke,** alive. **1016 cote-armures,** cloth vests bearing the heraldic arms worn over armor, hence the term "coat of arms." **gere,** gear (equipment). **1021 softe,** gently. **1024 raunsoun,** ransom here and below is not mentioned in *Tes.* The object of warfare by Chaucer's time had become less political or military victory than monetary gain through pillage and the ransom of prisoners. In 1193 Richard I had been held for an enormous ransom by the Emperor of Germany and in 1357 both King John of France and King David of Scotland were being held as prisoners for ransom in the English court. **1027 laurer,** laurel.

Terme of his lyf; what nedeth wordes mo?
And in a tour, in angwissh and in wo, 1030
This Palamon and his felawe Arcite
For everemoore; ther may no gold hem quite.
   This passeth yeer by yeer and day by day
Til it fil ones, in a morwe of May,
That Emelye, that fairer was to sene 1035
Than is the lylie upon his stalke grene,
And fressher than the May with floures newe—
For with the rose colour stroof hire hewe,
I noot which was the fyner of hem two—
Er it were day, as was hir wone to do, 1040
She was arisen and al redy dight,
For May wole have no slogardie a-nyght.
The sesoun priketh every gentil herte,
And maketh hym out of his slep to sterte,
And seith, "Arys, and do thyn observaunce."
This maked Emelye have remembraunce 1046
To doon honour to May, and for to ryse.
Yclothed was she fressh, for to devyse.
Hir yelow heer was broyded in a tresse
Bihynde hir bak, a yerde long, I gesse. 1050
And in the gardyn, at the sonne upriste,
She walketh up and doun, and as hire liste
She gadereth floures, party white and rede,
To make a subtil gerland for hire hede.
And as an aungel hevenysshly she soong. 1055
   The grete tour that was so thikke and
     stroong,
Which of the castle was the chief dongeoun—
Ther as the knyghtes weren in prisoun
Of whiche I tolde yow and tellen shal—
Was evene joynant to the gardyn wal 1060
Ther as this Emelye hadde hir pleyynge.
Bright was the sonne and cleer that
     morwenynge,
And Palamoun, this woful prisoner,
As was his wone, by leve of his gayler,

Was risen and romed in a chambre an heigh,
In which he al the noble citee seigh,
And eek the gardyn, ful of braunches grene, 1066
Ther as this fresshe Emelye the shene
Was in hir walk, and romed up and doun.
This sorweful prisoner, this Palamoun, 1070
Goth in the chambre romynge to and fro,
And to hymself compleynynge of his wo.
That he was born, ful ofte he seyde, "Allas!"
   And so bifel, by aventure or cas, 1074
That thurgh a wyndow, thikke of many a
    barre
Of iren greet and square as any sparre,
He cast his eye upon Emelya.
And therwithal he bleynte and cride, "A!"
As though he stongen were unto the herte.
And with that cry Arcite anon up sterte, 1080
And seyde, "Cosyn myn, what eyleth thee,
That art so pale and deedly on to see?
Why cridestow? Who hath thee doon offence?
For Goddes love, taak al in pacience
Oure prisoun, for it may noon oother be. 1085
Fortune hath yeven us this adversitee.
Som wikke aspect or disposicioun
Of Saturne, by sum constellacioun, 1088
Hath yeven us this, although we hadde it sworn.
So stood the hevene whan that we were born.
We moste endure; this is the short and playn."
   This Palamon answerde and seyde agayn,
"Cosyn, for sothe, of this opinioun
Thow hast a veyn ymaginacioun.
This prison caused me nat for to crye, 1095
But I was hurt right now thurghout myn eye
Into myn herte, that wol my bane be.
The fairnesse of that lady that I see
Yond in the gardyn romen to and fro
Is cause of al my criyng and my wo. 1100
I noot wher she be womman or goddesse,

1029 *his lyf:* E&c *his* om. **1031** Hg&c *Dwellen this Palamon and eek Arcite.* **1032 quite,** redeem. **1034 morwe,** morning. **1038 stroof,** strove (vied). **1039** *fyner:* Hg&c *fairer.* **1040 wone,** habit. **1041 dight,** dressed. **1042 slogardie,** laziness. *Double entendre* here and in the following lines—May was the traditional season of fertility cults. **1044** *hym:* Hg *it.* **1048 devyse,** describe. **1049 broyded,** braided. **1054 subtil,** skilful. **1057 dongeoun,** the keep (strong tower). **1060 evene joynant,** directly adjoining. **1064 wone,** habit. **1065 an heigh,** on high (high up). **1068 shene,** bright (pretty). **1074 cas,** chance. **1075 thikke of,** heavily barred. **1076 sparre,** beam. **1077 eye,** in the courtly convention, love enters through the eye. **1078 bleynte,** blanched. **1079 stongen,** stung. **1082 deedly,** deathly. **1087 wikke aspect,** wicked (evil) disposition of the horoscope. **1088 Saturne,** a particularly malignant influence, as we see in Arcite's death. **constellacioun,** configuration of heavenly bodies. **1089 sworn,** a line filler, "although we had sworn the opposite." **1091** *endure:* Hg&c *endure it.* **1093 for sothe,** certainly. **1094 veyn ymaginacioun,** wrong conception. **1096 thurghout,** through. **1097 bane,** destruction.

But Venus is it soothly, as I gesse."
And therwithal on knees doun he fil,
And seyde, "Venus, if it be thy wil
Yow in this gardyn thus to transfigure   1105
Bifore me, sorweful, wrecched creature,
Out of this prisoun help that we may scapen.
And if so be my destynee be shapen
By eterne word to dyen in prisoun,
Of oure lynage have som compassioun,   1110
That is so lowe ybroght by tirannye."

    And with that word Arcite gan espye
Wher as this lady romed to and fro,
And with that sighte hir beautee hurte hym so
That, if that Palamon was wounded soore,   1115
Arcite is hurt as muche as he, or moore.
And with a sigh he seyde pitously,
"The fresshe beautee sleeth me sodeynly
Of hire that rometh in the yonder place,
And but I have hir mercy and hir grace,   1120
That I may seen hire atte leeste weye,
I nam but deed; ther nis namoore to seye."

    This Palamon, whan he tho wordes herde,
Dispitously he looked and answerde,   1124
"Wheither seistow this in ernest or in pley?"

    "Nay," quod Arcite, "in ernest, by my fey!
God helpe me so, me list ful yvele pleye."

    This Palamon gan knytte his browes tweye.
"It nere," quod he, "to thee no greet honour
For to be fals, ne for to be traitour   1130
To me, that am thy cosyn and thy brother
Ysworn ful depe, and ech of us til oother,
That nevere, for to dyen in the peyne
Til that deeth departe shal us tweyne,
Neither of us in love to hyndre oother,   1135
Ne in noon oother cas, my leeve brother,
But that thou sholdest trewely forthren me

In every cas, as I shal forthren thee:
This was thyn ooth, and myn also, certeyn.
I woot right wel, thou darst it nat withseyn.
Thus artow of my conseil, out of doute,   1141
And now thow woldest falsly been aboute
To love my lady, whom I love and serve,
And evere shal til that myn herte sterve.
Nay, certes, false Arcite, thow shalt nat so.   1145
I loved hire first, and tolde thee my wo
As to my conseil and to my brother sworn
To forthre me, as I have toold biforn.
For which thou art ybounden as a knyght
To helpen me, if it lay in thy myght,   1150
Or elles artow fals, I dar wel seyn."

    This Arcite ful proudly spak ageyn:
"Thow shalt," quod he, "be rather fals than I,
And thou art fals, I telle thee outrely,
For paramour I loved hire first er thow.   1155
What wiltow seyen? Thou wistest nat yet now
Wheither she be a womman or goddesse!
Thyn is affeccioun of hoolynesse,
And myn is love as to a creature,
For which I tolde thee myn aventure   1160
As to my cosyn and my brother sworn.
I pose that thow lovedest hire biforn:
Wostow nat wel the olde clerkes sawe,
That 'who shal yeve a lovere any lawe?'
Love is a gretter lawe, by my pan,   1165
Than may be yeve to any erthely man.
And therfore positif lawe and swich decree
Is broken alday for love in ech degree.
A man moot nedes love, maugree his heed.
He may nat flee it, thogh he sholde be deed,
Al be she mayde or wydwe or elles wyf.   1171
And eek it is nat likly al thy lif
To stonden in hir grace. Namoore shal I.

1109 **eterne,** eternal (divine). 1110 **lynage,** royalty was due special consideration. 1120 **but,** unless. 1121 **atte leeste weye,** at least. 1124 **Dispitously,** coldly. 1125 **seistow,** sayest thou. 1126 **fey,** faith. 1127 **list ful yvele pleye,** it pleases me very ill to play. 1132 **Ysworn,** swearing of blood brotherhood was another romantic convention that became fashionable in the 14th century twilight of chivalry. 1133 **the peyne,** by torture. 1134 **departe,** divide. Hg&c *the deeth.* 1136 **cas . . . leeve,** situation, dear. 1137 **forthren,** advance. 1140 **withseyn,** repudiate. 1141 **artow of my conseil,** you are sharer of my confidence. 1142 **been aboute,** go about (begin). 1144 **sterve,** die. 1147 **conseil,** confidant. *to my brother:* Hg&c to om. 1152 **spak ageyn,** spoke in reply. 1153 **rather,** sooner. 1155 **paramour,** sexual love. 1156 **wistest,** knew. Hg *woost;* other MSS *wotest, wyst,* etc. 1158 **affeccioun of hoolynesse,** adoration of a spiritual being. 1162 **I pose,** I pose (the question), i.e., suppose. **biforn,** earlier (than I). 1163 **sawe,** saying; Chaucer's translation of *Boece* III m.12, 55, has nearly identical wording; also *TC* IV.618 written at about the same time. The Boethian sentiments throughout this tale are Chaucer's embroidery on much simpler expressions in *Tes.* 1165 **pan,** skull. 1167 **positif lawe,** Lat. *lex positiva* or "placed" (hence displaceable), man-made law, *vs.* immutable natural law. **swich decree,** such rule(s). 1168 **alday,** all day (constantly). 1169 **maugree,** in spite of.

For wel thou woost thyselven, verraily,
That thou and I be dampned to prisoun   1175
Perpetuelly—us gayneth no raunsoun.
We stryven as dide the houndes for the boon.
They foughte al day, and yet hir part was noon.
Ther cam a kyte, whil that they weren so wrothe,
And baar awey the boon bitwixe hem bothe.
And therfore, at the kynges court, my brother,
Ech man for hymself, ther is noon oother.   1182
Love, if thee list, for I love and ay shal.
And soothly, leeve brother, this is al.
Heere in this prisoun moote we endure,   1185
And everich of us take his aventure."

  Greet was the strif and long bitwix hem tweye,
If that I hadde leyser for to seye,
But to th'effect. It happed on a day,
To telle it yow as shortly as I may,   1190
A worthy duc that highte Perotheus,
That felawe was unto Duc Theseus
Syn thilke day that they were children lite,
Was come to Atthenes his felawe to visite,
And for to pleye as he was wont to do,   1195
For in this world he loved no man so,
And he loved hym als tendrely agayn.
So wel they lovede, as olde bookes sayn,
That whan that oon was deed, soothly to telle,
His felawe wente and soughte hym doun in
          helle—   1200
But of that storie list me nat to write.
Duc Perotheus loved wel Arcite,
And hadde hym knowe at Thebes yeer by yere,
And finally at requeste and preyere
Of Perotheus, withouten any raunsoun,   1205
Duc Theseus hym leet out of prisoun
Frely to goon wher that hym liste over al,
In swich a gyse as I you tellen shal.
  This was the forward, pleynly for t'endite,
Bitwixen Theseus and hym Arcite,   1210
That if so were that Arcite were yfounde

Evere in his lif, by day or nyght or stounde,
In any contree of this Theseus,
And he were caught, it was acorded thus,
That with a swerd he sholde lese his heed.   1215
Ther nas noon oother remedie ne reed,
But taketh his leve, and homward he him
          spedde.
Lat hym be war. His nekke lith to wedde.
  How greet a sorwe suffreth now Arcite!
The deeth he feeleth thurgh his herte smyte.   1220
He wepeth, wayleth, crieth pitously;
To sleen hymself he waiteth prively.
He seyde, "Allas that day that I was born!
Now is my prisoun worse than biforn.
Now is me shape eternally to dwelle   1225
Nat in purgatorie, but in helle.
Allas, that evere knew I Perotheus!
For elles hadde I dwelled with Theseus,
Yfetered in his prisoun everemo.   1229
Thanne hadde I been in blisse and nat in wo.
Oonly the sighte of hire whom that I serve,
Though that I nevere hir grace may deserve,
Wolde han suffised right ynough for me.
O deere cosyn Palamon," quod he,
"Thyn is the victorie of this aventure.   1235
Ful blisfully in prison maistow dure—
In prison? Certes nay, but in paradys!
Wel hath Fortune yturned thee the dys,
That hast the sighte of hire, and I th'absence.
For possible is, syn thou hast hire presence,   1240
And art a knyght, a worthy and an able,
That by som cas, syn Fortune is chaungeable,
Thow maist to thy desir somtyme atteyne.
But I that am exiled and bareyne
Of alle grace, and in so greet dispeir   1245
That ther nys erthe, water, fir, ne eir,
Ne creature that of hem maked is,
That may me helpe or doon confort in this,
Wel oughte I sterve in wanhope and distresse.

1175 **dampned,** condemned. 1177 **stryven,** fight. In *Tes.* Emilia is aware of the knights' infatuation and sings when she sees them "not for love but for vanity of her beauty." 1180 **bitwixe,** from between. 1183 **ay,** always. 1184 **soothly, leeve,** truly, dear. 1189 **effect,** to the point. 1192 *unto:* E&c *to.* 1200 This reference is found in *RR* 8148ff. (Dunn-Robbins, 38.124). 1208 **gyse,** manner. 1209 **forward ... endite,** agreement, declare. 1212 **or stounde,** or moment. One MS (Dd.4.24) reads *o stounde* (a moment). Tyrwhitt adopted this reading and many editors have followed. 1216 **reed,** help. 1218 **wedde,** pledge. 1222 **waiteth,** awaits his time. 1225 **me shape,** I am destined. 1236 **maistow dure,** mayest thou remain. 1238 **dys,** dice. 1242 **cas,** chance. 1248 *helpe:* E&c *heele.* 1249 **sterve ... wanhope,** perish, despair.

Farwel my lif, my lust, and my gladnesse!   1250
  "Allas, why pleynen folk so in commune
On purveiaunce of God, or of Fortune,
That yeveth hem ful ofte in many a gyse
Wel bettre than they kan hemself devyse?
Som man desireth for to han richesse,   1255
That cause is of his moerdre or greet siknesse.
And som man wolde out of his prisoun fayn,
That in his hous is of his meynee slayn.
Infinite harmes been in this mateere.
We witen nat what thing we preyen heere: 1260
We faren as he that dronke is as a mous.
A dronke man woot wel he hath an hous,
But he noot which the righte wey is thider,
And to a dronke man the wey is slider.
And certes, in this world so faren we.   1265
We seken faste after felicitee,
But we goon wrong ful often, trewely.
Thus may we seyen alle, and namely I,
That wende and hadde a greet opinioun
That if I myghte escapen from prisoun,   1270
Thanne hadde I been in joye and perfit heele,
Ther now I am exiled fro my wele.
Syn that I may nat seen you, Emelye,
I nam but deed; ther nys no remedye."
  Upon that oother syde Palamon,   1275
Whan that he wiste Arcite was agon,
Swich sorwe he maketh that the grete tour
Resouneth of his youlyng and clamour.
The pure fettres on his shynes grete
Weren of his bittre salte teeres wete.   1280
"Allas," quod he, "Arcita, cosyn myn,
Of al oure strif, God woot, the fruyt is thyn.
Thow walkest now in Thebes at thy large,
And of my wo thow yevest litel charge.
Thou mayst, syn thou hast wisdom and man-
    hede,   1285
Assemblen alle the folk of oure kynrede,

And make a werre so sharp on this citee
That by som aventure or som tretee
Thow mayst have hire to lady and to wyf
For whom that I moste nedes lese my lyf.   1290
For, as by wey of possibilitee,
Sith thou art at thy large, of prisoun free,
And art a lord, greet is thyn avauntage
Moore than is myn, that sterve here in a cage.
For I moot wepe and wayle, whil I lyve,   1295
With al the wo that prison may me yeve,
And eek with peyne that love me yeveth also
That doubleth al my torment and my wo."
Therwith the fyr of jalousie up sterte   1299
Withinne his brest, and hente him by the herte
So woodly that he lyk was to biholde
The boxtree or the asshen dede and colde.
  Thanne seyde he, "O crueel goddes that
    governe
This world with byndyng of youre word eterne,
And writen in the table of atthamaunt   1305
Youre parlement and youre eterne graunt,
What is mankynde moore unto you holde
Than is the sheep that rouketh in the folde?
For slayn is man right as another beest,
And dwelleth eek in prison and arreest,   1310
And hath siknesse and greet adversitee,
And ofte tymes giltelees, pardee.
  "What governance is in this prescience,
That giltelees tormenteth innocence?
And yet encresseth this al my penaunce,   1315
That man is bounden to his observaunce,
For Goddes sake, to letten of his wille,
Ther as a beest may al his lust fulfille.
And whan a beest is deed he hath no peyne,
But after his deeth man moot wepe and pleyne,
Though in this world he have care and wo.   1321
Withouten doute it may stonden so.
The answere of this lete I do dyvynys,

1250 lust . . . gladnesse, joy, happiness. **1251 in commune,** commonly. **1252 purveiaunce,** providence. These Boethian sentiments reflect *Boece* III pr.2. **1253 gyse,** way. **1255 han,** have. **1256 moerdre,** murder. **1257 fayn,** happily. **1258 meynee,** servants. **1260 preyen,** pray for, cf. Romans 8:26. **1264 slider,** slippery. The illustration is from a gloss in *Boece* III pr.2, 88. **1268 namely,** especially. **1269 wende,** thought. **1271 heele,** well-being. **1272 Ther,** where. E&c *That.* **wele,** good fortune. **1275 Upon . . . syde,** on the other hand. **1276 wiste,** knew. **1278 youlyng,** yowling. **1279 pure,** very. **1283 large,** at large (free). **1284 charge,** care. **1290 moste,** must. **1294 sterve,** die. **1301 woodly . . . lyk was,** madly, looked like. **1302 boxtree . . . asshen,** white as boxwood, grey as ashes. **1305 atthamaunt,** adamant. This passage resembles *Boece* I m.5. **1306 parlement,** saying, verdict. **1307 What . . . holde,** in what way is man worth more. **1308 rouketh,** cowers. **1313 governance . . . prescience,** theory of government, providence. **1316 observaunce,** duty. **1317 letten,** refrain. **1320 man,** appears in the MSS in various places in the line. An insertion?

But wel I woot that in this world greet pyne ys.
Allas, I se a serpent or a theef,   1325
That many a trewe man hath doon mescheef,
Goon at his large, and where hym list may turne.
But I moot been in prisoun thurgh Saturne,
And eek thurgh Juno, jalous and eek wood,
That hath destroyed wel ny al the blood   1330
Of Thebes with his waste walles wyde.
And Venus sleeth me on that oother syde
For jalousie and fere of hym Arcite."

   Now wol I stynte of Palamon a lite,
And lete hym in his prisoun stille dwelle,   1335
And of Arcita forth I wol yow telle.
The somer passeth, and the nyghtes longe
Encressen double wise the peynes stronge
Bothe of the lovere and the prisoner.
I noot which hath the wofuller mester.   1340
For, shortly for to seyn, this Palamoun
Perpetuelly is dampned to prisoun,
In cheynes and in fettres to been deed.
And Arcite is exiled upon his heed
For, evere mo, as out of that contree,   1345
Ne nevere mo he shal his lady see.

   Yow loveres axe I now this questioun:
Who hath the worse, Arcite or Palamoun?
That oon may seen his lady day by day,
But in prison he moot dwelle alway;   1350
That oother wher hym list may ride or go,
But seen his lady shal he nevere mo.
Now demeth as yow liste, ye that kan,
For I wol telle forth as I bigan.

Explicit prima pars. Sequitur pars secunda.

   Whan that Arcite to Thebes comen was,   1355
Ful ofte a day he swelte and seyde "Allas!"

For seen his lady shal he nevere mo.
And shortly to concluden al his wo,
So muche sorwe hadde nevere creature   1359
That is, or shal, whil that the world may dure.
His slep, his mete, his drynke, is hym biraft,
That lene he wex and drye as is a shaft;
His eyen holwe and grisly to biholde,
His hewe falow and pale as asshen colde,
And solitarie he was and evere allone,   1365
And waillynge al the nyght, makynge his mone.
And if he herde song or instrument,
Thanne wolde he wepe, he myghte nat be stent.
So feble eek were his spiritz, and so lowe,   1369
And chaunged so, that no man koude knowe
His speche nor his voys, though men it herde.
And in his geere for al the world he ferde,
Nat oonly lik the loveris maladye
Of hereos, but rather lyk manye,
Engendred of humour malencolik   1375
Biforen, in his celle fantastik.
And shortly, turned was al up so doun
Bothe habit and eek disposicioun
Of hym, this woful lovere daun Arcite.

   What sholde I al day of his wo endite?   1380
Whan he endured hadde a yeer or two
This crueel torment and this peyne and wo,
At Thebes, in his contree, as I seyde,
Upon a nyght in sleep as he hym leyde,
Hym thoughte how that the wynged god Mer-
   curie   1385
Biforn hym stood and bad hym to be murie.
His slepy yerde in hond he bar uprighte,
An hat he werede upon his heris brighte.
Arrayed was this god, as he took keep,
As he was whan that Argus took his sleep.   1390

1325 serpent, poisonous person. **1327 large,** free. **1329 Juno,** Juno's animosity against Thebes is from the tradition of the *Thebiad.*
See l. 2966n. below. **1340 noot . . . mester,** know not, mystery (occupation). **1342 dampned,** condemned. **1344 upon . . . heed,**
upon pain of losing. **1347 questioun,** "questiones d'amour" such as this were a mainstay of chivalric dalliance, as exemplified by
Andreas Cappalanus in *De Amore* (c.1175), and elsewhere. **1353 demeth,** decide. **1356 swelte,** fainted. **1361 His slep,** &c. The
following are symptoms of the malady of "er(e)os" which by false etymology became "hereos," and hence "amor hereos" or "the
loveris maladye of hereos" (l. 1373 below). The disease is described by both Arab and European medieval medical authorities. See
J. L. Lowes, *Modern Philology,* 11 (1910), 491–546. **1362 shaft,** stick. E&c *wexeth.* **1363 grisly,** dreadful. **1364 falow,** yellow. **1368
stent,** stopped. **1370 knowe,** recognize. **1372 geere,** manner. **1374 manye,** if "amor hereos" was not checked it led to mania and
death. **1375–76 malencolik . . . Biforen, in,** So Hg, but E&c read *Biforn his owne celle.* Chaucer appears to be referring to the usual
medieval division of the brain into three cells: the rear, memory; the middle, reason; and the front, fantasy. Mania was an affliction
of the front cell; melancholia was usually considered an affliction of the middle cell. **1377 shortly,** in short. **1379 daun,** Lat. *dom(inus),*
master. **1389 he . . . keep,** he (i.e., Arcite), heed. **1390 Argus,** Mercury put hundred-eyed Argus to sleep, then killed him, Ovid,
Met. 1.670.

And seyde hym thus, "To Atthenes shaltou
    wende,
Ther is thee shapen of thy wo an ende."
And with that word Arcite wook and sterte.
"Now trewely, hou soore that me smerte," 1394
Quod he, "to Atthenes right now wol I fare,
Ne for the drede of deeth shal I nat spare
To se my lady that I love and serve.
In hire presence I recche nat to sterve."
    And with that word he caughte a greet
    mirour
And saugh that chaunged was al his colour, 1400
And saugh his visage al in another kynde.
And right anon it ran hym in his mynde
That, sith his face was so disfigured
Of maladye the which he hadde endured,
He myghte wel, if that he bar hym lowe, 1405
Lyve in Atthenes everemoore unknowe
And seen his lady wel ny day by day.
And right anon he chaunged his array,
And cladde hym as a poure laborer,
And al allone, save oonly a squier 1410
That knew his privetee and al his cas,
Which was disgised pourely as he was,
To Atthenes is he goon the nexte way.
And to the court he wente upon a day,
And at the gate he profreth his servyse 1415
To drugge and drawe, what so men wol
    devyse.
And shortly of this matere for to seyn,
He fil in office with a chamberleyn
The which that dwellynge was with Emelye,
For he was wys and koude soone espye 1420
Of every servaunt which that serveth here.
Wel koude he hewen wode and water bere,
For he was yong and myghty for the nones
And therto he was long and big of bones
To doon that any wight kan hym devyse. 1425
    A yeer or two he was in this servyse,

Page of the chambre of Emelye the brighte,
And Philostrate he seyde that he highte.
But half so wel biloved a man as he
Ne was ther nevere in court of his degree. 1430
He was so gentil of condicioun
That thurghout al the court was his renoun.
They seyden that it were a charitee
That Theseus wolde enhauncen his degree,
And putten hym in worshipful servyse, 1435
Ther as he myghte his vertu exercise.
And thus withinne a while his name is spronge,
Bothe of his dedes and his goode tonge,
That Theseus hath taken hym so neer
That of his chambre he made hym a squier, 1440
And gaf hym gold to mayntene his degree.
And eek men broghte hym out of his contree,
From yeer to yeer, ful pryvely his rente,
But honestly and slyly he it spente, 1444
That no man wondred how that he it hadde.
And thre yeer in this wise his lif he ladde,
And bar hym so, in pees and eek in werre,
Ther was no man that Theseus hath derre.
And in this blisse lete I now Arcite,
And speke I wole of Palamon a lite. 1450
    In derknesse and horrible and strong
    prisoun
Thise seven yeer hath seten Palamoun
Forpyned, what for wo and for distresse.
Who feeleth double soor and hevynesse
But Palamon, that love destreyneth so 1455
That wood out of his wit he goth for wo?
And eek therto he is a prisoner
Perpetuelly, noght oonly for a yer.
    Who koude ryme in Englyssh proprely
His martirdom? For sothe it am nat I. 1460
Therfore I passe as lightly as I may.
    It fel that in the seventhe yer, of May
The thridde nyght, as olde bookes seyn,
That al this storie tellen moore pleyn,

1394 hou . . . smerte, however sorely I suffer. **1398 recche . . . sterve,** care not if I die. **1405 lowe,** discreetly. **1411 privetee . . . cas,** confidence, fortune. **1413 nexte,** nearest. **1416 drugge and drawe,** drag (drudge) and pull. **1418 office . . . chamberleyn,** employment, personal attendant. In *Tes.* Emilia recognized Arcita, but let no one know it. **1425 devyse,** command. **1428 Philostrate,** in *Tes.* the assumed name was Penteo, perhaps related to "penitent." Chaucer for some reason altered it to resemble Boccaccio's title for *TC, Il Filostrato,* "the one vanquished by love." **highte,** was called. **1430 degree,** status. **1431 condicioun,** disposition. **1433 were a charitee,** would be a charitable act. **1435 worshipful,** honorable. **1437 spronge,** sprung widely. **1443 rente,** income. **1448 derre,** dearer. **1453 Forpyned,** agonized. **1454 soor:** Gg&c *sorowe.* **1455 destreyneth,** afflicts. **1456 wood,** insane. **1462 of May:** E&c *in May.* **1463 thridde,** May 3 is also the date the fox seized Chanticleer (NPT vii.3190), and the night before Pandarus made his first approach to Criseyde on Troylus' behalf (*TC* ii.56). It was an "unlucky day" in the medieval calendar.

Were it by aventure or destynee—   1465
As whan a thyng is shapen it shal be—
That soone after the mydnyght Palamoun,
By helpyng of a freend, brak his prisoun
And fleeth the citee faste as he may go.
For he hadde yeve his gayler drynke so   1470
Of a clarree maad of a certeyn wyn,
With nercotikes and opie of Thebes fyn,
That al that nyght, thogh that men wolde him
          shake,
The gayler sleep—he myghte nat awake.
And thus he fleeth as faste as evere he may.   1475
The nyght was short and faste by the day
That nedes cost he moot hymselven hyde,
And til a grove faste ther bisyde
With dredeful foot thanne stalketh Palamoun.
For, shortly, this was his opinioun,   1480
That in that grove he wolde hym hyde al day,
And in the nyght thanne wolde he take his way
To Thebes-ward, his freendes for to preye
On Theseus to helpe hym to werreye.
And shortly, outher he wolde lese his lif,   1485
Or wynnen Emelye unto his wyf.
This is th'effect and his entente pleyn.
    Now wol I turne to Arcite ageyn,
That litel wiste how ny that was his care   1489
Til that Fortune had broght him in the snare.
    The bisy larke, messager of day,
Salueth in hir song the morwe gray,
And firy Phebus riseth up so brighte
That al the orient laugheth of the lighte,
And with his stremes dryeth in the greves   1495
The silver dropes hangynge on the leves.
And Arcita, that in the court roial
With Theseus is squier principal,
Is risen and looketh on the myrie day.
And for to doon his observaunce to May,   1500
Remembrynge on the poynt of his desir,
He on a courser, startlynge as the fir,

Is riden into the feeldes hym to pleye,
Out of the court were it a myle or tweye.
And to the grove of which that I yow tolde 1505
By aventure his wey he gan to holde,
To maken hym a gerland of the greves
Were it of wodebynde or hawethorn leves.
And loude he song ayeyn the sonne shene,
"May, with alle thy floures and thy grene,   1510
Welcome be thou, faire, fresshe May,
In hope that I som grene gete may."
And from his courser, with a lusty herte,
Into the grove ful hastily he sterte,
And in a path he rometh up and doun   1515
Theras by aventure this Palamoun
Was in a bussh, that no man myghte hym se,
For soore afered of his deeth was he.
Nothyng ne knew he that it was Arcite,
God woot he wolde have trowed it ful lite.   1520
But sooth is seyd, gon sithen many yeres,
That "feeld hath eyen and the wode hath eres."
It is ful fair a man to bere hym evene
For alday meeteth men at unset stevene.
Ful litel woot Arcite of his felawe   1525
That was so ny to herknen al his sawe,
For in the bussh he sitteth now ful stille.
    Whan that Arcite hadde romed al his fille,
And songen al the roundel lustily,
Into a studie he fil sodeynly,   1530
As doon thise loveres in hir queynte geres,
Now in the crope, now doun in the breres,
Now up, now doun, as boket in a welle.
Right as the Friday, soothly for to telle,
Now it shyneth, now it reyneth faste,   1535
Right so kan geery Venus overcaste
The hertes of hir folk. Right as hir day
Is gereful, right so chaungeth she array.
Selde is the Friday al the wowke ylike.   1539
    Whan that Arcite had songe, he gan to sike,
And sette hym doun withouten any moore.

1471 clarree, wine punch. **1472 opie . . . Thebes,** opium of (Egyptian) Thebes. **1477 nedes cost,** at any cost. **1479 dredeful,** fearful. **1484 werreye,** make war. **1492 Salueth . . . morwe,** greets, morning. **1495 stremes . . . greves,** beams, bushes. **1498** *is:* E&c *his.* **1502 startlynge,** capering. **1507 greves,** bushes. **1509 ayeyn . . . shene,** to the bright sun. **1512 grene gete,** possibly an allusion to some sort of Maying custom. **1516 by aventure,** in *Tes.,* Palemone learns in prison that Arcita has returned to Thebes and goes frequently to the grove to meditate his woe. Palemone purposely breaks out of prison to meet him there. **1518** E&c *deeth thanne was he.* **1520 woot . . . trowed,** knows, believed. **1521 sithen,** since. **1523 evene,** evenly (calmly). **1524 unset stevene,** unplanned meeting. **1526 sawe.** saying. **1531 geres,** manners. **1532 crope . . . breres,** leaves, briars. **1536 geery,** changeable. **Venus,** Friday was Venus' day, named for the Scandinavian goddess of fertility and love, Frigg. **1539 wowke,** week. **1540 sike,** sigh.

"Allas," quod he, "that day that I was bore!
How longe, Juno, thurgh thy crueltee,
Woltow werreyen Thebes the citee?
Allas, ybroght is to confusioun   1545
The blood roial of Cadme and Amphioun—
Of Cadmus, which that was the firste man
That Thebes bulte, or first the toun bigan,
And of the citee first was crouned kyng.
Of his lynage am I and his ofspryng   1550
By verray ligne, as of the stok roial,
And now I am so caytyf and so thral
That he that is my mortal enemy,
I serve hym as his squier pourely.
And yet dooth Juno me wel moore shame,   1555
For I dar noght biknowe myn owene name,
But ther as I was wont to highte Arcite
Now highte I Philostrate, noght worth a myte.
Allas, thou felle Mars! Allas, Juno!
Thus hath youre ire oure lynage al fordo,   1560
Save oonly me and wrecched Palamoun,
That Theseus martireth in prisoun.
And over al this, to sleen me outrely,
Love hath his firy dart so brennyngly
Ystiked thurgh my trewe, careful herte,   1565
That shapen was my deeth erst than my sherte.
Ye sleen me with youre eyen, Emelye!
Ye been the cause wherfore that I dye.
Of al the remenant of myn oother care
Ne sette I nat the montance of a tare,   1570
So that I koude doon aught to youre plesaunce."
And with that word he fil doun in a traunce
A longe tyme, and after he up sterte.
    This Palamoun, that thoughte that thurgh his
        herte
He felte a coold swerd sodeynliche glyde,   1575
For ire he quook, no lenger wolde he byde.
And whan that he had herd Arcites tale,
As he were wood, with face deed and pale,

He stirte hym up out of the buskes thikke,
And seide, "Arcite, false traytour wikke,   1580
Now artow hent, that lovest my lady so,
For whom that I have al this peyne and wo,
And art my blood, and to my conseil sworn,
As I ful ofte have told thee heerbiforn,
And hast byjaped heere Duc Theseus,   1585
And falsly chaunged hast thy name thus!
I wol be deed, or elles thou shalt dye.
Thou shalt nat love my lady Emelye,
But I wol love hire oonly and namo,
For I am Palamon, thy mortal foo.   1590
And though that I no wepene have in this place,
But out of prison am astert by grace,
I drede noght that outher thow shalt dye,
Or thow ne shalt nat loven Emelye.
Chees which thou wolt, or thou shalt nat
        asterte!"   1595
    This Arcite, with ful despitous herte,
Whan he hym knew and hadde his tale herd,
As fiers as leon pulled out his swerd,
And seyde thus, "By God that sit above,
Nere it that thou art sik and wood for love,   1600
And eek that thow no wepne hast in this place,
Thou sholdest nevere out of this grove pace,
That thou ne sholdest dyen of myn hond.
For I defye the seurete and the bond   1604
Which that thou seist that I have maad to thee.
What, verray fool, thynk wel that love is free,
And I wol love hire mawgree al thy myght!
But for as muche thou art a worthy knyght,
And wilnest to darreyne hire by bataille,
Have heer my trouthe, tomorwe I wol nat faille,
Withoute wityng of any oother wight,   1611
That heere I wol be founden as a knyght,
And bryngen harneys right ynough for thee,
And ches the beste, and leve the worste for me.
And mete and drynke this nyght wol I brynge

1543 **Juno,** Juno's enmity against Thebes was noted in connection with l. 1329n. above. 1546 **Cadme . . . Amphioun,** Cadmus and Amphion were the legendary founders of Thebes. 1552 **caytyf . . . thral,** wretched, enslaved. 1556 **biknowe,** reveal. 1557 **highte,** be called. 1559 **felle,** cruel. 1560 **fordo,** destroyed. *lynage:* E *kynrede.* 1565 **trewe, careful,** sincere, sorrowful. 1566 **shapen . . . sherte,** the notion that his death was foreordained before his shirt was woven suggests the classical figure of the weaving Fates (Parcæ). 1567 **sleen me,** dying for love is a principal sentiment of the troubadour "complaint," variously transmuted by Dante, Petrarch, Machaut, Chaucer, etc. 1570 **montance of a tare,** value of a weed. 1576 **quook,** quaked. 1578 **wood,** insane. 1579 **buskes,** bushes. 1580 **wikke,** wicked. 1581 **artow hent,** art thou caught. 1585 **byjaped,** fooled. 1592–95 **asterte,** escape. 1596 **despitous,** merciless. 1600 **Nere . . . wood,** were it not, insane. 1602 **pace,** pass. 1604 **defye . . . seurete,** renounce, pledge. 1607 **mawgree,** in spite of. 1609 **darreyne,** decide the right to. 1610 **trouthe,** pledge. 1611 **wityng . . . wight,** knowledge, person. 1613 **harneys,** armor and arms.

Ynough for thee, and clothes for thy beddynge.
And if so be that thou my lady wynne,   1617
And sle me in this wode ther I am inne,
Thow mayst wel have thy lady as for me."
   This Palamon answerde, "I graunte it
     thee."
And thus they been departed til amorwe,   1621
Whan ech of hem had leyd his feith to borwe.
   O Cupide, out of alle charitee!
O regne, that wolt no felawe have with thee!
Ful sooth is seyd that love ne lordshipe   1625
Wol noght, his thankes, have no felaweshipe.
Wel fynden that Arcite and Palamoun.
Arcite is riden anon unto the toun,
And on the morwe, er it were dayes light,
Ful prively two harneys hath he dight,   1630
Bothe suffisaunt and mete to darreyne
The bataille in the feeld bitwix hem tweyne,
And on his hors, allone as he was born,
He carieth al the harneys hym biforn.
And in the grove, at tyme and place yset,   1635
This Arcite and this Palamon ben met.
To chaungen gan the colour in hir face,
Right as the hunters in the regne of Trace,
That stondeth at the gappe with a spere,
Whan hunted is the leon or the bere,   1640
And hereth hym come russhyng in the greves,
And breketh bothe bowes and the leves,
And thynketh, "Heere cometh my mortal
     enemy!
Withoute faile, he moot be deed, or I,
For outher I moot sleen hym at the gappe,   1645
Or he moot sleen me, if that me myshappe."
So ferden they in chaungyng of hir hewe,
As fer as everich of hem oother knewe.
   Ther nas no good day, ne no saluyng,
But streight, withouten word or rehersyng,   1650
Everich of hem heelp for to armen oother

As freendly as he were his owene brother,
And after that, with sharpe speres stronge
They foynen ech at oother wonder longe.
Thou myghtest wene that this Palamoun   1655
In his fightyng were as a wood leoun,
And as a crueel tigre was Arcite.
As wilde bores gonne they to smyte,
That frothen whit as foom for ire wood.
Up to the ancle foghte they in hir blood.   1660
And in this wise I lete hem fightyng dwelle,
And forth I wole of Theseus yow telle.
   The destinee, ministre general,
That executeth in the world over al   1664
The purveiaunce that God hath seyn biforn,
So strong it is that, though the world had
     sworn
The contrarie of a thyng by ye or nay,
Yet somtyme it shal fallen on a day
That falleth nat eft withinne a thousand yeere.
For certeinly, oure appetites heere,   1670
Be it of werre, or pees, or hate, or love,
Al is this reuled by the sighte above.
   This mene I now by myghty Theseus,
That for to hunten is so desirus,
And namely at the grete hert in May,   1675
That in his bed ther daweth hym no day
That he nys clad, and redy for to ryde
With hunte and horn and houndes hym bisyde.
For in his huntyng hath he swich delit
That it is al his joye and appetit   1680
To been hymself the grete hertes bane,
For after Mars he serveth now Dyane.
   Cleer was the day, as I have toold er this,
And Theseus with alle joye and blis,
With his Ypolita, the faire queene,   1685
And Emelye, clothed al in grene,
On huntyng be they riden roially.
And to the grove that stood ful faste by,

1619 as for me, as far as I am concerned. **1622 to borwe,** as pledge. **1624 regne,** rule. **1626 his thankes,** willingly. **1630 harneys . . . dight,** arms and armor, prepared. This touch is Chaucer's, for in *Tes.* Palemone comes to the grove prepared to fight. **1631 suffisaunt and mete to darreyne,** sufficient and appropriate to decide. **1637** *To chaungen:* Some MSS *Tho chaungen.* **1638 regne of Trace,** kingdom of Thrace (Greece). **1639 the gappe,** the hunter who stands by the gap toward which the animal is driven by the circle of beaters. **1640** *or the:* E&c *and the.* **1641 greves,** bushes. **1646 me myshappe,** bad luck comes to me. **1654 foynen,** thrust at **1656** *as* om in all MSS. **1659 ire wood,** insane anger. **1663ff.** Another of the Boethian asides which characterize this tale, cf. *Boece* IV pr.6; v m.1. **1665 purveiaunce . . . seyn,** providence, seen. **1668 fallen,** happen. **1669 eft,** again. **1670 appetites,** desires. **1673 This mene I by . . . Theseus,** i.e., this must explain why Theseus happened to come by just then. **1675 namely,** especially. **1676 daweth,** dawns. **1678 hunte,** huntsman. **1681 bane,** slayer. **1682 Mars . . . Dyane,** god of war, goddess of hunting. **1688 faste,** near.

In which ther was an hert, as men hym tolde,
Duc Theseus the streighte wey hath holde. 1690
And to the launde he rideth hym ful right,
For thider was the hert wont have his flight,
And over a brook, and so forth on his weye.
This duc wol han a cours at hym or tweye
With houndes swiche as that hym list
    comaunde. 1695
   And whan this duc was come unto the launde,
Under the sonne he looketh, and anon
He was war of Arcite and Palamon,
That foughten breme as it were bores two.
The brighte swerdes wenten to and fro 1700
So hidously that with the leeste strook
It semed as it wolde felle an ook.
But what they were, nothyng he ne woot.
This duc his courser with his spores smoot,
And at a stert he was bitwix hem two, 1705
And pulled out a swerd and cride, "Hoo!
Namoore, up peyne of lesynge of youre heed!
By myghty Mars, he shal anon be deed
That smyteth any strook that I may seen.
But telleth me what myster men ye been 1710
That been so hardy for to fighten heere
Withouten juge or oother officere,
As it were in a lystes roially?"
   This Palamon answerde hastily,
And seyde, "Sire, what nedeth wordes mo? 1715
We have the deeth disserved bothe two.
Two woful wrecches been we, two caytyves,
That been encombred of oure owene lyves.
And as thou art a rightful lord and juge,
Ne yeve us neither mercy ne refuge. 1720
But sle me first, for seinte charitee!
But sle my felawe eek as wel as me,
Or sle hym first, for though thow knowest it lite,
This is thy mortal foo, this is Arcite,

That fro thy lond is banysshed on his heed, 1725
For which he hath deserved to be deed.
For this is he that cam unto thy gate
And seyde that he highte Philostrate.
Thus hath he japed thee ful many a yer,
And thou hast maked hym thy chief squier. 1730
And this is he that loveth Emelye.
For sith the day is come that I shal dye,
I make pleynly my confessioun
That I am thilke woful Palamoun
That hath thy prisoun broken wikkedly. 1735
I am thy mortal foo, and it am I
That loveth so hoote Emelye the brighte
That I wol dye present in hir sighte.
Wherfore I axe deeth and my juwise;
But sle my felawe in the same wise, 1740
For bothe han we deserved to be slayn."
   This worthy duc answerde anon agayn,
And seyde, "This is a short conclusioun.
Youre owene mouth, by youre confessioun,
Hath dampned yow, and I wol it recorde. 1745
It nedeth noght to pyne yow with the corde.
Ye shal be deed, by myghty Mars the rede!"
   The queene anon, for verray wommanhede,
Gan for to wepe, and so dide Emelye,
And alle the ladyes in the compaignye. 1750
Greet pitee was it, as it thoughte hem alle,
That evere swich a chaunce sholde falle,
For gentil men they were of greet estaat,
And no thyng but for love was this debaat;
And saugh hir blody woundes wyde and soore, 1755
And alle crieden, bothe lasse and moore, 1756
"Have mercy, Lord, upon us wommen alle!"
And on hir bare knees adoun they falle,
And wolde have kist his feet ther as he stood,
Til at the laste aslaked was his mood, 1760
For pitee renneth soone in gentil herte.

1691 launde, clearing. **1694 a cours,** a chase. **1695 houndes . . . comaunde,** hounds he wished to select (for each chase). **1697 Under,** toward (shading his eyes?). In *Tes.* it is Emilia who discovers the two knights fighting. **1699 breme,** fiercely. **1703 what,** who—in the medieval sense of status; see "which," *CT* I.40. **1707 EHg&c *upon*,** but some MSS have the older form *up peyne*. **1710 myster,** craft, i.e., "what kind of"—see l. 1703 above. **1711 hardy,** foolhardy. **1717 caytyves,** wretches. **1718 encombred,** burdened. **1723 lite,** little. **1725 on his,** on penalty of losing his. **1729 japed,** duped. **1732 sith,** since. **1735 broken,** broken out of. **1739 juwise,** sentence. **1745 dampned . . . recorde,** condemned, take note of. **1746 pyne,** torture. **1748 verray,** genuine. **1752 chaunce . . . falle,** event, occur. **1756 lasse . . . moore,** lesser and higher estate. **1760 aslaked,** satisfied. *Tes.* does not picture Theseus as angry nor the Queen as interceding. Scholars have cited actual intercessions by both Queen Philippa and Queen Anne that may have suggested to Chaucer this alteration. *LGW* l. 341ff. offers a parallel study of princely behavior. **1761** "Amor, che al cor gentil ratto s'apprende" (Dante, *Inf.* v.100). This was a favorite sentiment of the Italian poets of the "dolce stil nuovo." It was repeated by Chaucer in MLT II.660, MerchT IV.1986, SqT v.479, *TC* III.5, and *LGW* l.503.

And though he first for ire quook and sterte,
He hath considered shortly, in a clause,
The trespas of hem bothe, and eek the cause,
And although that his ire hir gilt accused,   1765
Yet in his resoun he hem bothe excused,
As thus: he thoghte wel that every man
Wol helpe hymself in love, if that he kan,
And eek delivere hymself out of prisoun.
And eek his herte hadde compassioun   1770
Of wommen, for they wepen evere in oon,
And in his gentil herte he thoughte anon,
And softe unto hymself he seyde, "Fy
Upon a lord that wol have no mercy,
But been a leon, bothe in word and dede,   1775
To hem that been in repentaunce and drede,
As well as to a proud, despitous man
That wol mayntene that he first bigan.
That lord hath litel of discrecioun,
That in swich cas kan no divisioun,   1780
But weyeth pride and humblesse after oon."
And shortly, whan his ire is thus agoon,
He gan to looken up with eyen lighte,
And spak thise same wordes al on highte:
    "The god of love, a, benedicite!   1785
How myghty and how greet a lord is he!
Ayeyns his myght ther gayneth none obstacles.
He may be cleped a god for his myracles,
For he kan maken, at his owene gyse,
Of everich herte as that hym list divyse.   1790
Lo heere this Arcite and this Palamoun,
That quitly weren out of my prisoun,
And myghte han lyved in Thebes roially,
And witen I am hir mortal enemy,
And that hir deth lith in my myght also,   1795
And yet hath love, maugree hir eyen two,
Broght hem hyder bothe for to dye.
Now looketh, is nat that an heigh folye?
    "Who may been a fool but if he love?
Bihoold, for Goddes sake that sit above,   1800
Se how they blede! Be they noght wel arrayed?
Thus hath hir lord, the god of love, ypayed

Hir wages and hir fees for hir servyse!
And yet they wenen for to been ful wyse
That serven love, for aught that may bifalle.
But this is yet the beste game of alle,   1806
That she for whom they han this jolitee
Kan hem therfore as muche thank as me.
She woot namoore of al this hoote fare,
By God, than woot a cokkow or an hare!   1810
But all moot ben assayed, hoot and coold.
A man moot ben a fool, or yong or oold—
I woot it by myself ful yore agon,
For in my tyme a servant was I oon.
And therfore, syn I knowe of loves peyne,   1815
And woot hou soore it kan a man distreyne,
As he that hath ben caught ofte in his laas,
I yow foryeve al hoolly this trespaas,
At requeste of the queene, that kneleth heere,
And eek of Emelye, my suster deere.   1820
And ye shul bothe anon unto me swere
That nevere mo ye shal my contree dere,
Ne make werre upon me nyght ne day,
But been my freendes in al that ye may.
I yow foryeve this trespas every deel."   1825
And they hym sworen his axyng faire and weel,
And hym of lordshipe and of mercy preyde,
And he hem graunteth grace, and thus he
      seyde,
    "To speke of roial lynage and richesse,
Though that she were a queene or a princesse,
Ech of you bothe is worthy, doutelees,   1831
To wedden whan tyme is, but nathelees—
I speke as for my suster Emelye,
For whom ye have this strif and jalousye—
Ye woot yourself she may nat wedden two   1835
Atones, though ye fighten everemo.
That oon of you, al be hym looth or lief,
He moot go pipen in an yvy leef.
This is to seyn, she may nat now han bothe,
Al be ye never so jalouse ne so wrothe.   1840
And forthy I yow putte in this degree,
That ech of yow shal have his destynee

1771 **evere in oon,** continuously. 1777 **despitous,** cruel. 1780 **kan no divisioun,** recognizes no difference. 1781 **after oon,** the same. 1784 **on highte,** on high (aloud). 1785ff. A familiar medieval sentiment, cf. *RR* 4221ff. (Dunn–Robbins, 21.6ff.) 1787 **gayneth,** avail. 1788 **cleped . . . for,** called, because of. 1789 **gyse,** inclination. 1794 **witen,** know. 1796 **maugree,** in spite of. 1799 **but if,** unless. 1804 **wenen,** think themselves. 1808 **Kan,** knows (gives). 1809–10 **woot,** knows. *cokkow or:* E&c *cokkow of.* 1811–12 **moot,** must. 1813 **yore agon,** long ago. 1816 **distreyne,** afflict. 1817 **laas,** noose. 1822 **dere,** harm. 1837 **lief,** happy. 1841 **forthy . . . degree,** therefore, condition.

As hym is shape, and herkneth in what wyse:
Lo heere youre ende of that I shal devyse.

    "My wyl is this, for plat conclusioun,   1845
Withouten any repplicacioun—
If that you liketh, take it for the beste:
That everich of you shal goon where hym leste
Frely, withouten raunson or daunger,
And this day fifty wykes fer ne ner,   1850
Everich of you shal brynge an hundred knyghtes
Armed for lystes up at alle rightes,
Al redy to darreyne hire by bataille.
And this bihote I yow withouten faille,
Upon my trouthe, and as I am a knyght,   1855
That wheither of yow bothe that hath myght—
This is to seyn, that wheither he or thow
May with his hundred, as I spak of now,
Sleen his contrarie, or out of lystes dryve,
Thanne shal I yeve Emelya to wyve   1860
To whom that Fortune yeveth so fair a grace.
The lystes shal I maken in this place.
And God so wisly on my soule rewe,
As I shal evene juge been and trewe,
Ye shul noon oother ende with me maken   1865
That oon of yow ne shal be deed or taken.
And if yow thynketh this is weel ysayd,
Seyeth youre avys and holdeth you apayd.
This is youre ende and youre conclusioun."

    Who looketh lightly now but Palamoun?
Who spryngeth up for joye but Arcite?   1871
Who kouthe telle, or who kouthe endite
The joye that is maked in the place
Whan Theseus hath doon so fair a grace?   1874
But doun on knees wente every maner wight,
And thonken hym with al hir herte and myght,
And namely the Thebans often sithe.
And thus with good hope and with herte blithe
They taken hir leve, and homward gonne they
    ride

To Thebes, with his olde walles wyde.   1880

Explicit secunda pars. Sequitur pars tercia.

    I trowe men wolde deme it necligence
If I foryete to tellen the dispence
Of Theseus, that gooth so bisily
To maken up the lystes roially,
That swich a noble theatre as it was,   1885
I dar wel seyn in this world ther nas.
The circuit a myle was aboute,
Walled of stoon, and dyched al withoute.
Round was the shape, in manere of compas,
Ful of degrees, the heighte of sixty pas,   1890
That whan a man was set on o degree,
He lette nat his felawe for to see.

    Estward ther stood a gate of marbul whit,
Westward right swich another in the
    opposit.
And shortly to concluden, swich a place   1895
Was noon in erthe, as in so litel space.
For in the lond ther was no crafty man
That geometrie or ars-metrik kan,
Ne portreitour, ne kervere of ymages,
That Theseus ne yaf mete and wages,   1900
The theatre for to maken and devyse.
And for to doon his ryte and sacrifise,
He estward hath, upon the gate above,
In worshipe of Venus, goddesse of love,
Doon make an auter and an oratorie.   1905
And on the gate westward, in memorie
Of Mars, he maked hath right swich another,
That coste largely of gold a fother.
And northward, in a touret on the wal,
Of alabastre whit and reed coral,   1910
An oratorie, riche for to see,
In worshipe of Dyane of chastitee,
Hath Theseus doon wroght in noble wyse.
    But yet hadde I foryeten to devyse

1843 shape, foreordained. **1845 plat,** plain. **1846 repplicacioun,** rejoinder. **1850 fifty . . . fer ne ner,** fifty, more nor less. This is taken to be poetic expression for exactly a year. *Tes.* has "un anno intero" (a year entire). **1852 up,** intensive, as in "dressed up." **1853 darreyne,** establish claim to. **1854 bihote,** promise. **1856 wheither,** whichever. **1863 rewe,** have pity. **1864 evene,** fair, as in "even hand." **1865 ende,** conclusion. **1868 avys . . . apayd,** view, satisfied. **1872 kouthe,** could. **1877 namely . . . sithe,** especially, times. **1882 dispence,** expenditure. **1886 nas,** was not. **1887** In *Tes.* the lists (not described until the tournament in Book VII) were built in the shape of a Roman circus rather than the usual rectangular wooden stockades. **1890 degrees . . . pas,** steps, paces. **1892 lette,** hindered. **1898 ars-metrik kan,** arithmetic knows. **1905 Doon make an auter,** caused an altar to be made. In *Tes.* the three temples are scattered about Athens and the temple of Diana is not described. Joining them to the lists and equalizing the descriptions are features of the unity and symmetry which characterize Chaucer's adaptation. **1906** E&c *gate* om. **1908 fother,** load. **1911 oratorie,** chapel. **1914 devyse,** describe.

The noble kervyng and the portreitures,   1915
The shape, the contenaunce, and the figures,
That weren in thise oratories thre.

   First in the temple of Venus maystow se
Wroght on the wal, ful pitous to biholde,
The broken slepes and the sikes colde,   1920
The sacred teeris and the waymentynge,
The firy strokes of the desirynge
That loves servantz in this lyf enduren,
The othes that hir covenantz assuren;
Plesaunce and Hope, Desir, Foolhardynesse,   1925
Beautee and Youthe, Bauderie, Richesse,
Charmes and Force, Lesynges, Flaterye,
Despense, Bisynesse, and Jalousye
That wered of yelewe gooldes a gerland
And a cokkow sittynge on hir hand;   1930
Festes, instrumentz, caroles, daunces,
Lust and array, and alle the circumstaunces
Of love, whiche that I rekned and rekne shal
By ordre, weren peynted on the wal,
And mo than I kan make of mencioun.   1935
For soothly al the mount of Citheroun,
Ther Venus hath hir principal dwellynge,
Was shewed on the wal in portreyynge,
With al the gardyn and the lustynesse.
Nat was foryeten the porter, Ydelnesse,   1940
Ne Narcisus the faire of yore agon,
Ne yet the folye of Kyng Salamon,
Ne yet the grete strengthe of Ercules,
Th'enchauntementz of Medea and Circes,
Ne of Turnus, with the hardy fiers corage,   1945
The riche Cresus, kaytyf in servage.

Thus may ye seen that wysdom ne richesse,
Beautee ne sleighte, strengthe ne hardynesse,
Ne may with Venus holde champartie,
For as hir list the world than may she gye.   1950
Lo, alle thise folk so caught were in hir las,
Til they for wo ful ofte seyde allas.
Suffiseth heere ensamples oon or two,
And though I koude rekene a thousand mo.

   The statue of Venus, glorious for to se,   1955
Was naked, fletynge in the large see,
And fro the navele doun al covered was
With wawes grene, and brighte as any glas.
A citole in hir right hand hadde she,
And on hir heed, ful semely for to se,   1960
A rose gerland, fressh and wel smellynge;
Above hir heed hir dowves flikerynge.
Biforn hire stood hir sone Cupido;
Upon his shuldres wynges hadde he two,
And blynd he was, as it is often seene;   1965
A bowe he bar and arwes brighte and kene.

   Why sholde I noght as wel eek telle yow al
The portreiture that was upon the wal
Withinne the temple of myghty Mars the rede?
Al peynted was the wal, in lengthe and brede,
Lyk to the estres of the grisly place   1971
That highte the grete temple of Mars in Trace,
In thilke colde, frosty regioun
Ther as Mars hath his sovereyn mansioun.

   First on the wal was peynted a forest,   1975
In which ther dwelleth neither man ne best,
With knotty, knarry, bareyne trees olde,
Of stubbes sharpe and hidouse to biholde,

1916 contenaunce, appearance. **1918ff.** This description is modeled upon *Tes.* VII.53ff. and other sources. Chaucer had twice before handled this material, in *PF* ll. 211–94 (a close translation) and *HF* ll. 119–39. **1920 sikes,** sighs. **1921 waymentynge,** lamenting. **1925 Plesaunce,** pleasure. **1926 Bauderie,** procuring. **1927 Lesynges,** lies. **1928 Despense, Bisynesse,** expenditure, attention. **1929 gooldes,** marigolds; yellow was the color of jealousy. **1932 Lust,** pleasure. **1933 reckne,** enumerate. **1936 Citheroun,** confused in *RR* 15662 (Dunn–Robbins, 75.4) and elsewhere with the island of Cythera where Venus rose from the sea. **1940 Ydelnesse,** gatekeeper of the Garden of Love in *RR* 561 (Dunn–Robbins, 3.40). **1941 Narcisus,** Narcissus, who fell in love with his own reflection, also in *RR* 1439ff. (Dunn–Robbins 6.1ff.). **1942 folye of Kyng Salamon,** his harem and its results, I Kings 11. *Ne:* E *And.* **1943 strengthe of Ercules,** in spite of which strength, he was killed through the love and jealousy of Deianira; see below MkT VII.2119ff. *Ne yet:* E&c *And eek.* **1944 Medea,** sorceress who helped Jason secure the Golden Fleece and later in love and jealousy killed their children and Jason's second wife. **Circes,** Circe, the sorceress who turned men to swine in the *Odyssey,* 10–12. **1945 Turnus,** opponent killed by Aeneas in *Aeneid* XII. **1946 Cresus,** Croesus, unfortunate king of Lydia, see MkT VII.2727 below. **kaytyf in servage,** miserable in captivity. **1948 sleighte,** trickery. **1949 holde champartie,** contend successfully. **1950 list . . . gye,** desires, guide. **1951 las,** noose. **1954 rekene,** enumerate. **1956 fletynge . . . large,** floating, broad; the traditional figure of Venus rising from the waves. **1959 citole,** pear-shaped, stringed musical instrument. **1971 estres . . . grisly,** interior, dreadful. **1972 highte . . . Trace,** is called, Thrace. **1974 sovereyn,** supreme. **1977 knarry,** gnarled.

In which ther ran a rumbel and a swough,   1979
As though a storm sholde bresten every bough.
And dounward from an hille, under a bente,
Ther stood the temple of Mars armypotente,
Wroght al of burned steel, of which the entree
Was long and streit and gastly for to see.
And therout cam a rage and swich a veze   1985
That it made al the gate for to rese.
The northren lyght in at the dores shoon,
For wyndowe on the wal ne was ther noon,
Thurgh which men myghten any light discerne.
The dore was al of adamant eterne,   1990
Yclenched overthwart and endelong
With iren tough; and for to make it strong,
Every pyler, the temple to sustene,
Was tonne-greet, of iren bright and shene.
    Ther saugh I first the dirke ymaginyng   1995
Of Felonye, and al the compassyng;
The crueel Ire, reed as any gleede;
The pykepurs, and eek the pale Drede;
The smylere with the knyfe under the cloke;
The shepne brennynge with the blake
        smoke;   2000
The tresoun of the mordrynge in the bedde;
The open werre, with woundes al bibledde;
Contek, with blody knyf and sharp manace.
Al ful of chirkyng was that sory place.
    The sleere of hymself yet saugh I ther—   2005
His herte-blood hath bathed al his heer;
The nayl ydryven in the shode a-nyght;
The colde deeth, with mouth gapyng upright.
Amyddes of the temple sat Meschaunce,
With disconfort and sory contenaunce.   2010

Yet saugh I Woodnesse, laughynge in his rage,
Armed Compleint, Outhees, and fiers Outrage;
The careyne in the busk, with throte ycorve;
A thousand slayn, and nat of qualm ystorve;
The tiraunt, with the pray by force yraft;   2015
The toun destroyed, ther was nothyng laft.
    Yet saugh I brent the shippes hoppesteres;
The hunte strangled with the wilde beres;
The sowe freten the child right in the cradel;
The cook yscalded, for al his longe ladel.   2020
    Noght was foryeten by the infortune of Marte
The cartere overryden with his carte—
Under the wheel ful lowe he lay adoun.
    Ther were also, of Martes divisioun,   2024
The barbour, and the bocher, and the smyth,
That forgeth sharpe swerdes on his styth.
    And al above, depeynted in a tour,
Saugh I Conquest, sittynge in greet honour,
With the sharpe swerd over his heed
Hangynge by a soutil twynes threed.   2030
    Depeynted was the slaughtre of Julius,
Of grete Nero, and of Antonius—
Al be that thilke tyme they were unborn,
Yet was hir deth depeynted ther-biforn
By manasynge of Mars, right by figure.   2035
So was it shewed in that portreiture
As is depeynted in the sterres above
Who shal be slayn or elles deed for love.
Suffiseth oon ensample in stories olde;
I may nat rekene hem alle though I wolde.   2040
    The statue of Mars upon a carte stood
Armed, and looked grym as he were wood,
And over his heed ther shynen two figures

1979 swough, sough (murmur). *and a:* Hg&c *in a.* **1980 bresten,** break. **1981 under a bente,** beside a heath. **1982 armypotente,** potent in arms (evidently here first introduced into English from *Tes.* VII.32). **1983 burned ... entree,** burnished, entrance. **1984 streit,** narrow. **1985 rage ... veze,** roar, blast. **1986 rese,** shake. **1987 northren,** the temple was oriented toward the north, away from the sun, whereas most temples point east. **1993 sustene,** support. **1994 tonne-greet ... shene,** large around as a barrel, shining. **1995 dirke ymaginyng,** in *Tes.* the prayers of Arcite, Palamon, and Emelye take human form. **1996 compassyng,** plotting. **1997 gleede,** live coal. **2000 shepne brennynge,** barn burning. **2003 Contek ... manace,** strife, menace. **2004 chirkyng,** jarring sounds. **2005 hymself,** perhaps in an earlier version "hir husband"? Lines 2006–8 (suggestive of Judges 4:17ff.) do not describe suicide, and see below *CT,* III.765–70. **2011 Woodnesse,** madness. **2012 Outhees,** outcry. **2013 careyne ... busk ... ycorve,** corpse, bush, cut. **2014 qualm ystorve,** plague dead. **2015 pray ... yraft,** booty, seized. **2017 brent ... hoppesteres,** burned, dancers (feminine suffix). *Tes.* has "navi bellatrici" (fighting ships), which was read by Chaucer or his source "navi ballatrici" (dancing ships). **2018 hunte,** hunter. **2019 freten,** having eaten. **2021 Noght ... infortune,** not, evil influence. **2022 overryden,** run over. **2024 divisioun,** category of persons. **2025** *barbour:* E&c *laborer.* **2026 styth,** anvil. **2029 swerd,** the sword of Damocles; see *Boece* III pr.5. **2030 soutil,** thin. **2031 slaughtre ... Julius,** killing, Julius Caesar. **2032 Antonius,** Marc Antony, who committed suicide just before Cleopatra. **2033 thilke,** at that. **2035 manasynge ... by figure,** threatening prediction, by horoscope. **2042 wood,** insane.

Of sterres, that been cleped in scriptures
That oon Puella, that oother Rubeus.   2045
This god of armes was arrayed thus.
A wolf ther stood biforn hym at his feet
With eyen rede, and of a man he eet.
With soutil pencel was depeynt this storie
In redoutynge of Mars and of his glorie.   2050

   Now to the temple of Dyane the chaste
As shortly as I kan I wol me haste,
To telle yow al the descripsioun.
Depeynted been the walles up and doun
Of huntyng and of shamefast chastitee.   2055

   Ther saugh I how woful Calistopee,
Whan that Diane agreved was with here,
Was turned from a womman til a bere,
And after was she maad the loode-sterre;   2059
Thus was it peynted, I kan sey yow no ferre.
Hir sone is eek a sterre, as men may see.

   Ther saugh I Dane, yturned til a tree—
I mene nat the goddesse Diane,
But Penneus doghter, which that highte Dane.

   Ther saugh I Attheon an hert ymaked,   2065
For vengeaunce that he saugh Diane al naked.
I saugh how that his houndes have hym caught
And freeten hym, for that they knewe hym
   naught.

   Yet peynted was a litel forther moor
How Atthalante hunted the wilde boor,   2070
And Meleagre, and many another mo,
For which Dyane wroghte hym care and wo.
Ther saugh I many another wonder storie,
The whiche me list nat drawen to memorie.

   This goddesse on an hert ful hye seet,   2075
With smale houndes al aboute hir feet,
And undernethe hir feet she hadde a moone,
Wexynge it was and sholde wanye soone.
In gaude grene hir statue clothed was,

With bowe in honde and arwes in a cas.   2080
Hir eyen caste she ful lowe adoun,
Ther Pluto hath his derke regioun.

   A womman travaillynge was hire biforn;
But for hir child so longe was unborn,
Ful pitously Lucyna gan she calle,   2085
And seyde, "Help, for thou mayst best of alle!"
Wel koude he peynten lifly that it wroghte;
With many a floryn he the hewes boghte.

   Now been thise lystes maad, and Theseus,
That at his grete cost arrayed thus   2090
The temples and the theatre every deel,
Whan it was doon, hym lyked wonder weel.
But stynte I wole of Theseus a lite,
And speke of Palamon and of Arcite.

   The day approcheth of hir retournynge,   2095
That everich sholde an hundred knyghtes
   brynge
The bataille to darreyne, as I yow tolde.
And til Atthenes, hir covenantz for to holde,
Hath everich of hem broght an hundred
   knyghtes,
Wel armed for the werre at alle rightes.   2100
And sikerly ther trowed many a man
That nevere sithen that the world bigan,
As for to speke of knyghthod of hir hond,
As fer as God hath maked see or lond,
Nas of so fewe so noble a compaignye.   2105
For every wight that lovede chivalrye,
And wolde, his thankes, han a passant name,
Hath preyed that he myghte been of that game;
And wel was hym that therto chosen was.
For if ther fille tomorwe swich a cas,   2110
Ye knowen wel that every lusty knyght
That loveth paramours and hath his myght,
Were it in Engelond or elleswhere,
They wolde, hir thankes, wilnen to be there—

2044 **scriptures,** written records. 2045 **Puella . . . Rubeus,** patterns of dots in geomancy described in detail by Skeat, Manly, and Robinson. 2049 **soutil,** clever. 2050 **redoutynge,** honor. 2055 **shamefast,** modest. 2056 **Calistopee,** transformed by Diana into the constellation of the Great Bear (Ursa Major) for surrendering her virginity to Jove. 2059 **loode-sterre,** pole star, actually in Ursa Minor, created from Calistopee's son. 2060 **ferre,** further. 2062 **Dane,** Daphne, transformed into a laurel to escape Apollo. 2065 **Attheon,** Acteon, transformed into a stag, because he saw Diana bathing naked, and killed by his own hounds. 2068 **freeten,** eaten. 2070–71 **Atthalante, Meleagre.** Meleager killed the Calydonian boar, first wounded by Atalanta. 2075 E&c *ful wel hye.* 2079 **gaude,** yellowish. 2082 **Pluto,** god of the underworld. 2083 **travaillynge,** in labor (childbirth). 2085 **Lucyna,** goddess of childbirth (another manifestation of Diana). 2087 **lifly,** lifelike. 2088 **floryn . . . hewes,** a gold coin originally issued in Florence, paints. 2097 **darreyne,** decide. 2098 **covenantz,** agreements. 2101 **sikerly . . . trowed,** certainly, thought. 2102 **sithen,** since. 2103 **knyghthod . . . hond,** valor of their deeds. 2107 **passant,** surpassing. 2110 **cas,** event. 2111 **lusty,** happy (spirited). 2112 **paramours,** with sexual love. 2114 **wilnen,** desire.

To fighte for a lady, benedicitee! 2115
It were a lusty sighte for to see.
    And right so ferden they with Palamon.
With hym ther wenten knyghtes many on;
Som wol ben armed in an haubergeoun,
And in a bristplate and a light gypoun; 2120
And somme woln have a paire plates large;
And somme woln have a Pruce sheeld or a targe;
Somme woln ben armed on hir legges weel,
And have an ax, and somme a mace of steel—
Ther is no newe gyse that it nas old. 2125
Armed were they, as I have yow told,
Everych after his opinioun.
    Ther maistow seen comynge with Palamoun
Lygurge hymself, the grete kyng of Trace.
Blak was his berd and manly was his face; 2130
The cercles of his eyen in his heed,
They gloweden bitwixen yelow and reed,
And lik a grifphon looked he aboute,
With kempe heeris on his browes stoute; 2134
His lymes grete, his brawnes harde and stronge,
His shuldres brode, his armes rounde and longe.
And as the gyse was in his contree,
Ful hye upon a chaar of gold stood he,
With foure white boles in the trays.
Instede of cote-armure over his harnays, 2140
With nayles yelewe and brighte as any gold,
He hadde a beres skyn, col-blak for old.
His longe heer was kembd bihynde his bak—
As any ravenes fethere it shoon for blak; 2144
A wrethe of gold, arm-greet, of huge wighte,
Upon his heed, set ful of stones brighte,
Of fyne rubyes and of dyamauntz.
Aboute his chaar ther wenten white alauntz,
Twenty and mo, as grete as any steer,

To hunten at the leoun or the deer, 2150
And folwed hym with mosel faste ybounde,
Colered of gold, and tourettes fyled rounde.
An hundred lordes hadde he in his route,
Armed ful wel, with hertes stierne and stoute.
    With Arcite, in stories as men fynde, 2155
The grete Emetreus, the kyng of Inde,
Upon a steede bay trapped in steel,
Covered in clooth of gold, dyapred weel,
Cam ridynge lyk the god of armes, Mars.
His cote-armure was of clooth of Tars 2160
Couched with perles white and rounde and
        grete;
His sadel was of brend gold newe ybete;
A mantel upon his shulder hangynge,
Bratful of rubyes rede as fyr sparklynge;
His crispe heer lyk rynges was yronne, 2165
And that was yelow, and glytered as the sonne.
His nose was heigh, his eyen bright citryn,
His lippes rounde, his colour was sangwyn;
A fewe frakenes in his face yspreynd,
Bitwixen yelow and somdel blak ymeynd; 2170
And as a leoun he his lookyng caste.
Of fyve and twenty yeer his age I caste.
His berd was wel bigonne for to sprynge;
His voys was as a trompe thonderynge.
Upon his heed he wered of laurer grene 2175
A gerland, fressh and lusty for to sene.
Upon his hand he bar for his deduyt
An egle tame, as any lilye whyt.
An hundred lordes hadde he with hym there,
Al armed, save hir heddes, in al hir gere, 2180
Ful richely in alle maner thynges.
For trusteth wel that dukes, erles, kynges
Were gadered in this noble compaignye,

2115 **benedicitee,** bless me (pronounce in three syllables). 2119 **haubergeoun,** chain mail. 2120 **gypoun,** cloth tunic. E&c *in bristplate and in a.* 2121 **paire plates,** set of plate armor. 2122 **Pruce sheeld . . . targe,** Prussian shield, shield. 2123 *hir:* Hg&c *his.* 2124 **mace,** spiked club. 2125 **gyse,** fashion. 2133 **grifphon,** griffin. 2134 **kempe . . . stoute,** shaggy, strong. 2135 **brawnes,** muscles. 2137 **gyse,** fashion. 2138 **chaar,** chariot. 2139 **boles . . . trays,** bulls, trace. 2140 **cote-armure,** coat of arms. 2141 **nayles yelewe,** i.e., the bearskin's. 2142 **for old,** for (from) age. 2143 **kembd,** combed. 2145 **wighte,** weight. 2148 **alauntz,** wolfhounds. 2151 **mosel . . . ybounde,** muzzled. 2152 **Colered . . . tourettes fyled,** collared, leash rings filed smooth. Some MSS *colers.* 2153 **route,** train. 2154 **stierne,** stern. 2156 **Emetreus,** not mentioned in *Tes.* 2157 **trapped,** with trappings of. 2158 **dyapred,** with crisscross quilting. 2160 **cote-armure . . . clooth of Tars,** cloth vest bearing his coat of arms, silk imported from China through Tartary. 2161 **couched,** set. 2162 **brend . . . ybete,** burnished, embroidered. 2164 **Bratful,** brimfull. 2165 **yronne,** run (transitive vb., fashioned). 2167 **heigh . . . citryn,** high (patrician), amber. 2168 **sangwyn,** reddish (i.e., of the four humors). 2169 **frakenes . . . yspreynd,** freckles, sprinkled. Amber eyes and freckles are marks of the Martian type, since Arcite was under the protection of Mars. The description of Lycurgus (above ll. 2128ff.) has been called Saturnalian, since Palamon was under the protection of Saturn. See W. C. Curry, *Chaucer and the Medieval Sciences* (1960 ed.), p. 130ff. 2170 **somdel . . . ymeynd,** somewhat, mingled. 2175 **laurer,** laurel. 2177 **deduyt,** pleasure.

For love and for encrees of chivalrye.
Aboute this kyng ther ran on every part 2185
Ful many a tame leoun and leopart.
And in this wise thise lordes, alle and some,
Been on the Sonday to the citee come
Aboute pryme, and in the toun alight. 2189
This Theseus, this duc, this worthy knyght,
Whan he had broght hem into his citee,
And inned hem, everich at his degree,
He festeth hem, and dooth so greet labour
To esen hem and doon hem al honour,
That yet men wenen that no mannes wit 2195
Of noon estaat ne koude amenden it.
The mynstralcye, the service at the feeste,
The grete yiftes to the meeste and leeste,
The riche array of Theseus paleys,
Ne who sat first ne last upon the deys, 2200
What ladyes fairest been or best daunsynge,
Or which of hem kan carole best and synge,
Ne who moost felyngly speketh of love,
What haukes sitten on the perche above,
What houndes liggen on the floor adoun— 2205
Of al this make I now no mencioun,
But al th'effect, that thynketh me the beste.
Now cometh the point, and herkneth if yow
      leste.
The Sonday nyght, er day bigan to sprynge,
Whan Palamon the larke herde synge, 2210
Although it nere nat day by houres two,
Yet song the larke; and Palamon right tho
With hooly herte and with an heigh corage,
He roos to wenden on his pilgrymage
Unto the blisful Citherea benigne, 2215
I mene Venus, honurable and digne.
And in hir houre he walketh forth a pas

Unto the lystes ther hire temple was,
And doun he kneleth, and with humble cheere
And herte soor, he seyde as ye shal heere: 2220
"Faireste of faire, O lady myn, Venus,
Doughter to Jove, and spouse of Vulcanus,
Thow gladere of the mount of Citheron,
For thilke love thow haddest to Adoon,
Have pitee of my bittre teeris smerte, 2225
And taak myn humble preyere at thyn herte.
Allas! I ne have no langage to telle
Th'effectes ne the tormentz of myn helle.
Myn herte may myne harmes nat biwreye.
I am so confus that I kan noght seye 2230
But, 'Mercy, lady bright, that knowest weele
My thought, and seest what harmes that I feele!'
Considere al this and rewe upon my soore
As wisly as I shal for everemoore,
Emforth my myght, thy trewe servant be, 2235
And holden werre alwey with chastitee.
That make I myn avow, so ye me helpe.
I kepe noght of armes for to yelpe,
Ne I ne axe nat tomorwe to have victorie,
Ne renoun in this cas, ne veyne glorie 2240
Of pris of armes blowen up and doun.
But I wolde have fully possessioun
Of Emelye, and dye in thy servyse.
Fynd thow the manere hou, and in what wyse.
I recche nat, but it may bettre be, 2245
To have victorie of hem, or they of me,
So that I have my lady in myne armes.
For though so be that Mars is god of armes,
Youre vertu is so greet in hevene above
That if yow list, I shal wel have my love. 2250
"Thy temple wol I worshipe everemo,
And on thyn auter, where I ride or go,

2185 **this kyng,** i.e., Emetreus. 2188 **Sonday,** Chaucer seems very precise about dates in KT: May 3 *after midnight* Palamon breaks prison (l. 1467). Hence it is on Friday, May 4, that Palamon comes to the grove (l. 1534). Hence it is on Saturday, May 5, that they fight (l. 1629). Theseus sets the tournament for a year later (l .1850), and it is on Sunday that the knights now assemble. Skeat pointed out that May 5 fell on Sunday in 1387 (Manly pointed out that it also fell on Sunday in 1381). See above, *CT* I.8n., for Skeat's parallel dating of Gen Pro. 2189 **pryme,** 6–9 A.M., first quarter of the day. 2191 **broght,** conducted. 2192 **inned . . . at his degree,** lodged, according to his rank. 2193 **festeth,** feasts. 2194 **esen,** put at ease. 2195 **wenen,** suppose. 2196 **estaat . . . amenden,** standing (authority), improve on. 2200 **first . . . last . . . deys,** diplomatic precedence, head table. 2202 *carole:* EHg&c repeat *dauncen.* Manly suggests *chaunten.* 2207 **al th' effect,** the total effect. 2211 **houres two,** the twenty-third hour of Sunday belongs to Venus; see *Astrolabe* II.12 for explanation of this, and below the prayer hours of Emelye (l. 2273) and Arcite (l. 2367). 2212 *right tho:* E&c *also.* 2215 **Citherea,** Venus, see l. 1936 above. 2216 **digne,** worshipful. 2219 **cheere,** expression. 2220 E *and seyde in this manere.* 2224 **Adoon,** Adonis. 2229 **biwreye,** betray. 2233 **rewe,** have pity. 2235 **Emforth,** to the extent of. 2236 **holden werre,** be at war. 2238 **kepe . . . yelpe,** care, boast. 2241 **pris . . . blowen,** excellence, announced by the heralds with fanfare of trumpets. 2245 **recche,** reck (care). 2249 **vertu,** potency.

I wol doon sacrifice and fires beete.
And if ye wol nat so, my lady sweete,
Thanne preye I thee, tomorwe with a spere 2255
That Arcita me thurgh the herte bere.
Thanne rekke I noght, whan I have lost my lyf,
Though that Arcita wynne hire to his wyf.
This is th'effect and ende of my preyere:
Yif me my love, thow blisful lady deere." 2260
    Whan the orison was doon of Palamon,
His sacrifice he dide and that anon,
Ful pitously with alle circumstaunce,
Al telle I noght as now his observaunce.
But atte laste the statue of Venus shook, 2265
And made a signe, wherby that he took
That his preyere accepted was that day.
For thogh the signe shewed a delay,
Yet wiste he wel that graunted was his boone;
And with glad herte he wente hym hoom ful
    soone. 2270
    The thridde houre inequal that Palamon
Bigan to Venus temple for to gon,
Up roos the sonne and up roos Emelye,
And to the temple of Dyane gan hye.
Hir maydens, that she thider with hir ladde,
Ful redily with hem the fyr they hadde, 2276
Th'encens, the clothes, and the remenant al
That to the sacrifice longen shal,
The hornes fulle of meeth, as was the gyse—
Ther lakked noght to doon hir sacrifise. 2280
    Smokynge the temple, ful of clothes faire,
This Emelye, with herte debonaire,
Hir body wessh with water of a welle.
But hou she dide hir ryte I dar nat telle,
But it be anything in general, 2285
And yet it were a game to heeren al.
To hym that meneth wel it were no charge,
But it is good a man been at his large.

Hir brighte heer was kembd, untressed al;
A coroune of a grene ook cerial 2290
Upon hir heed was set ful fair and meete.
Two fyres on the auter gan she beete,
And dide hir thynges, as men may biholde
In Stace of Thebes and thise bookes olde.
Whan kyndled was the fyr, with pitous cheere
Unto Dyane she spak as ye may heere: 2296
    "O chaste goddesse of the wodes grene,
To whom bothe hevene and erthe and see is sene,
Queene of the regne of Pluto derk and lowe,
Goddesse of maydens, that myn herte hast
    knowe 2300
Ful many a yeer, and woost what I desire,
As keep me fro thy vengeaunce and thyn ire,
That Attheon aboughte cruelly.
Chaste goddesse, wel wostow that I
Desire to ben a mayden al my lyf, 2305
Ne nevere wol I be no love ne wyf.
I am, thow woost, yet of thy compaignye,
A mayde, and love huntynge and venerye,
And for to walken in the wodes wilde,
And noght to ben a wyf and be with childe. 2310
Noght wol I knowe the compaignye of man.
Now help me, lady, sith ye may and kan,
For tho thre formes that thou hast in thee.
And Palamon, that hath swich love to me,
And eek Arcite, that loveth me so soore— 2315
This grace I preye thee withoute moore,
As sende love and pees bitwixe hem two,
And fro me turne awey hir hertes so
That al hire hoote love and hir desir,
And al hir bisy torment and hir fir 2320
Be queynt, or turned in another place.
And if so be thou wolt do me no grace,
Or if my destynee be shapen so
That I shal nedes have oon of hem two,

2253 **beete,** kindle. 2256 **bere,** bear (i.e., pierce). 2261 **orison,** prayer. 2263 **pitously . . . circumstaunce,** pitifully (reflecting his lovelorn condition), ceremony. 2269 **boone,** request. 2271 **thridde houre inequal that,** third hour after; inequal because only at the equinox are the twelve daylight and twelve dark hours equal. 2276 *hadde:* E&c *ladde.* 2277 **clothes, remenant,** hangings, other things. 2278 **longen shal,** should belong. 2279 **meeth . . . gyse,** mead, custom. 2281 **Smokynge,** censing. 2282 **debonaire,** gentle. 2286 **game,** pleasure. 2287 **charge,** matter. 2288 **at his large,** at liberty (to include only what he wishes). 2289 **kembd, untressed,** combed, unbraided. 2290 **cerial,** evergreen. 2292 **beete,** kindle. 2293 **dide hir thynges,** performed her observances. 2294 **Stace,** Statius, author of the *Thebaid,* the source of some of Boccaccio's *Tesaide,* which does not contain the account of Palamon and Arcite, nor, of course, Emelye's ritual. 2295 **pitous cheere,** pitiful expression. 2298 **sene,** visible. 2299 **regne of Pluto,** kingdom of the underworld; identified with the Greek moon goddess Hecate, Diana was also a goddess of the underworld. 2303 **Attheon aboughte,** Acteon (see 1.2065 above) paid for. 2308 **venerye,** hunting. 2313 **thre formes,** Luna in the heavens, Diana on earth, Hecate in the underworld. 2317 *As:* E&c *And.* 2321 **queynt,** quenched; *or:* Hg&c *and.*

As sende me hym that moost desireth me. 2325
Bihoold, goddesse of clene chastitee,
The bittre teeris that on my chekes falle.
Syn thou art mayde and kepere of us alle,
My maydenhede thou kepe and wel conserve,
And whil I lyve, a mayde I wol thee serve." 2330
 The fires brenne upon the auter cleere,
Whil Emelye was thus in hir preyere.
But sodeynly she saugh a sighte queynte,
For right anon oon of the fyres queynte,
And quyked agayn, and after that anon 2335
That oother fyr was queynt and al agon,
And as it queynte it made a whistelynge
As doon thise wete brondes in hir brennynge,
And at the brondes ende out ran anon
As it were blody dropes many oon. 2340
For which so soore agast was Emelye
That she was wel ny mad, and gan to crye,
For she ne wiste what it signyfied,
But oonly for the feere thus hath she cried,
And weep that it was pitee for to heere. 2345
And therwithal Dyane gan appeere,
With bowe in honde, right as an hunteresse,
And seyde, "Doghter, stynt thyn hevynesse.
Among the goddes hye it is affermed, 2349
And by eterne word writen and confermed,
Thou shalt ben wedded unto oon of tho
That han for thee so muchel care and wo,
But unto which of hem I may nat telle.
Farwel, for I ne may no lenger dwelle.
The fires whiche that on myn auter brenne 2355
Shulle thee declaren, er that thou go henne,
Thyn aventure of love, as in this cas."
And with that word, the arwes in the caas
Of the goddesse clateren faste and rynge,
And forth she wente and made a vanysshynge
For which this Emelye astoned was, 2361
And seyde, "What amounteth this, allas?
I putte me in thy proteccioun,

Dyane, and in thy disposicioun."
And hoom she goth anon the nexte weye. 2365
This is th'effect; ther is namoore to seye.
 The nexte houre of Mars folwynge this,
Arcite unto the temple walked is
Of fierse Mars, to doon his sacrifise
With alle the rytes of his payen wyse. 2370
With pitous herte and heigh devocioun,
Right thus to Mars he seyde his orisoun:
 "O stronge god, that in the regnes colde
Of Trace honoured art and lord yholde,
And hast in every regne and every lond 2375
Of armes al the brydel in thyn hond,
And hem fortunest as thee lyst devyse,
Accepte of me my pitous sacrifise.
If so be that my youthe may deserve,
And that my myght be worthy for to serve 2380
Thy godhede, that I may been oon of thyne,
Thanne preye I thee to rewe upon my pyne.
For thilke peyne and thilke hoote fir
In which thow whilom brendest for desir,
Whan that thow usedest the beautee 2385
Of faire, yonge, fresshe Venus free,
And haddest hire in armes at thy wille—
Although thee ones on a tyme mysfille,
Whan Vulcanus hadde caught thee in his las,
And foond thee liggynge by his wyf, allas— 2390
For thilke sorwe that was in thyn herte,
Have routhe as wel upon my peynes smerte.
I am yong and unkonnynge, as thow woost,
And, as I trowe, with love offended moost
That evere was any lyves creature. 2395
For she that dooth me al this wo endure
Ne reccheth nevere wher I synke or fleete.
And wel I woot, er she me mercy heete,
I moot with strengthe wynne hire in the place.
And wel I woot, withouten help or grace 2400
Of thee, ne may my strengthe noght availle.
Thanne help me, lord, tomorwe in my bataille

2331 cleere, brightly. **2333 queynte,** quaint (strange). **2334 queynte,** quenched (went out). **2335 quyked . . . anon,** came alive, immediately. **2336 agon,** gone. **2338 brondes,** firewood. **2341 agast,** frightened. **2348 stynt . . . hevynesse,** stop, sorrow. **2358 caas,** quiver. **2365 nexte,** nearest. **2367 houre of,** hour, that of Mars (i.e., the fourth hour). **2370 payen,** pagan. **2372 orisoun,** prayer. **2373 regnes,** regions. **2377 fortunest,** gives fortune to. **2382 rewe . . . pyne,** have mercy on, suffering. **2384 whilom,** formerly. **2386 Venus free,** generous Venus. **2388–89 mysfille . . . las,** Vulcan, Venus' husband, with a net (las, lasso) trapped her and Mars together in bed. **2391 thilke,** that. **2392 routhe,** compassion. **2393 unkonnynge . . . woost,** inexperienced, know. **2394 trowe . . . offended,** believe, hurt. **2395 lyves,** living. **2396 dooth,** makes. **2397 reccheth . . . wher . . . fleete,** cares, whether, float. **2398 woot . . . heete,** know, promise. **2399 moot . . . place,** must, public square (lists).

For thilke fyr that whilom brente thee
As wel as thilke fyr now brenneth me,
And do that I tomorwe have victorie.   2405
Myn be the travaille, and thyn be the glorie!
Thy sovereyn temple wol I moost honouren
Of any place, and alwey moost labouren
In thy plesaunce and in thy craftes stronge,
And in thy temple I wol my baner honge   2410
And alle the armes of my compaignye,
And everemo, unto that day I dye,
Eterne fir I wol biforn thee fynde.
And eek to this avow I wol me bynde:
My beerd, myn heer, that hongeth long adoun,
That nevere yet ne felte offensioun   2416
Of rasour nor of shere, I wol thee yeve,
And ben thy trewe servant whil I lyve.
Now, lord, have routhe upon my sorwes soore.
Yif me the victorie, I aske thee namoore."   2420
    The preyere stynt of Arcita the stronge,
The rynges on the temple dore that honge,
And eek the dores, clatereden ful faste,
Of which Arcita somwhat hym agaste.
The fyres brenden upon the auter brighte,   2425
That it gan al the temple for to lighte.
A sweete smel the ground anon up yaf,
And Arcita anon his hand up haf,
And moore encens into the fyr he caste,
With othere rytes mo; and atte laste   2430
The statue of Mars bigan his hauberk rynge,
And with that soun he herde a murmurynge
Ful lowe and dym, and seyde thus, "Victorie!"
For which he yaf to Mars honour and glorie
And thus with joye and hope wel to fare   2435
Arcite anon unto his in is fare,
As fayn as fowel is of the brighte sonne.
    And right anon swich strif ther is bigonne,
For thilke grauntyng, in the hevene above,

Bitwixe Venus, the goddesse of love,   2440
And Mars, the stierne god armypotente,
That Juppiter was bisy it to stente,
Til that the pale Saturnus the colde,
That knew so manye of aventures olde,
Foond in his olde experience an art   2445
That he ful soone hath plesed every part.
As sooth is seyd, elde hath greet avantage;
In elde is bothe wysdom and usage;
Men may the olde atrenne, and noght atrede.
Saturne anon, to stynten strif and drede,   2450
Al be it that it is agayn his kynde,
Of al this strif he gan remedie fynde.
    "My deere doghter Venus," quod Saturne,
"My cours, that hath so wyde for to turne,
Hath moore power than woot any man.   2455
Myn is the drenchyng in the see so wan;
Myn is the prison in the derke cote;
Myn is the stranglyng and hangyng by the
    throte;
The murmure and the cherles rebellyng;
The groynynge, and the pryvee empoysonyng.
I do vengeance and pleyn correccioun,   2461
Whil I dwelle in the signe of the leoun.
Myn is the ruyne of the hye halles;
The fallynge of the toures and of the walles
Upon the mynour or the carpenter.   2465
I slow Sampsoun, shakynge the piler;
And myne be the maladyes colde,
The derke tresons, and the castes olde;
My lookyng is the fader of pestilence.
Now weep namoore, I shal doon diligence   2470
That Palamon, that is thyn owene knyght,
Shal have his lady, as thou hast him hight.
Though Mars shal helpe his knyght, yet
    nathelees
Bitwixe yow ther moot be som tyme pees,

2409 In thy plesaunce, to do your pleasure. **2416 offensioun,** damage; dedication of hair and beards was an ancient custom, cf. Nazarites and Greek heroes. **2419 routhe,** compassion. **2421 stynt,** ended. **2424 hym agaste,** was frightened. **2428 haf,** lifted. **2431 hauberk,** armor. **2436 his in,** his inn. **2437 fayn,** happy. **2439 grauntyng,** promises. **2441 armypotente,** potent in arms, see 1.1982 above. **2442 stente,** stop. **2447 sooth,** truth. **2448 usage,** experience. **2449 atrenne . . . atrede,** outrun, outwit. **2451 kynde,** nature. **2454 cours . . . wyde,** wide orbit. In the Middle Ages, the planet Saturn was thought to have the largest orbit. Chaucer, here as elsewhere, blends notions of divine powers with notions of planetary influence—mythology with astrology. **2456 drenchyng,** drowning. **2457 cote,** hut. **2459 cherles rebellyng,** perhaps one of Chaucer's few allusions to the Peasants' Revolt of 1381. **2460 groynynge . . . pryvee,** complaining, secret. **2461 pleyn correccioun,** full punishment. **2462 leoun,** the influence of Saturn was particularly evil when it was in the zodiacal sign of Leo. **2463 ruyne,** ruin. **2465 mynour,** miner (especially one who undermines a fortress). **2467 colde,** as opposed to fevers. **2468 castes,** plots. **2469 lookyng is the fader,** astrological aspect is the cause. **2472 hight,** promised.

Al be ye noght of o compleccioun, 2475
That causeth al day swich divisioun.
I am thyn aiel, redy at thy wille;
Weep now namoore, I wol thy lust fulfille."
    Now wol I stynten of the goddes above,
Of Mars and of Venus, goddesse of love, 2480
And telle yow as pleynly as I kan
The grete effect for which that I bygan.

Explicit tercia pars. Sequitur pars quarta.

    Greet was the feeste in Atthenes that day,
And eek the lusty seson of that May 2484
Made every wight to been in swich plesaunce
That al that Monday justen they and daunce,
And spenden it in Venus heigh servyse.
But by the cause that they sholde ryse
Eerly, for to seen the grete fight,
Unto hir reste wenten they at nyght. 2490
And on the morwe, whan that day gan sprynge,
Of hors and harneys noyse and claterynge
Ther was in hostelryes al aboute,
And to the paleys rood ther many a route
Of lordes upon steedes and palfreys. 2495
Ther maystow seen devisynge of harneys
So unkouth and so riche, and wroght so weel
Of goldsmythrye, of browdynge, and of steel,
The sheeldes brighte, testeres, and trappures,
Gold-hewen helmes, hauberkes, cote-armures,
Lordes in parementz on hir courseres, 2501
Knyghtes of retenue, and eek squieres
Nailynge the speres, and helmes bokelynge,
Giggynge of sheeldes, with layneres lacynge—
There as nede is they weren nothyng ydel.
The fomy steedes on the golden brydel 2506
Gnawynge, and faste the armurers also
With fyle and hamer prikynge to and fro,
Yemen on foote, and communes many oon

With shorte staves, thikke as they may goon;
Pypes, trompes, nakers, clariounes, 2511
That in the bataille blowen blody sounes;
The paleys ful of peple up and doun,
Heere thre, ther ten, holdynge hir questioun,
Dyvynynge of thise Thebane knyghtes two. 2515
Somme seyden thus, somme seyde, "It shal be
    so."
Somme helden with hym with the blake berd,
Somme with the balled, somme with the thikke
    herd;
Somme seyde he looked grymme, and he wolde
    fighte:
"He hath a sparth of twenty pound of wighte."
Thus was the halle ful of divynynge, 2521
Longe after that the sonne gan to sprynge.
    The grete Theseus, that of his sleep awaked
With mynstralcie and noyse that was maked,
Heeld yet the chambre of his paleys riche
Til that the Thebane knyghtes, bothe yliche
Honured, were into the paleys fet. 2527
Duc Theseus was at a wyndow set,
Arrayed right as he were a god in trone.
The peple preesseth thiderward ful soone 2530
Hym for to seen, and doon heigh reverence,
And eek to herkne his heste and his sentence.
    An heraud on a scaffold made an "Oo!"
Til al the noyse of peple was ydo, 2534
And whan he saugh the peple of noyse al stille,
Tho shewed he the myghty dukes wille.
    "The lord hath of his heigh discrecioun
Considered that it were destruccioun
To gentil blood to fighten in the gyse
Of mortal bataille now in this emprise. 2540
Wherfore, to shapen that they shal nat dye,
He wol his firste purpos modifye.
No man therfore, up peyne of los of lyf,

2475 **o compleccioun,** the same complexion (humor). 2476 **That,** which. 2477 **aiel,** grandfather. 2478 **lust,** pleasure. 2479 **stynten,** stop. 2486 **justen,** joust. 2494 **route,** group. 2496 **devisynge,** preparing. 2497 **unkouth,** unfamiliar. 2498 **browdynge,** embroidering (ornamenting). 2499 **testeres . . . trappures,** helmets, horse armor. 2501 **parementz,** rich robes. 2502 **retenue,** service. 2503 **Nailynge,** fastening the heads on. 2504 **Giggynge . . . layneres,** fitting out, lacing them with straps. 2505 **they,** i.e., the attendants. 2508 **prikynge,** spurring their horses. 2509 **Yemen . . . communes,** yeomen (attendants of the nobility), the common people (the curious mob). 2511 **nakers,** kettledrums. 2515 **Dyvynynge of,** speculating about. This whole scene resembles the excitement preceding any major athletic event. 2518 **balled . . . thikke herd,** bald, thick-haired. 2520 **sparth,** battle-ax. 2525 **Heeld yet,** still stayed in. 2527 **fet,** fetched. 2532 **heste . . . sentence,** command, judgment. 2540 **mortal . . . emprise,** to the death, enterprise. These humane rules for the tournament are not found in *Tes.,* where the battle is to the death and many contestants are killed. 2541 **shapen,** arrange it.

No maner shot, ne polax, ne short knyf
Into the lystes sende, or thider brynge,   2545
Ne short swerd, for to stoke with poynt bitynge,
No man ne drawe, ne bere it by his syde.
Ne no man shal unto his felawe ryde
But o cours, with a sharpe ygrounde spere,
Foyne, if hym list, on foote, hymself to were.
And he that is at meschief shal be take   2551
And noght slayn, but be broght unto the stake
That shal ben ordeyned on either syde;
But thider he shal by force, and there abyde.
And if so falle the chieftayn be take   2555
On outher syde, or elles sleen his make,
No lenger shal the turneiynge laste.
God spede you! Gooth forth, and ley on faste!
With long swerd and with maces fighteth youre
     fille.
Gooth now youre wey, this is the lordes wille."
     The voys of peple touchede the hevene,   2561
So loude cride they with murie stevene,
"God save swich a lord, that is so good!
He wilneth no destruccion of blood."
Up goon the trompes and the melodye,   2565
And to the lystes rit the compaignye,
By ordinance, thurghout the citee large,
Hanged with clooth of gold, and nat with sarge.
     Ful lik a lord this noble duc gan ryde,
Thise two Thebans upon either syde,   2570
And after rood the queene, and Emelye,
And after that another compaignye
Of oon and oother, after hir degree.
And thus they passen thurghout the citee,
And to the lystes come they by tyme.   2575
It nas nat of the day yet fully pryme
Whan set was Theseus ful riche and hye,
Ypolita the queene, and Emelye,
And othere ladys in degrees aboute.

Unto the seetes preesseth al the route.   2580
And westward, thurgh the gates under Marte,
Arcite and eek the hondred of his parte
With baner reed is entred right anon.
     And in that selve moment Palamon
Is under Venus, estward in the place,   2585
With baner whyt and hardy chiere and face.
In al the world, to seken up and doun,
So evene, withouten variacioun,
Ther nere swiche compaignyes tweye,
For ther was noon so wys that koude seye   2590
That any hadde of oother avauntage
Of worthynesse, ne of estaat, ne age,
So evene were they chosen, for to gesse.
And in two renges faire they hem dresse.
Whan that hir names rad were everichon,   2595
That in hir nombre gyle were ther noon,
Tho were the gates shet, and cried was loude,
"Do now youre devoir, yonge knyghtes proude!"
     The heraudes lefte hir prikyng up and doun;
Now ryngen trompes loude and clarioun.   2600
Ther is namoore to seyn, but west and est
In goon the speres ful sadly in arrest;
In gooth the sharpe spore into the syde.
Ther seen men who kan juste and who kan
     ryde.   2604
Ther shyveren shaftes upon sheeldes thikke;
He feeleth thurgh the herte-spoon the prikke;
Up spryngen speres twenty foot on highte;
Out goon the swerdes as the silver brighte;
The helmes they tohewen and toshrede;   2609
Out brest the blood with stierne stremes rede;
With myghty maces the bones they tobreste;
He thurgh the thikkeste of the throng gan
     threste;
Ther stomblen steedes stronge, and doun gooth
     al;

2544 shot, polax, crossbow bolt, battle-ax. **2546 stoke,** stab. **2548 unto . . . felawe,** against, opponent. **2549 o cours,** one charge. **2550 Foyne . . . were,** Let him thrust, defend. **2551 at meschief,** disobeying the rules. **2552 stake,** Skeat quotes Strutt: "And for to assertayne the more of the tourney, there was on eche side a stake; and at eche stake two kynges of armes, with penne, and inke, and paper, to write the names of all that were yolden [i.e., surrendered], for they shold no more tournay." These technicalities of the tournament are not found in *Tes.* **2556 make,** mate (i.e., the opposing leader). **2559 maces,** war clubs. **2562 stevene,** voice. **2567 By ordinance,** by rank. **2568 sarge,** serge (wool worsted). **2576 pryme,** 6:00–9:00 A.M., the first quarter of the day. **2580 route,** crowd. **2586 hardy chiere,** courageous expression. **2588 evene,** equal. **2594 renges . . . dresse,** lines, arrange. **2595 rad,** read. **2596 gyle,** deceit. **2598 devoir,** duty. **2602 sadly in arrest,** firmly in their rests (i.e., against their breastplates). **2605 shyveren,** shatter. **2606 herte-spoon,** breastbone. **2607 Up spryngen,** fly up. **2610 brest . . . stierne,** bursts, dreadful. **2611 maces . . . tobreste,** war clubs, break. **2612 He . . . threste,** impersonal "This one," to push. **2613** *stomblen:* E&c *semblen.*

He rolleth under foot as dooth a bal;
He foyneth on his feet with his tronchoun; 2615
And he hym hurtleth with his hors adoun;
He thurgh the body is hurt and sithen ytake,
Maugree his heed, and broght unto the stake.
As forward was, right ther he moste abyde.
Another lad is on that oother syde. 2620
  And somtyme dooth hem Theseus to reste,
Hem to fresshen and drynken, if hem leste.
Ful ofte a day han thise Thebanes two
Togydre ymet and wroght his felawe wo;
Unhorsed hath ech oother of hem tweye. 2625
Ther nas no tygre in the vale of Galgopheye,
Whan that hir whelp is stole whan it is lite,
So crueel on the hunte as is Arcite
For jelous herte upon this Palamoun.
Ne in Belmarye ther nys so fel leoun 2630
That hunted is, or for his hunger wood,
Ne of his praye desireth so the blood,
As Palamon to sleen his foo Arcite.
The jelous strokes on hir helmes byte;
Out renneth blood on bothe hir sydes rede. 2635
  Somtyme an ende ther is of every dede.
For er the sonne unto the reste wente,
The stronge kyng Emetreus gan hente
This Palamon, as he faught with Arcite,
And made his swerd depe in his flessh to
     byte,
And by the force of twenty is he take, 2641
Unyolden, and ydrawe unto the stake.
And in the rescus of this Palamoun
The stronge kyng Lygurge is born adoun,
And Kyng Emetreus, for al his strengthe, 2645
Is born out of his sadel a swerdes lengthe,
So hitte him Palamoun er he were take.
But al for noght—he was broght to the stake.
His hardy herte myghte hym helpe naught:
He most abyde, whan that he was caught, 2650
By force and eek by composicioun.

Who sorweth now but woful Palamoun,
That moot namoore goon agayn to fighte?
And whan that Theseus hadde seyn this
     sighte,
Unto the folk that foghten thus echon 2655
He cryde, "Hoo! namoore, for it is doon!
I wol be trewe juge, and no partie.
Arcite of Thebes shal have Emelie,
That by his fortune hath hire faire ywonne."
Anon ther is a noyse of peple bigonne 2660
For joye of this, so loude and heighe withalle,
It semed that the lystes sholde falle.
  What kan now faire Venus doon above?
What seith she now? What dooth this queene of
     love,
But wepeth so, for wantynge of hir wille, 2665
Til that hir teeres in the lystes fille?
She seyde, "I am ashamed, doutelees."
  Saturnus seyde, "Doghter, hoold thy pees!
Mars hath his wille, his knyght hath al his
     boone, 2669
And, by myn heed, thow shalt been esed soone."
  The trompours with the loude mynstralcie,
The heraudes that ful loude yolle and crie,
Been in hire wele for joye of daun Arcite.
But herkneth me, and stynteth noyse a lite,
Which a myracle ther bifel anon. 2675
  This fierse Arcite hath of his helm ydon,
And on a courser, for to shewe his face,
He priketh endelong the large place,
Lokynge upward upon this Emelye,
And she agayn hym caste a freendlich eye—
For wommen, as to speken in comune, 2681
Thei folwen alle the favour of Fortune—
And was al his chiere as in his herte.
  Out of the ground a furie infernal sterte,
From Pluto sent at requeste of Saturne, 2685
For which his hors for fere gan to turne,
And leep aside, and foundred as he leep;

2615 **foyneth . . . tronchoun,** parries, shaft of spear. 2617 **sithen ytake,** then captured. 2618 **Maugree his heed,** in spite of his efforts. 2619 **forward,** agreement. 2620 **lad,** led. 2622 *fresshen:* some MSS *refresshe.* 2623 **a day,** during the day. 2625 **tweye,** twice. 2626 **Galgopheye,** Gargaphie, where Acteon was killed by his hounds (Ovid, *Met.* iii.155ff.). 2628 **hunte,** hunter. 2630 **Belmarye,** in North Africa (see *CT,* i.57 above). **fel,** cruel. 2631 **wood,** insane. 2638 **hente,** seize. 2642 **Unyolden,** unyielded. 2643 **rescus,** attempt to rescue. 2651 **composicioun,** agreement. 2653 **moot,** must (may). 2655 This line is omitted in many MSS and a new 1.2657 supplied: *Ne non shal lenger unto his felawe gon.* 2657 **partie,** partisan. 2665 **wantynge,** lacking. 2668 **Saturnus,** in *Tes.* Venus herself sent Erinis to frighten Arcita's horse. 2669 **boone,** petition. 2671 *trompours:* E&c *trompes.* 2672 **yolle,** yell. 2673 **wele,** joy. 2674 **stynteth,** stop. 2678 **priketh endelong,** spurs his horse the length of. 2681–82 Lines omitted in E and some other good MSS. Manly suggests that Chaucer had marked them for excision. 2683 This line has various readings in other MSS, e.g., *his in chiere.* 2687 **foundred,** fell.

And er that Arcite may taken keep,
He pighte hym on the pomel of his heed,
That in the place he lay as he were deed,   2690
His brest tobrosten with his sadel-bowe.
As blak he lay as any cole or crowe,
So was the blood yronnen in his face.
Anon he was yborn out of the place,
With herte soor, to Theseus paleys.   2695
Tho was he korven out of his harneys,
And in a bed ybrought ful faire and blyve,
For he was yet in memorie and alyve,
And alwey criynge after Emelye.

    Duc Theseus, with al his compaignye,   2700
Is comen hoom to Atthenes his citee,
With alle blisse and greet solempnitee.
Al be it that this aventure was falle,
He nolde noght disconforten hem alle.
Men seyde eek that Arcite shal nat dye,   2705
He shal been heeled of his maladye.
And of another thyng they weren as fayn,
That of hem alle was ther noon yslayn,
Al were they soore yhurt, and namely oon
That with a spere was thirled his brest-boon.
To othere woundes and to broken armes   2711
Somme hadden salves, and somme hadden
    charmes.
Fermacies of herbes and eek save
They dronken, for they wolde hir lymes have.
For which this noble duc, as he wel kan,   2715
Conforteth and honoureth every man,
And made revel al the longe nyght
Unto the straunge lordes, as was right.
Ne ther was holden no disconfitynge,
But as a justes or a tourneiynge,   2720
For soothly ther was no disconfiture.
For fallyng nys nat but an aventure,

Ne to be lad by force unto the stake
Unyolden, and with twenty knyghtes take,
O persone allone, withouten mo,   2725
And haryed forth by arme, foot, and too,
And eke his steede dryven forth with staves
With footmen, bothe yemen and eek knaves—
It nas arretted hym no vileynye;
Ther may no man clepen it cowardye.   2730

    For which anon Duc Theseus leet crye,
To stynten alle rancour and envye,
The gree as wel of o syde as of oother,
And eyther syde ylik as ootheres brother;
And yaf hem yiftes after hir degree,   2735
And fully heeld a feeste dayes three,
And convoyed the kynges worthily
Out of his toun a journee largely.
And hoom wente every man the righte way.
Ther was namoore but "Farewel, have good
    day!"   2740
Of this bataille I wol namoore endite,
But speke of Palamon and of Arcite.

    Swelleth the brest of Arcite, and the soore
Encreesseth at his herte moore and moore.
The clothered blood, for any lechecraft,   2745
Corrupteth and is in his bouk ylaft,
That neither veyne-blood, ne ventusynge,
Ne drynke of herbes may ben his helpynge.
The vertu expulsif, or animal,
Fro thilke vertu cleped natural   2750
Ne may the venym voyden ne expelle.
The pipes of his longes gonne to swelle,
And every lacerte in his brest adoun
Is shent with venym and corrupcioun.
Hym gayneth neither, for to gete his lif,   2755
Vomyt upward, ne dounward laxatif.
Al is tobrosten thilke regioun;

2688 **keep,** care. 2689 **pighte . . . pomel,** threw, crown. 2691 **sadel-bowe,** sharp front projection. 2694 **Anon,** at once. 2696 **korven,** cut. 2697 **blyve,** quickly. 2698 **in memorie,** conscious. 2702 **blisse,** splendor. 2707 **fayn,** happy. 2710 **thirled,** pierced. 2713 **Fermacies . . . save,** medicines, herb tea. 2714 *lymes:* other MSS *lyves.* 2718 **straunge,** i.e., visitors. 2719 **disconfitynge,** discomfiture (embarrassment). 2720 **But as,** i.e., but recognizing it as a game. 2721 **disconfiture,** defeat. 2722 **fallyng . . . aventure,** falling off his horse, accident. 2726 **haryed,** dragged. 2727 **dryven forth,** driven out of the melee. 2729 **arretted . . . vileynye,** imputed, disgrace (some irony here). 2730 **clepen,** call. 2731 **leet crye,** caused to be announced. 2732 **stynten,** stop. 2733 **gree,** esteem. 2738 **journee largely,** fully a day's journey. 2739 **righte way,** right away. 2745 **clothered . . . lechecraft,** clotted, medical skill. 2746 **Corrupteth . . . bouk,** becomes infected, body. 2747 **veyne-blood . . . ventusynge,** bleeding, cupping (or else setting up a counter-irritant). 2749 **vertu expulsif,** power of the body to expel infection. **animal,** medieval technical name of this cleansing power, believed to be seated in the brain. 2750 **Fro . . . vertu . . . natural,** "natural" power, seated in the liver, controlled the bodily functions. For discussion see Curry, *Chaucer and the Medieval Sciences.* 2752 **longes,** lungs. 2753 **lacerte,** muscle. 2754 **shent,** destroyed. 2755 **Hym gayneth,** It helps him. 2757 **tobrosten,** shattered (*to–* is an intensifier).

Nature hath now no dominacioun.
And certeinly, ther Nature wol nat wirche,
Farewel phisik—go ber the man to chirche!
This al and som, that Arcita moot dye;   2761
For which he sendeth after Emelye,
And Palamon, that was his cosyn deere.
Thanne seyde he thus, as ye shal after heere:

"Naught may the woful spirit in myn herte
Declare o point of alle my sorwes smerte   2766
To yow, my lady, that I love moost,
But I biquethe the servyce of my goost
To yow aboven every creature,
Syn that my lyf may no lenger dure.   2770
Allas, the wo, allas, the peynes stronge
That I for yow have suffred, and so longe;
Allas, the deeth, allas, myn Emelye,
Allas, departynge of oure compaignye;
Allas, myn hertes queene, allas, my wyf,   2775
Myn hertes lady, endere of my lyf !
What is this world? What asketh men to have?
Now with his love, now in his colde grave,
Allone, withouten any compaignye.
Farewel, my swete foo, myn Emelye.   2780
And softe taak me in youre armes tweye,
For love of God, and herkneth what I seye.

"I have heer with my cosyn Palamon
Had strif and rancour many a day agon
For love of yow, and for my jalousye.   2785
And Juppiter so wys my soule gye
To speken of a servaunt proprely,
With alle circumstances trewely—
That is to seyn, trouthe, honour, knyghthede,
Wysdom, humblesse, estaat, and heigh
    kynrede,
Fredom, and al that longeth to that art—   2791
So Juppiter have of my soule part,
As in this world right now ne knowe I non
So worthy to ben loved as Palamon,
That serveth yow, and wol doon al his lyf.   2795

And if that evere ye shul ben a wyf,
Foryet nat Palamon, the gentil man."
And with that word his speche faille gan,
For from his feet up to his brest was come
The coold of deeth, that hadde hym overcome,
And yet moore over, for in his armes two   2801
The vital strengthe is lost and al ago.
Oonly the intellect withouten moore,
That dwelled in his herte syk and soore,
Gan faillen whan the herte felte deeth.   2805
Dusked his eyen two, and failled breeth,
But on his lady yet caste he his eye;
His laste word was, "Mercy, Emelye!"
His spirit chaunged hous and wente ther
As I cam nevere, I kan nat tellen wher.   2810
Therfore I stynte, I nam no divinistre;
Of soules fynde I nat in this registre,
Ne me ne list thilke opinions to telle
Of hem, though that they writen wher they
    dwelle.
Arcite is coold, ther Mars his soule gye.   2815
Now wol I speken forth of Emelye.

Shrighte Emelye, and howleth Palamon,
And Theseus his suster took anon
Swownynge, and baar hire fro the corps away.
What helpeth it to tarien forth the day   2820
To tellen how she weep bothe eve and
    morwe?
For in swich cas wommen have swich sorwe,
Whan that hir housbondes ben from hem ago,
That for the moore part they sorwen so,
Or ellis fallen in swich maladye   2825
That at the laste certeinly they dye.

Infinite been the sorwes and the teeres
Of olde folk and folk of tendre yeeres
In al the toun for deeth of this Theban.
For hym ther wepeth bothe child and man.   2830
So greet wepyng was ther noon, certayn,
Whan Ector was ybroght, al fressh yslayn,

2758 Hg&c *now* om. 2759 **wirche,** work. 2766 **o point . . . smerte,** one bit, pain. 2768 **goost,** spirit. 2774 **departynge,** the parting. 2775 **wyf,** in *Tes.,* Arcite marries Emelye immediately after the tournament; here the term is a moving emotional climax (cf. Shakespeare, *Antony and Cleopatra,* v.ii.290). 2776 **endere,** ender (one who ends). Like "swete foo" below, this is troubadour oxymoron. 2781 **softe . . . tweye,** softly, two. 2786 **so wys . . . gye,** so wisely, guide. 2787 **of a servaunt,** about a lover. 2788 Hg&c *circumstances alle.* 2791 **Fredom . . . that art,** generosity, the art of love. 2799 E&c *And from his herte up to.* 2811 **stynte . . . divinistre,** stop, theologian. This cryptic observation replaces the description of the flight of Arcite's soul to heaven in *Tes.* XI (which, however, Chaucer did use to describe Troylus' death, *TC* v.1807–27). 2813 **me ne list thilke,** it does not please me those. 2815 **ther . . . gye,** wherever, may lead. 2823 E&c *housbond is from.* 2828 E *and eek of.*

To Troye. Allas, the pitee that was ther,
Cracchynge of chekes, rentynge eek of heer.
"Why woldestow be deed," thise wommen
    crye,   2835
"And haddest gold ynough, and Emelye?"
    No man myghte gladen Theseus,
Savynge his olde fader Egeus,
That knew this worldes transmutacioun,
As he hadde seyn it chaunge bothe up and doun,
Joye after wo, and wo after gladnesse,   2841
And shewed hem ensamples and liknesse.
    "Right as ther dyed nevere man," quod he,
"That he ne lyvede in erthe in som degree,
Right so ther lyvede never man," he seyde, 2845
"In al this world, that som tyme he ne deyde.
This world nys but a thurghfare ful of wo,
And we been pilgrymes, passynge to and fro.
Deeth is an ende of every worldly soore."
And over al this yet seyde he muchel moore 2850
To this effect, ful wisely to enhorte
The peple that they sholde hem reconforte.
    Duc Theseus, with al his bisy cure,
Caste now wher that the sepulture
Of goode Arcite may best ymaked be,   2855
And eek moost honurable in his degree.
And at the laste he took conclusioun
That ther as first Arcite and Palamoun
Hadden for love the bataille hem bitwene,
That in that selve grove, swoote and grene, 2860
Ther as he hadde his amorouse desires,
His compleynte, and for love his hoote fires,
He wolde make a fyr in which the office
Funeral he myghte al accomplice.
And leet comande anon to hakke and hewe 2865
The okes olde, and leye hem on a rewe
In colpons wel arrayed for to brenne.
His officers with swifte feet they renne
And ryden anon at his comandement.
And after this, Theseus hath ysent   2870
After a beere, and it al overspradde

With clooth of gold, the richeste that he hadde.
And of the same suyte he cladde Arcite.
Upon his hondes hadde he gloves white,
Eek on his heed a coroune of laurer grene, 2875
And in his hond a swerd ful bright and kene.
He leyde hym, bare the visage, on the beere;
Therwith he weep that pitee was to heere.
And for the peple sholde seen hym alle,
Whan it was day, he broghte hym to the halle,
That roreth of the criyng and the soun.   2881
    Tho came this woful Theban Palamoun,
With flotery berd and ruggy, asshy heeres,
In clothes blake, ydropped al with teeres;
And, passynge othere of wepynge, Emelye,
The rewefulleste of al the compaignye.   2886
In as muche as the servyce sholde be
The moore noble and riche in his degree,
Duc Theseus leet forth thre steedes brynge,
That trapped were in steel al gliterynge, 2890
And covered with the armes of daun Arcite.
Upon thise steedes grete and white
Ther sitten folk, of whiche oon baar his sheeld,
Another his spere up on his hondes heeld,
The thridde baar with hym his bowe
    Turkeys—
Of brend gold was the caas and eek the
    harneys—   2896
And riden forth a paas with sorweful cheere
Toward the grove, as ye shul after heere.
The nobleste of the Grekes that ther were
Upon his shuldres caryeden the beere   2900
With slak paas, and eyen rede and wete,
Thurghout the citee by the maister strete,
That sprad was al with blak, and wonder hye
Right of the same is the strete ywrye.
Upon the right hond wente olde Egeus, 2905
And on that oother syde Duc Theseus,
With vessels in hir hand of gold ful fyn,
Al ful of hony, milk, and blood, and wyn;
Eek Palamon, with ful greet compaignye;

2834 Cracchynge, scratching. **2840** E&c *chaunge bothe* om. Manly considered *chaunge* scribal. **2851 enhorte,** exhort. **2852 hem reconforte,** take comfort. **2853 cure,** care. **2854 Caste,** searched about. **2860 swoote,** sweet. **2866 rewe,** row. **2867 colpons,** in piles. **2871 beere,** bier. **2873 suyte,** suit (material). **2874 gloves white,** funeral emblems for an unmarried person. Manly would emend *hadde* to *putte.* **2883 flotery . . . ruggy, asshy heeres,** fluttering, shaggy ash-covered hair. *ruggy:* E&c *rugged.* **2885 passynge,** surpassing. **2886 rewefulleste,** most sorrowful. **2892** An eight-syllable line. Later MSS have various emendations, e.g., *steedes that weren.* **2894 up on:** E&c *in.* **2895 Turkeys,** Turkish. **2896 brend . . . caas . . . harneys,** burnished, quiver, fittings. **2897 a paas . . . cheere,** apace (slowly), expression. **2902 maister,** main. **2903 That sprad,** i.e., the bier. **2904 ywrye,** draped. **2907** E&c *vessel.*

And after that cam woful Emelye,   2910
With fyr in honde, as was that tyme the gyse,
To do the office of funeral servyse.

Heigh labour and ful greet apparaillynge
Was at the service and the fyr-makynge,   2914
That with his grene top the heven raughte;
And twenty fadme of brede the armes
    straughte—
This is to seyn, the bowes weren so brode.
Of stree first ther was leyd ful many a lode.
But how the fyr was maked upon highte,
Ne eek the names that the trees highte,   2920
As ook, firre, birch, asp, alder, holm, popler,
Wylugh, elm, plane, assh, box, chasteyn, lynde,
    laurer,
Mapul, thorn, bech, hasel, ew, whippeltree,
How they weren fild, shal nat be toold for me;
Ne hou the goddes ronnen up and doun,   2925
Disherited of hire habitacioun,
In which they woneden in reste and pees,
Nymphus, fawnes, and amadrides;
Ne hou the beestes and the briddes alle
Fledden for fere, whan the wode was falle;   2930
Ne how the ground agast was of the light,
That was nat wont to seen the sonne bright;
Ne how the fyr was couched first with stree,
And thanne with drye stikkes cloven a thre,
And thanne with grene wode and spicerye,   2935
And thanne with clooth of gold and with perrye,
And gerlandes, hangynge with ful many a flour;
The mirre, th'encens, with al so greet odour;
Ne how Arcite lay among al this,
Ne what richesse aboute his body is;   2940
Ne how that Emelye, as was the gyse,
Putte in the fyr of funeral servyse;
Ne how she swowned whan men made the fyr,

Ne what she spak, ne what was hir desir;
Ne what jeweles men in the fyre caste,   2945
Whan that the fyr was greet and brente faste;
Ne how somme caste hir sheeld, and somme hir
    spere,
And of hire vestimentz, whiche that they were,
And coppes fulle of wyn, and milk, and blood,
Into the fyr, that brente as it were wood;   2950
Ne how the Grekes, with an huge route,
Thries riden al the fyr aboute
Upon the left hand, with a loud shoutynge,
And thries with hir speres claterynge;
And thries how the ladyes gonne crye;   2955
Ne how that lad was homward Emelye;
Ne how Arcite is brent to asshen colde;
Ne how that lyche-wake was yholde
Al thilke nyght; ne how the Grekes pleye
The wake-pleyes, ne kepe I nat to seye;   2960
Who wrastleth best naked with oille enoynt,
Ne who that baar hym best, in no disjoynt.
I wol nat tellen eek how that they goon
Hoom til Atthenes, whan the pley is doon;
But shortly to the point thanne wol I wende,
And maken of my longe tale an ende.   2966

By processe and by lengthe of certeyn yeres,
Al stynted is the moornynge and the teres
Of Grekes, by oon general assent.
Thanne semed me ther was a parlement   2970
At Atthenes, upon certein pointz and caas,
Among the whiche pointz yspoken was
To have with certein contrees alliaunce,
And have fully of Thebans obeisaunce.
For which this noble Theseus anon   2975
Leet senden after gentil Palamon,
Unwist of hym what was the cause and why,
But in his blake clothes sorwefully

2911 **fyr . . . gyse**, i.e., to light the pyre, custom. 2913 **Heigh . . . apparaillynge**, great, preparation. 2915 **his . . . raughte**, i.e., the funeral pyre, reached. 2916 **fadme . . . brede . . . straughte**, fathom (six feet), broad, stretched. 2918 **stree**, straw. 2920 **highte**, were called. 2921 **asp . . . holm**, aspen, holly. 2922 **Wylugh . . . chasteyn**, willow, chestnut. 2923 **whippeltree**, dogwood. 2924 **fild**, felled. 2927 **woneden**, lived. 2928 **amadrides**, hamadryads (wood nymphs), not found in *Tes*. This unfamiliar word appears in a bewildering variety of forms in the MSS. 2930 *for fere*: Hg&c *forferd* (frightened). 2932 **wont**, accustomed. 2933 **couched . . . stree**, laid, straw. 2934 **cloven**, split. 2936 **perrye**, jewels. 2948 **whiche**, whatever kind; "hir(e)" in these lines refers to the mourners. 2950 **wood**, mad. 2951 **route**, company. 2952 *fyr*: E *place*. 2958 **lyche-wake**, funeral wake. 2960 **wake-pleyes**, athletic contests celebrating the death of the hero. **kepe**, care. 2962 **no disjoynt**, any predicament. 2963 *eek how*: Hg&c *al how*. 2966 In *Tes*., Palemone builds a temple to Juno over Arcite's ashes, with carvings depicting his deeds. 2967 **processe**, course of events. **yeres**, in *Tes*., the marriage is arranged after several *days* and the kings did not leave Athens until after the wedding (cf. l.2737 above). 2968 **stynted**, stopped. 2971 **pointz and caas**, problems and cases. 2973–4 **alliaunce . . . Thebans**, the political motivation for the marriage of Palamon and Emelye is not found in *Tes*. 2977 **Unwist**, unknown.

He cam at his comandement in hye.
Tho sente Theseus for Emelye.   2980
Whan they were set, and hust was al the
     place,
And Theseus abiden hadde a space
Er any word cam fram his wise brest,
His eyen sette he ther as was his lest.
And with a sad visage he siked stille,   2985
And after that right thus he seyde his wille:
   "The Firste Moevere of the cause above,
Whan he first made the faire cheyne of love,
Greet was th'effect and heigh was his entente.
Wel wiste he why and what therof he mente,
For with that faire cheyne of love he bond   2991
The fyr, the eyr, the water, and the lond
In certeyn boundes, that they may nat flee.
That same Prince and that same Moevere,"
     quod he,
"Hath stabilissed in this wrecched world
     adoun
Certeyn dayes and duracioun   2996
To al that is engendred in this place,
Over the whiche day they may nat pace,
Al mowe they yet tho dayes wel abregge.
Ther nedeth noght noon auctoritee allegge,   3000
For it is preeved by experience,
But that me list declaren my sentence.
Thanne may men by this ordre wel discerne
That thilke Moevere stable is and eterne.
Wel may men knowe, but it be a fool,   3005
That every part dirryveth from his hool,
For nature hath nat taken his bigynnyng
Of no partie or cantel of a thyng,
But of a thyng that parfit is and stable,
Descendynge so til it be corrumpable.   3010

And therfore, of his wise purveiaunce,
He hath so wel biset his ordinaunce,
That speces of thynges and progressiouns
Shullen enduren by sucessiouns,
And nat eterne, withouten any lye.   3015
This maystow understonde and seen at eye.
   "Loo the ook, that hath so long a norisshynge
From tyme that it first bigynneth sprynge,
And hath so long a lif, as we may see,
Yet at the laste wasted is the tree.   3020
   "Considereth eek how that the harde stoon
Under oure feet, on which we trede and goon,
Yet wasteth it as it lyth by the weye.
The brode ryver somtyme wexeth dreye.
The grete tounes se we wane and wende.   3025
Thanne may ye se that al this thyng hath
     ende.
   "Of man and womman seen we wel also
That nedeth, in oon of thise termes two,
This is to seyn in youthe or elles age,
He moot be deed, the kyng as shal a page,   3030
Som in his bed, som in the depe see,
Som in the large feeld, as men may see—
Ther helpeth noght, al goth that ilke weye.
Thanne may I seyn that al this thyng moot deye.
   "What maketh this but Juppiter, the
     kyng,   3035
That is prince and cause of alle thyng,
Convertynge al unto his propre welle
From which it is dirryved, sooth to telle?
And heer-agayns no creature on lyve,
Of no degree, availleth for to stryve.   3040
   "Thanne is it wysdom, as it thynketh me,
To maken vertu of necessitee,
And take it weel that we may nat eschue,

2979 in hye, in haste. **2980 Tho,** then. **2981 hust,** hushed. **2984 eyen sette . . . lest,** fixed his eyes, habit. **2985 sad visage . . . siked stille,** sober expression, sighed quietly. **2987 Firste Moevere,** God, the *primum mobile* of *Boece* I.m.5, III.pr.12, etc. **2988** The Platonic notion of the great chain of being descending from God through man to other forms of animate and inanimate nature, all held together by love, appears in *Boece* II.m.8, as well as frequently elsewhere (including the opening of the Gen Pro, ll. 1–12). **2995 world adoun,** down in this world. **2996 duracioun,** space of time to endure. **2998 Over . . . pace,** beyond, pass. **2999 Al mowe . . . abregge,** although they may, shorten. **3000 allegge,** to call upon. Hg&c *noght* om. **3001 preeved,** proved. **3002 But . . . me list . . . my sentence,** except, it pleases me, my point of view. **3003 ordre,** organization of the universe and of society. **3006 dirryveth . . . hool,** is derived from, whole (i.e., perfect original). *Boece* III.pr.10. **3008 partie or cantel,** part or portion (i.e., imperfect example). E&c *or of cantel.* **3010 corrumpable,** corruptible (i.e., an imperfect manifestation of the Platonic ideal). **3011 purveiaunce,** providence. **3012 biset his ordinaunce,** set his regulations. **3013 progressiouns,** series (categories). **3014 by sucessiouns,** successively. **3015 eterne, withouten . . . lye,** eternally, certainly. **3025 wende,** pass away. *tounes:* E&c *toures.* **3028 That nedeth . . . termes,** who must be, periods (of life). Some MSS *nedes.* **3033 ilke,** same. **3034 seyn,** say. **3035 What maketh,** who causes. **3037 Convertynge . . . his propre welle,** returning, its own source. **3038 dirryved, sooth,** derived, truth. **3039 on lyve,** alive. **3043 weel . . . eschue,** well, avoid.

And namely that to us alle is due.
And whoso gruccheth ought, he dooth folye,
And rebel is to hym that al may gye.   3046
And certeinly a man hath moost honour
To dyen in his excellence and flour,
Whan he is siker of his goode name;
Thanne hath he doon his freend, ne hym, no
    shame.   3050
And gladder oghte his freend been of his deeth,
Whan with honour up yolden is his breeth,
Than whan his name apalled is for age,
For al forgeten is his vassellage.
Thanne is it best, as for a worthy fame,   3055
To dyen whan that he is best of name.
   "The contrarie of al this is wilfulnesse.
Why grucchen we, why have we hevynesse,
That goode Arcite, of chivalrie flour,
Departed is with duetee and honour   3060
Out of this foule prisoun of this lyf?
Why grucchen heere his cosyn and his wyf
Of his welfare, that loved hem so weel?
Kan he hem thank—nay, God woot, never a
    deel—
That bothe his soule and eek hemself offende?
And yet they mowe hir lustes nat amende.   3066
   What may I concluden of this longe serye?
But after wo I rede us to be merye,
And thanken Juppiter of al his grace.
And er that we departen from this place   3070
I rede we make of sorwes two
O parfit joye, lastynge everemo.
And looketh now wher moost sorwe is herinne,
Ther wol we first amenden and bigynne.
   "Suster," quod he, "this is my fulle assent,

With al th'avys heere of my parlement,   3076
That gentil Palamon, youre owene knyght,
That serveth yow with wille, herte, and myght,
And ever hath doon syn ye first hym knewe,
That ye shul of youre grace upon hym rewe,
And taken hym for housbonde and for lord.   3081
Lene me youre hond, for this is oure accord.
Lat se now of youre wommanly pitee.
He is a kynges brother sone, pardee,
And though he were a poure bacheler,   3085
Syn he hath served yow so many a yeer,
And had for yow so greet adversitee,
It moste been considered, leeveth me,
For gentil mercy oghte to passen right."   3089
   Thanne seyde he thus to Palamon the
    knight,
"I trowe ther nedeth litel sermonyng
To make yow assente to this thyng.
Com neer, and taak youre lady by the hond."
   Bitwixen hem was maad anon the bond
That highte matrimoigne or mariage,   3095
By al the conseil and the baronage.
And thus with alle blisse and melodye
Hath Palamon ywedded Emelye.
And God, that al this wyde world hath wroght,
Sende hym his love that hath it deere aboght,
For now is Palamon in alle wele,   3101
Lyvynge in blisse, in richesse, and in heele,
And Emelye hym loveth so tendrely,
And he hire serveth also gentilly,
That nevere was ther no word hem bitwene   3105
Of jalousie or any oother teene.
Thus endeth Palamon and Emelye,
And God save al this faire compaignye. Amen.

Heere is ended the Knyghtes Tale.

3044 **namely that,** especially that which. 3045 **gruccheth ought,** complains at all. 3046 **gye,** guide. 3049 **siker,** sure. 3050 **ne hym,** nor himself. 3052 **yolden,** yielded. 3053 **apalled,** worn out. 3054 **vassellage,** service. 3057 **wilfulnesse,** wrongheadedness. 3058 **grucchen . . . hevynesse,** complain, sorrow. 3060 **duetee,** respect. 3063 *loved:* Hg&c *loveth.* 3065 **offende,** injure. 3066 **mowe hir lustes nat amende,** cannot achieve their happiness. 3067 **serye,** series (of observations). 3068 **rede,** advise. 3072 **parfit,** perfect. 3075 **assent,** desire. 3079 E&c *syn that ye.* 3080 **rewe,** have pity. 3082 **Lene,** lend (give). 3083 **Lat se,** reveal. 3088 **moste . . . leeveth,** ought to, believe. 3089 **passen right,** surpass prerogative. 3090 *the knight:* E&c *ful right.* 3091 **trowe,** believe. 3099 Hg&c *wyde* om. 3100 *hath* om. in E and placed variously in other MSS—evidently a marginal insertion. 3101 **wele,** happiness. 3102 **heele,** health. 3104 *also:* EHg&c *so.* 3106 **teene,** vexation.

MILLER'S TALE

cf. p. 19

PROLOGUE

Heere folwen the wordes bitwene the Hoost and the Millere.

Whan that the Knyght had thus his tale
    ytoold,
In al the route ne was ther yong ne oold   3110
That he ne seyde it was a noble storie
And worthy for to drawen to memorie,
And namely the gentils everichon.
Oure Hooste lough and swoor, "So moot I gon,
This gooth aright; unbokeled is the male.   3115
Lat se now who shal telle another tale.
For trewely the game is wel bigonne.
Now telleth ye, sire Monk, if that ye konne
Somwhat to quite with the Knyghtes tale."
    The Millere, that fordronken was al pale   3120
So that unnethe upon his hors he sat,
He nolde avalen neither hood ne hat,
Ne abyde no man for his curteisie,
But in Pilates voys he gan to crie,

And swoor, "By armes and by blood and bones,
I kan a noble tale for the nones,   3126
With which I wol now quite the Knyghtes tale."
Oure Hooste saugh that he was dronke of ale,
And seyde, "Abyd, Robyn, my leeve brother,
Som bettre man shal telle us first another.   3130
Abyd, and lat us werken thriftily."
    "By Goddes soule," quod he, "that wol nat I,
For I wol speke or elles go my wey."
Oure Hoost answerde, "Tel on, a devele wey!
Thou art a fool; thy wit is overcome."   3135
    "Now herkneth," quod the Millere, "alle and
    some.
But first I make a protestacioun:
That I am dronke, I knowe it by my soun.
And therfore if that I mysspeke or seye,
Wyte it the ale of Southwerk, I you preye.   3140

3110 route, company. Hg&c *compaignye nas.* **3113 namely the gentils,** especially the gentle (aristocratic) people. **3114 So moot I gon,** so might I go ("might I do as well"). **3115 unbokeled is the male,** untied is the money bag. **3119 quite,** compete. **3120 fordronken,** drunk ("for" is an intensifier). **3121 unnethe,** barely. **3122 avalen,** doff. **3123 abyde,** tolerate. **3124 Pilates voys,** Pontius Pilate was a roaring part in the mystery plays. **3125 armes . . . blood,** God's arms and blood. **3126 kan,** know. **3127 quite,** requite (surpass). **3129 leeve,** dear. **3131 thriftily,** properly. **3136 some,** one. **3138 soun,** sound of voice. **3140 Wyte,** recognize. EHg *you* om.

For I wol telle a legende and a lyf
Bothe of a carpenter and of his wyf,
How that a clerk hath set the wrightes cappe."
    The Reve answerde and seyde, "Stynt thy
      clappe!
Lat be thy lewed dronken harlotrye. 3145
It is a synne and eek a greet folye
To apeyren any man, or hym defame,
And eek to bryngen wyves in swich fame.
Thou mayst ynogh of othere thynges seyn."
    This dronke Millere spak ful soone ageyn
And seyde, "Leve brother Osewold, 3151
Who hath no wyf, he is no cokewold.
But I sey nat therfore that thou art oon.
Ther been ful goode wyves many oon, 3154
And evere a thousand goode ayeyns oon badde.
That knowestow wel thyself, but if thou madde.
Why artow angry with my tale now?
I have a wyf, pardee, as wel as thow,
Yet nolde I, for the oxen in my plogh,
Take upon me moore than ynogh, 3160
As demen of myself that I were oon.
I wol bileve wel that I am noon.
An housbonde shal nat been inquisityf

Of Goddes pryvetee, nor of his wyf.
So he may fynde Goddes foyson there, 3165
Of the remenant nedeth nat enquere."
    What sholde I moore seyn, but this
      Millere
He nolde his wordes for no man forbere,
But tolde his cherles tale in his manere.
M'athynketh that I shal reherce it heere. 3170
And therfore every gentil wight I preye,
For Goddes love, demeth nat that I seye
Of yvel entente, but that I moot reherce
Hir tales alle, be they bettre or werse,
Or elles falsen som of my mateere. 3175
And therfore, whoso list it nat yheere,
Turne over the leef and chese another tale;
For he shal fynde ynowe, grete and smale,
Of storial thyng that toucheth gentillesse,
And eek moralitee and hoolynesse. 3180
Blameth nat me if that ye chese amys.
The Millere is a cherl, ye knowe wel this,
So was the Reve and other manye mo,
And harlotrie they tolden bothe two.
Avyseth yow, and put me out of blame; 3185
And eek men shal nat maken ernest of game.

Heere bigynneth the Millere his tale.

    Whilom ther was dwellynge at Oxenford
A riche gnof that gestes heeld to bord,
And of his craft he was a carpenter. 3189
With hym ther was dwellynge a poure scoler,
Hadde lerned art, but al his fantasye
Was turned for to lerne astrologye,

And koude a certeyn of conclusiouns,
To demen by interrogaciouns,
If that men asked hym in certein houres 3195
Whan that men sholde have droghte or elles
    shoures,
Or if men asked hym what sholde bifalle

Of every thyng—I may nat rekene hem alle.
   This clerk was cleped hende Nicholas.
Of deerne love he koude and of solas,   3200
And therto he was sleigh and ful privee,
And lyk a mayden meke for to see.
A chambre hadde he in that hostelrye
Allone, withouten any compaignye,
Ful fetisly ydight with herbes swoote,   3205
And he hymself as sweete as is the roote
Of lycorys or any cetewale.
His Almageste and bookes grete and smale,
His astrelabie longynge for his art,
His augrym stones layen faire apart,   3210
On shelves couched at his beddes heed;
His presse ycovered with a faldyng reed;
And al above ther lay a gay sautrie,
On which he made a-nyghtes melodie
So swetely that al the chambre rong,   3215
And *Angelus ad virginem* he song,
And after that he song the Kynges Noote.
Ful often blessed was his myrie throte.
And thus this sweete clerk his tyme spente
After his freendes fyndyng and his rente.   3220
   This carpenter hadde wedded newe a wyf,
Which that he lovede moore than his lyf.
Of eighteteene yeer she was of age.
Jalous he was, and heeld hire narwe in cage,
For she was yong and wylde, and he was old,
And demed hymself been lik a cokewold.   3226
He knew nat Catoun, for his wit was rude,
That bad man sholde wedde his simylitude.
Men sholde wedden after hire estaat,
For youthe and elde is often at debaat.   3230

But sith that he was fallen in the snare,
He moste endure, as oother folk, his care.
   Fair was this yonge wyf, and therwithal
As any wezele hir body gent and smal.
A ceynt she werede, ybarred al of silk,   3235
A barmclooth eek as whit as morne milk
Upon hir lendes, ful of many a goore;
Whit was hir smok, and broyden al bifoore
And eek bihynde, on hir coler aboute,
Of col-blak silk, withinne and eek withoute;
The tapes of hir white voluper   3241
Were of the same suyte of hir coler;
Hir filet brood of silk, and set ful hye.
And sikerly she hadde a likerous eye.
Ful smale ypulled were hire browes two,   3245
And tho were bent and blake as any sloo.
She was ful moore blisful on to see
Than is the newe pere-jonette tree,
And softer than the wolle is of a wether.
And by hir girdel heeng a purs of lether,   3250
Tasseled with silk and perled with latoun.
In al this world, to seken up and doun,
Ther nys no man so wys that koude thenche
So gay a popelote or swich a wenche.
Ful brighter was the shynyng of hir hewe   3255
Than in the Tour the noble yforged newe.
   But of hir song, it was as loude and yerne
As any swalwe sittynge on a berne.
Therto she koude skippe and make game
As any kyde or calf folwynge his dame.   3260
Hir mouth was sweete as bragot or the meeth,
Or hoord of apples leyd in hey or heeth.
Wynsynge she was as is a joly colt,

3199 hende, handy (adroit). **3200 deerne . . . solas,** secret, sexual satisfactions. **3204** Cf. KT, I.2779. **3205 fetisly ydight . . . swoote,** elegantly furnished, sweet. **3207 cetewale,** zedoary (a spice). **3208 Almageste,** book on astrology (originally the Arabic title of a treatise by Ptolemy). **3209 astrelabie,** an instrument for ascertaining the positions of the stars; see Chaucer's own *Treatise on the Astrolabe.* **longynge for,** belonging to. **3210 augrym stones,** cubes marked with arabic numerals for calculation; arabic numerals and the decimal system (called algorism or augrim) were not introduced into Europe until after 1200. **3211 couched,** arranged. **3212 presse . . . faldyng,** cupboard, coarse cloth. **3213 sautrie,** psaltery (harp). **3216 *Angelus ad virginem,*** a hymn on the angel's Annunciation of the coming birth of Jesus (to a virgin whose husband was a carpenter). **3217 Kynges Noote,** an unidentified air or song. **3220 After . . . fyndyng . . . rente,** in accordance with what his friends provided and his income. **3225** Hg&c *wylde and yong.* **3227 Catoun,** *Distichia Catonis de Moribus,* a collection of hexameter maxims used as school exercises. **3229 estaat,** condition. **3234 gent and smal,** slender and delicate. **3235 ceynt . . . ybarred,** girdle, striped. **3236 barmclooth,** apron. EHg *eek* om. **3237 lendes . . . goore,** loins, triangular inserts of cloth (flounces). **3238 smok . . . broyden,** undergarment, embroidered. **3239 coler,** collar. **3241 tapes . . . voluper,** ties, bonnet. **3242 suyte,** design. **3243 filet,** hairband. **3244 sikerly . . . likerous,** truly, sexy. **3245 ypulled,** plucked. **3246 tho . . . sloo,** those, sloeberry. **3248 newe pere-jonette,** blossoming pear tree. Elsewhere in literature the blossoming pear tree is a symbol of awakening sexuality. **3249 wether,** sheep (ram). **3251 latoun,** brass. **3254 popelote . . . wenche,** doll; wench was already taking on its disparaging sense. **3256 Tour,** Tower of London, site of the mint. **noble yforged,** gold coin, minted. **3257 yerne,** lively. **3261 bragot . . . meeth,** ale made with honey, mead. **3262 heeth,** heather. **3263 Wynsynge,** skittish.

Long as a mast, and upright as a bolt.
A brooch she baar upon hir lowe coler   3265
As brood as is the boos of a bokeler.
Hir shoes were laced on hir legges hye.
She was a prymerole, a piggesnye,
For any lord to leggen in his bedde,
Or yet for any good yeman to wedde.   3270

   Now sire, and eft sire, so bifel the cas
That on a day this hende Nicholas
Fil with this yonge wyf to rage and pleye,
Whil that hir housbonde was at Oseneye—
As clerkes ben ful subtile and ful queynte—
And prively he caughte hire by the queynte, 3276
And seyde, "Ywis, but if ich have my wille,
For deerne love of thee, lemman, I spille,"
And heeld hire harde by the haunche-bones,
And seyde, "Lemman, love me al atones,   3280
Or I wol dyen, also God me save!"
And she sproong as a colt dooth in the trave,
And with hir heed she wryed faste awey,
And seyde, "I wol nat kisse thee, by my fey.
Why, lat be," quod she, "lat be, Nicholas,
Or I wol crie, 'out, harrow' and 'allas'!   3286
Do wey youre handes, for youre curteisye."

   This Nicholas gan mercy for to crye,
And spak so faire, and profred him so faste,
That she hir love hym graunted atte laste,   3290
And swoor hir ooth by Seint Thomas of Kent
That she wol been at his comandement,
Whan that she may hir leyser wel espie.
"Myn housbonde is so ful of jalousie
That but ye wayte wel and been privee,   3295
I woot right wel I nam but deed," quod she.

"Ye moste been ful deerne, as in this cas."
   "Nay, therof care thee noght," quod
      Nicholas.
"A clerk hadde litherly biset his whyle,
But if he koude a carpenter bigyle."   3300
And thus they been accorded and ysworn
To wayte a tyme, as I have told biforn.

   Whan Nicholas had doon thus everideel,
And thakked hire aboute the lendes weel,
He kist hire sweete and taketh his sawtrie, 3305
And pleyeth faste, and maketh melodie.

   Thanne fil it thus, that to the paryssh chirche,
Cristes owene werkes for to wirche,
This goode wyf wente on an haliday.
Hir forheed shoon as bright as any day,   3310
So was it wasshen whan she leet hir werk.

   Now was ther of that chirche a parissh clerk,
The which that was ycleped Absolon.
Crul was his heer, and as the gold it shoon,
And strouted as a fanne large and brode—
Ful streight and evene lay his joly shode.   3316
His rode was reed, his eyen greye as goos.
With Poules wyndow corven on his shoos,
In hoses rede he wente fetisly.
Yclad he was ful smal and proprely   3320
Al in a kirtel of a lyght waget—
Ful faire and thikke been the poyntes set—
And therupon he hadde a gay surplys
As whit as is the blosme upon the rys.
A myrie child he was, so God me save.   3325
Wel koude he laten blood, and clippe, and
      shave,
And maken a chartre of lond or acquitaunce.

3264 **upright . . . bolt,** straight, arrow. 3266 **boos,** boss (the metal center piece of a wooden shield). 3268 **prymerole . . . piggesnye,** primrose, "pig's eye" (a folk term of endearment not regularly identified with any flower). 3271 **eft,** again. 3273 **rage,** romp. 3274 **Oseneye,** town near Oxford where there was an abbey of Augustinian canons whose church the carpenter was evidently helping to build (see ll. 3361, 3366 below). 3275 **queynte,** clever. 3276 **queynte,** female genitalia. 3278 **deerne . . . spille,** secret, die (*double entendre,* ejaculate). 3280 **Lemman . . . atones,** mistress, right now. 3282 **trave,** box into which an unruly horse is put to be shod. 3283 **wryed,** twisted. 3285 *she:* EHg&c *ich.* 3286 **out, harrow . . . allas,** cries of rape. 3289 **profred him,** put himself forward. 3293 **leyser,** leisure (opportunity). 3295 **wayte,** guard. 3297 **deerne,** secret. 3299 **litherly biset his whyle,** poorly passed his time. 3304 **thakked . . . lendes,** patted, loins. 3305 **sawtrie,** harp. 3309 **haliday,** holy day. 3311 **leet,** left. 3312 **parissh clerk,** assistant to the parson. 3313 **Absolon,** Absalom, who was killed because his long hair caught in an oak as he rode under (II Samuel, 18:9ff.), was regarded as a type of effeminate beauty and vanity. 3314 **Crul,** curly. 3315 **strouted,** spread out. 3316 **joly shode,** pretty (hair) parting. 3317 **rode . . . reed . . . greye,** complexion, rosy, blue (see I.152). 3318 **Poules wyndow,** the high fashion was to have designs cut into the upper leather through which the bright color of the hose could be seen; St. Paul's cathedral had elaborate windows. 3319 **fetisly,** elegantly. 3320 **smal . . . proprely,** daintily, finely. 3321 **kirtel . . . lyght waget,** tunic, light blue. 3322 **faire and thikke . . . poyntes,** close together, laces for fastening. 3323 **surplys,** surplice (outer robe). 3324 **rys,** branch. 3325 **child,** young man. 3326 **laten blood . . . clippe,** let blood; note that in the Middle Ages barbers were also surgeons. 3327 **chartre . . . acquitaunce,** legal deed, quittance (legal release).

In twenty manere koude he trippe and daunce
After the scole of Oxenforde tho,
And with his legges casten to and fro, 3330
And pleyen songes on a smal rubible,
Therto he song somtyme a loud quynyble,
And as wel koude he pleye on a giterne.
In al the toun nas brewhous ne taverne
That he ne visited with his solas, 3335
Ther any gaylard tappestere was.
But sooth to seyn, he was somdeel squaymous
Of fartyng, and of speche daungerous.

    This Absolon, that jolif was and gay,
Gooth with a sencer on the haliday, 3340
Sensynge the wyves of the parisshe faste.
And many a lovely look on hem he caste,
And namely on this carpenteris wyf.
To looke on hire hym thoughte a myrie lyf,
She was so propre and sweete and likerous. 3345
I dar wel seyn, if she hadde been a mous,
And he a cat, he wolde hire hente anon.
This parissh clerk, this joly Absolon,
Hath in his herte swich a love-longynge
That of no wyf took he noon offrynge— 3350
For curteisie, he seyde, he wolde noon.

    The moone, whan it was nyght, ful brighte
        shoon,
And Absolon his gyterne hath ytake,
For paramours he thoghte for to wake.
And forth he gooth, jolif and amorous, 3355
Til he cam to the carpenteres hous
A litel after cokkes hadde ycrowe,
And dressed hym up by a shot-wyndowe
That was upon the carpenteris wal.
He syngeth in his voys gentil and smal, 3360
"Now, deere lady, if thy wille be,
I praye yow that ye wole rewe on me,"
Ful wel acordaunt to his gyternynge.

This carpenter awook and herde him synge,
And spak unto his wyf and seyde anon, 3365
"What, Alison, herestow nat Absolon,
That chaunteth thus under oure boures wal?"
And she answerde hir housbonde therwithal,
"Yis, God woot, John, I heere it every deel."
    This passeth forth; what wol ye bet than
        weel? 3370
Fro day to day this joly Absolon
So woweth hire that hym is wobigon.
He waketh al the nyght and al the day;
He kembeth his lokkes brode, and made hym
        gay;
He woweth hire by meenes and brocage, 3375
And swoor he wolde been hir owene page;
He syngeth, brokkynge as a nyghtyngale;
He sente hire pyment, meeth, and spiced ale,
And wafres, pipyng hoot out of the gleede;
And, for she was of towne, he profreth
        meede—
For som folk wol ben wonnen for richesse, 3381
And somme for strokes, and somme for
        gentillesse.
    Somtyme, to shewe his lightnesse and
        maistrye,
He pleyeth Herodes upon a scaffold hye.
But what availleth hym as in this cas? 3385
She loveth so this hende Nicholas
That Absolon may blowe the bukkes horn;
He ne hadde for his labour but a scorn.
And thus she maketh Absolon hire ape,
And al his ernest turneth til a jape. 3390
Ful sooth is this proverbe, it is no lye,
Men seyn right thus, "Alwey the nye slye
Maketh the ferre leeve to be looth."
For though that Absolon be wood or wrooth,
By cause that he fer was from hire sighte, 3395

3329 Oxenforde, perhaps the Oxford manner of dancing was also regarded as fashionable. **3331 rubible,** rebec (fiddle). **3332 quynyble,** high treble. **3333 giterne,** guitar. **3335 solas,** satisfactions (with sexual overtones). **3336 gaylard tappestere,** lively barmaid. **3337 squaymous,** squeamish. **3338 daungerous,** fastidious. **3340 sencer,** portable incense burner. Some scholars have argued that he went about the parish censing the homes. **3343 namely,** especially. **3345 likerous,** sexy. **3347 hente,** seize. **3350** Hg&c *ne took.* **3354 paramours,** sexual desire. **3358 dressed hym . . . shot-wyndowe,** stationed himself, hinged (shutter) window. **3360 smal,** dainty. **3362 rewe,** have pity: E&c *thynke.* **3363 acordaunt,** in harmony. **3364** E&c *him* om. **3367 boures,** bedroom's. **3369 woot,** knows. **3370 bet than weel,** better than well. **3372 woweth . . . wobigon,** woos, woebegone. **3374 kembeth . . . gay,** combs, gaily dressed. **3375 meenes . . . brocage,** go-betweens, agents. **3377 brokkynge,** trilling. **3378 pyment, meeth,** wine mixed with honey, mead. **3379 wafres . . . gleede,** cakes, coals. **3380 of towne . . . meede,** a city girl, money. **3381 for,** by. **3382 strokes,** blows (force). **3383 lightnesse and maistrye,** agility and virtuosity. **3384 Herodes . . . scaffold,** Herod, the roaring bully in the mystery plays, outdoor platform. **3387 blowe . . . horn,** i.e., go whistle. **3390 til a jape,** to a joke. **3392 nye slye,** sly one nearby. **3393 ferre leeve . . . looth,** distant love, disliked. **3394 wood or wrooth,** crazy or angry.

This nye Nicholas stood in his lighte.

Now bere thee wel, thou hende Nicholas,
For Absolon may waille and synge, "Allas!"
And so bifel it on a Saterday
This carpenter was goon til Osenay,   3400
And hende Nicholas and Alisoun
Acorded been to this conclusioun,
That Nicholas shal shapen hym a wyle
This sely jalous housbonde to bigyle,
And if so be the game wente aright,   3405
She sholde slepen in his arm al nyght,
For this was his desir and hire also.
And right anon, withouten wordes mo,
This Nicholas no lenger wolde tarie,
But dooth ful softe unto his chambre carie   3410
Bothe mete and drynke for a day or tweye,
And to hire housbonde bad hire for to seye,
If that he axed after Nicholas,
She sholde seye she nyste where he was,
Of al that day she saugh hym nat with eye;   3415
She trowed that he was in maladye,
For for no cry hir mayde koude hym calle,
He nolde answere for thyng that myghte falle.

This passeth forth al thilke Saterday,
That Nicholas stille in his chambre lay,   3420
And eet and sleep, or dide what hym leste,
Til Sonday, that the sonne gooth to reste.

This sely carpenter hath greet merveyle
Of Nicholas, or what thyng myghte hym eyle,
And seyde, "I am adrad, by Seint Thomas,   3425
It stondeth nat aright with Nicholas.
God shilde that he deyde sodeynly!
This world is now ful tikel, sikerly.
I saugh today a cors yborn to chirche
That now, on Monday last, I saugh hym
         wirche.   3430
"Go up," quod he unto his knave anoon,
"Clepe at his dore, or knokke with a stoon.

Looke how it is, and tel me boldely."

This knave gooth hym up ful sturdily,   3434
And at the chambre dore whil that he stood
He cride and knokked as that he were wood,
"What? How? What do ye, maister Nicholay?
How may ye slepen al the longe day?"

But al for noght; he herde nat a word.
An hole he foond, ful lowe upon a bord,   3440
Ther as the cat was wont in for to crepe,
And at that hole he looked in ful depe,
And at the laste he hadde of hym a sighte.
This Nicholas sat capyng evere uprighte,
As he had kiked on the newe moone.   3445
Adoun he gooth and tolde his maister soone
In what array he saugh this ilke man.

This carpenter to blessen hym bigan,
And seyde, "Help us, Seinte Frydeswyde!
A man woot litel what hym shal bityde.   3450
This man is falle, with his astromye,
In som woodnesse or in som agonye.
I thoghte ay wel how that it sholde be—
Men sholde nat knowe of Goddes pryvetee.
Ye, blessed be alwey a lewed man   3455
That noght but oonly his bileve kan!
So ferde another clerk with astromye;
He walked in the feeldes for to prye
Upon the sterres, what ther sholde bifalle,
Til he was in a marle-put yfalle—   3460
He saugh nat that. But yet, by Seint Thomas,
Me reweth soore of hende Nicholas.
He shal be rated of his studiyng,
If that I may, by Jhesus, hevene kyng!
Get me a staf, that I may underspore,   3465
Whil that thou, Robyn, hevest up the dore.
He shal out of his studiyng, as I gesse."
And to the chambre dore he gan hym dresse.
His knave was a strong carl for the nones,
And by the haspe he haaf it of atones;   3470

3403 **shapen . . . wyle,** devise, scheme. 3404 **sely,** foolish. 3407 Hg&c *hir desire and his.* 3410 **softe,** quietly (secretly). 3414 **nyste,** didn't know. 3416 **trowed,** believed. 3418 **myghte falle,** might happen. 3419 **passeth forth al thilke,** goes on all that. 3423 **sely . . . merveyle,** foolish (innocent), wonder. 3424 **eyle,** ail. 3427 **shilde,** shield (forbid). 3428 **tikel,** insecure (ticklish). 3429 **cors,** corps. 3431 **knave,** boy servant. 3432 **Clepe,** call. 3436 **wood,** crazy. 3444 **capyng,** gaping. Hg&c *evere capyng.* 3445 **kiked,** stared. 3446 **soone,** immediately. 3447 **array,** condition. 3448 **blessen hym,** cross himself. 3449 **Frydeswyde,** patron saint of Oxford. 3450 **woot . . . bityde,** knows, befall. 3451 **astromye,** like "Nowelis" (l. 3818 below) a malapropism. 3453 **I thoghte ay,** I always thought. 3454 **pryvetee,** secrets. 3455 **lewed,** ignorant. 3456 **bileve kan,** beliefs knows. 3460 **marle-put,** pit from which fertilizer is dug. 3462 **reweth,** have pity. 3463 **rated of,** scolded for. 3465 **underspore,** pry up (medieval doors were on gate hinges). 3468 **hym dresse,** to address himself. 3469 **carl,** farmer (Scandinavian form of churl). 3470 **haspe he haaf,** hinged fastener, heaved.

Into the floor the dore fil anon.
This Nicholas sat ay as stille as stoon,
And evere caped upward into the eir.
This carpenter wende he were in despeir,
And hente hym by the sholdres myghtily,   3475
And shook hym harde and cride spitously,
"What, Nicholay, what? How? What, looke
    adoun!
Awake and thenk on Cristes passioun!
I crouche thee from elves and fro wightes."
Therwith the nyght-spel seyde he anon-rightes
On foure halves of the hous aboute,   3481
And on the threshfold of the dore withoute:
"Jhesu Crist and Seint Benedight,
Blesse this hous from every wikked wight,
For nyghtes verye, the White Pater Noster.   3485
Where wentestow, Seint Petres soster?"

    And atte laste this hende Nicholas
Gan for to sike soore, and seyde, "Allas,
Shal al the world be lost eftsoones now?"   3489

    This carpenter answerde, "What seystow?
What! Thynk on God, as we doon, men that
    swynke."
    This Nicholas answerde, "Fecche me drynke,
And after wol I speke in pryvetee
Of certeyn thyng that toucheth me and thee.
I wol telle it noon oother man, certeyn."   3495

    This carpenter goth doun and comth ageyn,
And broghte of myghty ale a large quart.
And whan that ech of hem had dronke his part,
This Nicholas his dore faste shette,
And doun the carpenter by hym he sette.   3500

    He seyde, "John, myn hooste, lief and deere,
Thou shalt upon thy trouthe swere me heere
That to no wight thou shalt this conseil wreye,

For it is Cristes conseil that I seye.
And if thou telle it man, thou art forlore,   3505
For this vengeaunce thou shalt han therfore,
That if thou wreye me, thou shalt be wood."
    "Nay, Crist forbede it, for his hooly blood,"
Quod tho this sely man. "I nam no labbe,
Ne, though I seye, I nam nat lief to gabbe.   3510
Sey what thou wolt, I shal it nevere telle
To child ne wyf, by hym that harwed helle!"

    "Now, John," quod Nicholas, "I wol nat lye.
I have yfounde in myn astrologye,
As I have looked in the moone bright,   3515
That now a Monday next, at quarter nyght,
Shal falle a reyn, and that so wilde and wood
That half so greet was nevere Noees flood.
This world," he seyde, "in lasse than an hour
Shal al be dreynt, so hidous is the shour.   3520
Thus shal mankynde drenche, and lese hir lyf."

    This carpenter answerde, "Allas, my wyf!
And shal she drenche? Allas, myn Alisoun!"
For sorwe of this he fil almoost adoun,   3524
And seyde, "Is ther no remedie in this cas?"

    "Why, yis, for Gode," quod hende Nicholas,
"If thou wolt werken after loore and reed.
Thou mayst nat werken after thyn owene heed,
For thus seith Salomon, that was ful trewe,
'Werk al by conseil, and thou shalt nat rewe.'
And if thou werken wolt by good conseil,   3531
I undertake, withouten mast and seyl,
Yet shal I saven hire and thee and me.
Hastow nat herd hou saved was Noe,
Whan that oure Lord hadde warned hym
    biforn   3535
That al the world with water sholde be lorn?"
    "Yis," quod this Carpenter, "ful yoore ago."

3474 **wende . . . despeir,** thought, a depression. 3475 **hente,** seized. 3476 **spitously,** roughly. 3477 *What, looke:* Hg&c *What* om.; other MSS *Man/ Now look.* 3479 **crouche . . . wightes,** make the sign of the cross, creatures. 3480 **nyght-spel,** bedtime prayer or charm. 3485–86 These lines follow EHg&c. Wording varies in other MSS. Clearly the scribes were as mystified as we are. **verye,** Skeat derives it from Old English "for nihte werigum" (against the evil spirits of the night); Donaldson reads "nerye" (defend us). **White Pater Noster,** a bedtime prayer, the "Patenôtre Blanche." **Seint Petres soster,** perhaps a substitution for St. Peter's daughter, St. Petronilla (sometimes the night charms read "St. Peter's brother"). 3488 **sike,** sigh. 3489 **eftsoones,** a second time. 3491 **swynke,** work. 3497 **myghty,** strong. 3499 **shette,** shut. (Evidently Robin had put the door back on its hinges.) 3501 **lief,** loved. 3503 **wreye,** reveal. 3505 **forlore,** lost. E *it* om. 3507 **wreye . . . wood,** betray, crazy. 3509 **sely . . . labbe,** innocent, blabber. 3510 **lief . . . gabbe,** prone, gossip (gab). 3512 **harwed,** harrowed (i.e., Christ). 3516 **quarter nyght,** a quarter of the way through, i.e., about 9 P.M. 3518 *Noees:* Hg&c *Nowelles* (but this misses the point of the carpenter's malapropism). Noah's Flood began April 17 (see Genesis 7:11), the first day of the Canterbury Pilgrimage (see *CT* I.8n above). In exegetical tradition, the purpose of the Flood was to separate the righteous from the sinful. 3520 **dreynt,** drowned. 3521 **drenche,** drown. 3527 **werken after loore and reed,** do according to wisdom and advice. 3528 **heed,** head. 3530 **rewe,** regret. 3536 **lorn,** lost. 3537 **yoore,** long.

"Hastou nat herd," quod Nicholas, "also
The sorwe of Noe with his felaweshipe,
Er that he myghte gete his wyf to shipe? 3540
Hym hadde be levere, I dar wel undertake,
At thilke tyme, than alle his wetheres blake
That she hadde had a ship hirself allone.
And therfore, woostou what is best to doone?
This asketh haste, and of an hastif thyng 3545
Men may nat preche or maken tariyng.

"Anon go gete us faste into this in
A knedyng trogh, or ellis a kymelyn,
For ech of us, but looke that they be large,
In which we mowe swymme as in a barge, 3550
And han therinne vitaille suffisant
But for a day—fy on the remenant!
The water shal aslake and goon away
Aboute pryme upon the nexte day. 3554
But Robyn may nat wite of this, thy knave,
Ne eek thy mayde Gille I may nat save.
Axe nat why, for though thou aske me,
I wol nat tellen Goddes pryvetee.
Suffiseth thee, but if thy wittes madde,
To han as greet a grace as Noe hadde. 3560
Thy wyf shal I wel saven, out of doute.
Go now thy wey, and speed thee heer-aboute.

"But whan thou hast for hire and thee and me
Ygeten us thise knedyng tubbes thre, 3564
Thanne shaltow hange hem in the roof ful hye,
That no man of oure purveiaunce spye.
And whan thou thus hast doon as I have seyd,
And hast oure vitaille faire in hem yleyd,
And eek an ax to smyte the corde atwo, 3569
Whan that the water comth that we may go,
And breke an hole an heigh upon the gable,
Unto the gardyn-ward, over the stable,
That we may frely passen forth oure way,
Whan that the grete shour is goon away,
Thanne shaltou swymme as myrie, I undertake,

As dooth the white doke after hire drake. 3576
Thanne wol I clepe, 'How, Alison! How, John!
Be myrie, for the flood wol passe anon.'
And thou wolt seyn, 'Hayl, maister Nicholay!
Good morwe, I se thee wel, for it is day.' 3580
And thanne shul we be lordes al oure lyf
Of al the world, as Noe and his wyf.

"But of o thyng I warne thee ful right:
Be wel avysed on that ilke nyght
That we ben entred into shippes bord, 3585
That noon of us ne speke nat a word,
Ne clepe, ne crie, but been in his preyere,
For it is Goddes owene heeste deere.

"Thy wyf and thou moote hange fer atwynne,
For that bitwixe yow shal be no synne, 3590
Namoore in lookyng than ther shal in deede.
This ordinance is seyd. Go, God thee speede.
Tomorwe at nyght, whan folk ben alle aslepe,
Into oure knedyng tubbes wol we crepe,
And sitten there, abidyng Goddes grace. 3595
Go now thy wey, I have no lenger space
To make of this no lenger sermonyng.
Men seyn thus, 'sende the wise, and sey
        nothyng.'
Thou art so wys it needeth thee nat teche.
Go, save oure lyf, and that I the biseche." 3600
    This sely carpenter goth forth his wey.
Ful ofte he seith "allas" and "weylawey,"
And to his wyf he tolde his pryveetee,
And she was war and knew it bet than he,
What al this queynte cast was for to seye. 3605
But nathelees she ferde as she wolde deye,
And seyde, "Allas! go forth thy wey anon,
Help us to scape, or we been dede echon!
I am thy trewe, verray wedded wyf— 3609
Go, deere spouse, and help to save oure lyf."
    Lo, which a greet thyng is affeccioun!
Men may dyen of ymaginacioun,

3540 **wyf to shipe,** in the mystery plays the reluctance of Noah's wife to board the Ark is a traditional comic scene. *gete:* E *brynge.*
3541 **levere,** happier. 3542 **thilke . . . wetheres,** that, rams. 3544 **woostou,** do you know. 3547 **in,** house. 3548 **knedyng trogh . . .
kymelyn,** long wooden tub for kneading large quantities of dough, metal tub for brewing beer. 3550 **mowe,** may. 3551 **vitaille,** food
(victuals). 3552 **remenant,** i.e., any more food. 3553 **aslake,** diminish (slack off). 3554 **pryme,** 9 A.M. 3555 **wite,** know. 3565 **in the
roof,** among the exposed rafters of the hall ceiling. 3566 **purveiaunce,** preparedness. 3571 **breke an hole . . . gable,** cut a hole in
the gable. 3575 *shaltou:* E *shal I* (a Freudian slip on the part of the scribe). 3576 *hire:* Hg&c *his* (i.e., its). 3577 **clepe,** call. 3584 **ilke,**
same. 3588 **heeste,** command. 3589 **atwynne,** apart. 3593 *folk:* Hg&c *men.* 3599 *nat teche:* E *nat to preche.* 3603 **pryveetee,** secret.
3604 **war,** aware. 3605 **queynte cast . . . seye,** ingenious plan, see (but "queynte" may always be suspected of having *double entendre*
in Chaucer, cf. ll. 3275–76 above). 3606 **ferde,** acted. 3608 *dede:* E *lost.* 3611 **affeccioun,** emotion.

So depe may impressioun be take.
This sely carpenter bigynneth quake.
Hym thynketh verraily that he may see 3615
Noees flood come walwynge as the see
To drenchen Alisoun, his hony deere.
He wepeth, weyleth, maketh sory cheere;
He siketh with ful many a sory swogh;
He gooth and geteth hym a knedyng trogh, 3620
And after that a tubbe and a kymelyn,
And pryvely he sente hem to his in,
And heng hem in the roof in pryvetee.
His owene hand he made laddres thre
To clymben by the ronges and the stalkes 3625
Into the tubbes hangynge in the balkes,
And hem vitailleth, bothe trogh and tubbe,
With breed and chese and good ale in a jubbe,
Suffisynge right ynogh as for a day.
But er that he hadde maad al this array, 3630
He sente his knave and eek his wenche also
Upon his nede to London for to go.
And on the Monday, whan it drow to nyght,
He shette his dore withoute candel lyght,
And dresseth alle thyng as it shal be. 3635
And shortly, up they clomben alle thre;
They seten stille wel a furlong way.
    "Now, Pater Noster, clom!" seyde Nicolay,
And "Clom," quod John, and "Clom," seyde
    Alisoun.
This carpenter seyde his devocioun, 3640
And stille he sit and biddeth his preyere,
Awaitynge on the reyn, if he it heere.
    The dede sleep, for wery bisynesse,
Fil on this carpenter right as I gesse
Aboute corfew-tyme, or litel moore. 3645
For travaille of his goost he groneth soore,
And eft he routeth, for his heed myslay.
Doun of the laddre stalketh Nicholay,
And Alisoun ful softe adoun she spedde.
Withouten wordes mo they goon to bedde,

Ther as the carpenter is wont to lye. 3651
Ther was the revel and the melodye,
And thus lith Alison and Nicholas,
In bisynesse of myrthe and of solas,
Til that the belle of laudes gan to rynge, 3655
And freres in the chauncel gonne synge.
    This parissh clerk, this amorous Absolon,
That is for love alwey so wobigon,
Upon the Monday was at Oseneye 3659
With compaignye, hym to disporte and pleye,
And axed upon cas a cloisterer
Ful prively after John the carpenter.
And he drough hym apart out of the chirche
And seyde, "I noot, I saugh hym heere nat
    wirche
Syn Saterday. I trowe that he be went 3665
For tymber, ther our abbot hath hym sent.
For he is wont for tymber for to go
And dwellen at the grange a day or two.
Or elles he is at his hous, certeyn.
Where that he be, I kan nat soothly seyn." 3670
    This Absolon ful joly was and light,
And thoghte, "Now is tyme to wake al nyght,
For sikirly I saugh hym nat stirynge
Aboute his dore syn day bigan to sprynge.
    "So moot I thryve, I shal at cokkes crowe
Ful pryvely knokke at his wyndowe 3676
That stant ful lowe upon his boures wal.
To Alison now wol I tellen al
My love-longynge, for yet I shal nat mysse
That at the leeste wey I shal hire kisse. 3680
Som maner confort shal I have, parfay.
My mouth hath icched al this longe day—
That is a signe of kissyng atte leeste.
Al nyght me mette eek I was at a feeste. 3684
Therfore I wol go slepe an houre or tweye,
And al the nyght thanne wol I wake and pleye."
    Whan that the firste cok hath crowe, anon
Up rist this joly lovere Absolon,

3616 walwynge, billowing. **3617 drenchen,** drown. **3618 sory cheere,** sad countenance. **3619 siketh . . . swogh,** sighs, groan. **3625 stalkes,** the shafts. **3626 balkes,** beams. **3628 jubbe,** jug. **3632 his nede,** an errand. **3635** Hg&c *dressed . . . sholde.* **3637 furlong way,** time it takes to walk a furlong (220 yards). **3638 clom,** be quiet ("clam up"). **3641 biddeth,** pray. **3645 corfew,** curfew, about 9 P.M. when fires were to be covered. **3646 travaille of his goost,** affliction of his spirit. **3647 routeth,** snores. **3653** E *lith* om. **3654 solas,** sexual satisfaction. **3655 laudes,** the first service of the day, after midnight but before daybreak. **3656 chauncel,** chancel (church). **3661 upon cas,** by chance. **cloisterer,** member of the abbey of Augustinian canons (see l. 3274n. above). **3664 wirche,** work. **3668 grange,** farm. **3673 sikirly,** truly. **3675 thryve,** thrive (succeed). **3677 boures,** bedroom's. **3684 mette,** dreamed.

And hym arraieth gay at poynt devys.
But first he cheweth greyn of lycorys,   3690
To smellen sweete, er he hadde kembd his heer.
Under his tonge a trewe-love he beer,
For therby wende he to ben gracious.
He rometh to the carpenteres hous,   3694
And stille he stant under the shot-wyndowe—
Unto his brest it raughte, it was so lowe—
And softe he cougheth with a semy soun:
"What do ye, honycomb, sweete Alisoun,
My faire bryd, my sweete cynamome?   3699
Awaketh, lemman myn, and speketh to me!
Wel litel thynken ye upon my wo,
That for youre love I swete ther I go.
No wonder is thogh that I swelte and swete;
I moorne as dooth a lamb after the tete.   3704
Ywis, lemman, I have swich love-longynge
That lik a turtel trewe is my moornynge.
I may nat ete na moore than a mayde."
    "Go fro the wyndow, Jakke fool," she sayde.
"As help me God, it wol nat be 'com pa me.'
I love another—and elles I were to blame—
Wel bet than thee, by Jhesu, Absolon.   3711
Go forth thy wey or I wol caste a ston,
And lat me slepe, a twenty devel wey!"
    "Allas," quod Absolon, "and weylawey,
That trewe love was evere so yvel biset!   3715
Thanne kysse me, syn it may be no bet,
For Jhesus love and for the love of me."
    "Wiltow thanne go thy wey therwith?"
        quod she.
    "Ye, certes, lemman," quod this Absolon.
    "Thanne make thee redy," quod she, "I come
        anon."   3720
And unto Nicholas she seyde stille,
"Now hust, and thou shalt laughen al thy fille."
    This Absolon doun sette hym on his knees
And seyde, "I am a lord at alle degrees,

For after this I hope ther cometh moore.   3725
Lemman, thy grace, and sweete bryd, thyn
        oore!"
    The wyndow she undoth and that in haste.
"Have do," quod she, "com of, and speed the
        faste,
Lest that oure neighebores thee espie."   3729
    This Absolon gan wype his mouth ful drie.
Dirk was the nyght as pich, or as the cole,
And at the wyndow out she putte hir hole,
And Absolon, hym fil no bet ne wers,
But with his mouth he kiste hir naked ers
Ful savourly, er he were war of this.   3735
    Abak he stirte, and thoughte it was amys,
For wel he wiste a womman hath no berd.
He felte a thyng al rough and long yherd,
And seyde, "Fy! allas! what have I do?"
    "Tehee," quod she and clapte the wyndow to.
And Absolon gooth forth a sory pas.   3741
    "A berd, a berd!" quod hende Nicholas.
"By Goddes corpus, this goth faire and weel."
    This sely Absolon herde every deel,
And on his lippe he gan for anger byte,   3745
And to hymself he seyde, "I shal thee quyte."
    Who rubbeth now, who froteth now his lippes
With dust, with sond, with straw, with clooth,
        with chippes,
But Absolon, that seith ful ofte, "Allas."
"My soule bitake I unto Sathanas,   3750
But me were levere than al this toun," quod he,
"Of this despit awroken for to be.
Allas," quod he, "allas, I ne hadde ybleynt!"
His hoote love was coold and al yqueynt,
For fro that tyme that he hadde kist hir ers   3755
Of paramours he sette nat a kers,
For he was heeled of his maladie.
Ful ofte paramours he gan deffie,
And weep as dooth a child that is ybete.

3689 gay at poynt devys, gaily to perfection. **3690 greyn,** grain of paradise (the spice cardamom). **3691 kembd,** combed. **3692 trewe-love,** four-leaf clover. **3693 wende,** thought. **3694 rometh,** wanders. **3695 shot-wyndowe,** see l. 3358n above. **3696 raughte,** reached. **3697 semy,** thin (cf. Lat. *semisonus*). **cougheth:** E *knokketh.* **3698 honycomb,** the association of the following lines with the Song of Solomon (Ps. 19:10, etc.) has been noted. **3699 bryd . . . cynamome,** bird (also bride), cinnamon. **3700 lemman,** lover. **3702 swete,** sweat. **3703 swelte,** melt. **3704 tete,** tit. **3706 turtel,** turtledove. **3709 com pa me,** come kiss me. **3718** E&c *therwith* om. **3721–22** Lines found only in E&c. **stille,** quietly. **3724 degrees,** ways. **3726 bryd . . . oore,** bird (or bride), favor. **3735 war,** aware. **3738 yherd,** haired. **3741 pas,** step. **3742 berd,** prank, but *double entendre.* **3743 corpus,** body. **3746 quyte,** repay. **3747 froteth,** wipes. **3750 bitake . . . Sathanas,** promise, Satan. **3752 despit . . . awroken,** insult, avenged. **3753 ybleynt,** abstained. **3754 yqueynt,** quenched. **3756 paramours . . . kers,** sexual love, (water)cress. **3758 deffie,** denounce.

A softe paas he wente over the strete 3760
Until a smyth men cleped daun Gerveys,
That in his forge smythed plough harneys;
He sharpeth shaar and kultour bisily.
This Absolon knokketh al esily, 3764
And seyde, "Undo, Gerveys, and that anon."
    "What, who artow?" "It am I, Absolon."
"What, Absolon, for Cristes sweete tree,
Why rise ye so rathe? Ey, benedicitee,
What eyleth yow? Som gay gerl, God it woot,
Hath broght yow thus upon the viritoot. 3770
By Seinte Note, ye woot wel what I mene."
    This Absolon ne roghte nat a bene
Of al his pley; no word agayn he yaf.
He hadde moore tow on his distaf
Than Gerveys knew, and seyde, "Freend so
        deere, 3775
That hoote kultour in the chymenee heere,
As lene it me, I have therwith to doone,
And I wol brynge it thee agayn ful soone."
    Gerveys answerde, "Certes, were it gold
Or in a poke nobles alle untold, 3780
Thou sholdest have, as I am trewe smyth.
Ey, Cristes foo, what wol ye do therwith?"
    "Therof," quod Absolon, "be as be may.
I shal wel telle it thee tomorwe day"—
And caughte the kultour by the colde stele.
Ful softe out at the dore he gan to stele, 3786
And wente unto the carpenteris wal.
He cogheth first and knokketh therwithal
Upon the wyndowe, right as he dide er.
    This Alison answerde, "Who is ther 3790
That knokketh so? I warante it a theef."
    "Why, nay," quod he, "God woot, my sweete
        leef,
I am thyn Absolon, my deerelyng.
Of gold," quod he, "I have thee broght a ryng.

My mooder yaf it me, so God me save. 3795
Ful fyn it is and therto wel ygrave.
This wol I yeve thee, if thou me kisse."
    This Nicholas was risen for to pisse,
And thoughte he wolde amenden al the jape;
He sholde kisse his ers er that he scape. 3800
And up the wyndowe dide he hastily,
And out his ers he putteth pryvely
Over the buttok, to the haunche-bon.
And therwith spak this clerk, this Absolon,
"Spek, sweete bryd, I noot nat where thou art."
    This Nicholas anon leet fle a fart 3806
As greet as it had been a thonder-dent
That with the strook he was almoost yblent,
And he was redy with his iren hoot,
And Nicholas amydde the ers he smoot. 3810
    Of gooth the skyn an hande-brede aboute,
The hoote kultour brende so his toute,
And for the smert he wende for to dye.
As he were wood, for wo he gan to crye, 3814
"Help! Water! Water! Help, for Goddes herte!"
    This carpenter out of his slomber sterte,
And herde oon crien "water" as he were wood,
And thoughte, "Allas, now comth Nowelis
        flood!"
He sit hym up withouten wordes mo,
And with his ax he smoot the corde atwo, 3820
And doun gooth al; he foond neither to selle
Ne breed ne ale til he cam to the celle,
Upon the floor, and ther aswowne he lay.
    Up stirte hire Alison and Nicholay, 3824
And criden "out" and "harrow" in the strete.
The neighebores, bothe smale and grete,
In ronnen for to gauren on this man,
That aswowne lay bothe pale and wan,
For with the fal he brosten hadde his arm.
But stonde he moste unto his owene harm, 3830

3760 **softe paas,** subdued walk. 3761 **daun,** dom(inus). Contemporary records show that the blacksmiths did work all night. 3763 **shaar, kultour,** plowshare (blade), turf cutter. 3764 **esily,** quietly. 3765 **anon,** at once. 3766 E *I am heere, Absolon.* 3768 **rathe,** early. 3770 **viritoot,** term not found elsewhere, (?) prowl. 3771 **Note,** St. Neot of Glastonbury. 3772 **roghte . . . bene,** cared, bean. 3777 **lene,** lend. 3778 Hg&c *And* om. 3780 **poke . . . untold,** bag, uncounted. 3782 **foo,** (?) Satan. Editors suggest that this is a euphemism for "God's foot." 3785 **stele,** handle (not "steel," cf. rime). 3789 **er,** before. 3792 **leef,** beloved. 3796 **ygrave,** engraved. 3799 **amenden . . . jape,** improve on, joke. 3800 E *ers* om. 3807 **dent,** blast. 3808 **yblent,** blinded. 3810 *amydde:* Hg&c *in;* E *the* om. 3811 **brede,** breadth. 3812 **toute,** rump. 3814 **wood,** crazy. 3815 **herte,** heart. 3818 **Nowelis,** Noel's for Noah's, another malapropism. 3821 **to selle,** Tyrwhitt pointed out that this is a French expression, "Ainc tant come il mist a descendre,/ Ne trouva pas point de pain a vendre." 3822 **celle,** sill (floor). 3823 **aswowne,** unconscious. 3824 **hire,** her (or perhaps them). 3827 **gauren,** stare. 3828 E&c *That yet aswowne he lay.* 3829 **brosten,** broken. 3830 **stonde . . . moste . . . harm,** i.e., he must be held responsible for his own injury.

For whan he spak, he was anon bore doun
With hende Nicholas and Alisoun.
They tolden every man that he was wood,
He was agast so of Nowelis flood
Thurgh fantasie, that of his vanytee   3835
He hadde yboght hym knedyng tubbes thre,
And hadde hem hanged in the roof above;
And that he preyed hem, for Goddes love,
To sitten in the roof, *par compaignye.*

    The folk gan laughen at his fantasye.   3840
Into the roof they kiken and they cape,
And turned al his harm unto a jape.
For what so that this carpenter answerde,

It was for noght, no man his reson herde.
With othes grete he was so sworn adoun   3845
That he was holde wood in al the toun,
For every clerk anonright heeld with other.
They seyde, "The man is wood, my leeve
    brother,"
And every wight gan laughen at this stryf.
Thus swyved was this carpenteris wyf,   3850
For al his kepyng and his jalousye,
And Absolon hath kist hir nether eye,
And Nicholas is scalded in the towte.
This tale is doon, and God save al the
    rowte!

Heere endeth the Millere his Tale.

3833 wood, crazy. **3835 fantasie . . . vanytee,** delusion, folly. **3837** *roof:* E *roue.* **3839** *par,* for. **3841 kiken . . . cape,** gaze, gape. **3842 harm . . . jape,** injury, joke. **3847 clerk . . . heeld with other,** it was conventional in the fabliaux for clever clerks to outwit stupid laymen. **3848** *is:* EHg&c *was.* **3850 swyved,** copulated with. **3851 kepyng,** guarding. **3854 rowte,** company.

REEVE'S TALE

PROLOGUE

The Prologe of the Reves Tale.

Whan folk hadde laughen at this nyce cas
Of Absolon and hende Nicholas, 3856
Diverse folk diversely they seyde,
But for the moore part they loughe and pleyde.
Ne at this tale I saugh no man hym greve,
But it were oonly Osewold the Reve. 3860
By cause he was of carpenteris craft,
A litel ire is in his herte ylaft.
He gan to grucche, and blamed it a lite.
"So theek," quod he, "ful wel koude I yow
  quite
With bleryng of a proud milleres eye, 3865
If that me liste speke of ribaudye.
But ik am oold, me list no pley for age—
Gras tyme is doon, my fodder is now forage;

This white top writeth myne olde yeris;
Myn herte is mowled also as myne heris— 3870
But if I fare as dooth an open-ers.
That ilke fruyt is ever lenger the wers,
Til it be roten in mullok or in stree.
We olde men, I drede, so fare we:
Til we be roten, kan we nat be rype; 3875
We hoppen ay whil that the world wol pype.
For in oure wyl ther stiketh evere a nayl,
To have an hoor heed and a grene tayl,
As hath a leek; for thogh oure myght be goon,
Oure wyl desireth folie evere in oon. 3880
For whan we may nat doon, than wol we speke;
Yet in oure asshen olde is fyr yreke.
 "Foure gleedes han we, whiche I shal devyse,

3855 **nyce cas,** funny incident. **3863 grucche,** complain. **3864 So theek,** so might I prosper (*thee ik,* northern dialect forms). **quite,** repay. *yow:* Hg&c *thee.* **3865 bleryng . . . eye,** i.e., getting the better of, *double entendre,* cuckolding. **3866 me liste . . . ribaudrye,** pleased me, ribaldry. **3867 ik,** I (northern form). *no pley* thus in EHg; other MSS *not pley.* **3868 fodder . . . forage,** (cattle) food, skimpy winter gleanings. **3869 writeth,** writes (reveals). **3870 mowled,** moulded. **3871 open-ers,** medlar fruit, gathered after the first frost and stored until soft enough to be edible. **3872 ilke,** same. *lenger:* E *leng* (archaic form). **3873 mullok . . . stree,** compost, straw. **3874 drede,** fear. **3876 hoppen ay whil,** dance as long as. **3877 nayl,** i.e., the "thorn in the flesh" of sexual desire; cf. II Cor. 12:7. **3878** *heed:* Hg&c *heer.* **3880 in oon,** continually. **3882 yreke,** raked up. **3883 gleedes . . . devyse,** live coals, describe.

Avauntyng, liyng, anger, coveitise.
Thise foure sparkles longen unto eelde. 3885
Oure olde lemes mowe wel been unweelde,
But wyl ne shal nat faillen, that is sooth.
And yet ik have alwey a coltes tooth,
As many a yeer as it is passed henne
Syn that my tappe of lif bigan to renne. 3890
For sikerly, whan I was bore, anon
Deeth drough the tappe of lyf and leet it gon,
And ever sithe hath so the tappe yronne
Til that almoost al empty is the tonne. 3894
The streem of lyf now droppeth on the chymbe.
The sely tonge may wel rynge and chymbe
Of wrecchednesse that passed is ful yoore;
With olde folk, save dotage, is namoore!"
    Whan that our Hoost hadde herd this
      sermonyng,
He gan to speke as lordly as a kyng. 3900
He seide, "What amounteth al this wit?

What shul we speke alday of hooly writ?
The devel made a reve for to preche,
Or of a soutere a shipman or a leche.
Sey forth thy tale, and tarie nat the tyme. 3905
Lo Depeford, and it is half-wey pryme.
Lo Grenewych, ther many a shrewe is inne.
It were al tyme thy tale to bigynne."
    "Now, sires," quod this Osewold the Reve,
"I pray yow alle that ye nat yow greve 3910
Thogh I answere and somdeel sette his howve,
For leveful is with force force of-showve.
    "This dronke Millere hath ytoold us heer
How that bigyled was a carpenteer—
Peraventure in scorn, for I am oon. 3915
And, by youre leve, I shal hym quite anoon.
Right in his cherles termes wol I speke.
I pray to God his nekke mote tobreke.
He kan wel in myn eye seen a stalke,
But in his owene he kan nat seen a balke." 3920

Heere bigynneth the Reves Tale.

    At Trumpyngtoun, nat fer fro Cantebrigge,
Ther gooth a brook, and over that a brigge,
Upon the whiche brook ther stant a melle;
And this is verray sooth that I yow telle.
A millere was ther dwellynge many a day; 3925
As eny pecok he was proud and gay.
Pipen he koude, and fisshe, and nettes beete,
And turne coppes, and wel wrastle and sheete.
Ay by his belt he baar a long panade,
And of a swerd ful trenchant was the blade.

A joly poppere baar he in his pouche— 3931
Ther was no man, for peril, dorste hym touche.
A Sheffeld thwitel baar he in his hose.
Round was his face, and camuse was his nose;
As piled as an ape was his skulle. 3935
He was a market-betere atte fulle—
Ther dorste no wight hand upon hym legge
That he ne swoor he sholde anon abegge.
A theef he was forsothe of corn and mele,
And that a sly, and usaunt for to stele. 3940

3884 Avauntyng, boasting. **3886 lemes mowe . . . unweelde,** limbs may be incapable. **3888 coltes tooth,** youthful desire (cf. WB III.602). **3890 tappe,** spigot in the bunghole of a wine cask. **3891 sikerly . . . bore, anon,** truly, born, at once. **3894 tonne,** cask. **3895 chymbe,** cask rim. **3896 sely . . . chymbe,** foolish, chime. **3897 wrecchednesse . . . yoore,** wickedness, long ago. **3904 soutere . . . leche,** shoemaker, physician. E&c *And of [a] shipman* (*a* om.). **3905 tarie,** delay. **3906 Depeford,** Deptford, four miles along the road from Southwark. **half-wey pryme,** halfway through prime taken as 6:00–9:00 A.M., the first quarter of the day; i.e., 7:30 A.M. **3907 Grenewych,** Greenwich in Kent, where Chaucer himself may have been living when he wrote these lines. **shrewe,** rascal. **3911 howve,** hood, "get the best of" (like *set hir cappe* I.586, 3143). **3912 leveful . . . of-showve,** permissible, shove off. **3916 quite,** requite. **3918 mote tobreke,** may break ("to" is an intensifier). E&c. **breke. 3919 stalke,** stem, Vulgate Mat. 7:3 *festucum* (which becomes English "fescue," grass); the King James "mote" is a loose translation. **3920 balke,** beam (Lat. *trabs*). **3921 Trumpyngtoun . . . Cantebrigge,** Trumpington, two miles south of Cambridge on the London road. The site of the old mill can still be located. **3927 beete,** mend. **3928 turne coppes,** Skeat glossed this, to carve wooden cups on a turning lathe; Pratt suggests, to engage in a drinking contest in which the winner is the one who first sets his tankard on the table bottom up. **sheete,** shoot. **3929 panade,** cutlass. *Ay:* EHg&c *And.* **3930 trenchant,** sharp. **3931 poppere,** little dagger. **3933 thwitel,** knife (now "whittle"). Sheffield is famous for its steel. **3934 camuse,** flat; a plebeian characteristic. **3935 piled,** bald. **3936 market-betere,** street corner loafer. **3937 legge,** lay. **3938 abegge,** pay for it. **3939 E&c** *was of corn and eek.* **3940 usaunt,** accustomed.

His name was hoote deynous Symkyn.
A wyf he hadde, ycomen of noble kyn—
The person of the toun hir fader was.
With hire he yaf ful many a panne of bras,
For that Symkyn sholde in his blood allye. 3945
She was yfostred in a nonnerye;
For Symkyn wolde no wyf, as he sayde,
But she were wel ynorissed and a mayde,
To saven his estaat of yomanrye.
And she was proud, and peert as is a pye. 3950
A ful fair sighte was it upon hem two:
On halydayes biforn hire wolde he go
With his typet bounde aboute his heed,
And she cam after in a gyte of reed;
And Symkyn hadde hosen of the same. 3955
Ther dorste no wight clepen hire but "dame";
Was noon so hardy that wente by the weye
That with hire dorste rage or ones pleye,
But if he wolde be slayn of Symkyn
With panade, or with knyf, or boidekyn. 3960
For jalous folk ben perilous everemo—
Algate they wolde hire wyves wenden so.
And eek, for she was somdel smoterlich,
She was as digne as water in a dich,
And ful of hoker and of bisemare. 3965
Hir thoughte that a lady sholde hire spare,
What for hire kynrede and hir nortelrie
That she hadde lerned in the nonnerie.
    A doghter hadde they bitwixe hem two
Of twenty yeer, withouten any mo, 3970
Savynge a child that was of half yeer age;
In cradel it lay and was a propre page.
This wenche thikke and wel ygrowen was,

With kamuse nose and eyen greye as glas,
Buttokes brode and brestes rounde and
    hye, 3975
But right fair was hire heer, I wol nat lye.
    This person of the toun, for she was feir,
In purpos was to maken hire his heir,
Bothe of his catel and his mesuage,
And straunge he made it of hir mariage. 3980
His purpos was for to bistowe hire hye
Into som worthy blood of auncetrye,
For hooly chirches good moot been despended
On hooly chirches blood, that is descended.
Therfore he wolde his hooly blood
    honoure, 3985
Though that he hooly chirche sholde devoure.
    Greet sokene hath this millere, out of doute,
With whete and malt of al the land aboute;
And nameliche ther was a greet collegge, 3989
Men clepen the Soler Halle at Cantebregge,
Ther was hir whete and eek hir malt ygrounde.
And on a day it happed, in a stounde,
Sik lay the maunciple on a maladye.
Men wenden wisly that he sholde dye, 3994
For which this millere stal bothe mele and corn
And hundred tyme moore than biforn;
For therbiforn he stal but curteisly,
But now he was a theef outrageously,
For which the wardeyn chidde and made fare.
But therof sette the millere nat a tare; 4000
He craketh boost, and swoor it was nat so.
    Thanne were ther yonge poure clerkes two,
That dwelten in this halle, of which I seye.
Testif they were, and lusty for to pleye,

3941 hoote deynous Symkyn, called conceited; Symkyn is the diminutive of Simon, the original "simonist" (Acts 8:18). The name may have been suggested to Chaucer by the ensuing portrait of Symkyn's wife. **3944 bras,** money. The parson was willing to provide a handsome dowry to marry off his illegitimate daughter. **3945 allye,** enter into alliance (marry). **3948 ynorissed . . . mayde,** educated, virgin. **3949 saven his estaat of yomanrye,** maintain his estate as a freeman. Millers were looked down on because they had traditionally been serfs operating mills which were the monopolies of manorial lords. This miller is evidently a freeman and in busi- ness for himself. **3950 peert . . . pye,** pert, magpie. **3952 go,** walk. **3953 typet,** scarf. Hg&c *wounde.* **3954 gyte . . . reed,** cloak, red. **3958 rage . . . ones pleye,** flirt, once frolic. **3960 boidekyn,** bodkin (dagger). **3963 smoterlich,** soiled (by her illegitimacy). **3964 digne,** proud. **3965 hoker . . . bisemare,** scorn, contempt. **3966 hire spare,** be aloof. **3967 kynrede . . . nortelrie,** relatives, nur- ture. **3972 page,** boy. **3974–75 kamuse . . . greye,** flat, blue; the humor lies in the mixture of plebeian and aristocratic features. Hg&c *With buttokes.* **3976 heer,** hair. **3977** Hg&c *so feir.* **3979 catel . . . mesuage,** chattels (possessions), land. **3980 straunge,** raise problems about. **3982 auncetrye,** ancestry. **3987 Greet sokene,** a large monopoly (see note to l. 3949). **3989 nameliche,** especially. **3990 Soler Halle,** Skeat suggested that this was King's Hall, now part of Trinity College, named for its numerous upstairs rooms built with bay windows (Lat. *solaria,* sun chambers). **3992 stounde,** time. **3994 wenden wisly,** thought certainly. **3995 corn,** grain. **3999 wardeyn,** warden (head of the college). **made fare,** made a fuss. **4000 tare,** weed. **4001 craketh boost,** spoke boastfully. **4002 clerkes:** Hg&c *scolers.* **4004 Testif . . . lusty,** headstrong, happy.

And, oonly for hire myrthe and reverye,   4005
Upon the wardeyn bisily they crye
To yeve hem leve but a litel stounde
To goon to mille and seen hir corn ygrounde;
And hardily they dorste leye hir nekke   4009
The millere sholde nat stele hem half a pekke
Of corn by sleighte, ne by force hem reve;
And at the laste the wardeyn yaf hem leve.
John highte that oon, and Aleyn highte that
    oother;
Of o toun were they born, that highte Strother,
Fer in the north, I kan nat telle where.   4015

This Aleyn maketh redy al his gere,
And on an hors the sak he caste anon.
Forth goth Aleyn the clerk and also John
With good swerd and bokeler by hir side.
John knew the wey—hem nedede no gyde—
And at the mille the sak adoun he layth.   4021
Aleyn spak first, "Al hayl, Symond, y-fayth!
Hou fares thy faire doghter and thy wyf?"

"Aleyn, welcome," quod Symkyn, "by my
    lyf.
And John also, how now, what do ye heer?"   4025

"Symond," quod John, "by God, nede has na
    peer.
Hym boes serve hymselve that has na swayn,
Or elles he is a fool, as clerkes sayn.
Oure manciple, I hope he wil be deed,
Swa werkes ay the wanges in his heed;   4030
And forthy is I come, and eek Alayn,
To grynde oure corn and carie it ham agayn.
I pray yow spede us heythen that ye may."

"It shal be doon," quod Symkyn, "by my
    fay!   4034

What wol ye doon whil that it is in hande?"

"By God, right by the hopur wil I stande,"
Quod John, "and se how that the corn gas in.
Yet saugh I nevere, by my fader kyn,
How that the hopur wagges til and fra."

Aleyn answerde, "John, and wiltow swa?
Thanne wil I be bynethe, by my croun,   4041
And se how that the mele falles doun
Into the trough; that sal be my disport.
For John, yfaith, I may been of youre sort;
I is as ille a millere as ar ye."   4045

This millere smyled of hir nycetee,
And thoghte, "Al this nys doon but for a wyle.
They wene that no man may hem bigyle,
But by my thrift, yet shal I blere hir eye,
For al the sleighte in hir philosophye.   4050
The moore queynte crekes that they make,
The moore wol I stele whan I take.
Instide of flour yet wol I yeve hem bren.
The gretteste clerkes been noght wisest men,
As whilom to the wolf thus spak the mare.   4055
Of al hir art ne counte I noght a tare."

Out at the dore he gooth ful pryvely,
Whan that he saugh his tyme, softely.
He looketh up and doun til he hath founde
The clerkes hors, ther as it stood ybounde   4060
Bihynde the mille, under a lefesel,
And to the hors he goth hym faire and wel;
He strepeth of the brydel right anon.
And whan the hors was laus, he gynneth gon
Toward the fen ther wilde mares renne,   4065
And forth with "wehee," thurgh thikke and
    thurgh thenne.

This millere gooth agayn, no word he seyde,

4005 reverye, wantonness. Some MSS *revelrye*. **4007 stounde,** time (opportunity). **4009 hardily . . . leye,** confidently, bet. **4011 reve,** rob. **4013 highte,** was named. **4014 o toun . . . Strother,** one (the same) town. The town has not been identified; Tolkien suggested that *strother* was a dialect term for "marsh" and so helped characterize the rusticity of the two students. **4019** Hg&c *and with bokeler by his*. **4020 hem:** Hg&c *hym*. **4023 *fares,*** in glosses, the northern dialect forms, which further characterize the students' rusticity, are marked by an asterisk. In this dialect, the 3rd person sing. and pl. ending is (e)s. **4026 *na,*** no. Hg&c *By God, quod John, Symond.* **4027 *boes . . . swayn,*** behooves, servant. Hg&c *bihoves*. **4028** *fool:* some MSS **folt/*fon*. **4029 hope,** expect. **4030 *werkes . . . *wanges,** work (ache), molar teeth. **4031 *is I,** am I (another northern construction). Hg&c *therfore; *is:* in some MSS **es*. **4032 *ham,** home. **4033 *heythen,** hence. **that ye,** i.e., as fast as. **4036 hopur,** hopper (holds the grain dropping into the millstones). **4037 *gas,** goes. Hg&c *that* om; some MSS *how *gates the.* **4039 *til and *fra,** to and fro. **4040 *swa,** so. EHg&c *and* om. **4043 *sal . . . disport,** shall, sport. *Into:* some MSS **Intil.* **4045 *is . . . *ar,** both northern constructions. **4046 nycetee,** ignorance. **4047 wyle,** wile (stratagem). **4048 wene . . . bigyle,** think, deceive. **4049 blere hir eye,** i.e., trick them. **4051 crekes,** tricks. **4055 whilom,** once. **wolf thus spak,** one of the Reynard stories: the mare told the fox who wanted to buy her colt that the price was written on its back hoof. When he went to read it, the colt kicked him, whereupon the mare made the observation about "greatest clerks," etc. **4056 hir,** their (i.e., the students'). **tare,** weed. EHg&c *ne* om. **4057 at:** Hg&c *of.* **4058 softely,** quietly. **4061 lefesel,** arbor. **4063 strepeth of,** strips off. **4064 laus,** loose. Some MSS *loos.*

But dooth his note and with the clerkes pleyde
Til that hir corn was faire and weel ygrounde.
And whan the mele is sakked and ybounde, 4070
This John goth out and fynt his hors away,
And gan to crie "Harrow!" and "Weylaway!
Oure hors is lorn, Alayn, for Goddes banes,
Step on thy feet! Com of, man, al at anes!
Allas, oure wardeyn has his palfrey lorn." 4075
This Aleyn al forgat bothe mele and corn;
Al was out of his mynde his housbondrie.
"What, whilk way is he gane?" he gan to crie.
    The wyf cam lepynge inward with a ren.
She seyde, "Allas! youre hors goth to the fen
With wilde mares, as faste as he may go. 4081
Unthank come on his hand that boond hym so,
And he that bettre sholde han knyt the reyne!"
    "Allas," quod John, "Aleyn, for Cristes peyne,
Lay doun thy swerd, and I wil myn alswa.
I is ful wight, God waat, as is a raa; 4086
By Goddes herte, he sal nat scape us bathe.
Why nadstow pit the capul in the lathe?
Il-hayl, by God, Alayn, thou is a fonne!"
    This sely clerkes han ful faste yronne 4090
Toward the fen, bothe Aleyn and eek John.
    And whan the millere saugh that they were gon,
He half a busshel of hir flour hath take
And bad his wyf go knede it in a cake.
He seyde, "I trowe the clerkes were aferd. 4095
Yet kan a millere make a clerkes berd
For al his art; now lat hem goon hir weye.
Lo, wher they goon! Ye, lat the children pleye.
They gete hym nat so lightly, by my croun."
    Thise sely clerkes rennen up and doun 4100

With "Keep! Keep! Stand! Stand! Jossa! Warderere!
Ga whistle thou, and I sal kepe hym heere!"
But shortly, til that it was verray nyght,
They koude nat, though they dide al hir myght,
Hir capul cacche, he ran alwey so faste, 4105
Til in a dych they caughte hym atte laste.
    Wery and weet, as beest is in the reyn,
Comth sely John, and with him comth Aleyn.
"Allas," quod John, "the day that I was born!
Now are we dryve til hethyng and til scorn.
Oure corn is stoln, men wil us fooles calle, 4111
Bathe the wardeyn and oure felawes alle,
And namely the millere, weylaway!"
    Thus pleyneth John as he gooth by the way
Toward the mille, and Bayard in his hond.
The millere sittynge by the fyr he fond, 4116
For it was nyght, and forther myghte they noght.
But for the love of God they hym bisoght
Of herberwe and of ese, as for hir peny. 4119
    The millere seyde agayn, "If ther be eny,
Swich as it is, yet shal ye have youre part.
Myn hous is streit, but ye han lerned art.
Ye konne by argumentes make a place
A myle brood of twenty foot of space.
Lat se now if this place may suffise, 4125
Or make it rowm with speche as is your gise."
    "Now, Symond," seyde John, "by Seint Cutberd,
Ay is thou myrie, and this is faire answered.
I have herd seyd, man sal taa of twa thynges
Slyk as he fyndes, or taa slyk as he brynges.
But specially I pray thee, hooste deere, 4131
Get us som mete and drynke and make us cheere,

4068 note, task. 4073 lorn . . . *banes, lost, bones. Hg&c *lost*. 4074 at *anes, at once. *of:* E&c out; other MSS on. 4077 housbondrie, responsible management. 4708 *whilk, which. *gane:* E geen (according to Tolkien, not authentic dialect, but cf. 1. 4185 below). 4082 Unthank come, bad luck come to. 4084 E *John* om. 4085 *alswa, also. 4086 *wight . . . *waat . . . *raa, fast, knows, roe. 4087 *bathe, both. E *God*. 4088 nadstow *pit the capul . . . *lathe, had (did) you not put the horse, barn; *capul* is in Chaucer's usage pejorative. Hg&c *ne had thow*, E *hadtow*. 4089 Il-hayl . . . *fonne, bad luck to you, fool. 4096 make . . . berd, trick. 4097 *now:* Hg&c *ye*. 4098 *they goon:* Hg&c *he gooth*. 4099 lightly, easily. 4101 Keep! . . . Jossa! Warderere!, watch out, down here, watch out behind. 4102 *Ga . . . *sal, go, shall. *whistle:* some MSS *wightly (lively)/swiftly;* E&c *shall*. 4103 verray nyght, i.e., really dark. 4104 *dide:* E&c *do*. 4110 dryve *til *hethyng, driven to derision. 4111 *men:* E&c *me*. 4113 namely, especially. 4114 pleyneth, complains. 4115 Bayard, heroic name for a horse. 4119 herberwe . . . peny, lodging, for money. The college gate would be locked after dark. 4120 agayn, in reply. 4122 streit, cramped. 4126 rowm . . . gise, more roomy, fashion. 4127 Cutberd, patron saint of Northumberland (but also an apt pun considering the ensuing events of the evening). 4129 *sal *taa, shall take. 4130 *Slyk, such (a form narrowly localized to Northumberland). The proverb evidently means "must put up with what he can get." Hg&c *Swilk*. 4132 Get us som: some MSS *Gar us have*.

And we wil payen trewely atte fulle.
With empty hand men may none haukes tulle.
Loo, heere oure silver, redy for to spende.''

This millere into toun his doghter sende   4136
For ale and breed, and rosted hem a goos,
And boond hire hors, it sholde namoore go loos,
And in his owene chambre hem made a bed
With sheetes and with chalons faire yspred,   4140
Noght from his owene bed ten foot or twelve.
His doghter hadde a bed al by hirselve
Right in the same chambre by and by.
It myghte be no bet, and cause why?   4144
Ther was no roumer herberwe in the place.
They soupen and they speke, hem to solace,
And drynken evere strong ale atte beste.
Aboute mydnyght wente they to reste.

Wel hath this millere vernysshed his heed;
Ful pale he was fordronken and nat reed.   4150
He yexeth and he speketh thurgh the nose
As he were on the quakke or on the pose.
To bedde he goth, and with hym goth his wyf.
As any jay she light was and jolyf,
So was hir joly whistle wel ywet.   4155
The cradel at hir beddes feet is set,
To rokken, and to yeve the child to sowke.
And whan that dronken al was in the crowke,
To bedde wente the doghter right anon.
To bedde gooth Aleyn and also John—   4160
Ther nas na moore; hem nedede no dwale.
This millere hath so wisly bibbed ale
That as an hors he fnorteth in his sleep,
Ne of his tayl bihynde he took no keep.
His wyf bar hym a burdon, a ful strong;   4165
Men myghte hir rowtyng heere two furlong;
The wenche rowteth eek, *par compaignye.*

Aleyn the clerk, that herde this melodye,
He poked John, and seyde, ''Slepestow?
Herdestow evere slyk a sang er now?   4170
Lo, whilk a complyn is ymel hem alle.
A wilde fyr upon thair bodyes falle!
Wha herkned evere slyk a ferly thyng?
Ye, they sal have the flour of il endyng.
This lange nyght ther tydes me na reste;   4175
But yet, na fors, al sal be for the beste.
For, John,'' seyde he, ''als evere moot I thryve,
If that I may, yon wenche wil I swyve.
Som esement has lawe yshapen us,
For, John, ther is a lawe that says thus,   4180
That gif a man in a point be ygreved,
That in another he sal be releved.
Oure corn is stoln, sothly, it is na nay,
And we han had an il fit al this day,
And syn I sal have neen amendement   4185
Agayn my los, I wil have esement.
By Goddes saule, it sal neen other bee!''

This John answerde, ''Alayn, avyse thee.
The millere is a perilous man,'' he seyde,
''And gif that he out of his sleep abreyde,   4190
He myghte doon us bathe a vileynye.''

Aleyn answerde, ''I counte hym nat a flye.''
And up he rist, and by the wenche he crepte.
This wenche lay uprighte and faste slepte,
Til he so ny was er she myghte espie   4195
That it had been to late for to crie,
And shortly for to seyn, they were aton.
Now pley, Aleyn, for I wol speke of John.

This John lith stille a furlong wey or two,
And to hymself he maketh routhe and wo.   4200
''Allas,'' quod he, ''this is a wikked jape.
Now may I seyn that I is but an ape.

4134 tulle, lure. **none:** Hg&c *na.* **4138 namoore:** E&c *nat.* **4140 chalons,** blankets. **4143 by and by,** alongside. **4144 bet,** better. **4145 herberwe,** lodging. **4146 solace,** satisfy. **4149 vernysshed his heed,** slang for ''had a lot to drink.'' **4151 yexeth,** hiccoughs. **4152 quakke . . . pose,** hoarse, cold in the head. **4157 sowke,** suck. **4158 crowke,** crock. **4160 gooth:** E *wente.* **4161 dwale,** sleeping potion. **4163** *fnorteth,* thus EHg&c; other MSS *snorteth/snoreth/rowtith.* **4164 keep,** care. **4165 burdon,** accompaniment. **4166 rowtyng,** snoring. **two:** Hg&c *a.* **4170** E *Herdtow* ; **slyk* in EHg&c, cf. l. 4130 above. **4171 *whilk . . . complyn . . . *ymel,** which (what), compline (the last service before retiring), among. Hg&c **swilk;* some MSS **slik.* EHg&c *cowplyng* (copulation). **4172 wilde fyr,** erysipelas (a painful skin disease). **4173 *Wha . . . *slyk . . . *ferly,** who, such, strange. Hg&c **swilk.* **4174 *sal . . . flour . . . *il,** shall, flower (end product), bad. **4175 *tydes,** comes to. **4176 *na fors,** no matter. **4177 als . . . moot I thryve,** as, may I prosper. **4178 swyve,** copulate with. All MSS have southern form *If;* cf. ll. 4181, 4190. **4179 esement . . . yshapen,** recompense, provided. **4181** *ygreved:* Hg&c **agreved.* **4183** *sothly:* E&c *shortly.* **4184 *il fit,** bad time. *al this day:* Hg&c *today.* **4185 neen,** none (southern form). **4187 neen other bee,** be not otherwise. **4188 avyse thee,** be careful. **4190 abreyde,** awakened. **4192 counte . . . *nat,** consider him no more than. **4194 uprighte,** on her back. **4197 aton,** at one (in agreement). **4199 furlong wey,** 220 yards (two or three minutes). **4200 routhe,** pity. **4201 jape,** joke.

Yet has my felawe somwhat for his harm;
He has the milleris doghter in his arm.
He auntred hym, and has his nedes sped,   4205
And I lye as a draf-sek in my bed.
And when this jape is tald another day,
I sal been halde a daf, a cokenay.
I wil arise and auntre it, by my fayth.
Unhardy is unseely, thus men sayth."   4210
And up he roos, and softely he wente
Unto the cradel, and in his hand it hente,
And baar it softe unto his beddes feet.

  Soone after this the wyf hir rowtyng leet,
And gan awake, and wente hire out to pisse,   4215
And cam agayn, and gan hir cradel mysse,
And groped heer and ther, but she foond noon.
"Allas," quod she, "I hadde almoost mysgoon.
I hadde almoost goon to the clerkes bed.
Ey, benedicite, thanne hadde I foule ysped."
And forth she gooth til she the cradel fond.   4221
She gropeth alwey forther with hir hond,
And foond the bed, and thoghte noght but
     good,
By cause that the cradel by it stood,
And nyste wher she was, for it was derk,   4225
But faire and wel she creep in to the clerk,
And lith ful stille, and wolde han caught a
     sleep.
Withinne a while this John the clerk up leep,
And on this goode wyf he leith on soore.
So myrie a fit ne hadde she nat ful yoore;   4230
He priketh harde and depe as he were mad.
This joly lyf han thise two clerkes lad
Til that the thridde cok bigan to synge.

  Aleyn wax wery in the dawenynge,
For he had swonken al the longe nyght,   4235
And seyde, "Fareweel, Malyne, sweete wight.
The day is come, I may no lenger byde;
But everemo, wherso I go or ryde,

I is thyn awen clerk, swa have I seel!"
  "Now, deere lemman," quod she, "go,
     fareweel.   4240
But er thow go, o thyng I wol thee telle:
Whan that thou wendest homward by the
     melle,
Right at the entree of the dore bihynde
Thou shalt a cake of half a busshel fynde
That was ymaked of thyn owene mele,   4245
Which that I heelp my fader for to stele.
And, goode lemman, God thee save and kepe."
And with that word almoost she gan to wepe.

  Aleyn up rist, and thoughte, "Er that it dawe,
I wol go crepen in by my felawe,"   4250
And fond the cradel with his hand anon.
"By God," thoughte he, "al wrang I have
     mysgon.
Myn heed is toty of my swynk tonyght;
That maketh me that I go nat aright.
I woot wel by the cradel I have mysgo;   4255
Heere lith the millere and his wyf also."
And forth he goth, a twenty devel way,
Unto the bed ther as the millere lay.
He wende have cropen by his felawe John,
And by the millere in he creep anon,   4260
And caughte hym by the nekke, and softe he
     spak.
He seyde, "Thou John, thou swynes-heed,
     awak,
For Cristes saule, and heer a noble game.
For by that lord that called is Seint Jame,
As I have thries in this shorte nyght   4265
Swyved the milleres doghter bolt upright,
Whil thow hast, as a coward, been agast."

  "Ye, false harlot," quod the millere, "hast?
A, false traitour, false clerk," quod he,
"Thow shalt be deed, by Goddes dignitee!   4270
Who dorste be so boold to disparage

4205 **auntred ... nedes sped,** ventured, needs provided for. 4206 **draf-sek,** sack of chaff. 4208 **daf, cokenay,** fool, cockney (cock's eggs, simpleton). 4209 **auntre,** venture. 4210 **Unhardy ... unseely,** uncourageous, unlucky. 4212 **hente,** took. 4214 **rowtyng leet,** snoring stopped. 4225 **nyste,** did not know. 4230 **fit ... yoore,** bout, since long ago. 4231 **depe:** E&c *soore.* 4233 **thridde cok,** i.e., just before daylight. 4235 **swonken,** labored. 4236 **wight,** creature. The following exchange is a burlesque of the Provençal *alba,* the dawn song in which the lovers lament their parting. The form is used seriously in *TC,* III.1422ff. 4238 **go,** walk; "no," "mo," "so," "go," note the frequent lapse into southernisms from here on. 4239 ***awen ... *swa ... *seel,** own, so, good fortune. 4240 **lemman,** lover. 4241 **o thyng,** one thing. 4242 **wendest,** go. 4243 **bihynde,** behind the door. 4246 *fader:* Hg&c *sire.* 4249 **dawe,** dawn. 4253 **toty ... swynk,** dizzy, work. 4255 **woot ... mysgo,** knows, misgone. 4259 **wende ... cropen,** thought, crept. 4267 **agast,** afraid. 4269 **A,** ah. 4270 **deed,** dead.

My doghter, that is come of swich lynage?''
And by the throte-bolle he caughte Alayn,
And he hente hym despitously agayn,   4274
And on the nose he smoot hym with his fest;
Doun ran the blody streem upon his brest.
And in the floor, with nose and mouth tobroke,
They walwe as doon two pigges in a poke,
And up they goon, and doun agayn anon,
Til that the millere sporned at a stoon,   4280
And doun he fil bakward upon his wyf
That wiste nothyng of this nyce stryf—
For she was falle aslepe a lite wight
With John the clerk, that waked hadde al
     nyght—
And with the fal out of hir sleep she
     breyde.   4285
"Help, hooly croys of Bromeholm!" she seyde,
"*In manus tuas!* Lord, to thee I calle!
Awak, Symond, the feend is on us falle.
Myn herte is broken; help, I nam but deed!
Ther lyth oon upon my wombe and on myn
     heed.   4290
Help, Symkyn, for the false clerkes fighte!"
     This John stirte up as soone as ever he
        myghte,
And graspeth by the walles to and fro
To fynde a staf; and she stirte up also,
And knew the estres bet than dide this John,
And by the wal a staf she foond anon,   4296

And saugh a litel shymeryng of a light,
For at an hole in shoon the moone bright,
And by that light she saugh hem bothe two,
But sikerly she nyste who was who,   4300
But as she saugh a whit thyng in hir eye.
And whan she gan the white thyng espye,
She wende the clerk hadde wered a volupeer,
And with the staf she drow ay neer and neer,
And wende han hit this Aleyn at the fulle,   4305
And smoot the millere on the pyled skulle
That doun he gooth, and cride, "Harrow! I
        dye!"
Thise clerkes beete hym weel and lete hym lye,
And greythen hem, and tooke hir hors anon,
And eek hire mele, and on hir wey they gon,
And at the mille yet they tooke hir cake   4311
Of half a busshel flour ful wel ybake.
     Thus is the proude millere wel ybete,
And hath ylost the gryndynge of the whete,
And payed for the soper everideel   4315
Of Aleyn and of John, that bette hym weel.
His wyf is swyved, and his doghter als.
Lo, swich it is a millere to be fals!
And therfore this proverbe is seyd ful sooth:
Hym thar nat wene wel that yvele dooth.
A gylour shal hymself bigyled be.   4321
And God, that sitteth heighe in magestee,
Save al this compaignye, grete and smale.
Thus have I quyt the Millere in my tale.   4324

Heere is ended the Reves Tale.

4273 **throte-bolle,** Adam's apple. 4274 **he hente . . . despitously agayn,** he (Alayn) grasped, fiercely in return. 4278 **poke,** bag. 4280 **sporned,** tripped. 4282 **nyce,** ignorant (crazy). 4283 **lite wight,** little while. 4285 **breyde,** started. 4286 **croys of Bromeholm,** cross of Bromholm. In 1223 a piece of the true cross was reputed to have been brought to the priory there. 4287 *In manus,* into thy hands (cf. Luke 23:46). 4288 *us:* Hg&c *me.* 4290 **wombe,** stomach. 4292 *soone:* Hg&c *faste.* 4293 **graspeth,** searches around. 4295 **estres,** interior of the house. 4300 **sikerly . . . nyste,** truly, did not know. 4301 **But as . . . in,** but that, with. 4302 *the:* Hg&c *this.* 4303 **wende . . . volupeer,** thought, nightcap. 4305 **wende han,** thought to have. 4306 **pyled,** bald. 4307 *That:* E&c *And.* 4309 **greythen,** dressed. 4313 **ybete,** beaten. 4314 **ylost,** lost (payment for, i.e., a share of the flour). 4318 **swich,** such. 4320 **Hym . . . wene,** he (may) not expect. 4321 **gylour,** deceiver. 4322 *magestee:* E *Trinitee.* 4324 **quyt,** repayed.

COOK'S TALE

PROLOGUE

The Prologe of the Cokes Tale.

The Cook of Londoun, whil the Reve spak,
For joye him thoughte he clawed him on the
    bak.
"Haha," quod he, "for Cristes passioun,
This millere hadde a sharp conclusioun
Upon his argument of herbergage!
Wel seyde Salomon in his langage,   4330
"Ne brynge nat every man into thyn hous";
For herberwynge by nyghte is perilous.
Wel oghte a man avysed for to be
Whom that he broghte into his pryvetee.
I pray to God so yeve me sorwe and care   4335
If evere, sitthe I highte Hogge of Ware,
Herde I a millere bettre yset a werk.
He hadde a jape of malice in the derk.
But God forbede that we stynte heere;

And therfore, if ye vouchesauf to heere   4340
A tale of me, that am a poure man,
I wol yow telle as wel as evere I kan
A litel jape that fil in oure citee."
    Oure Hoost answerde and seide, "I graunte
    it thee.
Now telle on, Roger, looke that it be good,
For many a pastee hastow laten blood,   4346
And many a Jakke of Dovere hastow soold
That hath been twies hoot and twies coold.
Of many a pilgrym hastow Cristes curs
For of thy percely yet they fare the wors,   4350
That they han eten with thy stubbel goos,
For in thy shoppe is many a flye loos.
Now telle on, gentil Roger by thy name.
But yet I pray thee, be nat wroth for game:

4326 clawed, scratched; i.e., he enjoyed the tale so much it felt as pleasant as if the Reve were scratching his back. **4328 sharp,** painful. **4329 argument of herbergage,** experience with lodging. **4330 Salomon,** cf. Ecclesiastes 11:29. **4333 avysed,** careful. **4336 sitthe I highte,** since I was called. **Hogge of Ware,** Roger of Ware (small town outside of London in Hertfordshire). A "Roger Ware, Cook," has been identified in the London records. **4337 yset a werk,** i.e., "do a job on." **4338 jape of malice,** malicious joke. **4339 stynte,** stop. **4340 vouchesauf,** consent. **4346 pastee . . . laten blood,** meat pie, removed the filling (to reuse it). **4347 Jakke of Dovere,** evidently a stale pie. **4350 perceley,** parsley. **4351 stubbel,** stubble-fed (tough). **4352 flye,** the flies evidently got mixed with the parsley stuffing.

A man may seye ful sooth in game and pley."
   "Thou seist ful sooth," quod Roger, "by my
      fey.   4356
But sooth pley, quaad pley, as the Flemyng
      seith.
And therfore, Herry Bailly, by thy feith,

Be thou nat wrooth, er we departen heer,
Though that my tale be of an hostileer.   4360
But nathelees I wol nat telle it yit,
But er we parte, ywis, thou shalt be quit."
And therwithal he lough and made cheere,
And seyde his tale as ye shul after heere.

Heere bigynneth the Cookes Tale.

A prentys whilom dwelled in our citee,   4365
And of a craft of vitailliers was hee.
Gaillard he was as goldfynch in the shawe,
Broun as a berye, a propre short felawe,
With lokkes blake, ykembd ful fetisly;
Dauncen he koude so wel and jolily   4370
That he was cleped Perkyn Revelour.
He was as ful of love and paramour
As is the hyve ful of hony sweete—
Wel was the wenche with hym myghte meete.
At every bridale wolde he synge and
      hoppe.   4375
He loved bet the taverne than the shoppe,
For whan ther any ridyng was in Chepe
Out of the shoppe thider wolde he lepe—
Til that he hadde al the sighte yseyn,
And daunced wel, he wolde nat come ayeyn—
And gadered hym a meynee of his sort   4381
To hoppe and synge and maken swich disport.

And ther they setten stevene for to meete
To pleyen at the dys in swich a streete.
For in the toun nas ther no prentys   4385
That fairer koude caste a paire of dys
Than Perkyn koude, and therto he was free
Of his dispense in place of pryvetee.
That fond his maister wel in his chaffare,
For often tyme he foond his box ful bare.   4390
For sikerly a prentys revelour
That haunteth dys, riot, or paramour,
His maister shal it in his shoppe abye,
Al have he no part of the mynstralcye.
For thefte and riot, they been convertible,   4395
Al konne he pleye on gyterne or ribible.
Revel and trouthe, as in a lowe degree,
They been ful wrothe al day, as men may see.
   This joly prentys with his maister bood
Til he were ny out of his prentishood,   4400
Al were he snybbed bothe erly and late,

4355 sooth, truth. **4357 sooth . . . quaad,** a true joke is a bad (no) joke. **Flemyng,** native of Flanders (Belgium). **4358 Herry Bailly,** a "Henricus Bayliff, Ostyler" is listed in the 1380–81 subsidy roll for Southwark, but there is no evidence to explain why Chaucer should have included him among the *CT* Pilgrims. It is appropriate that the Host's name be revealed in an exchange with the Cook. **4359 departen,** separate. *nat:* E *na.* **4362 quit,** repaid. The Cook was evidently saving his tale about an innkeeper for later, since the original plan allowed each pilgrim to have four turns. **4365 prentys whilom,** apprentice once. **4366 vitailliers,** it has been argued that Chaucer was on the side of the nonvictualing guilds in their struggle for power against the victualing guilds in London in the 1380's, and hence his unflattering picture of the Cook and the apprentice victualer. **4367 Gaillard . . . shawe,** lively, woods. **4368 propre,** handsome. **4369 ykembd . . . fetisly.** combed, elegantly. **4371 Perkyn,** diminutive of Peter. **4372 paramour,** sexual desire. **4375 bridale . . . hoppe,** wedding (bride-ale), dance. **4376 bet . . . shoppe,** better, shop where he was apprenticed to learn to prepare and sell food. **4377 ridyng . . . Chepe,** parade, Cheapside (the main market street of medieval London). **4381 meynee,** following. **4382 swich disport,** such sport. **4383 setten stevene,** made appointment. **4387 therto,** in addition. **4388 dispense, pryvetee,** expenditure, privacy. **4389 fond . . . chaffare,** found, business. **4390 box,** money box. **4391 sikerly,** truly. **4393 abye,** pay for. **4395 riot . . . convertible,** debauchery, interchangeable. **4396 Al konne . . . gyterne or ribible,** even though he can, guitar or fiddle. **4397 as in a lowe,** in one of low. **4398 ful wrothe,** always at odds. **4399 bood,** stayed. **4400 ny out,** nearly through. Apprentices were contracted (bound) for a stipulated number of years to learn a trade. **4401 snybbed,** scolded.

And somtyme lad with revel to Newegate.
But atte laste his maister hym bithoghte,
Upon a day, whan he his papir soghte,
Of a proverbe that seith this same word: 4405
Wel bet is roten appul out of hoord
Than that it rotie al the remenaunt.
So fareth it by a riotous servaunt;
It is wel lasse harm to lete hym pace   4409
Than he shende alle the servantz in the place.
Therfore his maister yaf hym acquitance,
And bad hym go with sorwe and with
   meschance.

And thus this joly prentys hadde his
   leve.
Now lat hym riote al the nyght or leve.   4414
And for ther is no theef withoute a lowke
That helpeth hym to wasten and to
   sowke
Of that he brybe kan or borwe may,
Anon he sente his bed and his array
Unto a compier of his owene sort,
That lovede dys and revel and disport,   4420
And hadde a wyf that heeld for contenance
A shoppe, and swyved for hir sustenance . . .

4402 **lad . . . revel . . . Newegate,** led to Newgate prison. Skeat points out that when unruly persons were taken to prison, they were preceded by musicians to call attention to their disgrace. 4403 **hym bithoghte,** thought to himself. 4404 **his papir,** his articles of indenture—evidently Perkyn was seeking release from his contract. 4406 **bet . . . out of hoord,** better, (to be) out of the barrel (hoard). 4407 **rotie,** make rotten. 4408 **riotous,** depraved. 4409 **pace,** pass. *wel:* Hg&c *ful.* 4410 **shende,** ruin. 4411 **acquitance,** quittance (release). 4414 **riote . . . leve,** dissipate, leave off. 4415 **lowke,** accomplice. 4416 **sowke,** suck. 4417 **brybe,** steal. 4419 **compier,** comrade. 4421 **contenance,** countenance (appearance). 4422 **swyved . . . sustenance,** had intercourse, living.

INTRODUCTION

Canterbury Tales, Part II

T IS APPROPRIATE THAT the Man of Law's Tale be Part II of the Canterbury collection because its prologue sets the date of the pilgrimage (line II.5 below, and I.8 note above) and recapitulates the terms of the Host's story-telling contest (II.33ff). The Man of Law's assertion that he will tell a tale in prose (II.96), the "poverty prologue" (II.99 note), and the references to law and philosophy in the epilogue (II.1188 note) all suggest that the tale originally assigned to the Man of Law might have been the *Tale of Melibee* (now in Part VII), which would actually be more appropriate for a lawyer than the tale of Constance.

Aesthetically, however, the style and sentiment of the lay saint's tale of Constance provide an effective transition from the "love" stories of Part I to the "marriage" stories of Parts III-IV-V. The tale of Constance shifts the focus from the chivalric view of woman merely as a motive for action to woman as an actor. This perspective combines some of the most ancient ideas of folklore with more recent ideals of Christianity. Margaret Schlauch's *Constance and Accused Queens* (1927) reveals how Chaucer's tale transforms the widespread folk themes of the flight of the princess from a father who threatens incest, wishing to beget an heir upon his daughter through whom the matrilineal succession descends, and conflict between the daughter and the mother-in-law through whom the patrilineal succession descends. These themes are blended with Christianity which, from its inception, had stressed the importance of women. Marina Warner, *Alone of All Her Sex: The Myth and Cult of the Virgin Mary* (1976), details in the emergence of the cult of the Virgin the development of the maternal and tutelary roles of women. Mary the savior was set alongside Eve the temptress. In countless miracles of the Virgin and female saints' lives, feminine psychology was explored and the spiritual supremacy of women was extolled.

Chaucer's direct source for the story of Constance was the Anglo-Norman *Chronicle* of Nicholas Trivet, written (c1335) for Princess Marie, daughter of King Edward I of England, a nun at Almesbury. E. A. Block, "Originality, Controlling Purpose, and Craftsmanship in the Man of Law's Tale," *PMLA* (1953), shows how Chaucer made the treatment even more devotional than Trivet's by emphasizing the miraculous in the narrative and the pathos of Constance's situation. Morton Bloomfield, "The Man of Law's Tale: A Tragedy of Victimization and Christian Comedy," *PMLA* (1972), perceives the emergence of a genre of the "pathetic" in the Man of Law's, Clerk's, Physician's, and Second Nun's Tales that has persisted in such novels as Thomas Hardy's *Tess of the d'Urbervilles* and Theodore Dreiser's *Sister Carrie*. Chaucer evidently felt that pathos and miracle were the best ways to rationalize an inherently improbable plot. Just as important, they enabled him to compose the Man of Law's Tale in an elevated style quite different from the matter-of-fact narratives of Part I and the Wife of Bath's brilliant argument in Part III.

Although this sequence of tales is effective, we cannot be sure that it was Chaucer's intention. The textual evidence suggesting that the Man of Law originally told the *Tale of Melibee* and that his epilogue originally introduced what is now the Shipman's Tale (II.1163-90 and notes) point to an earlier stage in the evolution of the plan of the *Canterbury Tales*. However, the fact that the epilogue is lacking in twenty-two of the fifty-seven complete manuscripts indicates that Chaucer probably marked it for excision in the exemplar from which the early scribes worked.

Michael Paull, "The Influence of the Saint's Legend Genre in The Man of Law's Tale," *ChauR* (1971), Susan Clark and Julian Wasserman, "Constance as Romance and Folk Heroine in Chaucer's Man of Law's Tale," *Rice University Studies* (1978), and Paul M. Clogan, "The Narrative Style of The Man of Law's Tale," *M&H* (1977), all examine the combination of styles and genres.

Canterbury Tales

PART II

MAN OF LAW'S TALE

PROLOGUE

The wordes of the Hoost to the compaignye.

Oure Hooste saugh wel that the brighte sonne
The ark of his artificial day hath ronne
The ferthe part, and half an houre and moore,
And though he were nat depe ystert in loore,
He wiste it was the eightetethe day   5
Of Aprill, that is messager to May;
And saugh wel that the shadwe of every tree
Was as in lengthe the same quantitee
That was the body erect that caused it.
And therfore by the shadwe he took his wit   10

That Phebus, which that shoon so clere and
    brighte,
Degrees was fyve and fourty clombe on highte,
And for that day, as in that latitude,
It was ten at the clokke, he gan conclude;
And sodeynly he plighte his hors aboute.   15
    "Lordynges," quod he, "I warne yow, al this
    route,
The fourthe party of this day is gon.
Now, for the love of God and of Seint John,

---

2 artificial, from sunrise to sunset (vs. the natural day of 24 hours). See *Astrolabe* II.7. **3 ferthe part,** Skeat observed that on April 26, 1874 (the day he made the calculation, which would be equivalent to April 18, 1386, in Chaucer's calendar), the sun stood 56° from the south (one fourth of the *astrological* arc) at 9:20 A.M. Add "half an houre and moore" and we get about 10 A.M. At 9:58 that day the sun stood at 45° from the horizon making shadows exactly the same length as their objects (see ll. 7, 12 below). But, as Manly observes, if the Host had not known the date he could not have known the time or vice versa. **4 ystert in loore,** penetrated into learning. *ysterte:* some MSS *expert.* **5** E&c *eighte and twentithe.* In many MSS the numbers are in roman numerals and an x could be added or dropped. But April 28 does not fit the astrological calculations as well as April 18. **10 wit,** knowledge. **15 plighte,** pulled (plucked). **16 route,** company.

Leseth no tyme as ferforth as ye may.

Lordynges, the tyme wasteth nyght and day, 20

And steleth from us, what pryvely slepynge,

And what thurgh neccligence in oure wakynge,

As dooth the streem that turneth nevere agayn,

Descendynge fro the montaigne into playn.

Wel kan Senec and many a philosophre 25

Biwaillen tyme moore than gold in cofre,

For "los of catel may recovered be,

But los of tyme shendeth us," quod he.

It wol nat come agayn, withouten drede,

Namoore than wole Malkynes maydenhede, 30

Whan she hath lost it in hir wantownesse.

Lat us nat mowlen thus in ydelnesse.

 "Sire Man of Lawe," quod he, "so have ye
  blis,

Telle us as tale anon, as forward is. 34

Ye been submytted, thurgh youre free assent,

To stonden in this cas at my juggement.

Acquiteth yow now of youre biheeste;

Thanne have ye do youre devoir atte leeste."

 "Hooste," quod he, "depardieux, ich assente;

To breke forward is nat myn entente. 40

Biheste is dette, and I wole holde fayn

Al my biheste; I kan no bettre sayn.

For swich lawe as a man yeveth another wight,

He sholde hymselven usen it, by right;

Thus wole oure text. But nathelees, certeyn, 45

I kan right now no thrifty tale seyn

That Chaucer, thogh he kan but lewedly

On metres and on rymyng craftily,

Hath seyd hem in swich Englissh as he kan

Of olde tyme, as knoweth many a man. 50

And if he have noght seyd hem, leve brother,

In o book, he hath seyd hem in another.

For he hath toold of loveris up and doun

Mo than Ovide made of mencioun

In his *Episteles* that been ful olde. 55

What sholde I tellen hem, syn they ben tolde?

 "In youthe he made of Ceys and Alcione,

And sitthen hath he spoken of everichone

Thise noble wyves and thise loveris eke.

Whoso that wole his large volume seke 60

Cleped the Seintes Legende of Cupide,

Ther may he seen the large woundes wyde

Of Lucresse, and of Babilan Tesbee;

The swerd of Dido for the false Enee;

The tree of Phillis for hire Demophon; 65

The pleinte of Dianire and of Hermyon,

Of Adriane, and of Isiphilee—

The bareyne yle stondynge in the see—

The dreynte Leandre for his Erro;

The teeris of Eleyne, and eek the wo 70

Of Brixseyde, and the, Ladomya;

---

19 Leseth . . . ferforth, lose, far. **21 what pryvely,** secretly while (we are). **25 Senec,** Seneca at the beginning of his *Epistle I,* but the sentiment is proverbial. **28 shendeth,** ruins. **29 drede,** doubt. **32 mowlen,** mould. **34 forward,** agreement. **36 stonden . . . cas,** stand in this case; for the next few lines, the terminology of the Host and Man of Law grows legalistic. **37 Acquiteth . . . biheeste,** acquit (fulfill), promise (contract). **38 devoir,** obligation. **39 depardieux, ich,** Fr. "in the name of God," I (southern dialect form). **41 fayn,** gladly. **43 swich . . . wight,** such, person. **45 oure text,** the statement is proverbial, but Robinson traces it to the Justinian *Digests,* part of the *Corpus Juris Civilis* which provided the theoretical basis of medieval legal theory. **46 thrifty,** fitting. **47 kan but lewedly,** knows little. **48 On metres . . . rymyng craftily,** about meter, skillful rhyming. **50 Of olde tyme,** long ago. **51 leve,** dear. **52 o book,** one book. It has been suggested that Chaucer is here defending himself for not completing *LGW.* Gower evidently reproached him for this at the end of his *Confessio Amantis,* VIII.*2953ff. **55 Episteles,** Ovid's *Heroides,* which contains many of the stories listed below. **57 Ceys,** in the introduction to *BD.* **58 sitthen,** since then. **61 Cleped . . . Seintes Legende,** called; *LGW* is here referred to as a "large volume" and complete, which, of course, it is neither. Furthermore, the following purported list of its contents omits two ladies whose tales are included in *LGW* (Cleopatra, Philomela), and names eight whose tales are not found in *LGW.* The inaccuracy must have been deliberate since "Cleopatra" is the first tale in *LGW.* Those treated in *LGW* are indicated in the following notes by asterisks. **63 Lucresse,** the Rape of Lucrece. ***Tesbee,** Pyramus and Thisbe. **64 swerd of *Dido,** Dido, who killed herself with a sword for Aeneas. **65 *Phillis,** she hanged herself and was changed to a nut tree when deserted by Demophon. **66 pleinte of Dianire,** Ovid's epistle in *Heroides* in which she laments causing the death of Hercules. **Hermyon,** Ovid's epistle of the lament of Hermione at the banishment of Orestes. *Dianire:* E&c *Diane.* **67 *Adriane,** Ovid's epistle of Ariadne lamenting the falseness of Theseus. ***Isiphilee,** Ovid's epistle of Hypsipile lamenting the falseness of Jason. **68 bareyne yle,** Naxos on which Theseus abandoned Ariadne. **69 dreynte Leandre,** Leander, drowned swimming the Hellespont to visit Hero. **70 Eleyne,** Helen of Troy. E *eek* om. **71 Brixseyde,** the original name of the heroine in the Troylus story, which Boccaccio changed to Criseyde. **the, Ladomya,** thee, Laodamia; she killed herself because of the death of her husband in the Trojan War.

The crueltee of the, queene Medea,
Thy litel children hangynge by the hals,
For thy Jason, that was in love so fals!
O Ypermystra, Penelopee, Alceste,   75
Youre wifhede he comendeth with the
          beste.

     "But certeinly no word ne writeth he
Of thilke wikke ensample of Canacee,
That loved hir owene brother synfully—
Of swiche cursed stories I sey fy!   80
Or ellis of Tyro Appollonius,
How that the cursed kyng Antiochus
Birafte his doghter of hir maydenhede.
That is so horrible a tale for to rede—

Whan he hir threw upon the pavement.   85
And therfore he, of ful avysement,
Nolde nevere write in none of his sermons
Of swiche unkynde abhomynacions,
Ne I wol noon reherce, if that I may.

     "But of my tale how shal I doon this day?   90
Me were looth be likned, doutelees,
To muses that men clepe Pierides—
Methamorphosios woot what I mene;
But nathelees, I recche noght a bene
Though I come after hym with hawebake.   95
I speke in prose, and lat him rymes make."
And with that word he, with a sobre cheere,
Bigan his tale, as ye shal after heere.

The Prologe of the Mannes Tale of Lawe.

O hateful harm, condicion of poverte,
With thurst, with coold, with hunger so
          confounded!   100
To asken help thee shameth in thyn herte;
If thou noon aske, so soore artow ywounded
That verray nede unwrappeth al thy wounde
          hid.
Maugree thyn heed, thou most for indigence
Or stele, or begge, or borwe thy despence.   105

Thow blamest Crist and seist ful bitterly

He mysdeparteth richesse temporal,
Thy neighebore thou wytest synfully
And seist thou hast to lite and he hath al.
"Parfay," seistow, "somtyme he rekene shal, 110
Whan that his tayl shal brennen in the gleede,
For he noght helpeth needfulle in hir neede."

     Herke what is the sentence of the wise:
Bet is to dyen than have indigence;
Thy selve neighebor wol thee despise.   115
If thou be poure, farwel thy reverence.

72 *Medea, who killed their children when deserted by Jason. 75 *Ypermystra, who was killed by her father because sne would not kill her husband. Peneloppe, who waited for the return of Ulysses. Alceste, who died in place of her husband; this is the name of the heroine of *LGW*. 78 Canacee, since Tyrwhitt, Chaucer's criticisms of the incests in "Canace" and in "Apollonius of Tyre" (l. 81 below), have been taken as flings at his moral friend John Gower, who told both tales in the *Confessio Amantis* (III.143ff., VIII.271ff.). The reason for the references is not known. Perhaps it was in reply to Gower's reproach (see note to l. 52 above). 85 threw...pavement, this detail is not in Gower. 86 he...avysement, i.e., Chaucer, consideration. 87 sermons, discourses, but perhaps with a slight fling at Gower's didacticism. 88 unkynde, unnatural. 91 likned, compared. 92 Pierides, the nine daughters of Pierus who were transformed into magpies for presuming to compete with the muses, *Met.* 5.302. The Man of Law does not want to be compared with Chaucer; hence he proposes to tell a tale in prose (l. 96). 93 woot, knows. 94 recche...bene, care, bean. 95 hym... hawebake, i.e., Chaucer, baked hawthorn berries (barely edible). Some late MSS *halvebake* (half-baked). 96 prose, since MLT is in verse, this is either a joke or is left over from a time when the Man of Law was assigned a prose tale such as *Melibee*. See below ll. 99, 1779–89. 97 cheere, expression. 99 O hateful harm..., the "poverty prologue" (ll. 99–121) is a paraphrase from *De Contemptu Mundi* of Pope Innocent III (*PL* 217.708ff.), which in *LGW*, G414, Chaucer says he translated. There are other echoes of the work below at ll. 421, 771, 925, 1132, and elsewhere in *CT*, but no complete Chaucerian translation has been found. Because the first stanza (ll. 99–105) is found in *Mel* (VII, l. 1577ff.), some scholars have suggested that this prologue is left over from a time when *Mel* was the prose tale told by the Man of Law. However, the fact that the prologue is in verse and includes more than the corresponding passage in *Mel* raises problems. It is hard to see how the poverty motif makes an appropriate introduction either to *Mel* or MLT. 100 confoundid, mixed up. 102 Hg&c *aske, with nede artow so woundid.* 103 verray, genuine. 104 Maugree...heed, i.e., in spite of yourself. 105 despence, expenditure. 107 mysdeparteth, unjustly distributes. 108 wytest, blame. 110 rekene, i.e., make up for it. 111 brennen...gleede, burn, live coal(s). 112 needfulle, the needy. 115 selve, very (even your). 116 reverence, dignity.

Yet of the wise man take this sentence:
Alle the dayes of poure men been wikke.
Bewar, therfore, er thou come to that prikke!

If thou be poure, thy brother hateth thee, 120
And alle thy freendes fleen from thee, allas.
O riche marchauntz, ful of wele been yee;
O noble, O prudent folk, as in this cas,
Youre bagges been nat fild with ambes as
But with sys cynk that renneth for youre
    chaunce. 125

At Cristemasse myrie may ye daunce!

Ye seken lond and see for yowre wynnynges;
As wise folk ye known al th'estaat
Of regnes; ye been fadres of tidynges
And tales bothe of pees and of debaat. 130
I were right now of tales desolaat
Nere that a marchant, goon is many a
    yeere,
Me taughte a tale which that ye shal
    heere.

Heere bigynneth the Man of Lawe his Tale.

In Surrye whilom dwelte a compaignye
Of chapmen riche, and therto sadde and trewe,
That wyde-where senten hir spicerye, 136
Clothes of gold, and satyns riche of hewe.
Hir chaffare was so thrifty and so newe
That every wight hath deyntee to chaffare
With hem, and eek to sellen hem hire ware.

Now fil it that the maistres of that sort 141
Han shapen hem to Rome for to wende,
Were it for chapmanhode or for disport.
Noon oother message wolde they thider sende,
But comen hemself to Rome, this is the ende,
And in swich place as thoughte hem avantage
For hire entente, they take hir herbergage. 147

Sojourned han thise marchantz in that toun
A certein tyme, as fil to hire plesance.
And so bifel that th'excellent renoun 150
Of the Emperoures doghter, dame Custance,
Reported was with every circumstance
Unto thise Surryen marchantz in swich wyse,
Fro day to day, as I shal yow devyse. 154

This was the commune voys of every man:
"Oure Emperour of Rome—God hym see—
A doghter hath that syn the world bigan,
To rekene as wel hir goodnesse as beautee,
Nas nevere swich another as is shee.
I prey to God in honour hire susteene, 160
And wolde she were of al Europe the queene.

"In hire is heigh beautee withoute pride,
Yowthe withoute grenehede or folye;
To alle hire werkes vertu is hir gyde;
Humblesse hath slayn in hire al tirannye; 165
She is mirour of alle curteisye;
Hir herte is verray chambre of hoolynesse;
Hir hand, ministre of fredam for almesse."

And al this voys was sooth, as God is trewe.
But now to purpos lat us turne agayn. 170
Thise marchantz han doon fraught hir shippes
    newe,
And whan they han this blisful mayden sayn,
Hoom to Surrye been they went ful fayn,
And doon hir nedes as they han doon yoore,

---

118 wikke, evil. **121 fleen,** flee. **122 wele,** prosperity. **123 cas,** instance. **124 ambes as,** double aces (in dice, a losing throw). **125 sys cynk,** six and five (eleven, a winning throw). **that renneth ... chaunce,** i.e., so run your fortune(s). **127 seken ... wynnynges,** seek over, profits. **128 estaat,** condition. **129 regnes,** kingdoms. **131 desolaat,** desolate (lacking). **132 Nere,** were it not. **134 Surrye whilom,** Syria, once. **135 chapmen ... sadde,** merchants, serious. **136 wyde-where,** far and wide. **138 chaffare ... thrifty,** merchandise, attractive. **139 wight ... deyntee ... chaffare,** person, pleasure, trade. **141 sort,** group. **142 shapen,** decided. **143 Were it ... chapmanhode ... disport,** either for, business, pleasure. **144 message,** messenger. **146 thoughte hem avantage,** seemed to them advantageous. **147 herbergage,** lodging. **149 fil ... plesance,** befell, pleasure. **152 circumstance,** supporting detail. **156 see,** see to him (protect). **161 wolde,** would that. **163 grenehede,** immaturity. **168 fredam ... almesse,** generosity, almsgiving. **169 voys ... sooth,** report, true. **171 fraught ... newe,** freighted (loaded), again. **172 sayn,** seen. **173 fayn,** happy. **174 nedes ... yoore,** business, before.

And lyven in wele; I kan sey yow namoore. 175

Now fil it that thise marchantz stode in
    grace
Of hym that was the Sowdan of Surrye,
For whan they cam from any strange place
He wolde, of his benigne curteisye,
Make hem good chiere, and bisily espye 180
Tidynges of sondry regnes for to leere
The wondres that they myghte seen or heere.

Amonges othere thynges, specially,
Thise marchantz han hym toold of dame
    Custance
So greet noblesse, in ernest, ceriously, 185
That this Sowdan hath caught so greet
    plesance
To han hir figure in his remembrance
That al his lust and al his bisy cure
Was for to love hire whil his lyf may dure.

Paraventure in thilke large book 190
Which that men clipe the hevene ywriten
    was
With sterres, whan that he his birthe took,
That he for love sholde han his deeth, allas!
For in the sterres, clerer than is glas,
Is writen, God woot, whoso koude it rede, 195
The deeth of every man, withouten drede.

In sterres many a wynter therbiforn
Was writen the deeth of Ector, Achilles,
Of Pompei, Julius, er they were born;
The strif of Thebes; and of Ercules, 200
Of Sampson, Turnus, and of Socrates
The deeth; but mennes wittes ben so dulle
That no wight kan wel rede it atte fulle.

This Sowdan for his privee conseil sente,
And, shortly of this matiere for to pace, 205

He hath to hem declared his entente,
And seyde hem, certein, but he myghte have
    grace
To han Custance withinne a litel space
He nas but deed; and charged hem in hye
To shapen for his lyf som remedye. 210

Diverse men diverse thynges seyden.
They argumenten, casten up and doun.
Many a subtil resoun forth they leyden.
They speken of magyk and abusioun.
But finally, as in conclusioun, 215
They kan nat seen in that noon avantage,
Ne in noon oother wey, save mariage.

Thanne sawe they therinne swich difficultee
By wey of reson, for to speke al playn,
By cause that ther was swich diversitee 220
Bitwene hir bothe lawes, that they sayn
They trowe, "that no Cristen prince wolde
    fayn
Wedden his child under oure lawes sweete
That us were taught by Mahoun, oure
    prophete."

And he answerde, "Rather than I lese 225
Custance, I wol be cristned, doutelees.
I moot been hires, I may noon oother chese.
I prey yow hoold youre argumentz in pees.
Saveth my lyf, and beth noght recchelees
To geten hire that hath my lyf in cure; 230
For in this wo I may nat longe endure."

What nedeth gretter dilatacioun?
I seye, by tretys and embassadrie,
And by the popes mediacioun,
And al the chirche, and al the chivalrie, 235
That in destruccioun of maumettrie,
And in encrees of Cristes lawe deere,
They been acorded, so as ye shal heere:

---

175 wele, prosperity. **177 Sowdan,** sultan (king). **180 Make . . . chiere . . . espye,** entertain, seek information. **181 sondry regnes . . . leere,** different countries, learn. **185 So . . . ceriously,** such, in detail (serially). **186 caught . . . plesance,** i.e., taken such a fancy. **188 lust . . . cure,** pleasure, concern. **190 thilke,** that. **191 clipe,** call. **201 Turnus,** Aeneas' rival in Italy. **205 pace,** pass. **207 grace,** permission (good fortune). **208 han . . . space,** have, while. **209 deed . . . hye,** dead, haste. **212 casten,** argued. **214 abusioun,** deception (how the Sowdan had been bewitched by Constance). **218 swich,** such. **221 hir bothe,** both their. **222 trowe . . . fayn,** believed, willingly. **224 Mahoun,** Mahomet. **226 cristned, doutelees,** christened, without hesitation. **229 Saveth . . . recchelees,** save (imp.), negligent. **230 cure,** keeping. **232 dilatacioun,** amplification. **236 destruccioun of maumettrie,** defeat of Mohammedanism.

How that the Sowdan and his baronage
And alle his liges sholde ycristned be,   240
And he shal han Custance in mariage,
And certein gold, I noot what quantitee;
And heer-to founden sufficient suretee.
This same accord was sworn on eyther syde.
Now, faire Custance, almyghty God thee gyde!

Now wolde som men waiten, as I gesse,   246
That I sholde tellen al the purveiance
That th'Emperour, of his grete noblesse,
Hath shapen for his doghter, dame Custance.
Wel may men knowen that so greet ordinance
May no man tellen in a litel clause   251
As was arrayed for so heigh a cause.

Bisshopes been shapen with hire for to wende,
Lordes, ladies, knyghtes of renoun,
And oother folk ynogh, this is th'ende;   255
And notified is thurghout the toun
That every wight, with greet devocioun,
Sholde preyen Crist that he this mariage
Receyve in gree, and spede this viage.

The day is comen of hir departynge—   260
I seye, the woful day fatal is come,
That ther may be no lenger tariynge,
But forthward they hem dressen, alle and
    some.
Custance, that was with sorwe al overcome,
Ful pale arist, and dresseth hire to wende;   265
For wel she seeth ther is noon oother ende.

Allas, what wonder is it thogh she wepte,
That shal be sent to strange nacioun
Fro freendes that so tendrely hire kepte,

And to be bounden under subjeccioun   270
Of oon she knoweth nat his condicioun?
Housbondes been alle goode, and han ben
    yoore.
That knowen wyves—I dar sey yow na moore.

"Fader," she seyde, "thy wrecched child
    Custance,
Thy yonge doghter fostred up so softe,   275
And ye, my mooder, my soverayn plesance
Over alle thyng, out-taken Crist on-lofte,
Custance youre child hire recomandeth ofte
Unto youre grace, for I shal to Surrye,
Ne shal I nevere seen yow moore with eye.   280

"Allas, unto the Barbre nacioun
I moste goon, syn that it is youre wille;
But Crist, that starf for our savacioun
So yeve me grace his heestes to fulfille!
I, wrecche womman, no fors though I spille!   285
Wommen are born to thraldom and penance,
And to been under mannes governance."

I trowe at Troye, whan Pirrus brak the wal,
Or Ilion brende, at Thebes the citee,
N'at Rome, for the harm thurgh Hanybal   290
That Romayns hath venquysshed tymes thre,
Nas herd swich tendre wepyng for pitee
As in the chambre was for hire departynge;
But forth she moot, wher so she wepe or synge.

O firste moevyng, crueel firmament,   295
With thy diurnal sweigh that crowdest ay
And hurlest al from est til occident
That naturelly wolde holde another way,
Thy crowdyng set the hevene in swich array

---

240 **liges,** subjects. 243 **heer-to ... suretee,** hitherto committed, guarantee(s). 246 **waiten,** expect. 247 **purveiance,** provision (*double entendre,* God's providence). 249 **shapen,** planned. 250 **ordinance,** preparation. 252 **arrayed,** arranged. 253 **shapen,** prepared. 259 **gree ... spede,** favor, bring success to. 263 **forthward ... dressen ... some,** forward (on the way), proceed, one. 265 **dresseth,** prepares. 269 **kepte,** cared for. 271 **condicioun,** nature. 272 **yoore,** always. 273–87 Lines not in Trivet. 276 **soverayn plesance,** supreme pleasure. 277 **out-taken,** excepting. 278 **recomandeth,** commends herself. 281 **Barbre,** Barbary (north coast of Africa), or barbarian (heathen). The word is capitalized in E. 282 **goon**: Hg&c *anon.* 283 *savacioun*: Hg&c *redempcioun.* 284 **heestes,** commands. 285 **wrecche ... fors ... spille,** wretched, matter, die. 289 **Or Ilion,** before the citadel of Troy. EHg&c *at* om. 291 **thre,** evidently an allusion to the three Punic wars. 294 **wher so,** whether. 295–315 Lines not in Trivet, added by Chaucer in keeping with his persistent Boethian and astrological embroidering. 295 **firste moevyng,** *primum mobile,* the outermost sphere which impelled all the others. Hg&c *moevere* (i.e., God); some late MSS *frosty morning* (!). **crueel,** because it has arranged the stars unfavorably for Constance's departure. 296–97 **diurnal ... est ... occident,** daily motion; the *primum mobile* moved from east to west. 298 **naturelly,** in astrology the sun advances through the signs of the zodiac from west to east. 299 **crowdyng ... array,** impulsion, arrangement.

At the bigynnyng of this fiers viage   300
That crueel Mars hath slayn this mariage.

Infortunat ascendent tortuous,
Of which the lord is helplees falle, allas,
Out of his angle into the derkeste hous!
O Mars, o atazir, as in this cas!   305
O fieble moone, unhappy been thy paas.
Thou knyttest thee ther thou art nat receyved;
Ther thou were weel, fro thennes artow weyved.

Inprudent Emperour of Rome, allas,
Was ther no philosophre in al thy toun?   310
Is no tyme bet than oother in swich cas?
Of viage is ther noon eleccioun,
Namely to folk of heigh condicioun?
Noght whan a roote is of a burthe yknowe?
Allas, we been to lewed or to slowe!   315

To ship is brought this woful faire mayde
Solempnely, with every circumstance.
"Now Jhesu Crist be with yow alle!" she sayde.
Ther nys namoore but "Farewel, faire Cus-
    tance!"
She peyneth hire to make good contenance;
And forth I lete hire saille in this manere,   321
And turne I wole agayn to my matere.

The mooder of the Sowdan, welle of vices,
Espied hath hir sones pleyn entente,
How he wol lete his olde sacrifices;   325
And right anon she for hir conseil sente,
And they been come to knowe what she mente.
And whan assembled was this folk in-feere,
She sette hire doun, and seyde as ye shal heere.

"Lordes," she said, "ye knowen everichon,
How that my sone in point is for to lete   331
The hooly lawes of oure Alkaron,
Yeven by Goddes message Makomete.
But oon avow to grete God I heete:
The lyf shall rather out of my body sterte   335
Than Makometes lawe out of myn herte.

"What sholde us tyden of this newe lawe
But thraldom to oure bodies and penance,
And afterward in helle to be drawe
For we reneyed Mahoun oure creance?   340
But, lordes, wol ye maken assurance,
As I shal seyn, assentynge to my loore,
And I shal make us sauf for everemoore?"

They sworen and assenten, every man,
To lyve with hire and dye, and by hire stonde,
And everich, in the beste wise he kan,   346
To strengthen hire shal alle his frendes fonde.
And she hath this emprise ytake on honde
Which ye shal heren that I shal devyse,
And to hem alle she spak right in this wyse: 350

"We shul first feyne us Cristendom to take—
Coold water shal nat greve us but a lite!
And I shal swich a feeste and revel make
That, as I trowe, I shal the Sowdan quite.
For thogh his wyf be cristned never so white,   355
She shal have nede to wasshe awey the rede,
Thogh she a font-ful water with hire lede."

O Sowdanesse, roote of iniquitee!
Virago, thou Semyrame the secounde!
O serpent under femynynytee,   360

---

300 fiers, dangerous. **301 Mars,** Mars was in the ascendant. **302–05 Infortunat . . . tortuous,** etc. Mars has by the *primum mobile* been forced out of his proper ascendant position into a weak position. Slightly differing explanations are offered by Skeat, Curry, Manly, etc. **atazir,** influence (Arabic). **306 fieble moone,** the position of the moon was evidently similarly inauspicious. **paas,** pace (course). **307 knyttest,** join yourself (in conjunction with). **receyved,** welcomed. **308 weel . . . weyved,** propitious, moved. **312 eleccioun,** choice of time. **313 Namely . . . heigh condicioun,** especially for the nobility, who could have the advice of the best astrologers. **314 roote,** basis for calculation—in the case of an individual's horoscope, the date of birth. **315 lewed,** ignorant. **316 brought:** E *come.* **320 good contenance,** i.e., put a good face on it. **325 lete,** abandon. **326 conseil,** council. **328 in-feere,** together. **330 Hg&c** *quod she.* **331 in point,** on the point of. **332 Alkaron,** al (the) Koran (Mohammedanism). **333 message Makomete,** messenger Mahomet. **334 avow . . . grete . . . heete,** vow, great, promise. **337 tyden,** betide (befall). **340 reneyed . . . creance,** denied, faith. **342 loore,** wisdom. **343 sauf,** safe. **347 fonde,** induce. **348 emprise . . . on honde,** enterprise, in hand. **351 feyne,** pretend. **352 Coold water,** baptism. **354 trowe . . . quite,** believe, repay. **357 font . . . lede,** baptismal font, bring. **359 Virago . . . Semyrame,** bullying woman; Semiramis, an Assyrian queen who murdered her husband. **360 serpent . . . femynynytee,** in medieval iconography the serpent in Eden had the face of a woman.

Lik to the serpent depe in helle ybounde!
O feyned womman, al that may confounde
Vertu and innocence, thurgh thy malice,
Is bred in thee, as nest of every vice.

O Sathan, envious syn thilke day   365
That thou were chaced from oure heritage,
Wel knowestow to wommen the olde way.
Thou madest Eva brynge us in servage;
Thou wolt fordoon this Cristen mariage.   369
Thyn instrument so—weylawey the while—
Makestow of wommen, whan thou wolt bigile.

This Sowdanesse, whom I thus blame and
     warye,
Leet prively hire conseil goon hire way.
What sholde I in this tale lenger tarye?
She rydeth to the Sowdan on a day   375
And seyde hym that she wolde reneye hir lay,
And Cristendom of preestes handes fonge,
Repentynge hire she hethen was so longe;

Bisechynge hym to doon hire that honour
That she moste han the Cristen folk to feeste—
"To plesen hem I wol do my labour."   381
The Sowdan seith, "I wol doon at youre heeste,"
And knelynge thanketh hire of that requeste.
So glad he was he nyste what to seye.
She kiste hir sone, and hoom she gooth hir
     weye.   385

Explicit prima pars. Sequitur pars secunda.

Arryved been this Cristen folk to londe
In Surrye, with a greet solempne route,
And hastifliche this Sowdan sente his sonde
First to his mooder, and al the regne aboute,
And seyde his wyf was comen, out of doute,   390
And preyde hire for to ryde agayn the queene,

The honour of his regne to susteene.

Greet was the prees and riche was th'array
Of Surryens and Romayns met yfeere.
The mooder of the Sowdan, riche and gay,   395
Receyveth hire with also glad a cheere
As any mooder myghte hir doghter deere,
And to the nexte citee ther bisyde
A softe paas solempnely they ryde.

Noght trowe I the triumphe of Julius,   400
Of which that Lucan maketh swich a boost,
Was roialler or moore curius
Than was th'assemblee of this blisful hoost.
But this scorpioun, this wikked goost,
The Sowdanesse, for al hire flaterynge   405
Caste under this ful mortally to stynge.

The Sowdan comth hymself soone after this
So roially that wonder is to telle,
And welcometh hire with alle joye and blis.
And thus in murthe and joye I lete hem dwelle;
The fruyt of this matiere is that I telle.   411
Whan tyme cam, men thoughte it for the
     beste;
The revel stynte and men goon to hir reste.

The tyme cam this olde Sowdanesse
Ordeyned hath this feeste of which I tolde, 415
And to the feeste Cristen folk hem dresse
In general, ye, bothe yonge and olde.
Heere may men feeste and roialtee biholde,
And deyntees mo than I kan yow devyse;
But al to deere they boghte it er they ryse. 420

O sodeyn wo, that evere art successour
To worldly blisse, spreynd with bitternesse,
The ende of the joye of oure worldly labour!

362 **feyned,** counterfeit. 365 **Sathan . . . thilke,** Satan, that. 366 **chaced . . . heritage,** chased, salvation (since the day Satan fell from grace with God). 369 **wolt fordoon,** will destroy. 371 **Makestow . . . bigile,** makest thou, mislead. 372 **warye,** curse. 376 **reneye . . . lay,** deny, law. 377 **fonge,** receive. 380 **moste,** might. 382 **heeste,** request. 387 **solempne route,** impressive company. 388 **sonde,** messenger(s). 391 **agayn,** toward (to meet). 394 **yfeere,** together. 396 **also . . . cheere,** as, expression. 398 **nexte,** nearest. 399 **softe paas,** slow pace. 400 **trowe . . . Julius,** believe, Caesar. 401 In *Pharsalia*, III.79, Lucan laments that Caesar did not have a triumph, but French versions of Lucan supply triumphs. 402 **curius,** elaborate. *or:* Hg&c *ne.* 404 **scorpioun,** the scorpion was reputed to "make vayr mid the heavede and envenyme mid the tayle" (*Ayenbite of Inwyt*). **goost,** spirit. 406 **Caste,** prepared. 411 **fruyt,** essence. 415 **Ordeyned,** ordered. 416 **hem dresse,** go. 421–27 Another echo of *De Contemptu Mundi* and other medieval commonplaces, added by Chaucer, cf. note to l. 99 above. 422 **spreynd,** sprinkled.

Wo occupieth the fyn of oure gladnesse.
Herke this conseil for thy sikernesse: 425
Upon thy glade day have in thy mynde
The unwar wo or harm that comth bihynde.

For shortly for to tellen, at o word,
The Sowdan and the Cristen everichone
Been al tohewe and stiked at the bord,   430
But it were oonly dame Custance allone.
This olde Sowdanesse, cursed krone,
Hath with hir freendes doon this cursed dede,
For she hirself wolde al the contree lede.

Ne was ther Surryen noon that was converted,
That of the conseil of the Sowdan woot,   436
That he nas al tohewe er he asterted.
And Custance han they take anon, foot-hoot,
And in a ship al steerelees, God woot,
They han hir set, and bidde hire lerne saille 440
Out of Surrye agaynward to Ytaille.

A certein tresor that she with hire ladde,
And, sooth to seyn, vitaille greet plentee
They han hire yeven, and clothes eek she
    hadde,
And forth she sailleth in the salte see.   445
O my Custance, ful of benignytee,
O Emperoures yonge doghter deere,
He that is Lord of Fortune be thy steere!

She blesseth hire, and with ful pitous voys
Unto the croys of Crist thus seyde she,   450
"O cleere, o welful auter, hooly croys,
Reed of the Lambes blood ful of pitee,
That wessh the world fro the olde iniquitee,
Me fro the feend and fro his clawes kepe,
That day that I shal drenchen in the depe. 455

Victorious tree, proteccioun of trewe,
That oonly worthy were for to bere
The Kyng of Hevene with his woundes newe,
The white Lamb, that hurt was with a spere,
Flemere of feendes out of hym and here   460
On which thy lymes feithfully extenden,
Me helpe, and yif me myght my lyf
    t'amenden.''

Yeres and dayes fleet this creature
Thurghout the See of Grece unto the Strayte
Of Marrok, as it was hire aventure;   465
On many a sory meel now may she bayte;
After hir deeth ful often may she wayte,
Er that the wilde wawes wol hire dryve
Unto the place ther she shal arryve.   469

Men myghten asken why she was nat slayn
Eek at the feeste, who myghte hir body save?
And I answere to that demande agayn,
Who saved Danyel in the horrible cave
Ther every wight save he, maister and knave,
Was with the leon frete er he asterte?   475
No wight but God, that he bar in his herte.

God liste to shewe his wonderful myracle
In hire, for we sholde seen his myghty werkis.
Crist, which that is to every harm triacle,
By certeine meenes ofte, as knowen clerkis, 480
Dooth thyng for certein ende that ful derk is
To mannes wit, that for oure ignorance
Ne konne noght knowe his prudent
    purveiance.

Now sith she was nat at the feeste yslawe,
Who kepte hire fro the drenchyng in the see?
Who kepte Jonas in the fisshes mawe   486

---

425 **sikernesse,** security. 427 **unwar,** unexpected. 430 **tohewe . . . stiked . . . bord,** cut to pieces, stabbed, banquet table. 431 **But,** except. 434 **lede,** govern. 435 *ther*: E&c om.; variously placed in other MSS; Hg&c *ther nas*. 436 **conseil . . . woot,** counsel . . . knew. 437 **asterted,** escaped. 439 **steerelees,** rudderless. 442 **ladde,** brought. *with hire*: Hg&c *thider*. 443 **vitaille,** food. 448 **steere,** rudder (guide). 449–62 Not in Trivet or Gower. Addresses to the Cross were a familiar medieval lyric type. 449 **blesseth hire,** crosses herself. 451 **cleere . . . welful auter,** shining, bountiful altar. *welful*: E&c *woful*. 452 **Reed of,** red with. 455 **drenchen,** drown. 456 **trewe,** true Christians. 460 **Flemere,** one who puts to flight. 460–61 **hym . . . here . . . extenden,** men and women who wear the Cross as talisman. 462 *helpe*: Hg&c *kepe*. 463 **fleet,** floated. 464 **See of Grece,** eastern Mediterranean. 465 **Strayte of Marrok,** Strait of Morocco (of Gibraltar). **aventure,** lot (chance). 466 **bayte,** eat. 467 **After . . . wayte,** await. 470–504 Not in Trivet. 474 **wight . . . knave,** person, servant. 475 **frete . . . asterte,** eaten (cf. Ger. *fressen*), escape. 477 **liste,** chose. 478 **for we,** in order that we. 479 **triacle,** medicine (treacle). 481 **ende . . . derk,** purpose, mysterious. 483 **purveiance,** providence. 485 **drenchyng,** drowning. 486 **Jonas . . . mawe,** Jonah, mouth.

Til he was spouted up at Nynyvee?
Wel may men knowe it was no wight but he
That kepte the peple Ebrayk from hir
    drenchynge,
With drye feet thurghout the see passynge.   490

Who bad the foure spirites of tempest
That power han t'anoyen lond and see,
Bothe north and south and also west and est,
"Anoyeth, neither see, ne land, ne tree"?
Soothly, the comandour of that was he   495
That fro the tempest ay this womman kepte
As wel whan she wook as whan she slepte.

Where myghte this womman mete and
    drynke have
Thre yeer and moore? How lasteth hire vitaille?
Who fedde the Egipcien Marie in the cave,   500
Or in desert? No wight but Crist, sanz faille.
Fyve thousand folk it was as greet mervaille
With loves fyve and fisshes two to feede.
God sente his foyson at hir grete neede.

She dryveth forth into oure occian   505
Thurghout oure wilde see, til atte laste
Under an hoold that nempnen I ne kan
Fer in Northhumberlond the wawe hire caste,
And in the sond hir ship stiked so faste
That thennes wolde it noght of al a tyde;   510
The wyl of Crist was that she sholde abyde.

The constable of the castel doun is fare
To seen this wrak, and al the ship he soghte,
And foond this wery womman ful of care;
He foond also the tresor that she broghte.   515
In hir langage mercy she bisoghte,
The lyf out of hire body for to twynne,

Hire to delivere of wo that she was inne.

A maner Latyn corrupt was hir speche,
But algates therby was she understonde.   520
The constable, whan hym lyst no lenger seche,
This woful womman broghte he to the londe.
She kneleth doun and thanketh Goddes sonde;
But what she was she wolde no man seye,
For foul ne fair, thogh that she sholde deye.   525

She seyde she was so mazed in the see
That she forgat hir mynde, by hir trouthe.
The constable hath of hire so greet pitee,
And eek his wyf, that they wepen for routhe.
She was so diligent, withouten slouthe,   530
To serve and plesen everich in that place
That alle hir loven that looken in hir face.

This constable and dame Hermengyld, his
    wyf,
Were payens, and that contree everywhere;
But Hermengyld loved hire right as hir lyf,   535
And Custance hath so longe sojourned there,
In orisons, with many a bitter teere,
Til Jhesu hath converted thurgh his grace
Dame Hermengyld, constablesse of that place.

In al that lond no Cristen dorste route;   540
Alle Cristen folk been fled fro that contree
Thurgh payens that conquereden al aboute
The plages of the north by land and see.
To Walys fledde the Cristyanytee
Of olde Britons dwellynge in this ile;   545
Ther was hir refut for the meene while.

But yet nere Cristene Britons so exiled
That ther nere somme that in hir privetee

---

487 **Nynyvee,** Nineveh (Jonah 2:10). 489 **Ebrayk,** Hebrew. EHg&c *the* om. 490 **see passynge,** crossing the Red Sea (Exodus 14:22). 491 **foure spirites,** Rev. 7:1–3. 492 **anoyen,** disturb. 496 **ay,** always. 500 **Egipcien Marie,** St. Maria Egiptiaca, a legendary recluse who lived after a misspent youth 47 years in the desert beyond Jordan. 503 **loves . . . fisshes,** Matt. 14:17 etc. 504 **foyson,** plenty. 505 **oure,** i.e., the English. 507 **hoold . . . nempnen,** castle, name. 508 **Northhumberlond,** i.e., the Old English area of Yorkshire north of the Humber River. **wawe,** wave(s). 510 **wolde . . . noght of al,** would not move even at high tide. 513 **wrak . . . al,** wreck, all over. 517 **twynne,** separate. 519 **Latyn corrupt,** according to Trivet she spoke to the constable in Saxon; Chaucer evidently knew that the language of a 6th century Roman princess would be Vulgar (popular) Latin. 520 **algates,** nevertheless. 521 **seche,** search. 523 **sonde,** dispensation. 524 **what,** rank, status, cf. *CT* I.40. 526 **mazed,** dazed. 527 **by hir trouthe,** i.e., upon her word. 529 **routhe,** pity. 530 **slouthe,** sloth. 534 **payens,** pagans. Chaucer's knowledge of the relations between the pagan Angles and Saxons and the Romanized Britons in 6th century England could have come from Geoffrey of Monmouth or William of Malmesbury. 537 **orisons,** prayers. 540 **route,** assemble. 543 **plages,** coastal regions (Fr. *plage*). 547 **nere,** i.e., were not completely. 548 **privetee,** privacy (secrecy).

Honoured Crist and hethen folk bigiled,
And ny the castel swiche ther dwelten three. 550
That oon of hem was blynd and myghte nat see,
But it were with thilke eyen of his mynde
With whiche men seen, whan that they ben
    blynde.

Bright was the sonne as in that someres day,
For which the constable and his wyf also   555
And Custance han ytake the righte way
Toward the see a furlong wey or two,
To pleyen and to romen to and fro.
And in hir walk this blynde man they mette,
Croked and oold, with eyen faste yshette.   560

"In name of Crist," cride this blinde Britoun,
"Dame Hermengyld, yif me my sighte agayn!"
This lady weex affrayed of the soun,
Lest that hir housbonde, shortly for to sayn,
Wolde hire for Jhesu Cristes love han slayn,   565
Til Custance made hire boold, and bad hire
    wirche
The wyl of Crist, as doghter of his chirche.

The constable weex abasshed of that sight,
And seyde, "What amounteth al this fare?"
Custance answerde, "Sire, it is Cristes myght,
That helpeth folk out of the feendes snare."   571
And so ferforth she gan oure lay declare
That she the constable, er that it was eve,
Converteth, and on Crist maketh hym bileve.

This constable was nothyng lord of this place
Of which I speke, ther he Custance fond,   576
But kepte it strongly many wyntres space
Under Alla, kyng of al Northhumbrelond,
That was ful wys and worthy of his hond
Agayn the Scottes, as men may wel heere.   580
But turne I wole agayn to my mateere.

Sathan, that evere us waiteth to bigile,
Saugh of Custance al hire perfeccioun,
And caste anon how he myghte quite hir while,
And made a yong knyght that dwelte in that
    toun   585
Love hire so hoote of foul affeccioun
That verraily hym thoughte he sholde spille
But he of hire myghte ones have his wille.

He woweth hire, but it availleth noght;
She wolde do no synne, by no weye.   590
And for despit he compassed in his thoght
To maken hire on shameful deeth to deye.
He wayteth whan the constable was aweye,
And pryvely upon a nyght he crepte
In Hermengyldes chambre, whil she slepte.   595

Wery, forwaked in hire orisouns,
Slepeth Custance and Hermengyld also.
This knyght, thurgh Sathanas temptaciouns,
Al softely is to the bed ygo,
And kitte the throte of Hermengyld atwo,   600
And leyde the blody knyf by dame Custance,
And wente his wey, ther God yeve hym
    meschance!

Soone after cometh this constable hoom
    agayn,
And eek Alla, that kyng was of that lond,
And saugh his wyf despitously yslayn,   605
For which ful ofte he weep and wroong his hond.
And in the bed the blody knyf he fond
By dame Custance. Allas, what myghte she
    seye?
For verray wo hir wit was al aweye.

To Kyng Alla was toold al this meschance,   610
And eek the tyme, and where, and in what wise
That in a ship was founden dame Custance,

---

549 **bigiled,** deceived. 553 *whan:* Hg&c *after.* 557 **furlong,** 220 yards. 561 *blinde:* E&c olde. 563 **weex,** waxed (became). 565 **for . . . love,** for her love of. 566 **wirche,** perform. 569 **amounteth . . . fare,** means, business. 572 **ferforth . . . lay,** to such length, law. 575 **nothyng,** not at all. 577 **kepte . . . strongly,** defended, with strength. 578 **Alla,** Ælla, historical 6th century king of Deira (Northumbria). 579 **wys . . . worthy,** "sapientia et fortitudo," cf. *CT,* I.68. 580 **Scottes,** from Roman times on, the office of the northern rulers was to protect England against incursions of the Picts and Scots. 582 **bigile,** lead astray. 583 **Saugh,** saw. 584 **caste . . . quite hir while,** planned, repay her time (i.e., get even with her). 587 **spille,** die. 591 **despit . . . compassed,** spite (rage), planned. 596 **forwaked . . . orisouns,** from being awake, prayers. 602 **ther,** where (i.e., may). 605 **despitously,** cruelly. 612 *dame:* Hg&c *this.*

As heerbiforn that ye han herd devyse.
The kynges herte of pitee gan agryse
Whan he saugh so benigne a creature   615
Falle in disese and in mysaventure.

For as the lomb toward his deeth is broght,
So stant this innocent bifore the kyng.
This false knyght, that hath this tresoun wroght,
Berth hire on hond that she hath doon thys
    thyng.   620
But nathelees, ther was greet moornyng
Among the peple, and seyn they kan nat gesse
That she had doon so greet a wikkednesse,

For they han seyn hire evere so vertuous,
And lovynge Hermengyld right as hir lyf.   625
Of this baar witnesse everich in that hous,
Save he that Hermengyld slow with his knyf.
This gentil kyng hath caught a greet motyf
Of this witnesse, and thoghte he wolde enquere
Depper in this, a trouthe for to lere.   630

Allas, Custance, thou hast no champioun,
Ne fighte kanstow noght, so weylaway!
But he that starf for oure redempcioun,
And boond Sathan—and yet lith ther he
    lay—
So be thy stronge champion this day.   635
For, but if Crist open myracle kithe,
Withouten gilt thou shalt be slayn as swithe.

She sette hire doun on knees, and thus she sayde,
"Immortal God, that savedest Susanne
Fro false blame, and thou, merciful mayde,   640
Marie I meene, doghter of Seint Anne,
Bifore whos child angeles synge Osanne,
If I be giltees of this felonye,
My socour be, for ellis shal I dye!"

Have ye nat seyn somtyme a pale face   645
Among a prees, of hym that hath be lad
Toward his deeth, wher as hym gat no grace,
And swich a colour in his face hath had,
Men myghte knowe his face that was bistad
Amonges alle the faces in that route?   650
So stant Custance, and looketh hire aboute.

O queenes, lyvynge in prosperitee,
Duchesses, and ye ladyes everichone,
Haveth som routhe on hire adversitee!
An Emperoures doghter stant allone;   655
She hath no wight to whom to make hire mone.
O blood roial, that stondest in this drede,
Fer been thy freendes at thy grete nede!

This Alla kyng hath swich compassioun,
As gentil herte is fulfild of pitee,   660
That from his eyen ran the water doun.
"Now hastily do fecche a book," quod he,
"And if this knyght wol sweren how that she
This womman slow, yet wol we us avyse
Whom that we wole that shal been oure
    justise."   665

A Britoun book written with Evaungiles
Was fet, and on this book he swoor anoon
She gilty was. And in the meene whiles,
An hand hym smoot upon the nekke-boon,
That doun he fil atones as a stoon,   670
And bothe his eyen broste out of his face
In sighte of everybody in that place.

A voys was herd in general audience,
And seyde, "Thou hast desclaundred, giltelees,
The doghter of hooly chirche in heigh presence;
Thus hastou doon, and yet holde I my pees?"   676
Of this mervaille agast was al the prees;

---

614 agryse, feel compassion. **616 disese,** distress. **620 Berth . . . on hond,** accuses. **621** *moornyng:* Tyrwhitt emended to *murmuring* to fill out the line. **622 seyn,** saying (they said). **630 lere,** learn. **631–32 champioun . . . fighte,** one way of proving innocence was to fight, or have a champion fight, with the accuser. **631–58** Lines not in Trivet. **633 starf,** died. **634 ther he,** where he (Satan). **636 kithe,** show. **637 swithe,** quickly. **638** *sette:* E&c *sit.* **639 Susanne,** falsely accused of adultery by two elders in the Apocryphal account of "Susannah and the Elders." **646 prees,** crowd. The sight of a condemned person being conducted to public execution was not uncommon in the Middle Ages. **649 bistad,** beset (convicted). **650 route,** company. **654 routhe,** pity. **660 gentil herte,** the familiar sentiment, cf. *CT,* I.1761. **664–65 us avyse . . . justise,** i.e., we will reconsider and appoint a judge. **666 Britoun . . . Evaungiles,** this specification is Chaucer's addition; evidently he knew that there were Celtic and Anglo-Saxon versions of the Gospels. **668 meene whiles,** immediately (in the act). **671 broste,** burst. **673 audience,** hearing of all present. **674 desclaundred,** slandered.

As mazed folk they stoden everichone
For drede of wreche, save Custance allone.

Greet was the drede and eek the repentance
Of hem that hadden wrong suspecioun   681
Upon this sely innocent, Custance.
And for this miracle, in conclusioun,
And by Custances mediacioun,
The kyng, and many another in that place, 685
Converted was, thanked be Cristes grace!

This false kynght was slayn for his untrouthe
By juggement of Alla hastifly;
And yet Custance hadde of his deeth greet
     routhe.
And after this Jhesus, of his mercy,   690
Made Alla wedden ful solempnely
This hooly mayden, that is so bright and sheene;
And thus hath Crist ymaad Custance a queene.

But who was woful, if I shal nat lye,
Of this weddyng but Donegild, and namo, 695
The kynges mooder, ful of tirannye?
Hir thoughte hir cursed herte brast atwo.
She wolde noght hir sone had do so;
Hir thoughte a despit that he sholde take
So strange a creature unto his make.   700

Me list nat of the chaf, ne of the stree,
Maken so long a tale as of the corn.
What sholde I tellen of the roialtee
At mariage; or which cours goth biforn;
Who bloweth in a trumpe or in an horn?   705
The fruyt of every tale is for to seye
They ete, and drynke, and daunce, and synge,
     and pleye.

They goon to bedde, as it was skile and right;
For thogh that wyves be ful hooly thynges,

They moste take in pacience at nyght   710
Swiche manere necessaries as been plesynges
To folk that han ywedded hem with rynges,
And leye a lite hir hoolynesse aside,
As for the tyme—it may no bet bitide.

On hire he gat a knave child anon,   715
And to a bisshop and his constable eke
He took his wyf to kepe, whan he is gon
To Scotlond-ward, his foomen for to seke.
Now faire Custance, that is so humble and
     meke,
So longe is goon with childe til that stille 720
She halt hire chambre, abidyng Cristes wille.

The tyme is come a knave child she beer;
Mauricius at the font-stoon they hym calle.
This constable dooth forth come a messageer,
And wroot unto his kyng, that cleped was
     Alle,
How that this blisful tidyng is bifalle,   726
And othere tidynges spedeful for to seye.
He taketh the lettre, and forth he gooth his
     weye.

This messager, to doon his avantage,
Unto the kynges mooder rideth swithe,   730
And salueth hire ful faire in his langage.
"Madame," quod he, "ye may be glad and
     blithe,
And thanketh God an hundred thousand sithe.
My lady queene hath child, withouten doute,
To joye and blisse to al this regne aboute. 735

"Lo, heere the lettres seled of this thyng,
That I moot bere with al the haste I may.
If ye wol aught unto youre sone the kyng,
I am youre servant, bothe nyght and day."
Donegild answerde, "As now at this tyme, nay;

---

678 **mazed**, dazed. 679 **wreche**, revenge. 682 **sely**, blessed (OE *gesǣlig*). 689 **routhe**, pity. 692 **sheene**, shining. 695 **namo**, no more (no other). 697 **brast**, burst. 699 **despit**, disgrace. 700 **make**, mate. 701 **stree**, straw. 702 **corn**, grain. 704 EHg&c *mariages*. 706 **fruyt . . . seye**, essence, say. 708 **skile**, proper. 714 **bet bitide**, better happen. *bet:* Hg&c *oother*. 715 **gat . . . knave . . . anon**, begot, boy, immediately. *knave:* E altered to *man;* so also l. 722 and *CT* IV.444, 447. 717 **kepe**, care for. 718 **Scotlond**, cf. note to l. 580. 720 **stille**, constantly. 722 **knave:** E *man*, see l. 715 above. 723 **font-stoon**, baptismal font. 724 **dooth forth**, causes to be sent. 727 **spedeful**, useful. 729 **avantage**, i.e., to get a reward for carrying the good news. 730 **swithe**, quickly. 731 **salueth**, greets. 733 **sithe**, times, 736 **seled**, sealed.

But heere al nyght I wol thou take thy reste. 741
Tomorwe wol I seye thee what me leste.''

This messager drank sadly ale and wyn,
And stolen were his lettres pryvely
Out of his box, whil he sleep as a swyn; 745
And countrefeted was ful subtilly
Another lettre, wroght ful synfully,
Unto the kyng direct, of this mateere,
Fro his constable, as ye shal after heere.

The lettre spak the queene delivered was 750
Of so horrible a feendly creature
That in the castel noon so hardy was
That any while dorste ther endure.
The mooder was an elf, by aventure
Ycomen—by charmes or by sorcerie— 755
And everich wight hateth hir compaignye.

Wo was this kyng whan he this lettre had
     sayn,
But to no wight he tolde his sorwes soore,
But of his owene hand he wroot agayn,
"Welcome the sonde of Crist for everemoore
To me that am now lerned in his loore. 761
Lord, welcome be thy lust and thy plesaunce;
My lust I putte al in thyn ordinaunce.

"Kepeth this child, al be it foul or feir,
And eek my wyf, unto myn hoom-comynge.
Crist, whan hym list, may sende me an heir 766
Moore agreable than this to my likynge.''
This lettre he seleth, pryvely wepynge,
Which to the messager was take soone,
And forth he gooth; ther is na moore to doone.

O messager, fulfild of dronkenesse, 771
Strong is thy breeth, thy lymes faltren ay,

And thou biwreyest alle secreenesse.
Thy mynde is lorn, thou janglest as a jay,
Thy face is turned in a newe array. 775
Ther dronkenesse regneth in any route,
Ther is no conseil hyd, withouten doute.

O Donegild, I ne have noon Englissh digne
Unto thy malice and thy tirannye!
And therfore to the feend I thee resigne; 780
Lat hym enditen of thy traitorie!
Fy, mannysh, fy!—O nay, by God, I lye—
Fy, feendlych spirit, for I dar wel telle
Thogh thou heere walke thy spirit is in helle.

This messager comth fro the kyng agayn, 785
And at the kynges moodres court he lighte,
And she was of this messager ful fayn,
And plesed hym in al that ever she myghte.
He drank and wel his girdel underpighte;
He slepeth and he fnorteth in his gyse 790
Al nyght, til the sonne gan aryse.

Eft were his lettres stolen everychon,
And countrefeted lettres in this wyse:
"The king comandeth his constable anon,
Up peyne of hangyng, and on heigh juyse, 795
That he ne sholde suffren in no wyse
Custance in-with his reawme for t'abyde
Thre dayes and o quarter of a tyde.

"But in the same ship as he hire fond,
Hire, and hir yonge sone, and al hir geere, 800
He sholde putte, and croude hire fro the lond,
And chargen hire that she never eft coome
     theere.''
O my Custance, wel may thy goost have feere,
And slepynge, in thy dreem, been in penance,
Whan Donegild cast al this ordinance. 805

---

742 me leste, i.e., it pleases me to say. **743 sadly,** seriously (i.e., he was a "serious" drinker). **748 direct,** directed. **751 feendly,** monstrous. **753 endure,** remain. **754 elf . . . aventure,** fairy (evil spirit), (mis)chance. **756 wight,** person. So E; other MSS have various other words, so it must have been lacking in the original. **757 sayn,** seen. **760 sonde,** that which is sent. **761 lerned . . . loore,** i.e., (by this misfortune) have been instructed in his mystery. **762 lust . . . plesaunce,** desire, pleasure. **764 Kepeth,** preserve. **771–77** Again from *De Contemptu Mundi,* cf. note to l. 99 above. **773 biwreyest . . . secreenesse,** betray, secrecy. **774 lorn . . . janglest,** lost, babble. **775 array,** appearance. **776 Ther . . . route,** where, company. **778 digne,** worthy. **781 enditen,** indict (accuse). **782 mannysh,** like a man (rather than a woman). **787 fayn,** gracious. **789 underpighte,** stuffed. **790 gyse,** manner. *fnorteth:* other MSS *snoreth,* cf. *CT* I.4163. **792 Eft,** again. **795 juyse,** justice. **798 tyde,** presumably again measuring time by the tides. **801 croude,** crowd (push). **802 Hg&c** *charge hire that.* **803 feere,** fear.

This messager on morwe whan he wook
Unto the castel halt the nexte way,
And to the constable he the lettre took.
And whan that he this pitous lettre say,
Ful ofte he seyde "allas" and "weylaway."　810
"Lord Crist," quod he, "how may this world
　　endure,
So ful of synne is many a creature?

　"O myghty God, if that it be thy wille,
Sith thou art rightful juge, how may it be
That thou wolt suffren innocentz to spille,　815
And wikked folk regnen in prosperitee?
O goode Custance, allas, so wo is me
That I moot be thy tormentour or deye
On shames deeth; ther is noon oother weye."

Wepen bothe yonge and olde in al that
　　place
Whan that the kyng this cursed lettre sente,　821
And Custance, with a deedly pale face,
The ferthe day toward hir ship she wente.
But nathelees she taketh in good entente　824
The wyl of Crist, and knelynge on the stronde
She seyde, "Lord, ay welcome be thy sonde!

"He that me kepte fro the false blame
While I was on the lond amonges yow,
He kan me kepe from harm and eek fro shame
In salte see, althogh I se noght how.　830
As strong as evere he was, he is yet now.
In hym triste I, and in his mooder deere,
That is to me my seyl and eek my steere."

Hir litel child lay wepyng in hir arm,
And knelynge, pitously to hym she seyde,　835
"Pees, litel sone, I wol do thee noon harm."
With that hir coverchief of hir heed she
　　breyde,
And over his litel eyen she it leyde,
And in hir arm she lulleth it ful faste,
And into hevene hire eyen up she caste.　840

"Mooder," quod she, "and mayde bright,
　　Marie,
Sooth is that thurgh wommanes eggement
Mankynde was lorn, and dampned ay to dye,
For which thy child was on a croys yrent.
Thy blisful eyen sawe al his torment.　845
Thanne is ther no comparison bitwene
Thy wo and any wo man may sustene.

"Thow sawe thy child yslayn bifore thyne
　　eyen,
And yet now lyveth my litel child, parfay.　849
Now, lady bright, to whom alle woful cryen,
Thow glorie of wommanhede, thow faire may,
Thow haven of refut, brighte sterre of day,
Rewe on my child, that of thy gentillesse
Rewest on every reweful in distresse.

"O litel child, allas, what is thy gilt,　855
That nevere wroghtest synne as yet, pardee?
Why wil thyn harde fader han thee spilt?
O mercy, deere constable," quod she,
"As lat my litel child dwelle heer with thee;
And if thou darst nat saven hym, for blame,　860
Yet kys hym ones in his fadres name."

Therwith she looked bakward to the londe,
And seyde, "Farewel, housbonde routhelees!"
And up she rist, and walketh doun the stronde
Toward the ship—hir folweth al the prees.　865
And evere she preyeth hire child to holde his
　　pees;
And taketh hir leve, and with an hooly entente
She blissed hire, and into ship she wente.

Vitailled was the ship, it is no drede,
Habundantly for hire ful longe space,　870
And othere necessaries that sholde nede
She hadde ynogh, heryed be Goddes grace.
For wynd and weder, almyghty God purchace,
And brynge hire hoom! I kan no bettre seye,
But in the see she dryveth forth hir weye.　875

807 nexte, nearest. **813–26** Not in Trivet. A familiar sentiment, in *Boece* I. m.5, etc. **815 spille**, die. **824 entente**, spirit. **826 sonde**, that which is sent. **833 steere**, rudder. **835–75** Not in Trivet. **837 of . . . breyde**, off, pulled. **842 eggement**, instigation. **843 lorn**, lost. **849** E *litel* om. **851 may**, maid. **852 refut**, refuge. **853 Rewe**, have pity. **857 spilt**, killed. **860 saven . . . blame**, preserve; for fear of blame. *for*: some MSS *fro*. **863 routhelees**, pitiless. **865 prees**, crowd. **868 blissed**, crossed herself. **869 no drede**, no doubt. **872 heryed**, praised. **873 For . . . purchace**, As to, provide.

Explicit secunda pars. Sequitur pars tercia.

Alla the kyng comth hoom soone after this
Unto his castle, of the which I tolde,
And asketh where his wyf and his child is.
The constable gan aboute his herte colde,
And pleynly al the manere he hym tolde   880
As ye han herd—I kan telle it no bettre—
And sheweth the kyng his seel and eek his lettre,

And seyde, "Lord, as ye comanded me
Up peyne of deeth, so have I doon, certein."
This messager tormented was til he   885
Moste biknowe and tellen, plat and pleyn,
Fro nyght to nyght, in what place he had leyn.
And thus, by wit and sotil enquerynge,
Ymagined was by whom this harm gan sprynge.

The hand was knowe that the lettre wroot,
And al the venym of this cursed dede,   891
But in what wise, certeinly, I noot.
Th'effect is this, that Alla, out of drede,
His mooder slow—that may men pleynly rede—
For that she traitoure was to hire ligeance.   895
Thus endeth olde Donegild, with meschance.

The sorwe that this Alla nyght and day
Maketh for his wyf, and for his child also,
Ther is no tonge that it telle may.
But now wol I unto Custance go,   900
That fleteth in the see, in peyne and wo,
Fyve yeer and moore, as liked Cristes sonde,
Er that hir ship approched unto the londe.

Under an hethen castel, atte laste,   904
Of which the name in my text noght I fynde,
Custance, and eek hir child, the see up caste.
Almyghty God, that saved al mankynde,
Have on Custance and on hir child som mynde,
That fallen is in hethen hand eftsoone,

In point to spille, as I shal telle yow soone.   910

Doun fro the castle comth ther many a wight
To gauren on this ship and on Custance.
But shortly, from the castle, on a nyght,
The lordes styward—God yeve hym
     meschance—
A theef that hadde reneyed oure creance,   915
Cam into the ship allone, and seyde he sholde
Hir lemman be, wher so she wolde or nolde.

Wo was this wrecched womman tho bigon;
Hir child cride, and she cride pitously.
But blisful Marie heelp hire right anon,   920
For with hir struglyng wel and myghtily
The theef fil overbord al sodeynly,
And in the see he dreynte for vengeance.
And thus hath Crist unwemmed kept Custance.

O foule lust of luxurie, lo, thyn ende!   925
Nat oonly that thou feyntest mannes mynde,
But verraily thou wolt his body shende.
Th'ende of thy werk, or of thy lustes blynde,
Is compleynyng. Hou many oon may men
     fynde
That noght for werk somtyme, but for
     th'entente   930
To doon this synne, been outher slayn or shente!

How may this wayke womman han this
     strengthe
Hire to defende agayn this renegat?
O Golias, unmesurable of lengthe,
Hou myghte David make thee so maat,   935
So yong and of armure so desolaat?
Hou dorste he looke upon thy dredful face?
Wel may men seen, it nas but Goddes grace.

Who yaf Judith corage or hardynesse
To sleen hym Oloferne in his tente,   940

---

885 tormented, tortured. **886 biknowe . . . plat**, reveal, flat. **889 Ymagined**, deduced. **890 knowe**, ascertained. **893 drede**, without doubt. **894 slow**, slew. In Trivet the execution is more graphically detailed. **896 meschance**, bad fate (or "bad luck to her"). **901 fleteth**, floats. **902 sonde**, dispensation. **910 point to spille**, danger of death. **912 gauren**, stare. **915 reneyed . . . creance**, renounced, belief. **917 lemman**, lover. **922 theef fil**, in Trivet she pushes him overboard. The change is in line with Chaucer's general refinement of the action; cf. note to l. 894 above. **923 dreynte**, drowned. **924 unwemmed**, unblemished. **925–31** Again from *De Contemptu Mundi*, cf. note to l. 99 above. **926 feyntest**, make faint. **927 shende**, destroy. **929 compleynyng**, i.e., misery. **930 werk . . . entente**, action vs. intention. **932 wayke**, weak. **934 Golias**, Goliath, I Samuel 17:4ff. **935 maat**, dead. **939–40 Judith . . . Oloferne**, Judith killed Holofernes in the Apocryphal Book of Judith; cf. MkT, VII.2251 below.

And to deliveren out of wrecchednesse
The peple of God? I seye, for this entente,
That right as God spirit of vigour sente
To hem, and saved hem out of meschance,
So sente he myght and vigour to Custance.   945

   Forth gooth hir ship thurghout the narwe
     mouth
Of Jubaltare and Septe, dryvynge ay
Somtyme west and somtyme north and south
And somtyme est, ful many a wery day,
Til Cristes mooder—blessed be she ay—   950
Hath shapen, thurgh hir endelees goodnesse,
To make an ende of al hir hevynesse.

   Now lat us stynte of Custance but a throwe,
And speke we of the Romayn Emperour,
That out of Surrye hath by lettres knowe   955
The slaughtre of Cristen folk, and dishonour
Doon to his doghter by a fals traytour,
I mene the cursed wikked Sowdanesse
That at the feeste leet sleen both moore and
     lesse.

For which this Emperour hath sent anon   960
His senatour, with roial ordinance,
And othere lordes, God woot, many oon,
On Surryens to taken heigh vengeance.
They brennen, sleen, and brynge hem to
     meschance
Ful many a day; but shortly, this is th'ende, 965
Homward to Rome they shapen hem to
     wende.

   This senatour repaireth with victorie
To Rome-ward, saillynge ful roially,
And mette the ship dryvynge, as seith the storie,
In which Custance sit ful pitously.   970
Nothyng knew he what she was, ne why
She was in swich array, ne she nyl seye
Of hire estaat, althogh she sholde deye.

He bryngeth hire to Rome, and to his wyf
He yaf hire and hir yonge sone also;   975
And with the senatour she ladde hir lyf.
Thus kan Oure Lady bryngen out of wo
Woful Custance, and many another mo.
And longe tyme dwelled she in that place,
In hooly werkes evere, as was hir grace.   980

The senatoures wyf hir aunte was,
But for al that she knew hire never the
     moore.
I wol no lenger tarien in this cas,
But to Kyng Alla, which I spak of yoore,
That wepeth for his wyf and siketh soore,   985
I wol retourne, and lete I wol Custance
Under the senatoures governance.

   Kyng Alla, which that hadde his mooder
     slayn,
Upon a day fil in swich repentance
That, if I shortly tellen shal and playn,   990
To Rome he comth to receyven his penance,
And putte hym in the Popes ordinance
In heigh and logh, and Jhesu Crist bisoghte
Foryeve his wikked werkes that he wroghte.

   The fame anon thurghout the toun is born,
How Alla kyng shal comen in pilgrymage,   996
By herbergeours that wenten hym biforn;
For which the senatour, as was usage,
Rood hym agayns, and many of his lynage,
As wel to shewen his heighe magnificence   1000
As to doon any kyng a reverence.

   Greet cheere dooth this noble senatour
To Kyng Alla, and he to hym also;
Everich of hem dooth oother greet honour.
And so bifel that inwith a day or two   1005
This senatour is to Kyng Alla go
To feste, and shortly, if I shal nat lye,
Custances sone wente in his compaignye.

947 **Jubaltare and Septe,** Gibraltar and Ceuta (opposite, on the North African coast). 953 **stynte . . . throwe,** stop, while. 964 **brennen,** burn. 969 **dryvynge,** i.e., driven by the sea. 971 Hg&c *Nothyng ne.* 972 **nyl,** will not. 973 *althogh:* EHg&c *thogh.* 984 **yoore,** earlier. 985 **siketh,** sighs. 986 **lete,** leave. 995 Hg&c *anon thurgh Rome toun.* 997 **herbergeours,** advance agents who secured lodgings for a large retinue. 998 **usage,** custom. 999 **agayns,** to meet him. 1000–01 **As wel . . . As,** both, and. 1002 **cheere,** welcome. 1005 **inwith,** Hg *in;* other MSS *within/on.*

Som men wolde seyn at requeste of Custance
This senatour hath lad this child to feeste;   1010
I may nat tellen every circumstance:
Be as be may, ther was he at the leeste.
But sooth is this, that at his moodres heeste
Biforn Alla, durynge the metes space,   1014
The child stood, lookyng in the kynges face.

This Alla kyng hath of this child greet wonder,
And to the senatour he seyde anon,
"Whos is that faire child that stondeth yonder?"
"I noot," quod he, "by God, and by Seint John.
A mooder he hath, but fader hath he noon   1020
That I of woot"; but and shortly, in a stounde,
He tolde Alla how that this child was founde.

"But God woot," quod this senatour also,
"So vertuous a lyvere in my lyf
Ne saugh I nevere as she, ne herde of mo,   1025
Of worldly wommen, mayde, ne of wyf.
I dar wel seyn hir hadde levere a knyf
Thurghout hir brest than ben a womman
   wikke;
There is no man koude brynge hire to that
   prikke."

Now was this child as lyk unto Custance   1030
As possible is a creature to be.
This Alla hath the face in remembrance
Of dame Custance, and ther on mused he
If that the childes mooder were aught she
That is his wyf, and pryvely he sighte,   1035
And spedde hym fro the table that he myghte.

"Parfay," thoghte he, "fantome is in myn heed.
I oghte deme, of skilful juggement,
That in the salte see my wyf is deed."
And afterward he made his argument: 1040

"What woot I if that Crist have hyder ysent
My wyf by see, as wel as he hire sente
To my contree fro thennes that she wente?"

And after noon, hoom with the senatour
Goth Alla, for to seen this wonder chaunce.   1045
This senatour dooth Alla greet honour,
And hastifly he sente after Custaunce.
But trusteth weel, hire liste nat to daunce
Whan that she wiste wherfore was that sonde;
Unnethe upon hir feet she myghte stonde.   1050

Whan Alla saugh his wyf, faire he hire grette,
And weep that it was routhe for to see;
For at the firste look he on hire sette,
He knew wel verraily that it was she.
And she, for sorwe, as doumb stant as a tree,
So was hir herte shet in hir distresse,   1056
Whan she remembred his unkyndenesse.

Twyes she swowned in his owene sighte.
He weep, and hym excuseth pitously.
"Now God," quod he, "and alle his halwes
   brighte   1060
So wisly on my soule as have mercy,
That of youre harm as giltelees am I
As is Maurice my sone, so lyk youre face;
Elles the feend me fecche out of this place!"

Long was the sobbyng and the bitter peyne,
Er that hir woful hertes myghte cesse;   1066
Greet was the pitee for to heere hem pleyne,
Thurgh whiche pleintes gan hir wo encresse.
I pray yow alle my labour to relesse;
I may nat telle hir wo until tomorwe,   1070
I am so wery for to speke of sorwe.

But finally, whan that the sothe is wist

1009 **Som men,** since Tyrwhitt this and the reference at l. 1086 below have been interpreted by all editors as disparaging allusions to Gower's version of the story, which, Chaucer seems to be implying, was less decorous. Gower, following Trivet, here merely says that Constance instructed the child how he should act at the feast. **1013 heeste,** command. **1014 metes space,** duration of the meal. **1021 shortly . . . stounde,** a short while (briefly). **1025 mo,** more (another). **1028 Thurghout . . . wikke,** (were thrust) through, wicked. **1029 prikke,** point. **1034 aught,** at all. **1035 sighte,** sighed. **1036 that he,** as soon as he. **1037 fantome,** delusion. **1038 deme,** judge. **1041 What woot I if,** how do I know but. **1045 wonder chaunce,** wondrous possibility. **1048 liste,** wanted. **1049 wiste . . . sonde,** knew, summons. **1050 Unnethe,** barely. **1052 routhe,** pity. **1058 swowned,** fainted. **1060 halwes brighte,** shining saints. E *alle* om. **1061 wisly,** truly. **1067 pleyne,** lament. **1069 labour . . . relesse,** release me from. **1072 sothe . . . wist,** truth, known.

That Alla giltelees was of hir wo,
I trowe an hundred tymes been they kist,
And swich a blisse is ther bitwix hem two   1075
That, save the joye that lasteth everemo,
Ther is noon lyk that any creature
Hath seyn or shal, whil that the world may dure.

Tho preyde she hir housbonde mekely,
In relief of hir longe, pitous pyne,   1080
That he wolde preye hir fader specially
That of his magestee he wolde enclyne
To vouchesauf som day with hym to dyne.
She preyde hym eek he sholde by no weye
Unto hir fader no word of hire seye.   1085

   Som men wolde seyn how that the child
      Maurice
Dooth this message unto this Emperour;
But, as I guesse, Alla was nat so nyce
To hym that was of so sovereyn honour
As he that is of Cristen folk the flour,   1090
Sente any child, but it is bet to deeme
He wente hymself, and so it may wel seeme.

   This Emperour hath graunted gentilly
To come to dyner, as he hym bisoughte;
And wel rede I he looked bisily   1095
Upon this child, and on his doghter thoghte.
Alla goth to his in, and as hym oghte,
Arrayed for this feste in every wise
As ferforth as his konnyng may suffise.   1099

   The morwe cam, and Alla gan hym dresse,
And eek his wyf, this Emperour to meete.
And forth they ryde in joye and in gladnesse.
And whan she saugh hir fader in the strete,
She lighte doun and falleth hym to feete.
"Fader," quod she, "youre yonge child
      Custance   1105
Is now ful clene out of youre remembrance.

"I am youre doghter Custance," quod she,
"That whilom ye han sent unto Surrye.
It am I, fader, that in the salte see
Was put allone and dampned for to dye.   1110
Now, goode fader, mercy I yow crye!
Sende me namoore unto noon hethenesse,
But thonketh my lord heere of his kyndenesse."

   Who kan the pitous joye tellen al
Bitwixe hem thre, syn they been thus
      ymette?
But of my tale make an ende I shal;   1116
The day goth faste, I wol no lenger lette.
This glade folk to dyner they hem sette;
In joye and blisse at mete I lete hem dwelle
A thousand foold wel moore than I kan telle.

   This child Maurice was sithen Emperour 1121
Maad by the Pope, and lyved cristenly.
To Cristes chirche he dide greet honour.
But I lete al his storie passen by;
Of Custance is my tale specially.   1125
In the olde Romayn geestes may men fynde
Maurices lyf; I bere it noght in mynde.

   This Kyng Alla, whan he his tyme say,
With his Custance, his hooly wyf so sweete,
To Engelond been they come the righte way,
Wher as they lyve in joye and in quiete.   1131
But litel while it lasteth, I yow heete,
Joye of this world, for tyme wol nat abyde.
Fro day to nyght it changeth as the tyde.

   Who lyved evere in swich delit o day   1135
That hym ne moeved outher conscience,
Or ire, or talent, or somkynnes affray,
Envye, or pride, or passion, or offence?
I ne seye but for this ende this sentence.
That litel while in joye or in plesance   1140
Lasteth the blisse of Alla with Custance.

1082 enclyne, consent. **1083 vouchesauf,** be willing. **1086** See note to l. 1009 above. Here Trivet and Gower do have Maurice convey the invitation. **1088 nyce,** ignorant. **1091 deeme,** assume. **1093 graunted,** agreed. **1095 bisily,** intently. **1097 in,** lodging. **1099 ferforth . . . konnyng,** as far, ability. **1100 morwe,** morning. **1108 whilom,** earlier. **1117 lette,** delay. **1121 sithen,** later. **1126 geestes,** stories. The life of Maurice is found in Trivet's *Chronicle* along with that of Constance, in the section entitled "Les gestes des apostles, emperours, et rois." **1128 say,** saw. **1132–38** From *De Contemptu Mundi,* see note to l. 99 above. **1132 heete,** promise. **1135 o day,** one day. **1136 moeved,** agitate. **1137 talent . . . affray,** ambition, alarm. **1138 offence,** injury. **1139 sentence,** observation.

For deeth, that taketh of heigh and logh his
rente,
Whan passed was a yeer, evene as I gesse,
Out of this world this Kyng Alla he hente,
For whom Custance hath ful greet hevynesse.
Now lat us praye to God his soule blesse.   1146
And dame Custance, finally to seye,
Toward the toun of Rome goth hire weye.

    To Rome is come this hooly creature,
And fyndeth hire freendes hoole and sounde.
Now is she scaped al hire aventure.   1151
And whan that she hir fader hath yfounde,

Doun on hir knees falleth she to grounde;
Wepynge for tendrenesse in herte blithe,
She heryeth God an hundred thousand sithe.

    In vertu and in hooly almus-dede   1156
They lyven alle, and nevere asonder wende;
Til deeth departed hem, this lyf they lede.
And fareth now weel, my tale is at an ende.
Now Jhesu Crist, that of his myght may sende
Joy after wo, governe us in his grace,   1161
And kepe us alle that been in this place!

                                Amen.

Heere endeth the Tale of the Man of Lawe.

[EPILOGUE]

Owre Hoost upon his stiropes stood anon,
And seyde, "Goode men, herkeneth everych on!
This was a thrifty tale for the nones!   1165
Sir Parisshe Prest," quod he, "for Goddes
bones,
Telle us a tale, as was thi forward yore.
I se wel that ye lerned men in lore
Can moche good, by Goddes dignite!"
    The Parson him answerde, "Benedicite!   1170
What eyleth the man, so synfully to swere?"
Oure Host answerde, "O Jankin, be ye there?
I smelle a Lollere in the wynd," quod he.

"Now, goode men," quod oure Host,
    "herkeneth me;
Abydeth, for Goddes digne passioun,   1175
For we schal han a predicacioun;
This Lollere heer wil prechen us somwhat."
    "Nay, by my fader soule, that schal he nat!"
Seyde the Wif of Bath; "he schal nat preche;
He schal no gospel glosen here ne teche.   1180
We leven alle in the grete God," quod she;
"He wolde sowen som difficulte,
Or springen cokkel in our clene corn.
And therfore, Hoost, I warne thee biforn,

1142 **rente,** tribute. 1145 **hevynesse,** sorrow. 1155 **heryeth . . . sithe,** praises, times. 1156 **almus-dede,** almsgiving. EHg&c *in* om.
1162 **kepe,** protect. 1163–90 Lines omitted in EHg and 47 other MSS, so evidently marked for excision in the original. Found in 35
MSS. Here based on MS. Corpus Christi 198. 1165 **thrifty,** appropriate, skillful. 1167 **forward yore,** agreement earlier. 1169 **Can,**
know. 1172 **Jankin,** i.e., Johnny; diminutive of John, a traditional name for a priest. 1173 **Lollere,** Lollard, the popular name for a
follower of John Wycliff, 14th century puritanical church reformer, whose followers objected to swearing as well as to other forms of
license. 1176 **predicacioun,** preaching. 1179 **Wif of Bath.** This reading is not found in any MS. All read "Squyer," "Sumnour," or
"Shipman." "Wif of Bath" is assumed to have been Chaucer's original reading when this link connected with the ShT, vII.1ff. With
this conjectural emendation, the passage can serve as a link to Part III (following), which begins with the prologue and tale Chaucer
eventually assigned to the Wife of Bath. For further discussion, see ML headnote above. When Chaucer substituted "Shipman" for
"Wif of Bath," he had to supply a syllable; in the MSS *heer* is found in various positions in the line, indicating that it must have been
written with a caret in the margin of the original. 1180 **glosen,** gloss (explain). 1181 **leven,** believe. *she: he* in all MSS. 1182 **sowen,**
i.e., create. 1183 **springen cokkel,** sow weeds. 1184 **warne,** inform.

My joly body schal a tale telle,   1185
And I schal clynken you so mery a belle,
That I schal waken al this compaignie.

But it schal not ben of philosophie,
Ne phislyas, ne termes queinte of lawe.
Ther is but litel Latyn in my mawe!"   1190

1185 joly, pretty, merry (Fr. *jolie*); less appropriate for the Shipman, Squire, or Summoner than for the Wife of Bath, and found in ShT vii.423. **1188–90 philosophie . . . phislyas . . . lawe . . . Latyn,** terms all more appropriate to *Mel* than ShT; see note to ii.96, 99 above. **phislyas,** of the many possible explanations, the best is that it is the Wife of Bath's malapropism for the legal term "filace," file of documents. Other MSS have *philyas, fisleas,* etc. OED gives "filas," "fylas" as variants.

Plate 2.   The opening of *Troylus and Criseyde,* MS. Morgan 817, fol. 1. The Pierpont Morgan Library, New York

INTRODUCTION

Canterbury Tales, Part III

ARTS III-IV-V of the *Canterbury Tales* must come in this order because of the way that the Wife of Bath is referred back to in the Clerk's Tale (IV.1170) and Merchant's Tale (IV.1685), and because of the thematic continuity between the Wife's Prologue and Tale in III, the Clerk's and Merchant's Tales in IV, and the Franklin's Tale in V. Eleanor Prescott Hammond long ago dubbed these the "marriage group" since they all deal with the tensions between married people. But it is well to bear in mind that in the Middle Ages, marriage was a general figure for the well-ordered, hierarchical society, in which the husband is responsible for his wife and rules over his household. Christ was thought of as married to the Church; the bishop to the diocese; the king to the commonwealth; reason to the senses. When the "wife" rebelled against the "husband" in any of these situations, it was a form of "adultery." Walter Ullman, *The Individual and Society in the Middle Ages* (1966), describes this disposition as the principle of *Munt*. The Clerk's Tale is the best expression of Munt and the Wife of Bath's Prologue is the most explicit rebellion against it, but the Merchant's, Franklin's, Man of Law's, Physician's, Nun's Priest's, Second Nun's, *Melibee*, and perhaps other tales explore various aspects of acceptance and rejection of the principle of Munt.

So for Chaucer's audience, the tales about marriage had connotations of law and order in society over and above the details in any particular narrative. Since Chaucer was a poet and not a philosopher, the philosophical points were made by implication, while major attention was directed to the characters and the stories. The Wife of Bath's Prologue, which sets this argument in motion, is regarded by many critics as Chaucer's most sophisticated achievement. In spite of the fact that the Wife is the "realest" person on the pilgrimage—she is the only one referred to by other pilgrims in the tales (see above) or referred to by Chaucer outside the tales (see short poem 16, l.29)—she is modeled on a literary character and represents the distillation of a thousand years of antifeminist satire. Virtually every line in her Prologue is a quotation from some familiar authority, yet it is rendered with marvelous colloquial ease and in some of Chaucer's surest verse. In spite of the serious social criticism, no part of the Canterbury collection exhibits more gusto and salacious delight.

The Wife of Bath's Prologue is suggested by the "confession" of the Duenna in Jean de Meun's part of the *Roman de la Rose* (Dunn-Robbins trans., 64). The first 150 lines are largely a pastiche of quotations from St. Jerome's *Epistola adversus Jovinianum*; ll. 198-298 from Theophrastus' *Liber de Nuptiis* (included in Jerome); ll. 198-398 perhaps from Eustace Deschamps, *Miroir de Mariage*; and the examples after l. 642 from Walter Map, *Disuasio Valerii ad Ruffinum ne uxorem ducat*. These and other antifeminist materials were collected in anthologies like the one that belonged to the Wife's last husband (l.685), largely to convince young clerics that their celibate existence was better than marriage. (There were similar antimatrimonial materials, like the so-called "Katherine group," intended for nuns.)

The obsession of the Church with virginity was a facet of the general medieval ascetic ideal which sought to control all the natural drives: pride by humility, possession by poverty, mastery by obedience, shelter by discomfort, hunger by fasting—and sex by celibacy. Sex received more attention than the others because it was so interesting and so hard to control. For the other drives, the admonition of the church was to moderation. Human beings could not survive without some food, some shelter, and some self-esteem. In the fourth century, a Roman monk Jovinian had described marriage, the normal channel for sex, as equal in virtue to virginity. But after the crushing *Epistola* of St. Jerome, a succession of church synods established the official superiority of virginity.

This painful doctrine Chaucer satirized in hilarious fashion, by having the Wife of Bath distort for her own purpose the familiar antifeminist arguments. After l. 193, her harangue, like that of the Duenna, grows autobiographical, and we see in her life cycle the various permutations of relationships between the sexes. If Chaucer knew when he mentioned her deafness in the General Prologue (I.446) that he was going to describe in her own prologue how she became deaf, it is one of the most striking evidences of planning ahead we have in the *Canterbury Tales*. Possibly, however, it was serendipity, for the Wife of the General Prologue in Part I shows none of the complexity and learning of the Wife of the Prologue and Tale in Part III. More likely, the Shipman's Tale, now at the beginning of Part VII, had been originally intended for her, before Chaucer was inspired to develop her more fully and create the marriage group.

The Wife of Bath's Tale is the development of a "disenchanting" folktale in which a curse has transformed a beautiful maiden into a hideous shape from which she can be released only through the ministration of a hero. In the analogues, this tale had already been merged with the riddle of what women most desire. But the important addition, found in no other version, is the Loathly Lady's concluding lecture on true gentilesse. This introduces the second theme of the marriage argument. The message of the Wife's Prologue had been that marriage is a Darwinian struggle for "maistrie." The rape with which her tale begins continues this theme; but the resolution of the tale teaches that "gentilesse"—consideration, politeness—is more effective than competition.

The transformation of the concept of gentilesse from aristocratic birth to decorous behavior is one of the principal shifts between the medieval and modern world views. The sentiments expressed by the Loathly Lady echo those of Boethius, Dante, and the *Roman de la Rose*. The theme has been discussed by Donald C. Baker, "Chaucer's Clerk and the Wife of Bath on the Subject of Gentilesse," *Studies in Philology* (1962),

and the transformation by Ruth Kelso, *The Doctrine of the English Gentleman in the Sixteenth Century* (1929).

Part III shows the same pattern of contrasting styles as Part I. In both, a creditable pilgrim begins with an elevated story which piques two disreputable pilgrims to quarrel and tell vulgar stories to retaliate against each other. But the Friar's Tale of the summoner and the devil (built around a folktale type called "the three wishes") and the Summoner's Tale of the friar and the fart (a typical fabliau "dirty joke") do not appear to provide the same sort of thematic continuity as in Part I. The Friar's breaking into the Wife's Prologue at l. 830 shows that Part III was constructed as a whole, and critics are reluctant to view these tales simply as digressions. If there is a thematic connection, it probably results from the wider medieval view of the meaning of marriage. The Wife of Bath's Prologue is an examination of authority in marriage; the Friar's and Summoner's Tales are exposés of the corruption of moral and spiritual authority in society. The connection may appear forced to us, but it probably appeared less so to Chaucer and his audience.

The structure of Part III is analyzed by P.R. Szittya, "The Green Yeoman as Loathly Hag," *PMLA* (1975). W.G. East, "By Preeve Which That is Demonstratif," *Chaucer Review* (1977), and N. F. Blake, "The Wife of Bath and Her Tale," *Leeds Studies in English* (1982) argue the thematic unity of the three stories in Part III. The thematic unity of the marriage group as a whole is surveyed by Donald R. Howard, *The Idea of the Canterbury Tales* (1976). The moral pattern of the *Canterbury* collection is treated by Paul A. Olson, *The Canterbury Tales and the Good Society* (1986). Robert A. Pratt, "Jankyn's Book of Wikked Wyves: Medieval Anti- Matrimonial Propaganda in the Universities," *Annuale Mediaevale* (1962), surveys the antifeminist collections. William Matthews, "The Wife of Bath and All Her Sect," *Viator* (1974), traces the roots of Chaucer's characterization in classical and medieval tradition.

Canterbury Tales

PART III

WIFE OF BATH'S TALE

PROLOGUE

The Prologe of the Wyves Tale of Bathe.

Experience though noon auctoritee
Were in this world is right ynogh for me
To speke of wo that is in mariage.
For, lordynges, sith I twelve yeer was of age,
Thonked be God that is eterne on lyve,   5
Housbondes at chirche dore I have had fyve—
If I so ofte myghte have ywedded bee—

And alle were worthy men in hir degree.
But me was toold, certeyn, nat longe agoon is,
That sith that Crist ne wente nevere but onis
To weddyng in the Cane of Galilee,   11
That by the same ensample taughte he me
That I ne sholde wedded be but ones.
Herkne eek, which a sharp word for the nones:

1 **Experience . . . auctoritee,** since the MilT and RvT of Part I represent "experience," and MLT represents "authority," this is an appropriate line to connect Part III with I and II. The tension between these two ideals is the essential theme of the WB Prologue. The phrasing may have been suggested by the confession of the Duenna in *RR* 12,794ff. (Dunn-Robbins, 59.33), which serves as a model for the whole WBP. And see the character of the Wife of Bath in the Gen. Pro. 475–76. 2 *is/ for:* E&c *were/to.* 3 **wo . . . mariage,** the unhappiness of marriage was a staple of the medieval antifeminist tradition upon which WBP draws for material, especially St. Jerome, *Epistola adversus Jovinianum*; Theophrastus, *Liber de Nuptiis* (lost, but partially preserved in Jerome); Walter Map, *Dissuasio Valerii ad Ruffinum ne uxorem ducat*; and Eustace Deschamps, *Miror de mariage.* However, the theme is equally cogent in antimasculine literature intended for nuns, such as the Middle English *Hali Meidenhad.* Cf. notes to ll. 671–80 below. 4 **sith,** since. **twelve,** the canonical age at which girls could marry. 6 **chirche dore,** the marriage was performed at the church door, after which the couple went into the church for the nuptial mass, cf. *CT* I.460. 7 **If I so ofte,** in the next 150 lines St. Jerome's arguments against marriage and remarriage are hilariously turned inside out. E&c *For I so ofte have.* 10 **sith . . . onis,** since, once. 11 **Cane,** Cana, John 2:1, but the argument is from Jerome. 12 E *By the same ensample thoughte me.* 14 Hg&c *Herke eek, lo.*

Biside a welle, Jhesus, God and man,   15
Spak in repreeve of the Samaritan,
"Thou hast yhad fyve housbondes," quod he,
"And that man the which that hath now thee
Is noght thyn housbonde." Thus seyde he
   certeyn.
What that he mente therby, I kan nat seyn,   20
But that I axe why that the fifthe man
Was noon housbonde to the Samaritan?
How manye myghte she have in mariage?
Yet herde I nevere tellen in myn age
Upon this nombre diffinicioun.   25
Men may devyne and glosen up and doun,
But wel I woot, expres, withoute lye,
God bad us for to wexe and multiplye;
That gentil text kan I wel understonde.
Eek wel I woot, he seyde myn housbonde   30
Sholde lete fader and mooder and take to me.
But of no nombre mencioun made he,
Of bigamye or of octogamye.
Why sholde men speke of it vileynye?
   Lo, heere the wise kyng, daun Salomon,   35
I trowe he hadde wyves mo than oon.
As wolde God it were leveful unto me
To be refresshed half so ofte as he.
Which yifte of God hadde he for alle his wyvys!
No man hath swich that in this world alyve is.
God woot, this noble kyng, as to my wit,   41
The firste nyght had many a myrie fit
With ech of hem, so wel was hym on lyve.
Yblessed be God that I have wedded fyve,
Of whiche I have pyked out the beste,   44a
Bothe of here nether purs and of here cheste.
Diverse scoles maken parfyt clerkes,
And diverse practyk in many sondry werkes

Maketh the werkman parfit sekirly;
Of fyve husbondes scoleiyng am I.   44f
Welcome the sixte, whan that evere he shal.
For sothe, I wol nat kepe me chaast in al.   46
Whan myn housbonde is fro the world ygon,
Som Cristen man shal wedde me anon,
For thanne th'apostle seith that I am free
To wedde, a Goddes half, where it liketh me.
He seith that to be wedded is no synne;   51
Bet is to be wedded than to brynne.
What rekketh me, thogh folk seye vileynye
Of shrewed Lameth and his bigamye?
I woot wel Abraham was an hooly man,   55
And Jacob eek, as forferth as I kan,
And ech of hem hadde wyves mo than two,
And many another holy man also.
Wher can ye seye, in any manere age,
That hye God defended mariage   60
By expres word? I pray yow, telleth me.
Or where comanded he virginitee?
I woot as wel as ye, it is no drede,
Th'apostel, whan he speketh of maydenhede,
He seyde that precept therof hadde he noon.   65
Men may conseille a womman to been oon,
But conseillyng is nat comandement.
He putte it in oure owene juggement;
For hadde God comanded maydenhede,
Thanne hadde he dampned weddyng with the
   dede.   70
And certain, if ther were no seed ysowe,
Virginitee wherof thanne sholde it growe?
Poul dorste nat comanden, atte leeste,
A thyng of which his maister yaf noon heeste.
The dart is set up for virginitee: 75
Cacche whoso may; who renneth best lat see.

16 repreeve, reproof, John 4:5, but still from Jerome. **18** Hg&c *And that ilke man that now hath thee.* **25 diffinicioun,** Jerome, *non esse uxorum definitum.* **26 devyne . . . glosen,** speculate, explain. **27 expres,** specifically. **28 wexe . . . multiplye,** Gen. 1:28, but also from Jerome. **29** E *wel* om. **30 woot,** know. **31 lete,** leave; Matt. 19:5. The line is hypermetric, E&c *to* om. **33 octogamye,** the term is St. Jerome's. The canonists use these terms to designate successive marriages. **34** Hg&c *thanne speke.* **35 daun,** from Lat. *dom(inus).* I Kings 11:3. **36 trowe,** vow. **37 leveful,** lawful. Hg&c *leveful were.* **39 yifte,** gift—the Wife's Rabelesian imagination at work. **44a–f** Lines not found in EHg&c. Manly III.454 accepts them as later additions by Chaucer; so also ll. 575–84, 605–12, 619–26, 717–20 below. **44b nether . . . cheste,** lower, money box (both terms have *double entendre*). **44d practyk . . . sondry,** practice, different. **44e sekirly,** certainly. **44f scoleiyng,** studying. **46 sothe:** Hg&c *sith,* afterwards (which, with a change in punctuation, produces an interesting reading). **48 anon,** at once. I Cor. 7:9ff., but from Jerome. **51** E&c *that* om. **52 brynne,** burn. **53 rekketh,** do I care. **54 Lameth,** Gen. 4:19; Jerome. **56 forferth . . . kan,** far, know. Hg&c *as fer as ever.* **58** E *holy* om. **59 seye,** say. E&c *Whanne saugh ye evere.* **60 defended,** forbad. **61 expres,** specific. **64 maydenhede,** virginity. E&c *Whan th'apostle speketh.* **65 precept,** divine commandment, cf. I Cor. 7:25, and Jerome. **67 nat:** Hg&c *no.* **70 dampned,** condemned. **71 certain,** Hg&c *certes.* **72** Hg&c *thanne werof sholde.* **74 yaf . . . heeste,** gave, command. **75 dart,** the prize. *for:* E&c *of.*

But this word is nat taken of every wight,
But ther as God lust gyve it of his myght.
I woot wel that th'apostel was a mayde, 79
But nathelees, thogh that he wroot and sayde
He wolde that every wight were swich as he,
Al nys but conseil to virginitee.
And for to been a wyf he yaf me leve
Of indulgence; so it is no repreve
To wedde me if that my make dye, 85
Withoute excepcioun of bigamye.
Al were it good no womman for to touche—
He mente as in his bed or in his couche—
For peril is bothe fyr and tow t'assemble—
Ye knowe what this ensample may resemble. 90
This is al and som: he heeld virginitee
Moore parfit than weddyng in freletee.
Freletee clepe I, but if that he and she
Wolde leden al hir lyf in chastitee.

I graunte it wel, I have noon envie, 95
Thogh maydenhede preferre bigamye.
Hem liketh to be clene, body and goost.
Of myn estaat I nyl nat make no boost,
For wel ye knowe, a lord in his houshold
He nath nat every vessel al of gold; 100
Somme been of tree, and doon hir lord servyse.
God clepeth folk to hym in sondry wyse,
And everich hath of God a propre yifte,
Som this, som that, as hym liketh shifte.

Virginitee is greet perfeccioun, 105
And continence eek with devocioun,
But Crist, that of perfeccioun is welle,
Bad nat every wight he sholde go selle
Al that he hadde and gyve it to the poore,
And in swich wise folwe hym and his foore. 110

He spak to hem that wolde lyve parfitly;
And lordynges, by youre leve, that am nat I.
I wol bistowe the flour of al myn age
In the actes and in fruyt of mariage.

Telle me also, to what conclusioun 115
Were membres ymaad of generacioun,
And of so parfit wys a wight ywroght?
Trusteth right wel, they were nat maad for
noght.
Glose whoso wole and seye bothe up and doun
That they were maked for purgacioun 120
Of uryne, and oure bothe thynges smale
Were eek to knowe a femele from a male,
And for noon oother cause—say ye no?
The experience woot wel it is noght so.
So that the clerkes be nat with me wrothe, 125
I sey this, that they beth maked for bothe,
This is to seye, for office and for ese
Of engendrure, ther we nat God displese.
Why sholde men elles in hir bookes sette
That a man shal yelde to his wyf hire dette? 130
Now wherwith sholde he make his paiement,
If he ne used his sely instrument?
Thanne were they maad upon a creature
To purge uryne, and eek for engendrure.

But I seye noght that every wight is holde,
That hath swich harneys as I to yow tolde, 136
To goon and usen hem in engendrure.
Thanne sholde men take of chastitee no cure.
Crist was a mayde and shapen as a man,
And many a seint sith that the world bigan, 140
Yet lyved they evere in parfit chastitee.
I nyl nat envye no virginitee.
Lat hem be breed of pured whete seed,

77 word . . . taken of, command, enjoined upon. **78 lust . . . myght,** desires, through his strength. **79 woot,** know. E&c *that om.* **84 indulgence,** *Haec autem dico secundum indulgentiam,* I Cor. 7:6. **repreve,** disgrace. Other MSS *nys it/is it.* **85 make,** mate. **86 excepcioun of,** criticism for. **87 womman . . . touche,** I Cor. 7:1; Jerome. **89 tow,** unspun flax. **91** Hg&c *This al.* E&c *that virginitee.* **92 parfit . . . freletee,** perfect, frailty. *parfit:* E&c *profiteth.* **93 clepe,** call it. **96 preferre,** be considered better. **bigamye,** it must be born in mind that in WBP this always means remarriage of a widowed spouse. **97 goost,** spirit. Hg&c *It liketh hem to be clene in.* **98** Hg&c *estaat ne wol I.* **100 nath:** other MSS *ne hath nat/he hath nat.* **101 tree,** wood, cf. II Tim. 2:20. **102 clepeth . . . sondry,** calls, diverse. I Cor. 7:7. **103 propre yifte,** special gift. **104 shifte,** to distribute. **105 perfeccioun,** cf. Rev. 14:4. **107 welle,** source. **108 wight,** person. Matt. 19:21. All of this is from Jerome. E&c *he om;* other MSS *that he.* **110 foore,** footsteps. **113 flour . . . age,** best part, life. **115 conclusioun,** purpose. **117 a wight,** i.e., And created by so wise a Being *or else* And in such perfect manner created a human being. E&c *And for what profit was a;* other MSS have other readings. **119 Glose,** gloss (explain). **121** E&c *Of uryne bothe and thynges smale;* other MSS have other readings. **124 woot,** knows. **125 the:** some MSS *ye.* **126 this:** E *yis.* Hg&c *maked been.* **127 office,** excretion. **130 dette,** i.e., an obligation; cf. I Cor. 7:3–5. Hg&c *a om.* **hire:** some MSS *his.* **132 sely,** a *triple entendre,* innocent, foolish, blessed (OE *gesǣlig*). **135 holde,** obligated. **136 harneys,** equipment. *to yow:* E&c *of.* **138 cure,** care. E *They shul not take.* **139 mayde,** virgin. **143 pured,** refined.

And lat us wyves hoten barly-breed;
And yet with barly-breed, Mark telle kan, 145
Oure Lord Jhesu refresshed many a man.
In swich estaat as God hath cleped us
I wol persevere; I nam nat precius.
In wyfhode I wol use myn instrument
As frely as my Makere hath it sent. 150
If I be daungerous, God yeve me sorwe.
Myn housbonde shal it have bothe eve and
    morwe,
Whan that hym list com forth and paye his
    dette.
An housbonde I wol have, I nyl nat lette,
Which shal be bothe my dettour and my thral,
And have his tribulacioun withal 156
Upon his flessh whil that I am his wyf.
I have the power durynge al my lyf
Upon his propre body, and noght he.
Right thus the Apostel tolde it unto me, 160
And bad oure housbondes for to love us weel.
Al this sentence me liketh every deel—

Up stirte the PARDONER, and that anon:
"Now, dame," quod he, "by God and by Seint
    John,
Ye been a noble prechour in this cas. 165
I was aboute to wedde a wyf. Allas,
What sholde I bye it on my flessh so deere?
Yet hadde I levere wedde no wyf to-yeere."
    "Abyde," quod she, "my tale is nat bigonne.
Nay, thou shalt drynken of another tonne 170
Er that I go, shal savoure wors than ale.
And whan that I have toold thee forth my tale

Of tribulacioun in mariage,
Of which I am expert in al myn age— 174
This is to seyn, myself have been the whippe—
Than maystow chese wheither thou wolt sippe
Of thilke tonne that I shal abroche.
Be war of it, er thou to ny approche,
For I shal telle ensamples mo than ten.
'Whoso that nyl be war by othere men, 180
By hym shul othere men corrected be.'
The same wordes writeth Ptholomee;
Rede in his Almageste and take it there."
    "Dame, I wolde praye yow, if youre wyl it
    were,"
Seyde this Pardoner, "as ye bigan, 185
Telle forth youre tale; spareth for no man,
And teche us yonge men of youre praktike."
    "Gladly," quod she, "sith it may yow like.
But yet I praye to al this compaignye
If that I speke after my fantasye 190
As taketh not agrief of that I seye,
For myn entente nys but for to pleye."

    Now, sire, now wol I telle forth my tale:
As evere moote I drynken wyn or ale,
I shal seye sooth, of tho housbondes that I
    hadde, 195
As thre of hem were goode, and two were
    badde.
The thre men were goode, and riche, and olde.
Unnethe myghte they the statut holde
In which that they were bounden unto me.
Ye woot wel what I meene of this, pardee. 200
As help me God, I laughe whan I thynke

---

144 hoten, be called. **145 Mark,** really John 6:9, and Jerome. **146** E&c *Jhesu* om. **147 cleped,** called. **148 precius,** *double entendre,* i.e., gold (wheat bread), and fastidious. **151 daungerous,** aloof. **152 morwe,** morning. **154 lette,** stop. **155 thral,** slave. **156 tribulacioun,** I Cor. 7:28. **160 Apostel,** Paul, I Cor. 7:4–5 again. **161 love,** Eph. 5:25. **162 sentence me liketh,** pronouncement pleases me. **166 wedde,** recall that in the Gen Pro I.691, the Pardoner is described as impotent. **167 What sholde** etc., i.e., Why should I inflict it on myself at such a cost? **168 levere . . . to-yeere,** rather, this year. **170 tonne,** wine cask. The casks of sweet and bitter wine are described in *RR* 6762ff. (Dunn-Robbins, 32.131); by Gower, *Confessio Amantis* 6.333, 8.2253; and elsewhere. **172** E&c *thee* om. **173** E&c *tribulacioun that is in.* **174 expert . . . age,** expert throughout my life. **177 abroche,** tap (broach). *thilke:* E *that.* **180–81 be war . . . By hym,** i.e., be admonished by other man's experience, by his experience. **182 Ptholomee,** this proverb and that at l. 326 are found in the preface to the 1515 Venice edition of Ptolemy's *Almageste* (cf. *CT,* I.3280). EHg&c *Protholomee,* possibly from a careless flourish on the original P, but see III.2289 below. **184** E&c *yow* om. **186 spareth,** spare (stop). **187 praktike,** experience (practice). **188 sith . . . yow like,** since, you please. *quod she:* E&c *sires.* **189** *yet:* Hg&c *that.* **190 fantasye,** fancy (whim). **191 agrief,** amiss. E&c *of* om. **192** *nys:* E&c *is.* **193 forth my tale,** at this point, the text begins to incorporate illustrations from Deschamps and Matheolus, with *RR* always in the background. *now wol/forth:* Hg&c *thanne wol/yow forth.* **195** Hg&c *of* om. **197** *men* found in various places in MSS—inserted with a caret in the margin of the original? **198 Unnethe . . . statut,** barely, obligation (the marriage debt, cf. l. 130 above.)

How pitously a-nyght I made hem swynke!
And, by my fey, I tolde of it no stoor;
They had me yeven hir lond and hir tresoor.
Me neded nat do lenger diligence 205
To wynne hir love, or doon hem reverence.
They loved me so wel, by God above,
That I ne tolde no deyntee of hir love.
A wys womman wol sette hire evere in oon
To gete hire love, ye, ther as she hath noon. 210
But sith I hadde hem hoolly in myn hond,
And sith they hadde me yeven al hir lond,
What sholde I taken heede hem for to plese
But it were for my profit and myn ese?
I sette hem so a-werke, by my fey, 215
That many a nyght they songen "weilawey."
The bacon was nat fet for hem, I trowe,
That som men han in Essex at Dunmowe.
I governed hem so wel, after my lawe,
That ech of hem ful blisful was and fawe 220
To brynge me gaye thynges fro the fayre.
They were ful glad whan I spak to hem faire,
For, God it woot, I chidde hem spitously.
    Now herkneth hou I baar me proprely,
Ye wise wyves, that kan understonde. 225
Thus shul ye speke and bere hem wrong on
    honde,
For half so boldely kan ther no man
Swere and lyen as a womman kan.
I sey nat this by wyves that been wyse,
But if it be whan they hem mysavyse. 230
A wys wyf, if that she kan hir good,
Shal beren hym on hond the cow is wood,
And take witnesse of hir owene mayde
Of hir assent. But herkneth how I sayde:
    Sire olde kaynard, is this thyn array? 235

Why is my neighebores wyf so gay?
She is honoured over al ther she gooth;
I sitte at hoom; I have no thrifty clooth.
What dostow at my neighebores hous?
Is she so fair? Artow so amorous? 240
What rowne ye with oure mayde, benedicite?
Sire olde lecchour, lat thy japes be.
And if I have a gossib or a freend
Withouten gilt, thou chidest as a feend
If that I walke or pleye unto his hous. 245
Thou comest hoom as dronken as a mous
And prechest on thy bench with yvel preef.
Thou seist to me it is a greet meschief
To wedde a poure womman for costage;
And if that she be riche, of heigh parage, 250
Thanne seistow that it is a tormentrie
To suffren hire pride and hire malencolie.
And if that she be fair, thou verray knave,
Thou seyst that every holour wol hire have;
She may no while in chastitee abyde 255
That is assailled upon ech a syde.
    Thou seyst som folk desire us for richesse,
Somme for oure shap, and somme for oure
    fairnesse,
And som for she kan synge and daunce,
And som for gentillesse and daliaunce, 260
Som for hir handes and hir armes smale—
Thus goth al to the devel, by thy tale.
Thou seyst men may nat kepe a castel wal
It may so longe assailed been over al.
    And if that she be foul, thou seist that she 265
Coveiteth every man that she may se,
For as a spaynel she wol on hym lepe
Til that she fynde som man hire to chepe.
Ne noon so grey goos gooth ther in the lake

202 **swynke**, labor. 203 **tolde ... stoor**, took no account. 204 *lond:* E *gold.* 205 **do ... diligence**, make an effort. 208 **tolde no deyntee**, placed no value. 209 **in oon**, constantly. *sette:* Hg&c *bisye.* 210 **gete hire ... ther**, get for herself, where. E&c *ye* om. 212 Hg&c *sith that/yeven me.* 213 *heede:* Hg&c *keep.* 215 **fey**, faith. 217 **fet ... trowe**, fetched, vow. 218 **Essex**, At Dunmow in Essex, and at other places, a couple who had not quarreled for a year could claim a side of bacon. 220 **fawe**, eager. 223 **chidde ... spitously**, scolded, spitefully. 226 **bere ... honde**, accuse falsely. *shul:* Hg&c *scholde;* E&c *wrong* om. 228 E&c *as kan a womman.* 229 **by**, about. 230 **mysavyse**, i.e., make a misstep. 231 **kan hir good**, i.e., knows what's good for her. 232 **beren ... hond, cow is wood**, argue falsely, chough (crow) is crazy—an allusion to the tale of the bird who tattled on his mistress. This is the theme of MancT, Part IX below. 234 **Of hir assent**, that she (the maid) agrees. 235 **kaynard ... array**, sluggard, arrangement (or literally "clothes," in view of the next three lines). Parallels to what follows are in Deschamps and Mathelous, as well as Theophrastus and Jerome. 236 **gay**, gaily dressed. 238 **thrifty clooth**, suitable clothes. 241 **rowne**, whisper. 242 **japes**, jokes. 243 **gossib**, intimate friend ("God-relation," like "Godchild"). 244 Hg&c *ye chiden.* 247 **with yvel preef**, with poor proof (i.e., for no reason). 248ff. Illustrations from Deschamps, *RR,* and Theophrastus. 249 **costage**, expense. 250 **parage**, peerage (lineage). E&c *that* om., *and of.* 251 **tormentrie**, a torment. E&c *that* om. 252 **malencolie**, sullenness (one of the four humors). Hg&c *suffre.* 254 **holour**, fornicator. 258 E&c *and* om. 259 Hg&c *kan either synge or.* 260 **gentillesse and daliaunce**, refinement and pleasantness. 263 **kepe**, defend. 265 **foul**, ugly. 268 **chepe**, take (do business with). 269 E&c *ther* om.

As, seistow, wol been withoute make.   270
And seyst it is an hard thyng for to welde
A thyng that no man wole, his thankes, helde.
Thus seistow, lorel, whan thow goost to bedde,
And that no wys man nedeth for to wedde,
Ne no man that entendeth unto hevene—   275
With wilde thonder-dynt and firy levene
Moote thy welked nekke be tobroke!
    Thow seyst that droppyng houses and eek
        smoke
And chidyng wyves maken men to flee
Out of hir owene hous—a, benedicitee!   280
What eyleth swich an old man for to chide?
    Thow seyst we wyves wol oure vices hide
Til we be fast, and thanne we wol hem
        shewe—
Wel may that be a proverbe of a shrewe!
    Thou seist that oxen, asses, hors, and houndes,
They been assayed at diverse stoundes;   286
Bacyns, lavours, er that men hem bye,
Spoones and stooles, and al swich housbondrye,
And so been pottes, clothes, and array;
But folk of wyves maken noon assay,   290
Til they be wedded—olde dotard shrewe!
Thanne, seistow, we wol oure vices shewe.
    Thou seist also that it displeseth me
But if that thou wolt preyse my beautee,
And but thou poure alwey upon my face   295
And clepe me "faire dame" in every place,
And but thou make a feeste on thilke day
That I was born, and make me fressh and gay,
And but thou do to my norice honour,
And to my chamberere withinne my bour,   300
And to my fadres folk and his allyes—
Thus seistow, olde barelful of lyes!
    And yet of oure apprentice Janekyn,
For his crisp heer, shynynge as gold so fyn,

And for he squiereth me bothe up and doun,
Yet hastow caught a fals suspicioun.   306
I wol hym noght, thogh thou were deed
        tomorwe.
    But tel me, why hydestow with sorwe
The keyes of thy cheste awey fro me?
It is my good as wel as thyn, pardee.   310
What, wenestow to make an ydiot of oure dame?
Now by that lord that called is Seint Jame,
Thou shalt nat bothe, thogh that thou were
        wood,
Be maister of my body and of my good;   314
That oon thou shalt forgo, maugree thyne eyen.
What needeth thee of me to enquere or spyen?
I trowe thou woldest loke me in thy chiste.
Thou sholdest seye, "Wyf, go where thee liste;
Taak youre disport, I wol nat leve no talys.
I knowe yow for a trewe wyf, dame Alys."   320
We love no man that taketh kepe or charge
Wher that we goon; we wol ben at oure large.
    Of alle men yblessed moot he be,
The wise astrologien, daun Ptholome,
That seith this proverbe in his Almageste,   325
"Of alle men his wysdom is the hyeste
That rekketh nevere who hath the world in
        honde."
By this proverbe thou shalt understonde,
Have thou ynogh, what thar thee recche or
        care
How myrily that othere folkes fare?   330
For certeyn, olde dotard, by youre leve,
Ye shul have queynte right ynogh at eve.
He is to greet a nygard that wolde werne
A man to lighte a candle at his lanterne;
He shal have never the lasse light, pardee.   335
Have thou ynogh, thee thar nat pleyne thee.
Thou seyst also that if we make us gay

270 make, mate. **271–72 welde . . . his thankes, helde,** use, willingly, hold. Hg&c *wolde/holde.* **273 lorel,** wretch. **275 entendeth,** wants to go. **276 dynt . . . levene,** blow, lightning. **277 Moote . . . welked,** may, withered. **278 droppyng,** leaking. A widely repeated aphorism, cf. *Mel.* VII.1086, and Prov. 27:15. **279 chidyng,** scolding. **282** E&c *that we.* **283 fast,** secure (married). **286 assayed . . . stoundes,** tried out, occasions. **287 Bacyns, lavours,** basins, washbowls. **288** *and stooles:* Hg&c *and om.* **289 array,** equipment. **292** Hg&c *And thanne.* **294 But if,** unless. **295 poure,** pore (gaze). **299 norice,** nurse. **300 chamberere . . . bour,** chambermaid, bedroom. **301 allyes,** relatives. **304–05 For . . . for,** because of, because. **307 wol,** desire. **308 hydestow . . . sorwe,** do you hide, pain (irritation). Hg&c *tel me this.* **310 good,** goods (property). **311 wenestow,** do you think. Hg&c *to om.* **313 wood,** mad (furious). E&c *that om.* **315 maugree,** in spite of. **316** Hg&c *helpeth it of me enquere.* **317 loke,** lock. **318 liste,** please. **319 disport . . . leve . . . talys,** pleasure, believe, tales. E&c *nat om.;* Hg&c *nyl leve no.* **320 Alys,** Alice. **321 kepe or charge,** notice or heed. **322 at . . . large,** free. **324 Ptholome,** see note to l. 182 above. **327 rekketh . . . honde,** cares, in control. *nevere:* Hg&c *nat.* **329 Have thou . . . recche,** if you have, care. **331** *certeyn:* Hg&c *certes.* **332 queynte,** sex. **333 werne,** refuse. **334** E&c *his candle.* **336 pleyne,** complain.

With clothyng and with precious array
That it is peril of oure chastitee;
And yet with sorwe, thou most enforce thee, 340
And seye thise wordes in the Apostles name,
"In habit maad with chastitee and shame
Ye wommen shul apparaille yow," quod he,
"And noght in tressed heer and gay perree,
As perles, ne with gold, ne clothes riche." 345
After thy text, ne after thy rubriche,
I wol nat wirche as muchel as a gnat.

　　Thou seydest this, that I was lyk a cat;
For whoso wolde senge a cattes skyn
Thanne wolde the cat wel dwellen in his in, 350
And if the cattes skyn be slyk and gay
She wol nat dwelle in house half a day,
But forth she wole, er any day be dawed,
To shewe hir skyn and goon a-caterwawed.
This is to seye, if I be gay, sire shrewe, 355
I wol renne out my borel for to shewe.

　　Sire olde fool, what helpeth thee to spyen?
Thogh thou preye Argus with his hundred
　　eyen
To be my warde-cors, as he kan best,
In feith, he shal nat kepe me but me lest; 360
Yet koude I make his berd, so moot I thee!

　　Thou seydest eek that ther been thynges thre
The whiche thynges troublen al this erthe,
And that no wight may endure the ferthe—
O leeve sire shrewe, Jhesu shorte thy lyf! 365
Yet prechestow and seyst an hateful wyf
Yrekened is for oon of thise meschances.
Been ther none othere maner resemblances
That ye may likne youre parables to,
But if a sely wyf be oon of tho? 370

　　Thou liknest eek wommenes love to helle,
To bareyne lond, ther water may nat dwelle.

Thou liknest it also to wilde fyr,
The moore it brenneth, the moore it hath desir
To consume every thyng that brent wole be.
Thou seyest, right as wormes shende a tree, 376
Right so a wyf destroyeth hire housbonde;
This knowe they that been to wyves bonde.

　　Lordynges, right thus, as ye have understonde,
Baar I stifly myne olde housbondes on honde
That thus they seyden in hir dronkenesse—
And al was fals, but that I took witnesse 382
On Janekyn and on my nece also.
O Lord, the peyne I dide hem and the wo,
Ful giltelees, by Goddes sweete pyne! 385
For as an hors I koude byte and whyne.
I koude pleyne, thogh I were in the gilt,
Or elles often tyme hadde I been spilt.
Whoso comth first to mille, first grynt;
I pleyned first, so was oure werre ystynt. 390
They were ful glad to excuse hem blyve
Of thyng of which they nevere agilte hir lyve.

　　Of wenches wolde I beren hym on honde,
Whan that for syk unnethes myghte he stonde.
Yet tikled it his herte, for that he 395
Wende that I hadde of hym so greet chiertee.
I swoor that al my walkynge out by nyghte
Was for t'espye wenches that he dighte.
Under that colour hadde I many a myrthe.
For al swich wit is yeven us in oure byrthe: 400
Deceite, wepyng, spynnyng God hath yeve
To wommen kyndely whil that they may lyve.
And thus of o thyng I avaunte me,
Atte ende I hadde the bettre in ech degree,
By sleighte or force, or by som maner thyng,
As by continueel murmur or grucchyng. 406
Namely abedde hadden they meschaunce.
Ther wolde I chide and do hem no plesaunce;

340 sorwe . . . enforce, miserably, reinforce. **342 habit,** clothes, cf. I Tim. 2:9, but from Deschamps. **344 tressed . . . perree,** dressed, jewels. **346 After . . . rubriche,** according to, the portion of the text is red for emphasis. **347 wirche,** behave. **349 senge,** singe; the figure is in both Deschamps and Matheolus. **350 wel . . . in,** completely, dwelling. **353 dawed,** dawned. **354 a-caterwawed,** caterwauling. **355 gay,** gaily attired. **356 borel,** wardrobe (really a kind of coarse cloth). **357 helpeth:** E&c *eyleth.* **358 Argus,** hundred-eyed watchman over Io in Ovid, *Met.* 1.625. **359 warde-cors,** bodyguard. **360 kepe . . . lest,** guard, desire. **361 make . . . berd,** deceive. **thee,** prosper. **364 wight . . . ferthe,** person, fourth; Prov. 30:21–23, again quoting Jerome. **365 leeve . . . shorte,** dear, shorten. **367 Yrekened is,** is counted. **368 resemblances,** comparisons. **370 But if . . . sely . . . tho,** but must, innocent, those (comparisons). **371** E&c *eek* om; Hg&c *wommanes.* **374 brenneth,** burns. **375 brent wole,** can be burned. **380 Baar . . . honde,** accuse. **382 but that,** except that. **385 pyne,** pain. **387** Hg&c *and I was in.* **388 spilt,** ruined. **389 grynt,** grinds. Hg&c *that first to mille comth.* **390 pleyned . . . werre ystynt,** complained, war stopped. **391 blyve,** quickly. **392 agilte hir lyve,** guilty in their lives. **393 beren . . . honde,** accuse. Hg&c *hem.* **394 syk unnethes,** illness (feebleness) barely. Hg&c *they myghte unnethe.* **395 it:** Hg&c *I.* **396 Wende . . . chiertee,** thought, love. **398 dighte,** meddle with (had intercourse). **399 colour,** pretense. **402 kyndely,** naturally. **403 avaunte,** boast. **405 sleighte,** trickery. **406 grucchyng,** complaining. **408 chide . . . plesaunce,** scold, pleasure.

I wolde no lenger in the bed abyde
If that I felte his arm over my syde 410
Til he had maad his raunsoun unto me;
Thanne wolde I suffre hym do his nycetee.
And therfore every man this tale I telle,
Wynne whoso may, for al is for to selle;
With empty hand men may none haukes lure.
For wynnyng wolde I al his lust endure 416
And make me a feyned appetit—
And yet in bacon hadde I nevere delit.
That made me that evere I wolde hem chide;
For thogh the pope hadde seten hem biside, 420
I wolde nat spare hem at hir owene bord,
For, by my trouthe, I quitte hem word for
     word.
As helpe me verray God omnipotent,
Though I right now sholde make my testament,
I ne owe hem nat a word that it nys quit. 425
I broghte it so aboute by my wit
That they moste yeve it up as for the beste,
Or elles hadde we nevere been in reste.
For thogh he looked as a wood leoun,
Yet sholde he faille of his conclusioun. 430
     Thanne wolde I seye, "Goode lief, taak keep,
How mekely looketh Wilkyn, oure sheep!
Com neer, my spouse, lat me ba thy cheke!
Ye sholde been al pacient and meke,
And han a sweete spiced conscience, 435
Sith ye so preche of Jobes pacience.
Suffreth alwey, syn ye so wel kan preche;
And but ye do, certein we shal yow teche
That it is fair to have a wyf in pees.
Oon of us two moste bowen, doutelees, 440
And sith a man is moore resonable
Than womman is, ye moste been suffrable.
What eyleth yow to grucche thus and grone?

Is it for ye wolde have my queynte allone?
Wy, taak it al—lo, have it every deel. 445
Peter, I shrewe yow, but ye love it weel.
For if I wolde selle my bele chose,
I koude walke as fressh as is a rose,
But I wol kepe it for youre owene tooth.
Ye be to blame, by God, I sey yow sooth." 450
     Swiche manere wordes hadde we on honde.
Now wol I speken of my fourthe housbonde.
     My fourthe housbonde was a revelour—
This is to seyn, he hadde a paramour,
And I was yong and ful of ragerye, 455
Stibourne and strong, and joly as a pye.
Wel koude I daunce to an harpe smale,
And synge, ywis, as any nyghtyngale,
Whan I had dronke a draughte of sweete wyn.
Metellius, the foule cherl, the swyn, 460
That with a staf birafte his wyf hir lyf
For she drank wyn, thogh I hadde been his wyf,
He sholde nat han daunted me fro drynke!
And after wyn on Venus moste I thynke,
For al so siker as cold engendreth hayl, 465
A likerous mouth moste han a likerous tayl.
In wommen vinolent is no defence—
This knowen lecchours by experience.
     But, Lord Crist, whan that it remembreth me
Upon my yowthe and on my jolitee, 470
It tikleth me about myn herte roote.
Unto this day it dooth myn herte boote
That I have had my world as in my tyme.
But age, allas, that al wole envenyme,
Hath me biraft my beautee and my pith. 475
Lat go, farewel, the devel go therwith!
The flour is goon, ther is namoore to telle;
The bren, as I best kan, now moste I selle;
But yet to be right myrie wol I fonde.

---

411 maad . . . raunsoun, i.e., given in to. **412 nycetee,** foolishness (sex). **414 for to selle,** for sale. **416 wynnyng,** i.e., in the abstract, but also money (material gain). **417 feyned,** pretended. **418 bacon,** old meat (vs. fresh meat), a euphemism. **419 chide,** scold. **420 seten . . . biside,** sat beside them. **422 quitte,** repaid. **424 testament,** last will. **429 wood,** mad. **430 faille . . . conclusioun,** i.e., not get what he wants. **431 Goode lief . . . keep,** good friend, heed. **432 Wilkyn,** condescending diminutive of William. **433 ba,** kiss. **435 spiced conscience,** affected conscience (i.e., able to put up with anything). **439 fair,** well. **440 moste bowen,** must bow. **442 suffrable,** patient. **443 grucche,** complain. **444 queynte,** genitalia. **446 Peter . . . shrewe,** St. Peter (*double entendre?*), curse. **447 bele chose,** Fr. *lovely thing,* a euphemism. **450 sooth,** truth. **453 revelour,** reveler. **454 paramour,** mistress. **455 ragerye,** high spirits (passion). **456 Stibourne . . . pye,** stubborn (wild), magpie. **457 smale,** wantonly. *Wel:* other MSS *How/ Lord how.* **460 Metellius,** an incident from a medieval schoolbook, the *Memorabilium Exempla* of Valerius Maximus. Chaucer quotes from the same chapter (vi c.3) at ll. 642 and 647 below. **463 daunted,** frightened. *He:* Hg&c *Ne.* **464 Venus,** i.e., sex. **moste,** must. **465 siker,** surely. **466 likerous,** lecherous (*double entendre* with *licour,* drink). **467 vinolent,** intoxicated. Hg&c *womman.* **472 boote,** good. **474 envenyme,** poison. **477–78 flour . . . bren,** flour, bran. **479 fonde,** strive.

Now wol I tellen of my fourthe housbonde.   480
  I seye, I hadde in herte greet despit
That he of any oother had delit.
But he was quit, by God and by Seint Joce.
I made hym of the same wode a croce—
Nat of my body, in no foul manere,   485
But certeinly, I made folk swich cheere
That in his owene grece I made hym frye
For angre, and for verray jalousye.
By God, in erthe I was his purgatorie,
For which I hope his soule be in glorie.   490
For, God it woot, he sat ful ofte and song
Whan that his shoo ful bitterly hym wrong.
There was no wight save God and he that
    wiste,
In many wise, how soore I hym twiste.
He deyde whan I cam fro Jerusalem,   495
And lith ygrave under the roode beem,
Al is his tombe noght so curyus
As was the sepulcre of hym Daryus,
Which that Appelles wroghte subtilly;
It nys but wast to burye hym preciously.   500
Lat hym fare wel; God yeve his soule reste.
He is now in his grave and in his cheste.
  Now of my fifthe housbonde wol I telle.
God lete his soule nevere come in helle—
And yet was he to me the mooste shrewe;   505
That feele I on my ribbes al by rewe,
And evere shal unto myn endyng day.
But in oure bed he was so fresshe and gay,
And therwithal so wel koude he me glose,
Whan that he wolde han my bele chose,   510
That thogh he hadde me bet on every bon,
He koude wynne agayn my love anon.
I trowe I loved hym best for that he
Was of his love daungerous to me.
We wommen han, if that I shal nat lye,   515
In this matere a queynte fantasye:

Wayte what thyng we may nat lightly have,
Therafter wol we crie al day and crave.
Forbede us thyng, and that desiren we;
Preesse on us faste, and thanne wol we fle.   520
With daunger oute we al oure chaffare;
Greet prees at market maketh deere ware,
And to greet cheep is holde at litel prys.
This knoweth every womman that is wys.
  My fifthe housbonde—God his soule
    blesse—   525
Which that I took for love and no richesse,
He somtyme was a clerk of Oxenford,
And hadde left scole, and wente at hom to
    bord
With my gossib, dwellynge in oure toun—
God have hir soule—hir name was Alisoun;
She knew myn herte and eek my privetee   531
Bet than oure parisshe preest, so moot I thee!
To hire biwreyed I my conseil al.
For hadde myn housbonde pissed on a wal,
Or doon a thyng that sholde han cost his lyf,
To hire, and to another worthy wyf,   536
And to my nece, which that I loved weel,
I wolde han toold his conseil every deel.
And so I dide ful often, God it woot,
That made his face ful often reed and hoot   540
For verray shame, and blamed hymself for he
Had toold to me so greet a pryvetee.
  And so bifel that ones in a Lente—
So often tymes I to my gossyb wente,
For evere yet I loved to be gay,   545
And for to walke in March, Averill, and May,
Fro hous to hous, to heere sondry talys—
That Jankyn clerk and my gossyb dame Alys
And I myself into the feeldes wente.
Myn housbonde was at Londoun al the Lente;
I hadde the bettre leyser for to pleye,   551
And for to se, and eek for to be seye

---

481 despit, resentment. **483 quit,** repaid. **Seint Joce,** a Breton saint. **484 croce,** stick (to beat him with), *double entendre* cross (to hang him on). **486 cheere,** amorous invitation. **489 purgatorie,** a common figure for marriage in the antifeminist tradition, cf. esp. Matheolus iii.1673ff. **492 wrong,** wrung (pinched). **493 wiste,** knew. **496 ygrave . . . roode beem,** buried; the beam between nave and chancel on which hung a crucifix. **497 Al . . . curyus,** Although, elaborate. **498–99 Daryus . . . Appelles,** as indicated by a marginal gloss in E, Chaucer's knowledge of Darius' legendary tomb is from Gautier de Chatillon's *Alexandreis.* **500 preciously,** expensively. **505 mooste shrewe,** most quarrelsome person. **506 by rewe,** in a row. **508** *so:* E&c *ful.* **509 glose,** beguile (cajole). **510 bele chose,** cf. l. 447 above. **512 anon,** immediately. **514 daungerous,** aloof. **516 queynte fantasye,** strange desire. **517 Wayte what . . . lightly have,** whatever, easily get. **520 Preesse on,** chase after. **521 daunger . . . chaffare,** standoffishness, merchandise. **522 prees . . . deere,** crowd, expensive. **523 cheep,** a bargain. **529 gossib,** intimate friend, cf. l. 243 above. **532 thee,** prosper. **533 biwreyed . . . conseil,** revealed, confidences. **540** Hg&c *ful* om. **550** *the:* Hg&c *that.* **552 be seye,** be seen.

Of lusty folk. What wiste I wher my grace
Was shapen for to be, or in what place?
Therfore I made my visitaciouns 555
To vigilies and to processiouns,
To prechyng eek, and to thise pilgrimages,
To pleyes of myracles, and to mariages,
And wered upon my gaye scarlet gytes—
Thise wormes, ne thise motthes, ne thise mytes,
Upon my peril, frete hem never a deel; 561
And wostow why? For they were used weel.
    Now wol I tellen forth what happed me.
I seye that in the feeldes walked we,
Til trewely we hadde swich daliance, 565
This clerk and I, that of my purveiance
I spak to hym and seyde hym how that he,
If I were wydwe, sholde wedde me.
For certeinly, I sey for no bobance,
Yet was I nevere withouten purveiance 570
Of mariage, n'of othere thynges eek.
I holde a mouses herte nat worth a leek
That hath but oon hole for to sterte to,
And if that faille, thanne is al ydo.
    I bar hym on honde he hadde enchanted
        me— 575
My dame taughte me that soutiltee.
And eek I seyde I mette of hym al nyght:
He wolde han slayn me as I lay upright,
And al my bed was ful of verray blood,
But yet I hope that he shal do me good, 580
For blood bitokeneth gold, as me was
        taught—
And al was fals; I dremed of it right naught,
But I folwed ay my dames loore,
As wel of this as of othere thynges moore.
    But now, sire, lat me se, what I shal seyn?
Aha, by God, I have my tale ageyn! 586

Whan that my fourthe housbonde was on
        beere,
I weep algate and made sory cheere,
As wyves mooten for it is usage,
And with my coverchief covered my visage, 590
But for that I was purveyed of a make,
I wepte but smal, and that I undertake.
    To chirche was myn housbonde born
        a-morwe
With neighebores that for hym maden sorwe,
And Jankyn oure clerk was oon of tho. 595
As help me God, whan that I saugh hym go
After the beere, me thoughte he hadde a paire
Of legges and of feet so clene and faire
That al myn herte I yaf unto his hoold.
He was, I trowe, a twenty wynter oold, 600
And I was fourty, if I shal seye sooth;
But yet I hadde alwey a coltes tooth.
Gat-tothed I was, and that bicam me weel;
I hadde the prente of Seinte Venus seel.
As help me God, I was a lusty oon, 605
And faire and riche and yong and wel bigon,
And trewely, as myne housbondes tolde me,
I hadde the beste quonyam myghte be.
For certes, I am al Venerien
In feelynge, and myn herte is Marcien. 610
Venus me yaf my lust, my likerousnesse,
And Mars yaf me my sturdy hardynesse.
Myn ascendent was Taur, and Mars
        therinne—
Allas, allas, that evere love was synne!
I folwed ay myn inclinacioun 615
By vertu of my constellacioun,
That made me I koude noght withdrawe
My chambre of Venus from a goode felawe.
Yet have I Martes mark upon my face,

553 **What wiste . . . grace,** how did I know, good fortune. 554 **shapen,** destined. 556 **vigilies,** services preceding religious holidays. 559 **wered upon . . . gytes,** wore, gowns. 561 **frete,** ate, cf. *CT* II.475. 566 **purveiance,** providence (planning ahead). 569 **bobance,** boast. 575–84 Lines found only in E&c. 575 **bar . . . honde,** persuaded him to think. 576 **dame,** mother. 577 **mette,** dreamed. 578 **upright,** on my back. 579 **verray,** real. 583 Some E-related MSS have *But as.* 585 *sha :* some MSS *should.* 587 **beere,** bier. 588 **algate . . . cheere,** continuously, behavior. 589 **mooten . . . usage,** must, customary. 591 **for that . . . purveyed . . . make,** because, provided, mate. 592 **undertake,** guarantee. 596 **go,** walk. 599 **hoold,** possession. 602 **coltes tooth,** youthful desires, cf. *CT* I.3888. 603 **Gat-tothed,** gap-toothed, evidence of a sensuous nature, cf. *CT* I.468. 604 **seel,** a birthmark. 606 **wel bigon,** well situated. 608 **quonyam,** Lat. *quoniam* meaning "because," "whereas," used like *bele chose* (l. 510) as a euphemism for genitalia. 609–12 Lines found only in E&c. 609 **Venerien,** under the influence of Venus (sex). Curry, *Chaucer and the Medieval Sciences,* Ch. 5, argues that the character of the Wife of Bath is based directly upon her horoscope. 610 **Marcien,** under the influence of Mars (courage). 611 **likerousnesse,** sensuousness (with *double entendre* of promiscuity). 612 **hardynesse,** vigor, audacity. 613 **ascendent . . . Taur,** favorable sign of the zodiac, Taurus (the bull). 616 **constellacioun,** i.e., influence of a special configuration of the stars. 619–26 Lines found only in E&c. 619 **Martes mark,** Mars's, cf. l. 604.

And also in another privee place.   620
For God so wys be my savacioun,
I ne loved nevere by no discrecioun,
But evere folwede myn appetit,
Al were he short, or long, or blak, or whit;
I took no kepe, so that he liked me,   625
How poore he was, ne eek of what degree.

What sholde I seye but at the monthes ende
This joly clerk Jankyn that was so hende
Hath wedded me with greet solempnytee,
And to hym yaf I al the lond and fee   630
That evere was me yeven therbifoore—
But afterward repented me ful soore.
He nolde suffre nothyng of my list;
By God, he smoot me ones on the lyst,
For that I rente out of his book a leef,   635
That of the strook myn ere wax al deef.
Stibourne I was as is a leonesse,
And of my tonge a verray jangleresse,
And walke I wolde, as I had doon biforn,   639
From hous to hous, although he had it
    sworn;
For which he often tymes wolde preche,
And me of olde Romayn geestes teche;
How he Symplicius Gallus lefte his wyf,
And hire forsook for terme of al his lyf,
Noght but for open-heveded he hir say   645
Lokynge out at his dore upon a day.

Another Romayn tolde he me by name
That for his wyf was at a someres game
Withouten his wityng, he forsook hire eke.
And thanne wolde he upon his Bible seke   650
That ilke proverbe of Ecclesiaste
Where he comandeth and forbedeth faste
Man shal nat suffre his wyf go roule aboute.

Thanne wolde he seye right thus, withouten
    doute:
"Whoso that buyldeth his hous al of salwes,
And priketh his blynde hors over the
    falwes,   656
And suffreth his wyf to go seken halwes,
Is worthy to been hanged on the galwes."
But al for noght; I sette noght an hawe
Of his proverbes n'of his olde sawe,   660
Ne I wolde nat of hym corrected be.
I hate hym that my vices telleth me,
And so doo mo, God woot, of us than I.
This made hym with me wood al outrely.
I nolde noght forbere hym in no cas.   665

Now wol I seye yow sooth, by Seint Thomas,
Why that I rente out of his book a leef,
For which he smoot me so that I was deef.

He hadde a book that gladly, nyght and day,
For his desport he wolde rede alway.   670
He cleped it Valerie and Theofraste,
At which book he lough alwey ful faste.
And eek ther was somtyme a clerk at Rome,
A cardinal, that highte Seint Jerome,
That made a book agayn Jovinian;   675
In which book eek ther was Tertulan,
Crisippus, Trotula, and Helowys,
That was abbesse nat fer fro Parys;
And eek the Parables of Salomon,
Ovides Art, and bookes many on.   680
And alle thise were bounden in o volume,
And every nyght and day was his custume,
Whan he hadde leyser and vacacioun
From oother worldly occupacioun,
To reden on this book of wikked wyves.   685
He knew of hem mo legendes and lyves

625 kepe, heed. **628 hende,** handy (adroit), cf. hende Nicholas, *CT* I.3199ff. **630 fee,** wealth. **633 list,** desire. **634 lyst,** ear (OE "hlyst," hearing; cf. "listen"). **638 jangleresse,** loud mouth. **640 sworn,** i.e., forsworn, forbidden. **642 Romayn geestes,** the allusions here and at l. 647 are to Valerious Maximus, as at l. 460 above. **645 open-heveded,** bare-headed. **648 someres game,** midsummer revels. **649 wityng,** knowledge. **652 faste,** firmly; Eccl.25:25. **653 roule,** roam. **655 salwes,** willow withes—this jingle was proverbial. **656 falwes,** fallow (plowed) fields. **657 suffreth . . . halwes,** allows, shrines. **658 galwes,** gallows. **659 hawe,** hawthorne berry. **660** *sawe:* E&c *lawe.* **664 wood . . . outrely,** mad, utterly. **665 nolde . . . forbere,** would not, tolerate. **668 deef,** cf. *CT* I.466. **670 desport,** relaxation. **671 Valerie and Theofraste,** Walter Map's *Disuasio Valerii ad Rufinum* and Theophrastus' *Liber de Nuptiis,* see note to l. 3 above. More than 60 medieval manuscripts are extant containing various combinations of and selections from the anti-feminist materials listed in ll. 671–80. These were evidently compiled to promote celibacy of the clergy and to persuade young men to take holy orders rather than marry. **672 lough,** laughed. **674–75 Jerome . . . Jovinian,** St. Jerome, *Epistola adversus Jovinianum.* **676 Tertulan,** Tertullian, mentioned by Jerome as an antifeminist writer, although his treatises are not quoted in WBP. **677 Crisippus,** mentioned by Jerome, but otherwise unidentified. **Trotula,** identified as a woman physician of Salerno who wrote a treatise on the diseases of women. **Helowys,** Heloise, whose *Letters* gave reasons for her not wanting to marry Abelard. **679 Parables,** the Book of Proverbs. **680 Ovides Art,** Ovid's *Ars Amatoria.*

Than been of goode wyves in the Bible.
For trusteth wel, it is an inpossible
That any clerk wol speke good of wyves,
But if it be of hooly seintes lyves,   690
Ne of noon oother womman never the mo.
Who peyntede the leon, tel me who?
By God, if wommen hadde writen stories,
As clerkes han withinne hire oratories,
They wolde han writen of men moore
      wikkednesse   695
Than al the mark of Adam may redresse.
The children of Mercurie and of Venus
Been in hir wirkyng ful contrarius:
Mercurie loveth wysdam and science,
And Venus loveth ryot and dispence,   700
And for hire diverse disposicioun
Ech falleth in otheres exaltacioun.
And thus, God woot, Mercurie is desolat
In Pisces wher Venus is exaltat,
And Venus falleth ther Mercurie is reysed. 705
Therfore no womman of no clerk is preysed.
The clerk, whan he is oold and may noght do
Of Venus werkes worth his olde sho,
Thanne sit he doun and writ in his dotage
That wommen kan nat kepe hir mariage.   710
   But now to purpos, why I tolde thee
That I was beten for a book, pardee!
Upon a nyght Jankyn, that was oure sire,
Redde on his book, as he sat by the fire,
Of Eva first, that for hir wikkednesse   715
Was al mankynde broght to wrecchednesse,
For which that Jhesu Crist hymself was slayn
That boghte us with his herte blood agayn—

Lo, heere expres of womman may ye fynde
That womman was the los of al mankynde.   720
Tho redde he me how Sampson loste his heres:
Slepynge, his lemman kitte it with hir sheres,
Thurgh which treson loste he bothe his eyen.
   Tho redde he me, if that I shal nat lyen,
Of Hercules and of his Dianyre,   725
That caused hym to sette hymself afyre.
   Nothyng forgat he the sorwe and the wo
That Socrates hadde with his wyves two,
How Xantippa caste pisse upon his heed.
This sely man sat stille as he were deed;   730
He wiped his heed, namoore dorste he seyn
But "Er that thonder stynte, comth a reyn!"
   Of Phasifpha, that was the queene of Crete,
For shrewednesse hym thoughte the tale swete.
Fy! Spek namoore—it is a grisly thyng—   735
Of hire horrible lust and hir likyng.
   Of Clitermystra, for hire lecherye,
That falsly made hire housbonde for to dye,
He redde it with ful good devocioun.
   He tolde me eek for what occasioun   740
Amphiorax at Thebes loste his lyf.
Myn housbonde hadde a legende of his wyf
Eriphilem, that for an ouche of gold
Hath prively unto the Grekes told
Wher that hir housbonde hidde hym in a place
For which he hadde at Thebes sory grace.   746
   Of Lyvia tolde he me, and of Lucye:
They bothe made hir housbondes for to dye,
That oon for love, that oother was for hate.
Lyvia hir housbonde, upon an even late,   750
Empoysoned hath for that she was his fo;

---

689 clerk, man in holy orders. **692 peyntede the leon,** in Aesop's Fables, when the lion saw the picture of a man killing a lion, he remarked that if the lion had painted the picture, it would have been different. **694 oratories,** prayer chapels. **696 mark,** image (i.e., men). **697 Mercurie . . . Venus,** god and planet associated with learning and literature, goddess and planet associated with love and sex. EHg&c *and Venus.* **698 contrarius,** opposite. **699 science,** knowledge. **700 ryot . . . dispence,** revel, extravagance. **701 for hire diverse disposicioun,** because of their different placements in the heavens. **702 exaltacioun,** rising (as the planets revolve through the signs of the zodiac). **703 woot . . . desolat,** knows, powerless. **704 Pisces,** sign of the Fish, associated with religion and life after death. **711 to purpos,** i.e., to get on with it. **713 sire,** husband. **715** The examples that follow are largely from Walter Map. **717–20** Lines found only in E&c. **719 expres,** specifically. **720 los,** (cause of) loss. **721 heres,** hair, Judges 16:15ff. and MkT, VII.2015. **725 Hercules . . . Dianyre,** see ML Prologue II.66 and MkT VII.2095. **727 sorwe:** other MSS *care* or *penaunce. The wo:* E&c *the* om. **729 Xantippa,** the episode is from Jerome. **730 sely,** the usual range of meanings, from foolish to blessed. **732 stynte,** stops. **733 Phasifpha,** Pasiphae's passion for the bull which led to the birth of the Minotaur, related by both Ovid and Jerome. **734 shrewednesse,** evilness. **737 Clitermystra,** Clytemnestra, with the help of her lover, murdered her husband Agamemnon on his return from Troy—from Jerome. **741 Amphiorax,** Amphiaraus, whose wife Eriphyle betrayed his hiding place for a gold necklace so that he had to go to war and was killed in the siege of Thebes. **743 ouche,** jeweled brooch. **747 Lyvia,** Livia murdered her husband at the instigation of her lover Sejanus, the subject of Ben Jonson's play. **Lucye,** Lucilla poisoned her husband, the poet Lucretius, with a supposed love potion. *Lyvia:* Hg&c *Lyma* by a misreading of the minims.

Lucia, likerous, loved hire housbonde so
That for he sholde alwey upon hire thynke,
She yaf hym swich a manere love-drynke
That he was deed er it were by the morwe—
And thus algates housbondes han sorwe. 756

Thanne tolde he me how that oon Latumyus
Compleyned unto his felawe Arrius
That in his gardyn growed swich a tree
On which he seyde how that his wyves thre 760
Hanged hemself for herte despitus.
"O leeve brother," quod this Arrius,
"Yif me a plante of thilke blissed tree,
And in my gardyn planted it shal bee."

Of latter date, of wyves hath he red 765
That somme han slayn hir housbondes in hir
     bed
And lete hir lecchour dighte hire al the nyght,
Whan that the corps lay in the floor upright.
And somme han dryve nayles in hir brayn
Whil that they slepte, and thus they han hem
     slayn. 770
Somme han hem yeve poysoun in hire drynke.

He spak moore harm than herte may
     bithynke,
And therwithal he knew of mo proverbes
Than in this world ther growen gras or herbes.
"Bet is," quod he, "thyn habitacioun 775
Be with a leoun or a foul dragoun
Than with a womman usynge for to chyde."
"Bet is," quod he, "hye in the roof abyde
Than with an angry wyf doun in the hous;
They been so wikked and contrarious, 780
They haten that hir housbondes loveth ay."
He seyde, "A womman cast hir shame away
Whan she cast of hir smok," and forthermo,
"A fair womman, but she be chaast also,
Is lyk a gold ryng in a sowes nose." 785
Who wolde leeve or who wolde suppose
The wo that in myn herte was, and pyne?

And whan I saugh he wolde nevere fyne

To reden on this cursed book al nyght,
Al sodeynly thre leves have I plyght 790
Out of his book right as he radde, and eke
I with my fest so took hym on the cheke
That in oure fyr he fil bakward adoun.
And he up stirte as dooth a wood leoun,
And with his fest he smoot me on the heed 795
That in the floor I lay as I were deed.
And whan he saugh how stille that I lay,
He was agast and wolde han fled his way,
Til atte laste out of my swogh I breyde.
"O, hastow slayn me, false theef?" I seyde, 800
"And for my land thus hastow mordred me?
Er I be deed yet wol I kisse thee."

And neer he cam and kneled faire adoun,
And seyde, "Deere suster Alisoun,
As help me God, I shal thee nevere smyte. 805
That I have doon, it is thyself to wyte.
Foryeve it me, and that I thee biseke."
And yet eftsoones I hitte hym on the cheke,
And seyde, "Theef, thus muchel am I wreke.
Now wol I dye; I may no lenger speke." 810
But atte laste with muchel care and wo
We fille acorded by us selven two.
He yaf me al the bridel in myn hond,
To han the governance of hous and lond,
And of his tonge, and of his hond also; 815
And made hym brenne his book anon right tho.
And whan that I hadde geten unto me
By maistrie al the soveraynetee,
And that he seyde, "Myn owene trewe wyf,
Do as thee lust the terme of al thy lyf; 820
Keep thyn honour, and keep eek myn estaat."
After that day we hadden never debaat.
God helpe me so, I was to hym as kynde
As any wyf from Denmark unto Ynde,
And also trewe, and so was he to me. 825
I prey to God that sit in magestee
So blesse his soule for his mercy deere.
Now wol I seye my tale if ye wol heere.

---

752 likerous, sexually desirous. **755 morwe,** morning. **756 algates,** in every way. **757–58 Latumyus . . . Arrius,** the story is found, with other names, in Walter Map. **761 despitus,** spitefulness of heart. **762 leeve,** dear. **765 latter date,** later on. **767 lecchour dighte,** lover (lecher), have intercourse with. **777 usynge . . . chyde,** who habitually, scolds. **781 that,** what. **782 cast,** throws. **783 smok,** undergarment. **786 leeve,** believe. *leeve:* Hg&c *wene.* **788 fyne,** finish. **790 plyght,** tore. **794 wood,** mad. **799 swogh . . . breyde,** swoon (faint), started. **806 wyte,** blame. **807 biseke,** beseech. **808 eftsoones,** again. **809 wreke,** revenged. **816 And made . . . brenne . . . anon , . , tho,** and (I) made, burn, immediately, then. **818 maistrie . . . soveraynetee,** mastery, control. **820 lust . . . terme,** desire, duration. **821 Keep . . . estaat,** protect, (masculine) status.

Biholde the wordes bitwene the Somonour and the Frere.

The Frere lough whan he hadde herd al this.
"Now dame," quod he, "so have I joye or blis,
This is a long preamble of a tale." 831
And whan the Somonour herde the Frere gale,
"Lo," quod the Somonour, "Goddes armes two,
A frere wol entremette hym everemo.
Lo, goode men, a flye and eek a frere 835
Wol falle in every dyssh and eek mateere.
What spekestow of preambulacioun?
What, amble or trotte or pees or go sit doun!
Thou lettest oure disport in this manere."
    "Ye, woltow so, sire Somonour?" quod the Frere. 840
"Now, by my feith, I shal er that I go
Telle of a somonour swich a tale or two
That alle the fok shal laughen in this place."
    "Now elles, Frere, I bishrewe thy face,"
Quod this Somonour, "and I bishrewe me 845
But if I telle tales two or thre
Of freres er I come to Sidyngborne,
That I shal make thyn herte for to morne,
For wel I woot thy pacience is gon."
    Oure Hoost cride, "Pees, and that anon!" 850
And seyde, "Lat the womman telle hire tale.
Ye fare as folk that dronken ben of ale.
Do, dame, telle forth youre tale, and that is best."
    "Al redy, sire," quod she, "right as yow lest,
If I have licence of this worthy Frere." 855
    "Yis, dame," quod he, "tel forth and I wol heere."

Heere endeth the Wyf of Bathe hir Prologe and bigynneth hir Tale.

In th'olde dayes of the Kyng Arthour,
Of which that Britons speken greet honour,
Al was this land fulfild of fairye.
The elf-queene with hir joly compaignye 860
Daunced ful ofte in many a grene mede.
This was the olde opinion, as I rede—
I speke of manye hundred yeres ago.
But now kan no man se none elves mo,
For now the grete charitee and prayeres 865
Of lymytours and othere hooly freres,
That serchen every lond and every streem
As thikke as motes in the sonne-beem,
Blessynge halles, chambres, kichenes, boures,
Citees, burghes, castels, hye toures, 870
Thropes, bernes, shipnes, dayeryes—
This maketh that ther been no fairyes.
For ther as wont to walken was an elf
Ther walketh now the lymytour hymself,
In undermeles and in morwenynges, 875
And seyth his matyns and his hooly thynges
As he gooth in his lymytacioun.
Wommen may go now saufly up and doun;
In every bussh or under every tree
Ther is noon oother incubus but he, 880
And he ne wol doon hem but dishonour.
    And so bifel that this Kyng Arthour
Hadde in his hous a lusty bacheler
That on a day cam ridynge fro ryver,
And happed that, allone as he was born, 885
He saugh a mayde walkynge hym biforn,

829 **lough,** laughed. 832 **gale,** exclaim. 834 **entremette,** meddle. 836 EHg&c *eek* om. 837 **preambulacioun,** preambling (*double entendre* with perambulation, i.e., walking in front of and walking around). 838 **pees,** pace (i.e., walk; the term for the gait is not recorded before the 17th century). 839 **lettest . . . disport,** hinder, sport. 844 **bishrewe,** curse. 847 **Sidyngborne,** Sittingbourne, 40 miles from London. The reference to Rochester, only 30 miles out, later on at *CT* vii.1926, offers a problem: see Introduction on the order of the Tales. 850 **Pees . . . anon,** peace, immediately. 852 *ben:* E&c *were.* 855 **licence,** permission. 858 **Britons,** Celtic Britons. 861 **mede,** meadow. 866 **lymytours,** begging friars with assigned territories (limits); cf. i. 209 note. 868 **motes,** dust particles. 871 **Thropes, bernes, shipnes, dayeryes,** villages, barns, cowsheds, dairies. 873 **wont,** accustomed. 875 **undermeles . . . morwenynges,** afternoons, mornings. 876 **matyns,** morning prayers. 878 EHg&c *now* om. 880 **incubus,** evil spirits whose intercourse with human beings was always fertile. 881 **dishonour,** as contrasted with making them pregnant with demon children. 885 *he:* other MSS *she.*

Of whiche mayde anon, maugree hir heed,
By verray force he rafte hire maydenhed;
For which oppressioun was swich clamour
And swich pursute unto the Kyng Arthour, 890
That dampned was this knyght for to be deed,
By cours of lawe, and sholde han lost his heed—
Paraventure swich was the statut tho—
But that the queene and othere ladyes mo
So longe preyeden the kyng of grace 895
Til he his lyf hym graunted in the place,
And yaf hym to the queene, al at hir wille,
To chese wheither she wolde hym save or spille.
  The queene thanketh the kyng with al hir
    myght,
And after this thus spak she to the knyght, 900
Whan that she saugh hir tyme upon a day,
"Thou standest yet," quod she, "in swich array
That of thy lyf yet hastow no suretee.
I grante thee lyf if thou kanst tellen me 904
What thyng is it that wommen moost desiren.
Bewar and keep thy nekke-boon from iren.
And if thou kanst nat tellen it anon,
Yet shal I yeve thee leve for to gon
A twelf-month and a day to seche and leere
An answere suffisant in this mateere; 910
And suretee wol I han er that thou pace,
Thy body for to yelden in this place."
  Wo was this knyght and sorwefully he
    siketh.
But what, he may nat do al as hym liketh;
And at the laste he chees hym for to wende 915
And come agayn right at the yeres ende
With swich answere as God wolde hym
    purveye,
And taketh his leve and wendeth forth his
    weye.

He seketh every hous and every place
Where as he hopeth for to fynde grace 920
To lerne what thyng wommen loven moost,
But he ne koude arryven in no coost
Wher as he myghte fynde in this mateere
Two creatures accordynge in-feere. 924
  Somme seyde wommen loven best richesse,
Somme seyde honour, somme seyde jolynesse,
Somme riche array, somme seyden lust a-bedde,
And oftetyme to be wydwe and wedde.
Somme seyde that oure hertes been moost esed
Whan that we been yflatered and yplesed—
He gooth ful ny the sothe, I wol nat lye. 931
A man shal wynne us best with flaterye,
And with attendance and with bisynesse
Been we ylymed, bothe moore and lesse.
  And somme seyn that we loven best 935
For to be free and do right as us lest,
And that no man repreve us of oure vice,
But seye that we be wise and nothyng nyce.
For trewely ther is noon of us alle,
If any wight wol clawe us on the galle, 940
That we nel kike for he seith us sooth;
Assay, and he shal fynde it that so dooth,
For be we never so vicious withinne,
We wol been holden wise and clene of synne.
  And somme seyn that greet delit han we 945
For to been holden stable, and eek secree,
And in o purpos stedefastly to dwelle,
And nat biwreye thyng that men us telle.
But that tale is nat worth a rake-stele.
Pardee, we wommen konne nothyng hele: 950
Witnesse on Myda—wol ye heere the tale?
  Ovyde, amonges othere thynges smale,
Seyde Myda hadde under his longe heres
Growynge upon his heed two asses eres,

---

887 maugree hir heed, i.e., in spite of anything she could do. **888 rafte,** ravished. *he rafte:* E&c *birafte.* **889 oppressioun,** violence. **891 dampned . . . deed,** condemned, dead. **893 statut tho,** law then. **897 at hir wille,** i.e., for her to determine his punishment. **898 spille,** destroy. **902 array,** situation. **903 suretee,** assurance. **904 I grante,** I (will) grant. **906 iren,** axe. **907 anon,** now (immediately). *it:* Hg&c *me|it me.* **908 leve,** permission. *shal:* Hg&c *wol.* **909 leere,** learn. **911 suretee,** security (pledge). **912 for to yelden,** that you will yield. **913 siketh,** sighs. **914** E&c *what* om. **915 chees . . . wende,** choose, go. **917 purveye,** provide. **922 coost,** coast (region). **924 accordynge in-feere,** agreeing together. **929 esed,** comforted. Hg&c *herte is.* **931 ny,** nigh (near). **933 attendance . . . bisynesse,** attention, solicitude. **934 ylymed,** captured (with birdlime). **937 repreve,** reprove. **938 nyce,** ignorant. **940 wight . . . clawe . . . galle,** person scratch our sore spot. **941 kike . . . seith . . . sooth,** kick, speaks, truth. **942 Assay,** try. **944 been holden,** be considered. **946 stable . . . secree,** dependable, able to keep a secret. **947 o purpos . . . dwelle,** stay with one purpose. **948 biwreye . . . men,** betray; "man" is the impersonal, i.e., we are told. **949 rake-stele,** rake handle. **950 hele,** hide. **951 Myda,** Midas; in *Metamorphoses* 11. 174ff., Midas is betrayed by his barber and not his wife. The Wife of Bath (Chaucer) adapted the story.

The which vice he hydde as he best myghte 955
Ful subtilly from every mannes sighte,
That save his wyf ther wiste of it namo.
He loved hire moost and trusted hire also.
He preyde hire that to no creature
She sholde tellen of his disfigure. 960
    She swoor him nay for al this world to
      wynne,
She nolde do that vileynye or synne
To make hir housbonde han so foul a name;
She nolde nat telle it for hir owene shame.
But nathelees, hir thoughte that she dyde 965
That she so longe sholde a conseil hyde;
Hir thoughte it swal so soore aboute hir herte
That nedely som word hire moste asterte.
And sith she dorste telle it to no man,
Doun to a mareys faste by she ran— 970
Til she cam there hir herte was afyre—
And as a bitore bombleth in the myre,
She leyde hir mouth unto the water doun:
"Biwreye me nat, thou water, with thy soun,"
Quod she; "to thee I telle it and namo; 975
Myn housbonde hath longe asses erys two.
Now is myn herte al hool, now is it oute.
I myghte no lenger kepe it, out of doute."
Heere may ye se, thogh we a tyme abyde,
Yet out it moot; we kan no conseil hyde. 980
The remenant of the tale if ye wol heere,
Redeth Ovyde and ther ye may it leere.
    This knyght of which my tale is specially,
Whan that he saugh he myghte nat come
      therby— 984
This is to seye, what wommen love moost—
Withinne his brest ful sorweful was the goost.
But hoom he gooth, he myghte nat sojourne;
The day was come that homward moste he
      tourne.
And in his wey it happed hym to ryde
In al this care under a forest syde, 990

Wher as he saugh upon a daunce go
Of ladyes foure and twenty and yet mo;
Toward the whiche daunce he drow ful yerne,
In hope that som wysdom sholde he lerne.
But certeinly, er he cam fully there, 995
Vanysshed was this daunce, he nyste where.
Ne creature saugh he that bar lyf
Save on the grene he saugh sittynge a wyf—
A fouler wight ther may no man devyse.
Agayn the knyght this olde wyf gan ryse, 1000
And seyde, "Sire knyght, heer forth ne lith no
      wey.
Tel me what that ye seken, by youre fey.
Paraventure it may the bettre be;
Thise olde folk kan muchel thyng," quod she.
    "My leeve mooder," quod this knyght,
      "certeyn 1005
I nam but deed but if that I kan seyn
What thyng it is that wommen moost desire.
Koude ye me wisse, I wolde wel quite youre
      hire."
    "Plight me thy trouthe heere in myn hand,"
      quod she,
"The nexte thyng that I requere thee 1010
Thou shalt it do, if it lye in thy myght,
And I wol telle it yow er it be nyght."
    "Have heer my trouthe," quod the knyght.
      "I grante."
    "Thanne," quod she, "I dar me wel avante
Thy lyf is sauf, for I wol stonde therby. 1015
Upon my lyf, the queene wol seye as I.
Lat se which is the proudeste of hem alle
That wereth on a coverchief or a calle
That dar seye nat of that I shal thee teche.
Lat us go forth withouten lenger speche." 1020
Tho rowned she a pistel in his ere
And bad hym to be glad and have no fere.
    Whan they be comen to the court, this
      knyght

---

955 vice, flaw. **956 subtilly,** cleverly. **957 namo,** no one. **958** *trusted:* E&c *trist.* **965 she dyde,** she would die. **966 conseil,** confidence. **967 swal,** swelled. **968 nedely . . . hire . . . asterte,** necessarily some word must escape from her. **969 dorste,** dared. **970 mareys,** marsh. **972 bitore bombleth . . . myre,** bittern makes a bellowing noise in the mud. **974 Biwreye . . . soun,** betray, sound. **978 kepe . . . out of doute,** contain, without doubt. **980 moot . . . conseil,** must, confidence. **982 leere,** learn; in Ovid the reeds betrayed the secret. **984 come therby,** come by it (attain the answer). **986 goost,** spirit. **987 sojourne,** stay. **993 yerne,** eagerly. **996 nyste,** did not know. **998 wyf,** woman. **999 fouler wight . . . devyse,** uglier creature, imagine. **1000 Agayn,** i.e., to greet. **1001 heer forth,** i.e., there's no road here. **1004 kan muchel,** know many. **1005 leeve,** dear. **1006 deed . . . seyn,** dead, say. **1008 wisse . . . quite,** instruct, repay. **1009 Plight . . . trouthe,** promise, troth. **1010 requere,** demand of. **1014 avante,** boast. **1016 seye as I,** say as I do. **1018 calle,** caul (headdress). **1021 rowned . . . pistel,** whispered, message (epistle).

Seyde he had holde his day as he hadde hight,
And redy was his answere, as he sayde.   1025
Ful many a noble wyf, and many a mayde,
And many a wydwe—for that they been
     wise—
The queene hirself sittynge as justise,
Assembled been, his answere for to heere;
And afterward this knyght was bode appeere.

    To every wight comanded was silence,   1031
And that the knyght sholde telle in audience
What thyng that worldly wommen loven best.
This knyght ne stood nat stille as doth a best,
But to his questioun anon answerde   1035
With manly voys that al the court it herde.

    "My lige lady, generally," quod he,
"Wommen desiren to have sovereynetee
As wel over hir housbond as hir love,
And for to been in maistrie hym above.   1040
This is youre mooste desir thogh ye me kille.
Dooth as yow list; I am heer at youre wille."

    In al the court ne was ther wyf ne mayde
Ne wydwe that contraried that he sayde,
But seyden he was worthy han his lyf.   1045

    And with that word up stirte the olde wyf
Which that the knyght saugh sittynge on the
     grene:
"Mercy," quod she, "my sovereyn lady queene!
Er that youre court departe, do me right.
I taughte this answere unto the knyght,   1050
For which he plighte me his trouthe there
The firste thyng I wolde hym requere
He wolde it do, if it lay in his myght.
Bifore the court thanne preye I thee, sir
     knyght,"   1054
Quod she, "that thou me take unto thy wyf,
For wel thou woost that I have kept thy lyf.
If I seye fals, sey nat, upon thy fey."

    This knyght answerde, "Allas and weylawey!
I woot right wel that swich was my biheste.

For Goddes love, as chees a newe requeste;   1060
Taak al my good and lat my body go."

    "Nay thanne," quod she, "I shrewe us bothe
     two!
For thogh that I be foul and oold and poore,
I nolde for all the metal ne for oore
That under erthe is grave or lith above,   1065
But if thy wyf I were, and eek thy love."

    "My love?" quod he, "nay, my
     dampnacioun!
Allas, that any of my nacioun
Sholde evere so foule disparaged be."

    But al for noght; th'ende is this, that he   1070
Constreyned was, he nedes moste hire wedde;
And taketh his olde wyf and gooth to bedde.

    Now wolden som men seye, paraventure,
That for my necligence I do no cure
To tellen yow the joye and al th'array   1075
That at the feeste was that ilke day.
To which thyng shortly answere I shal:
I seye ther nas no joye ne feeste at al.
Ther nas but hevynesse and muche sorwe.
For prively he wedded hire on morwe,   1080
And al day after hidde hym as an owle,
So wo was hym, his wyf looked so foule.

    Greet was the wo the knyght hadde in his
     thoght.
Whan he was with his wyf abedde ybroght
He walweth and he turneth to and fro.   1085
His olde wyf lay smylynge everemo,
And seyde, "O deere housbonde, benedicitee,
Fareth every knyght thus with his wyf as ye?
Is this the lawe of Kyng Arthures hous?
Is every knyght of his so dangerous?   1090
I am youre owene love and eek youre wyf;
I am she which that saved hath youre lyf,
And certes yet ne dide I yow nevere unright;
Why fare ye thus with me this firste nyght?
Ye faren lyk a man had lost his wit.   1095

1024 holde . . . hight, held to, promised. **1030 bode,** bidden (to). The assemblage with the queen presiding is one of the "courts of love" described by Andreas Capellanus, and by modern scholars such as C. S. Lewis, *The Allegory of Love*, and Amy Kelly, *Eleanor of Aquitaine*. **1032 audience,** public. **1034 stille,** i.e., speechless. **1035 anon,** immediately. **1038 E** *to* om. **1039 love,** lover. **1042 list,** desire. **1045 han,** to have. **1046 stirte,** started. **1049 me right,** i.e., do right by me. **1056 kept,** saved. **1059 woot . . . biheste,** know, promise. **1062 shrewe,** curse. **1063** *foul and:* EHg&c *and* om. **1065 grave,** buried. **1068 nacioun,** i.e., family. **1069 disparaged,** foully degraded. **1074 cure,** i.e., am at no pains. **1080 morwe,** morning. E&c *on a morwe;* other MSS *on the.* **1090 dangerous,** standoffish. **1091 EHg&c** *eek* om. **1093** The words are in different order in various MSS. **1095 lost his wit,** to be put to bed with a virgin was a test for sanity, cf. Hamlet and Ophelia, *Hamlet,* III.i.

What is my gilt? For Goddes love, tel it,
And it shal been amended, if I may."
  "Amended?" quod this knyght, "allas, nay,
    nay,
It wol nat been amended nevere mo.
Thou art so loothly, and so oold also,   1100
And therto comen of so lough a kynde,
That litel wonder is thogh I walwe and wynde.
So wolde God myn herte wolde breste!"
  "Is this," quod she, "the cause of youre
    unreste?"
  "Ye, certeinly," quod he, "no wonder is."
  "Now sire," quod she, "I koude amende al
    this,   1106
If that me liste, er it were dayes thre,
So wel ye myghte bere yow unto me.
  "But, for ye speken of swich gentillesse
As is descended out of old richesse,   1110
That therfore sholden ye be gentil men,
Swich arrogance is nat worth an hen.
Looke who that is moost vertuous alway,
Pryvee and apert, and moost entendeth ay
To do the gentil dedes that he kan,   1115
Taak hym for the grettest gentil man.
Crist wole we clayme of hym oure gentillesse,
Nat of oure eldres for hire old richesse.
For thogh they yeve us al hir heritage,   1119
For which we clayme to been of heigh parage,
Yet may they nat biquethe for no thyng
To noon of us hir vertuous lyvyng,
That made hem gentil men ycalled be,
And bad us folwen hem in swich degree.
  "Wel kan the wise poete of Florence   1125
That highte Dant speken in this sentence.
Lo, in swich maner rym is Dantes tale:
'Ful selde up riseth by his branches smale
Prowesse of man, for God of his goodnesse

Wole that of hym we clayme oure
    gentillesse.'   1130
For of oure eldres may we no thyng clayme
But temporel thyng that man may hurte and
    mayme.
  "Eek every wight woot this as wel as I,
If gentillesse were planted natureelly
Unto a certeyn lynage doun the lyne,   1135
Pryvee and apert, thanne wolde they nevere
    fyne
To doon of gentillesse the faire office—
They myghte do no vileynye or vice.
  "Taak fyr and ber it in the derkeste hous
Bitwix this and the mount of Kaukasous,   1140
And lat men shette the dores and go thenne,
Yet wole the fyr as faire lye and brenne
As twenty thousand men myghte it biholde;
His office natureel ay wol it holde,
Up peril of my lyf, til that it dye.   1145
  "Heere may ye se wel how that genterye
Is nat annexed to possessioun,
Sith folk ne doon hir operacioun
Alwey, as dooth the fyr, lo, in his kynde.
For God it woot men may wel often fynde   1150
A lordes sone do shame and vileynye;
And he that wole han pris of his gentrye—
For he was born of a gentil hous
And hadde his eldres noble and vertuous—
And nel hymselven do no gentil dedis   1155
Ne folwen his gentil auncestre that deed is,
He nys nat gentil, be he duc or erl,
For vileyns synful dedes make a cherl.
For gentillesse nys but renomee   1159
Of thyne auncestres for hire heigh bountee,
Which is a strange thyng to thy persone.
Thy gentillesse cometh fro God allone.
Thanne comth oure verray gentillesse of grace;

1100 loothly, loathsome. **1101 lough a kynde,** low a lineage. **1102 wynde,** twist. **1103 breste,** burst. **1107 me liste,** pleased me. **1108 So wel . . . bere,** if well, behave. **1109 swich gentillesse,** such nobility. Parallels to this excursus have been pointed out in Dante's *Convivio* IV, *Boece* III, pr. 6, m.6., and *RR* 18607–946 (Dunn-Robbins 86.1ff.). But none of these puts the medieval commonplace about natural gentilesse in the context of marriage the way Gower does in *Mirour de l'omme* 17329ff. As in choosing to retell the tales of Constance and Florent in the first place, Chaucer may have been influenced by his old friend to include the gentilesse motif in the marriage argument. **1110 old richesse,** Dante uses the term "antica ricchezza." **1114 Pryvee . . . apert . . . entendeth ay,** privately, publicly, always tries. **1120 parage,** lineage. **1124 bad . . . swich degree,** (they) commanded, in the same manner. **1127 Dantes tale,** the quotation is from *Purgatorio* 7. 121–23. **1128 branches smale,** i.e., later branches of the family tree. **1129** *goodnesse:* Hg&c *prowesse.* **1136 fyne,** cease. *and:* E&c *nor.* **1140 Kaukasous,** Caucasus, in Russia. **1141 thenne,** thence (away). **1148 operacioun,** action. **1149 kynde,** nature. **1152 pris,** recognition. **1159 gentillesse . . . renomee,** i.e., hereditary nobility, fame. **1160 bountee,** magnanimity. **1161 strange,** alien. **1163 verray,** genuine.

It was no thyng biquethe us with oure place.

　"Thenketh hou noble, as seith Valerius,　1165
Was thilke Tullius Hostillius
That out of poverte roos to heigh noblesse.
Reed Senek, and redeth eek Boece;
Ther shul ye seen expres that it no drede is
That he is gentil that dooth gentil dedis.　1170
And therfore, leeve housbonde, I thus conclude:
Al were it that myne auncestres were rude,
Yet may the hye God—and so hope I—
Grante me grace to lyven vertuously.
Thanne am I gentil whan that I bigynne　1175
To lyven vertuously and weyve synne.

　"And there as ye of poverte me repreeve,
The hye God, on whom that we bileeve,
In wilful poverte chees to lyve his lyf.
And certes every man, mayden, or wyf,　1180
May understonde that Jhesus, hevene kyng,
Ne wolde nat chese a vicious lyvyng.
Glad poverte is an honeste thyng, certeyn;
This wole Senec and othere clerkes seyn.
Whoso that halt hym payd of his poverte,　1185
I holde hym riche al hadde he nat a sherte.
He that coveiteth is a poure wight,
For he wolde han that is nat in his myght;
But he that noght hath, ne coveiteth have,
Is riche, although ye holde hym but a knave.

　"Verray poverte it syngeth proprely.　1191
Juvenal seith of poverte myrily,
'The poure man, whan he goth by the weye,
Bifore the theves he may synge and pleye.'
Poverte is hateful good and, as I gesse,　1195
A ful greet bryngere out of bisynesse;
A greet amendere eek of sapience
To hym that taketh it in pacience.

Poverte is this, although it seme alenge,
Possessioun that no wight wol chalenge.　1200
Poverte ful ofte, whan a man is lowe,
Maketh his God and eek hymself to knowe.
Poverte a spectacle is, as thynketh me,
Thurgh which he may his verray freendes see.
And therfore, sire, syn that I noght yow greve,
Of my poverte namoore ye me repreve.　1206

　"Now, sire, of elde ye repreve me;
And certes, sire, thogh noon auctoritee
Were in no book, ye gentils of honour
Seyn that men sholde an oold wight doon
　　favour　1210
And clepe hym fader for youre gentillesse—
And auctours shal I fynden, as I gesse.

　"Now ther ye seye that I am foul and old,
Than drede you noght to been a cokewold,
For filthe and eelde, also moot I thee,　1215
Been grete wardeyns upon chastitee.
But nathelees, syn I knowe youre delit,
I shal fulfille youre worldly appetit.

　"Chese now," quod she, "oon of thise
　　thynges tweye:
To han me foul and old til that I deye　1220
And be to yow a trewe humble wyf,
And nevere yow displese in al my lyf,
Or elles ye wol han me yong and fair,
And take youre aventure of the repair
That shal be to youre hous by cause of me, 1225
Or in som oother place, may wel be.
Now chese yourselven, wheither that yow
　　liketh."

　　This knyght avyseth hym and sore siketh,
But atte laste he seyde in this manere,
"My lady and my love, and wyf so deere,　1230

1164 place, station in life. **1165–66 Valerius . . . Tullius,** Valerius Maximus, III.4, on Tullius Hostillius, who according to legend rose from a peasant hut to become the third king of Rome. **1168 Senek,** Seneca, Epist. 44. **1169 expres . . . no drede,** specifically, no doubt. EHg&c *it* om. **1171 leeve,** dear. **1176 weyve,** avoid. **1177 repreeve,** reproach. **1179 wilful poverte,** voluntary poverty, the requirement of both the Benedictine rule for monks and the Franciscan rule for friars, had become a major issue with critics of the Church in the 14th century because many of the orders had grown so wealthy. Cf. the Parson, I. 486. **1182 chese,** choose. **1184 Senec,** Seneca, Epist. 17. **1185 halt hym payd of,** considers himself rewarded by. **1187 wight,** creature. **1189 have,** to have. **1191 Verray . . . syngeth proprely,** true, sings of its own nature (?). The latter reading gave the scribes trouble: Hg&c *is synne;* other variations in other MSS. **1192 Juvenal,** Satire 10.21. **1196 bryngere out of bisynesse,** encourager of industry ("curarum remocio"). **1197 amendere of sapience,** improver of wisdom. **1199 alenge,** wearisome (OE "lǣnge," tiresome). **1203 spectacle,** a magnifying glass. **1205 syn . . . greve,** since, make unhappy. **1206 repreve,** reproach. **1215 thee,** prosper (an exclamation). (219) **Chese now,** Chaucer significantly alters the choice offered by Gower and the other versions of the tale from foul by day and fair by night or vice versa, to foul but true or fair but false. **1224 aventure . . . repair,** chance, visiting. **1226 Other MSS** *wel may be.* **1227 wheither,** whichever. **1228 avyseth . . . siketh,** ponders, sighs.

I put me in youre wise governance;
Cheseth youreself which may be moost plesance
And moost honour to yow and me also.
I do no fors the wheither of the two,
For as yow liketh it suffiseth me."   1235
  "Thanne have I gete of yow maistrie,"
    quod she,
"Syn I may chese and governe as me lest?"
  "Ye, certes, wyf," quod he. "I holde it best."
  "Kys me," quod she. "We be no lenger
    wrothe,
For, by my trouthe, I wol be to yow bothe—
This is to seyn, ye, bothe fair and good.   1241
I prey to God that I moote sterven wood
But I to yow be also good and trewe
As evere was wyf syn that the world was newe.
And but I be tomorn as fair to seene   1245
As any lady, emperice, or queene,

That is bitwixe the est and eke the west,
Dooth with my lyf and deth right as yow lest.
Cast up the curtyn, looke how that it is."
  And whan the knyght saugh verraily al this,
That she so fair was, and so yong therto,   1251
For joye he hente hire in his armes two.
His herte bathed in a bath of blisse,
A thousand tyme a-rewe he gan hire kisse,
And she obeyed hym in every thyng   1255
That myghte doon hym plesance or likyng.
  And thus they lyve unto hir lyves ende
In parfit joye. And Jhesu Crist us sende
Housbondes meeke, yonge, and fressh abedde,
And grace t'overbyde hem that we wedde.   1260
And eek I pray Jhesu shorte hir lyves
That wol nat be governed by hir wyves.
And olde and angry nygardes of dispence,
God sende hem soone verray pestilence!

Heere endeth the Wyves Tale of Bathe.

1232 **plesance,** agreeable. 1234 **do no fors,** do not mind. 1241 **ye,** yes. 1242 **moote sterven wood,** may die insane. 1249 **Cast up the curtyn,** i.e., and let in light; the foregoing has been a "curtain lecture," after the drapes in the canopy bed had been drawn for privacy. 1252 **hente,** seized. 1254 **a-rewe,** in a row. 1260 **t'overbyde,** outlive. 1261 **shorte,** shorten. 1263 **dispence,** expenditure.

FRIAR'S TALE

PROLOGUE

The Prologe of the Freres Tale.

This worthy lymytour, this noble Frere,   1265
He made alwey a maner louryng chiere
Upon the Somonour, but for honestee
No vileyns word as yet to hym spak he.
But atte laste he seyde unto the wyf,
"Dame," quod he, "God yeve yow right good
    lyf.   1270
Ye han heer touched, also moot I thee,
In scole-matere greet difficultee.
Ye han seyd muche thyng right wel, I seye.
But dame, heere as we ryde by the weye
Us nedeth nat to speken but of game,   1275
And lete auctoritees, on Goddes name,
To prechyng and to scole of clergye.
But if it lyke to this compaignye,
I wol yow of a somonour telle a game.
Pardee, ye may wel knowe by the name   1280
That of a somonour may no good be sayd;

I praye that noon of you be yvele apayd.
A somonour is a rennere up and doun
With mandementz for fornicacioun,
And is ybet at every townes ende."   1285
    Oure Hoost tho spak, "A, sire, ye sholde be
    hende
And curteys, as a man of youre estaat;
In compaignye we wol have no debaat.
Telleth youre tale and lat the Somonour be."
    "Nay," quod the Somonour, "lat hym seye
    to me   1290
Whatso hym list. Whan it comth to my lot,
By God, I shal hym quiten every grot.
I shal hym tellen which a greet honour
It is to be a flaterynge lymytour,
And of many another manere cryme   1295
Which nedeth nat rehercen for this tyme.
And his office I shal hym telle, ywis."

1265 **lymytour ... Frere,** a begging friar with an assigned territory (limit; cf. 1. 209 note); "friar" is an anglicization of Fr.
frere, brother. 1266 **louryng chiere,** lowering (sullen) expression (manner). 1267 **honestee,** propriety. 1268 **vileyns,** rude. 1271 **thee,**
prosper. 1272 **scole-matere ... difficultee,** i.e., on difficult scholastic questions. 1275 **game,** entertainment. 1276 **lete,** leave. 1278
But if: E&c *And if.* 1280 **name,** i.e., from the term itself. 1282 **yvele apayd,** be displeased. 1284 **mandementz,** summonses, literally
to come before the ecclesiastical court, but with the suggestion of coming to fornication itself. 1285 **ybet,** beaten. 1286 **hende,** gracious.
1288 **debaat,** quarrel. 1292 **quiten ... grot,** repay, groat (silver fourpence). 1295–96 These lines in some MSS follow l. 1308. 1297
office, function.

127

Oure Hoost answerde, "Pees, namoore of this."

And after this he seyde unto the Frere,   1299
"Tel forth youre tale, leeve maister deere."

Heere bigynneth the Freres Tale.

Whilom ther was dwellynge in my contree
An erchedekene, a man of heigh degree,
That boldely dide execucioun
In punysshynge of fornicacioun,
Of wicchecraft, and eek of bawderye,   1305
Of diffamacioun, and avowtrye,
Of chirche reves, and of testamentz,
Of contractes, and of lakke of sacramentz,
Of usure, and of symonye also.   1309
But certes, lecchours dide he grettest wo—
They sholde syngen if that they were hent—
And smale tytheres weren foule yshent
If any persone wolde upon hem pleyne.
Ther myghte asterte hym no pecunyal peyne.
For smale tithes and for smal offrynge   1315
He made the peple pitously to synge,
For er the bisshop caughte hem with his hook,
They were in the erchedeknes book.
And thanne hadde he, thurgh his jurisdiccioun,
Power to doon on hem correccioun.   1320
He hadde a somonour redy to his hond—
A slyer boye nas noon in Engelond,
For subtilly he hadde his espiaille
That taughte hym wher that hym myghte
    availle.
He koude spare of lecchours oon or two   1325

To techen hym to foure and twenty mo.
For thogh this somonour wood was as an hare,
To telle his harlotrye I wol nat spare,
For we been out of his correccioun.
They han of us no jurisdiccioun,   1330
Ne nevere shullen, terme of alle hir lyves.
    "Peter, so been wommen of the styves,"
Quod the Somonour, "yput out of my cure!"
    "Pees, with myschance and with
        mysaventure,"
Thus seyde oure Hoost, "and lat hym telle his
    tale.   1335
Now telleth forth, thogh that the Somonour
    gale,
Ne spareth nat, myn owene maister deere."
    This false theef, this somonour, quod the
        Frere,
Hadde alwey bawdes redy to his hond,
As any hauk to lure in Engelond,   1340
That tolde hym al the secree that they knewe,
For hire acqueyntance was nat come of newe.
They weren his approwours prively.
He took hymself a greet profit therby;
His maister knew nat alwey what he wan.   1345
Withouten mandement a lewed man
He koude somne, on peyne of Cristes curs,

1302 erchedekene, archdeacon, the disciplinary officer of a diocese, who administered its ecclesiastical court, charged with overseeing the moral health of the community as summarized in ll. 1304–10. **1305 bawderye,** procuring. **1306 diffamacioun . . . avowtrye,** slander, adultery. **1307 chirche reves,** church wardens (i.e., their behavior), or possibly church robberies. **1307–08 testamentz . . . contractes,** i.e., abuses in connection with wills, marriage contracts, etc. **1308 lakke of sacramentz,** failure to observe any of the seven sacraments: baptism, confirmation, communion, marriage, ordination, penance, and extreme unction. EHg&c *and eek of*. **1309 usure,** loaning money for interest was prohibited by canon law. **symonye,** the buying and selling of church offices. **1311 syngen . . . hent,** i.e., wail, caught. **1312 smale tytheres,** the tithe was officially a tax of 10 percent of one's income. **foule yshent,** treated harshly. **1313 persone,** i.e., parson (priest). **1314 asterte hym . . . ,** i.e., the tithe cheater could in no way escape financial punishment (a fine). **1315 offrynge,** voluntary contribution (in addition to the tithe). *and for:* E&c *for* om. **1317 hook,** the bishop's pastoral crook here assumes a sinister aspect. **1323 subtilly . . . espiaille,** secretly, network of spies. **1324 availle,** profit. E *that* om. **1326 techen,** lead. **1327 wood,** crazy. **1328 harlotrye,** wickedness, however, the modern sense of sexual immorality was already developing. **1329 we . . . correccioun,** we (i.e., friars), authority. **1332 styves,** brothels (stews). **1333 cure,** responsibility. **1334 myschance . . . mysaventure,** "and bad luck to you." **1336 gale,** makes a commotion. **1339 bawdes,** procurers. **1340 lure,** the feathers at the end of a thong by which a falcon was recalled to its master. **1343 approwours,** profit makers (from O. Fr. *prou,* profit). **1346 mandement . . . lewed,** official document, ignorant. **1347 curs,** excommunication.

And they were glade for to fille his purs
And make hym grete feestes atte nale.
And right as Judas hadde purses smale,   1350
And was a theef, right swich a theef was he;
His maister hadde but half his duetee.
He was, if I shal yeven hym his laude,
A theef and eek a somnour and a baude.
He hadde eek wenches at his retenue   1355
That wheither that Sir Robert or Sir Huwe,
Or Jakke, or Rauf, or whoso that it were
That lay by hem, they tolde it in his ere.
Thus was the wenche and he of oon assent;
And he wolde fecche a feyned mandement   1360
And somne hem to chapitre bothe two,
And pile the man and lete the wenche go.
   Thanne wolde he seye, "Freend, I shal for thy
     sake
Do striken hire out of oure lettres blake.
Thee thar namoore, as in this cas, travaille;   1365
I am thy freend ther I thee may availle."
Certeyn he knew of briberyes mo
Than possible is to telle in yeres two.
For in this world nys dogge for the bowe
That kan an hurt deer from an hool knowe   1370
Bet than this somnour knew a sly lecchour
Or an avowtier or a paramour.
And for that was the fruyt of al his rente,
Therfore on it he sette al his entente.
   And so bifel that ones on a day   1375
This somnour evere waityng on his pray
Rood for to somne an old wydwe, a ribibe,
Feynynge a cause, for he wolde brybe.
And happed that he saugh bifore hym ryde
A gay yeman under a forest syde.   1380
A bowe he bar and arwes brighte and kene;

He hadde upon a courtepy of grene;
An hat upon his heed with frenges blake.
   "Sire," quod this somnour, "hayl, and wel
     atake."
   "Welcome," quod he, "and every good
     felawe.   1385
Wher rydestow, under this grenewode shawe?"
Seyde this yeman, "Wiltow fer to day?"
   This somnour hym answerde and seyde,
     "Nay.
Heere faste by," quod he, "is myn entente
To ryden for to reysen up a rente   1390
That longeth to my lordes duetee."
   "Artow thanne a bailly?" "Ye," quod he.
He dorste nat, for verray filthe and shame
Seye that he was a somnour, for the name.
   "Depardieux," quod this yeman, "deere
     broother,   1395
Thou art a bailly, and I am another.
I am unknowen as in this contree;
Of thyn aqueyntance I wolde praye thee
And eek of bretherhede, if that yow leste.
I have gold and silver in my cheste;   1400
If that thee happe to comen in oure shire,
Al shal be thyn, right as thou wolt desire."
   "Grantmercy," quod this somonour, "by my
     feith!"
Everych in oothores hand his trouthe leith,
For to be sworne bretheren til they deye.   1405
In daliance they ryden forth hir weye.
   This somonour, that was as ful of jangles
As ful of venym been thise waryangles
And evere enqueryng upon everythyng,
"Brother," quod he, "where is now youre
     dwellyng   1410

1349 atte nale, at the ale (house) (from O.E. *æt tham*). **1350 purses,** Judas carried the purse for the disciples, cf. John 12:6. **1352 duetee,** amount due him. **1353 laude,** praise (deserts). **1354 baude,** procurer. **1359 oon assent,** in a collusion. **1360 feyned mandement,** spurious summons. **1361 chapitre,** the chapter (ecclesiastical) court. **1362 pile,** pluck (despoil). **1364 striken hire,** erase her name. *hire:* other MSS *thee.* **1365 thar . . . travaille,** about it, trouble (yourself). **1366 availle,** help. **1369 dogge . . . bowe,** dog trained to hunt with a bowman. **1372 avowtier . . . paramour,** adulterer, lover (with sexual implication). **1373 fruyt . . . rente,** the best part of his income. **1376 pray,** prey (victim). **1377 ribibe,** fiddle, cf. l. 1573. Halliwell suggested that this slang term for an old woman may have come from a confusion of Lat. *vetula,* old woman, and *vitula,* viol. EHg&c *Rood* om. **1379** EHg&c *And* om. **1382 courtepy of grene,** short coat; cf. the Yeoman, *CT* I.103, but it has been observed that the devil is also a hunter (after souls) and wears green. **1383 frenges,** fringes (or bindings). **1384 wel atake,** well met (overtaken). **1386 shawe,** grove. **1390 reysen,** collect. **1391 longeth . . . duetee,** belongs to what is owed. **1392 bailly,** bailiff (farm supervisor). **1395 Depardieux,** "in God's name"—an interesting oath from a devil; cf. ll. 1483ff. **1399 leste,** are agreeable. **1404 trouthe,** troth; i.e., they shook hands on it. **1406 daliance,** merriment. *hir weye:* Hg&c *and pleye.* **1407 jangles,** idle chatter. **1408 venym . . . waryangles,** poison, shrikes or butcher-birds who impaled their prey on thorns which were thereafter considered poisonous.

Another day if that I sholde yow seche?"
This yeman hym answerde in softe speche,
  "Brother," quod he, "fer in the north contree,
Where as I hope som tyme I shal thee see.
Er we departe I shal thee so wel wisse   1415
That of myn hous ne shaltow nevere mysse."
  "Now, brother," quod this somonour, "I yow preye,
Teche me whil that we ryden by the weye—
Syn that ye been a baillif as am I—
Som subtiltee, and tel me feithfully   1420
In myn office how that I may moost wynne;
And spareth nat for conscience ne synne,
But as my brother tel me how do ye."
  "Now by my trouthe, brother deere," seyde he,
"As I shal tellen thee a feithful tale: 1425
My wages been ful streite and ful smale.
My lord is hard to me and daungerous,
And myn office is ful laborous,
And therfore by extorcions I lyve.
For sothe, I take al that men wol me yeve.   1430
Algate, by sleyghte or by violence
Fro yeer to yeer I wynne al my dispence.
I kan no bettre telle, feithfully."
  "Now certes," quod this somonour, "so fare I.
I spare nat to taken, God it woot,   1435
But if it be to hevy or to hoot.
What I may gete in conseil prively,
No maner conscience of that have I.
Nere myn extorcioun, I myghte nat lyven,
Nor of swiche japes wol I nat be shryven.   1440
Stomak ne conscience ne knowe I noon;
I shrewe thise shrifte-fadres everychoon.
Wel be we met, by God and by Seint Jame!
But, leeve brother, tel me thanne thy name,"
Quod this somonour. In this meene while   1445
This yeman gan a litel for to smyle.
  "Brother," quod he, "wiltow that I thee telle?

I am a feend; my dwellyng is in helle.
And heere I ryde about my purchasyng
To wite where men wold me yeven anythyng.
My purchas is th'effect of al my rente.   1451
Looke how thou rydest for the same entente—
To wynne good, thou rekkest nevere how.
Right so fare I, for ryde I wold right now
Unto the worldes ende for a preye."   1455
  "A," quod this somonour, "benedicite, what sey ye?
I wende ye were a yeman trewely.
Ye han a mannes shap as wel as I.
Han ye a figure thanne determinat
In helle, ther ye been in youre estat?"   1460
  "Nay, certeinly," quod he, "ther have we noon;
But whan us liketh we kan take us oon,
Or elles make yow seme we been shape.
Somtyme lyk a man, or lyk an ape,
Or lyk an angel kan I ryde or go.   1465
It is no wonder thyng thogh it be so;
A lowsy jogelour kan deceyve thee,
And pardee, yet kan I moore craft than he."
  "Why," quod this somonour, "ryde ye thanne or goon
In sondry shap and nat alwey in oon?"   1470
  "For we," quod he, "wol us swiche formes make
As moost able is oure preyes for to take."
  "What maketh yow to han al this labour?"
  "Ful many a cause, leeve sire somonour,"
Seyde this feend, "but alle thyng hath tyme.
The day is short and it is passed pryme,   1476
And yet ne wan I nothyng in this day.
I wol entende to wynnen, if I may,
And nat entende oure wittes to declare.
For, brother myn, thy wit is al to bare   1480
To understonde althogh I tolde hem thee.
But, for thou axest why labouren we,

1413 north contree, hell was considered to be in the north. **1415 wisse,** inform. **1420 subtiltee,** trick. **1421** E *that* om. **1426 streite,** strait (narrow). **1427 daungerous,** demanding. **1431 Algate,** always. **1432 wynne . . . dispence,** earn, expenditure. **1437 conseil,** secret. **1439 Nere,** were it not for. **1440 japes . . . shryven,** tricks, absolved (cured). **1442 shrewe . . . shrifte-fadres,** curse, confessors. **1444 leeve,** dear. **1449 purchasyng,** acquiring. **1450 wite where,** know whether. **1451 purchas is th'effect . . . rente,** acquisition is the sum total of my income. **1453 wynne good . . . rekkest,** gain wealth, care. **1454** Hg&c *ryde wold I now.* **1457 wende,** thought. **1459 determinat,** since it was known that devils could assume any shape, it was a question for theological debate as to what their natural form was in hell. **1463 make yow seme,** make it seem to you. **1468 kan . . . craft,** know, skill. **1470 sondry,** different shape(s). **1475** The devil quotes scripture, Ecclesiastes 3:1. **1476 pryme,** 9:00 A.M. **1478 entende to wynnen,** i.e., attend to business (capturing souls). Hg&c *wynnyng.* **1479 wittes to declare,** intellect to display.

For somtyme we been Goddes instrumentz
And meenes to doon his comandementz,
Whan that hym list, upon his creatures,   1485
In divers art and in diverse figures.
Withouten hym we have no myght, certayn,
If that hym list to stonden ther-agayn.
And somtyme, at oure prayere, han we leve
Oonly the body and nat the soule greve: 1490
Witnesse on Job, whom that we diden wo.
And somtyme han we myght of bothe two,
This is to seyn, of soule and body eke.
And somtyme be we suffred for to seke
Upon a man and doon his soule unreste,   1495
And nat his body, and al is for the beste.
Whan he withstandeth oure temptacioun,
It is a cause of his savacioun,
Al be it that it was nat oure entente
He sholde be sauf but that we wolde hym
      hente.   1500
And somtyme be we servant unto man,
As to the erchebisshop Seint Dunstan,
And to the apostles servant eek was I."
    "Yet tel me," quod the somonour, "feithfully,
Make ye yow newe bodies thus alway   1505
Of elementz?" The feend answerde, "Nay.
Somtyme we feyne, and somtyme we aryse
With dede bodyes in ful sondry wyse,
And speke as renably and faire and wel
As to the Phitonissa dide Samuel—   1510
And yet wol som men seye it was nat he;
I do no fors of youre dyvynytee.
But o thyng warne I thee, I wol nat jape:
Thou wolt algates wite how we been shape;
Thou shalt herafterwardes, my brother deere,
Come there thee nedeth nat of me to leere,   1516

For thou shalt by thyn owene experience
Konne in a chayer rede of this sentence
Bet than Virgile while he was on lyve,
Or Dant also. Now lat us ryde blyve,   1520
For I wole holde compaignye with thee
Til it be so that thou forsake me."
    "Nay," quod this somonour, "that shal nat
      bityde.
I am a yeman knowen is ful wyde;
My trouthe wol I holde, as in this cas.   1525
For though thou were the devel Sathanas,
My trouthe wol I holde to thee my brother,
As I am sworn—and ech of us til oother—
For to be trewe brother in this cas.
And bothe we goon abouten oure purchas.   1530
Taak thou thy part, what that men wol thee
      yeve,
And I shal myn; thus may we bothe lyve.
And if that any of us have moore than oother,
Lat hym be trewe and parte it with his
      brother."   1534
    "I graunte," quod the devel, "by my fey."
And with that word they ryden forth hir wey.
And right at the entryng of the townes ende,
To which this somonour shoop hym for to
      wende,
They saugh a cart that charged was with hey,
Which that a cartere droof forth in his wey.   1540
Deep was the wey, for which the carte stood.
The cartere smoot and cryde as he were wood,
"Hayt, Brok! Hayt, Scot! What, spare ye for the
      stones?
The feend," quod he, "yow fecche, body and
      bones,
As ferforthly as evere were ye foled,   1545

1485 hym list, it pleases him. **1486 art . . . figures,** method(s), shapes. **1488 list . . . agayn,** it pleases him to oppose (what we do). **1489 prayere . . . leve,** entreaty, permission. **1490 greve,** to punish. **1491 Job,** Job 1:12, 2:6. **1492 myght of,** power over. **1496 body:** E *soule.* **1500 sauf . . . hente,** saved, get. **1502 Dunstan,** St. Dunstan, Archbishop of Canterbury (961–88), was reputed to have subjected demons. **1503 apostles,** in saints legends, the apostles subject demons to their service. **1506 elementz,** i.e., are your temporal shapes created of substance (or merely illusions)? **1507 feyne,** pretend (create illusions). **1508 dede bodyes,** enter into corpses. **sondry wyse,** various ways. **1509 renably,** reasonably. **1510 Phitonissa . . . Samuel,** In the Vulgate the Witch of Endor is called "pythonissam" (I Par. 10:13). The spirit called up in I Sam. 28:11ff. (Vulgate I Kings) was reputed to be not Samuel but a fiend. **1512 no fors . . . dyvynytee,** no regard, study of theology. **1513 jape,** joke. **1514 wolt . . . wite,** i.e., always want to know. **1516 leere,** learn. **1518 Konne . . . chayer rede,** will know how to deliver lectures on the subject. **1519–20 Virgile . . . Dant,** both the *Aeneid* and *Inferno* describe the underworld. **1520 blyve,** briskly. **1523 bityde,** happen. **1525 trouthe,** troth (promise). **1527 E&c** *thee* om. **1534 parte,** share. **1538 shoop . . . wende,** planned to go. **1539 charged,** loaded. **1541 Deep . . . stood,** deep with mud, stuck. **1543 spare ye,** i.e., do you spare yourselves (OED, "refrain from action because of difficulty"). **1545 ferforthly . . . foled,** i.e., sure as you were born.

So muche wo as I have with yow tholed!
The devel have al, bothe hors and cart and
    hey."
    This somonour seyde, "Heere shal we have a
        pley."
And neer the feend he drough, as noght ne were,
Ful prively, and rowned in his ere,   1550
"Herkne, my brother, herkne, by thy feith!
Herestow nat how that the cartere seith?
Hent it anon, for he hath yeve it thee,
Bothe hey and cart, and eek his caples thre."
    "Nay," quod the devel, "God woot, never a
        deel.   1555
It is nat his entente, trust thou me weel.
Axe hym thyself, if thou nat trowest me;
Or elles stynt a while, and thou shalt see."
    This cartere thakketh his hors upon the
        croupe,
And they bigonne drawen and to stoupe.   1560
"Heyt now," quod he, "ther Jhesu Crist yow
        blesse,
And al his handwerk, bothe moore and lesse!
That was wel twight, myn owene lyard boy.
I pray God save thee, and Seinte Loy!
Now is my cart out of the slow, pardee."   1565
    "Lo, brother," quod the feend, "what tolde I
        thee?
Heere may ye se, myn owene deere brother,
The carl spak oon, but he thoghte another.
Lat us go forth abouten oure viage;
Heere wynne I nothyng upon cariage."   1570
    Whan that they coomen somwhat out of
        towne,
This somonour to his brother gan to rowne:
"Brother," quod he, "heere woneth an old
        rebekke
That hadde almoost as lief to lese hire nekke

As for to yeve a peny of hir good.   1575
I wole han twelf pens, though that she be wood,
Or I wol sompne hire unto oure office;
And yet, God woot, of hire knowe I no vice.
But for thou kanst nat, as in this contree,   1579
Wynne thy cost, taak heer ensample of me."
    This somonour clappeth at the wydwes gate.
"Com out," quod he, "thou olde virytrate!
I trowe thou hast som frere or preest with thee."
    "Who clappeth?" seyde this wyf,
        "Benedicitee,
God save you, sire; what is youre sweete
        wille?"   1585
    "I have," quod he, "of somonce here a bille.
Upon peyne of cursyng, looke that thou be
Tomorn bifore the erchedeknes knee
T'answere to the court of certeyn thynges."
    "Now, Lord," quod she, "Crist Jhesu, kyng
        of kynges,   1590
So wisly helpe me, as I ne may.
I have been syk, and that ful many a day.
I may nat go so fer," quod she, "ne ryde,
But I be deed, so priketh it in my syde.
May I nat axe a libel, sire somonour,   1595
And answere there by my procuratour
To swich thyng as men wole opposen me?"
    "Yis," quod this somonour, "pay anon—
        lat se—
Twelf pens to me, and I wol thee acquite.
I shal no profit han therby but lite;   1600
My maister hath the profit and nat I.
Com of, and lat me ryden hastily;
Yif me twelf pens; I may no lenger tarye."
    "Twelf pens!" quod she, "Now, lady Seinte
        Marie
So wisly help me out of care and synne,   1605
This wyde world thogh that I sholde wynne,

1546 **tholed,** suffered. 1548 **a pley,** some fun. 1459 **noght ne were,** i.e., casually. 1550 **rowned,** whispered. 1553 **Hent . . . anon,** take, at once. 1554 **caples,** cart horses. 1555 **woot, never a deel,** knows, not at all. 1557 **trowest,** believe. 1558 **stynt,** stop (be quiet) 1559 **thakketh . . . croupe,** pats, rump. *thakketh:* E&c *taketh.* 1562 **handwerk,** creations. 1563 **twight . . . lyard,** pulled, gray. 1564 **Loy,** the patron saint of carters, but see the Prioress, I. 120 note. E&c *pray to God.* 1565 **slow,** slough (mud). 1568 *oon:* Hg&c *o thyng.* 1570 **cariage,** technical term for a feudal lord's claim on the use of his tenant's horses and carts, which could be commuted by money payment called *cariage;* i.e., the devil will make no profit on this cart and horses. 1572 **rowne,** whisper. 1573 **woneth . . . rebekke,** lives, fiddle (cf. note to l. 1377 above). 1576 **wood,** mad. 1577 **sompne . . . office,** summon, court. 1580 **Wynne . . . cost,** earn, expenses. 1582 **virytrate,** hag. 1586 **bille,** document. 1587 **cursyng,** excommunication. *Upon:* Hg&c *Up.* 1591 **ne may,** can not. 1595 **libel,** written copy of the accusation. 1596 **procuratour,** proxy. EHg&c *procutour* (proctor). 1597 **opposen,** bring against. 1598 **anon,** now. 1605 EHg&c *help me God.*

Ne have I nat twelf pens withinne myn hoold.
Ye knowen wel that I am poure and oold;
Kithe youre almesse on me, poure wrecche."
   "Nay thanne," quod he, "the foule feend me
     fecche   1610
If I th'excuse, though thou shul be spilt!"
   "Allas!" quod she, "God woot, I have no
     gilt."
   "Pay me," quod he, "or by the sweete Seinte
     Anne,
As I wol bere awey thy newe panne
For dette which that thou owest me of old. 1615
Whan that thou madest thyn housbonde
     cokewold,
I payde at hoom for thy correccioun."
   "Thou lixt," quod she, "by my savacioun,
Ne was I nevere er now, wydwe ne wyf,
Somoned unto youre court in al my lyf;   1620
Ne nevere I nas but of my body trewe.
Unto the devel, blak and rough of hewe,
Yeve I thy body and my panne also!"
   And whan the devel herde hire cursen so
Upon hir knees, he seyde in this manere,   1625
"Now Mabely, myn owene moder deere,
Is this youre wyl in ernest that ye seye?"
   "The devel," quod she, "so fecche hym er he
     deye,
And panne and al, but he wol hym repente!"
   "Nay, olde stot, that is nat myn entente,"   1630
Quod this somonour, "for to repente me
For any thyng that I have had of thee.
I wolde I hadde thy smok and every clooth."
   "Now brother," quod the devel, "be nat
     wrooth;

Thy body and this panne been myne by right.
Thou shalt with me to helle yet tonyght,   1636
Where thou shalt knowen of oure privetee
Moore than a maister of dyvynytee."
And with that word this foule feend hym hente;
Body and soule he with the devel wente   1640
Where as that somonours han hir heritage.
And God, that maked after his ymage
Mankynde, save and gyde us alle and some,
And leve thise somonours goode men bicome!

   Lordynges, I koude han toold yow, quod this
     Frere,   1645
Hadde I had leyser for this Somnour heere,
After the text of Crist, Poul, and John,
And of oure othere doctours many oon,
Swiche peynes that youre hertes myghte
     agryse,
Al be it so no tonge may it devyse,   1650
Thogh that I myghte a thousand wynter telle,
The peynes of thilke cursed hous of helle.
But for to kepe us fro that cursed place,
Waketh and preyeth Jhesu for his grace
So kepe us fro the temptour Sathanas.   1655
Herketh this word, beth war as in this cas:
The leoun sit in his awayt alway
To sle the innocent, if that he may.
Disposeth ay youre hertes to withstonde
The feend that yow wolde make thral and
     bonde.   1660
He may nat tempte yow over youre myght,
For Crist wol be youre champion and knyght.
And prayeth that thise somonours hem repente
Of hir mysdedes er that the feend hem hente!

Heere endeth the Freres Tale.

1607 **hoold**, possession. 1609 **Kithe . . . almesse**, show, charity. 1611 **spilt**, ruined. 1617 **correccioun**, fine. 1618 **lixt**, lie. 1630 **stot**, cow. 1633 **smok . . . clooth**, i.e., underclothes and every rag. 1636 **with me**, cf. Luke 23:43. 1639 **hente**, grabbed. 1644 **leve**, let. 1646 **leyser for**, permission of. 1649 **agryse**, terrify. 1650 **Al be it so**, Nevertheless. 1657 **leoun sit . . . awayt**, lies in wait, Ps. 10:9. 1660 **thral**, slave. 1663–64 Some MSS *this somonour/hym/hys/hym.*

SUMMONER'S TALE

PROLOGUE

The Prologe of the Somonours Tale.

This Somonour in his styropes hye stood;
Upon this Frere his herte was so wood   1666
That lyk an aspen leef he quook for ire.

    "Lordynges," quod he, "but o thyng I desire:
I yow biseke that, of youre curteisye,
Syn ye han herd this false Frere lye,   1670
As suffreth me I may my tale telle.
This Frere bosteth that he knoweth helle,
And God it woot that it is litel wonder—
Freres and feendes been but lyte asonder.
For, pardee, ye han ofte tyme herd telle   1675
How that a frere ravysshed was to helle
In spirit ones by a visioun,
And as an angel ladde hym up and doun
To shewen hym the peynes that ther were
In al the place saugh he nat a frere;   1680
Of oother folk he saugh ynowe in wo.
Unto this angel spak the frere tho,

    'Now, sire,' quod he, 'han freres swich a grace
That noon of hem shal come to this place?'

    'Yis,' quod this angel, 'many a millioun.'   1685
And unto Sathanas he ladde hym doun.

    'And now hath Sathanas,' seith he, 'a tayl
Brodder than of a carryk is the sayl.
Hold up thy tayl, thou Sathanas,' quod he.
'Shewe forth thyn ers, and lat the frere se   1690
Where is the nest of freres in this place!'
And er that half a furlong wey of space,
Right so as bees out swarmen from an hyve,
Out of the develes ers ther gonne dryve
Twenty thousand freres in a route,   1695
And thurghout helle swarmeden aboute,
And comen agayn as faste as they may gon,
And in his ers they crepten everychon.
He clapte his tayl agayn and lay ful stille.
This frere, whan he hadde looke al his fille   1700
Upon the tormentz of this sory place,
His spirit God restored, of his grace,
Unto his body agayn, and he awook.
But natheles for fere yet he quook,
So was the develes ers ay in his mynde—   1705
That is his heritage of verray kynde.
God save yow alle, save this cursed Frere!
My prologe wol I ende in this manere."

1666 **wood,** mad. 1671 **suffreth,** permit. 1674 **lyte asonder,** i.e., nearly the same. 1677 **visioun,** in a dream. 1682 **tho,** then. 1688 **carryk,** big ship. 1692 **furlong,** 220 yards, but as usual a measure of time, cf. *CT,* ɪ.3637. 1695 **route,** swarm. 1706 **verray kynde,** true nature.

Heere bigynneth the Somonour his Tale.

Lordynges, ther is in Yorkshire, as I gesse,
A mersshy contree called Holdernesse 1710
In which ther wente a lymytour aboute
To preche and eek to begge, it is no doute.
And so bifel that on a day this frere
Hadde preched at a chirche in his manere,
And specially, aboven every thyng, 1715
Excited he the peple in his prechyng
To trentals, and to yeve for Goddes sake
Wherwith men myghte hooly houses make
Ther as divine servyce is honoured,
Nat ther as it is wasted and devoured, 1720
Ne ther it nedeth nat for to be yeve,
As to possessioners that mowen lyve,
Thanked be God, in wele and habundaunce.
"Trentals," seyde he, "deliveren fro penaunce
Hir freendes soules, as wel olde as yonge, 1725
Ye, whan that they been hastily ysonge,
Nat for to holde a preest joly and gay—
He syngeth nat but o masse in a day.
Delivereth out," quod he, "anon the soules.
Ful hard it is with flesshhook or with oules 1730
To been yclawed, or to brenne or bake.
Now spede yow hastily, for Cristes sake!"
And whan this frere had seyd al his entente,
With *qui cum patre* forth his wey he wente.
  Whan folk in chirche had yeve him what hem
    leste, 1735
He wente his wey—no lenger wholde he
    reste—
With scrippe and tipped staf, ytukked hye.
In every hous he gan to poure and prye,
And beggeth mele and chese, or elles corn.

His felawe hadde a staf tipped with horn, 1740
A peyre of tables al of yvory,
And a poyntel polysshed fetisly,
And wroot the names alwey, as he stood,
Of alle folk that yaf hym any good,
Ascaunces that he wolde for hem preye. 1745
"Yif us a busshel whete, malt, or reye,
A Goddes kechyl, or a tryp of chese,
Or elles what yow lyst—we may nat
    cheese—
A Goddes halfpeny, or a masse peny,
Or yif us of youre brawn, if ye have eny, 1750
A dagon of youre blanket—leeve dame,
Oure suster deere—lo, heere I write youre
    name—
Bacon or boef, or swich thyng as ye fynde."
  A sturdy harlot wente ay hem bihynde,
That was hir hostes man, and bar a sak, 1755
And what men yaf hem, leyde it on his bak.
And whan that he was out at dore, anon
He planed awey the names everichon
That he biforn had writen in his tables;
He served hem with nyfles and with fables. 1760
  "Nay, ther thou lixt, thou Somonour!" quod
    the Frere.
  "Pees," quod oure Hoost, "for Cristes
    mooder deere.
Tel forth thy tale, and spare it nat at al."
  "So thryve I," quod this Somonour, "so I
    shal."
  So longe he wente, hous by hous, til he 1765
Cam til an hous ther he was wont to be
Refresshed moore than in an hundred placis.

1710 **Holdernesse,** a district north of Hull. Note that Chaucer makes no effort here to reproduce the Yorkshire accent, as he does in RvT. 1711 **lymytour,** a begging friar with an assigned territory (a limit; cf. l. 1265 above and *CT,* I.209). 1717 **trentals,** (the money paid for) masses said for thirty days to release souls from Purgatory. 1718 **make,** build. 1722 **possessioners,** monastic orders and beneficed clergy living on endowments. 1723 **wele,** prosperity. 1726 **hastily,** the friar advises that the 30 trentals be sung at one time. 1727 **holde,** keep (support, by the 30 days' payments). 1729 **out . . . anon,** out (of Purgatory), at once. 1730 **flesshhook . . . oules,** meathooks, awls (instruments by which souls in Purgatory are punished). 1731 **brenne,** burned. 1734 *qui cum patre,* opening formula for the benediction. 1735 **leste,** pleased. 1737 **scrippe, tipped staf, ytukked,** bag (for alms); staff tipped with metal or horn as a badge of authority (cf. OED tipstaff); with robe tucked up into his girdle for easier walking. 1738 **poure,** pore (search). 1739 **corn,** grain (wheat or barley, not maize). 1740 **felawe,** friars had to go about in pairs, cf. l. 1862 below. 1741 **tables,** folding writing tablets coated with wax. 1742 **poyntel . . . fetisly,** stylus, elegantly. 1744 **hym:** Hg&c **hem.** 1745 **Ascaunces,** as if. 1746 **us:** E **hym.** 1747 **kechyl . . . tryp,** cake, bit. 1749 **masse peny,** penny to pay toward a mass. 1750 **brawn,** pork. 1751 **dagon . . . blanket,** piece, blanket (being woven?). 1754 **harlot,** servant. 1755 **hostes man,** servant to guests in the convent(?). 1758 **planed,** smoothed. 1760 **nyfles,** trifles. 1761 **lixt,** lie. 1766 **wont,** accustomed. 1767 **Refresshed,** replenished.

Syk lay the goode man whos that the place is;
Bedrede upon a couche lowe he lay.
"*Deus hic!*" quod he, "O Thomas, freend, good
  day,"   1770
Seyde this frere, curteisly and softe.
"Thomas," quod he, "God yelde yow. Ful ofte
Have I upon this bench faren ful weel;
Heere have I eten many a myrie meel."
And fro the bench he droof awey the cat 1775
And leyde adoun his potente and his hat,
And eek his scrippe, and sette hym softe adoun.
His felawe was go walked into toun
Forth with his knave into that hostelrye
Where as he shoop hym thilke nyght to lye. 1780
 "O deere maister," quod this sike man,
"How han ye fare sith that March bigan?
I saugh yow noght this fourtenyght or moore."
 "God woot," quod he, "laboured I have ful
  soore,
And specially for thy savacioun   1785
Have I seyd many a precious orisoun,
And for oure othere freendes, God hem blesse!
I have to day been at youre chirche at messe,
And seyd a sermon after my symple wit,
Nat al after the text of hooly writ; 1790
For it is hard to yow, as I suppose,
And therfore wol I teche yow al the glose.
Glosynge is a glorious thyng, certeyn,
For lettre sleeth, so as we clerkes seyn.
There have I taught hem to be charitable, 1795
And spende hir good ther it is resonable;
And there I saugh oure dame—a, where is she?"
 "Yond in the yerd I trowe that she be,"
Seyde this man, "and she wol come anon."
 "Ey, maister, welcome be ye, by Seint
  John!"   1800
Seyde this wyf, "How fare ye, hertely?"
 The frere ariseth up ful curteisly
And hire embraceth in his armes narwe,

And kiste hire sweete, and chirketh as a sparwe
With his lyppes. "Dame," quod he, "right weel,
As he that is youre servant every deel, 1806
Thanked be God that yow yaf soule and lyf.
Yet saugh I nat this day so fair a wyf
In al the chirche, God so save me!"
 "Ye, God amende defautes, sire," quod she.
"Algates, welcome be ye, by my fey!" 1811
 "Graunt mercy, dame, this have I founde
  alwey.
But of youre grete goodnesse, by youre leve,
I wolde prey yow that ye nat yow greve,
I wole with Thomas speke a litel throwe. 1815
Thise curatz been ful necligent and slowe
To grope tendrely a conscience
In shrift; in prechyng is my diligence,
And studie in Petres wordes and in Poules.
I walke and fisshe Cristen mennes soules 1820
To yelden Jhesu Crist his propre rente;
To sprede his word is set al myn entente."
 "Now, by your leve, O deere sire," quod she,
"Chideth him weel, for seinte Trinitee.
He is as angry as a pissemyre   1825
Though that he have al that he kan desire.
Though I hym wrye a-nyght and make hym
  warm,
And on hym leye my leg outher myn arm,
He groneth lyk oure boor lith in oure sty.
Oother desport right noon of hym have I; 1830
I may nat plese hym in no maner cas."
 "O Thomas, *je vous dy*, Thomas! Thomas!
This maketh the feend; this moste ben amended.
Ire is a thyng that hye God defended,
And therof wol I speke a word or two." 1835
 "Now, maister," quod the wyf, "er that I go,
What wol ye dyne? I wol go theraboute."
 "Now, dame," quod he, "now *je vous dy sanz
  doute*,
Have I nat of a capon but the lyvere,

1769 Bedrede, bedridden. **1770 *Deus hic,*** God be here (pastoral blessing on a house). **1772 yelde,** reward. **1776 potente,** staff. **1780 shoop,** planned. **1786 orisoun,** prayer. **1793 Glosynge,** glossing (*double entendre,* explaining, but also lying, Mod.E. glozing). **1794 lettre sleeth,** II Cor. 3:6. *we:* E&c *thise.* **1795 There,** i.e., in church, where he was preaching. **1798 trowe,** believe. **1803 narwe,** closely. **1804 chirketh,** chirps. EHg&c *chirteth.* **1810 amende defautes,** repair (my) faults. **1811 Algates,** Always. **1815 throwe,** while. **1816 curatz,** resident priests, cf. l. 219. **1817 grope,** search, but cf. l. 2148 below. **1818 shrift,** confession. **1821 propre rente,** due income. **1824 Chideth,** admonish. **1825 pissemyre,** contemptuous term for an ant. **1827 wrye,** cover. **1832 *je vous dy,*** I say to you (French phrases were a mark of social affection in the 14th century, cf. the Prioress, l. 124). **1834 Ire,** one of the Seven Deadly Sins. **defended,** forbidden.

And of youre softe breed nat but a shyvere, 1840
And after that a rosted pigges heed—
But that I nolde no beest for me were deed—
Thanne hadde I with yow hoomly suffisaunce.
I am a man of litel sustenaunce;
My spirit hath his fostryng in the Bible. 1845
The body is ay so redy and penyble
To wake that my stomak is destroyed.
I prey yow, dame, ye be nat anoyed,
Though I so freendly yow my conseil shewe.
By God, I wolde nat telle it but a fewe." 1850
  "Now, sire," quod she, "but o word er I go.
My child is deed withinne thise wykes two,
Soone after that ye wente out of this toun."
  "His deeth saugh I by revelacioun,"
Seith this frere, "at hoom in oure dortour. 1855
I dar wel seyn that er that half an hour
After his deeth I saugh hym born to blisse
In myn avisioun, so God me wisse.
So dide oure sexteyn and oure fermerer,
That han been trewe freres fifty yeer; 1860
They may now—God be thanked of his loone—
Maken hir jubilee and walke allone.
And up I roos, and al oure covent eke,
With many a teere trillyng on my cheke,
Withouten noyse or claterynge of belles; 1865
Te Deum was oure song, and nothyng elles,
Save that to Crist I seyde an orisoun,
Thankynge hym of his revelacioun.
For, sire and dame, trusteth me right weel,
Oure orisons been moore effectueel, 1870
And moore we seen of Cristes secree thynges,
Than burel folk, although they weren kynges.
We lyve in poverte and in abstinence,
And burell folk in richesse and despence
Of mete and drynke, and in hir foul delit. 1875

We han this worldes lust al in despit.
Lazar and Dives lyveden diversly,
And diverse gerdon hadden they therby.
Whoso wol preye, he moot faste and be clene,
And fatte his soule, and make his body lene. 1880
We fare as seith th'apostle; clooth and foode
Suffisen us, though they be nat ful goode.
The clennesse and the fastynge of us freres
Maketh that Crist accepteth oure preyeres.
  "Lo, Moyses fourty dayes and fourty nyght
Fasted er that the heighe God of myght 1886
Spak with hym in the Mount of Synay.
With empty wombe, fastynge many a day,
Receyved he the lawe that was writen
With Goddes fynger; and Elye, wel ye witen, 1890
In Mount Oreb, er he hadde any speche 1891
With hye God that is oure lyves leche,
He fasted longe and was in contemplaunce.
  "Aaron, that hadde the temple in
      governaunce,
And eek the othere preestes everichon 1895
Into the temple whan they sholde gon
To preye for the peple and do servyse,
They nolden drynken in no maner wyse
No drynke which that myghte hem dronke
      make,
But there in abstinence preye and wake 1900
Lest that they deyden. Taak heede what I seye.
But they be sobre that for the peple preye,
War that I seye—namoore, for it suffiseth.
  "Oure Lord Jhesu, as hooly writ devyseth,
Yaf us ensample of fastynge and preyeres. 1905
Therfore we mendynantz, we sely freres,
Been wedded to poverte and continence,
To charite, humblesse, and abstinence,
To persecucioun for rightwisnesse,

1840 shyvere, sliver. **1842 I nolde . . . deed,** I would not have, killed. **1843 hoomly suffisaunce,** family fare. **1844 litel sustenaunce,** i.e., who eats lightly. **1845 fostryng,** is sustained by. **1846 ay so redy and penyble,** always so willing and (long) suffering. **1847 To wake,** to stay awake (in prayer and meditation). **stomak,** appetite. **1849 conseil,** secrets. **1855 dortour,** dormitory (in the convent). **1858 wisse,** witness. **1859 sexteyn . . . fermerer,** sacristan (in charge of the room housing sacred vessels and vestments), in charge of the infirmary. **1861 loone,** gift (loan). **1862 jubilee . . . allone,** fiftieth anniversary, go about alone (instead of in pairs). **1864** *trillyng:* EHg&c *triklyng.* **1865 noyse . . . belles,** the friars were usually called to service by bells. **1866 Te Deum,** hymn of praise, usually sung at matins. **1867 orisoun,** prayer. **1870** *moore:* EHg&c *wel moore.* **1872 burel,** laymen (really a coarse cloth). **1876 lust . . . despit,** pleasure, detestation. **1877 Lazar . . . Dives,** the poor man and the rich man, cf. Luke 16:19–26. **1878 diverse gerdon,** different rewards. **1879 clene,** pure. **1881 apostle,** cf. I Tim. 6:8. **1887 Synay,** Sinai, cf. Exodus 34:28. **mount:** Hg&c *mountain.* **1890 Elye,** Elijah, cf. I Kings 19:8. **1892 leche,** physician. **1893 contemplaunce,** contemplation. **1894 Aaron,** cf. Levit. 10:9. **1901 deyden,** died. **1903 War,** beware. **1906 mendynantz,** mendicants (the orders of friars—Franciscan, Dominicans, etc., cf. *CT,* i.210—were supposed to live on alms). **sely,** the usual range, from blessed to foolish. **1909 for,** i.e., for the sake of.

To wepynge, misericorde, and clennesse.   1910
And therfore may ye se that oure preyeres—
I speke of us, we mendynantz, we freres—
Been to the hye God moore acceptable
Than youres, with youre feestes at the table.
Fro Paradys first, if I shal nat lye,   1915
Was man out chaced for his glotonye—
And chaast was man in Paradys, certeyn.
    "But herkne now, Thomas, what I shal seyn.
I ne have no text of it, as I suppose,
But I shal fynde it in a maner glose   1920
That specially oure sweete Lord Jhesus
Spak this by freres whan he seyde thus,
'Blessed be they that povere in spirit been.'
And so forth al the gospel may ye seen
Wher it be likker oure professioun   1925
Or hirs that swymmen in possessioun.
Fy on hire pompe and on hire glotonye,
And for hir lewednesse I hem diffye.
    "Me thynketh they been lyk Jovinyan,
Fat as a whale and walkynge as a swan,   1930
Al vinolent as botel in the spence.
Hir preyere is of ful greet reverence
Whan they for soules seye the psalm of Davit:
Lo, 'buf!' they seye, '*cor meum eructavit!*'
Who folweth Cristes gospel and his foore   1935
But we that humble been, and chaast, and poore,
Werkeris of Goddes word, nat auditours?
Therfore, right as an hauk up at a sours
Up springeth into th'eir, right so prayeres
Of charitable and chaste bisy freres   1940
Maken hir sours to Goddes eres two.
Thomas, Thomas, so moote I ryde or go,
And by that lord that clepid is Seint Yve,

Nere thou oure brother, sholdestou nat thryve.
In oure chapitre praye we day and nyght   1945
To Crist that he thee sende heele and myght
Thy body for to weelden hastily."
    "God woot," quod he, "nothyng therof
        feele I!
As help me Crist, as I in a fewe yeres
Have spended upon diverse manere freres   1950
Ful many a pound, yet fare I never the bet.
Certeyn, my good I have almoost biset.
Farwel, my gold, for it is al ago."
    The frere answerde, "O Thomas, dostow so?
What nedeth yow diverse freres seche?   1955
What nedeth hym that hath a parfit leche
To sechen othere leches in the toun?
Youre inconstance is youre confusioun.
Holde ye thanne me, or elles oure covent,
To praye for yow been insufficient?   1960
Thomas, that jape nys nat worth a myte.
Youre maladye is for we han to lyte.
A, yif that covent half a quarter otes!
A, yif that covent foure and twenty grotes!
A, yif that frere a peny and lat hym go!   1965
Nay, nay, Thomas, it may no thyng be so!
What is a ferthyng worth parted in twelve?
Lo, ech thyng that is oned in itselve
Is moore strong than whan it is toscatered.
Thomas, of me thou shalt nat been yflatered;
Thou woldest han oure labour al for noght.   1971
The hye God, that al this world hath wroght,
Seith that the werkman worthy is his hyre.
Thomas, noght of youre tresor I desire
As for myself, but that al oure covent   1975
To preye for yow is ay so diligent,

1910 misericorde...clennesse, mercy, purity. **1916 chaced,** chased (*double entendre* with next line). **glotonye,** i.e., eating the forbidden fruit. **1917 chaast,** chaste. **1918** EHg&c *now* om. **1920 glose,** gloss, but again the *double entendre* with gloze, lie, because the friars were notorious in the 14th century for their self-indulgence; cf. l. 208ff. **1925 it be likker,** it, i.e., the scriptural admonition, more resembles; the famous medieval mystical treatise *Imitatio Christi* was attributed to the Augustinian canon Thomas à Kempis. **1926 possessioun,** cf. l. 1722n. above. **1928 lewednesse,** ignorance, but shading over into immorality. **diffye,** scorn. **1929 Jovinyan,** Jovinian is so described by Jerome, cf. *CT,* III.3n. above. **1931 spence,** pantry. **1934 buf,** a belch. *cor meum eructavit,* "My heart has uttered"—opening words to Ps. 45, but *double entendre* because Lat. *eructavi* also meanst belched. *buf:* E&c *but;* other MSS *buth.* **1935 foore,** track. **1937 Werkeris...nat auditours,** doers, not hearers. **1938 up...sours,** with a soar. **1944 brother,** religious institutions granted letters of fraternity to selected lay people, as Lincoln Cathedral did to Philippa Chaucer in 1386. **1946 heele,** health. **1947 weelden,** use (wield). **1949–50** E&c *as in a few yeres/I han.* **1952 biset,** spent. Hg&c *have* I. **1955 diverse,** different. **1956 leche,** physician. **1958 inconstance,** inconstancy (changing about). **1959 Holde ye,** do you think. **1961 jape...myte,** foolish behavior, least valuable coin. **1962 han...lyte,** have received too little. **1963 quarter,** quarter of a bushel (?). In this and the next two lines, the friar is mimicking what he regards as Thomas's niggardly donations. **1964 grotes,** groats (silver fourpence). **1967 ferthyng...parted,** cf. l. 2243ff. below. **1968 oned,** united. *itselve:* Hg&c *himselve.*

And for to buylden Cristes owene chirche.
Thomas, if ye wol lernen for to wirche,
Of buyldynge up of chirches may ye fynde
If it be good in Thomas lyf of Inde.   1980
Ye lye heere ful of anger and of ire,
With which the devel set youre herte afyre,
And chiden heere the sely innocent,
Youre wyf, that is so meke and pacient.   1984
And therfore, Thomas, trowe me if thee leste,
Ne stryve nat with thy wyf, as for thy beste.
And ber this word awey now, by thy feith,
Touchynge this thyng, lo, what the wise seith:
'Withinne thyn hous ne be thou no leoun;
To thy subgitz do noon oppressioun;   1990
Ne make thyne aqueyntance nat for to flee.'
And, Thomas, yet eftsoones I charge thee,
Bewar from ire that in thy bosom slepeth,
Bewar fro the serpent that so slily crepeth
Under the gras and styngeth subtilly.   1995
Bewar, my sone, and herkne paciently
That twenty thousand men han lost hir lyves
For stryvyng with hir lemmans and hir wyves.
Now sith ye han so hooly meke a wyf,
What nedeth yow, Thomas, to maken stryf?
Ther nys, ywys, no serpent so cruel   2001
Whan man tret on his tayl, ne half so fel
As womman is, whan she hath caught an ire;
Vengeance is thanne al that they desire.
Ire is a synne, oon of the grete of sevene,   2005
Abhomynable unto the God of hevene;
And to hymself it is destruccioun.
This every lewed viker or persoun
Kan seye, how ire engendreth homycide.
Ire is, in sooth, executour of pryde.   2010
I koude of ire seye so muche sorwe
My tale sholde laste til tomorwe.
And therfore preye I God bothe day and nyght
An irous man, God sende hym litel myght!
It is greet harm and certes greet pitee   2015

To sette an irous man in heigh degree.
    "Whilom ther was an irous potestat,
As seith Senek, that durynge his estaat
Upon a day out ryden knyghtes two,
And as Fortune wolde that it were so   2020
That oon of hem cam hoom that oother noght.
Anon the knyght bifore the juge is broght,
That seyde thus, 'Thou hast thy felawe slayn
For which I deme thee to the deeth, certayn.'
And to another knyght comanded he,   2025
'Go lede hym to the deeth, I charge thee.'
And happed as they wente by the weye
Toward the place ther he sholde deye,
The knyght cam which men wenden had be
    deed.
Thanne thoughte they it were the beste reed   2030
To lede hem bothe to the juge agayn.
They seiden, 'Lord, the knyght ne hath nat slayn
His felawe; heere he standeth hool alyve.'
'Ye shul be deed,' quod he, 'so moot I thryve,
That is to seyn, bothe oon, and two, and thre.'
And to the firste knyght right thus spak he,   2036
'I dampned thee; thou most algate be deed.
And thou also most nedes lese thyn heed
For thou art cause why thy felawe deyth.'   2039
And to the thridde knyght right thus he seith,
'Thou hast nat doon that I comanded thee.'
And thus he dide doon sleen hem alle thre.
    "Irous Cambises was eek dronkelewe
And ay delited hym to been a shrewe.
And so bifel, a lord of his meynee   2045
That loved vertuous moralitee
Seyde on a day bitwene hem two right thus,
'A lord is lost if he be vicius,
And dronkenesse is eek a foul record
Of any man, and namely in a lord.   2050
Ther is ful many an eye and many an ere
Awaityng on a lord and he noot where.
For Goddes love, drynk moore attemprely!

1978 **lernen ... wirche,** i.e., learn to do good works. 1980 **Thomas lyf,** St. Thomas of India was reputed to have built churches.
1983 **chiden ... sely,** scold, blessed. 1985 **trowe ... leste,** believe, will. 1986 **beste,** which will be best (for you). 1988 *this/wise:*
Hg&c *swich/wise man.* 1991 *aqueyntance:* EHg&c *aqueyntances* except that Chaucer appears never to have used the plural elsewhere as a
concrete noun. 1993 *ire:* EHg&c *hire.* 1994 *Bewar:* Hg&c *War.* 1995 **subtilly,** secretly. 1998 **lemmans,** lovers. 2002 **fel,** dangerous.
Whan: E *What.* 2005 *of sevene:* other MSS *of* om. What follows is a typical sermon against the sin of ire (wrath). 2008 **viker, persoun,**
vicar, parson. 2018 **Senek,** these illustrations are from Seneca's *De Ira.* 2024 **deme,** condemn. 2030 **reed,** idea. 2034 **thryve,** prosper.
2037 **dampned ... algate,** condemned, anyway. 2043 **dronkelewe,** drunkard. 2044 **shrewe,** evil person. 2045 **meynee,** household.
2047 **bitwene ... two,** confidentially. 2050 **namely,** especially. 2052 **noot,** doesn't know. 2053 **attemprely,** temperately.

Wyn maketh man to lesen wrecchedly
His mynde and eek his lymes everichon.' 2055
  'The revers shaltou se,' quod he, 'anon,
And preve it by thyn owene experience,
That wyn ne dooth to folk no swich offence.
Ther is no wyn bireveth me my myght
Of hand ne foot, ne of myne eyen sight.' 2060
And for despit he drank ful muchel moore
An hondred part than he hadde bifoore;
And right anon this irous, cursed wrecche
Leet this knyghtes sone bifore hym fecche,
Comandynge hym he sholde bifore hym stonde.
And sodeynly he took his bowe in honde, 2066
And up the streng he pulled to his ere,
And with an arwe he slow the child right there.
'Now wheither have I a siker hand or noon?'
Quod he. 'Is al my myght and mynde agon?
Hath wyn byreved me myn eyen sight?' 2071
  "What sholde I telle th'answere of the knyght?
His sone was slayn, ther is namoore to seye.
Beth war, therfore, with lordes how ye pleye.
Syngeth *Placebo* and 'I shal if I kan,' 2075
But if it be unto a poure man.
To a poure man men sholde his vices telle,
But nat to a lord thogh he sholde go to helle.
  "Lo irous Cirus, thilke Percien,
How he destroyed the ryver of Gysen 2080
For that an hors of his was dreynt therinne
Whan that he wente Babiloigne to wynne.
He made that the ryver was so smal
That wommen myghte wade it over al.
Lo, what seyde he that so wel teche kan: 2085
Ne be no felawe to an irous man,
Ne with no wood man walke by the weye,
Lest thee repente—I wol no ferther seye.
  "Now, Thomas, leeve brother, lef thyn ire;
Thou shalt me fynde as just as is a squyre. 2090

Hoold nat the develes knyf ay at thyn herte—
Thyn angre dooth thee al to soore smerte—
But shewe to me al thy confessioun."
  "Nay," quod the sike man, "by Seint
    Symoun,
I have be shryven this day at my curat. 2095
I have hym toold hoolly al myn estat.
Nedeth namoore to speken of it," seith he,
"But if me list, of myn humylitee."
  "Yif me thanne of thy gold, to make oure
    cloystre,"
Quod he, "for many a muscle and many an
    oystre, 2100
Whan othere men han ben ful wel at eyse,
Hath been oure foode, oure cloystre for to reyse.
And yet, God woot, unnethe the fundement
Parfourned is, ne of oure pavement
Nys nat a tyle yet withinne oure wones. 2105
By God, we owen fourty pound for stones.
  "Now help, Thomas, for hym that harwed
    helle!
For elles moste we oure bookes selle.
And if yow lakke oure predicacioun,
Thanne goth the world al to destruccioun. 2110
For whoso wolde us fro this world bireve,
So God me save, Thomas, by youre leve,
He wolde bireve out of this world the sonne.
For who kan teche and werchen as we konne?
And that is nat of litel tyme," quod he, 2115
"But syn Elye was, or Elise,
Han freres been, that fynde I of record,
In charitee, ythanked be oure Lord.
Now Thomas, help, for seinte charitee!"
And doun anon he sette hym on his knee. 2120
  This sike man wax wel ny wood for ire;
He wolde that the frere had been on fire,
With his false dissymulacioun.

2054 **lesen**, lose. 2056 **revers . . . anon**, opposite, at once. 2059 **bireveth**, deprives. 2061 **despit**, spite. 2062 **part**, times. *hadde:* Hg&c *hadde don.* 2064 **Leet**, caused. 2069 **wheither . . . siker . . . noon**, do, sure (secure), not. 2075 *Placebo*, "I will please," Vulgate Ps. 114:9, part of the office for the dead. The term came to mean to be complaisant; cf. MerchT, iv.1476ff. below. 2079 **Cirus**, this illustration is from Seneca's *De Ira.* 2085 **he**, Solomon, Prov. 22:24–25. 2087 **wood**, crazy. 2088 E *there is namoore to seye.* 2090 **squyre**, carpenter's square. 2095 **curat**, local priest, cf. l. 1816 above. 2096 **estat**, spiritual condition. 2098 **list**, choose. 2100 **muscle**, mussels and oysters, represented by the friar as penitential fare. 2103 **fundement**, foundation. 2104 **Parfourned . . . pavement**, completed, (paved) floor. 2105 **wones**, building. 2107 **harwed**, harrowed. 2108 *For:* Hg&c *Or.* 2109 **predicacioun**, preaching. 2111 **bireve**, deprive. 2115 **of litel**, i.e., not only today. 2116 **syn**, since. **Elye . . . Elise**, Elijah, Elisha—not true, of course, since the mendicant orders were created in the 12th century. But the Carmelites claimed that their order was founded by Elijah on Mt. Carmel; hence this friar would appear to be a Carmelite. *Elye:* E *Ennok.* 2121 **wood**, insane.

"Swich thyng as is in my possessioun," 2124
Quod he, "that may I yeven, and noon oother.
Ye sey me thus, that I am youre brother?"

"Ye, certes," quod the frere, "trusteth weel.
I took oure dame oure lettre and oure seel."

"Now wel," quod he, "and somwhat shal I yeve
Unto youre hooly covent whil I lyve; 2130
And in thyn hand thou shalt it have anon
On this condicion and oother noon,
That thou departe it so, my leeve brother,
That every frere have also muche as oother.
This shaltou swere on thy professioun, 2135
Withouten fraude or cavillacioun."

"I swere it," quod this frere, "by my feith!"
And therwithal his hand in his he leith,
"Lo, heer my feith; in me shal be no lak."

"Now thanne, put in thyn hand doun by my
bak," 2140
Seyde this man, "and grope wel bihynde.
Bynethe my buttok ther shaltow fynde
A thyng that I have hyd in pryvetee."

"A," thoghte this frere, "this shal go with
me!"
And doun his hand he launcheth to the clifte
In hope for to fynde there a yifte. 2146
And whan this sike man felte this frere
Aboute his tuwel grope there and heere,
Amydde his hand he leet the frere a fart—
Ther nys no capul drawynge in a cart 2150
That myghte have lete a fart of swich a soun.

The frere up stirte as dooth a wood leoun,
"A, false cherl," quod he, "for Goddes bones!
This hastow for despit doon for the nones.
Thou shalt abye this fart, if that I may." 2155

His meynee, whiche that herden this affray,
Cam lepynge in and chaced out the frere.

And forth he gooth with a ful angry cheere
And fette his felawe, ther as lay his stoor.
He looked as it were a wilde boor; 2160
He grynte with his teeth, so was he wrooth.
A sturdy paas doun to the court he gooth
Wher as ther woned a man of greet honour
To whom that he was alwey confessour.
This worthy man was lord of that village. 2165
This frere cam as he were in a rage
Where as this lord sat etyng at his bord.
Unnethes myghte the frere speke a word,
Til atte laste he seyde, "God yow see!" 2169

This lord gan looke, and seide, "Benedicitee,
What, Frere John, what maner world is this?
I se wel that some thyng ther is amys;
Ye looken as the wode were ful of thevys.
Sit doun anon and tel me what youre grief is,
And it shal been amended, if I may." 2175

"I have," quod he, "had a despit this day,
God yelde yow, adoun in youre village,
That in this world is noon so poure a page
That he nolde have abhomynacioun
Of that I have receyved in youre toun. 2180
And yet ne greveth me nothyng so soore
As that this olde cherl with lokkes hoore
Blasphemed hath oure hooly covent eke."

"Now, maister," quod this lord, "I yow
biseke—"

"No maister, sire," quod he, "but servitour,
Thogh I have had in scole that honour. 2186
God liketh nat that 'Raby' men us calle
Neither in market ne in youre large halle."

"No fors," quod he, "but tel me al youre
grief."

"Sire," quod this frere, "an odious meschief
This day bityd is to myn ordre and me, 2191
And so, *per consequens*, to ech degree

2128 **and oure**: Hg&c *with oure*. 2133 **departe**, divide. *leeve*: Hg&c *deere*. 2136 **cavillacioun**, quibbling. 2145 **clifte**, cleft. 2148 **tuwel**, anus. 2150 **capul**, cart horse. 2152 **wood**, mad. 2154 **despit**, spite. 2155 **abye**, regret. 2156 **meynee**, household. 2158 **cheere**, expression. In 7 MSS the tale ends here with the following conclusion: *He had noght elles for his longe sermoun | To parte amonge his bredern when he come home. | And thus is this tale of the Frere ydon, | For we were almost at the toune.* 2159 **fette . . . stoor**, fetched, store (collections). 2162 **sturdy paas . . . court**, quick pace, manor house. 2163 **woned**, lived. 2165 **lord**, i.e., feudal lord. 2168 **Unnethes**, scarcely. 2170 **gan**: E *bigan to*. 2171 **what . . . world**, what in the world is the matter. 2172 E *I trowe som maner thyng ther is amys*. 2175 **if**: E&c *if that*. 2176 **despit**, insult (spite). 2178 **poure a page**, lowly a serving boy. *is noon*: Hg&c *ther nys*. 2179 **abhomynacioun**, loathing. 2181 E&c *ne* om. 2184 **biseke**, beseech. 2185 **maister**, the friar mistakes a courteous greeting for a university degree, master of arts. 2186 **that**: E *swich*. 2187 **Raby**, Rabbi; cf. Matt. 23:7. 2191 **bityd**, happened. 2192 *per consequens*, in consequence. *to*: E&c *in*.

Of hooly chirche, God amende it soone."
  "Sire," quod the lord, "ye woot what is to
    doone.
Distempre yow noght; ye be my confessour;
Ye been the salt of the erthe and the savour. 2196
For Goddes love, youre pacience ye holde!
Tel me youre grief." And he anon hym tolde
As ye han herd biforn, ye woot wel what.
    The lady of the hous ay stille sat   2200
Til she had herd what the frere sayde.
  "Ey, Goddes mooder," quod she, "blisful
    mayde!
Is ther oght elles? Telle me feithfully."
  "Madame," quod he, "how thynke ye
    herby?"
  "How that me thynketh?" quod she. "So
    God me speede,   2205
I seye, a cherl hath doon a cherles dede.
What shold I seye? God lat hym nevere thee.
His sike heed is ful of vanytee;
I holde hym in a manere frenesye."
  "Madame," quod he, "by God, I shal nat lye,
But I on hym oother weyes be wreke,   2211
I shal disclaundre hym over al ther I speke,
This false blasphemour that charged me
To parte that wol nat departed be
To every man yliche, with meschaunce!"   2215
    The lord sat stille as he were in a traunce,
And in his herte he rolled up and doun,
"How hadde the cherl this ymaginacioun
To shewe swich a probleme to the frere?   2219
Nevere erst er now herde I of swich mateere.
I trowe the devel putte it in his mynde.
In ars-metrik shal ther no man fynde
Biforn this day of swich a questioun.
Who sholde make a demonstracioun
That every man sholde have yliche his part 2225
As of the soun or savour of a fart?

O nyce, proude cherl, I shrewe his face!
Lo, sires," quod the lord, "with harde grace,
Who herde evere of swich a thyng er now?
To every man ylike, tel me how?   2230
It is an inpossible, it may nat be.
Ey, nyce cherl, God lete him nevere thee!
The rumblynge of a fart, and every soun,
Nis but of eir reverberacioun,
And evere it wasteth litel and litel awey.   2235
Ther is no man kan deemen, by my fey,
If that it were departed equally.
What, lo, my cherl, lo, yet how shrewedly
Unto my confessour today he spak.
I holde hym certeyn a demonyak!   2240
Now ete youre mete and lat the cherl go pleye;
Lat hym go honge hymself a devel weye."

The wordes of the lordes squier and his kervere for
departynge of the fart on twelve.

    Now stood the lordes squier at the bord,
That karf his mete, and herde word by word
Of alle thynges whiche I have yow sayd.   2245
"My lord," quod he, "beth nat yvele apayd,
I koude telle, for a gowne-clooth,
To yow, sire frere, so ye be nat wrooth,
How that this fart sholde evene ydeled be
Among youre covent, if it lyked me."   2250
  "Tel," quod the lord, "and thou shalt have
    anon
A gowne-clooth, by God and by Seint John!"
  "My lord," quod he, "whan that the weder
    is fair,
Withouten wynd or perturbynge of air,   2254
Lat brynge a cartwheel heere into this halle—
But look that it have his spokes alle;
Twelve spokes hath a cartwheel comunly—
And bryng me thanne twelve freres, woot ye
    why?

2194 woot, know. **2195 Distempre,** i.e., don't lose your temper. **2196 salt,** cf. Matt. 5:13. **2200** *ay:* E *al.* **2207 thee,** prosper. **2211 wreke,** revenged. Hg&c *But I on oother wise be.* **2212 disclaundre:** Hg&c *diffame.* **2214 parte,** divide. **2215 yliche,** alike (equally). **2218** Hg&c *this cherl ymaginacioun.* **2219 shewe ... to,** set, for. **2220 erst,** before. **2221 trowe,** believe. **2222 ars-metrik,** arithmetic, but *double entendre: metrik* means measurement. **2224** E *certes, it was a shrewed conclusioun.* **2225 yliche,** equally. **2226 savour,** flavor. **2227 nyce ... shrewe,** foolish, curse. *nyce:* E *vyle.* **2228 harde grace,** general exclamation like "bad luck to it." **2229** Hg&c *evere herde.* **2232 thee,** prosper. *him:* E *thee.* **2235 evere:** Hg&c *ther/therwith;* Hg&c *lite and life.* **2236 deemen,** judge. **2240 demonyak,** demon possessed. **2243 kervere,** the squire carved for his lord, cf. l. 100. **2245 thynges:** Hg&c *thyng of.* **2246 beth:** Hg&c *be ye.* **2247 gowne-clooth,** cloth to make a gown. **2249 ydeled,** divided. E *evene delt shall.* **2250 covent,** convent (12 friars and a superior). **2255 E&c *heere* om.**

For thrittene is a covent, as I gesse.   2259
Youre confessour heere, for his worthynesse,
Shal parfourne up the nombre of his covent.
Thanne shal they knele doun by oon assent
And to every spokes ende, in this manere,
Ful sadly leye his nose shal a frere.
Youre noble confessour—there God hym
    save—   2265
Shal holde his nose upright under the nave.
Thanne shal this cherl, with bely stif and
    toght
As any tabour, been hyder ybroght;
And sette hym on the wheel right of this cart,
Upon the nave, and make hym lete a fart.   2270
And ye shul seen, up peril of my lyf,
By preeve which that is demonstratif,
That equally the soun of it wol wende,
And eke the stynk, unto the spokes ende,
Save that this worthy man, youre confessour,

By cause he is a man of greet honour,   2276
Shal have the first fruyt, as resoun is.
As yet the noble usage of freres is
The worthy men of hem shul first be served,
And certeinly he hath it weel disserved.   2280
He hath today taught us so muche good
With prechyng in the pulpit ther he stood
That I may vouchesauf, I sey for me,
He hadde the firste smel of fartes thre;
And so wolde al his covent hardily,   2285
He bereth hym so faire and hoolily.''
    The lord, the lady, and ech man save the frere
Seyde that Jankyn spak in this matere
As wel as Euclide or Protholomee.
Touchynge this cherl, they seyde, subtiltee 2290
And heigh wit made hym speke as he spak;
He nys no fool, ne no demonyak.
And Jankyn hath ywonne a newe gowne—
My tale is doon; we been almoost at towne.

Heere endeth the Somonours Tale.

2259 *thrittene:* E&c *twelve/dosen.* **2260** *Youre:* E&c *The;* other MSS *Youre noble.* **2261 parfourne,** complete. *his:* Hg&c *this.* **2264 sadly,** firmly. **2266 nave,** hub. **2267 toght,** taut. **2268 tabour,** drum. Hg&c *hyder been.* **2277 resoun,** right. **2278** Hg&c *The noble usage of freres yet is this.* **2285** *his:* E *the.* **2287** *ech man:* E *alle men.* **2289 Euclide or Protholomee,** Euclid, the Greek geometrician; Ptolemy, the astronomer, but for spelling see *CT,* III.182 above. **2290 subtiltee,** cleverness.

INTRODUCTION

Canterbury Tales, Part IV

THE CLERK'S and Merchant's Tales are the center of the marriage group. The most interesting question about the Clerk's Tale is the reason for its popularity. There are at least nine versions of this story in the fourteenth century, four of them by the most famous authors of the age. Boccaccio used it to conclude the *Decameron* (c1355); Petrarch translated it into Latin to give it wider circulation (1373); Sercambi did another Italian version (1374); there is an anonymous Latin version and four translations of Petrarch into French. Chaucer worked from Petrarch and an anonymous French version.

Why should this story—so grotesque and offensive by modern standards—have been so popular in Chaucer's day? One reason probably is that it is one of the few stories exemplifying natural gentilesse. Clerks might preach till they were blue in the face that true nobility was the gift of God, not inheritance from aristocratic ancestors, but people—authors—could not, and still cannot, really believe that a low-born character can be a convincing hero. Foundlings in stories and plays nearly always turn out, like Tom Jones, to have been gently born. The story of Griselda is a virtually unique account illustrating the theory of natural gentilesse.

The ambivalent attitude towards natural gentility makes for the ambiguity of the tale. Although it is a story of natural nobility in a woman, it is set in the context of masculine authoritarianism. Poetic justice makes it implicit that Griselda must pay for her good fortune. The role of the Markys is especially enigmatic. On the allegorical level, he is like God testing a mortal creature. This is the rationale of Boethius and the Book of Job for the existence of suffering in the world, or the parable of the Master of the Vineyard (Matt. 20:1-16) about Divine authority. On this allegorical level, the behavior of the Markys is finally unexceptionable. But on the human level, he is a capricious and cruel husband repudiating all the principles of gentilesse.

Chaucer was obviously aware of the inherent difficulties of his material, and dealt with it in the rhetorical fashion that Daniel Defoe made famous in "The Apparition of Mrs. Veal"—by sharing the audience's disbelief, yet insisting on his own reliability as a narrator. Because the birth of Jesus (who was, however, descended from the royal house of David) in a stable is the archetype of God-given nobility in Christian thought, the Griselda story is filled with images and echoes of the Biblical Annunciation and Nativity. Finally, after his four testings, the Markys acknowledges Griselda's perfection in language reminiscent of Christ sitting in judg-ment. At l. 1114 the ladies clothe her again in majesty, as they had before at l. 372, but this time she has earned her place and so lives happily ever after. Like the authorial demurrals at the beginnings of Parts 3 and 4, the moral at the end of the tale reveals Chaucer still wrestling with its improbability. The humorous "Envoy" may date from a time when the tale was recited independent of the Canterbury collection.

Bernard S. Levy in "Gentilesse in Chaucer's Clerk's and Merchant's Tales," *Chaucer Review* (1977), traces the continuity of the theme of gentilesse, while John P. McCall in "The Clerk's Tale and the Theme of Obedience," *MLQ* (1966), elucidates its clerical authoritarianism. James Sledd, "The Clerk's Tale: The Monsters and the Critics," *MP* (1953), and Mary J. Carruthers, "The Lady, the Swineherd, and Chaucer's Clerk," *Chaucer Review* (1983), examine the reactions of the audience.

The other piece in Part IV has the sharpest satire in the marriage discussion. Each of the first three tales is based on a warped idea of marriage. The Wife of Bath sees sex as the will to power. As in Jean de Meun's *Roman de la Rose* and Bernard Shaw's *Man and Superman*, men and women compete in a naturalistic struggle from which woman, as the true continuator of the species, must emerge victorious. The Clerk presents the essentially Manichean view of the

Church: that sex is sin. All of the temporal world is evil; birth into this evil world is a misfortune; woman, because she tempts man to lust after procreation, must be disciplined. Neither naturalistic nor ascetic, the Merchant's view of sex is psychotic. The old knight, with his back-to-the-womb dependence on woman, is sick; and the references to the "gentilesse" of Damyan and May (ll.1924, 2202) make mockery of the ideal.

The movement from the medieval to the modern world involves the change from a spiritual to a psychological conception of personality. Dreams are equally important in both conceptions. In the medieval, mystical view of personality, dreams are windows opening outward from the soul to heaven, through which spiritual truths are revealed. In modern psychoanalysis, dreams are windows opening inward to the psyche, through which psychological truths are perceived. In his early poems Chaucer used dream visions in their medieval manifestations as epiphanies. By the Merchant's Tale, he has come to the modern conception, showing January's fantasies as self-deception. As with Oedipus, the physical blindness that strikes January is merely a dramatic underscoring of his psychological blindness. As with Irene in Galsworthy's *Man of Property*, May's infidelity is impelled by January's callous possessiveness. How else can she establish her identity?

Much has been written about whether this tale is appropriately assigned to the Merchant. Lines 1251 and 1322 seem to imply that the narrator is not himself a secular. It has been suggested that the tale would suit either the worldly Monk or Friar of the General Prologue better than the tales they finally tell. However, in the true Christian "marriage" to God, desire for temporal things is regularly referred to as "fornicatio." The desire for money is equated with sexual desire in the Wife of Bath's Prologue, the Shipman's Tale, and most significantly in the resolution of the Franklin's Tale. Since merchants typify the desire for money, Chaucer may have decided that the Merchant was the most appropriate pilgrim to tell this bitter story of fornication.

The first part of the Merchant's Tale is based on the same body of antifeminist material as the Wife of Bath's Prologue. Although perhaps suggested by Folie and Franc Vouloir in Deschamps' *Miroir de Mariage* and Ami and Raison in *Roman de la Rose*, Placebo and Justinius are Chaucer's own creations. Like so many of the vices and virtues represented by the characters in the tales of Canterbury, Placebo reappears in his literal manifestation (though in a context highly elucidative of the personification) in the Parson's Tale (X.615). The unpleasant description of January's love-making has vivid parallels in Boccaccio's *Ameto* and the French fabliaux.

The pear-tree fabliau that begins at l. 2207 has many European and Oriental parallels. Its earthiness contrasts with the more ironical antifeminist materials. Perhaps to refine and give depth to the anecdote, as Pope refined *The Rape of the Lock* by introducing the sylphs and gnomes, Chaucer introduced the mock-heroic involvement of Pluto and Proserpine, who had presided over the wedding of the Seven Deadly Sins in his friend John Gower's *Miroir de l'omme* (l.961). Giving the blind man back his sight is the "point" of the original pear-tree fabliau, which here provides an ironical confirmation of January's psychological blindness.

The garden that January creates reflects the medieval figurative view of the meaning of gardens, extending from Eden, where man lost his innocence, to Gethsemane, where he secured salvation. This tradition is discussed by D. W. Robertson, "The Doctrine of Charity in Medieval Gardens," *Speculum* (1951). The classic explication of style and psychology of the tale is still J.S.P. Tatlock, "Chaucer's Merchant's Tale," *MP* (1935), and no one has discussed the problem of the original teller better than A.C. Baugh, "The Original Teller of the Merchant's Tale," *MP* (1937). Karl P. Wentersdorf treats the "Theme and Structure in the Merchant's Tale: The Function of the Pluto Episode," *PMLA* (1965).

Canterbury Tales

PART IV

CLERK'S TALE

PROLOGUE

Heere folweth the Prologe of the Clerkes Tale of Oxenford.

"Sire Clerk of Oxenford," oure Hooste sayde,
"Ye ryde as coy and stille as dooth a mayde
Were newe spoused, sittynge at the bord;
This day ne herde I of youre tonge a word.
I trowe ye studie aboute som sophyme, 5
But Salomon seith, everythyng hath tyme.
"For Goddes sake, as beth of bettre cheere!
It is no tyme for to studien heere.
Telle us som myrie tale, by youre fey,

For what man that is entred in a pley, 10
He nedes moot unto the pley assente.
But precheth nat, as freres doon in Lente,
To make us for oure olde synnes wepe,
Ne that thy tale make us nat to slepe.
"Telle us som murie thyng of aventures. 15
Youre termes, youre colours, and youre figures,
Keepe hem in stoor til so be that ye endite
Heigh style, as whan that men to kynges write.

---

2 coy, shy (Lat. *quietus*). **3 bord,** dinner table. **5 sophyme,** academic (useless or specious) argument. **6 Salomon seith,** cf. Eccles. 3:1. **7 cheere,** expression (mood). **10 pley,** game. **13 olde,** former (habitual). **16 termes,** technical jargon; **colours,** rhetorical flourishes (repetitions of words and sounds, double meanings, etc.); **figures,** figures of speech (similes, metaphors, etc.). **17 endite,** compose (in). **18 Heigh style ... to kynges write,** in the Middle Ages style was largely a feature of epistolary technique, the *ars dictaminis*, which taught that a letter should be couched in high, middle, or low style, depending on its subject matter and the status of its recipient. Only after the Renaissance did style become the province of belles lettres—poetry and prose fiction. In classical times it had been the province of oratory.

Speketh so pleyn at this tyme, we yow preye,
That we may understonde what ye seye." 20
   This worthy clerk benignely answerde,
"Hooste," quod he, "I am under youre yerde.
Ye han of us as now the governance,
And therfore wol I do yow obeisance
As fer as resoun axeth, hardily. 25
I wol yow telle a tale which that I
Lerned at Padwe of a worthy clerk,
As preved by his wordes and his werk.
He is now deed and nayled in his cheste—
I prey to God so yeve his soule reste. 30
   "Frauceys Petrak, the lauriat poete,
Highte this clerk, whos rethorike sweete
Enlumyned al Ytaille of poetrie,
As Lynyan dide of philosophie,
Or lawe, or oother art particuler; 35
But deeth, that wol nat suffre us dwellen heer,
But as it were a twynklyng of an eye,

Hem bothe hath slayn, and alle shul we dye.
   "But forth to tellen of this worthy man
That taughte me this tale, as I bigan 40
I seye that first with heigh stile he enditeth,
Er he the body of his tale writeth,
A prohemye, in the which discryveth he
Pemond and of Saluces the contree,
And speketh of Apennyn, the hilles hye, 45
That been the boundes of West Lumbardye,
And of Mount Vesulus in special
Where as the Poo out of a welle smal
Taketh his firste spryngyng and his sours,
That estward ay encresseth in his cours 50
To Emele-ward, to Ferrare, and Venyse,
The which a long thyng were to devyse.
And trewely, as to my juggement,
Me thynketh it a thyng impertinent,
Save that he wole convoyen his mateere. 55
But this his tale, which that ye may heere."

Heere bigynneth the Tale of the Clerk of Oxenford.

Ther is at the west syde of Ytaille,
Doun at the roote of Vesulus the colde,
A lusty playne, habundant of vitaille,
Where many a tour and toun thou mayst
      biholde 60
That founded were in tyme of fadres olde,
And many another delitable sighte,
And Saluces this noble contree highte.

A markys whilom lord was of that lond,

As were his worthy eldres hym bifore; 65
And obeisant, ay redy to his hond,
Were alle his liges, bothe lasse and moore.
Thus in delit he lyveth and hath doon yoore,
Biloved and drad thurgh favour of Fortune
Bothe of his lordes and of his commune. 70

Therwith he was, to speke as of lynage,
The gentilleste yborn of Lumbardye:
A fair persone, and strong, and yong of age,

19 *we:* some MSS *I.* 22 **yerde,** authority (yardstick, for punishment). 24 **obeisance,** obedience. 25 **axeth,** demands. 27 **Padwe,** Padua. 29 **deed,** Petrarch died in 1374. Chaucer might have met him on his first trip to Italy in 1372–73. 30 *reste:* some MSS *good reste.* 31 **Petrak, the lauriat,** one of Petrarch's greatest triumphs was being crowned by the Roman Senate on Easter Sunday, 1341, with the poetic laurel. 33 **Enlumyned al Ytaille,** Petrarch was famous for bringing to perfection poetry in the Italian vernacular as Chaucer was attempting to do in English—but Chaucer's Griselda story is from Petrarch's Latin prose translation of Boccaccio's Italian prose, and a French prose translation of Petrarch. 34 **Lynyan,** Giovanni di Lignano (d.1383), professor of canon law at Bologna, who once visited England as a papal legate. **philosophie,** moral philosophy; "philosophia moralis," the study of human behavior, and "philosophia naturalis," the study of natural science, were the two recognized branches of temporal learning down to the 19th century. 36 E *suffre us* om. 41 **heigh stile,** this seems to reflect Petrarch's prefatory letter explaining that he was submitting Boccaccio's "vulgar style" (i.e., Italian vernacular) to "the more valid discipline of the rhetoricians" (i.e., Latin). 43 **prohemye,** prologue. 44 **Pemond . . . Saluces,** Piedmont, Saluzzo. 45 **Apennyn,** the Apennines. 47 **Vesulus,** Viso. 48 **welle,** spring. 51 **Emele, Ferrare, Venyse,** Emilia, Ferrara, Venice. 54 **impertinent,** irrelevant. 55 **convoyen,** introduce; some MSS *conveyen.* 57 *at:* some MSS *right at.* 58 **the colde,** these words, all of l. 61, and all of the next stanza, ll. 64–70, are added by Chaucer, suggesting the way in which he was pointing up the contrast between the sterility of the ancient nobility and the fecundity of the teeming populace. 59 **vitaille,** produce. 62 **sighte,** site. 64 **markys,** marquis (third in rank of nobility, just below a duke). **whilom,** formerly. 66 **obeisant,** obedient. *ay:* E&c *and.* 70 **commune,** common people.

And ful of honour and of curteisye,
Discreet ynogh his contree for to gye— 75
Save in somme thynges that he was to blame.
And Walter was this yonge lordes name.

I blame hym thus, that he considered noght
In tyme comynge what hym myghte bityde,
But on his lust present was al his thoght, 80
As for to hauke and hunte on every syde.
Wel ny alle othere cures leet he slyde.
And eek he nolde—and that was worst of alle—
Wedde no wyf for noght that may bifalle.

Oonly that point his peple bar so soore 85
That flokmeele on a day they to hym wente,
And oon of hem, that wisest was of loore,
Or elles that the lord best wolde assente
That he sholde telle hym what his peple mente,
Or elles koude he shewe wel swich mateere, 90
He to the markys seyde as ye shul heere:

"O noble markys, youre humanitee
Asseureth us to yeve us hardinesse
As ofte as tyme is of necessitee
That we to yow mowe telle oure hevynesse. 95
Accepteth, lord, now for youre gentillesse,
That we with pitous herte unto yow pleyne,
And lat youre eres nat my voys desdeyne.

"Al have I noght to doone in this mateere
Moore than another man hath in this place, 100
Yet for as muche as ye, my lord so deere,
Han alwey shewed me favour and grace,
I dar the bettre aske of yow a space
Of audience to shewen oure requeste,
And ye, my lord, to doon right as yow leste.

"For certes, lord, so wel us liketh yow 106
And al youre werk, and evere han doon, that we
Ne koude nat us self devysen how

We myghte lyven in moore felicitee,
Save o thyng, lord, if it youre wille be, 110
That for to been a wedded man yow leste—
Thanne were youre peple in sovereyn hertes
        reste.

"Boweth youre nekke under that blisful yok
Of soveraynetee, noght of servyse,
Which that men clepe spousaille or wedlok. 115
And thenketh, lord, among youre thoghtes wyse
How that oure dayes passe in sondry wyse,
For thogh we slepe, or wake, or rome, or ryde,
Ay fleeth the tyme; it nyl no man abyde. 119

"And thogh youre grene youthe floure as yit,
In crepeth age alwey as stille as stoon,
And deeth manaceth every age, and smyt
In ech estaat, for ther escapeth noon.
And also certein as we knowe echoon
That we shul deye, as uncerteyn we alle 125
Been of that day whan deeth shal on us falle.

"Accepteth thanne of us the trewe entente,
That nevere yet refuseden youre heeste,
And we wol, lord, if that ye wole assente,
Chese yow a wyf in short tyme atte leeste, 130
Born of the gentilleste and of the meeste
Of al this land, so that it oghte seme
Honour to God and yow, as we kan deeme.

"Delivere us out of al this bisy drede
And taak a wyf, for hye Goddes sake! 135
For if it so bifelle, as God forbede,
That thurgh youre deeth youre lyne sholde slake,
And that a straunge successour sholde take
Youre heritage, O wo were us alyve.
Wherfore we pray you hastily to wyve." 140

Hir meeke preyere and hir pitous cheere
Made the markys herte han pitee.

---

75 Discreet . . . gye, wise, guide. **78** E&c *considereth.* **79** Hg&c *myghte hym:* other MSS *hym* om. **80 lust,** pleasure. *on:* E *in.* **82 cures,** responsibilities. **85 bar . . . soore,** i.e., took badly. **86 flokmeele,** in a group (cf. piecemeal). **88 elles that,** i.e., else (him to whom) that. **93 hardinesse,** courage. *to yeve:* Hg&c *and yeveth.* **95 mowe . . . hevynesse,** may, concern. **96 for:** Hg&c *of.* **97** Some MSS *That we to yow with petous herte complayne.* **105 leste,** choose. **108 devysen,** imagine. **112 sovereyn,** perfect. **114 soveraynetee,** domination. **117 sondry wyse,** various ways. **122 manaceth,** menaces. **127 entente,** intent (intention). **128 heeste,** command. *youre* (more formal, cf. l. 113ff.): EHg&c *thyn.* **131 meeste,** most (greatest). **133 deeme,** judge. **134 bisy,** i.e., constant. **137** *lyne:* some MSS *lynage.* **141 pitous cheere,** pitiful manner.

"Ye wol," quod he, "myn owene peple deere,
To that I nevere erst thoughte streyne me.
I me rejoysed of my liberte,   145
That seelde tyme is founde in mariage.
Ther I was free I moot been in servage.

"But nathelees I se youre trewe entente,
And truste upon youre wit, and have doon ay;
Wherfore of my free wyl I wole assente   150
To wedde me as soone as evere I may.
But ther as ye han profred me today
To chese me a wyf, I yow relesse
That choys, and prey yow of that profre cesse.

"For God it woot that children ofte been   155
Unlyk hir worthy eldres hem bifore;
Bountee comth al of God, nat of the streen
Of which they been engendred and ybore.
I truste in Goddes bountee, and therfore
My mariage and myn estaat and reste   160
I hym bitake; he may doon as hym leste.

"Lat me allone in chesynge of my wyf.
That charge upon my bak I wole endure.
But I yow preye, and charge upon youre lyf,
What wyf that I take, ye me assure   165
To worshipe hire whil that hir lyf may dure,
In word and werk, bothe heere and everywheere,
As she an emperoures doghter weere.

"And forthermoore, this shal ye swere, that ye
Agayn my choys shul neither grucche ne stryve.
For sith I shal forgoon my libertee   171
At youre requeste, as evere moot I thryve,
Ther as myn herte is set, ther wol I wyve.
And but ye wole assente in swich manere,   174
I prey yow spekëth namoore of this matere."

With hertely wyl they sworen and assenten

To al this thyng—ther seyde no wight
     nay—
Bisekynge hym of grace, er that they wenten,
That he wolde graunten hem a certein day
Of his spousaille, as soone as evere he may,   180
For yet alwey the peple somwhat dredde,
Lest that the markys no wyf wolde wedde.

He graunted hem a day swich as hym leste
On which he wolde be wedded sikerly,
And seyde he dide al this at hir requeste.   185
And they with humble entente buxomly,
Knelynge upon hir knees ful reverently,
Hym thonken alle, and thus they han an
     ende
Of hire entente and hoom agayn they wende.

And heerupon he to his officeres   190
Comaundeth for the feste to purveye,
And to his privee knyghtes and squieres
Swich charge yaf as hym liste on hem leye;
And they to his comandement obeye,
And ech of hem dooth al his diligence   195
To doon unto the feeste reverence.

Explicit prima pars. Incipit secunda pars.

Noght fer fro thilke paleys honurable
Ther as this markys shoop his mariage
There stood a throop of site delitable,
In which that poure folk of that village   200
Hadden hir beestes and hir herbergage,
And of hire labour tooke hir sustenance,
After that the erthe yaf hem habundance.

Amonges thise poure folk ther dwelte a
     man
Which that was holden pourest of hem alle,
But hye God somtyme senden kan   206
His grace into a litel oxes stalle.

144 **erst ... streyne me,** before, constrain myself. **146 seelde,** seldom. **147 Ther,** where. **149 wit ... ay,** wisdom, always. **152** *today:* E *this day.* **154 cesse,** cease (desist). **157 Bountee ... streen,** virtue, strain (family). **161 bitake ... leste,** entrust, desires. **163 charge,** responsibility. **165** *What:* Hg&c *That what/That that.* **166 worshipe,** honor. **168 As,** as if. **170 grucche ... stryve,** complain, resist. **174** *swich:* E *this.* **176 hertely,** hearty (sincere). **178 Bisekynge,** beseeching. **179 graunten ... day,** name the day. **183 leste,** pleased him. **184 sikerly,** certainly. **186 buxomly,** meekly. **191 feste ... purveye,** wedding feast, prepare. **192 privee,** confidential (cf. Privy Council). **196 doon ... reverence,** show solicitude (for his part of the preparations for) the wedding feast. **197 thilke,** that. **198 shoop,** planned. *Ther:* Hg&c *Wher.* **199 throop,** thorp (village). **201 herbergage,** dwelling. **207 oxes stalle,** this comparison was added by Chaucer, who likewise pointed up the similarity between the selection of Griselda and the Annunciation, ll. 274ff.

Janicula men of that throop hym calle.
A doghter hadde he, fair ynogh to sighte,
And Grisildis this yonge mayden highte.   210

But for to speke of vertuous beautee,
Thanne was she oon the faireste under sonne.
For poureliche yfostred up was she,
No likerous lust was thurgh hire herte yronne.
Wel ofter of the welle than of the tonne   215
She drank, and for she wolde vertu plese
She knew wel labour but noon ydel ese.

But thogh this mayde tendre were of age,
Yet in the brest of hire virginitee
Ther was enclosed rype and sad corage;   220
And in greet reverence and charitee
Hir olde poure fader fostred shee.
A fewe sheep, spynnynge, on feeld she kepte;
She wolde noght been ydel til she slepte.

And whan she homward cam, she wolde
      brynge
Wortes or othere herbes tymes ofte,   226
The whiche she shredde and seeth for hir
      lyvynge,
And made hir bed ful harde and nothyng softe;
And ay she kepte hir fadres lyf on-lofte
With everich obeisaunce and diligence   230
That child may doon to fadres reverence.

  Upon Grisilde, this poure creature,
Ful ofte sithe this markys caste his eye
As he on huntyng rood, paraventure;
And whan it fil that he myghte hire espye,   235
He noght with wantowne lookyng of folye
His eyen caste on hire, but in sad wyse
Upon hir chiere he wolde hym ofte avyse,

Commendynge in his herte hir wommanhede,

And eek hir vertu, passynge any wight   240
Of so yong age, as wel in chiere as dede.
For thogh the peple have no greet insight
In vertu, he considered ful right
Hir bountee, and disposed that he wolde   244
Wedde hire oonly, if evere he wedde sholde.

  The day of weddyng cam, but no wight kan
Telle what womman that it sholde be.
For which merveille wondred many a man,
And seyden whan they were in privetee,
"Wol nat oure lord yet leve his vanytee?   250
Wol he nat wedde? Allas, allas, the while!
Why wole he thus hymself and us bigile?"

  But natheless this markys hath doon make,
Of gemmes set in gold and in asure,
Brooches and rynges for Grisildis sake;   255
And of hir clothyng took he the mesure
By a mayde lyk to hire stature,
And eek of othere aornementes alle
That unto swich a weddyng sholde falle.

  The time of undren of the same day   260
Approcheth that this weddyng sholde be,
And al the paleys put was in array,
Bothe halle and chambres, ech in his degree—
Houses of office stuffed with plentee
Ther maystow seen, of deynteuous vitaille   265
That may be founde as fer as last Ytaille.

  This roial markys richely arrayed,
Lordes and ladyes in his compaignye,
The whiche that to the feeste weren
      yprayed,
And of his retenue the bachelrye,   270
With many a soun of sondry melodye,
Unto the village of the which I tolde
In this array the righte wey han holde.

208 **Janicula,** Lat. *little gate;* the name is from Boccaccio and Petrarch; it may have suggested to Chaucer the themes of the Annunciation and Nativity. 211–17 Again, much expanded by Chaucer. 211 *beautee:* E *bountee* (an abbreviation). 214 **likerous lust,** sensual pleasure. 215 **tonne,** wine cask. 220 **rype and sad corage,** mature and sober spirit. 223 **spynnynge,** spinning all the while. 226 **Wortes,** medicinal herbs. 227 **seeth,** boiled. 230 **obeisaunce,** obedience. 233 **sithe,** times. *caste:* Hg&c *sette.* 237 **sad,** serious. 238 **chiere,** expression (behavior). *wolde:* E *gan.* 240 **passynge ... wight,** surpassing, creature. 242 **peple,** the populace. *have:* E&c *hadde,* Hg&c *hath.* 250 **vanytee,** foolishness. 253 **hath doon make,** had had made. 254 **asure,** lapis lazuli. 260 **undren,** midmorning. 264 **Houses of office,** service buildings (kitchens and pantries were originally in separate buildings). 266 **last,** the end of. Some MSS *lasteth.* 269 **yprayed,** invited. 270 **bachelrye,** young knights. 273 **righte,** nearest.

Grisilde of this, God woot, ful innocent
That for hire shapen was al this array,   275
To fecchen water at a welle is went,
And comth hoom as soone as ever she may;
For wel she hadde herd seyd that thilke day
The markys sholde wedde, and if she myghte
She wolde fayn han seyn som of that sighte.   280

She thoghte, "I wole with othere maydens stonde,
That been my felawes, in oure dore and se
The markysesse, and therfore wol I fonde
To doon at hoom as soone as it may be
The labour which that longeth unto me,   285
And thanne I may at leyser hire biholde
If she this wey unto the castel holde."

And as she wolde over hir thresshfold gon,
The markys cam and gan hire for to calle,
And she set doun hir water pot anon,   290
Biside the thresshfold, in an oxes stalle,
And doun upon hir knes she gan to falle,
And with sad contenance kneleth stille
Til she had herd what was the lordes wille.

  This thoghtful markys spak unto this mayde
Ful sobrely, and seyde in this manere,   296
"Where is youre fader, O Grisildis?" he sayde.
And she with reverence, in humble cheere,
Answerde, "Lord, he is al redy heere."
And in she gooth withouten lenger lette,   300
And to the markys she hir fader fette.

  He by the hand thanne took this olde man
And seyde thus whan he hym hadde asyde,
"Janicula, I neither may ne kan
Lenger the plesance of myn herte hyde.   305
If that thou vouchesauf, what so bityde,
Thy doghter wol I take er that I wende

As for my wyf, unto hir lyves ende.

  "Thou lovest me, I woot it wel certeyn,
And art my feithful lige man ybore,   310
And al that liketh me, I dar wel seyn
It liketh thee, and specially therfore
Tel me that poynt that I have seyd bifore,
If that thou wolt unto that purpos drawe
To take me as for thy sone-in-lawe."   315

  The sodeyn cas this man astonyed so
That reed he wax; abayst and al quakynge
He stood. Unnethes seyde he wordes mo
But oonly thus, "Lord," quod he, "my willynge
Is as ye wole, ne ayeyns youre likynge   320
I wol no thyng. Ye be my lord so deere,
Right as yow lust, governeth this mateere."

  "Yet wol I," quod this markys softely,
"That in thy chambre I and thou and she
Have a collacioun. And wostow why?   325
For I wol axe if it hire wille be
To be my wyf and reule hire after me.
And al this shal be doon in thy presence;
I wol noght speke out of thyn audience."

  And in the chambre whil they were aboute
Hir tretys which as ye shal after heere,   331
The peple cam unto the hous withoute,
And wondred hem in how honeste manere
And tentifly she kepte hir fader deere.
But outrely Grisildis wondre myghte,   335
For nevere erst ne saugh she swich a sighte.

  No wonder is thogh she were astoned
To seen so greet a gest come in that place;
She nevere was to swiche gestes woned,
For which she looked with ful pale face.   340
But shortly forth this matere for to chace,

---

274 God woot, God knows, a conventional expression, but significant in terms of the Annunciation motif. **275 shapen,** prepared. **283 fonde,** i.e., find (a way). **285 longeth,** belongs. **286 leyser,** leisure. **287 holde,** takes. **288 wolde,** was about to. *hir:* Hg&c *the.* **291 thresshfold . . . stalle,** threshold; here the motifs of Annunciation and Nativity are joined. The iconography of each would be recalled. **293 sad,** sober. **294 lordes,** *double entendre.* **297** Some MSS *O* om. **300 lette,** hindrance (tarrying). **301 fette,** fetched. **303 asyde,** had taken him aside. **305 plesance,** pleasure (desire). **308** *hir:* Hg&c *my.* **311 liketh me,** pleases me. **316 cas,** event. *The:* E&c *This.* **317 reed . . . abayst,** red, abashed. **318 Unnethes,** scarcely. **320 wole,** will (desire). **322** *lust:* Hg&c *list.* **325 collacioun,** colloquy (conference). **327 reule hire,** i.e., obey. **331 tretys,** treaty (negotiation). **333 how honeste,** what a virtuous. **334 tentifly . . . kepte,** attentively, cared for. **335 outrely,** utterly (greatly). **336 erst,** before. **339 woned,** accustomed. **341 chace,** chase (pursue). *matere:* E *tale.*

Thise arn the wordes that the markys sayde
To this benigne, verray, feithful mayde.

"Grisilde," he seyde, "ye shal wel understonde
It liketh to youre fader and to me   345
That I yow wedde, and eek it may so stonde,
As I suppose, ye wol that it so be.
But thise demandes axe I first," quod he,
"That, sith it shal be doon in hastif wyse,
Wol ye assente, or elles yow avyse?   350

"I seye this, be ye redy with good herte
To al my lust, and that I frely may
As me best thynketh do yow laughe or smerte,
And nevere ye to grucche it, nyght ne day?
And eek whan I sey 'ye' ne sey nat 'nay,'   355
Neither by word ne frownyng contenance?
Swere this, and heere I swere oure alliance."

Wondrynge upon this word, quakynge for
          drede,
She seyde, "Lord, undigne and unworthy
Am I to thilke honour that ye me beede,   360
But as ye wole yourself, right so wol I.
And heere I swere that nevere willyngly
In werk ne thoght I nyl yow disobeye,
For to be deed, though me were looth to
          deye."

"This is ynogh, Grisilde myn," quod he.   365
And forth he gooth with a ful sobre cheere
Out at the dore, and after that cam she,
And to the peple he seyde in this manere,
"This is my wyf," quod he, "that standeth
          heere.
Honoureth hire and loveth hire, I preye,   370
Whoso me loveth; ther is namoore to seye."

And for that nothyng of hir olde geere
She sholde brynge into his hous, he bad

That wommen sholde dispoillen hire right
          theere;
Of which thise ladyes were nat right glad   375
To handle hir clothes wherinne she was clad.
But nathelees this mayde bright of hewe
Fro foot to heed they clothed han al newe.

Hir heris han they kembd, that lay untressed
Ful rudely, and with hir fyngres smale   380
A corone on hire heed they han ydressed,
And sette hire ful of nowches grete and smale.
Of hire array what sholde I make a tale?
Unnethe the peple hir knew for hire fairnesse
Whan she translated was in swich richesse.   385

This markys hath hire spoused with a ryng
Broght for the same cause, and thanne hire sette
Upon an hors snow-whit and wel amblyng,
And to his paleys er he lenger lette   389
With joyful peple that hire ladde and mette
Convoyed hire, and thus the day they spende
In revel til the sonne gan descende.

And shortly forth this tale for to chace,
I seye that to this newe markysesse
God hath swich favour sent hire of his grace
That it ne semed nat by liklynesse   396
That she was born and fed in rudenesse,
As in a cote or in an oxe-stalle,
But norissed in an emperoures halle.

To every wight she woxen is so deere   400
And worshipful that folk ther she was bore,
And from hire birthe knew hire yeer by yeere,
Unnethe trowed they—but dorste han swore—
That to Janicle, of which I spak bifore,
She doghter were, for as by conjecture   405
Hem thoughte she was another creature.

For though that evere vertuous was she,

---

343 **verray,** true. 345 **It liketh,** it pleases. 348 **demandes,** cf. the Fr. *questions.* 350 **avyse,** i.e., think about it. 352 **lust,** desire. 354 **grucche,** complain about. 356 *frownyng*: some MSS *froward* (disobedient), which term is, however, found only in *RR.* From this point on Chaucer's text follows the French version almost exclusively. 360 **beede,** offer. 366 **sobre cheere,** serious expression. 372 **geere,** equipment (clothing). 374 **dispoillen,** undress. 379 **kembd ... untressed,** combed, undressed. 381 **corone,** nuptial garland. 382 **nowches,** brooches. 384 **Unnethe,** scarcely. 385 **translated,** transformed; the term is used for sanctification and deification. 389 **er he ... lette,** i.e., without delay. 391 *Convoyed*: some MSS *Conveyed.* 398 **cote,** cottage. 403 **Unnethe trowed,** scarcely could believe. 404 E *That she to.*

She was encressed in swich excellence
Of thewes goode, yset in heigh bountee,
And so discreet and fair of eloquence,   410
So benigne and so digne of reverence,
And koude so the peples herte embrace,
That ech hire lovede that looked on hir face.

Noght oonly of Saluces in the toun
Publiced was the bountee of hir name,   415
But eek biside in many a regioun,
If oon seide wel, another seyde the same;
So spradde of hire heighe bountee the fame
That men and wommen, as wel yonge as olde,
Goon to Saluce upon hire to biholde.   420

Thus Walter lowely—nay, but roially—
Wedded with fortunat honestetee,
In Goddes pees lyveth ful esily
At hoom, and outward grace ynogh had he;
And for he saugh that under low degree   425
Was ofte vertu hid, the peple hym heelde
A prudent man, and that is seyn ful seelde.

Nat oonly this Grisildis thurgh hir wit
Koude al the feet of wyfly hoomlinesse,
But eek, whan that the cas required it,   430
The commune profit koude she redresse.
Ther nas discord, rancour, ne hevynesse
In al that land that she ne koude apese,
And wisely brynge hem alle in reste and ese.

Though that hire housbonde absent were, anon
If gentil men or othere of hire contree   436
Were wrothe, she wolde bryngen hem aton;
So wise and rype wordes hadde she,
And juggementz of so greet equitee,
That she from hevene sent was, as men wende,
Peple to save and every wrong t'amende.   441

Nat longe tyme after that this Grisild
Was wedded, she a doghter hath ybore,
Al had hire levere have born a knave child.
Glad was this markys and the folk therfore,   445
For though a mayde child coome al bifore,
She may unto a knave child atteyne
By liklihede, syn she nys nat bareyne.

Explicit secunda pars. Incipit tercia pars.

Ther fil, as it bifalleth tymes mo,
Whan that this child had souked but a
    throwe,
This markys in his herte longeth so   451
To tempte his wyf, hir sadnesse for to knowe,
That he ne myghte out of his herte throwe
This merveillous desir his wyf t'assaye—
Nedelees, God woot, he thoghte hire for
    t'affraye.   455

He hadde assayed hire ynogh bifore
And foond hire evere good. What neded it
Hire for to tempte, and alwey moore and moore,
Though som men preise it for a subtil wit?
But as for me, I seye that yvele it sit   460
To assaye a wyf whan that it is no nede,
And putten hire in angwyssh and in drede.

For which this markys wroghte in this
    manere:
He cam allone a-nyght ther as she lay,   464
With stierne face and with ful trouble cheere,
And seyde thus, "Grisilde," quod he, "that day
That I yow took out of youre pouere array
And putte yow in estaat of heigh noblesse—
Ye have nat that forgeten, as I gesse?

"I seye, Grisilde, this present dignitee   470
In which that I have put yow, as I trowe,

Maketh yow nat foryetful for to be
That I yow took in poure estaat ful lowe,
For any wele ye moot yourselven knowe.
Taak heede of every word that Y yow seye; 475
Ther is no wight that hereth it but we tweye.

"Ye woot youreself wel how that ye cam heere
Into this hous, it is nat longe ago;
And though to me that ye be lief and deere,
Unto my gentils ye be no thyng so. 480
They seyn to hem it is greet shame and wo
For to be subgetz and been in servage
To thee, that born art of a low lynage.

"And namely sith thy doghter was ybore
Thise wordes han they spoken, doutelees. 485
But I desire, as I have doon bifore,
To lyve my lyf with hem in reste and pees.
I may nat in this caas be recchelees;
I moot doon with thy doghter for the beste—
Nat as I wolde, but as my peple leste. 490

"And yet, God woot, this is ful looth to me.
But nathelees withoute youre wityng
I wol nat doon. But this wol I," quod he,
"That ye to me assente as in this thyng. 494
Shewe now youre pacience in youre werkyng
That ye me highte and swore in youre village
That day that maked was oure mariage."

Whan she had herd al this she noght ameved
Neither in word or chiere or contenaunce,
For, as it semed, she was nat agreved. 500
She seyde, "Lord, al lyth in your plesaunce.
My child and I, with hertely obeisaunce,
Been youres al, and ye mowe save or spille
Youre owene thyng; werketh after youre wille.

"Ther may nothyng, God so my soule save,
Liken to yow that may displese me; 506
Ne I desire nothyng for to have,
Ne drede for to leese, save oonly yee.
This wyl is in myn herte and ay shal be;
No lengthe of tyme or deeth may this deface,
Ne chaunge my corage to another place." 511

Glad was this markys of hire answeryng,
But yet he feyned as he were nat so;
Al drery was his cheere and his lookyng
Whan that he sholde out of the chambre go.
Soone after this, a furlong wey or two, 516
He prively hath toold al his entente
Unto a man, and to his wyf hym sente.

A maner sergeant was this privee man, 519
The which that feithful ofte he founden hadde
In thynges grete, and eek swich folk wel kan
Doon execucioun in thynges badde—
The lord knew wel that he hym loved and
    dradde.
And whan this sergeant wiste his lordes wille,
Into the chambre he stalked hym ful stille. 525

"Madame," he seyde, "ye moote foryeve it me
Though I do thyng to which I am constreyned.
Ye been so wys that ful wel knowe ye
That lordes heestes mowe nat been yfeyned;
They mowe wel been biwailled and compleyned,
But men moote nede unto hire lust obeye, 531
And so wol I; ther is namoore to seye.

"This child I am comanded for to take—"
And spak namoore, but out the child he hente
Despitously, and gan a cheere make 535
As though he wolde han slayn it er he wente.

472–74 Maketh . . . yourselven knowe, i.e., I trust that your present dignity won't make you forget your low estate, in spite of (for) any good fortune (any wele) you presently experience (knowe). **476 tweye,** two. **479 lief,** loved. **482** *been:* E&c *to been.* **483** *low lynage:* EHg&c *small village;* Fr. *basse lignie.* The "thee-thy" here and in the next stanza are disrespectful. **484 namely,** especially. **488 recchelees,** heedless. **490 leste,** desire. **492 wityng,** knowledge. **495 werkyng,** behavior. **496 highte,** promised. **498 ameved,** moved. **502 hertely obeisaunce,** hearty (sincere) obedience. **503 mowe . . . spille,** may, destroy. **504** Some MSS *Youre owene thyng whether that ye wille.* **506 Liken to yow,** be pleasing to you. **507 Ne I:** EHg *Ne I ne.* **508 Yee:** EHg&c *thee* (which is less respectful; E has "vel yee" in margin). **509 wyl . . . ay,** determination, always. **511 corage,** affection. **513 feyned,** pretended. **516 furlong,** 220 yards, but a measure of time. **519 sergeant,** a servant, or (OED 4) an officer whose duty it is to enforce the commands of a person in authority. **privee,** confidential. **522** *in:* E&c *on.* **523 dradde,** dreaded (respected). **525 stille,** quietly. **529 yfeyned,** evaded. **530 mowe,** may. **531 lust,** desire. **534 hente,** seized. **535 Despitously . . . cheere,** pitilessly, motions.

Grisildis moot al suffren and consente,
And as a lamb she sitteth meke and stille
And leet this crueel sergeant doon his wille.

Suspecious was the diffame of this man,   540
Suspect his face, suspect his word also,
Suspect the tyme in which he this bigan.
Allas, hir doghter that she loved so,
She wende he wolde han slawen it right tho.
But nathelees she neither weep ne syked,   545
Conformynge hire to that the markys lyked.

But atte laste to speken she bigan,
And mekely she to the sergeant preyde
So as he was a worthy gentilman
That she moste kisse hire child er that it deyde.
And in hir barm this litel child she leyde   551
With ful sad face, and gan the child to blisse,
And lulled it, and after gan it kisse.

And thus she seyde in hire benigne voys,
"Fareweel, my child! I shal thee nevere see.   555
But sith I thee have marked with the croys
Of thilke Fader—blessed moote he be—
That for us deyde upon a croys of tree,
Thy soule, litel child, I hym bitake,
For this nyght shaltow dyen for my sake."   560

I trowe that to a norice in this cas
It had been hard this reuthe for to se;
Wel myghte a mooder thanne han cryd "allas."
But nathelees so sad stidefast was she
That she endured al adversitee,   565
And to the sergeant mekely she sayde,
"Have heer agayn youre litel yonge mayde.

"Gooth now," quod she, "and dooth my
    lordes heeste.
But o thyng wol I prey yow of youre grace,

That, but my lord forbad yow, atte leeste   570
Burieth this litel body in som place
That beestes ne no briddes it torace."
But he no word wol to that purpos seye,
But took the child and wente upon his weye.

This sergeant cam unto his lord ageyn,   575
And of Grisildis wordes and hire cheere
He tolde hym point for point, in short and pleyn,
And hym presenteth with his doghter deere.
Somwhat this lord hath routhe in his manere,
But nathelees his purpos heeld he stille,   580
As lordes doon whan they wol han hir wille.

And bad his sergeant that he pryvely
Sholde this child softe wynde and wrappe,
With alle circumstances tendrely,
And carie it in a cofre or in a lappe;   585
But upon peyne his heed of for to swappe
That no man sholde knowe of his entente,
Ne whenne he cam, ne whider that he wente;

But at Boloigne to his suster deere,
That thilke tyme of Panik was countesse,   590
He sholde it take and shewe hire this mateere,
Bisekynge hire to doon hire bisynesse
This child to fostre in alle gentillesse;
And whos child that it was he bad hire hyde
From every wight, for oght that may bityde.

The sergeant gooth and hath fulfild this
    thyng.   596
But to this markys now retourne we.
For now gooth he ful faste ymaginyng
If by his wyves cheere he myghte se,
Or by hire word aperceyve, that she   600
Were chaunged. But he nevere hire koude
    fynde
But evere in oon ylike sad and kynde.

---

537 *consente:* Hg&c *al consente.* 540 **diffame,** evil reputation. 544 **wende . . . slawen . . . tho,** thought, slain, then. 546 *Conformynge:* E *Consentynge.* 550 **moste,** might. 551 **barm,** breast. 552 **sad . . . blisse,** serious, bless (make the sign of the cross). 552–53 E transfers *blisse* and *kisse.* 559 **bitake,** entrust. 561 **norice,** nurse. 562 **reuthe,** pathos. 564 **sad stidefast,** solidly steadfast. 568 **heeste,** command. 572 **torace,** tear it to pieces. 579 **routhe,** pity. 582 *his:* Hg&c *this.* 583 *softe:* some MSS *ful* or *wel softe.* 584 **circumstances,** care. 585 **cofre,** box (crib). 586 **swappe,** cut. 588 E *he cam* om. 589 **Boloigne,** Bologna. 590 *Panik:* E&c *Pavik;* n and u (v) are much alike in the MSS. The place has not been identified: Boccaccio, *Panago;* Petrarch, *Panico;* Fr. *Paniquo.* 591 **shewe . . . mateere,** reveal, this whole story. 592 **Bisekynge,** beseeching. 595 **oght . . . bityde,** anything, happen. 598 **faste ymaginyng,** intently examining. 599 **cheere,** behavior. 602 **in oon . . . sad,** alike, steadfast.

As glad, as humble, as bisy in servyse
And eek in love as she was wont to be,
Was she to hym in every maner wyse,   605
Ne of hir doghter noght a word spak she.
Noon accident for noon adversitee
Was seyn in hire, ne nevere hir doghter name
Ne nempned she, in ernest nor in game.   609

Explicit tercia pars. Sequitur pars quarta.

In this estaat ther passed been foure yeer
Er she with childe was, but as God wolde
A knave child she bar by this Walter,
Ful gracious and fair for to biholde.
And whan that folk it to his fader tolde,
Nat oonly he but al his contree merye   615
Was for this child, and God they thanke and
    herye.

Whan it was two yeer old, and fro the brest
Departed of his norice, on a day
This markys caughte yet another lest
To tempte his wyf yet ofter if he may.   620
O nedelees was she tempted in assay!
But wedded men ne knowe no mesure
Whan that they fynde a pacient creature.

"Wyf," quod this markys, "ye han herd er
    this
My peple sikly berth oure mariage,   625
And namely sith my sone yboren is,
Now is it worse than evere in al oure age.
The murmur sleeth myn herte and my corage,
For to myne eres comth the voys so smerte
That it wel ny destroyed hath myn herte.   630

"Now sey they thus, 'Whan Walter is agon,
Thanne shal the blood of Janicle succede
And been oure lord, for oother have we noon.'
Swiche wordes seith my peple, out of drede.
Wel oughte I of swich murmur taken heede,
For certeinly I drede swich sentence,   636
Though they nat pleyn speke in myn audience.

"I wolde lyve in pees, if that I myghte;
Wherfore I am disposed outrely,
As I his suster servede by nyghte   640
Right so thenke I to serve hym pryvely.
This warne I yow that ye nat sodeynly
Out of youreself for no wo sholde outreye;
Beth pacient, and therof I yow preye."

"I have," quod she, "seyd thus, and evere
    shal: 645
I wol no thyng, ne nyl no thyng, certayn,
But as yow list. Naught greveth me at al
Though that my doughter and my sone be
    slayn—
At youre comandement, this is to sayn.   649
I have noght had no part of children tweyne
But first siknesse and after wo and peyne.

"Ye been oure lord—dooth with youre owene
    thyng
Right as yow list; axeth no reed at me.
For as I lefte at hoom al my clothyng,
Whan I first cam to yow, right so," quod she,
"Lefte I my wyl and al my libertee,   656
And took youre clothyng; wherfore I yow preye,
Dooth youre plesaunce; I wol youre lust obeye.

"And certes, if I hadde prescience   659
Youre wyl to knowe er ye youre lust me tolde,
I wolde it doon withouten necligence.
But now I woot youre lust and what ye wolde,
Al youre plesance ferme and stable I holde.
For wiste I that my deeth wolde do yow ese,
Right gladly wolde I dyen yow to plese.   665

"Deth may noght make no comparisoun
Unto youre love." And whan this markys say
The constance of his wyf, he caste adoun
His eyen two, and wondreth that she may
In pacience suffre al this array.   670
And forth he goth with drery contenance,
But to his herte it was ful greet plesance.

607 **accident,** accidental evidence. 609 **nempned,** named. 610 **estaat,** condition. 612 *knave:* see l. 444 above. 615 **merye,** merry. 616 **herye,** praise. 619 **lest,** desire. 620 **tempte,** test. 625 **sikly berth,** ill bear. 626 **namely,** especially. 627 **oure age,** our time. 629 **smerte,** sharply. 636 **sentence,** opinion. 637 **pleyn,** openly. 639 **disposed outrely,** decided firmly. 640 **servede,** treated. 643 **outreye,** burst out. 646 **wol . . . nyl,** desire, will not (desire). 653 **reed,** advice. 659 **prescience,** foreknowledge. 664 **wiste,** i.e., if I thought. 670 **array,** treatment.

This ugly sergeant in the same wyse
That he hire doghter caughte, right so he—
Or worse, if men worse kan devyse—   675
Hath hent hire sone that ful was of beautee.
And evere in oon so pacient was she
That she no chiere maade of hevynesse,
But kiste hir sone and after gan it blesse.

Save this, she preyde hym that if he myghte   680
Hir litel sone he wolde in erthe grave,
His tendre lymes, delicaat to sighte,
Fro foweles and fro beestes for to save.
But she noon answere of hym myghte have.
He wente his wey as hym no thyng ne roghte,
But to Boloigne he tendrely it broghte.   686

This markys wondred evere lenger the moore
Upon hir pacience, and if that he
Ne hadde soothly knowen therbifoore
That parfitly hir children loved she,   690
He wolde have wend that of som subtiltee,
And of malice, or for crueel corage,
That she hadde suffred this with sad visage.

But wel he knew that next hymself, certayn,
She loved hir children best in every wyse.   695
But now of wommen wolde I axen fayn
If thise assayes myghte nat suffise?
What koude a sturdy housbonde moore devyse
To preeve hir wyfhod and hir stedefastnesse,
And he continuynge evere in sturdinesse?   700

But ther been folk of swich condicioun
That whan they have a certein purpos take,
They kan nat stynte of hire entencioun,
But right as they were bounded to that stake
They wol nat of that firste purpos slake.   705
Right so this markys fulliche hath purposed
To tempte his wyf as he was first disposed.

He waiteth if by word or contenance

That she to hym was changed of corage,
But nevere koude he fynde variance.   710
She was ay oon in herte and in visage,
And ay the forther that she was in age,
The moore trewe—if that it were possible—
She was to hym in love, and moore penyble.

For which it semed thus, that of hem two   715
Ther nas but o wyl, for as Walter leste
The same lust was hire plesance also.
And, God be thanked, al fil for the beste.
She shewed wel for no worldly unreste
A wyf, as of hirself, nothing ne sholde   720
Wille in effect, but as hir housbonde wolde.

The sclaundre of Walter ofte and wyde
    spradde
That of a crueel herte he wikkedly,
For he a poure womman wedded hadde,
Hath mordred bothe his children prively.   725
Swich murmur was among hem comunly;
No wonder is, for to the peples ere
Ther cam no word but that they mordred
    were.

For which, where as his peple therbifore
Hadde loved hym wel, the sclaundre of his
    diffame   730
Made hem that they hym hatede therfore—
To been a mordrere is an hateful name.
But nathelees, for ernest ne for game,
He of his crueel purpos nolde stente;
To tempte his wyf was set al his entente.   735

Whan that his doghter twelve yeer was of age,
He to the court of Rome, in subtil wyse
Enformed of his wyl, sente his message,
Comaundynge hem swiche bulles to devyse
As to his crueel purpos may suffyse—   740
How that the pope, as for his peples reste,
Bad hym to wedde another if hym leste.

677 in oon, anon (constantly). **678 chiere . . . hevynesse,** expression, unhappiness. **681 grave,** bury. **685 as hym . . . roghte,** as if, cared. **691 wend . . . of . . . subtiltee,** thought, from treachery. **692 crueel corage,** cruel spirit. **693 sad visage,** composed countenance. **694 next,** next to. **697 thise assayes,** these trials. **700 sturdinesse,** cruelty. **704** *that:* some MSS *a.* **709 corage,** spirit (attitude). **714 penyble,** painstaking. **716 leste,** list (desired). **719 worldly unreste,** earthly distress. **721 Wille in effect,** i.e., make a decision. **722 sclaundre,** evil reputation. **734 stente,** stop. **737 subtil,** secret. **738 message,** messenger. **739 bulles . . . devyse,** papal edicts (Lat. *bulla,* lead seal), compose. **741 reste,** contentment.

I seye, he bad they sholde countrefete
The popes bulles, makynge mencioun
That he hath leve his firste wyf to lete   745
As by the popes dispensacioun,
To stynte rancour and dissencioun
Bitwixe his peple and hym; thus seyde the bulle,
The which they han publiced atte fulle.

The rude peple, as it no wonder is,   750
Wenden ful wel that it hadde be right so;
But whan thise tidynges cam to Grisildis,
I deeme that hire herte was ful wo.
But she, ylike sad for everemo,
Disposed was, this humble creature,   755
The adversitee of Fortune al t'endure,

Abidynge evere his lust and his plesance
To whom that she was yeven herte and al
As to hire verray worldly suffisance.
But shortly if this storie I tellen shal,   760
This markys writen hath in special
A lettre in which he sheweth his entente,
And secreely he to Boloigne it sente.

To the Erl of Panyk, which that hadde tho
Wedded his suster, preyde he specially   765
To bryngen hoom agayn his children two
In honourable estaat al openly.
But o thyng he hym preyede outrely,
That he to no wight, though men wolde
    enquere,
Sholde nat telle whos children that they
    were,   770

But seye the mayden sholde ywedded be
Unto the Markys of Saluce anon.
And as this erl was preyed so dide he;
For at day set he on his wey is goon
Toward Saluce, and lordes many oon   775
In riche array, this mayden for to gyde,
Hir yonge brother ridynge hire bisyde.

Arrayed was toward hir mariage
This fresshe mayde, ful of gemmes cleere;
Hir brother, which that seven yeer was of age,
Arrayed eek ful fressh in his manere.   781
And thus in greet noblesse and with glad
    cheere,
Toward Saluces shapynge hir journey,
Fro day to day they ryden in hir wey.

Explicit quarta pars. Sequitur pars quinta.

Among al this after his wikke usage,   785
This markys yet his wyf to tempte moore
To the outtreste preeve of hir corage,
Fully to han experience and loore
If that she were as stidefast as bifoore,
He on a day in open audience   790
Ful boistously hath seyd hire this sentence:

"Certes, Grisilde, I hadde ynogh plesance
To han yow to my wyf for youre goodnesse,
As for youre trouthe and for youre obeisance,
Noght for youre lynage ne for youre richesse;
But now knowe I in verray soothfastnesse   796
That in greet lordshipe, if I wel avyse,
Ther is greet servitude in sondry wyse.

"I may nat doon as every plowman may.
My peple me constreyneth for to take   800
Another wyf, and crien day by day;
And eek the pope, rancour for to slake,
Consenteth it, that dar I undertake.
And treweliche thus muche I wol yow seye,
My newe wyf is comynge by the weye.   805

"Be strong of herte and voyde anon hir place,
And thilke dowere that ye broghten me,
Taak it agayn; I graunte it of my grace.
Retourneth to youre fadres hous," quod he.
"No man may alwey han prosperitee.   810
With evene herte I rede yow t'endure
The strook of Fortune or of aventure."

745 leve . . . lete, permission, leave. **747 stynte,** stop. **749 publiced atte fulle,** published fully. **750 rude,** ignorant. **751 Wenden,** believed. **754 ylike sad,** uniformly steadfast. **759 verray worldly suffisance,** total earthly resources. **764 tho,** then. *Panyk:* see l. 590n. **767 honourable estaat . . . openly,** handsomely arrayed, publicly. **768 outrely,** utterly (completely). **779 cleere,** bright. **785 Among,** i.e., meanwhile. **786 tempte,** test. **787 outtreste preeve . . . corage,** furthest proof, spirit. **788 loore,** knowledge. **791 boistously,** harshly. **792 plesance,** pleasure. **794 obeisance,** obedience. **796 soothfastnesse,** truth. **803 undertake,** assert. **805 by the,** (already) on the. **807 thilke dowere,** that dowery. **811 evene . . . rede,** tranquil, counsel. **812 aventure,** chance.

And she answerde agayn in pacience,
"My lord," quod she, "I woot, and wiste
   alway,
How that bitwixen youre magnificence   815
And my poverte no wight kan ne may
Maken comparisoun; it is no nay.
I ne heeld me nevere digne in no manere
To be youre wyf, no, ne youre chamberere.

"And in this hous, ther ye me lady maade,   820
The heighe God take I for my witnesse,
And also wysly he my soule glaade,
I nevere heeld me lady ne maistresse
But humble servant to youre worthynesse,
And evere shal whil that my lyf may dure,   825
Aboven every worldly creature.

"That ye so longe of youre benignitee
Han holden me in honour and nobleye,
Where as I was noght worthy for to bee,
That thonke I God and yow, to whom I preye
Foryelde it yow; ther is namoore to seye.   831
Unto my fader gladly wol I wende,
And with hym dwelle unto my lyves ende.

"Ther I was fostred of a child ful smal,
Til I be deed my lyf ther wol I lede,   835
A wydwe clene in body, herte, and al.
For sith I yaf to yow my maydenhede,
And am youre trewe wyf, it is no drede,
God shilde swich a lordes wyf to take
Another man to housbonde or to make.   840

"And of youre newe wyf God of his grace
So graunte yow wele and prosperitee.
For I wol gladly yelden hire my place,
In which that I was blisful wont to bee.
For sith it liketh yow, my lord," quod shee,   845
"That whilom weren al myn hertes reste,
That I shal goon, I wol goon whan yow leste.

"But ther as ye me profre swich dowaire
As I first broghte, it is wel in my mynde
It were my wrecched clothes nothyng faire,   850
The whiche to me were hard now for to
   fynde—
O goode God, how gentil and how kynde
Ye semed by youre speche and youre visage
The day that maked was oure mariage!

"But sooth is seyd—algate I fynde it trewe,   855
For in effect it preeved is on me—
Love is noght oold as whan that it is newe.
But certes, lord, for noon adversitee,
To dyen in the cas, it shal nat bee
That evere in word or werk I shal repente   860
That I yow yaf myn herte in hool entente.

"My lord, ye woot that in my fadres place
Ye dide me streepe out of my poure weede,
And richely me cladden of youre grace.
To yow broghte I noght elles, out of drede,   865
But feith, and nakednesse, and maydenhede.
And heere agayn your clothyng I restoore,
And eek my weddyng ryng, for everemore.

"The remenant of youre jueles redy be
Inwith youre chambre, dar I saufly sayn.   870
Naked out of my fadres hous," quod she,
"I cam, and naked moot I turne agayn.
Al youre plesance wol I folwen fayn.
But yet I hope it be nat youre entente
That I smoklees out of youre paleys wente.   875

"Ye koude nat doon so dishonest a thyng
That thilke wombe in which youre children leye
Sholde biforn the peple in my walkyng
Be seyn al bare; wherfore I yow preye,
Lat me nat lyk a worm go by the weye.   880
Remembre yow, myn owene lord so deere,
I was youre wyf, though I unworthy weere.

[margin note: Job]

---

813 Hg&c *agayn answerde*. 814 **woot . . . wiste**, know, knew. 818 **digne**, worthy. 819 **chamberere**, chambermaid. 828 **nobleye**, nobility. 831 **Foryelde**, repay. 834 *of a*, from a. 839 **shilde**, shield (forbid). 845 **liketh**, is pleasing to. 846 **whilom**, formerly. 850 **nothyng faire**, not at all attractive. 856 **effect**, i.e., its truth. 857 **oold as whan**, i.e., not the same when it is old as when. 859 **To dyen**, i.e., even if I should die. 863 **weede**, clothes. 867 *your clothyng*: EHg&c *my*. Manly cites Sir William McCormick as believing that in ll. 867–68, Griselda distinguishes between her clothes, which are her husband's, and her ring, which is her own. 870 **Inwith . . . saufly**, within, safely. 873 **fayn**, happily. 875 **smoklees**, without undergarment.

"Wherfore, in gerdon of my maydenhede,
Which that I broghte and noght agayn I bere,
As voucheth sauf to yeve me, to my meede,
But swich a smok as I was wont to were,   886
That I therwith may wrye the wombe of here
That was youre wyf. And heer take I my leeve
Of yow, myn owene lord, lest I yow greve."

"The smok," quod he, "that thou hast on thy
       bak,   890
Lat it be stille and bere it forth with thee."
But wel unnethes thilke word he spak,
But wente his wey, for routhe and for pitee.
Biforn the folk hirselven strepeth she,
And in hir smok, with heed and foot al bare, 895
Toward hir fader hous forth is she fare.

The folk hire folwe, wepynge in hir weye,
And Fortune ay they cursen as they goon.
But she fro wepyng kepte hire eyen dreye,
Ne in this tyme word ne spak she noon.   900
Hir fader, that this tidynge herde anoon,
Curseth the day and tyme that Nature
Shoop hym to been a lyves creature.

For out of doute this olde poure man
Was evere in suspect of hir mariage;   905
For evere he demed sith that it bigan
That whan the lord fulfild hadde his corage,
Hym wolde thynke it were a disparage
To his estaat so lowe for t'alighte,
And voyden hire as soone as ever he myghte.

Agayns his doghter hastiliche goth he,   911
For he by noyse of folk knew hire comynge,
And with hire olde coote as it myghte be
He covered hire, ful sorwefully wepynge.
But on hire body myghte he it nat brynge,   915

For rude was the clooth, and she moore of age
By dayes fele than at hire mariage.

Thus with hire fader for a certeyn space
Dwelleth this flour of wyfly pacience,
That neither by hire wordes ne hire face,   920
Biforn the folk, ne eek in hire absence,
Ne shewed she that hire was doon offence,
Ne of hire heighe estaat no remembraunce
Ne hadde she, as by hire contenaunce.

No wonder is, for in hire grete estaat   925
Hire goost was evere in pleyn humylitee;
No tendre mouth, noon herte delicaat,
No pompe, no semblant of roialtee,
But ful of pacient benyngnytee,
Discreet and prideless, ay honurable,   930
And to hire housbonde evere meke and stable.

Men speke of Job, and moost for his
       humblesse,
As clerkes whan hem list konne wel endite,
Namely of men, but as in soothfastnesse,
Though clerkes preise wommen but a lite,   935
Ther kan no man in humblesse hym acquite
As womman kan, ne kan been half so trewe
As wommen been, but it be falle of newe.

[*Pars sexta.*]

Fro Boloigne is this Erl of Panyk come,
Of which the fame up sprang to moore and
       lesse,
And in the peples eres alle and some   941
Was kouth eek that a newe markysesse
He with hym broghte, in swich pompe and
       richesse
That nevere was ther seyn with mannes eye
So noble array in al West Lumbardye.   945

---

883 **gerdon**, recompense. 885 **meede**, reward. 886 **But**, only. 887 **wrye**, cover. 892 **unnethes**, barely (with difficulty). 893 **routhe**, pity. 903 **Shoop . . . lyves**, created, living, cf. Job 3:3. 905 **suspect**, suspicious. 906 **demed**, judged. 907 **corage**, spirit (here sexual desire). 908 **disparage**, disgrace. 910 **voyden**, dismiss. After this line, the Lat. and Fr. add that for this reason, the father preserved her old coat (see l. 913). 911 **Agayns**, towards. 913 **as**, as well as. 915 **on**, i.e., around. 916 **rude**, rough. 916–17 **she . . . age . . . fele**, i.e., it no longer fit because she was much older. Some MSS om. *she*, which makes it the cloth of the coat that is older, as in the Lat., *tunicam eius hespidam, et attritam senio*. 924 **as by**, as (far as one could tell) by. 926 **goost . . . pleyn**, spirit, complete. 931 **stable**, faithful. 933 **list . . . endite**, wish, compose. 934 **Namely . . . soothfastnesse**, especially, truth. 937 *womman*: Hg&c *wommen*. 938 **falle of newe**, happened just recently. 939 *Panyk*, cf. l. 590n. 941 *in*: Hg&c *to*. 942 **kouth**, known.

The markys, which that shoop and knew al
    this,
Er that this erl was come sente his message
For thilke sely poure Grisildis,
And she with humble herte and glad visage,
Nat with no swollen thoght in hire corage,   950
Cam at his heste and on hire knees hire sette,
And reverently and wisely she hym grette.

    "Grisilde," quod he, "my wyl is outrely
This mayden, that shal wedded been to me,
Received be tomorwe as roially   955
As it possible is in myn hous to be,
And eek that every wight in his degree
Have his estaat in sittyng and servyse
And heigh plesaunce, as I kan best devyse.

    "I have no wommen suffisaunt, certayn,   960
The chambres for t'arraye in ordinaunce
After my lust, and therfore wolde I fayn
That thyn were al swich manere governaunce.
Thou knowest eek of old al my plesaunce.
Thogh thyn array be badde and yvel biseye,   965
Do thou thy devoir at the leeste weye."

    "Nat oonly, lord, that I am glad," quod she,
"To doon youre lust, but I desire also
Yow for to serve and plese in my degree
Withouten feyntyng, and shal everemo;   970
Ne nevere, for no wele ne no wo,
Ne shal the goost withinne myn herte stente
To love yow best with al my trewe entente."

And with that word she gan the hous to dighte,
And tables for to sette, and beddes make,   975
And peyned hire to doon al that she myghte,
Preyynge the chambereres, for Goddes sake,
To hasten hem and faste swepe and shake,

And she, the mooste servysable of alle,
Hath every chambre arrayed and his halle.   980

    Abouten undren gan this erl alighte,
That with hym broghte thise noble children
    tweye,
For which the peple ran to seen the sighte
Of hire array so richely biseye;
And thanne at erst amonges hem they seye   985
That Walter was no fool, thogh that hym
    leste
To chaunge his wyf, for it was for the beste.

    For she is fairer, as they deemen alle,
Than is Grisilde, and moore tendre of age,
And fairer fruyt bitwene hem sholde falle,   990
And moore plesant, for hire heigh lynage.
Hir brother eek so fair was of visage
That hem to seen the peple hath caught
    plesaunce,
Commendynge now the markys governaunce.

    "O stormy peple, unsad and evere untrewe!
Ay undiscreet and chaungynge as a vane,   996
Delitynge evere in rumbul that is newe,
For lyk the moone ay wexe ye and wane!
Ay ful of clappyng, deere ynogh a jane,
Youre doom is fals, youre constance yvele
    preeveth,   1000
A ful greet fool is he that on yow leeveth."

    Thus seyden sadde folk in that citee,
Whan that the peple gazed up and doun
For they were glad right for the noveltee
To han a newe lady of hir toun.   1005
Namoore of this make I now mencioun,
But to Grisilde agayn wol I me dresse,
And telle hir constance and hir bisynesse.

---

946 shoop, shaped (planned). **947 message,** messenger. **948 sely,** innocent (overtones of "blessed"). **950 corage,** spirit. **951 heste,** behest (command). **953 outrely,** utterly. **957–58 degree . . . estaat,** that proper precedence be observed at banquets and in all other arrangements. **959 heigh plesaunce,** lofty pleasures. *I:* some MSS *ye.* **960 suffisaunt,** competent. **961 in ordinaunce,** in proper order. **962 lust . . . fayn,** desire, wish. **965 array . . . biseye,** clothing, in appearance. **966 devoir . . . leeste weye,** duty, at least. **968 lust,** pleasure. **970 feyntyng,** flagging. **972 goost . . . stente,** spirit, stop. **974 dighte,** prepare. **979 mooste serysable,** i.e., working hardest. **981 undren,** midmorning. **984 biseye,** in appearance. **986 leste,** wished. **990 fruyt,** offspring. **993 caught plesaunce,** were pleased. **994 governaunce,** behavior. **995 unsad,** inconstant. **996 undiscreet . . . vane,** thoughtless, weathervane. **997 rumbul,** tumult (rumor). **999 clappyng, deere . . . jane,** chattering, expensive enough at a halfpenny. **1000 doom . . . constance,** judgment, stability. **1001 leeveth,** believes. **1002 sadde,** sober (steadfast). **1007 dresse,** address.

Ful bisy was Grisilde in everythyng
That to the feeste was apertinent. 1010
Right noght was she abayst of hire clothyng,
Thogh it were rude and somdeel eek torent,
But with glad cheere to the yate is went
With oother folk, to greete the markysesse,
And after that dooth forth hire bisynesse. 1015

With so glad chiere his gestes she receyveth,
And konnyngly, everich in his degree,
That no defaute no man aperceyveth,
But ay they wondren what she myghte bee
That in so poure array was for to see 1020
And koude swich honour and reverence,
And worthily they preisen hire prudence.

In al this meenewhile she ne stente
This mayde and eek hir brother to commende
With al hir herte, in ful benyngne entente, 1025
So wel that no man koude hir pris amende.
But atte laste, whan that thise lordes wende
To sitten doun to mete, he gan to calle
Grisilde as she was bisy in his halle. 1029

"Grisilde," quod he, as it were in his pley,
"How liketh thee my wyf, and hire beautee?"
"Right wel," quod she, "my lord, for in good
    fey
A fairer saugh I nevere noon than she.
I prey to God yeve hire prosperitee,
And so hope I that he wol to yow sende 1035
Plesance ynogh unto youre lyves ende.

"O thyng biseke I yow, and warne also,
That ye ne prikke with no tormentynge
This tendre mayden as ye han doon mo,
For she is fostred in hire norissynge 1040
Moore tendrely, and to my supposynge
She koude nat adversitee endure
As koude a poure fostred creature."

And whan this Walter saugh hire pacience,

Hir glade chiere, and no malice at al, 1045
And he so ofte had doon to hire offence,
And she ay sad and constant as a wal,
Continuynge evere hire innocence overal,
This sturdy markys gan his herte dresse
To rewen upon hire wyfly stedfastnesse. 1050

"This is ynogh, Grisilde myn," quod he.
"Be now namoore agast ne yvele apayed.
I have thy feith and thy benyngnytee
As wel as evere womman was assayed,
In greet estaat and poureliche arrayed. 1055
Now knowe I, dere wyf, thy stedfastnesse"—
And hire in armes took and gan hire kesse.

And she for wonder took of it no keep;
She herde nat what thyng he to hire seyde;
She ferde as she had stert out of a sleep, 1060
Til she out of hir mazednesse abreyde.
"Grisilde," quod he, "by God that for us deyde,
Thou art my wyf, ne noon oother I have,
Ne nevere hadde, as God my soule save.

"This is thy doghter, which thou hast
    supposed 1065
To be my wyf; that oother feithfully
Shal be myn heir, as I have ay disposed—
Thou bare hym in thy body trewely.
At Boloigne have I kept hem prively. 1069
Taak hem agayn, for now maystow nat seye
That thou hast lorn noon of thy children tweye.

"And folk that ootherweys han seyd of me,
I warne hem wel that I have doon this deede
For no malice ne for no crueltee, 1074
But for t'assaye in thee thy wommanheede,
And nat to sleen my children—God forbeede—
But for to kepe hem pryvely and stille,
Til I thy purpos knewe and al thy wille."

Whan she this herde, aswowne doun she
    falleth

1011 **abayst,** ashamed. 1012 **torent,** torn. 1013 *is went:* EHg&c *is she went.* 1017 **konnyngly,** skillfully. EHg&c *so konnyngly.* 1018 **defaute,** mistake. 1021 **koude,** understood. 1023 **stente,** stop. 1026 **pris amende,** praise surpass. 1030 **pley,** playfully. 1037 **biseke,** beseech. 1039 **mo,** more (others). 1045 **chiere,** expression. 1047 **sad,** stable. 1049 **dresse,** address. 1050 **rewen,** take pity. 1052 **agast . . . apayed,** afraid, treated. 1056 *deer:* E *goode.* 1058 **took . . . keep,** paid attention. 1061 **mazednesse abreyde,** dazedness awoke. 1063 EHg&c *ne* om. 1067 **disposed,** arranged. EHg&c *supposed.* 1071 **lorn,** lost.

For pitous joye, and after hire swownynge 1080
She bothe hire yonge children to hire calleth,
And in hire armes, pitously wepynge,
Embraceth hem, and tendrely kissynge
Ful lyk a mooder, with hire salte teeres
She bathed bothe hire visage and hire heeres.

O which a pitous thyng it was to se 1086
Hir swownyng, and hire humble voys to heere!
"Grauntmercy, lord, God thanke it yow,"
quod she,
"That ye han saved me my children
deere. 1089
Now rekke I nevere to been deed right heere,
Sith I stonde in youre love and in youre grace,
No fors of deeth ne whan my spirit pace.

"O tendre, O deere, O yonge children myne!
Youre woful mooder wende stedfastly
That crueel houndes or som foul vermyne 1095
Hadde eten yow; but God of his mercy,
And youre benyngne fader tendrely
Hath doon yow kept"—and in that same
stounde
Al sodeynly she swapte adoun to grounde.

And in hire swough so sadly holdeth she 1100
Hire children two whan she gan hem
t'embrace
That with greet sleighte and greet difficultee
The children from hire arm they gonne arace.
O many a teere on many a pitous face
Doun ran of hem that stooden hire bisyde; 1105
Unnethe abouten hire myghte they abyde.

Walter hire gladeth and hire sorwe slaketh.
She riseth up abaysed from hire traunce,
And every wight hire joye and feeste maketh
Til she hath caught agayn hire contenaunce.
Walter hire dooth so feithfully plesaunce 1111

That it was deyntee for to seen the cheere
Bitwixe hem two, now they been met yfeere.

Thise ladyes, whan that they hir tyme say,
Han taken hire and into chambre gon, 1115
And strepen hire out of hire rude array,
And in a clooth of gold that brighte shoon,
With a coroune of many a riche stoon
Upon hire heed, they into halle hire broghte,
And ther she was honured as hire oghte. 1120

Thus hath this pitous day a blisful ende,
For every man and womman dooth his myght
This day in murthe and revel to dispende
Til on the welkne shoon the sterres lyght.
For moore solempne in every mannes
syght 1125
This feste was, and gretter of costage,
Than was the revel of hire mariage.

Ful many a yeer in heigh prosperitee
Lyven thise two in concord and in reste,
And richely his doghter maryed he 1130
Unto a lord, oon of the worthieste
Of al Ytaille; and thanne in pees and reste
His wyves fader in his court he kepeth
Til that the soule out of his body crepeth.

His sone succedeth in his heritage 1135
In reste and pees after his fader day,
And fortunat was eek in mariage,
Al putte he nat his wyf in greet assay.
This world is nat so strong, it is no nay,
As it hath been in olde tymes yoore, 1140
And herkneth what this auctour seith
therfoore.

This storie is seyd, nat for that wyves sholde
Folwen Grisilde as in humylitee,
For it were inportable though they wolde,

1081 *to:* EHg&c *unto.* **1088** E *lord, that thanke I yow.* **1090 rekke . . . to been,** care if I should be. **1092 pace,** pass (die). **1094 wende stedfastly,** supposed truly. **1098 doon yow kept . . . stounde,** had you cared for, moment. **1099 swapte,** collapsed. **1100 swough . . . sadly,** swoon, firmly. **1103 arace,** extricate. **1106 Unnethe abouten,** scarcely about (in her company). **1108 abaysed,** disoriented. **1109 feeste maketh,** provides her with diversion. **1110 caught . . . contenaunce,** i.e., composed herself. **1112 deyntee,** delightful. **1113 yfeere,** as partners. **1114 say,** saw. **1124 welkne,** sky. **1126 feste . . . costage,** feast, expense. **1138 Al,** although. **1144 inportable . . . wolde,** intolerable, wished to.

But for that every wight in his degree   1145
Sholde be constant in adversitee
As was Grisilde. Therfore Petrak writeth
This storie, which with heigh stile he enditeth.

For sith a womman was so pacient
Unto a mortal man, wel moore us oghte   1150
Receyven al in gree that God us sent.
For greet skile is he preeve that he wroghte.
But he ne tempteth no man that he boghte
As seith Seint Jame, if ye his pistel rede;
He preeveth folk al day, it is no drede,   1155

And suffreth us, as for oure exercise,
With sharpe scourges of adversitee
Ful ofte to be bete in sondry wise,
Nat for to knowe oure wyl, for certes he
Er we were born knew al oure freletee,   1160
And for oure beste is al his governaunce.
Lat us thanne lyve in vertuous suffraunce.

But o word, lordynges, herkneth er I go:
It were ful hard to fynde now-a-dayes
In al a toun Grisildis thre or two,   1165
For if that they were put to swiche assayes,
The gold of hem hath now so badde alayes
With bras, that thogh the coyne be fair at eye,
It wolde rather breste a-two than plye.

For which, heere for the Wyves love of
          Bathe—   1170
Whos lyf and al hire secte God mayntene
In heigh maistrie, and elles were it scathe—
I wol with lusty herte, fressh and grene,
Seyn yow a song to glade yow, I wene.

And lat us stynte of ernestful matere.   1175
Herkneth my song that seith in this manere:

Lenvoy de Chaucer.

Grisilde is deed, and eek hire pacience,
And bothe atones buryed in Ytaille,
For which I crie in open audience
No wedded man so hardy be t'assaille   1180
His wyves pacience in hope to fynde
Grisildis, for in certein he shal faille.

O noble wyves, ful of heigh prudence,
Lat noon humylitee youre tonge naille,
Ne lat no clerk have cause or diligence   1185
To write of yow a storie of swich mervaille
As of Grisildis, pacient and kynde,
Lest Chichevache yow swelwe in hire entraille.

Folweth Ekko, that holdeth no silence,
But evere answereth at the countretaille.   1190
Beth nat bidaffed for youre innocence,
But sharply taak on yow the governaille.
Emprenteth wel this lessoun in youre mynde
For commune profit, sith it may availle.

Ye archewyves, stondeth at defense,   1195
Syn ye be strong as is a greet camaille;
Ne suffreth nat that men yow doon offense.
And sklendre wyves, fieble as in bataille,
Beth egre as is a tygre yond in Ynde;
Ay clappeth as a mille, I yow consaille.   1200

Ne dreed hem nat; doth hem no reverence.
For though thyn housbonde armed be in
          maille,

1145 degree, station in life. **1151 gree,** in good spirit. **1152 greet skile is he preeve . . . wroghte,** it is most reasonable that he test, created. **1153 tempteth . . . boghte,** tests (as severely as Walter did), redeemed; cf. James 1:13. **1160 freletee,** frailty (weakness). E&c *al* om. **1161 governaunce,** arrangement of affairs. **1162** The paraphrase of Petrarch and the French version ends here. **1166 assayes,** trials (note appropriateness to "gold" in the next line). **1167 alayes,** alloys. **1169 breste . . . plye,** break, bend (one test for the purity of gold). **1170–76** This stanza is lacking in one family of MSS, and the Envoy ends with stanza 1195–1200, both suggesting a version of the ClT earlier than the *Canterbury* collection: see Manly III.473. **1171 secte,** *double entendre* sect (category of persons), and sex. **1172 scathe,** too bad; cf. Wife of Bath; 1.446. **1174 wene,** hope. **1175 stynte . . . ernestful,** stop, serious. **1178 atones,** together. **1179 open audience,** public. **1180 assaille,** test. **1181** *hope:* Hg&c *trust.* **1188 Chichevache,** the cow in the French fable whose food is patient wives, and who is very lean, compared with Bicorne, whose food is patient husbands, and who is very fat. **swelwe,** swallow. **1190 countretaille,** reply (counter tally). **1191 bidaffed for,** tricked because of. **1192 sharply . . . governaille,** firmly, governance. **1196 camaille,** camel (an exotic and grotesque animal in Britain and northern Europe). **1198 sklendre,** thin. **1200 clappeth,** chatter. **1202 maille,** armor.

The arwes of thy crabbed eloquence
Shal perce his brest and eek his aventaille.
In jalousie I rede eek thou hym bynde,   1205
And thou shalt make hym couche as doth a
    quaille.

If thou be fair, ther folk been in presence,
Shewe thou thy visage and thyn apparaille;
If thou be foul, be fre of thy dispence;
To gete thee freendes ay do thy travaille;   1210
Be ay of chiere as light as leef on lynde,
And lat hym care and wepe and wrynge and
    waille.

**Bihoolde the murye wordes
of the Hoost.**

This worthy Clerk whan ended was his
    tale,   1212ᵃ
Oure Hoost seyde and swoor by Goddes
    bones,
"Me were levere than a barel ale
My wyf at hoom had herd this legende ones.
This is a gentil tale for the nones
As to my purpos, wiste ye my wille.
But thyng that wol nat be, lat it be
    stille."   1212ᵍ

Heere endeth the Tale of the Clerk of Oxenford.

1204 **aventaille,** helmet. 1205 **rede,** advise. 1206 **couche,** cower. **quaille,** partridge. 1207 **in presence,** when others are present. 1209 **dispence,** expenditure. 1210 **do . . . travaille,** to do your will. 1211 **lynde,** linden tree. 1212a–g Perhaps a cancelled link; in any event found only in EHg and 20 other MSS. See Hammond, p. 303; Brusendorff, p. 76.

MERCHANT'S TALE

PROLOGUE

The Prologe of the Marchantes Tale.

"Wepyng and waylyng, care and oother sorwe
I knowe ynogh, on even and a-morwe," 1214
Quod the Marchant, "and so doon othere mo
That wedded been. I trowe that it be so,
For wel I woot it fareth so with me.
I have a wyf, the worste that may be;
For thogh the feend to hire ycoupled were,
She wolde hym overmacche, I dar wel swere.
What sholde I yow reherce in special 1221
Hir hye malice? She is a shrewe at al.
Ther is a long and large difference
Bitwix Grisildis grete pacience
And of my wyf the passyng crueltee. 1225
Were I unbounden, also moot I thee,
I wolde nevere eft comen in the snare.
We wedded men lyve in sorwe and care.
Assaye whoso wole and he shal fynde
I seye sooth, by Seint Thomas of Ynde, 1230
As for the moore part—I sey nat alle.
God shilde that it sholde so bifalle!
"A, goode sire Hoost, I have ywedded bee
Thise monthes two, and moore nat, pardee,
And yet, I trowe, he that al his lyve 1235
Wyflees hath been, though that men wolde him ryve
Unto the herte, ne koude in no manere
Tellen so muchel sorwe as I now heere
Koude tellen of my wyves cursednesse."
"Now," quod oure Hoost, "Marchaunt, so God yow blesse, 1240
Syn ye so muchel knowen of that art,
Ful hertely I pray yow telle us part."
"Gladly," quod he, "but of myn owene soore
For soory herte I telle may namoore."

1213–44 These lines occur only in E&c. They are lacking in Hg&c. 1213 **Wepyng and waylyng**, the echo of l. 1212 above indicates the way the prologues and tales can, at their best, be interwoven. 1215 **othere mo**, more others. 1216 **trowe**, believe. 1217 **woot**, know. 1219 **feend . . . hire ycoupled**, the folk theme of the shrewish wife who is more than a match for the devil who carries her off is widespread. 1223 *and:* other MSS *and a.* 1226 **thee**, prosper. 1227 **eft**, again. This is the theme of *Lenvoy de Chaucer a Bukton* (short poem 16). 1230 **sooth**, truth. **Thomas of Ynde**, cf. SumT, III.1980n. above. Perhaps this was merely a convenient rhyme. Other MSS *That I seye.* 1231 **moore**, greater. 1236 **ryve**, pierce. 1241 **that art**, cf. echo of Wife of Bath, I.476, III.44ff., etc. 1242 **hertely**, heartily (sincerely). 1243 **soore**, suffering.

Heere bigynneth the Marchantes Tale.

Whilom ther was dwellynge in Lumbardye
A worthy knyght that born was of Pavye,   1246
In which he lyved in greet prosperitee;
And sixty yeer a wyflees man was hee,
And folwed ay his bodily delyt
On wommen ther as was his appetyt,   1250
As doon thise fooles that been seculeer.
And whan that he was passed sixty yeer,
Were it for hoolynesse or for dotage
I kan nat seye, but swich a greet corage
Hadde this knyght to been a wedded man   1255
That day and nyght he dooth al that he kan
T'espien where he myghte wedded be,
Preyinge oure Lord to graunten him that he
Mighte ones knowe of thilke blisful lyf
That is bitwixe an housbonde and his wyf,   1260
And for to lyve under that hooly boond
With which that first God man and womman
    bond.
"Noon oother lyf," seyde he, "is worth a
    bene,
For wedlok is so esy and so clene
That in this world it is a paradys."   1265
Thus seyde this olde knyght, that was so wys.
   And certeinly, as sooth as God is kyng,
To take a wyf it is a glorious thyng,
And namely whan a man is oold and hoor;
Thanne is a wyf the fruyt of his tresor.   1270
Thanne sholde he take a yong wyf and a feir,
On which he myghte engendren hym an heir,
And lede his lyf in joye and in solas,
Where as thise bacheleris synge allas,
Whan that they fynden any adversitee   1275
In love, which nys but childyssh vanytee.
And trewely it sit wel to be so

That bacheleris have often peyne and wo.
On brotel ground they buylde, and brotelnesse
They fynde whan they wene sikernesse.   1280
They lyve but as a bryd or as a beest,
In libertee and under noon arreest,
Ther as a wedded man in his estaat
Lyveth a lyf blisful and ordinaat
Under this yok of mariage ybounde.   1285
Wel may his herte in joye and blisse habounde.
For who kan be so buxom as a wyf?
Who is so trewe and eek so ententyf
To kepe hym, syk and hool, as is his make?
For wele or wo she wole hym nat forsake.   1290
She nys nat wery hym to love and serve
Thogh that he lye bedrede til he sterve.
And yet somme clerkes seyn it nys nat so,
Of whiche he Theofraste is oon of tho.
What force though Theofraste liste lye?   1295
   "Ne take no wyf," quod he, "for housbondrye,
As for to spare in houshold thy dispence.
A trewe servant dooth moore diligence
Thy good to kepe than thyn owene wyf,
For she wol clayme half part al hir lyf.   1300
And if that thou be syk, so God me save,
Thy verray freendes or a trewe knave
Wol kepe thee bet than she that waiteth ay
After thy good and hath doon many a day.
And if thou take a wyf unto thyn hoold,   1305
Ful lightly maystow been a cokewold."
This sentence and an hundred thynges worse
Writeth this man, ther God his bones corse!
But take no kepe of al swich vanytee;
Deffie Theofraste and herke me.   1310
   A wyf is Goddes yifte verraily;
Alle othere manere yiftes hardily,

1245 **Whilom,** formerly. 1246 **Pavye,** Pavia, near Milan. No reason has been advanced for setting the story in Italy. 1251 **seculeer,** laymen. Some commentators have suggested that this remark would come most appropriately from the mouth of one of the religious pilgrims (see also l. 1322 below), and therefore that the tale might have been assigned originally to the Monk. 1254 **corage,** longing. 1259 **ones knowe of thilke,** once experience that. 1269 **namely,** especially. 1270 **fruyt,** *double entendre,* best part, but also outgrowth (harvest). 1273 **solas,** pleasure (sexual overtone). 1277 **sit,** sitteth (i.e., is fitting). 1279 **brotelnesse,** brittleness. 1280 **wene siker-nesse,** expect security. 1282 **arreest,** restraint. 1284 **ordinaat,** regulated. 1288 **ententyf,** attentive. 1289 **kepe . . . make,** care for, mate. 1292 **sterve,** die. 1294 **Theofraste,** author of the lost *Liber de Nuptiis,* part of which is preserved in *Jerome adversus Jovinianum,* cf. *CT* III.3n above. 1296 **housbondrye,** domestic management. 1297 **spare . . . dispence,** to spare (save) expenses. 1299 **good,** goods. 1302 **verray . . . knave,** mere, serving man. 1304 **After,** i.e., to inherit. 1305 **hoold,** keeping. 1305–06 **unto . . . cokewold:** these words are found only in EGg; in Hg&c there is a blank; other MSS have other adjustments. The exemplar evidently had a gap. 1312 **hardily,** certainly. This and much that follows is from Albertano de Brescia, *Liber de Amore Dei.*

As londes, rentes, pasture, or commune,
Or moebles, alle been yiftes of Fortune,
That passen as a shadwe upon a wal.   1315
But drede nat, if pleynly speke I shal,
A wyf wol laste and in thyn hous endure
Wel lenger than thee list, paraventure.
      Mariage is a ful greet sacrement.
He which that hath no wyf, I holde hym shent.
He lyveth helplees and al desolat—   1321
I speke of folk in seculer estaat.
And herke why, I sey nat this for noght,
That womman is for mannes help ywroght.
The hye God, whan he hadde Adam maked,
And saugh him al allone, bely-naked,   1326
God of his grete goodnesse seyde than,
"Lat us now make an help unto this man
Lyk to hymself," and thanne he made him Eve.
Heere may ye se, and heerby may ye preve,
That wyf is mannes help and his confort,   1331
His paradys terrestre and his disport.
So buxom and so vertuous is she
They moste nedes lyve in unitee.
O flessh they been, and o flessh, as I gesse,   1335
Hath but oon herte in wele and in distresse.
      A wyf, a Seinte Marie, benedicite,
How myghte a man han any adversitee
That hath a wyf? Certes, I kan nat seye.
The blisse which that is bitwixe hem tweye
Ther may no tonge telle or herte thynke.   1341
If he be poure, she helpeth hym to swynke;
She kepeth his good, and wasteth never a deel;
Al that hire housbonde lust, hire liketh weel;
She seith nat ones nay, whan he seith
      ye.   1345
"Do this," seith he. "Al redy, sire," seith she.
O, blisful ordre of wedlok precious,
Thou art so murye and eek so vertuous,
And so commended and approved eek

That every man that halt hym worth a leek
Upon his bare knees oughte al his lyf   1351
Thanken his God that hym hath sent a wyf,
Or elles preye to God hym for to sende
A wyf to laste unto his lyves ende,
For thanne his lyf is set in sikernesse.   1355
He may nat be deceyved, as I gesse,
So that he werke after his wyves reed.
Thanne may he boldely beren up his heed—
They been so trewe and therwithal so wyse.
For which, if thou wolt werken as the wyse,
Do alwey so as wommen wol thee rede.   1361
      Lo how that Jacob, as thise clerkes rede,
By good conseil of his mooder Rebekke
Boond the kydes skyn aboute his nekke,
Thurgh which his fadres benysoun he wan.   1365
      Lo Judith, as the storie eek telle kan,
By wys conseil she Goddes peple kepte,
And slow hym Olofernus whil he slepte.
      Lo Abigayl, by good conseil how she
Saved hir housbonde Nabal whan that he   1370
Sholde han be slayn. And looke Ester also
By good conseil delyvered out of wo
The peple of God, and made hym Mardochee
Of Assuere enhaunced for to be.
      Ther nys nothyng in gree superlatyf,   1375
As seith Senek, above an humble wyf.
      Suffre thy wyves tonge, as Catoun bit;
She shal comande, and thou shalt suffren it,
And yet she wole obeye of curteisye.
A wyf is kepere of thyn housbondrye.   1380
Wel may the sike man biwaille and wepe
Ther as ther nys no wyf the hous to kepe.
I warne thee, if wisely thou wolt wirche,
Love wel thy wyf as Crist loved his chirche.
If thou lovest thyself, thou lovest thy wyf.   1385
No man hateth his flessh, but in his lyf
He fostreth it, and therfore bidde I thee

1313 **commune,** common rights (for grazing, woodcutting, etc.). 1314 **moebles,** movable belongings. 1316 *drede nat:* E&c *dredelees* (in E a correction). 1318 **list,** wish. 1320 **shent,** lost. 1322 **seculer estaat,** cf. l. 1251n. 1326 Hg&c *al* om. 1332 **disport,** delight (entertainment). 1333 **buxom,** obedient. 1335 **O flessh,** one flesh, Gen. 2:23, Matt. 19:5, etc. 1342 **swynke,** work. 1343 **kepeth,** guards. 1344 **lust, hire liketh,** desires, pleases her. 1355 **sikernesse,** security. 1357 **reed,** advice. 1358–61 Lines omitted in E&c; no gap in MS. 1358 *beren:* Hg&c *kepen.* 1361 **rede,** advice. 1362 **rede,** advise, cf. Gen. 27. The examples in 1362–74 are again from Albertano of Brescia, and reappear in *Mel* vii.1098. 1365 **benysoun,** blessing. 1367 **kepte,** protected, cf. Apocrypha, Judith 11. 1369 **Abigayl,** cf. I Sam. (Vulgate I Kings) 25. 1374 **enhaunced,** advanced, cf. Esther 7. 1375 **in gree superlatyf,** in degree better. 1377 **Suffre . . . Catoun bit,** endure, Cato commanded. Reference to *Distiches of Cato,* but through Albertano. 1379 **of,** out of. 1380 **housbondrye,** domestic arrangements. 1384–86 cf. Ephes. 5:25, 28, 29.

Cherisse thy wyf or thou shalt nevere thee.
Housbonde and wyf, whatso men jape or
    pleye,
Of worldly folk holden the siker weye.   1390
They been so knyt ther may noon harm bityde,
And namely upon the wyves syde.
For which this Januarie, of whom I tolde,
Considered hath, in with his dayes olde,
The lusty lyf, the vertuous quyete,   1395
That is in mariage hony-sweete,
And for his freendes on a day he sente
To tellen hem th'effect of his entente.
    With face sad his tale he hath hem toold.
He seyde, "Freendes, I am hoor and oold,   1400
And almoost, God woot, on my pittes brynke;
Upon my soule somwhat moste I thynke.
I have my body folily despended.
Blessed be God that it shal been amended,
For I wol be, certeyn, a wedded man,   1405
And that anoon in al the haste I kan,
Unto som mayde fair and tendre of age.
I prey yow, shapeth for my mariage
Al sodeynly, for I wol nat abyde;
And I wol fonde t'espien, on my syde,   1410
To whom I may be wedded hastily.
But forasmuche as ye been mo than I,
Ye shullen rather swich a thyng espyen
Than I, and where me best were to allyen.
    "But o thyng warne I yow, my freendes deere,
I wol noon oold wyf han in no manere.   1416
She shal nat passe twenty yeer, certayn.
Oold fissh and yong flessh wolde I have fayn.
Bet is," quod he, "a pyk than a pykerel,
And bet than old boef is the tendre veel.   1420
I wol no womman thritty yeer of age;
It is but bene-straw and greet forage.

And eek thise olde wydwes, God it woot,
They konne so muchel craft on Wades boot,
So muchel broken harm whan that hem
    leste,   1425
That with hem sholde I nevere lyve in reste.
For sondry scoles maken sotile clerkis:
Womman of manye scoles half a clerk is.
But certeynly, a yong thyng may men gye
Right as men may warm wex with handes plye.
Wherfore I sey yow pleynly, in a clause,   1431
I wol noon oold wyf han right for this cause.
For if so were I hadde swich myschaunce
That I in hire ne koude han no plesaunce,
Thanne sholde I lede my lyf in avoutrye,   1435
And streight unto the devel whan I dye.
Ne children sholde I none upon hire geten,
Yet were me levere houndes had me eten
Than that myn heritage sholde falle
In straunge hand. And this I telle yow alle: 1440
I dote nat, I woot the cause why
Men sholde wedde, and forthermoore woot I
Ther speketh many a man of mariage
That woot namoore of it than woot my page
For whiche causes man sholde take a wyf.   1445
Siththe he may nat lyven chaast his lyf,
Take hym a wyf with greet devocioun
By cause of leveful procreacioun
Of children, to th'onour of God above,
And nat oonly for paramour or love;   1450
And for they sholde leccherye eschue
And yelde hir dette whan that it is due;
Or for that ech of hem sholde helpen oother
In meschief, as a suster shal the brother,
And lyve in chastitee ful holily—   1455
But sires, by youre leve, that am nat I.
For, God be thanked, I dar make avaunt,

I feele my lymes stark and suffisaunt
To do al that a man bilongeth to;
I woot myselven best what I may do.　　　1460
Though I be hoor, I fare as dooth a tree
That blosmeth er that fruyt ywoxen bee,
And blosmy tree nys neither drye ne deed.
I feele me nowhere hoor but on myn heed;
Myn herte and alle my lymes been as grene　　1465
As laurer thurgh the yeer is for to sene.
And syn that ye han herd al myn entente,
I prey yow to my wyl ye wole assente.''
　　Diverse men diversely hym tolde
Of mariage manye ensamples olde.　　　1470
Somme blamed it, somme preysed it, certeyn,
But atte laste, shortly for to seyn,
As alday falleth altercacioun
Bitwixen freendes in disputisoun,
Ther fil a stryf bitwixe his bretheren two,　　1475
Of whiche that oon was cleped Placebo.
Justinus soothly called was that oother.
　　Placebo seyde, "O Januarie, brother,
Ful litel nede hadde ye, my lord so deere,
Conseil to axe of any that is heere,　　　1480
But that ye been so ful of sapience
That yow ne liketh, for youre heighe
　　prudence,
To weyven fro the word of Salomon.
This word seyde he unto us everychon:
'Wirk alle thyng by conseil,' thus seyde he,　　1485
'And thanne shaltow nat repente thee.'
But though that Salomon spak swich a word,
Myn owene deere brother and my lord,
So wysly God my soule brynge at reste,
I holde youre owene conseil is the beste.　　1490
For, brother myn, of me taak this motyf,
I have now been a court-man al my lyf,
And God it woot, though I unworthy be,
I have stonden in ful greet degree
Abouten lordes of ful heigh estaat;　　　1495
Yet hadde I nevere with noon of hem debaat.
I nevere hem contraried, trewely;

I woot wel that my lord kan moore than I.
What that he seith, I holde it ferme and
　　stable;
I seye the same or elles thyng semblable.　　1500
A ful greet fool is any conseillour
That serveth any lord of heigh honour
That dar presume, or elles thenken it,
That his conseil sholde passe his lordes wit.
Nay, lordes been no fooles, by my fay.　　1505
Ye han youreselven shewed heer today
So heigh sentence, so holily and weel,
That I consente and conferme everydeel
Youre wordes alle and youre opinioun.
By God, ther nys no man in al this toun,　　1510
N'yn Ytaille, that koude bet han sayd!
Crist halt hym of this conseil ful wel apayd.
And trewely, it is an heigh corage
Of any man that stapen is in age
To take a yong wyf. By my fader kyn,　　1515
Youre herte hangeth on a joly pyn!
Dooth now in this matiere right as yow leste,
For finally I holde it for the beste.''
　　Justinus that ay stille sat and herde
Right in this wise he to Placebo answerde:　　1520
"Now, brother myn, be pacient I preye,
Syn ye han seyd, and herkneth what I seye.
Senek among his othere wordes wyse
Seith that a man oghte hym right wel avyse
To whom he yeveth his lond or his catel.　　1525
And syn I oghte avyse me right wel
To whom I yeve my good awey fro me,
Wel muchel moore I oghte avysed be
To whom I yeve my body for alwey.
I warne yow wel, it is no childes pley　　1530
To take a wyf withouten avysement.
Men moste enquere, this is myn assent,
Wher she be wys, or sobre, or dronkelewe,
Or proud, or elles ootherweys a shrewe,
A chidestere, or wastour of thy good,　　1535
Or riche, or poore, or elles mannyssh wood.
Al be it so that no man fynden shal

Noon in this world that trotteth hool in al,
Ne man, ne beest, swich as men koude devyse.
But nathelees it oghte ynough suffise   1540
With any wyf, if so were that she hadde
Mo goode thewes than hire vices badde.
And al this axeth leyser for t'enquere.
For, God it woot, I have wept many a teere
Ful pryvely syn I have had a wyf.   1545
Preyse whoso wole a wedded mannes lyf,
Certein I fynde in it but cost and care,
And observances of alle blisses bare.
And yet, God woot, my neighebores aboute,
And namely of wommen many a route,   1550
Seyn that I have the mooste stedefast wyf,
And eek the mekeste oon that bereth lyf—
But I woot best where wryngeth me my sho.
Ye mowe, for me, right as yow liketh do.
Avyseth yow—ye been a man of age—   1555
How that ye entren into mariage,
And namely with a yong wyf and a fair.
By hym that made water, erthe, and air,
The yongeste man that is in al this route
Is bisy ynough to bryngen it aboute   1560
To han his wyf allone. Trusteth me,
Ye shul nat plesen hire fully yeres thre—
This is to seyn, to doon hire ful plesaunce.
A wyf axeth ful many an observaunce.
I prey yow that ye be nat yvele apayd."   1565
  "Wel," quod this Januarie, "and hastow
      ysayd?
Straw for thy Senek, and for thy proverbes.
I counte nat a panyer ful of herbes
Of scole-termes. Wyser men than thow,
As thou hast herd, assenteden right now   1570
To my purpos. Placebo, what sey ye?"
  "I seye it is a cursed man," quod he,
"That letteth matrimoigne, sikerly."
And with that word they rysen sodeynly
And been assented fully that he sholde   1575
Be wedded whanne hym liste and where he
      wolde.

  Heigh fantasye and curious bisynesse
Fro day to day gan in the soule impresse
Of Januarie aboute his mariage.
Many fair shap and many a fair visage   1580
Ther passeth thurgh his herte nyght by
      nyght.
As whoso tooke a mirour, polisshed bryght,
And sette it in a commune market-place,
Thanne sholde he se ful many a figure pace
By his mirour, and in the same wyse   1585
Gan Januarie inwith his thoght devyse
Of maydens whiche that dwelten hym bisyde.
He wiste nat wher that he myghte abyde.
For if that oon have beaute in hir face,
Another stant so in the peples grace   1590
For hire sadnesse and hire benyngnytee
That of the peple grettest voys hath she;
And somme were riche and hadden badde
      name.
But nathelees, bitwixe ernest and game,
He atte laste apoynted hym on oon,   1595
And leet alle othere from his herte goon,
And chees hire of his owene auctoritee—
For love is blynd alday and may nat see.
And whan that he was in his bed ybroght,
He purtreyed in his herte and in his thoght 1600
Hir fresshe beautee and hir age tendre,
Hir myddel smal, hire armes longe and
      sklendre,
Hir wise governaunce, hir gentillesse,
Hir wommanly berynge, and hire sadnesse.
And whan that he on hire was condescended,
Hym thoughte his choys myghte nat ben
      amended.   1606
For whan that he hymself concluded hadde,
Hym thoughte ech oother mannes wit so badde
That inpossible it were to repplye
Agayn his choys—this was his fantasye.   1610
His freendes sente he to at his instaunce,
And preyed hem to doon hym that plesaunce
That hastily they wolden to hym come;

1538 trotteth hool in al, i.e., goes perfect in every respect. **1539 devyse,** imagine. **swich:** E *which.* **1542 thewes,** qualities. **1548 observances,** duties. **1550 namely . . . route,** especially, company. **1551 Seyn,** say. **1553 wryngeth,** i.e., pinches. **1554 mowe, for me,** may, as far as I am concerned. **1565 yvele apayd,** displeased. **1568 counte . . . panyer,** value, a wicker basket. **1569 scole-termes,** i.e., "educated talk." **1573 letteth,** hinders. **1577 Heigh fantasye,** exaggerated imagination. **curious bisynesse,** irrational concern. **1587 E&c** *dwellen.* **1588 abyde,** stop. **1591 sadnesse . . . benyngnytee,** seriousness, graciousness. **1595 apoynted hym,** decided. **1597 auctoritee,** responsibility. **1603 governaunce,** behavior. **1605 condescended,** settled. **1609 repplye,** reply. **1611 instaunce,** initiative.

He wolde abregge hir labour alle and some.
Nedeth namoore for hym to go ne ryde;   1615
He was apoynted ther he wolde abyde.

　Placebo cam and eek his freendes soone
And alderfirst he bad hem alle a boone,
That noon of hem none argumentes make
Agayn the purpos which that he hath take,   1620
Which purpos was plesant to God, seyde he,
And verray ground of his prosperitee.

　He seyde ther was a mayden in the toun,
Which that of beautee hadde greet renoun.
Al were it so she were of smal degree,   1625
Suffiseth hym hir yowthe and hir beautee.
Which mayde, he seyde, he wolde han to his
　wyf,
To lede in ese and hoolynesse his lyf;
And thanked God that he myghte han hire al,
That no wight his blisse parten shal.   1630
And preyde hem to laboure in this nede
And shapen that he faille nat to spede;
For thanne, he seyde, his spirit was at ese.
"Thanne is," quod he, "nothyng may me
　displese,
Save o thyng priketh in my conscience   1635
The which I wol reherce in youre presence.

　"I have," quod he, "herd seyd ful yoore ago,
Ther may no man han parfite blisses two—
This is to seye, in erthe and eek in hevene.
For though he kepe hym fro the synnes sevene
And eek from every branche of thilke tree,   1641
Yet is ther so parfit felicitee
And so greet ese and lust in mariage,
That evere I am agast now in myn age
That I shal lede now so myrie a lyf,   1645
So delicat, withouten wo and stryf,
That I shal have myn hevene in erthe heere.
For sith that verray hevene is boght so deere
With tribulacioun and greet penaunce,

How sholde I thanne, that lyve in swich
　plesaunce,   1650
As alle wedded men doon with hire wyvys,
Come to the blisse ther Crist eterne on lyve
　ys?
This is my drede, and ye, my bretheren tweye,
Assoilleth me this questioun, I preye."

　Justinus, which that hated his folye,   1655
Answerde anon right in his japerye;
And for he wolde his longe tale abregge,
He wolde noon auctoritee allegge,
But seyde, "Sire, so ther be noon obstacle
Oother than this, God of his hygh myracle   1660
And of his mercy may so for yow wirche
That er ye have youre right of hooly chirche
Ye may repente of wedded mannes lyf,
In which ye seyn ther is no wo ne stryf.
And elles, God forbede but he sente   1665
A wedded man hym grace to repente
Wel ofte rather than a sengle man.
And therfore, sire, the beste reed I kan:
Dispeire yow noght, but have in youre
　memorie
Paraunter she may be youre purgatorie!   1670
She may be Goddes meene and Goddes
　whippe.
Thanne shal youre soule up to hevene skippe
Swifter than dooth an arwe out of the bowe.
I hope to God herafter shul ye knowe
That ther nys no so greet felicitee   1675
In mariage, ne nevere mo shal bee,
That yow shal lette of youre savacioun,
So that ye use, as skile is and resoun,
The lustes of youre wyf attemprely,
And that ye plese hire nat to amorously,   1680
And that ye kepe yow eek from oother synne.
My tale is doon for my wit is thynne.
Beth nat agast herof, my brother deere,

1614 **abregge,** shorten (abridge). 1615 **go . . . ryde,** walk, ride (i.e., search around). 1616 **apoynted . . . abyde,** settled (upon whom), stay. 1618 **boone,** request. 1622 **verray ground,** true basis. 1625 **smal degree,** humble class. 1630 **parten,** share. 1632 **shapen . . . spede,** arrange, succeed. 1637 **yoore ago,** long ago. 1638 **parfite,** perfect. 1640 **synnes sevene,** the Seven Deadly Sins; they are the staple of the ParsT, x.387ff. 1643 **lust,** pleasure. 1644 **agast,** terrified. 1646 **delicat,** delightful. 1654 **Assoilleth,** solve. 1656 **in . . . japerye,** in mockery. 1657 **abregge,** shorten. 1658 **allegge,** appeal to. 1661 E *hygh mercy.* 1662 **right,** rite(s), i.e., extreme unction. 1666 **hym grace,** i.e., him reasons. 1668 **reed I kan,** advice I know. 1670–71 **purgatorie, whippe,** these are the Wife of Bath's figures, III.175, 489. 1673 *the bowe:* Hg&c *a bowe.* 1677 **lette,** hinder. 1678 **skile,** proper. 1679 **lustes . . . attemprely,** pleasures, moderately. 1683–88 These lines cannot properly be assigned to Justinus. They are sometimes treated as parenthetical remarks by the Merchant. Manly III.475 suggests that they may have been a marginal memorandum by Chaucer in connection with the genesis of the *Lenvoy a Bukton* (short poem 16).

But lat us waden out of this mateere.
The Wyf of Bathe, if ye han understonde,   1685
Of mariage, which ye have on honde,
Declared hath ful wel in litel space.
Fareth now wel. God have yow in his grace."
    And with that word this Justyn and his
        brother
Han take hir leve, and ech of hem of
        oother.   1690
For whan they saugh that it moste nedes be,
They wroghten so, by sly and wys tretee,
That she, this mayden, which that Mayus
        highte,
As hastily as evere that she myghte
Shal wedded be unto this Januarie.   1695
I trowe it were to longe yow to tarie
If I yow tolde of every scrit and bond
By which that she was feffed in his lond,
Or for to herknen of hir riche array.
But finally ycomen is the day   1700
That to the chirche bothe be they went
For to receyve the hooly sacrement.
Forth comth the preest, with stole aboute his
        nekke,
And bad hire be lyk Sarra and Rebekke
In wysdom and in trouthe of mariage,   1705
And seyde his orisons, as is usage,
And croucheth hem, and bad God sholde hem
        blesse,
And made al siker ynogh with hoolynesse.
    Thus been they wedded with solempnitee,
And at the feeste sitteth he and she   1710
With othere worthy folk upon the deys.
Al ful of joye and blisse is the paleys,
And ful of instrumentz and of vitaille,

The mooste deynteuous of al Ytaille.
Biforn hem stoode instrumentz of swich soun
That Orpheus ne of Thebes Amphioun   1716
Ne maden nevere swich a melodye.
At every cours thanne cam loud mynstralcye
That nevere tromped Joab for to heere,
Nor he Theodomas yet half so cleere   1720
At Thebes whan the citee was in doute.
Bacus the wyn hem skynketh al aboute,
And Venus laugheth upon every wight,
For Januarie was bicome hir knyght
And wolde bothe assayen his corage   1725
In libertee and eek in mariage;
And with hire fyrbrond in hire hand aboute
Daunceth biforn the bryde and al the route.
And certeinly, I dar right wel seyn this,
Ymeneus that god of weddyng is   1730
Saugh nevere his lyf so myrie a wedded man.
Hoold thou thy pees, thou poete Marcian,
That writest us that ilke weddyng murie
Of hire Philologie and hym Mercurie,
And of the songes that the Muses songe!   1735
To smal is bothe thy penne, and eek thy tonge
For to descryven of this mariage
Whan tendre youthe hath wedded stoupyng
        age.
Ther is swich myrthe that it may nat be writen.
Assayeth it youreself, thanne may ye witen   1740
If that I lye or noon in this matiere.
    Mayus, that sit with so benyngne a chiere,
Hire to biholde it semed fairye.
Queene Ester looked nevere with swich an eye
On Assuer, so meke a look hath she.   1745
I may yow nat devyse al hir beautee,
But thus muche of hire beautee telle I may,

1684 waden, wade (move). **1686** *ye:* Hg&c *we.* **1689** *that:* E&c *this.* **1691** E *nedes* om. **1692 wroghten . . . sly . . . tretee,** arranged it, skillful, negotiation. **1696 tarie,** delay. **1697 scrit,** deed (writing). **1698 feffed,** enfeoffed (put in possession of). **1704 Sarra,** Sarah: these lines refer to commonplaces of the marriage ceremony, with some irony in view of the purpose of it all. **1705 trouthe,** fidelity. **1706 orisons . . . usage,** prayers, customary. **1707 croucheth,** made the sign of the cross. **1708 siker,** secure. **1711 deys,** dais (at the high table). **1713 vitaille,** food. **1714 deynteuous,** dainty (extraordinary). **1715** Hg&c *such instrumentz of soun.* **1716 Orpheus,** mythic Greek musician whose music charmed Pluto to release his wife from the Underworld. **Amphioun,** mythic musician who built Thebes by playing so beautifully that the stones moved into place of their own accord. **1719 Joab,** King David's trumpeter, II Sam. (Vulgate II Kings) 2:28. **1720 Theodomas,** seer in *Thebaid* (8.343) whose auguries are announced by a trumpet. **1722** *skynketh:* Hg&c *shenketh* (OE *scencan,* to pour). **1725 corage,** spirit. but the *double entendre* "penis" must be borne in mind here and at ll. 1759, 1808, etc. **1727 fyrbrond,** symbol of sexual desire, cf. *RR,* 3434, 21248 (Dunn-Robbins 17.17, 98.33). **1730 Ymeneus,** Hymen. **1732 Marcian,** Marcianus Capella, whose allegorical poem about the wedding of the liberal arts, *De Nuptiis Philologiae et Mercurii* (5th century), is at the opposite extreme from the libidinous marriage here being described. **1742 benyngne . . . chiere,** serene, expression. **1743 fairye,** i.e., enchanting. **1744 Ester,** Esther married King Ahasuerus in order to manipulate him, Esther 4ff.

That she was lyk the brighte morwe of May,
Fulfild of alle beautee and plesaunce.

 This Januarie is ravysshed in a traunce   1750
At every tyme he looked on hir face;
But in his herte he gan hire to manace
That he that nyght in armes wolde hire streyne
Harder than evere Parys dide Eleyne.
But nathelees yet hadde he greet pitee   1755
That thilke nyght offenden hire moste he,
And thoughte, "Allas, O tendre creature,
Now wolde God ye myghte wel endure
Al my corage, it is so sharp and keene!
I am agast ye shul it nat susteene—   1760
But God forbede that I dide al my myght!
Now wolde God that it were woxen nyght,
And that the nyght wolde lasten everemo.
I wolde that al this peple were ago."
And finally he dooth al his labour,   1765
As he best myghte, savynge his honour,
To haste hem fro the mete in subtil wyse.

 The tyme cam that resoun was to ryse,
And after that men daunce and drynken faste,
And spices al aboute the hous they caste,   1770
And ful of joye and blisse is every man—
Al but a squyer highte Damyan,
Which carf biforn the knyght ful many a day.
He was so ravysshed on his lady May   1774
That for the verray peyne he was ny wood.
Almoost he swelte and swowned ther he stood,
So soore hath Venus hurt hym with hire brond,
As that she bar it daunsynge in hire hond,
And to his bed he wente hym hastily.
Namoore of hym as at this tyme speke I,   1780
But there I lete hym wepe ynogh and pleyne,
Til fresshe May wol rewen on his peyne.

 O perilous fyr that in the bedstraw bredeth!
O famulier foo that his servyce bedeth!
O servant traytour, false hoomly hewe,   1785
Lyk to the naddre in bosom sly untrewe!
God shilde us alle from youre aqueyntaunce.
O Januarie, dronken in plesaunce
In mariage, se how thy Damyan,
Thyn owene squier and thy boren man,   1790
Entendeth for to do thee vileynye.
God graunte thee thy hoomly fo t'espye!
For in this world nys worse pestilence
Than hoomly foo al day in thy presence.   1794

 Parfourned hath the sonne his ark diurne;
No lenger may the body of hym sojurne
On th'orisonte as in that latitude.
Night with his mantel that is derk and rude
Gan oversprede the hemysperie aboute,
For which departed is this lusty route   1800
Fro Januarie with thank on every syde.
Hoom to hir houses lustily they ryde,
Where as they doon hir thynges as hem leste,
And whan they sye hir tyme goon to reste.
Soone after that, this hastif Januarie   1805
Wolde go to bedde, he wolde no lenger tarye.
He drynketh ypocras, clarree, and vernage
Of spices hoote t'encreessen his corage,
And many a letuarie hath he ful fyn,
Swiche as the cursed monk daun Constantyn
Hath writen in his book *De Coitu*;   1811
To eten hem alle he nas no thyng eschu.
And to his privee freendes thus seyde he,
"For Goddes love, as soone as it may be,
Lat voyden al this hous in curteys wyse."   1815
And they han doon right as he wol devyse.
Men drynken and the travers drawe anon.
The bryde was broght abedde as stille as stoon;
And whan the bed was with the preest yblessed,

1748 **morwe,** morning. 1752 **manace,** menace (threaten). 1756 **offenden,** hurt physically. 1759 **corage,** see l. 1725n. 1760 **agast . . . susteene,** afraid, endure. 1767 **mete . . . subtil,** (wedding) feast, indirectly. 1768 **resoun,** it was logical. 1769 **men,** impersonal "people." 1772 **highte,** named. 1773 **carf,** carved, i.e., was the old knight's personal retainer. 1775 **wood,** crazy. 1776 **swelte,** fainted. 1777 **Venus . . . brond,** see l. 1727n. 1780 EHg&c *as* om.; E *I* om. 1782 **rewen,** have pity. 1783 **bredeth,** begins (breeds). 1784 **bedeth,** proffers. 1785 **hoomly hewe,** domestic servant. 1786 **naddre . . . sly untrewe,** snake, secretly false. In *Gesta Romanorum,* Tale 174, and frequently elsewhere, is found the story of the man who put a frozen serpent in his bosom to warm it only to have it bite him just as soon as it thawed out. 1788 **plesaunce,** pleasure. 1790 **boren,** i.e., your servant since he was born. E *born.* 1792 **hoomly fo,** domestic (familiar) enemy. 1795 **Parfourned . . . diurne,** performed, daily. 1797 **On th'orisonte,** above the horizon. 1800 **route,** company. 1806 Hg&c *Wol/wol.* 1807 **ypocras, clarree, vernage,** wine drinks mixed with spices to make them aphrodisiac. 1808 **corage,** see l. 1725n. 1809 **letuarie,** medicine (electuary). 1810 **Constantyn,** Constantinus Africanus, mentioned in *CT* I.433 above, author of a treatise on diet and potions to enhance virility. E *cursed* om. 1812 **nas . . . eschu,** was not averse. 1815 **voyden,** empty. 1817 **travers,** curtain across the hall, making a private bedchamber; see *TC* III.659–76 and notes.

Out of the chambre hath every wight hym
    dressed. 1820
And Januarie hath faste in armes take
His fresshe May, his paradys, his make.
He lulleth hire, he kisseth hire ful ofte.
With thikke brustles of his berd unsofte—
Lyk to the skyn of houndfyssh, sharp as brere,
For he was shave al newe in his manere— 1826
He rubbeth hire aboute hir tendre face,
And seyde thus, "Allas, I moot trespace
To yow, my spouse, and yow greetly offende
Er tyme come that I wil doun descende. 1830
But nathelees, considereth this," quod he,
"Ther nys no werkman, whatsoevere he be,
That may bothe werke wel and hastily.
This wol be doon at leyser parfitly.
It is no fors how longe that we pleye; 1835
In trewe wedlok coupled be we tweye,
And blessed be the yok that we been inne,
For in oure actes we mowe do no synne.
A man may do no synne with his wyf,
Ne hurte hymselven with his owene knyf, 1840
For we han leve to pleye us by the lawe."
Thus laboureth he til that the day gan dawe,
And thanne he taketh a soppe in fyn clarree,
And upright in his bed thanne sitteth he,
And after that he sang ful loude and cleere, 1845
And kiste his wyf, and made wantown cheere.
He was al coltissh, ful of ragerye,
And ful of jargon as a flekked pye.
The slakke skyn aboute his nekke shaketh 1849
Whil that he sang, so chaunteth he and
    craketh.
But God woot what that May thoughte in hir
    herte
Whan she hym saugh up sittynge in his sherte,
In his nyght-cappe, and with his nekke lene.
She preyseth nat his pleyyng worth a bene.
Thanne seide he thus, "My reste wol I take.
Now day is come I may no lenger wake." 1856

And doun he leyde his heed and sleep til
    pryme.
And afterward whan that he saugh his tyme
Up ryseth Januarie. But fresshe May
Heeld hire chambre unto the fourthe day, 1860
As usage is of wyves for the beste,
For every labour somtyme moot han reste
Or elles longe may he nat endure,
This is to seyn, no lyves creature
Bc it of fyssh or bryd or beest or man. 1865
    Now wol I speke of woful Damyan,
That langwissheth for love, as ye shul heere.
Therfore I speke to hym in this manere,
I seye, "O sely Damyan, allas,
Andswere to my demaunde, as in this cas. 1870
How shaltow to thy lady, fresshe May,
Telle thy wo? She wole alwey seye nay.
Eek if thou speke, she wol thy wo biwreye.
God be thyn help! I kan no bettre seye."
    This sike Damyan in Venus fyr 1875
So brenneth that he dyeth for desyr,
For which he putte his lyf in aventure.
No lenger myghte he in this wise endure,
But prively a penner gan he borwe,
And in a lettre wroot he al his sorwe, 1880
In manere of a compleynt or a lay,
Unto his faire, fresshe lady May;
And in a purs of sylk heng on his sherte
He hath it put, and leyde it at his herte.
    The moone, that at noon was thilke day 1885
That Januarie hath wedded fresshe May
In two of Tawr, was into Cancre glyden.
So longe hath Mayus in hir chambre byden
As custume is unto thise nobles alle.
A bryde shal nat eten in the halle 1890
Til dayes foure, or thre dayes atte leeste,
Ypassed been; thanne lat hire go to feeste.
The fourthe day compleet fro noon to noon,
Whan that the heighe masse was ydoon,
In halle sit this Januarie and May 1895

1824 *thikke:* EHg&c *thilke.* **1825 houndfyssh,** spiny dogfish. **1826 shave . . . manere,** a shaven face was unusual in Chaucer's day. **1828 trespace,** do injury. **1829 offende,** displease, but also physically hurt. **1830 descende,** get down off of. **1835 fors,** matter. **1836** *coupled:* E *wedded.* **1839 synne . . . wyf,** the ParsT x.859 gives the traditional medieval religious point of view, which is somewhat different. **1843 soppe . . . clarree,** bread soaked in wine. **1846 cheere,** behavior. **1847 ragerye,** i.e., "cutting up." **1848 jargon . . . pye,** chattering, magpie. **1850 craketh,** croaks. **1857 pryme,** 9 A.M. **1869 sely,** foolish. **1870 demaunde,** question. **1873 biwreye,** betray. **1878** *wise:* some MSS *wo/worlde.* **1879 penner,** a case containing pen and ink. **1881 compleynt . . . lay,** lyric forms; cf. Chaucer's short poems. **1883 heng,** which hung. **1887 two of Tawr,** the second degree of Taurus.

As fressh as is the brighte someres day.
And so bifel how that this goode man
Remembred hym upon this Damyan,
And seyde, "Seynte Marie, how may this be
That Damyan entendeth nat to me? 1900
Is he ay syk, or how may this bityde?"
His squieres whiche that stooden ther bisyde
Excused hym by cause of his siknesse,
Which letted hym to doon his bisynesse; 1904
Noon oother cause myghte make hym tarye.
  "That me forthynketh," quod this Januarie.
"He is a gentil squier, by my trouthe. *qualities of a lover*
If that he deyde, it were harm and routhe.
He is as wys, discreet, and as secree
As any man I woot of his degree, 1910
And therto manly and eek servysable,
And for to been a thrifty man right able.
But after mete as soone as evere I may,
I wol myself visite hym, and eek May,
To doon hym al the confort that I kan." 1915
And for that word hym blessed every man
That of his bountee and his gentillesse
He wolde so conforten in siknesse
His squier, for it was a gentil dede. 1919
"Dame," quod this Januarie, "taak good hede,
At after-mete ye with youre wommen alle,
Whan ye han been in chambre out of this halle,
That alle ye go se this Damyan.
Dooth hym disport—he is a gentil man;
And telleth hym that I wol hym visite, 1925
Have I no thyng but rested me a lite.
And spede yow faste, for I wole abyde
Til that ye slepe faste by my syde."
And with that worde he gan to hym to calle
A squier that was marchal of his halle 1930
And tolde hym certeyn thynges what he wolde.
  This fresshe May hath streight hir wey yholde
With alle hir wommen unto Damyan.

Doun by his beddes syde sit she than,
Confortynge hym as goodly as she may. 1935
This Damyan, whan that his tyme he say,
In secree wise his purs and eek his bille,
In which that he ywriten hadde his wille,
Hath put into hire hand withouten moore,
Save that he siketh wonder depe and soore, 1940
And softely to hire right thus seyde he,
"Mercy, and that ye nat discovere me,
For I am deed if that this thyng be kyd."
This purs hath she in with hir bosom hyd
And wente hire wey—ye gete namoore of me.
But unto Januarie ycomen is she 1946
That on his beddes syde sit ful softe.
He taketh hire and kisseth hire ful ofte,
And leyde hym doun to slepe, and that anon.
She feyned hire as that she moste gon 1950
Ther as ye woot that every wight moot neede,
And whan she of this bille hath taken heede,
She rente it al to cloutes atte laste,
And in the pryvee softely it caste.
  Who studieth now but faire fresshe May?
Adoun by olde Januarie she lay, 1956
That sleep til that the coughe hath hym awaked. *un-couth lover*
Anon he preyde hire strepen hire al naked;
He wolde of hire, he seyde, han som plesaunce,
He seyde hir clothes dide hym encombraunce,
And she obeyeth, be hire lief or looth. 1961
But lest that precious folk be with me wrooth,
How that he wroghte I dar nat to yow telle,
Or wheither hire thoughte it paradys or helle.
But heere I lete hem werken in hir wyse 1965
Til evensong rong and that they moste aryse.
  Were it by destynee or by aventure,
Were it by influence or by nature,
Or constellacioun, that in swich estaat
The hevene stood, that tyme fortunaat 1970
Was for to putte a bille of Venus werkes—

1904 letted, prevented. **1906 forthynketh,** makes me worry. **1908 routhe,** pity. **1909 secree,** confidential. **1911 manly,** like "secree," "manly" and "servysable" lay on the irony with a pretty heavy hand. **1912 thrifty,** effective. **1921** E *after-noon.* **1923** *se* : Hg&c *To.* **1924 disport . . . gentil,** amusement; the play on the term "gentilesse" in the other tales of the Marriage Group gives special irony to its appearance in this tale. **1927 abyde,** wait. **1935 goodly,** pleasantly. **1936 say,** saw. **1937 bille,** document. **1938 wille,** desire, but perhaps with *double entendre,* cf. l. 1943. **1940 siketh,** sighs. **1942 discovere,** reveal. **1943 kyd,** known. **1949 anon,** soon. **1950 feyned,** pretended. **1951 woot . . . moot,** know, must. **1953 cloutes,** bits. **1954 softely,** quietly. **1955 studieth,** thinks, ponders. **1961 lief,** willing. **1962 precious,** prim. E *lest ye.* **1966 evensong,** the evening religious service (vespers). **1968 influence,** divine intervention. **1971 putte a bille,** put forward a petition.

For alle thyng hath tyme, as seyn thise
    clerkes—
To any womman for to gete hire love,
I kan nat seye, but grete God above
That knoweth that noon act is causelees,   1975
He deme of al, for I wole holde my pees.
But sooth is this, how that this fresshe May
Hath take swich impressioun that day
For pitee of this sike Damyan
That from hire herte she ne dryve kan   1980
The remembrance for to doon hym ese.
"Certeyn," thoghte she, "whom that this thyng
    displese,
I rekke noght, for heere I hym assure
To love hym best of any creature,   1984
Though he namoore hadde than his sherte."
Lo, pitee renneth soone in gentil herte!
    Heere may ye se how excellent franchise
In wommen is whan they hem narwe avyse.
Som tyrant is, as ther be many oon,
That hath an herte as hard as any stoon,   1990
Which wolde han let hym sterven in the place
Wel rather than han graunted hym hire grace,
And hem rejoysen in hire crueel pryde,
And rekke nat to been an homycide.
    This gentil May, fulfilled of pitee,   1995
Right of hire hand a lettre made she
In which she graunteth hym hire verray grace.
Ther lakketh noght oonly but day and place
Wher that she myghte unto his lust suffise,
For it shal be right as he wole devyse.   2000
And whan she saugh hir tyme upon a day,
To visite this Damyan gooth May,
And sotilly this lettre doun she threste
Under his pilwe: rede it if hym leste.
She taketh hym by the hand and harde hym
    twiste   2005
So secrely that no wight of it wiste,

And bad hym been al hool, and forth she wente
To Januarie whan that he for hire sente.
    Up riseth Damyan the nexte morwe.
Al passed was his siknesse and his sorwe.   2010
He kembeth hym, he preyneth hym and
    pyketh,
He dooth al that his lady lust and lyketh,
And eek to Januarie he gooth as lowe
As evere dide a dogge for the bowe.
He is so plesant unto every man—   2015
For craft is al, whoso that do it kan—
That every wight is fayn to speke hym good,
And fully in his lady grace he stood.
Thus lete I Damyan aboute his nede,
And in my tale forth I wol procede.   2020
    Somme clerkes holden that felicitee
Stant in delit, and therfore certeyn he,
This noble Januarie, with al his myght
In honest wyse as longeth to a kynght,
Shoop hym to lyve ful deliciously.   2025
His housynge, his array, as honestly
To his degree was maked as a kynges.
Amonges othere of his honeste thynges,
He made a gardyn walled al with stoon.
So fair a gardyn woot I nowher noon,   2030
For out of doute I verraily suppose
That he that wroot the *Romance of the Rose*
Ne koude of it the beautee wel devyse,
Ne Priapus ne myghte nat suffise,
Though he be god of gardyns, for to telle   2035
The beautee of the gardyn and the welle
That stood under a laurer alwey grene.
Ful ofte tyme he Pluto and his queene
Proserpina and al hire fairye
Disporten hem and maken melodye   2040
Aboute that welle, and daunced, as men
    tolde.
    This noble knyght, this Januarie the olde,

1976 deme, let him judge. **1979** *For:* Hg&c *Of.* **1981 doon hym ese,** make him comfortable. **1983 rekke . . . assure,** care, promise.
1986 Lo, pitee, the frequently repeated chivalric sentiment, here in an ironic context; cf. *CT* i.1761n. **1987 franchise,** generosity.
1988 narwe avyse, consider carefully. **1991 sterven,** die. **1998** Other MSS *noght elles but* or *but oonly.* **2000 wole devyse,** as he will
wish. **2004 leste,** wished. **2007–08** *she/hire:* E *he/hym.* **2009 morwe,** morning. **2011 kembeth, preyneth, pyketh,** combs, preens, cleans.
2013 lowe, ears and belly low (docile, obedient). **2014 bowe,** trained for hunting with a bow. **2016 craft,** skill, *double entendre* trickery.
2017 wight . . . fayn, person, eager. **2021–22 felicitee . . . delit,** supreme happiness, temporal pleasure—the Epicurean philosophy.
2024 honest, honorable; the word in its repetition takes on a tinge of irony. **2025 shoop,** shaped, arranged. **2032** *Romance of the*
Rose, the Chaucerian text describing the garden in *RR* is included in this edition. **2033 devyse,** describe. **2036 welle,** spring.

Swich deyntee hath in it to walke and pleye
That he wol no wight suffren bere the keye
Save he hymself; for of the smale wyket   2045
He baar alwey of silver a clyket
With which, whan that hym leste, he it
  unshette.
And whan he wolde paye his wyf hir dette
In somer seson, thider wolde he go,   2049
And May his wyf, and no wight but they two,
And thynges whiche that were nat doon
  abedde,
He in the gardyn parfourned hem and spedde.
And in this wyse many a murye day
Lyved this Januarie and fresshe May.
But worldly joye may nat alwey dure   2055
To Januarie, ne to no creature.
  O sodeyn hap, O thou Fortune unstable,
Lyk to the scorpion so deceyvable,
That flaterest with thyn heed whan thou wolt
  stynge!
Thy tayl is deeth, thurgh thyn envenymynge.
O brotil joye, O sweete venym queynte,   2061
O monstre that so subtilly kanst peynte
Thy yiftes under hewe of stidefastnesse,
That thou deceyvest bothe moore and lesse,
Why hastow Januarie thus deceyved,   2065
That haddest hym for thy fulle freend
  receyved?
And now thou hast biraft hym bothe his eyen
For sorwe of which desireth he to dyen.
  Allas, this noble Januarie free
Amydde his lust and his prosperitee   2070
Is woxen blynd, and that al sodeynly.
He wepeth and he wayleth pitously;
And therwithal the fyr of jalousie
Lest that his wyf sholde falle in som folye
So brente his herte that he wolde fayn   2075

That som man bothe hym and hire had
  slayn.
For neither after his deeth nor in his lyf
Ne wolde he that she were love ne wyf,
But evere lyve as wydwe in clothes blake
Soul as the turtle that lost hath hire make.   2080
But atte laste, after a month or tweye,
His sorwe gan aswage, sooth to seye.
For whan he wiste it may noon oother be,
He paciently took his adversitee
Save, out of doute, he may nat forgoon   2085
That he nas jalous everemoore in oon.
Which jalousye it was so outrageous
That neither in halle n'yn noon oother hous,
N'yn noon oother place neverthemo,
He nolde suffre hire for to ryde or go   2090
But if that he had hond on hire alway;
For which ful ofte wepeth fresshe May
That loveth Damyan so benyngnely
That she moot outher dyen sodeynly
Or elles she moot han hym as hir leste.   2095
She wayteth whan hir herte wolde breste.
  Upon that oother syde Damyan
Bicomen is the sorwefulleste man
That evere was, for neither nyght ne day
Ne myghte he speke a word to fresshe May,   2100
As to his purpos of no swich mateere,   2101
But if that Januarie moste it heere,
That hadde an hand upon hire everemo.
But nathelees, by writyng to and fro
And privee signes wiste he what she mente,
And she knew eek the fyn of his entente.   2106
  O Januarie, what myghte it thee availle,
Thogh thou myghtest se as fer as shippes
  saille?
For as good is blynd deceyved be
As to be deceyved whan a man may se.   2110

2043 Swich deyntee hath, some scholars have suggested that the "garden of delight" in which January so enjoyed to desport himself, and to which he would let no one but himself carry the key, until Damyan got hold of a duplicate and enjoyed himself there likewise— that all of this has elaborate sexual and indeed religious overtones reminiscent of the Garden of Eden, the Garden of Gethsemane, and the womb of the Virgin Mary which was sometimes referred to as the "hortus inclusus." Undoubtedly it does heighten the effect of some lines and images to keep the possibility of such *double entendre* in mind. **2045 wyket,** gate. **2046 clyket,** key. **2048 dette,** cf. l. 1452n. **2057 sodeyn hap,** sudden happening. E *instable*. **2059** *stynge:* E *synge*. **2061 brotil,** brittle, short-lived. **queynte,** strange, but *double entendre* genitalia. **2062 peynte,** color. **2063 yiftes,** gifts, i.e., misfortune. **2064 That . . . moore and lesse,** so that, great and small. **2067 biraft,** deprived of. **2070 lust,** joy. **2075 brente . . . fayn,** burned, been happy. **2076** Hg&c *hire and hym.* **2080 Soul . . . turtle . . . make,** sole (solitary), turtledove, mate. **2085 forgoon,** cease. **2090 go,** walk. **2093 benyngnely,** graciously. **2094 outher,** either. **2095 leste,** desired. **2096 She wayteth,** i.e., she is forced to stand and wait while her heart bursts with desire. **2106 fyn,** end (purpose).

Lo Argus, which that hadde an hondred eyen,
For al that evere he koude poure or pryen,
Yet was he blent, and God woot so been mo
That wenen wisly that it be nat so.
Passe over is an ese, I sey namoore.   2115

This fresshe May that I spak of so yoore,
In warm wex hath emprented the clyket
That Januarie bar of the smale wyket,
By which into his gardyn ofte he wente;
And Damyan, that knew al hire entente,   2120
The cliket countrefeted pryvely.
Ther nys namoore to seye, but hastily
Som wonder by this clyket shal bityde,
Which ye shul heeren, if ye wole abyde.   2124

O noble Ovyde, ful sooth seystou, God woot,
What sleighte is it, thogh it be long and hoot,
That he nyl fynde it out in som manere?
By Piramus and Tesbee may men leere,
Thogh they were kept ful longe streite overal,
They been accorded rownynge thurgh a
        wal,   2130
Ther no wight koude han founde out swich a
        sleighte.

But now to purpos: er that dayes eighte
Were passed, er the month of Juyl, bifille
That Januarie hath caught so greet a wille,   2134
Thurgh eggyng of his wyf, hym for to pleye
In his gardyn, and no wight but they tweye,
That in a morwe unto his May seith he,
"Rys up, my wyf, my love, my lady free;
The turtles voys is herd, my dowve sweete;
The wynter is goon with alle his reynes
        weete.   2140
Com forth now, with thyne eyen columbyn.
How fairer been thy brestes than is wyn!
The gardyn is enclosed al aboute;
Com forth, my white spouse! Out of doute

Thou hast me wounded in myn herte, O wyf.
No spot of thee ne knew I al my lyf.   2146
Com forth and lat us taken oure disport;
I chees thee for my wyf and my confort."
    Swiche olde lewed wordes used he.
On Damyan a signe made she   2150
That he sholde go biforn with his cliket.
This Damyan thanne hath opened the wyket
And in he stirte, and that in swich manere
That no wight myghte it se neither yheere,
And stille he sit under a bussh anon.   2155

    This Januarie, as blynd as is a stoon,
With Mayus in his hand, and no wight mo,
Into his fresshe gardyn is ago,
And clapte to the wyket sodeynly.
    "Now wyf," quod he, "heere nys but thou
        and I,   2160
That art the creature that I best love.
For by that Lord that sit in hevene above
Levere ich hadde to dyen on a kynf
Than thee offende, trewe deere wyf.
For Goddes sake, thenk how I thee chees,   2165
Noght for no coveitise, doutelees,
But oonly for the love I had to thee.
And though that I be oold and may nat see,
Beth to me trewe, and I wol telle yow why:
Thre thynges, certes, shal ye wynne therby.   2170
First, love of Crist, and to yourself honour,
And al myn heritage, toun and tour—
I yeve it yow, maketh chartres as yow leste;
This shal be doon tomorwe er sonne reste,
So wisly God my soule brynge in blisse.   2175
I prey yow first, in covenant ye me kisse,
And though that I be jalous, wyte me noght.
Ye been so depe enprented in my thoght
That whan that I considere youre beautee
And therwithal the unlikly elde of me,   2180

2111 Argus, Argos of the hundred eyes, set by Hera to watch over Io, was killed by Hermes (Ovid, *Met.* 1.722). **2112 poure,** pore, look intently. **2113 blent,** blinded, deceived. **2114 wenen,** think. **2115 Passe . . . ese,** perhaps "things may easily be passed over (overlooked)." **2117 clyket,** key. **2120** *hire:* Hg&c *his.* **2123 bityde,** happen. **2125 Ovyde,** in Pyramus and Thisbe, *Met.* 4.55, "Quid non sentit amor?" **2126 sleighte,** (deceitful) procedure. **2127** *he:* some MSS *Love.* **2129 streite,** strictly (protected). **2130 accorded rownynge,** came to an agreement whispering. **2131 Ther . . . wight . . . sleighte,** where, person, method (deceit). **2133 Juyl,** an error in the exemplar, found in all MSS; cf. 1. 2222. Some editors emend *of the month of Juyn.* **2138 Rys up,** January's speech is full of echoes of the Song of Solomon, which are found also in *Jerome adversus Jovinianum.* **2139 turtles . . . dowve,** turtledove, dove. **2141 columbyn,** dovelike. **2146 spot,** blemish. **2147** *oure:* E *som.* **2149 lewed,** multiple meanings in this context, secular, lascivious, and ignorant, all in contrast to the scriptural origin of January's words. **2151 cliket,** key. **2152 wyket,** gate. **2163 Levere,** rather. **2165 chees,** chose. **2166 coveitise,** covetousness. **2169** *wol:* E *shal.* **2173 chartres . . . leste,** legal documents, wish. **2176 covenant,** agreement. **2177 wyte,** blame. **2179 E&c** *That* om. **2180 unlikly elde,** unsuitable age.

I may nat, certes, though I sholde dye,
Forbere to been out of youre compaignye
For verray love. This is withouten doute.
Now kys me, wyf, and lat us rome aboute."
    This fresshe May, whan she thise wordes
      herde, 2185
Benyngnely to Januarie answerde,
But first and forward she bigan to wepe.
"I have," quod she, "a soule for to kepe
As wel as ye, and also myn honour,
And of my wyfhod thilke tendre flour 2190
Which that I have assured in youre hond,
Whan that the preest to yow my body bond.
Wherefore I wole answere in this manere,
By the leve of yow, my lord so deere:
I prey to God that nevere dawe the day 2195
That I ne sterve, as foule as womman may,
If evere I do unto my kyn that shame,
Or elles I empeyre so my name,
That I be fals; and if I do that lakke,
Do strepe me and put me in a sakke, 2200
And in the nexte ryver do me drenche.
I am a gentil womman and no wenche.
Why speke ye thus? But men been evere
    untrewe,
And wommen have repreve of yow ay newe.
Ye han noon oother contenance, I leeve, 2205
But speke to us of untrust and repreeve."
    And with that word she saugh wher Damyan
Sat in the bussh, and coughen she bigan,
And with hir fynger signes made she
That Damyan sholde clymbe upon a tree 2210
That charged was with fruyt, and up he wente.
For verraily he knew al hire entente,
And every signe that she koude make,
Wel bet than Januarie, hir owene make,
For in a lettre she hadde toold hym al 2215

Of this matere, how he werchen shal.
And thus I lete hym sitte upon the pyrie,
And Januarie and May romynge ful myrie.
    Bright was the day and blew the firmament.
Phebus hath of gold his stremes doun ysent
To gladen every flour with his warmnesse. 2221
He was that tyme in Geminis, as I gesse,
But litel fro his declynacion
Of Cancer, Jovis exaltacion.
And so bifel that brighte morwe-tyde 2225
That in that gardyn in the ferther syde
Pluto, that is kyng of Fairye,
And many a lady in his compaignye,
Folwynge his wyf the queene Proserpyne,
Which that he ravysshed out of Ethna 2230
Whil that she gadered floures in the mede—
In Claudyan ye may the stories rede,
How in his grisely carte he hire fette—
This kyng of Fairye thanne adoun hym sette
Upon a bench of turves, fressh and grene, 2235
And right anon thus seyde he to his queene,
    "My wyf," quod he, "ther may no wight
      seye nay,
Th'experience so preveth every day
The tresons whiche that wommen doon to man.
Ten hondred thousand stories tellen I kan 2240
Notable of youre untrouthe and brotilnesse.
O Salomon, wys and richest of richesse,
Fulfild of sapience and of worldly glorie,
Ful worthy been thy wordes to memorie
To every wight that wit and reson kan. 2245
Thus preiseth he yet the bountee of man:
'Amonges a thousand men yet foond I oon,
But of wommen alle foond I noon.'
    "Thus seith the kyng that knoweth youre
      wikkednesse.
And Jhesus filius Syrak, as I gesse, 2250

2186 Benyngnely, graciously. **2191 assured,** entrusted. **2195 dawe,** dawn. **2196 sterve . . . foule,** die, shamefully. **2198 empeyre,** injure (impair). **2199 lakke,** lack (misdeed). **2201 drenche,** drown. **2204 repreve,** reproof. **2205 contenance . . . leeve,** manner, believe. **2217 pyrie,** pear tree. **2218** EHg *ful* om; some MS emend by writing *Mayus.* **2219 blew,** blue. **2222 Geminis,** sign of Gemini, May 11–June 11. **2223 litel fro . . . declynacion,** shortly before entering Cancer on June 12. Skeat argues on various grounds that it was June 8. **2224 Jovis exaltacion,** Cancer, the sign of the zodiac over which Jupiter exerted most influence. **2225 morwe,** morning. **2230** Line evidently lacking in Chaucer's exemplar. Hg leaves a blank. E&c supply *Ech after other right as a (any) lyne.* Other MSS have *Which that he ravysshed out of Proserpyna* (sic) or other places of ravishment. Only MSS Harl. 7335 and Paris have *Ethna,* which is no doubt scribal, from Claudian (see l. 2232 below). **2232 Claudyan,** *De Raptu Proserpinae* (4th century A.D.). **2233** *How:* E *And; fette:* EHg&c *sette.* **2240** EHg&c *stories* om.; other MSS *samples tales.* This refers to the antifeminist materials also used in connection with WBP. **2241 brotilnesse,** brittleness, untrustworthiness. **2245 kan,** knows. **2247 a thousand,** Eccles. 7:28. **2250 filius Syrak,** supposed author of the Apocryphal Book of Ecclesiasticus.

Ne speketh of yow but seelde reverence.
A wylde fyr and corrupt pestilence
So falle upon youre bodyes yet tonyght!
Ne se ye nat this honurable knyght,
By cause, allas, that he is blynd and old,   2255
His owene man shal make hym cokewold.
Lo, where he sit, the lechour in the tree!
Now wol I graunten, of my magestee,
Unto this olde, blynde, worthy knyght
That he shal have ayeyn his eyen syght   2260
Whan that his wyf wold doon hym vileynye.
Thanne shal he knowen al hire harlotrye,
Bothe in repreve of hire and othere mo.”

"Ye shal?" quod Proserpyne, "Wol ye so?
Now by my moodres sires soule I swere   2265
That I shal yeven hire suffisant answere,
And alle wommen after, for hir sake,
That though they be in any gilt ytake   2268
With face boold they shulle hemself excuse,
And bere hem doun that wolden hem accuse.
For lakke of answere noon of hem shal dyen.
Al hadde man seyn a thyng with bothe his eyen,
Yit shul we wommen visage it hardily,
And wepe, and swere, and visage it subtilly,
So that ye men shul been as lewed as gees.   2275
What rekketh me of youre auctoritees?

"I woot wel that this Jew, this Salomon,
Foond of us wommen fooles many oon.
But though that he ne foond no good womman,
Yet hath ther founde many another man   2280
Wommen ful trewe, ful goode, and vertuous.
Witnesse on hem that dwelle in Cristes hous;
With martirdom they preved hire constance.
The Romayn geestes eek maken remembrance
Of many a verray, trewe wyf also.   2285
But sire, ne be nat wrooth, al be it so
Though that he seyde he foond no good
      womman;

I prey yow take the sentence of the man;
He mente thus, that in sovereyn bontee
Nis noon but God that sit in Trinitee.   2290
Ey, for verray God that nys but oon.

"What make ye so muche of Salomon?
What though he made a temple, Goddes hous?
What though he were riche and glorious?
So made he eek a temple of false goddis;   2295
How myghte he do a thyng that moore
      forbode is?
Pardee, as faire as ye his name emplastre,
He was a lecchour and an ydolastre,
And in his elde he verray God forsook;
And if that God ne hadde, as seith the book,   2300
Yspared hym for his fadres sake, he sholde
Have lost his regne rather than he wolde.
I sette right noght of al the vileynye
That ye of wommen write a boterflye.
I am a womman, nedes moot I speke   2305
Or elles swelle til myn herte breke.
For sithen he seyde that we been jangleresses,
As evere hool I moote brouke my tresses,
I shal nat spare for no curteisye   2309
To speke hym harm that wolde us vileynye.”

"Dame," quod this Pluto, "be no lenger
      wrooth.
I yeve it up! But sith I swoor myn ooth
That I wolde graunten hym his sighte ageyn,
My word shal stonde, I warne yow certeyn.
I am a kyng; it sit me noght to lye.”   2315

"And I," quod she, "a queene of Fairye.
Hir answere shal she have, I undertake.
Lat us namoore wordes heerof make.
For sothe, I wol no lenger yow contrarie.”

Now lat us turne agayn to Januarie   2320
That in the gardyn with his faire May
Syngeth ful murier than the papejay,
"Yow love I best, and shal, and oother noon.”

2251 seelde reverence, seldom honor. **2252 wylde fyr,** itching skin disease (erysipelas). **2257 lechour,** lecher, but perhaps *double entendre* with "leech," heal. St. Damian was the patron saint of physicians and the episode did restore to January his sight! *where:* E *heere.* **2263 repreve . . . othere mo,** reproof, other women. **2265 moodres sires,** grandfather's, i.e., Saturn, oldest and wisest of the gods. **2273 visage it hardily,** face it out boldly. **2274 subtilly,** secretly. *visage it:* Hg&c *chyde.* **2275 lewed,** silly (ignorant). **2276 rekketh me,** do I care. **2277 woot,** know. **2283 constance,** constancy. **2284 Romayn geestes,** Roman history. **2288 sentence,** higher meaning. **2289 sovereyn bontee,** supreme goodness. **2290** Hg&c *but God,* but neither he ne she. **2295 of,** to, I Kings (Vulgate III Kings) 11:7. **2296 forbode,** forbidden. **2297 emplastre,** plaster over, whitewash. **2300** EHg&c *that* om. **2301** E *hym* om. **2302 rather . . . wolde,** sooner, wanted. **2303–04 sette . . . noght . . . boterflye,** don't care a butterfly. **2307 sithen . . . jangleresses,** since, chatterboxes. **2308 hool I moote brouke,** I may keep whole (undamaged). **2315 sit,** befits. **2319 contrarie,** contradict.

So long aboute the aleyes is he goon
Til he was come agayns thilke pyrie 2325
Where as this Damyan sitteth ful myrie
An heigh among the fresshe leves grene.
    This fresshe May, that is so bright and
        sheene,
Gan for to syke and seyde, "Allas, my syde!
Now sire," quod she, "for aught that may
        bityde, 2330
I moste han of the peres that I see,
Or I moot dye, so soore longeth me
To eten of the smale peres grene.
Help, for hir love that is of hevene queene.
I telle yow wel, a womman in my plit 2335
May han to fruyt so greet an appetit
That she may dyen but she of it have."
    "Allas," quod he, "that I ne had heer a knave
That koude clymbe! Allas, allas," quod he,
"That I am blynd!" "Ye sire, no fors," quod
        she, 2340
"But wolde ye vouchesauf, for Goddes sake,
The pyrie inwith youre armes for to take—
For wel I woot that ye mystruste me—
Thanne sholde I clymbe wel ynogh," quod she,
"So I my foot myghte sette upon youre
        bak." 2345
    "Certes," quod he, "theron shal be no lak,
Mighte I yow helpen with myn herte blood."
He stoupeth doun, and on his bak she stood,
And caughte hire by a twiste, and up she
        gooth—
Ladyes, I prey yow that ye be nat wrooth,
I kan nat glose, I am a rude man— 2351
And sodeynly anon this Damyan
Gan pullen up the smok and in he throng.
    And whan that Pluto saugh this grete wrong,
To Januarie he gaf agayn his sighte, 2355
And made hym se as wel as evere he myghte.
And whan that he hadde caught his sighte
        agayn
Ne was ther nevere man of thyng so fayn
But on his wyf his thoght was everemo.

Up to the tree he caste his eyen two 2360
And saugh that Damyan his wyf had dressed
In swich manere it may nat been expressed,
But if I wolde speke uncurteisly;
And up he yaf a roryng and a cry, 2364
As dooth the mooder whan the child shal dye.
"Out! Help! Allas! Harrow!" he gan to crye,
"O stronge lady stoore, what dostow?"
    And she answerde, "Sire, what eyleth yow?
Have pacience and resoun in youre mynde.
I have yow holpe on bothe youre eyen blynde.
Up peril of my soule, I shal nat lyen, 2371
As me was taught, to heele with youre eyen,
Was no thyng bet, to make yow to see,
Than strugle with a man upon a tree.
God woot, I dide it in ful good entente." 2375
    "Strugle!" quod he, "Ye, algate in it wente!
God yeve yow bothe on shames deth to dyen!
He swyved thee; I saugh it with myne eyen;
And elles be I hanged by the hals."
    "Thanne is," quod she, "my medicyne fals.
For certeinly if that ye myghte se, 2381
Ye wolde nat seyn thise wordes unto me.
Ye han som glymsyng and no parfit sighte."
    "I se," quod he, "as wel as evere I myghte,
Thonked be God, with bothe myne eyen two,
And by my trouthe, me thoughte he dide thee
        so." 2386
    "Ye maze, maze, goode sire," quod she.
"This thank have I for I have maad yow see.
Allas," quod she, "that evere I was so kynde!"
    "Now, dame," quod he, "lat al passe out of
        mynde. 2390
Com doun, my lief, and if I have myssayd,
God helpe me so as I am yvele apayd.
But by my fader soule, I wende han seyn 2393
How that this Damyan hadde by thee leyn,
And that thy smok hadde leyn upon his brest."
    "Ye, sire," quod she, "ye may wene as yow
        lest.
But, sire, a man that waketh out of his sleep
He may nat sodeynly wel taken keep

2324 **aleyes,** garden paths (alleys). 2325 **pyrie,** pear tree. 2329 **syke,** sigh. 2340 *That:* Hg&c *For.* 2349 **twiste,** branch. 2351 **glose,** gloss (over). 2353 **throng,** thrust. 2358 **fayn,** happy, eager. 2361 **dressed,** addressed (treated). 2367 **stronge ... stoore,** strong (bold), great (impudent). 2373 **bet,** better, more effective. 2376 **algate,** completely, nevertheless. 2378 **swyved,** copulated with. 2379 **hals,** neck. 2380 Hg&c *al fals.* 2387 **maze,** are dazed. 2391 **lief,** love. 2392 **yvele apayd,** ill repaid, sorry. 2393 **wende han,** thought to have. 2396 **wene ... lest,** think, wish. 2398 **taken keep,** take heed.

Upon a thyng, ne seen it parfitly,
Til that he be adawed verraily.   2400
Right so a man that longe hath blynd ybe
Ne may nat sodeynly so wel yse
First whan his sighte is newe come ageyn
As he that hath a day or two yseyn.
Til that youre sighte ysatled be a while   2405
Ther may ful many a sighte yow bigile.
Beth war, I prey yow, for by hevene kyng,
Ful many a man weneth to seen a thyng,

And it is al another than it semeth.
He that mysconceyveth, he mysdemeth."   2410
And with that word she leep doun fro the tree.
    This Januarie, who is glad but he?
He kisseth hire and clippeth hire ful ofte,
And on hire wombe he stroketh hire ful softe,
And to his palays hoom he hath hire lad.   2415
Now, goode men, I pray yow to be glad.
Thus endeth heere my tale of Januarie.
God blesse us, and his mooder Seinte Marie.

Heere is ended the Marchants Tale of Januarie.

[EPILOGUE]

"Ey, Goddes mercy," seyde oure Hoost tho,
"Now swich a wyf I pray God kepe me fro!
Lo whiche sleightes and subtilitees   2421
In wommen been, for ay as bisy as bees
Been they us sely men for to deceyve,
And from a sooth evere wol they weyve
By this Marchauntes tale it preveth weel.   2425
But doutelees, as trewe as any steel
I have a wyf, though that she poure be,
But of hir tonge a labbyng shrewe is she,
And yet she hath an heep of vices mo—

Therof no fors. Lat alle swiche thynges go. 2430
But wyte ye what? In conseil be it seyd,
Me reweth soore I am unto hire teyd.
For and I sholde rekenen every vice
Which that she hath, ywis I were to nyce.
And cause why? It sholde reported be   2435
And toold to hire of somme of this meynee—
Of whom, it nedeth nat for to declare
Syn wommen konnen outen swich chaffare.
And eek my wit suffiseth nat therto
To tellen al, wherfore my tale is do."   2440

2400 **adawed,** awake. 2410 **mysconceyveth . . . mysdemeth,** misapprehends, misjudges. 2413 **clippeth,** hugs. 2416 E *to* om. 2419–40 These lines are found here only in E&c. With alterations to adapt them to their context, they are found in Hg&c between MerchT and FrankT. In some MSS they are reduced to two crude seven-line stanzas quite evidently not by Chaucer. See Manly III.480. 2424 **sooth . . . weyve,** truth, turn aside. 2430 **no fors,** no matter. 2431 **wyte ye . . . conseil,** do you know, confidence. 2432 **Me reweth,** it pains me. 2434 **nyce,** foolish. 2436 **meynee,** company. 2438 **konnen outen . . . chaffare,** know how to reveal such matters.

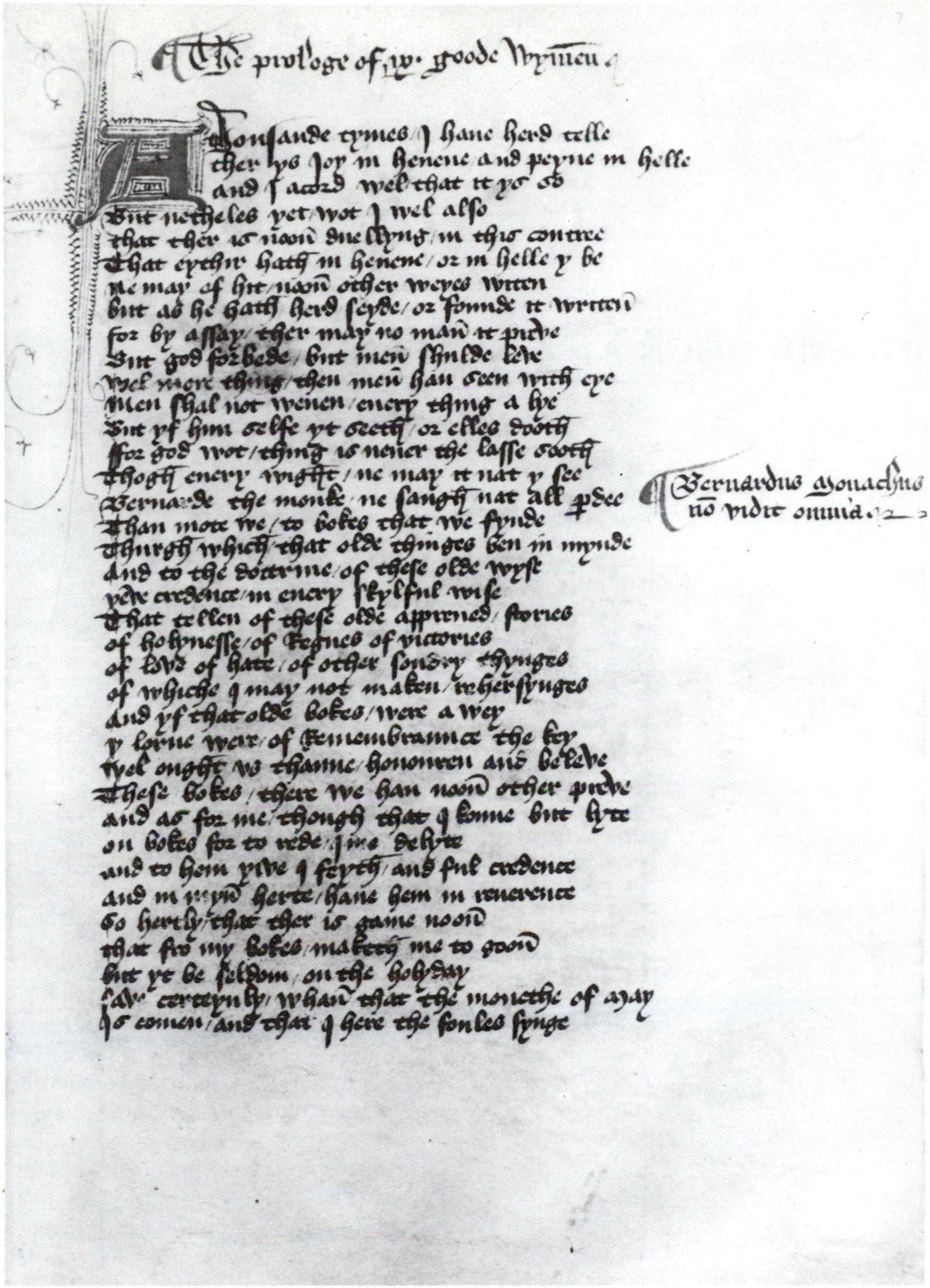

Plate 3. The opening of the *Legend of Good Women*, MS. Fairfax 16, fol. 83ʳ. Bodleian Library, Oxford

INTRODUCTION

Canterbury Tales, Part V

HE FIRST PUZZLE of this part is the nature and purpose of the incomplete Squire's Tale. It is an awkward agglomeration of materials from Oriental sources of the sort later made famous by the *Arabian Knights*. Crusaders came back with such stories, and there are suggestive parallels to various parts in Bryan and Dempster's *Sources and Analogues*. But the general consensus is that Chaucer was not following a source. Does this mean that the author of such narrative masterpieces as *Troylus* and the Miller's Tale could not invent an original plot? John Gardner in *The Poetry of Chaucer* (1977) goes so far as to hypothesize that Chaucer may here have been experimenting with "intentionally bad art." The faults in the Squire's Tale are elementary: too many motifs are introduced when the strange knight enters (in a scene so reminiscent of the entrance of the Green Knight in *Gawain and the Green Knight*); then, though more than enough had been introduced, Pars Secunda turns to a totally different topic—the lament of the falcon. At l. 401 the narrator acknowledges that the story is going badly. And the conclusion reads like notes a writer makes to himself about how he plans to continue.

Why did one as conscious of technique and

audience reaction as Chaucer include such a piece in the tales of Canterbury? Perhaps because its very deficiency was intended to make a dramatic contribution. In the epilogue, the Franklin praises the Squire and makes an unflattering comparison between his "gentil" performance and the behavior of his own good-for-nothing son. This evaluation exposes the Franklin's own lack of judgment. "Straw for your gentilesse!" says the Host, and then invites him to tell his tale. With this depreciation of the teller, we launch into the tale of Arvergus and Dorigen.

Earlier critics, and some still today, interpret the Franklin's Tale as the idealistic resolution of the marriage argument. But recent critics are not so sure. One of the delightful qualities of the *Canterbury Tales* is that we can never be sure who the joke is on. No source has been found for the plot. Although it claims to be a Breton lai, the closest analogues are in Boccaccio's *Filocolo* and *Decameron*. The local color suggests that the source was French. The opening section proposes that the solution of the maistrie-gentilesse tension is mutual consideration. The complication in the plot (symbolized by the rocks in the sea) indicates that the voyage of marriage is not always easy. There is always a serpent in the garden to test the integrity of the partners. Dorigen (Eve) slips when she makes her "rash promise." But in the end, all the estates display

their capacity for gentilesse. Money is again equated with sex, since Aurelius is going to have to pay the magician to achieve his desire; and money is absolved when the magician releases Aurelius from his bond. So it appears that the Franklin's Tale does provide a resolution to the marriage argument.

But does it? Is the simplistic "moralitee" of the story confirmed by the "experience" of the previous marriage tales? Is the ideal of chivalry being criticized when Arvergus goes off for two years "To seke in armes worshipe" (l.811), and is away when Aurelius makes his final onslaught (l.1460)? Is courtly love being satirized in Aurelius' illicit passion and two-year illness (l.1102)? Is Dorigen's weakness being criticized in her over-long complaint about the suicides of heroines she cannot emulate (ll.1355)? And how are we to take all of the impostures in the tale: that Arvergus still insisted on "the name of soveraynetee" (l.751); that it only "*semed* that alle the rokkes were aweye" (l.1296); that Arvergus told Dorigen to fulfill her promise, but added "I yow forbede, up peyne of deeth . . . To no wight telle thou of this aventure" (l.1483)? These are the kinds of questions that nag modern critics like Alfred David, "Sentimental Comedy in the Franklin's Tale," *Annuale Medievale* (1965), and Derek Traversi in *The Literary Imagination* (1982).

Canterbury Tales

PART V

SQUIRE'S TALE

PROLOGUE

"Squier, com neer, if it youre wille be,
And sey somwhat of love, for certes ye
Konnen theron as muche as any man."
  "Nay, sire," quod he, "but I wol seye as I kan

With hertly wyl, for I wol nat rebelle   5
Agayn your lust. A tale wol I telle;
Have me excused if I speke amys.
My wyl is good, and lo, my tale is this."

Heere bigynneth the Squieres Tale.

  At Sarray, in the land of Tartarye,
Ther dwelte a kyng that werreyed Russye,   10
Thurgh which ther dyde many a doughty man.
This noble kyng was cleped Cambyuskan,
Which in his tyme was of so greet renoun

That ther was nowher in no regioun
So excellent a lord in alle thyng.   15
Hym lakked noght that longeth to a kyng.
And of the secte of which that he was born
He kepte his lay, to which that he was sworn.

1–8 Lines found before SqT only in E&c. They go with iv.2419–40 in Hg&c, *Squier* being changed to *Marchaunt* or *Frankeleyn* in other MSS as the context requires; see Manly iv.3. **2** *somwhat of love:* Hg&c *us a tale.* **3 Konnen,** know. **6 lust,** pleasure: Hg&c *wille.* **9 Sarray,** Sarai on the Volga, capital city of the Kipchak Mongols of the Golden Horde who conquered Russia in the 13th century. **11 dyde,** died. The ferocity of the Mongol massacres was legendary. **12 Cambyuskan,** Genghis Khan (1162–1227; Lat. *Camius Khan*), founder of the Mongol empire. The actual conqueror of Russian and Eastern Europe was his grandson Batu Khan (1198–1255). **14** *was:* Hg&c *has.* **16 longeth,** belongs (is appropriate to). **17 secte,** religion, culture. *And:* Hg&c *As.* **18 his lay,** its law.

And therto he was hardy, wys, and riche,
And pitous and just, alwey yliche;   20
Sooth of his word, benigne, and honurable;
Of his corage as any centre stable;
Yong, fressh, strong, and in armes desirous
As any bacheler of al his hous.
A fair persone he was and fortunat,   25
And kepte alwey so wel roial estat
That there was nowher swich another man.
    This noble kyng, this Tartre Cambyuskan,
Hadde two sones on Elpheta his wyf,
Of whiche the eldeste highte Algarsyf,   30
That oother sone was cleped Cambalo.
A doghter hadde this worthy kyng also
That yongest was, and highte Canacee.
But for to telle yow al hir beautee,
It lyth nat in my tonge n'yn my konnyng.   35
I dar nat undertake so heigh a thyng;
Myn Englissh eek is insufficient.
It moste been a rethor excellent
That koude his colours longynge for that art
If he sholde hire discryven every part.   40
I am noon swich; I moot speke as I kan.
    And so bifel that whan this Cambyuskan
Hath twenty wynter born his diademe,
As he was wont fro yeer to yeer, I deme,
He leet the feeste of his nativitee   45
Doon cryen thurghout Sarray his citee,
The laste Idus of March, after the yeer.
Phebus the sonne ful joly was and cleer,
For he was neigh his exaltacioun
In Martes face, and in his mansioun   50
In Aries, the colerik hoote signe.

Ful lusty was the weder and benigne,
For which the foweles agayn the sonne sheene,
What for the sesoun and the yonge grene,
Ful loude songen hire affecciouns.   55
Hem semed han geten hem protecciouns
Agayn the swerd of wynter, keene and coold.
    This Cambyuskan, of which I have yow
        toold,
In roial vestiment sit on his deys,
With diademe, ful heighe in his paleys,   60
And halt his feeste so solempne and so ryche
That in this world ne was ther noon it lyche.
Of which if I shal tellen al th'array,
Thanne wolde it occupie a someres day,
And eek it nedeth nat for to devyse   65
At every cours the ordre of hire servyse.
I wol nat tellen of hir strange sewes,
Ne of hir swannes, ne of hire heronsewes.
Eek in that lond, as tellen knyghtes olde,
Ther is som mete that is ful deynte holde   70
That in this lond men recche of it but smal.
Ther nys no man that may reporten al.
    I wol nat taryen yow for it is pryme
And for it is no fruyt but los of tyme.
Unto my firste I wole have my recours.   75
    And so bifel that after the thridde cours,
Whil that this kyng sit thus in his nobleye,
Herknynge his mynstrales hir thynges pleye
Biforn hym at the bord deliciously,
In at the halle dore al sodeynly   80
Ther cam a knyght upon a steede of bras,
And in his hand a brood mirour of glas,
Upon his thombe he hadde of gold a ryng,

---

20 yliche, alike (consistent). Hg&c *Pietous and just and evermore yliche.* These lines may have been an indirect admonition to King Richard; cf. *Lack of Steadfastnesse* (short poem no. 14) and notes. **23** Hg&c *and strong.* **29–33 Elpheta . . . Canacee,** no significant Mongol or literary association has been discovered for these four names. **39 koude his colours,** knew his figures of speech. **47 Idus of March,** i.e., after March 15, as it fell that year. **49 exaltacioun,** point of greatest influence. **50–51 Martes face . . . Aries,** Aries is the sign of the zodiac associated with the sun; the face of Mars was the first third (10°) of that sign. **52 lusty,** invigorating. **53 sheene,** shine (warmth). **54 What for,** what with. **63 if I shal tellen,** the "occuptio" (the rhetorical device giving information while protesting "I have no time to tell") reflected in the following lines and elsewhere throughout this tale, as well as inartistic handling of details and narrative themes, suggests padding and reveals the insecure narrative technique of the piece. **67 strange sewes,** strange soups. Oriental foods were then as now considered exotic, although swan and hernshaw were European delicacies. **68 heronsewes,** hernshaws (young herons). **71 recche,** value. **73 pryme,** 9 A.M. **74 fruyt,** i.e., "This disquisition is not fruitful." **81 Ther cam a knyght,** in the romances, King Arthur's feasts customarily began with some "adventure" (happening); for example, the beginning of *Gawain and the Green Knight* somewhat resembles this episode, as Chaucer himself evidently recalled, see l. 95 below. **81–84 steede . . . mirour . . . ryng . . . swerd,** the multiplication of talismans, any one of which would make a story, is another indication of the inept conception of this tale.

And by his syde a naked swerd hangyng.
And up he rideth to the heighe bord.   85
In al the halle ne was ther spoken a word
For merveille of this knyght; hym to biholde
Ful bisily ther wayten yonge and olde.

    This strange knyght, that cam thus sodeynly,
Al armed save his heed ful richely,   90
Saleweth kyng and queene and lordes alle,
By ordre as they seten in the halle,
With so heigh reverence and obeisaunce,
As wel in speche as in contenaunce,
That Gawayn with his olde curteisye,   95
Though he were comen ayeyn out of Fairye,
Ne koude hym nat amende with a word.
And after this, biforn the heighe bord,
He with a manly voys seith his message,
After the forme used in his langage,   100
Withouten vice of silable or of lettre,
And for his tale sholde seme the bettre
Accordant to his wordes was his cheere,
As techeth art of speche hem that it leere.
Al be that I kan nat sowne his stile,   105
Ne kan nat clymben over so heigh a style,
Yet seye I this, as to commune entente,
Thus muche amounteth al that evere he mente,
If it so be that I have it in mynde.

    He seyde, "The kyng of Arabe and of Inde,
My lige lord, on this solempne day   111
Saleweth yow, as he best kan and may,
And sendeth yow, in honour of youre feeste,
By me that am al redy at youre heeste,
This steede of bras, that esily and weel   115
Kan in the space of o day natureel—
This is to seyn, in foure and twenty houres—
Wher so yow lyst, in droghte or elles shoures,
Beren youre body into every place
To which youre herte wilneth for to pace,   120
Withouten wem of yow, thurgh foul or fair,

Or if yow lyst to fleen as hye in the air
As dooth an egle whan hym list to soore,
This same steede shal bere yow evere moore,
Withouten harm, til ye be ther yow leste,   125
Though that ye slepen on his bak or reste,
And turne ayeyn with writhyng of a pyn.
He that it wroghte koude ful many a gyn.
He wayted many a constellacioun
Er he had doon this operacioun,   130
And knew ful many a seel and many a bond.

    "This mirour eek, that I have in myn hond,
Hath swich a myght that men may in it see
Whan ther shal fallen any adversitee
Unto youre regne or to youreself also,   135
And openly who is youre freend or foo.
And over al this, if any lady bright
Hath set hire herte on any maner wight,
If he be fals, she shal his tresoun see,
His newe love, and al his subtiltee,   140
So openly that ther shal no thyng hyde.
Wherfore, ageyn this lusty someres tyde,
This mirour and this ryng that ye may see,
He hath sent unto my lady Canacee,
Youre excellente doghter that is heere.   145

    "The vertu of the ryng, if ye wol heere,
Is this, that if hire lust it for to were
Upon hir thombe, or in hir purs it bere,
Ther is no fowel that fleeth under the hevene
That she ne shal wel understonde his stevene,   150
And knowe his menyng openly and pleyn,
And answere hym in his langage ageyn;
And every gras that groweth upon roote
She shal eek knowe, and whom it wol do boote,
Al be his woundes never so depe and wyde.   155

    "This naked swerd that hangeth by my syde
Swich vertu hath that what man so ye smyte
Thurghout his armure it wole kerve and byte,
Were it as thikke as is a branched ook.   159

---

88 *ther:* Hg&c *they.* 92 **By ordre,** in order (by precedence). 94 Hg&c, *his speche, his contenaunce.* 96 **Fairye,** fairyland. 101 **vice,** error. 103 **cheere,** expression, manner. 105 **sowne . . . stile,** sound (echo), style. 106 **style,** stile (for climbing over a fence). 107 **commune,** general. 110 **Arabe . . . Inde,** simply exotic Eastern regions; not territories particularly associated with the Mongol Hordes. 114 **heeste,** command. 115 **steede of bras,** magic conveyances (birds, carpets, boats, etc.) abound in folklore. 121 **wem,** injury. 127 **turne . . . writhyng . . . pyn,** return, twisting, pin (a switch). 128 **koude . . . gyn,** knew, artifice (but here technical skill). 129 **constellacioun,** i.e., he waited for the proper configurations of the horoscope. 131 **seel . . . bond,** seals and contracts were ways of binding genie and devils to do one's will, as in the *Arabian Nights* and *Dr. Faustus.* 133 **myght,** power. 135 **regne,** kingdom. 142 **ageyn . . . lusty someres,** in anticipation of; pleasant (but with overtones of amorous) summers; summer in Middle English included spring (as winter included fall). 147 **hire lust,** it pleases her. 149 **fleeth,** flies. 150 **stevene,** voice (language). 153 **gras,** i.e., growing plant. 154 **boote,** help, cure.

And what man that is wounded with the strook
Shal never be hool til that yow list, of grace,
To stroke hym with the plat in thilke place
Ther he is hurt; this is as muche to seyn,
Ye moote with the platte swerd ageyn
Stroke hym in the wounde and it wol close; 165
This is a verray sooth, withouten glose.
It failleth nat whils it is in youre hoold."
    And whan this knyght hath thus his tale
      toold,
He rideth out of halle and doun he lighte.
His steede, which that shoon as sonne brighte,
Stant in the court stille as any stoon. 171
This knyght is to his chambre lad anoon,
And is unarmed, and unto mete yset.
    The presentes been ful roially yfet—
This is to seyn, the swerd and the mirour— 175
And born anon into the heighe tour
With certeine officers ordeyned therfore;
And unto Canacee this ryng was bore
Solempnely, ther she sit at the table.
But sikerly, withouten any fable, 180
The hors of bras that may nat be remewed,
It stant as it were to the ground yglewed.
Ther may no man out of the place it dryve
For noon engyn of wyndas ne polyve;
And cause why? For they kan nat the craft. 185
And therfore in the place they han it laft
Til that the knyght hath taught hem the manere
To voyden hym, as ye shal after heere.
    Greet was the prees that swarmeth to and fro
To gauren on this hors that stondeth so, 190
For it so heigh was, and so brood and long,
So wel proporcioned for to been strong,
Right as it were a steede of Lumbardye;
Therwith so horsly and so quyk of eye,
As it a gentil Poilleys courser were. 195

For certes, fro his tayl unto his ere,
Nature ne art ne koude hym nat amende
In no degree, as al the peple wende.
But everemoore hir mooste wonder was
How that it koude gon, and was of bras. 200
It was a fairye, as the peple semed.
Diverse folk diversely they demed;
As many heddes as manye wittes ther been.
They murmureden as dooth a swarm of been
And maden skiles after hir fantasies, 205
Rehersynge of thise olde poetries,
And seyde that it was lyk the Pegasee,
The hors that hadde wynges for to flee,
Or elles it was the Grekes hors Synoun
That broghte Troie to destruccioun, 210
As men mowe in thise olde geestes rede.
    "Myn herte," quod oon, "is everemoore in
      drede.
I trowe som men of armes been therinne,
That shapen hem this citee for to wynne.
It were right good that al swich thyng were
      knowe." 215
    Another rowned to his felawe lowe
And seyde, "He lyeth; it is rather lyk
An apparence ymaad by som magyk,
As jogelours pleyen at thise feestes grete."
Of sondry doutes thus they jangle and trete. 220
As lewed peple demeth comunly
Of thynges that been maad moore subtilly
Than they kan in hir lewednesse comprehende,
They demen gladly to the badder ende.
    And somme of hem wondred on the mirour
That born was up into the maister tour, 226
Hou men myghte in it swiche thynges se.
    Another answerde and seyde it myghte wel
      be
Naturelly, by composiciouns

---

162 plat, flat side of the sword; weapons that produce wounds that can only be healed by the weapons themselves are common in folklore. *thilke:* E *that.* **164** E *plat.* **165** *Stroke:* E&c *Strike.* **166 glose,** lie. **167 hoold,** possession. **174 yfet,** fetched. **180 sikerly,** truly. **181 remewed,** removed (moved). **184 wyndas . . . polyve,** windlass, pulley. **188 voyden,** remove. **190 gauren,** stare. **194 quyk,** lively. **195 Poilleys,** Apulia in southern Italy and Lombardy in the north were both famous for their horses. **198 wende,** thought. **200 koude gon,** was able to move. **201 a fairye,** a magic thing. **202** Hg&c *han demed.* **205 skiles,** explanations. **207 Pegasee,** Pegasus, the winged steed of the Muses. **208 flee,** fly. **209 Grekes . . . Synoun,** the horse of the Greek Sinon (the pretended deserter who persuaded the Trojans to take the wooden horse into the city). This divided possessive form persisted sporadically until after Malory. **211 geestes,** stories. EHg&c *mowe* om. **213 trowe,** believe. **214 shapen hem,** plan. **216 rowned,** whispered. **220 doutes . . . jangle . . . trete,** doubts (possibilities), chatter, argue. **221 lewed . . . demeth,** ignorant, judge. **224 badder ende,** worst possibility. **226 maister tour,** principal stronghold. *maister:* E&c *hye.* **229 Naturelly,** i.e., not by magic. **229–30 composiciouns/Of anglis . . . slye,** arrangement of angles, skillfully contrived.

Of anglis and of slye reflexiouns,   230
And seyden that in Rome was swich oon.
They speken of Alocen, and Vitulon,
And Aristotle, that writen in hir lyves
Of queynte mirours and of perspectives,
As knowen they that han hir bookes herd.   235
   And oother folk han wondred on the swerd
That wolde percen thurghout everythyng,
And fille in speche of Thelophus the kyng,
And of Achilles with his queynte spere,
For he koude with it bothe heele and dere   240
Right in swich wise as men may with the
    swerd
Of which right now ye han youreselven herd.
They speken of sondry hardyng of metal,
And speke of medicynes therwithal,
And how and whanne it sholde yharded be,   245
Which is unknowe, algates unto me.
   Tho speeke they of Canacees ryng,
And seyden alle that swich a wonder thyng
Of craft of rynges herde they nevere noon,
Save that he Moyses and Kyng Salomon   250
Hadde a name of konnyng in swich art.
Thus seyn the peple and drawen hem apart.
   But natheless somme seiden that it was
Wonder to maken of fern-asshen glas,
And yet nys glas nat lyk asshen of fern.   255
But for they han knowen it so fern,
Therfore cesseth hir janglyng and hir wonder.
   As soore wondren somme on cause of
    thonder,
On ebbe, on flood, on gossomer, and on myst,
And on alle thyng, til that the cause is wyst. 260
Thus jangle they, and demen, and devyse,
Til that the kyng gan fro the bord aryse.
   Phebus hath laft the angle meridional,

And yet ascendynge was the beest roial,
The gentil Leon, with his Aldrian,   265
Whan that this Tartre kyng, this Cambyuskan,
Roos fro his bord, ther as he sat ful hye.
Toforn hym gooth the loude mynstralcye,
Til he cam to his chambre of parementz,
Ther as they sownen diverse instrumentz   270
That it is·lyk an hevene for to heere.
Now dauncen lusty Venus children deere,
For in the Fyssh hir lady sat ful hye,
And looketh on hem with a freendly eye.
   This noble kyng is set up in his trone.   275
This strange knyght is fet to hym ful soone,
And on the daunce he gooth with Canacee.
Heere is the revel and the jolitee
That is nat able a dul man to devyse.
He most han knowen love and his servyse,   280
And been a feestlych man as fressh as May,
That sholde yow devysen swich array.
   Who koude telle yow the forme of daunces
So unkouthe, and so fresshe contenaunces,
Swich subtil lookyng and dissymulynges   285
For drede of jalouse mennes aperceyvynges?
No man but Launcelot, and he is deed.
Therfore I passe of al this lustiheed;
I sey namoore, but in this jolynesse
I lete hem til men to the soper dresse.   290
   The styward bit the spices for to hye,
And eek the wyn, in al this melodye.
The usshers and the squiers been ygoon,
The spices and the wyn is come anoon.
They ete and drynke, and whan this hadde an
    ende,   295
Unto the temple, as reson was, they wende.
   The service doon, they soupen al by day.
What nedeth yow rehercen hire array?

232 **Alocen . . . Vitulon,** Alhazen, Arabian physicist whose treatise on optics was translated into Latin by the Polish physicist Witelo. 234 **perspectives,** lenses. 238 **Thelophus,** Telephus, who was both wounded and healed by the spear of Achilles. 240 **dere,** do injury. 243 **hardyng,** hardening (tempering). 246 **algates,** in any way. 249 **craft,** i.e., magic. 250 **Moyses . . . Salomon,** according to tradition Moses and Solomon both possessed magical rings. 254 **fern-asshen,** ashes of ferns were evidently an ingredient in making glass. *RR* 16081 (Dunn-Robbins 78.76) uses the same contrast between fern ash and clear glass. 256 **so fern,** so far (for such a long time). 258 **soore,** sorely (much). 259 **On ebbe, on flood, on gossomer,** of the tides, of cobwebs. 260 **wyst,** known. E *on* om. 261 **jangle . . . demen,** chatter, judge. 263 **angle meridional,** i.e., was past noon. 265 **Leon . . . Aldrian,** the constellation Leo; Aldira (plural Aldiran?) may refer to Castor and Pollux in Leo's forepaws. E has *Aldrian:* Hg&c *Aldiran.* 266 **this Cambyuskan:** EHg&c *this* om. 269 **parementz,** reception (audience). 270 *they:* Hg&c *ther.* 272 **Venus children,** lovers. 273 **Fyssh,** zodiac sign of Pisces in which Venus exerted the most influence. 276 **fet,** fetched. 279 **devyse,** imagine. 280 **most,** must. 281 **feestlych,** accustomed to feasts (parties). 282 **yow devysen . . . array,** describe for you, affair. 285 **subtil . . . dissymulynges,** secret, dissemblings. 290 **dresse,** address themselves (prepare for). 291 **bit . . . hye,** ordered, bring. *the spices:* EHg&c *the* om. 297 **by day,** by daylight. 298 *yow:* &c *me.*

Ech man woot wel that a kynges feeste 299
Hath plentee to the mooste and to the leeste,
And deyntees mo than been in my knowyng.
At after-soper gooth this noble kyng
To seen this hors of bras, with al the route
Of lordes and of ladyes hym aboute.
  Swich wondryng was ther on this hors of
    bras 305
That syn the grete sege of Troie was,
Theras men wondreden on an hors also,
Ne was ther swich a wondryng as was tho.
But fynally the kyng axeth this knyght
The vertu of this courser and the myght, 310
And preyde hym to telle his governaunce.
  This hors anoon bigan to trippe and
    daunce
Whan that this knyght leyde hand upon his
    reyne,
And seyde, "Sire, ther is namoore to seyne
But whan yow list to ryden anywhere, 315
Ye mooten trille a pyn stant in his ere,
Which I shal yow telle bitwix us two.
Ye moote nempne hym to what place also,
Or to what contree, that yow list to ryde.
And whan ye come ther as yow list abyde, 320
Bidde hym descende and trille another
    pyn—
For therin lith th'effect of al the gyn—
And he wol doun descende and doon youre
    wille,
And in that place he wol abyden stille.
Though al the world the contrarie hadde
    yswore, 325
He shal nat thennes been ydrawe ne ybore.
Or if yow liste bidde hym thennes goon,
Trille this pyn and he wol vanysshe anoon
Out of the sighte of every maner wight,
And come agayn, be it by day or nyght, 330
Whan that yow list to clepen hym ageyn
In swich a gyse as I shal to yow seyn

Bitwixe yow and me and that ful soone.
Ride whan yow list, ther is namoore to
    doone."
  Enformed whan the kyng was of that
    knyght, 335
And hath conceyved in his wit aright
The manere and the forme of al this thyng,
Ful glad and blithe this noble doughty kyng
Repeireth to his revel as biforn.
The brydel is unto the tour yborn 340
And kept among his jueles leeve and deere.
The hors vanysshed, I noot in what manere,
Out of hir sighte; ye gete namoore of me.
But thus I lete in lust and jolitee
This Cambyuskan his lordes festeiynge 345
Til wel ny the day bigan to sprynge.

Explicit pars prima. Sequitur pars secunda.

  The norice of digestioun, the sleep,
Gan on hem wynke and bad hem taken keep
That muchel drynke and labour wolde han
    reste,
And with a galpyng mouth hem alle he keste,
And seyde it was tyme to lye adoun, 351
For blood was in his domynacioun.
"Cherisseth blood, natures freend," quod he.
They thanken hym galpynge, by two, by
    thre,
And every wight gan drawe hym to his reste
As sleep hem bad; they tooke it for the beste.
  Hire dremes shul nat been ytoold for me; 357
Ful were hire heddes of fumositee
That causeth dreem of which ther nys no
    charge.
They slepen til that it was pryme large, 360
The mooste part, but it were Canacee.
She was ful mesurable as wommen be,
For of hir fader hadde she take leve
To goon to reste soone after it was eve.
Hir liste nat appalled for to be 365

---

303 route, company. **308 tho,** then. **310 vertu,** capabilities. **311 governaunce,** i.e., how it was controlled. **316 trille,** turn. **318 nempne,** name (tell). **322 effect . . . gyn,** method, contrivance. E *in* om. **324** *abyden:* E *stonde.* **326 ybore,** carried. **329 wight,** person. **331 clepen,** call. **332 gyse,** manner. **336 conceyved,** understood. **338** *Ful:* E *Thus;* E *doughty* om. **341 leeve,** beloved. **345 festeiynge,** feasting. **347 norice,** nurse. **348 keep,** care. **350 galpyng . . . keste,** yawning, kissed. **352 blood . . . domynacioun,** i.e., physical requirements must be satisfied; blood (as a humor) was in domination during the hours of darkness. **357** Hg&c *nat now been told.* **358 furmositee,** fumes arising from drinking. **359 no charge,** no significance. **360 pryme large,** 9 A.M. **361 but it were,** except for. **362 mesurable,** moderate. **363** Other MSS *take hir leve.* **365 appalled,** to grow pale (hence, tired, listless).

Ne on the morwe unfeestlich for to se.
And slepte hire firste sleep and thanne awook,
For swich a joye she in hir herte took
Bothe of hir queynte ryng and hire mirour
That twenty tyme she changed hir colour,   370
And in hire sleep right for impressioun
Of hire mirour, she hadde a visioun.
Wherfore, er that the sonne gan up glyde
She cleped on hir maistresse hire bisyde,
And seyde that hire liste for to ryse.   375

　Thise olde wommen that been gladly wyse,
As is hire maistresse, answerde hire anon
And seyde, "Madame, whider wil ye goon
Thus erly, for the folk been alle on reste?"

　"I wol," quod she, "arise, for me leste   380
No lenger for to slepe, and walke aboute."

　Hire maistresse clepeth wommen a greet
　　route,
And up they rysen, wel a ten or twelve.
Up riseth fresshe Canacee hirselve,
As rody and bright as dooth the yonge
　　sonne   385
That in the Ram is foure degrees up ronne—
Noon hyer was he whan she redy was—
And forth she walketh esily a pas,
Arrayed after the lusty seson soote
Lightly, for to pleye and walke on foote,   390
Nat but with fyve or sixe of hir meynee,
And in a trench forth in the park gooth she.

　The vapour which that fro the erthe glood
Made the sonne to seme rody and brood,
But nathelees it was so fair a sighte   395
That it made alle hire hertes for to lighte,
What for the seson and the morwenynge,
And for the foweles that she herde synge.
For right anon she wiste what they mente,   399
Right by hir song, and knew al hire entente.

The knotte why that every tale is toold,
If it be taried til that lust be coold
Of hem that han it after herkned yoore,
The savour passeth ever lenger the moore
For fulsomnesse of his prolixitee.   405
And by the same resoun, thynketh me,
I sholde to the knotte condescende,
And maken of hir walkyng soone an ende.

　Amydde a tree, fordrye as whit as chalk,
As Canacee was pleyyng in hir walk,   410
Ther sat a faucon over hire heed ful hye
That with a pitous voys so gan to crye
That all the wode resouned of hire cry.
Ybeten hath she hirself so pitously
With bothe hir wynges til the rede blood   415
Ran endelong the tree ther as she stood.
And evere in oon she cryde alwey and
　　shrighte,
And with hir beek hirselven so she prighte,
That ther nys tygre ne noon so crueel beest
That dwelleth outher in wode or in forest   420
That nolde han wept, if that he wepe koude,
For sorwe of hire, she shrighte alwey so loude.
For ther nas nevere man yet on lyve—
If that I koude a faucon wel discryve—
That herde of swich another of fairnesse   425
As wel of plumage as of gentillesse
Of shap, and al that myghte yrekened be.
A faucon peregryn thanne semed she
Of fremde land, and everemoore as she stood
She swowneth now and now for lakke of
　　blood,   430
Til wel neigh is she fallen fro the tree.

　This faire kynges doghter, Canacee,
That on hir fynger baar the queynte ryng
Thurgh which she understood wel everythyng
That any fowel may in his leden seyn,   435

---

366 morwe unfeestlich, morning, unfestive (jaded). **371 impressioun,** the effect produced (by). **374 cleped . . . maistresse,** called, governess. **376 gladly wyse,** i.e., would gladly learn what is on her charge's mind. **380 leste,** desire. **382 clepeth . . . route,** calls, company. **383** *a:* E *an.* **385–86 yonge sonne . . . Ram,** the early spring sun in Aries, the first zodiacal sign after the vernal equinox, i.e., about March 16. *foure:* in many MSS *x* instead of *iv.* **389 lusty . . . soote,** pleasant, mild (sweet). **391 meynee,** retinue. **392 trench,** path through the shrubbery. **393 glood,** glided. **399 wiste,** knew. **402 lust,** pleasure. **403 after herkned yoore,** listened to (after) it for a long time. **404 savour,** relish. **405 fulsomnesse,** surfeit (boredom). **409 fordrye,** completely dry ("for" is an intensifier). E&c *fordryed.* **418 prighte,** pricked. **423** Defective line; MSS have *yet* in various places. **424 discryve,** describe. **425 of . . . of,** i.e., of another so beautiful. **427 and al:** Hg&c *of al.* **428 peregryn,** a species of falcon, literally "pilgrim" because young peregrines were caught in passage from their breeding grounds rather than taken from the nest. **429 fremde,** foreign. **435 leden,** language (OE derived from "Latin").

And koude answeren hym in his ledene ageyn,
Hath understonde what this faucon seyde,
And wel neigh for the routhe almoost she
  deyde.
And to the tree she gooth ful hastily,
And on this faukon looketh pitously,   440
And heeld hir lappe abrood, for wel she wiste
The faukon moste fallen fro the twiste,
Whan that it swowned next, for lakke of blood.
A longe while to wayten hire she stood
Til atte laste she spak in this manere   445
Unto the hauk, as ye shal after heere:
  "What is the cause, if it be for to telle,
That ye be in this furial pyne of helle?"
Quod Canacee unto the hauk above.
"Is this for sorwe of deeth or los of love?   450
For as I trowe thise been causes two
That causen moost a gentil herte wo;
Of oother harm it nedeth nat to speke.
For ye yourself upon yourself yow wreke,
Which proveth wel that outher ire or drede   455
Moot been enchesoun of youre cruel dede,
Syn that I see noon oother wight yow chace.
For love of God, as dooth youreselven grace,
Or what may been youre help? For west nor est
Ne saugh I nevere er now no bryd ne beest   460
That ferde with hymself so pitously.
Ye sle me with youre sorwe verraily,
I have of yow so greet compassioun.
For Goddes love, com fro the tree adoun;
And as I am a kynges doghter trewe,   465
If that I verraily the cause knewe
Of youre disese, if it lay in my myght,
I wolde amenden it er that it were nyght,
As wisly helpe me the grete God of kynde!
And herbes shal I right ynowe yfynde   470
To heele with youre hurtes hastily."
  Tho shrighte this faucon yet moore pitously

Than ever she dide, and fil to grounde anon,
And lith aswowne, deed and lyk a stoon,
Til Canacee hath in hire lappe hire take   475
Unto the tyme she gan of swough awake.
  And after that she of hir swough gan breyde,
Right in hir haukes ledene thus she seyde:
"That pitee renneth soone in gentil herte,
Feelynge his similitude in peynes smerte,   480
Is preved alday, as men may it see,
As wel by werk as by auctoritee,
For gentil herte kitheth gentillesse.
I se wel ye han of my distresse
Compassion, my faire Canacee,   485
Of verray wommanly benignytee
That Nature in youre principles hath yset.
But for noon hope for to fare the bet,
But for to obeye unto youre herte free,
And for to maken othere bewar by me,   490
As by the whelp chasted is the leoun,
Right for that cause and that conclusioun,
Whil that I have a leyser and a space,
Myn harm I wol confessen er I pace."
  And evere, whil that oon hir sorwe tolde,   495
That oother weep as she to water wolde,
Til that the faucon bad hire to be stille,
And with a syk right thus she seyde hir wille:
"That I was bred—allas, that ilke day—
And fostred in a roche of marbul gray   500
So tendrely that nothyng eyled me,
I nyste nat what was adversitee,
Til I koude flee ful hye under the sky.
Tho dwelte a tercelet me faste by
That semed welle of alle gentillesse.   505
Al were he ful of treson and falsnesse,
It was so wrapped under humble cheere,
And under hewe of trouthe in swich manere,
Under plesance and under bisy peyne,
That no wight koude han wend he koude feyne,

438 routhe, pity. **441 lappe,** the hanging part of a garment. **442 twiste,** branch. **448 furial pyne,** furious pain. **451 trowe,** believe. **454 wreke,** revenge. **455 outher,** either. *ire:* E *love.* **456 enchesoun,** reason. **458 dooth . . . grace,** have mercy. **463** *compassioun:* E *com* om. **467 disese,** distress. **469 kynde,** nature (the universe). Hg&c *the* om. **470 ynowe,** enough. *yfynde:* Hg&c *fynde.* **472** E *moore yet.* **475 lappe,** see l. 441n. **476 swough,** swoon. **477** Hg&c *of swow gan abreyde.* **479 pitee renneth** etc., the frequently uttered sentiment, cf. I.1761n. **481 preved.** proved. **483 kitheth,** reveals. **487 principles,** innate disposition. **489 free,** generous. **491 chasted,** punished, i.e., beating the dog to punish the lion, cf. *Othello* II. iii. 272. **492** EHg&c *and for.* **493 leyser,** leisure (time). **496 to water,** turn to water. **498 syk,** sigh. What follows greatly resembles *Anelida and Arcite* (short poem no. 2), ll. 105ff., and there are many verbal resemblances. **499** *That:* Hg&c *Ther; ilke:* E *harde.* **500 roche,** rock. **501 eyled,** troubled. **502 nyste,** did not know. **503 flee,** fly. **504 Tho . . . tercelet,** Then, male peregrine falcon. **509 bisy peyne,** busy solicitude. **510 wend . . . feyne,** believed, pretend. E *That I ne koude.*

So depe in greyn he dyed his coloures. 511
Right as a serpent hit hym under floures
Til he may seen his tyme for to byte,
Right so this god of loves ypocryte
Dooth so his cerymonyes and obeisaunces, 515
And kepeth in semblaunt alle his observaunces
That sownen into gentillesse of love.
As in a toumbe is al the faire above
And under is the corps, swich as ye woot,
Swich was the ypocrite, bothe coold and hoot.
And in this wise he served his entente, 521
That, save the feend, noon wiste what he
        mente,
Til he so longe hadde wopen and compleyned,
And many a yeer his service to me feyned,
Til that myn herte, to pitous and to nyce, 525
Al innocent of his corouned malice,
For fered of his deeth, as thoughte me,
Upon his othes and his seuretee,
Graunted hym love upon this condicioun,
That everemoore myn honour and renoun 530
Were saved, bothe privee and apert;
This is to seyn, that after his desert
I yaf hym al myn herte and al my thoght—
God woot and he, that ootherwise noght—
And took his herte in chaunge of myn for ay. 535
But sooth is seyd, goon sithen many a day,
A trewe wight and a theef thenken nat oon.
And whan he saugh the thyng so fer ygoon
That I hadde graunted hym fully my love
In swich a gyse as I have seyd above, 540
And yeven hym my trewe herte as free
As he swoor he yaf his herte to me,
Anon this tigre, ful of doublenesse,
Fil on his knees with so devout humblesse,
With so heigh reverence, and as by his
        cheere
So lyk a gentil lovere of manere, 546
So ravysshed, as it semed, for the joye

That nevere Jason ne Parys of Troye—
Jason? Certes, ne noon oother man
Syn Lameth was, that alderfirst bigan 550
To loven two, as writen folk biforn—
Ne nevere, syn the firste man was born,
Ne koude man by twenty thousand part
Countrefete the sophymes of his art,
Ne were worthy unbrokelen his galoche 555
Ther doublenesse or feynyng sholde approche,
Ne so koude thonke a wight as he dide me!
His manere was an hevene for to see
Til any womman, were she never so wys,
So peynted he and kembde at point-devys, 560
As wel his wordes as his contenaunce.
And I so loved hym for his obeisaunce,
And for the trouthe I demed in his herte,
That if so were that any thyng hym smerte,
Al were it never so lite, and I it wiste, 565
Me thoughte I felte deeth myn herte twiste.
And shortly so ferforth this thyng is went
That my wyl was his willes instrument;
This is to seyn, my wyl obeyed his wyl
In alle thyng as fer as reson fil, 570
Kepynge the boundes of my worship evere.
Ne nevere hadde I thyng so lief, ne levere,
As hym, God woot, ne nevere shal namo.

    "This lasteth lenger than a yeer or two
That I supposed of hym noght but good. 575
But finally, thus atte laste it stood,
That Fortune wolde that he moste twynne
Out of that place which that I was inne.
Wher me was wo, that is no questioun.
I kan nat make of it discripsioun; 580
For o thyng dar I tellen boldely,
I knowe what is the peyne of deeth therby.
Swich harm I felte for he ne myghte bileve.
So on a day of me he took his leve
So sorwefully eek that I wende verraily 585
That he had felt as muche harm as I,

<hr/>

511 in greyn, i.e., so deep that it seemed natural, not dyed. **512 hit,** hides. **514** E&c *this god of love, this ypocryte.* **516 kepeth in semblaunt,** keeps up appearances. **517 sownen into,** are in harmony with. **522 wiste . . . mente,** knew, intended. **523 wopen,** wept. **525 nyce,** foolish. **526 corouned,** crowned (sovereign). **528 seuretee,** assurance. **531 saved . . . apert,** preserved, publicly. **533 and al:** EHg *al* om. **534 that ootherwise noght,** i.e., that on other terms I would not have done so. **535** E&c *for myn.* **537 oon,** alike. **545 cheere,** expression, appearance. **548 Jason,** deserted Medea, cf. LGW, iv, Legend of Hypsipyle and Medea. **Parys** deserted Oenone. *Jason:* E&c *Troilus.* **550 Lameth,** took two wives, Gen. 4:19. **554 sophymes,** sophisms, deceits. **557 thonke,** thank. **560 kembde . . . point-devys,** combed, to perfection. **562 obeisaunce,** humility. **564 smerte,** pained. **567 ferforth,** far. **571 worship,** honor. **572 lief . . . levere,** dear, dearer. **577 twynne,** depart. **583 harm . . . bileve,** pain, remain. **585 wende,** thought.

Whan that I herde hym speke, and saugh his
   hewe.
But nathelees, I thoughte he was so trewe;
And eek that he repaire sholde ageyn
Withinne a litel while, sooth to seyn; 590
And resoun wolde eek that he moste go
For his honour, as ofte it happeth so;
That I made vertu of necessitee
And took it wel, syn that it moste be.
As I best myghte, I hidde fro hym my sorwe, 595
And took hym by the hond, Seint John to
   borwe,
And seyde hym thus, 'Lo, I am youres al.
Beth swich as I to yow have been and shal.'
What he answerde, it nedeth noght reherce.
Who kan sey bet than he, who kan do werse? 600
Whan he hath al wel seyd, thanne hath he doon.
Therfore bihoveth hire a ful long spoon
That shal ete with a feend, thus herde I seye.
So atte laste he moste forth his weye,
And forth he fleeth til he cam ther hym leste. 605
   "Whan it cam hym to purpos for to reste,
I trowe he hadde thilke text in mynde,
That alle thyng, repeirynge to his kynde,
Gladeth hymself—thus seyn men, as I gesse.
Men loven of propre kynde newefangelnesse,
As briddes doon that men in cages fede. 611
For though thou nyght and day take of hem
   hede,
And strawe hir cage faire and softe as silk,
And yeve hem sugre, hony, breed, and milk,
Yet right anon as that his dore is uppe, 615
He with his feet wol spurne adoun his cuppe,
And to the wode he wole and wormes ete.
So newefangel been they of hire mete,
And loven novelries of propre kynde;
No gentillesse of blood ne may hem bynde. 620

"So ferde this tercelet, allas the day!
Though he were gentil born, and fressh and
   gay,
And goodlich for to seen, humble and free,
He saugh upon a tyme a kyte flee,
And sodeynly he loved this kyte so 625
That al his love is clene fro me ago,
And hath his trouthe falsed in this wyse.
Thus hath the kyte my love in hire servyse,
And I am lorn withouten remedie."
And with that word this faucon gan to crie 630
And swowned eft in Canacees barm.

   Greet was the sorwe for the haukes harm
That Canacee and alle hir wommen made.
They nyste hou they myghte the faucon glade.
But Canacee hom bereth hire in hir lappe, 635
And softely in plastres gan hire wrappe,
Ther as she with hire beek hadde hurt hirselve.
Now kan nat Canacee but herbes delve
Out of the ground, and make salves newe
Of herbes preciouse and fyne of hewe, 640
To heelen with this hauk. Fro day to nyght
She dooth hire bisynesse and al hire myght,
And by hire beddes heed she made a mewe,
And covered it with velvettes blewe
In signe of trouthe that is in wommen sene. 645
And al withoute, the mewe is peynted grene,
In which were peynted alle thise false fowles
As beth thise tidyves, tercelettes, and owles;
Right for despit were peynted hem bisyde
Pyes, on hem for to crie and chyde. 650
   Thus lete I Canacee hir hauk kepyng;
I wol namoore as now speke of hir ryng
Til it come eft to purpos for to seyn
How that this faucon gat hire love ageyn
Repentant, as the storie telleth us, 655
By mediacioun of Cambalus,

---

589 repaire, return. **596 Seint John to borwe,** St. John, the Apostle of Truth, as a pledge. **601** E&c *wel* om. **602 bihoveth hire,** she needs. **605 leste,** wished. **608 repeirynge to his kynde,** from *Boece* III m. 2.42, where Chaucer translates it "alle thinges rejoysen hem of her retorninge ayein to her nature." **610 propre kynde,** natural disposition. **620 gentillesse,** i.e., strength of character (responsibility, gratitude). EHg&c *ne* om. **622** *and fressh:* E&c *and* om. **623 free,** generous. **624 kyte,** kite, in England a scavenger bird (formerly abundant but now nearly extinct). **flee,** fly. **627 trouthe,** troth, promise. **631 barm,** lap. **634 glade,** gladden. **636 plastres,** curative bandages. **638 kan nat . . . but,** can do nothing but. **641** E *hauk* om. **642** E *hire fulle myght.* **643 mewe,** mew (hawk's cage). **648 tidyves,** an unidentified variety of bird, evidently reputed to be inconstant, cf. LGW l. 154. **649 despit,** scorn. **650 Pyes,** magpies. EHg&c *And pyes.* **653 eft,** again. **656ff. Cambalus** is perhaps the same son as Cambalo (l. 31), but ll. 667–69 seem confused. This summary listing of an unmanageable number of possible plots, like the unmanageable number of talismans at the beginning (ll. 81ff.), is evidence of lack of control of his material on the part either of the Squire or the poet himself.

The kynges sone, of which that I yow tolde.
But hennesforth I wol my proces holde
To speke of aventures and of batailles
That nevere yet was herd so grete mervailles. 660
   First wol I telle yow of Cambyuskan,
That in his tyme many a citee wan;
And after wol I speke of Algarsif,
How that he wan Theodera to his wif,
For whom ful ofte in greet peril he was, 665

Ne hadde he been holpen by the steede of bras;
And after wol I speke of Cambalo,
That faught in lystes with the bretheren two
For Canacee er that he myghte hire wynne.
And ther I lefte I wol ayeyn bigynne. 670

Explicit secunda pars. Incipit pars tercia.

   Appollo whirleth up his chaar so hye,
Til that the god Mercurius hous, the slye—

Heere folwen the wordes of the Frankeleyn to the Squier, and the wordes of the Hoost to the Frankeleyn.

"In feith, Squier, thow hast thee wel yquit
And gentilly. I preise wel thy wit,"
Quod the Frankeleyn, "considerynge thy
   yowthe, 675
So feelyngly thou spekest, sire, I allow the.
As to my doom, ther is noon that is heere
Of eloquence that shal be thy peere,
If that thou lyve—God yeve thee good
   chaunce,
And in vertu sende thee continuaunce, 680
For of thy speche I have greet deyntee.
I have a sone, and by the Trinitee,
I hadde levere than twenty pound worth lond,
Though it right now were fallen in myn hond,
He were a man of swich discrecioun 685
As that ye been. Fy on possessioun,
But if a man be vertuous withal!
I have my sone snybbed, and yet shal,
For he to vertu listeth nat entende,
But for to pleye at dees, and to despende 690
And lese al that he hath is his usage.

And he hath levere talken with a page
Than to comune with any gentil wight
There he myghte lerne gentillesse aright."
   "Straw for youre gentillesse!" quod oure
   Hoost. 695
"What, Frankeleyn, pardee sire, wel thou
   woost
That ech of yow moot tellen atte leste
A tale or two, or breken his biheste."
   "That knowe I wel, sire," quod the
   Frankeleyn.
"I prey yow, haveth me nat in desdeyn, 700
Though to this man I speke a word or two."
   "Telle on thy tale withouten wordes mo."
   "Gladly, sire Hoost," quod he, "I wole
   obeye
Unto your wyl. Now herkneth what I seye.
I wol yow nat contrarien in no wyse 705
As fer as that my wittes wol suffyse.
I prey to God that it may plesen yow;
Thanne woot I wel that it is good ynow."

657 EHg&c *that* om. **663–64 Algarsif,** Cambyuskan's other son (1. 30), but, as of him, there is nothing known of **Theodera. 671–72** Lines found in EHg and 26 other MSS. In E the rest of the page is blank. **671 chaar,** chariot. **672 Mercurius hous … slye,** zodiacal mansion of Mercury the cunning. **675** *Frankeleyn: Merchant* in MSS which have SqT following MerchT; see Manly iv.30, 484. **676 allow,** praise. **677 doom,** judgment. **679 chaunce,** luck. **681 deyntee,** pleasure. **683 twenty pound worth,** land which would yield £20 income annually. **688 synbbed,** scolded. **689 listeth … entende,** desires, attend (pursue). **690 dees … despende,** dice, spend. **692 levere,** rather. **694** *There:* Hg&c *Where.* **696 Frankeleyn,** see 1. 675n. above. **woost,** know. **698 biheste,** promise. **699 Frankeleyn,** see 1. 675n. above. **705 contrarien,** oppose. **708 woot … ynow,** know, enough.

FRANKLIN'S TALE

PROLOGUE

The Prologe of the Frankeleyns Tale.

Thise olde gentil Britouns in hir dayes
Of diverse aventures maden layes,   710
Rymeyed in hir firste Briton tonge,
Whiche layes with hir instrumentz they songe
Or elles redden hem for hir plesaunce;
And oon of hem have I in remembraunce,
Which I shal seyn with good wyl as I kan.   715
    But, sires, by cause I am a burel man,
At my bigynnyng first I yow biseche,
Have me excused of my rude speche.

I lerned nevere rethorik, certeyn.
Thyng that I speke, it moot be bare and pleyn.
I sleep nevere on the Mount of Pernaso,   721
Ne lerned Marcus Tullius Scithero.
Colours ne knowe I none, withouten drede,
But swiche colours as growen in the mede,
Or elles swich as men dye or peynte.   725
Colours of rethoryk been to queynte;
My spirit feeleth noght of swich mateere.
But if yow list, my tale shul ye heere.

Heere bigynneth the Frankeleyns Tale.

In Armorik, that called is Britayne,
Ther was a knyght that loved and dide his
        payne   730
To serve a lady in his beste wise;

And many a labour, many a greet emprise
He for his lady wroghte er she were wonne,
For she was oon the faireste under sonne,
And eek therto comen of so heigh kynrede   735

709 **Britouns,** Bretons, Celtic peoples of Brittany through whom the Arthurian legend and other Celtic stories are thought to have been transmitted to the French. **710 layes,** short romances sung by minstrels. **711 Rymeyed . . . firste Briton tonge,** rhymed (composed), original Celtic language of Brittany. **713 plesaunce,** pleasure. **716 burel,** ignorant. **721 Pernaso,** Mt. Parnassus, sacred to the Muses. Some MSS have Parnaso, but most simply have a crossed P. **722 Scithero,** Cicero, supreme exemplar of Latin rhetoric. **723–24 colours,** *double entendre,* rhetorical devices and the real colors of flowers or paint. **726 queynte,** strange. **729–30** Lines reversed in some MSS. **729 Armorik,** Armorica, ancient name for Brittany. **732 emprise,** enterprise. **735 kynrede,** kindred.

That wel unnethes dorste this knyght for drede
Telle hire his wo, his peyne, and his distresse.
But atte laste she for his worthynesse,
And namely for his meke obeysaunce,
Hath swich a pitee caught of his penaunce   740
That pryvely she fil of his accord
To take hym for hir housbonde and hir lord,
Of swich lordshipe as men han over hir wyves.
And for to lede the moore in blisse hir lyves,
Of his free wyl he swoor hire as a knyght   745
That nevere in al his lyf he day ne nyght
Ne sholde upon hym take no maistrie
Agayn hir wyl, ne kithe hire jalousie,
But hire obeye and folwe hir wyl in al,
As any lovere to his lady shal,   750
Save that the name of soveraynetee,
That wolde he have for shame of his degree.
 She thanked hym, and with ful greet
  humblesse
She seyde, "Sire, sith of youre gentillesse
Ye profre me to have so large a reyne,   755
Ne wolde nevere God bitwixe us tweyne,
As in my gilt, were outher werre or stryf.
Sire, I wol be youre humble trewe wyf—
Have heer my trouthe—til that myn herte
 breste."
Thus been they bothe in quiete and in reste.   760
 For o thyng, sires, saufly dar I seye,
That freendes everych oother moot obeye
If they wol longe holden compaignye.
Love wol nat been constreyned by maistrye.
Whan maistrie comth, the God of Love anon
Beteth his wynges and farewel, he is gon.   766
Love is a thyng as any spirit free.
Wommen, of kynde, desiren libertee,
And nat to been constreyned as a thral—
And so doon men, if I sooth seyen shal.   770

Looke who that is moost pacient in love,
He is at his avantage al above.
Pacience is an heigh vertu, certeyn,
For it venquysseth, as thise clerkes seyn,
Thynges that rigour sholde nevere atteyne.   775
For every word men may nat chide or pleyne.
Lerneth to suffre, or elles so moot I goon,
Ye shul it lerne wher so ye wole or noon.
For in this world, certein, ther no wight is
That he ne dooth or seith somtyme amys.   780
Ire, siknesse, or constellacioun,
Wyn, wo, or chaungynge of complexioun
Causeth ful ofte to doon amys or speken.
On every wrong a man may nat be wreken.
After the tyme moste be temperaunce   785
To every wight that kan on governaunce.
And therfore hath this wise, worthy knyght
To lyve in ese suffrance hire bihight,
And she to hym ful wisly gan to swere
That nevere sholde ther be defaute in here.   790
 Heere may men seen an humble, wys accord;
Thus hath she take hir servant and hir lord—
Servant in love and lord in mariage.
Thanne was he bothe in lordshipe and servage.
Servage? Nay, but in lordshipe above   795
Sith he hath bothe his lady and his love;
His lady, certes, and his wyf also,
The which that lawe of love acordeth to.
And whan he was in this prosperitee,
Hoom with his wyf he gooth to his contree,   800
Nat fer fro Pedmark ther his dwellyng was,
Where as he lyveth in blisse and in solas.
 Who koude telle but he hadde wedded be
The joye, the ese, and the prosperitee
That is bitwixe an housbonde and his wyf?   805
A yeer and moore lasted this blisful lyf,
Til that the knyght of which I speke of thus,

---

736 unnethes, hardly. **739 namely ... obeysaunce,** especially, obedience. **740 penaunce,** suffering. **741 pryvely ... fil of ...
accord,** privately agreed. **747 maistrie,** authority. **748 kithe,** show. **752 shame of his degree,** i.e., regard for his position. **755 large
a reyne,** free a rein. **757 As in my gilt ... outher,** through my fault, either. **759 trouthe ... breste,** promise, break. **761 saufly,**
safely. **765 anon,** at once. **768 of kynde,** by nature. **769 thral,** slave. **770 sooth,** truth. **772 avantage,** has the advantage. E *avantate.*
775 rigour, severity. **776 For ... pleyne,** at, complain. **777 suffre ... moot I goon,** tolerate, as I am able to walk. **778 ye wole,**
you wish to. **781 constellacioun,** influence of the stars. **782 complexioun,** balance of humors in the body (sanguinary, phlegmatic,
choleric, melancholic). **784 On ... wreken,** for, revenged. **785 After ... moste ... temperaunce,** according to, (there) must,
tolerance (moderation). **786 kan on governaunce,** knows about governing. **788 suffrance ... bihight,** tolerance, promised. **790
defaute in here,** i.e., failure on her part. **801 Pedmark,** Penmarch in Brittany. J. S. P. Tatlock and others have discussed both the
historical background and the poetic license of the Breton geography in this tale. **802 solas,** physical pleasure (with the usual sexual
overtone).

That of Kayrrud was cleped Arveragus,
Shoop hym to goon and dwelle a yeer or tweyne
In Engelond, that cleped was eek Briteyne, 810
To seke in armes worship and honour—
For al his lust he sette in swich labour—
And dwelled there two yeer, the book seith
    thus.

   Now wol I stynten of this Arveragus,
And speken I wole of Dorigen his wyf 815
That loveth hire housbonde as hire hertes lyf.
For his absence wepeth she and siketh,
As doon thise noble wyves whan hem liketh.
She moorneth, waketh, wayleth, fasteth,
    pleyneth.
Desir of his presence hire so destreyneth 820
That al this wyde world she sette at noght.
Hire freendes, whiche that knewe hir hevy
    thoght,
Conforten hire in al that ever they may.
They prechen hire, they telle hire nyght and
    day
That causelees she sleeth hirself, allas, 825
And every confort possible in this cas
They doon to hire with al hire bisynesse,
Al for to make hire leve hire hevynesse.

   By proces, as ye knowen everichoon,
Men may so longe graven in a stoon 830
Til som figure therinne emprented be.
So longe han they conforted hire, til she
Receyved hath, by hope and by resoun,
The emprentyng of hire consolacioun,
Thurgh which hir grete sorwe gan aswage; 835
She may nat alwey duren in swich rage.

   And eek Arveragus in al this care
Hath sent hire lettres hoom of his welfare,
And that he wol come hastily agayn;
Or elles hadde this sorwe hir herte slayn. 840

   Hire freendes sawe hir sorwe gan to slake,
And preyde hire on knees, for Goddes sake,
To come and romen hire in compaignye,
Awey to dryve hire derke fantasye.

And finally she graunted that requeste, 845
For wel she saugh that it was for the beste.
   Now stood hire castel faste by the see,
And often with hire freendes walketh shee
Hire to disporte upon the bank an heigh
Where as she many a ship and barge seigh 850
Seillynge hir cours, where as hem liste go.
But thanne was that a parcel of hire wo,
For to hirself ful ofte, "Allas," seith she,
"Is ther no ship of so manye as I se
Wol bryngen hom my lord? Thanne were myn
    herte 855
Al warisshed of his bittre peynes smerte."
   Another tyme ther wolde she sitte and
    thynke,
And caste hir eyen dounward fro the brynke.
But whan she saugh the grisly rokkes blake
For verray feere so wolde hir herte quake 860
That on hire feet she myghte hire noght sustene.
Thanne wolde she sitte adoun upon the grene
And pitously into the see biholde,
And seyn right thus with sorweful sikes colde:
   "Eterne God, that thurgh thy purveiaunce
Ledest the world by certein governaunce, 866
In ydel, as men seyn, ye no thyng make.
But, Lord, thise grisly, feendly rokkes blake,
That semen rather a foul confusioun
Of werk than any fair creacioun 870
Of swich a parfit wys God and a stable,
Why han ye wroght this werk unresonable?
For by this werk, south, north, ne west, ne
    eest,
Ther nys yfostred man, ne bryd, ne beest;
It dooth no good, to my wit, but anoyeth. 875
Se ye nat, Lord, how mankynde it destroyeth?
An hundred thousand bodyes of mankynde
Han rokkes slayn, al be they nat in mynde,
Which mankynde is so fair part of thy werk
That thou it madest lyk to thyn owene merk.
   "Thanne semed it ye hadde a greet chiertee 881
Toward mankynde; but how thanne may it bee

---

808 Kayrrud, Karru, or "red house," is found as a place name in modern Brittany, but not near Penmarch. **811 worship and honour,** uxoriousness was an abiding danger to the chivalric code, as illustrated by Chrétien de Troyes' two romances dealing with the subject, *Erec* and *Yvain.* **812 lust,** delight. **814 stynten,** leave off. **819 waketh,** lies awake. **820 destreyneth,** grips. **829 By proces,** in process of time. **830 graven,** engrave (cut). **835 gan aswage,** began to be assuaged (cured). **836 duren,** endure. **837 care,** sorrowfulness. **843 romen,** walk about. **852 parcel,** part. **856 warisshed,** cured. **864 sikes,** sighs. **865 purveiaunce,** providence. **867 In ydel,** i.e., to no purpose. **868 feendly,** fiendish. **874 nys yfostred,** i.e., is not benefited. **880 merk,** image. **881 chiertee,** charity (love).

That ye swiche meenes make it to destroyen,
Whiche meenes do no good but evere anoyen?
I woot wel clerkes wol seyn as hem leste, 885
By argumentz, that al is for the beste
Though I ne kan the causes nat yknowe.
But thilke God that made wynd to blowe
As kepe my lord! This my conclusion.
To clerkes lete I al disputison. 890
But wolde God that alle thise rokkes blake
Were sonken into helle for his sake!
Thise rokkes sleen myn herte for the feere."
Thus wolde she seyn, with many a pitous
      teere.

Hire freendes sawe that it was no disport 895
To romen by the see, but disconfort,
And shopen for to pleyen somwher elles.
They leden hire by ryveres and by welles,
And eek in othere places delitables;
They dauncen and they pleyen at ches and
      tables. 900

So on a day, right in the morwetyde,
Unto a gardyn that was ther bisyde,
In which that they hadde maad hir ordinaunce
Of vitaille and of oother purveiaunce,
They goon and pleye hem al the longe day. 905
And this was on the sixte morwe of May,
Which May hadde peynted with his softe
      shoures
This gardyn ful of leves and of floures;
And craft of mannes hand so curiously
Arrayed hadde this gardyn, trewely, 910
That nevere was ther gardyn of swich prys
But if it were the verray paradys.
The odour of floures and the fresshe sighte
Wolde han maked any herte lighte
That evere was born but if to greet siknesse 915
Or to greet sorwe helde it in distresse,
So ful it was of beautee with plesaunce.
At after-dyner gonne they to daunce,
And synge also, save Dorigen allone,
Which made alwey hir compleint and hir
      moone, 920
For she ne saugh hym on the daunce go
That was hir housbonde and hir love also.
But nathelees she moste a tyme abyde,
And with good hope lete hir sorwe slyde.

Upon this daunce, amonges othere men, 925
Daunced a squier biforn Dorigen,
That fressher was and jolyer of array,
As to my doom, than is the monthe of May.
He syngeth, daunceth, passynge any man
That is or was sith that the world bigan. 930
Therwith he was, if men sholde hym discryve,
Oon of the beste farynge man on lyve:
Yong, strong, right vertuous, and riche, and
      wys,
And wel biloved, and holden in greet prys.
And shortly, if the sothe I tellen shal, 935
Unwityng of this Dorigen at al
This lusty squier, servant to Venus,
Which that ycleped was Aurelius,
Hadde loved hire best of any creature
Two yeer and moore, as was his aventure, 940
But nevere dorste he tellen hire his grevaunce.
Withouten coppe he drank al his penaunce.
He was despeyred; nothyng dorste he seye,
Save in his songes somwhat wolde he wreye
His wo, as in a general compleynyng. 945
He seyde he lovede and was biloved no
      thyng.
Of swich matere made he manye layes,
Songes, compleintes, roundels, virelayes,
How that he dorste nat his sorwe telle,
But langwissheth as a furye dooth in helle; 950
And dye he moste, he seyde, as dide Ekko
For Narcisus, that dorste nat telle hir wo.
In oother manere than ye heere me seye
Ne dorste he nat to hire his wo biwreye,

---

885 **woot . . . leste,** know, wish. 889 **kepe,** protect. 895 **disport,** diversion. 897 **shopen,** arranged. 898 **welles,** springs. 900 **tables,** backgammon. 901 **morwetyde,** morning. 903 **ordinaunce,** arrangement(s). 904 **purveiaunce,** provision(s). 909 **curiously,** skill-fully. 910 **Arrayed,** arranged. 911 **prys,** excellence (price). 912 **verray,** true (genuine). 915 **but if to greet,** unless too great. 920 **moone,** moan. 927 **jolyer,** gayer (cf. Fr. *joli*). 928 **doom,** judgment. 929 **passynge,** surpassing. 932 **beste farynge,** most attractive. 936 **Unwityng,** unknown. 940 **aventure,** lot. 942 **Withouten coppe,** i.e., the hard way. 944 **wreye,** reveal. 948 **Songes, compleintes, roundels, virelayes,** songs translates Fr. *chanson (d'amor)*; complaints is a troubadour thematic designation (see many of Chaucer's own short poems); roundels and virelays are now thought of as stanzaic types, but they originate as dance songs with stanzas for a soloist and an answering refrain for a chorus. 951–52 **Ekko . . . Narcisus,** Echo's death for love of Narcissus who could love only himself is recounted by Ovid, *Met.* 3.407, *RR,* and elsewhere. E has a marginal note *Methamorposis.* 954 **biwreye,** betray.

Save that paraventure somtyme at daunces, 955
Ther yonge folk kepen hir observaunces,
It may wel be he looked on hir face
In swich a wise as man that asketh grace;
But nothyng wiste she of his entente.
Nathelees it happed, er they thennes wente, 960
By cause that he was hire neighebour,
And was a man of worship and honour,
And hadde yknowen hym of tyme yoore,
They fille in speche; and forthe moore and
    moore
Unto his purpos drough Aurelius, 965
And whan he saugh his tyme, he seyde thus:
   "Madame," quod he, "by God that this world
    made,
So that I wiste it myghte youre herte glade,
I wolde that day that youre Arveragus
Wente over the see, that I, Aurelius, 970
Hadde went ther nevere I sholde have come
    agayn.
For wel I woot my servyce is in vayn;
My gerdon is but brestyng of myn herte.
Madame, reweth upon my peynes smerte,
For with a word ye may me sleen or save. 975
Heere at youre feet God wolde that I were
    grave!
I ne have as now no leyser moore to seye;
Have mercy, sweete, or ye wol do me deye!"
   She gan to looke upon Aurelius: 979
"Is this youre wyl," quod she, "and sey ye thus?
Nevere erst," quod she, "ne wiste I what ye
    mente.
But now, Aurelie, I knowe youre entente,
By thilke God that yaf me soule and lyf
Ne shal I nevere been untrewe wyf
In word ne werk, as fer as I have wit. 985
I wol been his to whom that I am knyt.
Taak this for fynal answere as of me."
But after that in pley thus seyde she:

   "Aurelie," quod she, "by heighe God above,
Yet wolde I graunte yow to been youre love, 990
Syn I yow se so pitously complayne.
Looke what day that endelong Britayne
Ye remoeve alle the rokkes, stoon by stoon,
That they ne lette ship ne boot to goon—
I seye, whan ye han maad the coost so clene 995
Of rokkes that ther nys no stoon ysene,
Thanne wol I love yow best of any man.
Have heer my trouthe in al that evere I kan."
   "Is ther noon oother grace in yow?" quod he.
   "No, by that Lord," quod she, "that maked
    me! 1000
For wel I woot that it shal never bityde.
Lat swiche folies out of youre herte slyde.
What deyntee sholde a man han in his lyf
For to go love another mannes wyf,
That hath hir body whan so that hym liketh?"
   Aurelius ful ofte soore siketh; 1006
Wo was Aurelie whan that he this herde,
And with a sorweful herte he thus answerde:
   "Madame," quod he, "this were an
    inpossible.
Thanne moot I dye of sodeyn deth horrible."
And with that word he turned hym anon. 1011
Tho coome hir othere freendes many oon
And in the aleyes romeden up and doun,
And nothyng wiste of this conclusioun,
But sodeynly bigonne revel newe 1015
Til that the brighte sonne loste his hewe,
For th'orisonte hath reft the sonne his lyght—
This is as muche to seye as it was nyght.
And hoom they goon in joye and in solas,
Save oonly wrecche Aurelius, allas! 1020
He to his hous is goon with sorweful herte.
He seeth he may nat fro his deeth asterte;
Hym semed that he felte his herte colde.
Up to the hevene his handes he gan holde,
And on his knowes bare he sette hym doun, 1025

---

956 observaunces, rituals (of courtship, etc.: i.e., the mimetic significance of the dance). **959 wiste,** knew. **960 happed,** happened. **963 hadde...of tyme yoore,** (she) had, since old times. **964–65 forthe...drough,** nearer drew. **968 wiste...glade,** knew, gladden. **969 wolde,** wish. **972 woot,** know. **973 gerdon...brestyng,** reward, bursting (breaking). **974 reweth,** have pity. **975 sleen,** slay. **976 grave,** buried. **977 leyser,** time (leisure). **980 wyl,** desire. **981 erst...wiste,** before, knew. **983 yaf,** gave. **992 endelong,** along the whole length of. **994 lette,** hinder. **998 trouthe,** troth (promise). **1001–06** In some MSS these lines come between 998 and 999. Manly IV.485 suggests that they were in the margin of Chaucer's exemplar and actually intended to go after 998. **1001 woot...bityde,** know, happen. **1003 deyntee,** relish. **1004** Hg&c *go* om. **1006 siketh,** sighs. **1010 moot,** must. **1011 turned hym,** turned away. **1013 aleyes,** paths (alleys). **1014 conclusioun,** occurrence. **1017 orisonte...reft,** horizon had deprived. **1022 asterte,** escape. **1023 colde,** grow cold. **1025 knowes,** knees.

And in his ravyng seyde his orisoun.
For verray wo out of his wit he breyde.
He nyste what he spak, but thus he seyde;
With pitous herte his pleynt hath he bigonne
Unto the goddes, and first unto the sonne: 1030
 He seyde, "Appollo, god and governour
Of every plaunte, herbe, tree, and flour,
That yevest after thy declinacioun
To ech of hem his tyme and his sesoun,
As thyn herberwe chaungeth lowe or heighe,
Lord Phebus, cast thy merciable eighe 1036
On wrecche Aurelie which that am but lorn.
Lo, lord, my lady hath my deeth ysworn
Withoute gilt, but thy benignytee
Upon my dedly herte have som pitee. 1040
For wel I woot, lord Phebus, if yow lest,
Ye may me helpen, save my lady, best.
Now voucheth sauf that I may yow devyse
How that I may been holpen and in what
  wyse.
 "Youre blisful suster, Lucina the sheene, 1045
That of the see is chief goddesse and queene—
Though Neptunus have deitee in the see,
Yet emperisse aboven hym is she—
Ye knowen wel, lord, that right as hir desir
Is to be quyked and lightned of youre fir, 1050
For which she folweth yow ful bisily,
Right so the see desireth naturelly
To folwen hire, as she that is goddesse
Bothe in the see and ryveres moore and lesse.
Wherfore, lord Phebus, this is my requeste—
Do this miracle, or do myn herte breste— 1056
That now next at this opposicioun
Which in the signe shal be of the Leoun,
As preieth hire so greet a flood to brynge 1059
That fyve fadme at the leeste it oversprynge
The hyeste rokke in Armorik Briteyne;

And lat this flood endure yeres tweyne.
Thanne certes to my lady may I seye,
'Holdeth youre heste, the rokkes been aweye.'
 "Lord Phebus, dooth this miracle for me. 1065
Preye hire she go no faster cours than ye;
I seye, preyeth youre suster that she go
No faster cours than ye thise yeres two.
Thanne shal she been evene atte fulle alway,
And spryng flood laste bothe nyght and day.
And but she vouchesauf in swich manere 1071
To graunte me my sovereyn lady deere,
Prey hire to synken every rok adoun
Into hir owene dirke regioun
Under the ground ther Pluto dwelleth inne,
Or nevere mo shal I my lady wynne. 1076
Thy temple in Delphos wol I barefoot seke.
Lord Phebus, se the teeris on my cheke,
And of my peyne have som compassioun."
And with that word in swowne he fil adoun,
And longe tyme he lay forth in a traunce. 1081
 His brother, which that knew of his
  penaunce,
Up caughte hym, and to bedde he hath hym
  broght.
Dispeyred in this torment and this thoght
Lete I this woful creature lye; 1085
Chese he, for me, wheither he wol lyve or dye.
 Arveragus, with heele and greet honour,
As he that was of chivalrie the flour,
Is comen hoom, and othere worthy men.
O blisful artow now, thou Dorigen, 1090
That hast thy lusty housbonde in thyne armes,
The fresshe knyght, the worthy man of armes,
That loveth thee as his owene hertes lyf.
No thyng list hym to been ymaginatyf
If any wight hadde spoke, whil he was oute, 1095
To hire of love; he hadde of it no doute.

1026 **orisoun,** prayer. 1027 **breyde,** started (jumped). 1028 **nyste,** did not know. 1033 **yevest after thy declinacioun,** give according to your angle above the equator (i.e., the season of the year). 1035 **herberwe,** house (in the zodiac). 1037 **wrecche . . . lorn,** wretched, lost. 1039 **Withoute gilt,** i.e., guilt on my part. 1041 **woot . . . lest,** know, wish. 1042 **save,** except for. 1043 **yow devyse,** explain to you. 1045 **Lucina the sheene,** Diana the beautiful. 1050 **quyked,** brought to life. Hg&c *lighted.* 1054 **moore and lesse,** greater and smaller. 1056 **do . . . breste,** make, break. 1057 **opposicioun,** in opposite signs of the zodiac; the highest tides occur when the gravity of the sun and the moon are pulling together (in conjunction) or against one another (in opposition). 1058 **Leoun,** if the sun is in Leo, the moon would be opposite in Aquarius. 1059 **hire,** i.e., Diana, the moon. **flood,** flood tide. 1060 **fadme,** fathom (6 feet). 1064 **heste,** promise. 1067 Hg&c *seye thus/this.* 1069 **evene atte fulle,** completely at full tide. 1071 **vouchesauf,** consent. 1074–75 **dirke regioun . . . Pluto,** Diana was recognized in three forms, as Lucina the moon goddess, Artemis the earth goddess, and Hecate the goddess of the underworld. 1077 **Delphos,** Delphi (with which Diana had no special connection). 1086 **for me,** as far as I am concerned. 1087 **heele,** prosperity.

He noght entendeth to no swich mateere,
But daunceth, justeth, maketh hire good cheere.
And thus in joye and blisse I let hem dwelle,
And of the sike Aurelius I wol yow telle.   1100
   In langour and in torment furyus
Two yeer and moore lay wrecche Aurelyus
Er any foot he myghte on erthe gon;
Ne confort in this tyme hadde he noon
Save of his brother, which that was a clerk.
He knew of al this wo and al this werk,   1106
For to noon oother creature, certeyn,
Of this matere he dorste no word seyn.
Under his brest he baar it moore secree
Than evere dide Pamphilus for Galathee.   1110
His brest was hool withoute for to sene,
But in his herte ay was the arwe kene.
And wel ye knowe that of a sursanure
In surgerye is perilous the cure,
But men myghte touche the arwe or come
      therby.   1115
His brother weep and wayled pryvely
Til atte laste hym fil in remembraunce
That whiles he was at Orliens in Fraunce,
As yonge clerkes that been lykerous
To reden artes that been curious   1120
Seken in every halke and every herne
Particuler sciences for to lerne,
He hym remembred that upon a day
At Orliens in studie a book he say
Of magyk natureel, which his felawe,   1125
That was that tyme a bacheler of lawe—
Al were he ther to lerne another craft—
Hadde pryvely upon his desk ylaft.
Which book spak muchel of the operaciouns
Touchynge the eighte and twenty mansiouns
That longen to the moone, and swich folye   1131
As in oure dayes is nat worth a flye,
For hooly chirches feith in oure bileve

Ne suffreth noon illusioun us to greve.
And whan this book was in his remembraunce,
Anon for joye his herte gan to daunce,   1136
And to hymself he seyde pryvely:
"My brother shal be warisshed hastily,
For I am siker that ther be sciences
By whiche men make diverse apparences   1140
Swiche as thise subtile tregetoures pleye.
For ofte at feestes have I wel herd seye
That tregetours withinne an halle large
Have maad come in a water and a barge,
And in the halle rowen up and doun.   1145
Somtyme hath semed come a grym leoun;
And somtyme floures sprynge as in a mede;
Somtyme a vyne and grapes white and rede;
Somtyme a castel, al of lym and stoon;
And whan hym lyked, voyded it anon.   1150
Thus semed it to every mannes sighte.
   "Now thanne conclude I thus, that if I
      myghte
At Orliens som oold felawe yfynde
That hadde thise moones mansions in mynde,
Or oother magyk natureel above,   1155
He sholde wel make my brother han his love.
For with an apparence a clerk may make
To mannes sighte that alle the rokkes blake
Of Britaigne weren yvoyded everichon,
And shippes by the brynke comen and gon,   1160
And in swich forme enduren a wowke or two.
Thanne were my brother warisshed of his wo;
Thanne moste she nedes holden hire biheste,
Or elles he shal shame hire atte leeste."
   What sholde I make a lenger tale of this?   1165
Unto his brotheres bed he comen is,
And swich confort he yaf hym for to gon
To Orliens that he up stirte anon
And on his wey forthward thanne is he fare
In hope for to been lissed of his care.   1170

1097 entendeth, pays attention. **1103 gon,** walk. **1105 clerk,** person in holy orders, scholar. **1110 Pamphilus . . . Galathee,** the popular 13th-century Latin poem *Pamphilus de Amore* details Pamphilus' love for, and ultimately seduction of, Galatea. **1111 hool withoute,** whole outwardly. **1112 ay,** always. **1113 sursanure,** a wound with the foreign object (e.g., arrowhead) left within, but healed on the surface. **1115 But,** unless. **1118 Orliens,** Orleans, site of a famous university in the Middle Ages. **1119 lykerous,** eager (lecherous). **1120 reden . . . curious,** study, exotic (occult). **1121 halke . . . herne,** nook, corner. **1122 Particuler,** specialized. **1124 say,** saw. **1125 magyk natureel,** astrology (vs. black magic, which trafficked with demons). **1128 pryvely,** secretly. **1130 mansiouns,** the 28 daily positions of the lunar month. **1133 bileve,** creed. **1138 warisshed,** healed. **1139 siker,** sure (secure). **1141 tregetoures,** magicians. **1149 lym,** lime (mortar). **1153 felawe,** companion. **1157 apparence,** illusion. **1161 wowke,** week. Hg&c *day.* **1162 warisshed,** healed. **1163 holden . .. biheste,** keep, promise. **1167 confort,** encouragement. **1170 lissed,** relieved.

Whan they were come almoost to that citee,
But if it were a two furlong or thre,
A yong clerk romynge by hymself they mette,
Which that in Latyn thriftily hem grette,
And after that he seyde a wonder thyng: 1175
"I knowe," quod he, "the cause of youre
        comyng."
And er they ferther any foote wente,
He told hem al that was in hire entente.

    This Briton clerk hym asked of felawes   1179
The whiche that he had knowe in olde dawes,
And he answerde hym that they dede were,
For which he weep ful ofte many a teere.

    Doun of his hors Aurelius lighte anon,
And with this magicien forth is he gon   1184
Hoom to his hous, and maden hem wel at ese.
Hem lakked no vitaille that myghte hem plese.
So wel arrayed hous as ther was oon
Aurelius in his lyf saugh nevere noon.

    He shewed hym, er he wente to sopeer,
Forestes, parkes ful of wilde deer: 1190
Ther saugh he hertes with hir hornes hye,
The gretteste that evere were seyn with eye.
He saugh of hem an hondred slayn with
        houndes,
And somme with arwes blede of bittre woundes.

    He saugh, whan voyded were thise wilde deer,
Thise fauconers upon a fair ryver   1196
That with hir haukes han the heron slayn.

    Tho saugh he knyghtes justyng in a playn.
And after this he dide hym swich plesaunce
That he hym shewed his lady on a daunce,   1200
On which hymself he daunced, as hym
        thoughte.
And whan this maister that this magyk
        wroughte
Saugh it was tyme, he clapte his handes two,
And farewel, al oure revel was ago.   1204
And yet remoeved they nevere out of the hous
Whil they saugh al this sighte merveillous,
But in his studie, ther as his bookes be,

They seten stille, and no wight but they thre.

    To hym this maister called his squier
And seyde hym thus: "Is redy oure soper?   1210
Almoost an houre it is, I undertake,
Sith I yow bad oure soper for to make,
Whan that thise worthy men wenten with me
Into my studie, ther as my bookes be."

    "Sire," quod this squier, "whan it liketh yow,
It is al redy, though ye wol right now."   1216

    "Go we thanne soupe," quod he, "as for the
        beste.
Thise amorous folk somtyme moote han hir
        reste."

    At after-soper fille they in tretee
What somme sholde this maistres gerdon be
To remoeven alle the rokkes of Britayne,   1221
And eek from Gerounde to the mouth of Sayne.

    He made it straunge, and swoor, so God hym
        save,
Lasse than a thousand pound he wolde nat have,
Ne gladly for that somme he wolde nat goon.

    Aurelius, with blisful herte anoon,   1226
Answerde thus: "Fy on a thousand pound!
This wyde world, which that men seye is
        round,
I wolde it yeve if I were lord of it.
This bargayn is ful dryve, for we been knyt.   1230
Ye shal be payed trewely, by my trouthe.
But looketh now, for no necligence or slouthe
Ye tarie us heere no lenger than to-morwe."

    "Nay," quod this clerk, "have heer my feith
        to borwe."

    To bedde is goon Aurelius whan hym leste,
And wel ny al that nyght he hadde his reste.   1236
What for his labour and his hope of blisse,
His woful herte of penaunce hadde a lisse.

    Upon the morwe whan that it was day
To Britaigne tooke they the righte way,   1240
Aurelius and this magicien bisyde,
And been descended ther they wolde abyde.
And this was, as thise bookes me remembre,

1172 **furlong,** eighth of a mile. 1174 **Latyn,** Latin was the international language of universities and scholars. **thriftily,** suitably. 1175 **wonder,** wonderful (causing wonder). 1179 **Briton,** Breton. 1187 **arrayed,** provided for. 1196 **fauconers,** falconers. 1216 **wol,** wish (it). 1219 **tretee,** negotiation (treaty). 1220 **gerdon,** reward. 1222 **Gerounde . . . Sayne,** the rivers Gironde and Seine (an expanse that took in much of the coast of Poitou and Normandy, as well as Brittany proper). 1223 **straunge,** difficult. 1224 **thousand pound,** one pound was worth perhaps $200 in modern money. 1230 **dryve,** concluded (driven). 1231 **trouthe,** troth (honor). 1234 **borwe,** pledge. 1238 **lisse,** release. 1239 **morwe,** morning. 1240 **righte,** nearest. 1242 **descended,** dismounted.

The colde, frosty seson of Decembre.
    Phebus wax old and hewed lyk latoun, 1245
That in his hoote declynacioun
Shoon as the burned gold with stremes brighte;
But now in Capricorn adoun he lighte,
Where as he shoon ful pale, I dar wel seyn.
The bittre frostes, with the sleet and reyn, 1250
Destroyed hath the grene in every yerd.
Janus sit by the fyr with double berd
And drynketh of his bugle horn the wyn.
Biforn hym stant brawen of the tusked swyn,
And "Nowel" crieth every lusty man. 1255
    Aurelius in al that evere he kan
Dooth to this maister chiere and reverence,
And preyeth hym to doon his diligence
To bryngen hym out of his peynes smerte,
Or with a swerd that he wolde slitte his
    herte. 1260
    This subtil clerk swich routhe had of this
    man
That nyght and day he spedde hym that he kan
To wayten a tyme of his conclusioun—
This is to seye, to maken illusioun
By swich an apparence of jogelrye 1265
(I ne kan no termes of astrologye)
That she and every wight sholde wene and seye

That of Britaigne the rokkes were aweye,
Or ellis they were sonken under grounde.
So atte laste he hath his tyme yfounde 1270
To maken his japes and his wrecchednesse
Of swich a supersticious cursednesse.
His tables Tolletanes forth he brought,
Ful wel corrected; ne ther lakked nought,
Neither his collect ne his expans yeeris, 1275
Ne his rootes, ne his othere geeris,
As been his centris and his argumentz,
And his proporcioneles convenientz
For his equaciouns in everythyng.
And by his eighte speere in his wirkyng 1280
He knew ful wel how fer Alnath was shove
Fro the heed of thilke fixe Aries above,
That in the ninthe speere considered is;
Ful subtilly he kalkuled al this. 1284
    Whan he hadde founde his firste
    mansioun,
He knew the remenaunt by proporcioun,
And knew the arisyng of his moone weel,
And in whos face, and terme, and everydeel;
And knew ful weel the moones mansioun
Acordaunt to his operacioun, 1290
And knew also his othere observaunces
For swiche illusiouns and swiche meschaunces

1245 latoun, brass. **1246 hoote declynacioun,** high (summer) deflection. **1247 burned,** burnished. **1248 Capricorn,** zodiacal sign closest to the winter solstice. **1252 Janus,** Roman god of the gateway with two faces, one looking inward and the other outward, from which January, the gateway month, takes its name. **1253 bugle horn,** wild ox horn (large). **1254 brawen,** the traditional Christmas boar's head. This Christmas miniature appears to have no connection with the plot; perhaps it is a remnant of the occasion for which the poem was first composed. **1257 chiere,** hospitality. *This:* E&c *his.* **1261 routhe,** pity. **1263 wayten . . . conclusioun,** determine, accomplishment. **1265** *of:* Hg&c *or.* **1266 kan,** know. **1267 wene,** believe. **1271 japes . . . wrecchednesse,** tricks, despicable acts. **1273 tables Tolletanes,** widely used astrological tables composed by order of Alphonso X, King of Castile, and calculated for Toledo in Spain. The exhibition of astrological knowledge in the lines that follow reminds one that Chaucer was author of the *Treatise on the Astrolabe* and probably of the *Equatorie of the Planets,* both of which deal in a technical manner with similar data. **1274 corrected,** astrological and astronomical tables had to be calibrated for the particular location at which they were to be used; e.g., calculations in the *Astrolabe* are based on the latitude of Oxford, those in the *Equatorie* upon Westminster. **1275 collect,** a table showing the number of degrees of motion of a planet in multiples of 100 years. **expans yeeris,** a table showing the number of degrees in a single year. **1276 rootes,** the basis from which planetary motion is calculated, usually the position of the planet at the time of the birth of Christ, but the phrase "defferentia Christi et Radix Chaucer" in the *Equatorie,* whose root is December 1392, indicates that the term can mean the special basis for calculation in any set of tables or problems. **othere geeris,** other equipment. **1277 centris,** table indicating positions of planetary centers by months, days, hours, minutes. **argumentz,** angles and arcs used in calculating planetary motion. **1278 proporcioneles convenientz,** table of planetary motions by fractional parts of a year. **1279 equaciouns,** the process of dividing the sphere into equal "houses" for astrological purposes. **1280–83 eighte speere . . . Alnath . . . Aries . . . ninthe speere.** Alnath is a bright star in the constellation Aries by which the gradual westward shift of the equinoxes over long periods of time (the precession of the equinoxes) can be measured. Alnath was considered to be in the eighth sphere in the heavens, and the "fixed head of Aries," the true equinoctial point, in the ninth sphere. **1284** E *hadde kalkuled.* **1285 firste mansioun,** i.e., that of the moon. **1286 remenaunt,** remaining positions. **proporcioun,** codified relations among the movements of the heavenly bodies; cf. l. 1278 and note. **1288 face,** first third of zodiacal sign. **terme,** one of five unequal divisions of a zodiacal sign. **everydeel,** everything. **1290 Acordaunt,** in relation. **1291 observaunces,** procedures. **1292 For,** i.e., to achieve. **meschaunces,** misdoings.

As hethen folk useden in thilke dayes.
For which no lenger maked he delayes,
But thurgh his magik, for a wyke or tweye, 1295
It semed that alle the rokkes were aweye.

Aurelius, which that yet despeired is
Wher he shal han his love or fare amys,
Awaiteth nyght and day on this myracle; 1299
And whan he knew that ther was noon obstacle,
That voyded were thise rokkes everychon,
Doun to his maistres feet he fil anon
And seyde, "I woful wrecche, Aurelius,
Thanke yow, lord, and lady myn Venus,
That me han holpen fro my cares colde." 1305
And to the temple his wey forth hath he holde,
Where as he knew he sholde his lady see.
And whan he saugh his tyme, anon-right hee
With dredful herte and with ful humble cheere
Salewed hath his sovereyn lady deere: 1310

"My righte lady," quod this woful man,
"Whom I moost drede and love as I best kan,
And lothest were of al this world displese,
Nere it that I for yow have swich disese 1314
That I moste dyen heere at youre foot anon
Noght wolde I telle how me is wo bigon.
But certes outher moste I dye or pleyne;
Ye sle me giltelees for verray peyne.
But of my deeth thogh that ye have no routhe,
Avyseth yow er that ye breke youre trouthe.
Repenteth yow, for thilke God above, 1321
Er ye me sleen by cause that I yow love.
For, madame, wel ye woot what ye han hight—
Nat that I chalange any thyng of right
Of yow, my sovereyn lady, but youre grace—
But in a gardyn yond, at swich a place, 1326
Ye woot right wel what ye bihighten me,
And in myn hand youre trouthe plighten ye
To love me best—God woot, ye seyde so,
Al be that I unworthy am therto. 1330

Madame, I speke it for the honour of yow
Moore than to save myn hertes lyf right now.
I have do so as ye comanded me,
And if ye vouchesauf, ye may go see. 1334
Dooth as yow list; have youre biheste in mynde;
For, quyk or deed, right there ye shal me fynde.
In yow lith al to do me lyve or deye—
But wel I woot the rokkes been aweye."

He taketh his leve, and she astoned stood;
In al hir face nas a drope of blood. 1340
She wende nevere han come in swich a trappe.
"Allas," quod she, "that evere this sholde
    happe!
For wende I nevere by possibilitee
That swich a monstre or merveille myghte be.
It is agayns the proces of nature." 1345
And hoom she goth a sorweful creature.
For verray feere unnethe may she go.
She wepeth, wailleth, al a day or two,
And swowneth that it routhe was to see.
But why it was to no wight tolde shee, 1350
For out of towne was goon Arveragus.
But to hirself she spak and seyde thus,
With face pale and with ful sorweful cheere,
In hire compleynt, as ye shal after heere:

"Allas," quod she, "on thee, Fortune, I
    pleyne, 1355
That unwar wrapped hast me in thy cheyne,
Fro which t'escape woot I no socour
Save oonly deeth or elles dishonour;
Oon of thise two bihoveth me to chese.
But nathelees, yet have I levere to lese 1360
My lif than of my body to have a shame,
Or knowe myselven fals, or lese my name;
And with my deth I may be quyt, ywis.
Hath ther nat many a noble wyf er this,
And many a mayde, yslayn hirself, allas, 1365
Rather than with hir body doon trespas?

1293 useden, were accustomed to do. **1295 wyke,** week. **1298 Wher,** whether. **1299 on,** for. **1305 holpen,** helped (relieved). **1308 anon-right,** at once. **1309 dredful . . . cheere,** fearful, manner. **1310 Salewed,** greeted (saluted). **1313 lothest,** most reluctant (loath). **1314 disese,** dis-ease (agony). **1316 Noght wolde I,** unless I would. **1317 outher,** either. **1318 for verray peyne,** through sheer pain. **1319 routhe,** pity. **1320 Avyseth yow . . . trouthe,** be advised, promise. **1323 hight,** promised. **1324 chalange,** claim. **1327 woot . . . bihighten,** know, promised. **1334 vouchesauf,** consent. **1335 biheste,** promise. **1336 quyk,** alive. **1338 woot,** know. **1344 monstre,** wonder. **1347 unnethe . . . go,** hardly, walk. **1348 al,** a whole. **1349 routhe,** pity. **1353 cheere,** expression. **1356 unwar,** unaware (unexpectedly). **1357 woot . . . socour,** know, help. *Fro:* EHg&c *For;* E *scour.* **1358 EGg&c** *elles* om. **1361 E&c** *to* om. **1363 quyt,** acquitted (freed).

"Yis, certes, lo, thise stories beren witnesse.
Whan thritty tirauntz ful of cursednesse
Hadde slayn Phidon in Atthenes atte feste,
They comanded his doghtres for t'areste,   1370
And bryngen hem biforn hem in despit,
Al naked, to fulfille hir foul delit,
And in hir fadres blood they made hem daunce
Upon the pavement, God yeve hem
          myschaunce!   1374
For which thise woful maydens, ful of drede,
Rather than they wolde lese hir maydenhede,
They prively been stirt into a welle
And dreynte hemselven, as the bookes telle.

"They of Mecene leete enquere and seke
Of Lacedomye fifty maydens eke,   1380
On whiche they wolden doon hir lecherye.
But was ther noon of al that compaignye
That she nas slayn, and with a good entente
Chees rather for to dye than assente
To been oppressed of hir maydenhede.   1385
Why sholde I thanne to dye been in drede?

"Lo, eek the tiraunt Aristoclides,
That loved a mayden heet Stymphalides,
Whan that hir fader slayn was on a nyght,
Unto Dianes temple goth she right   1390
And hente the ymage in hir handes two,
Fro which ymage wolde she nevere go.
No wight ne myghte hir handes of it arace
Til she was slayn right in the selve place.

"Now sith that maydens hadden swich despit
To been defouled with mannes foul delit,   1396
Wel oghte a wyf rather hirselven slee
Than be defouled, as it thynketh me.

"What shal I seyn of Hasdrubales wyf
That at Cartage birafte hirself hir lyf?   1400
For whan she saugh that Romayns wan the
          toun,
She took hir children alle and skipte adoun

Into the fyr, and chees rather to dye
Than any Romayn dide hire vileynye.

"Hath nat Lucresse yslayn hirself, allas,   1405
At Rome whan that she oppressed was
Of Tarquyn, for hire thoughte it was a shame
To lyven whan that she had lost hir name?

"The sevene maydens of Melesie also
Han slayn hemself for verrey drede and wo   1410
Rather than folk of Gawle hem sholde oppresse.
Mo than a thousand stories as I gesse
Koude I now telle as touchynge this mateere.

"Whan Habradate was slayn, his wyf so deere
Hirselven slow and leet hir blood to glyde   1415
In Habradates woundes depe and wyde,
And seyde, 'My body, at the leeste way,
Ther shal no wight defoulen, if I may.'

"What sholde I mo ensamples heerof sayn,
Sith that so manye han hemselven slayn   1420
Wel rather than they wolde defouled be?
I wol conclude that it is bet for me
To sleen myself than been defouled thus.
I wol be trewe unto Arveragus,
Or rather sleen myself in som manere,   1425
As dide Demociones doghter deere
By cause that she wolde nat defouled be.

"O Cedasus, it is ful greet pitee
To reden how thy doghtren deyde, allas,
That slowe hemself for swich a manere cas.   1430

"As greet a pitee was it, or wel moore,
The Theban mayden that for Nichanore
Hirselven slow right for swich manere wo.

"Another Theban mayden dide right so   1434
For oon of Macidonye hadde hire oppressed;
She with hire deeth hir maydenhede redressed.

"What shal I seye of Nicerates wyf
That for swich cas birafte hirself hir lyf?
How trewe eek was to Alcebiades
His love, that rather for to dyen chees   1440

1369 **Phidon,** this account and the 22 examples that follow—the sheer number has led some critics to accuse Chaucer of levity in a serious situation—are all from *Jerome adversus Jovinianum,* as is indicated by glosses in E. *atte:* E *at.* 1371 **despit,** cruelty (spite). 1377 **prively been stirt,** i.e., leaped without warning. 1379–80 **Mecene . . . Lacedomye,** Jerome reports that Messene and Sparta (Lacedaemonia) exchanged virgins in connection with religious observances. 1385 **oppressed,** ravished. 1391 **hente,** grasped. 1393 **arace,** tear away. 1395 **sith . . . despit,** since, abhorrence (spite). 1399 **Hasdrubales wyf,** when Scipio conquered Carthage, the king's wife burned herself and her children. 1406 **oppressed,** ravished, cf. *LGW* 1680ff. 1409 **Melesie,** Miletus, Asia Minor. 1410 E *verrey* om. 1411 **Gawle,** Galatians. 1430 EHg&c *a* om. 1434 **Theban mayden,** Jerome gives no name. These instances are all taken from Jerome, although some of them may be verified from other sources. Skeat in the notes to the Oxford edition (v, 395ff.) quotes the relevant passages from Jerome. 1435 **oppressed,** ravished. 1436 **redressed,** i.e., made up for.

Than for to suffre his body unburyed be.

    "Lo, which a wyf was Alceste," quod she.

"What seith Omer of goode Penalopee?

Al Grece knoweth of hire chastitee.

Pardee, of Laodomya is writen thus,   1445

That whan at Troie was slayn Protheselaus,

No lenger wolde she lyve after his day.

    "The same of noble Porcia telle I may;

Withoute Brutus koude she nat lyve,

To whom she hadde al hool hir herte yeve. 1450

    "The parfit wyfhod of Arthemesie

Honured is thurgh al the barbarie.

O Teuta, queene, thy wyfly chastitee

To alle wyves may a mirour bee.

The same thyng I seye of Bilyea,   1455

Of Rodogone, and eek Valeria."

    Thus pleyned Dorigen a day or tweye,

Purposynge evere that she wolde deye.

But nathelees, upon the thridde nyght   1459

Hoom cam Arveragus, this worthy knyght,

And asked hire why that she weep so soore,

And she gan wepen ever lenger the moore.

    "Allas," quod she, "that evere I was born!

Thus have I seyd," quod she, "thus have I

    sworn—"

And toold hym al as ye han herd bifore;   1465

It nedeth nat reherce it yow namoore.

    This housbonde with glad chiere in freendly

    wyse

Answerde and seyde as I shal yow devyse,

"Is ther oght elles, Dorigen, but this?"

    "Nay, nay," quod she, "God helpe me so as

    wys!   1470

This is to muche, and it were Goddes wille."

    "Ye, wyf," quod he, "lat slepen that is stille.

It may be wel, paraventure, yet today.

Ye shul youre trouthe holden, by my fay,

For God so wisly have mercy upon me,   1475

I hadde wel levere ystiked for to be,

For verray love which that I to yow have,

But if ye sholde youre trouthe kepe and save.

Trouthe is the hyeste thyng that man may

    kepe."

But with that word he brast anon to wepe, 1480

And seyde, "I yow forbede, up peyne of deeth,

That nevere whil thee lasteth lyf ne breeth

To no wight telle thou of this aventure.

As I may best I wol my wo endure,

Ne make no contenance of hevynesse,   1485

That folk of yow may demen harm or gesse."

    And forth he cleped a squier and a mayde:

"Gooth forth anon with Dorigen," he sayde,

"And bryngeth hire to swich a place anon."

They take hir leve and on hir wey they gon,

But they ne wiste why she thider wente.   1491

He nolde no wight tellen his entente.

    Paraventure an heep of yow, ywis,

Wol holden hym a lewed man in this,

That he wol putte his wyf in jupartie.   1495

Herkneth the tale er ye upon hire crie.

She may have bettre fortune than yow semeth;

And whan that ye han herd the tale, demeth.

    This squier, which that highte Aurelius,

On Dorigen that was so amorus,   1500

Of aventure happed hire to meete

Amydde the toun, right in the quykkest strete,

As she was bown to goon the wey forth right

Toward the gardyn ther as she had hight.

And he was to the gardyn-ward also,   1505

For wel he spyed whan she wolde go

Out of hir hous to any maner place.

But thus they mette, of aventure or grace,

And he saleweth hire with glad entente,

And asked of hire whiderward she wente. 1510

    And she answerde, half as she were mad,

"Unto the gardyn, as myn housbonde bad,

My trouthe for to holde, allas, allas!"

    Aurelius gan wondren on this cas,

And in his herte hadde greet compassioun 1515

Of hire and of hire lamentacioun,

1442 **Alceste,** died in her husband's place; this is the name of the heroine of *LGW* ll. 510ff. 1445 *Laodomya:* E&c *Lacedomya.* 1450 **al hool,** wholly. 1452 **barbarie,** heathendom. 1455–56 Lines found only in E and Additional 35286. 1457 E *pleyne.* 1467 **glad chiere,** pleasant expression. 1474 **trouthe,** troth (promise). 1476 **ystiked,** stabbed. 1480 **brast anon,** burst immediately. 1481 *of deeth:* E *of* om. 1485 **make . . . contenance of hevynesse,** give appearance of sorrow. 1486 **demen,** judge. 1491 **wiste,** knew. 1493–98 Lines only in E and Additional 35286. 1494 **lewed,** ignorant (stupid, evil). 1495 **jupartie,** jeopardy. 1496 **upon,** against. 1498 **demeth,** judge. 1501 **aventure happed,** chance happened. 1502 **quykkest,** busiest (most alive). 1503 **bown,** bound (preparing). 1504 **hight,** promised. 1509 **saleweth . . . glad entente,** greets, happy expectation. 1513 **trouthe . . . holde,** promise, keep. 1514 **cas,** case, situation.

And of Arveragus, the worthy knyght,
That bad hire holden al that she had hight,
So looth hym was his wyf sholde breke hir
   trouthe;
And in his herte he caughte of this greet routhe,
Considerynge the beste on every syde, 1521
That fro his lust yet were hym levere abyde
Than doon so heigh a cherlyssh wrecchednesse
Agayns franchise and alle gentillesse;
For which in fewe wordes seyde he thus: 1525
   "Madame, seyth to youre lord Arveragus
That sith I se his grete gentillesse
To yow, and eek I se wel youre distresse,
That him were levere han shame—and that
   were routhe—
Than ye to me sholde breke thus youre trouthe,
I have wel levere evere to suffre wo 1531
Than I departe the love bitwix yow two.
I yow relesse, madame, into youre hond
Quyt every serement and every bond
That ye han maad to me as heerbiforn, 1535
Sith thilke tyme which that ye were born.
My trouthe I plighte, I shal yow never repreve
Of no biheste, and heere I take my leve
As of the treweste and the beste wyf
That evere yet I knew in al my lyf. 1540
But every wyf be war of hire biheeste;
On Dorigen remembreth atte leeste.
Thus kan a squier doon a gentil dede
As wel as kan a knyght, withouten drede."
   She thonketh hym upon hir knees al bare, 1545
And hoom unto hir housbonde is she fare,
And tolde hym al, as ye han herd me sayd;
And be ye siker, he was so weel apayd
That it were inpossible me to wryte.
What sholde I lenger of this cas endyte? 1550
   Arveragus and Dorigen his wyf
In sovereyn blisse leden forth hir lyf.
Nevere eft ne was ther angre hem bitwene.

He cherisseth hire as though she were a
   queene,
And she was to hym trewe for everemoore. 1555
Of thise two folk ye gete of me namoore.
   Aurelius, that his cost hath al forlorn,
Curseth the tyme that evere he was born:
"Allas," quod he, "allas that I bihighte
Of pured gold a thousand pound of wighte 1560
Unto this philosophre. How shal I do?
I se namoore but that I am fordo.
Myn heritage moot I nedes selle
And been a beggere. Heere may I nat dwelle
And shamen al my kynrede in this place, 1565
But I of hym may gete bettre grace.
But nathelees, I wole of hym assaye,
At certeyn dayes, yeer by yeer, to paye,
And thanke hym of his grete curteisye.
My trouthe wol I kepe, I wol nat lye." 1570
   With herte soor he gooth unto his cofre,
And broghte gold unto this philosophre
The value of fyve hundred pound, I gesse,
And hym bisecheth of his gentillesse
To graunte hym dayes of the remenaunt, 1575
And seyde, "Maister, I dar wel make avaunt,
I failled nevere of my trouthe as yit.
For sikerly my dette shal be quyt
Towardes yow, howevere that I fare
To goon a-begged in my kirtle bare. 1580
But wolde ye vouchesauf, upon seuretee,
Two yeer or thre for to respiten me,
Thanne were I wel, for elles moot I selle
Myn heritage; ther is namoore to telle."
   This philosophre sobrely answerde, 1585
And seyde thus, whan he thise wordes herde,
"Have I nat holden covenant unto thee?"
   "Yes, certes, wel and trewely," quod he.
"Hastow nat had thy lady as thee liketh?"
"No, no," quod he, and sorwefully he siketh.
"What was the cause? Tel me if thou kan."

1518 **hight,** promised. 1520 **routhe,** pity. 1522 **lust . . . levere abyde,** desire (pleasure), rather refrain. 1523 **heigh,** great. 1524 **franchise,** frankness, sincerity. 1529 **levere . . . routhe,** rather, a pity. 1534 **serement,** oath (Fr. *sairement*). 1537 **repreve,** reproach (reprove). 1538 **biheste,** promise. 1541–44 Lines evidently again misplaced in EHg&c. In two late MSS they come after l. 1550; see Manly iv.488. 1541 **be war,** should beware. 1544 **withouten drede,** without doubt. 1548 **siker . . . apayd,** sure, pleased. 1556 E&c *two* om. 1557 **forlorn,** lost. 1559 **bihighte,** promised. 1560 **pured . . . wighte,** refined (pure), weight. 1562 **fordo,** i.e., "done for." 1566 **But I . . . grace,** unless I, consideration. 1567 **assaye,** try. 1575 **dayes of,** i.e., time to make payments. 1576 **avaunt,** boast. 1577 **trouthe,** promise (obligation). 1578 **sikerly . . . quyt,** certainly, acquitted (paid). 1579–80 **howevere . . . a-begged,** i.e., even if I have to go beg. **kirtle,** underwear. 1581 **vouchesauf . . . seuretee,** consent, security. 1582 **respiten,** respite (an extension of time to pay). 1587 **covenant,** my promise.

Aurelius his tale anon bigan, 1592
And tolde hym al as ye han herd bifoore;
It nedeth nat to yow reherce it moore.

He seide, "Arveragus, of gentillesse, 1595
Hadde levere dye in sorwe and in distresse
Than that his wyf were of hir trouthe fals."
The sorwe of Dorigen he tolde hym als,
How looth hire was to been a wikked wyf, 1599
And that she levere had lost that day hir lyf,
And that hir trouthe she swoor thurgh
    innocence,
She nevere erst hadde herd speke of apparence.
"That made me han of hire so greet pitee;
And right as frely as he sente hire me,
As frely sente I hire to hym ageyn. 1605
This al and som; ther is namoore to seyn."

This philosophre answerde, "Leeve brother,
Everich of yow dide gentilly til oother.

Thou art a squier, and he is a knyght;
But God forbede, for his blisful myght, 1610
But if a clerk koude doon a gentil dede
As wel as any of yow, it is no drede.

"Sire, I releesse thee thy thousand pound
As thou right now were cropen out of the
    ground
Ne nevere er now ne haddest knowen me. 1615
For, sire, I wol nat taken a peny of thee
For al my craft, ne noght for my travaille.
Thou hast ypayed wel for my vitaille.
It is ynogh, and farewel, have good day." 1619
And took his hors, and forth he goth his way.

Lordynges, this question, thanne, wol I aske
    now,
Which was the mooste fre, as thynketh yow?
Now telleth me, er that ye ferther wende.
I kan namoore; my tale is at an ende.

Heere is ended the Frankeleyns Tale.

1598 als, also. **1601 innocence,** i.e., lack of wisdom and caution. **1602 erst . . . apparence,** before, illusion. **1607 Leeve,** dear. **1612 drede,** doubt. **1614 As . . . cropen,** As if, crept. **1615 er now,** before. **1617 craft . . . travaille,** skill, work. **1618 vitaille,** food (expenses). **1622 fre,** generous. **1624 kan,** know.

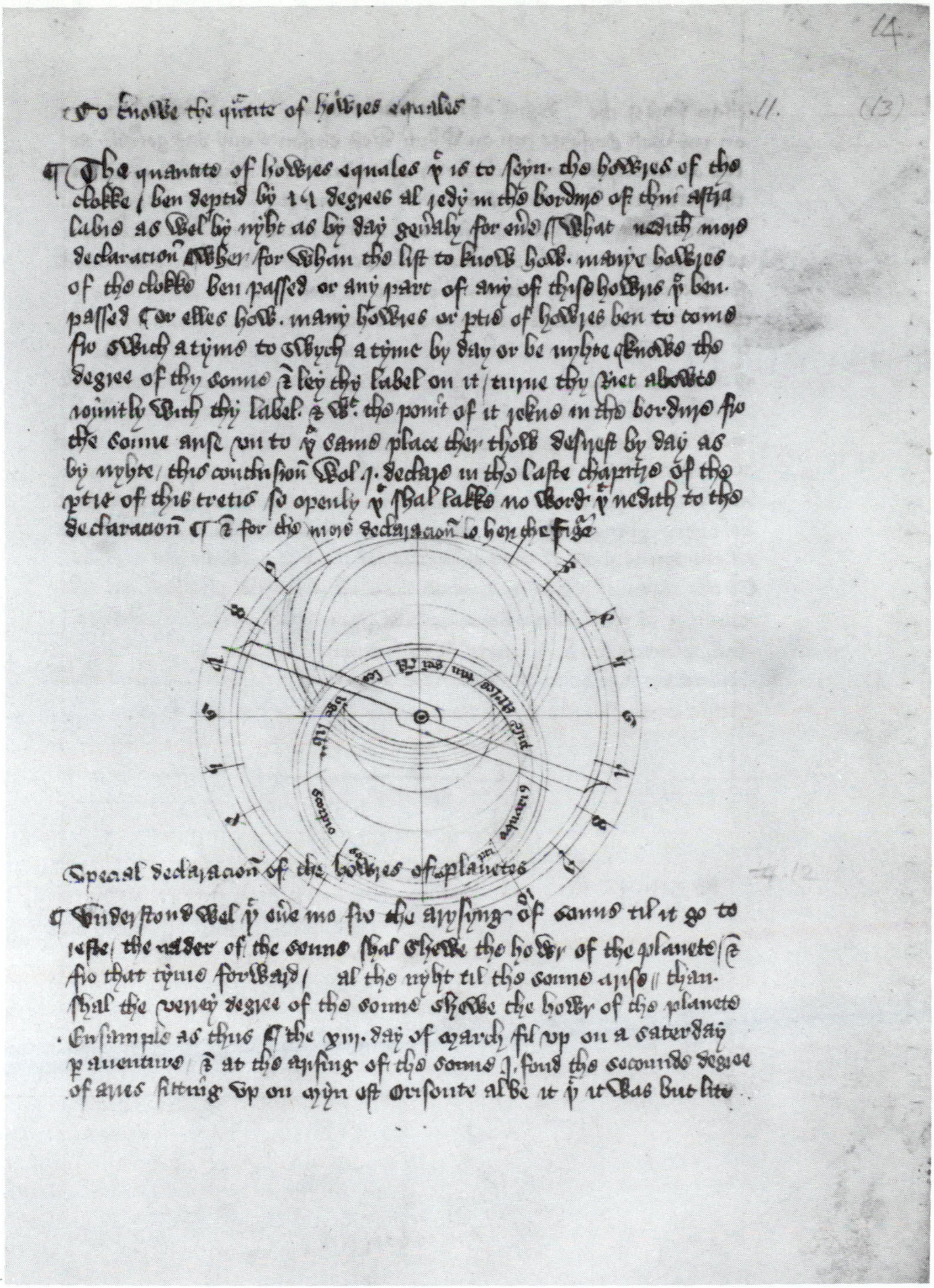

INTRODUCTION

Canterbury Tales, Part VI

HERE IS NO evidence where Part VI should come in the Canterbury sequence. The Physician's Tale begins without reference to narrator or the frame (the incipit and explicit are scribal, but the Physician is identified as the narrator in the Pardoner's Prologue), and is followed by a vividly dramatic prologue and tale. If the ten "parts" of the *Canterbury Tales* were really ten fascicles left on Chaucer's desk when he died, with no indication as to their order, it almost seems that this fascicle had been begun before he thought of the Canterbury frame, and was picked up and added to after he had begun work on the roadside drama.

Aesthetically it is quite satisfactory to leave Part VI in the Ellesmere order. The tale of Appius and Virginia is an appropriate sequel to Dorigen's lament about unfortunate women at the end of Part V. Chaucer's tale is based principally on the version in the *Roman de la Rose*, with some details taken from the ultimate source of all medieval versions, Livy's *History of Rome*. Emerson Brown, "What is Chaucer Doing with The Physician and His Tale?" *PQ* (1981) surveys the criticism.

The impersonal Physician's Tale leads into the vivdly personal Prologue of the Pardoner's

Tale. More that any other in the collection, the Pardoner and his Tale invite figurative interpretation. The eunuchism of the Pardoner (I.691) symbolizes the impotence of the pardons he sells. Like the Wife of Bath, the Pardoner adopts the confessional mode to reveal his own defects. The inspiration is again from the *Roman de la Rose*, this time the confession of Fals Semblant (Hypocrisy; ll.6135ff in the Middle English translation in this volume; Dunn-Robbins 52ff). Like the Friar's, Summoner's, and Canon's Yeoman's Tales, the Pardoner's Prologue is an exposé of fraud. Unlike these others, however, this does not represent merely individual transgression, but the corruption of the system. Chaucer never questions the Catholic Church's essential doctrine of penance and absolution. But circumvention of this honored sacrament by money payment to as cynical a mediary as the Pardoner was horrifying to thinking people of the time. A.L. Kellogg and L.A. Haselmayer in "Chaucer's Satire on the Pardoner," *PMLA* (1951), cite numerous admonitions from papal and episcopal encyclicals against exactly the sort of deceptions the Pardoner describes. But, as they point out, the authorities could not abolish the sale of pardons because the Church had allowed itself to become dependent on this revenue. It was the sale of pardons (Indulgences) that eventually led to Martin Luther's break with the Church of Rome.

The antithesis between impotent pardons and potent absolution is reinforced by the contrast between the vicious Pardoner and his virtuous sermon. The exemplum of the search for Death which forms the heart of the sermon is ultimately Oriental, but there are many medieval and modern analogues. The most interesting addition Chaucer makes is the Old Man (ll.710ff) who points the way to Death, who has been interpreted as Old Age, Death, or the Wandering Jew.

The conclusion of the tale re-emphasizes its contradictions. At l. 915 the Pardoner appears for a moment to be aware of the fraudulence of his merchandise in contrast to true salvation. Then—motivated by what demon no critic can explain—he invites the pilgrims to buy his pardons. This provokes the crudest rebuff of the pilgrimage. For a moment the Host loses control of himself, and the Knight, as the natural leader, has to intervene to restore peace. Melvin Storm, "The Pardoner's Invitation: Quaestor's Bag or Becket's Shrine," *PMLA* (1982), explores the significance of the Pardoner's performance. The summary of criticism by G.G. Sedgwick, "The Pardoner's Progress, 1880-1940," *MLQ* (1940), is continued by John Halverson, "Chaucer's Pardoner and the Progress of Criticism," *Chaucer Review* (1970).

Canterbury Tales

PART VI

PHYSICIAN'S TALE

Heere folweth the Phisiciens Tale.

Ther was, as telleth Titus Livius,
A knyght that called was Virginius,
Fulfild of honour and of worthynesse,
And strong of freendes and of greet richesse.

This knyght a doghter hadde by his wyf;   5
No children hadde he mo in al his lyf.
Fair was this mayde in excellent beautee
Aboven every wight that man may see,
For Nature hath with sovereyn diligence
Yformed hire in so greet excellence,   10
As though she wolde seyn, "Lo, I, Nature,
Thus kan I forme and peynte a creature
Whan that me list. Who kan me countrefete?
Pigmalion noght, though he ay forge and bete,

Or grave or peynte, for I dar wel seyn   15
Apelles, Zanzis, sholde werche in veyn
Outher to grave or peynte or forge or bete,
If they presumed me to countrefete.
For He that is the formere principal
Hath maked me his vicaire general,   20
To forme and peynten erthely creaturis
Right as me list, and ech thyng in my cure is
Under the moone that may wane and waxe,
And for my werk right no thyng wol I axe.
My lord and I been ful of oon accord.   25
I made hire to the worship of my lord.
So do I alle myne othere creatures,
What colour that they han or what figures."

1 **Titus Livius**, the story of Appius and Virginia goes back to the Roman historian Livy, but Chaucer evidently took this version from *RR*, 5589ff. (Dunn-Robbins 27.1ff.), with his own additions—see Introduction. 2 E *was called*; other MSS *cleped*. 6 *No children*: other MSS *And never*. 13 **countrefete**, emulate. 14–16 **Pigmalion . . . Apelles, Zanzis**, Pygmalion, Apelles, and Zeuxis are mentioned together as examples of famous artists in *RR* 1645–55 (Dunn-Robbins 78.140–50). 17 **Outher . . . grave**, either, carve. 19 **formere**, creator. 20 **vicaire general**, general deputy; this phrase is found in *RR*, 16768, 19505ff. (Dunn-Robbins 81.61, 91.1), and in Chaucer's *PF* 379, where it comes from Alanus ab Insulis, *De Planctu Naturæ*. 22 **me list . . . cure**, pleases me, charge. 26 **to the worship**, in honor of.

216

Thus semeth me that Nature wolde seye.
This mayde of age twelve yeer was and
   tweye, 30
In which that Nature hadde swich delit.
For right as she kan peynte a lilie whit
And reed a rose, right with swich peynture
She peynted hath this noble creature
Er she were born, upon hir lymes fre, 35
Where as by right swiche colours sholde be.
And Phebus dyed hath hire tresses grete
Lyk to the stremes of his burned heete.
And if that excellent was hire beautee,
A thousand foold moore vertuous was she. 40
In hire ne lakked no condicioun
That is to preyse, as by discrecioun.
As wel in goost as body chast was she,
For which she floured in virginitee
With alle humylitee and abstinence, 45
With alle attemperaunce and pacience,
With mesure eek of beryng and array.
Discreet she was in answeryng alway,
Though she were wis as Pallas, dar I seyn,
Hir facound eek ful wommanly and pleyn. 50
No countrefeted termes hadde she
To seme wys, but after hir degree
She spak, and alle hire wordes moore and lesse
Sownynge in vertu and in gentillesse. 54
Shamefast she was in maydens shamefastnesse,
Constant in herte, and evere in bisynesse
To dryve hire out of ydel slogardye.
Bacus hadde of hir mouth right no maistrie;
For wyn and youthe dooth Venus encresse
As men in fyr wol casten oille or greesse. 60
And of hir owene vertu, unconstreyned,
She hath ful ofte tyme syk hire feyned
For that she wolde fleen the compaignye
Where likly was to treten of folye,

As is at feestes, revels, and at daunces, 65
That been occasions of daliaunces.
Swich thynges maken children for to be
To soone rype and boold, as men may se,
Which is ful perilous and hath been yoore.
For al to soone may she lerne loore 70
Of booldnesse, whan she woxen is a wyf.
And ye maistresses, in youre olde lyf,
That lordes doghtres han in governaunce,
Ne taketh of my wordes no displesaunce.
Thenketh that ye been set in governynges 75
Of lordes doghtres oonly for two thynges,
Outher for ye han kept youre honestee,
Or elles ye han falle in freletee
And knowen wel ynough the olde daunce,
And han forsaken fully swich meschaunce 80
For everemo; therfore for Cristes sake,
To teche hem vertu looke that ye ne slake.
A theef of venysoun that hath forlaft
His likerousnesse and al his olde craft
Kan kepe a forest best of any man. 85
Now kepeth wel, for if ye wole, ye kan.
Looke wel that ye unto no vice assente
Lest ye be dampned for youre wikke entente,
For whoso dooth, a traitour is certeyn.
And taketh kepe of that that I shal seyn: 90
Of alle tresons sovereyn pestilence
Is whan a wight bitrayseth innocence.
Ye fadres and ye moodres eek also,
Though ye han children, be it oon or mo,
Youre is the charge of al hire surveiaunce 95
Whil that they been under youre governaunce.
Beth war if by ensample of youre lyvynge
Or by youre necligence in chastisynge
That they perisse; for I dar wel seye
If that they doon ye shul it deere abeye. 100
Under a shepherde softe and necligent

---

34 peynted, i.e., created the shape as well as the color. **35 fre,** gracious. **38 burned heete,** burnished heat (sunshine). **42 discrecioun,** discrimination. **43 goost,** spirit. **46 attemperaunce,** temperance. **47 mesure eek,** moderation also. **49 Pallas,** goddess of wisdom. EHg&c *as* om. **50 facound,** manner of speaking (eloquence). *and:* E *a.* **51 countrefeted,** pretentious (pretended). **52 degree,** station. **54 Sownynge,** resounding (reflecting). **55 Shamefast,** modest. E *in* om. **56 Constant,** steadfast. **57 hire . . . slogardye,** herself, laziness. **58 Bacus,** god of wine. **59 Venus,** i.e., sexual desire. Some MSS *will and thought.* **60 men:** E *man.* **62 syk . . . feyned,** ill, pretended. **66 daliaunces,** amorous play. **69 yoore,** long (always). **72 maistresses,** governesses. **77 honestee,** virtue. **78 falle in freletee,** fallen in weakness. **79 olde daunce,** i.e., lovemaking. **80 meschaunce,** misconduct. **82 slake,** slack. For this line some MSS have *Kepeth wel tho that ye undertake.* **83 theef of venysoun . . . forlaft,** poacher, left off (*for* is an intensifier). **84 likerousnesse,** greed (lecherousness). **85 kepe,** protect. **88 dampned . . . wikke entente,** condemned, wicked intention. **91 sovereyn pestilence,** supreme wickedness. **92 bitrayseth,** betrays. **94 mo:** E&c *two.* **95 surveiaunce,** surveillance (protection). **97–99 if . . . perisse:** other MSS *that . . . ne perisse.* **100 deere abeye,** dearly pay for. *deere:* some MSS *sore.*

The wolf hath many a sheep and lamb torent.
Suffiseth oon ensample now as heere,
For I moot turne agayn to my matere.

   This mayde, of which I wol this tale expresse,
So kepte hirself hir neded no maistresse,   106
For in hir lyvyng maydens myghten rede
As in a book every good word or dede
That longeth to a mayden vertuous,
She was so prudent and so bounteuous.   110
For which the fame out sprong on every syde
Bothe of hir beautee and hir bountee wyde,
That thurgh that land they preised hire echone
That loved vertu, save Envye allone
That sory is of oother mennes wele,   115
And glad is of his sorwe and his unheele—
The doctour maketh this descripcioun.

   This mayde upon a day wente in the toun
Toward a temple, with hire mooder deere,
As is of yonge maydens the manere.   120

   Now was ther thanne a justice in that toun
That governour was of that regioun.
And so bifel this juge his eyen caste
Upon this mayde, avysynge hym ful faste
As she cam forby ther as this juge stood.   125
Anon his herte chaunged and his mood,
So was he caught with beautee of this mayde,
And so hymself ful pryvely he sayde,
"This mayde shal be myn, for any man!"

   Anon the feend into his herte ran   130
And taughte hym sodeynly that he by slyghte
The mayden to his purpos wynne myghte.
For certes, by no force ne by no meede,
Hym thoughte, he was nat able for to speede.
For she was strong of freendes and eek she   135
Confermed was in swich soverayn bountee
That wel he wiste he myghte hire nevere wynne
As for to make hire with hir body synne.
For which, by greet deliberacioun,

He sente after a cherl, was in the toun,   140
Which that he knew for subtil and for boold.
This juge unto this cherl his tale hath toold
In secree wise, and made hym to ensure
He sholde telle it to no creature,
And if he dide, he sholde lese his heed.   145
Whan that assented was this cursed reed,
Glad was this juge, and maked him greet
   cheere,
And yaf hym yiftes preciouse and deere.

   Whan shapen was al hire conspiracie
Fro point to point, how that his lecherie   150
Parfourned sholde been ful subtilly,
As ye shul heere it after openly,
Hoom gooth the cherl, that highte Claudius.
This false juge, that highte Apius—
So was his name, for this is no fable,   155
But knowen for historial thyng notable;
The sentence of it sooth is out of doute—
This false juge gooth now faste aboute
To hasten his delit al that he may.

   And so bifel soone after on a day   160
This false juge, as telleth us the storie,
As he was wont, sat in his consistorie,
And yaf his doomes upon sondry cas.
This false cherl cam forth a ful greet pas,
And seyde, "Lord, if that it be youre wille,   165
As dooth me right upon this pitous bille
In which I pleyne upon Virginius;
And if that he wol seyn it is nat thus,
I wol it preeve and fynde good witnesse
That sooth is that my bille wol expresse."   170

   The juge answerde, "Of this, in his absence,
I may nat yeve diffynytyve sentence.
Lat do hym calle, and I wol gladly heere.
Thou shalt have al right and no wrong heere."

   Virginius cam to wite the juges wille,   175
And right anon was rad this cursed bille.

---

102 torent, torn to pieces. **103–4** Lines lacking in E. **105** *wol:* some MSS *telle.* **106 kepte . . . maistresse,** took care of, governess. **109 longeth,** belongs. **110 bounteuous,** excellent. **115 wele,** prosperity. **116 unheele,** misfortune. **117 doctour,** EHg have a marginal gloss *Augustinius,* and PsT x.484 reads "and after the word of Seint Augustyn it is sorwe of oother mennes wele, and joye of othere mennes harm." **124 avysynge hym ful faste,** apprising himself intently (i.e., staring at her). **125 forby,** past. **129 for,** in spite of. **130 Anon,** at once. **131 slyghte,** trickery. **133 meede,** bribery. **136 soverayn bountee,** supreme goodness. **139 by,** with. **140 cherl,** rascal. Some MSS *clerk,* but cf. *RR,* 5596, "Li ribauz" (Dunn-Robbins 27.8, "The ribald"). **146 reed,** plan. **147 maked . . . cheere,** i.e., "was nice to." **149 shapen,** planned out. **151 subtilly,** secretly. **153 highte,** was named. **156 historial,** historical (true). **157 sentence . . . sooth,** substance, true. **162 wont . . . consistorie,** accustomed, law court. **163 doomes,** judgments. **164 ful greet pas,** hurriedly. **166 bille,** list (of complaints). **167 pleyne,** complain. **170 sooth,** true. **172 diffynytyve,** final. **175 wite,** know. **176 rad,** read out.

The sentence of it was as ye shul heere:
"To yow, my lord, sire Apius so deere,
Sheweth youre poure servant Claudius
How that a knyght, called Virginius,   180
Agayns the lawe, agayn al equitee,
Holdeth, expres agayn the wyl of me,
My servant, which that is my thral by right,
Which fro myn hous was stole upon a nyght,
Whil that she was ful yong—this wol I
     preeve   185
By witnesse, lord, so that it nat yow greeve.
She nys his doghter nat, what so he seye.
Wherfore to yow, my lord the juge, I preye,
Yeld me my thral, if that it be youre wille."
Lo, this was al the sentence of his bille.   190

    Virginius gan upon the cherl biholde,
But hastily, er he his tale tolde
And wolde have preeved it as sholde a knyght,
And eek by witnessyng of many a wight,
That al was fals that seyde his adversarie,   195
This cursed juge wolde nothyng tarie
Ne heere a word moore of Virginius,
But yaf his juggement, and seyde thus:
"I deeme anon this cherl his servant have;
Thou shalt no lenger in thyn hous hir save.   200
Go bryng hire forth and put hire in oure warde.
The cherl shal have his thral. This I awarde."

    And whan this worthy knyght Virginius
Thurgh sentence of this justice Apius
Moste by force his deere doghter yeven   205
Unto the juge, in lecherie to lyven,
He gooth hym hoom and sette him in his halle,
And leet anon his deere doghter calle,
And with a face deed as asshen colde
Upon hir humble face he gan biholde,   210
With fadres pitee stikynge thurgh his herte,
Al wolde he from his purpos nat converte.

    "Doghter," quod he, "Virginia, by thy name,
Ther been two weyes, outher deeth or shame,
That thou most suffre. Allas, that I was bore!

For nevere thou deservedest wherfore   216
To dyen with a swerd or with a knyf.
O deere doghter, endere of my lyf,
Which I have fostred up with swich plesaunce
That thou were nevere out of my
     remembraunce!   220
O doghter, which that art my laste wo,
And in my lyf my laste joye also,
O gemme of chastitee, in pacience
Take thou thy deeth, for this is my sentence.
For love, and nat for hate, thou most be
     deed;   225
My pitous hand moot smyten of thyn heed.
Allas, that evere Apius the say!
Thus hath he falsly jugged the today."
And tolde hire al the cas, as ye bifore
Han herd; nat nedeth for to telle it moore.   230

    "O mercy, deere fader!" quod this mayde,
And with that word she bothe hir armes layde
Aboute his nekke, as she was wont to do.
The teeris bruste out of hir eyen two,
And seyde, "Goode fader, shal I dye?   235
Is ther no grace, is ther no remedye?"

    "No, certes, deere doghter myn," quod he.

    "Thanne yif me leyser, fader myn," quod
    she,
"My deeth for to compleyne a litel space;
For, pardee, Jepte yaf his doghter grace   240
For to compleyne er he hir slow, allas!
And God it woot, nothyng was hir trespas
But for she ran hir fader first to see
To welcome hym with greet solempnitee."
And with that word she fil aswowne anon,   245
And after whan hir swownyng is agon
She riseth up and to hir fader sayde,
"Blissed be God that I shal dye a mayde.
Yif me my deeth er that I have a shame.
Dooth with youre child youre wyl, a Goddes
    name!"   250
And with that word she preyed hym ful ofte

---

181 **equitee,** justice. 182 **expres,** specifically. 183 **thral,** slave. 185 **preeve,** prove. 186 **greeve,** displease (grieve). 187 **what so,** whatever. 191 **biholde,** i.e., stare. 192 **er he,** before he (Virginius). 195 *al:* EHg&c *it.* 196 **nothyng tarie,** i.e., wait for nothing. 199 **deeme anon,** adjudge, at once. 200 **save,** keep. 201 **warde,** wardship, custody. 204 *sentence:* some MSS *thassent.* 207 **halle,** main hall of the mansion. All versions except Chaucer's have Virginia killed in the public square before the people. 208 **leet . . . calle,** had, called. 212 **converte,** change. 215 **bore,** born. 218 **endere,** one who ends. 219 **plesaunce,** pleasure. 223 *of:* E *o.* 227 **say,** saw. 238 **leyser,** leisure (time). 240 **Jepte,** Jephthah in Judg. 11:30ff. vowed, if he were given victory in battle, to sacrifice whoever came out of his house first to meet him. His daughter was the one, and he allowed her two months to bewail her fate. 243 *first:* EHg&c *for;* in other MSS om.

That with his swerd he wolde smyte softe.
And with that word aswowne doun she fil.
Hir fader, with ful sorweful herte and wil,
Hir heed of smoot, and by the top it hente, 255
And to the juge he gan it to presente
As he sat yet in doom in consistorie.
And whan the juge it saugh, as seith the storie,
He bad to take hym and anhange hym faste.
But right anon a thousand peple in thraste 260
To save the knyght, for routhe and for pitee,
For knowen was the false iniquitee.
The peple anon had suspect in this thyng,
By manere of the cherles chalangyng,
That it was by the assent of Apius; 265
They wisten wel that he was lecherus.
For which unto this Apius they gon
And caste hym in a prisoun right anon,
Ther as he slow hymself; and Claudius,
That servant was unto this Apius, 270

Was demed for to hange upon a tree,
But that Virginius of his pitee
So preyde for hym that he was exiled,
And elles, certes, he had been bigyled.
The remenant were anhanged, moore and
    lesse, 275
That were consentant of this cursednesse.
  Heere may men seen how synne hath his
    merite.
Beth war, for no man woot whom God wol
    smyte
In no degree, ne in which manere wyse
The worm of conscience may agryse 280
Of wikked lyf, though it so pryvee be
That no man woot therof but God and he.
For be he lewed man or ellis lered
He noot how soone that he shal been afered.
Therfore I rede yow this conseil take: 285
Forsaketh synne er synne yow forsake.

Heere endeth the Phisiciens Tale.

255 **hente**, took. 257 **doom . . . consistorie**, judgment, court. 260 **thraste**, thrust. 263 *had/in*: E *hath/of*. 269 **slow**, slew (killed). *Ther as*: some MSS *Wher as*. 271 **demed**, judged (sentenced). 272 Some MSS *greet pitee*. 274 **bigyled**, tricked (out of his life). 276 **consentant**, consenting. 277 **his merite**, its reward. 279 **degree . . . wyse**, i.e., of what class or in what manner. 280 **agryse**, be terrified of. 281 **pryvee**, secret. 283 **lewed . . . lered**, ignorant, learned. 284 **afered**, terrified (by the approach of death). 285 **rede**, advise. 286 **yow forsake**, i.e., leaves you (damned), cf. PsT x.93.

PARDONER'S TALE

PROLOGUE

The wordes of the Hoost to the Phisicien and the Pardoner.

Oure Hooste gan to swere as he were wood,
"Harrow," quod he, "by nayles and by blood!
This was a fals cherl and a fals justise.
As shameful deeth as herte may devyse   290
Come to thise false juges and hire advocatz.
Algate this sely mayde is slayn, allas!
Allas, to deere boughte she beautee!
Wherfore I seye al day as men may see
That yiftes of Fortune and of Nature   295
Been cause of deeth to many a creature.
Of bothe yiftes that I speke of now
Men han ful ofte moore for harm than prow.

   "But trewely, myn owene maister deere,   301

This is a pitous tale for to heere.
But nathelees, passe over, is no fors.
I pray to God so save thy gentil cors,
And eek thyne urynals and thy jurdones,   305
Thyn ypocras, and eek thy galiones,
And every boyste ful of thy letuarie;
God blesse hem, and oure lady Seinte Marie.

   "So moot I theen, thou art a propre man,
And lyk a prelat, by Seint Ronyan!   310
Seyde I nat wel? I kan nat speke in terme;
But wel I woot thou doost myn herte to erme
That I almoost have caught a cardynacle.
By corpus bones, but I have triacle,

287–328 Manly IV.78ff. finds two versions of the Physician-Pardoner link, that in EHg&c and an earlier from Harl 7334&c. The main difference in the latter is in ll. 289–92: *This was a cursed thef, a fals justice. | As schendful deth as herte can devise | So falle upon his body and his bones. | The devel I bykenne him al at oones.* **287 wood,** crazy. **288 Harrow,** exclamation from an ancient Norman warning cry. **nayles . . . blood,** the strongest oaths were for centuries those related to the Crucifixion. **291 advocatz,** attorneys. *false juges,* Hg&c *false* om. **292 Algate . . . sely,** at any rate, innocent (blessed). **297–98** Many editions insert here a couplet from the early version: *Hir beaute was hir deth, I dar wel sayn. | Allas, so pitously as she was slain!* The early version of the link ends with l. 298, but there are a number of variations in its readings through l. 328. **300 prow,** profit. **303 fors,** matter. **304 cors,** body. **305 jurdones,** chamber pots. **306 ypocras . . . galiones,** medicines named for the famous physicians Hippocrates and Galen; the former was a recognized term; the latter is evidently Herry Bailley's invention. **307 boyste . . . letuarie,** box, electuary (medicine in syrup). **309 theen,** prosper. **310 Ronyan,** a Scottish saint, Ronan, but taken to be *double entendre* on *runnion,* kidney, sexual organ. **311 terme,** in learned terms. **312 erme,** grieve. **313 cardynacle,** evidently the Host's error, which many MSS correct to *cardiacle,* heart attack. **314 corpus bones,** an ignorant mistake for *Corpus Dei.* **triacle,** medicine.

Or elles a draughte of moyste and corny ale, 315
Or but I heere anon a myrie tale,
Myn herte is lost for pitee of this mayde.
Thou beel amy, thou Pardoner," he sayde,
"Telle us som myrthe or japes right anon."
  "It shal be doon," quod he, "by Seint
    Ronyon. 320
But first," quod he, "heere at this ale stake

I wol bothe drynke and eten of a cake."
  And right anon thise gentils gonne to crye,
"Nay, lat hym telle us of no ribaudye! 324
Telle us som moral thyng that we may leere
Som wit, and thanne wol we gladly heere."
  "I graunte, ywis," quod he, "but I moot
    thynke
Upon som honest thyng while that I drynke."

Heere folweth the Prologe of the Pardoners Tale.

Lordynges, quod he, in chirches whan I
    preche,
I peyne me to han an hauteyn speche 330
And rynge it out as round as gooth a belle,
For I kan al by rote that I telle.
My theme is alwey oon, and evere was:
Radix malorum est cupiditas.
  First I pronounce whennes that I come, 335
And thanne my bulles shewe I, alle and some.
Oure lige lordes seel on my patente,
That shewe I first my body to warente,
That no man be so boold, ne preest ne clerk,
Me to destourbe of Cristes hooly werk. 340
And after that thanne telle I forth my tales.
Bulles of popes and of cardynales,
Of patriarkes and bisshopes I shewe,
And in Latyn I speke a wordes fewe,
To saffron with my predicacioun, 345
And for to stire hem to devocioun.
Thanne shewe I forth my longe cristal stones,
Ycrammed ful of cloutes and of bones—
Relikes been they, as wenen they echoon.
Thanne have I in latoun a sholder-boon 350
Which that was of an hooly Jewes sheep.
"Goode men," I seye, "taak of my wordes keep;

If that this boon be wasshe in any welle,
If cow, or calf, or sheep, or oxe swelle
That any worm hath ete or worm ystonge, 355
Taak water of that welle and wassh his tonge,
And it is hool anon; and forthermoor,
Of pokkes and of scabbe and every soor
Shal every sheep be hool that of this welle
Drynketh a draughte. Taak kepe eek what I
    telle: 360
If that the goode man that the beestes oweth
Wol every wyke, er that the cok hym croweth,
Fastynge, drynken of this welle a draughte,
As thilke hooly Jew oure eldres taughte,
His beestes and his stoor shal multiplie. 365
  "And, sires, also it heeleth jalousie;
For though a man be falle in jalous rage,
Lat maken with this water his potage,
And nevere shal he moore his wyf mystriste,
Though he the soothe of hir defaute wiste, 370
Al had she taken preestes two or thre.
  "Heere is a miteyn eek, that ye may se.
He that his hand wol putte in this mitayn,
He shal have multiplyng of his grayn,
Whan he hath sowen, be it whete or otes— 375
So that he offre pens, or elles grotes.

315 **moyste and corny,** fresh. 316 **anon,** immediately. 318 **beel amy,** Fr. feminine, *belle amie,* sweetheart. Some MSS *John Pardoner.* 319 **japes,** jokes. 321 **ale stake,** projecting pole hung with a garland or bush as the sign of an alehouse. 323 **gentils,** gentlefolk. 324 **ribaudye,** ribaldry (coarse humor). 325 **leere,** learn. 328 **Upon . . . honest,** about, moral. 330 **peyne me . . . hauteyn,** take pains, dignified. 332 **kan . . . by rote,** know, by heart. 333–34 These lines appear between 346–47 in some MSS. 333 **oon,** one (the same). 334 *malorum:* some MSS *omnium malorum.* 335 **pronounce whennes,** tell whence (i.e., Rome). 336 **bulles,** official documents (from Lat. *bulla,* seal). 337 **lige lordes seel . . . patente,** pope's seal, licence (short for "letters patent," i.e., to be shown publicly). 338 **my body to warente,** to protect myself. 339 **ne . . . ne,** neither, nor. 345 **saffron,** yellow condiment used to spice and adorn food. **predicacioun,** preaching. 346 *hem:* some MSS *men/folke.* 347 **cristal,** cf. I.700. 348 **cloutes,** rags. 349 **wenen,** believe. 350 **latoun,** brass. E&c *I* om. 352 **keep,** heed. 355 **worm,** snake. 358 **pokkes,** pox. 361 **oweth,** owns. 362 **wyke,** week. 364 **thilke,** the same. 365 **stoor,** livestock. 366 EHg&c *sire.* 368 **potage,** soup. 370 **soothe . . . defaute,** truth, fault. 371 **Al,** although. 372 **miteyn,** mitten. 376 **pens . . . grotes,** pence, groats (silver coins worth fourpence).

"Goode men and wommen, o thyng warne I
    yow:
If any wight be in this chirche now
That hath doon synne horrible, that he
Dar nat for shame of it yshryven be,   380
Or any womman, be she yong or old,
That hath ymaked hir housbonde cokewold,
Swich folk shal have no power ne no grace
To offren to my relikes in this place.   384
And whoso fyndeth hym out of swich blame,
They wol come up and offre in Goddes name,
And I assoille hem by the auctoritee
Which that by bulle ygraunted was to me."

    By this gaude have I wonne, yeer by yeer,
An hundred mark sith I was pardoner.   390
I stonde lyk a clerk in my pulpet,
And whan the lewed peple is doun yset,
I preche so as ye han herd bifoore,
And telle an hundred false japes moore.   394
Thanne peyne I me to strecche forth the nekke,
And est and west upon the peple I bekke,
As dooth a dowve sittynge on a berne.
Myne handes and my tonge goon so yerne
That it is joye to se my bisynesse.
Of avarice and of swich cursednesse   400
Is al my prechyng, for to make hem free
To yeven hir pens, and namely unto me,
For myn entente is nat but for to wynne,
And nothyng for correccioun of synne.   404
I rekke nevere, whan that they been beryed,
Though that hir soules goon a-blakeberyed!
For certes, many a predicacioun
Comth ofte tyme of yvel entencioun;
Som for plesance of folk and flaterye,
To been avaunced by ypocrisye,   410
And som for veyne glorie, and som for hate.
For whan I dar noon oother weyes debate,

Thanne wol I stynge hym with my tonge
    smerte
In prechyng, so that he shal nat asterte
To been defamed falsly, if that he   415
Hath trespased to my bretheren or to me.
For though I telle noght his propre name,
Men shal wel knowe that it is the same
By signes and by othere circumstances.
Thus quyte I folk that doon us displesances;   420
Thus spitte I out my venym under hewe
Of hoolynesse, to semen hooly and trewe.
    But shortly myn entente I wol devyse:
I preche of nothyng but for coveityse.
Therfore my theme is yet, and evere was,   425
Radix malorum est cupiditas.
Thus kan I preche agayn that same vice
Which that I use, and that is avarice.
But though myself be gilty in that synne,
Yet kan I maken oother folk to twynne   430
From avarice, and soore to repente.
But that is nat my principal entente—
I preche nothyng but for coveitise.
Of this mateere it oghte ynogh suffise.
    Thanne telle I hem ensamples many oon   435
Of olde stories longe tyme agoon.
For lewed peple loven tales olde;
Swiche thynges kan they wel reporte and holde.
What, trowe ye the whiles I may preche,
And wynne gold and silver for I teche,   440
That I wol lyve in poverte wilfully?
Nay, nay, I thoghte it nevere, trewely,
For I wol preche and begge in sondry landes;
I wol nat do no labour with myne handes,
Ne make baskettes and lyve therby,   445
By cause I wol nat beggen ydelly.
I wol noon of the apostles countrefete;
I wol have moneie, wolle, chese, and whete,

---

380 yshryven, absolved. **382 cokewold**, cuckold. Other MSS *ymaad/made*. **384 offren**, make offering. **385 fyndeth hym out**, i.e., is not guilty. *blame:* E *fame*. **386** *They:* Hg&c *He. in:* E&c *on/a*. **387 assoille**, (will) absolve. **389 gaude**, trick. **390 mark**, formerly worth two-thirds of a pound. **392 lewed**, ignorant (lay). **394 japes**, tricks. **395 peyne I**, I am careful. **396 bekke**, nod. **397 berne**, barn. **398 yerne**, eagerly. **399 bisynesse**, gesticulation (as in "stage business"). **401 free**, open-handed. **402 namely**, especially. **403 wynne**, accumulate. **405 rekke . . . beryed**, care, buried. **406 a-blakeberyed**, a-blackberrying. **407 predicacioun**, sermon (preaching). **409 plesance**, pleasing. **412 debate**, fight. **414 asterte**, escape. **416 trespased**, injured. **420 quyte**, requite (repay). **423 devyse**, reveal. **426** *Radix malorum*, The root of evil is cupidity—the love of money. I Tim. 6:10. **430 twynne**, separate. **437 lewed**, ignorant. **438 reporte . . . holde**, repeat, remember. **439 trowe**, believe. **441 wilfully**, voluntarily. Voluntary poverty had become a major issue in the church by the 14th century; see WBT III.1179ff. and notes. **444 labour with . . . handes**, like voluntary poverty, manual labor had been one of the ideals of original monastic Christianity; see I.187 and note. **447 countrefete**, imitate.

Al were it yeven of the povereste page,
Or of the povereste wydwe in a village,   450
Al sholde hir children sterve for famyne.
Nay, I wol drynke licour of the vyne
And have a joly wenche in every toun.
   But herkneth, lordynges, in conclusioun:
Youre likyng is that I shal telle a tale.   455

Now have I dronke a draughte of corny ale,
By God, I hope I shal yow telle a thyng
That shal by reson been at youre likyng.
For though myself be a ful vicious man,
A moral tale yet I yow telle kan,   460
Which I am wont to preche for to wynne.
Now hoold youre pees; my tale I wol bigynne.

Heere bigynneth the Pardoners Tale.

In Flaundres whilom was a compaignye
Of yonge folk that haunteden folye,
As riot, hasard, stywes, and tavernes,   465
Where as with harpes, lutes, and gyternes
They daunce and pleyen at dees bothe day and
   nyght,
And eten also and drynken over hir myght,
Thurgh which they doon the devel sacrifise
Withinne that develes temple in cursed wise
By superfluytee abhomynable.   471
Hir othes been so grete and so dampnable
That it is grisly for to heere hem swere.
Oure blissed Lordes body they totere—
Hem thoughte that Jewes rente hym noght
   ynough—   475
And ech of hem at otheres synne lough.
And right anon thanne comen tombesteres
Fetys and smale, and yonge frutesteres,
Syngeres with harpes, baudes, wafereres,
Whiche been the verray develes officeres   480
To kyndle and blowe the fyr of lecherye
That is annexed unto glotonye.
   The hooly writ take I to my witnesse
That luxurie is in wyn and dronkenesse.
Lo, how that dronken Looth, unkyndely,   485
Lay by his doghtres two, unwityngly;

So dronke he was, he nyste what he wroghte.
Herodes, whoso wel the stories soghte,
Whan he of wyn was repleet at his feeste,
Right at his owene table he yaf his heeste   490
To sleen the Baptist John, ful giltelees.
   Senec seith a good word doutelees;
He seith he kan no difference fynde
Bitwix a man that is out of his mynde
And a man which that is dronkelewe   495
But that woodnesse, fallen in a shrewe,
Persevereth lenger than dooth dronkenesse.
O glotonye, ful of cursednesse!
O cause first of oure confusioun!
O original of oure dampnacioun,   500
Til Crist hadde boght us with his blood agayn!
Lo, how deere, shortly for to sayn,
Aboght was thilke cursed vileynye!
Corrupt was al this world for glotonye.
   Adam oure fader and his wyf also   505
Fro Paradys to labour and to wo
Were dryven for that vice, it is no drede.
For whil that Adam fasted, as I rede,
He was in Paradys; and whan that he
Eet of the fruyt deffended on the tree,   510
Anon he was out cast to wo and peyne.
O glotonye, on thee wel oghte us pleyne!

---

449 of . . . page, by, servant. **451 Al . . . sterve,** even though, die. **452 vyne,** wine was much more expensive than beer. **463 Flaundres,** Flanders, in present Belgium. **whilom,** once (formerly). **464 haunteden,** haunted, practiced. **465 riot, hasard, stywes,** wild parties, gambling, brothels. **466 gyternes,** guitars. **468 over hir myght,** beyond their strength. **471 superfluytee,** overindulgence. **474 totere,** tear. Oaths were traditionally thought to tear Christ's body to pieces; this idea was related to the fact that oaths were so often upon aspects of the Crucifixion. **476 lough,** laughed. **477–78 tombesteres . . . frutesteres,** female tumblers and fruit peddlers ("ster" is a feminine suffix, cf. tappster, spinster, Baxter). **Fetys,** shapely. **479 baudes, wafereres,** procurers, cake peddlers. **484 luxurie,** lechery. **485 Looth, unkyndely,** Lot, unnaturally, Gen. 19:30–38. **488 whoso . . . soghte,** i.e., whoever might seek out his story. **490 heeste,** command, Matt. 14:1–12. **492 Senec,** Seneca (in his *Letters,* no. 83). **495 dronkelewe,** habitually drunk. **496 shrewe,** twisted personality. **499 cause first,** i.e., Adam, Eve, and the apple. **501 boght,** redeemed. **510 deffended,** forbidden. Hg&c *a tree.*

O, wiste a man how manye maladyes
Folwen of excesse and of glotonyes,
He wolde been the moore mesurable   515
Of his diete, sittynge at his table.
Allas, the shorte throte, the tendre mouth,
Maketh that est and west and north and south,
In erthe, in eir, in water, men to swynke
To gete a glotoun deyntee mete and drynke. 520
Of this matiere, O Paul, wel kanstow trete:
"Mete unto wombe, and wombe eek unto
         mete,
Shal God destroyen bothe," as Paulus seith.
Allas, a foul thyng is it, by my feith,
To seye this word, and fouler is the dede,   525
Whan man so drynketh of the white and rede
That of his throte he maketh his pryvee
Thurgh thilke cursed superfluitee.

   The apostel wepyng seith ful pitously,
"Ther walken manye of whiche yow toold
         have I—   530
I seye it now wepyng, with pitous voys—
They been enemys of Cristes croys,
Of whiche the ende is deeth; wombe is hir
         god!"
O wombe, O bely, O stynkyng cod,
Fulfilled of donge and of corrupcioun!   535
At either ende of thee foul is the soun.
How greet labour and cost is thee to fynde!
Thise cookes, how they stampe and streyne
         and grynde
And turnen substaunce into accident
To fulfille al thy likerous talent.   540
Out of the harde bones knokke they
The mary, for they caste noght awey
That may go thurgh the golet softe and swoote.
Of spicerie of leef and bark and roote
Shal been his sauce ymaked by delit,   545

To make hym yet a newer appetit.
But certes, he that haunteth swiche delices
Is deed whil that he lyveth in tho vices.
   A lecherous thyng is wyn, and dronkenesse
Is ful of stryvyng and of wrecchednesse.   550
O dronke man, disfigured is thy face,
Sour is thy breeth, foul artow to embrace,
And thurgh thy dronke nose semeth the soun
As though thou seydest ay "Sampsoun,
         Sampsoun."
And yet, God woot, Sampsoun drank nevere no
         wyn.   555
Thou fallest as it were a styked swyn;
Thy tonge is lost, and al thyn honeste cure;
For dronkenesse is verray sepulture
Of mannes wit and his discrecioun.
In whom that drynke hath dominacioun   560
He kan no conseil kepe, it is no drede.
Now kepe yow fro the white and fro the rede,
And namely fro the white wyn of Lepe,
That is to selle in Fysshstrete or in Chepe.
This wyn of Spaigne crepeth subtilly   565
In othere wynes, growynge faste by,
Of which ther ryseth swich fumositee
That whan a man hath dronken draughtes thre,
And weneth that he be at hoom in Chepe,
He is in Spaigne right at the toune of Lepe—
Nat at the Rochele, ne at Burdeux toun—   571
And thanne wol he seye "Sampsoun,
         Sampsoun!"
   But herkneth, lordynges, o word I yow preye,
That alle the sovereyn actes, dar I seye,
Of victories in the Olde Testament,   575
Thurgh verray God that is omnipotent,
Were doon in abstinence and in preyere.
Looketh the Bible and ther ye may it leere.
   Looke Attilla, the grete conquerour,   579

---

513 **wiste,** if a person knew. 515 **mesurable,** moderate. 519 **swynk,** work. 522 **wombe,** stomach; cf. Paul, I Cor. 6:13. 523 Some MSS *Paule us.* 526 **white and rede,** wine. 527 **pryvee,** privy (by vomiting). 532 *They:* EHg&c *Ther;* other MSS *That they.* 533 **wombe,** stomach; cf. Phil. 3:18–19. 534 **cod,** bag (here stomach). 536 **soun,** sound. 537 **fynde,** provide for. 539 **substaunce . . . accident,** a philosophical joke: in scholastic terminology "substance" is the ideal Platonic reality, and "accident" the imperfect material manifestation of that ideal. 540 **likerous talent,** greedy (lecherous) nature. 542 **mary . . . noght,** marrow, nothing. 543 **swoote,** blandly (sweetly); cf. I. ln. 545 **by,** for. 547 **swiche delices,** such delicacies. 550 **stryvyng,** quarreling. 552 *Sour:* some MSS *Foule.* 555 **woot,** knows. 556 **styked swyn,** stuck pig. 557 **honeste cure,** seemly behavior (self-control). 558 **verray sepulture,** really (the) burial. 561 **conseil,** confidence. 563 **Lepe,** in Spain. 564 **Fysshstrete . . . Chepe,** London streets. 565 **crepeth subtilly,** the practice of adulterating expensive French wines with cheaper wines from Spain and elsewhere is evidently very old. 569 **weneth,** thinks. 571 **Rochele . . . Burdeux,** homes of the expensive French wines. 573 E *lordes.* 578 **leere,** learn.

Deyde in his sleep with shame and dishonour,
Bledynge ay at his nose in dronkenesse.
A capitayn sholde lyve in sobrenesse.
And over al this, avyseth yow right wel
What was comaunded unto Lamwel—
Nat Samuel, but Lamwel, seye I—   585
Redeth the Bible, and fynde it expresly
Of wyn-yevyng to hem that han justise.
Namoore of this, for it may wel suffise.

    And now that I have spoken of glotonye,
Now wol I yow deffenden hasardrye.   590
Hasard is verray mooder of lesynges,
And of deceite, and cursed forswerynges,
Blaspheme of Crist, manslaughtre, and wast
    also
Of catel and of tyme; and forthermo,
It is repreeve and contrarie of honour   595
For to ben holde a commune hasardour.
And ever the hyer he is of estaat,
The moore is he yholden desolaat.
If that a prynce useth hasardrye,
In alle governaunce and policye   600
He is, as by commune opinioun,
Yholde the lasse in reputacioun.

    Stilboun, that was a wys embassadour,
Was sent to Corynthe in ful greet honour
Fro Lacidomye to make hire alliaunce.   605
And whan he cam, hym happede par chaunce
That alle the gretteste that were of that lond
Pleyynge atte hasard he hem fond.
For which as soone as it myghte be
He stal hym hoom agayn to his contree   610
And seyde, "Ther wol I nat lese my name,
Ne I wol nat take on me so greet defame
Yow for to allie unto none hasardours.
Sendeth othere wise embassadours,
For by my trouthe me were levere dye   615

Than I yow sholde to hasardours allye.
For ye that been so glorious in honours
Shul nat allyen yow with hasardours
As by my wyl, ne as by my tretee."
This wise philosophre, thus seyde hee.   620
    Looke eek that to the kyng Demetrius
The kyng of Parthes, as the book seith us,
Sente him a paire of dees of gold in scorn,
For he hadde used hasard ther-biforn,
For which he heeld his glorie or his renoun 625
At no value or reputacioun.
Lordes may fynden oother maner pley
Honeste ynough to dryve the day awey.
    Now wol I speke of othes false and grete
A word or two, as olde bookes trete.   630
Gret sweryng is a thyng abhominable,
And fals sweryng is yet moore reprevable.
The heighe God forbad sweryng at al,
Witnesse on Mathew, but in special
Of sweryng seith the hooly Jeremye,   635
"Thou shalt swere sooth thyne othes and nat
    lye,
And swere in doom and eek in rightwisnesse,
But ydel sweryng is a cursednesse."
Bihoold and se that in the firste table
Of heighe Goddes heestes honurable   640
Hou that the seconde heeste of hym is this,
"Take nat my name in ydel or amys."
Lo, rather he forbedeth swich sweryng
Than homycide or many a cursed thyng—
I seye that as by ordre thus it stondeth, 645
This knoweth that his heestes understondeth
How that the seconde heeste of God is that.
And fortherover I wol thee telle al plat
That vengeance shal nat parten from his
    hous
That of his othes is to outrageous.   650

581 Hg&c *ay* om. **584 Lamwel,** see Prov. 31:4–5, "It is not for kings, O Lemuel, it is not for kings to drink wine; not for princes strong drink; / Lest they drink, and forget the law, and pervert the judgment of any of the afflicted." **590 deffenden hasardrye,** censure gambling. **591 lesynges,** lyings. **592 forswerynges,** perjuries. **593 Blaspheme of . . . wast,** blasphemy against, waste. **594 catel,** chattels (property). **595 repreeve,** shame. **598 yholden,** considered. EHg&c *holden.* **603 Stilboun,** this and the following exemplum are from John of Salisbury's *Policraticus* via John of Wales's *Communiloquium.* In *Policraticus,* the ambassador is called "Chilon." *was:* some MSS *was holde.* **605 Lacidomye,** Sparta (famous for its "Spartan" life style). **611 lese,** lose. **612 Ne I:** Hg&c *Ny.* **621 Demetrius,** his identity is unknown; Skeat suggests Demetrius Nikator, King of Syria. E&c *to* om. **622 Parthes,** Parthians (Persians). **book,** formerly taken to mean *Policraticus,* but R. A. Pratt now argues for *Communiloquium.* **634 Mathew;** cf. Matt. 5:34. **636 sooth,** true. *swere:* E *seye.* **637 in doom,** with judgment. **639 firste table,** the stone tablet containing the first five of the Ten Commandments. **640 heestes,** commandments. **641 seconde,** second in Vulgate; third in the King James version. **644 many a:** E&c *any other.* **645 by ordre,** in order (i.e., second from the beginning). **646 knoweth,** (he) knows. E&c *knowen.* **648 plat,** plainly (flat). **649 parten,** depart.

"By Goddes precious herte and by his nayles,"
And "By the blood of Crist that is in Hayles,
Sevene is my chaunce and thyn is cynk and
    treye,"
"By Goddes armes, if thou falsly pleye   654
This daggere shal thurghout thyn herte go,"
This fruyt cometh of the bicched bones two—
Forsweryng, ire, falsnesse, homycide.
Now for the love of Crist, that for us dyde,
Lete youre othes bothe grete and smale.
But, sires, now wol I telle forth my tale.   660

    Thise riotoures thre of whiche I telle,
Longe erst er prime rong of any belle,
Were set hem in a taverne for to drynke,
And as they sat they herde a belle clynke
Biforn a cors was caried to his grave.   665
That oon of hem gan callen to his knave,
"Go bet," quod he, "and axe redily
What cors is this that passeth heer forby,
And looke that thou reporte his name weel."
    "Sire," quod this boy, "it nedeth never-a-
        deel;   670
It was me toold er ye cam heer two houres.
He was, pardee, an old felawe of youres,
And sodeynly he was yslayn tonyght,
Fordronke as he sat on his bench upright.
Ther cam a privee theef men clepeth Deeth 675
That in this contree al the peple sleeth,   *pride*
And with his spere he smoot his herte atwo
And wente his wey withouten wordes mo.
He hath a thousand slayn this pestilence.
And, maister, er ye come in his presence,   680
Me thynketh that it were necessarie
For to be war of swich an adversarie.
Beth redy for to meete hym everemoore—
Thus taughte me my dame. I sey namoore."
    "By Seinte Marie," seyde this taverner,   685

"The child seith sooth, for he hath slayn this
    yeer
Henne over a mile withinne a greet village
Bothe man and womman, child, and hyne, and
    page.
I trowe his habitacioun be there.
To been avysed greet wysdom it were   690
Er that he dide a man a dishonour."
    "Ye, Goddes armes," quod this riotour,
"Is it swich peril with hym for to meete?
I shal hym seke by wey and eek by strete,
I make avow to Goddes digne bones!   695
Herkneth, felawes, we thre been al ones;
Lat ech of us holde up his hand til oother,
And ech of us bicomen otheres brother,
And we wol sleen this false traytour Deeth.
He shal be slayn, he that so manye sleeth,   700
By Goddes dignitee, er it be nyght."
    Togidres han thise thre hir trouthes plight
To lyve and dyen ech of hem for oother
As though he were his owene ybore brother.
And up they stirte, al dronken in this rage,   705
And forth they goon towardes that village
Of which the taverner hadde spoke biforn.
And many a grisly ooth thanne han they
    sworn,
And Cristes blessed body they torente—   709
Deeth shal be deed, if that they may hym hente!
    Whan they han goon nat fully half a mile,
Right as they wolde han troden over a stile,
An oold man and a poure with hem mette.
This olde man ful mekely hem grette,
And seyde thus, "Now, lordes, God yow see!"
    The proudeste of thise riotoures three   716
Answerde agayn, "What, carl with sory grace,
Why artow al forwrapped save thy face?
Why lyvestow so longe in so greet age?"

651 **Goddes . . . herte,** on oaths see l. 474 and note. 652 **Hayles,** Hayles Abbey in Gloucestershire which claimed to have a vial of Christ's blood. 653 **cynk . . . treye,** five, three; combinations in dice (craps). 656 **bicched bones,** bitched (i.e., cursed) dice. 657 **Forsweryng, ire,** perjury, anger. 659 *Lete:* some MSS *Leveth.* 662 **prime,** 9 A.M. 663 *for to:* EHg&c *to.* 664 **belle,** hand-bell carried before the corpse at a funeral. 665 **cors,** corpse. 666 **knave,** servant boy. 667 **Go bet . . . redily,** go at once, quickly. 674 **Fordronke,** "for" is an intensifier. 675 **clepeth,** call. 679 **pestilence,** the frantic escapism of the rioters in this tale and the ritual quality of their search for death are associated with the frenzy of despair that swept Europe during the plague years. 686 **sooth,** truth. 687 **Henne,** hence. 688 **hyne . . . page,** farm laborer, court attendant. 689 **trowe,** believe. 690 **avysed,** prepared. 694 **wey . . . strete,** byway, highway. 695 **digne,** honored. 696 **al ones,** all of one mind. 697 **holde up . . . til,** hold up to (as a sign of swearing fidelity). 700 *he that:* E *which that.* 702 **trouthes plight,** made their promises (plighted their troth). 704 **ybore,** born. 705 *al:* E&c *and.* 709 **torente,** cf. l. 474 and note. 710 **hente,** take, grasp. 712 **troden . . . stile,** climbed, stile to get over a fence. 715 **yow see,** i.e., see to you (care for you). 717 **carl,** fellow (churl, a disparaging reference). 718 **forwrapped,** completely wrapped ("for" is an intensifier).

This olde man gan looke in his visage, 720
And seyde thus: "For I ne kan nat fynde
A man, though that I walked into Ynde,
Neither in citee ne in no village,
That wolde chaunge his youthe for myn age;
And therfore moot I han myn age stille 725
As longe tyme as it is Goddes wille.
Ne Deeth, allas, ne wol nat han my lyf.
Thus walke I lyk a restelees kaityf,
And on the ground, which is my moodres gate,
I knokke with my staf bothe erly and late, 730
And seye, 'Leeve mooder, leet me in!
Lo, how I vanysshe, flessh and blood and skyn.
Allas, whan shul my bones been at reste?
Mooder, with yow wolde I chaunge my cheste *never*
That in my chambre longe tyme hath be, 735 *enough*
Ye, for an heyre clowt to wrappe me.'
But yet to me she wol nat do that grace,
For which ful pale and welked is my face.
    "But, sires, to yow it is no curteisye
To speken to an old man vileynye 740
But he trespasse in word or elles in dede.
In Hooly Writ ye may yourself wel rede,
'Agayns an oold man, hoor upon his heed,
Ye sholde arise.' Wherfore I yeve yow reed,
Ne dooth unto an oold man noon harm
        now 745
Namoore than that ye wolde men did to yow
In age, if that ye so longe abyde.
And God be with yow, where ye go or ryde.
I moot go thider as I have to go."
    "Nay, olde cherl, by God thou shalt nat so,"
Seyde this oother hasardour anon. 751
"Thou partest nat so lightly, by Seint John!
Thou spak right now of thilke traytour Deeth,
That in this contree alle oure freendes sleeth.
Have heer my trouthe, as thou art his espye,
Telle where he is or thou shalt it abye, 756
By God and by the hooly sacrement!
For soothly thou art oon of his assent

To sleen us yonge folk, thou false theef!" 759
    "Now, sires," quod he, "if that ye be so leef
To fynde Deeth, turne up this croked wey,
For in that grove I lafte hym, by my fey,
Under a tree and there he wole abyde.
Noght for youre boost he wole him nothyng
        hyde.
Se ye that ook? Right there ye shal hym
        fynde. 765
God save yow, that boghte agayn mankynde,
And yow amende." Thus seyde this olde man.
And everich of thise riotoures ran
Til he cam to that tree, and ther they founde
Of floryns fyne of gold ycoyned rounde 770
Wel ny an eighte busshels as hem thoughte.
No lenger thanne after Deeth they soughte,
But ech of hem so glad was of that sighte,
For that the floryns been so faire and brighte,
That doun they sette hem by this precious
        hoord. 775
The worste of hem he spak the firste word.
    "Bretheren," quod he, "taak kepe what I
        seye;
My wit is greet, though that I bourde and
        pleye.
This tresor hath Fortune unto us yeven
In myrthe and jolitee oure lyf to lyven, 780
And lightly as it comth so wol we spende.
Ey, Goddes precious dignitee, who wende
Today that we sholde han so fair a grace?
But myghte this gold be caried fro this place
Hoom to myn hous—or elles unto
        youres— 785
For wel ye woot that al this gold is oures,
Thanne were we in heigh felicitee.
But trewely, by daye it may nat bee.
Men wolde seyn that we were theves stronge,
And for oure owene tresor doon us honge. 790
This tresor moste ycaried be by nyghte
As wisely and as slyly as it myghte.

---

724 chaunge, exchange. **728 kaityf,** wretch. **731 Leeve,** dear. **734 chaunge my cheste,** exchange my chest (of worldly property). **736 heyre clowt,** haircloth burial sheet. Some MSS *wrappe in me.* **738 welked,** withered. **741 But,** unless. **743 Agayns,** in the presence of; Lev. 19:32. **744 reed,** advice. **748 where ye go,** whither you walk. **751 hasardour,** gambler. **752 partest . . . lightly,** depart (get away), so easily. **755 trouthe . . . espye,** word (troth), spy. **756 abye,** pay for. **758 assent,** i.e., in agreement with. **760 leef,** eager. *ye:* Hg&c *yow.* **762 fey,** faith. **764 nothyng,** not at all. **765 ook,** oak. **766 boghte agayn,** redeemed. **767 amende,** correct. **769** Other MSS *they cam.* **770 floryns,** gold coins worth six or more silver shillings. **771** *eighte:* other MSS *seven/vij.* **778 bourde,** joke. **779 Fortune,** according to the Boethian world view, Fortune grants only mutable, temporal felicity; God alone grants eternal felicity: cf. *Boece* Bks. II and III. **781 lightly,** easily. **782 wende,** thought. **786 woot,** know. **790 honge,** hanged.

Wherfore I rede that cut among us alle
Be drawe, and lat se wher the cut wol falle;
And he that hath the cut with herte blithe   795
Shal renne to towne, and that ful swithe,
And brynge us breed and wyn ful prively.
And two of us shul kepen subtilly
This tresor wel. And if he wol nat tarie,
Whan it is nyght we wol this tresor carie   800
By oon assent where as us thynketh best."
That oon of hem the cut broghte in his fest
And bad hem drawe and looke where it wol
    falle,
And it fil on the yongeste of hem alle,
And forth toward the toun he wente anon.   805
    And also soone as that he was gon
That oon of hem spak thus unto that oother,
"Thow knowest wel thou art my sworn
    brother;
Thy profit wol I telle thee anon.
Thou woost wel that oure felawe is agon.   810
And heere is gold, and that ful greet plentee,
That shal departed been among us thre.
But nathelees, if I kan shape it so
That it departed were among us two,   814
Hadde I nat doon a freendes torn to thee?"
    That oother answerde, "I noot hou that may
    be.
He woot wel that the gold is with us tweye.
What shal we doon? What shal we to hym
    seye?"
    "Shal it be conseil?" seyde the firste shrewe,
"And I shal tellen in a wordes fewe   820
What we shal doon, and brynge it wel aboute."
    "I graunte," quod that oother, "out of doute,
That by my trouthe I shal thee nat biwreye."
    "Now," quod the firste, "thou woost wel we
    be tweye,
And two of us shul strenger be than oon.   825
Looke whan that he is set that right anoon
Arys as though thou woldest with hym pleye,

And I shal ryve hym thurgh the sydes tweye
Whil that thou strogelest with hym as in game,
And with thy daggere looke thou do the same.
And thanne shal al this gold departed be,   831
My deere freend, bitwixen me and thee.
Thanne may we bothe oure lustes all fulfille,
And pleye at dees right at oure owene wille."
    And thus acorded been thise shrewes tweye   835
To sleen the thridde, as ye han herd me seye.
    This yongeste, which that wente unto the
    toun,
Ful ofte in herte he rolleth up and doun
The beautee of thise floryns newe and brighte.
"O Lord," quod he, "if so were that I myghte
Have al this tresor to myself allone   841
Ther is no man that lyveth under the trone
Of God that sholde lyve so murye as I."
And atte laste the feend, oure enemy,   844
Putte in his thought that he sholde poyson beye
With which he myghte sleen his felawes
    tweye—
Forwhy the feend foond hym in swich lyvynge
That he hadde leve hem to sorwe brynge.
For this was outrely his fulle entente,   *damnacion*
To sleen hem bothe and nevere to repente.   850
And forth he gooth, no lenger wolde he tarie,
Into the toun unto a pothecarie,
And preyde hym that he hym wolde selle
Som poyson that he myghte his rattes quelle,
And eek ther was a polcat in his hawe   855
That, as he seyde, his capouns hadde yslawe,
And fayn he wolde wreke hym, if he myghte,
On vermyn that destroyed hym by nyghte.
    The pothecarie answerde, "And thou shalt
    have
A thyng that, also God my soule save,   860
In al this world ther is no creature
That eten or dronken hath of this confiture
Noght but the montance of a corn of whete
That he ne shal his lif anon forlete—

---

793 rede . . . cut, advise, draw straws. **798 kepen subtilly,** protect secretly. **801 oon assent,** common agreement. **812 departed,** divided. **816 noot,** don't know. **817** *wel that:* E *how that;* Hg&c *that.* **819 conseil . . . shrewe,** confidential, wretch (bad-tempered animal). **820** Other MSS *tellen thee.* **822 graunte . . . doute,** agree (promise), without a reservation. **823 trouthe . . . biwreye,** word (troth), betray. **826** *whan that:* other MSS *that* om. **828 ryve,** stab. **833 lustes,** pleasures. **843 murye,** merry. **847 lyvynge,** condition of life. **848 leve,** permission (leave). *hem:* Hg&c *hym.* **852 a pothecarie,** an apothecary (druggist). **854 quelle,** kill. **855 polcat . . . hawe,** weasel (OF, *poule,* fowl + cat), yard. **857 wreke,** revenge. **862 confiture,** concoction. **863 montance . . . corn,** amount, grain. **864 anon forlete,** immediately give up.

Ye, sterve he shal and that in lasse while   865
Than thou wold goon a paas nat but a mile,
The poysoun is so strong and violent.''

   This cursed man hath in his hond yhent
This poysoun in a box, and sith he ran
Into the nexte strete unto a man   870
And borwed of hym large botels thre,
And in the two his poyson poured he.
The thridde he kepte clene for his owene
    drynke
For al the nyght he shoop hym for to swynke
In cariynge of the gold out of that place.   875
And whan this riotour, with sory grace,
Hadde filled with wyn his grete botels thre,
To his felawes agayn repaireth he.

   What nedeth it to sermone of it moore?   879
For right as they hadde cast his deeth bifoore,
Right so they han hym slayn, and that anon.
And whan that this was doon, thus spak that
    oon,
"Now lat us sitte and drynke and make us
    merie,
And afterward we wol his body berie.''
And with that word it happed hym par cas   885
To take the botel ther the poyson was,
And drank, and yaf his felawe drynke also,
For which anon they storven bothe two.

   But certes, I suppose that Avycen
Wroot nevere in no canon ne in no fen   890
Mo wonder signes of empoisonyng
Than hadde thise wrecches two er hir endyng.
Thus ended been thise homycides two
And eek the false empoysonere also.

   O cursed synne of alle cursednesse!   895
O traytours homycide, O wikkednesse!
O glotonye, luxurie, and hasardrye!
Thou blasphemour of Crist with vileynye
And othes grete of usage and of pride!

Allas, mankynde, how may it bitide   900
That to thy creatour, which that the wroghte
And with his precious herte-blood thee boghte,
Thou art so fals and so unkynde, allas?

   Now goode men, God foryeve yow youre
    trespas,
And ware yow fro the synne of avarice.   905
Myn hooly pardoun may yow alle warice—
So that ye offre nobles or sterlynges
Or elles silver broches, spoones, rynges.
Boweth youre heed under this hooly bulle!
Com up, ye wyves, offreth of youre wolle!   910
Youre names I entre heer in my rolle anon;
Into the blisse of hevene shul ye gon.
I yow assoille by myn heigh power,
Yow that wol offre, as clene and eek as cleer
As ye were born.—And lo, sires, thus I preche.
And Jhesu Crist, that is oure soules leche,   916
So graunte yow his pardoun to receyve,
For that is best—I wol yow nat deceyve.

   But, sires, o word forgat I in my tale:
I have relikes and pardoun in my male   920
As faire as any man in Engelond,
Whiche were me yeven by the popes hond.
If any of yow wole of devocioun
Offren, and han myn absolucioun,
Com forth anon and kneleth heere adoun   925
And mekely receyveth my pardoun,
Or elles taketh pardoun as ye wende
Al newe and fressh at every miles ende—
So that ye offren, alwey newe and newe,
Nobles or pens whiche that be goode and trewe.
It is an honour to everich that is heer   931
That ye mowe have a suffisant pardoneer
T'assoille yow in contree as ye ryde
For aventures whiche that may bityde.
Paraventure ther may fallen oon or two   935
Doun of his hors and breke his nekke atwo.

---

865 sterve, die. **866 goon a paas,** walk at a footpace. **868 yhent,** taken. **869 sith,** then. **871** *of* not found in any MS. **874 shoop hym
. . . swynke,** planned, work. **880 cast,** planned. **881 anon,** at once. **885 par cas,** Fr., by chance. **888 storven,** died. **889 Avycen,**
Avicenna, famous ancient Persian physician. **890 canon . . . fen,** Avicenna's most famous treatise, *Liber Canonis Medicinae,* was divided
into fens (Arabic *fann,* a unit of technical exposition). Lib. IV, fen vi treats of poisons. **891 wonder,** wonderful (awesome). **897 luxurie
. . . hasardrye,** lechery, gambling. **899 usage,** habit. **905 ware,** beware. **906 warice,** save. **907 So that . . . nobles . . . sterlynges,**
if, gold coins, silver coins. **910 wolle,** wool—the Pardoner will take any sort of offering. **913 assoille,** absolve of sin. **916 leche,**
physician. **920 male,** bag. **923 of devocioun,** out of (through). **927 taketh . . . wende,** take (receive), ride along. **928** *miles*: other
MSS *tounes.* **929 So that,** i.e., as long as. **930** *or pens*: other MSS *and pens.* **932 mowe . . . suffisant,** can, capable. **934 aventures,**
experiences; this could allude to the sort of picaresque adventures which are made so much of in novels like *Don Quixote* and *Tom Jones.*

Looke which a seuretee is it to yow alle
That I am in youre felaweship yfalle,
That may assoille yow bothe moore and lasse
Whan that the soule shal fro the body passe. 940
I rede that oure Hoost heere shal bigynne,
For he is moost envoluped in synne.
Com forth, sire Hoost, and offre first anon,
And thou shalt kisse my relikes everychon—
Ye, for a grote: unbokele anon thy purs." 945
  "Nay, nay," quod he, "thanne have I Cristes
    curs.
Lat be," quod he, "it shal nat be, so theech!
Thou woldest make me kisse thyn olde breech
And swere it were a relyk of a seint, 949
Though it were with thy fundement depeint.
But by the croys which that Seint Eleyne fond
I wolde I hadde thy coillons in myn hond

Instide of relikes or of seintuarie.
Lat kutte hem of, I wol thee helpe hem carie.
They shul be shryned in an hogges toord." 955
  This Pardoner answerde nat a word.
So wrooth he was, no word ne wolde he seye.
  "Now," quod oure Hoost, "I wol no lenger
    pleye
With thee ne with noon oother angry man."
But right anon the worthy Knyght bigan, 960
Whan that he saugh that al the peple lough,
"Namoore of this, for it is right ynough.
Sire Pardoner, be glad and myrie of cheere;
And ye, sire Hoost, that been to me so deere,
I prey yow that ye kisse the Pardoner. 965
And Pardoner, I prey thee drawe thee neer,
And as we diden lat us laughe and pleye."
Anon they kiste and ryden forth hir weye.

Heere is ended the Pardoners Tale.

937 **seuretee,** assurance. 940 **body passe,** extreme unction, like baptism, absolution, and marriage, was one of the sacraments of the Church reserved to ordained clergy like the Parson. Chaucer is voicing his criticism of the system of pardons and pardoners by having the Pardoner claim this vital privilege. 941 **rede,** advise. Hg&c *heere* om. 942 **envoluped,** enveloped (involved). 944 *my:* Hg&c *the.* 945 **grote,** silver coin worth fourpence. 946 **have I,** i.e., I would have. 947 **theech,** may I prosper. 948 **breech,** underpants. 950 **fundement depeint,** bottom (anus), stained (painted). 951 **Eleyne,** St. Helena, Mother of the Emperor Constantine, was believed to have found the true cross. 952 **coillons,** testicles, but cf. I.691. 953 **seintuarie,** box for relics (sanctuary). 954 **Lat kutt hem,** let them be. *thee helpe hem:* E *with thee hem;* Hg&c *thee hem;* other MSS *helpe hem.* 955 **shryned . . . toord,** enshrined, turd. 961 **lough,** laughed.

INTRODUCTION

Canterbury Tales, Part VII

ART VII IS THE longest section of the *Canterbury Tales.* As observed in the Introduction to Part II, the epilogue to Part II may at one time have been the link connecting *Melibee* told by the Man of Law with the Shipman's Tale told by the Wife of Bath. At l. 12 of the Shipman's Tale, the narrator refers to himself as a woman. Part VII thus appears to be a compilation of pieces independently composed. *Sir Thopas, Melibee,* and the Monk's Tale can hardly have been written especially for the Canterbury collection. The Prioress's Tale is not especially suited to the worldly Prioress of the General Prologue. Only at the end, in the Nun's Priest's Prologue and Tale, do we find the reciprocal interplay between teller, tale, and audience that characterizes Parts I-VI. We see Chaucer's conception of dramatic interplay emerging as the section progresses.

In the Shipman's Tale, Chaucer uses the same technique of characterization and local color to convert an anecdote into a story that he does in the Miller's and Reeve's Tales, although with less brilliance of execution. The Shipman's plot is the widespread folktale type called "the lover's gift regained." The analogues closest to Chaucer are in the *Decameron* and Sercambi's *Novelle,*

though there is no evidence that Chaucer knew either one. In relation to the themes of the marriage group, the most interesting aspect of the Shipman's Tale is the specific identification of sex with money, as discussed by A.H. Silverman, "Sex and Money in Chaucer's Shipman's Tale," *PQ* (1953). As previously observed, in the exegetical language of the time, preoccupation with temporal instead of spiritual matters was called "fornicatio." It is precisely this preoccupation with money that leads to the fornication in the tale.

The Prioress's Tale is an exquisite retelling of a popular miracle of the Virgin which had, however, unpleasant appositions in real life. If Chaucer shared the modern perspective, this assignment is institutional criticism second in bitterness only to the satire on the Pardoner. Like her sympathy only for mice and small dogs at a time when human beings were dying from war, hunger, and the plague, the Prioress's tenderness for the little clergeon ignores the underlying antisemitism of the story. But, as pointed out by Robert W. Frank, "Miracles of the Virgin, Medieval Anti-Semitism, and the Prioress's Tale" in *The Wisdom of Poetry* (1982), Chaucer was probably no more than faintly aware of the stereotype he was perpetuating. Yet the assignment of this bloody tale to the Prioress and the equally paradoxical martyrdom of St. Cecelia to the Second Nun can hardly avoid being seen as some sort of comment on the way their institution distorted the humanity of these well-meaning women. Florence Ridley, *The Prioress and the Critics* (1965), summarizes the criticism to 1963.

The dramatic interplay by which Chaucer the Pilgrim gets to tell the next two tales is worth study. The plump, preoccupied persona who appears in the headlink to the *Tale of Sir Thopas* (l.700) is much like the one who appears in the *House of Fame* (ll.574,660) and "Scogan" (short poem 17, ll.27,31). The first tale the author-persona tells is a burlesque on popular romances. This is the third incomplete piece in the Canterbury collection, and, like the Cook's and Squire's Tales, it is effective in its incompleteness. One of the finest chapters in *Sources and Analogues* is that by Laura Hibbard Loomis which discusses the nature and inspiration of the satire. Her conclusion is that *Thopas* was not created around a plot but around a catalog of clichés suitable for satire. When Chaucer had run through the clichés, the piece was finished.

The *Thopas* joke and the interruption by the Host (l.919) provide an introduction to the long prose *Tale of Melibee*. There is a twinkle in the persona's eye when, to the Host's demand for a more serious tale, he responds that he will tell "a litel thyng in prose" (l.937). The inclusion of such a long and heavy treatise as *Melibee* is a

233

commentary on medieval taste. It hardly reinforces the verisimilitude of the roadside drama. But regardless of its appropriateness, it is of intrinsic cultural interest. *Melibee* is a serious discussion of governance, concluding that a ruler will succeed better with love and arbitration than with force. It foreshadows or reflects (depending on one's view of the sequence in which the parts of the *Canterbury Tales* were compiled) the marriage argument, since the spokesperson for peace is Melibeus' wife Prudence, and at first he says he will not be governed by the counsel of a woman (ll.1055ff). Some critics have suggested that the treatise was originally directed to John of Gaunt or Richard II, who, contemporary chronicles report, were both counselled by Richard's mother, Joan of Kent. That may be, but the tale is a faithful translation of a long treatise by an Italian judge, Albertano de Brescia, with only minor adaptations—such as the omission of a reference to the lack of wisdom in young kings which might have offended young Richard. Gardiner Stillwell, "The Political Meaning of Chaucer's Tale of Melibeus," *Speculum* (1944), explores the political implications.

The variety which is the hallmark of Part VII moves next to the Monk's Tale, introduced by the longest and most dramatic link so far encountered in this section. It is particularly interesting for the light it throws on the personality of the Host. Indeed, as Alan T. Gaylord has shown, "*Sentence* and *Solaas* in Fragment VII of the *Canterbury Tales*," *PMLA* (1967), Part VII provides the fullest view of the Host's aesthetic.

The most significant literary observation in this headlink is the Monk's identifying his biographies as "tragedies." This identification, and the rubric "De casibus virorum illustrium" that appears in many of the manuscripts, reveal Chaucer's medieval conception of tragedy. There was no tragedy of "little people," only the fall of great people from high places. The connection of this idea with fortune has been traced by Willard Farnham, *The Medieval Heritage of Elizabethan Tragedy* (1936).

The "De casibus" rubric originated with Boc-

caccio, who wrote a collection of Latin prose tragedies under that title. But, as always, the connection between Boccaccio's work and Chaucer's is obscure. It may have served as a model, but Chaucer's collection shares only five lives with it, none derived from Boccaccio, yet with lines that certainly suggest that he knew Boccaccio's work. At l. 2325 Chaucer seems to refer to Petrarch as his authority, but his real sources seem to be the Bible, *Roman de la Rose*, and his other familiar reading.

The link between the Monk's Tale and the Nun's Priest's Tale reveals the dramatic interplay of the Canterbury frame at its full maturity. After the comments on the previous tale, the Host turns to the Nun's Priest with unkind remarks about his bad horse and forced gaiety. These remarks provide a context for interpreting the tale of the lordly cock and his harem of hens as humorous revenge by the Priest for his servile situation in a convent of nuns. The attitude of the teller thus becomes an ingredient in the reception of the story, as it is in most of the tales in Parts I-VI. A.T. Broes, "Chaucer's Disgruntled Cleric: The Nun's Priest's Tale," *PMLA* (1963) explores the relations of the Nun's Priest to his tale.

The Nun's Priest's Tale is based on the popular beast-fable cycle of Reynard the Fox, treated by N.F. Blake, "Reynard the Fox in England," *Aspects of the Medieval Animal Epic* (1975), and Morton W. Bloomfield, "The Wisdom of the Nun's Priest's Tale," *Chaucerian Problems* (1979). Chaucer here begins to develop a style brought to its zenith by Sterne in *Tristram Shandy*, in which the digressions are more interesting than the plot itself. The tale of Reynard and the cock is told from a Boethian perspective and embroidered with medical lore, dream lore, rhetoric, and philosophy, yet narrated with a colloquial ease that rivals that of the Wife of Bath's Prologue. Michael Hoy in *Chaucer's Major Tales* (1969), and John B. Friedman in "The Nun's Priest's Tale: The Preacher and the Mermaid's Song," *Chaucer Review* (1973), illuminate the stylistic variety.

Canterbury Tales

PART VII

SHIPMAN'S TALE

Heere bigynneth the Shipmannes Tale.

A marchant whilom dwelled at Seint Denys,
That riche was, for which men helde hym wys.
A wyf he hadde of excellent beautee,
And compaignable and revelous was she,
Which is a thyng that causeth more dispence   5
Than worth is al the chiere and reverence
That men hem doon at festes and at dethces.
Swiche salutaciouns and contenaunces
Passen as dooth a shadwe upon the wal.
But wo is hym that payen moot for al!   10
The sely housbonde algate he moot paye,
He moot us clothe, and he moot us arraye,
Al for his owene worship, richely—
In which array we daunce jolily.
And if that he noght may, par aventure,   15

Or ellis list no swich dispence endure,
But thynketh it is wasted and ylost,
Thanne moot another payen for oure cost,
Or lene us gold—and that is perilous.
    This noble marchaunt heeld a worthy hous,
For which he hadde alday so greet repair   21
For his largesse, and for his wyf was fair,
That wonder is. But herkneth to my tale:
Amonges alle his gestes grete and smale
Ther was a monk, a fair man and a boold—   25
I trowe a thritty wynter he was oold—
That evere in oon was drawynge to that
    place.
This yonge monk that was so fair of face
Aqueynted was so with the goode man

1 whilom . . . Seint Denys, once, a monastic town just north of Paris. For spurious prologues to ShipT see Manly IV.495. 4 revelous, loving revels (parties). Other MSS *reverent*. 5 dispence, expense. 6 chiere . . . reverence, notice, respect. 8 contenaunces, expressions of approval. 11 sely . . . algate, foolish (innocent), always; ll. 11–19 still read as though the ShipT were told by the Wife of Bath. 13 worship, credit, esteem. 16 list, chooses. 19 lene, lend. 20 heeld, maintained. 21 repair, i.e., so many visitors. 22 largesse, generosity. 26 *a*: E *of*. 27 in oon, constantly. *drawynge*: E *conynge*. 29 goode man, the usual term for the master of a household.

Sith that hir firste knoweliche bigan, 30
That in his hous as famulier was he
As it is possible any freend to be.
And for as muchel as this goode man
And eek this monk of which that I bigan
Were bothe two yborn in o village, 35
The monk hym claymeth as for cosynage;
And he agayn, he seith nat ones nay
But was as glad therof as fowel of day,
For to his herte it was a greet plesaunce.
Thus been they knyt with eterne alliaunce, 40
And ech of hem gan oother for t'assure
Of bretherhede whil that hir lyf may dure.

Free was daun John and namely of dispence
As in that hous, and ful of diligence
To doon plesaunce and also greet costage. 45
He noght forgat to yeve the leeste page
In al the hous, but after hir degree
He yaf the lord and sitthe al his meynee,
Whan that he cam, som manere honest thyng,
For which they were as glad of his comyng 50
As fowel is fayn whan that the sonne up riseth.
Namoore of this as now, for it suffiseth.

But so bifel, this marchant on a day
Shoop hym to make redy his array
Toward the toun of Brugges for to fare 55
To byen there a porcioun of ware.
For which he hath to Parys sent anon
A messager, and preyed hath daun John
That he sholde come to Seint Denys to pleye
With hym and with his wyf a day or tweye, 60
Er he to Brugges wente, in alle wise.

This noble monk of which I yow devyse
Hath of his abbot as hym list licence,
By cause he was a man of heigh prudence

And eek an officer, out for to ryde 65
To seen hir graunges and hire bernes wyde,
And unto Seinte Denys he comth anon.
Who was so welcome as my lord daun John,
Oure deere cosyn, ful of curteisye?
With hym broghte he a jubbe of malvesye, 70
And eek another, ful of fyn vernage,
And volatyl, as ay was his usage.
And thus I lete hem ete and drynke and pleye,
This marchant and this monk, a day or tweye.

The thridde day this marchant up ariseth 75
And on his nedes sadly hym avyseth,
And up into his countour-hous gooth he
To rekene with hymself, wel may be,
Of thilke yeer how that it with hym stood,
And how that he despended hadde his good, 80
And if that he encressed were or noon.
His bookes and his bagges many oon
He leith biforn hym on his countyng-bord.
Ful riche was his tresor and his hord, 84
For which ful faste his countour-dore he shette;
And eek he nolde that no man sholde hym lette
Of his acountes for the meene tyme;
And thus he sit til it was passed pryme.

Daun John was rysen in the morwe also
And in the gardyn walketh to and fro 90
And hath his thynges seyd ful curteisly.

This goode wyf cam walkynge pryvely
Into the gardyn there he walketh softe,
And hym saleweth as she hath doon ofte.
A mayde child cam in hire compaignye 95
Which as hir list she may governe and gye
For yet under the yerde was the mayde.
"O deere cosyn myn, daun John," she sayde,
"What eyleth yow so rathe for to ryse?"

---

30 knoweliche, acquaintance. **36 cosynage**, kinship. **43 Free . . . namely . . . dispence**, generous, especially, spending money. *namely*: Hg&c *manly*. **45 doon . . . costage**, make expenditure. **47 after . . . degree**, according to their station. **48 sitthe . . . meynee**, afterward, household. **49 honest**, appropriate. **51 fayn**, happy. **54 Shoop hym**, prepared. **55 Brugges**, Bruges in Flanders (Belgium). **59** Hg&c *and pleye*. **63 list licence**, desired permission. Monks were supposed to be restricted to their monasteries, cf. I.179–88 and notes; like that monk, daun John is an "outrider," I.166. **66 seen . . . wyde**, oversee, throughout a large region. **67 anon**, immediately, refers back to ll. 58–59. **70 jubbe of malvesye**, jug of malmsey (sweet white Greek wine). **71 vernage**, sweet white Italian wine. **72 volatyl**, game fowl for eating. **76 sadly**, soberly, but *double entendre* regretfully. **hymn avyseth**, takes thought. **77 countour-hous**, counting house, office; since money in the Middle Ages was largely in coins, it had to be stored and counted in a secure place. **78** *wel*: other MSS *as wel*. **79 thilke**, that. **80 despended . . . good**, spent, wealth. **83 countyng-bord**, board or table cloth divided into squares on which accounts were reckoned by means of counters. This came to be called the "exchequer" (i.e., chess board), which in turn became the name for the king's treasury. **86 lette**, hinder. **88 pryme**, 9 A.M. **89 morwe**, morning. **91 thynges . . . curteisly**, devotions. Is "curteisly" ironic? How should a monk say his breviary under the circumstances? **94 saleweth**, greets. **96 gye**, guide. **97 under the yerde**, subject to discipline by spanking with a yardstick. **99 rathe**, early.

"Nece," quod he, "it oghte ynough suffise
Fyve houres for to slepe upon a nyght　101
But it were for an old appalled wight,
As been thise wedded men that lye and dare
As in a fourme sit a wery hare
Were al forstraught with houndes grete and
　　smale.　105
But deere nece, why be ye so pale?
I trowe, certes, that oure goode man
Hath yow laboured sith the nyght bigan
That yow were nede to resten hastily."
And with that word he lough ful murily,　110
And of his owene thought he wax al reed.

　This faire wyf gan for to shake hir heed
And seyde thus, "Ye, God woot al," quod she.
"Nay, nay, cosyn myn, it stant nat so with me;
For by that God that yaf me soule and lyf,　115
In al the reawme of France is ther no wyf
That lasse lust hath to that sory pley.
For I may synge 'allas and weylawey
That I was born,' but to no wight," quod she,
"Dar I nat telle how that it stant with me.　120
Wherfore I thynke out of this land to wende,
Or elles of myself to make an ende,
So ful am I of drede and eek of care."

　This monk bigan upon this wyf to stare,
And seyde, "Allas, my nece, God forbede　125
That ye for any sorwe or any drede
Fordo youreself. But telleth me youre grief—
Paraventure I may in youre meschief
Conseille or helpe; and therfore telleth me
Al youre anoy, for it shal been secree.　130
For on my porthors I make an ooth
That nevere in my lyf, for lief ne looth,
Ne shal I of no conseil yow biwreye."

　"The same agayn to yow," quod she, "I seye.
By God and by this porthors I yow swere,　135
Though men me wolde al into pieces tere,
Ne shal I nevere, for to goon to helle,
Biwreye a word of thyng that ye me telle,

Nat for no cosynage ne alliance
But verraily for love and affiance."　140
Thus been they sworn, and heerupon they kiste
And ech of hem tolde oother what hem liste.

　"Cosyn," quod she, "if that I hadde a space,
As I have noon, and namely in this place,
Thanne wolde I telle a legende of my lyf,　145
What I have suffred sith I was a wyf
With myn housbonde, al be he youre cosyn."
　"Nay," quod this monk, "by God and Seint
　　Martyn,
He is na moore cosyn unto me
Than is this leef that hangeth on the tree.　150
I clepe hym so, by Seint Denys of Fraunce,
To have the moore cause of aqueyntaunce
Of yow, which I have loved specially
Aboven alle wommen, sikerly.
This swere I yow on my professioun.　155
Telleth youre grief, lest that he come adoun,
And hasteth yow, and gooth youre wey anon."
　"My deere love," quod she, "O my daun
　　John,
Ful lief were me this conseil for to hyde,
But out it moot; I may namoore abyde.　160
Myn housbonde is to me the worste man
That evere was sith that the world bigan.
But sith I am a wyf, it sit nat me
To tellen no wight of oure privetee,
Neither abedde ne in noon oother place;　165
God shilde I sholde it tellen, for his grace!
A wyf ne shal nat seyn of hir housbonde
But al honour, as I kan understonde—
Save unto yow thus muche I tellen shal:
As helpe me God, he is noght worth at al　170
In no degree the value of a flye.
But yet me greveth moost his nygardye.
And wel ye woot that wommen naturelly
Desiren thynges sixe as wel as I:
They wolde that hir housbondes sholde be　175
Hardy, and wise, and riche, and therto free,

---

102 But it were . . . appalled, unless it were, fatigued. **103 dare,** cower (opposite to "dare," be bold). **104 fourme,** burrow. **105 forstraught,** distraught. **109 hastily,** soon. **117 lust,** desire. **121 wende,** go. **127 Fordo,** do for (kill). E *tel me of.* **128** E *I yow may.* **131 porthors,** breviary, trisyllabic *portehors* in Fr. Some MSS have *here I make* to add a syllable. **133 conseil,** confidence. **135** Hg&c *yow* om., which might have been Chaucer's reading if *portehors* were again trisyllabic. **144 namely,** especially. **147** *cosyn:* E *kyn.* **148** E&c *by seint.* **154 sikerly,** truly. **155 professioun,** monastic vows. **157** *youre wey:* Hg&c *awey.* **159 lief . . . conseil,** happy, secret. **162 sith,** since. **163 sit,** becomes. **166 shilde,** forbid. **171 In no degree,** in any way. **172 nygardye,** stinginess. **176 Hardy . . . free,** resolute (bold), generous.

And buxom unto his wyf, and fressh abedde.
But by that ilke Lord that for us bledde,
For his honour myself for to arraye,
A Sonday next I most nedes paye   180
An hundred frankes, or ellis I am lorn.
Yet were me levere that I were unborn
Than me were doon a sclaundre or vileynye.
And if myn housbonde eek it myghte espye,
I nere but lost. And therfore I yow preye,   185
Lene me this somme, or ellis moot I deye.
Daun John, I seye lene me thise hundred
     frankes.
Pardee, I wol nat faille yow my thankes,
If that yow list to doon that I yow praye.
For at a certeyn day I wol yow paye,   190
And doon to yow what plesance and service
That I may doon, right as yow list devise.
And but I do, God take on me vengeance
As foul as evere hadde Genylon of France."
     This gentil monk answerde in this manere,
"Now trewely, myn owene lady deere,   196
I have," quod he, "on yow so greet a routhe
That I yow swere and plighte yow my trouthe
That whan youre housbonde is to Flaundres
     fare,
I wol delyvere yow out of this care,   200
For I wol brynge yow an hundred frankes."
And with that word he caughte hire by the
     flankes,
And hire embraceth harde, and kiste hire ofte.
"Gooth now youre wey," quod he, "al stille and
     softe,
And lat us dyne as soone as that ye may,   205
For by my chilyndre it is pryme of day.
Gooth now, and beeth as trewe as I shal be."
     "Now elles God forbede, sire," quod she,
And forth she gooth as jolif as a pye,

And bad the cookes that they sholde hem hye
So that men myghte dyne, and that anon.   211
Up to hir housbonde is this wyf ygon,
And knokketh at his countour boldely.
     "Qui la?" quod he. "Peter, it am I,"
Quod she; "what sire, how longe wol ye faste?
How longe tyme wol ye rekene and caste   216
Youre sommes, and youre bookes, and youre
     thynges?
The devel have part on alle swiche rekenynges!
Ye have ynough, pardee, of Goddes sonde.
Com doun today, and lat youre bagges stonde.
Ne be ye nat ashamed that daun John   221
Shal fasting al this day alenge goon?
What, lat us heere a messe and go we dyne."
     "Wyf," quod this man, "litel kanstow devyne
The curious bisynesse that we have.   225
For of us chapmen, also God me save,
And by that lord that clepid is Seint Yve,
Scarsly amonges twelve tweye shul thryve
Continuelly, lastynge unto oure age.
We may wel make chiere and good visage,   230
And dryve forth the world as it may be,
And kepen oure estaat in pryvetee
Til we be deed, or elles that we pleye
A pilgrymage, or goon out of the weye.
And therfore have I greet necessitee   235
Upon this queynte world t'avyse me,
For everemoore we moote stonde in drede
Of hap and fortune in oure chapmanhede.
     "To Flaunders wol I go tomorwe at day,
And come agayn as soone as evere I may.   240
For which, my deere wyf, I thee biseke
As be to every wight buxom and meke,
And for to kepe oure good be curious,
And honestly governe wel oure hous.
Thou hast ynough, in every maner wise,   245

That to a thrifty houshold may suffise.
Thee lakketh noon array ne no vitaille;
Of silver in thy purs shaltow nat faille."
And with that word his countour-dore he shette,
And doun he gooth, no lenger wolde he lette.
But hastily a messe was ther seyd, 251
And spedily the tables were yleyd,
And to the dyner faste they hem spedde,
And richely this monk the chapman fedde.

At after-dyner daun John sobrely 255
This chapman took apart, and prively
He seyde hym thus, "Cosyn, it standeth so
That wel I se to Brugges wol ye go.
God and Seint Austyn spede yow and gyde!
I prey yow, cosyn, wisely that ye ryde. 260
Governeth yow also of youre diete
Atemprely, and namely in this hete.
Bitwix us two nedeth no strange fare.
Farewel, cosyn. God shilde yow fro care.
And if that any thyng by day or nyght, 265
If it lye in my power and my myght,
That ye me wol comande in any wyse,
It shal be doon right as ye wol devyse.

"O thyng, er that ye goon, if it may be:
I wolde prey yow for to lene me 270
An hundred frankes for a wyke or tweye,
For certein beestes that I moste beye,
To stoore with a place that is oures.
God helpe me so, I wolde it were youres!
I shal nat faille surely at my day, 275
Nat for a thousand frankes, a mile way.
But lat this thyng be secree, I yow preye,
For yet tonyght thise beestes moot I beye.
And fare now wel, myn owene cosyn deere;
Graunt mercy of youre cost and of youre
    cheere." 280

This noble marchant gentilly anon
Answerde and seyde, "O cosyn myn, daun John,
Now sikerly this is a smal requeste.
My gold is youres whan that it yow leste,

And nat oonly my gold but my chaffare. 285
Take what yow list, God shilde that ye spare.

"But o thyng is, ye knowe it wel ynogh,
Of chapmen that hir moneie is hir plogh.
We may creaunce whil we have a name,
But goldlees for to be it is no game. 290
Paye it agayn whan it lith in youre ese;
After my myght ful fayn wolde I yow plese."

Thise hundred frankes he fette forth anon,
And prively he took hem to daun John.
No wight in al this world wiste of this lone 295
Savynge this marchant and daun John allone.
They drynke, and speke, and rome a while and
    pleye,
Til that daun John rideth to his abbeye.

The morwe cam, and forth this marchant
    rideth
To Flaundres-ward; his prentys wel hym
    gydeth 300
Til he cam into Brugges murily.
Now gooth this marchant faste and bisily
Aboute his nede, and byeth and creaunceth.
He neither pleyeth at the dees ne daunceth,
But as a marchaunt, shortly for to telle, 305
He let his lyf, and there I lete hym dwelle.

The Sonday next this marchant was agon,
To Seint Denys ycomen is daun John,
With crowne and berd al fressh and newe
    yshave.
In al the hous ther nas so litel a knave, 310
Ne no wight elles, that he nas ful fayn
That my lord daun John was come agayn.
And shortly to the point right for to gon,
This faire wyf acorded with daun John
That for thise hundred frankes he sholde al
    nyght 315
Have hire in his armes bolt upright.
And this acord parfourned was in dede;
In myrthe al nyght a bisy lyf they lede
Til it was day, that daun John wente his way,

---

247 **array**, clothes. 250 **lette**, delay. 262 **Atemprely . . . namely**, moderately, especially. 271 **wyke**, week. 273 **stoore**, furnish. 275 *at my:* Hg&c *of my.* 280 **Graunt mercy . . . cost . . . cheere**, many thanks, expense (in entertaining), friendliness. 281 **gentilly anon**, courteously at once. 284 **leste**, desire. 285 **chaffare**, merchandise. 288 **plogh**, plowing and seeding were metaphors for having sexual intercourse and impregnating. The use to which the merchant's money will be put lends irony to his discourse. 289 **creaunce**, obtain credit. 292 **myght . . . fayn**, ability, gladly. 293 **fette**, fetched. E *fette hym forth.* 295 **lone**, loan. 300 **prentys**, apprentice. 303 **creaunceth**, buys on credit. 306 **let**, contracted third person present of *leadeth*. 311 **fayn**, happy. 312 Some MSS: *For that.* 316 **bolt upright**, flat on her back.

And bad the meynee, "Farewel, have good
    day," 320
For noon of hem, ne no wight in the toun,
Hath of daun John right no suspecioun.
And forth he rydeth hoom to his abbeye,
Or where hym list; namoore of hym I seye.
   This marchant, whan that ended was the
    faire, 325
To Seint Denys he gan for to repaire,
And with his wyf he maketh feeste and cheere,
And telleth hire that chaffare is so deere
That nedes moste he make a chevyssaunce,
For he was bounded in a reconyssaunce 330
To paye twenty thousand sheeld anon.
For which this marchant is to Parys gon
To borwe of certeine freendes that he hadde
A certeyn frankes, and somme with him he
    ladde.
And whan that he was come into the toun, 335
For greet chiertee and greet affeccioun,
Unto daun John he gooth hym first—to pleye,
Nat for to axe or borwe of hym moneye,
But for to wite and seen of his welfare,
And for to tellen hym of his chaffare, 340
As freendes doon whan they been met yfeere.
Daun John hym maketh feeste and murye
    cheere,
And he hym tolde agayn, ful specially,
How he hadde wel yboght and graciously,
Thanked be God, al hool his marchandise, 345
Save that he moste, in alle maner wise,
Maken a chevyssaunce as for his beste,
And thanne he sholde been in joye and reste.
   Daun John answerde, "Certes, I am fayn
That ye in heele ar comen hom agayn. 350
And if that I were riche, as have I blisse,
Of twenty thousand sheeld sholde ye nat mysse,
For ye so kyndely this oother day
Lente me gold; and as I kan and may,

I thanke yow, by God and by Seint Jame. 355
But nathelees, I took unto oure dame
Youre wyf at hom the same gold ageyn
Upon youre bench; she woot it wel, certeyn,
By certeyn tokenes that I kan yow telle.
Now, by youre leve, I may no lenger dwelle.
Oure abbot wole out of this toun anon, 361
And in his compaignye moot I goon.
Grete wel oure dame, myn owene nece sweete,
And fare wel, deere cosyn, til we meete."
   This marchant, which that was ful war and
    wys, 365
Creanced hath, and payd eek in Parys
To certeyn Lumbardes redy in hir hond
The somme of gold, and gat of hem his bond,
And hoom he gooth murie as a papejay,
For wel he knew he stood in swich array 370
That nedes moste he wynne in that viage
A thousand frankes aboven al his costage.
   His wyf ful redy mette hym atte gate,
As she was wont of oold usage algate,
And al that nyght in myrthe they bisette, 375
For he was riche and cleerly out of dette.
Whan it was day, this marchant gan embrace
His wyf al newe, and kiste hire on hir face,
And up he gooth and maketh it ful tough.
   "Namoore," quod she, "by God, ye have
    ynough!" 380
And wantownely agayn with hym she pleyde,
Til atte laste thus this marchant seyde,
"By God," quod he, "I am a litel wrooth
With yow, my wyf, although it be me looth.
And woote ye why? By God, as that I gesse 385
That ye han maad a manere straungenesse
Bitwixen me and my cosyn daun John.
Ye sholde han warned me, er I had gon,
That he yow hadde an hundred frankes payed
By redy tokene; and heeld hym yvele apayed
For that I to hym spak of chevyssaunce— 391

---

320 meynee, household. **325 faire,** he was evidently at a trade fair in Bruges. **328 chaffare,** merchandise. **329 chevyssaunce,** borrow money. **330 reconyssaunce,** legal obligation. **331 sheeld,** shield, French gold coin, *écu.* **334 somme . . . he ladde,** i.e., some money, he took. **336 chiertee,** friendship. **339 wite,** know. **340 chaffare,** trading. **341 yfeere,** together. **344 graciously,** favorably. **345 al hool,** all of. **347 chevyssaunce . . . his beste,** borrow money, as best he could. **349 fayn,** happy. **350 heele,** health. **358 woot,** knows. **359 tokenes,** evidences. *yow:* other MSS *hir.* **360 dwelle,** stay. **365 war,** prudent. **366 Creanced,** borrowed on credit. **367 Lumbardes,** the Northern Italians from Milan and the surrounding territories had by the 14th century become bankers for Europe; they would transmit the payment to his creditors in Bruges. **368** *gat:* E *hadde.* **369 papejay,** parrot. **371 wynne . . . viage,** earn a profit, trip. **372 costage,** expenses. **374 wont . . . algate,** accustomed (ready), always (in every way); this line and the following ones are heavy with sexual and psychological *double entendre.* **382** EHg&c *thus* om. **384 be:** E *were.* **386 straungenesse,** estrangement, coolness. **390 redy tokene,** i.e., with available evidence. **yvele apayed,** treated badly. **391 chevyssaunce,** borrowing money.

Me semed so as by his contenaunce.
But nathelees, by God oure hevene kyng,
I thoughte nat to axen hym no thyng.
I prey thee, wyf, as do namoore so;   395
Telle me alwey er that I fro thee go
If any dettour hath in myn absence
Ypayed thee, lest thurgh thy necligence
I myghte hym axe a thing that he hath payed."

    This wyf was nat afered nor affrayed,   400
But boldely she seyde, and that anon,
"Marie, I deffie the false monk, daun John!
I kepe nat of his tokenes never a deel.
He took me certeyn gold, that woot I weel.
What, yvel thedam on his monkes snowte,   405
For, God it woot, I wende withouten doute
That he hadde yeve it me bycause of yow,
To doon therwith myn honour and my prow,
For cosynage, and eek for beele cheere
That he hath had ful ofte tymes heere.   410
But sith I se I stonde in this disjoynt,
I wol answere yow shortly to the poynt:
Ye han mo slakkere dettours than am I!

For I wol paye yow wel and redily
Fro day to day, and if so be I faille,   415
I am youre wyf; score it upon my taille
And I shal paye as soone as ever I may.
For by my trouthe, I have on myn array,
And nat on wast, bistowed every deel,
And for I have bistowed it so weel   420
For youre honour, for Goddes sake, I seye
As be nat wrooth, but lat us laughe and pleye.
Ye shal my joly body have to wedde.
By God, I wol nat paye yow but a-bedde!
Forgyve it me, myn owene spouse deere;   425
Turne hiderward, and maketh bettre cheere."

    This marchant saugh ther was no remedie,
And for to chide it nere but greet folie
Sith that the thyng may nat amended be.
"Now wyf," he seyde, "and I foryeve it thee;
But by thy lyf, ne be namoore so large.   431
Keep bet my good, that yeve I thee in charge."
Thus endeth now my tale, and God us sende
Taillynge ynough unto oure lyves ende.
                                          Amen.

Heere endeth the Shipmannes Tale.

Bihoold the murie wordes of the Hoost to the Shipman
and to the Lady Prioresse.

"Wel seyd, by corpus dominus," quod oure
    Hoost,   435
"Now longe moote thou saille by the cost,
Sire gentil maister, gentil maryneer!
God yeve this monk a thousand last quade yeer.
Aha, felawes, beth war of swich a jape!
The monk putte in the mannes hood an ape,
And in his wyves eek, by Seint Austyn.   441
Draweth no monkes moore unto youre in.
    "But now passe over and lat us seke aboute:

Who shal now telle first of al this route
Another tale?" And with that word he sayde,
As curteisly as it had been a mayde,   446
"My lady Prioresse, by youre leve,
So that I wiste I sholde yow nat greve,
I wolde demen that ye tellen sholde
A tale next, if so were that ye wolde.   450
Now wol ye vouchesauf, my lady deere?"
    "Gladly," quod she, and seyde as ye shal
        heere.

Explicit.

392 Me semed so, it seemed so to me. **395 as do:** Hg&c *ne do/do.* **400 affrayed,** afraid. **402 Marie . . . deffie,** oath by the Virgin Mary, defy. **403 kepe,** care about. **404 took,** gave. **405 thedam,** luck. **406 wende,** thought. **408 prow,** advantage. **409 cosynage . . . beele cheere,** kinship, lovely disposition. **411 disjoynt,** difficult situation. **413 mo,** more. **416 taille,** *double entendre,* tally (charge account), and tail. **419 wast,** waste. **423 wedde,** as a pledge. **428 nere,** would not be. **431 large,** spendthrift. **432 charge,** i.e., I instruct you. *my:* E *oure.* **434 Taillynge,** the same pun as at l. 416. Some MSS *Toylyng/Tellyng.* **435 corpus dominus,** body of the Lord (the Host mistakes *dominus* for *domini*). **438 last quade yeer,** cartloads of bad years. **439 beth war . . . jape,** beware, trick. **440 hood . . . ape,** i.e., has made a fool of him. **442 in,** inn (house). **449 demen,** judge. **451 vouchesauf,** consent.

PRIORESS'S TALE

PROLOGUE

The Prologe of the Prioresses Tale.

Domine dominus noster.

O Lord, oure Lord, thy name how
    merveillous
Is in this large world ysprad, quod she,
For noght oonly thy laude precious   455
Parfourned is by men of dignitee,
But by the mouth of children thy bountee
Parfourned is, for on the brest soukynge
Somtyme shewen they thyn heriynge.

Wherfore in laude, as I best kan or may,   460
Of thee and of the white lylye flour
Which that the bar, and is a mayde alway,
To telle a storie I wol do my labour—

Nat that I may encreessen hir honour,
For she hirself is honour and the roote   465
Of bountee, next hir Sone, and soules boote.

O mooder mayde, O mayde mooder free!
O bussh unbrent, brennynge in Moyses sighte,
That ravysedest doun fro the deitee,

Thurgh thyn humblesse, the goost that in
    th'alighte,   470
Of whos vertu whan he thyn herte lighte
Conceyved was the Fadres sapience,
Help me to telle it in thy reverence.

---

453 Domini dominus noster, beginning of Psalm 8:1 (Vulgate 8:2). This prologue is made up of phrases drawn from the Psalms and the liturgy of the Blessed Virgin. There are interesting parallels with Dante's *Paradiso*, 33:1–21, both here and in the prologue to 2nd NT. **454 quod she,** l. 453 carries on without a break from the last line of the Shipman's epilogue (l. 452 above). **455 laude**, praise. **456 Parfourned**, performed (celebrated). **457 bountee**, bounty (generosity). **458 soukynge**, sucking. **459 heriynge**, praising. **461–62 lylye flour . . . Which that the bar,** a reference to the Immaculate Conception, still a controversial dogma in the 14th century. **466 boote**, remedy. **467 free**, bountiful. **468 bussh unbrent**, the bush which burned without being consumed (Ex. 3:2) was a symbol of Mary's virginal motherhood. **469 ravysedest**, drew (ravished). **470 goost**, spirit. **471 vertu**, potency, the original Lat. meaning of *virtus*. **lighte**, illuminated. **472 sapience**, wisdom (i.e., Christ); cf. I Cor. 1:24.

Lady, thy bountee, thy magnificence,
Thy vertu, and thy grete humylitee, 475
Ther may no tonge expresse in no science,
For somtyme, Lady, er men praye to thee,
Thou goost biforn of thy benyngnytee,
And getest us the lyght of thy preyere
To gyden us unto thy Sone so deere. 480

My konnyng is so wayk, O blisful queene,
For to declare thy grete worthynesse
That I ne may the weighte nat susteene,
But as a child of twelf monthe oold or lesse
That kan unnethe any word expresse, 485
Right so fare I, and therfore I yow preye,
Gydeth my song that I shal of yow seye.

Explicit.

Heere bigynneth the Prioresses Tale.

Ther was in Asye in a greet citee
Amonges Cristene folk a Jewerye
Sustened by a lord of that contree 490
For foul usure and lucre of vileynye,
Hateful to Crist and to his compaignye;
And thurgh the strete men myghte ride or
    wende,
For it was free and open at eyther ende.

A litel scole of Cristen folk ther stood 495
Doun at the ferther ende, in which ther were
Children an heep ycomen of Cristen blood,
That lerned in that scole yeer by yere
Swich manere doctrine as men used there,
This is to seyn, to syngen and to rede, 500
As smale children doon in hire childhede.

Among thise children was a wydwes sone,
A litel clergeoun seven yeer of age,
That day by day to scole was his wone,
And eek also, where as he saugh th'ymage 505

Of Cristes mooder, hadde he in usage,
As hym was taught, to knele adoun and seye
His *Ave Marie* as he goth by the weye.

Thus hath this wydwe hir litel sone ytaught
Oure blisful Lady, Cristes mooder deere, 510
To worshipe ay, and he forgat it naught,
For sely child wol alday soone leere.
But ay whan I remembre on this mateere,
Seint Nicholas stant evere in my presence,
For he so yong to Crist dide reverence. 515

This litel child his litel book lernynge,
As he sat in the scole at his prymer,
He *Alma redemptoris* herde synge,
As children lerned hire antiphoner;
And as he dorste, he drough hym ner and ner,
And herkned ay the wordes and the noote, 521
Til he the firste vers koude al by rote.

Noght wiste he what this Latyn was to seye,

476 **science,** factual way. 478 **benyngnytee,** generosity. 479 *the:* E *thurgh; of:* some MSS *thurgh.* 480 **gyden,** guide. 481 **konnyng,** ability. 485 **unnethe,** hardly. 488 **Asye,** Asia. 490–91 **Sustened . . . For . . . usure,** Jews were often bankers and as such enjoyed special royal protection in England and in other countries. But banking charges and interest could all too easily be interpreted as "usury." 492 **Hateful to Crist,** usury was forbidden by the Church, although there was no agreement on the percentage at which usury began. 493 **the strete,** i.e., the Jewry (ghetto). 503 **clergeoun seven,** diminutive of clergy, i.e., pupil. In other accounts the child is ten and in the first year of school, and there is no older "felawe" (l. 1720) who interprets for him; this may somewhat alter audiences' sympathies in the tale. 504 **wone,** habit. 506 E&c *he hadde.* 508 **Ave Marie,** Hail Mary, the most popular prayer to the Virgin Mary, constructed from words of the Annunciation, Luke 1:28, 42. 511 **ay,** always. 512 **sely . . . wol alday . . . leere,** i.e., an innocent child is always ready to learn. *alday:* Hg&c *alwey.* 514 **Seint Nicholas,** who was reputed from precocious piety to have sucked at his mother's breast only on Wednesday and Friday. He was the patron saint of schoolboys. 517 **prymer,** first schoolbook, made up of the alphabet, Lord's Prayer, Ten Commandments, etc. 518 *Alma redemptoris,* Mother of the Redeemer—a Latin anthem used especially in the service of the Advent to Candlemass. 519 **antiphoner,** hymnal, so called because the hymns and chants were sung responsively (antiphonally), one part of the choir to the other. 520 **dorste . . . ner,** durst (dared), nearer. 522 **vers . . . koude al by rote,** line, knew by heart. 523 **to seye,** i.e., what it meant.

For he so yong and tendre was of age.
But on a day his felawe gan he preye   525
T'expounden hym this song in his langage,
Or telle hym why this song was in usage;
This preyde he hym to construe and declare
Ful often tyme upon his knowes bare.

His felawe, which that elder was than he,   530
Answerde hym thus, "This song, I have herd
   seye,
Was maked of oure blisful Lady free,
Hire to salue, and eek hire for to preye
To been oure help and socour whan we deye.
I kan namoore expounde in this mateere;   535
I lerne song, I kan but smal grammeere."

  "And is this song maked in reverence
Of Cristes mooder?" seyde this innocent.
"Now, certes, I wol do my diligence
To konne it al er Cristemasse be went—   540
Though that I for my prymer shal be shent,
And shal be beten thries in an houre,
I wol it konne Oure Lady for to honoure."

His felawe taughte hym homward prively,
Fro day to day, til he koude it by rote,   545
And thanne he song it wel and boldely.
Fro word to word, acordynge with the note.
Twies a day it passed thurgh his throte,
To scoleward and homward whan he wente;
On Cristes mooder set was his entente.   550

  As I have seyd, thurghout the Juerie
This litel child, as he cam to and fro,
Ful murily than wolde he synge and crie
O Alma redemptoris everemo.
The swetnesse his herte perced so   555
Of Cristes mooder that to hire to preye
He kan nat stynte of syngyng by the weye.

Oure firste foo, the serpent Sathanas,
That hath in Jues herte his waspes nest,
Up swal and seide, "O Hebrayk peple, allas,   560
Is this to yow a thyng that is honest,
That swich a boy shal walken as hym lest
In youre despit, and synge of swich sentence,
Which is agayn youre lawes reverence?"

Fro thennes forth the Jues han conspired   565
This innocent out of this world to chace.
An homycide therto han they hyred
That in an aleye hadde a privee place;
And as the child gan forby for to pace,
This cursed Jew hym hente and heeld hym
   faste,   570
And kitte his throte and in a pit hym caste.

I seye that in a wardrobe they hym threwe
Where as thise Jewes purgen hire entraille.
O cursed folk of Herodes al newe,
What may youre yvel entente yow availle?   575
Mordre wol out, certeyn, it wol nat faille,
And namely ther th'onour of God shal sprede;
The blood out crieth on youre cursed dede.

  O martir sowded to virginitee,
Now maystow syngen, folwynge evere in oon   580
The white Lamb celestial—quod she—
Of which the grete evaungelist Seint John
In Pathmos wroot, which seith that they that
   goon
Biforn this Lamb and synge a song al newe,
That nevere flesshly wommen they ne
   knewe.   585

  This poure wydwe awaiteth al that nyght
After hir litel child, but he cam noght;
For which, as soone as it was dayes lyght,
With face pale of drede and bisy thoght,

She hath at scole and elleswhere hym soght, 590
Til finally she gan so fer espie
That he last seyn was in the Juerie.

With moodres pitee in hir brest enclosed,
She gooth, as she were half out of hir mynde,
To every place where she hath supposed 595
By liklihede hir litel child to fynde;
And evere on Cristes mooder meeke and kynde
She cride, and atte laste thus she wroghte,
Among the cursed Jues she hym soghte.

She frayneth and she preyeth pitously 600
To every Jew that dwelte in thilke place
To telle hire if hir child wente oght forby.
They seyde "nay"; but Jhesu of his grace
Yaf in hir thoght in with a litel space
That in that place after hir sone she cryde 605
Where he was casten in a pit bisyde.

O grete God, that parfournest thy laude
By mouth of innocentz, lo heere thy myght!
This gemme of chastite, this emeraude,
And eek of martirdom the ruby bright, 610
Ther he with throte ykorven lay upright,
He *Alma redemptoris* gan to synge
So loude that al the place gan to rynge.

The Cristene folk that thurgh the strete wente
In coomen for to wondre upon this thyng, 615
And hastily they for the provost sente.
He cam anon withouten tariyng,
And herieth Crist that is of hevene kyng,
And eek his mooder, honour of mankynde,
And after that the Jewes leet he bynde. 620

This child with pitous lamentacioun
Up taken was, syngynge his song alway,
And with honour of greet processioun
They carien hym unto the nexte abbay.

His mooder swownynge by his beere lay; 625
Unnethe myghte the peple that was theere
This newe Rachel brynge fro his beere.

With torment and with shameful deeth echon
This provost dooth the Jewes for to sterve
That of this mordre wiste, and that anon. 630
He nolde no swich cursednesse observe.
Yvele shal he have that yvele wol deserve;
Therfore with wilde hors he dide hem drawe,
And after that he heng hem by the lawe.

Upon this beere ay lith this innocent 635
Biforn the chief auter, whil the masse laste;
And after that the abbot with his covent
Han sped hem for to burien hym ful faste;
And whan they hooly water on hym caste,
Yet spak this child, whan spreynd was hooly
water, 640
And song *O Alma redemptoris mater.*

This abbot which that was an hooly man
As monkes been—or elles oghte be—
This yonge child to conjure he bigan,
And seyde, "O deere child, I halse thee, 645
In vertu of the Hooly Trinitee,
Tel me what is thy cause for to synge,
Sith that thy throte is kut to my semynge?"

"My throte is kut unto my nekke-boon,"
Seyde this child, "and as by wey of kynde 650
I sholde have dyed, ye, longe tyme agon.
But Jesu Crist, as ye in bookes fynde,
Wil that his glorie laste and be in mynde;
And for the worship of his Mooder deere
Yet may I synge *O Alma* loude and cleere. 655

"This welle of mercy, Cristes mooder sweete,
I loved alwey as after my konnynge;
And whan that I my lyf sholde forlete,

---

598 wroghte, worked (did). **600 frayneth,** asks. **602 wente . . . forby,** i.e., had gone by. **604 Yaf . . . thoght . . . litel space,** i.e., put it in her mind, in a little while. **607 laude,** praise. **611 Ther . . . ykorven . . . upright,** where, cut, on his back. **615 In coomen,** came in (to the enclosure). **616 provost,** magistrate. **618 herieth,** praises. **620 leet,** caused to be. **624 nexte,** nearest. **626 Unnethe,** scarcely. **627 Rachel,** in Matt. 2:18 Rachel is named as an example of the mothers whose children were killed at Herod's command. **629 sterve,** die. **631 observe,** countenance. **632** Hg&c, *schal have.* **635** *this:* Hg&c *his.* **636 auter,** altar. **637 covent,** convent of monks. **640 spreynd,** sprinkled. **644 conjure,** beseech. **645 halse,** entreat. EHg&c *halsen.* **650 wey of kynde,** in the course of nature. **653 Wil,** wills (wishes). **be in,** i.e., be kept in. **657 konnynge,** knowledge, perception. **658 forlete,** leave ("for" is an intensifier).

To me she cam, and bad me for to synge
This anthem verraily in my deyynge,   660
As ye han herd, and whan that I hadde songe,
Me thoughte she leyde a greyn upon my tonge.

"Wherfore I synge and synge I moot, certeyn,
In honour of that blisful Mayden free
Til fro my tonge of taken is the greyn;   665
And afterward thus seyde she to me,
'My litel child, now wol I fecche thee
Whan that the greyn is fro thy tonge ytake.
Be nat agast, I wol thee nat forsake.' "

  This hooly monk, this abbot, hym meene I,   670
His tonge out caughte and took awey the greyn,
And he yaf up the goost ful softely.
And whan this abbot hadde this wonder seyn,
His salte teeris trikled doun as reyn,

And gruf he fil al plat upon the grounde,   675
And stille he lay as he had leyn ybounde.

The covent eek lay on the pavement
Wepynge, and heryen Cristes mooder deere,
And after that they ryse and forth been went,
And tooken awey this martir from his beere;   680
And in a tombe of marbul stones cleere
Enclosen they his litel body sweete.
Ther he is now, God leve us for to meete!

  O yonge Hugh of Lyncoln, slayn also
With cursed Jewes—as it is notable,   685
For it is but a litel while ago—
Preye eek for us, we synful folk unstable,
That of his mercy, God so merciable
On us his grete mercy multiplie,
For reverence of his mooder Marie. Amen.   690

Heere is ended the Prioresses Tale.

662 **greyn,** grain, seed. 663 **I moot,** I must. Hg&c *I om.* 666 *afterward:* Hg&c *after that.* 675 **gruf . . . plat,** groveling, flat. 676 *leyn:* other MSS **been.** 678 **heryen,** they praise. Other MSS *herying.* 681 *tombe:* E *temple.* 683 **Ther . . . leve,** where, grant. E *us alle.* 684 **Hugh of Lyncoln,** a supposed child-murder for which nineteen Jews were executed by Henry III in 1255. 686 *is:* other MSS *nys.*

TALE OF SIR THOPAS

PROLOGUE

Bihoold the murye wordes of the Hoost to Chaucer.

Whan seyd was al this miracle, every man
As sobre was that wonder was to se,
Til that oure Hooste japen tho bigan,
And thanne at erst he looked upon me,   694
And seyde thus, "What man artow?" quod he.
"Thou lookest as thou woldest fynde an hare,
For evere upon the ground I se thee stare.

"Approche neer and looke up murily.
Now war yow, sires, and lat this man have
    place—
He in the waast is shape as wel as I!   700
This were a popet in an arm t'enbrace

For any womman, smal and fair of face.
He semeth elvyssh by his contenaunce,
For unto no wight dooth he daliaunce.   704

"Sey now somwhat, syn oother folk han sayd.
Telle us a tale of myrthe, and that anon."
"Hooste," quod I, "ne beth nat yvele apayd,
For oother tale certes kan I noon,
But of a rym I lerned longe agoon."
"Ye, that is good," quod he. "Now shul we
    heere   710
Som deyntee thyng, me thynketh by his
    cheere."

Explicit.

693 japen tho, joke then. tho: EHg&c to. 694 at erst, for the first time. 699 war yow, i.e., be aware. have place, i.e., make room for him. 700 waast, waist. Chaucer makes fun of his own plumpness in HF ll. 574, 660, and Lenvoy a Scogan (short poem 21), ll. 27, 31. 701 popet, doll. 703 elvyssh, abstracted (like someone in fairyland). 704 daliaunce, small talk. 707 yvele apayd, displeased. 708 kan, know. 711 deyntee . . . cheere, delightful, expression.

Heere bigynneth Chaucers Tale of Thopas.

Listeth, lordes, in good entent,
And I wol telle verrayment
   Of myrthe and of solas;
Al of a knyght was fair and gent   715
In bataille and in tourneyment—
   His name was Sire Thopas.

Yborn he was in fer contree,
In Flaundres al biyonde the see,
   At Poperyng in the place.   720
His fader was a man ful free,
And lord he was of that contree,
   As it was Goddes grace.

Sire Thopas wax a doghty swayn;
Whit was his face as payndemayn,   725
   His lippes rede as rose;
His rode is lyk scarlet in grayn,
And I yow telle in good certayn,
   He hadde a semely nose.

His heer, his berd was lyk saffroun,   730
That to his girdel raughte adoun,
   His shoon of cordewane.
Of Brugges were his hosen broun,
His robe was of syklatoun,
   That coste many a jane.   735

He koude hunte at wilde deer,
And ride an haukyng for river
   With grey goshauk on honde;

Therto he was a good archeer,
Of wrastlyng was ther noon his peer,   740
   Ther any ram shal stonde.

Ful many a mayde bright in bour,
They moorne for hym paramour,
   Whan hem were bet to slepe.
But he was chaast and no lechour,   745
And sweete as is the brembul flour
   That bereth the rede hepe.

And so bifel upon a day,
Forsothe as I yow telle may,
   Sire Thopas wolde out ride.   750
He worth upon his steede gray,
And in his hand a launcegay,
   A long swerd by his side.

He priketh thurgh a fair forest
Therinne is many a wilde best,   755
   Ye, bothe bukke and hare;
And as he priketh north and est,
I telle it yow, hym hadde almest
   Bitidde a sory care.

Ther spryngen herbes grete and smale,   760
The lycorys and cetewale,
   And many a clowe-gylofre,
And notemuge to putte in ale,
Wheither it be moyste or stale,
   Or for to leye in cofre.   765

712 Listeth, lordes, listen, lords. *Thopas* is a pastiche of clichés and formulas from the popular minstrel romances; these opening lines are the conventional attention-getter of the oral performer. **714 solas,** pleasure (solace), but with sexual innuendo; *Thopas* is back in the world of sexual *double entendre*. **715 gent,** handsome (genteel). **717 Thopas,** topaz, a yellow semiprecious stone. **718–19 fer contree . . . Flaundres,** to have the knight errant come from a far country is a cliché, but Flanders (in modern Belgium) was the most bourgeois and least chivalric country in Europe in Chaucer's day. **720 Poperyng,** a Flemish market town. **place,** city square (hardly an aristocratic birthplace). **721 free,** noble, aristocratic. The humor in this piece comes partly from juxtaposing chivalric and antichivalric markers. **724 doghty swayn,** bold servant. **725 payndemayn,** fine white bread. **727 rode . . . in grayn,** complexion, deep-dyed. **728 And:** Hg&c *As.* **729 semely nose,** handsome nose (an aristocratic feature). **731 raughte,** reached. **732 cordewane,** Cordovan (Spanish) leather. **733 hosen,** laced tights covering legs and hips (yeoman's garb). **734 syklatoun,** costly material woven with silk and gold. **735 jane,** small silver coin from Genoa. **736 deer,** animals. **737 river,** waterfowl (extension from Fr. *riviere,* bank of a stream where the fowl are found). **738 goshauk,** an inferior sort of hawk "fit only for a yeoman." **739–40** Hunting and hawking were aristocratic sports; archery and wrestling plebeian. **741 ram . . . stonde,** the ram was the wrestling prize. **742 bour,** bower (bed chamber). **743 paramour,** with sexual desire. **746–47 brembul flour . . . rede hepe,** wild rose, red rose berry (hip). **748 bifel:** Hg&c *it fil.* **751 worth . . . steede gray,** got; gray horses were workhorses—chargers might be black or white, but were preferably bay. **752 launcegay,** a parade lance, not intended for battle. **754 priketh,** spurs. **759 Bitidde,** happened to him. **761 cetewale,** setwall (zedoary); of course none of the herbs mentioned in these lines is native to Flanders. **762 clowe-gylofre,** clove. **764 moyste,** fresh. **765 cofre,** a chest.

The briddes synge, it is no nay,
The sparhauk and the papejay,
  That joye it was to heere;
The thrustelcok made eek hir lay,
The wodedowve upon a spray   770
  She sang ful loude and cleere.

Sire Thopas fil in love-longynge,
Al whan he herde the thrustel synge,
  And pryked as he were wood.
His faire steede in his prikynge   775
So swatte that men myghte him wrynge;
  His sydes were al blood.

Sire Thopas eek so wery was
For prikyng on the softe gras,
  So fiers was his corage,   780
That doun he leyde him in that plas
To make his steede som solas,
  And yaf hym good forage.

"O Seinte Marie, benedicite,
What eyleth this love at me   785
  To bynde me so soore?
Me dremed al this nyght, pardee,
An elf-queene shal my lemman be
  And slepe under my goore.

"An elf-queene wol I love, ywis,   790
For in this world no womman is
  Worthy to be my make
    In towne;
Alle othere wommen I forsake,
And to an elf-queene I me take   795
  By dale and eek by downe."

Into his sadel he clamb anon,
And priketh over stile and stoon

An elf-queene for t'espye,
Til he so longe hadde riden and goon 800
That he foond in a pryve woon
  The contree of Fairye
    So wilde;
For in that contree was ther noon
That to him durste ride or goon,   805
  Neither wyf ne childe.

Til that ther cam a greet geaunt,
His name was Sire Olifaunt,
  A perilous man of dede.
He seyde, "Child, by Termagaunt,   810
But if thou prike out of myn haunt,
  Anon I sle thy steede
    With mace.
Heere is the queene of Fairye,
With harpe and pipe and symphonye,   815
  Dwellynge in this place."

The child seyde, "Also moote I thee,
Tomorwe wol I meete with thee,
  Whan I have myn armoure;
And yet I hope, *par ma fay*,   820
That thou shalt with this launcegay
  Abyen it ful sowre.
    Thy mawe
Shal I percen if I may,
Er it be fully pryme of day,   825
  For heere thow shalt be slawe."

Sire Thopas drow abak ful faste;
This geant at hym stones caste
  Out of a fel staf-slynge;
But faire escapeth Sir Thopas,   830
And al it was thurgh Goddes gras,
  And thurgh his fair berynge.

---

767 **sparhauk . . . papejay,** sparrow hawk, parrot—hardly singing birds. 769 **thrustelcok,** male thrush. *hir:* Hg&c *his.* 770 **wode-dowve,** wood dove. 774 **pryked . . . wood,** the echo of a memorable line from the ReT, i.4231, reinforces the sexual *double entendre* of the next eight lines. 776 **swatte,** sweated. 780 **fiers . . . corage,** spirit, but *double entendre*, "penis," as in MerchT, iv.1725. 782 **solas,** see above, l. 714. 783 Other MSS *For he was so savage.* 784 **benedicite,** pronounced trisyllabic *bencité.* 785 **eyleth . . . at me,** has against me. 788 **lemman,** lover (mistress). 789 **goore,** garment, generally skirt. 790 *love:* Hg&c *have.* 792 **make,** mate; love for a heroine one has not seen is another romance cliché. 793 **In towne,** these tag lines with only one accented syllable were favorites in the romances, e.g., *Gawain and the Green Knight.* 796 **downe,** hill. 801 **pryve woon,** secret place. 805 Line missing in EHg&c; this, from other MSS, is perhaps scribal. 807 **geaunt,** giant. 808 **Olifaunt,** elephant. 810 **Child,** knight. **Termagaunt,** Saracen idol in *The King of Tars* and other romances. 812 **steede,** killing the horse was not chivalrous. 813 **mace,** spiked war club. 817 **thee,** prosper. 822 **Abyen . . . sowre,** pay for it, sourly (bitterly). 823 **mawe,** stomach. 823 E&c *Thyn hauberk.* 829 **fel staf-slynge,** deadly slingshot (recall David and Goliath). 830 *Sir:* Hg&c *Child.*

Yet listeth, lordes, to my tale,
Murier than the nightyngale,
   For now I wol yow rowne 835
How Sir Thopas with sydes smale,
Prikyng over hill and dale,
   Is comen agayn to towne.

His myrie men comanded he
To make hym bothe game and glee, 840
   For nedes moste he fighte
With a geaunt with hevedes three,
For paramour and jolitee
   Of oon that shoon ful brighte.

"Do come," he seyde, "my mynstrales, 845
And geestours for to tellen tales,
   Anon in myn armynge,
Of romances that been roiales,
Of popes and of cardinales,
   And eek of love-likynge." 850

They fette hym first the sweete wyn,
And mede eek in a mazelyn,
   And roial spicerye
Of gyngebreed that was ful fyn,
And lycorys, and eek comyn, 855
   With sugre that is trye.

He dide next his white leere
Of clooth of lake fyn and cleere,
   A breech and eek a sherte,
And next his sherte an aketoun, 860
And over that an haubergeoun
   For percynge of his herte.

And over that a fyn hawberk,
Was al ywroght of Jewes werk,

Ful strong it was of plate; 865
And over that his cote-armour
As whit as is a lilye flour,
   In which he wol debate.

His sheeld was al of gold so reed,
And therinne was a bores heed, 870
   A charbocle bisyde.
And there he swoor on ale and breed
How that the geaunt shal be deed,
   Bityde what bityde!

His jambeux were of quyrboilly, 875
His swerdes shethe of yvory,
   His helm of latoun bright;
His sadel was of rewel-boon,
His brydel as the sonne shoon,
   Or as the moone light. 880

His spere was of fyn ciprees,
That bodeth werre and nothyng pees,
   The heed ful sharpe ygrounde;
His steede was al dappull gray,
It gooth an ambil in the way 885
   Ful softely and rounde
         In londe.
Loo, lordes myne, heere is a fit!
If ye wol any moore of it,
   To telle it wol I fonde. 890

[The Second Fit]

Now holde youre mouth, *par charitee*,
Bothe knyght and lady free,
   And herkneth to my spelle.
Of bataille and of chivalry

---

835 **rowne,** tell (really "whisper"). EHg&c *For now* om. 836 **sydes smale,** a feminine detail suggesting a slender waist. 840 **glee,** music, entertainment. 842 **hevedes,** heads. 843 **paramour,** love (sex). 845 **Do come,** summon—this begins to sound like the Mother Goose rhyme "Old King Cole." 847 **armynge,** the arming of the knight for battle was another cherished formula in the romances. 850 **love-likynge,** love delights. 852 **mede, mazelyn,** honey wine, mazer (wooden bowl). 855 **comyn,** cumin (a spice). 856 **trye,** excellent. E *so trye*. 857 **leere,** flesh. 858 **clooth of lake . . . cleere,** linen, bright. 860 **aketoun,** padded jacket. 861 **haubergeoun,** coat of chain mail. 862 **For,** against. 863 **hawberk,** plate mail. 864 **Jewes werk,** the Jews were traditionally expert metal craftsmen and dealers in armor and weapons. 866 **cote-armour,** surcoat bearing his heraldic design. 868 **debate,** fight. 871 **charbocle,** carbuncle, in heraldry an eight-pointed star. *bisyde:* Hg&c *by his syde.* 875 **jambeux,** leg-armor. **quyrboilly,** leather shaped by being boiled and dried over forms. 877 **latoun,** brass alloy (showy, but too weak for a helmet). 878 **rewel-boon,** whalebone. 881 **ciprees,** lances were traditionally of ash; cypress trees were planted in cemeteries and symbolized death. E *spere it was.* 884–85 **dappull gray . . . ambil,** neither the color nor the gait of a war-horse. 888 **fit,** canto. 890 **fonde,** try. 891 **holde yonre mouth,** such brusqueness is *not* part of the minstrel tradition. 893 **spelle,** narrative.

And of ladyes love-drury   895
  Anon I wol yow telle.

Men speken of romances of prys,
Of Horn Child and of Ypotys,
  Of Beves and of Sir Gy,
Of Sir Lybeux and Pleyndamour—   900
But Sir Thopas, he bereth the flour
  Of roial chivalry!

His goode steede al he bistrood,
And forth upon his wey he glood
  As sparcle out of the bronde;   905
Upon his creest he bar a tour,

And therinne stiked a lilie flour—
  God shilde his cors fro shonde!

And for he was a knyght auntrous,
He nolde slepen in noon hous,   910
  But liggen in his hoode;
His brighte helm was his wonger,
And by hym baiteth his dextrer
  Of herbes fyne and goode.

Hymself drank water of the well,   915
As dide the knyght Sire Percyvell
  So worthy under wede,
Til on a day . . .

895 love-drury, love service (in the courtly love sense). **898 Horn Child,** the romance *King Horn.* Several of these romances are found together in the Auchinleck MS, which suggests that Chaucer may have had a similar anthology. **Ypotys,** not a romance, but a dialogue in which a Christian child, Ypotis, converts the pagan emperor of Rome. **899 Beves,** *Bevis of Hampton.* **Sir Gy,** *Guy of Warwick.* **900 Sir Lybeux,** *Libeus Desconus* (*Li Beaux Desconous,* The Fair Unknown). **Pleyndamour,** "filled with love," but this romance has not been identified. **904 glood,** glided, E&c *rood.* **905 sparcle . . . bronde,** spark, (burning) brand. **906 tour,** tower. **908 cors . . . shonde,** body, harm. **909 auntrous,** adventurous. **911 liggen,** lie. **912 wonger,** pillow. **913 baiteth . . . dextrer,** grazes, war-horse. **916 Sire Percyvell,** in *Sir Perceval de Galles,* Sir Perceval lived for a time in the forest by a spring. **917 wede,** clothes.

TALE OF MELIBEE

PROLOGUE

Heere the Hoost stynteth Chaucer of his Tale of Thopas.

"Namoore of this, for Goddes dignitee,"
Quod oure Hooste, "for thou makest me   920
So wery of thy verray lewednesse
That, also wisly God my soule blesse,
Myne eres aken of thy drasty speche.
Now swich a rym the devel I biteche!
This may wel be rym dogerel," quod he.   925

   "Why so?" quod I, "why wiltow lette me
Moore of my tale than another man,
Syn that it is the beste rym I kan?"

   "By God," quod he, "for pleynly, at o word,
Thy drasty rymyng is nat worth a toord!   930
Thou doost noght elles but despendest tyme.
Sire, at o word, thou shalt no lenger ryme.
Lat se wher thou kanst tellen aught in geeste,
Or telle in prose somwhat at the leeste,
In which ther be som murthe or som doc-
      tryne."   935

   "Gladly," quod I, "by Goddes sweete pyne,
I wol yow telle a litel thyng in prose

That oghte liken yow, as I suppose,
Or elles certes ye been to daungerous.
It is a moral tale vertuous,   940
Al be it told somtyme in sondry wyse
Of sondry folk as I shal yow devyse.

   "As thus: ye woot that every Evaungelist
That telleth us the peyne of Jhesu Crist
Ne seith nat alle thyng as his felawe dooth,   945
But nathelees hir sentence is al sooth,
And alle acorden as in hire sentence,
Al be ther in hir tellyng difference.
For somme of hem seyn moore and somme
      seyn lesse
Whan they his pitous passioun expresse—   950
I meene of Mark, Mathew, Luc, and John—
But doutelees hir sentence is al oon.

   "Therfore, lordynges alle, I yow biseche,
If that yow thynke I varie as in my speche,
As thus, though that I telle somwhat moore
Of proverbes than ye han herd bifoore   956

---

stynteth, stops. **921 verray lewednesse,** genuine ignorance. **922 also wisly,** as truly. **923 drasty,** worthless (drast, dregs). **924 biteche,** bestow. **926 lette,** hinder. **928 kan,** know. *rym:* E *tale.* **929** *o:* E&c *a.* **931 despendest,** spend (waste). **933 wher . . . geeste,** whether, prose romance. **936 pyne,** pain. **938 liken,** please. **939 daungerous,** critical. **941** *told:* E *take.* **942 devyse,** describe. **946 hir sentence,** their meaning. **952 oon,** the same (one).

Comprehended in this litel tretys heere,
To enforce with th'effect of my mateere,
And though I nat the same wordes seye
As ye han herd, yet to yow alle I preye   960
Blameth me nat, for as in my sentence

Shul ye nowher fynden difference
Fro the sentence of this tretys lyte
After the which this murye tale I write.
And therfore herkneth what that I shal seye
And lat me tellen al my tale I preye."   966

Explicit.

Here biginneth Chaucers Tale of Melibee.

A yong man called Melibeus, mighty and riche, bigat upon his wyf, that called was Prudence, a doghter which that called was Sophie. /

Upon a day bifel that he for his desport is went into the feeldes hym to pleye. / His wyf and eek his doghter hath he left inwith his hous of which the dores weren fast yshette. / Thre of his olde foes han it espyed, and setten laddres to the walles of his hous, and by the wyndowes been entred, / and betten his wyf, and   970 wounded his doghter with fyve mortal woundes in fyve sondry places— / this is to seyn, in hir feet, in hire handes, in hir erys, in hir nose, and in hire mouth—and leften hire for deed, and wenten awey. /

Whan Melibeus retourned was into his hous and saugh al this meschief, he lyk a mad man, rentinge his clothes, gan to wepe and crye. /

Prudence his wyf, as ferforth as she dorste, bisoghte hym of his wepyng for to stynte, / but nat forthy he gan to crie and wepen ever lenger the moore. /   975

This noble wyf Prudence remembered hire upon the sentence of Ovide, in his book that cleped is *The Remedie of Love,* wher as he seith, / "He is a fool that destourbeth the mooder to wepen in the deeth of hire child til she have wept hir fille as for a certein tyme, / and thanne shal man doon his diligence with amyable wordes hire to reconforte, and preyen hire of hir weping for to stynte." /

For which resoun this noble wyf Prudence suffred hir housbond for to wepe and crie as for a certein space, / and whan she saugh hir tyme she seyde hym in this wise, "Allas, my lord," quod she, "why make ye yourself for to be lyk a fool? / For sothe, it aperteneth nat to   980 a wys man to maken swiche a sorwe. / Youre doghter, with the grace of God, shal warisshe and escape. / And al were it so that she right now were deed, ye ne oughte nat as for hir deeth yourself to destroye. / Senek seith, 'The wise man shal nat take to greet disconfort for the deeth of his children, / but certes he sholde suffren it in pacience, as wel as he abideth the deeth of his owene propre persone.' /   985

This Melibeus answerde anon and seyde, "What man," quod he, "sholde of his wepyng stente that hath so greet a cause for to wepe? /

---

958 To enforce . . . effect, to reinforce, conclusion. **967 Melibeus,** "the one who drinks honey," see l. 1410 below. **Sophie,** "wisdom." The name is not found in Chaucer's sources. From classical times, prudence and wisdom were usually personified as feminine, courage and strength as masculine. Line numbers follow the traditional Tyrwhitt line divisions. *Sophie:* other MSS *Sapience.* **968 desport,** recreation. **969 hous,** i.e., his body. **970 Thre . . . foes,** the world, the flesh, and the devil; traditional temptations in the medieval ascetic tradition. See ll. 1420–26 below. **971 fyve . . . woundes,** wounds in the five senses, by which temptation enters the soul. Note the marked rhythm of the opening lines. **974 as ferforth,** as much (far). **975 nat forthy,** nevertheless. **976 Ovide,** *Remedia Amoris,* ll. 127–30. **977 destourbeth . . . to wepen,** i.e., disturbs (prevents) from weeping. **981 aperteneth nat,** i.e., is not becoming. **982 warisshe,** recover. **983 al were it so,** even though. **984 Senek,** Seneca, *Epistolae* 74.30. **986 anon,** immediately.

Jesu Crist oure lord hymself wepte for the deeth of Lazarus hys freend." /

Prudence answerde, "Certes, wel I woot attempree wepyng is nothing deffended to hym that sorweful is, amonges folk in sorwe, but it is rather graunted hym to wepe. / The Apostle Paul unto the Romayns writeth, 'Man shal rejoyse with hem that maken joye, and wepen with swich folk as wepen.' / But though attempree wepyng be ygraunted, outrageous wepyng certes is deffended. / 990 Mesure of wepyng sholde be considered, after the loore that techeth us Senek. / 'Whan that thy frend is deed,' quod he, 'lat nat thyne eyen to moyste been of teeres, ne to muche drye. Although the teeres come to thyne eyen, lat hem nat falle.' / And whan thou hast forgoon thy freend, do diligence to gete another freend; and this is moore wysdom than for to wepe for thy freend which that thou hast lorn, for therinne is no boote. / And therfore if ye governe yow by sapience put awey sorwe out of your herte. / Remembre yow that Jesus Syrak seith, 'A man that is joyous and glad in herte, it hym conserveth florisshyng in his age, but soothly sorweful herte maketh his bones drye.' / He seith eek thus, that sorwe in 995 herte sleeth ful many a man. / Salomon seith that right as motthes in the shepes flees anoyeth to the clothes, and the smale wormes to the tree, right so anoyeth sorwe to the herte. / Wherfore us oghte as wel in the deeth of oure children as in the losse of oure goodes temporels have pacience. / Remembre yow upon the pacient Job. Whan he hadde lost his children and his temporel substance, and in his body endured and receyved ful many a grevous tribulacioun, yet seyde he thus, / 'Oure Lord hath yeven it me, our Lord hath biraft it me.

Right as our Lord hath wold, right so it is doon. Blessed be the name of our Lord.' " / 1000

To thise foreseide thinges answerde Melibeus unto his wyf Prudence, "Alle thy wordes," quod he, "been sothe and therwith profitable. But trewely myn herte is troubled with this sorwe so grevously that I noot what to doone." /

"Lat calle," quod Prudence, "thy trewe freendes alle and thy lynage whiche that been wise. Telleth your cas and herkneth what they seye in conseillyng, and yow governe after hire sentence. / Salomon seith, 'Werk alle thy thinges by conseil and thou shalt never repente.' " /

Thanne, by the conseil of his wyf Prudence, this Melibeus leet callen a greet congregacioun of folk, / as surgiens, phisiciens, olde folk and yonge, and somme of his olde enemys reconsiled as by hir semblaunt to his love and into his grace. / And ther with al ther coomen 1005 somme of his neighebores that diden hym reverence more for drede than for love, as it happeth ofte. / Ther coomen also ful many subtille flatereres, and wise advocatz lerned in the lawe. /

And whan this folk togidre assembled weren, this Melibeus in sorweful wise shewed hem his cas, / and by the manere of his speche it semed wel that in herte he baar a crueel ire, redy to doon vengeaunce upon his foes, and sodeynly desired that the werre sholde bigynne. / But nathelees yet axed he hire conseil upon this matiere. / A surgien, by licence and 1010 assent of swiche as weren wise, up roos and to Melibeus seyde as ye may heere. /

"Sire," quod he, "as to us surgiens aperteneth that we do to every wight the beste that we kan, wher as we been withholde and to our pacientz

987 Lazarus, John 11:35. **988 attempree . . . deffended,** temperate, forbidden. **989 Paul,** Rom. 12:15. **991 Mesure,** moderation. **Senek,** *Epistolae* 63.1.11. **993 forgoon . . . lorn . . . boote,** lost, lost, remedy. **994 sapience,** wisdom (as contrasted to emotion). **995 Jesus Syrak,** Ecclesiasticus in the Septuagint is called "The Wisdom of Jesus, son of Sirach," but this passage comes from Prov. 17:22. **996 He seith,** Ecclus. 30:23 (Vulgate). **997 flees,** wool (fleece). **998 goodes temporels,** adj. following the noun and agreeing in number is in imitation of Fr. usage. *oure goodes:* E&c *othere goodes.* **1000** *hath yeven—as our Lord* E om. (by eyeskip). Job 1:21. **1001 noot,** don't know (ne wot). **1002 lynage . . . sentence,** relatives, advice. **1003 Salomon,** Ecclus. 32:24 (Vulgate). **1005 as . . . semblaunt,** in appearance (apparently). **1006 ther with al,** also. **1009** *semed wel:* Hg&c *wel* om. **1012 aperteneth . . . wight . . . withholde,** belongs (the responsibility), person, retained.

that we do no damage, / wherfore it happeth many tyme and ofte that whan twey men han everich wounded oother, oon same surgien heleth hem bothe. / Wherfore unto our art it is nat pertinent to norice werre, ne parties to supporte. / But certes, as to the warisshynge of youre doghter, al be it so that she perilously be wounded, we shullen do so ententif bisynesse fro day to nyght that with the grace of God she shal be hool and sound as soone as is possible." / Almoost right in the same wise   1015 the phisiciens answerden, save that they seyden a fewe woordes moore, / that "right as maladies been cured by hir contraries, right so shul men warisshe werre by vengeaunce." / His neighebores ful of envye, his feyned freendes that semeden reconsiled, and his flatereres / maden semblant of wepyng, and empeireden and agreggeden muchel of this matiere in preising greetly Melibee of myght, of power, of richesse, and of freendes, despisynge the power of his adversaries, / and seiden outrely that he anon sholde wreken hym on his foes and bigynne werre. /   1020

Up roos thanne an advocat that was wys, by leve and by conseil of othere that were wise, and seide, / "Lordynges, the nede for which we been assembled in this place is a ful hevy thyng and an heigh matiere, / by cause of the wrong and of the wikkednesse that hath be doon, and eek by resoun of the grete damages that in tyme comynge been possible to fallen for this same cause, / and eek by resoun of the grete richesse and power of the parties bothe, / for the whiche resouns it were a ful greet peril to erren in this matiere. / Wherfore,   1025

Melibeus, this is our sentence: we conseille yow aboven alle thing that right anon thou do thy diligence in kepynge of thy propre persone in swich a wise that thou wante noon espie ne wacche thy body for to save. / And after that we conseille that in thyn hous thou sette sufficeant garnisoun so that they may as wel thy body as thyn hous defende. / But certes, for to moeve werre, or sodeynly for to doon vengeaunce, we may nat demen in so litel tyme that it were profitable. / Wherfore we axen leyser and espace to have deliberacioun in this cas to deme. / For the commune proverbe seith thus, 'He that sone deemeth, soone shal repente.' / And eek men seyn that thilke   1030 juge is wys that soone understondeth a matiere and juggeth by leyser. / For al be it so that alle tariyng be anoyful, algates it is nat to repreve in yevynge of juggement, ne in vengeance-takyng, whan it is sufficeant and resonable. / And that shewed oure lord Jesu Crist by ensample, for whan that the womman that was taken in avowtrie was broght in his presence, to knowen what sholde be doon with hire persone, al be it so that he wiste wel hymself what that he wolde answere, yet ne wolde he nat answere sodeynly, but he wolde have deliberacioun, and in the ground he wroot twies. / And by thise causes we axen deliberacioun, and we shal thanne, by the grace of God, conseille thee thyng that shal be profitable." /

Up stirten thanne the yonge folk at ones, and the mooste partie of that compainye scorned the olde wise men, and bigonnen to make noyse, and seyden that / right so as whil   1035

1014 norice . . . parties to supporte, encourage (nourish), support either party. **1015 warisshynge . . . ententif,** healing, diligent (attentive). **1017 cured by . . . contraries,** the medieval belief that the "humors" (phlegm, blood, choler, and melancholy) must be preserved in balance for good health. *by vengaunce* a non sequitur not found in the original Lat. but added by the Fr. translation. **1018 feyned,** pretended. **1019 semblant . . . empeireden . . . agreggeden,** appearance, made worse, aggravated. **Melibee of myght,** i.e., the might of Melibee. **1020 outrely . . . wreken,** without reserve (utterly), revenge. **1022 hevy,** serious. **1023 eek . . . fallen,** also, occur. **1025 to erren,** to make a mistake. **1026 do . . . diligence . . . kepynge . . . wante . . . wacche,** take pains, guarding, lack, guard (watchman). *thou wante:* Hg&c *thou ne wante; body:* E *persone.* **1027 garnisoun,** garrison (guards). **1028 moeve werre . . . demen,** i.e., move to war (begin), decide. *or sodeynly:* Hg&c *be sodeynly.* **1029 espace,** space of time. Some MSS *a space/space.* **1030 commune proverbe,** various parallels to this and subsequent proverbs are listed in the Skeat and Robinson editions. **soone,** quickly. **1032 algates . . . to repreve,** nevertheless, to be reproved. **1033 avowtrie,** adultery, John 8:3–8. **1035 the olde:** Hg&c *this olde.*

that iren is hoot men sholden smyte, right so men sholde wreken hir wronges while that they been fresshe and newe. And with loud voys they criden, 'Werre! Werre!' /

Up roos tho oon of thise olde wise, and with his hand made contenaunce that men sholde holden hem stille and yeven hym audience. / "Lordynges," quod he, "ther is ful many a man that crieth 'werre, werre,' that woot ful litel what werre amounteth. / Werre at his bigynnyng hath so greet an entryng and so large that every wight may entre whan hym liketh, and lightly fynde werre. / But certes what ende that shal therof bifalle, it is nat light to knowe. / 1040 For soothly, whan that werre is ones bigonne, ther is ful many a child unborn of his mooder that shal sterve yong by cause of that ilke werre, or elles lyve in sorwe and dye in wrecchednesse. / And therfore, er that any werre bigynne, men moste have greet conseil and greet deliberacioun." /

And whan this olde man wende to enforcen his tale by resons, wel ny alle at ones bigonne they to rise for to breken his tale, and beden hym ful ofte his wordes for to abregge. / For soothly, he that precheth to hem that listen nat heeren his wordes, his sermon hem anoieth. / For Jesus Syrak seith that musik in wepynge is anoyous thing—this is to seyn, as muche availleth to speken bifore folk to whiche his speche anoyeth, as it is to synge biforn hym that wepeth. / And whan this wyse 1045 man saugh that hym wanted audience, al shamefast he sette him doun agayn. / For Salomon seith, "Ther as thou ne mayst have noon audience, enforce thee nat to speke." / "I see wel," quod this wise man, "that the commune proverbe is sooth, that good conseil wanteth whan it is most nede." /

Yet hadde this Melibeus in his conseil many folk that prively in his eere conseilled hym certeyn thing and conseilled hym the contrarie in general audience. /

Whan Melibeus hadde herd that the gretteste partie of his conseil weren accorded that he sholde maken werre, anoon he consented to hir conseilling and fully affermed hir sentence. / Thanne dame Prudence, when 1050 that she saugh how that hir housbonde shoop hym for to wreken hym on his foes and to bigynne werre, she in ful humble wise, when she saugh hir tyme, seide to hym thise wordes, / "My lord," quod she, "I yow biseche as hertely as I dar and kan, ne haste yow nat to faste, and for alle gerdons as yeveth me audience. / For Piers Alfonce seith, 'Whoso that dooth to thee oother good or harm, haste thee nat to quiten it; for in this wise thy freend wol abyde and thyn enemy shal the lenger lyve in drede.' / The proverbe seith, 'He hasteth wel that wisely kan abyde,' and in wikked haste is no profit." /

This Melibee answerde unto his wyf Prudence, "I purpose nat," quod he, "to werke by thy conseil for many causes and resouns. For certes, every wight wolde holde me thanne a fool— / this is to seyn, if I for thy 1055 conseilling wolde chaungen thynges that been ordeyned and affermed by so manye wyse. / Secoundly, I seye that alle wommen been wikke and noon good of hem alle. For of a thousand men, seith Salomon, I foond o good man, but, certes, of alle wommen, good womman foond I never. / And also certes, if I governed me by thy conseil, it sholde seme that I hadde yeve to thee over me the maistrie, and God forbede that it so weere. / For Jesus Syrak seith that if the wyf have maistrie, she is

1036 wreken, avenge. **1037 tho . . . made contenaunce,** then, made a gesture. **1038 woot . . . amounteth,** knows, means (amounts to). **1039 entryng . . . lightly,** entry, easily. Hg&c *entre*. **1041 ones . . . sterve . . . ilke,** once, die, same. **1042** *bigynne*: Hg&c *be bigonne*. **1043 wende to enforcen . . . breken,** thought (tried) to reinforce, interrupt. **1044 listen . . . heeren,** desire, to hear. **1045 Jesus Syrak,** Ecclus. 22:6 (Vulgate). **1046 hym wanted,** i.e., was lacking to him. E&c *whan* om. **1047 Salomon,** Ecclus. 32:6 (Vulgate). **1048 wanteth . . . nede,** lacking, needed. E *nede* om. **1049 general audience,** i.e., in public. **1051 shoop . . . wreken,** prepared (shaped), avenge. **1052 gerdons . . . audience,** rewards, i.e., for goodness' sake listen to me. **1053 Piers Alfonce,** Petrus Alphonsus, author of a popular collection of exempla, *Disciplina Clericalis* ("the education of clerks"); this ref. is in exemplum 24. **thee oother . . . quiten,** thee either, repay. E&c *that oother good*. **1057 noon . . . o good,** not one (none), one good. Eccles. 7:28. E&c *a good*. **1058** *God forbede*: Hg&c *goddes forbode* (God's prohibition). **1059 Jesus Syrak,** Ecclus. 25:30 (Vulgate).

contrarious to hir housbonde. / And Salomon seith, 'Never in thy lyf to thy wyf ne to thy child ne to thy freend ne yeve no power over thyself. For bettre it were that thy children aske of thy persone thynges that hem nedeth than thou be thyself in the handes of thy children.' / And if I wolde werke by thy conseilling, certes my conseilling moste somtyme be secree til it were tyme that it moste be knowe, and this ne may noght be. / For it is writen that the janglerie of wommen kan nat hyden thynges save that they witen noght. / Furthermore the philosophre seith, 'In wikked conseil wommen venquisshe men.' And for thise resouns I ne owe nat usen thy conseil.'' /

Whanne dame Prudence ful debonairly and with greet pacience hadde herd al that hir housbonde lyked for to seye, thanne axed she of hym licence for to speke, and seyde in this wyse. / "My lord," quod she, "as to your firste resoun, certes it may lightly been answered. For I seye that it is no folie to chaunge conseil whan the thyng is chaunged, or elles whan the thyng semeth otherweyes than it was biforn. / And mooreover I seye that though ye han sworn and bihight to parfourne youre emprise, and nathelees ye weyve to parfourne thilke same emprise by juste cause, men sholde nat seyn therfore that ye were a lier ne forsworn. / For the book seith that the wise man maketh no lesyng whan he turneth his corage to the bettre. / And al be it so that your emprise be establissed and ordeyned by greet multitude of folk, yet thar ye nat accomplice thilke ordinaunce but yow lyke. / For the trouthe of thynges and the profit been rather founden in fewe folk that been wise and ful of resoun than by greet multitude of folk ther

every man crieth and clatereth what that hym liketh. Soothly swich multitude is nat honeste. / As to the seconde resoun, where as ye seyn that alle wommen been wikke, save your grace, certes ye despisen alle wommen in this wyse; and he that alle despyseth alle displeseth, as seith the book. / And Senec seith that who so wole have sapience shal no man dispreise, but he shal gladly techen the science that he kan withouten presumpcioun or pryde. / And swiche thynges as he nought ne kan, he shal nat been ashamed to lerne hem and enquere of lasse folk than hymself. / And sire, that ther hath been many a good womman may lightly be preved. / For certes, sire, oure lord Jesu Crist wolde nevere have descended to be born of a womman if alle wommen hadden ben wikke. / And after that, for the grete bountee that is in wommen, our lord Jesu Crist, whan he was risen fro deeth to lyve, appeered rather to a womman than to his apostles. / And though that Salomon seith that he ne fond never womman good, it folweth nat therfore that alle wommen ben wikke. / For though that he ne fond no good womman, certes, ful many another man hath founden many a womman ful good and trewe. / Or elles peraventure the entente of Salomon was this, that as in sovereyn bountee he foond no womman— / this is to seyn, that ther is no wight that hath sovereyn bountee save God allone, as he hymself recordeth in hys Evaungelie. / For ther nys no creature so good that hym ne wanteth somwhat of the perfeccioun of God that is his maker. / Your thridde resoun is this: ye seyn if ye governe yow by my conseil, it sholde seme that ye hadde yeve me the maistrie and the lordshipe over your persone. / Sire,

1060 Salomon seith, Ecclus. 33:19–21 (Vulgate). *be thyself:* Hg&c *see* thyself. **1061 moste somtyme,** must for a time. **1062 janglerie . . . witen,** babbling, know. **1063 ne owe nat usen,** ought not follow. Lines 1062–63 om. from all MSS and therefore probably from Chaucer's source; trans. by Skeat from Fr. original (here slightly emended). **1064 debonairly,** courteously. **1065 lightly . . . conseil,** easily, purpose (or counselor). **1066 bihight . . . emprise . . . weyve,** promised, enterprise, refrain (charge). **1067 the book,** Seneca, *De Beneficiis* 4.38.1. **lesyng . . . turneth his corage,** lying, changes his mind. **1068 thar . . . ordinaunce but yow lyke,** need, plan unless it pleases you. **1069 rather . . . ther every man . . . honeste,** sooner, where everyone, dependable. **1070** *As to:* Hg&c *And to.* E *and he that—book* om. **1071 Senec,** erroneously attributed to Seneca; found in Martinus Dumiensis, *Formula Honestae Vitae,* Chap. 3. **dispreise,** i.e., shall disparage no one. **1072 nought ne kan,** does not know. **1073 lightly,** easily. **1078 sovereyn bountee,** supreme goodness. **1079 Evaungelie,** gospel, e.g., Matt. 19:17, Luke 18:19. **1080 wanteth,** lacks.

save your grace, it is nat so. For if it were so, that no man sholde be conseilled but oonly of hem that hadden lordshipe and maistrie of his persone, men wolden nat be conseilled so ofte. / For soothly, thilke man that asketh conseil of a purpos, yet hath he free choys, wheither he wole werke by that conseil or noon. / And as to youre fourthe resoun, ther ye seyn that the janglerie of wommen kan nat hyd thynges save that they wiste noght, as who seith that a womman kan nat hyde that she woot, / sire, thise wordes been understonde of wommen that been jangleresses and wikked, / of whiche 1085 wommen men seyn that three thinges dryven a man out of his hous, that is to seyn, smoke, dropping of reyn, and wikked wyves. / And of swiche wommen seith Salomon that it were bettre dwelle in desert than with a womman that is riotous. / And sire, by youre leve, that am nat I. / For ye haan ful ofte assayed my grete silence and my gret pacience, and eek how wel that I kan hyde and hele thynges that men oghte secreely to hyde. / And soothly, as to youre fifthe resoun, wher as ye seyn that in wikked conseil wommen venquisshe men, God woot thilke resoun stant heere in no stede. / For understoond now, ye 1090 asken conseil to do wikkednesse; / and if ye wole werken wikkednesse and your wyf restreyneth thilke wikked purpos and overcometh yow by resoun and by good conseil, / certes, youre wyf oghte rather to be preised than yblamed. / Thus sholde ye understonde the philosophre that seith, 'In wikked conseil wommen venquisshen hir housbondes.' / And ther as ye blamen alle wommen and hir resouns, I shal shewe yow by manye ensamples

that many a womman hath ben ful good, and yet been, and hir conseils ful hoolsome and profitable. / Eek som men han seyd 1095 that the conseillinge of wommen is outher to deere or elles to litel of prys. / But al be it so that ful many a womman is badde and hir conseil vile and noght worth, yet han men founde ful many a good womman and ful discrete and wise in conseillinge. / Loo Jacob by good conseil of his mooder Rebekka wan the benysoun of Ysaak his fader and the lordshipe over alle his bretheren. / Judith by hire good conseil delivered the citee of Bethulie, in which she dwelled, out of the handes of Olofernus that hadde it biseged and wolde have al destroyed it. / Abygail delivered Nabal hir housbonde fro David the kyng that wolde have slayn hym, and apaysed the ire of the kyng by hir wit and by hir good conseillyng. / Hester en- 1100 haunced greetly by hir good conseil the peple of God in the regne of Assuerus the kyng. / And the same bountee in good conseilling of many a good womman may men telle. / And mooreover, whan our Lord hadde creat Adam our formefader, he seyde in this wyse, 'It is nat good to been a man alloone. Make we to hym an help semblable to hymself.' / Heere may ye se that if that wommen were nat goode, and hir conseils goode and profitable, / 1105 oure lord God of hevene wolde neither han wroght hem, ne called hem help of man, but rather confusioun of man. / And ther seyde oones a clerk in two vers: 'What is bettre than gold? Jaspre. What is bettre than jaspre? Wisedoom. / And what is bettre than wisedoom? Womman. And what is bettre than a good womman? Nothyng.' / And sire, by manye of

---

1083 of a purpos . . . noon, about a plan, not. **1084 wiste . . . woot,** know, know. *kan nat hyd:* Hg&c *kan hyd,* E *hath hyd. save that:* all MSS *save* om. **1085 jangleresses,** female gossips. **1086 three thinges,** a favorite proverb in the Middle Ages, used by Chaucer in WBP, III.278, and ParsT, x.631. For parallels and Biblical sources see Skeat and Robinson editions. **1087 Salomon,** Prov. 21:9. **riotous,** quarrelsome. **1088 that am nat I,** see WBP, III.112. The similarities in phrasing in this section suggest the influence of *Melibee* on the development of the marriage argument in *CT,* III–v. **1089 assayed . . . hele,** tested, conceal. **1090 venquisshe . . . no stede,** surpass, no account. **1095 hir resouns . . . yet been,** their arguments, still are. **1096 outher to deere,** either too costly. **1098 Jacob,** Gen. 27. **wan . . . benysoun,** won, blessing. Jacob, Judith (Jth. 11–13), Abygail (I Sam. 25:14), and Esther (Esther 7) are cited in the same order in MerchT, IV.1362ff. **1100 apaysed,** appeased. **1101 enhaunced,** advanced (the condition of). **1102 bountee,** virtues. **1103 formefader,** first father. **1104 help semblable,** helpmate (companion), similar. **1106 confusioun,** see NPT, VII.3164. *neither:* E&c *nevere.*

othre resons may ye seen that manye wommen been goode and hir conseils goode and profitable. / And therfore, sire, if ye wol triste to my conseil, I shal restoore yow youre doghter hool and sound. / And eek I wol do to yow so muche that ye shul have honour in this cause." / 1110

Whan Melibee hadde herd the wordes of his wyf Prudence he seyde thus, / "I se wel that the word of Salomon is sooth. He seith that wordes that been spoken discreetly by ordinaunce been honycombes, for they yeven swetnesse to the soule and hoolsomnesse to the body. / And wyf, by cause of thy swete wordes and eek for I have assayed and preved thy grete sapience and thy grete trouthe, I wol governe me by thy conseil in alle thing." /

"Now sire," quod dame Prudence, "and syn ye vouchesauf to been governed by my conseil, I wol enforme yow how ye shul governe yourself in chesynge of your conseillours. / 1115 Ye shul first in alle youre werkes mekely biseken to the heighe God that he wol be your conseillour; / and shapeth yow to swich entente that he yeve yow conseil and confort, as taughte Thobie his sone: / 'At alle tymes thou shalt blesse God, and praye hym to dresse thy weyes.' And looke that alle thy conseils been in hym for evermoore. / Seint Jame eek seith, 'If any of yow have nede of sapience, axe it of God.' / And afterward thanne shul ye taken conseil of yourself and examyne wel your thoghtes of swich thyng as yow thynketh that is best for your profit. / And thanne 1120 shul ye dryve fro your herte thre thynges that been contrariouse to good conseil, / that is to seyn, ire, coveitise, and hastifnesse. /

"First, he that axeth conseil of hymself, certes he moste been withouten ire, for manye causes. / The firste is this: he that hath greet ire and wratthe in hymself, he weneth alwey that he may do thyng that he may nat do. / And secoundely, he that is irous and wrooth, he ne may nat wel deme; / and he that 1125 may nat wel deme may nat wel conseille. / The thridde is this, that he that is irous and wrooth, as seith Senec, ne may nat speke but blameful thynges; / and with his viciouse wordes he stireth oother folk to angre and to ire. / And eek, sire, ye moste dryve coveitise out of youre herte. / For the apostle seith that coveitise is roote of alle harmes. / And 1130 trust wel that a coveitous man ne kan noght deme ne thynke, but oonly to fulfille the ende of his coveitise. / And certes, that ne may never been accompliced, for ever the moore habundaunce that he hath of richesse, the moore he desireth. / And sire, ye moste also dryve out of youre herte hastifnesse, for certes, / ye may nat deeme for the beste by a sodeyn thought that falleth in youre herte, but ye moste avyse yow on it ful ofte. / For as ye herde biforn, the commune proverbe is this, that he that soone demeth, soone repenteth. / 1135

"Sire, ye ne be nat alwey in lyke disposicioun / for certes somthyng that somtyme semeth to yow that it is good for to do another tyme it semeth to yow the contrarie. /

"Whan ye han taken conseil of yourself, and han deemed by good deliberacion swich thyng as you list best, / thanne rede I yow that ye kepe it secree. / Biwrey nat youre conseil to no persone but if so be that ye wenen sikerly that, thurgh your biwreying, your condicioun shal be to yow the moore profitable. / For 1140 Jesus Syrak seith, 'Neither to thy foe ne to thy frend discovere nat thy secree ne thy folie, / for they wol yeve yow audience and looking and supportacioun in thy presence and scorne thee in thyn absence.' / Another clerk seith that

1113 Salomon, Prov. 16:24. **by ordinaunce,** rationally (by plan). **1114 trouthe,** integrity (loyalty). **1115 syn ye vouchesauf,** since you agree. At this point the Fr. text omits 10 pages of the Lat. original. **1116 biseken,** beseech (northern dialect). **1117 shapeth yow ... Thobie,** bend yourself, Tobias 4:20 (Vulgate). **1118 dresse,** guide. **1119 Seint Jame,** James 1:5. **1124 weneth,** thinks. **1125 deme,** judge (reason). **1127 Senec,** not from Seneca's *De Ira,* but from Pubilius Syrus, *Sententiae* 281. **blameful thynges:** E *he blame thynges;* Fr. *choses crimineuses.* **1130 apostle,** I Tim. 6:10. **1131 deme,** judge. **1134 avyse yow,** deliberate. **beste by:** Hg&c *by* om. **1138 list,** pleases, Hg&c *semeth.* **1139 rede,** advise. **1140 Biwrey ... conseil ... wenen sikerly,** reveal, decision, believe truly (securely, northern dialect). **1141 Jesus Syrak,** Ecclus. 19:8–9 (Vulgate).

scarsly shaltou fynden any persone that may kepe conseil sikerly. / The book seith, 'Whil that thou kepest thy conseil in thyn herte, thou kepest it in thy prisoun, / and whan thou biwreyest thy conseil to any wight, he holdeth thee in his snare.' / And therefore 1145 yow is bettre to hyde your conseil in your herte than praye hem to whom ye han biwreyed youre conseil that he wole kepen it cloos and stille. / For Seneca seith, 'If so be that thou ne mayst nat thyn owene conseil hyde, how darstou prayen any oother wight thy conseil sikerly to kepe?' / But nathelees, if thou wene sikerly that the biwreiyng of thy conseil to a persone wol make thy condicioun to stonden in the bettre plyt, thanne shaltou tellen hym thy conseil in this wise. / First, thou shalt make no semblant wheither thee were levere pees or werre, or this or that, ne shewe hym nat thy wille and thyn entente. / For trust wel, that comenli thise conseillours been flatereres, / 1150 namely the conseillours of grete lordes, / for they enforcen hem alwey rather to speken plesante wordes, enclynynge to the lordes lust, than wordes that been trewe or profitable. / And therfore men seyn that the riche man hath seeld good conseil but if he have it of hymself. / And after that, thou shalt considere thy freendes and thyne enemys. / And as touchynge thy freendes, thou shalt considere wiche of hem that been moost feithful and moost wise, and eldest and most approved in con-seilling. / And of hem shalt thou aske thy 1155 conseil, as the caas requireth. /

"I seye that first ye shul clepe to youre conseil your freendes that been trewe. / For Salomon seith that right as the herte of a man deliteth in savour that is soote, right so the conseil of trewe freendes yeveth swetenesse to the soule. / He seith also, 'Ther may nothing be likned to the trewe freend.' / For certes, gold ne silver beth nat so muche worth as the goode wyl of a trewe freend. / And eek he 1160 seith that a trewe freend is a strong deffense; whoso that hym fyndeth, certes he fyndeth a greet tresour. / Thanne shul ye eek considere if that your trewe freendes been discrete and wyse. For the book seith, 'Axe alwey thy conseil of hem that been wise.' / And by this same resoun shul ye clepen to youre conseil of youre freendes that been of age, swiche as han seyn and been expert in manye thynges, and been approved in conseillinges. / For the book seith that in the olde men is the sapience and in longe tyme the prudence. / And Tullius seith that grete thynges ne been nat ay accompliced by strengthe, ne by delivernesse of body, but by good conseil, by auctoritee of persones, and by science, the whiche thre thynges ne been nat fieble by age, but certes they enforcen and encreesen day by day. / And thanne shul ye kepe this for a 1165 general reule. First shul ye clepen to your conseil a fewe of your freendes that been especiale, / for Salomon seith, 'Manye freendes have thou, but among a thousand chese thee oon to be thy conseillour.' / For al be it so that thou first ne telle thy conseil but to a fewe, thou mayst afterward telle it to mo folk if it be nede. / But looke alwey that thy conseillours have thilke thre condiciouns that I have seyd bifore, that is to seyn, that they be trewe, wise, and of oold experience. / And werke nat alwey in every nede by oon counseillour allone, for somtyme bihooveth it to been conseilled by manye. / For Salomon seith, 'Salvacioun 1170 of thynges is wher as ther been manye conseillours.' /

"Now sith I have toold yow of which folk ye sholde been counseilled, now wol I teche yow

1143 sikerly, securely, Hg&c *secrely.* **1146 praye,** beg. **1147 Seneca,** not from Seneca, but pseudo-Martinus Dumiensis, *De Moribus* 16. *sikerly:* Hg&c *secrely.* **1148 wene . . . biwreiyng,** think, revealing. **1149 semblant . . . levere,** hint (gesture), more desirable. **1151 namely,** especially. **1152 enforcen hem . . . lust,** try, desire. **1153 seeld,** seldom. **1157 clepe,** summon (call). **1158 Salomon,** Prov. 27:9. **soote,** sweet. **1159 likned,** compared. Ecclus. 6:15 (Vulgate). **1161 he seith,** Ecclus. 6:14 (Vulgate). *hym fyndeth:* Hg&c it *findeth.* **1162 if that,** whether. **the book,** Tobias 4:19 (Vulgate). **1163 swiche . . . seyn,** such, seen. **1164 the book,** Job 12:12. **1165 Tullius,** Cicero, *De Senectute* 6.17. **delivernesse . . . science . . . enforcen,** agility, knowledge, grow stronger. **1167 Salomon,** Ecclus. 6:6 (Vulgate). **1168 mo,** more. **1169 looke . . . thilke,** see, those. **1170 werke,** act. **1171 Salomon,** Prov. 11:14. **Salvacioun,** rectifying.

which conseil ye oghte to eschewe. / First ye shul escheue the conseillyng of fooles. For Salomon seith, 'Taak no conseil of a fool, for he ne kan noght conseille but after his owene lust and his affeccioun.' / The book seith that the propretee of a fool is this: he troweth lightly harm of every wight, and lightly troweth alle bountee in hymself. / Thou shalt eek escheue the conseillyng of flatereres, swiche as enforcen hem rather to preise your persone by flaterye than for to telle yow the sothfastnesse of thinges. /   1175

"Wherfore Tullius seith, 'Amonges alle the pestilences that been in freendshipe, the gretteste is flaterie.' And therfore is it moore nede that thou escheue and drede flatereres than any oother peple. / The book seith, 'Thou shalt rather drede and flee fro the sweete wordes of flaterynge preiseres than fro the egre wordes of thy freend that seith thee thy sothes.' / Salomon seith that the wordes of a flaterere is a snare to cacche with innocents. / He seith also that he that speketh to his freend wordes of swetnesse and of plesaunce setteth a net biforn his feet to cacche hym. / And therfore seith Tullius, 'Enclyne nat thyne eres to flatereres, ne taaketh no conseil of the wordes of flaterye.' / And Caton seith, 'Avyse thee   1180 wel and escheue the wordes of swetnesse and of plesaunce.' / And eek thou shalt escheue the conseillyng of thyne olde enemys that been reconsiled. / The book seith that no wight retourneth saufly into the grace of hys olde enemy. / And Isope seith, 'Ne trust nat to hem to whiche thou hast had somtyme werre or enemytee, ne telle hem nat thy conseil.' / And Seneca telleth the cause why: 'It may nat be,' seith he, 'that where greet fyr hath longe tyme

endured that ther ne dwelleth som vapour of warmnesse.' / And therfore seith   1185 Salomon, 'In thyn olde foo trust nevere.' / For sikerly though thyn enemy be reconsiled and maketh thee chiere of humylitee and lowteth to thee with his heed, ne trust him nevere. / For certes, he maketh thilke feyned humilitee moore for his profit than for any love of thy persone, by cause that he deemeth to have victorie over thy persone by swich feyned contenance, the which victorie he mighte nat wynne by strif or werre. / And Peter Alfonce seith, 'Make no felawshipe with thyne olde enemys, for if thou do hem bountee, they wol perverten it into wikkednesse.' / And eek thou most escheue the conseilling of hem that been thy servants and beren thee greet reverence, for peraventure they doon it moore for drede than for love. / And therfore seith a   1190 philosophre in this wise, 'Ther is no wight parfitly trewe to hym that he to soore dredeth.' / And Tullius seith, 'Ther nys no myght so greet of any emperour that longe may endure but if he have moore love of the peple than drede.' / Thou shalt also escheue the conseiling of folk that been dronkelewe, for they kan no conseil hyde. / For Salomon seith, 'Ther is no privetee ther as regneth dronkenesse.' / Ye shul also han in suspect the conseillyng of swich folk as conseille yow o thyng prively and conseille yow the contrarie openly. / For Cassidorie   1195 seith that it is a manere sleighte to hyndre whan he sheweth to doon o thyng openly and werketh prively the contrarie. / Thou shalt also have in suspect the conseillyng of wikked folk. For the book seith, 'The conseillyng of wikked folk is alwey full of fraude.' / And David seith, 'Blisful is that man that hath nat folwed the

---

1172 **eschewe,** avoid. 1173 **Salomon,** Ecclus. 8:17 (Vulgate). **lust . . . affeccioun,** desire, gratification. 1174 **The book,** Cicero, *Disputationes Tusculanae* 3.30.73. **propretee . . . troweth . . . bountee,** quality (property), believes, goodness. 1175 **enforcen . . . sothfastnesse,** try, truth. 1176 **Tullius,** Cicero, *Laelius* 25.91. 1177 **sothes,** truths. 1178 **Salomon,** Prov. 29:5. Hg&c *to cacchen innocentz.* 1180 **Tullius,** Cicero, *De Officiis* 1.26.91. 1181 **Caton,** Dionysius Cato, *Disticha* 3.4. **Avyse,** consider. 1183 **The book,** Pubilius Syrus, *Sententiae* 91. 1185 **Seneca,** Publius Syrus, *Sententiae* 389. 1186 **Salomon,** Ecclus. 12:10 (Vulgate). 1187 **chiere . . . lowteth,** appearance, bows. 1188 **thilke,** that (sort of). *wynne:* Hg&c *have.* 1189 **Peter Alfonce,** *Disciplina Clericalis* 4.4. **bountee,** goodness. 1190 *doon:* Hg&c *seyn* (say). 1191 **to soore,** too much (sorely). 1192 **Tullius,** Cicero, *De Officiis* 2.7. E *for drede.* 1193 **dronkelewe,** drunkards. 1194 **Salomon,** Prov. 31.4. 1195–96 *o thyng:* EHg&c *a thyng.* 1196 **Cassidorie,** Cassiodorus, *Variae* 10.18. **a manere sleighte,** a kind of trick. 1197 **the book,** Prov. 12:5. 1198 **David,** Ps. 1.1.

conseilyng of shrewes.' / Thou shalt also escheue the conseillyng of yong folk, for hir conseil is nat rype. /

"Now sire, sith I have shewed yow of which folk ye shul take your conseil, and of which folk ye shul folwe the conseil, / now wol I 1200 teche yow how ye shal examyne your conseil, after the doctrine of Tullius. / In the examynynge thanne of your conseillour, ye shul considere manye thynges. / Alderfirst thou shalt considere that in thilke thyng that thou purposest, and upon what thyng thou wolt have conseil, that verray trouthe be seyd and conserved, this is to seyn, telle trewely thy tale. / For he that seith fals may nat wel be conseilled in that cas of which he lieth. / And after this, thou shalt considere the thynges that acorden to that thou purposest for to do by thy conseillours, if resoun accorde therto, / 1205 and eek if thy myght may atteine therto, and if the moore part and the bettre part of thy conseillours accorde therto or noon. / Thanne shaltou considere what thyng shal folwe after hir conseillyng, as hate, pees, werre, grace, profit, or damage, and manye othere thynges. / Thanne of alle thise thynges thou shalt chese the beste and weyve alle othere thynges. / Thanne shaltow considere of what roote is engendred the matiere of thy conseil and what fruyt it may conceyve and engendre. / Thou shalt eek considere alle thise causes fro whennes they been spronged. / And whan 1210 ye han examyned youre conseil as I have seyd, and which partie is the bettre and moore profitable, and hast approved it by manye wise folk and olde, / thanne shaltou considere if thou mayst parfourne it and maken of it a good ende. / For certes, resoun wol nat that any man sholde bigynne a thyng but if he myghte parfourne it as hym oghte. / Ne no wight sholde

take upon hym so hevy a charge that he myghte nat bere it. / For the proverbe seith, he that to muche embraceth, distreyneth litel. / 1215 And Catoun seith, 'Assay to do swich thing as thou hast power to doon lest that the charge oppresse thee so soore that thee bihoveth to weyve thyng that thou hast bigonne.' / And if so be that thou be in doute wheither thou mayst parfourne a thyng or noon, chese rather to suffre than bigynne. / And Piers Alphonce seith, 'If thou hast myght to doon a thyng of which thou most repente thee, it is bettre nay than ye.' / This is to seyn that thee is bettre holde thy tonge stille than for to speke. / Thanne may ye understonde by strenger resons that if thou hast power to parfourne a werk of which thou shalt repente, thanne is it bettre that thou suffre than bigynne. / Wel seyn they 1220 that defenden every wight to assaye anything of which he is in doute, wheither he may parfourne it or noon. / And after, whan ye han examyned youre conseil as I have seyd biforn and knowen wel that ye may parfourne youre emprise, conferme it thanne sadly til it be at an ende. /

"Now is it resoun and tyme that I shewe yow whanne and wherfore that ye may chaunge your conseil withouten youre repreve. / Soothly a man may chaungen his purpos and his conseil if the cause cesseth or whan a newe caas bitydeth. / For the lawe seith that upon thinges that newely bityden bihoveth newe conseil. / And Senec seith, 'If thy conseil 1225 is comen to the eres of thyn enemy, change thy conseil.' / Thou mayst also chaunge thy conseil if so be that thou mayst fynde that by errour or by oother cause harm or damage may bityde. / Also, if thy conseil be dishonest or ellis cometh of dishoneste cause, chaunge thy conseil. / For the lawes seyn that alle bihestes

1198 shrewes, villains. **1201–10 Tullius,** Cicero, *De Officiis* 2.5.18, paraphrase. **1203 Alderfirst,** first of all (archaic genitive). **1204 cas of which,** matter about which. **1205 acorden,** suit (agree with). **1207** *after hir:* Hg&c *of that.* **1208 weyve,** avoid. *Thanne of:* Hg&c *And in.* **1209 shaltow,** shalt thou. *conceyve:* E *conserve.* **1211 approved it,** i.e., had it approved. **1215 distreyneth,** keeps. **1216 Catoun,** Dionysius Cato *Disticha* 3.14. **charge . . . weyve,** burden, abandon. **1217 to suffre,** to endure (it). **1218 Piers Alphonce,** *Disciplina Clericalis* 4. **1221 defenden,** forbid. *anything:* Hg&c *a thyng.* **1222 emprise, conferme . . . sadly,** enterprise, pursue, steadfastly. **1223 repreve,** reproof. **1224 bitydeth,** occurs. **1225 bihoveth,** is necessary. **1229 bihestes,** promises.

that been dishoneste been of no value. / And eek, if so be that it be inpossible or may nat goodly be parfourned or kept. / 1230

"And take this for a general reule that every conseil that is affermed so strongly that it may nat be chaunged for no condicioun that may bityde, I seye that thilke conseil is wikked." /

This Melibeus, whanne he hadde herd the doctrine of his wyf dame Prudence, answerde in this wyse. / "Dame," quod he, "as yet into this tyme ye han wel and convenably taught me as in general how I shal governe me in the chesynge and in the withholdynge of my conseillours. / But now wolde I fayn that ye wolde condescende in especial / and telle me how liketh yow, or what semeth yow, by oure conseillours that we han chosen in oure present nede." / 1235

"My lord," quod she, "I biseke yow in al humblesse that ye wol nat wilfully replie agayn my resouns, ne distempre youre herte thogh I speke thyng that yow displese. / For God woot that, as in myn entente, I speke it for your beste, for youre honour, and for youre profite eke. / And soothly, I hope that youre benygnytee wol taken it in pacience. / Trusteth me wel," quod she, "that your conseil as in this caas ne sholde nat, as to speke properly, be called a conseilling, but a mocioun or a moevyng of folye, / in which conseil ye han erred in many a sondry wise. / 1240

"First and forward, ye han erred in th'assemblynge of youre conseillours. / For ye sholde first have cleped a fewe folk to your conseil, and after ye myghte han shewed it to mo folk, if it hadde been nede. / But certes, ye han sodeynly cleped to your conseil a greet multitude of peple ful chargeant and ful anoyous for to heere. / Also ye han erred for there as ye sholden oonly have cleped to youre conseil youre trewe frendes olde and wise, / ye han ycleped straunge folk and yong folk, false flatereres and enemys reconsiled, and folk that doon yow reverence withouten love. / And eek also ye have erred for ye han broght with yow to youre conseil ire, coveitise, and hastifnesse, / the whiche thre thynges been contrariouse to every conseil honeste and profitable, / the whiche thre ye han nat anientissed or destroyed hem, neither in yourself ne in your conseillours as yow oghte. / Ye han erred also for ye han shewed to your conseillours youre talent, and youre affeccioun to make werre anon and for to do vengeance. / They han espied by your wordes to what thyng ye been enclyned. / 1250 And therfore han they rather conseilled yow to your talent than to your profit. / Ye han erred also for it semeth that it suffiseth to han been conseilled by thise conseillours oonly and with litel avys, / wher as in so greet and so heigh a nede it hadde been necessarie mo conseillours and moore deliberacioun to parfourne your emprise. / Ye han erred also for ye ne han nat examyned youre conseil in the forseyde manere, ne in due manere as the caas requireth. / Ye han erred also, for ye han nat maked no divisioun bitwixe your conseillours—this is to seyn bitwixen your trewe freendes and your feyned conseillours, / ne ye han nat knowe 1255 the wil of youre trewe freendes olde and wise, / but ye han cast alle hire wordes in an hochepot and enclyned youre herte to the moore partie and to the gretter nombre, and ther been ye condescended. / And sith ye woot wel that men shal alwey fynde a gretter nombre of fooles than of wise men, / and therfore the conseils that been at congragaciouns and multitudes of folk ther as men take moore reward to the nombre than to the sapience of persones, / ye se wel that in swiche conseillynges fooles han the maistrie." / 1260

1230 **goodly,** satisfactorily. 1233 **convenably,** properly. 1235 **liketh . . . by oure conseillours,** pleases, about our counselors. 1236 **replie,** object. 1242 **cleped,** called. 1243 **chargeant,** burdensome. 1248 **anientissed,** nullified. *thre:* Hg&c *thre thynges.* 1249 **talent . . . affeccioun . . . anon,** inclination, desire, immediately. 1252 **avys,** advice. *that it:* Hg&c *that yow.* 1253 **it hadde been,** it would (should) have been. 1257 **moore partie . . . condescended,** larger part, settled. 1259 **been at . . . reward,** are from, regard.

Melibeus answerde agayn, and seyde, "I graunte wel that I have erred; / but ther as thou hast toold me heerbiforn that he nys nat to blame that chaungeth his conseillours in certein caas and for certeine juste causes, / I am al redy to chaunge my conseillours, right as thow wolt devyse. / The proverbe seith that for to do synne is mannyssh, but certes for to persevere longe in synne is werk of the devel." /

To this sentence answerde anon dame Prudence and seyde, / "Examineth," 1265 quod she, "your conseil, and lat us see the whiche of hem han spoken most resonably and taught yow best conseil. / And for as muche as that the examynacioun is necessarie, lat us bigynne at the surgiens and at the phisiciens, that first speeken in this matiere. / I sey yow that the surgiens and phisiciens han seyd yow in your conseil discreetly, as hem oughte, / and in hir speche seyd ful wisely, that to the office of hem aperteneth, to doon to every wight honour and profit and no wight for to anoye, / and in hire craft, to doon greet diligence unto the cure of hem whiche that they han in hire governaunce. / And sire, right as they han 1270 answered wisely and discreetly, / right so rede I that they been heighly and sovereynly gerdoned for hir noble speche, / and eek for they sholde do the moore ententif bisynesse in the curacioun of your doghter deere. / For al be it so that they been your freendes, therfore shal ye nat suffren that they serve yow for noght, / but ye oghte the rather gerdone hem and shewe hem your largesse. / And as 1275 touchynge the proposicioun which that the phisiciens encreesceden in this caas, this is to seyn, / that in maladies that oon contrarie is warisshed by another contrarie, / I wolde fayn knowe hou ye understonde this text and what is youre sentence." /

"Certes," quod Melibeus, "I understonde it in this wise: / that right as they han doon me a contrarie, right so sholde I doon hem another. / For right as they han venged 1280 hem on me and doon me wrong, right so shal I venge me upon hem and doon hem wrong, / and thanne have I cured oon contrarie by another." /

"Lo, lo," quod dame Prudence, "how lightly is every man enclined to his owene desir and to his owene plesaunce! / Certes," quod she, "the wordes of the phisiciens ne sholde nat han been understonden in thys wise. / For certes, wikkednesse is nat contrarie to wikkednesse, ne vengeaunce to vengeaunce, ne wrong to wrong, but they been semblable. / And 1285 therfore, o vengeaunce is nat warisshed by another vengeaunce, ne o wrong by another wrong, / but everich of hem encreesceth and aggreggeth other. / But certes, the wordes of the phisiciens sholde been understonden in this wise: / for good and wikkednesse been two contraries, and pees and werre, vengeaunce and suffraunce, discord and accord, and manye othere thynges. / But certes, wikkednesse shal be warisshed by goodnesse, discord by accord, werre by pees, and so forth of othere thinges. / And heerto accordeth Seint 1290 Paul the apostle in manye places. / He seith, 'Ne yeldeth nat harm for harm, ne wikked speche for wikked speche, / but do wel to hym that dooth thee harm, and blesse hym that seith to thee harm.' / And in manye othere places he amonesteth pees and accord. / But now wol I speke to yow of the conseil which that was yeven to yow by the men of lawe and the wise folk / that seyden alle by oon 1295 accord as ye han herd bifore, / that over alle thynges ye sholde doon youre diligence to kepen youre persone and to warnestoore youre hous. / And seyden also that in this caas yow oghten for to werken ful avysely and with greet

1262 **ther as,** since (because). 1264 **mannyssh,** human. 1265 **sentence,** axiom. 1270 **in hire craft,** by their professional ability. 1272 **rede . . . gerdoned,** advise, rewarded. 1275 **gerdone . . . largesse,** reward, generosity. 1276 **encreesceden,** developed: some MSS *entreteden.* 1277 **warisshed,** cured. 1278 **sentence,** opinion. 1283 **lightly,** readily. 1285 **semblable,** similar. 1287 **aggreggeth,** aggravates. 1291 **accordeth Seint Paul,** agrees, Rom. 12:17. 1297 **diligence . . . kepen . . . warnestoore,** diligent effort, protect, defend (fortify). 1298 **avysely,** advisedly.

deliberacioun. / And sire, as to the firste point that toucheth to the kepyng of youre persone, / ye shul understonde that he that hath werre shal evermore mekely and devoutly preyen biforn alle thynges / that Jesus Crist of his 1300 grete mercy wol han hym in his proteccioun and been his sovereyn helpyng at his nede. / For certes, in this world ther is no wight that may be conseilled ne kept sufficeantly withouten the keping of oure lord Jesu Crist. / To this sentence accordeth the prophete David that seith, / 'If God ne kepe the citee, in ydel waketh he that it kepeth.' / Now sire, thanne shul ye comitte the kepyng of youre persone to youre trewe freendes that been approved and yknowe, / and of hem shul ye axen 1305 help youre persone for to kepe. For Catoun seith, 'If thou hast nede of help, axe it of thy freendes, / for ther nys noon so good a phisicien as thy trewe freend.' / And after this, thanne shul ye kepe yow fro alle straunge folk and fro lyeres, and have alwey in suspect hir compaignye. / For Piers Alfonce seith, 'Ne taak no compaignye by the weye of straunge men but if so be that thou have knowe hym of a lenger tyme. / And if so be that he be falle into thy compaignye paraventure withouten thyn assent, / enquere thanne as subtilly as thou 1310 mayst of his conversacioun and of his lyf bifore, and feyne thy wey. Seye that thou goost thider as thou wolt nat go. / And if he bereth a spere, hoold thee on the right syde, and if he bere a swerd, hoold thee on the lift syde.' / And after this, thanne shul ye kepe yow wisely from alle swich manere peple as I have seyd bifore, and hem and hir conseil escheue. / And after this, thanne shul ye kepe yow in swich manere / that for any presumpcioun of youre strengthe that ye ne dispise nat, ne acounte nat the myght of your adversarie so litel that ye lete the kepyng of youre persone for your presumpcioun, / for every wys man dredeth his 1315 enemy. / And Salomon seith, 'Weleful is he that of alle hath drede, / for certes he that thurgh the hardynesse of his herte and thurgh the hardynesse of hymself hath to greet presumpcioun, hym shal yvel bityde.' / Thanne shul ye evermoore countrewayte embusshementz and alle espiaille. / For Senec seith that the wyse man that dredeth harmes escheueth harmes, / ne he ne falleth into perils that 1320 perils escheueth. / And al be it so that it seme that thou art in siker place, yet shaltow alwey do thy diligence in kepynge of thy persone, / this is to seyn ne be nat necligent to kepe thy persone nat oonly fro thy gretteste enemys but fro thy leeste enemy. / Senek seith, 'A man that is wel avysed, he dredeth his leste enemy.' / Ovyde seith that the litel wesele wol slee the grete bole and the wilde hert. / 1325 And the book seith, 'A litel thorn may prikke a greet kyng ful soore, and an hound wol holde the wilde boor.' / But nathelees, I sey nat thou shalt be so coward that thou doute ther wher as is no drede. / The book seith that somme folk han greet lust to deceyve, but yet they dreden hem to be deceyved. / Yet shaltou drede to been empoisoned and kepe yow from the compaignye of scorneres. / For the book seith, 'With scorneres make no compaignye, but flee hire wordes as venym.' / 1330

"Now as to the seconde point, wher as youre wise conseillours conseilled yow to warnestoore youre hous with gret diligence, / I wolde fayn knowe how that ye understonde thilke wordes and what is your sentence." /

Melibeus answerde and seyde, "Certes I understande it in this wise, that I shal

---

1301 **sovereyn,** highest. 1302 **keping,** protection. 1303 **David,** Ps. 127:1. 1304 **waketh,** stays awake. 1306 **Catoun,** *Disticha* 4:13. 1308 **kepe yow,** keep away from. 1309 **Piers Alfonce,** *Disciplina Clericalis* 17. 1311 **feyne,** pretend. 1312 *the lift* (left): E&c *his lift.* 1313 **kepe yow,** protect yourself. 1315 **presumpcioun,** i.e., don't overestimate your strength. **lete,** neglect. *acounte:* Hg&c *attempte.* 1317 **Salomon,** Prov. 28:14. **Weleful,** fortunate. 1318 **bityde,** occur. 1319 **countrewayte,** be on watch against. 1320 **Senec,** Pubilius Syrus, *Sententiae* 607. E *he dredeth harmes ne he ne falleth.* 1321 **siker,** safe. 1322 *nat oonly fro . . . fro:* E *for/for.* 1324 **Senek,** Pubilius Syrus, *Sententiae* 255. **leste,** least. 1325 **Ovyde,** *Remedia Amoris* 421. **bole,** bull. *wesele,* apparently Chaucer's mistranslation of Fr. *vivre,* Lat. *vipera,* viper, for Lat. *viverra,* ferret. 1326 **litel thorn . . . soore,** this line was interpolated by Chaucer; note the rhyme. 1327 **doute,** fear. *so coward:* E *so* om. 1328 **The book,** Seneca, *Epistolae* 3.3. **lust,** desire. 1331 **warnestoore,** protect. 1332 **sentence,** opinion.

warnestoore myn hous with toures swiche as han castelles and othere manere edifices, and armure, and artelries, / by whiche thinges I may my persone and myn hous so kepen and deffenden that myne enemys shul been in drede myn hous for to approche." /

To this sentence answerde anon Prudence, "Warnestooryng," quod she, "of heighe toures and of grete edifices apperteneth somtyme to pryde, / and eek men make heighe 1335 toures and grete edifices with grete costages and with greet travaille, and whan that they been accompliced yet be they nat worth a stree but if they be defended by trewe freendes that been olde and wise. / And understoond wel that the gretteste and the strongeste garnyson that a riche man may have as wel to kepen his persone as his goodes is / that he be biloved amonges hys subgetz and with his neighebores. / For thus seith Tullius that ther is a manere garnyson that no man may venquysse ne disconfite and that is / a lord to be biloved of his citezeins and of his peple. / 1340

"Now sire, as to the thridde point: wher as your olde and wise conseillours seyden that yow ne oghte nat sodeynly ne hastily proceden in this nede, / but that yow oghte purveyen and apparaillen yow in this caas with greet diligence and greet deliberacioun, / trewely I trowe that they seyden right wisely and right sooth. / For Tullius seith, 'In every nede er thou bigynne it, apparaille thee with greet diligence.' / Thanne seye I that in vengeance takyng, in werre, in bataille, and in warnestooryng, / er 1345 thow bigynne, I rede that thou apparaille thee ther to, and do it with greet deliberacioun. / For Tullius seith that longe apparaillyng biforn the bataille maketh short victorie. / And Cassidorus seith, 'The garnyson is stronger whan it is longe tyme avysed.' /

"But now lat us speken of the conseil that was accorded by your neighebores swiche as doon yow reverence withouten love, / youre olde enemys reconsiled, your flatereres / 1350 that conseilled yow certeyne thynges prively, and openly conseilleden yow the contrarie, / the yonge folk also that conseilleden yow to venge yow and make werre anon. / And certes, sire, as I have seyd biforn, ye han greetly erred to han cleped swich maner folk to youre conseil, / which conseillours been ynogh repreved by the resouns aforeseyd. / But nathelees lat us now descende to the special. Ye shuln first procede after the doctrine of Tullius. / Certes, the trouthe of this 1355 matiere or of this conseil nedeth nat diligently enquere, / for it is wel wist whiche they been that han doon to yow this trespas and vileynye, / and how manye trespassours, and in what manere they han to yow doon al this wrong and al this vileynye. / And after this thanne shul ye examyne the seconde condicioun, which that the same Tullius addeth in this matiere. / For Tullius put a thing which that he clepeth 'consentynge'; this is to seyn, / who been they, and how manye, 1360 and whiche been they that consenteden to thy conseil in thy wilfulnesse to doon hastif vengeance. / And lat us considere also who been they, and how manye been they, and whiche been they that consenteden to your adversaries. / And certes, as to the firste poynt, it is wel knowen whiche folk been they that consenteden to youre hastif wilfulnesse, / for trewely alle tho that conseilleden yow to maken sodeyn werre ne been nat youre freendes. / Lat us now considere whiche been they that ye holde so greetly youre freendes as to youre persone. / For 1365 al be it so that ye be mighty and riche, certes ye ne been but allone. / For certes, ye ne

1335 of heighe . . . apperteneth . . . to, with high, is related to. *apperteneth somtyme—grete edifices,* passage omitted (by eyeskip?) in EHg&c, but preserved in other, less authoritative MSS. **1336 costages . . . travaille . . . stree,** expense, effort, straw. **1337 kepen,** protect. **1339 Tullius,** Seneca, *De Clementia* 1.19.5. **1342 purveyen and apparaillen yow,** provide and prepare yourself. **1343 trowe,** believe. **1344 Tullius,** Cicero, *De Officiis* 1.21. **1346 rede,** advise. **1347 apparaillyng,** preparing. *seith that:* E *seith the.* **1348 Cassidorus,** *Variae* 1.17. **garnyson . . . longe tyme avysed,** garrison, warned long before. **1352 werre anon,** war immediately. **1353 cleped,** called. **1354 repreved,** discredited (reproved). **1355 Tullius,** Cicero, *De Officiis* 2.5. **1356 nat . . . enquere,** not be inquired about. **1357 wist,** known. **1360 Tullius put,** added. **1361** E *and whiche been they* om. **1362 consenteden to,** agreed with. **1365 whiche been they,** i.e., what they are like. **1366** E *ne been nat.*

han no child but a doghter; / ne ye ne han bretheren ne cosyns germayns ne noon oother neigh kynrede, / wherfore that youre enemys for drede sholde stinte to plede with yow or to destroye youre persone. / Ye knowen also that youre richesses mooten been dispended in diverse parties; / and whan that every 1370 wight hath his part, they ne wollen taken but litel reward to venge thy deeth. / But thyne enemys been thre, and they han manie children, bretheren, cosyns, and oother ny kynrede. / And though so were that thou haddest slayn of hem two or thre, yet dwellen ther ynowe to wreken hire deeth and to sle thy persone. / And though so be that youre kynrede be moore siker and stedefast than the kyn of youre adversarie, / yet nathelees youre kynrede nys but a fer kynrede; they been but litel syb to yow, / and the kyn of your enemys been 1375 ny syb to hem. And certes, as in that, hire condicioun is bet than youres. / Thanne lat us considere also if the conseillyng of hem that conseilleden yow to taken sodeyn vengeaunce, wheither it accorde to resoun. / And certes, ye knowe wel nay. / For as by right and resoun, ther may no man taken vengeance on no wight but the juge that hath the jurisdiccioun of it, / whan it is graunted hym to take thilke vengeance hastily or attemprely as the lawe requireth. / And yet mooreover of 1380 thilke word that Tullius clepeth 'consentynge,' / thou shalt considere if thy might and thy power may consenten and suffise to thy wilfulnesse and to thy conseillours. / And certes, thou mayst wel seyn that nay. / For sikerly, as for to speke proprely, we may do nothing but oonly swich thyng as we may doon rightfully. / And certes, rightfully ne mowe ye take no vengeance as of your propre auctoritee. / Thanne mowe ye seen that 1385 youre power ne consenteth nat ne accordeth nat with your wilfulnesse. / Lat us now examyne the thridde point that Tullius clepeth 'consequent.' / Thou shalt understonde that the vengeance that thou purposest for to take is the consequent. / And therof folweth another vengeaunce, peril, and werre, and other damages withoute nombre of whiche we be nat war as at this tyme. / And as touchynge the fourthe point, that Tullius clepeth 'engendrynge,' / thou shalt considere that 1390 this wrong which that is doon to thee is engendred of the hate of thyne enemys; / and of the vengeance takinge upon that wolde engendre another vengeance and muchel sorwe and wastinge of richesses, as I seyde. /

"Now sire, as to the point that Tullius clepeth 'causes,' which that is the laste point, / thou shalt understonde that the wrong that thou hast receyved hath certeine causes / whiche that clerkes clepen *oriens* and *efficiens*, and *causa longinqua* and *causa propinqua*, this is to seyn, the fer cause and the ny cause. / The 1395 fer cause is Almighty God, that is cause of alle thinges. / The neer cause is thy thre enemys. / The cause accidental was hate. / The cause material been the fyve woundes of thy doghter. / The cause formal is the manere of hire werkynge that broghten laddres and cloumben in at thy wyndowes. / The cause 1400 final was for to sle thy doghter; it letted nat in as muche as in hem was. / But for to speken of the fer cause, as to what ende they shul come, or what shal finally bityde of hem in this caas, ne kan I nat deme but by conjectynge and by supposinge. / For we shul suppose that they shul come to a wikked ende, / by cause that the Book of Decrees seith, 'Seelden or with greet peyne been causes ybroght to good ende whanne they been baddely bigonne.' /

"Now sire, if men wolde axe me, why that God suffred men to do yow this vileinye,

---

1368 **cosyns germayns,** first cousins. 1369 **wherfore that,** i.e., because of whom (an echo of the primitive clan spirit). 1370 **mooten,** must (after your death). **dispended,** divided. 1373 **so were that thou,** i.e., even if you. **dwellen . . . wreken,** remain, avenge. 1374 **siker,** dependable (secure). 1375 **fer kynrede . . . syb,** distant relations, blood relation (sibling). 1380 **hastily or attemprely,** harshly or moderately. 1382 **consenten,** accord (with). 1384 **sikerly,** surely. 1385 **mowe,** may. 1387 **consequent,** the consequences. 1390 **engendrynge,** causing (stimulating). 1395 *oriens,* etc., the Latin terms do not occur in the sources and may have been added by Chaucer. 1401 **letted,** lacked (i.e., they suceeded as far as they were able). 1402 **bityde of . . . deme,** happen to, judge. 1404 **Book of Decrees,** *Decretum Gratiani* (Decrees of the Roman Emperor Gratian), 2.1 qu.1.c.25.

certes I kan nat wel answere as for no sothfastnesse. / For th'apostle seith that the sciences and the juggementz of oure lord God Almighty been ful depe. / Ther may no man comprehende ne serchen hem suffisantly. / Nathelees, by certeyne presumpciouns and conjectynges I holde and bileeve / that God which that is ful of justice and of rightwisenesse hath suffred this bityde by juste cause resonable. /

"Thy name is Melibee, this is to seyn, 'a man that drynketh hony.' / Thou hast ydronke so muchel hony of sweete temporeel richesses and delices and honours of this world / that thou art dronken and hast forgeten Jesu Crist thy creatour. / Thou ne hast nat doon to hym swich honour and reverence as thee oughte. / Ne thou ne hast nat wel ytaken kepe to the wordes of Ovide that seith, / 'Under the hony of the goodes of the body is hyd the venym that sleeth the soule.' / And Salomon seith, 'If thou hast founden hony, ete of it that suffiseth, / for if thou ete of it out of mesure thou shalt spewe,' and be nedy and poure. / And peraventure Crist hath thee in despit and hath turned awey fro thee his face and his eereis of misericorde, / and also he hath suffred that thou hast been punysshed in the manere that thow has ytrespassed. / Thou has doon synne agayn our lord Crist, / for certes the thre enemys of mankynde, that is to seyn, the flessh, the feend, and the world, / thou hast suffred hem entre into thyn herte wilfully by the wyndowes of thy body, / and hast nat defended thyself suffisantly agayns hire assautes and hire temptaciouns, so that they han wounded thy soule in fyve places, / this is to seyn, the deedly synnes that been entred into thyn herte by thy fyve wittes. / And in the same manere our lord Crist hath woold and suffred that thy three enemys been entred into thyn hous by the wyndowes / and han ywounded thy doghter in the forseyde manere." /

"Certes," quod Melibee, "I se wel that ye enforce yow muchel by wordes to overcome me in swich manere that I shal nat venge me of myne enemys, / shewynge me the perils and the yveles that myghten falle of this vengeance. / But whoso wolde considere in alle vengences the perils and yveles that myghte sewe of vengeance takynge, / a man wolde never take vengeance, and that were harm. / For by the vengeance takinge been the wikked men disseevered fro the goode men. / And they that han wyl to do wikkednesse restreyne hir wikked purpos whan they seen the punyssynge and chastisynge of the trespassours." /

And to this answerde dame Prudence, "Certes," seyde she, "I graunte wel that of vengeaunce cometh muchel yvel and muchel good, / but vengeaunce taking aperteneth nat unto everichoon but only unto juges and unto hem that han jurisdiccioun upon the trespassours. / And yet seye I moore, that right as a singuler persone synneth in takynge vengeance of another man, / right so synneth the juge if he do no vengeance of hem that it han disserved. / For Senec seith thus, 'That maister,' he seith, 'is good that proveth shrewes.' / And as Cassidore seith, 'A man dredeth to do outrages whan he woot and knoweth that it displeseth to the juges and sovereyns.' / Another seith, 'The juge that dredeth to do right maketh men shrewes.' / And Seint Paule the apostle seith in his Epistle, whan he wryteth unto the Romayns, that the juges beren nat the spere withouten cause, / but they beren it to punysse the shrewes and mysdoeres and to defende the goode men. / If ye wol thanne take

1405 as for no sothfastnesse, with no certainty. **1409 bityde,** to happen. **1414 ytaken kepe,** taken heed. **Ovide,** *Amores* 1.8.104. **1416 Salomon,** Prov. 25:16. **1417 spewe,** vomit. **1418 despit . . . misericorde,** contempt, mercy. **1419 suffred . . . ytrespassed,** permitted, sinned. **1425 woold,** willed. **1427 enforce yow,** i.e., try. **1429 sewe of,** result from (ensue). **1431 disseevered,** separated (divided). **1433–34** *And—trespassours,* line omitted in all MSS; trans. by Skeat from the Fr. **1434 aperteneth nat,** is not appropriate. **1435 singuler,** individual. **1436 of hem,** upon them. **1437 Senec,** pseudo-Seneca, *De Moribus* 5. **proveth shrewes,** test scoundrels. **1438 Cassidore,** *Variae* 1.4. **1440 Seint Paule,** Rom. 13.4. *Spere* is a mistake for *swerd.*

vengeance of youre enemys, ye shul retourne or have your recours to the juge that hath the jurisdiccion upon hem, / and he shal punysse hem as the lawe axeth and requireth." /

"A," quod Melibee, "this vengeance liketh me nothyng. / I bithenke me now and take heede, how fortune hath norissed me fro my childhede, and hath holpen me to passe many a stroong paas. / Now wol I assayen 1445 hir, trowynge with Goddes helpe, that she shal helpe me my shame for to venge." /

"Certes," quod Prudence, "if ye wol werke by my conseil, ye shul nat assaye fortune by no wey, / ne ye shul nat lene or bowe unto hir after the word of Senec / for 'thynges that been folily doon and that been in hope of fortune shullen never come to good ende.' / And as the same Senec seith, 'The moore cleer and the moore shynyng that fortune is, the moore brotil and the sonner broken she is.' / 1450 Trusteth nat in hire, for she nys nat stidefast ne stable, / for whan thow trowest to be moost seur and siker of hire help, she wol faille thee and deceyve thee. / And where as ye seyn that fortune hath norissed yow fro youre childhede, / I seye that in so muchel shul ye the lasse truste in hire and in hir wit. / For Senec seith, 'What man that is norissed by fortune, she maketh hym a greet fool.' / 1455 Now thanne, syn ye desire and axe vengeance, and the vengeance that is doon after the lawe and bifore the juge ne liketh yow nat, / and the vengeance that is doon in hope of fortune is perilous and uncertein, / thanne have ye noon oother remedie but for to have youre recours unto the sovereyn juge that vengeth alle vileynyes and wronges, / and he shal venge yow after that hymself witnesseth, where as he seith, / 'Leveth the vengeance to me and I shal do it.' " / 1460

Melibee answerde, "If I ne venge me nat of the vileynye that men han doon to me, / I sompne or warne hem that han doon to me that vileynye and alle othere to do me another vileynye. / For it is writen, 'If thou take no vengeance of an oold vileynye, thou sompnest thyne adversaries to do thee a newe vileynye.' / And also, for my suffrance, men wolden do to me so muchel vileynye that I myghte neither bere it ne susteene, / and so sholde I been put and holden over lowe. / For men seyn, 1465 'In muchel suffrynge shul manye thynges falle unto thee whiche thou shalt nat mowe suffre.' " /

"Certes," quod Prudence, "I graunte yow that over muchel suffraunce nys nat good, / but yet ne folweth it nat therof that every persone to whom men doon vileynye take of it vengeance, / for that aperteneth and longeth al oonly to the juges, for they shul venge the vileynyes and injuries. / And therfore tho two auctoritees that ye han seyd above been oonly understonden in the juges, / for whan 1470 they suffren over muchel the wronges and the vileynyes to be doon withouten punys-shynge, / they sompne nat a man al oonly for to do newe wronges, but they comanden it. / Also a wys man seith that the juge that correcteth nat the synnere comandeth and biddeth hym do synne. / And the juges and sovereyns myghten in hire land so muchel suffre of the shrewes and mysdoeres, / that they sholden by swich suffrance, by proces of tyme, wexen of swich power and myght that they sholden putte out the juges and the sovereyns from hire places / and atte laste maken hem lesen 1475 hire lordshipes. /

"But lat us now putte that ye have leve to

1444 liketh me nothyng, pleases me not at all. **1445 passe . . . stroong paas,** endure, difficult situation. **1446 assayen hir, trowynge,** try her (Fortune), believing. **1447 shul nat,** i.e., won't have to. **1448 Senec,** Pubilius Syrus, *Sententiae* 320. **1449 folily,** foolishly. **1450 Senec,** Pubilius Syrus, *Sententiae* 189. **brotil,** brittle. **1452 trowest . . . siker,** believe (think you are), secure. **1455 Senec,** Pubilius Syrus, *Sententiae* 172. *a greet:* Hg&c *to greet a;* Fr. *trop elle le fait.* **1456 ne liketh yow,** doesn't please you. **1459 after that,** as; Rom. 12:19. **1462 sompne or warne,** summon or notify. **1463 it is writen,** Pubilius Syrus, *Sententiae* 645. **1466 men seyn,** Pubilius Syrus, *Sententiae* 487. **nat mowe suffre,** i.e., cannot endure. **1467 over muchel suffraunce,** too much patient endurance. **1469 aperteneth . . . longeth,** belongs, belongs. **1470 tho . . . auctoritees,** those, maxims. **1471 suffren,** permit. **1473 wys man,** Caecilius Balbus, *De Nugis Philosophorum* 41.4. **1474 so muchel suffre . . . shrewes,** i.e., be so lenient toward scoundrels. **1475 by proces of tyme,** eventually. **1477 putte,** assume.

venge yow. / I seye ye been nat of myght and power as now to venge yow. / For if ye wole maken comparisoun unto the myght of youre adversaries, ye shul fynde in manye thynges that I have shewed yow er this that hire condicioun is bettre than youres. / And therfore seye I that it is good as now that ye suffre and be pacient. / 1480

"Forthermoore, ye knowen wel that, after the commune sawe, it is a woodnesse a man to stryve with a strenger or a moore myghty man than he is hymself, / and for to stryve with a man of evene strengthe—that is to seyn, with as strong a man as he—it is peril, / and for to stryve with a weyker man it is folie. / And therfore sholde a man flee stryvynge as muchel as he myghte. / For Salomon seith, 'It is a greet worship to a man to kepen him fro noyse and stryf.' / And if it so bifalle or happe that a man of gretter myght and strengthe than thou art do thee grevaunce, / studie and bisye thee rather to stille the same grevaunce than for to venge thee. / For Senec seith that he putteth hym in greet peril that stryveth with a gretter man than he is hymself. / And Catoun seith, 'If a man of hyer estaat or degree or moore myghty than thou do thee anoy or grevaunce, suffre hym, / for he that oones hath greved thee another tyme may releeve thee and helpe.' / Yet sette I caas, 1490 ye have bothe myght and licence for to venge yow. / I seye that ther be ful manye thynges that shul restreyne yow of vengeance takinge, / and make yow for to enclyne to suffre, and for to han pacience in the thynges that han been doon to yow. / First and foreward, if ye wole considere the defautes that been in youre owene persone, / for whiche defautes God hath suffred yow have this tribulacioun, as I have seyd yow heer biforn. / For the 1495 poete seith that we oghte paciently taken the tribulacions that comen to us, whan we thynken and consideren that we han disserved to have hem. / And Seint Gregorie seith that whan a man considereth wel the nombre of his defautes and of his synnes, / the peynes and the tribulaciouns that he suffreth semen the lesse unto hym; / and inasmuche as hym thynketh his synnes moore hevy and grevous, / insomuche semeth his peyne the lighter and the esier unto hym. / Also ye owen for to enclyne 1500 and bowe youre herte to take the pacience of oure lord Jesu Crist, as seith Seint Peter in his Epistles. / 'Jesu Crist,' he seith, 'hath suffred for us and yeven ensample to every man to folwe and sewe him, / for he dide never synne, ne nevere cam ther a vileynous word out of his mouth. / Whan men cursed hym, he cursed hem noght, and whan men betten hym, he manaced hem noght.' / Also the grete pacience which the seintes that been in paradys han had in tribulaciouns that they han ysuffred withouten hir desert or gilt / oghte muchel 1505 stiren yow to pacience. / Forthermoore, ye sholde enforce yow to have pacience, / consider-ynge that the tribulaciouns of this world but litel while endure and soone passed been and goone. / And the joye that a man seketh to have by pacience in tribulaciouns is perdurable, after that the apostle seith in his Epistle. / 'The joye of God,' he seith, 'is perdurable,' that is to seyn, everlastinge. / Also troweth and 1510 bileveth stedefastly that he nys nat wel ynorissed ne wel ytaught that kan nat have pacience or wol nat receyve pacience. / For Salomon seith that the doctrine and the wit of a man is knowen by pacience. / And in another place he seith that he that is pacient governeth hym by greet prudence. / And the same Salomon seith, 'The angry and wrathful man maketh noyses, and the pacient man atempreth hym and stilleth.' / He seith also, 'It is moore

1481 sawe . . . woodnesse, proverb, madness. **1482 evene,** ordinary. **1485 Salomon,** Prov. 20:3. **worship,** credit. **1488 Senec,** Pubilius Syrus, *Sententiae* 483. **1489. Catoun,** *Disticha* 4.39. **1491 sette I caas,** make the assumption. **1493 thynges:** Hg&c *wronges.* **1494 defautes,** defects. **1501 owen,** ought (owe to). **Seint Peter,** I Peter 2:21–23. **1502 sewe,** imitate (pursue). **1504 manaced,** threatened. **1506 stiren,** encourage (stir). **1509 perdurable,** everlasting. **apostle seith,** II Cor. 4:17. **1511 troweth,** (you should) believe. **1512 Salomon,** Prov. 19:11 (Vulgate). **doctrine . . . wit,** learning, wisdom. **1513 another place,** Prov. 19:29 (Vulgate). **1514 Salomon seith,** Prov. 15:18. **atempreth hym . . . stilleth,** restrains himself, remains quiet. *hym:* EHg&c *hem.* **1515 seith also,** Prov. 16:32.

worth to be pacient than for to be right strong; / and he that may have the lordshipe of his owene herte is moore to preyse than he that by his force or strengthe taketh grete citees.' / And therfore seith Seint Jame in his Epistle that pacience is a greet vertu of perfeccioun." /

"Certes," quod Melibee, "I graunte yow, dame Prudence, that pacience is a greet vertu of perfeccioun. / But every man may nat have the perfeccioun that ye seken; / ne I nam nat of the nombre of right parfite men, / for myn herte may never been in pees unto the tyme it be venged. / And al be it so that it was greet peril to myne enemys to do me a vileynye in takinge vengeance upon me, / yet tooken they noon heede of the peril but fulfilleden hire wikked wyl and hir corage. / And therfore methynketh men oghten nat repreve me though I putte me in a litel peril for to venge me, / and though I do a greet excesse, that is to seyn, that I venge oon outrage by another." /

"A," quod dame Prudence, "ye seyn youre wil and as yow lyketh; / but in no caas of the world a man sholde nat doon outrage ne excesse for to vengen hym. / For Cassidore seith that as yvel dooth he that vengeth hym by outrage as he that dooth the outrage. / And therfore ye shul venge yow after the ordre of right, that is to seyn by the lawe, and noght by excesse ne by outrage. / And also, if ye wol venge yow of the outrage of youre adversaries in oother manere than right comandeth, / ye synnen. / And therfore seith Senec that a man shal nevere vengen shrewednesse by shrewednesse. / And if ye seye that right axeth a man to defenden violence by violence and fightyng by fightyng, / certes ye seye sooth whan the defense is doon anon withouten intervalle or withouten tariyng or delay / for to deffenden

hym and nat for to vengen hym. / And it bihoveth that a man putte swich attemperance in his deffense, / that men have no cause ne matiere to repreven hym that deffendeth hym of excesse and outrage, for ellis were it agayn resoun. / Pardee, ye knowen wel that ye maken no deffense as now for to deffende yow, but for to venge yow, / and so seweth it that ye han no wyl to do youre dede attemprely. / And therfore, methynketh that pacience is good. For Salomon seith that he that is nat pacient shal have greet harm." /

"Certes," quod Melibee, "I graunte yow that whan a man is inpacient and wrooth of that that toucheth him noght and that aperteneth nat unto hym though it harme him, it is no wonder. / For the lawe seith that he is coupable that entremetteth or medleth with swych thyng as aperteneth nat unto hym. / And Salomon seith that he that entremetteth hym of the noyse or strif of another man is lyk to hym that taketh an hound by the eris. / For right as he that taketh a straunge hound by the eris is outherwhile biten with the hound, / right in the same wise is it resoun that he have harm that by his inpacience medleth hym of the noyse of another man wher as it aperteneth nat unto hym. / But ye knowen wel that this dede—that is to seyn, my grief and my disese—toucheth me right ny. / And therfore, though I be wrooth and inpacient, it is no merveille. / And savynge youre grace, I kan nat seen that it mighte greetly harme me though I tooke vengeaunce, / for I am richer and moore myghty than myne enemys been. / And wel knowen ye that by moneye and by havynge grete possessions been all the thynges of this world governed. / And Salomon seith that alle thynges obeyen to moneye." /

Whan Prudence hadde herd hir hous-

1515 moore worth, worth more. **1517 Seint Jame,** James 1:4. **1521 unto,** until. **1523 corage,** inclination. **1524 methynketh,** it seems to me. **1526 yow lyketh,** it pleases you. **1528 Cassidore,** *Variae* 1.30. **1531 Senec,** pseudo-Seneca, *De Moribus* 6. **shrewednesse,** villainy. **1535 putte . . . attemperance,** use, moderation. **1536 to repreven hym . . . deffendeth hym,** to reprove him, defends himself. **1538 seweth,** follows: E&c *sheweth.* **1539 Salomon,** Prov. 19:19. **1540 toucheth . . . aperteneth,** involves, concerns. **1541 coupable . . . entremetteth,** culpable, interferes. **1542 Salomon,** Prov. 26:17. **1543 outherwhile,** sometimes. **1544 noyse,** commotion. **1545 disese,** disaster (i.e., the attack by the three enemies). **1550 Salomon,** Eccles. 10:19.

bonde avanten hym of his richesse and of his moneye, dispreisynge the power of his adversaries, she spak and seyde in this wise, / "Certes, dere sire, I graunte yow that ye been riche and myghty, / and that the richesses been goode to hem that han wel ygeten hem and wel konne usen hem. / For right as the body of a man may nat lyven withoute the soule, namore may it live withouten temporeel goodes. / And for richesses may a man gete hym grete freendes. / And therfore seith Pamphilles, ¹⁵⁵⁵ 'If a netherdes doghter,' seith he, 'be riche, she may chesen of a thousand men which she wol take to hir housbonde, / for of a thousand men oon wol nat forsaken hire ne refusen hire.' / And this Pamphilles seith also, 'If thou be right happy (that is to seyn, if thou be right riche) thou shalt fynd a greet nombre of felawes and freendes. / And if thy fortune change that thou wexe poure, farewel freendshipe and felaweshipe, / for thou shalt be al alloone withouten any compaignye, but if it be the compaignye of poure folk.' / And ¹⁵⁶⁰ yet seith this Pamphilles moreover that they that been thralle and bonde of lynage shullen been maad worthy and noble by the richesses. / And right so as by richesses ther comen manye goodes, right so by poverte come ther manye harmes and yveles. / For greet poverte constreyneth a man to do manye yveles. / And therfore clepeth Cassidore poverte 'the moder of ruyne,' / that is to seyn the mooder of overthrowynge or fallynge doun. / And therfore seith Piers Alfonce, ¹⁵⁶⁵ 'Oon of the gretteste adversitees of this world is / whan a free man by kynde or by burthe is constreyned by poverte to eten the almesse of his enemy.' / And the same seith

Innocent in oon of his bookes. He seith that sorweful and myshappy is the condicioun of a poure begger, / for if he axe nat his mete he dyeth for hunger, / and if he axe he dyeth for shame; and algates necessitee constreyneth hym to axe. / And therfore seith Salomon ¹⁵⁷⁰ that bet it is to dye than for to have swich poverte. / And as the same Salomon seith, 'Bettre it is to dye of bitter deeth than for to lyven in swich wise.' / By thise resons that I have seid unto yow, and by manye othere resons that I koude seye, / I graunte yow that richesses been goode to hem that geten hem wel, and to hem that wel usen tho richesses. / And therfore wol I shewe yow hou ye shul have yow, and how ye shul bere yow in gaderynge of richesses, and in what manere ye shul usen hem. / ¹⁵⁷⁵

"First, ye shul geten hem withouten greet desir, by good leyser sokyngly, and nat over hastily. / For a man that is to desirynge to gete richesses abaundoneth hym first to thefte and to alle other yveles. / And therfore seith Salomon, 'He that hasteth hym to bisily to wexe riche shal be noon innocent.' / He seith also that the richesse that hastily cometh to a man soone and lightly gooth and passeth fro a man, / but that richesse that cometh litel and litel wexeth alwey and multiplieth. / ¹⁵⁸⁰ And sire, ye shul geten richesses by youre wit and by youre travaille unto youre profit, / and that withouten wrong or harmdoinge to any oother persone. / For the lawe seith that ther maketh no man himselven riche if he do harm to another wight, / this is to seyn that nature deffendeth and forbedeth by right that no man make hymself riche unto the harm of another persone. / And Tullius seith that no sorwe ne no drede of deeth, ne nothing

---

1551 avanten, boast. **1556 Pamphilles**, Pamphilius, hero of a popular Latin poetic dialogue on the nature of love, *Pamphilus de Amore* (12th cent.). **netherdes**, cowherd's; so in EHg&c, but the term puzzled the scribes, and in other MSS it comes out *nygardes*, *any goddes, an erlis*, etc. E *which—housbonde* om. **1558 Pamphilles**, not from *Pamphilus*, but perhaps Ovid, *Tristia* 1.9.5–6. **felawes**, companions. **1561 Pamphilles**, Petrus Alfonsus, *Disciplina Clericalis* 4. **thralle and bonde**, i.e., serfs. **1564 Cassidore**, *Variae* 2.13. **1566 Piers Alfonce**, *Disciplina Clericalis* 2. **1567 kynde ... eten the almesse**, nature, live on the charity. **1568 Innocent**, Pope Innocent III, *De Contemptu Mundi* 1.16. **1570 axe ... algates**, ask for (beg), nevertheless. **1571 Salomon**, *Ecclus.* 40:28 (Vulgate). **1572 Salomon**, Ecclus. 30:17 (Vulgate). **1574 geten hem wel**, i.e., gain them fairly. **1575 have yow**, behave yourself. **1576 sokyngly**, gradually: E&c *sekyngly*. **1578 Salomon**, Prov. 28:20. **1579 He seith**, Prov. 13:11. **1584 deffendeth**, prohibits. **1585 Tullius**, Cicero, *De Officiis* 3.5.21.

that may falle unto a man / is so muchel 1585
agayns nature as a man to encressen his
owene profit to the harm of another man. / And
though the gretc men and the myghty men
geten richesses moore lightly than thou, / yet
shaltou nat been ydel ne slow to do thy profit,
for thou shalt in alle wise flee ydelnesse. / For
Salomon seith that ydelnesse techeth a man to
do manye yveles. / And the same Salomon seith
that he that travailleth and bisieth hym to
tilien his land shal eten breed, / but he 1590
that is ydel and casteth hym to no bisynesse
ne occupacioun shal falle into poverte and dye
for hunger. / And he that is ydel and slow kan
never fynde covenable tyme for to doon his
profit. / For ther is a versifiour seith that the
ydel man excuseth hym in wynter by cause of
the grete cold, and in somer by enchesoun of
the heete. / For thise causes seith Caton,
'Waketh and enclyneth nat yow over muchel
for to slepe, for over muchel reste norisseth and
causeth manye vices.' / And therfore seith Seint
Jerome, 'Dooth somme goode dedes that the
devel which is oure enemy ne fynde yow
nat unoccupied.' / For the devel ne taketh 1595
nat lightly unto his werkynge swiche as he
fyndeth occupied in goode werkes.' /

"Thanne thus in getynge richesses ye mosten
flee ydelnesse. / And afterward ye shul use the
richesses whiche ye have geten by youre wit and
by youre travaille / in swich a manere that men
holde nat yow to scars, ne to sparynge, ne to
fool large, that is to seyn over large a spender. /
For right as men blamen an avaricious
man by cause of his scarsetee and
chyncherye, / in the same wise is he to 1600
blame that spendeth over largely. / And
therfore seith Caton, 'Use,' he seith, 'thy
richesses that thou hast geten / in swich a

manere that men have no matiere ne cause to
calle thee neither wrecche ne chynche, / for it is
a greet shame to a man to have a pouere herte
and a riche purs.' / He seith also, 'The goodes
that thou hast ygeten, use hem by mesure,'
that is to seyn, spende hem mesurably. / 1605
For they that folily wasten and despenden
the goodes that they han, / whan they han
namore propre of hire owene, they shapen hem
to take the goodes of another man. / I seye
thanne that ye shul fleen avarice / usynge youre
richesses in swich manere that men seye nat
that youre richesses been yburyed, / but that ye
have hem in youre myght and in youre
weeldynge. / For a wys man repreveth the 1610
avaricious man and seith thus in two
vers: / 'Wherto and why burieth a man his
goodes by his grete avarice, and knoweth wel
that nedes moste he dye, / for deeth is the ende
of every man as in this present lyf?' / And for
what cause or enchesoun joyneth he hym or
knytteth he hym so faste unto his goodes, / that
alle his wittes mowen nat disseveren hym
or departen hym from his goodes, / and 1615
knoweth wel, or oghte knowe, that whan
he is deed he shal nothing bere with hym out of
this world? / And therfore seith Seint Augustin
that the avaricious man is likned unto helle, /
that the moore it swelweth, the moore desir it
hath to swelwe and devoure. / And as wel as ye
wolde eschewe to be called an avaricious man
or chynche, / as wel sholde ye kepe yow and
governe yow in swich a wise that men calle
yow nat fool large. / Therfore seith 1620
Tullius, 'The goodes,' he seith, 'of thyn
hous ne sholde nat been hyd, ne kept so cloos
but that they mighte been opened by pitee
and debonairetee'— / that is to seyn, to yeven
part to hem that han greet nede— / 'ne thy

1588 to do . . . profit, to make profit. **1589 Salomon,** *Ecclus.* 33:27 (Vulgate). **1590 Salomon,** Prov. 28:19. **tilien,** till. **1592 slow . . . convenable,** slothful, convenient. **1593 versifiour,** Prov. 20:4. **enchesoun,** reason. **1594 Caton,** *Disticha* 1.2. **Waketh,** stay awake. **1595 Seint Jerome,** *Epistolae* 125:11. *goode dedes:* E *goodes.* **1599 scars . . . fool large,** stingy, foolishly generous. **1600 chyncherye,** stinginess: E *chyngerie.* **1602 Caton,** *Disticha* 4.16. **1605 by mesure,** in moderation. **1607 propre . . . shapen,** belonging (property), scheme. **1609 yburyed,** buried; a reference to the parable of the talents, Matt. 25:14–30. **1610 myght . . . weeldynge,** power, control. **1614 enchesoun,** reason. **1615 mowen nat disseveren,** can not separate. **1617 Seint Augustin,** Prov. 27:20. **likned,** compared. **1618 swelweth,** swallows. **1619 chynche,** miser. **1621 Tullius,** Cicero, *De Officiis,* 2.15.55. **debonairetee,** graciousness.

goodes shullen nat been so opene to been every mannes goodes.' /

"Afterward, in getynge of youre richesses and in usynge hem ye shul alwey have thre thynges in youre herte, / that is to seyn, our lord God, conscience, and good name. / First, ye shul have God in youre herte, / and for no richesse ye shullen do nothyng which may in any manere displese God that is youre creatour and maker. / For after the word of Salomon, 'It is bettre to have a litel good with the love of God / than to have muchel good and tresour and lese the love of his lord God.' / And the prophete seith that bettre it is to been a good man and have litel good and tresour / than to been holden a shrewe and have grete richesses. / And yet seye I ferthermoore that ye sholde alwey doon your bisynesse to gete yow richesses, / so that ye gete hem with good conscience. / And th'apostle seith that ther nys thyng in this world of which we sholden have so greet joye as whan oure conscience bereth us good witnesse. / And the wise man seith, 'The substance of a man is ful good whan synne is nat in mannes conscience.' / Afterward in getynge of youre richesses and in usynge of hem, / yow moste have greet bisynesse and greet diligence that youre goode name be alwey kept and conserved. / For Salomon seith that bettre it is and moore it availleth a man to have a good name than for to have grete richesses. / And therfore he seith in another place, 'Do greet diligence,' seith Salomon, 'in kepyng of thy freend and of thy goode name, / for it shal lenger abide with thee than any tresour be it never so precious.' / And certes he sholde nat be called a gentilman that after God and good conscience, alle thynges left, ne dooth his diligence and bisynesse to kepen his good

name. / And Cassidore seith that it is signe of a gentil herte whan a man loveth and desireth to han a good name. / And therfore seith Seint Augustyn that ther been two thynges that arn necessarie and nedefulle, / and that is good conscience and good loos— / that is to seyn, good conscience to thyn owene persone inward and good loos for thy neighebore outward. / And he that trusteth hym so muchel in his goode conscience / that he displeseth and setteth at noght his goode name or loos, and rekketh noght though he kepe nat his goode name, nys but a crueel cherl. /

"Sire, now have I shewed yow how ye shul do in getynge richesses, and how ye shullen usen hem, / and I se wel that for the trust that ye han in youre richesses ye wole moeve werre and bataille. / I conseille yow that ye bigynne no werre in trust of youre richesses for they ne suffisen noght werres to mayntene. / And therfore seith a philosophre, 'That man that desireth and wole algates han werre shal never have suffisaunce, / for the richer that he is the gretter despenses moste he make if he wole have worship and victorie.' / And Salomon seith that the gretter richesses that a man hath the mo despendours he hath. / And deere sire, al be it so that for youre richesses ye mowe have muchel folk, / yet bihoveth it nat, ne it is nat good, to bigynne werre where as ye mowe in oother manere have pees unto youre worship and profit. / For the victories of batailles that been in this world lyen nat in greet nombre or multitude of the peple ne in the vertu of man, / but it lith in the wyl and in the hand of oure lord God Almyghty. / And therfore Judas Machabeus, which was Goddes knight, / whan he sholde fighte agayn his adversarie that hadde a greet nombre and a gretter multitude of folk and strenger than was

1628 Salomon, Prov. 15:16. **1630 the prophete,** Ps. 37:16. **1631 shrewe,** evil person. **1633 so that,** so long as. **1634 th'apostle,** II Cor. 1:12. **1635 wise man,** Ecclus. 13:30. (Vulgate). **substance,** property. **1637 bisynesse . . . kept,** care, protected. **1638 Salomon,** Prov. 22:1. **1639 another place,** Ecclus. 41:15 (Vulgate). **Do . . . diligence,** make an effort. *freend,* so in all MSS, but Fr. reads *ton bon nom et ta bonne fame.* **1641 after God,** next to God. **1642 Cassidore,** *Variae* 1.4. **1643 Seint Augustyn,** *Sermo* 355.1. This citation is not in the Latin. **1644 loos,** reputation. **1647 rekketh . . . crueel,** cares, crude. **1649 moeve,** commence. **1651 algates,** under any circumstance. **1653 Salomon,** Eccles. 5:11, not in the Latin. **despendours,** spenders (wasters). **1654 for . . . mowe,** because of, can (may). **1658 Judas Machabeus,** I Maccabees 3:18–19 (Vulgate).

this peple of Machabee, / yet he reconforted his litel compaignye, and seyde right in this wise: / 'Als lightly,' quod he, 'may oure 1660 lord God Almighty yeve victorie to a fewe folk as to many folk, / for the victorie of bataile comth nat by the grete nombre of peple / but it come from our lord God of Hevene.' / And deere sire, for as muchel as there is no man certein if he be worthy that God yeve hym victorie, namore than he is certein whether he be worthy of the love of God or naught, after that Salomon seith, / therfore every man sholde greetly drede werres to bigynne. / 1665 And by cause that in batailles fallen manye perils, / and happeth outher while that as soone is the grete man slayn as the litel man, / and as it is writen in the Seconde Book of Kynges, 'The dedes of batailles been aventurouse and nothing certeyne,' / for as lightly is oon hurt with a spere as another. / And for ther is gret peril in werre, therfore sholde a man flee and escheue werre in as muchel as a man may goodly. / For 1670 Salomon seith, 'He that loveth peril shal falle in peril.' " /

After that dame Prudence hadde spoken in this manere, Melibee answerde and seyde, / "I see wel, dame Prudence, that by youre faire wordes and by youre resons that ye han shewed me, that the werre liketh yow nothing. / But I have nat yet herd youre conseil, how I shal do in this nede." /

"Certes," quod she, "I conseille yow that ye accorde with youre adversaries, and that ye have pees with hem. / For Seint Jame 1675 seith in his Epistles that by concord and pees the smale richesses wexen grete, / and by debaat and discord the grete richesses fallen doun. / And ye knowen wel that oon of the gretteste and moost sovereyn thyng that is in this world is unytee and pees. / And therfore seyde oure lord Jesu Crist to his apostles in this wise, / 'Wel, happy, and blessed been they that loven and purchacen pees, for they been called children of God.' " / 1680

"A," quod Melibee, "now se I wel that ye loven nat myn honour ne my worshipe. / Ye knowen wel that myne adversaries han bigonnen this debaat and bryge by hire outrage; / and ye see wel that they ne requeren ne preyen me nat of pees, ne they asken nat to be reconsiled. / Wol ye thanne that I go and meke me and obeye me to hem and crie hem mercy? / Forsothe, that were nat my worship. / For 1685 right as men seyn that over greet hoomlynesse engendreth dispreisynge, so fareth it by to greet humylitee or mekenesse." /

Thanne bigan dame Prudence to maken semblant of wratthe and seyde, / "Certes, sire, sauf youre grace, I love youre honour and youre profit as I do myn owene, and ever have doon; / ne ye ne noon oother syen nevere the contrarie. / And yit, if I hadde seyd that ye sholde han purchaced the pees and the reconsiliacioun, I ne hadde nat muchel mystaken me ne seyd amys. / For the wise 1690 man seith the dissensioun bygynneth by another man, and the reconsilyng bygynneth by thyself. / And the prophete seith, 'Flee shrewednesse and do goodnesse; / seke pees and folwe it, as muchel as in thee is.' / Yet seye I nat that ye shul rather pursue to youre adversaries for pees than they shuln to yow, / for I knowe wel that ye been so hard herted, that ye wol do nothing for me. / And Salomon 1695 seith, 'He that hath over hard an herte, atte laste he shal myshappe and mystyde.' " /

Whanne Melibee hadde herd dame Prudence maken semblant of wratthe, he seyde in this wise, / "Dame, I prey yow that ye be nat

---

1664 Salomon, Ecclus. 9:1 (Vulgate). *namore—God* om. from all MSS; trans. by Skeat from Fr. **1666 fallen,** befall. **1667 as soone,** as often (quickly). **1668 Kynges,** II Sam. 11:25 (Vulgate, Liber Secundus Regum). **aventurouse,** haphazard. **1669 lightly,** easily. **1671 Salomon,** Ecclus. 3:27 (Vulgate). **1673 liketh yow nothing,** pleases you not at all. **1675 accorde,** make peace (accord). **1676 Seint Jame,** Seneca, *Epistolae* 94:46. *Seneque* in Fr. and Lat. **1679 Jesu Crist,** Matt. 5:9. **1680 purchacen,** obtain. **1682 bryge,** strife. **1685 worship,** credit. **1686 hoomlynesse,** familiarity. **1687 semblant,** appearance. **1689 syen,** saw. **1690 mystaken,** done amiss. **1691 wise man,** Martinus Dumiensis, *De Moribus* 49. **1692 the prophete,** Ps. 33:15. **shrewednesse,** evil. **1694 rather,** more quickly (before). **1696 Salomon,** Prov. 28:14. **atte laste ... myshappe and mystyde,** in the end, (come to) misfortune and calamity.

displesed of thynges that I seye, / for ye knowe wel that I am angry and wrooth and that is no wonder, / and they that been wrothe witen nat wel what they don ne what they seyn. / Therfore the prophete seith that troubled eyen han no cleer sighte. / But seyeth and conseileth me as yow liketh for I am redy to do right as ye wol desire, / and if ye repreve me of my folye I am the moore holden to love yow and preyse yow. / For Salomon seith that he that repreveth hym that dooth folye, / he shal fynde gretter grace than he that deceyveth hym by sweete wordes." /

Thanne seide dame Prudence, "I make no semblant of wratthe ne anger but for youre grete profit. / For Salomon seith, 'He is moore worth that repreveth or chideth a fool for his folye shewynge hym semblant of wratthe, / than he that supporteth hym and preyseth hym in his mysdoynge and laugheth at his folye.' / And this same Salomon seith afterward that by the sorweful visage of a man—that is to seyn, by the sory and hevy countenaunce of a man— / the fool correcteth and amendeth himself." /

Thanne seyde Melibee, "I shal nat konne answere to so manye faire resouns as ye putten to me and shewen. / Seyeth shortly youre wyl and youre conseil, and I am al ready to fulfille and parfourne it." /

Thanne dame Prudence discovered al hir wyl to hym, and seyde, / "I conseille yow," quod she, "aboven alle thynges, that ye make pees bitwene God and yow, / and beth reconsiled unto hym and to his grace. / For as I have seyd yow heerbiforn, God hath suffred yow to have this tribulacioun and disese for youre synnes. / And if ye do as I sey yow, God wol sende youre adversaries unto yow, / and maken hem fallen at youre feet, redy to do youre wyl and youre comandementz. / For Salomon seith, 'Whan the condicioun of man is plesaunt and likynge to God, / he chaungeth the hertes of the mannes adversaries, and constreyneth hem to biseken hym of pees and of grace.' / And I prey yow, lat me speke with youre adversaries in privee place, / for they shul nat knowe that it be of youre wyl or of youre assent. / And thanne, whan I knowe hire wil and hire entente, I may conseille yow the moore seurely." /

"Dame," quod Melibee, "dooth youre wil and youre likynge, / for I putte me hoolly in youre disposicioun and ordinaunce." /

Thanne dame Prudence, whan she saugh the goode wil of hire housbonde, delibered and took avys in hirself, / thinkynge how she myghte brynge this nede unto a good conclusioun and to a good ende. / And whan she saugh hire tyme, she sente for thise adversaries to come unto hire into a pryvee place, / and shewed wisely unto hem the grete goodes that comen of pees, / and the grete harmes and perils that been in werre; / and seyde to hem in a goodly manere, hou that hem oughten have greet repentaunce / of the injurie and wrong that they hadden doon to Melibee hire lord, and to hire, and to hire doghter. /

And whan they herden the goodliche wordes of dame Prudence, / they weren so surpprised and ravysshed, and hadden so greet joye of hire, that wonder was to telle. / "A, lady," quod they, "ye han shewed unto us the blessynge of swetnesse, after the sawe of David the prophete; / for the reconsilynge which we been nat worthy to have in no manere, / but we oghte requeren it with greet contricioun and humylitee, / ye of youre grete goodnesse have presented unto us. / Now se we wel that the science and the konnynge of Salomon is ful

1700 seyn, say. 1702 yow liketh, pleases you. 1703 repreve . . . holden, reprove, bound (compelled). 1704 Salomon, Prov. 28:23. 1705 gretter grace, greater honor. 1707 Salomon, Ecclus. 7:4–6 (Vulgate). moore worth, more worthy. 1709 hevy, somber. 1711 konne, be able to. 1713 discovered, revealed. 1716 disese, discomfort. 1719 Salomon, Prov. 16:7. condicioun . . . likyng, spiritual condition, agreeable. 1720 biseken hym, beseech of him. biseken, northern form. 1722 be . . . youre wyl, is, your desire. 1723 seurely, certainly. 1726 delibered, deliberated. 1729 goodes, benefits. 1731 goodly, kind. 1732 hire lord . . . hire . . . hire, their lord, her, their (or her). 1734 surpprised and ravysshed, captivated and entranced. 1735 sawe, saying. David, Ps. 20:4 (Vulgate). 1737 requeren, request. 1738 ye, (which) you. 1739 science and . . . konnynge, wisdom and knowledge. Salomon, Ecclus. 6:5 (Vulgate).

trewe. / For he seith that sweete wordes multiplien and encreesen freendes, and maken shrewes to be debonaire and meeke. / 1740

"Certes," quod they, "we putten oure dede and al oure matere and cause al hoolly in youre goode wyl, / and been redy to obeye to the speche and comandement of my lord Melibee. / And therfore, deere and benygne lady, we preien yow and biseke yow as mekely as we konne and mowen / that it lyke unto youre grete goodnesse to fulfillen in dede youre goodliche wordes, / for we consideren and knowlichen that we han offended and greved my lord Melibee out of mesure / so 1745 ferforth that we be nat of power to maken his amendes. / And therfore we oblige and bynden us and oure freendes to doon all his wyl and his comandementz. / But peraventure he hath swich hevynesse and swich wratthe to us-ward by cause of oure offense / that he wole enjoyne us swich a peyne as we mowe nat bere ne susteene. / And therfore, noble lady, we biseke to youre wommanly pitee / to taken 1750 swich avysement in this nede that we ne oure freendes be nat desherited ne destroyed thurgh our folye." /

"Certes," quod Prudence, "it is an hard thyng and right perilous / that a man putte hym al outrely in the arbitracioun and juggement and in the myght and power of his enemys. / For Salomon seith, 'Leeveth me, and yeveth credence to that I shal seyn. I seye,' quod he, 'ye peple, folk and governours of hooly chirche, / to thy sone, to thy wyf, to thy freend, ne to thy broother / ne yeve 1755 thou nevere myght ne maistrie of thy body whil thou lyvest.' / Now sithen he deffendeth that man shal nat yeven to his broother ne to his freend the might of his body, / by strenger resoun he deffendeth and forbedeth a man to yeven hymself to his enemy. / And nathelees I conseille you that ye mystruste nat my lord. / For I woot wel and knowe verraily that he is debonaire and meeke, large, curteys, / 1760 and nothing desyrous ne coveitous of good ne richesse. / For ther nys nothing in this world that he desireth save oonly worship and honour. / Forthermoore I knowe wel and am right seur that he shal nothyng doon in this nede withouten my conseil. / And I shal so werken in this cause that by grace of oure lord God ye shul been reconsiled unto us." /

Thanne seyden they with o voys, "Worshipful lady, we putten us and our goodes al fully in youre wil and disposicioun / and been 1765 redy to comen, what day that it lyke unto youre noblesse to lymyte us or assigne us, / for to maken oure obligacioun and boond as strong as it liketh unto youre goodnesse / that we mowe fulfille the wille of yow and of my lord Melibee." /

Whan dame Prudence hadde herd the answeres of thise men, she bad hem goon agayn prively, / and she retourned to hire lord Melibee and tolde hym how she foond his adversaries ful repentant, / knowlechynge 1770 ful lowely hire synnes and trespas, and how they were redy to suffren all peyne, / requirynge and preiynge hym of mercy and pitee. /

Thanne seyde Melibee, "He is wel worthy to have pardoun and foryifnesse of his synne that excuseth nat his synne / but knowlecheth it and repenteth hym, axinge indulgence. / For Senec seith, 'Ther is the remissioun and foryifnesse where as confessioun is.' / For 1775 confessioun is neighebore to innocence. / And he seith in another place, 'He that hath shame for his synne and knowlecheth it is worthy remissioun.' And therfore I assente and conferme me to have pees. / But it is good that

1741 dede . . . matere, (mis)deed, affair. 1746 ferforth, far. 1747 oblige, obligate. 1748 hevynesse, resentment. 1749 enjoyne . . . peyne, impose, punishment. 1751 taken . . . avysement, i.e., consider. 1754 Salomon, Ecclus. 33:19–20 (Vulgate). Leeveth, believe. 1756 maistrie of, authority over. 1757 sithen . . . deffendeth, since, forbids. 1760 large, generous. 1762 worship, respect. 1766 lymyte, appoint. 1772 requirynge, requesting. 1775 Senec, Martinus Dumiensis, *De Moribus* 4. 1777 *And he seith—remissioun* (*De Moribus* 4), E&c om., supplied by Skeat and Manly from other MSS where it occurs with many variations. *conferme*: E&c *conforme* (E *corforme*).

we do it nat withouten the assent and wyl of oure freendes." /

Thanne was Prudence right glad and joyeful, and seyde, / "Certes, sire," quod she, "ye han wel and goodly answered. / For right 1780 as by the conseil, assent, and help of youre freendes ye han been stired to venge yow and maken werre, / right so withouten hire conseil shul ye nat accorden yow, ne have pees with youre adversaries. / For the lawe seith, 'Ther nys nothing so good by wey of kynde as a thyng to been unbounde by hym that it was ybounde.' " /

And thanne dame Prudence, withouten delay or tariynge, sente anon hire messages for hire kyn, and for hyr olde freendes whiche that were trewe and wyse, / and tolde hem by ordre, in the presence of Melibee, al this mateere as it is aboven expressed and declared, / and 1785 preyden that they wolde yeven hire avys and conseil what best were to doon in this nede. / And whan Melibees freendes hadde taken hire avys and deliberacioun of the forseide mateere, / and hadden examyned it by greet bisynesse and greet diligence, / they yave ful conseil for to have pees and reste, / and that Melibee sholde receyve with good herte his adversaries to foryifnesse and mercy. / 1790

And whan dame Prudence hadde herd the assent of hir lord Melibee and the conseil of his freendes / accorde with hire wille and hire entencioun, / she was wonderly glad in hire herte, and seyde, / "Ther is an old proverbe," quod she, "seith that the goodnesse that thou mayst do this day, do it, / and abide nat ne delaye it nat til tomorwe. / 1795 And therfore I conseille that ye sende youre messages, swiche as been discrete and wise, / unto youre adversaries tellynge hem on youre bihalve / that if they wole trete of pees and of accord, / that they shape hem withouten delay or tariyng to comen unto us." / Which thyng parfourned was in dede. / 1800 And whanne thise trespassours and repentynge folk of hire folies—that is to seyn, the adversaries of Melibee— / hadden herd what thise messagers seyden unto hem / they weren right glad and joyeful, and answereden ful mekely and benignely, / yeldynge graces and thankynges to hire lord Melibee and to al his compaignye, / and shopen hem withouten delay to go with the messagers and obeye to the comandement of hire lord Melibee. / 1805

And right anon they tooken hire wey to the court of Melibee, / and tooken with hem somme of hire trewe freendes to maken feith for hem and for to been hire borwes. / And whan they were comen to the presence of Melibee, he seyde hem thise wordes, / "It standeth thus," quod Melibee, "and sooth it is, that ye / causelees and withouten skile and resoun / 1810 han doon grete injuries and wronges to me and to my wyf Prudence and to my doghter also. / For ye han entred into myn hous by violence, / and have doon swich outrage, that alle men knowen wel that ye have disserved the deeth. / And therfore wol I knowe and wite of yow / wheither ye wol putte the punyssement and the chastisynge and the vengeance of this outrage in the wyl of me and of my wyf Prudence, or ye wol nat?" / 1815

Thanne the wiseste of hem thre answerde for hem alle, and seyde, / "Sire," quod he, "we knowen wel that we been unworthy to comen unto the court of so greet a lord and so worthy as ye been. / For we han so greetly mystaken us and han offended and agilt in swich a wise agayn youre heigh lordshipe / that trewely we han disserved the deeth. / But yet for the grete goodnesse and debonairetee that al the world witnesseth in youre persone, / we submytten us to the 1820 excellence and benignitee of youre gracious lordshipe, / and been redy to obeie to alle youre comandementz, / bisekynge yow that of youre merciable pitee ye wol considere oure grete repentaunce and lough submyssioun, / and graunten us foryevenesse of oure outrageous

---

1783 lawe seith, Justinian, *Digesta* 1.17.35. **by wey of kynde ... unbounde ... ybounde,** in the world, revoked (withdrawn), stipulated (promised). **1784 messages,** messengers. **1785 by ordre,** in order. **1793 wonderly,** wonderfully. **1798 trete,** negotiate. **1799 shape,** prepare. **1807 maken feith ... borwes,** give assurance, securities. **1810 skile,** cause. **1818 agilt,** been guilty.

trespas and offense. / For wel we knowe that youre liberal grace and mercy strecchen hem ferther into goodnesse than doon oure outrageouse giltes and trespas into wikkednesse, / al be it that cursedly and 1825 dampnably we han agilt agayn your heigh lordshipe." /

Thanne Melibee took hem up fro the ground ful benignely, / and receyved hire obligaciouns and hir boondes by hire othes upon hire plegges and borwes, / and assigned hem a certeyn day to retourne unto his court / for to accepte and receyve the sentence and jugement that Melibee wolde comande to be doon on hem by the causes aforeseyd; / whiche 1830 thynges ordeyned, every man retourned to his hous. /

And whan that dame Prudence saugh hire tyme, she freyned and axed hir lord Melibee / what vengeance he thoughte to taken of his adversaries. /

To which Melibee answerde and seyde, "Certes," quod he, "I thynke and purpose me fully / to desherite hem of al that ever they han, and for to putte hem in exil forever." / 1835

"Certes," quod dame Prudence, "this were a crueel sentence, and muchel agayn resoun. / For ye been riche ynough, and han no nede of oother mennes good. / And ye mighte lightly in this wise gete yow a coveitous name, / which is a vicious thyng and oghte been escheued of every good man. / For after the sawe of the word of the apostle, 'Coveitise is roote of alle harmes.' / And therfore it 1840 were bettre for yow to lese so muchel good of youre owene than for to taken of hire good in this manere. / For bettre it is to lesen good with worshipe than it is to wynne good with vileynye

and shame. / And everi man oghte to doon his diligence and his bisynesse to geten hym a good name. / And yet shal he nat oonly bisie hym in kepynge of his good name, / but he shal also enforcen hym alwey to do somthing by which he may renovelle his good name. / 1845 For it is writen that the olde good loos and good name of a man is soone goon and passed whan it is nat newed ne renovelled. / And as touchynge that ye seyn ye wole exile youre adversaries, / that thynketh me muchel agayn resoun and out of mesure, / considered the power that they han yeve yow upon hemself. / And it is writen that he is worthy to lesen his privilege that mysuseth the myght and the power that is yeven hym. / And I sette 1850 cas ye myghte enjoyne hem that peyne by right and by lawe, / which I trowe ye mowe nat do, / I seye ye mighte nat putten it to execucioun peraventure, / and thanne were it likly to retourne to the werre as it was biforn. / And therfore, if ye wole that men do yow obeisance, ye moste deemen moore curteisly— / this is to seyn, ye moste 1855 yeven moore esy sentences and juggementz. / For it is writen that he that moost curteisly comandeth, to hym men moost obeyen. / And therfore, I prey yow that in this necessitee and in this nede, ye caste yow to overcome youre herte. / For Senec seith that he that overcometh his herte, overcometh twies. / And Tullius seith, 'Ther is nothyng so comendable in a greet lord / as whan he is 1860 debonaire and meeke, and appeseth hym lightly.' / And I prey yow that ye wole forbere now to do vengeance / in swich a manere that youre goode name may be kept and conserved; / and that men mowe have cause and mateere to preyse yow of pitee and of mercy; / and that ye

---

1828 **receyved . . . borwes,** accepted, securities. 1830 **by . . . causes,** for, reasons. 1832 **freyned,** inquired; Hg&c *feyned.* 1837 **good,** goods (possessions). 1838 **lightly . . . coveitous name,** easily, name (reputation) for covetousness. 1839 **vicious,** evil. 1840 **sawe,** saying, I Tim. 6:10. 1842 **lesen good,** lose property. *lesen good/wynne good:* E *good* om. 1845 **enforcen hym . . . renovelle,** make himself, renew. 1846 **olde . . . loos,** established, reputation. 1847 **touchynge . . . seyn,** concerning, say. 1848 **thynketh me . . . out of measure,** seems to me, excessive. 1850 **lesen,** lose. 1851 **sette cas . . . enjoyne . . . peyne,** suppose, assign, punishment. 1852 **trowe . . . mowe,** trust, will (may). 1853 **mighte,** i.e., may. 1854 **and thanne,** i.e., for then. 1855 **wole . . . deemen . . . curteisly,** desire, adjudge, mildly. 1858 **caste yow,** try. 1859 **Senec,** Pubilius Syrus, *Sententiae* 64. **twies,** twice. 1860 **Tullius,** Cicero, *De Officiis,* 1.25.88. 1861 **appeseth hym lightly,** i.e., is easily satisfied (mollified). E *hym* om.

have no cause to repente yow of thyng that ye doon. / For Senec seith, 'He 1865 overcometh in an yvel manere that repenteth hym of his victorie.' / Wherfore I pray yow, lat mercy been in youre mynde and in your herte / to th'effect and entente that God Almyghty have mercy on yow in his laste juggement. / For Seint Jame seith in his Epistle, 'Juggement withouten mercy shall be doon to hym that hath no mercy of another wight.' " /

Whanne Melibee hadde herd the grete skiles and resouns of dame Prudence, and hir wise informaciouns and techynges, / 1870 his herte gan enclyne to the wil of his wif, considerynge hire trewe entente, / and conformed hym anon, and assented fully to werken after hire conseil, / and thonked God of whom procedeth al vertu and alle goodnesse that hym sente a wif of so greet discrecioun. / And whan the day cam that his adversaries sholde appieren in his presence, / he spak unto hem ful goodly, and seyde in this wyse, / "Al be it 1875 so that of youre pride and presumpcioun and folie and of youre necligence and unkonnynge, / ye have mysborn yow and trespassed unto me, / yet for as much as I see and biholde your grete humylitee, / and that ye been sory and repentant of youre giltes, / it constreyneth me to doon yow grace and mercy. / Therfore I receyve yow to my 1880 grace / and foryeve yow outrely alle the offenses, injuries, and wronges, that ye have doon agayn me and myne / to this effect and to this ende that God of his endelees mercy / wole at the tyme of oure dyinge foryeven us oure giltes that we han trespassed to hym in this wrecched world. / For doutelees, if we be sory and repentant of the synnes and giltes whiche we han trespassed in the sighte of oure lord God, / he is so free and so merciable / 1885 that he wole foryeven us our giltes / and bryngen us to his blisse that never hath ende. Amen." /

Heere is ended Chaucers Tale of Melibee and of Dame Prudence.

1866 Senec, Pubilius Syrus, *Sententiae* 366. **1867** Hg&c *in youre mynde* om. **1869 Seint Jame,** James 2:13. **of . . . wight,** upon, person. **1870 skiles,** arguments. **1875 goodly,** pleasantly. **1880 constreyneth,** persuades. **1886 free,** generous.

MONK'S TALE

PROLOGUE

The murye wordes of the Hoost to the Monk.

Whan ended was my tale of Melibee
And of Prudence and hire benignytee,   1890
Oure Hooste seyde, "As I am feithful man,
And by that precious corpus Madrian,
I hadde levere than a barel ale
That Goodelief, my wyf, hadde herd this tale.
She nys nothyng of swich pacience   1895
As was this Melibeus wyf Prudence.
By Goddes bones, whan I bete my knaves,
She bryngeth me forth the grete clobbed
    staves,
And crieth, 'Slee the dogges everichoon,
And brek hem bothe bak and every boon!'
And if that any neighebore of myne   1901
Wol nat in chirche to my wyf enclyne,
Or be so hardy to hire to trespace,
Whan she comth hoom she rampeth in my
    face,

And crieth, 'False coward, wrek thy wyf !   1905
By corpus bones, I wol have thy knyf,
And thou shalt have my distaf and go spynne!'
Fro day to nyght right thus she wol bigynne.
'Allas,' she seith, 'that evere I was shape
To wedden a milksop, or a coward ape,   1910
That wol been overlad with every wight.
Thou darst nat stonden by thy wyves right.'

    "This is my lif but if that I wol fighte;
And out at dore anon I moot me dighte,
Or elles I am but lost but if that I   1915
Be lik a wilde leoun, fool-hardy.
I woot wel she wol do me slee somday
Som neighebore, and thanne go my way,
For I am perilous with knyf in honde
Al be it that I dar hire nat withstonde,   1920
For she is byg in armes, by my feith—
That shal he fynde that hire mysdooth or seith.

1890 **beynignytee,** graciousness. 1892 **corpus Madrian,** body, but "Madrian" has not been explained; perhaps it is another of Herry Bailly's malapropisms. 1894 **Goodelief:** E&c *good lief.* Some editions take this to mean merely "my dear wife," but the combination is found as a name in Kentish records. In Southwark records, the real Herry Bailly's wife was named "Christian." 1895 *She:* other MSS *For she.* 1897 **knaves,** servant boys. 1898 Hg&c *forth* om. 1902 **enclyne,** bow. 1903 **trespace,** do offence (e.g., step in front of her). 1904 **rampeth,** rages. EHg&c *hoom* om. Manly II.409 points out that the exemplar of the MkT for EHg&c must have been faulty; the text of Harley 7334&c is much better. In the notes that follow the obvious errors in EHg&c are not listed. 1905 **wrek,** avenge. 1911 **overlad ... wight,** pushed around by everyone. 1914 **anon ... me dighte,** immediately, must take myself. 1918 **go my way,** run away.

But lat us passe awey fro this mateere.

"My lord, the Monk," quod he, "be myrie of
cheere,

For ye shul telle a tale trewely.   1925

Loo, Rouchestre stant heer faste by.

Ryde forth, myn owene lord, brek nat oure
game.

But by my trouthe, I knowe nat youre name.

Wher shal I calle yow my lord daun John,

Or daun Thomas, or elles daun Albon?   1930

Of what hous be ye, by youre fader kyn?

I vowe to God, thou hast a ful fair skyn;

It is a gentil pasture ther thow goost.

Thou art nat lyk a penant or a goost.

Upon my feith, thou art som officer,   1935

Som worthy sexteyn, or som celerer,

For by my fader soule, as to my doom,

Thou art a maister whan thou art at hoom,

No poure cloysterer ne no novys,

But a governour, wily and wys,   1940

And therwithal of brawnes and of bones,

A wel farynge persone for the nones.

I pray to God, yeve hym confisioun

That first thee broghte unto religioun!

Thou woldest han been a tredefowel aright.

Haddestow as greet a leeve as thou hast
myght   1946

To parfourne al thy lust in engendrure,

Thou haddest bigeten ful many a creature.

Allas, why werestow so wyd a cope?

God yeve me sorwe but, and I were a pope,   1950

Nat oonly thou, but every myghty man,

Though he were shorn ful hye upon his pan,

Sholde have a wyf, for al the world is lorn—

Religioun hath take up al the corn   1954

Of tredyng, and we borel men been shrympes.

Of fieble trees ther comen wrecched ympes.

This maketh that oure heires been so sklendre

And feble that they may nat wel engendre.

This maketh that oure wyves wole assaye

Religious folk, for ye mowe bettre paye   1960

Of Venus paiementz than mowe we.

God woot, no lussheburgh payen ye!

But be nat wrooth, my lord, though that I
pleye.

Ful ofte in game a sooth I have herd seye."

This worthy Monk took al in pacience,   1965

And seyde, "I wol doon al my diligence—

As fer as sowneth into honestee—

To telle yow a tale, or two, or three,

And if yow list to herkne hyderward,

I wol yow seyn the lyf of Seint Edward—   1970

Or ellis, first, tragedies wol I telle

Of whiche I have an hundred in my celle.

"Tragedie is to seyn a certeyn storie,

As olde bookes maken us memorie,

Of hym that stood in greet prosperitee   1975

And is yfallen out of heigh degree

Into myserie, and endeth wrecchedly.

And they ben versified communely

Of six feet which men clepen exametron.

In prose eek been endited many oon,   1980

And eek in meetre, in many a sondry wyse.

Lo, this declaryng oghte ynogh suffise.

"Now herkneth, if yow liketh for to heere.

But first I yow biseeke in this mateere,

Though I by ordre telle nat thise thynges,   1985

Be it of popes, emperours, or kynges,

1926 Rouchestre, Rochester, 30 miles from Southwark, and a little over half way to Canterbury. **1929 daun,** from Lat. *dom(inus).*
In NP prologue, l. 2792, the Host knew that the Monk's name was "daun Piers." **1931 hous,** generally glossed "monastery," but in
view of **fader kyn,** it may here mean "noble family"—i.e., the Monk appears, like the Knight and the Prioress, to be of gentle birth.
(Andreas Cappellanus asserts that his natural birth determines a cleric's status in love, not his religious status.) **1933 gentil pasture,**
i.e., you eat well. **1934 penant,** penitent (fasting). **1936 sexteyn . . . celerer,** officers in charge of buildings and grounds and of
food and wine. **1937 doom,** judgment. **1939 novys,** novice, one who has newly entered a religious order. **1941 brawnes,** flesh.
1942 wel farynge, well appearing. **1945 tredefowel,** rooster (breeding fowl). The virility of the clergy is commonplace in all ages.
It is one of the themes of Swift's satiric *Argument against Abolishing Christianity.* **1949 cope,** here probably cowl. **1952 shorn,** tonsure,
sign of religious vocation. **1953 lorn,** lost. **1954 corn,** valuable (fertile) part. **1955 tredyng . . . borel,** copulation, laymen. **1956
ympes,** offshoots. **1957–58** Lines omitted in E. **1957 sklendre,** slender (puny). **1960 mowe,** can. **1962 lussheburgh,** counterfeit
coin (from Luxembourg). **1963** *though:* E *for.* **1964 sooth,** truth. **1967 sowneth into honestee,** conforms to propriety. **1970** E *yow* om.
1973 Tragedie, a similar definition of tragedy is found in a gloss in Chaucer's translation of *Boece,* II pr. 2, 72; and the final lines
of the final tale of Cresus, 2761–66, echo *Boece* II pr. 2, III pr. 5. Thus, the Boethian conception of tragedy provides a frame for the
MkT. **1979 exametron,** hexameters, the meter of the Latin heroic poetry of Virgil, Lucan, &c. **1980 endited,** composed. **1985
ordre,** i.e., chronological order.

After hir ages, as men writen fynde,
But tellen hem som before and som bihynde,

As it now comth unto my remembraunce,
Have me excused of myn ignoraunce."   1990

Heere bigynneth the Monkes Tale De Casibus Virorum Illustrium.

I wol biwaille in manere of tragedie
The harm of hem that stoode in heigh degree,
And fillen so that ther nas no remedie
To brynge hem out of hire adversitee.
For certein, whan that Fortune list to flee,   1995
Ther may no man the cours of hire withholde.
Lat no man truste on blynd prosperitee;
Be war by thise ensamples trewe and olde.

LUCIFER

At Lucifer, though he an angel were
And nat a man, at hym wol I bigynne.   2000
For though Fortune may noon angel dere,
From heigh degree yet fel he for his synne
Doun into helle where he yet is inne.
O Lucifer, brightest of angels alle,   2004
Now artow Sathanas, that mayst nat twynne
Out of miserie, in which that thou art falle.

ADAM

Loo Adam, in the feeld of Damyssene
With Goddes owene fynger wroght was he,
And nat bigeten of mannes sperme unclene,
And welte al paradys savynge o tree.   2010
Hadde nevere worldly man so heigh degree
As Adam, til he for mysgovernaunce
Was dryven out of hys hye prosperitee
To labour, and to helle, and to meschaunce.

SAMPSON

Loo Sampsoun, which that was annunciat
By the angel longe er his nativitee,   2016
And was to God Almyghty consecrat,

And stood in noblesse whil he myghte see.
Was nevere swich another as was hee,
To speke of strengthe and therwith hardynesse;
But to his wyves toolde he his secree,   2021
Thurgh which he slow hymself for
    wrecchednesse.

Sampsoun, this noble almyghty champioun,
Withouten wepen save his handes tweye,
He slow and al torente the leoun,   2025
Toward his weddyng walkynge by the weye.
His false wyf koude hym so plese and preye
Til she his conseil knew; and she untrewe
Unto his foos his conseil gan biwreye,   2029
And hym forsook and took another newe.

Thre hundred foxes took Sampson for ire,
And alle hir tayles he togydre bond,
And sette the foxes tayles alle on fire,
For he on every tayl had knyt a brond.   2034
And they brende alle the cornes in that lond,
And alle hire olyveres, and vynes eke.
A thousand men he slow eek with his hond,
And hadde no wepen but an asses cheke.

Whan they were slayn, so thursted hym that he
Was wel ny lorn, for which he gan to preye
That God wolde on his peyne han som pitee   2041
And sende hym drynke or elles moste he deye,
And of this asses cheke that was dreye,
Out of a wang-tooth sprang anon a welle,
Of which he drank anon shortly to seye,   2045
Thus heelp hym God, as Judicum can telle.

De Casibus, the title is the same as that of Boccaccio's famous "Fall of Illustrious Men," but there is evidently little direct relation between Chaucer's content and Boccaccio's. **1992 heigh degree,** high station. **1998 by:** E&c *of.* **1999 though ... were,** although, was. **2001 dere,** harm. **2005 twynne,** escape. **2007–14** The Adam stanza is omitted in Hg&c. **2007 Damyssene,** Damascus, reputed to be built on the site where Adam was created. **2010 welte ... o,** ruled (wielded), one. **2015 annunciat,** announced, cf. Judges 13:3. **2018 whil,** as long as. **2020 hardynesse,** courage. **2022 slow,** slew. **2023** Some MSS *noble and myghty.* **2025 torente,** tore to pieces. The account of Sampson follows mainly Judges 13ff. **2027 preye,** beseech (pray). **2028 conseil,** secret. **2029 biwreye,** betray. **2030 took another,** Sampson's wife was given to a friend, Judges 14:20. **2031 ire,** anger. **2034 knyt a brond,** attached a firebrand. **2035 cornes,** grain crops. **2036 olyveres,** olive trees. **2038 cheke,** i.e., jawbone. **2040 lorn,** lost. **2044 wang-tooth ... welle,** molar, spring. **2046 Judicum,** Book of Judges (*Liber Judicum*).

By verray force at Gazan on a nyght,
Maugree Philistiens of that citee,
The gates of the toun he hath up plyght
And on his bak ycaryed hem hath hee   2050
Hye on an hill wher as men myghte hem see.
O noble, almyghty Sampsoun, lief and deere,
Had thou nat toold to wommen thy secree,
In al this world ne hadde been thy peere!

This Sampson nevere ciser drank ne wyn,   2055
Ne on his heed cam rasour noon ne sheere,
By precept of the messager divyn,
For alle his strengthes in his heeres weere.
And fully twenty wynter, yeer by yeere,
He hadde of Israel the governaunce.   2060
But soone shal he wepe many a teere,
For wommen shal hym bryngen to meschaunce.

Unto his lemman Dalida he tolde
That in his heeris al his strengthe lay,
And falsely to his foomen she hym solde.   2065
And slepynge in hir barm upon a day,
She made to clippe or shere his heres away,
And made his foomen al this craft espyen,
And whan that they hym foond in this array,
They bounde hym faste and putten out his
          eyen.   2070

But er his heer were clipped or yshave,
Ther was no boond with which men myghte
          him bynde.
But now is he in prison in a cave,
Where as they made hym at the queerne
          grynde.   2074
O noble Sampsoun, strongest of mankynde,
O whilom juge, in glorie and in richesse,

Now maystow wepen with thyne eyen blynde,
Sith thou fro wele art falle in wrecchednesse.

The ende of this caytyf was as I shal seye.
His foomen made a feeste upon a day,   2080
And made hym as hire fool biforn hem pleye,
And this was in a temple of greet array.
But atte laste he made a foul affray,   2083
For he two pilers shook and made hem falle,
And doun fil temple and al, and ther it lay,
And slow hymself, and eek his foomen alle.

This is to seyn, the prynces everichoon
And eek thre thousand bodyes were ther slayn
With fallynge of the grete temple of stoon.
Of Sampson now wol I namoore sayn.   2090
Beth war by this ensample oold and playn
That no men telle hir conseil til hir wyves
Of swich thyng as they wolde han secree fayn,
If that it touche hir lymes or hir lyves.

HERCULES

Of Hercules, the sovereyn conquerour,   2095
Syngen his werkes laude and heigh renoun,
For in his tyme of strengthe he was the flour.
He slow and rafte the skyn fro the leoun;
He of centauros leyde the boost adoun;
He arpies slow, the crueel bryddes felle;   2100
He golden apples rafte of the dragoun;
He drow out Cerberus, the hound of helle;

He slow the crueel tyrant Busirus,
And made his hors to frete hym, flessh and boon;
He slow the firy serpent venymus;   2105
Of Acheloys hornes two he brak oon;

2049 plyght, plucked, torn. **2051** *wher as:* E *that.* **2052** *almyghty:* some MSS *o myhty.* **2054 peere,** peer (equal). **2055 ciser,** strong drink (Lat. *sicera,* cider). **2056 sheere,** shears. **2063 lemman,** mistress. **2066 barm,** lap. **2074 queerne,** handmill. **2076 whilom,** sometime. **2078 Sith . . . wele,** since, prosperity. **2079 caytyf,** wretch. **2081 hire:** E&c *a.* **2083 foul affray,** horrible commotion. **2084 two:** E *the;* *pilers:* other MSS *postis.* **2086 slow,** slew. **2092 conseil,** secrets. **2093 fayn,** gladly. **2094 touche . . . lymes,** concerns, limbs. **2095 sovereyn,** supreme. The account of Hercules follows mainly *Boece* IV m.7, which mentions only five of Hercules' traditional twelve labors. **2096 laude,** praise. **2097 was:** other MSS *bar.* **2098 slow . . . rafte,** slew, peeled (took)—the traditional first labor of Hercules was to slay the Nemean lion. *fro:* E&c *of.* **2099 centauros,** in performing his fourth labor, Hercules killed two centaurs (half-horse, half-man) over a cask of wine. **2100 arpies . . . felle,** harpies, dreadful. Hercules' sixth labor was killing these man-eating birds. **2101 rafte,** took. Hercules' eleventh labor was to bring back the golden apples of the Hesperides. **2102 Cerberus,** Hercules' twelfth labor was to bring into the upper world the three-headed dog that guarded the gates of Hades. **2103 Busirus,** the name in the *Boece* gloss is Dyomedes; the account of Busirus is at II pr.6, 68. Chaucer has conflated the two stories. **2104 frete,** eat. **2105 firy:** other MSS *verray,* which Manly considers more probable since in *Boece* (and mythology) the Hydra was not fiery. **2106 Acheloys,** river god who fought Hercules in the form of a bull (the account is mostly from the gloss in *Boece*).

And he slow Cacus in a cave of stoon;
He slow the geant Antheus the stronge;
He slow the grisly boor, and that anon;
And bar the hevene on his nekke longe.   2110

Was nevere wight sith that this world bigan
That slow so manye monstres as dide he.
Thurghout this wyde world his name ran,
What for his strengthe and for his heigh
  bountee,
And every reawme wente he for to see.   2115
He was so stroong that no man myghte hym
  lette.
At bothe the worldes endes, seith Trophee,
In stide of boundes he a pileer sette.

A lemman hadde this noble champioun,
That highte Dianira, fressh as May,   2120
And as thise clerkes maken mencioun,
She hath hym sent a sherte, fressh and gay.
Allas, this sherte, allas and weylaway,
Envenymed was so subtilly withalle
That er that he had wered it half a day   2125
It made his flessh al from his bones falle.

But nathelees somme clerkes hire excusen
By oon that highte Nessus that it maked.
Be as be may, I wol hire noght accusen—
But on his bak this sherte he wered al naked
Til that his flessh was for the venym blaked.   2131
And whan he saugh noon oother remedye,
In hoote coles he hath hymselven raked,
For with no venym deigned hym to dye.

Thus starf this worthy, myghty Hercules.   2135

Lo, who may truste on Fortune any throwe?
For hym that folweth al this world of prees
Er he be war is ofte yleyd ful lowe.
Ful wys is he that kan hymselven knowe!   2139
Beth war, for whan that Fortune list to glose,
Thanne wayteth she her man to overthrowe
By swich a wey as he wolde leest suppose.

NABUGODONOSOR

The myghty trone, the precious tresor,
The glorious ceptre, and roial magestee
That hadde the Kyng Nabugodonosor   2145
With tonge unnethe may discryved bee.
He twyes wan Jerusalem the citee;
The vessel of the temple he with hym ladde.
At Babiloigne was his sovereyn see,
In which his glorie and his delit he hadde.   2150

The faireste children of the blood roial
Of Israel he leet do gelde anoon,
And maked ech of hem to been his thral.
Amonges othere Daniel was oon
That was the wiseste child of everychon,   2155
For he the dremes of the kyng expowned,
Where as in Chaldeye clerk ne was ther noon
That wiste to what fyn his dremes sowned.

This proude kyng leet maken a statue of gold,
Sixty cubites long and sevene in brede,   2160
To which ymage bothe yong and oold
Comanded he to loute and have in drede,
Or in a fourneys ful of flambes rede
He shal be brent that wolde noght obeye.
But nevere wolde assente to that dede   2165
Daniel ne his yonge felawes tweye.

2107 **Cacus,** giant son of Vulcan who stole Hercules' oxen. 2108 **Antheus,** wrestler whose strength increased each time he touched the earth. 2109 **boor,** reference back to the fourth labor (l. 2099) in which Hercules captured (not slew) the Erymanthian bear. 2110 **hevene,** heavens; in his eleventh labor, Hercules held up the heavens while Atlas took the golden apples from his daughters, the Hesperides. 2115 **reawme,** realm. 2116 **lette,** prevent. 2117 **Trophee,** this author has not been identified. 2118 **boundes,** boundary markers. 2120 **highte,** was called. 2124 **Envenymed,** poisoned. 2128 **Nessus,** centaur rival for Dianira. When he attempted to carry her off, Hercules killed him. Dying, he told her to keep some of his blood to use as a charm to preserve Hercules' love for her. Later, jealous of Iole, she sent Hercules a shirt dipped in Nessus' blood. 2133 **raked,** raked over with hot coals. 2136 **throwe,** length of time. 2137 **prees,** press (busy world). 2140 **glose,** beguile. 2146 **unnethe . . . discryved,** scarcely, described. The parallel accounts of Nebuchadnezzar and Belshazzar are taken largely from Daniel 1–5. 2148 **vessel . . . ladde,** vessels (treasure), carried off. 2149 **sovereyn see,** royal seat (capitol). 2152 **gelde,** castrate;,this detail is not in the biblical account. 2153 **thral,** slave. 2156 **expowned,** expounded, interpreted. 2157 **Chaldeye,** Chaldea; Babylonians were traditionally versed in occult learning. 2158 **fyn . . . sowned,** end, tended. 2160 **cubites,** measure of the length of a forearm, 17–22 inches. **brede,** breadth. 2161 *To/bothe:* EHg&c *The/he bothe.* 2162 **loute . . . drede,** bow, awe. EHg&c *he* om.

This kyng of kynges proud was and elaat.
He wende that God that sit in magestee
Ne myghte hym nat bireve of his estaat.
But sodeynly he loste his dignytee,   2170
And lyk a beest hym semed for to bee,
And eet hey as an oxe, and lay theroute
In reyn; with wilde beestes walked hee
Til certein tyme was ycome aboute.

And lik an egles fetheres wax his heres;   2175
His nayles lyk a briddes clawes weere;
Til God relessed hym a certeyn yeres,
And yaf hym wit, and thanne with many a
    teere
He thanked God; and evere his lyf in feere
Was he to doon amys or moore trespace;   2180
And til that tyme he leyd was on his beere,
He knew that God was ful of myght and grace.

BALTHASAR

His sone, which that highte Balthasar,
That heeld the regne after his fader day,
He by his fader koude noght be war,   2185
For proud he was of herte and of array,
And eek an ydolastre he was ay.
His hye estaat assured hym in pryde;
But Fortune caste hym doun, and ther he lay,
And sodeynly his regne gan divide.   2190

A feeste he made unto his lordes alle
Upon a tyme, and bad hem blithe bee,
And thanne his officeres gan he calle.
"Gooth, bryngeth forth the vesseles," quod he,
"Whiche that my fader in his prosperitee   2195
Out of the temple of Jerusalem birafte;
And to oure hye goddes thanke we
Of honour that oure eldres with us lafte."

Hys wyf, his lordes, and his concubynes
Ay dronken whil hire appetites laste   2200
Out of thise noble vessels sondry wynes.

And on a wal this kyng his eyen caste,
And saugh an hand, armlees, that wroot ful
    faste,
For feere of which he quook and siked soore.
This hand that Balthasar so soore agaste   2205
Wroot *Mane, techel, phares* and namoore.

In al that land magicien was noon
That koude expoune what this lettre mente,
But Daniel expowned it anoon,
And seyde, "Kyng, God to thy fader lente   2210
Glorie and honour, regne, tresour, rente,
And he was proud, and nothyng God ne
    dradde,
And therfore God greet wreche upon hym
    sente,
And hym birafte the regne that he hadde.

"He was out cast of mannes compaignye—
With asses was his habitacioun,   2216
And eet hey as a beest in weet and drye,
Til that he knew, by grace and by resoun,
That God of hevene hath domynacioun
Over every regne and every creature.   2220
And thanne hadde God of hym compassioun,
And hym restored his regne and his figure.

"Eek thou that art his sone art proud also,
And knowest alle thise thynges verraily,
And art rebel to God, and art his foo.   2225
Thou drank eek of his vessels boldely;
Thy wyf eek, and thy wenches, synfully
Dronke of the same vessels sondry wynys;
And heryest false goddes cursedly.
Therfore to thee yshapen ful greet pyne ys.   2230

"This hand was sent from God that on the wal
Wroot *Mane, techel, phares,* truste me.
Thy regne is doon, thou weyest noght at al.
Dyvyded is thy regne, and it shal be
To Medes and to Perses yeven," quod he.   2235

2167 **elaat,** arrogant. 2168 **wende,** thought. 2169 **bireve,** deprive. 2179 **evere,** i.e., for the rest of. 2185 **koude . . . be war,** could be warned. 2187 **ydolastre,** idol worshipper. 2190 **gan divide,** began to break up. 2192 *bad:* Hg&c *made.* 2196 **birafte,** carried off. 2204 **siked,** sighed. 2205 **agaste,** frightened. 2208 **expoune,** explain. 2210 *lente:* E&c *sente.* 2211 **regne . . . rente,** dominion, income. 2212 **nothyng . . . ne dradde,** dreaded not at all. 2213 **wreche,** wretchedness (misery). 2222 **figure,** (human) form. 2227 **wyf eek,** wife, also. 2229 **heryest,** worship. 2230 **yshapen . . . pyne,** prepared, punishment. 2233 **weyest,** weigh (i.e., are of no importance). 2234 **Dyvyded . . . regne,** broken up, kingdom. 2235 **Perses,** Persians.

And thilke same nyght this kyng was slawe,
And Darius occupieth his degree,
Thogh he therto hadde neither right ne lawe.

Lordynges, ensample heerby may ye take
How that in lordshipe is no sikernesse, 2240
For whan Fortune wole a man forsake,
She bereth awey his regne and his richesse,
And eek his freendes, bothe moore and lesse.
For what man that hath freendes thurgh
     Fortune,
Mishap wol maken hem enemys as I gesse; 2245
This proverbe is ful sooth and ful commune.

CENOBIA

Cenobia, of Palymerie queene,
As writen Persiens of hir noblesse,
So worthy was in armes and so keene
That no wight passed hire in hardynesse, 2250
Ne in lynage, nor in oother gentillesse.
Of kynges blood of Perce is she descended—
I seye nat that she hadde moost fairnesse,
But of hir shape she myghte nat been amended.

From hire childhede I fynde that she fledde 2255
Office of wommen, and to wode she wente,
And many a wilde hertes blood she shedde
With arwes brode that she to hem sente.
She was so swift that she anon hem hente.
And whan that she was elder, she wolde
     kille 2260
Leouns, leopardes, and beres al torente,
And in hir armes weelde hem at hir wille.

She dorste wilde beestes dennes seke,
And rennen in the montaignes al the nyght,
And slepen under a bussh, and she koude
     eke 2265

Wrastlen by verray force and verray myght
With any yong man, were he never so wight.
Ther myghte no thyng in hir armes stonde.
She kepte hir maydenhod from every wight;
To no man deigned hire for to be bonde. 2270

But atte laste hir freendes han hire maried
To Odenake, a prynce of that contree,
Al were it so that she hem longe taried.
And ye shul understonde how that he
Hadde swiche fantasies as hadde she. 2275
But natheless, whan they were knyt in feere,
They lyved in joye and in felicitee,
For ech of hem hadde oother lief and deere.

Save o thyng, that she wolde nevere assente
By no wey that he sholde by hire lye 2280
But ones, for it was hir pleyn entente
To have a child the world to multiplye.
And also soone as that she myghte espye
That she was nat with childe with that dede,
Thanne wolde she suffre hym doon his
     fantasye 2285
Eftsoone and nat but oones, out of drede.

And if she were with childe at thilke cast,
Namoore sholde he pleyen thilke game
Til fully fourty wikes weren past.
Thanne wolde she ones suffre hym do the same.
Al were this Odenake wilde or tame, 2291
He gat namoore of hire, for thus she seyde,
It was to wyves lecherie and shame,
In oother caas if that men with hem pleyde.

Two sones by this Odenake hadde she 2295
The whiche she kepte in vertu and lettrure.
But now unto oure tale turne we:
I seye, so worshipful a creature,

2236 slawe, slain. **2237 degree,** station. **2240 sikernesse,** security. **2246 sooth . . . commune,** true, widespread. **2247 Cenobia . . . Palymerie,** Zenobia, Palmyra (northeast of Damascus). This account is evidently related to Boccaccio's *De Claris Mulieribus,* which is odd in view of the fact that none of the accounts is drawn from the more appropriate *De Casibus* (see l. 1991n.). **2250 passed . . . hardynesse,** surpassed, courage. **2252 Perce,** Persia (Boccaccio says Egypt). **2254 amended,** improved. **2256 Office,** duties. **2257 hertes,** hart's (deer's). **2261 torente,** torn to pieces. **2262 weelde,** handle (wrestle). **2267 wight,** strong. **2268 in . . . armes stonde,** i.e., stand (the strength of) her arms. **2269 wight,** person. **2272 *Odenake:*** EHg&c have *Onedake* wherever the name appears. **2273 taried,** i.e., kept them waiting. **2275 fantasies,** desires, interests. **2276 in feere,** in companionship. **2281 ones,** once. **2285 fantasye,** desire. **2286 Eftsoone . . . out of drede,** again, without a doubt. **2289 *wikes:*** EHg&c *dayes.* Boccaccio speaks of "post partus purgationes," which indicates the period of gestation, 40 weeks. **2294 caas,** situation. **2296 lettrure,** learning.

And wys therwith, and large with mesure,
So penyble in the werre, and curteis eke,   2300
Ne moore labour myghte in werre endure,
Was noon, though al this world men wolde seke.

Hir riche array ne myghte nat be told,
As wel in vessel as in hire clothyng.
She was al clad in perree and in gold,   2305
And eek she lafte noght, for noon huntyng,
To have of sondry tonges ful knowyng,
Whan that she leyser hadde; and for to entende
To lerne bookes was al hire likyng,
How she in vertu myghte hir lyf dispende.   2310

And shortly of this proces for to trete,
So doghty was hir housbonde and eek she
That they conquered manye regnes grete
In the orient, with many a fair citee
Apertenaunt unto the magestee   2315
Of Rome, and with strong hond held hem ful
        faste,
Ne nevere myghte hir foomen doon hem flee
Ay whil that Odenakes dayes laste.

Hir batailles, whoso list hem for to rede,
Agayn Sapor the kyng and othere mo,   2320
And how that al this proces fil in dede,
Why she conquered, and what title had therto,
And after, of hir meschief and hire wo,
How that she was biseged and ytake;
Lat hym unto my maister Petrak go,   2325
That writ ynough of this, I undertake.

Whan Odenake was deed, she myghtily
The regnes heeld, and with hire propre hond
Agayn hir foos she faught so cruelly
That ther nas kyng ne prynce in al that lond
That he nas glad, if he that grace fond,   2331
That she ne wolde upon his lond werreye.

With hire they maden alliance by bond
To been in pees, and lete hire ride and pleye.

The Emperour of Rome Claudius,   2335
Ne hym bifore the Romayn Galien,
Ne dorste nevere been so corageus,
Ne noon Ermyn, ne noon Egipcien,
Ne Surrien, ne noon Arabyen,
Withinne the feeldes that dorste with hire
        fighte,   2340
Lest that she wolde hem with hir handes slen,
Or with hir meignee putten hem to flighte.

In kynges habit wente hir sones two,
As heires of hir fadres regnes alle,
And Hermanno and Thymalao   2345
Hir names were, as Persiens hem calle.
But ay Fortune hath in hire hony galle:
This myghty queene may no while endure.
Fortune out of hir regne made hire falle
To wrecchednesse and to mysaventure.   2350

Aurelian, whan that the governaunce
Of Rome cam into his handes tweye,
He shoop upon this queene to doon vengeaunce.
And with his legions he took his weye
Toward Cenobie, and shortly for to seye,   2355
He made hire flee, and atte laste hire hente,
And fettred hire, and eek hire children tweye,
And wan the land, and hoom to Rome he
        wente.

Amonges othere thynges that he wan,
Hir chaar that was with gold wroght and
        perree   2360
This grete Romayn, this Aurelian,
Hath with hym lad, for that men sholde it see.
Biforen his triumphe walketh shee,
With gilte cheynes on hire nekke hangynge.

2299 **large with mesure,** estimable in moderation. 2300 **penyble,** hard-working. 2303 **array,** equipment. 2304 **vessel,** dishware, flatware. 2305 **perree,** jewels. 2307 **sondry tonges,** i.e., she knew languages. 2308 **entende,** try (books were clearly thought of as instructive, not entertaining). 2311 *proces:* Hg&c *storie.* 2312 **doghty,** courageous. 2313 **regnes,** kingdoms. 2315 **Apertenaunt,** belonging. 2320 **Sapor,** Shapur, King of Persia. 2323 **meschief,** misfortune. 2325 **Petrak,** as usual, Chaucer denies Boccaccio as his source, this time attributing it to Petrarch. 2327 **myghtily,** powerfully. 2328 **propre,** own. 2332 **werreye,** make war. 2335–36 The Emperor Claudius (A.D. 268–70), the Emperor Gallienus (A.D. 253–68). 2338 **Ermyn . . . Egipcien,** Armenian, Egyptian. 2342 **meignee,** army (retinue). 2347 **galle,** gall (bile, bitterness). 2351 **Aurelian,** The Emperor Aurelianus (A.D. 270–75). 2353 **shoop,** prepared. 2356 **hente,** captured. 2360 **chaar . . . perree,** chariot, jewels.

Coroned was she, as after hir degree,   2365
And ful of perree charged hire clothynge.

Allas, Fortune! She that whilom was
Dredeful to kynges and to emperoures
Now gaureth al the peple on hire, allas.
And she that helmed was in starke stoures,   2370
And wan by force townes stronge and toures,
Shal on hir heed now were a vitremyte;
And she that bar the ceptre ful of floures
Shal bere a distaf hire costes for to quyte.

DE PETRO REGE ISPANNIE

O noble, O worthy Petro, glorie of Spayne,
Whom Fortune heeld so hye in magestee,   2376
Wel oghten men thy pitous deeth complayne.
Out of thy land thy brother made thee flee,
And after at a seege, by subtiltee,
Thou were bitraysed and lad unto his tente,   2380
Where as he with his owene hand slow thee,
Succedynge in thy regne and in thy rente.

The feeld of snow, with th'egle of blak therinne,
Caught with the lymerod coloured as the
     gleede,
He brew this cursednesse and al this synne.   2385
The wikked nest was werkere of this nede.
Noght Charles Olyver, that took ay heede
Of trouthe and honour, but of Armorike

Genylon Olyver, corrupt for meede,
Broghte this worthy kyng in swich a brike.   2390

DE PETRO REGE DE CIPRO

O worthy Petro, kyng of Cipre, also,
That Alisandre wan by heigh maistrie,
Ful many an hethen wroghtestow ful wo,
Of which thyne owene liges hadde envie,
And for no thyng but for thy chivalrie   2395
They in thy bed han slayn thee by the morwe.
Thus kan Fortune hir wheel governe and gye,
And out of joye brynge men to sorwe.

DE BARNABO DE LUMBARDIA

Off Melan grete Barnabo Viscounte,
God of delit and scourge of Lumbardye,   2400
Why sholde I nat thyn infortune acounte,
Sith in estaat thow cloumbe were so hye?
Thy brother sone, that was thy double allye,
For he thy nevew was and sone-in-lawe,
Withinne his prisoun made thee to dye—   2405
But why ne how noot I that thou were slawe.

DE HUGELINO COMITE DE PIZE

Off the Erl Hugelyn of Pyze the langour
Ther may no tonge telle for pitee.
But litel out of Pize stant a tour
In which tour in prisoun put was he,   2410

2365 **degree,** station. 2369 **gaureth,** stare. 2370 **stoures,** battles. E *shoures*. 2372 **vitremyte,** a nonce word; Baugh suggests that it means something like "fool's cap." 2374 **costes . . . quyte,** i.e., to pay her keep. 2375–2462 The "modern instances" came at the end in the faulty MkT exemplar of EHg&c (see l. 1904n.). Context, particularly the various resonances of the Cresus conclusion (ll. 2761–66), favors their placement here, where they appear in other MSS. See Manly IV.511. 2375 **Petro,** Pedro the Cruel, King of Castile (1350–69), probably known to Chaucer when he was in Spain in 1366, whose daughter Constance married John of Gaunt in 1371. 2378 Other MSS *thy bastard brother;* Manly IV.511 considers this emendation Chaucer's own and politically motivated. (The throne was wrested from Pedro by one of his nine illegitimate half brothers.) 2379 **subtiltee,** i.e., treachery. 2380 **bitraysed,** betrayed. 2382 **rente,** income. 2384 **lymerod,** rod smeared with birdlime for catching birds. These lines describe the coat of arms of Bertrand du Guesclin, the French general who assisted in the overthrow of Pedro and had much to do with ending the English military domination of France. **gleede,** live coal (red). 2385 **brew,** brewed. 2387 **Charles Olyver,** Charlemagne's Oliver, Roland's devoted comrade in the *Chanson de Roland.* 2389 **Genylon Olyver,** the Ganelon Oliver, i.e., traitor Oliver; Ganelon betrayed Roland in the *Chanson de Roland.* **meede,** bribery. 2390 **brike,** trap. 2391 **Petro, kyng of Cipre,** Pierre de Lusignan, who visited the English court in 1363 seeking support for his conquest of Alexandria (1365; I.51), and was assassinated in 1369. Chaucer's account of his death does not accord with history but appears to be taken from Machaut's *La Prise d'Alexandrie.* 2393 **wroghtestow,** did you bring misery upon. 2394 **liges,** followers. 2399 **Barnabo Viscounte,** Lord of Milan, with whom Chaucer did business on his 1378 trip to Italy, and who was related by marriage to Chaucer's earliest patron, Prince Lionel, second son of King Edward III. 2406 **why ne how,** Gian Galeazzo Visconti imprisoned and executed his uncle in 1385; the precise means of death is not known. 2407 **Hugelyn,** Count Ugolino. Chaucer cites Dante (l. 2461) as the source for this account, which appears in *Inferno* 33, but the variations indicate either that he did not know Dante well or had additional information. **langour,** plight. 2409 **litel out,** only a little way outside of Pisa (50 miles west of Florence, near the sea).

And with hym been his litel children thre—
The eldeste scarsly fyf yeer was of age.
Allas, Fortune, it was greet crueltee
Swiche briddes for to putte in swich a cage!

Dampned was he to dyen in that prisoun,   2415
For Roger, which that bisshop was of Pize,
Hadde on hym maad a fals suggestioun
Thurgh which the peple gan upon hym rise,
And putten hym to prisoun in swich wise
As ye han herd, and mete and drynke he
      hadde   2420
So smal that wel unnethe it may suffise,
And therwithal it was ful poure and badde.

And on a day bifil that in that hour
Whan that his mete wont was to be broght,
The gayler shette the dores of the tour.   2425
He herde it wel, but he spak right noght,
And in his herte anon ther fil a thoght
That they for hunger wolde doon hym dyen.
"Allas," quod he, "allas, that I was wroght!"
Therwith the teeres fillen from his eyen.   2430

His yonge sone that thre yeer was of age
Unto hym seyde, "Fader, why do ye wepe?
Whanne wol the gayler bryngen oure potage?
Is ther no morsel breed that ye do kepe?
I am so hungry that I may nat slepe.   2435
Now wolde God that I myghte slepen evere!
Thanne sholde nat hunger in my wombe crepe.
Ther is nothyng but breed that me were levere."

Thus day by day this child bigan to crye,
Til in his fadres barm adoun it lay   2440
And seyde, "Farewel, fader, I moot dye."
And kiste his fader, and dyde the same day.
And whan the woful fader deed it say,
For wo his armes two he gan to byte.

And seyde, "Allas, Fortune, and weylaway!
Thy false wheel my wo al may I wyte."   2446

His children wende that it for hunger was
That he his armes gnow, and nat for wo,
And seyde, "Fader, do nat so, allas,
But rather ete the flessh upon us two.   2450
Oure flessh thou yaf us, take oure flessh us fro,
And ete ynogh." Right thus they to hym seyde,
And after that, withinne a day or two,
They leyde hem in his lappe adoun and deyde.

Hymself, despeired, eek for hunger starf.   2455
Thus ended is this myghty Erl of Pize.
From heigh estaat Fortune awey hym carf.
Of this tragedie it oghte ynough suffise;
Whoso wol here it in a lenger wise,
Redeth the grete poete of Ytaille   2460
That highte Dant, for he kan al devyse
Fro point to point, nat o word wol he faille.

NERO

Although that Nero were as vicius
As any feend that lith in helle adoun,
Yet he, as telleth us Swetonius,   2465
This wyde world hadde in subjeccioun,
Bothe est and west, south, and septemtrioun.
Of rubies, saphires, and of peerles white
Were alle his clothes brouded up and doun,
For he in gemmes greetly gan delite.   2470

Moore delicaat, moore pompous of array,
Moore proud was nevere emperour than he.
That ilke clooth that he hadde wered o day
After that tyme he nolde it nevere see.   2474
Nettes of gold threed hadde he greet plentee
To fisshe in Tybre whan hym liste pleye.
His lustes were al lawe in his decree
For Fortune as his freend hym wolde obeye.

2411 thre, Dante says four. **2415 Dampned,** condemned. **2416 Roger,** Archbishop Ruggiero, leader of the opposing political faction in Pisa. **2417 suggestioun,** accusation. This false accusation is not mentioned by Dante. **2421 unnethe,** barely. **2422 therwithal,** in addition. **2424 wont,** customary. **2426** *spak right:* other MSS *saugh it.* **2428 doon,** make. **2431 thre yeer,** Dante does not give the ages. **2432** EHg&c *Fader, fader.* **2433 potage,** stew. **2437 wombe,** stomach. **2438 levere,** more desirable. **2440 barm,** breast. **2446 wyte,** blame. **2448 gnow,** gnawed. **2455 starf,** died. **2461 devyse,** compass. **2463** EHg&c *as* om. **2464** *in helle:* Hg&c *ful lowe.* **2465 Swetonius,** Suetonius in Book I of *The Lives of the Twelve Caesars.* But all of Chaucer's details could come from *RR* 6183ff. (Dunn-Robbins 30.1ff.), in Jean de Meun's section on Fortune, which influenced various parts of MkT. **2467 septemtrioun,** north. *south:* EHg&c *north,* om. in other MSS; perhaps from a marginal gloss on *septemtrioun.* **2469 brouded,** embroidered. **2471 delicaat,** sensual. **2477 lustes,** desires. *al:* other MSS *as.*

He Rome brende for his delicasie;
The senatours he slow upon a day   2480
To heere how men wolde wepe and crie;
And slow his brother, and by his suster lay.
His mooder made he in pitous array,
For he hire wombe slitte to biholde
Where he conceyved was—so weilaway,   2485
That he so litel of his mooder tolde!

No teere out of his eyen for that sighte
Ne cam, but seyde, "A fair womman was she."
Greet wonder is how that he koude or myghte
Be domesman of hire dede beautee.   2490
The wyn to bryngen hym comanded he,
And drank anon—noon oother wo he made.
Whan myght is joyned unto crueltee,
Allas, to depe wol the venym wade.

In yowthe a maister hadde this emperour   2495
To teche hym letterure and curteisye,
For of moralitee he was the flour,
As in his tyme, but if bookes lye,
And whil this maister hadde of hym
          maistrye,
He maked hym so konnyng and so sowple   2500
That longe tyme it was er tirannye
Or any vice dorste on hym uncowple.

This Seneca, of which that I devyse,
By cause Nero hadde of hym swich drede,
For he fro vices wolde hym ay chastise   2505
Discreetly, as by word and nat by dede:
"Sire," wolde he seyn, "an emperour moot
          nede
Be vertuous and hate tirannye";
For which he in a bath made hym to blede
On bothe his armes, til he moste dye.   2510

This Nero hadde eek of acustumaunce
In youthe agayns his maister for to ryse,

Which afterward hym thoughte greet
          grevaunce;
Therfore he made hym dyen in this wise.
But natheless this Seneca the wise   2515
Chees in a bath to dye in this manere
Rather than han any oother tormentise.
And thus hath Nero slayn his maister deere.

Now fil it so that Fortune liste no lenger
The hye pryde of Nero to cherice,   2520
For though that he was strong, yet was she
          strenger.
She thoughte thus, "By God, I am to nyce
To sette a man that is fulfild of vice
In heigh degree, and emperour hym calle.
By God, out of his sete I wol hym trice.   2525
Whan he leest weneth, sonnest shal he falle."

The peple roos upon hym on a nyght
For his defaute, and whan he it espied
Out of his dores anon he hath hym dight
Allone, and ther he wende han been allied   2530
He knokked faste, and ay the moore he cried
The fastere shette they the dores alle.
Tho wiste he wel he hadde himself mysgyed,
And wente his wey; no lenger dorste he calle.

The peple cride and rombled up and doun,   2535
That with his erys herde he how they seyde,
"Where is this false tiraunt, this Neroun?"
For fere almoost out of his wit he breyde,
And to his goddes pitously he preyde
For socour, but it myghte nat bityde.   2540
For drede of this, hym thoughte that he deyde,
And ran into a gardyn hym to hyde.

And in this gardyn foond he cherles tweye
That seten by a fyr ful greet and reed.
And to thise cherles two he gan to preye   2545
To sleen hym and to girden of his heed,

That to his body whan that he were deed
Were no despit ydoon for his defame.
Hymself he slow, he koude no bettre reed,   2549
Of which Fortune lough and hadde a game.

DE OLOFERNO

Was nevere capitayn under a kyng
That regnes mo putte in subjeccioun,
Ne strenger was in feeld of alle thyng,
As in his tyme, ne gretter of renoun,   2554
Ne moore pompous in heigh presumpcioun
Than Oloferne, which Fortune ay kiste
So likerously, and ladde hym up and doun
Til that his heed was of er that he wiste.

Nat oonly that this world hadde hym in awe
For lesynge of richesse or libertee,   2560
But he made every man reneyen his lawe.
"Nabugodonosor was god," seyde hee.
"Noon oother god sholde adoured bee."
Agayns his heeste no wight dorste trespace
Save in Bethulia, a strong citee,   2565
Where Eliachim a preest was of that place.

But taak kepe of the deeth of Oloferne:
Amydde his hoost he dronke lay a-nyght,
Withinne his tente, large as is a berne,
And yet, for al his pompe and al his myght,   2570
Judith, a womman, as he lay upright
Slepynge, his heed of smoot and from his tente
Ful pryvely she stal from every wight,
And with his heed unto hir toun she wente.

DE REGE ANTHIOCHO ILLUSTRI

What nedeth it of Kyng Anthiochus   2575
To telle his hye roial magestee,
His hye pride, his werkes venymus?
For swich another was ther noon as he.
Rede which that he was in Machabee,

And rede the proude wordes that he seyde,   2580
And why he fil fro heigh prosperitee,
And in an hill how wrecchedly he deyde.

Fortune hym hadde enhaunced so in pride
That verraily he wende he myghte attayne
Unto the sterres upon every syde,   2585
And in balance weyen ech montayne,
And alle the floodes of the see restrayne.
And Goddes peple hadde he moost in hate;
Hem wolde he sleen in torment and in payne
Wenynge that God ne myghte his pride abate.

And for that Nichanore and Thymothee   2591
Of Jewes weren venquysshed myghtily,
Unto the Jewes swich an hate hadde he
That he bad greithen his chaar ful hastily,
And swoor and seyde ful despitously   2595
Unto Jerusalem he wolde eftsoone
To wreken his ire on it ful cruelly,
But of his purpos he was let ful soone.

God for his manace hym so soore smoot
With invisible wounde, ay incurable,   2600
That in his guttes carf it so and boot
That his peynes weren importable.
And certeinly the wreche was resonable
For many a mannes guttes dide he peyne.   2604
But from his purpos cursed and dampnable,
For al his smert, he wolde hym nat restreyne,

But bad anon apparaillen his hoost;
And sodeynly, er he was of it war,
God daunted al his pride and al his boost.
For he so soore fil out of his char   2610
That it his limes and his skyn to-tar,
So that he neyther myghte go ne ryde,
But in a chayer men aboute hym bar
Al forbrused bothe bak and syde.

The wreche of God hym smoot so cruelly   2615
That thurgh his body wikked wormes crepte,
And therwithal he stank so horribly
That noon of al his meynee that hym kepte,
Wheither so he wook, or ellis slepte,
Ne myghte noght the stynk of hym endure.   2620
In this meschief he wayled and eek wepte,
And knew God lord of every creature.

To al his hoost and to hymself also
Ful wlatsom was the stynk of his careyne.
No man ne myghte hym bere to ne fro.   2625
And in this stynk and this horrible peyne
He starf ful wrecchedly in a monteyne.
Thus hath this robbour and this homycide,
That many a man made to wepe and pleyne,
Swich gerdoun as bilongeth unto pryde.   2630

DE ALEXANDRO

The storie of Alisaundre is so commune
That every wight that hath discrecioun
Hath herd somwhat or al of his fortune.
This wyde world, as in conclusioun,   2634
He wan by strengthe, or for his hye renoun
They weren glad for pees unto hym sende.
The pride of man and beest he leyde adoun
Wher so he cam unto the worldes ende.

Comparisoun myghte nevere yet been maked
Bitwixe hym and another conquerour   2640
For al this world for drede of hym hath quaked.
He was of knyghthod and of fredom flour.
Fortune hym made the heir of hire honour.
Save wyn and wommen, no thing myghte
    aswage
His hye entente in armes and labour,   2645
So was he ful of leonyn corage.

What pris were it to hym, though I yow tolde
Of Darius and an hundred thousand mo

Of kynges, princes, erles, dukes bolde
Whiche he conquered, and broghte hem into
    wo?   2650
I seye, as fer as man may ryde or go
The world was his—what sholde I moore
    devyse?
For though I write or tolde yow everemo
Of his knyghthode, it myghte nat suffise.

Twelf yeer he regned, as seith Machabee.   2655
Philippes sone of Macidoyne he was,
That first was kyng in Grece the contree.
O worthy, gentil Alisandre, allas,
That evere sholde fallen swich a cas!
Empoysoned of thyn owene folk thou weere;
Thy *sys* Fortune hath turned into *aas*,   2661
And for thee ne weep she never a teere.

Who shal me yeven teeris to compleyne
The deeth of gentillesse and of franchise,
That al the world weelded in his demeyne,
And yet hym thoughte it myghte nat suffise?
So ful was his corage of heigh emprise.   2667
Allas, who shal me helpe to endite
False Fortune, and poyson to despise,
The whiche two of al this wo I wyte?   2670

DE JULIO CESARE

By wisedom, manhede, and by greet labour,
From humble bed to roial magestee
Up roos he Julius, the conquerour,
That wan al th'occident by land and see,
By strengthe of hand, or elles by tretee,   2675
And unto Rome made hem tributarie.
And sitthe of Rome the emperour was he
Til that Fortune weex his adversarie.

O myghty Cesar, that in Thessalie
Agayn Pompeus, fader thyn in lawe,   2680
That of the orient hadde al the chivalrie

2615 **wreche,** vengeance. 2618 **meynee,** household. 2624 **wlatsom,** loathsome. 2627 **starf,** died. 2630 **gerdoun,** reward. 2634 **conclusioun,** finally. No single source can be identified for the familiar story of Alexander the Great. 2637 **adoun,** low. 2642 **fredom,** generosity. 2644 **aswage,** divert, lessen. *thing:* E *man.* 2647 **pris,** praise. 2655 **Machabee,** I Macc. 1:1–7. 2661 **sys . . . aas,** six (highest throw in dice), ace (lowest). 2664 **gentillesse . . . franchise,** nobility, magnanimity. 2665 **demeyne,** dominion. 2667 **emprise,** endeavor. 2668 **endite,** indict (accuse). 2670 **wyte,** blame. 2677 **sitthe . . . emperour,** afterwards; Julius Caesar was, of course, never emperor. This account, like the previous one, is so familiar that it cannot be traced to any single source. 2680 **Pompeus,** Pompey was actually Caesar's son-in-law. Is this not evidence that Chaucer was working from general knowledge?

As fer as that the day bigynneth dawe,
Thou thurgh thy knyghthod hast hem take and
　　slawe,
Save fewe folk that with Pompeus fledde,
Thurgh which thou puttest al th'orient in awe.
Thanke Fortune, that so wel thee spedde.　2686

But now a litel while I wol biwaille
This Pompeus, this noble governour
Of Rome, which that fleigh at this bataille.
I seye, oon of his men, a fals traitour,　2690
His heed of smoot, to wynnen hym favour
Of Julius, and hym the heed he broghte.
Allas, Pompeye, of th'orient conquerour,
That Fortune unto swich a fyn thee broghte.

To Rome agayn repaireth Julius　2695
With his triumphe, lauriat ful hye;
But on a tyme Brutus Cassius,
That evere hadde of his hye estaat envye,
Ful prively hath maad conspiracye
Agayns this Julius in subtil wise,　2700
And caste the place in which he sholde dye
With boydekyns, as I shal yow devyse.

This Julius to the Capitolie wente
Upon a day, as he was wont to goon,
And in the Capitolie anon hym hente　2705
This false Brutus and his othere foon,
And stiked hym with boydekyns anoon
With many a wounde, and thus they lete hym
　　lye;
But nevere gronte he at no strook but oon,
Or elles at two, but if his storie lye.　2710

So manly was this Julius of herte,
And so wel lovede estaatly honestee,

That though his deedly woundes soore smerte,
His mantel over his hypes castyth he
For no man sholde seen his privetee,　2715
And as he lay of diyng in a traunce,
And wiste verraily that deed was hee,
Of honestee yet hadde he remembraunce.

Lucan, to thee this storie I recomende,
And to Swetoun, and to Valerius also,　2720
That of this storie writen word and ende,
How that to thise grete conqueroures two
Fortune was first freend and sitthe foo.
No man ne truste upon hire favour longe,
But have hire in awayt for everemoo.　2725
Witnesse on alle thise conqueroures stronge.

CRESUS

This riche Cresus, whilom kyng of Lyde,
Of which Cresus Cirus soore hym dradde,
Yet was he caught amyddes al his pryde,
And to be brent men to the fyr hym ladde.　2730
But swich a reyn doun fro the welkne shadde
That slow the fyr and made hym to escape;
But to be war no grace yet he hadde,
Til Fortune on the galwes made hym gape.

Whanne he escaped was, he kan nat stente
For to bigynne a newe werre agayn.　2736
He wende wel, for that Fortune hym sente
Swich hap that he escaped thurgh the rayn,
That of his foos he myghte nat be slayn,
And eek a swevene upon a nyght he mette,　2740
Of which he was so proud and eek so fayn
That in vengeance he al his herte sette.

Upon a tree he was, as that hym thoughte,
Ther Juppiter hym wessh, bothe bak and syde,

2682 dawe, dawn; Pompey was ruler of the eastern portion of the Roman Empire. **2683 take and slawe,** Caesar defeated Pompey in Thessaly in 48 B.C. **2689 fleigh,** fled. **2691 heed . . . smoot,** Pompey was actually stabbed to death in Egypt. **2696 lauriat,** crowned with laurel, after the fashion of the victor in a Roman triumph. **2701 caste,** planned. **2702 boydekyns,** daggers. **2705 hente,** seized. **2709 gronte . . . strook,** groaned, stroke (stab). **2712 estaatly honestee,** dignified decorum. **2713 deedly,** deathly. **2715 privetee,** private parts. **2719–20 Lucan . . . Swetoun . . . Valerius,** Lucan's *Pharsalia* is a poem narrating the struggle between Caesar and Pompey; Suetonius' *Lives of the Twelve Caesars* has been noted before (l. 2465n.); Valerius Maximus, *Factorum ac Dictorum Memorabilium* contains anecdotes about Caesar. Perhaps Chaucer was acquainted with these works. **2723 sitthe,** afterwards. **2725 awayt,** i.e., keep an eye on her. **2727 Lyde,** Croesus, King of Lydia; Chaucer's story again comes from Jean de Meun's discussion of Fortune, *RR* 6489ff. (Dunn-Robbins 31.1ff.). **2728 Cirus,** Cyrus the Great, King of Persia. **2731 welkne,** slay. **2732 slow,** quenched (slew). **2735 stente,** stop, desist. **2737 wende,** thought. **2738 hap,** luck. **2740 swevene . . . mette,** dream, dreamed. **2741 fayn,** happy. **2744 wessh,** washed.

And Phebus eek a fair towaille hym
    broughte   2745
To dryen hym with. And therfore wax his
    pryde,
And to his doghter that stood hym bisyde,
Which that he knew in heigh sentence
    habounde,
He bad hire telle hym what it signyfyde,   2749
And she his dreem bigan right thus expounde:

"The tree," quod she, "the galwes is to meene,
And Juppiter bitokneth snow and reyn,
And Phebus with his towaille so clene,
Tho been the sonne stremes for to seyn.
Thou shalt anhanged be, fader, certeyn;   2755

Reyn shal thee wasshe, and sonne shal thee
    drye."
Thus warned hym ful plat and eek ful pleyn
His doghter, which that called was Phanye.

Anhanged was Cresus, the proude kyng;
His roial trone myghte hym nat availle.   2760
Tragedies noon oother maner thyng
Ne kan in syngyng crie ne biwaille
But that Fortune alwey wole assaille
With unwar strook the regnes that been
    proude;
For whan men trusteth hire, thanne wol she
    faille,   2765
And covere hire brighte face with a clowde.

Explicit Tragedia.

Heere stynteth the Knyght the Monk of his tale.

2745 **towaille,** towel. 2748 **sentence habounde,** wisdom abounded. *sentence:* E&c *science.* 2754 *stremes:* E&c *bemes.* 2757 **plat,** flat (directly). *warned/eek:* other MSS *warned she/eek* om. 2761–64 Paraphrase of *Boece* II pr. 2.69. 2764 **unwar strook,** unexpected blow.

NUN'S PRIEST'S TALE

PROLOGUE

The Prologe of the Nonnes Preestes Tale.

"Hoo," quod the Knyght, "good sire,
    namoore of this!
That ye han seyd is right ynough, ywis,
And muchel moore, for litel hevynesse
Is right ynough to muche folk, I gesse.   2770
I seye for me, it is a greet disese,
Where as men han been in greet welthe and ese,
To heeren of hire sodeyn fal, allas.
And the contrarie is joye and greet solas,
As whan a man hath been in poure estaat   2775
And clymbeth up and wexeth fortunat,
And there abideth in prosperitee.
Swich thyng is gladsom, as it thynketh me,
And of swich thyng were goodly for to telle."
    "Ye," quod oure Hooste, "by Seint Poules
    belle,   2780
Ye seye right sooth. This Monk he clappeth
    lowde.

He spak how Fortune covered with a clowde
I noot nevere what; and also of a tragedie
Right now ye herde; and pardee, no remedie
It is for to biwaille ne compleyne   2785
That that is doon, and als it is a peyne,
As ye han seyd, to heere of hevynesse.
    "Sire Monk, namoore of this, so God yow
    blesse!
Youre tale anoyeth al this compaignye.
Swich talkyng is nat worth a boterflye,   2790
For therinne is ther no desport ne game.
Wherfore, sire Monk, daun Piers by youre
    name,
I pray yow hertely telle us somwhat elles;
For sikerly, nere clynkyng of youre belles
That on youre bridel hange on every syde,   2795
By Hevene Kyng that for us alle dyde,
I sholde er this han fallen doun for sleep,

2767 *Knyght:* seven MSS (but not E or Hg) read *Host,* making him the interrupter; 14 MSS (including Hg but not all of the seven above—there is much contamination here) omit ll. 2771–90 giving a "short form" of this prologue. Note the significance of what Chaucer evidently added in revision. For further discussion see Manly II.410, IV.513. **2768 right ynough,** good enough. **2769 hevynesse,** seriousness (sadness). **2771 disese,** dis-ease (discomfort). **2774 solas,** pleasure. **2780 Poules belle,** the bell of St. Paul's Cathedral, London. **2781 clappeth,** chatters (like a bell clapper). **2783 noot,** know not. **2784 pardee,** a mild oath, "by god." **2786 That that . . . als,** that which, also. **2791** Hg and other short form MSS read *Your tales doon us no desport ne game.* **2794 nere,** were it not for. **2796 dyde,** died.

296

Althogh the slough had never been so deep.
Thanne hadde youre tale al be toold in veyn,
For certeinly, as that thise clerkes seyn,   2800
Where as a man may have noon audience,
Noght helpeth it to tellen his sentence.
And wel I woot the substance is in me,
If any thyng shal wel reported be.
[Sire, sey somwhat of huntyng, I yow preye."
"Nay," quod this Monk, "I have no lust to
    pleye.   2806
Now lat another telle, as I have toold."
    Thanne spak oure Hoost with rude speche and
    boold,

And seyde unto the Nonnes Preest anon,
"Com neer, thou preest, com hyder, thou sir
    John!   2810
Telle us swich thyng as may oure hertes glade.
Be blithe, though thou ryde upon a jade.
What thogh thyn hors be bothe foul and lene?
If he wol serve thee, rekke nat a bene.
Looke that thyn herte be murie everemo."   2815
    "Yis, sire," quod he, "yis, Hoost, so moot I go.
But I be myrie, ywis I wol be blamed."
And right anon his tale he hath attamed,
And thus he seyde unto us everichon,   2819
This sweete preest, this goodly man sir John.

Explicit.

Heere bigynneth the Nonnes Preestes Tale of the Cok and Hen, Chauntecleer and Pertelote.

A poure wydwe somdeel stape in age
Was whilom dwellyng in a narwe cotage,
Biside a grove, stondynge in a dale.
This wydwe, of which I telle yow my tale,
Syn thilke day that she was last a wyf,   2825
In pacience ladde a ful symple lyf.
For litel was hir catel and hir rente,
By housbondrie of swich as God hire sente
She foond hirself and eek hir doghtren two.
Thre large sowes hadde she and namo,   2830
Three keen, and eek a sheep that highte Malle.
Ful sooty was hir bour and eek hir halle,
In which she eet ful many a sklendre meel.
Of poynaunt sauce hir neded never a deel—

No deyntee morsel passed thurgh hir throte.   2835
Hir diete was accordant to hir cote.
Repleccioun ne made hire nevere sik;
Attempree diete was al hir phisik,
And exercise, and hertes suffisaunce.
The goute lette hire nothyng for to daunce,   2840
N'apoplexie shente nat hir heed.
No wyn ne drank she, neither whit ne reed.
Hir bord was served moost with whit and blak—
Milk and broun breed, in which she foond no
    lak;
Seynd bacoun, and somtyme an ey or tweye,   2845
For she was, as it were, a maner deye.
A yeerd she hadde enclosed al aboute

2798 slough, mud. **2802 sentence,** message, meaning. **2803 substance,** i.e., I have the capacity to appreciate. **2806 lust,** desire. **2811 glade,** gladden. **2812 jade,** wretched horse. **2813 foul,** foul (not curried). **2814 rekke ... bene,** care, bean. **2815 murie,** merry. **2817 blamed,** reprimanded. **2818 attamed,** commenced. **2821 stape,** advanced. **2822 whilom ... narwe,** once, small. **2827 catel ... rente,** chattels (possessions), income. **2828 housbondrie,** economy. **2829 foond,** provided for. **2831 keen ... highte,** cows (kine), was named. **2832 sooty ... bour ... halle,** i.e., so simple that it did not have a chimney and smoke had to find its way out through the thatch. Dignifying the main room where the animals slept and the lean-to where the widow and her daughter slept as "hall" and "bower" may be part of the Nun's Priest's ironic contrast between this simple dwelling and rich St. Leonard's Convent (1.125n.). **2833 sklendre,** slender. **2834 poynaunt,** sharp, tangy. **2836 cote,** cottage. **2837 Repleccioun,** overeating. **2838 Attempree,** moderate. **2839 hertes suffisaunce,** heart's content. **2840 lette,** hinder. **2841 shente,** injured. **2844 no lak,** no fault. **2845 Seynd ... ey,** smoked (singed), egg. **2846 deye,** dairywoman.

Eden With stikkes, and a drye dych withoute,
In which she hadde a cok hight Chauntecleer.
In al the land of crowyng nas his peer.   2850
His voys was murier than the murie orgon
On messe-dayes that in the chirche gon.
Wel sikerer was his crowyng in his logge,
Than is a clokke or an abbey orlogge.
By nature he knew ech ascencioun   2855
Of the equynoxial in thilke toun;
For whan degrees fiftene weren ascended,
Thanne crew he that it myghte nat been
      amended.
His coomb was redder than the fyn coral,
And batailled as it were a castel wal;   2860
His byle was blak, and as the jeet it shoon;
Lyk asure were his legges and his toon;
His nayles whitter than the lylye flour;
And lyk the burned gold was his colour.
This gentil cok hadde in his governaunce   2865
Sevene hennes for to doon al his plesaunce,
Whiche were his sustres and his paramours,
And wonder lyk to hym as of colours;
Of whiche the faireste hewed on hir throte
Was cleped faire damoysele Pertelote.   2870
Curteys she was, discreet, and debonaire,
And compaignable, and bar hyrself so faire,
nobiety Syn thilke day that she was seven nyght oold,
That trewely she hath the herte in hoold
Of Chauntecleer, loken in every lith.   2875
He loved hire so that wel was hym therwith.
But swich a joye was it to here hem synge,
Whan that the brighte sonne bigan to sprynge,
In sweete accord, "My lief is faren in londe"—
For thilke tyme, as I have understonde,   2880
Beestes and briddes koude speke and synge.
    And so bifel that in a dawenynge,

As Chauntecleer among his wyves alle
Sat on his perche that was in the halle—
And next hym sat this faire Pertelote—   2885
This Chauntecleer gan gronen in his throte,
As man that in his dreem is drecched soore.
And whan that Pertelote thus herde hym roore,
She was agast and seyde, "O herte deere,
What eyleth yow to grone in this manere?   2890
Ye been a verray sleper; fy, for shame!"
    And he answerde and seyde thus, "Madame,
I pray yow that ye take it nat agrief.
By God, me mette I was in swich meschief
Right now that yet myn herte is soore
      afright.   2895
Now God," quod he, "my swevene recche
      aright,
And kepe my body out of foul prisoun!
Me mette how that I romed up and doun
Withinne our yeerd, wheer as I saugh a beest
Was lyk an hound, and wolde han maad
      areest   2900
Upon my body, and wolde han had me deed.
His colour was bitwixe yelow and reed,
And tipped was his tayl and bothe his eeris
With blak, unlyk the remenant of his heeris;
His snowte smal, with glowynge eyen tweye.
Yet of his look for feere almoost I deye;   2906
This caused me my gronyng, doutelees."
    "Avoy," quod she, "fy on yow, hertelees!
Allas," quod she, "for by that God above,
Now han ye lost myn herte and al my love.   2910
I kan nat love a coward, by my feith!
For certes, what so any womman seith,
We alle desiren, if it myghte bee,
To han housbondes hardy, wise, and free,
And secree, and no nygard, ne no fool,   2915

2849 hight, called. **2853 sikerer . . . logge,** surer (more accurate), station (again the Nun's Priest's ironic inflation). **2854 orlogge,** clock. **2855–56 nature . . . ascencioun . . . equynoxial in thilke toun,** instinctively he knew the revolution of each of the 24 artificial clock hours as calculated for that latitude. *knew:* EHg&c *crew/krew.* **2857 degrees fiftene,** the number of degrees per hour in the artificial equator by which the clock hours were calculated. **2858 amended,** improved upon. **2860 batailled,** notched with indentations like battlements. **2862 asure . . . toon,** blue (lapis lazuli), toes. **2866 pleasaunce,** pleasure. **2867 paramours,** mistresses. **2869 hewed,** colored. **2870 cleped,** called. **2871 debonaire,** obliging. **2875 loken . . . lith,** locked, limb. **2878 bigan:** Hg&c *gan.* **2879 accord . . . "My lief is faren in londe,"** harmony, "My love has gone away"—an unidentified popular song. **2880 thilke,** that. **2882 dawenynge,** dawn; according to medieval dreamlore the best time for premonition. *a:* E&c *the.* **2887 drecched,** troubled. **2889 agast,** afraid. *O herte:* Hg&c *O* om. **2891 verray,** sound. **2894 mette,** dreamed. E&c *thoughte.* **2896 swevene recche aright,** dream interpret favorably. **2900 maad areest,** seized; like "prisoun" (l. 2897), this is the inflated language of the mock heroic. **2901 EHg&c wolde** om. **2902 yelow:** several MSS *white.* **2906 Yet,** still. **2908 Avoy . . . hertelees,** fie, coward. **2914 hardy . . . free,** bold, generous. **2915 secree,** discreet.

Ne hym that is agast of every tool,
Ne noon avauntour. By that God above,
How dorste ye seyn, for shame, unto youre love
That any thyng myghte make yow aferd?
Have ye no mannes herte, and han a berd?   2920
  "Allas, and konne ye been agast of
    swevenys?
Nothyng, God woot, but vanitee in swevene is.
Swevenes engendren of repleccciouns,
And ofte of fume and of compleccciouns,   2924
Whan humours been to habundant in a
    wight.
Certes this dreem which ye han met tonyght
Cometh of the greet superfluytee
Of youre rede colera, pardee,
Which causeth folk to dreden in hir dremes
Of arwes, and of fyr with rede lemes,   2930
Of rede beestes, that they wol hem byte,
Of contek, and of whelpes grete and lyte;
Right as the humour of malencolie
Causeth ful many a man in sleep to crie
For feere of blake beres, or boles blake,   2935
Or elles blake develes wole hem take.
Of othere humours koude I telle also
That werken many a man in sleep ful wo;
But I wol passe as lightly as I kan.
Lo Catoun, which that was so wys a man,   2940
Seyde he nat thus, 'Ne do no fors of dremes'?
  "Now, sire," quod she, "whan ye flee fro the
    bemes,
For Goddes love, as taak som laxatyf.
Up peril of my soule and of my lyf,
I conseille yow the beste, I wol nat lye,   2945
That bothe of colere and of malencolye
Ye purge yow; and for ye shal nat tarie,
Though in this toun is noon apothecarie,
I shal myself to herbes techen yow

That shul been for youre heele and for youre
    prow;   2950
And in oure yeerd tho herbes shal I fynde
The whiche han of hire propretee by kynde
To purge yow bynethe and eek above.
Foryet nat this, for Goddes owene love,
Ye been ful coleryk of compleccccioun.   2955
Ware the sonne in his ascencioun
Ne fynde yow nat repleet of humours hoote.
And if it do, I dar wel leye a grote
That ye shul have a fevere terciane,
Or an agu that may be youre bane.   2960
A day or two ye shul have digestyves
Of wormes, er ye take youre laxatyves
Of lawriol, centaure, and fumetere,
Or elles of ellebor, that groweth there,
Of katapuece, or of gaitrys beryis,   2965
Of herbe yve, growyng in oure yeerd ther
    mery is—
Pekke hem up right as they growe and ete hem
    yn.
Be myrie, housbonde, for youre fader kyn!
Dredeth no dreem; I kan sey yow namoore."
  "Madame," quod he, "graunt mercy of
    youre loore.   2970
But nathelees, as touchyng daun Catoun,
That hath of wysdom swich a greet renoun,
Though that he bad no dremes for to drede,
By God, men may in olde bookes rede
Of many a man moore of auctorite   2975
Than evere Caton was, so moot I thee,
That al the revers seyn of this sentence,
And han wel founden by experience
That dremes been significaciouns
As wel of joye as of tribulaciouns   2980
That folk enduren in this lif present.
Ther nedeth make of this noon argument;

2916 agast . . . tool, afraid, weapon. **2917 avauntour,** boaster. **2921 swevenys,** dreams. **2922 vanitee,** illusion. **2923 engendren of repleccciouns,** spring from overeating. **2924 fume . . . compleccciouns,** gas, bodily disposition (result of the volatile mixture of the sanguine, choleric, phlegmatic, and melancholic humors). **2925 wight,** person. **2926 met,** dreamed. **2928 rede colera,** red bile, which causes sanguine and choleric humors. **2930 lemes,** flames. **2931** *rede:* E&c **grete. 2932 contek . . . whelpes,** conflict, dogs. EHg&c *conteks.* **2933 Right as,** just as. **2935** *blake:* other MSS **grete. 2938 werken,** cause. **2940 Catoun,** Dionysius Cato, supposed author of *Disticha,* a book of maxims used as a schoolbook; this is II.31. **2941 do no fors,** pay no heed. **2942 flee . . . bemes,** fly (down), rafters. *ye:* Hg&c *we.* **2949 techen,** lead. **2950 heele . . . prow,** health, benefit. **2952 propretee by kynde,** natural properties. **2956 Ware,** beware that. **2957 repleet . . . hoote,** full, hot. **2958 leye a grote,** bet a groat (silver fourpence). **2959 fevere terciane,** fever that rises on alternate days, attributed to an excess of red and black bile. **2960 agu . . . bane,** ague (chills and fever), death. **2961 digestyves,** foods that promote digestion. **2963–65 lawriol** &c, W. C. Curry, *Chaucer and the Medieval Sciences,* and others have shown that these purgatives are all authentic and discussed by contemporary medical authorities. **2966 herbe yve . . . mery,** ivy, pleasant. **2970 graunt mercy . . . loore,** many thanks, instruction. **2976 thee,** prosper.

The verray preeve sheweth it in dede.

"Oon of the gretteste auctour that men rede
Seith thus, that whilom two felawes wente   2985
On pilgrimage in a ful good entente,
And happed so they coomen in a toun
Wher as ther was swich congregacioun
Of peple, and eek so streit of herbergage,
That they ne founde as muche as o cotage   2990
In which they bothe myghte logged bee.
Wherfore they mosten of necessitee,
As for that nyght, departen compaignye.
And ech of hem gooth to his hostelrye,
And took his loggyng as it wolde falle.   2995
That oon of hem was logged in a stalle,
Fer in a yeerd, with oxen of the plough;
That oother man was logged wel ynough,
As was his aventure or his fortune
That us governeth alle as in commune.   3000

"And so bifel that longe er it were day,
This man mette in his bed, ther as he lay,
How that his felawe gan upon hym calle,
And seyde, 'Allas, for in an oxes stalle
This nyght I shal be mordred ther I lye.   3005
Now help me, deere brother, or I dye!
In alle haste com to me!" he sayde.

"This man out of his sleep for feere abrayde;
But whan that he was wakened of his sleep,
He turned hym, and took of it no keep.   3010
Hym thoughte his dreem nas but a vanitee.
Thus twies in his slepyng dremed hee,
And atte thridde tyme yet his felawe
Cam, as hym thoughte, and seide, 'I am now
     slawe.
Bihold my bloody woundes depe and wyde.   3015
Arys up erly in the morwe tyde,
And at the west gate of the toun,' quod he,
'A carte ful of donge ther shaltow se,
In which my body is hid ful prively.
Do thilke carte arresten boldely.   3020

My gold caused my mordre, sooth to sayn.'
And tolde hym every point how he was slayn,
With a ful pitous face, pale of hewe.
And truste wel, his dreem he foond ful trewe,
For on the morwe as soone as it was day   3025
To his felawes in he took the way,
And whan that he cam to this oxes stalle,
After his felawe he bigan to calle.

"The hostiler answerede hym anon,
And seyde, 'Sire, youre felawe is agon.   3030
As soone as day he wente out of the toun.'

"This man gan fallen in suspecioun,
Remembrynge on his dremes that he mette,
And forth he gooth—no lenger wolde he lette—
Unto the west gate of the town, and fond   3035
A dong-carte, wente as it were to donge lond,
That was arrayed in that same wise
As ye han herd the dede man devyse.
And with an hardy herte he gan to crye
Vengeance and justice of this felonye.   3040
'My felawe mordred is this same nyght,
And in this carte heere he lith gapyng upright.
I crye out on the ministres,' quod he,
'That sholden kepe and reulen this citee.
Harrow, allas, heere lith my felawe slayn!'   3045
What sholde I moore unto this tale sayn?
The peple out sterte and caste the carte to
     grounde,
And in the myddel of the dong they founde
The dede man that mordred was al newe.

"O blisful God, that art so just and trewe,   3050
Lo, how that thou biwreyest mordre alway!
Mordre wol out, that se we day by day.
Mordre is so wlatsom and abhomynable
To God, that is so just and resonable,
That he ne wol nat suffre it heled be,   3055
Though it abyde a yeer, or two, or thre.
Mordre wol out, this my conclusioun.
And right anon, ministres of that toun

Han hent the cartere and so soore hym pyned,
And eek the hostiler so soore engyned,   3060
That they biknewe hire wikkednesse anon,
And were anhanged by the nekke-bon.
Heere may men seen that dremes been to drede.
"And certes in the same book I rede,
Right in the nexte chapitre after this—   3065
I gabbe nat, so have I joye or blis—
Two men that wolde han passed over see
For certeyn cause, into a fer contree,
If that the wynd ne hadde been contrarie
That made hem in a citee for to tarie   3070
That stood ful myrie upon an haven-syde.
But on a day, agayn the eventyde,
The wynd gan chaunge and blew right as hem
   leste.
Jolif and glad they wente unto hir reste,
And casten hem ful erly for to saille.   3075
But, herkneth, to that o man fil a greet
   mervaille:
That oon of hem, in slepyng as he lay,
Hym mette a wonder dreem agayn the day.
Hym thoughte a man stood by his beddes syde,
And hym comanded that he sholde abyde,   3080
And seyde hym thus, 'If thou tomorwe wende,
Thow shalt be dreynt; my tale is at an ende.'
"He wook and tolde his felawe what he mette,
And preyde hym his viage to lette;
As for that day, he preyde hym to byde.   3085
His felawe that lay by his beddes syde
Gan for to laughe, and scorned him ful faste.
'No dreem,' quod he, 'may so myn herte agaste
That I wol lette for to do my thynges.
I sette nat a straw by thy dremynges,   3090
For swevenes been but vanytees and japes.

Men dreme alday of owles and of apes,
And eek of many a maze therwithal;
Men dreme of thyng that nevere was ne shal.
But sith I see that thou wolt heere abyde,   3095
And thus forslewthen wilfully thy tyde,
God woot, it reweth me; and have good day!'
And thus he took his leve and wente his way.
But er that he hadde half his cours yseyled,
Noot I nat why, ne what myschaunce it
   eyled,   3100
But casuelly the shippes botme rente,
And ship and man under the water wente
In sighte of othere shippes it bisyde,
That with hem seyled at the same tyde.
"And therfore, faire Pertelote so deere,   3105
By swiche ensamples olde yet maistow leere
That no man sholde been to recchelees
Of dremes; for I seye thee, doutelees,
That many a dreem ful soore is for to drede.
Lo, in the lyf of Seint Kenelm I rede,   3110
That was Kenulphus sone, the noble kyng
Of Mercenrike, how Kenelm mette a thyng
A lite er he was mordred. On a day
His mordre in his avysioun he say.
His norice hym expowned every deel   3115
His swevene, and bad hym for to kepe hym
   weel
For traisoun; but he nas but seven yeer oold,
And therfore litel tale hath he toold
Of any dreem, so hooly was his herte.
By God, I hadde levere than my sherte   3120
That ye hadde rad his legende, as have I.
Dame Pertelote, I sey yow trewely,
Macrobeus, that writ the avisioun
In Affrike of the worthy Cipioun,

3059 pyned, tortured. **3060 engyned,** tortured on machines, e.g., the rack. **3061 biknewe,** revealed. **3065 nexte chapitre,** no source has been identified that has the two stories in this specific order. **3066 gabbe,** lie. **3071 myrie . . . haven-syde,** i.e., pleasantly by a harbor. **3072 agayn,** on toward. **3073 leste,** wished. **3075 casten,** made plans. **3076** Hypermetrical *herkneth* is found in EHg&c; om. in other MSS. **3078 mette . . . agayn the day,** dreamed, toward morning (when dreams are most valid). **3080 abyde,** wait. **3081 wende,** go (travel). **3082 dreynt,** drowned. **3084 lette,** put off (hinder). **3088 agaste,** frighten. **3089 lette,** put off (hinder). **3091 swevenes . . . vanytees . . . japes,** dreams, illusions, jokes. **3092 owles . . . apes,** i.e., fanciful illusions. *and:* EHg&c *or.* **3093 maze,** amazement. EHg&c *eek* om. **3095 sith,** since. **3096 forslewthen wilfully,** waste (by sloth) deliberately. **3097 reweth,** i.e., makes me sorry. **3100 myschaunce it eyled,** accident ailed it. **3101 casuelly . . . rente,** accidentally, split open. **3106 leere,** learn. Hg&c *yet* om. **3107 recchelees,** heedless. **3110 Kenelm,** according to tradition, in 821 as a child of seven, he succeeded his father Kenulph on the throne of the Mercians. He was murdered at the instigation of his aunt and his body was miraculously revealed by a heavenly ray of light. He had had a dream foretelling his own death. **3114 say,** saw. **3115 norice,** nurse. **3116 kepe,** protect. **3117 For,** against. **3123 Macrobeus,** author of a commentary on Cicero's lost *Somnium Scipionis;* see *PF* ll. 31ff. and notes.

Affermeth dremes, and seith that they been 3125
Warnynge of thynges that men after seen.

"And forthermoore, I pray yow, looketh wel
In the Olde Testament of Daniel,
If he heeld dremes any vanitee.
Reed eek of Joseph and ther shul ye see 3130
Wher dremes be somtyme—I sey nat alle—
Warnynge of thynges that shul after falle.
Looke of Egipte the kyng, daun Pharao,
His bakere and his butiller also,
Wher they ne felte noon effect in dremes. 3135
Whoso wol seken actes of sondry remes
May rede of dremes many a wonder thyng.

"Lo Cresus, which that was of Lyde kyng,
Mette he nat that he sat upon a tree,
Which signified he sholde anhanged bee? 3140
Lo heere Andromacha, Ectores wyf,
That day that Ector sholde lese his lyf,
She dremed on the same nyght biforn
How that the lyf of Ector sholde be lorn
If thilke day he wente into bataille. 3145
She warned hym but it myghte nat availle.
He wente for to fighte natheles,
But he was slayn anon of Achilles.
But thilke tale is al to longe to telle,
And eek it is ny day, I may nat dwelle. 3150
Shortly I seye, as for conclusioun,
That I shal han of this avisioun
Adversitee—and I seye forthermoor
That I ne telle of laxatyves no stoor,
For they been venymes, I woot it weel; 3155
I hem diffye, I love hem never a deel!

"Now lat us speke of myrthe and stynte al this.
Madame Pertelote, so have I blis,
Of o thyng God hath sent me large grace,

For whan I se the beautee of youre face— 3160
Ye been so scarlet reed aboute youre eyen—
It maketh al my drede for to dyen.
For al so siker as *In principio,*
Mulier est hominis confusio—
Madame, the sentence of this Latyn is 3165
'Womman is mannes joye and al his blis.'
For whan I feele a-nyght youre softe syde—
Al be it that I may nat on yow ryde
For that oure perche is maad so narwe, allas—
I am so ful of joye and of solas 3170
That I diffye bothe swevene and dreem."

And with that word he fley doun fro the beem,
For it was day, and eek his hennes alle,
And with a chuk he gan hem for to calle,
For he hadde founde a corn lay in the yerd.
Real he was, he was namoore aferd. 3176
He fethered Pertelote twenty tyme,
And trad hire eke as ofte, er it was pryme.
He looketh as it were a grym leoun,
And on his toos he rometh up and doun; 3180
Hym deigned nat to sette his foot to grounde.
He chukketh whan he hath a corn yfounde,
And to hym rennen thanne his wyves alle.
Thus roial, as a prince is in an halle,
Leve I this Chauntecleer in his pasture, 3185
And after wol I telle his aventure.

Whan that the monthe in which the world
bigan,
That highte March, whan God first maked man,
Was compleet, and passed were also
Syn March bigan thritty dayes and two, 3190
Bifel that Chauntecleer in al his pryde,
His sevene wyves walkynge by his syde,
Caste up his eyen to the brighte sonne

3125 **Affermeth,** confirms. 3129 **vanitee,** illusion; Dan. 7. 3130 **Joseph,** Gen. 37, 40, 41. 3135 **Wher . . . effect in,** whether, effect from. 3136 **actes . . . remes,** accounts (histories), realms. 3138 **Cresus . . . Lyde,** Croesus, Lydia, cf. MkT, ll. 2727ff. 3141 **Andromacha,** Hector's wife's dream is reported by Dares, but not in classical accounts. 3144 **lorn,** lost. 3145 **thilke,** that. 3149 E *tale* om. *for to.* 3155 **venymes,** poisons. Other MSS *venemyous.* 3157 **stynte,** stop. 3163 **In principio,** as Manly points out, part of the humor here is the assertion that the Latin is "so siker (certain) as *In Principio*," i.e., as the opening of the Gospel of St. John, the essential tenet of Christianity. 3164 *Mulier est* etc., woman is man's confusion, a medieval commonplace beginning with Eve. 3165 **sentence,** meaning. 3171 **diffye . . . swevene,** reject, dream. 3175 **corn,** grain. 3176 **Real,** royal. Other MSS *Royal.* 3177 **fethered,** i.e., embraced. 3178 **trad . . . pryme,** trod (copulated with), 9 A.M. EHg&c *And trad as oft er.* 3184 **an:** Hg&c *his.* 3190 **thritty dayes and two,** according to medieval tradition, the world was created at the vernal equinox, i.e., March 12 because of the error in the Julian calendar; add 32 days and we are back to Chaucer's favorite date of May 3. Pratt proposes *March was gon* as a more logical reading although it does not appear in any MS. It has been several times demonstrated that Chaunticleer's method for inferring that it was prime (9 A.M.) is quite accurate. 3192 Hg&c *hym bisyde.*

That in the signe of Taurus hadde yronne 3194
Twenty degrees and oon and somwhat moore,
And knew by kynde and by noon oother loore
That it was pryme, and crew with blisful stevene.
"The sonne," he seyde, "is clomben up on
    hevene
Fourty degrees and oon, and moore ywis.
Madame Pertelote, my worldes blis, 3200
Herkneth thise blisful briddes how they synge,
And se the fresshe floures how they sprynge!
Ful is myn herte of revel and solas."
But sodeynly hym fil a sorweful cas,
For evere the latter ende of joye is wo. 3205
God woot that worldly joye is soone ago,
And if a rethor koude faire endite
He in a cronycle saufly myghte it write
As for a sovereyn notabilitee.
Now every wys man, lat him herkne me: 3210
This storie is also trewe, I undertake,
As is the book of Launcelot de Lake,
That wommen holde in ful greet reverence.
Now wol I torne agayn to my sentence.
    A colfox ful of sly iniquitee, 3215
That in the grove hadde woned yeres three,
By heigh ymaginacioun forncast,
The same nyght thurghout the hegges brast
Into the yerd ther Chauntecleer the faire
Was wont, and eek his wyves, to repaire, 3220
And in a bed of wortes stille he lay
Til it was passed undren of the day,

Waitynge his tyme on Chauntecleer to falle,
As gladly doon thise homycides alle
That in await liggen to mordre men. 3225
O false mordrour, lurkynge in thy den!
O newe Scariot, newe Genylon,
False dissymulour, O Greek Synon,
That broghtest Troye al outrely to sorwe!
O Chauntecleer, acursed be that morwe 3230
That thou into that yerd flaugh fro the
    bemes!
Thou were ful wel ywarned by thy dremes
That thilke day was perilous to thee;
But what that God forwoot moot nedes bee,
After the opinioun of certein clerkis. 3235
Witnesse on hym that any parfit clerk is
That in scole is greet altercacioun
In this mateere, and greet disputisoun,
And hath been of an hundred thousand
    men.
But I ne kan nat bulte it to the bren, 3240
As kan the hooly doctour Augustyn,
Or Boece, or the bisshop Bradwardyn,
Wheither that Goddes worthy forwityng
Streyneth me nedely for to doon a thyng—
"Nedely" clepe I symple necessitee— 3245
Or elles if free choys be graunted me
To do that same thyng or do it noght
Though God forwoot it er that it was wroght;
Or if his wityng streyneth never a deel
But by necessitee condicioneel. 3250

3196 kynde . . . loore, instinct, learning. **3197 stevene,** voice. **3204 cas,** event (case). **3207 rethor . . . endite,** rhetorician, compose. **3212 Launcelot,** this may be a backhanded slap (humorous, of course) at the improbity of the romances. **3214** *torne:* E *come.* **3215 colfox,** fox with black tips on ears, tail, feet (see l. 2903). Leslie Hotson has suggested a complicated allegory in which the fox represents one Nicholas Colfax in the political infighting of 1397, shortly before the deposition of Richard II. **3216 woned,** lived. **3217 heigh ymaginacioun forncast,** predestined by divine foresight. **3218 brast,** burst (broke). **3221 wortes,** cabbages. **3222 undren,** midmorning (undark). **3227–28 Scariot,** Judas Iscariot. **Genylon,** Ganelon, traitor to Roland. **Synon,** traitor to Troy. **3230 morwe,** morning. **3234 forwoot,** foreknows. **3240 bulte . . . bren,** sift, bran. **3241–42 Augustyn . . . Boece . . . Bradwardyn.** The original controversy over the relations between the divine and human will, and the related concepts of foreknowledge and free will, was in the 4th century between St. Augustine, who maintained that man was born in original sin and could be saved only by divine grace, and his contemporary Pelagius, who maintained that man was born innocent and had the free will to do good or evil. Boethius attempted to reconcile the Augustinian and Pelagian positions. In Chaucer's own time, Thomas Bradwardine, Oxford professor and at the time of his death Archbishop of Canterbury (1349), showed that the controversy was still very much alive by writing a major theological treatise *De causa Dei contra Pelagium et de virtute causarum* ("The cause of God versus Pelagius and concerning the nature of causation" [in the world]). Chaucer uses NPT playfully to explore these concepts. **3243 worthy forwityng,** valuable foreknowledge. **3244 Streyneth,** constrains. *nedely for:* E&c *nedefully.* **3245 symple necessitee,** constraint through simple cause and effect: the Augustinian position. **3246 free choys,** no constraint: the Pelagian position. **3248** Hg&c *I was.* **3250 necessitee condicioneel,** Boethius' compromise: foreknowledge combined with free will because to the divine perception all action is simultaneous, cf. *Boece,* Bk. v.

I wol nat han to do of swich mateere.
My tale is of a cok, as ye may heere,
That took his conseil of his wyf, with sorwe,
To walken in the yerd upon that morwe
That he hadde met that dreem that I yow
    tolde.
Wommennes conseils been ful ofte colde; 3256
Wommannes conseil broghte us first to wo
And made Adam fro Paradys to go
Ther as he was ful myrie and wel at ese.
But for I noot to whom it myght displese 3260
If I conseil of wommen wolde blame,
Passe over, for I seyde it in my game.
Rede auctours, where they trete of swich
    mateere,
And what they seyn of wommen ye may
    heere.
Thise been the cokkes wordes and nat myne;
I kan noon harm of no womman divyne. 3266
    Faire in the soond to bathe hire myrily
Lith Pertelote, and alle hire sustres by,
Agayn the sonne, and Chauntecleer so free
Soong murier than the mermayde in the
    see— 3270
For Phisiologus seith sikerly
How that they syngen wel and myrily.
And so bifel that as he caste his eye
Among the wortes on a boterflye,
He was war of this fox that lay ful lowe. 3275
Nothyng ne liste hym thanne for to crowe,
But cride anon, "Cok, cok!" and up he sterte
As man that was affrayed in his herte.
For natureelly a beest desireth flee
Fro his contrarie if he may it see, 3280
Though he never erst hadde seyn it with his eye.

This Chauntecleer whan he gan hym espye
He wolde han fled, but that the fox anon
Seyde, "Gentil sire, allas, wher wol ye gon?
Be ye affrayed of me that am youre freend?
Now, certes, I were worse than a feend 3286
If I to yow wolde harm or vileynye.
I am nat come youre conseil for t'espye,
But trewely the cause of my comynge
Was oonly for to herkne how that ye synge. 3290
For trewely, ye have as myrie a stevene
As any aungel hath that is in hevene.
Therwith ye han in musyk moore feelynge
Than hadde Boece, or any that kan synge.
My lord youre fader—God his soule blesse—
And eek youre mooder, of hire gentillesse, 3296
Han in myn hous ybeen to my greet ese.
And certes, sire, ful fayn wolde I yow plese.
    "But for men speke of syngyng, I wol
    seye,
So moote I brouke wel myne eyen tweye, 3300
Save yow, herde I nevere man so synge
As dide youre fader in the morwenynge.
Certes, it was of herte al that he song.
And for to make his voys the moore strong,
He wolde so peyne hym that with bothe his
    eyen 3305
He moste wynke, so loude he wolde cryen,
And stonden on his tiptoon therwithal,
And strecche forth his nekke long and smal.
And eek he was of swich discrecioun
That ther nas no man in no regioun 3310
That hym in song or wisedom myghte
    passe.
I have wel rad in *Daun Burnel the Asse*,
Among his vers, how that ther was a cok

3252 cok, the juxtaposition of the abstruse theological problems with Chauntecleer and Pertelote nicely illustrates Boethius' final contrast between divine and human knowledge. Like God, we have foreknowledge of Chauntecleer's fate and yet cannot prevent it. **3255** *yow*: E&c *of*. **3256 colde,** fatal; the line is proverbial. **3266 divyne,** conceive. **3267 soond,** sand. **3269 Agayn . . . free,** in, noble. **3270–71 mermayde . . . Phisiologus,** identified with the sirens as described in the *Bestiary* (Lat. title *Phisiologus*), an ancient collection of fanciful animal descriptions with morals appended. **sikerly,** certainly. **3276 liste,** desired. **3280 contrarie,** enemy. **3281 erst,** before. **3283 anon,** immediately. **3288 conseil,** to intrude (spy) on your secrets. **3291 stevene,** voice. **3294 Boece,** the standard textbook on musical theory in the Middle Ages was Boethius' *De Musica*. **3299** E *wol yow Seye*. **3300 brouke,** as I may enjoy (a mild oath). **3301** *so*: E *yet*. **3303 of,** from the. **3311 passe,** surpass. **3312** *Daun Burnel,* the *Speculum Stultorum* (*Mirror of Fools*), a popular Latin satire of the donkey who was dissatisfied with the length of his tail. Most of the medieval universities and religious orders are satirized in connection with his travels seeking to get it lengthened. In the *Speculum,* the boy had hit a cock with a stick; years later when the boy was about to be ordained as a priest, the cock failed to crow causing him to oversleep and thus lose his benefice.

For that a preestes sone yaf hym a knok
Upon his leg whil he was yong and nyce, 3315
He made hym for to lese his benefice.
But certeyn, ther nys no comparisoun
Bitwixe the wisedom and discrecioun
Of youre fader and of his subtiltee.
Now syngeth, sire, for seinte charitee; 3320
Lat se, konne ye youre fader countrefete?"
    This Chauntecleer his wynges gan to bete,
As man that koude his traysoun nat espie,
So was he ravysshed with his flaterie.
Allas, ye lordes, many a fals flatour 3325
Is in youre courtes, and many a losengeour,
That plesen yow wel moore, by my feith,
Than he that soothfastnesse unto yow seith.
Redeth Ecclesiaste of flaterye;
Beth war, ye lordes, of hir trecherye. 3330
    This Chauntecleer stood hye upon his toos,
Strecchynge his nekke, and heeld his eyen
    cloos,
And gan to crowe loude for the nones.
And daun Russell the fox stirte up atones,
And by the gargat hente Chauntecleer, 3335
And on his bak toward the wode hym
    beer,
For yet ne was ther no man that hym sewed.
    O destinee that mayst nat been eschewed!
Allas that Chauntecleer fleigh fro the bemes!
Allas his wyf ne roghte nat of dremes! 3340
And on a Friday fil al this meschaunce.
    O Venus, that art goddesse of plesaunce,
Syn that thy servant was this Chauntecleer,
And in thy servyce dide al his poweer,
Moore for delit than world to multiplye, 3345

Why woldestow suffre hym on thy day to
    dye?
    O Gaufred, deere maister soverayn,
That whan thy worthy Kyng Richard was
    slayn
With shot, compleynedest his deeth so soore,
Why ne hadde I now thy sentence and thy
    loore, 3350
The Friday for to chide, as diden ye?
For on a Friday, soothly, slayn was he.
Thanne wolde I shewe yow how that I koude
    pleyne
For Chauntecleres drede and for his peyne.
    Certes, swich cry ne lamentacioun 3355
Was nevere of ladyes maad whan Ylioun
Was wonne, and Pirrus with his streite swerd
Whan he hadde hent Kyng Priam by the berd
And slayn hym, as seith us *Eneydos*,
As maden alle the hennes in the clos, 3360
Whan they had seyn of Chauntecleer the
    sighte.
But sovereynly dame Pertelote shrighte
Ful louder than dide Hasdrubales wyf
Whan that hir housbonde hadde lost his lyf,
And that the Romayns hadde brend
    Cartage.
She was so ful of torment and of rage 3366
That wilfully into the fyr she sterte
And brende hirselven with a stedefast herte.
    O woful hennes, right so criden ye
As whan that Nero brende the citee 3370
Of Rome cryden senatoures wyves
For that hir husbondes losten alle hir lyves—
Withouten gilt this Nero hath hem slayn.

3315 nyce, foolish. **3320 seinte,** holy. **3321 countrefete,** imitate. **3323 traysoun,** treachery. **3325 ye lordes,** the court situation, or even Inns of Court situation, in which Chaucer first read his individual tales, surfaces only occasionally in the rhetoric. This appears to be one such occasion. **3326 losengeour,** liar. **3328 soothfastnesse,** truth. **3329 Ecclesiaste,** the closest reference that has been found is in the apocryphal Ecclus. 12:10ff. **3335 gargat,** throat. **3337 sewed,** pursued. **3338 eschewed,** avoided. **3340 roghte,** cared. **3341–47 Friday . . . Venus . . . Gaufred,** Friday was Venus' day, and Chauntecleer with his seven wives was Venus' servant; but Friday was also in popular superstition the bad-luck day—the day that Adam was driven from Paradise, that the Flood began, that Jesus was crucified, etc. Geoffrey de Vinsauf was the author of a rhetoric popular in the schools, and his specimen lament on the death of Richard the Lion-Hearted (slain on Friday) is burlesqued in ll. 3350–73. **3345** Other MSS *the world.* **3350 sentence, . . . loore** sentiment, learning. **3353 pleyne,** complain (in poetic lament; of Chaucer's own "complaints"). **3356 Ylioun,** the citadel of Troy. **3357 Pirrus . . . streite,** son of Achilles, drawn. **3359** *Eneydos, Aeneid* II.469ff. **3360 clos,** enclosure. **3362 sovereynly . . . shrighte,** supremely, shrieked. E&c *sodeynly.* **3363 Hasdrubales,** King of Carthage, defeated by Scipio (146 B.C.). **3367 wilfully,** deliberately.

Now turne I wole to my tale agayn.
    This sely wydwe and eek hir doghtres two
Herden thise hennes crie and maken wo,   3376
And out at dores stirten they anon
And syen the fox toward the grove gon,
And bar upon his bak the cok away,
And cryden, "Out, harrow, and weylaway!   3380
Haha, the fox!" and after hym they ran,
And eek with staves many another man.
Ran Colle oure dogge, and Talbot and Gerland,
And Malkyn with a dystaf in hir hand;
Ran cow and calf, and eek the verray hogges,
So fered for the berkyng of the dogges   3386
And shoutyng of the men and wommen eke;
They ronne so hem thoughte hir herte breke.
They yolleden as feendes doon in helle;
The dokes cryden as men wolde hem quelle;   3390
The gees for feere flowen over the trees;
Out of the hyve cam the swarm of bees.
So hydous was the noyse, a benedicitee,
Certes, he Jakke Straw and his meynee
Ne made nevere shoutes half so shrille   3395
Whan that they wolden any Flemyng kille
As thilke day was maad upon the fox.
Of bras they broghten bemes, and of box,
Of horn, of boon, in whiche they blewe and
        powped,
And therwithal they skriked and they
        howped.   3400
It seemed as that hevene sholde falle.
Now, goode men, I prey yow herkneth alle.
    Lo, how Fortune turneth sodeynly
The hope and pryde eek of hir enemy.
This cok that lay upon the foxes bak   3405
In al his drede unto the fox he spak,
And seyde, "Sire, if that I were as ye,
Yet wolde I seyn, as wys God helpe me,

'Turneth agayn, ye proude cherles alle!
A verray pestilence upon yow falle!   3410
Now I am come unto the wodes syde.
Maugree youre heed, the cok shal heere
        abyde.
I wol hym ete, in feith, and that anon!' "
    The fox answerde, "In feith, it shal be don."
And as he spak that word, al sodeynly   3415
This cok brak from his mouth delyverly,
And heighe upon a tree he fleigh anon.
And whan the fox saugh that the cok was gon,
"Allas," quod he, "O Chauntecleer, allas!
I have to yow," quod he, "ydoon trespas,   3420
In as muche as I maked yow aferd
Whan I yow hente and broghte out of the yerd.
But, sire, I dide it of no wikke entente.
Com doun, and I shal telle yow what I
        mente.
I shal seye sooth to yow, God help me so."   3425
    "Nay thanne," quod he, "I shrewe us bothe
        two.
And first I shrewe myself bothe blood and
        bones
If thou bigyle me any ofter than ones.
Thou shalt namoore thurgh thy flaterye
Do me to synge and wynke with myn eye;   3430
For he that wynketh whan he sholde see,
Al wilfully, God lat him nevere thee!"
    "Nay," quod the fox, "but God yeve hym
        meschaunce
That is so undiscreet of governaunce
That jangleth whan he sholde holde his pees."
    Lo, swich it is for to be recchelees   3436
And necligent, and truste on flaterye.
But ye that holden this tale a folye,
As of a fox, or of a cok and hen,
Taketh the moralite, goode men.   3440

3375 **sely,** innocent. *This:* Hg&c *The.* 3378 **syen,** saw. 3383 **Colle . . . Talbot . . . Gerland,** names of dogs. 3384 **distaf,** staff wound with unspun wool—just as she had come rushing from her spinning. 3385 E&c *eek* om. 3386 *for the:* EHg&c *the* om. 3389 **yolleden,** yelled. Hg&c *yelleden.* 3390 **quelle,** kill. 3394 **Jakke Straw,** one of the leaders in the Peasants' Revolt of 1381, in which many Flemish (Belgian) workers were killed because they were considered to be in competition with the English workers. This is one of Chaucer's very few references to this cataclysmic event. **meynee,** followers. 3398 **bemes . . . box,** trumpets, boxwood. 3399 **boon,** bone. 3400 **howped,** whooped. 3403 **turneth,** reverses. 3409 **agayn,** back. 3412 **Maugree,** i.e., in spite of anything you can do. 3416 **delyverly,** agilely (*double entendre* on "deliver," set free). 3426 **shrewe,** curse. 3428 **bigyle,** deceive. 3432 **thee,** prosper. 3435 **jangleth,** chatters. 3436 **recchelees,** careless.

For Seint Paul seith that al that writen is,
To oure doctrine it is ywrite, ywis.
Taketh the fruyt and lat the chaf be stille.

Now, goode God, if that it be thy wille,
As seith my Lord, so make us alle goode men,
And brynge us to his heighe bliss. Amen.   3446

Heere is ended the Nonnes Preestes Tale.

[Epilogue]

"Sire Nonnes Preest," oure Hooste seide anoon,
"Iblessed be thy breche, and every stoon!
This was a murie tale of Chauntecleer.
But by my trouthe, if thou were seculer,   3450
Thou woldest ben a trede-foul aright.
For if thou have corage as thou hast myght,
Thee were nede of hennes, as I wene,

Ya, moo than seven tymes seventene.
See, which braunes hath this gentil preest,   3455
So gret a nekke, and swich a large breest!
He loketh as a sperhauk with his eyen;
Him nedeth nat his colour for to dyen
With brasile, ne with greyn of Portyngale.
Now, sire, faire falle yow for youre tale!"   3460
    And after that he, with ful merie chere,
Seide unto another, as ye shuln heere.

3441 Paul, Rom. 15:4. **3443 fruyt . . . chaf,** traditional terms for the doctrinal meaning versus the narrative account. This line is the best evidence that Chaucer was acquainted with the exegetical techniques of scriptural interpretation and—at least playfully—implied that these techniques might be applied to the *Canterbury Tales*. Such techniques would be particularly appropriate to a character like the Nun's Priest. **3447–62** Lines not found in EHg&c, but only in Additional 5140 and nine other MSS. Like the epilogue to MLT, II.1163–90, they were probably marked for excision in Chaucer's exemplar. Perhaps this occurred when the prologue came to depict a different personality for the Nun's Priest, since these lines sound like those addressed to the Monk: cf. VII.1943–64 and VII.2807–20. **3448 breche . . . stoon,** breeches (or thighs?), testicles. **3450 seculer,** layman. **3451 trede-foul,** rooster (breeding fowl). **3452 corage,** spirit. **3455 braunes,** muscles. **3457 sperhauk,** sparrowhawk, i.e., repacious. **3459 brasile . . . greyn of Portyngale,** red dyes. **3460 faire falle yow,** good luck to you.

INTRODUCTION

Canterbury Tales, Part VIII

IKE PARTS VI AND VII, this part of the *Canterbury Tales* begins without reference to the frame. The "Invocacio ad Mariam" in the Prologue to the Second Nun's Tale is Chaucer's most beautiful devotional lyric, replete, like the rest of the Prologue, with echoes of the liturgy. The oxymora in ll. 36ff reveal how similar the expression of devotional poetry could be to medieval love poetry. The resemblance of this poem to St. Bernard's prayer in Dante's *Paradiso* 33 has been remarked, but the similarities are commonplaces of the Cult of the Virgin. The rubric of the "Interpretacio" acknowledges the influence of the life of St. Cecilia in Jacobus de Voragine's *Legenda Aurea*, but Chaucer must have used an expanded version not yet identified. Sherry L. Reames, "The Cecelia Legend as Chaucer Inherited It and Retold It," *Speculum* (1980), examines Chaucer's adaptations.

The martyrdom of St. Cecelia is a very old story, of considerable anthopological interest. It depicts Christianity when it was a small and persecuted sect. (Cecelia is supposed to have died in Sicily between 176 and 180 A.D.) The story reveals the fanaticism by which the sect maintained discipline among its embattled adherents. Marriage has always been recognized as an important means for securing converts. In this legend, that tradition is merged with the early Church's obsession with virginity and with the sort of militant feminism that enabled St. Catharine of Sienna or Joan of Arc to have such enormous influence on political affairs. By the time these traditions had reached the tales of Constance and Griselda, and even the Wife of Bath's Prologue, they had become watered down. In the martyrdom of St. Cecelia, we witness them in their awful, pristine purity.

The Canon's Yeoman's Prologue and Tale can be linked with the Second Nun's Tale by the sort of special pleading by which the Wife of Bath's Prologue and Tale are linked with the other two in Part III. Joseph E. Grennen, "Saint Cecelia's 'Chemical Wedding'," *JEGP* (1966); Russell A. Peck, "The Ideas of 'Entente' and Translation in Chaucer's Second Nun's Tale," *Annuale Mediaevale* (1967); and Bruce A. Rosenberg, "The Contrary Tales of the Second Nun and Canon's Yeoman," *Chaucer Review* (1968) are three interesting attempts.

The Canon's Yeoman's Prologue represents an exceptional stage in the development of the Canterbury drama. We speak constantly of dramatic interplay in the frame, but it is noteworthy that Chaucer never really went beyond drama of situation to drama of character. Critics may argue whether the Wife of Bath, Monk, and other pilgrims are the same characters in their tales as they are in the General Prologue, but no one has suggested that the differences are dramatic developments brought about by confrontations which the audience can observe. But one episode in which we can observe a bit of character development is the Canon's Yeoman's Prologue, in which we see the Yeoman, in response to questions from the Host, moving from pride in his master's accomplishment (ll.600ff) to chagrin that it has not paid off (ll.648ff) to grievance and revelation of his master's fraud (ll.668ff).

The Canon's Yeoman's Tale falls in with the Friar's and Summoner's Tales and Pardoner's Prologue as muck raking, an exposé of fraudulent professional behavior. The first part is a survey of the mysteries of alchemy. The naive belief of laymen in the Middle Ages was that alchemists—who were really the early chemists—must be searching for something of material value, especially for ways to make gold. This belief led to "confidence" rackets that were condemned in countless episcopal decretals. The second part of the Yeoman's tale is just such a sting operation. Edgar H. Duncan, "The Literature of Alchemy and Chaucer's Canon's Yeoman's Tale: Framework, Theme, and Characters," *Speculum* (1968) documents Chaucer's borrowings and adaptations.

Canterbury Tales

PART VIII

SECOND NUN'S TALE

PROLOGUE

The Prologe of the Seconde Nonnes Tale.

The ministre and the norice unto vices,
Which that men clepe in Englissh ydelnesse,
That porter of the gate is of delices,
To eschue and by hire contrarie hire
    oppresse—
That is to seyn, by leveful bisynesse—   5
Wel oughten we to doon al oure entente
Lest that the feend thurgh ydelnesse us hente.

For he that with his thousand cordes slye
Continuelly us waiteth to biclappe,
Whan he may man in ydelnesse espye,   10
He kan so lightly cacche hym in his trappe—
Til that a man be hent right by the lappe
He nys nat war the feend hath hym in honde.
Wel oghte us werche and ydelnesse with-
    stonde.

---

1 ministre ... norice, servant, nurse. **2 clepe ... ydelnesse,** call, idleness. The four "idleness" stanzas are a commonplace introduction in monastic literature since idleness—Sloth—was one of the Seven Deadly Sins to which the contemplative life was most vulnerable ("the devil finds work for idle hands"). Translating, copying, illuminating, like manual labor in the fields, were regarded as therapeutic. **3 porter of the gate,** in contrast to the religious view, idleness was considered essential to the pursuit of courtly love, and Lady Idleness is gatekeeper to the Garden of Love in the *Roman de la Rose,* l. 560 (Dunn-Robbins 3.40). **delices,** sensual delights. **4 eschue ... oppresse,** avoid, overcome. **5 leveful,** permissible. **6 doon ... entente,** work energetically (attentively). **7 hente,** seize. **8 cordes slye,** i.e., his net. **9 biclappe,** entrap. **11 lightly,** easily. **12 lappe,** hanging part of the garment (hem).

And though men dradden nevere for to dye, 15
Yet seen men wel by resoun, doutelees,
That ydelnesse is roten slogardye
Of which ther nevere comth no good
    n'encrees;
And seen that slouthe hire holdeth in a lees
Oonly to slepe, and for to ete and drynke, 20
And to devouren al that othere swynke.

And for to putte us fro swich ydelnesse,
That cause is of so greet confusioun,
I have heer doon my feithful bisynesse
After the legende in translacioun 25
Right of thy glorious lif and passioun—
Thou with thy gerland wroght of rose and
    lilie,
Thee meene I, mayde and martyr Seint Cecilie.

Invocacio ad Mariam.

And thow that flour of virgines art alle,
Of whom that Bernard list so wel to write, 30
To thee at my bigynnyng first I calle;
Thou confort of us wrecches, do me endite
Thy maydens deeth, that wan thurgh hire
    merite
The eterneel lyf, and of the feend victorie,
As man may after reden in hire storie. 35

Thow mayde and mooder, doghter of thy
    sone,
Thow welle of mercy, synful soules cure,
In whom that God for bountee chees to wone,
Thow humble and heigh over every creature,

Thow nobledest so forferth oure nature 40
That no desdeyn the Makere hadde of kynde
His sone in blood and flessh to clothe and
    wynde.

Withinne the cloistre blisful of thy sydis
Took mannes shap the eterneel love and pees
That of the tryne compas lord and gyde is, 45
Whom erthe and see and hevene out of relees
Ay heryen; and thou, virgine wemmelees,
Baar of thy body—and dweltest mayden
    pure—
The creatour of every creature.

Assembled is in thee magnificence 50
With mercy, goodnesse, and with swich pitee
That thou that art the sonne of excellence
Nat oonly helpeth hem that preyen thee,
But often tyme of thy benygnytee
Ful frely, er that men thyn help biseche, 55
Thou goost biforn and art hir lyves leche.

Now help, thow meeke and blisful faire mayde,
Me, flemed wrecche, in this desert of galle;
Thynk on the womman Cananee that sayde
That whelpes eten somme of the crommes alle
That from hir lordes table been yfalle; 61
And though that I, unworthy sone of Eve,
Be synful, yet accepte my bileve.

And for that feith is deed withouten werkis,
So for to werken yif me wit and space, 65
That I be quit fro thennes that most derk is.

---

17 slogardye, sluggishness (sloth). **18 encrees,** profit. **19 hire . . . lees,** i.e., idleness, leash. *seen:* other MSS *syn/sithens.* **20** Hg&c *Oonly for to.* **21 swynke,** work for. **26 passioun,** martyrdom. **27 of:** E&c *with.* **28 martyr:** E *mooder.* **29–77** The Invocation to Mary begins (ll. 36–56) with echoes of the prayer of St. Bernard in Dante's *Paradiso* 23.1ff., to which are added materials from the liturgy and other poems in praise of the Virgin. It may be compared with the Invocation at the beginning of the Prioress' Tale. **30 Bernard list,** Bernard chose; St. Bernard of Clairvaux (1090–1153) was a notable figure in the development of medieval Mariolatry. **32 do me endite,** cause me to write. **38 bountee . . . wone,** graciousness, live. **40 nobledest . . . forferth,** ennobled, greatly. **41 kynde,** (human) nature. **42 wynde,** envelope. **45 tryne compas,** threefold universe (see the next line). **46 out of relees,** without ceasing. **47 heryen . . . wemmelees,** praise, spotless. **52 sonne,** sun. **54 benygnytee,** graciousness. **56 goost biforn . . . leche,** i.e., anticipate their needs, physician. **58 flemed wrecche . . . galle,** banished exile, gall (bitterness). **59 womman Cananee,** Canaanite woman, Matt. 15:21–28. **60 crommes,** crumbs. **62 sone of Eve,** this has been taken by most scholars to reflect a stage when this piece was composed to be read separately (when the "sone" would refer to the poet), or intended for a male pilgrim (such as the Monk or Parson). Pratt notes, however, that it echoes a line in the antiphon of our Lady, *Salve Regina,* which the Nun sang every day, "Ad te clamamus exules filii Evae" (To thee we cry, exiled sons of Eve), where "son" means simply "descendant." **63 bileve,** devotion. **64 deed,** dead. **65 yif . . . space,** grant, time. **66 quit . . . thennes . . . derk,** saved; i.e., from Hell.

O thou that art so fair and ful of grace,
Be myn advocat in that heighe place
Theras withouten ende is songe Osanne,
Thow Cristes mooder, doghter deere of Anne.

And of thy light my soule in prison lighte,   71
That troubled is by the contagioun
Of my body, and also by the wighte
Of erthely lust and fals affeccioun;
O havene of refut, O salvacioun   75
Of hem that been in sorwe and in distresse,
Now help, for to my werk I wol me dresse.

Yet preye I yow that reden that I write,
Foryeve me that I do no diligence
This ilke storie subtilly to endite,   80
For bothe have I the wordes and sentence
Of hym that at the seintes reverence
The storie wroot, and folwen hire legende,
And I pray yow that ye wole my werk amende.

Interpretacio nominis Cecilie quam ponit Frater Jacobus Januensis in Legenda

First wolde I yow the name of Seinte Cecilie   85
Expowne, as men may in hir storie see.
It is to seye in Englissh "hevenes lilie,"
For pure chaastnesse of virginitee;
Or for she whitnesse hadde of honestee,
And grene of conscience, and of good fame   90
The soote savour, "lilie" was hir name.

Or Cecilie is to seye "the wey to blynde,"
For she ensample was by good techynge.
Or elles Cecile, as I writen fynde,
Is joyned by a manere conjoynynge   95
Of "hevene" and "Lia"; and heere in figurynge
The "hevene" is set for thoght of hoolynesse,
And "Lia" for hire lastynge bisynesse.

Cecile may eek be seyd in this manere,
"Wantynge of blyndnesse," for hir grete light
Of sapience, and for hire thewes cleere;   101
Or elles, loo, this maydens name bright
Of "hevene" and "leos" comth, for which by right
Men myghte hire wel "the hevene of peple" calle,
Ensample of goode and wise werkes alle.   105

For "leos" "peple" in Englissh is to seye,
And right as men may in the hevene see
The sonne and moone and sterres every weye,
Right so men goostly in this mayden free
Seyen of feith the magnanymytee,   110
And eek the cleernesse hool of sapience,
And sondry werkes brighte of excellence.

And right so as thise philosophres write
That hevene is swift and round and eek brennynge,
Right so was faire Cecilie the white   115

---

69 Osanne, Hosanna (in Heaven). **72–73 contagioun/Of my body,** this sentiment, like the sentiment of this entire legend, comes close to the heresy of Manichaeism (the belief that all physical matter is evil) against which the Church fought throughout the Middle Ages. One wonders whether its very grotesquery may not have been what attracted Chaucer to this story; see the Introduction. **wighte,** weight. **74 lust,** pleasure. **75 refut,** refuge. *havene:* other MSS *hevene.* **77 dresse,** address. **78 reden,** read; evidently this piece was not written originally for oral presentation. **79 do no diligence,** take no pains. **80 subtilly to endite,** presumably this means just what it says: that the poet was apologizing for the lack of subtlety in the narrative, its incredible motivations, its heavy didacticism. **81 sentence,** meaning. **82 at . . . reverence,** out of reverence for. **84 amende,** correct. E&c *And* om; Hg&c *I* om; other MSS *I* in various positions (from the margin in the exemplar?) **Jacobus Januensis,** Jacobus de Voragine, author of the *Legenda Aurea (Golden Legend),* the most famous medieval collections of saints' lives. Chaucer follows this account for his "Interpretacio" and through l. 357. The rest of his account comes from various sources. **85** E&c *yow* om. **86 Expowne,** expound (explain). *in:* Hg&c *on.* All of the etymologies that follow are false. **89 Or,** or else. **91 soote savour,** sweet odor. **92 wey to blynde,** Lat. *caecis via.* **96 hevene,** Lat. *caelum,* Fr. *ciel.* **Lia,** Leah, symbol of the active life, Gen. 29:32ff. **100 Wantynge,** lack. **101 sapience . . . thewes . . . cleere,** wisdom, virtues, bright. **103 leos,** people (Gk.). **109 goostly,** spiritually. **110 Seyen . . . magnanymytee,** see, generosity. **112 sondry,** various. **114 swift . . . round . . . brennynge,** swiftly turning round (the topmost sphere, the Primum Mobile), burning (the area beyond the nine spheres where fire alone subsists, the Empyrean, abode of saints and angels).

Ful swift and bisy evere in good werkynge,
And round and hool in good perseverynge,

And brennynge evere in charite ful brighte.
Now have I yow declared what she highte.

Explicit

Here bigynneth the Seconde Nonnes Tale of the Lyf of Seinte Cecile.

This mayden bright Cecilie, as hir lif
   seith,   120
Was comen of Romayns and of noble kynde,
And from hir cradel up fostred in the feith
Of Crist, and bar his gospel in hir mynde.
She nevere cessed, as I writen fynde,
Of hir preyere, and God to love and drede, 125
Bisekynge hym to kepe hir maydenhede.

And whan this mayden sholde unto a man
Ywedded be, that was ful yong of age,
Which that ycleped was Valerian,
And day was comen of hir marriage,   130
She ful devout and humble in hir corage,
Under hir robe of gold that sat ful faire,
Hadde next hire flessh yclad hire in an haire.

And whil the orgnes maden melodie,
To God allone in herte thus sang she,   135
"O Lord, my soule and eek my body gye
Unwemmed, lest that it confounded be."
And for his love that dyde upon a tree,
Every seconde and thridde day she faste,
Ay biddynge in hire orisons ful faste.   140

The nyght cam and to bedde moste she gon
With hire housbonde, as ofte is the manere,
And pryvely to hym she seyde anon,
"O sweete and wel biloved spouse deere,

Ther is a conseil, and ye wolde it heere,   145
Which that right fayn I wolde unto yow
   seye,
So that ye swere ye shul it nat biwreye."

Valerian gan faste unto hire swere
That for no cas, ne thyng that myghte be,
He sholde nevere mo biwreyen here.   150
And thanne at erst to hym thus seyde she,
"I have an aungel which that loveth me,
That with greet love, wherso I wake or sleepe,
Is redy ay my body for to keepe.

"And if that he may feelen, out of drede, 155
That ye me touche, or love in vileynye,
He right anon wol sle yow with the dede,
And in youre yowthe thus ye shullen dye,
And if that ye in clene love me gye,   159
He wol yow loven as me, for youre clennesse,
And shewen yow his joye and his brightnesse."

Valerian, corrected as God wolde,
Answerde agayn, "If I shal trusten thee,
Lat me that aungel se and hym biholde,
And if that it a verray angel bee,   165
Thanne wol I doon as thou hast prayed me;
And if thou love another man, for sothe,
Right with this swerd thanne wol I sle yow
   bothe."

117 **perseverynge,** steadfastness. 119 **highte,** was named. 121 **comen . . . kynde,** descended, nature (stock). 126 **Bisekynge . . . kepe,** beseeching, protect (save). 131 **corage,** heart. 133 **haire,** hair shirt. 134 *orgnes:* Hg&c *organs.* St. Cecilia did not become the patron saint of music until the Renaissance. The occurrence of the word *organis* in this context is evidently what led to that association, which appeared first in painting and eventually in literature. 135 Hg&c *in hir herte.* 136 **gye,** guide (protect). 137 **Unwemmed . . . confounded,** spotless, condemned. *it:* Hg&c *I.* 138 *a tree:* Hg&c *the tree.* 140 **Ay biddynge . . . orisons,** always praying, prayers. 143 **pryvely,** privately. 145 **conseil,** secret. 146 **fayn,** happily. 147 **biwreye,** betray. *it:* E *me.* 149 **for no cas,** i.e., in no event. 151 Hg&c *thus* om. 154 **keepe,** protect. 155 **out of drede,** without doubt. 156 **vileynye,** shamefully (i.e., sexually). 157 **with the dede,** i.e., at the moment of. 158 *shullen:* E&c *sholden.* 159 **gye,** guide. 161 *shewen:* Hg&c *shew to.* 162 **corrected,** admonished.

Cecile answerde anon-right in this wise,
"If that yow list the angel shul ye see   170
So that ye trowe in Crist and yow baptize.
Gooth forth to Via Apia," quod shee,
"That fro this toun ne stant but miles three,
And to the poure folkes that ther dwelle
Sey hem right thus as that I shal yow telle.   175

"Telle hem that I, Cecile, yow to hem sente
To shewen yow the goode Urban the olde
For secree nedes and for good entente.
And whan that ye Seint Urban han biholde,
Telle hym the wordes whiche that I to yow
          tolde.   180
And whan that he hath purged yow fro
          synne,
Thanne shul ye se that angel er ye twynne."

   Valerian is to the place ygon,
And right as hym was taught by his lernynge
He foond this hooly olde Urban anon   185
Among the seintes buryeles lotynge.
And he anon withouten tariynge
Dide his message, and whan that he it tolde
Urban for joye his handes gan up holde.

The teeris from his eyen leet he falle.   190
"Almyghty Lord, O Jhesu Crist," quod he,
"Sowere of chaast conseil, hierde of us alle,
The fruyt of thilke seed of chastitee
That thou hast sowe in Cecile, taak to thee!
Lo, lyk a bisy bee, withouten gile,   195
Thee serveth ay thyn owene thral Cecile.

"For thilke spouse that she took riht now,
Ful lyk a fiers leoun, she sendeth heere,
As meke as evere was any lomb, to yow."
And with that word anon ther gan appeere 200
An oold man clad in white clothes cleere

That hadde a book with lettre of gold in honde,
And gan bifore Valerian to stonde.

Valerian as deed fil doun for drede   204
Whan he hym saugh, and he up hente hym tho,
And on his book right thus he gan to rede,
"O Lord, O feith, O God, withouten mo,
O Cristendom, and Fader of alle also,
Aboven alle and over alle everywhere."
Thise wordes al with gold ywriten were.   210

Whan this was rad, thanne seyde this olde man,
"Leevestow this thyng or no? Sey ye or nay."
"I leeve al this thyng," quod Valerian,
"For sother thyng than this, I dar wel say,
Under the hevene no wight thynke may."   215
Tho vanysshed this olde man, he nyste where,
And Pope Urban hym cristened right there.

   Valerian gooth hoom and fynt Cecilie
Withinne his chambre with an angel stonde.
This angel hadde of roses and of lilie   220
Corones two, the whiche he bar in honde,
And first to Cecile, as I understonde,
He yaf that oon, and after gan he take
That oother to Valerian hir make.   224

"With body clene and with unwemmed thoght
Kepeth ay wel thise corones," quod he.
"Fro Paradys to yow have I hem broght,
Ne nevere mo ne shal they roten bee,
Ne lese hir soote savour, trusteth me;
Ne nevere wight shal seen hem with his eye 230
But he be chaast and hate vileynye.

"And thow, Valerian, for thow so soone
Assentedest to good conseil also,
Sey what thee list, and thou shalt han thy boone.
"I have a brother," quod Valerian tho,   235

---

171 trowe, believe. **172 Via Apia,** the Appian Way leads south from Rome past the catacombs where the Christians secreted themselves when Rome was still pagan. **177 Urban,** Pope Urban I, beheaded in A.D. 230. **178 nedes:** E *thynges.* **182 twynne,** depart. **183** Hg&c *This Valerian.* **186 seintes buryeles lotynge,** burial places of the saints lying hidden (i.e., in the catacombs). **192 hierde,** shepherd. **196 thral,** slave. **197 riht:** Hg&c *but.* **201 cleere,** shining. Probably St. Paul in view of ll. 207–09. **205 hente . . . tho,** lifted, then. **207 O Lord . . . ,** One Lord, one faith, etc.; cf. Eph. 4:5–6. **212 Leevestow,** do you believe. **214 sother,** truer. E&c *oother.* **224 make,** mate. **225 unwemmed,** unblemished. **226 Kepeth,** guard. *quod he:* E *three.* **229 soote savour,** sweet odor. **231 But he,** unless he. **234 list . . . boone,** desire, wish.

"That in this world I love no man so.
I pray yow that my brother may han grace
To knowe the trouthe, as I do, in this place."

The angel seyde, "God liketh thy requeste,
And bothe with the palm of martirdom   240
Ye shullen come unto his blisful feste."
And with that word Tiburce his brother coom.
And whan that he the savour undernoom,
Which that the roses and the lilies caste,
Withinne his herte he gan to wondre faste,   245

And seyde, "I wondre, this tyme of the yeer,
Whennes that soote savour cometh so
Of rose and lilies that I smelle heer?
For though I hadde hem in myne handes two,
The savour myghte in me no depper go.   250
The sweete smel that in myn herte I fynde
Hath chaunged me al in another kynde."

Valerian seyde, "Two corones han we,
Snow white and rose reed that shynen cleere,
Whiche that thyne eyen han no myght to see;
And as thou smellest hem thurgh my preyere,
So shaltow seen hem, leeve brother deere,   257
If it so be thou wolt, withouten slouthe,
Bileve aright and knowen verray trouthe."

Tiburce answerde, "Seistow this to me   260
In soothnesse, or in dreem I herkne this?"
"In dremes," quod Valerian, "han we be
Unto this tyme, brother myn, ywis.
And now at erst in trouthe oure dwellyng is."
"How woostow this," quod Tiburce, "and in
    what wyse?"   265
Quod Valerian, "That shal I thee devyse.

"The aungel of God hath me the trouthe
    ytaught
Which thou shalt seen if that thou wolt reneye

The ydoles and be clene, and elles naught."
And of the myracle of thise corones tweye   270
Seint Ambrose in his preface list to seye;
Solempnely this noble doctour deere
Commendeth it, and seith in this manere:

"The palm of martirdom for to receyve,
Seinte Cecile, fulfild of Goddes yifte,   275
The world and eek hire chambre gan she
    weyve—
Witnesse Tyburces and Valerians shrifte,
To whiche God of his bountee wolde shifte
Corones two of floures wel smellynge,   279
And made his angel hem the corones brynge.

"The mayde hath broght thise men to blisse
    above;
The world hath wist what it is worth, certeyn,
Devocioun of chastitee to love."
Tho shewed hym Cecile al open and pleyn
That alle ydoles nys but a thyng in veyn,   285
For they been dombe and therto they been deve,
And charged hym his ydoles for to leve.

"Whoso that troweth nat this, a beest he is,"
Quod tho Tiburce, "if that I shal nat lye."
And she gan kisse his brest, that herde this,   290
And was ful glad he koude trouthe espye.
"This day I take thee for myn allye,"
Seyde this blisful faire mayde deere,
And after that she seyde as ye may heere: 294

"Lo, right so as the love of Crist," quod she,
"Made me thy brotheres wyf, right in that wise
Anon for myn allye heer take I thee,
Syn that thou wolt thyne ydoles despise.
Go with thy brother now and thee baptise,
And make thee clene so that thou mowe
    biholde   300
The angeles face of which thy brother tolde."

---

243 **savour undernoom**, odor perceived. 251 *sweete*: other MSS *sote/swote*. 252 **in**, into. 258 **slouthe**, sloth, hesitation. 261 **soothnesse**, reality. 264 **in trouthe**, i.e., in actuality. 265 **woostow**, do you know. 268 **reneye**, renounce. 271 **Ambrose in his preface**, the preface to the mass for St. Cecelia's day in the Ambrosian liturgy. **list to seye**, chooses to tell. 273 *it*: E *hym*. 276 **chambre . . . weyve**, bedroom (i.e., the marriage bed), give up. 277 **shrifte**, conversion. EHg&c read *Tyburces and Cecilies*, which is corrected in late MSS. 278 **shifte**, assign. 281 E&c *thise* om. 282 **wist what it is worth**, i.e., learned what devotion to chastity is worth. 284 **hym**, i.e., Tiburce. 286 **deve**, deaf. 288 **troweth**, believes.

Tiburce answerde and seyde, "Brother deere,
First tel me whider I shal and to what man?"
"To whom?" quod he, "Com forth with right
    good cheere.
I wol thee lede unto the Pope Urban."   305
"Til Urban? Brother myn Valerian,"
Quod tho Tiburce, "woltow me thider lede?
Me thynketh that it were a wonder dede.

"Ne menestow nat Urban," quod he tho,
"That is so ofte dampned to be deed,   310
And woneth in halkes alwey to and fro,
And dar nat ones putte forth his heed?
Men sholde hym brennen in a fyr so reed
If he were founde, or that men myghte hym
    spye,
And we also, to bere hym compaignye.   315

"And whil we seken thilke divinitee
That is yhid in hevene pryvely,
Algate ybrend in this world shul we be!"
To whom Cecile answerde boldely,
"Men myghten dreden wel and skilfully   320
This lyf to lese, myn owene deere brother,
If this were lyvynge oonly and noon oother.

"But ther is bettre lif in oother place
That nevere shal be lost, ne drede thee noght,
Which Goddes Sone us tolde thurgh his
    grace.
That Fadres Sone hath alle thyng ywroght,   326
And al that wroght is with a skilful thoght,
The Goost that fro the Fader gan procede
Hath sowled hem, withouten any drede.

By word and by myracle Goddes Sone,   330
Whan he was in this world, declared heere
That ther was oother lyf ther men may wone."
To whom answerde Tiburce, "O suster deere,
Ne seydestow right now in this manere,

Ther nys but o God, lord in soothfastnesse?   335
And now of three how maystow bere
    witnesse?"

"That shal I telle," quod she, "er I go.
Right as a man hath sapiences three,
Memorie, engyn, and intellect also,
So in o beynge of divinitee   340
Thre persones may ther right wel bee."
Tho gan she hym ful bisily to preche
Of Cristes come, and of his peynes teche,

And manye pointes of his passioun:
How Goddes Sone in this world was
    withholde
To doon mankynde pleyn remissioun,   346
That was ybounde in synne and cares colde.
Al this thyng she unto Tiburce tolde.
And after this, Tiburce in good entente
With Valerian to Pope Urban he wente,   350

That thanked God, and with glad herte and
    light
He cristned hym and made hym in that place,
Parfit in his lernynge, Goddes kynght.
And after this Tiburce gat swich grace
That every day he saugh in tyme and space   355
The aungel of God; and every maner boone
That he God axed, it was sped ful soone.

It were ful hard by ordre for to seyn
How manye wondres Jhesus for hem wroghte,
But atte laste, to tellen short and pleyn,   360
The sergeantz of the toun of Rome hem
    soghte,
And hem biforn Almache the prefect broghte,
Which hem apposed, and knew al hire entente,
And to the ymage of Juppiter hem sente,

And seyde, "Whoso wol nat sacrifise,   365

---

303 EHg&c *whider that.* 310 **dampned,** condemned. 311 **woneth in halkes,** lives in corners (crevices). 315 **we also,** i.e., and burn us too. 318 **Algate,** meanwhile. 326 **ywroght,** created. 327 **skilful thoght,** endowed with reason. 328 **Goost,** spirit. 329 **sowled,** endowed them with souls. **withouten . . . drede,** without doubt. 330 *Goddes:* Hg&c *he|heigh Goddes.* 332 **wone,** live. 335 **soothfastnesse,** truth. 338 **sapiences,** mental faculties. 339 **engyn,** imagination (ingenuity). 340 **o beynge,** one being. E *o* om. 343 **come . . . teche,** coming, to teach. 345 **withholde,** retained. 346 **pleyn,** full. 356 **boone,** request. 357 Here direct dependence on the *Legenda Aurea* ends, and other materials begin to be employed. 362 **prefect,** chief of police. 363 **apposed,** questioned. EHg&c *opposed.*

Swap of his heed; this my sentence heer."
Anon thise martirs that I yow devyse,
Oon Maximus, that was an officer
Of the prefectes and his corniculer,
Hem hente, and whan he forth the seintes
    ladde   370
Hymself he weep for pitee that he hadde.

Whan Maximus had herd the seintes loore,
He gat hym of the tormentoures leve,
And ladde hem to his hous withoute moore;
And with hir prechyng er that it were eve   375
They gonnen fro the tormentours to reve,
And fro Maxime, and fro his folk echone,
The false feith, to trowe in God allone.

  Cecile cam, whan it was woxen nyght,
With preestes that hem cristned alle
    yfeere;   380
And afterward, whan day was woxen light,
Cecile hem seyde with a ful stedefast cheere,
"Now, Cristes owene knyghtes leeve and
    deere,
Cast alle awey the werkes of derknesse,
And armeth yow in armure of brightnesse.   385

"Ye han forsothe ydoon a greet bataille,
Youre cours is doon, youre feith han ye
    conserved.
Gooth to the corone of lif that may nat
    faille;
The rightful Juge, which that ye han
    served,
Shal yeve it yow as ye han it deserved."   390
And whan this thyng was seyd as I devyse,
Men ledde hem forth to doon the sacrefise.

But whan they weren to the place broght,
To tellen shortly the conclusioun,
They nolde encense ne sacrifise right noght,   395

But on hir knees they setten hem adoun
With humble herte and sad devocioun,
And losten bothe hir hevedes in the place.
Hir soules wenten to the Kyng of Grace.

This Maximus, that saugh this thyng bityde,
With pitous teeris tolde it anon-right,   401
That he hir soules saugh to hevene glyde
With aungels ful of cleernesse and of light,
And with this word converted many a wight;
For which Almachius dide hym so tobete   405
With whippe of leed til he his lif gan lete.

  Cecile hym took and buryed hym anon
By Tiburce and Valerian softely
Withinne hire buriyng place under the
    stoon;
And after this Almachius hastily   410
Bad his ministres fecchen openly
Cecile, so that she myghte in his presence
Doon sacrifice and Juppiter encense.

But they, converted at hir wise loore,
Wepten ful soore and yaven ful credence   415
Unto hire word, and cryden moore and
    moore,
"Crist, Goddes sone, withouten difference,
Is verray God—this is al oure sentence—
That hath so good a servant hym to serve.
This with o voys we trowen, thogh we
    sterve."   420

  Almachius, that herde of this doynge,
Bad fecchen Cecile that he myghte hire see;
And alderfirst, lo, this was his axynge,
"What maner womman artow?" tho quod he.
"I am a gentil womman born," quod she.   425
"I axe thee," quod he, "though it thee
    greeve,
Of thy religioun and of thy bileeve."

367 **devyse,** narrate. 369 **corniculer,** assistant. 372 **loore,** teaching. 373 **tormentoures leve,** torturers permission. 376 **reve,** remove. 378 **trowe,** believe. 380 **yfeere,** together. 385 **armeth yow,** cf. Eph. 6:11–13. 386–90 **Ye han . . . ydoon,** cf. II Tim. 4:7–8. 395 **nolde,** would not offer. 398 **bothe,** i.e., Valerian and Tiburce. 400 **bityde,** happen. 401 **anon-right,** immediately. 403 **cleernesse,** brightness. 404 *this:* Hg&c *his.* 405 *tobete:* Hg&c *to* om. 406 **lete,** give up. 408 **softely,** secretly. 409 **hire,** their. 414 **at . . . loore,** by, teaching. 417 **difference,** distinction (i.e., between the authority of the Father and the Son). 418 **verray,** true. 420 **o voys . . . trowen . . . sterve,** a single voice, believe, die. 423 **alderfirst,** first of all.

"Ye han bigonne youre questioun folily,"
Quod she, "that wolden two answeres conclude
In o demande; ye axed lewedly.''   430
Almache answerde unto that similitude,
"Of whennes comth thyn answeryng so rude?"
"Of whennes?" quod she whan that she was
    freyned,
"Of conscience and of good feith unfeyned."

Almachius seyde, "Ne takestow noon heede
Of my power?" And she answerde hym
    this: 436
"Youre myght," quod she, "ful litel is to
    dreede,
For every mortal mannes power nys
But lyk a bladdre ful of wynd, ywys.
For with a nedles poynt, whan it is blowe,   440
May al the boost of it be leyd ful lowe."

"Ful wrongfully bigonne thow," quod he,
"And yet in wrong is thy perseveraunce.
Wostow nat how oure myghty princes free
Han thus comanded and maad ordinaunce   445
That every Cristen wight shal han penaunce
But if that he his Cristendom withseye,
And goon al quit if he wole it reneye?"

"Yowre princes erren, as youre nobleye
    dooth,"
Quod tho Cecile, "and with a wood sentence
Ye make us gilty, and it is nat sooth.   451
For ye, that knowen wel oure innocence,
For as muche as we doon a reverence
To Crist, and for we bere a Cristen name,
Ye putte on us a cryme and eek a blame.   455

But we that knowen thilke name so
For vertuous, we may it nat withseye."
Almache answerde, "Chees oon of thise two:

Do sacrifice, or Cristendom reneye,   459
That thou mowe now escapen by that weye."
At which the hooly blisful faire mayde
Gan for to laughe, and to the juge sayde:

"O juge, confus in thy nycetee,
Woltow that I reneye innocence
To make me a wikked wight?" quod shee.   465
"Lo, he dissymuleth heere in audience;
He stareth and woodeth in his advertence."
To whom Almachius, "Unsely wrecche,
Ne woostow nat how fer my myght may
    strecche?

"Han noght oure myghty princes to me yiven,
Ye, bothe power and auctoritee   471
To maken folk to dyen or to lyven?
Why spekestow so proudly thanne to me?"
"I speke noght but stedfastly," quod she,
"Nat proudly, for I seye, as for my syde,   475
We haten deedly thilke vice of pryde.

"And if thou drede nat a sooth to heere,
Thanne wol I shewe al openly, by right,
That thou hast maad a ful gret lesyng heere.
Thou seyst thy princes han thee yeven myght
Bothe for to sleen and for to quyken a wight,
Thou that ne mayst but oonly lyf bireve;   482
Thou hast noon oother power ne no leve.

"But thou mayst seyn thy princes han thee
    maked
Ministre of deeth, for if thou speke of mo,   485
Thou lyest, for thy power is ful naked."
"Do wey thy booldnesse," seyde Almachius
    tho,
"And sacrifice to oure goddes er thou go.
I recche nat what wrong that thou me profre,
For I kan suffre it as a philosophre,   490

428 folily, foolishly; Cecile is giving the police chief a lesson in scholastic argumentation. **430 lewedly,** ignorantly. **431 similitude,** comparison (statement). **433 freyned,** questioned. **434 unfeyned,** frank, unfeigned. **441 boost,** boast. **442 bigonne,** you began. **443 perseveraunce,** continuing (in the argument). **446 han,** do. **447 withseye,** deny. **448 And goon,** and shall go. **449 nobleye,** nobility. **450 wood,** insane. **451** *it is:* EHg&c *it* om. **456 thilke,** that. **462** Hg&c *she sayde.* **463 nycetee,** folly. **466 dissymuleth . . . audience,** dissembles, public. **467 stareth . . . woodeth . . . advertence,** stares, raves, mental control. **468 Unsely,** unfortunate. **474 stedfastly,** resolutely. **475** *seye:* E *speke.* **477 sooth,** truth. **479 lesyng,** lying. **481 quyken,** bring to life. **482 bireve,** remove. **483 leve,** permission. **489 recche,** care.

"But thilke wronges may I nat endure
That thou spekest of oure goddes heere," quod
   he.
Cecile answerde, "O nyce creature!
Thou seydest no word syn thou spak to me
That I ne knew therwith thy nycetee;   495
And that thou were, in every maner wise,
A lewed officer and a veyn justise.

"Ther lakketh no thyng to thyne outter eyen
That thou n'art blynd, for thyng that we seen
   alle
That it is stoon—that men may wel espyen—
That ilke stoon a god thow wolt it calle.   501
I rede thee, lat thyn hand upon it falle
And taste it wel and stoon thou shalt it fynde,
Syn that thou seest nat with thyne eyen
   blynde.

"It is a shame that the peple shal   505
So scorne thee and laughe at thy folye,
For communly men woot it wel overal
That myghty God is in his hevenes hye.
And thise ymages, wel thou mayst espye
To thee ne to hemself ne mowen noght profite,
For in effect they been nat worth a myte."   511

   Thise wordes and swiche othere seyde she,
And he weex wrooth and bad men sholde hir
   lede
Hom til hir hous, and "In hire hous," quod he,
"Brenne hire right in a bath of flambes rede."
And as he bad, right so was doon in dede;   516
For in a bath they gonne hire faste shetten,
And nyght and day greet fyr they under
   betten.

The longe nyght and eek a day also

For al the fyr and eek the bathes heete   520
She sat al coold and feelede no wo;
It made hire nat a drope for to sweete.
But in that bath hir lyf she moste lete,
For he Almachius, with ful wikke entente,
To sleen hire in the bath his sonde sente.   525

Thre strokes in the nekke he smoot hire tho,
The tormentour, but for no maner chaunce
He myghte noght smyte al hir nekke atwo.
And for ther was that tyme an ordinaunce
That no man sholde doon man swich penaunce
The ferthe strook to smyten, softe or soore,   531
This tormentour ne dorste do namoore,

But half deed, with hir nekke ycorven there,
He lefte hir lye, and on his wey he went.
The Cristen folk which that aboute hire were
With sheetes han the blood ful faire yhent.   536
Thre dayes lyved she in this torment,
And nevere cessed hem the feith to teche
That she hadde fostred. Hem she gan to preche,

And hem she yaf hir moebles and hir thyng,   540
And to the Pope Urban bitook hem tho,
And seyde, "I axed this at Hevene Kyng,
To han respit thre dayes and namo,
To recomende to yow er that I go
Thise soules, lo, and that I myghte do werche
Heere of myn hous perpetuelly a cherche."   546

   Seint Urban with his deknes prively
The body fette and buryed it by nyghte
Among his othere seintes honestly.
Hir hous the chirche of Seinte Cecilie highte.   550
Seint Urban halwed it as he wel myghte,
In which into this day in noble wyse
Men doon to Crist and to his seinte servyse.

Heere is ended the Seconde Nonnes Tale.

493 **nyce,** foolish. 497 **lewed ... veyn,** ignorant, ineffectual (in vain). 498 **outter,** outer; i.e., you are physically blind. 500 *it is:* Hg&c *is a.* 502 **rede,** advise. 517–18 **bath ... fyr,** bath in the Roman sense: a hypocaust, a room with a space under the floor where the heat from the furnace accumulated to heat it. **betten,** fed. 521 *feelede:* EHg&c *feeled;* other MSS *felt of it.* 525 **sonde,** emissary. 530 **penaunce,** punishment. 540 **moebles ... thyng,** furniture, things (possessions). 541 **bitook hem,** entrusted them (i.e., the Christians). 545 **do werche,** have created. 547 **deknes,** deacons. 548 *The body:* E *This body.*

CANON'S YEOMAN'S TALE

PROLOGUE

The Prologe of the Chanouns Yemannes Tale.

Whan ended was the lyf of Seinte Cecile,
Er we hadde riden fully fyve mile,   555
At Boghtoun-under-Blee us gan atake
A man that clothed was in clothes blake,
And undernethe he hadde a whyt surplys.
His hakeney, that was al pomely grys,
So swatte that it wonder was to see;   560
It semed as he had priked miles three.
The hors eek that his yeman rood upon
So swatte that unnethe myghte it gon.
Aboute the peytrel stood the foom ful hye;

He was of foom al flekked as a pye.   565
A male tweyfoold upon his croper lay.
It semed that he caried lite array.
Al light for somer rood this worthy man.
And in myn herte to wondren I bigan
What that he was til that I understood   570
How that his cloke was sowed to his hood,
For which, whan I hadde longe avysed me,
I demed hym som chanoun for to be.
His hat heeng at his bak doun by a laas,
For he hadde riden moore than trot or paas;

---

554 *ended was:* E *toold was al.* 555 **riden fully fyve mile,** Skeat observed that this is the distance from Boughton back to Ospringe, the customary final lodging place on the three-night journey from London to Canterbury, and from this he deduced that this is where the Pilgrims had spent the night; see l. 589 below. 556 **Boghtoun-under-Blee,** Boughton-under-Blean, five miles out of Canterbury, in Blean Forest. 558 E&c *undernethe he wered a surplys.* 559 **hakeney ... pomely grys,** hired horse, dappled gray. *that:* E&c *whiche that.* 560 **swatte,** sweated (from being overridden). 561 **priked,** spurred. 562 *hors:* E&c *hakeny.* 563 **unnethe,** hardly. 564–65 Lines omitted in E&c; ll. 562–63 omitted in one MS and transposed with ll. 564–65 in others. Manly IV.522 suggests that in the exemplar 564–65 may have stood as alternates for 562–63. 564 **peytrel ... foom,** breast harness, foamy sweat. 565 **pye,** magpie (a black bird with white markings). 566 **male tweyfoold ... croper,** saddlebag (double bag), crupper (harness extending from saddle under the tail). 567 **lite array,** little baggage (equipment). 568 **light for somer,** lightly equipped as if for summer; like the sweating horses, the lack of luggage bespeaks culprits on the run; cf. short poem no. 20, l. 20n. 572 **avysed me,** reflected. 573 **demed,** judged. **chanoun,** canon, strictly speaking a priest who lived in a community of priests in the precincts of a cathedral, renounced private property, and ordered his life according to the canons of the Church. These were known as canons regular. Some canons, who served as parish priests or teachers, were granted episcopal permission to live alone and own private property. These were known as canons secular. This character would appear to be a canon secular. 574 **laas,** cord (lace). 575 **paas,** (foot) pace.

He hadde ay priked lik as he were wood. 576
A clote-leef he hadde under his hood
For swoot, and for to kepe his heed from
    heete—
But it was joye for to seen hym swete!
His forheed dropped as a stillatorie 580
Were ful of plantayne and of paritorie.
And whan that he was come he gan to crye,
"God save," quod he, "this joly compaignye!
Faste have I priked," quod he, "for youre sake,
By cause that I wolde yow atake, 585
To riden in som myrie compaignye."
His yeman eek was ful of curteisye
And seyde, "Sires, now in the morwe-tyde
Out of youre hostelrie I saugh yow ryde,
And warned heer my lord and my soverayn, 590
Which that to ryden with yow is ful fayn
For his desport; he loveth daliaunce."
    "Freend, for thy warnyng God yeve thee
      good chaunce,"
Thanne seyde oure Hoost, "for certein it wolde
    seme
Thy lord were wys, and so I may wel deme. 595
He is ful jocunde also, dar I leye!
Can he oght telle a myrie tale or tweye,
With which he glade may this compaignye?"
    "Who, sire? My lord? Ye, ye withouten lye.
He kan of murthe and eek of jolitee 600
Nat but ynough; also, sire, trusteth me,
And ye hym knewe as wel as do I,
Ye wolde wondre how wel and craftily
He koude werke, and that in sondry wise.
He hath take on hym many a greet emprise, 605
Which were ful hard for any that is heere
To brynge aboute, but they of hym it leere.
As hoomly as he rit amonges yow,
If ye hym knewe, it wolde be for youre prow.
Ye wolde nat forgoon his aqueyntaunce 610

For muchel good, I dar leye in balaunce
Al that I have in my possessioun.
He is a man of heigh discrecioun;
I warne yow wel, he is a passyng man."
    "Wel," quod oure Hoost, "I pray thee, tel me
    than, 615
Is he a clerk or noon? Telle what he is."
    "Nay, he is gretter than a clerk, ywis,"
Seyde this Yeman, "and in wordes fewe,
Hoost, of his craft somwhat I wol yow shewe.
    "I seye, my lord kan swich subtilitee— 620
But al his craft ye may nat wite at me,
And somwhat helpe I yet to his wirkyng—
That al this ground on which we been ridyng
Til that we come to Caunterbury toun,
He koude al clene turnen up so doun, 625
And pave it al of silver and of gold!"
    And whan this Yeman hadde this tale ytold
Unto oure Hoost, he seyde, "Benedicitee,
This thyng is wonder merveillous to me,
Syn that thy lord is of so heigh prudence, 630
By cause of which men sholde hym reverence,
That of his worshipe rekketh he so lite.
His oversloppe nys nat worth a myte,
As in effect, to hym, so moot I go.
It is al baudy and totore also. 635
Why is thy lord so sluttissh, I the preye,
And is of power bettre clooth to beye,
If that his dede accorde with they speche?
Telle me that, and that I thee biseche."
    "Why?" quod this Yeman, "Wherto axe ye
    me? 640
God help me so, for he shal nevere thee—
But I wol nat avowe that I seye,
And therfore keep it secree, I yow preye—
He is to wys, in feith, as I bileeve.
That that is overdoon, it wol nat preeve 645
Aright, as clerkes seyn; it is a vice.

---

576 priked . . . wood, spurred, crazy. **577 clote,** burdock (which has large, heart-shaped leaves). **578 swoot,** sweat. **580 stillatorie,** still. **581 plantayne . . . paritorie,** plantain, pellitory; herbs distilled to make medicine. **585 atake:** Hg&c *overtake.* **586 som:** Hg&c *this.* **588 morwe-tyde,** early morning. **590 warned,** alerted. **591 fayn,** happy (eager). E&c *that* om. **592 daliaunce,** social conversation. **593 good chaunce,** good luck. **595 deme,** judge. **596 jocunde . . . leye,** cheerful, bet. **600 kan,** knows. **601 Nat but,** quite. **603** *craftily:* other MSS *thriftily.* **605 emprise,** enterprise. **607 leere,** learn. **608 hoomly . . . rit,** informally, rides. **609 prow,** profit. **614 passyng,** surpassing (superior). **620 kan . . . subtilitee,** knows, complexity. **621** *at me:* E *for me;* Hg&c *of me.* **625** *turnen:* E&c *turn it.* **627** *this tale:* Hg&c *thus.* **632 worshipe,** honor (appearance). **633 oversloppe . . . myte,** surplice (outer garment), smallest coin. **634 moot I go,** as I have power to walk. **635 baudy,** dirty. **641 thee,** prosper. **642 avowe,** admit openly. **645 That that . . . preeve,** that which, prove (turn out well). **646** *Aright:* Hg&c *And right.*

Wherfore in that I holde hym lewed and nyce.
For whan a man hath over-greet a wit,
Ful oft hym happeth to mysusen it.   649
So dooth my lord, and that me greveth soore.
God it amende! I kan sey yow namoore."
        "Therof no fors, good Yeman," quod oure
            Hoost;
"Syn of the konnyng of thy lord thow woost,
Telle how he dooth, I pray thee hertely,
Syn that he is so crafty and so sly.   655
Where dwelle ye, if it to telle be?"
        "In the suburbes of a toun," quod he,
"Lurkynge in hernes and in lanes blynde,
Where as thise robbours and thise theves by
            kynde
Holden hir pryvee, fereful residence,   660
As they that dar nat shewen hir presence;
So faren we, if I shal seye the sothe."
        "Now," quod oure Hoost, "yit lat me talke
            to the.
Why artow so discoloured of thy face?"
        "Peter," quod he, "God yeve it harde
            grace!
I am so used in the fyr to blowe   666
That it hath chaunged my colour, I trowe.
I am nat wont in no mirour to prie,
But swynke soore and lerne multiplie.
We blondren evere and pouren in the fir,   670
And for al that we faille of oure desir,
For evere we lakken oure conclusioun.
To muchel folk we doon illusioun,
And borwe gold, be it a pound or two,
Or ten, or twelve, or manye sommes mo,   675
And make hem wenen at the leeste weye
That of a pound we koude make tweye.
Yet is it fals, but ay we han good hope
It for to doon, and after it we grope.
But that science is so fer us biforn,   680

We mowen nat, although we hadden sworn,
It overtake, it slit awey so faste.
It wole us maken beggers atte laste."
        Whil this Yeman was thus in his talkyng,
This Chanoun drough hym neer and herde al
            thyng   685
Which this Yeman spak, for suspecioun
Of mennes speche evere hadde this Chanoun.
For Catoun seith that he that gilty is
Demeth alle thyng be spoke of hym, ywis.
That was the cause he gan so ny hym drawe   690
To his Yeman, to herknen al his sawe.
And thus he seyde unto his Yeman tho,
"Hoold thou thy pees and spek no wordes mo,
For if thou do, thou shalt it deere abye.   694
Thou sclaundrest me heere in this compaignye,
And eek discoverest that thou sholdest hyde."
        "Ye," quod oure Hoost, "telle on what so
            bityde.
Of al his thretyng rekke nat a myte."
        "In feith," quod he, "namoore I do but lyte."
        And whan this Chanoun saugh it wolde nat
            bee,   700
But his Yeman wolde telle his pryvetee,
He fledde awey for verray sorwe and shame.
        "A," quod the Yeman, "heere shal arise
            game;
Al that I kan anon now wol I telle.
Syn he is goon, the foule feend hym
            quelle!   705
For nevere heerafter wol I with hym meete
For peny ne for pound, I yow biheete.
He that me broghte first unto that game,
Er that he dye, sorwe have he and shame.
For it is ernest to me, by my feith;   710
That feele I wel, what so any man seith.
And yet for al my smert and al my grief,
For al my sorwe, labour, and meschief,

---

647 **lewed . . . nyce,** ignorant, foolish. 651 **amende,** correct. 652 **no fors,** no matter. 656 **telle be,** i.e., can be told. 658 **hernes,** corners. 659 **by kynde,** naturally (instinctively). 660 **pryvee,** secret. 663 E&c *yit lat me telle.* 665 **Peter,** i.e., "by St. Peter." 668 **wont . . . prie,** accustomed, pry (examine). 669 **swynke,** work. **multiplie,** the alchemical term for transmuting base metals into gold. The important point for the confidence man was that, as indicated by the term itself, some gold had to be present to start the process working. 670 **blondren . . . pouren,** blunder, pore (stare into). 672 **lakken,** i.e., fail to create gold. Hg&c *lakke of.* 674 **pound,** a pound's worth in money value, or is the yeoman simply hyperbolizing? 676 **wenen,** think. 678 *but:* Hg&c *and.* 681 Hg&c *hadde it.* 682 **slit,** slides. 688 **Catoun,** the Latin school text *Dionysii Catonis Disticha de Moribus,* I.17. 691 **sawe,** saying. 694 **deere abye,** pay for it dearly. 696 **discoverest,** reveal. 697 **bityde,** happens. 704 Hg&c *now* om. 705 **quelle,** kill. 707 **biheete,** promise. 711 E&c *what that.*

I koude nevere leve it in no wise.
Now wolde God my wit myghte suffise 715
To tellen al that longeth to that art.

And nathelees yow wol I tellen part.
Syn that my lord is goon, I wol nat spare;
Swich thyng as that I knowe, I wol declare."

Heere endeth the Prologe of the Chanouns Yemannes Tale.

Heere bigynneth the Chanouns Yeman his Tale.

With this Chanoun I dwelt have seven yeer,
And of his science am I never the neer. 721
Al that I hadde I have lost therby,
And God woot so hath many mo than I.
Ther I was wont to be right fressh and gay
Of clothyng and of oother good array, 725
Now may I were an hose upon myn heed;
And wher my colour was bothe fressh and reed,
Now is it wan and of a leden hewe—
Whoso it useth, soore shal he rewe—
And of my swynk yet blered is myn eye. 730
Lo, which avantage is to multiplie!
That slidyng science hath me maad so bare
That I have no good wher that evere I fare;
And yet I am endetted so therby
Of gold that I have borwed, trewely, 735
That whil I lyve I shal it quite nevere.
Lat every man bewar by me forevere!
What maner man that casteth hym therto,
If he continue I holde his thrift ydo.
For so helpe me God, therby shal he nat
    wynne, 740
But empte his purs and make his wittes thynne.
And whan he thurgh his madnesse and folye
Hath lost his owene good thurgh jupartye,
Thanne he exciteth oother folk therto

To lesen hir good, as he hymself hath do. 745
For unto shrewes joye it is and ese
To have hir felawes in peyne and disese.
Thus was I ones lerned of a clerk—
Of that no charge, I wol speke of oure werk.
Whan we been there as we shul exercise 750
Oure elvysshe craft we semen wonder wise,
Oure termes been so clergial and so queynte.
I blowe the fir til that myn herte feynte.
What sholde I tellen ech proporcioun
Of thynges whiche that we werche upon, 755
As on fyve or sixe ounces, may wel be,
Of silver, or som oother quantitee,
And bisye me to telle yow the names
Of orpyment, brent bones, iren squames,
That into poudre grounden been ful smal; 760
And in an erthen pot how put is al,
And salt yput in, and also papeer,
Biforn thise poudres that I speke of heer;
And wel ycovered with a lampe of glas;
And of muche oother thyng which that ther
    was; 765
And of the pot and glasses enlutyng,
That of the eyr myghte passe out nothyng;
And of the esy fir, and smart also,
Which that was maad; and of the care and wo

721 **science . . . neer,** knowledge, nearer. 726 **hose,** stocking cap. 728 E&c *a* om. 729 **it useth,** i.e., practices alchemy. **rewe,** repent. 730 **swynk . . . blered . . . eye,** work, my eyes are bleared (but probably *double entendre,* I have been cheated). 732 **slidyng,** slippery. 733 **good,** goods (property). 734 **endetted,** in debt. 736 **quite,** never be quit of the debt. 738 **casteth,** devotes himself to alchemy. 744 **exciteth,** incites. 746 **shrewes,** rascals. 748 **ones lerned,** once taught. 751 **elvysshe,** mysterious, magical. 752 **clergial,** learned (clerical). 754 **What sholde I tellen,** why should I tell: an example of *occupatio* because he goes on to tell. The alchemical details, which Chaucer obviously enjoyed manipulating just as he did astrological details, have been explained at length by W. C. Curry, E. H. Duncan, J. W. Spargo, and others, and in some detail in the Skeat and Robinson editions. 759 **orpyment . . . squames,** arsenic, scales. 762 **papeer,** paper (for lining?). 764 **lampe,** sheet (Fr. *lame*). 765 *of muche:* E&c *muchel.* 766 **enlutyng,** sealing with cement (lute). 768 **esy . . . smart,** moderate, brisk.

That we hadden in oure matires sublymyng; 770
And in amalgamyng and calceniyng
Of quyksilver, yclept mercurie crude?
For alle oure sleightes we kan nat conclude.
Oure orpyment and sublymed mercurie,
Oure grounden litarge eek in the porfurie, 775
Of ech of thise of ounces a certeyn,
Noght helpeth us. Oure labour is in veyn.
Ne eek oure spirites ascencioun,
Ne oure matires that lyen al fix adoun, 779
Mowe in oure werkyng nothyng us availle,
For lost is al oure labour and travaille;
And al the cost, a twenty devel way,
Is lost also which we upon it lay.

   Ther is also ful many another thyng
That is unto oure craft apertenyng. 785
Though I by ordre hem nat reherce kan
By cause that I am a lewed man,
Yet wol I telle hem as they come to mynde,
Thogh I ne kan nat sette hem in hir kynde,
As boole armonyak, vertgrees, boras, 790
And sondry vessels maad of erthe and glas,
Oure urynals and oure descensories,
Violes, crosletz, and sublymatories,
Cucurbites and alambikes eek,

And othere swiche, deere ynough a leek— 795
Nat nedeth it for to reherce hem alle—
Watres rubifiyng, and boles galle,
Arsenyk, sal armonyak, and brymstoon;
And herbes koude I telle eek many oon,
As egremoyne, valerian, and lunarie, 800
And othere swiche, if that me liste tarie;
Oure lampes brennyng bothe nyght and day,
To brynge aboute oure purpos, if we may;
Oure fourneys eek of calcinacioun,
And of watres albificacioun; 805
Unslekked lym, chalk, and gleyre of an ey,
Poudres diverse, asshes, donge, pisse, and cley,
Cered pottes, sal peter, vitriole,
And diverse fires maad of wode and cole;
Sal tartre, alkaly, and sal preparat, 810
And combust matires and coagulat;
Cley maad with hors or mannes heer, and oille
Of tartre, alum glas, berme, wort, and argoille,
Resalgar, and oure matires enbibyng,
And eek of oure matires encorporyng, 815
And of oure silver citrinacioun,
Oure cementyng and fermentacioun,
Oure yngottes, testes, and many mo.

---

770 sublymyng, vaporizing (sublimation). **771 amalgamyng . . . calceniyng,** fusing with mercury (amalgamating), heating until a substance becomes powder (calcinate). **772 quyksilver,** mercury; in alchemy regarded as the essential element in all metals. **773 sleightes . . . conclude,** tricks (procedures), succeed. As John Spargo observed, many of the experiments described in this and other alchemical discussions could be regarded as straightforward attempts at chemical analysis. The specifically alchemical interpretation may often have been assigned by uncomprehending laymen seeking to explain the tedious experimentation. **775 litarge . . . porfurie,** protoxide of lead, mortar made of porphyry (purple stone) in which to grind ingredients. **in:** Hg&c *on*. **776 Of ech:** E&c *And ech.* **778 spirites,** gasses; the four kinds of spirits are detailed in ll. 822–24 below. **779 matires,** substances that are left at the bottom of the flask after the gasses have been distilled. **789 kynde,** i.e., can't classify them. **790 boole armonyak,** medicinal earth supposedly from Armenia. **vertgrees,** copper acetate. **boras,** borax. Hg&c *verclegrees.* **792 urynals,** chemical flasks. **descensories,** retorts for distilling. **793 Violes,** vials (glass bottles). **crosletz,** crucibles (porcelain vessels for melting or calcining). **sublymatories,** vessels for vaporizing solids. **794 Cucurbites,** the lower part of a distilling apparatus that holds the original substance. **alambikes,** alembic, the upper part of the apparatus that receives the vapor and drains off the distillate. **795 deere ynough a leek,** usually interpreted as dear enough at the price of a leek. **797 rubifiyng,** turning red by heat and chemical action. **boles galle,** bull's gall (i.e., the bitter liver extract)—the yeoman's list grows haphazard at this point. **798 Arsenyk,** etc., these are three of the four spirits detailed at l. 822. **800 egremoyne,** agrimony. **valerian,** plant of that name. **lunarie,** the fern moonwort. **803** *purpos:* Hg *craft.* **805 albificacioun,** turning white (cf. l. 797 above); "waters" in these lines probably means liquids in a generic sense. **806 Unslekked lym,** unslaked lime (caustic). **chalk,** slaked lime. **gleyre of . . . ey,** egg white. **808 Cered pottes,** waxed pots. **sal peter,** saltpeter. **vitriole,** sulphuric acid. *pottes:* Hg&c *pocketz,* which editors interpret as waxed (waterproof) bags. **810 Sal tartre,** salt of tartar (prepared from cream of tartar). **alkaly,** raw salt (sodium carbonate). **sal preparat,** purified salt (i.e., domestic). **811 combust matires,** burnt (calcined) substance. **coagulat,** congealed. **812** *or:* E&c *and.* **812–13 oille/Of tartre,** cream of tartar (potassium bitartarate). **alum glas,** rock alum. **berme,** yeast. **wort,** malt. **argoille,** tartar deposited as a crust on wine casks. **814 Resalgar,** red arsenic (ratsbane). **matires enbibyng,** materials for moistening or liquefying. *oure:* Hg&c *othere.* **815 matires encorporyng,** materials for precipitating or solidifying. **816 silver citrinacioun,** imparting a yellow color to silver (which made it look like gold). **817 cementyng,** fusing at high temperature. **fermentacioun,** physical and chemical changes produced by heat. E *And of oure.* **818 yngottes,** ingots. **testes,** experiments.

I wol yow telle, as was me taught also,
The foure spirites and the bodies sevene   820
By ordre, as ofte I herde my lord hem
  nevene.
The firste spirit quyksilver called is,
The seconde orpyment, the thridde, ywis,
Sal armonyak, and the ferthe brymstoon.
The bodyes sevene eek, lo, hem heere anoon:
Sol gold is, and Luna silver we threpe,   826
Mars iren, Mercurie quyksilver we clepe,
Saturnus leed, and Juppiter is tyn,
And Venus coper, by my fader kyn.
This cursed craft whoso wole exercise,   830
He shal no good han that hym may suffise,
For al the good he spendeth theraboute
He lese shal, therof have I no doute.
Whoso that listeth outen his folie,
Lat hym come forth and lerne multiplie.   835
And every man that oght hath in his cofre,
Lat hym appiere and wexe a philosophre.
Ascauns that craft is so light to leere—
Nay, nay, God woot, al be he monk or frere,
Preest or chanoun, or any oother wyght,   840
Though he sitte at his book bothe day and
  nyght
In lernyng of this elvysshe nyce loore,
Al is veyn, and parde, muchel moore.
To lerne a lewed man this subtiltee—
Fy, spek nat therof, for it wol nat bee.   845
And konne he letterure or konne he noon,
As in effect he shal fynde it al oon.
For bothe two, by my savacioun,
Concluden in multiplicacioun
Ylike wel, whan they han al ydo—   850
This is to seyn, they faillen bothe two.

Yet forgat I to maken rehersaille
Of watres corosif, and of lymaille,
And of bodies mollificacioun,
And also of hire induracioun,   855
Oilles, ablucions, and metal fusible—
To tellen al wolde passen any bible
That owher is. Wherfore, as for the beste,
Of alle thise names now wol I me reste.
For, as I trowe, I have yow toold ynowe   860
To reyse a feend, al looke he never so rowe.
A, nay, lat be! The philosophres stoon,
Elixer clept, we sechen faste echoon,
For hadde we hym, thanne were we siker
  ynow.
But unto God of hevene I make avow,   865
For al oure craft whan we han al ydo,
With al oure sleighte he wol nat come us to.
He hath ymaad us spenden muchel good
For sorwe of which almoost we wexen wood,
But that good hope crepeth in oure herte   870
Supposynge evere, though we sore smerte,
To be releeved by hym afterward.
Swich supposyng and hope is sharp and hard.
I warne yow wel, it is to seken evere,
That futur temps hath maad men dissevere   875
In trust therof from al that evere they hadde.
Yet of that art they kan nat wexen sadde,
For unto hem it is a bitter sweete—
So semeth it—for nadde they but a sheete
Which that they myghte wrappe hem inne
  a-nyght,   880
And a brat to walken inne by daylyght,
They wolde hem selle and spenden on this craft.
They kan nat stynte til nothyng be laft.
And everemoore where that evere they goon

---

820 spirites, substances that can be vaporized by heat. **bodies,** metals that are reacted upon. **822–24 firste spirit,** the four "spirits" of alchemy were quicksilver (mercury), orpyment (arsenic), sal armonyalc (ammonia), and brymstoon (sulphur). **826–29 Sol,** alchemy and astrology come together in that the seven metals correspond to the seven planets. **threpe,** assert. These four lines have the appearance of a mnemonic jingle. **834 outen,** reveal. **838 Ascauns . . . light . . . leere,** as though, easy, learn. **846 konne he letterure,** knows he book learning. **847 al oon,** all the same. **848 bothe two,** i.e., the literate and the illiterate. **853 watres corosif,** acids. **lymaille,** metal filings. **854 mollificacioun,** being made soft and pliable. **855 induracioun,** being made hard. **856 ablucions,** baths, **fusible,** meltable. **858 owher,** anywhere. **861 reyse a feend,** call up a devil, cf. Marlow's *Dr. Faustus,* III.ii. **rowe,** rough. **862 philosophres stoon,** a talisman by which base metals could be transmuted to gold. **863 Elixer,** another name for the talisman, which was not always thought of as a stone; it could be a liquid or a powder. When brandy was first produced by distillation, some thought the elixir had been discovered. **864 hym,** the pronouns in this and the following lines refer to the talisman. **siker,** secure. **867 sleighte,** trickery (process). **With:** Hg&c *And.* **868** E&c **maad. 869 wood,** crazy. **870 But that,** except that. **871** E *evere* om. **872 releeved,** repaid. **875–76 dissevere . . . from,** separate themselves from. Hg&c *to dissevere.* **877 wexen sadde,** become satisfied. **880** E&c *at nyght.* **881 brat,** coat made of coarse cloth. **882** *this:* E&c *the.* **883 stynte,** stop.

Men may hem knowe by smel of brymstoon. 885
For al the world they stynken as a goot;
Hir savour is so rammyssh and so hoot
That though a man a mile from hem be,
The savour wole infecte hym, trusteth me.
And thus by smell and threedbare array,   890
If that men liste this folk they knowe may.
And if a man wole aske hem pryvely
Why they been clothed so unthriftily,
They right anon wol rownen in his ere
And seyn if that they espied were   895
Men wolde hem slee by cause of hir science.
Lo, thus this folk bitrayen innocence!
    Passe over this; I go my tale unto.
Er that the pot be on the fir ydo,
Of metals with a certeyn quantitee,   900
My lord hem trempeth, and no man but he—
Now he is goon, I dar seyn boldely—
For, as men seyn, he kan doon craftily.
Algate I woot wel he hath swich a name,
And yet ful ofte he renneth in a blame.   905
And wite ye how? Ful ofte it happeth so
The pot tobreketh, and farewel, al is go.
Thise metals been of so greet violence
Oure walles mowe nat make hem resistence,
But if they weren wroght of lym and stoon;   910
They percen so, and thurgh the wal they goon.
And somme of hem synke into the ground—
Thus han we lost by tymes many a pound—
And somme are scatered al the floor aboute;
Somme lepe into the roof. Withouten doute,   915
Though that the feend noght in oure sighte
        hym shewe,
I trowe he with us be, that ilke shrewe!
In helle, where that he lord is and sire,
Nis ther moore wo ne moore rancour ne ire.
Whan that oure pot is broke, as I have sayd, 920
Every man chit and halt hym yvele apayd.

Somme seyde it was long on the fir makyng.
Somme seyde nay, it was on the blowyng—
Thanne was I fered, for that was myn office.
"Straw," quod the thridde, "ye been lewed and
        nyce!   925
It was nat tempred as it oghte be."
"Nay," quod the fourthe, "stynt and herkne
        me.
By cause oure fir ne was nat maad of beech,
That is the cause and oother noon, so theech!"
I kan nat telle wheron it was along,   930
But wel I woot greet strif us is among.
    "What," quod my lord, "ther is namoore to
        doone.
Of thise perils I wol be war eftsoone.
I am right siker that the pot was crased.
Be as be may, be ye nothyng amased;   935
As usage is, lat swepe the floor as swithe.
Plukke up youre hertes and beeth glad and
        blithe."
    The mullok on an heep ysweped was,
And on the floor ycast a canevas,
And al this mullok in a syve ythrowe,   940
And sifted and ypiked many a throwe.
    "Pardee," quod oon, "somwhat of oure
        metal
Yet is ther heere, though that we han nat al.
And though this thyng myshapped have as now,
Another tyme it may be wel ynow.   945
Us moste putte oure good in aventure.
A marchant, pardee, may nat ay endure,
Trusteth me wel, in his prosperitee.
Somtyme his good is drenched in the see,
And somtyme comth it sauf unto the londe."   950
    "Pees," quod my lord, "the nexte tyme I wol
        fonde
To bryngen oure craft al in another plite,
And but I do, sires, lat me han the wite.

885 brymstoon, sulphur. **887 rammyssh . . . hoot**, ramlike, intense. **889** E *truste*. **890** *And/smell*: Hg&c *Lo/smellyng*. **893 unthriftily**, badly. **894 rownen**, whisper. **895** E *that if that*. **896 science**, knowledge. **897 bitrayen**, deceive. **901 trempeth**, blends (mixes). **904 Algate**, even though. **905 renneth . . . blame**, i.e., makes mistakes. **915** E *lepte*. **917 ilke shrewe**, same wretch. **921 chit . . . yvele apayd**, chides (complaining), badly treated. **922 long on . . . makyng**, i.e., on account of how the fire was made. *long*: E&c *along*. **923 blowyng**, i.e., blowing on the charcoal to increase the heat. **925 lewed . . . nyce**, ignorant, foolish. **927 stynt**, stop. **929 theech**, may I prosper. **930 wheron . . . along**, i.e., what it was about. *along*: Hg&c *long*. **933 eftsoone**, after this. **934 siker . . . crased**, sure, cracked. **936 swithe**, promptly. **938 mullok**, refuse. **941 many a throwe**, repeatedly; the litter has bits of gold and silver in it, of course. **944** *And*: E *Al*. **946 Us . . . aventure**, we must risk. **947 ay endure**, always persist. **949** *drenched*: Hg&c *drowned*. **951 wol fonde**, will try. **953 wite**, blame. E&c *sires* om.

Ther was defaute in somwhat, wel I woot."
    Another seyde the fir was over-hoot. 955
But be it hoot or coold, I dar seye this,
That we concluden everemoore amys.
We faille of that which that we wolden have,
And in oure madnesse everemoore we rave.
And whan we been togidres everichoon, 960
Every man semeth a Salomon.
But al thyng which that shyneth as the gold
Nis nat gold, as that I have herd told;
Ne every appul that is fair to eye
Nis nat good, what so men clappe or crye. 965
    Right so, lo, fareth it amonges us;
He that semeth the wiseste, by Jhesus,
Is moost fool whan it cometh to the preef,
And he that semeth trewest is a theef.
That shul ye knowe er that I fro yow wende 970
By that I of my tale have maad an ende.

Explicit prima pars. Et sequitur pars secunda.

    Ther is a chanoun of religioun
Amonges us wolde infecte al a toun,
Thogh it as greet were as was Nynyvee,
Rome, Alisaundre, Troye, and othere three. 975
His sleightes and his infinite falsenesse
Ther koude no man writen, as I gesse,
Though that he lyve myghte a thousand yeer.
In al this world of falshede nis his peer,
For in his termes so he wole hym wynde, 980
And speke his wordes in so sly a kynde,
Whanne he commune shal with any wight,
That he wol make hym doten anon-right,
But it a feend be as hymselven is.
Ful many a man hath he bigiled er this, 985
And wole if that he lyve may a while.
And yet men ride and goon ful many a mile
Hym for to seke and have his aqueyntaunce,
Noght knowynge of his false governaunce.

And if yow list to yeve me audience, 990
I wol it tellen heere in youre presence.
    But worshipful chanons religious,
Ne demeth nat that I sclaundre youre hous,
Although that my tale of a chanoun bee.
Of every ordre som shrewe is, pardee, 995
And God forbede that al a compaignye
Sholde rewe o singuleer mannes folye.
To sclaundre yow is nothyng myn entente,
But to correcten that is mys I mente.
This tale was nat oonly toold for yow, 1000
But eek for othere mo. Ye woot wel how
That among Cristes aposteles twelve
Ther nas no traytour but Judas hymselve.
Thanne why sholde al the remenant have a
    blame
That giltlees were? By yow I seye the same, 1005
Save oonly this, if ye wol herkne me,
If any Judas in youre covent be,
Remoeveth hym bitymes, I yow rede,
If shame or los may causen any drede.
And beeth nothyng displesed, I yow preye, 1010
But in this cas herkeneth what I shal seye.
    In Londoun was a preest, an annueleer,
That therinne had dwelled many a yeer,
Which was so plesaunt and so servysable
Unto the wyf, where as he was at table, 1015
That she wolde suffre hym no thyng for to paye
For bord ne clothyng, wente he never so gaye,
And spendyng silver hadde he right ynow.
Therof no fors; I wol procede as now,
And telle forth my tale of the chanoun 1020
That broghte this preest to confusioun.
    This false chanoun cam upon a day
Unto this preestes chambre, wher he lay,
Bisechynge hym to lene hym a certeyn
Of gold, and he wolde quite it hym ageyn. 1025
"Leene me a marc," quod he, "but dayes three,

---

954 defaute in somwhat, defect in something. **962** *al/shyneth:* E *every/seineth;* other MSS *seemeth.* **964** *to:* Hg&c *at.* **965 clappe,** jabber. **966** E&c *lo* om. **972** *is:* E&c *was.* **979** *falshede:* Hg&c *falsenesse.* **980** Hg&c *he wol hym so wynde.* **981 kynde,** manner. **983 doten,** behave foolishly. **984 But it . . . as hymselven,** i.e., unless he is as fiendlike himself. **992 religious,** regular, cf. 573n. This apostrophe may be simply rhetorical, or may date from a time when Chaucer composed this piece to be read before an audience like the canons of King's Chapel at Windsor. **993** *sclaundre:* E *desclaundre.* **997 rewe,** suffer for. **1004** EHg&c *al* om. **1008 bitymes . . . rede,** promptly advise. **1012 annueleer,** a priest employed to sing daily masses in the chantry chapels of city churches, called "annuals" because they were endowed anniversary memorial services. E&c *an* omitted by haplology. **1014 servysable,** helpful. **1015 wyf . . . table,** woman with whom he boarded. **1019 no fors,** no matter. **1024 lene,** lend. **1025 quite,** repay (requite).

And at my day I wol it quiten thee.
And if so be that thow me fynde fals,
Another day do hange me by the hals."
    This preest hym took a marc, and that as
      swithe, 1030
And this chanoun hym thanked ofte sithe,
And took his leve, and wente forth his weye,
And at the thridde day broghte his moneye,
And to the preest he took his gold agayn 1034
Wherof this preest was wonder glad and fayn.
    "Certes," quod he, "nothyng anoyeth me
To lene a man a noble, or two, or thre,
Or what thyng were in my possessioun,
Whan he so trewe is of condicioun
That in no wise he breke wole his day. 1040
To swich a man I kan never seye nay."
    "What," quod this chanoun, "sholde I be
      untrewe?
Nay, that were thyng yfallen al of newe.
Trouthe is a thyng that I wol evere kepe
Unto that day in which that I shal crepe 1045
Into my grave, and ellis God forbede.
Bileveth this as siker as your Crede.
God thanke I, and in good tyme be it sayd
That ther was nevere man yet yvele apayd
For gold ne silver that he to me lente, 1050
Ne nevere falshede in myn herte I mente.
And sire," quod he, "now of my pryvetee,
Syn ye so goodlich han been unto me,
And kithed to me so greet gentillesse,
Somwhat to quyte with youre kyndenesse 1055
I wol yow shewe, if that yow list to leere,
I wol yow teche pleynly the manere
How I kan werken in philosophie.
Taketh good heede, ye shul wel seen at eye,
That I wol doon a maistrie er I go." 1060
    "Ye," quod the preest, "ye, sire, and wol
      ye so?
Marie, therof I pray yow hertely."
    "At youre comandement, sire, trewely,"
Quod the chanoun, "and ellis God forbeede."

    Loo, how this theef koude his service beede!
Ful sooth it is that swich profred servyse 1066
Stynketh, as witnessen thise olde wyse,
And that ful soone I wol it verifie
In this chanoun, roote of al trecherie, 1069
That everemoore delit hath and gladnesse—
Swiche feendly thoghtes in his herte impresse—
How Cristes peple he may to meschief brynge.
God kepe us from his false dissymulynge!
    Noght wiste this preest with whom that he
      delte,
Ne of his harm comynge he nothyng felte. 1075
O sely preest, O sely innocent!
With coveitise anon thou shalt be blent!
O gracelees, ful blynd is thy conceite.
Nothyng ne artow war of the deceite
Which that this fox yshapen hath to thee. 1080
His wily wrenches thou ne mayst nat flee.
Wherfore to go to the conclusioun
That refereth to thy confusioun,
Unhappy man, anon I wol me hye,
To tellen thyn unwit and thy folye, 1085
And eek the falsnesse of that oother wrecche
As ferforth as my konnyng may strecche.
    This chanoun was my lord ye wolden weene?
Sire hoost, in feith, and by the hevenes queene,
It was another chanoun and nat hee, 1090
That kan an hundred foold moore subtiltee.
He hath bitrayed folkes many tyme.
Of his falsnesse it dulleth me to ryme.
Evere whan that I speke of his falshede,
For shame of hym my chekes wexen rede—
Algates they bigynnen for to glowe, 1096
For reednesse have I noon right wel I knowe
In my visage; for fumes diverse
Of metals, which ye han herde me reherce,
Consumed and wasted han my reednesse. 1100
Now taak heed of this chanons cursednesse.
    "Sire," quod he to the preest, "lat youre man
      gon
For quyksilver, that we hadde it anon;

1029 **hals**, neck. 1030 **took . . . swithe**, gave, quickly. 1035 **fayn**, happy. 1040 **breke . . . day**, i.e., breaks his agreement. 1043 E&c *a thing*. 1045 *Unto*: E&c *Into*. 1047 **siker**, certain. *your*: E&c *the*. 1052 **pryvetee**, confidence. 1054 **kithed**, shown. 1055 **quyte**, repay. 1056 **leere**, learn. 1058 **philosophie**, i.e., alchemy. 1060 **maistrie**, a demonstration of skill. 1061 E *sire, quod he*. 1065 **beede**, volunteer. 1066 "Proffered service stinketh" is proverbial. 1076 **sely**, foolish (silly). 1077 **blent**, blinded. 1080 **yshapen**, planned. *to*: E *for*. 1081 **wrenches**, devices. 1085 *thy*: E *his*. 1087 **ferforth**, far. *may*: Hg&c *wol*. 1088 **weene**, think. 1093 **dulleth**, depresses. *falsnesse*: E *falshede*. 1096 **Algates**, in any event. 1102 **man**, servant.

And lat hym bryngen ounces two or three;
And whan he comth, as faste shal ye see 1105
A wonder thyng, which ye saugh nevere er
    this."
    "Sire," quod the preest, "it shal be doon,
    ywis."
He bad his servant fecchen hym this thyng;
And he al redy was at his biddyng
And wente hym forth and cam anon agayn 1110
With this quyksilver, shortly for to sayn,
And took thise ounces thre to the chanoun.
And he hem leyde faire and wel adoun,
And bad the servant coles for to brynge
That he anon myghte go to his werkynge. 1115
    The coles right anon weren yfet,
And this chanoun took out a crosselet
Of his bosom and shewed it to the preest.
"This instrument," quod he, "which that thou
    seest,
Taak in thyn hand and put thyself therinne 1120
Of this quyksilver an ounce, and heer bigynne,
In name of Crist, to wexe a philosofre.
Ther been ful fewe to whiche I wolde profre
To shewen hem thus muche of my science.
For ye shul seen heer, by experience, 1125
That this quyksilver I wol mortifye
Right in youre sighte anon, withouten lye,
And make it as good silver and as fyn
As ther is any in youre purs or myn,
Or elleswhere, and make it malliable, 1130
And elles holdeth me fals and unable
Amonges folk forevere to appeere.
I have a poudre heer that coste me deere
Shal make al good, for it is cause of al 1134
My konnyng, which that I to yow shewen shal.
Voyde youre man and lat hym be theroute,
And shette the dore whils we been aboute
Oure pryvetee, that no man us espie
Whils that we werke in this philosophie."
    Al as he bad fulfilled was in dede. 1140
This ilke servant anonright out yede,

And his maister shette the dore anon,
And to hire labour spedily they gon.
    This preest at this cursed chanons biddyng
Upon the fir anon sette this thyng, 1145
And blewe the fir, and bisyed hym ful faste.
And this chanoun into the crosselet caste
A poudre, noot I wherof that it was
Ymaad, outher of chalk, or of glas,
Or somwhat elles, was nat worth a flye, 1150
To blynde with this preest, and bad hym hye
The coles for to couchen al above
The crosselet. "For in tokenyng I thee love,"
Quod this chanoun, "thyne owene handes two
Shul werche al thyng which shal heer be
    do." 1155
    "Graunt mercy," quod the preest and was
    ful glad,
And couched coles as that the chanoun bad.
And while he bisy was, this feendly wrecche,
This false chanoun—the foule feend hym
    fecche—
Out of his bosom took a bechen cole 1160
In which ful subtilly was maad an hole,
And therinne put was of silver lemaille
An ounce, and stopped was withouten faille,
This hole with wex, to kepe the lemaille in.
And understondeth that this false gyn 1165
Was nat maad ther, but it was maad bifore;
And othere thynges I shal tellen moore
Herafterward, whiche that he with hym
    broghte.
Er he cam there, hym to bigile he thoghte.
And so he dide, er that they wente atwynne;
Til he had terved hym, he koude nat blynne.
It dulleth me whan that I of hym speke. 1172
On his falshede fayn wolde I me wreke
If I wiste how, but he is heere and there;
He is so variaunt, he abit nowhere. 1175
    But taketh heede now, sires, for Goddes
    love.
He took this cole of which I spak above,

1111 *shortly*: E *soothly*. 1117 **crosselet**, crucible. 1122 **philosofre**, alchemist. 1126 **mortifye**, transform (i.e., "kill" from quicksilver—quick (live) silver—to silver. 1127 *withouten*: E *I wol nat*. 1128 E *it* om. 1136 **Voyde**, i.e., send him out. 1138 **pryvetee**, secret business. 1141 **yede**, went. 1149 *or*: Hg&c *outher*. 1152 **couchen**, pile (couch). 1157 E *cole as that Chanoun*. 1160 **bechen cole**, piece of charcoal made of beechwood. E *he took*. 1162 **silver lemaille**, silver filings. 1165 **gyn**, contrivance. 1171 **terved ... blynne**, skinned, stop. 1172 **dulleth**, depresses. 1173 **fayn ... wreke**, happily, take revenge. 1175 **variaunt ... abit**, shifty, stays. E *that he abit*. 1177 *this*: Hg&c *his*.

And in his hand he baar it pryvely.
And whiles the preest couched bisily
The coles, as I tolde yow er this,   1180
This chanoun seyde, "Freend, ye doon amys.
This is nat couched as it oghte be.
But soone I shal amenden it," quod he.
"Now lat me medle therwith but a while,
For of yow have I pitee, by Seint Gile.   1185
Ye been right hoot; I se wel how ye swete.
Have heere a clooth, and wipe awey the wete."
And whiles that the preest wiped his face,
This chanoun took his cole—with sory grace—
And leyde it above upon the myddeward   1190
Of the crosselet, and blew wel afterward,
Til that the coles gonne faste brenne.
      "Now yeve us drynke," quod the chanoun
            thenne.
"As swithe al shal be wel, I undertake.
Sitte we doun and lat us myrie make."   1195
And whan that this chanounes bechen cole
Was brent, al the lemaille out of the hole
Into the crosselet fil anon adoun—
And so it moste nedes, by resoun,
Syn it so evene aboven it couched was.   1200
But therof wiste the preest nothyng, alas.
He demed alle the coles yliche good,
For of that sleighte he nothyng understood.
And whan this alkamystre saugh his tyme,
"Ris up," quod he, "sire preest, and stondeth
            by me;   1205
And for I woot wel ingot have ye noon,
Gooth, walketh forth, and bryng us a chalk
            stoon.
For I wol make it of the same shap
That is an ingot, if I may han hap.
And bryngeth eek with yow a bolle or a panne
Ful of water, and ye shul se wel thanne   1211
How that oure bisynesse shal thryve and preeve.
And yet, for ye shul han no mysbileeve
Ne wrong conceite of me in youre absence,
I ne wol nat been out of youre presence,   1215

But go with yow and come with yow ageyn."
The chambre dore, shortly for to seyn,
They opened and shette and wente hir weye.
And forth with hem they carieden the keye
And coome agayn withouten any delay.   1220
What sholde I tarien al the longe day?
He took the chalk and shoop it in the wise
Of an ingot as I shal yow devyse.
     I seye, he took out of his owene sleeve
A teyne of silver—yvcle moot he cheeve—   1225
Which that ne was nat but an ounce of weighte.
And taaketh heede now of his cursed sleighte.
     He shoop his ingot in lengthe and in breede
Of this teyne, withouten any drede,
So slyly that the preest it nat espide,   1230
And in his sleve agayn he gan it hide,
And fro the fir he took up his mateere,
And in th'yngot putte it with myrie cheere,
And in the water-vessel he it caste
Whan that hym luste, and bad the preest as
            faste,   1235
"Loke what ther is; put in thyn hand and grope.
Thow fynde shalt ther silver, as I hope."
What, devel of helle, sholde it elles be?
Shaving of silver silver is, pardee!
He putte his hand in and took up a teyne   1240
Of silver fyn, and glad in every veyne
Was this preest whan he saugh that it was so.
"Goddes blessyng, and his moodres also,
And alle halwes, have ye, sire chanoun,"
Seyde the preest, "and I hir malisoun,   1245
But, and ye vouchesauf to techen me
This noble craft and this subtilitee,
I wol be youre in al that evere I may."
     Quod the chanoun, "Yet wol I make assay
The seconde tyme that ye may taken heede   1250
And been expert of this, and in youre neede
Another day assaye in myn absence
This disciplyne and this crafty science.
Lat take another ounce," quod he tho,
"Of quyksilver, withouten wordes mo,   1255

1189 sory grace, bad luck (grace) to him. **1194 swithe,** soon. **1200 evene,** directly. Hg&c *it* om. **1203 sleighte,** trick. **1204 alkamystre,** alchemist (Arabic *al,* the). **1205** *stondeth:* E&c *sit/syttyth.* **1206 ingot,** mold. **1207 chalk stoon,** a soft chunk of chalk, or else powdered lime to be molded. **1208** *it of:* E *oon of.* **1209 hap,** success. **1212 preeve,** prove. **1225 teyne ... cheeve,** small piece, fare. **1226** E *ne* om; other MSS *ne/nat* both om. **1228** E *and eek in.* **1232 mateere,** molton substance. **1235 luste,** desired. **1236** E&c *What that heer is.* **1238–39** Lines omitted in E&c. **1245 hir malisoun,** their curse. *the:* E&c *this.* **1249** *chanoun:* E *preest.*

And do therwith as ye han doon er this
With that oother, which that now silver is.''

This preest hym bisieth in al that he kan
To doon as this chanoun, this cursed man,
Comanded hym, and faste he blew the fir   1260
For to come to th'effect of his desir.
And this chanoun right in the meene while
Al redy was the preest eft to bigile,
And for a contenaunce in his hand he bar
An holwe stikke—taak kepe and bewar—   1265
In the ende of which an ounce, and namoore,
Of silver lemaille put was, as bifore
Was in his cole, and stopped with wex weel
For to kepe in his lemaille every deel.
And whil this preest was in his bisynesse,   1270
This chanoun with his stikke gan hym dresse
To hym anon, and his poudre caste in
As he dide er—the devel out of his skyn
Hym terve, I pray to God, for his falshede!
For he was evere fals in thoght and dede—   1275
And with this stikke, above the crosselet,
That was ordeyned with that false jet,
He stired the coles til relente gan
The wex agayn the fir, as every man
But it a fool be woot wel it moot nede,   1280
And al that in the stikke was out yede,
And in the crosselet hastily it fel.

Now, goode sires, what wol ye bet than wel?
Whan that this preest thus was bigiled ageyn,
Supposynge noght but treuthe, sooth to seyn,
He was so glad that I ne kan nat expresse   1286
In no manere his myrthe and his gladnesse;
And to the chanoun he profred eftsoone
Body and good. ''Ye,'' quod the chanoun soone,
''Though poure I be, crafty thou shalt me fynde.
I warne thee, yet is ther moore bihynde.   1291
Is ther any coper herinne?'' seyde he.

''Ye,'' quod the preest, ''sire, I trowe wel ther
be.''

''Elles go bye us som, and that as swithe.
Now, good sire, go forth thy wey and hy
the.''   1295

He wente his wey, and with the coper cam,
And this chanon it in his handes nam,
And of that coper weyed out but an ounce.

Al to symple is my tonge to pronounce
As ministre of my wit the doublenesse   1300
Of this chanoun, roote of alle cursednesse.
He semed freendly to hem that knewe hym
noght,
But he was feendly bothe in werk and thoght.
It weerieth me to telle of his falsnesse,
And nathelees yet wol I it expresse,   1305
To th'entente that men may bewar therby,
And for noon oother cause, trewely.

He putte the ounce of coper in the crosselet,
And on the fir as swithe he hath it set,
And caste in poudre, and made the preest to
blowe,   1310
And in his werkyng for to stoupe lowe
As he dide er—and al nas but a jape.
Right as hym liste, the preest he made his ape.
And afterward in the ingot he it caste,
And in the panne putte it at the laste   1315
Of water, and in he putte his owene hand,
And in his sleve (as ye biforen-hand
Herde me telle) he hadde a silver teyne.
He slyly took it out, this cursed heyne,
Unwityng this preest of his false craft,   1320
And in the pannes botme he hath it laft;
And in the water rombled to and fro,
And wonder pryvely took up also
The coper teyne, noght knowynge this preest,
And hidde it, and hym hente by the breest,
And to hym spak, and thus seyde in his game:
''Stoupeth adoun, by God, ye be to blame! 1327
Helpeth me now, as I dide yow whileer;
Putte in youre hand, and looketh what is theer.''

This preest took up this silver teyne anon,   1330
And thanne seyde the chanoun, ''Lat us gon
With thise thre teynes whiche that we han
wroght
To som goldsmyth, and wite if they been oght.
For by my feith I nolde, for myn hood,

1260 Hg&c *he* om. 1263 **eft,** again. 1264 **contenaunce,** appearance. 1268 E&c *Was* om. 1271 **dresse,** address (talk to). 1274 **terve,** flay (vb. skin). 1277 **ordeyned . . . jet,** prepared, device. 1278 **relente,** melt. 1281 **yede,** went (poured). 1286 Hg&c *ne* om. 1288 **eftsoone,** at once. 1295 **hy the,** hurry. 1297 **nam,** took. 1300 **ministre,** servant. 1303 *werk:* E&c *herte.* 1309 **swithe,** quickly. 1316 E *Of the water in he.* 1318 E&c *he* om. 1319 **heyne,** wretch. 1333 **oght,** (worth) anything. 1334 **nolde, for myn hood,** bet by my head.

But if that they were silver fyn and good,   1335
And that as swithe preeved it shal bee."
 Unto the goldsmyth with thise teynes three
They wente, and putte thise teynes in assay
To fir and hamer. Myghte no man seye nay
But that they weren as hem oghte be.   1340
 This sotted preest, who was gladder than he?
Was nevere brid gladder agayn the day,
Ne nyghtyngale in the sesoun of May.
Nas nevere man that luste bet to synge,
Ne lady lustier in carolynge.   1345
Or for to speke of love and wommanhede,
Ne knyght in armes to doon an hardy dede,
To stonden in grace of his lady deere,
Than hadde this preest this soory craft to leere,
And to the chanoun thus he spak and seyde,   1350
"For love of God, that for us alle deyde,
And as I may deserve it unto yow,
What shal this receite coste? Telleth now!"
 "By oure Lady," quod this chanon, "it is
  deere,
I warne yow wel; for save I and a frere,   1355
In Engelond ther kan no man it make."
 "No fors," quod he, "now, sire, for Goddes
  sake,
What shal I paye? Telleth me, I preye."
 "Ywis," quod he, "it is ful deere, I seye.
Sire, at o word, if that thee list it have,   1360
Ye shul paye fourty pound, so God me save.
And nere the freendshipe that ye dide er this
To me, ye sholde paye moore, ywis."
 This preest the somme of fourty pound anon
Of nobles fette, and took hem everichon   1365
To this chanoun for this ilke receit.
Al his werkyng nas but fraude and deceit.
 "Sire preest," he seyde, "I kepe han no loos
Of my craft, for I wolde it kept were cloos;
And as ye love me kepeth it secree.   1370

For and men knewen al my soutiltee,
By God they wolden han so greet envye
To me by cause of my philosophye
I sholde be deed—ther were noon oother
  weye."
 "God it forbeede," quod the preest, "what
  sey ye?   1375
Yet hadde I levere spenden al the good
Which that I have, or elles wexe I wood,
Than that ye sholden falle in swich mescheef."
 "For youre good wyl, sire, have ye right
  good preef,"   1379
Quod the chanoun, "and farwel, grant mercy."
He wente his wey, and never the preest hym sy
After that day. And whan that this preest
  shoolde
Maken assay at swich tyme as he wolde
Of this receit, farwel, it wolde nat be.
Lo, thus byjaped and bigiled was he.   1385
Thus maketh he his introduccioun
To brynge folk to hir destruccioun.
 Considereth, sires, how that in ech estaat
Bitwixe men and gold ther is debaat
So ferforth that unnethe is ther noon.   1390
This multiplying blent so many oon
That in good feith I trowe that it bee
The cause grettest of swich scarsetee.
Philosophres speken so mystily
In this craft that men kan nat come therby.   1395
For any wit that men han now-a-dayes
They mowe wel chiteren as doon thise jayes,
And in hir termes sette hir lust and peyne,
But to hir purpos shul they nevere atteyne.
A man may lightly lerne, if he have aught,   1400
To multiplie and brynge his good to naught!
 Lo, swich a lucre is in this lusty game.
A mannes myrthe it wol turne unto grame,
And empten also grete and hevye purses,

1336 **swithe preeved,** quickly proved. 1338 **assay,** test of the purity of precious metal. 1340 *be:* Hg&c *to be.* 1341 **sotted,** besotted (hypnotized). 1342 **agayn,** i.e., at the coming of. 1344 *Nas/man:* Hg&c *Was/noon.* 1349 **leere,** learn. 1352 **unto,** from. 1353 **receite,** recipe (formula). 1361 **fourty pound,** one pound was the equivalent of perhaps $200 today. 1365 **nobles,** gold coins. 1368 **kepe . . . loos,** care to have no fame. 1369 **cloos,** secret. Hg&c *it were kept.* 1371 **and . . . soutiltee,** if, cleverness. 1387 E&c *hir* om. 1389 **debaat,** strife, i.e., over gold. 1390 **forferth . . . unnethe,** so extreme, that scarcely is there any (left). 1391 **multiplying,** alchemical promise to increase the supply of gold. **blent,** blinds. 1392 **trowe,** believe. 1394 **Philosophres,** alchemists. 1395 **In . . . come therby,** about, catch on. 1397 **mowe wel chiteren,** might as well chatter. E&c *as that doon jayes;* E *joyes.* 1398 **in hir termes,** i.e., get their pleasures and pains from their jargon. 1400 **lightly,** easily. 1402 **lucre,** profit (money). 1403 **grame,** grief.

And maken folk for to purchacen curses 1405
Of hem that han hir good therto ylent.
O, fy, for shame, they that han been brent,
Allas, kan they nat flee the fires heete?
Ye that it use, I rede ye it leete
Lest ye lese al, for bet than nevere is late. 1410
Nevere to thryve were to long a date.
Though ye prolle ay, ye shul it nevere fynde.
Ye been as boold as is Bayard the blynde
That blondreth forth and peril casteth noon.
He is as boold to renne agayn a stoon 1415
As for to goon bisides in the weye.
So faren ye that multiplie, I seye.
If that youre eyen kan nat seen aright,
Looke that youre mynde lakke noght his sight.
For though ye looken never so brode and stare,
Ye shul nothyng wynne on that chaffare, 1421
But wasten al that ye may rape and renne.
Withdraweth the fir lest it to faste brenne;
Medleth namoore with that art, I mene, 1424
For if ye doon, youre thrift is goon ful clene.
And right as swithe I wol yow tellen heere
What philosophres seyn in this mateere.
  Lo, thus seith Arnold of the Newe Toun,
As his *Rosarie* maketh mencioun;
He seith right thus, withouten any lye: 1430
"Ther may no man mercurie mortifie
But it be with his brother knowlechyng."
How be that he which that first seyde this thyng
Of philosophres fader was, Hermes.
He seith how that the dragon, doutelees, 1435
Ne dyeth nat but if that he be slayn

With his brother; and that is for to sayn,
By the dragon, Mercurie, and noon oother
He understood, and brymstoon by his brother,
That out of Sol and Luna were ydrawe. 1440
"And therfore," seyde he—taak heede to my
    sawe—
"Lat no man bisye hym this art for to seche
But if that he th'entencioun and speche
Of philosophres understonde kan.
And if he do, he is a lewed man. 1445
For this science and this konnyng," quod he,
"Is of the secree of secretes, pardee."
  Also ther was a disciple of Plato
That on a tyme seyde his maister to,
As his book *Senior* wol bere witnesse, 1450
And this was his demande in soothfastnesse,
"Telle me the name of the privee stoon?"
  And Plato answerde unto hym anoon,
"Take the stoon that Titanos men name."
  "Which is that?" quod he. "Magnasia is the
    same," 1455
Seyde Plato. "Ye sire, and is it thus?
This is *ignotum per ignocius*.
What is Magnasia, good sire, I yow preye?"
  "It is a water that is maad, I seye,
Of elementes foure," quod Plato. 1460
  "Telle me the roote, good sire," quod he tho,
"Of that water, if it be youre wille."
  "Nay, nay," quod Plato, "certein, that I nylle.
The philosophres sworn were everychoon
That they sholden discovere it unto noon, 1465
Ne in no book it write in no manere.

1407 E&c *O* om. 1409 use . . . rede . . . leete, practice, advise, leave. 1412 prolle ay, prowl forever. 1413 Bayard the blynde, proverbial; the horse was brave because he could not see the danger. 1414 casteth, notices. 1415 agayn, into. 1416 bisides, aside from an obstacle in the road. 1420 brode, wide-eyed. 1421 chaffare, exchange. 1422 rape and renne, seize and clutch, a folk idiom. 1425 thrift, prosperity. 1427 philosophres, alchemists. EHg&c *What that the.* 1428 Arnold of the Newe Toun, Arnaldus de Villanova, 13th century French physician and alchemist. 1429 *Rosarie,* Arnaldus wrote the *Rosarium Philosophorum,* but ll. 1428–47 echo his *De Lapide Philosophorum,* not the *Rosarium.* 1431 mercurie mortifie, convert mercury; but in this passage the metals are again identified with the planets. 1432 brother knowlechyng, help of his brother (sulphur). 1433 No MS includes the essential *be.* 1434 Hermes, Hermes Trismegistus, identified with the Egyptian god Toth, reputed to be the founder of alchemy. His name is preserved in the adjective "hermetic." E *fader first.* 1435–40 This is the typical figurative language that gave the sense of "sealed off" or "occult" to the hermetic science of alchemy: The dragon (mercury) may not be slain (mortified, transmuted) except by his brother (brymstoon, sulphur), that (i.e., the mercury) is extracted from sol (gold) and luna (silver). 1441 sawe, saying. 1445 lewed, rash (misguided). 1447 secree of secretes, this is the title (*Secreta Secretorum*) of the popular pseudo-Aristotelian advice to Alexander about how to be a good king, but here it evidently means simply "most secret of secrets." 1450 *Senior,* an alchemical treatise *Senioris Zadith fil. Hamuelis Tabula Chemica,* which includes this anecdote of Solomon, attributed to Plato because the name of Plato occurs shortly afterward. 1452 privee, secret (i.e., the philosopher's stone that transmutes base metal to gold). 1454 Titanos, Thitarios in *Senior.* 1457 *ignotum per ignocius,* explaining the unknown by the unknown. 1461 roote, essential nature.

For unto Crist it is so lief and deere
That he wol nat that it discovered bee
But where it liketh to his deitee
Men for t'enspire, and eek for to deffende   1470
Whom that hym liketh—lo, this is the
      ende."
   Thanne conclude I thus, sith that God of
      hevene
Ne wil nat that the philosophres nevene

How that a man shal come unto this stoon,
I rede, as for the beste, lete it goon.   1475
For whoso maketh God his adversarie,
As for to werken anythyng in contrarie
Of his wil, certes never shal he thryve,
Thogh that he multiplie terme of his lyve.
And there a poynt, for ended is my tale.   1480
God sende every trewe man boote of his bale.
                                    Amen.

Heere is ended the Chanouns Yemannes Tale.

1469 it liketh, it is pleasing. **1470 deffende,** forbid (it to). **1473 nevene,** reveal (name). **1475 rede,** counsel. *as:* E&c *us.* **1479** E&c *his* om. **1480 poynt,** period (full stop). **1481 boote ... bale,** help, suffering.

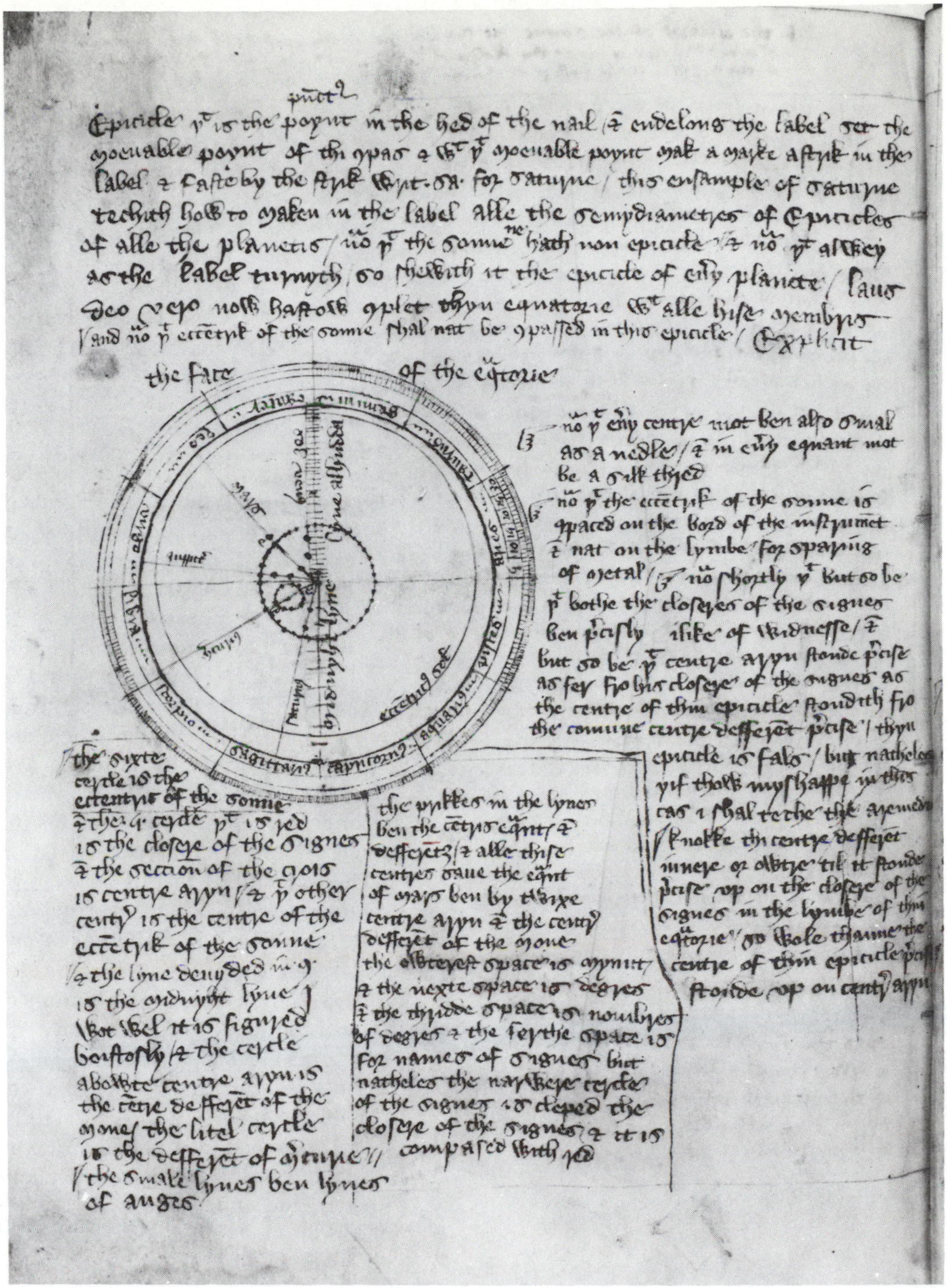

Plate 5. A page from the *Equatorie of the Planets*, MS. Peterhouse 75, fol. 73ᵛ. Cambridge University Library, Cambridge

INTRODUCTION

Canterbury Tales, Part IX

THE CANON AND HIS Yeoman join the pilgrimage at Boughton in the Blean forest, just four miles from Canterbury (VIII.556). The Manciple begins his tale at "Bobbe-up-and-down, / Under the Blee," identified with Harbledown on the edge of the Blean forest, two miles from Canterbury (IX.2). And in the Parson's Prologue, the pilgrims are entering a town, presumably Canterbury (X.12). So the three parts are linked together by indications that the pilgrimage is approaching its destination.

The Manciple's Tale is an exemplum from the *Metamorphoses* by Chaucer's favorite author, Ovid. R.W. Frank in *Chaucer and the Legend of Good Women* (1972) argues that the Ovidian tales in the *Legend* were Chaucer's training ground for the technique of brief narrative that distinguishes his Canterbury period. *Troylus* and the Knight's Tale, written earlier, had contributed to his mastering of plot and characterization, but not to his selection of detail and command of pithy expression, which are displayed to best effect in the short stories in the Canterbury collection. The Manciple's Tale may, therefore, date from the period of the *Legend of Good Women*, when Chaucer was experimenting with retelling these Ovidian stories in English verse.

This early date is supported by the parallels with the version of the story found in John Gower's *Confessio Amantis*. Solomon's admonition in the Manciple's Tale, "My sone, keep wel thy tonge" (l.319), is curiously similar to the first line of Genius's admonition to the Lover in the *Confessio Amantis*, "Mi Sone ... hold thi tunge" (III.768-69). The *Confessio*, which dates from 1386-89, has interesting parallels with the frame and occasion of the *Legend* (see that Introduction, p. 618 below). So the Manciple's Tale may be another piece composed earlier and subsequently adapted to the frame of the *Canterbury Tales*.

In this instance, adaptation meant adding a prologue nearly half as long as the tale itself. The style of the prologue is dramatic and colloquial, in contrast to the impersonality of the tale. Like the early links in Part VII, this one is concerned largely with characterization of the Host and offers little interplay with the tale. The dramatic action is built around the quarrel between the Manciple and the Cook. These two are professional associates, like the other quarreling pairs of pilgrims, the Miller and Reeve and Friar and Summoner. But this exchange is not integrated into the fabric and does not result in a pair of retaliatory stories like the others, and it does not seem to cast much light on the tale that follows. Several critics, like Chauncey Wood, "Speech, the Principle of Contraries, and Chaucer's Tales

of the Manciple and the Parson," *Mediaevalia* (1980), have recently argued, however, for an association between the Host's remark that the Manciple's garrulity might get him in trouble with the Cook and his masters (ll.69ff) and the crow's garrulity that got him in trouble in the tale (ll.319ff). And quite aside from the relations between prologue and tale, the comments on fidelity in marriage (ll.148ff) make a connection between this tale and the marriage argument that runs through so much of the Canterbury collection.

In spite of the many acknowledgements of Ovid, no story in the Canterbury collection appears to be adopted directly from Ovid. The Manciple's Tale is the closest, but its sententious commentary appears to be taken from some expanded version like the French *Ovid Moralisé*. Nevertheless, Ovid's influence appears to permeate the entire Canterbury compilation. Richard L. Hoffman, *Ovid and the Canterbury Tales* (1966), traces to the *Metamorphoses* the quarrels and story-telling contests of Chaucer's frame, and John M. Fyler, *Chaucer and Ovid* (1979), finds Chaucer's ironic, debunking tone and world view similar to Ovid's. Hence, in addition to the Manciple's Tale and countless individual allusions, Ovid may have helped to shape the dramatic structure and the satiric voice of the *Canterbury Tales*.

337

Canterbury Tales

PART IX

MANCIPLE'S TALE

PROLOGUE

Heere folweth the Prologe of the Maunciples Tale.

Woot ye nat where ther stant a litel toun
Which that ycleped is Bobbe-up-and-doun,
Under the Blee, in Caunterbury weye?
Ther gan oure Hooste for to jape and pleye,
And seyde, "Sires, what, Dun is in the myre! 5
Is ther no man for preyere ne for hyre
That wole awake oure felawe al bihynde?
A theef myghte hym ful lightly robbe and
    bynde.
See how he nappeth! See how, for cokkes bones,
That he wol falle fro his hors atones! 10
Is that a cook of Londoun, with meschaunce?
Do hym come forth—he knoweth his
    penaunce—
For he shal telle a tale, by my fey,
Although it be nat worth a botel hey.
"Awake, thou Cook," quod he, "God yeve
    thee sorwe! 15
What eyleth thee to slepe by the morwe?
Hastow had fleen al nyght, or artow dronke?

1–104 Lines lacking in several MSS, see Manly II.445 and IV.525. The contrast in style suggests that they were late additions to a tale written earlier; however, note that MancT itself develops themes that appear elsewhere in *CT.* **2 Bobbe-up-and-doun,** identified with Harbledown, two miles from Canterbury, on the edge of Blean Forest. **3 Blee, in Caunterbury weye,** Blean, on the Canterbury road. **4 jape,** joke. **5 Dun . . . myre,** Dun (the horse) is stuck in the mud; i.e., things have come to a standstill. **8 lightly,** easily. **9 cokkes bones,** euphemistic substitute for "God's bones." After NPT, the Host twice uses this oath. **12 Do hym,** have him. **14 botel hey,** bundle of hay. **16 morwe,** morning. **17 fleen,** fleas.

Or hastow with som quene al nyght yswonke,
So that thow mayst nat holden up thyn heed?"
　This Cook, that was ful pale and nothyng
　　reed,　20
Seyde to oure Hoost, "So God my soule blesse,
As ther is falle on me swich hevynesse—
Noot I nat why—that me were levere slepe
Than the best galon wyn in Chepe."
　"Wel," quod the Maunciple, "if it may doon
　　ese　25
To thee, sire Cook, and to no wight displese,
Which that heere rideth in this compaignye,
And that oure Hoost wole of his curteisye,
I wol as now excuse thee of thy tale.
For in good feith thy visage is ful pale,　30
Thyne eyen daswen eek, as that me thynketh,
And wel I woot thy breeth ful soure stynketh—
That sheweth wel thou art nat wel disposed.
Of me, certeyn, thou shalt nat been yglosed.
See how he ganeth, lo, this dronken wight,　35
As though he wolde swolwe us anonright.
Hoold cloos thy mouth, man, by thy fader kyn!
The devel of helle sette his foot therin!
Thy cursed breeth infecte wole us alle.
Fy, stynkyng swyn, fy, foule moote thee falle!
A, taketh heede, sires, of this lusty man.　41
Now, sweete sire, wol ye justen atte fan?
Therto me thynketh ye been wel yshape!
I trowe that ye dronken han wyn ape,
And that is whan men pleyen with a straw."　45
And with this speche the Cook wax wrooth and
　wraw,
And on the Manciple he gan nodde faste
For lakke of speche, and doun the hors hym
　caste,

Where as he lay til that men up hym took.
This was a fair chyvachee of a cook!　50
Allas, he nadde holde hym by his ladel!
And er that he agayn were in his sadel,
Ther was greet showvyng bothe to and fro
To lifte hym up, and muchel care and wo,
So unweeldy was this sory palled goost.　55
And to the Manciple thanne spak oure
　Hoost:
　"By cause drynke hath dominacioun
Upon this man, by my savacioun,
I trowe lewedly he wolde telle his tale.
For were it wyn or oold or moysty ale　60
That he hath dronke, he speketh in his nose,
And fneseth faste, and eek he hath the pose.
He hath also to do moore than ynough
To kepen hym and his capul out of the
　slough.
And if he falle from his capul eftsoone,　65
Thanne shal we alle have ynogh to doone
In liftyng up his hevy dronken cors.
Telle on thy tale; of hym make I no fors.
　"But yet, Manciple, in feith thou art to nyce,
Thus openly repreve hym of his vice.　70
Another day he wole, peraventure,
Reclayme thee and brynge thee to lure—
I meene, he speke wole of smale thynges,
As for to pynchen at thy rekenynges
That were nat honeste, if it cam to preef."　75
　"No," quod the Manciple, "that were a greet
　mescheef!
So myghte he lightly brynge me in the snare.
Yet hadde I levere payen for the mare
Which he rit on than he sholde with me stryve.
I wol nat wratthen hym, also moot I thryve!　80

---

18 quene . . . yswonke, quean (prostitute), labored. **23 levere,** rather. **24 Than the best . . . Chepe,** i.e., than have the best, Cheapside (the chief market street of London). **31 daswen,** are dazed. **34 yglosed,** flattered. **35 ganeth,** yawns. **40 falle,** befalle. *thee:* E&c *thou* (nom.). **42 justen atte fan,** tilt at a quintain: a pivoted board with a club or bag of sand attached to the back end. The contestant tried to hit the front end (the fan) and agilely get out of the way to avoid being struck by the back end. **43 Therto . . . yshape,** For that, in good shape. **44 wyn ape,** the four traditional stages of drunkenness were sheep-drunk (sheepish), lion-drunk (belligerent), ape-drunk (playful), and hog-drunk (stupefied). The Manciple's remark is sarcastic, because the Cook is obviously beyond wine ape into wine hog. **46 wraw,** angry. *this:* Hg&c *his.* **47** Hg&c *bygan he nodde.* **50 chyvachee,** exhibition of horsemanship. **51 holde . . . ladel,** i.e., stuck to his cooking ladle. **55 palled,** pallid (pale). **59 lewedly,** ignorantly, crudely. Hg&c *he lewedly telle wolde;* other MSS *he lewedly wolde telle.* **60 moysty,** new. **62 fneseth . . . pose,** snorts (an onomatopoeia), head cold. **64 capul . . . slough,** (cart)horse, mud. **65 eftsoone,** again. **69 nyce,** foolish. **72 Reclayme . . . lure,** the language of falconry, i.e., get you back, get back at you. **74 pynchen . . . rekenynges,** object, accounts. As business agent for an institution, the Manciple purchased from the Cook and submitted his accounts for reimbursement to his superiors at the Inn (I.567–74). Obviously, he made money in the transaction. **75 preef,** proof. **77 lightly,** easily. **78 levere,** rather. **79 stryve,** quarrel. E&c *which that.* **80 thryve,** prosper.

That that I spak, I seyde it in my bourde.
And wite ye what? I have heer in a gourde
A draghte of wyn, ye, of a ripe grape,
And right anon ye shul seen a good jape.
This Cook shal drynke therof, if I that may. 85
Up peyne of deeth, he wol nat seye me nay."
    And certeynly, to tellen as it was,
Of this vessel the Cook drank faste, allas.
What neded hym? He drank ynough biforn.
And whan he hadde pouped in this horn 90
To the Manciple he took the gourde agayn.
And of that drynke the Cook was wonder fayn,
And thanked hym in swich wise as he koude.

Thanne gan oure Hoost to laughen wonder loude,
And seyde, "I se wel it is necessarie, 95
Where that we goon, good drynke we with us carie.
For that wol turne rancour and disese
T'acord and love, and many a wrong apese.
    O Bacus, yblessed be thy name,
That so kanst turnen ernest into game! 100
Worship and thank be to thy deitee!
Of that mateere ye gete namoore of me.
Telle on thy tale, Manciple, I thee preye."
    "Wel, sire," quod he, "now herkneth what I seye."

Heere bigynneth the Maunciples Tale of the Crowe.

Whan Phebus dwelled heere in this erthe adoun, 105
As olde bookes maken mencioun,
He was the mooste lusty bachiler
In al this world, and eek the beste archer.
He slow Phitoun the serpent as he lay
Slepynge agayn the sonne upon a day, 110
And many another noble worthy dede
He with his bowe wroghte, as men may rede.
    Pleyen he koude on every mynstralcie,
And syngen that it was a melodie
To heeren of his cleere voys the soun. 115
Certes the kyng of Thebes Amphioun,
That with his syngyng walled that citee,
Koude nevere syngen half so wel as hee.
Therto he was the semelieste man
That is or was sith that the world bigan. 120
What nedeth it his fetures to discryve?
For in this world was noon so fair on-lyve.
He was therwith fulfild of gentillesse,
Of honour, and of parfit worthynesse.
    This Phebus that was flour of bachilrie, 125

As wel in fredom as in chivalrie,
For his desport in signe eek of victorie
Of Phitoun, so as telleth us the storie,
Was wont to beren in his hand a bowe. 129
    Now hadde this Phebus in his hous a crowe
Which in a cage he fostred many a day,
And taughte it speke as men teche a jay.
Whit was this crowe as is a snowwhit swan,
And countrefete the speche of every man
He koude whan he sholde telle a tale. 135
Therwith in al this world no nyghtyngale
Ne koude, by an hondred thousand deel,
Syngen so wonder myrily and weel.
    Now hadde this Phebus in his hous a wyf
Which that he lovede moore than his lyf, 140
And nyght and day dide evere his diligence
Hir for to plese, and doon hire reverence—
Save oonly, if I the sothe shal sayn,
Jalous he was and wolde have kept hire fayn.
For hym were looth byjaped for to be, 145
And so is every wight in swich degree.
But al in ydel, for it availleth noght.

---

81 bourde, humor. *E&c speke.* **84 jape,** joke. **89** *hym:* Hg&c *it.* **90 pouped,** lit. blown; the *double entendre* for the drunken Cook is not pleasant to contemplate. **96** *good:* E *that. we with:* other MSS *we* om. **97 disese,** discomfort. **105** *erthe:* E&c *worlde.* **107 lusty bachiler,** vigorous knight. **109 Phitoun,** the Python. **110 agayn,** in. **113 mynstralcie,** musical instrument. **116 Amphioun,** played his lyre (not sang) so beautifully that the stones moved into place of their own accord. **119 semelieste,** most handsome. **126 fredom,** generosity. **133** E&c *is* om. **134 countrefete,** imitate. **143** Reading from Bodley 686&c. EHg&c show great variety, particularly in word order. **144 kept hire fayn,** guarded her happily. **145 byjaped,** deceived. **147** *al in ydel:* Hg&c *al for naught.*

A good wyf that is clene of werk and thoght
Sholde nat been kept in noon awayt, certayn,
And trewely the labour is in vayn   150
To kepe a shrewe, for it wol nat bee.
This holde I for a verray nycetee
To spille labour for to kepe wyves;
Thus writen olde clerkes in hir lyves.

   But now to purpos as I first bigan: 155
This worthy Phebus dooth al that he kan
To plesen hire, wenynge for swich plesaunce,
And for his manhede and his governaunce,
That no man sholde han put hym from hir
    grace.
But God it woot, ther may no man embrace
As to destreyne a thyng which that nature   161
Hath natureelly set in a creature.

   Taak any bryd and put it in a cage,
And do al thyn entente and thy corage
To fostre it tendrely with mete and drynke   165
Of alle deyntees that thou kanst bithynke,
And keep it al so clenly as thou may,
Although his cage of gold be never so gay,
Yet hath this brid by twenty thousand foold
Levere in a forest that is rude and coold   170
Goon ete wormes and swich wrecchednesse.
For evere this brid wol doon his bisynesse
To escape out of his cage, if he may.
His libertee this brid desireth ay.   174

   Lat take a cat and fostre hym wel with milk
And tendre flessh, and make his couche of silk,
And lat hym seen a mous go by the wal,
Anon he weyveth milk and flessh and al,
And every deyntee that is in that hous,
Swich appetit hath he to ete a mous.   180
Lo, heere hath lust his dominacioun,
And appetit fleemeth discrecioun.

   A she-wolf hath also a vileyns kynde.
The lewedeste wolf that she may fynde,
Or leest of reputacioun, that wol she take   185

In tyme whan hir lust to han a make.

   Alle thise ensamples speke I by thise men
That been untrewe and nothyng by wommen.
For men han evere a likerous appetit
On lower thyng to parfourne hire delit   190
Than on hire wyves, be they never so faire,
Ne never so trewe, ne so debonaire.
Flessh is so newefangel, with meschaunce,
That we ne konne in nothyng han plesaunce
That sowneth into vertu any while.   195

   This Phebus, which that thoghte upon no
    gile,
Deceyved was for al his jolitee.
For under hym another hadde shee,
A man of litel reputacioun,
Nat worth to Phebus in comparisoun.   200
The moore harm is, it happeth ofte so,
Of which ther cometh muchel harm and wo.

   And so bifel, whan Phebus was absent,
His wyf anon hath for hir lemman sent.   204
Hir lemman? Certes, this is a knavyssh speche!
Foryeveth it me, and that I yow biseche.

   The wise Plato seith, as ye may rede,
The word moot nede accorde with the dede.
If men shal telle proprely a thyng,
The word moost cosyn be to the werkyng.   210
I am a boystous man, right thus seye I,
Ther nys no difference, trewely,
Bitwixe a wyf that is of heigh degree,
If of hir body dishonest she bee,
And a poure wenche, oother than this—   215
If it so be they werke bothe amys—
But that the gentile in hire estaat above,
She shal be cleped his lady, as in love;
And for that oother is a poure womman,   219
She shal be cleped his wenche or his lemman.
And, God it woot, myn owene deere brother,
Men leyn that oon as lowe as lith that oother.

   Right so bitwixe a titlelees tiraunt

---

148 **clene,** pure. 149 **kept . . . awayt,** kept, surveillance. 151 **wol nat bee,** can't be done. 152 **verray nycetee,** real foolishness.
154 **in,** during. 157 **wenynge . . . plesaunce,** thinking, pleasure. *for:* E&c *that,* other MSS *by.* 158 **governaunce,** behavior. 161
destreyne, restrain. 163 The following illustrations are from *RR.* 170 *rude:* other MSS *wilde.* 178 **weyveth,** abandons. 180 E *he hath.*
182 **fleemeth,** drives out. 183 **vileyns kynde,** base nature. 184 **lewedeste,** a usage such as this shows the term already in Chaucer's
time degenerating from "ignorant" to "immoral." 185 *that:* other MSS *hym.* 186 **lust . . . make,** desires, mate. 187 **by,** about. 189
likerous, lecherous. 193 **newefangel,** eager for novelty. 194 **plesaunce,** pleasure. 195 **sowneth,** conduces to. 200 **Nat,** nought,
i.e., worth nothing. 204 **lemman,** lover. 211 **boystous,** rough, crude. 222 **leyn,** lay; *double entendre,* consider and lay. 223 **titlelees,**
without a legal title, a usurper.

And an outlawe or a theef erraunt
The same I seye—ther is no difference.   225
To Alisaundre was toold this sentence,
That, for the tirant is of gretter myght,
By force of meynee for to sleen dounright,
And brennen hous and hoom, and make al playn,
Lo, therfore is he cleped a capitayn;   230
And for the outlawe hath but smal meynee,
And may nat doon so greet an harm as he,
Ne brynge a contree to so greet mescheef,
Men clepen hym an outlawe or a theef.
But for I am a man noght textueel,   235
I wol noght telle of textes never a deel.
I wol go to my tale as I bigan.
Whan Phebus wyf had sent for hir lemman
Anon they wroghten al hire lust volage.   239
  The white crowe that heeng ay in the cage
Biheeld hire werk and seyde never a word.
And whan that hoom was come Phebus, the lord,
This crowe sang "Cokkow! Cokkow! Cokkow!"
  "What, bryd?" quod Phebus, "What song syngestow?
Ne were thow wont so myrily to synge   245
That to myn herte it was a rejoysynge
To heere thy voys? Allas, what song is this?"
  "By God," quod he, "I synge nat amys.
Phebus," quod he, "for al thy worthynesse,
For al thy beautee and thy gentilesse,   250
For al thy song and al thy mynstralcye,
For al thy waityng, blered is thyn eye
With oon of litel reputacioun,
Noght worth to thee as in comparisoun   254
The montance of a gnat, so moote I thryve!
For on thy bed thy wyf I saugh hym swyve."
  What wol ye moore? The crowe anon hym tolde
By sadde tokenes and by wordes bolde
How that his wyf had doon hire lecherye

Hym to greet shame and to greet vileynye,   260
And tolde hym ofte he saugh it with his eyen.
  This Phebus gan aweyward for to wryen.
Hym thoughte his sorweful herte brast atwo.
His bowe he bente and sette therinne a flo,
And in his ire his wyf thanne hath he slayn—   265
This is th'effect, ther is namoore to sayn—
For sorwe of which he brak his mynstralcie,
Bothe harpe, and lute, and gyterne, and sautrie,
And eek he brak his arwes and his bowe,
And after that thus spak he to the crowe: 270
  "Traitour," quod he, "with tonge of scorpioun,
Thou hast me broght to my confusioun.
Allas, that I was wroght! Why nere I deed?
O deere wyf, O gemme of lustiheed,
That were to me so sad and eek so trewe,   275
Now listow deed with face pale of hewe
Ful giltelees, that dorste I swere, ywys!
O rakel hand, to doon so foule amys!
O trouble wit, O ire recchelees,
That unavysed smyteth giltelees!   280
O wantrust, ful of fals suspicioun,
Where was thy wit and thy discrecioun?
O every man, bewar of rakelnesse!
Ne trowe nothyng withouten strong witnesse.
Smyt nat to soone er that ye witen why,   285
And beeth avysed wel and sobrely
Er ye doon any execucioun
Upon youre ire for suspecioun.
Allas, a thousand folk hath rakel ire
Fully fordoon and broght hem in the mire.   290
Allas, for sorwe I wol myselven slee."
  And to the crowe, "O false theef," seyde he,
"I wol thee quite anon thy false tale!
Thou songe whilom lyk a nyghtyngale;
Now shaltow, false theef, thy song forgon,   295
And eek thy white fetheres everichon,
Ne nevere in al thy lif ne shaltou speke.

---

224 theef erraunt, roving robber. **228 meynee,** retinue. **229 playn,** i.e., level everything to the ground. **239 lust volage,** transient (volatile) desire. **243 Cokkow,** the term "cuckold" is supposedly derived from "cuckoo" (OF *cucu, cucuald*). **252 waityng, blered . . . eye,** watching, you have been hoodwinked (cuckolded). **255 montance . . . thryve,** amount, prosper. **256 swyve,** copulate with. **258 sadde tokenes,** strong evidence. **262 wryen,** turn. **263 Hym:** EHg&c *And.* **264 flo,** arrow. **266 effect,** outcome. **268 sautrie,** psaltery (a small harp). **274 lustiheed,** delight. **276 listow,** you lie. **278 rakel,** rash. **280 unavysed,** thoughtless. **281 wantrust,** distrust. **283 rakelnesse,** rashness. **284 trowe,** believe. **290, fordoon,** i.e., done for. **293 quite,** repay. **294 whilom,** formerly.

Thus shal men on a traytour been awreke;
Thou and thyn ofspryng evere shul be blake,
Ne nevere sweete noyse shul ye make,   300
But evere crie agayn tempest and rayn,
In tokenynge that thurgh thee my wyf is slayn."
And to the crowe he stirte and that anon
And pulled his white fetheres everychon,   304
And made hym blak, and refte hym al his song,
And eek his speche, and out at dore hym slong
Unto the devel, which I hym bitake—
And for this caas been alle crowes blake.

Lordynges, by this ensample I yow preye
Beth war and taketh kepe what ye seye,   310
Ne telleth nevere no man in youre lyf
How that another man hath dight his wyf.
He wol yow haten mortally, certeyn.
Daun Salomon, as wise clerkes seyn,
Techeth a man to kepen his tonge weel.   315
But, as I seyde, I am noght textueel,
But nathelees thus taughte me my dame:
"My sone, thenk on the crowe, a Goddes name!
My sone, keep wel thy tonge, and keep thy
          freend.
A wikked tonge is worse than a feend,   320
My sone; from a feend men may hem blesse.
My sone, God of his endelees goodnesse
Walled a tonge with teeth and lippes eke,
For man sholde hym avyse what he speeke.
My sone, ful ofte for to muche speche   325
Hath many a man been spilt, as clerkes teche,
But for litel speche avysely
Is no man shent, to speke generally.
My sone, thy tonge sholdestow restreyne   329
At alle tymes but whan thou doost thy peyne

To speke of God in honour and preyere.
The firste vertu, sone, if thou wolt leere,
Is to restreyne and kepe wel thy tonge;
Thus lerne children whan that they been yonge.
My sone, of muchel spekyng yvele avysed,   335
Ther lasse spekyng hadde ynough suffised,
Comth muchel harm; thus was me toold and
          taught.
In muchel speche synne wanteth naught.
Wostow wherof a rakel tonge serveth?
Right as a swerd forkutteth and forkerveth   340
An arm a-two, my deere sone, right so
A tonge kutteth freendshipe al a-two.
A janglere is to God abhomynable.
Reed Salomon, so wys and honurable,
Reed David in his psalmes, reed Senekke.   345
My sone, spek nat, but with thyn heed thou
          bekke.
Dissimule as thou were deef if that thou heere
A janglere speke of perilous mateere.
The Flemyng seith, and lerne it if thee leste,
That litel janglyng causeth muchel reste.   350
My sone, if thou no wikked word hast seyd,
Thee thar nat drede for to be biwreyd
But he that hath mysseyd, I dar wel sayn,
He may by no wey clepe his word agayn.   354
Thyng that is seyd is seyd, and forth it gooth,
Though hym repente or be hym nevere so looth.
He is his thral to whom that he hath sayd
A tale of which he is now yvele apayd.
My sone, bewar and be noon auctour newe
Of tidynges, wheither they been false or trewe.
Wherso thou come, amonges hye or lowe,   361
Kepe wel thy tonge and thenk upon the crowe."

Heere is ended the Maunciples Tale of the Crowe.

298 awreke, avenged. **300 noyse:** E *voys*. **301 agayn,** in anticipation of. **307 which . . . bitake,** to whom, commit. **308 caas,** cause. **312 dight,** treated (had intercourse with). **314 Salomon,** Prov. 21:23. **315 kepen,** guard. **320** Parallels to these proverbs are cited by Skeat and Robinson. **321 blesse,** protect by making the sign of the cross. **324 avyse,** consider. **328 shent,** hurt. **330 but whan,** except when. **332 leere,** learn. **335 yvele avysed,** poorly considered. **336 Ther,** where. **339 Wostow . . . rakel,** do you know, rash. **340 forkutteth . . . forkerveth,** "for" is an intensifier. **343 janglere,** boisterous talker. **346 bekke,** nod. **347 Dissimule,** pretend. **349 Flemyng,** Flemish man (Belgian); Chaucer evidently thought of this as a Flemish apothegm. **352 biwreyd,** betrayed. **354 clepe,** call back. **356** Reading from Bodley 686; EHg&c *leef or looth*. **358 yvele apayd,** repentant, conscience-smitten. **362 Kepe,** guard.

INTRODUCTION

Canterbury Tales, Part X

N SPITE OF its obvious incompleteness, the *Canterbury Tales* has always been regarded as a complete work of art. This is because the frame is complete. Hugh Kenner, "Art in a Closed Field," *Virginia Quarterly Review* (1962), points out that art requires a restricted field within which materials can be arranged for maximum effect. Only this limitation allows us to speak of "composition" or "texture." Quite probably at the same time that he was working on the General Prologue and Man of Law's Prologue, or certainly with these introductions in mind, Chaucer wrote the conclusion to his work, providing a conceptually satisfying frame within which he could compose and rearrange at will.

At the beginning of the Man of Law's Prologue, the date of the pilgrimage and the time of day had been established by a complicated astronomical calculation (II.2ff). Here in the Parson's Prologue the calculation is repeated (X.2ff). There the time had been 10 a.m.; here it is 4 p.m. Evening is the archetypal figure for completion and death, just as morning is for commencement and birth. The morning figure in the Man of Law's Prologue reinforces the springtime and germination imagery at the beginning of the General Prologue. The death imagery of the Parson's Prologue is further pointed up by "my shadwe," whose proportion on the ground is eleven feet to six—six being suggestive of the dimension of a grave. It has always been a puzzle why in the General Prologue Chaucer used the indirect reference to the zodiacal sign Aries when the commencement of the pilgrimage was really in Taurus (I.8 note). Aries was the sign of the spring equinox and the beginning of the year, which is here balanced by the reference to Libra (X.11), the sign of the fall equinox and the end of the year. Libra, the sign of the scales, is also associated with Judgment and (because of its shape) the Crucifixion.

By l. 12 of the Parson's Prologue, the pilgrims are entering a "thropes ende." In medieval imagery, Heaven is always a city, "Jerusalem celestial" as the Parson designates it (l.51). Although "thorp" means "village," presumably the town they were entering was their destination, Canterbury. The Host's words here and throughout the prologue are replete with what rhetoricians call "signals of closure." Never mind that his statements are not strictly in accord with the plan he had set forth in the General Prologue (I.788ff), they permit no doubt that we are approaching the conclusion. Chaucer's decision to begin his series in Part I with the Knight may represent a dissent from the traditional medieval hierarchy, which would

place the religious pilgrims first, but his placing the conclusion in the hands of the Church is strictly orthodox. We observe that the "artificial" governance of the Host operates within the "natural" boundaries of the Knight and the Parson—the social contract between hereditary aristocracy and religion.

The words of the Parson in reply to the Host identify "this viage" with "thilke glorious pilgymage" (ll.49, 51). However, the poet-persona must have a smile on his face when the Parson promises a "myrie tale in prose." This is reminiscent of the "litel thyng in prose" called *Melibee* that he himself had proposed (VII.937). But if one can overlook the disproportion, the subject matter of the Parson's Tale is an appropriate summation of the vices and virtues depicted in what has gone before.

The Parson's Tale is not a sermon but a "penitential," an "examination of conscience" of a sort which devout people read or had read to them to prepare themselves for confession. It seems unlikely that such a technical treatise on the nature of sin would have been composed by a layman. More likely Chaucer was translating a penitential manual into English for the use of some member of the royal family, following the tradition of Friar Lorens Gallus who translated his *Le somme le roi* into French for the King of France (1297). Lee W. Patterson, "The Parson's

Tale and the Quitting of the *Canterbury Tales*," *Traditio* (1978), discusses the Parson's Tale in the context of the penitential tradition.

If the Parson's Tale was indeed composed as a separate work, its opening was revised after Chaucer decided to make it the concluding piece in his compilation, for the beginning of the tale (ll.75ff) describes the "wey" through penitence to the "Jerusalem celestial" which had provided the emotional climax of the prologue (l.51). The tale is ostensibly structured around the discussion of Contrition, Confession, and Satisfaction (Absolution). "Prima pars" is devoted to Contrition. "Secunda pars" introduces the subject of Confession with a discussion of Concupiscence as the root of all sin. Into the middle of Confession is inserted an independent treatise on the Seven Deadly Sins and their corresponding virtues. The 600 lines of this section are quite out of proportion to the 900 lines of the entire piece. Many years ago Frederick Tupper, *PMLA* (1914), developed the theory that all of the characters and tales in the Canterbury compilation were exemplifications of the Seven Sins, which were then summed up in the Parson's Tale. After this argument was demolished by J.L. Lowes, *PMLA* (1915), scholars hesitated to posit a systematic conceptual basis for the collection until this view was resurrected by such modern critics as D.W. Robertson, Ralph Baldwin, and most recently Paul Olson. It is true that the vices and virtues in the tales do sometimes represent closely the sins and remedies in the Tale. "Pride of dress" (X.415ff) suggests the Squire and Monk; "pride of table" (X.440ff) suggests the Prioress and Franklin; Placebo of the Merchant's Tale is mentioned in connection with flattery (X.615); the marriage argument comes up in "Remedium contra luxurie" (X.930ff). But in spite of these and other specific parallels, the variety of the *Canterbury Tales* cannot be confined within this or any other unified scheme. In the Middle Ages the Seven Deadly Sins were the moral spectacles through which human behavior was viewed, just as we today view human behavior through the psychological spectacles of Nietzche and Freud. It is significant that Chaucer chose to conclude his vivid characterizations and dramatizations with an abstract treatise on the nature of sin, but there is no evidence that his compilation is a systematic exemplification of this or any other abstract system.

At the end of the treatise on the Seven Deadly Sins, the discussion returns to Confession, and "Tercia pars" takes up the final topic, Satisfaction.

The problem of integrating the Parson's Tale into the fabric of the *Canterbury Tales* applies even more acutely to the Retraction. Both the Tale and the Retraction are in a sense anticlimactic after the effective conclusion in the Parson's Prologue. However, the Retraction is found in so many good manuscripts that there is no doubt that it was the conclusion of Part X in Chaucer's exemplar. Looking at these two last items from the vantage point of the General Prologue, one is impressed by how much the conception of Chaucer's poem has changed. The "game" proposed by the Host in the Prologue envisaged a jolly, festive conclusion. Instead we conclude with a penitential and a prayer. Setting aside biographical reasons for the Retraction (that Chaucer felt death approaching), or conventional (that this was the customary medieval way to end a weighty work), or practical (that it gave Chaucer a final opportunity to list his works), perhaps the best reason for ending the Parson's Tale with the Retraction is aesthetic. In *The Anatomy of Criticism* (1957), Northrop Frye says that in all literature there is only one plot, the passage from birth to death, of which the structure of the Bible is the archetype. The integrity of the *Canterbury Tales* derives as much from its somber ending as from its joyful beginning. Despite the problems of internal order and loose ends, the Canterbury collection "feels" complete because it embodies this archetypal pattern. The reader's aesthetic response to the completeness of the work is elucidated in Donald R. Howard's *The Idea of the Canterbury Tales* (1976).

Canterbury Tales

PART X

PARSON'S TALE

PROLOGUE

Heere folweth the Prologe of the Persouns Tale.

By that the Maunciple hadde his tale al ended,	For ellevene foot, or litel moore or lesse,
The sonne fro the south lyne was descended	My shadwe was at thilke tyme, as there
So lowe that he nas nat to my sighte	Of swiche feet as my lengthe parted were
Degrees nyne and twenty as in highte.	In sixe feet equal of proporcioun.
Foure of the clokke it was tho, as I gesse, 5	Therwith the moones exaltacioun— 10
	I meene Libra—alwey gan ascende

1 **By that,** By (the time) that. *Maunciple:* Hg writes it over an erasure; other MSS have *Marchaunt* or *Yeman* depending on the order of the tales; see Manly IV.527. **2 south lyne,** the meridian. Chaucer's method of calculating the time of day here parallels the method in MLT, II.2–14. **4 nyne and twenty,** Skeat calculated that the altitude of the sun would be approximately 29° from the horizon at 4:00 P.M. in mid-April. EHg&c read 29, but the numbers vary in other MSS due to misreading of the roman numerals. **5** *Foure:* E&c *Ten,* again due to misreading; see Manly IV.528. *tho:* Hg&c *so.* **6 ellevene foot,** the angle of the sun at 4:00 P.M. would make a six-foot vertical (see l. 9) cast an eleven-foot horizontal shadow. See MLT, II.3–12. **7 thilke,** that. **10 moones exaltacioun,** the exaltation was the presence of a planet in the sign of the zodiac where it was believed to exert the greatest influence. In astrological tables, the moon's exaltation is Taurus and Libra is Saturn's, but all MSS have the present reading. **11 Libra,** zodiacal sign of the scales, associated with the Crucifixion (cross, the shape of scales), with judgment (the scales), freedom of choice (Lat. *liber*). Libra was the sign of the fall equinox as Aries was the sign of the spring equinox (Gen. Pro., I.8).

As we were entryng at a thropes ende.
For which oure Hoost, as he was wont to gye
As in this caas oure joly compaignye,
Seyde in this wise, "Lordynges everichoon,   15
Now lakketh us no tales mo than oon.
Fulfilled is my sentence and my decree.
I trowe that we han herd of ech degree.
Almoost fulfild is al myn ordinaunce.
I pray to God, so yeve hym right good
     chaunce   20
That telleth this tale to us lustily.

     "Sire preest," quod he, "artow a vicary,
Or arte a person? Sey sooth, by thy fey.
Be what thou be, ne breke thou nat oure pley,
For every man save thou hath toold his tale. 25
Unbokele and shewe us what is in thy male,
For trewely me thynketh by thy cheere
Thou sholdest knytte up wel a greet mateere.
Telle us a fable anon, for cokkes bones!"

     This Persoun answerde al atones,   30
"Thou getest fable noon ytoold for me,
For Paul, that writeth unto Thymothee,
Repreveth hem that weyven soothfastnesse,
And tellen fables and swich wrecchednesse.
Why sholde I sowen draf out of my fest   35
Whan I may sowen whete, if that me lest?
For which I seye, if that yow list to heere
Moralitee and vertuous mateere,
And thanne that ye wol yeve me audience,
I wol ful fayn at Cristes reverence   40
Do yow plesaunce leefful, as I kan.
But trusteth wel, I am a southren man.

I kan nat geeste 'rum, ram, ruf,' by lettre,
Ne, God woot, rym holde I but litel bettre.
And therfore, if yow list—I wol nat glose—   45
I wol yow telle a myrie tale in prose
To knytte up al this feeste and make an ende.
And Jhesu for his grace wit me sende
To shewe yow the wey in this viage
Of thilke parfit glorious pilgrymage   50
That highte Jerusalem celestial.
And if ye vouchesauf, anon I shal
Bigynne upon my tale, for which I preye
Telle youre avys; I kan no bettre seye.
     "But nathelees, this meditacioun   55
I putte it ay under correccioun
Of clerkes, for I am nat textueel.
I take but the sentence, trusteth weel.
Therfore I make protestacioun
That I wol stonde to correccioun."   60
     Upon this word we han assented soone,
For as us seemed it was for to doone
To enden in som vertuous sentence,
And for to yeve hym space and audience,
And bede oure Hoost he sholde to hym seye   65
That alle we to telle his tale hym preye.
     Oure Hoost hadde the wordes for us alle,
"Sire preest," quod he, "now faire yow bifalle!
Telleth," quod he, "youre meditacioun.
But hasteth yow, the sonne wole adoun;   70
Beth fructuous and that in litel space,
And to do wel God sende yow his grace.
Sey what yow list, and we wol gladly heere."
And with that word he seyde in this manere.

Explicit prohemium.

12 **thropes ende,** village's outskirts. 13 **gye,** guide (direct). 19 **ordinaunce,** scheme (law). 20 **chaunce,** fortune. 21 **lustily,** pleasingly. 22 **vicary,** vicar, a priest acting in the place of the original holder of a benefice. *artow:* EHg *arte.* 23 **person,** parson, the original holder of the benefice. **sooth . . . fey,** truth, faith. 24 **breke . . . pley,** i.e., don't spoil our game. 25 **his tale,** Chaucer (or the Host) evidently changed his mind about the number of tales each pilgrim would tell, see i.792, v.698. 26 **male,** wallet. 27 **cheere,** appearance (expression). 29 **cokkes bones,** after NPT, the Host uses this expression, see ix.9. 30 **al atones,** at once. 31 **fable . . . for,** fiction (Lat. *fabula*), by. 32 **Paul,** I Tim. 1:4, 4:7; II Tim. 4:4. 33 **weyven,** turn aside from (waive). 35 **draf . . . fest,** chaff, fist. 36 **me lest,** it pleases me. 37 **list,** wish. 40 **fayn,** happily. *ful:* E&c om.; other MSS *right*/*wel.* 41 **Do yow plesaunce leefful,** please you legitimately (lawfully). 42–43 **kan nat geeste,** cannot recite a romance. **southren . . . rum, ram, ruf,** in the south of England, alliterative verse had given way to rhyme. 45 **glose,** lie. 51 **Jerusalem celestial,** see Rev. 21:2. With this allusion, Chaucer points to a metaphoric interpretation for the *Canterbury Tales;* see ll. 79–80 below. 54 **avys,** view (advice). 56 **ay,** always. 57 **textueel,** i.e., a textual (exact) scholar. 58 **sentence,** general meaning. 62 **us seemed . . . for to doone,** it seems to us, necessary to do. 64 **space and audience,** time and attention. 65 **bede,** bade. 71 **fructuous,** fruitful. 73–74 In all MSS these lines follow 69; editors have moved them to the end because of context.

Heere bigynneth the Persounes Tale.

Jer. 6. State super vias et videte et interrogate de viis antiquis, que sit via bona; et ambulate in ea, et invenietis refrigerium animabus vestris, &c.

Our sweete lord God of hevene, that wole no man perisse but wole that we comen alle to the knoweleche of hym and to the blissful lif that is perdurable, / amonesteth us by the prophete Jeremie and seith in thys wyse, / "Stondeth upon the weyes and seeth and axeth of olde pathes (that is to seyn, of olde sentences) which is the goode wey; / and walketh in that wey, and ye shal fynde refresshynge for youre soules, &c." / Manye been the weyes espirituels that leden folk to oure lord Jesu Crist and to the regne of glorie. / Of whiche weyes, ther is a ful noble wey and a ful covenable, which may nat fayle to no man ne to womman, that thurgh synne hath mysgoon fro the righte wey of Jerusalem celestial. / And this wey is cleped penitence, of which man sholde gladly herknen and enquere with al his herte / to wyten what is penitence, and whennes it is cleped penitence, and in how manie maneres been the acciouns or werkynges of penitence, / and how manie speces ther been of penitence, and whiche thynges apertenen and bihouven to penitence, and whiche thynges destourben penitence. /

Seint Ambrose seith that penitence is the pleynynge of man for the gilt that he hath doon, and namore to do anythyng for which hym oghte to pleyne. / And som doctour seith, "Penitence is the waymentynge of man that sorweth for his synne and pyneth hymself for he hath mysdoon." / Penitence, with certeyne circumstances, is verray repentance

of a man that halt hymself in sorwe and oother peyne for his giltes. / And for he shal be verray penitent, he shal first biwaylen the synnes that he hath doon and stidefastly purposen in his herte to have shrift of mouthe and to doon satisfaccioun, / and never to doon thyng for which hym oghte moore to biwayle or to compleyne, and continue in goode werkes, or elles his repentance may nat availle. / For as seith Seint Ysidre, "He is a japer and a gabbere and no verray repentant that eftsoone dooth thyng for which hym oghte repente." / Wepynge and nat for to stynte to synne may nat avaylle. / But nathelees men shal hope that every tyme that man falleth, be it never so ofte, that he may arise thurgh penitence if he have grace—but certeinly it is greet doute. / For as seith Seint Gregorie, "Unnethe ariseth he out of synne that is charged with the charge of yvel usage." / And therfore repentant folk that stynte for to synne and forlete synne er that synne forlete hem, Hooly Chirche holdeth hem siker of hire savacioun. / And he that synneth and verraily repenteth hym in his laste, Hooly Chirche yet hopeth his savacioun by the grete mercy of oure lord Jesu Crist, for his repentaunce—but taak the siker wey. /

And now sith I have declared yow what thyng is penitence, now shul ye understonde that ther been three acciouns of penitence. / The firste accioun of penitence is that a man be baptized after that he hath synned. / Seint Augustyn seith, "But he be penytent for his olde synful lyf, he may nat bigynne the newe clene lif." / For certes if he

---

Jer. 6. Jeremiah 6:16, "Stondeth up-on weies, and seeth, and asketh of the olde pathis, what is the goode weie; and goth in it, and yee shul fynde refreshinge to youre soules" (Wyclif). **75 wole ... perdurable,** wishes, forever lasting. *and to:* E&c *to* om. **76 amonesteth,** admonishes. **77 sentences,** teachings. **80 ful convenable,** very appropriate: E&c *ful* om. **wey of,** way toward. **81 cleped,** named. **82 wyten,** know. **83 apertenen and bihouven,** belong (appertain) and are needed. **84 Seint Ambrose,** *Sermo* 25.1. **pleynynge,** lamenting. **85 waymentynge,** lamenting. **86 verray ... halt,** genuine, holds. **87 shrift ... satisfaccioun,** confession, penance. **88 oghte moore,** i.e., ought ever again. **89 Seint Ysidre,** Isidore of Seville; not identified. **japer ... gabbere ... eftsoone,** jokester, boaster, immediately. **90 stynte,** cease. **92 Seint Gregorie,** *In Septem Psalmas Poenitentiales Expositio,* Ps. 37:5.8. **Unnethe ... charged ... usage,** scarcely (with difficulty), burdened, habit. **93 stynte ... forlete ... siker of,** cease, abandon, sure of. **94 repenteth hym,** see Chaucer's own Retraction, below, ll. 1081ff. **laste,** last day. **95 acciouns,** effects. **97 Seint Augustyn,** *Sermo* 351.c.2.

be baptized withouten penitence of his olde gilt, he receyveth the mark of baptesme but nat the grace ne the remission of his synnes, til he have repentance verray. / Another defaute is this, that men doon deedly synne after that they han receyved baptesme. / .The thridde defaute is that men fallen in venial synnes after hir baptesme fro day to day. / Therof seith Seint Augustyn that penitence of goode and humble folk is the penitence of every day. /

The speces of penitence been three. That oon of hem is solempne, another is commune, and the thridde is privee. / Thilke penance that is solempne is in two maneres, as to be put out of Hooly Chirche in Lente for slaughtre of children, and swich maner thyng. / Another thyng is whan a man hath synned openly, of which synne the fame is openly spoken in the contree, and thanne Hooly Chirche by juggement destreyneth hym for to do open penaunce. / Commune penaunce is that preestes enjoynen men comunly in certeyn caas, as for to goon, peraventure, naked in pilgrimages, or barefoot. / Pryvee penaunce is thilke that men doon alday for privee synnes, of whiche they shryve hem prively and receyve privee penaunce. /

Now shaltow understande what is bihovely and necessarie to verray perfit penitence. And this stant on three thynges: / contricioun of herte, confessioun of mouth, and satisfaccioun. / For which seith Seint John Crisostom, "Penitence destreyneth a man to accepte benygnely every peyne that hym is enjoyned, with contricioun of herte, and shrift of mouth, with satisfaccioun, and in werkynge of alle maner humylitee." / And this is fruytful penitence agayn three thynges in whiche we wratthe

oure lord Jesu Crist, / this is to seyn, by delit in thynkynge, by recchelesnesse in spekynge, and by wikked synful werkynge. / And agayns thise wikkede giltes is penitence, that may be likned unto a tree. /

The roote of this tree is contricioun, that hideth hym in the herte of hym that is verray repentaunt, right as the roote of a tree hydeth hym in the erthe. / Of the roote of contricion spryngeth a stalke that bereth braunches and leves of confessioun, and fruyt of satisfaccioun. / For which Crist seith in his gospel, "Dooth digne fruyt of penitence." For by this fruyt may men knowe this tree, and nat by the roote that is hyd in the herte of man, ne by the braunches ne by the leves of confessioun. / And therfore oure lord Jesu Crist seith thus, "By the fruyt of hem ye shul knowen hem." / Of this roote eek spryngeth a seed of grace, the which seed is mooder of sikernesse, and this seed is egre and hoot. / The grace of this seed spryngeth of God thurgh remembrance of the day of doome and on the peynes of helle. / Of this matere seith Salomon that in the drede of God man forleteth his synne. / The heete of this seed is the love of God and the desiryng of the joye perdurable. / This heete draweth the herte of a man to God and dooth hym haten his synne. / For soothly, ther is nothing that savoureth so wel to a child as the milk of his norice, ne nothing is to him moore abhomynable than thilke milk whan it is medled with oother mete. / Right so the synful man that loveth his synne, hym semeth that it is to him moost sweete of anything. / But fro that tyme that he loveth sadly oure lord Jesu Crist, and desireth the lif perdurable, ther nys to him nothing moore abhomynable. / For soothly, the

---

99 defaute, fault; editors differ on whether *defaute* is a non sequitur to the "three actions" (l. 95) or merely a shift in terminology. **100 venial,** pardonable. **101 Seint Augustyn,** *Epistola* 265.8. **102 speces . . . solempne . . . commune . . . privee,** kinds, serious, public, private. **104 destreyneth,** compels. **105 enjoynen men comunly . . . caas,** command people (to do penance) in a group, cases. *men comunly:* E *comunly* om. **106 they shryve hem,** they obtain absolution: Hg&c *we shryve us.* **107 bihovely . . . verray,** needful, genuine. **109 destreyneth . . . peyne,** compels, punishment. **110 agayn . . . wratthe,** against, anger. **111 delit in thynkynge,** i.e., erotic thoughts. **recchelesnesse,** carelessness. **113 verray . . . right as,** truly, just as. **115 Crist seith,** John the Baptist, Matt. 3:8. **Dooth digne,** produce exemplary (dignified). **116 Jesu Crist,** Matt. 7:20. **117 sikernesse . . . egre . . . hoot,** safety, tart, hot (tasting). *of grace:* E *a grace.* **119 Salomon,** Prov. 16:6. **forleteth,** rejects. **121 dooth hym,** makes him. **122 savoureth . . . norice . . . medled . . . mete,** tastes, nurse, mixed, food. E *is to him* om.; different order in other MSS. **124 sadly,** firmly.

lawe of God is the love of God; for which David the prophete seith, "I have loved thy lawe and hated wikkednesse and hate." He that loveth God kepeth his lawe and his word. / 125 This tree saugh the prophete Daniel in spirit upon the avysioun of the king Nabugodonosor, whan he conseiled hym to do penitence. / Penaunce is the tree of lyf to hem that it receyven, and he that holdeth hym in verray penitence is blessed, after the sentence of Salomon. /

In this penitence or contricioun man shal understonde foure thinges, that is to seyn: what is contricioun; and whiche been the causes that moeven a man to contricioun; and how he sholde be contrit; and what contricioun availleth to the soule. / Thanne is it thus, that contricioun is the verray sorwe that a man receyveth in his herte for his synnes, with sad purpos to shryve hym, and to do penaunce and nevermoore to do synne. / And this sorwe shal been in this manere, as seith Seint Bernard, "It shal been hevy and grevous, and ful sharpe and poynaunt in herte." / First, for man hath 130 agilt his lord and hys creatour; and moore sharpe and poynaunt for he hath agilt hys fader celestial; / and yet moore sharpe and poynaunt for he hath wrathed and agilt hym that boghte hym, which with his precious blood hath delivered us fro the bondes of synne and fro the crueltee of the devel and fro the peynes of helle. /

The causes that oghte moeve a man to contricioun been six. First, a man shal remembre hym of his synnes. / But looke he that thilke remembraunce ne be to hym no delit by no wey, but greet shame and sorwe for his gilt. For Job seith, "Synful men doon werkes worthy of confusion." / And therfore seith Ezechie, "I wol

remembre me alle the yeres of my lyf in bitternesse of myn herte." / And God seith 135 in the Apocalips, "Remembreth yow fro whennes that ye been falle." For biforn that tyme that ye synned ye were the children of God and lymes of the regne of God, / but for youre synne ye been woxen thral and foul, and membres of the feend, hate of aungels, sclaundre of Hooly Chirche, and foode of the false serpent, perpetueel matere of the fir of helle. / And yet moore foul and abhomynable, for ye trespassen so ofte tyme as dooth the hound that retourneth to eten his spewyng. / And yet be ye fouler for youre longe continuyng in synne and youre synful usage, for which ye be roten in youre synne as a beest in his dong. / Swiche manere of thoghtes maken a man to have shame of his synne and no delit, as God seith by the prophete Ezechiel, / "Ye shal remembre 140 yow of youre weyes and they shuln displese yow." Soothly, synnes been the weyes that leden folk to helle. /

The seconde cause that oghte make a man to have desdeyn of synne is this, that as seith Seint Peter, "Whoso that dooth synne is thral of synne," and synne put a man in greet thraldom. / And therfore seith the prophete Ezechiel, "I wente sorweful in desdayn of myself." And certes, wel oghte a man have desdayn of synne, and withdrawe hym from that thraldom and vileynye. / And lo, what seith Seneca in this matere? He seith thus, "Though I wiste that neither God ne man ne sholde nevere knowe it, yet wolde I have desdayn for to do synne." / And the same Seneca also seith, "I am born to gretter thynges than to be thral to my body, or than for to maken of my body a thral." / 145 Ne a fouler thral may no man ne womman maken of his body than for to yeven his body

125 **David,** Ps. 119:113. 126 **Daniel,** Daniel 4:10–27. **upon the avysioun,** after the vision. 127 **Salomon,** Prov. 28:13. 129 **verray sorwe . . . sad . . . shryve hym,** genuine sorrow, serious, receive absolution. 131 **agilt,** sinned against. 134 **looke he,** he must look out. *confusion,* so other MSS and Raymund de Penneforte, but EHg&c *confession.* The quotation has not been found in Job. 135 **Ezechie,** King Hezekiah, Isa. 38:15. **remembre me,** i.e., remind myself (of my sins). 136 **Apocalips,** Rev. 2:5. **been falle,** have fallen. **lymes of the regne,** members (limbs) of the kingdom. 137 **been woxen thral,** have become enslaved. **hate of . . . sclaundre . . . matere of,** hated by, denounced, material for. 138 **trespassen . . . spewyng,** sin, vomit, II Pet. 2:22. 139 **usage,** habitual action. 140 **Ezechiel,** Ezek. 20:43. 142 **Seint Peter,** II Pet. 2:19, but closer to John 8:34. 143 **Ezechiel,** not identified, but see Job 42:6. 144 **Seneca,** unidentified; in Pennefort merely "Philosophus." **wiste,** thought.

to synne. / Al were it the fouleste cherl or the fouleste womman that lyveth, and leest of value, yet is he thanne moore foule and moore in servitute. / Evere fro the hyer degree that man falleth, the moore is he thral, and moore to God and to the world vile and abhomynable. / O goode God, wel oghte man have desdayn of synne sith that thurgh synne ther he was free, now is he maked bonde. / And therfore seyth Seint Augustin, "If thou hast desdayn of thy servant, if he agilte or synne, have thou thanne desdayn that thou thyself sholdest do synne." / Take reward of thy value, that 150 thou ne be to foul to thyself. / Allas, wel oghten they thanne have desdayn to been servauntz and thralles to synne, and soore been ashamed of hemself, / that God of his endelees goodnesse hath set hem in heigh estaat, or yeven hem wit, strengthe of body, heele, beautee, prosperitee, / and boghte hem fro the deeth with his herte blood, that they so unkyndely agayns his gentilesse quiten hym so vileynsly, to slaughtre of hir owene soules. / O goode God, ye wommen that been of so greet beautee, remembreth yow of the proverbe of Salomon, that seith, / 155 "Likneth a fair womman that is a fool of hire body lyk to a ryng of gold that were in the groyn of a soughe." / For right as a soughe wroteth in everich ordure, so wroteth she hire beautee in the stynkynge ordure of synne. /

The thridde cause that oghte moeve a man to contricioun is drede of the Day of Doome and of the horrible peynes of helle. / For as Seint Jerome seith, "At every tyme that me remembreth of the Day of Doome, I quake, / for whan I ete or drynke or whatso that I do, evere semeth me that the trompe sowneth in myn ere: / 'Riseth up, ye that been dede, and 160 cometh to the juggement.' " / O goode God, muchel oghte a man to drede swich a jugge-ment, "ther as we shullen been alle," as Seint Poul seith, "biforn the seete of oure lord Jesu Crist," / where as he shal make a general congregacioun, where as no man may been absent. / For certes, there availleth noon essoyne ne excusacioun. / And nat oonly that oure defautes shullen be jugged, but eek that alle oure werkes shullen openly be knowe. / And 165 as seith Seint Bernard, "Ther ne shal no pledynge availle, ne sleighte. We shullen yeven rekeninge of everich ydel word." / Ther shul we han a juge that may nat been deceyved ne corrupt. And why? For certes, alle oure thoghtes been discovered as to hym, ne for preyere ne for meede he shal nat been corrupt. / And therfore seith Salomon, "The wratthe of God ne wol nat spare no wight for preyere ne for yifte." / And therfore at the Day of Doom ther nys noon hope to escape. / Wherfore, as seith Seint Anselm, "Ful greet angwyssh shul the synful folk have at that tyme. / Ther shal the stierne and wrothe juge sitte above, and under hym the horrible put of helle open to destroyen hym that noot biknowen his synnes, whiche synnes openly been shewed biforn God and biforn every creature. / And in the left syde, 170 mo develes than herte may bithynke, for to harye and drawe the synful soules to the peyne of helle. / And withinne the hertes of folk shal be the bitynge conscience, and withoute forth shal be the world al brennynge. / Whider shal thanne the wrecched synful man flee to hiden hym? Certes, he may nat hiden hym; he moste come forth and shewen hym." / For certes, as seith Seint Jerome, "The erthe shal casten hym out of hym, and the see also, and the eyr also, that shal be ful of thonder clappes and light-nynges." / Now soothly, whoso wel remembreth hym of thise thynges, I gesse that his synne shal nat turne hym in delit, but to greet sorwe for

---

148 E *vile and* om. **149 ther he,** where(as) he. **150 Seint Augustin,** *Sermo* 9:16. **151 reward,** regard. **153 heele,** health. **154 unkyndely . . . quiten,** unnaturally, requite. **155 Salomon,** Prov. 11:22. *that seith:* EHg&c *he seith/he* om. **156 groyn,** snout; cf. WBP III.784. **157 wroteth . . . ordure,** roots, filth. **162 Seint Poul,** Rom. 14:10. **164 essoyne,** excuse from appearance in court. **166 Seint Bernard,** *Sermo ad Prelatos in Concilio* 5. **sleighte,** pretense. **167 discovered . . . meede,** revealed, bribery. **168 Salomon,** Prov. 1:28. **169 Seint Anselm,** *Meditatio Secunda,* paraphrase. **170 wrothe . . . put . . . noot biknowen,** angry, pit, will not ack-knowledge. *noot:* Hg&c *moot.* **174 Seint Jerome,** quotation not identified, see Ps. 97:3–4.

drede of the peyne of helle. / And therfore 175
seith Job to God, "Suffre, Lord, that I may
a while biwaille and wepe er I go withoute
returning to the derke lond covered with the
derknesse of deeth, / to the lond of mysese and
of derknesse where as is the shadwe of deeth,
where as ther is noon ordre or ordinaunce, but
grisly drede that evere shal laste." / Loo, heere
may ye seen that Job preyde respit a while, to
biwepe and waille his trespas, for soothly a day
of respit is bettre than al the tresor of the world. /
And forasmuche as a man may acquiten hymself
biforn God by penitence in this world, and nat
by tresor, therfore sholde he preye to God to
yeve him respit a while, to biwepe and biwaillen
his trespas. / For certes, al the sorwe that a man
myghte make fro the bigynnyng of the world
nys but a litel thyng at regard of the sorwe
of helle. / The cause why that Job clepeth 180
helle "the lond of derknesse," / understondeth that he clepeth it "londe" or erthe for
it is stable and nevere shal faille; "dirk," for
he that is in helle hath defaute of light material. /
For certes, the derke light that shal come out of
the fyr that evere shal brenne shal turne hym
al to peyne that is in helle; for it sheweth hym
to the horrible develes that hym tormenten. /
"Covered with the derknesse of deeth"—that is
to seyn that he that is in helle shal have defaute
of the sighte of God, for certes the sighte of God
is the lyf perdurable. / "The derknesse of deeth"
been the synnes that the wrecched man hath
doon whiche that destourben hym to see the
face of God, right as dooth a derk clowde
bitwixe us and the sonne. / "Lond of misese," 185
by cause that ther been three maneres of
defautes agayn three thynges that folk of this
world han in this present lyf, that is to seyn,
honours, delices, and richesses. / Agayns honour
have they in helle shame and confusioun. / For
wel ye woot that men clepen "honour" the
reverence that man doth to man; but in helle
is noon honour ne reverence. For certes, namoore reverence shal be doon there to a kyng
than to a knave. / For which God seith by the
prophete Jeremye, "Thilke folk that me despisen
shul been in despit." / "Honour" is eek cleped
greet lordshipe; ther shal no man serven other
but of harm and torment. "Honour" is eek
cleped greet dignitee and heighnesse, but
in helle shul they been al fortroden of
develes. / And God seith, "The horrible 190
develes shulle goon and comen upon the
hevedes of the dampned folk." And this is
forasmuche as the hyer that they were in this
present lyf the more shulle they been abated
and defouled in helle. / Agayns the richesses of
this world shul they han mysese of poverte. And
this poverte shal been in foure thinges: / in
defaute of tresor, of which that David seith,
"The riche folk that embraceden and oneden
al hire herte to tresor of this world shul slepe in
the slepynge of deeth; and nothyng ne shal they
fynden in hir handes of al hir tresor." / And
mooreover the myseyse of helle shal been in
defaute of mete and drinke. / For God seith
thus by Moyses, "They shul been wasted with
hunger, and the briddes of helle shul devouren
hem with the bitter deeth, and the galle of the
dragon shal been hire drynke, and the
venym of the dragon hire morsels." / And 195
fortherover, hire myseyse shal been in
defaute of clothyng, for they shulle be naked in
body as of clothyng, save the fyr in which they
brenne and othere filthes. / And naked shul
they been of soule as of alle manere vertues,
which that is the clothyng of the soule. Where
been thanne the gaye robes and the softe shetes
and the smale shertes? / Loo, what seith God of
hem by the prophete Ysaye, that under hem
shul been strawed motthes, and hire covertures
shulle been of wormes of helle. / And forther-

176 Job, Job 10:20–22. **177 ordinaunce,** law. **180 at regard of,** compared with. **182 light material,** physical (in contrast to spiritual) light. **185 destourben,** hinder. **186 delices,** temporal delights. **189 Jeremye,** I Sam. 2:30. **190 but of . . . fortroden,** but with, trod upon ("for" is an intensifier). *ther—dignitee,* E&c om. **191 God seith,** Job 20:25. **hevedes . . . abated,** heads, degraded. **192 Agayns,** in contrast to. **193 David,** Ps. 75:6 (Vulgate). **defaute . . . oneden,** lack (default), united. **194 mete,** food. **195 Moyses,** Deut. 32:24, 33. **197 smale,** fine textured; other MSS *softe;* Hg&c *small clothes.* **198 Ysaye,** Isa. 14:11. **strawed . . . covertures,** strewn, blankets (coverlets).

over, hir myseyse shal been in defaute of freendes, for he nys nat poure that hath goode freendes. But there is no frend, / for neither God ne no creature shal been freend to hem, and everich of hem shall haten oother with deedly hate. / "The sones and the doghtren 200 shullen rebellen agayns fader and mooder, and kynrede agayns kynrede, and chiden and despisen everich of hem oother," bothe day and nyght, as God seith by the prophete Michias. / And the lovynge children, that whilom loveden so flesshly everich oother, wolden everich of hem eten oother if they myghte. / For how sholden they love togidre in the peyne of helle, whan they hated ech of hem oother in the prosperitee of this lyf? / For truste wel, hir flesshly love was deedly hate, as seith the prophete David, "Whoso that loveth wikked-nesse, he hateth his soule." / And whoso hateth his owene soule, certes he may love noon oother wight in no manere. / And therfore 205 in helle is no solas ne no freendshipe, but evere the moore flesshly kynredes that been in helle, the moore cursynges, the moore chidynges, and the moore deedly hate ther is among hem. / And fortherover, they shul have defaute of alle manere delices. For certes, delices been after the appetites of the fyve wittes, as sighte, herynge, smellynge, savorynge, and touchynge. / But in helle hir sighte shal be ful of derknesse and of smoke, and therfore ful of teeres; and hir herynge ful of waymentynge and of gryntynge of teeth, as seith Jesu Crist; / hir nosethirles shullen be ful of stynkynge stynk. And as seith Ysaye the prophete, "Hir savoryng shal be ful of bitter galle." / And touchynge of al hir body ycovered with "fir that nevere shal quenche and with wormes that nevere shul dyen," as God seith by the mouth of Ysaye. / And for as 210

muche as they shul nat wene that they may dyen for peyne, and by hir deeth flee fro peyne, that may they understonden by the word of Job that seith, "Ther as is the shadwe of deeth." / Certes a shadwe hath the liknesse of the thyng of which it is shadwe, but shadwe is nat the same thyng of which it is shadwe. / Right so fareth the peyne of helle. It is lyk deeth for the horrible anguissh, and why? For it peyneth hem evere as though they sholde dye anon; but certes they shal nat dye. / For as seith Seint Gregorie, "To wrecche caytyves shal be deeth withoute deeth, and ende withouten ende, and defaute withoute failynge. / For hir deeth shal alwey lyven, and hir ende shal everemo bigynne, and hir defaute shal nat faille." / 215 And therfore seith Seint John the Evaungelist, "They shullen folwe deeth and they shul nat fynde hym, and they shul desiren to dye and deeth shal flee fro hem." / And eek Job seith that in helle is noon ordre of rule. / And al be it so that God hath creat alle thynges in right ordre, and nothing withouten ordre, but alle thynges been ordeyned and nombred, yet nathelees they that been dampned been nothyng in the ordre, ne holden noon ordre, / for the erthe ne shal bere hem no fruyt. / For as the prophete David seith, "God shal destroie the fruyt of the erthe as fro hem," ne water ne shal yeve hem no moisture, ne the eyr no refresshyng, ne fyr no light. / For as seith 220 Seint Basilie, "The brennynge of the fyr of this world shal God yeven in helle to hem that been dampned, / but the light and the cleernesse shal be yeven in hevene to his children," right as the goode man yeveth flessh to his children and bones to his houndes. / And for they shullen have noon hope to escape, seith Seint Job atte laste that ther shal horrour and grisly drede

---

dwellen withouten ende. / Horrour is alwey drede of harm that is to come, and this drede shal evere dwelle in the hertes of hem that been dampned. And therfore han they lorn al hire hope for sevene causes. / First, for God that is hir juge shal be withouten mercy to hem, and they may nat plese hym ne noon of his halwes; ne they ne may yeve nothyng for hir raunsoun; / ne they have no voys to speke 225 to hym; ne they may nat fle fro peyne; ne they have no goodnesse in hem that they mowe shewe to delivere hem fro peyne. / And therfore seith Salomon, "The wikked man dyeth, and whan he is deed he shal have noon hope to escape fro peyne." / Whoso thanne wolde wel understande these peynes, and bithynke hym weel that he hath deserved thilke peynes for his synnes, certes, he sholde have moore talent to siken and to wepe than for to syngen and to pleye. / For as that seith Salomon, "Whoso that hadde the science to knowe the peynes that been establissed and ordeyned for synne, he wolde make sorwe." / "Thilke science," as seith Seint Augustyn, "maketh a man to waymenten in his herte." /   230

The fourthe point that oghte maken a man to have contricioun is the sorweful re- membraunce of the good that he hath left to doon heere in erthe, and eek the good that he hath lorn. / Soothly, the goode werkes that he hath lost, outher they been the goode werkes that he hath wroght er he fel into deedly synne, or elles the goode werkes that he wroghte while he lay in synne. / Soothly, the goode werkes that he dide biforn that he fil in synne been al mortefied and astoned and dulled by the ofte synnyng. / The othere goode werkes that he wroghte whil he lay in deedly synne, thei been outrely dede as to the lyf perdurable in hevene. / Thanne thilke goode werkes that been mortefied

by ofte synnyng, whiche goode werkes he dide whil he was in charitee, ne mowe nevere quyken agayn withouten verray penitence. / 235 And therof seith God by the mouth of Ezechiel that if the rightful man returne agayn from his rightwisnesse and werke wikkednesse, shal he live? / Nay, for alle the goode werkes that he hath wroght ne shul nevere been in remembraunce, for he shal dyen in his synne. / And upon thilke chapitre seith Seint Gregorie thus, that we shulle understonde this prin- cipally, / that whan we doon deedly synne, it is for noght thanne to rehercen or drawen into memorie the goode werkes that we han wroght biforn. / For certes, in the werkynge of the deedly synne, ther is no trust to no good werk that we han doon biforn, that is for to seyn as for to have therby the lyf perdurable in hevene. / But nathelees, the goode werkes 240 quyken agayn, and comen agayn, and helpen, and availlen to have the lyf perdurable in hevene whan we han contricioun. / But soothly, the goode werkes that men doon whil they been in deedly synne, for as muche as they were doon in deedly synne, they may nevere quyke agayn. / For certes, thyng that nevere hadde lyf may nevere quykene; and nathelees, al be it that they ne availle noght to han the lyf perdurable, yet availlen they to abregge of the peyne of helle, or elles to geten temporal rich- esse, / or elles that God wole the rather enlumyne and lightne the herte of the synful man to have repentance; / and eek they availlen for to usen a man to doon goode werkes that the feend have the lasse power of his soule. / And thus 245 the curteis lord Jesu Crist wole that no good werk be lost, for in somwhat it shal availle. / But for as muche as the goode werkes that men doon whil they been in good lyf been al mortified by synne folwynge, and eek sith that alle the

---

224 lorn, lost. **225 halwes . . . raunsoun,** saints, ransom. **226 mowe shewe,** may show (use). **227 Salomon,** Prov. 11:7. **228 bithynke hym . . . that,** think that. **talent . . . siken,** inclination, sigh. **229 science . . . peynes,** knowledge, punishments. **231 left to doon . . . lorn,** left undone, lost. **232** *lost:* EHg&c *left.* **233 mortefied,** killed. **235 in charitee . . . quyken,** in (God's) love, come to life. **236 Ezechiel,** Ezek. 18:24. **returne agayn,** turns away. **243 availle . . . abregge,** help, shorten. **244 rather,** sooner. **245 usen,** accustom.

goode werkes that men doon whil they been in deedly synne been outrely dede as for to have the lyf perdurable, / wel may that man that no good werke ne dooth synge thilke newe Frenshe song, *Jay tout perdu mon temps et mon labour.* / For certes, synne bireveth a man bothe goodnesse of nature and eek the goodnesse of grace. / For soothly, the grace of the Holy Goost fareth lyk fyr that may nat been ydel; for fyr fayleth anoon as it forleteth his wirkynge, and right so grace fayleth anoon as it forleteth his werkynge. / 250 Then leseth the synful man the goodnesse of glorie, that oonly is bihight to goode men that labouren and werken. / Wel may he be sory thanne that oweth al his lif to God as longe as he hath lyved, and eek as longe as he shal lyve, that no goodnesse ne hath to paye with his dette to God, to whom he oweth al his lyf. / For trust wel, "He shal yeven acountes," as seith Seint Bernard, "of alle the goodes that han be yeven hym in this present lyf, and how he hath hem despended, / noght so muche that ther shal nat perisse an heer of his heed, ne a moment of an houre ne shal nat perisse of his tyme, that he ne shal yeve of it a rekening." /

The fifthe thyng that oghte moeve a man to contricioun is remembrance of the passioun that oure lord Jesu Crist suffred for oure synnes. / For as seith Seint Bernard, "Whil 255 that I lyve I shal have remembrance of the travailles that oure lord Crist suffred in prechyng, / his werynesse in travaillyng, his temptaciouns whan he fasted, his longe wakynges whan he preyde, his teeres whan that he weepe for pitee of good peple, / the wo and the shame and the filthe that men seyden to hym, of the foule spittyng that men spitte in his face, of the buffettes that men yaven hym, of the foule mowes, and of the repreves that men to hym seyden, / of the nayles with whiche he was nayled to the croys, and of al the remenant of his passioun that he suffred for my synnes, and nothing for his gilt." / And ye shul understonde that in mannes synne is every manere of ordre or ordinaunce turned upsodoun. / For 260 it is sooth that God and resoun and sensualitee and the body of man been ordeyned that everich of thise foure thynges sholde have lordshipe over that oother. / As thus: God sholde have lordshipe over resoun, and resoun over sensualitee, and sensualitee over the body of man. / But soothly whan man synneth, al this ordre or ordinaunce is turned upsodoun. / And therfore thanne, for as muche as the resoun of man ne wol nat be subget ne obeisant to God, that is his lord by right, therfore leseth it the lordshipe that it sholde have over sensualitee, and eek over the body of man. / And why? For sensualitee rebelleth thanne agayns resoun, and by that wey leseth resoun the lordshipe over sensualitee and over the body. / For right as resoun is rebel to God, 265 right so is bothe sensualitee rebel to resoun and the body also. / And certes, this disordinaunce and this rebellioun oure lord Jesu Crist aboghte upon his precious body ful deere, and herkneth in which wise. / For as muche thanne as resoun is rebel to God, therfore is man worthy to have sorwe and to be deed. / This suffred oure lord Jesu Crist for man, after that he hadde be bitraysed of his disciple, and distreyned and bounde, so that his blood brast out at every nayle of his handes, as seith Seint Augustyn. / And forther over, for as muchel as resoun of man ne wol nat daunte sensualitee whan it may, therfore is man worthy to have shame. And this suffred oure lord Jesu Crist for man whan they spetten in his visage. / 270 And forther over, for as muchel thanne as the caytyf body of man is rebel bothe to resoun

---

248 *Jay tout perdu,* "I have completely lost my time and my work"; evidently the refrain of a popular song, used again in "Fortune" (short poem no. 10). **249 bireveth,** robs. **250 anoon as it forleteth,** as soon as it ceases. **251 bihight,** promised. **252 paye with his dette,** pay his debt with. **253 despended,** spent. **256 Seint Bernard,** *Sermones in Cantica* 43, quoted many places. **travailles,** troubles. **258 mowes ... repreves,** scowls, reproofs. **259 nothing for his,** not at all for his. **267 disordinaunce ... aboghte upon,** disorder, redeemed with. **269 bitraysed ... distreyned,** betrayed, arrested. **270 daunte,** tame.

and to sensualitee, therfore is it worthy the deeth. / And this suffred oure lord Jesu Crist for man upon the croys, where as ther was no part of his body free withouten greet peyne and bitter passioun. / And al this suffred Jesu Crist that nevere forfeted. "To muchel am I peyned for the thynges that I nevere deserved, and to muche defouled for shendshipe that man is worthy to have." / And therfore may the synful man wel seye, as seith Seint Bernard, "Acursed be the bitternesse of my synne, for which ther moste be suffred so muchel bitternesse." / For certes, after the diverse disordinaunces of oure wikkednesses was the passioun of Jesu Crist ordeyned in diverse thynges, / as thus. 275 Certes, synful mannes soule is bitraysed of the devel by coveitise of temporeel prosperitee, and scorned by deceite whan he cheseth flesshly delices; and yet is it tormented by inpacience of adversitee, and bispet by servage and subjeccioun of synne; and atte laste it is slayn fynally. / For this disordinaunce of synful man was Jesu Crist bitraysed, and after that was he bounde that cam for to unbynden us of synne and peyne. / Thanne was he byscorned, that oonly sholde han been honoured in alle thynges and of alle thynges. / Thanne was his visage, that oghte be desired to be seyn of al mankynde, in which visage aungels desiren to looke, vileynsly bispet. / Thanne was he scourged that nothing hadde agilt. And finally thanne was he crucified and slayn. / Thanne was 280 acompliced the word of Ysaye that seith that he was wounded for oure mysdedes and defouled for oure felonies. / Now sith that Jesu Crist took upon hymself the peyne of alle oure wikkednesses, muchel oghte synful man wepen and biwayle that for his synnes Goddes sone of hevene sholde al this peyne endure. /

The sixte thyng that oghte moeve a man to contricioun is the hope of three thynges: that is to seyn, foryifnesse of synne, and the yifte of grace wel for to do, and the glorie of hevene with which God shal guerdone a man for his goode dedes. / And for as muche as Jesu Crist yeveth us thise yiftes of his largesse and of his sovereyn bountee, therfore is he cleped *Iesus Nazarenus rex Iudeorum.* / *Iesus* is to seyn "saveour" or "salvacioun," on whom men shul hope to have foryifnesse of synnes, which that is proprely salvacioun of synnes. / And ther- 285 fore seyde the aungel to Joseph, "Thou shalt clepen his name Jesus, that shal saven his peple of hir synnes." / And heerof seith Seint Peter, "Ther is noon other name under hevene that is yeve to any man by which a man may be saved, but only Jesus." / *Nazarenus* is as muche for to seye as "florisshynge," in which a man shal hope that he that yeveth hym remission of synnes shal yeve hym eek grace wel for to do. For in the flour is hope of fruit in tyme comynge, and in foryifnesse of synnes hope of grace wel for to do. / "I was atte dore of thyn herte," seith Jesus, "and cleped for to entre. He that openeth to me shal have foryifnesse of synne. / I wol entre into hym by my grace and soupe with hym" by the goode werkes that he shal doon, whiche werkes been the foode of God, "and he shal soupe with me" by the grete joye that I shal yeven hym. / Thus shal man hope for 290 his werkes of penaunce that God shall yeven hym his regne, as he bihooteth hym in the gospel. /

Now shal a man understonde in which manere shal been his contricioun. I seye that it shal been universal and total, this is to seyn a man shal be verray repentant for alle his synnes that he hath doon in delit of his thoght, for delit is ful perilous. / For ther been two manere of consentynges. That oon of hem is cleped con-

---

273 forfeted ... peyned ... shendshipe, sinned, caused to suffer pain, disgrace. **275** *disordinaunces:* E *diconcordances;* Hg&c *discordaunces.* **276 bispet,** spat upon: E *dispeir.* **280 agilt,** sinned. **281 Ysaye,** Isa. 53:5. **283 guerdone,** reward. **284 largesse ... *rex Iudeorum,*** generosity, king of the Jews. **286 aungel,** Matt. 1:20–21. **287 Seint Peter,** Acts 4:12. **289 Jesus,** Rev. 3:20. **cleped,** called. **291 for his ... regne ... bihooteth,** because of his, kingdom, promises. **292 verray ... delit,** genuinely, sensual pleasure. Note the parallel to the steps by which Troylus fell in love, *TC,* 1.365ff.

sentynge of affeccioun, whan a man is moeved to
do synne and deliteth hym longe for to thynke
on that synne, / and his reson aperceyveth it
wel that it is synne agayns the lawe of God, and
yet his resoun refreyneth nat his foul delit or
talent, though he se wel apertly that it is agayns
the reverence of God. Although his resoun ne
consente noght to doon that synne in dede, / yet
seyn somme doctours that swich delit that
dwelleth longe it is ful perilous al be it
nevere so lite. / And also a man sholde 295
sorwe, namely, for al that evere he hath
desired agayn the lawe of God with perfit consentynge of his resoun, for therof is no doute
that it is deedly synne in consentynge. / For
certes, ther is no deedly synne that it nas first
in mannes thought and after that in his delit,
and so forth into consentynge and into dede. /
Wherfore I seye that many men ne repenten
hem nevere of swiche thoghtes and delites, ne
nevere shryven hem of it, but oonly of the dede
of grete synnes outward. / Wherfore I seye that
swiche wikked delites and wikked thoghtes been
subtile bigileres of hem that shullen be
dampned. / Mooreover man oghte to sorwe for
his wikkede wordes as wel as for his wikkede
dedes, for certes the repentaunce of a synguler
synne and nat repente of alle his othere synnes,
or elles repenten him of alle his othere synnes
and nat of a synguler synne, may nat
availle. / For certes, God Almighty is al 300
good, and therfore he foryeveth al or elles
right noght. / And heerof seith Seint Augustyn,
"I woot certeinly / that God is enemy to everich
synnere." And how thanne, he that observeth o
synne, shal he have foryifnesse of the remenaunt
of his othere synnes? Nay. / And fortherover,
contricioun sholde be wonder sorweful and
angwissous. And therfore yeveth hym God
pleynly his mercy. And therfore whan my soule
was angwissous withinne me, I hadde remembrance of God that my preyere myghte
come to hym. / Fortherover, contricioun moste

be continueel, and that man have stedefast
purpos to shriven hym, and for to amenden
hym of his lyf. / For soothly, whil con- 305
tricioun lasteth man may evere have hope
of foryifnesse. And of this comth hate of synne
that destroyeth synne bothe in himself and
eek in oother folk, at his power. / For which
seith David, "Ye that loven God hateth
wikkednesse." For trusteth wel, to love God
is for to love that he loveth and hate that he
hateth. /

The laste thyng that man shal understonde in
contricioun is this: wherof avayleth contricioun?
I seye that somtyme contricioun delivereth a
man fro synne, / of which that David seith, "I
seye," quod David, that is to seyn, "I purposed
fermely to shryve me and thow, Lord, relessedest
my synne." / And right so as contricion availleth noght withouten sad purpos of shrifte, if
man have oportunitee, right so litel worth is
shrifte or satisfaccioun withouten contricioun. / And mooreover, contricion 310
destroyeth the prisoun of helle; and maketh
wayk and fieble alle the strengthes of the
develes; and restoreth the yiftes of the Hooly
Goost and of alle goode vertues. / And it clenseth
the soule of synne, and delivereth the soule fro
the peyne of helle, and fro the compaignye of
the devel, and fro the servage of synne, and
restoreth it to alle goodes espirituels, and to
the compaignye and communyoun of Hooly
Chirche. / And fortherover, it maketh hym that
whilom was sone of ire to be sone of grace. And
alle thise thynges been preved by hooly writ. /
And therfore, he that wolde sette his entente to
thise thynges, he were ful wys, for soothly he ne
sholde nat thanne in al his lyf have corage to
synne, but yeven his body and al his herte to
the service of Jesu Crist, and therof doon hym
hommage. / For soothly, oure sweete lord Jesu
Crist hath spared us so debonairly in our folies
that if he ne hadde pitee of mannes soule,
a sory song we mighten alle singe. / 315

293 **affeccioun,** emotion. 294 **talent...apertly,** appetite, clearly. 296 **namely,** especially. 298 **shryven,** seek absolution. 302
Seint Augustyn, *De Vera et Falsa Poenitentia* 1.9.24. E *I—certeinly* om. 303 **observeth o,** adheres to one. 304 **wonder,** wonderfully.
307 **David,** Ps. 97:10. 309 **David,** Ps. 32:5. 310 **sad,** steadfast. 313 **whilom,** formerly. 315 **debonairly,** graciously.

Explicit prima pars Penitentie et sequitur secunda pars eiusdem.

The seconde partie of penitence is confessioun, that is signe of contricioun. / Now shul ye understonde what is confessioun, and wheither it oghte nedes be doon or noon, and whiche thynges been covenable to verray confessioun. /

First shaltow understonde that confessioun is verray shewinge of synnes to the preest. / This is to seyn "verray" for he moste confessen hym of alle the condiciouns that bilongen to his synne, as ferforth as he kan. / Al moot be seyd, and nothyng excused ne hyd ne forwrapped; and noght avaunte thee of thy goode werkes. / And fortherover, it is necessarie to ₃₂₀ understonde whennes that synnes spryngen, and how they encreessen, and whiche they been. /

Of the spryngynge of synnes seith Seint Paul in this wise, that right as by a man synne entred first into this world, and thurgh that synne deeth, right so thilke deeth entred into alle men that synneden. / And this man was Adam, by whom synne entred into this world whan he brak the comaundementz of God. / And therfore he that first was so mighty that he sholde nat have dyed bicam swich oon that he moste nedes dye, wheither he wolde or noon, and all his progenye in this world that in thilke man synneden. / Looke that in th'estaat of innocence, whan Adam and Eve naked weren in paradys, and nothing ne hadden shame of hir nakednesse, / how that the serpent that was ₃₂₅ moost wily of alle othere beestes that God hadde maked seyde to the womman, "Why comaunded God to yow, ye sholde nat eten of every tree in paradys?" / The womman answerde, "Of the fruyt," quod she, "of the trees in paradys we feden us, but soothly of the fruyt of the tree that is in the myddel of paradys God forbad us for to ete, and nat touchen it, lest peraventure we should dyen." / The serpent seyde to the womman, "Nay, nay, ye shul nat dyen of deeth, for sothe! God woot that what day that ye eten therof, youre eyen shul opene and ye shul been as goddes knowynge good and harm." / The womman thanne saugh that the tree was good to feedyng, and fair to the eyen, and delitable to the sighte. She took of the fruyt of the tree and eet it, and yaf to hire housbonde and he eet, and anoon the eyen of hem bothe openeden. / And whan that they knewe that they were naked, they sowed of figeleves a maner of breches to hiden hire membres. / ₃₃₀ There may ye seen that deedly synne hath first suggestion of the feend, as sheweth heere by the naddre; and afterward, the delit of the flessh, as sheweth heere by Eve; and after that, the consentynge of resoun, as sheweth heere by Adam. / For trust wel, though so were that the feend tempted Eve, that is to seyn the flessh, and the flessh hadde delit in the beautee of the fruyt defended, yet certes, til that resoun, that is to seyn Adam, consented to the etynge of the fruyt, yet stood he in th'estaat of innocence. / Of thilke Adam tooke we thilke synne original; for of hym flesshly descended be we alle, and engendred of vile and corrupt matiere. / And whan the soule is put in oure body, right anon is contract original synne, and that that was erst but oonly peyne of concupiscence is afterward bothe peyne and synne. / And therfore be we alle born sones of wratthe and of dampnacioun perdurable, if it nere baptesme that we receyven which bynymeth us the culpe. But for

---

316 that is signe, which is evidence. **317 covenable,** appropriate. **319 condiciouns,** circumstances; note the light these lines cast on the confessional background to the descriptions of the Pilgrims in *CT*, Gen. Pro., l.38–41ff. **320 forwrapped . . . avaunte,** wrapped up (intensive "for"), boast. *thee/thy:* Hg&c *hym/his.* **322 spryngynge,** origin. **325 Adam and Eve,** Gen. 3:1–7. **328 God woot . . . harm,** God knows, evil. **330 membres,** genitals. **331 naddre,** serpent. Note the light that the figurative interpretations of Eve and Adam (ll. 331–57) cast upon the relations of Troylus and Criseyde, the Wife of Bath, and other lovers in medieval narrative. **332 fruyt defended,** forbidden fruit. **333 tooke we . . . flesshly,** we derived, physically. **334 anon is contract . . . peyne . . . concupiscence,** immediately is incurred (contracted), affliction, sexual desire. **335 perdurable, if it nere . . . bynymeth . . . culpe,** everlasting, if it were not for, removes, guilt.

sothe, the peyne dwelleth with us as to temptacioun, which peyne highte concupiscence. / And this concupiscence whan 335 it is wrongfully disposed or ordeyned in man, it maketh hym coveite, by coveitise of flessh, flesshly synne by sighte of his eyen as to erthely thynges, and coveitise of hynesse by pride of herte. /

Now as for to speken of the firste coveitise, that is concupiscence after the lawe of oure membres that weren lawefulliche ymaked and by rightful juggement of God, / I seye for as muche as man is nat obeisaunt to God that is his lord, therfore is the flessh to hym disobeisaunt thurgh concupiscence, which yet is cleped norissynge of synne and occasioun of synne. / Therfore, al the while that a man hath in hym the peyne of concupiscence, it is impossible but he be tempted somtime and moeved in his flessh to synne. / And this thyng may nat faille as longe as he lyveth. It may wel wexe fieble and faille by vertu of baptesme and by the grace of God thurgh penitence, / but 340 fully ne shal it nevere quenche that he ne shal somtyme be moeved in hymself, but if he were al refreyded by siknesse, or by malefice of sorcerie, or colde drynkes. / For lo, what seith Seint Paul, "The flessh coveiteth agayn the spirit, and the spirit agayn the flessh; they been so contrarie and so stryven that a man may nat alwey doon as he wolde." / The same Seint Paul, after his grete penaunce in water and in lond (in water by night and by day in greet peril and in greet peyne, in lond in famyne, in thurst, in coold and cloothlees, and ones stoned almoost to the deeth), / yet seyde he, "Allas, I, caytyf man, who shal delivere me fro the prisoun of my caytyf body?" / And Seint Jerome, whan he longe tyme hadde woned in desert where as he hadde no compaignye but of wilde beestes, where as he ne hadde no mete but herbes and water to his drynke, ne no bed but the naked erthe, for which his flessh was blak as an Ethiopeen for heete and ny destroyed for coold, / yet seyde he that the brennynge of 345 lecherie boyled in al his body. / Wherfore I woot wel sykerly that they been deceyved that seyn that they ne be nat tempted in hir body. / Witnesse on Seint Jame the apostel that seith that every wight is tempted in his owene concupiscence, that is to seyn that everich of us hath matere and occasioun to be tempted of the norissynge of synne that is in his body. / And therfore seith Seint John the Evaungelist, "If that we seyn that we beth withoute synne, we deceyve us-selve and trouthe is nat in us." /

Now shal ye understonde in what manere that synne wexeth or encreesseth in man. The firste thyng is thilke norissynge of synne of which I spak biforn, thilke flesshly concupiscence. / And after that comth the 350 subjeccioun of the devel, this is to seyn the develes bely, with which he bloweth in man the fir of flesshly concupiscence. / And after that, a man bithynketh hym wheither he wol doon or no thilke thing to which he is tempted. / And thanne, if that a man withstonde and weyve the first entisynge of his flessh and of the feend, thanne is it no synne. And if it so be that he do nat so, thanne feeleth he anoon a flambe of delit. / And thanne is it good to bewar and kepen hym wel, or elles he wol falle anon into consentynge of synne; and thanne wol he do it if he may have tyme and place. / And of this matere seith Moyses by the devel in this manere, "The feend seith. I wole chace and pursue the man by wikked suggestioun, and I wole hente him by moevynge or stirynge of synne. I wol departe my prise or my praye by deliberacioun, and my lust shal been accompliced in delit.

---

335 **highte,** called. 336 **hynesse,** high place (in the world). E&c *And—concupiscence* om. 337 **firste coveitise,** first sort of covetousness. **lawe of oure membres,** demands (law) of our genitals. 341 **refreyded . . . malefice,** chilled, wicked work. 342 **Seint Paul,** Gal. 5:17. 343 **same Seint Paul,** II Cor. 11:25, Rom. 7:24. 344 **caytyf,** miserable. 345 **Seint Jerome,** *Epistola 22 ad Eustachium, De Virginitate* 7. **woned,** lived. 347 **woot . . . sykerly,** know, certainly. 348 **Seint Jame,** James 1:14. 349 **Seint John,** I John 1:8. 351 **subjeccioun . . . bely,** suggestion, bellows. 353 **weyve,** turn aside. 354 **kepen hym,** guard himself. 355 **Moyses,** Exod. 15:9. **hente . . . departe . . . prise . . . praye . . . lust . . . delit,** capture, single out, prize, prey, desire, sexual pleasure.

I wol drawe my swerd in consentynge." / 355 For certes, right as a swerd departeth a thyng in two pcces, right so consentynge departeth God fro man. "And thanne wol I sleen hym with myn hand in dede of synne," thus seith the feend. / For certes, thanne is a man al deed in soule. And thus is synne accompliced by temptacioun, by delit, and by consentynge; and thanne is the synne cleped actueel. /

For sothe, synne is in two maneres: outher it is venial or deedly sinne. Soothly, whan man loveth any creature moore than Jesu Crist oure creatour, thanne is it deedly sinne. And venial synne is it if man love Jesu Crist lasse than hym oghte. / For sothe, the dede of this venial synne is ful perilous, for it amenuseth the love that men sholde han to God moore and moore. / And therfore, if a man charge hymself with manye swiche venial synnes, certes, but if so be that he somtyme descharge hym of hem by shrifte, they mowe ful lightly amenuse in hym al the love that he hath to Jesu Crist. / 360 And in this wise skippeth venial into deedly synne. For certes, the moore that a man chargeth his soule with venial synnes, the moore is he enclyned to fallen into deedly synne. / And therfore, lat us nat be necligent to deschargen us of venial synnes. For the proverbe seith that manye smale maken a greet. / And herkne this ensample. A greet wawe of the see comth somtyme with so greet a violence that it drencheth the shipe. And the same harm dooth somtyme the smale dropes of water that entren thurgh a litel crevace into the thurrok, and into the botme of the shipe, if men be so necligent that they ne descharge hem nat bytyme. / And therfore, althogh ther be a difference bitwixe thise two causes of drenchynge, algates the shipe is dreynt. / Right so fareth it somtyme of deedly synne, and of anoyouse veniale synnes,

whan they multiplie in a man so greetly that thilke worldly thynges that he loveth, thurgh whiche he synneth venyally, is as greet in his herte as the love of God, or moore. / And 365 therfore, the love of everything that is nat biset in God ne doon principally for Goddes sake, although that a man love it lasse than God, yet is it venial synne. / And deedly synne whan the love of anythyng weyeth in the herte of man as muchel as the love of God, or moore. / "Deedly synne," as seith Seint Augustyn, "is whan a man turneth his herte fro God, which that is verray sovereyn bountee that may nat chaunge, and yeveth his herte to thyng that may chaunge and flitte." / And certes, that is everything save God of hevene. For sooth is that if a man yeve his love the which that he oweth al to God with al his herte unto a creature, certes, as muche as he yeveth of his love to thilke creature, so muche he bireveth fro God; / and therfore doth he synne. For he that is dettour to God ne yeldeth nat to God al his dette, that is to seyn al the love of his herte. / 370

Now sith man understondeth generally which is venial synne, thanne is it covenable to tellen specially of synnes whiche that many a man peraventure ne demeth hem nat synnes, and ne shryveth hym nat of the same thynges, and yet nathelees they becn synnes / soothly, as thise clerkes writen. This is to seyn that at every tyme that a man eteth or drynketh moore than suffyseth to the sustenaunce of his body, in certein he dooth synne. / And eek, whan he speketh moore than nedeth, it is synne. Eke whan he herkneth nat benignely the compleint of the poure. / Eke whan he is in heele of body and wol nat faste whan hym oghte faste, withouten cause resonable. Eke whan he slepeth moore than nedeth, or whan he comth by thilke

---

356 departeth . . . in dede, parts, by the dede. **357 al deed . . . cleped,** completely dead, called. **358 venial . . . deedly,** pardonable, unpardonable (deadly). **359 amenuseth,** decreases. **360 charge,** load. **363 wawe . . . drencheth . . . thurrok . . . bytyme,** wave, drowns, hold, in time. **364 algates . . . dreynt,** nevertheless, drowned. **365 anoyouse,** annoying. **367 weyeth,** weighs. E&c *wexeth.* **368 sovereyn bountee,** supreme goodness. **369 bireveth,** steals. **371 convenable,** appropriate. *hym:* E&c *hem.* **374 heele,** health. *hym oghte:* Hg&c *oother folk.*

enchesoun to late to chirche, or to othere werkes
of charite. / Eke whan he useth his wyf withouten sovereyn desir of engendrure to the
honour of God, or for the entente to yelde to
his wyf the dette of his body. / Eke whan 375
he wol nat visite the sike and the prisoner,
if he may. Eke if he love wyf or child or oother
worldly thyng moore than resoun requireth.
Eke if he flatere or blandishe moore than hym
oghte for any necessitee. / Eke if he amenuse or
withdrawe the almesse of the poure. Eke if he
apparailleth his mete moore deliciously than
nede is or ete to hastily by likerousnesse. / Eke
if he tale vanytees at chirche or at Goddes
service, or that he be a talkere of ydel wordes of
folye or of vileynye, for he shal yelden acountes
of it at the day of doome. / Eke whan he
biheteth or assureth to do thynges that he may
nat perfourne. Eke whan that he by lightnesse
or folie mysseyeth or scorneth his neighebore. /
Eke whan he hath any wikked suspecioun of
thyng ther he ne woot of it no soothfastnesse. / Thise thynges and mo withoute 380

nombre been synnes, as seith Seint
Augustyn. /
Now shal men understonde, that al be it so
that noon erthely man may eschue alle venial
synnes, yet may he restreyne hym by the brennynge love that he hath to oure lord Jesu Crist,
and by preyeres and confessioun and othere
goode werkes, so that it shal but litel greve. /
For as seith Seint Augustyn, "If a man love
God in swich manere that al that evere he dooth
is in the love of God, and for the love of God
verraily, for he brenneth in the love of God, /
looke how muche that a drope of water that
falleth in a fourneys ful of fyr anoyeth or
greveth, so muche anoyeth a venial synne unto
a man that is parfit in the love of Jesu Crist." /
Men may also refreyne venial synne by re-
ceyvynge worthily of the precious body of
Jesu Crist, / by receyvyng eek of hooly 385
water, by almesdede, by general confessioun
of *Confiteor* at masse and at complyn, and by
blessynge of bisshopes and of preestes and
oothere goode werkes. /

Sequitur de Septem Peccatis Mortalibus et eorum dependenciis circumstanciis et speciebus.

De Superbia.

Now is it bihovely thyng to telle whiche been
the Deedly Synnes, this is to seyn chieftaynes of
synnes. Alle they renne in o lees, but in diverse
maneres. Now been they cleped chieftaynes for
as muche as they been chief, and spryngers of
alle othere synnes. / Of the roote of thise sevene
synnes thanne is pride the general roote of alle

374 **enchesoun,** reason. 375 **sovereyn . . . engendrure,** principal, begetting offspring; distorted in MerchT, IV.1838. **yelde . . . the dette,** the marital obligation to sexual intercourse, I Cor. 7:3; see WBP, III.130. 377 **amenuse . . . apparailleth his mete . . . likerousnesse,** reduce, prepares his food, gluttony (lechery). 378 **tale vanytees,** regale nonsense (scandal). 379 **biheteth . . . lightnesse,** promises, thoughtlessness. 380 **woot . . . soothfastnesse,** know, truth. 382 **greve,** hurt (him). *restreyne:* Hg&c *refreyne.* 384 **fourneys,** furnace. 385 **refreyne . . . precious body,** curb, the communion wafer. 386 *Confiteor,* "I confess," ritual beginning of the confession. **complyn,** last of the canonical hours, devoted to prayers before going to sleep. E has rubric *Explicit secunda pars penitentie* here, but repeats it again at l. 1027 where it occurs in most MSS. **Sequitur de Septem** &c, "Here follow the Seven Deadly Sins and their subdivisions, circumstances, and varieties." **De Superbia,** "Concerning Pride." No direct source has been found for the combination of materials in the Parson's Tale. The portion on the Seven Sins has verbal echoes of various redactions of Guilielmus Peraldus' *Summa de vitiis et virtutibus* made in England. Although the closest parallels are to treatises in Latin, Chaucer's prose style and vocabulary suggest that he was working from French. 387 **bihovely . . . chieftaynes,** necessary, capital (chief), Fr. *capitous.* See Bryan and Dempster, *Sources and Analogues,* p. 745, for a French treatise on the sins somewhat like that used by Chaucer, which begins with an explanation "Pur quei les set pechez sunt appellez pechez capitous," i.e., because from these seven, like seven heads, come all the other sins. This led to the Deadly Sins sometimes being called Capital Sins. **Alle they renne in o lees,** they all run on one leash. In other discussions, the Seven Sins are described as the "dogs of hell," with which the devil hunts his prey. **spryngers,** sources; Hg&c *spring,* E&c *spryngen.*

harmes, for of this roote spryngen certein braunches, as ire, envye, accidie or slewthe, avarice or coveitise (to commune understondynge), glotonye, and lecherye. / And everich of thise chief synnes hath his braunches and his twigges, as shal be declared in hire chapitres folwinge. /

And thogh so be that no man kan outrely telle the nombre of the twigges and of the harmes that cometh of pride, yet wol I shewe a partie of hem, as ye shul understonde. / 390 Ther is inobedience, avauntynge, ypocrisie, despit, arrogance, inpudence, swellynge of herte, insolence, elacioun, inpacience, strif, contumacie, presumpcioun, irreverence, pertinacie, veyne glorie, and many another twig that I kan nat declare. / Inobedient is he that disobeyeth for despit to the comandementz of God, and to his sovereyns, and to his goostly fader. / Avauntour is he that bosteth of the harm or of the bountee that he hath doon. / Ypocrite is he that hideth to shewe hym swich as he is and sheweth hym swiche as he noght is. / Despitous is he that hath desdeyn of his neighebore, that is to seyn of his evene-Cristene, or hath despit to doon that hym oghte to do. / 395 Arrogant is he that thynketh that he hath thilke bountees in hym that he hath noght, or weneth that he sholde have hem by his desertes, or elles he demeth that he be that he nys nat. / Inpudent is he that for his pride hath no shame of his synnes. / Swellynge of herte is whan a man rejoyseth hym of harm that he hath doon. / Insolent is he that despiseth in his juggement alle othere folk as to regard of his value, and of his konning, and of his spekyng, and of his beryng. / Elacioun is whan he ne may neither suffre to have maister ne felawe. / 400

Inpacient is he that wol nat been ytaught ne undernome of his vice, and by strif werreieth trouthe wityngly, and deffendeth his folye. / *Contumax* is he that thurgh his indignacion is agayns everich auctoritee or power of hem that been his sovereyns. / Presumpcioun is whan a man undertaketh an emprise that hym oghte nat do, or elles that he may nat do, and this is called surquidrie. Irreverence is whan men do nat honour there as hem oghte to doon, and waiten to be reverenced. / Pertinacie is whan man deffendeth his folies, and trusteth to muchel in his owene wit. / Veyne glorie is for to have pompe and delit in his temporeel hynesse, and glorifie hym in this worldly estaat. / 405 Janglynge is whan men speken to muche biforn folk, and clappen as a mille, and taken no kepe what they seye. /

And yet is ther a privee spece of pride that waiteth first for to be salewed er he wole salewe, al be he lasse worth than that oother is peraventure; and eek he waiteth or desireth to sitte, or elles to goon above hym in the wey, or kisse pax, or been encensed, or goon to offryng biforn his neighebore, / and swiche semblable thynges agayns his duetee, peraventure, but that he hath his herte and his entente in swich a proud desir to be magnified and honoured biforn the peple. /

Now been ther two maneres of pride, that oon of hem is withinne the herte of man and that oother is withoute. / Of whiche soothly thise forseyde thynges, and mo than I have seyd, apertenen to pride that is in the herte of man; and that othere speces of pride been withoute. / But natheles that oon of thise speces 410 of pride is signe of that oother, right as the gaye leefsel atte taverne is signe of the wyn that

---

388 accidie or slewthe, sloth. **390 outrely telle,** completely count. **391 avauntynge . . . despit . . . swellynge of herte,** boasting, disdain, insolence. **elacioun . . . contumacie . . . pertinacie,** arrogance, insubordination, obstinacy. **392 goostly,** spiritual (ghostly). **393 bountee,** the good things. **395 evene-Cristene,** fellow Christian. **396 weneth . . . demeth,** believes, judges. **401 undernome . . . werreieth trouthe,** reproved, wars against truth. **403 emprise,** enterprise. *surquidrie:* E&c *surquidie.* **406 clappen as a mille,** clatter like a mill (constantly). Hg&c *a man speketh,* with singular following. **407 privee . . . salewed,** secret, greeted. **sitte, or . . . goon above hym,** sit in higher place at table, or precede in walking. **kisse pax,** i.e., be the first in church to kiss the pax, a tablet bearing the representation of the Crucifixion, kissed as part of the ritual of Mass. **been encensed,** censing was likewise part of the Mass. **goon to offryng,** see the Wife of Bath, Gen. Pro., 1.450. **410 apertenen,** appertain. **411 leefsel,** arbor.

is in the celer. / And this is in manye thynges, as in speche and contenaunce, and in outrageous array of clothyng. / For certes, if ther ne hadde be no synne in clothyng, Crist wolde nat have noted and spoken of the clothyng of thilke riche man in the gospel. / And as seith Seint Gregorie that precious clothyng is cowpable for the derthe of it, and for his softenesse, and for his strangenesse and degisynesse, and for the superfluitee, and for the inordinat scantnesse of it. / Allas, may men nat seen, as in oure dayes, the synful costlewe array of clothynge, and namely in to muche superfluitee, or elles in to desordinat scantnesse? /   415

As to the firste sinne, that is in superfluitee of clothynge which that maketh it so deere, to harm of the peple, / nat oonly the cost of embrowdynge, the degise endentynge, barrynge, owndynge, palynge, wyndynge, or bendynge, and semblable wast of clooth in vanitee, / but ther is also costlewe furrynge in hir gownes, so muche pownsonynge of chisels to maken holes, so muche daggynge of sheres, / forthwith the superfluitee in lengthe of the forseide gownes, trailynge in the dong and in the mire, on horse and eek on foote, as wel of men as of wommen, that al thilke trailyng is verraily as in effect wasted, consumed, thredbare, and roten with donge, rather than it is yeven to the poure, to greet damage of the forseyde poure folk. / And that in sondry wise. This is to seyn that the moore that clooth is wasted, the moore it costeth to the peple for the scantnesse. /   420 And fortherover, if so be that they wolde yeven swich pownsoned and dagged clothyng to the poure folk, it is nat convenient to were for

hire estaat, ne suffisant to beete hire necessitee, to kepe hem fro the distemperance of the firmament. / Upon that oother side, to speken of the horrible disordinat scantnesse of clothyng, as been thise kutted sloppes or haynselyns, that thurgh hire shortnesse ne covere nat the shameful membres of man, to wikked entente. / Allas, somme of hem shewen the boce of hir shape and the horrible swollen membres that semeth lik the maladie of hirnia, in the wrappynge of hir hoses, / and eek the buttokes of hem faren as it were the hyndre part of a she-ape in the fulle of the mone. / And mooreover the wrecched swollen membres that they shewe thurgh the degisynge, in departynge of hire hoses in whit and reed semeth that half hir shameful privee membres weren flayne. /   425 And if so be that they departen hire hoses in othere colours, as is whit and blak, or whit and blew, or blak and reed, and so forth, / thanne semeth it as by variaunce of colour that half the partie of hire privee membres were corrupt by the fir of Seint Antony, or by cancre, or by oother swich meschaunce. / Of the hyndre part of hir buttokes, it is ful horrible for to see. For certes, in that partie of hir body ther as they purgen hir stynkynge ordure, / that foule partie shewe they to the peple prowdly in despit of honestitee, the which honestitee that Jesu Crist and his freendes observede to shewen in hir lyve. / Now as of the outrageous array of wommen, God woot that though the visages of somme of hem seme ful chaast and debonaire, yet notifie they in hire array of atyr likerousnesse and pride. / I sey nat that   430 honestitee in clothynge of man or womman

---

413 clothyng ... in the gospel, Luke 16:19; recall the descriptions of the Squire, the Monk, etc., in the Gen. Pro. **414 Seint Gregorie,** *Homiliarum in Evangelia* 2.40.3. **cowpable ... derthe,** blameworthy, scarcity (i.e., expensiveness). **strangenesse ... degisynesse,** oddness, fashionableness ("disguisedness"). **415 costlewe,** costly. **416 deere ... harm,** expensive, detriment. **417 degise endentynge,** fashionable notching. **barrynge, owndynge, palynge, wyndynge, bendynge,** decorating with bars, undulating stripes, vertical stripes, coils, borders. **418 pownsonynge of chisels,** perforation with blades. **daggynge of sheres,** cutting fringes with shears. **419 forthwith,** as well as. *as wel of men:* E *as wel* om. **420 scantnesse,** brevity (tightness). **421 beete ... distemperance ... firmament,** supply, inclemency, weather (sky). **422 kutted sloppes ... haynselyns ... membres,** short cut coats, brief jackets, genitals. The complaint here is against the immodesty of short jackets when decorum decreed that men should wear cloaks to their knees or ankles. **423 boce ... hoses,** swelling, tight pants (leggings). *boce of hir shape and:* Hg&c *shap and the boce of.* **425 departynge,** contemporary high fashion decreed that the two legs of hose should be different colors. **flayne,** cut off (flayed). **427 fir of Seint Antony,** erysipelas (which causes a scarlet rash). **429 despit of honestitee,** contempt of decency. **430 as of ... notifie ... likerousnesse,** as to, signal, sensuality (lechery).

is uncovenable, but certes the superfluitee or disordinat scantitee of clothynge is reprevable. /

Also the synne of aornement or of apparaille is in thynges that apertenen to rydynge, as in to manye delicat horses that been hoolden for delit, that been so faire, fatte, and costlewe; / and also to many a vicious knave that is sustened by cause of hem; in to curious harneys, as in sadeles, in crouperes, peytrels, and bridles covered with precious clothyng and riche, barres and plates of gold and of silver. / For which God seith by Zakarie the prophete, "I wol confounde the ryderes of swiche horses." / This folk taken litel reward of the rydynge of Goddes sone of hevene, and of his harneys whan he rood upon the asse and ne hadde noon oother harneys but the poure clothes of his disciples; ne we ne rede nat that evere he rood on oother beest. / I speke this for the synne of super- 435 fluitee, and nat for reasonable honestitee whan reson it requireth. / And forther, certes, pride is greetly notified in holdynge of greet meynee whan they be of litel profit or of right no profit. / And namely, whan that meynee is felonous and damageous to the peple, by hardy-nesse of heigh lordshipe or by wey of offices. / For certes, swiche lordes sellen thanne hir lord-shipe to the devel of helle whanne they sustenen the wikkednesse of hir meynee. / Or elles whan this folk of lowe degree, as thilke that holden hostelries, sustenen the thefte of hire hos-tilers, and that is in many manere of deceites. / Thilke manere of folk been the 440 flyes that folwen the hony, or elles the houndes that folwen the careyne. Swiche for-seyde folk stranglen spiritually hir lordshipes. /

For which thus seith David the prophete, "Wikked deeth moote come upon thilke lord-shipes, and God yeve that they moote descenden into helle al doun, for in hire houses been iniquitees and shrewednesses," and nat God of hevene. / And certes, but if they doon amende-ment, right as God yaf his benisoun to Laban by the service of Jacob, and to Pharao by the service of Joseph, right so God wol yeve his malisoun to swiche lordshipes as sustenen the wikkednesse of hir servauntz, but if they come to amendement. /

Pride of the table appeereth eek ful ofte, for certes riche men been cleped to festes, and poure folk been put awey and rebuked. / Also in excesse of diverse metes and drynkes, and namely swiche manere bake metes and dissh metes, brennynge of wilde fyr, and peynted and castelled with papir, and semblable wast so that it is abusioun for to thynke. / And eek 445 in to greet preciousnesse of vessel and curiositee of mynstralcie, by whiche a man is stired the moore to delices of luxurie, / if so be that he sette his herte the lasse upon oure lord Jesu Crist, certeyn it is a synne. And certeinly the delices myghte been so grete in this caas that man myghte lightly falle by hem into deedly synne. / The especes that sourden of pride, soothly whan they sourden of malice ymagined, avised, and forncast, or elles of usage, been deedly synnes, it is no doute. / And whan they sourden by freletee unavysed sodeynly, and sodeynly withdrawen ayeyn, al been they grevouse synnes, I gesse that they ne been nat deedly. /

Now myghte men axe wherof that pride

---

431 uncovenable . . . reprevable, unsuitable, reprehensible. **432 aornement . . . delicat,** adornment, elegant; recall the Monk in the Gen. Pro., I.168. **433 sustened,** retained (to groom the horses). **curious . . . crouperes, peytrels, . . . barres and plates,** ornate, cruppers (tail straps), breast shields, metal adornments. **434 Zakarie,** Zech. 10:5. **435 reward,** regard. **rydynge of Goddes sone,** the way Christ rode on Palm Sunday, Matt. 21. **436 for,** i.e., against. **437 notified . . . holdynge . . . meynee,** indicated, maintaining, body of retainers. **438 namely,** especially. **hardynesse of heigh lordshipe . . . offices,** insolence of high position, official positions. **439 lordshipe . . . sustenen,** authority, support. **441 Thilke manere,** this kind. **442 David,** Ps. 55:15. **God yeve,** God grant. **houses been . . . shrewednesses,** homes are, wickednesses. *al doun:* E *al doun al doun;* Hg&c *al doun adown.* **443 benisoun . . . malisoun,** blessing, curse. *Laban/Pharao* reversed in EHg&c. **444 cleped . . . put awey,** invited, turned away. Recall the Franklin, Gen. Pro., I.336. **445 metes . . . dissh metes,** foods, foods in serving dishes (e.g., stews). **wilde fyr . . . castelled,** flambéed dishes, decorated with battlements. **abusioun for to thynke,** outrage to think of. **446 curiositee of mynstralcie,** elaborateness of the music accompanying the meal. **delices,** the delights. **447 lightly,** easily. **448 especes . . . sourden,** subdivisions, arise. **malice ymagined,** premeditated evil (malice). **avised . . . forncast . . . usage,** considered, planned, habit. **449 freletee unavysed,** unpremeditated weakness.

sourdeth and spryngeth, and I seye somtyme it spryngeth of the goodes of nature, and somtyme of the goodes of fortune, and somtyme of the goodes of grace. / Certes, the goodes 450 of nature stonden outher in goodes of body or in goodes of soule. / Certes, goodes of body been heele of body, as strengthe, delivernesse, beautee, gentries, franchise. / Goodes of nature of the soule been good wit, sharpe understondynge, subtil engyn, vertu natureel, good memorie. / Goodes of fortune been richesses, highe degrees of lordships, preisinges of the peple. / Goodes of grace been science, power to suffre spiritueel travaille, benignitee, vertuous contemplacion, withstondynge of temptacion, and semblable thynges. / Of whiche 455 forseyde goodes, certes it is a ful greet folye a man to priden hym in any of hem alle. / Now as for to speken of goodes of nature, God woot that somtyme we han hem in nature as muche to oure damage as to oure profit. / As for to speken of heele of body, certes it passeth ful lightly, and eek it is ful ofte enchesoun of the siknesse of oure soule. For God woot, the flessh is a ful greet enemy to the soule, and therfore the moore that the body is hool, the moore be we in peril to falle. / Eke for to pride hym in his strengthe of body it is an heigh folye, for certes the flessh coveiteth agayn the spirit, and ay the moore strong that the flessh is the sorier may the soule be. / And over al this, strengthe of body and worldly hardynesse causeth ful ofte many a man to peril and meschaunce. / Eek for to 460 pride hym of his gentrie is ful greet folie, for oftetyme the gentrie of the body binymeth the gentrie of the soule. And eek we ben alle of o fader and of o mooder, and alle we been of o nature roten and corrupt, bothe riche and poure. / For sothe, o manere gentrie is for to preise, that apparailleth mannes corage with vertues and moralitees and maketh hym Cristes child. / For truste wel that over what man that synne hath maistrie, he is a verray cherl to synne. /

Now been ther generale signes of gentillesse, as eschewynge of vice and ribaudye and servage of synne, in word, in werk, and contenaunce, / and usynge vertu, curteisye, and clennesse, and to be liberal—that is to seyn, large by mesure, for thilke that passeth mesure is folie and synne. / Another is to remembre hym of 465 bountee that he of oother folk hath receyved. / Another is to be benigne to his goode subgetis. Wherfore seith Senek, "Ther is nothing moore covenable to a man of heigh estaat than debonairetee and pitee. / And therfore thise flyes that men clepeth bees, whan they maken hire kyng, they chesen oon that hath no prikke wherwith he may stynge." / Another is, a man to have a noble herte and a diligent, to attayne to heighe vertuouse thynges. / Now certes, a man to pride hym in the goodes of grace is eek an outrageous folie, for thilke yiftes of grace that sholde have turned hym to goodnesse and to medicine turneth hym to venym and to confusioun, as seith Seint Gregorie. / Certes 470 also, whoso prideth hym in the goodes of fortune, he is a ful greet fool. For somtyme is a man a greet lord by the morwe that is a caytyf and a wrecche er it be nyght. / And somtyme the richesse of a man is cause of his deth. Somtyme the delices of a man is cause of the grevous maladye thurgh which he dyeth. / Certes, the commendacion of the peple is somtyme ful fals and ful brotel for to triste. This day they preyse, tomorwe they blame. / God woot, desir to have commendacioun eek of the peple hath caused deeth to many a bisy man. /

---

450 goodes, gifts (benefits). **452 heele . . . delivernesse . . . gentries . . . franchise,** health, agility, high birth, freedom. *gentries:* some MSS *gentrice, gentrye.* **453 wit . . . engyn,** intelligence, ingenuity. **455 science . . . benignitee . . . semblable,** knowledge, kindness, similar. **458 passeth . . . lightly . . . enchesoun,** departs, easily, cause. **459 coveiteth,** struggles. **461 binymeth,** takes away. Recall the sermon on gentilesse in WBT, iii.109ff. **464 ribaudye . . . servage . . . contenaunce,** ribaldry (debauchery), bondage, manner. **465 large by mesure . . . passeth,** generous with discretion, surpasses. **467 Senek,** Seneca, *De Clementia* 1.3.3., 1.9.2. **covenable . . . debonairetee,** suitable, graciousness. **470 goodes of grace . . . medicine,** i.e., unearned benefits, improvement. **471 morwe . . . caytyf,** morning, outcast. **472 delices,** sensual pleasures. **473 commendacion . . . peple . . . brotel . . . triste,** approbation, populace, brittle, trust.

Remedium contra peccatum Superbie.

Now sith that so is, that ye han understonde what is pride, and whiche been the speces of it, and whennes pride sourdeth and springeth, / now shul ye understonde which 475 is the remedie agayns the synne of pride, and that is humylitee or mekenesse. / That is a vertu thurgh which a man hath verray knoweleche of hymself, and holdeth of hymself no pris ne deyntee as in regard of his desertes, considerynge evere his freletee. / Now been ther three maneres of humylitee, as humylitee in herte, and another humylitee in his mouth, the thridde in his werkes. / The humilitee in herte is in foure maneres: that oon is whan a man holdeth hymself as noght worth biforn God of hevene. Another is whan he ne despiseth noon oother man. / The thridde is whan he rekketh nat though men holde him noght worth. The ferthe is whan he nys nat sory of his humiliacioun. / Also the humilitee of mouth 480 is in foure thynges: in attempree speche, and in humblesse of speche, and whan he biknoweth with his owene mouth that he is swich as hym thynketh that he is in his herte. Another is whan he preiseth the bountee of another man and nothyng therof amenuseth. / Humilitee eek in werkes is in foure maneres: the firste is whan he putteth othere men biforn hym. The seconde is to chese the loweste place overal. The thridde is gladly to assente to good conseil. / The ferthe is to stonde gladly to the award of his sovereyns or of hym that is in hyer degree. Certein, this is a greet werk of humylitee. /

Sequitur de Invidia.

After pryde wol I speken of the foule synne of envye, which is, as by the word of the philosophre, sorwe of oother mennes prosperitee, and after the word of Seint Augustyn it is sorwe of oother mennes wele, and joye of othere mennes harm. / This foule synne is platly agayns the Hooly Goost. Al be it so that every synne is agayns the Hooly Goost, yet nathelees for as muche as bountee aperteneth proprely to the Hooly Goost, and envye comth proprely of malice, therfor it is proprely agayn the bountee of the Hooly Goost. / Now hath 485 malice two speces, that is to seyn, hardnesse of herte in wikkednesse, or elles the flessh of man is so blynd that he considereth nat that he is in synne or rekketh nat that he is in synne, which is the hardnesse of the devel. / That oother spece of malice is whan a man werreyeth trouthe whan he woot that it is trouthe, and eek whan he werreyeth the grace that God hath yeve to his neighebore, and al this is by envye. / Certes, thanne is envye the worste synne that is. For soothly, alle othere synnes been somtyme oonly agayns o special vertu. / But certes, envye is agayns alle vertues and agayns alle goodnesses. For it is sory of alle the bountees of his neighebore, and in this manere it is divers from alle othere synnes. / For wel unnethe is ther any synne that it ne hath som delit in itself, save only envye that evere hath in itself angwissh and sorwe. / The speces of envye 490 been thise: there is first sorwe of other mannes goodnesse and of his prosperitee. And prosperitee is kyndely matere of joye, thanne is envye a synne agayns kynde. / The secounde spece of envye is joye of oother mannes harm, and that is proprely lyk to the devel that evere rejoyseth hym of mannes harm. / Of thise two speces comth bakbityng, and this synne of bakbityng or detraccion hath certeine speces, as thus. Som man preiseth his neighebore by a

---

475 E puts *Remedium* heading in midsentence, after *springeth.* **sith . . . sourdeth,** since, arises. **478 maneres,** kinds. **481 attempree . . . biknoweth . . . amenuseth,** temperate, confesses, detracts. **482 gladly,** cheerfully. E *good* om. **483 award of his sovereyns,** decision of his rulers. **484 sorwe of . . . wele,** sorrow at, good fortune. **Seint Augustyn,** *Enarrationes in Psalmos* Ps. 105:25 (Vulgate). E&c *mannes/mannes/mennes.* **485 platly . . . bountee,** directly, generosity. E&c *foule* om. **486 rekketh,** cares. **487 werreyeth . . . woot,** wars against, knows. *malice:* Hg&c *envye.* **489 sory of . . . bountees . . . divers,** sorry about, advantages, different. **490 unnethe,** hardly. **491 kyndely,** naturally.

wikke entente, / for he maketh alwey a wikked knotte atte laste ende. Alwey he maketh a "but" atte laste ende, that is digne of moore blame than worth is al the preisynge. / The seconde spece is that if a man be good and dooth or seith a thing to good entente, the bakbiter wol turne all thilke goodnesse upsodoun to his shrewed entente. / The thridde is to amenuse the bountee of his neighebore. / The fourthe spece of bakbityng is this, that if men speke goodnesse of a man thanne wol the bakbitere seyn, "Pardee, swich a man is yet bet than he," in dispreisynge of hym that men preise. / The fifte spece is this, for to consente gladly and herkne gladly to the harm that men speke of oother folk. This synne is ful greet and ay encreeseth after the wikked entente of the bakbiter. / After bakbityng cometh grucching or murmuracion; and somtyme it spryngeth of inpacience agayns God and somtyme agayns man. / Agayns God it is whan a man gruccheth agayn the peynes of helle, or agayns poverte, or los of catel, or agayn reyn or tempest, or elles grucccheth that shrewes han prosperitee, or elles for that goode men han adversitee. / And alle thise thynges sholde men suffre paciently, for they comen by the rightful jugge- ment and ordinaunce of God. / Somtyme comth grucching of avarice, as Judas grucched agayns the Magdaleyne whan she enoynte the hevede of oure lord Jesu Crist with hire precious oyne- ment. / This maner murmure is swich as whan man gruccheth of goodnesse that hymself dooth, or that oother folk doon of hir owene catel. / Somtyme comth murmure of pride, as whan Simon the Pharisee grucched agayn the Magdaleyne whan she approched to Jesu Crist and weep at his feet for hire synnes. / And somtyme grucchyng sourdeth of envye, whan men discovereth a mannes harm that was pryvee, or bereth hym on hond thyng that

is fals. / Murmure eek is ofte amonges ser- vauntz, that grucchen whan hir sovereyns bidden hem doon leveful thynges, / and for as muche as they dar nat openly withseye the comaundementz of hir sovereyns yet wol they seyn harm and grucche and murmure prively for verray despit, / whiche wordes men clepen the develes Pater Noster, though so be that the devel ne hadde nevere Pater Noster, but that lewed folk yeven it swich a name. / Somtyme grucchyng comth of ire or prive hate that norisseth rancour in herte, as afterward I shal declare. / Thanne cometh eek bitternesse of herte, thurgh which bitternesse every good dede of his neighebor semeth to hym bitter and unsavory. / Thanne cometh discord that unbyndeth alle manere of freendshipe. Thanne comth scornynge of his neighebore, al do he never so weel. / Thanne comth accusynge, as whan man seketh occasioun to anoyen his neighebor, which that is lyk to the craft of the devel that waiteth bothe night and day to accusen us alle. / Thanne comth malignitee, thurgh which a man anoyeth his neighebor prively if he may, / and if he noght may, algate his wikked wil ne shal nat wante as for to brennen his hous pryvely, or empoysone or sleen his bestes, and semblable thynges. /

Remedium contra peccatum Invidie.

Now wol I speken of the remedie agayns the foule synne of envye. First is the love of God principal, and loving of his neighebor as hym- self, for soothly that oon ne may nat been withoute that oother. / And truste wel that in the name of thy neighebore thou shalt understonde the name of thy brother; for certes alle we have o fader flesshly and o mooder, that is to seyn Adam and Eve; and eek o fader espiritueel, and that is God of hevene. / Thy neighebore artow holden for to love and wilne

494 digne of, deserving of. **495 shrewed,** evil. **496 amenuse,** diminish. **497 Pardee,** Fr. "by god." Hg&c *Parfey.* **499 grucching,** complaining. **500 catel . . . shrewes,** property (chattels), evil people. **502 hevede,** head, John 12:4–6; not Mary Magdalen but Mary, sister of Martha. **504 Simon,** Luke 7:39. **505 sourdeth . . . discovereth . . . bereth hym on hond,** arises, reveals, accuses him of. **506 leveful,** legitimate (lawful). **507 withseye,** refuse. **508 Pater Noster,** the Lord's Prayer. **lewed,** ignorant. **511 al do he,** although he may do. **514 algate . . . wante,** nevertheless, lack. **515 principal,** most important. **517 holden . . . wilne,** obliged, desire. E&c *bothe* om.

hym alle goodnesse. And therfore seith God, "Love thy neighebore as thyselve," that is to seyn, to salvacioun bothe of lyf and of soule. / And mooreover thou shalt love hym in word and in benigne amonestynge and chastisynge, and conforten hym in his anoyes, and preye for hym with al thyn herte. / And in dede thou shalt love hym in swich wise that thou shalt doon to hym in charitee as thou woldest that it were doon to thyn owene persone. / And therfore thou ne shalt doon hym no damage in wikked word, ne harm in his body, ne in his catel, ne in his soule, by entissyng of wikked ensample. / Thou shalt nat desiren his wyf 520 ne none of his thynges. Understoond eek that in the name of neighebor is comprehended his enemy. / Certes man shal loven his enemy by the comandement of God; and soothly thy freend shaltow love in God. / I seye, thyn enemy shaltow love for Goddes sake, by his comandement. For if it were reson that a man sholde haten his enemy, forsothe God nolde nat receyven us to his love that been his enemys. / Agayns three manere of wronges that his enemy dooth to hym, he shal doon three thynges, as thus. / Agayns hate and rancour of herte, he shal love hym in herte. Agayns chiding and wikkede wordes, he shal preye for his enemy. And agayn the wikked dede of his enemy, he shal doon hym bountee. / For Crist seith, 525 "Loveth youre enemys, and preyeth for hem that speke yow harm, and eek for hem that yow chacen and pursewen, and doth bountee to hem that yow haten." Loo, thus comaundeth us oure lord Jesu Crist to do to oure enemys. / For soothly, nature dryveth us to loven oure freendes, and parfey oure enemys han moore nede to love than oure freendes. And they that moore nede have, certes to hem shal men doon goodnesse, / and certes in thilke dede have we remembraunce of the love of

Jesu Crist that deyde for his enemys. / And inasmuche as thilke love is the moore grevous to parfourne, insomuche is the moore gretter the merite, and therfore the lovynge of oure enemy hath confounded the venym of the devel. / For right as the devel is disconfited by humylitee, right so is he wounded to the deeth by love of oure enemy. / Certes, 530 thanne is love the medicine that casteth out the venym of envye fro mannes herte. / The speces of this paas shullen be moore largely in hir chapitres folwynge declared. /

Sequitur de Ira.

After envye wol I discryven the synne of ire. For soothly, whoso hath envye upon his neighebor, anon he wole comunly fynde hym a matere of wratthe, in word or in dede, agayns hym to whom he hath envye. / And as wel comth ire of pryde as of envye; for soothly, he that is proude or envyous is lightly wrooth. / This synne of ire, after the discryvyng of Seint Augustyn, is wikked wil to been avenged by word or by dede. / Ire, after the 535 philosophre, is the fervent blood of man yquiked in his herte thurgh which he wole harm to hym that he hateth. / For certes the herte of man by eschawfynge and moevynge of his blood wexeth so trouble that he is out of alle juggement of resoun. / But ye shal understonde that ire is in two maneres, that oon of hem is good, and that oother is wikked. / The goode ire is by jalousye of goodnesse, thurgh which a man is wrooth with wikkednesse and agayns wikkednesse; and therfore seith a wys man that ire is bet than pley. / This ire is with debonairetee, and it is wrooth withouten bitternesse; nat wrooth agayns the man, but wrooth with the mysdede of the man, as seith the prophete David, *Irascimini et nolite peccare.* / Now 540

---

518 benigne amonestynge, gentle admonishing. **520 catel,** property. Note the echoes of the Ten Commandments. **523 reson,** i.e., reasonable. **524** *wronges:* E *thynges.* **525 bountee,** goodness: E *bonte* or *boute* (also in l. 526). **526 Crist seith,** Matt. 5:44. **yow chacen,** chase you. **527 nede to,** need of. **532 paas,** section. **533 discryven,** describe. **534 lightly,** easily. **535 after,** according to. **536 yquiked,** awakened. **537 eschawfynge,** heating. **539 jalousye of . . . pley,** zeal for, good humor. **540 David,** Ps. 4:5 (Vulgate), "Be ye angry, and sin not."

understondeth that wikked ire is in two maneres, that is to seyn, sodeyn ire or hastif ire, withouten avisement and consentynge of resoun. / The menyng and the sens of this is that the resoun of man ne consente nat to thilke sodeyn ire and thanne it is venial. / Another ire is ful wikked that comth of felonie of herte avysed and cast biforn, with wikked wil to do vengeance; and therto his resoun consenteth, and soothly this is deedly synne. / This ire is so displesant to God that it troubleth his hous and chaceth the Hooly Goost out of mannes soule, and wasteth and destroyeth the liknesse of God—that is to seyn the vertu that is in mannes soule— / and put in hym the liknesse of the devel, and bynymeth the man fro God that is his rightful lord. / This ire is a ful 545 greet plesaunce to the devel, for it is the develes fourneys that is eschawfed with the fir of helle. / For certes, right so as fir is moore mighty to destroyen erthely thynges than any oother element, right so ire is mighty to destroyen alle spiritueel thynges. / Looke how that fir of smale gleedes that been almoost dede under asshen wollen quike agayn whan they been touched with brymstoon. Right so ire wol everemo quyken agayn whan it is touched by the pride that is covered in mannes herte. / For certes fir ne may nat comen out of nothing, but if it were first in the same thyng natureelly, as fir is drawen out of flyntes with steel. / And right so as pride is ofte tyme matere of ire, right so is rancour norice and keper of ire. / 550 Ther is a maner tree as seith Seint Ysidre that whan men maken fir of thilke tree, and covere the coles of it with asshen, soothly the fir of it wol lasten al a yeer or moore. / And right so fareth it of rancour. Whan it is ones conceyved in the hertes of som men, certein it wol lasten peraventure from oon Estre day unto

another Estre day, and moore. / But certes thilke man is ful fer fro the mercy of God al thilke while. /

In this forseyde develes fourneys ther forgen three shrewes: pride that ay bloweth and encreesseth the fir by chidynge and wikked wordes. / Thanne stant envye and holdeth the hoote iren upon the herte of man with a peire of longe toonges of long rancour. / 555 And thanne stant the synne of contumelie, or strif and cheeste, and batereth and forgeth by vileyns reprevynges. / Certes, this cursed synne anoyeth bothe to the man hymself and eek to his neighebor. For soothly, almoost al the harm that any man dooth to his neighebore comth of wratthe. / For certes, outrageous wratthe dooth al that evere the devel hym comaundeth, for he ne spareth neither Crist ne his sweete mooder. / And in his outrageous anger and ire, allas, allas, ful many oon at that tyme feeleth in his herte ful wikkedly bothe of Crist and of alle his halwes. / Is nat this a cursed vice? Yis, certes. Allas, it bynymeth from man his wit and his resoun, and al his debonaire lif espiritueel that sholde kepen his soule. / Certes, it bynymeth eek goddes 560 due lordshipe, and that is mannes soule and the love of his neighebores. It stryveth eek alday agayn trouthe. It reveth hym the quiete of his herte and subverteth his soule. /

Of ire comen thise stynkynge engendrures: first hate that is oold wratthe; discord, thurgh which a man forsaketh his olde freend that he hath loved ful longe. / And thanne cometh werre, and every manere of wrong that man dooth to his neighebore in body or in catel. / Of this cursed synne of ire cometh eek manslaughtre. And understonde wel that homycide, that is manslaughtre, is in diverse wise. Som manere of homycide is spiritueel, and som is

542 venial, pardonable. 543 avysed . . . cast biforn, considered, planned ahead (malice aforethought). 545 bynymeth, removes. 546 fourneys . . . eschawfed, furnace, heated. 548 gleedes . . . quike . . . brymstoon, coals, come to life, brimstone (sulphur). 550 norice, nurse. 551 maner, kind. Seint Ysidre, St. Isidore, *Etymologiae* 17.7.35. The etymology is for "juniper," derived from Gk. for "fire." 552 Estre day, an allusion to the ritual kindling of the new fire on Holy Saturday. 554 forgen . . . shrewes, i.e., three scoundrels work the forge. 556 contumelie . . . cheeste, rebelliousness, quarreling. 559 of Crist . . . halwes, toward Christ, saints. 560 bynymeth . . . kepen, removes, protect. 561 reveth hym, steals from him. 562 engendrures, offspring. 563 catel, property.

bodily. / Spiritueel manslaughtre is in thre thynges. First, by hate, as Seint John seith, "He that hateth his brother is homycide." / 565 Homycide is eek by bakbitynge. Of whiche bakbiteres seith Salomon that they han two swerdes with whiche they sleen hire neighe-bores. For soothly, as wikke is to bynyme his good name as his lyf. / Homycide is eek in yevynge of wikked conseil by fraude, as for to yeven conseil to areysen wrongful custumes and taillages. / Of whiche seith Salomon, "Leon rorynge and bere hongry been like to the crueel lordshipes," in withholdynge or abreggynge of the shepe, or the hyre, or of the wages of servauntz, or elles in usures or in withdrawynge of the almesse of poure folk. / For which the wise man seith, "Fedeth hym that almoost dyeth for honger," for soothly but if thow feede hym, thou sleest hym. And alle thise been deedly synnes. / Bodily manslaughtre is whan thow sleest him with thy tonge in oother manere, as whan thou comandest to sleen a man, or elles yevest hym conseil to sleen a man. / 570 Manslaughtre in dede is in foure maneres. That oon is by lawe, right as a justice dampneth hym that is coupable to the deeth. But lat the justice bewar that he do it rightfully, and that he do it nat for delit to spille blood, but for kepynge of rightwisenesse. / Another homycide is that is doon for necessitee, as whan o man sleeth another in his defendaunt, and that he ne may noon ootherwise escape from his owene deeth. / But certeinly, if he may escape with-outen manslaughtre of his adversarie, and sleeth hym, he doth synne, and he shal bere penance as for deedly synne. / Eek if a man by caas or aventure shete an arwe or caste a stoon with which he sleeth a man, he is homycide. / Eek if a womman by necligence overlyeth hire child

in hir slepyng, it is homycide and deedly synne. / Eek whan man destourbeth con- 575 cepcioun of a child, and maketh a womman outher bareyne by drynkinge venemouse herbes, thurgh which she may nat conceyve, or sleeth a child by drynkes wilfully, or elles putteth certeine material thynges in hire secree places to slee the child, / or elles doth unkyndely synne by which man or womman shedeth hire nature in manere or in place ther as a child may nat be conceived, or elles if a womman have con-ceyved and hurt hirself and sleeth the child, yet is it homycide. / What seye we eek of wommen that mordren hir children for drede of worldly shame? Certes, an horrible homycide. / Homycide is eek if a man approcheth to a womman by desir of lecherye, thurgh which the child is perissed, or elles smyteth a womman wityngly, thurgh which she leseth hir child. Alle thise been homycides and horrible deedly synnes. / Yet comen ther of ire manye mo synnes, as wel in word as in thoght and in dede; as he that arretteth upon God, or blameth God of thyng of which he is hymself gilty; or despiseth God and alle his halwes, as doon thise cursede hasardours in diverse con-trees. / This cursed synne doon they whan 580 they feelen in hir hertes ful wikkedly of God and of his halwes. / Also, whan they treten unreverently the sacrement of the auter, thilke sinne is so greet that unnethe may it been releessed, but that the mercy of God passeth alle his werkes; it is so greet and he so benigne. / Thanne comth of ire attry angre. Whan a man is sharply amonested in his shrifte to forleten his synne, / than wole he be angry and answeren hokerly and angrily, and deffenden or excusen his synne by unstedefastnesse of his flessh, or elles he dide it for to holde compaignye with

565 Seint John, I John 3:15. *thre:* MSS have *vj,* misread for *iij* (?). **566 Salomon,** Prov. 25:18. **sleen . . . as wikke is . . . bynyme,** slay, it is as wicked, take. **567 areysen . . . custumes and taillages,** impose, duty and taxes. **568 Salomon,** Prov. 28:15. **lord-shipes . . . abreggynge . . . shepe,** authorities, reducing, wages. **569 wise man,** Prov. 25:21. **570 with thy tonge,** i.e., by direct command. **571 dampneth,** condemns. **572 defendaunt,** defense. **574 caas,** chance. **575 overlyeth,** lies on (smothers). **576 outher,** either. **venemouse:** E&c *venenouse.* **577 unkyndely . . . nature,** nature, semen (sexual fluid). *hirself:* E *hir child.* **579 a womman,** i.e., a pregnant woman. **580 arretteth . . . halwes . . . hasardours,** blames, saints, gamblers. **581 of God,** against God. **582 auter . . . unnethe . . . passeth,** altar, scarcely, surpasses. **583 attry . . . amonested . . . shrifte . . . forleten,** poisonous, admonished, confession, leave. **584 hokerly . . . unstedefastnesse,** scornfully, weakness.

his felawes, or elles, he seith, the feend enticed hym, / or elles he dide it for his youthe, or elles his compleccioun is so corageous that he may nat forbere, or elles it is his destinee, as he seith, unto a certein age, or elles, he seith, it cometh hym of gentillesse of his auncestres, and semblable thynges. / Alle this manere of 585 folk so wrappen hem in hir synnes that they ne wol nat delivere hemself. For soothly, no wight that excuseth hym wilfully of his synne may nat been delivered of his synne til that he mekely biknoweth his synne. / After this thanne cometh sweryng that is expres agayn the comandement of God, and this bifalleth ofte of anger and of ire. / God seith, "Thow shalt nat take the name of thy lord God in veyn or in ydel." Also oure lord Jesu Crist seith by the word of Seint Mathew, / "Ne wol ye nat swere in alle manere, neither by hevene for it is Goddes trone, ne by erthe for it is the bench of his feet, ne by Jerusalem for it is the citee of a greet king, ne by thyn heed for thou mayst nat make an heer whit ne blak. / But seyeth by youre word, ye, ye, and nay, nay. And what that is moore, it is of yvel," seith Crist. / For 590 Cristes sake, ne swereth nat so synfully in dismembrynge of Crist by soule, herte, bones, and body. For certes, it semeth that ye thynke that the cursede Jewes ne dismembred nat ynough the preciouse persone of Crist, but ye dismembre hym moore. / And if so be that the lawe compelle yow to swere, thanne rule yow after the lawe of God in youre sweryng, as seith Jeremye *4 capitulo,* "Thou shalt kepe three condicions: thou shalt swere in trouthe, in doom, and in rightwisnesse." / This is to seyn, thou shalt swere sooth, for every lesynge is agayns Crist, for Crist is verray trouthe. And thynk wel this, that every greet swerere nat compelled lawefully to swere, the wounde shal nat departe from his hous whil he useth swich unleveful sweryng. / Thou shalt sweren eek in doom whan thou art constreyned by thy domesman to witnessen the trouthe. / Eek thow shalt nat swere for envye, ne for favour, ne for meede, but for rightwisnesse and for declaracioun of it to the worship of God and helpyng of thyne evene-Cristene. / And therfore, every 595 man that taketh Goddes name in ydel, or falsly swereth with his mouth, or elles taketh on hym the name of Crist, to be called a Cristene man, and lyveth agayns Cristes lyvynge and his techynge, alle they taken Goddes name in ydel. / Looke eek what Seint Peter seith, *Actuum 4 capitulo, Non est aliud nomen sub celo,* &c.: "Ther nys noon oother name," seith Seint Peter, "under hevene yeven to men in which they mowe be saved." That is to seyn, but the name of Jesu Crist. / Take kepe eek how that the precious name of Crist, as seith Seint Paul *ad Philipenses 2, In nomine Iesu,* &c.: that in the name of Jesu every knee of hevenely creatures, or erthely, or of helle sholden bowe, for it is so heigh and so worshipful that the cursede feend in helle sholde tremblen to heeren it ynempned. / Thanne semeth it that men that sweren so horribly by his blessed name, that they despise hym moore booldely than dide the cursede Jewes, or elles the devel that trembleth whan he heereth his name. /

Now certes, sith that sweryng, but if it be lawefully doon, is so heighly deffended, muche worse is forsweryng falsly and yet nedelees. / What seye we eek of hem that 600 deliten hem in sweryng, and holden it a gentrie or a manly dede to swere grete othes? And what of hem that of verray usage ne cesse nat to swere grete othes, al be the cause nat worth a straw? Certes, it is horrible synne. / Swerynge sodeynly withoute avysement is eek a

<hr />

585 **compleccioun,** temperament (complexion, following the medieval theory of the "humors"; see *CT,* 1.333 note). **gentillesse,** high birth. 586 **delivere . . . biknoweth,** free, acknowledges. 587 **expres,** expressly. 588 **God seith,** Exod. 20:7. **Seint Mathew,** Matt. 5:34–37. 591 **in dismembrynge,** so as to dismember. 592 **Jeremye,** Jer. 4:2. **doom,** justice. 593 **lesynge,** lying. **wounde . . . unleveful,** plague, illegitimate; Ecclus. 23:12 (Vulgate). 594 **doom . . . domesman,** court, judge. 595 **evene-Cristene,** fellow-Christian. 596 **ydel,** vain. 597 **Seint Peter,** Acts 4:12. **mowe,** may. 598 **Seint Paul,** Phil. 2:10. **ynempned,** named. 600 **but if . . . deffended . . . forsweryng,** unless, forbidden, perjury. 601 **gentrie,** fashionable thing. **verray usage,** simple habit. 602 **avysement,** thinking.

synne. / But lat us go now to thilke horrible sweryng of adjuracioun and conjuracioun, as doon thise false enchauntours or nigromanciens in bacyns ful of water, or in a bright swerd, in a cercle, or in a fir, or in a shulder boon of a sheep. / I kan nat seye but that they doon cursedly and dampnably, agayns Crist and al the feith of Hooly Chirche. /

What seye we of hem that bileeven in divynailes, as by flight or by noyse of briddes, or of beestes, or by sort, by nygromancye, by dremes, by chirkynge of dores, or crakynge of houses, by gnawynge of rattes, and swich manere wrecchednesse? / Certes, al this 605 thyng is deffended by God and by al Hooly Chirche. For which they been acursed til they come to amendement that on swich filthe setten hire bileeve. / Charmes for woundes or maladie of men or of beestes, if they taken any effect it may be peraventure that God suffreth it, for folk sholden yeve the moore feith and reverence to his name. /

Now wol I speken of lesynges, which generally is fals significacioun of word in entente to deceyven his evene-Cristene. / Some lesynge is of which ther comth noon avantage to no wight, and som lesynge turneth to the ese and profit of o man and to disese and damage of another man. / Another lesynge is for to saven his lyf or his catel. Another lesynge comth of delit for to lye, in which delit they wol forge a long tale, and peynten it with alle circumstaunces, where al the ground of the tale is fals. / 610 Som lesynge comth for he wole sustene his word; and som lesynge comth of recchelees-nesse, withouten avisement; and semblable thynges. /

Lat us now touche the vice of flaterynge, which ne comth nat gladly but for drede or for coveitise. / Flaterye is generally wrongful preisynge. Flatereres been the develes norices, that norissen his children with milk of losen-gerie. / For sothe, Salomon seith that flaterie is wors than detraccioun. For somtyme detraccion maketh an hauteyn man be the moore humble, for he dredeth detraccion. But certes flaterye, that maketh a man to enhauncen his herte and his contenaunce. / Flatereres been the develes enchauntours, for they make a man to wene of hymself be lyk that he nys nat lyk. / They 615 been lyk to Judas that bitraysen a man to sellen hym to his enemy, that is to the devel. / Flatereres been the develes chapelleyns, that syngen evere *Placebo*. / I rekene flaterie in the vices of ire for ofte tyme if o man be wrooth with another, thanne wol he flatere som wight to sustene hym in his querele. /

Speke we now of swich cursynge as comth of irous herte. Malisoun generally may be seyd every maner power or harm. Swich cursynge bireveth man fro the regne of God, as seith Seint Paul. / And ofte tyme swich cursynge wrongfully retorneth agayn to hym that curseth, as a bryd that retorneth agayn to his owene nest. / And over alle thyng men oghten 620 eschewe to cursen hire children and yeven to the devel hire engendrure, as ferforth as in hem is. Certes, it is greet peril and greet synne. /

Lat us thanne speken of chidynge and re-proche, whiche been ful grete woundes in mannes herte, for they unsowen the semes of freendshipe in mannes herte. / For certes, unnethes may a man pleynly been accorded with hym that hath hym openly revyled and

---

603 adjuracioun … conjuracioun, exorcism, incantation. **bacyns … swerd,** basins of water, polished objects, and fire were used for divination; circles and animal bones were likewise used for divination and casting spells. *nigromanciens:* E *nigromanens.* **605 divynailes … sort … chirkynge,** divination, drawing lots, creaking. *nygromancye:* E&c *geomancie* (divination by dots in the dust). **606 deffended,** forbidden. **they … amendement,** those who engage in such magic, correction. **607 for folk,** so that people. **608 lesynges,** lies. **610 ground,** basis. *Another lesynge comth:* E&c *Another lesynge* om. **611 for … sustene,** because, support. **recchelees-nesse … avisement,** thoughtlessness, consideration. **612 gladly,** willingly. **613 norices … losengerie,** nurses, deceit. **614 hauteyn … enhauncen … contenaunce,** arrogant, be more haughty, expression (manner). **615 wene,** think. **616** *bitraysen:* EHg&c *bitraysed,* but Peraldus indicates that *They* is the subject of *betray.* **617** *Placebo,* "I will please," see SumT, III.2075 note, and MerchT, IV.1476. **618 in the vices,** among the vices. **619 Malisoun … bireveth,** placing a curse upon, removes. **Seint Paul,** I Cor. 6:10. **620 cursynge … retorneth,** this is the theme of SumT. **621 engendrure, as ferforth,** offspring, as far as possible. **623 unnethes … pleynly,** scarcely, fully.

repreved in disclaundre. This is a ful grisly synne, as Crist seith in the gospel. / And taak kepe now that he that repreveth his neighebor outher he repreveth hym by som harm of peyne that he hath on his body, as "mesel," "croked harlot," or by som synne that he dooth. / Now if he repreve hym by harm of peyne, thanne turneth the repreve to Jesu Crist, for peyne is sent by the rightwys sonde of God, and by his suffrance, be it meselrie, or maheym, or maladie. / And if he repreve 625 hym uncharitably of synne, as "thou holour," "thou dronkelewe harlot," and so forth, thanne aperteneth that to the rejoysynge of the devel that evere hath joye that men doon synne. / And certes, chidynge may nat come but out of a vileyns herte. For after the habundance of the herte speketh the mouth ful ofte. / And ye shul understonde that looke, by any wey, whan any man shal chastise another, that he bewar from chidynge and reprevynge. For trewely, but he bewar he may ful lightly quyken the fir of angre and of wratthe, which that he sholde quenche, and peraventure sleeth hym which that he myghte chastise with benignitee. / For as seith Salomon, "The amyable tonge is the tree of lyf," that is to seyn, of lyf espiritueel. And soothly, a deslavee tonge sleeth the spirites of hym that repreveth and eek of hym that is repreved. / Loo, what seith Seint Augustyn, "Ther is nothyng so lyk the develes child as he that ofte chideth." Seint Paul seith eek, "The servant of God bihoveeth nat to chide." / And how that 630 chidynge be a vileyns thyng bitwixe alle manere folk, yet is it certes moost uncovenable bitwixe a man and his wyf, for there is nevere reste. And therfore seith Salomon, "An hous that is uncovered and droppynge, and a chidynge wyf been lyke." / A man that is in a droppynge hous in manye places, though he eschewe the droppynge in o place, it droppeth on hym in another place; so fareth it by a chidynge wyf. But she chide hym in o place, she wol chide hym in another. / And therfore, "Bettre is a morsel of breed with joye than an hous ful of delices with chidynge," seith Salomon. / Seint Paul seith, "O ye wommen, be ye subgetes to youre housbondes as bihoveth in God; and ye men, loveth youre wyves." *Ad Colossenses 3.* /

Afterward speke we of scornynge, which is a wikked synne, and namely whan he scorneth a man for his goode werkes. / For 635 certes, swiche scorneres faren lyk the foule tode that may nat endure to smelle the soote savour of the vyne whanne it florissheth. / Thise scorneres been partyng felawes with the devel, for they han joye whan the devel wynneth and sorwe whan he leseth. / They been adversaries of Jesu Crist, for they haten that he loveth, that is to seyn salvacion of soule. /

Speke we now of wikked conseil, for he that wikked conseil yeveth is a traytour. He deceyveth hym that trusteth in hym, *ut Achitofel ad Absolonem.* But natheles, yet is his wikked conseil first agayn hymself. / For as seith the wise man, every fals lyvynge hath this propertee in hymself, that he that wole anoye another man he anoyeth first hymself. / And men 640 shul understonde that man shal nat taken his conseil of fals folk, nor of angry folk, or grevous folk, ne of folk that loven specially to muchel hir owene profit, ne to muche worldly folk, namely, in conseilynge of soules. /

Now comth the synne of hem that sowen and maken discord amonges folk, which is a synne that Crist hateth outrely; and no wonder is.

---

623 Crist, Matt. 5:22. **624 repreveth . . . mesel,** scolds, leper. **625 repreve hym by harm of peyne,** i.e., threatens him with affliction. **sonde . . . meselrie . . . maheym,** visitation, leprosy, maiming. **626 holour . . . dronkelewe harlot . . . aperteneth,** lecher, drunken good-for-nothing, adds. E&c *thou holour* om. **627 after the habundance,** Matt. 12:34. **629 Salomon,** Prov. 15:4. **deslavee,** foul (Fr. *deslaver,* unwashed). **630 Seint Paul,** II Tim. 2:24. **bihoveth,** ought. *The servant:* MSS *I servant* with various emendations. Manly suggests misreading of thorn as *y* (for *I*). **631 unconvenable . . . uncovered . . . droppynge . . . lyke,** inappropriate, roofless, leaking, the same. **Salomon,** Prov. 27:5. See *Mel,* VII.1086, note. **633 Salomon,** Prov. 17:1. **634 Seint Paul,** Col. 3:18–19. **bihoveth,** is requisite. E *as—God* om. **636 tode . . . soote savour,** toad, sweet odor. **637 partyng felawes,** partners. **639 ut Achitofel ad,** as Achitophel to, II Sam. 17:1. **640 fals lyvynge,** evil liver. **641 E&c *ne of folk* om.**

For he deyde for to make concord. / And moore shame do they to Crist than dide they that hym crucifiede, for God loveth bettre that freendshipe be amonges folk than he dide his owene body, the which that he yaf for unitee. Therfore been they likned to the devel, that evere been aboute to maken discord. /

Now comth the synne of double tonge, swiche as speken faire byforn folk and wikkedly bihynde, or elles they maken semblant as though they speeke of good entencioun, or elles in game and pley, and yet they speke of wikked entente. /

Now comth biwreying of conseil, thurgh which a man is defamed. Certes, unnethe may he restoore the damage. /   645

Now comth manace, that is an open folye, for he that ofte manaceth, he threteth moore than he may parfourne ful ofte tyme. /

Now cometh ydel wordes, that is withouten profit of hym that speketh tho wordes and eek of hym that herkneth tho wordes. Or elles ydel wordes been tho that been nedelees or withouten entente of natureel profit. / And al be it that ydel wordes been somtyme venial synne, yet sholde men douten hem, for we shul yeve rekenynge of hem bifore God. /

Now comth janglynge, that may nat been withoute synne. And as seith Salomon, "It is a synne of apert folye." / And therfore a philosophre seyde, whan men axed hym how that men sholde plese the peple, and he answerde, "Do manye goode werkes, and spek fewe jangles." /   650

After this comth the synne of japeres, that been the develes apes, for they maken folk to laughe at hire japerie, as folk doon at the gawdes of an ape. Swiche japeres deffendeth Seint Paul. / Looke how that vertuouse wordes and hooly conforten hem that travaillen in the service of Crist. Right so conforten the vileyns wordes and knakkes of japeris hem that travaillen in the service of the devel. / Thise been the synnes that comen of the tonge, that comen of ire, and of othere synnes mo. /

Sequitur remedium contra peccatum Ire.

The remedie agayns ire is a vertu that men clepen mansuetude, that is debonairetee, and eek another vertu that men callen pacience or suffrance. /

Debonairetee withdraweth and refreyneth the stirynges and the moevynges of mannes corage in his herte in swich manere that they ne skippe nat out by angre ne by ire. / Suf- 655 france suffreth swetely alle the anoyaunces and the wronges that men doon to man outward. / Seint Jerome seith thus of debonairetee that it dooth noon harm to no wight, ne seith; ne for noon harm that men doon or seyn, he ne eschawfeth nat agayns his resoun. / This vertu somtyme comth of nature, for as seith the philosophre, a man is a quyk thyng, by nature debonaire and tretable to goodnesse, but whan debonairetee is enformed of grace, thanne is it the moore worth. /

Pacience that is another remedie agayns ire is a vertu that suffreth swetely every mannes goodnesse, and is nat wrooth for noon harm that is doon to hym. / The philosophre seith that pacience is thilke vertu that suffreth debonairely alle the outrages of adversitee and every wikked word. / This vertu 660 maketh a man lyk to God, and maketh hym Goddes owene deere child, as seith Crist. This vertu disconfiteth thyn enemy. And therfore seith the wise man, if thow wolt venquysse thyn enemy, lerne to suffre. / And thou shalt understonde that man suffreth foure manere of

---

645 conseil . . . unnethe, confidences, hardly. **646 manace,** threats. **647 natureel,** usual. **648 venial . . . douten,** pardonable, mistrust. Matt. 12:36. **649 janglynge . . . apert,** gossiping, evident. Salomon, Eccles. 5:3. **651 japeres . . . gawdes . . . deffendeth,** people who tell jokes, tricks, forbids. **Seint Paul,** Eph. 5:4. **652 travaillen . . . knakkes,** labor, quips ("cracks"). **hooly:** E *hooly woordes*. **654 mansuetude,** meekness. **655 corage,** disposition (spirit). **657 eschawfeth,** becomes heated. **658 quyk . . . tretable . . . enformed,** sensitive, amenable, formed (molded). **661 seith Crist,** Matt. 5:9. **wise man,** Dionysius Cato, *Disticha de Moribus* 1.38. **suffre,** endure.

grevances in outward thynges, agayns the whiche foure he moot have foure manere of paciences. /

The firste grevance is of wikkede wordes. Thilke suffrede Jesu Crist withouten grucchyng, ful paciently, whan the Jewes despised and repreved hym ful ofte. / Suffre thou therfore paciently, for the wise man seith if thou stryve with a fool, though the fool be wrooth or though he laughe, algate thou shalt have no reste. / That oother grevance outward is to have damage of thy catel. Theragayns suffred Crist ful paciently, whan he was despoyled of al that he hadde in this lyf, and that nas but his clothes. / The thridde grevance is 665 a man to have harm in his body. That suffred Crist ful paciently in al his passioun. / The fourthe grevance is in outrageous labour in werkes. Wherfore I seye that folk that maken hir servantz to travaillen to grevously, or out of tyme as on haly dayes, soothly they do greet synne. / Heer agayns suffred Crist ful paciently, and taughte us pacience, whan he baar upon his blissed shulder the croys upon which he sholde suffren despitous deeth. / Heer may men lerne to be pacient, for certes noght only Cristen men been pacient for love of Jesu Crist, and for gerdoun of the blisful lyf that is perdurable, but certes the olde payens that nevere were Cristene commendeden and useden the vertu of pacience. /

A philosophre upon a tyme, that wolde have beten his disciple for his grete trespas, for which he was greetly amoeved and broghte a yerde to scoure with the child, / and whan 670 this child saugh the yerde, he seyde to his maister, "What thenke ye to do?" "I wol bete thee," quod the maister, "for thy correccioun." / "For sothe," quod the child, "ye oghten first correcte yourself, that han lost al youre pacience for the gilt of a child." / "For sothe," quod the maister al wepynge, "thow seyst sooth. Have thow the yerde, my deere sone, and correcte me for myn inpacience." / Of pacience comth obedience, thurgh which a man is obedient to Crist and to alle hem to whiche he oghte to been obedient in Crist. / And understond wel that obedience is perfit whan that a man dooth gladly and hastily, with good herte entierly, al that he sholde do. / 675 Obedience generally is to parfourne the doctrine of God and of his sovereyns, to whiche hym oghte to ben obeisaunt in alle rightwisnesse. /

Sequitur de Accidia.

After the synne of envye and of ire, now wol I speken of the synne of accidie. For envye blyndeth the herte of a man, and ire troubleth a man, and accidie maketh hym hevy, thoghtful, and wrawful. / Envye and ire maken bitternesse in herte, which bitternesse is mooder of accidie, and bynymeth hym the love of alle goodnesse. Thanne is accidie the angwissh of troubled herte. And Seint Augustyn seith, "It is anoy of goodnesse and joye of harm." / Certes, this is a dampnable synne, for it dooth wrong to Jesu Crist inasmuche as it bynymeth the service that men oghte doon to Crist with alle diligence, as seith Salomon. / But accidie dooth no swich diligence; he dooth alle thyng with anoy, and with wrawnesse, slaknesse, and excusacioun, and with ydelnesse and unlust. For which the book seith, acursed be he that dooth the service of God necligently. / Thanne is accidie enemy 680 to everich estaat of man, for certes, the estaat of man is in three maneres. / Outher it is th'estaat of innocence, as was th'estaat of Adam biforn that he fil into synne, in which estaat he was holden to wirche, as in heriynge and

---

663 **grucchyng**, complaining. 664 **wise man**, Prov. 29:9. **algate**, nevertheless. 665 **catel**, property. 666 **passioun**, crucifixion. 667 **labour in werkes**, i.e., physical labor. 668 **Heer agayns**, against this. 669 **gerdoun ... perdurable ... payens**, reward, everlasting, pagans. 670 **amoeved ... scoure with**, provoked, with which to whip. 675 **gladly**, willingly. 676 **sovereyns**, superiors. 677 **hevy**, sluggish. 678 **bynymeth hym**, takes from him. **anoy of**, annoyance at. **Seint Augustyn**, see l. 484 and note. 679 **Salomon**, Eccles. 9:10. 630 **wrawnesse ... unlust**, peevishness, lack of zest. **the book**, Jer. 48:10 (Vulgate "fradulenter," A.V. "deceitfully," for "necligently.") 682 **holden ... heriynge ... adowrynge**, obliged, praising, adoring.

adowrynge of God. / Another estaat is the estaat of synful men, in which estaat men been holden to laboure in preiynge to God for amendement of hire synnes, and that he wole graunte hem to arysen out of hire synnes. / Another estaat is th'estaat of grace, in which estaat he is holden to werkes of penitence. And certes, to alle thise thynges is accidie enemy and contrarie. For he loveth no bisynesse at al. / Now certes, this foule swyn accidie is eek a ful greet enemy to the lyflode of the body, for it ne hath no purveaunce agayn temporeel necessitee, for it forsleweth and forsluggeth, and destroyeth alle goodes temporeles by reccheleesnesse. / 685

The fourthe thynge is that accidie is lyk to hem that been in the peyne of helle, by cause of hir slouthe and of hire hevynesse, for they that been dampned been so bounde that they ne may neither wel do ne wel thynke. / Of accidie comth first that a man is anoyed and encombred for to doon any goodnesse, and maketh that God hath abhomynacion of swich accidie, as seith Seint Johan. /

Now comth slouthe that wol nat suffre noon hardnesse ne no penaunce. For soothly, slouthe is so tendre and so delicaat, as seith Salomon, that he wol nat suffre noon hardnesse ne penaunce, and therfore he shendeth al that he dooth. / Agayns this roten-herted synne of accidie and slouthe sholde men exercise hemself to doon goode werkes, and manly and vertuously cacchen corage wel to doon, thynkynge that oure lord Jesu Crist quiteth every good dede be it never so lite. / Usage of labour is a greet thyng, for it maketh, as seith Seint Bernard, the laborer to have stronge armes and harde synwes, and slouthe maketh hem feble and tendre. / Thanne comth drede to bigynne 690 to werke anye goode werkes, for certes he

that is enclyned to synne, hym thynketh it is so greet an emprise for to undertake to doon werkes of goodnesse, / and casteth in his herte that the circumstaunces of goodnesse been so grevouse and so chargeaunt for to suffre that he dar nat undertake to do werkes of goodnesse, as seith Seint Gregorie. /

Now comth wanhope that is despeir of the mercy of God, that comth somtyme of to muche outrageous sorwe, and somtyme of to muche drede, ymaginynge that he hath doon so muche synne that it wol nat availlen hym, though he wolde repenten hym and forsake synne, / thurgh which despeir or drede he abaundoneth al his herte to every maner synne, as seith Seint Augustyn. / Which dampnable synne, if that it continue unto his ende, it is cleped synnyng in the Hooly Goost. / This horrible synne is 695 so perilous that he that is despeired, ther nys no felonye ne no synne that he douteth for to do, as sheweth wel by Judas. / Certes, aboven alle synnes thanne is this synne moost displesant to Crist, and moost adversarie. / Soothly, he that despeireth hym is lyk the coward champioun recreant that seith creant withoute nede. Allas, allas, nedelees is he recreant and nedelees despeired. / Certes, the mercy of God is evere redy to every penitent and is aboven alle his werkes. / Allas, kan a man nat bithynke hym on the gospel of Seint Luc, 15, where as Crist seith that as wel shal ther be joye in hevene upon a synful man that dooth penitence, as upon nynety and nyne rightful men that neden no penitence? / Looke forther in the 700 same gospel, the joye and the feeste of the goode man that hadde lost his sone, whan his sone with repentaunce was retourned to his fader. / Kan they nat remembren hem eek that, as seith Seint Luc 23, how that the theef that

---

685 **swyn,** swine; the Deadly Sins were often depicted as animals, or riding on symbolic animals. **lyflode** . . . **purveaunce** . . . **forsleweth** . . . **reccheleesnesse,** life support, provision, is slothful ("for" is an intensifier), negligence (indolence). *swyn:* Hg&c *synne.* **687 Seint Johan,** Rev. 3:16. **688 hardnesse** . . . **shendeth,** hardship, destroy. **Salomon,** Prov. 18:9, 20:4, 21:25. **689 manly** . . . **cacchen corage** . . . **quiteth,** manfully, take courage (spirit), rewards. **691 emprise,** enterprise. **692 casteth** . . . **chargeaunt,** considers, burdensome. **694 Seint Augustin,** *De Natura Gratia* 35; *Sermo* 20.3. **695 cleped,** called. **696 despeired** . . . **douteth,** in despair, hesitates. **698 recreant** . . . **creant,** admitting defeat, mercy (Fr. "I throw myself on your mercy"). E *that seith—recreant* om. **700 Seint Luc,** Luke 15:7. *nyne:* EHg&c *nynetene.* **701 same gospel,** vv. 22–24. **702 Luc 23,** vv.42–43.

was hanged bisyde Jesu Crist seyde "Lord, remembre of me whan thow comest into thy regne"? / "For sothe," seyde Crist, "I seye to thee, today shaltow been with me in Paradys." / Certes, ther is noon so horrible synne of man that it ne may, in his lyf, be destroyed by penitence, thurgh vertu of the passion and of the deeth of Crist. / Allas, what nedeth man thanne to been despeired, sith that his mercy so redy is and large? Axe and have. / 705 Thanne cometh sompnolence, that is sluggy slombrynge, which maketh a man be hevy and dul in body and in soule, and this synne comth of slouthe. / And certes, the tyme that by wey of resoun men sholde nat slepe, that is by the morwe, but if ther were cause resonable. / For soothly, the morwetyde is moost covenable a man to seye his preyeres, and for to thynken on God, and for to honoure God, and to yeven almesse to the poure, that first cometh in the name of Crist. / Lo, what seith Salomon, "Whoso wolde by the morwe awaken and seke me, he shal fynde." / Thanne cometh necligence or recchelesnesse that rekketh of nothyng. And how that ignoraunce be mooder of alle harm, certes, necligence is the norice. / 710 Necligence ne dooth no fors, whan he shal doon a thyng, wheither he do it weel or baddely. /

Of the remedie of thise two synnes, as seith the wise man that he that dredeth God, he spareth nat to doon that hym oghte doon. / And he that loveth God, he wol doon diligence to plese God by his werkes and abaundone hymself with al his myght wel for to doon. / Thanne comth ydelnesse that is the yate of alle harmes. An ydel man is lyk to a place that hath no walles; the develes may entre on every syde and sheten at hym at discovert by temptacion on every syde. / This ydelnesse is the thurrok of

alle wikked and vileyns thoghtes, and of alle jangles, trufles, and of alle ordure. / Certes, 715 the hevene is yeven to hem that wol labouren, and nat to ydel folk. Eek David seith that they ne been nat in the labour of men, ne they shul nat been whipped with men, that is to seyn, in purgatorie. / Certes, thanne semeth it they shul be tormented with the devel in helle, but if they doon penitence. /

Thanne comth the synne that men clepen *tarditas*, as whan a man is to laterede or tariynge er he wole turne to God, and certes that is a greet folie. He is lyk to him that falleth in the dych and wol nat arise. / And this vice comth of a fals hope, that he thynketh that he shal lyve longe, but that hope faileth ful ofte. /

Thanne comth lachesse, that is he that whan he biginneth any good werk anon he shal forleten it and stynten, as doon they that han any wight to governe and ne taken of hym namore kepe anon as they fynden any contrarie or any anoy. / Thise been the 720 newe sheepherdes that leten hir sheep wityngly go renne to the wolf that is in the breres, or do no fors of hir owene governaunce. / Of this comth poverte and destruccioun, bothe of spiritueel and temporeel thynges. Thanne comth a manere cooldnesse that freseth al the herte of a man. / Thanne comth undevocioun, thurgh which a man is so blent, as seith Seint Bernard, and hath swiche langour in soule, that he may neither rede ne singe in hooly chirche, ne heere ne thynke of no devocioun, ne travaille with his handes in no good werk, that it nys hym unsavoury and al apalled. / Thanne wexeth he slough and slombry, and soone wol be wrooth, and soone is enclyned to hate and to envye. / Thanne comth the synne of worldly sorwe which as is cleped *tristicia* that sleeth man, as Seint Paul seith. / For certes, swich 725

702 regne, kingdom. **703** E *seyde* om. **705 large,** generous. **707 morwe,** morning. E *the morwe* om. **708 convenable,** appropriate. **709 Salomon,** Prov. 8:17. **710 recchelesnesse ... norice,** carelessness, nurse. **711 dooth no fors,** does not care. **714 sheten ... at discovert,** shoot, in the open. **715 thurrok ... jangles, trufles,** ship's bilge, gossip, trifles. **716 hevene,** Matt. 11:12. **David,** Ps. 73:5. "They are not in trouble as other men; neither are they plagued like other men." **718 laterede,** tardy. **720 lachesse, forleten ... stynten,** laziness, leaves, stops. **wight to governe ... kepe anon,** person to supervise, notice, as soon. **721 sheepherdes,** i.e., parsons. **wityngly,** deliberately. **722 freseth,** freezes. **723 blent ... unsavoury ... apalled,** blinded, unattractive, boring.

sorwe werketh to the deeth of the soule and of the body also, for therof comth that a man is anoyed of his owene lif. / Wherfore swich sorwe shorteth ful ofte the lif of man, er that his tyme be come by wey of kynde. /

Remedium contra peccatum Accidie.

Agayns this horrible synne of accidie, and the branches of the same, ther is a vertu that is called *fortitudo* or strengthe, that is an affeccioun thurgh which a man despiseth anoyouse thynges. / This vertu is so myghty and so vigorous that it dar withstonde myghtily, and wisely kepen hymself fro perils that been wikked, and wrastle agayn the assautes of the devel. / For it enhaunceth and enforceth the soule, right as accidie abateth it and maketh it fieble. For this *fortitudo* may endure by long suffraunce the travailles that been covenable. / 730

This vertu hath manye speces, and the firste is cleped magnanimitee, that is to seyn greet corage. For certes, ther bihoveth greet corage agains accidie lest that it ne swolwe the soule by the synne of sorwe, or destroye it by wanhope. / This vertu maketh folk to undertake harde thynges and grevouse thynges, by hir owene wil, wysely and resonably. / And for as muchel as the devel fighteth agayns a man moore by queyntise and by sleighte than by strengthe, therfore men shal withstonden hym by wit and by resoun and by discrecioun. / Thanne arn ther the vertues of feith and hope in God and in his seintes, to acheve and acomplice the goode werkes in the whiche he purposeth fermely to continue. / Thanne comth seuretee or sikernesse, and that is whan a man ne douteth no travaille in tyme comynge of the goode werkes that a man hath bigonne. / 735 Thanne comth magnificence, that is to seyn, whan a man dooth and parfourneth grete werkes of goodnesse, and that is the ende why that men sholde do goode werkes. For in the acomplissynge of grete goode werkes lith the grete gerdoun. / Thanne is ther constaunce, that is stablenesse of corage, and this sholde been in herte by stedefast feith, and in mouth, and in berynge, and in chiere, and in dede. / Eke ther been mo speciale remedies agains accidie in diverse werkes, and in consideracioun of the peynes of helle, and of the joyes of hevene, and in trust of the grace of the Hooly Goost, that wole yeve hym myght to parfourne his goode entente. /

Sequitur de Avaricia.

After accidie wol I speke of avarice and of coveitise, of which synne seith Seint Paule that the roote of alle harmes is coveitise, *ad Timotheum 6.* / For soothly, whan the herte of a man is confounded in itself and troubled, and that the soule hath lost the confort of God, thanne seketh he an ydel solas of worldly thynges. / 740

Avarice, after the descripcion of Seint Augustyn, is likerousnesse in herte to have erthely thynges. / Som oother folk seyn that avarice is for to purchacen manye erthely thynges, and nothyng yeve to hem that han nede. / And understond that avarice ne stant nat oonly in lond ne catel, but somtyme in science and in glorie, and in every manere of outrageous thyng is avarice and coveitise. / And the difference bitwixe avarice and coveitise is this. Coveitise is for to coveite swiche thynges as thou hast nat, and avarice is for to withholde and kepe swiche thynges as thou hast withoute rightful nede. / Soothly, this avarice is a synne that is ful dampnable, for al hooly writ curseth it and speketh agayns that vice, for it dooth wrong to Jesu Crist. / For it bireveth hym   745 the love that men to hym owen, and turneth it bakward agayns alle resoun, / and maketh that the avaricious man hath moore hope in his catel than in Jesu Crist, and dooth moore observance in kepynge of his tresor than he

---

726 **anoyed of,** annoyed with. 727 **kynde,** nature. 730 **convenable,** suitable. 731 **greet corage,** greatness of heart. **bihoveth,** is needed. 733 **queyntise,** craft. 735 **seuretee ... sikernesse,** assurance, security. **douteth ... travaille,** fears, hardship. 736 **gerdoun,** reward. 737 **constaunce ... chiere,** constancy, manner. 739 **Seint Paule,** I Tim. 6:10. 741 **Seint Augustyn,** *Enerratio in Psalmum* 31.2.5. **likerousnesse,** desire. 743 **catel ... science ... outrageous,** property, knowledge, excessive. 746 **bireveth,** robs. 747 **dooth ... observance,** pays attention.

dooth to service of Jesu Crist. / And therfore seith Seint Paul *ad Ephesios 5*, that an avaricious man is in the thraldom of ydolatrie. /

What difference is bitwixe an ydolastre and an avaricious man, but that an ydolastre per-aventure ne hath but o mawmet or two and the avaricious man hath manye? For certes, every florin in his cofre is his mawmet. / And certes, the synne of mawmetrye is the firste thyng that God deffended in the Ten Comaundmentz, as bereth witnesse *Exodi 20*, / "Thou shalt 750 have no false goddes bifore me, ne thou shalt make to thee no grave thyng." Thus is an avaricious man that loveth his tresor biforn God an ydolastre / thurgh this cursed synne of avarice. Of coveitise comen thise harde lord-shipes, thurgh whiche men been distreyned by taylages, custumes, and cariages, moore than hire duetee or resoun is. And eek they taken of hire bondemen amercimentz, whiche myghten moore resonably ben cleped extorcions than amercimentz. / Of whiche amercimentz and raunsonynge of bondemen, somme lordes sty-wardes seyn that it is rightful for as muche as a cherl hath no temporeel thyng that it ne is his lordes, as they seyn. / But certes, thise lordshipes doon wrong that bireven hire bondefolk thynges that they nevere yave hem, *Augustinus de Civitate, libro 9*. / Sooth is that the condicioun of thraldom and the firste cause of thraldom is for synne, *Genesis, 5*. / 755

Thus may ye seen that the gilt disserveth thraldom, but nat nature. / Wherfore thise lordes ne sholde nat muche glorifien hem in hir lordshipes, sith that by natureel condicion they been nat lordes of thralles, but for that thraldom comth first by the desert of synne. / And forther-over, ther as the lawe seith that temporeel goodes of boondefolk been the goodes of hir lordshipes, ye that is for to understonde the goodes of the emperour, to deffenden hem in hir right, but nat for to robben hem ne reven hem. / And therfore seith Seneca, "Thy prudence sholde lyve benignely with thy thralles." / Thilke that thou clepest thy thralles been Goddes peple, for humble folk been Cristes freendes; they been contubernyal with the Lord. / 760

Thynk eek that of swich seed as cherles spryngeth, of swich seed spryngen lordes. As wel may the cherl be saved as the lord. / The same deeth that taketh the cherl, swich deeth taketh the lord. Wherfore I rede, do right so with thy cherl as thou woldest that thy lord dide with thee, if thou were in his plit. / Every synful man is a cherl to synne. I rede thee, certes, that thou, lord, werke in swiche wise with thy cherles that they rather love thee than drede. / I woot wel ther is degree above degree, as reson is; and skile it is that men do hir devoir ther as it is due; but certes, extorcions and despit of youre underlynges is dampnable. /

And fortherover, understoond wel that thise conquerours or tirauntz maken ful ofte thralles of hem that been born of as roial blood as been they that hem conqueren. / This name 765 of thraldom was nevere erst kowth til that Noe seyde that his sone Canaan sholde be thral to his bretheren for his synne. / What seye we thanne of hem that pilen and doon extorcions to Hooly Chirche? Certes, the swerd that men yeven first to a knyght whan he is newe dubbed signifieth that he sholde deffenden Hooly Chirche, and nat robben it ne pilen it. And whoso dooth is traitour to Crist. / And as seith Seint Augustyn, "They been the develes wolves that stranglen the sheepe of Jesu Crist"—and doon worse than wolves. / For soothly, whan the wolf hath ful his wombe, he stynteth to strangle sheepe. But soothly, the pilours and destroyours of goodes of Hooly Chirche ne do nat so, for they ne stynte nevere to pile. / Now, as I have seyd,

748 Seint Paul, Eph. 5:5. **749 mawmet,** idol (corruption of Mahomet). **750 deffended,** forbade, Exod. 20:3–4. **751 grave,** graven (carved). **752 harde lordshipes,** harsh rule. **taylages . . . cariages,** taxes, tolls. **bondemen amercimentz,** serfs, fines. **753 raun-sonynge,** ransoming. **754 *Augustinus,* De Civitate Dei** 19.15. **755 Genesis,** 9:18–27. **758 deffenden . . . reven,** protect, steal. **759 Seneca,** *Epistola* 47. **760 contubernyal,** intimate. **762 rede,** advise; recall the Wife of Bath's lecture on gentilesse, WBT, III.1109ff. **764 skile . . . devoir . . . despit,** right, duty, scorn. **766 kowth,** known (couth), Gen. 9:25. **767 pilen,** pillage. *to:* E *in.* **769 wombe . . . stynteth . . . pilours,** stomach, stops, pillagers. *goodes of:* E *goddes.*

sith so is that synne was first cause of thraldom, thanne is it thus, that thilke tyme that al this world was in synne, thanne was al this world in thraldom and subjeccioun. / But 770 certes, sith the time of grace cam, God ordeyned that som folk sholde be moore heigh in estaat and in degree, and some folk moore lough, and that everich sholde be served in his estaat and in his degree. / And therfore, in somme contrees ther they byen thralles, whan they han turned hem to the feith they maken hire thralles free out of thraldom. And therfore, certes, the lord oweth to his man that the man oweth to his lord. / The Pope calleth hymself servant of the servauntz of God; but for as muche as the estaat of Hooly Chirche ne myghte nat han be, ne the commune profit myghte nat han be kept, ne pees and reste in erthe, but if God hadde ordeyned that som men hadde hyer degree and som men lower, / therfore was sovereyntee ordeyned to kepe and mayntene and deffenden hire underlynges or hire subgetz in resoun, as ferforth as it lith in hire power, and nat to destroyen hem ne confounde. / Wherfore I seye that thilke lordes that been lyk wolves, that devouren the possessiouns or the catel of poure folk wrongfully, withouten mercy or mesure, / they 775 shul receyven by the same mesure that they han mesured to poure folk the mercy of Jesu Crist, but if it be amended. /

Now comth deceite bitwixe marchant and marchant. And thow shalt understonde that marchandise is in manye maneres: that oon is bodily, and that oother is goostly. That oon is honeste and leveful, and that oother is deshoneste and unleveful. / Of thilke bodily marchandise that is leveful and honeste is this, that there as God hath ordeyned that a regne or a contree is suffisaunt to hymself, thanne is it honeste and leveful that of habundaunce of this contree that men helpe another contree that is moore nedy. / And therfore, ther moote been marchantz to bryngen fro that o contree to that oother hire marchandises. / That oother marchandise that men haunten with fraude and trecherie and deceite, with lesynges and false othes, is cursed and dampnable. / Espiritueel 780 marchandise is proprely symonye, that is ententif desir to byen thyng espirituel, that is thyng that aperteneth to the seintuarie of God and to cure of the soule. / This desir, if so be that a man do his diligence to parfournen it, al be it that his desir ne take noon effect, yet is it to hym a deedly synne; and if he be ordred, he is irreguleer. / Certes, symonye is cleped of Symon Magus, that wolde han boght for temporeel catel the yifte that God hadde yeven by the Hooly Goost to Seint Peter and to the apostles. / And therfore understoond that bothe he that selleth and he that beyeth thynges espirituels been cleped symonials, be it by catel, be it by procurynge, or by flesshly preyere of his freendes, flesshly freendes or espiritueel freendes. / Flesshly in two maneres, as by kynrede or othere freendes. Soothly, if they praye for hym that is nat worthy and able, it is symonye if he take the benefice, and if he be worthy and able, ther nys noon. / That 785 oother manere is whan a man or womman preyen for folk to avauncen hem oonly for wikked flesshly affeccioun that they han unto the persone, and that is foul symonye. / But certes, in service for which men yeven thynges espiritueels unto hir servantz, it moot been understonde that the service moot been honeste, and elles nat; and eek that it be withouten bargaynynge; and that the persone be able. / For as seith Seint Damasie, "Alle the synnes of the world at regard of this synne arn as thyng of noght," for it is the gretteste synne that may be, after the synne of Lucifer and Antecrist. / For by this synne, God forleseth the chirche and the soule that he boghte with his precious

---

771 E *and in his degree* om. **772 ther,** where. *byen:* Hg&c *ben.* **777 marchandise . . . bodily . . . goostly . . . leveful,** marketing, material, spiritual, lawful. **778 regne,** kingdom. **780 haunten . . . lesynges,** exercise, lies. **782 ordred . . . irreguleer,** in holy orders, unfit to perform holy office. **784 procurynge . . . flesshly,** persuasion, worldly (secular). **785 praye,** intercede. **787 thynges espitueels . . . servantz,** i.e., ecclesiastical preferments, retainers. **788 Seint Damasie,** Pope Damasus I, in Jerome, *Contra Hierosolymitanum* 8. **789 forleseth,** completely loses.

blood by hem that yeven chirches to hem that been nat digne. / For they putten in theves that stelen the soules of Jesu Crist and destroyen his patrimoyne. / By swiche undigne preestes 790 and curates han lewed men the lasse reverence of the sacramentz of Hooly Chirche. And swiche yeveres of chirches putten out the children of Crist, and putten into the chirche the develes owene sone. / They sellen the soules that lambes sholde kepen to the wolf that strangleth hem. And therfore shul they nevere han part of the pasture of lambes, that is the blisse of hevene. /

Now comth hasardrie with his apurtenaunces, as tables and rafles, of which comth deceite, false othes, chidynges, and alle ravynes, blasphemynge and reneiynge of God, and hate of his neighebores, wast of goodes, mysspendynge of tyme, and somtyme manslaughtre. / Certes, hasardours ne mowe nat been withouten greet synne whyles they haunte that craft. / Of avarice comen eek lesynges, thefte, fals witnesse, and false othes. And ye shul understonde that thise been grete synnes, and expres agayn the comaundementz of God, as I have seyd. / 795 Fals witnesse is in word and eek in dede.

In word, as for to bireve thy neighebores goode name by thy fals witnessyng, or bireven hym his catel or his heritage by thy fals witnessyng, whan thou for ire, or for meede, or for envye berest fals witnesse, or accusest hym, or excusest hym by thy fals witnesse, or elles excusest thyself falsly. / Ware yow, questemongeres and notaries! Certes, for fals witnessyng was Susanna in ful gret sorwe and peyne, and many another mo. / The synne of thefte is eek expres agayns Goodes heeste, and that in two maneres, corporeel or espiritueel. / Corporeel, as for to take thy neighebores catel agayn his wyl, be it by force or by sleighte, be it by met or by

mesure. / By stelyng eek of false enditementz upon hym, and in borwynge of thy neighebores catel, in entente nevere to payen it agayn, and semblable thynges. / Espiritueel thefte 800 is sacrilege, that is to seyn hurtynge of hooly thynges or of thynges sacred to Crist in two maneres: by reson of the hooly place, as chirches or chirche hawes, / for which every vileyns synne that men doon in swiche places may be cleped sacrilege, or every violence in the semblable places. Also they that withdrawen falsly the rightes that longen to Hooly Chirche. / And pleynly and generally, sacrilege is to reven hooly thyng fro hooly place, or unhooly thyng out of hooly place, or hooly thyng out of unhooly place. /

Relevacio contra peccatum Avaricie.

Now shul ye understonde that the releevynge of avarice is misericorde and pitee largely taken. And men myghten axe, why that misericorde and pitee is releevinge of avarice? / Certes, the avaricious man sheweth no pitee ne misericorde to the nedeful man, for he deliteth hym in the kepynge of his tresor, and nat in the rescowynge ne releevynge of his evene-Cristene. And therfore speke I first of misericorde. / Thanne is misericorde, as seith the 805 philosophre, a vertu by which the corage of man is stired by the mysese of hym that is mysesed. / Upon which misericorde folweth pitee in parfournynge of charitable werkes of misericorde. / And certes, thise thynges moeven a man to misericorde of Jesu Crist: that he yaf hymself for oure gilt, and suffred deeth for misericorde, and forgaf us oure originale synnes, / and therby relessed us fro the peynes of helle, and amenused the peynes of purgatorie by penitence, and yeveth grace wel to do, and atte laste the blisse of hevene. / The speces of

791 **By . . . undigne . . . lewed,** because of, unworthy, laymen (ignorant). 792 **kepen,** protect. Recall the description of the Parson in the Gen. Pro., 1.501ff. 793 **hasardrie . . . tables . . . rafles,** gambling, backgammon, dice. **ravynes . . . reneiynge,** stealing, denying. 794 E&c *whyles—craft* om. 795 **expres,** expressly. 796 **bireve . . . meede,** steal, bribery. 797 **questemongeres,** lawyers (holders of inquests for pay). **Susanna,** Dan. 13 and the apocryphal Book of Susanna. 798 **expres . . . heeste,** expressly, command. 799 EHg&c *Corporeel* om. 800 **stelyng of,** stealing by means of. 801 **chirche hawes,** churchyards. 802 **longen,** belong. 803 **reven,** steal. 804 **releevynge . . . misericorde . . . largely taken,** relieving (remedying), mercy, generously employed. 806 **mysese . . . mysesed,** distress, distressed. 809 **amenused,** reduced.

misericorde been as for to lene, and for to yeve, and to foryeven and relesse, and for to han pitee in herte, and compassioun of the meschief of his evene-Cristene, and eek to chastise there as nede is. / Another manere of 810 remedie agayns avarice is resonable largesse. But soothly, heere bihoveth the consideracioun of the grace of Jesu Crist and of his temporeel goodes, and eek of the goodes perdurables that Crist yaf to us; / and to han remembrance of the deeth that he shal receyve, he noot whanne, where, ne how; and eek that he shal forgon al that he hath save oonly that he hath despended in goode werkes. /

But for as muche as som folk been un-mesurable, men oughten eschue fool largesse, that men clepen wast. / Certes, he that is fool large ne yeveth nat his catel, but he leseth his catel. Soothly, what thyng that he yeveth for veyne glorie, as to mynstrals and to folk, for to beren his renoun in the world, he hath synne therof and noon almesse. / Certes, he leseth foule his good that ne seketh with the yifte of his good nothing but synne. / He is lyk 815 to an hors that seketh rather to drynken drovy or trouble water than for to drynken water of the clere welle. / And for as muchel as they yeven ther as they sholde nat yeven, to hem aperteneth thilke malisoun that Crist shal yeven at the day of doome to hem that shullen been dampned. /

Sequitur de Gula.

After avarice comth glotonye, which is expres eek agayn the comandement of God. Glotonye is unmesurable appetit to ete or to drynke, or elles to doon ynogh to the un-mesurable appetit and desordeynee coveitise to eten or to drynke. / This synne corrumped al this world as is wel shewed in the synne of Adam and of Eve. Looke eek what seith Seint Paul of glotonye. / "Manye," seith Seint Paul, "goon, of whiche I have ofte seyd to yow and now I seye it wepynge that they been the enemys of the croys of Crist, of whiche the ende is deeth, and of whiche hire wombe is hire god, and hire glorie in confusioun of hem that so devouren erthely thynges." / He that is usaunt to this 820 synne of glotonye, he ne may no synne withstonde. He moot been in servage of alle vices, for it is the develes hoord ther he hideth hym and resteth. / This synne hath manye speces. The firste is dronkenesse, that is the horrible sepulture of mannes resoun. And ther-fore whan a man is dronken, he hath lost his resoun, and this is deedly synne. / But soothly, whan that a man is nat wont to strong drynke, and peraventure ne knoweth nat the strengthe of the drynke, or hath feblesse in his heed, or hath travailed, thurgh which he drynketh the moore, al be he sodeynly caught with drynke, it is no deedly synne, but venyal. / The seconde spece of glotonye is that the spirit of a man wexeth al trouble, for dronkenesse bireveth hym the discrecioun of his wit. / The thridde spece of glotonye is whan a man devoureth his mete and hath no rightful manere of etynge. / 825 The fourthe is whan thurgh the grete habundaunce of his mete the humours in his body been destempred. / The fifthe is foryetel-nesse by to muchel drynkynge, for which som-tyme a man foryeteth er the morwe what he dide at even or on the nyght biforn. /

In oother manere been distinct the speces of glotonye, after Seint Gregorie. The firste is for to ete biforn tyme to ete. The seconde is whan a man get hym to delicaat mete or drynke. / The

---

810 lene . . . relesse, lend, release (from obligations). **811 resonable largesse,** moderate generosity. **bihoveth . . . perdurables,** is needed, everlasting. **813 unmesurable,** immoderate. **815 leseth foule . . . good,** loses sinfully, property (goods). **816 drovy . . . welle,** muddy, spring. **817 malisoun,** malediction. **818 doon ynogh,** i.e., do enough to satisfy. **desordeynee,** immoderate. **819 corrumped,** corrupted. **Seint Paul,** Phil. 3:18–19. **820 Manye . . . goon,** i.e., many people are now walking around. **wombe,** stomach. *devouren:* other MSS *saveren.* **821 usaunt . . . servage . . . hoord,** accustomed, bondage, collection (treasury). **823 wont,** accustomed. **825 mete . . . rightful,** food, proper (good manners). **826 humours . . . been destempred,** see *Mel,* vii.1017 note. **827 foryetelnesse,** forgetfulness. **828 after,** according to. **Seint Gregorie,** *Moralium* 30.18.60. **delicaat,** fine (gourmet).

thridde is whan men taken to muche over mesure. The fourthe is curiositee with greet entente to maken and apparaillen his mete. The fifthe is for to eten to gredily. / Thise been the fyve fyngres of the develes hand by whiche he draweth folk to synne. /   830

Remedium contra peccatum Gule.

Agayns glotonye is the remedie abstinence, as seith Galien, but that holde I nat meritorie if he do it oonly for the heele of his body. Seint Augustyn wole that abstinence be doon for vertu and with pacience. / Abstinence, he seith, is litel worth but if a man have good wil therto, and but it be enforced by pacience and by charitee, and that men doon it for Godes sake, and in hope to have the blisse of hevene. / The felawes of abstinence been attemperaunce that holdeth the meene in alle thynges; eek shame that eschueth alle deshonestee; suffisance that seketh no riche metes ne drynkes, ne dooth no fors of to outrageous apparailynge of mete; / mesure also that restreyneth by resoun the deslavee appetit of etynge; sobrenesse also that restreyneth the outrage of drynke; / sparynge also that restreyneth the delicaat ese to sitte longe at his mete and softely, wherfore som folk stonden of hir owene wyl to eten at the lasse leyser. /   835

Sequitur de Luxuria.

After glotonye thanne comth lecherie, for thise two synnes been so ny cosyns that ofte tyme they wol nat departe. / God woot, this synne is ful displesaunt thyng to God, for he seyde hymself, "Do no lecherie." And therfore he putte grete peynes agayns this synne in the olde lawe. / If womman thral were taken in this synne, she sholde be beten with staves to the deeth. And if she were a gentil womman, she sholde be slayn with stones. And if she were a bisshoppes doghter, she sholde been brent by Goddes comandement. / Fortherover, by the synne of lecherie God dreynte al the world at the diluge. And after that, he brente fyve citees with thonder-leyt, and sank hem into helle. /

Now lat us speke thanne of thilke stynkynge synne of lecherie that men clepe avowtrie of wedded folk, that is to seyn if that oon of hem be wedded, or elles bothe. / Seint John   840 seith that avowtiers shullen been in helle in a stank brennynge of fyr and of brymston— in fyr for the lecherie, in brymston for the stynk of hire ordure. / Certes, the brekynge of this sacrement is an horrible thyng. It was maked of God hymself in paradys, and confermed by Jesu Crist, as witnesseth Seint Mathew in the gospel, "A man shal lete fader and mooder, and taken hym to his wif, and they shullen be two in o flessh." / This sacrement bitokneth the knyttynge togidre of Crist and of Hooly Chirche. / And nat oonly that God forbad avowtrie in dede, but eek he comanded that thou sholdest nat coveite thy neighebores wyf. / In this heeste, seith Seint Augustyn, is forboden alle manere coveitise to doon lecherie. Lo what seith Seint Mathew in the gospel, that whoso seeth a womman to coveitise of his lust, he hath doon lecherie with hire in his herte. /   845 Heere may ye seen that nat oonly the dede of this synne is forboden, but eek the desir to doon that synne. / This cursed synne anoyeth grevousliche hem that it haunten. And first to hire soule, for he obligeth it to synne and to

---

829 over mesure . . . curiositee . . . apparaillen, beyond moderation, complexity, garnish. **831 Galien,** Galen, famous Greek physician (2nd cent. A.D.). **meritorie . . . heele,** meritorious (spiritually), health. **833 meene,** mean (average). **suffisance . . . dooth no fors,** contentment, does not care. **834 mesure . . . deslavee . . . sobrenesse,** moderation, foul (see l. 629), sobriety. **835 sparynge . . . delicaat . . . hir owene wyl,** frugality, voluptuous, voluntarily. **836 departe,** separate. **837 seyde hymself,** Exod. 20:14, Lev. 19:20. **peynes,** punishments. **838 thral,** bondwoman. **839 by . . . dreynte . . . brente . . . thonder-leyt,** for, drowned (Noah's flood), burned (Sodom and Gomorrah), lightning (not "light," but OE *liget,* "flash"). **840 avowtrie,** adultery. **841 Seint John,** Rev. 21:8. **stank . . . ordure,** pool, filth. *stank:* other MSS *stynke/stenche,* etc. E&c *in fyr—brymston* om. **842 maked of God,** Gen. 2:22. **Seint Mathew,** Matt. 19:5. **lete,** leave. **845 heeste,** commandment. **Seint Mathew,** Matt. 5:28. **847 haunten . . . obligeth,** indulge, compels.

peyne of deeth that is perdurable. / Unto the body anoyeth it grevously also, for it dreyeth hym, and wasteth, and shent hym, and of his blood he maketh sacrifice to the feend of helle; it wasteth his catel and his substaunce. / And certes, if it be a foul thyng a man to waste his catel on wommen, yet is it a fouler thyng whan that for swich ordure wommen dispenden upon men hir catel and substaunce. / This synne, as seith the prophete, bireveth man and womman hir goode fame and al hire honour, and it is ful pleasaunt to the devel, for therby wyn- neth he the mooste partie of this world. / 850 And right as a marchant deliteth hym moost in chaffare that he hath moost avantage of, right so deliteth the fend in this ordure. /

This is that other hand of the devel, with fyve fyngres to cacche the peple to his vileynye. / The firste fynger is the fool lookynge of the fool womman and of the fool man, that sleeth right as the basilicok sleeth folk by the venym of his sighte, for the coveitise of eyen folweth the coveitise of the herte. / The seconde fynger is the vileyns touchynge in wikkede manere, and therfore seith Salomon that whoso toucheth and handleth a womman, he fareth lyk hym that handleth the scorpioun that styngeth and sodeynly sleeth thurgh his envenymynge. As whoso toucheth warm pych is shent his fyngres. / The thridde is foule wordes that fareth lyk fyr, that right anon brenneth the herte. / The fourthe fynger is the kyssinge, 855 and trewely he were a greet fool that wolde kisse the mouth of a brennynge ovene or of a fourneys. / And moore fooles been they that kissen in vileynye, for that mouth is the mouth of helle—and namely, thise olde dotardes holours, yet wol they kisse though they may nat do, and smatre hem. / Certes, they been lyk to houndes, for an hound whan he comth by the roser or by othere beautees, though he may nat pisse yet wole he heve up his leg and make a contenaunce to pisse. / And for that many man weneth that he may nat synne for no likerous- nesse that he dooth with his wyf, certes, that opinion is fals. God woot, a man may sleen hymself with his owene knyf, and make hym- selven dronken of his owene tonne. / Certes, be it wyf, be it child, or any worldly thyng that he loveth biforn God, it is his mawmet and he is an ydolastre. / Man sholde loven hys 860 wyf by discrecioun, paciently and atemprely, and thanne is she as though it were his suster. / The fifthe fynger of the develes hand is the stynkinge dede of leccherie. / Certes, the fyve fyngres of glotonie the feend put in the wombe of a man, and with his fyve syngres of lecherie he gripeth hym by the reynes for to throwen hym into the fourneys of helle / ther as they shul han the fyr and the wormes that evere shul lasten, and wepynge and wailynge, sharpe hunger and thurst, and grymnesse of develes that shullen al to-trede hem, withouten respit and withouten ende. / Of leccherie, as I seyde, sourden diverse speces, as fornicacioun that is bitwixe man and womman that been nat maried, and this is deedly synne and agayns nature. / Al that is enemy and destruccioun 865 to nature is agayns nature. / Parfay, the resoun of a man telleth eek hym wel that it is deedly synne for as muche as God forbad leccherie. And Seint Paul yeveth hem the regne that nys dewe to no wight but to hem that doon deedly synne. / Another synne of leccherie is to bireve a mayden of hir maydenhede, for he that so dooth, certes he casteth a mayden out of the hyeste degree that is in this present lif / and bireveth hire thilke precious fruyt that the

---

848 dreyeth . . . shent . . . catel, dries (drains), ruins, property. **849 ordure,** filth. **850 bireveth . . . mooste partie,** robs, greatest part. **851 chaffare . . . avantage,** trading, profit. **852 cacche . . . to,** i.e., draw to. **853 fool,** foolish. **basilicok,** mythical beast with head of a cock and body of a serpent, supposed to kill with a glance. **854 Salomon,** Ecclus. 26:10 (Vulgate). **pych . . . shent,** pitch, soils, Ecclus. 13:1 (Vulgate). **857 holours . . . smatre,** lechers, defile. **858 *beautees:*** most eds. substitute *busshes,* not found in any MS. **859 likerousnesse . . . tonne,** lechery, wine cask. Recall MerchT, v.1840. **860 mawmet,** idol. **863 wombe,** belly. **864 to-trede,** trample. *grymnesse:* Hg&c *grislynesse.* **865 sourden,** arise. **867 Seint Paul,** Gal. 5:19–21. **regne . . . dewe,** kingdom (reward), due.

book clepeth "the hundred fruyt." I ne kan seye it noon oother weyes in Englissh, but in Latyn it highte *centesimus fructus*. / Certes, he that so dooth is cause of manye damages and vileynyes, mo than any man kan rekene, right as he somtyme is cause of alle damages that beestes don in the feeld that breketh the hegge or the closure thurgh which he destroyeth that may nat been restoored. / For certes, 870 namore may maydenhede be restoored than an arm that is smyten fro the body may retourne agayn to wexe. / She may have mercy, this woot I wel, if she do penitence; but nevere shal it be that she nas corrupt. / And al be it so that I have spoken somwhat of avowtrie, it is good to shewen mo perils that longen to avowtrie, for to eschue that foule synne. / Avowtrie in Latin is for to seyn approchynge of oother mannes bed, thurgh which tho that whilom weren o flessh abawndone hir bodyes to othere persones. / Of this synne, as seith the wise man, folwen manye harmes. First, brekynge of feith; and certes, in feith is the keye of Cristendom. / 875 And whan that feith is broken and lorn, soothly Cristendom stant veyn and withouten fruyt. / This synne is eek a thefte, for thefte generally is for to reve a wight his thyng agayns his wille. / Certes, this is the fouleste thefte that may be, whan a womman steleth hir body from hir housbonde and yeveth it to hire holour to defoulen hire, and steleth hir soule fro Crist and yeveth it to the devel. / This is a fouler thefte than for to breke a chirche and stele the chalice, for thise avowtiers breken the temple of God spiritually and stelen the vessel of grace, that is the body and the soule, for which Crist shal destroyen hem, as seith Seint Paul. / Soothly of this thefte douted gretly Joseph, whan that his lordes wyf preyed hym of vileynye, whan he seyde, "Lo, my lady, how my lord hath take to me under my warde al that he hath in this world, ne nothyng of his thynges is out of my power but oonly ye that been his wyf. / And 880 how sholde I thanne do this wikkednesse and synne so horrible agayns God and agayns my lord? God it forbeede." Allas, al to litel is swich trouthe now yfounde! / The thridde harm is the filthe thurgh which they breken the comandement of God and defoulen the auctour of matrimoyne, that is Crist. / For certes, insomuche as the sacrement of mariage is so noble and so digne, so muche is it gretter synne for to breken it. For God made mariage in paradys, in the estaat of innocence, to multiplye mankynde to the service of God. / And therfore is the brekynge moore grevous. Of which brekynge comen false heires ofte tyme, that wrongfully occupien folkes heritages. And therfore wol Crist putte hem out of the regne of hevene, that is heritage to goode folk. / Of this brekynge comth eek ofte tyme that folk unwar wedden or synnen with hire owene kynrede, and namely thilke harlotes that haunten bordels of thise fool wommen that mowe be likned to a commune gonge where as men purgen hire ordure. / What seye we eek of putours that 885 lyven by the horrible synne of putrie, and constreyne wommen to yelden to hem a certeyn rente of hire bodily puterie, ye somtyme of his owene wyf or his child, as doon as this bawdes? Certes, thise been cursede synnes. / Understood eek that avowtrie is set gladly in the Ten Comandementz bitwixe thefte and manslaughtre, for it is the gretteste thefte that may be, for it is thefte of body and of soule. / And it is lyk to homycide, for it kerveth a-two and breketh a-two hem that first were maked o flessh, and therfore by the olde lawe of God they sholde be slayn. / But nathelees, by the lawe of Jesu Crist, that is lawe of pitee, whan he seyde to the womman that was founden in avowtrie and sholde han been slayn with stones

869 hundred fruyt, virginity, widowhood, and matrimony were compared by St. Jerome, *Contra Jovinianum* 1.3, with the grain that brought forth a hundredfold, sixtyfold, and thirtyfold, Matt. 13:8. **874 whilom,** formerly. **876 lorn,** last. **877 reve,** rob. **878 holour,** lecher. **879 avowtiers,** adulterers. **Seint Paul,** I Cor. 3:17. **880 douted . . . take . . . warde,** feared, given, control. Gen. 39:8–9. **882 auctour,** author. **885 unwar . . . harlotes . . . bordels . . . mowe . . . commune gonge,** unaware, lechers, brothels, may, public toilet. **886 putours . . . putrie . . . bawdes,** pimps, prostitution, pimps. **887 gladly,** appropriately.

after the wyl of the Jewes as was hir lawe, "Go," quod Jesu Crist, "and have namoore wyl to synne," or "wille namore to do synne." / Soothly, the vengeaunce of avowtrie is awarded to the peynes of helle, but if so be that it be destourbed by penitence. / Yet been ther 890 mo speces of this cursed synne, as whan that oon of hem is religious, or elles bothe; or of folk that been entred into ordre, as subdekne, or dekne, or preest, or hospitaliers. And evere the hyer that he is in ordre, the gretter is the synne. / The thynges that gretly agreggen hire synne is the brekynge of hire avow of chastitee, whan they receyved the ordre. / And forther-over, sooth is that hooly ordre is chief of al the tresorie of God, and his especial signe and mark of chastitee, to shewe that they been joyned to chastitee, which that is moost precious lyf that is. / And thise ordred folk been specially titled to God, and of the special meignee of God, for which whan they doon deedly synne, they been the special traytours of God and of his peple; for they lyven of the peple to preye for the peple, and whyle they been suche traitours hire preyers availen nat to the peple. / Preestes been aungeles, as by the dignitee of hir mysterye, but for sothe, Seint Paul seith that Sathanas transformeth hym in an aungel of light. / 895 Soothly, the preest that haunteth deedly synne, he may be likned to the aungel of derk-nesse transformed in the aungel of light—he semeth aungel of light but for sothe he is aungel of derknesse. / Swiche preestes been the sones of Helie, as sheweth in the Book of Kynges that they weren the sones of Belial, that is the devel. / Belial is to seyn "withouten juge," and so faren they. Hem thynketh they been free and han no juge, namore than hath a free bole that

taketh which cow that hym liketh in the town. / So faren they by wommen. For right as a free bole is ynough for al a town, right so is a wikked preest corrupcioun ynough for al a parisshe or for al a contree. / Thise preestes, as seith the book, ne konne nat the mysterie of preesthode to the peple, ne God ne knowe they nat. They ne holde hem nat apayd, as seith the book, of soden flesh that was to hem offred but they tooke by force the flessh that is rawe. / 900 Certes, so thise shrewes ne holden hem nat apayed of roosted flessh and sode flessh with which the peple fedden hem in greet reverence, but they wole have raw flessh of folkes wyves and hir doghtres. / And certes, thise wommen that consenten to hire harlotrie doon greet wrong to Crist and to Hooly Chirche and alle halwes and to alle soules, for they bireven alle thise hym that sholde worshipe Crist and Hooly Chirche and preye for Cristene soules. / And therfore han swiche preestes, and hire lemmanes eek that consenten to hir leccherie, the malisoun of al the court Cristiene, til they come to amendement. / The thridde spece of avowtrie is somtyme bitwixe a man and his wyf; and that is whan they take no reward in hire assemblynge, but oonly to hire flesshly delit, as seith Seint Jerome, / and ne rekken of nothyng but that they been assembled. By cause that they been maried al is good ynough, as thynketh to hem. / But in swich folk hath 905 the devel power, as seyde the aungel Raphael to Thobie, for in hire assemblynge they putten Jesu Crist out of hire herte, and yeven hemself to alle ordure. / The fourthe spece is the assemblee of hem that been of hire kynrede, or of hem that been of oon affynytee, or elles with hem with whiche hir fadres or hir

889 quod Jesu Crist, John 8:11. **891 ordre . . . hospitaliers,** holy orders, Knights Hospitalers. E&c *or dekne* om. **892 agreggen,** aggravate. **894 titled . . . meignee . . . lyven of,** belonging (as by legal title), household retainers, live off of (are supported by). E&c *to preye—peple* om. **895 mysterye . . . transformeth hym in,** profession, transforms himself into. **897 Helie,** Eli, I Sam. 2:12 (Vulgate, Liber Primus Regum). *Helie:* Hg&c *Belie.* **898 withouten juge,** in Vulgate Judg. 19:22 "Belial" is interpreted as *absque iugo* (without a yoke); in Fr. *sans ioug,* which could be misread *sans iuge.* Note that the explanation fits the correct reading. **900 konne . . . mysterie.** know, duty. **apayd . . . soden,** paid (satisfied), boiled, I Sam. 2:15. **901 shrewes,** evil people. **902 halwes . . . bireven . . . thise hym,** saints, rob these of him. **903 lemmanes . . . malisoun . . . court Cristiene,** lovers, malediction, ecclesi-astical court. **904 reward . . . assemblynge,** regard, sexual intercourse. **Seint Jerome,** *Contra Jovinianum* 1:49. See again MerchT, v.1836ff. **906 in swich,** over such. **Thobie,** Tob. 6:17 (Vulgate). **907 oon affynytee,** related by marriage.

kynrede han deled in the synne of leccherie. This synne maketh hem lyk to houndes that taken no kepe to kynrede. / And certes, parentele is in two maneres, outher goostly or flesshly. Goostly as for to deelen with his godsibbes, / for right so as he that engendreth a child is his flesshly fader, right so is his godfader his fader espiritueel. For which a womman may in no lasse synne assemblen with hire godsib than with hir owene flesshly brother. / The fifthe spece is thilke abhomynable synne of which that no man unnethe oghte speke ne write, nathelees it is openly reherced in hooly writ. / This cursednesse doon men and wommen in diverse entente and in diverse manere. But though that hooly writ speke of horrible synne, certes, hooly writ may nat been defouled namore than the sonne that shyneth on the mixne. / Another synne aperteneth to leccherie that comth in slepynge, and this synne cometh ofte to hem that been maydenes, and eek to hem that been corrupt, and this synne men clepen polucioun, that comth in foure maneres. / Somtyme of langwissynge of body, for the humours been to ranke and habundaunt in the body of man. Somtyme of infermetee, for the fieblesse of the vertu retentif as phisik maketh mencioun. Somtyme for surfeet of mete and drynke. / And somtyme of vileyns thoghtes that been enclosed in mannes mynde whan he gooth to slepe, which may nat been withoute synne. For which men moste kepen hem wisely, or elles may men synnen ful grevously. /

Remedium contra peccatum Luxurie.

Now comth the remedie agayns leccherie, and that is, generally, chastitee and continence that restreyneth alle the desordeynee moevinges that comen of flesshly talentes. / And evere the gretter merite shal he han that moost restreyneth the wikkede eschawfynges of the ardour of this synne. And this is in two maneres, that is to seyn chastitee in mariage and chastitee of widwehode. / Now shaltow understonde that matrimoyne is leefful assemblynge of man and of womman that receyven by vertu of the sacrement the boond thurgh which they may nat be departed in al hir lyf, that is to seyn whil that they lyven bothe. / This, as seith the book, is a ful greet sacrement. God maked it, as I have seyd, in paradys, and wolde hymself be born in mariage. / And for to halwen mariage, he was at a weddynge, where as he turned water into wyn, which was the firste miracle that he wroghte in erthe biforn his disciples. / Trewe effect of mariage clenseth fornicacioun and replenysseth Hooly Chirche of good lynage, for that is the ende of mariage and it chaungeth deedly synne into venial synne bitwixe hem that been ywedded, and maketh the hertes al oon of hem that been ywedded, as wel as the bodies. / This is verray mariage, that was establissed by God er that synne bigan, whan natureel lawe was in his right poynt in paradys. And it was ordeyned that o man sholde have but o womman, and o womman but o man, as seith Seint Augustyn, by manye resouns. /

First, for mariage is figured bitwixe Crist and Hooly Chirche. And that oother is for a man is heved of a womman, algate by ordinaunce it sholde be so. / For if a womman hadde mo men than oon, thanne sholde she have moo hevedes than oon, and that were an horrible thyng biforn God, and eek a womman ne myghte nat plese to many folk at oones. And also ther ne

908 parentele ... godsibbes, kinship, children of one's godparents or godchildren of one's parents. **910 unnethe,** hardly. **hooly writ,** Rom. 1:26–27. **911 mixne,** manure pile. **912 maydenes,** virgins. *foure:* E&c *iij.* **913 langwissynge,** i.e., pining with desire. **vertu retentif,** ability to retain seminal fluid. **914 moste kepen,** must guard. **915 talentes,** desires. **916 eschawfynges,** inflaming. *ardour:* all MSS but one *ordure;* the emendation is Robinson's. **917 leefful,** legitimate. **918 the book,** Eph. 5:32 (Vulgate). **God,** Gen. 2:24. **919 halwen,** hallow. **weddynge,** John 2:1–11. **921 verray ... his right poynt,** true, its right state. **922 figured ... heved ... algate by ordinaunce,** represented, head, at any rate by (divine) law; Eph. 5:25, I Cor. 11:13.

sholde nevere be pees ne reste amonges hem, for everich wolde axen his owene thyng. / And fortherover, no man ne sholde knowe his owene engendrure, ne who sholde have his heritage, and the womman sholde been the lasse biloved fro the tyme that she were conjoynt to many men. /

Now comth how that a man sholde bere hym with his wif, and namely in two thynges, that is to seyn in suffraunce and reverence, as shewed Crist whan he made first womman. / 925 For he ne made hire nat of the heved of Adam, for she sholde nat clayme to greet lordshipe. / For ther as the womman hath the maistrie, she maketh to muche desray. Ther neden none ensamples of this; the experience of day by day oghte suffise. / Also certes, God ne made nat womman of the foot of Adam for she ne sholde nat been holden to lowe, for she kan nat paciently suffre. But God made womman of the ryb of Adam, for womman sholde be felawe unto man. / Man sholde bere hym to his wyf in feith, in trouthe, and in love, as seith Seint Paul, that a man sholde loven his wyf as Crist loved Hooly Chirche, that loved it so wel that he deyde for it. So sholde a man for his wyf if it were nede. /

Now how that a womman sholde be subget to hire housbonde, that telleth Seint Peter. First, in obedience. / And eek, as seith the 930 decree, a womman that is wyf, as longe as she is a wyf, she hath noon auctoritee to swere ne bere witnesse withoute leve of hir housbonde that is hire lord, algate he sholde be so by resoun. / She sholde eek serven hym in alle honestee and been attempree of hire array. I woot wel that they sholde setten hire entente to plesen hir housbondes, but nat by hire queyntise of array. / Seint Jerome seith that wyves that been apparailled in silk and in precious purpre ne mowe nat clothen hem in

Jesu Crist. What seith Seint John eek in thys matere? / Seint Gregorie eek seith that no wight seketh precious array but oonly for veyne glorie to been honoured the moore biforn the peple. / It is a greet folye, a womman to have a fair array outward and in hirself be foul inward. / A wyf sholde eek be mesurable 935 in lookinge and in berynge and in lawghynge, and discreet in alle hire wordes and hire dedes. / And aboven alle worldly thyng she sholde loven hire housbonde with al hire herte, and to hym be trewe of hir body. / So sholde an housbonde eek be to his wyf. For sith that al the body is the housbondes, so sholde hire herte been, or elles ther is bitwixe hem two as in that no parfit mariage. / Thanne shal men understonde that for thre thynges a man and his wyf flesshly mowen assemble. The firste is in entente of engendrure of children to the service of God, for certes that is the cause final of matrimoyne. / Another cause is to yelden everich of hem to oother the dette of hire bodies, for neither of hem hath power over his owene body. The thridde is for to eschewe leccherye and vileynye. The ferthe is for sothe deedly synne. / As to the firste, it is meritorie. The 940 seconde also, for as seith the decree that she hath merite of chastitee that yeldeth to hire housbonde the dette of hir body, ye though it be agayn hir lykynge and the lust of hire herte. / The thridde manere is venyal synne, and trewely scarsly may ther any of thise be withoute venial synne for the corrupcion and for the delit. / The fourthe manere is for to understonde, if they assemble oonly for amorous love and for noon of the forseyde causes, but for to accomplice thilke brennynge delit, they rekke nevere how ofte, soothly it is deedly synne. And yet with sorwe somme folk wol peynen hem moore to doon than to hire appetit suffiseth. /

The seconde manere of chastitee is for to

925 suffraunce, consideration. **927 desray,** disorder. Recall the theme of the "marriage argument" in *CT*. **929 bere hym to,** behave toward. **Seint Paul,** Eph. 5:25. **930 Seint Peter,** I Pet. 3:1. **931 decree . . . algate,** canon law, at least. **932 attempree . . . array . . . queyntise,** moderate, dress, elaborateness. **933 purpre,** purple. **Seint John,** Rev. 17:4, 18:16. **934 Seint Gregorie,** see l. 414 and note. **936 mesurable,** modest. **940 dette,** see l. 375 and note. **941 meritorie . . . lust,** meritorious, desire. E *merite of chastitee* om. **943 with sorwe,** unfortunately.

been a clene wydewe and eschue the embracynges of man, and desiren the embracynge of Jesu Crist. / Thise been tho that han been wyves and han forgoon hire housbondes, and eek wommen that han doon leccherie and been releeved by penitence. / And certes, 945 if that a wyf koude kepen hire al chaast by licence of hir housbonde so that she yeve nevere noon occasion that he agilte, it were to hire a greet merite. / This manere wommen that observen chastitee moste be clene in herte as well as in body and in thoght, and mesurable in clothynge and in contenaunce, and been abstinent in etynge and drynkynge, in spekynge, and in dede. They been the vessel or the boyste of the blissed Magdelene, that fulfilleth Hooly Chirche of good odour. / The thridde manere of chastitee is virginitee, and it bihoveth that she be hooly in herte and clene of body; thanne is she spouse to Jesu Crist, and she is the lyf of angeles. / She is the preisynge of this world, and she is as thise martirs in egalitee; she hath in hire that tonge may nat telle ne herte thynke. / Virginitee baar oure lord Jesu Crist, and virgine was hymselve. / 950

Another remedie agayns leccherie is specially to withdrawen swiche thynges as yeve occasion to thilke vileynye, as ese, etynge, and drynkynge, for certes whan the pot boyleth strongly, the beste remedie is to withdrawe the fyr. / Slepynge longe in greet quiete is eek a greet norice to leccherie. /

Another remedie agayns leccherie is that a man or a womman eschue the compaignye of hem by whiche he douteth to be tempted, for al be it so that the dede is withstonden, yet is ther greet temptacioun. / Soothly a whit wal, although it ne brenne noght fully by stikynge of a candele, yet is the wal blak of the leyt. / Ful ofte tyme I rede that no man truste in his owene perfeccioun but he be stronger than Sampson, and hoolier than Danyel, and wiser than Salomon. / 955

Now after that I have declared yow as I kan the Sevene Deedly Synnes, and somme of hire braunches and hire remedies, soothly, if I koude, I wolde telle yow the Ten Comandementz. / But so heigh a doctrine I lete to divines. Nathelees, I hope to God they been touched in this tretice, everich of hem alle. /

Sequitur secunda pars Penitencie.

Now for as muche as the second partie of penitence stant in confessioun of mouth, as I bigan in the firste chapitre, I seye, Seint Augustyn seith, / "Synne is every word and every dede and al that men coveiten agayn the lawe of Jesu Crist." And this is for to synne in herte, in mouth, and in dede, by thy five wittes, that been sighte, herynge, smellynge, tastynge or savourynge, and feelynge. / Now is it good to understonde that that agreggeth muchel every synne. / Thow shalt considere what 960 thow art that doost the synne, wheither thou be male or femele, yong or oold, gentil or thral, free or servant, hool or syk, wedded or sengle, ordred or unordred, wys or fool, clerk or seculeer, / if she be of thy kynrede bodily or goostly or noon, if any of thy kynrede have synned with hire or noon, and manye mo thynges. /

Another circumstaunce is this: wheither it be

---

945 forgoon, lost, **946 licence . . . agilte,** permission, sinned. **947 manere . . . moste be,** kind of, must be. E&c *moste be—mesurable* om. **boyste,** box (of precious ointment), Matt. 26:7. **949 in egalitee,** i.e., equal in merit. Hg&c *ne herte thynke* om. **951 ese,** comfort. **952 norice,** nurse (nourishment). **953 douteth,** fears. **954 stikynge . . . leyt,** touching against it, flame (see l. 839 note). **955 rede . . . but,** advise, unless. **960 agreggeth,** intensifies. Hg&c *the circumstaunces that aggreggen.* **961 Thow shalt considere,** see l. 319 and note. **ordred . . . clerk,** both mean a person in holy orders.

doon in fornicacioun or in avowtrie or noon, incest or noon, mayden or noon, in manere of homicide or noon, horrible grete synnes or smale, and how longe thou hast continued in synne. / The thridde circumstaunce is the place ther thou hast do synne, wheither in oother mennes hous or in thyn owene, in feeld or in chirche or in chirche hawe, in chirche dedicat or noon. / For if the chirche be halwed and man or womman spille his kynde in with that place by wey of synne, or by wikked temptacioun, the chirche is entredited til it be reconciled by the bishop; / and the preest 965 that dide swich a vileynye, to terme of al his lif he sholde namore synge masse, and if he dide he sholde doon deedly synne at every tyme that he so songe masse. / The fourthe circumstaunce is by whiche mediatours or by whiche messagers as for enticement or for consentement to bere compaignye with felaweshipe, for many a wrecche for to bere compaignye shal go to the devel of helle. / Wherfore they that eggen or consenten to the synne been parteners of the synne, and of the dampnacioun of the synnere. / The fifthe circumstaunce is how manye tymes that he hath synned, if it be in his mynde, and how ofte that he hath falle. / For he that ofte falleth in synne, he despiseth the mercy of God, and encreesseth hys synne, and is unkynde to Crist; and he wexeth the moore fieble to withstonde synne, and synneth the moore lightly, / and the latter ariseth, and is the 970 moore eschew for to shryven hym, namely, to hym that is his confessour. / For which that folk whan they falle agayn in hir olde folies, outher they forleten hir olde confessours al outrely, or elles they departen hir shrift in diverse places. But soothly, swich departed shrift deserveth no mercy of God of his synnes. / The sixte circumstaunce is why that a man synneth, as by whiche temptacioun, and if hymself procure thilke temptacioun, or by the excitynge of oother folk; or if he synne with a womman by force, or by hire owene assent; / or if the womman, maugree hir heed, hath been afforced, or noon. This shal she telle, for coveitise or for poverte, and if it was hire procurynge or noon, and swiche manere harneys. / The seventhe circumstaunce is in what manere he hath doon his synne, or how that she hath suffred that folk han doon to hire. / And the 975 same shal the man telle pleynly with alle circumstaunces, and wheither he hath synned with comune bordel wommen or noon, / or doon his synne in hooly tymes or noon, in fastyng tymes or noon, or biforn his shrifte, or after his latter shrifte, / and hath peraventure broken therfore his penance enjoyned, by whos help and whos conseil, by sorcerie or craft, al moste be toold. / Alle thise thynges, after that they been grete or smale, engreggen the conscience of man, and eek the preest that is thy juge may the bettre been avysed of his juggement in yevynge of thy penaunce, and that is after thy contricioun. / For understond wel that after tyme that a man hath defouled his baptesme by synne, if he wole come to salvacioun ther is noon other wey but by penitence and shrifte and satisfaccioun, / 980 and namely by the two if ther be a confessour to which he may shriven hym, and the thridde if he have lyf to parfournen it. /

Thanne shal man looke and considere that if he wole maken a trewe and a profitable confessioun ther moste be foure condiciouns. / First, it moot been in sorweful bitternesse of

---

964 chirche hawe . . . dedicat, churchyard, consecrated. **965 kynde . . . entredited . . . reconciled,** seminal fluid, defiled (interdicted), reconsecrated. E&c *til it—bishop* om. **967 messagers . . . to bere compaignye,** messengers (go-betweens), (is the sinner) brought to keep company (with other sinners). **970 lightly,** easily. **971 latter . . . moore eschew . . . shryven,** tardily (later), more likely to avoid, confess. **972 forleten . . . departen,** abandon, divide. **974 maugree hir heed,** in spite of all she could do. **coveitise,** i.e., whether the sin was for greed. **harneys,** related matters (trappings). **976 pleynly . . . bordel,** fully, brothel. **977 hooly tymes,** religious holidays. **978 broken . . . penance enjoyned,** i.e., failed to discharge the penance assigned by the confessor. **979 engreggen,** burden.

herte, as seyde the King Ezechye to God, "I wol remembre me alle the yeres of my lif in bitternesse of myn herte." / This condicioun of bitternesse hath fyve signes. The firste is that confessioun moste be shamefast, nat for to covere ne hyden his synne, for he hath agilt his God and defouled his soule. / And therof seith Seint Augustyn, "The herte travailleth for shame of his synne." And for he hath greet shamefastnesse, he is digne to have greet mercy of God. / Swich was the confessioun of the puplican that wolde nat heven up his eyen to hevene for he hadde offended God of hevene, for which shamefastnesse he hadde anon the mercy of God. / And therof seith Seint Augustyn that swich shamefast folk been next foryevenesse and remissioun. / Another signe is humylitee in confessioun. Of which seith Seint Peter, "Humbleth yow under the might of God." The hond of God is mighty in confessioun, for therby God foryeveth thee thy synnes, for he allone hath the power. / And this humylitee shal been in herte and in signe outward, for right as he hath humylitee to God in his herte, right so sholde he humble his body outward to the preest that sit in Goddes place. / For which in no manere, sith that Crist is sovereyn, and the preest meene and mediatour bitwixe Crist and the synnere, and the synnere is the laste by wey of resoun, / thanne sholde nat the synnere sitte as heighe as his confessour, but knele biforn hym or at his feet but if maladie destourbe it. For he shal nat taken kepe who sit there, but in whos place that he sitteth. / A man that hath trespased to a lord, and comth for to axe mercy and maken his accord, and set him doun anon by the lord, men wolde holden hym outrageous and nat worthy so soone for to have remissioun ne mercy. / The thridde signe is how that thy shrift sholde be ful

of teeres, if man may, and if man may nat wepe with his bodily eyen, lat hym wepe in herte. / Swich was the confession of Seint Peter, for after that he hadde forsake Jesu Crist, he wente out and weepe ful bitterly. / The fourthe signe is that he ne lette nat for shame to shewen his confessioun. / Swich was the confessioun of the Magdelene that ne spared for no shame of hem that weren atte feeste for to go to oure lord Jesu Crist and biknowe to hym hire synnes. / The fifthe signe is that a man or a womman be obeisant to receyven the penaunce that hym is enjoyned for his synnes, for certes Jesu Crist, for the giltes of a man, was obedient to the deeth. /

The seconde condicion of verray confession is that it be hastily doon, for certes if a man hadde a deedly wounde, evere the lenger that he taried to warisshe hymself, the moore wolde it corrupte and haste hym to his deeth, and eek the wounde wolde be the wors for to heele. / And right so fareth synne that longe tyme is in a man unshewed. / Certes, a man oghte hastily shewen his synnes for manye causes, as for drede of deeth that cometh ofte sodenly and is in no certeyn what tyme it shal be, ne in what place. And eek the drecchynge of o synne draweth in another, / and eek the lenger that he tarieth, the ferther he is fro Crist. And if he abide to his laste day, scarsly may he shryven hym or remembre hym of his synnes or repenten hym for the grevous maladie of his deeth. / And for as muche as he ne hath nat in his lyf herkned Jesu Crist whanne he hath spoken, he shal crie to Jesu Crist at his laste day and scarsly wol he herkne hym. / And understond that this condicioun moste han foure thynges. Thi shrift moste be purveyed bifore and avysed, for wikked haste dooth no profit. And that a man konne shryve hym of his synnes, be it of pride, or of

983 Ezechye, Hezekiah, Isa. 38:15. E&c *Ezechiel.* **984 agilt,** sinned against. **985 Seint Augustyn,** *Liber de Vera et Falsa Poenitentia* 1.10.25 (attributed to Augustine). **travailleth for . . . digne,** labors under, worthy. **986 puplican . . . heven . . . anon,** publican (Luke 18:13), raise, immediately. **987 next,** nearest to. **988 Seint Peter,** I Peter 5:6. **993 wepe with his bodily eyen,** recall the Friar, Gen. Pro., I.230. **994 Seint Peter,** Matt. 26:75. **995 lette,** refrain. **996 biknowe,** reveal, Luke 7:37. **998 warisshe,** cure. **999 unshewed,** unrevealed. **1000 drecchynge,** continuing. **1001 for the . . . maladie,** because of the sickness. **1003 purveyed . . . avysed,** arranged, considered.

envye, and so forth of the speces and circumstances; / and that he have comprehended in
hys mynde the nombre and the greetnesse of his
synnes, and how longe that he hath leyn in
synne; / and eek that he be contrit of his synnes
and in stidefast purpos, by the grace of God,
nevere eft to falle in synne; and eek that he
drede and countrewaite hymself that he fle the
occasiouns of synne to whiche he is enclyned. / Also thou shalt shryve thee of alle   1005
thy synnes to o man, and nat a parcel to o
man and a parcel to another, that is to understonde, in entente to departe thy confessioun as
for shame or drede, for it nys but stranglynge of
thy soule. / For certes, Jesu Crist is entierly al
good; in hym nys noon inperfeccioun; and
therfore outher he foryeveth al parfitly or never
a deel. / I seye nat that if thow be assigned to
the penitauncer for certein synne that thow art
bounde to shewen hym al the remenaunt of thy
synnes, of whiche thow hast be shryven to thy
curaat, but if it like to thee of thyn humylitee.
This is no departynge of shrifte. / Ne I seye nat,
theras I speke of divisioun of confessioun, that if
thou have licence for to shryve thee to a discreet
and an honeste preest, where thee liketh, and
by licence of thy curat, that thow ne mayst wel
shryve thee to him of alle thy synnes. / But lat
no blotte be bihynde; lat no synne been
untoold, as fer as thow hast remembraunce. / And whan thou shalt be shriven   1010
to thy curaat, telle hym eek alle the synnes
that thow hast doon syn thou were last yshryven.
This is no wikked entente of divisioun of shrifte. /

Also the verray shrifte axeth certeine condiciouns. First, that thow shryve thee by thy
free wil, noght constreyned, ne for shame of folk,
ne for maladie, ne swiche thynges. For it is
resoun that he that trespasseth by his free wyl,
that by his free wyl he confesse his trespas, / and
that noon oother man telle his synne but he

hymself. Ne he shal nat nayte ne denye his
synne, ne wratthe hym agayn the preest for his
amonestynge to leve synne. / The seconde condicioun is that thy shrift be laweful, that is to
seyn, that thow that shryvest thee, and eek the
preest that hereth thy confessioun, been verraily
in the feith of Hooly Chirche, / and that a man
ne be nat despeired of the mercy of Jesu
Crist, as Caym or Judas. / And eek a man   1015
moot accusen hymself of his owene trespas,
and nat another; but he shal blame and wyten
hymself and his owene malice of his synne, and
noon oother. / But nathelees, if that another
man be occasioun or enticere of his synne, or
the estaat of a persone be swich thurgh which
his synne is agregged, or elles that he may nat
pleynly shryven hym but he telle the persone
with which he hath synned, thanne may he
telle, / so that his entente ne be nat to bakbite
the persone, but oonly to declaren his confessioun. /

Thou ne shalt nat eek make no lesynges in
thy confessioun, for humylitee peraventure to
seyn that thou hast doon synnes of whiche that
thou were nevere gilty. / For Seint Augustyn
seith if thou by cause of thyn humylitee makest
lesynges on thyself, though thow ne were nat in
synne biforn, yet artow thanne in synne
thurgh thy lesynges. / Thou most eek   1020
shewe thy synne by thyn owene propre
mouth, but thow be woxe dowmb, and nat by
no lettre; for thow that hast doon the synne,
thou shalt have the shame therfore. / Thow
shalt nat eek peynte thy confessioun by faire
subtile wordes, to covere the moore thy synne,
for thanne bigylestow thyself and nat the preest.
Thow most tellen it pleynly, be it nevere so foul
ne so horrible. / Thow shalt eek shryve thee to
a preest that is discreet to conseille thee, and
eek thou shalt nat shryve thee for veyne glorie,
ne for ypocrisye, ne for no cause, but oonly for

1005 eft ... countrewaite, again, be on watch. **1008 penitauncer,** priest who assigns penance. **but if it like,** unless it please. **1009 licence,** permission. **1010 bihynde,** i.e., left behind. **1012 verray ... resoun,** genuine, reasonable. **1013 nayte,** deny. **wratthe ... amonestynge,** be angry, admonishing. **1015 as Caym or Judas,** like Cain or Judas, Gen. 4:14, Matt. 27:5. **1016 moot ... wyten,** must, accuse. **1017 agregged ... pleynly,** increased, fully. **1019 lesynges,** lies. **1020 Seint Augustyn,** *Sermo* 181.4. **1022 peynte ... moore,** conceal (paint), greater part. *pleynly:* Hg&c *plathy.*

the doute of Jesu Crist and the heele of thy soule. / Thow shalt nat eek renne to the preest sodeynly to tellen hym lightly thy synne, as whoso telleth a jape or a tale, but avysely and with greet devocioun. / And generally, shryve thee ofte. If thou ofte falle, ofte thou arise by confessioun. / And thogh thou shryve thee ofter than ones of synne of which thou 1025

hast be shryven, it is the moore merite. And, as seith Seint Augustyn, thow shalt have the moore lightly relessyng and grace of God, bothe of synne and of peyne. / And certes, oones a yeere atte leeste wey it is laweful for to been housled, for certes oones a yeere alle thynges renovellen. /

Now have I toolde you of verray confessioun, that is the seconde partie of penitence. /

Explicit secunda pars Penitencie et sequitur tercia pars eiusdem de Satisfaccione.

The thridde partie of penitence is satisfaccioun, and that stant moost generally in almesse and in bodily peyne. / Now been ther three manere of almesses: contricion of herte, where a man offreth hymself to God; another is to han pitee of defaute of his neighebores; and the thridde is in yevynge of good conseil and comfort goostly and bodily, where men han nede, and namely in sustenaunce of mannes foode. / And tak kepe that a man hath 1030 nede of thise thinges generally: he hath nede of foode, he hath nede of clothyng and herberwe, he hath nede of charitable conseil and visitynge in prisone and in maladie, and sepulture of his dede body. / And if thow mayst nat visite the nedeful with thy persone, visite him by thy message and by thy yiftes. / Thise been generally almesses or werkes of charitee of hem that han temporeel richesses or discrecioun in conseilynge. Of thise werkes shaltow heren at the day of doome. /

Thise almesses shaltow doon of thyne owene propre thynges, and hastily and prively if thow mayst; / but nathelees if thow mayst nat doon it prively, thow shalt nat forbere to doon almesse

though men seen it; so that it be nat doon for thank of the world, but oonly for thank of Jesu Crist. / For as witnesseth Seint 1035 Mathew, *capitulo 5*, "A citee may nat been hyd that is set on a montayne. Ne men lighte nat a lanterne and put it under a busshel, but men sette it on a candlestikke to yeve light to the men in the hous. / Right so shal youre light lighten bifore men, that they may seen youre goode werkes, and glorifie youre fader that is in hevene." /

Now as to speken of bodily peyne, it stant in preyeres, in wakynges, in fastynges, in vertuouse techynges of orisouns. / And ye shul understonde that orisouns or preyeres is for to seyn a pitous wyl of herte that redresseth it in God, and expresseth it by word outward to remoeven harmes and to han thynges espiritueel and durable, and somtyme temporele thynges. Of whiche orisouns, certes, in the orisoun of the Pater Noster hath Jesu Crist enclosed moost thynges. / Certes, it is privyleged of thre thynges in his dignytee for which it is moore digne than any oother preyere: for that Jesu Crist hymself maked it; / and it is short for it 1040

1023 doute . . . heele, fear, health. **1024 lightly,** easily. **1026 Seint Augustyn,** *De Vera et Falsa Poenitentia*, 1.9.24. **peyne,** punishment. **1027 to been housled,** to receive communion; this requirement was laid down by the Fourth Lateran Council of 1215–16, which inspired penitentials like those of St. Raymond of Pennafort and Guilielmus Peraldus, from which Chaucer's ParsT ultimately derived. **renovellen,** renew (themselves). E *de Satisfaccione* om. from heading. **1029 almesse,** alms giving. **1030 defaute,** faults. **1031 tak kepe . . . herberwe,** take note, shelter. **1033 heren,** hear. **1034 propre thynges,** personal property. **1036 Seint Mathew** 5:14–16. *to yeve light:* Hg&c *to lighten.* **1038 bodily peyne . . . wakynges,** i.e., physical acts of penance, vigils. **1039 redresseth it in . . . han thynges . . . enclosed,** addresses itself to, procure things, included. **1040 privyleged of,** endowed with.

sholde be koud the moore lightly, and for to withholden it the moore esily in herte, and helpen hymself the ofter with the orisoun, / and for a man sholde be the lasse wery to seyen it, and for a man may nat excusen hym to lerne it, it is so short and so esy; and for it comprehendeth in itself alle goode preyeres. / The exposicioun of this hooly preyere, that is so excellent and digne, I bitake to thise maistres of theologie, save thus muchel wol I seyn: that whan thou prayest that God sholde foryeve thee thy giltes as thow foryevest hem that agilten to thee, be ful wel war that thow ne be nat out of charitee. / This hooly orisoun amenuseth eek venyal synne, and therfore it aperteneth specially to penitence. /

This preyere moste be trewely seyd and in verray feith, and that men preye to God ordinatly and discreetly and devoutly; and alwey a man shal putten his wyl to be subget to the wille of God. / This orisoun 1045 moste eek been seyd with greet humblesse and ful pure, honestly and nat to the anoyaunce of any man or womman. It moste eek been continued with the werkes of charitee. / It avayleth eek agayn the vices of the soule, for as seith Seint Jerome, "By fastynge been saved the vices of the flessh, and by preyere the vyces of the soule." /

After this thou shalt understonde that bodily peyne stant in wakynge, for Jesu Crist seith, "Waketh and preyeth that ye ne entre in wikked temptacioun." / Ye shul understanden also that fastynge stant in thre thynges, in forberynge of bodily mete and drynke, and in forberynge of worldly jolitee, and in forberynge of deedly synne. This is to seyn that a man shal kepen hym fro deedly synne with al his myght. / And thou shalt understanden eek that God

ordeyned fastynge. And to fastynge appertenen foure thinges: / largenesse to 1050 poure folk, gladnesse of herte espiritueel, nat to been angry ne anoyed, ne grucche for he fasteth, and also resonable houre for to ete by mesure. That is for to seyn, a man shal nat ete in untyme ne sitte the lenger at his table to ete for he fasteth. /

Thanne shaltow understonde that bodily peyne stant in disciplyne or techynge by word, or by writynge, or in ensample. Also in werynge of heyres, or of stamyn, or of haubergeons on hir naked flessh, for Cristes sake, and swiche manere penances. / But war thee wel that swiche manere penaunces on thy flessh ne make thee nat bitter or angry or anoyed of thyself. For bettre is to caste awey thyn heyre than for to caste away the sikernesse of Jesu Crist. / And therfore seith Seint Paul, "Clothe yow, as they that been chosen of God, in herte of misericorde, debonairetee, suffraunce, and swich manere of clothynge"; of whiche Jesu Crist is moore apayed than of heyres, or haubergeouns, or hauberkes. /

Thanne is disciplyne eek in knokkynge of thy brest, in scourgynge with yerdes, in knelynges, in tribulacions, / in suffrynge 1055 paciently wronges that been doon to thee, and eek in pacient suffraunce of maladies, or lesynge of worldly catel, or of wyf, or of child, or othere freendes. /

Thanne shaltow understonde whiche thynges destourben penaunce, and this is in foure maneres, that is, drede, shame, hope, and wanhope, that is, desperacion. / And for to speke first of drede, for which he weneth that he may suffre no penaunce, / ther agayns is remedie for to thynke that bodily penaunce is but short and litel at regard of the peynes of helle, that is so

---

1041 **koud . . . lightly,** learned, easily. 1043 **bitake,** leave. 1044 **amenuseth,** reduces. 1045 **trewely . . . verray . . . ordinatly,** sincerely, genuine, methodically. 1046 **continued,** supplemented. 1047 *vices of the soule:* E&c *vertues of the soule.* 1048 **Jesu Crist,** Matt. 26:41. 1049 **forberynge of,** abstaining from. 1051 **mesure . . . untyme . . . for,** moderation, irregular time, because. 1052 **werynge of heyres,** wearing of hair shirts. **stamyn . . . haubergeons,** coarse cloth, shirts of mail. 1053 **sikernesse,** security. *thee nat:* Hg&c *nat thyn herte. sikernesse:* Hg&c *swetenesse.* E *bitter* om. 1054 **Seint Paul,** Col. 3:12. **misericorde, debonairetee,** mercy, graciousness. **apayed . . . hauberkes,** repaid, chain mail. 1055 **disciplyne . . . knokkynge,** the discipline of penance, beating. 1056 **lesynge . . . catel,** losing, property. 1057 **destourben . . . wanhope,** impede, despair. 1058 **weneth,** thinks. E *demeth.*

crueel and so long that it lasteth withouten ende. /

Now again the shame that a man hath to shryven hym, and namely thise ypocrites that wolden been holden so parfite that they han no nede to shryven hem, / agayns that shame sholde a man thynke that by wey of resoun that he that hath nat been shamed to doon foule thynges, certes hym oghte nat been ashamed to do faire thynges, and that is confessiouns. / A man sholde eek thynke that God seeth and woot alle his thoghtes and alle his werkes. To hym may nothyng been hyd ne covered. / Men sholden eek remembren hem of the shame that is to come at the day of doome to hem that been nat penitent and shryven in this present lyf. / For alle the creatures in hevene, in erthe, and in helle shullen seen apertly al that they hyden in this world. /

Now for to speken of the hope of hem that been necligent and slowe to shryven hem, that stant in two maneres: / that oon is that he hopeth for to lyve longe and for to purchacen muche richesse for his delit, and thanne he wol shryven hym, and as he seith, hym semeth thanne tymely ynough to come to shrifte. / Another is surquidrie that he hath in Cristes mercy. / Agayns the firste vice, he shal thynke that oure lif is in no sikernesse, and eek that alle the richesses in this world ben in aventure and passen as a shadwe on the wal. / And as seith Seint Gregorie that it aperteneth to the grete rightwisnesse of God, that nevere shal the peyne stynte of hem that nevere wolde withdrawen hem fro synne hir thankes, but ay continue in synne. For thilke perpetueel wil to do synne shul they han perpetueel peyne. /

Wanhope is in two maneres: the firste wanhope is in the mercy of Crist, that oother is

that they thynken that they ne myghte nat longe persevere in goodnesse. / The firste wanhope comth of that he demeth that he hath synned so greetly and so ofte, and so longe leyn in synne that he shal nat be saved. / Certes, agayns that cursed wanhope sholde he thynke that the passion of Jesu Crist is moore strong for to unbynde than synne is strong for to bynde. / Agayns the seconde wanhope, he shal thynke, that as ofte as he falleth he may arise agayn by penitence. And though he never so longe have leyn in synne, the mercy of Crist is alwey redy to receiven hym to mercy. / Agayns the wanhope that he demeth that he sholde nat longe persevere in goodnesse, he shal thynke that the feblesse of the devel may nothing doon but if men wol suffren hym; / and eek he shal han strengthe of the helpe of God, and of al Hooly Chirche, and of the proteccioun of aungels, if hym list. /

Thanne shal men understonde what is the fruyt of penaunce, and after the word of Jesu Crist it is the endelees blisse of hevene, / ther joye hath no contrarioustee of wo ne grevaunce, ther alle harmes been passed of this present lyf, ther as is the sikernesse fro the peyne of helle, ther as is the blisful compaignye that rejoysen hem everemo everich of otheres joye, / ther as the body of man that whilom was foul and derk is moore cleer than the sonne, ther as the body that whilom was syk, freele, and fieble, and mortal, is inmortal, and so strong and so hool that ther may nothing apeyren it, / ther as ne is neither hunger, thurst, ne coold, but every soule replenyssed with the sighte of the parfit knowynge of God. / This blisful regne may men purchace by poverte espiritueel, and the glorie by lowenesse, the plentee of joye by hunger and thurst, and the reste by travaille, and the lyf by deeth and mortificacion of synne. /

1070

1075

1080

1060

1065

1062 woot, knows. **1064 apertly,** openly. E&c *in hevene* om. **1066 purchacen,** acquire. **1067 surquidrie,** overconfidence. **1068 sikernesse ... in aventure,** certainty, uncertain. **1069 Seint Gregorie,** *Moralium* 34.19.36. **aperteneth ... stynte ... hir thankes,** relates, cease, voluntarily. **1074 suffren,** allow. **1077 sikernesse,** security. **1078 whilom ... cleer ... apeyren,** formerly, bright, harm. **1080 lowenesse ... mortificacion,** humility, expunging (killing). Observe the spirit of the "New Jerusalem" with which *Canterbury Tales* concludes.

RETRACTION

Heere taketh the makere of this book his leve.

Now preye I to hem alle that herkne this litel tretys or rede, that if ther be anythyng in it that liketh hem that therof they thanken oure lord Jhesu Crist, of whom procedeth al wit and al goodnesse. / And if ther be anythyng that displese hem, I preye hem also that they arrette it to the defaute of myn unkonnynge, and nat to my wyl that wolde ful fayn have seyd bettre if I hadde had konnynge. / For oure book seith, "Al that is writen is writen for oure doctrine," and that is myn entente. / Wherfore I biseke yow mekely, for the mercy of God, that ye preye for me that Crist have mercy on me and foryeve me my giltes, / and namely of my translacions and enditynges of worldly vanitees, the whiche I revoke in my retracciouns: / as is the Book of Troilus; the Book also of Fame; the Book of the xxv Ladies; the Book of the Duchesse; the Book of Seint Valentynes Day of the Parlement of Briddes; the Tales of Caunter- bury, thilke that sownen into synne; / the Book of the Leoun; and many another book, if they were in my remembrance, and many a song and many a leccherous lay, that Crist for his grete mercy foryeve me the synne. / But of the trans- lacioun of Boece de Consolacione and othere bookes of legendes of seintes, and omelies, and moralitee, and devocioun, / that thanke I oure lord Jhesu Crist and his blisful mooder, and alle the seintes of hevene, / bisekynge hem that they from hennes forth unto my lyves ende sende me grace to biwayle my giltes and to studie to the salvacioun of my soule, and graunte me grace of verray penitence, confessioun and satisfaccioun to doon in this present lyf, / thurgh the benigne grace of hym that is kyng of kynges and preest over alle preestes, that boghte us with the precious blood of his herte, / so that I may been oon of hem at the day of doome that shulle be saved. *Qui cum patre* &c.

Heere is ended the book of The Tales of Caunterbury compiled by Geffrey Chaucer of whos soule Jhesu Christ have mercy. Amen.

1081 rede ... liketh hem ... wit, read, pleases them, wisdom. **1082 arrette ... unkonnynge,** ascribe, lack of skill. **1085 namely ... enditynges,** especially, writings. This list of Chaucer's writings may be compared with the list in *LGW,* ll. 329–34, 417–30; **1086 xxv Ladies,** there are nineteen ladies mentioned in *LGW;* some of the late MSS have here xix, xv, etc. **sownen into,** tend toward. **1087 Book of the Leoun,** an unidentified work by Chaucer, assumed to be a translation of Machaut's *Dit dou Lyon* or Deschamps' *Dict du Lyon.* **1088 omelies ... moralitee,** homilies, moral treatises. **1092 *Qui cum patre,*** the full formula is "Qui cum Patre et Spiritu Sancto vivit et regnat in saeccula saeculorum."

Troylus and Criseyde

INTRODUCTION

Troylus and Criseyde

THE WORKMANSHIP of *Troylus and Criseyde* suggests that it was more fully "finished" than anything else that Chaucer wrote. The elegance of its design, the refinement of its sentiments, and the polish of its rhyme royal stanzas indicate that Chaucer intended it as a major accomplishment, and, indeed, until the eighteenth century, it was considered his best poem. Only as the novel became popular did the realism of the *Canterbury Tales* begin to eclipse the romance of *Troylus.*

Symmetry and decorum mark the design of this poem as they do the design of the Knight's Tale, Chaucer's other adaptation from Boccaccio. The consummation of the love occurs at just about the middle of the third book. In tension with this symmetrical curve is another movement which does not reach its climax until Troylus receives "occular proof" of Criseyde's infidelity near the end of the poem (V.1661). Thus the "double sorrow" of Troylus in loving and losing provides a double movement for the poem. Other parallels may be noted: Criseyde enters sorrowing the loss of her father and exits lamenting her falsity to Troylus. Troylus enters laughing at the foolishness of lovers and exits laughing at the triviality of the world. The acceptance of love by both Troylus and Criseyde is punctuated by song. The progress of their affair and its termination are marked by dreams and the exchanges of letters. Gerry Brenner, "Narrative Structure in Chaucer's *Troilus and Criseyde*," *Annuale Mediaevale* (1965), argues that the summetry evokes a metaphor of harmony and grace. Ida Gordon, *The Double Sorrow of Troilus* (1970), sees the duality as producing irony. And there are many other discussions of metaphorical quality of the design.

The treatment refashions the story of Boccaccio's *Filostrato*. Unlike the Knight's Tale, which is reduced to one quarter its original length, *Troylus* is increased by one third, from 5740 to 8239 lines. Boccaccio alleges that his uncomplicated story in which the man loses out when his lady takes another lover reflects his own unhappy love affair with Maria d'Aquino. Chaucer's account follows *Filostrato* fairly closely to II.1155, but from the time Pandarus thrusts Troylus' letter into Criseyde's bosom to the end of Book III (some 2400 lines, more than a fourth of the poem), the plot is original. In Boccaccio's version, Criseide accepts the letter voluntarily and within 400 lines takes Troilo as her lover. On the next feast night she sends for him and there follows a straightforward assignation scene. All of Pandarus' elaborate arrangements for the meeting at Deiphebus' house and for the con-

summation at his own house in Book III, by which Criseyde's resistance is overcome and her good name preserved, are Chaucer's addition to the plot.

These changes in the plot reflect very different roles for the characters from those in *Filostrato*. Criseyde is refined and elevated. Her recognition of the significance of her faithlessness (V.1054ff) makes her defection harder for the audience to accept and endure. Pandarus is changed from Criseyde's irresponsible young cousin to her guardian uncle. His recognition of the significance of his breach of trust (III.253ff) has given the term "to pander" to the English language as it did not to Italian. The only character that does not recognize the significance of his role is Troylus, who is reduced in Chaucer's version to such impotent passivity that he threatens to become a laughing stock to the modern reader.

These changes in plot and character are glossed by lyrical commentary—Boethian meditations, appeals to the stars, moral and theological reflections, especially the wonderful prohems—which transform Boccaccio's "novella" into a very different kind of production. Chaucer calls attention to this difference by dedicating his poem to "moral Gower" and "philosophical Strode." However these epithets may have characterized his two friends in real life, they elucidate the intention of his poem. As a result of the moral and intellectual alterations and elaborations, *Troylus and Criseyde* achieves the catharsis of great tragedy, as Chaucer himself recognizes (V.1786ff). Monica E. McAlpine, *The Genre of Troilus and Criseyde* (1978), and Donald W. Rowe, *O Love O Charite!* (1976), are two of many discussions of its tragic sublimity.

The tension between the erotic matter and philosophical manner of Chaucer's *Troylus* has led to a variety of critical interpretations which are classified and evaluated by Alice R. Kaminsky, *Chaucer's Troylus and Criseyde and the Critics* (1980). James I. Wimsatt, "Medieval and Modern in Chaucer's *Troilus and Criseyde*," *PMLA* (1977), explores the interaction between realism and convention in the motivation, which led earlier critics to debate whether it is the "first English novel" or a sophisticated medieval romance. Chauncey Wood, *The Elements of Chaucer's Troilus* (1984), traces the transformation of the erotic acceptance of sex in *Filostrato* to the subordination of sex to will, as exemplified in the poems of Chaucer's friend John Gower, to whom *Troylus* is dedicated. Recent discussions of the narrator's influence on the reader's reception have been summarized by Richard Waswo, "The Narrator of *Troilus and Criseyde*," *ELH* (1983). The connections between the existential tragedy of the story and the narrator's spiritual epilogue have been explored by John Steadman, *Disembodied Laughter: Troilus and the Apotheosis Tradition* (1970).

The effect of *Troylus and Criseyde* results not only from the quality of its narrative, but from the effectiveness of the verse in which it is recounted. Martin Stevens, "The Royal Stanza in Early English Literature," *PMLA* (1979), has pointed out that rhyme royal was in the Middle Ages associated with ceremonial literature. Paull Baum, *Chaucer's Verse* (1961), has discussed Chaucer's technical virtuosity. As he says, Chaucer could command the whole diapason, all the stops from vox humana to full organ, to suit the needs of his subjects. Nowhere is his virtuosity more evident than in *Troylus*. The

handling of lines and stanzas enhances the liveliness of the first two books in contrast to the more subdued tone of Book V. Book III shows the variety to best advantage. When Pandarus lectures Troylus on the sin of boasting, he is diffuse (and aware of it, ll.295ff), but the verse is firm and rhetorical. But when Troylus replies (ll.360ff) he is almost incoherent and the stanzas run together until l. 386 where he recovers his poise. The tone becomes sonorous as Criseyde reflects on the unstableness of temporal joy (l.813ff), but the meter picks up again when Troylus swoons (ll.1093ff). The variations in tone and rhythm reflect the quality of the actions as accurately as movie music, and Baum cites interesting evidence from the manuscripts that shows Chaucer adjusting and polishing as he goes along.

All of this is far indeed from the Trojan War that forms a background to the poem. In both literature and life, the shadow of war makes the Freudian drives toward sex and death (*eros* and *thanatos*) particularly urgent, as we are made aware when Troylus first rides by Criseyde's window (II.624ff). Chaucer knew Boccaccio's source, the *Roman de Troie* by a twelfth-century trouvère, Benoit de Sainte Maure, and may have been influenced by Benoit in his use of the historian-narrator, his concern with fortune, and his employment of proverbs. Benoit had evidently invented the story of Troilus and Briseida (*sic*) as love interest on the Trojan side, to match that of Achilles and Polyxena on the Greek side, but in his version the narrative begins with Briseida's departure from Troy and concentrates on the wooing of Diomede. Most of his long poem (23,126 lines) is devoted to the siege and combats of the war itself. From this account, transmitted through the Latin prose translation of Guido delle Collone, Boccaccio about 1340 abstracted the love story of Troilo and Criseide (evidently altering the initial in the process). The development of the story and its English versions have been traced by C. David Benson, *The History of Troy in Middle English Literature* (1980).

Troylus and Criseyde

BOOK I

Incipit liber primus

The double sorwe of Troylus to tellen,
That was the Kyng Priamus sone of Troye,
In lovynge, how his aventures fellen
Fro wo to wele, and after out of joye,
My purpos is, er that I parte fro ye.   5
Thesiphone, thow help me for t'endite
These woful vers, that wepen as I write.

To the clepe I, thow goddesse of torment,
Thow cruel Furie, sorwynge evere yn peyne,
Help me, that am the sorwful instrument   10
That helpeth loveres, as I kan, to pleyne.
For wel sit it, the sothe for to seyne,
A woful wight to han a drery feere,
And to a sorwful tale, a sory cheere.

For I, that God of Loves servauntz serve,   15
Ne dar to Love, for myn unliklynesse,
Preyen for sped, al sholde I therfor sterve,
So fer am I fro his help in derknesse.

But natheles, if this may don gladnesse
Unto ony lovere, and his cause avayle,   20
Have he my thank, and myn be his
    travayle.

But ye loveres, that bathen in gladnesse,
If ony drope of pite in yow be,
Remembreth yow on passed hevynesse
That ye han felt, and on the adversite   25
Of othere folk, and thenketh how that ye
Han felt that Love dorste yow displese,
Or ye han wonne hym with to grete an ese.

And preyeth for hem that ben yn the cas
Of Troylus, as ye may after here,   30
That Love hem brynge in hevene to solas.
And ek for me, preyeth to God so dere
That I have myght to shewe in som manere
Swych peyne and wo as Loves folk endure,
In Troylus unsely aventure.   35

Text based on MS Morgan 817 (M), formerly the Campsall, with variants from Corpus Christi Coll., Cambridge, MS 61 (C). Unrevised readings (A) and revised (B) follow the principles laid down by R. K. Root: see "The Text of This Edition," p. 966. **2 Kyng Priamus sone of Troye,** the son of King Priam of Troy, the split form of the possessive used as late as Malory. **4 wele,** prosperity. This line corresponds with Chaucer's definition of tragedy in MkT vii. 1976, and the gloss to *Boece* ii pr. 2, 73: "Tragedye is to seyn, a dite of a prosperite for a tyme that endeth in wrecchednesse." **5 er that I parte,** along with "tellen" in l. 1, this line represents the narrator as reciting the story orally to his audience, as Chaucer evidently recited most of his poems to the court and to other audiences. **6 Thesiphone,** one of the Furies, invoked as being "goddess of torment." The proems to Books ii, iii, iv were evidently composed separately. They are omitted in some MSS and treated as conclusions to i, ii, iii in others (see Root ed.). But the invocations to Books i and v, which are much like these proems in tone, are incorporated in all the texts. Chaucer omitted Boccaccio's proem addressed to Fiametta. He picks up the translation after the invocation, l. 21, *Fil.* i.5. **endite,** compose. **8 clepe,** call. **9 Furie, sorwynge:** *A wighte that sorowist.* **11 pleyne,** lament. **12 sit it,** it is appropriate. **13 wight . . . feere,** creature (person), companion. **14 cheere,** expression (manner), i.e., on the part of the narrator. **15 servauntz serve,** the narrator (poet), imitating the papal title "servus servorum dei," adopts the pose of the pope of love. **16 myn unliklynesse,** the Chaucerian persona as unsuccessful lover appears at *HF* 640–60, *CT* vii.700–701, *Lenvoy a Scogan* (short poem no. 17), 27–32. Pandarus was likewise unsuccessful in love, *TC* i.622, ii.1107, etc. **17 sped . . . sterve,** success, die. **19** A *myght I do yit gladnesse.* **20 avayle,** assist. **21 travayle,** labor. *his:* C&c *this.* **24–28** Revised from very inferior reading in A. **24 hevynesse,** sadness. **28 Or,** or else. **31 solas,** joy (satisfaction). **33** A *He yeve me myghte.* **34** A *Some peyn or woo such as his folk endure.* **35 unsely,** unhappy.

And biddeth ek for hem that ben despeyred
In love, that nevere nyl recovered be,
And ek for hem that falsly ben apeyred
Thorugh wykked tonges, be it he or she;
Thus biddeth God, for his benignite,   40
So graunte hem soone out of this world to pace,
That ben despeyred out of Loves grace.

And biddeth ek for hem that ben at ese,
That God hem graunte ay good perseveraunce,
And sende hem myght hire ladies so to plese   45
That it to Love be worship and plesaunce.
For so hope I my soule best avaunce,
To prey for hem that Loves servauntz be,
And write hire wo, and lyve in charite.

And for to have of hem compassioun,   50
As though I were hire owne brother deere.
Now herkneth with a good entencioun,
For now wol I gon streyght to my matere,
In which ye may the double sorwes here
Of Troylus, in lovynge of Criseyde,   55
And how that she forsok hym er she deyde.

Yt is wel wyst how that the Grekes stronge
In armes with a thousand shippes wente
To Troyewardes, and the cite longe
Assegeden, neigh ten yer er they stente;   60
And in diverse wyse and oon entente,
The raveshyng to wreken of Eleyne,
By Paris don, thei wroughten al hire peyne.

Now fil it so that in the town ther was
Dwellyng a lord of gret auctorite,   65

A gret devyn, that clepid was Calkas,
That in science so expert was that he
Knew wel that Troye sholde destroyed be,
By answere of his god that highte thus
Daun Phebus or Appollo Delphicus.   70

So whan this Calkas knew by calkulynge,
And ek by answer of this Appollo,
That Grekes sholden swych a peple brynge
Thorugh which that Troye moste ben fordo,
He caste anoon out of the town to go.   75
For wel wyste he by sort that Troye sholde
Destroyed ben, ye, wolde whoso nolde.

For which for to departen softely
Took purpos ful this forknowyng wyse,
And to the Grekes ost ful pryvely   80
He stal anoon; and they in curteys wyse
Hym deden bothen worship and servyse,
In trust that he hath konnyng hem to rede
In every peril which that is to drede.

The noyse up ros, whanne it was first aspied,   85
Thorugh al the town, and generally was
    spoken
That Calkas, traitour fals, fled was and allyed
With hem of Grece; and casten to ben wroken
On hym that falsly hadde his feith so broken,
And seyden he and al his kyn at onys   90
Ben worthi for to brennen, fel and bones.

Now hadde Calkas left in this meschaunce,
Al unwist of this false and wikked dede,
His douhter, which that was in gret penaunce,
For of hire lyf she was ful sore in drede,   95

---

36 biddeth, pray. *despeyred:* MC *desespeyred* (hypermetrical). **38 apeyred,** damaged. **39 wykked tonges,** gossip, a principal enemy to love in *RR,* cf. 3499ff. (Dunn-Robbins 18.1), and see *TC* III.281ff., v.1610ff. **40 benignite,** graciousness. **41 pace,** pass. **42 despeyred out of,** in despair of; cf. l. 36. **44 perseveraunce,** continuance (in love). **45 ladies:** MA&c *loves.* **46 Love:** A *them.* **47 soule avaunce,** the narrator maintains the fiction of the religion of love. **51 hire,** their. **52 entencioun,** attention. **53** Some A MSS *For I will now go.* **58** A *With armys in.* **60 Assegeden . . . stente,** beseiged, stopped. **61 diverse wyse,** different ways. **62 raveshyng . . . wreken,** abduction, avenge. **66 devyn,** soothsayer (diviner). **67 science,** abstruse knowledge. **69 highte,** was called. **70 Delphicus,** of Delphi. M *Delphebus.* **71 calkulynge,** one of Chaucer's nicer puns, "Calkas" and "calculating" (i.e., by astrology). **72 And ek,** and also. **73 swych a peple,** such an army. **74 fordo,** destroyed. **75 caste anoon,** decided at once. **76 by sort,** by casting lots. **77 wolde . . . nolde,** willy-nilly. **78 softely,** secretly. **79 Took purpos . . . this . . . wyse,** i.e., this wise, foreknowing person took full purpose. **80 ost,** host. **81 stal,** stole. **82 worship,** honor. **83 trust . . . konnyng . . . rede,** confidence, ability, advise. **85** A *Grete rumour gan whan.* **88 casten . . . wroken,** (the Trojans) determined, to be revenged. **89** *feith:* A *trouthe.* **91 brennen, fel,** burn, skin. **93 Al unwist** completely uninformed. A *Unknowyng.* **94 penaunce,** distress.

As she that nyste what was best to rede,
For bothe a wydewe was she and allone
Of ony frend to whom she dorste hire mone.

Criseyde was this lady name al right.
As to my dome, in al Troyes cyte   100
Nas non so fair, forpassyng every wyght
So angelik was hire natyf beaute
That lyk a thing inmortal semed she,
As doth an hevenysh parfit creature   104
That down were sent in scornynge of nature.

This lady, which that alday herd at ere
Hire fadres shame, his falsnesse and tresoun,
Wel nygh out of hire wit for sorwe and fere,
In widewes habit large of samyt broun,
On knees she fil byforn Ector adoun;   110
With pitous voys and tendrely wepynge,
His mercy bad, hireselven excusynge.

Now was this Ector pitous of nature,
And saugh that she was sorwfully bigon,
And that she was so fair a creature;   115
Of his goodnesse he gladed hire anon,
And seyde, "Lat youre fadres treson gon
Forth with mischaunce, and ye yourself in joye
Dwelleth with us, whil yow good lyst, in
        Troye.

"And al th'onour that men may don yow have,
As ferforth as youre fader dwelled here, 121
Ye shul han, and youre body shal men save
As fer as I may ought enquere or here."
And she hym thonked with ful humble chere,

And ofter wolde and it hadde ben his wylle, 125
And took hire leve home and held hire stille.

And in hire hous she abod with swych meyne
As to hire honour nede was to holde,
And whil she was dwelled yn that cyte
Kepte hire estat, and bothe of yong and olde 130
Ful wel beloved, and wel men of hire tolde—
But whether that she children hadde or noon,
I rede it naught, therfore I late it goon.

The thinges fellen as thei don of werre
Bitwixen hem of Troye and Grekes ofte,   135
For som day boughten they of Troye it derre,
And eft the Grekes founde nothing softe
The folk of Troye; and thus Fortune on lofte
Now up, now down gan hem to whilen bothe
After hire cours, ay whil that thei were
        wrothe.   140

But how this town com to destruccion
Ne falleth naught to purpos me to telle,
For it were here a long digression
Fro my matere, and yow to long to dwelle.
But the Troian gestes as thei felle,   145
In Omer, or yn Dares, or in Dite,
Whoso that kan may rede hem as thei write.

But though that Grekes hem of Troye
        shetten,
And hire cyte bisegede al aboute,
Hire olde usage wolde thei not letten   150
As for to honoure hire goddes ful devoute;
But aldermost yn honour out of doute,

---

96 nyste . . . rede, didn't know, think (i.e., do). **98 mone,** moan. M *dorst make hire mone.* **99** *al right:* C&c *aright.* **100 dome,** judgment. **101 forpassyng . . . wyght,** surpassing, person. A *So fair was none, for over every wight.* **108** A *for pure fere.* **109 large . . . samyt,** full-cut, rich silk cloth. *large:* other MSS *blak.* **111** A *With chere and voys ful pytous and wepyng.* **112 bad,** prayed (for). **114 sorwfully bigon,** overwhelmed by sorrow. **116 gladed,** cheered him up. **117 Lat . . . treson gon,** Let (all thought of) your father's treason go. **118 with mischaunce,** i.e., with bad luck. A *To sory hap, and ye.* **119 yow good lyst,** it pleases you. **120 don yow have,** caused you to have. **121 ferforth,** i.e., as much as when. **124 chere,** expression. **125 ofter,** repeatedly. **126 held . . . stille,** lived quietly. **127 meyne,** attendants. **128** *to hire:* C&c *till hire.* **130 Kepte hire estat,** lived appropriately to her station. **132 children . . . noon,** *Fil.* 1.15 states specifically at just this point that she had no children; Chaucer's reason for making the change is not known. M *hadde children.* **133 rede,** read. **136 boughton . . . derre,** bought more dearly (had the worst). **137 eft,** again. **138–40 Fortune on lofte . . . to whilen . . . wrothe,** Fortune on high wheeled them now up, now down, while they fought (were wrothe, angry); so reads C. *Now up, now down:* M&c *And wonder oft/weylen;* other MSS *And under eft/whielen.* **143** M&c *here* om. **145 gestes,** deeds. **146 Omer . . . Dares . . . Dite,** Homer, Dares, Dictys, the sources for knowledge of the Trojan War: see Introduction. **148 shetten,** shut in. **150 letten,** give up. A *nold they of Troy lettyn.* **151** A *hire goddis and to loute* (bow down). **152 aldermost,** most of all.

Thei hadde a relyk hight Palladion
That was hire tryst aboven everichon.

And so bifell, whan comen was the tyme   155
Of Aperil, whan clothed is the mede
With newe grene of lusti ver the pryme,
And swoote smellen floures white and rede,
In sondry wyses shewed, as I rede,
The folk of Troye hire observaunces olde,   160
Palladiones feste for to holde.

And to the temple yn al hire beste wyse,
In general there went many a wight,
To herknen of Palladion the servyse,
And namely so many a lusti knyght,   165
So many a lady fresch, and mayden bright,
Ful wel arayed, bothe meste and leste,
Ye, bothe for the seson and the feste.

Among these othere folk was Criseyda,
In widewes habit blak. But natheles,   170
Right as oure first lettre is now an A,
In beaute first so stod she makeles.
Hire goodly lokyng gladede al the prees.
Nas nevere yet thing seyn to ben preysed derre,
Nor under cloude blak so bright a sterre,   175

As was Criseyde, as folk seyde everichone
That hire behelden in hire blake wede.
And yet she stod ful lowe and stille allone,
Byhynden other folk, in litel brede,
And neigh the dore, ay under shames drede,   180
Symple of atyre and debonaire of chere,
With ful assuryd lokyng and manere.

This Troylus, as he was wont to gyde
His yonge knyghtes, ladde hem up and doun
In thilke large temple on every syde,   185
Byholding ay the ladyes of the toun,
Now here, now there, for no devocioun
Hadde he to noon, to reven hym his reste,
But gan to preyse and lakken whom hym leste.

And yn his walk ful faste he gan to wayten   190
If knyght or squyer of his compaignie
Gan for to sike, or lete his eien beyten
On any woman that he koude aspye,
He wolde smyle and holden it folye,
And sey hym thus, "God wot, she slepeth
     softe   195
For love of the, whan thou turnest ofte.

"I have herd told, pardieux, of youre lyvynge,
Ye loveres, and youre lewede observaunces,
And swich labour as folk han yn wynnynge   199
Of love, and yn the kepyng which doutaunces;
And whan youre prey is lost, woo and
     penaunces.
O verray fooles, nyce and blynde be ye!
Ther nys not oon kan war by other be."

And with that word he gan caste up the
     browe
Ascaunces, "Lo, is this nought wysely spoken?"
At which the God of Love gan loken rowe   206
Right for despit, and shop for to ben wroken,
And kyd anoon his bowe nas not broken,
For sodeynly he hit hym at the fulle—
And yet as proud a pekok kan he pulle.   210

---

153 hight, called. C&c *heet.* **Palladion,** a statue of Pallas Athene upon which the safety of Troy depended. **154 tryst,** i.e., the talisman upon which they trusted. **everichon,** everyone (i.e., every other god). **157 ver . . . pryme,** springtime, beginning. **158 swoote,** sweet. **159 sondry wyses,** various ways. **161** Mc&c *Palladions.* **162** M&c *here goodly beste wyse.* **163–67** Revised considerably from A: see Root. **165 namely,** especially. **167** M&c *bothe meene, meste.* **168** M *and for the feste.* **171 now an A,** substituted for "And as much as the rose outdeth the violet in beauty, so much fairer was she than other ladies," *Fil.* 1.19. Lowes suggested that Chaucer's change was intended to compliment Queen Anne. **172 makeles,** matchless. **173 lokyng . . . prees,** appearance, crowd. **174 seyn . . . derre,** seen, dearer. **177 wede,** garments (widow's weeds). **178 lowe . . . stille,** humbly, always. **179 brede,** apart (breadth). **181 debonaire of chere,** gentle of expression. **183** *This Troylus:* A *Daun Troyllus.* **185 thilke,** that. **188 reven,** deprive. **189 lakken . . . leste,** find fault with, wished to. **190 faste . . . wayten,** closely, watch. **192 sike . . . beyten,** sigh, feast (bait). **196 ofte:** C&c *ful ofte.* **198 lewede,** ignorant. M&c *lewede* om. **199 swich,** such (what). C&c *which a labour folk han.* **200 doutaunces,** uncertainties (doubts). **202–03** Revised from inferior readings in A. **202 nyce,** foolish. *fooles:* M *loves.* **203 war,** taught (warned). **205 Ascaunces,** as if to say. **206–09** Revised from A. **206 rowe,** rough (angry). **207 despit . . . shop . . . wroken,** contempt, prepared, avenged. **208 kyd anoon,** showed immediately. **209 at the fulle,** squarely. **210 And yet . . . pulle,** and to this day, pull (the feathers out of).

O blynde world, O blynde entencioun!
How often falleth al th'effect contraire
Of surquidrie and foul presumpcioun;
For caught is proud, and caught is debonaire.
This Troylus is clomben on the staire,   215
And litel weneth that he most descenden—
But alday faileth thyng that foles wenden.

As proude Bayard gynneth for to skyppe
Out of the wey, so priketh hym his corn,
Til he a lasshe have of the longe whippe,   220
Than thenketh he, "Though I praunce al byforn,
First yn the trays, ful fat and newe shorn,
Yet am I but an hors, and horses lawe
I moot endure, and with my feres drawe";

So ferde it by this ferse and proude knyght: 225
Though he a worthi kynges sone were,
And wende nothing hadde had swych myght
Ayens his wil that shold his herte stere,
Yet with a lok his herte wax afere,
That he that now was most in pride above   230
Wax sodeynly most subget unto love.

Forthi ensample taketh of this man,
Ye wyse, proude, and worthi folkes alle,
To scornen Love, which that so soone kan
The fredom of youre hertes to hym thralle;   235
For evere it was, and evere it shal bifalle
That Love is he that alle thing may bynde,
For may no man fordo the lawe of kynde.

That this be soth hath preved and doth yet,
For this trowe I ye knowen alle or some.   240
Men reden nat that folk han gretter wit

Than they that han be most with love ynome,
And strengest folk ben therwith overcome,
The worthiest and grettest yn degre—
This was and is and yet men shal it se.   245

And trewelich it sit wel to be so,
For alderwisest han therwith ben plesed,
And thei that han ben aldermost in wo
With love han ben comforted most and esed;
And ofte it hath the cruel herte apesed,   250
And worthi folk maad worthier of name,
And causeth most to dreden vice and shame.

Now sith it may not goodly be withstonde,
And is a thyng so vertuous yn kynde,
Refuseth not to Love for to be bonde,   255
Syn as hymselven lyste he may yow bynde.
The yerde is bet that bowen wole and wynde
Than that that brest, and therfor I yow rede
To folowen hym that so wel kan yow lede.

But for to tellen forth yn special   260
As of this kynges sone of which I tolde,
And letten other thing collateral,
Of hym thenk I my tale forth to holde,
Bothe of his joies and of his cares colde,
And al his werk, as touchyng this matere,   265
For I it gan, I wil therto refere.

Withinne the temple he went hym forth
        pleyinge,
This Troylus, of every wyght aboute,
On this lady and now on that lokynge,
Where so she were of towne or of withoute;   270
And upon cas bifel that thorugh a route

211 **entencioun**, understanding. 212 **th'effect**, the result; ll. 206–10 and ll. 214–66 have no counterpart in *Fil.* Introducing these editorializing, universalizing passages begins to change the tone of Chaucer's poem. 213 **surquidrie**, pride; the term appears most often in connection with the Seven Deadly Sins. 214 **debonaire**, meek (in contrast to proud). 215 *This Troylus: A Daun Troyllus.* 216 **weneth**, supposes. 217 M *falleth thyng that foles ne wenden.* 218 **Bayard gynneth**, traditional name for a fine stallion, begins. 219 **corn**, oats (corn means simply "grain"). 222 **trays**, trace (harness). 224 **feres**, companions. M *felawes.* 227 **wende**, believed. 228 **stere**, stir, or steer (control). M *dere*, hurt. 229 **wax afere**, took fire. 232 **ensample**, example, but in this context, warning. 234 *scornen:* C&c *serven.* 235 **thralle**, enslave. 238 **fordo . . . kynde**, undo, nature. 239 **soth . . . preved**, truth, proved. 242 **ynome**, captured. 244 *yn:* C&c *of.* 246 **sit wel**, is appropriate. 247 **alderwisest**, the wisest of all. 252 **causeth . . . dreden vice**, this is another of the traditional excellences of courtly love. 253 **goodly**, easily. 255 A *Ne grucchith not to Love.* 256 **lyste**, wishes. 257 **yerde . . . bowen . . . wynde**, rod, bow, bend. A *Betir is the wand.* 258 **brest . . . rede**, breaks, counsel. 261 *As of:* M *As om.* 262 **letten**, leave aside. 263 *forth:* M *for.* 266 **refere**, return. Here ends Chaucer's excursus. 267 **pleyinge**, making fun of. 271 **upon cas . . . route**, by chance, crowd.

His eye percede, and so depe it wente
Til on Criseyde it smot, and ther it stente.

And sodeynly he wax therwith astoned,
And gan hire bet biholde yn thrifty wyse.   275
"O mercy God," thoughte he, "wher hastow
   woned,
That art so fair and goodly to devyse?"
Therwith his herte gan to sprede and ryse,
And softe sighed lest men myghte hym here,
And caught ayen his firste pleyinge chere.   280

She nas not with the leste of hire stature,
But alle hire lymes so wel answerynge
Weren to womanhode that creature
Was nevere lasse mannyssh in semynge.
And ek the pure wyse of hire mevynge   285
Shewed wel that men myght in hire gesse
Honour, estat, and wommanly noblesse.

To Troylus right wonder wel with alle
Gan for to lyke hire mevynge and hire chere,
Which somdel deynous was, for she leet falle
Hire look a lite aside in swych manere,   291
Ascaunces, "What, may I nat stonden here?"
And after that hire lokynge gan she lyghte,
That nevere thought hym seen to fair a
   sighte.

And of hire look yn hym ther gan to quyken   295
So gret desir and such affeccioun
That in his hertes botme gan to stiken
Of hire his fixe and depe impressioun.
And though he erst hadde poured up and doun,
He was to glad his hornes yn to shrynke—   300
Unnethes wyste he how to loke or wynke.

Lo, he that leet hymselven so konnynge,
And scorned hem that Loves peynes dryen,
Was ful unwar that Love hadde his dwellynge
Withinne the subtile stremes of hire eyen,   305
That sodeynly hym thoughte he felte dyen
Right with hire look the spirit in his herte.
Blyssyd be Love that kan thus folk converte!

She, this in blak, lykynge to Troylus
Over al thyng, he stood for to byholde;   310
Ne his desir, ne wherfor he stod thus,
He neither chere ne made, ne worde tolde;
But from afer, his manere for to holde,
On other thing his look somtyme he caste,
And eft on hire, while that the servise laste.   315

And after this, not fullych al awhaped,
Out of the temple al esilych he wente,
Repentynge hym that he hadde evere yjaped
Of Loves folk, lest fully the descente   319
Of scorn fille on hymself. But what he mente,
Lest it were wyst on any maner side,
His wo he gan dissimulen and hide.

Whan he was fro the temple thus departed,
He streyght anoon unto his paleys turneth,
Right with hire look thorugh-shoten and
   thorugh-darted,   325
Al feyneth he yn lust that he sojorneth;
And al his speche and cher also he borneth,
And ay of Loves servantz every while,
Hymself to wrye, at hem he gan to smyle,

And seyde, "Lord, so ye lyve al yn lest,   330
Ye loveres, for the konnyngeste of yow,
That serveth most ententiflych and best,

272 *percede:* M *procede.* 273 **stente,** stopped. 274 **astoned,** astonished. 275 **bet biholde . . . thrifty wyse,** look at her better, careful manner. 276 **woned,** lived. A *O verray God.* 277 **devyse,** observe (look at). 279 A and many G MSS *And softe he.* 280 **caught ayen . . . pleyinge chere,** resumed, joking manner. 285 **pure wyse,** very manner. 289 **lyke . . . mevynge . . . chere,** i.e., her movement and her expression pleased Troylus. 290 **deynous,** disdainful. 291 **lite,** little. 292 **Ascaunces,** as if to say. 293 **lyghte,** light up (brighten). 294 *fair:* C&c *good.* 295 **quyken,** germinate. 298 **fixe,** fixed. 299 **poured,** gazed (pored). 300 **hornes . . . shrynke,** the figure is of a snail. 301 **Unnethes wyste . . . wynke,** Hardly knew he . . . blink (i.e., not look). 302 **leet,** considered. 303 **dryen,** suffer. 305 **subtile stremes,** secret beams. The mysterious power in the rays of Criseyde's eyes made Troylus feel that he was about to die. 306 *he felte:* M&c *that he sholde.* 309–10 Perhaps the wrenched word order is intended to convey something of Troylus' agitation. 312 **chere ne made,** revealed nothing by his expression. *ne made:* C&c *ne om.* 313 **manere . . . holde,** maintain his (usual) behavior. 315 **eft,** again. C&c *oft.* 316 **awhaped,** stupefied. 317 **esilych,** calmly. 318 **yjaped,** made fun. 319 **descente,** weight (descent). 320 **what he mente,** i.e., what he really felt. 324 *his:* A *the.* 326 **Al feyneth . . . lust,** although he pretended, joy. 327 **cher . . . borneth,** expression, smooths over (burnishes). 329 **wrye,** conceal. 330 **lest,** pleasure (lust). 331 **konnyngeste,** wisest.

Hym tyt as often harm therof as prow.
Youre hire is quyt ayeyn, ye God wot how—
Nought wel for wel, but scorn for good service.
In feith, youre ordre is ruled in good wyse! 336

"In nouncerteyn ben alle youre observaunces,
But it a sely fewe poyntes be.
Ne nothing asketh so grete attendaunces
As doth youre lay, and that knowe alle ye. 340
But that is not the worste, as mote I the—
But tolde I yow the worste point, I leve,
Al seyde I soth, ye wolden at me greve.

"But take this: that ye loveres ofte eschuwe,
Or elles doon of good entencioun, 345
Ful ofte thi lady wole it mysconstrue,
And deme it harm yn hire opinyoun;
And yet if she for other enchesoun
Be wroth, than shalt thou han a groyn anoon.
Lord, wel is hym that may ben of yow oon!" 350

But for al this, whanne he say his tyme,
He held his pes; noon other bote hym gayned.
For love bygan his fetheres so to lyme
That wel unnethe unto his folk he feyned
That other besy nedes hym destrayned; 355
For wo was hym that what to doon he nyste,
But bad his folk to gon wher that hem lyste.

And whan that he in chambre was allone,
He down upon his beddes feet hym sette,
And first he gan to syke and eft to grone, 360
And thoughte ay on hire so withouten lette,

That as he sat and wok his spirit mette
That he hire saw a-temple, and al the wyse
Right of hire lok, and gan it newe avyse.

Thus gan he make a myrrour of his mynde, 365
In which he saugh alle holly hire figure,
And that he wel koude yn his herte fynde.
It was to hym a right good aventure
To love swych on, and yf he dede his cure
To serven hire yet myghte he falle in grace, 370
Or elles for on of hire servauntz pace;

Ymagynge that travaylle nor grame
Ne myghte for so goodly on be lorn
As she, ne hym for his desir no shame,
Al were it wist, but yn prys and upborn 375
Of alle lovers wel more than byforn.
Thus argumented he yn his gynnynge,
Ful unavysed of his wo comynge.

Thus tok he purpos loves craft to suwe,
And thoughte he wolde werken pryvely, 380
First to hiden his desir in muwe
From every wight yborn, al outrely,
But he myghte ought recovered be therby;
Remembryng hym that love to wyde yblowe
Yelt bittre fruyt, though swete seed be sowe. 385

And over all this, yet muche more he thoughte
What for to speke and what to holden inne;
And what to arten hire to love he soughte;
And on a song anoon right to bygynne,
And gan loude on his sorwe for to wynne; 390

---

333 tyt . . prow, befalls (tideth), profit. **334 hire . . . quyt . . . ye,** payment, repaid, yes. **335 wel,** i.e., good for good. **336 ordre,** the order of courtly lovers, whose "rules" are developed in the next two stanzas. **337 nouncerteyn,** uncertainty. **338 sely fewe poyntes,** i.e., except for a few foolish details, the rules of love are all uncertain. **339 attendaunces,** attention (close observance). **340 lay,** law. **341 the,** prosper. **342 leve,** believe. **343 Al,** although. **344 eschuwe,** avoid doing (eschew). **345** A *For good, or done of good intencioun.* **348 enchesoun,** reason. **349 groyn,** complaint: this is the courtly tradition of *la belle dame sans merci.* C&c *shaltow have.* **351 say,** saw. **352 bote,** profit. **353 fetheres . . . lyme,** smear with sticky birdlime, by which birds are trapped. **354 unnethe . . . feyned,** hardly, pretended (i.e., could he pretend). **355 destrayned,** occupied. **357 lyste,** wherever they wished. *hem:* M *hym.* **360 syke . . . eft,** sigh, then. **361 lette,** ceasing (hindrance). M *withouten ony.* **362 and wok . . . mette,** i.e., awake, dreamed. **363 wyse,** manner. *a-temple:* C&c *and temple.* **364 avyse,** ponder. **366 holly,** wholly, but *double entendre* holy. **368 aventure,** fortune. **369 cure,** care (i.e., did his best). **370 in,** into (her). **371 pace,** pass. **372 travaylle . . . grame,** labor, pain. *grame:* C *grace;* other MSS *game.* **373 lorn,** lost. **374 hym,** to him. **375 wist . . . prys . . . upborn,** known (secrecy was a fetish of courtly love, see l. 39 above), praised, exalted. **378 unavysed,** unaware. **379 suwe,** pursue. **381 muwe,** concealment (mew, a private cage for moulting falcons). **383 But . . . ought recovered,** unless he might gain anything (?). **385 M** *seed* om. The secrecy *topos* again. **387** *What for:* M *For what.* **388 what . . . arten,** how, induce. **390 wynne,** overcome (?); this is an OED spelling for "whine," but it is not found elsewhere in the Chaucer Concordance.

For with good hope he gan fully assente
Criseyde for to love, and nought repente.

And of his song nought only the sentence,
As writ myn auctour called Lollyus,
But pleynly, save oure tonge deference,   395
I dar wel seyn yn al that Troylus
Seyde yn his song, lo every word right thus
As I shal seyn; and whoso lyst it here,
Lo next this vers he may it fynden here.

Cantus Troili

"If no love is, O God, what fele I so?   400
And if love is, what thyng and which is he?
If love be good, from whenes cometh my wo?
If it be wykke, a wonder thenketh me
Whenne every torment and adversite
That cometh of hym may to me savory thynke,
For ay thurst I, the more that ich it drynke.   406

"And yf that at myn owene lust I brenne,
Fro whennes cometh my waylyng and my
   pleynte?
If harm agree me, wherto pleyne I thanne?—
I not; ne whi unweri that I feynte.   410
O quyke deth, O swete harm so queynte,
How may of the yn me swich quantite,
But if that I consente that it be?

"And if that I consente, I wrongfully
Compleyne, iwys. Thus possed to and fro,   415
Al sterles withinne a bot am I

Amyd the see, bitwixen wyndes two
That in contrarye stonden evere mo.
Allas, what is this wondre maladye?
For hete of cold, for cold of hete, I deye."   420

And to the God of Love thus seyde he
With pitous vois, "O lord, now youres is
My spirit, which that aughte youre be.
Yow thank I, lord, that han me brought to
   this,
But whether goddesse or womman, iwys,   425
She be, I not, which that ye do me serve;
But as hire man I wol ay leve and sterve.

"Ye stonden yn hire eyen myghtily,
As yn a place unto your vertu digne,
Wherfore, my lord, if my servyse or I   430
May lyke yow, so beth to me benygne;
For myn estat royal here I resigne
Into hire hond, and with ful humble chere
Bycome hire man, as to my lady dere."

In hym ne deyned spare blood royal   435
The fyr of love—the wherfro God me blysse—
Ne hym forbar in no degre, for al
His vertu or his excellent prowesse,
But held hym as his thral lowe yn distresse,
And brende hym so in sondry wyse ay newe,   440
That sixty tyme a day he loste his hewe.

So muche day by day his owene thought
For lust to hire gan quyken and encrese,
That every other charge he sett at nought.

394 Lollyus, the song is actually a paraphrase of Petrarch's Sonnet 88. Chaucer's failure to mention Boccaccio as the author of the *Filostrato,* and the identity of the "Lollius" whom he cites as his source here and at v.1653 are unexplained. **399 M&c** *Cantus Troili* heading omitted; other MSS *The Song of Troylus.* **400 M** *no* om. **401 which,** what sort of. **405 savory thynke,** seem sweet. M&c *may me so goodly.* **406 ich:** M *I.* **407 lust . . . brenne,** desire, burn. **411 quyke . . . queynte,** living, strange. **413 consente,** D. W. Robertson discerns Troylus' three steps toward the "sin" of love as suggestion (the view of Criseyde in the temple), excessive contemplation (the meditation in his chamber), and consent. The consent of Criseyde is likewise punctuated by song, II.827ff.; and see ParsT x.292ff. **415 iwys . . . possed,** indeed, tossed. **416 sterles,** rudderless. **417** *bitwixen:* M *bytwen.* **418 contrarye stonden,** blow from opposite directions. **420 hete of cold,** burning for passion while freezing from the lady's indifference is a favorite troubadour figure, which came to be thought of as typically Petrarchan. **426 not . . . do me,** don't know (ne wot), make me. **427 sterve,** die. **428 stonden . . . eyen,** stand in her esteem. **429 vertu digne,** power worthy. **430** *my lord:* C&c *my* om. **431 lyke,** please. **433 chere,** manner. **435–36 blood royal . . . fyr,** i.e., the fire of love did not spare the royal blood. This is from *Fil.* 1.40, but the *incendium amoris* was also a medieval mystical concept, as in the piece of that name by Richard Rolle. **437 hym forbar,** spared him. **440 brende,** burned. **441 loste . . . hewe,** became pale—one of the typical symptoms of chivalric love. **443 lust . . . quyken,** desire, grow lively. **444 charge,** responsibility.

Forthi ful ofte his hote fyr to cese, 445
To seen hire goodly look he gan to prese,
For therby to ben esed wel he wende—
And ay the ner he was, the more he brende.

For ay the ner the fyr, the hotter is—
This, trowe I, knoweth al this compaignye. 450
But were he fer or neer, I dar seye this,
By nyght or day, for wysdom or folye,
His herte, which that is his brestes eye,
Was ay on hire that fairer was to sene
Than evere was Eleyne or Polixene. 455

Ek of the day ther passed nought an houre
That to hymself a thousand tymes he seyde,
"Good goodly, to whom serve I and laboure
As I best kan, now wolde God, Criseyde,
Ye wolden on me rewe er that I deyde! 460
My dere herte, allas, myn hele and hewe
And lyf is lost but ye wole on me rewe."

Alle other dredes weren from hym fledde,
Bothe of th'assege and his salvacioun;
Ne yn hym desir noon other fownes bredde 465
But argumentes to this conclusioun,
That she of hym wolde han compassioun,
And he to be hire man while he may dure.
Lo, here his lyf, and from the deth his cure.

The shoures sharpe felle of armes preve, 470
That Ector or his othere bretheren diden,
Ne made hym oonly therfore ones meve;
And yet was he wherso men wente or riden
Founde oon the beste, and lengest tyme
        abyden
Ther peril was, and dide ek such travayle 475
In armes, that to thenke it was mervayle.

But for non hate he to the Grekes hadde,
Ne also for the rescous of the town,
Ne made hym thus yn armes for to madde,
But oonly, lo, for this conclusioun, 480
To lyken hire the bet for his renoun.
Fro day to day yn armes so he spedde
That the Grekes as the deth hym dredde.

And fro this forth tho refte hym love his sleep,
And made his mete his foo, and ek his sorwe 485
Gan multiplie, that whoso took keep,
It shewed in his hewe bothe eve and morwe.
Therfor a title he gan hym for to borwe
Of other syknesse, lest of hym men wende
That the hote fyr of love hym brende, 490

And seyde he hadde a fevere and ferde amys.
But how it was, certeyn, kan I not seye,
If that his lady understod not this,
Or feynede hire she nyste, oon of the tweye.
But wel I rede that by no manere weye 495
Ne semed it as that she of hym roughte,
Nor of his peyne, or whatsoevere he thoughte.

But thanne felt this Troylus such wo
That he was wel neigh wood, for ay his drede
Was this, that she som wyght hadde loved so 500
That nevere of hym she wolde han taken hede.
For which hym thoughte he felt his herte blede,
Ne of his wo ne dorste he nat bygynne
To tellen hir for al this world to wynne.

But whanne he hadde a space fro his care, 505
Thus to hymself ful ofte he gan to pleyne;
He seyde, "O fool, now art thow in the snare,
That whilom japedest at loves peyne.
Now artow hent, now gnaw thin owen cheyne.

445 Forthi . . . cese, therefore, extinguish. **446 goodly look,** lovely face (appearance). **447 esed . . . wende,** relieved, thought. **448 ay . . . ner . . . brende,** always, nearer, burned. **455 Eleyne . . . Polixene,** Helen of Troy; Polyxena, daughter of Priam (sister of Troylus). **458 Good:** C&c *God.* C&c *and om.* **460 rewe,** have pity. **461 hele . . . hewe,** health, color. **464 assege . . . salvacioun,** seige, safety. **465 fownes,** offspring (until 1600 "fawn" meant simply young animal, cub). *hym:* other MSS *his.* **469 cure,** remedy. **470 preve,** proofs (feats) of arms. **472 made hym . . . meve,** i.e., did not once make him move in emulation. **476 to thenke,** to think on it. **478 rescous,** rescue, protection. **479 madde,** rage (in battle). **481 lyken,** please. **483 the deth,** the plague. **484 tho refte,** then deprived. **485 mete,** food. **486 took keep,** took note. **488 title,** name. **490 Other MSS** *so sore him brende.* **494 nyste,** did not know; the indifference of the lady was a *topos* of the courtly situation. **496 roughte,** cared. **499 wood . . . ay,** crazy, always. **502** *For which:* M *For such.* **504** M *tellen it.* **505 space,** time to spare. **508 whilom japedest,** earlier made fun of. **509 hent,** captured.

Thow were ay wont eche lovere reprehende   510
Of thing fro which thow kanst the nought
   defende.

"What wol now every lovere seyn of the
If this be wist, but evere yn thyn absence
Laughen yn skorn, and seyn, "Lo, ther goth he
That is the man of so gret sapience;   515
That held us loveres lest yn reverence.
Now, thonked be God, he may goon in the
   daunce
Of hem that Love lyst febely for to avaunce.

"But O thow woful Troylus, God wolde,
Syn thow most loven thurgh thy destene,   520
That thow beset were on swych oon that
   sholde
Know al thi wo, al lakked hire pite.
But also cold yn love towardes the
Thi lady is as frost in wynter mone,
And thow fordon as snow yn fyre is soone.   525

"God wolde I were aryved in the port
Of deth, to which my sorwe wil me lede!
A, Lord, to me it were gret comfort.
Than were I quyt of langwysshyng in drede.
For be myn hidde sorwe iblowe on brede,   530
I shal byjaped ben a thousand tyme
More than that fol of whos folye men ryme.

"But now help, God, and ye, swete for whom
I pleyne, icaught, ye, nevere wyght so faste!
O mercy, dere herte, and help me from   535
The deth, for I while that my lyf may laste,
More than myself, wol love yow to my laste.
And with som frendly look gladeth me, swete,
Though nevere more thyng ye me byhete."

Thise wordes and ful many an other to   540
He spak, and called evere yn his compleynte
Hire name, for to tellen hire his woo,
Til neigh that he in salte teres dreynte.
Al was for nought; she herde nought his pleynte.
And whan that he bithought on that folye,   545
A thousandfold his wo gan multiplie.

Bywayling yn his chambre thus allone,
A frend of his that called was Pandare
Com onys in unwar and herde hym grone,
And say his frend in swych distresse and care.
"Allas," quod he, "who causeth al this fare?   551
O mercy God, what unhap may this mene?
Han now thus soone Grekes maad yow lene?

"Or hastow som remors of conscience,
And art now fallen yn som devocioun,   555
And waylest for thi synne and thyn offence,
And hast for ferde caught attricioun?
God save hem that byseged han oure toun,
That so kan leye oure jolyte on presse,
And brynge oure lusty folk to holynesse!"   560

These wordes seyde he for the nones alle
That with swych thing he myght hym angry
   maken,
And with an angre don his wo to falle
As for the tyme, and his corage awaken.
But wel he wiste, as fer as tonges spaken,   565
Ther nas a man of grettere hardinesse
Thanne he, ne more desirede worthinesse.

"What cas," quod Troylus, "or what aventure
Hath gided the to se me langwysshynge,
That am refus of every creature?   570
But for the love of God, at my preyinge,

510 **reprehende,** to scold. 513 **wist,** known. 515 **sapience,** wisdom. *That:* C&c *And.* 520 **Syn . . . destene,** since, destiny. This line is found in *Fil.* 1.53, but Chaucer consistently increases the emphasis on destiny in his version, particularly in his revision. 521 **beset,** fixated. 522 **al,** although. 525 **fordon,** destroyed, cf. l. 420n. 530 **be . . . iblowe on brede,** if it be, blown abroad (made public). **be:** MC&c *by.* **hidde:** M *hed.* 531 **byjaped,** made fun of. 533 **for whom,** because of whom. 534 **ye,** yea (yes). *ye:* M *yet.* 536 *may:* M *wol.* 539 **more thyng . . . byhete,** anything more, promise. 543 **dreynte,** drowned. 545 **bithought . . . folye,** reflected, absurdity. 550 **say,** saw. The Friend (go-between, procurer or procuress) was another stock character in both the chivalric and Ovidian tableaux. 553 **lene,** lean (for fear). 557 **ferde . . . attricioun,** fear, contrition. 559 **jolyte on presse,** high spirits, aside (as in a closet). 561 **for the nones alle,** all for the purpose. 568 **cas . . . aventure,** chance, accident. 569 *me:* MA *my.* 570 **refus of,** rejected by. 571 **preyinge,** request.

Go hennes awey, for certes my deyinge
Wol the dishese, and I mot nedes deye.
Therfor go wey; ther is na more to seye.

"But if thou wene I be thus sike for drede,   575
It is not so, and therfore scorne nought.
Ther is another thing I take of hede
Wel more than ought the Grekes han yet
    wrought,
Which cause is of my deth for sorowe and
    thought.
But though that I now telle it the ne leste,   580
Be thow naught wroth; I hide it for the beste."

This Pandare, that neigh malt for sorwe and
    routhe,
Ful often seyde, "Allas, what may this be?
Now, frend," quod he, "yf evere love or trouthe
Hath ben, or is, bytwyxen the and me,   585
Ne do thou nevere such a cruelte
To hide fro thi frend so gret a care.
Wostow nought wel that it am I, Pandare?

"I wole parten with the al thyn peyne—
If it be so I do the no comfort—   590
As it is frendes right, soth for to seyne,
To entreparten wo as glad desport.
I have and shal, for trewe or fals report,
In wrong and right iloved the al my lyve
Hyd not thi wo fro me, but telle it blyve."   595

Than gan this Troylus sorwfully to syke,
And seyde hym thus, "God leve it be my
    beste
To telle it the; for sith it may the lyke,
Yet wol I telle it thowh myn herte breste.
And wel wot I thow mayst don me no reste,   600

But lest thow deme I truste not to the,
Now herke, frend, for thus it stant with me.

"Love, ayens the which whoso defendeth
Hymselven most hym alderlest avayleth,
With desespeir so sorwfully me offendeth   605
That streyght unto the deth myn herte
    fayleth,
Therto desir so brennyngly me assayleth,
That to ben slayn it were a gretter joye
To me than kyng of Grece ben and Troye.

"Suffiseth this, my fulle frend Pandare,   610
That I have seyd, for now wostow my wo.
And for the love of God, my colde care
So hyd it wel, I telle it nevere to mo.
For harmes myghte folwen mo than two
If it were wyst; but be thou in gladnesse,   615
And lat me sterve unknowe of my distresse."

"How hastow thus unkyndely and longe
Hid this fro me, thow fool?" quod Pandarus.
"Paraunter thow myghte after swych on
    longe
That myn avys anoon may helpen us."   620
"This were a wonder thyng," quod Troylus.
"Thow koudest nevere yn love thynselven
    wysse.
How devel maystow bryngen me to blysse?"

"Ye, Troilus, now herke," quod Pandare,
"Though I be nyce, it happeth ofte so   625
That on that excesse doth ful yvele fare
By good counseyl kan kepe his frend therfro.
I have myself ek seyn a blynd man go
Ther as he fel that koude loke wyde.
A fool may ek ofte a wys man gyde.   630

---

573 **dishese,** distress (disease). 575 **wene,** believe. 576 A *scorne me nought.* 580 **telle . . . ne leste,** I don't choose to tell. 581 M *Ne be thow.* 582 **malt . . . routhe,** melted, pity. 589 **parten,** share. 590 **If it be so,** i.e., even though I may. 591 **soth,** truth. 592 **entreparten . . . desport,** share, pleasure. 595 **blyve,** quickly. 596 **syke,** sigh. C&c *sorwful Troylus.* 597 **leve,** grant. 598 **lyke,** please. A *for* om. 599 A&c *telle it the.* 600 **wot . . . don . . . reste,** know, give me relief. *And:* M *But.* 601 **deme,** think (judge). 604 **alderlest avayleth,** i.e., is least of all successful. 605 **desespeir,** despair. 606 *fayleth* so MC&c: other MSS *sayleth.* 607 **brennyngly,** burningly. 614 **mo than two,** i.e., many. *folwen:* C&c *fallen.* 616 **sterve unknowe,** i.e., die with my distresses unknown. 617 **unkyndely,** cruelly. 619 **Paraunter,** peradventure. 620 **avys,** advice. 621 **were . . . wonder thyng,** would be, thing of wonder. 622 **wysse,** instruct. 625 **nyce,** foolish. 626 **excesse doth,** intemperance (this is an intriguing sidelight on Pandarus which is never followed up), causes to fare badly. 628 **go,** walk. 629 **wyde,** widely (wide-eyed).

"A wheston is no kervyng instrument,
But yet it maketh sharpe kervyng tolys.
And there thow wost that I have ought myswent,
Eschewe thou that, for swych thyng to the
    scole is—
Thus ofte wyse men ben war by folys. 635
If thou do so, thi wit is wel bywared.
By his contrari is everything declared.

"For how myght evere swetnesse have be knowe
To hym that nevere tasted bitternesse?
Ne no man may be inly glad, I trowe, 640
That nevere was yn sorwe or som distresse.
Ek whit by blak, by shame ek worthinesse,
Ech set by other, more for other semeth,
As men may se, and so the wyse it demeth.

"Sith thus of two contraries is o lore, 645
I, that have in love so ofte assayed,
Grevaunces oughte konne, and wel the more
Counsayllen the of that thow art amayed.
Ek the ne oughte not ben yvel apayed,
Thowh I desire with the for to bere 650
Thyn hevy charge—it shal the lasse dere.

"I wot wel that it fareth thus by me
As to thi brother Parys: an hierdesse
Which that icleped was Oenone
Wrot yn a compleynt of hire hevynesse. 655
Ye say the lettre that she wrot, I gesse?"
"Nay nevere yet, ywis," quod Troylus.
"Now," quod Pandare, "herkene, it was thus:

"'Phebus, that first fond art of medecyne,'

Quod she, 'and koude in every wyghtes care 660
Remede and red by erbess he knew fyne;
Yet to hymself his konnyng was ful bare,
For love hadde hym so bounden yn a snare,
Al for the doughter of the kyng Amete,
That al his craft ne koude his sorwe bete.' 665

"Ryght so fare I, unhappily for me.
I love oon best, and that me smerteth sore,
And yet peraunter kan I rede the,
And not myself—repreve me no more.
I have no cause, I wot wel, for to sore 670
As doth an hauk that lysteth for to pleye.
But to thyn help yet somwhat kan I seye.

"And of o thyng right siker maystow be,
That certayn, for to dyen in the peyne,
That I shal nevere more discoveren the. 675
Ne by my trouthe, I kepe not restreyne
The fro thi love, they that it were Eleyne
That is thi brotheres wif, if ich it wyste—
Be what she be, and love hire as the liste!

"Therfore, as a frend, fullich yn me assure, 680
And telle me plat what is thyn enchesoun
And final cause of wo that ye endure?
For douteth nothyng, myn entencioun
Nys nought to yow of reprehencioun,
To speke as now, for no wyght may bireve 685
A man to love tyl that hym lyst to leve.

"And weteth wel that bothe two ben vices:
Mystrusten alle, or elles alle leve.
But wel I wot, the meene of it no vice is,

---

631 wheston: some MSS *whetston(e)*. This and much of what follows is Chaucer's addition, as Pandarus' learning of Criseyde's identity is expanded from 200 lines in *Fil.* to 500 in *TC.* **633 there ... wost ... ought myswent,** where, perceive, at all gone astray. *ought:* M *out.* **636 bywared,** put to use. **637 declared,** revealed (explained). *his:* M *eche.* **640 trowe,** believe. A *Ne no man wrote what gladnes ys, I trowe.* **645 o lore,** one knowledge. **647 oughte konne,** ought to know the reasons for. **wel the more,** all the better. **648 amayed,** concerned. **649 yvel apayed,** ill pleased. **651 charge ... dere,** responsibility, hurt. **653 hierdesse,** shepherdess. **655 hevynesse,** unhappiness. **656 the lettre,** Oënone's letter to Paris after he deserted her for Helen is one of Ovid's *Heroides* (v). **658 *Now:*** M *No.* **659 Phebus,** This detail about Apollo is evidently from a gloss in an expanded version of the Oënone letter. **fond,** discovered. **660 koude ... care,** knew for the care of every person. **661 red ... erbess,** advice, herbs. *he:* M *she.* **662 bare,** i.e., of little use. **665 bete,** heal. **667 that me smerteth,** that (one) pains me. **668 rede,** counsel. **673 siker,** sure. **674 dyen ... peyne,** as may die by torture. **675 discoveren,** reveal. **676 kepe not restreyne,** i.e., will not restrain. **677 they,** though. **680 assure,** have confidence. **681 plat ... enchesoun,** plainly, reason. **682 *final:*** M *finally.* **684 reprehencioun,** reproof. **685 bireve,** prevent. **686 lyst to leve,** wishes to stop. **687 weteth,** know. **688 Mystrusten ... leve,** to mistrust, to believe. *leve:* other MSS *to leve/believe.* **689 meene,** mean (middle-way).

For for to trusten sum wight is a preve 690
Of trouth; and forthi wolde I fayn remeve
Thy wrong conseyte, and do the som wyght
    tryste
Thi wo to telle—and telle me, yf thow
    lyste.

"Thise wyse seyth, 'Wo hym that is allone,
For, and he falle, he hath noon helpe to ryse'. 695
And sith thou hast a felawe, tel thi moone;
For this nys not, yn certeyn, the nexte wyse
To wynnen love, as techen us the wyse—
To walwe and wepe as Niobe the queene,
Whos terys yet yn marbel ben yseene. 700

"Lat be thi wepyng and thi drerynesse,
And lat us lyssen wo with other speche.
So may thy woful tyme seme lesse.
Delite not in wo thi wo for to seche,
As doon these foles that hire sorwes eche 705
With sorwe when they han mysaventure,
And lysten nought to sechen other cure.

"Men seyn, to wrecche is consolacioun
To have another felawe yn his peyne.
That oughte wel ben oure opynyoun, 710
For bothe thow and I, of love we pleyne.
So ful of sorwe am I, soth for to seyne,
That certaynly no more harde grace
May sitte on me, forwhi ther is no space.

"If God wol, thow art not agast of me 715
Lest I wold of thi lady the bygyle.
Thow wost thiself whom that I love, parde,
As I best kan, gon sithen longe while.
And sith thow wost I do it for no wyle,

And sithen I am he in whom thou tristest
    most, 720
Tel me sumwhat syn al my wo thow wost."

Yet Troylus for al this no word seyde,
But longe he lay as stylle as he ded were;
And after this with sikynge he abreyde,
And to Pandarus voys he lente his eere, 725
And up his eyen caste he, that in feere
Was Pandarus lest that in frenesye
He sholde falle or elles soone dye,

And cride, "Awake!" ful wonderly and
    sharpe.
"What, slombrestow as yn a lytargie? 730
Or artow lyk an asse to the harpe,
That hereth soun whan men the strenges plye,
But yn his mynde of that no melodye
May synken hym to glade, for that he
So dul is of his bestialite?" 735

And with that Pandare of his wordes stente,
And Troylus yet hym nothyng answerde,
Forwhy to telle nas not his entente
To nevere man for whom that he so ferde.
For it is seyd, man maketh ofte a yerde 740
With which the makere is hymself ybeten
In sondry manere—as thise wyse treten;

And namelich yn his counseyl tellynge
That toucheth love, that oughte ben secre,
For of hymself it wol ynough out sprynge 745
But yf that it the bet governed be.
Ek somtyme it is a craft to seme fle
Fro thyng which yn effect men hunte faste—
Al this gan Troylus in his herte caste.

---

690 *For for:* M&c second *for* om. **691 fayn,** happily. **692 conseyte … do,** conceit (idea), make. **693 lyste,** wish. **694 wyse,** wise people. Other MSS *Wo is hym.* **696 moone,** moan (grief). **697 nexte wyse,** nearest way. **699 Niobe,** weeping for her seven sons and seven daughters, was turned to marble, Ovid, *Met.* 6.312. She was a stock example of bereavement in art and rhetoric. **702 lyssen,** soothe. **704 thi:** M *this.* **705 eche,** increase (eke out). **707 lysten,** desire. **709 felawe,** companion **711 pleyne,** complain. **713 harde grace,** misfortune. **714 forwhi,** because. **715 agast,** afraid. *If God wol:* A *A God wil.* **716 bygyle,** rob (deceive). **718 gon sithen,** (and have) for a very long while. **719 sith … wyle,** since, deception. **720 sithen,** since. C&c *And sey I am he that thow trustest moost.* **724 sikynge … abreyde,** sighing, rose up. **726 up his eyen caste,** i.e., rolled back his eyes. **730 lytargie,** lethargy (stupor). **731 asse to the harpe,** from *Boece* I pr. 4. A *unto an harpe.* **732 plye,** ply (use). C&c *pleye.* **734 synken:** M&c *synk in.* **736 stente,** stopped. **737 nothyng:** M&c *no word.* **738 Forwhy,** because. **739 nevere man … so ferde,** no man, on whose account he fared so. **740 yerde,** yardstick. **742 treten,** tell. **743 namelich … counseyl tellynge,** especially, telling his secrets. **745 of hymself … out sprynge,** of its own accord, become known. M *it wolde not ought sprynge.* **746 But yf,** unless. **749 caste,** ponder.

But natheles, whan he hadde herd hym crye
"Awake," he gan to syke wonder sore,   751
And seyde, "Frend, though that I stille lye,
I am not def. Now pes and cry no more,
For I have herd thi wordes and thi lore;
But suffre me my myschef to bywayle,   755
For thi proverbes may me nought avayle.

"Nor other cure canstow noon for me.
Eke I nyl not be cured; I wol deye.
What knowe I of the queene Niobe?
Lat be thyne olde ensamples, I the preye."   760
"No," quod tho Pandarus, "therfore I seye,
Such is delit of foles to bywepe
Hire wo, but seken bote thei ne kepe.

"Now knowe I that ther reson yn the fayleth.
But telle me, yf I wyste what she were   765
For whom that the al this mysaunter ayleth?
Dorstestow that I telle in hire eere
Thi wo, sith thow darst not thiself for feere,
And hire bysoughte on the to han som routhe?"
"Why, nay," quod he, "by God and by my
      trouthe!"   770

"What, nat as bisily," quod Pandarus,
"As though myn owen lyf lay on this nede?"
"No, certes, brother," quod this Troylus.
"And why?"—'For that thow sholdest nevere
      spede."
"Wostow that wel?"—"Ye, that is out of
      drede,"   775
Quod Troylus. "For al that evere ye konne,
She nyl to no swych wrecche as I be wonne."

Quod Pandarus, "Allas, what may this be,
That thow despered art thus causeles?

What, lyveth not thi lady, bendiste?   780
How wostow so that thow art graceles?
Such yvel is not alwey boteles.
Why, put not impossible thus thi cure,
Syn thyng to come is oft yn aventure.

"I graunte wel that thow endurest wo   785
As sharp as doth he Ticius yn helle,
Whos stomak foughles tiren everemo,
That highte volturis, as bokes telle.
But I may not endure that thow dwelle
In so unskilful an opynyoun   790
That of thi wo is no curacioun.

"But ones nyltow for thy coward herte,
And for thyn ire and folessh wilfulnesse,
For wantrust, tellen of thi sorwes smerte,
Ne to thyn owen help do bysynesse   795
As muche as speke a resoun more or lesse,
But lyest as he that lest of nothyng recche—
What womman koude loven such a wrecche?

"What may she demen other of thi deth,
If thou thus deye and she not whi it is,   800
But that for fere is yolden up thi breth,
For Grekes han byseged us, ywys?
Lord, which a thonk then shaltow han of this!
Thus wol she seyn, and al the toun atones,
'The wrecche is ded, the devil have his
      bones!'   805

"Thow mayst allone here wepe and crie and
      knele,
But love a womman that she wot it nought,
And she wole quyte that thow shalt not fele—
Unknowe, unkyst, and lost, that is unsought.
What, many a man hath love ful dere ybought

---

751 **syke,** sigh. 754 **lore,** wisdom. 755 **myschef,** misfortune. 760 *ensamples:* other MSS *proverbes/paroles.* 763 **bote . . . ne kepe,** remedy, care not. 764 **ther,** with respect to that. M&c *ther* om. 765 **what,** who. 766 **mysaunter,** misadventure. 767 **Dorstestow,** would you dare. C&c *told hir in hire.* 769 **routhe,** pity. 771 **nat as bisily,** i.e., not if I proffered as diligently. 774 **spede,** be successful. 775 **Wostow . . . wel . . . drede,** know you, for sure, doubt. 777 M *nyl not to no swych wrecche be.* 779 M *desespered.* 780 M&c *benedicite.* 781 **wostow . . . graceles,** do you know, without favor. 782 **yvel . . . boteles,** trouble, hopeless. 784 **yn aventure,** subject to chance. 786 **Ticius,** Titius who for attempting to ravish Diana lay stretched out in Hades where two vultures perpetually tore at his liver. Chaucer appears here to be quoting his own translation of *Boece* III m. 12.42. **he:** MA *the.* 787 **foughles tiren,** fowls tear. 790 **unskilful,** unreasonable. 792 **But ones nyltow for,** But you will not once because of. 794 **wantrust . . . smerte,** lack of trust, pain. 795 **do bysynesse,** take action. 797 **lyest . . . lest . . . recche,** lie down, wishes, care. **lyest:** M *lyk.* 798 **koude:** M *wolde.* 799 **demen,** conclude. 800 **not,** not know (ne wot). 801 **yolden,** yielded. 808 **quyte,** repay. 810 **dere ybought,** dearly bought (with devoted service).

Twenty wynter that his lady wyste, 811
That nevere yet his lady mouth he kyste.

"What, shulde he therfore fallen in despeyr,
Or be recreaunt for his owene tene,
Or slen hymself, al be his lady feyr? 815
Nay, nay, but evere yn oon be fressh and
    greene
To serve and love hys dere hertes queene,
And thenk it is a guerdoun hire to serve
A thowsandfold more than he kan deserve."

And of that word tok hede Troylus, 820
And thought anoon what folye he was inne,
And how that hym soth seyde Pandarus,
That for to slen hymself myght he nat wynne,
But bothe doon unmanhod and a synne,
And of his deth his lady nought to wyte, 825
For of his wo, God woot, she knew ful lyte.

And with that thought he gan ful sore syke,
And seyde, "Allas, what is me best to do?"
To whom Pandare answerde, "Yf the lyke,
The beste is that thow telle me al thi wo. 830
And have my trowthe, but thow it fynde so
I be thi bote or that it be ful longe,
To pieces do me drawe and sithen honge."

"Ye, so thow seyst," quod Troylus tho, "allas,
But God wot, it is not the rather so. 835
Ful hard were it to helpen yn this cas,
For wel fynde I that Fortune is my fo,
Ne alle the men that riden konne or go
May of hire cruel whiel the harm wythstonde,
For as hire lyst she pleyeth with free and
    bonde." 840

Quod Pandarus, "Than blamestow Fortune
For thow art wroth? Ye, now at erst I se.
Wostow not wel that Fortune ys comune
To every maner wight yn som degre?
And yet thow hast this comfort, lo, parde, 845
That as hire joyes moten overgone,
So mote hire sorwes passen everychone.

"For yf hire whiel stynte anythyng to torne,
Thanne cessed she Fortune anoon to be.
Now, sith hire whiel by no wey may sojourne,
What wostow if hire mutabilite 851
Ryght as thiselven lyst wol don by the,
Or that she be not fer fro thyn helpynge?
Paraunter thow hast cause for to synge.

"And therfore wostow what I the beseche? 855
Lat be thi wo and turnyng to the grounde,
For whoso lyst have helyng of his leche,
To hym byhoveth first unwrye his wounde.
To Cerberus yn helle ay be I bounde,
Were it for my suster, al thy sorwe, 860
By my wil she sholde al be thyn tomorwe.

"Lok up, I seye, and telle me what she is,
Anoon that I may goon aboute thin nede.
Knowe ich hire ought? For my love, telle me
    this.
Thenne wolde I hopen rather for to spede." 865
Tho gan the veyne of Troylus to blede,
For he was hit and wax al red for shame.
"Aha," quod Pandare, "here bygynneth
    game."

And with that word he gan hym for to shake,
And seyde, "Thef, thow shalt hire name telle."

---

811 wyste, knew of. **812 he:** M *yet*. **814 recreaunt . . . tene,** disloyal, grief. **816 yn oon,** always (anon). **818 guerdoun,** reward. This is a statement of the most idealistic form of courtly love, "amor purus," which is purely platonic. **823 wynne,** profit. **826** M *For of his wo, God knoweth ful lyte.* **827 syke,** sigh. **829 the lyke,** you please. **831 trowthe,** promise. **832 bote or,** assistance before (ere). **833 do me drawe . . . sithen,** have me drawn (i.e., pulled apart), afterwards. **834–56** Not found in *Fil.;* inserted by Chaucer as part of his emphasis upon the influence of Fortune and Destiny in the poem. **835 rather,** sooner. **840 lyst,** desires. **842 at erst,** for the first time. M *Ye* om. **843 comune,** in common (i.e., treats equally). **846–47** *Boece* II pr. 3.76. **848 stynte anythyng,** stopped at all; *Boece* II pr. 1.115. **850 sojourne,** stop. **851–52 What . . . if . . . by the,** i.e., how do you know her changeableness won't do for you as you wish? The ultimate danger of the circular motion is, however, suggested early, at *TC* I.4, where Chaucer first introduces the notion of the counter influences of Fortune. **853 not fer fro,** i.e., not far from helping you. **856 turnyng to,** turning toward. **857 lyst . . . leche,** desires, physician. *helyng:* M&c *helpyng.* **858 unwrye,** uncover. **859 Cerberus,** the three-headed watchdog at the gate of Hades. **ay . . . bounde,** may I ever be tied. **862 what,** who. **865 rather . . . spede,** more quickly, have success. M&c *the rathere.*

But tho gan sely Troylus for to quake 871
As though men sholde han lad hym into helle,
And seyde, "Allas, of al my wo the welle,
Than is my swete fo called Criseyde." 874
And wel neygh with the word for fere he deyde.

And whan that Pandare herd hire name nevene,
Lord, he was glad, and seyde, "Frend so dere,
Now fare aright, for Joves name yn hevene.
Love hath beset the wel; be of good chere.
For of good name and wysdom and manere 880
She hath ynough, and ek of gentilesse—
If she be fayr, thow wost thyself, I gesse.

"Ne nevere saw I a more bounteuous
Of hire estat, ne a gladder, ne of speche
A frendliour, ne a more gracious 885
For to do wel, ne lasse hadde nede to seche
What for to doon; and al this bet to eche
In honour, to as fer as she may strecche,
A kynges herte semeth by hires a wrecche.

"And forthy loke of good comfort thou be, 890
For certainly, the firste poynt is this,
Of noble corage and wel ordayne,
A man to have pees with himself, ywis.
So oughtest thou, for nought but good it is
To loven wel and in a worthy place. 895
The oughte nat to clepe it hap, but grace.

"And also thenk and therwith glade the
That sith thy lady vertuous is al,
So foloweth it that there is som pite
Amonges alle thyse other in general; 900

And forthy se that thow in special
Requere not that is ayen hire name,
For vertu streccheth not hymself to shame.

"But wel is me that evere I was born
That thou biset art yn so good a place, 905
For by my trouthe, yn love I dorste have sworn
The sholde nevere han tyd so fayr a grace.
And wostow whi? For thow were wont to chace
At Love yn scorn, and for despit hym calle
Seynt Idyot, lord of these foles alle. 910

"How ofte hastow mad thi nyce japes
And seyd that Loves servantz everychone
Of nycete ben verray Goddes apes;
And some wole mucche hire mete allone, 914
Lyggyng abedde, and make hem for to grone;
And som, thow seydest, hadde a blaunche fevere,
And preydest God he sholde nevere kevere;

"And som of hem toke on hem for the colde,
More than ynough, so seydestow ful ofte;
And som han feyned ofte tyme and tolde 920
How that they wake whan thei slepen softe—
And thus thei wolde han brought hemself
   alofte,
And natheles were under at the laste.
Thus seidestow, and japedest ful faste.

"Yet seidestow that for the more part 925
These loveres wolden speke in general,
And thoughte that it was a siker art
For faylyng for to assayn overal.
Now may I jape of the if that I shal;

But natheles, though that I sholde deye,   930
That thow art none of tho I dorste saye.

"Now beet thi brest and seye to God of Love,
'Thi grace, lord, for now I me repente
If I mysspak, for now myself I love.'
Thus sey with al thyn herte yn good entente."
Quod Troylus, "A, lord, I me consente,   936
And pray to the my japes thow foryeve,
And I shal nevere more whil I leve."

"Thow seyst wel," quod Pandarus, "and now I
    hope
That thow the goddes wrathe hast al apesed;   940
And sithen that thow hast wepen many a drope,
And seyd swych thyng wherwith thi god is
    plesed,
Now wolde nevere god but thow were esed.
And thynk wel, she of whom rist al thi wo
Hereafter may thy comfort be also.   945

"For thilke ground that bereth the wedys wykke
Bereth eke these holsome herbes as ful ofte;
Next the foule netle, rough and thikke,
The rose waxeth swote and smothe and softe;
And next the valey is the hil alofte;   950
And next the derke nyght the glade morwe—
And also joye is next the fyn of sorwe.

"Now loke that atempre be thy brydel,
And for the beste ay suffre to the tyde,
Or elles alle oure labour is on ydel: 955
He hasteth wel that wisely kan abyde.
Be diligent and trewe, and ay wel hide,
Be lusty, fre, persevere yn thyn servyce,
And al is wel if thou werk in this wyse.

"But he that departed is yn every place   960
Is nowher hool, as writen clerkes wyse.
What wonder is though swich on have no grace?
Ek wostow how it fareth on som service—
As plaunte a tre or herbe yn sondry wyse,
And on the morwe pulle it up as blyve—   965
No wonder is though it mow nevere thrive.

"And sith that God of Love hath the bystowed
In place digne unto thi worthynesse,
Stond faste, for to good port hastow rowed.
And of thyself, for any hevynesse,   970
Hope alwey wel; for but if drerynesse
Or over-haste oure bothe labour shende,
I hope of this to maken a good ende.

"And wostow whi I am the lasse afered
Of this matere with my nece trete?   975
For this have I herd seyd of wyse ylered:
Was nevere man ne womman yet bygete
That was unapt to suffren loves hete,
Celestial, or elles love of kynde—
Forthi som grace I hope in hire to fynde.   980

"And for to speke of hire in special,
Hire beaute to bythynke and hire youthe,
It sit hire nought to be celestial
As yet, though that hire lyste bothe and kouthe;
But trewly, it sate hire wel right nowthe   985
A worthy knyght to loven and cherice—
And but she do I holde it for a vice.

"Wherfore I am and wole ben ay redy
To peyne me to do yow this servyse.
For bothe yow to plese thus hope I   990
Herafterward, for ye beth bothe wyse

---

931 M *tho that dorste I seye.* 933 **Thi grace,** give me thy grace. 937 **japes,** ridicule. *thow:* other MSS *to/now/me.* 941 *wepen:* C&c *wopen.* 943 **wolde nevere god,** would to God that. 946 **wykke,** evil. 949 A *The lilie wexith white, smothe, and softe.* 952 M *next after sorwe.* 953 **atempre...brydel,** moderate, self-control (bridle). 954 **beste...tyde,** for the best (outcome) endure the (present) time. 955 **on ydel,** in vain. 957 **ay...hide,** always, secret (hidden). 958 **lusty, fre...servyce,** happy, generous, (love) service. 960 **departed,** disintegrated. 962 M *that such.* 963 **som service,** some (love) service. 965 **blyve,** readily. 966 **mow,** may. *though:* M *thow.* 968 **digne...worthynesse,** suitable to your own worth. With this stanza Chaucer returns to the text of *Fil.* 970 **for...hevynesse,** in spite of, grief. 971 **drerynesse,** melancholy (hopelessness). 972 **shende,** spoil. 975 **trete,** negotiate. 976 **ylered,** sages. A *olde ylered;* C&c *lered.* 977 **bygete,** born (begotten). 978 **unapt,** unsuited. 979 **Celestial...kynde,** i.e., divine, sexual. 980 **Forthi,** therefore. 983 **It sit,** it is not appropriate. 984 **lyste bothe and kouthe,** both wished to and could. 985 **sate...nowthe,** would be appropriate, now. 987 **vice,** flaw. Chaucer has considerably refined Pandarus' statement. In *Fil.* 2.27 he says flatly, "My cousin is a widow and hath desires; if she should deny it, I would not believe her." 990 **bothe yow,** i.e., Troylus and Criseyde.

And konne it counseyl kepe in such a wyse
That no man shal of it the wiser be.
And so we may ben gladed alle thre.

"For by my trowthe, I have right now of the   995
A good conceyte yn my wit, as I gesse,
And what it is I wol now that thow se.
I thenke, sith that Love of his goodnesse
Hath the converted out of wikkednesse,
That thow shalt ben the best post, I leve,   1000
Of al his lay, and most his foos to greve.

"Ensample whi, se now these wyse clerkes
That erren aldermost ayen the lawe,
And ben converted from hire wikked werkes
Thorugh grace of God that lyst hem to hym
    drawe,   1005
Than arn thei folk that han most God in awe,
And strengest feythed ben, I understonde,
And konne an errour alderbest withstonde."

Whanne Troylus had herd Pandare assentyd
To ben his help yn lovyng of Cryseyde,   1010
Wex of his wo, as who seyth, untormentyd,
But hotter weex his love, and thus he seyde
With sobre chere although his herte pleyde,
"Now blyssful Venus, help er that I sterve!
Of the, Pandare, I may som thank deserve.   1015

"But, dere frend, how shal myn wo be lesse
Til this be don? And, good, eke telle me thisse:
How wyltow seyn of me and my destresse,
Lest she be wroth—this drede I most, iwysse—
Or nyl nat heren or trowen how it ysse?   1020
Al this drede I, and ek for the manere
Of the, hire em, she nyl no swych thyng here."

Quod Pandarus, "Thou hast a ful grete care
Lest that the cherl may falle out of the
    mone!
Whi, Lord, I hate of the thi nyce fare.   1025
Whi, entremete of that thow hast to done.
For Goddes love, I bydde the a bone:
So lat me allone, and it shal be thi beste."
"Whi, frend," quod he, "now do right as the
    leste.

"But herke, Pandare, o word, for I nolde   1030
That thow in me wendest so gret folye
That to my lady I desiren sholde
That toucheth harm or ony vilenye,
For dredles me were levere dye
Than she of me ought elles understode   1035
But that that myghte sownen ynto gode."

Tho lough this Pandare and anoon answerde,
"And I thi borwh? Fy, no wyght doth but so.
I roughte nought though that she stod and
    herde
How that thow seyst. But farewel, I wol go.   1040
Adieu. Be glad. God spede us bothe two.
Yeve me this labour and this besynesse,
And of my spede be thyn al that swetnesse."

Tho Troylus gan doun on knees to falle,
And Pandare yn his armes hente faste,   1045
And seyde, "Now fy on the Grekes alle.
Yet, parde, God shal helpe us atte laste.
And dredeles, yf that my lyf may laste,
And God toforn, lo, som of hem shal
    smerte;
And yet m'athynketh that this avant me
    asterte.   1050

"Now, Pandare, I kan no more seye,
But thow wys, thow wost, thow mayst, thow
    art al!
My lyf, my deth, hool yn thyn hond I leye.
Help now!"—Quod he, "Yis, by my trouthe I
    shal."
"God yelde the, frend, and this yn special,"   1055
Quod Troylus, "that thou me recomaunde
To hire that to the deth me may comaunde."

This Pandarus, tho desirous to serve
His fulle frend, thenne seyde yn this manere,
"Fairwel, and thenk I wole thi thank
    deserve,   1060
Have here my trouthe, and that thou shalt wel
    here."—
And went his wey, thenkyng on this matere,
And how he best myghte hire beseche of
    grace,
And fynde a tyme therto, and a place.

For every wyght that hath an hows to founde
Ne renneth nought the werk for to bygynne   1066
With rakel hond, but he wol byde a stounde,
And send his hertes lyne out fro withinne
Alderfirst his purpos for to wynne.

Al this Pandare yn his herte thoughte,   1070
And caste his werk ful wysly or he wroughte.

But Troylus lay tho no lengere down,
But up anoon upon his stede bay,
And in the feld he pleyde tho lyoun.
Wo was that Grek that with hym mette that day!
And yn the town his manere tho forth ay   1076
So goodly was, and gat hym so yn grace,
That eche hym loved that loked on his face.

For he bycom the frendlyeste wyght,
The gentileste, and ek the moste fre,   1080
The thriftieste and oon the beste knyght
That yn his tyme was or myghte be.
Dede were his japes and his cruelte,
His heighe port, and his manere estraunge—
And ech of tho gan for a vertu chaunge.   1085

Now lat us stynte of Troylus a stounde,
That fareth lyk a man that hurt is sore,
And is somdel of akynge of his wounde
Ilissed wel, but heled no deel moore,
And as an esy pacient the lore   1090
Abit of hym that goth aboute his cure.
And thus he drieth forth his aventure.

Explicit liber primus.

1052 wys . . . wost . . . mayst . . . art, but you, wise one, you know, can do, and are everything. Cf. *Fil.* 2.33 "Thou philosopher, thou friend, etc." **1055 yelde,** reward. **1058 tho,** then. **1060 thenk . . . deserve,** i.e., think how to deserve. **1061 trouthe . . . here,** promise, hear (how). **1063** M *best* om. **1064** *place:* A *space.* **1067 rakel . . . stounde,** rash, while. This nice passage is a translation from Geoffrey de Vinsauf, *Poetria Nova,* one of the Latin rhetorics Chaucer must have studied in school. It begins "Si quis habet fundare domum, non currit ad actum," etc. (ll. 43–45). **1068 hertes lyne,** i.e., imaginary projection (plan). **1069 Alderfirst . . . purpos . . . wynne,** first of all, intention, attain. **1071 caste . . . or . . . wroughte,** planned, before, worked (performed). **1073 bay,** red-brown (traditional color for a war-horse). **1074 tho** (then): other MSS *the.* **1075** *Wo:* C&c *Who. That day:* C&c *a-day.* **1076 tho forth ay,** forever thenceforth. A *his name sprong for ay.* **1080 fre,** generous. **1081 thriftieste,** most effective. A *trustiest.* **1083 japes,** jokes. **1084 heighe port,** arrogant manner. **1085 tho,** those (flaws). **1086 stynte . . . stounde,** stop, while. **1089 Ilissed,** relieved (of the pain). **1090 esy pacient,** patient at ease (not in pain). **1091 Abit . . . cure,** i.e., awaits the wisdom of the one who is curing him. **1092 drieth** (endures): other MSS *driveth.*

BOOK II

Incipit prohemium secundi libri.

Owt of these blake wawes for to sayle,
O wynd, O wynd, the weder gynneth clere,
For in this see the bot hath swych travaylle
Of my connyng that unneth I it stere—
This see clepe I the tempestous matere 5
Of disesper that Troilus was inne—
But now of hope the kalendes bygynne.

O lady myn, that called art Cleo,
Thow be my sped fro this forth, and my muse,
To ryme wel this book til I have do; 10
Me nedeth here noon other art to use.
Forwhi to every lovere I me excuse
That of no sentement I this endite,
But out of Latyn in my tunge it write.

Wherfore I nel have neyther thank ne blame 15
Of al this werk, but pray yow mekely,
Disblameth me if ony word be lame,
For as myn auctour seyde, so sey I.
Ek though I speke of love unfelyngly,
No wonder is, for it nothyng of newe is; 20
A blynd man kan not juggen wel in hewys.

Ye knowe ek that in forme of speche is
    chaunge
Withinne a thousand yer, and wordes tho
That hadden prys now wonder nyce and
    straunge
Us thenketh hem, and yet they spake hem so,
And sped as wel in love as men now do. 26
Eke for to wynnen love in sondry ages,
In sondry londes, sondry ben usages.

And forthi if it happe yn ony wyse
That here be ony lovere yn this place, 30
That herkneth as the story wol devyse,
How Troylus com to hys lady grace,
And thenketh, "So nold I nat love purchace,"
Or wondreth on his speche or his doynge,
I not, but it is me no wonderynge; 35

For every wyght which that to Rome went
Halt nat o path, or alwey o manere.
Ek in some lond were al the game shent
If that thei ferde yn love as men don here,
As thus, in open doyng or in chere, 40

1–6 Parallels between these lines and the opening lines of Dante's *Purgatorio* have been noted. On the nature of this proem in comparison with the invocation to Bk. I, see 1.6n. The invocations and proems to all five books treat the artist's problems in handling his material, as well as with the nature of the material itself. **wawes**, waves. **3 bot . . . travaylle**, boat, difficulty. **4 connyng . . . unneth**, skill, barely. *connyng*: MCA *com(m)yng(e)*. **5 clepe,** call. **6 disesper**: M *desper*. **7 kalendes,** the day of the new moon and the beginning of the month in the ancient Roman calendar. **8 Cleo,** the muse of history. **9 sped,** help. **11 MA** *other om.* **12 Forwhi,** therefore. **13 sentement,** knowledge based on personal emotional experience. Chaucer is maintaining his pose as reporter on love, cf. 1.10ff. above. **14 Latyn,** Chaucer's deliberate obfuscation of his sources was never plainer; *Il Filostrato* is in Italian, and Chaucer was probably working from a French translation (see the Introduction). Where either Latin or "myn auctour" come into it, no one can tell. **20 it nothyng of newe is,** "it" evidently refers to his story, which, he says, is not striking or original. This is a conventional medieval "modesty" demurral. **23 tho,** then. **24 prys . . . nyce,** value, foolish. **26 sped,** succeeded. **27 sondry,** different. **29–42** In two A MSS these stanzas follow l. 49. **29 happe,** happen. **32 grace,** favor. **35 not . . . me,** do not know, to me. **37 o path,** one path. M *al o path.* **38 shent,** lost. **40 open doyng or in chere,** public behavior or in manner. *doyng*: A *delyng*.

In vysitynge, in forme, or seyde hire sawes;
Forthi men seyn, ech contre hath his lawes.

Ek scarsly ben ther in this place thre
That han yn love seyd lyk and don yn al,

For to thi purpos this may lyken the,   45
And the right nought; yet al is seyd or shal.
Ek som men grave in tre, some in ston wal,
As it bitit. But syn I have bigonne,
Myn auctour shal I folwe if I konne.

Explicit prohemium secundi libri.

Incipit liber secundus.

In May, that moder is of monthes glade,   50
That fresshe floures blew and white and rede
Ben quike agayn, that wynter dede made,
And ful of bawme is fletyng every mede,
Whan Phebus doth his bryghte bemes sprede
Right in the white Bole, it so bytydde,   55
As I shal synge, on Mayes day the thridde,

That Pandarus, for al his wyse speche,
Felt ek his part of loves shotes keene,
That koude he nevere so wel of lovyng preche,
It made his hewe a-day ful ofte grene.   60
So shop it that hym fil that day a tene
In love, for which yn wo to bedde he wente,
And made er it was day ful many a wente.

The swalwe Proigne with a sorowful lay,
Whan morwe com gan make hire
     waymentynge,   65

Whi she forshapen was; and ever lay
Pandare abedde, half yn a slomberynge,
Til she so neigh hym made hire cheterynge,
How Tireux gan forth hire suster take,
That with the noyse of hire he gan awake,   70

And gan to calle and dresse hym up to ryse,
Remembryng hym his erand was to done
From Troylus, and ek his gret emprise,
And cast and knew yn good plyt was the mone
To don viage, and tok his weye ful sone   75
Unto his neces palays ther bysyde.
Now Janus, god of entre, thow hym gyde!

Whan he was come unto his neces place,
"Wher is my lady?" to hire folk seyde he.
And they hym tolde, and he yn forth gan pace,
And fond two othere ladyes sette, and she,   81
Withinne a paved parlour, and thei thre

---

41 in forme, or seyde hire sawes, in formal etiquette, or said their speeches. **42 Forthi . . . his,** therefore, its ("his" was the possessive of "it" until the 17th century). **44 lyk . . . don yn al,** alike, done (alike) in all (things). *and:* A *or.* **45 lyken,** please; i.e., for in furthering your purpose, this speech may please one and not another. **46 al is seyd or shal,** i.e., all kinds of speeches must be uttered. **47 grave,** carve. **48 bitit,** happens. **50 May,** this is the *reverdi* (returning of spring) introduction typical of so many lyrics and romances, including the beginning of *CT.* But the time scheme of *TC,* including the conjunction of Jupiter and Saturn with the crescent moon (after 13 May 1385; cf. iii.624n.) is carefully worked out. **52 quike,** alive. **53 bawme . . . fletyng,** balm (fragrance), floating. **55 Bole,** bull, Taurus, sign of the zodiac for April–May. **56 Mayes day the thridde,** the reason for Chaucer's affinity for May 3 is not known, but many important things seem to happen on that day; see *CT,* i.1463. **59** A *nevere of love so wele;* M *of lovyng* om. **61 shop it . . . tene,** it came about, a pang. *fil:* M *felt.* **63 wente,** turn. **64–69 Proigne . . . Tireux,** Procne was changed into the swallow for taking vengeance on her husband Tereus for violating her sister Philomela. Philomela was transformed into the nightingale and Tereus into the hoopoe, Ovid, *Met.* 6.438ff. **65 waymentynge,** lamenting. **66 forshapen,** transformed in shape. **71 calle,** i.e., his servants. **dresse,** prepare (address). **73 emprise,** enterprise. **74 cast . . . plyt,** examined his horoscope, position. **75 don viage,** take a trip. M *his/ful* om. **76 bysyde,** nearby. **77 Janus,** Roman god of gates and entrances (two-faced, looking in and out). **80** C&c *forth in.* The matter beginning Bk. ii, through the scene of the three ladies listening to the reading of the romance, was added by Chaucer. In *Fil.* 2.34, Pandarus goes immediately from Troylus' bedchamber to Criseyde's house, and the conversation picks up at about *TC,* ii.120, but in a much more candid and businesslike tone than in *TC.* **82 paved parlour,** tile-floored private sitting room.

Herden a mayden reden hem the geste
Of the sege of Thebes while hem leste.

Quod Pandarus, "Madame, God yow see,   85
With yowre faire book and al the compaignye."
"Ey, uncle myn, welcome ywys," quod she.
And up she ros, and by the hond in hye
She tok hym faste, and seyde, "This nyght
    thrie—
To goode mot it turne—of yow I mette."   90
And with that word she doun on bench hym
    sette.

"Ye, nece, ye shal fare wel the bet,
If God wole, al this yer," quod Pandarus.
"But I am sory that I have yow let
To herken of youre book ye preysen thus.   95
For Goddes love, what seith it? Telle it us.
Is it of love? Som good ye me lere!"
"Uncle," quod she, "youre maystresse is nat
    here."

With that thei gonnen laughe, and tho she
    seyde,
"This romaunce is of Thebes that we rede;   100
And we han herd how that Kyng Layus deyde
Thorugh Edyppus his sone, and al that dede;
And here we stenten at these lettres rede,
How the bisshop, as the book kan telle,   104
Amphiorax fil thorugh the ground to helle."

Quod Pandarus, "Al this knowe I myselve,
And al the assege of Thebes and al the care,

For herof ben there maked bokes twelve.
But lat be this and telle me how ye fare.
Do wey youre barbe and shewe youre face
    bare.   110
Do wey youre book, rys up, and lat us daunce,
And lat us don to May som observaunce."

"I? God forbede!" quod she. "Be ye mad?
Is that a wydewes lyf, so God you save?
By God, ye maken me ryght sore adrad.   115
Ye ben so wylde, it semeth that ye rave.
It sate me wel bet ay in a cave
To bydde and rede on holy seyntes lyves.
Lat maydens gon to daunce, and yonge wyves."

"As evere thrive I," quod this Pandarus,   120
"Yet kowde I telle a thyng to doon yow pleye."
"Now, uncle deere," quod she, "tel it us,
For Goddes love. Is than the assege aweye?
I am of Grekes so fered that I deye."
"Nay, nay," quod he, "as evere mot I thryve,
It is a thyng wel bet than swyche fyve."   126

"Ye, holy God," quod she, "what thyng is that?
What? Bet than swyche fyve? I, nay, iwys!
For al this world ne kan I reden what
It sholde ben. Som jape, I trowe, is this.   130
And but youreselven telle us what it is,
My wit is for to arede it al to lene.
As help me God, I not nat what ye mene."

"And I youre borugh, ne nevere shal for me   134
This thing be told to yow, as mote I thryve."

84 sege of Thebes, Statius' *Thebaid,* known to the Middle Ages through the French *Roman de Thèbes,* has an ironic appropriateness for victims of the seige of Troy, and also, it turns out, because Diomede, who replaces Troylus as Criseyde's lover, is the son of Tideus, who was killed in the seige of Thebes; see v.1480ff. below and notes. **85 God . . . see,** watch over you. A *Madame, quod Pandare.* **86** MC&c *al yowre faire;* other MSS om. *al* or *faire.* **88 in hye,** in haste. **90 mot . . . mette,** may, dreamed. **92 wel the bet,** the better. **94 let,** hindered. **97 lere,** teach. CA *O, som.* **99 tho,** then. **100 Thebes,** the allusions to the narrative are partly to Statius and partly to the *Roman.* **101–02 Layus . . . Edyppus,** King Laius of Thebes, slain by his son Oedipus. **103 stenten . . . rede,** stopped, red (the "rubric," red lettering that marks section headings, etc.). **104–05 bisshop . . . Amphiorax,** Amphiaraus, in Statius called *vates* (seer), is in the *Roman* called *Un arcevesque mout corteis* (a most courteous archbishop); he was one of the seven who laid seige to Thebes, and— as he himself predicted—fell living into Hades. **110 barbe,** headdress covering everything but the face. Other MSS *wympel.* **112 May . . . observaunce,** pagan fertility rites gave May observances a licentious connotation; cf. *CT* i.1045, 1500. The teasing, hinting technique by which Pandarus reveals his mission to Criseyde is much expanded by Chaucer; ll. 106–595, is expressed by Boccaccio in 25 stanzas (200 lines). **113 I:** M&c *A/Eighe* (interjection). **115** A *Ye make me, by Jovis, sore adrad.* **117 sate me . . . ay,** would be more fitting for me, always. **118 bydde,** pray. **120 thrive,** prosper. **121 doon . . . pleye,** make you play. **126 bet . . . fyve,** i.e., five times better. M *thyng is worth such fyve.* **129 reden,** say. **130 jape . . . trowe,** joke, believe. **131** M *us* om. **132 arede . . . lene,** explain, weak (lean). **133** *what:* M *whan.* **134 borugh,** pledge (borrow). **135 thryve,** prosper.

"And why so, uncle myn? Why so?" quod she.
"By God," quod he, "that wol I telle as blyve.
For proudder womman were ther noon on lyve,
And ye it wyst, yn al the toun of Troye.
I jape nought, as evere have I joye." 140

Tho gan she wondren more than byforn
A thousandfold, and doun hire eyen caste,
For nevere sith the tyme that she was born
To knowe thyng desired she so faste.
And with a syk she seyde hym at the laste, 145
"Now, uncle myn, I nel yow nowght displese,
Nor axen more that may do yow disese."

So after this, with many wordes glade,
And frendly tales, and with mery chere,
Of this and that they pleyde, and gunnen wade
In many an unkouth, glad, and dep matere, 151
As frendes don whanne thei ben met yfere,
Til she gan axen hym how Ector ferde,
That was the townes wal and Grekes yerde.

"Ful wel, I thanke it God," quod
  Pandarus, 155
"Save in his arm he hath a litel wownde—
And ek his fresshe brother Troylus,
The wyse, worthi Ector the secounde,
In whom that alle vertu lyst abounde,
As alle trowth and alle gentilesse, 160
Wysdom, honour, fredom, and worthinesse."

"In good feyth, em," quod she, "that lyketh me.
They faren wel, God save hem bothe two.
For trewely I holde it gret deynte,
A kynges sone in armes wel to do, 165
And ben of goode condicions therto.
For gret power and moral vertu here
Is seelde yseye in o persone yfere."

"In good fayth, that is soth," quod Pandarus.
"But by my trouthe, the kyng hath sones
  tweye— 170
That is to mene, Ector and Troylus—
That certeynly, though that I sholde deye,
They ben as voyde of vices, dar I seye,
As ony men that lyven under the sonne.
Hire myght is wyde yknowe, and what they
  konne. 175

"Of Ector nedeth it no more for to telle:
In al this world ther nys a bettre knyght
Than he, that is of worthinesse welle,
And he wel more vertu hath than myght.
This knoweth many a wis and worthi wyght.
The same pris of Troylus I seye— 181
God help me so, I knowe not swyche tweye."

"Be God," quod she, "of Ector that is soth.
Of Troylus the same thing trowe I;
For dredeles, men tellen that he doth 185
In armes day by day so worthily,
And bereth hym here at hom so gentilly
To every wight, that alle prys hath he
Of hem that me were levest preysed be."

"Ye sey right soth, ywys," quod Pandarus, 190
"For yesterday whoso hadde with hym ben,
He myghte han wondred upon Troylus,
For nevere yet so thikke a swarm of ben
Ne fleygh, as Grekes gonne fro hym flen,
And thorugh the feld in every wightes ere 195
There nas no cry but 'Troylus is there!'

"Now here, now ther, he hunted hem so faste,
Ther nas but Grekes blood, and Troylus.
Now hym he hurte, and hym al down he
  caste;

---

137 blyve, immediately. **139 wyst,** knew. **140 jape,** joke. **145 syk,** sigh. **147 disese,** discomfort. **150 pleyde ... gunnen wade,** bantered (chaffed); i.e., began to discuss. **151 unkouth, glad, and dep matere,** unfamiliar, joyous, and serious subject. **152 yfere,** together. **154 townes wal ... Grekes yerde,** i.e., protection of Troy, scourge of the Greeks. **159 alle:** A *every.* **161 fredom,** generosity. **162 em ... lyketh,** uncle, pleases. **163 faren wel,** do well. **164 gret deynte,** very estimable. **166 condicions therto,** character also. **168 o ... yfere,** one, together. **175 konne,** can do. **178 welle,** wellspring (source). **179 wel more,** even more. **181 pris,** worth. **182 swyche tweye,** such two. **184 trowe I,** I believe. **185 dredeles,** doubtless. **188 prys,** praise. **189 me were levest,** I would be happiest to be praised by. **193 ben,** bees. **194 Ne fleygh ... gonne ... flen,** never flew, as fled. **195 ere,** ear. **199 hym/hym:** MC hem/hem.

Ay wher he wente, it was arayed thus: 200
He was hire deth, and lyf and sheld for us;
That al that day ther dorste noon withstonde,
Whil that he held his blody swerd in honde.

"Therto he is the frendlyeste man
Of gret estat that evere I sawh my lyve,   205
And wher hym lyst, best felawshipe kan
To suche as hym thenketh able for to thryve."
And with that word tho Pandarus as blyve
He tok his leve and seyde, "I wol go henne."
"Nay, blame have I, myn uncle," quod she
    thenne.   210

"What eyleth yow to be thus wery soone,
And namelych of womman? Wol ye so?
Nay, sitteth down. By God, I have to done
With yow, to speke of wysdom er ye go."
And every wight that was aboute hem tho,   215
That herde that gan fer awey to stonde,
Whil they two hadde al that hem liste yn
    honde.

Whan that hire tale al brought was to an ende
Of hire estat and of hire governaunce,
Quod Pandarus, "Now is it tyme I wende.   220
But yet, I say, aryseth and lat us daunce,
And cast youre wydewes habit to myschaunce.
What lyst yow thus youreself to disfigure,
Sith yow is tyd thus faire an aventure?"   224

"A, wel bithought, for love of God," quod she,
"Shal I nat wete what ye mene of this?"
"No, this thyng axeth layser," tho quod he,
"And eke me wolde muche greve, iwys,
If I it tolde, and ye it toke amys.

Yet were it bet my tonge for to stille   230
Than sey a soth that were ayeyns youre
    wylle.

"For, nece, by the goddesse Mynerve,
And Juppiter that maketh the thonder rynge,
And by the blysful Venus that I serve,
Ye be the womman in this world
    lyvynge—   235
Withoute paramours to my wyttynge—
That I best love and lothest am to greve,
And that ye wete wel yourself, I leve."

"Iwis, myn uncle," quod she, "grant mercy,
Youre frendshipe have I founden evere yit.   240
I am to no man holden, trewely,
So muche as yow, and have so litel quyt,
And with the grace of God, emforth my wit,
As in my gilt I shal yow nevere offende,
And yf I have er this, I wol amende.   245

"But, for the love of God, I yow biseche,
As ye ben he that most I love and triste,
Lat be to me youre fremde manere speche,
And sey to me, youre nece, what yow lyste."
And with that word hire uncle anoon hire kiste,
And seyde, "Gladly, leve nece dere;   251
Tak it for good that I shal sey yow here."

With that she gan hire eyen down to caste,
And Pandarus to koghe gan a lyte,
And seyde, "Nece, alwey, lo, to the laste,   255
How so it be that som men hem delite
With subtil art hire tales for to endite,
Yet for al that in hire entencioun
Hire tale is al for som conclusioun.

---

202 *al:* C&c *as.* **206 wher hym lyst . . . kan,** where he wants to, can (show). M *wher that.* **207 able . . . to thryve,** able to prosper (i.e., competent, deserving). **208 as blyve,** promptly. **212 namelych,** especially. *womman:* C&c *wommen.* **214 wysdom,** serious business. **215** *tho:* M&c *two.* **217 hadde al that hem liste yn honde,** concerned themselves with what they wished. **219 hire governaunce,** her (household) management. **220** A *Now, quod Pandarus, is it tyme.* **222 to myschaunce,** i.e., bad luck to it. **223 What lyst,** why do you wish. **224 tyd . . . aventure,** befallen, happening. **225 A, wel bithought,** i.e., ah, a happy thought. **226 wete,** know. **227 layser,** leisure. **231 soth,** truth. **232 Mynerve,** Minerva, goddess of wisdom. **236 paramours,** Skeat proposed "excepting sweethearts," but other eds. prefer "having no lover(s)" cf. l. 241. **wyttynge,** knowledge. **238 wete . . . leve,** know, believe. **240 founden,** i.e., found secure. **241 holden,** beholden (owe so much). **242 quyt,** repaid. **243 emforth,** to the extent of. **244 As in . . . gilt,** i.e., purposely. **245 amende,** made amends. **247 triste,** trust. **248 fremde,** strange (obscure). *fremde:* MC&c *frend/frendly.* **249 yow lyste,** pleases you. **251 leve,** dear. **255 to the laste,** i.e., in the end. M *lo* om. **257 endite,** compose. **259 conclusioun,** purpose, point.

"And sithen the ende is every tales strengthe,
And this matere is so byhovely,   261
What sholde I poynte or drawen it on lenghthe
To yow that ben my frend so feithfully?"
And with that word he gan right inwardly
Byholden hire and loken on hire face,   265
And seyde, "On suche a mirour, goode grace!"

Thanne thought he thus: "Yf I my tale endite
Ought hard, or make a proces ony while,
She shal no savour han theryn but lite,
And trowe I wold hire in my wyl bygile,   270
For tendre wittes wenen al be wyle
Thereas they kan not pleynly understonde.
Forthi hire wit to serven wol I fonde."

And loked on hire yn a besy wyse,
And she was war that he byheld hire so,   275
And seyde, "Lord, so faste ye me avyse!
Sey ye me nevere er now? What, sey ye no?"
"Yes, yes," quod he, "and bet wole er I go.
But be my trowthe, I thoughte now yf ye
Be fortunat, for now men shal it se;   280

"For to every wight som goodly aventure
Som tyme is shape, if he it kan receyven.
And if that he wol take of it no cure
Whan that it cometh, but wylfully it weyven,
Lo, neyther cas nor fortune hym deseyven,   285
But right his verray slouthe and wrecched-
        nesse—
And swich a wyght is for to blame, I gesse.

"Good aventure, O bele nece, have ye
Ful lightly founden, and ye konne it take;
And for the love of God, and ek of me,   290
Cache it anoon lest aventure slake.

What sholde I lenger proces of it make?
Yif me youre hond, for yn this world is noon—
If that yow lyst—a wyght so wel bygon.

"And sith I speke of good entencioun,   295
As I to yow have told wel heretoforn,
And love as wel youre honour and renoun
As creature yn al this world yborn,
By alle the othes that I have yow sworn,
And ye be wroth therfore, or wene I lye,   300
Ne shal I nevere seen yow eft with eye.

"Beth nought agast, ne quaketh not. Wherto?
Ne chaungeth not for fere so youre hewe.
For hardely the werst of this is do,
And though my tale as now be to yow
        newe,   305
Yet trist alwey ye shal me fynde trewe.
And were it thyng that me thoughte unsittynge,
To yow nolde I no such tales brynge."

"Now, good em, for Goddes love, I prey,"
Quod she, "com of, and telle me what it is.   310
For both I am agast what ye wol sey,
And ek me longeth it to wyte, ywys;
For whether it be wel or be amys,
Say on, lat me not yn this fere dwelle."
"So wol I don; now herkeneth. I shal yow
        telle: 315

"Now, nece myn, the kynges dere sone,
The goode, wyse, worthi, fresshe, and fre,
Which alwey for to don wel is his wone,
The noble Troylus, so loveth the,
That, bot ye helpe, it wol his bane be.   320
Lo, here is al. What sholde I more seye?
Doth what yow lyst to make hym lyve or deye.

---

261 byhovely, beneficial. **262 poynte**, expatiate. C&c *peynte*. **264 inwardly**, deeply, intensely. **267–68 endite/Ought hard**, make it complicated. **268 proces ony while**, make a long story of it. **269 savour . . . lite**, pleasure, little. **270 trowe . . . wyl bygile**, believe, intentionally deceive. **271 wenen al be wyle**, think everything is deception. **272 Thereas**, which. **273 Forthi . . . fonde**, therefore, try. **274 besy**, intent. **276 faste . . . avyse**, steadily, stare at. M *faste* om. **277 Sey . . . sey**, saw, say. **278 bet**, better. **279 thoughte**, wondered. **282 shape**, designed. **283 cure**, care (advantage). *And:* M *But*. **284 wylfully . . . weyven**, deliberately, ignore. *weyven:* M *weylen*. **285 cas**, luck. **286 right his verray**, i.e., but his very own. **289 lightly**, easily, without effort on your part. **291 anoon . . . aventure slake**, immediately, fortune wane. *Cache it:* A *Takith*. **294 lyst . . . wel bygon**, are pleased, fortunate. **295 of**, with. **300 And ye . . . wene**, if you, think. **301 eft**, again. **302 agast . . . Wherto**, frightened, What for? **303 chaungeth . . . hewe**, i.e., blush and grow pale. **304 hardely . . . do**, truly, done. **305 as now**, at present, just now. **306 trewe**, dependable. **307 unsittynge**, unfitting. **311 agast**, afraid. **312 wyte**, know. **318 wone**, habit. **320 bane**, death.

"But if yow late hym deye, I wol sterve.
Have here my trouthe, nece, I nel not lyen,
Al sholde I with this knyf my throte kerve."
With that the teres braste out of his eyen,   326
And seyde, "Yf that ye doon us bothe dyen,
Thus gilteles, than have ye fysshed faire.
What mende ye though that we both apeyre?

"Allas, he which that is my lord so dere,   330
That trewe man, that noble, gentil knyght,
That nought desireth but youre frendly chere,
I se hym deye ther he goth upright,
And hasteth hym with al his fulle myght
For to be slayn, yf fortune wole assente.   335
Allas, that God yow swich a beaute sente!

"If it be so that ye so cruel be
That of his deth yow lyst nought to recche—
That is so trewe and worthi, as ye se—
No more than of a japere or a wrecche,   340
If it be swych, youre beaute may nat strecche
To make amendes of so cruel a dede.
Avysement is good byfore the nede.

"Wo worth the faire gemme vertules!
Wo worth that herbe also that doth no bote!
Wo worth that beaute that is routheles!   346
Wo worth that wight that tret ech under fote!
And ye that ben of beaute crop and rote,
If therwithal in you there be no routhe,
Than is it harm ye lyven, by my trouthe.   350

"And also thenk wel that this is no gaude;
For me were levere thow and I and he
Were hanged than I sholde be his baude,
As heygh as men myghte on us alle yse.

I am thyn em; the shame were to me   355
As wel as the, yf that I sholde assente
Thorugh myn abet that he thyn honour shente.

"Now understonde, for I yow nought requere
To bynde yow to hym thorugh no beheste,
But oonly that ye make hym bettre chere   360
Than ye han don er this, and more feste,
So that his lyf be saved atte leste—
This al and som and playnly oure entente.
God help me so, I nevere other mente!

"Lo, this requeste is not but skyle, ywys,   365
Ne doute of reson, pardee, is ther noon.
I sette the worste that ye dredden this:
Men wolden wondren to se hym come or goon.
Ther-ayens answere I thus anoon,
That every wight, but he be fool of kynde,   370
Wol deme it love of frendshipe yn his mynde.

"What, who wol demen though he se a man
To temple go that he th'ymages eteth?
Thenk ek how wel and wysely that he kan   374
Governe hymself, that he nothyng foryeteth,
That wher he cometh, he prys and thank hym
    geteth.
And ek therto he shal come here so selde,
What fors were it though al the town behelde?

"Swych love of frendes regneth al this town!
And wre yow yn that mantel everemo,   380
And, God so wys be my salvacioun,
As I have seyd, youre beste is to do so.
But alwey, goode nece, to stynte his wo,
So lat youre daunger sucred ben a lyte,
That of his deth ye be nought for to wyte."   385

323 **sterve**, die. 324 **trouthe . . . nel**, promise, will not. 325 **Al sholde I**, even if I should have to. M *my owene throte.* 327 **doon us**, make us. 328 **fysshed faire**, fished well (i.e., made a great catch). 329 **mende . . . apeyre**, profit, perish. 332 **chere**, expression. 333 **ther he goth**, where he walks. 335 C&c *yf his fortune assente.* 338 **recche**, care. 339 *ye:* some MSS *we.* 340 **japere**, trickster. 343 **Avysement**, forethought. 344 **Wo worth**, woe be to. **gemme . . . vertules**, jewels were thought to possess magic power. 345 **bote**, cure. 346 **routheles**, pitiless. 347 **tret ech**, treads everyone. 348 **crop**, leaves (top). 349 **routhe**, pity. 350 M *that ye lyven.* 351 **gaude**, trick. 353 **baude**, procurer. 355 **em**, uncle. 357 **abet . . . shente**, assistance, destroyed. 359 **beheste**, promise. 360 **bettre chere**, more favor. 361 **feste**, encouragement. 363 **al and som**, entire sum. A *This is al.* 365 **skyle**, reasonable. 366 **reson:** some MSS *tresoun.* 370 **fool of kynde**, a born idiot. 371 **deme**, judge. 372 M *What* om. 375 **Governe . . . nothyng foryeteth**, control, never forgets (himself). 376 **prys**, praise. 377 **therto . . . selde**, in addition, seldom. 378 **What fors**, what matter. *though:* A *if.* 379 **regneth**, exists throughout. 380 **wre**, wrap (conceal). 382 **beste**, i.e., best course. 383 **stynte**, in order to stop. 384 **daunger sucred**, aloofness sugared (sweetened). 385 **wyte**, blame.

Criseyde, which that herd hym yn this wyse,
Thought, "I shal fele what he meneth, ywis."
"Now, em," quod she, "what wole ye devyse?
What is youre red I shal don of this?"
"That is wel seyd," quod he, "certayn, best is
That ye hym love ayen for his lovynge,   391
As love for love is skylful guerdonynge.

"Thenk ek how elde wasteth every houre
In eche of yow a partie of beaute;
And therfore, er that age the devoure,   395
Go love; for olde, ther wil no wight of the.
Lat this proverbe a lore unto yow be:
To late ywar, quod beaute whan it paste,
For elde daunteth daunger at the laste.

"The kynges fool is wonted to cryen lowde   400
Whan that hym thenketh a womman bereth
     hire heighe,
'So longe mot ye lyve, and alle prowde,
Til crowes feet be growen under youre eye,
And sende yow thanne a myrrour yn to prye
In which that ye may se youre face a-morwe.'
Nece, I bidde, wisshe yow no more sorwe."   406

With this he stente, and caste adown the hed,
And she bygan to breste a-wepe anoon,
And seyde, "Allas for wo, why nere I ded?
For of this world the feyth is al agoon.   410
Allas, what sholde straunge to me doon,
Whan he that for my beste frend y wende
Ret me to love, and sholde it me defende?

"Allas, I wolde han trusted, douteles,
That if that I thurgh my disaventure   415

Had loved other hym or Achilles,
Ector, or ony mannes creature,
Ye nolde han had no mercy ne mesure
On me, but alwey had me in repreve.
This false world, allas, who may it leve?   420

"What, is this al the joye and al the feste?
Is this youre red? Is thys my blyssful cas?
Is this the verray mede of youre byheste?
Is al this peynted proces seyd, allas,
Right for this fyn? O lady myn, Pallas,   425
Thow in this dredful cas for me purveye,
For so astoned am I that I deye."

Wyth that she gan ful sorwfully to syke.
"Ay, may it be no bet?" quod Pandarus.   429
"By God, I shal no more come here this wyke,
And God toforn, that am mystrusted thus.
I se ful wel that ye sette lite of us,
Or of oure deth. Allas, I, woful wrecche!
Might he yet lyve, of me is nought to recche.

"O cruel god, O dispitouse Marte,   435
O Furyes thre of helle, on yow I crye!
So lat me nevere out of this hous departe
If I mente harm or ony vilenye!
But sith I se my lord mot nedes dye,
And I with hym, here I me shryve, and seye
That wikkedly ye don us bothe deye.   441

"But sith it lyketh yow that I be ded,
By Neptunus, that god is of the se,
Fro this forth shal I nevere eten bred
Til I myn owen herte blood may se.   445
For certayn I wol deye as sone as he."

387 *he:* some MSS *ye.* 388 **devyse,** recommend. 389 **red,** advice. 392 **skylful guerdonynge,** reasonable recompense. 393 **elde wasteth,** age destroys. 396 **Go love,** one of the oldest of poetic commonplaces: "Gather ye rosebuds . . ." 397 **lore,** lesson. 398 **ywar,** made aware (warned). 399 **daunteth daunger,** overcomes aloofness. 400 **is wonted,** is in the habit of. 401 **hym thenketh . . . bereth hire heighe,** it seems to him, behaves arrogantly. 402 **mot . . . alle prowde,** may, always be proud. 404 **prye,** peer. 405 **a-morwe,** in the morning. 406 **bidde, wisshe yow,** pray, wish yourself. 407 **stente,** stopped. 408 **breste a-wepe,** burst out weeping. 411 **straunge,** strangers. 412 **wende,** considered. 413 **Ret . . . defende,** advises, forbid. 416 **other hym,** i.e., either Troylus. 419 **repreve,** reproof. 420 **leve,** believe. 421 **feste,** delight. *this:* M *that.* 422 **red . . . blyssful cas,** advice, happy situation. 423 **verray mede . . . byheste,** real fulfillment, promise. 424 **peynted proces,** painted (i.e., sham, not real) argument. 425 **fyn,** conclusion (objective). **Pallas,** Pallas Athene, goddess of wisdom (same as the Roman goddess Minerva). 426 **purveye,** provide. 428 **syke,** sigh. 429 *Ay:* C&c *A.* 430 **wyke,** week. 431 **God toforn,** before God. 432 **sette lite,** think little of. 434 **Might he . . . to recche,** if he might, no one should care. 435 **dispitouse Marte,** pitiless Mars, god of war; Troylus is, after all, in daily combat, and the sex-death syndrome (*eros-thanatos*) of the romance tradition lies behind this narrative. 438 MC&c *If that.* 439 **sith . . . mot,** since, must. 440 **shryve,** confess myself (to receive absolution). 441 **don,** cause. 442 **lyketh yow,** pleases you.

And up he sterte and on his weye he raughte
Til she hym agayn by the lappe caughte.

Criseyde, which that wel neigh starf for fere,
So as she was the ferfulleste wyght   450
That myghte be, and herde ek with hire ere,
And saw the sorwful ernest of the knyght,
And in his preyer eke saw noon unright,
And for the harm that myghte ek fallen more,
She gan to rewe and dradde hire wonder
           sore,   455

And thoughte thus, "Unhappes fallen thikke
Alday for love, and in such manere cas
As men ben cruel yn hemself and wykke.
And yf this man sle here hymself, allas,
In my presence, it wyl be no solas.   460
What men of hit wolde deme I kan nat seye:
It nedeth me ful sleyghly for to pleye."

And with a sorowful syk she sayde thrie,
"A, Lord, what me is tyd a sory chaunce!
For myn estat now lyth in jupartie,   465
And ek myn emes lif lyth in balaunce.
But natheles, with Goddes governaunce,
I shal don so myn honour shal I kepe,
And ek his lyf"—and stynte for to wepe.

"Of harmes two, the lesse is for to chese.   470
Yet have I levere maken hym good chere
In honour than myn emes lyf to lese—
Ye seyn ye nothyng elles me requere?"
"No, ywys," quod he, "myn owene nece
           dere."
"Now wel," quod she, "and I wol don my
           peyne.   475
I shal myn herte ayens my lust constreyne.

"But that I nyl not holden hym yn honde,
Ne love a man ne kan I not ne may
Ayens my wil; but elles wol I fonde,
Myn honour sauf, plesen hym fro day to day.
Therto nolde I nought onys have seyd nay   481
But that I drede, as yn my fantasye.
But cesseth cause, ay cesseth maladye.

"And here I make a protestacioun,
That yn this proces yf ye depper go,   485
That certaynly for no salvacioun
Of yow, though that ye sterve bothe two,
Though al the world on o day be my fo,
Ne shal I nevere on hym han other routhe."
"I graunte wel," quod Pandare, "by my
           trouthe.   490

"But may I truste wel therto," quod he,
"That of this thyng that ye han hight me
           here,
Ye wole it holden trewly unto me?"
"Ye, doutlees," quod she, "myn uncle dere."
"Ne that I shal han cause in this matere,"   495
Quod he, "to pleyne, or ofter yow to preche?"
"Why no, parde, what nedeth more speche?"

Tho fillen thei yn other tales glade,
Til at the laste, "O good em," quod she tho,
"For his love which that us bothe made,   500
Tel me how first ye wysten of his wo.
Wot noon of hit but ye?"—He seyde, "No."—
"Kan he wel speke of love?" quod she. "I preye,
Tel me for I the bet me shal purveye."

Tho Pandarus a litel gan to smyle,   505
And seyde, "By my trouthe, I shal yow telle.
This other day nought go ful longe while,

447 **raughte,** started off (reached). 448 **agayn . . . lappe caughte,** pulled him back by the hanging part of the garment (hem, sleeve). 449 **starf,** died. 452 **ernest,** serious(ness). 455 **rewe,** be sorry. 456 **Unhappes,** misfortunes. 457 **such manere cas,** such situations. 460 **solas,** comfort, relief. 461 **deme,** judge. 462 **sleyghly . . . pleye,** cautiously, act (play). 463 **syk . . . thrie,** sigh, three times. 464 **tyd,** befallen. 465 **estat,** condition. 466 *lyth:* C&c *is* (or om.). 467 **governaunce,** guidance. *Goddes:* in some A MSS *good.* 468–69 **kepe . . . stynte,** protect, stopped. 470 **for to chese,** i.e., the one to choose. 471 **levere,** rather. *have:* other MSS *hadde.* 473 **me,** i.e., of me. 474 C&c *No wis.* 475 **my peyne,** i.e., make an effort. 476 **lust,** desire. 477 **holden . . . yn honde,** deceive. 478 *a man:* two A MSS *no man;* A *that can no wight.* 479 **elles . . . fonde,** aside from that, try. *my:* A&c *his.* 480 **plesen,** to please. 481 **Therto nolde . . . onys,** to that I would not, once. 482 **drede . . . fantasye,** was afraid, imagination. 483 **cesseth,** i.e., when the cause ceases. 485 **proces,** matter. 487 **sterve,** die. 489 **routhe,** i.e., greater pity. 492 **hight,** promised. 496 **pleyne . . . ofter,** complain, more often. 498 **tales glade,** cheerful conversation. 501 **wysten,** learned. 502 **Wot,** know. 504 **purveye,** prepare. 505 M *bygan for to.*

In-with the paleys gardyn by a welle,
Gan he and I wel half a day to dwelle,
Right for to speken of an ordinaunce 510
How we the Grekes myghten disavaunce.

"Soon after that bigonne we to lepe,
And casten with oure dartes to and fro,
Tyl at the laste he seyde he wolde slepe,
And on the gres adoun he leyde hym tho. 515
And I afer gan romen to and fro,
Til that I herd, as that I welk allone,
How he bygan ful wofully to grone.

"Tho gan I stalke softly hym byhynde,
And sikerly, the sothe for to seyne, 520
As I kan clepe ayen now to my mynde,
Right thus to Love he gan hym for to pleyne:
He seyde, 'Lord, have routhe upon my peyne,
Al have I ben rebel yn myn entente.
Now, *mea culpa*, lord, I me repente. 525

" 'O god, that at thi disposicioun
Ledest the fyn—by juste purveyaunce—
Of every wyght, my lowe confessioun
Accepte in gre, and sende me swych penaunce
As liketh the; but from desesperaunce 530
That may my gost departe awey fro the,
Thow be my sheld for thy benignite.

" 'For certes, lord, so sore hath she me
      wounded,
That stod in blak, wyth lokyng of hire eyen,
That to myn hertes botme it is ysounded, 535
Thorugh which I wot that I mot nedes deyen.

This is the werste, I dar me not bywreyen,
And wel the hotter ben the gledes rede
That men hem wrien with asshen pale and
      dede.'

"Wyth that he smot adown his hed anoon, 540
And gan to motre, I not what, trewly.
And I awey with that stille gan to goon,
And let therof as nothyng wyst hadde I,
And com ayen anoon, and stod hym by,
And seyde, 'Awake, ye slepen al to longe. 545
It semeth not that love doth yow longe,

" 'That slepen so that no man may yow wake.
Who sey evere er this so dul a man?'
'Ye, frend,' quod he, 'do ye yowre hedes ake
For love, and lat me lyven as I kan.' 550
But though that he for wo was pale and wan,
Yet made he tho as fressh a countenaunce
As though he shulde have led the newe daunce.

"This passed forth til now this other day
It fel that I com romynge al allone 555
Into his chaumbre, and fond how that he lay
Upon his bed; but man so sore grone
Ne herd I nevere, and what that was his mone
Ne wyst I nought, for as I was comynge
Al sodeynly he lefte his compleynynge. 560

"Of which I tok somwhat suspecioun,
And ner I com, and fond he wepte sore;
And God so wys be my salvacioun,
As nevere of thyng hadde I no routhe more.
For neither with engyn ne with no lore 565

508 **paleys gardyn,** this account is not mentioned at 1.547ff. Perhaps it really happened, or perhaps—as is amply demonstrated as the narrative proceeds—one of Pandarus' characteristics is his proclivity for invention even when the truth would do just as well. 510 **ordinaunce,** plan. 511 **disavaunce,** set back. 513 **casten … dartes,** throw spears. 516 **afer,** afar. MC&c *therafter/aftir.* 520 **sikerly,** truly. 521 **clepe,** call. 523 **routhe,** pity. 525 *mea culpa,* I am at fault, a stock phrase of the confessional formula. Pandarus has Troylus making a confession in the tradition of the religion of love. Gower's *Confessio Amantis* is an extended application of the device. 526 **god … disposicioun,** the god of love, disposal. 527 **Ledest the fyn … purveyaunce,** determine the conclusion, predestination. 528 **wyght … lowe,** creature, humble. 529 **in gre,** graciously. 530 **liketh the … desesperaunce,** pleases you, despair. 531 **may … gost … departe,** i.e., that my ghost may depart. 532 **benignite,** graciousness. 534–35 **lokyng … eyen … hertes botme … ysounded,** as at 1.305, this again refers to the mysterious beams from Criseyde's eyes that probed (ysounded) Troylus to the bottom of his heart. 536 **wot … mot,** know, must. 537 **This … werste … bywreyen.** The worst of it is, reveal myself. 538 **gledes,** coals. 539 **wrien,** cover. 541 **motre … not,** mutter, know not. 542 C&c *And I with that gan stille away to goon.* 543 **let … wyst,** pretended, been aware. 546 **doth yow longe,** makes you pine (lie awake). 548 **sey … dul,** saw, apathetic. 549 **do ye,** you make. 551 *wo:* some MSS *love.* 552 **made … fressh … countenaunce,** put on, bright, expression. 556 *his:* M *a.* 564 **routhe,** pity. 565 **engyn … lore,** tricks, wisdom.

Unnethes myghte I fro the deth hym kepe,
That yet fele I myn herte for hym wepe.

"And God woot, nevere sith that I was born
Was I so bysy no man for to preche,
Ne nevere to wyght so depe was isworn,   570
Er he me tolde who myghte ben his leche.
But now to yow rehersen al his speche,
Or alle his woful wordes for to sowne,
Ne bid me not, but ye wol se me swowne.

"But for to save his lif, and elles nought,   575
And to noon harm of yow, thus am I dreven.
And for the love of God, that us hath wrought,
Swych cher hym doth that he and I may lyven!
Now have I plat to yow myn herte shryven,
And syn ye wot that myn entent is clene,   580
Take hede therof, for I noon yvel mene.

"And right good thryft I pray to God have ye,
That han swych on ycaught withoute net.
And be ye wys as ye ben fair to se,
Wel yn the ryng than is the ruby set.   585
There were nevere two so wel imet,
Whanne ye ben his al hool as he is youre—
Ther myghty God yet graunte us se that
     houre!"

"Nay, therof spak I not, ha, ha!" quod she.
"As helpe me God, ye shenden every deel."   590
"O, mercy, dere nece," anoon quod he,
"What so I spak, I mente nought but wel,
By Mars, the god that helmed is of stel,
Now beth nought wroth, my blod, my nece
     dere."   594
"Now, wel," quod she, "foryeven be it here."

With this he tok his leve, and home he wente,
And, Lord so he was glad and wel bygon.
Criseyde aros, no lenger she ne stente,
But streght into hire closet wente anoon,
And sette hire down as stille as ony ston,   600
And every word gan up and down to wynde
That he hadde seyd, as it com hire to mynde;

And was somdel astonyed in hire thought
Right for the newe cas. But whanne that she
Was ful avised, tho fond she right nought   605
Of peril why she ought afered be.
For a man may love of possibilite
A womman so his herte may tobreste,
And she naught love ayen but yf hire leste.

But as she sat allone and thoughte thus,   610
Ascry aros at skarmyssh al withoute,
And men cryde in the strete, "Se, Troylus
Hath right now put to flighte the Grekes route!"
With that gan al hire meyne for to shoute,
"A, go we se! Cast up the yates wyde!   615
For thurgh this strete he mot to palays ryde.

"For other weye is fro the yate noon
Of Dardanus, there opyn is the cheyne."
With that come he and al his folk anoon,
An esy pas rydynge yn routes tweyne,   620
Right as his happy day was, soth to seyne,
For which men sayn may nought disturbed be
That shal bytyden of necessitee.

This Troylus sat on his baye stede,
Al armed, save his hed, ful richely,   625
And wounded was his hors, and gan to blede,
On which he rod a pas ful softely.

---

570 **isworn,** i.e., committed to help him. 571 **leche,** physician. 575 **elles nought,** nothing else. 578 **cher hym doth,** favor show to him. 579 **plat . . . shryven,** openly, confessed. 582 **thryft,** success. 587 **al hool,** wholly. 588 *yet graunte:* C&c *yet* om., with various readings, e.g., *to see.* 589 **spak,** spoke. M *ha, ha* om. 590 **shenden every deel,** spoil everything. 597 **wel bygon,** well pleased. MC&c *so* om. 598 **stente,** stopped, waited. 599 **closet,** private room. 601 **wynde,** i.e., turn over. 603 **astonyed,** astonished (amazed). *was:* A *wax.* 604 **cas,** situation. 605 **Was ful avised,** had considered fully. 607 *a man:* MC&c *a* om. 608 **tobreste,** break into pieces. 611 **Ascry . . . skarmyssh,** outcry, skirmish. The ensuing scene, ll. 603–94, is Chaucer's insertion at *Fil.* 2.68. 613 **route,** troop. 614 **meyne,** household. 615 **Cast up . . . yates,** open, gates. Root remarks that *latis* (lattice) would fit better with *cast up*; but this reading is found in only one unreliable MS. 618 *Dardanus:* M *Gardanus.* 620 **esy pas . . . routes tweyne,** easy pace, two companies. 621 **happy day,** fortunate day. 622 **disturbed,** hindered. 623 **bytyden,** befall; again the fortune-destiny motif is emphasized by Chaucer. 624 *This:* M *Thus.* 626 **wounded was his hors,** the sex-death imagery is overt in this striking passage. The details of wounds and blood are transferred from Troylus to his accoutrements, leaving his body unimpaired "To don that thing" (l. 634). See also l. 435 and note.

But swich a knyghtly sighte trewely
As was on hym was nought, withouten faile,
To loke on Mars that god is of bataile.　　　630

So lyk a man of armes and a knyght
He was to sen, fulfild of heigh prowesse;
For bothe he hadde a body and a myght
To don that thing, as wel as hardynesse;
And ek to sen hym yn his gere hym dresse,　635
So fressh, so yong, so weldy semed he,
It was an hevene upon hym for to se.

His helm tohewen was yn twenty places,
That by a tissew heng his bak byhynde;
His sheld todasshed was with swerdes and
　　　maces,　　　640
In which men myghte many an arwe fynde
That thirlled hadde horn and nerf and
　　　rynde;
And ay the peple cryde, "Here cometh oure
　　　joye,
And next his brother, holder up of Troye!"

For which he wex a litel reed for shame,　645
Whan he the peple upon hym herde cryen,
That to biholde it was a noble game,
How sobrelich he caste doun his eyen.
Cryseyde gan al his chere aspien,
And let it so softe yn hire herte synke,　650
That to hireself she seyde, "Who yaf me
　　　drynke?"

For of hire owene thought she wex al red,
Remembryng hire right thus, "Lo, this is he
Which that myn uncle swereth he mot be ded,
But I on hym have mercy and pite."　655
And with that thought for pure ashamed she

Gan in hire hed to pulle, and that as faste,
Whil he and al the peple forby paste;

And gan to caste and rollen up and down
Withinne hire thought his excellent
　　　prowesse,　　　660
And his estat, and also his renoun,
His wit, his shap, and ek his gentillesse,
But most hir favour was for his distresse
Was al for hire, and thoughte it was a
　　　routhe
To slen swich oon, yf that he mente trouthe.

Now myghte som envious jangle thus,　666
"This was a sodeyn love. How myght it be
That she so lightly loved Troylus,
Right for the firste syghte, ye, parde?"
Now whoso seith so, mot he nevere the!　670
For everythyng a gynnyng hath it nede
Er al be wrought, withouten ony drede.

For I sey nought that she so sodeynly
Yaf hym hire love, but that she gan enclyne
To lyke hym first, and I have told yow
　　　why.　　　675
And after that, his manhod and his pyne
Made love withinne hire herte for to myne,
For which by proces and by good servise
He gat hire love, and in no sodeyn wyse.

And also blisful Venus wel arayed　680
Sat in hire seventhe hows of hevene tho,
Disposed wel and with aspectes payed,
To helpen sely Troilus of his wo.
And soth to seyn she nas not al a fo
To Troilus in his natyvite;　685
God wot that wel the sonner spedde he.

634 hardynesse, spirit. **636 weldy,** vigorous. *weldy:* B&c *worthy.* **638 tohewen,** hacked open. **640 todasshed ... maces,** badly battered, spiked war clubs. **642 thirlled,** pierced. **horn ... nerf ... rynde,** bone, sinew, skin; these painfully physical particulars were the actual components of a shield. M *thrilled.* **646** A&c *Whan he so herd the peple on hym crien.* **649 chere,** appearance. C&c *Criseyda;* A *Cryseyd.* **650** Some MSS *so softe it.* **651 hireself:** M *hirselven.* **653 Remembryng,** reflecting. **658 forby paste,** passed by. M *forth by.* **659 caste,** consider. **663 for his,** because. **664 routhe,** pity. **665 mente trouthe,** had honest intentions. **666 envious jangle,** envious person complain. **668 lightly,** easily. **670 mot ... the,** may, prosper. C&c *ythe* (from OE *geþēon*). **672 drede,** doubt. **676 pyne,** pain. **677 myne,** mine (burrow). MC&c *herte* om. **678 by proces,** in time. **679 gat:** A&c *wan.* **680 arayed,** situated. **681 seventhe hows,** the portion of the heavens just above the western horizon, presided over by Venus. But note that at v.1016ff. Venus is quite impartial, and encourages the consummation of any love. **682 aspectes payed,** the positions (aspects) of other planets were disposed favorably toward Venus. **683 sely,** foolish, but this is a word with varying connotations in ME. OE *gesælig* (blessed) came to mean blessed, innocent, and finally foolish. It could have the full range, or any part of it, in ME. **686 spedde,** succeeded.

Now lat us stynte of Troylus a throwe,
That rideth forth, and lat us tourne faste
Unto Criseyde that heng hire hed ful lowe
Ther as she sat allone, and gan to caste 690
Whereon she wolde apoynte hire atte laste,
If it so were hire em ne wolde cesse
For Troilus upon hire for to presse.

And Lord, so she gan in hire thought argue
In this matere of which I have yow told, 695
And what to done best were, and what eschue,
That plited she ful ofte in many folde;
Now was hire herte warm, now was it colde.
And what she thoughte, somwhat shal I write,
As to myn auctour lysteth for to endite. 700

She thoughte wel that Troylus persone
She knew by sighte, and ek his gentilesse,
And thus she seyde, "Al were it nat to done
To graunte hym love, yet for his worthynesse
It were honour with pley and with gladnesse
In honeste with swych a lord to dele, 706
For myn estat, and also for his hele.

"Ek wel wot I my kynges sone is he;
And sith he hath to se me swych delit,
If I wolde outreliche his sighte flee, 710
Peraunter he myghte have me in dispit,
Thorugh which I myghte stonde in worse plyt.
Now were I wys me hate to purchace
Withouten nede there I may stonde in grace?

"In everythyng I wot, there lith mesure. 715
For though a man forbede dronkenesse,
He nought forbet that every creature
Be drynkeles for alwey, as I gesse.

Ek sith I wot for me is his distresse,
I ne oughte nat for that thyng hym despise, 720
Sith it is so he meneth in good wyse.

"And eke I knowe of longe tyme agon
His thewes goode, and that he is nat nyse.
Ne avaunter, certeyn, seyth men, is he non;
To wys is he to doon so gret a vyse— 725
Ne als I nel hym nevere so cherise
That he may make avaunt by juste cause.
He shal me nevere bynde in swich a clause.

"Now sette a cas: the hardest is, ywys,
Men myghten demen that he loveth me. 730
What dishonour were it unto me, this?
May ich hym lette of that? Why, nay, parde!
I knowe also, and alday heere and se,
Men loven women al byside hire leve, 734
And whanne hem leste no more, lat hem byleve.

"I thenke ek how he able is for to have
Of al this noble town the thryftiest
To ben his love, so she hire honour save.
For out and out he is the worthyest,
Save only Ector which that is the best; 740
And yet his lif al lyth now in my cure.
But swych is love, and ek myn aventure.

"Ne me to love, a wonder is it nought,
For wel wot I myself, so God me spede—
Al wolde I that noon wyste of this
      thought— 745
I am oon the faireste, out of drede,
And goodliest whoso taketh hede—
And so men seyn—in al the town of Troye.
What wonder is though he of me have joye?

---

687 stynte . . . throwe, stop, while. **690 caste,** consider. The text here returns to *Fil.* 2.69. **691 Whereon . . . apoynte,** i.e., what course she would decide on. **694** M *So she yn thought gan to argue.* **696 eschue,** avoid. **697 plited,** pleated. **700 myn auctour,** actually Chaucer treated Criseyde's internal argument very freely, expanding it from 10 stanzas (80 lines, *Fil.* 2.69–78), to 230 lines (700–931), including Antigone's song (ll. 813ff.) and the dream of the white eagle (ll. 925ff.). **702** M *ek by gentilesse.* **703 nat to done,** i.e., "it won't do." **705 pley . . . gladnesse,** i.e., cheerful exchange of pleasantries. **706 honeste,** decorum. **707 estat . . . hele,** practical advantage, health. **710** *outreliche:* M *uttirly.* **711 dispit,** disfavor. **714 there,** where. **715 wot . . . mesure,** know, moderation. **719** M *Ek for me sith I wot is al his.* **722 eke,** also. **723 thewes . . . nyse,** habits, foolish. **724 avaunter,** boaster (about his amorous conquests). **725 vyse,** vice. **726 als . . . cherise,** also, cherish. M *cherishe.* **729 sette a cas,** imagine a situation. **730 demen,** guess. **732 lette,** prevent. *ich:* M *I.* **734 byside,** without. **735 byleve,** leave, abandon. A *leve.* **736** M&c *for* om. **737 thryftiest,** most attractive. **741 cure,** care. **742 aventure,** fortune. **744 wot I myself,** I know myself. **745 wyste,** knew. **746 oon the . . . drede,** one of the, doubt. **747 goodliest,** most pleasing. **749** M&c *is it/ist.*

"I am myn owene womman, wel at ese—   750
I thank it God—as after myn estat,
Right yong, and stonde untyd in lusty lese,
Withouten jalousye or swich debat.
Shal non housbonde seyn to me "Chekmat."
For either they ben ful of jalousye,   755
Or maisterful, or loven novelrie.

"What shal I don? To what fyn lyve I thus?
Shal I nat love in cas yf that me leste?
What, pardieux, I am not religious!
And though that I myn herte sette at reste   760
Upon this knyght, that is the worthieste,
And kep alwey myn honour and my name,
By alle right, it may do me no shame."

But ryght as whanne the sonne shyneth bright
In March, that chaungeth ofte tyme his face,   765
And that a cloud is put with wynd to flyght,
Which oversprat the sonne as for a space,
A cloudy thought gan thorugh hire soule pace,
That overspradde hire brighte thoughtes alle,
So that for fere almost she gan to falle.   770

That thought was this: "Allas, syn I am fre,
Sholde I now love and put in jupartie
My sikernesse, and thrallen liberte?
Allas, how dorst I thenken that folye?
May I naught wel in other folk aspie   775
Hire dredfull joye, hire constreynte, and hire
          peyne?
Ther loveth noon, that she nath why to pleyne.

"For love is yet the mooste stormy lyf,
Right to hymself, that evere was bygonne;
For evere som mystrust or nyce stryf   780
Ther is in love, som cloud is over that sonne.

Therto we wrecched wommen nothyng konne,
Whan us is wo, but wepe and sitte and thynke.
Oure wreche is this, oure owen wo to drynke.

"Also these wikked tonges ben so prest   785
To speke us harm; ek men ben so untrewe
That right anoon as sesed is hire lest,
So cesseth love, and forth to love an newe.
But harm idon is don, whoso it rewe;
For though these men for love hem ferst torende,
Ful sharp bygynnyng breketh ofte at ende.   791

"How ofte tyme hath it yknowe be
The treson that to wommen hath ben do.
To what fyn is swych love I kan nat se,
Or wher bycomth it whenne it is ago.   795
Ther is no wyght that wot, I trowe so,
Where it bycometh. Lo, no wyght on it
          sporneth!
That erst was nothyng, into nought it torneth.

"How bysy, if I love, ek most I be   799
To plesen hem that jangle of love and dremen,
And coye hem that they seye noon harm of me.
For though there be no cause, yet hem semen
Al be for harm that folk hire frendes quemen.
And who may stoppen every wikked
          tungen—   804
Or sown of belles, whil that thei be rungen?"

And after that hire thought bygan for to clere,
And seyde, "He which that nothyng under-
          taketh,
Nothyng n'acheveth, be hym loth or dere."
And with another thought hire herte quaketh.
Than slepeth hope, and after drede
          awaketh,   810

---

751 **as after myn estat,** with respect to my wealth. 752 **lusty lese,** pleasant pasture. 756 **novelrie,** novelty, i.e., new women. 757 **fyn,** end. 758 **in case yf . . . me leste,** in the event that it pleases me. 759 **religious,** a nun. 767 **space,** time. 768 *soule,* A&c *herte.* 773 **sikernesse . . . thrallen,** security, enslave. 776 **dredfull,** fearful (because of love's problems). 777 *why:* MC&c *weye.* 778 *mooste:* M *meste.* 780 **nyce,** foolish. 782 **konne,** can do. 784 **wreche,** misery. 785 **prest,** ready. 787 **sesed . . . lest,** ceased (finished), desire. 789 **rewe,** regret. 790 **torende,** tear to pieces. 791 **Ful sharp,** i.e., too eager; apparently a proverb. One MS has the gloss *Acriores in principio franguntur in fine* ("Sharp at the beginning, fragments at the end.") 792 M *knowe.* 794 **fyn,** purpose. 795 **bycomth . . . whenne . . . ago,** what becomes of it, gone. 796 **wot . . . trowe,** knows, believe. 797 **sporneth,** stumbles. 800 **jangle . . . dremen,** gossip, imagine things. *dremen:* A&c *demen* (judge). 801 **coye,** quiet. M *that* om. 803 **quemen,** (do) to please. 805 *whil:* M *whanne.* 808 **hym loth . . . dere,** i.e., be (the outcome) to him pleasant or unpleasant.

Now hot, now cold; but thus, bytwyxen
    tweye,
She rist hire up and went hire for to pleye.

Adoun the steyre anoon-right tho she wente
Into the gardeyn, with hire neces thre,
And up and doun ther made many a wente,
Flexippe, she, Tharbe, and Antigone,   816
To pleyen, that it joye was to se;
And othere of hire wommen a gret rowte
Hire foloweden in the gardeyn al abowte.

This yerd was large, and rayled alle the
    aleyes,   820
And shadwed wel with blosmy bowes grene,
And benched newe, and sonded alle the
    weyes,
In which she walketh arm yn arm bytwene,
Til at the laste Antigone the shene
Gan on a Troian song to syngen clere,   825
That it an heven was hire voys to here.

She seyd, "O Love, to whom I have and shal
Ben humble subgit, trewe yn myn entente,
As I best kan, to yow, lord, yeve ych al,
For everemore, myn herte lust to rente.   830
For nevere yet thi grace no wight sente
So blyssful cause as me my lyf to lede
In alle joye and surete out of drede.

"Ye, blissful god, han me so wel beset
In love, ywys, that al that bereth lyf   835
Ymagynen ne kowde how to ben bet.
For, lord, withouten jalousye or stryf,

I love oon which that is most ententyf
To serven wel, unwery or unfeyned,   839
That evere was, and lest with harm distreyned.

"As he that is the welle of worthinesse,
Of trouthe ground, myrour of goodlyhed,
Of wit Appollo, ston of sikernesse,
Of vertu rote, of lust fyndere and hed,
Thurgh which is alle sorwe fro me ded.   845
Iwys, I love hym best, so doth he me.
Now good thryft have he, wherso that he be!

"Whom sholde I thanken but yow, God of
    Love,
Of al this blysse in which to bathe I gynne?
And thonked be ye, lord, for that I love.   850
This is the righte lyf that I am inne,
To flemen alle manere vice and synne;
This doth me so to vertu for t'entende,
That day by day I in my wil amende.

"And whoso seyth that for to love is vice   855
Or thraldom, though he fele in it destresse,
He outher is envyous or right nyce,
Or is unmyghty for his shrewednesse
To loven. For swich manere folk, I gesse,
Defamen Love as nothing of him knowe;   860
They speken, but they benten nevere his bowe.

"What, is the sonne wers of kynde right
Though that a man, for feeblesse of his eyen,
May nought endure on it to se for bryght?
Or love the wers, though wrecches on it crien?
No wele is worth that may no sorwe dryen.   866

---

812 pleye, relaxation. **813 anoon-right,** promptly. **815 wente,** turn. *ther:* A *they.* The three nieces and their lovely names are Chaucer's addition. **818 rowte,** band. **820 rayled . . . aleyes,** bordered, paths. *yerd:* M *gardeyn.* **821** M *with bowes blosmy and grene.* **822 benched,** provided with turf-covered mounds to sit on. **sonded,** sanded. **824 shene,** fair. **825** *song:* some MSS *lay.* This song, punctuating Criseyde's "consent" to love, parallels Troylus' song at 1.400. But this one can be traced to no definite source, although it somewhat resembles a song in Machaut's *Paradis d'Amour.* **828 subgit,** a humble subject. **829 yeve,** give. **830 herte lust to rente,** heart's joy as tribute. **833 surete out of drede,** security without fear. **834 beset,** settled. **838** *which that:* M *that* om. **840 distreyned,** misled: C&c *disteyned* (stained). **841 welle,** source. **842 ground . . . goodlyhed,** foundation, virtue. **843 Appollo,** god of wisdom. **ston of sikernesse,** rock of reliability. *sikernesse:* M&c *secrenesse.* **844 lust fyndere . . . hed,** pleasure discoverer, source. **847 thryft,** prosperity. **849 Of . . . gynne,** for, begin. **850 for that,** because. **852 flemen,** banish. **857 right nyce,** very foolish. **858 unmyghty . . . shrewednesse,** unable, wickedness. **860** *him:* M&c *it.* **861 benten . . . bowe,** as scribes of some of the MSS recognized, this is a variation on a popular proverb, "Thei spekyn of Robynhod but thei bente never his bowe" (marginal gloss from Harleian 2392). Phillipps 8250 notes in a contemporary hand, "of Robyn hood." **862 What . . . kynde right,** how, proper nature. **864 se for bryght,** look because of brightness. *it:* other MSS *hym.* **866 wele . . . dryen,** prosperity, endure.

And forthi, who that hath an hed of verre,
Fro caste of stones war hym in the werre!

"But I with al myn hert and al my myght,
As I have seyd, wole love unto my laste   870
My dere hert and al myn owen knyght,
In which myn herte growen is so faste,
And his in me, that it shal evere laste.
Al dredde I first to love hym to bygynne,
Now wot I wel ther is no peril inne."   875

And of hire song right with that word she
    stynte.
And therwithal, "Now, nece," quod Criseyde,
"Who made this song now with so good
    entente?"
Antigone answerde anoon and seyde,
"Madame, iwys, the goodlyeste mayde   880
Of gret estat in al the town of Troye,
And led hire lif in most honour and joye."

"Forsothe, so it semeth by hire song,"
Quod tho Criseyde, and gan therwith to syke,
And seyde, "Lord, is ther such blysse
    among   885
These loveres as they konne faire endite?"
"Ye, wys," quod fresshe Antigone the white,
"For alle the folk that han or ben on lyve
Ne konne wel the blysse of love dyscrive.

"But wene ye that every wrecche wot   890
The parfite blysse of love? Whi, nay, ywys.
They wenen al be love yf oon be hot.
Do wey, do wey, they wot nothyng of this!
Men mosten axe at seyntes if it is
Aught faire yn hevene—why? for they kan
    telle—   895
And axen fendes is it foul yn helle."

Criseyde unto that purpos nought answerde,
But seyde, "Ywys, it wole be nyght as faste."
But every word which that she of hire herde
She gan to prenten in hire herte faste,   900
And ay gan love hire lasse for to agaste
Than it dide erst, and synken in hire herte,
That she wax somwhat able to converte.

The dayes honour and the hevenes eye,
The nyghtes fo—al this clepe I the sonne—   905
Gan westren faste and downward for to wrye
As he that hadde his dayes cours yronne,
And white thynges wexen dymme and donne
For lak of lyght, and sterres for to appere,
That she and alle hire folk in went yfere.   910

So whan it liked hire to gon to reste,
And voyded were they that voyden oughte,
She seyde that to slepe wel hire leste.
Hire wommen soone til hire bed hire broughte.
Whan al was hust, thanne lay she stille and
    thoughte   915
Of al this thyng the manere and the wyse—
Reherce it nedeth nought for ye ben wyse.

A nyghtyngale upon a cedre grene
Under the chambre wal there as she lay
Ful loude sang ayen the mone shene,   920
Peraunter, yn his bryddes wyse, a lay
Of love, that made hire herte fressh and gay.
That herkened she so longe yn good entente,
Til at the laste the dede slep hire hente.

And as she slep, anoon-right tho hire mette   925
How that an egle, fethered whit as bon,
Under hire brest his longe clawes sette,
And out hire herte he rente, and that anoon,
And dide his herte into hire brest to goon—

---

867 forthi . . . verre, therefore, glass. *hed,* "helmet," which appears in some other forms of the proverb, might be preferable in context. **868 werre,** battle. **872 faste,** firmly. **876 stynte,** stopped. **878** M&c *now* om. **881 gret estat,** if Antigone means Helen, irony is involved. **884 syke,** sigh. **886 endite,** describe. **887** *wys:* other MSS *ywis.* **890 wene . . . wot,** think, knows. **891** A&c *Whi* om. **892 wenen,** think. **896** *is it:* other MSS *if it be.* **897** Other MSS *therto nothing hir answerde.* **900 prenten . . . faste,** imprint, firmly. **901 agaste,** frighten. **903** *wax:* M *was.* **906 wrye,** turn. **908 donne,** dun (dull gray). **910 That . . . yfere,** so that, together. **911 liked hire,** pleased her. **912 voyded,** departed. **917 wyse,** informed. **920 ayen . . . shene,** in, bright. **921 Peraunter,** perhaps. **922** A&c *love, which that made his herte gay.* **924 hente,** seized. **925 mette,** dreamed. **929 dide . . . goon,** i.e., put his heart in her breast. The dream of the exchange of hearts, a familiar figure in troubadour lyrics, is another Chaucerian addition.

Of which she nought agros, ne nothing
    smerte—   930
And forth he fleygh with herte left for herte.

Now lat hire slepe, and we oure tales holde
Of Troylus, that is to palays ryden
Fro the skarmuch of the which I tolde,
And yn his chaumbre sit and hath abyden   935
Til two or thre of his messages yeden
For Pandarus, and soughten hym ful faste
Til they hym founde and broughte hym at the
    laste.

This Pandarus com lepyng in atones,
And seide thus, "Who hath ben wel ybete   940
Today with swerdes and with slynge-stones,
But Troylus that hath caught hym now an
    hete?"
And gan to jape, and seyde, "Lord, ye so swete!
But rys, and late us soupe and go to reste."
And he answerd hym, "Do we as the leste." 945

With al the haste goodly that they myghte,
They spedde hem fro the soper unto bedde;
And every wyght out at the dore hym dyghte,
And wher hym lyst upon his wey he spedde.
But Troilus, that thoughte his herte bledde   950
For wo til that he herde som tydynge,
He seyde, "Frend, shal I now wepe or synge?"

Quod Pandarus, "Ly stylle and lat us slepe.
And don thyn hod; thy nedes spedde be.
And chese if thow wolt synge or daunce or lepe.
At shorte wordes, thow shalt trowe me: 956
Sire, my nece wol do wel by the,
And love the best, by God and by my trouthe,
But lak of pursuyt make it in thi slouthe.

"For thus ferforth I have thi werk bygonne,
Fro day to day, til this day by the morwe   961
Hire love of frendshipe have I to the wonne,
And also hath she leyd hire feyth to borwe.
Algate a fot is hameled of thi sorwe!"
What sholde I lenger sermon of it holde?   965
As ye han herd byfore, al he hym tolde.

But right as floures, thorugh the cold of nyght
Yclosed, stoupen on hire stalkes lowe,
Redressen hem ayen the sonne bryght,
And spreden on hire kynde cours by rowe,   970
Right so gan tho his eyghen up to throwe
This Troylus, and seyde, "O Venus dere,
Thi myght, thi grace, yhered be it here!"

And to Pandare he held up bothe his hondes,
And seyde, "Lord, al thyn be that I have!   975
For I am hol; al brosten ben my bondes.
A thousand Troyes whoso that me yave,
Ech after other, God so wys me save,
Ne myghte me so gladen. Lo myn herte,
It spredeth so for joye it wol tosterte.   980

"But, Lord, how shal I don? How shal I lyven?
Whanne shal I next my dere herte se?
How shal this longe tyme awey be dryven
Til that thow be ayen at hire fro me?
Thow mayst answere, 'Abyd, abyd,' but he   985
That hangeth by the nekke, soth to seyne,
In grete dishese abydeth for the peyne."

"Al esily now, for the love of Marte,"
Quod Pandarus, "for everythyng hath tyme.
So longe abyd til that the nyght departe;   990
For al so syker as thow lyst here by me,
And God toforn, I wol be there at pryme.

---

930 **agros . . . smerte,** feared, felt pain. 934 **skarmuch,** skirmish. 935 **abyden,** waited. 936 **messages,** messengers. 940 **ybete,** beaten. 941 *slynge:* other MSS *slynging/sleynge.* 942 **hete,** fever. 943 **jape . . . swete,** joke, sweat. 948 **hym dyghte,** i.e., took himself. 950 A&c *But* om.; MC&c *that* om. 953 *us:* C&c *me.* 954 **don thyn hod . . . spedde,** i.e., keep your hat on, successful. 956 **trowe,** believe. *trowe(n):* A *truste(n).* 959 **But . . . make it in . . . slouthe,** unless, make it (turn out otherwise), (because of) your sloth. 960 **ferforth,** far. 961 **morwe,** morning. 963 **to borwe,** as pledge. *also:* A *therto.* 964 **hameled,** maimed. Dogs living near forest preserves had to have a foot lamed so that they would not chase game. The implication here is that Troylus' sorrow can no longer pursue him so fast. 968 **stoupen,** droop. 970 **on hire kynde cours by rowe,** in their natural manner in a row. 973 **yhered,** praised. 975 **that,** whatever. 976 **hol . . . brosten,** whole, burst. 977 *Troyes:* MC&c *Troians.* 980 **tosterte,** burst. 983 *be dryven:* M *ben ydreven.* 988 **Marte,** Mars. 991 **syker . . . lyst,** sure, lie. 992 **toforn . . . pryme,** before, 9 A.M.

And forthi, werk somwhat as I shal seye,
Or on som other wyght this charge leye.

"For parde, God wot I have evere yit 995
Ben redy the to serve, and to this nyght
Have I nought fayned, but emforth my wit
Don al thi lust, and shal with al my myght.
Do now as I shal seye and fare aryght.
And if thow nylt, wyte al thiself thy care; 1000
On me ys nought ylong thyn yvel fare.

"I wot wel that thow wyser art than I
A thousand fold, but yf I were as thow,
God help me so, as I wolde outrely
Of myn owene hond write hire right now 1005
A lettre in which I wolde hire telle how
I ferde amys, and hire beseche of routhe.
Now help thiself and leve it not for slouthe.

"And I mynself wil therwith to hire gon;
And whanne thow wost that I am with hire
there, 1010
Worth thow upon a courser right anon,
Ye, hardyly, ryght in thi beste gere,
And ryd forth by the place as nought ne
were
And thow shalt fynde us, if I may, sittynge
At som wyndowe ynto the strete lokynge. 1015

"And yf the lyst, than maystow us saluwe,
And upon me make thi contenaunce.
But by thy lyf bewar and faste eschuwe
To taryen ought—God shilde us fro
myschaunce—

Ride forth thi wey and hold thy governaunce.
And we shal spek of the somwhat, I trowe, 1021
Whan thow art goon, to don thyne eeres
glowe.

"Towchyng thi lettre, thow art wys ynowh:
I wot thow nylt it digneliche endite,
As make it with thise argumentez towh; 1025
Ne scryvenyssh or craftyly thow it wryte;
Biblotte it with thi teeris eke a lyte;
And yf thow write a goodly word al softe,
Though it be good, reherce it not to ofte.

"For though the beste harpour upon lyve 1030
Wolde on the beste souned joly harpe
That evere was, with alle his fyngres fyve
Touche ay o streng, or ay o werbul harpe,
Were his nayles poynted nevere so sharpe,
It shulde maken every wyght to dulle 1035
To here his gle, and of his strokes fulle.

"Ne jompre ek no discordant thyng yfere,
As thus, to usen termes of phisyk
In loves termes; hold of thy matere
The forme alwey, and do that it be lyk. 1040
For if a peyntour wolde peynte a pyk
With asses feet and hede it as an ape,
It cordeth nought, so were it but a jape."

This counseyl liked wel unto Troylus,
But, as a dredful lovere, he seyde this, 1045
"Allas, my dere brother Pandarus,
I am ashamed for to write, ywys,
Lest of myn innocence I seyde amys,

---

993 forthi, werk, therefore, do. **994 charge,** responsibility. **997 fayned . . . emforth,** pretended, to the extent of. **998 lust,** pleasure. **999** *fare:* M *do.* **1000 wyte,** blame. **1001 ylong . . . yvel fare,** dependent, misfortune. **1005** A *Right of myn . . . write her now.* **1007 ferde amys . . . routhe,** fared badly, pity. **1008 leve it,** i.e., don't neglect it. **1011 Worth,** get. M&c *thow* om. **1012 hardyly,** bravely. **1016 saluwe,** greet. **1017 make . . . contenaunce,** look toward. C&c *make thow.* **1018 eschuwe,** avoid. **1019 taryen ought,** linger at all. **1020 governaunce,** self-control. **1022 don,** make. **1023 Towchyng thi lettre,** the circumstance of writing the letter is from *Fil.* 2.91ff., but the explicit directions are Chaucer's addition from various classical rhetoricians and the medieval masters of *ars dictaminis* (the art of formal Latin correspondence). **1024–25 digneliche endite . . . argumentez towh,** loftily compose, arguments tough (difficult). Making the style of the letter appropriate to the station and condition of the recipient was a cardinal principle of the *ars dictaminis.* **1026 scryvenyssh . . . craftyly,** like a professional secretary (scrivener), skillfully. Other MSS *scryvenliche.* **1027 Biblotte,** blot. **1028 softe,** tender. **1033 ay o werbul,** always one strain. **1035 dulle,** be bored. **1036 gle . . . fulle,** music, satiated. **1037 jompre . . . thyng yfere,** jumble, things together. **1038 As thus . . . phisyk,** for example, medicine. **1039 In . . . matere,** in the midst of, subject matter. **1040 forme,** i.e., regularity (consistency). **do . . . lyk,** see that it is consistent (suitable). **1041 pyk,** pike (fish). **1042 hede it,** give it a head. **1043 cordeth . . . jape,** it is not compatible, joke. **1045 dredful,** timid.

Or that she nolde it for despit receyve.
Thanne were I ded; ther myght it nothyng
    weyve."   1050

To that Pandare answered, "Yf the lest,
Do that I seye, and lat me therwith gon;
For by that Lord that formede est and west,
I hope of it to brynge answere anon
Ryght of hire hond. And yf that thow nylt non
Lat be, and sory mot he ben his lyve   1056
Ayens thi lust that helpeth the to thryve."

Quod Troylus, "Depardieux, ich assente.
Syn that the lyst, I wyl aryse and wryte;
And blysful God I pray with good entente   1060
The viage, and the lettre I shal endite
So spede it; and thow, Mynerva the white,
Yef thow me wit my lettre to devyse."
And sette hym down and wrot ryght yn this
    wyse.

Fyrst he gan hire his righte lady calle,   1065
His hertes lyf, his lust, his sorwes leche,
His blysse, and ek this othere termes alle
That yn such cas alle these loveres seche;
And yn ful humble wyse as in his speche   1069
He gan hym recomaunde unto hire grace—
To telle al how, it axeth muche space.

And after this, ful lowely he hire prayde
To be nought wroth thogh he of his folye
So hardy was to hire to write; and seyde
That love it made, or elles most he dye;   1075
And pitously gan mercy for to crye;
And after that he seyde—and ley ful loude—
Hymself was lytel worth, and lesse he koude;

And that she sholde han his konnyng excused,
That litel was; and ek he dredde hire so;   1080
And his unworthynesse he ay acused;
And after that than gan he telle his wo—
But that was endeles, withouten ho—
And seyde he wolde yn trouthe alwey hym
    holde;
And radde it over, and gan the lettre folde.

And with his salty terys gan he bathe   1086
The ruby yn his signet, and it sette
Upon the wex delyverlyche and rathe.
Therwith a thousand tymes er he lette,
He cussed tho the lettre that he shette,   1090
And seyde, "Lettre, a blysful destene
The shapen is; my lady shal the se."

This Pandare tok the lettre and that bytyme
A-morwe, and to his neces paleys sterte,   1094
And faste he swor that it was passed pryme,
And gan to jape, and seyde, "Ywys, myn herte
So fressh it is, although it sore smerte,
I may not slepe nevere a Mayes morwe;
I have a joly wo, a lusty sorwe."

Criseyde, whan that she hire uncle herde,   1100
With dredful herte and desirous to here
The cause of his comynge, thus answerde,
"Now, by youre feyth, myn uncle," quod she,
    "dere,
What manere wyndes gydeth yow now here?
Tel us youre joly wo and youre penaunce.   1105
How ferforth be put ye in loves daunce?"

"By God," quod he, "I hoppe alwey byhynde!"
And she to-laugh, it thoughte hire herte breste.

1049 despit, scorn. **1050 weyve,** avoid. **1051 the lest,** it pleases you. **1053** *that Lord:* M *hym.* **1054 anon,** soon. **1055 nylt non,** will not (write a letter). MC&c *Ryght* om. **1057 lust . . . thryve,** pleasure, prosper. **1058** *ich:* M *I.* **1061 viage,** the venture. **1062 spede,** assist. **Mynerva . . . white,** Roman parallel to Athene, goddess of wisdom; bright (shining). **1065 righte,** own. **1066 lust . . . leche,** joy, physician. **1074 hardy,** foolhardy. **1075 it made,** i.e., made him do it. **1077 ley,** lied. **1078 lesse . . . koude,** i.e., was less able than worthy. **1079** *sholde:* M *wolde.* **1081 unworthynesse . . . acused,** the lover's self-abasement in these opening lines, an essential convention of the courtly tradition, is very briefly touched on in Boccaccio's version of the letter, which details far more fully than Chaucer's the torments of love that Troylus feels, *Fil.* 2.96–106. **1083 ho,** halt. **1084 trouthe,** fidelity to his lady. **1088 delyverlyche . . . rathe,** deftly, quickly. **1089 lette,** stopped. **1090 cussed . . . shette,** kissed, sealed. **1092 The shapen,** prepared for you. **1093 bytyme,** early. A&c *Pandare up therwith and that.* **1094 A-morwe,** in the morning. **1095 pryme,** 9 A.M. A&c *And seide, "Slepe ye and it is pryme?"* **1097 fressh,** youthful. **1099 joly . . . lusty,** pleasant, pleasurable (typical troubadour oxymorons). **1101 dredful,** fearful. **1103** *feyth:* C&c *fey.* **1106 ferforth . . . put,** far, got. **1108 breste,** would break. *it thoughte:* A *as thogh.*

Quod Pandarus, "Lok alwey that ye fynde
Game in myn hod. But herkneth, yf yow leste,
There is right now ycome into towne a
    geste,   1111
A Griek espie, and telleth newe thynges,
For which I come to telle yow new tidynges.

"Into the gardyn go we and ye shal here
Al prevely of this a long sermon."   1115
With that they wenten arm in arm yfere
Into the gardeyn from the chaumbre doun.
And whan that he so fer was that the soun
Of that they spoke no man here myghte,   1119
He seyde hire thus, and out the lettre plighte,

"Lo, he that is al holly youres fre,
Hym recomaundeth lowly to youre grace,
And sent you this lettre here by me.
Aviseth yow on it, whan ye han space,
And of som goodly answere yow purchace, 1125
Or helpe me God, so pleynly for to seyne,
He may nat longe lyven for his peyne."

Ful dredfully tho gan she stonde stille,   1128
And tok it nought, but al hire humble chere
Gan for to chaunge, and seyde, "Scrit ne bille,
For love of God, that toucheth swich matere,
Ne brynge me noon; and also, uncle dere,
To myn estat have more rewarde, I preye,
Than to his lust. What sholde I more seye?

"And loketh now yf this be resonable,   1135
And letteth nought for favour ne for slouthe

To seyn a soth; now were it covenable
To myn estat, by God and by youre trouthe,
To taken it, or to han of hym routhe,
In harmyng of myself, or in repreve?   1140
Ber it ayen, for hym that ye on leve!"

This Pandarus gan on hire for to stare,
And seyde, "Now is this the grettest wonder
That evere I sey! Lat be this nyce fare.
To dethe mot I be smet with thonder   1145
If for the cite whiche that stondeth yonder
Wold I a lettre unto yow brynge or take
To harm of yow! What lyst yow thus to make?

"But thus ye faren wel nyh al and some
That he that most desireth yow to serve, 1150
Of hym ye recche lest wher he bycome,
And whether that he lyve or elles sterve.
But for al that that ever I may deserve,
Refuse it nought," quod he, and hent hire faste,
And yn hire bosom the lettre doun he thraste,

And seyde hire, "Now cast it awey anon, 1156
That folk may sen and gauren on us tweye."
Quod she, "I kan abyde til they be gon";
And gan to smyle, and seyde hym, "Em, I
    preye,
Swych answere as yow lyst youreself purveye,
For trewely I wol no lettre write."   1161
"No? Than wol I," quod he, "so ye endite."

Therwith she lough, and seyde, "Go we dyne."
And he gan at hymself to jape faste,

1109 Lok, i.e., see to it. MC&c *that* om. **1110 Game . . . hod,** amusement, hood (i.e., reason to laugh at me). **1111 geste,** stranger. **1113 A&c** *new* om. **1116 yfere,** together. **1120 plighte,** plucked. **1121 holly,** wholly. **1122 lowly,** humbly. **1124 Aviseth yow,** peruse. **1125 yow purchace,** provide yourself. **1127 for,** because of. **1128 dredfully,** fearfully. **1129 chere,** manner. **1130 Scrit ne bille,** i.e., don't put anything in writing. **1133 estat . . . rewarde,** position (social, economic, etc.), regard. **1134 lust,** desire. **1135 loketh,** see. **1136 letteth . . . slouthe,** desist, sloth (negligence, timidity). **1137 seyn a soth,** speak the truth. **convenable,** suitable. **1139 routhe,** pity. **1140 In harmyng . . . repreve,** i.e., to my own harm or reproach. **1141 leve,** believe (God). **1142 A** *This* om.; *began* or *upon*. **1143 grettest:** some MSS *moste*. **1144 nyce fare,** foolish behavior. **1145 mot . . . smet,** may, smitten. C&c *smyten be*. **1149 ye . . . nyh al and some,** i.e., nearly all of you women. **1152 sterve,** die. *And:* other MSS *Or*. **1154 hent . . . faste,** seized, quickly. **1155 lettre doun he thraste,** this scene marks the dividing point between Chaucer's and Boccaccio's versions. In *Fil.* 2.113, Criseida takes the letter and herself puts it into her bosom. Pandarus leaves and she goes to her room where she reads the letter with delight and at once resolves to accept Troilo as her lover. From this point, it is only 400 lines until she arranges to have him come to her house for an uncomplicated assignation scene. Chaucer replaced this material with 1800 lines of manipulation by Pandarus and the stars which give his poem a totally different aura. **1156** *anon:* M *or noon.* **1157 gauren,** gape. **1159 M&c** *hym* om. **1162 endite,** compose (it). **1164 jape,** joke.

And seyde, "Nece, I have so gret a pyne   1165
For love that everich other day I faste—"
And gan his beste japes forth to caste,
And made hire so to laughe at his folye
That she for laughter wende for to dye.

And whan that she was comen into halle,   1170
"Now, em," quod she, "we wol go dyne
        anon."
And gan som of hire wommen to hire calle,
And streyght into hire chaumbre gan she gon;
But of hire byesynesses this was on,
Amonges othere thynges, out of drede,   1175
Ful prevyly this lettre for to rede.

Avysed word by word in every lyne
And fond no lak, she thoughte he koude good;
And up it putte, and went hire yn to dyne.
But Pandarus, that in a study stood,   1180
Or he was war, she took hym by the hood,
And seyde, "Ye were caught er that ye wyste."
"I vouchesauf," quod he. "Do what yow lyste."

Tho wesshen they, and sette hem doun, and ete;
And after noon ful sleyly Pandarus   1185
Gan drawe hym to the wyndowe next the
        strete,
And seyde, "Nece, who hath arayed thus
The yonder hous, that stont aforyeyn us?"
"Which hous?" quod she, and gan for to
        byholde,   1189
And knew it wel, and whos it was hym tolde;

And fillen forth yn speche of thynges smale,
And seten yn the wyndowe bothe tweye.
Whan Pandarus sawe tyme unto his tale,

And sawh wel that hire folk were alle aweye,
"Now, nece myn, tel on," quod he. "I seye,
How liketh yow the lettre that ye wot?   1196
Kan he theron? For by my trouthe, I not."

Therwith al rosy hewed tho wax she,
And gan to humme, and seyde, "So I trowe."
"Aquyte hym wel, for Goddes love," quod he;
"Myself to medes wol the lettre sowe."   1201
And held his hondes up, and fel on knowe.
"Now, goode nece, be it nevere so lyte,
Yif me the labour it to sowe and plyte."

"Ye, for I kan so writen," quod she tho,   1205
"And ek I not what I sholde to hym seye."
"Nay, nece," quod Pandare, "sey nat so.
Yet at the leste, thanketh hym, I preye,
Of his good wil, and doth hym not to deye.
Now, for the love of me, my nece dere,   1210
Refuseth not at this tyme my preyere!"

"Depardieux," quod she, "God leve al be wel.
God help me so, this is the firste lettre
That evere I wrot, ye, al or ony del."
And into a closet for to avyse hire bettre   1215
She wente allone, and gan hire herte unfettre
Out of disdaynes prison but a lyte,
And sette hire doun, and gan a lettre write.

Of which to telle in short is myn entente
Th' effect, as fer as I kan understonde.   1220
She thonked hym of al that he wel mente
Towardes hire, but holden hym in honde
She wolde nought ne make hireselven bonde
In love, but as his suster, hym to plese,
She wolde ay fayn to don his herte an ese.   1225

1165 **pyne,** pain. 1169 **wende,** thought. 1171 **anon,** here "soon." This is the process by which the word changed from "immediately" to "in a little while." 1175 **out of drede,** doubtless. 1177 **Avysed,** considered. 1178 **koude good,** knew proper decorum. 1180 **study,** lost in thought (a brown study). 1181 **Or,** ere. 1182 **wyste,** knew. 1183 **vouchesauf,** agree. 1184 **wesshen they,** in a basin held by an attendant. 1185 **sleyly,** casually. 1187 **arayed,** decorated (e.g., tiled or painted). 1188 M *aforn yeyn.* 1193 **his tale,** his question. 1194 M *weren awaye.* 1196 *ye wot:* other MSS *he wrote.* 1197 **Kan he theron,** does he know about things like that. 1199 **trowe,** believe. 1200 **Aquyte,** repay. 1201 **to medes . . . lettre sowe,** as a bonus, sew the parchment leaves after they are written to make a scroll. 1202 **knowe,** knees. *fel:* MC&c *sat.* 1204 **plyte,** fold. 1209 **doth,** make. 1212 **leve,** grant. 1214 **ye . . . del,** yes, part. 1215 **closet . . . avyse hire,** private room, concentrate. 1222 **holden . . . in honde,** deceive. 1224 **as his suster,** Boccaccio gives the letter in full, *Fil.* 2.121–27, and it ends with Criseida promising that Troilo "couldst and canst have" her "more than a thousand times, an the cruel fire do not burn me" *Fil.* 2.127. Criseyde's remark about being a sister to Troylus marks the extent to which Chaucer's conception of her character differed from Boccaccio's. 1225 **ay fayn,** always be happy. MC&c *ay om.*

She shette it, and in to Pandarus gan gon
Ther as he sat and loked into the strete,
And doun she sette hire by hym on a ston
Of jaspre, upon a quysshon gold-ybete,
And seyde, "As wysly help me God the grete,
I nevere dide thing with more peyne   1231
Than write this, to which ye me constreyne,"

And tok it hym. He thonked hire and seyde,
"God wot, of thing ful ofte loth bygonne
Comth ende good. And nece myn, Criseyde,
That ye to hym of hard now be ywonne   1236
Oughte he be glad, by God and yonder sonne,
For-whi men seyth, impressiones lyghte
Ful lyghtly ben ay redy to the flyghte.

"But ye han played tyrant neigh to longe,   1240
And hard was it youre herte for to grave.
Now stynt that ye no lengere on it honge,
Al wolde ye the forme of daunger save;
But hasteth yow to don hym joye have.
For trusteth wel, to longe ydon hardnesse   1245
Causeth despit ful often for distresse."

And right as they declamed this matere,
Lo, Troylus, right at the stretes ende,
Com rydyng with his tenthe som yfere,
Al softly, and thederward gan bende   1250
There as they sete, as was his way to wende
To palays-ward. And Pandarus hym aspyde
And seyde, "Nece, yse who comth here ryde.

"O fle naught in—he seeth us, I
          suppose—   1254
Lest he may thynken that ye hym eschuwe."
"Nay, nay," quod she, and waxe as red as rose.

With that he gan hire humbly to saluwe
With dredful chere, and oft his hewes muwe,
And up his look debonairly he caste,
And bekked on Pandare, and forth he paste.

God wot yf he sat on his hors aright,   1261
Or goodly was beseyn, that ilke day!
God wot wher he was lyk a manly knyght!
What sholde I drecche or telle of his aray?
Criseyde, which that alle these thynges say,   1265
To telle in short, hire lyked al yfere,
His person, his aray, his look, his chere,

His goodly manere, and his gentilesse,
So wel that nevere sith that she was born
Ne hadde she swych a routhe of his destresse. 1270
And how so she hath hard ben here byforn,
To God hope I she hath now kaught a thorn,
She shal nat pulle it out this nexte wyke.
God sende mo swich thornes on to pyke!

Pandare, which that stod hire faste by,   1275
Felt iren hot, and he bygan to smyte
And seyde, "Nece, I pray yow hertely,
Telle me that I shal axen yow a lyte.
A womman that were of his deth to wyte,   1279
Withouten his gilt, but for hire lakked routhe,
Were it wel don?" Quod she, "Nay, by my
          trouthe!"

"God help me so," quod he, "ye sey me soth.
Ye felen wel yourself that I not lye.
Lo, yond he rit." "Ye," quod she, "so he doth."
"Wel," quod Pandare, "as I have told yow
          thrye,   1285
Lat be youre nice shame and youre folye,

1229 **quysshon gold-ybete,** cushion gold-embroidered. Other MSS *with gold/of gold.* 1236 **of hard,** with difficulty. 1238 **For-whi**
. . . lyghte, therefore, slight (superficial). 1240 Other MSS *the tyrant.* 1241 **grave,** carve (i.e., make an impression on). 1242 **stynt . . .**
honge, stop, hang (hesitate). 1243 **forme of daunger,** the appearance of aloofness. 1244 **don,** make. 1245 **ydon hardnesse,** hard-
heartedness maintained. 1246 **despit . . . for,** hatred because of. 1247 **declamed,** discussed. A&c *declared.* 1249 **tenthe som yfere,**
group of ten together (cf. ModE, foursome). 1250 **softly . . . bende,** slowly, tend (go forward). 1253 **ryde,** riding. This episode
resembles the one time Troilo passes by Criseida's window at *Fil.* 2.82, but Chaucer increases the episodes to two and makes each
a psychological experience. 1255 **eschuwe,** avoid. 1257 **saluwe,** greet. 1258 **dredful chere . . . muwe,** timid expression, change.
1259 **debonairly,** meekly. 1260 **bekked,** nodded. 1262 **beseyn,** to see. 1263 **wher,** whether. 1264 **drecche,** be tiresome. 1265 **say,**
saw. 1266 **yfere,** together. 1270 **routhe,** pity. 1271 **how so,** although. 1272 **thorn,** the "thorn in the flesh," i.e., sexual desire; cf.
II Cor. 12:7, *CT* I.3877n. *God:* A&c *good.* 1276 A&c *the iryn.* 1279 **wyte,** blame. 1280 **for . . . routhe,** because, pity. Other MSS
or hire lakke of routhe. 1284 **rit,** rides. M&c *yend, rat/Ye om.* 1285 **thrye,** thrice. 1286 **nice,** foolish.

And spek with hym in esyng of his herte.
Lat nicete not do yow bothe smerte."

But theron was to heven and to done.
Considered alle thyng, it may not be.   1290
And whi? For shame, and it were ek to
          soone
To graunten hym so gret a liberte.
For playnly hire entente, as seyde she,
Was for to love hym unwist, if she myghte,
And guerdone hym with nothyng but with
          sighte.   1295

But Pandarus thoughte, "It shal not be so.
Yf that I may, this nyce opinioun
Shal not be holde fully monthes two."
What sholde I make of this a long sermoun?
He moste assente on that conclusioun,   1300
As for the tyme; and whanne that it was
          eve,
And al was wel, he ros and tok his leve.

And on his wey ful faste homward he spedde,
And right for joye he felte his herte daunce;
And Troylus he fond alone abedde,   1305
That lay as doth these loveres in a traunce,
Bytwixen hope and derk desesperaunce.
But Pandarus right at his in-comynge,
He song, as who seyth, "Somwhat I brynge,"

And seyde, "Who is in his bed so soone   1310
Yburyed thus?" "It am I, frend," quod he.
"Who, Troylus? Nay, help me so the mone,"
Quod Pandarus, "thow shalt arise and se
A charme that was sent right now to the,
The which kan helen the of thyn accesse,   1315
Yf thow do forthwith al thi besynesse."

"Ye, thorugh the myght of God," quod Troylus.
And Pandarus gan hym the lettre take,
And seyde, "Parde, God hath holpen us.
Have here a lyght and loke on al this blake."
But ofte gan the herte glade and quake   1321
Of Troylus whil that he gan it rede
So as the wordes yaf hym hope or drede.

But fynally, he tok al for the beste   1324
That she hym wrot, for sumwhat he byheld
On which hym thoughte he myghte his herte
          reste,
Al covered she the wordes under sheld.
Thus to the more worthi part he held,
That what for hope and Pandarus byheste,
His grete wo foryede he at the leste.   1330

But as we may alday oureselven se,
Thorugh more wode or col the more fyr,
Right so encrees of hope, of what it be,
Therwith ful ofte encresseth ek desir;
Or as an ok cometh of a litel spir,   1335
So thorugh this lettre which that she hym
          sente
Encressen gan desir, of which he brente.

Wherfore I seye alwey that day and nyght
This Troylus gan to desiren more
Thanne he dide erst, thorugh hope, and dide
          his myght   1340
To pressen on, as by Pandarus lore,
And writen to hire of his sorwes sore.
Fro day to day he leet it nought refreyde
That by Pandare he wrot somwhat or seyde;

And dide also his othere observaunces   1345
That to a lovere longeth yn this cas.

1288 do, make. **1289 heven . . . done,** heave, do—i.e., effort. **1290 Considered alle thyng,** all things considered. **1291 were ek,** would also be. *shame:* other MSS *speche.* **1294 unwist,** unknown (to him). **1295 guerdone,** reward. **1297 nyce,** foolish. **1298 monthes,** this is the reading of the less reliable MSS and no doubt scribal. MC&c read *yeres,* which, while possibly Chaucerian, stretches credulity. **1307 desesperaunce,** despair. **1312 mone,** editors have interpreted this as another astrological allusion, but it is easier to suppose that in pre-electric days, Pandarus used moonlight to show Troylus the letter he was carrying, before he lighted a light (l. 1320) so that he could read it. **1315 accesse,** fever. **1316 forthwith . . . besynesse,** immediately, make an effort (to read it). Other MSS *So that thow do. al* om. **1320 blake,** black (ink). Two A MSS *thes lettres blake.* **1321 glade,** be glad. **1323 So as,** i.e., according to whether. *or:* other MSS *and.* **1327 Al,** although. *the:* C&c *tho.* **1329 byheste,** promise. **1330 grete . . . foryede . . . leste,** i.e., he put aside at least his greatest grief. **1333 of what,** i.e., whatever it is for. **1335 spir,** shoot. **1337 brente,** burned. **1341 lore,** instruction. **1343 refreyde,** grow cool. **1344 Other MSS** *he somwhat* or *somwhat he.* **1346 longeth,** belong.

And after that thise dees torned on chaunces,
So was he outher glad or seyde allas,
And held after his gistes ay his pas;
And after swyche answeres as he hadde,   1350
So were his dayes sory outher gladde.

But to Pandarus alwey was his recours,
And pitously gan ay til hym to pleyne,
And hym bisoughte of red and som socours;
And Pandarus, that sey his wode peyne,   1355
Wex wel neigh ded for ruthe, soth to seyne,
And bysily with al his herte caste
Som of his wo to slen, and that as faste;

And seyde, "Lord, and frend, and brother dere,
God wot that thi dishese doth me wo.   1360
But wiltow stynten al this woful chere,
And, by my trouthe, er it be dayes two,
And God toforn, yet shal I shape it so
That thou shalt come into a certeyn place
There as thow mayst thiself hire preye of grace.

"And certeynly—I not if thow it wost,   1366
But tho that ben expert in love it seye—
It is oon of the thynges furthereth most,
A man to have a leyser for to preye,
And syker place his wo for to bywreye.   1370
For in good herte it mot som routhe impresse
To here and se the giltlees in distresse.

"Peraunter thynkestow: though it be so
That Kynde wolde don hire to bygynne
To han a manere routhe upon my wo,   1375
Seyth Daunger, 'Nay, thow shalt me nevere
     wynne.'

So reuleth hire hire hertes gost withinne
That though she bende, yet she stant on rote.
What in effect is this unto my bote?   1379

"Thenk hereayens, whan that the stordy ok,
On which men hakketh ofte for the nones,
Receyved hath the happy fallyng strok,
The grete sweigh doth it come al at onys,
As doth these rokkes or thise mylnestones;
For swifter cours cometh thyng that is of
     wighte,   1385
Whan it descendeth, than don thynges lyghte.

"And ried that boweth down for every blast,
Ful lightly, cesse wynd, it wol aryse;
But so nyl nought an ok whan it is cast.
It nedeth me nought the longe to forbyse.   1390
Men shal rejoyssen of a gret emprise
Acheved wel, and stant withouten doute,
Al han men ben the lenger theraboute.

"But, Troylus, yet telle me yf the lest,
A thing now which that I shal axen the: 1395
Which is thi brother that thou lovest best,
As yn thi verray hertes prevyte?"
"Iwys, my brother Deyphebus," quod he.
"Now," quod Pandare, "er owres twyes
     twelve,
He shal the ese, unwyst of it hymself.   1400

"Now lat me alone, and werken as I may,"
Quod he. And to Deiphebus wente he tho
Which hadde his lord and grete frend ben ay;
Save Troylus, no man he loved so.
To telle in short, withouten wordes mo,   1405

1347 **after . . . dees . . . chaunces,** i.e., as the fortunes of these throws of dice turned out. *thise:* other MSS *his.* 1349 **gistes,** stages of his journey. A *giftes.* 1354 **red,** advice. 1355 **wode peyne,** insane agony. 1356 **ruthe,** pity. 1358 **slen,** slay (end). 1361 **But . . . stynten,** if only, leave off. 1363 **God toforn,** before God. 1366 **not . . . wost,** don't, know. 1368 **furthereth,** that furthers one. 1369 **leyser . . . preye,** an opportunity to plead. 1370 **syker . . . bywreye,** secure (private), reveal. 1371 **routhe,** pity. 1373 **Peraunter,** perhaps. 1374 **Kynde . . . don,** Nature, cause. 1375 **manere routhe,** kind of pity. 1376 **Daunger,** aloofness. These are the personifications from the "psychomachia" (internal warfare) in *RR;* see the Introduction to the Chaucerian translation in this volume. 1377 **gost,** spirit. M second *hire* om. 1378 **stant on rote,** stands firmly rooted. 1379 **my bote,** my assistance. 1382 **happy fallyng,** final felling. 1383 **sweigh . . . doth . . . come,** sway (falling motion), makes, come down (fall). 1384 **mylnestones,** millstones, examples of great weight. M *mylstones.* 1385 **swifter cours,** this Aristotelian doctrine was, of course, disproved by the classic experiments of Galileo which demonstrated (c. 1600) that bodies of different weights fall with equal velocity. 1390 **forbyse,** give examples. 1391 **emprise,** enterprise. 1393 **Al,** although. 1399 **owres,** hours. *twyes:* A *thries.* 1400 **unwyst,** unaware. The whole episode in Diephebus' house is Chaucer's invention.

Quod Pandarus, "I pray yow that ye be
Frend to a cause which that toucheth me."

"Yis, parde," quod Deiphebus, "wel thow wost,
In al that evere I may, and God tofore,
Al nere it but for man I love most,   1410
My brother Troylus. But sey wherfore
It is, for sith that day that I was bore,
I nas, ne nevere mo to ben I thynke,
Ayens a thyng that myghte the forthynke."

Pandare gan hym thonke and to hym seyde,
"Lo, sire, I have a lady yn this town   1416
That is my nece and called is Criseyde,
Which som men wolden don oppressioun,
And wrongfully have hire possessioun.
Wherfore I of youre lordship yow byseche   1420
To ben oure frend, withouten more speche."

Deiphebus hym answerde, "O, is not this
That thow spekest of to me so straungely
Criseyda, my frend?" He seyde, "Yis."
"Than nedeth," quod Deiphebus, "hardely,
No more to speke, for trusteth wel that I   1426
Wol be hire chaumpioun with spore and yerde;
I roughte nought though alle hire foos it herde.

"But telle me, thow that wost alle this matere,
How I myght best avaylen."—"Now lat se,"
Quod Pandarus; "yf ye, my lord so dere,   1431
Wolden as now do this honour to me,
To prayen hire tomorwe, lo, that she
Come unto yow hire pleyntes to devyse,
Hire adversaries wolde of it agryse.   1435

"And yf I more dorste preye yow as now,
And chargen yow to have so gret travayle,

To han som of youre bretheren here with yow,
That myghten to hire cause bet avayle,
Than wot I wel she myghte nevere fayle   1440
For to ben holpen, what at youre instaunce,
What with hire other frendes governaunce."

Deiphebus, which that comen was of kynde
To al honour and bounte to consente,
Answerd, "It shal be don; and I kan fynde   1445
Yet grettere help to this yn myn entente.
What wiltow seyn yf I for Eleyne sente
To speke of this? I trowe it be the beste,
For she may ledyn Parys as hire leste.   1449

"Of Ector, which that is my lord my brother,
It nedeth nought to prey hym frend to be,
For I have herd hym o tyme ek and other
Speke of Criseyde swich honour that he
May seyn no bet, swich hap to hym hath she.
It nedeth nought his helpes for to crave;   1455
He shal be swych right as we wol hym have.

"Spek thow thiself also to Troylus
On my byhalve, and pray hym with us dyne."
"Sire, al this shal be don," quod Pandarus,
And tok his leve; and nevere wold he
      fyne,   1460
But to his neces hous, as streyht as lyne,
He com, and fond hire fro the mete aryse,
And sette hym down, and spak right in this
      wyse.

He seyde, "O verray God, so have I ronne!
Lo, nece myn, se ye nought how I swete?   1465
I not whether ye me the more thank konne.
Be ye nought war how false Polyphete
Is now abowte eftsoones for to plete,

1407 **toucheth**, concern. 1409 **God tofore**, before God. 1410 **Al nere**, i.e., more for you than anyone except the man I love most. 1414 **the forthynke**, displease you. 1419 **possessioun**, property. 1421 **frend**, in an aristocratic society "friend" in this sense means protector. 1427 **spore ... yerde**, spur, whip (i.e., eagerly). Other MSS *spere ... swerde*. 1428 **roughte**, care. 1429–30 Other MSS *But telle me how—thow woost of this matere—|It myghte best avaylen....* 1434 **devyse**, tell. 1435 **agryse**, be frightened. 1436 A&c *If that more y durst.* 1437 **chargen ... to have ... travayle**, persuade you to take, trouble. 1439 **avayle**, assist. 1441 **what at ... instaunce**, what with, urging. 1442 **governaunce**, management. 1443 **comen ... kynde**, i.e., was of such a nature. 1444 **bounte**, generosity. 1447 **Eleyne**, Helen of Troy. 1449 **ledyn**, lead (influence). 1454 **hap to**, favor with. 1455 *It*: other MSS *She*. 1460 *wold he*: C&c *gan to*. 1465 **swete**, sweat. 1466 **not ... thank konne**, don't know, will feel grateful. 1467 **Polyphete**, how much there actually is to the Poliphete threat and how much is Pandarus' invention we do not know; there is no hint of it in *Filostrato*. 1468 **eftsoones ... plete**, very soon, go to court.

And brynge on yow advocacies newe?"
"I? No," quod she, and chaunged al hire
    hewe.   1470

"What is he more aboute me to drecche
And don me wrong? What shal I do, allas?
Yet of hymself nothyng nolde I recche
Nere it for Antenor and Eneas
That ben his frendys yn swych manere cas. 1475
But for the love of God, myn uncle dere,
No fors of that; lat hym han al yfere;

"Withouten that I have ynowh for us."
"Nay," quod Pandare, "it shall nothynge
    be so,
For I have ben right now at Deiphebus, 1480
At Ector, and myn other lordes mo,
And shortly maked eche of hem his fo,
That, by my thryft, he shal it nevere wynne,
For ought he kan, whan that so he bygynne."

And as they casten what was best to done, 1485
Deiphebus, of his owene curtasie,
Com hire to preye yn his propre persone,
To holde hym on the morwe compaignye
At dyner; which she nolde not denye,
But goodly gan to his preyere obeye. 1490
He thonked hire, and wente upon his weye.

Whan this was don, this Pandare up anoon,
To tellen in short, and forth gan for to wende
To Troylus, as stille as ony ston.
And al this thing he tolde hym, word and
    ende,   1495
And how that he Deiphebus gan to blende,
And seyde hym, "Now is tyme, if that thow
    konne,
To bere the wel tomorwe, and al is wonne.

"Now spek, now prey, now pitously compleyne;
Lat not for nice shame, or drede, or
    slouthe,   1500
Somtyme a man mot telle his owen peyne.
Bileve it, and she shal han on the routhe.
Thow shalt be saved, by thi feyth, in trouthe.
But wel wot I thow art now yn drede,
And what it is I ley I kan arede. 1505

"Thow thinkest now, 'How sholde I don al
    this?
For by my cheres mosten folk aspye
That for hire love is that I fare amys;
Yet hadde I levere unwyst for sorwe dye.'
Now thenk not so for thou dost gret folye, 1510
For right now have I founden o manere
Of sleyghte for to coveren al thi chere.

"Thow shalt gon over nyght, and that blyve,
Unto Deiphebus hous, as the to pleye,
Thi maladye awey the bet to dryve— 1515
For-why thou semest syk, soth for to seye.
Soone after that, doun in thi bed the leye,
And sey thow mayst no lengere up endure,
And lye right there and byde thyn aventure.

"Sey that thi fevre is wont the for to take 1520
The same tyme and lasten til amorwe;
And lat se now how wel thow kanst it make,
For, parde, syk is he that is in sorwe.
Go now, farewel, and Venus here to borwe,
I hope and thow this purpos holde ferme, 1525
Thi grace she shal fully ther conferme."

Quod Troylus, "Ywys, thow nedeles
Conseylest me that syklych I me feyne,
For I am syk yn ernest, douteles,
So that wel neygh I sterve for the peyne." 1530

1469 advocacies, lawsuit. **1471 drecche,** harass. **1473 recche,** care. **1474 Antenor . . . Eneas,** these were ultimately the traitors who caused the fall of Troy, and the exchange for Antenor caused Troylus to lose Criseyde, cf. IV.133ff. **1477 No fors . . . al yfere,** no matter, altogether. **1484 ought he kan,** anything he can do. Other MSS *so that.* **1489 denye,** refuse. **1493** Other MSS *forth he gan to.* **1494 as stille,** i.e., secretly. **1496 blende,** blind (deceive). **1500 nice,** foolish. Other MSS *Leve not.* **1502 routhe,** pity. **1505 ley . . . arede,** bet, tell. **1507 cheres,** looks. **1509 unwyst,** undetected. **1511–12 o manere/Of sleyghte,** a kind of trick. **1512 coveren . . . chere,** conceal, appearance. **1513 nyght . . . blyve,** (to)night, immediately. **1516 For-why,** because. **1517** *Soone:* MC&c *And.* **1519 byde,** await. **1520 wont,** accustomed. **1521 amorwe,** tomorrow. **1524 to borwe,** as pledge. **1525 and thow,** if thou. **1526** M *there fully.* **1528 feyne,** pretend. **1530 sterve,** die.

Quod Pandarus, "Thow shalt the bettre
    pleyne,
And hast the lasse nede to countrefete,
For hym men demen hot that men seen swete.

"Lo, hold the at thi tryste clos, and I
Shal wel the der unto thi bowe dryve."   1535
Therwith he tok his leve al softely,
And Troylus to palays wente blyve.
So glad ne was he nevere in al his lyve,
And to Pandarus reed gan all assente,
And to Deiphebus hous at nyght he wente.   1540

What nedeth yow to tellen al the chere
That Deiphebus unto his brother made,
Or his accesse, or his sykliche manere—
How men gan hym with clothes for to lade
Whanne he was leyd, and how men wolde hym
    glade?   1545
But al for nought; he held forth ay the wyse
That ye han herd Pandare er this devyse.

But certayn is, er Troylus hym leyde,
Deiphebus had hym prayed over-nyght
To ben a frend and helpyng to Criseyde.   1550
God wot that he it graunted anoon right,
To ben hire fulle frend with al his myght—
But swych a nede was to prey hym thenne,
As for to bydde a wood man for to renne.

The morwen com and neyhen gan the tyme
Of meltid that the faire queene Eleyne   1556
Shoop hire to ben, an owre after the pryme,
With Deiphebus, to whom she nolde feyne;
But as his suster, homly, soth to seyne,
She com to dyner yn hire playne
    entente—   1560
But God and Pandare wyst what al this
    mente.

Come ek Criseyde, al innocent of this,
Antigone, hire sister Tarbe also.
But fle we now prolixite best is,
For love of God, and lat us faste go   1565
Right to th'effect withoute tales mo,
Whi al this folk assembled in this place,
And lat us of hire saluynges pace.

Gret honour dide hem Deiphebus, certeyn,   1569
And fedde hem wel with al that myghte like.
But evere more "Allas" was his refreyn,
"My goode brother Troylus the syke
Lyth yet," and therwithal he gan to syke,
And after that he peyned hym to glade
Hem as he myghte, and chere good he made.

Compleyned ek Eleyne of his syknesse   1576
So feythfully that pite was to here;
And every wight gan waxen for accesse
A leche anon, and seyde, "In this manere
Men curen folk."—"This charme I wol yow
    lere."   1580
But ther sat oon, al lyst hire nought to teche,
That thoughte, "Best koude I yet ben his
    leche."

After compleynt, hym gonnen thei to preyse,
As folk don yet whan som wyght hath bygonne
To preyse a man, and up with prys hym
    reyse   1585
A thousandfold yet hyer than the sonne:
"He is, he kan, that fewe lordes konne."
And Pandarus, of that they wolde afferme,
He naught forgat hire preysynge to conferme.

Herde al this thyng Criseyde wel ynowh,   1590
And every word gan for to notefye,
For which with sobre chere hire herte lowh,
For who is that ne wolde hire glorifye,

1531 bettre pleyne, all the better complain. **1533 demen,** judge. **1534 tryste,** hunting station. **1536 softely,** quietly. **1539 reed,** counsel. **1543 accesse,** fever. **1544 lade,** cover (load). **1545 leyd . . . glade,** laid in bed, gladden (cheer up). **1546** *the wyse:* some MSS *his gyse.* **1554 wood . . . renne,** crazy, run. **1557 Shoop hire . . . pryme,** arranged, 9 A.M. MC&c *Shapt.* **1558 feyne,** pretend (accept the invitation but not appear). **1559 homly,** familiarly. **1560 playne entente,** frank manner. **1561 But God,** only God. **1568 pace,** pass (over). **1573 syke,** sigh. A *gan he sike.* **1575 A** *good chere hem made.* **1578 accesse,** fever. **1579 leche,** physician. **1580 lere,** teach. *yow:* A&c *the.* **1581 lyst hire,** it pleased her. **1583 gonnen,** began. **1585 MC&c** *up* om. **1588 of that,** of that which. **1590 Other MSS** *Herde alwey this Criseyde.* **1591 notefye,** take note of. **1592 sobre chere . . . lowh,** demure expression, laughed.

To mowen swych a knyght don lyve or dye?
But al passe I, lyst ye to longe dwelle, 1595
For for o fyn is al that evere I telle.

The tyme com fro dyner for to ryse,
And as hem oughte arysen everychon,
And gonne a while of this and that devyse.
But Pandarus brak al this speche anoon, 1600
And seide to Deiphebus, "Wol ye gon,
If youre wille be, as I yow preyde,
To speke here of the nedes of Criseyde?"

Eleyne, which that by the hond hire held,
Took first the tale and seyde, "Go we blyve,"
And goodly on Criseyde she byheld, 1606
And seyde, "Joves lat hym nevere thryve
That doth yow harm, and brynge hym soone
of lyve,
And yeve me sorwe but he shal it rewe,
If that I may, and alle folk be trewe." 1610

"Telle thow thi neces cas," quod Deiphebus
To Pandarus, "for thow kanst best it telle."
"My lordes and my ladyes, it stant thus.
What sholde I lengere," quod he, "do yow
dwelle?"
He rong hem out a proces lyk a belle 1615
Upon hire fo, that highte Poliphete,
So heynous, that men myghte on it spete.

Answerde of this ech worse of hem than other,
And Poliphete they gonnen thus to waryen:
"Anhonged be swych on, were he my
brother!" 1620
"And so he shal, for it ne may not varyen!"
What shold I lengere yn this tale taryen?
Pleynly alle at ones they hire hyghten
To ben hire helpe in al that evere they myghten.

Spak than Eleyne, and seyde, "Pandarus, 1625
Woot ought my lord, my brother, this matere,
I mene Ector? Or wot it Troylus?"
He seyde, "Ye, but wole ye now me here?
Me thenketh this, sith that Troylus is here,
It were good, if that ye wolde assente, 1630
She tolde hireself hym al this er she wente.

"For he wol have the more hir grief at herte,
By cause, lo, that she a lady is.
And, by youre leve, I wol but yn right sterte
And do yow wete, and that anoon, ywys, 1635
If that he slepe or wol ought here of this."
And yn he lepte, and seyde hym in his ere,
"God have thi soule, ibrought have I thi
bere!"

To smylen of this gan tho Troylus,
And Pandarus withoute rekenynge 1640
Out wente anoon to Eleyne and Deiphebus,
And seyde hem, "So ther be no taryinge,
Ne more pres, he wol wel that ye brynge
Criseyda, my lady, that is here;
And as he may enduren, he wol here. 1645

"But wel ye wot, the chaumbre is but lite,
And fewe folk may lightly make it warm.
Now loketh ye—for I wol have no wyte
To brynge yn pres that myghte don hym
harm,
Or hym dishesen, for my bettre arm— 1650
Where it be bet she byde til eftsonys?
Now loketh ye that knowen what to don is.

"I sey for me, best is as I kan knowe
That no wight yn ne wente but ye tweye,
But it were I, for I kan in a throwe 1655
Reherce hire cas unlyk that she kan seye.

1594 mowen . . . don, be able to make. *don:* M om., other MSS *to.* **1596 o fyn,** one conclusion. **1605 Go we blyve,** let's begin at once. **1607 thryve,** prosper. **1608 of lyve,** to death (out of life). **1609 rewe,** regret. **1614** C&c *quod he* om., making the line metrically defective, but assigning the statement to the narrator. **1615 proces,** case (argument). **1618 ech . . . of hem,** each of those present. **1619 waryen,** curse. **1621 varyen,** be otherwise. **1623 Pleynly . . . ones . . . hyghten,** i.e., to put it simply, together, promised. **1624** *helpe:* other MSS *frend.* **1634** M&c *right yn.* **1635 do yow wete,** let you know. **1638 bere,** *double entendre,* coffin (bier) and pillow (pillowbere). *thi:* M *the.* **1640 rekenynge,** accounting (of details). **1642 So . . . taryinge,** provided, lingering. **1643 more pres,** more of a crowd. **1647 lightly,** easily. **1648 loketh . . . wyte,** consider, blame. **1650 bettre arm,** good arm (mild expletive). **1651 Where . . . byde . . . eftsonys,** whether, wait, later. **1655 throwe,** moment.

And after this, she may hym ones preye
To ben good lord, yn short, and take hire leve.
This may not mechel of his ese hym reve.

"And ek for she is straunge he wol forbere   1660
His ese, which that hym thar nought for yow.
Ek other thing that toucheth not to here,
He wol yow telle—I wot it wel right now—
That secret is, and for the townes prow."   1664
And they, that nothing knewe of this entent,
Withoute more to Troylus yn they went.

Eleyne in al hire goodly softe wyse
Gan hym saluwe, and wommanly to pleye,
And seyde, "Ywis, ye moste alweyes arise;
Now, faire brother, beth al hool, I preye!"   1670
And gan hire arm right over his sholder leye,
And hym with al hire wit to reconforte.
As she best kowde, she gan hym to disporte.

So after this quod she, "We yow byseke,
My dere brother Deiphebus and I,   1675
For love of God—and so doth Pandare eke—
To ben good lord and frend right hertely
Unto Criseyde, which that certeynly
Receyveth wrong—as wot wel here Pandare,
Than kan hire cas wel bet than I declare."   1680

This Pandarus gan newe his tong affyle,
And al hire cas reherce, and that anoon.
Whan it was seyd, soone after in a while,
Quod Troylus, "As sone as I may gon,   1684
I wol right fayn with al my myght ben oon—
Have God my trouthe—hire cause to
       susteyne."
"Good thryft have ye," quod Eleyne the
       queene.

Quod Pandarus, "And it youre wille be,
That she may take hire leve, er that she go?"
"O, elles God forbede," tho quod he,   1690
"If that she vouchesauf for to do so."
And with that word quod Troylus, "Ye two,
Deiphebus and my suster leef and dere,
To yow have I to speke of o matere,

To ben avysed by youre red the bettre."   1695
And fond, as hap was, at his beddes hed
The copye of a tretes and a lettre
That Ector hade hym sent to axen red
If swych a man was worthi to ben ded—
Woot I nought who; but in a grysly wyse   1700
He preyede hem anoon on it avyse.

Deiphebus gan this lettre to unfolde
In ernest gret; so did Eleyne the queene;
And romyng outward, faste it gonne byholde,
Downward a steyre, into an herber grene.   1705
This ilke thing thei redden hem bytwene,
And largely the mountance of an owre,
Thei gon on it to reden and to powre.

Now lat hem rede, and turne we anoon
To Pandarus, that gan ful faste prye   1710
That al was wel, and out he gan to gon
Into the grete chaumbre and that in hye,
And seyde, "God save al this compaynye.
Come, nece myn, my lady queene Eleyne
Abydeth yow, and ek my lordes tweyne.   1715

"Rys, take with yow yowre nece Antigone,
Or whom yow list—or no fors, hardyly,
The lasse pres, the bet—com forth with me,
And loke that ye thonken humbely
Hem alle thre; and whan ye may goodly   1720

1659 **mechel . . . hym reve,** much, deprive him of. 1661 **hym . . . nought,** there is no (need to do). 1662 **toucheth not to here,** don't concern her. 1663 **yow:** MC&c *me;* other MSS *it.* 1664 **prow,** profit. 1665 *this:* other MSS *his.* 1668 **pleye,** be playful. 1669 **alweys arise,** by all means get up (get well). *arise:* M *avyse.* 1673 **disporte,** joke with. 1681 **affyle,** file (make smooth). *newe:* A *now.* 1684 **gon,** walk. 1685 **fayn . . . ben oon,** happily, be one (of her supporters). 1686 **trouthe,** promise. 1687 **thryft,** luck. 1690 **elles God forbede,** unless God prevents it (a stock phrase of consent). O: A&c *Or;* C&c *forbede it;* M&c *tho* om. 1691 **vouchesauf,** consent. 1693 **leef,** dear. 1695 **red,** counsel. 1697 **tretes,** document. 1700 **grysly,** terrifyingly serious. A&c *Note y not who.* 1701 **avyse,** ponder. 1704 **romyng outward,** wandering out. 1705 **herber,** arbor or garden. *into:* other MSS *and in.* 1707 **mountance . . . owre,** extent, hour. 1708 **powre,** pore. 1710 **prye,** spy. 1712 **hye,** haste. 1717 **no fors, hardyly,** no matter, truly. 1718 **pres,** crowd.

Youre tyme se, taketh of hem youre leve
Lest we to longe his reste hym byreve."

Al innocent of Pandarus entente,
Quod tho Criseyde, "Go we, uncle dere."
And arm in arm inward with hym she wente,
Avysed wel hire wordes and hire chere.   1726
And Pandarus yn ernestful manere
Seyde, "Alle folk, for Goddes love, I preye,
Stynteth right here, and softely yow pleye.

"Aviseth yow what folk ben here withinne,   1730
And in what plit oon is, God hym amende!"
And inward thus ful softely bygynne,
"Nece, I conjure, and heighly yow defende,
On his byhalf which that us al sowle sende,
And in the vertue of corounes tweyne,   1735
Sle naught this man, that hath for yow this
       peyne.

"Fy on the devel! Thenk which on he is,
And in what plyt he lith. Com of anoon!

Thenk al swych taried tid but lost it nys;
That wol ye bothe seyn whan ye ben oon.   1740
Secoundelich, ther yet devyneth noon
Upon yow two. Com of now, if ye konne;
While folk is blent, lo, al the tyme is wonne.

"In titeryng and pursuyte and delayes
The folk devyne at waggyng of a stre.   1745
And though ye wolden han after merye dayes,
Than dar ye nought. And why? For she and she
Spak swych a word; thus loked he and he.
Allas tyme ylost! I dar not with yow dele.
Com of, therfore, and bryngeth hym to hele."

But now to yow, ye loveres that ben here,   1751
Was Troylus nought in a kankedort,
That lay and myghte whysprynge of hem here,
And thought, "O Lord, ryght now renneth my
       sort
Fully to dye or han anoon comfort!"   1755
And was the firste tyme he shulde hire preye
Of love: O myghti God, what shal he seye?

Explicit secundus liber.

1722 **byreve,** deprive him of. M *reve.* 1726 **Avysed,** having considered. 1729 **Stynteth,** stop. 1730 **Aviseth,** consider. 1732 **softely bygynne,** softly began. 1733 **heighly ... defende,** strictly, forbid. 1735 **corounes tweyne,** an obscure allusion; none of the explanations is very plausible. 1737 **which on,** what sort of a person. 1739 **taried tid,** delayed time. 1740 **seyn ... oon,** say, united. 1741 **devyneth,** suspects. 1743 **blent,** blinded (deceived). 1744 **titeryng ... pursuyte,** hesitations, entreaty. 1745 **devyne ... waggyng ... stre,** surmise, moving of a straw; i.e., while you are hesitating, people will be surmising. 1746 **wolden han,** would like to have. 1747 **Than,** yet. A&c *For why?* 1749 **dele,** argue. 1752 **kankedort,** a nonce word—predicament. A *kankerdort.* 1754 **sort,** fortune.

BOOK III

Incipit prohemium tercii libri.

O blysful light, of which the bemes clere
Adorneth al the thridde heven faire,
O sonnes lyef, O Joves doughter dere,
Plesaunce of love, O goodly debonaire,
In gentil hertes ay redy to repaire,　　　　5
O verray cause of hele and of gladnesse,
Iheried be thi myght and thi goodnesse.

In hevene and helle, in erthe and salte se,
Is felt thi myght, if that I wel descerne;
As man, bryd, best, fissh, herbe, and grene tree
The fele in tymes with vapour eterne.　　　11
God loveth, and to love wol nought werne;
And in this world no lyves creature
Withouten love is worth or may endure.

Ye Joves first to thilke effectes glade,　　　15
Thorough which that thinges lyven alle and be,
Comeveden, and amorous hym made
On mortal thyng, and as yow lyst ay ye
Yeve hym in love ese or adversite,
And in a thousand formes doun hym sente　　20
For love in erthe, and whom yow lyste he
　　hente.

Ye fierse Mars apeysen of his ire,
And as yow lyst, ye maken hertes digne;
Algates hem that ye wol sette afyre,
Thei dreden shame and vices thei resigne;　25
Ye do hem corteys be, fresche and benigne;
And hye or lowe, after a wyght entendeth,
The joyes that he hath, youre myght hym
　　sendeth.

Ye holden regne and hous in unite;
Ye sothfast cause of frendshipe ben also;　　30
Ye knowe al thilke covered qualite
Of thynges, which that folk on wondren so,
Whan they kan noght construe how it may jo
She loveth hym, or whi he loveth here,
As whi this fissh and nought that comth to
　　were.　　　　　　　　　　　　　　　　35

1–38 prohemium, like the proems to Bks. ii and iv, this appears to be a composition independent of the body of the text; cf. i.6n. It follows *Fil.* 3.74–79, Troilo's hymn of joy after he has won the love of Criseida, which is, in turn, based on *Boece* ii m.8. **2 thridde heven,** in the Ptolemaic cosmography, sun, moon, planets, and stars revolved about the earth in seven concentric spheres, of which Venus' was the third from the bottom; cf. v.1809 below. **3 sonnes lyef,** beloved of the sun, because astronomically Venus is close to the sun. **Joves doughter,** because mythologically Venus was the daughter of Jove. **4 Plesaunce . . . debonaire,** delight, agreeable. **5 In gentil hertes,** one of Chaucer's favorite sentiments; cf. *CT* i.1761n. *Fil.* 3.74 has "Benigna donna d'ogni gentil core" (Kindly mistress of every gentle heart). A&c *ay* om. **6 verray . . . hele,** true, well-being. **7 Iheried,** praised. **9 wel:** M&c *wole.* **11 The fele . . . vapour eterne,** feel (apprehend) you at times through an eternal (universal) influence. *The fele:* M *The feld;* C&c *They fele.* **12 werne,** refuse. **13 lyves,** living. **14 worth,** valuable (worth anything). **15–17 Ye Joves . . . Comeveden,** you first moved Jove to those pleasurable effects, etc. *Comeveden:* C&c *Comended/Comenden.* **20 thousand formes,** a reference to the different shapes Jove took when wooing mortal women, a swan, a bull, etc. *hym:* M&c *hem.* **21 hente,** took. **22 apeysen,** appease. **23 digne,** honorable. **24 Algates,** always. **26 do . . . fresche . . . benigne,** make, eager, gracious. **27 entendeth,** aims (desires). **28 hym:** M *it.* **29 regne and hous,** this is the Empedoclean philosophy that sees love as an expression of the force which holds the material as well as the spiritual elements of the universe in their places. **31 covered,** secret. **33 jo,** another nonce word, spelled *Io* or *Ioo* in all MSS. Skeat suggested a derivation from OF *joer,* to play, hence, "it may happen." **35 were,** wier (fish trap).

Ye folk a lawe han sett in universe,
And this knowe I by hem that loveres be,
That whoso stryveth with yow hath the
  werse.
Now, lady bryght, for thi benignite,
At reverence of hem that serven the,   40
Whos clerc I am, so techeth me devyse
Som joye of that is felt in thi servyse.

Ye in my naked herte sentement
Inhelde, and do me shewe of thy swetnesse.
Caliope, thi voys be now present,   45
For now is nede. Sestow not my destresse,
How I mot telle anon-right the gladnesse
Of Troylus, to Venus heriynge?
To which gladnesse, who nede hath, God hym
  brynge!

Explicit prohemium tercii libri.

Incipit liber tercius.

Lay al this menewhile Troylus   50
Recordyng his lesson in this manere:
"Mafay," thought he, "thus wole I sey, and
  thus;
Thus wole I pleyne unto my lady dere;
That word is good, and this shal be my
  chere;
This nyl I not foryeten in no wyse."   55
God leve hym werken as he kan devyse!

And Lord, so that his herte gan to quappe,
Heryng hire come, and shorte for to syke!
And Pandarus, that lad hire by the lappe,
Com ner and gan in at the curtyn pyke,   60
And seyde, "God do bot on all syke.
Se who is here yow comen to visite;
Lo, here is she that is youre deth to wyte."

Therwith it semed as he wepte almost.
"A-ha," quod Troylus so rufully,   65

"Wher me be wo, O myghty God, thow
  woost!
Who is al there? I se nought trewely."
"Sire," quod Criseyde, "it is Pandare and I."
"Ye, swete herte? Allas, I may nought ryse
To knele and do yow honour in some wyse." 70

And dressed hym upward, and she right tho
Gan bothe hire hondes softe upon hym leye.
"O, for the love of God, do ye not so
To me," quod she, "I, what is this to seye?
Sire, comen am I to yow for causes tweye: 75
First, yow to thonke, and of youre lordshipe eke
Continuance I wolde yow biseke."

This Troylus, that herde his lady preye
Of lordship hym, wax neyther quyk ne ded,
Ne myghte o word for shame to it seye,   80
Although men sholde smyten of his hed.
But Lord, so he wex sodeynliche red,

---

36 Ye folk, you, for people, have set. M *universite*. **39 benignite,** graciousness. The conclusion of the proem is Chaucer's. **40 At reverence,** out of respect for. **41 devyse,** narrate. **42** *thi:* M *this.* **43** *herte:* A&c *hertis.* **44 Inhelde . . . do,** infuse, make. **45 Caliope,** the muse of epic poetry and eloquence whom Chaucer evidently considered the appropriate inspiration for the triumph of love to be described in this book. **48 heriynge,** i.e., to the praise of Venus. **49** MC&c *gladnesse* om. **51 Recordyng,** rehearsing. **52 Mafay,** my faith. **53 pleyne,** complain. *lady:* A *herte.* **54 chere,** expression. **56 leve,** permit. *kan:* M&c *gan.* **57 so that . . . quappe,** how, beat. **58 syke,** sigh. **59 lappe,** hanging part of the garment, e.g., sleeve. **60 curtyn pyke,** curtain peek; the bed was, of course, the typical canopy bed provided with curtains for privacy. **61 bot,** assistance. **63 wyte,** blame for. **65** *A-ha:* C&c *Ha-a.* **66 Wher me,** whether to me. *O myghty:* other MSS *almighty.* **67 Who is al,** i.e., who all is. **69 Ye,** you. **71 dressed,** raised. **74 I,** oh (exclamation). **76 lordshipe eke,** protection also. *lordshipe:* M *mercy.* **77 Continuance,** continued protection. **79 hym . . . quyk,** him for protection, alive. Two A MSS *Hym of lordship.*

And sire, his lesson that he wende konne
To preyen hire is thurgh his wit yronne.

Cryseyde al this aspied wel ynowgh,   85
For she was wys, and loved hym nevere the lasse
Al nere he malapert or made it towgh
Or was to bold to synge a fol a masse.
But whan his shame gan somwhat to passe,
His resons, as I may my rymes holde,   90
I yow wol telle as techen bokes olde.

In chaunged voys, right for his verray drede,
Which voys ek quook, and therto his manere
Goodly abayst, and now his hewes rede,
Now pale, unto Criseyde his lady dere,   95
With look douncast and humble yolden chere,
Lo, the alderfirste word that hym asterte
Was twyes, "Mercy, mercy, swete herte!"

And stynte awhile, and whan he myghte
      outbrynge,
The nexte word was, "God wot that I have,   100
As ferforthly as I have had konnynge,
Ben yowres al, God so my sowle save,
And shal til that I, woful wyght, be grave.
And though I ne dar ne kan unto yow pleyne,
Iwys, I suffre nought the lasse peyne.   105

"Thus muche as now, O wommanlyche wyf,
I may out-brynge, and yf this yow displese,
That shal I wreke upon myn owen lyf
Right sone, I trowe, and don youre herte an ese,
If with my deth youre wreththe I may apese.   110
But syn that ye han herd me somwhat seye,
Now recche I nevere how sone that I deye."

Therwith his manly sorwe to byholde,

It myght han mad an herte of ston to rewe;
And Pandare wep as he to water wolde,   115
And poked evere his nece newe and newe,
And seyde, "Wobygon ben hertes trewe!
For love of God, make of this thyng an ende,
Or sle us bothe at ones er that ye wende."

"I, what?" quod she, "By God and by my
      trowthe,   120
I not nought what ye wille that I shol seye."
"I, what?" quod he. "That ye han on hym
      routhe,
For Goddes love, and doth hym nought to
      deye."
"Now thanne thus," quod she, "I wolde hym
      preye
To telle me the fyn of his entente.   125
Yet wyst I nevere wel what that he mente."

"What that I mene, O swete herte dere?"
Quod Troylus, "O goodly fresshe fre,
That with the stremes of youre eyen clere
Ye wolde somtyme frendly on me se,   130
And thanne agreen that I may ben he,
Withoute braunche of vyce on ony wyse,
In trowthe alwey to don yow my servyse,

"As to my lady right and chief resort,
With al my wit and al my deligence;   135
And I to han right as yow lyst comfort,
Under yowre yerde egal to myn offence,
As deth, if that I breke youre defence;
And that ye deigne me so muche honoure
Me to comaunden ought yn any owre;   140

"And I to ben yowre verray, humble, trewe,
Secret, and yn myn paynes pacient,

83 **wende konne,** thought he knew. 87 **malapert . . . made it towgh,** presumptuous, acted arrogant. 88 **fol a masse,** a mass for a fool (the implication seems clear though no one has been able satisfactorily to explain the specific figure). 90 **resons,** speeches. *resons:* other MSS *wordes/werkis.* 91 **bokes olde,** as previously remarked, this entire episode appears to be Chaucer's creation and to owe nothing to "bokes olde." 92 **verray,** genuine. 94 **Goodly abayst,** attractively abashed. 96 **yolden,** submissive (yielded). C&c *iyolden.* 97 **alderfirste,** first of all. 99 **stynte,** stopped. 100 *that:* C&c *for.* 101 **ferforthly,** far. MC&c *feythfully.* 102 *al:* M *also.* 103 **grave,** buried. 104 *ne dar:* MC&c *ne om.* 106 **wommanlyche wyf,** (most) womanly woman. 107 **out-brynge,** speak out. 108 **That . . . wreke,** then, avenge (it). 109 **trowe . . . don . . . an ese,** believe, put, at ease. 110 **wreththe,** wrath. MC&c *herte.* 112 **recche,** care. 114 **rewe,** have pity. 120 **I,** oh (exclamation). 122 **routhe,** pity. 125 **fyn,** object. 131 **agreen,** consent. 134 **resort,** source of help. 136 MC&c *I* om. 137 **yerde egal,** correction (with a yardstick), appropriate. 138 **defence,** prohibition. 139 *deigne:* M *digne.* 140 **ought . . . owre,** of anything, hour. 142 **paynes pacient,** patient in my love miseries.

And everemo desiren fresshly newe
To serven, and ben ay ilyke diligent,
And with good herte al holly youre talent 145
Receyven wel, how sore that me smerte—
Lo, this mene I, myn owene swete herte."

Quod Pandarus, "Lo, here an hard requeste,
A resonable lady for to werne!
Now, nece myn, by natal Joves feste, 150
Were I a god ye sholden sterve as yerne,
That heren wel this man wol nothyng yerne
But youre honour, and sen hym almost sterve,
And ben so loth to suffren hym yow serve."

With that she gan hire eyen on hym caste 155
Ful esyly and ful debonairly,
Avysyng hire, and hied not to faste
With nevere a word, but seyde hym softely,
"Myn honour sauf, I wol wel trewely,
And in swych forme as he gan now devyse, 160
Receyven hym fully to my servyse,

"Bysechyng hym for Goddes love that he
Wolde in honour of trouthe and gentilesse,
As I wel mene, eke mene wel to me,
And myn honour with wit and besynesse 165
Ay kepe. And yf I may don hym gladnesse,
From hennesforth, iwys, I nyl not feyne.
Now beth al hol; no lenger ye ne pleyne.

"But nathelees, this warne I yow," quod she,
"A kynges sone although ye be, iwys, 170
Ye shul no more have soveraynete
Of me in love than right in that cas is;
Ne I nyl forbere, yf that ye don amys,

To wrathen yow; and whil that ye me serve,
Cherycen yow right after ye deserve. 175

"And shortly, dere herte and al my knyght,
Beth glad and draweth yow to lustynesse,
And I shal trewely with al my myght
Youre bittre tornen al into swetnesse.
If I be she that may yow do gladnesse, 180
For every wo ye shal recovere a blysse."
And hym in armes tok, and gan hym kysse.

Fil Pandarus on knees, and up his eyen
To hevene threw, and held his hondes hye,
"Inmortal god," quod he, "that mayst nought
    dyen, 185
Cupide I mene, of this mayst glorifie;
And Venus, thow mayst make melodie.
Withouten hond, me semeth in the towne,
For this merveyle ich here ech belle sowne.

"But ho, no more as now of this matere, 190
Forwhi this folk wol comen up anoon
That han the lettre red—lo, I hem here.
But I conjure the, Criseyde and oon,
And two thow Troylus, whan thow mayst
    goon,
That at myn hows ye ben at my warnynge, 195
For I ful wel shal shape youre comynge;

"And eseth there youre hertes right ynough,
And lat se which of yow shal bere the belle
To speke of love aright"—therwith he
    lough—
"For ther have ye a layser for to telle." 200
Quod Troylus, "How longe shal y dwelle

---

145 holly . . . talent, wholly, wishes. **146 how sore,** however sorely. **149 werne,** refuse. C&c *And resonable, a lady for to.* **150 natal Joves,** Jove was patron of nativities, but Root interprets this as Jove's natal feast, i.e., birthday (like Christmas). **151 sterve . . . yerne,** die as quickly. **152 wol . . . yerne,** desires. **154 suffren,** permit. **156 esyly . . . debonairly,** softly, gently. **157 Avysyng . . . hied,** deliberating, hastened. A *hyed her.* **158** *softely:* other MSS *sobrely/sekyrly.* **160 forme . . . devyse,** manner, describe. *And/gan:* M&c *But/can; he:* A *y.* **165 besynesse,** diligence. **167 feyne,** evade (pretend). **168 hol,** whole (well). A *That ye pleyn.* **174 wrathen,** be angry with. **175 Cherycen,** cherish (treat with affection). **176** M *my dere.* **177 lustynesse,** good spirits. **178** Other MSS *with my ful.* **180** *yow:* M *now;* other MSS *do yow.* **186 mayst glorifie,** you may glory in (be proud of). A *mayst thou.* **188 me semeth,** it seems to me. Church bells ringing spontaneously to celebrate special events are a commonplace in ballads and saints' lives. **189** *merveyle:* other MSS *miracle; ich:* M *I.* **190** MA *as* om. **191 Forwhi,** because. **193–94 and oon . . . And two,** M&c read so, which eds. interpret as "both the one and the other"; C&c have *anon* and *to,* which would mean "from now on" and "also." **195 warnynge,** summons. **196 shape,** plan. **198 bere the belle,** i.e., take the lead (be the bellwether). **199 lough,** laughed. **200 have . . . layser . . . telle,** will have, time, talk. **201 dwelle,** wait.

Er this be don?" Quod he, "Whan thow mayst
   ryse,
This thing shal be right as I yow devyse."

With that Eleyne and also Deiphebus   204
Tho comen upward right at the steyres ende.
And Lord, so thanne gan grone Troylus
His brother and his suster for to blende.
Quod Pandarus, "It tyme is that we wende.
Tak, nece myn, youre leve at alle thre,
And lat hem speke, and cometh forth with
   me."   210

She tok hire leve at hem ful thryftyly,
As she wel koude, and they hire reverence
Unto the fulle deden hardely,
And wonder wel speken, in hire absence,
Of hire in preysing of hire excellence: 215
Hire governaunce, hire wit, and hire manere
Comendeden that it was joye to here.

Now lat hire wende unto hire owen place,
And torne we to Troylus ayen,
That gan ful lyghtly of the lettre pace   220
That Deiphebus hadde yn the gardeyn seyn;
And of Eleyne and hym he wolde feyn
Delyvered ben, and seyde that hym leste
To slepe and after tales have reste.

Eleyne hym kyste and tok hire leve blyve,   225
Deiphebus ek, and hom wente every wyght;
And Pandarus, as faste as he may dryve,
To Troylus tho com as lyne right,
And on a paillet al that glade nyght
By Troylus he lay with mery chere   230
To tale, and wel was hem thei were yfere.

Whan every wyght was voyded but they two,

And alle the dores were faste yshette,
To telle in shorte withoute wordes mo,
This Pandarus withouten ony lette   235
Up roos, and on his beddes side hym sette,
And gan to speken in a sobre wyse
To Troylus, as I shal yow devyse:

"Myn alderlevest lord and brother dere,
God wot, and thow, that it sat me so sore   240
When I the saw so langwysshyng to-yere
For love, of which thi wo wax alwey more,
That I with al my myght and al my lore
Have evere sethen do my bysynesse
To brynge the to joye out of distresse;   245

"And have it brought to swich plit as thow
   wost,
So that thorugh me thow stondest now in weye
To faren wel—I sey it for no bost—
And wostow whi? For shame it is to seye,
For the have I a game bygonne to pleye   250
Which that I nevere don shal eft for other,
Although he were a thousandfold my brother.

"That is to seye, for the am I becomen
Bytwixen game and ernest swych a mene
As maken wommen unto men to comen—   255
Al sey I nought, thow wost wel what I mene.
For the have I my nece of vices clene
So fully mad thi gentilesse triste,
That al shal ben right as thiselve lyste.

"But God that al wot take I to wytnesse   260
That nevere I this for coveytise wroughte,
But oonly for t'abrygge that destresse
For which wel nygh thow deydest, as me
   thoughte.
But, gode brother, do now as the oughte,

---

206 Two A MSS *so gronith.* 207 **blende,** deceive. 211 **thryftyly,** properly. 212 **hire reverence,** to her respects. 220 **pace,** pass over.
222 **feyn,** happily. 223 **Delyvered,** released. 225 **blyve,** quickly. 228 **as lyne right,** like a straight line. A *com tho/as blyve.* 229 **paillet,**
pallet (mattress on the floor). 230 *mery:* other MSS *blisful.* 231 **tale . . . yfere,** talk, together. 235 **lette,** hesitation. 239–87 Chaucer
turns back to *Fil.* 3.5–10 for this part of Pandarus' discussion, but then expands it with 65 lines of his own (287–343). 239 **alderlevest,**
dearest of all. 240 **sat,** affected. 243 **lore,** wisdom. *myght:* A *wit.* 244 **bysynesse,** effort. 246 **plit,** plight (state). 247 **stondest . . .
in weye,** are on the way to. 250 C&c *For the have I bigonne a gamen pleye.* 251 **eft,** again. A *shal nevere do.* 254 **mene,** means (instrument).
256 Other MSS *Thow woost thiselven what I wolde meene.* 259 **lyste,** desire. 261 **coveytise,** desire for material gain. 262 **abrygge,** abridge
(reduce). A *for* om.; *thy distresse.*

For Goddes love, and kep hire out of blame, 265
Syn thow art wys, and save alwey hire name.

"For wel thow woost, the name as yet of hire
Among the peple, as who seyth, halwed is,
For that man is unbore, dar I swere,
That evere wyste that she dide amys. 270
But wo is me that I, that cause al this,
May thenken that she is my nece dere,
And I hire em, and traytour eke yfere!

"And were it wyst that I thorugh myn engyn
Hadde in my nece iput this fantasye, 275
To do thi lust and holly to be thyn,
Why, al the world upon it wolde crye,
And seyn that I the worste trecherye
Dide yn this cas that evere was bygonne,
And she forlost, and thow right nought ywonne.

"Wherfore, er I wol ferther gon a pas, 281
Yet eft I the byseche and fully seye
That prevete go with us in this cas—
That is to seyn, that thow us nevere wreye;
And be nought wroth though I the ofte preye
To holden secre swych an heigh matere, 286
For skylful is, thow wost wel, my preyere.

"And thenk what wo ther hath bytyd er this
For makyng of avauntes, as men rede,
And what myschaunce in this world yet is 290
Fro day to day right for that wykked dede.
For which these wise clerkes that ben dede
Han evere yet proverbed to us yonge,
That first vertu is to kepe tonge.

"And nere it that I wilne as now t'abregge 295
Diffusion of speche, I koude almost

A thousand olde storyes the alegge
Of wommen lost through fals and foles bost.
Proverbes kanst thyselve ynowe and wost
Ayens that vice for to ben a labbe, 300
Al seyde men soth as often as they gabbe.

"O tonge, allas, so often here byforn
Hastow made many a lady bright of hewe
Seyd 'Welaway the day that I was born!'
And manye a maydes sorwe for to newe. 305
And for the more part, al is untrewe
That men of yelpe, and it were brought to
     preve.
Of kynde noon avauntours is to leve.

"Avauntoure and a lyere al is on,
As thus: I pose a womman graunte me 310
Hire love, and seyth that other wol she non,
And I am sworn to holden it secre,
And after I go telle it two or thre;
Iwys, I am avauntour at the leste,
And a lyere, for I breke my biheste. 315

"Now loke thanne yf they be nought to
     blame,
Swych manere folk—what shal I clepe hem?
     what?—
That hem avaunte of wommen, and by name,
That nevere yet byhyghte hem this ne that,
Ne knewe hem more than myn olde hat! 320
No wonder is, so God me sende hele,
Though wommen drede with us men to dele.

"I sey this not for no mystrust of yow,
Ne for no wyse men, but for foles nice,
And for the harm that in the world is now, 325
As wel for folye ofte as for malice;

---

266 save . . . name, protect, reputation. Other MSS *so save/kepe*, etc. **268 halwed**, deeply respected (hallowed). M *alwed*. **269 unbore**, unborn. Other MSS *For never was ther wight, I dar wel swere.* **270 wyste**, knew. **273 yfere**, at the same time (together). **274 engyn**, contriving. **275 fantasye**, desire (notion). **276 lust**, pleasure. **277 wolde crye**, cry out against. A *al the peeple wolde upon it.* **280 forlost . . . nought ywonne**, utterly lost (ruined), nothing won. A&c *fordon.* **281 pas**, step. **282** Other MSS *The preye ich eft, althogh thow sholdest deye.* **283 prevete**, secrecy. **284 wreye**, reveal. **287 skylful**, reasonable. **288 bytyd**, occurred. **289 avauntes**, boasts. **290** *myschaunce*: A *mischef.* **293** Other MSS *Han writen or this, as yit men teche us yonge.* **294 kepe**, guard. **295 wilne . . . t'abregge**, wish, to shorten. **297 alegge**, cite (allege). **298 foles**, foolish (of fools). **300 labbe**, gossip. A *blabbe.* **301 Al seyde . . . gabbe**, even though men said, lie. Other MSS *Though men soth seyde.* **303** Other MSS *Hath made ful.* **308 Of kynde . . . avauntours . . . leve**, by nature, boaster, believe. *kynde*: M *kyng.* **309 is on**, is the same (one). **310 I pose**, suppose. **315 biheste**, promise. M *myn heste.* **316 be nought**: other MSS *ben ought.* **319 byhyghte**, promised. C&c *yet bihyghte hem nevere.* **321 hele**, health. **324 nice**, foolish.

For wel wot I in wyse folk that vice
No womman drat, if she be wel avised,
For wyse ben by foles harm chastised.

"But now to purpos: leve brother dere,⁣ 330
Have al this thing that I have seyd in
    mynde,
And kep the clos, and be now of good chere,
For at thi day thow shalt me trewe fynde.
I shal thi proces sette yn swych a kynde,
And God toforn, that it shal the suffise,⁣ 335
For it shal ben right as thow wolt devyse.

"For wel I wot thow menest wel, parde;
Therfore I dar this fully undertake.
Thow wost eke what thi lady graunted the;
And day is set the chartres up to make.⁣ 340
Have now good nyght, I may no lengere
    wake.
And byd for me, syn thow art now yn blysse,
That God me sende deth or soone lysse."

Who myghte telle half the joye or feste
Whiche that the sowle of Troylus tho felte⁣ 345
Herynge th'effect of Pandarus byheste?
His olde wo that made his herte swelte
Gan tho for joye wasten and tomelte,
And al the richesse of his sikes sore
At ones fledde; he felte of hem no more.⁣ 350

But right so as these holtes and these hayis,
That han in wynter dede ben and dreye,
Revesten hem in grene when that May is,
Whan every lusti lyketh best to pleye,
Right in that selve wyse, soth for to seye,⁣ 355
Wax sodeynlyche his herte ful of joye,
That gladder was there nevere man in Troye.

And gan his lok on Pandarus up caste,
Ful sobrely and frendly for to se,
And seyde, "Frend, in Aperil the laste—⁣ 360
As wel thow wost, if it remembreth the—
How neigh the deth for wo thow founde me,
And how thow dedest al thi bysynesse
To knowe of me the cause of my distresse;

"Thow wost how longe ich it forbar to seye⁣ 365
To the, that art the man that I best triste;
And peril was it noon to the bywreye,
That wyst I wel; but telle me, yf the lyste,
Sith I so loth was that thiself it wyste,
How dorst I mo tellen of this matere,⁣ 370
That quake now and no wyght may us here?

"But natheles, by that God I the swere,
That as hym lyst may al this world governe,
And, yf I lye, Achilles with his spere
Myn herte cleve al were my lyf eterne,⁣ 375
As I am mortal, if I late or yerne
Wolde it bywreye, or dorst, or sholde konne,
For al the good that God made under sonne,

"That rather deye I wolde and determyne,
As thenketh me, now stokked yn presoun,⁣ 380
In wrecchednesse, in filthe, and yn vermine,
Caytif to cruel Kyng Agamenoun—
And this yn all the temples of this town,
Upon the goddes alle, I wol the swere
Tomorwe day, if that it lyketh the here.⁣ 385

"And that thow hast so muche ido for me
That I ne may it nevere more deserve,
This knowe I wel, al myghte I now for the
A thowsand tymes on a morwe sterve.
I kan no more but that I wol the serve⁣ 390

---

327 that vice, i.e., boasting of their conquests. **328 drat,** dreads. A *dredith.* **330 leve,** dear. **332 clos,** secret. **333 thi day,** the fitting time. **334 proces . . . kynde,** affair, fashion. **335 toforn,** before. **336 devyse,** wish. **340 day is set . . . chartres,** the day is set to draw up the final papers (highly figurative language in the present situation). **342 byd,** pray. **343 lysse,** comfort. **344 or:** M *and.* **346 effect . . . byheste,** gist, promise. *th'effect:* M *the feyth.* **347 swelte,** faint. *herte:* M *sorwe.* **348 wasten . . . tomelte,** shrink, melt (*to* is an intensifier). **349 richesse . . . sikes,** abundant sighs. **350 ones,** once. **351 holtes . . . hayis,** woods, hedges. **352 dreye,** dry. **354 lusti,** joyful person. **359 for to:** A *on to.* **365 forbar,** refrained. **366 triste,** trust. *best:* A *most.* **367 bywreye,** reveal. **371 wyght:** other MSS *man.* **376 late or yerne,** late or early. **377 Wolde . . . dorst . . . sholde konne,** wanted to, should dare, should be able to. **378 good,** wealth. **379 determyne,** come to an end. B *But rather wold I dye.* **380 stokked,** confined in stocks. **382 Agamenoun,** Agamemnon, leader of the Greek forces. *Caytif:* M *Castif.* **385 Tomorwe day . . . here,** tomorrow morning, you (to) hear (it). **386 muche ido:** M *meche don.* **389 on a morwe sterve,** in a day die.

Right as thi sclave, whider so thow wende,
For everemore, unto my lyves ende.

"But here with al myn herte I the byseche
That nevere in me thow deme swych folye
As I shal seyn; me thowghte by thi speche 395
That this which thow me dost for compaignye,
I sholde wene it were a bauderye.
I am nought wood, al if I lewed be.
It is not so; that wot I wel, parde.

"But he that goth for gold or for richesse 400
On swych message, calle hym what the lyst;
And this that thow dost, calle it gentilesse,
Compassioun, and felawship, and trist.
Departe it so, for wydewhere is wyst
How that ther is dyversite requered 405
Bytwyxen thynges lyk, as I have lered.

"And that thow knowe I thenke nought, ne
wene,
That this servise a shame be or a jape,
I have my faire suster Polixene,
Cassandre, Eleyne, or ony of the frape, 410
Be she nevere so faire or wel ishape,
Tel me which thow wylt of everychone
To han for thyn, and lat me thanne allone.

"But sith thow hast idon me this servyse
My lyf to save, and for noon hope of mede, 415
So for the love of God, this grete emprise
Performe it out, for now is moste nede.
For hygh and low, withouten ony drede,
I wol alwey thye hestes alle kepe.
Have now good nyght, and lat us bothe
slepe." 420

Thus held hym eche of other wel apayed,
That al the world me myghte it bet amende.
And on the morwe, whan they were arayed,
Ech to his owen nedes gan entende.
But Troylus, though as the fyr he brende 425
For sharp desir of hope and of plesaunce,
He not forgat his gode governaunce.

But in hymself with manhood gan restreyne
Ech rakel dede and ech unbrydled chere,
That alle tho that lyven, soth to seyne, 430
Ne sholde han wyst by word or by manere
What that he mente, as towchyng this matere.
From every wyght as fer as is the clowde
He was, so wel dissimulen he kowde.

And al the while which that I yow devyse, 435
This was hys lyf: with al his fulle myght
By day he was in Martes highe servyse—
This is to seyn, in armes as a kynght—
And for the more part, the longe nyght
He lay and thoughte how that he myghte
serve 440
His lady best, hire thank for to deserve.

Nyl I nought swere, although he lay ful softe,
That in his thought he nas sumwhat dishesed,
Ne that he torned on his pylwes ofte, 444
And wold of that hym myssed han ben sesed.
But yn swych cas man is nought alwey yplesed,
For ought I wot, no more than was he;
That kan I deme of possibilite.

But certeyn is, to purpos for to go,
That in this while, as wreten is in geste, 450
He say his lady somtyme, and also

391 **sclave**, slave. M&c *knave* (in M a later correction). 394 **deme . . . folye**, suppose, stupidity. 395 **seyn**, say. 396 **compaignye**, friendship (comradeship). 397 **wene . . . bauderye**, think, pimping. 398 **wood . . . lewed**, crazy, ignorant. 401 **swych message**, such an errand. 403 **trist**, trust. 404 **Departe it so**, i.e., keep the distinction clear. **wydewhere is wyst**, it is widely known. Root points out that distinguishing between "likeness" and "identity" of nature was a common scholastic exercise. 405 **dyversite**, distinction. 406 **lered**, learned. 407 **wene**, believe. 408 **a jape**, a joke. MC&c *a* om. 410 **frape**, group. 415 **mede**, material reward. 416 **emprise**, enterprise. 418 **drede**, doubt. 419 **hestes**, commands. 421 **apayed**, satisfied. 425 *though*: M&c *thoughte*. 427 **governaunce**, decorum. 429 **rakel . . . chere**, rash, expression. 432 **mente**, intended (thought). 435 **devyse**, describe. 437 **Martes**, Mars'. 439 *more*: A&c *most*. 442 B *I nyl nat seyn that though he lay ful softe*; MC&c *ful* om. For other variations in this stanza see Root. 445 **that hym myssed . . . sesed**, what he lacked, put in possession (seise). *sesed*: other MSS *esed*; in M the first *s* has been erased. 448 **deme of**, imagine a. 449 **purpos**, i.e., to get on with the story. 450 **geste**, story. Other MSS, *This mene while*. 451 **say**, saw.

She with hym spak whan that she dorst and
    leste;
And by hire bothe avys, as was the beste,
Apoynteden full warly in this nede,
So as they dorste, how they wolde procede.   455

But it was spoken in so short a wyse,
In swych awayt alwey, and in swych fere,
Lest ony wyght dyvynen or devyse
Wolde of hem two, or to it leye an eere,
That al this world so lef to hem ne were   460
As that Cupido wolde hem grace sende
To maken of hire speche aryght an ende.

But thilke lytel that they spake or wroughte,
His wyse gost tok ay of al swych hede,
It semed hire he wyste what she thoughte   465
Withouten word, so that it was no nede
To bidde hym ought to don, or ought
    forbede;
For which she thoughte that love, al coom it late,
Of alle joye hadde opned hire the yate.

And shortly of this proces for to pace,   470
So wel his werk and wordes he bysette
That he so ful stod in his lady grace
That twenty thousand tymes, er she lette,
She thonked God she evere with hym mette.
So koude he hym governe in swych
    servyse   475
That al the world ne myght it bet devyse.

For whi she fond hym so dyscret in al,
So secret, and of swych obeysaunce,
That wel she felte he was to hire a wal
Of stel, and sheld from every dysplesaunce;   480
That to ben in his goode governaunce,

So wys he was, she nas no more afered—
I mene as fer as oughte ben requered.

And Pandarus to quyke alwey the fyr
Was evere ylyke prest and dyligent;   485
To ese his frend was set al his desir.
He shof ay on, he to and fro was sent,
He lettres bar whan Troylus was absent,
That nevere man, as in his frendes nede,
Ne bar hym bet than he withouten drede.   490

But now, paraunter, som man wene wolde
That every word, or sonde, or lok, or chere
Of Troylus that I rehersen sholde,
In al this while unto his lady dere:
I trowe it were a long thing for to here,   495
Or of what wyght that stont in swych
    disjoynte,
His wordes alle, or every lok, to poynte.

Forsothe, I have not herd it don er this
In storye noon, ne no man here, I wene.
And though I wolde, I koude not, iwys,   500
For ther was som epistel hem bytwene
That wolde, as seyth myn autour, wel
    contene
Neigh half this book, of which hym lyste not
    write.
How sholde I thanne a lyne of it endite?

But to the grete effect: Than sey I thus,   505
That stondyng in concord and in quiete,
Thise ilke two, Criseyde and Troylus,
As I have told, and in this tyme swete—
Save only often myghte they nought mete,
Ne layser have hire speches to fulfille—   510
That it befel right as I shal yow telle,

---

452 leste, wished. **453 bothe avys,** mutual agreement. **454 Apoynteden . . . warly,** arranged, cautiously. **455 dorste,** dared. Other MSS *In everything now.* **457 awayt,** watchfulness. **458 dyvynen . . . devyse,** guess, conjecture. **459** B *Wolde on this thing, or.* **460 lef,** dear. **461** *Cupido:* C&c *Cupide.* grace: other MSS *space.* **462 aryght . . . ende,** a speedy conclusion (i.e., in action). **463 wroughte,** did. **464 gost . . . ay,** spirit, always. **470** A *forth to pace.* **473 lette,** stopped. **478 obeysaunce,** obedience. **481 governaunce,** control (care for). **483 as fer as . . . requered,** i.e., within the limits of decorum. **484 quyke,** quicken. **485 prest,** available. **487** Some MSS *to and fro he went.* **489 man:** some MSS *wight.* **490** Some MSS: *Ne bar hym bet to don his frend to spede.* **491 wene,** think. C&c *wayten.* **492 sonde . . . chere,** message, expression. **495 trowe . . . were,** believe (think), would be. **496 Or . . . wyght . . . disjoynte,** either, person, difficult situation. **497 or . . . to poynte,** to point out. **499 no man here, I wene,** no one here (has heard such detail), I suppose. **501 epistel,** letters. **503** *Neigh half this book:* other MSS *An hondred vers.* **505 grete effect,** main point.

That Pandarus, that evere dide his myght
Right for the fyn that I shal speke of here,
As for to bryngen to his hous som nyght
His faire nece and Troylus yfere, 515
Wher as at leyser al this heigh matere
Towchyng hire love were at the fulle
  upbounde,
Hadde out of doute a tyme to it founde.

For he with gret deliberacioun
Hadde everything that herto myghte avayle 520
Forncast and put in execucioun,
And neither laft for cost ne for travayle.
Come yf hem lest, hem sholde nothing fayle;
And for to ben in ought espied there,
That, wyst he wel, an inpossible were. 525

Dredeles it clere was in the wynd
From every pye and every lette-game.
Now al is wel, for al the world is blynd
In this matere, bothe fremed and tame.
This tymbur is al redy up to frame; 530
Us lakketh nought but that we weten wolde
A certeyn houre in whiche she comen sholde.

And Troylus, that al this purvyaunce
Knew at the fulle and waytede on it ay,
Hadde hereupon ek made gret ordinaunce, 535
And found his cause, and therto his aray,
Yf that he were myssed nyght or day,
Ther while he was abowte this servyse,
That he was gon to don his sacrifise,

And most at swych a temple alone wake, 540
Answered of Apollo for to be,

And first to sen the holy laurer quake,
Er that Apollo spake out of the tre
To telle hym next whan Grekes sholden fle—
And forthy lette hym no man, God forbede, 545
But prey Apollo helpen in this nede.

Now is ther litel more for to done,
But Pandare up, and shortly for to seyne,
Right soone upon the chaungyng of the moone,
Whan lyghtles is the world a nyght or tweyne,
And that the wolken shop hym for to reyne, 551
He straught amorwe unto his nece wente;
Ye han wel herd the fyn of his entente.

Whanne he was come, he gan anoon to pleye
As he was woned, and of hymself to jape; 555
And fynally he swor and gan hire seye,
By this and that, she sholde hym not escape,
Ne lenger don hym after hire to gape,
But certeynly she moste, by hire leve,
Come soupen in his hous with hym at eve. 560

At which she lough and gan hire faste excuse,
And seyde, "It rayneth, lo. How sholde I gon?"
"Lat be," quod he, "ne stond not thus to muse.
This mot be don. Ye shal be ther anoon."
So at the laste herof they felle atoon, 565
Or elles, softe he swor hire in hire ere,
He nolde nevere comen ther she were.

Soone after this, she to hym gan to rowne,
And axed hym yf Troylus were there.
He swor hire nay, for he was out of towne, 570
And seyde, "Nece, I pose that he were,
Yow thurste han nevere the more fere;

For rather than men myghte hym ther aspie,
Me were levere a thousand fold to dye."

Nought list myn auctour fully to declare   575
What that she thoughte whan that he seyde so,
That Troylus was out of towne yfare,
As yf he seyde therof soth or no;
But that withouten awayt with hym to go
She graunted hym, sith he hire that bisoughte,
And, as his nece, obeyed as hire oughte.   581

But natheles yet gan she hym byseche,
Although with hym to gon it was no fere,
For to bewar of goosish poeples speche,
That dremen thynges whiche that nevere
    were,   585
And wel avyse hym whom he broughte there;
And seyde hym, "Em, syn I moste on yow triste,
Loke al be wel, and do now as yow liste."

He swor hire yis by stokkes and by stones,
And by the goddes that in hevene dwelle,   590
Or elles were hym levere, fel and bones,
With Pluto kyng as depe ben yn helle
As Tantalus. What sholde I more telle?
Whan al was wel, he ros and tok his leve,
And she to souper com whan it was eve,   595

With a certeyn of hire owene men,
And with hire faire nece Antigone,
And othere of hire wommen nyne or ten.
But who was glad now? Who, as trowe ye,
But Troylus, that stod and myght it se   600

Thoroughout a lytel wyndowe in a stuwe,
Ther he byshet syn mydnyght was in mewe,

Unwist of every wight but of Pandare.
But to the poynt. Now whanne she was
    ycome,
With alle joye and alle frendes fare,   605
Hire em anoon in armes hath hire nome,
And after to the souper alle and some,
Whan tyme was, ful softe they hem sette.
God wot, ther was no deynte for to fette.

And after souper gonnen they to ryse,   610
At ese wel with hertes fresshe and glade,
And wel was hym that koude best devyse
To liken hire, or laughen that hire made.
He song, she pleyde, he tolde tales of Wade.
But at the laste, as everything hath ende,   615
She tok hire leve, and nedes wolde wende.

But O Fortune, executrice of wyrdes!
O influences of thise hevenes hye!
Soth is that under God ye ben oure hierdes,
Though to us bestez ben the causes wrie.   620
This mene I now for she gan homward hye;
But execut was al byside hire leve
The goddes wil, for which she moste bleve.

The bente mone with hire hornes pale,
Saturne, and Jove in Cancro joyned were,   625
That swych a rayn from heven gan avale
That every maner womman that was there
Hadde of that smoky reyn a verray fere;

579–80 Lines transposed in B and Root ed. **579 awayt,** delay. B MSS *Withoute await, syn that he hire bisoughte.* **580** B MSS *But that she graunted with hym for to go.* **584 goosish:** M *gosylyche.* **587 moste,** must. **588** Other MSS *for I do as yow liste.* **589 yis:** other MSS *this.* **591 fel,** skin. MC&c *soule.* **593 Tantalus,** in classical mythology, condemned to punishment in Hades with food and drink forever just out of reach (hence "tantalize"). M *Tatalus. more telle:* other MSS *lenger duelle.* **599 trowe,** believe (think). **601 Thoroughout . . . stuwe,** out through, heated room (by Chaucer's time, already used for "brothel," cf. *CT* III.1332). A *Thurghout an hole within a litil stewe.* **602 byshet . . . mewe,** shut up, in a coop. **603 Unwist,** unknown. **605 frendes fare,** friendly ceremony. **606 nome,** taken. **608 softe,** comfortably. **609 for to fette,** that needed to be fetched. **612 wel was hym . . . devyse,** he was fortunate, devise entertainment. *devyse:* M *avyse.* **613 liken,** please. **614 Wade,** the mythical hero of Germanic legend known only by allusions such as this. Chaucer's only other reference to him may have salacious overtones, cf. *CT* IV.1424 and note. **617 wyrdes,** fate; glossed "destine" in M. **618 influences,** astrological influence of the stars. **619 under God . . . hierdes,** i.e., the fates are under God's power, guardians (herdsmen). **620 wrie,** hidden. A *cause ywrye.* **621** A *I mene it now for she gan home to hye.* **622 byside hire leve,** without her consent. **623 bleve,** remain. **624–25 bente mone . . . Saturne . . . Jove . . . Cancro.** This is the famous conjunction of the new moon, Saturn, and Jupiter in the zodiacal sign of Cancer which occurred in May 1385 after a lapse of 600 years, and so helps to date the composition of the poem. **626** A *That madyn such a reyne fro hevyn avale.*

At which Pandare tho lough and seyde
    thenne,
"Now were it tyme a lady to go henne!   630

"But goode nece, yf I myghte evere plese
Yow any thing, thanne prey ich yow," quod he,
"To don myn herte as now so grete an ese
As for to dwelle here al this nyght with me,
For whi this is youre owene hous, parde.   635
For, by my trouthe, I sey it for no game,
To wende now it were to me a shame."

Criseyde, which that kowde as muche good
As half a world, tok hede of his preyere,
And syn it ron, and al was on a flod,   640
She thoughte, "As good chep may I dwellen
    here,
And graunte it gladly with a frendes chere,
And have a thank, as grucche and thanne
    abyde—
For hom to gon, it may noght wel betyde."

"I wol," quod she, "myn uncle lef and dere. 645
Syn that yow lyst, it skile is to be so.
I am right glad with yow to dwellen here.
I seyde but a-game I wolde go."
"Iwys, graunt mercy, nece," quod he tho,
"Were it a-game or no, soth for to telle,   650
Now am I glad syn that yow lyst to dwelle."

Thus al is wel. But tho bygan aright
The newe joye and al the feste agayn.
But Pandarus, yf goodly hadde he myght,
He wolde han hyed hire to bedde fayn,   655
And seyde, "Lord, this is an huge rayn!

This were a weder for to slepen inne,
And that I rede us soone to bygynne.

"And, nece, wot ye wher I wol yow leye,
For that we shul nat lyggen fer asonder,   660
And for ye neither shullen, dar I seye,
Heren noyse of reynes nor of thonder?
By God, right in my litel closet yonder.
And I wole in that outer hous allone
Be wardeyn of youre wommen everychone. 665

"And in this myddel chaumbre that ye se
Shul youre wommen slepen wel and softe.
And there I seyde shal youreselven be—
And yf ye liggen wel tonyght, com ofte,
And careth not what weder is on lofte.   670
The wyn anon, and whan so that yow leste,
So go we slepe; I trowe it be the beste."

Ther nys no more, but hereafter soone,
The voyde dronke and travers drawe anoon,
Gan every wight that hadde nought to done 675
More in the place out of the chaumber gon.
And evermo so sternelyche it ron,
And blew therwith so wondirliche loude,
That wel neigh no man heren other koude.

Tho Pandarus, hire em, right as hym oughte, 680
With women swyche as were hire most aboute,
Ful glad unto hire beddes syde hire broughte,
And tok his leve, and gan ful lowe lowte,
And seyde, "Here at this closet dore withoute,
Right overthwart, youre wommen liggen alle,
That whom yow lyst of hem, ye may hire
    calle."   686

---

636 C&c *sey it nought a-game.* **641 chep,** as easily (cheaply). **643 grucche,** grumble. **646 lyst, it skile,** desire, it is reason (enough). **654 goodly . . . myght,** i.e., had been well able to. **655 fayn,** happily. **658 rede,** advise. **659 wot ye,** do you know. **660 lyggen . . . asonder,** lie, apart. **661** A *sholdyn neither.* **663–66 litel closet . . . outer hous . . . myddel chaumbre,** the design of a typical London city house included a small private room (the closet) behind the dais in the main hall, and a traverse curtain (l. 674) across the middle of the hall that could divide it into a section near the entrance (the outer chamber), and a section between this and the closet (the middle chamber). A cellar extended beneath the whole floor, with (in this instance) a trapdoor into the closet through which Pandarus and Troylus could enter without disturbing the attendants in the middle chamber. **664 outer:** M *other.* **665 wardeyn,** guardian. **668 there,** where. Other MSS *And all withinne shal.* **671 The wyn anon:** in A the imperative had been *Goth yn anone.* **672** Other MSS *Than is it tyme for to gon to reste.* **674 voyde,** wine drunk before retiring, called the "voide." **travers,** curtain which could be drawn to divide the hall into two parts, cf. ll. 663ff. Two A MSS *They voydid and drunk and curtyns drew anone.* **677** Other MSS *And alweye in this meene while it ron* (rained). **681 most aboute,** i.e., her closest attendants. **683 lowte,** bow. **685 overthwart,** across the door (so one would have to step over them to enter).

So whan that she was yn the closet leyd,
And alle hire wommen forth by ordenaunce
Abedde weren, ther as I have seyd,
There was nomore to skippen nor to
    traunce,   690
But boden go to bedde with myschaunce,
If ony wight was steryng onywhere,
And lat hem slepen that abedde were.

But Pandarus, that wel koude eche a del
The olde daunce and every poynt therinne, 695
Whan that he sey that alle thyng was wel,
He thought he wolde upon his werk bygynne,
And gan the stewe doore al softe unpynne,
And stille as ston, withouten lenger lette,
By Troylus adown right he hym sette.   700

And shortly to the poynt ryght for to gon,
Of alle this werk he told hym word and ende,
And seyde, "Make the redy right anoon,
For thow shalt into hevene blysse wende."
"Now blisful Venus, thow me grace sende," 705
Quod Troylus, "for nevere yet no nede
Hadde ich er now, ne halvendel the drede."

Quod Pandarus, "Ne drede the nevere a del,
For it shal ben right as thow wylt desire.
So thrive I, this nyght shal I make it wel, 710
Or casten al the gruwel in the fyre."
"Yit, blisful Venus, this nyght thow me
    enspire,"

Quod Troylus, "As wys as I the serve,
And evere bet and bet shal til I sterve.

"And yf ich hadde, O Venus ful of myrthe, 715
Aspectes badde of Mars or of Saturne,
Or thow combest or let were in my byrthe,
Thy fader prey al thilke harm disturne
Of grace, and that I glad ayen may turne,
For love of hym thow lovedest yn the
    shawe—   720
I mene Adoon, that with the bor was slawe.

"Jove ek, for the love of faire Europe,
The whiche in forme of bole awey thow fette,
Now help! O Mars, thow with thi blody cope,
For love of Cipris, thow me noght ne lette! 725
O Phebus, thenk whan Dane hireselven shette
Under the bark, and laurer wax for drede;
Yet for hire love, O help now at this nede!

"Mercurie, for the love of Hierse ek,
For which Pallas was with Aglawros wroth, 730
Now help! And ek Diane, I the bysek
That this viage be not to the loth.
O fatal sustren, which er ony cloth
Me shapen was, my destene me sponne,
So helpeth to this werk that is bygonne." 735

Quod Pandarus, "Thow wrecched mouses
    herte,
Artow agast so that she wol the byte?

688 ordenaunce, command. **690 skippen . . . traunce,** skipping, tramping around. *skippen:* M *speken.* **691 boden . . . with myschaunce,** ordered, with abuse. **692** *wight:* A&c *man.* **694 eche a del,** each (every) part. **695 olde daunce,** the game of love—a favorite Chaucerian phrase, cf. *CT* I.476, VI.79. **696 sey,** saw. **698 unpynne,** unfasten. **699 stille . . . lette,** quiet, delay. *lenger:* A *more.* **702** *werk:* other MSS *thing.* **705 blisful:** B *seint.* **706 nevere . . . nede,** never (such) need. **707 halvendel the drede,** half the fear. **708 a del,** a bit. **710 thrive,** prosper. **711 casten . . . gruwel,** spill the porridge (proverbial). **712 blisful:** A *seynt.* **714 sterve,** die. **716 Aspectes badde . . . Mars . . . Saturne,** bad horoscopes; Mars and Saturn were planets detrimental to love, as Venus and Jupiter were beneficial. **717 combest . . . let,** when too close to the sun, Venus was considered burnt up (combust) and her influence hindered (let). *combest:* A *cumbrid;* C&c *combust.* **718 fader . . . disturne,** Jupiter, turn away. **719 Of grace . . . turne,** through (his) graciousness, become. **720 shawe,** woods. **721 Adoon,** Adonis, killed hunting the wild boar, Ovid, *Met.* 10.708ff. **722–23 Europe . . . bole,** Europa, whom Jupiter carried off after assuming the shape of a bull. Ovid, *Met.* 2.833ff. Troylus invokes the planets in order from the outermost inward (omitting baleful Saturn and sympathetic Venus). **724 blody cope,** bloody (because he was god of war) cloak. **725 Cipris,** name for Venus because she was born from the sea near the island of Cyprus; in mythology she was the lover of Mars. **lette,** hinder. **726 Phebus . . . Dane,** Phoebus Apollo, god of the sun, pursued the nymph Daphne, who to escape him was transformed into a laurel tree, Ovid, *Met.* 1.452ff. **729–30 Mercurie . . . Hierse . . . Pallas . . . Aglawros,** Pallas Minerva, angry with Aglauros, made her envious of Mercury's love for her sister Hierse; when Aglauros tried to thwart the love, Mercury turned her to stone, Ovid, *Met.* 2.708ff. **731 Diane,** Diana, goddess of chastity. **733 fatal sustren . . . cloth,** the fates spin the thread of life and weave the cloth of an individual's destiny. **735 A** *Now helpith;* M *help.* **737 agast,** afraid. M *Art thow.*

Why, don this furred cloke above thi sherte,
And folwe me, for I wol have the wyte.
But byde, and lat me go byforn a lyte." 740
And with that word he gan undon a trappe,
And Troylus he brought in by the lappe.

The sterne wynd so lowde gan to route
That no wight other noyse myghte here,
And they that layen at the dore withoute, 745
Ful sikerly they slepten al yfere.
And Pandarus, with a ful sobre chere,
Goth to the dore anoon withowten lette,
There as they laye, and softely it shette.

And as he come ayeynward prevely, 750
His nece awook and axed, "Who goth there?"
"My dere nece," quod he, "it am I.
Ne wondreth not, ne have of it no fere."
And ner he com and seyde hire yn hire ere,
"No word, for love of God, I yow byseche! 755
Lat no wight rysen and heren of oure speche."

"What? Which wey be ye comen, bendiste?"
Quod she. "And how thus unwyst of hem
     alle?"
"Here at this secre trappe dore," quod he.
Quod tho Criseyde, "Lat me som wight
     calle." 760
"I, God forbede that it sholde falle,"
Quod Pandarus, "that ye swych folye
     wroughte—
They myghte demen thyng they nevere er
     thoughte.

"It is nought good a slepyng hound to wake,
Ne yeve a wyght a cause to devyne. 765
Youre wommen slepen alle, I undertake,

So that for hem the hous men myghte myne,
And slepen wolen til the sonne shyne.
And whan my tale al brought is to an ende,
Unwist, right as I com, so wol I wende. 770

"Now, nece myn, ye shul wel understonde,"
Quod he, "so as ye wommen demen alle,
That for to holde in love a man in honde,
And hym hire lef and dere herte calle,
And maken hym an howve above a calle— 775
I mene, as love another in this while—
She doth hireself a shame and hym a gyle.

"Now, wherby that I telle yow al this:
Ye wot yourself as wel as ony wyght
How that youre love al fully graunted is 780
To Troylus, the worthieste kynght
On of this world, and therto trouthe yplight,
That but it were on hym along, ye nolde
Hym nevere falsen while ye lyven sholde.

"Now stant it thus, that sith I fro yow wente,
This Troylus, right platly for to seyn, 786
Is thurgh a goter by a prevy wente
Into my chaumbre come in al this reyn,
Unwyst of every manere wyght, certeyn,
Save of myself, as wysly have I joye, 790
And by that feith I shal Pryam of Troye.

"And he is come in swich peyne and distresse
That but he be al fully wod by this,
He sodeynly mot falle into wodnesse,
But yf God helpe—and cause whi is this. 795
He seyth hym told is of a frend of his
How that ye loven sholde on hatte Horaste,
For sorwe of which this nyght shal ben his
     laste."

---

738 don, put on. M *do on.* **739 wyte,** blame. **740 byde,** wait. **741 trappe,** trap door, cf. l. 663n. **742 lappe,** hanging part of the garment, e.g., sleeve. **743 route,** roar. **746 sikerly . . . yfere,** securely, together. **747 sobre chere,** serious expression. **748 anoon . . . lette,** immediately, hesitation. **757 bendiste:** MC&c *benedicite.* **758** MC&c *thus* om.; *hem:* M *us.* **759** *secre:* other MSS *litill.* **763 demen . . . er,** judge, before. **765 devyne,** guess. **767 for hem . . . myne,** as far as they are concerned, dig through into (undermine). **770 Unwist,** undetected. **772 demen,** know (judge). **773 holde in . . . honde,** pretend. *in love:* other MSS *in longe.* **775 howve above a calle,** hood above a cap, i.e., deceive. **776** MC&c *another this mene while.* **778 wherby,** wherefore. **783 on hym along,** by his fault. **786 platly,** flatly (directly). **787 goter . . . prevy wente,** gutter, secret passage. One scholar suggests that this was actually the passage into the privy—with degrading connotations for the whole love affair. **791** *shal:* other MSS *owe.* **793 but he be . . . this,** unless he is, by this time. **794 wodnesse,** madness. **797 hatte,** called. MC&c *on that hatte.*

Criseyde, which that al this wonder herde,
Gan sodeynly aboute hire herte colde,   800
And with a syk she sorwfully answerde,
"Allas, I wende whoso tales tolde,
My dere herte wolde me not holde
So lyghtly fals! Allas, conseytes wronge,
What harm they don, for now lyve I to
        longe!   805

"Horaste, allas, and falsen Troylus?
I knowe hym not, God helpe me so," quod she.
"Allas, what wykked spirit tolde hym thus?
Now certes, em, tomorwe and I hym se,
I shal therof as fully excusen me   810
As evere dide womman, yf hym lyke."
And with that word she gan ful sore syke.

"O God," quod she, "so worldly selynesse,
Which clerkes callen fals felicite,
Ymedled is with many a bitternesse.   815
Ful angwysshous than is, God wot," quod she,
"Condicioun of veyn prosperite.
For either joyes comen nought yfere,
Or elles no wight hath hem alwey here.

"O brotel wele of mannes joye unstable,   820
With what wyght so thow be, or how thow
        pleye,
Either he wot that thow, joye, art muable,
Or wot it not; it mot ben on of tweye.
Now yf he wot it not, how may he seye
That he hath verray joye and selynesse,   825
That is of ignoraunce ay in derknesse?

"Now yf he wot that joye is transitorie,
As every joye of worldly thyng mot fle,

Than every tyme he that hath in memorie,
The drede of lesyng maketh hym that he   830
May in no parfit selynesse be.
And yf to lese his joye he set a myte,
Than semeth it that joye is worth but lyte.

"Wherfore I wol deffyne in this matere,
That trewely, for ought I kan espie,   835
Ther is no verray wele in this world here.
But O thow wykked serpent jalousye,
Thow mysbeleved and envyous folye,
Whi hastow mad Troylus to me untriste,
That nevere yet agylt hym that I wyste?"   840

Quod Pandarus, "Thus fallen is this cas—"
"Whi, uncle myn," quod she, "who tolde hym
        this?
Whi doth my dere herte thus, allas?"
"Ye wot, ye, nece myn," quod he, "what is.
I hope al shal be wel that is amys.   845
For ye may quenche al this yf that yow leste.
And doth right so, for I holde it the beste."

"So shal I do tomorwe, ywys," quod she,
"And God toforn, so that it shal suffise."
"Tomorwe? Allas, that were a fayr!" quod he.
"Nay, nay, it may nat stonden yn this wyse.   851
For, nece myn, thus writen clerkes wyse,
That peril is with drecchyng in idrawe.
Nay, swyche abodes be nought worth an hawe.

"Nece, alle thing hath tyme, I dar avowe;   855
For whan a chaumbre afyre is, or an halle,
More nede is it sodeynly to rescowe
Than to dispute and axe amonges alle
How this candele in the straw is falle.

799 *this wonder:* M *these thynges.* **800** *sodeynly:* other MSS *therwithal.* **801 syk,** sigh. *sorwfully:* other MSS *sodeynly.* **802 wende,** thought. **804 conseytes,** conceits (imaginings). **809** *tomorwe and:* M *to more yf.* **811 hym lyke,** it pleases him. M *yf he lyke;* A *if that hym lyke.* **813 selynesse,** from OE *gesælig,* blessed, happy, with Chaucer's usual range of connotation from happy through innocent to silly. These sentiments follow *Boece* II pr. 4 and are, like this whole episode, Chaucer's addition to the poem and to Criseyde's character. **814 fals felicite,** the Boethian concept of happiness founded upon mutable temporal pleasures. **815 Ymedled,** mingled. **817 veyn,** worthless. **818 yfere,** together. *either:* M *other.* **819** *alwey:* A *long.* **820 brotel wele,** brittle good fortune. *of mannes:* other MSS *O worldly.* **822 wot . . . muable,** knows, mutable. **823** M *Other he wot.* **826 ay,** always. **829** MC&c *that* om. **830 lesyng,** losing (it). **832 set a myte,** cares a bit. **834 deffyne,** conclude. *matere:* M&c *manere.* **836 verray wele,** true prosperity. **838 mysbeleved,** disbelieving. **839 me untriste,** not to trust me. **840 agylt,** wronged. **842** *hym:* M *yow.* **849 toforn . . . suffise,** before, in a satisfactory way. **853 peril . . . drecchyng . . . idrawe,** i.e., danger is caused by delay (proverbial). **854 abodes . . . hawe,** delays, hawthorn berry (inedible). **857** C&c *Wel more nede/Hit nedith more,* etc. **859** C&c *How is this . . . yfalle,* etc.

A, bendiste, for al among that fare   860
The harm is don, and farewel feldefare.

"And nece myn—ne take it not agref—
If that ye suffre hym al nyght in this wo,
God help me so, ye hadde hym nevere lef—
That dar I seyn, now there is but we two.   865
But wel I wot that ye wol nat do so;
Ye ben to wys to do so gret folye,
To putte his lyf al nyght in jupartie."

"Hadde I hym nevere lef? By God, I wene
Ye hadde nevere thing so lief!" quod she.   870
"Now by my thryft," quod he, "that shal be
     sene,
For syn ye make this ensaumple of me,
If ich al nyght wolde hym in sorwe se,
For al the tresour yn the town of Troye
I bidde God I nevere mote have joye.   875

"Now loke thanne, if ye that ben his love
Shul putte al nyght his lyf in jupartie
For thing of nought, now by that God above,
Naught only this delay cometh of folye,
But of malis, if that I shal nought lye.   880
What, platly, and ye suffre hym in distresse,
Ye neyther bounte don ne gentilesse."

Quod tho Criseyde, "Wole ye don o thing,
And ye therwith shal stynte al his disese?
Have here, and bereth hym this blewe
     ryng,   885
For there is nothing myghte hym bettre plese,
Save I myself, ne more his herte apese.
And sey my dere herte that his sorwe
Is causeles, that shal ben sene tomorwe."

"A ryng?" quod he. "Ye, haselwodes shaken!   890
Ye, nece myn, that ryng moste han a ston
That myhte a dede man alyve maken,

And swych a ryng I trowe that ye have non.
Discrecioun out of youre hed is gon—
That fele I now," quod he, "and that is
     routhe.   895
O tyme ylost, wel maystow coursen slouthe!

"Wot ye not wel that noble and heigh corage
Ne sorweth not—ne stenteth ek—for lyte?
But yf a fol were in a jalous rage,
I nolde not sette at his sorwe a myte,   900
But feffe hym with a fewe wordes white
Another day, whan that I myghte hym
     fynde—
But this thing stont al in another kynde.

"This is so gentil and so tendre of herte
That with his deth he wole his sorwes
     wreke.   905
For trusteth wel, how sore that hym smerte,
He wol to yow no jalous wordes speke.
And forthi, nece, er that his herte breke,
So speke youreself to him of this matere,
For with o word ye may his herte stere.   910

"Now have I told what peril he is inne,
And his comyng unwyst is to every wyght.
Ne, parde, harm may ther be non, ne synne;
I wol myself be with yow al this nyght.
Ye knowe ek how it is youre owen knyght,   915
And that by right ye moste upon hym triste,
And I al prest to fecche hym whan yow liste."

This accident so petous was to here,
And ek so lyke a soth at pryme face,
And Troylus hire knyght to hire so dere,   920
His preve comyng, and the siker place,
That, though that she dide hym as thanne a
     grace,
Considered alle thinges as they stode,
No wonder is, syn she dide al for gode.

---

860 fare, business (argument). **861 feldefare,** a thrush (i.e., and meanwhile the bird has flown). **862 agref,** amiss. **864 hadde . . . lef,** i.e., you never loved him. **869 wene,** believe. *I:* M *ye.* **870** *Ye:* M I. **872 ensaumple,** comparison. **875 bidde,** pray. **882 bounte,** generosity. Other MSS *wisdom.* **884 stynte,** stop. **887** *more:* M *bettre.* **889** *causeles:* A *nedeles; ben sene:* other MSS *he see.* **890 Ye, haselwodes shaken,** yes, shake the hazelnut trees (i.e. "nuts"). A *hasilwode is.* **895 routhe,** a pity. **898 stenteth,** stops. **901 feffe,** endow (bestow on him). **905 wreke,** banish. **910 stere,** steer (control). **915** A *wele eke how he is.* **917 prest,** ready. **918 accident,** incident. **919 pryme face,** first sight. **921 siker,** secure. **922 grace,** favor.

Cryseide answerde, "As wysly God at reste 925
My sowle brynge, as me is for hym wo!
And, em, ywys, fayn wolde I do the beste,
Yf that I hadde a grace to do so.
But whether that ye dwelle or for hym go,
I am, til God me bettre mynde sende, 930
At dulcarnon, right at my wittes ende."

Quod Pandarus, "Ye, nece, wol ye here?
Dulcarnon called is 'flemyng of wrecches'—
It semeth hard, for wrecches nel hit lere
For verray slouthe or other wilful tacches; 935
This seyd by hem that ben not worth two
    facches.
But ye ben wys, and that we han on honde
Nis neither hard ne skylful to withstonde."

"Thanne, em," quod she, "doth herof as yow
    lyst.
But er he come I wil up first aryse, 940
And, for the love of God, syn al my trist
Is on yow two, and ye ben bothe wyse,
So wyrcheth now in so discret a wyse
That I honour may have, and he plesaunce;
For I am here al yn youre governaunce." 945

"That is wel seyd," quod he, "my nece deere.
Ther good thryft on that wyse gentil herte.
But liggeth stille, and taketh hym ryght here.
It nedeth not no ferther for hym sterte.
And eche of yow ese otheres sorwes smerte, 950
For love of God. And Venus, I the herye,
For soone, hope I, we shul ben alle merye."

This Troylus ful sone on knes hym sette,
Ful sobrely, ryght be hire beddes hed,
And yn his beste wyse his lady grette. 955

But Lord, so she wax sodeynlyche red!
Ne though men sholden smyten of hire hed,
She kowde nought a word aryght out-brynge
So sodeynly, for his sodeyn comynge.

But Pandarus, that so wel koude fele 960
In everythyng, to pleye anoon bygan,
And seyde, "Nece, se how this lord kan knele!
Now, fore youre trouthe, seth this gentil man!"
And with that word he for a quysshon ran,
And seyde, "Kneleth now, while that yow
    leste, 965
There God youre hertes brynge soone at reste."

Kan I not seyn, for she bad hym not ryse,
If sorwe it put out of hire remembraunce,
Or elles if she tok it in the wyse
Of deuete, as for his observaunce; 970
But wel fynde I she dide hym this pleasaunce,
That she hym kyste, although she siked sore,
And bad hym sytte adown withowten more.

Quod Pandarus, "Now wol ye wel bygynne.
Now doth hym sitte, gode nece dere, 975
Upon youre beddes side al there withinne,
That eche of yow the bet may other here."
And with that word he drow hym to the fyre,
And tok a lyght, and fond his contenaunce
As for to loke upon an old romaunce. 980

Criseyde, that was Troylus lady right,
And cler stod on a ground of sykernesse,
Al thoughte she hire servaunt and hire knyght
Ne sholde of right noon untrouthe in hire gesse,
Yet natheles, considered his distresse, 985
And that love is in cause of swych folye,
Thus to hym spak she of his jelousye:

925–26 **As wysly . . . as me,** as surely as God will save me, I am sorry for him. **927 fayn,** happily. **930** *mynde:* other MSS *wit.* **931 dulcarnon,** dilemma (from Arabic "two-horned," used as the designation for the 47th proposition of Euclid). **933 flemyng of wrecches,** banishment of wretches. Euclid's 5th proposition was called "fuga miserorum"; Pandarus conflates the epithets for the 5th and 47th. **934** *nel hit:* MC&c *wol not.* **935 tacches,** vices. **936 seyd by . . . facches,** is said about, beans (vetches). **938 skylful,** reasonable. **943 wyrcheth,** behave. **945 governaunce,** control. *al:* other MSS *as/now.* **947 thryft,** prosperity (simply an expression of approbation). **951 herye,** praise. **953** A *Troilus on knees sone.* **954 sobrely,** solemnly. **956** A *And thogh she sholde anon have be dede.* **957 Ne though,** even though. **962** A *Nece, how wel, lord, kan he knele.* **972 siked,** sighed. **975 doth,** make. **976 withinne,** again we must recall the canopy bed, whose curtains could be drawn for privacy. **978** *fyre:* a false rhyme in M; Kentish *fe(e)re* in C&c. **979 fond,** arranged. **980 As for to loke upon,** as if to read. **982 cler . . . sykernesse,** clear, security (innocence). **983 Al thoughte she,** she thought.

"Lo, herte myn, as wolde the excellence
Of love ayeyns the which that no man may—
Ne oughte ek—goudly make resistence,   990
And ek bycause I felte wel and say
Youre grete trouthe and servyse every day,
And that yowre herte al myn was, soth to
      seyne,
This drof me first to rewe upon yowre peyne.

"And youre goodnesse have I founde alwey yit,
Of which, my dere herte and al my knyght,   996
I thonke it yow as fer as I have wit,
Al kan I nought as muche as it were right;
And I emforth my konnyng and my myght
Have and ay shal, how sore that me smerte,   1000
Ben to yow trewe and hol with al myn herte;

"And dredles that shal be founde at preve.
But, herte myn, what al this is to seyne
Shal wel be told, so that ye yow not greve,
Though I to yow right on yourself compleyne.
For therwith mene I fynally the peyne   1006
That halt youre herte and myn in hevynesse
Fully to slen, and every wrong redresse.

"My goode myn, not I for-whi ne how
That jalousye, allas, that wikkede wyvere,   1010
Thus causeles is cropen into yow,
The harm of which I wolde fayn delyvere.
Allas, that he, al hool or of hym slyvere,
Shuld have his refuyt in so digne a place,
Ther Jove soone out of youre herte hym race.

"But O, thow Jove, O auctor of nature,   1016
Is this an honour to thi deite,

That folk ungiltyf suffren hire injure,
And who that gyltyf is, al quyt goth he?
O were it leful for to pleyn on the,   1020
That undeserved suffrest jalousie,
Of that I wolde upon the pleyne and crye!

"Ek al my wo is this, that folk now usen
To seyn right thus, 'Ye, jalousye is love!'
And wolde a busshel venym al excusen   1025
For that o greyn of love is on it shove.
But that wot heighe God that sit above,
If it be likere love or hate or grame;
And after that it oughte bere his name.

"But certeyn is, som manere jalousye   1030
Is excusable more than som, iwys,
As whanne cause is; and som swych fantasye
With pite so wel repressed is
That it unnethe doth or seyth amys,
But goodly drynketh up al his distresse.   1035
And that excuse I for the gentilesse.

"And som so ful of furye is and despit
That it sourmounteth his repressioun.
But, herte myn, ye be not in that plyt,
That thanke I God, for which yowre passioun
I wol not calle it but illusioun   1041
Of habundaunce of love and bysy cure,
That doth youre herte this disese endure,

"Of which I am right sory, but not wroth.
But for my devoir and youre hertes reste,   1045
Wherso yow lyste, by ordal or by oth,
By sort, or in what wyse so yow leste,
For love of God, lat preve it for the beste,

994 rewe, have pity. *first:* C&c *for.* **999 emforth . . . konnyng,** to the extent of, understanding. **1002 dredles . . . at preve,** doubtless, by experience. **1005 on,** about. **1008 slen,** kill (drive out). **1009** *myn* (mine): M *love* (correction in the MS); A *good herte myn.* **1010 wyvere,** viper. **1011 is cropen,** has crept. **1013 slyvere,** in part (sliver). **1014 refuyt . . . digne,** refuge, worthy. **1015 Ther . . . race,** where, root out. *Ther:* A *That; race:* C&c *arace.* **1020 leful . . . pleyn on the,** lawful (permissible), complain about you (Jove). M *that I pleyn of.* **1021 undeserved suffrest jalousie,** permit undeserved jealousy (to exist). **1022 upon,** to. **1023 usen,** are accustomed. **1024 jalousye is love,** one of the axioms of courtly love, as set forth in Andreas Capellanus' *De Amore,* is that love cannot exist without jealousy. **1028 likere . . . grame,** more nearly like, anger. **1029 after that . . . his,** according to that (i.e., the emotion it most resembles), its ("it" did not have a separate possessive form until the 17th century). **1031 than som,** than others. **1032 swych fantasye,** such imaginings (of jealousy). **1033 pite,** pity (for the loved one). **1034 unnethe,** scarcely. **1035 goodly,** with good behavior (politely). **1041 calle:** A *clepe.* **1042 cure,** care. **1043 doth,** makes. **1045 devoir,** duty. **1046 ordal . . . oth,** trial by ordeal (some such test as walking on coals or grasping hot metal), oath (on the Bible or some holy relic, in which case perjury would call down God's vengeance, cf. *CT* ii.670). *Yow lyste:* A *ye wil.* **1047 sort,** drawing lots (sortilege).

And yf that I be gyltyf, do me deye!
Allas, what myght I more do or seye?" 1050

With that a fewe brighte terys newe
Owt of hire eyen fille, and thus she seyde,
"Now God, thow wost, in thought ne dede
    untrewe
To Troylus was nevere yet Criseyde." 1054
With that hire hed into the bed down she leyde,
And with the shete it wreygh, and sighed sore,
And held hire pes; not o word spak she
    more.

But now help God to quenchen al this sorwe—
So hope I that he shal, for he best may.
For I have seyn of a ful mysty morwe 1060
Folwen ful ofte a merye someres day;
And after wynter foloweth grene May;
Men sen alday, and reden ek in storyes,
That after sharpe shoures ben victories.

This Troylus, whan he hire wordes herde, 1065
Have ye no care, hym lyste not to slepe,
For it thought hym no strokes of a yerde
To here or sen Criseyde his lady wepe.
But wel he felte aboute his herte crepe,
For every teere which that Criseyde asterte, 1070
The crampe of deth to streyne hym by the
    herte.

And in his mynde he gan the tyme acorse
That he cam there, and that he was born,
For now is wykke iturned unto worse,
And al the labour he hath don byforn, 1075
He wend it lost; he thoughte he nas but lorn.
"O Pandarus," thoughte he, "allas, thi wyle
Serveth of nought, so welaway the while."

And therwithal he heng adown the hed,
And fil on knes, and sorwfully he sighte. 1080

What myghte he seyn? He felte he nas but ded,
For wroth was she that shulde his sorwes lyghte.
But natheles, whenne that he speken myghte,
Than seyde he thus, "God wot that of this
    game,
Whan al is wyst, than am I not to blame." 1085

Therwith the sorwe so his herte shette
That from his eyen fil there not a tere,
And every spirit his vigour yn-knette,
So they astoned and oppressed were.
The felyng of his sorwe, or of his fere, 1090
Or of ought elles, fled was out of towne,
And doun he fel al sodeynly aswowne.

This was no litel sorwe for to se—
But al was hust, and Pandare up as faste,
"O nece, pes, or we be lost," quod he. 1095
"Beth nought agast." But certeyn, at the laste,
For this or that he into bedde hym caste,
And seyde, "O thef, is this a mannes herte?"
And of he rente al to his bare sherte,

And seyde, "Nece, but ye helpe us now, 1100
Allas, youre owen Troylus is lorn."
"Iwys, so wolde I and I wiste how,
Ful fayn," quod she. "Allas that I was born!"
"Ye, nece, wole ye pullen out the thorn
That stiketh in his herte?" quod Pandare. 1105
"Sey 'al foryeve,' and stynt is al this fare."

"Ye, that to me," quod she, "ful levere were
Than al the good the sonne aboute goth."
And therwithal she swor hym in his ere,
"Iwis, my dere herte, I am nought wroth, 1110
Have here my trouthe," and many another
    oth.
"Now speke to me, for it am I, Cryseyde!"
But al for nought; yet myght he nought
    abreyde.

1049 do me, make me. **1056 wreygh,** covered. **1060 morwe,** morning. **1064 shoures,** battles. **1067 no strokes,** not merely strokes. *For:* A *Eke.* **1070 asterte,** escaped from. **1074 wykke,** bad. **1076 wend,** thought. *he nas:* A *it nas.* **1082 sorwes:** A *daies.* **1084** A *Thus seide he,* "*Yet God woot of this game.*" **1088 spirit . . . yn-knette,** each of his vital spirits, retracted. **1089 astoned,** astonished (stunned). **1090 felyng,** feeling (consciousness). **1094 hust,** hushed (quiet). **1096 agast,** afraid. *certeyn:* other MSS *alwey.* **1099 rente . . . sherte,** tore, undershirt. **1101 lorn,** lost. **1103 fayn,** happily. **1104 thorn,** the thorn of sexual need, cf. II.1272 above and note. **1106 stynt . . . fare,** stop, business. **1107 levere,** more desirable. **1113 abreyde,** regain consciousness.

Therwith his pows and pawmes of his hondes
They gan to frote, and wete his temples
    tweyne;   1115
And for to delyveren hym fro bittre bondes
She ofte hym kyste; and shortly for to seyne,
Hym to revoken she dide al hire peyne.
And at the laste, he gan his breth to drawe,
And of his swough sone after that adawe,   1120

And bet gan mynde and reson to hym take.
But wonder sore he was abayst, iwys,
And with a syk, whan he gan bet awake,
He seyde, "O mercy, God, what thing is
    this?"
"Whi do ye with yowreselven thus amys?"   1125
Quod tho Criseyde. "Is this a mannes game?
What, Troylus, wol ye do thus for shame?"

And therwithal hire arm over hym she leyde,
And al foryaf, and ofte tyme hym keste.
He thonked hire, and to hire spak and seyde
As fil to purpos for his hertes reste,   1131
And she to that answerde hym as hire leste,
And with hire goodly wordes hym disporte
She gan, and ofte his sorwes to comforte.

Quod Pandarus, "For ought I kan espyen,   1135
This lyght nor I ne serven here of nought.
Lyght is not good for syke folkes eyen!
And for the love of God, syn ye ben brought
In thus good plit, lat now non hevy thought
Ben hangynge in the hertes of yow tweye"—
And bar the candele to the chimeneye.   1141

Soone after this, though it no nede were,
Whan she swyche othes as hire lyste devyse
Hadde of hym take, hire thoughte tho no fere,
Ne cause ek non to bidde hym thennes ryse.   1145
Yet lesse thyng than othes may suffise

In many a cas, for every wyght, I gesse,
That loveth wel, meneth but gentilesse.

But in effect she wolde wite anoon
Of what man, and ek wher, and also why   1150
He jalous was, syn there was cause non;
And ek the signe that he tok it by,
She bad hym that to telle hire bysily,
Or elles, certeyn, she bar hym on honde
That this was don of malys, hire to fonde.   1155

Withouten more, shortly for to seyne,
He most obeye unto his lady heste;
And for the lasse harm, he moste feyne.
He seyde hire whanne she was at swyche a
    feste,
She myght on hym han loked at the leste—   1160
Noot I not what, al dere ynow a rysshe,
As he that nedes most a cause fysshe.

And she answerde, "Swete, al were it so,
What harm was that, syn I noon yvel mene?
For by that God that bought us bothe two,   1165
In alle thyng is myn entente clene.
Swyche argumentz ne ben not worth a bene.
Wol ye the chyldyssh jalous contrefete?
Now were it worthy that ye were ybete."

Tho Troylus gan sorwfully to syke—   1170
Lest she be wroth, hym thoughte his herte
    deyde—
And seyde, "Allas, upon my sorwes syke
Have mercy, swete herte myn Cryseyde!
And yf that in tho wordes that I seyde
Be ony wrong, I wol no more trespace.   1175
Doth what yow lyst, I am al in youre grace."

And she answerde, "Of gilt mysericorde.
That is to seyn that I foryeve al this.

1114 pows, pulse. **1115 frote,** rub. *wete:* other MSS *ek.* **1118 revoken,** revive. **1119** *And:* other MSS *So.* **1120 adawe,** to awaken. **1122, abayst,** abashed (embarrassed). **1123 syk,** sigh. **1126 game,** behavior. **1127** A *Wole Troilus do thus allas for schame?* **1131 reste,** i.e. to ease his heart. **1133 disporte,** cheer up. **1136** Other MSS *I nor this candel ne.* **1152 tok,** suspected. **1153** B *This bad she hym to telle.* **1154 bar . . . on honde,** accused him. **1155 malys . . . fonde,** malice, test. **1157 heste,** command. **1158 lasse harm . . . feyne,** less discord, pretend. **1161 dere ynow a rysshe,** i.e., worth as little as a rush (reed). **1162 nedes most a cause fysshe,** i.e., must fish for a reason. **1163** Other MSS *Criseyde answerde.* **1165** *bought:* other MSS *wrought.* **1168 jalous,** jealous person. M&c *jalousye.* **1169 ybete,** beaten. **1170 syke,** sigh. **1172 syke,** sickly. **1177 mysericorde,** mercy. Other MSS *Criseyde answerde.*

And evere more on this nyght yow recorde,
And beth wel war ye do no more amys." 1180
"Nay, dere herte myn," quod he, "iwys."
"And now," quod she, "that I have don yow
    smerte,
Foryeve it me, myn owene swete herte."

This Troylus, with blysse of that supprised,
Put al in Goddes hand, as he that mente 1185
Nothyng but wel, and sodeynly avysed
He hire in armes faste to hym hente.
And Pandarus with a ful good entente
Leyd hym to slepe, and seyde, "If ye ben
    wyse,
Swowneth not now, lest more folk aryse!" 1190

What myght or may the sely larke seye
Whan that the sperhauk hath it in his fot?
I kan no more, but of thise ilke tweye,
To whom this tale sucre be or sot,
Though that I tarye a yer, somtyme I
    mot 1195
After myn auctour tellen hire gladnesse,
As wel as I have told hire hevynesse.

Criseyde, which that felte hire thus itake,
As writen clerkes in hire bokes olde,
Right as an aspes lef she gan to quake 1200
Whan she hym felte hire in his armes folde.
But Troylus, al hool of cares colde,
Gan thanken tho the blysful goddes sevene.
Thus sondry peynes bryngen folk to hevene.

This Troylus yn armes gan hire streyne, 1205
And seyde, "O swete, as evere mot I gon,
Now be ye kaught, now is ther but we tweyne.
Now yeldeth yow, for other bote is non."

To that Criseyde answerde thus anon,
"Ne hadde I er now, my swete herte dere, 1210
Ben yold, ywys, I were now not here!"

O soth is seyd, that heled for to be
As of a fevre or other gret syknesse,
Men moste drynke, as men may ofte se,
Ful bittre drynke; and for to han gladnesse, 1215
Men drynken ofte peyne and gret distresse—
I mene it here, as for this aventure,
That thorugh a peyne hath founden al his cure.

And now swetnesse semeth more swete
That bitternesse assayed was byforn, 1220
For out of wo in blysse now they flete—
Non swych they felten sith that they were
    born.
Now is this bet than bothe two be lorn.
For love of God, take every womman hede
To werken thus, yf it come to the nede. 1225

Criseyde, al quyt from every drede and tene,
As she that just cause hadde hym to tryste,
Made hym swych feste it joye was to sene,
Whan she his trowthe and clene entente
    wyste;
And as abowte a tre, with many a twyste, 1230
Bytrent and wryth the soote wodebynde,
Gan eche of hem in armes other wynde.

And as the newe abayssed nyghtyngale,
That stynteth first whan she gynneth to synge,
Whan that she hereth any herde tale, 1235
Or in the hegges ony wight sterynge,
And after siker doth hire voys out rynge,
Right so Criseyde, whan hire drede stente,
Opened hire herte and tolde hym hire entente.

1183 *swete:* A *dere.* 1184 **supprised,** seized. 1186 **avysed,** fully conscious. 1191 **sely,** innocent; cf. l. 813n. 1194 **sucre . . . sot,** sugar (sweet), soot (bitter); this is the reading in C and the majority of MSS, but M took *sot* as *swote* (sweet) and so changed *sucre* to *sour,* i.e., *sour be or sot.* 1195 **tarye a yer,** Chaucer was aware of the agonizing protraction of the foreplay in his poem (which is not over yet). This was a deliberate device in troubadour poetry, which saw anticipation as a more effective impulse for poetry than consummation—as Keats likewise recognized in *Ode on a Grecian Urn.* With Chaucer's complicated, drawn-out account, one may compare the alacrity with which the affair is consummated in *Fil.* 3.28–32 (40 lines). 1200 *aspes:* A&c *aspen.* 1203 **sevene,** the seven planets that control man's destiny. *blysful:* other MSS *bryghte.* 1208 **bote,** alternative. 1211 **yold,** yielded. 1214 M *often;* other MSS *ofte* or *alday.* 1220 **assayed,** experienced. 1221 **flete,** float. 1223 **lorn,** lost. 1225 *yf:* other MSS *whan.* 1226 **tene,** grief. 1231 **Bytrent . . . wryth . . . soote,** encircles, twines, sweet. 1233 **abayssed,** startled. 1234 **stynteth,** stops. 1235 **herde tale,** shepherd talk. 1237 **siker,** reassured (secure). 1238 **stente,** stopped.

And right as he that seth his deth yshapen,   1240
And deye mot, in ought that he may gesse,
And sodeynly rescous doth hym escapen
And from his deth is brought in sykernesse,
For al this world, yn swych present gladnesse
Was Troylus, and hath his lady swete.   1245
With worse hap God lat us nevere mete!

Hire armes smale, hire streyghte bak and softe,
Hire sydes longe, flesshly, smothe, and white,
He gan to stroke, and good thryft bad ful ofte
Hire snowysshe throte, hire brestes rounde and
   lyte.   1250
Thus in this hevene he gan hym to delyte,
And therwithal a thowsand tyme hire kyste,
That what to don for joye unnethe he wyste.

Than seyde he thus, "O Love, O Charite,
Thi moder ek, Citherea the swete,   1255
After thiself next heried be she—
Venus mene I, the wel-willy planete—
And next the, Imeneus, I the grete,
For nevere man was to yow goddes holde
As I, which ye han brought fro cares
   colde.   1260

"Benygne Love, thow holy bond of thynges,
Whoso wol grace and lyst the nought honouren,
Lo, his desir wol fle withouten wynges.
For noldestow of bounte hem socouren
That serven best and most alwey labouren,   1265
Yet were al lost, that dar I wel seyn certes,
But yf thi grace passed oure desertes.

"And for thow me, that lest kowde deserve
Of hem that noumbred ben unto thi grace,
Hast holpen, ther I lykly was to sterve,   1270
And me bistowed in so heygh a place

That thilke boundes may no blysse pace,
I kan namore but laude and reverence
Be to thy bounte and thyn excellence!"

And therwithal Criseyde anoon he kyste,   1275
Of which, certeyn, she felte no dishese.
And thus seyde he, "Now wolde God I wyste,
Myn herte swete, how I yow myght plese.
What man," quod he, "was evere thus at ese
As I, on which the faireste and the beste   1280
That evere I say deyneth hire herte reste?

"Here may men se that mercy passeth ryght;
The experience of that is felt in me,
That am unworthi to so swete a wyght.
But herte myn, of youre benyngnite,   1285
So thynketh, thowgh that I unworthi be,
Yet mot I nede amenden in som wyse,
Right thorugh the vertu of yowre heygh
   servyse.

"And for the love of God, my lady dere,
Syn God hath wrought me for I shal yow
   serve—   1290
As thus I mene, that ye wol be my stere,
To do me lyve, if that yow lyste, or sterve—
So techeth me how that I may deserve
Youre thank so that I thorugh myn
   ignoraunce
Ne do nothing that yow be displesaunce.   1295

"For certes, fresshe wommanliche wyf,
This dar I seye, that trouthe and diligence,
That shal ye fynden in me al my lyf;
Ne I wol nat, certeyn, breken youre defence;
And if I do, present or in absence,   1300
For love of God, lat sle me with the dede,
If that it lyke unto youre wommanhede."

1240 **yshapen,** planned out; M *is shapen.* 1241 **deye mot,** etc., i.e., is certain to die for all that he can tell. 1242 **doth hym,** causes him. 1243 **sykernesse,** safety. 1245 *Was:* other MSS *Is.* 1246 **hap,** luck. 1248 *flesshly:* C *flesshy.* 1249 **thryft bad,** blessing invoked. 1250 *snowysshe:* A *snowe whit.* 1251 M *hevene* om. 1253 **unnethe . . . wyste,** hardly, knew. 1255 **Citherea,** Venus. 1256 **heried,** praised. 1257 **wel-willy,** well-willing (benevolent—to lovers). 1258 **Imeneus,** Hymen, god of marriage. 1259 **holde,** indebted (beholden). 1262 **wol grace,** desires favor. 1263 **his desir . . . fle,** what he desires, fly. 1267 **passed,** surpassed. 1268 **for thow,** because you. 1270 **sterve,** die. 1272 **thilke boundes . . . pace,** the bounds of it, surpass. 1273 **laude,** praise. 1282 **passeth,** surpasses. 1284 Other MSS *to yow, lady bright.* 1286 M *So thenk.* 1287 **amenden,** improve. 1291 **stere,** guide. C&c *he wol ye be,* and variations. 1292 **do . . . sterve,** make, die. 1295 Other MSS *that do yow.* 1299 **breken . . . defence,** transgress, prohibition. 1301 **lat sle me,** let me be slain.

"Iwys," quod she, "myn owene hertes lyst,
My ground of ese, and al myn herte dere,
Gramercy, for on that is al my trist.   1305
But lat us falle awey fro this matere,
For it suffisith this that seyd is here,
And at o word, withouten repentaunce,
Welcome, my knyght, my pes, my suffisaunce."

Of hire delyt or joyes oon the leste   1310
Were impossible to my wyt to seye;
But juggeth, ye that han ben at the feste
Of swych gladnesse, yf that hem lyste pleye.
I kan no more, but thus thise ilke tweye
That nyght, betwixen drede and sikernesse,   1315
Felten in love the grete worthynesse.

O blysful nyght, of hem so longe ysought,
How blithe unto hem bothe two thow
         were!
Why nad I swych on with my soule ybought,
Ye, or the leeste joye that was there?   1320
Awey, thow fowle daunger and thow fere,
And lat hem in this hevene blysse dwelle,
That is so heygh that al ne kan I telle.

But soth is, though I kan nat tellen al,
As kan myn auctour of his excellence,   1325
Yet have I seyd, and God toforn, and shal
In everythyng the grete of his sentence;
And yf that ich, at Loves reverence,
Have ony word in eched for the beste,
Doth therwithal right as youreselven leste.   1330

For myne wordes, here and every part,
I speke hem alle under correccioun
Of yow that felyng han in loves art,
And putte it al in youre discrecioun
T'encresse or maken dyminucioun   1335

Of my langage, and that I yow byseche.
But now to purpos of my rather speche.

Thise ilke two, that ben in armes laft,
So loth to hem asonder gon it were,
That ech from other wenden ben byraft,   1340
Or elles, lo, this was hir moste fere,
That al this thyng but nyce dremes nere;
For which ful ofte ech of hem seyde, "O swete,
Clippe ich yow thus, or elles I it mete?"

And Lord, so he gan goodly on hire se   1345
That nevere his lok ne blente from hire face,
And seyde, "O dere herte, may it be
That it be soth that ye ben in this place?"
"Ye, herte myn, God thank I of his grace,"
Quod tho Criseyde, and therwithal hym kyste,
That where his spirit was for joye he nyste.   1351

This Troylus ful ofte hire eyen two
Gan for to kysse, and seyde, "O eyen clere,
It weren ye that wroughte me swych wo,
Ye humble nettes of my lady dere.   1355
Though there by mercy wreten yn youre
         chere,
God wot, the text ful hard is, soth, to fynde.
How koude ye withouten bond me bynde?"

Therwith he gan hire faste in armes take,
And wel an hundred tymes gan he syke—   1360
Nought swyche sorwful sykes as men make
For wo, or elles whanne that folk ben syke,
But esy sykes swyche as ben to lyke,
That shewed his affeccion withinne;
Of swyche sikes koude he nought bilynne.   1365

Sone after this they speke of sondry thynges,
As fil to purpos of this aventure,

1304 **ground,** foundation. 1310 **joyes oon the leste,** one of the least of their joys. 1315 **sikernesse,** assurance. 1317–18 These two lines, from *Fil.* 3.33, are nearly the only echo of Boccaccio's consummation scene in Chaucer. 1321 **daunger,** aloofness. 1322 M *blyssyd.* 1323 Other MSS *that no man kan it telle.* 1324–37 In the B version these stanzas are shifted to between ll. 1414–15, where they do not interrupt the love scene. 1326 **toforn,** before. 1327 **grete . . . sentence,** main part, meaning. *grete:* MC&c *al hoolly his.* 1329 **in eched,** added in. 1334 *it al:* other MSS *hem hool.* 1337 **rather,** earlier. 1342 **nyce,** foolish. 1344 **Clippe . . . mete,** embrace, dream. 1345 M *A, lord . . . gan gladly.* 1346 **blente,** wavered (turned away). 1349 *Ye:* A *we.* 1355 **nettes,** i.e., the agents through which Troylus has been caught. 1356 **chere,** expression. 1357 **text,** meaning. 1360 **syke,** sigh. Other MSS *a thousand.* 1362 *For wo:* other MSS *For sorwe.* 1363 **to lyke,** pleasant. 1365 **bilynne,** cease. M *blynne.* 1367 *this:* other MSS *hire.*

And pleyinge entrechaungeden hire rynges,
Of which I kan nought tellen no scripture;
But wel I wot, a broche, gold and asure, 1370
In whiche a ruby set was lyk an herte,
Criseyde hym yaf, and stak it on his sherte.

Lord, trowe ye a coveytous or a wrecche,
That blameth love and holt of it despit,
That of the pens that he kan mokre and
    krecche 1375
Was evere yet yyeve hym swych delyt
As ys in love, in oo poynt in som plyt?
Nay, douteles, for also God me save,
So perfit joye may no nygard have.

They wol sey "yis," but, Lord, so that they
    lye, 1380
Tho bysy wrecches ful of wo and drede!
They callen love a woodnesse or folye,
But it shal falle hem as I shal yow rede:
They shul forgo the white and ek the rede,
And leve in wo, there God yeve hem
    myschaunce, 1385
And every lovere yn his trouthe avaunce.

As wolde God tho wrecches that dispise
Servyse of love hadde eerys also longe
As hadde Myda, ful of coveytise,
And therto drenken hadde as hoot and stronge
As Crassus dide for his affectis wronge, 1391
To techen hem that they ben in the vice,

And loveres nought although they holde hem
    nyce.

Thise ilke two of whom that I yow seye,
Whan that hire hertes wel assured were, 1395
Tho gonne they to speken and to pleye,
And ek rehercen how and whanne and where
They knewe hem first, and every wo and
    feere
That passed was; but al swych hevynesse,
I thank it God, was tourned to gladnesse. 1400

And everemo, when that hem fille to speke
Of onything of swych a tyme agoon,
With kyssing al that tale sholde breke
And fallen in a newe joye anoon;
And deden al hire myght, syn they were
    oon, 1405
For to recoveren blysse and ben at eyse,
And passed woo with joye contrepeyse.

Reson wol not that I speke of slep,
For it accordeth nought to my matere.
God wot, they tok of that ful lytel kep! 1410
But lest this nyght, that was to hem so dere,
Ne sholde in veyn escape in no manere,
It was byset in joye and bysynesse
Of al that sowneth into gentilesse.

But whanne the kok, comune astrologer, 1415
Gan on his brest to bete and after crowe,

1368 **pleyinge entrechaungeden,** playfully exchanged. *Pleyinge* must be understood in contrast to formal exchanges of rings in marriage, which this was not. This exchange of tokens is not found in *Fil.* 1369 **scripture,** inscription. 1370 **broche,** this is not the brooch found on Diomede's armor (v.1661), but it foreshadows that fateful jewel (which is found in *Fil.* 8.9–10) and further contributes to the symmetry of Chaucer's poem. 1373 **trowe ye . . . coveytous,** can you believe (imagine), miser. Lines 1373–86 reflect *Fil.* 3.38–39. 1374 **despit,** contempt. 1375 **of the pens . . . mokre and krecche,** for pence (money), dig in dung (muck) and scratch. M *moke and kecche,* and many other variants in C&c. 1377 **oo poynt . . . som plyt,** i.e., as is given by love at a single point in certain circumstances. 1382 **woodnesse,** madness. *callen:* A *clepen.* 1383 **rede,** advise. 1384 **white . . . rede,** *Fil.* 3.39 has "they will lose themselves and their money," which has led editors to interpret this as "white silver" and "red gold." But at *CT* vi.526 and vii.2842 "white and red" means white and red wine; so it may be that Chaucer meant that misers forget other pleasures. 1389 **Myda,** Midas, who was granted his wish that whatever he touched would turn to gold and was punished for his folly by growing ass's ears. Ovid, *Met.* 11. 100ff. *ful of:* A *for his.* 1391 **Crassus,** a Roman general so greedy for wealth that after he was conquered and killed by the Parthians they poured molten gold into his mouth saying, "Now satisfy yourself with the metal for which you were so greedy in life." Crassus and Midas were common examples of the vice of covetousness. 1392–93 Other MSS *To techen hem that coveytise is vice,/And love is vertu, though men holde it nyce.* 1393 **nyce,** foolish. 1394ff. The text here returns to *Fil.* 3.40ff., but with many verbal alterations, particularly in the aubade. The astrological allusions are all Chaucer's additions. 1402 *onything:* other MSS *any wo.* 1407 **contrepeyse,** to counterbalance. 1413 **byset,** occupied. 1414 **sowneth,** conduces to. 1415 **comune,** popular (because he proclaims the coming of sunrise to the populace). Marginal glosses in some MSS call him *"vulgaris astrologus,"* so this was evidently a familiar epithet.

And Lucifer, the dayes messager,
Gan for to ryse and out hire bemys throwe,
And estward ros (to hym that kowde it knowe)
Fortuna Major, that anoon Criseyde,   1420
With herte sor, to Troylus thus seyde:

"Myn hertes lyf, my tryst, and my plesaunce,
That I was born, allas, what me is wo,
That day of us mot make desseveraunce.
For tyme it is to ryse and hens to go,   1425
Or ellys I am lost for everemo.
O nyght, allas, whi nyltow over us hove
As longe as whanne Almena lay by Jove?

"O blake nyght, as folk in bokes rede,
That shapen art by God this world to hide   1430
At certeyn tymes wyth thi derke wede,
That under that men myghte in reste abyde,
Wel oughte bestes pleyne and folk the chide
That there as day wyth labour wolde us breste,
That thow thus flest, and deynest us nought
      reste.   1435

"Thow dost, allas, to shortly thyn office,
Thow rakle nyght, there God, maker of kynde,
The for thyn hast and thyn unkynde vice
So faste ay to oure hemyspere bynde
That neveremore under the ground thow
      wynde!   1440
For now, for thow so hyest out of Troye,
Have I forgon thus hastely my joye."

This Troylus, that with tho wordes felte,
As thoughte hym tho, for pitous distresse

The blody teerys from his herte melte,   1445
As he that nevere yet swych hevynesse
Assayed hadde out of so gret gladnesse,
Gan therwithal Criseyde, his lady dere,
In armes streyne, and seyde in this manere:

"O cruel day, accusour of the joye   1450
That nyght and love han stole and faste
      ywryen,
Acursed be thi comyng into Troye,
For every bore hath oon of thi bryghte eyen.
Envyous day, what lyst the so to spyen?
What hastow lost? Why sekestow this place? 1455
Ther God thi lyght so quenche, for his grace!

"Allas, what han these loveres the agilt,
Dispitous day? Thyn be the pyne of helle!
For many a lovere hastow shent, and wilt;
Thi pouryng in wol nowhere lat hem dwelle.
What profrestow thi light here for to selle? 1461
Go selle it hem that smale selys graven;
We wol the nought; us nedeth no day haven."

And ek the sonne, Tytan, gan he chyde,
And seyde, "O fol, wel may men the dispise,
That hast the Dawyng al nyght by thi syde, 1466
And suffrest hire so soone up fro the ryse,
For to disesen loveres yn this wyse.
What, hold youre bed ther, thow and ek thi
      Morwe;
I bidde God so yeve yow bothe sorwe!"   1470

Therwith ful sore he sighte, and thus he seyde,
"My lady right, and of my wele or wo

1417 Lucifer, another name for Venus as the morning star. **1418** *bemys:* other MSS *stremys.* **1419** *estward:* M&c *afterward.* **1420 Fortuna Major.** Skeat, Root, Robinson, and Curry discuss what this may mean: it is either the sun (Curry), a morning constellation (Root), or the planet Jupiter (Skeat). **1427–42** These lines are not found in the parting lament in *Fil.* 3.43ff. They represent an aubade, or dawn song, a recognized lyric type derived from the Provençal poetry of the 12th century. **1427 hove,** linger. **1428 Almena,** when Jove lay with Alcmena and begot Hercules, he miraculously extended the night, in one version to the length of three nights. **1431 wede,** garment. *tymes/derke:* other MSS *termes/blake.* **1433 pleyne,** complain. **1434 there as . . . breste,** because, crush. **1435 flest,** flee. **1436 office,** duty. C&c *so shortly.* **1437 rakle . . . there . . . kynde,** hasty (impetuous), may, nature. **1438** Other MSS *For thow so downward hastest of malice.* **1441** Other MSS *For thorugh thy rakel hying out.* **1444 tho,** then. **1450–70** Troylus' response in the aubade is adapted from *Fil.* 3.44–47. **1451 ywryen,** hidden. **1453 bore,** hole (through which the sun shines). **1456 Ther,** may. **1457 agilt,** offended. **1458 Dispitous . . . pyne,** cruel, pain. **1459** *shent:* C&c *slayn.* **1462 smale selys graven,** engrave small seals (and so need a bright light). **1463 wol,** desire. **1464ff. Tytan . . . Dawyng,** in classical mythology, the mortal lover for whom Aurora (the dawn) obtained immortality was Tithonus, not Titan, but this was a common confusion. **1467** *so:* other MSS *to.* **1470 bidde,** pray. Other MSS *prey to.*

The welle and rote, O goodly myn Criseyde,
And shal I ryse, allas, and shal I go?
Now fele I that myn herte mot a-two.   1475
For how sholde I an houre my lyf save,
Syn that with yow is al the lyf ich have?

"What shal I don, for, certes, I not how,
Ne whanne, allas, I shal the tyme se
That yn this plit I may ben eft with yow?   1480
And of my lyf, God wot how that shal be,
Syn that desir ryght now so brenneth me
That I am ded anoon but I retorne.
How shold I longe, allas, fro yow sojourne?

"But natheles, myn owene lady bryght,   1485
Yit were it so that I wiste outrely
That I, youre humble servant and youre knyght,
Were in youre herte iset so fermely
As ye in myn—the which thyng, trewely,
Me levere were than these worldes
          tweyne—   1490
Yet sholde I bet enduren al my peyne."

To that Cryseyde answerde right anoon,
And with a syk she seyde, "O herte dere,
The game, ywys, so ferforth now is gon
That first shal Phebus falle fro his spere,   1495
And everich egle ben the dowves fere,
And every roche out of his place sterte,
Er Troylus out of Criseydes herte.

"Ye ben so depe in-with myn herte grave,
That though I wolde it turne out of my thought,
As wysly verray God my soule save,   1501
To dyen in the peyne, I kowde nowght.
And for the love of God that us hath wrought,
Lat in youre brayn noon other fantasye
So crepe that it cause me to dye.   1505

"And that ye me wolde han as faste in mynde
As I have yow, that wold I yow byseche;
And yf I wyste sothly that to fynde,
God myghte not a poynt my joyes eche.
But herte myn, withoute more speche,   1510
Beth to me trewe, or elles were it routhe—
For I am thyn, by God and by my trouthe!

"Beth glad, forthi, and lyve in sykernesse;
Thus seyde I nevere er this, ne shal to mo.
And yf to yow it were a gret gladnesse   1515
To turne ayen soone after that ye go,
As fayn wolde I as ye that it were so,
As wysly God myn herte brynge at reste."
And hym in armes toke and ofte keste.

Agayns his wil, syn it mot nedes be,   1520
This Troylus up ros, and faste hym cledde,
And in his armes tok his lady fre
An hondred tyme, and on his wey hym spedde;
And with swyche voys as though his herte
          bledde,
He seyde, "Farewel, myn herte and dere
          swete,   1525
There God us graunte sounde and soone to
          mete!"

To which no word for sorwe she answerde,
So sore gan his partyng hire destreyne.
And Troylus unto his palays ferde
As wobygon as she was, soth to seyne.   1530
So hard hym wrong of sharp desir the peyne
For to ben eft there he was in plesaunce,
That it may nevere out of his remembraunce.

Retorned to his palais real soone,
He softe into his bedde gan for to slynke,   1535
To slepe longe, as he was woned to done.

1473 Other MSS *The verray roote.* 1474 go: C&c *so.* 1480 **plit**, situation. *A place.* 1482 *brenneth*: C&c *biteth*; other MSS *streyneth.* 1483 **but**, unless. 1486 **wiste outrely**, knew completely. 1487 *humble*: other MSS *owen.* 1490 **levere . . . these worldes tweyne**, more valuable, twice this world. 1493 **syk**, sigh. 1494 **ferforth**, far. 1495 **Phebus . . . spere**, the sun, sphere. 1496 **fere**, friend. *dowves*: other MSS *haukes.* 1499 *grave*, buried. 1502 **To dyen . . . peyne**, even if I were to die, torture. 1509 **a poynt . . . eche**, an iota, increase. 1511 **routhe**, a pity. 1513 **forthi . . . sykernesse**, therefore, confidence. 1514 **seyde I nevere er this**, since according to courtly conventions, marriages were not love matches, this may be taken as a valid statement—until we hear Criseyde with Diomede, v.975–78. *this*: other MSS *now.* 1516 **turne**, return. 1517 **fayn**, happy. 1524 MC&c *swyche wordes as his herte.* 1525 C&c *my dere herte swete.* 1528 **destreyne**, distress. 1531 **wrong**, wrung. 1532 **eft there**, again where. 1534 **real**, royal.

But al for nought; he may wel lygge and wynke,
But slep ne may ther in his herte synke
Thenkynge how she, for whom desir hym
    brende,
A thousandfold was worth more than he
    wende.   1540

And in his thought gan up and doun to wynde
Hire wordes alle, and every countenaunce,
And fermely impressen yn his mynde
The leste poynt that to hym was plesaunce;
And verraylich of thilke remembraunce   1545
Desir al newe hym brende, and lust to brede
Gan more than erst, and yet tok he non hede.

Criseyde also, right in the same wyse,
Of Troylus gan in hire herte shette
His worthinesse, his lust, his dedes wyse,   1550
His gentilesse, and how she with hym mette,
Thonkynge Love he so wel hire bysette,
Desirying eft to have hire herte dere
In swych a plyt she dorste make hym chere.

Pandare, a-morwe which that comen was   1555
Unto his nece and gan hire fayre grete,
Seyde, "Al this nyght so reyned it, allas,
That al my drede is that ye, nece swete,
Han litel layser had to slepe and mete.
Al nyght," quod he, "hath reyn so do me wake,
That som of us, I trowe, hire hedes ake."   1561

And ner he come and seyde, "How stont it now,
This murye morwe? Nece, how kan ye fare?"
Criseyde answerde, "Nevere the bet for yow,
Fox that ye ben. God yeve youre herte care!
God help me so, ye caused al this fare,   1566
Trow I," quod she, "for alle youre wordes
    whyte.
O, whoso seth yow, he knoweth yow ful lite."

With that she gan hire face for to wrye
With the shete, and wax for shame al red;   1570
And Pandarus gan under for to prye,
And seyde, "Nece, yf that I shal be ded,
Have here a swerd and smyteth of myn hed!"
With that his arm al sodeynly he thriste   1574
Under hire nekke, and at the laste hire kyste.

I passe al that which chargeth nought to seye.
What, God foryaf his deth, and she also
Foryaf, and with hire uncle gan to pleye,
For other cause was ther noon but so.
But of this thing right to the effect to go,   1580
Whan tyme was, hom til hire hous she wente,
And Pandarus hath fully his entente.

Now torne we ayen to Troylus,
That resteles ful longe abedde lay,
And prevely sente after Pandarus,   1585
To hym to com in al the haste he may.
He com anoon, nought onyes seyde he nay,
And Troylus ful sobrely he grette,
And doun upon his beddes syde hym sette.

This Troylus, with al th'affeccioun   1590
Of frendes love that herte may devyse,
To Pandarus on knees fil adown,
And er that he wolde of the place aryse,
He gan hym thonken in his beste wyse
An hondred sithe, and gan the tyme blysse   1595
That he was born to brynge hym fro distresse.

He seyde, "O frend, of frendes the alderbeste
That evere was, the sothe for to telle,
Thow hast in hevene ybrought my soule at reste
Fro Flegiton, the fery flood of helle,   1600
That though I myght a thousand tymes selle
Upon a day my lyf in thy servise,
It myght nought a mote in that suffise.

1537 lygge, lie. **1539 brende,** burned. **1542** *Hire:* M *His.* **1543** *his:* M *hire.* **1546 lust . . . brede,** desire, grow. **1550 lust,** vigor. **1554 plyt . . . dorste,** situation, dared (i.e., could again). **1559 mete,** dream. **1561** Other MSS *of us, for God, our hede may ake.* **1563 morwe,** morning. *murye:* other MSS *brighte.* **1565** *youre herte:* other MSS *yow harde.* **1569 wrye,** hide. **1573** *smyteth:* MC&c *smyte/ smyten.* **1576 chargeth nought,** is not important. Other MSS *nedeth nought.* **1577 his deth,** i.e., those who crucified him. **1579 cause,** i.e., course of action. **1580 effect,** point. **1582** *fully:* other MSS *holly.* **1588 sobrely,** seriously. **1592** *knees:* C&c *knowes.* **1595** *hondred/ tyme:* other MSS *thousand/day.* **1597 alderbeste,** best of all. **1600 Flegiton,** Phlegethon, the river of fire in Hades, cf. Virgil, *Aeneid* 6.550. **1603 mote,** particle.

"The sonne, which that al the world may se,
Sawh nevere yet my lyf, that dar I leye,   1605
So inly feyr and goodly as is she,
Whos I am al, and shal til that I deye.
And that I thus am hires, dar I seye
That thanked be the heighe worthynesse
Of Love, and ek thi kynde bysynesse.   1610

"Thus hastow me no lytel thyng yyeve,
For which to the obliged be for ay
My lyf. And whi? For thorugh thyn help I leve,
Or elles ded hadde I be many a day."   1614
And with that word doun in his bed he lay.
And Pandarus ful sobrely hym herde
Til al was seyd, and thanne he hym answerde:

"My dere frend, yf I have don for the
In ony cas, God wot, it is me lief,
And am as glad as man may of it be,   1620
God help me so. But tak it not a-grief
That I shal seyn: bewar of this myschief,
That there as thow now brought art into thy
    blysse,
That thow thiself ne cause it nought to mysse.

"For of Fortunes sharpe adversite   1625
The worste kynde of infortune is this,
A man to have ben in prosperite,
And it remembren whan it passed is.
Thow art wys ynowh, forthi do nought amys;
Be not to rakel, though thou sitte warme,   1630
For if thow be, certeyn, it wol the harme.

"Thow art at ese, and hold the wel therinne.
For also seur as red is every fir,
As gret a craft is kepe wel as wynne.
Bridle alwey wel thi speche and thi desir,   1635
For worldly joye halt not but by a wir.

That preveth wel it brest alday so ofte;
Forthi nede is to werke with it softe."

Quod Troylus, "I hope, and God toforn,
My dere frend, that I shal so me bere   1640
That in my gilt ther shal nothing be lorn,
Ne I nyl not rakle as for to greven hire.
It nedeth not this matere ofte stere,
For wistestow myn herte wel, Pandare,
God wot of this thow woldest litel care."   1645

Tho gan he telle hym of his glade nyght,
And wherof first his herte dredde, and how,
And seyde, "Frend, as I am trewe knyght,
And by that feyth I shal to God and yow,
I hadde it never half so hote as now;   1650
And ay the more that desir me biteth,
To love hire best the more it me delyteth.

"I not myself not wisly what it is,
But now I fele a newe qualite,
Ye, al another than I dede er this."   1655
Pandare answered, and seyde thus, that "He
That onys may in hevene blysse be,
He feleth other weyes, dar I leye,
Than thilke tyme he first herde of it seye."

This is o word for al. This Troylus   1660
Was nevere ful to speke of this matere,
And for to preysen unto Pandarus
The bounte of his righte lady dere,
And Pandarus to thanke and maken chere.
This tale was ay span-newe to bygynne   1665
Til that the nyght departed hem atwynne.

Soone after this, for that Fortune it wolde,
Icomen was the blysful tyme swete
That Troylus was warned that he sholde,

1605 my lyf . . . leye, in my life, bet. **1606 inly,** inwardly (naturally). **1607 shal,** shall be. **1612 for ay,** forever. **1619 lief,** pleasing. **1622** Other MSS *For love of God bewar of.* **1625–28** "There is no sorrow like remembered pleasure," a medieval commonplace, *Boece* II pr. 4,7; Dante, *Inf.* 5.121–23, and elsewhere. **1629 forthi,** therefore. **1630 rakel,** rash (impetuous), **1634 craft is kepe wel,** i.e., art it is to preserve (love). **1636 halt . . . wir,** hangs, wire (thread). **1637 preveth . . . brest alday,** i.e., which is proved by the fact that it breaks so often. **1638 Forthi . . . softe,** therefore, softly (gently). **1639 toforn,** before. **1641 in my gilt . . . lorn,** through my fault, lost. **1642 rakle,** behave rashly. **1643 stere,** raise (stir up). MC&c *tere* (tear). **1644 wistestow,** if you knew. **1653 I not,** I do not know. **1661 ful to,** i.e., could never talk enough about. **1662 preysen,** praise. **1665 span-newe,** brand new (i.e., each time he told it again).

There he was erst, Criseyde his lady mete, 1670
For which he felt his herte in joye flete,
And feythfully gan alle the goddes herye.
And lat se now yf that he kan be merye.

And holden was the forme and al the wyse
Of hire commynge, and ek of his also, 1675
As it was erst, whych nedeth nought devyse.
But playnly to the effect right for to go,
In joye and seurte Pandarus hem two
Abedde brought whan that hem bothe leste,
And thus thei ben in quyete and yn reste. 1680

Nought nedeth it to yow, syn they ben met,
To axe at me yf that they blythe were.
For yf it erst was wel, tho was it bet
A thousandfold; this nedeth not enquere.
Agon was every sorwe and every fere, 1685
And bothe, ywys, they hadde, and so they
    wende,
As muche joye as herte may comprende.

This is no litel thyng of for to seye,
This passeth every wyt for to devyse,
For eche of hem gan otheres lust obeye. 1690
Felicite, which that thise clerkes wyse
Commenden so, ne may not here suffise.
This joye may not ywrete ben with inke;
This passeth al that herte may bythenke.

But cruel day, so welawey the stounde, 1695
Gan for to aproche, as they by synes knewe,
For which hem thoughte felen dethes wounde.
So wo was hem that changen gan hire hewe,
And day they gonnen to dispise al newe,
Callyng it traytour, envyous, and worse, 1700
And bitterly the dayes light they corse.

Quod Troilus, "Allas, now am I war
That Piros and tho swyfte stedes thre,
Which that drawen forth the sonnes char,
Han gon som bypath in despit of me. 1705
That maketh it so soone day to be.
And for the sonne hym hasteth thus to ryse,
Ne shal I nevere don hym sacrifise."

But nedes day departe hem moste soone, 1709
And whanne hire speche don was and hire chere,
They twynne anoon, as they were woned
    to done,
And setten tyme of metyng eft yfere.
And many a nyght they wrought yn this manere.
And thus Fortune a tyme ledde in joye
Criseyde and ek this kynges sone of Troye. 1715

In suffisaunce, in blisse, and in syngynges,
This Troylus gan al his lyf to lede.
He spendeth, justeth, maketh festeynynges,
He yeveth frely ofte, and chaungeth wede,
And held aboute hym alwey, out of drede, 1720
A world of folk as kam hym wel of kynde,
The fresshest and the beste he koude fynde.

That swych a voys was of hym and a stevene
Thorughout the world, of honour and largesse,
That it up rong unto the yate of hevene. 1725
And, as in love, he was in swych gladnesse,
That in his herte he demede as I gesse
That ther nys lovere in this world at ese
So wel as he; and thus gan love hym plese.

The goodlihede or beaute which that Kynde
In ony other lady hadde yset 1731
Kan not the mountaunce of a knot unbynde
Aboute his herte of al Criseydes net.

1670 **erst,** first (before). 1671 **flete,** float. 1672 **herye,** praise. 1674 **forme,** decorum. 1678 **seurte,** security. 1682 M *aske.* A *that* om. 1683 **tho,** then. 1686 **wende,** believed. 1687 *comprende:* M *complende;* other MSS *comprehende.* 1690 **lust,** desire (pleasure). 1691 **Felicite,** the Boethian term for supreme happiness. The Boethian contrast between mutable earthly felicity and immutable divine felicity is the theme of Bks. IV and V of the poem, culminating in Troylus' final epiphany, v.1818–21. 1695 **stounde,** hour. 1697 *felen:* A *thei felt (en).* 1703 **Piros,** Pyrois was the name of one of the four horses that pulled the chariot (**char**) of the sun, Ovid, *Met.* 2.153. 1705 **bypath . . . despit,** shortcut, in spite. 1708 *hym:* MC&c *hire.* 1709 **departe . . . moste,** must separate. 1710 **chere,** pleasure. 1711 **twynne . . . woned,** separated, accustomed. 1712 **yfere,** together. 1714 **a tyme,** for a time. 1716 **suffisaunce,** contentment. 1718 **festeynynges,** celebrations. C&c *festynges.* 1719 **wede,** clothes. 1721 **world of folk as kam hym . . . kynde,** i.e., surrounded by a large group of followers, as was natural to him. 1723 **voys . . . stevene,** report, celebrity. 1729 **So wel as,** as well as. 1730 **Kynde,** nature. 1732 **mountaunce,** extent (of a single knot).

He was so narwe ymasked and yknet,
That it undon on any manere syde, 1735
That nyl not ben, for ought that may betide.

And by the hond ful ofte he wolde take
This Pandarus, and into garden lede,
And swych a feste and swych a proces make
Hym of Criseyde, and of hire womanhede, 1740
And of hire beaute, that withouten drede
It was an hevene his wordes for to here;
And thanne he wolde synge in this manere:

"Love, that of erthe and se hath governaunce,
Love, that his hestes hath in hevenes hye, 1745
Love, that with an holsom alliaunce
Halt peples joyned as hym lyst hem gye,
Love, that knetteth lawe of compaignye,
And couples doth in vertu for to dwelle,
Bynd this acord that I have told and
      telle. 1750

"That that the world with feyth, which that is
      stable,
Dyverseth so his stoundes concordynge,
That elementes that ben so discordable
Holden a bond perpetuely durynge, 1754
That Phebus mote his rosy day forth brynge,
And that the mone hath lordshipe over the
      nyghtes—
Al this doth Love, ay heryed be his myghtes.

"That that the se, that gredy is to flowen,
Constreyneth to a certeyn ende so
His flodes that so fiersly they ne growen 1760
To drenchen erthe and al for everemo.
And yf that Love ought lat his bridel go,

Al that now loveth asondre sholde lepe,
And al were lost that Love halt now to-hepe.

"So wolde God, that auctour is of Kynde, 1765
That with his bond Love of his vertu liste
To cerclen hertes alle and faste bynde,
That from his bond no wight the weye out
      wyste.
And hertes colde, hem wolde I that he twyste
To make hem love, and that hem leste ay
      rewe 1770
On hertes sore, and kep hem that ben trewe."

In alle nedes for the townes werre
He was and ay the firste in armes dight,
And certaynly, but if that bokes erre,
Save Ector most ydrad of ony wight. 1775
And this encres of hardinesse and myght
Cam hym of love, his ladyes thank to wynne,
That altered his spirit so withinne.

In tyme of trewe, on haukyng wolde he ride,
Or elles hunten bor, ber, or lyoun— 1780
The smale bestes leet he gon bysyde.
And whan that he com rydynge into town,
Ful ofte his lady from hire wyndow down,
As freshe as fawkon comen out of muwe,
Ful redy was hym goodly to saluwe. 1785

And most of love and vertu was his speche,
And in despit hadde alle wrecchednesse.
And douteles, no nede was hym byseche
To honouren hem that hadde worthynesse,
And esen hem that weren in distresse. 1790
And glad was he yf any wyght wel ferde,
That lovere was, whan he it wyste or herde.

1734 **narwe ymasked,** narrowly (closely) enmeshed. 1739 **feste . . . proces,** feast of words, discourse. 1744–71 These stanzas from *Boece* II.m.8 provide a philosophical preparation for the proem of Bk. IV and what follows, for if the love of Troylus and Criseyde is equated so directly with temporal, natural phenomena, it follows that, like other natural phenomena, it too must change with time. These stanzas do not occur in some of the A MSS and hence may have been added by Chaucer in revision. If so, it would indicate that in revision Chaucer pointed up the philosophical basis for Criseyde's infidelity. 1745 **hestes,** commands. Mc&c *heste/hevene.* 1747 **hym lyst hem gye,** it pleases him to govern them. 1748 **compaignye,** companionship. **knetteth:** other MSS *enditeth.* 1752 **Dyverseth . . . stoundes concordynge,** so varies its times harmoniously. 1753 **discordable,** discordant. 1757 **heryed,** praised. 1759 **Constreyneth . . . certeyn ende,** i.e., confines within certain limits. 1760 *fiersly:* M *freshly.* 1761 **drenchen,** drown. 1762 **ought,** at all. 1764 **to-hepe,** together. 1765 **wolde . . . Kynde,** would to God, Nature. 1766 **vertu,** power. 1767 *cerclen:* M&c *cerchen/serchyn.* 1769 *twyste:* M *wyste.* 1770 **hem lest ay rewe,** it pleased them to have pity. 1771 **kep,** look after. 1773 **ay . . . dight,** always, arrayed. 1779 **trewe,** truce. 1781 **gon bysyde,** escape. 1784 **muwe,** coop. 1787 **despit,** contempt.

For soth to seyn, he lost held every wyght
But yf he were in Loves heyhe servyse—
I mene folk that oughte it ben of right.   1795
And over al this, so wel koude he devyse
Of sentement—and in so unkouth wyse—
Al his aray, that every lovere thoughte
That al was wel, whatso he seyde or wroughte.

And though that he be come of blod royal,   1800
Lyst hym of pride at no wyght for to chase.
Benygne he was to ech yn general,
For which he gat hym thank in every place.
Thus wolde Love—yheryed be his grace—
That pride, envye, ire, and avaryce   1805
He gan to fle, and everich other vice.

Thow lady bryght, the doughter to Dyone,
Thy blynde and wynged sone ek, daun Cupide,
Ye sustren nyne ek that by Elycone
In hil Pernaso lysten for to abide,   1810
That ye thus fer han deyned me to gyde—
I kan no more, but syn that ye wol wende,
Ye heryed ben for ay withouten ende.

Thorugh yow have I seyd fully in my song
Th'effect and joye of Troylus servyse,   1815
Al be that there were som dishese among,
As to myn auctour listeth to devyse.
My thridde book now ende ich in this wyse,
And Troylus, in lust and in quiete,
Is with Criseyde, his owne herte swete.   1820

Explicit liber tercius.

1795 folk that oughte, i.e., not those for whom, for some reason, love affairs were inappropriate. **1796–98 devyse ... unkouth wyse ... aray,** i.e., compose all his behavior to exhibit love, but in a concealed fashion (so as not to be discerned by wicked tongues). **1801 chase,** persecute (chase). **1804 yheryed,** praised. **1807 Dyone,** Venus, daughter of Jove and Dione. **1809 sustren nyne ... Elycone,** the nine Muses, Mt. Helicon (abode of the Muses). **1810 hil Pernaso,** Mt. Parnassus, sacred to the Muses. Like others in his time, Chaucer evidently thought of Helicon as the spring Hippocrene, the inspiration of poets (on Mt. Helicon), and that the spring was on Mt. Parnassus. **1813 heryed,** praised. **1816 among,** as well. **1817 listeth,** it pleases. **1820** The Explicit and Incipit come at IV.28 in MC&c: see IV.1n.

BOOK IV

Incipit prohemium quarti libri.

But al to litel, weylaway the whyle,
Lasteth swych joye, ythonked be Fortune,
That semeth trewest whanne she wol bygyle,
And kan to foles so hire song entune, 4
That she hem hent and blent, traytour comune.
And whan a wyght is from hire whiel ythrowe,
Than laugheth she and maketh hym the mowe.

From Troylus she gan hire brighte face
Awey to writhe, and tok of hym noon hede,
But caste hym clene oute of his lady grace, 10
And on hire whiel she sette up Diomede;
For which ryght now myn herte gynneth blede,
And now my penne, allas, with which I write,
Quaketh for drede of that I moste endite.

For how Criseyde Troylus forsook, 15
Or at the leste how that she was unkynde,
Mot hennesforth ben matere of my book,
As writen folk thorugh which it is in mynde.
Allas, that they shulde evere cause fynde
To speke hire harm—and yf they on hire lye,
Ywys, hemself sholde han the vilonye. 21

O ye Herynes, Nyghtes doughtren thre,
That endeles compleygnen evere in pyne,
Megera, Alete, and ek Thesiphone,
Thow cruel Mars ek, fader to Quyryne, 25
This ilke ferthe book me helpeth fyne,
So that the losse of lyf and love yfere
Of Troylus be fully shewed here.

Incipit quartus liber.

Liggyng yn ost, as I have seyd er this,
The Grekys stronge aboute Troye town, 30
Byfel that whanne that Phebus shynyng is
Upon the brest of Hercules lyoun,
That Ector with many a bold baroun
Caste on a day with Grekes for to fighte,
As he was woned, to greve hem what he myghte.

Not I how longe or short it was bytwene 36
This purpos and that day they fighte mente,
But on a day, wel armed, bright and shene,
Ector and many a worthi wight out wente,
With spere yn honde and bygge bowes bente, 40
And in the berd, withouten lenger lette,
Hire fomen in the feld anon hem mette.

1–28 MC&c (the G group in Root's classification) treat this proem as a conclusion to Bk. III. "Incipit" and "Prohemium" are found at this point only in two "other" MSS. **2 ythonked be,** thanks to. **3 bygyle,** deceive. **5 hent . . . blent . . . comune,** seizes, blinds, common to all men. **6 whiel,** the wheel of Fortune is a Boethian concept, II pr. 1, etc. **7 mowe,** mocking face (moue), *hym:* M *here; the:* other MSS *a.* **9 writhe,** turn. Other MSS *wrye.* **20 on,** about. **21 vilonye,** shame. **22 Herynes,** Erinyes, the Furies, named Megaera, Alecto, and Tisiphone (see I.6 above). **25 Quyryne,** one name for Romulus, founder of Rome. *Mars/to:* A *god/of.* **26 fyne,** finish. **27 yfere,** together. **29ff.** The text here returns to follow *Fil.* 4.1ff. **32 Hercules lyoun,** the sun, Phoebus, entered the zodiacal sign of Leo in July. **34 Caste,** decided. **35 woned,** accustomed. **36 Not I,** I don't know. **37 fighte mente,** meant to fight. **38 shene,** shining. **39–40** Lines transposed in other MSS. **41 in the berd . . . lette,** i.e., face to face, hesitation. **42** Other MSS *hem faste mette.*

The longe day, with speres sharpe ygrounde,
With arwes, dartes, swerdes, maces felle,
They fyghte and bryngen hors and man to
  grounde,   45
And with hire axes out the braynes quelle.
But in the laste shour, soth for to telle,
The folk of Troye hemselven so mysledden
That with the worse at nyght homward they
  fledden.

At whiche day was taken Antenor, 50
Maugre Polydamas or Monesteo,
Santippe, Sarpedon, Polynestor,
Polyte, or eke the Trojian daun Rupheo,
And other lasse folk as Phebuseo;
So that for harm that day the folk of Troye 55
Dredden to lese a gret part of hire joye.

Of Pryamus was yeve at Grekes requeste
A tyme of trewe, and tho they gonnen trete.
Hire prisoners to chaungen, moste and leste,
And for the surplus yeven sommes grete. 60
This thing anoon was kouth in every strete,
Bothe in th'assege, in town, and everywhere.
And with the firste it com to Calkas ere.

Whan Calkas knew this tretys sholde holde,
In consistorie among the Grekes soone 65
He gan in thrynge forth with lordes olde,
And sette hym there as he was woned to done;
And with a chaunged face hem bad a bone,
For love of God, to don that reverence,
To stynte noyse and yeve hym audyence. 70

Thanne seyde he thus, "Lo, lordes myne, ich was
Troian, as it is knowen out of drede,

And, if that yow remembre, I am Calkas,
That alderfirst yaf comfort to youre nede
And tolde wel how that ye sholden spede. 75
For dredeles thorugh yow shal in a stounde
Ben Troye ybrend and bete doun to grounde.

"And in what forme or in what manere wyse,
This town to shende and al youre lust to
  acheve,
Ye han er this wel herd it me devyse. 80
This knowe ye, my lordes, as I leve.
And for the Grekes weren me so leve,
I com myself, in my propre persone,
To teche in this how yow was best to done,

"Havyng unto my tresour ne my rente 85
Right no resport to respect of youre ese.
Thus al my good I lefte and to yow wente,
Wenyng in this you, lordes, for to plese.
But al that losse ne doth me no dishese.
I vouchesaf, as wysly have I joye, 90
For you to lese al that I have in Troye,

"Save of a doughter that I lafte, allas,
Slepynge at hom whanne out of Troye I sterte.
O sterne and cruwel fader that I was,
How myghte I have yn that so hard an herte?
Allas I ne hadde ybrought hire in hire sherte! 96
For sorwe of which I wol not lyve tomorwe
But yf ye lordes rewe upon my sorwe.

"For by that cause I say no tyme er now
Hire to delyvere, ich holden have my pes, 100
But now or nevere, yif that it lyke yow,
I may hire have right sone, douteles.
O help and grace amonges al this pres!

---

44 maces felle, cruel maces (spiked war clubs). **46 quelle,** kill (bash out). **47 shour,** assault (shower). **51 Maugre Polydamas,** etc. In *Fil.* 4.3 Polydamas and the others are captured along with Antenor. Chaucer has returned to the version of Benoit and Guido in which Antenor alone is captured. **57 yeve,** given. **58 trewe . . . trete,** truce, negotiate. **59 chaungen,** exchange. **60 surplus . . . sommes,** i.e., those for whom exchanges were not available had to be ransomed. **63 with,** among. **64 tretys,** negotiation. **65 consistorie,** council of rulers. **66 in thrynge forth,** to press in among. **67 woned,** accustomed. **68 chaunged face,** his face expressing his deep concern. **bad a bone,** asked a favor (boon). **70 stynte,** stop. **72 out of drede,** without doubt. **74 alderfirst . . . comfort,** first of all, support. **75 spede,** succeed; Calkas was a seer, cf. 1.71ff. **76 dredeles . . . stounde,** doubtless, time. **77 ybrend,** burned. **79 shende,** destroy. **80 it me:** other MSS *me yow.* **81 leve,** believe. **82 leve,** lief (dear). **83 propre,** own. **84 yow was best,** it would be best for you. **85 rente,** income. **86 resport to respect of,** regard in comparison with. **87 lefte:** M&c *loste.* **88 Other MSS,** *this, my lordes, yow to plese.* **90 vouchesaf,** am willing. **93 Troye:** A *toun.* **96 ne hadde . . . sherte,** that I did not, undershirt. **98 rewe,** take pity. **99 say,** saw. **100 holden,** have held.

Rewe on this olde caytyf in destresse,
Syn I for yow have al this hevynesse.   105

"Ye have now kaught and fetered in preson
Troians ynowe; and yf youre wille be,
My chyld with on may have redempcion.
Now, for the love of God and of bounte,
On of so fele, allas, so yeve hym me!   110
What nede were it this preyere for to werne,
Syn ye shul bothe han folk and town as yerne?

"On peril of my lyf, I shal not lye,
Appollo hath me told it feythfully;
I have ek founden be astronomye,   115
By sort, and by augurye ek, trewely;
And dar wel seye the tyme is faste by
That fir and flaumbe on al the toun shal
     sprede,
And thus shal Troye turne to asshen dede.

"For certeyn, Phebus and Neptainus bothe,   120
That makeden the walles of the toun,
Ben with the folk of Troye alwey so wrothe
That thei wol brynge it to confusioun,
Right in despit of Kyng Lameadoun—
By cause he nolde payen hem here hire,   125
The town of Troye shal ben set on fire."

Tellyng his tale alwey, this olde greye,
Humble in his speche and yn his lokyng eke,
The salte terys from his eyen tweye
Ful faste ronnen doun by eyther cheke.   130
So longe he gan of socour hem byseke
That for to hele hym of his sorwes sore,
They yaf hym Antenor withoute more.

But who was glad ynowh but Calkas tho?
And of this thing ful sone his nedes leyde   135

On hem that sholden for the tretis go,
And hem for Antenor ful ofte preyde
To bryngen hom Kyng Toas and Criseyde.
And whan Pryam his savegarde sente,
The ambassiatours to Troye streyght thei wente.

The cause ytold of hire comyng, the olde   141
Pryam the kyng ful soone in general
Let hereupon his parlement to holde,
Of which the effect rehersen yow I shal:
Th'embassadours ben answerd for fynal,   145
Th'eschaunge of prisoners and al this nede
Hem lyketh wel, and forth in they procede.

This Troylus was present in the place
Whan axed was for Antenor Criseyde,
For which ful soone chaungen gan his face   150
As he that with tho wordes wel neygh deyde.
But natheles he no word to it seyde,
Lest men sholde his affeccioun espye.
With mannes herte he gan his sorwes drye,

And ful of angwyssh and of grysly drede   155
Abod what lordes wolde unto it seye.
And yf they wolde graunte—as God
     forbede—
Th'eschaunge of hire, than thoughte he thynges
     tweye,
First how to save hire honour, and what weye
He myghte best th'eschaunge of hire with-
     stonde.   160
Ful faste he cast how al this myghte stonde.

Love hym made al prest to don hire byde,
And rather dye than she sholde go;
But resoun seyde hym, on that other syde,
"Withoute assent of hire ne do not so,   165
Lest for thi werk she wolde be thi fo,

104 **Rewe . . . caytyf,** have pity on, wretch. 105 *for:* C&c *through; have al this hevynesse: A am broght in wrecchidnes.* 111 **werne,** refuse. 112 **yerne,** soon. 114 A *hath me told sikirly.* 117 **faste,** near. 120 **Neptainus,** Neptune and Apollo were reputed to have built the walls of Troy and not been paid by King Laomedon, father of Priam. 124 **despit,** spite (anger) toward. 131 **socour,** help. A *mercy.* 135 **nedes leyde,** i.e., entrusted his commission. 136 **tretis,** negotiation. 138 **Toas,** Chaucer is again conflating his sources. In *Fil.* 4.12ff., Antenore is exchanged for Criseida on even terms, but in Benoit 13079ff. he is exchanged for Thoas, and Criseida is sent to her father without exchange. **bryngen hom:** M&c *bryng hem.* 139 **savegarde:** other MSS *safe conduyt.* 143 **Let,** caused. 146 **this nede,** that is necessary. 156 **Abod,** waited. Other MSS *Abood what oother lordes wolde seye.* 160 **th'eschaunge:** A *the grauntyng.* 161 A *This cast he tho how.* 162 **prest . . . don,** eager (ready), make. 166 Other MSS *If thow debate it, lest she be thy fo.*

And seyn that thorugh thi medlyng is yblowe
Yowre bothere love there it was erst unknowe."

For which he gan deliberen for the beste
That though the lordes wolde that she wente,
He wolde lat hem graunte what hem leste,   171
And telle his lady fyrst what that they mente;
And whanne that she hadde seyd hym hire
    entente,
Therafter wolde he werken also blyve,
Though al the world ayen it wolde stryve.   175

Ector, which that wel the Grekis herde,
For Antenor how they wolde han Criseyde,
Gan it withstonde, and sobrely answerde,
"Sires, she nys no presoner," he seyde.
"I not on yow who that this charge leyde,   180
But on my part ye may eftsone hym telle
We usen here no wommen for to selle."

The noyse of peple up stirte thanne at onys,
As breme as blase of straw yset on fyre;
For infortune it wolde, for the nonys,   185
They sholden hire confusioun desire.
"Ector," quod they, "what gost may yow enspire
This womman thus to shilde, and don us lese
Daun Antenor? A wrong wey now ye chese!

"That is so wys and ek so bold baroun,   190
And we han nede to folk, as men may se.
He is ek on the grettest of this town.
O Ector, lat tho fantasyes be!
O Kyng Pryam," quod they, "thus seggen we,
That al oure voys is to forgon Criseyde."   195
And to delyveren Antenor they preyde.

O Juvenal, lord, trewe is thi sentence,
That litel wyten folk what is to yerne,
That they ne fynde in hire desir offence,
For cloude of errour lat hem not descerne   200
What best is. And lo, here ensample as yerne:
This folk desiren now delyveraunce
Of Antenor, that brought hem to myschaunce.

For he was after traytour to the town
Of Troye—allas, they quyt hym out to rathe!
O nyce world, lo thy dyscressioun!   206
Criseyde, which that nevere dede hem skathe,
Shal now no lengere in hire blysse bathe;
But Antenor, he shal come hom to towne,
And she shal out—thus seyden here and howne.

For which delibered was by parlement   211
For Antenor to yelden up Criseyde,
And it pronounced by the president,
Althey that Ector "nay" ful ofte preyede.
And fynaly, what wyght that it withseyde,   215
It was for nought; it moste ben and sholde,
For substaunce of the parlement it wolde.

Departed out of parlement echone,
This Troylus withoute wordes mo
Unto his chambre spede hym faste allone,   220
But yf it were a man of his or two
The which he bad out faste for to go
Bycause he wolde slepen, as he seyde;
And hastily upon his bed hym leyde.

And as yn wynter leves ben byraft,   225
Eche after other, til the tre be bare,
So that ther nys but bark and braunche ylaft,

Lyth Troylus, byraft of ech welfare,
Ibounden in the blake bark of care,
Disposed wod out of his wit to breyde, 230
So sore hym sat the chaungynge of Criseyde.

He rist hym up, and every dore he shette,
And wyndow ek, and tho this sorwful man
Upon his beddes side adoun hym sette,
Ful lyk a ded ymage, pale and wan. 235
And in his brest the heped wo bygan
Out brest, and he to werken yn this wyse
In his woodnesse, as I shal yow devyse.

Ryght as the wylde bole bygynneth sprynge,
Now her, now ther, idarted to the herte, 240
And of his deth roreth yn compleynynge,
Right so gan he aboute the chaumbre sterte,
Smytyng his brest ay with his festes smerte;
His hed to the wal, his body to the grounde
Ful ofte he swapte, himselven to confounde. 245

Hys eyen two for pite of his herte
Out stremeden as swyfte welles tweye.
The heyghe sobbes of his sorwes smerte
His speche hym rafte. Unnethes myghte he
        seye,
"O deth, allas, whi nyltow do me deye? 250
Acursed be the day which that Nature
Shop me to ben a lyves creature!"

But after, whan the furye and the rage,
Which that his herte twyste and faste threste,
By lengthe of tyme somwhat gan aswage, 255
Upon his bed he leyde hym down to reste.
But tho bygonne his terys more out breste,
That wonder is the body may suffise
To half this wo which that I yow devyse.

Thanne seyde he thus, "Fortune, allas the while!
What have I don? What have I thus agilt? 261
How myghtestow for reuthe me bygyle?
Is ther no grace, and shal I thus be spilt?
Shal thus Criseyde awey, for that thow wylt?
Allas, how maystow in thyn herte fynde 265
To ben to me thus cruwel and unkynde?

"Have I the nought honoured al my lyve,
As thow wel wost, above the goddes alle?
Why wiltow me fro joye thus depryve?
O Troylus, what may men the now calle 270
But wrecche of wrecches, out of honour falle
Into myserie, yn which I wol bywayle
Criseyde, allas, til that the breth me fayle?

"Allas, Fortune, yf that my lyf yn joye
Displesed hadde unto thi foule envye, 275
Why ne haddestow my fader, kyng of Troye,
Byraft the lyf, or don my bretheren deye,
Or slayn myself that thus compleyne and
        crye—
I, combre-world, that may of nothing serve,
But evere dye, and nevere fully sterve? 280

"Yf that Criseyde allone were me laft,
Nought roughte I wheder thow woldest me
        stere!
And hire, allas, than hastow me byraft!
But everemore, lo, this is thi manere,
To reve a wyght that most is to hym dere, 285
To preve yn that thi gerful violence.
Thus am I lost; there helpeth no defence.

"O verrey lord of love, O god, allas,
That knowest best myn herte and al my thought,
What shal my sorwful lyf don in this cas, 290

---

230 wod . . . breyde, insane, rush (go). **231** *chaungynge:* other MSS *eschaunge.* **237 brest,** burst. **238 woodnesse,** madness. A *distresse.*
239 bole, bull. This episode is in *Fil.* 4.27ff., but the lover's running mad, beating his head against the wall, etc., is a set piece in
the Tristan and Lancelot epitomes of the behavior of courtly lovers. **240 idarted,** pierced. **245 swapte,** dashed. **246** *pite:* other MSS
piete; C&c *his* om. **247 welles,** springs. A *So wepyn that they semyn welles tweye.* **249 hym rafte. Unnethes,** deprived him, barely.
250 do, make. **252 Shop,** created. **253** Other MSS *Whan al this furye and (al) this rage.* **254 threste,** pierced. **261 agilt,** offended.
The following lament (ll. 260–336) parallels Troilo's lament in *Fil.* 4.30–40, but makes some interesting changes. **262 reuthe . . .
bygyle,** pity, deceive. **263 grace . . . spilt,** favor (relief), destroyed. **266** *thus:* A *so.* **269** A *thanne of joye me deprive.* **279 combre-world,**
(useless) encumberer of the world. **280 sterve,** perish. *evere:* other MSS *alwey.* **282 roughte,** would care. Other MSS *whiderward
thow woldest steere.* **285 reve,** deprive. **286 preve . . . gerful,** demonstrate, changeable. A *gery.*

Yf I forgo that I so dere have bought?
Syn ye Cryseyde and me han fully brought
Into youre grace, and bothe oure hertes seled,
How may ye suffre, allas, it be repeled?

"What may I don? I shal whil I may dure,   295
On lyve in torment and yn cruwel peyne,
This infortune of this disaventure,
Allone as I was born, ywys, compleyne;
Ne nevere wyl I seen it shyne or reyne,
But ende I wil, as Edippe, yn derknesse   300
My sorwful lyf, and dyen in dystresse.

"O wery goost that errest to and fro,
Why nyltow fle out of the wofulleste
Body that evere myghte on grounde go?
O soule, lurkynge in this wo, unneste,   305
Fle forth out of myn herte and lat it breste,
And folowe alwey Criseyde, thi lady dere.
Thi righte place is now no lenger here.

"O wofulle eyen two, syn youre desport
Was al to seen Criseydes eyen bryght,   310
What shal ye don but for my discomfort
Stonden for nought, and wepen out youre
      sight,
Syn she is queynt that wont was yow to light?
In vayn fro this forth have ich eyen tweye
Yformed, syn youre vertu is aweye.   315

"O my Criseyde, O lady sovereyne
Of thilke woful soule that thus crieth,
Who shal now yeven comfort to the peyne?
Allas, no wight; but whan myn herte dyeth,
My spirit, which that so unto yow hyeth,   320
Receyve in gre, for that shal ay yow serve;
Forthi no fors is, though the body sterve.

"O ye loveres, that heyhe upon the whiel
Ben set of Fortune, yn good aventure,
God leve that ye fynde ay love of stel,   325
And longe mot youre lyf yn joye endure!
But whanne ye comen by my sepulture,
Remembreth that youre felawe resteth there—
For I loved ek, though ich unworthi were.

"O old, unholsom, and myslyved man,   330
Calkas I mene, allas, what eyleth the
To ben a Grek syn thou art born Troian?
O Calkas, which that wilt my bane be,
In cursed tyme was thow born for me!
As wolde blisful Jove for his joye   335
That I the hadde where as I wolde in Troye!"

A thousand sykes hottere than the glede
Out of his brest eche after other wente,
Meddled with pleyntes new his wo to fede,
For which his woful terys nevere stente.   340
And shortly, so his peynes hym torente
And wex so mat that joye nor penaunce
He feleth noon, but lyth forth in a traunce.

Pandare, which that in the parlement
Hadde herd what every lord and burgeys seyde,
And how ful graunted was by on assent   346
For Antenor to yelden so Criseyde,
Gan wel neygh wod out of his wit to breyde,
So that for wo he nyste what he mente,
But in a res to Troylus he wente.   350

A certeyn knyght that for the tyme kepte
The chaumbre door undede it hym anoon;
And Pandare that ful tendreliche wepte
Into the derke chambre, as stille as ony ston,
Toward the bed gan softely to gon,   355

---

294 repeled, repealed. *allas:* A *that.* **295 dure,** endure. Other MSS *What shal;* M *What I may.* **296 On lyve,** alive. **297 infortune . . . disaventure,** ill fortune, calamity. A *mysaventure.* **298 Allone:** MA *Allas.* **300 Edippe,** Oedipus, who died blind. **302 goost . . . errest,** spirit, wanders. *wery:* M&c *verray.* **305 unneste,** depart from your nest. **306 Fle,** fly. A *Fle forth anon and do myn herte brest.* **309 desport,** pleasure. **312 Stonden for nought,** be of no use. **313 queynt,** quenched. **315 Yformed . . . vertu,** i.e., have I been formed with eyes, (power) use. **318 the:** other MSS *my/thy/your.* **321 gre,** favor. **322 Forthi no fors . . . sterve,** therefore no matter, perish. **325 leve . . . stel,** permit, (durable as) steel. *fynde:* other MSS *graunte/lende.* **326 mot,** may. *youre:* A *ye.* **330 myslyved,** evil-living. MA *mysbyleved.* **333 bane,** death. **337 sykes . . . glede,** sighs, live coal. **339 Meddled,** mixed. **340 stente,** stopped. **341** *peynes:* A&c *sorwis.* **342 mat,** exhausted. **347** *yelden:* A *chaungyn.* **348 wod . . . breyde,** run crazy. **350 res,** rush. **351 kepte,** guarded. **354** C&c *ony om.*

So confus that he nyste what to seye;
For verray wo his wit was neigh aweye.

And with his chere and lokyng al totorn
For sorwe of this, and with his armes folden,
He stod this woful Troylus byforn,   360
And on his pitous face he gan byholden.
But Lord, so ofte gan his herte colden,
Seyng his frend in wo, whose hevynesse
His herte slow, as thought hym, for
    distresse.

This woful wight, this Troylus, that felte   365
His frend Pandare ycomen hym to se,
Gan as the snow ayen the sonne melte,
For whych this sorwful Pandare of pyte
Gan for to wepe as tendrelyche as he,
And specheles thus ben this ilke tweye,   370
That neyther myghte o word for sorwe
    seye.

But at the laste this woful Troylus,
Ney ded for smert, gan bresten out to rore,
And with a sorwful noyse he seyde thus,
Among his sobbes and his sikes sore,   375
"Lo, Pandare, I am ded withouten more.
Hastow nought herd at parlement," he seyde,
"For Antenor how lost is my Criseyde?"

This Pandarus, ful dede and pale of hewe,
Ful pytously answerde and seyde, "Yis,   380
As wysly were it fals as it is trewe,
That I have herd and wot al how it is.
O mercy God, who wolde have trowed this?
Who wolde have wend that yn so lytel a
    throwe
Fortune oure joye wolde han overthrowe?   385

"For yn this world there is no creature,
As to my dom, that ever saw ruyne
Straunger than this, thorugh cas or aventure.
But who may al eschewe or al devyne?
Swych is this world! Forthi I thus defyne: 390
Ne trust no wyght to fynden in Fortune
Ay proprete—hire yeftes ben comune.

"But tel me this: whi thou art now so mad
To sorwen thus? Whi listow in this wyse,
Syn thi desir al holly hastow had,   395
So that by right it oughte ynow suffise?
But I, that nevere felte in my servyse
A frendly chere, or lokyng of an eye,
Lat me thus wepe and wailen til I dye.

"And over al this, as thow wel wost thiselve,   400
This town is ful of ladyes al aboute;
And, to my dom, fairer than swyche twelve
As evere she was shal I fynde yn som route,
Ye oon or two, withouten any doute.
Forthi be glad, myn owen dere brother.   405
If she be lost, we shul recovere another.

"What, God forbede alwey that ech plesaunce
In o thyng were and in noon other wyght.
Yf oon kan synge, another kan wel daunce;
Yf this be goodly, she is glad and lyght;   410
And this is fayr, and that kan good aright.
Ech for his vertu holden is for dere,
Bothe heroner and faukoun for ryvere.

"And ek, as writ Zanzis that was ful wys,
The newe love out chaceth ofte the olde,   415
And upon newe cas lyth newe avys.
Thenk ek, thi lif to saven thow art holde.
Swych fyr by proces shal of kynde colde;

357 neigh: A *al.* **358 chere . . . totorn,** face, ravaged. **359** A *Ny dede for wo and with.* **363 hevynesse,** sadness. **364 slow,** slew. **373 bresten,** burst. A *For crewel smert.* **374** noyse: other MSS *voys.* **375 sikes,** sighs. **383 trowed,** believed. **384 wend . . . throwe,** thought, time. **386** For: A *O.* **387 dom,** judgment. **388 cas,** chance. Straunger: A *Strengere.* **389 eschewe . . . devyne,** escape, foresee. **392 Ay proprete . . . yeftes . . . comune,** always his own possession (proprietary), gifts, common (belonging to everyone). hire: M *his.* **394 listow,** do you lie (down). **397 servyse,** love-service. felte: A *fond.* **398 chere,** expression. lokyng: A *castyng.* **402 dom . . . swyche twelve,** judgment, twelve times as fair. **403 route,** group. **404** A *to or thre.* **407 plesaunce,** pleasure. **411** And/And that: A *Yf /sche that.* **412** for dere: other MSS *ful dere.* **413 heroner . . . faukoun for ryvere,** large falcon for herons, smaller falcon for waterfowl. **414 Zanzis,** the quotation is from Ovid by way of *Fil.* 4.49, but Ovid and Boccaccio assign no author for the adage. No one knows why Chaucer chose Zanzis. M&c *Zauzis;* other MSS *Zenes,* etc. **416 cas lyth . . . avys,** situation requires, consideration. **417 holde,** bound. lif: M *self.* thow art: C&c *artow.* **418 of kynde,** naturally. shal: other MSS *moot.*

For syn it is but casuel plesaunce,
Som cas shal putte it out of remembraunce.   420

"For also seur as day cometh after nyght,
The newe love, labour, or other wo,
Or ellys selde seynge of a wyght,
Don olde affecciouns al overgo.
And for thi part, thow shalt have one of tho   425
To abrigge with thi bittre peynes smerte;
Absence of hire shal dryve hire out of herte."

Thise wordes seyde he for the nones alle,
To helpe his frend lest he for sorwe deyde.
For douteles, to don his wo to falle,   430
He roughte nought what unthryft that he
    seyde.
But Troylus, that neigh for sorwe deyde,
Tok litel hed of al that evere he mente;
Oon eere it herde, at the other out it wente.

But at the laste he answerde and seyde,
    "Frend,   435
This lechecraft, or heled thus to be,
Were wel sittyng if that I were a fend—
To traysen hire that trewe is unto me.
I pray to God lat this consayl nevere the,
But do me rathere anon sterve right here,   440
Er I thus do as thow me woldest lere.

"She that I serve, ywys, what so thow seye,
To whom myn herte enhabyt is by right,
Shal han me holly hires til that I deye.
For, Pandarus, syn I have trouthe hire hight,
I wol nat ben untrewe for no wyght,   446
But as hire man I wole ay lyve and sterve,
And nevere other creature serve.

"And ther thow seyst thow shalt as faire fynde
As she, lat be. Make no comparysoun   450
To creature yformed here by kynde.
O leve Pandare, in conclusion,
I wol nat ben of thyn opynyon
Towchyng al this. For whiche I the byseche,
So hold thi pes; thow slest me with thi
    speche!   455

"Thow biddest me I sholde love another
Al fresshly newe, and lat Criseyde go.
It lith nat in my power, leve brother;
And though I myght, I wolde not do so.
But kanstow pleyen raket, to and fro,   460
Nettle in, dokke out, now this, now that,
    Pandare?
Now fowle falle hire that for thi wo hath care!

"Thow farest ek by me, thow Pandarus,
As he that whan a wyght is wobygon,   464
He cometh to hym a pas and seyth right thus,
'Thenk not on smert, and thow shalt fele noon.'
Thow most me first transmewen in a ston,
And reve me my passiones alle,
Er thow so lightly do my wo to falle.

"The deth may wel out of my brest departe   470
The lyf, so longe may this sorwe myne;
But fro my sowle shal Criseydes darte
Out neveremo. But down with Proserpyne,
Whan I am ded, I wol go wone in pyne,
And ther I wol eternally compleyne   475
My wo, and how that twynned be we tweyne.

"Thow hast here mad an argument for fyn,
How that it sholde a lasse peyne be

419 **casuel,** due to chance (transitory). This observation is not found in Pandaro's speech in *Fil.* 4.49. Chaucer's adding it here may be less to paint Pandarus as a cynic than to reinforce the Boethian view of the insufficiency of temporal love, cf. *Boece* III.814, 1691, 1744. 420 **cas,** chance event. 423 **selde seynge,** seldom seeing. 424 **Don . . . overgo,** make, go away. 425 **one of tho,** i.e., those chance events (including new ladies). 426 **abrigge,** reduce. 430 **don . . . falle,** make, disappear. *don:* A *make; wo:* M *sorwe.* 431 **roughte . . . unthryft,** cared, foolishness. 436 **lechecraft,** physician-craft. 438 **traysen,** betray. 439 **the,** prosper. C&c *ythe.* 440 **sterve,** perish. 441 **lere,** instruct. *thus do:* other MSS *so werke.* 443 **enhabyt,** devoted. 445 **hight,** promised. A *What, Pandarus, syn I have hir bihight.* 447 **sterve,** die. 451 **kynde,** nature. 459 *wolde:* M *wil.* 460 **raket,** court tennis, played off the walls. 461 **Nettle . . . dokke,** first words of a charm in which dock leaves are used to wipe out the sting of nettle, and a proverbial expression for inconstancy. Other MSS *now her, now ther.* 465 **a pas,** apace (promptly). 467 **transmewen,** change. 468 **reve,** relieve of. 469 **do . . . falle,** make, depart. 471 **myne,** undermine. 473 **Proserpyne,** queen of Hades. 474 **wone,** live. 476 **twynned,** parted. A *this wo.* 477 **for fyn,** to the conclusion. Other MSS *ful fyn.*

Criseyde to forgon for she was myn
And lyved in ese and yn felicite. 480
Whi gabbestow that seydest thus to me,
That 'hym is wors that is fro wele ythrowe,
Than he hadde erst non of that wele yknowe?'

"But tel me now, syn that the thenketh so
   lyght
To chaungen so in love ay to and fro, 485
Whi hastow not don bysyly thi myght
To chaungen hire that doth the al thi wo?
Why neltow lete hire fro thyn herte go?
Whi neltow love another lady swete,
That may thin herte setten in quyete? 490

"If thow hast had in love ay yet myschaunce,
And kanst it not out of thyn herte dryve,
I that levede yn lust and in plesaunce
With hire as muche as creature on lyve,
How sholde I that foryete, and that so blyve?
O, where hastow ben hid so longe in muwe, 496
That kanst so wel and formaly arguwe?

"Nay, God wot, nought worth is al thi red.
For which, for what that evere may byfalle,
Withouten wordes mo, I wol be ded. 500
O deth, that endere art of sorwes alle,
Com now, syn I so ofte after the calle;
For sely is that deth, soth for to seyne,
That, ofte ycleped, cometh and endeth peyne.

"Wel wot I, whil my lyf was in quyete, 505
Er thow me slowe, I wolde have yeven hire;
But now thi comynge is to me so swete
That in this world I nothing so desire.
O deth, syn with this sorwe I am afyre,
Thou other do me anoon yn teris drenche, 510
Or with thi colde strok myn hete quenche.

"Syn that thou sleest so fele in sondry wyse,
Ayens hire wil, unpreyed, day and nyght,
Do me at my requeste this servise:
Delyvere now the world, so dostow right, 515
Of me that am the wofulleste wyght
That evere was, for tyme is that I sterve,
Syn in this world of right nought may I serve."

This Troylus in teris gan distille,
As licour out of a lambyc ful faste. 520
And Pandarus gan holde his tunge stille,
And to the ground his eyen doun he caste.
But natheles, thus thought he at the laste,
"What, parde, rather than my felawe deye,
Yet shal I somwhat more unto hym seye." 525

And seyde, "Frend, syn thow hast swych
   distresse,
And syn thee list myn argumentes blame,
Why nylt thiself helpen don redresse,
And with thy manhod letten al this grame?
To ravysshe hire ne kanstow not? For shame! 530
And other lat hire out of towne fare,
Or hold hire stille, and leve thi nyce fare.

"Artow in Troye, and hast noon hardiment
To take a womman which that loveth the,
And wolde hireselven ben of thyn assent? 535
Now is nat this a nyce vanyte?
Rys up anoon, and lat this wepyng be,
And kyth thow art a man, for yn this owre
I wil be ded or she shal bleven oure."

To this answerde hym Troylus ful softe, 540
And seyde, "Parde, leve brother dere,
Al this have I myself yet thought ful ofte,
And more thyng than thow devysest here.
But whi this thyng is laft thow shalt wel here,

---

480 lyved, (we) lived. M *leve*. **481 gabbestow,** do you talk foolishness. **482 wele,** prosperity, cf. III.1625n. **484 lyght,** easy. *tel:* A *sey. now:* other MSS *this.* **495 blyve,** quickly. **496 muwe,** coop. **498 red,** advice. Other MSS *Nay, nay;* A *Nay, Pandarus naught worth.* **499** A *But douteles for ought that may bifalle.* **503 sely,** happy. **504 ycleped,** called. **506 hire,** ransom (hire). *thow:* A *deth.* **507 thi:** A *his.* **510 other,** either. M *yn this teris.* **512 fele,** many. **515 so:** A *thanne.* **517 sterve,** die. **519 This:** other MSS *Thus.* **520 lambyc,** alembic; retort used in distilling. **527** C&c *argumentz to.* **528** Other MSS *help to don.* **529 letten . . . grame,** prevent, grief. **530 ravysshe,** abduct. *To:* C&c *Go.* **531 other . . . fare,** either, go. **532 leve . . . nyce fare,** leave off, foolish behavior. *thi/fare:* other MSS *this/care.* **533 hardiment,** courage. **536 nyce vanyte,** foolish futility. **537 wepyng:** A *sorwe.* **538 kyth . . . owre,** show, hour. **539 bleven oure,** remain ours. **543 devysest,** suggest. **544 laft,** i.e., not performed.

And whan thow me hast yeve an audience, 545
Therafter maystow telle al thi sentence.

"Fyrst, syn thow wost this town hath al this
    werre
For ravysshyng of womman so by myght,
It sholde not be suffred me to erre,
As it stant now, ne don so gret unright. 550
I sholde han also blame of every wyght
My fadres graunt yf that I so withstode,
Syn she is chaunged for the townes goode.

"I have ek thought, so it were hire assent,
To axe hire at my fader, of his grace; 555
Than thenke I this were hire accusement,
Syn wel I wot I may hire nought purchace.
For syn my fader in so heigh a place
As parlement hath hire eschaunge enseled,
He nyl for me his lettre be repeled. 560

"Yet drede I moost hire herte to pertourbe
With violence, yf I do swych a game.
For yf I wolde it openly distourbe,
It moste ben disclaundre to hire name,
And me were levere ded than hire defame—
As nolde God but yf I sholde have 566
Hire honour levere than my lyf to save!

"Thus am I lost, for ought that I kan se.
For certeyn is, syn that I am hire knyght,
I moste hire honour levere han than me 570
In every cas, as lovere ought of right.
Thus am I with desir and reson twyght:
Desir for to destourben hire me redeth,
And reson nyl not, so myn herte dredeth."

Thus wepyng that he koude nevere cesse, 575

He seyde, "Allas, how shal I, wrecche, fare?
For wel fele I alwey my love encresse,
And hope is lasse and lasse alway, Pandare.
Encressen ek the causes of my care.
So welawey, whi nyl myn herte breste? 580
For as in love ther is but litel reste."

Pandare answerde, "Frend, thow mayst, for me,
Don as the list; but hadde ich it so hote,
And thyn estat, she sholde go with me,
Though al this town criede on this thyng by
    note. 585
I nolde sette at al that noyse a grote.
For when men han wel cried, than wol they
    rowne—
A wonder last but nyne nyght nevere yn towne.

"Devyne not in reson ay so depe
Ne curteysly, but help thiself anoon. 590
Bet is that othere than thiselven wepe,
And namly syn ye two ben al oon.
Rys up, for by myn hed she shal not goon!
And rather be in blame a lite yfounde
Than sterve here as a gnat, withowten wounde.

"It is no shame unto yow, ne no vice, 596
Hire to withholden that ye loveth most.
Peraunter, she myghte holden the for nyce
To late hire go thus unto the Greke ost.
Thenk ek Fortune, as wel thiselven wost, 600
Helpeth hardy man to his enprise,
And weyveth wrecches for hire cowardise.

"And though thi lady wolde a lite hire greve,
Thow shalt thi pes ful wel hereafter make,
But as for me, certeyn, I kan not leve 605
That she wolde it as now for yvel take.

---

546 **sentence**, opinion. 548 **ravysshyng**, according to tradition, the Trojan War was brought on by the Greek Telamon's abduction of Priam's sister Hesione, and Paris' retaliatory abduction of Menelaus' wife Helen (Benoit, 2793, 4059, etc.). 553 **chaunged**, exchanged. 555 **axe hire**, i.e., request her of him as a favor. 556 **hire accusement**, accusation of her (i.e., that she is his mistress). 557 **purchace**, obtain. 559 **enseled**, sealed (granted officially). 560 **lettre**, decree. A *his honour*. 566 **nolde God**, God forbid. 567 **levere**, preferably. 570 A *I have hir honour levere yit than me*. 572 **twyght**, pulled. 573 **redeth**, counsels. 581 A *For why in love is litel hertes reste*. 585 **by note**, in unison. 586 **grote**, the smallest coin. 587 **rowne** quiet down (whisper). *wol they*: A *lat hem*. 588 *A*: C&c *Ek*. 589 **Devyne**, inquire. 590 *curteysly*: A *preciously*. 592 **namly . . . al oon**, especially, in agreement. 594 *lite*: M *litel*; other MSS *litel stounde* (time). 596 A *It is no rape in my dom, ne no vice*. 597 **withholden**, i.e., from the Greeks. 598 **nyce**, foolish. 600 **wost**, know. 602 **weyveth**, abandons: A *fleeth fro*. 604 C&c *Thow shalt thiself thi pees hereafter make*. 605 **leve**, believe.

Whi sholde thanne of fered thyn herte quake?
Thenk ek how Parys hath, that is thi brother,
A love; and whi shaltow nat have another?

"And Troylus, o thyng I dar the swere, 610
That if Criseyde, whiche that is thi lef,
Now loveth the as wel as thow dost hire,
God helpe me so, she nyl not take a-gref,
Theigh thou do bote anoon in this myschef.
And yf she wilneth fro the for to passe, 615
Thanne is she fals; so love hire wel the lasse.

"Forthi tak herte, and thenk right as a knyght,
Thorugh love is broken alday every lawe.
Kith now somwhat thi corage and thi myght,
Have mercy on thiself for ony awe. 620
Lat nat this wrecched wo thyn herte gnawe,
But manly set the world on sixe and sevene,
And yf thow deye a martir, go to hevene.

"I wol myself ben with the at this dede,
Theygh ich and al my kyn upon a stounde 625
Shulle in a strete as dogges liggen dede,
Thorugh-girt with many a wyd and blody
 wounde.
In every cas I wol a frend be founde.
And yf the lyst here sterven as a wrecche,
Adieu—the devel spede hym that it recche." 630

This Troylus gan with tho wordes quyken,
And seyde, "Frend, graunt mercy, ich assente.
But certeynly thow mayst not me so priken,
Ne peyne noon ne may me so tormente,
That for no cas it is not myn entente, 635
At shorte wordes, though I dyen sholde,
To ravysshen hire but yf hireself it wolde."

"Why, so mene I," quod Pandarus, "al this
 day.
But telle me thanne, hastow hire wil assayed,

That sorwest thus?" And he answerde hym,
 "Nay." 640
"Wherof artow," quod Pandare, "than
 amayed,
That nost not that she wol ben evele apayed
To ravysshen hire, syn thow hast not ben there,
But if that Jove told it yn thyn eere?

"Forthi rys up as nought ne were, anoon, 645
And wassh thi face, and to the kyng thow wende,
Or he may wondren whider thow art goon.
Thow most with wysdom hym and othere
 blende,
Or, upon cas, he may after the sende,
Er thow be war. And shortly, brother dere, 650
Be glad, and lat me werke in this matere.

"For I shal shappe it so that sikerly
Thow shalt this nyght somtyme in som
 manere
Com speke with thi lady prevely,
And by hire wordes ek, and by hire chere, 655
Thow shalt ful sone aparceyve and wel here
Al hire entente, and in this cas the beste.
And fare now wel, for in this point I reste."

The swyfte Fame, which that false thynges
Egal reporteth lyk the thynges trewe, 660
Was thoroughout Troye yfled with preste wynges
Fro man to man and made this tale al newe,
How Calkas doughter with hire brighte hewe,
At parlement, withoute wordes more,
Igraunted was yn chaunge of Antenore. 665

The whiche tale anoon-right as Criseyde
Had herd, she which that of hire fader roughte,
As in this cas, right nought, ne whanne he
 deyde,
Ful bysily to Juppiter bysoughte
Yeve hym myschaunce that this tretis broughte.

607 fered, being frightened. **611 lef,** love. **614 bote,** remedy. *Theigh* (though): M *They.* **615 wilneth,** wishes. **619 Kith,** show. M *Kygh.* **624 dede:** M&c *nede.* **625 a stounde,** at one time. **627 Thorugh-girt,** pierced through. **629 the lyst . . . sterven,** it pleases you to die. **630 recche,** cares. **631 quyken,** revive. **638** A *Pandare answerde, Of that be as be may.* **639 wil:** M&c *wel.* **641 amayed,** dismayed. **642 evele apayed,** displeased. **644** A *But any aungel told.* **648 most . . . blende,** must, blind (deceive). **649 upon cas,** perhaps. **652 sikerly,** surely. **655 chere,** manner. *and/cheere:* other MSS *as/cheere.* **659 swyfte Fame,** i.e., rumor. **660 Egal,** equally. **661 preste,** swift. **666 anoon-right,** as soon as. **667 roughte,** cared. **670 tretis,** negotiation.

But shortly, lest this tales sothe were,   671
She dorste at no wyght asken it for fere,

As she that hadde hire herte and al hire mynde
On Troilus yset so wonder faste
That al the world ne koude hire love unbynde, 675
Ne Troylus out of hire herte caste—
She wol ben his, whil that hire lyf may laste.
And thus she brenneth bothe in love and drede,
So that she nyste what was best to rede.

But as men sen in towne and al aboute   680
That wommen usen frendes to visite,
So to Criseyde of wommen come a rowte,
For pitous joye, and wenden hire delite.
And with hire tales, dere ynowh a myte,   684
These wommen, whiche that yn the cite dwelle,
Thei sette hem doun and seyde as I shal telle.

Quod first that oon, "I am glad, trewely,
By cause of yow, that ye shal youre fader se."
Another seyde, "Iwys, so am not I,
For al to litel hath she with us be."   690
Quod tho the thridde, "I hope, ywys, that she
Shal bryngen us the pes on every side,
That whanne she gooth, Almyghty God hire
      gide."

Tho wordes and tho wommanysshe thynges,
She herd hem ryght as though she thennes
      were,   695
For God it wot, hire herte on other thing is.
Although the body sat among hem there,
Hire advertence is alwey ellyswhere,
For Troylus ful faste hire soule soughte.   699
Withouten word, alwey on hym she thoughte.

This wommen, that thus wenden hire to plese,

Aboute nought gonne alle hire tales spende.
Swych vanite ne kan don hire non ese,
As she that al this menewhile brende
Of other passioun than that they wende,   705
So that she felte almost hire herte deye
For wo and wery of that companye.

For which no lenger myghte she restreyne
Hire teeris, so they gonnen up to welle,
That yaven signes of the bittre peyne   710
In which hir spirit was, and moste dwelle,
Remembryng hire fro heven into which helle
She fallen was syn she forgoth the syghte
Of Troylus; and sorwfully she sighte.

And thilke fooles sittynge hire aboute   715
Wenden that she wepte and syked sore
By cause that she sholde out of that route
Departe, and nevere pleye with hem more.
And they that hadde yknowen hire of yore
Seygh hire so wepe and thoughte it
      kyndenesse,   720
And eche of hem wepte eke for hire distresse.

And bisily they gonnen hire comforten
Of thing, God wot, on which she litel
      thoughte,
And with hire tales wenden hire disporten,
And to be glad they often hire bysoughte.   725
But swich an ese therwith they hire wroughte,
Right as a man is esed for to fele
For ache of hed to clawen hym on his hele!

But after al this nyce vanyte
They tok hire leve and hom they wenten alle.   730
Cryseyde, ful of sorwful pite,
Into hire chaumbre up went out of the halle,
And on hire bed she gan for ded to falle,

---

671 **lest**, i.e., for fear. 674 **faste**, firmly. **yset**: A *biset*. 678 **brenneth**, burns. 679 **rede**, the best advice. 681 **usen**, are accustomed. 682 **rowte**, great company. 683 **pitous . . . wenden . . . delite**, compassionate, thought, to please. 684 **dere . . . myte**, i.e., too expensive at the price of the smallest value in money. 688 C&c *ye* om. 689 **seyde**: M *answered*. 691 M *tho* om.; A *The thridde answerede*. 695 **thennes**, far away. 696 A *For al this while hir herte*. 698 **advertence**, attention. A *God wot hir advertence is elliswhere*. 699 **soule**: M *herte*. 701 **wenden**, thought. *thus*: A *so*, omitted in M. 702 **Aboute nought gonne . . . tales spende**, to no purpose, went about, making conversation. 704 **brende**, burned. 705 **wende**, knew. 706 A *So that she wende anonright for to dye*. 708–14 Stanza omitted from C&c. 713 **forgoth**, is deprived of (forgoes). 716 **syked**, sighed. 717 **route**, company. 724 **wenden . . . disporten**, thought, amuse. *tales*: A *wordes*. 733 A *for ded she gan*.

In purpos nevere thennes for to ryse.
And thus she wroughte as I shal yow devyse. 735

Hire ownded heer that sonnyssh was of hewe
She rente, and ek hire fyngres longe and smale
She wrong ful ofte, and bad God on hire rewe,
And with the deth to don bote on hire bale.
Hire hewe, whilom bryght that tho was pale, 740
Bar witnesse of hire wo and hire constreynte.
And thus she spak, sobbynge in hire
　　compleynte:

"Allas," quod she, "out of this regioun
I, woful wrecche and infortuned wight, 745
And born in corsed constellacioun,
Mot gon, and thus departen fro my knyght.
Wo worth, allas, that ilke dayes lyght
On which I saw hym first with eyen tweyne,
That causeth me, and ich hym, al this peyne!"

Therwith the terys from hire eighen two 750
Doun fille, as shour in Aperill ful swythe.
Hire white brest she bet, and for the wo
After the deth she cried a thousand sithe,
Syn he that wont hire wo was for to lythe
She mot forgon; for which disaventure 755
She held hireself a forlost creature.

She seyde, "How shal he don, and ich also?
How sholde I lyve, yf that I from hym twynne?
O dere herte ek, that I love so,
Who shal that sorwe sleen that ye ben inne? 760
O Calkas, fader, thyn be al this synne!
O moder myn, that cleped were Argyve,
Wo worth that day that thow me bere on lyve!

"To what fyn sholde I lyve and sorwen thus?
How sholde a fyssh withoute water dure? 765
What is Criseyde worth, from Troylus?
How sholde a plaunte or lyves creature
Lyve withouten his kynde noriture?
For which ful oft a byword here I seye,
That 'roteles mot grene sone deye.' 770

"I shal don thus, syn neyther swerd ne darte
Dar I noon handle for the crueltee:
That ilke day that I from yow departe,
If sorwe of that nyl not my bane be,
Than shal no mete or drynke come in me 775
Til I my soule out of my breste unshethe;
And thus myselven wil I don to dethe.

"And, Troylus, my clothes everychon
Shul blake ben in tokenyng, herte swete,
That I am as out of this world agon, 780
That wont was yow to setten in quiete.
And of myn ordre, ay til deth me mete,
The observance evere, yn youre absence,
Shal sorwe ben, compleynte, and abstinence.

"Myn herte and ek the woful gost therinne 785
Biquethe I with youre spirit to compleyne
Eternally, for they shul nevere twynne.
For though in erthe ytwynned be we tweyne,
Yet in the feld of pite out of peyne,
That hight Elysos, shul we ben yfere, 790
As Orpheus with Erudice his fere.

"Thus, herte myn, for Antenor, allas,
I soone shal be chaunged, as I wene.
But how shul ye don in this sorwful cas?

---

734 In purpos, intending. **736 ownded,** wavy. Other MSS *ornyd, undid, owene, yelowe.* In A, ll. 750–56 come here. **737 smale,** slender. **738 rewe,** have pity. **739 bote . . . bale,** remedy, harm. **740 whilom,** formerly. **744 infortuned,** unfortunate. **747 worth,** be to. A *Wo worth that day and namely that nyght.* **750** A *The salte teeris from his eyne tweyne.* **751 swythe,** fast. A *Out roone as shoure;* M *ful* om. **752 the wo:** A *the peyne.* **753 sithe,** times. **754 wont . . . to lythe,** accustomed to ease. **757 How,** what. A *What shal he don? What shal I do also?* **758 twynne,** separate. **760 sleen,** comfort (end). **762 Argyve,** this name was added by Chaucer. There seems no connection with the Argive followers of Agamemnon. In Statius' *Theb.* ii.297 Argia is the name of Polynices' wife; Chaucer calls her Argyve at v.1509 below. **767 lyves,** living. A *oother.* **768 kynde,** natural. **769 byword,** proverb. **770 grene,** green plant. *roteles:* A *ertheles.* **774 bane,** destroyer. **781 setten in quiete,** give peace. *setten:* A *holden.* **782 ordre,** religious sect. **785 gost,** spirit. **787 twynne,** part. **790 Elysos . . . yfere,** Elysian fields (classical paradise), together. A *Ther Pluto regneth shal we.* **791 As Orpheus . . . Erudice,** like Orpheus, a musician so talented in classical legend that he descended into Hades, seeking by his music to recover his dead wife Eurydice. He failed, but after his death they were reunited in Hades. **fere,** companion (mate). **793 wene,** believe. *chaunged:* A *yolden.*

How shal youre tendre herte this sustene?   795
But, herte myn, foryete this sorwe and tene,
And me also; for sothly for to seye,
So ye wel fare, I recche not to deye."

How myghte it evere yred ben or ysonge
The pleynte that she made in hire distresse,   800
I not. But as for me, my litel tonge,
If I discreven wolde hire hevynesse,
It sholde make hire sorwe seme lesse
Than that it was, and chyldisshly deface
Hire heyghe compleynte, and therfore ich it
        pace.   805

Pandare, which that sent from Troylus
Was to Criseyde—as ye han herd devyse
That for the beste it was acorded thus,
And he ful glad to don hym that servise—
Unto Criseyde in a ful secree wyse,   810
Ther as she lay in torment and in rage,
Com hire to telle al hoolly his message,

And fond that she hireselven gan to trete
Ful pitously, for with hire salte terys
Hire brest, hire face, ybathed was ful wete;   815
The myghty tresses of hire sonnysshe herys
Unbroyden hangen al aboute hire eris,
Which yaf hym verray signal of martire
Of deth, which that hire herte gan desire.

Whan she hym saw, she gan for sorwe
        anoon   820
Hire tery face atwixe hire armes hyde,
For which this Pandare is so wobygon
That in the hous he myghte unnethe abyde,
As he that pyte felte on every syde.
For yf Criseyde hadde erst compleyned sore,   825
Tho gan she pleyne a thousand tymes more.

And in hire aspre pleynt thus she seyde,
"Pandare first of joyes mo than two
Was cause causyng unto me, Criseyde,
That now transmewed ben in cruel wo.   830
Wher shal I seye to yow welcom or no,
That alderferst me brought into servise
Of love, allas, that endeth in this wyse?

"Endeth thanne love in wo? Ye, or men lieth!
And alle worldly blysse, as thenketh me.   835
The ende of blisse ay sorwe it occupieth;
And who that troweth not that it so be,
Lat hym upon me, woful wrecche, yse,
That myself hate and ay my birthe accorse,
Felynge alwey fro wikke I go to worse.   840

"Whoso me seth, he seth sorwe al atonys,
Peyne, torment, pleynte, wo, and distresse.
Out of my woful body harm ther non is,
As angwyssh, langour, cruel bitternesse,
Anoy, smert, drede, fury, and ek siknesse.   845
I trowe, iwys, from hevene teris reyne
For pite of myn aspre and cruwel peyne."

"And thow, my suster, ful of discomfort,"
Quod Pandarus, "what thynkestow to do?
Whi ne hastow to thiselven som resport?   850
Whi woltow thus thiselve, allas, fordo?
Lef al this werk, and take now hede to
That I shal seyn, and herkene of good entente
This which by me thi Troylus the sente."

Tornede hire tho Criseyde, a wo makynge   855
So gret that it a deth was for to se.
"Allas," quod she, "what wordes may ye
        brynge?
What wold my dere herte seyn to me,
Which that I drede nevere mo to se?"

---

796 **tene,** grief. 798 **recche,** i.e., care not whether I. 801 **not,** don't know. 805 **pace,** pass over. 808 **acorded,** agreed. 813 **trete,** treat. 817 **Unbroyden,** unbraided. 818 **verray . . . martire,** sure, martyrdom. *martire:* M&c *matere.* 819 A *which that for wo she gan desire.* 820 *sorwe:* A shame. 823 *hous:* A *chambre.* 827 **aspre,** bitter. 828 A *Myn em Pandare, of joyes.* 829 **cause causyng,** a scholastic distinction, "causa causans," primary cause, vs. "causa causata," secondary cause. 830 **transmewed,** transformed. 831 **Wher,** whether (i.e., I wonder whether). 832 **alderferst,** first of all. 835 A *And every worldly joye, as.* 837 **troweth,** believes. 840 **wikke,** bad. M *wo.* 841 **sorwe al atonys,** all kinds of sorrow at once. 843 **Out . . . non is,** i.e., no sort of misery is lacking. 846 **trowe,** vow. 847 **aspre,** bitter. 850 **resport,** regard. 851 **fordo,** destroy. M *allas* om.; other MSS *allas, thyself.* 852 **Lef,** leave. 854 C&c *This message.*

Wol he han pleynte or terys er I wende? 860
I have ynowe yf he therafter sende!"

She was right swych to sen in hire visage
As is that wight that men on bere bynde;
Hire face, lyk of Paradys the ymage,
Was al ichaunged in another kynde; 865
The pleye, the laughtre, men was wont to fynde
In hire, and ek hire joyes everychone,
Ben fled; and thus lith now Criseyde allone.

Aboute hire eyen two a purpre ryng
Bytrent, in sothfast tokenynge of hire peyne, 870
That to byholde it was a dedly thing;
For which Pandare myght not restreyne
The terys from his eyen for to reyne.
But natheles as he best myghte he seyde
From Troilus thise wordes to Criseyde: 875

"Lo, nece, I trowe wel ye han herd al how
The kyng with othere lordes, for the beste,
Hath mad eschaunge of Antenor and yow,
That cause is of this sorwe and this unreste.
But how this cas doth Troylus moleste, 880
That may non erthely mannes tonge seye;
For verray wo his wit is al aweye.

"For which we han so sorwed, he and I,
That into litel bothe it hadde us slawe;
But thurgh my conseyl this day fynally 885
He somwhat is fro wepyng now withdrawe.
It semeth me that he desireth fawe
With yow to ben al nyght for to devyse
Remede in this yf ther were any wyse.

"This, short and pleyn, th'effect of my message,
As ferforth as my wit may comprehende; 891
For ye that ben of torment in swych rage

May to no long prologe as now entende.
And herupon ye may answere hym sende.
And for the love of God, my nece dere, 895
So lef this wo er Troylus be here!"

"Gret is my wo," quod she, and sighed soore
As she that feleth dedly sharp distresse,
"But yet to me his sorwe is muche more,
That loveth hym bet than he hymself, I gesse. 900
Allas, for me hath he swych hevynesse?
Kan he for me so pitously compleyne?
Iwis, this sorwe doubleth al my peyne.

"Grevous to me, God wot, is for to twynne,"
Quod she, "but yet it harder is to me 905
To sen that sorwe which that he is inne,
For wel wot I it wol my bane be,
And deye I wol in certeyn," tho quod she.
"But bidde hym come, er deth that thus me
   threteth
Dryf out the gost which in myn herte
   beteth." 910

Thise wordes seyd, she on hire armes two
Fil gruf, and gan to wepen pitously.
Quod Pandarus, "Allas, whi do ye so
Syn wel ye wot the tyme is faste by
That he shal come? Arys up hastely, 915
That he yow nat bywopen thus ne fynde,
But ye wol han hym wod out of his mynde.

"For wist he that ye ferde in this manere,
He wolde hymselve sle. And yf I wende
To han this fare, he sholde nat come here 920
For al the good that Pryam may despende.
For to what fyn he wolde anoon pretende,
That knowe ich wel; and forthi yet I seye,
So lef this sorwe or platly he wol deye.

---

860 *he:* M&c *ye.* 861 **therafter sende,** i.e., if he sends for any. 863 **bere,** bier (i.e., a corpse). 864 **lyk ... ymage,** i.e., (when composed) the image of Paradise. 865 **ichaunged,** i.e., misshapen with grief. 867 *and ek hire:* A *and oother.* 868 Other MSS *now* om. 870 **Bytrent,** encircled. 871 **dedly,** dreadful. 882 Other MSS *As he that shortly shapeth hym to deye.* 884 **into litel,** very nearly. 887 **fawe,** eagerly. 891 **ferforth,** far. 893 M *as to*/*prologe now.* 896 **lef,** leave off. 904 **twynne,** separate. 906 A *To sen hym in that wo that he is inne.* 907 **bane,** destruction. 909 **threteth,** threatens. M *treteth.* 910 **Dryf,** drives. MC&c *he beteth.* 912 **gruf,** prone (groveling). 914 **faste,** near. 915 *hastely:* A *softly.* 916 **bywopen,** i.e., tear-stained. Other MSS *you finde.* 917 **wod,** crazy. 918 **wist he,** if he knew. 919–20 **wende ... To han this fare,** i.e., thought to find such behavior. 922 **fyn ... pretende,** end he would see (i.e., death). 923 **forthi,** therefore. 924 **platly,** plainly speaking. A *Lat be this sorwe.*

"And shappeth yow his sorwe for to abregge,   925
And nought encresse, leve nece swete.
Beth rather to hym cause of flat than egge,
And with som wysdom ye his sorwes bete.
What helpeth it to wepen ful a strete,
Or though ye bothe in salte teris dreynte?   930
Bet is a tyme of cure ay than of pleynte.

"I mene thus: whan ich hym hider brynge,
Syn ye ben wyse and bothe of on assent,
So shappeth how distourbe this goynge,
Or come ayen soone after ye be went.   935
Women ben wyse in short avysement;
And lat sen how youre wit shal now avayle,
And what that I may helpe, it shal nat fayle."

"Go," quod Criseyde, "and uncle, trewely,
I shal don al my myght me to restreyne   940
From wepyng in his sighte, and bysily
Hym for to glade I shal don al my peyne,
And in myn herte seken every veyne.
If to this sor ther may be founden salve,
It shal nat lakken, certein, on myn halve."   945

Goth Pandarus and Troylus he soughte
Til in a temple he fond hym al allone,
As he that of his lyf no lenger roughte,
But to the petouse goddes everychone
Ful tendrely he preyed and made his mone,   950
To don hym sone out of this world to pace,
For wel he thouhte ther was noon other grace.

And shortly, al the sothe for to seye,
He was so fallen in despeyr that day

That outrely he shop hym for to deye,   955
For right thus was his argument alway.
He seyde, "I am but lorn, so weylaway!
For al that cometh, comth by necessite;
Thus to ben lorn, it is my destyne.

"For certeynly, this wot I wel," he seyde,   960
"That forsight of dyvyne purveyaunce
Hath seyn alwey me to forgon Criseyde,
Syn God seth everything, out of doutaunce,
And hem desponeth thourgh his ordenaunce,
In hire merites sothly for to be,   965
As they shul comen by predestine.

"But natheles, allas, whom shal I leve?
For ther ben clerkes grete many on
That destyne thorugh argumentez preve;
And som men seyn that nedely ther is
noon,   970
But that fre choys is yeven us everychon.
O welaway, so sley arn clerkes olde
That I not whos opynyoun I may holde.

"For som men seyn, yf God seth al byforn—
Ne God may nat deceyved ben, parde—   975
Than mot it falle theigh men hadde it sworn
That purveyance hath seighen byfore to be.
Wherfor I seye that from eterne yf he
Hath wyst byforn oure thought ek as oure
dede,
We have no fre choys, as these clerkes rede.   980

"For other thought, nor other dede also,
Myghte nevere ben but swych as purveyaunce,

---

925 **shappeth . . . abregge,** arrange, reduce. 926 **leve,** dear. 927 **flat . . . egge,** flat of the sword (which in myth healed), edge. *Beth:* M *Buth;* M *cause of* om. 928 **bete,** heal. 929 **strete,** a street full. 930 **dreynte,** drowned. 931 **tyme of . . . pleynte,** time spent on, complaint. 932 M *I/here.* 934 **shappeth . . . distourbe,** plan, circumvent (prevent). 936 **short avysement,** quick decisions. 937 M&c *sen now how.* 942 **glade,** gladden. 943 **veyne,** editors interpret this literally as "search every vein for illness." By 1500 NED gives the abstract meaning "course of action," which would fit well in this context. 944 **this:** other MSS *his.* 948 **roughte,** cared. 949 **petouse,** pitying. 951 **don,** make. 952 **grace,** mercy. 955 **outrely . . . shop,** utterly, prepared. 957 **lorn,** lost. *I am:* MC&c *he nas.* This long passage on predestination, not found in *Filostrato,* and not found in the A version of the poem, is a paraphrase of *Boece* v pr.3; but whereas *Boece* v pr. 4–6 goes on to defend freedom of the will in terms of "conditional necessity," Troylus here stops short with a deterministic conclusion. Addition of this passage shows Chaucer again pointing up the "naturalistic" view of human nature by which the defection of Criseyde is rationalized, cf. III.1744–71 above and notes. 961 **purveyaunce,** providence. 962 **seyn . . . forgon,** seen that I would lose. 964 **desponeth . . . ordenaunce,** arranges, decree. *desponeth:* other MSS *disposeth.* 965 **In . . . sothly,** according to, correctly. 966 **As . . . predestine,** i.e., as they shall eventually come out according to their predestiny. 967 **leve,** believe. 970 **nedely . . . noon,** i.e., there is no necessary predestination. 972 **sley,** clever. 974 **seyn . . . seth,** say, sees. 976 **mot it falle theigh . . . sworn,** must it happen though men had sworn (it would not). *theigh:* M *they.* 977 **That purveyance,** what providence. 979 **wyst,** known. 980 **rede,** advise. 982 **purveyaunce,** providence.

Which may nat ben deceyved nevere mo,
Hath feled biforn withouten ignoraunce.
For yf ther myghte ben a variaunce 985
To writhen out fro Goddes purveyinge,
Ther nere no prescience of thyng comynge,

"But it were rathere an opynyoun
Uncerteyn, and no stedfast forseynge.
And certes, that were an abusioun 990
That God shulde han no parfit cler witynge
More than we men that han doutous wenynge.
But swych an errour upon God to gesse
Were fals and foul and corsed wykkednesse.

"Ek this is an opynyoun of some 995
That han hire top ful heighe and smothe
    yshore:
They seyn right thus, that thyng is nat to come
For that the prescience hath seyghen byfore
That it shal come. But they seyn that therfore
That it shal come, therfore the purveyaunce 1000
Wot it byforn, withouten ignoraunce.

"And in this manere this necessite
Retorneth in his part contrarie agayn.
For nedfully byhoveth it nat to be
That thilke thinges fallen in certayn 1005
That ben purveyed; but nedely, as they sayn,
Byhoveth it that thinges whiche that falle,
That they in certayn ben purveyed alle.

"I mene as though I laboured me in this,
To enqueren which thyng cause of which thyng
    be, 1010
As wheyther that the prescience of God is
The certeyn cause of the necessite
Of thinges that to comen ben, parde,

Or yf necessite of thing comynge
Be cause certeyn of the purveyinge. 1015

"But now n'enforce I me nought in shewynge
How the ordre of causes stant; but wel wot I
That it byhoveth that the byfallynge
Of thinges wyste byforen certeynly
Be necessarie, al seme it not therby 1020
That prescience put fallyng necessaire
To thing to come, al falle it foule or fayre.

"For if ther sit a man yond on a see,
Than by necessite byhoveth it
That, certes, thin opynyon soth be 1025
That wenest or conjectest that he sit.
And ferther over now ayeynward yit,
Lo, right so is it of the part contrarie
As thus—nowe herkne, for I wol nat tarie—

"I seye, that yf the opynion of the 1030
Be soth for that he sit, than seye I this,
That he mot sitten by necessite;
And thus necessite in eyther is.
For yn hym nede of syttynge is, ywys,
And in the nede of soth. And thus, forsothe, 1035
Ther mot necessite ben in yow bothe.

"But thow maist seyn the man sit not therfore
That thyn opynyoun of his sittynge soth is,
But rather for the man sit ther byfore;
Therfore is thyn opynyoun soth, ywys. 1040
And I seye, though the cause of soth of this
Comth of his sittyng, yet necessite
Is entrechaunged both in hym and the.

"Thus on this same wyse, out of doutaunce,
I may wel maken, as it semeth me, 1045

984 feled biforn ... ignoraunce, i.e., anticipated, error. **985 variaunce,** i.e., various possible courses of action. **986 writhen ... purveyinge,** squirm, foreseeing. **987 prescience,** foreknowledge. **990 abusioun,** slander. **991 cler witynge,** clear knowledge. **992 doutous wenynge,** doubtful supposing. **993 upon ... gesse,** about, suppose. **994** C&c *wikked corsednesse.* **996 smothe yshore,** smoothly shorn, i.e., tonsured; in the Middle Ages, the sign of a cleric. Until the Renaissance virtually all scholars were clerics. **998 seyghen byfore,** foreseen. **999 therfore,** because. **1000-01 purveyaunce/Wot,** providence knows. **1002-03ff. necessite/ Retorneth,** i.e., necessity turns inside out, since things don't happen because they have been foreseen, but everything that happens must have been foreseen. **1011 prescience,** foreknowledge. **1015 purveyinge,** foreseeing. **1016 n'enforce,** i.e., I won't strive. **1019** C&c *by for.* **1020 al seme it,** although it seems. **1021 put fallyng,** makes occurring. **1023 see,** seat. The illustration is from Boethius. **1026 wenest ... conjectest,** think (conjecture). **1033 eyther is,** i.e., in the necessity of sitting and in the necessity of truth: see next lines and *Boece* v pr. 3.55. **1037 therfore,** because. **1038 soth,** true. **1039 for the ... sit,** because, was sitting. **1043 entrechaunged,** reciprocal.

My resonynge of Goddes purveyaunce
And of the thynges that to comen be.
By which resoun may men wel yse
That thilke thinges that in erthe falle,
That by necessite they comen alle.   1050

"For although that for thyng shal come, ywys,
Therfore it is purveyed, certaynly—
Nought that it comth for it purveyed is.
Yet natheles, byhoveth it nedfully
That thing to come be purveyed, trewely,   1055
Or elles thinges that purveyed be,
That they bytiden by necessite.

"And this suffiseth right ynow, certeyn,
For to destroye oure fre choys every del.
But now is this abusioun to seyn   1060
That fallynge of the thinges temporel
Is cause of Godes prescience eternel.
Now trewely, that is a fals sentence,
That thyng to come sholde cause his prescience.

"What myght I wene, and ich hadde swych a
      thought,   1065
But that God purveyeth thyng that is to come
For that it is to come, and ellis nought?
So myghte I wene that thynges alle and some,
That whylom ben byfalle and overcome,
Ben cause of thilke soveyren purveyaunce   1070
That forwot al withouten ignoraunce.

"And over al this, yet sey I more therto,
That right as whan I wot ther is a thing,
Iwys, that thing mot nedefully be so.
Ek right so, whan I wot a thyng comyng,   1075
So mot it come. And thus the byfallyng
Of thynges that ben wyst byfore the tyde,
They mowe not ben eschewed on no syde."

Thanne seyde he thus, "Almyghty Jove in
      trone,
That wost of alle thyng the sothfastnesse,   1080
Rewe on my sorwe, or do me deye sone,
Or bryng Criseyde and me fro this destresse!"
And whil he was in al this hevynesse,
Disputyng with hymself in this matere,
Com Pandare in, and seyde as ye may here.   1085

"O myghti God," quod Pandarus, "in trone,
I, who seygh evere a wys man faren so?
Whi, Troylus, what thenkestow to done?
Hastow swych lust to ben thyn owen fo?
What, parde, yet is nat Criseyde ago!   1090
Whi lust the so thynself fordon for drede,
That in thyn hed thyn eyghen semen dede?

"Hastow not lyved many a yer byforn
Withouten hire, and ferd ful wel at ese?
Artow for hire and for noon other born?   1095
Hath Kynde the wrought al oonly hire to plese?
Lat be, and thenk right thus in thi disese,
That in the des right as there fallen chaunces,
Right so in love ther com and gon plesaunces.

"And yet this is a wonder most of alle,   1100
Whi thow thus sorwest, syn thow nost not yit,
Touchyng hire goyng, how that it shal falle,
Ne yif she kan hireself destuorben it.
Thow hast nat yet assayed al hire wit.
A man may al bytyme his nekke bede   1105
Whan it shal of, and sorwen at the nede.

"Forthi take hede of that that I shal the seye:
I have with hire yspoke and longe ybe,
So as accorded was bytwyxe us tweye,
And everemo me thenketh thus, that she   1110
Hath somwhat in hire hertes prevete

1046 **purveyaunce,** providence (foreknowledge). 1052 **purveyed,** foreseen. 1054 **byhoveth . . . nedfully,** is necessary, necessarily. 1057 **bytiden,** come about. 1060 **abusioun,** a slander. 1061 **fallynge,** occurring. 1062 **prescience,** foreknowledge. 1065 **wene,** believe. 1067 **For that,** because. 1069 **whylom . . . byfalle and overcome,** formerly, happened and gone by. 1070 **soveyren purveyaunce,** supreme providence. 1071 **forwot . . . ignoraunce,** foreknows, error. 1073 M *That* om. 1075 **wot,** know. 1077 **wyst,** known. 1078 **eschewed,** escaped. 1079 **Almyghty Jove,** Troylus' concluding prayer seems to open the door to divine intervention, even though his philosophical discourse has been purely deterministic. 1081 **Rewe,** have pity. 1087 **faren,** behave. 1089 **lust,** desire. 1091 **fordon,** destroy. 1093 A *lyved al thy lyf biforn.* 1096 **Kynde,** nature. Other MSS *iwrought the.* 1097 A *Kanstow nat thinken thus.* 1098 **des,** dice. 1099 A *In love also ther com.* 1101 **nost,** don't know. 1103 **destourben,** alter. 1105 **al bytyme . . . bede,** soon enough, offer. 1106 **shal of,** must be cut off.

Wherwith she kan, if I shal right arede,
Destorbe al this of which thow art in drede.

"For which my counseyl is, whan it is nyght
Thow to hire go and make of this an ende.   1115
And blisful Juno thorugh hire grete myght
Shal, as I hope, hire grace unto us sende.
Myn herte seyth, 'Certeyn, she shal not wende.'
And forthi put thyn herte a whyle in reste,
And hold thi purpos, for it is the beste."   1120

This Troylus answerde, and sighte sore,
"Thow seyst right wel, and I wil do right so."
And what hym lyste he seyde unto it more.
And whan that it was tyme for to go,
Ful prevely hymself withouten mo   1125
Unto hire com, as he was wont to done.
And how thei wroughte, I shal yow telle sone.

Soth it is whanne they gonne first to mete,
So gan the peynes hire hertes for to twyste
That neyther of hem other myghte grete,   1130
But hem in armes tok and after kyste.
The lasse wofulle of hem bothe nyste
Wher that he was, ne myghte o word out
       brynge,
As I seyde erst, for wo and for sobbynge.

Tho woful teris that they leten falle   1135
As bittre weren out of teris kynde,
For peyne, as is ligne aloes or galle—
So bittre teris weep nought, as I fynde,
The woful Myrra thorough the bark and
       rynde—
That in this world ther nys so hard an herte   1140
That nolde han rewed on hire peynes smerte.

But whanne hire woful wery gostes tweyne

Retorned ben ther as hem oughte to dwelle,
And that somwhat to wayken gan the peyne
By lengthe of pleynte, and ebben gan the welle
Of hire teris, and the herte unswelle,   1146
With broken voys, al hoors forshright, Criseyde
To Troylus thise ilke wordes seyde,

"O Jove, I deye, and mercy I beseche!
Help, Troylus!" And therwithal hire face   1150
Upon his brest she leyde and loste speche,
Hire woful spirit from his propre place
Right with the word alwey o poynt to pace.
And thus she lith with hewes pale and grene,
That whilom fressh and fairest was to sene.   1155

This Troylus, that on hire gan byholde,
Clepynge hire name—and she lay as for ded—
Withouten answere, and felte hir lymes colde,
Hire eyen throwen upward to hire hed,
This sorwful man kan now noon other red   1160
But ofte tyme hire colde mouth he kyste.
Wher hym was wo, God and hymself it wyste.

He rist hym up and long streyght he hire leyde,
For signe of lyf, for ought he kan or may,
Kan he non fynde in nothyng on Criseyde,   1165
For which his song ful ofte is "Weylaway!"
But whan he sawgh that specheles she lay,
With sorweful voys, and herte of blysse al bare,
He seyde how she was fro this world yfare.   1169

So after that he longe hadde hire compleyned,
His hondes wrong, and seyde that was to seye,
And with his teris salte hire brest byreyned,
He gan tho teris wypen of ful dreye,
And pitously gan for the soule preye,   1174
And seyde, "O Lord, that set art in thy trone,
Rewe ek on me, for I shal folwe hire sone."

1113 Destorbe, prevent (change). A *Stynt al this thing of which.* **1114** *which:* M *swych.* **1118 wende,** go. **1120** *thi:* other MSS *this.*
1121 sighte, sighed. **1123 hym lyste,** was pleasing to him. **1131** A *armes hente and softe kiste.* **1132 nyste,** didn't know. **1133** A *What for to don, ne.* **1134** *wo:* other MSS *sorwe.* **1136 kynde,** nature. **1137 ligne aloes,** a nauseous bitter purgative made from the juice of the aloe plant. **1139 Myrra,** the story of Myrrha, metamorphosed into a myrrh tree (because of her incestuous love) that weeps tears of aromatic gum through its bark, is told by Ovid, *Met.* 10.298ff. **1141 rewed,** had pity. **1144 wayken,** weaken. Other MSS *lesse.* **1147 hoors forshright,** hoarse from shrieking. M *forbright Criseyde.* **1153 o poynt to pace,** on the point of passing away. **1157 Clepynge,** calling. **1160 red,** remedy. *noon other:* other MSS *no manner.* **1162** *Wher:* other MSS *Whether.* **1163 long streyght,** stretched out. **1165** *in nothyng:* A *in no case.* **1173** *ful:* other MSS *and.* **1176 Rewe,** have pity.

She cold was and withouten sentement,
For ought he wot, for breth ne felte he non;
And this was hym a preignant argument
That she was forth out of this world agon. 1180
And whan he seygh ther was non other won
He gan hire lymes dresse in swych manere
As men don hem that shul be leyd on bere.

And after this, with sterne and cruwel herte,
His swerd anoon out of his shethe he
    twyghte, 1185
Hymself to slen, how sore that hym smerte,
So that his sowle hire sowle folwen myghte
Ther as the dom of Mynos wolde it dyghte,
Syn Love and cruwel Fortune it ne wolde
That in this world he lenger lyven sholde. 1190

Thanne seyde he thus, "Fulfilled of heigh
    desdayn,
O cruwel Jove, and thow, Fortune adverse,
This al and som, that falsly have ye slayn
Criseyde. And syn ye may do me no werse,
Fy on youre myght and werkes so diverse! 1195
Thus cowardly ye shul me nevere wynne—
Ther shal no deth me fro my lady twynne.

"For I this world, syn ye han slayn hire thus,
Wol lete and folwe hire spirit lowe or hye.
Shal nevere lovere seyn that Troylus 1200
Dar nat for fere with his lady dye,
For certeyn I wol bere hire companye.
But syn ye wol nat suffren us lyven here,
Yet suffreth that oure soules ben yfere.

"And thow, cite, whiche that I leve in wo; 1205
And thow, Pryam, and bretheren al yfere;
And thow, my moder, farewel, for now I go.
And Attropos, make redy thow my bere.

And thow, Criseyde, O swete herte dere,
Receyve now my spirit," wold he seye, 1210
With swerd at herte, al redy for to deye.

But as God wolde, of swough therwith
    sh'abreyde
And gan to syke, and "Troylus" she cride.
And he answerde, "Lady myn, Cryseyde,
Lyve ye yet?" and let his swerd doun
    glide. 1215
"Ye, herte myn, that thanked be Cipride,"
Quod she. And therwithal she sore syghte,
And he bygan to glade hire as he myghte,

Took hire in armes two, and kyste hire ofte,
And hire to glade he dide al his entente, 1220
For which hire gost, that flikered ay on lofte,
Into hire woful herte ayeyn it wente.
But at the laste, as that hire eyen glente
Asyde anoon she gan his swerd aspye,
As it lay bare, and gan for fere crie, 1225

And asked hym whi he hadde it out drawe.
And Troylus anoon the cause hire tolde,
And how hymself therwith he wolde han
    slawe;
For which Criseyde upon hym gan byholde,
And gan hym in hire armes faste folde, 1230
And seyde, "O mercy, God, lo swych a dede!
Allas, how neigh we were bothe dede!

"Thenne yf I nadde spoken, as grace was,
Ye wolde han slayn youreself anoon?" quod she.
"Ye, douteles." And she answerde, "Allas, 1235
For by that ilke Lord that made me
I nolde a forlong wey on lyve han be
After youre deth, to han be crowned quene
Of al the londes the sonne on shyneth shene.

1177 sentement, feeling. **1178** A *and breth;* M *For I wot.* **1179 preignant,** compelling. **1181 won,** hope. **1182 dresse,** arrange. **1183**
hem: A *folk.* **1185 twyghte,** plucked. **1188 dom of Mynos . . . dyghte,** judgment of Minos (the judge of spirits in Hades), decree.
1190 Other MSS *no more he lyven.* **1193 al and som,** i.e., is the sum total of my complaint. **1196 wynne,** defeat. **1197 twynne,** separate.
1199 lete, leave. A *forth in hye.* **1204 yfere,** together. **1205 leve,** leave. C&c *lyve* (live). **1208 Attropos,** third of the three Fates, who
cuts the thread and ends a person's life. **1212 swough . . . abreyde,** swoon, awoke. **1213 syke,** sigh. **1214 Lady:** A *Herte.* **1216 Cipride,**
Venus, so called because she was born from the sea near the island of Cyprus. M&c *Cupide.* **1218 glade,** cheer her up. A *conforte.*
1221 gost . . . flikered, spirit, wavered out of her body. **1222** A *Ayein into hir herte al softe wente.* **1223 glente,** glanced. **1231 dede,**
deed. **1237 forlong,** 220 yards, but, as usual, a measure of time. **1238 to han be,** even for the sake of being.

"But with this selve swerd whiche that here is
Myselve I wolde have slayn," quod she tho. 1241
"But ho, for we han right ynow of this,
And lat us rise, and streyght to bedde go,
And there lat us speken of oure wo.
For by the morter which that I se brenne, 1245
Knowe I right wel that day is not far henne."

Whanne they were in hire bed, in armes
    folde,
Nought was yt lyk the nyghtes herebyforn.
For pitously eche other gan byholde,
As thei that hadden al hire blisse ylorn, 1250
Bywaylinge ay the day that they were born;
Til at the last this sorwful wyght Criseyde
To Troylus these ilke wordes seyde.

"Lo, herte myn, wel wot ye this," quod she,
"That yf a wyght alwey his wo compleyne, 1255
And seketh nought how holpen for to be,
It is but folye and encres of peyne;
And syn that here assembled be we tweyne
To fynde bote of wo that we ben inne,
It were al tyme sone to bygynne. 1260

"I am a womman, as ful wel ye wot,
And as I am avised sodeynly,
So wole I telle yow whil it is hot.
Me thenketh thus, that neyther ye ne I
Ought half this wo to maken, skilfully. 1265
For ther is art ynow for to redresse
That yet is mys, and slen this hevynesse.

"Soth is, the wo the which that we ben inne,
For ought I wot, for nothyng elles is
But for the cause that we sholden twynne. 1270
Considered al, ther nys no more amys.
But what is thanne a remede unto this,
But that we shape us sone for to mete?
This al and som, my dere herte swete.

"Now, that I shal wel bryngen it aboute 1275
To come ayen, soone after that I go,
Therof am I no manere thyng in doute.
For dredeles, withinne a wowke or two
I shal ben here; and that it may be so,
By alle right and in a wordes fewe, 1280
I shal yow wel an hep of weyes shewe.

"For which I wol not make long sermon,
For tyme ylost may not recovered be;
But I wol gon to my conclusyon,
And to the beste, in ought that I kan se. 1285
And for the love of God, foryeve it me
If I speke ought ayeyn youre hertes reste,
For trewely I speke it for the beste,

"Makyng alwey a protestacion
That now these wordes which that I shal
    seye 1290
Nys but to shewen yow my mocion
To fynde unto oure help the beste weye;
And taketh it non other wyse, I preye.
For yn effect, what so ye me comaunde,
That wol I don, for that is no demaunde. 1295

"Now herkneth this: ye han wel understonde
My goyng graunted is by parlement
So ferforth that it may nat be withstonde
For al this world, as by my juggement.
And syn ther helpeth noon avisement 1300
To letten it, lat it passe out of mynde,
And lat us shape a bettre wey to fynde.

"The soth is that the twynnyng of us tweyne
Wol us dishese and cruweliche anoye;
But hym byhoveth somtyme han a peyne 1305
That serveth Love, yf that he wol have joye.
And syn I shal no ferther out of Troye
Than I may ride ayen on half a morwe,
It oughte the lasse causen us to sorwe.

1242 **ho,** stop. 1245 **morter,** bowl of wax with a wick. 1250 A *hir joyes alle lorn.* 1251 A *Seying allas that evere they.* 1259 **bote,** remedy. 1260 **al tyme,** high time. 1262 **am avised sodeynly,** i.e., have concluded impulsively. 1265 **skilfully,** reasonably. 1267 **mys,** amiss. **slen . . . hevynesse,** i.e., end, grief. 1269 **wot,** know. 1270 **twynne,** separate. 1273 **shape,** plan. 1278 **dredeles . . . wowke,** doubtless, week. 1284 *to my:* A *right to.* 1287 **hertes reste,** i.e., peace of mind. 1291 **mocion,** motion (proposal). 1295 **demaunde,** i.e., there is no question about that. 1298 **ferforth,** far (firmly). 1301 **letten,** prevent. 1303 *that:* C&c om.; other MSS *this.* 1308 **ayen,** back.

"So as I shal not so ben hid in muwe, 1310
That day by day, myn owne herte dere,
Syn wel ye wot that it is now a truwe,
Ye shul ful wel al myn estat yhere.
And er that truwe is don, I shal ben here.
And thanne have ye both Antenor ywonne 1315
And me also. Beth glad now, yf ye konne,

"And thenk right thus, 'Criseyde is now
agon.
But what, she shal come hastiliche ayen!'
And whanne, allas? By God, lo, right anoon,
Er dayes ten, this dar I saufly seyn. 1320
And thanne at erst shal we be so fayn,
So as we shal togederes evere dwelle,
That al this world ne myghte oure blysse telle.

"I se that ofte tyme, there as we ben now,
That for the beste, oure counseyl for to hide,
Ye speke not with me, nor I with yow, 1326
In fourtenyght, ne se yow go ne ryde.
May ye not ten dayes thanne abyde
For myn honour, yn swych an aventure?
Iwys, ye mowen ellys lite endure. 1330

"Ye knowe ek how that al my kyn is here
But yf that onlyche it my fader be,
And ek myn othere thinges alle yfere,
And namelyche, my dere herte, ye,
Whom that I nolde leven for to se 1335
For al this world, as wyd as it hath space,
Or elles se ich nevere Joves face!

"Whi trowe ye my fader yn this wyse
Coveyteth so to se me but for drede
Lest yn this town that folkes me despise 1340
By cause of hym, for his unhappy dede?
What wot my fader what lyf that I lede?
For if he wyste in Troy how wel I fare,
Us neded for my wendyng nought to care.

"Ye sen that every day ek, more and more, 1345
Men trete of pees, and it supposid is
That men the queene Eleyne shal restore,
And Grekes us restoren that is mys.
So, though there nere comfort noon but this,
That men purposen pes on every syde, 1350
Ye may the bettre at ese of herte abyde.

"For yf that it be pes, myn herte dere,
The nature of the pes mot nedes dryve
That men most entrecomunen yfere,
And to and fro ek ryde and gon as blyve 1355
Alday as thikke as ben flen from an hyve,
And every wight han liberte to bleve
Where as hym lyste the bet, withouten leve.

"And though so be that pes ther may be noon,
Yet hider, though there nevere pes ne
were, 1360
I moste come; for wheder sholde I gon,
Or how, myschaunce, sholde I dwellen there,
Among tho men of armes evere in fere?
For which, as wysly God my soule rede,
I kan nat sen wherof ye sholden drede. 1365

"Have here another wey, if it so be
That al this thing ne may yow not suffise:
My fader, as ye knowen wel, parde,
Is old, and elde is ful of coveytise,
And I right now have founden al the gyse 1370
Withoute net wherwith I shal hym hente.
And herkeneth how, if that ye wol assente.

"Lo, Troylus, men seyn that hard it is
The wolf ful and the wether hol to have;
This is to seyn, that men ful ofte, ywys, 1375
Mote spenden part, the remnaunt for to save.
For ay with gold men may the herte grave
Of hym that set is upon coveitise;
And how I mene, I shal it yow devyse.

1310 **muwe,** cage. 1312 **truwe,** truce. 1313 **estat,** condition. 1321 **fayn,** happy. 1323 *blysse:* A *joys.* 1327 **go,** walk. 1330 **mowen . . . lite,** can, little. *lite:* M *litel.* 1333 **yfere,** together. 1334 **namelyche,** especially. 1335 **leven,** leave off. 1337 **se ich,** may I never see. 1338 **trowe,** think. 1342 **wot,** knows. 1344 **wendyng,** returning. 1348 **mys,** amiss. 1349 **nere,** if there were no comfort. 1354 **entrecomunen yfere,** communicate with each other. 1355 **gon . . . blyve,** walk, readily. 1356 **ben flen,** bees fly. 1357 **bleve,** live. 1364 **rede,** counsel. 1370 **gyse,** method. 1371 **hente,** capture. 1372 *how:* C&c *now.* 1374 **wether,** sheep (ram). 1377 **grave,** influence (engrave). 1379 **devyse,** explain.

"The moeble which that I have in this town
Unto my fader shal I take, and seye   1381
That right for trust and for savacioun
It sent is from a frend of his or tweye;
The wheche frendes ferventlyche hym preye
To senden after more, and that in hye,   1385
Whil that this town stant thus in jupartie.

"And that shal ben an huge quantite—
Thus shal I seyn—but lest it folk aspide,
This may be sent by no wyght but by me.
I shal ek shewen hym, yf pes bytyde,   1390
What frendes that ich have on every syde
Toward the court, to don the wrathe pace
Of Priamus, and don hym stonde in grace.

"So, what for o thyng and for other, swete,
I shal hym so enchaunten with my sawes,   1395
That right in hevene his sowle is shal he mete.
For al Appollo, or his clerkes lawes,
Or calkullyng avayleth nought thre hawes;
Desir of gold shal so his soule blende
That as me lyst I shal wel make an ende.   1400

"And yf he wolde aught by hys sort it preve
If that I lye, in certayn I shal fonde
Distourben hym and plukke hym by the sleve,
Makynge his sort, and beren hym on honde
He hath not wel the goddes understonde—
For goddes speken in amphibologies,   1406
And for o soth they tellen twenty lyes.

"Eke drede fond first goddes, I suppose—
Thus shal I seyn—and that his coward herte
Made hym amys the goddes text to glose,   1410
Whan he for fered out of Delphos sterte.
And but I make hym soone to converte,
And don my red withinne a day or tweye,
I wol to yow oblige me to deye."

And trewelyche, as wreten wel I fynde,   1415
That al this thyng was seyd of good entente,
And that hire herte trewe was and kynde
Towardes hym, and spak right as she mente,
And that she starf for wo neigh whan she
    wente,
And was in purpos evere to be trewe: 1420
Thus writen they that of hire werkes knewe.

This Troylus, with herte and eerys spradde,
Herde al this thing devysen to and fro.
And verraylich hym semed that he hadde
The same wit, but yet to lat hire go   1425
His herte mysforyaf hym everemo.
But fynally he gan his herte wreste
To trusten hire, and tok it for the beste.

For which the grete fury of his penaunce
Was queynt with hope, and therwith hem
    bitwene   1430
Bygan for joye the amorouse daunce.
And as the briddes, whanne the sonne is
    shene,
Deliten in hire song yn leves grene,
Right so the wordes that they spake yfere
Deliten hem and made hire hertes clere.   1435

But natheles, the wendyng of Criseyde
For al this world may nought out of his
    mynde;
For which ful ofte he pitously hire preyde
That of hire heste he mighte hire trewe fynde,
And seyde hire, "Certes, yf ye be unkynde,   1440
And but ye come at day set into Troye,
Ne shal I nevere have hele, honour, ne joye.

"For also soth as sonne uprist on morwe,
And God, so wisly thow me, woful wrecche,
To reste brynge out of this cruwel sorwe,   1445

1380 **moeble,** personal possessions ("movables"). 1382 **savacioun,** security. 1385 **in hye,** quickly. 1390 **bytyde,** should come. 1392 **don . . . pace,** make, pass (away). 1395 **sawes,** sayings. 1396 **mete,** dream (think). 1397 **Appollo . . . clerkes lawes,** i.e., wisdom, scholarly precepts. 1398 **calkullyng . . . hawes,** calculation, hawthorn berries. 1399 **blende,** blind. 1401 **sort,** augury. 1402–03 **fonde/Distourben,** find a way to interrupt. 1404 **beren . . . honde,** fooling him into believing. 1406 **amphibologies,** ambiguities. 1408 **fond,** created. 1410 **glose,** interpret (gloss). 1411 **fered,** fear. 1413 **red,** i.e., take my advice. 1419 **starf . . . neigh,** nearly died. 1422 **spradde,** receptive (open). 1425 **same wit,** same idea. 1426 **misforyaf,** misgave. 1427 **wreste,** constrain. 1429 **penaunce,** suffering. 1430 **queynt,** quenched. 1434 **yfere,** together. 1436 **wendyng,** departing. 1442 **hele,** health. 1444 **thow me,** i.e., in God's wisdom, you can bring me to rest.

I wol myselven sle yf that ye drecche.
But of my deth though litel be to recche,
Yet, er that ye me cause so to smerte,
Dwelle rathere here, myn owene swete herte.

"For trewely, myn owne lady deere,   1450
Tho sleyghtes yet that I have herd yow stere
Ful shaply ben to fayllen alle yfere.
For thus men seyn, 'that oon thenketh the bere,
But al another thenketh his ledere.'
Youre sire is wys; and seyd is, out of drede,   1455
'Men may the wyse at-renne, but not
          at-rede.'

"It is ful hard to halten unespied
Byfore a crepul, for he kan the craft.
Youre fader is in sleyght as Argus eyed;
For al be that his moeble is hym byraft,   1460
His olde sleyghte is yet so with hym laft
Ye shal nat blende hym for youre
          womanhede,
Ne feyne aright; and that is alle my drede.

"I not if pes shal evere mo bytyde;
But pes or no, for ernest ne for game,   1465
I wot, syn Calkas on the Grekes syde
Hath ones ben and lost so foule his name,
He dar no more come here ayen for shame;
For which that wey, for ought I kan espye,
To trusten on nys but a fantasye.   1470

"Ye shal ek sen, yowre fader shal yow glose
To ben a wyf; and as he kan wel preche,
He shal som Grek so preyse and wel alose
That ravysshen he shal yow with his speche,
Or do yow don by force as he shal teche.   1475

And Troylus, of whom ye nyl han routhe,
Shal causeles so sterven in his trouthe.

"And over al this, youre fader shal despise
Us alle and seyn this cite nys but lorn,
And that th'assege nevere shal aryse,   1480
For-why the Grekes han it alle sworn,
Til we be slayn and doun oure walles torn.
And thus he shal you with his wordes fere,
That ay drede I that ye wol bleven there.

"Ye shul ek seen so mani a lusty knyght   1485
Among the Grekes, ful of worthynesse,
And eche of hem with herte, wit, and myght
To plesen yow don al his besynesse,
That ye shul dullen of the rudenesse
Of us sely Troians, but yf routhe   1490
Remorde yow, or vertue of youre trouthe.

"And this to me so grevous is to thenke
That fro my brest it wole my soule rende.
Ne, dredles, in me ther may not synke
A good opynyoun yf that ye wende;   1495
For why youre fadres sleyghte wole us
          shende.
And yf ye gon, as I have told yow yore,
So thenk I nam but ded, withoute more.

"For which with humble, trewe, and pitous
          herte,
A thousand tymes mercy I yow preye;   1500
So reweth on myn aspre peynes smerte,
And doth somwhat as that I shal yow seye,
And lat us stele awey bytwext us tweye.
And thenk that folye is, whan man may chese,
For accident his substaunce ay to lese.   1505

1446 **drecche**, delay (beyond the promised 10 days). 1451 **sleyghtes .. stere**, schemes, devise. 1452 **shaply . . . yfere**, likely, together. 1453 **oon . . . bere**, one way, bear. 1455 **out of drede**, without doubt. 1456 **at-renne . . . at-rede**, outrun, outthink. M *arede;* other MSS *out renne/out rede.* 1457 **halten unespied**, limp undetected. 1458 **crepul**, cripple. 1459 **sleyght**, trickery. **Argus**, hundred-eyed watchman over Io in Ovid, *Met.* 1.625. 1460 **moeble**, possessions (wealth). 1462 **blende . . . for**, blind, with (in spite of). 1463 **feyne aright**, pretend successfully. 1464 **not**, don't know. 1471 **glose**, flatter (persuade). 1473 **alose**, praise. 1475 **do yow don by,** make you do with. 1476 **routhe**, pity. *ye:* M&c *he.* 1477 **sterven . . . trouthe**, die, fidelity (troth). 1478 A *al* om. 1479 **lorn**, lost. 1481 **For-why**, because. 1483 **fere**, frighten. *And:* M *Al.* 1484 **bleven**, remain. 1489 **dullen**, grow weary. 1490 **routhe**, pity. 1491 **Remorde . . . vertue . . . trouthe**, cause you remorse, strength, fidelity. 1493 **rende**, tear out. 1495 **good opynyoun**, favorable expectation. 1496 **sleyghte . . . shende**, trickery, destroy. 1501 **reweth . . . aspre**, have pity, bitter. 1505 **accident . . . substaunce**, scholastic language for the variable superficial qualities versus the permanent essential qualities. Troylus' usage appears to be antichivalric: decorum and honor are the accidents, love is the substance.

"I mene this, that syn we mowe er day
Wel stele awey and ben togedere so,
What nede were it to putten in assay,
In cas ye sholde to youre fader go,
If that ye myghte come ayen or no?   1510
Thus mene I, that it were a gret folye
To putte that sikernesse in jupartie.

"And vulgarly to speken of substaunce,
Of tresour may we bothe with us lede
Ynowh to lyve in honour and plesaunce   1515
Til into tyme that we shul ben dede.
And thus we may eschewen al this drede.
For everych other wey ye kan recorde,
Myn herte, ywys, may not therwith acorde.

"And hardely, ne dredeth no poverte,   1520
For I have kyn and frendes elleswhere
That though we comen in oure bare sherte
Us sholde neyther lakke golde ne gere,
But ben honured while we dwelten there.
And go we anoon; for as yn myn entente,   1525
This is the beste, yf that ye wole assente."

Criseyde with a syk right in this wyse
Answerde, "Ywys, my dere herte trewe,
We may wel stele awey as ye devyse,
And fynden swyche unthryfty weyes
    newe;   1530
But afterward ful sore it wole us rewe.
And helpe me God so at my moste nede,
As causeles ye suffren al this drede.

"For thilke day that I for cherysshynge
Or drede of fader, or for other wight,   1535
Or for estat, delit, or for weddynge,
Be fals to yow, my Troylus, my knyght,

Saturnes doughter Juno, thorugh hire myght,
As wod as Athamante do me dwelle
Eternaly in Stix, the put of helle!   1540

"And this on every god celestial
I swere it yow, and ek on eche goddesse,
On every nymphe and diete infernal,
On satiry and fawny more and lesse
That halve-goddes ben of wildernesse.   1545
And Attropos, my thred of lif thow breste
If I be fals! Now trowe me if ye leste.

"And thow, Symoys, that as an arwe clere
Thorugh Troye ay rennest downward to the se,
Ber witnesse of this word that seyd is here: 1550
That thilke day that ich untrewe be
To Troylus, myn owene herte fre,
That thow retorne bakwarde to thi welle,
And I with body and soule synke in helle!

"But that ye speke awey thus for to go   1555
And leten alle youre frendes, God forbede
For ony womman that ye sholden so,
And namly syn Troye hath now swych nede
Of help. And ek of o thyng taketh hede:
If this were wist, my lif lay in balaunce,   1560
And youre honour. God shilde us fro
    myschaunce!

"And if so be that pes hereafter take,
As alday happeth after anger game,
Why, Lord, the sorwe and wo ye wolden
    make
That ye ne dorste come ayen for shame.   1565
And er that ye juparten so youre name,
Beth nought to hastyf in this hote fare,
For hastyf man ne wanteth nevere care.

1506 mowe, may. *this:* C&c *thus.* **1508 nede:** C&c *wit.* **1512 sikernesse,** security. **1513 substaunce,** a nice play on words, since "substance" here changes from a philosophical to a quite practical meaning. **1514 may we . . . lede,** we can, take. **1517 eschewen,** escape. **1518 recorde,** suggest. **1525 anoon,** immediately. **1527 syk,** sigh. **1529 devyse,** outline. **1530 unthryfty,** unprofitable. **1531 us rewe,** make us regret. **1534 cherysshynge,** devotion to. **1535** *other:* C&c *any other.* **1539 wod . . . Athamante,** insane, Athamas, King of Thebes, driven mad by Juno, and an example of the "falsifiers" in the eighth circle of Dante's *Inferno,* 30.1–12. **1540 Stix . . . put,** river Styx in Hades, pit. **1544 satiry . . . fawny,** satyrs, fauns. **1546 Attropos,** the one of the three Fates who cuts the thread of life. *thow breste:* C&c *tobreste.* **1547 trowe,** believe. *ye:* M&c *thow/yow.* **1548 Symoys,** a river in Troy. **1553 thow retorne,** i.e., flow backward to your source. **1555 speke,** propose. *awey:* M&c *alwey.* **1556 leten,** leave. **1558 namly,** especially. **1560 lay,** would lie. **1563 game,** i.e., joy. **1566 juparten,** endanger. **1567–68** *hastyf:* M&c *hasty.* **1568 ne wanteth . . . care,** never lacks, trouble.

"What trowe ye the peple ek al aboute
Wolde of it seye? It is ful light t'arede.   1570
They wolden seye, and swere it out of doute,
That love ne drof yow nought to don this dede,
But lust voluptuous and coward drede.
Thus were al lost, ywys, myn herte dere,
Yowre honour, which that now shyneth so
          clere.   1575

"And also thenketh on myn honeste,
That floureth yet, how foule I sholde it shende,
And with what filthe it spotted sholde be,
If in this forme I sholde with yow wende.
Ne though I lyved unto the worldes ende,   1580
My name sholde I nevere ayenward wynne.
Thus were I lost, and that were routhe and
          synne.

"And forthi sle with reson al this hete.
Men seyn 'the suffraunt overcomith,' parde;
Ek 'whoso wol han leef, he leef mot lete.'   1585
Thus maketh vertu of necessite
By pacience, and thenk that lord is he
Of Fortune ay, that nought wole of hire recche;
And she ne daunteth no wight but a wrecche.

"And trusteth this, that certes, herte swete,   1590
Er Phebus suster, Lucyna the shene,
The Leoun passe out of this Ariete,
I wol ben here withouten any wene.
I mene, as helpe me Juno, hevenes quene,
The tenthe day, but if that deth me assayle,   1595
I wol yow sen withouten ony fayle."

"And now, so this be soth," quod Troylus,
"I shal wel suffre unto the tenthe day,
Syn that I se that nede it mot be thus.

But for the love of God, yf it be may,   1600
So late us stelen pryvely away;
For evere in oon, as for to lyve in reste,
Myn herte seyth that it wol ben the beste."

"O mercy God, what lyf is this?" quod she.
"Allas, ye sle me thus for verray tene!   1605
I se wel now that ye mystrusten me,
For by youre wordes it is wel isene.
Now for the love of Cynthia the shene,
Mistrust me nought thus causeles, for routhe,
Syn to be trewe I have yow plyght my
          trouthe.   1610

"And thenketh wel that somtyme it is wit
To spende a tyme, a tyme for to wynne.
Ne, parde, lorn am I nought fro yow yit,
Though that we ben a day or two atwynne.
Dryf out the fantasies yow withinne,   1615
And trusteth me, and leveth ek youre sorwe,
Or her my trouthe, I wol not lyve til morwe.

"For if ye wiste how sore it doth me smerte,
Ye wolde cesse of this; for God, thow wost,
The pure spirit wepeth in myn herte   1620
To se yow wepen that I love most,
And that I mot gon to the Grekes ost.
Ye, nere it that I wiste remedie
To come ayeyn, right here I wolde dye.

"But certes, I am not so nyce a wyght   1625
That I ne kan ymagynen a weye
To come ayen that day that I have hight.
For who may holde thing that wole awey?
My fader nought, for al his queynte pley.
And by my thryft, my wendyng out of Troye
Another day shal torne us alle to joye.   1631

1569 **trowe,** think. 1570 **light . . . arede,** easy, foretell. 1576 **honeste,** honor (chastity). 1577 **shende,** spoil. 1581 **name,** good name. 1582 **routhe,** a pity. 1583 **sle . . . hete,** banish (kill), eagerness (heat). 1584 **suffraunt,** long-suffering person. 1585 **leef . . . lete,** something valuable, give up. 1587 *pacience:* M *pacient;* other MSS *Be pacient.* 1588 **recche,** care—the Boethian notion that the person who does not care for temporal things is not subject to the domination of Fortune. 1589 **daunteth,** frightens. 1591 **Lucyna,** the moon. 1592 **Leoun . . . Ariete,** i.e., passes from the zodiacal sign of Aries, in which it then stands, through Leo—a passage that will require 10 days. Criseyde promises to return at the next new moon, cf. v.652–57. Such astrological allusion is not found in *Filostrato;* it is an element of Chaucer's individual voice. 1593 **wene,** doubt. 1597 **so,** i.e., so long as. 1602 **in oon,** continually. 1605 **tene,** vexation. 1608 **Cynthia,** the moon. 1609 **routhe,** pity. 1611 **wit,** wise. 1613 **lorn,** lost. 1614 **atwynne,** apart. 1618 **wiste . . . smerte,** knew, pain. 1623 **nere,** were it not. 1625 **nyce,** foolish. 1626 **ymagynen,** devise. 1627 **hight,** promised. 1630 **thryft,** skill (cunning).

"Forthy with al myn herte I yow biseke,
Yf that yow lyst don ought for my preyere,
And for the love which that I love yow eke,
That er that I departe fro yow here,   1635
That of so good a confort and a chere
I may yow sen that ye may brynge at reste
Myn herte, which that is o poynt to breste.

"And over al this I pray yow," quod she tho,
"Myn owen hertes sothfast suffisaunce,   1640
Syn I am thyn al hool, withouten mo,
That whil that I am absent, no plesaunce
Of other do me fro youre remembraunce.
For I am evere agast, forwhi men rede
That love is thing ay ful of bysy drede.   1645

"For yn this world ther lyveth lady noon,
If that ye were untrewe—as God defende—
That so bytraysed were or wobygon
As I, that al trouthe in yow entende.
And douteles, yf that ych other wende,   1650
I nere but ded, and er ye cause fynde,
For Goddes love, so beth me not unkynde."

To this answerde Troylus and seyde,
"Now God, to whom ther nys no cause ywrye,
Me glade, as wys I nevere unto Criseyde,   1655
Syn thilke day I saw hire first with eye,
Was fals, ne nevere shal til that I dye.
At shorte wordes, wel ye may me leve:
I kan no more; it shal be founde at preve."

"Graunt mercy, goode myn, ywys," quod she,
"And blysful Venus lat me nevere sterve,   1661
Er I may stonde of plesaunce in degre
To quyte hym wel that so wel kan deserve.
And whil that God my wit wol me conserve,

I shal so don—so trewe I have yow founde,
That ay honour to me-ward shal rebounde.   1666

"For trusteth wel that youre estat royal,
Ne veyn delit, nor oonly worthinesse
Of yow in werre or torney marcial,
Ne pompe, array, nobley, or ek richesse   1670
Ne made me to rewe on youre destresse.
But moral vertu, grounded upon trouthe,
That was the cause I first hadde on yow routhe.

"Ek gentil herte and manhod that ye hadde;
And that ye hadde, as me thoughte, in despit
Everythyng that souned into badde,   1676
As rudenesse and pepelyssh appetit;
And that yowre reson brydled youre delit—
This made aboven every creature
That I was youre, and shal while I may dure.

"And this may lengthe of yeres not fordo,   1681
Ne remuable Fortune deface;
But Juppiter, that of his myght may do
The sorwful to be glad, so yeve us grace
Er nyghtes ten to meten in this place,   1685
So that it may youre herte and myn suffise.
And fareth now wel, for tyme is that ye ryse."

And after that they longe ypleyned hadde,
And ofte ikist, and streyght in armes folde,
The day gan ryse, and Troylus hym cladde,   1690
And rewfullych his lady gan byholde,
As he that felte dethes cares colde,
And to hire grace he gan hym recomaunde.
Wher hym was wo, this holde I no demaunde.

For mannes hed ymagynen ne kan,   1695
N'entendement considere, ne tonge telle

1632 biseke, beseech. **1638 o poynt . . . breste,** on the point, break (burst). **1639 over al,** beyond. **1642 plesaunce,** pleasure. **1643 other do,** another put. **1644 agast, forwhi . . . rede,** afraid, because, say (advise). **1645 bysy drede,** anxiety. **1647 defende,** forbid. **1648 bytraysed were,** would be so betrayed. **1649 entende,** depend on. **1650 other wende,** believed otherwise. **1651 er ye,** i.e., before you could find out why. **1654 ywrye,** hidden. *cause:* A thought. **1655 wys,** surely. **1657** Other MSS *was nevere fals ne schal.* **1658 leve,** believe. **1659 kan . . . preve,** can say, proof (i.e., by actions). **1661 sterve,** die. **1662 plesaunce in degre,** in the happy condition. **1663 quyte,** repay. **1666 ay,** forever. **1667–82 For trusteth wel,** this passage follows *Fil.* 4.164–44, but there it is spoken by Troilo to Criseida; the shift considerably alters the resonances of their relationship. **1668 veyn delit,** worthless (i.e., sensual) delight. **1671 rewe,** have pity. **1673 routhe,** pity. **1675 despit,** contempt. **1677 pepelyssh,** vulgar. **1681 fordo,** destroy. **1682 remuable,** mutable. **1683 do,** make. **1685 Er,** ere (before). **1688 ypleyned,** lamented. **1689 streyght,** tight. **1691 rewfullych,** sadly. **1696 entendement,** understanding.

The cruwel peynes of this sorwful man
That passen every torment doun in helle.
For whan he saugh that she ne myghte dwelle,
Which that his soule out of his herte rente,   1700
Withouten more out of the chaumbre he
    wente.

Explicit liber quartus.

1698 **passen,** surpassed.

BOOK V

Incipit liber quintus.

Aprochen gan the fatal destyne
That Joves hath in disposicioun,
And to yow, angry Parcas, sustren thre,
Comytteth to don execucioun;
For which Criseyde moste out of the toun, 5
And Troylus shal dwellen forth yn pyne
Til Lachesis his threed no lengere twyne.

The gold-tressed Phebus heighe on lofte
Thries hadde al with his bemes clene
The snowes molte, and Zephirus as ofte 10
Ybrought ayen the tendre leves grene,
Syn that the sone of Ecuba the queene
Bygan to love hire first for whom his sorwe
Was al that she departe sholde o-morwe.

Ful redy was at pryme Dyomede 15
Criseyde unto the Grekes ost to lede,
For sorwe of which she felte hire herte blede
As she that nyste what was best to rede.
And trewely, as men in bokes rede,
Men wyste nevere womman han the care, 20
Ne was so loth out of a town to fare.

This Troylus, withouten red or lore,
As man that hath his joyes ek forlore,

Was waytyng on his lady everemore
As she that was the sothfast crop and more 25
Of al his lust or joyes here-byfore.
But Troylus, now farwel al thi joye,
For shaltow nevere sen hire eft in Troye.

Soth is that while he bod in this manere,
He gan his wo ful manly for to hyde, 30
That wel unnethe it sene was in his chere;
But at the yate there she sholde out ryde,
With certeyn folk he hovede hire t'abyde,
So wobygon al wolde he nought hym pleyne
That on his hors unnethe he sat for peyne. 35

For ire he quok, so gan his herte gnawe,
Whan Diomede on hors gan hym dresse,
And seyde to hymself this ilke sawe,
"Allas," quod he, "thus foul a wrecchednesse,
Why suffre ich it? Whi nyl ich it redresse? 40
Were it not bet at onys for to dye
Than everemore in langour thus to drye?

"Whi nyl I make at onys ryche and pore
To have ynowh to done er that she go?
Why nyl I brynge al Troye upon a rore? 45
Whi nyl I slen this Diomede also?

---

3 Parcas, Parcae, the three Fates. The lyric prologue of ll. 1–14 is not paralleled in *Fil.* 5.1ff. **4** *Comytteth:* M *Comytted.* **6 forth yn pyne,** henceforth in pain. **7 Lachesis . . . twyne,** the Fate who controls the length of human life by spinning (**twyne,** twist), until Atropos cuts it off (cf. iv.1546). **9** *clene:* MC&c *clere;* other MSS *shene.* **10 molte,** melted, i.e., the love affair had lasted for three years; this detail is added by Chaucer. **12 Ecuba,** Hecuba, Priam's queen. **15 pryme,** 9:00 A.M. Here the text begins to follow *Fil.* 5.1ff. **18 nyste . . . rede,** didn't know, think. **20 Men . . . han . . . care,** i.e., never was a woman known to have such sorrow ("men" is the impersonal subj.). **22 red . . . lore,** counsel, wisdom. **23 forlore,** lost. **25 crop and more,** crown (of a tree) and everything. **26 lust,** pleasure. **27** M&c *farewel now.* **28 eft,** again. **29 bod,** waited. **31 unnethe . . . chere,** scarcely, expression. **32 there,** where. **33 hovede,** lingered. **34** *hym pleyne:* other MSS *compleyne.* **35 unnethe,** scarcely (could be). **37 dresse,** approach. *hym:* other MSS *hir.* **38 sawe,** speech. **42 drye,** suffer. **45 upon a rore,** set in an uproar.

Why nyl I rathere with a man or two
Stele hire away? Whi wol I this endure?
Whi nyl I helpen to myn owene cure?"

But why he nolde don so fel a dede, 50
That shal I seyn, and why hym lyst it spare:
He hadde in herte alweys a manere drede
Lest that Cryseyde, yn rumour of this fare,
Sholde han ben slayn; lo, this was al his care.
And elles, certeyn, as I seyde yore, 55
He hadde it don, withouten wordes more.

Criseyde, whan she redy was to ryde,
Ful sorwfully she sighte and seyde allas.
But forth she mot, for ought that may bytyde,
And forth she rit ful sorwfully a pas. 60
Ther nys non other remedye yn this cas.
What wonder is, though that hire sore smerte,
Whan she forgoth hire owene swete herte?

This Troylus, in wyse of curtasie, 64
With hauke on honde and with an huge route
Of knyghtes, rod and did hire compaynye,
Passynge al the valey fer withoute,
And ferthere wold han ryden, out of doute,
Ful fayn, and wo was hym to gon so sone;
But torne he moste, and it was ek to done. 70

And right with that was Antenor icome
Out of the Grekes ost, and every wyght
Was of it glad and seyde he was welcome.
And Troylus, al nere his herte lyght,
He peyned hym with al his fulle myght 75
Hym to withholde of wepynge atte leste,
And Antenor he kyste and made feste.

And therwithal he moste his leve take,
And caste his eye upon hire pitously,
And ner he rod his cause for to make, 80
To take hire by the honde al sobrely.

And Lord, so she gan wepen tendrely!
And he ful softe and sleyghly gan hire seye,
"Now holde yowre day, and doth me not to
    deye."

With that his courser torned he aboute, 85
With face pale, and unto Diomede
No word he spak, ne non of al his route;
Of which the sone of Tydeus tok hede,
As he that koude more than the crede
In swych a craft, and by the reyne hire hente. 90
And Troylus to Troye homward he wente.

This Diomede, that ladde hire by the bridel,
Whan that he saw the folk of Troye aweye,
Thoughte, "Al my labour shal nat ben on ydel,
If that I may, for somwhat shal I seye, 95
For at the worste it may yet shorte oure weye.
I have herd seyd ek tymes twyes twelve,
'He is a fool that wole foryete hymselve.'"

But natheles, this thoughte he wel ynowh,
That "Certaynlich I am aboute nought 100
If that I speke of love or make it tough,
For douteles, yf she have in hire thought
Hym that I gesse, he may nat ben ybrought
So son awey. But I shal fynde a mene
That she shal not as yet wete what I mene." 105

This Diomede as he that koude his good,
Whan this was don, gan fallen forth in speche
Of this and that, and axed whi she stood
In swych dishese, and gan hire ek byseche
That yf that he encrese myghte or eche 110
With onythyng hire ese, that she sholde
Comaunde it hym, and seyde he don it wolde.

For treweliche he swor hire as a knyght
That ther nas thyng with whiche he myghte
    hire plese,

---

50 fel, wicked. **55 yore**, earlier. **60–61** Lines transposed in other MSS. **64 wyse of curtasie**, i.e., as a guard of honor (not dressed for battle). **65 route**, company. **67** *valey*: other MSS *wallys*. **69 fayn**, happily. **77 feste**, i.e., made much of. **80 cause . . . to make**, case, to urge. **82** *she*: C&c *he*. **83 sleyghly**, secretly. **84 holde . . . day**, i.e., keep to the date (you promised to return). **87 route**, company. **88 Tydeus**, Diomede; for his genealogy see ll. 1464ff. below. **89 koude . . . crede**, i.e., knew more than creed (elementary knowledge). **90 swych a craft**, i.e., the craft of love. **100 aboute nought**, i.e., will accomplish nothing. **101 make it tough**, i.e., be too insistent. **105 wete**, realize. **106 koude his good**, i.e., knew what was best for him. **107** Other MSS *Whan tyme was*. **110 eche**, add to.

That he nolde don his peyne and al his myght
To don it, for to done hire herte an ese; 116
And preyede hire she wolde hire sorwe apese,
And seyde, "Ywys, we Grekes kon have joye
To honouren yow as wel as folk of Troye."

He seyde ek thus, "I wot yow thenketh
    straunge— 120
Ne wonder is, for it is to yow newe—
Th'aquayntaunce of these Troians to chaunge
For folk of Grece that ye nevere knewe.
But wolde nevere God but if as trewe
A Grek ye shulde among us alle fynde 125
As ony Troian is, and ek as kynde.

"And by the cause I swor yow right, lo, now,
To ben youre frend, and helply to my myght,
And for that more aquayntaunce ek of yow
Have ich had than another straunger wight, 130
So fro this forth, I pray yow, day and nyght
Comaundeth me, how sore that me smerte,
To don al that may like unto youre herte;

"And that ye me wolde as youre brother trete,
And taketh not my frendshipe in despit. 135
And though youre sorwes be for thinges
    grete—
Not I not whi—but out of more respit
Myn herte hath for to amende it gret delit.
And yf I may youre harmes nat redresse,
I am right sory for youre hevynesse. 140

"For though ye Troians with us Grekes wrothe
Han many a day ben, alwey yet, parde,
O god of Love in soth we serven bothe.
And for the love of God, my lady fre, 144
Whomso ye hate, as beth not wroth with me,
For trewely, ther kan no wyght yow serve
That half so loth yowre wraththe wold deserve.

"And nere it that we been so neigh the tente
Of Calkas, which that sen us bothe may,

I wolde of this yow telle al myn entente. 150
But this enseled til another day—
Yeve me youre hond. I am and shal ben ay,
God helpe me so, while that my lyf may dure,
Youre owene aboven every creature.

"Thus seyde I nevere er now to womman
    born, 155
For, God myn herte as wysly glade so,
I loved never womman here-byforn
As paramours, ne nevere shal no mo.
And for the love of God, beth not my fo,
Al kan I not to yow, my lady dere, 160
Compleyne aryght, for I am yet to lere.

"And wondreth not, myn owen lady bryght,
Though that I speke of love to you thus blyve,
For I have herd er this of many a wyght
Hath loved thyng he nevere saugh his lyve. 165
Ek I am not of power for to stryve
Ayeyns the god of Love, but hym obeye
I wole alwey, and mercy I yow preye.

"Ther ben so worthi knyghtes in this place,
And ye so feyr, that everich of hem alle 170
Wol peynen hym to stonden in youre grace.
But myghte me so faire a grace falle
That ye me for youre servant wolde calle,
So lowely ne so trewely yow serve
Nil noon of hem as I shal til I sterve." 175

Criseyde unto that purpos lite answerde,
As she that was with sorwe oppressed so
That in effect she nought his tales herde
But her and there, now here a word or two.
Hire thoughte hire sorwful herte brast a-two,
For whan she gan hire fader fer aspye 181
Wel neigh doun of hire hors she gan to sye.

But natheles she thonked Diomede
Of al his travayle and his goode chere,
And that hym lyst his frendshipe hire to bede.

---

115 *peyne:* other MSS *herte.* 117 **apese,** appease (calm). 124 **wolde nevere God,** God forbid. 128 **helply to,** helpfully to the extent of. 135 **despit,** contempt. 137 **Not I . . . out of . . . respit,** I don't know, without delay. 139 **redresse,** remedy. 143 **O god,** one god. 145 **Whomso,** whomsoever. 151 **enseled,** i.e., be sealed up. 161 **Compleyne aryght . . . lere,** i.e., pay homage in proper language. 163 **blyve,** quickly. 165 **saugh his,** saw in his. 166 *Ek:* other MSS *Nor/For.* 175 **sterve,** die. 176 *lite:* M *litel.* 182 **sye,** sink. 184 **travayle,** effort. 185 **bede,** offer.

And she accepteth it in goode manere,   186
And wold do fayn that is hym lef and dere,
And trusten hym she wolde, and wel she
    myghte,
As seyde she, and from hire hors sh'alighte.

Hire fader hath hire in his armes nome,   190
And tweynty tyme he kyste his doughter swete,
And seyde, "O dere doughter myn, welcome."
She seyde ek she was fayn with hym to mete,
And stod forth mewet, mylde, and mansuete.
But here I leve hire with hire fader dwelle,   195
And forth I wole of Troylus yow telle.

To Troye is come this woful Troylus,
In sorwe aboven alle sorwes smerte,
With felon lok and face dispitous.
Tho sodeynly doun from his hors he sterte,   200
And thorough his paleys, with a swollen herte,
To chambre he wente. Of nothing tok he hede,
Ne noon to hym dar speke a word for drede.

And there his sorwes that he spared hadde
He yaf an yssue large, and "Deth" he cride;   205
And in his throwes frenetyk and madde
He curssed Jove, Appollo, and ek Cupide,
He curssed Ceres, Bacus, and Cipryde,
His burthe, hymself, his fate, and ek nature,
And, save his lady, every creature.   210

To bedde he goth and walwith there and
    torneth
In furye, as doth he Ixion in helle.
And in this wyse he neigh til day sojourneth.
But tho bygan a lyte his herte unswelle
Thorough teris which that gonnen up to welle.
And pitously he cride upon Criseyde,   216
And to hymself right thus he spak and seyde:

"Wher is myn owene lady lief and dere?
Wher is hire white brest? Wher is it? Where?

Wher ben hire armes and hire eyen clere   220
That yesternyght this tyme with me were?
Now may I wepe allone many a tere,
And graspe aboute I may, but in this place
Save a pilwe I fynde nought t'enbrace.

"How shal I do? Whan shal she come ayen?   225
I not, allas! Whi let ich hire to go?
As wolde God ich hadde as tho be sleyn!
O herte myn, Criseyde, O swete fo!
O lady myn that I love and no mo,
To whom for evermo myn herte I dowe,   230
Se how I deye; ye nyl me not rescowe!

"Who seeth yow now, my righte lode-sterre?
Who sit right now, or stant in yowre presence?
Who kan conforten now youre hertes werre?
Now I am gon, whom yeve ye audience?   235
Who speketh for me right now in myn absence?
Allas, no wight, and that is al my care,
For wel I wot as yvele as I ye fare.

"How shulde I thus ten dayes ful endure,
Whan I the firste nyght have al this tene?   240
How shal she don ek, sorwful creature?
For tendernesse how shal she ek sustene
Swich wo for me? O pitous pale and grene
Shal ben youre fresshe wommanlyche face
For langour, er ye torne unto this place."   245

And whan he fil in ony slomberynges,
Anoon bygonne he sholde for to grone,
And dremen of the dredefulleste thinges
That myghte ben: as mete he were allone
In place horrible, makyng ay his mone,   250
Or meten that he was amonges alle
His enemys, and in hire hondes falle.

And therwithal his body sholde sterte,
And with the stert al sodeynlich awake,
And swich a tremor fele aboute his herte   255

187 **fayn** . . **lef**, i.e., happily do what is pleasing to him. 190 **nome**, took. 193 **fayn**, happy. 194 **mewet** . . . **mansuete**, mute, gentle. 199 **dispitous**, cruel (harsh). 202 *nothing:* A *no wight.* 204 **spared**, suppressed. 206 **throwes**, throes. 211 **walwith**, wallows. M&c *weyleth/waileth.* 212 **Ixion**, chained in Hades to an ever-revolving wheel. 226 **not**, don't know. 227 **as tho**, at that time. 230 **dowe**, give (endow). 232 **lode-sterre**, guiding star. 238 M&c *wot I.* 240 **tene**, grief. 241 **don**, i.e., endure (make out). 242 M *tendresse;* *ek:* MC&c *this.* 245 **torne**, return. 249 **mete**, dream. 253 **sholde**, would.

That of the feere his body sholde quake,
And therwithal he sholde a noyse make,
And seme as though he sholde falle depe
From heighe o-lofte—and than he wolde
   wepe,

And rewen on hymself so pytously   260
That wonder was to here his fantasye.
Another tyme he sholde myghtily
Conforte hymself, and seine it was folye
So causeles swych drede for to drye—
And eft bygynne his aspre sorwes newe,   265
That every man myghte on his sorwes rewe.

Who koude telle aright or ful discryve
His wo, his pleynt, his langour, and his peyne?
Nought al the men that han or ben on lyve.
Thow, redere, mayst thyself ful wel devyne   270
That swych a wo my wit kan nat defyne.
On ydel for to write it sholde I swynke,
Whan that my wit is wery it to thenke.

On hevene yet the sterres weren sene,
Although ful pale ywoxen was the moone;   275
And whiten gan the orisonte shene
Al estward, as it woned is to done;
And Phebus with his rosy carte sone
Gan after that to dresse hym up to fare,
Whan Troylus hath sent after Pandare.   280

This Pandare, that of al the day biforn
Ne myghte have comen Troylus to se,
Although he on his hed it hadde isworn—
For with the kyng Pryam alday was he,
So that it lay not in his liberte   285
Nowher to gon—but on the morwe he
   wente
To Troylus whan that he for hym sente.

For in his herte he koude wel devyne
That Troylus al nyght for sorwe wook,
And that he wolde telle hym of his peyne,   290
This knew he wel ynough withoute book.
For which to chaumbre streyght the wey he
   took,
And Troylus tho sobrelych he grette,
And on the bed ful soone he gan hym sette.

"My Pandarus," quod Troilus, "the sorwe   295
Which that I drye I may not longe endure.
I trowe I shal nat lyven til tomorwe.
For whiche I wolde alwey, on aventure,
To the devysen of my sepulture
The forme, and of my moeble thow dispone   300
Right as the semeth best is for to done.

"But of the fyr and flaumbe funeral
In whiche my body brenne shal to glede,
And of the feste and pleyes palestral
At my vigile, I pray the take good hede   305
That that be wel; and offre Mars my stede,
My swerd, myn helm, and, leve brother dere,
My sheld to Pallas yef, that shyneth clere.

"The poudre in which myn herte ybrend shal
   torne,
That prey I the thow take and it conserve   310
In a vessel that men clepeth an urne
Of gold, and to my lady that I serve,
For love of whom thus pitously I sterve,
So yeve it hire, and do me this plesaunce,
To preyen hire to kepe it for a remembraunce.

"For wele I fele by my maladye,   316
And by my dremes now and yore ago,
Al certeynly that I mot nedes dye.
The owle ek which that hatte Escaphilo

---

260 rewen, have pity. **261 fantasye,** hallucination(s). **262 sholde,** would. **264 drye,** suffer. **265 eft ... aspre,** again, bitter. **266 rewe,** have pity. **270 redere,** note that in spite of the Corpus frontispiece, Chaucer here conceives of the poem as being read. **272 swynke,** labor. **276 orisonte shene,** bright horizon. **278 Phebus ... carte,** Phoebus who drives his chariot, the sun. **279 dresse,** prepare. **282 Ne myghte have,** was not able. **286 morwe,** morning. **296 drye,** suffer. **297 trowe,** believe. **298 on aventure,** against that event. **299 devysen ... sepulture,** arrange, funeral. **300 moeble ... dispone,** possessions, dispose. **303 glede,** coals (ashes). **304 palestral,** athletic. The "palaestra" was the stadium; funeral games occur in *Iliad* 23, *Thebiad* 6, etc. **306** *That that:* M&c *That al.* **308 sheld:** C&c *swerde.* **313 sterve,** die. **317 yore ago,** past. **319 hatte Escaphilo,** is called Ascalaphus, who was changed into an owl by Proserpina, Ovid, *Met.* 5.533.

Hath after me shright alle thise nyghtes two. 320
And god Mercurye, of me now, woful wrecche,
The soule gide, and whan the lyste it fecche!"

Pandare answerde and seyde, "Troylus,
My dere frend, as I have told the yore,
That it is folye for to sorwen thus, 325
And causeles, for which I kan no more.
But whoso wole not trowen rede ne lore,
I kan nat seen in hym no remedye,
But late hym worthen with his fantasye.

"But, Troylus, I pray the telle me now 330
If that thow trowe, er this, that ony wyght
Hath loved paramours as wel as thow?
Ye, God wot, and fro many a worthi knyght
Hath his lady gon a fourtenyght,
And he nat yet made halvendel the fare. 335
What nede is the to maken al this care?

"Syn day by day thow mayst thiselven se
That from his love, or elles from his wyf
A man mot twynnen of necessite,
Ye, though he love hire as his owene lif, 340
Yet nyl he with hymself thus maken stryf.
For wel thou wost, my leve brother dere,
That alwey frendes may not ben yfere.

"How don this folk that seen hire loves
    wedded
By frendes myght, as it bytyt ful ofte, 345
And sen hem in hire spouses bed ybedded?
God wot, they take it wysly, faire and softe,
Forwhy good hope halt up hire herte o-lofte.
And for they kan a tyme of sorwe endure,
As tyme hem hurt a tyme doth hem cure. 350

"So sholdestow endure, and late slyde
The tyme, and fonde to ben glad and lyght.
Ten dayes nys not so longe to abyde.
And syn she the to come hath byhyght,
She nyl not hire hestes breken for no wight. 355
For drede that not that she nyl fynden weye
To come ayen; my lyf that dorste I leye.

"Thy swevenes ek and al swich fantasye
Dryf out, and lat hem faren to myschaunce,
For thei proceden of thi malencolye, 360
That doth the fele in slep al this penaunce.
A straw for alle swevenes signifiaunce;
God helpe me so, I counte hem not a bene!
Ther wot no man aright what dremes mene.

"For prestes of the temple tellen this, 365
That dremes ben the revelacions
Of goddes, and as wel they telle, ywys,
That they ben infernals illusions;
And leches seyn that of complexions
Proceden thei, or fast, or glotonye. 370
Who wot in soth thus what thei signifie?

"Ek other seyn that thorugh impressions,
As yf a wight hath faste a thing in mynde,
That therof cometh swich avysions;
And othere seyn, as they in bokes fynde, 375
That after tymes of the yer, by kynde,
Men dreme, and that th'effect goth by the
    mone.
But lef no drem, for it is nought to done.

"Wel worth of dremes ay these olde wyves!
And treweliche ek augurye of these fowles, 380
For fere of which men wenen lese here lyves,

---

320 shright, the screech owl, traditionally regarded as an omen of death. **321 Mercurye,** in classical mythology Mercury guided souls on their way to Hades (cf. v.1827). **322 the lyste,** it pleases you. **324 yore,** before. **327 rede ... lore,** advice, wisdom. **329 worthen,** dwell. **331 trowe,** believe. **332 paramours,** sexually. **339 twynnen,** separate. **343 yfere,** together. **345 frendes myght,** the power of others. Medieval marriages were always arranged; this was the genesis of the courtly love doctrine that love was not compatible with marriage. **bytyt,** happens. **348 Forwhy,** because. **352 fonde,** try. **353** MC&c *hys so long nought t'abide.* **354 byhyght,** promised. **355 hestes,** promises. **358 swevenes,** dreams. The clinical detail about the causes and variety of dreams (a preoccupation of Chaucer's, cf. *HF* 1ff.; *CT* vii.2922ff.) is not found at *Fil.* 5.32. **361 doth,** makes. **363 not a bene,** not worth a bean. **369 leches ... complexions,** physicians, balance of the humors in the system at any given time. **373 faste ... in mynde,** i.e., compulsive preoccupation. **374 avysions,** visions. **376 kynde,** nature. **378 lef,** believe. **379 worth,** become; i.e., leave dreams to old women. **380 augurye ... fowles,** the most characteristic signs by which Roman diviners told whether the gods approved of proposed actions were given by birds. These might be chickens, which were carried by armies into the field for the purpose, or flights and cries of wild birds. **381 wenen lese,** think to lose.

As ravenes qualm, or shrykyng of these
    owles—
To trowen on it bothe fals and foule is.
Allas, allas, so noble a creature
As is a man shal drede swich ordure!   385

"For which with al myn herte I the beseche,
Unto thiself that al this thow foryeve.
And rys now up withoute more speche,
And lat us caste how forth may best be dreve
This tyme, and ek how fresshly we may leve 390
Whan that she cometh, the which shal be right
    sone.
God help me so, the beste is thus to done.

"Rys, lat us speke of lusti lyf in Troye
That we han led, and forth the tyme dryve,
And ek of tyme comynge us rejoye,   395
That bryngen shal oure blysse now so blyve.
And langour of these twyes dayes fyve
We shal therwith so foryete or oppresse
That wel unneth it don shal us duresse.

"This town is ful of lordes al aboute,   400
And trewes lasten al this mene while.
Go we pleye us in som lusti route—
To Sarpedon, not hennes but a myle.
And thus thow shalt the tyme wel bygile,
And dryve it forth unto that blisful morwe 405
That thow hire se that cause is of thi sorwe.

"Now rys, my dere brother Troylus,
For certes, it noon honour is to the
To wepe and in thi bed to jowken thus.
For trewely, of o thing thow trust to me: 410
If thow thus ligge a day or two or thre,
The folk wol wene that thou for cowardyse
The feynest syk, and that thow darst nat ryse."

This Troylus answerde, "O brother dere,
This knowen folk that han ysuffred peyne, 415

That though he wepe and make sorwful chere
That feleth harm and smert yn every veyne,
No wonder is. And though ich evere pleyne,
Or alwey wepe, I am nothing to blame,
Syn I have lost the cause of al my game. 420

"But syn of fyne force I mot aryse,
I shal aryse as soone as evere I may—
And God, to whom myn herte I sacrifise,
So sende us hastely the tenthe day!
For was ther nevere foule so fayn of May 425
As I shal ben, whan that she comth in Troye,
That cause is of my torment and my joye.

"But whider is thi red," quod Troylus,
"That we may pleye us best in al this town?"
"By God, my conseyl is," quod Pandarus, 430
"To ryde and pley us with Kyng Sarpedoun."
So longe of this they speken up and doun
Til Troylus gan at the laste assente
To ryse, and forth to Sarpedoun they wente.

This Sarpedoun, as he that honourable 435
Was evere his lyve, and ful of heigh largesse,
With al that myghte yserved ben on table
That deynte was, al coste it gret richesse,
He fedde hem day by day, that swich noblesse,
As seyden bothe the meste and ek the leste, 440
Was nevere er that day wyst at ony feste.

Nor in this world ther is noon instrument
Delicious, thorugh wynd or touche of corde,
As fer as ony wyght hath evere ywent,
That tonge telle or herte may recorde, 445
That at that feste it nas wel herd accorde;
Ne of ladyes ek so fayr a companye
On daunce, er tho, was nevere yseyn with eye.

But what avayleth this to Troylus,
That for his sorwe nothing of it roughte? 450
For evere in oon his herte pitous

382 **qualm,** croak. 383 **trowen,** believe. 385 **ordure,** filth. This strong statement against divination reflects the Christian resistance to classical custom. 387 **thiself . . . foryeve,** i.e., be kind to yourself. 389 **caste . . . dreve,** plan, spent (driven). 390 **fresshly,** i.e., with renewed vigor. 393 **lusti,** gay. 396 **blyve,** soon. 398 *or:* MC&c *oure.* 399 **unneth,** hardly. 401 **trewes,** truce. 402 **route,** company. 409 **jowken,** rest (roost, Fr. *jouquier,* used in falconry). 412 **wene:** other MSS *seyn.* 413 **feynest,** pretend. 420 **game,** joy. 421 **fyne force,** sheer necessity. 425 **fayn,** happy. 428 **red,** advice. 436 *largesse:* MC&c *prowesse.* 443 M&c *touche or corde.* 448 **er tho,** before then. 450 **roughte,** cared.

Ful bysily Criseyde, his lady, soughte.
On hire was evere al that his herte thoughte,
Now this, now that, so faste ymagynynge,
That glad, ywys, kan hym no festeyinge.   455

These ladyes ek that at this feste ben,
Syn that he saw his lady was aweye,
It was his sorwe upon hem for to sen,
Or for to here on instruments so pleye.
For she that of his herte berth the keye   460
Was absent, lo, this was his fantasye,
That no wight sholde make melodye.

Nor ther nas houre in al the day or nyght,
Whan he was there as no wight myghte hym
          here,
That he ne seyde, "O lufsom lady bryght,   465
How have ye faren syn that ye were here?
Welcome, ywys, myn owne lady dere!"
But weylaway, al this nas but a maze.
Fortune his howve entendeth bet to glaze.

The lettres ek that she of olde tyme   470
Had hym ysent he wolde allone rede
An hondred sithe atwixen noon and pryme,
Refiguryng hire shap, hire wommanhede,
Withinne his herte, and every word and dede
That passed was. And thus he drof to an
          ende   475
The ferthe day, and seyde he wolde wende.

And seyde, "Leve brother Pandarus,
Intendestow that we shul here bleve
Til Sarpedoun wol forth congeyen us?
Yet were it fairer that we toke oure leve.   480
For Godes love, lat us now sone at eve
Oure leve take, and homward lat us torne,
For trewely, I wol not thus sojourne."

Pandare answerde, "Be we comen hider
To fecchen fyr and rennen hom ayen?   485
God helpe me so, I kan nat tellen whider
We myghten gon, yf I shal sothly seyn,
Ther ony wyght is of us more fayn
Than Sarpedoun; and if we hennes hye
Thus sodeynly, I holde it vilanye,   490

"Syn that we seyden that we wolde bleve
With hym a wowke; and now thus sodeynly
The ferthe day to take of hym oure leve,
He wolde wondren on it, trewely.
Lat us holde forth oure purpos fermely.   495
And syn that ye bihighten hym to byde,
Holde forward now, and after lat us ryde."

Thus Pandarus with alle peyne and wo
Made hym to dwelle, and at the wykes ende
Of Sarpedoun thei toke hire leve tho,   500
And on hire wey they spedden hem to wende.
Quod Troylus, "Now God me grace sende
That I may fynden at myn hom-comynge
Criseyde comen," and therwith gan he synge.

"Ye, haselwode," thoughte this Pandare,   505
And to hymself ful softelich he seyde,
"God wot, refreyden may this hote fare
Er Calkas sende Troylus Cryseyde!"
But natheles, he japed thus and pleyde,
And swor, ywys, his herte hym wel byhighte 510
She wolde come as soone as evere she myghte.

Whan they unto the paleys were ycomen
Of Troylus, thei down of hors alighte,
And to the chambre hire wey than han they
          nomen,
And into tyme that it gan to nyghte,   515
They spaken of Criseyde the brighte.

---

455 glad . . . no festeyinge, i.e., no celebration can make him glad. M *festenynge*. **460 For,** because. **464 there,** where. **466** *here*: M&c *there*. **468 maze,** delusion. **469 howve . . . glaze,** to glaze one's hood (give a person a glass helmet) meant to hoodwink (delude). **472 sithe . . . noon and pryme,** times, 12:00 to 3:00 P.M., 6:00 to 9:00 A.M. (the order for metrical convenience?). **476** A *and thennes wolde he wende.* **478 bleve,** remain. *bleve:* other MSS *be leve.* **479 congeyen,** dismiss. Other MSS *convien.* **485 fecchen fyr,** before the days of matches "borrowing fire" was a necessity, and one had to hurry home before the coals died. **488 of us . . . fayn,** i.e., more glad to have us. **491 bleve,** stay. **496 bihighten,** promised. **497 forward,** agreement. **505 haselwode,** Pandarus' way of saying "nuts." **506** *softelich:* M&c *sobrelich.* **507 refreyden,** be cooled off. **509 japed,** joked. *pleyde:* MC&c *seyde.* **510 byhighte,** assured. **513** M *of hire hors.* **514 nomen,** taken.

And after this, whan that hem bothe leste,
Thei spedde hem fro the soper unto reste.

O-morwe as soone as day bygan to clere,
This Troylus gan of his slep t'abreyde, 520
And to Pandare, his owen brother dere,
"For love of God," ful pitously he seyde,
"As go we seen the paleys of Criseyde;
For syn we yet may have no more feste,
So lat us seen hire paleys atte leste." 525

And therwithal, his meyne for to blende,
A cause he fond in towne for to go,
And to Criseyde hous thei gonnen wende.
But Lord, this sely Troylus was wo! 529
Hym thoughte his sorwful herte braste a-two.
For whan he saugh hire dorres sperid alle,
Wel neigh for sorwe adown he gan to falle.

Therwith whan he was ware and gan byholde
How shet was every wyndowe of the place,
As frost hym thoughte his herte gan to colde, 535
For which with chaunged deedlych pale face,
Withouten word, he forthby gan to pace,
And, as God wolde, he gan so faste ryde
That no wight of his contenaunce aspide.

Than seyde he thus, "O paleys desolat, 540
O hous of houses whilom best yhight,
O paleys empty and disconsolat,
O thou lanterne of which queynt is the light,
O paleys whilom day that now art nyght,
Wel oughtestow to falle, and I to dye, 545
Syn she is went that wont was us to gye.

"O paleys whilom crowne of houses alle,
Enlumyned with the sonne of alle blysse,
O ryng fro which the ruby is out falle,
O cause of wo that cause hast ben of lisse, 550

Yet syn I may no bet, fayn wolde I kysse
Thy colde dores, dorste I for this route;
And farewel shryne, of which the seynt is oute!"

Therwith he caste on Pandarus his eye,
With chaunged face, and pitous to byholde; 555
And whan he myght his tyme aright aspye,
Ay as he rod, to Pandarus he tolde
His newe sorwe and ek his joyes olde,
So pitously and with so dede an hewe
That every wight myghte on his sorwe rewe. 560

Fro thennesforth he rideth up and down,
And everything cam hym to remembraunce
As he rod forby places of the toun
In whiche he whilom hadde al his plesaunce.
"Lo, yende saugh I myn owene lady daunce, 565
And in that temple, with hire eyen clere,
Me kaughte first my righte lady dere.

"And yender have I herd ful lustily
Me dere herte laugh; and yender pleye
Saugh ich hire ones ek ful blysfully; 570
And yender ones to me gan she seye,
'Now goode swete, love me wel, I preye.'
And yond so goodly gan she me byholde
That to the deth myn herte is to hire holde.

"And at that corner in the yonder hous 575
Herde I myn alderlevest lady dere,
So wommanly with vois melodious,
Syngen so wel, so goodly, and so clere,
That in my soule yet me thenketh ich here
The blisful sown. And in that yonder place 580
My lady first me tok unto hire grace."

Thanne thought he thus, "O blisful lord Cupide,
Whanne I the proces have in memorie,

520 **abreyde,** wake up. 526 **meyne . . . blende,** household, deceive (blind). 529 **sely,** the usual spectrum of meaning: silly, innocent, blessed. 530 **braste,** would break (burst). 531 **sperid,** barred. 537 **forthby . . . pace,** pass by. 541 **whilom . . . yhight,** formerly, called. Harley 1239 has *best ylyght,* which might seem better to translate *Fil.* 5.53 *quanto luminoso/Era* except cf. ll. 545–53, which were added by Chaucer. 543 **queynt,** quenched. 546 **gye,** guide. 550 **lisse,** joy. M *blysse.* 551 **fayn,** happily. 552 **route,** crowd. 560 **rewe,** have pity. 563 **forby,** by. M *forth by;* other MSS *the places/paleisis.* 565 Other MSS *yonder saugh ich last my lady daunce.* 566 **clere,** bright. 567 **kaughte,** caught sight of. 568 **lustily,** gaily. 570 *blysfully:* other MSS *busily.* 574 **holde,** bound. 575 **yonder,** more distant. 576 **alderlevest,** dearest of all. 580 **yonder place,** i.e., Diephebus' house.

How thow me hast waryed on every syde,
Men myght a book mak of it lyk a storie.   585
What nede is the to seke on me victorie,
Syn I am thyn and holly at thi wille?
What joye hastow thyn owene folk to spille?

"Wel hastow, lord, ywroke on me thin ire,
Thow myghty god and dredful for to greve.   590
Now mercy, lord, thow wost wel I desire
Thi grace most of alle lustes leeve,
And leve and deye I wol in thy byleeve;
For which I n'axe in guerdoun but o bone—
That thow Criseyde ayen me sende soone.   595

"Distreyne hire herte as faste to retorne
As thow dost myn to longen hire to se.
Than wot I wel that she nyl not sojourne.
Now blisful lorde, so cruwel thow ne be
Unto the blod of Troye, I preye the,   600
As Juno was unto the blood Thebane,
For which the folk of Thebes caughte hire
      bane."

And after this he to the yates wente
There as Criseyde out rood a ful good paas,
And up and doun ther made he many a
      wente,   605
And to hymself ful ofte he seyde, "Allas,
Fro hennes rood my blysse and my solas;
As wolde blisful God now for his joye,
I myghte hire seen ayen come into Troye!

"And to the yonder hill I gan hire gyde,   610
Allas, and ther I tok of hire my leve.
And yond I saugh hire to hire fader ryde,
For sorwe of which myn herte shal tocleve.
And heder hom I com whan it was eeve,

And here I dwelle outcast from alle joye,   615
And shal til I may sen hire eft in Troye."

And of hymself ymagyned he ofte
To ben defet, and pale, and woxen lesse
Than he was wont, and that men seyde softe,
"What may it be? Who kan the sothe gesse   620
Whi Troylus hath al this hevynesse?"
And al this nas but his malencolye,
That he hadde of hymself swich fantasye.

Another tyme ymagynen he wolde
That every wight that wente by the weye   625
Had of hym routhe, and that thei seyen
      sholde,
"I am right sory Troylus wol deye."
And thus he drof a day yet forth or tweye,
As ye have herd. Swich lyf right gan he lede
As he that stood bitwixen hope and drede.   630

For which hym liked in his songes shewe
Th'encheson of his wo, as he best myghte,
And make a song of wordes but a fewe,
Somwhat his woful herte for to lyghte.
And whan he was from every mannes sighte, 635
With softe voys he of his lady dere,
That absent was, gan synge as ye may here.

Canticus Troili

"O sterre of which I lost have al the light,
With herte sor wel oughte I to bewayle
That evere derk in torment, nyght by nyght, 640
Toward my deth with wynd in stere I sayle;
For which the tenthe nyght, if that I fayle
The gydyng of thi bemes bright an houre,
My ship and me Carybdes wol devoure."

---

584 waryed, made war on. **588 spille,** destroy. **589 ywroke,** wreaked. **590 dredful . . . to greve,** terrible, to offend. **592 lustes leeve,** dear delights. **593 byleeve,** belief (religion). **594 guerdoun . . . bone,** reward, request. **596 Distreyne,** force (constrain). **598 sojourne,** linger. **601 blood Thebane,** Juno's hostility, because of Jove's infidelities with Theban women, was one of the causes for the fall of Thebes in the *Teseida.* **602 bane,** death. **604 good paas,** good distance. **605 wente,** turn (pacing). **607 solas,** comfort. **610 yonder,** more distant. **613 tocleve,** split apart. **616 eft,** again. **618 defet . . . lesse,** disfigured, smaller. **621 hevynesse,** despondency. **626 routhe,** pity. **628 drof,** drove. **632 encheson,** reason. Other MSS *th'entencion.* **633 make:** C&c *made.* **637 M** *was absent, gan to syngen.* **638 Canticus Troili** omitted from M; found in C&c. This is quite different from the corresponding passage in *Fil.,* 5.62–66. **641 in stere,** astern. **643 bright an,** bright for an. M *Thy gydyng.* **644 Carybdes,** Charybdis, in classical mythology a whirlpool off the Sicilian coast, opposite the rocks of Scylla.

This song when he thus songen hadde, soone 645
He fil ayen into his sikes olde.
And every nyght, as was his wone to done,
He stod the bryghte mone to beholde,
And al his sorwe he to the mone tolde,
And seyde, "Iwis, whan thow art horned newe,
I shal be glad, if al the world be trewe. 651

"I saugh thyn hornes olde ek by the morwe
Whan hennes rod my ryghte lady dere,
That cause is of my torment and my sorwe,
For which, O brighte Lathona the clere, 655
For love of God, ren faste aboute thy spere!
For whanne thyne hornes newe gynne sprynge,
Than shal she come that may me blisse brynge."

The dayes more and lengere every nyght 659
Than they ben wont to be, hym thoughte tho,
And that the sonne wente his cours unright
By lenger wey than it was wont to go;
And seyde, "Iwis, me dredeth everemo
The sonnes sone, Pheton, be on lyve,
And that his fadres carte amys he dryve." 665

Upon the walles faste ek wolde he walke,
And on the Grekes ost he wolde se,
And to hymself right thus he wolde talke,
"Lo, yender is myn owene lady fre,
Or elles yender, there tho tenten be. 670
And thennes comth this eyr that is so soote
That in my soule I fele it doth me boote.

"And hardely, this wynd that more and more
Thus stoundemele encreseth in my face
Is of my ladyes depe sikes sore. 675
I preve it thus: for in noon othere place
Of al this town save onlyche in this space

Feele I no wynd that sowneth so lik peyne—
It seyth, 'Allas, why twynned be we
     tweyne?' "

This longe tyme he dryveth forth right thus, 680
Til fully passed was the nynthe nyght.
And ay bisyde hym was this Pandarus,
That bysily did alle his fulle myght
Hym to comforte, and make his herte lyght,
Yevyng hym hope alwey the tenthe morwe 685
That she shal come and stynten al his sorwe.

Upon the tother side ek was Criseyde,
With wommen fewe, among the Grekes
     stronge,
For whiche ful ofte a day "Allas," she seyde,
"That I was born! Wel may myn herte
     longe 690
After my deth, for now lyve I to longe.
Allas, and I ne may it not amende,
For now is wors than evere yet I wende.

"My fader nyl for nothing do me grace
To goon ayen for ought I kan hym queme; 695
And yf so be that I my terme passe,
My Troylus shal in his herte deme
That I am fals, and so it may wel seme.
Thus shal ich have unthank on every side.
That I was born so weylaway the tyde! 700

"And yf that I me put in jupartie
To stele awey by nyght, and it byfalle
That I be caught, I shal be hold a spie.
Or elles—lo, this drede I most of alle—
Yf in the hondes of som wreche I falle, 705
I am but lost, al be myn herte trewe.
Now, myghty God, thow on my sorwe rewe!"

---

646 **sikes olde,** former sighs. 647 **wone,** custom. 650 **horned newe,** i.e., the new moon, which was to signal the passage of the ten days, cf. IV.1592 and note. 652 **hornes olde,** i.e., the last quarter of the old moon. Although nearly all the astrological allusions were added by Chaucer, in *Fil.* 5.69, Troilo had seen the old moon early in the morning as he was leaving Criseida's house. **morwe** morning. 655 *Lathona,* one MS and some eds. have *Lucinia* (the moon), but Diana, the moon goddess, is also called *Latonia.* 656 **spere,** sphere. 662 *go:* C&c *do.* 664 **Pheton,** an allusion to Phaëton who, attempting to drive the sun-chariot of his father Phoebus, nearly set the earth on fire, until Zeus killed him with a thunderbolt. 671 **soote,** sweet. 672 **boote,** remedy. 673 **hardely,** surely. 674 **stoundemele,** gradually (cf. piecemeal). 675 **sikes,** sighs. M *It is of.* 676–77 Other MSS *place-space* transposed. 678 **sowneth,** sounds. 679 **twynned,** separated. 686 **stynten,** end. 693 **wende,** thought. 694 **grace,** favor (consent). 695 **hym queme,** to please him. 696 **terme,** i.e., the term of my agreement.

Ful pale ywoxen was hire brighte face,
Hire lymes lene, as she that al the day   709
Stod, whan she dorste, and loked on the place
Ther she was born and ther she dwelt hadde ay,
And al the nyght wepyng, allas, she lay.
And thus despeired out of alle cure
She ladde hire lif, this woful creature.

Ful ofte a day she syked for destresse,   715
And in hireself she wente ay portraynge
Of Troylus the grete worthinesse,
And alle his goodly wordes recordynge
Syn first that day hire love bygan to sprynge.
And thus she sette hire woful herte afyre   720
Thorugh remembraunce of that she gan desire.

In al this world ther nys so cruwel herte
That hire hadde herd compleynen in hire sorwe,
That nolde han wopen for hire peynes smerte,
So tendrely she wepte, both eve and morwe.   725
Hire nedede no teris for to borwe!
And this was yet the worste of al hire peyne,
Ther nas no wight to whom she dorste hire
    pleyne.

Ful rewfully she loked upon Troye,
Byheld the toures heygh and ek the halles.   730
"Allas," quod she, "the plesaunce and the joye,
The whiche that now al torned into galle is,
Have ich had ofte withinne tho yonder wallys.
O Troylus, what dostow now?" she seyde.
"Lord, wheyther yet thow thenke upon
    Criseyde?   735

"Allas, I ne hadde trowed on youre lore,
And went with yow, as ye me redde er this,
Thenne had I now not siked half so sore.
Who myght have seyd that I had don amys
To stele awey with swich on as he is?   740

But al to late cometh the letuarye
Whan men the cors unto the grave carye.

"To late is now to speke of this matere.
Prudence, allas, oon of thyne eyen thre
Me lakked alwey, er that I cam here!   745
On tyme ypassed wel remembred me,
And present tyme ek koud ich wel yse,
But futur tyme, er I was in the snare,
Koude I not seen—that causeth now my care.

"But natheles, bytyde what bityde,   750
I shal tomorwe at nyght, by est or west,
Out of this ost stele on som manere syde,
And gon with Troylus where as hym lest.
This purpos wol ich holde, and this is best.
No fors of wykked tonges janglerye,   755
For evere on love han wrecches had envye.

"For whoso wold of every word take hede,
Or rewelyn hym by every wightes wit,
Ne shal he nevere thryven, out of drede;
For that that som men blamen evere yit,   760
Lo, other manere folk comenden it.
And as for me, for al swych variaunce,
Felicite clepe I my suffisaunce.

"For which, withouten ony wordes mo,
To Troye I wole, as for conclusion."   765
But God it wot, er fully monthes two
She was ful fer fro that entencion.
For bothe Troylus and Troye toun
Shal knotteles thoroughout hire herte slyde,
For she wol take a purpos for t'abyde.   770

This Diomede, of whom yow telle I gan,
Gooth now withinne hymself ay arguynge,
With al the sleighte and al that evere he kan,
How he may best, with shortest taryinge,

711 MC&c *and ther* om. **713 out of,** of. **715 syked,** sighed. **716** *hireself:* other MSS *hir sowle.* **720** *woful:* M *wo* om. **728 pleyne,** complain (confide). **729 rewfully,** sadly. **730** *halles:* other MSS *walles.* **735 wheyther . . . thow,** do you. **736 trowed . . . lore,** trusted, advice. **737 redde,** advised. **738 siked,** sighed. **741 letuarye,** medicine. **744 eyen thre,** in medieval art Prudence is sometimes depicted with three eyes looking to the past, present, and future. *thre:* M *two.* **750 bytyde,** come. **752** *ost stele:* other MSS *ostel.* **755 fors . . . janglerye,** heed (care), gossiping. **758 rewelyn,** rule. **759 thryven, out of drede,** prosper, without doubt. **760 that,** that which. M *somme han blamed evere yit.* **763 Felicite . . . suffisaunce,** i.e., I call it happiness when I have what satisfies me. cf. *Boece* III. pr. 2,68. **769 knotteles,** i.e., like a thread without knots. *slyde:* other MSS *glyde.* **773 sleighte,** guile.

Into his net Criseydes herte brynge.   775
To this entent he koude nevere fyne;
To fysshen hire he leyde out hook and lyne.

But natheles, wel in his herte he thoughte
That she nas nat withoute a love in Troye.
For nevere sythen he hire thennes broughte, 780
Ne koude he sen hire laughen or maken joie.
He nyst how best hire herte for t'acoye.
"But for to assaye," he seyde, "it nought ne
    greveth,
For he that nought n'assayeth, nought
    n'acheveth."

Yet seide he to hymself upon a nyght,   785
"Now am I not a fool that wot wel how
Hire wo for love is of another wight,
And hereupon to gon assaye hire now?
I may wel wite, it nyl nat ben my prow.
For wyse folk in bokes it expresse,   790
'Men shal nat wowe a wight in hevynesse.'

But whoso myghte wynnen swych a flour
From hym for whom she morneth nyght and
    day,
He myghte seyn he were a conquerour."
And right anoon, as he that bold was ay,   795
Thoughte in his herte, "Happe how happe may.
Al sholde I deye, I wole hire herte seche.
I shal no more lesen but my speche."

This Diomede, as bokes us declare,
Was in his nedes prest and corageous,   800
With sterne voys and myghty lymes square,

Hardy, testyf, strong, and chevalrous
Of dedes, lyk his fader Tideus;
And som men seyn he was of tunge large.
And heyr he was of Calydoyne and Arge.   805

Criseyde mene was of hire stature;
Therto of shap, of face, and ek of chere,
Ther myghte ben no fayrer creature.
And ofte tyme this was hire manere,
To gon ytressed with hire heerys clere   810
Doun by hire coler at hire bak byhynde,
Which with a thred of gold she wolde bynde.

And save hire browes joyneden yfere,
Ther nas no lak in ought I kan espyen.
But for to speken of hire eyen clere,   815
Lo, trewely, thei writen that hire syen
That Paradys stood formed in hire eyen.
And with hire riche beaute everemore
Strof love in hire ay which of hem was more.

She sobre was, ek symple, and wys withal,   820
The beste ynorisshed ek that myghte be,
And goodly of hire speche in general;
Charitable, estatlych, lusty, and fre,
Ne nevere mo ne lakkede hire pyte;
Tendre-herted, slydynge of corage;   825
But trewely, I kan nat telle hire age.

And Troylus wel woxen was in highte,
And complet formed by proporcion
So wel that kynde it not amenden myghte;
Yong, fresch, strong, and hardy as lyon;   830
Trewe as stel in ech condicion;

---

776 fyne, cease. **780 sythen,** since. **782 nyst . . . acoye,** didn't know, tame (quiet). **789 prow,** profit. **791 hevynesse,** i.e., who is sad. **799–840** The portraits of Diomede, Criseyde, and Troylus are not found in *Fil*. They represent a conventional rhetorical type of which the portraits of the pilgrims in *CT* are supreme examples. The convention dates back to the "characters" of Theophrastas and leads on to the character writers of the 17th century, the character sketches in the *Spectator Papers*, etc. The ultimate source for this addition is Joseph of Exeter, *Frigii Daretis Ylias*, combined with details from Benoit and other parts of the *Filostrato*; but the portraits circulated independently, and what intermediaries Chaucer may have used has not been ascertained. **800 nedes prest,** actions, prompt. **802 Hardy, testyf . . . chevalrous,** brave, impetuous, loving chivalric combat. **804 tunge large,** tongue lax. **805 heyr of Calydoyne . . . Arge,** Calydon and Argos, cf. v.1464ff. **806 mene,** average height, but cf. i.281. **807 chere,** expression. **810–11 ytressed/Doun . . . byhynde,** i.e., hanging in braids down her back. **813 browes joyneden,** her brows met; a defect in beauty to Europeans, but a special mark of beauty in Greece and the Near East. **816 syen,** saw. **821 ynorisshed,** brought up. **823 estatlych, lusty . . . fre,** dignified, gay, generous. **825 slydynge of corage,** unstable of will; C. S. Lewis takes this to be the essential characteristic of Criseyde, which explains all of her behavior—irresolution resulting from fear. **829 kynde,** nature. **830 hardy,** brave. **831 condicion,** situation.

On of the beste enteched creature
That is or shal whil that the world may dure.

And certeynly in storye it is founde
That Troylus was nevere unto no wight,   835
As in his tyme, in no degre secounde
In dorryng don that longeth to a knyght.
Al myghte a geaunt passen hym of myght,
His herte ay with the ferste and with the beste
Stod paregal, to dorre don that hym leste.   840

But for to tellen forth of Diomede:
It fil that after, on the tenthe day
Syn that Criseyde out of the cite yede,
This Diomede, as fressh as braunche in May,
Com to the tente ther as Calkas lay,   845
And feyned hym with Calkas han to doon;
But what he mente, I shal yow telle soon.

Criseyde, at shorte wordes for to telle,
Welcomed hym and doun hym by hire sette—
And he was ethe ynowh to maken dwelle!   850
And after this, withouten more lette,
The spices and the wyn men forth hem fette,
And forth thei speke of this and that yfere,
As frendes don, of which som shal ye here.

He gan first fallen of the werre in speche   855
Bytwyxen hem and the folk of Troye toun,
And of th'assege he gan hire ek byseche
To telle hym what was hire opynyoun.
Fro that demaunde he so descendeth doun
To axen hire yf that hire straunge thoughte   860
The Grekes gyse and werkes that they
          wroughte;

And whi hire fader tarieth so longe
To wedden hire unto som worthi wight.
Criseyde, that was in hire peynes stronge
For love of Troylus, hire owene knyght,   865

As ferforth as she konnyng hadde or myght,
Answerde hym tho; but, as of his entente,
It semed not she wiste what he mente.

But natheles this ilke Diomede
Gan in hymself assure, and thus he seyde,   870
"If ich aright have taken of yow hede,
Me thenketh thus, O lady myn, Criseyde,
That syn I first hond on youre bridel leyde,
Whan ye out come of Troye by the morwe,
Ne koude I nevere sen yow but in sorwe.   875

"Kan I nat seyn what may the cause be
But if for love of som Troian it were,
The which right sore wolde athynken me
That ye for ony wight that dwelleth there
Sholden spille a quarter of a tere,   880
Or pitously yourselven so bygile,
For dredles, it is nought worth the while.

"The folk of Troye, as who seyth, alle and
          some
In preson ben, as ye youreselven se;
Fro thennes shal nat oon on-lyve come   885
For al the gold bytwixen sonne and se.
Trusteth wel and understondeth me:
Ther shal nat on to mercy gon on-lyve,
Al were he lord of worldes twyes fyve.

"Swyche wreche on hem for fecchyng of
          Eleyne   890
Ther shal ben take, er that we hennes wende,
That Manes, which that goddes ben of peyne,
Shul ben agast that Grekes wol hem shende.
And men shul drede unto the worldes ende
From hennesforth the ravesshynge of a
          queene,   895
So cruel shal oure wreche on hem be seene.

"And but if Calkas lede us with ambages—

That is to seyn, with dowble wordes sleye,
Swich as men clepe a word with two
    visages—
Ye shul wel knowen that I nought ne lye,   900
And al this thing right sen it with youre eye,
And that anoon; ye nyl not trowe how soone.
Now taketh hede, for it is for to doone.

"What, wene ye youre wyse fader wolde
Han yeven Antenor for yow anoon   905
If he ne wiste that the cite sholde
Destroyed ben? Whi nay, so mote I gon.
He knew ful wel ther shal not skapen on
That Troian is; and for the grete fere,
He dorste not ye dwelte lenger there.   910

"What wole ye more, lufsom lady dere?
Lat Troye and Troian fro youre herte pace.
Dryf out that bittre hope, and make good
    chere,
And clepe ayen the beaute of youre face,
That ye with salte terys so deface.   915
For Troye is brought in swych a jupartie
That it to save is now no remedye.

"And thenketh wel, ye shal in Grekes fynde
A more parfit love er it be nyght
Than ony Troian is, and more kynde,   920
And bet to serven yow wol don his myght.
And yf ye vouchesauf, my lady bryght,
I wol ben he to serven yow myselve,
Ye, levere than be lord of Greces twelve."

And with that word he gan to waxen red,   925
And in his speche a litel wight he quok,
And caste asyde a litle wight his hed,
And stynte a while, and afterward awok,
And sobrelych on hire he threw his lok,
And seyde, "I am, al be it yow no joye,   930
As gentil man as ony wight in Troye.

"For yf my fader Tideus," he seide,

"Ilyved hadde, ich hadde ben er this
Of Calydoyne and Arge a kyng, Criseyde,
And so hope I that I shal yet, ywys.   935
But he was slayn, allas, the more harm is,
Unhappyly at Thebes al to rathe,
Polymyte and many a man to skathe.

"But herte myn, syn that I am youre man—
And ben the ferste of whom I seche grace—   940
To serven yow as hertely as I kan,
And evere shal whil I to lyve have space,
So er that I departe out of this place,
Ye wol me graunte that I may tomorwe,
At bettre leyser, tellen yow my sorwe."   945

What shold I telle his wordes that he seyde?
He spak ynow for o day at the meste.
It preveth wel, he spak so that Criseyde
Graunted on the morwe at his requeste
For to speken with hym at the leste—   950
So that he nolde speke of swych matere.
And thus she to hym seyde as ye may here,

As she that hadde hire herte on Troylus
So faste that there may non it arace,
And strangely she spak and seyde thus,   955
"O Diomede, I love that ilke place
Ther I was born, and Joves, for his grace,
Delivere it soone of al that doth it care.
God, for thi might, so leve it wel to fare!

"That Grekes wolde hire wrath on Troye
    wreke,   960
If that thi myghte. I knowe it wel, ywys.
But it shal not bifallen as ye speke.
And God toforn, and ferther over this,
I wot my fader wys and redy is,
And that he me hath bought, as ye me tolde,
So dere; I am the more unto hym holde.   966

"That Grekes ben of heigh condicion
I wot ek wel; but certeyn, men shal fynde

---

902 trowe, believe. **904 wene,** think. **912 pace,** pass. **922 vouchesauf,** consent. **924 levere,** rather. *lord:* other MSS *kyng.* **926 wight . . . quok,** bit, shook. **928 stynte,** stopped. *awok:* C&c *he woke.* **931 gentil,** i.e., nobly born. **937 rathe,** soon, cf. v.1501. **938 Polymyte . . . skathe,** Polynices, Tydeus' ally in the war against Thebes; i.e., to the harm (*skathe*) of Polynices and many a man. **954 arace,** tear up by the roots. **958 Delivere . . . doth . . . care,** rescue, cause, hardship. **959 leve,** let. **963 toforn,** before. **966 holde,** obliged.

As worthi folk withinne Troye town,
As konnyng, and as parfit, and as kynde   970
As ben bitwyxen Orcades and Inde.
And that ye koude wel youre lady serve,
I trowe ek wel, hire thank for to deserve.

"But as to speke of love, ywys," she seyde,
"I hadde a lord, to whom I wedded was,   975
The whos myn herte al was, til that he deyde;
And other love, as help me here Pallas,
Ther in myn herte nys, ne nevere was.
And that ye ben of noble and heigh kynrede,
I have wel herd it tellen, out of drede.   980

"And that doth me to han so gret a wonder
That ye wol scornen ony womman so.
Ek God wot, love and I ben fer asonder!
I am disposed bet, so mot I go,
Unto my deth to pleyne and maken wo.   985
What I shal after don, I kan nat seye;
But trewelich, as yet me lyst not pleye.

"Myn herte is now in tribulacion,
And ye in armes bisy day by day.
Hereafter, whan ye wonnen han the town,   990
Peraunter thanne so it happen may
That whan I se that nevere yit I say,
Than wol I werke that I nevere wroughte.
This word to yow ynough suffisen oughte.   994

"Tomorwe ek wol I speke with yow feyn—
So that ye touchen nought of this matere.
And whan yow list, ye may come here
      ayeyn—
And er ye gon, thus muche I sey yow here:
As helpe me Pallas with hire heres clere,

If that I sholde of any Grek han routhe,   1000
It shulde be yourselven, by my trouthe.

"I sey not therfore that I wol yow love,
Ne sey not nay; but in conclusion,
I mene wel, by God that sit above!"
And therwithal she cast hire eyen down,   1005
And gan to syke, and seyde, "O Troye town,
Yet bidde I God in quiete and in reste
I may yow sen, or do myn herte breste."

But in effect, and shortly for to seye,
This Diomede al fresshly newe ayeyn   1010
Gan pressen on, and faste hire mercy preye;
And after this, the sothe for to seyn,
Hire glove he tok, of which he was ful feyn.
And fynally, whan it was woxen eeve,
And al was wel, he ros and tok his leeve.   1015

The bryghte Venus folewede and ay taughte
The wey there brode Phebus doun alighte;
And Cynthea hire charhors overraughte
To whirle out of the Lyon yf she myghte;
And Sygnyfer his candels shewed bryghte,   1020
When that Criseyde unto hire bedde wente
Inwith hire fadres faire bryghte tente,

Retornyng in hire soule ay up and doun
The wordes of this sodeyn Diomede,
His grete estat, and peril of the toun,   1025
And that she was allone and hadde nede
Of frendes help. And thus bygan to brede
The cause whi, the sothe for to telle,
That sche tok fully purpos for to dwelle.

The morwen come, and gostly for to speke,   1030

---

971 **Orcades,** Orkney Islands and India, i.e., the ends of the earth. 973 *ek:* other MSS *it.* 977 **Pallas,** Pallas Athene, patron goddess of Troy. 982 **scornen,** mock. 984 **disposed bet, so mot I go,** more inclined, if I might so do. 985 **Unto . . . pleyne,** until, complain. 986 **after,** afterward. 987 **me lyst,** pleases me. M *trewely/to pleye.* 989 *bisy:* M *ben.* 992 **say,** saw. M&c *that I nevere er say;* other MSS various readings. 993 **werke . . . wroughte,** i.e., do, done (work, worked). 995 **feyn,** happily. 1000 **routhe,** pity. 1006 **syke,** sigh. M *O Troylus and Troye town.* 1007 **bidde,** pray. 1008 **breste,** break (burst). 1013 **glove,** the detail of the glove, lacking in *Fil.,* is found in both Benoit and Guido, but when Diomede first delivers Criseyde to her father's tent. 1016–17 **taughte . . . brode Phebus,** Venus, the evening star, pointed to (*taughte*) the direction in which the sun had set. Venus, as goddess of love, had no interest in fidelity but encouraged any love. 1018–19 **Cynthea . . . the Lyon,** Cynthia, the moon, urged on (*overraughte,* reached over) her chariot horse to reach the end of the zodiacal sign of Leo, at which point the ten days would be over, cf. iv.1592n. 1020 **Sygnyfer . . . candels . . . bryghte,** the belt of sky bearing the signs of the zodiac, whose stars (*candels*) shine brightly because Leo is the dark of the moon. *bryghte:* other MSS *lighte.* 1021 *bedde:* other MSS *reste.* 1030 **gostly,** spiritually, i.e., truly.

This Diomede is come unto Criseyde;
And shortly, lest that ye my tale breke,
So wel for hymself he spak and seyde
That alle hire sore sykes adoun he leyde.
And finally, the sothe for to seyne,   1035
He refte hire of the grete of al hire peyne.

And after this the story telleth us
That she hym yaf the fayre baye stede,
The which he onys wan of Troylus;
And ek a broche—and that was litel nede—   1040
That Troylus was, she yaf this Diomede.
And ek, the bet from sorwe hym to releve,
She made hym were a pencel of hire sleve.

I fynde ek in storyes ellyswhere,
Whan thorugh the body hurt was Diomede 1045
Of Troylus, tho wepte she many a tere,
Whan that she saugh his wyde wowndes blede;
And that she tok to kepen hym good hede;
And for to helen hym of his sorwes smerte,
Men seyn—I not—that she yaf hym hire
        herte.   1050

But trewely, the story telleth us,
Ther made nevere woman more wo
Than she whan that she falsed Troylus.
She seyde, "Allas, for now is clene ago
My name of trouthe in love for everemo!   1055
For I have falsed oon the gentileste
That evere was, and oon the worthieste.

"Allas, of me unto the worldes ende
Shal neyther ben ywriten nor isonge
No good word, for these bokes wol me shende.
O, rolled shal I ben on many a tonge;   1061
Thoroughout the world my belle shal be ronge!
And wommen most wol hate me of alle.
Allas, that swych a cas me sholde falle!

"Thei wol seyn, inasmuche as in me is,   1065
I have hem don dishonour, weylaway!
Al be I not the firste that dide amys,
What helpeth that to don my blame awey?
But syn I se ther is no bettre way,
And that to late is now for me to rewe,   1070
To Diomede algate I wol be trewe.

"But, Troylus, syn I no beter may,
And syn that thus departen ye and I,
Yet preye I God so yeve yow right good day
As for the gentileste, trewely,   1075
That evere I say to serven feythfully,
And best kan ay his lady honour kepe."
And with that word she brast anon to wepe.

"And certes, yow ne haten shal I nevere;
And frendes love, that shal ye han of me,   1080
And my good word, al myght y lyven evere.
And, trewely, I wolde sory be
For to sen yow in adversite;
And gilteles, I wot wel, I yow leve.
But al shal passe; and thus take I my leve." 1085

But trewely, how longe it was bytwene
That she forsok hym for this Diomede,
Ther is noon auctour telleth it, I wene.
Tak every man now to his bokes hede:
He shal no terme fynden, out of drede.   1090
For though that he gan for to wowe hire
        sone,
Er he hire wan yet was ther more to done.
Ne me ne lyst this sely womman chyde
Ferther than this story wol devyse.
Hire name, allas, is punysshed so wyde   1095
That for hire gilt it oughte ynow suffise.
And yf I myghte excuse hire ony wyse,
For she so sory was for hire untrouthe,
Iwys, I wolde excuse hire yet for routhe.

1032 breke, interrupt. **1036 refte ... grete,** relieved, greater part. **1038 baye stede,** this enigmatic detail is not found in *Fil.,* but adopted from Benoit, *Roman de Troie,* 15079ff., where it is told in more detail. Diomede had captured Troylus' charger and presented it to Criseida; when he loses his own, he asks her to return the gift. **1039 he|wan:** other MSS *she|had.* **1043 pencel,** strip (pencil); a typical lady's favor in the romances. This detail again is in Benoit (l. 15176) but not in *Fil.* **1048 kepen,** tend. **1050 not,** don't know. **1060 shende,** disgrace. **1065 inasmuche ... is,** i.e., in so far as I can. **1070 rewe,** be sorry. M *for* om. **1071 algate,** at least. **1076 say,** saw. **1079 ne haten:** M *to haten.* **1081 M** *Almyghty leven;* C&c *al sholde I lyven.* **1084 leve,** believe. **1090 out of drede,** without doubt. **1091** *wowe:* other MSS *love.* **1093 sely,** foolish. **1094 devyse,** relate. **1095** *punysshed:* other MSS *published.* **1099 routhe,** pity.

This Troylus, as I byforn have told,   1100
Thus dryveth forth as wel as he hath myght.
But often was his herte hot and cold,
And namely that ilke nynthe nyght
Which on the morwe she hadde hym byhight
To come ayeyn. God wot, ful litel reste   1105
Hadde he that nyght—nothing to slepe hym
      leste.

The laurer-crowned Phebus with his hete
Gan in his course, ay upward as he wente,
To warmen of the Est See the wawes wete,
And Nisus doughter song with fressh entente,
Whan Troylus his Pandare after sente,   1111
And on the walles of the toun they pleyde,
To loke if they kan sen ought of Criseyde.

Til it was noone thei stoden for to se
Who that ther come, and every maner wight
That kam fro fer, thei seyden it was she   1116
Til that thei koude knowen hym aright.
Now was hire herte dul, now was it light.
And thus byjaped stonden for to stare
Aboute nought this Troylus and Pandare.   1120

To Pandarus this Troylus tho seyde,
"For ought I wot, byfor noon, sykerly,
Into this town ne cometh nought Criseyde.
She hath ynow to done, hardyly,
To twynnen from hire fader, so trowe I.   1125
Hire olde fader wole yet make hire dyne
Er that she go—God yeve hys herte pyne!"

Pandare answerde, "It may wel be, certeyn.
And forthi lat us dyne, I the byseche.   1129
And after noon than maystow come ayeyn."
And hom thei go withoute more speche,
And comen ayen. But longe may they seche

Er that they fynde that they after gape—
Fortune hem bothe thenketh for to jape.

Quod Troylus, "I se wel now that she   1135
Is taried with hire olde fader so
That er she come it wol neygh even be.
Com forth; I wole unto the yate go.
Thise porterys ben unkonnynge everemo,
And I wol don hem holden up the yate   1140
As nought ne were, although she come late."

The day goth faste, and after that come eve,
And yet com nought to Troylus Criseyde.
He loketh forth by hegge, by tree, by greve,
And fer his hed over the wal he leyde,   1145
And at the laste he torned hym and seyde,
"By God, I wot hire menyng now, Pandare—
Almost, ywys, al newe was my care—

"Now douteles, this lady kan hire good.
I wot she meneth ryden pryvely.   1150
I comende hire wysdom, by myn hood!
She wol not maken peple nicely
Gaure on hire whan she comth, but softely
By nyghte into the toun she thenketh ryde.
And, dere brother, thenk not to longe
      t'abyde—   1155

"We han not ellys for to don, ywys.
And Pandarus, now woltow trowen me?
Have here my trouthe, I se hire! Yond she is!
Heve up thyn eyen, man! Maystow not se?"
Pandare answerede, "Nay, so mot I the.   1160
Al wrong, by Gode. What seystow, man,
      where arte?
That I se yond nys but a fare-carte."

"Allas, thow seist right soth," quod Troylus.

1103 *nynthe:* other MSS *tenthe/selven.* **1104 byhight,** promised. **1106 hym leste,** he desired. **1107 laurer . . . Phebus,** laurel, the sun. **1110 Nisus doughter,** metamorphosed into a lark for killing her father, Ovid, *Met.* 8.11ff. **1112 pleyde,** diverted themselves. **1118 hire,** their. C&c *his.* **1119 byjaped,** tricked. **1122 sykerly,** surely. **1125 twynnen . . . trowe,** separate (get away), believe. C&c *wynnen.* **1129 forthi,** therefore. **1133 gape,** stare. M&c *cape.* **1134 jape,** trick. **1139 porterys . . . unkonnynge,** gatekeepers, stupid. **1140 don . . . holden up,** make; Chaucer obviously thought of the gate as being a portcullis that was hoisted and lowered. **1141 As nought ne were,** i.e., casually; gates ordinarily had to be shut at a specified time. **1144 greve,** thicket. **1147 menyng,** intention. **1149 hire good,** knows what is best for her. **1152 nicely,** foolishly. **1153 Gaure . . . softely,** stare, quietly (secretly). **1155 t'abyde,** to wait. **1157 trowen,** believe. **1159 Heve,** raise. **1160 the,** prosper. **1161 seystow,** do you see (?). C&c *saistow* (do you say). **1162 fare-cart,** work cart.

"But, hardely, it is not all for nought
That in myn herte I now rejoyse thus.   1165
It is ayen som good I have a thought.
Not I not how, but syn that I was wrought
Ne felt I swich a confort, dar I seye.
She comth tonyght, my lyf that dorste I
      leye!"   1169

Pandare answerde, "It may be, wel ynowh,"
And held with hym of al that evere he seyde.
But in his herte he thoughte, and softe lough,
And to hymself ful sobreliche he seyde,
"From haselwode, there joly Robyn pleyde,
Shal come al that that thow abydest here.   1175
Ye, farewel al the snow of ferne yere!"

The wardeyn of the yates gan to calle
The folk which that withoute the yates were,
And bad hem dryven in hire bestes alle,
Or al the nyght they moste bleven there.   1180
And fer withinne the nyght, with many a tere,
This Troylus gan homward for to ryde,
For wel he seth it helpeth nought t'abyde.

But natheles, he gladed hym yn thys:
He thought he mysacounted hadde his day, 1185
And seyde, "I understonde have al amys.
For thilke nyght I last Criseyde say,
She seyde, 'I shal ben here, yf that I may,
Er that the mone, O dere herte swete,
The Lyon passe out of this Ariete.'   1190

"For which she may yet holde al hire byheste."
And on the morwe unto the yate he wente,
And up and down, by west and ek by este,
Upon the walles made he many a wente—   1194
But al for nought; his hope alwey hym blente.
For which at nyght yn sorwe and sykes sore
He wente hym hom withouten ony more.

His hope al clene out of his herte is fledde,
He nath wheron now lenger for to honge,
But for the peyne hym thoughte his herte
      bledde,   1200
So were his throwes sharpe and wonder stronge.
For when he saugh that she abood so longe,
He nyste what he juggen of it myghte,
Syn she hath broken that she hym byhyghte.

The thridde, ferthe, fifthe, sixte day   1205
After tho dayes ten of which I tolde,
Bytwyxen hope and drede his herte lay,
Yet somwhat trustyng on hire hestes olde.
But whan he saugh she nolde hire terme holde,
He kan now sen noon other remedye   1210
But for to shape hym soone for to dye.

Therwith the wykked spyrit—God us
      blesse—
Which that men clepeth the wode jalousye,
Gan in hym crepe, in al this hevynesse,
For whiche, by cause he wold soone dye,   1215
He ne eet ne dronk, for his malencolye,
And ek from every compaignye he fledde—
This was the lyf that al the tyme he ledde.

He so defet was that no manere man
Unneth myghte hym knowe ther he wente; 1220
So was he lene, and therto pale and wan,
And feble, that he walketh by potente;
And with his ire he thus hymselve shente.
And whoso axed hym wherof hym smerte,
He seyde his harm was al aboute his herte. 1225

Pryam ful ofte, and ek his moder dere,
His bretheren and his sustren, gonne hym freyne
Why he so sorwful was in al his chere,
And what thyng was the cause of al his peyne.
But al for nought: he nolde his cause pleyne,

1171 held, agreed. **1172 lough,** laughed. **1174 haselwode . . . Robyn,** i.e., from the land of make-believe. Robin and Marion were the names of the protagonists in saccharine French *pastourelles* and the English Robin Hood ballads, which were already current by Chaucer's time. **1175 abydest,** wait for. **1176 snow of ferne yere,** one is reminded of Villon's "*Mais où sont les neiges d'antan!*" **1180 bleven,** remain. **1186 understonde,** understood. **1187 say,** saw. **1191 byheste,** promise. **1195 blente,** deceived. **1196 sykes,** sighs. **1199 nath,** has nothing. **1201 throwes,** agonies (throes). **1204 byhyghte,** promised. **1208 hestes olde,** former promises. **1211 shape,** prepare. **1213 wode,** insane. **1219 defet,** disfigured. **1220 Unneth,** scarcely. **1222 potente,** crutch. **1223 shente,** destroyed. **1227 freyne,** inquire. **1228 chere,** expression, behavior. **1230 pleyne,** lament (reveal).

But seyde he felte a grevous maledye 1231
Aboute his herte, and fayn he wolde dye.

So on a day he leyde hym doun to slepe,
And so byfel that yn his slep hym thoughte
That in a forest faste he welk to wepe 1235
For love of here that hym these peynes
    wroughte,
And up and doun as he the forest soughte,
He mette he saugh a bor with tuskes grete,
That slepte ayeyn the bryghte sonnes hete.

And by this bor, faste in hir armes folde, 1240
Lay kyssyng ay his lady bryght Criseyde.
For sorwe of which, whan he it gan byholde,
And for despit, out of his slep he breyde,
And loude he cride on Pandarus and seyde,
"O Pandarus, now know I crop and rote! 1245
I n'am but ded; ther nys non other bote!

"My lady bryght Criseyde hath me bytrayed,
In whom I trusted most of ony wight.
She elliswhere hath now here herte apayed.
The blysful goddes thorugh here grete myght
Han in my drem yshewed it ful right. 1251
Thus in my drem Criseyde I have byholde"—
And al this thing to Pandarus he tolde.

"O my Criseyde, allas, what subtilte, 1254
What newe lust, what beaute, what science,
What wratthe of juste cause have ye to me?
What gilt of me, what fel experience,
Hath fro me raft, allas, thyn advertence?
O trust, O feyth, O depe aseuraunce! 1259
Who hath me reft Criseyde, al my plesaunce?

"Allas, whi leet I you from hennes go,

For which wel neigh out of my wit I breyde?
Who shal now trowe on ony othes mo?
God wot, I wende, O lady bright Criseyde,
That every word was gospel that ye seyde! 1265
But who may bet bigile, yf hym lyste,
Than he on whom men wenen best to triste?

"What shal I don, my Pandarus? Allas,
I fele now so sharp a newe peyne,
Syn that ther is no remedye in this cas, 1270
That bet were it I with myn hondes tweyne
Myselven slowh alwey than thus compleyne.
For thorugh my deth my wo shal han an ende,
Ther every day with lyf myself I shende."

Pandare answerde and seyde, "Allas the while
That I was born. Have I not seyd er this 1276
That dremes many a maner man bygyle?
And whi? For folk expounden hem amys.
How darstow seyn that fals thi lady ys
For ony drem right for thyn owene drede? 1280
Lat be this thought; thow kanst no dremes rede.

"Peraunter, there thow dremest of this bor,
It may so be that it may signyfie
Hire fader, which that old is and ek hor,
Ayen the sonne lith o poynt to dye, 1285
And she for sorwe gynneth wepe and crye,
And kysseth hym, there he lyth on the
    grounde—
Thus sholdestow thi drem aright expounde."

"How myghte I thanne do," quod Troylus, 1289
"To knowe of this, ye, were it nevere so lite?"
"Now seystow wysly," quod this Pandarus.
"My reede is this: syn thow kanst wel endite,
That hastely a lettre thow hire write,

1232 fayn, gladly. **1235 faste . . . welk,** dense, walked. *welk:* other MSS *wente/walked.* **1239 ayeyn,** in. **1240** *hir:* M&c *his.* **1243 despit . . . breyde,** chagrin, started. **1245 crop and rote,** i.e., beginning and end. **1246 bote,** remedy. **1254 subtilte,** guile. **1255 lust . . . science,** desire, knowledge. **1256 wratthe,** i.e., just cause of wrath. **1257 gilt of me . . . fel,** guilt of mine, dreadful. **1258 raft . . . advertence,** torn, attention. **1259 aseuraunce,** assurance. **1260 me reft,** i.e., deprived me of (torn from me). **1262 breyde,** start (go). **1264 wende,** believed. **1266 bet bigile,** better deceive. **1274 shende,** destroy. **1277 bygyle,** deceive. In *Fil.* 7.27ff., Troilo understands at once from the dream that Diomede is Criseida's lover, and Pandaro merely suggests that he test the validity of the dream by writing to her. **1278** *folk:* M *men.* **1280 For ony . . . right for . . . drede,** because of, just because of, fear (that she may be false). **1282 there,** where. **1285** *o poynt:* other MSS *on/in/up.* **1290 were it nevere so lite,** i.e., though what I might learn were ever so little. **1292 reede . . . endite,** advice, compose.

Thorugh which thow shalt wel bryngen it
    aboute
To knowe a soth of that thow art in doute. 1295

"And se now why: for this I dar wel seyn,
That if so is that she untrewe be,
I kan nat trowen that she wol write ayeyn.
And yf she write, thow shalt ful soone se
As wheyther she hath ony liberte 1300
To come ayen; or ellys yn som clause,
If she be let, she wol assigne a cause.

"Thow hast nat wreten hire syn that she wente,
Nor she to the; and this I dorste leye,
There may swych cause ben in hire entente 1305
That, hardely, thow wolt thiselven seye
That hire abod the beste is for yow tweye.
Now write hire thanne, and thow shalt fele sone
A soth of al. Ther is no more to done."

Accorded ben to this conclusioun, 1310
And that anoon, these ilke lordes two;
And hastely sit Troylus adoun,
And rolleth yn his herte to and fro
How he may best discryven hire his wo.
And to Criseyde, his owene lady dere, 1315
He wrot right thus, and seyde as ye may here.

Litera Troili

"Right fresshe flour, whos I ben have and shal,
Withouten part of elliswhere servise,
With herte, body, lyf, lust, thought, and al,
I, woful wight, in everich humble wyse 1320
That tonge telle or herte may devyse,
As ofte as matere occupieth place,
Me recomaunde unto youre noble grace.

"Liketh it yow to witen, swete herte,
As ye wel knowe, how longe tyme agon 1325

That ye me lafte yn aspre peynes smerte,
Whan that ye went, of which yet bote non
Have I non had, but evere wors bygon
Fro day to day am I, and so mot dwelle,
While it yow lyst, of wele and wo my
    welle. 1330

"For which to yow with dredful herte trewe
I wryte, as he that sorwe dryfth to wryte,
My wo, that everich houre encreseth newe,
Compleynyng, as I dar or kan endite.
And that defaced is, that may ye wyte 1335
The terys which that fro myn eyen reyne,
That wolde speke, yf that they koude, and
    pleyne.

"Yow first biseche I that youre eyen clere
To look on this defouled ye not holde,
And over al this, that ye, my lady dere, 1340
Wol vouchesauf this lettre to byholde.
And by the cause ek of my cares colde,
That sleth my wit, if ought amys m'asterte,
Foryeve it me, myn owene swete herte.

"Yf ony servant dorste or oughte of ryght 1345
Upon hys lady pytously compleyne,
Thanne wene I that ich oughte be that wyght,
Considered this, that ye these monethes
    tweyne
Han taried there ye seyden, soth to seyne,
But dayes ten ye nolde in ost sojourne— 1350
But yn two monethes yet ye nat retourne.

"But for as muche as me mot nedes lyke
Al that yow lyste, I dar not pleyne more,
But humbely, with sorwful sykes syke,
Yow wryte ich myn unresty sorwes sore, 1355
Fro day to day desyryng everemore
To knowen fully, yf youre wil it were,
How ye han ferd and don whyl ye be there;

1295 Other MSS *ther thow art now in.* 1302 **let,** prevented. 1304 **leye,** bet. 1306 **hardely,** certainly. 1309 **A soth,** i.e., the truth. 1314 **discryven,** describe. 1318 **part . . . elliswhere,** i.e., with no part of my service given elsewhere. 1322 **ofte,** i.e., long (always). 1326 **aspre,** bitter. 1327 **bote,** remedy. 1330 **yow lyst,** pleases you. 1331 **dredful,** fearful. 1332 **dryfth,** drives. 1335 **that defaced . . . wyte,** that (the letter) is defaced, blame. 1337 **pleyne,** lament. 1339 **defouled,** i.e., that you don't consider your eyes befouled by looking on this letter. 1341 **vouchesauf,** consent. 1342 **by the cause,** because. 1343 **sleth . . . m'asterte,** slays, escapes from me. 1350 **in ost,** (the Greek) host. 1352 **me . . . lyke,** please me. *me:* M *I.* 1354 **sykes syke,** sighs sick. 1355 **unresty,** unquiet.

"The whos welfare and hele ek God encresse
In honour swych that upward in degre   1360
It growe alwey, so that it nevere cesse.
Right as youre herte ay kan, my lady fre,
Devyse, I prey to God, so mot it be,
And graunte it that ye soone upon me rewe,
As wysly as in al I am yow trewe.   1365

"And if yow lyketh knowen of the fare
Of me, whos wo ther may no wit discryve,
I kan no more but, chyste of every care,
At writyng of this letre I was on-lyve,
Al redy out my woful gost to dryve,   1370
Which I delaye, and holde hym yet in honde,
Upon the sighte of matere of youre sonde.

"Myn eyen two, in veyn with which I se,
Of sorweful teres salte arn woxen wellys;
My song yn pleynte of myn adversite;   1375
My good yn harme; myn ese ek woxen helle ys;
My joye yn wo. I kan sey yow nought ellys,
But turned ys—for which my lyf I warye—
Everych joye or ese in his contrarye.   1379

"Which with youre comyng hom ayen to Troye
Ye may redresse, and more a thousand sithe
Than evere ych hadde encressen yn me joye.
For was there nevere herte yet so blythe
To han his lyf as I shal ben as swythe
As I yow se. And though no manere routhe 1385
Commeve yow, yet thynketh on youre trouthe.

"And yf so be my gilt hath deth deserved,
Or yf yow lyst no more upon me se,
In guerdoun yet of that I have yow served,
Biseche I yow, myn hertes lady fre,   1390
That hereupon ye wolden wryte me,
For love of God, my righte lode-sterre,
That deth may make an ende of al my werre.

"If other cause aught dothe yow for to dwelle,
That with youre lettre ye me recomforte,   1395
For though to me youre absence is an helle,
With pacience I wol my wo comporte,
And with youre lettre of hope I wol desporte.
Now writeth, swete, and lat me thus not
    pleyne,
With hope or deth delyvereth me fro peyne.

"Ywys, myn owene dere herte trewe,   1401
I wot that whan ye next upon me se,
So lost have I myn hele and ek myn hewe,
Criseyde shal nought konne knowen me.
Iwys, myn hertes day, my lady fre,   1405
So thursteth ay myn herte to biholde
Youre beaute that my lyf unnethe I holde.

"I say no more, al have I for to seye
To yow wel more than I telle may,
But whether that ye do me lyve or deye,   1410
Yet pray I God, so yeve yow right good day.
And fareth wel, goodly, fayre, fresshe may,
As ye that lyf and deth me may comaunde.
And to youre trouthe ay I me recomaunde,

"With hele swych but that ye yeven me   1415
The same hele, I shal noon hele have.
In yow lyth, whan yow lyst that it so be,
The day yn which me clothen shal my grave;
In yow my lyf, in yow myght for to save
Me fro dyshese of alle peynes smerte;   1420
And fare now wel, myn owene swete herte.
                    le vostre T."

This lettre forth was sent unto Criseyde,
Of which hire answere yn effect was this:
Ful pytously she wrot ayen and seyde
That also soone as that she myghte, ywys, 1425
She wolde come and mende al that was mys;

1359 **hele,** health (well-being). 1363 **Devyse,** determine. 1364 **rewe,** have pity. 1366 **the fare,** the progress (i.e., how I am getting along). 1367 **wit:** M *wight.* 1368 **chyste,** (like a) chest (receptacle). 1369 **on-lyve,** alive. 1370 **gost,** spirit. 1372 **sighte . . . sonde,** i.e., in anticipation of the content (*matere*) of your message (*sonde*). 1373–79 The letter offers an opportunity for another series of troubadourlike oxymora. 1378 **warye,** curse. 1381 **sithe,** times. 1384 **swythe,** soon. 1385 **routhe,** pity. 1386 **Commeve . . . trouthe,** move, promise (troth). 1388 **no more:** M *no manere.* 1389 **guerdoun,** reward. 1390 *hertes:* C&c *owen.* 1392 **lode-sterre,** guiding star. 1394 **dothe,** compels. 1398 **desporte,** take comfort. 1403 **hele,** health. 1404 **konne,** be able. 1407 **unnethe,** scarcely. 1408 **al,** although. 1412 **may,** maid. 1413 *ye:* other MSS *she.* 1415 **hele,** health. 1418 **clothen,** enclose (clothe). 1419 **myght,** power. 1421 M omits *le vostre T.*

And fynally she wrot and seyde hym thanne,
She wolde come, ye, but she nyste whanne.

But yn hire lettre made she swyche festes
That wonder was, and swereth she loveth hym
    best;   1430
Of which he fond but botmeles byhestes.
But Troylus, thow mayst now, est or west,
Pype yn an ivy lef, yf that the lest.
Thus goth the world, God shylde us fro
    myschaunce,
And every wight that meneth trouthe avaunce!

Encressen gan the wo fro day to nyght   1436
Of Troylus for taryinge of Criseyde,
And lessen gan his hope and ek his myght,
For which al doun he yn his bed hym leyde.
He ne eet, ne dronk, ne slep, ne word ne seyde,
Ymagynyng ay that she was unkynde,   1441
For which wel neigh he wax out of his
    mynde.

This drem of which I told have ek byforn
May nevere come out of his remembraunce.
He thought ay wel he hadde his lady lorn,   1445
And that Joves, of his purveyaunce,
Hym shewed hadde in sleep the signyfyaunce
Of hire untrothe and his disaventure,
And that the bor was shewed hym yn figure.

For which he for Sibille his suster sente,   1450
That called was Cassandre ek al aboute,
And al his drem he tolde hire er he stente,
And hire bisoughte assoylen hym the doute
Of the stronge bor with tuskes stoute;
And fynally, withinne a lytel stounde,   1455

Cassandre hym gan right thus hys drem
    expounde.

She gan first smyle, and seyde, "O brother dere,
If thow a soth of this desirest knowe,
Thow most a fewe of olde storyes here,
To purpos how that Fortune overthrowe   1460
Hath lordes olde, thorugh which, withinne a
    throwe,
Thow wel this bor shalt knowe, and of what
    kynde
He comen is, as men yn bokes fynde.

"Diane, which that wroth was and yn ire
For Grekes nolde don hire sacrifise,   1465
Ne encens upon hire auter sette afyre,
She, for that Grekes gonne hire so dispise,
Wrak hire in a wonder cruwel wyse:
For with a bor as grete as oxe in stalle
She made up frete hire corn and vynes alle.   1470

"To sle this bor was al the contre reysed,
Amonges which ther com this bor to se
A mayde, on of this world the beste ypreysed.
And Meleagre, lord of that contre,
He loved so this fresshe mayde fre,   1475
That with his manhod, er he wolde stente,
This bor he slow, and hire the hed he sente.

"Of which, as olde bokes tellen us,
Ther ros a contek and a gret envye.
And of this lord descendede Tydeus   1480
By ligne, or ellys olde bokes lye.
But how this Meleagre gan to dye
Thorugh his moder wol I yow not telle,
For al to longe it were for to dwelle."

1429 festes, sweetnesses. **1431 botmeles byhestes,** baseless (bottomless) promises. **1433 Pype . . . ivy lef,** "go whistle." **1446 purveyaunce,** providence (foreknowledge). **1448** *his:* M *here.* **1449 yn figure,** symbolically. **1450 Sibille,** "sibyl" means simply prophetess, but medieval writers took it as an alternative name for Cassandra. **1452 stente,** stopped. **1453 assoylen,** absolve (remove from). **1455 stounde,** while. **1461 throwe,** little while. **1462 kynde,** lineage. **1464ff. Diane,** Diane, Atalanta, and the story of the Calydonian boar is told, among others, by Ovid, *Met.* 8.271ff. **1467 gonne,** began. **1468 Wrak,** revenged. **1470 frete hire,** eat (cf. Ger. distinction between *essen* and *fressen*) their. **corn,** grain. **1471 reysed,** roused to arms. **1474 Meleagre,** son of the Calydonian king, who led the band that slew the boar and fell in love with Atalanta. **1476 stente,** stop. **1479 contek,** strife. Meleager's uncles protested his giving the boar's head to Atalanta, for which he killed them. **1480 Tydeus,** Tydeus was actually Meleager's half-brother. The error is found in *Fil.* 7.27 although Boccaccio has the relationship correct in *De Geneologia Deorum* 9. **1482 gan to dye,** the Fates had indicated at his birth that he would live as long as a piece of wood in the fire was unconsumed. His mother seized it and hid it. When he killed her brothers in the quarrel over the boar's head, she brought it out in anger and threw it on the fire.

She tolde ek how Tydeus, er she stente, 1485
Unto the stronge cite of Thebes,
To cleymen kyngdom of the cite, wente,
For his felawe daun Polymytes,
Of which the brother daun Ethyocles
Ful wrongfully of Thebes held the strengthe—
This tolde she by proces al the lengthe. 1491

She tolde ek how Hemonydes asterte
Whan Tydeus slowh fifty knyghtes stoute;
She tolde ek alle the prophesies by herte,
And how that seven kynges with hire route 1495
Bysegeden the cite al aboute;
And of the holy serpent, and the welle,
And of the furyes, al she gan hym telle;

Of Archymoris burynge and the pleyes,
And how Amphiorax fil thorugh the grounde;
How Tydeus was slayn, lord of Argeyes, 1501
And how Ypomedon y lytel stounde
Was dreynt, and ded Parthonope of wounde;
And also how Cappaneus the proude
With thonder-dynt was slayn, that cryde
loude. 1505

She gan ek telle hym how that eyther brother,
Ethyocles and Polymyte also,
At a scarmyche eche of hem slowh other,
And of Argyves wepynge and hire wo; 1509
And how the town was brent, she tolde ek tho.
And so descendeth doun from gestes olde
To Diomede, and thus she spak and tolde:

"This ilke bor bytokeneth Diomede,
Tydeus sone, that down descended is
Fro Meleagre, that made the bor to blede. 1515
And thy lady, where that she be, ywis,
This Dyomede hire herte hath and she his.
Wep if thow wolt, or leef, for out of doute,
This Diomede is inne and thow art oute."

"Thow seyst nat soth," quod he, "thou
sorceresse! 1520
With al thi fals gost of prophesie,
Thow wenest ben a grete devyneresse!
Now seystow not this fol of fantasye
Peyneth hire on ladyes for to lye? 1524
Awey," quod he, "ther Joves yeve the sorwe!
Thow shalt be fals, peraunter, yet tomorwe!

"As wel thow myghtest lyen on Alceste,
That was of creatures—but men lye—
That evere weren, kyndest and the beste.
For whanne hire housbonde was in jupartie 1530
To dye hymself, but yf she wolde dye,
She ches for hym to dye and go to helle,
And starf anoon, as us the bokes telle."

Cassandre goth, and he with cruwel herte
Foryat his wo, for angre of hire speche, 1535
And from his bed al sodeynly he sterte
As though al hol hym hadde ymade a leche.
And day by day he gan enquere and seche
A sooth of this with al his fulle cure;
And thus he drieth forth his aventure. 1540

1485ff. Here we have a brief summary of the *Thebaid* of Statius, the source of the material for Boccaccio's *Teseida* and, ultimately, Chaucer's *Knight's Tale*. **stente,** stopped. **1487 cleymen kyngdom,** claim kingship. **1488–89 daun Polymytes . . . Ethyocles,** don or dom (from Lat. *dominus,* master). In *Theb.* Polynices and Eteocles, sons of Oedipus, were to be alternate rulers of Thebes. But Eteocles would not relinquish the rule when his turn was up, so Polynices secured the assistance of six other champions, among them Tydeus, to wrest it from him. All but one were killed in the conflict. **1491 by proces,** in detail. *the*: C&c *by*. **1492 Hemonydes asterte,** a Theban warrior escaped. **1494 prophesies,** perhaps an allusion to the prophecies at the end of Bk. III of *Theb.* **1495 route,** company. **1497 holy serpent . . . welle,** in another episode in *Theb.* v; while a seeress is directing the attacking army to Thebes, Jupiter sends a serpent that kills her infant son, Archemorus. **1500 Amphiorax,** Amphiaraus, one of the seven kings, was swallowed by the earth just as he was about to be taken prisoner. At this point nearly all MSS have a 12-line Latin verse summary of *Theb.,* which Root attributes to Chaucer himself. **1501ff. Tydeus . . . Ypomedon . . . Parthonope . . . Cappaneus,** these lines detail the deaths of the other four of the seven kings. For Polynices see l. 1507 below. Only Adrastus emerged alive from the disastrous war. **1501 Argeyes,** Argives, inhabitants of Argos. **1502 stounde,** while. *y*: C&c *a/in.* **1503 dreynt,** drowned. **1505 dynt,** bolt, from Jupiter. **1509 Argyves,** Argia's (wife of Polynices). **1518 leef,** leave off weeping. **1521 gost,** spirit. **1522 devyneresse,** diviner (fore-teller). **1523 seystow . . . fol of fantasye,** do you not see (rhetorical question, not addressed to Cassandra), deluded fool. **1524 Peyneth hire on,** takes pains about. **1527 Alceste,** the type of a perfect wife, cf. Alceste in *LGW.* **1533 starf,** died. **1537 leche,** physician. **1539 A sooth . . . cure,** i.e., the truth, care (attention). **1540 drieth forth,** suffers through.

Fortune, whiche that permutacioun
Of thinges hath, as it is hire commytted
Thorugh purveyaunce and disposicioun
Of heyghe Jove, as regnes shal ben flytted 1544
Fro folk yn folk, or when they shal ben smytted,
Gan pulle awey the fetheres brighte of Troye
Fro day to day, til they ben bare of joye.

Among al this, the fyn of the parodye
Of Ector gan aprochen wonder blyve.
The fate wolde his soule sholde unbodye, 1550
And shapen hadde a mene it out to dryve,
Ayeyns which fate hym helpeth not to stryve;
But on a day to fyghten gan he wende,
At which, allas, he caught his lyves ende.

For which methenketh every manere wight 1555
That haunteth armes oughte to bywayle
The deth of hym that was so noble a knyght;
For as he drough a kyng by th'aventayle,
Unwar of this, Achilles thorugh the mayle 1559
And thorugh the body gan hym for to ryve;
And thus this worthi knyght was brought of
    lyve.

For whom, as olde bokes tellen us,
Was mad swych wo that tonge may it not telle,
And namely the sorwe of Troylus,
That next hym was of worthinesse welle. 1565
And yn this wo gan Troylus to dwelle,
That, what for sorwe, and love, and for unreste,
Ful ofte a day he bad his herte breste.

But natheles, though he gan hym dispeyre,
And dradde ay that his lady was untrewe, 1570
Yet ay on hire his herte gan repeyre.
And as thise loveres don, he soughte ay newe
To gete ayen Criseyde, bright of hewe;
And in his herte he wente hire excusynge

That Calkas caused al hire taryinge. 1575

And ofte tyme he was yn purpose grete
Hymselven lyk a pylgrym to desgyse
To sen hire, but he may not contrefete
To ben unknowen of folk that weren wyse,
Ne fynde excuse aright that may suffise, 1580
Yf he among the Grekes knowen were,
For which he wep ful ofte many a tere.

To hire he wrot yet ofte tyme al newe
Ful pitously—he lefte it nought for slouthe—
Bisechyng hire, syn that he was trewe, 1585
That she wolde come ayeyn and holde hire
    trowthe.
For which Criseyde upon a day, for routhe—
I take it so—towchyng this matere,
Wrot hym ayeyn, and seyde as ye may here:

Litera Criseydis

"Cupides sone, ensample of goodlihede, 1590
O swerd of knyghthod, sours of gentilesse,
How myght a wyght in torment and in drede
And heeleles, yow sende as yet gladnesse—
I herteles, I syke, I yn distresse?
Syn ye with me nor I with yow may dele, 1595
Yow neyther sende ich herte may nor hele.

"Youre lettres ful, the papir al ypleynted,
Conseyved hath myn hertes piete.
I have ek seyn with terys al depeynted
Youre lettre, and how that ye requeren me 1600
To come ayen, which yet ne may not be.
But why, lest that this lettre founden were,
No mencion ne make I now, for fere.

"Grevous to me, God wot, is youre unreste,
Youre haste, and that the goddes ordenaunce

1541 **permutacioun**, i.e., responsibility for change. 1543 **purveyaunce**, foresight (providence). 1544 **regnes . . . flytted**, kingdoms, transferred. 1545 **smytted**, smutted (tarnished). *brighte:* M *out of.* 1548 **parodye**, period. C&c gloss this as *duracioun*. For the episode of Hector's death, not in *Fil.*, Chaucer turned to Benoit, *Roman de Troie*, 16007ff. 1549 **blyve**, quickly. 1551 **shapen**, prepared. 1556 **haunteth**, occupies oneself with. 1558 **aventayle**, movable mouthpiece of a helmet. 1560 **ryve**, pierce. 1561 **of lyve**, from life (to death). 1564 **namely**, especially. 1565 **welle**, wellspring (source). 1568 **breste**, break. 1571 **on hire . . . repeyre**, to her, return. 1584 **lefte . . . slouthe**, left off, sloth (neglect). 1586 **trowthe**, promise. 1587 **routhe**, pity. 1593 **heeleles**, ill (healthless). Criseyde's letter is not found in *Fil.* 1594 **syke**, sick. 1595 **dele**, deal (meet). 1597 **ypleynted**, covered with complaints. 1598 **piete**, pity. 1605 **haste**, impatience.

It semeth not ye take it for the beste;   1606
Nor other thyng nys in youre remembraunce,
As thenketh me, but oonly youre plesaunce.
But beth not wroth, and that I yow byseche:
For that I tarye is al for wykked speche.   1610

"For I have herd wel more than I wende
Towchynge us two, how thynges han ystonde,
Which I shal with dissimulynge amende.
And—beth nought wroth—I have eke
          understonde
How ye ne don but holden me in honde.   1615
But now no fors—I kan not in yow gesse
But alle trouthe and alle gentilesse.

"Come I wole, but yet in swich disjoynte
I stonde as now that what yer or what day
That this shal be that kan I not apoynte.   1620
But yn effect I pray yow as I may
Of youre good word and of yowre frendship ay.
For trewely, while that my lyf may dure,
As for a frend ye may in me assure.

"Yet preye ich yow, on yvyl ye ne take   1625
That it is short which that I to yow write.
I dar nat ther I am wel lettres make,
Ne nevere yet ne koude I wel endite.
Ek gret effect men write yn place lite:
Th'entente is al, and nought the lettres
          space.   1630
And fareth now wel, God have yow in his grace.
          la vostre C."

This lettre this Troylus thoughte al straunge,
Whan he it saugh, and sorwfullich he sighte;
Hym thoughte it lyk a kalendes of chaunge.
But fynally, he ful ne trowen myghte   1635

That she ne wolde hym holden that she
          highte;
For with ful yvel wil lyst hym to leve
That loveth wel, yn swich cas, though hym
          greve.

But natheles, men seyn that at the laste,
For ony thyng, men shal the sothe se.   1640
And swych a cas bytidde, and that as faste,
That Troylus wel understod that she
Nas not so kynde as that hire oughte be.
And fynally, he wot now out of doute
That al is lost that he hath ben aboute.   1645

Stod on a day in his malencolye
This Troylus, and yn suspecioun
Of hire for whom he wende for to dye,
And so bifel that thorughout Troye town,
As was the gyse, yborn was up and down   1650
A manere cote-armure, as seyth the storye,
Byforn Deiphebe yn signe of his victorye,

The whiche cote, as telleth Lollius,
Deiphebe it had yrent fro Diomede
The same day. And whan this Troylus   1655
It saugh, he gan to taken of it hede,
Avysyng of the lengthe and of the brede,
And al the werk; but as he gan byholde,
Ful sodeynly his herte gan to colde,

As he that on the coler fond withinne   1660
A broch that he Criseyde yaf that morwe
That she from Troye moste nedes twynne,
In remembraunce of hym and of his sorwe,
And she hym leyde ayen hire feyth to borwe
To kepe it ay! But now ful wel he wiste   1665
Hys lady nas no lengere on to tryste.

1607 M *nys not.* 1608 **thenketh me . . . plesaunce**, it seems to me, pleasure. 1610 **wykked speche**, gossip, one of the principal sins, and fears, of the courtly convention. cf. III.266ff. 1611 **wende**, supposed. 1612 **ystonde**, stood. 1615 **holden . . . in honde**, deceive. 1618 **disjoynte**, predicament. 1622 **ay**, always. 1627 **ther**, where. 1628 **endite**, compose. 1629 **place lite**, small space. 1634 **kalendes**, beginning (lit., the first day of the month). 1635 **trowen**, believe. 1636 **highte**, promised. 1637 **yvel wil . . . leve**, reluctance, believe. 1640 **For**, in spite of. 1643 *kynde:* M *trewe.* 1645 *ben:* M&c *gon.* 1650 **gyse**, custom. 1651 **manere cote-armure**, kind of cloth tunic emblazoned with a coat of arms (worn over armor). Chaucer's wording may reflect the vagueness of *Fil.* 8.8 "*uno ornato vestimento.*" 1653 **Lollius**, Chaucer's second reference to his hypothetical source, cf. I.394. 1654 **yrent**, ripped. 1657 **Avysyng**, studying. 1658 **werk**, workmanship. 1660 **As he . . . coler**, when he, collar. In *Fil.* 8.9 the brooch is not concealed but used as a clasp. 1661 **yaf that morwe**, in *Fil.* 8.10 Troilo had given Criseida the brooch the last time he passed the night with her. 1662 **twynne**, depart. 1664 **to borwe**, as a pledge. 1666 **on to tryste**, to be trusted in.

He goth hym hom and gan ful soone sende
For Pandarus, and al this newe chaunce,
And of this broche, he told hym word and ende,
Compleynynge of hire hertes variaunce,   1670
His longe love, his trouthe, and his penaunce;
And after deth, withouten wordes more,
Ful faste he cride, his reste hym to restore.

Thanne spak he thus, "O lady myn
        Criseyde,
Wher is youre feyth, and where is youre
        byheste?   1675
Where is youre love? Where is youre trouthe?"
        he seyde.
"Of Diomede have ye now al this feste?
Allas, I wolde have trowed atte leste
That syn ye nolde in trouthe to me stonde,
That ye thus nolde han holden me in honde.

"Who shal now trowe on any othes mo?   1681
Allas, I nevere wolde han wend er this
That ye, Criseyde, koude han chaunged so;
Ne, but I hadde agilt or don amys,
So cruwel wende I not youre herte, ywys,   1685
To sle me thus! Allas, youre name of trouthe
Is now fordon, and that is al my routhe.

"Was there noon other broche yow lyste lete
To feffe with youre newe love," quod he,
"But thilke broch that I, with terys wete,   1690
Yow yaf as for a remembraunce of me?
Non other cause, allas, ne hadde ye
But for despit, and ek for that ye mente
Al outrely to shewe youre entente.

"Thorugh which I se that clene out of youre
        mynde   1695
Ye han me cast; and I ne kan nor may,
For al this world, withinne myn herte fynde

To unloven yow a quarter of a day.
In cursed tyme I born was, weylaway,
That ye that do me al this wo endure   1700
Yet love I best of any creature!

"Now God," quod he, "me sende yet the grace
That I may meten with this Diomede.
And trewely, yf I have myght and space,
Yet shal I make, I hope, his sides blede.   1705
O God," quod he, "that oughtest taken hede
To fortheren trouthe and wronges to punyce,
Whi nyltow don a vengeaunce on this vice?

"O Pandarus, that in dremes for to triste
Me blamed hast, and wont art ofte upbreyde,
Now maystow se thiself yf that thow lyste   1711
How trewe is now thi nece, bryght Cryseyde!
In sondry formes, God it wot," he seyde,
"The goddes shewen bothe joye and tene
In slep, and by my drem it is now sene.   1715

"And certeynly, withoute more speche,
From hennesforth, as ferforth as I may,
Myn owene deth in armes wol I seche.
I recche nat how soone be the day.
But trewely, Criseyde, swete may,   1720
Whom I have ay with al my myght iserved,
That ye thus don, I have it nought deserved."

This Pandarus, that alle these thynges herde,
And wist wel he seyde a soth of this,
He nought a word ayen to hym answerde,   1725
For sory of his frendes sorwe he is,
And shamed for his nece hath don amys,
And stant astoned of these causes tweye
As stille as ston—a word ne koude he seye.

But at the laste thus he spak and seyde,   1730
"My dere brother, I may the do no more.

1671 trouthe, fidelity. **1672 after deth,** for death. **1674** *myn:* other MSS *bright*. **1675 byheste,** promise. **1677 feste,** feast (delight). **1678 trowed,** believed. **1679 syn,** since (i.e., although). **1680 holden . . . in honde,** deceive. **1681 trowe,** believe. *othes:* M *other*. **1682 wend,** believed. **1684 agilt,** offended. **1687 routhe,** sorrow. **1688 yow lyste lete,** pleased you to let go. **1689 feffe,** endow. **1693 despit,** spite (contempt). **1698 unloven,** Troylus' continued devotion in the face of the ultimate "ocular proof" is another change from *Fil.* 8.16ff., where he at once calls down curses on Criseida. **1700 do me,** make me. **1707 fortheren trouthe . . . punyce,** advance fidelity, punish. **1714 tene,** sorrow. **1717 ferforth,** far. **1719 recche,** care. **1720 may,** maid. **1724 wist . . . soth,** knew, truth. **1731 the do,** do for you.

What shulde I seyen? I hate, ywys, Criseyde,
And God wot I wol hate hire everemore.
And that thow me bysoughtest don of yore,
Havynge unto myn honour ne my reste   1735
Right no reward, I dede al that the leste.

"If I dede ought that myghte lyken the,
It is me lef; and of this treson now,
God wot that it a sorwe is unto me.
And dredles, for hertes ese of yow,   1740
Right fayn wolde I amende it, wist I how.
And fro this world almyghti God I preye
Delyvere hire soon—I kan no more seye."

Gret was the sorwe and pleynte of Troylus,
But forth hire cours Fortune ay gan to holde:
Criseyde loveth the sone of Tydeus,   1746
And Troylus mot wepe in cares colde.
Swich is this world, whoso it kan biholde.
In ech estat is litel hertes reste.
God leve us for to take it for the beste!   1750

In many cruwel batayle out of drede
Of Troylus, this ilke noble knyght,
As men may in these olde bokes rede,
Was sen his knyghthod and his grete myght.
And dredles, his yre, day and nyght,   1755
Ful cruwely the Grekes ay aboughte;
And alwey most this Diomede he soughte.

And ofte tyme I fynde that they mette
With blody strokes and with wordes grete,
Assayinge how hire speres weren whette;   1760
And God it wot, with many a cruwel hete
Gan Troylus upon his helm to bete.

But natheles, Fortune it nought ne wolde
Of others hond that eyther deyen sholde.

And yf I hadde ytaken for to writen   1765
The armes of this ilke worthi man,
Than wolde ich of his batayles enditen,
But for that I to writen first bygan
Of his love, I have seyd as I kan—
His worthi dedes, whoso list hem here,   1770
Red Dares, he kan telle hem alle yfere—

Bysechyng every lady bryght of hewe
And every gentil womman, what she be,
That al be that Criseyde was untrewe,
That for that gylt she be nat wroth with me—
Ye may hire gilte in other bokes se;   1776
And gladlyer I wol write, yf yow leste,
Penelopees trouthe and goode Alceste.

Ne I sey not this alonly for these men,
But most for wommen that bytraysed be   1780
Thorugh false folk—God yeve hem sorwe,
    amen!—
That with hire grete wit and subtilte
Bytrayse yow. And this commeveth me
To speke, and yn effect yow alle I preye,
Beth war of men, and herkneth what I seye. 1785

Go litel bok, go litel myn tragedye,
Ther God thi makere yet, er that he dye,
So sende myght to make yn som comedye.
But litel bok, no makyng thow n'envye,
But subgit be to alle poesye,   1790
And kys the steppes where as thow seest pace
Virgile, Ovyde, Omer, Lukan, and Stace.

1732 I hate, at *Fil.* 8.24 Pandaro prays that Criseida be punished, but he makes no such flat statement of hate as this. **1734 by-soughtest don,** begged me to do. **1736 reward,** regard. **1737 lyken the,** please you. **1738 me lef,** pleasing to me. **1740 dredles,** without doubt. **1741 fayn,** happily. **1744 pleynte,** lament. **1750 leve,** grant. **1756 ay aboughte,** ever paid. **1766 armes,** warlike deeds. **1771 Dares,** up to l. 1764 Chaucer followed the details in *Fil.* 8 fairly closely. With this stanza he turns to his own conclusion, returning to *Fil.* 8.27 for ll. 1800–06, and playing some interesting variations on Boccaccio's final exhortation to young men in his concluding lines. He omits completely Boccaccio's Book 9, addressed like Boccaccio's proem to Fiametta. *Dares* was one of the medieval sources for the Troy story, cf. I.146n. **1775** *she:* other MSS *ye.* **1778 Penelopees trouthe . . . goode Alceste,** Chaucer did just this in *LGW*, evidently written shortly after *TC*. **1779 this,** i.e., *TC*. **1780 bytraysed,** betrayed. **1783 commeveth,** persuades. **1786–88 tragedye . . . comedye,** the existential character of the love of Troylus and Criseyde, frequently referred to throughout the poem, marks its pagan-tragic nature. It is hard to say whether Chaucer already had in mind a poem in which a pilgrimage toward a New Jerusalem would suggest a Christian comedy. **1787 Ther God,** may God. **1789** Other MSS *ne make thow noon envie.* **1791** *where:* M *there; pace:* C&c *space.* **1792 Virgile,** &c. Virgil, Ovid, Homer, Lucan, and Statius were the great names of classical narrative poetry; Chaucer would here appear to be making his bid to be included in their company.

And for ther is so gret dyversite
In Englyssh and yn wrytyng of oure tonge,
So prey I God that noon myswryte the,　　1795
Ne the mysmetre for defaute of tonge.
And red wherso thow be, or elles songe,
That thow be understonde, God I beseche—
But yet to purpos of my rathere speche:

The wraththe, as I bigan yow for to seye,　　1800
Of Troylus the Grekes boughten dere,
For thousandys his hondes maden deye,
As he that was withouten any pere
Save Ector, yn his tyme, as I kan here.
But weylawey, save only Goddes wille,　　1805
Despitously hym slowh the fiers Achille.

And whan that he was slayn yn this manere,
His lighte gost ful blysfully is went
Up to the holughnesse of the eighte spere,
In convers lettynge everich element;　　1810
And ther he saugh with ful avysement
The erratyk sterres, herkenynge armonye
With sownes ful of hevenyssh melodye.

And doun from thennes faste he gan avyse
This litel spot of erthe, that with the se　　1815
Enbraced is, and fully gan despise
This wrecched world, and held al vanite
To respect of the pleyn felicite
That is yn hevene above; and at the laste,
Ther he was slayn his lokyng down he
　　caste.　　1820

And yn hymself he lough right at the wo
Of hem that wepten for his deth so faste,
And dampned al oure werk that foloweth so
The blynde lust, the which that may not laste,
And shulden al oure herte on heven caste.　　1825
And forth he wente, shortly for to telle,
Ther as Mercurye sorted hym to dwelle.

Swich fyn hath, lo, this Troylus for love;
Swych fyn hath al his grete worthynesse;
Swich fyn hath his estat real above;　　1830
Swich fyn his lust, swich fyn hath his noblesse;
Swych fyn hath false worldes brotelnesse!
And thus bigan his lovyng of Criseyde,
As I have told, and yn this wyse he deyde.

O yonge, fresshe folkes, he or she,　　1835
In which that love up groweth with youre
　　age,
Repeyreth hom fro worldly vanyte,
And of youre herte up casteth the visage
To thilke God that after his ymage
Yow made; and thynketh al nys but a fayre　1840
This world that passeth soone as floures fayre.

And loveth hym, the which that right for love
Upon a cros, oure soules for to beye,
First starf, and ros, and sit yn hevene above;
For he nyl falsen no wight, dar I seye,　　1845
That wole his herte al holly on hym leye.
And syn he best to love is, and most meke,
What nedeth feyned loves for to seke?

1795 A *So prey to God.* **1796 mysmetre . . . defaute of tonge,** make the lines unmetrical because of a faulty dialect (since each scribe tended to write in his own dialect, and both meter and rhyme depended on following Chaucer's London English). **1799 rathere,** earlier. **1801 boughten,** paid for. **1806 Despitously,** cruelly. **1808–27 His lighte gost,** light spirit. These lines are suggested by the death of Arcita in Boccaccio's *Teseida* 11. 1–3. **1809 holughnesse,** hollowness. *eighte:* MC&c *seventhe,* but *Tes.* has *ottava.* There has been much written about why Chaucer would have chosen the eighth sphere. Counting outward, this is the sphere of the fixed stars, where the souls of the Church assemble (which does not seem particularly appropriate for pagan Troylus). Counting inward the eighth is the sphere of the moon, where spirits go whose vows have been broken through no fault of their own (cf. Dante's Piccarda Donati, *Paradiso* III). The reading of *LGW* 2236 makes it probable that Chaucer was counting inward, although some scholars argue still for the sphere of fixed stars where Troylus can undergo penance. **1810 convers lettynge everich element,** leaving on the other side (behind) all other (temporal) elements. **1811 avysement,** deliberation. **1812 erratyk . . . armonye,** moving (as opposed to fixed), the harmony of the spheres as they move through the heavens. **1814 faste . . . avyse,** intently, stare at. **1818 pleyn felicite,** perfect joy, in contrast to the false felicity of temporal pleasures: this is Boethian and Christian doctrine, contrasting to the physical, pagan love of Troylus and Criseyde, cf. III.814 and note. **1820 Ther,** where. **1823 dampned,** condemned. **1824 lust,** desire (pleasure). **1825 And shulden,** when we should. **1827 Mercurye,** a curious anachronism since Mercury was the classical guide of souls to the underworld. **sorted,** allotted. **1831** *his lust:* other MSS *hath lust.* **1832 brotelnesse,** brittleness (insecurity), cf. III.820. **1836** *that love:* other MSS *any love.* **1840 a fayre,** a fair (i.e., Vanity Fair). **1843 beye,** buy. **1844 starf,** died. **1845 falsen,** betray. **1848 feyned,** pretended (pseudo-).

Lo here of payens corsed olde rytes;
Lo here what alle hire goddes may avayle;   1850
Lo here these wrecched worldes appetites;
Lo here the fyn and guerdon for travayle
Of Jove, Appollo, of Mars, of swich rascayle!
Lo here the forme of olde clerkes speche
In poetrie, if ye hire bokes seche.   1855

O moral Gower, this bok I directe
To the, and to the, philosophical Strode,
To vouchen sauf ther nede is to corecte
Of youre benygnites and zeles goode.   1859

And to that sothefast Crist, that starf on rode,
With al myn herte of mercy evere I preye,
And to the Lord right thus I speke and seye:

Thow oon and two and thre eterne on lyve,
That regnest ay yn thre and two and oon,
Uncircumscript and al mayst circumscryve,   1865
Us from visible and invysible foon
Defende, and to thy mercy everychon
So make us, Jesus, for thi mercy digne,
For love of mayde and moder thyn benigne.
                                          Amen.

Explicit liber Troili et Criseide.

1849 corsed, cursed. **1852 guerdon . . . travayle,** reward, work (service). **1853 rascayle,** a worthless mob. **1856ff.** MS. Harley 1239 heads these final lines "Lenvoye de Chaucer." **1856–57ff. moral Gower . . . philosophical Strode,** John Gower, the poet, and Ralph Strode, the lawyer, were personal friends of Chaucer and important figures at court and in the City of London. However, more than any personal gesture, this dedication called attention to the two values implicit in Chaucer's poem: "morality," i.e., teaching concerning the principles of human conduct, of which Gower's poems are themselves exemplars; "philosophy," i.e., Boethian discussions about freedom of the will, astrological allusions, quotations from the classics, proverbs, and the like, of which Strode (who had both a university and a legal education) must have been considered a fitting exemplar. Distinction between moral and intellectual virtues was a commonplace in classical and medieval commentary. For example, St. Thomas Aquinas begins Quaestio LVIII of the *Summa Theologica,* "If virtue perfects man's speculative or practical intellect in order that his action may be good, it will be intellectual virtue: if it perfects his appetitive part, it will be moral virtue." **1857** M&c second *to* om. **1858 vouchen sauf ther,** consent where. **1859 benygnites,** kindnesses. **1860 starf . . . rode,** died, cross. **1865 Uncircumscript . . . circumscryve,** uncircumscribed, circumscribe (unlimited, limit; uncomprisable, comprise). **1868 digne,** worthy.

Book of the Duchess

INTRODUCTION

Book of the Duchess

T HE ONLY ONE of Chaucer's poems of whose date and occasion we can be reasonably sure is *Book of the Duchess.* As indicated by the names worked into its conclusion (ll.1318-19), it is an elegy on the death of Blanche, Duchess of Lancaster, the first wife of John of Gaunt, third son of Edward III and one of the principal patrons to both Geoffrey and Philippa Chaucer. Blanche died in September 1368, when Chaucer was about 26 years old.

Chaucer's poetic achievement in *Book of the Duchess* was to produce an English equivalent to the polished poetry of the French court, which had evolved over a period of 250 years from the poetry of the troubadours. Since the Norman Conquest, French had been the language of the Anglo-Norman aristocracy, but by Chaucer's time, England had been separated from Normandy, and English was becoming the spoken language of the aristocracy, as it had always continued to be of the lower classes. It was a courageous act for Chaucer to write an elegy for a princess in a disdained vulgate—somewhat as if Robert Frost had chosen to write a poem for President Kennedy's inauguration in Appalachian English. That he got away with it, and launched a tradition of sophisticated poetry in

English, is a commentary on the sociolinguistic situation of the day.

French and Latin were still the official languages of England. The aristocracy and government bureaucracy were essentially trilingual, speaking English, but reading and writing French and Latin. For this audience, Chaucer and other fourteenth-century London writers created a new literary language, half French and half English. *Book of the Duchess* is the first notable achievement in the new idiom. Its vocabulary and syntax reward study. Although 914 of its 1334 lines have direct parallels in the *Roman de la Rose* and the poems of Machaut and Froissart, it is thoroughly idiomatic. It never reads like "translation English." But the meter is French, and it has the simple elegance of expression that we find in French court poetry.

The realization continues to grow as to how effectively Chaucer managed to animate an occasional poem in a conventional mode. Machaut and Froissart do not rank high on the scale of French poets, and their *dits amoreux* that Chaucer was imitating have impressed modern readers as affected and insipid. An important reason for the superiority of Chaucer's poem is that it deals with a genuine tragedy—the death of a beautiful woman. At a stroke, this converts the insincere troubadour whining about "dying for love" into poignant reality, as discussed by Phillip C. Boardman, "Courtly Language and the Strategy of Consolation in the *Book of the Duchess*," *ELH* (1977). In addition, Chaucer managed to endow the conventions of "complaint" and "debate" in the exchanges between the dreamer and the knight with dramatic verisimilitude that foreshadows the triumphs of the *Canterbury Tales*.

In spite of attempts to find a relationship, the introductory story of Seyes and Alcyone remains a distraction. The poem does not get started until the dream begins at l. 291. But from there to the end, the pattern of consolation is flawless. In the persona of the dreamer, we have the beginning of Chaucerian irony—the pose of naiveté which leads other characters to reveal their inner beings. The dreamer's questioning, and the sorrowing knight's thrice-repeated "I have lost more than thou wenest," culminating in the stark "She ys ded!" reveal Chaucer's instinctive command of the process of psychological analysis. B.H. Bronson, "*The Book of the Duchess* Re-opened," *PMLA* (1952), first perceived the psychological depth of the poem. James Wimsatt, *Chaucer and the French Love Poets* (1968), is a study of Chaucer's relation to his French models. W. Clemen, *Chaucer's Early Poetry* (1963), is the fullest study of the linguistic and prosodic transformations in the early poems and the emergence of Chaucer's individual voice.

Book of the Duchess

[handwritten: iambic tetrameter]

I have gret wonder, be this lyghte,
How that I lyve, for day ne nyghte
I may nat slepe wel nygh noght.
I have so many an ydel thoght
Purely for defaute of slepe   5
That, by my trouthe, I take no kepe
Of nothing, how hyt cometh or gooth,
Ne me nys nothyng leve nor looth.
Al is ylyche good to me,
Joy or sorowe, wherso hyt be,   10
For I have felynge in nothynge,
But as yt were a mased thynge,
Alway in poynt to falle adoun;
For sorwful ymagynacioun
Ys alway hooly in my mynde.   15
And wel ye woot, agaynes kynde
Hyt were to lyven in thys wyse,
For nature wolde nat suffyse
To noon erthly creature
Nat longe tyme to endure   20
Withoute slepe and be in sorwe.
And I ne may, ne nyght ne morwe,
Slepe; and thus melancolye   *[handwritten: neither nor]*
And drede I have for to dye.   *[handwritten: physecal condition]*
Defaute of slepe and hevynesse   25
Hath sleyn my spirit of quyknesse
That I have lost al lustyhede.

Suche fantasies ben in myn hede.
So I not what is best to doo.
But men myght axe me why soo   30
I may not sleepe, and what me is.
But natheles, who aske this
Leseth his asking trewely.
Myselven can not telle why
The sothe; but trewly, as I gesse,   35
I hold hit be a sicknesse   *[handwritten: love-sick]*
That I have suffred this eight yeere—
And yet my boote is never the nere,
For there is phisicien but oon   *[handwritten: his lover]*
That may me hele. But that is don;   40
Passe we over untill efte.
That wil not be mot nede be lefte.
Our first mater is good to kepe.
    So when I saw I might not slepe
Til now late this other night,   45
Upon my bedde I sat upright
And bad oon reche me a booke,
A romaunce, and he it me toke,
To rede and drive the night away,
For me thought it beter play   50
Then play either at chesse or tables.
And in this boke were written fables
That clerkes had in olde tyme,
And other poets, put in rime

[handwritten left margin: ay = ai]
[handwritten left margin: a = ah]

Text based on MS Fairfax 16 (F) with variants from the Thynne edition, 1532 (T), Tanner 346 (Ta), and Bodley 638 (B). See "The Text of This Edition," p. 966.

1–8 These lines, modeled upon ll. 1–9 of Froissart's *Paradys d'Amour*, reveal how these early pieces were exercises in adapting the French poetic idiom to English: "*Je sui de moi en grant merveille | Comment je vifs, quant tant je veille, | Et on ne porrait en veillant | Trouver de moi plus travaillant,*" etc. **5 defaute,** lack, spelled *defaulte* throughout F. **6 trouthe . . . take no kepe,** troth (word, promise), don't care. F *noo thinge.* **8 me . . . leve nor looth,** pleasant to me nor unpleasant (loath). **9 ylyche,** alike. **12 mased,** dazed. **13 in poynt,** on the point of. *Alway:* T *Alday.* **14 ymagynacioun,** imaginings (mental images). **15 hooly,** wholly; a *double entendre* with "holy" is not impossible considering that the poem is an elegy. **16 kynde,** nature. **22 ne . . . ne morwe,** neither, nor morning. **23** *thus:* TF&c *this.* **25 Defaute . . . hevynesse,** lack, sadness. **26 quyknesse,** vitality. F *sleyn* om. **27 lustyhede,** enthusiasm. **29 not,** don't know (*ne wot*). **31–96** These lines, along with 288, 480, 886, originally lacking from all the MSS, are found in Thynne's edition, and from T were copied into F by a later hand. **33 Leseth,** loses. **35 sothe,** truth. **36 hold hit be,** hold that it is. This protestation of being sick with love is a troubadour convention found in Chaucer's French models, but Margaret Galway has proposed that it is a specific tribute to Joan of Kent, mother of Richard II, who may have been Chaucer's principal patron until her death in 1385. In 1369, she had been married for eight years to the Black Prince, eldest son of Edward III. **38 boote . . . nere,** remedy, nearer. **41 efte,** later (another time). **43 mater . . . kepe,** subject, stick to. **51 tables,** backgammon.

To rede and for to be in minde, 55
While men loved the lawe of kinde.
This boke ne spak but of such thinges,
Of quenes lives and of kinges,
And many other thinges smale.
Amonge al this I fond a tale 60
That me thoughte a wonder thing.
  This was the tale: There was a king
That hight Seyes, and had a wife,
The beste that mighte bere lyfe,
And this quene hight Alcyone. 65
So it befil thereafter soone
This king wol wenden over see.
To tellen shortly, whan that he
Was in the see, thus in this wise,
Suche a tempest gan to rise 70
That brak her maste and made it fal,
And clefte her ship and dreinte hem al,
That never was founde, as it telles,
Bord ne man ne nothing elles.
Right thus this king Seyes loste his life. 75
  Now for to speke of Alcyone his wife:
This lady that was left at home,
Hath wonder that the king ne come
Hom, for it was a longe terme.
Anone her herte began to erme; *yearn* 80
And for that her thoughte evermo
It was not wele—her thoghte so—
She longed so after the king
That certes it were a pitous thing
To tell her hertely sorowfull life 85
That she had, this noble wife,
For him, alas, she loved alderbeste.
Anon she sent bothe eeste and weste
To seke him, but they founde nought.
"Alas!" quoth shee, "that I was wrought! 90

And where my lord, my love, be deed? *1 st*
Certes, I nil never eate breed— *lament*
I make avowe to my god here—
But I mowe of my lord here."
Such sorowe this lady to her took 95
That trewly I, which made this book,
Had such pittee and such rowthe
To rede hir sorwe, that by my trowthe
I ferde the worse al the morwe
Aftir, to thenken on hir sorwe. 100
  So whan this lady koude here noo word
That no man myghte fynde hir lord,
Ful ofte she swouned and sayed "Alas."
For sorwe ful nygh wood she was,
Ne she koude no rede but oon, 105
But doun on knees she sat anoon
And wepte that pittee was to here.
  "A, mercy, swete lady dere,"
Quod she to Juno, hir goddesse,
"Helpe me out of thys distresse, *prayer in the* 110
And yeve me grace my lord to se *form of a*
Soone, or wete wher so he be, *complaint*
Or how he fareth, or in what wise,
And I shal make yow sacrifise,
And hooly youres become I shal 115
With good wille, body, herte, and al.
And but thow wilt this, lady swete,
Send me grace to slepe, and mete
In my slepe som certeyn sweven
Wherthorgh that I may knowe even 120
Whether my lord be quyke or ded."
With that word she henge doun the hed
And felle aswowne as colde as ston.
Hyr women kaught hir up anoon,
And broghten hir in bed al naked, 125
And she, forweped and forwaked,

---

55 be in, i.e., be kept in. **56 While . . . kinde,** i.e., as long as . . . nature (forever). **of:** F *in.* **59 thinges smale,** an early example of Chaucerian humor, since, more certainly than for any other piece he ever wrote, the audience of *BD* was the royal family. **63 Seyes,** the story of Ceyx and Alcione is found in Ovid, *Met.* 11. 410ff., and also Machaut, *La Fonteinne Amoureuse,* upon both of which Chaucer drew for the following account. *Seyes:* T *Seys.* **64 bere:** F *beare.* **65 hight,** was named. **71 her,** their. **72 dreinte,** drowned. **79 terme,** time. **80 erme,** grieve. FT&c *yerne;* eds. have substituted *erme* for the rhyme. **81 her thoughte,** it seemed to her. **82 *her thoghte:*** Skeat &c replace this FT reading with *he dwelte,* Koch with *he taried.* **85 hertely,** heartfelt. **87 alderbeste,** best of all. Some critics have suggested that Alcione was an example of *tristitia,* the sin of excessive grief, against which John of Gaunt was being warned throughout *BD.* **91 where . . . be,** i.e., whether, is. **92 nil,** will not. F *will.* **94 mowe . . . here,** may, hear. **97 rowthe,** pity. **98 rede,** read about. **100 Aftir:** F *And aftir.* **104 wood,** crazy. **105 rede,** counsel (course of action). **112 wete,** know. **118 mete,** dream (vb.). **119 sweven,** dream (n.). **120 even,** exactly. **121 quyke,** alive. **123 aswowne,** in a swoon (faint). **124 anoon,** immediately. **126 forweped,** i.e., wept out ("for" is an intensifier and completive).

Was wery, and thus the dede slepe
Fil on hir or she tooke kepe,
Throgh Juno, that had herd hir bone,
That made hir to slepe sone. 130
For as she prayede, ryght so was done
In dede, for Juno ryght anone
Called thus hir messagere
To doo hir erande, and he come nere.
Whan he was come, she bad hym thus: 135
   "Go bet," quod Juno, "to Morpheus—
Thou knowest hym wel, the god of slepe;
Now understond wel and tak kepe—
Sey thus on my halfe, that he
Go faste into the Grete Se, 140
And byd hym that on alle thyng
He take up Seyes body, the kyng
That lyeth ful pale and nothyng rody.
Bid hym crepe into the body
And doo hit goon to Alcione 145
The quene, ther she lyeth allone,
And shewe hir shortly, hit ys no nay,
How hit was dreynt thys other day;
And do the body speke ryght soo,
Ryght as hyt was woned to doo 150
The whiles that hit was alyve.
Goo now faste, and hye the blyve."
   This messager tok leve and went
Upon hys wey, and never ne stent
Til he com to the derke valey 155
That stant betwexe roches twey
Ther never yet grew corn ne gras,
Ne tre, ne noght that oughte was,
Beste, ne man, ne noght elles,
Save ther were a fewe welles 160
Came rennynge fro the clyffes adoun,
That made a dedely slepynge soun,
And ronnen doun ryght by a cave

That was under a rokke ygrave
Amydde the valey, wonder depe. 165
There these goddes lay and slepe,
Morpheus and Eclympasteyre,
That was the god of slepes heyre,
That slepe and did noon other werk.
This cave was also as derk 170
As helle pitte overal aboute.
They had good leyser for to route,
To envye who myght slepe beste.
Somme henge her chyn upon hir breste
And slept upryght, hir hed yhedde, 175
And somme lay naked in her bedde
And slepe whiles the dayes laste.
   This messager come fleynge faste
And cried, "O ho, awake anoon!"
Hit was for noght; there herde hym non. 180
"Awake!" quod he. "Whoo ys lyth there?"
And blew his horn ryght in here eere,
And cried "Awaketh" wonder hye.
This god of slep with hys oon eye
Caste up and axed, "Who clepeth there?" 185
   "Hyt am I," quod this messager.
"Juno bad thow shuldest goon"—
And tolde hym what he shulde doon,
As I have told yow here-to-fore—
Hyt ys no nede reherse hyt more— 190
And went hys wey, whan he had sayde.
Anoon this god of slepe abrayede
Out of hys slepe, and gan to goon,
And dyd as he had bede hym doon:
Tooke up the dreynt body sone 195
And bar hyt forth to Alcione,
Hys wif the quene, ther as she lay
Ryght even a quarter before day,
And stood ryght at hyr beddes fete,
And called hir ryght as she hete 200

128 **or . . . tooke kepe,** before, was aware. 129 **bone,** prayer. 136 **bet,** quickly (better). 138 **kepe,** heed. 140 **Grete Se,** the Mediterranean. 141 **on alle thyng,** i.e., without fail. 142 F&c *That he take.* 143 **rody,** ruddy. 145 **doo,** make. *Alcione:* F&c *Alchione* throughout, as in Machaut. 146 **ther,** where. 150 **woned,** accustomed. 152 **blyve,** quickly. 154 **stent,** stopped. 160 **welles,** springs. 164 **ygrave,** carved out. 166 *and slepe:* T *aslepe.* 167 **Eclympasteyre,** one of the sons of Morpheus, god of sleep, in Froissart's *Le Paradys d'Amour,* upon which the opening lines of *BD* were modeled (see l. 1n.). 168 **heyre,** heir. F *eyre.* 172 **route,** snore. 173 **envye,** contend. TTa *To vye,* but OED does not record the aphetic form before 1533. 175 **upryght . . . yhedde,** flat on their backs, hidden. 177 *the:* T *theyr,* again an unusual Chaucerian form (attested to only by *CT* I.4172). 178 *fleynge:* T *rennyng.* 179 F&c *O how;* T *Ho, ho.* 181 TB *ys* om.; Ta *is it that.* 182 *eere:* F *heere.* 184 *eye:* F *ye.* 185 **Caste . . . clepeth,** looked, calls. 192 **abrayede,** started up. 195 **dreynt,** drowned. T *deed.* 198 **a quarter,** the last quarter of the day (i.e., three hours before dawn). 199 *hyr:* F&c *hys.* 200 **she hete,** she was named.

By name, and sayede, "My swete wyfe,
Awake, let be your sorwful lyfe,
For in your sorwe there lyth no rede,
For certes, swete, I am but dede—
Ye shul me never on lyve yse.   205
But good swete herte, that ye
Bury my body, for suche a tyde
Ye mowe hyt fynde the see besyde.
And farewel, swete, my worldes blysse.
I pray God youre sorwe lysse.   210
To lytel while oure blysse lasteth!"
With that hir eyen up she casteth
And sawe noght. "Allas," quod she for sorwe,
And deyde within the thridde morwe.
But what she sayede more in that swow   215
I may not telle yow as now—
Hyt were to longe for to dwelle.
My first matere I wil yow telle,
Wherfore I have tolde this thynge
Of Alcione and Seys the kynge.   220
For thus moche dar I say welle,
I had be dolven everydelle,
And ded, ryght thorgh defaute of slepe,
Yif I ne had redde and take kepe
Of this tale next before.   225
And I wol telle yow wherfore:
For I ne myght for bote ne bale
Slepe or I had redde thys tale
Of this dreynte Seys the kynge,
And of the goddes of slepynge.   230
    Whan I had redde thys tale wel
And overloked hyt everydel,
Me thoght wonder yf hit were so.
For I had never herde speke or tho
Of noo goddes that koude make   235
Men to slepe ne for to wake,
For I ne knew never god but oon.

And in my game I sayede anoon—
And yet me lyst ryght evel to pley—
"Rather then that y shulde dey
Thorgh defaute of slepynge thus,
I wolde yive thilke Morpheus,
Or hys goddesse, dame Juno,
Or some wight elles, I ne roghte who,
To make me slepe and have som reste—   245
I wil yive hym the alderbeste
Yifte that ever he abode hys lyve,
And here on warde, ryght now as blyve,
Yif he wol make me slepe a lyte,
Of down of pure dowves white   250
I wil yif hym a fether-bedde,
Rayed with gold and ryght wel cledde
In fyn blak satyn doutremere,
And many a pelowe, and every bere
Of clothe of Reynes, to slepe softe—   255
Hym thar not nede to turnen ofte.
And I wol yive hym al that falles
To a chambre, and al hys halles
I wol do peynte with pure gold
And tapite hem ful many-fold   260
Of oo sute. This shal he have—
Yf I wiste where were hys cave—
Yf he kan make me slepe sone,
As did the goddesse quene Alcione.
And thus this ylke god Morpheus   265
May wynne of me moo fees thus
Than ever he wan; and to Juno,
That ys hys goddesse, I shal soo do
I trow that she shal holde hir payede."
    I hadde unneth that word ysayede,   270
Ryght thus as I have tolde hyt yow,
That sodeynly, I nyste how,
Such a lust anoon me tooke
To slepe that ryght upon my booke

[marginal note:] narr. wants the same gift as Alcione.

203 rede, advantage (counsel). **204** T *swete love.* **207 for . . . tyde,** for at, time. **208 mowe,** may. **210 lysse,** comfort. **215 swow,** swoon. F *sorowe.* **222 dolven,** buried (dug). **224 redde . . . take kepe,** read, paid attention. **227 bote . . . bale,** good, bad. **228 or,** ere (until). **234 or tho,** before then. **237 god but oon,** i.e., the God of Love, who kept him awake. **244 roghte,** cared. **246 alderbeste,** best of all. **247 abode,** experienced, expected. **248 on warde . . . blyve,** as pledge, quickly. **251 fether-bedde,** in Machaut's *La Fonteinne Amoureuse* (l. 63n. above), the poet promises the God of Sleep a hat and a bed of gyrfalcon feathers. F *feder.* **252 Rayed,** striped. **253 doutremere,** imported (from over the sea). F *de owtre mere.* **254 bere,** pillowcase. **255 Reynes,** Rennes, France, center of medieval linen weaving; cotton cloth was scarcely known in Europe before 1500 (though centuries old in India and Arabia), and linen was the softest cloth. T *to slepe on.* **257 falles,** belongs. **258** T *To his chambre and to his.* **260 tapite,** hang with tapestries. **269 trow,** believe. **270 unneth,** hardly. **273 lust anoon,** desire immediately.

Y fil aslepe; and therwith evene   275
Me mette so ynly swete a swevene,
So wonderful that never yitte
Y trowe no man had the wytte
To konne wel my sweven rede—
No, not Joseph, withoute drede,   280
Of Egipte, he that redde so
The kynges metynge Pharao,
No more than koude the lest of us;
Ne nat skarsly Macrobeus
(He that wrot al th'avysyoun   285
That he mette, Kyng Scipioun,
The noble man, the Affrikan—
Suche marvayles fortuned than)
I trowe arede my dremes even.
Loo, thus hyt was, thys was my sweven.   290

  Me thoghte thus, that hyt was May,
And in the dawenynge I lay—
Me mette thus—in my bed al naked
And loked forth, for I was waked
With smale foules a gret hepe   295
That had affrayed me out of my slepe,
Thorgh noyse and swetnesse of her songe.
And as me mette, they sate amonge
Upon my chambre roof wythoute,
Upon the tyles overal aboute,   300
And songen everych in hys wyse
The moste solempne servise
By noote that ever man, y trowe,
Had herd; for some of hem song lowe,
Some high, and al of oon acorde.   305

To telle shortly att oo worde,
Was never herd so swete a steven
But hyt had be a thyng of heven,
So mery a soun, so swete entewnes,
That certes for the toune of Tewnes   310
I nolde but I had herd hem synge;
For al my chambre gan to rynge
Thurgh syngynge of her armonye;
For instrument nor melodye
Was nowhere herd yet half so swete,   315
Nor of acorde half so mete;
For ther was noon of hem that feyned
To synge, for ech of hem hym peyned
To fynde out mery crafty notes.
They ne spared not her throtes.   320
And sooth to seyn, my chambre was
Ful wel depeynted, and with glas
Were al the wyndowes wel yglased
Ful clere, and nat an hoole ycrased,
That to beholde hyt was grete joye.   325
For hoolly al the story of Troye
Was in the glasynge ywroght thus,
Of Ector and of Kyng Priamus,
Of Achilles and Kyng Lamedon,
And eke of Medea and of Jason,   330
Of Paris, Eleyne, and of Lavyne.
And alle the walles with colouris fyne
Were peynted, bothe text and glose,
Of al the *Romaunce of the Rose.*
My wyndowes were shette echon,   335
And throgh the glas the sonne shon

---

275 **evene,** directly (immediately). 276 **mette . . . ynly . . . swevene,** dreamed, inwardly, dream. 278 **trowe,** believe. 279 **konne . . . rede,** know how, to interpret. 281 **redde,** interpreted. 282 **metynge,** dreaming (about). 284–87 **Macrobeus . . . Scipioun . . . Affrikan,** Macrobius wrote a commentary on Cicero's *Dream of Scipio.* The reference here is evidently secondhand, cf. *Romaunt* 7–10 (Dunn-Robbins 1. 4–6), and Chaucer did not know that the piece was by Cicero nor that the dream was *by* Scipio the Younger *about* his illustrious ancestor Scipio Africanus. By the time he wrote *PF,* however, Chaucer had read Macrobius and could make extensive, firsthand reference to it. 285 **avysyoun,** vision. 288 See l. 31n. 289 **trowe arede . . . even,** believe interpret, correctly. 291ff. The lines describing the beginning of the dream are modeled on the opening lines of *RR,* cf. *Romaunt* in this edition and Sutherland and Dunn-Robbins for the original. 292 FT&c *dawning;* T *there I.* 296 **affrayed,** startled. 298 **amonge,** here and there. 301 T *And everyche songe.* 303 **By noote,** i.e., in their birdsongs (*OED,* sb.² I. 2b). 307 **steven,** sound (voice). **herd:** F *harde.* 309 **swete entewnes,** sweetly harmonious. 310 **Tewnes,** Tunis (?), chosen for the rhyme. 311 **nolde but,** would not but, i.e., wouldn't have missed. 316 **acorde . . . mete,** musical concord, suitable (successful). 317 **feyned,** pretended. 318 **hym peyned,** took pains. 319 **fynde out,** i.e., produce. F *out of;* T *many crafty.* 324 **ycrased,** broken. 328 **Ector . . . Priamus,** Hector, principal Trojan hero; Priam, King of Troy. 329 **Achilles . . . Lamedon,** principal Greek hero; Laomedon, father of Priam. 330 **Medea . . . Jason,** the witch maiden who helped Jason secure the Golden Fleece, with eventual tragic results. 331 **Paris, Eleyne, Lavyne,** Paris and Helen, whose elopement caused the Trojan War; Lavinia, the princess Aeneas married in Italy after deserting Dido. 333 **glose,** gloss (commentary). 334 *Romaunce of the Rose,* acknowledgment of one of the major influences upon Chaucer's and other 14th-century French and English poetry. Wall paintings of famous narratives were common in palaces and churches (see *HF,* Bk. 1). FT&c *And al.*

Upon my bed with bryghte bemes,
With many glade gilde stremes;
And eke the welken was so faire—
Blew, bryght, clere was the ayre—   340
And ful attempre for sothe hyt was,
For nother to cold nor hoot yt nas,
Ne in al the welken was a clowde.

  And as I lay thus, wonder lowde
Me thoghte I herde an hunte blowe   345
T'assay hys horn, and for to knowe
Whether hyt were clere or hors of soune,
And I herde goynge bothe up and doune
Men, hors, houndes, and other thynge;
And al men speken of huntynge,   350
How they wolde slee the hert with strengthe,
And how the hert had upon lengthe
So moche embosed—y not now what.
Anoon-ryght, whan I herde that—
How that they wolde on-huntynge goon—   355
I was ryght glad, and up anoon
Took my hors, and forth I went
Out of my chambre. I never stent
Til I com to the feld withoute.
Ther overtok y a grete route   360
Of huntes and eke of foresteres,
With many relayes and lymeres,
And hyed hem to the forest faste,
And I with hem. So at the laste
I asked oon, ladde a lymere,   365
"Say, felowe, whoo shal hunte here?"
Quod I, and he answered ageyn,

"Syr, th'emperour Octovyen,"
Quod he, "and ys here faste by."
  "A Goddes halfe, in good tyme," quod I,   370
"Go we faste," and gan to ryde.
Whan we came to the forest syde,
Every man didde ryght anoon
As to huntynge fille to doon.
The mayster-hunte, anoon fot-hote,   375
With a gret horn blewe thre mote
At the uncouplynge of hys houndes.
Withynne a while the hert yfounde ys,
Yhalowed, and rechased faste
Longe tyme. And so at the laste   380
This hert rused and staal away
Fro alle the houndes a prevy way.
The houndes had overshette hym alle,
And were upon a defaute yfalle.
Therwyth the hunte wonder faste   385
Blewe a forloyn at the laste.
  I was go walked fro my tree,
And as I wente ther cam by mee
A whelp, that fauned me as I stoode,
That hadde yfolowed and koude no goode.   390
Hyt come and crepte to me as lowe
Ryght as hyt hadde me yknowe,
Held doun hys hede and joyned hys eres,
And leyde al smothe doun hys heres.
I wolde have kaught hyt, and anoon   395
Hyt fled and was fro me goon;
And I hym folwed, and hyt forthe went
Doun by a floury grene went

338 gilde, golden (gilt) streams through the small lead panes. **339 welken,** sky. **341 attempre,** temperate. **342 nas:** F&c *was.* **343 *a:*** T *no.* **345 hunte blowe,** huntsman blow his horn. Some scholars have commented on the verisimilitude of the ensuing description, which is full of the technical terminology of medieval hunting. Others have pointed to the telescoping of events (at l. 356 he gets from his bed to his horse; at l. 387 he is off his horse and standing under a tree) as typical dream psychology. **346 T'assay,** to try out. **351 slee the hert,** the hunt as an allegory for the pursuit of love, both human and divine, is familiar in iconography and literature, from the unicorn tapestries and *Gawain and the Green Knight* to Francis Thompson's "The Hound of Heaven." The repetition of *hert* (*e*) throughout *BD* has many overtones: it is the "hart" (the stag; by extension, the lady), the wounded "heart" of the lover, and the verb "hurt." These various meanings are subtly interwoven. **352 upon,** at. **353 embosed,** hidden itself (OF *embuschier*). **354 Anoon-ryght,** immediately. **358 stent,** stopped. **360 route,** hunters. **361 huntes,** huntsmen. **362 relayes . . . lymeres,** packs of fresh hounds, scent hounds. **365 ladde,** led; scent hounds were kept on leash. **368 Octovyen,** Octavian, original name of Caesar Augustus (63 B.C.–A.D. 14), adopted son of Julius Caesar and founder of the imperial Roman government. At ll. 1314–19 he is called "this kynge" and rides home to a castle whose "significatio" is Blanche of Lancaster and John of Richmond. Hence, some scholars have taken "Octavian" to be a complimentary reference to Edward III. The reference also maintains dream psychology by connecting with the material the poet had been reading about before he fell asleep, cf. l. 58 above. **370 Goddes halfe,** God's sake. **376 mote,** notes. **378 hert,** hart, but cf. l. 350n. *yfounde:* FT&c *founde.* **379 Yhalowed . . . rechased,** yelled at, headed off. **381 rused,** evaded by deception. **382 prevy,** secret. **383 overshette,** overshot. **384 defaute,** failure (to catch the hart). **385 hunte,** huntsman. **386 forloyn,** recall to hounds and huntsmen. F *forleygne.* **387 my tree,** huntsmen were posted around the perimeter to head the stag back into the hunting area by yelling and "rechasing" (l. 379), and to shoot at it if they could. **389 fauned,** fawned on. Scholars have observed that animal guides frequently lead knights to adventures in the romances, but they are seldom so realistically depicted as this. **390 yfolowed and koude,** i.e., followed the pack but could do no good. **397 And:** T *As.* **398 went,** path.

Ful thikke of gras, ful softe and swete,
With floures fele faire under fete, 400
And litel used—hyt semed thus;
For both Flora and Zephirus,
They two that make floures growe,
Had mad her dwellynge ther, I trowe.
For hit was, on to beholde, 405
As thogh the erthe envye wolde
To be gayer than the heven,
To have moo floures swiche seven
As in the welken sterres bee;
Hyt had forgete the povertee 410
That wynter, thorgh hys colde morwes,
Had mad hyt suffre, and his sorwes.
All was forgeten, and that was sene,
For al the woode was waxen grene;
Swetnesse of dewe had mad hyt waxe. 415
Hyt ys no nede eke for to axe
Wher there were many grene greves,
Or thikke of trees so ful of leves;
And every tree stood by hymselve
Fro other wel ten foot or twelve— 420
So grete trees, so huge of strengthe,
Of fourty or fifty fadme lengthe,
Clene withoute bowgh or stikke,
With croppes brode and eke as thikke—
They were nat an ynche asonder— 425
That hit was shadewe overal under.
And many an hert and many an hynde
Was both before me and behynde.
Of founes, sowres, bukkes, does
Was ful the woode, and many roes, 430
And many sqwirelles that sete
Ful high upon the trees and ete,
And in hir maner made festes.
Shortly, hyt was so ful of bestes,

That thogh Argus, the noble countour, 435
Sete to rekene in hys countour,
And rekene with his figures ten—
For by tho figures mowe al ken,
Yf they be crafty, rekene and noumbre,
And tel of everything the noumbre— 440
Yet shoulde he fayle to rekene evene
The wondres me mette in my swevene.
    But forth I romed ryght wonder faste
Doun the woode; so at the laste
I was war of a man in blak 445
That sete and had yturned his bak
To an ooke, an huge tree.
"Lord," thoght I, "who may that be?
What ayleth hym to sitten here?"
Anoon-ryght I wente nere; 450
Than found I sitte even upryght
A wonder wel farynge knyght—
By the maner me thoghte so—
Of good mochel, and ryght yong therto,
Of the age of foure and twenty yere, 455
Upon hys berde but lytel here,
And he was clothed al in blake.
I stalked even unto hys bake,
And there I stood as stille as ought
That, soth to saye, he saw me nought, 460
For-why he heng hys hed adoune,
And with a dedely sorwful soune
He made of ryme ten vers or twelfe
Of a compleynt to hymselfe—
The moste pitee, the moste rowthe, 465
That ever I herde; for by my trowthe,
Hit was gret wonder that nature
Myght suffre any creature
To have such sorwe and be not ded.
Ful petous pale and nothyng red, 470

400 **fele**, many. 402 **Flora . . . Zephirus**, goddess of flowers, the west wind (cf. *CT* 1.5n.). 404 **trowe**, believe. 406 **envye**, contend, cf. l. 173n. 408 **swiche seven**, seven times. 409 **welken**, sky. F *walkene*. 417 **Wher . . . greves**, whether, branches. 420 *foot*: F *fete*. 422 **fadme**, fathom (6 feet). 424 **croppes**, i.e., branches and foliage. *brode*: F&c *bothe*. 427 **hert . . . hynde**, male and female deer. 429 **founes, sowres**, fawns, sorrels (3–4 year old bucks). 434 **Shortly**, i.e., in short. 435 **Argus, the . . . countour**, Algus (perhaps confused with the 100-eyed Argus), the 9th-century Arabian mathematician through the translation of whose writings arabic numerals and the decimal system (called alegorism or augrim) were introduced into Europe after 1200; cf. *CT* 1.3210n. 436 **countour**, counting-house. 438 **mowe**, may. 441 **evene**, fully. 443 *I*: F&c *they*. 446 **sete**: T *sate*; F *turned*. 451 **even upryght**, quite erect. 452 **wel farynge**, attractive seeming. 454 **good mochel**, good size. 455 **foure and twenty**, John of Gaunt, Blanche's bereaved husband—to whom *BD* is mainly addressed, whatever incidental compliments it may pay to Joan of Kent or Edward III—was 29 in 1369, about the same age as Chaucer himself. Manly suggested that 24 may have resulted from scribal misreading of XXIV for XXIX, but the next line suggests a deliberate juvenation. Perhaps, as sometimes today, it was a compliment to underestimate the age of a prince. 458 **stalked**, crept. 460 *That*: T *The*. 461 **For-why**, because. 463 T *verses*. 465 **rowthe**, sorrow.

He sayed a lay, a maner songe,
Withoute noote, withoute songe,
And was thys, for ful wel I kan
Reherse hyt ryght. Thus hyt began:

I have of sorwe so grete wone   475
That joye gete I never none
Now that I see my lady bryght,
Which I have loved with al my myght,
Is fro me ded, and ys agoon.   479

Allas, dethe, what ayleth the   481
That thou noldest have taken me,
Whan thou toke my lady swete,
That was so faire, so freshe, so fre,
So goode, that men may wel se   485
Of al goodnesse she had no mete?

Whan he had mad thus his complaynt
Hys sorwful hert gan faste faynt,
And his spirites wexen dede;
The blood was fled for pure drede   490
Doun to hys herte to make hym warme,
For wel hyt feled the herte had harme,
To wete eke why hyt was adrad,
By kynde and for to make hyt glad,
For hit ys membre principal   495
Of the body; and that made al
Hys hewe chaunge and wexe grene
And pale, for ther noo blood ys sene
In no maner lym of hys.
Anoon therwith whan y sawgh this   500
He ferde thus evel there he sete,
I went and stoode ryght at his fete
And grette hym, but he spake noght,
But argued with his oune thoght,
And in hys wytte disputed faste   505
Why and how hys lyfe myght laste—

Hym thought hys sorwes were so smerte,
And lay so colde upon hys herte.
So throgh hys sorwes and hevy thoght
Made hym that he herde me noght,   510
For he had wel nygh lost hys mynde,
Thogh Pan, that men clepe God of Kynde,
Were for hys sorwes never so wroth.
    But at the last, to sayn ryght soth,
He was war of me, how y stoode   515
Before hym and did of myn hoode,
And had ygret hym as I best koude,
Debonayrly and nothyng lowde.
He sayde, "I prey the, be not wroth.
I herde the not, to seyn the soth,   520
Ne I sawgh the not, syr, trewely."
    "A, goode sire, no fors," quod y,
"I am ryght sory yif I have oughte
Destroubled yow out of your thoughte.
Foryive me yif I have mystake."   525
    "Yis, th'amendes is lyght to make,"
Quod he, "for ther lyeth noon therto.
There ys nothyng myssayd nor do."
Loo, how godoely spak thys knyghte,
As hit had be another wyghte: 530
He made hyt nouther towgh ne queynte.
And I saw that and gan me aqueynte
With hym, and fonde hym so tretable,
Ryght wonder skylful and resonable,
As me thoght, for al hys bale.   535
Anoon-ryght I gan fynde a tale
To hym, to loke wher I myght oughte
Have more knowynge of hys thoughte.
    "Sir," quod I, "this game is doon.
I holde that this hert be goon;   540
These huntes konne hym nowher see."
    "Y do no fors therof," quod he.

---

471 **maner songe,** kind of song. 472 **noote . . . songe,** musical notes, music. 475 **wone,** plenty. 480 T adds a line: *And thus in sorwe lefte me alone.* This line has generally been regarded as spurious and omitted. (Cf. l.31n). Koch suggests that 478 might follow 480 to achieve the aabaab scheme of the second stanza. However, the *agoon–alone* rhyme is not Chaucerian and the shift strains the syntax. 481 **Allas, dethe,** the apostrophe to Death is a commonplace of the *"Planctus Mariae,"* the lament of Mary at the foot of the cross. 482 T *Whan that.* 486 **mete,** equal. 493 **To wete eke,** also to learn. 494 **By kynde,** i.e., the blood all flowed to the heart by natural impulse. 499 **lym,** limb. 501 **He ferde thus evel,** (that) he fared so badly. 507 **smerte,** painful. 509 *hevy:* T *holi.* 512 **Pan . . . Kynde,** Pan, god of Nature, a typical medieval view of pagan "pantheism." F *the god.* 516 **did of,** i.e., doffed. 518 **Debonayrly,** politely. 522 **no fors,** no matter. 525 **mystake,** done wrong. 526 **lyght,** easy. 527 **lyeth noon therto,** none is needed. 529 **goodely,** pleasantly. 530 **be another wyghte,** be (to) another person. 531 **towgh ne queynte,** arrogant nor affected—in this line we observe Chaucer's "good ear" for voice as a clue to character. 533 **tretable,** approachable. 534 **skylful,** sensible. 535 **bale,** grief. 536 **fynde a tale,** i.e., think of something to say. 537 **to loke wher,** to discover whether. 538 *knowynge:* T *knowlegyng.* 539 **game,** i.e., the hunt. 542 **do no fors,** don't care.

"My thought ys thereon never a dele."

  "By oure Lorde," quod I, "y trow yow wele;
Ryght so me thenketh by youre chere.   545
But sir, oo thyng wol ye here?
Me thynketh in gret sorowe I yow see,
But certes, sir, yif that yee
Wolde ought discure me youre woo,
I wolde, as wys God helpe me soo,   550
Amende hyt, yif I kan or may.
Ye mowe preve hyt be assay.
For, by my trouthe, to make yow hool
I wol do alle my power hool.
And telleth me of your sorwes smerte.   555
Paraunter hyt may ese youre herte
That semeth ful seke under your syde."

  With that he loked on me asyde,
As who sayth, "Nay, that wol not be."
"Graunt mercy, goode frend," quod he,   560
"I thanke thee that thow woldest soo,
But hyt may never the rather be doo.
No man may my sorwe glade;
That maketh my hewe to fal and fade,
And hath myn understondynge lorne,   565
That me ys wo that I was borne.
May noght make my sorwes slyde
Nought al the remedyes of Ovyde,
Ne Orpheus, god of melodye,
Ne Dedalus with his playes slye;   570
Ne hele me may noo phisicien,
Noght Ypocras ne Galyen.
Me ys woo that I lyve oures twelve.
But whooso wol assay hymselve
Whether his hert kan have pitee   575

Of any sorwe, lat hym see me—
Y wrecchhe, that deth hath made al naked
Of alle blysse that ever was maked,
Yworthe worste of alle wyghtes,
That hate my dayes and my nyghtes.   580
My lyf, my lustes, be me loothe,
For al welfare and I be wroothe.
The pure deth ys so ful my foo
That I wolde deye—hyt wolde not soo,
For whan I folwe hyt, hit wol flee.   585
I wolde have hym, hyt nyl nat me.
This ys my peyne, wythoute rede,
Alway deynge and be not dede,
That Thesiphus that lyeth in helle
May not of more sorwe telle.   590
And whoso wiste al, be my trouthe,
My sorwe, but he hadde rowthe
And pitee of my sorwes smerte,
That man hath a fendely herte.
For whoso seeth me first on morwe   595
May seyn he hath mette with sorwe,
For y am sorwe and sorwe ys y.

  "Allas, and I wol tel the why
My song ys turned to pleynynge,
And al my lawghtre to wepynge,   600
My glade thoghtes to hevynesse:
In travayle ys myn ydelnesse
And eke my reste; my wele is woo,
My goode ys harme, and evermoo
In wrathe ys turned my pleynge,   605
And my delyt into sorwynge.
Myn hele ys turned into seknesse,
In drede ys al my sykernesse,

---

544 trow, believe. **545 chere,** behavior. 549 **discure,** reveal. Although there has been much critical writing around the topic, the pattern of consolation in *BD* is evident. The Dreamer purposely misunderstands the reason for the Black Knight's grief (which he had heard stated clearly at ll. 475–83) to get him to talk about it, which is itself a step toward assuaging it—a technique that Chaucer comments on directly in connection with Pandarus and Troylus, *TC* i.561ff. **552 mowe preve,** may test (prove). **553 hool,** whole. **556** *Paraunter:* F&c *Peraventure.* **562 rather,** sooner. **565 lorne,** impaired (lost). **567 slyde,** go away. **568 remedyes of Ovyde,** the ironic, antifeminist suggestions in Ovid's *Remedia Amoris* suggest that the less one knows about the contents, the more the title seems appropriate to this context. **569 Orpheus,** whose harping eased the tortures of the sufferers in Hades—music cannot help the mourner. **570 Dedalus,** tried to invent wings to escape the earth—mechanical contrivances cannot help the mourner. **playes slye,** clever creations. **572 Ypocras . . . Galyen,** Hippocrates, Galen, classical Greek founders of medicine. **579 Yworthe,** (have) become. **581 lustes, be me,** pleasures are to me. **582 be wroothe,** are angry with each other. **587 rede,** remedy. **589 Thesiphus,** either Tityus, who lay stretched out over 9 acres with a vulture tearing at his liver (Ovid, *Met.* 4.450), or Sisyphus, whose punishment was eternally to roll a stone up a hill (ibid., 454). **592 rowthe,** sympathy. **594 fendely,** fiendish. **595 morwe,** morning. **599 song . . . pleynynge,** the oxymora in this and the following lines are characteristic of troubadour convention. *song:* FT&c *sorowe.* **603 wele,** good fortune. **607 hele,** health. **608 sykernesse,** security.

To derke ys turned al my lyghte,
My wytte ys foly, my day ys nyghte,   610
My love ys hate, my slepe wakynge,
My merthe and meles ys fastynge,
My countenaunce ys nycete,
And al abawed whereso I be
My pees, in pledynge and in werre.   615
Allas, how myghte I fare werre?
My boldenesse ys turned to shame
For fals Fortune hath pleyde a game
Atte chesse with me, allas the while!
The trayteresse fals and ful of gyle,   620
That al behoteth and nothyng halte,
She geth upryght and yet she halte,
That baggeth foule and loketh faire,
The dispitouse debonaire,
That skorneth many a creature.   625
An ydole of fals portrayture
Ys she, for she wol sone wrien.
She is the mowstres hed ywrien,
As fylthe over-ystrawed with floures.
Hir moste worshippe and hir flour ys   630
To lyen, for that ys hyr nature,
Withoute feyth, lawe, or mesure.
She ys fals and ever lawghynge
With one eye, and that other wepynge.
That ys broght up, she sette al doun.   635
I lykne hyr to the scorpioun
That ys a fals, flaterynge beste,
For with his hede he maketh feste,

But al amydde his flaterynge
With hys tayle he wol stynge   640
And envenyme—and so wol she.
She ys th'envyouse charite
That ys ay fals and seemeth wele,
So turneth she hyr false whele
Aboute, for hyt ys nothyng stable,   645
Now by the fire, now at table.
For many oon hath she thus yblent;
She ys pley of enchauntement,
That semeth oon and ys not soo.
The false thef, what hath she doo,   650
Trowest thou? By oure Lord, I wol the seye.
At the chesse with me she gan to pleye;
With hir fals draughtes dyvers
She staal on me and toke my fers.
And whan I sawgh my fers away,   655
Allas, I kouthe no lenger play,
But seyde, 'Farewel, swete, ywys,
And farewel al that ever ther ys!'
Therwith Fortune seyde, 'Chek here!'
And mate in myd poynt of the chekkere   660
With a poune errant. Allas,
Ful craftier to pley she was
Than Athalus that made the game
First of the chesse—so was hys name.
But God wolde I had oones or twyes   665
Ykoud and knowe the jeupardyes
That kowde the Greke Pictagores!
I shulde have pleyd the bet at ches,

---

609 *lyghte:* T *syght.* **613 countenaunce . . . nycete,** seriousness, foolishness. **614 abawed,** abashed. **615 pledynge,** lawsuit(s). **616 werre,** worse. **619 chesse,** chess was a favorite game with the medieval warrior aristocracy as the designations for the pieces still reveal. It was both a war game and an exposition of the Boethian idea of "conditional necessity," because, while the movements of individual pieces were severely circumscribed, the variety of moves on the board was limitless. The second book Caxton printed in English was his moralizing *Game and Play of Chess* (Bruges, 1475). **619** *Atte:* T *At the.* **621 behoteth . . . halte,** promises, holds (fulfills). **622 halte,** limps. F&c *is halte.* **623 baggeth foule,** squints repulsively. **624 dispitouse debonaire,** cruel gracious one—more oxymoron. **626 fals portrayture,** false representation. **627 wrien,** turn away. F&c *urien.* **628 mowstres . . . ywrien,** monster's, concealed. **629 over-ystrawed,** overstrewn. **630 moste worshippe . . . flour,** greatest renown, achievement (flower). **632 mesure,** restraint. **636 scorpioun,** this figure was a favorite with Chaucer, cf. *CT* II.404, IV.58, IX.271, X.854, and is referred to frequently elsewhere in medieval writings. **638 maketh feste,** is pleasant. **640** *he:* F&c *hyt.* **643 wele,** well (agreeable). **644 false whele,** the wheel of Fortune, which carried temporal fortunes up, then down, was another favorite medieval figure, beginning perhaps with Boethius, II pr. 1. **647 yblent,** blinded. *For:* T *Ful.* **651 Trowest thou,** would you believe. **653 draughtes,** moves. T *ful dyvers.* **654 fers,** the OF term for the queen, from the original Persian *ferzan,* counsellor or companion. In Europe, the *fers* came to be designated the queen, the only feminine piece among the chessmen. **655 fers away,** in chess the function of the queen is to protect the king; its loss leaves the king vulnerable. **659–60 Chek . . . mate,** another relic of Persian terminology: "check" from *shah,* "mate" from *mat(a),* is dead. **660 chekkere,** chessboard. **661 poune errant,** to be checkmated in the middle of the board by a stray pawn is to lose rather ignominiously. **663 Athalus,** in *RR* 6675 (Dunn-Robbins 32.44) cited as the inventor of chess. Several of Chaucer's lines are lifted directly from this passage (*RR* 6647ff.). **667 Pictagores,** an eponym for wisdom—and a good rhyme. T *Pithagores.*

And kept my fers the bet therby.
And thogh wherto? For trewely,
I holde that wyssh nat worth a stree.
Hyt had be never the bet for me.
For Fortune kan so many a wyle
Ther be but fewe kan hir begile.
And eke she ys the lasse to blame;
Myself I wolde have do the same,
Before God, hadde I ben as she;
She oghte the more excused be.
For this I say yet more therto,
Had I be God and myghte have do
My wille, whan she my fers kaughte,
I wolde have drawe the same draughte.
For, also wys God yive me reste,
I dar wel swere she took the beste.
But through that draughte I have lorn
My blysse. Allas that I was born,
For evermore, y trowe trewly,
For al my wille, my lust holly
Ys turned. But yet what to doone?
Be oure Lord, hyt ys to deye soone—
For nothyng I leve hyt noghte,
But lyve and deye ryght in this thoghte.
For there nys planete in firmament,
Ne in ayr ne in erthe noon element,
That they ne yive me a yifte echone
Of wepynge whan I am allone.
For whan that I avise me wel,
And bethenke me every del,
How that ther lyeth in rekenyng
Inne my sorwe for nothyng,
And how ther leveth no gladnesse
May glade me of my distresse,
And how I have lost suffisance,
And therto I have no plesance,
Thanne may I say I have ryght noghte.
And whan al this falleth in my thoghte,

Allas, than am I overcome,
For that ys doon ys not to come.
I have more sorowe than Tantale."
    And whan I herde hym tel thys tale
Thus pitously, as I yow telle,
Unnethe myght y lenger duelle—
Hyt dyde myn hert so moche woo.
"A, goode sir," quod I, "say not soo.
Have some pitee on your nature
That formed yow to creature.
Remembre yow of Socrates,
For he ne counted nat thre strees
Of noght that Fortune koude doo."
    "No," quod he, "I kan not soo."
    "Why so, good syr, parde?" quod y.
"Ne say noght soo, for trewely,
Thogh ye had lost the ferses twelve,
And ye for sorwe mordred yourselve,
Ye sholde be dampned in this cas
By as goode ryght as Medea was,
That slowgh hir children for Jason;
And Phyllis also for Demophon
Henge hirselfe, so weylaway,
For he had broke his terme-day
To come to hir. Another rage
Had Dydo, the quene eke of Cartage,
That slough hirself for Eneas
Was fals—which a fool she was—
And Ecquo died for Narcisus
Nolde nat love hir. And ryght thus
Hath many another foly doon;
And for Dalida died Sampson,
That slough hymself with a pilere.
But ther is no man alyve here
Wolde for a fers make this woo."
    "Why so?" quod he, "hyt ys nat soo.
Thou woste ful lytel what thou menest.
I have lost more than thow wenest."

670
675
680
685
690
695
700
705
710
715
720
725
730
735
740

---

669 **kept,** guarded. 671 **stree,** straw. 672 **had be,** would have been. 673 **kan,** knows. 677 F *God, as I be as* 682 **drawe . . . draughte,** made, move. 684 *she:* F&c *he.* 685 **lorn,** lost. 688 **lust,** joy. 689 **turned,** reversed. **yet:** T *ye.* 691 **leve,** believe (trust in). 697 **avise me,** consider. 699–700 **rekenyng . . . for nothyng,** i.e., there is no sorrow owing to my account. 701 **leveth,** remains. 703 **suffisance,** contentment. 709 **Tantale,** Tantalus, whose punishment in Hades was to stand for eternity with food and drink just beyond his grasp. 711 **Thus:** F *This.* 712 **Unnethe . . . duelle,** scarcely, stay (there). 718 **strees,** straws; for this view of Socrates cf. *RR* 5832ff. (Dunn-Robbins, 28.37ff.). 721 FT&c *yis parde.* 726 **Medea,** who helped Jason secure the Golden Fleece, eloped with him, and killed their children when he deserted her. These stock examples of overreaction are all found in various parts of *RR.* 730 **terme-day,** agreed-upon day: Demophon, Theseus' son, did not return to his wife, Phyllis, at the time he had promised. 735 **Ecquo,** Echo, who was loved by Narcissus even though he was indifferent to her. 738 **Dalida,** Delilah. 744 **wenest,** know.

"Loo, sey how that may be," quod y. 745
"Good sir, telle me al hooly
In what wyse, how, why, and wherfore
That ye have thus youre blysse lore."

"Blythely," quod he. "Come sytte adoun.
I telle hyt the upon condicioun 750
That thou shalt hooly with all thy wytte
Doo thyn entent to herkene hitte."

"Yis, syr."—"Swere thy trouthe therto."

"Gladly."—"Do thanne holde hereto."

"I shal ryght blythely, so God me save, 755
Hooly, with al the witte I have,
Here yow as wel as I kan."

"A Goddes half," quod he, and began.

"Syr," quod he, "sith firste I kouthe
Have any maner wyt fro youthe, 760
Or kyndely understondynge
To comprehende in any thynge
What love was, in myn oune wytte,
Dredeles, I have ever yitte
Be tributarye and yiven rente 765
To Love, hooly with good entente,
And throgh plesaunce become his thralle,
With good wille, body, hert, and alle.
Al this I putte in his servage,
As to my lord, and did homage, 770
And ful devoutely I prayed hym to
He shulde besette myn herte so
That hyt plesance to hym were,
And worship to my lady dere.
And this was longe and many a yere 775
Or that myn herte was set owhere,
That I dide thus, and nyste why;
I trowe hit came me kyndely.
Paraunter I was therto most able,
As a white walle or a table, 780

For hit ys redy to cachche and take
Al that men wil theryn make,
Whethir so men wil portreye or peynt,
Be the werkes never so queynt.

"And thilke tyme I ferde ryght so 785
I was able to have lerned tho
And to have kende as wel or better
Paraunter other art or letre,
But for love came first in my thoghte,
Therfore I forgat hyt noghte. 790
I ches love to my firste crafte,
Therfore hit ys with me lafte,
Forwhy I tok hyt of so yonge age
That malyce hadde my corage
Nat that tyme turned to nothynge 795
Thorgh to mochel knowlechynge.
For that tyme Yowthe, my maistresse,
Governed me in ydelnesse,
For hyt was in my firste youthe,
And thoo ful lytel good y couthe, 800
For al my werkes were flyttynge
That tyme, and al my thoght varyinge.
Al were to me ylyche goode
That I knew thoo. But thus hit stoode:

"Hit happed that I came on a day 805
Into a place ther that I say
Trewly the fayrest companye
Of ladyes that evere man with eye
Had seen togedres in oo place.
Shal I clepe hyt happe other grace 810
That broght me there? Nay, but Fortune,
That ys to lyen ful comune,
The false trayteresse pervers!
God wolde I koude clepe hir wers,
For now she worcheth me ful woo, 815
And I wol telle sone why soo.

---

745 F&c *Loo she that may be*; T *How that may be.* 748 **lore**, lost. 749 **Blythely**, happily. 750 F *up a*; T *telle the upon a.* 754 *hereto*: F&c *here, lo.* 761 **kyndely**, natural. 764 **Dredeles**, doubtless. 767 **throgh plesaunce**, with pleasure (willingly). 772 **besette**, dispose of. 773 **plesance to hym**, i.e., as it pleased him. 776 **Or . . . owhere**, before (ere), anywhere. 777 **nyste**, didn't know. 778 **trowe . . . kyndely**, believe, naturally (i.e., he had a natural aptitude for love). 779 **able**, i.e., prepared, ready. F&c *Peraventure.* 780 **white walle**, this figure of the *tabula rasa*, which we associate with the philosophy of John Locke, is found in Boethius, v m. 4, and can be traced to antiquity. Chaucer modeled his phrasing on Machaut's *Remede de Fortune*, ll.26–30. **table**, (wax) tablet. 783 **portreye**, draw. 786 **was able . . . tho**, i.e., would have been (as) able, then. 787 **kende**, understood. 793 **Forwhy**, because. 794 **That malyce . . . corage**, when trouble (cf. OED "malease"), spirit (courage). 799 **firste youthe**, John of Gaunt married Blanche of Lancaster at the age of 19. 803 **Al . . . ylyche**, all (things) . . . equally. 804 **thoo**, then. *But:* T *For.* 806 **say**, saw. 807 **fayrest companye**, the "vision of fair ladies," an icon of Western poets from the troubadours to Yeats and Eliot. 810 **clepe . . . happe other**, call, chance or. 811 *Nay*: T *Not.* 812 **comune**, accustomed.

"Among these ladyes thus echon,
Soth to seyen y sawgh oon
That was lyk noon of the route,
For I dar swere, withoute doute,   820
That as the someres sonne bryghte
Ys fairer, clere, and hath more lyghte
Than any other planete in hevene,
The moone, or the sterres sevene,
For al the world so hadde she   825
Surmounted hem al of beaute,
Of maner and of comelynesse,
Of stature and of wel sette gladnesse,
Of godlyhede so wel besey,
Shortly—what shal y more sey—   830
By God and by his halwes twelve,
Hyt was my swete, ryght al hirselve.
She had so stedfast countenaunce,
So noble port and meyntenaunce,
And Love, that had wel herd my boone,   835
Had espyed me thus soone,
That she ful sone in my thoght,
As helpe me God, so was ykaught
So sodenly, that I ne tok
No maner counseyl but at hir loke,   840
And at myn herte. Forwhy hir eyen
So gladly, I trow, myn herte seyen
That purely tho myn oune thoghte
Seyde hit were beter serve hir for noghte
Than with another to be wel.   845
And hyt was soth, for everydel
I wil anoon ryght telle thee why:
I sawgh hyr daunce so comelely,
Carole and synge so swetely,
Lawghe and pleye so womanly,   850
And loke so debonairly,

So goodely speke and so frendly,
That certes y trowe that evermore
Nas seyn so blysful a tresore.
For every heer on hir hede,   855
Soth to seyne hyt was not rede,
Ne nouther yelowe ne broune hyt nas;
Me thoghte most lyk gold hyt was.
And whiche eyen my lady hadde—
Debonair, goode, glade, and sadde,   860
Symple, of good mochel, noght to wyde.
Therto hir look nas not asyde,
Ne overthwert, but beset so wele
Hyt drewh and took up everydele
Al that on hir gan beholde.   865
Hir eyen semed anoon she wolde
Have mercy—foolys wenden soo—
But hyt was never the rather doo.
Hyt nas no countrefeted thynge,
Hyt was hir oune pure lokynge   870
That the goddesse dame Nature
Had made hem opene by mesure,
And cloos; for were she never so glad,
Hyr lokynge was not foly sprad,
Ne wildely, thogh that she pleyde.   875
But ever me thoght hir eyen seyde,
'Be God, my wrathe ys al foryive.'
    "Therwith hir lyste so wel to lyve
That dulnesse was of hir adrad.
She nas to sobre ne to glad.   880
In alle thynges more mesure
Had never, I trowe, creature.
But many oon with hire loke she hert,
And that sat hyr ful lytel at hert,
For she knew nothynge of her thoght.   885
But whither she knew or knew it nowght,

---

819 **route,** crowd. The following moving description of the lady is in fact pieced together from lines translated from *RR*, poems of Machaut and Deschamps that Chaucer has used throughout, and examples in Geoffrey of Vinsauf's handbook of rhetoric, *Poetria Nova,* ll. 563ff. 824 **sterres sevene,** evidently the Pleiades. 828 **stature . . . wel sette gladnesse,** bodily shape, suitable gaiety. F *so wel.* 829 **godlyhede . . . besey,** beauty (attractiveness), provided. 830 F&c *more* om. 831 **halwes,** i.e., Christ and his apostles. F&c *his* om. 833 **stedfast,** steady (not giddy). 835 **boone,** prayer. 841 **Forwhy,** because. *herte:* F *hest.* 842 **seyen,** looked at. 853 T *nevermore.* 858 F&c *gold* om. 860 **Debonair . . . sadde,** gracious, serious. 861 **good mochel,** good size. 863 **overthwert,** across. F&c *over twert, overtwhart.* 867 *foolys:* T *folly.* 868 **rather doo,** sooner done (i.e., in spite of her merciful manner, she was not too quick to do mercy). 870 **pure,** i.e., not assisted by cosmetics, etc. 872 **by mesure,** just right. 874 **lokynge . . . foly sprad,** countenance, foolishly (fatuously) spread—she kept an aristocratic "closed countenance." *foly:* T *folyche.* 875 **pleyde,** joked. 877 **wrathe,** i.e., "daunger"—the courtly lady's protective aloofness. 878 **lyste . . . lyve,** i.e., enjoyed life. 881 **mesure,** moderation (suitable emphasis on the various facets of life). 883–84 **hert . . . hert,** hurt, heart, cf. l. 350n. 884 **sat hyr,** affected her. 885 **her,** their. 886 Line originally lacking in F&c; cf. l. 3n.

Algate she ne rought of hem a stree.
To gete hyr love noo nerre was he
That woned at hom than he in Ynde;
The formest was alway behynde.   890
But goode folk over al other
She loved as man may do hys brother,
Of whiche love she was wonder large
In skilful places that bere charge.
    "But which a visage had she thertoo!   895
Allas, myn herte ys wonder woo
That I ne kan discryven hyt.
Me lakketh both Englyssh and wit
For to undo hyt at the fulle,
And eke my spirites be so dulle   900
So gret a thyng for to devyse.
I have no witte that kan suffise
To comprehenden hir beaute.
But thus moche dar I sayn, that she
Was rody, fressh, and lyvely hewed,   905
And every day hir beaute newed.
And negh hir face was alderbest,
For certes, Nature had swich lest
To make that faire that trewly she
Was hir chefe patron of beaute,   910
And chefe ensample of al hir werke,
And moustre; for be hyt never so derke,
Me thynketh I se hir evermoo.
And yet moreover, thogh alle thoo
That ever levede were not alyve,   915
Ne sholde have founde to diskryve
Yn al hir face a wikked sygne,
For hit was sad, symple, and benygne.
    "And which a goodely, softe speche
Had that swete, my lyves leche!   920
So frendly, and so wel ygrounded,
Up al resoun so wel yfounded,
And so tretable to alle goode,

That I dar swere wel, by the roode,
Of eloquence was never founde   925
So swete a sownynge facounde,
Ne trewer tonged, ne skorned lasse,
Ne bet koude hele, that, by the masse,
I durste swere, thogh the pope hit songe,
That ther was never yet throgh hir tonge   930
Man ne woman gretely harmed—
As for her, was al harm hyd.
Ne lasse flaterynge in hir word,
That purely hir symple record
Was founde as trewe as any bonde,   935
Or trouthe of any mannes honde,
Ne chyde she koude never a dele;
That knoweth al the world ful wele.
    "But swiche a fairenesse of a nekke
Had that swete that boon nor brekke   940
Nas ther non seene that myssatte.
Hyt was smothe, streght, and pure flatte,
Wythouten hole, or canel-boon,
As be semynge, had she noon.
Hyr throte, as I have now memoyre,   945
Semed a round tour of yvoyre,
Of good gretenesse and noght to grete.
    "And goode faire White she hete,
That was my lady name ryghte.
She was bothe faire and bryghte;   950
She hadde not hir name wronge.
Ryght faire shuldres and body longe
She had, and armes, every lyth
Fattyssh, flesshy, not grete therwith;
Ryght white handes and nalyes rede;   955
Rounde brestes; and of good brede
Hyr hippes were; a streight flat bakke.
I knewe on hir noon other lakke
That al hir lymmes nere pure sywynge
In as ferre as I had knowynge.   960

---

887 rought . . . stree, cared, straw. **888 nerre,** nearer. **889 woned,** stayed. **893 large,** generous. **894 skilful . . . bere charge,** reasonable (suitable), bear the weight (deserved it). **899 undo,** reveal. **904 T** *I dar.* **905 FT&c** *whit, rody.* **907 negh . . . alderbest,** nearly, best of all. **912 moustre,** model. **916 diskryve,** discern. **917 wikked sygne,** i.e., sign of wickedness. **918 sad,** sober. **920 leche,** physician. **921 ygrounded,** educated. **922 Up,** upon. **923 tretable . . . goode,** fair-spoken, good (people or topics). **924 roode,** cross. **926 sownynge facounde,** sounding (an) eloquence. **927 skorned,** mocked. **928 hele,** heal. **932 As for her,** as far as she was concerned. *her:* F *hit.* **934 record,** statement. **937 chyde . . . dele,** scold, bit. **939–60,** esp. ll. 958–60, which might appear to reflect the reticence of a court poet describing the wife of his prince, are modeled upon Geoffrey of Vinsauf, ll. 586–600. **940 boon . . . brekke,** bone, flaw. **942 FT&c** *white, smothe,* etc. **943 canel-boon,** collarbone. **944 As be semynge,** as apparently. *As:* Th *And.* **948 White,** Blanche (of Lancaster); cf. ll. 1318–19. This and *LGW* (l. 496) are the only poems in which Chaucer so clearly identifies his royal patrons. **950** *bothe:* T *therto.* **953 lyth,** limb. **956 brede,** breadth. **959 nere pure sywynge,** were not perfectly proportioned (suitable).

"Therto she koude so wel pley,
Whan that hir lyst, that I dar sey
That she was lyk to torche bryghte
That every man may take of lyghte
Ynogh, and hyt hath never the lesse. 965
Of maner and of comlynesse
Ryght so ferde my lady dere,
For every wight of hir manere
Myght cachche ynogh, yif that he wolde,
Yif he had eyen hir to beholde. 970
For I dar swere wel yif that she
Had amonge ten thousande be,
She wolde have be, at the lest,
A chef meroure of al the fest,
Thogh they had stonden in a rowe 975
To mennes eyen koude have knowe.
For wher so men had pleyed or waked,
Me thoghte the felawsshyppe as naked
Withouten hir, that sawgh I oones,
As a corowne withoute stones. 980
Trewly she was to myn eye
The soleyn fenix of Arabye;
For ther levyth never but oon,
Ne swich as she ne knowe I noon.

"To speke of godenesse, trewly she 985
Had as moche debonairyte
As ever had Hester in the Bible,
And more yif more were possyble.
And soth to seyn, therwythalle
She had a wytte so generalle, 990
So hoole enclyned to alle goode,
That al hir wytte was set, by the rode,
Withoute malyce, upon gladnesse.
And therto I sawgh never yet a lesse
Harmful than she was in doynge— 995

I sey nat that she ne had knowynge
What harm was, or elles she
Had koude no good, so thenketh me.
And trewly, for to speke of trouthe,
But she had had, hyt hadde be routhe. 1000
Therof she had so moche hyr dele—
And I dar seyn and swere hyt wele—
That Trouthe hymselfe over al and alle
Had chose hys maner principalle
In hir, that was his restyng place. 1005
Therto she hadde the moste grace
To have stedefast perseveraunce,
And esy, attempry governaunce,
That ever I knew or wyste yitte,
So pure suffraunt was hir wytte. 1010
And reson gladly she understood—
Hyt folowed wel she koude good;
She used gladly to do wel.
These were hir maners everydel.

"Therwith she loved so wel ryght, 1015
She wrong do wolde to no wyght.
No wyght myght doo hir noo shame,
She loved so wel hir oune name.
Hyr lust to holde no wyght in honde,
Ne, be thou siker, she wolde not fonde 1020
To holde no wyght in balaunce
By halfe word ne by countenaunce,
But yf men wolde upon hir lye;
Ne sende men into Walakye,
To Pruyse, and into Tartarye, 1025
To Alysaundre, ne into Turkye,
And byd hym faste anoon that he
Goo hoodles into the Drye Se
And come hom by the Carrenare,
And seye, 'Sir, be now ryght ware 1030

---

961 pley, jest (exchange pleasantries). **962** *Whan:* T *What.* **974 chef meroure,** i.e., mirror as the point of focus. **976 eyen koude . . . knowe,** eyes that could discriminate. T *that coulde.* **979** T *I sawe.* **982 soleyn fenix,** solitary (unique) phoenix. The phoenix, which, in the bestiaries, dies in flames and rises from the ashes, is a type of Christ. Like the Black Knight's lament (l. 475ff.), this figure contributes to the pathos by which the chivalric cliché of dying for love is in this poem revivified. **986 debonairyte,** graciousness (attractiveness). **987 Hester,** biblical Esther. **990 wytte . . . generalle,** mind, broad. **992 rode,** cross. **998 koude no good,** i.e., would not have recognized virtue. **1000 had had . . . routhe,** had had (integrity), pity. **1001 dele,** share. **1004 maner,** residence (manor). **1008 attempry governaunce,** moderate behavior. **1010 suffraunt,** tolerant. **1012 koude,** recognized. **1019 lust . . . wyght in honde,** desired, to deceive no one. **1020 siker,** sure. **1022 countenaunce,** i.e., by ambiguous word or look. **1023 But yf . . . upon hir lye,** unless, lied about her. **1024 Walakye,** Wallachia in Roumania—unimaginably distant, like Timbuktu today. The convention that suitors be assigned difficult tasks was derived from folklore; in romances these tasks were usually assigned by *"la belle dame sans merci"* herself. **1025 Pruyse . . . Tartarye,** Prussia, Tartary (Mongolia). **1026 Alysaundre,** Alexandria (Egypt). **1028 hoodles . . . Drye Se,** there is debate about this allusion, but a logical explanation is "without a hat into the Gobi Desert." **1029 Carrenare,** Lake Kara Nor (Black Lake), east of the Gobi, on the trade route from China to the West. **1030 ware,** alert.

That I may of yow here seyn
Worshyppe or that ye come ageyn.'
She ne used no suche knakkes smale.
    "But wherfore that y tel my tale?
Ryght on thys same, as I have seyde,　　1035
Was hooly al my love leyde.
For certes she was, that swete wife,
My suffisaunce, my luste, my lyfe,
Myn happe, myn hele, and al my blysse,
My worldes welfare, and my goddysse,　　1040
And I hooly hires and everydel."
    "By oure Lord," quod I, "y trowe yow wel.
Hardely, your love was wel besette.
I not how ye myght have doo bette."
    "Bette? Ne no wyght so wel!" quod he.　　1045
    "Y trowe hyt, sir," quod I, "parde."
    "Nay, leve hyt wel!"—"Sire, so do I;
I leve yow wel, that trewely
Yow thoghte that she was the best,
And to beholde the alderfayrest,　　1050
Whosoo had loked hir with your eyen."
    "With myn? Nay, alle that hir seyen
Seyde and sworen hyt was soo.
And thogh they ne hadde, I wolde thoo
Have loved best my lady free.　　1055
Thogh I had hadde al the beaute
That ever had Alcipyades,
And al the strengthe of Ercules,
And therto had the worthynesse
Of Alysaunder, and al the rychesse　　1060
That ever was in Babyloyne,
In Cartage, or in Macedoyne,
Or in Rome, or in Nynyve;
And therto also as hardy be
As was Ector, so have I joye,　　1065
That Achilles slough at Troye—
And therfore was he slayn alsoo
In a temple, for bothe twoo

Were slayne, he and Antylegyus,
And so seyth Dares Frygius,　　1070
For love of hir Polixena—
Or ben as wis as Mynerva,
I wolde ever, withoute drede,
Have loved hir, for I moste nede.
Nede! Nay, trewly, I gabbe nowe.　　1075
Noght nede, and I wol telle howe.
For of good wille myn herte hyt wolde,
And eke to love hir I was holde
As for the fairest and the beste.
She was as good, so have I reste,　　1080
As ever was Penelopee of Grece,
Or as the noble wife Lucrece,
That was the best—he telleth thus,
The Romayn, Tytus Lyvyus—
She was as good, and nothyng lyke,　　1085
Thogh hir stories be autentyke;
Algate she was as trewe as she—
But wherfore that I telle the?
    "Whan I first my lady say,
I was ryght yong, soth to say,　　1090
And ful gret nede I hadde to lerne;
Whan my herte wolde yerne
To love, hyt was a gret empryse.
But as my wytte koude best suffise,
After my yonge childely wytte,　　1095
Withoute drede, I besette hytte
To love hir in my beste wyse,
To do hir worshippe and the servise
That I koude thoo, be my trouthe,
Withoute feynynge outher slouthe,　　1100
For wonder feyn I wolde hir se.
So mochel hyt amended me
That whan I saugh hir first a-morwe
I was warysshed of al my sorwe
Of al day after, til hyt were eve;　　1105
Me thoghte nothyng myghte me greve,

1031 here seyn, hear said. **1032 Worshyppe or,** military fame, before. **1033 knakkes,** tricks. **1037 wife,** woman, but also wife, and the *double entendre* on the lips of the Black Knight, John of Gaunt, is poignant. **1038 luste,** joy. **1039 happe . . . hele,** good fortune, well-being. **happe:** T *hope.* **1042 trowe,** believe. **1043 Hardely,** truly. **1044 not,** don't know. **1045** *no wyght:* T *noghte.* **1046** F *hyt wel,* **sir. 1047 leve,** believe. **1050 alderfayrest,** fairest of all. **1054 thoo,** still (then). **1055 free,** generous. **1057 Alcipyades,** Alcibiades, Athenian famous for his beauty. The comparisons are commonplaces. **1059 worthynesse,** eminence. **1064 hardy,** brave. **1069 Antylegyus . . . Dares Frygius,** Chaucer cannot resist going beyond the commonplace to an esoteric detail from the Troy story. It is in Dares, but also in Benoit, etc., all of whom are discussed in the Introduction to *TC.* **1071** FT&c *hir* om. **1074 moste nede,** must needs (am compelled to). **1075 gabbe,** talk foolishly. **1078 holde,** bound. **1089 say,** saw. **1093 empryse,** undertaking. **1094 koude:** T *wolde.* **1095 childely,** childish. **1096 besette,** employed. **1100 feynynge outher,** pretense or. **1101 wonder feyn,** wonderfully gladly. **1103 a-morwe,** in the morning. **1104 warysshed,** cured.

Were my sorwes never so smerte.
And yet she syt so in myn herte
That, by my trouthe, y nolde noghte,
For al thys worlde, out of my thoghte   1110
Leve my lady. Noo, trewely!"
    "Now, by my trouthe, sir," quod I,
"Me thynketh ye have such a chaunce
As shryfte wythoute repentaunce."
    "Repentaunce? Nay, fy!" quod he,   1115
"Shulde y now repente me
To love? Nay, certes, than were I wel
Wers than was Achetofel,
Or Anthenor, so have I joye,
The traytor that betraysed Troye,   1120
Or the false Genelloun,
He that purchased the tresoun
Of Rowlande and of Olyvere.
Nay, while I am alyve here,
I nyl foryete hir nevermoo."   1125
    "Now, good syr," quod I thoo,
"Ye han wel told me herebefore—
Hyt ys no nede to reherse hit more—
How ye sawgh hir firste, and where.
But wolde ye tel me the manere   1130
To hire which was your firste speche,
Therof I wolde yow beseche;
And how she knewe first your thoghte,
Whether ye loved hir or noghte?
And telleth me eke what ye have lore,   1135
I herde yow telle herebefore."
    "Yee," seyde he, "thow nost what thou
        menest.
I have lost more than thou wenest."
    "What losse is that?" quod I thoo.
"Nyl she not love yow? Ys hyt soo?   1140
Or have ye oght doon amys,
That she hath left yow? Ys hyt this?
For Goddes love, telle me alle."

"Before God," quod he, "and I shalle.
I say ryght as I have seyde,   1145
On hir was al my love leyde,
And yet she nyste hyt nat never a del
Noght longe tyme, leve hyt wel.
For be ryght siker, I durste noght,
For al this world tel hir my thoght,   1150
Ne I wolde have wraththed hir, trewely.
For wostow why? She was lady
Of the body—she had the hert,
And who hath that may not astert.
But for to kepe me fro ydelnesse,   1155
Trewly I did my besynesse
To make songes, as I best koude,
And ofte tyme I songe hem loude,
And made songes this a gret dele—
Althogh I koude not make so wele   1160
Songes, ne knewe the art alle,
As koude Lamekes sone Tuballe
That founde out first the art of songe,
For as hys brothres hamers ronge
Upon hys anvelt up and doun,   1165
Therof he took the firste soun—
But Grekes seyn Pictagoras,
That he the firste fynder was
Of the art, *Aurora* telleth soo.
But therof no fors, of hem twoo.   1170
Algates songes thus I made
Of my felynge, myn herte to glade;
And lo, this was the altherferst—
I not wher hyt were the werst:

Lord, hyt maketh min herte lyght,   1175
Whan I thenke on that swete wyght
That is so semely on to see;
And wisshe to God hit myght so bee
That she wolde holde me for hir knyght,
My lady, that is so fair and bryght!   1180

1108 **syt**, remains (sits). 1113–14 **chaunce**, i.e., about as much of a chance of forgetting her as of receiving absolution without doing penance. 1118 **Achetofel**, Achitophel, King David's counselor who led his son to rebel. What follows is a commonplace list of traitors. 1135 **lore**, lost. 1137 F *he seyde.* 1147 **nyste**, didn't know. 1148 **leve**, believe. 1149 **siker**, sure. 1154 **who hath that . . . astert**, i.e., if one has that, the captive may not escape. 1155 F *me so fro.* 1161 **knewe**: F *knowe.* 1162 **Tuballe**, in Gen. 4:21 Jubal is called the father of music; Tubalcain, his brother, invented metalwork. 1165 **anvelt**, anvil. 1167–69 **Pictagoras . . . Aurora**, Pythagoras, but Chaucer indicates that his information comes from the 12th century omnibus of classical and biblical lore, the *Aurora* of Peter Riga. 1171 **Algates**, nevertheless. 1173 **altherferst**, first of all (expression of his love). 1174 *werst*: F *first* (rhyme *altherfirst*).

"Now have I told thee, soth to say,
My firste song. Upon a day
I bethoghte me what woo
And sorwe that I suffred thoo
For hir, and yet she wyste hyt noght, 1185
Ne telle hir durst I nat my thoght.
'Allas,' thoghte I, 'y kan no rede,
And but I telle hir, I nam but dede;
And yif I telle hyr, to seye ryght sothe,
I am adred she wol be wrothe. 1190
Allas, what shal I thanne doo?'

"In this debat I was so woo
Me thoghte myn herte braste atweyne.
So at the laste, soth to sayne,
I bethoghte me that Nature 1195
Ne formed never in creature
So moche beaute, trewely,
And bounte, wythoute mercy.
In hope of that my tale I tolde,
With sorwe, as that I never sholde; 1200
For nedes, and mawgree my hede,
I most have told hir or be dede.
I not wel how that I beganne—
Ful evel rehersen hyt I kanne,
And eke, as helpe me God withalle, 1205
I trowe hyt was in the dismalle
That was the ten woundes of Egipte—
For many a word I overskipte
In my tale, for pure fere
Lest my wordes myssette were. 1210
With sorweful herte and woundes dede,
Softe and quakynge for pure drede
And shame, and styntynge in my tale
For ferde, and myn hewe al pale,
Ful ofte I wex bothe pale and rede. 1215
Bowynge to hir, I heng the hede,
I durste nat ones loke hir on,
For witte, maner, and al was goon.
I seyde 'Mercy,' and no more.

Hyt nas no game, hyt sat me sore. 1220
"So at the laste, sothe to seyn,
Whan that myn herte was come ageyn,
To telle shortly al my speche,
With hool herte I gan hir beseche
That she wolde be my lady swete, 1225
And swore, and gan hir hertely hete
Ever to be stedfast and trewe,
And love hir alwey fresshly newe,
And never other lady have,
And al hir worship for to save 1230
As I best koude—I swor hir this:
'For youres is alle that ever ther ys
For evermore, myn herte swete!
And never to false yow, but I mete,
I nyl, as wys God helpe me soo.' 1235
"And whan I had my tale ydoo,
God wot, she acounted nat a stree
Of al my tale, so thoghte me.
To telle shortly ryght as hyt ys,
Trewly hir answere hyt was this— 1240
I kan not now wel counterfete
Hyr wordes, but this was the grete
Of hir answere: she sayde 'Nay,'
Alle outerly. Allas, that day
The sorowe I suffred, and the woo, 1245
That trewly Cassandra, that soo
Bewayled the destruccioun
Of Troye and of Ilyoun,
Had never swich sorwe as I thoo.
I durste no more say thertoo 1250
For pure fere, but stal away.
And thus I lyved ful many a day,
That trewely I hadde no nede
Ferther than my beddes hede
Never a day to seche sorwe. 1255
I fond hyt redy every morwe
For-why I loved hyr in no gere.
"So hit befel, another yere

1185 **wyste**, knew. 1187 **kan no rede**, know no remedy. 1188 *nam:* FT&c *am.* 1200 **never sholde**, i.e., as if I never should have told it. 1203 **not**, don't know. 1204 **evel rehersen**, badly repeat it. 1206 **dismalle**, *double entendre*, evil days (Lat. *dies mali*), and ten evils (Fr. *dix mals*). There were two evil days each month, and these were associated in popular superstition with the ten plagues (Lat. *plaga*, wound) of Egypt, Exodus 7–12. The Black Knight is saying that it was on one of these unlucky days that he made his first profession of love. 1211 **dede**, deadly. 1213 **styntynge . . . tale**, halting, speech. 1214 **ferde**, fear. 1220 **game . . . sat me sore**, joke, was painful to me. 1226 **hete**, promise. 1230 **worship**, honor. 1234 **mete**, dream (i.e., unless I'm out of my mind). 1237 **stree**, straw. 1242 **grete**, substance. 1246 **Cassandra**, seeress daughter of Priam. 1256 **morwe**, morning. 1257 **gere**, changeable spirit.

I thoughte ones I wolde fonde
To do hir knowe and understonde 1260
My woo; and she wel understode
That I ne wilned nothyng but gode
And worshippe and to kepe hir name
Over all thynges, and drede hir shame,
And was so besy hyr to serve, 1265
And pitee were I shulde sterve,
Syth that I wilned noon harm, ywys.
So whan my lady knewe al thys,
My lady yaf me al hooly
The noble yifte of hir mercy, 1270
Savynge hir worshippe, by al weyes—
Dredles, I mene noon other weyes.
And therwith she yaf me a rynge;
I trowe hyt was the firste thynge.
But yf myn herte was iwaxe 1275
Glad, that is no nede to axe.
As helpe me God, I was as blyve
Reysed as fro deth to lyve,
Of al happes the alderbeste,
The gladdest, and the moste at reste. 1280
For trewely that swete wyght,
Whan I had wrong and she the ryght,
She wolde alway so goodely
Foryeve me, so debonairly.
In al my yowthe, in al chaunce, 1285
She took me in hir governaunce.
Therwyth she was alway so trewe,
Our joye was ever ylyche newe.
Oure hertes wern so evene a payre
That never nas that oon contrayre 1290
To that other for noo woo.
Forsothe, ylyche they suffred thoo
Oo blysse, and eke oo sorwe bothe,
Ylyche they were bothe glad and wrothe.
Al was us oon, withoute were. 1295
And thus we lyved ful many a yere

So wel I kan nat telle how."
"Sir," quod I, "where is she now?"
"Now?" quod he, and stynte anoon.
Therwith he waxe as dede as stoon, 1300
And seyde, "Allas that I was bore,
That was the losse that here before
I tolde the that I hadde lorne.
Bethenke how I seyde herebeforne,
'Thow wost ful lytel what thow menest. 1305
I have lost more than thow wenest'—
God wot, allas, ryght that was she!"
"Allas, sir, how? What may that be?"
"She ys ded."—"Nay!"—"Yis, be my trouthe!"
"Is that youre losse? Be God, hyt ys routhe."
And with that worde ryght anoon 1311
They gan to strake forth; al was doon,
For that tyme, the herte-huntynge.
With that me thoghte that this kynge
Gan homwarde for to ryde 1315
Unto a place was there besyde,
Which was from us but a lyte,
A longe castel with walles white,
Be Seynt Johan, on a ryche hille,
As me mette. But thus hyt fille, 1320
Ryght thus me mette, as I yow telle,
That in the castell ther was a belle,
As hyt hadde smyten oures twelve.
Therwith I awook myselve
And fonde me lyinge in my bedde, 1325
And the book that I hadde redde
Of Alcione and Seyes the kyng,
And of the goddes of slepynge,
I fond hyt in myn honde ful evene.
Thoghte I, "Thys ys so queynt a swevene 1330
That I wol, be processe of tyme,
Fonde to put this swevene in ryme
As I kan best, and that anoon."
This was my swevene; now hit ys doon.

1259 **fonde,** try. 1260 **do,** make. 1262 **wilned,** intended. 1266 **were I . . . sterve,** (it) would be (if) I, die. 1271 **Savynge . . . weyes,** i.e., assuming that her honor would be protected in every way. 1272 **Dredles,** doubtless. 1276 T *it is.* 1277 **blyve,** quickly. 1279 **happes . . . alderbeste,** happinesses, best of all. 1280 **moste at reste,** most satisfying. 1285 **chaunce,** situation. 1295 **were,** doubt. 1299 **stynte anoon,** stopped immediately. 1300 **waxe,** became. 1303 **lorne,** lost. 1310 **routhe,** sad. 1312 **They . . . strake forth,** the huntsmen, return from the hunt. 1314 **this kynge,** i.e., Octavian, cf. l. 368n. 1318 **longe castel . . . white,** Lancaster, Blanche. Blanche was the daughter of Henry, Duke of Lancaster, and John of Gaunt acceded to the title through his marriage to her. 1319 **Johan . . . ryche hille,** until his marriage to Blanche, John was Earl of Richmond. 1320 **mette,** dreamed. 1323 **smyten oures twelve,** striking tower clocks were known in Chaucer's day, but the tolling of a funeral bell may also be suggested. 1329 **evene,** straight, as if he were still reading it. 1330 **queynt a swevene,** strange a dream. 1331 **processe of tyme,** due course. 1332 **Fonde,** try.

Parliament
of Fowls

INTRODUCTION

Parliament of Fowls

HE OCCASIONS and dates of the *Parliament of Fowls* and *House of Fame* are not known. Scholars are agreed that both are occasional poems associated with the protracted efforts to arrange a suitable marriage for young King Richard, in which Chaucer was personally involved. The order in this edition is based on Haldeen Braddy, *Chaucer's Parlement of Fowles in Relation to Contemporary Events* (2nd. ed, 1969), which sets the *Parliament* in 1377-78 in connection with the unsuccessful effort to secure Richard's betrothal to Marie, daughter of King Charles V of France, and *Fame* in 1381 to celebrate his actual betrothal to Anne of Bohemia. But Larry Benson, "The Occasion of the *Parliament of Fowls*," in *Wisdom of Poetry* (1982), has reviewd the evidence and argues that *Fame* should be dated about December 10, 1379 (see ll.63,111), when England received word that negotiations for the hand of Caterina Visconti were off, and *Parliament* about May 1, 1381, when a marriage settlement with Anne was ratified. The various arguments are summed up by Donald Howard, *Chaucer* (1987). The pentameter line of the *Parliament* is, indeed, more mature than the octosyllabic of *Fame*. Nevertheless, *Fame* appears to be a more appropriate transition to *Troylus and Criseyde*, as will be

argued in the next Introduction.

Whatever the occasions, these poems, like the *Book of the Duchess*, speak with a personal voice and touch upon larger issues. All three of the early poems are dream visions in which the poet-narrator falls asleep troubled about his own situation, and in the dream has an educational experience. From one poem to the next, we can see Chaucer growing away from courtly love exemplified in Guillaume de Lorris' part of the *Roman de la Rose* toward social and intellectual satire exemplified in Jean de Meun's continuation, an evolution traced by Charles Muscatine, *Chaucer and the French Tradition* (1957).

The *Parliament of Fowls* takes a step in this direction. It begins with another appeal to classical authority not directly related to the real subject of the poem, but the dream of Scipio is better integrated than the dream of Alcyone since it introduces the idea of "common profit" which develops as the central theme of the poem (ll.47, 75, 507). The conceptual satire turns on the contrast between the icons of sterile, unnatural courtly love that the dreamer first encounters in the temple of Venus and the fertile, natural love of the mating birds gathered about Dame Nature, elucidated by C.O. McDonald, "An Interpretation of Chaucer's *Parliament of Fowls*," *Speculum* (1955). But even more delightful to the modern reader is the perceptual satire of the ar-gument between the royal eagles and the common birds. The humor and variety of the voices and points of view in the *Parliament of Fowls* are the seeds from which the variety of *Canterbury Tales* will eventually grow. As in *Canterbury Tales*, the satire of *Parliament* is not simplistic. It is hard to tell whether the gentles or the commons come out ahead. Both are ridiculed, but both are also approved.

The literary backgrounds of the *Parliament of Fowls* are broader than those of the *Book of the Duchess*. In *Book of the Duchess* Chaucer gives no indication of knowing any poetry beyond the courtly French *dits amoreux* and the Latin poems of Ovid and Virgil that he had studied in school, and he thinks that Macrobius himself had the dream about Scipio (*BD* ll.284-87 and note). In the *Parliament* he has read and summarizes Macrobius' *Commentary* (*PF* ll.31ff and notes) and he has discovered the literature of the Italian Renaissance to which he pays tribute (ll.15-25). Chaucer's knowledge of Dante's *Divine Comedy* remains something of a mystery. The more closely it is studied the more ephemeral it appears. But there can be little doubt that the guide "Affrican" and the "gate, with letteres large iwroughte" show an acquaintance with *Inferno* 1-3. The best general interpretation of the poem is J.A.W. Bennett, *The Parlement of Fowls: An Interpretation* (2nd ed. 1965).

Parliament of Fowls

Here begynyth the Parlement of Foulys.

The lyf so short, the craft so long to lerne,
Th'assay so hard, so sharp the conquerynge,
The dredful joye alwey that slit so yerne—
Al this mene I be Love that my felynge
Astonyeth with his wondyrful werkynge   5
So sore, iwis, that whan I on hym thynke,
Nat wot I wel wher that I flete or synke.

For al be that I knowe nat Love in dede,
Ne wot how that he quiteth folk her hyre,
Yit happeth me ful ofte in bokes rede   10
Of his myrakles and his crewel yre.
There rede I wel he wol be lord and syre—
I dar nat seyn, his strokes been so sore,
But "God save swich a lord!" I can no
      more.

Of usage, what for lust and what for lore,   15
On bokes rede I ofte, as I yow tolde.
But wherfore that I speke al this? Nat yore
Agon it happede me for to beholde
Upon a bok, was write with letteres olde;
And therupon, a certeyn thing to lerne,   20

The longe day ful faste I redde and yerne.

For out of olde feldes, as men seyth,
Cometh al this newe corn fro yer to yere,
And out of olde bokes, in good feyth,
Cometh al this newe science that men lere.   25
But now to purpos as of this matere:
To rede forth hit gan me so delite
That al that day me thoughte but a lyte.

This bok of which I make of mencioun
Entytled was al thus as I shal telle: 30
"Tullyus of the Drem of Scipioun."
Chapitres sevene it hadde of hevene and helle
And erthe and soules that theryn dwelle,
Of whiche, as shortly as I can it trete,
Of his sentence I wol yow seyn the grete.   35

Fyrst telleth it, whan Scipion was come
In Affrik, how he meteth Massynisse,
That hym for joie in armes hath inome;
Thanne telleth it here speche and al the blysse
That was betwix hem til the day gan mysse;   40

Text based on MS Cambridge Gg. 4.27 (G), with variants from Fairfax 16 (F). See "The Text of This Edition," p. 966. Title in F: *The Parlement of Briddes.*

1 lyf so short, "*ars longa, vita brevis,*" an aphorism that can be traced back to Hippocrates. **2 assay,** attempt. F&c transpose *sharp/hard.* **3 dredful,** frightening—a troubadour oxymoron. **slit . . . yerne,** slips away, quickly. F *slyder* (slippery) *joye that alwey slyd.* **5 Astonyeth,** is astonished. G&c *Astonyed;* F *so with a dredeful worchyng.* **6 sore, iwis,** sorely, I declare. **7 wher . . . flete,** whether, float. G *slete.* F&c *wake or wynke.* **9 quiteth . . . her hyre,** pays, their wages. **10** F *in bookes ofte to.* **12 There:** G *That.* **13** F&c *Dar I.* **14 I can,** I can (say). **can:** G&c *seye.* **15 usage . . . lust . . . lore,** habit, pleasure, knowledge. **17 yore,** long. **wherfore:** F&c *why that.* **21 ȝerne,** eagerly. **redde:** F&c *rad.* **22 men,** impersonal, "is said." **out:** GF *ofte.* rhyme *seyth/feyth:* G&c *sey/fey.* **23 corn,** grain (nourishment). **25 science,** learning; this would appear to be Chaucer's tribute to the revival of learning that he could have observed on his trip to Italy in 1372–73. **lere,** learn. **26** F&c *purpose of my first matere.* **27** G *forth so gan me to.* **28** F *thought me.* **30** G&c *Entylt;* F&c *there I shal yow telle.* **31 Tullyus,** Cicero's *Somnium Scipionis (Dream of Scipio)* was written as an epilogue to his *De Re Publica.* Most of the latter has been lost, but the *Somnium* was preserved independently by Macrobius along with an extensive commentary. Chaucer evidently knew it only by name from *RR* and mistook its nature in *BD* 284–87. But by this time he has clearly read it and summarizes it in detail. *Scipioun:* G *Sothion;* F *Cipion.* **32** F&c *hyt had vij.* **33** G *theryn* altered to *theron.* **34** F&c *it* om. **35 sentence . . . grete,** meaning, substance. *seyn:* F *tel.* **36 Scipion,** called Scipio Africanus Minor, the destroyer of Carthage in the Punic Wars. His dream is of his grandfather Scipio Africanus Major, conqueror of Hannibal in the same wars. Cicero describes Scipio Minor as a great general, patriot, patron of letters, and exemplary friend. **37 Massynisse,** Masinissa, King of Numidia (present-day Libya), and long-time adherent of Scipio Major. F *Into Aufryke/mette.* **38 inome,** taken. **39 it:** all MSS *he; al the:* G&c *of the.* **40 mysse,** end. G&c *betwixsyn/ betwen; the:* G&c *that.*

And how his auncestre, Affrycan so dere,
Gan in his slep that nyght to hym apere.

Thanne telleth it that from a sterry place
How Affrycan hath hym Cartage shewed,
And warnede hym beforn of al his grace, 45
And seyde what man, lered other lewed,
That lovede comoun profyt, wel ithewed,
He shulde into a blysful place wende
There as joye is that last withouten ende.

Thanne axede he if folk that here been dede 50
Han lyf and dwellynge in another place.
And Affrican seyde, "Ye, withouten drede,"
And that oure present worldes lyves space
Nys but a maner deth, what wey we trace.
And rightful folk shul gon after they deye 55
To hevene; and shewede hym the Galaxye.

Thanne shewede he hym the litel erthe that here is,
At regard of the hevenes quantite;
And after shewede he hym the nyne speris;
And after that the melodye herde he 60
That cometh of thilke speres thryes thre,
That welle is of musik and melodye
In this world here, and cause of armonye.

Than bad he hym, syn erthe was so lyte,
And ful of torment and of harde grace, 65

That he ne shulde hym in the world delyte.
Thanne tolde he hym, in certeyn yeres space
That every sterre shulde come into his place,
Ther it was first, and al shulde out of mynde
That in this world is don of al mankynde. 70

Thanne preyede hym Scypyon to telle hym al
The wey to come into that hevene blysse.
And he seyde, "Know thyself first inmortal,
And loke ay besily thow werche and wysse
To comoun profit, and thow shalt not mysse 75
To comen swiftly to that place deere
That ful of blysse is and of soules cleere.

"But brekers of the lawe, soth to seyn,
And lykerous folk, after that they ben dede,
Shul whirle aboute th'erthe alwey in peyn, 80
Tyl manye a world be passed, out of drede,
And than, foryeven al her weked dede,
Than shul they come into that blysful place
To which to comen God the sende his grace."

The day gan faylen, and the derke nyght, 85
That reveth bestes from her besynesse,
Berafte me myn bok for lak of lyght,
And to my bed I gan me for to dresse,
Fulfyld of thought and busy hevynesse;
For bothe I hadde thyng which that I nolde, 90
And ek I ne hadde that thyng that I wolde.

---

41 F *Aufrikan* throughout. **43** F&c *told he hym that.* **45 warnede . . . grace,** apprised, fortune (in destroying Carthage and ending the Punic Wars). **46 lered . . . lewed,** learned, unlearned. F&c *seyde hym; lered:* G *lernyd.* **47 comoun profyt,** an important social and political concept as Europe near the end of the Middle Ages began to grope its way toward a more participatory society. "Common profit" had formed the basis for the Roman concept of *res publica,* and was coming to form the basis of the English notion of "commonwealth." The conflict between the "common profit" of fertile married love and the destructiveness of sterile courtly love is a central theme in *PF.* **ithewed,** endowed with virtues. **47–48** F&c *loveth/shal.* **49** F *There joy is that lasteth without ende.* **50** *here:* G *now; been:* F *be.* **51** *Han:* F *Have.* **52 drede,** doubt. **53** *that:* F om.; other MSS *here. worldes,* om. in some A MSS. **54** *Nys:* F&c *Meneth.* **55** F *goo whan.* **56 Galaxye,** the Milky Way. G *Galylye;* F *Galoxye.* **57** G *litel* om. **59 speris,** spheres; the nine spheres that constituted the Ptolemaic heavens. **60 melodye,** the *Somnium* asserts that the spheres produce the eight tones of the diatonic scale; Chaucer misses this subtlety by having all nine spheres produce tones. **64** F&c *hym see the erthe that is.* **65** F&c *somedel fulle.* G *And was somedel disseyvable and ful of.* **68 sterre . . . come into his place,** the so-called "great" or "mundane" year, the length of time it takes all the heavenly bodies to return together to an original position. Baugh says the period is about 26,000 years. **69 shulde out of mynde,** should be forgotten. **71** *hym:* F *he.* G *Cypyon.* **72** *into:* F&c *to.* **73** F&c *mortale.* **74 wysse,** lead. **75 comoun profit,** here, as at l. 47, Chaucer's term; at l. 47 for *patriam,* "native land," and here for *salute patriae,* "health of the nation." *not:* F *never.* **76** *that:* G *this.* **77 cleere,** shining. **78** F *soth for to.* **79 lykerous,** lecherous. F&c *lecherous.* Lechery does not here mean sexual immorality per se, but mortal depravity—what St. Augustine and some modern critics have termed "cupidity" in contrast to divine "charity." **80 whirle,** this has sometimes been taken as an allusion to the punishment of Paolo and Francesca in Dante, *Inferno* 5, but the *Somnium,* c. ix.2, has the same figure. F *shul alwey. th'erthe:* G *there;* other MSS *the worlde.* **82** F *foryeven hem;* G *that foryeven is his.* **83** *that:* G *this.* **84** *the sende his:* F&c *sende ech lover;* G *send us.* **85 day gan faylen,** cf. *Inferno* 2.1–3, but Dante was borrowing from the *Aeneid,* 4.522, 9.224, which Chaucer also knew. *faylen:* F *faile;* G *folwyn.* **86 reveth,** relieves. **87 Berafte,** deprived (of). **88 dresse,** prepare. *bed:* G *self.* **89 busy hevynesse,** restless sadness. **90 nolde,** did not want (wouldn't). G&c *which* om. **91** *that thyng:* FG *that* om.; other MSS *the thyng.*

But fynally, my spirit at the laste,
For-wery of my labour al the day,
Tok reste, that made me to slepe faste;
And in my slep I mette as that I lay   95
How Affrican, ryght in the selfe aray
That Scipion hym say byfore that tyde,
Was come and stod right at myn bedes syde.

The wery huntere slepynge in his bed,
To wode ayen his mynde goth anon;   100
The juge dremeth how his plees been sped;
The cartere dremeth how his carte is gon;
The riche, of gold; the knyght fyght with his
    fon;
The syke met he drynketh of the tonne;
The lovere met he hath his lady wonne.   105

Can I nat seyn yf that the cause were
For I hadde red of Affrican byforn
That made me to mete that he stod there,
But thus seyde he, "Thow hast the so wel born
In lokynge of myn olde bok totorn,   110
Of which Macrobye roughte nat a lyte,
That sumdel of thy labour wolde I quyte."

Cytherea, thow blysful lady swete,
That with thy ferbrond dauntest whom the
    lest,
And madest me thys swevene for to mete,   115

Be thow myn helpe in this, for thow mayst best!
As wisly as I seye the north-north-west
Whan I began myn swevene for to write,
So yif me myght to ryme and ek t'endyte.

This forseyde Affrican me hente anon,   120
And forth with hym unto a gate broughte
Ryght of a park walled of grene ston,
And over the gate, with letteres large iwroughte,
There were vers iwreten, as me thoughte,
On eyther half of ful gret difference,   125
Of which I shal now seyn the pleyn sentence:

"Thorw me men gon into that blysful place
Of hertes hele and dedly woundes cure;
Thorw me men gon unto the welle of grace,   129
There grene and lusty May shal evere endure.
This is the wey to al good aventure.
Be glad, thow redere, and thy sorwe of-caste.
Al open am I; passe in, and sped the faste."

"Thorw me men gon," than spak that other
    side,
"Unto the mortal strokes of the spere,   135
Of which Disdayn and Daunger is the gyde,
There nevere tre shal fruyt ne leves bere.
This strem yow ledeth to the sorweful were
There as the fish in prysoun is al drye—
Th'eschewyng is only the remedye."   140

---

93 **For,** i.e., completely ("for" is an intensifier). 95 **mette,** dreamed. 96 **selfe,** same. *selfe:* G&c *same/ilk.* 97 **hym say . . . tyde,** saw him (in), time. *say:* F&c *saw(e).* 99 **wery huntere,** this dream psychology (which has a bearing on the dreamwork of *BD, HF,* and *LGW*) is familiar in classical and medieval discussions from Claudian to Macrobius' own commentary on the *Somnium.* 101 **plees,** cases. 102 *carte is:* F&c *cartes.* 104 **tonne,** wine cask. 107 F&c *redde had.* 108 **mete,** dream. 110 **of . . . totorn,** at, tattered. F&c *al totorn;* G *byforn.* 111 **roughte,** cared. 112 **quyte,** repay. F *the quyte.* 113 **Cytherea,** Venus. 114 **dauntest . . . lest,** defeat, wish. F&c *firy bronde.* 115 **swevene . . . to mete,** dream, to dream. 117 **wisly . . . seye . . . north-north-west,** truly, saw; the compass reading has been taken either as Chaucer's ironic comment on the tenor of the whole poem (north-north-west being a deviant position: cf. Hamlet, "I am but mad north-north-west," II.ii.396), or else as a means of dating the poem, Venus having been visible as an evening star in a northwesterly position in 1374, 1377, and 1382. Of these, 1377 agrees with the dating proposed by the betrothal to Marie of France; see the Introduction. *seye:* F&c *saw(e).* G *north nor west* (i.e., south or east), which opens up a whole new series of possible dates. 119 **endyte,** compose. 120 **hente,** grasped. The gate into the garden suggests the gate of Hell in *Inferno* 3, and African's physically leading the dreamer in and being able to read the questions in his face (l. 155) parallel similar aspects of Virgil. However, Chaucer has adapted the material to develop his own theme, which is very different from that of Dante. 123 G *gatis.* 125 G *eythir syde.* 126 **pleyn sentence,** full meaning. *now:* F&c *yow.* 128 **hele,** well-being. In contrast to *Inferno,* Chaucer's gate has two aspects symbolizing the traditional interpretations of heavenly and earthly love, or Nature and Venus, or, as some recent critics have suggested, the beneficence of fertile married love and the malevolence of sterile eroticism. "Grene and lusty May" would represent natural love for the purpose of procreation. 132 *of-caste:* G *over caste.* 133 *sped:* F&c *hye.* 136 **Disdayn and Daunger,** these personifications of aspects of the courtly mistress represent the pains of chivalric love. 137 F&c *tree shal never;* G *That never yit shal freut.* 138 **were,** fish trap (weir). 140 G *Ther shewyng is.*

These vers of gold and blak iwreten were,
Of whiche I gan astonyed to beholde,
Forwhi that oon encresede ay my fere,
And with that other gan myn herte bolde;
That oon me hette, that other dede me
    colde.   145
No wit hadde I, for errour, for to chese
To entre or flen, or me to save or lese.

Right as betwixen adamauntes two
Of evene myght, a pece of yren set
Ne hath no myght to meve to ne fro—   150
For what that on may hale, that other let—
Ferde I, that nyste whether me was bet
To entre or leve, til Affrycan my gide
Me hente and shof in at the gates wide,

And seyde, "It stondeth writen in thy face,   155
Thyn errour, though thow telle it not to me.
But dred the not to come into this place,
For this writyng nys nothyng ment bi the,
Ne by non but he Loves servaunt be.
For thow of love hast lost thy tast, I gesse,   160
As sek man hath of swete and bytternesse.

"But natheles, althow that thow be dul,
Yit that thow canst not do, yit mayst thow se.
For manye a man that may nat stonde a pul,
It liketh hym atte wrastlyng for to be,   165
And demen yit wher he do bet or he.
And if thow haddest cunnyng for t'endite,
I shal the shewe mater for to wryte."

With that myn hand he tok in his anon,   169
Of whiche I confort kaughte, and went in faste.
But, Lord, so I was glad and wel begoon,
For overal where that I myn eyen caste
Were trees clad with leves that ay shal laste,
Eche in his kynde, of colour fresh and greene
As emeroude, that joye was to seene.   175

The byldere ok; and ek the hardy assh;
The piler elm, the cofere unto carayne;
The boxtre pipere; holm to whippes lasch;
The saylynge firre; the cipresse, deth to pleyne;
The shetere ew; the asp for shaftes pleyne;   180
The olyve of pes; and ek the dronke vyne;
The victor palm; the laurer to devyne.

A gardyn saw I ful of blosmy bowes
Upon a rever in a grene mede,
There as swetnesse everemore inow is,   185
With floures white, blewe, yelwe, and rede,
And colde welle-stremes, nothyng dede,
That swymmen ful of smale fisches lyghte,
With fynnes rede and skales sylver bryghte.

On every bow the foules herde I synge,   190
With voys of aungel in here armonye;
Some besyede hem here bryddes forth to
    brynge.
The litele conyes to here pley gunne hye.
And ferther al aboute I gan aspye   194
The dredful ro, the buk, the hert and hynde,
Squyreles, and bestes smale of gentil kynde.

---

142 *astonyed:* F&c *a stounde* (a while). **143** F&c *For with.* **144** F&c *to bolde.* **145 hette,** inflamed. **146 chese,** choose. **147 flen . . . lese,** flee, lose. **148 adamauntes,** lodestones (magnets). **149** F&c *ysette.* **150** F&c *That hath.* **151 hale . . . let,** attract, repel. **152** F *that I ne wiste wher that.* **154 hente,** seized. **155** *stondeth:* G *stant.* **158 bi,** for. **160** *tast:* G *stat.* **161 of swete,** i.e., the dreamer has lost his ability to taste, not necessarily his desire. **166 demen . . . wher,** to judge, whether. **167** G *And there if.* **169 hand he tok,** at *Inferno* 3.19 Virgil places his hand on Dante's, comforts him, and leads him through the gates of Hell. **170** *went in:* G *that as.* **171 wel begoon,** happy. **175** *joye:* G *sothe.* **176 byldere ok,** the catalog of trees with their epithets is a rhetorical convention. There is such a list in Boccaccio's *Teseida* (11.22ff.), which Chaucer knew in connection with the KT, but this list is more like the one in Joseph of Exeter's *Iliad,* i.505ff. However, many of the epithets appear to be original with Chaucer. **hardy,** courageous (because it was used to make spears). **177 piler,** because it supports vines. **cofere,** because it was used to make coffins. **178 pipere,** boxwood is used to make flutes and recorders. F *The box pipe tre.* **holm,** holly, small-grained, suitable for carving into whip handles, etc. **179 saylynge firre** fir was used for masts and spars. **pleyne,** complain; cypresses were planted in graveyards. **180 shetere,** yew was used to make bows. **asp,** aspen to make arrows. **pleyne,** straight (flat). **181** F *drunken.* **182 devyne,** i.e., used for divination; it was said that when laurel leaves were eaten they imparted oracular powers. **183** G *blospemy;* F *blossomed.* Lines 183–294 are modeled on Boccaccio's *Teseida* 7.51–66. **186** G *and yelwe.* **187 welle-stremes . . . dede,** streams flowing from springs, still. **188** F&c *And swynnynge.* G *lite.* **190** *foules:* all MSS *bryddes,* but cf. ll. 192, 203. **192 bryddes,** their young ones. *Some:* G&c *So;* F&c *That.* **193 conyes,** rabbits. **195 dredful . . . hynd,** timid, female deer.

Of instrumentes of strenges in acord
Herde I so pleye a ravyshyng swetnesse,
That God that makere is of al and lord
Ne herde nevere beter, as I gesse. 200
Therwith a wynd, unnethe it myghte be lesse,
Made in the leves grene a noyse softe
Acordaunt to the foules song alofte.

The aire of that place so attempre was 204
That nevere was ther grevaunce of hot ne cold.
Ther wex ek every holsum spice and gras;
Ne no man may there waxe sek ne old.
Yit was there joye more a thousentfold
Than man can telle; ne nevere wolde it nyghte,
But ay cler day to any manes syghte. 210

Under a tre besyde a welle I say
Cupide oure lord his arwes forge and file.
And at his fet his bowe al redy lay,
And Wille his doughter temperede al this whyle
The hevedes in the welle, and with hire wile 215
She couchede hem after as they shulde serve,
Some for to sle, and some to wounde and kerve.

Tho was I war of Plesaunce anon-ryght,
And of Aray, and Lust, and Curteysie, 219
And of the Craft that can and hath the myght
To don by force a wight to don folye—
Disfigurat was she, I nyl nat lye.

And by hemself under an ok, I gesse,
Saw I Delyt that stod with Gentilesse.

I saw Beute withouten any atyr, 225
And Youthe ful of game and jolyte,
Foolhardynesse and Flaterye and Desyr,
Messagerye and Meede and other thre—
Here names shul not here be told for me.
And upon pileres greete of jasper longe 230
I saw a temple of bras ifounded stronge.

Aboute that temple daunseden alwey
Wemen inowe, of whiche some ther weere
Fayre of hemself, and some of hem were gay;
In kerteles, al dishevele wente they there; 235
That was here offys alwey, yer by yeere.
And on the temple, of doves white and fayre
Saw I syttynge manye an hunderede peyre.

Byfore the temple dore ful sobyrly
Dame Pes sat with a curtyn in hire hond, 240
And by hire syde, wonder discretly,
Dame Pacience syttynge there I fond,
With face pale, upon an hil of sond;
And aldirnext, withinne and ek withoute,
Byheste and Art, and of here folk a route. 245

Withinne the temple, of sykes hoote as fyr
I herde a swow that gan aboute renne.

197 *of:* F&c *on.* **198** F&c *so om.; a: and.* **201 unnethe,** scarcely. **203 Acordaunt,** in harmony with. *foules:* G *bryddis.* **204** *aire:* G *erthe.* **205** F&c *was grevance ther.* **207** *Ne no:* GF *Ne om.* **209** F&c *No man kan|ne om.* **211 say,** saw. **212 Cupide,** through l. 294 are listed icons of chivalric love. This would appear to be Chaucer's first handling of material from Boccaccio's *Teseida* 7.53ff., Bersuire, *Ovidiana Moraliter,* and Albricus Philosophus, *Libellus de Deorum,* which he repeated in *HF* ll. 119–39 and *CT,* 1.1918–66. **214 Wille,** perhaps a misreading of the name of Cupid's daughter as "Voluntade" for "Vollutade" (*Tes.* 7.54), sensual pleasure (from Lat. *voluptas*). G&c *Welle* (prosperity). **215 hevedes . . . wile,** heads, skill. F&c *hedes; hire wile: harde file.* **216 couchede . . . after,** arranged according to how. *couchede:* other MSS *touchede.* **218 Plesaunce,** pleasure; these are personifications from the *RR* tradition, but suggested by Boccaccio *Tes.* 7.55. **219 Lust,** desire. **221 don,** make. F&c *To goo before a wight.* **224 Delyt,** *Tes. Diletto,* vain delight. **225 withouten . . . atyr,** this is Chaucer's vision; in *Tes.* she is merely *Sanz ornamento.* **228 Messagerye,** messengerhood— the icon of the go-between in love affairs. **other thre,** Chaucer once again used this number without a referent to fill out a rhyme: *CT* 1.164. **229** *not here:* F *here om.* **230 jasper,** a green semiprecious quartz. **231** *bras:* F *glas,* which misses the parallel with I Cor. 1, equating this kind of love with sounding brass or a tinkling cymbal. The parallel is Chaucer's, since the temple in *Tes.* is made of copper (metal precious to Venus). **234 gay,** carefree. **235 kerteles . . . dishevele,** kirtles (straight dresses), unbound hair. **236 here offys,** their function. The static, iconographic nature of each of these figures here becomes very clear. F *fro yere to yere.* **237–38** F&c *saugh I white and fayre|Of dowves white.* **238** *hunderede:* other MSS *thowsand.* **239 sobyrly,** i.e., somberly. **240 curtyn in . . . hond,** in *Tes.* at the entrance, she lightly moved a curtain at the door. While the purpose of this is obscure enough, it makes more sense than Chaucer's version. F&c *with om.* **241** F&c *And hir beside.* **243 face pale . . . hil of sond,** the pale face is in *Tes.,* but Chaucer added the hill of sand which again suggests sterility and contrasts with Dame Nature's hill of flowers, l. 302 below. **244 aldirnext,** next of all. **245 Byheste . . . Art,** Promise, Craft (i.e., deceitful promises?). **route,** company. **246 sykes,** sighs. **247 swow,** murmur.

Whiche sikes were engendered with desyr
That maden every auter for to brenne
Of newe flaume; and wel espyed I thennc 250
That al the cause of sorwe that they drye
Cam of the bittere goddesse Jelosye.

The god Priapus saw I, as I wente,
Withinne the temple in sovereyn place
stonde,
In swich aray as whan the asse hym shente 255
With cri by nyghte, and with sceptre in his
honde.
Ful besyly men gunne assaye and fonde
Upon his hed to sette, of sundery hewe,
Garlondes ful of freshe floures newe.

And in a prive corner in desport 260
Fond I Venus and hire porter Richesse,
That was ful noble and hautayn of hyre
port—
Derk was that place, but afterward lightnesse
I saw a lyte, unnethe it myghte be lesse—
And on a bed of gold she lay to reste 265
Tyl that the hote sunne gan to weste.

Hyre gilte heres with a goldene thred
Ibounden were, untressed as she lay;
And naked from the brest up to the hed
Men myghte hyre sen—and sothly for to
say, 270
The remenaunt was wel kevered to myn pay

Ryght with a subtyl covercheif of Valence.
Ther nas no thikkere cloth of no defense.

The place yaf a thousand savouris sote,
And Bachus, god of wyn, sat hire besyde, 275
And Ceres next, that doth of hunger boote,
And as I seyde, amyddes lay Cypride,
To whom on knees two yonge folk there cryde
To ben here helpe. But thus I let hir lye,
And ferthere in the temple I gan espie 280

That, in dispit of Dyane the chaste,
Ful many a bowe ibroke heng on the wal
Of maydenes swich as gunne here tymes waste
In hyre servyse. And peynted overal
Ful many a story, of which I touche shal 285
A fewe, as of Calyxte and Athalante,
And manye a mayde of whiche the name I
wante.

Semyramis, Candace, and Hercules,
Biblis, Dido, Thisbe, and Piramus,
Tristram, Isaude, Paris, and Achilles, 290
Eleyne, Cliopatre, and Troylus,
Silla, and ek the moder of Romulus—
Alle these were peynted on that other syde,
And al here love, and in what plyt they
deyde.

Whan I was come ayen unto the place 295
That I of spak, that was so sote and grene,

249 **maden . . . auter . . . brenne,** the breeze from the sighs made the altars flare up. 251 **drye,** suffer. 253 **Priapus,** Roman fertility god, represented as a wizened little man with an enormous phallus, often found in Italian gardens. 254 **sovereyn,** conspicuous. 255 **asse . . . shente,** the ass ruined him. The ass was sacred to Priapus as a symbol of stupid lust. In Ovid's *Fasti*, 1.415ff., it brayed just as Priapus was about to embrace the nymph Lotis, enabling her to escape and turn into a water flower, and subjecting him to derision. 256 **sceptre,** i.e., penis. F&c *his ceptre in honde.* G *septure.* 257 **fonde,** try. 260 **desport,** enjoying herself (or themselves). In *Tes.* 7.63–64, there is no ambiguity; Richezza is merely guarding the door. 261 *Venus:* G *febz.* 262 **hautayn of hyre port,** haughty of her manner. 264 **unnethe,** scarcely. 268 **untressed,** unbound. 269 F&c *unto.* 271 F&c *was om./kevered wel.* 272 **subtyl . . . Valence,** fine, city in France famous for weaving. Its name survives in modern curtain "valance." 273 **of no defense,** for any protection. 274 **sote,** sweet smelling. cf. *CT* 1.1n. Other MSS *swete.* 276 **Ceres,** goddess of agriculture. G *Sereis.* **boote,** remedy. 277 **Cypride,** Venus, so called because she was reputed to have been born from the waves near Cyprus. Other MSS *Cupide.* 278 **two:** F&c *the/ there om.* 279 *hir:* G *hem.* 281 **dispit,** defiance. 282 **bowe ibroke,** the broken bows symbolize lost chastity. 284 **hyre servyse,** i.e., the service of Venus. *And peynted:* G *ipeyntede were.* 285 F *Of many.* 286 **Calyxte,** Callisto, nymph beloved of Jove and changed to a bear, Ovid *Met.* 2.401ff. **Athalante,** who had to be beaten in a footrace to be won. This list of famous lovers begins with, but develops beyond, that in *Tes.* 7.61–62. For the device of wall paintings, cf. *HF* Bk. 1. 288 **Semyramis,** queen of Assyria and traditional founder of Babylon. **Candace,** Indian queen in the Alexander romances. 289 **Biblis,** because of incestuous love for her brother changed into a fountain, Ovid, *Met.* 9.454ff. **Dido,** Carthaginian queen who loved Aeneas. 292 **Silla,** for love of Minos brought about her father's death, Ovid, *Met.* 8.8ff. 295 F *that place.* 296 **sote,** sweet smelling.

Forth welk I tho myselven to solace.
Tho was I war wher that ther sat a queene
That, as of lyght the someres sonne shene
Passeth the sterre, right so over mesure   300
She fayrer was than any creature.

And in a launde, upon an hil of floures,
Was set this noble Goddesse of Nature.
Of braunches were hire halles and hire boures
Iwrought after hire cast and hire mesure,   305
Ne there nas foul that cometh of engendrure
That they ne were prest in hire presence
To take hire dom and yeve hire audyence.

For this was on Seynt Valentynes day,
Whan every foul cometh there to chese his
    make,   310
Of every kynde that men thynke may;
And that so huge a noyse gan they make
That erthe and eyr and tre and every lake
So ful was that unethe was there space
For me to stonde, so ful was al the place.   315

And right as Aleyn in the *Pleynt of Kynde*
Devyseth Nature of aray and face,
In swich aray men myghte hire there fynde.
This noble emperesse, ful of grace,

Bad every foul to take his owne place,   320
As they were woned alwey, fro yer to yeere,
Seynt Valentynes day to stonden theere.

That is to seyn, the foules of ravyne
Were heyest set, and thanne the foules smale
That eten as hem Nature wolde enclyne—   325
As werm or thyng of which I telle no tale;
And water-foul sat loueste in the dale;
But foul that lyveth by sed sat on the grene,
And that so fele that wonder was to sene.

There myghte men the ryal egle fynde,   330
That with his sharpe lok perseth the sunne,
And othere egles of a lowere kynde,
Of whiche that clerkes wel devyse cunne.
Ther was the tiraunt with his federys dunne
And grey, I mene the goshauk, that doth
    pyne
To bryddes for his outrageous ravyne.   336

The gentyl faucoun that with his feet
    distrayneth
The kynges hand; the hardy sperhauk eke,
The quayles foo; the merlioun that payneth
Hymself ful ofte the larke for to seke;   340
There was the douve with hire eyen meke;

297 **welk . . . solace,** walked, compose (i.e., after witnessing the tensions and agonies of love). Other MSS *walked*. 299 **sonne shene,** bright sun. G *someris sonnys*; F&c *sommer sonne*. 300 **Passeth,** surpasses. 302 **launde,** plain. 303 G&c *of* om. 304 **boures,** bowers. 305 **cast . . . mesure,** design, proportion. *cast:* F&c *crafte*. 306 **nas:** G&c *was*. 307 **prest,** ready. *they:* F&c *there*. 308 **dom . . . audyence,** judgment, listen to her. This tableau was suggested to Chaucer (as acknowledged in l. 316) by Alanus ab Insulis, *De Planctu Naturae,* which also, among other things, contrasts ennobling spiritual love with distorting human passions (see the Introduction). In *De Planctu,* the birds are depicted as decorations on Dame Nature's robe and described with epithets somewhat as in ll. 337ff. However, Nature's robe is so ethereal that the creatures appear to move about in a council of animals ("*animalium celebratur concilium*"). This might have helped suggest to Chaucer his "parlement of foules," except that assemblies of birds are themselves a commonplace in medieval poetry, especially on St. Valentine's day. 309 **Valentynes day,** poems celebrating St. Valentine's day were a recognized genre. Chaucer's *Complaint of Mars, Complaint of Venus,* and *Complaint Made at Windsor* (short poems 3, 4, and 22) are Valentine poems, and there are examples by Gower, Lydgate, etc. In *LGW* small birds defy the fowler and praise St. Valentine, and immediately the God of Love appears with Alceste who taught "the craft of fyn lovynge,/ And namely of wyfhood the lyvynge" (ll. 544–45). There, as here, St. Valentine is associated with wedded rather than courtly love. 310 **make,** mate. *foul:* G&c *bryd.* 311 **kynde,** species. 313 *eyr,* F&c *see.* 314 **unethe,** scarcely. 316 **Aleyn,** see l. 308n. 317 **Devyseth,** describes. There may be some typically Chaucerian humor here, since Alanus' description is exceedingly long and tedious. 320 *his* (i.e., its): F&c *her* (i.e., their). 321–22 **woned . . . to stonden,** accustomed to stand. The birds' observance of strict hierarchy is an ingredient in the debate that follows. 323 **foules of ravyne,** birds of prey. There have been various efforts to make the classes of birds fit classes in society, but the results are not really satisfactory. If birds of prey are nobility, water fowl merchants, and seed fowl agricultural workers, then worm fowl must be the church. This may be another bit of Chaucerian humor, like the position of the water fowl. 325 **as hem:** F&c *as that/as their.* 326 *werm:* F&c *worm.* G *thyng I telle myn tale.* 329 **fele,** numerous. 330 F&c *Royal Egle* (capitalized). 331 **perseth,** in the bestiary tradition, the eagle can look straight into the sun. 333 **devyse cunne,** are able to describe. 335 **pyne,** pain (injury). 336 **ravyne,** rapaciousness. 337 **distrayneth,** grasps. 338 **sperhauk,** sparrow hawk. F *hardy* om. 339 **merlioun,** merlin (small hawk).

The jelous swan, ayens his deth that syngeth;
The oule ek that of deth the bode bryngeth;

The crane, the geaunt, with his trompes soun;
The thef, the chough; and ek the jangelynge
    pye;   345
The skornynge jay; the eles fo, heroun;
The false lapwynge, ful of trecherye;
The stare that the conseyl can bewreye;
The tame roddok; and the coward kyte;
The kok, that orloge is of thorpes lyte;   350

The sparwe, Venus sone; the nyghtyngale
That clepeth forth the grene leves newe;
The swalwe, mortherere of the foules smale
That maken hony of floures freshe of hewe;
The wedded turtil with hire herte trewe;   355
The pecok with his aungels fetheres bryghte;
The fesaunt, skornere of the cok by nyghte;

The waker goos; the cokkow ever unkynde;
The popynjay ful of delicasye;
The drake, stroyere of his owene kynde;   360
The stork, the wrekere of avouterye;
The hote cormeraunt of glotenye;
The raven wys; the crowe with vois of
    care;
The thrustil old; the frosty feldefare.

What shulde I seyn? Of foules every kynde   365
That in this world hath federes and stature,
Men myghten in that place assemblede fynde
Byfore the noble Goddesse of Nature,
And everiche of hem ded his besy cure
Benygnely to chese or for to take,   370
By hire acord, his formel or his make.

But to the poynt: Nature held on hire hond
A formel egle, of shap the gentilleste
That evere she among hire werkes fond,
The moste benygne and the goodlieste.   375
In hire was everi vertu at his reste
So ferforth that Nature hireself hadde blysse
To loke on hire and ofte hire bek to kysse.

Nature, the vicarye of the almyghty Lord,   379
That hot, cold, hevy, lyght, moyst, and dreye
Hath knyt with evene noumberes of acord,
In esy voys began to speke and seye,
"Foules, tak hed of my sentence, I preye,
And for youre ese, in fortheryng of youre nede,
As faste as I may speke, I wol yow speede.   385

"Ye knowe wel how, Seynt Valentynes day,
By my statute and thorw my governaunce,
Ye come for to cheese—and fle youre wey—
Youre makes, as I prike yow with plesaunce.

---

342 **ayens**, at the approach of. *his:* G&c *hire*. 343 **bode**, warning. 344 **trompes**, trumpet's. 345 **chough . . . jangelynge pye**, a kind of crow, chattering magpie. *chough:* G&c *crow*. 346 *eles* (eel's): F&c *egles;* some MSS *the heroun*. 347 **false lapwynge**, the lapwing's practice of distracting intruders who venture near its nest by pretending to have a broken wing made it a figure for fraud. 348 **stare . . . conseyl**, starling, secrets. G *starlyng*. 349 **roddok**, ruddock (European robin). F&c *ruddok*. 350 **orloge . . . thorpes**, town clock, village. 351 **Venus sone**, the sparrow, sacred to Venus, was a figure for sexual desire. 352 **clepeth forth**, calls forth (by singing in the springtime). *grene:* F&c *fresshe*. 353 **mortherere of foules smale**, murderer of bees. *foules:* other MSS *bryddis/flyes.* 355 **wedded turtil**, according to the bestiary tradition, the turtledove never takes a second mate. *hire:* F *hys*. 356 G *aungilis clothis.* 357 **skornere . . . cok,** the pheasant was supposed to breed with the domestic hen. 358 **waker goos**, geese are called more vigilant guardians even than dogs; those kept on the Capitoline Hill in Rome are always cited as examples. **ever unkynde,** always unnatural (because it deposits its eggs in other birds' nests, cf. *King Lear* I.iv.205). *ever:* G *most.* 359 **delicasye**, the parrot was reputed to have a weakness for wine. F *papjay.* 360 **stroyere**, drakes were supposed to kill the ducklings. 361 **wrekere of avouterye**, revenger of adultery; storks were supposed to kill their adulterous mates. 362 **hote . . . glotenye**, the cormorant was supposed to be burning of its own gluttony. 363 F&c *The ravens and the crowes with her voys of care.* 364 **thrustil old,** the thrush was supposed to live to be very old. G *thurstil;* F&c *throstil.* **frosty feldefare**, another kind of thrush, "frosty" because it wintered in England. 368 **the:** F&c *that;* G *of* om. 369 **besy cure**, eager business. 370 **Benygnely**, with good will. F *Benyngle.* 371 **formel . . . make**, female bird, mate. 373 **gentilleste**, most refined. 375 **benygne . . . goodlieste**, gracious, most beautiful. 376 **at his reste**, i.e., familiar. 379 **vicarye**, deputy (vicar). This is the role of Nature in both *De Planctu Naturae* and de Meun's part of *RR.* F&c *vyker/vicaire.* 381 **knyt with evene noumberes**, joined with just proportions; ll. 379–81 are from *De Planctu*, but cf. *Boece* III. m.9, 17ff. This is the so-called Empedoclean theory of love and nature which makes the two nearly interchangeable, as they are here in *PF.* 382 **esy voys**, note Chaucer's ear for just the right tone in which Nature should begin to address her unruly audience. *began:* G *gan for.* 385 *yow:* F&c *me.* 387–90 Other MSS transpose *ordenaunce/governaunce.* 389 **plesaunce**, desire.

But natheles, myn ryghtful ordenaunce   390
May I nat lete for al this world to wynne,
That he that most is worthi shal begynne.

"The tersel egle, as that ye knowe ful wel,
The foul ryal, above yow in degre,
The wyse and worthi, secre, trewe as stel,   395
Whiche I have formed, as ye may wel se,
In every part as it best liketh me—
It nedeth not his shap yow to devyse—
He shal ferst chese and speken in his gyse.

"And after hym by order shul ye chese,   400
After youre kynde, everiche as yow lyketh,
And as youre hap is shul ye wynne or lese—
But which of yow that love most entriketh,
God sende hym hire that sorest for hym
   syketh."
And therwithal the tersel gan she calle,   405
And seyde, "My sone, the choys is to the falle.

"But natheles, in this condicioun
Mot be the choys of everich that is heere,
That she agre to his eleccioun
Whatso he be that shulde be hire feere.   410
This is oure usage alwey, from yer to yeere,
And whoso may at this tyme have his grace
In blisful tyme he cam into this place."

With hed enclyned and with ful humble cheere
This ryal tersel spak, and tariede noht: 415
"Unto my sovereyn lady, and not my fere,
I chese, and chese with wil and hert and
   thought,
The formel on youre hond, so wel iwrought,
Whos I am al, and evere wol hire serve,
Do what hire lest to do me lyve or sterve;   420

"Besekynge hire of merci and of grace,
As she that is myn lady sovereyne;
Or let me deye present in this place.
For certes, longe I may nat lyve in payne,
For in myn herte is korven every veyne.   425
And havynge reward only to my trouthe,
My deere herte, have of my wo sum routhe.

"And if that I to hyre be founde untrewe,
Disobeysaunt, or wilful necligent,
Avauntour, or in proces love a newe,   430
I preye to yow this be my jugement:
That with these foules be I al torent
That ilke day that evere she me fynde
To hire untrewe, or in my gilt unkynde.

"And syn that hire loveth non so wel as I—   435
Al be she nevere of love me behette—
Thanne ouhte she be myn thourh hire mercy,
For other bond can I non on hire knette.
Ne nevere for no wo ne shal I lette
To serven hire, how fer so that she wende;   440
Say what yow lest, my tale is at an ende."

Ryght as the freshe, rede rose newe
Ayen the somer sunne coloured is,
Ryght so for shame al wexen gan the hewe
Of this formel whan she herde al this;   445
She neyther answerde wel ne seyde amys,
So sore abashed was she, tyl that Nature
Seyde, "Doughter, drede the nought, I yow
   assure."

Another tersel egle spak anon,   449
Of lower kynde, and seyde, "That shal nat be!
I love hire bet than ye don, by Seynt John,
Or at the leste I love as wel as ye,

---

391 lete . . . wynne, hinder, i.e., for anything in the world. *lete:* G *breke.* **392 most is worthi,** Chaucer is clearly having Dame Nature assert that aristocratic hierarchy is the law of nature. **393 tersel,** a male hawk or eagle. G *terslet.* F&c *ful* om. **394** G *abovyn every degre* (status). **396** F&c *The whiche/wel* om. **398 devyse,** describe. **399 chese . . . gyse,** choose (his mate), fashion. **402 hap,** luck. **403 entriketh,** entraps. **404 syketh,** sighs. *sorest:* G *soryest.* **406 to the:** G *to yow.* **407 in,** on. **408 Mot,** must. **410 shulde . . . feere,** would, companion (mate). F&c *Whoso.* Nature's concession of veto power to the lady was not the "usage" (custom) in medieval society. **412 grace,** good fortune. **413 blisful,** happy. **414 cheere,** expression. G&c *ful* om. **420 do . . . sterve,** make, die. *lest:* F&c *lyst/lust.* **421 of,** for. **423 present,** now. **425 korven,** cut. **426 trouthe,** fidelity. G *only reward to.* **427 routhe,** pity. **428** F *And yf I be founde to hir.* **430 Avauntour . . . proces,** boaster (about love), time. **432 with . . . torent,** by, torn to pieces. **433 ilke,** same. **436 behette,** promised. G *[s]he me nevere;* other MSS various readings: see Koch. **438 knette,** fasten. G *areete* (attribute). **439 lette,** stop. *Ne:* F&c *For;* other MSS *Yit.* **440 wende,** go. **444 the:** G *hire.* **446** F *Neyther she.* **447 abashed:** G *abashat.* **450 shal:** F&c *shulde.* **452** F&c *love hire.*

And longer have served hire in my degre;
And if she shulde have loved for long lovynge,
To me ful longe hadde be the gerdonynge.   455

"I dar ek seyn, if she me fynde fals,
Unkynde, janglere, or rebel in any wyse,
Or jelous, do me hangen by the hals.
And but I bere me in hire servyse
As wel as that my wit can me suffyse,   460
From poynt to poynt, hyre honour for to
    save,
Take she my lif and al the good I have!"

The thredde tercel egle answerde tho,
"Now, sires, ye seen the lytel leyser heere,
For every foul cryeth out to ben ago   465
Forth with his mak, or with his lady deere;
And ek Nature hireself ne wol not heere,
For taryinge here, not half that I wolde seye.
And but I speke, I mot for sorwe deye.

"Of long servyse avaunte I me nothing—   470
But as possible is me to deye today
For wo as he that hath ben languysshyng
This twenty wynter; and wel happen may
A man may serven bet, and more to pay,
In half a yer, althow it were no moore,   475
Than sum man doth that hath served ful
    yoore.

"I sey not this by me, for I ne can
Don no servyse that may my lady plese.
But I dar seyn, I am hire treweste man,
As to my dom, and faynest wolde hire ese,   480
At shorte wordes, til that deth me sese.

I wol ben hires, whether I wake or wynke,
And trewe in al that herte may bethynke."

Of al my lyf, syn that day I was born,
So gentil ple in love or other thyng   485
Ne herde nevere no man me beforn—
Who that hadde leyser and cunnyng
For to reherse hyre cher and hire spekyng.
And from the morwe gan this speche laste
Tyl dounward drow the sunne wonder faste.   490

The noyse of foules for to ben delyvered
So loude ronge, "Have don, and lat us wende!"
That wel wende I the wode hadde al toshyvered.
"Cum of," they crieden, "allas, ye wol us
    shende!
Whan shal youre cursede pletynge have an
    ende?   495
How shulde a juge eyther partie leve
For ye or nay withouten other preve?"

The goos, the cokkow, and the doke also
So cryede, "Kek kek, kokkow, quek quek,"
    hye,
That thourw myne eres the noyse wente tho.   500
The goos seyde, "Al this nys not worth a flye.
But I can shappe herof a remedie,
And I wol seye my verdit fayre and swythe
For water-foul, whoso be wroth or blythe!"

"And I for werm-foul," quod the fol
    kokkow,   505
"For I wol of myn owene autorite
For comun spede take on the charge now,
For to delyvere us is gret charite."

453 **my degre,** probably "my condition" of love, rather than "my rank." *longer:* F *lenger.* 454 *shulde have:* G *shulde a.* 455 **gerdonynge,** reward. *ful longe:* F&c *allone.* 457 **janglere,** gossiper. GF&c *in* om. 458 **hals,** neck. 460 F&c *that* om. 462 *she:* G *the;* other MSS *ye.* 463 **tho,** then. 464 **lytel leyser,** little leisure (for this sort of courtly declaration). 465 **ago,** gone. 466 **mak . . . lady,** mate, mistress. 468 **For taryinge,** i.e., because of the delay it causes. 469 **but . . . mot,** unless, must. 470 **avaunte,** boast. 471 **But as,** but (it is) as. G *That possible is.* 474 **more to pay,** pay more. 476 **yoore,** long. F *ful* om.; other MSS *men doon/have.* 477 **by me,** about myself. 480 **dom . . . faynest,** judgment, most eager. *ese:* F&c *plese.* 485 **ple,** plea (technically an argument in court). 488 **hyre,** their. 489 **morwe,** morning. 490 *drow:* F&c *went.* 492 **wende,** go. 493 **wende . . . toshyvered,** thought, broken to pieces. G *toslyvered.* 494 **shende,** ruin. 495 **pletynge,** pleading, cf. l. 485n. F&c *pledynge.* 496 **leve,** believe. 497 **preve,** proof. *other:* F&c *any.* 498 All MSS (except G) *The duk and the cukkowe also,* but cf. l. 499. 501 F&c *seyde tho/not* om. 502 **shappe herof,** create for this. 503 **verdit . . . swythe,** verdict, quickly. F&c *I* om. 504 **blythe,** happy. 505 **fol,** foolish. *quod:* F&c *seyde;* F&c *fool/foule.* 507 **comun spede,** this appears to hark back to *comoun profit* of ll. 47, 75, but those who would give it a serious interpretation in this poem must reckon that this time the allusion is put in the mouth of the foolish cuckoo. **charge,** responsibility. *spede:* G&c *profit.* F&c *take on me the.*

"Ye may onbyde a while yit, parde,"
Quod the turtil, "if it be youre wille.   510
A wight may speke hym were as fayr be stylle.

"I am a sed-foul, oon the unworthieste,
That wot I wel, and litel of cunnynge,
But bet is that a wyghtes tunge reste
Than entermeten hym of such doinge   515
Of which he neyther rede can ne synge;
And whoso it doth ful foule hymself acloyeth,
For offys uncommytted ofte anoyeth."

Nature, which that alwey hadde an ere
To murmur of the lewedenesse behynde,   520
With facound voys seyde, "Hold youre tonges
          there!
And I shal sone, I hope, a conseyl fynde
Yow to delyvere, and from this noyse
          unbynde:
I juge, of every folk men shul oon calle
To seyn the verdit for yow foules alle."   525

Assented were to this conclusioun
The briddes alle; and foules of ravyne
Han chosen fyrst, by pleyn eleccioun,
The terselet of the faucoun to diffyne
Al here sentence, as him lest to termyne,   530
And to Nature hym gunne to presente,
And she accepteth hym with glad entente.

The terslet seyde thanne, "In this manere
Ful hard were it to prove by resoun
Who loveth best this gentil formel heere,   535
For everych hath swich replicacioun
That non by skilles may be brought adoun.
I can not se that argumentes avayle:
Thanne semeth it there moste be batayle."

"Al redy!" quod these egles tercels tho.   540
"Nay, sires," quod he, "if that I durste it seye;
Ye don me wrong, my tale is not ido.
For, sires, ne taketh not agref, I preye,
It may not gon as ye wolde in this weye.
Oure is the voys that han the charge on honde,
And to the juges dom ye moten stonde.   546

"And therfore, pes. I seye, as to myn wit,
Me wolde thynke how that the worthieste
Of knyghthod, and lengest had used it,
Most of estat, of blod the gentilleste,   550
Were sittyngest for hire, if that hir leste;
And of these thre she wot hireself, I trowe,
Which that he be, for it is light to knowe."

The water-foules han here hedes leid
Togedere, and of a short avysement,   555
Whan everych hadde his large golee seyd,
They seyden sothly, al by oon assent,
How that the goos, with hire facounde gent,
"That so desyreth to pronounce oure nede,
Shal telle oure tale," and preyede "God hir
          spede."   560

And for these water-foules tho began
The goos to speke, and in hir kakelynge
She seyde, "Pes, now tak kep, every man,
And herkeneth which a resoun I shal forth
          brynge—
My wit is sharp, I love no taryinge—   565
I seye I rede hym, thow he were my brother,
But she wol love hym, let hym love another."

"Lo, here a parfit resoun of a goos,"
Quod the sperhauk. "Nevere mot she thee!
Lo, siche it is to have a tunge loos.   570

---

509 **onbyde**, wait. F&c *abyde*. 510 **if it be youre wille**, i.e., if you don't mind. 511 **wight may speke**, i.e., some people talk who might better be quiet. *fayr:* F&c *good*. 513 **wot**, know. 514 *bet:* F&c *better*. 515 **entermeten**, meddle. 517 **foule . . . acloyeth**, badly, overreaches. 518 **offys uncommytted**, i.e., assumed (unasked-for) service. *uncommytted:* G *onquit*. 520 **lewedenesse**, rabble (ignorant parties). G *behynde* om; other MSS *blynde/by kynde*. 521 **facound**, authoritative; cf. l. 382—more evidence of Chaucer's sensitive ear. 524 **I juge**, I rule. 529 **diffyne**, express. 530 **sentence . . . termyne**, opinion, determine. *him:* G *hem*. 533 G *thanne* om.; other MSS *that.* 534 F&c *preve(n) (h)it.* 536 **replicacioun**, ability to reply. 537 **skilles**, arguments. F&c *That by/may non.* 540 G *this eglis terslet.* 544 **wolde**, wish. 545 **charge**, responsibility. 546 **dom**, decision. 548 **Me wolde thynke**, i.e., it would seem to me. 551 **sittyngest**, most fitting. *hir leste:* G *he leste.* 553 **light**, easy. *it:* G *here; light:* other MSS *ethe.* 556 **golee**, mouthful. 558 **facounde gent**, genteel eloquence. G *so gent.* 560 F&c *to God. hir:* G *hym.* 562 *hir:* G *his.* 563 **kep**, care. *She:* G *He.* 564 G *forth* om. 565 *love:* G *take.* 566 **rede**, advise. 567 **wol**, unless. 569 **thee**, prosper. *she:* G *he.*

Now, parde, fol, yit were it bet for the
Han holde thy pes than shewed thyn nycete.
It lyth nat in his wit ne in his wille,
But soth is seyd, a fol can not ben stille."

The laughtere aros of gentil foules alle,　575
And right anon the sed-foul chosen hadde
The turtle trewe, and gunne hire to hem calle,
And preyeden hire to seyn the sothe sadde
Of this matere, and axede what she radde.
And she answerde that pleynly hire entente　580
She wolde shewe, and sothly what she mente.

"Nay, God forbede a lovere shulde chaunge,"
The turtle seyde, and wex for shame al red.
"Thow that his lady everemore be straunge,
Yit lat hym serve hire til that he be ded.　585
Forsoth, I preyse nat the goses red.
For thow she deyede, I wolde non other make;
I wol ben hire til that the deth me take."

"Wel bourded," quod the doke, "by myn hat!
That men shulde loven alwey causeles,　590
Who can a resoun fynde or wit in that?
Daunseth he murye that is myrtheles?
What shulde I rekke of him that is recheles?
Ye quek," yit seyde the doke, ful wel and fayre,
"There been mo sterres, God wot, than a
　　payre!"　595

"Now fy, cherl," quod the gentil terselet,
"Out of the donghil cam that word ful right!
Thow canst nat seen what thyng is wel beset.
Thow farst by love as oules don by lyght:　599
The day hem blent, but wel they sen by nyght.
Thy kynde is of so low a wrechednesse
That what love is thow canst nat seen ne gesse."

Tho gan the kokkow putte hym forth in pres
For foul that eteth werm, and seyde blyve,
"So I," quod he, "may have my make in pes,　605
I reche nat how longe that ye stryve.
Lat ech of hem be soleyn al here lyve!
This is my red, syn they may nat acorde.
This shorte lessoun nedeth nat recorde."

"Ye, have the glotoun fild inow his paunche,　610
Thanne are we wel," seyde the merlioun.
"Thow mortherere of the heysoge on the
　　braunche
That broughte the forth, thow rewful glotoun,
Lyve thow soleyn, wermes corupcioun!
For no fors is of lak of thy nature.　615
Go, lewed be thow whil the world may dure!"

"Now pes," quod Nature, "I comaunde here;
For I have herd al youre opynyoun,
And in effect yit be we nevere the nere.
But fynally, this is my conclusioun,　620
That she hireself shal han the eleccioun
Of whom hire lest; and who be wroth or blythe,
Hym that she cheseth, he shal hire han as
　　swithe.

"For syn it may not here discussed be
Who loveth hire best, as seyth the terselet,　625
Thanne wol I don hire this favour, that she
Shal han right hym on whom hire herte is set,
And he hire that his herte hath on hire knet.
Thus juge I, Nature, for I may not lye;
To non estat I have non other eye.　630

"But as for conseyl for to chese a make,
If I were Resoun, certes, thanne wolde I
Conseyle yow the ryal tersel take—

---

571 *yit:* G *now.* 572 **nycete,** foolishness. 573 *wit:* G *mygh*[*t*]. 577 *turtle:* G *tersel.* 578 **sadde,** sober. 579 **radde,** advised. 581 G *wolde it.*
583 *turtle:* G *tersel.* 585 *til that:* F&c *ever til.* 586 **red,** advice. 589 **bourded,** joked. G *bordit.* 593 **rekke . . . recheles,** care, doesn't care.
F&c *Who shulde recche of that is recheles?* 594 G *Kek, kek yit seith.* **doke:** other MSS *goos.* 596 *fy:* G *sey.* 598 **wel beset,** suitable (proper).
600 **blent,** blinds. *but:* F&c *ful.* 602 *nat:* F&c *neyther.* 603 **in pres,** in the crowd. 604 **blyve,** eagerly. G *blythe.* 606 **stryve,** contest.
607 **soleyn,** single. 608 **red,** advice. 609 **recorde,** no record. 611 G *seyde thanne a.* 612 **heysoge,** hedge sparrow. The eggs of the cuckoo
were deposited in the hedge sparrow's nest; after she had hatched and cared for the young, they killed her—cf. l. 358n. 613 **rewful,**
pitiful. G *reufulles.* 614 **soleyn,** solitary. 615 **no fors . . . nature,** i.e., it doesn't matter if your line perishes. 616 **lewed,** ignorant.
619 **in effect . . . nere,** to our conclusion, nearer. *nevere:* G *not.* 621 **eleccioun,** choice. **han the:** F *have hir.* 622 *and who:* F&c *whoso.*
623 **as swithe,** immediately. **cheseth:** F&c *cheest.* *as:* G *a.* 626 F&c *this favour to hir, that she.* 627 G *right om.* 628 **knet,** fastened (knit).
629 *Thus:* F&c *This.* 630 **non estat,** no (other) estate (except coupling). 632 *I:* other MSS *hit;* F&c *certes* om.

As seyde the terselet ful skylfully—
As for the gentilleste and most worthi,   635
Which I have wrought so wel to my plesaunce,
That to yow oughte to been a suffisaunce."

With dredful vois the formel tho answerde,
"My rightful lady, Goddesse of Nature,
Soth is that I am evere under youre yerde,   640
As is another lyves creature,
And mot ben youre whil that my lyf may dure,
And therfore graunteth me my ferste bone,
And myn entent yow wol I sey right sone."

"I graunte it yow," quod she. And right anon
This formel egle spak in this degre,   646
"Almyghty queen, unto this yer be gon
I axe respit for to avise me,
And after that to have my choys al fre—
This al and sum that I wol speke and seye;   650
Ye gete no more, althow ye do me deye.

"I wol nat serve Venus ne Cupide
Forsothe, as yit, by no manere weye."
"Now, syn it may non otherwise betyde,"
Quod tho Nature, "heere is no more to seye.   655
Thanne wolde I that these foules were aweye,
Eche with his make, for taryinge lengere
          heere."
And seyde hem thus, as ye shul after here.

"To yow speke I, ye terseletes," quod Nature,
"Beth of good herte, and serveth alle thre.   660
A yer ne is nat so longe to endure,
And ech of yow peyne hym in his degre

For to do wel, for, God wot, quyt is she
Fro yow this yer; what after so befalle,
This entremes is dressed for yow alle."   665

And whan this werk al brought was to an ende,
To every foul Nature yaf his make
By evene acord, and on here wey they wende.
But, Lord, the blisse and joye that they make!
For ech gan other in his wynges take,   670
And with here nekkes eche gan other wynde,
Thankynge alwey the noble queen of Kynde.

But fyrst were chosen foules for to synge,
As yer by yer was alwey hir usaunce
To synge a roundel at here departynge,   675
To don to Nature honour and plesaunce.
The note, I trowe, imaked was in Fraunce;
The wordes were swich as ye may here fynde,
The nexte vers as I now have in mynde.

Now welcome, somor, with thy sonne softe,   680
That hast this wintres wedres overshake,
And drevyne away the longe nyghtes blake!
Saynt Valentyn, that art ful hye on-lofte,
Thus syngen smale foules for thy sake:
Now welcome, somer, with thy sonne softe,   685
That hast this wintres wedres overshake.

Well han they cause for to gladen ofte,
Sith ech of hem recovered hath hys make,
Ful blisseful mowe they synge when they wake:
Now welcome, somer, with thy sonne softe,   690
That hast this wintres wedres overshake,
And driven away the longe nyghtes blake!

---

634 skylfully, reasonably. **635 As for the,** i.e., as the. **637** F&c *hit oughte.* **638 dredful,** timid. *tho:* F&c *hir.* **640 under . . . yerde,** subject to your discipline (literally, to be beaten with a yardstick). **641** *another lyves:* F&c *everich other.* **642** *mot:* F&c *moste;* F&c *youres whil my.* **643 bone,** request. **644** G *that wele I seyn wol sone.* **645** *right:* G *that.* **646 degre,** manner. **647** *gon:* F&c *don.* **648 avise me,** i.e., think about it. **651 do me,** make me. **652** *Cupide:* F *Cipride.* **654** F&c *other weyes.* **657 for taryinge,** i.e., rather than. **662 his degre,** his situation. *peyne hym:* G *peignynge.* **665 entremes,** intermission (literally, a course served between main courses). **666** *brought:* F&c *wroght.* **668 evene acord,** mutual agreement. **670** F *ech of hem/his* om. **672 Kynde,** nature. *queen:* F&c *goddesse.* **674 usaunce,** custom. *hir:* G *the.* **675 roundel,** originally a dance song with a repeated refrain; by Chaucer's time a French song like a "round," and a stanza type. **677 note . . . Fraunce,** tune was French. Some MSS have the French line *Que bien ayme a tarde oublie* (Who loves well forgets slowly) in the margin, but no tune to go with such a French song is known. The English rondel can be sung to Machaut's music. **678** G *sweche/here* om. **680–92** The words of the rondel are lacking in most MSS. The most nearly complete text is in a later hand in G, but the words and refrain were put in this order by Skeat, *Oxford Chaucer,* I.524. **680** *thy,* so Digby; G om. **682** *longe,* so Digby; G *large.* **683** G *ert/o-lofte.* **688** G *Sethe.* **689** *synge:* G *ben.* Digby *synge and endless joy thei make.*

And with the shoutyng, whan the song
    was do,
That foules maden at here flyght awey,
I wok, and othere bokes tok me to,   695

To reede upon, and yit I rede alwey
In hope, iwis, to rede so sum day
That I shal mete sumthyng for to fare
The bet, and thus to rede I nel nat spare.

Parliamentum avium in die Sancti Valentini tentum secundum Galfridum Chaucer. Deo gracias.

693 *the:* F&c *hir.* **697** *In:* F&c *I.* **699** *nel:* F&c *wol;* other MSS *nyl.*

House of Fame

INTRODUCTION

House of Fame

NONE OF Chaucer's poems tempts one to autobiographical interpretation more than the *House of Fame.* It provides our most intimate picture of the bureaucrat at work in his office and the poet at work in his study (ll.641-60) and of his personal relations with someone very close to him (ll.556-66). The eagle calls him "Geffrey" (l.729) and speaks to him in a familiar voice (ll.562-66). Critics are generally agreed that the poem addresses a crisis in his artistic development: What does the future hold for Geoffrey the poet? What sort of poetry should he write to secure "fame"? What *is* "fame" in contrast to "rumor" and "tidings"? It is reasonable to assume that soon after asking these questions, he turned to *Troylus and Criseyde,* the Knight's Tale, and the Canterbury compilation, upon which his true fame rests. This interpretation is elucidated by Donald Howard, *Chaucer* (1987).

Unlike the two previous poems, the classical prologue this time falls within the dream. It takes the form of wall paintings in a temple depicting the story of Dido as an exemplum against falsehood in love, like the stories of the unhappy lovers referred to in the temple of Venus in the *Parliament of Fowls* (ll.281-94). After viewing this sequence, the dreamer goes out of the temple and finds himself in a wasteland. As he stands there wondering, a golden eagle swoops down upon him, resembling the eagle that carried Dante's body to the first ledge of the mountain of Purgatory (*Purgatorio* 9). This suggests a connection between Chaucer's wasteland and the artistic and spiritual wasteland in which Dante found himself at the beginning of the *Divine Comedy,* from which Dante was rescued by his transcendental journey.

When Book II begins, the difference between Chaucer and Dante becomes evident. The English poet's genius is not for epiphany but for satire. He cannot take spiritual wastelands and swooping eagles seriously. In his hands, they are converted to wry allusions to domestic discord and caricatures of intimate friends. Like the whelp and Affrican in the earlier visions, the eagle here is a guide, sent to teach the detached dreamer more "tydinges" (i.e., news) about love than he ever imagined. This may be a reference to an announcement of Richard's betrothal that was being prepared for at the end of the poem—although it is hard to imagine the 2158 lines of the piece being read as a prologue to such an announcement. The version for that or any other occasion would have had to be severely cut.

But, as noted before, the dream visions went beyond whatever occasions may have inspired them. Books II and III of *House of Fame* are discussions of the nature of poetry and the function of the poet. The eagle is the epitome of the dull professor whose facts are accurate but irrelevant. Finally deposited before the castle of Fame, the dreamer sees first the entertainers—purveyors of other men's art—then Fame herself surrounded by all the great poets of antiquity. When at l. 1529, Chaucer might logically have been invited, like Dante in *Inferno* 4, to become a member of that illustrious group, a "ryght gret companye…of sondry regiouns, / Of alleskynnes condiciouns" (ll.1528-32) bursts in, foreshadowing the band of "sondry folk" (*CT* I.25) upon whom Chaucer's immortality eventually rests. Serendipity no doubt, but the development of Chaucer's art reflects so many presentiments that one is left wondering.

The rest of the poem is a study of the unreliability of fame and rumor, ending with preparation for an announcement by a "man of greet auctorite." The conceit on how truth and falsehood are commingled as they emerge from the spinning house of Rumor (ll. 2088 ff) is one of Chaucer's most interesting figures. J.A.W. Bennett, *Chaucer's Book of Fame* (1968), and Piero Boitani, *Chaucer and the Imaginary World of Fame* (1984), are two of the best general introductions.

House of Fame

BOOK I

Proem

God turne us every dreme to goode,
For hyt is wonder, be the roode,
To my wytte, what causeth swevenes,
Eyther on morwes or on evenes;
And why th'effect folweth of somme,   5
And of somme hit shal never come;
Why that is an avisioun,
And this a revelacioun,
Why this a dreme, why that a swevene,
And noght to every man lyche evene;   10
Why this a fantome, why these oracles,
I not. But whoso of these meracles
The causes knoweth bet then I,
Devyne he, for I certenly
Ne kan hem noght, ne never thinke   15
To besely my wytte to swinke,
To knowe of hir signifiaunce
The gendres, neyther the distaunce
Of tymes of hem, ne the causis,
Or why this more then that cause is—   20
As yf folkys complexions
Make hem dreme of reflexions,
Or ellis thus, as other sayne,
For to gret feblenesse of her brayne,
By abstinence or by sekenesse,   25
Prison, stewe, or gret distresse,
Or ellis by dysordynaunce
Of naturell acustumaunce,
That somme man is to curiouse
In studye, or melancolyouse,   30
Or thus so inly ful of drede
That no man may hym bote bede;
Or ellis that devocion
Of somme, and contemplacion
Causen suche dremes ofte;   35
Or that the cruelle lyfe unsofte
Which these ilke lovers leden
That hopen over muche or dreden,
That purely her impressions
Causen hem avisions;   40
Or yf that spirites have the myght
To make folk to dreme a-nyght;
Or yf the soule, of propre kynde
Be so parfit, as men fynde,
That yt forwot that ys to come,   45
And that hyt warneth al and some
Of everych of her aventures
Be avisions or be figures,

Text based on MS. Fairfax 16(F) with variants from Pepys 2006 (P), Caxton (Cx), and Thynne (Th). See "The Text of This Edition," p. 966.

2 P&c *wonder thynge*. 3 **swevenes,** dreams. This discussion has been compared with that in *RR* 18240ff. (Dunn-Robbins, 84 and 85). The varieties of dreams may owe something to the five kinds distinguished in Macrobius' Commentary on Cicero's *Somnium Scipionis*, which Chaucer used so extensively at the beginning of *PF*. Macrobius types are *somnium*, the enigmatic dream; *visio*, the prophetic dream; *oraculum*, the oracular dream; *insomnium*, the nightmare; and *phantasma (visum)*, the apparition. It is not easy to equate all of Chaucer's terminology with this classification, and there are no precise distinctions for some of the English terms he uses. **4 morwes,** mornings. *Eyther on:* P&c *On the.* **5 th'effect,** i.e., the predicted outcome. **8** All authorities: *And why.* **10 lyche evene,** the same. **14 Devyne he,** let him know by intuition. P&c *Defyne.* **15 kan,** know. **16 To . . . swinke,** too, belabor. **17** P&c *significacions.* **18 gendres . . . distaunce,** varieties, intervals. Cx *gendres ne dystinctions.* **19** P&c *Of the tymes.* **20 more then that cause,** i.e., why one cause for a dream is more influential than another. F&c *For why.* All authorities: *this is.* **21 complexions,** temperaments. *As:* Cx *Or.* **22 reflexions,** i.e., reflections of their own temperaments. **24 to** (too): P&c *the.* **26 stewe,** brothel. Cx *stryf.* **28 acustumaunce,** routine. **29** P&c *men ben.* **32 bote bede,** offer help. *bede:* P&c *rede* (suggest). **39 impressions,** reactions (emotions). **40** P&c *hem have visions.* **43 propre kynde,** of its own nature. **45 forwot,** foreknows. **48 figures,** symbols.

But that oure flessh ne hath no myght
To understonde hyt aryght, 50
For hyt is warned to derkly—
But why the cause is, noght wot I.
Wel worth of this thyng grete clerkes
That trete of this and other werkes,
For I of noon opinion 55
Nyl as now make mensyon,
But oonly that the holy roode
Turne us every dreme to goode.
For never sith that I was borne,
Ne no man elles me beforne, 60
Mette, I trowe stedfastly,
So wonderful a dreme as I,
The tenthe day now of Decembre,
The which as I kan now remembre
I wol yow tellen everydel. 65
   But at my gynnynge, trusteth wel,
I wol make invocacion,
With special devocion,
Unto the god of slepe anoon,
That duelleth in a cave of stoon 70
Upon a streme that cometh fro Lete,
That is a floode of helle unswete,
Besyde a folke men clepeth Cymerie.
There slepeth ay this god unmerie
With his slepy thousand sones, 75
That alwey for to slepe hir wone is.
And to this god that I of rede
Prey I that he wol me spede
My swevene for to telle aryght,
Yf every dreme stonde in his myght. 80
And he that mover ys of alle,
That is and was and ever shalle,
So yive hem joye that hyt here

Of alle that they dreme to-yere,
And for to stonden al in grace 85
Of her loves, or in what place
That hem were levest for to stonde,
And shelde hem fro poverte and shonde,
And fro unhappe and eche disese,
And sende hem alle that may hem plese, 90
That take hit wel and skorne hyt noghte,
Ne hyt mysdemen in her thoghte
Thorgh malicious entencion.
And whoso thorgh presumpcion,
Or hate, or skorne, or thorgh envye, 95
Dispit, or jape, or vilanye,
Mysdeme hyt, pray I Jesus God,
That dreme he barefot, dreme he shod,
That every harm that any man
Hath had syth the world began 100
Befalle hym therof or he sterve.
And graunte he mote hit ful deserve,
Loo, with suche a conclusion
As had of his avision
Cresus that was kyng of Lyde, 105
That high upon a gebet dyde.
This prayer shal he have of me—
I am no bet in charyte!
Now herkeneth, as I have yow seyde,
What that I mette or I abreyde. 110

The Dream

   Of Decembre the tenthe day,
Whan hit was nyght to slepe I lay
Ryght ther as I was wont to done,
And fille on slepe wonder sone,
As he that wery was forgoo 115

49 **But,** except. 51 **derkly,** indistinctly. 53 **Wel worth,** good luck (to). 54 *this and:* P&c *that and of.* 57 **roode,** cross. 61 **Mette,** dreamed. 62 Cx *as dide I.* 63 **tenthe day,** various explanations of the date have been offered. Because of the error in the Julian calendar, the winter solstice was then on December 11. If one theme of *HF* is Chaucer's searching for a more worthwhile kind of poetry (see Introduction) he might wish to set the dream at the dawn of the new year. Or, if *HF* was an occasional poem, the 10th might have been the day ambassadors were actually appointed to arrange Richard's marriage with Anne of Bohemia (December 12 in the records). Such explanations are not mutually exclusive, and the date was evidently conventional—at least it is also used in Machaut's poems. 64 *now* CxTh om.; F *yow.* 65–66 Lines lacking in PCx. 68 P&c *With devoute special.* 71 **Lete,** Lethe, the river of forgetfulness in Hades. P&c *streme that men clepen.* 73 **Cymerie,** near whose gloomy land Ovid placed Morpheus' cave, *Met* 11.592ff. This is the same passage used in *BD* 137ff. 76 **wone,** custom. 88 **shonde,** harm. 89 **unhappe . . . disese,** mischance, dis-ease. P&c *And from every unhappe and disese.* 91 P&c *That taketh wel and scorneth nought.* 92 **mysdemen,** misjudge. 96 *vilanye:* P&c *felonye.* 98 **barefot . . . shod,** i.e., at night or by day. P&c *That* om. 101 **or he sterve,** before he dies. 102 **mote,** may. 105 **Lyde,** Lydia, cf. *CT* vii.2727. 110 **or I abreyde,** before I awoke. 115 **wery . . . forgoo,** i.e., completely weary.

On pilgrymage myles two
To the corseynt Leonard,
To make lythe of that was hard.
But as I slepte, me mette I was
Withyn a temple ymad of glas,   120
In whiche ther were moo ymages
Of golde, stondynge in sondry stages,
And moo ryche tabernacles,
And with perre moo pynacles,
And moo curiouse portreytures,   125
And queynte maner of figures
Of olde werke then I sawgh ever.
For certeynly, I nyste never
Wher that I was. But wel wyste I
Hyt was of Venus redely,   130
The temple, for in portreyture
I sawgh anoon-ryght hir figure
Naked fletynge in a see,
And also on hir hed, pardee,
Hir rose garlond white and rede,   135
And hir comb to kembe hyr hede,
Hir dowves, and daun Cupido
Hir blynde sone, and Vulcano
That in his face was ful broune.
   But as I romed up and doune,   140
I fond that on a wall ther was
Thus writen on a table of bras:
"I wol now singen, yif I kan,
The armes and also the man
That first came, thorgh his destinee,   145

Fugityf of Troy contree,
In Itayle, with ful moche pyne,
Unto the strondes of Lavyne."
And tho began the story anoon
As I shal telle yow echon.   150
   First sawgh I the destruction
Of Troy throgh the Greke Synon,
That with his false forswerynge,
And his chere and his lesynge,
Made the hors broght into Troye   155
Thorgh which Troyens lost al her joye.
And aftir this was grave, allas,
How Ilyon assayled was,
And wonne, and Kyng Priam yslayne,
And Polite his sone, certayne,   160
Dispitously, of daun Pirrus.
And next that sawgh I how Venus,
Whan that she sawgh the castel brende,
Doun fro the hevene gan descende,
And bad hir sone Eneas flee;   165
And how he fled, and how that he
Escaped was from al the pres,
And tooke his fader Anchises,
And bar hym on hys bakke away,
Cryinge, "Allas, and welaway!"   170
The whiche Anchises in hys honde
Bar the goddes of the londe,
Thilke that unbrende were.
   And I saugh next in al thys fere
How Creusa, daun Eneas wif,   175

---

117 corseynt Leonard, no one knows why two miles on a pilgrimage to St. Leonard should be so exhausting. Skeat's *Oxford Chaucer*, III.249, takes this as a reference to unhappy marriage (see below ll. 560–66; 654–66), since St. Leonard was reputed to free prisoners (Skeat reads "married people") who have repented. This reading would give added meaning to the next line. Cx *corps of seynt*. **118 lythe of that was hard,** easy what was hard. **122 stages,** stations (however, the Stations of the Cross date from the 17th century). *sondry:* P&c *divers*. **123 tabernacles,** canopies, like those over tombs. **124 perre . . . pynacles,** jeweled, obelisklike decorations. **125 curiouse,** intricate. P&c *ryche*. **127** P&c *golde werk(is)*. **130 redely,** truly. **133 Naked fletynge,** floating. This description is modeled upon Boccaccio's *Teseida* 7.53ff. and other sources. Chaucer handled the same material in *PF* ll. 211–94, and *CT*, KT I.1918ff. **135–36** Gap in P. Cx *Rose garlondes smellynge as a mede | And also fleyng aboute her hede*. **138 Vulcano,** Vulcan, god of metal work (his face brown from working over the forge), mythological husband of Venus. **140 romed,** wandered. **142 bras,** as in *PF* l. 231, this allusion to brass may be a reflection on the inadequacy of conventional chivalric love as the theme for great poetry, because that is the only aspect of the *Aeneid* treated in the following account. **143 I wol now singen,** this is the first translation into English of Virgil's famous opening lines, but cast in couplets. *singen:* F&c *say*. **148 Lavyne,** Lavinium, where Aeneas landed in Italy. F&c *Labyne*. **154 chere . . . lesynge,** (deceptive) manner, lying. **157 grave,** carved. **158 Ilyon,** the citadel of Troy. These memorable details down to l. 240 are drawn largely from the *Aeneid*, except that instead of beginning *in medias res* and recounting the fall of Troy and escape of Aeneas in a flashback, Chaucer puts the events in sequence. **159** P&c *Pryamis(us) slayne*. **160** *Polite:* P *Plite*; Th *Polites*, cf. *Aeneid* 2.526. **161 Dispitously . . . daun,** cruelly, don (Lat. *dominus,* master). *of:* F *and*. **163 brende,** burned, cf. *Aeneid* 2.589ff. **167 pres,** crowd. **172 Bar the goddes,** i.e., the household gods, the "Lares and Penates." **174 fere,** peril, cf. *Aeneid* 2.736ff. *thys:* F&c *hys*.

Which that he lovede as hys lyf,
And hir yonge sone Iulo,
And eke Askanius also,
Fledden eke with drery chere,
That hyt was pitee for to here; 180
And in a forest as they went,
At a turnynge of a went,
How Creusa was ylost, allas,
That ded—not I how—she was;
How he hir soughte, and how hir goste 185
Bad hym to flee the Grekes oste,
And seyde he most unto Itayle,
As was hys destynee, sauns faille;
That hyt was pitee for to here,
When hir spirite gan appere, 190
The wordes that she to hym seyde,
And for to kepe hir sone hym preyde.
Ther sawgh I grave eke how he,
Hys fader eke, and his meynee,
With hys shippes gan to saylle 195
Towardes the contree of Itaylle
As streight as that they myghte goo.
Ther saugh I the, cruel Junoo,
That art daun Jupiteres wife,
That hast yhated al thy lyfe 200
Alle the Troianysshe bloode,
Renne and crye as thou were woode
On Eolus the god of wyndes
To blowen out of alle kyndes
So lowde that he shulde drenche 205
Lorde and lady, grome and wenche,
Of al the Troian nacion,
Withoute any savacion.
    Ther saugh I such tempeste aryse

That every herte myght agryse 210
To see hyt peynted on the walle.
Ther saugh I graven eke withalle
Venus, how ye, my lady dere,
Wepynge with ful woful chere,
Prayen Jupiter on hye 215
To save and kepe that navye
Of the Troian Eneas
Syth that he hir sone was.
Ther saugh I Joves Venus kysse,
And graunted of the tempest lysse. 220
Ther saugh I how the tempest stent,
And how with alle pyne he went,
And prevely toke arryvage
In the contree of Cartage;
And on the morwe, how that he 225
And a knyght highte Achate
Mette with Venus that day,
Goynge in a queynt array
As she had ben an hunteresse,
With wynde blowynge upon hir tresse; 230
How Eneas gan hym to pleyne,
When that he knew hir, of his peyne;
And how his shippes dreynte were,
Or elles lost, he nyste where;
How she gan hym comforte thoo, 235
And bad hym to Cartage goo,
And ther he shulde his folke fynde
That in the see were left behynde.
    And, shortly of this thyng to pace,
She made Eneas so in grace 240
Of Dido quene of that contree
That, shortly for to tellen, she
Became hys love and let hym doo

---

178 **Askanius,** another name for Julius; cf. *Aeneid* 1.267, 690. In *LGW* l. 941 Chaucer gets it right, so this is merely a slip. (Koch proposed *That highte* for *And eke,* but this has no MS authority.) 179 **chere,** expression. 180 **here,** hear. Throughout this section Chaucer ignores the limitations on movement and sound implied by wall paintings. 182 **went,** path. 185 **goste,** spirit, cf. *Aeneid* 2.772. 192 **kepe . . . sone,** protect, son. 194 **meynee,** retainers. 198 **Junoo,** Juno was the perpetual enemy of Troy because Paris had judged Venus more beautiful. Here Chaucer returns to *Aeneid* Bk. 1. P&c *I eke the.* 201 P&c *Trogeans, Troian.* 202 **woode,** insane. 204 **blowen . . . alle kyndes,** blow all kinds of winds. 205 **drenche,** drown. 206 **grome . . . wenche,** manservant, maidservant. 209 **tempeste aryse,** this is the beginning of Virgil's *Aeneid.* 210 **agryse,** terrify. 213 **Venus,** Chaucer increases her influence; in *Aeneid* she does not appear until Neptune has calmed the storm. 215 P&c *Praynge.* 219 **Joves,** Jove (the *s* ending is OF nom.). 220 **lysse,** relief. 222 **pyne,** pain. 223 **prevely . . . arryvage,** secretly landing. 226 **Achate,** companion of Aeneas—not his son, cf. 1.178n. 231 P&c *began.* 232 P&c *that* om. 233 **dreynte,** drowned. 239 **pace,** pass (over). From this point, the treatment abandons Virgil to follow the conception of Ovid's *Heroides* 7, which depicts Aeneas as a philanderer and Dido as the woman wronged. This is likewise the conception of the legend of Dido in *LGW,* l. 924ff.

Al that weddynge longeth too.
What shulde I speke more queynte, 245
Or peyne me my wordes peynte
To speke of love? Hyt wol not be;
I kan not of that faculte.
And eke to telle the manere
How they aqueynteden in-fere, 250
Hyt were a long proces to telle,
And over-long for yow to dwelle.
Ther sawgh I grave how Eneas
Tolde Dido every caas
That hym was tyd upon the see. 255
And after grave was how shee
Made of hym shortly at oo worde
Hyr lyf, hir love, hir luste, hir lorde,
And did hym al the reverence
And leyde on hym al the dispence 260
That any woman myghte do,
Wenynge hyt had al be so
As he hir swor; and herby demed
That he was good, for he suche semed.
Allas, what harm doth apparence 265
Whan hit is fals in existence!
For he to hir a traytour was;
Wherfore she slowe hirself, allas.
Loo, how a woman dothe amys
To love him that unknowe ys. 270
For be Cryste, lo, thus yt fareth,
Hyt is not al gold that glareth.
For also browke I wel myn hed,
Ther may be under godlyhed
Kevered many a shrewed vice. 275
Therfore be no wyght so nyce
To take a love oonly for chere,
Or speche, or for frendly manere.
For this shal every woman fynde,
That some man, of his pure kynde, 280

Wol shewen outward the fayreste,
Tyl he have caught that what him leste,
And thanne wol he causes fynde,
And swere how that she ys unkynde,
Or fals, or prevy, or double was. 285
Al this sey I be Eneas,
And Dido and hir nyce lest,
That loved al to sone a gest.
Therfore I wol seye a proverbe,
That he that fully knoweth th'erbe 290
May savely ley hyt to his eye—
Withoute drede, this ys no lye.
But let us speke of Eneas,
How he betrayed hir, allas,
And lefte hir ful unkyndely. 295
So when she saw al-utterly,
That he wolde hir of trouthe fayle,
And wende fro hir to Itayle,
She gan to wringe hir hondes two.
"Allas," quod she, "what me ys woo! 300
Allas, is every man thus trewe,
That every yere wolde have a newe,
Yf hit so longe tyme dure,
Or elles three, peraventure?
As thus, of oon he wolde have fame 305
In magnyfyinge of hys name;
Another for frendshippe, seyth he;
And yet ther shal the thridde be
That shal be take for delyte,
Loo, or for synguler profite." 310
In suche wordes gan to pleyne
Dydo of hir grete peyne,
As me mette redely—
Non other auctour alegge I.
"Allas," quod she, "my swete hert, 315
Have pitee on my sorwes smert,
And slee mee not! Goo noght awey!

---

244 *Al that:* F&c *That that.* 245 **queynte,** mysteriously. 246 P&c *for to peynte.* 248 **kan,** know. 250 **in-fere,** together. P&c *furst aqueynted were.* 252 **dwelle,** dwell on. 254 **caas,** adventure. This is the flashback in *Aeneid* 3 and 4, in which are recounted the fall of Troy and Aeneas' escape. P&c *Tolde to.* 255 **tyd,** befallen. 258 **luste,** delight. 259 P&c *to hym; the* om. 260 **leyde . . . dispence,** i.e., lavished expenditure. 262 **Wenynge,** believing. 263 *herby:* P&c *hertly.* 268 **slowe,** slew. 271 PCx *For eny* (every) *trust, lo.* 273 **browke I,** as I may enjoy. 274 **godlyhed,** handsomeness. 276 **nyce,** foolish. 277 **chere,** looks (expression). 278 All except Th: *Or for speche.* 280–83 Lines found only in Th. 280 **pure kynde,** essential nature. 282 **leste,** desires. 285 **prevy . . . double was,** sexually intimate (cf. *Romaunt* l. 5964), was double dealing. 286 **be,** about. 287 **nyce lest,** foolish desire. 287–88 P&c *nece lest/gost.* 291 *savely:* P&c *sa(u)fly.* 300 *me:* P&c *myn hert.* 303 P&c *endure.* 305 *As:* P&c *And.* *oon:* F&c *love.* 310 **synguler profite,** special advantage. P&c *or els.* 313 **mette redely,** dreamed truly. 314 **alegge,** do I cite. What can be the reason for this demurral at this point?

O woful Dido, welaway,"
Quod she to hirselve thoo,
"O Eneas, what wol ye doo? 320
O that your love, ne your bonde
That ye have sworn with your ryght honde,
Ne my crewel deth," quod she,
"May holde yow stille here with me.
O haveth of my deth pitee! 325
Iwys, my dere herte, ye
Knowen ful wel that never yit,
As ferforth as I hadde wyt,
Agylte I yowe in thoght ne dede.
O men, have ye suche godlyhede 330
In speche, and never a dele of trouthe?
Allas, that ever hadde routhe
Any woman on any man.
Now see I wel, and telle kan,
We wrechched wymmen konne noon arte, 335
For certeyne, for the more parte,
Thus we be served everychon.
How sore that ye men konne groon,
Anoon as we have yow receyved,
Certaynly we ben deceyvyd. 340
For though your love laste a seson,
Wayte upon the conclusyon,
And eke how that ye determynen,
And for the more part diffynen.
    "O welawey that I was borne, 345
For thorgh yow is my name lorne,
And al myn actes red and songe
Over al thys londe, on every tonge.
O wikke Fame, for ther nys
Nothing so swift, lo, as she is! 350
O, sothe ys, everything ys wyste,
Though hit be kevered with the myste.
Eke, though I myghte duren ever,

That I have don rekever I never,
That I ne shal be seyd, allas, 355
Yshamed be thourgh Eneas,
And that I shal thus juged be,
'Loo, ryght as she hath don, now she
Wol doo eftesones, hardely'—
Thus seyth the peple prevely." 360
    But that is don, is not to done.
Al hir compleynt ne al hir mone,
Certeyn, avayleth hir not a stre.
And when she wiste sothly he
Was forthe unto his shippes goon, 365
She into hir chambre wente anoon
And called on hir suster Anne,
And gan hir to compleyne thanne;
And seyde that she cause was
That she first loved him, allas, 370
And thus counseylled hir thertoo.
But what, when this was seyde and doo,
She rof hirselve to the herte,
And deyde thorgh the wounde smerte.
And al the maner how she deyde, 375
And al the wordes that she seyde,
Whoso to knowe hit hath purpos,
Rede Virgile in *Eneydos*
Or the *Epistle* of Ovyde,
What that she wrot or that she dyde, 380
And nere hyt were to long t'endyte,
Be God, I wolde hyt here write.
But welaway, the harm, the routhe,
That hath betyd for suche untrouthe,
As men may ofte in bokes rede, 385
And al day se hyt yet in dede,
That for to thynk hyt, a tene is.
    Loo Demophon, duk of Athenys,
How he forswore hym ful falsly,

---

328 ferforth, far. P&c *as ever* I. **329 Agylte,** wronged. All authorities: *I* om. **330 godlyhede,** attractiveness. F&c *have ye men.* **332 routhe,** pity. **335 konne,** know. **337 be served,** are treated. **338 How sore,** however sorely. **339 receyved,** accepted. **340** Line lacking in F. **342–44 Wayte . . . determynen . . . diffynen,** i.e., wait and see how you will decide, and generally end it. **346 lorne,** lost. As Clemen points out, Chaucer's Dido utters the plaintive lamentations of a middle-class girl who has been let down, not the passionate grief of an imperious queen. **347** F&c *youre actes.* **359 eftesones,** again. **361 to done,** yet to be done. **362** All authorities *But al.* P&c *ne hir.* **363 stre,** straw. F&c *Certeynly.* **364 sothly,** truly. **365** F&c *agoon.* **369 she cause was,** this is just the opposite to Anna's role in *LGW,* l. 1183. **370** *first:* P&c *so.* FP *him* om. **373 rof,** pierced. **376** P *alle the maner how she.* **378–79** *Eneydos . . . Epistle,* Chaucer's acknowledgment of his two sources, *Aeneid,* and Epistle 7 of the *Heroides.* **381 nere:** F *nor.* Th *were* om. **383 routhe,** grief. P&c *and routhe.* **384 betyd,** occurred. **387 tene,** sorrow. P&c *thenken hit.* **388 Demophon,** these examples of false and unfortunate lovers are all in *Heroides.* Such lists are found in *CT,* I.57ff., *BD,* l. 726ff., *PF,* l. 285ff., and of course the stories attached to *LGW.* They form the staple of Gower's *Confessio Amantis* and are a convention in medieval literature generally (Dante, Boccaccio, etc.).

And trayid Phillis wikkidly, 390
That kynges doghtre was of Trace,
And falsly gan hys terme pace;
And when she wiste that he was fals,
She heng hirself ryght be the hals,
For he had doon hir suche untrouthe. 395
Loo, was not this a woo and routhe?
Eke lo how fals and reccheles
Was to Breseyda Achilles,
And Paris to Enone,
And Jason to Isiphile, 400
And eft Jason to Medea,
And Ercules to Dyanira,
For he left hir for Yole,
That made hym cache his deth, parde.
How fals eke was he Theseus, 405
That as the story telleth us
How he betrayed Adriane—
The devel be hys soules bane!
For had he lawghed, had he loured,
He moste have ben al devoured 410
Yf Adriane ne had ybe.
And for she had of hym pite,
She made hym fro the dethe escape,
And he made hir a ful fals jape,
For aftir this, withyn a while, 415
He lefte hir slepynge in an ile
Deserte allone, ryght in the se,
And stale away and let hir be,
And took hir suster Phedra thoo
With him, and gan to shippe goo. 420
And yet he had yswore to hire
On alle that ever he myghte swere,
That so she saved hym hys lyfe,
He wolde have take hir to hys wife,
For she desired nothing ellis, 425
In certeyne, as the book us tellis.

But to excusen Eneas
Fullyche of al his grete trespas,
The booke seyth Mercur, sauns fayle,
Bad hym goo into Itayle, 430
And leve Auffrikes regioun,
And Dido and hir faire toun.
Thoo sawgh I grave how to Itayle
Daun Eneas is goo to sayle;
And how the tempest al began, 435
And how he lost hys sterisman,
Which that the stere, or he tok kepe,
Smote overbord, loo, as he slepe.
And also sawgh I how Sybile
And Eneas besyde an yle 440
To helle went for to see
His fader, Anchyses the free;
How he ther fond Palinurus,
And Dido, and eke Deiphebus;
And every turment eke in helle 445
Saugh he, which is longe to telle;
Which whoso willeth for to knowe,
He most rede many a rowe
On Virgile or on Claudian,
Or Daunte, that hit telle kan. 450
Tho saugh I grave al the aryvayle
That Eneas had in Itayle;
And with Kyng Latyne hys tretee,
And alle the batayles that hee
Was at hymself, and eke hys knyghtis, 455
Or he had al ywonne hys ryghtis;
And how he Turnus reft his lyfe,
And wan Lavina to his wife,
And alle the mervelous signals
Of the goddys celestials— 460
How, mawgree Juno, Eneas,
For al hir sleight and hir compas,
Acheved al his aventure,

---

390 **trayid,** betrayed. P&c *trased.* 392 **terme pace,** appointed time pass. Demophon did not return from Athens at the time he had promised. 394 **hals,** neck. P&c *ryght* om. 396 **routhe,** pity. 397 **reccheles,** uncaring. *lo:* P&c *loke.* 399 P&c *Oenone.* 401 **eft,** again. 408 **bane,** destroyer. 409 **loured,** scowled. 410 **devoured,** Ariadne saved Theseus from the Minotaur. F&c *be; al* om. 411 P&c *Yef that/be.* 414 **jape,** trick. 426 F&c *as/us* om. 428 F&c *grete* om.; P&c *al* om. 429–30 Cx *The book saythe sauns faylle | The goddis bad hym go to Itaylle.* 432 Th *And fayre Dydo and her towne.* 433 **grave,** carved. 434 F&c *for to assaylle.* 437 **stere, or . . . tok kepe,** rudder (steering oar), ere, was aware. *Aeneid* 5.860. 438 P&c *over the bord. Lo how he.* 441 **To helle,** cf. *Aeneid* 6. 444 P&c *And also Dido and Deiphebus.* 447 *willeth for to:* P&c *listeth to.* 448 **rowe,** line. 449 **Claudian,** Claudian's *De Raptu Proserpinae* (A.D. 400) was another famous description of the underworld, along with Book 6 of the *Aeneid* and Dante's *Inferno.* 453 **tretee,** negotiation. 455 *eke:* P&c *alle.* 456 **Or,** ere. 457 **Turnus,** a king in Italy, rival suitor for Lavinia. 458 F *wanne Labina.* 462 **sleight . . . compas,** deceit, cunning.

For Jupiter took of hym cure
At the prayer of Venus— 465
The whiche I preye alwey save us,
And us ay of oure sorwes lyghte.
　When I had seen al this syghte
In this noble temple thus,
"A, Lord," thought I, "that madest us, 470
Yet sawgh I never such noblesse
Of ymages, ne such richesse,
As I saugh grave in this chirche;
But not wot I whoo did hem wirche,
Ne where I am, ne in what contree. 475
But now wol I goo out and see,
Ryght at the wiket, yf y kan
See owhere any stiryng man,
That may me telle where I am."
　When I out at the dores cam, 480
I faste aboute me behelde.
Then sawgh I but a large felde,
As fer as that I myghte see,
Withouten toun, or hous, or tree,
Or bush, or grass, or eryd londe, 485
For al the feld nas but of sonde

As smal as man may se yet lye
In the desert of Lybye.
Ne no maner creature
That ys yformed be Nature 490
Ne sawgh I, me to rede or wisse.
"O Crist," thoughte I, "that art in
　blysse,
Fro fantome and illusion
Me save," and with devocion
Myn eyen to the hevene I caste. 495
Thoo was I war, lo, at the laste
That faste be the sonne, as hye
As kenne myghte I with myn eye,
Me thoughte I sawgh an egle sore,
But that hit semed moche more 500
Then I had any egle seyn.
But this as sooth as deth, certeyn,
Hyt was of gold and shone so bryghte,
That never sawe men such a syghte,
But yf the heven had ywonne 505
Alle newe of gold another sonne,
So shone the egles fethers bryghte,
And somwhat dounward gan hyt lyghte.

BOOK II

Proem

　Now herkeneth, every maner man
That Englissh understonde kan, 510
And listeneth of my dreme to lere,

For now at erste shul ye here
So sely an avisyoun
That Isaye, ne Scipioun,
Ne Kynge Nabugodonosor, 515
Pharoo, Turnus, ne Elcanor,

464 **cure,** care. 467 **ay . . . lyghte,** always, lighten. 473 **grave,** carved. 474 **wirche,** who made them. 477 **wiket,** gate (the term used for the gate to the garden in the *Romaunt,* l. 528). 480 **at:** P&c *of; dore icam.* 485 **eryd,** plowed (cultivated). 486 F&c *of* om. 487 P&c *se at leye.* 488 **desert of Lybye,** Libya had a reputation in literature as a desert. In both biblical and classical tradition, such a desert symbolized a spiritual or emotional wasteland. Several commentators have taken this wasteland to represent Chaucer's own disillusion with the superficiality of conventional love-legends like Dido's and the others listed in ll. 385ff. 489 All authorities except Th: *Ne I no.* 491 **rede . . . wisse,** advise, inform. 499 **egle,** this passage appears to be suggested by the description of the eagle in *Purgatorio* 9.19ff., where Dante dreamed that a golden eagle carried his body to the gate of Purgatory. 500 **semed . . . more,** seemed larger. 502 P&c *This is as.* 504–07 Lines lacking in F&c. 506 **another sonne,** the passage from *Inferno* may have suggested another from *Paradiso* 1.61ff. 508 *somwhat:* P&c *sone.* **Book II.** The division into books is not found in the MSS, but first in Cx. Evidently it was made by Caxton rather than Chaucer. At l. 1093 the poem does refer to "This lytel laste bok." 511 **lere,** learn. P&c *listeth* (desire). 512 **at erste,** for the first time. P&c *For at the first.* 513 **sely,** marvelous. P&c *sely and dredfull a vision.* 514 **Isaye,** cf. Isaiah 1. **Scipioun,** cf. *PF* ll. 31ff. and notes. All of these are figures in biblical and classical lore associated with dreams. F&c *Cipion.* 515 **Nabugodonosor,** cf. Daniel 1–4. 516 **Pharoo,** cf. Genesis 12. **Turnus,** evidently *Aeneid* 9.1ff. where Iris warns Turnus of the coming of Aeneas. **Elcanor,** unidentified.

Ne mette such a dreme as this.
Now faire blisfull, O Cipris,
So be my favour at this tyme!
And ye, me to endite and ryme   520
Helpeth, that on Parnaso duelle,
Be Elicon, the clere welle.

 O Thought that wrot al that I mette,
And in the tresorye hyt shette
Of my brayn, now shal men se   525
Yf any vertu in the be
To tel al my drem aryght.
Now kythe thyn engyne and myght.

The Dream

 This egle, of whiche I have yow tolde,
That shone with fethres as of golde,   530
Which that so high gan to sore,
I gan beholde more and more,
To se the beaute and the wonder.
But never was ther dynt of thonder,
Ne that thyng that men calle fouder,   535
That smyte somtyme a tour to powder,
And in his swifte comynge brende,
That so swithe gan descende
As this foul, when hyt behelde
That I a-roume was in the felde.   540
And with hys grymme pawes stronge,
Withyn hys sharpe nayles longe,
Me, fleynge, in a swappe he hente,
And with hys sours ayen up wente,
Me caryinge in his clawes starke   545
As lyghtly as I were a larke,
How high I can not telle yow,

For I cam up y nyste how.
For so astonyed and asweved
Was every vertu in my heved,   550
What with his sours and with my drede,
That al my felynge gan to dede,
For-whi hit was to gret affray.

 Thus I longe in hys clawes lay
Til at the last he to me spake   555
In mannes vois, and seyde, "Awake,
And be not agaste so, for shame."
And called me tho by my name,
And for I shulde the bet abreyde,
Me mette "awake" to me he seyde,   560
Ryght in the same vois and stevene
That useth oon I koude nevene.
And with that vois, soth for to seyn,
My mynde cam to me ageyn,
For hyt was goodely seyd to me   565
So nas hyt never wont to be.
And herewithalle I gan to stere,
And he me in his fete to bere
Til that he felt that I had hete,
And felte eke tho myn herte bete.   570
And thoo gan he me to disporte,
And with wordes to comforte,
And sayde twyes, "Seynte Marye,
Thou art noyous for to carye,
And nothyng nedeth it, pardee!   575
For, also wis God helpe me,
As thou noon harme shalt have of this;
And this caas that betydde the is,
Is for thy lore and for thy prowe.
Let see! Darst thou yet loke nowe?   580
Be ful assured, boldely,

---

517 mette, dreamed. **518 Cipris,** Venus (from Cyprus, beside which she was born from the sea). **519 favour,** helper (favorer). **520 endite,** compose. **521–22 Parnaso . . . Elicon,** both mountains sacred to the muses, but many medieval writers took Helicon to be the name of a spring on Mt. Parnassus. **523 O Thought,** cf. Dante, *Inferno* 2.8. (Chaucer evidently used *Inferno* 2, 1–3 at *PF* 85–86). **mette,** dreamed. **526 vertu,** power. **528 kythe . . . engyne,** reveal, skill. **530 as:** P&c *alle*. **532 beholde more,** see larger. **533** P&c *To seen her* (their, i.e., of the feathers). **534 dynt,** crash. **535 fouder,** thunderbolt. These lines echo Machaut *Jugement du Roi de Nevarre* ". . . la foudre | Que mainte ville mist en poudre" (ll. 301–2), which in turn echoes *Boece* 1 m. 4. **thyng:** F&c *kyng.* **fouder:** F *founder.* **536 smyte/to:** F&c *smote/of.* **537 brende,** burned. F&c *be(e)nde.* **538 swithe,** swiftly. **540 a-roume,** roaming (unprotected). **541** All authorities *grym.* **543 swappe . . . hente,** swoop, grasped. **in:** P&c *at.* **544 sours,** rise (Mod. E. "source" from Lat. *surgere*). **545 starke,** cruel. **548** P&c *never how.* **549 astonyed . . . asweved,** astonished, bewildered. **552 dede,** be dead. **553 For-whi . . . affray,** because, fright. **to:** P&c *a.* **557** F&c *so* om. **558** FP&c *tho* (then) om. **559 bet abreyde,** better wake out of. P&c *the om.*; *bet(ter).* **560 mette,** dream. P&c *Me to awake.* **561 stevene,** tone. **562 nevene,** name. **koude:** P&c *can.* **565 goodely,** pleasantly. **566 wont,** accustomed. **567 stere,** stir. **569 hete,** heat (life). **570 tho:** F *that.* **571 disporte,** jolly along. **572** P&c *gentil wordes.* **574 noyous,** troublesome. This allusion, like l. 660 below and *To Scogan* (short poem 17) ll. 27, 31, confirms Chaucer's plumpness. P&c *a noyes thyng to.* **575 nedeth it,** i.e., there is no need for your anxiety. **578 betydde,** happened (to). **579 lore . . . prowe,** instruction, profit.

I am thy frend." And therwith I
Gan for to wondren in my mynde.
"O God," thoughte I, "that madest kynde,
Shal I noon other weyes dye?   585
Wher Joves wol me stellefye,
Or what thing may this sygnifye?
I neyther am Ennok ne Elye,
Ne Romulus, ne Ganymede,
That was ybore up, as men rede,   590
To hevene with daun Jupiter,
And made the goddys botiller."
Loo, this was thoo my fantasye.
But he that bare me gan espye
That I so thoughte, and seyde this,   595
"Thow demest of thyself amys,
For Joves ys not theraboute—
I dar wel put the out of doute—
To make of the as yet a sterre.
But er I bere the moche ferre,   600
I wol the telle what I am,
And whider thou shalt, and why I cam
To do thys, so that thou take
Good herte, and not for fere quake."
    "Gladly," quod I.—"Now wel," quod he,   605
"First, I that in my fete have the,
Of which thou hast a fere and wonder,
Am dwellynge with the god of thonder,
Whiche that men callen Jupiter,
That dooth me flee ful ofte fer   610
To do al hys comaundement.
And for this cause he hath me sent
To the. Now herke, be thy trouthe:
Certeyn, he hath of the routhe
That thou so longe trewely   615
Hast served so ententyfly
Hys blynde neviw Cupido,

And faire Venus also,
Withoute guerdon ever yitte,
And neverthelesse has set thy witte—   620
Although that in thy hed ful lyte is—
To make bookes, songes, dytees
In ryme or elles in cadence,
As thou best canst, in reverence
Of Love and of hys servantes eke   625
That have hys servyse soght, and seke,
And peynest the to preyse hys arte,
Although thou haddest never parte.
Wherfore, also God me blesse,
Joves halt hyt grete humblesse,   630
And vertu eke, that thou wolt make
A-nyght ful ofte thyn hede to ake
In thy studye, so thou writest
And evermo of love enditest,
In honour of hym and in preysynges,   635
And in his folkes furtherynges,
And in hir matere al devisest,
And noght hym nor his folk dispisest,
Although thou maist goo in the daunce
Of hem that hym lyst not avaunce.   640
    "Wherfore, as I seyde, ywys,
Jupiter considereth this,
And also, beau sir, other thynges,
That is that thou hast no tydynges
Of Loves folk yf they be glade,   645
Ne of noght elles that God made.
And noght oonly fro fer contree
That ther no tydynge cometh to thee,
But of thy verray neyghebores,
That duellen almost at thy dores,   650
Thou herist neyther that ne this;
For when thy labour doon al ys
And hast ymad thy rekenynges,

---

584 kynde, nature. *thoughte/kynde:* P&c *quod/alle kynde.* **585** P&c *otherwyse.* **586 Wher . . . stellefye,** whether, transform into a constellation (i.e., is Jove going to). **588 Ennok . . . Elye,** Enoch (Gen. 5:24), Elijah (II Kings 2:11), both of whom were translated into heaven. **589 Romulus . . . Ganymede,** one of the founders of Rome and a beautiful Trojan prince, both carried off to Olympus (Ovid, *Met.* 14.805, 10.155). **592 botiller,** butler (originally the person in charge of the bottles). Because of his beauty, Ganymede was carried to Olympus by Zeus in the form of an eagle to serve as his cupbearer. **595 thoughte,** Virgil could likewise read Dante's thoughts in the *Inferno.* **596 demest,** judge. **597 theraboute,** i.e., has no intention. **598 the:** P&c *ful.* **600 ferre,** farther. **607** *which:* P&c *whom.* **610 flee,** fly. **614 routhe,** pity. **615–16** P&c *has so truly/Longe served.* **616 ententyfly,** attentively. **619 guerdon,** reward. **621–22** F&c *lytel is/songes, dytees, bookys* (very ragged rhyme). **623 cadence,** prose rhythm (i.e., in verse or prose). **630 humblesse,** devotion (humility). **634 enditest,** compose. **636 in . . . furtherynges,** in furthering of. **642** P&c *wel this.* **646 noght:** P&c *nothyng.* **649** *verray:* F *werray.* **653** P&c *mad alle thy rekenynges.* During 1374–86 Chaucer was Controller of Wool Customs in the Port of London with the stipulation that he keep the accounts in *"manu sua propria"*—in his own hand. These lines appear to be a portrait of his existence during that period.

Instede of reste and newe thynges,
Thou goost hom to thy hous anoon 655
And, also dombe as any stoon,
Thou sittest at another book
Tyl fully daswyd ys thy look,
And lyvest thus as an heremyte,
Although thyn abstynence ys lyte. 660

"And therfore Joves, thorgh hys grace,
Wol that I bere the to a place
Which that hight the Hous of Fame,
To do the somme disport and game,
In somme recompensacion 665
Of labour and devocion
That thou has had, loo causeles,
To Cupido the rechcheles.
And thus this god, thorgh his merite,
Wol with somme maner thing the quyte, 670
So that thou wolt be of good chere.
For truste wel that thou shalt here,
When we be come there I seye,
Mo wonder thynges, dar I leye:
Of Loves folke moo tydynges, 675
Both sothe sawes and lesynges,
And moo loves newe begonne,
And longe yserved loves wonne,
And moo loves casuelly
That betyd no man wot why 680
But as a blynd man stert an hare,
And more jolytee and fare
While that they fynde love of stele,
As thinketh hem, and over-al wele;
Mo discordes, moo jelousies, 685
Mo murmures, and moo novelries,
And moo dissymulacions,
And feyned reparacions;

And moo berdys in two houres
Withoute rasour or sisoures 690
Ymad then greynes be of sondes;
And eke moo holdynge in hondes,
And also moo renovelaunces
Of olde forleten aqueyntaunces;
Mo love-dayes and acordes 695
Then on instrumentes be cordes;
And eke of loves moo eschaunges
Then ever cornes were in graunges—
Unnethe maistow trowen this?"
Quod he. "Noo, helpe me God so wys!" 700
Quod I. "Noo? Why?" quod he.—"For
    hytte
Were impossible, to my wytte,
Though that Fame had al the pies
In al a realme, and al the spies,
How that yet she shulde here al this, 705
Or they espie hyt."—"O yis, yis,"
Quod he to me, "that kan I preve
Be reson worthy for to leve,
So that thou yeve thyn advertence
To understonde my sentence: 710
    "First shalt thou here where she duelleth,
And so thyn oune boke hyt tellith.
Hir paleys stant, as I shal sey,
Ryght even in myddes of the wey
Betwexen hevene and erthe and see, 715
That whatsoever in al these three
Is spoken, either prevy or aperte,
The way therto ys so overte,
And stant eke in so juste a place,
That every soune mot to hyt pace, 720
Or what so cometh from any tonge,
Be hyt rouned, red, or songe,

---

658 daswyd, dazed. **663 hight,** is called. **664 disport,** diversion. **666** P&c *thy grete labour.* **667 causeles,** without reason. **668 rechcheles,** heedless (reckless). **670 quyte,** repay (requite). **674 leye,** i.e., lay a wager. **676 sothe sawes . . . lesynges,** true sayings, lies. **678** *loves:* P&c *love is.* **679 casuelly,** accidentally. **680 betyd,** happen. P&c *ben betyd.* **682 fare,** frolic (activity). P&c *welfare.* **683 of stele,** i.e., as true as steel. **684 over-al wele,** generally good. *hem:* P&c *men.* **688 feyned reparacions,** pretended reconciliations. **689 berdys,** "make a beard" (trick, deceive). **692 holdynge in hondes,** i.e., encouraging with false hopes. **693 renovelaunces,** renewals. **694 forleten,** abandoned. **695 love-dayes,** days set aside for conciliation outside the legal framework; eventually the "day" came to designate simply the practice, cf. *CT* I.258n. **696 cordes,** strings. F&c *be acordes* (harmonies). Chords in the modern sense were unknown in medieval music. **697 eschaunges,** exchanges. **698 cornes . . . graunges,** kernels of grain were in barns (bins). **699 Unnethe . . . trowen,** scarcely, believe. **703 pies,** magpies (symbols of gossip, rumor). **704** P&c *al aspies.* **705** *she:* FP&c *he.* **708 leve,** believe. **709 advertence,** attention. **710 sentence,** meaning. **712 oune boke,** Ovid's *Metamorphoses,* 12.39ff. This is acknowledgment of Chaucer's attachment to this work, which he refers to continuously in his poetry. **717 aperte,** openly. *either:* P&c *in.* **718** *way:* F&c *aire.* **720 pace,** pass (go). **722 rouned,** whispered.

Or spoke in suerte or in drede,
Certeyn, hyt most thider nede.
    "Now herkene wel, for-why I wille   725
Tellen the a propre skille
And a worthy demonstracioun
In myn ymagynacioun.
Geffrey, thou wost ryght wel this,
That every kyndely thyng that is   730
Hath a kyndely stede ther he
May best in hyt conserved be,
Unto which place everythyng
Thorgh his kyndely enclynyng
Moveth for to come to,   735
Whan that hyt is awey therfro—
As thus: loo, thou maist alday se
That anything that hevy be,
As stoon or led or thyng of wight,
And bere hyt never so hye on hight,   740
Lat goo thyn hand, hit falleth doun.
Ryght so seye I be fire or soun
Or smoke or other thynges lyght,
Alwey they seke upward on hight.
While ech of hem is at his large,   745
Lyght thing upward, and dounward charge.
And for this cause mayst thou see
That every ryver to the see
Enclyned ys to goo by kynde,
And by these skilles, as I fynde,   750
Hath fyssh duellynge in floode and see,
And trees eke in erthe bee.
Thus everything, by thys reson,
Hath his propre mansyon
To which hit seketh to repaire,   755
As there hit shulde not apaire.
Loo, this sentence ys knowen kouthe
Of every philosophres mouthe,
As Aristotile and daun Platon

And other clerkys many oon.   760
And to confirme my resoun,
Thou wost wel this, that spech is soun,
Or elles no man myght hyt here;
Now herke what y wol the lere.
    "Soune ys noght but eyr ybroken,   765
And every spech that ys yspoken,
Lowde or pryvee, foule or faire,
In his substaunce ys but aire,
For as flaumbe ys but lyghted smoke,
Ryght soo soune ys aire ybroke.   770
But this may be in many wyse,
Of which I wil the twoo devyse,
As soune that cometh of pipe or harpe.
For whan a pipe is blowen sharpe,
The aire ys twyst with violence   775
And rent—loo, thys ys my sentence—
Eke, whan men harpe-strynges smyte,
Whether hyt be moche or lyte,
Loo, with the stroke the ayr tobreketh;
And ryght so breketh it when men speketh.   780
Thus wost thou wel what thinge is speche.
    "Now hennesforth y wol the teche
How every speche, or noyse, or soun,
Thurgh hys multiplicacioun,
Thogh hyt were piped of a mous,   785
Mote nede come to Fames Hous.
I preve hyt thus—take hede now—
Be experience: for yf that thow
Throwe on water now a stoon,
Wel wost thou hyt wol make anoon   790
A litel roundell as a sercle,
Paraunter brod as a covercle;
And ryght anoon thow shalt see wel
That whele wol cause another whel,
And that the thridde, and so forth, brother,   795
Every sercle causynge other

723 suerte, confidence. **724 thider nede,** needs go thither. **725 for-why,** because. **726 skille,** reason. **730 kyndely,** natural. This technical description of how sound reaches the palace of Fame is the same as that in *Boece* III. pr. 11,136ff. **731 stede,** place. **739 wight,** weight. **745–46** Lines transposed in P&c. **ech:** P&c *ever(yche)*. **his:** P&c *her*. **745 at ... large,** i.e., to rise when they are free to move. **746 charge,** heavy (load). **747** P&c *thou maist well*. **750 skilles,** reasons. **756 As there ... apaire,** where, deteriorate, (i.e., be conserved). *As there:* P&c *Ther as*. **764 lere,** teach. The disquisition on the physics of sound is similar to that in Boethius *De Musica* 1.3, 14; Vincent of Beauvais, *Speculum Naturale* 4.14; and other familiar medieval textbooks. **770** P&c *is sown*. **771 wyse,** ways (i.e., that air is broken). **772 devyse,** describe. **773** *As:* F&c *Of*. **776 rent ... sentence,** torn, opinion. **780** Line lacking in F. **781 wost,** know. **789 on:** P&c *in a*. **791 roundell,** ring. **792 covercle,** potlid. **793 ryght anoon,** immediately. **794** All authorities *The whele sercle*.

Wydder than hymselfe was.
And thus fro roundel to compas,
Eche aboute other goynge,
Caused of othres sterynge,   800
And multiplyinge evermoo,
Til that hyt be so fer ygoo
That hyt at bothe brynkes bee.
Although thou mowe hyt not ysee,
Above hyt gooth yet alway under,   805
Although thou thenke hyt a gret wonder.
And whoso seyth of trouthe I varye,
Bid hym proven the contrarye.
And ryght thus every word, ywys,
That lowde or pryvee yspoken ys   810
Moveth first an ayre aboute,
And of thys movynge, out of doute,
Another ayre anoon ys meved,
As I have of the watir preved
That every cercle causeth other.   815
Ryght so of ayr, my leve brother;
Everych ayre in other stereth
More and more, and speche up bereth,
Or voys, or noyse, or word, or soun,
Ay through multiplicacioun,   820
Til hyt be atte Hous of Fame.
Take yt in ernest or in game.
   "Now have I tolde, yf ye have in mynde,
How speche or soun of pure kynde
Enclyned ys upward to meve—   825
This mayst thou fele wel ipreve.
And that same place, ywys,
That everythynge enclyned to ys,
Hath his kyndelyche stede.
That sheweth hyt, withouten drede,   830
That kyndely the mansioun
Of every speche, of every soun,
Be hyt eyther foule or faire,
Hath hys kynde place in ayre.
And syn that everythyng that is   835

Out of hys kynde place, ywys,
Moveth thidder for to goo
Yif hyt aweye be therfroo,
As I have before preved the,
Hyt seweth, every soun, parde,   840
Moveth kyndely to pace
Al up into his kyndely place.
And this place of which I telle,
Ther as Fame lyst to duelle,
Ys set amyddys of these three,   845
Heven, erthe, and eke the see
As most conservatyf the soun.
Than ys this the conclusyoun,
That every speche of every man,
As y the telle first began,   850
Moveth up on high to pace
Kyndely to Fames place.
   "Telle me this now feythfully,
Have y not preved thus symply,
Withouten any subtilite   855
Of speche, or gret prolixite
Of termes of philosophie,
Of figures of poetrie,
Or colours of rethorike?
Pardee, hit oughte the to lyke,   860
For hard langage and hard matere
Ys encombrous for to here
Attones. Wost thou not wel this?"
   And y answered and seyde, "Yis."
   "Aha" quod he, "lo, so I can   865
Lewedly to a lewed man
Speke, and shewe hym swyche skiles
That he may shake hem be the biles,
So palpable they shulden be.
But telle me this, now pray y the,   870
How thenketh the my conclusyon?"
   "A good persuasion,"
Quod I, "hyt is, and lyke to be
Ryght so as thou has preved me."

---

797 *Wydder:* P&c *Broder.* **798 roundel . . . compas,** small ring, large circle. **803 brynkes,** edges. *That:* F&c *Til.* **816 leve,** dear. **820 multiplicacioun,** amplification (in size, as the rings grow larger). **823** P&c *in* om. **824 pure kynde,** essential nature. **826 ipreve,** proved. F&c *wel I preve;* CxTh *by preve.* **827** F *And that sum place stide;* other MSS *And that some stede.* **829 kyndelyche stede,** natural home. **830 drede,** doubt. **831 kyndely,** naturally. **841 pace,** pass. **844 lyst to,** is pleased to. **847 conservatyf,** preservative (of) (i.e. in this place all sound is preserved). **852 Kyndely,** naturally. **860 the to lyke,** to please you. **863 Attones,** at the same time (at once) **866 Lewedly . . . lewed,** in layman's language to a layman (ignorant man). **867 skiles,** reasons (abstract arguments). **868 biles,** bills (beaks). **871 thenketh the,** what do you think of. **872** Metrically defective line in all the authorities. Modern eds. supply *Quod he* at the beginning, or *A right good.* **873** *I:* F&c *he. be:* F&c *me.*

"Be God," quod he, "and as I leve,   875
Thou shalt have yet, or hit be eve,
Of every word of thys sentence
A preve by experience,
And with thyn eres heren wel
Toppe and taylle and everydel,   880
That every word that spoken ys
Cometh into Fames Hous, ywys,
As I have seyd. What wilt thou more?"
And with this word upper to sore
He gan, and seyde, "Be Seynt Jame,   885
Now wil we speken al of game!
How farest thou?" quod he to me.
    "Wel," quod I.—"Now see," quod he,
"By thy trouthe, yonde adoun,
Wher that thou knowest any toun,   890
Or hous, or any other thinge.
And whan thou hast of ought knowynge,
Looke that thou warne me,
And y anoon shal telle the
How fer that thou art now therfro."   895
    And y adoun to loken thoo,
And beheld feldes and playnes,
And now hilles, and now mountaynes,
Now valeyes, now forestes,
And now unnethes grete bestes,   900
Now ryveres, now citees,
Now tounes, and now grete trees,
Now shippes seyllynge in the see.
But thus sone in a while hee
Was flowen fro the ground so hye   905
That al the worlde, as to myn eye,
No more semed than a prikke,
Or elles was the air so thikke
That y ne myghte not discerne.
With that he spak to me as yerne,   910

And seyde, "Seest thou any token
Or ought that in the world is of spoken?"
    I sayde, "Nay."—"No wonder nys,"
Quod he, "for half so high as this
Nas Alixandre of Macedo,   915
Kynge; ne of Rome daun Scipio
That saw in dreme, at poynt-devys,
Helle and erthe and paradys;
Ne eke the wrechche Didalus;
Ne his child, nyce Ykarus,   920
That fleegh so highe that the hete
Hys wynges malte, and he fel wete
In myd the see, and ther he dreynt,
For whom was maked moch compleynt.
    "Now turne upward," quod he, "thy face,
And behold this large space,   926
This eyr—but loke thou ne be
Adrad of hem that thou shalt se,
For in this region, certeyn,
Duelleth many a citezeyn,   930
Of which that speketh daun Plato.
These ben the eyryssh bestes, lo!"
And so saw y all that meynee
Boothe goon and also flee.
    "Now," quod he thoo, "cast up thyn
        eye.   935
Se yonder, loo, the Galaxie,
Which men clepeth the Melky Wey,
For hit ys whit—and somme, parfey,
Kallen hyt Watlynge Strete—
That ones was ybrent with hete,   940
Whan the sonnes sone, the rede,
That highte Pheton, wolde lede
Algate hys fader carte, and gye.
The carte-hors gonne wel espye
That he koude no governaunce,   945

---

875 leve, believe. **876 or,** ere. **886 game,** amusement. **887** P&c *thow now.* **890 Wher,** whether. **893 warne,** inform. **900 unnethes grete,** barely large. **901** P&c *now grete citees.* **907 prikke,** dot. **910–12** Lines lacking in F&c; reading from Cx. **910 yerne,** eagerly. **913** F&c *I sayde* om. **915–16** Reading from CxTh; F&c *Alixandre Macedo/Ne the kynge, daun Cipio.* **917 poynt-devys,** very clearly. **919–20 Didalus . . . Ykarus,** Daedalus, who made wings of wax and feathers for himself and his son to escape from the Labyrinth after he had built it; Icarus, his son; cf. Ovid, *Met.* 8.183ff. **nyce,** foolish. **wrechche:** P&c *wright.* **923 dreynt,** drowned. **924 moch:** P&c *a grete.* **926 space:** F&c *place.* **928 Adrad,** afraid. **932 eyryssh bestes,** probably the animals of the zodiac, though some scholars have argued that this means demons of the air more generally. **933 meynee,** company. **934 goon . . . flee,** i.e., both those that walk and those that fly. **935** *Now:* P&c *Lo.* P&c *thoo* om. **939 Watlynge Strete,** as Skeat points out, the Milky Way is called after an important road in each country: by Roman peasants "*strada di Roma,*" by the Spanish "*the road to Santiago.*" Watling Street was the major Roman road from Dover through London to Chester. **941 the rede,** i.e., son of the red sun. For the story of Phaëthon, see Ovid, *Met.* 2.31ff. **943 Algate . . . gye,** at any cost, guide (drive). **945 koude . . . governaunce,** knew (could exert), control.

And gonne for to lepe and launce,
And beren hym now up, now doun,
Til that he sey the Scorpioun,
Which that in heven a sygne is yit.
And he for ferde loste hys wyt 950
Of that, and lat the reynes gon
Of his hors; and they anoon
Gonne up to mounte and doun descende,
Til bothe the eyre and erthe brende;
Til Jupiter, loo, atte laste, 955
Hym slow, and fro the carte caste.
Loo, ys it not a gret myschaunce
To lat a fool han governaunce
Of thing that he can not demeyne?"
And with this word, soth for to seyne, 960
He gan upper alway to sore,
And gladded me ay more and more,
So feythfully to me spak he.
    Tho gan y loken under me
And beheld the ayerissh bestes, 965
Cloudes, mystes, and tempestes,
Snowes, hayles, reynes, wyndes,
And th'engendrynge in hir kyndes,
All the wey thrugh which I cam.
"O God," quod y, "that made Adam, 970
Moche ys thy myght and thy noblesse!"
And thoo thoughte y upon Boece,
That writ, "A thought may flee so hye
Wyth fetheres of Philosophye
To passen everych element, 975
And whan he hath so fer ywent,
Than may be seen behynde hys bak
Cloude"—and al that y of spak.
Thoo gan y wexen in a were,

And seyde, "Y wote wel y am here; 980
But wher in body or in gost
I not, ywys; but, God, thou wost!"
For more clere entendement
Nas me never yit ysent.
And than thoughte y on Marcian, 985
And eke on *Anteclaudian*,
That sooth was her descripsion
Of alle the hevenes region,
As fer as that y sey the preve.
Therfore y kan hem now beleve. 990
    With that this egle gan to crye,
"Lat be," quod he, "thy fantasye.
Wilt thou lere of sterres aught?"
    "Nay, certeynly," quod y, "ryght naught."
"And why?"—"For y am now to olde." 995
    "Elles I wolde the have tolde,"
Quod he, "the sterres names, lo,
And al the hevens sygnes therto,
And which they ben."—"No fors," quod y.
    "Yis, pardee," quod he. "Wostow why? 1000
For when thou redest poetrie,
How goddes gonne stellifye
Bridd, fissh, best, or him or here,
As the Ravene, or eyther Bere,
Or Arionis harpe fyn, 1005
Castor, Pollux, or Delphyn,
Or Athalantes doughtres sevene,
How al these arn set in hevene,
For though thou have hem ofte on honde,
Yet nostow not wher that they stonde." 1010
    "No fors," quod y, "hyt is no nede.
I leve as wel, so God me spede,
Hem that write of this matere,

As though I knew her places here;
And eke they shynen here so bryght,
Hyt shulde shenden al my syght
To loke on hem."—"That may wel be,"
Quod he. And so forth bare he me
A while, and than he gan to crye
That never herd I thing so hye,
"Now up the hed, for alle ys wel;
Seynt Julyan, loo, bon hostel!
Se here the Hous of Fame, lo!
Maistow not heren that I do?"

    "What?" quod I.—"The grete soun,"
Quod he, "that rumbleth up and doun
In Fames Hous, full of tydynges,
Bothe of feir speche and chidynges,
And of fals and soth compouned.
Herke wel—hyt is not rouned.
Herestow not the grete swogh?"

    "Yis, parde," quod y, "wel ynogh."
    "And what soun is it lyk?" quod hee.
    "Peter, lyk betynge of the see,"
Quod y, "ayen the roches holowe,
Whan tempest doth the shippes swalowe,
And lat a man stond, out of doute,
A myle thens and here hyt route;
Or elles lyk the last humblynge
After a clappe of oo thundringe,
Whan Joves hath the aire ybete.
But yt doth me for fere swete!"

    "Nay, dred the not thereof," quod he.
"Hyt is nothing will byten the.
Thou shalt non harme have trewely."
    And with this word both he and y
As nygh the place arryved were
As men may casten with a spere.
Y nyste how, but in a strete
He sette me fair on my fete,
And seyde, "Walke forth a pas,
And tak thyn aventure or cas

That thou shalt fynde in Fames place."
    "Now," quod I, "while we han space
To speke, or that I goo fro the,
For the love of God, telle me,
In sooth, that wil I of the lere,
Yf thys noyse that I here
Be as I have herd the tellen
Of folk that doun in erthe duellen,
And cometh here in the same wyse
As I the herde or this devyse;
And that there lives body nys
In al that hous that yonder ys,
That maketh al this loude fare."
    "Noo," quod he, "by Seynte Clare,
And also wis God rede me.
But o thing y will warne the
Of the whiche thou wolt have wonder:
Loo, to the Hous of Fame yonder,
Thou wost now how, cometh every
        speche—
Hyt nedeth noght eft the to teche.
But understond now ryght wel this,
Whan any speche ycomen ys
Up to the paleys, anon-ryght
Hyt wexeth lyk the same wight
Which that the word in erthe spak,
Be hyt clothed red or blak,
And hath so very hys lyknesse
That spak the word that thou wilt gesse
That it the same body be,
Man or woman, he or she.
And ys not this a wonder thynge?"
    "Yis," quod I tho, "by heven kynge!"
    And with this word, "Farewel," quod he,
"And here I wol abyden the,
And God of heven sende the grace
Some good to lernen in this place."
And I of him tok leve anon,
And gan forth to the paleys gon.

1015
1020
1025
1030
1035
1040
1045
1050
1055
1060
1065
1070
1075
1080
1086
1090

1015 *they shynen:* F&c *thy selven.* **1016 shenden,** ruin. *Hyt:* P&c *I.* **1020 hye,** loud. **1022 Seynt Julyan . . . bon hostel,** patron saint of hospitality; good lodging. **1024 that,** what. **1030 rouned,** whispered. **1031 swogh,** sough (murmuring sound). **1034** F *lyk* om.; Cx *lyke the.* **1038 route,** roar. **1042 doth . . . fere swete,** makes, fear to sweat. **1044** *byten:* FP&c *beten.* **1045** P&c *have no harme.* **1052 cas,** chance. **1057 lere,** learn. **1060 Of folk,** from people. **1062 or . . . devyse,** ere, describe. **1063 lives,** living. F&c *And* om. **1067 rede,** help. **1072 eft,** again. **1075 anon-ryght,** immediately. **1078** *hyt:* P&c *he.* **1079 very,** truly (verily). F&c *And so were hys.* **1080** *That:* F&c *And.*

BOOK III

Proem

O God of science and of lyght,
Appollo, thurgh thy grete myght,
This lytel laste bok thou gye!
Nat that I wilne for maistrye
Here art poetical be shewed,   1095
But for the ryme ys lyght and lewed,
Yit make hyt sumwhat agreable,
Though somme vers fayle in a sillable,
And that I do no diligence
To shewe craft, but o sentence.   1100
And yif, devyne vertu, thow
Wilt helpe me to shewe now
That in myn hed ymarked ys—
Loo, that is for to menen this,
The Hous of Fame for to descryve—   1105
Thou shalt se me go as blyve
Unto the nexte laure y see,
And kysse yt, for hyt is thy tree.
Now entreth in my brest anoon!

The Dream

Whan I was fro thys egle goon,   1110
I gan beholde upon this place.
And certein, or I ferther pace,
I wol yow al the shap devyse
Of hous and site, and al the wyse
How I gan to thys place aproche,   1115
That stood upon so hygh a roche,
Hier stant ther non in Spayne.

But up I clomb with alle payne,
And though to clymbe greved me,
Yit I ententyf was to see,   1120
And for to powren wonder low,
Yf I koude any weyes know
What maner stoon this roche was,
For hyt was lyk alum de glas,
But that hyt shoon ful more clere,   1125
But of what congeled matere
Hyt was, I nyste redely.
But at the laste aspied I,
And found that hit was every dele
A roche of yse, and not of stele.   1130
Thoughte I, "By Seynt Thomas of Kent,
This were a feble fundament
To bilden on a place hye.
He ought him lytel glorifye
That her-on bilt, God so me save!"   1135
    Tho sawgh I the half ygrave
With famous folkes names fele,
That had iben in mochel wele,
And her fames wide yblowe.
But wel unnethes koude I knowe   1140
Any lettres for to rede
Hir names by; for, out of drede,
They were almost of-thowed so
That of the lettres oon or two
Was molte away of every name,   1145
So unfamous was wox hir fame.
But men seyn, "What may ever laste?"
Thoo gan I in myn herte caste
That they were molte awey with hete,

1091 **science . . . lyght,** i.e., knowledge, inspiration. This invocation has been compared with Dante's *Paradiso,* 1, ll. 13–27, but the tone is playful rather than elevated. 1093 **gye,** guide. P&c *thow now.* 1094 **wilne . . . maistrye,** wish, superior achievement. 1096 **for . . . lyght and lewed,** because, trivial, unskilled. 1099 **do no diligence,** take no pains. 1100 **o sentence,** only meaning. 1101–02 F&c rhyme *nowe/yowe.* 1103 **That . . . ymarked,** what, marked out. 1104 **menen:** P&c *moven.* 1106 **blyve,** eagerly. **me:** F&c *men.* 1107 **laure,** laurel. Cx *lawrer.* 1114 **site:** all authorities *citee.* 1115 **thys:** F *hys;* P&c *the.* 1116 **roche,** rock. 1117 **Hier,** higher. 1120 **ententyf,** desirous. 1121 **powren . . . low,** stare (pore), closely. 1122 **weyes:** P&c *wyse.* 1124 **alum de glas,** a whitish, translucent, astringent mineral salt. F&c *a thynge of glas.* In Dante's *Commedia,* the Mountain of Purgatory is likewise white. P&c *alymde;* CxTh *a lymed.* 1125 **clere,** bright. 1127 **nyste redely,** i.e., didn't know at first. F&c *nyst I never.* 1131 **Thomas of Kent,** St. Thomas à Becket. See below ll. 1528–30 and note. Perhaps in some subliminal way, the design of the *Canterbury Tales* was already taking shape in Chaucer's mind. 1132 **fundament,** foundation. 1136 **the half ygrave,** one side carved. P&c *alle the half.* 1137 **fele,** many. 1138 **wele,** good fortune. 1140 **unnethes . . . knowe,** scarcely, make out. 1142 **by; for:** F&c *before.* 1143 **of-thowed,** thawed off. P&c *overthowed.*

And not awey with stormes bete, 1150
For on that other syde I say
Of this hille, that northward lay,
How hit was writen ful of names
Of folkes that hadden grete fames
Of olde tyme, and yet they were 1155
As fressh as men had writen hem here
The selfe day, ryght or that houre
That I upon hem gan to poure.
But wel I wiste what yt made,
Hyt was conserved with the shade— 1160
Al this writynge that I sigh—
Of a castel that stood on high,
And stood eke on so cold a place
That hete myghte hit not deface.

Thoo gan I up the hille to goon 1165
And fond upon the cop a woon
That al the men that ben on lyve
Ne han the kunnynge to descrive
The beaute of that ylke place,
Ne coude casten no compace 1170
Swich another for to make,
That myght of beaute ben hys make,
Ne so wonderlych ywrought,
That hit astonyeth yit my thought,
And maketh al my wyt to swynke, 1175
On this castel to bethynke,
So that the grete beaute,
The cast, craft, and curiosite
Ne kan I not to yow devyse—
My wit ne may me not suffise. 1180

But natheles alle the substance
I have yit in my remembrance,
For-whi me thoughte, be Seynt Gyle,
Alle was of ston of beryle,
Bothe the castel and the toure, 1185
And eke the halle and every boure,

Wythouten peces or joynynges.
But many subtil compassinges,
Babewynnes and pynacles,
Ymageries and tabernacles 1190
I say, and ful eke of wyndowes
As flakes falle in grete snowes.
And eke in ech of the pynacles
Weren sondry habitacles,
In which stoden, al withoute 1195
Ful the castel alle aboute,
Of alle maner of mynstralles
And gestiours that tellen tales,
Both of wepinge and of game
Of al that longeth unto Fame. 1200
Ther herde I pleye upon an harpe,
That sowned bothe wel and sharpe,
Orpheus ful craftely,
And on his syde, faste by,
Sat the harper Orion, 1205
And Eaycedis Chiron,
And other harpers many oon,
And the Bret Glascurion.
And smale harpers with her glees
Sate under hem in dyvers sees, 1210
And gunne on hem upward to gape,
And countrefete hem as an ape,
Or as craft countrefeteth kynde.

Tho saugh I stonden hem behynde,
Afer fro hem, al be hemselve, 1215
Many thousand tymes twelve,
That maden lowde mynstralcyes
In cornemuse and shalemyes,
And many other maner pipe,
That craftely begunne to pipe 1220
Bothe in doucet and in rede,
That ben at festes with the brede,
And many flowte and liltyng-horne,

1151 **say,** saw. 1154 *hadden:* P&c *had afore.* 1157 **or,** ere. 1161–62 Lines transposed in P&c. 1166 **cop a woon,** top a dwelling. 1170 **casten no compace,** i.e., couldn't go to the extent. *no:* P&c *the.* 1172 **make,** mate. 1175 **swynke,** toil. P&c *wyt for to thinke.* 1178 **cast . . . curiosite,** contrivance, complexity. F&c *craft* om. 1184 **beryle,** a blue-green silicate gemstone. 1188 **compassinges,** (architectural) exploits. 1189 **Babewynnes,** grotesque carvings (gargoyles). 1190 **tabernacles,** carved niches. 1191 P&c *say* (saw) *eke and ful.* 1194 **habitacles,** niches. 1195 F&c *stoden* om. 1203 Cx *Hym Orpheus.* 1204 **faste,** close. 1205 **Orion,** Arion, legendary harper of Corinth. 1206 **Eaycedis Chiron,** Chiron belonging to Aecaides, i.e., Achilles, so-called for his grandfather Aeacus. Chiron was the centaur who taught Achilles both music and horsemanship, cf. Ovid, *Ars Amatoria* 1.17. 1208 **Bret Glascurion,** Briton (Celt) Glasgerion, famous Welsh bard. *Bret:* F *gret:* CxTh *Bryton.* 1209 **glees,** instruments. 1210 **under . . . sees,** below, seats. 1210–14 *hem:* F&c *hym. gape:* F *jape.* 1212 **countrefete,** imitate. 1213 **craft . . . kynde,** art, nature. 1215 **Afer,** far away from. 1218 **cornemuse . . . shalemyes,** bagpipes, shawms (reed instruments). 1221 **doucet . . . rede,** flute, reed (instrument). 1222 **brede,** roast meat. 1223 **flowte . . . liltyng-horne,** flute, a variety of trumpet.

And pipes made of grene corne,
As han thise lytel herde-gromes 1225
That kepen bestis in the bromes.
Ther saugh I than Atiteris,
And of Athenes daun Pseustis,
And Marcia that loste her skyn,
Bothe in face, body, and chyn, 1230
For that she wolde envien, loo,
To pipen bet than Appolloo.
Ther saugh I famous, olde and yonge,
Pipers of the Duche tonge,
To lerne love-daunces, sprynges, 1235
Reyes, and these straunge thynges.
Tho saugh I in another place
Stonden in a large space
Of hem that maken blody soun
In trumpe, beme, and claryoun, 1240
For in fyght and blood-shedynges
Ys used gladly clarionynges.
Ther herde I trumpen Messenius,
Of whom that speketh Virgilius.
There herde I trumpe Joab also, 1245
Theodomas, and other mo.
And alle that used clarion
In Cataloigne and Aragon,
That in her tyme famous were
To lerne, saugh I trumpe there. 1250
There saugh I sitte in other sees,
Pleyinge upon sondry glees,

Which that I kan not nevene,
Moo than sterres ben in hevene,
Of whiche I nyl as now not ryme, 1255
For ese of yow, and losse of tyme.
(For tyme ylost, this knowen ye,
Be no way may recovered be.)
Ther saugh I pleye jugelours,
Magiciens, and tregetours, 1260
And phitonesses, charmeresses,
Olde wicches, sorceresses,
That usen exorsisacions,
And eke these fumygacions;
And clerkes eke, which konne wel 1265
Alle this magik naturel,
That craftely doon her ententes
To make, in certeyn ascendentes,
Ymages, lo, thrugh which magike
To make a man ben hool or syke. 1270
Ther saugh I the quene Medea,
And Circes eke, and Calipsa.
Ther saugh I Hermes Ballenus,
Limete, and eke Symon Magus.
There saugh I, and knew hem by name, 1275
That by such art don men han fame.
Ther saugh I Colle tregetour
Upon a table of sycamour
Pleye an uncouth thyng to telle—
Y saugh him carien a wyndmelle 1280
Under a walsh-note shale.

1224 grene corne, i.e., hollow grass or reeds (Pan's pipes). **1225 herde-gromes,** shepherd boys. **1226 bromes,** broom (grass). **1227–28** Lines transposed in F&c. **1227 Atiteris,** perhaps Tityrus in Virgil's first eclogue. P&c *daun Cytherus.* **1228 Pseustis,** a shepherd in Theodulus' *Ecloga,* which was used as a textbook in the Middle Ages. **1229 Marcia,** Marsyas, a satyr who was flayed for losing a musical contest with Apollo, Ovid, *Met.* 6.382. Chaucer may have been misled as to the satyr's sex by Dante's reference to the episode, *Inferno* 4.128. **1234 Duche,** i.e., German—a tribute to the reputation even then of the Germans as musicians. **1235 sprynges,** evidently a kind of dance. **1236 Reyes,** the Dutch term for ring dances (i.e., carols). F&c *Reus;* P *Reyths.* **1240 beme,** trumpet. **1243 Messenius,** Misenus, trumpeter to Hector and Aeneas, *Aeneid* 3.239, 6.162. **1245 Joab,** trumpeter in II Sam. 2:28. **1246 Theodomas,** evidently Thiodamas who incited the attack on Thebes, which was followed by a blare of trumpets, *Thebaid* 8.343ff. **1248 Cataloigne . . . Aragon,** Catalonia and Aragon in Spain, noted for their trumpet playing. P&c *Castellyon.* **1250 To lerne,** to learn about. **1251 sees,** seats. **1252 glees,** instruments. **1253 nevene,** name. **1255** F&c *nyl not now.* **1260 tregetours,** tricksters, sleight of hand artists. **1261 phitonesses,** witches, cf. *CT* III.1510n. **1262 wicches:** F *wrecches.* **1264 fumygacions,** using smoke as part of incantation. Th *eke subfumyacions.* **1266 magik naturel,** control over nature (largely through astrology, cf. *CT* I.414–18 and notes. **1268–69 ascendentes . . . Ymages,** presumably astrological representations related to the patient's horoscope. **1271 Medea,** Jason's wife, an enchantress (Ovid, *Met.* 7). **1272 Circes . . . Calipsa,** Circe and Calipso, enchantresses in the *Odyssey* (Ovid, *Met.* 14, *ex Ponto* 4.10). *Circes:* F&c *Artes.* **1273 Hermes Ballenus,** Balanus, disciple of Hermes Trismegistus, reputed to be the founder of alchemy, cf. *CT* VIII.1434n. **1274 Limete** (P&c *Limate*), probably the sorcerer Elymas, Acts 13:8. **Symon Magus,** magician, Acts 8:9. **1275–76** Lines lacking in F; reading from Bodley 368. **1276 don . . . han,** make, to have. **1277 Colle tregetour,** a notable magician, contemporary with Chaucer, in a 1396 French manual described as "*un Englois qu' estoit fort nigromancien qui est a nom Colin T.*" **1279 uncouth,** strange. **1281 walsh-note shale,** walnut shell (i.e., he was a master of the shell game).

What shuld I make lenger tale
Of alle the pepil y ther say,
Fro hennes into domes day?
Whan I had al this folk beholde, 1285
And fond me lous and nought yholde,
And eft I mused longe while
Upon these walles of berile,
That shoone ful lyghter than a glas,
And made wel more than hit was 1290
To semen everything, ywis,
As kynde thyng of Fames is,
I gan forth romen til I fond
The castel yate on my ryght hond,
Which that so wel corven was 1295
That never such another nas—
And yit it was be aventure
Iwrought as often as be cure.
Hyt nedeth noght yow more to tellen,
To make yow to longe duellen, 1300
Of this yates florisshinges,
Ne of compasses, ne of kervynges,
Ne how they hatte in masoneries,
As corbetz, ful of ymageries.
But, Lord, so fair yt was to shewe, 1305
For hit was alle with gold behewe.
But in I went, and that anoon.
Ther mette I cryinge many oon,
"A larges, larges, hold up wel!
God save the lady of thys pel, 1310
Our oune gentil Lady Fame,
And hem that wilnen to have name
Of us!" Thus herde y crien alle,
And faste comen out of halle,
And shoon nobles and sterlynges. 1315
And somme corouned were as kynges,
With corounes wroght ful of losenges,

And many ryban and many frenges
Were on her clothes trewely.
Thoo atte last aspyed y 1320
That pursevantes and heraudes,
That crien ryche folkes laudes,
Hyt weren alle; and every man
Of hem, as y yow tellen can,
Had on him throwen a vesture 1325
Which that men clepe a cote-armure,
Enbrowded wonderliche ryche,
Although they nere nought ylyche.
But noght nyl I, so mote y thryve,
Ben aboute to dyscryve 1330
Al these armes that ther weren,
That they thus on her cotes beren,
For hyt to me were impossible.
Men myghte make of hem a bible
Twenty foot thykke, as y trowe. 1335
For certeyn, whoso koude iknowe
Myghte ther alle the armes seen
Of famous folk that han ybeen
In Auffrike, Europe, and Asye,
Syth first began the chevalrie. 1340
Loo, how shulde I now telle al thys?
Ne of the halle eke what nede is
To tellen yow that every wal
Of hit, and flor, and roof, and al,
Was plated half a foote thikke 1345
Of gold, and that nas nothyng wikke
But for to prove in alle wyse
As fyne as ducat in Venyse—
Of which to lite al in my pouche is!
And they were set as thik of nouchis, 1350
Ful of the fynest stones faire
That men rede in the Lapidaire
As grasses growen in a mede.

1283 P&c *that I.* 1284 Cx *I coud not telle tyl domes.* 1286 **yholde,** held. F *yeolde.* lous: P&c *loos(e).* 1287 *eft:* F *oft. I mused:* eds. read *imused.* 1290 **made . . . more,** i.e., magnified. 1292 **kynde,** natural. 1293 *forth:* F&c *to.* 1297–98 **aventure . . . cure,** i.e., by chance as by intention. 1300 *longe:* P&c *lenger to.* 1301 **florisshinges,** decorations. 1302 **compasses,** contrivances. 1303 **how they hatte,** what they are called. 1304 **corbetz,** corbels. F *ful of ymageries* lacking. 1309 **larges,** largess (donation). Bromyard in *Summa Predicantium* says that this is the insatiable cry of the "*histrio*" (minstrel). 1310 **pel,** castle (peel). 1312 **wilnen,** wish. 1315 **shoon nobles . . . sterlynges,** gleamed (pt. of shine), gold and silver coins. *shoon:* P&c *shoke (n).* 1317 **losenges,** heraldic lozenges (diamond shapes). P&c *lesynges* (lies). 1318 *frenges:* P&c *thynges.* 1321 **pursevantes,** pursuivants (heralds of lesser rank). 1322 **laudes,** praises. 1326 **clepe . . . cote-armure,** call, cloth tunic worn over armor bearing the heraldic insignia—the "coat of arms." 1327 **Enbrowded,** embroidered. 1328 *Although:* F&c *As though.* 1335 F&c *as* om. 1346 **wikke,** inferior (wicked). 1348 **fyne as ducat in Venyse,** pure as Venetian gold coins. 1350 **nouchis,** jeweled ornaments. P&c *owches.* 1351 *Ful:* F&c *Fyne.* 1352 **Lapidaire,** any one of several popular treatises on precious stones.

But hit were al to longe to rede
The names, and therfore I pace.   1355
But in this lusty and ryche place,
That Fames halle called was,
Ful moche prees of folk ther nas,
Ne crowdyng for to mochil prees.
But al on hye, above a dees,   1360
Sit in a see imperiall,
That mad was of a rubee all,
Which that a carbuncle ys ycalled,
Y saugh, perpetually ystalled,
A femynyne creature,   1365
That never formed by Nature
Nas suche another thing yseye.
For altherfirst, soth for to seye,
Me thoughte that she was so lyte
That the lengthe of a cubite   1370
Was lengere than she semed be.
But thus sone in a whyle she
Hir tho so wonderliche streighte
That with hir fet she th'erthe reighte,
And with hir hed she touched hevene   1375
Ther as shynen sterres sevene.
And therto eke, as to my wit,
I saugh a gretter wonder yit
Upon her eyen to beholde;
But certeyn y hem never tolde,   1380
For as feele eyen hadde she
As fetheres upon foules be,
Or weren on the bestes foure
That Goddis trone gunne honoure,
As John writ in th'Apocalips.   1385
Hir heer, that oundy was and crips,
As burned gold hyt shoon to see.
And soth to tellen, also she

Had also fele upstondyng eres
And tonges as on bestes heres.   1390
And on hir fet wexen saugh y
Partriches wynges redely.
      But, Lord, the perry and the richesse
I saugh sittyng on this godesse!
And, Lord, the hevenyssh melodye   1395
Of songes ful of armonye
I herde aboute her trone ysonge,
That al the paleys walles ronge.
So song the myghty Muse, she
That cleped ys Caliope,   1400
And hir eighte sustren eke,
That in her face semen meke,
And evermo eternally
They songe of Fame, as thoo herd y:
"Heryed be thou and thy name,   1405
Goddesse of Renoun and of Fame!"
      Tho was I war, loo, atte laste,
As I myne eyen gan up caste,
That thys ylke noble quene
On her shuldres gan sustene   1410
Bothe the armes and the name
Of thoo that hadde large fame,
Alexander and Hercules,
That with a sherte hys lyfe les.
Thus fond y syttynge this goddesse   1415
In nobley, honour, and rychesse—
Of which I stynte a while now,
Other thing to tellen yow.
      Tho saugh I stonde on eyther syde,
Streight doun to the dores wide   1420
Fro the dees, many a peler
Of metal that shoon not ful cler.
But though they nere of no rychesse,

1355 pace, pass. **1356 lusty**, happy. **1360 dees**, dais, *above:* P *upon.* **1361 see**, seat. **1362 all:** Cx *ryal;* P&c om. **1367 yseye**, seen. **1368 altherfirst**, first of all. **1370 cubite**, 17 to 22 inches (originally, the length of the forearm). Fame's shifting size is modeled on *Boece* I pr. 1. **1371** F&c *semed be* om. **1372** F&c *This was gret marvaylle to me.* **1373 streighte**, stretched. P&c *Hir silf tho.* **1374 reighte**, reached. F&c *erthe.* **1376 sterres sevene**, the planets. **1378** P&c *saugh as grete a.* **1380 tolde**, counted. **1381 feele**, many. **1385 Apocalips**, Rev. 4.6. **1386 oundy … crips**, wavy (cf. surr-ound), crisp (curly). **1389 fele**, many. **1390 heres**, hairs. P&c *on an beste ben.* **1391 wexen**, growing. **1392 Partriches**, in addition to Boethius, Chaucer was evidently following the *Aeneid* 4.173ff. in this description. Virgil has Fame travel with *"pernicibus alis,"* swift wings, which Chaucer (or his source) took as *"perdicibus alis,"* partridge wings. Curiously, he translates this correctly at *TC* IV.661. **1393 perry**, jewelry. **1400 Caliope**, muse of epic poetry. **1401 eighte:** P&c *seven,* but there are nine muses. **1402 her**, their. **1404 thoo**, then. **1405 Heryed**, praised. **1406 and:** F&c *or.* **1411 armes**, emblems. In Chaucer's vision, Fame and the great authors of antiquity are the pillars that support the roof of Fame's palace. **1412 thoo**, those. **1414 sherte**, Hercules was killed when Deianira, thinking to preserve his love for her, gave him a poisoned shirt. **1417 stynte**, stop. **1421 peler**, pillar. **1422 cler**, bright.

Yet they were mad for gret noblesse,
And in hem hy and gret sentence, 1425
And folk of digne reverence,
Of whiche I wil yow telle fonde,
Upon the piler saugh I stonde.
Alderfirst, loo, ther I sighe
Upon a piler stonde on highe, 1430
That was of led and yren fyne,
Hym of secte saturnyne,
The Ebrayk Josephus the olde,
That of Jewes gestes tolde,
And he bare on hys shuldres hye 1435
The fame up of the Jewerye.
And by hym stonden other sevene,
Wise and worthy for to nevene,
To helpen hym bere up the charge,
Hyt was so hevy and so large. 1440
And for they writen of batayles,
As wel as other olde mervayles,
Therfor was, loo, thys piler
Of whiche that I yow telle her,
Of led and yren bothe, ywys, 1445
For yren Martes metal ys,
Which that god is of bataylle,
And the led, withouten faille,
Ys, loo, the metal of Saturne,
That hath a ful large whel to turne. 1450
  Thoo stoden forth on every rowe
Of hem which that I koude knowe,
Though I hem noght be ordre telle,
To make yow to longe to duelle,

These of whiche I gynne rede. 1455
There saugh I stonden, out of drede,
Upon an yren piler stronge
That peynted was al endelonge
With tigres blode in every place,
The Tholosan that highte Stace, 1460
That bar of Thebes up the fame
Upon his shuldres, and the name
Also of cruel Achilles.
And by him stood, withouten les,
Ful wonder hye on a piler 1465
Of yren, he, the gret Omer,
And with him Dares and Tytus
Before, and eke he Lollius,
And Guydo eke de Columpnis,
And Englyssh Gaufride eke, ywis— 1470
And eche of these, as have I joye,
Was besy for to bere up Troye.
So hevy therof was the fame
That for to bere hyt was no game.
But yet I gan ful wel espie, 1475
Betwex hem was a litil envye.
Oon seyde Omer was lyes,
Feynynge in hys poetries,
And was to Grekes favorable;
Therfor held he hyt but fable. 1480
  Tho saugh I stonde on a piler
That was of tynned yren cler
That Latyn poete Virgile,
That bore hath up a longe while
The fame of Pius Eneas. 1485

1425 in hem . . . sentence, i.e., in them (there was) great significance. All authorities *hy and* om. **1426** P&c *grete and digne*. **1427 telle fonde,** try to tell. **1429 Alderfirst . . . sighe,** first of all, saw. **1432 secte saturnyne,** Jewish religion, which, as the root of Christianity, was thought to have arisen from a conjunction of Saturn and Jupiter. **1433 Ebrayk Josephus,** Hebrew Josephus, author of *The History of the Jews*. **1435** P&c *he* om.; *upon*. **1436** F&c *up* om.; *Jurye*. **1439 charge,** load, responsibility. **1446 Martes,** Mars's. **1450 large whel,** Saturn had the largest orbit of any planet known in the Middle Ages. **1453 be ordre,** in order (i.e., in detail). **1455 These . . . rede,** i.e., (on) those whom I do discuss. **1456 out of drede,** without doubt. **1458 endelonge,** the entire length. **1459–60 tigres blode . . . Tholosan . . . Stace,** Skeat cites two tigers sacred to Bacchus which are wounded in Statius' *Thebaid* 7. Tholosan because Statius was incorrectly supposed to have been a native of Toulouse, cf. Dante, *Purg.* 21.89. **1466 Omer,** Homer. **1467 Dares . . . Tytus,** Dares, Dictys, authors of the prose accounts of the Trojan War best known in the Middle Ages. **1468 Lollius,** supposed writer on the Trojan War and cited as authority for *TC*. **1469 Guydo eke de Columpnis,** Guido delle Colonne, who translated Benoit de Sainte-Maure's *Roman de Troie* into Latin prose (c. 1287). **1470 Englyssh Gaufride,** Geoffrey of Monmouth, whose *Historia Regum Britanniae* links the settlement of England to the fall of Troy. **1477 Oon:** P&c *Other*. P&c *seide that Omer made*. **1478 Feynynge,** pretending (deceiving). **1479 Grekes favorable,** such allegations began with Dares and were repeated by Guido. **1482 tynned yren cler,** tin-plated, bright. Eds. quote the note from Bell's *Chaucer*, "Homer's iron is admirably represented as having been covered by Virgil over with tin." But this can hardly have been Chaucer's conscious meaning; he thought of the tin as adding beauty and as being the metal of Jupiter, who controlled Mars (iron) in the *Aeneid*. **1485 Pius,** pious, the epithet by which Aeneas is distinguished in both Virgil and pre-Virgilian literature; the term has the broader sense of faithful to one's trusts, parents, homeland, etc., as well as the gods.

And next hym on a piler was,
Of coper, Venus clerk Ovide,
That hath ysowen wonder wide
The grete god of Loves name.
And ther he bar up wel hys fame   1490
Upon his piler, also hye
As I myghte see hyt with myn eye.
For-why this halle, of which I rede,
Was woxen on highte, length, and brede,
Wel more be a thousand del   1495
Than hyt was erst, that saugh I wel.
   Thoo saugh I on a piler by
Of yren wroght ful sternely,
The grete poete daun Lucan,
And on hys shuldres bar up than,   1500
As high as that y myghte see,
The fame of Julius and Pompe.
And by him stoden alle these clerkes
That writen of Romes myghty werkes,
That yf y wolde her names telle,   1505
Al to longe most I dwelle.
And next him on a piler stoode
Of soulfre, lyke as he were woode,
Daun Claudian, the sothe to telle,
That bar up al the fame of helle,   1510
Of Pluto, and of Proserpyne
That quene ys of the derke pyne.
   What shulde y more telle of this?
The halle was al ful, ywys,
Of hem that writen olde gestes   1515
As ben on trees rokes nestes;
But hit a ful confus matere
Were al the gestes for to here
That they of write, or how they highte.
But while that y beheld thys syghte,   1520

I herd a noyse aprochen blyve
That ferde as been don in an hive
Ayen her tyme of out-fleynge—
Ryght such a maner murmurynge,
For al the world, hyt semed me.   1525
Tho gan I loke aboute and see
That ther come entryng into the halle
A ryght gret companye withalle,
And that of sondry regiouns,
Of alleskynnes condiciouns   1530
That duelle in erthe under the mone,
Pore and ryche. And also sone
As they were come in to the halle,
They gonne doun on knees falle
Before this ilke noble quene,   1535
And seyde, "Graunte us, lady shene,
Ech of us of thy grace a bone!"
And somme of hem she graunted sone,
And somme she werned wel and faire,
And some she graunted the contraire   1540
Of her axyng outterly.
But thus I seye yow, trewely,
What her cause was y nyste.
For of this folk ful wel y wiste
They hadde good fame ech deserved   1545
Although they were dyversly served
Ryght as her suster, dame Fortune,
Ys wont to serven in comune.
   Now herke how she gan to paye
That gonne her of her grace praye,   1550
And yit, lo, al this companye
Seyden sooth, and noght a lye.
   "Madame," seyde they, "we be
Folk that here besechen the
That thou graunte us now good fame,   1555

1487 **coper,** copper, metal of Venus. 1489–90 Cx *name/fame* transposed. 1491 **also,** as. 1493 **For-why . . . rede,** because, speak (advise). Like Fame herself, the hall could magically expand. 1494 F *high, the length.* 1497 **by,** near by. 1498 *sternely:* F *sturmely.* Lucan's *Pharsalia* treats the war between Caesar and Pompey. 1500 **And:** Cx *That.* 1508 **soulfre . . . woode,** sulphur (brimstone), crazy. Claudian wrote *De Raptu Proserpinae* in a rhapsodic (incoherent) style. 1512 **pyne,** pain (i.e., place of torment). 1515 **gestes,** stories. F&c *al of the olde.* 1516 **rokes,** rook's (crow's). 1519 **how . . . highte,** what they were called. 1521 **blyve,** quickly. 1522 **ferde . . . been,** behaved, bees. 1523 **Ayen,** in preparation for swarming. 1524 P&c *maner out comynge.* 1529–30 **sondry regiouns/Of alleskynnes condiciouns.** Is it possible that Chaucer, considering the kind of poetry that would bring him fame comparable with that of the great poets he has been naming, was already gestating a poem concerning "sondry folk" of many "condiciouns" (*CT* i.25, 38), or is the parallel coincidental? 1536 **shene,** bright. 1537 **bone,** boon (favor). 1538 **sone,** immediately. 1539 **werned,** refused. 1541 **her,** their. 1543 **cause . . . nyste,** reason, don't know. 1544 F&c *of* om. 1546 **served,** rewarded. Line lacking in F&c 1547 **suster,** Robinson suggests that Chaucer invented the notion that Fame was the sister of Fortune. F&c *daun Fortune.* 1550 **That gonne,** they that began. 1551 *yit:* F&c *ryght.* 1553 *seyde:* F *quod.*

And let our werkes han that name.
In ful recompensacioun
Of good werkes, yive us good renoun."
   "I werne yow hit," quod she anon.
"Ye gete of me good fame non, 1560
Be God, and therfore goo your wey."
   "Allas," quod they, "and welaway!
Telle us what may your cause be."
   "For me lyst hyt noght," quod she.
"No wyght shal speke of yow, ywis, 1565
Good ne harm, ne that ne this."
And with that word she gan to calle
Her messanger that was in halle,
And bad that he shulde faste goon,
Upon peyne to be blynd anon, 1570
For Eolus the god of wynde,
"In Trace, ther ye shal him fynde,
And bid him bring his clarioun,
That is ful dyvers of his soun,
And hyt is cleped Clere Laude, 1575
With which he wont is to heraude
Hem that me list ypreised be.
And also bid him how that he
Brynge his other clarioun,
That highte Sklaundre in every toun, 1580
With which he wont is to diffame
Hem that me liste, and do hem shame."
This messanger gan faste goon,
And found where in a cave of ston,
In a contree that highte Trace, 1585
This Eolus, with harde grace,
Held the wyndes in distresse,
And gan hem under him to presse,
That they gonne as beres rore,
He bond and pressed hem so sore. 1590
   This messanger gan faste crie,
"Ryse up," quod he, "and faste hye,

Til thou at my lady be,
And tak thy clariouns eke with the,
And spede the forth." And he anon 1595
Tok to a man that highte Triton
Hys clarions to bere thoo,
And let a certeyn wynd to goo,
That blew so hydously and hye
That hyt ne lefte not a skye 1600
In alle the welken longe and brode.
This Eolus nowhere abode
Til he was come to Fames fete,
And eke the man that Triton hete,
And ther he stod as stille as stoon. 1605
   And herwithal ther come anoon
Another huge companye
Of goode folk, and gunne crie,
"Lady, graunte us now good fame,
And lat oure werkes han that name 1610
Now in honour of gentilesse—
And also God your soule blesse—
For we han wel deserved hyt,
Therfore is ryght that we ben quyt."
   "As thryve I," quod she, "ye shal faylle! 1615
Good werkes shal yow noght availle
To have of me good fame as now.
But wete ye what? Y graunte yow
That ye shal have a shrewde fame,
And wikkyd loos, and worse name, 1620
Though ye good loos have wel deserved.
Now goo your wey for ye be served.
And thou, dan Eolus, let see,
Tak forth thy trumpe anon," quod she,
"That is ycleped Sklaundre lyghte, 1625
And blow her loos that every wighte
Speke of hem harme and shrewednesse
In stede of good and worthynesse.
For thou shalt trumpe alle the contrayre

1559 **werne . . . anon**, refuse, immediately. 1563 **cause**, reason. P&c *your cause may*. 1564 **lyst**, wish, desire. P&c *not it*. 1572 **Trace**, Thrace (Bulgaria). Line lacking in all MSS; evidently a Cx emendation, cf. l. 1585. 1573–82 The passage on the two trumpets of Fame parallels Gower, *Miroir de l'omme* ll. 22129–52. Recent scholarship accords priority to Gower, but the more important implication might be that both poets were pondering the nature of, and perhaps the accomplishments essential to, true fame. 1575 **Clere Laude**, shining praise. 1576 **heraude**, herald (proclaim). 1580 **Sklaundre**, slander. 1586–87 **harde grace . . . in distresse**, bad luck to him, in captivity. 1595 *forth*: P&c *faste*. *he*: F *hye*. 1596 **Tok to . . . Triton**, gave to; in classical art, Triton, a sea god, is always pictured blowing on a conch shell. 1600 **skye**, cloud (the original meaning). 1604 **eke . . . hete**, also, was named. 1611 **honour of gentilesse**, i.e., in honor of our worth. *of*: P *and*. 1614 **quyt**, recompensed. 1615 **thryve**, prosper. 1618 **wete ye**, do you know. 1619 **shrewde**, evil. 1620 **loos**, reputation. 1623 F&c *have doon Eolus. lat see*: P&c *quod she*. 1624 P&c *lette se*. 1625 **lyghte**, nimble, volatile.

Of that they han don wel or fayre." 1630
"Allas," thoughte I, "what aventures
Han these sory creatures!
For they, amonges al the pres,
Shul thus be shamed, gilteles.
But what, hyt moste nedes be." 1635
What did this Eolus, but he
Tok out hys blake trumpe of bras,
That fouler than the devel was,
And gan this trumpe for to blowe,
As al the world shulde overthrowe, 1640
That thrughout every regioun
Went this foule trumpes soun,
As swifte as pelet out of gonne
Whan fyr is in the poudre ronne.
And suche a smoke gan out-wende 1645
Out of his foule trumpes ende,
Blak, bloo, grenyssh, swartish red,
As doth where that men melte led,
Loo, alle on high fro the tuelle.
And therto oo thing saugh I welle, 1650
That the ferther that hit ran,
The gretter wexen hit began,
As dooth the ryver from a welle,
And hyt stank as the pit of helle.
Allas, thus was her shame yronge, 1655
And gilteles, on every tonge!
Tho come the thridde companye,
And gunne up to the dees to hye,
And doun on knes they fille anon,
And seyde, "We ben everychon 1660
Folke that han ful trewely
Deserved fame ryghtfully,
And pray yow, hit mot be knowe,
Ryghte as hit is, and forth yblowe."
"I graunte," quod she, "for me liste 1665
That now your goode werkes be wiste,
And yet ye shul han better loos,
Right in dispit of alle your foos,
Than worthy is, and that anoon.

Lat now," quod she, "thy trumpe goon, 1670
Thou Eolus, that is so blake,
And out thyn other trumpe take
That highte Laude, and blow yt soo
That thrugh the world her fame goo
Al esely, and not to faste, 1675
That hyt be knowen atte laste."
"Ful gladly, lady myn," he seyde.
And out hys trumpe of golde he brayde
Anon, and sette hyt to his mouthe,
And blew it est, and west, and southe, 1680
And northe, as lowde as any thunder,
That every wight hath of hit wonder,
So brode hyt ran or than hit stent.
And, certes, al the breth that went
Out of his trumpes mouthe smelde 1685
As men a potful bawme helde
Among a basket ful of roses.
This favour dide he til her loses.
And ryght with this y gan aspye,
Ther come the ferthe companye— 1690
But certeyn they were wonder fewe—
And gunne stonden in a rewe,
And seyden, "Certes, lady bryght,
We han don wel with al our myght,
But we ne kepen have no fame. 1695
Hide our werkes and our name,
For Goddys love, for certes we
Han certeyn doon hyt for bounte,
And for no maner other thinge."
"I graunte yow alle your askynge," 1700
Quod she; "let your werkes be dede."
With that aboute y clywe myn hede
And saugh anoon the fifte route
That to this lady gunne loute,
And doun on knes anoon to falle, 1705
And to hir thoo besoughten alle
To hyde her goode werkes ek,
And seyden they yeven noght a lek
For no fame ne for suche renoun,

1631 aventures, i.e., luck. **1633 For:** P&c *That.* **1643 pelet,** stone cannon ball. **1647 swartish,** darkish. F&c *swart.* **1649 tuelle,** chimney, but with a *double entendre* of anus, cf. *CT* III.2148. **1653 welle,** spring, source. **1661** F *ben ful cruelly.* **1662** F *righte fully.* **1667 loos,** reputation. **1669 worthy,** deserved. **1675** F&c *Al* om. **1678 brayde,** moved hastily (brandished). **1686 bawme helde,** balm poured out (Baugh cites OED "hield"). All authorities *potful of.* **1688 til her loses,** to their reputations. *favour:* ThB *savour.* **1692 rewe,** row. **1695 kepen,** care. **1698 bounte,** kindness. **1702 aboute y clywe,** i.e., I scratched my head (in perplexity) all around. *clywe* (clawed): P&c *turned.* **1703 route,** company. **1704 loute,** bow. **1708 lek,** leek.

For they for contemplacioun 1710
And Goddes love hadde ywrought,
Ne of fame wolde they nought.
   "What?" quod she, "and be ye wood?
And wene ye for to doo good,
And for to have of that no fame? 1715
Have ye dispit to have my name?
Nay, ye shul lyven everychon!
Blow thy trumpes, and that anon,"
Quod she, "thou Eolus, y hote,
And ryng this folkes werk be note, 1720
That al the world may of hyt here."
And he gan blowe her loos so clere
In his golden clarioun
That thrugh the world wente the soun
Also kenely and eke so softe; 1725
But atte last hyt was on-lofte.
   Thoo come the sexte companye,
And gunne faste on Fame crie.
Ryght verraly in this manere
They seyden: "Mercy, lady dere, 1730
To tellen certeyn as hyt is,
We han don neither that ne this,
But ydel al oure lyf ybe.
But natheles yet preye we
That we mowe han as good a fame, 1735
And gret renoun and knowen name,
As they that han doon noble gestes,
And acheved alle her lestes,
As wel of love as other thynge.
Al was us never broche ne rynge, 1740
Ne elles noght, from wymmen sent,
Ne ones in her herte yment
To make us oonly frendly chere,
But myghten temen us upon bere.
Yet lat us to the peple seme 1745
Suche as the world may of us deme
That wommen loven us for wode—
Hyt shal doon us as moche goode,

And to oure herte as moche avaylle,
To countrepese ese and travaylle, 1750
As we had wonne hyt with labour,
For that is dere boght honour
At regard of oure grete ese.
And yet thou most us more plese:
Let us be holden eke therto 1755
Worthy, wise, and goode also,
And riche, and happy unto love.
For Goddes love, that sit above,
Thogh we may not the body have
Of wymmen, yet, so God yow save, 1760
Leet men gliwe on us the name—
Sufficeth that we han the fame."
   "I graunte," quod she, "be my trouthe!
Now, Eolus, withouten slouthe.
Tak out thy trumpe of gold, let se, 1765
And blow as they han axed me,
That every man wene hem at ese,
Though they goon in ful badde lese."
This Eolus gan hit so blowe
That thrugh the world hyt was yknowe. 1770
   Thoo come the seventh route anoon,
And fel on knees everychoon,
And seyde, "Lady, graunte us sone
The same thing, the same bone,
That ye this nexte folk han doon." 1775
   "Fy on yow," quod she, "everychon!
Ye masty swyn, ye ydel wrechches,
Ful of roten, slowe techches!
What, false theves, wher ye wolde
Be famous good, and nothing nolde 1780
Deserve why, ne never ye roughte?
Men rather yow to hangen oughte.
For ye be lyke the sweynte cat
That wolde have fissh; but wostow what?
He wolde nothing wete his clowes. 1785
Yvel thrift come to your jowes,
And eke to myn, if I hit graunte,

1711 ywrought, i.e., worked for the love of God. **1713 wood,** crazy. **1716 dispit,** scorn. **1717** *lyven:* F&c *lyen.* **1719 hote,** command. **1725** *kenely:* P&c *kyndely.* **1734** *But:* F *That.* P&c *we preyen the.* **1738 lestes,** desires. P&c *bestes.* **1744 temen . . . bere,** i.e., would just as happily have seen us dead (brought to our biers). **1747 for wode,** like mad. **1750 countrepese,** balance. **1751 As,** as if. **1753 At regard . . . ese,** in comparison with, ease (laziness). **1760** *yow:* P&c *me.* **1761 gliwe,** glue, fasten. P&c *blaw.* **1765** F&c *now let se;* P&c *quod she.* **1768 lese,** pasture. **1775** All authorities *ye* om.; Cx *to thyse.* **1777 masty,** fat (on acorns, mast). F *maisty.* **1778 slowe techches,** defects of sloth. **1779 wher,** whether (i.e., would you). **1780 famous,** famously. **1781 roughte,** cared (pt. of reck). P&c *thoughte.* **1782** F&c *to* om. **1783 sweynte,** lazy. P&c *slepy.* **1785 clowes,** claws. **1786 thrift . . . jowes,** luck, jaws.

Or do yow favour, yow to avaunte!
Thou Eolus, thou kyng of Trace,
Goo blowe this folk a sory grace,"   1790
Quod she, "anon; and wostow how?
As I shal telle thee ryght now.
Sey: 'These ben they that wolde honour
Have, and do noskynnes labour,
Ne doo no good, and yet han lawde;   1795
And that men wende that bele Isawde
Ne coude hem noght of love werne,
And yet she that grynt at a querne
Ys al to good to ese her herte.' "
This Eolus anon up sterte,   1800
And with his blake clarioun
He gan to blasen out a soun
As lowde as beloweth wynd in helle.
And eke therwith, soth to telle,
This soun was so ful of japes,   1805
As ever mowes were in apes,
And that wente al the world about,
That every wight gan on hem shout,
And for to lawghe as they were wode—
Such game fonde they in her hode.   1810
   Tho come another companye,
That had ydoon the trayterye,
The harm, the grettest wikkednesse
That any herte kouthe gesse;
And prayed her to han good fame,   1815
And that she nolde doon hem no shame,
But yeve hem loos and good renoun,
And do hyt blowe in a clarioun.
"Nay, wis," quod she, "hyt were a vice.
Al be ther in me no justice,   1820
Me lyste not to doo hyt now,
Ne this nyl I not graunte yow."
   Tho come ther lepynge in a route,
And gunne choppen al aboute
Every man upon the crowne,   1825

That al the halle gan to sowne,
And seyden, "Lady, leefe and dere,
We ben suche folke as ye mowe here.
To tellen al the tale aryght,
We ben shrewes, every wyght,   1830
And han delyt in wikkednesse,
As good folk han in godenesse,
And joy to be knowen shrewes,
And ful of vices and wikked thewes.
Wherfore we praye yow, a-rowe,   1835
That oure fame such be knowe
In alle thing ryght as hit ys."
   "Y graunte hyt yow," quod she, "ywis.
But what art thow that seyst this tale,
That werest on thy hose a pale,   1840
And on thy tipet such a belle?"
   "Madame," quod he, "soth to telle,
I am that ylke shrewe, ywis,
That brende the temple of Ysidis
In Athenes, loo, that citee."   1845
   "And wherfor didest thou so?" quod she.
   "By my thrift," quod he, "madame,
I wolde fayn han had a fame,
As other folk hadde in the toune
Although they were of gret renoune   1850
For her vertu and for her thewes.
Thoughte y, as gret a fame han shrewes,
Though hit be for shrewednesse,
As good folk han for goodenesse;
And sith y may not have that oon,   1855
That other nyl y noght forgoon.
And for to gette of Fames hire,
The temple sette y alle afire.
Now do our loos be blowen swithe,
As wisly be thou ever blythe!"   1860
   "Gladly," quod she; "thow Eolus,
Herestow not what they prayen us?"
   "Madame, yis, ful wel," quod he,

1788 *avaunte*, extol. **1793** F&c *they om.; wolden.* **1794** *noskynnes,* of no kind (*nones kindes*). F *no skynnes,* P&c *no kynes.* **1795 lawde,** praise. **1796 Isawde,** Iseult (of Tristan and Iseult). **1797 werne,** refuse. **1798 querne,** hand mill; i.e., a serf. **1803** *beloweth:* P&c *bellyth.* **1805 so ful of japes,** as full of tricks. **1806 mowes,** grimaces (*moues*). **1809 wode,** crazy. **1810 game . . . in her hode,** i.e., spectators found the seventh company absurd. For another use of this figure see *TC* II.1109. **1812** *trayterye:* P&c *trecherye.* **1817 loos,** praise. **1824** *gunne choppen:* P&c *gan clappe(n).* **1826 sowne,** resound. **1828 mowe,** must. **1830 shrewes,** scoundrels. **1834 thewes,** habits. **1835 a-rowe,** in a row. **1836** P&c *be suche iknowe.* **1837** *ryght:* P&c *suche.* **1840 pale,** stripe (cf. paling fence). **1841 tipet,** hanging part of hood or sleeve. **1843** P breaks off here. **1844 Ysidis,** Lat. gen. of Isis; perhaps a faulty allusion to one Herostratus who, according to Plutarch, set fire to the temple of Diana at Ephesus to immortalize his name. **1847** *thrift:* Cx *trouthe.* **1853** F *hit be noght.* **1857 hire,** reward. **1859 do . . . loos . . . swithe,** make, praise, quickly. **1862** *they:* F&c *this folke.*

And I wil trumpen it, parde!"
And tok his blake trumpe faste,   1865
And gan to puffen and to blaste,
Til hyt was at the worldes ende.
    With that y gan aboute wende,
For oon that stood ryght at my bak
Me thoughte goodly to me spak,   1870
And seyde, "Frend, what is thy name?
Artow come hider to han fame?"
    "Nay, for sothe, frend," quod y.
"I cam noght hyder, graunt mercy,
For no such cause, by my hede.   1875
Sufficeth me, as I were dede,
That no wight have my name in honde.
I wot myself best how y stonde,
For what I drye, or what I thynke,
I wil myselfen al hyt drynke,   1880
Certeyn, for the more parte,
As ferforth as I kan myn arte."
    "But what doost thou here?" quod he.
    Quod y, "That wyl y tellen the,
The cause why y stonde here: 1885
Somme newe tydynges for to lere,
Somme newe thinges, y not what,
Tydynges other this or that,
Of love or suche thynges glade.
For certeynly, he that me made   1890
To comen hyder seyde me,
Y shulde bothe here and se
In this place wonder thynges.
But these be no suche tydynges
As I mene of."—"Noo?" quod he.   1895
    And I answered, "Noo, parde!
For wel y wiste ever yit,
Sith that first y hadde wit,
That somme folk han desired fame
Diversly, and loos, and name.   1900

But certeynly, y nyste how
Ne where that Fame duelled, er now,
And eke of her descripcioun,
Ne also her condicioun,
Ne the ordre of her dome,   1905
Unto the tyme y hidder come."
    "Whych than be, loo, these tydynges,
That thou now thus hider brynges,
That thou hast herd?" quod he to me.
"But now no fors, for wel y se   1910
What thou desirest for to here.
Com forth and stond no lenger here,
And y wil thee, withouten drede,
In such another place lede
Ther thou shalt here many oon."   1915
    Tho gan I forth with hym to goon
Out of the castel, soth to sey.
Tho saugh y stonde in a valey,
Under the castel, faste by,
An hous that Domus Dedaly,   1920
That Laboryntus cleped ys,
Nas mad so wonderlych, ywis,
Ne half so queyntelych ywrought.
And evermo, so swyft as thought
This queynt hous aboute went,   1925
That never mo stil hyt stent,
And therout com so gret a noyse
That had hyt stonden upon Oyse,
Men myghte hyt han herd esely
To Rome, y trowe sikerly.   1930
And the noyse which that I herde,
For al the world ryght so hyt ferde
As dooth the rowtynge of the ston
That from th'engyn ys leten gon.
And al thys hous of which y rede   1935
Was mad of twigges, falwe, rede,
And grene eke, and somme weren white,

1870 goodly, pleasantly. **1879 drye,** endure. **1880 hyt drynke,** an echo of the proverb, "As I brew, so must I drink." **1882 ferforth . . . kan myn arte,** far, know my business—unless Chaucer also has more specific reference to his fame and his art as a poet. **1883** Cx&c *here than.* **1886 lere,** learn. **1887** All authorities *thinge.* **1895 mene of,** speak of (i.e., have actually experienced). **1897 wiste,** knew. All authorities *wote.* **1900 loos,** praise. **1905 ordre . . . dome,** manner of her judgment. **1907–08** All authorities: *Why than; thus* om. Eds. trans. "What are the tidings you want to hear?" **1910 no fors,** no matter. **1920 Domus Dedaly,** Daedalus constructed the Labyrinth, Ovid, *Met.* 8.157ff. **1925 queynt,** strange. **1926 stent,** stopped (stood). **1928 Oyse,** Oise, French river flowing into Seine below Paris. **1931** F *whiche I have herde.* **1933–34 rowtynge . . . ston . . . engyn,** roaring of a stone released from a catapult. **1936 falwe,** reddish yellow. Houses woven of withes were known in Wales and Ireland, and whirling houses are common in the romances, but the combination seems to be Chaucer's. The company inside again resembles Ovid, *Met.* 12.39ff.

Swiche as men to these cages thwite,
Or maken of these panyers,
Or elles hottes or dossers,   1940
That for the swough and for the twygges,
This hous was also ful of gygges,
And also ful eke of chirkynges,
And of many other werkynges.
And eke this hous hath of entrees   1945
As fele as of leves ben in trees
In somer whan they grene been,
And on the roof men may yet seen
A thousand holes, and wel moo,
To leten wel the soun out goo.   1950
And be day in every tyde
Been al the dores opened wide,
And by nyght echon unshet;
Ne porter ther is noon to let
No maner tydynges in to pace.   1955
Ne never rest is in that place
That hit nys fild ful of tydynges,
Other loude or of whisprynges;
And over alle the houses angles
Ys ful of rounynges and of jangles   1960
Of werres, of pes, of mariages,
Of reste, of labour, of viages,
Of abood, of deeth, of lyfe,
Of love, of hate, acord, of stryfe,
Of loos, of lore, and of wynnynges,   1965
Of hele, of seknesse, of lesynges,
Of faire wyndes, and of tempestes,
Of qwalme of folk, and eke of bestes;
Of dyvers transmutacions
Of estats, and eke of regions;   1970
Of trust, of drede, of jelousye,
Of wit, of wynnynge, of folye;
Of plente, and of gret famyne,
Of chepe, of derthe, and of ruyne;

Of good or mys governement,   1975
Of fyr, and of dyvers accident.
And loo, thys hous of which I write,
Syker be ye, hit nas not lyte,
For hyt was sixty myle of lengthe.
Alle was the tymber of no strengthe,   1980
Yet hit is founded to endure
While that hit lyst to Aventure,
That is the moder of tydynges,
As the see of welles and of sprynges;
And hyt was shapen lyk a cage.   1985
   "Certys," quod y, "in al myn age,
Ne saugh y suche an hous as this."
And as y wondred me, ywys,
Upon this hous, tho war was y
How that myn egle faste by   1990
Was perched hye upon a stoon,
And I gan streghte to hym gon,
And seyde thus, "Y preye the
That thou a while abide me,
For Goddis love, and lete me seen   1995
What wondres in this place been,
For yit, paraunter, y may lere
Somme good thereon, or sumwhat here
That leef me were, or that y wente."
   "Petre, that is myn entente,"   2000
Quod he to me. "Therfore y duelle.
But certeyn, oon thyng I the telle,
That but I bringe the therinne,
Ne shalt thou never kunne gynne
To come into hyt, out of doute,   2005
So faste hit whirleth, lo, aboute.
But sith that Joves, of his grace,
As I have seyd, wol the solace
Fynally with these thinges,
Unkouthe syghtes and tydynges,   2010
To passe with thyn hevynesse,

1938 thwite, whittle (cut and fit). *Swiche:* F&c *Whiche.* **1939 panyers,** wicker baskets. **1940 hottes . . . dossers,** wicker baskets for carrying heavy loads on the human back, wicker baskets for carrying loads on each side of a horse. *hottes:* all authorities *hattes* or *hutches.* The emendation is from Skeat, who cites evidence. **1941 swough,** sough (murmuring noise). **1942 also . . . gygges,** as, creaking sounds (cf. OF *gigue,* fiddle). **1943 chirkynges,** creaking sounds. **1944** Defective line in F; reading from Cx. Koch proposed *As ful is, lo, a harpe of strynges* (cf. l. 696). **1946 fele,** many. **1946–47** Cx *ben grene/sene.* **1954 let,** hinder. **1960 rounynges . . . jangles,** whisperings, quarrels. **1965 loos,** praise. **1966 lesynges,** losses. F *bildynges* (? building houses). **1967** *wyndes:* Cx *wether.* **1968 qwalme,** plague. **1969 transmutacions,** changes. **1974 chepe,** low prices (because of surplus). **1978 Syker . . . lyte,** assured, little. **1980 Alle,** although. **1982 lyst to Aventure,** was pleasing to Chance. **1990 faste,** close. **1994 abide,** wait for (i.e., don't carry me back immediately). **1999 leef,** pleasing. **2000 Petre,** by St. Peter. **2001 duelle,** stay. **2003 but,** unless. **2004 kunne gynne,** know how to begin. **2010 Unkouthe,** unknown. **2011 passe with,** drive away.

Such routhe hath he of thy distresse
That thou suffrest debonairly,
And wost thyselfen outtirly
Disesperat of alle blys, 2015
Syth that Fortune hath mad amys
The fruit of al thyn hertys reste
Languysshe and eke in poynt to breste,
That he thrugh hys myghty merite
Wol do the an ese, al be hyt lyte, 2020
And yaf expres commaundement,
To which I am obedient,
To further the with al my myght,
And wisse and teche the aryght
Where thou maist most tidynges here. 2025
Shaltow here anoon many oon lere."
   With this word he ryght anoon
Hente me up bytweene hys toon
And at a wyndowe yn me broghte,
That in this hous was, as me thoghte— 2030
And therwithalle, me thoughte hit stent,
And nothing hyt aboute went—
And me sette in the flore adoun.
But which a congregacioun
Of folk, as I saugh rome aboute, 2035
Some wythin and some wythoute,
Nas never seen, ne shal ben eft,
That, certys, in the world nys left
So many formed be Nature,
Ne ded so many a creature, 2040
That wel unnethe in that place
Hadde y a fote-brede of space.
And every wight that I saugh there
Rouned everych in others ere
A newe tydynge prevely, 2045
Or elles tolde alle openly
Ryght thus, and seyde, "Nost not thou

That ys betyd, lo, late or now?"
   "No," quod he, "telle me what."
And than he tolde hym this and that, 2050
And swor therto that hit was sothe—
"Thus hath he sayd," and "Thus he dothe,"
"Thus shal hit be," "Thus herde y seye,"
"That shal be founde," "That dar I leye"—
That al the folk that ys alyve 2055
Ne han the kunnynge to discryve
The thinges that I herde there,
What aloude, and what in ere.
But al the wonder most was this:
Whan oon had herd a thinge, ywis, 2060
He come forth ryght to another wight,
And gan him tellen anon-ryght
The same that to him was tolde,
Or hyt a forlong way was olde,
But gan somwhat for to eche 2065
To this tydynge in this speche
More than hit ever was.
And nat so sone departed nas
Tho fro him, that he ne mette
With the thrid, and or he lette 2070
Any stounde he told him als.
Were the tydynge sothe or fals,
Yit wolde he telle hyt natheles,
And evermo with more encres
Than yt was erst. Thus north and south 2075
Wente every tydyng fro mouth to mouth,
And that encresing evermoo
As fire ys wont to quyke and goo
From a sparke spronge amys,
Til alle a citee brent up ys. 2080
And whan that was ful ysprong
And woxen more on every tong
Than ever hit was, hit went anoon

2012 **routhe,** pity. 2013 **debonairly,** meekly. 2014 **wost,** knowest. 2015 **Disesperat,** despairing. Cx. *Desperate.* 2016 **mad amys,** caused to go wrong. 2017 **fruit . . . hertys reste,** the outcome that would give your heart rest. *fruit:* F *frot;* Cx *swote.* 2018 **in poynt to breste,** on the point of breaking. *Languysshe:* F *Laugh.* 2019 **he . . . hys,** note the gender of Fortune here. 2023 **further,** assist. 2024 **wisse,** instruct. 2026 **lere,** learn. 2028 **Hente,** picked. Line lacking in F; supplied from Cx. 2031 **stent,** stopped. 2034 *which:* Th *suche.* 2036 Line lacking in F; supplied from Cx. 2037 **eft,** again. 2040 **ded,** Skeat cites Dante, *Inferno* 3.55–57: "and following came / Such a long train of spirits, I should n'er / Have thought that death so many had despoiled." 2041 **unnethe,** scarcely. 2042 **fote-brede,** footbreadth. 2044 **Rouned,** whispered. 2048 Line defective in F; Cx *lo ryght now.* Bodley *late or now.* 2053 All authorities: *And thus/And thus.* 2054 **leye,** lay a wager. 2061 *ryght:* Th *streyght.* 2062 **anon-ryght,** immediately. 2064 **forlong,** furlong, 220 yards, but as usual a measure of time—the time it takes to walk a furlong. 2065 **eche,** add to. 2067 Cx *than ever it spoken was.* 2069 **Tho,** that one. F garbled; supplied from Cx. 2070 **lette,** hesitated. 2071 **stounde . . . als,** moment, also 2076 **tydyng:** F *mouthe.* 2078 **quyke,** quicken. 2083 *hit:* FCx *and.*

Up to a wyndowe out to goon;
Or, but hit myght out there pace,   2085
Hyt gan out crepe at somme crevace,
And flygh forth faste for the nones.
And somtyme saugh I thoo at ones
A lesyng and a sad soth sawe,
That gonne of aventure drawe   2090
Out at a wyndowe for to pace,
And when they metten in that place,
They were acheked bothe two,
And neyther of hem most out goo
For other; so they gonne crowde   2095
Til ech of hem gan crien lowde,
"Lat me go first!"—"Nay, but let me!
And here I wol ensuren the
Wyth the nones that thou wolt do so,
That I shal never fro the go,   2100
But be thyn owne sworen brother!
We wil medle us eche with other,
That no man, be they never so wroth,
Shal han that oon of us two, but both
At ones, al besyde his leve,   2105
Come we a-morwe or on eve,
Be we cried or stille yrouned."
Thus saugh I fals and soth compouned
Togeder fle for oo tydynge.

Thus out at holes gunne wringe   2110
Every tydynge streght to Fame,
And she gan yeven ech hys name,
After hir disposicioun,
And yaf hem eke duracioun,
Somme to wexe and wane sone,   2115
As doth the faire, white mone,
And lete hem goon. Ther myght y seen
Wenged wondres faste fleen,
Twenty thousand in a route,

As Eolus hem blew aboute.   2120
And, Lord, this hous in alle tymes,
Was ful of shipmen and pilgrimes,
With scrippes bret-ful of lesynges,
Entremedled with tydynges.
And eke allone be hemselve,   2125
O many a thousand tymes twelve
Saugh I eke of these pardoners,
Currours, and eke messangers,
With boystes crammed ful of lyes
As ever vessel was with lyes.   2130
And as I altherfastest went
About, and dide al myn entent
Me for to pleye and for to lere,
And eke a tydynge for to here,
That I had herd of somme contre   2135
That shal not now be told for me—
For hit no nede is, redely;
Folk kan synge hit bet than I;
For al mot out, other late or rathe,
Alle the sheves in the lathe—   2140
I herde a grete noyse withalle
In a corner of the halle,
Ther men of love-tydynges tolde.
And I gan thiderward beholde,
For I saugh rennynge every wight,   2145
As faste as that they hadden myght,
And everych cried, "What thing is
     that?"
And somme sayde, "I not never what."
And whan they were alle on an hepe,
Tho behynde begunne up lepe,   2150
And clamben up on other fast,
And up the nose and eyen kast,
And troden fast on others heles,
And stampen as men doon aftir eles.

2085 **but . . . pace,** unless, pass. 2088 **thoo,** then. F *I* om. Cx *I sawe there at.* 2089 **lesyng . . . sad soth sawe,** lie, sober true report. 2090 **of aventure,** by chance. 2093 **acheked,** checked, stopped. 2094 **most,** could. *most:* Cx *myght.* Cx ends here and adds a spurious conclusion. 2095 **For,** because of. 2099 **Wyth the nones,** on the condition. 2102 **medle,** mingle. 2104 All authorities: *of us* om. 2105 **besyde . . . leve,** without, desire (permission). 2107 **cried . . . stille yrouned,** cried (aloud), quietly whispered. 2110 **wringe,** squeeze. 2111 **streght to,** (and go) straight to. 2118 **fleen,** to fly. 2119 **route,** company. 2122 **shipmen . . . pilgrimes,** traveling men who carry tales. 2123 **scrippes bret-ful . . . lesynges,** wallets, chock full, lies. 2124 **Entremedled . . . tydynges,** mingled, news. 2128 **Currours,** couriers. 2129 **boystes,** boxes. Th *boxes.* 2130 **lyes,** dregs (lees). 2131 **altherfastest,** fastest of all. 2133 **pleye . . . lere,** entertain, learn. 2139 **rathe,** hastily (soon). 2140 **sheves . . . lathe,** every sheaf in the barn has to come out to be thrashed (Skeat). 2141 **withalle,** therewith. 2152 F *noyse on highen.* 2154 **stampen . . . eles,** stamp as people do catching eels.

Atte laste y saugh a man,   2155   But he semed for to be
Which that y nevene nat ne kan,   A man of gret auctorite. . . .

2156 *nevene* (name) omitted in all authorities. 2158 F ends with 12 spurious lines in a later hand.

Legend of
Good Women

INTRODUCTION

Legend of Good Women

HE LIST OF Chaucer's works in the Prologue to the *Legend of Good Women* (ll.417-41) indicates that this poem follows *Troylus and Criseyde* and *Palamon and Arcite* (the Knight's Tale) and precedes the *Canterbury Tales* in the chronology of Chaucer's compositions. This is puzzling to critics, who see the development of Chaucer's art as incremental, and the *Legend* as a lapse back into a mode he had outgrown by the time of *Troylus*. In the Prologue to the *Legend* the narrator is himself a lover, a pose he had abandoned after *Book of the Duchess*; and not only are the tales in the *Legend* inferior in narrative art to *Troylus* and the Knight's Tale, but they are retellings of classical stories as exempla against falsehood in love, matter and motive that appear to be rejected at the end of Book I of the *House of Fame*.

The best explanation for Chaucer's lapse back into this earlier mode appears to be two external influences. At the end of the Prologue (ll.475ff), Alceste and the God of Love instruct the dreamer-narrator to produce, as penance for his sins against love, a "glorious legend" of women who had been betrayed in love, "And whan this book ys maad, yive it to the quene / On my byhalf, at Eltham or at Sheene" (F 496, excised in G). It is interesting that Chaucer's friend John Gower at about the same time attributed his *Confessio Amantis* to a command from the King (unrevised Prologue 35ff). Both poems are expressions of the "religion" of love, created by the troubadours to parallel the rituals of established religion. Like the collection of "legends" about love's martyrs, the *Confessio* is a love vision comprising a collection of exemplary stories motivated by the dreamer-narrator's "confession" of his sins against love. The visions of the King and Queen of Love and their attitudes toward the dreamers are very similar in the two poems. Although these and other parallels are not definitive, they make it probable that one of the reasons for Chaucer's undertaking this piece at this stage in his career was a direct command from King Richard and Queen Anne. The relations between Chaucer's and Gower's poems are detailed by John H. Fisher, *John Gower* (1964).

A second reason for composing this poem at this time may have been to reply to a complimentary balade Chaucer received from Eustace Deschamps in the spring of 1386. Deschamps was a civil servant and poet in the French court just as Chaucer was in the English. His poem is printed on p. 952 below. In reply to what amounted almost to a diplomatic communication, Chaucer evidently decided to kill two birds with one stone: to fulfill the royal demand for a collection of stories about love's martyrs, and to begin with a prologue complimenting the French court poets. Marguerite (French for daisy) poems were a rage in the French court at the time—as discussed by James I. Wimsatt, *The Marguerite Poetry of Guillaume de Machaut* (1970). The vision of the court of love and the devotion to the daisy reflect these models, which Chaucer acknowleges in ll. 66-80.

Even though it is so heavily in the French tradition, the Prologue to the *Legend of Good Women* is more mature and independent than the three early dream visions. The poet-persona has changed from a novice in search of instruction to a mature poet defending what he has written. Furthermore, Alceste's speech to the God of Love (ll.342-408) is as overt a political statement as we find in Chaucer's poetry. And recent critics have discerned in the Prologue and the tales that follow Chaucer's continued search for an *ars poetica*.

One interesting feature of the Prologue is that it exists in two forms. Much has been written about the differences, but the consensus is that the F text printed in this volume is the original and the G text recorded in the notes is the revised. Some of the changes appear arbitrary, but two principles are clear. The G text tones down the narrator's expressions of personal devotion to the daisy (F 56, 86, 103) and introduces references to his age and unaptness for love (G 262, 315, 400). Also, G excises the reference to the Queen and the royal manors (F 496). These changes cannot be explained solely on the basis of Chaucer's artistic or religious development. A possible explanation for the revised version is that the Prologue originally dedicated to Queen Anne was rewritten after Anne's death in 1394 to honor Richard's 1396 marriage to the seven-year-old Princess Isabel of France. Richard was so affected by Anne's death that he ordered that Shene manor be torn down, and that his lords wear the livery of the dead queen at his wedding to Isabel. The way that the changes in the Prologue accord with these events is detailed by John H. Fisher, "The Revision of the Prologue to the *Legend of Good Women*," *SAB* (1978).

The Prologue is the most interesting part of the *Legend* and has received the most attention. Except for R.W. Frank, Jr., *Chaucer and the Legend of Good Women* (1972), and Lisa J. Kiser, *Telling Classical Tales* (1983), most critics have regarded the tales themselves as perfunctory. All are from Ovid. Frank defends them as training for the technique of short narrative in the *Canterbury Tales*, and Kiser interprets both the Prologue and the tales as Chaucer's commentary on his indebtedness to classical literature. Scholars have proposed thematic continuities for the nine stories, but the trouble is that we do not know how many or what stories were intended. At ll. 554-57 the God of Love seems to imply that they will be about the nineteen ladies in the balade "Hyd, Absolon." Eight of the stories are about ladies there named, but Phyllis (no. 8) is not in the balade, and eleven of those in the balade, including Alceste herself, are not treated. Then in the Canterbury Retraction Chaucer calls the poem the "Book of the XXV Ladies" (*CT* X.1085). Donald Howard, *Chaucer* (1987), cites Bernard Witlieb's fascinating observation that in 1386 there were nineteen ladies in the Order of the Garter, and that by 1390 Richard had appointed the statutory number of twenty-five, but Witlieb can suggest no connection between the ladies of the Garter and love's martyrs. Howard himself takes Alceste's command that the legends be produced "yer by yere" (ll. 481-84) to mean that Chaucer was ordered to produce a poem each year, and, indeed, if he produced the first in 1386, he would have been at work on the ninth in 1394 when the Queen died.

Chaucer's difficulty in taking his material seriously and his boredom with his subject seem apparent as we pass from one legend to the next. Only the stories of Thisbe and Hypermnestra are treated sympathetically. Dido, Hypsipyle, Ariadne, and Phyllis are marred by incongruous touches of irony or humor. In Philomela the narrator says that he will hurry over his story "For I am wery of him for to telle" (l.2258); in Phyllis, he complains, "I am agroted [surfeited] here beforne / To write of hem that in love ben forsworne" (l. 2454). Frank and other critics have argued that these complaints by the persona should not be attributed to Chaucer the poet, that they represent the demurral by which he typically shortened his stories. Elaine Hansen, "Irony and the Antifeminist Narrator in Chaucer's Legend of Good Women," *JEGP* (1983) reads the legends as a parody of literature that falsely idealizes female passivity. But whether relieved of his obligation by the death of Queen Anne, or simply weary of the project, there seems little doubt that Chaucer turned from this to a compilation as remarkable for its diversity as the legends of good women are for their uniformity.

At the end of the *Confessio Amantis* (VIII. 2941ff), Venus commands "John Gower" to "gret wel Chaucer" and instruct him to complete his "testament of love, / As thou hast do thi schrifte above." If we take these words at face value, they mean that the Queen is telling Gower that he has finished his royally assigned task (as indeed he had) and is prompting Chaucer to get on with his. This allusion has been taken as the reason for Chaucer's defensiveness about the completeness of "his large volume . . . Cleped the Seintes Legende of Cupide" and his digs at Gower in the Man of Law's headlink (*CT* II.60ff).

Legend of Good Women

PROLOGUE

A thousand tymes have I herd men telle
That ther ys joy in hevene and peyne in helle,
And I acorde wel that it ys so.
But natheles, yet wot I wel also
That ther nis noon duellyng in this contree   5
That eyther hath in hevene or helle ybe,
Ne may of hit noon other weyes witen,
But as he hath herd seyde, or founde it writen—
For by assay ther may no man it preve.
But God forbede but men shulde leve   10
Wel more thing then men han seen with eye.
Men shal not wenen everything a lye
But yf himself yt seeth, or elles dooth,
For, God wot, thing is never the lasse sooth
Thogh every wight ne may it nat ysee.   15
Bernard the monk ne saugh nat all, pardee!
Than mote we to bokes that we fynde,
Thurgh which that olde thinges ben in mynde,
And to the doctrine of these olde wyse,
Yeve credence, in every skylful wise,   20
That tellen of these olde appreved stories
Of holynesse, of regnes, of victories,
Of love, of hate, of other sondry thynges,
Of whiche I may not maken rehersynges.

And yf that olde bokes were awey,   25
Yloren were of remembraunce the key.
Wel ought us thanne honouren and beleve
These bokes, there we han noon other preve.
    And as for me, though that I konne but lyte,
On bokes for to rede I me delyte,   30
And to hem yive I feyth and ful credence,
And in myn herte have hem in reverence
So hertely that ther is game noon
That fro my bokes maketh me to goon
But yt be seldom on the holyday,   35
Save, certeynly, whan that the month of May
Is comen, and that I here the foules synge,
And that the floures gynnen for to sprynge.
Fairwel my bok and my devocioun!
Now have I thanne eek this condicioun,   40
That of al the floures in the mede,
Thanne love I most thise floures white and rede,
Suche as men callen daysyes in oure toun.
To hem have I so gret affeccioun,
As I seyde erst, whanne comen is the May,   45
That in my bed ther daweth me no day
That I nam up and walkyng in the mede
To seen this flour ayein the sonne sprede,

Text based on Fairfax 16 (F), with variants from Cambridge Gg.4.27 (G) and Trinity R.3.19 (T). Lines in G not found in F are identified by an asterisk (*) in the notes; see "The Text of This Edition," p. 966.

1 *tymes:* G&c *sythes.* F&c *men* om. **2** F *That* om. **3** acorde, agree. T&c *acorde me.* **4** wot, know. *yet wot:* G *this wit.* **6** GT *helle or hevene.* **7** witen, know. *other weyes:* T *otherwyse.* **10** leve, believe. G *goddis forbode.* **12** wenen, imagine. **13–14** G 13–14 *For that he say it nat of yore ago | God wot . . . lesse so.* **16** Bernard, St. Bernard, noted mystic and theologian. **17** mote, must. **18** ben in mynde, i.e., are kept in memory. **19** wyse, seers (wise men). **20** skylful, reasonable. **21** appreved, confirmed (proved). G 21 *And trowyn on these.* **26** Yloren, lost. **27–28** preve, proof. G 27–28 *thanne on olde bokys leve | There as there is non othyr asay be preve.* **29** konne, know. G 29 *thow that myn wit be lite.* **31–32** transposed in G **32** *geve swich lust and swich credence.* **33** game, diversion. G 33 *That there is wel onethe game.* **35** But, unless. G 35 *be other upon the.* **36** G 36 *Or ellis in the joly tyme of May.* **37** G 37 *Whan that I here the smale.* **39** G 39 *Farwel myn stodye as lastynge that sesoun.* **40** F *thanne such a.* G 40 *have I therto this.* **42** white and rede, the outer petals of the English daisy are pink at the tips. **43** daysyes, on the cult of the daisy, the marguerite, see the Introduction. *oure:* F *her.* **45** erst, first. **46** daweth, dawns. **48** ayein, toward.

Whan it upryseth erly by the morwe.
That blisful sight softneth al my sorwe,   50
So glad am I, whan that I have presence
Of it, to doon it alle reverence,
As she that is of alle floures flour,
Fulfilled of al vertu and honour,
And evere ilyke faire and fressh of hewe,   55
And I love it, and ever ylike newe,
And evere shal, til that myn herte dye,
Al swere I nat—of this I wol nat lye—
Ther loved no wight hotter in his lyve.
And whan that hit ys eve, I renne blyve,   60
As sone as evere the sonne gynneth weste,
To seen this flour, how it wol go to reste,
For fere of nyght, so hateth she derknesse.
Hire chere is pleynly sprad in the brightnesse
Of the sonne, for ther yt wol unclose.   65
Allas that I ne had Englyssh, ryme or prose,
Suffisant this flour to preyse aryght!
But helpeth, ye that han konnyng and myght,
Ye lovers that kan make of sentement,
In this cas oghte ye be diligent   70
To forthren me somwhat in my labour,
Whethir ye ben with the leef or with the
    flour.
For wel I wot that ye han her-biforne
Of makyng ropen, and lad awey the corne,
And I come after, glenyng here and there,   75
And am ful glad yf I may fynde an ere
Of any goodly word that ye han left.

And thogh it happen me rehercen eft
That ye han in your fresshe songes sayde,
Forbereth me, and beth nat evele apayde,   80
Syn that ye see I do yt in the honour
Of love, and eke in service of the flour
Whom that I serve as I have witte or myght.
She is the clerenesse and the verray lyght   84
That in this derke world me wynt and ledeth.
The hert in-with my sorwfull brest yow
    dredeth
And loveth so sore that ye ben verrayly
The maistresse of my witte, and nothing I.
My word, my werk ys knyt so in youre bond
That, as an harpe obeieth to the hond,   90
And maketh it soune after his fyngerynge,
Ryght so mowe ye oute of myn herte bringe
Swich vois, ryght as yow lyst, to laughe or
    pleyne.
Be ye my gide and lady sovereyne!
As to myn erthely god to yow I calle,   95
Bothe in this werk and in my sorwes alle.

But wherfore that I spak, to yive credence
To olde stories and doon hem reverence,
And that men mosten more thyng beleve   99
Then men may seen at eighe or elles preve—
That shal I seyn, whanne that I see my tyme.
I may not al attones speke in ryme.
My besy gost that thursteth alwey newe
To seen this flour so yong, so fressh of hewe,
Constreyned me with so gledy desire   105

49 G 49 *upryseth be the morwe schene* | 50 **The longe day thus walkynge in the grene.* 50–52 Lines omitted in G. 53–56 in G transferred to 55–58. 53 G 55 *This dayeseye of alle.* 55 **ilyke,** equally. 56 T&c *And ever I.* G 58 *As wel in wyntyr as in somyr newe.* 57–60 Omitted in G. 60 **blyve,** quickly. 61–62 G 51–54 *And whan the sunne begynnys for to weste* | *Thanne closeth it and drawith it to reste* | *So sore it is aferid of the nygt* | **Til on the morwe that it is dayis lygt* | ll. 53–56 follow. 62 **go to reste,** the inner petals of the English daisy close at night. 64 **chere . . . pleynly,** face, openly. 64–66 Omitted in G. 66 **Englyssh,** the next twelve lines are generally interpreted as a tribute to Deschamps and the other French court poets from whom Chaucer learned his art; see the Introduction. 67 G 59–60 *Fayn wolde I preysyn if I coude aryht* | **But wo is me it lyth nat in myn myght.* 68–72 Omitted in G. 69 **make,** compose poetry. 70 T *In thys cause and cas.* 71 **forthren,** assist (further). 72 **leef . . . flour,** evidently an allusion to some sort of playful contest in the French and English courts; see the Introduction. 73 G 61 *folk han.* 74 **makyng ropen . . . corne,** composing poetry, reaped, wheat (usable grain). 77 G 65 *they han.* 78 **eft,** again. G 66 *And if.* 79 G 67 *That they/in here.* 80 **Forbereth . . . evele apayde,** bear with, displeased. G 68 *I hope that they wel nat ben evele apayd.* 81–82 G 69–70 *Sith it is seyd in fortheryng and honour* | *Of hem that eythir servyn lef or flour.* F 188–96 follow. 83 **I serve,** the apostrophe to the daisy is to Alceste, who is possibly Joan of Kent. See below, and Introduction. 83–96 Omitted in G. 84 **clerenesse,** brightness. 85 **wynt,** guides (winds). 88 *witte:* T *hert.* 89 **knyt in bond,** knit up in bonds (fetters). 97 **wherfore that,** i.e., why it is that. 98 G 82 *To bokys olde.* 99 T *thyng* om. G 83 *Is for men schulde autoriteis beleve.* 100 **at eighe . . . preve,** with eyes, prove. T&c *Then they.* G 84 *There as there lyth non othyr asay be preve.* 101 **see my tyme,** i.e., see that the time is right. 101–20 Omitted in G except 108, 119. G 85–89 **For myn entent is or I fro yow fare* | **The nakede tixt in Englis to declare* | **Of manye a story or ellis of manye a geste* | **As autourys seyn leuyth hem if yow lest.* | *Whan passed was almost the monyth of May.* F 180–212 follow, with omissions. 105 **gledy,** glowing. T&c *Constreyneth.*

That in myn herte I feele yet the fire
That made me to ryse er yt were day—
And this was now the first morwe of May—
With dredful hert and glad devocioun,
For to ben at the resureccioun   110
Of this flour, whan that yt shulde unclose
Agayn the sonne, that roos as red as rose,
That in the brest was of the beste that day
That Agenores doghtre ladde away.
And doun on knes anoon-ryght I me sette,   115
And as I koude, this fresshe flour I grette,
Knelyng alwey, til it unclosed was,
Upon the smale, softe, swote gras,
That was with floures swote enbrouded al,
Of swich swetnesse and swich odour overal,   120
That, for to speke of gomme, or herbe, or tree,
Comparisoun may noon ymaked bee,
For yt surmounteth pleynly alle odoures,
And of riche beaute alle floures.
Forgeten had the erthe his pore estat   125
Of wynter, that hym naked made and mat,
And with his swerd of cold so sore greved.
Now hath th'atempre sonne all that releved,
That naked was, and clad him new agayn.
The smale foules, of the sesoun fayn,   130
That from the panter and the net ben scaped,
Upon the foweler, that hem made awhaped
In wynter, and distroyed hadde hire broode,
In his dispit hem thoghte yt did hem goode
To synge of hym and in hir song despise   135
The foule cherl that for his coveytise
Had hem betrayed with his sophistrye.
This was hire song, "The foweler we deffye,

And al his craft." And somme songen clere
Layes of love, that joye it was to here,   140
In worshipynge and preysinge of hir make.
And for the newe blisful somers sake,
Upon the braunches ful of blosmes softe,
In hire delyte they turned hem ful ofte,
And songen, "Blessed be Seynt Valentyne,   145
For on his day I chees yow to be myne,
Withouten repentyng, myn herte swete!"
And therwithalle hire bekes gonnen meete,
Yeldyng honour and humble obeysaunces
To love, and diden hire other observaunces   150
That longeth onto love and to nature—
Construeth that as yow lyst, I do no cure.
And thoo that hadde doon unkyndenesse,
As dooth the tydif, for newfangelnesse,
Besoghte mercy of hir trespassynge,   155
And humblely songen hire repentynge,
And sworen on the blosmes to be trewe,
So that hire makes wolde upon hem rewe,
And at the laste maden hire acord.
Al founde they Daunger for a tyme a lord,   160
Yet Pitee, thurgh his stronge gentil myght,
Forgaf, and made Mercy passen Ryght,
Thurgh Innocence and ruled Curtesye.
But I ne clepe nat innocence folye,
Ne fals pitee, for vertu is the mene,   165
As *Etik* seith—in swich maner I mene.
And thus thise foweles, voide of al malice,
Acordeden to love, and laften vice
Of hate, and songen alle of oon acorde,
"Welcome, somer, oure governour and lorde."
     And Zepherus and Flora gentilly   171

---

108 firste morwe, in G 89 above, the date is changed to the end of May. **109 dredful,** fearful. **113–14 beste . . . Agenores doghtre,** the bull that carried off Europa, daughter of Agenor of Phoenicia. Chaucer was saying that the sun was in the middle of the zodiacal sign of Taurus on May 1 (Skeat says that he was stretching a point—that it was nearly out). **118** T&c *smale, swete, softe.* **119 enbrouded,** embroidered. G 108. **120** T *Of suche odour and suche swetnes.* The English daisy is not a fragrant flower; this attribution of sweetness in the marguerite poems is simply transferred from the usual allusions to the rose. **126 mat,** dead; cf. *BD* 660n. **128 atempre,** temperate (warm). **129** G 117 *And clothede hym in grene al newe ageyn.* **130 fayn,** joyous. **131 panter,** snare (cf. a boat's "painter"). **132 awhaped,** frightened. **134 dispit,** scorn. **137 sophistrye,** cleverness. **138 deffye,** defy. **139–40** G 127–28 *Some songyn on the braun his clere | Of love, and that joye.* **141 make,** mate. **143–44** Omitted in G. **146** G 132 *At his day I.* **149 obeysaunces,** obediences. G 135 *The honour and the.* **150** G 136 *And after dedyn othere.* **151 longeth,** belong. G 137–40 *Right onto love and to natures | *So eche of hem to cryaturys | *This song to herkenyn I ded al myn entent | *For-why I mette I wiste what they ment.* F 209 follows. **152 do no cure,** don't care. The sexual innuendo is evident. **152–187** Omitted in G, except 180, 182. **153 thoo . . . unkyndenesse,** those, unkindnesses. **154 tydif,** an unidentified variety of bird, evidently reputed to be inconstant, cf. *CT* vii.648. **158 makes . . . rewe,** mates, have pity. **160 Daunger,** the personification in *RR* of maidenly aloofness (disdain). **162 passen Ryght,** overcome justice. **164 clepe,** call. **165 mene,** ideal. **166 Etik,** Aristotle's *Ethics.* **171 Zepherus . . . Flora,** west wind, goddess of flowers, cf. *CT* i.5n.

Yaf to the floures softe and tenderly
Hire swoote breth, and made hem for to sprede,
As god and goddesse of the floury mede.
In which me thoghte I myghte, day by day,
Dwellen alwey, the joly month of May,   176
Withouten slep, withouten mete or drynke.
Adoun ful softely I gan to synke,
And lenynge on myn elbowe and my syde,
The longe day I shoop me for t'abide   180
For nothing elles, and I shal nat lye,
But for to loke upon the dayesie,
That wel by reson men it calle may
The "dayesye," or elles the "eye of day,"
The emperice and flour of floures alle.   185
I praye to God that faire mote she falle,
And alle that loven floures, for hire sake!

    But natheles, ne wene nat that I make
In preysing of the flour agayn the leef,
No more than of the corn agayn the sheef,   190
For as to me nys lever noon ne lother.
I nam withholden yit with never nother,
Ne I not who serveth leef, ne who the flour—
Wel browken they her service or labour.
For this thing is al of another tonne,   195
Of olde storye, er swich stryf was begonne.
    Whan that the sonne out of the south gan
          west,
And that this flour gan close and goon to rest
For derknesse of the nyght, the which she
          dred,
Hom to myn hous ful swiftly I me sped   200
To goon to reste, and erly for to ryse,

To seen this flour to sprede, as I devyse.
And in a litel herber that I have,
Ibenched newe with turves fressh ygrave,
I bad men sholde me my couche make,   205
For deyntee of the newe someres sake—
I bad hem strawen floures on my bed.
Whan I was leyd, and had myn eyen hed,
I fel on slepe in-with an houre or twoo.
Me mette how I lay in the medewe thoo,   210
To seen this flour that I so love and drede;
And from afer come walkyng in the mede
The God of Love, and in his hand a quene,
And she was clad in real habit grene.
A fret of gold she hadde next her heer,   215
And upon that a whyt corowne she beer
With flourouns smale. And I shal nat lye,
For al the world, ryght as a dayesye
Ycorouned ys with white leves lyte,
So were the flowrouns of hire coroune white.
For of o perle fyne, oriental,   221
Hire white coroune was ymaked al,
For which the white coroune above the grene
Made hire lyke a daysie for to sene,
Considered eke the fret of golde above.   225
    Yclothed was this myghty God of Love
In silk, enbrouded ful of grene greves,
In-with a fret of rede rose-leves,
The fresshest syn the world was first bygonne.
His gilte heer was corowned with a sonne,   230
Instede of gold, for hevynesse and wyghte.
Therwith me thoghte his face shoon so
          bryghte

---

180 shoop, prepared (shaped). G 90–91 *And I hadde romed al the somerys day | * The grene medewe of which that I yow tolde.* **182** G 92 *Upon the fresche dayseie to beholde.* **183** F&c *That men/wel it.* **186 faire mote . . . falle,** may good befall her. **188 wene . . . make,** think, compose poetry. **188–89** G 71–73 *For trustyth wel I ne have not undyrtake | As of the lef agayn the flour to make | Ne of the flour to make ageyn the lef.* **190–96** G 74–80. **191 lever . . . lother,** more pleasant, more unpleasant. **192 withholden . . . never nother,** retained (committed), to neither (the one) nor the other. T. *neyther nother.* **193 not,** don't know. G 77 *Ne om.* **194 browken they her,** may they enjoy their. G 78 *That nys nothyng the entent of myn labour.* **195 tonne,** wine cask. *thing:* G 79 *werk.* **196 stryf:** F *thinge.* **198** G 94 *And clothede was the flour and gon to reste.* **199–200** G 95–96. **201** Omitted in G. **203 herber,** arbor. G 97. **204 Ibenched . . . turves . . . ygrave,** provided with mounds of freshly dug turf on which to sit or lie. F *That benched was, on turves.* **206 deyntee,** delight. **208 hed,** hid. **209** T&c *aslepe/within.* **210 mette,** dreamed. *lay:* G 104 *was.* G 105–06 *And that I romede in the same gyse | To sen that flour as ye had herd devyse* (cf. F 202). G 141–43 * Tyl at the laste a larke song above above | * I se, quod she, the mighty God of Love | * Lo, yond he comyth. I se hise wyngis sprede.* **212** T *And fro me fer.* G 144 *Tho gan I loke endelong the mede.* **213** G 145 *And saw hym come, and in.* **214 real,** royal. G 146 *Clothid in ryal abyte al of grene.* **215 fret . . . next,** net, over. **217 flourouns,** little flowers. **218** *a:* G 150 *the.* **221 o perle oriental,** a single exotic pearl. G 153 *fyn and oryental.* **225 Considered,** considering (i.e., the gold resembled the yellow center of the daisy). *the:* F&c *hir.* **227 enbrouded . . . greves,** embroidered, sprays (branches). **228 In-with . . . rose-leves,** intermingled with red rose petals. G 160 *A garlond on his hed of rose-levys.* **229–31** G 161–62 * Stekid al with lylye flourys newe | * But of his face I can not seyn the hewe.* **231 for hevynesse and wyghte,** i.e., because it would *not* be so heavy and weighty.

That wel unnethes myghte I him beholde.
And in his hand me thoghte I saugh him holde
Twoo firy dartes, as the gledes rede.   235
And aungelyke hys wynges saugh I sprede.
And al be that men seyn that blynd ys he,
Algate me thoghte that he myghte se,
For sternely on me he gan byholde,
So that his loking dooth myn herte colde.   240
And by the hand he held this noble quene,
Corowned with white, and clothed al in grene,
So womanly, so benigne, and so meke,
That in this world, thogh that men wolde seke,
Half hire beaute shulde men nat fynde   245
In creature that formed ys by kynde.
And therfore may I seyn, as thynketh me,
This song in preysyng of this lady fre.

Balade

Hyd, Absolon, thy gilte tresses clere;
Ester, ley thou thy mekenesse al adown;   250
Hyd, Jonathas, al thy frendly manere;
Penalopee and Marcia Catoun,
Make of youre wifhod no comparysoun;

Hyde ye youre beautes, Ysoude and Eleyne:
My lady cometh, that al this may disteyne.   255

Thy faire body, lat yt nat appere,
Lavyne; and thou, Lucresse of Rome toun,
And Polixene, that boghten love so dere,
And Cleopatre, with al thy passyoun,   259
Hyde ye your trouthe of love and your renoun;
And thou, Tesbe, that hast for love such peyne:
My lady cometh, that al this may disteyne.

Herro, Dido, Laudomia, alle yfere,
And Phillis, hangyng for thy Demophoun,
And Canace, espied by thy chere,   265
Ysiphile, betraysed with Jasoun,
Maketh of your trouthe neythir boost ne soun;
Nor Ypermystre or Adriane, ye tweyne:
My lady cometh, that al this may dysteyne.

This balade may ful wel ysongen be,   270
As I have seyd erst, by my lady free,
For certeynly al thise mowe nat suffise
To apperen wyth my lady in no wyse.

---

233 unnethes . . . beholde, i.e., scarcely bear to look at him. G 163–65 *For sekyrly his face schon so bryghte | *That with the glem astonede was the syhte. | A furlong wey I myhte hym not beholde.* **234** G 166 *But at the laste in hande I saugh.* **235 gledes,** live coals. **Twoo:** G 167 *Tho.* **236** G 168 *wengis gan he sprede.* **238 Algate,** nevertheless. G 170 *he myghte wel ise.* **240 dooth,** makes. **241** *this:* T&c *hys;* G 173 *the.* **246 kynde,** nature. **247 as thynketh me,** as it seems to me (i.e., reflecting my sentiment). **247–48** Omitted in G; instead G inserts F 276–95 at this point (with some variations, as noted below), followed by four new lines, G 199–202, *And aftyr that they wentyn in cumpas | *Daunsynge aboute this flour an esy pas | *And songyn as it were in carole wyse | *This balade whiche that I schal yow devyse.* According to these lines, the balade is sung by the nineteen ladies as part of the dramatic action instead of being, as in F, editorial comment by the author-dreamer. **248 fre,** generous. **249 Absolon,** son of David, a medieval archetype of physical beauty and its hazards, cf. II Sam. 18:9ff, and *CT* I.3313ff. and notes. Lists of this sort, exemplifying the virtues (or vices), are not uncommon in sermons. **250 Ester,** of the biblical Book of Esther. **251 Jonathas,** Jonathan, of David and Jonathan, I Sam. 19:1ff. **252 Penalopee,** wife of Ulysses. **Marcia Catoun,** either the wife or daughter of Cato, both named Marcia, and both famous examples of domestic fidelity. **254 Ysoude . . . Eleyne,** Iseult of Tristan and Iseult, Helen of Troy. **255 disteyne,** outshine. G 209 *Alceste is here that al this may disteyne.* For some reason, the revision relinquishes the suspense provided by concealing "my lady's" name until she herself announces it in l. 432. Alceste is simply another classical example of wifely fidelity (she died for her husband; her story is found in Gower's *Confessio Amantis* 7.1917ff.). If the suspense had any function, the name might possibly have been associated with someone in the court— (?) Joan of Kent, cf. l. 321n. **257 Lavyne,** Lavinia, wife of Aeneas. **Lucresse,** Lucrece, whose rape is recounted in the fifth legend, below, l. 1680ff. **258 Polixene,** daughter of Priam, beloved of Achilles and sacrificed on his tomb to be reunited with him. **260 trouthe,** faithfulness. **261 Tesbe,** of Pyramus and Thisbe. **262** G 216 *Alceste is here that.* **263 Herro,** of Hero and Leander. **Laudomia,** Laodomia, wife of Protesilaus, Ovid, *Heroides* 12. **yfere,** together. **264 Phillis . . . Demophoun,** whose story is the seventh legend below, l. 2394ff. **265 Canace,** whose incestuous love for her brothers is told by Ovid, *Heroides* 11, and Gower, *CA* 3.143ff., and disparaged in ML prologue, *CT* II.78ff. **chere,** face. **266 Ysiphile . . . Jasoun,** whose story is in the fourth legend below, l. 1368ff. TG&c 220 *betrayed.* **267 neythir:** G 221 *in love no.* **268 Ypermystre,** punished for being unwilling to kill her husband. Her story is the last legend (nine) below, l. 2562ff. **Adriane,** Ariadne, who helped Theseus slay the Minotaur and was later deserted by him. Her story is the sixth legend below, l. 1886ff. G 222 *Adriane ne pleyne.* **269** G 223 *Alceste is here that.* **270** G 224 *Whan that this balade al isongyn was.* **271–75** Omitted in G. **272 mowe,** may. **273 apperen,** be equal (peer).

For as the sonne wole the fyr disteyne,
So passeth al my lady sovereyne, 275
That ys so good, so faire, so debonayre—
I prey to God that ever falle hire faire!
For nadde comfort ben of hire presence,
I hadde ben ded, withouten any defence,
For drede of Loves wordes and his chere, 280
As, when tyme ys, herafter ye shal here.

Behynde this God of Love, upon the grene
I saugh comyng of ladyes nyntene,
In real habit, a ful esy paas, 284
And after hem coome of wymen swich a traas
That syn that God Adam hadde mad of erthe
The thridde part of mankynde, or the ferthe,
Ne wende I not by possibilitee
Had ever in this wide world ybee— 289
And trewe of love thise women were echon.
Now wheither was that a wonder thing or
    non,
That ryght anoon as that they gonne espye
Thys flour which that I clepe the dayesie,
Ful sodeynly they stynten al attones,
And kneled doun, as it were for the nones, 295
And songen with o vois, "Heel and honour
To trouthe of womanhede, and to this flour
That bereth our alder pris in figurynge.
Hire white corowne bereth the witnessynge."
And with that word, a-compas enviroun, 300
They setten hem ful softely adoun.
First sat the God of Love, and syth his quene
With the white corowne, clad in grene,

And sithen al the remenaunt by and by,
As they were of estaat, ful curteysly. 305
Ne nat a word was spoken in the place
The mountaunce of a furlong wey of space.

I, knelyng by this flour, in good entente,
Abood to knowen what this peple mente,
As stille as any ston, til at the last 310
This God of Love on me hys eyen cast
And seyde, "Who kneleth there?" And I
    answerde
Unto his askynge, whan that I it herde,
And seyde, "Sir, it am I," and com him nere,
And salwed him. Quod he, "What dostow
    here 315
So nygh myn oune floure, so boldely?
Yt were better worthy, trewely,
A worm to neghen ner my flour than thow."
    "And why, sire," quod I, "and yt lyke
    yow?"
    "For thow," quod he, "art therto nothyng
    able. 320
Yt is my relyke, digne and delytable,
And thow my foo, and al my folk werreyest,
And of myn olde servauntes thow mysseyest,
And hynderest hem with thy translacioun,
And lettest folk from hire devocioun 325
To serve me, and holdest it folye
To serve Love. Thou maist yt nat denye,
For in pleyn text, withouten nede of glose,
Thou hast translated the *Romaunce of the
    Rose*

That is an heresye ayeins my lawe,   330
And makest wise folk fro me withdrawe.
And of *Creseyde* thou hast seyde as the lyste,
That maketh men to wommen lasse triste,
That ben as trewe as ever was any steel.
Of thyn answere avise the ryght weel,   335
For thogh thou reneyed hast my lay,
As other wrecches han doon many a day,
By Seynt Venus, that my moder ys,
If that thou lyve, thou shalt repenten this
So cruelly that it shal wel be sene!''   340

Thoo spak this lady, clothed al in grene,
And seyde, "God, ryght of youre curtesye,
Ye moten herken yf he can replye
Agayns al this that ye have to him meved.
A god ne sholde nat be thus agreved,   345
But of hys deitee he shal be stable,
And therto gracious and merciable.

And yf ye nere a god that knowen al,
Thanne myght yt be as I yow tellen shal:
This man to yow may falsly ben accused,   350
That as by right him oughte ben excused.
For in youre court ys many a losengeour,
And many a queynte totelere accusour,
That tabouren in youre eres many a soun
Ryght after hire ymagynacioun   355
To have youre daliance, and for envie.
Thise ben the causes, and I shal not lye.
Envie ys lavendere of the court alway,
For she ne parteth neither nyght ne day
Out of the hous of Cesar—thus seith
   Dante.   360
Whoso that gooth, algate she wol nat
   wante.
And eke, peraunter, for this man ys nyce,
He myghte doon yt gessyng no malice,

332 the lyste, it pleases you. G here inserts 55 lines (258–312), 50 not in F: 258 **And thynkist in thyn wit that is ful cole* | **That he nys but a verray propre fole* | 260 **That lovyth paramouris to harde and hote* | **Wel wot I therby thow begynnyst dote* | **As olde folis whan here spryt faylyth* | **Thanne blame they folk and wete nat what hem ealyth* | **Hast thow nat mad in englys ek the bok* | 265 *How that Crisseyde Troylis forsok* | *In schewynge how that wemen han don mis* | **Bit natheles answere me now to this* | **Why noldist thow as wel a seyd goodnes* | **Of wemen as thow hast seyd wekedenes* | 270 **Was there no good matyr in thyn mynde* | **Ne in alle thyne bokys no coudist thow nat fynde* | **Sum story of wemen that were goode and trewe* | **Yis god wot .lx. bokys olde and newe* | **Hast thow thyn self alle ful of storyis grete* | 275 **That bothe romaynys and ek grekis trete* | **Of sundery wemen whiche lyf that they ledde* | **And evere an hunderede goode ageyn on badde* | **This knowith god and alle clerkis ek* | **That usyn sweche materis for to sek* | 280 **What seith Valerye, Titus, or Claudyan* | **What seith Jerome agayns Jouynyan* | **How clene maydenys and how trewe wyvys* | **How stedefaste wedewys durynge alle here lyvys* | **Tellyth Jerome and that nat of a fewe* | 285 **But I dar seyn an hunderede on a rewe* | **That it is pete for to rede and routhe* | **The wo that they endure for here trouthe* | *For to hyre love were they so trewe* | **That rathere than they wole take a newe* | 290 **They chose to be ded in sundery wyse* | **And deiedyn as the story wele devyse* | **And some were brend and some were cut the hals* | **And some dreynkt for thy woldyn not be fals* | **For alle kepid they here maydynhed* | 295 **Or ellis wedlok or here wedewehed* | **And this thing was nat kept for holynesse* | **But al for verray vertu and clennesse* | **And for men schulde sette on hem no lak* | **And yit they were hethene al the pak* | 300 **That were so sore adrad of alle schame* | **These olde wemen kepte so here name* | **That in this world I trowe men schal nat fynde* | **A man that coude be so trowe and kynde* | **As was the leste woman in that tyde* | 305 **What seyth also the epistelle of Ovyde* | **Of trewe wyvys and of here labour* | **What Vincent in his estoryal myrour* | **Ek al te world of autourys mayst tow here* | **Cristene and hethene trete of swich matere* | 310 **It nedyth nat al day thus for to endite* | **But yit I seye what eylyth the to wryte* | 312 **The draf of storyis and forgete the corn.* F 332–35 are G 265–67, 288. **333 to,** upon. 334 G 288 *For to hyr love were they so trewe; T as evyr was steele.* **335 avise the,** give careful thought. **336 reneyed . . . lay,** denied, law. G 314. 337 G 315 *As othere olde folys manye a day.* 338 G 313 *Be Seynt Venus of whom that I was born.* **339–40** G 316 *Thow shalt repenten it so that it schal be sene.* **341** G 317 *Thanne spak Alceste the worthyere queene.* **343 moten herken,** must listen. The address by Alceste has been interpreted by Margaret Galway and other scholars as an admonition by Joan of Kent to Richard II addressed through the medium of his dead father. It parallells contemporary criticisms of Richard's obstinacy and instability found in the Chronicles and in Gower's *Vox Clamantis* 6. **344 to him meved,** urged against him. al this: G 320 *these poyntys.* **346 deitee:** G 322 *dede.* **347 gracious:** G 323 *ryghtful.* **348–49** Omitted in G. T *And yef ye were nat a god and knew all.* G 324–27 **He schal nat ryghtfully his yre wreke* | **Or he have herd the tothyr partye speke* | **Al ne is nat gospel that is to yow pleynyd* | **The god of love hereth manye a tale ifeynyd.* **350 falsly:** G 338 *wrongly.* **351 That:** G 339 *There.* **352 losengeour,** liar. **353 queynte totelere,** cunning tattler. **354 tabouren,** drum (vb.). **soun:** F *swon;* G 330 *thyng.* **355** G 331 *For hate or for jelous ymagynyng.* **356 daliance,** i.e., to enjoy your attention (conversation). G 332 *And for to han with you sum dalyaunce.* **357** Omitted in G. **358 lavendere,** laundress (i.e., washes the dirty linen). G 333–34 *Envye, I preye to God yeve hire myschaunce, | Is lavender in the grete court alway.* **359 parteth,** departs. **360 Dante,** cf. *Inferno* 13.64. **361 Whoso . . . gooth, algate . . . wante,** whoever (comes or) goes, nevertheless, lack (material to tattle about—be envious of). G 337 *goth alwey sche mote wante.* **362 nyce,** foolish. G 340 *Or ellis, sere* [sir], *for that this.* **363 gessyng,** thinking. G 341 *He may translate a thyng.*

But for he useth thynges for to make—
Hym rekketh noght of what matere he take—
Or him was boden maken thilke tweye   366
Of somme persone, and durste yt nat withseye,
Or him repenteth outrely of this.
He ne hath nat doon so grevously amys,
To translaten that olde clerkes writen,   370
As thogh that he of malice wolde enditen
Despite of love, and had himself yt wroght.
This shoolde a ryghtwis lord have in his thoght,
And nat be lyk tirauntez of Lumbardye
That han no reward but at tyrannye,   375
For he that kynge or lord ys naturel,
Hym oghte nat be tiraunt ne crewel,
As is a fermour, to doon the harm he kan.
He moste thinke yt is his leege man,
And is his tresour, and his gold in cofre.   380
This is the sentence of the philosophre,
A kyng to kepe his leeges in justice—
Withouten doute, that is his office.
Al wol he kepe his lordes hire degree,
As it ys ryght and skilful that they bee   385
Enhaunced and honoured and most dere—
For they ben half-goddes in this world here—
Yit mot he doon bothe ryght to poore and
      ryche,
Al be that hire estaat be nat yliche,
And han of poore folk compassyoun.   390

For loo the gentil kynde of the lyoun,
For whan a flye offendeth him or biteth,
He with his tayle awey the flye smyteth
Al esely, for of hys genterye
Hym deyneth not to wreke hym on a flye,   395
As dooth a curre or elles another best.
In noble corage oughte ben arest,
And weyen everything by equytee,
And ever have reward to his owen degree.
For, syr, yt is no maistrye for a lorde   400
To dampne a man without answere of worde,
And for a lord, that is ful foul to use.
And if so be he may hym nat excuse,
But asketh mercy with a sorweful herte,
And profereth him ryght in his bare sherte   405
To ben ryght at your owen jugement,
Than oght a god, by short avysement,
Consydre his owne honour and hys trespas.
    "For syth no cause of deth lyeth in this caas,
Yow oghte to ben the lyghter merciable—   410
Leteth youre ire, and beth sumwhat tretable.
The man hath served yow of his kunnyng,
And furthred wel youre lawe in his makyng.
Al be hit that he kan nat wel endite,
Yet hath he maked lewed folk delyte   415
To serve yow, in preysing of your name.
He made the book that hight the *Hous of Fame*,
And eke the *Deeth of Blaunche the Duchesse*,

---

364 useth thynges . . . make, is accustomed to composing poetry. *thynges:* G 342 *bokis.* **365 Hym rekketh noght,** it matters not to him. G 343–45 *And takyth non hed of what matere he take | *Therfore he wrot the Rose and ek Crisseyde | *Of innocence and nyste what he seyde.* **366 boden,** commanded. **367 withseye,** refuse. **368** Omitted in G. G 348 *For he hath wrete manye a bok er this.* **371 enditen,** write. **As:** F&c *And.* **372 Despite . . . wroght,** scorn (unpleasantness), invented. G 352 *iwrouht.* **374 tirauntez of Lumbardye,** Italian tyrants like the Visconti, Capuletti, and Gonzaga. These were evidently commonplace examples of despotic rulers. Gower had used the same figure in *Mirour de l'omme,* l. 23233. **375 at,** through. G 355 *That usyn wilfulhed and tyrannye.* **376 naturel,** i.e., not by usurpation but by inheritance. **378 fermour,** renter. **379 leege,** free subject, i.e., subjects who owe service voluntarily, and not as slaves. G 360–64 adds **And that hym owith of verry duetee | *Schewyn hys peple pleyn benygnete | *And wel to heryn here excusacyouns | *And here compleyntys and petyciouns | *In duewe tyme whan they schal it profre.* **380** Omitted in G. **381 philosophre,** ll. 376–80 echo the *Secretum Secretorum* (EETS, p. 36), attributed to Aristotle, and parallel Gower, *Vox Clamantis* 6.581, 1001, and *Confessio Amantis* 7.2695ff. **383 office,** duty. G 368–69 adds **And therto is a kyng ful depe isworn | *Ful manye an hundrede wyntyr herebeforn.* **384 kepe . . . degree,** protect, estate(s) (dignities). T&c *As well hys lordes to kepe theyr.* G 370 *And for to kepe.* **385 skilful,** reasonable. **388 poore and ryche,** a commonplace of medieval discussions of kingship, but found in Gower's *Vox* 6.741ff., and *Confessio* 7.2743ff. G 374 *This schal be don bothe to.* **391 kynde,** nature. **394 esely . . . genterye,** gently, nobility. **395 wreke,** revenge. **397 arest,** restraint. **398 equytee,** impartiality. **399 reward,** regard. **400 no maistrye,** no achievement (i.e., easy). **401 dampne . . . without answere,** condemn, without (giving him an opportunity) to reply. **402** *ful foul:* T&c *ryght full.* **403** *if:* F&c *it.* **407 short avysement,** brief deliberation. **408 his owne . . . hys,** (both) the king's own, and the petitioner's. **409 syth . . . this caas,** since, this case—we now return to the accusation that the poet has defamed love in his writing. **410 the lyghter,** more easily. **411 Leteth . . . tretable,** slacken, open to entreaty. **412 of,** with. **413 makyng,** composing poetry. G 400–401 adds **Whil he was yong he kepte youre estat. | *I not where he be now a renegat.* **414** G 402 *But wel I wot with that he can endyte.* **415 lewed,** ignorant. G 403 *He hath . . . folk to delyte.* **416 in preysing,** by praising. **417 hight,** is called.

And the *Parlement of Foules,* as I gesse,
And al the love of *Palamon and Arcite*   420
Of Thebes, thogh the storye ys knowen lyte;
And many an ympne for your halydayes,
That highten balades, roundels, virelayes;
And for to speke of other holynesse,
He hath in prose translated *Boece,*   425
And maad the lyf also of *Seynt Cecile.*
He made also, goon ys a gret while,
Origenes upon the Maudeleyne.
Hym oughte now to have the lesse peyne;
He hath maad many a lay and many a
         thinge.   430
    "Now as ye be a god and eke a kynge,
I, your Alceste, whilom quene of Trace,
Y aske yow this man, ryght of your grace,
That ye him never hurte in al his lyve.
And he shal swere to yow, and that as blyve,   435
He shal no more agilten in this wyse,
But he shal maken as ye wol devyse,
Of wommen trewe in lovyng al hire lyf,
Wher so ye wol, of mayden or of wyf,
And forthren yow as muche as he mysseyde   440
Or in the *Rose* or elles in *Creseyde.*"
    The God of Love answerde hire thus anoon,
"Madame," quod he, "it is so long agoon
That I yow knew so charitable and trewe,
That never yit, syn that the world was newe,   445
To me ne found y better noon than yee.
If that I wol save my degree,
I may, ne wol, nat werne your requeste.

Al lyeth in yow; dooth wyth hym as yow
      leste.
I al foryeve withouten lenger space—   450
For whoso yeveth a yift, or dooth a grace,
Do it bytyme, his thank ys wel the more.
And demeth ye what he shal doo therfore.
Goo thanke now my lady here," quod he.
    I roos, and doun I sette me on my knee,   455
And seyde thus, "Madame, the God above
Foryelde yow that ye the God of Love
Han maked me his wrathe to foryive,
And yeve me grace so long for to lyve
That I may knowe soothly what ye bee,   460
That han me holpe and put in this degree.
But trewely I wende, as in this cas,
Naught have agilt, ne doon to love trespas.
For-why a trewe man, withouten drede,
Hath nat to parten with a theves dede;   465
Ne a trewe lover oght me not to blame,
Thogh that I speke a fals lovere som shame.
They oghte rather with me for to holde
For that I of Creseyde wroot or tolde,
Or of the Rose, what so myn auctour mente.
Algate, God woot, yt was myn entente   471
To forthren trouthe in love and yt cheryce,
And to ben war fro falsnesse and fro vice
By swich ensample—this was my menynge."
    And she answerde, "Lat be thyn arguynge,   475
For love ne wol nat countrepleted be
In ryght ne wrong; and lerne that of me.
Thow hast thy grace, and hold the ryght therto.

---

423 balades, roundels, virelayes, as in the Retraction to the *CT* (x.1087), Chaucer here claims to have written many independent lyrics. We have a few independent balades (see the short poems), an independent triple rondel (short poem 19), the rondel at the end of *PF,* and the possible examples of virelays in *Anelida* ll. 256–71, 317–32. But we have no evidence of Chaucer's having written many independent love songs and lyrics. **424 other,** other kinds of, or simply Chaucerian humor, since the previous "hymns" were to the holy days of Love. *holynesse:* G 412 *besynesse.* **425** T *Boes;* G 414–15 adds **And of the wrechede engendrynge of mankynde | *As man may in Pope Innocent ifynde.* This is Innocent III, *De Contemptu Mundi;* cf. *CT* II.99n. **426 Seynt Cecile,** i.e., The Second Nun's Tale, and evidence that some of the "Canterbury" pieces had been composed before the frame story was envisaged. **428 Origenes . . . Maudeleyne,** most scholars accept Tyrwhitt's suggestion that this refers to a popular medieval homily *De Maria Magdalena* attributed to Origen, but, like *De Contemptu* above, the *Dit de Leoun, CT,* X, 1087, and indeed the *Roman de la Rose* itself, it is a Chaucerian work that has not survived. **432 whilom . . . Trace,** formerly, Thrace (modern Bulgaria). The tradition of queens and ladies of the court interceding for those in trouble was a common feature in medieval romances (cf. *CT* I.1748; III.895) and no doubt in medieval life. **435 blyve,** promptly. **436 agilten,** offend. *no:* F&c *never.* **437 maken,** compose poetry. **440 forthren . . . mysseyde,** assist, spoken against. **441 Or,** either. **443 it is so long agoon,** i.e., for such a long time. **447 wol save . . . degree,** i.e., am to preserve my standing (as king). F *ye wolde;* G 437 *That if that I.* **448 werne,** refuse. **450** G 440 *And al foryeve.* **452 bytyme,** promptly. **453 demeth,** judge. **457 Foryelde,** repay. **461 degree,** state. **462 wende,** thought. **463 agilt,** offended. **464 For-why,** because. **465 parten . . . dede,** take part in, deed. **466** G 456 *may me nat blame.* **468 with me . . . holde,** agree with me. **471 Algate,** however. **473 ben war,** give warning. **476 countrepleted,** contradicted. **478 grace,** forgiveness.

Now wol I seyn what penance thou shalt do
For thy trespas, and understonde yt here:　480
Thow shalt, while that thou lyvest, yer by yere,
The most partye of thy tyme spende
In makyng of a glorious legende
Of goode wymmen, maydenes and wyves,
That weren trewe in lovyng al hire lyves;　485
And telle of false men that hem bytraien,
That al hir lyf do nat but assayen
How many women they may doon a shame;
For in youre world that is now holde a game.
And thogh the lyke nat a lovere bee,　490
Speke wel of love; this penance yive I thee.
And to the God of Love I shal so preye
That he shal charge his servantz by any weye
To forthren thee, and wel thy labour quyte.
Goo now thy wey; this penanuce ys but
　　lyte.　495
And whan this book ys maad, yive it the quene,
On my byhalf, at Eltham or at Sheene."
　　The God of Love gan smyle, and than he
　　　sayde:
"Wostow," quod he, "wher this be wyf or
　　mayde,
Or queene, or countesse, or of what degre,　500
That hath so lytel penance yiven thee,
That hast deserved sorer for to smerte?
But pite renneth soone in gentil herte;
That maistow seen—she kytheth what she ys."
　　And I answerd, "Nay, sire, so have I blys,　505
No moore but that I see wel she is good."
　　"That is a trewe tale, by myn hood,"
Quod Love, "and that thou knowest wel,
　　pardee,

If yt be so that thou avise the.
Hastow nat in a book, lyth in thy cheste,　510
The grete goodnesse of the quene Alceste,
That turned was into a dayesye—
She that for hire housbonde chees to dye,
And eke to goon to helle, rather than he,
And Ercules rescowed hire, parde,　515
And broght hir out of helle agayn to blys?"
　　And I answerd ageyn, and sayde, "Yis,
Now knowe I hire. And is this good Alceste,
The dayesie, and myn owene hertes reste?
Now fele I weel the goodnesse of this wyf,　520
That both aftir hir deth and in hir lyf
Hir grete bounte doubleth hire renoun.
Wel hath she quyt me myn affeccioun,
That I have to hire flour, the dayesye.
No wonder ys thogh Jove hire stellyfye,　525
As telleth Agaton, for hire goodnesse!
Hire white corowne berith of hyt witnesse;
For also many vertues hadde shee
As smale florouns in hire corowne bee.
In remembraunce of hire and in honour　530
Cibella maade the daysye and the flour
Ycrowned al with white, as men may see;
And Mars yaf to hire corowne reed, pardee,
Instede of rubyes, sette among the white."
　　Therwith this queene wex reed for shame a
　　　lyte,　535
Whan she was preysed so in hire presence.
Thanne seyde Love, "A ful gret necligence
Was yt to the, that ylke tyme thou made
'Hyd, Absolon, thy tresses,' in balade,
That thou forgate hire in this song to sette,　540
Syn that thou art so gretly in hire dette,

---

482 *tyme:* G 472 *lyf.* 485 *lovyng:* G 475 *levynge.* 490 **the lyke nat,** it does not please you. *lyke:* G 480 *lestyth.* 494 **forthren . . . quyte,** aid, repay. 495 *this:* G 485 *thyn.* 496–97 **Eltham . . . Sheene,** royal manors in Kent, favorite retreats of King Richard and Queen Anne. When Anne died in 1394, Richard was inconsolable. He would not return to the manors and indeed ordered Shene House torn down. These two lines are omitted in G—perhaps the best evidence that this is the revised version and that the revision was made after 1394. 499–500 **Wostow . . . wher . . . queene, or countesse,** do you know whether. This pointed question appears to support those who would identify Alceste as Joan of Kent. As the mother of Richard, Joan was dowager queen, even though her husband had never ruled, and she was Countess of Kent in her own right. 503 **pite renneth,** a favorite Chaucerian sentiment, cf. *CT* I.1761 and note. 504 **kytheth,** knows. 506 **No moore,** i.e., I know no more. 513 **chees to dye,** chose to die, cf. 255n. above. 521 G 509 *and ek hire lyf.* 523 **quyt,** repaid. 526 **Agaton,** Plato's *Symposium* was a banquet at Agathon's house and recounts the story of Alcestis as an example of love. 531 **Cibella,** Cybele, goddess of nature. 533 **corowne reed,** i.e., the pink tips of the petals (cf. l. 42n.); red was the color of Mars. 538 G 526 *to the, to write on stedefastnesse.* 539–41 Omitted in G, and replaced by G 527–32 **Of women sithe thow knowist here goodnesse | *By pref and ek by storyis here byforn | *Let be the chaf and writ wel of the corn | *Why noldist thow han writyn of Alceste | *And latyn Criseide ben aslepe and reste | *For Alceste schulde thyn wrytynge be.*

And wost so wel that kalender ys shee
To any woman that wol lover bee.
For she taught al the craft of fyn lovynge,
And namely of wyfhod the lyvynge,   545
And al the boundes that she oghte kepe.
Thy litel wit was thilke tyme aslepe.
But now I charge the, upon thy lyf,
That in thy legend thou make of thys wyf,
Whan thou hast other smale ymaad before;   550
And fare now wel; I charge the namore.
But er I goo, thus muche I wol the telle,
Ne shal no trewe lover come in helle.
Thise other ladies sittynge here arowe
Ben in thy balade, yf thou kanst hem
          knowe,   555
And in thy bookes alle thou shalt hem fynde.
Have hem now in thy legende al in mynde—
I mene of hem that ben in thy knowynge.
For here ben twenty thousand moo sittynge
Than thou knowest, goode wommen alle,   560

And trewe of love, for oght that may byfalle.
Make the metres of hem as the leste.
  "I mot goon hom—the sonne draweth
          weste—
To paradys, with al this companye,
And serve alwey the fresshe dayesye.   565
At Cleopatre I wol that thou begynne,
And so forth, and my love so shalt thou wynne.
For lat see now what man that lover be,
Wol doon so strong a peyne for love as she.
I wot wel that thou maist nat al yt ryme   570
That swiche lovers diden in hire tyme;
It were to long to reden and to here.
Suffiseth me thou make in this manere,
That thou reherce of al hir lyf the grete,
After thise olde auctours lysten for to trete. 575
For whoso shal so many a storye telle,
Sey shortly, or he shal to longe dwelle."
  And with that word my bokes gan I take,
And ryght thus on my legende gan I make.

542 **kalender,** guide. 543 Omitted in G. 544 G 534 *Of goodnesse, for sche taughte of fyn lovynge.* 545 **namely,** especially. T *And hyt was preved in dede doyng.* 546 **boundes,** rules (decorum). 550 **other smale,** i.e., composed other less important lives. Alcestis was to be the crowning story in the collection. 552–65 Omitted in G. 554ff. **Thise other ladies ... balade ... legende,** evidently the initial idea was that the subjects of the legends were to be those cited in the balade. Leaving aside the men, we have legends of Cleopatra, Thisbe, Dido, Hypsipyle and Medea, Lucrece, Ariadne (Philomena), Phyllis, and Hypermnestra. Philomena, however, does not appear in the balade. The names in the balade for which we lack legends are Penelope, Marcia, Iseult, Helen, Lavinia, Polyxena, Hero, Laodomia, Canace, and Alcestis. Furthermore, this list does not agree with that given for *LGW* in ML prologue, *CT* ii.61ff. 555 *thy:* F *my.* 558 **that ben in thy knowynge,** i.e., that you know about; Chaucer here leaves the door open to alter the original list. 560 *goode:* T&c *and good.* 562 **leste,** wish. 568–77 Omitted in G. 569 **doon ... peyne,** i.e., suffer so much pain. 574 **grete,** essence. 575 **After ... lysten,** as, are pleased. 577 **Sey shortly,** i.e., should be brief. 578 G 544 *of slep I gan awake.*

I

LEGEND OF CLEOPATRA

Incipit legenda Cleopatrie martiris, Egipti regine.

After the deth of Tholome the kyng,   580
That al Egipt hadde in his governyng,
Regned hys queene Cleopataras,
Til on a tyme befel ther swich a cas
That out of Rome was sent a senatour
For to conqueren regnes and honour   585
Unto the toun of Rome, as was usaunce,
To have the world at hir obeysaunce,
And sooth to seye, Antonius was his name.
So fil it, as Fortune hym ought ashame,
Whanne he was fallen in prosperitee,   590
Rebel unto the toun of Rome is hee.
And over al this, the suster of Cesar,
He lafte hir falsly er that she was war,
And wolde algates han another wyf;
For which he took with Rome and Cesar strif.

Natheles, forsooth, this ylke senatour   596
Was a ful worthy gentil werreyour,
And of his deeth it was ful gret damage.
But love had broght this man in swich a rage,
And him so narwe bounden in his laas,   600
Alle for the love of Cleopataras,
That al the world he sette at no value.
Him thoghte ther nas nothyng to him so due
As Cleopatras for to love and serve;
Him roghte nat in armes for to sterve   605
In the defence of hir and of hir ryght.
This noble queene ek lovede so this knyght,

Thurgh his desert and for his chivalrye,
As certeynly, but if that bookes lye,
He was of persone and of gentillesse   610
And of discrecioun and hardynesse,
Worthy to any wight that lyven may—
And she was fair as is the rose in May.
And for to maken shortly is the beste,
She wax his wif and hadde him as hir leste.   615

The weddyng and the feste to devyse,
To me that have ytake swich empryse
Of so many a story for to make,
It were to longe, lest that I sholde slake
Of thing that bereth more effect and charge,
For men may overlade a shippe or barge.   621
And forthy to th'effect than wol I skyppe,
And al the remenaunt, I wol lete it slyppe.

Octovyan, that woode was of this dede,
Shoop hym an oost on Antony to lede   625
Al outerly for his destruccioun.
With stoute Romayns, crewel as lyoun,
To shippe they wente, and thus I lat hem sayle.
Antonius was war, and wol nat fayle
To meten with thise Romayns—
      if he may—   630
Took eke his rede, and both upon a day
His wyf and he and al his oost forth went
To shippe anon; no lengere they ne stent.
And in the see hit happed hem to mete.

580 **Tholome,** Ptolemy, name of Cleopatra's father and also her two brothers. No source has been identified for Chaucer's version of this familiar story. 582 **hys queene,** Chaucer or his source mistakes the complicated relationship. Cleopatra did not marry her father; she was betrothed to her elder brother, who was killed in the war with Julius Caesar; she married her younger brother and had him murdered. T&c *Cleopatras* throughout. 585 **regnes,** kingdoms. 586 **usaunce,** custom. 587 *at:* G *unto;* T&c *under.* 588 **Antonius,** Mark Antony. 589 **hym ought,** owed (i.e., had prepared for) him. 590 **in,** from. 592 **over al . . . suster of Cesar,** especially, Octavia (Antony's wife, sister of Octavius Caesar). 593 **war,** aware. 594 **algates,** in any way possible. 599 **rage,** passion. 600 **narwe . . . laas,** closely, net. 603 G *to hym nothyng so.* 605 **roghte . . . sterve,** i.e., cared not if he should die. 611 **hardynesse,** bravery. 612 **wight,** person. 616 **devyse,** describe. 617 **swich empryse,** such (an) enterprise. 620 **effect . . . charge,** importance, weight. 621 **overlade,** overload. 622 **forthy . . . effect,** therefore, conclusion. 624 **woode,** mad. 625 **Shoop . . . oost,** prepared (shaped), host. 629 **war,** aware. 631 **rede,** counsel. 633 **stent,** stopped. 634 **happed,** happened (came about). This is, historically, the battle of Actium, but actually a stirring, alliterative description of a sea battle in Chaucer's own day.

Up gooth the trumpe, and for to shoute and
    shete, 635
And penyen hem to sette on with the sonne.
With grisly soun out gooth the grete gonne,
And heterly they hurtelen al attones,
And fro the top doun cometh the grete stones.
In gooth the grapenel, so ful of crokes; 640
Among the ropes renne the sheryng-hokes.
In with the polax preseth he and he;
Byhynde the mast begyneth he to fle,
And out agayn, and dryveth hym overborde.
He styngeth hym upon hys speres orde; 645
He rent the sayl with hokes lyke a sithe;
He bryngeth the cuppe, and biddeth hem be
    blithe;
He poureth pesen upon the hacches slidre;
With pottes ful of lyme they goon togidre.
And thus the longe day in fight they spende,
Til at the laste, as everything hath ende, 651
Antony is shent and put hym to the flyght,
And al hys folk to-goo that best goo myght.

    Fleeth ek the queene, with al hir purpre sayle,
For strokes which that went as thik as hayle. 655
No wonder was she myghte it nat endure.
And whan that Antony saugh that aventure,
"Allas," quod he, "the day that I was borne!
My worshippe in this day thus have I lorne."
And for dispeyr out of his wytte he sterte, 660
And rof hymself anoon thurghout the herte,
Er that he ferther wente out of the place.
Hys wyf, that koude of Cesar have no grace,
To Egipt is fled for drede and for distresse.
But herkeneth, ye that speken of kyndenesse,
Ye men that falsly sweren many an oothe 666
That ye wol dye if that youre love be wroothe,

Here may ye seen of women which a trouthe.
This woful Cleopatre hath mad swich routhe
That ther nys tonge noon that may it telle. 670
But on the morwe she wol no lenger dwelle,
But made hir subtil werkmen make a shryne
Of al the rubees and the stones fyne
In al Egipte that she koude espye,
And putte ful the shryne of spicerye, 675
And let the cors enbawme, and forth she fette
This dede cors, and in the shryne yt shette.
And next the shryne a pitte than dooth she grave,
And al the serpents that she myghte have,
She put hem in that grave, and thus she
    sayde, 680
"Now, love, to whom my sorweful hert
    obeyde
So ferforthely that fro that blisful houre
That I yow swor to ben al frely youre—
I mene yow, Antonius, my knyght—
That never wakyng, in the day or nyght, 685
Ye nere out of myn hertes remembraunce,
For wele or woo, for carole or for daunce;
And in myself this covenaunt made I thoo,
That ryght swich as ye felten, wel or woo,
As ferforth as it in my power lay, 690
Unreprovable unto my wifhood ay,
The same wolde I felen, life or deeth—
And thilke covenant, whil me lasteth breeth,
I wol fulfille; and that shal wel be seene,
Was never unto hir love a trewer queene." 695
    And with that worde, naked, with ful good
    herte,
Among the serpents in the pit she sterte,
And ther she chees to han hir buryinge.
Anoon the neddres gonne hir for to stynge,

---

635 trumpe . . . shete, trumpet, shoot. **636 peynen hem . . . sette on . . . sonne,** i.e., tried to attack with the sun at their back.
637 grisly . . . out gooth, terrifying. Cannon were extended through the gun ports only in time of war; otherwise they were rolled
back and the ports closed. **638 heterly . . . hurtelen,** violently, crash together. **639 the top,** i.e., the high deck of one ship onto the
low deck of the other. **640 grapenel,** grappling hook (to pull the ships together). **641 sheryng-hokes,** sickles (to cut the enemy's
rigging). *renne:* F&c *and.* **642 polax,** battle axe, used in hand-to-hand combat after boarding. *and he:* G *and sche.* **645 orde,** point.
646 rent . . . sithe, tears, scythe. **647 cuppe . . . blithe,** cup of woe, enjoy it (irony). **648 pesen,** peas. Pouring hard peas on them
made the decks so slippery that the attackers could not stand up. **649 lyme,** unslaked (burning) lime to throw in the enemy's
eyes. **652 shent,** destroyed. **653 to-goo,** disperse. **654 purpre,** purple. **655 For strokes,** i.e., because of the blows of battle. **659
lorne,** lost. *day:* T&c *world.* **661 rof,** pierced. Actually, Antony stabbed himself a year later in Alexandria. **668 which a trouthe,**
such fidelity. **669 routhe,** mourning. **676 let the cors,** had the corpse. **678 grave,** dig. **682 ferforthely,** completely. **688 thoo,**
then. **690 ferforth,** much. **691 Unreprovable,** not deserving reproof (i.e., enhancing). **697 in the pit,** this version of the death of
Cleopatra is peculiar to Chaucer and Gower (*Confessio Amantis,* 8.2573ff.).

And she hir deeth receveth with good chere 700
For love of Antony, that was hir so dere.
And this is storial sooth, it is no fable.

Now, er I fynde a man thus trewe and stable,
And wol for love his deeth so frely take,
I prey God let oure hedes nevere ake! 705

Explicit legenda Cleopatre martiris &c.

II

LEGEND OF THISBE

Incipit legenda Tesbe Babilonie, martiris.

At Babiloine whilom fil it thus,
The whiche toun the queen Semyramus
Leet dichen al about, and walles make
Ful hye of harde tiles wel ybake.
Ther were dwellinge in this noble toune 710
Two lordes, which that were of grete renoune,
And woneden so neigh upon a grene
That ther nas but a stoon wal hem bitwene,
As ofte in grette tounes is the wone.
And sooth to seyn, that o man had a sone, 715
Of al that londe oon of the lustieste.
That other had a doghter, the faireste
That esteward in the world was tho dwellinge.
The name of everych gan to other sprynge
By wommen that were neighbores aboute, 720
For in that contree yit, withouten doute,
Maydens ben ykept, for jelosye,
Ful streite lest they diden somme folye.
    This yonge man was cleped Piramus,
And Tesbe hight the maid, Naso seith thus. 725
And thus by report was hir name yshove
That as they wex in age, wex hir love,

And certein, as by reson of hir age,
Ther myghte have ben betwex hem mariage,
But that hir fadres nolde hit nat assente. 730
And boothe in love ylike soore they brente
That noon of al her frendes myghte hit lette,
But prevely somtyme yit they mette
By sleight, and speken somme of hir desire—
As wry the glede and hotter is the fire, 735
Forbede a love, and it is ten so woode.
    This wal, which that bitwix hem bothe stoode,
Was cloven a-twoo right fro the toppe adoune
Of olde tyme of his fundacioun,
But yit this clyft was so narwe and lyte 740
It was nat seene deere ynogh a myte.
But what is that, that love can nat espye?
Ye lovers twoo, if that I shal nat lye,
Ye founden first this litel narwe clyfte,
And with a soune as softe as any shryfte, 745
They lete hir wordes through the clyfte pace,
And tolden while that they stoden in the place
Al hir compleynt of love, and al hir woo,
At every tyme whan they dorste so.

---

702 storial sooth, historic truth. **707 Semyramus,** Semiramis, legendary queen and founder of Babylon. Chaucer's account closely follows Ovid, *Met.* 4.55ff. **712 upon a grene,** on a grassy plot (a very English touch for Babylon—added by Chaucer). **714 wone,** custom. **716 lustieste,** most vigorous (attractive). **718 esteward,** i.e., in the East (Ovid, *"quas Oriens habuit"*). G *That tho was in the lond estward dwellinge.* **720 By wommen,** the touch about the gossiping women is another Chaucerian addition to Ovid's account. **725 Naso,** Ovid; acknowledgment of the source. **726 yshove,** "boosted." **731 brente,** burned. **732 lette,** hinder (pacify). **734 sleight,** trickery. **735 wry . . . glede,** cover, coal. **736 ten so woode,** ten times as frenzied. **738 cloven,** split. **739 olde tyme . . . fundacioun,** i.e., ever since it had been built. **741 deere ynogh a myte,** i.e., even a little bit. **745 softe as shryfte,** a tone as low as when uttering confession—another Chaucerian touch. **746 pace,** pass.

Upon that o syde of the wal stood he,   750
And on that other syde stood Tesbe,
The swoote soun of other to receyve,
And thus her wardeyns wolde they deceyve.
And every day this walle they wolde threte,
And wisshe to God that it were doun ybete.   755
Thus wolde they seyn, "Allas, thou wikked walle,
Through thyn envye thou us lettest alle!
Why nyltow cleve or fallen al a-two?
Or at the leste, but thow woldest so,
Yit woldestow but ones let us meete,   760
Or ones that we mighte kisse sweete,
Than were we covered of our cares colde.
But natheles, yit be we to thee holde
Inasmuche as thou suffrest for to goon
Our wordes through thy lyme and ek thy
         stoon.   765
Yet oghte we with the ben wel apayde."
And whan these idel wordes weren sayde,
The colde wal they wolden kysse of stoon,
And take hir leve, and foorth they wolden goon.
And this was gladly in the evetyde,   770
Or wonder erly lest men it espyde.

   And longe tyme they wroght in this manere
Til on a day, whan Phebus gan to clere,
Aurora with the stremes of hir hete
Had dried up the dewe of herbes wete,   775
Unto this clyfte, as it was wont to be,
Come Pyramus, and after come Tesbe,
And plighten trouthe fully in here faye
That ilke same night to steele aweye,
And to begyle here wardeyns everychone,   780
And forth out of the citee for to gone,
And for the feeldes ben so broode and wyde,
For to meete in o place at o tyde.
They sette mark here metyng sholde be
Ther King Nynus was graven under a
         tree—   785

For olde payens that ydoles heried
Useden thoo in feeldes to ben beried—
And faste by this grave was a welle.
And shortly of this tale for to telle,
This covenaunt was affermed wonder faste.   790
And longe hem thoughte that the sonne laste,
That hit nere goon under the see adoune.

   This Tesbe hath so greete affeccioun,
And so grete lykynge Piramus to see,
That whan she seigh hir tyme mighte bee,   795
At night she stal awey ful prevely
With her face ywimpled subtilly,
For al hir frendes, for to save hir trouthe,
She hath forsake. Allas, and that is routhe
That ever woman wolde be so trewe   800
To trusten man but she the bet him knewe!
And to the tree she gooth a ful goode paas,
For love made her so hardy in this caas,
And by the welle adown she gan hir dresse.
Allas, than comith a wilde leonesse   805
Out of the woode, withouten more arreste,
With blody mouthe of strangeling of a beste,
To drynken of the welle ther as she sat.
And whan that Tesbe had espyed that,
She ryst hir up with a ful drery herte,   810
And in a cave with dredful foot she sterte,
For by the moone she saugh hit wel withalle.
And as she ran, hir wimpel leet she falle,
And tooke noon hede, so soore she was awhaped,
And eke so glad of that she was escaped.   815
And thus she sytte and darketh wonder stille.
Whan that this leonesse hath dronke hir fille,
Aboute the welle gan she for to wynde,
And ryght anoon the wimpel gan she fynde,
And with hir blody mouth hit al to-rente.   820
Whan this was don, no lenger she ne stente,
But to the woode hir wey than hath she nome.
   And at the laste, this Piramus is come;

---

752 **swoote**, gentle (sweet). 754 **threte**, threaten. 757 **us lettest alle**, i.e., deprive us of everything. 762 **covered**, recovered. 763 **holde**, indebted (beholden). 766 **wel apayde**, well pleased. 770 **gladly**, preferably. *Alle:* P&c *And.* 773–74 **Phebus . . . Aurora**, the sun, the dawn; their functions are here reversed. 778 **plighten trouthe . . . here faye**, promised (plighted troth), their faith. 785 **Nynus**, husband of Semiramis and legendary founder of Nineveh. **graven**, buried. 786 **payens . . . heried**, pagans, worshiped. 787 **Useden**, were accustomed, i.e., instead of in consecrated church grounds. 788 **welle**, spring. 792 **nere**, would not. F *goon* om. 794 *And:* F *Had.* 798 **trouthe**, promise (honor). 799 **routhe**, pity. 802 **goode paas**, quickly. 803 **hardy**, brave. 804 **dresse**, arrange (i.e., sit). 807 **of strangeling**, from killing (strangling). 810 **drery**, terrified. 811 **dredful**, fearful. 813 **wimpel**, head shawl. 814 **awhaped**, confounded (dazed). 815 F *of* om. 816 **darketh**, lies hidden. 821 **stente**, stayed. 822 **nome**, taken.

But al to longe, allas, at home was hee.
The moone shoon; men mighte wel ysee;   825
And in his wey, as that he come ful faste,
His eighen to the grounde adoun he caste,
And in the sonde, as he beheld adoune,
He seigh the steppes broode of a leoune,
And in his herte he sodeinly agroos,   830
And pale he wex, therwith his heer aroos.
And neer he come and found the wimpel torne.
"Allas," quod he, "the day that I was borne!
This oo nyght wole us lovers boothe sle.
How shulde I axen mercy of Tesbe   835
Whan I am he that have yow slain, allas?
My bydding hath yow slain, as in this caas.
Allas, to bidde a woman goon by nyghte
In place theras peril fallen myghte,
And I so slowe! Allas I ne hadde be   840
Here in this place a furlongwey or ye!
Now what leoun that be in this foreste,
My body mote he renden, or what beste
That wilde is, gnawen mote he now myn herte."
And with that worde he to the wimpel sterte,   845
And kyste hit ofte, and weep on it ful sore,
And seyde, "Wimpel, allas, ther nys no more
But thou shalt feele as wel the blod of me,
As thou hast felt the bledyng of Tesbe."   849
And with that worde he smot him to the herte.
The blood out of the wounde as brode sterte
As water whan the conduyt broken is.

    Now Tesbe, which that wyste nat of this,
But sytting in hir drede, she thoghte thus,
"If hit so falle that my Piramus   855
Be comen hider, and may me nat fynde,
He may me holden fals and ek unkynde."
And out she comith and after him gan espien
Booth with hir hert and with hir eighen,
And thoghte, "I wol him tellen of my drede 860
Booth of the leonesse and al my dede."
And at the laste hir love than hath she founde
Betyng with his helis on the grounde,

Al blody; and therwithal abak she sterte,
And lyke the wawes quappe gan her herte,   865
And pale as box she wex, and in a throwe
Avised hir, and gan him wel to knowe,
That it was Piramus, hir herte dere.
Who koude write whiche a dedely chere
Hath Tesbe now, and how hir heer she rente,   870
And how she gan hirselve to turmente,
And how she lyth and swowneth on the grounde,
And how she wepe of teres ful his wounde,
How medeleth she his blood with hir
          compleynte,
And with his blood hirselven gan she peynte,   875
How clippeth she the dede cors, allas!
How dooth this woful Tesbe in this cas;
How kysseth she his frosty mouth so colde!
"Who hath doon this, and who hath ben so bolde
To sleen my leef? O spek, my Piramus!   880
I am thi Tesbe, that thee calleth thus!"
And therwithal she lyfteth up his heed.

    This woful man, that was nat fully deed,
Whan that he herd the name of Tesbe crien,
On hir he caste his hevy dedely eyen,   885
And doune agayn, and yeldeth up the gooste.
Tesbe rist uppe withouten noyse or booste,
And saugh hir wimpel and his empty shethe,
And eke his swerd that him hath doon to dethe.
Than spak she thus, "My woful hand,"
          quod she,   890
"Is strong ynogh in swiche a werk to me,
For love shal yive me strengthe and hardynesse
To make my wounde large ynogh, I gesse.
I wol the folowen deed, and I wol be
Felawe and cause eke of thy deeth," quod she.   895
"And thogh that nothing save the deth oonly
Myghte the fro me departe trewely,
Thou shalt noo more now departe fro me
Than fro the deth, for I wol goo with the!
And now, ye wrecched jelous fadres oure,   900
We that weren whilom children youre,

---

828 beheld, looked. **830 agroos,** shivered. **834 oo nyght,** one (same) night. **837 bydding,** entreaty. **841 furlongwey or,** a furlong (220 yards, but a measure of time) before. **842 what leoun,** whatever lion. **843 mote,** must. F *body mote rente.* **855** F *hit* om. **861 dede,** deed, i.e., what I did. **865 quappe,** beat (palpitate). **866 box . . . throwe,** boxwood, moment. F&c *she was, in a throwe.* **867 Avised hir,** i.e., thought about it. **876 clippeth,** embraces. **882** *she:* G&c *he.* **885 dedely,** dying. **887 booste,** boast, the sort of pronouncement epic heroes make before undertaking difficult deeds, but ll. 890ff. is such a "boast." *noyse or:* G *ony.* **892 hardynesse,** courage. **895 Felawe . . . eke,** companion, also. **897 departe,** separate. **901 whilom,** formerly.

We prayen yow, withouten more envye,
That in oo grave yfere we moten lye,
Syn love hath brought us to this pitous
   ende.
And ryghtwis God to every lover sende, 905
That loveth trewely, more prosperite
Than ever hadde Piramus and Tesbe!
And lat noo gentil woman hir assure
To putten hir in swiche an aventure.
But God forbede but a woman kan 910
Ben as trewe and lovyng as a man!
And, for my part, I shal anoon it kythe."

And with that worde, his swerd she took as
   swythe,
That warme was of hir loves blood and hoote,
And to the herte she hirselven smoote. 915
   And thus ar Tesbe and Piramus agoo.
Of trewe men I fynde but fewe moo
In al my bookes save this Piramus,
And therfor have I spoken of him thus.
For hit is deyntee to us men to fynde 920
A man that kan in love be trewe and kynde.
Here may ye seen, what lover so he be,
A woman dar and kan as wel as he.

Explicit legenda Tesbe &c.

III

LEGEND OF DIDO

Incipit legenda Didonis martiris, Cartaginis regine.

Glorie and honour, Virgile Mantoan,
Be to thy name, and I shal, as I kan, 925
Folow thy lanterne, as thou gost byforn,
How Eneas to Dido was forsworn.
In thyne *Eneyd* and Naso wol I take
The tenour and the grete effectes make.
   Whan Troye broght was to destruccion 930
By Grekes sleight, and namely by Synon,
Feynyng the hors offred unto Mynerve,
Thurgh which that many a Troian moste
   sterve;
And Ector had after his deeth appered,
And fire so woode it mighte nat ben stered 935

In al the noble tour of Ilion,
That of the citee was the cheef dungeon;
And al the contree was so lowe ybroghte,
And Priamus the king fordoon and noghte;
And Eneas was charged by Venus 940
To fleen awey, he tooke Ascanius,
That was his sone, in his right hande and fledde,
And on his bakke he baar and with him ledde
His olde fader cleped Anchises,
And by the weye his wyf Creusa he lees. 945
And mochel sorwe hadde he in his mynde
Er that he koude his felawshippe fynde.
But at the last, whan he hadde hem founde,

903 yfere, together; om. in F. **908 hir assure**, assume (be so bold). **909 aventure**, chance. **912 kythe**, display. **913 swythe**, quickly. **920 deyntee**, pleasing. **924 Virgile Mantoan**, Mantua (in northern Italy) was Virgil's birthplace. This legend is based largely on the *Aeneid*, Bks. 1–4, but the character of Dido is influenced by Ovid's version of the story in the *Heroides* 8, as retold in Bk. 1 of *HF*. **927 forsworn**, swore falsely. **928 Naso**, Ovid, see above. **929 tenour . . . grete effectes make**, tenor (meaning), versify the main events. **931 namely**, especially. **932 Feynyng**, pretending. Sinon allowed himself to be taken prisoner by the Trojans, and then persuaded them to take the wooden horse within the walls as an atonement to Minerva, *Aeneid* 2.57ff. **933 sterve**, die. **934 Ector . . . appered**, the ghost of Hector appeared to Aeneas and told him to flee, *Aeneid* 2.268ff. **935 stered**, controlled. **936 Ilion**, originally an alternate name for Troy, but taken by medieval authors as the name of the Trojan citadel. **945 lees**, lost, *Aeneid* 2.738. **947 felawshippe**, companions.

He made him redy in a certeyn stounde,
And to the see ful faste he gan him hye,   950
And sayleth forth with al his companye
Towarde Itayle, as wolde destenee.
But of his aventures in the see
Nys nat to purpos for to speke of here,
For hit acordeth nat to my matere.   955
But, as I seyde, of him and of Dydo
Shal be my tale, til that I have do.

So longe he saylled in the salte see
Til in Lybye unnethe arryved he
With shippes seven and with no more
              navye,   960
And glad was he to londe for to hye,
So was he with the tempest al to-shake.
And whan that he the havene had ytake,
He had a knight was called Achates,
And him of al his felawshippe he ches   965
To goon with him the contree for t'espye;
He toke with him na more companye.
But forth they goon, and lafte his shippes ride,
His fere and he, withouten any gyde.
So longe he walketh in this wildernesse   970
Til at the laste he mette an hunteresse.
A bowe in honde and arwes hadde she,
Her clothes knytte were unto the knee,
But she was yit the fairest creature
That ever was yformed by nature.   975
And Eneas and Achates she grette,
And thus she to hem spak whan she hem mette:
"Sawe ye," quod she, "as ye han walked wide,
Any of my sustren walke yow besyde,
With any wilde boor or other beste   980
That they han hunted to in this foreste,
Ytukked up, with arwes in here cas?"
"Nay, soothly, lady," quod this Eneas,
"But by thy beaute, as hit thynketh me,
Thou myghtest never erthely woman be,   985
But Phebus suster artow, as I gesse.
And if so be that thou be a goddesse,
Have mercy on our labour and our woo."
"I nam no goddesse, soothely," quod she thoo,

"For maydens walken in this contree here   990
With arwes and with bowe in this manere.
This is the regne of Libie ther ye been,
Of which that Dido lady is and queen"—
And shortly tolde al the occasioun
Why Dido come into that regioun   995
Of which as now me lusteth nat to ryme;
It nedeth nat; it nere but los of tyme.
For this is al and somme, it was Venus,
His owene moder, that spake with him thus;
And to Cartage she bad he sholde him
              dighte,   1000
And vanyshed anoon out of his sighte.

I koude folwe word for worde Virgile,
But it wolde lasten al to longe a while.

This noble queen, that cleped was Dido,
That whilom was the wife of Sitheo,   1005
That fairer was than the bryghte sonne,
This noble toun of Cartage hath begonne,
In which she regneth in so greete honoure,
That she was holde of alle quenes floure,
Of gentilesse, of fredom, of beautee,   1010
That wel was him that might hir oones see;
Of kynges and of lordes so desired
That al the world hir beaute hadde yfired,
She stood so wel in every wyghtes grace.

Whan Eneas was come unto that place,   1015
Unto the maister temple of al the toun
Ther Dido was in her devocioun,
Ful prively his wey than hath he nome.
Whan he was in the large temple come;
I kan nat seyn if that hit be possible,   1020
But Venus hadde him maked invisible—
Thus seith the book, withouten any les.
And whan this Eneas and Achates
Hadden in this temple been over alle,
Than founde they depeynted on a walle,   1025
How Troye and al the lond destrued was.
"Allas that I was born," quod Eneas,
"Throughout the world our shame is kid so
              wide,
Now it is peynted upon every side.

---

949 **stounde**, time. 959 **Lybye unnethe**, i.e., he arrived in Libya (North Africa) with barely seven ships. **960–61** Lines omitted in F&c. 966 F *to spye*. 969 **fere**, companion. 973 *knytte:* G&c *cutte.* 982 **Ytukked up**, with robes tucked up. 984 **thynketh me**, seems to me. 1002 F *word by worde.* 1005 **whilom**, formerly. 1010 **fredom**, magnanimity. 1013 **yfired**, fired (aroused). 1016 **maister**, principal. 1017 **Ther**, to where. 1018 **nome**, taken. 1019 F *large* om. 1022 **les**, lies. At *Aeneid* 1.412 Venus covers Aeneas and Achates with a cloud. 1024 **over alle**, everywhere. 1028 **kid**, known.

We that weren in prosperitee 1030
Be now disclaundred, and in swiche degre!
No lenger for to lyven I ne kepe."
And, with that worde, he braste out for to wepe
So tendrely that routhe hit was to seene.
This fresshe lady of the citee queene 1035
Stoode in the temple in hir estaat royalle,
So richely and eke so fair withalle,
So yong, so lusty, with her eighen glade,
That if that God that hevene and erthe made
Wolde han a love for beaute and goodenesse, 1040
And womanhode, and trouthe and
    seemlynesse,
Whom sholde he loven but this lady swete?
There nys no womman to him half so mete.

    Fortune, that hath the worlde in governaunce,
Hath sodeynly broght in so newe a chaunce 1045
That never was ther yit so fremd a cas.
For al the companye of Eneas,
Which that he wende han loren in the see,
Aryved is noght fer fro that citee,
For which the grettest of his lordes some 1050
By aventure ben to the citee come,
Unto that same temple, for to seke
The queene, and of hir socour hir beseke,
Swich renown was ther spronge of hir
    goodenesse.
And whan they had told al here distresse, 1055
And al here tempest and here harde cas,
Unto the queene appered Eneas
And openly beknew that hit was hee.
Who hadde joye thanne but his menee,
That hadden founde here lord, here
    governour? 1060
    The queene saw they dide him swich honour,
And had herd ofte of Eneas er thoo,
And in her herte she hadde routhe and woo
That ever swich a noble man as hee
Shal been dishereted in swich degree, 1065
And sawgh the man, that he was lyke a knyghte,
And suffisaunt of persone and of mighte,

And lyke to ben a verray gentil man,
And wel his wordes he besette kan,
And hadde a noble visage for the nones, 1070
And formed wel of brawnes and of bones—
For after Venus hadde he swich fairnesse
That no man myght be half so fair, I gesse—
And wel a lorde him semed for to be.
And for he was a straunger, somwhat she 1075
Lyked him the bette, as God do boote,
To somme folk ofte newe thing is swoote.
Anoon hir herte hath pitee of his woo,
And with that pitee love come in alsoo.
And thus for pitee and for gentilesse, 1080
Refresshed mote he been of his distresse.
She seyde, certes, that she sory was
That he hath had swich peril and swich cas,
And in hir frendely speche, in this manere
She to him spak, and seide as ye may here: 1085
    "Be ye nat Venus sone and Anchises?
In good feyth, al the worshippe and encres
That I may goodly doon yow, ye shal have.
Youre shippes and your meynee shal I save."
And many a gentil word she spak him to, 1090
And comaunded hir messageres go
The same day, withouten any faylle,
His shippes for to seke, and hem vitaylle.
Ful many a beste she to the shippes sente,
And with the wyn she gan hem to presente, 1095
And to hir royall paleys she hir spedde,
And Eneas alwey with hir she ledde.
What nedeth yow the feste to discryve?
He never beter at ease was in his lyve.
Ful was the feste of deyntees and richesse, 1100
Of instruments, of song, and of gladnesse,
And many an amorous lokyng and devys.
This Eneas is come to paradys
Out of the swolowe of helle, and thus in joye
Remembreth him of his estaat in Troye. 1105
To daunsyng chambres ful of parements,
Of riche beddes, and of ornaments,
This Eneas is ladde after the mete.

1031 **in swiche**, to such a. 1032 **kepe**, care. 1034 **routhe**, pity. 1038 **lusty**, gay. 1041 **trouthe**, sincerity (troth). 1043 **mete**, suitable. 1046 **fremd**, strange. F *in cas*. 1048 **loren**, lost. 1053 **beseke**, beseech. 1058 **beknew**, acknowledged. 1059 **menee**, retinue. 1062 **thoo** then. 1063 **routhe ... woo**, pity, sorrow. F *she hadde* om. 1066 F *that he* om. 1068 **lyke to ... verray gentil**, likely to, true noble. 1071 **brawnes**, muscles. 1076 **do boote**, give help (Lord help us!). 1077 **swoote**, sweet. 1087 **worshippe ... encres**, honor, assistance. 1093 **vitaylle**, provision (vb.). 1104 **swolowe**, mouth or gulf (ME had both meanings). 1106 **parements**, hangings. 1107 *ornaments:* F&c *pavements*.

And with the queene whan that he hadde sete,
And spices parted, and the wyn agon,   1110
Unto his chambres was he lad anon
To take his ease and for to have his reste,
With al his folk, to doon what so hem leste.

Ther nas coursere wel ybrydled noon,
Ne stede for the justyng wel to goon,   1115
Ne large palfrey esy for the nones,
Ne juwel fretted ful of riche stones,
Ne sakkes ful of gold, of large wyghte,
Ne rubee noon that shyneth by nyghte,
Ne gentil hawteyn faucon heroneer,   1120
Ne hound for hert or wilde boor or deer,
Ne coupe of golde with floryns newe ybete,
That in the lond of Lybye may ben gete,
That Dido ne hath hit Eneas ysente.
And al is payed, what that he hath spente.   1125
Thus kan this noble queene hir gestes calle,
As she that kan in fredom passen alle.

Eneas soothly eke, withouten les,
Hath sent unto his shippe by Achates
After his sone, and after ryche thynges,   1130
Both ceptre, clothes, broches, and eke rynges,
Somme for to were, and somme for to presente
To hir that al thise noble thynges him sente;
And bad his sone, how that he sholde make
The presentyng, and to the queene hit
      take.   1135
Repeyred is this Achates agayne,
And Eneas ful blysful is and fayne
To seen his yonge sone Ascanius.
But natheles our autour telleth us
That Cupido, that is the god of love,   1140
At preyere of his moder, hye above,
Hadde the liknes of the childe ytake,
This noble queene enamoured to make
On Eneas—but as of that scripture,
Be as be may; I make of hit no cure.   1145

But sooth is this, the queene hath mad swich
      chere
Unto this child that wonder is to here,
And of the present that his fader sente
She thanked him ful ofte, in good entente.

Thus is this queene in plesaunce and in
      joye,   1150
With al this newe lusty folk of Troye.
And of the dedes hath she moore enquered
Of Eneas, and al the story lered
Of Troye; and al the longe day they twey
Entendeden to speke and for to pley,   1155
Of which ther gan to breden swich a fire
That sely Dido hath now swich desire
With Eneas, her newe gest, to dele
That she hath loste hir hewe and eke hir hele.
Now to th'effect, now to the fruyt of al,   1160
Why I have told this story, and tellen shal.

Thus I bygynne: hit fil upon a nyght,
Whan that the mone up-reyseth hath hir light,
This noble queene unto hir reste wente.
She siketh soore, and gan hirself turmente.   1165
She waketh, walweth, maketh many a brayde,
As doon thise loveres, as I have herd sayde.
And at the laste unto her suster Anne
She made her mone, and ryght thus spak she
      thanne.
"Now, dere suster myn, what may it be   1170
That me agasteth in my dreme?" quod she.
"This ilke Troian is so in my thoghte,
For that me thinketh he is so wel ywroghte,
And eke so likly for to ben a man,
And therwithal soo mykel good he kan,   1175
That al my love and lyf lyth in his cure.
Have ye nat herd him telle his aventure?
Now certes, Anne, if that ye rede it me,
I wolde fayn to him ywedded be—
This is th'effect; what sholde I more seye?   1180

1110 spices parted, spices departed (taken away). Wine and spices were served as a collation before retiring, cf. *CT* v.291. **1112** G *For hise ese and for to take hise reste.* **1120 hawteyn ... heroneer,** proud, for capturing herons. **1122 ybete,** struck (stamped). **1126** *noble,* Skeat's amendment; all authorities *honourable.* **calle,** i.e., treat. **1127 fredom,** generosity. **1128 withouten les,** without lies (i.e., truly). **1136 Repeyred,** returned. **1137 fayne,** happy. **1139** F&c *For to him yt was reported thus.* **1145 cure,** care. **1146 mad ... chere,** was so hospitable. **1151 newe lusty,** newly arrived, gay (engaging). **1153 lered,** learned. **1155 Entendeden,** i.e., were engaged in (attended). **1156 breden,** develop (breed). **1157 sely,** the usual spectrum from OE fortunate to Mod.E foolish. **1159 hewe ... hele,** color, health—the conventional signs of lovesickness. **1160 th'effect,** the outcome. **1165 siketh,** sighs. **1166 walweth ... brayde,** tosses, start. G *Sche waylith and sche makith.* **1171 agasteth,** frightens. **1175 kan,** knows. **1176 cure,** care. **1178 rede,** advise.

In him lith alle to do me lyve or deye."

Hir suster Anne, as she that kouth hir goode,
Seyde as hir thought, and somdel hit withstoode.
But herof was so longe a sermonynge,
Hit were to long to make rehersynge. 1185
But finally hit may nat be withstonde.
Love wol love—for no wyght wol hit wonde.

The dawenyng upryst out of the see;
This amorous queene chargeth hir meynee
The nettes dresse, and speres brode and kene. 1190
An huntyng wol this lusty fresshe quene,
So priketh hir this newe joly woo.
To hors is al hir lusty folke ygoo.
Unto the court the houndes ben ybroughte,
And upon coursers swyfte as any thoughte 1195
Hir yonge knyghtes hoven al aboute,
And of hir women eke an huge route.
Upon a thikke palfrey, paper whyt,
With sadel rede enbroudet with delyt,
Of gold the barres up-enbossed heighe, 1200
Sitte Dido al in gold and perrey wreighe.
And she is faire as is the brighte morwe
That heeleth seke folk of nyghtes sorwe.
Upon a courser startlyng as the fire—
Men mighte turne him with a lytel wire— 1205
Sitte Eneas, lyke Phebus to devyse,
So was he fressh arayed in hys wyse.
The fomy bridel with the bitte of golde
Governeth he right as himself hath wolde.
And foorth this noble quene, this lady ryde 1210
On hunting, with this Troian by hir syde.

The herd of hertes founden is anoon,
With "Hey! Goo bet! Prik thou! Lat goon,
lat goon!
Why nyl the leoun comen, or the bere,

That I mighte him ones meten with this
spere?" 1215
Thus seyn thise yonge folk, and up they kille
These hertes wilde, and han hem at here wille.

Among al this to romblen gan the hevene;
The thonder rored with a grisly stevene;
Doune come the rain with haile and sleet
so faste, 1220
With hevenes fire, that hit so sore agaste
This noble quene, and also hir meynee,
That yche of hem was glad awey to flee.
And shortly, fro the tempest hir to save,
She fled hirself into a lytel cave— 1225
And with hir went this Eneas also.
I not with hem yf ther went any moo;
The auctour maketh of hit no mencioun.
And here began the depe affeccioun
Betwix hem two. This was the firste morwe 1230
Of here gladnesse, and gynnyng of hir sorwe.
For ther hath Eneas ykneled soo,
And told hir al his herte and al his woo,
And swore so depe to hir to be trewe
For wele or woo and chaunge for noo newe, 1235
And as a fals lover so wel kan pleyne,
That sely Dido rewed on his peyne
And tok hym for housbond and became his wyf
For evermo while that hem laste lyf.
And after this, whan that the tempest stente, 1240
With myrth out as they comen, home they
wente.

The wikked fame up roos, and that anoon,
How Eneas hath with the queene ygoon
Into the cave; and demed as hem liste.
And whan the kynge that Yarbas hight hit
wiste, 1245

1182 **kouth hir goode,** i.e., knew Dido's best course. Chaucer cuts short 22 lines in the *Aeneid* 4.31–53. 1187 **wonde,** desist. 1189 **chargeth . . . meynee,** orders, retainers. 1190 **nettes dresse,** (hunting) nets to prepare. 1196 **hoven,** hover. F&c *heven.* 1197 **route,** company. 1198 **thikke palfrey,** sturdy riding horse. **paper whyt,** white as paper, an unusual figure for this early period. 1199 **enbroudet with delyt,** delightfully embroidered. 1200 **barres,** ornamental metal bands on saddles, harness, etc. 1201 **perrey wreighe,** jewels covered. 1202 **morwe,** morning. 1204 **startlyng,** moving suddenly, quickly. 1205 **lytel wire,** delicate bridle. 1206 **Phebus . . . devyse,** god of the sun, describe. 1209 **wolde,** desired, would (i.e., as he wished). 1210 F *noble* om. T *quene thus lat I ryde.* 1213 **Goo bet! Prik thou! Lat goon.** go better (faster), spur on, let go (the dogs). 1216–17 **kille . . . hertes,** hart-hunting was a familiar figure for the amorous chase in medieval literature (hart-heart; cf. *BD* 350n.), and here foreshadows the liaison between Aeneas and Dido. **hertes:** G *bestes.* 1218 **Among,** i.e., meanwhile. 1219 **grisly stevene,** frightening voice. 1221 **hit:** F *ys.* 1222 **meynee,** retinue. 1227 **not,** don't know. 1237 **sely . . . rewed,** foolish (innocent), had pity. 1240 **stente,** stopped. 1242 **wikked fame,** scandal. In the *Aeneid* at this point (4.173ff.), Virgil has the description of Fame which Chaucer had used in *HF* 1360ff. 1244 **demed . . . liste,** concluded, wished. 1245 **Yarbas hight,** was named Yarbas, *Aeneid* 4.196.

As he that had hir loved ever his lyf,
And wowed hir to have hir to his wyf,
Swich sorowe as he hath maked, and swich
    chere,
Hit is a rewthe and pitee for to here.
But as in love al day hit happeth soo,   1250
That oon shal lawghen at anothers woo,
Now lawgheth Eneas and is in joye,
And more riches than ever was in Troye.
    O sely wemen, ful of innocence,
Ful of pitee and trouthe and conscience,   1255
What maked yow to men to trusten soo?
Have ye suche rewthe upon here feyned woo,
And han suche ensamples olde yow biforne?
Se ye nat al how they ben forsworne?
Where se ye oon that he ne hath laft his leef,   1260
Or ben unkynde, or don hir som myscheef,
Or pilled hir, or bosted of his dede?
Ye may as wel hit seen as ye may rede.
Tak hede now of this grete gentilman,
This Troian, that so wel hir plesen kan,   1265
That feyneth him so trewe and obeysinge,
So gentil and so privy of his doynge,
And kan so wel doon al his obeysaunces,
And waiten hir at festes and at daunces,
And whan she gooth to temple and home
    agayne,   1270
And fasten til he hath his lady a sayne,
And beren in his devyses for hir sake—
Wot I nat what—and songes wolde he make,
Justen, and doon of armes many thynges,
Send hir lettres, tokens, broches, rynges—   1275
Now herkneth how he shal his lady serve!
Ther as he was in peril for to sterve
For hunger and for myscheef in the see,
And desolat, and fledde fro his contree,
And al his folk with tempeste al to-driven,   1280
She hath hir body and eke hir reame yiven

Into his hand, ther as she myghte have bene
Of other lond than of Cartage a quene,
And lyved in joye ynogh. What wolde ye more?
This Eneas that hath thus depe yswore   1285
Is wery of his craft within a throwe,
The hoote ernest is al over-blowe.
And prively he dooth his shippes dyghte,
And shapeth him to steele awey by nighte.
    This Dido hath suspecioun of thys,   1290
And thoughte wel that hit was al amys,
For in his bed he lyth anyght and siketh.
She asketh him anoon what him mysliketh—
"My dere hert, which that I love mooste?"
    "Certes," quod he, "thys myght my fadres
    gooste   1295
Hath in my sleep so sore me turmented,
And eke Mercure his message hath presented,
That nedes to the conquest of Itayle
My destany is soone for to sayle—
For whiche, methinketh, brosten is myn
    herte!"   1300
Therwith his fals teeres out they sterte,
And taketh hir within his armes twoo.
    "Is that in ernest?" quod she. "Wil ye soo?
Have ye nat sworn to wife me to take?
Alas, what womman wol ye of me make?   1305
I am a gentilwoman and a queen!
Ye wol nat fro your wife thus foule fleen!
That I was borne, allas, what shal I do?"
    To telle in short, this noble queen Dido,
She seketh halwes and dooth sacrifise,   1310
She kneleth, crieth that routhe is to devyse,
Conjureth him, and profreth him to bee
His thral, his servant in the lest degree;
She falleth him to foote and swowneth there
Dischevely with hir bryght gilte here,   1315
And seith, "Have mercy! Let me with yow ryde!
These lordes which that wonien me besyde

1246 **ever,** i.e., all. 1248 **chere,** expression. 1249 **rewthe,** pity. 1254 **sely,** foolish. F *woman.* 1257 **rewthe . . . feyned,** pity, pretended. 1259 **forsworne,** sworn falsely. 1260 **leef,** love. 1261 T&c *her shame or gryef.* 1262 **pilled,** robbed. 1266 **obeysinge,** obedient. 1267 **privy,** secret. 1268 **obeysaunces,** homages. 1269 **waiten hir,** wait (on) her. 1271 **sayne,** seen. 1272 **beren in his devyses,** i.e., select his fashion in dress. 1277 **sterve,** die. 1286 **throwe,** space of time. 1288 **dyghte,** prepared. 1289 **shapeth him,** prepared. 1292 **siketh,** sighs. 1295 **fadres gooste,** cf. *Aeneid* 4.351ff., but Chaucer (given his context) treats this divine admonition merely as a restless lover's excuse. 1306 **gentilwoman and a queen,** the pathetic feminine appeal of this passage is Chaucer's transformation of Virgil's vengeful, imperious queen. 1310 **halwes,** shrines. 1311 **routhe . . . devyse,** pity, describe. 1312 **profreth,** offers. 1313 G *leste gre.* 1315 **Dischevely,** with hair disordered. 1317 **wonien,** live.

Wol me destroien oonly for youre sake.
And ye wol me now to wife take,
As ye han sworn, than wol I yive yow leve   1320
To sleen me with your swerd now soone at eve!
For than shal I yet dien as your wife.
I am with childe, and yive my childe his lyfe!
Mercy, lord, have pitee in youre thought!"
But al this thing avayleth hir ryght nought,   1325
For on a nyght sleping he let hir lye,
And staal awey unto his companye,
And as a traytour forthe he gan to saile
Toward the large contree of Itayle.
And thus he lefte Dido in woo and pyne,   1330
And wedded ther a lady highte Lavyne.

    A cloth he lefte, and eke his swerd stondyng,
Whan he fro Dido staal in her sleping,
Ryght at hir beddes hed, so gan he hye,
Whan that he staal awey to his navye.   1335
Which cloth, whan sely Dido gan awake,
She hath hit kyst ful ofte for hys sake,
And seyde, "O cloth, while Jupiter hit leste,
Take now my soule, unbind me of this
    unreste!
I have fulfilled of Fortune al the cours."   1340
And thus, allas, withouten hys socours,
Twenty tyme yswowned hath she thanne.

And whan that she unto her suster Anne
Compleyned had, of which I may nat write—
So grete a routhe I have hit for t'endite—   1345
And bad hir noryce and hir suster goon
To fecchen fire and other thinges anoon,
And seyde that she wolde sacrifyee,
And whan she myght hir tyme wel espyee,
Upon the fire of sacrifice she sterte,   1350
And with his swerd she roof hir to the herte.

    But, as myn auctour seyth, yit thus she seyde,
Or she was hurt, beforne or she deyde,
She wroot a lettre anoon, that thus biganne:
"Ryght so," quod she, "as that the white
    swanne   1355
Ayenst his deeth begynneth for to synge,
Ryght so to yow make I my compleynynge.
Nat that I trowe to geten yow agayn,
For wel I woot that hit is al in vayn,
Syn that the goddes ben contraire to me.   1360
But syn my name is lost thurgh yow," quod she,
"I may wel lese a word on yow, or letter,
Al be it that I shal be never the better—
For thilke wynd that blew your shipe away,
The same wind hath blowe away your fay."

    But whoso wol al this letter have in mynde,
Rede Ovyde, and in him he shal hit fynde.   1367

Explicit legenda Didonis martiris, Cartaginis regine.

1319 And ye wol, and if you will. **1330** F&c *And thus hath he.* G *Thus hath he.* **1331 highte,** named. **1332 A cloth,** in *Aeneid* 4.648 his Trojan garments. **1334 gan he hye,** i.e., he was in such haste. **1338 while . . . leste,** i.e., when it pleases. **1341 hys socours,** i.e., Aeneas' help (attention). **1345 routhe,** pity. **1353 Or,** before. **1354 lettre,** the letter is based on the first eight lines of the 7th Epistle of Ovid's *Heroides*. **1356 Ayenst,** anticipating. **1358 trowe,** believe (I will). **1365 fay,** faith.

IV

LEGEND OF HYPSIPYLE AND MEDEA

Incipit legenda Ysiphile et Medee, martirum.

Legend of Hypsipyle

Thou roote of fals lovers, Duke Jasoun,
Thou slye devourer and confusyoun
Of gentilwomen, tender creatures, 1370
Thou madest thy reclaimyng and thy lures
To ladies of thy staately aparaunce,
And of thy wordes farsed with plesaunce,
And of thy feyned trouthe and thy manere,
With thyne obeysaunce and humble chere, 1375
And with thy counterfeted peyn and woo.
Ther oother falsen oon, thow falsest twoo!
O, ofte swore thou that thou woldest deye
For love, whan thou ne feltest maladeye
Save foul delyt, which that thou callest love. 1380
If that I lyve, thy name shal be shove
In Englyssh, that thy sekte shal be knowe!
Have at thee, Jason, now thyn horn is blowe!
But certes, it is both rowth and woo
That love with fals lovers werketh soo, 1385
For they shal have wel better and gretter chere
Than he that hath bought love ful dere,
Or had in armes many a blody box.
For ever as tendre a capoun eteth the fox,
Though he be fals and hath the foule
betrayed, 1390
As shal the goodman that therfor hath
payed—
Allethof he have to the capoun skille and
ryghte,

The false fox wil have his part at nyght.
On Jasoun this ensample is wel yseene
By Isiphile and Medea the queene. 1395
In Tessalye, as Guido telleth us,
Ther was a kyng that highte Pelleus,
That had a brother which that hight Eson,
And whan for age he myghte unnethes gon,
He yaf to Pelleus the governynge 1400
Of al his regne, and made him lorde and kynge,
Of which Eson this Jasoun geten was,
That in his tyme in al that land ther nas
Nat suche a famous kynght of gentilesse,
Of fredome, and of strengthe and lustynesse. 1405
After his fader deeth, he bare him soo
That there nas noon that lyste ben his foo,
But dide him al honour and companye;
Of which this Pelleus hath grete envye,
Imagynyng that Jasoun myghte be 1410
Enhaunced so and put in suche degre
With love of lordes of his regioun,
That from his regne he may be put adoun.
And in his witte anyghte compassed he
How Jasoun myghte best destroyed be, 1415
Withoute sclaunder of his compassemente.
And at the laste he took avysemente
To senden him into some fer contree
Ther as this Jasoun may distroyed be.
This was his witte, al made he to Jasoun 1420
Grete chere of love and of affeccioun,
For drede leste his lordes hit espyede.

1370 F&c *gentil creatures*: G *tendere wemen, gentil*. This legend depends most heavily upon Guido delle Colonne's *Historia Troiana*, but also Ovid, *Met.* 7 and *Heroides* 6 and 12. **1371 reclaimyng . . . lures,** enticement (calling back of a hawk). **1373 farsed,** stuffed. **1374 feyned,** pretended. **1375 obeysaunce . . . chere,** homage, expression. **1377 Ther,** where. **1381 shove,** i.e., made prominent. **1382 sekte,** suit leading to the legal process of outlawry. F *sleighte*. **1383 horn is blowe,** reference to the horn blowing which accompanied the "hue and cry" by which outlawry was proclaimed. **1384 rowth,** pity. **1386 G** *better love and chere*. **1388 box,** buffet. **1390 foule,** fowl. **1392 skille,** logic. **1396** *Guido* in G: F&c *Ovyde,* but cf. l. 1464. **1397** *kyng*: F&c *knyght*. **1399 unnethes gon,** hardly walk. **1402 geten,** begotten. **1405 fredome . . . lustynesse,** generosity, high spirits. **1414 compassed,** schemed. **1417 took avysemente,** i.e., decided. **1420 al made,** although he made.

So felle hit so, as fame renneth wyde,
Ther was suche tidynge overalle and suche los,
That in an ile that called was Colcos, 1425
Beyonde Troy, esteward in the see,
That therin was a ram that men myghte see
That had a flees of gold that shoon so bryght
That nowher was ther suche another sight.
But hit was kept alway with a dragoun, 1430
And many other mervels up and doun,
And with twoo booles maked al of bras,
That spitten fire, and muche thinge ther was.
But this was eke the tale, nathelees,
That whoso wolde wynne thilke flees, 1435
He moste bothe or he hit wynne myghte,
With the booles and the dragoun fyghte;
And King Oetes lord was of that ile.
    This Pelleus bethoughte upon this wyle,
That he his nevywe Jasoun wolde enhorte 1440
To saylen to that londe him to disporte,
And seyde, "Neviwe, if hit myghte be
That suche a worshippe myghte falle the
That thou this famous tresor myghte wynne,
And bryngen hit my regyoun wythinne, 1445
Hit were to me grette plesaunce and honoure;
Thanne were I holde to quyte thy laboure.
And al the costes I wole myselfe make;
And chese what folke thou wilt wyth the
    take;
Let see now, darstow taken this viage?" 1450
Jasoun was yonge and lusty of corage
And undertook to doon this ilke empryse.
    Anoon Argus his shippes gan devyse.
With Jasoun went the strong Ercules,
And many another that he with him ches. 1455
But whoso axeth who is with him gon,
Let him go reden *Argoniauticon*,
For he wol telle a tale long ynoughe.
Philotetes anoon the sayle up droughe,

Whan that the wynd was good, and gan him
    hye 1460
Out of his contree called Tessalye.
So longe he sayled in the salte see
Til in the ile of Lemnoun arryved he—
Al be this nat rehersed of Guydo,
Yet seyth Ovyde in his *Epistoles* so— 1465
And of this ile lady was and queene
The faire yonge Ysiphile the shene,
That whilom Thoas doughter was, the kynge.
    Ysiphile was goon in hir pleyinge,
And romyng on the clyves by the see, 1470
Under a banke anoon espied shee
Where that the shippe of Jasoun gan arryve.
Of hir goodnesse adoun she sendeth blyve
To weten yif that any straunge wyghte
With tempest thider were yblowe
    anyghte— 1475
To doon him socour, as was hir usaunce
To forthren every wyght, and don plesaunce
Of veray bountee and of curteysie.
This messagere adoun him gan to hye,
And found Jasoun, and Ercules also, 1480
That in a cogge to londe were ygo
Hem to refresshen and to take the eyre—
The morwenyng atempree was and faire.
And in his wey this messagere hem mette.
Ful kunnyngely these lordes two he grette, 1485
And did his message, axyng hem anoon
If they were broken or ought woo begoon
Or hadde nede of lodesmen or vitayle,
For of socoure they shulde nothing fayle,
For hit was outrely the quenes wille. 1490
    Jasoun ansuerde, mekely and stille,
"My lady," quod he, "thanke I hertely
Of hir goodnesse. Us nedeth, trewely,
Nothing as now, but that we wery bee,
And come for to pley out of the see 1495

1424 **los,** report (praise). 1430 **kept,** guarded. 1436 **or,** ere. 1438 F&c *Otes*. 1439 *wyle*: F *while*. 1440 **enhorte,** exhort. 1441 **disporte,** enjoy. 1447 **holde to quyte,** bound to repay. 1452 **empryse,** enterprise. 1453 **Argus,** Argos, legendary builder of the ship Argo, which gave the name to Jason's company of Argonauts, possibly known to Chaucer through the *Argonauticon* of Valerius Flaccus. 1457 F *him rede*. 1463 *Lemnoun*: F *Leonoun* (Lemnos). 1465 **Ovyde,** as Chaucer says, the story of Hypsipyle is not in the English MSS of Guido (Skeat observes that it is in the Spanish MSS); so he here switches to Ovid, *Heroides* 6. 1467 **shene,** fair. 1470 **clyves,** cliffs. 1471 *banke*: F *brake* (thicket). 1472 F&c *Where lay the shippe that Jasoun*. 1476 **usaunce,** habit. 1478 **veray bountee,** true generosity. 1481 **cogge,** cockboat (small boat). 1485 **kunnyngely,** skillfully. 1487 **they were broken,** i.e., their ship was damaged. 1488 **lodesmen,** pilots. 1490 Line found only in G. 1491 **stille,** quietly.

Til that the wynd be better in oure wey."
  This lady rometh by the clyffe to pley,
With hir meynee, endelong the stronde,
And fyndeth this Jasoun and these other stonde,
In spekyng of this thinge as I yow tolde.   1500
This Ercules and Jasoun gan beholde
How that the queene it was, and faire hir grette
Anoon ryght as they with this lady mette.
And she tooke hede, and knew by here manere,
By here aray, by wordes and by chere,   1505
That hit were gentilmen of grete degree.
And to the castel with hir ledeth she
These straunge folk, and dooth hem grete
    honour,
And axeth hem of travaylle and labour
That they han suffred in the salte see,   1510
So that, withynne a day, or two, or three,
She knew, by folk that in his shippes bee,
That hit was Jasoun, ful of renomee,
And Ercules, that hadde the grete los,
That soughten the aventures of Colcos,   1515
And did hem honour more than before,
And with hem deled ever lenger the more,
For they ben worthy folk, withouten les.
And namely, she spak most with Ercules,
To him hir herte bar, he shulde bee   1520
Sad, wise, and trewe, of wordes avysee,
Withouten any other affeccioun
Of love or evyl ymaginacioun.
  This Ercules hath so this Jasoun preysed
That to the sonne he hath him up areysed,   1525
That half so trewe a man ther nas of love
Under the cope of hevene that is above.
And he was wys, hardy, secree, and ryche—
Of these thre poyntes ther nas noon hym
    liche—
Of fredom passed he, and lustihede,   1530
Al thoo that lyven or ben dede.

Ther to so grete a gentilman was he,
And of Tessalye likly kyng to be.
Ther nas no lakke but that he was agaste
To love, and for to speke shamefaste;   1535
He had lever hymselfe to mordre and dye
Than that men shulde a lover him espye:
"As wolde God that I hadde yive
My blood and flessh so that I myghte lyve
With the nones that he hadde oghwher a wyf 1540
For his estaat, for suche a lusty lyf
She sholde lede with this lusty knyghte!"
And al this was compassed on the nyghte
Betwix him Jasoun and this Ercules.
Of these twoo her was mad a shrewed les   1545
To come to hous upon an innocent,
For to bedote this queen was here entent.
This Jasoun is as coy as is a mayde;
He loketh pitously, but noght he sayde,
But freely yaf he to hir counseileres   1550
Yiftes grete, and to hir officeres,
As wolde God I leyser hadde, and tyme,
By processe al his wowyng for to ryme.
But in this hous if any fals lover be,
Ryght as himself now doth, ryght so did he,   1555
With feynyng and with every sotil dede.
Ye gete no more of me, but ye wol rede
The original, that telleth al the cas.
  The sothe is this, that Jasoun weddid was
Unto this queene, and toke of hir substaunce   1560
Whatso him lyste, unto his purveyaunce.
And upon hir begat he children two,
And drough his sayle, and saugh hir nevermo.
  A letter sente she him certeyn,
Which were to long to written and to seyn,   1565
And him repreveth of his grete untrouthe,
And prayeth him on hir to have some routhe.
And of his children two, she sayede him this,
That they be lyke, of alle thing, ywis,

1498 meynee, endelong, retinue, along. **1508 straunge folk,** i.e., strangers. **1509 of,** about. **1513 renomee,** renown. **1514 los,** praise. **1517 deled,** had dealings. **1518 les,** lies. **1519 namely,** especially. **1520 bar . . . shulde bee,** (she) bared, ought to have been. This Pandaruslike role played by Hercules is unique to Chaucer's version. **1521 Sad . . . avysee,** serious, thoughtful. **1527 cope,** cloak. **1528 hardy, secree,** brave, discreet—the conventional virtues of the courtly lover. **1530 fredom passed . . . lustihede,** generosity, surpassed, gay disposition. **1534 agaste,** afraid. **1540 With the nones,** i.e., to see the time (for the nonce). **1541 For,** worthy of. **1543 compassed,** schemed. **1545 shrewed les,** cruel deceit (lie). **1547 to bedote,** to make her dote. *entent:* G *assent.* **1548 coy,** meek, but the *double entendre* is evident, cf. *CT* I.119. **1556 feynyng,** pretending. **1559 sothe:** G&c *somme.* **1560 substaunce,** belongings. **1561 him lyste . . . purveyaunce,** pleased him, provisioning (of his ship). **1564 letter,** the letter follows Ovid, *Heroides* 6.1569–75. **1567 routhe,** pity.

To Jasoun, save they coude nat begile; 1570
And prayed God, or hit were longe while,
That she, that had his herte yreft hir fro,
Most fynden him to hir untrewe also,
And that she moste bothe hir children spille,
And althoo that suffreth him his wille. 1575
And trew to Jasoun was she al hir lyf,
And ever kepte hir chast, as for his wyf;
Ne never had she joye at hir herte,
But dyed for his love of sorwes smerte.

Legend of Medea

 To Colcos comen is this Duke Jasoun, 1580
That is of love devourer and dragoun.
As matere appetyteth forme alwey,
And from forme into forme hit passen may,
Or as a welle that were botomles,
Ryght so kan fals Jasoun have no pes 1585
For to desiren, thurgh his appetyte,
To doon with gentilwymmen hys delyte—
This is his luste and his felicitee.
Jasoun is romed forth to the citee
That whilom cleped was Jaconitos, 1590
That was the maister toune of al Colcos,
And hath ytold the cause of his comynge
Unto Oetes, of that contree kynge,
Praying him that he most doon his assay
To gete the flees of gold, if that he may. 1595
Of which the kynge assentith to hys bone,
And doth him honour, as hit is to done,
So ferforth that his doghtre and his eyre,
Medea, which that was so wise and feyre,
That feyrer saugh ther never man with eye, 1600
He made her doon to Jasoun companye
Atte mete, and sitte by him in the halle.
 Now was Jasoun a semely man withalle,
And like a lorde, and had a grete renoun,
And of his loke as real as leoun, 1605

And goodly of his speche, and famulere,
And koude of love al craft and art plenere
Withoute boke, with everyche observaunce.
And as fortune hir oughte a foul meschaunce,
She wex enamoured upon this man. 1610
"Jasoun," quod she, "for oght I se or kan,
As of this thing the which ye ben aboute,
Ye han yourself iput in moche doute.
For whoso wol this aventure acheve,
He may nat wel asterten, as I leve, 1615
Withouten deth, but I his helpe be.
But nathelesse, hit is my wille," quod she,
"To furtheren yow, so that ye shal nat dye,
But turnen sound home to your Thessalye."
 "My ryghte lady," quod thys Jasoun thoo, 1620
"That ye han of my dethe or of my woo
Any rewarde, and doon me this honour,
I wot wel that my myght ne my labour
May nat deserve hit in my lyves day.
God thanke yow, ther I ne kan ne may. 1625
Youre man am I, and louly yow beseche
To ben my help, withoute more speche;
But certes, for my dethe shal I nat spare."
 Thoo gan this Medea to him declare
The peril of this cas, fro poynt to poynte, 1630
And of his batayle, and in what dysjoynte
He mote stonde, of which no creature
Save oonly she ne myght his lyfe assure.
And shortely ryght to the point for to go,
They ben accorded ful betwex hem two, 1635
That Jasoun shal hir wedde, as trewe knyght,
And terme ysette, to come soone at nyght
Unto hir chambre, and make ther his ooth
Upon the goddes, that he for leef no looth
Ne shulde hir never falsen, nyght ne day, 1640
To ben hir husbond while he lyve may,
As she that from his dethe him saved there.
And herupon, anight they mette yfere,

1571 or, ere. **1574 spille,** kill—a foreshadowing of Medea. **1582 appetyteth,** i.e., desires. The sentiment is from Guido's *Historia,* *"sicut appetit materia semper formann,"* etc., but it is there applied to the desire of women for men. *matere:* F *nature.* **1588 luste . . . felicitee,** desire, joy. **1590** *Jaconitos* in G&c: F&c *Jasonicos;* Guido *Iaconites.* **1591 maister,** principal. **1593** F&c *Otes.* **1594 most,** might. **1596 bone,** request (boon). **1598 So ferforth . . . eyre,** to such an extent, heir. **1605 real,** royal. **1606 famulere,** familiar (affable). **1607 koude . . . plenere,** knew fully. **1609 hir oughte,** owed her. **1611 kan,** know. **1613** F&c *Ye and/I put.* **1615 asterten . . . leve,** escape, believe. **1619 turnen,** return. **1621–22 han . . . rewarde,** have concern. **1625 ther,** where. **1628 for . . . spare,** i.e., because I might die, desist. **1631 dysjoynte,** peril. **1637 terme,** time. **1643 yfere,** together. Line omitted in F&c. G *up anyght/in feere.*

And doth his oothe, and gooth with hir
  to bed.
And on the morwe, upward he him sped.   1645
For she hath taught him how he shal nat faile
The flees to wynne, and stynten his batayle;
And saved him his lyf and his honour;
And gat him a name as a conquerour
Ryght through the sleyght of hir
    enchauntement.   1650
  Now hath Jasoun the flees, and home is went
With Medea and tresoures ful gret woon.
But unwiste of hir fader she is goon
To Thessaly with Duke Jasoun, hir leef,
That afterward hath broght hir to myscheef. 1655
For as a traytour he is from hir goo,
And with hir lefte his yonge children twoo,
And falsly hath betrayed hir, allas—
And ever in love a cheef traytour he was—
And wedded yet the thirdde wife anon,   1660

That was the doghtre of King Creon.
This is the mede of lovynge and guerdon
That Medea receyved of Jasoun
Ryght for hir trouthe and for hir kyndenesse,
That loved him better than hirselfe, I gesse, 1665
And lefte hir fader and hir heritage.
And of Jasoun this is the vassalage,
That in his dayes nas never noon yfounde
So fals a lover goynge on the grounde.
And therfor in hir letter thus she sayde,   1670
First whan she of his falsnesse him umbrayde,
"Why lyked me thy yelow heer to see
More then the boundes of myn honeste;
Why lyked me thy youthe and thy fairnesse,
And of thy tonge the infynyt graciousnesse? 1675
O, haddest thou in thy conquest ded ybe,
Ful mykel untrouthe had ther dyed with the!"
  Wel kan Ovyde hir letter in vers endyte,
Which were as now to long for me to wryte.

Explicit legenda Ysiphile et Medee, martirum.

V

LEGEND OF LUCRECE

Incipit legenda Lucrecie Rome, martiris.

Now mote I sayn th'exilynge of kynges   1680
Of Rome, for her horrible doynges,
And of the laste kyng, Tarquynius,
As saythe Ovyde and Titus Lyvius.
But for that cause ne telle I nat thys storie,
But for to preyse and drawen to memorie   1685

The verray wife, the verray trewe Lucresse,
That for hir wyfehode and hir stidfastnesse,
Nat oonly that these payens hir comende,
But he that cleped is in our legende
The grete Austyne hath grete compassyoun   1690
Of this Lucresse that starf at Rome toun.

1647 **stynten,** end. 1652 **woon,** won. 1653 **unwiste of,** unknown to. 1662 **mede,** reward. 1667 **vassalage,** prowess (irony). 1670 **hir letter,** Ovid, *Heroides* 12. 1671 **umbrayde,** reproached (upbraided). 1677 **mykel,** great (much). 1680 **mote I sayn,** must I tell. This legend is from Ovid, *Fasti* 2.721–852. Chaucer also refers to Livy, and Gower told the story in *CA* 3.251. 1684 *ne telle:* F&c *ne* om. 1686 **verray,** i.e., Fr. *vrai,* true. F *werray; trewe* om. 1690 **Austyne,** in *De Civitate Dei* 1.19, St. Augustine praises the purity of Lucrece but condemns her self-murder for a crime of which she was innocent. Chaucer could have known of Augustine's allusion through *Gesta Romanorum* or other intermediaries. 1691 **starf,** died.

And in what wise, I wol bot shortly trete;
And of this thing I touche but the grete.
   Whan Ardea beseged was aboute
With Romaynes that ful sterne were and
      stoute,   1695
Ful longe lay the sege and lytel wroghte,
So that they were half ydel, as hem thoghte.
And in his pley Tarquynius the yonge
Gan for to jape, for he was lyght of tonge,
And sayde that hit was an ydel lyfe,   1700
No man dide ther more than his wife:
"And lat us speke of wyves—that is best.
Preise every man his oune as him lest,
And with oure speche let us ease oure hert."
   A knyght that hyght Colatyne up stert   1705
And sayde thus, "Nay, for hit is no nede
To trowen on the word, but on the dede.
I have a wife," quod he, "that, as I trowe,
Is holden good of al that ever hir knowe.
Go we tonight to Rome, and we shul se."   1710
   Tarquynius answerde, "That lyketh me."
To Rome be they come, and faste hem dighte
To Colatynes hous, and doun they lyghte,
Tarquynius and eke this Colatyne.
The housbond knew the estres wel and fyne,   1715
And prevely into the hous they goon,
Nor at the gate porter was ther noon;
And at the chambre dore they abyde.
This noble wyf sat by hir beddys syde
Dischevely, for no malice she ne thoght,   1720
And softe wolle our boke sayeth that she wroght
To kepen hir fro slouthe and ydelnesse,
And bad hir servantes doon her besynesse,
And axeth hem, "What tydynges heren ye?
How sayne men of the sege? How shal hit be?
God wolde the walles werne fal adoune!   1726
Myn housbond is to longe out of this toune,
For which the drede doth me so to smerte.
Ryght as a swerd hit styngeth to myn herte
Whan I thenk on the sege or of that place.   1730

God save my lord. I pray him for his grace."
And therwithalle ful tendirly she wepe,
And of hir werk she toke no more kepe,
But mekely she let hir eyen falle.
And thilke semblant sat hir wel withalle,   1735
And eke hir teeres, ful of honestee,
Embelysshed hir wifely chastitee.
Hir countenaunce is to hir herte digne,
For they acordeden in dede and signe.
   And with that word hir husbond Colatyne,   1740
Or she of him was war, com stertyng ynne,
And sayde, "Drede the noght, for I am here!"
And she anoon up roos, with blysful chere,
And kyssed him, as of wyves is the wone.
   Tarquynius, this prowde kynges sone,   1745
Conceyved hath hir beautee and hir chere,
Hir yelow heer, hir shap, and hir manere,
Hir hew, hir wordes that she hath
      compleyned—
And by no crafte hir beautee nas nat feyned—
And kaughte to this lady suche desire   1750
That in his hert brent as any fire
So wodely that his witte was al foryeten.
For wel, thoghte he, she shulde nat be geten.
And ay the more that he was in dispaire,
The more he coveteth hir and thoght hir
      faire.   1755
His blynde lust was al his covetynge.
On morwe, whan the bird began to synge,
Unto the sege he cometh ful pryvely,
And by himself he walketh sobrely,
The ymage of hir recordyng alwey newe: 1760
"Thus lay hir heer, and thus fresh was hir
      hewe;
Thus sat, thus spak, thus span; this was hir
      chere;
Thus fair she was, and thys was hir manere."
Al thys conceyt his herte hath now ytake.
And as the see with tempest al toshake,   1765
That after whan the storm is al agoo

1693 grete, essence. Line omitted in F. **1694** From this point on Chaucer translates the *Fasti* very closely. **1696 wroghte,** accomplished. **1699 jape,** joke. **1706** *for:* G *sire.* **1707 trowen,** believe. **1711 lyketh me,** pleases me. **1715 estres,** interior. **1718 abyde,** stop. **1720 Dischevely,** disheveled (i.e., not formally groomed). **1721 wroght,** worked (spun wool yarn). **1723 bad . . . her besynesse,** ordered, their tasks. **1730** F *thenk on these or of.* **1731** *his:* F *my.* **1733 kepe,** care. **1735 semblant sat hir wel,** appearance became her. **1736** *honestee:* F *hevytee.* **1737** G *Emblemyschid.* **1738 digne,** suitable. **1741 Or,** ere. **1746 Conceyved,** observed (taken in). **1749 feyned,** artificial. **1752 wodely,** insanely. **1755** *coveteth hir:* F&c *hir* om. **1757 On morwe,** in the morning. **1762 span . . . chere,** spun, expression. **1764** *now:* F&c *newe.*

Yet wol the water quappe a day or twoo,
Ryght so, thogh that hir forme were absent,
The plesaunce of hir forme was present.
But natheles nat plesaunce but delyte,   1770
Or an unryghtful talent with despyte:
"For, mawgre hir, she shal my lemman be;
Happe helpeth hardy man alway," quod he.
"What ende that I make, hit shal be soo."
And gyrt him with his swerde, and gan
     to goo.   1775
And forth he rit til he to Rome is come,
And al aloon his way than hath he nome
Unto the house of Colatyne ful ryght.
Doun was the sonne, and day hath lost his
     lyght;
And in he come unto a prevy halke,   1780
And in the nyght ful thefely gan he stalke,
Whan every wight was to his reste broght,
Ne no wight had of tresoun suche a thoght.
Whether by wyndow or by other gynne,
With swerde ydraw, shortly he cometh ynne   1785
Ther as she lay, thys noble wife Lucresse.
And as she woke, her bed she felte presse.
"What beste is that," quod she, "that weyeth
     thus?"
     "I am the kynges sone, Tarquynius,"
Quod he, "but and thou crye, or noyse mak,   1790
Or if thou any creature awak,
By thilke God that formed man on lyve,
This swerde through thyn herte shal I ryve."
And therwithal unto hir throte he sterte,
And sette the poynt al sharpe unto hir herte.   1795
No word she spak; she hath no myght therto.
What shal she sayn? Hir wytte is al ago,
Ryght as a wolf that fynt a lomb allone.
To whom shal she compleyne or make mone?
What, shal she fyghte with an hardy knyght?   1800
Wel wot men a woman hath no myght.
What, shal she crye, or how shal she asterte

That hath hir by the throte, with swerde at
     herte?
She axeth grace, and seith al that she kan.
     "Ne wolt thou nat," quod he, this cruelle
     man,   1805
"As wisly Jupiter my soule save,
As I shal in the stable slee thy knave,
And lay him in thy bed, and lowde crye,
That I the finde in suche avowterye.
And thus thou shalt be ded, and also lese   1810
Thy name, for thou shalt non other chese."
     These Romayn wyves loveden so her name
At thilke tyme, and dredden so the shame,
That, what for fere of sklaundre and drede of
     dethe,
She loste bothe atones wytte and brethe,   1815
And in a swowgh she lay, and wex so ded
Men myghte smyten of hir arm or hed—
She feleth nothing, neither foul ne feyre.
Tarquynius, that art a kynges eyre,
And sholdest, as by lynage and by ryght,   1820
Doon as a lord and as a verray knight,
Why hastow doon dispit to chevalrye?
Why hastow doon this lady vylanye?
Allas, of the thys was a vileyn dede!
     But now to purpos. In the story I rede   1825
Whan he was goon al this myschaunce is falle.
Thys lady sent aftir hir frendes alle,
Fader, moder, husbond, al yfere,
And al dyschevelee, with her heres clere,
In habyt suche as wymmen used thoo   1830
Unto the buryinge of her frendes goo,
She sitte in halle with a sorwful syght.
Hir frendes axen what hir aylen might,
And who was dede? And she sytte ay wepynge;
A word for shame ne may she forth out
     brynge,   1835
Ne upon hem she durste nat beholde.
But atte last of Tarquyny she hem tolde

1767 **quappe,** palpitate. 1769 **plesaunce,** pleasure. 1771 **unryghtful talent with despyte,** sinful inclination (desire) with malice. 1772 **mawgre hir . . . lemman,** in spite of herself, lover. 1773 **Happe . . . hardy,** luck, brave. 1774 **What ende,** whatever end (i.e., however it comes out). 1776 F&c *way he fortheryght nome.* 1780 **halke,** corner. 1784 **gynne,** method. 1795 *poynt:* F&c *swerd.* 1796 **myght,** strength. 1798 F&c *wolf that fayneth a love.* 1807 **knave,** servant. 1809 **avowterye,** adultery. 1811 **chese,** i.e., have no other choice. *non other:* F&c *not.* 1812–26 These lines are original with Chaucer, and as Skeat remarks, "breathe the spirit of chivalry." 1816 **swowgh,** swoon. 1822 **dispit,** scorn (injury). 1824 **vileyn:** F&c *vilenouse.* 1828 **yfere,** together. 1829 **dyschevelee,** disheveled. 1830 **habyt . . . used thoo,** clothes, were accustomed to them. 1832 **syght,** expression. 1836 **upon hem . . . beholde,** look at them.

This rewful cas, and al thys thing horryble.
The woo to tellen hit were impossible,
That she and al hir frendes make attones.　　1840
Al had folkes hertes ben of stones,
Hit myghte have maked hem upon hir rewe,
Hir herte was so wyfley and so trewe.
She sayde that for hir gilt ne for hir blame
Hir husbond shulde nat have the foule
　　name—　　　　　　　　　　　　　1845
That nolde she nat suffre, by no wey.
And they answerden alle, upon her fey,
That they forgaf hit hir, for hit was ryght;
Hit was no gilt; hit lay nat in hir myght.
And seyden hir ensamples many oon.　　1850
But al for noght, for thus she seyde anoon:
"Be as be may," quod she, "of forgyvinge,
I wol nat have no forgyft for nothinge."
But pryvely she kaughte forth a knyf,
And therwithalle she rafte hirself her lyf;　1855
And as she felle adoun, she caste her look,
And of hir clothes yet she hede toke,
For in hir falling yet she hadde care
Lest that her fete or suche thyng lay bare—
So wel she loved clennesse and eke trouthe.　1860
　　Of hir had al the toun of Rome routhe.

And Brutus hath by hir chaste bloode swore
That Tarquyn shulde ybanysshed be therfore,
And al his kynne; and let the peple calle,
And openly the tale he tolde hem alle,　　1865
And openly let cary hir on a bere
Thurgh al the toun, that men may see and
　　here
The horryble dede of hir oppressyoun.
Ne never was ther kyng in Rome toun
Syn thilke day. And she was holden there　1870
A seynt, and ever hir day yhalwed dere
As in her lawe. And thus endeth Lucresse,
The noble wife, as Tytus bereth wittnesse.
　　I telle hit for she was of love so trewe,
Ne in hir wille she chaunged for no newe,　1875
And for the stable herte, sadde and kynde,
That in these wymmen man may alday fynde.
Ther as they kaste her hert, ther hit duelleth.
For wel I wot that Crist himselve telleth
That in Israel, as wyde as is the londe,　　1880
That so gret feythe in al the lond he ne fonde
As in a woman, and this is no lye.
And as of men, loketh which tirannye
They doon alday, assay hem whoso lyste—
The trewest is ful brotel for to triste.　　1885

Explicit legenda Lucrecie Rome, martiris.

1838 **rewful,** pitiful. 1840 **attones,** together (at once). 1842 **rewe,** have pity. 1860 **clennesse,** purity. 1864 **let . . . calle,** had, called (together). 1871 **yhalwed,** hallowed (worshiped). 1876 **sadde,** serious. *for the:* F&c *in hir.* 1885 **brotel,** brittle (not dependable).

VI

LEGEND OF ARIADNE

Incipit legenda Adriane de Athenes.

Juge infernal, Mynos, of Crete kynge,
Now cometh thy lot, now comestow on the
    rynge.
Nat for thy sake oonly wryte I this storie,
But for to clepe ageyn unto memorie
Of Theseus the grete untrouthe of love,   1890
For which the goddes of the heven above
Ben wrothe, and wreche han take for thy synne.
Be rede for shame, now I thy lyf begynne.
    Mynos that was the myghty kyng of Crete,
That hadde an hundred citees stronge
        and grete,   1895
To scole hath sent his sone Androgius
To Athenes, of the which hit happed thus,
That he was slayn, lernyng philosophye,
Ryght in that citee, nat but for envye.
The grete Mynos, of the whiche I speke,   1900
His sones dethe is comen for to wreke.
Alcathoe he besegeth harde and longe,
But natheles the walles be so stronge,
And Nysus that was kyng of that citee
So chevalrous that lytel dredeth he.   1905
Of Mynos or his ost toke he no cure,
Til on a day befel an aventure
That Nysus doghtre stode upon the walle
And of the sege saw the maner alle.
So happed hit that at a skarmysshynge   1910
She caste hir herte upon Mynos the kynge,

For his beaute and for his chevalrye,
So sore that she wende for to dye.
And shortly of this processe for to pace,
She made Mynos wynnen thilke place,   1915
So that the citee was al at his wille,
To saven whom him lyst, or elles spille.
But wikkedly he quytte hir kyndenesse,
And let hir drenche in sorowe and distresse,
Ner that the goddes hadde of hir pite—   1920
But that tale were to longe as now for me.
    Athenes wanne thys kyng Mynos also,
And Alcathoe, and other tounes mo,
And this th'effect, that Minos hath so dryven
Hem of Athenes that they mote him yiven   1925
Fro yere to yere hir oune children dere
For to be slayn, as ye shal after here.
Thys Mynos hath a monstre, a wikked beste,
That was so cruelle that without areste,
Whan that a man was broght in his presence,   1930
He wolde him ete, ther helpeth no defence.
And every thridde yere, withouten doute,
They casten lot, and as hit came aboute
On ryche, on pore, he moste his sone take,
And of his child he moste present make   1935
Unto Mynos, to save him or to spille,
Or lat his best devoure him at his wille.
And this hath Mynos doon, ryght in despyt.
To wreke his sone was sette al his delyt,

1886 Juge infernal, Mynos, Minos, judge of the lower world, was in Boccaccio's *De Genealogia Deorum* and other medieval accounts confused with Minos, king of Crete, who built the Labyrinth to house the Minotaur. Chaucer's version is evidently based upon expanded versions of Ovid's *Met.* 7.456ff., 8.6ff., and *Heroides* 10, with possible influences from Plutarch and other accounts of Theseus and the Minotaur. *Crete:* F&c *Greece.* G lacks the first leaf of this legend; T&c read *Crete,* and see l. 1894. **1887 lot . . . rynge,** chance, exhibition ring (i.e., now it's your turn to be exhibited). **1888** F&c *oonly for thy sake writen ys.* **1889 clepe,** call. **1892 wreche,** revenge. **1895** *hadde:* F&c *wanne.* **1898 lernyng,** studying. **1899 nat but for,** for nothing but (i.e., without provocation). **1901 wreke,** avenge. **1902 Alcathoe,** in Megara, just east of Attica in Greece. T *Alcathoe:* F&c *And (All) the citee.* **1906 cure,** care. **1914 processe . . . pace,** i.e., to pass through this business. **1917 spille,** destroy. **1918 quytte,** repaid. **1919 drenche,** drown. **1920 Ner,** were it not. **1923** *Alcathoe:* F&c *Al cites.* **1924 th'effect,** the result. **1925 mote,** must. **1929 areste,** hesitation. **1933 They casten,** i.e., the Athenians. **1938 despyt,** malice. **1939 wreke,** avenge.

And maken hem of Athenes his thralle 1940
Fro yere to yere, while he lyven shalle—
And home he saileth whan this toun is wonne.

This wikked custom is so longe yronne
Til that of Athenes Kyng Egeus
Moste sende his oune sone Theseus, 1945
Sith that the lotte is fallen him upon,
To be devoured, for grace is ther non.
And forth is lad thys woful yonge knyght
Unto the contree of Kyng Mynos ful of myght,
And in a prison, fetred, caste is he 1950
Til thilke tyme he shulde yfreten be.
Wel maystow wepe, O woful Theseus,
That art a kynges sone, and dampned thus.
Me thynketh this, that thow depe were yholde
To whom that saved the fro cares colde. 1955
And now, if any woman helpe thee,
Wel oughtestow hir servant for to be,
And ben her trewe lover yere by yere.
But now to come agayn to my matere.

The tour ther as this Theseus is throwe, 1960
Doun in the bothome, derke, and wonder lowe,
Was joynyng to the walle of a foreyne,
And hit was longyng to the doghtren tweyne
Of Kyng Mynos, that in her chambres grete
Dwelten above, toward the mayster strete, 1965
In mochel mirthe, in joye, and in solas.
Wot I nat how, hit happed ther, par cas,
As Theseus compleyned him by nyght,
The kynges doghtre that Adriane hyghte,
And eke hir suster Phedra, herden alle 1970
His compleynt as they stode on the walle
And lokeden upon the brighte mone;
Hem leste nat to goo to bed so sone.
And of his woo they had compassyoun:
A kynges sone to be in swich prisoun, 1975
And be devoured, thoughte hem gret pitee.

Than Adriane spak to hir suster free,
And seyde, "Phedra, leve suster dere,
This woful lordes sone may ye nat here,
How pitousely compleyneth he his kin, 1980
And eke his pore estat that he is in,
And gilteless? Certes now, hit is routhe!
And if ye wol assenten, by my trouthe,
He shal be holpen, how soo that we doo."

Phedra answerde, "Ywis, me is as woo 1985
For him as ever I was for any man.
And to his help, the best rede I kan
Is that we doon the gayler prively
To come, and speke with us hastely,
And doon this woful man with him to come. 1990
For if he may the monstre overcome,
Than were he quyt; ther is noon other bote.
Lat us wel taste him at his herte-rote,
That if so be that he a wepne have
Wher that his lyf he dar to kepe or save, 1995
Fighten with this fend, and him defende.
For in the prison ther he shal descende,
Ye wite wel that the beste is in a place
That nys nat derke, and hath roum and eke
  space
To welde an ax or swerd or staf or knyf, 2000
So that me thenketh he shulde save his lyf.
If that he be a man, he shal do soo!
And we shal make him balles eke alsoo
Of wexe and towe, that, whan he gapeth faste,
Into the bestes throte he shal hem caste 2005
To sleke his hunger and encombre his teeth.
And ryght anoon, whan that Theseus seeth
The beste achoked, he shal on him lepe
To sleen him or they comen more to hepe.
This wepen shal the gayler or that tyde 2010
Ful prively within the prison hyde;
And for the hous is crynkled to and fro,

And hath so queynte weyes for to go—
For hit is shapen as the mase is wroght—
Therto have I a remedy in my thoght,   2015
That by a clewe of twyne, as he hath goon,
The same way he may returne anoon,
Folwyng alwey the threde as he hath come.
And whan that he this beste hath overcome,
Then may he fleen away out of this stede,   2020
And eke the gayler may he with him lede,
And him avaunce at home in his contree,
Syn that so gret a lordes sone is he.
Thys is my rede, if that he dar hit take."
    What shulde I lenger sermoun of hit
        make?   2025
The gayler cometh, and with him Theseus.
And whan these thynges ben acorded thus,
Adoun sytte Theseus upon his knee,
"The ryghte lady of my lyf," quod he,
"I, sorwful man, ydampned to the deth,   2030
Fro yow, whiles that me lasteth lyf or breth,
I wol nat twynne, after this aventure,
But in your servise thus I wol endure,
That as a wrechche unknowe I wol yow serve
For evermore, til that myn herte sterve.   2035
Forsake I wol at home myn herytage,
And, as I seyde, ben of your court a page,
If that ye vouchesauf that in this place
Ye graunte me to have suche a grace
That I may have nat but my mete and
        drinke.   2040
And for my sustenance yet wol I swynke
Ryght as yow lyst, that Mynos ne no wyght—
Syn that he sawe me never with eighen syght—
Ne no man elles shal me konne espye.
So slyly and so wel I shal me gye,   2045
And me so wel disfigure and so lowe,
That in this world ther shal no man me knowe,
To han my lyf, and for to han presence
Of yow that doon to me this excellence.
And to my fader shal I senden here   2050
This worthy man that is your gaylere,

And him to guerdon that he shal wel bee
Oon of the gretest men of my contree.
And yif I durste sayne, my lady bryght,
I am a kynges sone, and eke a knyght,   2055
As wolde God, yif that hit myghte bee
Ye weren in my contree, alle three,
And I with yow, to bere yow companye,
Than shulde ye seen yif that I therof lye!
And if I profre yow in low manere   2060
To ben your page and serven yow ryght here,
But I yow serve as lowly in that place,
I prey to Mars to yeve me suche grace
That shames dethe on me ther mote falle,
And dethe and povert to my frendes alle,   2065
And that my spirit by nyghte mote goo
After my dethe, and walke to and froo,
That I mot of a traytour have a name,
For which my spirit mot go to do me shame!
And yif I ever yclaime other degre,   2070
But if ye vouchesauf to yeve hit me,
As I have seyde, of shames deth I deye!
And mercy, lady! I kan no more saye!"
    A semely knyght was Theseus to see,
And yong, but of twenty yere and three;   2075
But whoso hadde yseen his countenaunce,
He wolde have wept for routhe of his penaunce.
For which this Adriane in this manere
Answerde to his profre and to his chere:
    "A kynges sone and eke a knyght,"
        quod she,   2080
"To ben my servant in so low degre,
God shelde hit, for the shame of wymmen alle,
And leve me never suche a cas befalle!
But sende yow grace, and sleyghte of hert also,
Yow to defende and knyghtly sleen your fo,   2085
And leve herafter that I may yow fynde
To me and to my suster here so kynde
That I repente nat to geve yow lyf!
Yet wer hit better that I were your wyf,
Syn that ye ben as gentil borne as I,   2090
And have a realme nat but faste by,

2014 **mase,** maze. 2016 **clewe,** ball of twine. This usage gives the present meaning to clew/clue. 2024 **rede,** advice. 2025 F&c *sermoun* om. 2032 **twynne,** separate. 2035 **sterve,** die. 2038 **vouchesauf,** consent. 2041 **swynke,** labor. 2045 **me gye,** behave (guide myself). Theseus is here promising to be discreet and considerate after his escape. 2052 **guerdon,** reward. 2062 **But I . . . in that place,** i.e., if I am not just as attentive when we get to my country where I am a prince. 2070 **degre,** station in life. 2072 **I deye,** may I die. 2077 **routhe,** pity. 2079 **chere,** expression (mood). 2082 **shelde,** forbid. 2083 **leve,** grant (leave). 2084 **sleyghte,** skill, cunning. 2091 **nat but faste by,** i.e., nearby.

Then that I suffred your gentilesse to sterve,
Or that I let yow as a page serve;
Hit is not profit, as unto your kynrede,
But what is that that man wol nat do for drede? 2095
And to my suster, syn that hit is so
That she mot goon with me, if that I goo,
Or elles suffre deth as wel as I,
That ye unto your sone as trewely
Doon her be wedded at your home comynge. 2100
This is the fynal ende of al this thynge—
Ye swere hit here, on al that may be sworne."
    "Ye, lady myn," quod he, "or elles torne
Mote I be with the Mynatour tomorwe!
And haveth herof my herte-blood to borwe, 2105
Yif that ye wole. If I had knyf or spere,
I wolde hit laten out and ther-on swere,
For then at erst I wot ye wol me leve.
By Mars, that is the chefe of my beleve,
So that I myghte lyven and nat fayle   2110
Tomorwe for t'acheve my bataile,
I nolde never fro this place flee
Til that ye shuld the verray prefe see.
For now if that the sothe I shal yow say,
I have loved yow ful many a day,   2115
Thogh ye ne wiste hit nat, in my contree,
And aldermost desired yow to see
Of any erthly lyvyng creature.
Upon my trouthe I swere, and yow assure,
These seven yere I have your servant be;   2120
Now have I yow, and also have ye me,
My dere hert, of Athenes duchesse!"
    This lady smyleth at his stedfastnesse,
And at his hertly wordes, and at his chere,
And to hir suster sayde in this manere,   2125
Al softely, "Now, suster myn," quod she,
"Now be we duchesses, bothe I and ye,
And sykered to the regals of Athenes,
And both herafter lykly to be queenes,
And saved fro his deth a kynges sone,   2130
As ever of gentil wymmen is the wone
To save a gentil man, enforth her myght,

In honest cause, and namely in his ryght.
Me thinketh no wyght oughte us herof blame,
Ne beren us therfor an evel name."   2135
    And shortely of this matere for to make,
This Theseus of hir hath leve ytake.
And every point performed was in dede
As ye have in this covenant herd me rede.
His wepne, his clew, his thing that I have
    sayde,   2140
Was by the gayler in the hous ylayde
Ther as this Mynatour hath his duellinge,
Ryght faste by the dore at his entringe.
And Theseus is ladde unto his dethe,
And forthe unto this Mynatour he gethe,   2145
And by the techyng of this Adriane
He overcome this beste, and was his bane;
And oute he cometh by the clewe agayne
Ful prevely, whan he this beste hath slayne;
And by the gayler geten hath a barge,   2150
And of his wyves tresor gan hit charge,
And tok his wife, and eke hir suster fre,
And eke the gayler, and wyth hem alle thre
Is stole away out of the lond by nyghte,
And to the contree of Eunopye him dyghte   2155
There as he had a frende of his knowynge.
There festen they, there dauncen they and
    synge;
And in his armes hath this Adriane,
That of the beste hath kepte him from his bane;
And gat him ther a newe barge anoon,   2160
And of his contree folk a grete woon,
And taketh his leve, and homeward sayleth hee.
And in an yle, amydde the wilde see,
Ther as ther dwelleth creature noon
Save wilde bestes, and that ful many oon,   2165
He made his shippe alonde for to sette;
And in that yle half a day he lette,
And sayde that on the lond he moste him reste.
His maryners han don ryght as him leste,
And for to telle schortly in this cas,   2170
Whan Adriane his wyf aslepe was,

2092 *your gentilesse:* G&c *giltles yow to.* 2105 to borwe, as a pledge. 2107 hit laten out, i.e., draw my own blood (take a blood oath). 2108 leve, believe. 2111 t'acheve: F&c *to taken.* 2113 prefe, proof. 2128 sykered . . . regals, secured (united with), royalty. 2131 wone, custom. 2132 enforth, as far as (emforth). 2133 namely, especially. 2147 bane, death. 2150–51 Lines lacking in F. 2151 charge, load. 2153 F *And by the gayler.* 2155 Eunopye, Oenopia (the island of Aegina). 2157 festen . . . dauncen, in some traditions, Ariadne becomes engrossed in a Dionysiac orgy on the island. 2159 bane, death. 2160 newe: F&c *noble.* 2161 woon, number. 2167 lette, paused.

For that her suster fairer was than she,
He taketh hir in his hond, and forth gooth he
To shippe, and as a traitour stal his way
While that this Adriane aslepe lay,　　　2175
And to his contree-ward he sayleth blyve
(A twenty devel way the wynd him dryve!),
And fond his fader drenched in the see.
　Me list no more to speke of him, pardee.
These false lovers, poyson be her bane!　　2180
But I wol turne ageyn to Adriane,
That is with slepe for werynesse ytake.
Ful sorwefully hir herte may awake.
Allas, for the myn herte hath now pitee!
Ryght in the dawnyng awaketh shee　　　2185
And gropeth in the bed, and fond ryght
　　noght.
"Allas," quod she, "that ever I was wroght!
I am betrayed!" and hir heer to-rent,
And to the stronde barefot faste she went,
And cryed, "Theseus, myn herte swete,　　2190
Wher be ye, that I may nat wyth yow mete,
And myghte thus with bestes ben yslayn?"
The holwe rokkes answerde hir agayn.
No man she saw, and yet shone the mone,
And hye upon a rokke she wente sone,　　2195
And saw his barge saylyng in the see.
Cold wax hir hert, and ryght thus sayde she,
"Meker than ye fynde I the bestes wilde!"
Hadde he nat synne that hir thus begylde?
She cried, "O turne agayn, for routhe and
　　synne!　　　　　　　　　　　　　2200

Thy barge hath nat al his meyny inne!"
Hir kerchef on a pole up styked shee,
Ascaunce that he shulde hit wel ysee,
And him remembre that she was behynde,
And turne agayne, and on the stronde hir
　　fynde.　　　　　　　　　　　　　2205
But al for noght; his wey he is ygoon.
And doun she felle aswown upon a stoon,
And up she ryst, and kyssed in al hir care
The steppes of his fete ther he hath fare,
And to hir bedde ryght thus she spbeketh
　　thoo:　　　　　　　　　　　　　2210
"Thow bed," quod she, "that hast receyved
　　twoo,
Thou shalt answere of twoo, and nat of oon!
Wher is thy gretter part away ygoon?
Allas, wher shal I, wreched wyght, become?
For though so be that any bote here come,　2215
Home to my contree dar I nat for drede.
I kan myselven in this cas nat rede!"
　What shulde I telle more hir compleynynge?
Hit is so long, hit were an hevy thynge.
In hir epistil Naso telleth alle.　　　　　2220
But shortly to the ende I telle shalle.
The goddes have hir holpen, for pitee,
And in the signe of Taurus men may see
The stones of hir corown shyne clere.
I wol no more speke of this matere.　　　2225
But thus this false lover kan begile
His trewe love—the devel quyte him his
　　while!

Explicit legenda Adriane de Athenes.

2176 **blyve,** quickly. 2178 **drenched,** drowned. 2180 **bane,** death (slayer). 2193 Line lacking in F. 2200 **routhe,** pity. 2201 **meyny,** household (crew). *his:* F&c *thy.* 2203 **Ascaunce,** in case (hope) that. 2213 *thy:* F&c *the.* 2214 **wher . . . become,** where shall I go. 2215 Reading from Selden: FG&c *that botte noon here come.* 2217 **rede,** advise. 2220 **epistil Naso,** Ovid, *Heroides* 10. 2224 **hir corown,** Corona Borealis, the Northern Crown, opposite Taurus in the sky. See Ovid, *Met.* 8.176ff. 2226 F&c *these false lovers.* 2227 **quyte . . . his while,** repay him for the way he spent his time.

VII

LEGEND OF PHILOMENE

Incipit legenda Philomene.

Deus dator formarum.

Thow yiver of the formes that hast wroght
The faire worlde, and bare hit in thy thoght
Eternally, or thow thy werk began,   2230
Why madest thow, unto the sklaundre of man,
Or—al be that hit was not thy doynge,
As for that fyn to make such a thynge—
Why suffrest thow that Tereus was bore,
That is in love so fals and so forswore,   2235
That fro thys world up to the firste hevene
Corrumpeth whan that folk his name nevene?
And, as to me, so grisly was his dede
That whan that I his foule story rede,
Myn eyen wexen foule and sore also—   2240
Yet laste the venym of so longe ago,
That hit infecteth him that wol beholde
The story of Tereus, of which I tolde.
Of Trase was he lorde, and kynne to Marte,
The cruelle god that stant with blody darte,   2245
And wedded had he with a blisful chere
Kyng Pandyones faire doghter dere,
That hyghte Proygne, floure of hir contree,
Thogh Juno list nat at the feste bee,
Ne Ymeneus, that god of weddyng is;   2250
But at the feste redy ben, ywis,
The furies thre with al her mortel brond.
The owle al nyght about the balkes wond,

That prophet is of woo and of myschaunce.
This revel, ful of songe and ful of daunce,   2255
Laste a fourtenyght, or lytel lasse.
But shortly of this story for to passe—
For I am wery of him for to telle—
Fyve yere his wyf and he togedir dwelle,
Til on a day she gan so sore longe   2260
To seen her suster that she saugh nat longe,
That for desire she nyste what to sey.
But to hir husbond gan she for to prey,
For Goddys love, that she moste ones goon
Hir suster for to seen, and come anoon,   2265
Or elles but she moste to hir wende,
She preyde him that he wolde after hir sende;
And this was, day be day, al hir prayere
With al humblesse of wyfhod, worde and chere.
  This Tereus let make his shippes yare,   2270
And into Grece himself is forth yfare
Unto his fader-in-lawe, and gan him prey
To vouchesauf that for a moneth or twey,
That Philomene, his wyfes suster, myght
On Proigne his wyf but ones have a syght—   2275
"And she shal come to yow agayne anoon.
Myself with hir I wil bothe come and goon,
And as myn hertes lyf I wol hir kepe."
  This olde Pandeon, this kyng, gan wepe

Deus dator formarum, the Latin tag found in Bodley 638 and F (*. . . formatorum*) is doubtless from the unidentified source from which Chaucer translated the opening lines. The Platonic sentiment is familiar, cf. *Boece* III m.9 and *RR* 15995ff. (Dunn-Robbins 77.67ff.). The legend is based upon Ovid, *Met.* 6.424ff., and the expanded *Ovide Moralisé.* **2230 or,** ere. **2231 sklaundre,** slander (disgrace). **2233 fyn,** end (purpose). F&c *fende.* **2236 firste hevene,** outermost sphere. **2237 Corrumpeth,** everything is corrupted (impers. vb. without expressed subject, cf. "Bifil," *CT* I.19). **nevene,** name (vb.). **2239** *his:* F&c *this.* **2241 Yet laste,** so long lasts. **2244 Trase . . . Marte,** Tereus was King of Thrace and, according to Ovid, descended from Mars. **2247 Pandyones,** Pandion, king of Athens. **2249 Juno,** wife of Jupiter and guardian of marriage. *list* (desired): F&c *baste.* **2250 Ymeneus,** Hymen. **2252 mortel brond,** in Ovid (6.430), the Furies light the way with torches stolen from a funeral procession. **2253 balkes wond,** beams flew (wound). **2261 saugh nat,** had not seen. **2266 she . . . to hir wende,** she (Philomene), to her (Procne) come. **2270 yare,** ready. **2273 vouchesauf,** consent. **2278 kepe,** protect.

For tendernesse of herte for to leve 2280
His doghter goon, and for to yive hir leve.
Of al this world he loved nothing soo.
But at the laste leve hath she to goo,
For Philomene with salte teres eke
Gan of her fader grace to beseke 2285
To seen her suster that hir longeth soo,
And him enbraceth with hir armes twoo.
And therwithal, so yong and fair was she
That whan that Tereus sawgh hir beautee,
And of array that ther was noon hir lyche, 2290
And yet of bountee was she two so ryche,
He caste his firy herte upon hir soo
That he wol have hir, how soo that hit goo,
And with his wiles kneled and so preyde,
Til at the laste Pandeon thus seyde, 2295
"Now, sone," quod he, "that art to me so dere,
I the betake my yonge doghter here,
That bereth the key of al my hertes lyf.
And grete wel my doghter and thy wyf,
And yeve hir leve somtyme for to pleye, 2300
That she may seen me oones or I deye."
And sothly, he hath made him ryche feste,
And to his folk, the moste and eke the leste,
That with him com; and yaf him yiftes grete,
And him conveyeth thurgh the maister-strete 2305
Of Athenes, and to the see him broghte,
And turneth home—no malice he ne thoghte.

The ores pulleth forth the vessel faste,
And into Trace arryveth at the laste,
And up into a forest he hir ledde, 2310
And into a cave pryvyly him spedde;
And in this derke cave, yif hir leste,
Or leste noght, he bad hir for to reste;
Of which hir hert agrose, and seyde thus,
"Wher is my suster, brother Tereus?" 2315
And therwithal she wepte tenderly,
And quoke for fere, pale and pitously,

Ryght as the lamb that of the wolf is byten,
Or as the colver that of the egle is smyten,
And is out of his clawes forth escaped, 2320
Yet hit is aferde and awhaped
Lest hit be hent eft-sones, so sat she.
But utterly hit may non other be:
By force hath he, this traytour, done that dede,
That he hath reft hir of hir maydenhede, 2325
Maugree hir hede, by strengthe and by his myght.
Loo, here a dede of men, and that a ryght!
She crieth "Suster!" with ful loude stevene,
And "Fader dere!" and "Help me, God in Hevene!"
Al helpeth nat; and yet this false thefe 2330
Hath doon this lady get a more myschefe,
For fere lest she sholde his shame crye,
And done him openly a vilanye,
And with his swerd hir tonge of kerveth he,
And in a castel made hir for to be 2335
Ful privily in prison evermore,
And kept hir to his usage and to his store,
So that she myghte him nevermore asterte.
O sely Philomene, woo is in thyn herte;
God wreke the, and send the thy bone! 2340
Now is hit tyme I make an ende sone.

This Tereus is to his wyf ycome,
And in his armes hath his wyf ynome,
And pitously he wepe, and shook his hede,
And swor hir that he fond hir suster dede, 2345
For which the sely Proigne hath suche woo
That nygh hir sorwful herte brak atwoo.
And thus in teres lat I Proigne dwelle,
And of hir suster forth I wol yow telle.

This woful lady ylerned had in yowthe 2350
So that she werken and enbrowden cowthe,
And weven in her stole the radevore

2280 **leve,** let. 2286 **that hir longeth,** i.e., that so longs for her. G&c *she loveth.* 2291 **bountee,** goodness (generosity). G&c *beautee,* which corresponds to Ovid's *"divitior forma."* 2293 **that hyt goo:** G *evere he do.* 2294 **kneled and so:** G *so fayre hire.* 2297 **betake,** entrust. *here:* F&c *dere.* 2300 **to pleye,** to amuse herself (take a vacation). 2305 **maister-strete,** main street. 2314 **agrose,** was terrified. 2319 **colver,** dove. 2321 **awhaped,** terrified. 2322 **eft-sones,** again. 2328 **stevene,** voice. *loude:* F *longe.* 2332 **crye,** cry out (reveal). 2337 **to his store,** as his possession. 2338 **asterte,** escape. Line lacking in F&c. 2339 G *wo is.* F&c insert spurious line 2339a *Huges ben thy sorwes, and wonder smert.* 2340 **wreke . . . bone,** avenge, boon (request for vengeance). 2346 **sely,** foolish (innocent). 2351 **enbrowden,** embroider. 2352 **stole . . . radevore,** tapestry frame (Ger. *Weberstuhl,* loom), tapestry cloth (according to Skeat *rcs de Vaur,* cloth of Vaur, although other scholars object to this etymology); G&c *radvore, rady vore,* etc.

As hit of wymen hath be woved yore.
And, shortly for to seyn, she hath hir fille 2354
Of mete and drynke, of clothing at hir wille,
And koude eke rede wel ynogh and endyte,
But with a penne koude she nat wryte;
But lettres kan she weven to and froo,
So that by that the yere was agoo
She had ywoven in a stamen large 2360
How she was broght from Athenes in a barge,
And in a cave how that she was broght;
And al the thing that Tereus hath wroght,
She wave hit wel, and wrote the story above,
How she was served for hir suster love. 2365
And to a knave a ryng she yaf anoon,
And prayed him, by sygnes, for to goon
Unto the queene, and beren hir that clothe,
And by sygne sworne many an othe 2369
She shulde him yeve what she geten myghte.
  This knave anoon unto the queene him dyght,
And toke hit hir, and al the maner tolde.
And whan that Proigne hath this thing beholde,

No word she spak, for sorwe and eke for rage,
But feyned hir to goon a pilgrimage 2375
To Bachus temple, and in a lytel stounde
Hir dombe suster sytting hath she founde,
Weping in the castel hirself aloon.
Allas, the woo, the compleint, and the moon
That Proigne upon hir dombe suster
    maketh! 2380
In armes everych of hem other taketh,
And thus I lat hem in her sorwe duelle.
The remenant is no charge for to telle,
For this is al and somme, thus was she served
That never harm agylte ne deserved 2385
Unto this cruelle man that she of wyste.
Ye may bewar of men, yif that yow lyste.
For al be that he wol nat, for his shame,
Doon so as Tereus, to lese his name,
Ne serve yow as a morderere or a knave, 2390
Ful lytel while shul ye trewe hem have.
That wol I seyn, al were he now my brother,
But hit so be that he may have non other.

Explicit legenda Philomene.

2353 *woved yore:* F *woved wore;* G&c *wonid yore.* 2356 **endyte,** compose the substance of a message or poem. 2359 **by that,** by the time that. 2360 **stamen,** coarse wool cloth, tapestry cloth. 2364 **wave,** wove. 2365 **served . . . suster,** treated, love of her sister. 2366 **knave,** manservant. 2371 **dyght,** hastened. 2375 **feyned,** pretended. 2376 **stounde,** while. 2379 *compleint:* F&c *constreynt.* 2383 **charge,** importance. Chaucer omits Ovid's conclusion in which Procne kills their son and feeds his flesh to Tereus, and when Tereus retaliates by attacking the sisters, all three are transformed into birds. 2385 **agylte,** committed. 2386 **of wyste,** was aware of. 2393 **But hit so be,** i.e., unless he, for some reason, can have no other lover. *non other:* F&c *another.*

VIII

LEGEND OF PHYLLIS

Incipit legenda Phillis.

By preve as wel as by auctoritee,
That wikked frute cometh of a wikked
 tree, 2395
That may ye fynde, if that hit lyketh yow.
But for this ende I speke this as now,
To telle you of fals Demophon.
In love a falser herde I never non,
But if hit were his fader Theseus. 2400
God, for his grace, fro suche oon kepe us—
Thus may these wymen prayen that hit here.
Now to th'effect turne I of my matere.
 Destroyed is of Troye the citee.
This Demophon come sayling in the see 2405
Towarde Athenes, to his paleys large.
With him come many a shippe and many a
 barge
Ful of his folk, of which ful many oon
Is wounded sore, and seke, and woo begoon,
And they han at the sege longe ylayne. 2410
Behynde come a wynde and eke a rayne
That shofe so sore his saylle might not
 stonde.
Him were lever than al the world alonde,
So hunteth him the tempest to and fro.
So derk hit was, he kouth nowher go, 2415
And with a wawe brosten was his stere.
His shippe was rent so lowe in suche manere
That carpenter ne koude hit nat amende.
The see by nyght as any torche brende
For wode, and posseth him now up now
 doun, 2420

Till Neptunius hath of him compassyoun—
And Thetis, Chorus, Triton, and they alle—
And maden him upon a lond to falle
Wherof that Phillis lady was and quene,
Ligurgus doghter, fayrer on to sene 2425
Than is the flour ageyn the bryghte sonne.
Unnethe is Demophon to londe ywonne,
Wayk and eke wery, and his folk forpyned
Of werynesse, and also enfamyned,
And to the dethe he was almost ydreven. 2430
His wise folk to conseyl han him yeven
To seken help and socour of the quene,
And loken what his grace myghte bene,
And maken in that lond somme
 chevissaunce
To kepen him fro woo and fro myschaunce. 2435
For seke he was, and almost at the dethe;
Unneth myghte he speke or drawe brethe;
And lyeth in Rodopeya him for to reste.
Whan he may walke, him thought hit was the
 beste
Unto the court to seken for socour. 2440
Men knewe him wel, and diden him
 honour,
For at Athenes duke and lord was he,
As Theseus his fader hadde ybe,
That in his tyme was of grete renoun,
No man so grete in al his regyoun, 2445
And lyk his fader of face and of stature—
And fals of love. Hit came him of nature
As dooth the fox Renard, the foxes sone.

2396 hit lyketh, it pleases. This story is found in Ovid, *Heroides* 2, but the accounts of Chaucer and Gower (*Confessio Amantis* 4.731ff.) evidently derive from another unidentified source. *fynde:* G *wete.* **2398 Demophon,** son of Theseus and Phaedra. **2401 kepe,** protect. **2413 lever . . . alonde,** i.e., he would have been happier than anything to be on land. **2416 brosten . . . stere,** broken, rudder. **2417 rent,** breached (torn). **2419** G *it brende.* **2420 For wode . . . posseth,** like mad, pushes (tosses). F&c *hym up and.* **2422 Thetis,** etc., various sea gods. F&c *Tetes, Thorus.* **2425** F *Bygurgys.* **2427 Unnethe,** scarcely. **2428 forpyned,** tormented. **2429 enfamyned,** famished. **2434 chevissaunce,** borrowing. **2438 Rodopeya,** a mountain range in Thrace (modern Bulgaria). **2440** *court:* F&c *contree.*

Of kynde he koude his olde fadres wone
Withoute lore, as kan a drake swimme   2450
Whan hit is kaught and caried to the brymme.
  This honourable Phillis doth him chere,
Hir lyketh wel his porte and his manere—
But for I am agroted here beforne
To write of hem that in love ben forsworne,   2455
And eke to haste me in my legende,
Which to performe God me grace sende,
Therfore I passe shortly in this wyse:
Ye han wel herd of Theseus devyse
In the betraysing of fair Adriane,   2460
That of hir pite kepte him fro his bane.
At shorte wordes, ryght so Demophon
The same wey, the same path hath gon
That did his false fader Theseus.
For unto Phillis hath he sworne thus,   2465
To wedden hir, and hir his trouthe plyght,
And piked of hir al the good he myght,
Whan he was hole and sound and had his reste,
And doth with Phillis whatso that him leste.
And wel kouth I, yif that me lest soo,   2470
Tellen al his doing to and froo.
He sayde to his contree moste hym saylle
For ther he wolde hir wedding apparayle
As fille to hir honour and his also.
And openly he took his leve tho,   2475
And to hir sworne he wolde nat sojourne,
But in a moneth he wolde ageyn retourne.
And in that lond let make his ordynaunce
As verray lord, and toke the obeisaunce
Wel and homely, and let his shippes dyght,   2480
And home he gooth the nexte wey he myght.
But unto Phillis yet ne come he noght,
And that hath she so harde and sore yboght,
Allas, that, as the storye us recorde,
She was hir owne dethe ryght with a corde,   2485

Whan that she segh that Demophon hir trayed.
  But to him first she wrote and faste him
    prayed
He wolde come and delyver hir of peyne,
As I reherse shal oo word or tweyne.
Me lyste nat vouchesauf on him to swynke,   2490
Dispenden on him a penne ful of ynke,
For fals in love was he, ryght as his syre—
The devel set her soules both on fire!
But of the letter of Phillis wol I wryte
A word or tweyne, althogh hit be but lyte.   2495
"Thyn hostesse," quod she, "O Demophon,
Thi Phillis, which that is so woobegon,
Of Rodopeye, upon yow mot compleyne
Over the terme sette betwix us tweyne,
That ye ne holden forward, as ye seyde.   2500
Your anker, which ye in oure haven leyde,
Hyghte us that ye wolde comen, out of doute,
Or that the mone ones went aboute.
But tymes foure the mone hath hid hir face
Syn thylke day ye wente fro this place,   2505
And foure tymes lyght the world ageyn.
But for al that, yif I shal soothly seyn,
Yet hath the streme of Sitho nat ybroght
From Athenes the shippe; yet cometh hit noght.
And yif that ye the terme rekne wolde,   2510
As I or other trewe lovers sholde,
I pleyne nat, God wot, beforn my day."
  But al hir letter writen I ne may
By ordre, for hit were to me a charge.
Hir letter was ryght long and therto large.   2515
But here and there in ryme I have hit layde,
Ther as me thoghte that she wel hath sayde.
  She seyde, "Thy saylles comen nat ageyn,
Ne to thy word ther nys no fey certeyn;
But I wot why ye come nat," quod she,   2520
"For I was of my love to yow so fre.

2449 kynde . . . wone, nature, habits. *olde:* G *owene.* **2450 lore**, teaching. **2452 doth . . . chere**, makes welcome. *Phillis:* F&c *quene.* **2454 agroted**, surfeited. This is the passage which, along with the incompleteness of the final tale, leads some critics to feel that Chaucer may have found *LGW* an increasingly uncongenial task. **2455 forsworne**, false (falsely sworn). **2459 devyse**, narrate. *devyse:* F&c *the nyse.* **2461 of . . . bane**, because of, death. **2473 apparayle**, prepare. **2474 fille**, befitted (befell). **2475** Line lacking in F&c. **2478 ordynaunce**, preparations. **2479 verray lord**, i.e., as the real ruler. **2480 homely . . . dyght**, familiarly, be prepared. **2481 nexte**, nearest. **2482 yet**, again. *But:* FG&c *For.* **2483 sore yboght**, i.e., took it so badly. **2485 dethe . . . with a corde**, i.e., hanged herself. **2490 swynke**, labor. **2491 Dispenden**, to spend. G *Ne spende.* **2496** These lines are derived from *Heroides* 2. **2499 terme**, appointment. **2500 forward**, agreement. **2502 Hyghte**, promised. **2503 Or**, ere. **2507** *yif:* F&c *yet.* **2508 Sitho**, i.e., Thracian current (because Sitho, her father, was King of Thrace). *Sitho* is Skeat's emendation: FG&c *Sitoio*, etc. **2510 terme**, space of time. **2514 By ordre . . . charge**, at length (in order), burden. **2515 large**, free (rambling). **2518–19** *thy:* F&c *the.* **2519 fey**, faith. **2520 wot**, know.

And of the goddes that ye han forswore,
Yf that her vengeaunce fal on yow therfore,
Ye be nat suffisaunt to bere the peyne.
To moche trusted I, wel may I pleyne,   2525
Upon youre lynage and youre faire tonge,
And on youre teres falsly out ywronge.
How kouth ye wepe soo be craft?" quod she.
"May ther suche teres feyned be?
Now certes, yif ye wolde have in memorye, 2530
Hit oghte be to yow but lytel glorye
To have a sely mayde thus betrayed!
To God," quod she, "prey I, and ofte have
    prayed,
That hit be now the grettest prise of alle, 2534
And moste honour that ever yow shal befalle.
And when thyn olde auncestres peynted be,
In which men may her worthynesse se,
Than, pray I God, thow peynted be also,
That folk may reden, forthby as they go,
'Lo, this is he, that with his flaterye   2540
Betrayed hath and doon her vilanye

That was his trewe love in thoghte and dede.'
But sothely, of oo poynt yet may they rede,
That ye ben lyke youre fader as in this,
For he begiled Adriane, ywis,   2545
With suche an art and suche soteltee
As thou thyselven hast begiled me.
As in that poynt, althogh hit be nat fayr,
Thou folwest him, certeyn, and art his eyr.
But syn thus synfully ye me begile,   2550
My body mote ye seen within a while
Ryght in the haven of Athenes fletinge,
Withouten sepulture and buryinge,
Thogh ye ben harder then is any ston!"
    And whan this letter was forth sent
        anon,   2555
And knew how brotel and how fals he was,
She for dispeyr fordide hirself, allas.
Suche sorowe hath she for she beset hir so.
Bewar, ye wymmen, of your sotil fo,
Syn yet this day men may ensample se—   2560
And, as in love, trust no man but me.

Explicit legenda Phillis.

IX

LEGEND OF HYPERMNESTRA

Incipit legenda Ypermystre.

In Grece whilom weren brethren two
Of whiche that oon was called Danao,
That many a sone hath of his body wonne,
As suche false lovers ofte konne.   2565

Among his sones alle ther was oon
That aldermost he loved of everychon.
And whan this child was born, this Danao
Shope him a name, and called him Lyno.

2525 *pleyne:* F&c *seyne.* 2529 **feyned,** pretended. 2539 **forthby,** by; G *forby.* 2549 **eyr,** heir. 2556 **And knew ... brotel,** and (she) knew, brittle (undependable). 2557 **fordide,** killed. 2558 **beset hir,** bestowed herself. 2561 G&c *And trustyth as* (now) *in love.* 2563 **Danao,** Danous. F *Danoo* throughout. Again, the story is found in Ovid, *Heroides* 14, from which Chaucer's version is considerably different. 2567 **aldermost,** most of all. 2569 **Shope ... Lyno,** gave (created), Lynceus.

That other brother called was Egiste, 2570
That was in love as fals as ever him lyste,
And many a doghtre gat he in his lyve,
Of which he gat upon his righte wyve
A doghter dere, and dide hir for to calle
Ypermystra, yongest of hem alle. 2575
The whiche childe of hir natyvite
To al good thewes born was she,
As lyked to the goddes or she was borne
That of the shefe she shulde be the corne.
The Wirdes, that we clepen Destanee, 2580
Hath shapen hir that she most nedes be
Pitouse, sadde, wise, trewe as stele,
And to this woman hit acordeth wele.
For though that Venus yaf hir grete beaute,
With Jupiter compouned so was she 2585
That conscience, trouthe, and drede of
    shame,
And of her wyfehod for to kepe hir name,
This thoghte hir was felicite as here.
And rede Mars was that tyme of the yere
So feble that his malice is him rafte; 2590
Repressed hath Venus his cruelle crafte.
What with Venus and other oppressyoun
Of houses, Mars his venym is adoun
That Ypermystra dar nat handel a knyf
In malyce thogh she shulde lese hir lyf. 2595
But natheles, as heven gan thoo turne,
To badde aspectes hath she of Saturne,
That maked her to deyen in prisoun,
As I shal after make mencioun.
    To Danao and Egistes also— 2600
Althogh so be that they were brethren two,
For thilke tyme nas spared no lynage—
Hit lyketh hem to maken mariage
Betwix Ypermystra and him Lyno,

And casten suche a day hit shal be so. 2605
And ful acorded was hit uttirly:
The array is wroght, the tyme is faste by.
And thus Lyno hath of his fadres brother
The doghter wedded, and eche of hem hath
    other.
   The torches brennen and the lampes
    bryght, 2610
The sacrifices ben ful redy dyght,
Th'encence out of the fire reketh sote,
The flour, the lefe is rent up by the rote
To maken garlands and corounes hye,
Ful is the place of soun of mynstralcye, 2615
Of songes amorouse of mariage,
As thilke tyme was the pleyn usage.
And this was in the paleys of Egiste,
That in his hous was lord ryght as him liste.
And thus the day they dreven to an ende; 2620
The frendes taken leve, and home they wende.
The nyght is comen, the bride shal go to bed.
Egiste to his chambre fast him sped,
And prively he let his doghter calle.
Whan that the hous was voyded of hem alle,
He loked on his doghter with glad chere, 2626
And to hir spak as ye shal after here.
"My righte doghter, tresour of myn hert,
Syn first that day that shapen was my shert,
Or by the fatal sustren hadde my dom, 2630
So ny myn herte never thing me com
As thou, myn Ypermystra, doghter dere!
Tak heed what I thy fader sey thee here,
And wirk aftir thy wiser evermoo.
For alderfirste doghter, I love thee soo 2635
That al the world to me nys halfe so lefe,
Ne I nolde rede the to thy myschefe
For al the goode under the colde moone.

2570 **Egiste,** Aegyptus. 2573 **righte wyve,** lawful wife. 2576 **of,** from (the time of). 2577 **thewes,** qualities. 2578 **lyked . . . or,** pleased, before. F *goddesse.* 2580 **Wirdes,** fate. AS *wyrd.* 2582 **Pitouse, sadde,** compassionate, serious. 2583 **acordeth,** i.e., it became her. 2584–85 **Venus . . . Jupiter,** the reference is to influence of the planets. 2587 **wyfehod,** characteristics becoming a lady (refinement, modesty, etc.). **name,** reputation. 2588 **felicite as here,** i.e., the greatest earthly joy (phrase that takes its meaning with reference to the Boethian concept of heavenly joy, "pleyne felicite," *TC* v.1818). 2590 **him rafte,** taken from him. 2592 *What with:* F&c *And with;* G&c *That what with.* 2594 **Ypermystra dar nat,** the sense of the passage seems rather that because of the repression of Mars at her birth, she disliked handling a knife in conflict, even in self-defense. 2601 *Althogh:* F&c *And.* 2602 **nas spared no lynage,** i.e., kinship was no bar to marriage. 2611 **dyght,** prepared. 2612 **sote,** sweetly. 2620 *the:* F&c *that.* 2624 **let,** had. 2625 F&c *voyded was of alle.* 2626 **chere,** expression. 2629 **shapen . . . shert,** perhaps "since my first shirt was made for me" although the next line suggests a reference to the Fates who spin, weave, and cut off the thread of life. F *firste day.* 2633 F *what thy fader seythe.* 2634 **wirk aftir . . . wiser,** follow the advice of the wiser person. 2635 **alderfirste,** first of all. 2636 **lefe,** dear. 2637 **rede,** counsel.

And what I mene, hit shal be seyd ryght soone,
With protestacioun, as in this wyse, 2640
That but thou do as I shal the devyse,
Thou shalt be ded, by Him that al hath wrought!
At shorte wordes, thow nescapest nought
Out of my paleys or that thou be deed,
But thou consente and werke after my rede—
Tak this to the for ful conclusioun." 2646

This Ypermystra caste hir eyen doun,
And quoke as dooth the lefe of aspe grene.
Ded wex hir hewe, and lyk as ash to sene,
And seyde, "Lord and fader, al your wille 2650
After my myght, God wot, I shal fulfille,
So hit to me be no confusioun."

"I nyl," quod he, "have noon excepcioun."
And out he kaughte a knyf, as rasour kene,
"Hyd this," quod he, "that hit be nat ysene,
And whan thyn housbond is to bed ygo, 2656
While that he slepeth, kut his throte atwo.
For in my dremes hit is warned me
How that my nevywe shal my bane be,
But which I not, wherfor I wol be siker. 2660
Yif thou sey nay, we two shal have a biker
As I have seyd, by Him that I have sworn."

This Ypermystra hath nygh hir wytte forlorn,
And for to passen harmelesse of that place,
She graunted him; ther was noon other grace.
And therwythal a costrel taketh he tho 2666
And seyde, "Herof a draught or two
Yif him to drynke whan he gooth to reste,
And he shal slepe as longe as ever the leste,
The narcotiks and opies been so stronge. 2670
And goo thy wey, lest that him thynke longe."

Out cometh the bride and with ful sobre chere,
As is of maydens ofte the manere.
To chambre is brought with revel and with
    songe,
And shortly, lest this tale be to longe, 2675
This Lyno and she ben broght to bedde,

And every wight out at the dore him spedde.
    The nyght is wasted, and he felle aslepe.
Ful tenderly begynneth she to wepe.
She rist her up, and dredefully she quaketh, 2680
As doth the braunche that Zephirus shaketh,
And husht were al in Argon that citee.
As colde as any frost now wexeth she,
For pite by the herte hir streyneth so,
And drede of deth doth hir so moche woo, 2685
That thries doun she fel in swich a were.
She ryst hir up and stakereth here and there,
And on hir handes faste loketh she.
"Allas, and shal myn handes blody be?
I am a mayd, and as by my nature, 2690
And by my semblant, and by my vesture,
Myn handes ben nat shapen for a knyf,
As for to reve no man fro his lyf.
What devel have I with the knyf to do?
And shal I have my throte korve atwo? 2695
Than shal I blede, allas, and me beshende.
And nedes cost this thing not have an ende;
Or he or I mot nedes lese oure lyf.
Now certes," quod she, "syn I am his wyf,
And hath my feyth, yet is hit bet for me 2700
For to be ded in wyfly honeste
Than be a traytour lyving in my shame.
Be as be may, for erneste or for game,
He shal awake and ryse and go his way
Out at this goter or that hit be day!"— 2705
And wept ful tenderly upon his face,
And in hir armes gan him to embrace,
And him she roggeth and awaketh softe.

    And at the window lepe he fro the lofte
Whan she hath warned him, and doon him
    bote. 2710
This Lyno swyfte was, and lyght of fote,
And from his wyf he ran a ful good pas.
This sely woman is so wayk, allas,
And helples so that or that she fer went,

2640 **in this:** F&c *seyn these.* 2644 **or,** before. 2648 **aspe,** aspen. 2649 **ash,** i.e., pale as ashes. 2659 **bane,** death. 2660 **siker,** sure. 2661 *have:* F *make.* 2664 **for to,** in order to. 2665 **graunted,** agreed. 2666 **costrel,** flask. 2666–67 Defective in F&c. G&c *taketh he/two or thre.* 2670 **opies,** opiates. F&c *nartotikes and epies.* 2671 **thynke longe,** think (you are gone too) long. 2672 **chere,** expression. 2680 **dredefully,** fearfully. 2681 **Zephirus,** zephyr, the west wind. 2684 **hir streyneth:** F&c *streyv(n)eth hir.* 2686 **were,** turmoil (weir). 2696 **beshende,** ruin. F&c *and be shende.* 2697 **nedes cost,** it is essential. *And:* F *Or.* 2705 **goter,** channel for water. 2708 **roggeth,** shakes. 2710 **doon hym bote,** given him assistance. 2712 F&c *from hir ranne.* 2713 **sely ... wayk,** innocent (foolish), weak. 2714 **or,** ere.

Her crwel fader did hir for to hent.   2715
Allas, Lyno, why art thou so unkynde?
Why ne haddest thou remembred in thy
    mynde
And taken hir, and ledde hir forth with the?

For whan she saw that goon awey was he,
And that she myghte nat so faste go,   2720
Ne folwen him, she sate her doun ryght tho,
Til she was kaught and fetered in prisoun.
This tale is seid for this conclusion.

2715 **did . . . hent,** had her taken. **2723** The legend ends with this line in most complete MSS. Modern critics consider it unfinished and assume that Chaucer would have added a line or two of moralization, but many contemporary scribes evidently considered this a satisfactory concluding line.

Short Poems

INTRODUCTION

Short Poems

E VIDENCE FOR dating most of Chaucer's short poems is so uncertain that in this edition they have been grouped topically: *religious poems,* no. 1; *love poems,* nos. 2-8 and 19-22; *philosophical poems,* nos. 9-13; and *verse epistles,* nos. 14-18. Of course, some poems belong to more than one category.

On the basis of statements in the Prologue to the *Legend of Good Women* (ll.422-23) and Retraction to the *Canterbury Tales* (X.1087), these would appear to be only a few of the short poems Chaucer wrote. However, A.K. Moore, "Chaucer's Lost Songs," *JEGP* (1949), has argued that these statements refer largely to lyrics embedded in the narrative poems and that we have not really lost many poems. It would seem that in view of Chaucer's position and reputation as a poet in his own time, if he had composed other lyrics, they would have been preserved. The mystery with these poems, as with everything else Chaucer wrote, is why all of the texts are preserved in manuscripts that appeared after his death. This is not typical. Most medieval poets of Chaucer's stature, like Machaut, Deschamps, and Gower, took care to preserve their texts, but Chaucer evidently did not.

Not only do we lack some of Chaucer's lyrics,

some of those here printed are possibly not by Chaucer. Nos. 1-18 are attributed to him in the manuscripts, but nos. 7 and 8 may not be Chaucerian. Nos. 19-22 are not attributed to him in the manuscripts and the last two are not skillful. The authenticity of the canon is being reviewed by Alfred David and George B. Pace in Vol. 5 of the *Variorum Chaucer* (Part I, 1982; Part II still to appear).

When *Prier a Nostre Dame* (*ABC*, no 1) was first printed, two hundred years after Chaucer's death, Speght (1598) stated that it was composed "at the request of Blanche Duchesse of Lancaster, as a praier for her privat use." If this is true, the *Prier* is one of the first poems we have from Chaucer's hand. Its nature bears out its early date. As a close rendition from *Le pélerinage de la vie humaine*, written about 1330 by Guillaume Deguileville, a Cistercian monk in the French royal abbey of Chalis, the poem shows Chaucer learning his art through translation. The French is printed under the English in Skeat's *Oxford Chaucer* (I.261), and Alexander Weiss, "Chaucer's Early Translations from the French," in *Literary and Historical Perspectives of the Early Middle Ages* (1982), discusses the technique. The idiom is more French and the syntax more strained than in his later poems, yet the personal interjections and flexibility of meter and stanza show that, even in this derivative work, Chaucer was developing his own language and style.

The love poems are variations on the *complaintes d'amour* of the French court poets. Machaut, Deschamps, and Froissart were Chaucer's principal models, and scholars from Kittredge and Lowes to Wimsatt in our time have pointed out Continental originals for most of his themes and many of his lines. For *Anelida and Arcite* (no. 2) Chaucer creates a narrative frame into which the lyric complaint is set, bearing out Moore's observation on his disinclination toward independent lyrics. For the frame Chaucer used the backdrop of Greek epic, as he did in *Troylus and Criseyde* and the Knight's Tale. As with the Knight's Tale, his intermediary is Boccaccio's *Teseide*, although he claims (l. 21) to be following Statius' *Thebiad*. No source has been found for the thread of plot. Some scholars have read it as comment on a scandal in the English court, but for this there is no evidence. If inspiration was necessary, the desertion theme could have been suggested by the tale of Dido that Chaucer retold in the *Legend of Good Women*, and the epistolary form by Dido's letter in Ovid's *Heroides* 7 (or the many epistolary complaints by Machaut and Deschamps). The "complaint" part of the poem is really an excuse for elaborate metrical experiments. Here Chaucer the budding virtuoso practices his scales.

669

Complaint of Mars (no.3) has the same structure as *Anelida*, a classical love tragedy providing the frame for the lover's complaint. The story this time is the familiar myth of the adultery of Mars and Venus. John Shirley says in his manuscript that the poem was made at the command of John of Gaunt to censure a liaison between John Holland, Earl of Huntington, and Isabella, Duchess of York. Although most scholars discount this interpretation, A. Brusendorff, *The Chaucer Tradition* (1925), defended it in detail. In addition to the myth and possible occasion, the narrative has another level of meaning: description of an astrological conjunction between the planets Mars and Venus. On this level, the poem is a study of free will and determinism: as gods, the lovers appear to respond to voluntary impulses, while as planets they move to fixed laws. This hints at the world view explored more fully in *Troylus and Criseyde*. The complaint itself is composed of five sequences of three balade stanzas each, without the common refrain which marks the balade as a musical composition.

In many manuscripts, although not in those of Shirley, who evidently knew the lyrics best, *Complaint of Venus* (no.4) forms a conclusion to *Complaint of Mars*. It is made up of three balades adapted from the French of Oton de Graunson, a Savoyard knight attached to the English court, noteworthy for his melodramatic career (and see below under short poems 19-22). Although very conventional, these verses are interesting because we can compare them directly with their French original as edited in James I. Wimsatt, *Chaucer and the Poems of Ch* (1982).

A Complaint unto Pity (no.5) uses the personification of the allegory of love, popularized by *Roman de la Rose* and elucidated by C.S. Lewis, *The Allegory of Love* (1936). It is striking that Chaucer so seldom made use of personification in spite of its pervasive appearance in his French models. The structure is again narrative followed by a "bill of complaint" made up of three triplets of balade stanzas without the common refrain. The artificiality and conventionality of this poem is like the artificiality and conventionality of *Prier a Nostre Dame* and its interest is the same. Although no specific source has been identified, it shows Chaucer as translator, rendering into English the polished idiom of French court poetry.

The jottings that have been grouped by modern editors under the heading *A Balade of Pity* (no.6) are even more experimental than *A Complaint unto Pity* to which they are joined in Shirley's manuscripts. The first section comprises two stanzas in rhyme royal playing with phrases and rhymes that show up more effectively in *Book of the Duchess* and later poems. The second and third sections appear to be experiments in terza rima, perhaps reflecting an awareness of Italian poetry (and see no. 19). Neither of these experiments (which should come out *ababcbcdc*) is perfect. Perhaps Chaucer found English rhymes too "scarce" to work further in this form. The last section is in ten-line stanzas, again unique and again not perfect. There is no evidence that these experiments with prosody were composed at the same time.

Womanly Noblesse (no. 7) is attributed to Chaucer in the one manuscript in which it survives, but its genuineness is questioned since "Souvenaunce" (l.13), "outrance" (l. 25), and "unbuxumnesse" (l.26) occur nowhere else in Chaucer's poetry. It is a formulaic courtly love expression of the sovereignty of the lady and the humility of the lover.

To Rosemounde (no. 8) is a lovely balade, of a sort that can be sung to Machaut's music. Here French polish is perfectly wedded to English idiom. The sentiment is spiced with typical Chaucerian humor. Like *Womanly Noblesse* it is found in a single manuscript and contains words (mapamounde, l.2; tyne, l.9) not found in Chaucer's other poems. But this lyric is so delightful that it *should* be by Chaucer. Edith Rickert and others have proposed that it was addressed to Richard's child-wife, Isabel of France (see Introduction to *Legend of Good Women*), and the teasing, affectionate tone does seem appropriate for an old courtier addressing the little queen.

Poems 19, 20, 21, 22, not attributed to Chaucer in the manuscripts, have been since Skeat's edition included because of their "Chaucerian" manner. (To these we might now add fifteen poems in French initialed "Ch" that have recently turned up in MS French 15 at the University of Pennsylvania. The manuscript also contains the text of Oton de Gaunson's *Cinque balades* closest to Chaucer's *Complaint of Venus*. This anthology of 310 French poems is exactly the sort that would have circulated in the English court in Chaucer's time, and unlike the manuscripts of Chaucer's English poems, it dates from the fourteenth century. The "Ch" poems have been edited, translated, and discussed, by James I. Wimsatt, *Chaucer and the Poems of Ch*, 1982.)

Merciless Beaute (no. 19) is an experiment in interlaced triplet stanzas though not terza rima; this appears to be a triple roundel intended to be sung. *Against Women Unconstant* (no. 20), is an uncharacteristic balade of reproach, perhaps dealing with some social or political situation. *A Balade of Complaint* (no. 21) and *An Amorous Complaint* (no.22) are as formulaic as, but less successful than, *Womanly Noblesse,* and should probably be regarded as non-Chaucerian.

Among the philosophical poems, the authenticity of *Proverbe of Chaucer* (no. 9) has also been questioned since proverbial sayings have a way of becoming attached to famous names, but the polished language makes these memorable. They are two quatrains in which the first two lines pose a question, and the second two answer with a proverb. In B.J. Whiting, *Proverbs, Sentences, and Proverbial Phrases* (1968), the first is like H305 and the second like M774. The second also appears in *Melibee* (*CT* VII.1215), translated directly from its French source.

The others in this philosophical group are sometimes called the "Boethian poems" since they express sentiments found in the *Consolatio Philosophiae*. *Fortune* (no.10) is comprised of three balades on how to bear misfortune, similar to sections of *Boece* II. pr. 1-4 and 8. The envoy, which exists in only one of the ten manuscripts, seems to allude to an ordinance passed on March 8, 1390, and it has been suggested that the occasion for the poem was to ask relief from having to repay the money Chaucer lost in three robberies in September 1390 while serving as Clerk of the King's Works. But the three balades themselves are very general and the editors of the Variorum edition discount the topical explanation.

Balade de Bon Conseil (*Truth*, no. 11), surviving in thirty copies, was the most popular of Chaucer's short poems. Its rejection of temporal concerns is like that of *Boece*. The Shirley manuscript says that it was written by Chaucer "vppon his dethe bedde." As with *Fortune*, the envoy survives in only one manuscript, which may indicate two versions, one generalized and one for a special occasion. Chaucer could have added the envoy to the generalized version, but it would be more like him to take the opportunity of a specific occasion to express a universal sentiment. In this case, the occasion could have been the distress Chaucer shared with his friend Sir Philip de la Vache when they both lost their government emoluments in the "merciless" parliament of 1388.

Moral Balade (*Gentilesse*, no. 12), dealing with the theme of natural gentilesse made famous by the Wife of Bath's Tale (*CT*, III.1109 and note), is another expression of sentiments so timely that the entire balade was quoted in a poem by Henry Scogan (see no. 17 below). *Former Age* (no. 13) is a free translation of *Boece* II. met. 5. One wonders why Chaucer as a poet did not put all the metra of his translation of *Boece* into verse; but even though one of the two surviving texts of this poem is attached to a copy of Chaucer's translation, it does not suggest such an intention. It resembles too many other classical and medieval appeals to the Golden Age as criticism of the greed and violence of contemporary society. It could well reflect Chaucer's disillusionment with political events in the 1380s or 90s, but it lacks an objective correlative like the envoys to *Fortune* and *Balade de Bon Conseil*.

The final group is composed of poems addressed to individuals (*Bon Conseil* falls in this group as well as with the philosophical poems). *Lack of Steadfastnesse* (no. 14) is according to John Shirley's headnote addressed to King Richard and it parallels closely what contemporary chroniclers (and perhaps Chaucer himself in the Prologue to the *Legend of Good Women*—see that Introduction) were saying about Richard's reign. But if so Chaucer again uses such conventional language to make his specific points that J.E. Cross, "The Old Swedish *Trohetsvisan*," *Saga Book* (1965), can cite exact verbal parallels in a wide variety of poems in Latin and the various vernaculars.

To Adam Scryven (no. 15) is the sort of exasperated expostulation nearly every author has at one time or another addressed to his typist. It too survives in a unique text in one of John Shirley's manuscripts. The poem is important because it indicates that Chaucer did have fair copies of his poems made. Why not one of these has survived becomes even more mysterious. The linking of *Boece* and *Troylus* suggests that Chaucer was working on these at the same time (c1380-85), which is confirmed by the Boethian coloring of *Troylus*. Chaucer's plea that *Troylus* not be miswritten (*TC* V.1795) ties in with his admonition to Adam.

Lenvoy de Chaucer a Bukton (no. 16) and *Lenvoy a Scogan* (no. 17) are verse epistles like those that Machaut and Deschamps addressed to intimate friends. It has been observed that Bukton, Scogan, and Vache were all, like Chaucer himself, members of the emerging secular administrative class which would in the course of the next two centuries take over control of the nation from the barons and the bishops, and that this circle of active, talented, educated friends suggests the real audience for Chaucer's sophisticated poetry. The urbanity of the two verse epistles suggests the coffee-house society of the 18th century. *Bukton* is the kind of poem a middle-aged widower whose domestic life had not been idyllic might address to a middle-aged friend contemplating marriage. The phrasing and sentiment echo the Wife of Bath's Prologue, both in their good natured cynicism and their

learned allusions to antifeminist literature (ll.6, 18-22), and the Wife is referred to at l.29. Much ink has been spilled over just which Bukton is being addressed, but his identity has not yet been established.

Henry Scogan has been identified as a courtier who about 1400 was named tutor to the sons of Henry IV. About 1407 he addressed to his royal charges a "Moral Balade" in which he quoted the entire text of Chaucer's *Gentilesse* (no. 12). Chaucer's *Lenvoy a Scogan* (no. 17) is dated by its references to rainstorms between 1390 and 93, when Scogan was still a young attendant at court. As with *Bukton*, Chaucer is warning his friend against the dangers of love. He pokes fun at himself in the persona of the fat man unsuited for love that he had used first in the *House of Fame* (ll.31, 35, 40) and then in the headlink to *Thopas* (*CT* VII.700). But beneath the banter there is a somber note. Evidently Chaucer felt—as other poets have felt as they reached middle age—that his poetic gift was deserting him (ll.38ff). The envoy turns this into a begging poem. Scogan who is still living at the "stremes hed" in court is asked to intercede for Chaucer who is living in "solytarie wildernesse," perhaps in Greenwich.

Complaint of Chaucer to His Purse (no. 18) is probably the last poem Chaucer wrote. Its personal voice, mastery of idiom, and deft verbal play on the fiscal and sexual connotations of "light" and "heavy" reveal how far Chaucer had come as a poet since *Prier a Nostre Dame*. This poem was written between September 1399 when Henry was elected king (ll.22-23 note) and the time when Henry granted Chaucer a large annuity (most recently argued as February 1400, backdated to October 13, Henry's coronation day). Chaucer never lived to collect all of the pension due him, and he may have actually been in need; "this towne" (l.17) has been interpreted as Westminster Close, a refuge for debtors, where Chaucer signed the lease for his final residence on December 24, 1399. For details see Andrew J. Finnel, "The Poet as Sunday Man," *Chaucer Review* (1973).

Short Poems

Poems Attributed to Chaucer in the Manuscripts

1   **PRIER A NOSTRE DAME**

Of Our Lady the ABC.

Incipit carmen secundum ordinem litterarum alphabeticum.

Almyghty and al mercyable quene,
To whom that al this world fleeth for socour,
To have relees of synne, of sorwe, of tene,
Gloriouse virgyne, of alle floures flour,
To the I flee, confounded in errour.   5
Help and releve, thow myghty debonayre,
Have mercy of my perilouse langour.
Venquysshed hath me my cruel adversayre.

Bountee so fix hath in thine hert his tent,
That wel I wot, thow wolt my socour bee.   10
Thow kanst not werne him that with good
    entent
Axeth thyn help, thine herte is ay so free.
Thow art largesse of pleyn felicitee,
Haven of refut, of quiete, and of reste.
Loo, how that theves seven chasen me!   15
Help, lady bryght, er that my shippe
    to-breste.

Comfort is noon but in yow, lady dere,
For loo, my synne and my confusioun,
Which oughte not in thy presence appere,
Han take on me a grevouse accioun   20
Of verray ryght and desperacioun,
And, as by ryght, they myghten wel sustene
That I were worthy my dampnacioun,
Nere mercy of yow, blysful hevenes quene.

Doute is ther noon, quene of misericorde,   25
That thow nart cause of grace and mercy
    here.
God vouched sauf thurgh the with us
    t'acorde,
For certes, Cristes blysful moder dere,
Were now the bowe ybent in swich manere
As hit was first, of justice and of ire,   30
The ryghtful God nolde of no mercy here—
But thurgh thee han we grace, as we desire.

Text from MS Fairfax 16 (F), with variants from Cambridge Ff.5.30 (C); see "The Text of This Edition," p. 966. *Priere* title in MS Pepys 2006; *ABC* is Lydgate's title; *Incipit* is Shirley's title (see Brusendorff, *Chaucer Tradition*, p. 238). In F&c the piece is an independent work attributed to Chaucer; in C&c it is inserted without attribution into an anonymous translation of Deguilleville.

2 socour, help (rescue). F&c *that om.* **3** *of sorwe:* C&c *of sinne, sorwe, and teene.* **6 debonayre,** gracious lady. **9 Bountee,** goodness. **11 werne,** deny. **12 free,** generous. **13 largesse of pleyn felicitee,** generosity of perfect happiness. **14 refut,** refuge. *Pèlerinage,* "*de salu porte.*" **15 theves seven,** Seven Deadly Sins. *chasen:* F *chacen.* **20 accioun,** i.e., taken legal action against. *Pèlerinage,* "*Contre moy font une accion.*" The idea is that sin is accusing the sinner before the bar of heaven. The law court is a familiar figure in penitential literature. **21 verray ryght,** just right. **22 by ryght . . . sustene,** by the canon of justice, sustain (prove). **24 Nere,** were it not for. F&c *Ne.* **25 misericorde,** pity. C&c *thou queen.* **27 vouched sauf,** consented. **30 first,** i.e., before the Incarnation. **31 here,** hear.

673

Ever hath myn hope of refut in the be,
For here-beforn, ful ofte, in many a wyse,
Unto mercy hastow receyved me.   35
But mercy, lady, at the grete assise,
Whan we shul come before the hye justise.
So litel good shal thanne in me be founde
That but thou er that day correcte me,
Of verrey ryght my werk wol me confounde.   40

Fleeing, I flee for socour to thy tent,
Me for to hide fro tempest ful of drede,
Beseching yow that ye yow nat absent
Though I be wikke. O help yet at this nede!
Al have I ben a best in wytte and dede,   45
Yet, lady, thow me clothe wyth thy grace.
Thyn enemy and myn—lady, tak hede—
Unto my deth in poynt is me to chace.

Gloriouse mayde and moder, which that
          never
Were bitter, nor in erthe nor in see,   50
But ful of swetnesse and of mercy ever,
Help that my Fader be nat wroth with me.
Spek thow, for I ne dar nat him ysee.
So have I doon in erthe, allas the while,
That certes but that thou my socour bee,   55
To stynke eterne he wol my goost exile.

He vouched sauf, telle him, as was his wille,
Become a man as for our alliaunce,
And with his blood he wroot the blysful bille
Upon the crois as general acquytaunce   60
To every penytent in ful creaunce.
And therfor, lady bryght, thow for us pray.

Than shalt thou both stynte al his grevaunce,
And make our foo to faylen of his pray.

I wot hit wel, thow wolt ben oure socour,   65
That art so ful of bountee, in certeyne,
For whan a soule falleth in errour,
Thy pitee gooth and haleth him ageyne.
Than makestow his pees with his sovereyn,
And bringest him out of the crooked strete.   70
Whoso the loveth, he shal nat love in veyn—
That shal he fynde as he the life shal lete.

Kalenderes enlumyned ben they
That in this world ben lyghted with thi name,
And whoso gooth to yow the ryghte wey,   75
Him thar nat drede in soule to be lame.
Now, quene of comfort, sith thou art that same
To whom I seche for my medycine,
Lat not my foo no more my wounde entame.
Myn hele into thyn hand alle I resygne.   80

Lady, thy sorwe kan I nat purtreye
Under the crois, ne His grevous penaunce.
But for your bothe peynes, I yow preye,
Lat nat our aller foo make his bobaunce
That he hath in his lystes of meschaunce   85
Convict that ye both han boght so dere.
As I seyde erst, thou grounde of our substaunce,
Contynue on us thy pitous eyen clere.

Moises that saugh the bussh with flambes rede
Brenninge of which ther never a stikke brende,
Was signe of thyn unwemmed maydenhede.   91
Thou art the bussh on which ther gan discende

---

33 C&c *refuit been in thee.* **34** F *often;* a om. **35** C&c *Hast thou to misericorde,* but cf. *Pélerinage,* "Quant a merci m'as recu." **36 assise,** court (i.e., Last Judgment). **38 good:** C&c *fruit,* but *Pélerinage,* "bien." **39 correcte me,** note the false rhyme found in all MSS except C, which has *me chastyse* over an erasure. **43** *Beseching:* F&c *Besekyng.* **44 wikke,** wicked. **45 wytte:** C&c *wille.* **48 in poynt,** on the point of. **50 bitter,** this is word play on "Maria" and the Hebrew "*marah,*" bitterness; cf. *Pélerinage,* "Glorieuse vierge mere/Qui a nul onques amere (bitter)." **56 stynke eterne,** hell; this figure is Chaucer's addition. **58 as for:** C&c *to have our.* **59 bille,** legal document. C&c *precious blood/the bille.* **60 acquytaunce,** pardon. **61 creaunce,** i.e., in complete good faith. **63 stynte,** check (stop). **64 our foo,** Satan. **66** C&c *Thou art.* **68 haleth,** pulls him back out. **70** F *of the crooked strete* om. **72 lete,** give up. **73** Note that modern *J* is lacking in the sequence; cf. l. 153n. *ben:* F *bethe.* **73 Kalenderes enlumyned,** in church calendars, names of special festivals were written with illuminated letters. **74 lyghted,** made happy (illuminated). **75 ryghte wey,** direct way. **76 Him thar nat drede,** i.e., he need not dread. **79 entame,** reopen. **80 hele,** health. **84 bobaunce,** boast. *aller* (all, gen.,): G&c *alder.* **85 lystes of meschaunce,** wiles with bad luck. **86 Convict that,** etc., convicted (the soul) that you both (Mary and Jesus) have bought so dearly. **87 erst . . . grounde . . . substaunce,** first (before), basis, being. **88 on:** F *in.* **91 unwemmed,** unblemished. The burning bush (Exod. 3.2) was a recognized symbol of the virgin birth.

The Holy Gost, the which that Moises wende
Had ben afire, and this was in figure.
Now lady, fro the fire thou us defende   95
Which that in helle eternally shal dure.

Noble princesse that never haddest pere,
Certes if any comfort in us bee
That cometh of the, Cristes moder dere,
We han noon other melodie or glee   100
Us to rejoyse in our adversitee,
Ne advocat noon that wol and dar so prey
For us, and that for litel hyre as ye
That helpen for an Ave Marie or twey.

O verray light of eyen that ben blynde,   105
O verray lust of labour and distresse,
O tresorere of bounte to mankynde,
The whom God chees to moder for humblesse!
From his ancile he made the maistresse
Of heven and erthe, our bille up for to beede.
This worlde awaiteth ever on thy godenesse,   111
For thou ne failest never wight at neede.

Purpos I have sommetyme for t'enquere
Wherfore and why the Holy Goost the sought,
Whan Gabrieles voys cam to thyn ere.   115
He nat to werre us swich a wonder wrought,
But for to save us that he sithen bought.
Than nedeth us no wepene us for to save,
But oonly ther we did nat, as we ought,
Do penytence and mercy axe and have.   120

Queen of comfort, yet whan I me bethynke
That I agilt have bothe him and thee,
And that my soule is worthy for to synke,
Allas, I katyf, whider may I flee?
Who shal unto thy sone my mene be?   125
Who but thyself that art of pitee welle?

Thow hast more routhe on oure adversite
Than in this world myghte any tonge telle.

Redresse me, moder, and me chastise,
For certeynly my fadres chastisinge,   130
That dar I nat abiden in no wise,
So hidouse is his ryghtful rekeninge.
Moder, of whom our mercy gan to springe,
Beth ye my juge and eke my soules leche,
For ever in yow is pitee haboundinge   135
To ech that wol of pitee yow beseche.

Soth is that He ne graunteth noo pitee
Withoute the. For God of his goodnesse
Foryeveth noon, but hit lyke unto the.
He hath the maked vicaire and maistresse   140
Of alle this worlde, and eke governeresse
Of hevene; and he represseth his justise
Aftir thy wille, and therefore in witnesse
He hath the crowned in so riall wise.

Temple devout, ther God hath his woninge,   145
Fro which these mysbeleved pryved been,
To yow my soule penytent I brynge.
Receyve me; I kan no ferther fleen!
With thornes venymouse, O hevene queen,
For which the erthe acursed was ful yore,   150
I am so wounded, as ye may wel seen,
That I am lost almost, it smert so sore.

Virgyne, that art so noble of apparayle,
That ledest us into the hye toure
Of Paradys, thou me wysse and counsayle,   155
How I may have thy grace and thy socoure.
Al have I ben in filthe and in erroure,
Lady, unto that court thou me adjourne
That cleped is thy bench, O fresshe floue,
Ther as that mercy ever shal sojourne.   160

---

93 **wende,** thought. 99 C *thou Cristes.* 105 **of,** to. 106 **lust of,** joy to. 107 **tresorere of bounte,** treasurer (giver) of bounty. 109 **ancile,** serving maid (Luke 1.38 "*Ecce ancilla Domini*"). 110 **bille . . . beede,** petition, pray (present). 116 **to werre,** to (make) war (on). 117 **sithen,** afterward. 125 **mene,** mediator. 127 **routhe,** compassion. 129 **Redresse,** vindicate. 131 **abiden,** endure. 132 **ryghtful rekeninge,** just account-keeping. 134 **leche,** leech (physician). 135 **haboundinge,** abounding. 137 *He:* C&c *God.* 139 **hit lyke,** it is pleasing. 145 **woninge,** dwelling. 146 **mysbeleved pryved,** unbelievers excluded. *pryved* in St. John's &c: FC&c *deprived.* 153, 161 Note that modern *U* and *W* are lacking in the sequence, cf. l. 73n. 153 **apparayle,** bearing (behavior). 155 **wysse,** instruct. 158 **adjourne,** i.e., fix the day of appearance. Again the poem falls into legal terminology, cf. l. 20ff. 159 **bench,** the Middle English term for "court" (e.g., King's Bench), here introduced into the translation by Chaucer.

Xpūs, thy sone, that in this world alyghte
Upon the crois to suffre his passioun,
And eke that Longius his herte pighte
And made his herte blood to renne adoun,
And al was this for my salvacioun,   165
And I to him am fals and eke unkynde,
And yet he wol not my dampnacioun—
This thanke I yow, socour of al mankynde.

Ysaac was figure of His dethe, certeyne,
That so ferforth his fader wolde obeye   170
That him ne rought nothing to be sleyne,
Ryght so thy sone lyst, as a lamb, to deye.

Now lady, ful of mercy, I yow preye,
Sith he his mercy mesured so large,
Be ye nat skant, for al we synge and seye   175
That ye been fro vengeaunce ay oure targe.

Zakarye yow clepeth the open welle
To wasshe synful soule out of his gilt.
Therfore this lessoun oughte I wel to telle
That nere thy tender herte, we were spilt.   180
Now lady bryght, sith thou kanst and wilt
Been to the sede of Adam mercyable,
Bryng us to that palays that is bilt
To penytents that been to mercy able. Amen.   184

Explicit

2   ANELIDA AND ARCITE

The Compleynt of Feire Anelida and Fals Arcite.

Invocation

Thou fers god of armes, Mars the rede,
That in the frosty countre called Trace,
Within thy grisly temples ful of drede,
Honoured art as patroun of that place,
With thy Bellona, Pallas, ful of grace,   5
Be present, and my song contynew and gye.

At my begynning thus I to the crye.

For hit ful depe is sonken in my mynde,
With pitous hert in Englyssh to endyte
This olde storie in Latyn which I fynde,   10
Of Quene Anelida and fals Arcite,
That elde, which al can frete and bite,

---

161 Xpūs, Christus. The Greek *chi* followed by *rho* with a mark of abbreviation over *u* was a common contraction for Christus in medieval MSS (cf. Xmas). **163 Longius . . . pighte,** Longinus, pierced. This allusion was introduced by Chaucer. The account of Longinus, the blind centurion who pierced Jesus' side on the cross and had his sight restored by drops of the sacred blood, is found in the pseudoepigraphic Gospel of Nicodemus. **169 Ysaac was figure,** a reference to the medieval concept of figural interpretation according to which characters and events in the Old Testament were thought to prefigure characters and events in the New Testament; so the sacrifice of Isaac (Gen. 22; Hebrews 11:17–19) prefigured the death of Jesus. Cf. l. 94 above. **170 forforth,** far (completely). **171 rought,** cared about. **175 skant . . . al we,** niggardly, we all. **176 targe,** shield. **177 yow clepeth,** calls you (Mary). Zech. 13:1 is usually applied to the blood of Christ. **180 nere . . . spilt,** were it not for, lost. **181 F&c *bryght* om. 184 To penytents,** for penitents.

Text from MS Fairfax 16 (F) with corrections and variants from Caxton (C) up to the "Complaint," and Pepys 2006 (P) to the end. See "The Text of This Edition," p. 966. In F the *Complaint* precedes the *Invocation* and *Narrative.*

1 The first stanzas of this poem and the name Arcite are taken from Boccaccio's *Teseida,* which Chaucer was evidentaly perusing in preparation for the full-scale adaptation that eventually became the Knight's Tale. Stanza 1 here is indebted to *Tes.* 1.3. **2 Trace,** Thrace (modern Bulgaria). **5 Bellona, Pallas,** goddess of war, goddess of wisdom, evidently confused by Chaucer as by other medieval writers. These references are not in *Tes.,* but are found in its source, Statius' *Thebaid* (7.40), which describes Mars' temple in Thrace. *thy:* other MSS *the.* **6 gye,** guide. **10 storie in Latyn,** this is the medieval writer's familiar claim to classical authority (cf. Lollius, *TC*1.394). No source has been found for the plot of this poem. **12 elde . . . frete,** age, eat (cf. Ger. *fressen*).

As hit hath freten mony a noble storie,
Hath nygh devoured out of oure memorie.

Be favorable eke, thou Polymya, 15
On Parnaso that with thy sustres glade,
By Elycon, not fer from Cirrea,
Singest with vois memorial in the shade,
Under the laurer which that may not fade,
And do that I my shippe to haven wynne. 20
First folow I Stace, and after him Corynne.

Narrative

Iamque domos patrias, Cithice post aspera gentis, &c.

Whan Theseus with werres longe and grete
The aspre folke of Cithe had overcome,
With laurer crouned, in his char golde-bete,
Home to his contre houses is ycome, 25
For which the peple blisful al and somme
So criden that to the sterres hit went,
And him to honouren dide al her entent.

Beforn this duke, in signe of victorie,
The trompes come, and in his baner large 30
The ymage of Mars, and in token of glorie
Men myghte sene of tresour many a charge,
Many a bright helm, and many a spere and
    targe,
Many a fresh knyght, and many a blysful
    route,
On hors, on fote, in al the felde aboute. 35

Ipolita his wife, the hardy quene
Of Cithia, that he conquered had,
With Emelye hir yonge suster shene,
Faire in a char of golde he with him lad,

That al the grounde about hir char she sprad 40
With brightnesse of the beaute in hir face,
Fulfilled of largesse and of alle grace.

With his tryumphe and laurer corouned thus,
In al the floure of fortunes yeving,
Let I this noble prince Theseus 45
Towarde Athenes in his wey ryding,
And founde I wol in shortly for to bring
The sley wey of that I gan to write—
Of Quene Anelida and fals Arcite.

Mars which that thro his furiouse course of ire
The olde wrath of Juno to fulfille 51
Hath set the peples hertes bothe on fire
Of Thebes and Grece, everich other to kille
With blody speres, ne rested never stille,
But throng now her, now ther, among hem
    bothe, 55
That everych other slough, so wer they wrothe.

For whan Amphiorax and Tydeus,
Ipomedon and Parthonope also,
Were ded, and slayn proud Campaneus,
And whan the wrecches Thebans, bretheren
    two, 60
Were slayn, and Kyng Adrastus home ago,
So desolat stode Thebes and so bare
That no wyght coude remedie of his care.

And whan the olde Creon gan espye
How that the blood roial was broght adoun, 65
He held the cite by his tyrannye,
And dyd the gentils of that regioun
To ben his frendes, and duellen in the toun.
So what for love of him, and what for awe,
The noble folk wer to the toune idrawe. 70

---

14 *oure:* C *my.* **15 Polymya,** Polymnia, one of the Muses. **17 Elycon . . . Cirrea,** as elsewhere, Chaucer thinks of Helicon as the name of an inspirational spring on Mt. Parnassus instead of another mountain in Boetia sacred to the Muses. Cirra, an ancient town near Delphi, at the foot of Parnassus. **19 laurer,** laurel. **20 do,** i.e., arrange it so that. **21 Stace . . . Corynne,** Statius, *Thebaid,* on which the next stanzas are modeled; Corinnus, another legendary writer on the Trojan War. But see l. 10n. **22 *Cithice,*** Scythia. F&c here include three lines from *Theb.* 12.519–21, of which 519 and half of 520 are found also at the head of KT in *CT.* **23 aspre,** fierce. **24 laurer . . . char golde-bete,** laurel, chariot, gold-plated (i.e., with beaten gold). *With:* F&c *The.* **25 houses:** C *hool; Theb.* "*domos patrias,*" native homes. There are echoes of these lines in KT, *CT.* 1.965ff. **32 charge,** load. **33 targe,** shield. **34 blysful route,** happy company (of soldiers). **38 shene,** beautiful. **42 largesse,** generosity. **48 sley . . . of that,** deceitful, about which. **50** At this point, Chaucer returns to *Tes.* 2.10–12 as his source. **55 throng,** pressed. **57 Amphiorax,** etc., these are all characters in the famous siege of the seven against Thebes. Chaucer treats this in a little more detail in *TC* v.1485ff. **58** F&c *and* om.; *Prothonolope.* **63 *care:*** C *fare.* **68 duellen:** other MSS *wonnen;* C *women.*

Among al these, Anelida the quene
Of Ermony was in that toun duelling,
That fairer was then is the sunne shene.
Throughout the world so gan hir name spring,
That hir to seen had every wyght lyking,   75
For as of trouthe is ther noon hir lyche
Of al thes wymen in this worlde riche.

Yong was this quene, of twenty yer of elde,
Of mydel stature, and of suche fairenesse
That nature had a joye hir to behelde.   80
And for to speken of hir stidfastnesse,
She passed bothe Penolope and Lucresse,
And shortly, if she shal be comprehended,
In hir ne myght nothing been amended.

This Theban knyght Arcite eke, sothe to seyne,
Was yonge, and therwithal a lusty knyght,   86
But he was double in love and nothing pleyne,
And subtil in that crafte over any wyght,
And with his kunning wan this lady bryght,
For so forforth he gan hir trouthe assure,   90
That she him trusted over any creature.

What shuld I seyn? She loved Arcite so
That whan that he was absent any throw,
Anon hir thoght hir herte brast atwo;
For in hir sight to hir he bare him low,   95
So that she wende have al his herte yknow.
But he was fals; hit nas but feyned chere,
As nedeth not to men such craft to lere.

But nevertheles, ful mykel besynesse
Had he er that he myght his lady wynne,   100
And sworne he wolde dyen for distresse,
Or from his wit he seyde he wolde twynne—
Alas the whyle, for hit was routhe and synne
That she upon his sorowes wolde rewe!

But nothing thinketh the fals as doth the
      trewe.   105

Hir fredom fond Arcite in suche manere
That al was his that she hath, moche and lyte,
Ne to no creature made she chere
Ferther than that hit lyked to Arcite.
Ther was no lak with which he myghte hir wite,
She was so forforth yeven him to plese   111
That al that lyked him, hit did hir ese.

Ther nas to hir no maner lettre isent
That touched love from any maner wyght,
That she ne shewed hit him er hit was
      brent—   115
So pleyn she was, and did hir fulle myght
That she nyl hyden nothing from hir knyght
Lest he of any untrouthe hir upbreyde.
Withouten bode his heste she obeyde.

And eke he made him jelous over hire   120
That what that any man had to hir seyd
Anoon he wolde preyen hir to swere
What was that word, or make him evel apayd.
Than wende she out of hir wit have brayd.
But al this nas but sleght and flaterye—   125
Withoute love he feyned jelousye.

And al this toke she so debonerly
That al his wil hir thoghte hit skilful thing,
And ever the lenger she loved him tendirly,
And did him honour as he were a kyng.   130
Hir hert was wedded to him with a ring.
So forforth upon trouthe is hir entent
That wher he goth, hir herte with him went.

Whan she shal ete, on him is so hir thoght
That wel unnethe of mete toke she kepe,   135

---

72 Ermony, evidently Armenia, on the Black Sea; but from here on no source has been discovered for the poem. **75 wyght,** person. **77** *thes:* C&c *the.* **81 stidfastnesse,** constancy (faithfulness). **82 bothe:** C&c *hath.* **85** *Arcite* om. in all authorities. **87 double . . . pleyne,** devious, straightforward. **90 forforth,** far. **93 throw,** time. **95 bare . . . low,** i.e., was so humble. **96 wende,** thought. **97 chere,** manner (expression). **103 routhe,** grief. **104 rewe,** take pity. **105 nothing,** i.e., not at all. In what follows Anelida and Arcite resemble the falcon and tercelet in SqT, *CT* vII.499ff. **106 fredom,** generosity. **107** F&c *both moche.* **108 made . . . chere,** she was friendly (cheerful). **110 lak . . . wite,** i.e., he could know no shortcoming in her. **112** F&c *hir her an ese.* **118 upbreyde,** scold. **119 bode . . . heste,** bidding, command. *heste:* F *hert.* **123 evel apayd,** i.e., be in bad humor. **124 brayd,** started. **125 sleght,** deceit. F&c *this* om. **127 debonerly,** graciously. **128 wil . . . skilful,** desire, reasonable. **132** *So forforth:* F *For so.* **135 unnethe,** scarcely.

And whan that she was to hir rest ybroght,
On him she thoght alwey til that she slepe.
Whan he was absent, prevely she wepe.
Thus lyveth feir Anelida the quene
For fals Arcite that did hir al this tene. 140

This fals Arcite, of his newfangelnesse,
For she to him so lowly was and trewe,
Toke lesse deyntee for hir stidfastnesse,
And saw another lady, proud and newe,
And ryght anon he clad him in hir hewe, 145
Wot I not whether in white, rede, or grene,
And falsed fair Anelida the quene.

But neverthelesse, gret wonder was hit noon
Thogh he wer fals, for hit is kynde of man
Sith Lamek was, that is so longe agoon, 150
To ben in love as fals as ever he can.
He was the first fader that began
To loven two, and was in bigamye—
And he found tentes first, but if men lye.

This fals Arcite, sumwhat most he feyn 155
Whan he wex fals, to covere his traitorie,
Ryght as an hors that can both bite and pleyn,
For he bar hir on honde of trecherie,
And swore he coude hir doublenesse espie,
And al was falsnes that she to him ment. 160
Thus swore this thefe, and forth his way he
              went.

Alas, what hert myght enduren hit,
For routhe or wo, hir sorow for to telle?
Or what man hath the cunning or the wit?
Or what man myght within the chambre
              duelle
If I to him rehersen shal the helle 166

That suffreth feir Anelida the quene
For fals Arcite, that did hir al this tene?

She wepith, waileth, swowneth pitously;
To grounde dede she falleth as a ston; 170
Al crampyssheth hir lymes crokedly;
She speketh as hir wit were al agon;
Other colour then asshen hath she non;
Ne non other word speketh she moche or lyte
But, "Mercie, cruel herte myn, Arcite!" 175

And thus endureth til that she was so mate
That she nad foot on which she may sustene,
But forth languisshing ever in this estate,
Of whiche Arcite hath nouther routhe ne tene.
His herte was elleswher, newe and grene, 180
That on hir wo ne deyneth him not to thinke.
Him rekketh never wher she flete or synke.

His new lady holdeth him so narowe,
Up by the bridel, at the staves ende,
That every word he dred hit as an arowe. 185
Hir daunger made him bothe bowe and bende,
And as hir liste made him turne or wende,
For she ne graunted him in hir lyvinge
No grace why that he hath lust to singe,

But drof him forth. Unnethe list hir knowe 190
That he was servaunt unto hir ladishippe;
But lest that he wer proud she helde him lowe.
Thus serveth he withouten fee or shippe.
She sent him now to londe, now to shippe;
And for she yaf him daunger al his fille, 195
Therfor she had him at hir oune wille.

Ensample of this, ye thrifty wymmen alle,
Take here of Anelida and fals Arcite,

---

137 *alwey:* F&c *ay.* 140 **tene,** grief. 141 **newfangelnesse,** fickleness. 142 **lowly,** humble. 143 **Toke lesse deyntee for,** set less value on. 145 **clad . . . in . . . hewe,** a reminder that knights wore their ladies' colors. 146 **white,** etc., i.e., any color but blue, which was symbolic of constancy. 149 **kynde,** nature. 150 **Lamek,** cf. Gen. 4.19–20. 154 **found,** invented. Actually, the verse says it was Jabal, his son, who invented tents. 155 **feyn,** pretend. 158 **bar hir,** accused her. 163 **routhe,** pity. 165 F&c *myght* om. 171 **crampyssheth,** cramps together. FC&c *Al* om. F *craumpysshe.* 176 **mate,** exhausted (dead). 177 **nad:** F&c *ne hath.* 178 **forth,** i.e., goes forth (on). F *for.* 179 **routhe ne tene,** pity nor grief. 182 **flete,** floated. 183 **so narowe,** under such tight control. F&c *holdeth him up.* 184 **staves ende,** shaft's end, i.e., tightly reined in between the shafts. 186 **daunger,** imperiousness. 188 **lyvinge,** lifetime. 189 **grace why . . . lust,** i.e., favor that would cause him to want to sing. 190 **list hir,** did it please her. 193 **fee or shippe,** fee or reward. C&c *mete or sype/shepe.* 194 **londe . . . shippe,** i.e., on dangerous missions; cf. *BD* 1024ff. 197 **thrifty,** skillful. 198 *here:* C&c *hede.* F *of, fals* om.

That for hir liste him "der herte" calle,
And was so meke, therfor he loved hir
    lyte. 200
The kynde of mannes hert is to delyte
In thing that straunge is, also God me save!
For what he may not gete, that wolde he
    have.

Now turne we to Anelida ageyn,
That pyneth day by day in langwisshinge, 205
But whan she saw that hir ne gat no geyn,
Upon a day ful sorowfully wepinge
She caste hir for to make a compleyninge,
And with hir owne honde she gan hit write,
And sente hit to hir Theban knyght Arcite. 210

The Compleynt of Anelida the Quene upon Fals Arcite.

Proem

So thirleth with the poynt of remembraunce
The swerd of sorowe, ywhet with fals plesaunce,
Myn herte bare of blis and blake of hewe,
That turned is to quaking al my daunce,
My surete in awhaped countenaunce, 215
Sith hit availeth not for to ben trewe.
For whoso trewest is, hit shal hir rewe,
That serveth love and doth hir observaunce
Alwey to oon, and chaungeth for no newe.

Strophe

I wot myself as wel as any wight, 220
For I loved oon with al my herte and myght
More then myself, an hundred thousand sithe,
And cleped him my hertes life, my knyght,
And was al his, as fer as hit was ryght,
And whan that he was glad, than was I blithe,
And his disese was my deth as swithe, 226
And he ayen his trouthe me had iplyght
For evermore, his lady me to kythe.

Alas, now hath he left me causeles,
And of my wo he is so routheles 230
That with oo worde him list not ones deyne
To bring ayen my sorowful hert in pes,
For he is caught up in another les.
Ryght as him list, he laugheth at my peyne,
And I ne can myn herte not restreyne 235
That I ne love him alwey, nevertheles.
And of al this I not to whom me pleyne.

And shal I pleyne—alas, the harde stounde—
Unto my foo that yaf my hert a wounde,
And yet desireth that myn harm be more? 240
Nay, certes, ferther wol I never founde
Non other help, my sores for to sounde.
My destany hath shap hit so ful yore;
I wil non other medecyne ne lore.
I wil ben ay ther I was ones bounde; 245
That I have seid, be seid for evermore.

Alas, wher is become youre gentilesse,
Youre wordes ful of plesaunce and humblesse,
Youre observaunces in soo low manere,
And your awayting and your besynesse 250
Upon me that ye calden your maistresse,
Your sovereigne lady in this worlde here?

199 hir liste, it pleased her. **201 kynde,** nature. **202 straunge,** cold, aloof. **208 caste hir,** decided. **211 thirleth,** pierces. Skeat cites Dante, "*Per la puntura della rimembranza,*" *Purg.* 12.20. F&c *thirled.* The stanzas of the "compleynt" are elaborate and artificial. The first and last lines, 211 and 350, are similar. All stanzas save 5 (256ff.) and 11 (317ff.) are 9 lines, varying between 8 and 10 syllables, rhyming *a a b a a b b a b* (stanza 9, 299ff., is monorhyme). **212 ywhet . . . plesaunce,** sharpened, pleasure. **214** P *in quakynge.* **215 surete . . . awhaped,** security, stupified. F&c *into a w(h)aped.* **216 availeth,** helps (advances one). **217 rewe,** regret. *hir:* F&c *him.* **219 Alwey to oon,** always with integrity. **220 wot,** know. **222 sithe,** times. **223 cleped:** P&c *called.* **226 disese . . . swithe,** distress, immediately. **227 trouthe . . . iplyght,** plighted his troth (given his word). **228 kythe,** recognize. **229** P&c *Now is he fals, alas, and causeles.* **230 routheles,** pitiless. **231 him list . . . deyne,** it does not please him, to deign (condescend). **233 les,** snare (leash). **234** *him:* F *me.* **236** PC&c *For to love him nothertheless.* **237 not . . . me pleyne,** do not know to whom to complain. **238 stounde,** time. **241 founde,** seek after. All MSS *be founde.* P&c *certes, for ther shall never be founde.* **242 sounde,** heal. **243** F&c *shapen it ful.* **244 wil . . . lore,** desire, advice. **249 observaunces . . . low,** services, humble. **250 awayting . . . besynesse,** waiting up (serving), attentiveness. **252** F *worlde ne here.*

Alas, and is ther nother word ne chere
Ye vouchesauf upon myn hevynesse?
Alas, youre love, I bye hit al to dere!   255

Now certes, swete, thogh that ye
Thus causeles the causer be
Of my dedely adversyte,
Your manly resoun oghte it to respite
To slene your frend, and namely me,   260
That never yet in no degre
Offended yow, as wisly He
That al wot out of wo my soule quyte!
But for I shewed yow, Arcite,
Al that men wolde to me write,   265
And was so besy yow to delyte—
My honor safe—meke, kynde, and fre,
Therfor ye put on me the wite,
And of me rekke not a myte,
Thogh the swerd of sorow byte   270
My woful herte thro your cruelte.

My swete foo, / why do ye so? / For shame!
And thenke ye / that furthered be / your
        name,
To love a newe / and ben untrewe? / Nay!
And putte yow / in sclaunder now / and
        blame,
And do to me / adversite / and grame,   276
That love yow most, / God, wel thou wost, /
        alway?
Yet turn ayein / and be al pleyn / somme day,
And than shal this / that now is mis / be game,
And al foryive / while that I lyve / may.   280

Antistrophe

Loo, herte myn, al this is for to seyn
As wheder shal I prey or elles pleyn?
Whiche is the wey to doon yow to be trewe?
For either mot I have yow in my cheyn,
Or with the dethe ye mot departe us
        tweyn.   285
Ther ben non other mene weyes newe;
For God so wisly on my soule rewe,
As verrely ye sleen me with the peyn
That may ye se unfeyned of myn hewe.

For thus ferforth have I my dethe soght;   290
Myself I mordre with my prevy thoght.
For sorow and routhe of your unkyndenesse
I wepe, I wake, I fast. Al helpeth noght.
I weyve joy that is to speke of oght,
I voyde companye, I fle gladnesse.   295
Who may avaunte hir bet of hevynesse
Then I? And to this plyte have ye me
        broght
Withoute gilt. Me nedeth no witnesse.

And shal I preye and weyve womanhede?
Nay, rather deth then do so foul a dede!   300
And axe mercy giltles? What nede?
And if I pleyn what lyf that I lede,
Yow rekketh not; that know I, out of drede.
And if I unto yow myn othes bede
For myn excuse, a skorn shal be my mede.   305
Your chere floureth, but hit wol not sede.
Ful longe agoon I oght to have take hede.

---

253 F *and om.* P&c *ther now no word.* 254 **vouchesauf . . . hevynesse,** bestow, sadness. 255 **bye hit . . . dere,** i.e., I pay too much for it. 256–71 This 16-line stanza approaches the structure of a virelay. 257 *causer:* P&c *cause.* 259 **respite,** reprieve (desist). 263 **wot,** knows. 264 P&c *But for I was so pleyn, Arcite.* The Shirley MSS then skips to l. 269. P&c 265 *In all my werkes, muche and lite,* and so on to l. 266. 266 **delyte,** please. 267 **fre,** generous. 268 **wite,** judgment (?). 269 P&c *(And) als (alas) ye rekke not a myte.* 272 This stanza and the one ending the "antistrophe" (l. 333ff.; the designations are Skeat's) are decasyllabic with complicated internal rhyme. 274 *Nay:* other MSS *Ay.* 276 **grame,** grief. 278 *turn:* FP&c *come. be al:* P&c *yet be;* C *be thou.* 279 F&c *And turne at this/that hath be mys/to game.* 281 **seyn,** see. 283 **doon,** make. 285 **departe,** separate. 286 **mene,** middle. *ben:* P&c *lye* (n.). 287 **rewe,** have pity. 289 **unfeyned of . . . hewe,** i.e., without coloring of pretense. 290 **ferforth,** far. ll. 290–98 om. in PC&c. 291 **mordre . . . prevy,** kill, secret. 292 **routhe,** grief. 293 **Al helpeth noght,** nothing helps. 294 **weyve joy . . . to speke,** i.e., I relinquish the joy of talking about it (my passion). 295 **voyde,** avoid. 296 **avaunte . . . bet . . . hevynesse,** boast, better, sadness. 297 **plyte,** plight. 299 **weyve womanhede,** relinquish womanhood (by becoming the aggressor in passion). *shal:* P&c *sholde.* 300 *deth/foul:* P&c *die/cruell.* 301 *giltles:* P&c *causeles.* 302 **pleyn what,** complain what sort of. 303 **Yow rekketh . . . out of drede,** to you it matters, without doubt. P&c *Than woll ye laugh. I know it, out.* 304 **bede,** pray. 305 **mede,** reward. 306 **chere floureth . . . sede,** expression (manner) flowers (promises), but it will not seed (produce results). 307 *oght to:* P&c *ofte(n);* other MSS *might.*

For thogh I had yow tomorow ageyn,
I myght as wel holde Aprill fro reyn
As holde yow, to make yow be stidfast.   310
Almighty God, of trouthe sovereign,
Wher is the trouthe of man? Who hath hit
    sleyn?
Who that hem loveth, she shal hem fynde as
    fast
As in a tempest is a roten mast.
Is that a tame best that is ay feyn   315
To renne away when he is lest agast?

Now mercie, swete, if I missey;
Have I seyde oght amys, I prey?
I not; my wit is al awey.
I fare as doth the song of *Chaunte-pleure*.   320
For now I pleyne and now I pley;
I am so mased that I dey;
Arcite hath born awey the key
Of al my worlde, and my good aventure.
For in this worlde there is no creature   325
Wakinge in more discomfiture
Then I, ne more sorow endure.
And if I slepe a furlong-wey or twey,
Then thenketh me that your figure
Before me stant, clad in asure,   330
To swere yet eft a newe assure
For to be trewe, and mercie me to prey.

The longe nyght / this wonder sight / I drye,

And on the day / for this afray / I dye,
And of al this / right noght, ywis, / ye
    reche.   335
Ne never mo / myn eyen two / be drye,
And to your routhe / and to your trouthe / I
    crye.
But welawey, / to fer be they / to feche.
Thus holdeth me / my destany / a wreche.
But me to rede / out of this drede, / or gye,   340
Ne may my wit, / so weyk is hit, / not streche.

Than ende I thus, sith I may do no more.
I yeve hit up for now and evermore.
For I shal never eft put in balaunce
My sekernes, ne lerne of love the lore.   345
But as the swan, I have herd seyd ful yore,
Ayeins his deth shal singe in his penaunce,
So singe I here my destany or chaunce,
How that Arcite Anelida to sore
Hath thirled with the poynt of remem-
    braunce.   350

Narrative

Whan that Anelida this woful quene
Hath of hir hande writen in this wise,
With face dede, betwixe pale and grene,
She fel a-swow; and sith she gan to rise,
And unto Mars avoweth sacrifise   355
Within the temple, with a sorowful chere,
That shapen was as ye shal after here. . . .

309 holde . . . fro reyn, keep from raining. P *Averill;* F *Aprrile.* **311** P lacks the next leaf; C continues to the end. **313 fast,** dependable. **315 tame . . . feyn,** well-tamed, eager. F *This that.* **316 agast,** frightened. *renne:* C&c *fle(n).* **317–32** This virelay comes before the concluding stanza of the antistrophe, as did the earlier, ll. 256ff. **318** C&c *ought seyd out of the weye.* **319** C&c *half aweye.* **320** *Chaunte-pleure,* Fr. "sing-lament," a French moral poem saying that those who sing in this world will weep in the next. **322 mased,** dazed. C *marred.* **325** C&c *world nys creature.* **326** *Wakinge:* other MSS *Walkyng.* **328 furlong-wey,** 220 yards, but a measure of time. *or:* F *other.* **330** C *azure,* blue, the symbol of constancy. **331** C&c *To profren eft;* F *asure.* **332** C&c *trewe, and love me til he deye.* **333 drye,** endure. **334 afray,** fear. *this:* C&c *thilke, suche.* **335 reche,** care. **337 routhe . . . trouthe,** pity, promise (troth). **340 rede . . . gye,** advise, guide. **345 sekernes,** security. **347 Ayeins,** in anticipation of. **350 thirled,** pierced. FC&c have *Explicit* here. Other less authoritative MSS have the final awkward stanza, which may be a scribal addition, or may have been intended to introduce a description of the Temple of Mars, like that in the Knight's Tale. **354 sith,** then.

3   COMPLAINT OF MARS

The Brooch of Thebes.

Introduction

Gladeth, ye foules, of the morow gray,
Loo, Venus rysen among yon rowes rede;
And floures fresshe, honouren ye this day,
For when the sunne uprist, then wol ye
    sprede.
But ye lovers that lye in any drede,   5
Fleeth lest wikked tonges yow espye.
Loo, yond the sunne, the candel of jalosye!

Wyth teres blew, and with a wounded hert,
Taketh your leve, and with Seynt John to
    borow,
Apeseth sumwhat of your sorowes smert.   10
Tyme cometh eft that cese shal your sorow.
The glade nyght ys worth an hevy morow!—
Seynt Valentyne, a foule thus herd I synge
Upon your day, er sunne gan up-sprynge.

Yet sang this foul: I rede yow al awake.   15
And ye that han not chosen, in humble wyse
Without repenting cheseth yow your make.
And ye that han ful chosen as I devyse,
Yet at the leste renoveleth your servyse.
Confermeth hit perpetuely to dure,   20

And paciently taketh your aventure.

And for the worship of this highe fest
Yet wol I in my briddes wise synge
The sentence of the compleynt at the lest
That woful Mars made atte departynge   25
Fro fresshe Venus in a morwenynge,
Whan Phebus with his firy torches rede
Ransaked every lover in his drede.

Narrative

Whilom the thridde hevenes lord above,
As wel by hevenysh revolucion   30
As by desert, hath wonne Venus his love,
And she hath take him in subjeccion,
And as a maistresse taught him his lesson,
Commaunding him that never in hir servise
He nere so bold no lover to dispise.   35

For she forbad him jelosye at alle,
And cruelte, and bost, and tyrannye.
She made him at hir lust so humble and talle
That when hir deyned to caste on him her eye,
He toke in pacience to lyve or dye.   40
And thus she brydeleth him in hir manere
With nothing but with scourging of hir chere.

Text from MS Fairfax 16 (F) with variants from the complete version in Pepys 2006 (P); see "The Text of This Edition," p. 966. Shirley's title, MS Harl. 7333, is *The Broche of Thebes as of the Love of Mars and Venus.*

1 morow, morning. *ye:* P *the.* *foules/of:* F&c *lovers/on.* The speaker is a bird on St. Valentine's Day in the morning, cf. l. 13. **2 Venus,** both the goddess and the morning star. The familiar legend of the adultery of Mars and Venus (Ovid, *Met.* 4.171, *Ars Amatoria* 2.562) is used throughout the poem to personify an astrological conjunction of the two planets in the zodiacal sign of Taurus. **rowes,** rays (of light). *yon:* F&c *yow.* **3 ye:** F *the.* *day:* P&c *May.* **4 ye:** F&c *they, he.* **5 ye:** P *the.* **6 wikked tonges,** scandal, personified as one of the defenders of the Rose in *RR.* **7 candel of jalosye,** Phoebus, the sun, aroused Vulcan's jealousy by revealing his wife Venus in bed with Mars. These first 12 lines have been described as an "aube" or troubadour dawn song, cf. *TC* III.1422ff. **8 blew,** i.e., blue (livid) with tears. **9 Seynt John to borow,** St. John as a pledge, a familiar Chaucerian demi-oath. **11 eft,** again. **12 ys worth,** is worth, or possibly "has become." **15 rede,** urge (advise). **17 make,** mate; cf. *PF* 309ff. St. Valentine's day was associated with wedded rather than with courtly love. F l. 19 inserted after l. 16. FP&c *yow* om. **19 renoveleth . . . servyse,** renew, promise. *the leste:* F *this ferst.* **20** P *to endure.* **21 aventure,** i.e., what comes. **22 highe fest,** special holy days were so designated in the liturgical calendar. **24 sentence,** sense. **28 Ransaked,** searched out. F *Ransaked hath.* **29 thridde hevenes,** counting from the outermost sphere inward, the third sphere is that of Mars. **30–31 As wel by . . . As by,** Chaucer here specifically notes the poem's blending of astrology and mythology. **32 take,** i.e., caused to be. **35 nere,** were not (should not be). **38 talle,** agreeable (the original meaning of the word). F *him* om. *talle:* F&c *calle, in alle.* **42 scourging of hir chere,** i.e., the discipline of her expression. *scourging:* F&c *stering, strenght.*

Who regneth now in blysse but Venus,
That hath thys worthy knyght in governaunce?
Who syngeth now but Mars, that serveth thus 45
The faire Venus, causer of plesaunce?
He bynt him to perpetuall obeisaunce,
And she bynt hir to loven him forever,
But so be that his trespace hit desever.

Thus be they knyt, and regnen as in heven   50
Be loking moost, til hit fil on a tyde
That by her bothe assent was set a steven
That Mars shal entre as faste as he may glyde
Into hir nexte paleys, to abyde
Walking his cours til she had him atake.   55
And he preide hir to haste hir for his sake.

Then seyde he thus, "Myn hertes lady swete,
Ye knowe wel my myschef in that place;
For sikerly til that I with yow mete,
My lyf stant ther in aventure and grace.   60
But when I se the beaute of your face,
Ther ys no dred of deth may do me smert,
For alle your lust is ese to myn hert."

She hath so gret compassion on hir knyght,
That dwelleth in solitude til she come—   65
For hit stode so, that ylke tyme no wight
Counseyled him, ne seyde to him welcome—
That nygh hir wit for woo was overcome.
Wherfore she sped hir as faste in hir wey
Almost in oon day as he dyd in twey.   70

The grete joye that was betwex hem two
When they be met ther may no tunge tel.
Ther is no more, but unto bed thei go,
And thus in joye and blisse I let hem dwel.

This worthi Mars, that is of knyghthod wel,   75
The flour of feyrnes lappeth in his armes,
And Venus kysseth Mars, the god of armes.

Sojourned hath this Mars, of which I rede,
In chambre amyd the paleys prively
A certeyn tyme, til him fel a drede   80
Throgh Phebus that was comen hastely
Within the paleys yates ful sturdely,
With torche in honde of which the stremes
    bryghte
On Venus chambre knokkeden ful lyghte.

The chambre ther as ley this fresshe quene   85
Depeynted was with white boles grete,
And by the lyght she knew, that shone so shene,
That Phebus cam to bren hem with his hete.
This sely Venus, nygh dreynt in teres wete,
Enbraceth Mars and seyde, "Alas, I dye!   90
The torch is come that al this world wol wrye."

Up stert Mars; him liste not to slepe
When he his lady herde so compleyne.
But for his nature was not for to wepe,
Instid of teres fro his eyen tweyne   95
The firy sparkes brosten out for peyne;
And hente his hauberk that ley him besyde.
Fle wolde he not, ne myghte himselven hyde.

He throweth on his helme of huge wyght,
And girt him with his swerde, and in his honde
His myghty spere, as he was wont to fyght,   101
He shaketh so that almost hit towonde.
Ful hevy was he to walken over londe.
He may not holde with Venus companye,
But bad hir fleen lest Phebus hir espye.   105

49 **But so,** unless. 51 **Be loking moost,** in most favorable aspect to one another; "loking" translates Lat. astrological term *aspectus*. 52 **steven,** time. 54 **paleys,** zodiacal sign. F&c *and ther abide.* 55 **atake,** overtake. Venus travels about twice as fast as Mars in annual mean motion. In the poem, Venus starts behind, catches up for the planetary conjunction, and then passes on beyond Mars as Phoebus brings the conjunction to an end. 56 **haste:** F *faste.* 58 **myschef in that place,** Taurus (cf. l. 86) was not an auspicious sign for Mars. 62 **smert,** hurt. 63 **lust,** desire. 66–67 **no wight / Counseyled him,** scholars who argue that this poem deals with some scandal in the English court cite these lines as referring to the situation of Holland or Exeter or someone else. 68 *woo:* F&c *sorowe.* 82 P&c *ful* om. In Chaucer's time the sun entered Taurus on April 12, cf. l. 139 below. 84 F *knokken.* 87 **shene,** bright. 89 **dreynt,** drowned. Venus was reputed to be a cold, wet planet, and Mars hot and dry (ll. 94–96). *nygh:* P&c *ne* or om. 91 **wrye,** reveal. 92 **him liste,** it pleased him. *liste:* F&c *lust(eth).* 97 **hente . . . hauberk,** (he) took, armor. 99 F *thrwe,* P *throw.* 102 **towonde,** flew to pieces. 104 **holde . . . companye,** i.e., keep up with. 105 *Phebus:* P [Phebus?] *ded.*

O woful Mars, alas, what maist thou seyn,
That in the paleys of thy disturbaunce
Art left behynde in peril to be sleyn?
And yet therto is double thy penaunce,
For she that hath thin hert in governaunce   110
Is passed halfe the stremes of thin eyen.
That thou nere swift, wel maist thou wepe and
    cryen.

Now fleeth Venus into Cilinios toure
With voide cours, for fere of Phebus lyght.
Alas, and ther ne hath she no socoure,   115
For she ne found ne saugh no maner wyght,
And eke as ther she had but litil myght,
Wherfor hirselven for to hyde and save,
Within the gate she fledde into a cave.

Derk was this cave, and smoking as the
    hel;   120
Not but two pas within the yate hit stode.
A naturel day in derk I let hir dwel.
Now wol I speke of Mars, furiouse and
    wode.
For sorow he wolde have sene his herte blode
Sith that he myghte do hir no companye—
He ne roghte not a myte for to dye.   126

So feble he wex for hete and for his wo
That nygh he swelt; he myghte unnethe endure.
He passeth but oo steyre in dayes two,

But ner the lesse, for al his hevy armure,   130
He foloweth hir that is his lyves cure,
For whos departing he toke gretter ire
Then for al his brenning in the fire.

After he walketh softely a pas,
Compleyning that hit pite was to here.   135
He seyde, "O lady bryght, Venus, alas
That ever so wyde a compas is my spere!
Alas, when shal I mete yow, herte dere?
This twelfte day of Aprrile I endure
Throgh jelous Phebus this mysaventure."   140

Now God helpe sely Venus allone!
But, as God wolde, hit happed for to be
That, while that Venus weping made hir
    mone,
Cilinius ryding in his chevache—
Fro Venus valaunce mighte his paleys se—   145
And Venus he salueth and maketh chere,
And hir receyveth as his frend ful dere.

Mars dwelleth forth in his adversyte,
Compleyning ever on hir departinge,
And what his compleynt was remembreth
    me;
And therfore in this lusty morweninge,   151
As I best can, I wol hit seyn and singe,
And after that I wol my leve take.
And God yif every wyght, joye of his make!

---

107 **disturbaunce**, i.e., when you were disturbed. 108 F *Art thou.* 111 **passed halfe the stremes**, i.e., has passed through half the rays emanating from Mars. 112 **nere**, were not. 113 **Cilinios toure**, i.e., the zodiacal sign of Gemini, which is also the sign of Mercury, who was born on Mt. Cyllene. **into:** P&c *unto.* 114 **voide**, solitary; there was no other planet in Gemini at that time (l. 116). 115 F&c *ne* om. 117 **litil myght**, Gemini was not an auspicious sign for Venus. 119 **cave**, Skeat takes this to be trans. of Lat. astrological term *puteus* literally "pit," but used to designate "degree." Chaucer takes poetic advantage of the literal meaning. 120 **Derk . . . smoking**, *gradus tenebrosi* and *gradus fumosi* technically indicated degrees in which the light of the planet is obscured. Evidently there are none such for Venus in Gemini, and Chaucer was exercising poetic license. 121 **pas**, i.e., Lat. *gradus*, degree. **within the yate**, at the beginning of the zodiacal sign. **pas:** F *pales.* 122 **naturel day**, 24 hours (vs. artificial day, from sunup to sundown). 123 **wode**, mad. 124 **have sene . . . blode**, i.e., have done himself violence. **have sene:** P *aseien.* 125 F **have don her no.** 126 **roghte . . . for**, cared, whether. *roghte:* F *thoghte*, P *right.* 127 **feble he wex**, the light of Mars grew less as it approached the sun. 128 **swelt . . . unnethe**, died, scarcely. 129 **oo steyre**, one degree (stair). F *a sterre.* 130 **ner**, never. P *netheles; al* om. 131 **foloweth hir**, Venus and Mars are both moving in the same direction as the sun. 133 **brenning**, burning because of proximity to the sun. 137 **wyde a compas**, the fact that the orbit of Mars is larger than that of Venus is what makes its apparent motion slower. 139 F *This xij dayes.* 141 **sely**, innocent, foolish. 144 **Cilinius**, Mercury, cf. l. 113n. **chevache**, course (horseback ride). P *chyvalrie.* 145 **valaunce**, explained by Skeat as Fr. *fallance*, trans. of Lat. astrological term *detrimenta*, the zodiacal sign opposite to a planet's mansion. Gemini is the mansion of Mercury, which he could see from Venus' vallance, Aries. F *valaunses;* P&c *balaunce.* 146 **maketh chere**, is pleasant to.

Compleynt of Mars.

Introduction

The ordre of compleynt requireth skylfully 155
That if a wight shal pleyne pitously,
There mot be cause wherfore that men pleyne,
Or men may deme he pleyneth folely
And causeles—alas, that am not I!
Wherfore the ground and cause of al my
    peyne,
So as my troubled wit may hit ateyne, 161
I wol reherse, not for to have redresse,
But to declare my ground of hevynesse.

I

The firste tyme, alas, that I was wroght,
And for certeyn effectes hider broght 165
Be Him that lordeth ech intelligence,
I yaf my trewe servise and my thoght,
For evermore—how dere I have hit boght—
To hir that is of so gret excelence
That what wight that first sheweth his
    presence, 170
When she is wroth and taketh of him no cure,
He may not longe in joye of love endure.

This is no feyned mater that I telle;
My lady is the verrey sours and welle
Of beaute, lust, fredam, and gentilnesse, 175
Of riche aray—how dere men hit selle—
Of al disport in which men frendly dwelle,
Of love and pley, and of benigne humblesse,
Of soune of instrumentes, of al swetnesse,
And therto so wel fortuned and thewed 180
That throgh the world hir goodnesse is yshewed.

What wonder is then thogh that I beset
My servise on suche oon that may me knet
To wele or wo, sith hit lyth in hir myght?
Therfore my hert forever I to hir het. 185
Ne, truly, for my dethe I shal not let
To ben hir treuest servaunt and hir knyght.
I flater noght; that may wete every wyght.
For this day in hir servise shal I dye,
But grace be I see hir oonce wyth eye. 190

II

To whom shal I than pleyn of my distresse?
Who may me help; who may my harm redresse?
Shal I compleyn unto my lady fre?
Nay, certes, for she hath such hevynesse
For fere and eke for wo, that as I gesse 195
In lytil tyme hit wol hir bane be.
But were she safe, hit wer no fors of me.
Alas, that ever lovers mote endure
For love so many a perilous aventure!

For tho so be that lovers be as trewe 200
As any metal that is forged newe,
In many a cas hem tydeth ofte sorowe.
Somtyme hir ladies wil not on hem rewe;
Somtyme, if that jelosie hit knewe,
They myghten lyghtly ley her hede to borowe; 205
Somtyme envyous folk with tunges horowe 206
Depraven hem. Alas, whom may they plese?
But he be fals, no lover hath his ese.

But what availeth suche a long sermoun
Of aventures of love up and doun? 210
I wol returne and speken of my peyne.

---

155 **skylfully,** reasonably. 158 **deme . . . folely,** judge, foolishly. *Or:* F *Other.* 160 **ground,** basis. 161 **ateyne,** perceive (understand). 163 **hevynesse,** sadness. 164 **firste tyme,** i.e., when I was first. 165 **effectes,** purposes. Line lacking in P. 166 **Be Him that lordeth,** an anachronism since pagan Mars is here evidently speaking of God the Creator. 168 **dere . . . boght,** dearly paid for. Line om. in P. 169 F *That her that.* 170 **sheweth . . . presence,** i.e., approaches her. 171 **cure,** care (attention). 173 **feyned,** pretended. 175 **lust, fredam,** pleasure, generosity. 176 **dere . . . selle,** i.e., how much it costs; cf. l. 168. 180 **thewed,** disposed (having a good disposition). 182 **beset,** fixed. 183 **knet,** knit (join). 184 **wele . . . sith,** good fortune, since. 185 **het,** promise. FP&c *hight;* other MSS *set.* 186 **let,** stop. 188 **wete,** know (wit). 190 **But grace be,** i.e., unless I receive the favor. 194 **hevynesse,** sadness. 196 **bane,** death. 197 **But were she . . . hit wer no fors of,** if she were, it would not matter about. 201 **metal:** P *mortal.* 202 **tydeth,** betides (comes to). 203 **rewe,** have pity. *Somtyme:* F *Somme.* 204 **jelosie hit knewe,** i.e., jealousy knew about their love. 205 **lyghtly ley . . . to borowe,** easily lay (lose), a pledge. 206 **horowe,** filthy. 207 **Depraven,** calumniate. *Depraven:* F&c *Departen.*

The poynt is this of my distruccioun,
My righte lady, my savacyoun,
Is in affray, and not to whom to pleyne.
O herte swete, O lady sovereyne,   215
For your disese wel oght I swoune and swelt,
Thogh I non other harm ne drede felt!

III

To what fyn made the God that sit so hye
Benethen him love other companye,
And streyneth folk to love, malgre her
    hede?   220
And then her joye, for oght I can espye,
Ne lasteth not the twynkeling of an eye,
And somme han never joye til they be dede.
What meneth this? What is this mystihede?
Wherto constreyneth he his folk so fast   225
Thing to desyre, but hit shulde last?

And thogh he made a lover love a thing,
And maketh hit seme stidfast and during,
Yet putteth he in hit such mysaventure
That reste nys ther noon in his yevinge.   230
And that is wonder that so just a kynge
Doth such hardnesse to his creature.
Thus, whether love breke or elles dure,
Algates he that hath with love to done
Hath ofter wo then changed is the mone.   235

Hit semeth he hath to lovers enmyte,
And lyk a fissher, as men alday may se,
Bateth his angle-hoke with summe plesaunce
Til mony a fissch is wode to that he be
Sesed therwith. And then at erst hath he   240
Al his desire, and therwith al myschaunce;
And thogh the lyne breke, he hath penaunce.
For with the hoke he wounded is so sore
That he his wages hath for evermore.

IV The Brooch of Thebes.

The broche of Thebes was of suche a kynde,   245
So ful of rubies and of stones of Ynde,
That every wight that set on hit an eye
He wend anon to worthe out of his mynde.
So sore the beaute wold his herte bynde
Til he hit had, him thoght he moste dye,   250
And whan that hit was his, than shulde he drye
Such woo for drede, ay while that he hit had,
That welnygh for the fere he shulde mad.

And whan hit was fro his possessioun,
Than had he double woo and passioun   255
For he so feir a tresor had forgo.
But yet this broche, as in conclusioun,
Was not the cause of this confusioun,
But he that wroghte hit enfortune hit so
That every wight that had hit shuld have wo.
And therfore in the worcher was the vyce,   261
And in the covetour that was so nyce.

So fareth hit by lovers and by me,
For thogh my lady have so gret beaute
That I was mad til I had get hir grace,   265
She was not cause of myn adversite,
But he that wroghte hir, also mot I thee,
That put suche a beaute in hir face,
That made me coveten and purchace
Myn oune deth—him wyte I that I dye,   270
And myn unwit that ever I clomb so hye.

V

But to yow, hardy knyghtes of renoun,
Syn that ye be of my devisioun,
Al be I not worthy to so grete a name,
Yet seyn these clerkes I am your patroun.   275
Therfore ye oghte have somme compassioun
Of my disese, and take it not agame.

214 in affray ... not, frightened, does not know. **216 swelt,** die. F&c *I oght wel.* F *sowne.* **218 fyn,** purpose. *the God:* P&c *He.* **219 other companye,** or companionship. F *him* om. **220 streyneth ... malgre,** constrains, in spite of themselves. **224 mystihede,** mystery. **226 but,** unless. **228 during,** enduring. **230** F&c *noon* om. **234 Algates,** nevertheless. **239 wode to,** frenzied to (the extent that). **244 wages,** compensation (for falling in love). **245 broche of Thebes,** the following account is adapted from Statius, *Thebaid* 2.265ff. **248 worthe,** go. **251 drye,** suffer. F&c *that/his* om. **252 ay while,** all the while. **259 enfortune,** invested it with such power (fortune). **261 worcher,** creator (worker). **262 nyce,** foolish. **267 also mot I thee,** as I may prosper. *also:* F&c *as.* **270 wyte,** blame. **271 unwit,** foolishness. F *oune witte.* **273 devisioun,** group (class of people). Mars is speaking as the god of war. **277 agame,** in jest.

The proudest of yow may be mad ful tame.
Wherfore I prey yow, of your gentilesse,
That ye compleyne for myn hevynesse. 280

And ye, my ladyes, that ben treue and stable
By wey of kynde, ye oghten to be able
To have pite of folk that be in peyne.
Now have ye cause to clothe yow in sable,
Sith that your emperice, the honorable, 285
Is desolat; wel oght ye to pleyne.
Now shuld your holy teres falle and reyne.
Alas, your honour and your emperise

Negh ded for drede ne can hir not chevise.

Compleyneth eke ye lovers al in fere 290
For hir that with unfeyned humble chere
Was ever redy to do yow socour;
Compleyneth hir that ever hath had yow
 dere;
Compleyneth beaute, fredom, and manere;
Compleyneth hir that endeth your labour; 295
Compleyneth thilke ensample of al honour,
That never dide but al gentilesse;
Kytheth therfor on hir summe kyndenesse. 298

4   COMPLAINT OF VENUS

I

Ther nys so high comfort to my plesaunce,
When that I am in any hevynesse,
As for to have leyser of remembraunce
Upon the manhod and the worthynesse,
Upon the trouthe and on the stidfastnesse 5
Of him whos I am al whiles I may dure.
Ther oghte blame me no creature,
For every wight preiseth his gentilesse.

In him is bounte, wysdom, governaunce,
Wel more then any mannes witte can gesse, 10
For grace hath wold so ferforth him avaunce
That of knyghthode he is parfit richesse.
Honour honoureth him for his noblesse.
Therto so well hath formed him Nature
That I am his for ever, I him assure, 15
For every wight preyseth his gentilesse.

And notwithstanding al his suffisaunce,
His gentil hert is of so grete humblesse
To me in word, in werk, in contenaunce,
And me to serve is al his besynesse, 20
That I am set in verrey sikernesse.
Thus oght I blesse wel myn aventure,
Sith that him list me serven and honoure,
For every wight preiseth his gentilesse.

II

Now certes, Love, hit is ryght covenable 25
That men ful dere bye thy nobil thinge,
As wake abed, and fasten at the table,
Weping to laugh, and sing in compleyninge,
And doun to cast visage and lokinge,
Often to chaungen hewe and contenaunce, 30
Pleyne in sleping, and dremen at the daunce,
Al the revers of any glad felinge.

280 **compleyne ... hevynesse,** lament, sadness. 282 **By ... kynde,** naturally. 284 **sable,** black. 286 P *myghten ye compleyn.* 287 P *fall down.* 289 **chevise,** accomplish (her desire). 290 **in fere,** together. 291 **unfeyned ... chere,** unpretended, expression. 293 **Compleyneth,** lament for. 297 F&c *al* om. 298 **Kytheth ... on,** display toward.

Text from MS Fairfax 16 (F) with variants from Bodleian Ashmole 59 (A), or Trinity Coll. Camb. R3.2 (T) where A is lacking. In F, as in most MSS, this poem follows *The Complaint of Mars* without a break, even though it is clearly an independent adaptation of three French balades by Oton de Graunson; see Introduction, and "The Text of This Edition," p. 966.

8 A *Sith he is croppe and roote of gentylesse.* 9 **governaunce,** self-control. 11 **wold ... forforth,** willed, far. A *hath* om. 15 **assure:** A&c *ensure.* 17 **suffisaunce,** adequacy. 21 **sikernesse,** security. 22 **aventure,** luck. *adventure/honoure.* In poems certainly identified as Chaucer's, *ure* never rhymes with *oure,* but the rhyme scheme of Graundson's balade obviously presented problems. (cf. 1. 80 below). A *Thus aught me wel to blesse myn aventure.* 23 **him list,** it pleases him. 25 **covenable,** suitable. 26 **men,** impersonal "one." **nobil thinge,** i.e., noble love. **dere:** A *sore.* 27 **wake abed,** etc., this is a typical list of troubadour oxymora. 30 A *Offt sythes.* F *chaunge visage;* Graundson, *souvent changier couleur.* 31 **Pleyne:** FA&c *Pley;* Graundson, *Plaindre.* 32 **any:** A *my.*

Jelousye be hanged by a cable!
She wold al knowe thro hir espyinge.
Ther doth no wyght nothing so resonable   35
That al nys harm in hir ymageninge.
Thus dere abought is love in yevinge,
Which ofte he yifeth withouten ordynaunce,
As sorow ynogh and litel of plesaunce,
Al the revers of any glad felinge.   40

A lytel tyme his yift is agreable,
But ful encomberouse is the usinge;
For subtil jelosie, the deceyvable,
Ful oftentyme causeth destourbinge.
Thus be we ever in drede and sufferinge,   45
In nouncerteyn we languisshe in penaunce,
And han ful often many an hard meschaunce,
Al the revers of any glad felinge.

III

But certes, Love, I sey nat in such wise
That for t'escape out of youre lace I ment,   50
For I so longe have be in your servise
That for to lete of wil I never assent.
No fors thogh jelosye me turment.
Sufficeth me to se him when I may.
And therfore certes to myn ending day   55
To love him best ne shal I never repent.

And certes, Love, when I me wel avise
On any estat that man may represent,

Then have ye maked me, thro your fraunchise,
Chese the best that ever on erthe went.   60
Now love wel, hert, and loke thou never
    stent,
And let the jelouse put hit in assay
That for no peyne wille I not sey nay.
To love him best ne schal I never repente.

Hert, to the hit oght ynogh suffise   65
That Love so highe a grace to the sent
To chese the worthiest in alle wise
And most agreable unto myn entent.
Seche no ferther neyther wey ne went,
Sith I have suffisaunce unto my pay.   70
Thus wol I ende this compleynt or this lay.
To love him best ne shal I never repent.

Lenvoy

Princes, resseyveth this compleynt in gre,
Unto your excelent benignite.
Direct after my litel suffisaunce,   75
For eld that in my spirit dulleth me
Hath of endyting al the subtilite
Wel nyghe bereft out of my remembraunce.
And eke to me hit is a grete penaunce,
Syth ryme in Englissh hath such skarsite,   80
To folowe word by word the curiosite
Of Graunson, floure of hem that make in
    Fraunce.

33–40 Stanza om. in A. **33** T *Thaughe jalousye were hanged.* **37 yevinge,** giving. **38 ordynaunce,** consideration. **42 encomberouse,** burdensome. **43 deceyvable,** deceitful. *the:* A *is ful.* **46 nouncerteyn,** uncertainty. **47** *meschaunce:* F *penaunce;* Graundson, *meschance.* **50 lace,** snare (cf. lasso). **52 lete of,** stop. A *leet off wol.* **53 No fors,** it does not matter. **56** F&c *ne* om. **57 avise,** consider. **59 fraunchise,** generosity of spirit. **60 went,** walked. **61 stent,** stop. **62 put . . . assay,** put it (my love) to the test. F *jelousie.* **64 him:** F&c *yow.* A *ne never to repente.* **66 the:** F *yow.* A *hathe to thee sent.* **69 wey . . . went,** road, footpath. *Seche:* A *Serche.* **70 my pay,** my satisfaction. **I:** F *ye.* **72** FA&c *ne* om. A *and never to repente.* **73 Princes,** MSS A and T read *Pryncesse,* which led Skeat to support Shirley's statement that this piece was addressed to the Duchess of York, "princess" because she was the daughter of Pedro, King of Castile. However, the balade was a favorite form for court and civic literary contests, and it was customary for the envoy to be addressed to a "prince" who was to judge its merit. **in gre,** with favor. **75 Direct . . . suffisaunce,** guide (me), ability. **77 endyting,** composing. **81 curiosite,** intricacy.

5   A COMPLAINT UNTO PITY

Pite, that I have sought so yore agoo,
With herte soore and ful of besy peyne,
That in this world was never wight so woo
Withoute dethe, and yf I shal not feyne
My purpos was to Pite to compleyne   5
Upon the crueltee and tirannye
Of Love, that for my trouthe doth me dye.

And when that I, by lengthe of certeyn yeres,
Had ever in oon a tyme sought to speke,
To Pite ran I, al bespreynt with teres,   10
To preyen hir on Cruelte me awreke.
But er I myght with any worde outbreke,
Or tellen any of my peynes smerte,
I fond hir dede and buried in an herte.

Adoun I fel, when that I saugh the herse,   15
Dede as a stone while that the swogh me laste,
But up I roos, with colour ful dyverse,
And petously on hir myn eyen I caste,
And ner the corps I gan to presen faste,
And for the soule I shope me for to prey.   20
I was but lorn; ther was no more to sey.

Thus am I slayn, sith that Pite is dede.
Allas that day that ever hit shulde falle!
What maner man dar now holde up his hede?
To whom shal now any sorwful herte calle?   25
Now Cruelte hath cast to slee us alle
In ydel hope, folk redelees of peyne,
Syth she is dede to whom we shulde us pleyne.

But yet encreseth me this wonder newe,
That no wight woot that she is dede but I.   30
So many men as in her tyme hir knewe,
And yet she dyed not so sodeynly.
For I have sought hir ever ful besely
Sith first I hadde witte or mannes mynde,
But she was dede er that I koude hir fynde.   35

Aboute hir herse ther stoden lustely,
Withouten any woo, as thoughte me,
Bounte parfyt, wel armed and richely,
And fresshe Beaute, Lust, and Jolyte,
Assured Maner, Youthe, and Honeste,   40
Wisdom, Estaat, Drede, and Governaunce,
Confedred bothe by bonde and alliaunce.

A compleynt had I, writen in myn honde,
For to have put to Pite as a bille.
But whan I al this companye ther fonde,   45
That rather wolden al my cause spille
Than do me help, I held my pleynte stille.
For to that folk, withouten any fayle,
Withoute Pite ther may no bille availe.

Then leve I al vertues save oonly Pite   50
Keping the corps, as ye have herd me seyn,
Confedred alle by bonde of Cruelte,
And ben assented that I shal be sleyn.
And I have put my complaynt up ageyn;
For to my foes my bille I dar not shewe,   55
Th'effect of which seith thus in wordes fewe:

Text from Fairfax 16 (F) with substantive variants from B.M. MS Harley 78 (H); see "The Text of This Edition," p. 966. Title found in Bodl. 638.

1 yore agoo, i.e., for so long. The personifications in this poem have been compared with those in Statius, *Thebaid* 11, but the convention is more familiar in *Roman de la Rose* and other contemporary allegorical poems and plays. **4 Withoute dethe ... feyne,** without actually dying, pretend. **6 Upon,** about. **7 trouthe doth,** faithfulness causes me to. **9 ever in oon,** constantly (ever anon). F *soughte a tyme.* **10 bespreynt,** sprinkled. **11 awreke,** avenge. **15 herse,** bier. *that* om. in all MSS. **16 swogh,** faint (swoon). *a* om. in all MSS. **20 shope me,** began. **21 lorn,** lost. H *Me thought me lorne; ther was noon other weye.* **26 hath cast,** has planned. **27 In,** with. **redelees,** i.e., without hope of cure (advisorless). H *In ydel hope, we lyve redlesse of peyne.* **28 F** *to whom shul we compleyne?* **32 F** *she/so* om. **34 F** *hadde firste; mannes* om. **37 woo,** sorrow. H *doel.* **40 Youthe:** H *Thought.* **41 Drede ... Governaunce,** fear (awe), authority. **42 Confedred ... bonde,** confederated, oath. *alliaunce:* H *assurance.* **44 bille,** petition. F *For* om. **46 spille,** undo. **50 I:** F *we.* H *alle thees vertues sauf Pitee.* **51 Keping,** guarding. **54 put my complaynt up,** i.e., put it away.

The Bill of Complaint.

I

Humblest of herte, highest of reverence,
Benygne flour, coroune of vertues alle,
Sheweth unto your rialle excellence
Your servaunt, yf I durste me so calle,   60
His mortal harm, in which he is yfalle,
And noght al oonly for his evel fare,
But for your renoun, as he shal declare.

Hit stondeth thus: your contraire Cruelte
Allyed is ageynst your regalye   65
Under colour of womanly Beaute,
For men shulde not knowe hir tirannye,
With Bounte, Gentilesse, and Curtesye,
And hath depryved yow of your place
That hyght Beaute, apertenant to Grace.   70

For kyndly, by your herytage ryght,
Ye be annexed ever unto Bounte,
And verrely ye oughte do youre myght
To helpe Trouthe in his adversyte.
Ye be also the corowne of Beaute.   75
And certes, if ye wanten in these tweyne,
The worlde is lore; ther nis no more to seyne.

II

Eke what availeth Maner and Gentilesse
Withoute yow, benygne creature?
Shal Cruelte be your governeresse?   80
Allas, what herte may hit longe endure?
Wherfor but ye the rather take cure
To breke that perilous alliaunce,
Ye sleen hem that ben in your obeisaunce:

And further over, yf ye suffre this,   85
Youre renoun is fordoo than in a throwe.
Ther shal no man wete wel what Pite is.
Allas, that ever your renoun is fall so lowe!
Ye be also fro youre heritage ythrowe
By Cruelte, that occupieth youre place.   90
And we despeyred that seken to your grace.

Have mercy on me, thow Herenus quene,
That yow have sought so tendirly and yore.
Let somme streme of your lyght on me be sene,
That love and drede yow ever lenger the
          more.
For sothely for to seyne, I bere the soore,   96
And though I be not kunning for to pleyne,
For Goddes love, have mercy on my peyne!

III

My peyne is this, that whatso I desire,
That have I not, ne nothing lyk therto;   100
And ever set Desire myn hert on fire.
Eke on that other syde, wherso I goo,
What maner thing that may encrese woo,
That have I redy, unsoght, everywhere;
Me lakketh but my deth, and than my bere.   105

What nedeth to shewe parcel of my peyne
Sith every woo that herte may bethynke
I suffre, and yet I dar not to yow pleyne?
For wel I wot, although I wake or wynke,
Ye rekke not whether I flete or synke.   110
But natheles, my trouthe I shal sustene
Unto my deth, and that shal wel be sene.

59–60 Sheweth . . . Your servaunt, your servant (lover) shows you. *Sheweth* was the technical word employed in petitions. *rialle* (royal): H *souvereyne.* **62 evel fare,** unfortunate situation. **63** *he:* H *I.* **64** F&c *that your contrary Crueltee.* **65 regalye,** authority. **66 Under colour,** under the outward appearance. **67 For men,** so that people. **70 hyght . . . apertenant,** is termed, joined. F&c *your grace.* **71 kyndly,** by nature. **72 Bounte,** generosity. **76 wanten,** are lacking. **77 lore,** lost. **79** H *benigne and feyre.* **80** H *be nowe our.* **82 rather . . . cure,** sooner, pains. **83** H *breke of thoo persones the allyaunce.* **85 further over . . . suffre,** furthermore, permit. **86 fordoo . . . throwe,** destroyed (done for), moment. **87 wete,** know. *Pite:* H *the peyne.* **88** H *that youre renoune shoulde be.* **89 also:** H *thanne.* **91 seken:** F *speken.* **92 Herenus quene,** there has been much argument about this reading. If it means "Erinyes" (the Furies), the epithet would seem more appropriate to Cruelty than to Pity, who is here being addressed. Other MSS related to F read *heremus;* H&c *yee vertuouse.* **93 yore,** long. H *so truwely and so.* **94 somme:** H *the.* **95 ever:** H *ay.* **96 the soore:** F&c *so soore;* H *the hevy sore.* **100** H *ne nought that lythe therto.* **101** F *setteth.* **103** F *my woo.* **105 bere,** bier. **106 parcel,** portion. **110 flete,** float. **111 trouthe,** fidelity (to you).

This is to seyne, I wol be youres ever,
Though ye me slee by Cruelte, your foo;
Algate my spirit shal never dissever   115
Fro youre servise for any peyne or woo.

Sith ye be ded—allas that hit is soo—
Thus for your deth I may wel wepe and
      pleyne,
With herte sore and ful of besy peyne.   119

Explicit

6   A BALADE OF PITY

I *(rhyme royal)*

The longe nyght, whan every creature
Shuld have her rest in somwhat as by kynde,
Or elles ne may her lyf nought long endure,
Hit falleth most into my wooful mynde
How I so fer have brought myself behynde,   5
That sauf the deth ther may nothing me lisse,
So desespaired I am from alle blisse.

This same thought me lasteth til the morow,
And from the morow forth til hit be eve;
Ther nedeth me no care for to borow,   10
For both I have gode leyser and gode leve;
Ther is no wight that wil my wo bereve
To wepe inough, and wailen al my fille;
The sore spark of peyne now doth me spille.

II *(terza rima)*

The sore spark of peyne now doth me spille,   15
This Love that hath me set in suche a place
That my desire never wil fulfille;

For neither pite, mercy, neyther grace
Can I nat fynde; and yet my sorowful hert,
For to be dede, I can hit nat arace.   20

The more I love, the more she doth me smert,
Thurgh which I see withoute remedye
That from the dethe I may no wise astert.

III *(terza rima)*

Now sothly, what she hight I wil reherse:

Hir name is Bounte set in womanhede,   25
Sadnesse in yowth, and Beaute prideles,
And Plesaunce under governaunce and drede.

Hir surname is eke Faire Rewtheles
The Wise, iknyt unto Goode Aventure,
That for I love hir sleeth me gilteles.   30

Hir love I best, and shal while I may dure,
Bet than myself an hundred thousand dele,
Than al this worldes riches or creature.

Now hath nat Love me bestowed wele
To love ther I never shal have part?   35
Allas, right thus is turned me the whele!

Thus am I slayn with loves firy dart;
I can but love hir best, my swete foo;
Love hath me taught no more of his art

---

115 Algate, in any event. **116** H *How pitee, that I have sought so yoore agoo.* **119** In the two MSS in which it is found, *A Balade of Pity* (no. 6 below) follows without a break.

Text from MS B.M. Add. 34360 (A), with variants from Harley 78 (H). In these two MSS—the only ones in which these three metrical experiments are found—they are treated as a continuation of no. 5 above. In Shirley's MS H, they are labeled *The Balade of Pytee;* see "The Text of This Edition," p. 966.

1 *nyght:* AH *nyghtes.* **2 kynde,** nature. *her:* AH *theyr.* A *as* om. **3** *her:* AH *theyr.* **6 lisse,** comfort. **7** A *dispaired.* **8 morow,** morning. **11 leyser . . . leve,** opportunity, permission. *leve:* A *love.* **12 bereve,** deprive (relieve). *my:* H *me.* **14 spille,** perish. **15** This line is not in the MSS; Skeat repeated l. 14 to complete the terza rima pattern. **17** AH *wil (wol) never.* **20 arace,** root out. **22** A *I see* om. **23 astert,** escape. **24** No break in MSS between II and III. The terza rima pattern continues in III except for the introductory line. **hight,** is called. **25 Bounte,** generosity. **26 Sadnesse,** seriousness. **27 Plesaunce . . . governaunce . . . drede,** cheerfulness, self-control, fear (of scandal). **28 Rewtheles,** pitiless. **29 iknyt . . . Goode Aventure,** joined, pleasant experience. **30 for,** because. AH *she sleeth.* **34 bestowed,** treated (irony). **36 the whele,** Fortune's wheel.

But serve alwey, and stynte for no woo.   40

IV *(ten-line stanzas)*

In my trewe, careful herte there is
So moche woo and eke so litel blisse
That woo is me that ever I was bore,
For al that thyng whiche I desire I misse,
And al that ever I wolde nat, iwisse,   45
That fynde I redy to me evermore.
And of al this I not to whom me pleyne,
For she that myghte me out of this bring
Ne reccheth nought whether I wepe or sing,
So litel rewth hath she upon my peyne.   50

Allas, whan sleping-time is, lo than I wake,
Whan I shuld daunce, for feere lo than I qwake;
This hevy liff I leede lo for yowre sake,
Though ye therof in no wise heede take,
Myn hertes lady, and hoole my lives quene!   55
For trewly durste I sey as that I feele,
Me semeth that your swete herte of steele
Is whetted now ayens me to kene.

My dere hert and best beloved foo,
Why liketh yow to do me al this woo?   60
What have I don that greveth yow, or sayde,
But for I serve and love yow and no moo?
And while I live, I wil do ever soo.
And therfor, swete, ne beth nat evil apayd,
For so goode and so faire as that ye be,   65
Hit were a right grete wonder but ye had
Of al servauntes, both of goode and bad;
And lest worthy of al hem, I am he.

But nevertheles, my right lady swete,
Though that I be unkonning and unmete   70
To serve as I best kowde ay yowr hyenesse,
Yet is ther non fayner, that wolde I hete,
Than I to do yow ease or elles bete

Whatso I wist were to yow hevynesse.
And had I myght as goode as I have wil,   75
Than shuld ye fele wher it wer so or non,
For in this world than living is ther non
That fayner wolde youre hertes wil fulfil.

For both I love and eke drede yow so sore,
And algates mote, and have yow don ful
       yore,   80
That better loved is non, ne never shal.
And yet I wolde besechen yow of no more,
But leveth wel and be nat wroth therfore,
And let me serve yow forth—lo, this is al.
For I am nat so hardy ne so wood   85
For to desire that ye shuld love me,
For wel I wot, allas, that wil nat be,
I am so litel worthy, and ye so good.

For ye be oon the worthiest on lyve,
And I the most unlikly for to thryve.   90
Yet for al this, witeth ye right wele
That ye ne shul me from youre service dryve,
That I nil ay with al my wittes fyve
Serve yow trewly, what wo so that I fele.
For I am sette on yow in suche manere   95
That though ye never wil upon me rewe,
I muste yow love and ever been as trewe
As any man can or may on lyve here.

The more that I love yow, goodly free,
The lasse fynde I that ye loven me.   100
Allas, whan shal that hard witte amende?
Wher is now al your wommanly pite,
Youre gentilnesse, and your debonarite?
Wil ye nothing therof upon me spende?
And so holy, swete, as I am yowres al,   105
And so gret wil as I have yow to serve,
Now, certes, and ye lete me thus sterve,
Yet have ye wonne theron but a smal.

40 **stynte,** stop. 41 **careful,** full of care (feeling). 42 AH *eke om.* 47 **not,** don't know. 50 **rewth,** pity. 55 Following ll. 55 and 57 there should be lines with *b* rhyme to make this stanza match the others in the sequence. However, these stanzas are all clearly experimental, and this one is effective as it stands. 56 **durste,** if I dared. 58 **to kene,** too sharply. 63 AH *will ever do.* 64 **evil apayd,** angry. *ne:* A *me.* 65 AH *that om.* 66 AH *a om.* 67 **Of al,** of all (kinds of). 70 **unmete,** unfit. 71 **ay,** always. 72 **fayner . . . hete,** happier, promise. 73 **bete,** better (your condition). *yow:* A *youre.* 74 **hevynesse,** distress. AH *that were to youre hyenesse.* 80 **algates mote . . . have yow don,** in every event must, and for a long time have loved you. 83 **leveth,** believe. A *lovith.* 85 **wood,** crazy. 90 **thryve,** succeed. 91 **witeth,** know. 93 **nil:** AH *ne wil.* 96 **rewe,** have pity. 97 A *bien ever als trewe.* 98 AH *here om.* 99 AH *But the more.* 101 **hard witte amende,** i.e., cruel spirit improve. 107 **and . . . sterve,** if, die. 108 A *ye om.*

For at my knowing, I do nothing why,
And this I wil beseche yow hertely,   110
That therever ye finde, whiles ye live,
A trewer servaunt to yow than am I,
Leveth thanne, and sle me hardely,
And I my deth to yow wil al forgive.
And if ye finde no trewer, so verily,   115
Will ye suffre than that I thus spille,
And for no maner gilt but my good wille?
Als good wer thanne untrewe as trewe to be.

But I my lyf and deth to yow obey,
And with right buxom hert holy I prey   120
As is youre most plesure, so doth by me;
For wel lever is me liken yow and dey
Than for to anything or thynke or sey
That yow might offende in any tyme.
And therfor, swete, rewe on my peynes smert, 125
And of your grace granteth me som drope;
For elles may me last ne blisse ne hope,
Ne dwelle within my trouble, careful hert.

Explicit Pyte

Dan Chaucer l'auceire.

7 WOMANLY NOBLESSE

Balade That Chaucer Made.

So hath myn herte caught in remembraunce
Yowre beaute hoole, and stidefast
          governaunce,
Yowre vertues al, and yowre hie noblesse,
That yow to serve is sette al my plesaunce.
So wel me liketh youre womanly contenaunce, 5
Youre fresshe fetures, and youre comlynesse,
That whiles I live, myn hert to his maystresse
Yow hath ful chose in trewe perseveraunce,
Never to chaunge for no maner distresse.

And sith I shal do yow this observaunce   10
Al my lif, withouten displesaunce,
Yow for to serve with al my besynesse,

And have me somwhat in your souvenaunce.
My woful herte suffreth grete duresse,
And loke how humbly, with al symplesse,   15

My wil I conforme to youre ordynaunce
As yow best list, my peynes for to redresse.

Considryng eke how I hange in balaunce
In yowre service, such, lo, is my chaunce,
Abidyng grace, whan that yowr gentilnesse   20
Of my grete woo liste do allegeaunce,
And with youre pite me som wise avaunce,
In ful rebatyng of myn hevynesse,
And thynketh by raison that wommanly
          noblesse
Shuld nat desire for to do the outrance   25
Ther as she fyndeth non unbuxumnesse.

Lenvoye

Auctour of norture, lady of plesaunce,
Soveraigne of beaute, floure of wommanhede,

109 at my knowing, I do nothing why, i.e., as far as I know, I do nothing to cause (your cruelty). **nothing:** AH *nat, nought.* **111 therever,** if ever. **113** *Leveth:* A *Loveth.* **114** AH *I* om. **116 spille,** die. **118 Als good,** just as good. A *trewe trewly.* **119–28** The end of H is lost; final stanza only in A. **120 buxom,** obedient. **121** A *is* om. **122 liken,** to like. **125 rewe,** have pity.

Text from B.M. Add. 34360; see "The Text of This Edition," p. 966. Title assigned by Skeat. Shirley's title in the MS is *Balade that Chauncier (sic) made.*

2 governaunce, decorum. **5 me liketh,** pleases me. **7 to his,** as its. **8 perseveraunce,** constancy. MS *triue.* **10** MS *yow* om. **11** *lif:* MS *live.* **12** After l. 12, the rhyme calls for another line. Various suggestions have been made, e.g., Furnivall (used by Skeat, *Oxford Chaucer* iv.xxvi), *Taketh me, lady, in your obeisaunce.* **13 souvenaunce,** memory. **15** MS *loke* om. **17 list,** desire. **20 Abidyng,** awaiting. **21 Of...allegeaunce,** to, alleviation. **23 hevynesse,** grief. **24 by raison,** reasonably (logically). **25 outrance,** great injury. **to:** MS *til.* **26 unbuxumnesse,** disobedience. **27 Auctour of norture...plesaunce,** provider of sustenance (education), lady who delights.

Take ye non hede unto myn ignoraunce,

Thynkyng that I have caught in remembraunce

But this receyveth of yowre goodelyhede,   30

Yowr beaute hole, your stidefast governaunce.

8   TO ROSEMOUNDE

Madame, ye ben of alle beaute shryne

As fer as cercled is the mapamounde,

For as the cristall glorious ye shyne,

And lyke ruby ben your chekes rounde.

Therwyth ye ben so mery and so jocounde   5

That at a revell whan that I se you daunce,

It is an oynement unto my wounde,

Thogh ye to me ne do no daliaunce.

For thogh I wepe of teres ful a tyne,

Yet may that wo myn herte nat confounde.   10

Your semy voys, that ye so small out twyne,

Maketh my thoght in joy and blys habounde.

So curtaysly I go, with love bounde,

That to myself I sey, in my penaunce,

"Suffyseth me to love you, Rosemounde,   15

Thogh ye to me ne do no daliaunce."

Nas never pyk walwed in galauntyne

As I in love am walwed and iwounde,

For whych ful ofte I of myself devyne

That I am trewe Tristam the secounde.   20

My love may not refreyde nor affounde;

I brenne ay in an amorouse plesaunce.

Do what you lyst; I wyl your thral be founde,

Thogh ye to me ne do no daliaunce.

TREGENTIL.   CHAUCER.

9   PROVERBE OF CHAUCER

What shul these clothes thus manyfolde,

Loo, this hoote somers day?

After grete hete cometh colde;

No man caste his pilch away.

Of al this world the large compace,

Yt wil not in my armes tweyne.

Whooso mochel wol embrace,

Litel therof he shal distreyne.

31–32 Note the return to the opening lines.

Text from MS Bodl. Rawl. Poet. 163; see "The Text of This Edition," p. 966.

1 *alle:* MS *al.* **2 mapamounde,** map of the world; medieval maps of the world enclosed in frames were often so designated, or by the Lat. *mappa mundi.* **9 tyne,** tub. **11 semy . . . twyne,** thin (small), twist out. *small:* MS *fynall.* **17 walwed,** wallowed. **galauntyne,** a piquant wine sauce. **19 devyne,** divine (understand). **20 Tristam,** lover of Iseult, who drank the magic love potion. **21 refreyde . . . affounde,** grow cold, founder (sink). MS *be refreyde.* **Tregentil—Chaucer.** The colophon, in a later hand, offers no evidence of the authorship of the poem. It is in imitation of the colophon of the *Troylus* on the preceding verso of the manuscript.

Text from MS Fairfax 16 (A) with variants from B. M. Add. 16165 (A); see "The Text of This Edition," p. 966.

1 shul, i.e., use are. A *shal.* **3** A *grete* om. **4 caste . . . pilch,** should cast, fur garment. **5–7** *compace* (compass)/*embrace,* Chaucer's authorship has been doubted on the basis of this rhyme, but Brusendorff points out that it is the same as *plas/solas, Thopas/gras* in *CT.* A *al* om. *large:* A *wyde.* **6 wil not . . . tweyne,** i.e., it will not fit into my two arms. **8 distreyne,** hold on to (clutch).

10   FORTUNE

Balade de visage sanz peinture.

I Le Pleintif countre Fortune

This wrechched worldes transmutacioun,
As wele or woo, now poure and now honour,
Withouten ordre or wise discrecioun
Governed is by Fortunes errour;
But natheles, the lakke of hir favour   5
Ne may nat don me synge, though I dye,
Jay tout perdue mon temps et mon labour,
For fynaly, Fortune, I the diffye!

Yet is me left the light of my resoun,
To knowen frend fro foo in thy mirour.   10
So moche hath yet thy whirling up and doun
Ytaught me for to knowen in an hour.
But trewely, noo fors of thy reddour
To him that over himself hath the maistrye.
My suffisaunce shal be my socour,   15
For fynaly, Fortune, I thee dyffye!

O Socrates, thou stedfast champioun,
She mighte never be thy tormentour.
Thou never dreddest hir oppressioun,
Ne in hir chere founde thou noo savour.   20
Thow knewe wel the deceit of hir colour,
And that hir mooste worshipe is to lye.
I knowe hir eke a fals dissymulour,
For fynaly, Fortune, I thee diffye!

II La respons du Fortune au Pleintif

Noo man is wrechched but himself hit wene,   25
And he that hath himself hath suffisaunce.
Why seystow thanne I am to the so kene,
That hast thyself out of my governaunce?
Sey thus, "Grauntmercy of thyn habundaunce
That thou hast lent or this." Why wolt thou
          strive?   30
What woost thou yet how I the wol avaunce?
And eke thou hast thy beste frend alive.

I have the taught divisioun bitwene
Frend of effect and frend of countenaunce.
The nedeth nat the galle of noon hyene   35
That cureth eyen derke fro her penaunce.
Now seestow cleer, that were in ignoraunce.
Yet halt thin ankre and yet thow mayst arrive
Ther bounte berith the keye of my
          substaunce—
And eke thow hast thy beste frend alive.   40

How many have I refused to sustene,
Sith I the fostred have in thy plesaunce!
Woltow than make a statut on thy quene,
That I shal ben ay at thyn ordinaunce?
Thow borne art in my regne of variaunce.   45
Aboute the whele with other most thou drive.

Text from MS Bodl. Fairfax 16 (F), with corrections and variants from Cambridge Ii 3.21 (I), and Shirley's Bodl. Ashmole 59 (A).
See "The Text of This Edition," p. 966.

visage saunz peynture, an allusion to *Boece* II pr. 1, 58, "Thow has now knowen and ataynt the dowtous or dowble vysage of thilke blynde goddesse Fortune. She that yit covereth and wympleth hir to oother foolkes hath shewed hir everydel to the." This is an acknowledgment of the Boethian inspiration for these three balades, largely Bk. II pr.1–4 and 8. **2** F *and woo, now poverte and now riche honour.* **4** A *fals errour.* **7 Jay tout,** the same line is quoted in ParsT, *CT,* x.248. **8, 16, 24** Reading from I. F *the* om. A *now Fortune I defye.* Other MSS *yitte Fortune.* **9** *light:* F&c *sight.* **11** *whirling:* F&c *turnyng.* **13 noo fors . . . reddour,** no matter, violence. A *fals reddour.* **15 suffisaunce,** self-sufficiency. **18** I *never myght.* **19** A *Fortunes oppressioun.* **20 chere . . . savour,** favor, pleasure. A *thou fondest.* **21 colour,** i.e., surface appearance; cf. the *peynture* of the subtitle. **25 wene,** consider. See the gloss at *Boece* II pr. 4, 112, "thow thyself, ne no wyht elles, nis a wrechche, but whan he weneth hymself a wrechche." **26** *And:* A *For.* **27 kene,** sharp (harsh). **28 That hast thyself,** i.e., that exist (on the spiritual level) beyond the influence of Fortune. **30 or,** ere (before). F *Thou shalt not strive.* **31 What woost thou,** how do you know. A *how wel I wol th'avaunce.* **32 beste frend,** cf. note to l. 73 below. **33 divisioun,** the difference. **34 effect,** reality. **35 galle of . . . hyene.** Vincent of Beauvais and other medieval medical manuals state that the gall of a hyena restores keenness of sight. **36 penaunce,** i.e., weeping in penance. I *derk yd.* **38 halt,** holds. **43 statut on,** i.e., law for. **45 in,** into. **46** *most thou:* F *maisthow.*

My lore is bet than wikke is thy grevaunce;
And eke thow hast thy beste frend alive.

III Le Pleintif encountre Fortune

Thy lore I dampne; hit is adversite.
My frend maistow nat reve, blynd
    goddesse!   50
That I thy frendes knowe, I thanke hit the!
Tak hem ageyn; let hem goo lye on presse.
The negardye in keping her richesse
Prenostik is thow wolt her tour assayle.
Wikke appetit cometh ay before seknesse;   55
In general, this rule may nat fayle.

Fortune encountre le Pleintif

Thow pynchest at my mutabilite,
For I the lent a drope of my rychesse,
And now me liketh to withdrawe me.
Why shuldest thow my realte oppresse?   60
The see may ebbe and flowe more or lesse;

The welkene hath myght to shyne, reyn, or
    hayle.
Ryght so mot I kythe my brotelnesse;
In general, this rule may nat fayle.

Loo, th'execucion of the mageste   65
That al purveyeth of his rightwisnesse,
That same thing "Fortune" clepen ye,
Ye blynde bestes, ful of lewednesse.
The hevene hath proprete of sikernesse,
This world hath ever restelesse travayle.   70
Thi last day is ende of myn intresse;
In general, this rule may nat fayle.

Lenvoy du Fortune

Princes, I pray yow of your gentilesse,
Lat nat thys man on me thus crie and pleyne,
And I shal quyte yow your besynesse   75
At my requeste, as three of you or tweyne.
And but you list releve him of his peyne,
Preyeth his beste frend of his noblesse
That to som beter estat he may atteyne.   79

---

47 lore . . . wikke, teaching, injurious. **49** *dampne:* A *banne.* **50 reve,** steal. **51** *frendes:* F&c *frende.* A *I thank not the.* **52 on presse,** in a group. F *a presse* (a cupboard). **53 The,** i.e., their. F&c *negardes.* **54 Prenostik is . . . tour assayle,** forecasts, overthrow their good fortune. **57 pynchest,** complain. **59 me liketh,** it pleases me. *And now:* A *therfore.* **60 realte,** royalty (royal prerogative). **61** A&c *bothe more. or:* FI *and.* **63 kythe . . . brotelnesse,** show, undependability (brittleness). **65** All MSS attribute this stanza to *Le Pleintif.* **66 al purveyeth of,** provides for everything through. **67 clepen,** call. A *thing, loo.* **68 lewednesse,** ignorance. **69 sikernesse,** security. **70 travayle,** labor. **71 intresse,** interest. *Boece* III pr. 3, 89: "the laste day of a mannes lyf is a manere deth to Fortune." **73 Princes,** This reference is taken to refer to the dukes of Lancaster, York, and Gloucester, who, by Ordinance of the Privy Council of March 8, 1390, had to authorize any grant made by Richard II—who would then be the "best friend" (ll. 32, 78). But appealing to the arbiter prince in the envoy was a balade convention; see *Complaint of Venus* (short poem 4), l. 73 and note. **74 on me,** to me. The envoy turns this into a begging poem, but Patch has suggested that the envoy may have been added after 1390 to a series of balades written earlier. **75 quyte,** repay. *your:* F&c *this.* **76 as three . . . or tweyne,** the 1390 Ordinance (l. 73n.) states that the King could make no grant "saunz avys de consail et lassent des Ducs de Gyene [Gaunt, Lancaster], et Deverwyk [Langley, York], et de Gloucestre [Woodstock], et du chanceller *ou deux de eux*" (Brusendorff, *Chaucer Tradition,* p. 199). This line is found only in I.

11   BALADE DE BON CONSEIL

Truth.

Fle fro the prees and dwell with sothfastnesse,
Suffise unto thy good, though it be smal,
For hord hath hate, and clymbyng tykelnesse,
Prees hath envye, and wele blent overal.
Savour no more than the byhove shal.   5
Reule wel thiself, that other folk canst rede;
And trouthe the shal delivere, it is no drede.

Tempest the noght al croked to redresse,
In trust of hir that turneth as a bal.
Gret reste stant in lytel bisynesse.   10
Bewar also to sporne ayeyns an al.
Stryve noght as doth the crokke with the wal.
Daunte thiself, that dauntest otheres dede;
And trouthe the shal delivere, it is no drede.

That the is sent, receyve in boxomnesse.   15
The wrastling for this world axeth a fal.

Here nis non home, here nis but wyldernesse:
Forth, pilgrym, forth! Forth, beste, out of thi
   stal!
Know thi contree, lok up, thank God of al;
Hold the hye wey, and lat thi gost the
   lede;   20
And trouthe the shal delivere, it is no drede.

Envoy

Therfore, thou Vache, leve thine old
   wrechedenesse;
Unto the world leve now to be thral.
Crie Hym mercy, that of His hie godnesse
Made the of noght, and in especial   25
Draw unto Him, and pray in general
For the, and eke for other hevenlyche mede;
And trouthe the shal delivere, it is no drede.

Text from Ellesmere MS (E) with variants from the first of two versions in Bodl. Fairfax 16 (F) and B. M. Add. 16340 (A). The envoy is found only in A; see "The Text of This Edition," p. 966.

1 prees, crowd. There are Boethian overtones to the poem, cf. II pr.4, m.4; III pr.11, m.11; IV pr.6, m.6. **2 Suffise unto thy good,** in *Confessio Amantis* 5.7735ff. Gower has: "Senec conseileth in this wise, | And seith, '*Bot if thi good suffise* | Unto the liking of thi wille, | *Withdrawh thi lust* and hold the stille, | *And be to thi good suffisant,*' | For that thing is appourtenant | To trouthe and causeth to be fre," which (together with Gower's Latin gloss), Brusendorff and others take to be the inspiration for Chaucer's poem. A *Suffise thin owen thing.* unto: F *the. good:* other MSS *thing,* which Brusendorff (p. 204) takes to be Chaucer's own variant from Gower's trans. of *res—rebus* as "good" and "thing." **3 tykelnesse,** insecurity. **4 wele blent,** prosperity blinds. blent: E&c *blyndeth.* **5 Savour . . . byhove,** enjoy (desire), profit. **6 rede,** advise. Reule: E&c *Werke;* F *Do.* **7 delivere . . . no drede,** free, no fear; cf. John 8:32. the om. in ll. 7, 14, 21, 28 in EA&c; found in F&c. **8** *Tempest:* F *Peyne.* **9 hir that turneth,** i.e., Fortune and her wheel. **10** E *For gret.* **11 sporne . . . al,** kick, awl; cf. Acts 9:5. E&c *And ek bewar;* A *By war therfore.* **12 crokke with . . . wal,** the proverb usually counseled "spurn not against the wall," cf. B. J. Whiting, *Proverbs* W 20. **13 Daunte . . . dede,** govern, behavior (deeds). **15 boxomnesse,** humility. **16 a fal,** technical term for a defeat in wrestling. **17 non home,** *Boece* I pr. 5,10. **18 Forth, pilgrym,** this exhortation calls to mind the symbolic interpretations of the *Canterbury* pilgrimage, cf. *CT* x.50. **19** F&c *Loke up on hye, and thonke.* **20 gost,** spirit. F&c *Weyve* (put aside) *thy lust.* **22 Vache,** formerly taken as Fr. "cow," in context of l. 18, until Edith Rickert identified it as Chaucer's friend Sir Philip de la Vache, who, like Chaucer, lost his government emoluments when Gloucester and the Lords Appelant came to power after 1386, and recovered them when Richard resumed power in 1389. This poem may have been written to console Vache at some point during this discouraging period. **23 leve,** stop. **27 mede,** reward.

12   MORAL BALADE OF GENTILESSE

The firste stok, fader of gentilesse—
What man that claymeth gentil for to be
Must folowe his trace, and alle his wittes dresse
Vertu to sewe, and vices for to fle.
For unto vertu longeth dignite,   5
And nought the revers, savely dar I deme,
Al were he mytre, coroune, or dyademe.

This firste stok was full of rightwisenesse,
Trewe of his word, sobre, pitous, and fre,
Clene of his goost, and loved besynesse,   10
Ayenst the vyce of slouthe, in honeste;

And but his heir love vertu as did he,
He is nought gentil, though he riche seme,
Al were he mytre, coroune, or dyademe.

Vices may well be heir to old richesse,   15
But ther may no man—as men may well se—
Bequethe his heir his vertuous noblesse:
That is appropred unto no degre
But to the firste fader in mageste,
That maketh his heires hem that him
     queme,   20
Al were he mytre, coroune, or dyademe.

Explicit

13   THE FORMER AGE

Chawcer upon the fyfte metrum of the second book.

A blysful lyf, a paysyble and a swete,
Ledden the poeples in the former age.
They helde hem paied of the fructes that they
     ete,
Whiche that the feldes yave hem by usage.
They ne were nat forpampred with owtrage.   5

Unknowen was the quyerne and ek the melle;
They eten mast, hawes, and swych pownage,
And dronken water of the colde welle.

Yit nas the grownd nat wownded with the
     plowh,

Text from B.M. Cotton Cleopatra D. vii (C), with variants from B.M. Ashmole 59 (A). The familiar sentiment is inspired by *Boece* III pr. 6 and m. 6, but also by Dante, *RR,* Gower.

1 firste stok, clearly God in the first stanza, but shading over into Christ or even Adam in the second and third. C *stocke.* A&c *fader and founder (fynder).* **2 gentil,** the term contains within itself the tension between the ideals "nobly born" and "of virtuous behavior." *that claymeth:* C&c *desireth.* **3 trace ... dresse,** track (footsteps), direct (address). **4 sewe,** follow (pursue). *sewe:* C&c *love.* **5 longeth,** belongs. **6 savely ... deme,** safely, judge. **7 Al were,** although, wear. **mytre, coroune ... dyademe,** bishop, king, emperor. C *coroune, miter,* but cf. 1. 14. **8 full:** A&c *grounde.* **9 fre,** generous. **10 goost,** spirit. **13 is:** A&c *nys.* **15 old richesse,** Dante, *Convivio,* "*antica richezza*" (4.3, etc.), *RR* "*richcces ancienes*" (l. 20313); cf. *CT* III.1109–10n. A&c *Vyce;* C *Vycesse.* **16 as men:** A&c *as thou.* **17** C *vertues.* **18 appropred,** appropriated (made the privilege of). **19 But,** except. **20 queme,** please. A *heyre him.*

Text from MS Cambridge Ii 3.21 (I), with variants from the other version in Camb. Hh4.12 (H); see "The Text of This Edition," p. 966. This is a free translation of *Boece* II m. 5.

3 paied of, satisfied with. **4 by usage,** by custom (i.e., without being cultivated). **5 forpampred with owtrage,** outrageously pampered. **6 quyerne ... melle,** hand mill, mill. **7 mast, hawes, pownage,** acorns, hawthorn berries, swine's food.

But corn up-sprong, unsowe of mannes hond, 10
The which they gnodded, and eete nat half
　　inowh.
No man yit knew the forwes of his lond;
No man the fyr owt of the flynt yit fond;
Unkorven and ungrobbed lay the vyne;
No man yit in the morter spices grond 15
To clarre, ne to sawse of galentyne.

No mader, welde, or wod no litestere
Ne knew; the fles was of his former hewe.
No flessh ne wyste offence of egge or spere;
No coyn ne knew man which was fals or trewe;
No ship yit karf the wawes grene and blewe; 21
No marchaunt yit ne fette owtlandissh ware;
No batails trompes for the werres folk ne knewe,
No towres heye, and walles rownde or square.

What sholde it han avayled to werreye? 25
Ther lay no profyt, ther was no rychesse.
But corsed was the tyme, I dar wel seye,
That men fyrst dede her swety bysynesse
To grobbe up metal, lurkinge in derknesse,
And in the ryveres fyrst gemmes sowhte. 30
Allas, than sprong up al the cursednesse
Of covetyse, that fyrst owr sorwe browhte!

Thyse tyrauntz putte hem gladly nat in pres
No places wyldnesse ne no busshes for to wynne
Ther poverte is, as seith Diogenes, 35
Ther as vitayle is ek so skars and thinne

That noght but mast or apples is therinne.
But ther as bagges ben, and fat vitaile,
Ther wol they gon and spare for no synne
With al hir ost the cyte for t'assayle. 40

Yit were no paleis chaumbres, ne non halles;
In kaves and wodes softe and swete
Slepten this blyssed folk withowte walles,
On gras or leves in parfyt joye and quiete.
No down of fetheres ne no bleched shete 45
Was kyd to hem, but in surte they slepte.
Hir hertes were al oon withowte galles;
Everych of hem his feith to oother kepte.

Unforged was the hawberk and the plate;
The lambyssh poeple, voyd of alle vyce, 50
Hadden no fantasye to debate,
But eche of hem wolde oother wel cheryce.
No pryde, non envye, non avaryce,
No lord, no taylage by no tyranye:
Umblesse and pes; good feith the emperice. 55

Yit was nat Juppiter the lykerous,
That fyrst was fader of delicacie,
Come in this world; ne Nembrot, desyrous
To regne, had nat maad his towres hye.
Allas, allas, now may men wepe and crye! 60
For in owr dayes nis but covetyse,
Dowblenesse, and tresoun, and envye,
Poysoun, and manslawhtre, and mordre in
　　sondry wyse.

Finit etas prima. Chaucers.

10 **corn**, grain. 11 **gnodded**, rubbed (husked). 12 **forwes**, borders (holdings were marked off by dead furrows). 13 H *yit fier . . . flynt fand*. 14 **Unkorven . . . ungrobbed**, unpruned, uncultivated (i.e., ungrubbed). 16 **To clarre . . . galentyne**, for spiced wine, spiced sauce. 17 **mader, welde, wod . . . litestere**, madder, weld, woad: plants whose roots give red, yellow, and blue dye; dyer. 18 **former**, original (undyed). 19 **egge**, edge (sword). 20 **coyn . . . fals or trewe**, genuine or counterfeit coins. *was:* I *is*. 22 **fette owtlandissh**, fetched foreign. 25 **werreye**, make war. 28 H *dyd first*. 31 H *al owre*. 33 **in pres**, in effort. Scholars have cited as a source for this figure both John of Salisbury, *Policraticus* 8.6, and *Jerome Adversus Jovinianum* 2:11. 34 H *place of wyldnesse*. 35 **Ther**, where. 36 **vitayle**, food. H *eke is*. 37 **mast**, acorns. 38 **bagges**, bags (full of goods). 39–40 Lines transposed in I. 40 I *for to asayle*. 41 *were:* I *was*. 46 **kyd . . . surte**, known, security. 47 **galles**, twinges (of envy). 48 H *to odyr hys*. 49 **hawberk . . . plate**, armor. 50 **voyd:** I *voyded*. 51 **fantasye**, desire. 54 **taylage**, taxation. 55 **emperice**, empress. The stanza lacks a link in both MSS. 56 **lykerous**, lecherous (because of his many seductions). 57 **delicacie**, wantonness (sensuality). 58 **Nembrot**, Nimrod, according to medieval tradition builder of the "towres hye" of Babel, cf. Gen. 10.10. 60 I **men om**. 61 **nis:** H *is not*. 62 **and tresoun:** H *and om*. 63 H *and/and om*.

14   LACK OF STEADFASTNESSE

Envoy to King Richard.

Somtyme the world was so stedfast and stable
That mannes word was obligacioun,
And now it is so fals and deceivable
That word and dede, as in conclusioun,
Ben nothing lyk, for turned up so doun   5
Is al this world for mede and wilfulnesse,
That all is lost for lak of stedfastnesse.

What maketh this world to be so veriable
But lust that folk have in discencioun?
For among us now a man is holde unable,   10
But if he can by som collusioun
Do his neyghburgh wrong or oppressioun.
What causeth this but wilfull wrecchednesse,
That all is lost for lak of stedfastnesse?

Trouthe is putte doun, resoun is holden fable, 15

Vertu hath now no domynacioun;
Pite exiled, no man is merciable;
Through covetise is blent discrecioun.
The world hath mad a permutacioun
Fro right to wrong, fro trouthe to
      fikelnesse,   20
That all is lost for lak of stedfastnesse.

Lenvoy to King Richard

O prince, desire to be honourable;
Cherice thi folk and hate extorcioun.
Suffre nothing that may be reprevable
To thyn estaat don in thi regioun.   25
Shew forth thy swerd of castigacioun.
Dred God, do law, love trouthe and
      worthynesse,
And wed thy folk ageyn to stedfastnesse.

Explicit

Text from B.M. Cotton Cleopatra D.vii (C) with variants from B.M. Harley 7333 (H). In the latter is Shirley's note, "This balade made Geoffrey Chauciers the Laureall poete of albion and sent it to his soverain lorde Kynge Richarde the Secounde thane being in his castell of Windesore"; see Introduction above, and "The Text of This Edition," p. 966.

1 H&c *Somtyme* om. 2 H&c *was hold.* 3 **deceivable**, deceitful. 4 H&c *worde and werke.* 5 **up so doun,** the complaint against the topsy-turvy world is a conventional lament that can be traced back to classical literature; cf. *Boece* II m. 8 and the Prologue to Gower's *Confessio Amantis*, ll. 93ff. *Ben:* C *Is. lyk:* H&c *oon.* 6 **mede,** bribery. H&c *by wikked wilfulnesse.* 9 **lust,** joy. 10 **unable,** incompetent. H&c *For now adayes a man.* 11 **collusioun:** C *conclusion.* 13 **wrecchednesse,** wickedness. 18 **blent,** blinded. 19 **mad a:** C *made.* 22 **prince,** probably Richard, in view of the ascription of the poem and its appropriateness to the career of Richard II. However, in literary contests the balade was customarily addressed to an arbiter "prince," cf. *Complaint of Venus* (short poem 4) 1. 73 and note, and *Fortune* (short poem 10), l. 73 and note. The exhortation to Richard is paralleled by Alceste's admonition to the God of Love in *LGW*, ll. 373–408, and John Gower's epistle to the king in *Vox Clamantis*, VI.581ff. *to be:* H&c *for to be.* 24 **reprevable,** deserving of reproof. 28 H&c *And dryve thy people.*

15   TO ADAM SCRYVEN

Geffrey unto Adame his owen scryvene.

Adam scryveyn, if ever it thee byfalle
Boece or *Troylus* for to wryten newe,
Under thy long lokkes thow most have the
    scalle

But after my makyng thow wryte more trewe!
So ofte a daye I mot thy werk renewe   5
It to corecte and eke to rubbe and scrape;
And al is thorugh thy neglygence and rape!

16   LENVOY DE CHAUCER A BUKTON

My maister Bukton, whan of Criste our
    kyng
Was axed what is trouthe or sothefastnesse,
He nat a word answerde to that axing,
As who saith, "Noo man is al trew," I gesse.
And therfore, though I highte to expresse   5
The sorwe and woo that is in mariage,
I dar not writen of hit noo wikkednesse,
Lest I myself falle eft in swich dotage.

I wol nat seyn how that hit is the cheyne
Of Sathanas, on which he gnaweth evere;   10
But I dar seyn, were he out of his peyne,
As by his wille he wolde be bounde nevere.
But thilke doted fool that eft hath levere
Ycheyned be than out of prisoun crepe,
God lete him never fro his woo dissevere,   15
Ne noo man him bewayle, though he wepe.

But yet, lest thow doo worse, take a wyf!
Bet is to wedde than brenne in worse wise.
But thow shalt have sorwe on thy flessh thy lyf,
And ben thy wifes thral, as seyn these wise.   20
And yf that hooly writte may nat suffyse,
Experience shal the teche, so may happe,
That the were lever to be take in Frise
Than eft to falle of weddynge in the trappe.

Envoy

This lytel writte, proverbes or figure,   25
I sende yow; take kepe of hit, I rede:
Unwise is he that kan noo wele endure;
Yf thow be siker, put the nat in drede.
The Wyf of Bathe I pray yow that ye rede
Of this matere that we have on honde.   30
God graunte yow your lyf frely to lede
In fredam—for ful hard it is to be bonde.

Explicit

Text found only in MS Trinity Coll. Camb. R 3.20 and B.M. Stowe (S).

1 scryveyn, scrivener (copyist, i.e., the medieval equivalent of a typist). The term has become a family name, and has been taken by some scholars to be Adam's surname. S *scrivener.* **2 Boece . . . Troylus,** this linkage supports other evidence that these two pieces date from nearly the same period, c. 1380–85. **3 scalle,** parasitic skin infection (dermatophytosis). **4 makyng . . . trewe,** composing, correctly. **6 rubbe and scrape,** parchment was corrected by scraping off the old ink and then rubbing the surface smooth again. **7 rape,** haste.

Text only in MS Bodl. Fairfax 16 (F), and the Notary (N) and Thynne (T) editions; see "The Text of This Edition," p. 966.

1 maister, title of respect, eventually leading to "Mr." NT *Buketon.* **2 sothefastnesse,** truthfulness, cf. John 18.38. **4 As who saith,** i.e., as if to say. **5 highte,** promised. N *you texpresse.* **8 eft,** again. Philippa Chaucer died in 1387. **13 levere,** rather. *eft:* FN *oft(e).* **18 Bet . . . wedde,** cf. I Cor. 7.9. **19 thy lyf,** all your life. **20 wise,** sages. **23 take . . . Frise,** captured, Friesland. Froissart says that Frisians were known for executing their prisoners; an English expedition against them was mounted in 1396. **25 figure,** metaphor (indirect statement). **26 rede,** advise. **27 wele,** prosperity. **28 siker . . . drede,** secure, jeopardy. **29 Wyf of Bathe,** The Wife is the only character among the pilgrims to be referred to by Chaucer outside the context of her own tale (cf. MerchT, *CT* IV.1685), and here outside of the context of the *Canterbury* collection. **32 NT** *it* om.

17 LENVOY DE CHAUCER A SCOGAN

I

Tobroken been the statutez hye in hevene
That creat weren eternally to dure,
Syth that I see the bryghte goddis sevene
Mowe wepe and wayle, and passioun endure,
As may in erthe a mortal creature.   5
Allas, fro whennes may thys thing procede,
Of which errour I deye almost for drede?

By word eterne whilom was yshape
That fro the fyfte sercle, in no manere,
Ne myghte a drope of teeres doun eschape.   10
But now so wepith Venus in hir spere
That with hir teeres she wol drenche us here.
Allas, Scogan, this is for thyn offence;
Thow cawsest this diluge of pestilence.   14

Hastow not seyd, in blaspheme of the goddes,
Thurgh pride, or thrugh thy grete rekelnesse,
Swich thing as in the lawe of love forbede is,
That for thy lady sawgh nat thy distresse,
Therfore thow yave hir up at Mychelmesse?
Allas, Scogan, of olde folk ne yonge   20
Was never erst Scogan blamed for his tonge!

II

Thow drowe in skorn Cupide eke to recorde
Of thilke rebel word that thow hast spoken,
For which he wol no lenger be thy lorde.

And, Scogan, though his bowe be nat broken, 25
He wol nat with his arwes been ywroken
On the ne me ne noon of oure figure;
We shul of him have neyther hurt ne cure.

Now certes, frend, I dreed of thyn unhappe,
Lest for thy gilt the wreche of Love procede 30
On alle hem that ben hoor and rounde of
      shappe,
That ben so lykly folk in love to spede.
Than shal we for oure labour han no mede—
But wel I wot, thow wolt answere and saye,
"Loo, th'olde Grisel lyst to ryme and playe!" 35

Nay, Scogan, say not soo, for I m'excuse—
God helpe me soo—in no ryme, dowteles,
Ne thynke I never of slepe to wake my muse,
That rusteth in my shethe stille in pees.
While I was yong, I put hir forth in prees,   40
But alle shal passe that men prose or ryme.
Take every man his turn, as for his tyme.

Envoy

Scogan, that knelest at the stremes hed
Of grace, of alle honour and worthynesse,
In th'ende of which streme I am dul as ded,   45
Forgete in solytarie wildernesse—
Yet, Scogan, thenke on Tullius kyndenesse:
Mynne thy frend, there it may fructyfye!
Farewel, and loke thow never eft Love dyffye.

Text from MS Bodl. Fairfax 16 (F), with variants from Pepys 2006 (P) and Camb. Gg 4.27 (G); see "The Text of This Edition," p. 966.

1 statutez, laws. G *hye* om. **3 goddis sevene,** the seven planets. **4 wepe and wayle,** excessive rains are the "objective correlative" of the grief of the gods throughout this humorous begging poem. Attempts have been made to identify them as deluges and pestilences that occurred in 1391 and 1393. Then again, Chaucer was appointed a commissioner to oversee repair of the dikes and ditches around Greenwich as a result of a great storm which created havoc in March 1390. **6** *whennes:* P *hens.* **8 whilom . . . yshape,** formerly, decreed. PG *it shape.* **9 fyfte sercle,** the sphere of Venus. **13** G *Skogan.* **14** *diluge:* G *deluvye.* **15** F *this goddis* (= *goddess?*). **16 rekelnesse,** rashness. **17** *forbede:* G *forbode.* **18 for . . . sawgh,** because, heeded. **19 Mychelmesse,** Michaelmas, September 29, traditional beginning of the English fall business and social season. FP *Mighelmesse.* **21 erst,** before. **22 to recorde,** to take note. **25** *his:* F *thy.* G *his bowe, Scogan,* be. **26 ywroken,** avenged. **27** *oure:* F *youre.* **28** *him:* P *hem.* *ne:* F *nor.* **29 dreed . . . unhappe,** am frightened by your misfortune. **31 On . . . hoor,** against, hoar (white-headed). **32** P *in love* om. **33 mede,** reward. F *have.* **35 Grisel,** gray head. Caxton and Thynne read *renne and playe,* in which case Grisel would have its primary meaning, "old gray horse." *th'olde:* PG *olde.* **40 in prees,** in public. *hir:* FG *hyt.* **43 stremes hed,** MSS carry marginal note "i. a. Wyndesor." *stremes:* G *wellis* (i.e., source). **46 wildernesse,** MSS carry marginal note "i.a. Grenewich," which suggest that Chaucer may have lived there for a time before renting the house in Westminster in 1399. His sister Katherine was married to Simon Manning of Cudham and East Greenwich. **47 Tullius kyndenesse,** evidently a reference to Cicero *De Amicitia* as recalled in *Romaunt,* ll. 5285ff. **48 Mynne . . . there,** remember, where.

18   COMPLAINT OF CHAUCER TO HIS PURSE

A Supplication to King Henry.

To yow, my purs, and to non othir wyght
Complayne I, for ye ben my lady dere!
I am so sory, now that ye been lyght;
For certes, but yf ye make me hevy chere,
Me were as leef be leyd upon my bere;   5
For which unto your mercy thus I crye,
Beth hevy ayeyn, or elles mot I dye!

Now voucheth sauf this day, or hyt be nyght,
That I of yow the blisful soun may here,
Or se your colour lyk the sonne bryght,   10
That of yelownesse had never pere.
Ye be my lyf, ye be myne hertes stere,
Quene of comfort and of gode companye;
Beth hevy ayeyn, or elles mot I dye!

Now purs, that ben to me my lyves lyght   15
And saveour, as doun in this worlde here,
Out of this towne helpe me thurgh your
     myght,
Syn that ye wylle nat ben my tresorere;
For I am shave as nye as any frere.
But yet I pray unto youre curtesye,   20
Beth hevy ayeyn, or elles mot I dye!

Lenvoy de Chaucer

O conquerour of Brutes Albyoun,
Which that by lyne and fre eleccioun
Ben verray kyng, this song to you I sende;
And ye, that mowen alle oure harmes amende,
Have mynde upon my supplicacioun.   26

Text from MS Camb. Ff 1.6 (Ff), with corrections from Fairfax 16 (F) and variants from B.M. Add. 22139 (A). MS Pepys 2006 has the French heading *La Complainte de Chaucer a sa Bourse Voide.* Shirley's B.M. MS Harley 7333 has *A supplicacion to Kyng Richard by Chaucier,* but with the envoy to Henry; see Introduction, and "The Text of This Edition," p. 966.

1 wyght, creature. **3–4 lyght . . . hevy,** in addition to the weight of coins, in the mock love complaint "light" can mean fickle, and "heavy" serious (constant). **8 voucheth sauf . . . or,** consent, ere. **10 se:** A *shew.* **11 yelownesse:** Ff *lewdnesse.* **12 stere,** rudder. **13** A *gode* om. **15** A *Yee pursse.* **16** A *doune here.* **17 this towne,** there have been many conjectures about the meaning of this allusion. If Chaucer was still living in the "wildernesse" of Greenwich (cf. *Scogan,* short poem 17, l. 46n.), the grant from Henry may have enabled him to rent the house in Westminster on December 24, 1399. But Chaucer may have already retreated to the house in the Abbey close because it gave him sanctuary from his creditors. **19 shave . . . frere,** this figure for his insolvency is cited as evidence that the poem was written after he was living among the tonsured monks at Westminster. Ff *shave as ys any.* **22–23 conquerour . . . lyne . . . fre eleccioun,** conquest, inheritance, and election by Parliament were the three grounds upon which Henry IV claimed the throne from Richard II in the Parliament of 30 September 1399. **Brutes Albyoun,** Brutus, descendent of Aeneas, the legendary founder of Albion (Britain). **24 verray,** true. **25 mowen,** can (may). **26 Have mynde,** pay attention to. This seems peremptory language in which to address a sovereign. In a patent dated 13 October 1399, Henry granted Chaucer the sizable annuity of 40 marks a year; see Introduction for some of the complications.

Poems Not Attributed to Chaucer in the Manuscripts

19   MERCILESS BEAUTE

A triple roundel.

I

Yowr eyen two woll sle me sodenly;
I may the beaute of hem not sustene,
So woundeth hit throughout my herte
    kene.

And but your word woll helen hastely
My hertes wound, while that hit is grene,   5
Your eyen &c.

Upon my trouth, I sey yow feithfully
That ye ben of my lyf and deth the quene;
For with my deth the trouthe shal be sene.
Your eyen &c.   10

II

So hath yowr beaute fro your herte chaced
Pitee, that me navailleth not to pleyne;
For Danger halt your mercy in his cheyne.

Giltles my deth thus han ye me purchaced—

I sey yow soth; me nedeth not to feyne.   15
So hath yowr beaute &c.

Allas that Nature hath in yow compassed
So grete beaute that no man may atteyn
To mercy, though he sterve for the peyn.
So hath yowr beaute &c.   20

III

Syn I fro Love escaped am so fat,
I nevere thenk to ben in his prison lene;
Syn I am fre, I counte hym not a bene.

He may answere, and sey this and that.
I do no fors; I speke ryght as I mene.   25
Syn I fro Love &c.

Love hath my name istrike out of his sclat,
And he is strike out of my bokes clene
For evermo; ther is non other mene.
Syn I fro Love &c.   30

Explicit

Text found only in MS Pepys 2006.

1 MS *yowr two yen;* but cf. l. 6. **6 Your eyen,** first three lines are to be sung as a refrain. **8** MS *liffe.* **10 Your eyen,** first three lines as refrain. **13 Danger,** disdain. **15 feyne,** pretend. **19 sterve,** die. **21 fat,** despairing love makes lovers lean. **23 counte . . . bene,** count him not worth a bean. **25 do no fors,** don't care. **27 istrike . . . sclat,** erased, slate. **29 mene,** course. *ther:* MS *this.*

20   AGAINST WOMEN UNCONSTANT

Madame, that throgh your newfangelnesse
Many a servaunt have put out of your grace,
I take my leve of your unstedfastnesse,
For wel I woot, while ye have lyves space,
Ye kan not love ful half yere in a place;   5
To newe thing your lust is ay so kene;
Instede of blew, ye may wel were al grene.

Ryght as in a merour nothing may impresse,
But lyghtly as hit cometh, so mot it pace,
So fareth your love, your werkes beren witnesse.
Ther is noo feyth that may your hert embrace; 11

But as a wedercok that turneth ay his face
With every wynd ye fare, and that is sene;
Instede of blew, ye may wel were al grene.

Ye myght be shryned, for your brotelnesse,   15
Bet than Dalyda, Creseyde, or Candace;
Forever in chaungyng stant your sikernesse,
That tache may noo wyght fro your herte
     arace;
Yf ye lese oon, ye kan wel tweyn purchace.
Al lyght for somer—ye woot wel what I mene—
Insted of blew, ye may wel were al grene.   21

21   A BALADE OF COMPLAINT

Compleyne ne koude ne might myn herte never
My peynes halve ne what turment I have,
Though that I shoulde in youre presence ben
     ever,
My hertes lady, as wisely He me save
That bounte made, and beaute list to grave   5
In youre persone, and bad hem bothe in-fere
Ever t'awayte, and ay be wher ye were.

As wisely He gye alle my joyes here
As I am youres, and to yow sadde and trewe,
And ye, my lyf and cause of my gode chere,   10

And dethe also, whan ye my peynes newe,
My worldes joye, whom I wol serve and sewe,
My heven hole, and al my souffisaunce,
Whom for to serve is sette al my plesaunce.

Beseching yow in my most humble wyse   15
T'accepte in worth this lytel pore dyte,
And for my trouthe my service nat despyse,
Myn observaunce eke have nat in despyte,
Ne yit to long to suffren in this plyte,
I yow beseche, myn hertes lady dere,   20
Sith I yow serve, and so wil yere by yere.

Text from MS Bodl. Fairfax 16 (F), corrected from the other two MSS, Harley 7578 and Cotton Cleopatra D.vii.

6 **lust,** desire (pleasure). 7 **blew . . . grene,** blue, color of constancy, green of fickleness. 9 **lyghtly,** easily. 15 **shryned . . . brotelnesse,** enshrined, undependability (brittleness). 16 **Dalyda . . . Candace,** Delilah, Candace who deceived Alexander—all three types of faithless women. F *Better.* 17 **sikernesse,** security. F *stondeth.* 18 **tache . . . arace,** defect, eliminate (root out). F *from.* 20 **lyght for somer,** the implication of inconstancy may throw light on the appearance of the phrase in CYT, *CT* viii.568.

Text in MS B.M. Add. 16165 only.

1–2 **Compleyne . . . halve,** i.e., my heart cannot complain of half the pain it suffers. 5 **bounte . . . grave,** goodness, engrave. 6 **in-fere,** together. 8 **gye,** guide. 9 **sadde,** steadfast. 11 *newe,* in MS corrected from *rewe.* 12 **sewe,** follow. 16 **dyte,** poem (ditty). 17 **trouthe,** loyalty. 19 **long to suffren,** i.e., cause me to suffer. 20 *dere:* MS *here.* 21 **Sith,** since.

22 AN AMOROUS COMPLAINT MADE AT WINDSOR

Complaynt Damours.

I, which that am the sorwefullest man
That in this world was ever yet lyvinge,
And lest recoverer of himselven kan,
Begynne right thus my dedely compleyninge
On hir that may to lyf and deth me bringe, 5
Which hath on me no mercy ne noo routhe,
That love hir best, but sleeth me for my trouthe.

Can I noght doon to seyen that yow may lyke,
Ne certes, now, allas, allas, the while!
Your plesaunce is to lawghen whan I syke, 10
And thus ye me from al my blisse exile.
Ye han me cast in thilke spitous yle
Ther never man on lyve myghte asterte;
This have I for I love yow, swete herte.

Sothe is that wel I wot, by lyklynesse, 15
Yf that it were a thing possible to doo,
T'acompte youre beute and goodenesse.
I have no wonder thogh ye do me woo,
Sith I, the unworthiest that may ryde or goo,
Dorste never thynken in so high a place; 20
What wonder is, though ye do me noo
    grace?

Allas, thus is my lyf brought to an ende;
My deth I se is my conclusioun.
I may wel singe, "In sory tyme I spende
My lyf"—that song may have confusioun! 25
For mercy, pitee, and deep affeccioun,
I sey for me, for al my deedly chere,
Alle thise diden in that me love yow dere.

And in this wise and in dispeyre I lyve:
In love, nay, but in dispeyre I dye! 30
But shal I thanne my deth foryive,
That causeles doth me this sorwe drye?
Ye, certes, I! For she of my folye
Hath noght to doone, although she do me sterve.
Hit is nat with hir wil that I hir serve! 35

And sithen I am of my sorwe the cause
And sithen I have this withoute hir rede,
Than may I seyn ryght shortely in a clause
Hit is no blame unto hir womanhede
Though suche a wrecche as I be for hir dede. 40
Yet alwey two thinges doon me dye,
That is to seyn, hir beute and myn eye.

So that, algates, she is verray roote
Of my disese, and of my dethe alsoo;
For wyth a word she myghte be my boote, 45
Yf that she vouched sauf for to do soo.
But than is hir gladnesse at my woo;
Hit is hir wone plesaunce for to take
To seen hir servaunts dyen for hir sake.

But certes, than is al my wondering, 50
Sithen she is the fairest creature
As to my doome that ever was lyving,
The benygnest and best eke that Nature
Hath wrought or shal while that the world may
    dure.
Why that she lefte pitee all behinde? 55
Hit was, ywis, a grete defaute in kynde.

Text from MS B. M. Fairfax 16 (F) with corrections from Harley 7333 (H).
3 recoverer, heal (cure). **4 dedely,** deathly. **6 routhe,** pity. **7 sleeth me . . . trouthe,** slay myself, fidelity. **8** Skeat emended to *doon ne seye.* **10 plesaunce . . . syke,** pleasure, sigh. **12 spitous yle,** hateful isle. **13 on lyve . . . asterte,** alive, escape. **14** H *love yow best.* **15 wot . . . lyklynesse,** know, probability. **17 T'acompte,** to measure (value). **19 goo,** walk. **20 thynken in so high,** i.e., presume to love one of such high estate. **22** *my lyf:* F *mis[c]hefe.* **24–28** Line ends missing in F. Various readings in H&c. **27 deedly chere,** deathly expression. **28 diden . . . me love . . . dere,** made me love, dearly. **30** H *nay, nay.* **31** *thanne:* H *thus yow.* **32 drye,** suffer. **34 sterve,** die. **35 with,** by. This is something like the "Brooch of Thebes" motif in *The Complaint of Mars;* and see ll. 57ff. below. **36 sithen,** since. H *than sith.* **37 rede,** advice. H *sitthe that.* **41 doon,** make. **43 algates,** always. **45 boote,** remedy. **48 wone,** custom. F *wone to.* **52 doome,** judgment. **55** *all:* H *so.* **56 kynde,** nature.

Yet is this no lakke to hir, pardee,
But God or Nature, hem wolde I blame.
For though she shew no pitee unto me,
Sythen that she dooth other men the same   60
I ne oughte to despyse my ladies game.
Hit is hir pley to lawghen whan men syketh,
And I assente al that hir list and lyketh.

Yet wolde I, as I dar, with sorwful hert,
Beseche unto your meke womanhede   65
That I dorste my sharpe sorwes smerte
Shewe by word, that ye wolde ones rede
Compleynte of me, which ful sore I drede
That I have seid through myn unkonninge
In any worde to your displesinge.   70

Lothest of anything that ever was loothe
Were me, as wisly God my soule save,
To seyn a thing thorgh which ye myght be
          wroothe;

And to that day that I be leyd in grave,
A trewer servaunt shul ye never have.   75
And though that I on yow have pleyned here,
Foryiveth it me, myn owne lady dere.

Ever have I ben, and shal howso I wende,
Outher to lyve or dye your humble trewe;
Ye been to me my gynning and myn ende,   80
Sonne of the sterre, bryght and clere of hewe.
Alwey in oon, to love yow freshly newe,
By God and by my trouthe, is myn entente;
To lyve or dye, I wol it never repente.

This compleynt on Seint Valentynes day,   85
Whan every foul chesen shal his make,
To hir whos I am hool and shal alway,
This woful song and this compleynt I make,
That never yet wolde me to mercy take.
And yet wol I evermore hir serve   90
And love hir best although she do me sterve.

Explicit

57 H *al this.* **58** *hem:* H *sore.* **60 Sythen,** since. **62 syketh,** sigh. **66** H *now dorste. sorwes:* H *shoures.* **67 rede,** read. **68** *Compleynte:* H *The pleynt.* **69** H *seid here.* F *myn* om. **70** Line lacking in F. **76** H *have pleyned unto yow.* **77** *lady:* F *hert.* H *so dere.* **81** *of:* F *over; and clere* om. **82 in oon,** the same. **83** F *this is myn.* **87** F *hool* om. **91 sterve,** die.

Romaunt of the Rose

INTRODUCTION

Romaunt of the Rose

HAUCER'S ART was shaped, like that of his French courtly models, under the influence of the *Roman de la Rose.* The influence of the *Roman* was so profound because it combined the the idealism of courtly love with satire on human frailties. The first 4058 lines of the French poem, by Guillaume de Lorris (who died in 1237 with the work incomplete), are an idealized vision of the Court of Love as the icon of aristocratic society. It is no accident that this was an erotic fantasy. Henry Adams, *Mont-Saint-Michel and Chartres* (1904) remains the most cogent elucidation of the part love played in civilizing a warrior society, and C.S. Lewis, *The Allegory of Love* (1936), remains the most interesting treatment of the literary antecedents and psychological depth of the *Roman,* although D.W. Robertson, Jr., *A Preface to Chaucer* (1962), and his students have interpreted it as a Christian allegory of Temptation and the Fall. This interpretation is summarized in the introduction to the translation by Charles Dahlberg (1971).

As important as Guillaume's love vision is the good fortune that the work was completed (c1277, in 17,722 lines, for a total of 21,780) by Jean de Meun, master of the University of Paris, prolific author on many topics, whose perspective was very different from Guillaume's. Keeping the thread of the lover's assault on the virginity of the rose, Jean poured into his continuation irony gained from a lifetime of reading. The Robertsonians see the conflict between Jean's personifications of Raison (Reason), Amis (the Friend), La Vieille (the experienced old woman, prototype for the Wife of Bath), Faus-Semblant (Hypocrisy, prototype for the Pardoner), and the others as continuations of the moral allegory, but it is their perceptual satire on marriage, money, and manners and their conceptual satire on trendy philosophy and theology that most impressed the contemporary audience. In place of Guillaume's personifications of courtly etiquette, Jean created naturalistic personifications of sex as a biological function and of the fraud and avarice that govern human relations. As the style of Guillaume exemplifies the sensibility of romance, the style of Jean exemplifies the realism of satire. In a sense, Chaucer's poetic career from *Book of the Duchess* to the *Wife of Bath* is this movement from sensibility to satire. Charles Muscatine, *Chaucer and the French Tradition* (1957), bases his study of the development of Chaucer's style on the two parts of the *Roman.*

In the *Legend of Good Women* (1.329), Chaucer lists a translation of the *Romaunce of the Rose* among his compositions, and Deschamps praises him for it in his complimentary balade (p.952 below, 2nd stanza). This translation has not come down to us. What has come down is three fragments in different Middle English dialects. Ronald Sutherland, *The Romaunt of the Rose and Le Roman de la Rose* (1968), provides the most authoritative description of the text and the best French parallel. Of the three parts, only the first (to l.1705) is in Chaucer's dialect, but all have been included in collections of Chaucer's poetry since Thynne's edition (1532).

In the translation that has come down to us we have a spectrum of subjects and styles. Through l.4430, the English follows Guillaume's text fairly closely beginning with the vision of the garden of love that so profoundly influenced fourteenth-century court poetry. But of Jean's continuation it preserves only part of the discourse with Reason (ll.4431-5810) and then skips 5000 lines to pick up part of Love's barons' plans for war and part of the confession of Faus-Semblant (ll.5811ff; *RR* 10,679ff). All of the discussion with Friend, onslaught on the castle of Jealousy, confession of LaVieille, and discourse of Nature and Genius, from which Chaucer and his friend John Gower borrowed stories, images, and ideas, do not appear in the English translation. Chaucer's borrowings have all been identified by D.S. Fansler, *Chaucer and the Roman de la Rose* (1914).

Romaunt of the Rose

FRAGMENT A

Many men sayn that in sweveninges
Ther nys but fables and lesinges,
But men may some swevenes sene
Which hardely that false ne bene,
But afterward ben apparaunt.   5
This maye I drawe to warraunt
An authour that hight Macrobes,
That halt nat dremes false ne lees,
But undothe us the avysioun
That whilom mette Kyng Cipioun.   10
And whoso saith or weneth it be
A jape or eles a nycete
To wene that dremes after fal,
Lette whoso lyste a fole me cal.
For this trowe I, and say for me,   15
That dremes signifiaunce be
Of good and harme to many wightes
That dremen in her slepe anyghtes
Ful many thynges covertly
That fallen after al openly.   20

   Within my twenty yere of age,   **THE DREAM**
Whan that Love taketh his cariage
Of yonge folke, I went sone
To bedde, as I was wont to done,
And faste I slept; and in slepyng,   25
Me mette suche a swevenyng
That lyked me wonders wel.

But in that sweven is never a del
That it nys afterward befal,
Right as this dreme wol tel us al.   30
Now this dreme wol I ryme aright
To make your hertes gaye and lyght,
For Love it prayeth and also
Commaundeth me that it be so.
And if there any aske me,   35
Whether that it be he or she,
How this book whiche is here
Shal hatte, that I rede you here,
It is the *Romance of the Rose*,
In whiche al the arte of love I close.   40
The mater fayre is of to make;
God graunte me in gree that she it take
For whom that it begonnen is!
And that is she that hath, ywis,
So mochel prise, and therto she   45
So worthy is beloved to be
That she well ought, of prise and right,
Be cleped Rose of every wight.

   That it was May me thought tho—
It is fyve yere or more ago—   50
That it was May thus dremed me
In tyme of love and jolyte,
That al thyng gynneth waxen gay,
For ther is neyther busk nor hay

Text from Thynne edition (T) with variants from MS Glasgow, Hunterian Museum V 3.7 (G). French from Sutherland edition, see Introduction and "The Text of This Edition," p. 966.

1 sweveninges, dreams. Lines 1–44 lost from G. **2 lesinges,** lies. **3** T *sweven.* **5 apparaunt,** apparent (when they come to pass). **6 to warraunt,** as proof. **7 Macrobes,** Macrobius, author of commentary on Cicero's *Somnium Scipionis.* This obscure allusion led to Chaucer's mistaken reference in *BD,* ll. 284–87, which he corrected in *PF,* ll. 31ff. **8 lees,** lies. **9 undothe,** reveals. **10 whilom mette . . . Cipioun,** formerly dreamed, Scipio. The failure here to specify that Scipio the Younger dreamt of his ancestor Scipio Africanus led to Chaucer's initial confusion. **11 weneth,** thinks. **12 jape . . . nycete,** joke, foolishness. *a nycete:* TG *a* om. **13 fal,** happen (fall out). **19 covertly,** secretly. **22 cariage,** toll. T *corage.* Fr. *paage* (toll). **27 lyked me,** pleased me. **31** *Now:* T *Howe.* Fr. *Or.* **33 prayeth,** asks. **38 hatte,** be named. **40 close,** enclose. **41 mater . . . make,** subject matter, compose poetry. **42 gree,** good will. **45 prise,** price (value). *mochel:* T *mokel.* **54 busk . . . hay,** bush, hedge.

In May that it nyl shrouded bene,   55
And it with newe leves wrene.
These woddes eke recoveren grene
That drie in wynter ben to sene,
And the erthe wexeth proud withall
For swote dewes that on it fall,   60
And the poore estate forgette
In which that wynter had it sette.
And than becometh the grounde so proude
That it wol have a newe shroude,
And maketh so queynt his robe and fayre   65
That it hath hewes an hundred payre
Of grasse and floures, ynde and pers,
And many hewes ful dyvers—
That is the robe I mene, iwys,
Through which the ground to praysen is.   70
   The byrdes, that han left her songe
Whyl they han suffred cold ful stronge
In wethers grille and derke to sight,
Ben in May for the sonne bright
So gladde that they shewe in syngyng   75
That in her herte is suche lyking
That they mote syngen and be lyght.
Than doth the nightyngale hir myght
To maken noyse and syngen blythe.
Than is blysful many a sythe   80
The chelaundre and the popyngay.
Than yonge folke entenden ay
For to ben gay and amorous,
The tyme is than so savorous.
Harde is his herte that loveth nought   85
In May, whan al this myrthe is wrought,
Whan he may on these braunches here
The smale byrdes syngen clere
Her blysful swet song pytous.
   And in this seson delytous,   90
Whan love affraieth alle thyng,
Me thought one night in my slepyng,

Right in my bedde, ful redyly,
That it was by the morowe erly,
And up I rose and gan me clothe.   95
Anon I wyssh myn hondes bothe.
A sylver nedyl forthe I drowe
Out of an aguyler queynt ynowe,
And gan this nedyl threde anon,
For out of town me lyst to gon   100
The sowne of briddes for to here
That on these buskes syngen clere.
And in the swete seson that lefe is,
With a threde bastyng my slevys,
Alone I wente in my playing,   105
The smale foules song harkening
That payned hem ful many a payre
To synge on bowes blossomed fayre.
Jolyf and gay, ful of gladnesse,
Towarde a ryver gan I me dresse   110
That I herde renne faste by,
For fayrer playing non saugh I
Than playen me by that ryvere,
For from an hyl that stode ther nere,
Come down the streme full styffe and bold.   115
Clere was the water, and as cold
As any welle is, sothe to sayne;
And somdele lasse it was than Sayne,
But it was strayter wel away.
And never saugh I, er that day,   120
The water that so wel lyked me.
And wonder glad was I to se
That lusty place, and that ryvere.
And with that water that ran so clere
My face I wyssh. Tho sawe I wel   125
The botme ypaved everydel
With gravel, ful of stones shene.
The medowes softe, sote, and grene,
Beet right on the watersyde.
Ful clere was than the morow-tyde,   130

56 wrene, covered. **59 wexeth proud,** swells (cf. OED "proud flesh"). **64 shroude,** garment. **65 queynt,** intricate. **66 hath:** T *had*. **67 ynde . . . pers,** azure (India), blue (Persia). **69–72** G Beginnings of lines torn off. **70 to praysen,** to be praised. **72** *ful:* G *so*. **73 grille,** rough. **77 lyght,** happy. **78** *Than:* T *That*. **81 chelaundre . . . popyngay,** lark, parrot. **82 entenden,** are inclined. **85** G *the hert*. **91 affraieth,** arouses. T *affirmeth*. Fr. *s'esfroie*. **92** G *anyght*. **98 aguyler,** needlecase. Sleeves in the 14th century were laced. The figure of unlaced sleeves for emotional disorder persisted as late as "the ravell'd sleave of care" in *Macbeth* II.ii.34. **101** *sowne:* G *song* Fr. *les sons*. **103 lefe,** lief (dear), but *double entendre*, in English, with leaf. **105 playing,** enjoyment (amusing myself). **110 dresse,** direct (address) **117 welle,** spring. Lines 117–20 G torn. **118 lasse . . . Sayne,** smaller, Seine River (in France). **119 strayter,** either "narrower" or "straighter." (The Seine is famous for its meandering course.) Fr. *plus espandue* (broader). **127 shene,** glistening. **128 sote,** sweet-smelling, cf. *CT* I.1n. **129 Beet,** beat (bordered), Fr. *bastoit* (beat). **130 morow-tyde,** morning.

And ful attempre, out of drede.
Tho gan I walken thorowe the mede,
Downward aye in my playing,
The rivers side costeiyng.

    And whan I had a while ygone,   135
I sawe a garden right anone,   THE GARDEN
Ful longe and brode, and everydel
Enclosed it was, and walled wel,
With hye walles enbatayled,
Portrayed without and wel entayled   140
With many riche portreytures.
And bothe the ymages and peyntures
Gan I beholde besely.
And I wol tel you redely
Of thilke ymages the semblaunce,   145
As ferre as I have remembraunce.

    Amydde sawe I Hate stonde,   HATE
That for hir wrathe and yre and onde
Semed to been a mynoresse,
An angry wight, a chideresse;   150
And ful of gyle and fel corage
By semblaunt was that ylke ymage.
And she was nothyng wel arayde,
But lyk a wode woman afrayde;
Yfrounced foule was hir visage,   155
And grynnyng for dispitous rage;
Hir nose snorted up for tene.
Ful hydous was she for to sene;
Ful foule and rusty was she, this;
Hir heed ywrithen was, ywis,   160
Ful grymly with a great towayle.

    An ymage of another entayle   FELONY
A lyft half was hir faste by.
Hir name above hir heed sawe I,
And she was called Felonye.   165

    Another ymage that Villanye   VILLAINY
Ycleped was sawe I and fond

Upon the wall on hir right hond.
Vyllanye was lyk somdel
That other ymage, and trusteth wel,   170
She semed a wicked creature.
By countenaunce, in portreyture,
She semed be ful dispytous,
And eke ful proude and outragious.
Wel coude he paynt, I undertake,   175
That suche an ymage coude make.
Ful foule and cherlish semed she,
And eke vileynous for to be,
And lytel coude of norture
To worshippe any creature.   180

    And next was paynted Covetyse,
That eggeth folk in many a gyse   COVETOUSNESS
To take and yeve right nought agayn,
And gret tresours up to layn.
And that is she that for usure   185
Leneth to many a creature
The lasse for the more wynnyng,
So covetous is her brennyng.
And that is she, for pennes feele,
That techeth for to robbe and steele   190
These theves and these smale harlotes;
And that is routhe, for by her throtes
Ful many one hongeth at the last.
She maketh folk compasse and cast
To taken other folkes thynge   195
Through robberye or myscountyng.
And that is she that maketh trechours.
And she maketh false pledours,
That with her termes and her domes
Done maydens, children, and eke
    gromes   200
Her heritage to forgo.
Ful croked were hir hondes two,
For Covetyse is ever wode

---

131 **attempre**, temperate. 134 **costeiyng**, coasting (following the coast). T *coostyng*; Fr. *costoiant*. 139 **enbatayled**, battlemented. 140 **Portrayed . . . entayled**, painted, sculptured, Fr. *entaillié*. The following are icons of the qualities antithetic to the courtly virtues. 145 **semblaunce**, appearance. 147 **Amydde**, in the middle. 148 **onde**, envy. 149 **mynoresse**, Minorite nun. Skeat and other eds. have emended this on basis of context and the Fr. *meneresse* (agitator, ringleader) to *moveresse*. 150 **chideresse**, scolder. 151 **fel corage**, evil spirit. 154 **wode woman**, crazy woman. 155 **Yfrounced**, wrinkled (pleated). 156 **dispitous**, spiteful. 157 **tene**, vexation. 160 **ywrithen**, wrapped. 162 **entayle**, shape. 163 **lyft . . . faste**, left, near. G *faste* om. 173 **dispytous**, spiteful. 177 T *chorlych*. 179 **coude of norture**, knew of breeding. 185 **usure**, usury. 186 **Leneth**, lends. 188 **brennyng**, burning. 189 **feele**, many. 191 **harlotes**, rascals; Fr. *ribaudiaus*. 192 **routhe**, pity. 194 **compasse and cast**, scheme and plan. 196 *myscountyng*: GT *myscoveytyng*. 197 **trechours**, traitors. 198 **pledours**, lawyers. 199 **domes**, judgments. 200 **Done . . . gromes**, make, men. 203 **wode**, mad.

To grypen other folkes gode.
Covetyse for hir wynnyng   205
Ful lefe hath other mennes thyng.

   Another ymage set sawe I   AVARICE
Next Covetyse faste by,
And she was cleped Avarice.
Ful foul in payntyng was that vice;   210
Ful fadde and caytif was she eke,
And also grene as any leke.
So yvel hewed was hir colour,
Hir semed to have lyved in langour.
She was lyk thyng for hungre deed,   215
That ladde hir lyf onely by breed
Kneden with eysel strong and egre;
And therto she was leane and megre.
And she was cladde ful pourely
Al in an old torn courtepy,   220
As she were al with dogges torne;
And bothe behynde and eke beforne
Clouted was she beggarly.
A mantel hong hir faste by,
Upon a perche, weyke and smal;   225
A burnette cote hong therwithal.
Furred with no menyvere,
But with a furre rough of here,
Of lambe-skynnes hevy and blake—
It was ful old, I undertake.   230
For Avarice to clothe hir wel
Ne hasteth hir never a del,
For certainly it were hir lothe
To wearen ofte that ilke clothe.
And if it were forweared, she   235
Wolde have ful great necessite
Of clothyng er she boughte hir newe,
Al were it bad of wol and hewe.
This Avarice held in hir hande
A purs, that hong by a bande;   240
And that she hydde and bond so stronge,
Menne must abyde wonder longe
Out of the purs er ther come ought,

For that ne cometh in hir thought.
It was not, certayn, hir entente   245
That fro that purs a peny wente.

   And by that ymage, nygh ynough,   ENVY
Was paynted Envye, that never lough
Nor never wel in herte ferde
But if she eyther sawe or herde   250
Som great mischaunce or greet disese.
Nothyng may so moch hir plese
As mischef and misaventure,
Or whan she seeth discomfyture
Upon any worthy man fall,   255
Than lyketh hir ful wel withall.
She is ful glad in hir corage,
If she se any gret linage
Be brought to naught in shamful wyse.
And if a man in honour ryse,   260
Or by his wytte, or by prowesse,
Of that hath she gret hevynesse,
For trusteth wel, she goth nye wood
Whan any chaunce happeth good.
Envye is of suche cruelte   265
That fayth ne trouthe holdeth she
To frend ne felawe, badde or good.
Ne she hath kyn none of hir blood
That she nys ful her enemy.
She nolde, I dar sayn hardely,   270
Hir owne fader ferde wel.
And sore abyeth she everydel
Hir malyce and hir maletalent,
For she is in so great turment
And hath such wo whan folk doth good,   275
That nygh she melteth for pure wood.
Hir herte kerveth and so breketh
That God the people wel awreketh.
Envye, iwys, shal never let
Som blame upon the folk to set.   280
I trowe that if Envye, iwys,
Knewe the best man that is
On this syde or beyond the see,

---

205 **wynnyng,** gain. 206 **lefe hath,** dear holds. 211 **fadde,** wasted (faded). T *sadde*; Fr. *meigre*. 215 **deed,** dead. 217 **Kneden . . . eysel,** mixed, vinegar. 219 T *poorly*. 220 **courtepy,** short cape. 223 **Clouted,** patched. 225 **perche,** perch (projecting peg). T *benche*; Fr. *perche*. 226 **burnette,** brown (wool) cloth. 227 **menyvere,** miniver (fine pale fur, like ermine). 228 **here,** hair. 235 **forweared,** worn out. 236 **necessite:** T *nycete*. 238 **Al were it,** even though it were. 242 **abyde,** wait. 248 **lough,** laughed. 256 *ful wel:* GT *ful* om.; Fr. *plet mout*. 261 GT *by his.* 263 **wood,** crazy. 266 **trouthe,** promise (troth). 271 T *father.* 273 **maletalent,** ill will. 275 **hath:** T *hate.* GT *wo* om. Fr. *tel duel.* 276 **wood,** madness. 278 **awreketh,** avenges. 279 **let,** cease.

Yet somwhat lacken him wolde she.
And if he were so hende and wyse   285
That she ne mighte al abate his pryse,
Yet wolde she blame his worthynesse,
Or by hir wordes make it lesse.
I sawe Envye in that payntyng
Had a wonderful lokyng,   290
For she ne loked but awrie,
Or overthwarte al baggyngly.
And she had a foule usage;
She mighte loke in no visage
Of man or womman forthright playn,   295
But shette one eye for disdayn,
So for envye brenned she
Whan she might any man yse,
That fayre or worthy were, or wyse,
Or elles stood in folkes pryse.   300
      Sorowe was paynted next Envye   SORROW
Upon that wal of masonrye.
But wel was sene in hir colour
That she had lyved in langour;
Hir semed to have the jaunyce.   305
Not half so pale was Avaryce,
Ner nothyng lyk, as of leanesse;
For sorowe, thought, and great distresse,
That she had suffred day and nyght
Made hir ful yelowe and nothyng bryght,   310
Ful fade, pale, and megre also.
Was never wight yet half so wo
As that hir semed for to be,
Nor so fulfylled of yre as she.
I trowe that no wight mighte hir plese,   315
Nor do that thyng that mighte hir ese;
Nor she ne wolde hir sorowe slake,
Nor comfort none unto hir take,
So depe was hir wo begonne,
And eke hir herte in angre ronne—   320
A sorouful thyng wel semed she.
Nor she had nothyng slowe be
For to cracchen al hir face,

And for to rent in many place
Hir clothes, and for to teare hir swyre,   325
As she that was fulfylled of yre;
And al to-torn lay eke hir here
Aboute hir shuldres, here and there,
As she that hadde it al to-rent
For angre and for maletalent.   330
And eke I tel you certaynly
How that she wept ful tenderly.
In world nys wyght so harde of herte
That had sene hir sorowes smerte,
That nolde have had of hir pyte,   335
So wobegon a thyng was she.
She al to-dassht hirself for wo,
And smot togyder hir hondes two.
To sorowe was she ful ententyf,
That woful recheless caytyf.   340
Hir rought lytel of playing,
Or of clypping or kissing;
For whoso soroweful is in herte,
Him luste not to play ne sterte,
Ne for to dauncen, ne to synge,   345
Ne may his herte in temper bringe
To make joye on even or morowe,
For joye is contrarie unto sorowe.
      Elde was paynted after this,   OLD AGE
That shorter was a foote, ywis,   350
Than she was wonte in hir yonghede.
Unneth hirself she mighte fede.
So feble and eke so old was she
That faded was al hir beaute.
Ful salowe was waxen hir colour,   355
Hir heed forhor was, whyte as flour.
Iwys, great qualm ne were it none,
Ne synne, although hir lyf were gone.
Al woxen was hir body unwelde,
And drie, and dwyned al for elde.   360
A foul forwelked thyng was she
That whylom rounde and softe had be.
Hir eeres shoken fast withall,

---

284 lacken, disparage. **285 hende,** attractive. **286 pryse,** worth (price). **290 lokyng,** appearance; Fr. *laide esgardeure*. **292 over-thwarte . . . baggyngly,** sideways, askance. **293 usage,** custom. **296** G *her eien;* Fr. *i oil.* **299** G *fairer or worthier.* **300 pryse,** esteem (price). **305 jaunyce,** jaundice (yellow). **307** GT *as* om. **310** T *ful* om.; Fr. *mout.* **323 cracchen,** scratch. G *forcracchen* ("for" is an intensifier). **325 swyre,** throat. **330 maletalent,** ill will. **333–80** Lines omitted from G. **337 to-dassht,** bruised. **340 recheless,** hopeless. **341 rought . . . playing,** cared, amusing (herself). **342 clypping,** hugging. **344 sterte,** skip. **351 wonte . . . yonghede,** formerly, youth. **352 Unneth,** barely. **357 qualm,** evil (plague). **359 unwelde,** weak. **360 dwyned,** dwindled. **361 forwelked,** much wrinkled.

As from her heed they wolde fall.
Hir face frounced and forpyned, 365
And bothe hir hondes lorne, fordwyned.
So old she was that she ne wente
A foote, but it were by potente.
 The Tyme, that passeth nyght and day, TIME
And restelees travayleth ay, 370
And steleth from us so prively,
That to us seemeth sykerly
That it in one point dwelleth ever,
And certes, it ne resteth never,
But goth so faste, and passeth ay, 375
That ther nys man that thynke may
What tyme that now present is—
Asketh at these clerkes this;
For er men thynke it redily,
Thre tymes ben ypassed by. 380
The Tyme, that may not sojourne,
But goth and may never retourne,
As water that downe renneth ay,
But never droppe retourne may.
Ther may nothyng as Tyme endure, 385
Metal nor erthely creature,
For al thing it fret and shal.
The Tyme, eke, that chaungeth al,
And al doth waxe and fostred be,
And al thyng distroyeth he. 390
The Tyme that eldeth our auncestours
And eldeth kynges and emperours,
And that us al shal overcomen
Er that Dethe us shal have nomen.
The Tyme that hath al in welde 395
To elden folk had maad hir elde
So inly that, to my wetyng,
She might helpe hirself nothyng,
But turned ayen unto childhede;
She had nothing hirself to lede, 400
Ne wyt ne pyth in hir holde
More than a chyld of two yere olde.
But nathelesse, I trowe that she

Was fayr sumtyme, and fressh to se,
Whan she was in hir rightful age. 405
But she was past al that passage
And was a doted thyng becomen.
A furred cope on had she nomen;
Wel had she clad hirself and warme,
For colde might els done hir harme. 410
These olde folke have alway colde,
Hir kynde is suche, whan they ben olde.
 Another thyng was don ther writ
That semede lyk an ipocryt, POPE-HOLY
And it was cleped Pope-Holy. 415
That ilke is she that prively
Ne spareth never a wicked dede,
Whan men of hir taken non hede;
And maketh hir outward precious,
With pale vysage and pytous, 420
And semeth a symple creature;
But ther nys no misaventure
That she ne thynketh in hir corage.
Ful lyk to hir was thilke ymage
That maked was lyk hir semblaunce. 425
She was ful symple of countenaunce,
And she was clothed and eke shod
As she were, for the love of God,
Yolden to relygion—
Suche semed hir devocion. 430
A psauter held she faste in honde,
And besyly she gan to fonde
To make many a feynt prayere
To God and to his sayntes dere.
Ne she was gaye, fresshe, ne jolyf, 435
But semed to be ful ententyf
To good werkes and to fayre,
And therto she had on an hayre.
Ne certes, she was fatte nothyng,
But semed wery for fastyng; 440
Of colour pale and dede was she.
From hir the gates aye werned be
Of paradyse, that blysful place.

---

365 frounced . . . forpyned, pleated, much pained. **366 lorne . . . fordwyned,** lost, shrunken. **368 potente,** crutch. **379** GT *er* om.; Fr. *carançois.* **387 fret,** devours (cf. Ger. *fressen*). **389 doth waxe and fostred be,** makes to grow and be nourished. **391 eldeth,** ages (vb.). **394 nomen,** taken. **395 welde,** power (cf. wield). **396 hir,** i.e., Old Age. **397 inly . . . wetyng,** essentially, knowledge. **400 had nothing,** i.e., had no ability. **401 holde,** possession. **403 trowe,** believe. **408** *cope:* T *cappe.* **412 kynde,** nature. **413 don ther writ,** caused to be written (painted). **416 prively,** secretly. **421** *symple:* G *semely.* **423 corage,** spirit. **429 Yolden,** given (i.e., dressed like a nun). **432 fonde,** begin. **438 hayre,** hair shirt. **439 fatte nothyng,** not at all fat. **442 werned,** refused.

For suche folk maken leane her face,
As Christ sayth in his Evangyle, 445
To gette hem prise in town a whyle,
And for a lytel glory veine
They lesen God and eke his reigne.
 And alderlast of everychone POVERTY
Was paynted Povert al alone, 450
That not a peny had in holde
Although she hir clothes solde,
And though she shulde anhonged be;
For naked as a worm was she.
And if the wether stormy were, 455
For colde she shulde have dyed there.
She nadde on but a strayt olde sacke,
And many a cloute on it ther stacke—
This was hir cote and hir mantel.
No more was there never a del 460
To clothe hir with, I undertake.
Great leyser had she to quake.
And she was put, that I of talke,
Ferre fro these other, up in an halke.
Ther lurked and ther coured she, 465
For poore thyng, wherso it be,
Is shamfaste and dispysed ay.
Acursed may wel be that day
That poore man conceyved is,
For God wot, al to selde, iwys, 470
Is any poore man wel yfedde,
Or wel arayed, or wel ycledde,
Or wel beloved, in suche wyse
In honour that he may aryse.
 Al these thinges, wel avysed, 475
As I have you er this devysed,
With golde and asure over all
Depaynted were upon the wall.
Squar was the wall and hygh somdel;
Enclosed and ybarred wel 480
In stede of hegge was that gardyn;
Com never shepherde therin.
Into that gardyn, wel ywrought,

Whoso that me coude have brought,
By laddre or elles by degre, 485
It wolde wel have lyked me.
For suche solace, suche joy and pley,
I trowe that never man ne sey
As was in that place delycious.
The gardyn was not daungerous 490
To herberowe byrddes many one;
So ryche a yerd was never none
Of byrdes songe and braunches grene.
Therin were byrdes mo, I wene,
Than ben in al the realme of Fraunce. 495
Ful blysful was the accordaunce
Of swete and pytous songe they mad,
For al this worlde it ought glad.
And I myselfe so mery ferde,
Whan I her blysful songes herde, 500
That for an hundred pound nolde I—
If that the passage openly
Had be unto me fre—
That I nolde entren for to se
Th'assemblee—God kepe it fro care— 505
Of byrdes whiche therein ware,
That songen through her mery throtes
Daunces of love and mery notes.
 Whan I thus herde foules synge,
I fel faste in a waymentynge 510
By whiche art or by what engyn
I might come into that gardyn.
But way I couthe fynde none
Into that gardyn for to gone,
Ne nought wyst I if that ther were 515
Eyther hole or place owhere
By whiche I might have entre.
Ne ther was none to teche me,
For I was al alone, iwys,
Ful wo and anguissous of this. 520
Til atte laste bethoughte I me
That by no way ne might it be
That ther nas ladder or way to pace,

---

444 *face:* GT *grace;* Fr. *vis.* **446 prise,** praise (price, prize). G *hem* om. **448 lesen,** lose. G *eke* om. **449 alderlast,** last of all. **451** *holde :* G *wolde* (possession). **457 strayt,** i.e., shapeless. T *ne hadde.* **458 cloute . . . stacke,** patch, stuck. **464 halke,** corner. **465 coured,** cowered. **471** G *fedde.* **472 wel ycledde:** GT *wel* om.; Fr. *bien chauciez.* G *cled.* **476 devysed,** described. **483** GT *wrought.* **485 degre,** steps. **490 daungerous,** reluctant (aloof). **496 accordaunce,** harmony. **505–06** *care/ware.* Skeat pointed out that this is not a Chaucerian rhyme and proposed *God it kepe and were* (protect, Fr. *Dex guerisse*) / *were.* The identical rhyme is familiar in Chaucer. **510 waymentynge,** lamenting. **511 engyn,** ingenuity. **516** GT *where.* **520** *Ful:* GT *For;* Fr. *mout engoiseus.* **521** T *at.* **523 pace,** pass.

Or hole, into so fayre a place.
Tho gan I go a ful great paas   525
Envyroning even in compas
The closyng of the square wall,
Tyl that I fonde a wyket small
So shette that I ne mighte in gone,
And other entre was ther none.   530

  Upon this dore I gan to smyte,   THE GATE
That was fetys and so lyte,
For other way coude I not seke.
Ful longe I shof, and knocked eke,
And stode ful longe and oft herkenyng   535
If that I herde a wight comyng,
Tyl that the dore of thylke entre
A mayden curteys opened me.   IDLENESS
Hir heer was as yelowe of hewe
As any basen scoured newe.   540
Hir flesh tender as is a chyke,
With bent browes, smothe and slyke;
And by mesure large were
The openyng of hir eyen clere.
Hir nose of good proporcion;   545
Hir eyen gray as is a faucon;
With swete brethe and wel savoured.
Hir face whyt and wel coloured,
With lytel mouth, and round to se;
A clove chynne eke hadde she.   550
Hir necke was of good fassyon
In length and gretnesse, by reson,
Without bleyne, scabbe, or royne.
Fro Hierusalem unto Burgoyne
Ther nys a fayrer necke, iwys,   555
To fele how smothe and softe it is.
Hir throte also whyte of hewe
As snowe on braunche snowed newe.
Of body ful wel wrought was she;
Men neden not in no cuntre   560
A fayrer body for to seke.
And of fyne orfrays had she eke
A chapelet; so semly oon

Ne wered never mayde upon.
And fayre above that chapelet   565
A rose gerlande had she set.
She had in honde a gay mirrour,
And with a ryche gold tressour
Hir heed was tressed queyntely;
Hir sleves sewed fetisly.   570
And for to kepe hir hondes fayre,
Of gloves whyte she had a payre.
And she had on a cote of grene
Of cloth of Gaunt; withouten wene,
Wel semed by hir apparayle   575
She was not wont to great travayle.
For whan she kempt was fetisly,
And wel arayed and richely,
Than had she done al hir journee,
For mery and wel bigon was she.   580
She ladde a lusty lyf in May;
She had no thought, by night ne day,
Of nothing but it were onely
To grayth hir wel and uncouthly.

  Whan that this dore had opened me   585
This mayden semely for to se,
I thonked hir as I best myght,
And asked hir how that she hyght,
And what she was I asked eke.
And she to me was nought unmeke,   590
Ne of hir answer daungerous,
But fayre answerde, and sayde thus:
"Lo, sir, my name is Idelnesse;
So clepe men me, more and lesse.
Ful mighty and ful ryche am I,   595
And that of one thyng, namely,
For I entende to nothing
But to my joye and my playing,
And for to kembe and tresse me.
Acquaynted am I, and prive,   600
With Myrthe, lorde of this gardyn,
That fro the lande of Alexandryn
Made the trees hyther be fette

---

525 **paas,** distance (pace). 528 **wyket,** small gate for foot passage. 532 **fetys . . . lyte,** well made, little. 535 **oft:** G *of;* T *al;* F *maintes foiz.* 551 **fassyon,** formation. 552 **gretnesse,** size (thickness). 553 **bleyne . . . royne,** blemish, roughness. 560 G *neded.* 562 **orfrays,** embroidered cloth of gold. 567 GT *in honde* om.; Fr. *En sa main.* 568 **tressour,** ribbons or threads of gold to be plaited with the hair. 570 **sewed fetisly,** laced neatly, cf. l. 98n. T *fetously.* 574 **Gaunt,** Ghent (in modern Belgium), celebrated for its fine weaving. **wene,** doubt. 576 **wont . . . travayle,** used, work. 577 **kempt,** groomed. 579 **journee,** day's work. 580 **wel bigon,** carefree. 584 **grayth . . . uncouthly,** adorn, strikingly. 588 **hyght,** was called. 591 **daungerous,** disdainful. 597 **entende,** attend (care for). 602 **Alexandryn,** Alexandria (Egypt), i.e., the East, the original home of most fruit trees, and also, traditionally, of the sybaritic life.

That in this garden ben ysette.
And whan the trees were woxen on hyght,   605
This wal that stant here in thy syght
Dyde Myrthe enclosen al aboute.
And these ymages al without,
He dyd hem bothe entayle and peynte
That neyther ben jolyf ne queynte;   610
But they ben ful of sorowe and wo,
As thou hast sene a whyle ago.
   "And ofte tyme, him to solace,
Sir Myrthe cometh into this place,
And eke with him cometh his meyne,   615
That lyven in luste and jolyte.
And now is Myrthe therin, to here
The byrdes how they syngen clere,
The mavys and the nyghtyngale,
And other joly byrdes smale.   620
And thus he walketh to solace
Hym and his folk, for swetter place
To playen in he may not fynde
Although he sought one intyl Inde.
The alther-fayrest folk to se   625
That in this world may founde be
Hath Myrthe with him in his route,
That folowen him always aboute."
   Whan Idelnesse had told al this,
And I had herkned wel, iwys,   630
Than sayde I to Dame Idelnesse,
"Now also wisly God me blesse,
Syth Myrthe that is so fayre and fre
Is in this yerde with his meyne,
Fro thylke assemble if I may   635
Shal no man werne me today,
That I this nyght ne mote it se.
For wel wene I, ther with him be
A fayre and joly companye
Fulfylled of al curtesye."   640
   And forth without wordes mo
In at the wiket went I tho,
That Idelnesse had opened me,
Into that garden fayr to se.

And whan I was therin, iwys,   645
Myn herte was ful glad of this.   THE GARDEN
For wel wende I ful sykerly
Have been in paradys erthly.
So fayre it was that, trusteth well,
It semed a place espyrituell.   650
For certes, as at my devyse,
Ther is no place in paradyse
So good in for to dwell or be
As in that garden, thoughte me.
For ther was many a byrd singyng   655
Throughout the yerde al thringing.
In many places were nightyngales,
Alpes, fynches, and wodewales,
That in her swete song delyten
In thilke places as they habyten.   660
Ther might men se many flockes
Of turtles and laverokkes.
Chalaundres fele sawe I there,
That wery nigh forsongen were.
And thrustels, teryns, and mavise,   665
That songen for to wynne hem prise,
And eke to surmounte in her songe
That other byrdes hem amonge.
By note made fayr servyse
These byrdes that I you devyse;   670
They songe her songe as fayre and well
As angels doon espirituell.
And trusteth wel, whan I hem herde,
Full lustily and wel I ferde,
For never yet suche melodye   675
Was herd of man that mighte dye.
Suche swete song was hem amonge
That me thought it no byrdes songe,
But it was wonder lyk to be
Song of meermaydens of the see,   680
That for her synging is so clere,
Though we meermaydens clepe hem here
In Englisshe, as in our usaunce,
Men clepe hem sereyns in Fraunce.
   Ententyf weren for to syng   685

---

609 entayle, carve. **615 meyne**, retinue. **616 luste**, pleasure. **619 mavys**, song thrush. **625 alther**, archaic gen. pl. "of all." **636 werne**, restrict (debar). **638 wene**, know. **645** *therin*: GT *in*. **647 wende . . . sykerly**, believed, surely. **651 devyse**, supposition. **656 thringing**, thronging. **658 Alpes . . . wodewales**, bullfinches (awps), witwall (green woodpecker). **662 turtles . . . laverokkes**, turtle doves, larks. **663 Chalaundres**, variety of lark. **664 forsongen**, "sung out." **665 thrustels, teryns**, thrushes, siskin (Skeat). **673 wel**: T *me*; Fr. *bien sachiez*. **674** T *lusty*. **676 mighte dye**, i.e., mortal man.

These byrdes that not unkonnyng
Were of her craft, and aprentys,
But of her song subtyl and wys.
And certes, whan I herde her songe,
And saw the grene place amonge,   690
In herte I wext so wonder gay
That I was never erst, er that day,
So jolyf nor so wel bygo,
Ne mery in herte, as I was tho.
And than wyste I, and saw ful wel,   695
That Ydelnesse me served wel,
That me putte in suche jolyte.
Hir frend wel oughte I for to be
Syth she the dore of that gardyn
Had opened and me lette in.   700
    From henceforth how that I wrought,
I shall you tellen, as me thought.
First, whereof Myrthe served there,
And eke what folk ther with him were,
Without fable I wol discryve.   705
And of that garden eke as blyve
I wol you tellen after this.
The fayre fassyon al, iwys,
That wel ywrought was for the nones,
I may not tel you al at ones,   710
But as I may and can, I shal
By ordre tellen you it al.
    Ful fayre servyce and eke ful swete
These byrdes maden as they sete.
Layes of love ful wel sowning   715
They songen in her jargoning.
Some hye and some eke lowe songe
Upon the braunches grene ispronge.
The swetnesse of her melodye
Made al myn herte in revelrye.   720
And whan that I had herd, I trowe,
These byrdes synging on a rowe,
Than might I not withholde me
That I ne went in for to se

Sir Myrthe; for my desyring   725
Was him to sene, over al thing—
His countenaunce and his manere.
That syghte was to me ful dere.
    Tho went I forthe on my right honde,
Down by a lytel path I fonde,   730
Of myntes ful and fenell grene,
And faste by, withoute wene,
Syr Myrthe I founde; and right anon
Unto Sir Myrthe gan I gon,   SIR MIRTH
Ther as he was, him to solace.   735
And with him, in that lusty place,
So fayre folk and so fresshe had he
That whan I sawe I wondred me
Fro whence suche folk might come,
So fayre they weren, al and some.   740
For they were lyk, as to my syght,
To angels that been fethered bright.
    These folke, of whiche I tel you so,
Upon a karole wenten tho.
A lady karoled hem that hyght   745
Gladnes, the blysful and the lyght.   GLADNESS
Wel coude she synge and lustely,
Non half so wel and semely,
And make in song suche refraynynge,
It sat hir wonder wel to synge.   750
Hir voyce ful clere was and ful swete.
She was not rude ne unmete,
But couthe ynough of suche doyng
As longeth unto karolyng,
For she was wont in every place   755
To syngen fyrst folk to solace,
For synging moste she gave hir to;
No crafte had she so lefe to do.
    Tho mightest thou karolles sene,
And folke daunce and mery bene,   760
And make many a fayr tourning
Upon the grene gras springing.
Ther mightest thou se these flutours,

---

687 aprentys, novices (beginners). **688** *But:* G *For.* GT *her* om. **690 amonge**, as well. **693 bygo**, contented (begone). **703 whereof**, how. **706 as blyve**, very promptly. **708 fassyon**, appearance. **716 jargoning**, chattering (jargon). G *yarkonyng.* **720** *revelrye:* G *reverye;* Fr. *reverdie* (joy in the return of spring). **723 withholde me**, restrain myself. **731 fenell**, fennel, an herb with aromatic seeds. **732 wene**, doubt. **735 him to solace**, to please himself. **744 karole**, ring dance. **745 karoled...hyght**, sang a song to accompany the dance, was called. **746** *the blysful:* GT *the* om. *the lyght:* T *the* om. **749 refraynynge**, add refrains to her song. GT *couthe make.* **752 unmete**, discordant. **753 couthe**, knew. **754 longeth unto**, i.e., goes with. **755 wont**, accustomed. **756 solace**, please. **758 so lefe**, such pleasure. **759 Tho**, then. **763 flutours**, flute players.

Mynstrales, and eke joglours,
That wel to synge dyd her payne. 765
Som songe songes of Lorayne,
For in Lorayne her notes be
Ful swetter than in this countre.
Ther was many a tymbestere,
And saylours that I dar wel swere 770
Couthe her craft ful parfetly.
The tymbres up ful subtelly
They caste, and hente ful ofte
Upon a fynger fayre and softe,
That they ne fayled nevermo. 775
Ful fetys damosels two,
Right yonge and ful of semelyhede,
In kyrtles and none other wede,
And fayre tressed every tresse,
Had Myrthe done for his noblesse 780
Amydde the carole for to daunce.
But herof lyeth no remembraunce,
How that they daunsed queyntely.
That one wolde come al prively
Agayn that other, and whan they were 785
Togythre almost, they threwe yfere
Her mouthes so that through her play
It semed as they kyste alway.
To dauncen wel couthe they the gyse;
What shulde I more to you devyse? 790
Ne bede I never thence go,
Whyles that I saw hem daunce so.
  Upon the karol wonder faste
I gan beholde, tyl atte laste
A lady gan me for to espye, 795
And she was cleped Curtesye,   COURTESY
The worshypful, the debonayre—
I pray to God ever fall hir fayre!
Ful curteysly she called me,
"What do ye there, beau sire?" quod she, 800
"Come, and if it lyke you

To daunsen, daunseth with us now."
And I, without tarying,
Went into the karolling.
I was abasshed never a del, 805
But it me lykede right wel
That Curtesye me cleped so,
And bade me on the daunce go.
For if I had durst, certayne
I wolde have karoled right fayne, 810
As man that was to daunce right blythe.
Than gan I loken ofte sythe
The shap, the bodyes, and the cheres,
The countenaunce, and the maneres
Of al the folk that daunsed there, 815
And I shal telle what they were.
  Ful fayr was Myrthe, ful longe and hygh;
A fayrer man I never sygh.   MIRTH
As rounde as appel was his face,
Ful roddy and whyte in every place. 820
Fetys he was and wel besey,
With metely mouth and eyen grey;
His nose by mesure wrought ful right;
Crysp was his heer, and eke ful bright.
His shuldres of a large brede, 825
And smallysshe in the gyrdelstede.
He semed lyke a purtreyture,
So noble he was of his stature,
So fayr, so joly, and so fetyse,
With lymmes wrought at poynt devyse, 830
Delyver, smerte, and of great myght;
Ne sawe thou never man so lyght.
Of berde unnethe had he nothyng,
For it was in the firste spring;
Ful yong he was, and mery of
  thought. 835
And in samyt, with byrdes wrought,
And with gold beten ful fetysly,
His body was clad ful richely.

---

766 **Lorayne,** Lorraine, in eastern France (Alsace-Lorraine). 768 **this countre,** Fr. *nul aigne* (any country). 769 **tymbestere,** female player of the timbrel (tambourine). 770 **saylours,** dancers. 775 **ne fayled,** didn't miss. T *ne* om. 776 **fetys,** pretty. 778 **kyrtles,** short one-piece dresses. 779 **tressed,** with hair dressed. 780 **Had,** caused. 784 **prively,** stealthily. 785 **Agayn,** toward. 786 **yfere,** together. 789 **gyse,** manner. 791 **bede,** desired (prayed). GT *bode.* 798 **fall hir fayre,** fair fall to her. 801 **lyke you,** please you. 810 **fayne,** happily. 812 **sythe,** times. 813 **cheres,** expressions. 817 *longe and hygh:* Fr. *lonc et droiz* (tall and straight). 821 **Fetys . . . wel besey,** well-formed, good-looking. 822 **metely,** well-proportioned. 823 **by mesure,** by proportion. 826 **gyrdelstede,** waist. 830 **poynt devyse,** perfection. 831 **Delyver, smerte,** agile, quick. 833 **unnethe,** scarcely. 836 **samyt . . . wrought,** rich silk, embroidered. T *samette.* 837 **beten,** shaped.

Wrought was his robe in straunge gyse,
And al to-slyttered for queyntyse   840
In many a place, lowe and hye.
And shod he was with great maystrye,
With shoon decoped, and with lace.
By drucrye and by solace
His leefe a rosen chapelet   845
Had maad and on his heed it set.
    And wete ye who was his leefe?
Dame Gladnes ther was him so lefe,   GLADNESS
That syngeth so wel with glad corage
That from she was twelve yere of age   850
She of hir love graunt him made.
Sir Myrthe hir by the fynger hadde
In daunsyng, and she him also;
Great love was atwyxt hem two.
Bothe were they fayre and brighte of hewe.   855
She semed lyke a rose newe
Of colours, and hir flesshe so tendre
That with a brere smale and slendre
Mon mighte it cleve, I dar wel seyn.
Hir forheed, frounceles al pleyn;   860
Bent were hir browes two;
Hir eyen gray, and glad also,
That laugheden aye in hir semblaunt,
First or the mouth, by covenaunt.
I not what of hir nose descryve;   865
So fayre hath no woman alyve.
Hir heer was yelowe and clere shyning;
I wot no lady so lyking.
Of orfrayes fresshe was hir garlande;
I, whiche sene have a thousande,   870
Sawe never, iwys, no garland yet
So wel ywrought of sylke as it.
And in an overgylt samyte
Cladde she was by great delyte—
Of whiche hir leefe a robe werde,   875

The meryer she in hir herte ferde.
    And next hir wente, on hir other syde,
The God of Love, that can devyde   CUPID
Love, and as him lyketh it be.
But he can cherles daunten, he,   880
And maken folkes pride fallen.
And he can wel these lordes thrallen,
And ladyes put at lowe degre,
Whan he may hem to proude se.
    This God of Love of his fascioun   885
Was lyk no knave ne quystroun.
His beutie greatly was to prise.
But of his robe to devyse
I drede encombred for to be.
For not yclad in sylk was he,   890
But al in floures and flourettes,
Ypaynted al with amorettes,
And with losenges and scochons,
With byrddes, lyberdes, and lyons,
And other beestes wrought ful wel.   895
His garnement was everydel
Ypurtrayed and ywrought with flours,
By dyvers medeling of colours.
Floures ther were of many gyse
Yset by compas in assyse.   900
Ther lacked no floure, to my dome,
Ne not so moche as floure of brome,
Ne vyolet, ne eke pervynke,
Ne floure non that man can on thynke.
And many a rose-lefe ful longe   905
Was entermedled ther amonge,
And also on his heed was set
Of roses reed a chapelet.
But nightyngales, a ful great route,
That flyen over his heed aboute,   910
The leves felden as they flyen.
And he was al with byrdes wryen,

---

840 to-slyttered, slashed (with a different colored lining showing underneath). **842 maystrye,** elegance. **843 decoped,** slashed. **844 By druerye . . . by solace,** in love service, to please (comfort). **845 leefe,** love. **849 corage,** spirit. **853 GT** *In* om.; Fr. *A la querole.* **858** *slendre:* T *tendre* (repeated). **859 cleve,** cut. **859–60** T *sey|pley.* **860 frounceles,** without wrinkles. **863 semblaunt,** appearance. **864 or . . . covenaunt,** ere (before), previous agreement. **865 GT** *I wot not of.* T *nose I shal discryve.* **868 lyking,** pleasing. **869 orfrayes,** gold embroidery. **873 overgylt,** worked over in gold. **878 devyde,** dispense. **880 daunten,** subdue. **882 thrallen,** enslave. **886 knave . . . quystroun,** serving-boy, kitchen-boy. **889 encombred,** embarrassed. **891 G** *and in.* **892 amorettes,** love knots. Line omitted in G. **893 losenges . . . scochons,** lozenges (diamond shapes), escutcheons—heraldic figures. **894 lyberdes,** leopards. **897 Ypurtrayed and ywrought,** i.e., Cupid's garment itself and the decorations on it were wrought of varicolored flowers. **900 by compas in assyse,** by plan in position. **901 dome,** judgment. **903 pervynke,** periwinkle. **905 rose-lefe,** rose petal. **906 entermedled,** intermingled. **911 felden,** caused to fall (felled). **912 wryen,** hidden.

With popingay, with nightyngale,
With chalaundre, and with wodewale,
With fynch, with lark, and with archangell. 915
He semed as he were an angell
That down were comen fro heven clere.
    Love had with him a bachelere,
That he made alwayes with him be;
Swete-Loking cleped was he. 920
This bachelere stod beholding   SWEET-LOOKING
The daunce; and in his honde holding
Turke bowes two had he.
That one of hem was of a tree
That bereth a fruit of savour wicke. 925
Ful croked was that foule stycke,
And knotty here and there also,
And blacke as bery or any slo.
That other bowe was of a plante
Withoute wemme, I dar warante, 930
Ful even, and by proporcioun
Treitys and longe, of good facyoun.
And it was paynted wel and twhitten,
And over-al diapred and written
With ladyes and with bacheleres 935
Ful lyghtsom and glad of cheres.
These bowes two held Swete-Loking,
That semed lyk no gadeling.
And ten brode arowes held he there,
Of whiche fyve in his right hond were. 940
But they were shaven wel and dyght,
Nocked and fethered aryght,
And al they were with gold begon,
And stronge poynted everychon,
And sharpe for to kerven wel. 945
But yron was ther noon, ne steel,
For al was gold, men mighte it se,
Outtake the fethers and the tree.
    The swyftest of these arowes fyve
Out of a bowe for to dryve, 950

And best yfethered for to flye,
And fayrest eke, was cleped Beautie.   BEAUTY
That other arowe, that hurteth lesse,
Was cleped, as I trowe,
    Symplesse.   SIMPLICITY
The thyrde cleped was Fraunchyse 955
That fethered was in noble wyse   CANDOR
With valour and with curtesye.
The fourthe was cleped Companye   COMPANY
That hevy for to shoten is;
But whoso shoteth right, iwys, 960
May therwith don great harme and wo.
The fyfte of these and laste also
Fayr-Semblaunt men that arowe call,   FAIR-
The leest grevous of hem all;   APPEARANCE
Yet can it make a full great wounde. 965
But he may hope his sores sounde
That hurt is with that arowe, iwys.
His wo the bette bestowed is;
For he may soner have gladnesse,
His langour ought be the lesse. 970
    Five arowes were of other gyse,
That been ful foule to devyse,
For shafte and ende, soth for to tell,
Were also blacke as fende in hell. 974
    The first of hem is called Pride.   PRIDE
That other arowe next hym besyde,
It was cleped Vylanye.   VILLAINY
That arowe was al with felonye
Envenymed, and with spytous blame. 979
The thyrde of hem was cleped
    Shame.   SHAME
The fourthe, Wanhope cleped is;   DESPAIR
The fyfte, the Newe-Thought, iwys.   FICKLENESS
    These arowes that I speke of here
Were al fyve on one manere,
And al were they resemblable. 985
To hem was wel sytting and able

---

913 **popingay,** parrot. 914 **chalaundre ... wodewale,** lark, witwall (green woodpecker). 915 **archangell,** evidently titmouse, Fr. *mesanges.* 918 **bachelere,** young man. 920 **Swete-Loking,** alluring glances; Fr. *Douz Regart.* 923 **Turke,** Turkish. GT *Turke bowes two ful wel devysed had he.* The motif of the two aspects of love, agony and ecstasy, is a commonplace, cf. *PF,* l. 128. 925 **savour wicke,** evil taste. 928 **slo,** sloe berry. 930 **wemme,** blemish. 932 **Treitys,** graceful. 933 **twhitten,** shaped (cf. whittle). G *twythen.* 934 **diapred ... written,** decorated, inscribed (with figures of men and women). 936 **lightsom ... cheres,** gay, expressions. 938 **gadeling,** vagabond. 941 **shaven ... dyght,** planed smooth, decorated. 942 **Nocked,** notched. 943 **begon,** ornamented. 944 **stronge,** strongly. *poynted:* G *peynted.* 947 T *it* om. 948 **Outtake,** except. 957 **valour,** value. 966 **sounde,** heal. 970 *His:* G *Hir.* 978 *al:* GT *as.* 979 **spytous,** malicious. 984 **on one,** of one. 986 **wel sytting,** well-fitting.

The foule croked bowe hydous,
That knotty was and al roynous.
That bowe semed wel to shete
These arowes fyve that ben unmete,   990
And contrarye to that other fyve.
But though I telle not as blyve
Of her power, ne of her myght,
Herafter shal I tellen right
The sothe and eke signyfyaunce   995
As ferre as I have remembraunce.
Al shal be sayd, I undertake,
Er of this booke an ende I make.
    Now come I to my tale agayne.
But alderfirst I wol you sayne   1000
The fassyoun and the countenaunces
Of al the folk that on the daunce is.
The God of Love, jolyf and lyght,
Ladde on his honde a lady bright,
Of hygh prise and of great degre.   1005
This lady called was Beaute—   BEAUTY
As an arowe, of which I tolde.
Ful wel thewed was she holde.
Ne she was derk ne brown but bright
And clere as is the moonelyght,   1010
Agayn whom al the sterres semen
But smale candels, as we demen.
Hir flesshe was tendre as dewe of flour,
Hir chere was symple as byrde in bour,
As whyte as lylye or rose in ryse,   1015
Hir face, gentyl and tretyse.
Fetys she was and smal to see;
No wyndred browes hadde she,
Ne popped hir, for it neded nought
To wyndre hir or to paynte hir ought.   1020
Hir tresses yelowe and longe straughten,
Unto hir heles down they raughten.
Hir nose, hir mouthe, and eye, and cheke
Wel wrought, and al the remenaunt eke.

A ful gret savour and a swote   1025
Me toucheth in myn herte rote,
As helpe me God, whan I remembre
Of the fassyoun of every membre!
In worlde is none so fayre a wight,
For yonge she was and hewed bright,   1030
Sote, plesaunt, and fetys withall,
Gent, and in hir myddell small.
    Bisyde Beaute yede Rychesse,   RICHES
An hygh lady of great noblesse,
And great of prys in every place.   1035
But whoso durste to hir trespace,
Or tyl hir folke, in word or dede,
He were ful hardy, out of drede,
For bothe she helpe and hyndre may;
And that is not of yesterday   1040
That ryche folke have ful great myght
To helpe and eke to greve a wight.
The best and greattest of valour
Dydden Richesse ful great honour,
And besy weren hir to serve.   1045
For that they wolde hir love deserve,
They cleped hir "Lady," greate and smal.
This wyde worlde hir dredeth al;
This worlde is al in hir daungere.
Hir courte hath many a losengere,   1050
And many a traytour envyous,
That ben ful besy and curious
For to dispreysen and to blame
That best deserven love and name.
Toforne the folk, hem to begylen,   1055
These losyngeours hem preyse and smylen,
And thus the world with worde anoynten.
But afterwarde they pricke and poynten
The folk right to the bare bone,
Behynde her back whan they ben gone,   1060
And foule abaten the folkes pris.
Ful many a worthy man and wys

Han hyndred and ydon to dye
These losyngeours with her flaterye,
And maketh folk ful straunge be   1065
Ther as hem ought ben pryve.
Wel yvel mote they thryve and thee,
And yvel aryved mote they be,
These losyngeours, ful of envy!
No good man loveth her company.   1070

    Rychesse a robe of purple on hadde—
Ne trowe nat that I lye or madde,
For in this worlde is none it lyche,
Ne by a thousand dele so riche,
Ne non so fayr. For it ful wel   1075
With orfreys leyd was everydel,
And purtrayed in the rybanynges
Of dukes stories and of kynges,
And with a bend of gold tassyled,
And knoppes fyne of gold amyled.   1080
About hir necke of gentyl entayle
Was shette the riche chevesayle,
In whiche ther was ful great plente
Of stones clere and fayr to se.

    Richesse a gyrdel had upon,   1085
The bokell of it was of a ston
Of vertue great, and mokel of myght.
For whoso bar the ston so bright,
Of venym durst him nothyng dout
While he the ston had him about   1090
That ston was greatly for to love,
And tyl a riche mannes behove
Worthe al the golde in Rome and Fryse.
The mourdant, wrought in noble gyse,
Was of a ston ful precious,   1095
That was so fyne and vertuous
That whole a man it couthe make
Of palsye and of tothe-ake.

And yet the ston had suche a grace
That he was seker in every place   1100
Al thylke day not blynde to bene
That fastyng might that ston sene.
The barres were of gold ful fyne
Upon a tyssu of satyne,
Ful hevy, great, and nothyng lyght;   1105
In everych was a besaunt-wyght.

    Upon the tresses of Rychesse
Was set a cercle, for noblesse,
Of brende gold that ful lyght shone;
So fayr, trowe I, was never none.   1110
But he were konnyng, for the nones,
That coude devysen al the stones
That in that cercle shewen clere;
It is a wonder thyng to here.
For no man coude preyse or gesse   1115
Of hem the value or richesse.
Rubyes there were, saphirs, iagounces,
And emeraudes more than two ounces.
But al before, ful subtelly,
A fyn charboncle set sawe I.   1120
The stone so clere was and so bright
That also sone as it was nyght
Men myghte sene to go, for nede,
A myle or two in length and brede.
Suche lyght sprange out of the stone   1125
That Richesse wonder brighte shone,
Bothe hir heed and al hir face,
And eke aboute hir al the place.

    Dame Richesse on hir hond gan lede
A yonge man ful of semelyhede,   1130
That she best loved of any thyng.
His lust was moche in housholdyng;
In clothing was he ful fetys,
And lovede wel have hors of prys.

1063 G *An hundrid have to do.* 1065 **straunge,** i.e., hostile to each other. G *Have maad.* 1066 **pryve,** intimate. 1067 **mote . . . thee,** may, prosper. 1072 **madde,** rave. 1073 *it:* G *hir.* 1074 **thousand dele,** thousandth part. 1076 **orfreys,** gold embroidery. 1077 **rybanynges,** borders. 1079 **bend,** band (heraldic term). 1080 **knoppes . . . amyled,** buds, enameled. G *enameled.* 1081 **entayle,** shape (i.e., her neck). 1082 **chevesayle,** collar. 1084 *fayr:* G *bright.* 1087 **mokel,** great (*muchel*). 1089 **dout,** fear. 1092 **behove,** profit. 1093 **Fryse,** Friesland. 1094 **mourdant,** metal trimming, finishing off the end of a belt, in this case set with a magic jewel. *gyse:* G *wyse.* 1100 **seker,** sure (secure). 1102 **sene,** look at. 1103 **barres,** decorative—if the belt was satin, perhaps practical—metal strips fixed across the belt. The tongue of the buckle might have pressed against these to avoid tearing the cloth. 1105 **great,** large. 1106 **besaunt,** gold coin originally struck in Byzantium. 1109 **brende,** burnished. 1111 *he:* G *she.* 1112 **devysen,** describe. 1113 **that cercle,** i.e., the headband. 1117 **iagounces,** jaccinths (reddish brown zircons). GT *ragounces;* Fr. *iagonces.* 1119 **before,** in front. 1120 **charboncle,** carbuncle (ruby, garnet, or almandine). 1130 **semelyhede,** attractiveness. 1132 **lust . . . housholdyng,** pleasure, domestic occupation. 1133 **fetys,** handsome. 1134 **of prys,** valuable.

He wende to have reproved be 1135
Of thefte or murdre if that he
Had in his stable an hakeney.
And therfore he desyred ay
To ben aqueynted with Richesse.
For al his purpos, as I gesse, 1140
Was for to make great dispence
Withouten warning or defence.
And Richesse myghte it wel sustene,
And hir dispences wel mayntene,
And hym alway suche plentie sende 1145
Of golde and sylver for to spende
Without lacking or daungere,
As it were pourde in a garnere.
    And after on the daunce went   LARGESS
Largesse, that sette al hir entent 1150
For to be honorable and free.
Of Alexanders kynne was she.
Hir moste joye was, iwys,
Whan that she yaf, and seide, "Have this."
Nat Avarice, the foule caytif, 1155
Was half to grype so ententyf
As Largesse is to yeve and spende.
And God alway ynowe hire sende
So that the more she yave away,
The more, ywis, she had alwey. 1160
Gret loos hath Largesse, and gret prys,
For bothe wys folk and unwys
Were wholy to hir bandon brought,
So wel with yeftes hath she wrought.
And if she hadde an enemy, 1165
I trowe that she couth craftely
Make hym ful sone hir freend to be,
So large of yeftes and free was she.
Therfore she stode in love and grace
Of riche and poore in every place. 1170
A ful gret foole is he, ywis,
That bothe riche and nygarde is.
A lord may have no maner vyce

That greveth more than avarice.
For nygard never with strength of hande 1175
May wynne hym great lordship or lande,
For frendes al to fewe hath he
To done his wyl performed be.
And whoso wol have frendes here,
He maye nat holde his tresour dere. 1180
For by ensample tel I this:
Right as an adamant, ywis,
Can drawen to hym subtelly
The yron that is layd therby,
So draweth folkes hertes, ywis, 1185
Sylver and gold that yeven is.
    Largesse hadde on a robe fresshe
Of riche purpure Sarsynysshe.
Wel fourmed was hir face and clere,
And opened had she hir colere, 1190
For she right there had, in present,
Unto a lady mad present
Of a gold broche ful wel wrought.
And certes, it missat hir nought, 1194
For through hir smocke, wrought with sylke,
The flessh was sene as whyte as mylke.
Largesse, that worthy was and wys,
Held by the honde a knight of prys,
Was sybbe to Arthour of Breteigne.
And that was he that bar the enseigne 1200
Of worshyp, and the gounfanoun.
And yet he is of suche renoun
That men of hym say fayre thynges
Before barons, erles, and kynges.
This knyght was comen al newely 1205
Fro tourneyinge faste by.
There had he done great chyvalrye
Through his vertu and his maystrye,
And for the love of his lemman
He cast down many a doughty man. 1210
    And next hym daunced Dame Fraunchyse,
Arayed in ful noble gyse.   CANDOR

1135 **wende,** thought. 1137 **hakeney,** nag. 1140 *For:* G *And.* 1141 **dispence,** expenditure. 1142 **warning . . . defence,** heed, care. 1147 **daungere,** aloofness. 1148 **As it,** as if it. 1151 **free,** generous. 1152 **Alexanders,** Alexander was the medieval type for liberality. 1156 **grype,** grasp (hold on). 1161 **loos,** praise. 1162 G *wys* om. 1163 **bandon,** feudal service. 1166 *craftely:* G *tristely.* 1168 *free:* T *wyse.* 1172 T *riche and poore and nygarde.* 1182 **adamant,** magnet. 1188 **Sarsynysshe,** Saracenish cloth (brightly dyed). GT *Sarlynysshe.* 1192 **mad present,** Largesse's collar was open because she had just then given away the brooch she used to fasten it. 1194 **missat,** ill-suited. 1199 **sybbe to Arthour,** kin to King Arthur. 1201 **gounfanoun,** war banner. GT *gousfaucon* (goshawk?); Fr. *gonfanon.* 1208 **vertu . . . maystrye,** power, skill.

She nas not browne ne dunne of hewe,
But white as snowe yfallen newe.
Hir nose was wrought at poynt devyse,   1215
For it was gentyl and tretyse,
With eyen glade and browes bente.
Hir heer doun to hir heles wente.
And she was symple as dowve on tree.
Ful debonayre of hert was she;   1220
She durste never saye ne do
But that thing that hyr longeth to.
And if a man were in distresse,
And for hir love in hevynesse,
Hir herte wolde have ful great pitee,   1225
She was so amiable and free.
For were a man for hir bistadde,
She wolde ben right sore adradde
That she dyd over great outrage
But she hym holpe his harm t'aswage;   1230
Hir thoughte it elles a vylanye.
And she hadde on a suckenye
That nat of hempen herdes was;
So fayr was none in al Arras.
Lorde, it was ryddeled fetysly!   1235
Ther nas nat a poynt, trewely,
That it nas in his right assyse.
Ful wel yclothed was Fraunchyse,
For ther nys no clothe sytteth bette
On damosel than doth rokette.   1240
A womman wel more fetys is
In rokette than in cote, ywis.
The white rokette, ryddeled fayre,
Betokeneth that ful debonayre
And swete was she that it bere.   1245
    By hir daunced a bachelere;
I can nat tellen you what he hyght,
But fayr he was and of good hyght,
Al had he ben—I say no more—

The lordes sone of Wyndesore.   1250
    And next that daunced Curtesye,   COURTESY
That preysed was of lowe and hye,
For neither proud ne fole was she.
She for to daunce called me—
I pray God gyve hir right good grace!—   1255
Whan I come first into the place.
She nas not nyce ne outrageous,
But wys and war and vertuous,
Of fayre speche and fayre answere;
Was never wight myssayd of here;   1260
She bar no rancour to no wight.
Clere brown she was, and therto bright
Of face; of body avenaunt.
I wot no lady so plesaunt.
She were worthy for to bene   1265
An emperesse or crowned quene.
    And by hir went a knyght dauncing
That worthy was and wel speking,
And ful wel coude he done honour.
The knyght was fayre and styf in stour,   1270
And in armure a semely man,
And wel beloved of his lemman.
    Fair Idelnesse than saugh I   IDLENESS
That alway was me faste by.
Of hir have I, withouten fayle,   1275
Told you the shappe and appareyle,
For, as I sayde, lo, that was she
That dyd to me so great bounte,
That she the gate of that gardyn
Undid and let me passen in.   1280
    And after daunced, as I gesse,   YOUTH
Youthe, fulfyld of lustynesse,
That has not yet twelve yere of age,
With herte wylde and thought volage.
Nyce she was, but she ne mente   1285
None harm ne sleight in hir entente,

1215 poynt devyse, excellently. **1216 gentyl ... tretyse,** aristocratic, well-formed. **1220 debonayre,** gracious. **1222 longeth to,** is suitable to. GT *thing* om. **1226 free,** generous. **1227 bistadde,** beset (attacked). **1228 adradde,** frightened. **1230 But,** unless. **1231** *elles:* G *ell;* T *al.* **1232 suckenye,** loose coverall, usually of canvas or coarse cotton. **1233 hempen herdes,** coarse hemp. **1234 Arras,** French city, famous for its fine cloth (whence "arras"). **1235 ryddeled,** pleated (OF *ridel,* curtain). **1237 assyse,** position. **1240 rokette,** loose frock (cf. **suckenye**), now applied to bishop's surplice. **1247 hyght,** was called. **1250 lordes sone of Wyndesore,** archaic gen., "lord of Windsor's son." When de Lorris wrote the line, this would have been Henry III and his son Edward, but in his ed. of the French, Langlois points out that in romances, Arthur was also lord of Windsor, so that the reference may have been traditional. **1255** T *right* om. **1256** T *For whan.* **1257 nyce ... outrageous,** silly, hostile. **1258 war,** aware (observant). **1260 myssayd of here,** spoken ill of by her. **1262 Clere brown,** vivid brunette. **1263 avenaunt,** graceful. **1270 stour,** battle. **1282** *Youthe:* GT *And she;* Fr. *Joinece.* **1284 volage,** volatile (changeable). **1285 Nyce,** silly.

But onely lust and jolyte.
For yonge folk, wel weten ye,
Have lytel thought but on her play.
Hir lemman was besyde alway,   1290
In suche a gyse that he hir kyste
At al tymes that him lyste,
That al the daunce myghte it se;
They make no force of prevyte.
For whoso spak of hem yvel or wel,   1295
They were ashamed never-a-del,
But men mighte sene hem kysse there,
As it two yonge dowves were.
For yong was thylke bachelere;
Of beaute wot I non his pere;   1300
And he was right of suche an age
As Youthe his lefe, and suche corage.
  The lusty folk thus daunced there,
And also other that with hem were,
That weren al of her meyne;   1305
Ful hende folk, wys and fre,
And folk of fayr port, truely,
Ther weren al comenly.
Whan I had sene the countenaunces
Of hem that ladden thus these daunces,   1310
Than had I wyl to gon and se
The gardyn that so lyked me,
And loken on these fayre laureres,
On pyne-trees, cedres, and olmeres.
For daunces than ended were;   1315
For many of hem that daunced there
Were with her loves went away
Under the trees to have her play.
  A, lord, they lyved lustely!
A great fole were he, sykerly,   1320
That nolde, his thankes, suche lyf lede!
For this dare I sayn, out of drede,
That whoso myght so wel fare,
For better lyf durst him not care.
For ther nys so good paradyse   1325

As to have a love at his devyse.
  Out of that place went I tho,
And in that gardyn gan I go,
Playing along ful merily.
The God of Love ful hastely   1330
Unto him Swete-Lokyng clepte;
No lenger wolde he that he kepte
His bowe of golde, that shone so bright.
He bad him bende it anon right;
And he ful sone it sette anende,   1335
And at a brayd he gan it bende,
And toke him of his arowes fyve
Ful sharpe and redy for to dryve.
Now God that syt in magiste,
Fro deedly woundes he kepe me,   1340
If so be that he had me shete,
For if I with his arowe mete,
It had me greved sore, ywis!
But I, that nothing wyste of this,
Went up and downe ful many a way,   1345
And he me folowed faste alway,
But nowher wolde I reste me
Tyll I had in al the gardyn be.
  The gardyn was by mesuryng
Right even and square in compasyng;   1350
It as long was as it was large.
Of fruit hadde every tree his charge,   TREES
But it were any hydous tre
Of whiche ther were two or thre.
Ther were, and that wot I ful wel,   1355
Of pomegarnettes a ful great del;
That is a frute ful wel to lyke,
Namely to folk whan they ben syke.
And trees ther were, great foysoun,
That baren nuttes in her sesoun   1360
Suche as men notemygges call,
That swote of savour ben withall.
And almandres great plente,
Fygges, and many a date tre

1287 **lust,** pleasure. 1294 **make no force,** don't care. 1302 **suche corage,** similar spirit. 1303 *thus:* GT *there;* Fr. *Ensi.* 1305 **meyne,** retinue. 1306 **hende,** attractive. G *folk and wys.* 1307 **port,** comportment (behavior). 1312 **lyked,** pleased. 1313 **laureres,** laurels. G *loreyes;* T *laurelles;* Fr. *loriers.* 1314 **olmeres,** elms. 1321 **his thankes,** thankfully. 1326 **devyse,** wish (devices). 1328 **go,** walk. 1331 **clepte,** called. 1332 **kepte,** withheld (guarded). *he kepte:* GT *she kepte.* 1334 **anon right,** immediately. GT *had him bent anon.* 1335 GT *it* om. 1336 **at a brayd,** with a quick movement. 1337 **him of,** from him. 1339 *syt:* T *sytteth.* 1340 **kepe,** protect. 1348 **gardyn,** Fr. *vergier* (orchard). 1352 **charge,** burden. 1354 **two or thre,** i.e., the orchard had every kind of fruit tree except two or three that were too hideous. 1358 **Namely,** especially. 1359 **foysoun,** abundance. 1363 **almandres,** almond trees.

Ther weren, if men hadde nede,   1365
Through the gardyn in length and brede.
Ther was eke wexyng many a spyce,
As clow-gylofre and lycoryce,
Gingere and greyn de paradys,
Canell and setewale of prys,   1370
And many a spyce delytable
To eeten whan men ryse fro table.
　And many homely trees ther were
That peches, coynes, and apples bere,
Medlers, plommes, peeres, chesteynis,   1375
Cheryse, of whiche many one fayn is,
Notes, aleys, and bolas,
That for to sene it was solas;
With many hygh laurer and pyne
Was renged clene al that gardyne;   1380
With cipres and with olyveris,
Of which that nygh no plente here is.
Ther were elmes greate and stronge,
Maples, asshe, oke, asp, planes longe,
Fyne ewe, popler, and lindes fayre,   1385
And othere trees ful many a payre.
　What shulde I tel you more of it?
Ther were so many trees yit,
That I shulde al encombred be
Er I had rekened every tree.   1390
　These trees were set, that I devyse,
One from another in assyse
Fyve fadome or sixe, I trowe so.
But they were hye and great also,
And for to kepe out wel the sonne   1395
The croppes were so thicke yronne,
And every braunche in other knytte,
And ful of grene leves sytte,
That sonne myght there none descende
Lest it the tendre grasses shende.   1400
Ther myghte men does and roes yse,
And of squyrels ful great plente   ANIMALS
From bowe to bowe alway lepynge.

Conies ther were also playynge,
That comyn out of her claperes,   1405
Of sondrie colours and maneres,
And maden many a tourneying
Upon the fresshe grasse sprynging.
　In places sawe I welles there,   SPRINGS
In whiche ther no frogges were,   1410
And fayre in shadowe was every wel.
But I ne can the nombre tel
Of stremys smal that by devyse
Myrthe had don come through condyse,
Of which the water in renning   1415
Gan make a noyse ful lyking.
　About the brinkes of these welles,
And by the stremes over al elles,
Sprange up the grasse as thicke yset
And softe as any velvet,   1420
On which men myghte his lemman ley
As on a fetherbed to pley,
For the erthe was ful softe and swete.
Through moisture of the welle wete
Spronge up the sote grene gras   1425
As fayre, as thicke, as myster was.
But moche amended it the place
That th'erthe was of suche a grace
That it of floures hath plente,
That both in somer and wynter be.   1430
　Ther sprang the violet al newe,   FLOWERS
And fresshe pervynke, riche of hewe,
And floures yelowe, white, and rede;
Suche plente grewe there never in mede.
Ful gaye was al the grounde, and queynt,   1435
And poudred as men had it peynt
With many a fresshe and sondrie flour,
That casten up ful good savour.
　I wol nat longe holde you in fable
Of al this garden dilitable.   1440
I mote my tonge stynten nede,
For I ne maye, withouten drede,

1365 *weren:* G *wexen;* Fr. *i trovoit.* 1368 **clow-gylofre,** cloves. 1369 **greyn de paradys,** cardamom. *paradys:* GT *parys;* Fr. *paradis.* 1370 **Canell . . . setewale,** cinnamon, zedoary. 1374 **coynes,** quince. 1375 **Medlers . . . chesteynis,** pears, chestnuts. 1376 **Cheryse,** cherries. 1377 **aleys,** fruit of the wild service tree; Fr. *alies.* **bolas,** damson plum. 1379 **laurer,** laurel. 1380 **renged clene,** ringed completely. 1384 **asp,** aspen. 1387–1422 Lines lacking in G. 1392 **assyse,** position. 1393 **fadome,** fathom (length of outstretched arms—six feet). 1400 **shende,** destroy. T *it* om. 1404 T *Connes* (rabbits). 1405 **claperes,** burrows. 1409 **welles,** springs. 1413 **devyse,** ingenuity. 1414 **condyse,** conduits. 1416 **lyking,** pleasing. 1425 **sote,** sweet-smelling. 1426 **myster,** necessary (i.e., "as could be"). 1427 **amended,** improved. 1432 **pervynke,** periwinkle. 1439 **holde . . . in fable,** i.e., detain by description. 1441 **stynten,** stop.

Naught tellen you the beaute al,
Ne halfe the bounte therewithal.

I went on right honde and on lefte 1445
About the place; it was nat lefte,
Tyl I had al the garden bene,
In the estres that men myght sene.
And thus while I wente in my playe,
The God of Love me folowed aye, 1450
Right as an hunter can abyde
The beest, tyl he seeth his tyde
To shoten at good mes to the dere,
Whan that hym nedeth go no nere.

And so befyl, I rested me 1455
Besydes a wel, under a tree,
Whiche tree in Fraunce men cal a pyne.
But sithe the tyme of Kyng Pepyne,
Ne grewe there tree in mannes syght
So fayre, ne so wel woxe in hight; 1460
In al that yarde so high was none.
And springyng in a marble stone
Had Nature set, the sothe to tel,
Under that pyne tree a wel.
And on the border al without 1465
Was written in the stone about
Letters smal that sayden thus,
"Here starf the fayre Narcisus."

Narcisus was a bachelere NARCISUS
That Love had caught in his dangere, 1470
And in his nette gan hym so strayne,
And dyd him so to wepe and playne,
That nede him must his lyfe forgo,
For a fayre lady that hight Echo
Him loved over any creature, 1475
And gan for hym suche payne endure
That on a tyme she him tolde
That if he her loven nolde,
That her behoved nedes dye;
There laye none other remedy. 1480

But nathelesse for his beaute
So feirs and daungerous was he
That he nolde graunten her askyng,

For wepyng ne for fayre prayeng.
And whan she herde hym werne her so, 1485
She had in herte so great wo,
And toke it in so great dispyte,
That she withoute more respyte
Was deed anon. But er she deyde,
Ful pitously to God she prayde 1490
That proude herted Narcisus,
That was in love so daungerous,
Mighte on a day ben hampred so
For love, and ben so hot for wo,
That never he myghte to joye attayne; 1495
Than shulde he fele in every vayne
What sorowe trewe lovers maken
That ben so vilaynously forsaken.

This prayer was but resonable;
Therefor God held it ferme and stable. 1500
For Narcisus, shortly to tel,
By aventure came to that wel
To rest him in the shadowing,
A day whan he come from hunting.
This Narcisus had suffred paynes 1505
For renning al day in the playnes,
And was for thurst in great distresse,
Of hete and of his werynesse
That had his brethe almost benomen.
Whan he was to that wel ycomen, 1510
That shadowed was with braunches grene,
He thoughte of thilke water shene
To drinke and fresshe him wel withal.
And downe on knees he gan to fal,
And forth his necke and heed outstraught 1515
To drynke of that wel a draught.
And in the water anon was sene
His nose, his mouth, his eyen shene.
And he therof was al abasshed;
His owne shadowe had him betrasshed. 1520
For wel wende he the forme se
Of a chyld of great beaute.
Wel couthe Love him wreke tho
Of daunger and of pride also,

1444 **bounte**, graciousness. 1448 **estres**, inner areas. 1453 **good mes**, good advantage (Lat. *missum*, a throw). 1458 **Pepyne**, father of Charlemagne. 1468 **starf**, died. 1470 **dangere**, power. 1474 **hight**, was called. 1478 **nolde**, would not. 1482 **feirs and daungerous**, cruel and disdainful. 1485 **werne**, reject. 1493 **hampred**, burdened. 1496 G *And that he shulde*. 1502 **aventure**, chance. 1503 **shadowing**, shade. 1508 *hete*: T *herte*; Fr. *chaut*. 1509 **benomen**, taken. 1512 **shene**, clear (bright). 1515 **straught**, stretched. G *he straught*. 1519 **abasshed**, disconcerted. 1520 **betrasshed**, betrayed. 1521 **wende**, thought. 1523 **him wreke**, revenge himself.

That Narcisus somtyme him bere. 1525
He quytte him wel his guerdon there.
For he musede so in the well,
That shortely the sothe to tell,
He loved his owne shadowe so
That at laste he starf for wo. 1530
For whan he sawe that he his wyll
Might in no maner way fulfyll,
And that he was so faste caught
That he him couthe comfort naught,
He loste his wytte right in that place 1535
And deyde within a lytell space.
And thus his warysoun he toke
For the lady that he forsoke.
    Ladyes, I praye ensample taketh,
Ye that ayenst your love mistaketh, 1540
For if her dethe be you to wyte,
God can ful wel your whyle quyte.
    Whan that this lettre of whiche I tell
Had taught me that it was the well
Of Narcisus in his beaute, 1545
I gan anon withdrawe me,
Whan it fell in my remembraunce
That him betyd suche mischaunce.
But at the laste than thoughte I
That scatheles, ful sykerly, 1550
I myghte unto the welle go.   HER EYES
Wherof shulde I abasshen so?
Unto the welle than went I me,
And down I louted for to se
The clere water in the stone, 1555
And eke the gravel which that shone
Downe in the botome as sylver fyne,
For of the welle this is the fyne:
In world is none so clere of hewe.
The water is ever fresshe and newe 1560
That welmeth up with wawes bright
The mountenaunce of two fynger hight.
Abouten it is grasse springing,
For moyste so thycke and wel lyking

That it ne may in wynter dye 1565
No more than may the see be drye.
    Down at the botome set sawe I
Two cristall stones craftely
In thilke fresshe and fayre well.
But o thyng sothly dar I tell, 1570
That ye wol holde a great mervayle
Whan it is told, withouten fayle.
For whan the sonne clere in syght
Cast in that welle his bemes bright,
And that the heet discended is, 1575
Than taketh the cristall stone, ywis,
Agayne the sonne an hundred hewes,
Blewe, yelowe, and reed, that fressh and
    newe is.
Yet hath the mervaylous cristall
Suche strength that the place over all, 1580
Bothe flour and tree and leves grene
And al the yerd in it is sene.
And for to don you to understonde,
To make ensample wol I fonde:
Right as a myrrour openly 1585
Sheweth al thyng that stant therby,
As wel the colour as the fygure,
Withouten any coverture,
Right so the cristal stone shyning,
Withouten any disceyving, 1590
The estrees of the yerde accuseth
To him that in the water museth;
For ever, in whiche half that he be,
He may wel half the gardyn se,
And if he turne, he may right wel 1595
Sen the remenaunt everydel.
For ther is none so lytel thing
So hydde, ne closed with shytting,
That it ne is sen as though it were
Paynted in the cristall there. 1600
    This is the myrrour perillous
In which the proude Narcisus
Sey al his fayre face bright,

1526 **quytte him ... guerdon,** repaid him, reward. 1528 G *all the.* 1530 **starf,** died. 1534 **him couthe,** himself could. 1537 **warysoun,** requital. 1541 **wyte,** blame. 1542 **whyle quyte,** time repay. 1550 **scatheles ... sykerly,** without harm, securely. 1553 Line lacking in G. 1554 **louted,** bent. 1557 **fyne,** end (significant objective, the point), i.e., the eyeballs. 1561 **welmeth,** surges. 1562 **mountenaunce,** amount. 1568 **cristall stones,** i.e., the pupils of the eyes. 1577 **Agayne,** i.e., from the reflections of. 1581 *flour:* GT *foule;* Fr. *Arbres e flors.* 1586 *stant:* T *stondeth.* 1588 **coverture,** concealment. 1591 **estrees ... accuseth,** interior, reveals. GT *entrees;* Fr. *l'estre.* 1592 **in ... museth,** i.e., gazes into. 1593–94 *he ... He:* GT *ye ... Ye.* 1598 **closed with shytting,** connected by enclosure.

That made him sith to lye upright.
For whoso loke in that myrrour,   1605
There may nothyng ben his socour
That he ne shal there se somthing
That shal him lede into loving.
Ful many a worthy man hath it
Yblent, for folke of greatest wyt   1610
Ben soone caught here and awayted;
Withouten respyt ben they bayted.
Here cometh to folk of newe rage;
Here chaungeth many wight corage;
Here lyth no rede ne wytte therto;   1615
For Venus sone, Daun Cupido,
Hath sowen there of love the sede,
That help ne lyth there none, ne rede,
So cercleth it the welle aboute.
His gynnes hath he set withoute   1620
Right for to cacche in his panteres
These damosels and bacheleres;
Love wyl none other byrde catche
Though he set eyther nette or latche.
And for the sede that here was sowen,   1625
This welle is cleped, as wel is knowen,
The Welle of Love, of verray right,
Of which ther hath ful many a wight
Spoke in bokes dyversely.
But they shul never so verily   1630
Discripcion of the welle here,
Ne eke the sothe of this matere,
As ye shul, whan I have undo
The crafte that hir bylongeth to.
    Allway me lyked for to dwell   1635
To sene the christall in the well
That shewed me ful openly
A thousand thynges faste by.
But I may say, in sory houre
Stod I to loken or to powre,   1640

For sythen have I sore syked;
That myrrour hath me nowe entryked.
But had I first knowen in my wyt
The vertue and the strengthe of it,
I nolde not have mused there;   1645
Me hadde bet ben elleswhere.
For in the snare I fell anone
That hath bytraisshed many one.
    In thylke myrrour sawe I tho,
Amonge a thousand thynges mo,   1650
A roser charged ful of roses,   THE ROSE
That with an hedge aboute enclos is.   GARDEN
Tho had I suche lust and envye,
That for Parys ne for Pavye
Nolde I have left to gone and se   1655
Ther greatest heape of roses be.
Whan I was with this rage hent,
That caught hath many a man and shent,
Toward the roser gan I go.
And whan I was not ferre therfro,   1660
The savour of the roses swote
Me smote right to the herte rote,
As I had al enbaumed be.
And if I ne had endouted me
To have ben hated or assayled,   1665
My thankes, wol I not have fayled
To pull a rose of al that route
To beren in myn honde aboute,
And smellen to it wher I wente,
But ever I dredde me to repente   1670
And leste it greved or forthought
The lorde that thilke gardyn wrought.
Of roses ther were great wone,
So fayre ware never in rone.
Of knoppes clos some sawe I there;   1675
And some wel better woxen were;
And some ther been of other moyson

1604 sith to lye upright, afterward, to lie dead. **1606 socour,** aid. **1608** *loving:* GT *laughyng;* Fr. *d'amors.* **1610 Yblent,** blinded. **1611 awayted,** waylaid. T *wayted.* **1612 bayted,** tormented. **1613 of newe rage,** sudden passion. **1614 corage,** spirit (nature). **1615 rede,** wisdom. **1620 gynnes,** traps (engine). **1621 panteres,** nets. **1624 latche,** trap. **1627 Welle,** spring. T *wells.* **1630 verily,** truly. **1631 here,** hear. **1639 sory,** unfortunate. **1640 powre,** pore (ponder). **1641 sythen . . . syked,** since (then), sighed. GT *have* om. **1642 entryked,** deceived (entricked). **1644** *and the:* GT *the* om. **1648 bytraisshed,** betrayed. **1654 Pavye,** Pavia (N. Italy). **1655 left,** i.e., would I not have gone. **1656 Ther . . . heape,** where, quantity. **1657 rage hent,** passion caught. **1658 shent,** destroyed. **1661 savour . . . swote,** odor, sweet. **1663 enbaumed,** covered with balm (perfume). *be:* GT *me.* **1664 endouted,** feared. **1666** T *Me thankis.* **1667 pull . . . route,** pluck, company. **1671 And leste . . . forthought,** lest, displeased. **1673 great wone,** great quantity. **1674 rone,** possibly "rows" (s.v. *Prompt. Parv.* rowe, reenge). Skeat suggested Scottish "bush." *ware:* G *waxe.* **1675 knoppes,** buds. One principal evidence of a different translator for parts A and B is that instead of *knoppes,* B uses *bothum* (Fr. *bouton*), cf. l. 1721 etc. **1677 moyson,** size.

That drowe nygh to her seson,
And spedde hem faste for to sprede.
I love wel suche roses rede, 1680
For brode roses, and open also,
Ben passed in a day or two,
But knoppes wyl al fresshe be
Two dayes at leest, or els thre.
The knoppes greatly lyked me, 1685
For fayrer may ther no man se.
Whoso mighte have one of all,
It oughte him ben ful leef withall.
Mighte I a gerlond of hem geten, 1689
For no richesse I wold it leten. THE
Among the knoppes I chese one ROSEBUD

So fayr that of the remenaunt none
Ne preyse I half so wel as it,
Whan I avyse it in my wyt.
For it so wel was enlumyned 1695
With colour reed, as wel yfyned
As Nature couthe it make fayre.
And it hath leves wel foure payre
That Kynde hath set through his knowing
Aboute the redde roses sprynging. 1700
The stalke was as rysshe right,
And theron stode the knoppe upright
That it ne bowed upon no syde.
The swote smell sprong so wyde
That it dyed al the place aboute... 1705

FRAGMENT B

Whan I had smelled the savour swote,
No wyl had I fro thence yet go,
But somdele nere it went I tho
To take it; but myn honde, for drede,
Ne durste I to the rose bede, 1710
For thystels sharpe, of many maners,
Netles, thornes, and hoked THE DREAMER
briers; · PIERCED BY
For moche they distourbled me, BEAUTY
For sore I dradde to harmed be.
The God of Love, with bowe bent, 1715
That al day set had his talent
To pursuen and to spyen me,
Was stondyng by a fygge-tree.
And whan he sawe howe that I
Had chosen so ententifly 1720
The bothum, more unto my paye
Than any other that I say,
He toke an arowe ful sharply whette,
And in his bowe whan it was sette,
He streight up to his eere drough 1725

The stronge bowe, that was so tough,
And shotte at me so wonder smerte
That through myn eye unto myn herte
The takel smote, and depe it wente.
And therwithal suche colde me hente 1730
That under clothes warme and softe
Sythen that day I have chyvered ofte.
Whan I was hurte thus in a stounde,
I fell downe platte unto the grounde.
Myn herte fayled and faynted aye, 1735
And longe tyme aswoune I laye.
But whan I came out of swounyng,
And had wytte, and my felyng,
I was al mate, and wende ful wele
Of bloode have lorne a ful great dele. 1740
But certes, the arowe that in me stoode
Of me ne drewe no droppe of bloode,
For-why I founde my woundes al drey.
Than toke I with myn hondes twey
The arrowe, and ful faste it out-plyght, 1745
And in the pullyng sore I syght.

1683 GT *al* om.; F *tuit frois.* 1688 **him ben . . . leef,** been pleasing to him. 1689 GT *a* om. 1690 **leten,** hesitate. 1694 **avyse,** consider.
G *it* om. 1695 **enlumyned,** illuminated (tinted). 1696 **yfyned,** shaped. GT *y-* om. 1699 **Kynde,** nature. 1701 **rysshe right,** rush
straight. 1705 **dyed,** dyed (saturated); Fr. *replenist* (filled). 1710 **bede,** reach out (proffer). 1717 T *pursue.* 1718 **fygge-tree,** fig
(symbolic of genitalia). 1721 **bothum,** bud. G *botoun* throughout; Fr. *bouton, boton,* which section A translated *knoppe,* l. 1685 etc. **my
paye,** my pleasure. 1722 **say,** saw. 1727 *shotte:* G *shette* throughout. 1730 **hente,** seized. 1732 **Sythen . . . chyvered,** since, shivered.
G *Syth.* 1733 **stounde,** moment. GT *a* om. 1736 T *in swoune.* 1739 **mate . . . wende,** exhausted, thought. 1740 **lorne,** lost. 1745
plyght, plucked. 1746 **syght,** sighed.

So at the laste the shafte of tree
I drough out with the fethers thre,
But yet the hoked heed, ywis,
The whiche Beaute called is,　　　　　1750
Gan so depe in myn herte pace
That I it might not arace;
But in myn hert styl it stoode,
Al bledde I not a droppe of bloode.
I was bothe anguysshous and trouble　1755
For the peryll that I sawe double:
I nyste what to say or do,
Ne get a leche my woundes to;
For neyther through grasse ne rote
Ne had I helpe of hope ne bote.　　　1760
But to the bothum evermo
Myn herte drewe; for al my wo,
My thought was in none other thyng.
For had it ben in my kepyng,
It wolde have brought my lyfe agayne.　1765
For certes evenly, I dare wel sayne,
The sight onely, and the savoure,
Alegged moche of my langoure.
　　Than gan I for to drawe me
Towarde the bothom fayre to se;　　　1770
And Love had get him, in his throwe,
Another arowe into his bowe,
And for to shote gan hym dresse—
The arowes name was　　　　THE ARROW
　　Symplesse.　　　　　SIMPLICITY
And whan that Love gan nygh me nere,　1775
He drowe it up, withouten were,
And shotte at me with al his myght,
So that this arowe anon right
Throughout myn eygh, as it was founde
Into myn herte hath made a wounde.　1780
Than I anon dyd al my crafte
For to drawen out the shafte,
And therewithal I syghed efte;
But in myn herte the heed was lefte,
Whiche aye encresed my desyre.　　1785
Unto the bothom drowe I nere;

And evermo that me was wo,
The more desyre had I to go
Unto the roser, where that grewe
The fresshe bothom so bright of hewe.　1790
Better me were to have letten be,
But it behoved nede me
To don right as myn herte badde:
For ever the body muste be ladde
After the herte; in wele and wo,　　1795
Of force togyder they muste go.
But never this archer wolde fyne
To shote at me with al his pyne,
And for to make me to him mete.
The thirde arowe he gan to shete,　1800
Whan best his tyme he myght espye,
The whiche was named Curtesye.　THE ARROW
Into myn herte it dyd avale;　　COURTESY
Aswoune I fel, bothe deed and pale;
Longe tyme I lay and styrred nought,　1805
Tyl I abrayde out of my thought.
And faste than I avysed me
To drawe out the shafte of tree;
But ever the heed was lefte behynde
For aught I couthe pull or wynde.　　1810
　　So sore it stycked whan I was hytte
That by no crafte I myght it flytte;
But anguysshous and ful of thought,
I felte suche wo my wounde aye wrought,
That somoned me alway to go　　　1815
Towarde the rose that plesed me so;
But I ne durste in no manere,
Bycause the archer was so nere.
For evermore gladly, as I rede,
Brent chylde of fyre hath moche drede.　1820
And certes yet, for al my peyne,
Though that I sygh yet arowes reyne,
And grounde quarels sharpe of steele,
Ne for no payne that I might fele,
Yet might I not myselfe withholde　1825
The fayre roser to beholde;
For Love me yave suche hardyment

1749 *yet:* G *atte.* 1750 G *which it Beaute.* 1752 **arace**, root out. 1758 **leche**, physician. *to:* G *two.* 1759 **grasse ne rote**, i.e., medicinal herbs. 1766 **evenly**, even. 1768 **Alegged**, allayed. 1771 **throwe**, moment. 1773 **dresse**, prepare (address). 1774 **Symplesse**, i.e., sincere (artless). 1776 **were**, hesitation (inward turmoil, Fr. *guerre*). 1779 TG *myn* om. 1783 **efte**, again. 1797 **fyne**, finish. 1798 **pyne**, pain. 1799 **mete**, meet (i.e., succumb). 1803 **avale**, descend. 1806 **abrayde**, started up. 1812 **flytte**, escape. 1814 **felte**: TG *lefte.* 1816 *plesed me*, in BC this phrase is regularly used instead of the more Chaucerian *lyked me*, cf. A, l. 27 etc. 1820 **Brent**, burned. 1823 **grounde quarels**, sharpened crossbow bolts. 1827 **hardyment**, courage.

For to fulfyll his commaundement.
Upon my fete I rose up than
Feble as a forwounded man,   1830
And forthe to gon my might I sette,
And for the archer nolde I lette.
Towarde the roser faste I drowe;
But thornes sharpe mo than ynowe
There were, and also thystels thicke,   1835
And breres, brimme for to pricke,
That I ne myght get grace
The roughe thornes for to pace,
To sene the roses fresshe of hewe.
I muste abyde, though it me rewe,   1840
The hedge aboute so thycke was,
That closed the roses in compas.

But o thyng lyked me right wele:
I was so nyghe, I myght fele
Of the bothom the swote odoure,   1845
And also se the fresshe coloure;
And that right greatly lyked me,
That I so nere might it se.
Suche joye anon thereof had I,
That I forgate my maladye.   1850
To sene I had suche delyte,
Of sorowe and angre I was al quyte,
And of my woundes that I had thore.
For nothyng lyken me myght more
Than dwellen by the roser aye,   1855
And thence never to passe awaye.

But whan a whyle I had be thare,
The God of Love, whiche al toshare
Myn herte with his arowes kene,
Casteth him to yeve me woundes grene.   1860
He shotte at me ful hastely
An arowe named Company,   THE ARROW
The whiche takell is ful able   COMPANY
To make these ladyes merciable.
Than I anon gan chaungen hewe   1865
For grevaunce of my wounde newe,
That I agayne fel in swounyng,
And syghed sore in complaynyng.

Sore I complayned that my sore
On me gan greven more and more.   1870
I had non hope of allegeaunce,
So nygh I drowe to disperaunce.
I rought of dethe ne of lyfe,
Whether that Love wolde me drife,
If me a martyr wolde he make.   1875
I myght his power not forsake.
And whyle for anger thus I woke,   THE ARROW
The God of Love an arowe toke;   FAIR
Ful sharpe it was and pugnaunt,   APPEARANCE
And it was called Fayre-Semblaunt,   1880
The whiche in no wyse wol consent
That any lover hym repente
To serve his love with herte and all,
For any peryll that may befall.
But though this arowe was kene grounde   1885
As any rasour that is founde,
To cutte and kerve, at the poynte
The God of Love it had anoynt
With a precious oyntment,
Somdele to yeve alegement   1890
Upon the woundes that he hade
Through the body in my herte made,
To helpe her sores, and to cure,
And that they may the bette endure.
But yet this arowe, without more,   1895
Made in myn herte a large sore,
That in ful great payne I abode.
But aye the oyntement went abrode;
Throughout my woundes large and wyde
It spredde aboute in every syde,   1900
Thorough whose vertue and whose myght
Myn herte joyful was and lyght.
I had ben deed and al toshent
But for the precious oyntment.
The shafte I drowe out of the arowe,   1905
Rokyng for wo right wonder narowe;
But the heed, whiche made me smerte,
Lefte behynde in myn herte
With other foure, I dare wel say,

1831 **gon**, walk. TG *my* om. 1832 **lette**, hesitate. 1836 **brimme**, cruel. 1838 **pace**, pass. 1840 **abyde**, wait. 1843 **lyked me**, pleased me. 1853–54 Note the non-Chaucerian northern rhyme *thore* (there)/*more*. 1857–58 *thare*/*toshare* (lacerated), again non-Chaucerian rhyme. 1861–62 Non-Chaucerian rhyme *hastely*/*Company*(*e*). 1871 **allegeaunce**, alleviation. 1872 **disperaunce**, despair. 1873 **rought**, cared. 1874 **drife**, drive. 1879 **pugnaunt**, piercing. 1880 **Fayre-Semblaunt**, i.e., "charm." Fr. *Beau Semblant*. 1890 **alegement**, alleviation. 1892 G in later hand, to fill space left in original: *That he hadde the body hole made*. 1903 **toshent**, destroyed. 1906 **Rokyng... narowe**, i.e., moving it back and forth slightly (to get it out).

That never wol be take away.   1910
But the oyntment halpe me wele.
And yet suche sorowe dyd I fele
That al day I chaunged hewe,
Of my woundes fresshe and newe,
As men might se in my vysage.   1915
The arowes were so ful of rage,
So varyaunt of diversyte
That men in everyche might se
Bothe great anoye and eke swetnesse,
And joye meynt with bytternesse.   1920
Nowe were they easy, nowe were they wood.
In hem I felte bothe harme and good.
Nowe sore without aleggement,
Nowe softyng with oyntment;
It softned here, and pricketh there.   1925
Thus ease and anger togyther were.
    The God of Love delyverly   LOVE CLAIMS
Come lepande to me hastely,   HIS VICTIM
And sayd to me, in great rape,
"Yelde the, for thou may not escape!   1930
May no defence avayle the here;
Therfore I rede make no daungere.
If thou wolte yelde the hastely,
Thou shalt the rather have mercy.
He is a foole in sykernesse   1935
That with daunger or stoutnesse
Rebelleth there that he shulde plese;
In suche folye is lytel ese.
Be meke where thou muste nedes bowe;
To stryve ayen is nought thy prowe.   1940
Come at ones, and have ydo,
For I wol that it be so.
Than yelde the here debonairly."
    And I answered ful humbly,
"Gladly, sir, at your byddyng.   1945
I wol me yelde in al thyng.
To your servyce I wol me take.
For God defende that I shulde make
Ayen your byddyng resystence;

I wol not don so great offence,   1950
For if I dyd, it were no skyll.
Ye may do with me what ye wyll,
Save or spyll, and also slo;
Fro you in no wyse may I go.
My lyfe, my dethe, is in your honde;   1955
I may not laste out of your bonde.
Playne at your lyste I yelde me,
Hopyng in herte that somtyme ye
Comforte and ese shul me sende,
Or els, shortly, this is the ende.   1960
Withouten helthe I mote aye dure,
But if ye take me to your cure.
Comforte or helthe howe shulde I have,
Sythe ye me hurte, but ye me save?
The helthe of lovers mote be founde   1965
Where as they token first her wounde.
And if ye lyst of me to make
Your prisoner, I wol it take
Of herte and wyll, fully at gre.
Holy and playne I yelde me,   1970
Without feynyng or feyntyse,
To be governed by your emprise.
Of you I here so moche price,
I wol ben hole at your devyce
For to fulfyll your lykyng   1975
And repente for nothyng,
Hopyng to have yet in some tyde
Mercy; of that I abyde."
And with that covenaunt yelde I me
Anon, downe knelyng upon my kne,   1980
Proferyng for to kysse his fete.
    But for nothyng he wolde me lete,
And sayd, "I love the bothe and preise,
Sens that thyn answer dothe me ese,
For thou answered so curtesly.   1985
For nowe I wote wel utterly
That thou arte gentyl, by thy speche.
For though a man ferre wolde seche,
He shulde not fynden, in certayne,

1913–14 transposed order from Fr.; cf. Sutherland. **1920 meynt,** mixed (s.v. OED meng). **1921 wood,** mad. **1923 aleggement,** alleviation. **1927 delyverly,** nimbly. **1928 lepande,** leaping, with northern "–and" participial ending. **1929 rape,** haste. T *jape.* **1932 rede . . . daungere,** advise, resistance (disdain). **1934 rather,** sooner. TG *the* om. **1935 sykernesse,** state of security. **1940 ayen is nought thy prowe,** against (love) is not to your advantage. **1951 no skyll,** no use. **1953 spyll . . . slo,** destroy, slay. **1957 Playne . . . lyste,** fully, desire. **1962 cure,** care. **1964 Sythe . . . but,** since, unless. **1965 lovers:** TG *love.* **1969 at gre,** willingly. **1970 Holy and playne,** wholly and completely. **1971 feynyng . . . feyntyse,** pretending, pretence. **1972 emprise,** will. **1973 price,** prize (renown). **1974 devyce,** command. **1978 of . . . abyde,** for, await. **1982 for nothyng,** not at all. G *me* om. **1984** G line in a later hand, to fill in a space. **1986 wote,** know.

No suche answere of no vilayne. 1990
For suche a worde ne myght nought
Isse out of a vylayns thought.
Thou shalt not lesen of thy speche,
For to thy helpyng woll I eche,
And eke encresen that I maye. 1995
But first I wol that thou obaye
Fully, for thyn avauntage,
Anon to do me here homage.
And sythe kysse thou shalte my mouthe,
Whiche to no vilayne was never couthe 2000
For to aproche it, ne for to touche;
For saufe of cherles, I ne vouche
That they shal never neigh it nere.
For curteys, and of fayre manere,
Wel taught, and ful of gentylnysse 2005
He muste ben that shal me kysse,
And also of ful hygh fraunchyse,
That shal atteyne to that emprise.
And first of o thyng warne I the,
That payne and great adversyte 2010
He mote endure, and eke travayle,
That shal me serve, without fayle.
But there agaynst, the to comforte,
And with thy servyce to disporte,
Thou mayst ful glad and joyful be 2015
So good a mayster to have as me,
And lorde of so hygh renoun.
I beare of Love the gonfenoun,
Of Curtesy the banere.
For I am of the selfe manere, 2020
Gentyll, curteys, meke, and fre,
That whoever ententyfe be
Me to honoure, doute, and serve,
And also that he hym observe
Fro trespace and fro vilanye, 2025
And hym governe in curtesye
With wyll and with entencion.
For whan he first in my prison

Is caught, than muste he utterly,
Fro thence forthe ful besyly, 2030
Caste hym gentyll for to be,
If he desyre helpe of me."
    Anon without more delay,
Withouten daunger or affray,
I become his man anone, 2035
And gave hym thankes many a one,
And kneled downe with hondes joynt,
And made it in my port ful queynt;
The joye went to my hert rote.
Whan I had kyssed his mouthe so swote, 2040
I had suche myrthe and suche lykyng,
It cured me of languysshyng.   THE DREAMER
He asked of me than hostages: BECOMES
"I have," he sayd, "taken fele   A LOVER
    homages
Of one and other, where I have bene 2045
Disceyved ofte, withouten wene.
These felons, ful of falsyte,
Have many sythes begyled me,
And through falshede her luste acheved,
Whereof I repent and am agreved. 2050
And I hem get in my daungere,
Her falshede shul they bye ful dere.
But for I love the, I say the playne,
I wol of the be more certayne;
For the so sore I wol nowe bynde 2055
That thou away ne shalt not wynde
For to denyen the covenaunt,
Or done that is not avenaunt.
That thou were false it were great ruthe,
Sythe thou semest so ful of truthe." 2060
    "Sir, if the lyst to understande,
I mervayle the askyng this demande.
For why or wherfore shulde ye
Hostages or borowes aske of me,
Or any other sykernesse, 2065
Sythe ye wot, in sothfastnesse,

1990 vilayne, in its original sense of lowborn person. **1993 lesen of,** lose by. **1994 eche,** augment. TG *to* om. **1999 sythe,** afterward. **2000 couthe,** known. **2002 saufe of,** safely kept from churls (again, the lowborn). **2007 fraunchyse,** nobility. **2008 emprise,** achievement. **2014 disporte,** divert (please). **2018 gonfenoun,** symbolic banner. **2021 fre,** liberal. **2024 observe,** preserve. **2031 Caste hym,** devote himself. **2034 affray,** fear. **2038 port . . . queynt,** posture, curious (artful). This describes the traditional posture of a vassal, kneeling and placing his joined hands between those of his lord as a sign of homage. **2044 fele,** many. **2046** *Disceyved:* TG *Disteyned;* Fr. *deceu.* **2048 sythes,** times. **2049** TG *through her.* **2051 And I . . . daungere,** and if I, power. **2058 avenaunt,** becoming. **2059 ruthe,** pity. **2061 lyst,** please. **2064 borowes,** pledges. **2065 sykernesse,** security. **2066 sothfastnesse,** truth. *wot* (know): G *wole.*

That ye me have suprised so,
And hole myn herte taken me fro,
That it wol do for me nothyng
But if it be at your byddyng? 2070
Myn herte is yours, and myn right nought,
As it behoveth, in dede and thought,
Redy in al to worche your wyll,
Whether so it turne to good or yll.
So sore it lusteth you to plese, 2075
No man thereof may you disese.
Ye have theron sette such justyse
That it is werreyed in many wyse;
And if he doute it nolde obey,
Ye may therof do make a key, 2080
And holde it with you for hostage."
    "Nowe certes, this is none outrage,"
Quod Love, "and fully I accorde,
For of the body he is ful lorde
Than hath the herte in his tresore; 2085
Outrage it were to asken more."
    Thann of his aumener he drough
A lytel key, fetise ynough,
Whiche was of golde polysshed clere,
And sayd to me, "With this key here 2090
Thyne herte to me nowe wol I shette,
For al my jowels loke and knette   THE LOVER'S
I bynde under this lytel key,   HEART
That no wight maye cary awey;   LOCKED
This key is ful of great poeste." 2095
With whiche anon he touched me
Under the syde ful softely,
That he myne herte sodainly
Without anoye hadde speered,
That yet right nought it hath me deered. 2100
    Whan he hadde done his wyl al out,
And I had putte hym out of dout,
"Sir," I sayd, "I have right great wyl
Your luste and pleasure to fulfyl.
Loke ye my servyce take at gree, 2105
By thilke faythe ye owe to me.

I saye nought for recreaundyse,
For I nought doute of your servyce;
But the servaunt traveyleth in vayne
That for to serven doth his payne 2110
Unto that lorde whiche in no wyse
Conne hym no thanke for his servyce."
    Love sayde, "Dismay the nought,
Syth thou for socour hast me sought.
In thanke thy servyce wol I take, 2115
And highe of degree I wol the make,
If wyckednesse ne hynder the.
But as I hoope, it shal nought be:
To worshyppe no wight by aventure
Maye come but if he payne endure. 2120
Abyde and suffre thy distresse
That hurteth nowe. It shal be lesse.
I wotte myselfe what maye the save,
What medicyne thou woldest have.
And if thy trouthe to me thou kepe, 2125
I shal unto thyne helpyng eke,
To cure thy woundes and make hem clene
Whereso they be olde or grene;
Thou shalte be holpen, at wordes fewe.
For certainly thou shalte wel shewe 2130
Where that thou servest with good wyl
For to accomplysshen and fulfyl
My commaundements, daye and nyght,
Whiche I to lovers yeve of right."
    "Ah, sir, for Goddes love," sayd I, 2135
"Er ye passe hens, ententyfely
Your commaundements to me ye say,
And I shal kepe hem, if I may,
For hem to kepen is al my thought,
And if so be I wote hem nought, 2140
Than maye I erre unwyttingly.
Wherfore I praye you entierly,
With al myne herte, me to lere,
That I trespace in no manere."
    The God of Love than charged me 2145
Anon as ye shal here and se,

2067 **suprised,** captured. 2068 **hole,** wholly. 2074 TG *it* om. 2075 **lusteth,** desires. 2076 **disese,** dispossess; Fr. *dessaisir.* 2077 **justyse,** government. 2078 **werreyed,** battered (warred upon). 2085 **Than hath . . . tresore,** That has, treasury (power). 2087 **aumener,** purse (alms bag). 2088 **fetise,** neat. 2092 **loke and knette,** locked and bound (knit). TG *jowel.* 2095 **poeste,** power. T *poste.* 2099 **speered,** fastened. 2100 **deered,** injured. 2105 **at gree,** for granted. 2107 **recreaundyse,** cowardice. 2112 **Conne,** acknowledges. 2119 **worshyppe . . . aventure,** honor, accident. 2128 **Whereso . . . grene,** whether, fresh. 2132 G *compleysshen.* 2141 TG *erre* om. 2143 **lere,** teach. 2145 **charged,** instructed.

Worde by worde, by right emprise,
So as the *Romaunt* shal devyse.

    The maister leseth his tyme to lere
Whan the disciple wol nat here.   2150
It is but vayne on hym to swynke,
That on his lernynge wol nat thynke.
Whoso luste love, lette him entende,
For nowe the romance begynneth to amende.
Nowe is good to here, in faye,   2155
If any be that canne it saye,
And poynt it as the reason is
Sette; for other gate, ywis,
It shal nat wel in al thyng
Be brought to good understondyng.   2160
For a reder that poynteth yl
A good sentence maye ofte spyl.
The boke is good at the endyng,
Made of newe and lusty thyng;
For whoso wol the endyng here,   2165
The crafte of Love he shal mowe lere,
If that he wol so longe abyde,
Tyl I this romance maye unhyde,
And undo the signyfiaunce
Of this dreme into romaunce.   2170
The sothfastnesse that nowe is hydde
Without coverture shal be kydde   LOVE'S
Whan I undone have this dremyng,   COMMAND-
Wherein no worde is of leasyng.   MENTS

    "Villany, at the begynnyng,   2175
I wol," sayde Love, "over al thyng,
Thou leave, if thou wolte not be   AVOID
False and trespace ayenst me.   VILLAINY
I curse and blame generally
Al hem that loven villany;   2180
For villany maketh villayne,
And by his dedes a chorle is seyne.
These vilayns arne without pyte,
Frendshyp, love, and al bounte.
I nyl receyve unto my servyce   2185

Hem that ben vilayns of emprise.
But understond in thyn entent
That this is not myn entendement,
To clepe no wight in no ages
Onely gentyl for his lynages.   2190
But whoso is vertuous,
And in his porte not outragyous.
Whan suche one thou seest the beforne,
Though he be not gentyl borne,
Thou mayste wel seyne, this is in sothe,   2195
That he is gentyl by cause he dothe
As longeth to a gentylman;   NATURAL
Of hem none other deme I can.   GENTILESSE
For certaynly, withouten drede,
A chorle is demed by his dede,   2200
Of hye or lowe, as ye may se,
Or of what kynrede that he be.
    "Ne say nought, for none yvel wyll,
Thyng that is to holden styll;
It is no worshyp to missey.   2205
Thou mayste ensample take of Key,
That was somtyme for missayeng
Hated bothe of olde and yonge.
As ferre as Gaweyn the worthy
Was praysed for his curtesye,   2210
Kaye was hated, for he was fell
Of worde, dispytous and cruell.
    "Wherfore be wyse and aqueyntable,
Goodly of worde, and reasonable
Bothe to lesse and eke to mare.   2215
And whan thou comest there men are,
Loke that thou have in custome aye
First to salue hem, if thou may;
And if it fall that of hem somme
Salue the first, be not domme,   2220
But quyte hem curtesly anon
Without abydyng, er they gon.
    "For nothyng eke thy tonge applye
To speke wordes of rybaudye.

2147 emprise, design. **2149–52** In Fr. placed after 2144. **2151 swynke,** labor. **2154 romance,** by the 14th cent. already a generalized term for a narrative of chivalry and love. Eds. suggest *gynneth t'amende.* **2167** *he:* G *ye.* **2172 kydde,** revealed. **2174 leasyng,** lying. **2176** *sayde:* TG *say(e).* **2177** TG *not* om. **2186 emprise,** behavior. **2189 clepe,** call (to my service). **2191–2202** These lines are not found in the French. Their close parallel to WBT, *CT* III.1109ff. led Skeat, Brusendorff, and others to argue that they are evidence of Chaucer's authorship of this part of the text; but the ideas themselves are commonplace. **2198 deme,** judge. **2202 Or of,** rather than by (before by). **2204 to holden styll,** should be kept quiet. **2206 Key,** Sir Kay, the type of rudeness in Arthurian romance, as Sir Gawain was the type of courtesy. **2211 fell,** fierce. **2215–16** *mare/are,* again a northern rhyme. G *more.* **2218 salue,** greet. **2220 domme,** dumb. **2221 quyte,** repay.

To vilayne speche in no degre 2225
Late never thy lyppe unbounden be;
For I nought holde him, in good faythe,
Curteys that foule wordes saythe.

"And al women serve and preyse,
And to thy power her honour reyse. 2230
And if that any missayere
Dispyse women, that thou mayste here,
Blame him, and bydde him holde him styll.
And sette thy might and al thy wyll
Women and ladyes for to plese, 2235
And to do thyng that may hem ese,
That they ever speke good of the;
For so thou mayste best praysed be. AVOID

"Loke fro pride thou kepe the wele; PRIDE
For thou mayste bothe parceyve and fele 2240
That pride is bothe foly and synne;
And he that pride hath him within,
Ne may his herte in no wyse
Meken ne souplen to servyce,
For pride is founde in every parte 2245
Contrarye unto loves arte.

"And he that loveth trewly
Shulde him conteyne jolyly,
Without pride, in sondrie wyse,
And him disgysen in queyntyse. 2250
For queynte aray, without drede,
Is nothyng proude, who taketh hede;
For fresshe aray, as men may se,
Without pride may ofte be.
Mayntayne thyselfe after thy rent 2255
Of robe and eke of garnement;
For many sythe fayre clothyng
A man amendeth in moche thyng.
And loke alwaye that they be shape—
What garnement that thou shalte make— 2260
Of him that can best do
With al that parteyneth therto.
Poyntes and sleves be wel syttande,
Right and streight on the hande.
Of shone and bootes, newe and fayre, 2265

Loke at the leest thou have a payre,
And that they sytte so fetously,
That these rude may utterly
Mervayle, sythe that they sytte so playne,
Howe they come on or of agayne. 2270
Weare strayte gloves, with aumenere
Of sylke; and alway with good chere
Thou yeve, if thou have rychesse;
And if thou have naught, spende the lesse.
Alway be mery, if thou may, 2275
But waste not thy good alway.
Have hatte of floures as fresshe as May,
Chapelet of roses of Whitsonday;
For suche araye ne costneth but lyte.
Thyne hondes wasshe, thy tethe make white, 2280
And lette no fylthe upon the be.
Thy nayles blacke if thou mayst se,
Voyde it away delyverly.
And kembe thyne heed right jolyly.
Farce nat thy visage in no wyse, 2285
For that of love is nat th'emprise,
For love dothe haten, as I fynde,
A beaute that cometh nat of BE GRACIOUS
Kynde. AND MERRY

"Alwaye in hert I rede the
Gladde and mery for to be, 2290
And be as joyful as thou canne;
Love hath no joye of sorouful manne.
That yvel is ful of curtesy
That laugheth in his malady.
For ever of love the sicknesse 2295
Is meynte with swete and bytternesse.
The sore of love is mervaylous,
For now the lover is joyous,
Nowe can he playne, nowe can he grone,
Now can he syngen, nowe maken mone; 2300
Today he playneth for hevynesse,
Tomorowe he pleyeth for jolynesse.
The lyfe of love is ful contrarye,
Whiche stoundemeale can ofte varye.
But if thou canste myrthes make, 2305

2230 to thy power, according to your power. **2244 souplen,** bend (make supple). **2248 him conteyne,** bear himself. **2255 rent,** income. **2257 sythe,** times. **2263 Poyntes . . . syttande,** laced closures, fitting (northern form). **2267 fetously,** neatly. **2270 on:** T *an.* **2271 strayte . . . aumenere,** tight, purse. TG *au(w)mere.* **2283 delyverly,** quickly (nimbly). **2285 Farce,** paint (?). The word means "stuff"; Skeat suggests it is a miswriting for Fr. *farde,* to paint the face. **2286 emprise,** style. **2289 rede,** advise. **2293 That yvel,** that sick person. **2294 laugheth:** TG *knoweth;* Fr. *rit.* **2296 meynte,** mixed. **2297 sore,** soreness. Fr. *mal d'amer.* **2298 TG is om. 2302 TG playneth. 2304 stoundemeale,** from time to time.

That men in gre wol gladly take,
Do it goodly, I commaunde the.
For men shulde, wheresoever they be,
Do thynge that hem best syttyng is,
For therof cometh good loos and pris.　　2310
Wherof that thou be vertuous,
Ne be not straunge ne daungerous.
For if that thou good ryder be,
Pricke gladly, that men may se.
In armes also if thou conne,　　2315
Pursue tyl thou a name hast wonne.
And if thy voyce be fayre and clere,
Thou shalt maken no great daungere
Whan to synge they goodly pray;
It is thy worshyp for to obey.　　2320
Also to you it longeth aye
To harpe and gyterne, daunce and playe;
For if he can wel flute and daunce,
It may him greatly do avaunce.
Amonge eke for thy lady sake　　2325
Songes and complayntes that thou make,
For that wol meven in her herte
Whan they reden of thy smerte.

　　"Loke that no man for scarce　　AVOID
　　　the holde,　　MISERLINESS
For that may greve the many folde;　　2330
Reson wol that a lover be
In his yeftes more large and fre
Than chorles that ben not of lovyng.
For who thereof can anythyng,
He shal be lefe aye for to yeve—　　2335
In Loves lore whoso wolde leve.
For he that through a sodayne syght,
Or for a kyssyng anon ryght
Yave hole his herte in wyl and thought,
And to hymselfe kepeth right nought,　　2340
After so riche gift it is good reson
He yeve his good in abandon.
　　"Nowe wol I shortly here reherce

Of that I have sayd in verce,
Al the sentence by and by,　　2345
In wordes fewe compendously,
That thou the better mayste on hem thynke,
Whether so it be thou wake or wynke;
For the wordes lytel greve
A man to kepe whan it is breve.　　2350
Whoso with Love wol gon or ryde,
He mote be curteyes and voyde of pride,
Mery and ful of jolyte,
And of largesse alosed be.
　　"First I joyne the here in penaunce　　2355
That ever without　　RECAPITULATION
　　repentaunce,　　OF LOVE'S
Thou set thy thought in thy　　COMMANDS
　　lovyng,
To laste without repentyng;
And thinke upon thy myrthes swete
That shal folowe after whan ye mete.　　2360
　　"And for thou trewe to love shalt be,
I wyl and commaunde the
That in one place thou set, al hole,
Thyn herte, without halfen dole,
For trecherye and sykernesse;　　2365
For I loved never doublenesse.
To many his herte that wol departe,
Everyche shal have but lytel parte;
But of him drede I me right nought
That in one place setteth his thought.　　2370
Therfore in o place it sette,
And lette it never thens flette.
For if thou yevest it in lenyng,
I holde it but a wretched thyng.
Therfore yeve it hole and quyte,　　2375
And thou shalte have the more meryte.
If it be lent, than after soone
The bounte and the thanke is done;
But in love free yeven thyng
Requyreth a great guerdonyng.　　2380

2306 **in gre,** in good spirit. 2309 **best syttyng,** most suitable. TG *best* om.; Fr. *mieuz.* 2310 **loos . . . pris,** praise, reward. 2311 **vertuous,** skillful. 2312 **straunge . . . daungerous,** distant, aloof. 2318 G *no* om. 2320 **worshyp,** honor. 2322 **gyterne,** play the guitar. 2323 **flute:** TG *flote;* Fr. *flauter.* 2325 **Amonge,** from time to time. 2328 **they reden,** they inform. 2329 **scarce,** niggardly. 2334 **can,** knows. 2335 **lefe,** happy. 2336 *Loves:* TG *londes;* Fr. *d'amour.* 2338 **anon ryght,** at once. 2341 TG *After this swifte it is;* F *Après si riche don.* 2354 **alosed,** praised. 2355 G *that heere.* 2364 **halfen dole,** half portions (halfheartedness). 2365 **For trecherye,** i.e., divided between treachery and faithfulness (**sykernesse**). Fr. *ton cuer mis, | Si qui ne soit mie demis, | Mes tout entiers, sanz tricherie.* 2372 **flette,** flit (move). 2373 **lenyng,** lending. 2380 **guerdonyng,** rewarding.

Yeve it in yefte al quyte fully,
And make thy gifte debonairly;
For men that yefte holde more dere
That yeven is with gladsome chere;
That gifte nought to praysen is   2385
That man yeveth maugre his.
  "Whan thou hast yeven thyne hert, as I
Have sayde the here openly,
Than aventures shul the fal,
Whiche harde and hevy ben withal.   2390
For ofte whan thou bethynkest the
Of thy lovyng, whereso thou be,
Fro folke thou must departe in hye,
That none perceyve thy malady;
But hyde thyne harme thou must alone,   2395
And go forthe sole, and make thy mone.
Thou shalte no whyle be in o state,
But whylom colde and whilom hate,
Nowe reed as rose, nowe yelowe and fade;
Such sorowe, I trowe, thou never hade;   2400
Cotidien ne quarteyne,
It is nat so ful of peyne.
For often tymes it shal fal
In love, among thy paynes al,
That thou thyselfe, al holy,   2405
Foryeten shalte so utterly,
That many tymes thou shalte be
Styl as an ymage of tree,
Domme as a stone, without steryng
Of fote or honde, without spekyng.   2410
Than, soone after al thy payne,
To memorye shalte thou come agayne,
As man abasshed wonder sore,
And after syghen more and more.
For wytte thou wele, withouten wene,   2415
In suche astate ful ofte have bene
That have the yvel of love assayde,
Wherthrough thou arte so dismayde.
  "After, a thought shal take   MISERY OF
      the so   ABSENCE
That thy love is to ferre the fro,   2420
Thou shalte saye, 'God, what may this be,

That I ne maye my lady se?
Myne herte alone is to her go,
And I abyde al sole in wo,
Departed fro myne owne thought,   2425
And with myne eyen se right nought.
Alas, myne eyen sende I ne may,
My careful hert to convay!
Myne hertes gyde but they be,
I prayse nothyng whatever they se.   2430
Shul they abyde than? Nay,
But gone and visyten without delay
That myne herte desyreth so.
For certainly, but if they go,
A foole myselfe I maye wel holde,   2435
Whan I ne se what myne hert wolde.
Wherfore I wol gone her to sene,
Or eased shal I never bene
But I have some tokenyng.'
  "Than gost thou forthe without dwellyng;
But ofte thou faylest of thy desyre,   2441
Er thou mayst come her any nere,
And wastest in vayne thy passage.
Than fallest thou in a newe rage;
For want of syght thou gynnest murne,   2445
And homwarde pensyfe thou dost returne.
In great myschefe than shalte thou be,
For than agayne shal come to the
Sighes and playntes, with newe wo,
That no itchyng pricketh so.   2450
Who wote it nought, he maye go lere
Of hem that byen love so dere.
Nothynge thyne herte appesen maye
That ofte thou wolte gone and assaye
If thou mayst sene, by aventure,   2455
Thy lyves joye, thyne hertes cure;
So that by grace if thou myght
Attayne of her to have a syght,
Than shalte thou done none other dede
But with that syght thyne eyen fede.   2460
That fayre fresshe whan thou mayst se,
Thyne hert shal so ravysshed be,
That never thou woldest, thy thankes, lete

2386 **maugre his,** in spite of himself. 2395–2442 Leaf missing in G. 2392 **whereso,** wherever. 2393 **hye,** haste. 2398 **whilom . . . hate,** sometimes, hot (northern form). 2401 **Cotidien . . . quarteyne,** daily fever, every fourth day fever. 2413 **abasshed,** dazed. **As:** T *A*; Fr. *Ausi.* 2415 **wene,** doubt. 2427 **sende:** T *sene*; Fr. *envoier.* 2436 **wolde,** desires. 2439 **But,** unless. 2442 **nere,** nearer. 2451 **wote . . . lere,** knows, learn. 2452 **byen . . . dere,** i.e., pay so much for. 2463 **thy thankes,** willingly.

Ne remove for to se that swete.
The more thou seest in sothfastnesse,　　　2465
The more thou covytest of that swetnesse;
The more thyn herte brenneth in fyre,
The more thyn herte is in desyre.
For who consydreth every dele,
It may be lykened wonder wele,　　　2470
The payne of love, unto a fere.
For evermore thou neyghest nere
That, or whoso that it be,
For very soth I tel it the,
The hotter ever shal thou brenne,　　　2475
As experyence shal the kenne.
Whereso comest in any coste
Who is next fyre, he brenneth moste.
　　"And yet forsothe, for al thyn hete,
Though thou for love swelte and swete,　　　2480
Ne for nothyng thou felen may,
Thou shalt not wyllen to passe away.
And though thou go, yet muste the nede
Thynke al day on her fayre hede,
Whom thou behelde with so good wyll,　　　2485
And holde thyselfe begyled yll
That thou ne haddest none hardyment
To shewe her aught of thyn entent.
Thyn herte ful sore thou wolte dispyse,
And eke repreve of cowardyse,　　　2490
That thou, so dull in everythyng,
Were domme for drede, without spekyng.
Thou shalt eke thynke thou dyddest folye
That thou were her so faste bye,
And durste not auntre the to say　　　2495
Somethyng er thou came away.
For thou haddest no more wonne,
To speke of her whan thou begonne,
But yif she wolde, for thy sake,
In armes goodly the have take—　　　2500
It shulde have be more worthe to the
Than of tresour great plente.
　　"Thus shalte thou morne and eke complayne,
And get encheson to gon agayne
Unto thy walke, or to thy place,　　　2505

Where thou behelde her flesshly face.
And never, for false suspection,
Thou woldest fynde occasyon
For to gone unto her house.
So arte thou than desyrouse　　　2510
A syght of her for to have,
If thou thyn honour myghtest save,
Or any erande mightest make
Thyder for thy loves sake;
Ful fayne thou woldest, but for drede　　　2515
Thou goest not, leest that men take hede.
Wherfore I rede in thy goynge,
And also in thyn agayne-commynge,
Thou be wel ware that men ne wyt.
Feyne the other cause than it　　　2520
To go that waye, or faste bye;
To heale wel is no folye.
　　"And if so be it happe the　　　LOVE'S
That thou thy love there mayste se,　　　TORMENTS
In syker wyse thou her salewe,　　　2525
Wherwith thy coloure wol transmewe,
And eke thy bloode shal al to-quake,
Thy hewe eke chaungen for her sake.
But worde and wytte, with chere ful pale,
Shul wante for to tel thy tale;　　　2530
And if thou mayste so fer forthe wynne,
That thou reson durste begynne,
And woldest sayne thre thynges or mo,
Thou shalte ful scarsly sayne the two.
Though thou bethynke the never so wele,　　　2535
Thou shalt foryete yet somdele,
But if thou deale with trecherye.
For false lovers mowe al folye
Sayne, what hem luste, withouten drede;
They be so double in her falshede,　　　2540
For they in herte can thynke o thynge
And sayne another in her spekynge.
　　"And whan thy speche is ended all,
Right thus to the it shal befall,
If any worde than come to mynde,　　　2545
That thou to saye haste lefte behynde,
Than thou shalt brenne in great martyre,

2472 **neyghest nere**, draw nearer. 2473 *That, or:* TG *Thought or.* 2478 **next**, nearest to. 2480 **swelte**, languish (die). 2482 **passe away**, i.e., go from her presence. 2490 **repreve**, reprove (scold). 2495 **auntre**, (ad)venture. 2499 **But yif**, unless. TG *yet;* Fr. *si.* 2504 **encheson**, occasion (excuse). 2517 **rede**, advise. 2519 **wyt**, know. 2521 **faste**, near. 2525 **syker**, secure (i.e., secret). 2537 **But if . . . deale**, unless, deal (with her). 2538 **mowe**, can. 2547 **martyre**, martyrdom.

For thou shalt brenne as any fyre.
This is the stryfe and eke the affraye,
And the batell that lasteth aye. 2550
This batell ende may never take
But if that she thy peace wyl make.
  "And whan the nyght is comen anon,
A thousande angres shal come upon.
To bedde as faste thou wolte the dyght, 2555
Where thou shalt have but smal delyght.
For whan thou wenest for to slepe,
So ful of payne shalt thou crepe,
Sterte in thy bedde aboute ful wyde,
And turne ful ofte on every syde, 2560
Nowe downwarde groffe, and nowe upright,
And walowe in wo the longe nyght;
Thyn armes shalt thou sprede abrede
As man in werre were forwerede.
Than shal the come a remembraunce 2565
Of her shappe and her semblaunce,
Wherto non other may be pere.
And wete thou wel, without were,
That the shal seme, somtyme that nyght,
That thou haste her that is so bright 2570
Naked bytwene thyn armes there,
Al sothfastnesse as though it were.
Thou shalte make castels than in Spayne,
And dreme of joy, al but in vayne,
And the delyten of right nought, 2575
Whyle thou so slombrest in that thought
That is so swete and delytable,
The whiche, in sothe, nys but a fable,
For it ne shal no whyle laste.
Than shalte thou syghe and wepe faste, 2580
And say, 'Dere God, what thyng is this?
My dreme is turned al amys,
Which was ful swete and apparent,
But nowe I wake; it is al shent!
Nowe yede this mery thought away. 2585
Twenty tymes upon a day
I wolde this thought wolde come agayne,

For it alegeth wel my payne;
It maketh me ful of joyfull thought;
It sleeth me that it lasteth nought. 2590
Ah, Lorde, why nyl ye me socoure,
The joye, I trowe, that I langoure?
The dethe I wolde me shulde slo
Whyle I lye in her armes two.
Myne harme is harde, withouten wene; 2595
My great unease ful ofte I mene.
But wolde Love do so I might
Have fully joye of her so bright,
My payne were quytte me rychely.
Alas, to great a thyng aske I! 2600
It is but foly and wronge wenyng
To aske so outragyous a thyng.
And whoso asketh folily,
He mote be warned hastely.
And I ne wote what I may say, 2605
I am so ferre out of the way.
For I wolde have ful great lykyng
And ful great joy of lasse thyng:
For wolde she, of her gentylnesse,
Withouten more, me ones kesse, 2610
It were to me a great guerdon,
Relece of al my passyon.
But it is harde to come therto;
Al is but foly that I do,
So hygh I have myn herte sette, 2615
Where I may no comforte gette.
I not where I say wel or nought.
But this I wote wel in my thought,
That it were better of her alone,
For to stynte my wo and mone, 2620
A loke of her ycaste goodly,
Than for to have al utterly
Of another al hole the play.
Ah, Lorde, where I shal byde the day
That ever she shal my lady be? 2625
He is ful cured that may her se.
A, God, whan shal the dawnyng spring?

2551 *batell*: TG *barga(e)yne*; Fr. *guerre*. 2554 **angres**, vexations (angers). 2563 **abrede**, abroad. 2564 **forwerede**, defeated ("battled out"). 2568 **were**, doubt. 2569 *seme*: TG *se*; Fr. *avis*. 2573 **castels in Spayne**, the still-familiar proverbial metaphor. 2574 *in*: T *at*. 2578 G *a* om. 2584 **shent**, destroyed. 2585 **yede**, goes. 2588 **alegeth**, alleviates. 2591 **socoure**, assist me (to attain). 2592 **langoure**, languish for. 2596 **unease . . . mene**, misfortune, bemoan. 2599 **quytte**, repaid. 2601 **wenyng**, imagining. 2610 **kesse**, kiss (Kentish form). 2611 **guerdon**, reward. 2617 **not**, don't know (*ne wot*). TG *wote not*. 2619 **her alone**, i.e., from her only. 2621 TG *A loke on her I caste*; Fr. *de li uns regarz*. 2622 *Than*: TG *That*. 2624 **where . . . byde**, i.e., how, await.

To lyggen thus is an angry thyng;
I have no joy thus here to lye
Whan that my love is not me bye.   2630
A man to lyen hath great disese,
Whiche may not slepe ne rest in ese.
I wolde it dawed, and were nowe day,
And that the nyght were went away;
For were it day, I wolde upryse.   2635
Ah, slowe sonne, shewe thyne enprise!
Spede the to sprede thy beemes bright,
And chace the derknesse of the nyght
To put away the stoundes stronge
Whiche in me lasten al to longe.'   2640
    "The nyght shalt thou contynue so,
Without rest, in payne and wo.
If ever thou knewe of love distresse,
Thou shal mowe lerne in that sicknesse.
And thus enduryng shalt thou lye,   2645
And ryse on morowe up erly
Out of thy bedde, and harneys the
Er ever dawnyng thou mayst se.
Al prively than shalt thou gone,
What weder it be, thyselfe alone,   2650
For reyne or hayle, for snowe, for slete,
Thyder she dwelleth that is so swete—
The whiche may fall aslepe be,
And thynketh but lytel upon the.
Than shalt thou go ful foule aferde;   2655
Loke if the gate be unsperde,
And wayte without in wo and payne,
Ful yvel acolde in wynde and rayne.
Than shalt thou go the dore before;
If thou mayste fynde any score,   2660
Or hole, or refte, whatever it were,
Than shalte thou stoupe and lay to eere,
If they within aslepe be—
I mene al save thy lady free,
Whom wakyng if thou mayst aspye,   2665
Go put thyselfe in jupardye

To aske grace, and the bymene,
That she may wete, without wene,
That thou anyght no rest hast had,
So sore for her thou were bestad.   2670
Women wel ought pyte to take
Of hem that sorowen for her sake.
    "And loke, for love of that relyke,
That thou thynke none other lyke,
For whom thou haste so great annoy,   2675
Shal kysse the er thou go awey;
And holde that in ful great deynte,
And, for that no man shal the se
Before the house, ne in the way,
Loke thou be gon agayne er day.   2680
Suche commyng, and suche goyng,
Suche hevynesse, and suche wakyng,
Maketh lovers, withouten any wene,
Under her clothes pale and lene.
For love leveth colour ne cleernesse;   2685
Who loveth trewe hath no fatnesse.   DISMAL
Thou shalte wel by thyselfe se   EFFECTS
That thou must nedes assayed be.   OF LOVE
For men that shape hem other way
Falsely her ladyes for to betray,   2690
It is no wonder though they be fatte;
With false othes her loves they gatte;
For ofte I se suche losengeours
Fatter than abottes or priours.
    "Yet with o thynge I the charge,   2695
That is to saye, that thou be large
Unto the mayde that her dothe serve,
So best her thanke thou shalt deserve;
Yeve her yeftes, and get her grace,
For so thou may thanke purchace,   2700
That she the worthy holde and fre,
Thy lady, and al that may the se.
Also her servauntes worshyp aye,
And please as moche as thou may.
Great good through hem may come to the   2705

2633 **dawed,** dawned. 2636 **enprise,** enterprise. 2639 **stoundes,** hours. 2641 *contynue:* G *contene.* 2644 **mowe,** be able. 2647 **harneys,** dress. 2650 *weder:* TG *whyder.* 2655 **foule aferde,** shamefully afraid. 2656 **unsperde,** unbarred. 2660 **score,** crack. T *shore.* 2667 **bymene,** complain. 2668 **wete,** know. 2669 *anyght:* TG *nyght.* 2673 **relyke,** treasure (relic). 2675 *whom:* TG *whan(ne);* Fr. *De qui.* 2676 Kaluza suggested *Thou kisse the dore er;* Fr. *la porte bese.* 2677 **deynte,** dainty (i.e., privilege). 2682 **hevynesse,** sadness. *wakyng:* TG *walkyng.* 2683 **wene,** doubt. 2685 **cleernesse,** brightness (of face). 2689 **shape hem,** plan. 2692 **gatte,** obtained (got). 2693 **losengeours,** liars. 2696 **large,** generous. This advice is straight from Ovid, *Ars Amatoria,* as is much of the other material in this part of the poem. 2701 **fre,** generous. 2703 **worshyp,** honor.

Bycause with her they ben prive;
They shal her tel howe they the fande
Curteys and wyse and wel doande,
And she shal preyse wel the more.
Loke out of londe thou be not fore; 2710
And if suche cause thou have, that the
Behoveth to gone out of countre,
Leave hole thyn herte in hostage,
Tyl thou agayne make thy passage.
Thynke longe to se the swete thyng 2715
That hath thyn herte in her kepyng.
Nowe have I tolde the in what wise
A lover shal do me servyce.
Do it than, if thou wolte have
The mede that thou after crave." 2720

   Whan Love al this had   END OF LOVE'S
     boden me,   COMMANDMENTS
I sayd him: "Sir, howe may it be
That lovers may in suche manere
Endure the payn ye have said here?
I mervayle me wonder faste 2725
Howe any man may lyve or laste
In suche payne and suche brennyng,
In sorowe and thought and suche sighyng,
Aye unrelesed wo to make,
Whether so it be they slepe or wake, 2730
In suche anoy contynuelly.
As helpe me God, this mervayle I
Howe man, but he were made of stele,
Might lyve a monthe suche paynes to fele."

   The God of Love than sayd me: 2735
"Frende, by the faythe I owe to the,
May no man have good, but he   LOVE
    it bye.   CONTINUES
A man loveth more tenderlye
The thyng that he hath bought most dere.
For wete thou wel, without were, 2740
In thanke that thynge is taken more
For whiche a man hath suffred sore.   VIRTUES
Certes, no wo ne may attayne   OF HOPE
Unto the sore of loves payne;
None yvel therto ne may amounte, 2745

No more than a man may counte
The droppes that of the water be.
For drie as wel the great see
Thou myghtest as the harmes tell
Of hem that with Love dwell 2750
In servyce, for peyne hem sleeth.
And yet eche man wolde flye the dethe,
And trowe they shulde never escape,
Nere that Hoope couth hem make
Gladde as man in prison sete, 2755
And maye nat getten for to ete
But barlye breed and water pure,
And lyeth in vermyn and in ordure;
With al this, yet canne he lyve,
Good Hope suche comforte hath hym
    yeve, 2760
Whiche maketh wene that he shal be
Delyvered and come to lyberte;
In fortune is his ful trust.
Though he lye in strawe or dust,
In Hoope is al his systaynyng. 2765
And so for lovers, in her wenyng,
Whiche Love hath shytte in his prisoun,
Good Hope is her salvatioun.
Good Hope, howe sore that they smerte,
Yeveth hem bothe wyl and herte 2770
To profer her body to martyre;
For Hope so sore dothe hem desyre
To suffre eche harm that men devyse
For joye that afterwarde shal aryse.
Hoope in desyre catcheth victorie. 2775
In Hoope, of love is al the glorie,
For Hoope is al that love maye yeve;
Nere Hoope, there shulde no lover lyve.
Blessed be Hoope, whiche with desyre
Avaunceth lovers in suche manyre! 2780
Good Hope is curteyse for to please,
To kepe lovers from al disease.
Hoope kepeth his bonde, and wol abyde
For any peryll that may betyde;
For Hoope to lovers, as most chefe, 2785
Dother hem endure al myschefe.

2709–10 TG *more/fore*, probably originally northern *mare/fare*; cf. 2707–08 northern *fande/doande*. 2713 **hole**, wholly. 2715 **Thynke longe**, i.e., it will seem long. 2720 **mede**, reward. 2721 **boden**, commanded. 2740 **were**, doubt. 2744 **sore**, soreness. 2746 TG *may* om. 2752 **flye**, fly (flee from). *yet*: TG *that*. 2753 **trowe**, believe. 2761 **wene**, think. 2763 TG *his* om. 2772 **dothe**, makes. 2775 TG *catche*. 2778 **lover**: T *longer*; Fr. *amanz*. 2783 **bonde**: TG *londe*.

Hoope is her helpe, whan myster is.   LOVE's

"And I shal yeve the eke, ywis,   THREE

Thre other thynges that great solace   GIFTS

Dothe to hem that be in my lace.   2790

"The first good that maye be founde

To hem that in my lace be bounde

Is Swete-Thought, for to recorde   SWEET-

Thyng wherwith thou canst accorde   THOUGHT

Best in thyne herte where she be;   2795

Thynkyng in absence is good to the.

Whan any lover dothe complayne,

And lyveth in distresse and in payne,

Than Swete-Thought shal come as blyve

Awaye his angre for to dryve.   2800

It maketh lovers to have remembraunce

Of comforte, and of highe plesaunce,

That Hoope hath hight hym for to wynne.

For Thought anone than shal begynne,

As ferre, God wotte, as he can fynde,   2805

To make a myrrour of his mynde;

For to beholde he wol nat lette.

Her persone he shal afore hym sette,

Her laughyng eyen, persaunt and clere,

Her shappe, her forme, her goodly chere,   2810

Her mouthe that is so gratious,

So swete, and eke so saverous.

Of al her feyters he shal take hede,

His eyen with al her lymmes fede.

Thus Swete-Thynkyng shal aswage   2815

The payne of lovers and her rage.

The joye shal double, without gesse,

Whan thou thynkest on her semelynesse,

Or of her laughyng, or of her chere,

That to the made thy lady dere.   2820

This comforte wol I that thou take;

And if the nexte thou wolte forsake

Whiche is nat lesse saverous,

Thou shuldest ben to daungerous.   SWEET-

"The seconde shal be Swete-Speche,   SPEECH

That hath to many one be leche,   2826

To bringe hem out of wo and were,

And helpe many a bachelere.

And many a lady sent socour,

That have loved paramour,   2830

Through spekyng whan they might here

Of her lovers, to hem so dere.

To hem it voydeth al her smerte,

The whiche is closed in her herte.

In herte it maketh hem glad and lyght,   2835

Speche, when they ne mowe have syght.

And therfore nowe it cometh to mynde,

In olde dawes, as I fynde,

That clerkes writen that her knewe

There was a lady fresshe of hewe,   2840

Whiche of her love made a songe

On him for to remembre amonge,

In whiche she sayd, 'Whan that I here

Speken of him that is so dere,

To me it voydeth al smerte,   2845

Iwys, he sytteth so nere myn herte.

To speke of hem at eve or morowe,

It cureth me of al my sorowe.

To me is none so hygh plesaunce

As of his person dalyaunce.'   2850

She wyste ful wel that Swete-Spekyng

Comforteth in ful moche thyng.

Her love she had ful wel assayde;

Of him she was ful wel apayde;

To speke of him her joye was set.   2855

"Therfore I rede the that thou get

A felowe that can wel concele

And kepe thy counsayle, and wel hele,

To whom go shewe holly thyn herte,

Bothe wel and wo, joye and smerte;   2860

To gette comforte to him thou go,

And prively, bytwene you two,

Ye shal speke of that goodly thyng

That hath thyn herte in her kepyng,

Of her beaute and her semblaunce,   2865

And of her goodly countenaunce.

Of al thy state thou shalt him say,

And aske him counsayle howe thou may

2787 **myster,** (love) service. 2790 **lace,** net. 2793 **Swete-Thought,** Fr. *Douz Penser.* 2799 **blyve,** quickly. 2803 **hight,** promised. 2807 **lette,** stop (hesitate). 2809 **persaunt,** piercing. 2813 **feyters,** features. 2822–24 **And if the nexte . . . daungerous,** i.e., and if you don't accept the next comfort (also), which is no less pleasing, you are too disdainful. 2824 TG *nat ben.* 2825 **Swete-Speche,** Fr. *Douz Parlers.* 2826 **leche,** physician. 2827 **were,** doubt. 2830 **paramour,** sexual love. 2833 **hem:** TG *me.* 2836 **mowe,** may. TG *ne* om. 2842 **amonge,** constantly. In the Fr. ll. 2843–50 appear to be the words of a song. 2850 **dalyaunce,** small talk. 2856 **rede,** advise. 2857 **felowe,** companion. 2858 **hele,** hide.

Do anythyng that may her plese.
For it to the shal do great ese, 2870
That he may wete thou truste him so,
Bothe of thy wele and of thy wo.
And if his herte to love be sette,
His companye is moche the bette;
For reson wol he shewe to the 2875
Al utterly his privyte;
And what she is he loveth so
To the playnly he shal undo,
Without drede of any shame
Bothe tel her renoune and her name. 2880
Than shal he forther, ferre and nere,
And namely to thy lady dere,
In syker wyse. Ye, every other
Shal helpen as his owne brother,
In trouthe without doublenesse, 2885
And kepen close in sykernesse.
For it is noble thyng, in fay,
To have a man thou darste say
Thy prive counsayle every dele;
For that wol comforte the right wele; 2890
And thou shalt holde the wel apayed,
Whan suche a frende thou haste assayed.
    "The thirde good of great comforte
That yeveth to lovers moste disporte
Cometh of syght and beholdyng, 2895
That cleped is Swete-Lokyng, SWETE-
The whiche may none ese do LOOKING
Whan thou arte ferre thy lady fro;
Wherfore thou prese alway to be
In place where thou mayst her se. 2900
For it is thyng moste amerous,
Moste delytable and saverous,
For to aswage a mannes sorowe
To sene his lady by the morowe,
For it is a ful noble thyng 2905
Whan thyn eyen have metyng
With that relyke precious,
Whereof they be so desyrous.
But al day after, sothe it is,

They have no drede to faren amys. 2910
They dreden neyther wynde ne rayne,
Ne non other maner payne.
For whan thyn eyen were thus in blysse,
Yet of her curtesye, ywysse,
Alone they can not have her joye, 2915
But to the herte they it convoye;
Parte of her blysse to him they sende
Of al this harme to make an ende.
The eye is a good messangere,
Whiche can to the herte in suche manere 2920
Tydynges sende that he hath sene,
To voyde him of his paynes clene.
Whereof the herte rejoyseth so
That a great partye of his wo
Is voyded and put away to flyght. 2925
Right as the derknesse of the nyght
Is chased with clerenesse of the moone,
Right so is al his wo ful soone
Devoyded clene, whan that the syght
Beholden may that fresshe wight 2930
That the herte desyreth so,
That al his derknesse is ago;
For than the herte is al at ese,
Whan the eyen sene that may hem plese.
    "Nowe have I declared the al out 2935
Of that thou were in drede and doute;
For I have tolde the faythfully
What the may curen utterly,
And al lovers that wol be
Faythful, and ful of stabylite. 2940
Good-Hope alwaye kepe by thy syde,
And Swete-Thought; make eke abyde
Swete-Lokynge and Swete-Speche—
Of al thyne harmes they shal be leche,
Of every thou shalte have great plesaunce. 2945
If thou canst byde in sufferaunce,
And serve wel without fayntise,
Thou shalte be quyte of thyne emprise
With more guerdoun, if that thou lyve;
But at this tyme this I the yeve." 2950

2871 **wete,** understand. 2875 **For reson,** i.e., reasonably (in return for your confidence). 2881 **he forther,** he goes farther (in your behalf). 2882 **namely,** especially. 2883 **syker ... every other,** secret (secure), each of you the other. 2885 **doublenesse,** deceit. 2891 **apayed,** repaid. 2896 **Swete-Lokyng,** Fr. *Douz Regart.* 2916 TG *it* om. 2917 *they:* TG *thou.* 2921 TG *he* om.; Fr. *il.* 2922 **clene,** completely. 2927 **clerenesse,** brightness. 2934 *the eyen:* TG *they sene;* Fr. *li oeill.* 2947 **fayntise,** growing faint. 2948 **quyte ... emprise,** repaid, effort. 2949 **guerdoun,** reward. 2950 *at:* TG *al;* Fr. *des ia (déjà).*

The God of Love whan al the day   LOVE
Had taught me, as ye have herd say,   DEPARTS
And enformed compendously,
He vanysshed awaye al sodainly,
And I alone lefte, al soole,   2955
So ful of complaynt and of doole,
For I sawe no man there me by.
My woundes me greved wondersly;
Me for to curen nothyng I knewe,
Save the bothon bright of hewe,   2960
Whereon was sette hooly my thought;
Of other comforte knewe I nought,
But it were through the God of Love.
I knewe nat els to my behove
That myght me ease or conforte gete,   2965
But if he wolde hym entermete.
    The roser was, withouten dout,
Closed with an hedge without,
As ye toforne have herde me sayne;
And fast I besyed, and wolde fayne   2970
Have passed the haye, if I myght
Have getten in by any sleyght
Unto the bothom so fayre to se.
But ever I dradde blamed to be,
If men wolde have suspectioun   2975
That I wolde of ententioun
Have stole the roses that there were;
Therfore to entre I was in fere.
But at the laste, as I bethought
Wheder I shulde passe or nought,   2980
I sawe come with a gladde chere   FAIR-
To me, a lusty bachelere,   WELCOME
Of good stature, and of good height,   APPEARS
And Bialacoil forsoth he height.
Sonne he was to Curtesy,   2985
And he me graunted ful gladly
The passage of the utter hay,
And sayd, "Sir, nowe that ye may
Passe, if your wyl be,
The fresshe roser for to se,   2990

And ye the swete savour fele.
You warrant may I right wele;
So thou the kepe fro folye,
Shal no man do the vylanye.
If I may helpe you in ought,   2995
I shal not fayne, dredeth nought;
For I am bounde to your servyse,
Fully devoyde of feyntyse."
    Than unto Bialacoyl sayd I,
"I thanke you, sir, ful hertely,   3000
And your beheste take at gre,
That ye so goodly profer me;
To you it cometh of great fraunchyse,
That ye me profer your servyse."
Than after, ful delyverly,   3005
Through the breres anon went I,
Whereof encombred was the haye.
I was wel plesed, the sothe to saye,
To se the bothom fayre and swote,
So fresshe spronge out of the rote.   3010
And Bialacoyle me served wele,
Whan I so nyghe me myght fele
Of the bothon the swete odour,
And so lusty hewed of colour.
But than a chorle—foule him betyde—   3015
Besyde the roses gan him hyde,   DANGER
To kepe the roses of that rosere,   LIES
Of whom the name was Daungere.   HIDDEN
This chorle was hyd there in the greves,
Covered with grasse and with leves,   3020
To spye and take whom that he fonde
Unto that roser put an honde.
He was not soole, for there was mo,
For with him were other two
Of wicked maners and yvel fame.   3025
That one was cleped, by his name,
Wicked-Tonge, God yeve him sorowe! WICKED-
For neyther at eve ne at morowe   TONGUE
He can of no man good speke;
On many a juste man dothe he wreke.   3030

2960 bothon, (rose)bud (button). **2963 But,** unless. **2964 behove,** assistance. *els:* T *ele.* **2966 entermete,** intercede. **2970 besyed . . . fayne,** busied (myself), happily. **2971 haye,** the usual form for "hedge" in the B part of *Romaunt;* seldom used elsewhere in *Romaunt* or Chaucer's poems. **2987 utter,** outer. **2988** *nowe:* TG *howe.* **2992 warrant,** protect. GT *Youre warrans may right wele;* Fr. *Je vos i puis bien garentir.* **2993 So thou,** if thou. **2996 fayne,** be false (pretend). **2998 feyntyse,** pretense. **3001 at gre,** with pleasure. **3003 fraunchyse,** generosity. **3005 delyverly,** nimbly. **3007 encombred . . . haye,** equipped, hedge. **3015 betyde,** come to him. **3017 kepe,** guard. **3019 greves,** branches. **3023 soole,** alone (sole). **3027 Wicked-Tonge,** gossip. **3030 wreke,** mistreat (avenge).

There was a woman eke that hyght
Shame, that who can reken ryght.   SHAME
Trespace was her fathers name,
Her mother Reson; and thus was Shame
Brought of these ylke two.   3035
And yet had Trespasse never ado
With Reason, ne never ley her by,
He was so hydous and so ugly—
I meane this that Trespasse hight.
But Reason conceyveth of a sight   3040
Shame, of that I spake aforne.
And whan that Shame was thus borne,
It was ordayned that Chastite
Shulde of the roser lady be,
Whiche of the bothoms more and las,   3045
With sondrie folke assayled was,
That she ne wyste what to do.
For Venus her assayleth so
That nyght and day from her she stal
Bothoms and roses over al.   3050
To Reason than prayeth Chastyte,
Whom Venus hath flemed over the see,
That she her doughter wolde her lene
To kepe the roser fresshe and grene.
Anone Reason to Chastyte   3055
Is fully assented that it be,
And graunted her, at her request,
That Shame, bycause she is honest,
Shal keper of the roser be.
   And thus to kepe it there were thre,   3060
That none shulde hardy be ne bolde—
Were he yonge, or were he olde—
Agayne her wyl awaye to bere
Bothoms ne roses that there were.
I hadde wel spedde had I nat bene   3065
Awayted with these thre and sene.
For Bialacoil, that was so fayre,
So gratious and debonayre,
Quytte hym to me ful curtesly,
And, me to please, badde that I   3070
Shulde drawe me to the bothom nere;

Prese in to touche the rosere
Whiche bare the roses, he yafe me leve;
This graunt ne myght but lytel greve.
And for he sawe it lyked me,   3075
Right nygh the bothom pulled he   THE LOVER
A leafe al grene, and yave me   APPROACHES
   that,   THE ROSE
The whiche ful nyghe the bothom sat.
I made me of that leafe ful queynt,
And whan I felte I was aqueynt   3080
With Bialacoil, and so pryve,
I wende all at my wyl hadde be.
Than wext I hardy for to tel
To Bialocoil howe me befel
Of Love, that toke and wounded me,   3085
And sayd, "Sir, so mote I the,
I maye no joye have in no wyse,
Upon no syde, but it ryse;
For sithe (if I shal nat feyne)
In herte I have had so great peyne,   3090
So great annoye and suche affraye,
That I ne wotte what I shal saye;
I drede your wrathe to deserve.
Lever me were that knyves kerve
My body shulde in peces smal,   3095
Than in any wyse it shulde fal
That ye wrathed shulde ben with me."
   "Saye boldely thy wyl," quod he,
"I nyl be wrothe if that I maye,
For nought that thou shalte to me
   saye."   3100
   Than sayd I, "Sir, not you displease
To knowen of my great unese,
In whiche only Love hath me brought;
For paynes great, disese, and thought
Fro day to day he dothe me drie.   3105
Supposeth not, sir, that I lye.
In me fyve woundes dyd he make,
The sore of whiche shal never slake
But ye the bothom graunt me,
Whiche is moste passaunt of beaute—   3110

3039 **this that . . . hight,** this one that was called. 3044 **lady,** guardian. 3045 **Whiche of,** which because of the buds. 3052 **flemed,** banished. 3054 **kepe,** protect. 3065 **wel spedde,** succeeded well. 3066 **Awayted,** watched. 3069 **Quytte,** behaved. 3075 **lyked,** pleased. 3079 **queynt,** happy (strange). TG *me* om. 3081 **pryve,** intimate. 3082 **wende . . . wyl hadde be,** thought, desire would be fulfilled. 3083 **wext . . . hardy,** grew, bold. 3086 **the,** prosper. 3088 **but it ryse,** i.e., unless I recover. 3091 **affraye,** fear. 3105 **drie,** suffer. 3109 **But,** unless.

My lyfe, my dethe, and my martyre,
And tresour that I most desyre."
    Than Bialacoil, affrayde all,
Sayd, "Sir, it may not fall;
That ye desyre, it may not aryse.   3115
What, wolde ye shende me in this wyse?
A mokel foole than I were,
If I suffred you away to bere
The fresshe bothom, so fayre of syght.
For it were neyther skyll ne right   3120
Of the roser ye broke the rynde,
Or take the rose aforne his kynde.
Ye are not courteys to aske it;
Let it stylle on the roser syt,
And growe tyl it amended be,   3125
And parfetly come to beaute.
I nolde not that it pulled were
Fro the roser that it bere;
To me it is so lefe and dere."
    With that anon sterte out Daungere,   3130
Out of the place where he was hydde.
His malyce in his chere was kydde;   DANGER
Ful great he was the blacke of hewe,   AWAKENS
Sturdy and hydous, whoso him knewe;
Lyke sharpe urchons his heer was growe, 3135
His eyes reed sparclyng as the fyre-glowe;
His nose frounced, ful kyrked stode,
He come cryande as he were woode,
And sayd, "Bialacoyl, tel me why
Thou bringest hyder so boldely   3140
Him that so nyghe is the rosere?
Thou worchest in a wronge manere;
He thynketh to dishonour the.
Thou arte wel worthy to have maugre
To lette hym of the rosere wytte!   3145
Who serveth a felonne is yvel quytte.
Thou woldest have done great bounte,
And he with shame wolde quyte the.
Flye hence, felowe! I rede the go!
It wanteth lytel I wol the slo;   3150

For Bialacoyl ne knewe the nought,
Whan the to serve he sette his thought;
For thou wolte shame him, if thou
        myght,
Bothe agayne reason and right.
I wol no more in the affye,   3155
That comest so slyghly for t'espy;
For it proveth wonder wele,
Thy sleight and trayson every dele."
    I durst no more make there abode,
For the chorle he was so wode;   3160
So ganne he thrette and manace,
And through the haye he dyd me chace.
For feare of him I trymbled and quoke,
For chorlisshly his heed he shoke,
And sayd if efte he myght me take,   3165
I shulde nat from his hondes scape.
Than Bialacoil is fledde and mate,   THE LOVER
And I al soole, disconsolate,   REPULSED
Was lefte alone in payne and thought.
For shame to dethe I was nygh brought.   3170
Than thought I on my highe foly,
Howe that my body utterly
Was yeve to payne and to martyre;
And therto hadde I so great yre
That I ne durst the hayes passe;   3175
There was no hoope, there was no grace.
I trowe never man wyste of payne,
But he were laced in Loves chayne;
Ne no man wot, and sothe it is,
But if he love, what anger is.   3180
Love holdeth his heest to me right wele
Whan payne he sayd I shulde fele.
No herte maye thynke, no tonge sayne,
A quarter of my wo and payne
I myght nat with the angre last;   3185
Myne herte in poynt was for to brast
Whan I thought on the rose that so
Was through Daunger caste me fro.
    A longe whyle stoode I in that state,

3113 **affrayde**, afraid. 3115 **aryse**, happen. 3116 **shende**, destroy. 3117 **mokel**, great. 3120 **skyll**, reasonable. 3121 **rynde**, bark (skin). 3122 **aforne his kynde**, before its natural time (maturity). 3125 **amended**, improved. 3129 **lefe**, dear. 3130 **Daungere**, aloofness (disdain), on the part of the lady. 3132 **kydde**, revealed. 3135 **urchons**, hedgehogs. 3136 Line omitted in G; Fr. *sparclyng* om. 3137 **frounced . . . kyrked**, seamed, crooked. 3138 **cryande . . . woode**, yelling (northern form), crazy. 3141 TG *is* om. 3144 **maugre**, displeasure (Fr. *malgré*). 3145 **wytte**, know. 3146 **quytte**, repaid. 3149 **rede**, advise. 3150 **It wanteth**, i.e., it won't take much. *I*: T *he*; G *it*; Fr. *je*. 3155 **affye**, trust. 3164 *he*: G *it*. 3165 **efte**, again. 3167 **mate**, defeated. 3178 **laced**, secured. 3179 TG *wot* om. 3181 **heest**, promise. 3188 G *That was.*

Tyl that me sawe, so madde and mate, 3190
The lady of the highe warde,
Which from her towre loked thiderwarde.
Reason men clepe that lady,
Whiche from her toure delyverly
Come downe to me without more. 3195
But she was neyther yonge ne hore,
Ne hygh ne lowe, ne fatte ne lene,
But best as it were in a mene.
Her eyen two were clere and lyght
As any candell that brenneth bright, 3200
And on her heed she had a crowne.
Her semed wel an hygh person,
For rounde envyron her crownet
Was ful of ryche stones fret.
Her goodly semblant, by devyse, 3205
I trowe was made in paradyse,
For Nature had never suche a grace
To forge a werke of suche compace.
For certeyne, but if the letter lye,
God himselfe, that is so hye, 3210
Made her after his ymage,
And yafe her sythe suche avauntage
That she hath might and seignorie
To kepe men from al folye.
Whoso wol trowe her lore 3215
Ne may offenden nevermore.
    And whyle I stode thus derke and pale,
Reson began to me her tale.
She sayde: "Al hayle, my swete frende!
Foly and childhode wol the shende, 3220
Whiche the have put in great affray.
Thou haste bought dere the tyme of May
That made thyn herte mery to be.
In yvel tyme thou wentest to se
The gardyn, wherof Ydelnesse 3225
Bare the keye and was maistresse,
Whan thou yedest in the daunce
With her, and had aqueyntaunce.
Her aqueyntaunce is peryllous,

First softe, and after noyous; 3230
She hath the trasshed, without wene.
The God of Love hadde the nat sene,
Ne had Idelnesse the conveyde
In the verger where Myrthe him pleyde.
If folly have supprised the, 3235
Do so that it recovered be,
And be wel ware to take no more
Counsayle that greveth after sore.
He is wyse that wol hymselfe chastyse.
And though a yonge man in any wyse 3240
Trespasse amonge, and do folly,
Lette hym nat tary, but hastely
Lette hym amende what so be mys.
And eke I counsayle the, ywis,
The God of Love holly foryete, 3245
That hath the in suche payne sette,
And the in herte tourmented so.
I can nat sene howe thou maist go
Other wayes to garysoun;
For Daunger, that is so feloun, 3250
Felly purposeth the to werrey,
Whiche is ful cruel, the sothe to sey.
    "And yet of Dangere cometh no blame,
In rewarde of my doughter Shame,
Whiche hath the roses in her warde, 3255
As she that may be no musarde.
And Wicked-Tonge is with these two,
That suffreth no man thyder go;
For er a thynge be do, he shal,
Where that he cometh, over al, 3260
In fourty places, if it be sought,
Say thyng that never was don ne wrought;
So moche trayson is in his male,
Of falsnesse for to sayne a tale.
Thou delest with angry folke, ywis; 3265
Wherfore to the better is
From these folke awaye to fare,
For they wol make the lyve in care.
This is the yvel that love they cal,

3190 mate, dejected. **3191 warde,** watchtower. **3194 delyverly,** quickly. **3198 mene,** i.e., the golden mean. **3205 semblant,** appearance (esp., face). **3215 trowe ... lore,** believe, wisdom. **3217 T** *this.* **3220 shende,** destroy. **3221 affray,** distress. **3222 bought dere,** paid dearly for. **3230 softe ... noyous,** soft (attractive), annoying (repulsive). **3231 trasshed ... wene,** betrayed, doubt. TG *the* om. **3232 hadde ... nat,** would not have. **3234 verger,** orchard. **3238 after sore,** afterward, sorely. **3241 amonge,** from time to time. **3245 holly foryete,** wholly to forget. **3249 garysoun,** protection (garrison). **3251 Felly ... werrey,** cruelly, make war on. **3254 rewarde,** regard. **3256 musarde,** sluggard. **3263 trayson ... male,** falsehood, pouch.

Wherein there is but foly al,   3270
For love is folly everydell.
Who loveth, in no wyse maye do wel,
Ne sette his thought on no good werke;
His schole he leseth, if he be a clerke,
Or other crafte eke if that he be;   3275
He shal nat thryve therin, for he
In love shal have more passyoun
Than monke, hermyte, or chanoun.
This payne is herde, out of measure,
The joye maye eke no whyle endure;   3280
And in the possessyoun
Is moche trybulatioun;
The joye it is so shorte lastynge,
And but in happe is the gettyng;
For I se there many in travayle,   3285
That at laste foule fayle.
I was nothyng thy counsayler,
Whan thou were made the homager
Of God of Love to hastely;
There was no wysdom, but foly.   3290
Thyn herte was joly but not sage
Whan thou were brought in suche a rage
To yelde the so redily,
And to love of his great maystry.
I rede the love away to drive,   3295
That maketh the retche not of thy lyve.
The foly more fro day to day
Shal growe but thou it put away.
Take with thy tethe the bridel faste,
To daunte thyn herte; and eke the caste,   3300
If that thou mayst, to get the defence
For to redresse thy first offence.
Whoso his herte alway wol leve,
Shal fynde amonge that shal him greve."
    Whan I her herde thus me chastyse,   3305   THE
I answerde in ful angry wyse.   LOVER'S
I prayde her cesse of her speche,   REPLY
Eyther to chastyse me or teche,
To bydde me my thought refreyne,

Whiche Love hath caught in his demeyne: 3310
"What, wene ye Love wol consente,
That me assayleth with bowe bente,
To drawe myn herte out of his honde,
Which is so quickly in his bonde?
That ye counsayle may never be;   3315
For whan he first arested me,
He toke myne herte so sore him tyll
That it is nothyng at my wyll.
He taught it so him for to obey
That he it sparred with a key.   3320
I pray you let me be al styll,
For ye may wel, if that ye wyll,
Your wordes waste in ydelnesse;
For utterly, withouten gesse,
Al that ye sayne is but in vayne.   3325
Me were lever dye in the payne,
Than Love to me-warde shulde arette
Falshede, or treson on me sette.
I wol me get pris or blame,
And love trewe, to save my name;   3330
Who that me chastyseth, I him hate."
    With that worde Reson went her gate,
Whan she saw for no sermonyng
She myght me fro my foly bring.
Than dismayed, I lefte al soole,   3335
Forwery, forwandred as a foole,
For I ne knewe no chevysaunce.
Than I fel into my remembraunce
Howe Love bade me to purvey
A felowe to whom I might sey   3340
My counsell and my privyte,
For that shulde moche avayle me.
With that bethought I me that I
Had a felowe fast by,
Trewe and syker, curteys and hende,   3345   THE
And he was called by name a Frende;   FRIEND
A trewer felowe was nowhere non.
In haste to him I went anon,
And to him al my wo I tolde;

3274 schole, education. **3277 passyoun,** suffering. **3284 happe,** i.e., only by chance. **3286 foule,** miserably (foully). **3287 nothyng,** not at all. **3295 rede,** advise. **3296 retche,** care (reck). **3298 but,** unless. **3300 daunte,** defeat. **3303 wol leve,** will allow to leave. **3304 amonge,** from time to time. **3310 demeyne,** power. **3311 wene,** think. **3317 him tyll,** to him. **3319** *taught:* TG *thought.* **3320 sparred,** fastened. **3327 arette,** impute. **3329 pris,** reward (prize). **3332 gate,** way (a northernism). **3336 Forwery, forwandred,** "for" is an intensifier. **3337 chevysaunce,** trading for profit. TG *cherysaunce;* Fr. *chevissance.* **3339 purvey,** provide (seek out). **3345 syker . . . hende,** trusty (secure), competent ("handy").

Fro him right nought I wolde witholde.　3350
I tolde him al without were,
And made my compleynt on Daungere,
Howe for to se he was hydous,
And to me-warde contraryous;
The whiche through his cruelte　3355
Was in poynte to have meymed me,
With Bialacoil whan he me sey
Within the gardyn walke and pley.
Fro me he made him for to go,
And I belefte alone in wo;　3360
I durste no lenger with him speke,
For Daunger says he wolde be wreke,
Whan that he sawe howe I wente
The fresshe bothom for to hente,
If I were hardy to come nere　3365
Bytwene the hay and the rosere.
　This Frende, whan he wyst of my thought,
He discomforted me right nought,
But sayd, "Felowe, be not so madde,
Ne so abasshed nor bestadde.　3370
Myselfe I knowe ful wel Daungere,
And howe he is fiers of his chere
At prime temps love to manace;
Ful ofte I have ben in his case.
A felon first though that he be,　3375
After thou shalt him souple se.
Of longe passed I knew him wele;
Ungoodly first though men him fele,
He wol meke after in his bearynge
Ben, for servyce and obeyssynge.　3380
I shal the tel what thou shalt do:
Mekely I rede thou go him to;
Of herte pray him specially
Of thy trespace to have mercy;
And hote him wel, here to plese,　3385
That thou shalte nevermore him displese.
Who can best serve of flatery
Shal plese Daunger moste utterly."
My Frende hath sayd to me so wele
That he me eased hath somdele,　3390
And eke alegged of my turment;

For through him had I hardement
Agayne to Daunger for to go,
To preve if I might meke him so.
　To Daunger came I al ashamed,　3395
The whiche aforne me had blamed,
Desyring for to pese my wo—
But over hedge durste I not go,
For he forbode me the passage.
I founde him cruel in his rage,　3400
And in his honde a great burdown.
To him I kneled lowe adown,
Ful meke of porte, and symple of chere,
And sayd, "Sir I am comen here
Onely to aske of you mercy.　3405
That greveth me ful greatly
That ever my lyfe I wrathed you.
But for to amenden I am come now,
With al my might, bothe loude and styll,
To done right at your owne wyl;　3410
For Love made me for to do
That I have trespassed hiderto;
Fro whom I ne maye withdrawe myne hert.
Yet shal I never, for joye ne smert,
What so befal, good or il,　3415
Offende more agayne your wyl;
Lever I have endure disease
Than do that shulde you displease.
　"I you requyre and praye that ye
Of me have mercy and pyte,　3420
To stynt your yre that greveth so,
That I wol swere for evermo
To be redressed at your lykyng,
Yf I trespasse in anythyng—
Save that I praye the graunt me　3425
A thynge that maye nat warned be,
That I maye love, al onely;
None other thynge of you aske I.
I shal done al wel, ywis,
Yf of your grace ye graunt me this;　3430
And ye maye nat letten me,
For wel wote ye that love is free,
And I shal loven, sith that I wyl,

3351 **were**, doubt. 3362 **wreke**, avenged. 3370 **abasshed . . . bestadde**, confused, beset. 3372 **chere**, expression. T *his* om. 3373 **prime temps**, first off. 3374 **case**, plight. 3376 **After . . . souple**, later, flexible. 3379 **meke**: G *make*. 3385 **hote**, promise. 3391 **alegged**, allayed. 3392 **hardement**, courage. 3394 **meke**, soften; Fr. *soploier*. 3397 **pese**, appease. 3399 **forbode**, forbade; G *forbede*. 3401 **burdown**, cudgel. 3423 **redressed**, repaid. 3426 **warned**, denied. 3433 **sith**, since. T *suche*; G *sichen*.

Whoever lyke it wel or yl;
And yet ne wolde I, for al Fraunce, 3435
Do thynge to do you displesaunce."
   Than Daungere fyl in his entent
For to foryeve his maletalent;
But al his wrathe yet at last
He hath released, I prayde so fast. 3440
Shortely he sayd, "Thy request
Is nat to mokel dishonest;
Ne I wol nat werne it the,
For yet nothynge engreveth me.
For though thou love thus evermore, 3445
To me is neither softe ne sore.
Love where that the lyst: what retcheth me,
So thou ferre fro my roses be?
Trust nat on me, for none assaye,
If any tyme thou passe the haye." 3450
   Thus hath he graunted my prayere.
Than went I forthe, withouten were,
Unto my Frende, and tolde hym al,
Whiche was right joyful of my tale.
He sayd, "Nowe gothe wel thyne affayre. 3455
He shal to the be debonayre.
Though he aforne was dispitous,
He shal herafter be gratious.
If he were touched on some good veyne,
He shulde yet rewen on thy peyne. 3460
Suffre, I rede, and no boost make,
Tyl thou at good mes mayst him take.
By sufferaunce and wordes softe,
A man maye overcome ofte
Him that aforne he had in drede, 3465
In bokes sothely as I rede."
   Thus hath my Frende with great comforte
Avaunced me with high disporte,
Whiche wolde me good as moche as I.
And than anone ful sodainly 3470
I toke my leave, and streight I went
Unto the haye; for great talent
I hadde to sene the fresshe bothom,

Wherein laye my salvatioun.
And Daungere toke kepe, if that I 3475
Kepe him covenaunt trewly.
So sore I dradde his manasyng,
I durste nat breke his byddyng;
For lest that I were of him shent,
I brake nat his commaundement, 3480
For to purchase his good wyl.
It was hard for to come there-tyl,
His mercy was to ferre behynde.
I wepte for I ne myght it fynde,
I complayned and sighed sore, 3485
And languysshed evermore,
For I durst nat over go
Unto the rose I loved so.
Throughout my demyng utterly,
Tyl he had knowlege certainly, 3490
That Love me ladde in suche a wyse,
That in me there was no feyntise,
Falsheed, ne mo trechery.
And yet he, ful of villany,
Of disdayne, and cruelte, 3495
On me ne wolde have pyte,
His cruel wyl for to refrayne,
Tho I wepte alwaye, and me complayne.
   And while I was in this tourment
Were come of grace, by God sent, 3500
Fraunchise, and with her Pyte,   CANDOR
Fulfylde the bothen of bounte.   AND PITY
They go to Daungere anon-ryght   INTERCEDE
To forther me with al her myght,
And helpe in worde and in dede, 3505
For wel they sawe that it was nede.
First, of her grace, Dame Fraunchise
Hath taken word of this emprise.
She sayd, "Daungere, great wronge ye do
To worche this man so moche wo, 3510
Or pynen him so angerly;
It is to you great villany.
I canne nat se why, ne how,

3438 maletalent, ill humor. **3442 mokel dishonest,** much dishonorable. **3443 werne,** deny. **3444 engreveth,** displeases. **3448** TG *thou* om. **3449 assaye,** attempt. **3450** T *In any tyme to passe*; G *I ony tyme to.* **3452 were,** hesitation (doubt). **3460 rewen,** have pity. **3462 good mes,** favorable time. **3469 Whiche wolde,** who desired. **3472 talent,** desire. **3475 kepe,** care. **3477 manasyng,** menacing. **3479 shent,** destroyed. **3482** TG *hard* om. **3484** *wepte:* T *kepte;* Fr. *pleure.* **3489 Throughout my demyng,** i.e., to my judgment. **3490** *Tyl:* TG *That;* Fr. *taut qu'il.* **3491** *That:* TG *Than(ne).* **3492 feyntise,** deception. **3502 bothen:** TG *bothom.* **3508 emprise,** enterprise. TG *word* om.; Fr. *parole.*

That he hath trespassed agayne you,
Save that he loveth; wherfore ye shulde 3515
The more in cherete of him holde.
The force of Love maketh hym do this;
Who wolde him blame he dyd amys?
He leseth more than ye maye do;
His payne is harde, ye maye se, lo! 3520
And Love in no wyse wolde consent
That he have power to repent;
For though that quicke ye wolde him slo,
Fro Love his herte may nat go.
Nowe, swete sir, is it your ease 3525
Him for to angre or disease?
Alas, what maye it you avaunce
To done to him so great grevaunce?
What worshippe is it agayne him take,
Or on your man a werre make, 3530
Sithe he so lowly every wyse
Is redy, as ye luste devyse?
If Love hath caught him in his lace,
You for t'obey in every caas,
And ben your subjecte at your wyl, 3535
Shulde ye therfore wyllen him yl?
Ye shulde him spare more, al out,
Than him that is bothe proude and stout.
Curtesy wol that ye socure
Hem that ben meke under your cure. 3540
His hert is harde that wol nat meke,
Whan men of mekenesse him beseke."
    "This is certayne," sayd Pyte.
"We se ofte that humylyte
Bothe yre and also felony 3545
Venquyssheth, and also melancoly.
To stonde forthe in suche duresse,
Th'is cruelte and wickednesse.
Wherfore I pray you, Sir Daungere,
For to mayntene no lenger here 3550
Suche cruel werre agayne your man,
As holly yours as ever he can;
Nor that ye worchen no more wo
Upon this caytife that languyssheth so,
Whiche wol no more to your trespace, 3555

But put him holly in your grace;
His offence ne was but lyte.
The God of Love it was to wyte,
That he your thrall so greatly is,
And if ye harme him, ye done amys, 3560
For he hath had ful harde penaunce,
Syth that ye refte him th'aqueyntaunce
Of Bialacoil, his moste joye,
Whiche al his paynes might acoye.
He was before anoyed sore, 3565
But than ye doubled him wel more;
For he of blysse hath ben ful bare,
Sythe Bialacoil was fro hym fare.
Love hath to hym do great distresse;
He hath no nede of more duresse. 3570
Voydeth from him your yre, I rede;
Ye may not wynnen in this dede.
Maketh Bialacoil repayre agayne,
And haveth pyte upon his payne;
For Fraynchyse wol, and I, Pyte, 3575
That mercyful to him ye be.
And sythe that she and I accorde,
Have upon him misericorde,
For I you pray, and eke moneste,
Nought to refusen our requeste; 3580
For he is harde and fel of thought,
That for us two wol do right nought."
    Daunger ne might no more endure;
He meked him unto measure.
"I wol in no wyse," sayth Daungere, 3585
"Deny that ye have asked here;
It were to great uncurtesye.
I wol he have the companye
Of Bialacoil, as ye devyse;
I wol him let in no wyse." 3590
    To Bialacoil than went in hye
Fraunchise, and sayd ful curteslye,
"Ye have to longe be deignous
Unto this lover, and daungerous,
Fro him to withdrawe your presence, 3595
Whiche hath do to him great offence,
That ye not wolde upon him se;

3516 **cherete of him holde**, i.e., be charitable to him. 3522 *he*: TG *ye*; Fr. *il.* 3523 **quicke**, alive. 3532 **luste devyse**, desire to instruct. 3533 T *have.* 3540 **cure**, keeping. 3547 **duresse**, hardness. 3562 **refte**, deprived (of). 3564 **acoye**, quiet. 3569 T *do* om. 3572 **wynnen**, profit. 3573 **repayre**, come. 3579 **moneste**, admonish. 3581 **fel**, cruel. 3584 **measure**, moderation. 3588 *he*: TG *ye*; Fr. *il.* 3590 **let**, hinder. 3591 **hye**, haste. 3593 **deignous**, disdainful. 3595–3690 Lines lacking in G. 3597 **se**, look.

Wherfore a sorouful man is he.
Shape ye to paye him, and to please,
Of my love if ye wol have ease.   3600
Fulfyl his wyl, sithe that ye knowe   RETURN
Daunger is daunted and brought   OF FAIR-
    lowe   WELCOME
Through helpe of me and of Pyte;
You dare no more aferde be."
   "I shal do right as ye wyl,"   3605
Saith Bialacoil, "for it is skyl,
Sithe Daunger wol that it so be."
Than Fraunchise hath him sent to me.
Byalacoil at the begynnyng
Salued me in his commyng;   3610
No straungenesse was in him sene,
No more than he ne had wrathed bene.
As fayre semblaunt than shewed he me,
And goodly, as aforne dyd he;
And by the honde, without dout,   3615
Within the haye right al about
He ladde me, with right good chere,
Al envyron the vergere
That Daunger hadde me chased fro.
Nowe have I leave over al to go;   3620
Nowe am I raysed, at my devyse,
Fro hel unto paradyse.
Thus Bialacoil, of gentylnesse,
With al his payne and besynesse,
Hath shewed me onely of grace   3625
The estres of the swote place.
   I sawe the rose, whan I was nygh,
Was greatter woxen, and more high,
Fresshe, roddy, and fayre of hewe,
Of coloure ever yliche newe.   3630
And when I hadde it longe sene,
I sawe that through the leves grene
The rose spredde to spaunysshinge;
To sene it was a goodly thynge.
But it ne was so sprede on brede   3635
That men within myght knowe the sede;

For it covert was and close
Bothe with the leves and with the rose.
The stalke was even and grene upright;
It was theron a goodly syght,   3640
And wel the better, without wene,
For the seed was nat sene.
Ful fayre it spradde, God it blesse,
For suche another, as I gesse,
Aforne ne was, ne more vermayle.   3645
I was abawed for marveyle,
For ever the fayrer that it was,
The more I am bounden in Loves laas.
    Longe I abode there, sothe to saye,
Tyl Bialacoil I ganne to praye,   3650
Whan that I sawe him in no wyse
To me warnen his servyce,
That he me wolde graunt a thynge,
Whiche to remembre is wel syttynge—
This is to sayne that of his grace   3655
He wolde me yeve leysar and space,
To me that was so desyrous
To have a kyssynge precious
Of the goodly fresshe rose,
That so swetely smelleth in my nose: 3660
"For if it you displeased nought,
I wolde gladly, as I have sought,
Have a cosse therof freely
Of your yefte; for certainly
I wol none have but by your leve,   3665
So lothe me were you for to greve."
    He sayd, "Frende, so God me spede,
Of Chastite I have suche drede;
Thou shuldest nat warned be for me,
But I dare nat, for Chastyte.   3670
Agayne her dare I nat mysdo,
For alwaye byddeth she me so
To yeve no lover leave to kysse.
For who therto maye wynnen, ywisse,
He of the surplus of the praye   3675
May live in hoope to gette some daye.

3599 Shape, proceed. **3601 wyl,** desire. **3602 daunted,** defeated. **3606 skyl,** reasonable (right). **3610 Salued,** greeted. **3611 straungenesse,** hostility. **3613 semblaunt,** appearance. **3618 vergere,** orchard. **3621 devyse,** wish. **3626 estres,** interior. **3633 spaunys-shinge,** full expansion (full bloom). **3635 brede,** breadth. **3636 knowe,** see. **3641 wene,** doubt. **3642 For,** because. **3643** T *The god of blesse;* Fr. *Dex la benoie.* **3645 vermayle,** vermillion. **3646 abawed,** astonished. **3648 laas,** net. **3652 warnen,** withhold. **3654 syttynge,** appropriate. **3669 warned,** prevented. **3675 surplus...praye,** remainder, suit (with perhaps a *double entendre* of *prey,* "victim"). Fr. *atant remaindre.* **3676** *May live:* T *My lyfe.*

For whoso kyssynge maye attayne
Of loves payne hath, sothe to sayne,
The best and most avenaunt,
And ernest of the remenaunt." 3680
Of his answere I sighed sore;
I durst assaye him tho no more,
I hadde suche drede to greve him aye.
A man shulde nat to moche assaye
To chafe his frende out of measure, 3685
Nor putte his lyfe in aventure;
For no man at the first stroke
Ne maye nat fel downe an oke,
Nor of the reysyns have the wyne
Tyl grapes be rype and wel afyne 3690
Be sore empressed, I you ensure,
And drawn out of the pressure.
But I, forpeyned wonder stronge,
Thought that I abode right longe
After the kysse, in payne and wo, 3695
Sithe I to kysse desyred so;
Tyl that, rewyng on my distresse,
There to me Venus the goddesse,
Whiche aye werryeth Chastite,
Came of her grace to socour me, 3700
Whose myght is knowe ferre   VENUS ASSISTS
   and wyde,   THE LOVER
For she is mother of Cupyde,
The God of Love, blynde as stone,
That helpeth lovers many one.
This lady brought in her right honde 3705
Of brennynge fyre a blasyng bronde,
Wherof the flame and hote fyre
Hath many a lady in desyre
Of love brought, and sore hette,
And in her servyce her hertes sette. 3710
This lady was of good entayle,
Right wonderful of apparayle;
By her atyre so bright and shene,
Men myght perceyve wel and sene
She was nat of relygioun. 3715

Nor I nyl make mencioun
Nor of robe, nor of tresour,
Of broche, neither of her riche attour,
Ne of her gyrdel about her syde,
For that I nyl nat longe abyde; 3720
But knoweth wel that certainly
She was arrayed richely.
Devoyde of pride certayne she was.
To Bialacoil she went a paas,
And to hym shortely, in a clause, 3725
She sayd: "Sir, what is the cause
Ye ben of porte so daungerous
Unto this lover, and daynous,
To graunt him nothyng but a kysse?
To warne it him ye done amysse, 3730
Sithe wel ye wotte howe that he
Is Loves servant, as ye maye se,
And hath beaute, wherthrough he is
Worthy of love to have the blys.
Howe he is semely, beholde and se, 3735
Howe he is fayre, howe he is free,
Howe he is swote and debonayre,
Of age yonge, lusty, and fayre.
There is no lady so hawtayne,
Duchesse, countesse, ne chastelayne, 3740
That I nolde holde her ungoodly
For to refuce him utterly.
His brethe is also good and swete,
And eke his lyppes roddy, and mete
Onely to playne and to kysse. 3745
Graunt him a kysse of gentylnysse!
His teth arne also white and clene.
Me thynketh wronge, withouten wene,
If ye nowe warne him, trusteth me,
To graunt that a kysse have he. 3750
The lasse to helpe him that ye haste,
The more tyme shul ye waste."
Whan the flame of the very   THE KISS
   bronde   GRANTED
That Venus brought in her right honde

3679 **avenaunt,** pleasing. 3686 **his lyfe in aventure,** i.e., his friend's life in jeopardy. 3690 **afyne,** completely. 3692 **pressure,** (wine) press. 3694–95 **abode . . . After,** waited for. *Thought:* TG *Though.* 3697 **rewyng,** having pity. TG *rennyng(e).* 3698 *to me:* TG *come.* 3699 **werryeth,** makes war upon. 3709 **sore hette,** sorely heated. 3710 **her,** their. **hertes:** TG *hert is.* 3711 **entayle,** figure (sculpture). 3715 **of relygioun,** of a religious order. 3724 **a paas,** quickly (apace). 3727 **daungerous,** obdurate. 3728 **daynous,** disdainful. 3730 **warne,** withhold. 3733 T *he* om. 3737 **swote,** fragrant. 3739 **hawtayne,** haughty. 3744 **mete,** suitable. 3745 **playne,** complain (of love). 3749 **warne,** withhold. 3751 *to:* TG *ye.* 3752 T *And the more.* 3753 **very,** same.

Hadde Bialacoil with hete smete,   3755
Anone he badde, withouten lete,
Graunt to me the rose kysse.
Than of my payne I ganne to lysse,
And to the rose anone went I,
And kyssed it ful faithfully.   3760
There no man aske if I was blythe
When the savour softe and lythe
Stroke to myne hert without more,
And me allegged of my sore,
So was I ful of joye and blysse.   3765
It is fayre suche a floure to kysse,
It was so swote and saverous.
I myght nat be so anguysshous,
That I ne mote gladde and joly be,
Whan that I remembre me.   3770
Yet ever amonge, sothly to sayne,
I suffre noye and moche payne.
The see may never be so styl,
That a litel winde it wyl
Overwhelme and tourne also,   3775
As it were woode, in wawes go.
After the calme the trouble sonne
Mote folowe and chaunge as the moone.
Right so fareth Love, that selde in one
Holdeth his ancre; for right anone   3780
Whan they in ease wene best to lyve,
They ben with tempest al fordryve.
Who serveth Love canne tel of wo;
The stoundmele joye mote overgo.
Nowe he hurteth, and nowe he cureth,   3785
For selde in o poynte Love endureth.
   Nowe is it right me to procede,   DEFENSE
Howe Shame gan medle and take   OF THE
      hede,   ROSE
Through whom fel angres I have hade;
And howe the stronge wall was made,   3790
And the castell of brede and length,   SHAME

That God of Love wan with his strength.
Al this in romance wyll I sette,
And for nothyng ne wyll I lette,
So that it lykyng to her be,   3795
That is the flour of beaute;
For she may best my labour quyte,
That I for her love shal endyte.
   Wicked-Tonge, that the covyne
Of every lover can devyne   3800
Worste, and addeth more   WICKED-
      somdele—   TONGE
For Wicked-Tonge saythe never wele—
To me-warde bare he right great hate,
Espyeng me erly and late,
Tyl he hath sene the great chere   3805
Of Bialacoil and me yfere.
He might not his tonge withstonde
Worse to reporte than he fonde,
He was so ful of cursed rage;
It satte him wel of his lynage,   3810
For him an Irisshe woman bare.
His tongue was fyled sharpe and square,
Poignaunt and right kervyng,
And wonder bytter in spekyng.
For whan that he me gan espye,   3815
He swore affirmyng sykerly
Bytwene Bialacoil and me
Was yvel aquayntaunce and prive.
He spake thereof so folilye
That he awaked Jelousye,   JEALOUSY
Whiche, al afrayde in his risyng,   3821
Whan that he herde janglyng,
He ran anon as he were wode
To Bialacoil there that he stode,
Whiche had lever in this caas   3825
Have ben at Reynes or Amyas.
For foote-hote, in his felonye,
To hym thus sayd Jelousye:

3755 T *with his hete.* **3756 lete,** hesitation. TG *bad (de) me.* **3758 lysse,** be relieved. **3761** T *There nede no.* **3762 lythe,** delicate. **3764 allegged,** alleviated. **3769** TG *ne* om. **3771 ever amonge,** now and again. **3772 noye,** annoyance. **3774** T *at wyl.* **3776 woode,** mad. **3777 trouble,** troubled (bringing trouble). **3779 in one,** in stableness. **3781 wene,** think. **3784 stoundmele,** momentary. **3789 fel angres,** cruel anguishes. **3791 brede,** breadth. **3793 romance,** French (verse). **3794 lette,** stop. **3795 lykyng,** pleasing. **3797 quyte,** requite. **3798 endyte,** compose poetry. **3799 covyne,** secret plan. **3805 chere,** cordiality. **3806 yfere,** together. **3810 satte . . . wel,** was well-fitting. **3811 Irisshe,** probably a *double entendre,* "irous" (full of ire, anger), as well as a jibe at the Irish. **3820 Jelousye,** "le jalous" in the allegories of love was typically the husband. **3822 janglyng,** quarreling. **3823 wode,** crazy. **3826 Reynes . . . Amyas,** Rennes, Brittany, but "Amyas" has not been identified; Fr. *Estampes . . . Mieaux,* Etampes and Meaux, towns near Paris.

"Why haste thou ben so neglygent,
To kepen, whan I was absent, 3830
This verger here left in thy warde?
To me thou haddest no regarde,
To truste—to thy confusyon—
Him thus, to whom suspection
I have right great; for it is nede, 3835
It is wel shewed by the dede.
Great faute in the nowe have I founde;
By God, anone thou shalte be bounde,
And faste loken in a toure,
Without refuyte or socoure. 3840
For Shame to longe hath be the fro;
Over soone she was ago.
Whan thou hast lost bothe drede and fere,
It semed wel she was nat here.
She was besy in no wyse, 3845
To kepe the and to chastice,
And for to helpen Chastite
To kepe the roser, as thynketh me.
For than this boye-knave so boldly
Ne shulde nat have be hardy, 3850
Ne in this verger hadde suche game,
Whiche nowe me tourneth to great shame."
    Bialacoil nyst what to saye;
Ful fayne he wolde have fledde away,
For feare have hydde, nere that he 3855
Al sodainly toke him with me.
And whan I sawe he had so—
This Jelousye—take us two,
I was astoned and knewe no rede,
But fledde away for very drede. 3860
    Than Shame came forthe ful symply—
She wende have trespaced ful greatly—
Humble of her porte, and made it symple,
Wearyng a vayle in stede of wymple,
As nonnes done in her abbey. 3865
Bycause her herte was in affray,

She gan to speke within a throwe
To Jelousye, right wonder lowe.
First of his grace she besought,
And sayd, "Sir, ne leveth nought 3870
Wicked-Tonge, that false espye,
Whiche is so glad to fayne and lye.
He hath you made, through flateryng,
On Bialacoil a false leasyng.
His falsnesse is not nowe anewe; 3875
It is to longe that he him knewe.
This is not the first daye,
For Wicked-Tonge hath custome aye
Yonge folkes to bewrye,
And false lesynges on hem lye. 3880
Yet neverthelesse I se amonge
That the loigne it is so longe
Of Bialacoil, hertes to lure,
In Loves servyce for to endure,
Drawyng suche folke him to 3885
That he hath nothyng with to do.
But in sothnesse I trowe nought
That Bialacoil had ever in thought
To do trespace or vilanye,
But for his mother Curtesye 3890
Hath taught him ever to be
Good of acqueyntaunce and prive.
For he loveth none hevynesse,
But myrthe and play and al gladnesse.
He hateth al trecherous, 3895
Soleyne folke and envyous,
For ye weten howe that he
Wol ever glad and joyful be
Honestly with folke to pley.
I have be neglygent, in good fey, 3900
To chastyse him; therfore nowe I,
Of herte I crye you here mercy,
That I have ben so recheles
To tamen hym withouten lees.

3830 kepen, protect. **3831 verger . . . warde,** orchard, safekeeping. **in:** T *ein.* **3832** *regarde:* G *rewarde.* **3837 faute,** fault. **3839 loken,** locked up. **3846 kepe,** guard. TG *to* om. **3851** TG *Ne* om.; *verge.* **3855 nere that he,** i.e., if it had not been that Jealousy. **3856 toke,** caught. **3859 rede,** expedient. **3862 wende,** thought. **3864 vayle . . . wymple,** nun's veil, secular lady's wimple (pleated headdress). **3866 affray,** fright. **3867 throwe,** moment. **3870 leveth,** believe. **3871 espye,** spy. **3872 fayne,** pretend. **3874 leasyng,** lying. **3881 amonge,** constantly. **3882 loigne,** leash for a hawk. **3886 nothyng with to do,** i.e., Fair Welcome inspires love in folk of whom he is not even aware. **3892 Good of acqueyntaunce . . . prive,** sociable, intimate. **3893 hevynesse,** sadness. **3895** TG *trechours.* **3896 Soleyne,** solitary. **3903 recheles,** careless. **3904 To tamen . . . withouten lees,** about taming (Fair Welcome); without lies (truly); possibly also without (a) leash.

Of my foly I me repente;   3905
Nowe wol I hole set myn entente
To kepe, bothe lowde and styll,
Bialacoil to do your wyll."
   "Shame, shame," sayd Jelousy;
"To be bytrasshed great drede have I.   3910
Lecherye hath clombe so hye
That almoste blered is myn eye.
No wonder is if that drede have I;
Over al reigneth Lechery,
Whose myght groweth nyght and dey.   3915
Bothe in cloystre and in abbey
Chastyte is werreyed over all.
Therfore I wol with syker wall
Close bothe roses and rosere.
I have to long in this manere   3920
Left hem unclosed wylfully;
Wherfore I am right inwardly
Sorouful, and repente me.
But nowe they shal no lenger be
Unclosed; and yet I drede sore,   3925
I shal repent ferthermore,
For the game gothe al amys.
Counsayle I must newe, iwys.
I have to longe trusted the,
But nowe it shal no lenger be;   3930
For he may best, in every coste,
Disceyve, that men trusten moste.
I se wel that I am nyghe shent,
But if I sette my ful entent
Remedye to purvey.   3935
Wherfore close I shal the wey
Fro hem that wol the rose espye,
And come to wayte me vilonye.
For in good faythe and in trouthe,
I wol not let, for no slouthe,   3940
To lyve the more in sykernesse,
To make anon a fortresse,
T'enclose the roses of good savour.
In myddes shall I make a tour

To put Bialacoil in prison,   3945
For ever I drede me of treson.
I trowe I shal hym kepe so
That he shal have no might to go
Aboute to make companye
To hem that thynke of vilanye;   3950
Ne to no suche as hath ben here
Aforne, and founde in him good chere,
Whiche han assayled him to shende,
And with her trowandyse to blende.
A foole is eyth to begyle;   3955
But may I lyve a lytel while,
He shal forthynke his fayre semblaunt."
   And with that worde came Drede   DREAD
      avaunt,
Whiche was abasshed, and in great fere.
Whan he wyste Jelousye was there,   3960
He was for drede in suche affray
That not a worde durste he saye,
But quakyng stode ful styl alone
Tyl Jelousye his way was gone,
Save Shame, that him not forsoke.   3965
Bothe Drede and she ful sore quoke,
That at laste Drede abrayde,
And to his cosyn Shame sayde:
"Shame," he sayd, "in sothfastnesse,
To me it is great hevynesse   3970
That the noyse so ferre is go,
And the sclaunder of us two.
But sythe that it is befall,
We may it not agayne call,
Whan ones spronge is a fame.   3975
For many a yere withouten blame
We have ben, and many a day;
For many an Aprill and many a May
We han passed not shamed
Tyl Jelousye hath us blamed   3980
Of mystrust and suspection
Causelesse, without encheson.
Go we to Daunger hastely,

3906 hole, wholly. **3907 kepe,** constrain. *lowde:* TG *lowe.* **3910 bytrasshed,** betrayed. **3912 blered . . . eye,** the familiar Chaucerian image for cuckolding, cf. *CT* I.3865, IX.252, etc. **3917 werreyed,** warred upon. **3918 syker,** secure. **3928 Counsayle . . . newe,** i.e., I must have new advice. **3933 shent,** ruined. **3934 But if,** unless. **3938 wayte,** waylay (ambush). **3940 let,** hesitate. **3941 sykernesse,** security. **3942 To:** TG *Do.* **3943 T'enclose:** TG *Than(ne) clos;* Fr. *clorra entour.* **3953 assayled . . . shende,** attempted, destroy. **3954 trowandyse,** imposture. **3955 eyth,** easy. **3957 forthynke,** repent. **3958 avaunt,** forward. **3961 affray,** fright. **3967 abrayde,** recovered. **3974 agayne call,** call it back. **3982 encheson,** occasion.

And let us shewe hym openly
That he hath not aright wrought, 3985
Whan that he set not his thought
To kepe better the purprise;
In his doyng he is not wyse.
He hath to us do great wronge,
That hath suffred nowe so longe 3990
Bialacoil to have his wyll,
Al his lustes to fulfyll.
He muste amende it utterly,
Or els shal he vilaynously
Exyled be out of his londe, 3995
For he the werre may not withstonde
Of Jelousye, nor the grefe,
Sythe Bialacoil is at mischefe."
    To Daunger, Shame and Drede anon
The righte way ben gon.   DANGER
The chorle they founde hem aforne, 4001
Lyggyng under an hawethorne.
Under his heed no pylowe was,
But in the stede a trusse of gras.
He slombred and a nappe he toke 4005
Tyl Shame pitously him shoke,
And great manace on him gan make.
"Why slepest thou whan thou shulde wake?"
Quod Shame. "Thou doest us vilanye!
Who trusteth the, he dothe folye, 4010
To kepe roses or bothoms
Whan they ben fayre in her sesons.
Thou arte woxe to famyliere
Where thou shulde be straunge of chere,
Stoute of thy porte, redy to greve. 4015
Thou doest great folye for to leve
Bialacoil here-inne to call
The yonder man to shenden us all.
Though that thou slepe, we may here
Of Jelousye great noyse here. 4020
Arte thou nowe late? Ryse up in hye
And stoppe sone and delyverly
Al the gappes of the hay.

Do no favour, I the pray.
It falleth nothyng to thy name 4025
To make fayre semblant where thou mayste
        blame.
If Bialacoil be swete and free,
Dogged and fel thou shuldest be;
Frowarde and outragyous, iwys.
A chorle chaungeth that curteys is— 4030
This have I herde ofte in sayeng,
That man ne may, for no dauntyng,
Make a sperhauke of a bosarde.
Al men wol holde the for musarde,
That debonayre have founden the; 4035
It sytteth the nought curteys to be.
To do men plesaunce or servyse
In the it is recreaundyse.
Let thy werkes, ferre and nere,
Be lyke thy name, whiche is Daungere." 4040
    Than al abawed in shewyng,
Anon spake Drede, right thus sayeng,
And said, "Daunger, I drede me
That thou ne wolte besy be
To kepe that thou hast to kepe; 4045
Whan thou shuldest wake, thou art aslepe.
Thou shalte be greved certainly
If the aspye Jelousye,
Of if he fynde the in blame.
He hath today assayled Shame, 4050
And chased away with great manace
Bialacoil out of this place,
And swereth shortly that he shall
Enclose him in a sturdy wall;
And al is for thy wickydnesse, 4055
For that the fayleth straungenesse.
Thyn herte, I trowe, be fayled all;
Thou shalte repent in speciall,
If Jelousye the soth knewe;
Thou shalte forthynke and sore rewe." 4060
    With that the chorle his clubbe gan shake,
Frownyng his eyen gan to make,

And hydous chere, as man in rage.
For yre he brent in his visage
Whan that he herde him blamed so. 4065
He said, "Out of my wytte I go!
To be discomfyte I have great wronge.
Certes, I have nowe lyved to longe
Sithe I maye nat this closer kepe.
Al quycke I wolde be dolven depe 4070
If any man shal more repayre
Into this gardyn, for foule or fayre.
Myne herte for yre gothe afere,
That I lette any entre here.
Lever I had with swerdes twayne 4075
Throughout myn herte, in every vayne
Perced to be, with many a wounde,
Than slouthe shulde in me be founde.
I have do folly, nowe I se,
But nowe it shal amended be. 4080
Who setteth fote here any more,
Truly he shal repent it sore;
For no man more into this place
Of me to entre shal have grace.
From hensforthe, by nyght or day, 4085
I shal defende it, if I may,
Withouten any excepcion
Of eche maner condycion;
And if I it any man graunte,
Holdeth me for recreaunte." 4090
    Than Daunger on his fete gan stonde,
And hente a burdon in his honde.
Wrothe in his ire, ne lefte he nought,
But through the verger he hath sought
If he myght fynde hole or trace 4095
Where through that men mote fortheby
    pace,
Or any gappe, he dyd it close,
That no man might touche a rose
Of the roser all aboute;
He shytteth every man withoute. 4100
Thus day by day Daunger is wers,
More wonderfull and more dyvers,

And feller eke than ever he was.
For hym ful ofte I synge "Alas!"
For I ne may nought, through his yre, 4105
Recover that I moste desyre.
Myn herte, alas, wol brest atwo,
For Bialacoil I wrathed so;
For certaynly, in every membre
I quake, whan I me remembre 4110
Of the bothom, whiche I wolde
Ful ofte a day sene and beholde.
And whan I thynke upon the kysse,
And howe moche joye and blysse
I had through the savour swete, 4115
For wante of it I grone and grete.
Me thynketh I fele yet in my nose
The swete savour of the rose.
And nowe I wote that I mote go
So ferre the fresshe floures fro, 4120
To me ful welcome were the dethe!
Absence therof, alas, me slethe!
For whylom with this rose, alas,
I touched nose, mouthe, and face;
But nowe the dethe I must abyde. 4125
But Love consent another tyde
That ones I touche may and kysse,
I trowe my payne shal never lysse.
Theron is al my covetyse,
Whiche brent myn herte in many wyse. 4130
Nowe shal repayre agayne syghyng
Longe watche on nyghtes, and no slepyng,
Thought in wysshyng, turment, and wo,
With many a turnyng to and fro,
That halfe my payne I cannot tell, 4135
For I am fallen into hell
From paradyse and welthe. The more
My turment greveth, more and more
Anoyeth nowe the bytternesse,
That I toforne have felte swetnesse. 4140
And Wicked-Tonge, through his falshede,
Causeth al my wo and drede;
On me he leyeth a pytous charge,

4067 discomfyte, overcome (discomfited). **4069 closer,** enclosure. **4070 quycke ... dolven,** alive, buried (dug). **4073 afere,** on fire. **4075–78** Lines in TG misplaced between 4084–85. **4088 eche ... condycion,** i.e., any kind or class of person. **4092 burdon,** cudgel. **4095 trace,** track. **4096 men:** TG *me.* **4102 wonderfull ... dyvers,** strange, contradictory. **4103 feller,** more cruel. **4105 through,** because of. **4108 wrathed,** angered. **4116 grete,** lament. **4128 trowe,** believe. **4129 covetyse,** desire. **4140 felte,** felt (to be).

Bycause his tonge was to large.

Nowe it is tyme, shortly, that I 4145
Tell you somthyng of Jelousy, **THE TOWER**
That was in great suspection. **OF JEALOUSY**
Aboute him lefte he no mason
That stone coulde laye, ne querrour;
He hyred hem to make a tour. 4150
And first, the roses for to kepe,
Aboute hem made he a diche depe,
Right wonder large, and also brode;
Upon the whiche also stode
Of squared stone a sturdy wall, 4155
Whiche on a cragge was founded all;
And right great thicknesse eke it bare.
About it was founded square,
An hundred fadome on every syde;
It was al lyche longe and wyde. 4160
Lest any tyme it were assayled,
Ful wel about it was batayled,
And rounde envyron eke were sette
Ful many a riche and fayre tourette.
At every corner of this wall 4165
Was sette a toure ful principall;
And everiche hadde, without fable,
A port-colyse defensable,
To kepe of enemyes and to greve
That there her force wolde preve. 4170
And eke amydde this purprise
Was made a toure of great maistryse;
A fayrer saugh no man with syght,
Large and wyde and of great hyght.
They dradde none assaut 4175
Of gynne, gonne, nor skaffaut,
For the temprure of the mortere
Was made of lycour wonder dere:
Of quicke lyme, persaunt and egre,
The whiche was tempred with vynegre. 4180
The stone was harde as adamant,

Wherof they made the foundemant.
The toure was rounde made in compas;
In al this worlde no richer was,
Ne better ordayned therewithal. 4185
About the toure was made a wal,
So that betwixt that and the toure
Rosers were sette of swete savour,
With many roses that they bere.
And eke within the castel were 4190
Springoldes, gonnes, bowes and archers;
And eke above, at corners,
Men seyne over the wal stonde
Great engyns who were nere honde.
And in the kernels, here and there, 4195
Of arblasters great plentie were.
None armure myght her strok withstonde,
It were foly to preace to honde.
Without the dytche were lystes made,
With wal batayled large and brade, 4200
For men and horse shulde not attayne
To nyghe the dyche over the playne.

Thus Jelousye hath envyron **THE GARRISON**
Sette aboute his garnyson **OF THE TOWER**
With walles rounde, and dyche depe, 4205
Onely the roser for to kepe.
And Daunger erly and late
The keyes kepte of the utter gate,
The whiche openeth towarde the eest;
And he had with him at leest 4210
Thurty servauntes, echone by name.
That other gate kept Shame,
Whiche opened, as it was couthe,
Towarde the partie of the southe.
Sergeauntes assigned were her to 4215
Ful many, her wyl for to do.
Than Drede had in her baillye
The kepyng of the conestablerye
Towarde the northe, I understonde,

4149 **querrour**, stonecutter (quarrier). 4151 **kepe**, protect. 4159 **fadome**, fathom (6 feet). 4160 **al lyche**, equally. 4162 **batayled**, provided with battlements. 4168 **port-colyse**, portcullis (vertically suspended grill). 4171 **purprise**, enclosure. 4172 **maistryse**, strength. 4174 *hyght*: TG *myght*; Fr. *haute*. 4176 **gynne, gonne . . . skaffaut**, catapult (war engine), gun, scaffold (for scaling walls). 4177 **temprure**, mixture. TG *For* om.; Fr. *Car*. 4178 **lycour . . . dere**, liquid, expensive (sugar, ale, and other substances have been used to give mortar strength; vinegar is not a common additive). 4179 **persaunt . . . egre**, sharp, active (unslaked lime can burn badly). 4181 *as*: TG *of*; Fr. *come*. 4182 **foundemant**, foundation. 4185 **ordayned**, arranged. 4188 **Rosers**, rose trees. TG *Roses*; Fr. *rosier*. 4191 **Springoldes**, catapults. 4192 *above*: T *about*; Fr. *par desus*. 4195 **kernels**, battlements. 4196 **arblasters**, large crossbows. 4198 **preace to honde**, press close (to the castle). 4200 **wal batayled**, battlemented walls. 4201 **For**, so that. 4204 **garnyson**, protection (garrison). 4208 **utter**, outer. G *kepte* om. 4214 *partie*: TG *parte*. 4217 **baillye**, command.

That opened upon the lyfte honde; 4220
The whiche for nothyng may be sure,
But if she do besy cure
Erly on morowe and also late
Strongly to shette and barre the gate.
Of every thyng that she may se 4225
Drede is aferde, whereso she be;
For with a puffe of lytel wynde
Drede is astonyed in her mynde.
Therfore, for stealyng of the rose,
I rede her not the yate unclose. 4230
A foules flyght wol make her fle,
And eke a shadowe, if she it se.
Than Wicked-Tonge, full of envye,
With soudyours of Normandye,
As he that causeth al the bate, 4235
Was keper of the fourthe gate;
And also to the tother thre
He went ful ofte, for to se.
Whan his lotte was to wake anyght,
His instrumentes wolde he dyght, 4240
For to blowe and make sowne,
Ofter than he hath enchesoun;
And walken ofte upon the wall,
Corners and wickettes over all
Ful narowe serchen and espye; 4245
Though he naught fonde, yet wolde he lye.
Discordaunt ever fro armony,
And distoned from melodye,
Controve he wolde, and foule fayle,
With hornepypes of Cornewayle. 4250
In floytes made he discordaunce,
And in his musyke, with mischaunce,
He wolde seyne, with notes newe,
That he fonde no woman trewe,
Ne that he sawe never in his lyfe 4255
Unto her husbonde a trewe wyfe,
Ne none so ful of honeste,
That she nyl laughe and mery be
Whan that she hereth or may espye

A man speken of lecherye. 4260
Everyche of hem hath some vyce;
One is dishonest, another is nyce;
If one be ful of vilanye,
Another hath a lykerous eye;
If one be ful of wantonnesse, 4265
Another is a chyderesse.
Thus Wicked-Tonge—God yeve him shame—
Can put hem everychone in blame
Without deserte and causelesse;
He lyeth, though they ben gyltlesse. 4270
I have pyte to sene the sorowe
That waketh bothe eve and morowe,
To innocentes dothe suche grevaunce.
I pray God yeve him yvel chaunce,
That he ever so besye is 4275
Of any woman to seyne amys!
    Eke Jelousye God confounde,
That hath made a toure so rounde,
And made aboute a garyson
To sette Bealacoil in prison, 4280
The whiche is shette there in the tour,
Ful longe to holde there sojour,
There for to lyve in penaunce,
And for to do him more grevaunce—
There hath ordayned Jelousye 4285
And olde vecke for to espye   **THE**
The maner of his governaunce,   **DUENNA**
The whiche dyvel, in her enfaunce,
Had lerned of Loves arte,
And of his pleys toke her parte. 4290
She was so expert in his servyse,
She knewe eche wrenche and every gyse
Of Love, and every wyle;
It was harde her to begyle.
Of Bealacoil she toke aye hede, 4295
That ever he lyveth in wo and drede.
He kepte him koye and eke prive,
Leest in him she had se

4229 for stealyng, to prevent stealing. **4230 rede,** advise. **4234 soudyours,** soldiers. **4235 bate,** strife. **4239 lotte,** turn (i.e., when he was officer of the day). **4240 dyght,** prepare. **4242 enchesoun,** occasion. **4244 wickettes,** gates. **4245 narowe,** carefully. **4248 distoned,** untuned. **4249 Controve . . . foule fayle,** compose (music), miserably fail. **4250 hornepypes of Cornewayle,** i.e., Cornish horns; Fr. *estriuuenz de Cornouaille.* **4251 floytes,** flutes. **4262 nyce,** foolish. **4264 lykerous,** lecherous. **4266 chyderesse,** scolder. **4269** *deserte:* G *disseit.* **4272** *waketh:* TG *walketh.* **4274 yvel chaunce,** bad luck. **4285** *There:* TG *Which(e).* **4286 vecke,** old woman. **4291** *expert:* TG *except.* **4292 wrenche,** twist. **4294** *harde:* G *harder.* **4297 koye,** quiet (coy).

Any foly countenaunce,
For she knewe al the olde daunce.   4300
   And after this, whan Jelousye
Had Bealacoil in his baillie,
And shette him up that was so fre,
For sure of him he wolde be,
He trusteth sore in his castell;   4305
The stronge werke him lyketh well.
He dradde not that no glotons
Shulde steale his roses or bothoms—
The roses weren assured all,
Defenced with the stronge wall.   4310
Nowe Jelousye ful wel may be
Of drede devoyde in lyberte,
Whether that he slepe or wake;
For of his roses may none be take.
   But I, alas, nowe morne shal,   4315
Bycause I was without the wal.   COMPLAINT
Ful moche doole and mone I made.   OF THE
Who had wyste what wo I hade,   LOVER
I trowe he wolde have had pyte.
Love to dere had solde me   4320
The good that of his love had I.
I wende a bought it al queyntly,
But nowe, through doublyng of my payne,
If so he wolde it sell agayne,
And me a newe bargayne lere,   4325
The whiche al out the more is dere,
For the solace that I have lorne,
Than I had it never aforne.
Certayne I am ful lyke, indede,
To him that caste in erthe his sede,   4330
And hath joye of the newe spring,
Whan it greneth in the gynnyng,
And is also fayre and fresshe of floure,
Lusty to sene, swote of odoure;
But er he it in sheves shere,   4335
May fall a wether that shal it dere,

And make it to fade and fall,
The stalke, the greyne, and floures all,
That to the tyllers is fordone
The hope that he had to sone.   4340
I drede, certayne, that so fare I,
For hope and travayle sykerly
Ben me byrafte al with a storme;
The floure nyl seden of my corne.
For Love hath so avaunced me,   4345
Whan I began my privyte
To Bailacoil al for to tel,
Whom I ne founde frowarde ne fel,
But toke a gree al hole my play.
But Love is of so harde assaye   4350
That al at ones he reved me,
Whan I wende best aboven to have be.
It is of Love, as of Fortune,
That chaungeth ofte, and nyl contune;
Whiche whilom wol on folke smyle,   4355
And glombe on hem another while;
Nowe frende, nowe foe, shaltow her fele.
For in a twynclynge tourneth her whele.
She canne writhe her heed awaye;
This is the concourse of her playe.   4360
She canne areyse that doth mourne,
And whirle adowne, and overtourne
Who sytteth hyghest, but as her lust;
A foole is he that wol her trust.
For it is I that am come downe   4365
Through change and revolutioun!
Sithe Bialacoil mote fro me twynne,
Shette in the prison yonde withinne,
His absence at myne herte I fele,
For al my joye and al myne hele   4370
Was in him and in the rose,
That but yon wal, whiche him dothe close,
Openne, that I maye him se,
Love wol nat that I cured be

4299 **foly countenaunce,** foolish expression. 4302 **baillie,** power. 4303 **fre,** outgoing. 4306 **werke,** fortification. 4312 **Of drede devoyde,** free of dread. 4322 **wende a bought,** thought to have bought. TG *wente aboute;* Fr. *cuidoie les avoir achetez.* In the complicated syntax of ll. 4320–28, the Lover is complaining that he had already paid too dearly for love, but now sees that Love would sell it to him again at double the price, i.e., double the pain for the solace he has lost. 4325 **lere,** teach. 4336 **dere,** destroy. 4342 **travayle sykerly,** labor certainly. 4344 **seden . . . corne,** produce seed, grain. 4346 **privyte,** confidence. 4348 **frowarde . . . fel,** obstinate, cruel. 4349 **a gree,** in good spirit. 4350 **assaye,** endeavor. 4351 **reved,** bereaved. 4352 **wende . . . aboven,** thought, high (in luck). 4354 **contune,** continue. 4356 **glombe,** frown (glum). 4357 *shaltow:* TG *shalte.* 4358 TG *in* om.; G *turne.* 4359 **writhe,** twist. 4360 **concourse,** course (nature). 4363 **her lust,** pleases her. 4366 *change:* TG *charge.* 4367 **twynne,** (be) separate. 4370 **hele,** health. 4372 **but,** unless. *yon wal:* T *you wol;* G *wol;* Fr. *les murs.*

Of the paynes that I endure,   4375
Nor of my cruel aventure.
Ah, Bialacoil, myne owne dere!
Though thou be nowe a prisonere,
Kepe at leest thyne herte to me,
And suffre nat that it daunted be,   4380
Ne lette nat Jelousy in his rage
Putten thyne herte in no servage.
Although he chastice the without,
And make thy body unto him lout,
Have herte as harde as diamaunt,   4385
Stedfast, and naught plyaunt.
In prison though thy body be,
At large kept thyne herte free:
A trewe herte wol nat plye
For no manace that it maye drye.   4390
If Jelousye doth the payne,
Quyte him his while thus agayne,
To venge the, at leest in thought,
If other waye thou mayst nought.
And in this wyse subtelly   4395
Worche, and wynne the maistry.
But yet I am in great affraye
Lest thou do nat as I saye;
I drede thou canst me great maugre,
That thou enprisoned arte for me.   4400
But that is nat for my trespas,
For through me never discovered was

Yet thynge that ought be secree.
Wel more annoye is in me
Than is in the of this myschaunce,   4405
For I endure more harde penaunce
Than any canne sayne or thynke,
That for the sorowe almost I synke.
Whan I remembre me of my wo,
Ful nyghe out of my wytte I go.   4410
Inwarde myne herte I fele blede,
For comfortlesse the dethe I drede.
Owe I nat wel to have dystresse,
Whan false, through her wickednesse,
And traytours, that arne envyous,   4415
To noyen me be so curious?
Ah, Bialacoile, ful wel I se
That they hem shape to disceyve the,
To make the buxome to her lawe,
And with her corde the to drawe   4420
Wherso hem lust, right at her wyl;
I drede they have the brought thertyl.
Without comforte, thought me slethe;
This game wol bringe me to my dethe.
For if your good wyl I lese,   4425
I mote be deed; I maye nat chese.
And if that thou foryete me,
Myne hert shal never in lykynge be;
Nor elswhere fynde solace,
If I be putte out of your grace,   4430

Jean de Meun's Continuation.

As it shal never ben, I hoope;
Than shulde I fal in wanhope.
    Alas, in wanhope? Naye, parde!
For I wol never dispeyred be.
If Hope me fayle, than am I   4435
Ungratious and unworthy.
In Hoope I wol conforted be,   COMPLAINT
For Love, whan he betaught her me,   OF THE
Says that Hoope, whereso I go,   LOVER

Shulde aye be relees to my wo.   4440
But what and she my bales bete,
And be to me curteis and swete?
She is in nothynge ful certayne.
Lovers she putte in ful great payne.
And maketh hem with wo to dele.   4445
Her fayre behest disceyveth fele,
For she wol behote, sykerly,
And faylen after utterly.

4379 **Kepe**, i.e., keep faithful. 4380 **daunted**, defeated. 4384 **lout**, bow. 4388 **At large**, in liberty. 4389 **plye**, bend. 4390 **drye**, endure. 4392 **Quyte**, repay. 4397 **affraye**, fear. 4399 **maugre**, ill will. 4401 TG *is* om. 4405 **of**, for. 4411 **fele**, greatly. 4413 **Owe**, ought. 4414 **false . . . her**, false people, their. 4416 **curious**, eager. T *coragious*; G *coraious*; Fr. *curieus*. 4432 **wanhope**, despair. 4441 **But what . . . bales bete**, what if, sorrows cure. 4446 **behest . . . fele**, promise, many. 4447 **behote, sykerly**, promise, securely (faithfully).

Ah, that is a ful noyous thyng!
For many a lover, in lovyng,   4450
Hangeth upon her, and trusteth fast,
Whiche lese her traveyle at the last.
Of thyng to commen she wotte right nought;
Therfore, if it be wisely sought,
Her counsayle foly is to take.   4455
For many tymes, whan she wol make
A ful good sylogisme, I drede
That afterwarde there shal in dede
Folowe an yvel conclusyoun;
This putte me in confusyoun.   4460
For many tymes I have it sene,
That many have begyled bene,
For truste that they have sette in Hoope,
Whiche fel hem afterwards aslope.
But nathelesse yet, gladly she wolde   4465
That he that wol him with her holde,
Hadde al tymes his purpose clere,
Without disceyte or any were.
That she desyreth sykerly.
Whan I her blamed, I dyd foly.   4470
But what avayleth her good wyl,
Whan she ne maye staunche my stounde yl?
That helpeth lytel that she maye do,
Outtake beheest unto my wo.
And heest certayne, in no wyse,   4475
Without yefte, is nat to pryse.
Whan heest and dede asondre vary,
They done me have a great contrary.
Thus am I possed up and downe
With doole, thought, and confusyoune;   4480
Of my disease there is no nombre.
Daungere and Shame me encombre,
Drede also, and Jelousye,
And Wicked-Tonge, ful of envye,
Of whiche the sharpe and cruel ire   4485
Ful ofte me putte in great martyre.
They have my joye fully lette,

Sithe Bialacoil they have beshette
Fro me in prison wickedly,
Whome I love so entierly,   4490
That it wol my bane be,
But I the sooner maye him se.
And yet moreover, worste of al,
There is sette to kepe—foule her befal—
A rympled vecke, ferre ronne in age,   4495
Frownyng and yelowe in her visage,
Whiche in awayte lyeth day and nyght,
That none of hem may have a syght.
    Nowe mote my sorowe enforced be;
Ful sothe it is that Love yafe me   4500
Thre wonder yeftes of his grace,
Whiche I have lorne nowe in this place,
Sithe they ne maye, without drede,
Helpen but lytel, who taketh hede.
For here aveyleth no Swete-Thought,   4505
And Swete-Speche helpeth right nought.
The thirde was called Swete-Lokyng,
That nowe is lorne, without lesyng.
Yeftes were fayre, but nat forthy
They helpe me but symply   4510
But Bialacoil loosed be,
To gone at large and to be free.
For him my lyfe lyeth al in dout,
But if he come the rather out.
Alas, I trowe it wol nat bene,   4515
For howe shulde I evermore him sene?
He maye nat out, and that is wronge,
Bycause the toure is so stronge.
Howe shulde he out, or by whose prowesse,
Of so stronge a forteresse?   4520
By me, certayne, it nyl be do;
God wotte, I have no wytte therto!
But wel I wotte I was in rage,
Whan I to Love dydde homage.
Who was in cause, in sothfastnesse,   4525
But herselfe, Dame Idelnesse,

4452 **traveyle,** effort. 4457–59 **sylogisme ... conclusyoun,** a scholastic syllogism has a major premise, a minor premise, and a conclusion. Jean de Meun was associated with the University of Paris throughout his life. His continuation of the *Roman* (18,000 lines, compared with 4,058 by Guillaume de Lorris) makes it a vehicle for most of the social, philosophical, and scientific ideas of his period. 4464 **fel ... aslope,** fell askew. 4465 **wolde,** wished. 4467 *his:* TG *her.* 4468 **were,** doubt. 4472 **staunche ... stounde yl,** heal, bad time. 4474 **Outtake beheest,** except promise. 4476 **yefte ... pryse,** (tangible) gift, take (accept). TG *preyse.* 4478 TG *me have* om.; Fr. *avoir.* 4479 **possed,** pushed. 4487 **lette,** cut off (prevented). 4491 **bane,** death. 4495 **vecke,** old woman. *age:* T *rage.* 4499 **enforced,** reinforced. 4501 **yeftes,** gifts. 4502 **lorne,** lost. 4508 **lesyng,** lying. 4509 **forthy,** therefore. 4511 **But,** unless. 4514 **rather,** sooner. 4520 G *Out of so.*

Which me conveyde, through my prayere,
To entre into that fayre vergere?
She was to blame me to leve,
The whiche nowe dothe me sore greve. 4530
A fooles worde is nought to trowe,
Ne worthe an apple for to lowe;
Menne shulde him snybbe bitterly,
At prime temps of his foly.
I was a foole, and she me leved, 4535
Through whom I am right nought releved;
She accomplysshed al my wyll,
That nowe me greveth wonder yll.
Reason me sayde what shulde fall.
A foole myselfe I may wel call 4540
That love asyde I had nat layde,
And trowed that Dame Reson sayde.
Reson had bothe skyll and ryght
Whan she me blamed with al her myght
To medle of love, that hath me shent; 4545
But certayne nowe I wol repent.
    And shulde I repent? Nay, parde!
A false traytour than shulde I be.
The dyvels engyns wolde me take
If I my lorde wolde forsake, 4550
Or Bialacoil falsly betraye.
Shulde I at mischefe hate him? Naye,
Sythe he nowe, for his curtesye,
Is in prison of Jelousye.
Curtesye certayne dyd he me, 4555
So moche that it may not yolden be,
Whan he the hay passen me lete,
To kysse the rose, fayre and swete.
Shulde I therfore conne him maugre?
Nay, certaynly, it shal not be; 4560
For Love shal never, if God wyll,
Here of me, through worde or wyll,
Offence or complaynt, more or lesse,
Neyther of Hope nor Idelnesse.
For certes, it were wronge that I 4565
Hated hem for her curtesye.

There is not els but suffre and thynke,
And waken whan I shulde wynke,
Abyde in hope tyl Love, through chaunce,
Sende me socour or allegeaunce, 4570
Expectant aye tyl I may mete
To getten mercy of that swete.
    Whylom I thynke howe Love to me
Sayd he wolde take at gre
My servyce, if unpacience 4575
Ne caused me to done offence.
He sayd, "In thanke I shal it take,
And hygh mayster eke the make,
If wickednesse ne reve it the;
But sone, I trowe, that shal not be." 4580
These were his wordes by and by—
It semed he loved me trewly.
Nowe is there not but serve him wele,
If that I thynke his thanke to fele.
My good, myn harme, lythe hole in me; 4585
In Love may no defaute be.
For trewe Love ne fayled never man;
Sothly, the faute mote nedes than—
As God forbyd—be founde in me,
And howe it commeth, I cannot se. 4590
Nowe let it gone as it may go;
Whether Love wol socoure me or slo,
He may do hole on me his wyll.
I am so sore bounde hym tyll,
From his servyce I may not flene; 4595
For lyfe and dethe, withouten wene,
Is in his hande; I may not chese;
He may me do bothe wynne and lese.
And sythe so sore he dothe me greve,
Yet if my luste he wolde acheve, 4600
To Bialacoil goodly to be,
I yeve no force what fel on me.
For though I dye, as I mote nede,
I pray Love, of his goodlyhede,
To Bialacoil do gentylnesse, 4605
For whom I lyve in suche distresse

4527 *my:* TG *fayre;* Fr. *ma priere.* 4528 **vergere,** orchard. 4531 **trowe,** believe. 4532 **lowe,** value. 4533 **snybbe,** scold. 4534 **prime temps,** first time (springtime). 4535 **leved,** believed. 4537 **accomplysshed . . . wyll,** fulfilled, desire. 4539 **fall,** befall. 4543 **skyll,** reason. 4545 **shent,** destroyed. 4550 *lorde:* TG *love.* 4556 **yolden,** returned (yielded). 4557 **hay,** hedge. 4559 **conne him maugre,** shows him ill will. 4561 *if God wyll:* TG *yever good will(e);* Fr. *se Dieu plest.* 4574 **at gre,** with favor. 4576 *Ne caused:* TG *Ne* om. 4579 **reve,** steal from (bereave). 4580 **trowe,** believe. 4585 **hole,** wholly. 4586 **defaute,** fault. 4595 **flene,** flee. 4596 **wene,** doubt. 4602 **yeve no force,** i.e., care not.

That I mote dyen for penaunce.
But first, without repentaunce,
I wol me confesse in god entent,
And make in haste my testament, 4610
As lovers done that felen smerte:
To Bialacoil leave I myn herte
Al hole, without departyng,
Or doublenesse of repentyng.

Comment Raison vient a l'Amant

   Thus as I made my passage 4615
In compleynt, and in cruel rage,
And I not where to fynde a leche
That couthe unto myn helpyng eche.
Sodainly agayne comen doun   **REASON**
Out of her tour I sawe Reasoun,   **REAPPEARS**
Discrete, and wyse, and ful plesaunt, 4621
And of her porte ful avenaunt.
The right way she toke to me,
Whiche stode in great perplexite,
That was posshed in every syde, 4625
That I nyst where I myght abyde,
Tyl she, demurely sadde of chere,
Sayd to me, as she came nere:
   "Myne owne frende, arte thou yet greved?
Howe is this quarel yet atcheved 4630
Of Loves syde? Anone me tel.
Hast thou nat yet of love thy fyl?
Arte thou nat wery of thy servyce
That the hath pyned in suche wyse?
What joye haste thou in thy lovyng? 4635
Is it swete or bytter thyng?
Canst thou yet chese, lette me se,
What best thy socour myght be?
Thou servest a ful noble lorde,
That maketh the thral for thy rewarde, 4640
Whiche aye reneweth thy tourment,
With foly so he hath the blent;
Thou fel in myschefe thylke daye,
Whan thou dyddest, the sothe to saye,
Obeysaunce and eke homage; 4645

Thou wroughtest nothyng as the sage.
Whan thou became his liege man,
Thou dyddest a great foly than;
Thou wystest nat what fel therto,
With what lorde thou haddest to do. 4650
If thou haddest him wel knowe,
Thou haddest nought be brought so lowe.
For if thou wystest what it were,
Thou noldest serve him halfe a yere,
Nat a weke, nor halfe a daye, 4655
Ne yet an hour without delaye,
Ne never yloved paramours,
His lordshyppe is so ful of shours.
Knowest him ought?"
L'AMAUNT: "Ye, dame, parde!"
RAYSOUN: "Nay, nay."
L'AMAUNT: "Yes, I."
RAYSOUN: "Wherfore, lette se?"
L'AMAUNT: "Of that he sayd I shulde be 4661
Gladde to have suche lorde as he,
And maister of suche seignorie."
RAYSOUN: "Knowest him no more?"
L'AMAUNT: "Naye, certes, I,
Save that he yafe me rules there, 4665
And went his waye, I nyst where,
And I abode bounde in balaunce."
RAYSOUN: "Lo, there a noble conysaunce!
But I wol that thou knowe him nowe,
Gynnynge and ende, sithe that thou 4670
Arte so anguysshous and mate,
Disfygured out of astate;
There maye no wretche have more of wo,
Ne caytife none enduren so.
It were to every manne syttyng 4675
Of his lorde have knowlegyng.
For if thou knewe him, out of dout,
Lightly thou shuldest escapen out
Of thy prysone that marreth the."
L'AMAUNT: "Ye, dame, sithe my lorde is he, 4680
And I his manne, made with myne honde,
I wolde ryght fayne understonde
To knowe of what kynde he be,

4614 **Comment Raison**, heading in TG. 4617 **leche**, physician. 4622 **avenaunt**, pleasant. 4625 **posshed**, pushed. 4627 **sadde**, sober. 4629 **yet**, still. 4630 **atcheved**, settled. 4634 TG *pyned* om. 4640 **thral**, slave. 4641 **aye**, constantly. 4642 **blent**, blinded. 4649 **fel therto**, went along with it. 4657 **paramours**, (with) sexual love. 4658 **shours**, storms (showers). 4661 **Of that**, on the basis of what. 4668 **conysaunce**, acquaintanceship. 4671 **mate**, exhausted. 4675 **syttyng**, fitting.

If any wolde enforme me."
RAYSOUN: "I wolde," sayd Reason, "the lere, 4685
Sithe thou to lerne hast suche desyre,
And shewe the, withouten fable,
A thynge that is nat demonstrable:
Thou shalte wite withouten science,
And knowe withouten experience, 4690
The thyng that may nat knowen be,
Ne wyst, ne shewed, in no degree.
Thou mayst the sothe of it nat wytten,
Though in the it were written.
Thou shalte nat knowe therof more 4695
Whyle thou arte ruled by his lore;
But unto him that love wol flye
The knotte may unclosed be,
Whiche hath to the, as it is founde,
So longe be knytte and nat unbounde. 4700
Now sette wel thyne ententioun,
To here of love discriptioun:

"Love, it is an hateful pees, REASON'S
A free acquytaunce without relees, LECTURE
A trouthe frette ful of falshede, 4705
A sickernesse al sette in drede;
In herte is a dispeyryng hoope,
And ful of hoope, it is wanhoope;
Wyse woodnesse, and wode reasoun,
A swete peryl in to drowne, 4710
An hevy burthen lyght to beare,
A wicked wawe awaye to weare.
It is Carybdes perilous,
Disagreable and gratious.
It is descordaunce that can accorde, 4715
And accordaunce to discorde.
It is connynge without science,
Wysedom without sapyence,
Wytte without discretioun,
Havoyre without possessyoun. 4720

It is syke hele and hole sickenesse,
A thruste drowned in dronknesse,
An helthe ful of maladye,
And charyte ful of envye,
An hunger ful of habundaunce, 4725
And a gredy suffysaunce;
Delyte right ful of hevynesse,
And dreryhed ful of gladnesse;
Bytter swetnesse and swete errour,
Right yvel savoured good savour; 4730
Sen that pardone hath withinne,
And pardone spotted without with synne;
A payne also it is, joyous,
And felonye ryght pytous;
Also playe that selde is stable, 4735
And stedfast stat, right mevable;
A strength weyked to stonde upright,
And feblenesse ful of myght;
Wytte unavysed, sage folye,
And joye ful of tourmentrye; 4740
A laughter it is, wepynge aye,
Rest that traveyleth nyght and daye.
Also a swete helle it is,
And a sorouful paradys;
A pleasaunt gayle and easy prisoun, 4745
And, ful of frost, somer seasoun;
Pryme temps ful of frostes whyte,
And Maye devoyde of al delyte,
With seer braunches, blossoms ungrene;
And newe frute, fylled with wynter tene. 4750
It is a slowe, maye nat forbeare
Ragges rybaned with golde to weare;
For also wel wol love he sette
Under ragges as riche rochette;
And eke as wel be amorettes 4755
In mournyng blacke as bright burnettes.
For none is of so mokel prise,

4685 lere, teach. **4689 wite … science,** understand, knowledge. TG *wite* om. **4693 sothe,** truth. **4697 him … wol flye,** him who will fly from. **4700 be,** been. T *to.* **4701 ententioun,** attention. **4703 hateful pees,** what follows is a series of conventional troubadour-like oxymora. **4705 frette,** adorned. *A trouthe:* TG *And through the.* **4708 wanhoope,** despair. **4709 woodnesse,** insanity. *wode:* TG *vo(y)de.* **4712 wawe,** wave. **awaye to weare,** (?) always to beware. **4720 Havoyre,** to have (Fr. *avoir*). **4721 hele,** health. *syke:* TG *lyke.* **4722 thruste:** TG *trust(e)* ; Fr. *soif. in:* TG *and.* **4723 An:** TG *And.* **4725 An hunger:** TG *And angre;* Fr. *C'est faim.* **4728 dreryhed:** TG *dreryed.* **4731 Sen,** sin. **4732** TG *with* om. **4736** TG *stat* om.; Fr. *Estat.* **4737 weyked,** (too) weak. **4745 gayle,** jail (gaol). **4747 Pryme temps,** spring. **4750 newe … tene,** fresh, bitterness. **4751 slowe,** loafer (sluggard). Fr. *caigne* (useless dog). **4754 rochette,** cloak (bishop's vestment). **4755–56 amorettes … burnettes,** i.e., sweethearts are as good in black mourning as in bright robes. *be:* TG *by;* Fr. *sont.* **4757 mokel prise,** much value (price).

Ne no manne founden so wyse,
Ne none so highe is of parage,
Ne no manne founde of wytte so sage,　　4760
No manne so hardy ne so wight,
Ne no manne of so mokel myght,
None so fulfylled of bounte,
That ne with Love maye daunted be.
Al the worlde holdeth this waye;　　4765
Love maketh al to gone myswaye,
But it be they of yvel lyfe,
Whome Genius cursed, man and wyfe,
That wrongly werke agayne Nature.
None suche I love, ne have no cure　　4770
Of suche as Loves servauntes bene,
And wol nat by my counsayle flene.
For I ne preyse that lovynge
Wher-through men, at the laste endynge,
Shal cal hem wretches ful of wo.　　4775
Love greveth hem and shendeth so.
But if thou wolte wel Love eschewe,
For to escape out of his mewe,
And make al hoole thy sorowe to slake,
No better counsayle mayst thou take　　4780
Than thynke to fleen wel, ywis;
Maye nought helpe els, for wytte thou this:
If thou flye it, it shal flye the;
Folowe it, and folowen shal it the."
L'AMAUNT: Whan I hadde herde al Reason
　　sayne,　　4785
Whiche had spilte her speche in vayne,
"Dame," sayd I, "I dare wel saye
Of this avaunt me wel I maye
That from your schole so deviaunt
I am that never the more avaunt　　4790
Right nought am I, through your doctryne;

I dulle under your disciplyne;
I wotte no more than wyste I er,
To me so contrary and so fer
Is everythynge that ye me lere.　　4795
And yet I canne it al par cuere;
Myne herte foryeteth therof right nought,
It is so written in my thought;
And depe greven it is so tender
That al by herte I can it render,　　4800
And rede it over communely;
But to myselfe lewdest am I.
But sithe ye love discryven so,
And lacke and preise it bothe two,
Defyneth it into this letter　　4805
That I maye thynke on it the better.
For I herde never diffyne it ere,
And wylfully I wolde it lere."
　　"If love be serched well and sought,
It is a sickenesse of the thought　　4810
Annexed and knedde betwixt tweyne,　　REASON
Which male and female with o cheyne　　DESCRIBES
So frely byndeth that they nyl twynne,　　LOVE
Wheder so therof they lese or wynne.
The rote spryngeth through hoote brennynge
Into disordynate desyringe　　4816
For to kyssen and enbrace,
And at her luste them to solace.
Of other thynge love retcheth nought,
But setteth her herte and al her thought　　4820
More for delectatioun
Than any procreatioun
Of other fruite by engendrure,
Whiche love to God is nat pleasure.
For of her body fruyte to gette　　4825
They yeve no force, they are so sette

4759 **parage**, lineage. 4761 **wight**, active. 4764 **daunted**, overcome. *ne:* TG *he;* Fr. *ne soit.* 4766 **myswaye**, astray (i.e., his way). 4767 **But**, unless. 4768 **Genius**, the priest of Nature in *RR* 16249ff. (Dunn-Robbins 79ff.), and of Venus in Gower's *Confessio Amantis,* 1.190ff. In both cases, as in the philosophy of the "Chartrian" school, genius serves as priest of the fundamental sexual drive for procreation. 4769 **wrongly werke**, in Alanus ab Insulis, *De Planctu Naturae,* which greatly influenced *RR* (and Chaucer's *PF*), one of the principal complaints of Nature is against unnatural sex. 4770 **cure**, custody. 4772 **flene**, flee (from love). 4775 **hem**, themselves. 4776 **shendeth**, destroys. 4778 **mewe**, cage. 4782 **Maye nought**, nothing else can help. 4785 **sayne**, said. 4788 **avaunt**, boast. 4790 **avaunt**, successful (forward). 4792 **dulle**, grow dull. 4793 **er**, before. TG *wyst(e) ever.* 4795 **lere**, teach. 4796 **canne**, know. *al par cuere* (by heart): TG *al by partuere.* 4799 **greven**, engraved. 4800 **by:** T *myne.* 4801 **communely**, frequently. 4802 **lewdest**, most ignorant. 4803 **discryven**, describe. 4805 **letter**, i.e., statement (definition). 4807 *diffyne it ere:* TG *diffyned he(e)re;* Fr. *l'oi deffenir onques.* 4808 **wylfully ... lere**, deliberately, learn. 4811 **knedde**, knit. 4812 *Which:* TG *With.* 4813 **frely ... twynne**, of (their own) free will, part. TG *frely that.* 4814 **lese ... wynne**, lose, profit. 4818 **luste ... solace**, pleasure, enjoy (relieve). 4819 **retcheth**, cares. 4826 **no force**, no care.

Upon delyte, to playe in-fere.
And some have also this manere,
To faynen hem for love seke;
Suche love I preyse nat at a leke.   4830
For paramours they do but fayne;
To love trewly they disdayne.
They falsen ladyes traytoursly,
And swerne hem othes utterly
With many a leasyng and many a fable,   4835
And al they fynden disceyvable;
And whan they han her luste getten,
The hoote ernes they al foryetten.
Women the harme byen ful sore;
But menne this thynken evermore   4840
That lasse harme is, so mote I thee,
Disceyve them that disceyved be;
And namely, where they ne maye
Fynde none other meane waye.
For I wotte wel, in sothfastnesse,   4845
That who dothe nowe his besynesse
With any woman for to dele,
For any luste that he may fele,
But if it be for engendrure,
He dothe trespasse, I you ensure;   4850
For he shulde setten al his wyl
To getten a lykely thynge him tyl,
And to sustayne, if he myght,
And kepe forthe, by Kyndes ryght,
His owne lykenesse and semblable,   4855
For because al is corrumpable,
And fayle shulde successyoun,
Ne were their generatioun
Our sectes sterne for to save.
Whan father or mother arne in grave,   4860
Her chyldren shulde, whan they ben dede,
Ful dilygent bene in her stede

To use that warke on suche a wyse
That one may through another ryse.
Therfore sette Kynde therin delyte,   4865
For men therin shulde hem delyte,
And of that dede be nat erke,
But ofte sythes haunt that werke;
For none wolde drawe therof a draught
Ne were delyte whiche hath him caught.   4870
    "Thus hath subtylled Dame Nature;
For none gothe right, I the ensure,
Ne hath entent hoole ne parfyte;
For her desyre is for delyte,
The whiche fortened crease and eke   4875
The playe of love for-ofte seke,
And thral hemselfe, they be so nyce,
Onto the prynce of every vyce.
For of eche synne it is the rote,
Unleful luste, though it be sote,   4880
And of a yvel the racyne,
As Tullyus canne determyne,
Whiche in his tyme was ful sage,
In a booke he made *Of Age*,
Where that more he prayseth Elde,   4885
Though he be croked and unwelde,
And more of commendatioun,
Than Youthe in his discriptioun;
For Youthe sette bothe man and wyfe
In al parel of soule and lyfe;   4890
And parel is, but men have grace,
The tyme of youthe for to pace
Without any dethe or distresse,
It is so ful of wyldnesse;
So ofte it dothe shame or domage   4895
To him or to his lynage.
It ledeth man nowe up, nowe downe,
In mokel dissolutioun,

4827 in-fere, together. **4829 faynen . . . seke,** pretend, to attain. **4830 at a leke,** the value of a leek. **4831 paramours,** sexual love. **4835 leasyng,** lying. **4836 disceyvable,** deceptive. **4838 ernes,** ardor. **4839 byen,** pay for. **4841 thee,** prosper. **4843 namely,** especially. **4846** *who:* TG *what.* **4852 getten a lykely . . . tyl,** beget a thing like himself. This is the "natural" justification for sex in Chartrian philosophy. **4853 myght,** is able. **4854 Kyndes ryght,** natural right. **4856** Line omitted in G. **corrumpable,** destructible. **4857 successyoun,** succession of generations—all important in an hereditary society. **4858 their generatioun,** were there not procreation (regeneration). **4859 sectes sterne,** species' strain. **4867 erke,** weary (irked). **4868 sythes,** times. **4869 drawe . . . draught,** participate (take a sip). **4871 subtylled,** figured out. TG *This had subtyl;* Fr. *Ainsi Nature i soutiva.* **4875 fortened crease,** obstructed increase. **4876 for-ofte,** very often ("for" is an intensifier). **4877 thral . . . nyce,** enslave, foolish. **4878** *vyce:* G *wise.* **4880 Unleful luste,** unlawful pleasure (i.e., sexual pleasure not with the intention of procreation). **4881 racyne,** root. **4882 Tullyus,** Cicero's *De Senectute.* **4886 unwelde,** awkward (weak). **4887 of commendatioun,** to be praised. **4892** *tyme:* TG *parel.* **4898 mokel,** great.

And maketh him love yvel company,
And lede his lyfe disrulyly, 4900
And halte hym payde with ñone estate.
Within hymselfe is suche debate,
He chaungeth purpose and entent;
And yalte him into some covent,
To lyven after her emprise, 4905
And leseth fredom and fraunchyse
That Nature in him had sette,
The whiche agayne he may not gette,
If he there make his mansyon
For to abyde professyon. 4910
Though for a tyme his herte absente,
It may not fayle, he shal repente,
And eke abyde thilke day
To leave his abyte and gon his way,
And leseth his worshyp and his name, 4915
And dare not come agayne for shame.
But al his lyfe he dothe so mourne,
Bycause he dare nat home retourne.
Fredom of kynde so loste hath he
That never may recured be, 4920
But if that God him graunte grace
That he may, er he hence pace,
Conteyne under obedyence
Through the vertue of pacience.
For Youthe set man in al folye, 4925
In unthrifte and in ribaudye,
In lechery and in outrage,
So ofte it chaungeth of corage.
Youthe gynneth ofte suche bargayne
That may not ende without payne. 4930
In great parell is set youth-hede,
Delyte so doth his bridell lede.
Delyte thus hangeth, drede the nought,
Bothe mans body and his thought,
Onely through Youthe, his chamberere, 4935
That to done yvell is customere,

And of naught els taketh hede
But onely folkes for to lede
Into disporte and wyldenesse,
So is she frowarde from sadnesse. 4940
"But Elde draweth hem therfro.
Who wote it not, he may wel go
Demand of hem that nowe arne olde,
That whylom Youthe had in holde,
Whiche yet remembre of tender age, 4945
Howe it hem brought in many a rage,
And many a foly therein wrought.
But nowe that Elde hath hem through sought,
They repent hem of her folye,
That Youthe hem put in jeopardye, 4950
In parell and in moche wo,
And made hem ofte amysse to do,
And sewen yvell companye,
Ryot and avoutrye.
But Elde can agayne restrayne 4955
From suche foly, and refrayne
And set men by her ordynaunce
In good rule and in governaunce.
But yvel she spendeth her servyse,
For no man wol her love ne preyse; 4960
She is hated, this wote I wele.
Her acqueyntaunce wolde no man fele,
Ne han of Elde companye,
Men hate to be of her alye.
For no man wolde becomen olde, 4965
Ne dye whan he is yonge and bolde.
And Elde merveyleth right greatly,
Whan they remembre hem inwardly
Of many a perillous emprise,
Whiche that they wrought in sondrie wyse, 4970
However they might, without blame,
Escape away without shame,
In Youthe, without domage
Or reprefe of her lynage,

4901 **halte ... payde ... estate.** i.e., and considers himself satisfied with no situation. 4904 **yalte ... covent,** yields, convent (monastic order). TG *him* om. 4905 **emprise,** vow (undertaking). 4910 **abyde professyon,** await profession of holy orders (after his probationary period). 4911 **absente,** is absent (from sex and secular pleasures). 4914 **leave his abyte,** leave his (monk's) habit. 4915 **worshyp ... name,** honor, good name (for forsaking his vow). 4921 TG *But that if.* 4923 **Conteyne ... obedyence,** continue, monastic vows. 4926 T *ribaudue.* 4928 **corage,** spirit. 4933 *thus:* TG *this;* Fr. *Ensi.* 4935 TG *youthes chamb(e)re;* Fr. *Jonesce sa chambriere.* 4940 **frowarde from sadnesse,** obstinate against sobriety. TG *she* om. 4943 *Demand:* TG *And no(o);* Fr. *demande.* 4948 *hem:* TG *him.* 4953 **sewen,** to pursue. 4954 **avoutrye,** adultery. 4955 *can:* TG *gan.* 4959 **yvel ... spendeth ... servyse,** i.e., her efforts are unprofitable. 4960 *ne:* TG *neyther.* 4962 **fele,** make (feel). 4964 **alye,** alliance. 4974 **reprefe,** reproof.

Losse of membre, shedyng of blood,　　　　4975
Parell of dethe, or losse of good.
　"Woste thou not where Youthe abyt,
That men so preysen in her wyt?
With Delyte she halte sojour,
For bothe they dwellen in o tour.　　　　4980
As longe as Youthe is in season,
They dwellen in one mansyon.
Delyte of Youthe wol have servyce
To do what so he wol devyse;
And Youthe is redy evermore　　　　4985
For to obeye, for smerte of soore,
Unto Delyte, and him to yeve
Her servyce whyle that she may lyve.
　"Where Elde abytte I wol the tel
Shortly, and no while dwel,　　　　4990
For thyder behoveth the to go,
If dethe in youthe the nat slo;
Of this journey thou mayst nat fayle.
With her Labour and Travayle
Lodged ben, with Sorowe and Wo,　　　　4995
That never out of her courte go.
Payne and Dystresse, Syckenesse and Yre.
And Melancoly, that angry syre,
Bene of her paleys senatours;
Gronyng and Grutchyng, her herbegeours,　　5000
The daye and nyght, her to tourment,
With cruel Dethe they her present,
And tellen her, erlyche and late,
That Dethe stondeth armed at her gate.
Than brynge they to her remembraunce　　5005
The foly dedes of her enfaunce,
Whiche causen her to mourne in wo
That Youthe hath her begyled so,
Whiche sodainly awaye is hasted.
She wepeth the tyme that she hath wasted, 5010
Complaynynge of the preterytte,
And the present that nat abytte,
And of her olde vanyte,
That but aforne her she maye se
In the future some socoure,　　　　5015

To leggen her of her doloure,
To graunt her tyme of repentaunce,
For her synnes to do penaunce,
And at the laste so her governe
To wynne the joye that is eterne.　　　　5020
Fro whiche go backwarde Youthe her made,
In vanyte to drowne and wade,
For present tyme abydeth nought.
It is more swyfte than any thought;
So lytel whyle it dothe endure　　　　5025
That there nys compte ne measure.
　"But howe that ever the game go,
Who lyst to have joye and myrthe also
Of love, be it he or she,
Hye, or lowe, who it be,　　　　5030
In fruyte they shulde hem delyte.
Her parte they maye nat els quyte
To save hemselfe in honeste.
And yet ful many one I se
Of women, sothly for to sayne,　　　　5035
That desyre and wolde fayne
The playe of love, they be so wylde,
And nat coveyte to go with chylde.
And if with chylde they be perchaunce,
They wol it holde a great myschaunce;　　5040
But whatsoever wo they fele,
They wol nat playne, but concele,
But if it be any foole or nyce,
In whome that shame hath no justyce.
For to delyte echone they drawe,　　　　5045
That haunt this worke, bothe hye and lawe,
Save suche that arne worthe right nought,
That for money wal be bought.
Suche love I preyse in no wyse,
Whan it is goven for covetyse.　　　　5050
I preyse no woman, though she be woode,
That yeveth herselfe for any goode.
For lytel shulde a man telle
Of her that wol her body selle,
Be she mayde, be she wyfe,　　　　5055
That quycke wol selle her by her lyfe.

4977 abyt, abides. **4989 abytte,** lives. **4992 slo,** slay. **5000 Grutchyng . . . herbegeours,** complaining, hosts (as in an inn). **5006 foly,** foolish. **5010 TG** *weped.* **5011 preterytte,** time past. **5012 nat abytte,** abides not. **5016 leggen,** alleviate. **5021 go,** to go. *her:* TG *he.* **5026 compte,** count. **5028 lyst,** desires. *have:* TG *love.* **5031 fruyte,** i.e., children. **5032 parte . . . quyte,** action, make amends for. **5036 fayne,** eagerly. **5043 nyce,** foolish (woman). **5050 goven,** given. **5051 woode,** mad. *she:* TG *so.* **5053 telle,** account (value). **5054** *wol:* T *wel.* **5056 quycke,** alive.

Howe fayre chere that ever she make,
He is a wretch, I undertake,
That loveth suche one, for swete or soure,
Though she hym called her paramoure, 5060
And laugheth on him, and maketh him feest.
For certainly no suche beest
To be loved is nat worthy,
Or beare the name of drury.
None shulde her please but he were woode, 5065
That wol dispoyle him of his goode.
Yet nathelesse, I wol nat saye
But she for solace and for playe
Maye a jewel or other thynge
Take of her loves free yevynge— 5070
But that she aske it in no wyse,
For drede of shame or covetyse.
And she of hers maye him, certayne,
Without sclaunder, yeven agayne,
And joyne her hertes togyder so 5075
In love, and take and yeve also.
Trowe nat that I wol hem twynne
Whan in her love there is no synne;
I wol that they togyder go,
And done al that they hanne ado, 5080
As curteys shulde and debonayre,
And in her love beren hem fayre,
Without vyce, bothe he and she;
So that alwaye, in honeste,
Fro folly love they kepe hem clere 5085
That brenneth hertes with his fere;
And that her love in any wyse
Be devoyde of covetyse.
   "Good love shulde engendred be
Of trewe hert, juste and secree, 5090
And nat of suche as sette her thought
To have her luste and els nought;
So are they caught in Loves lace,
Trewly, for bodily solace.
Flesshely delyte is so present 5095
With the, that set al thyn entent,

Without more (what shulde I glose?)
For to get and have the rose,
Whiche maketh the so mate and wood
That thou desyrest none other good. 5100
But thou arte not an ynche the nerre,
But ever abydest in sorowe and werre,
As in thy face it is sene.
It maketh the bothe pale and lene;
Thy might, thy vertue gothe away. 5105
A sory gest, in good fay,
Thou herborest hem in thyn inne,
The God of Love whan thou let inne!
Wherfore I rede thou shette him oute,
Or he shal greve the, out of doute; 5110
For to thy profyte it wol turne,
If he nomore with the sojourne.
In great mischefe and sorowe sonken
Ben hertes that of love arne dronken,
As thou peraventure knowen shall, 5115
Whan thou hast lost thy tyme all,
And spent thy youthe in ydelnesse,
In waste and woful lustynesse.
If thou mayst lyve the tyme to se
Of Love for to delyvered be, 5120
Thy tyme thou shalte bewepe sore
The whiche never thou mayst restore.
For tyme loste, as men may se,
For nothyng may recovered be.
And if thou scape yet, at laste, 5125
Fro Love, that hath the so faste
Knytte and bounden in his lace,
Certayne I holde it but a grace.
For many one, as it is seyne,
Have loste and spent also in veyne 5130
In his servyce, without socour,
Body and soule, good and treasour,
Wytte and strength and eke rychesse,
Of whiche they had never redresse."
L'AMANT: Thus taught and preched hath
   Reason, 5135

5057 fayre chere, attractive welcome. **5059** TG *loved.* **5061 maketh . . . feest,** i.e., is good to him. **5064 drury,** chivalric love service. **5068** *But:* TG *That.* **5077 twynne,** separate. **5085 folly,** foolish (unnatural). *they:* TG *to.* **5093 lace,** net. **5097 more . . . glose,** more ado, lie. **5099 mate . . . wood,** dazed, mad. G *the* om. **5101 nerre,** nearer. **5102 werre,** anxiety (war). **5105 vertue,** potency. **5107** T *hem* om.; eds. emend to *than.* **5109 rede,** advise. **5116 thy:** TG *the;* Fr. *ton tens.* **5117** *thy youthe:* TG *by thought;* Fr. *ta jenesce.* **5118 lustynesse,** desire. **5120 Of . . . delyvered,** from, released. **5124** A commonplace found twice elsewhere in Chaucer, *HF* l. 1257; *CT* II.20. *recovered:* G *recured;* Fr. *recouvrer.*

But Love spylte her sermon,
That was so imped in my thought,
That her doctryne I set at nought.
And yet ne sayd she never a dele,
That I ne understode it wele,   5140
Worde by worde, the mater all.
But unto Love I was so thrall,
Whiche calleth over al his praye;
He chaseth so my thought aye,
And holdeth myne herte under his sele   5145
As trusty and trewe as any stele,
So that no devocion
Ne had I in the sermon
Of Dame Reason, ne of her rede;
It toke no sojour in myn heede.   5150
For al yede out at one ere
That in that other she dyd lere.
Fully on me she lost her lore;
Her speche me greved wonder sore.
    Than unto her for ire I sayde,   5155
For anger, as I dyd abrayde:
"Dame, and is it your wyl algate
That I not love, but that I hate
Al men, as ye me teche?
For if I do after your speche,   5160
Sythe that ye seyne love is not good,
Than must I nedes say with mode,
If I it leve, in hatred aye
Lyven; and voyde love awaye
From me wole I, a synful wretche,   5165
Hated of al that vertu tetche.
I may not go none other gate,
For eyther muste I love or hate.
And if I hate men of-newe,
More than love it wol me rewe,   5170
As by your prechyng semeth me,
For love nothyng ne prayseth the.
Ye yeve good counsayle, sykerly,
That precheth me al day that I
Shulde not Loves lore alowe—   5175
He were a foole, wolde you not trowe!

In speche also ye han me taught
Another love that knowen is naught,
Whiche I have herde you not repreve,
To love eche other. By your leve,   5180
If ye wolde diffyne it me,
I wolde gladly here, to se,
At the leest, if I may lere
Of sondrie loves the manere.
RAISON: "Certes, frende, a foole arte thou   5185
Whan that thou nothyng wolte alow
That I for thy profyte saye.
Yet wol I saye the more, in faye;
For I am redy, at the leest,
To accomplysshe thy request.   5190
But I not where it wol aveyle;
In vayne, pareventure, I shale traveyle.
Love there is in sondrye wyse,
As I shal the here devyse.
For some love leful is and goode—   5195
I meane nat that whiche maketh the woode,
And bringeth the in many a fytte,
And ravyssheth fro the al thy wytte,
It is so marveylous and queynt;
With suche love be no more aqueynt.   5200

Comment Raison diffinist amitie

    "Love of frendshippe also there is,   VARIOUS
Whiche maketh no man done amys,   KINDS
Of wyl knytte betwixte two,   OF LOVE
That wol nat breke for wele ne wo;
Whiche longe is lykely to contune,   5205
Whan wyl and goodes ben in commune;
Grounded by Goodes ordynaunce,
Hoole without discordaunce;
With hem holdynge commune
Of al her good charyte,   5210
That there be none excepcioun
Through chaungynge of ententioun;
That eche helpe other at her nede,
And wisely hele bothe worde and dede;

5136 **spylte,** spoiled. 5137 **imped,** planted. 5143 **praye,** prey. 5144 **aye,** continuously. 5145 **sele,** seal (authority). 5149 **rede,** advice. 5150 **sojour,** sojourn (dwelling place). 5152 **lere,** teach. 5155 *Than:* TG *That;* Fr. *Lors.* 5156 **abrayde,** start up. 5157 **algate,** in every way. 5162 **mode,** anger. 5165–66 Text follows Sutherland in adding *wole I* and *vertu.* 5167 **gate,** manner. 5168 *eyther:* G *other.* 5170 **rewe,** distress. 5176 **wolde . . . trowe,** i.e., who would not believe you. 5188 **faye,** faith. 5191 **where,** whether. 5194 **devyse,** describe. **amitie:** TG *aunsete.* 5203 **Of wyl,** deliberately. 5207 **Grounded by,** based upon. 5214 **hele,** conceal.

Trewe of meanyng, devoyde of slouthe, 5215
For wytte is nought without trouthe;
So that the tone dare al his thought
Sayne to his frende, and spare nought,
As to himselfe, without dredynge
To be discovered by wreying. 5220
For gladde is that conjunctioun
Whan there is none suspectioun
Ne lak in hem whome they wolde prove
That trewe and parfyte weren in love.
For no man maye be amyable, 5225
But if he be so ferme and stable
That Fortune chaunge him nat, ne blynde,
But that his frende alwaye him fynde,
Bothe poore and ryche, in o state.
For if his frende, through any gate, 5230
Wol complayne of his poverte,
He shulde nat byde so longe tyl he
Of his helpynge him requyre;
For good dede done through prayere
Is solde and bought to dere, ywis, 5235
To hert that of great value is.
For herte fulfylled of gentylnesse
Canne yvel demeane his distresse.
And man that worthy is of name
To askenne often hath great shame; 5240
A good manne brenneth in his thought
For shame, whan he asketh ought.
He hath great thought and dredeth aye
For his disease, whan he shal praye
His frende, lest that he warned be, 5245
Tyl that he preve his stabilyte.
But whan that he hath founden one
That trusty is and trewe as stone,
And assayed him at al,
And founde him stedfast as a wal, 5250
And of his frendshippe be certayne,
He shal him shewe bothe joye and payne,
And al that he dare thynke or saye,
Without shame, as he wel maye.
For howe shulde he ashamed be 5255

Of suche one as I told the?
For whan he wotte his secree thought,
The thirde shal knowe therof right nought;
For twey in nombre is bette than thre
In every counsayle and secree. 5260
Repreve he dredeth never a dele,
Who that besette his wordes wele,
For every wyse manne, out of drede,
Canne kepe his tonge tyl he se nede.
And fooles cannenat holde her tonge; 5265
A fooles belle is soone ronge.
Yet shal a trewe frende do more
To helpe his felowe of his sore,
And socour him whan he hath nede
In al that he maye done in dede, 2570
And gladder be that he him pleaseth
Than his felowe that he easeth.
And if he do nat his request,
He shal as moche him molest
As his felowe, for that he 5275
Maye nat fulfyl his volunte
Fully, as he hath requyred.
If bothe the hertes Love hath fyred,
Joye and wo they shal departe,
And take evenly eche his parte. 5280
Halfe his anoye he shal have aye,
And comforte him what that he maye;
And of his blysse parte shal he,
If Love wel departed be.
    "And whylom of this amyte 5285
Spake Tullius in a dyte:
'A man shulde maken his request
Unto his frende that is honest,
And he goodly shulde it fulfyll
But it the more were out of skyll, 5290
And otherwyse not graunte therto
Except only in cases two:
If men his frende to dethe wolde drive,
Let him be besy to save his lyve
Also if men wollen him assayle 5295
Of his worshyp to make him fayle,

5220 **discovered by wreying,** revealed by revelation. 5223 **Ne lak,** nor shortcoming (failure of friendship). TG *Ne lak in hem* om.
5230 **gate,** circumstance. 5236 **value,** worth. 5238 **yvel demeane,** ill endure. 5244 **disease,** distress. 5245 **warned,** denied. 5253
TG *he* om. 5257 **wotte,** knows. 5271 TG *be* om. 5276 **volunte,** desire. 5279 **departe,** divide. 5282 TG *him* om. 5283 *his:* TG *this.*
5284 *wel:* TG *wol.* 5285 *amyte:* TG *unyte;* Fr. *amitie.* 5287 *A man:* TG *And.* 5290 **But ... out of skyll,** unless, unreasonable. 5292
cases: TG *cause(s);* Fr. *cas.* 5296 **worshyp,** honor.

And hyndren him of his renoun,
Let him with ful entencioun,
His dever done in eche degre
That his frende ne shamed be.   5300
In this two cases with his might,
Takyng no kepe to skyll nor right,
As ferre as love may him excuse,
This ought no man to refuse.'
This love that I have tolde to the   5305
Is nothyng contrarye to me;
This wol I that thou folowe wele,
And leave the tother everydele.
This love to vertue al attendith,
The tother fooles blent and shendeth.   5310

"Another love also there is,
That is contrarye unto this,
Whiche desyre is so constrayned
That it is but wyl fayned.
Away fro trouthe it dothe so varye,   5315
That to good love it is contrarye;
For it maymeth in many wyse
Syke hertes with covetyse.
Al in wynnyng and in profyte
Suche love setteth his delyte.   5320
This love so hangeth in balaunce
That if it lese his hope parchaunce
Of lucre that he is set upon,
It wol fayle and quench anon.
For no man may be amorous,   5325
Ne in his lyvyng vertuous,
But he love more, in moode,
Men for hemselfe than for her goode.
For love that profyte dothe abyde
Is false, and bydeth not in no tyde.   5330
This love cometh of Dame Fortune,
That lytel whyle wol contune,
For it shal chaungen wonder soone,
And take eclyps right as the moone
Whan she is from us lette   5335
Through erthe, that betwixt is sette

The sonne and her, as it may fall,
Be it in partie or in all;
The shadowe maketh her bemes merke,
And her hornes to shewe derke,   5340
That parte where she hath loste her lyght
Of Phebus fully, and the syght,
Tyl whan the shadowe is overpaste,
She is enlumyned ageyn as faste,
Through the brightnesse of the sonne bemes 5345
That yeveth to her agayne her lemes.
That love is right of suche nature;
Nowe is fayre, and nowe obscure,
Nowe bright, nowe clipsy of manere,
And whilom dymme and whylom clere.   5350
As soone as Poverte gynneth take
With mantel and weedes blake
It hydeth of Love the light away,
That into nyght it turneth day;
It may not se Richesse shyne   5355
Tyl the blacke shadowes fyne.
For whan Rychesse shyneth bright,
Love recovereth ayen his lyght;
And whan it fayleth, he wol flyt,
And as she groweth, so groweth it.   5360

"Of this love, here what I saye:
The ryche men are loved aye,
And namely tho that sparande bene,
That wol not wasshe her hertes clene
Of the fylthe nor of the vyce   5365
Of gredy brennyng Avaryce.
The ryche man ful fonde is, ywis,
That weneth that he loved is.
If that his herte it understode,
It is not he, it is his good;   3570
He may wel weten in his thought,
His good is loved, and he right nought.
For if he be a nygarde eke,
Men wol nat set by him a leke,
But haten him; this is the sothe.   5375
Lo, what profyte his catel dothe!

5299 dever, duty (devoir). **5301** TG *case;* G *two* om. **5302 skyll,** reason. **5306 contrarye,** objectionable. **5309** *attendith:* TG *entendith:* Fr. *s'amort* (attaches itself). **5314 wyl fayned,** feigned desire. TG *it* om. **5323 lucre,** i.e., hope for money, material gain. **5327 moode,** spirit. **5329 abyde,** expect (await). **5330 bydeth,** lasts. G *bit.* **5331** TG *This* om.; Fr. *Ceste.* **5335 lette,** prevented (hidden). *she:* TG *he.* **5338 in partie,** partly (i.e., making a partial moon). **5339 merke,** dim. **5346 lemes,** rays. **5349 clipsy,** eclipsed. **5353** TG *It* om. **5360** *groweth:* TG *greveth;* Fr. *resaillent* (spout forth). **5363 sparande,** miserly (sparing; northern form). **5367 fonde,** foolish. **5368 weneth,** thinks. **5369** *it:* TG *is.* **5376 catel,** chattels (wealth). *his:* G *this.*

Of every man that may him se,
It getteth him nought but enmyte.
But he amende hym of that vyce,
And knowe himselfe, he is not wyse. 5380
"Certes, he shulde aye frendly be,
To get hym love also ben fre;
Or els he is not wyse ne sage
No more than is a gote ramage.
That he not loveth, his dede proveth, 5385
Whan he his richesse so wel loveth,
That he wol hyde it aye and spare,
His poore frendes sene forfare,
To kepen aye his purpose
Tyl for drede his eyen close, 5390
And tyl a wicked dethe him take.
Hym had lever asondre shake
And let al his lymmes asondre ryve,
Than leave his richesse in his lyve.
He thenketh parte it with no man; 5395
Certayne no love is in him than.
Howe shulde love within hym be,
Whan in his herte is no pyte?
That he trespaseth, wel I wate,
For eche man knoweth his estate; 5400
Ful wel him ought to be reproved
That loveth nought, ne is not loved.
"But sithe we arne to Fortune comen
And have our sermon of her nomen, FORTUNE
A wonder wyll I tel the nowe, 5405
Thou herdest never suche one, I trowe.
I not where thou me leven shall,
Though sothfastnesse it be all.
As it is written and is sothe
That unto men more profyte dothe 5410
The frowarde Fortune and contraire
Than the swote and debonaire.
And if the thynke it is doutable,
It is through argument provable,
For the debonayre and softe 5415

Falseth and begyleth ofte.
For lyche a mother she can cherishe
And mylken as dothe a norice;
And of her good to hem deles,
And yeveth hem parte of her joweles, 5420
With great rychesse and dignite.
And hem she hoteth stabylite
In a state that is not stable,
But chaungyng aye and variable;
And fedeth hem with glorie veyne 5425
And worldly blysse noncertayne,
Whan she hem setteth on her whele.
Than wene they to be right wele,
And in so stable state withall,
That never they wene for to fall. 5430
And whan they sette so hygh be,
They wene to have in certeynte
Of hertly frendes so great nombre
That nothyng might her state encombre.
They truste hem so on every syde, 5435
Wenyng with hem they wolde abyde
In every parel and mischaunce,
Without chaunge or variaunce,
Bothe of catel and of good;
And also for to spende her blood 5440
And al her membres for to spyll
Onely to fulfyll her wyll.
They maken it hole in many wyse,
And hoten hem her ful servyse,
Howe sore that it do hem smerte 5445
Into her very naked sherte!
Herte and al so hole they yeve
For the tyme that they may lyve
So that with her flaterye
They maken fooles glorifye 5450
Of her wordes spekyng,
And han therof a rejoysyng,
And trowe hem as the Evangyle;
And it is al falshede and gyle,

5379 **hym:** TG *hymselfe.* 5382 **love . . . fre,** i.e., love that is sincere. 5384 **gote ramage,** wild goat; Fr. *Sers* (stag). 5387 **spare,** hoard. 5388 **forfare,** perish. 5393 **ryve,** wrench (be wrenched). 5395 **parte,** to divide. 5399 **wate,** know. 5401 *Ful:* TG *For;* Fr. *mout.* 5404 **have:** TG *hath.* 5407 **leven,** believe. 5408 G *it be it al.* 5411 **frowarde,** obstinate. 5418 **mylken . . . norice,** provide milk, nurse. 5419–20, 25, 27, 36 **hem:** TG *hy(i)m;* Fr. *les.* **deles,** give (deal). 5422 **hoteth,** promises. 5425 G *glorie and weyne.* 5433 **hertly,** bosom (hearty). **so:** TG *to.* 5441 **spyll,** sacrifice (waste). 5443 **maken it hole,** i.e., promise their whole service. 5444 **hoten,** promise. 5445 **Howe sore,** however sorely. 5446 G *very* om. 5450 **fooles glorifye,** fools to be glorified. 5452 *ther:* TG *chere.* 5453 **trowe . . . Evangyle,** believe, Gospel.

As they shal afterwarde se, 5455
Whan they arne fall in poverte
And ben of good and catell bare;
Than shul they sene who frendes ware.
For of an hundred, certaynly,
Nor of a thousande ful scarsly, 5460
Ne shal they fynde unnethes one,
Whan poverte is comen upon.
For this Fortune that I of tell,
With men whan her lust to dwell,
Maketh hem to lese her conysaunce, 5465
And norissheth hem in ignoraunce.

"But frowarde Fortune and perverse,
Whan high estates she dothe reverse,
And maketh hem to tomble doune
Of her whele, with sodayne tourne, 5470
And from her rychesse dothe hem flye,
And plongeth hem in poverte,
As a stepmother envyous,
And layeth a playstre dolorous
Unto her hertes, wounded egre, 5475
Whiche is not tempred with vynegre,
But with poverte and indygence,
For to shewe, by experience,
That she is Fortune verilye
In whom no man shulde affye, 5480
Nor in her yeftes have fyaunce,
She is so ful of varyaunce.
Thus can she maken hye and lowe,
Whan they from rychesse arne throwe,
Fully to knowen, without were, 5485
Frende of affecte and frende of chere;
And whiche in love weren trewe and stable,
And whiche also weren varyable,
After Fortune, her goddesse,
In poverte, either in rychesse, 5490
For al she yeveth here, out of drede,
Unhappe bereveth it in dede.

For Infortune lette not one
Of frendes whan Fortune is gone—
I meane tho frendes that wol fle 5495
Anon as entreth poverte.
And yet they wol not leave hem so,
But in eche place where they go
They cal hem 'wretche', scorne and blame,
And of her mishappe hem diffame; 5500
And namely suche as in rychesse
Pretendeth moste of stablenesse,
Whan that they sawe hem set onlofte,
And weren of hem socoured ofte,
And moste yholpe in al her nede. 5505
But nowe they take no maner hede,
But seyne in voyce of flaterye
That nowe appereth her folye
Over al where so they fare,
And synge, 'Go, farewel feldefare!' 5510
Al suche frendes I beshrewe,
For of trewe there be to fewe;
But sothfaste frendes, what so betyde,
In every fortune wollen abyde.
They han her hertes in suche noblesse 5515
That they nyl love for no rychesse,
Nor for that Fortune may hem sende
They wollen hem socour and defende,
And chaunge for softe ne for sore,
For who is frende, loveth evermore. 5520
Though men drawe swerde his frende to slo,
He may not hewe her love atwo,
But in case that I shal say,
For pride and ire lese it he may,
And for reprove by nycete, 5525
And discoveryng of privyte,
With tonge woundyng, as felon,
Through venemous detraction.
Frende in this case wol gon his way,
For nothyng greve him more ne may; 5530

5457 **catell,** chattels. 5461 **unnethes,** scarcely. 5463 *this:* TG *thus;* Fr. *Ceste.* 5464 **lust,** desires. 5465 **conysaunce,** understanding. **hem:** G *men.* 5467 **frowarde,** obstinate. 5470 *Of* (off): G *Or with.* 5474 **playstre dolorous,** painful medicinal plaster. 5475 **egre,** sharply. 5476 **tempred with vynegre,** vinegar was used to soothe irritations. 5480 **affye,** trust. 5481 **fyaunce,** confidence. 5485 **were,** doubt. 5486 **affecte . . . chere,** i.e., true, false. 5489 **After,** i.e., like. 5491 **drede,** doubt. *she:* TG *that.* 5492 **Unhappe bereveth,** misfortune causes it to vanish (bereave). 5493 **lette,** leaves. 5501 **namely,** especially. 5503 *they:* G *the.* **hem:** TG *him.* 5504 **hem:** TG *him.* 5505 *yholpe:* G *I hope.* 5510 **feldefare,** a kind of thrush. The same phrase is found in *TC* III.861. 5511 **beshrewe,** curse. 5524 **lese it,** i.e., lose true friendship. 5525 **reprove by nycete,** foolish reproof. 5526 **discoveryng of privyte,** revealing confidence.

And for nought els wol he fle,
If that he love in stabylite.
And certayne he is wel begone
Amonge a thousande that fyndeth one.
For there may be no rychesse, 5535
Ayenst frendshyp of worthynesse;
For it ne may so hygh attayne
As may the valoure, sothe to sayne,
Of him that loveth trewe and well.
Frendshyp is more than is catell. 5540
For frende in courte aye better is
Than peny in purse, certis;
And Fortune, mishappyng,
Whan upon men she is fallyng,
Through misturnyng of her chaunce, 5545
And caste hem out of balaunce,
She maketh, through her adversyte,
Men ful clerely for to se
Hym that is frende in existence
From hym that is by apparence. 5550
For infortune maketh anone
To knowe thy frendes fro thy fone,
By experyence, right as it is;
The whiche is more to prayse, ywis,
Than is moche rychesse and tresour. 5555
For more doth profyte and valour
Povertie and suche adversyte
Before than dothe prosperyte;
For that one yeveth conysaunce,
And the tother ignoraunce. 5560
  "And thus in poverte is in dede
Trouthe declared fro falshede,
For faynte frendes it wol declare,
And trewe also, what way they fare.
For whan he was in his rychesse, 5565
These frendes, ful of doublenesse,
Offred him in many wyse,
Herte and body and servyce.
What wolde he than have yove to have bought
To knowen openly her thought, 5570

That he nowe hath so clerely sene?
The lasse begyled he shulde have bene
And he hadde than parceyved it,
But richesse nolde nat lette him wytte.
Wel more avauntage dothe him than, 5575
Sithe that it maketh him a wyse man,
The great myschefe that he receyveth
Than dothe richesse that him disceyveth.
  "Richesse riche ne maketh nought
Him that on treasour sette his thought; 5580
For richesse stonte in suffysaunce   DECEPTION
And nothynge in habundaunce;   OF RICHES
For suffysaunce al onely
Maketh menne to lyve richely.
For he that at mytches tweyne 5585
Ne valued is in his demayne
Lyveth more at ease, and more is riche,
Than dothe he that is chiche,
And in his berne hath, sothe to sayne,
An hundred mauys of whete grayne, 5590
Though he be chapman or marchaunt,
And have of golde many besaunt.
For in the gettyng he hath suche wo,
And in the kepyng drede also,
And sette evermore his besynesse 5595
For to encrease, and nat to lesse,
For to augment and multiplye.
And though on heapes it lye him by,
Yet never shal make his richesse
Asseth unto his gredynesse. 5600
But the poore that retcheth nought,
Save of his lyvelode, in his thought,
Whiche that he getteth with his traveyle,
He dredeth naught that it shal feyle,
Though he have lytel worldes goode, 5605
Meate and drynke and easy foode,
Upon his traveyle and lyvyng,
And also suffysaunt clothyng.
Or if in syckenesse that he fal,
And lothe meate and drynke withal, 5610

5533 wel begone, fortunate. **5543 mishappyng,** going wrong. **5544** *fallyng:* TG *fablyng;* Fr. *cheanz* (falling). **5555** *is:* TG *in.* **5556 doth profyte,** i.e., do poverty and adversity profit and enhance [true friendship]. *doth:* TG *depe.* **5559 conysaunce,** understanding. **5564 what way,** [by] what way. **5569** *yove* (given): T *you.* **5577** *receyveth:* TG *parceyveth;* Fr. *reçoit.* **5581 stonte in suffysaunce,** stands in sufficiency. **5585 mytches,** loaves of bread. *at:* TG *hath.* **5586** TG *Ne value in.* **5588 chiche,** niggardly. **5590 mauys,** Fr. *muis,* bushels (Lat. *medius*). **5592 besaunt,** gold coin, originally of Byzantium. **5593 gettyng,** learning. **5598** *it:* TG *that.* **5600 Asseth,** enough. **5601 retcheth,** cares. **5602 lyvelode,** livelihood. **5607 Upon his traveyle,** i.e., which he himself earns.

Though he have nat his meate to bye,
He shal bethynke him hastely,
To putte him out of al daungere,
That he of meate hath no mystere;
Or that he maye with lytel eke   5615
Be founden, whyle that he is seke;
Or that men shul hym berne in haste
To lyve tyl his syckenesse be paste,
To some maysondewe besyde.
He caste nought what shal him betyde.   5620
He thynketh nought that ever he shal
Into any syckenesse fal.
And though it fal, as it maye be,
That al betyme spare shal he,
As mokel as shal to hym suffyce,   5625
Whyle he is sycke in any wyse,
He dothe for that he wol be
Content with his poverte
Without nede of any manne.
So moche in lytel have he canne;   5630
He is apayde with his fortune.
And for he nyl be importune
Unto no wyght, ne onerous,
Nor of her goodesse coveytous,
Therfore he spareth, it maye wel bene,   5635
His poore estate for to sustene.
   "Or if hym luste nat for to spare,
But suffreth frost as hot ne ware,
At laste it hapneth, as it maye,
Right unto his laste daye,   5640
And take the worlde as it wolde be.
For ever in herte thynketh he,
The sooner that dethe hym slo,
To paradyse the sooner go
He shal, there for to lyve in blysse,   5645
Where that he shal no good mysse.
Thyder he hoopeth God shal him sende
After his wretched lyves ende.

Pythagoras himselfe reherses,
In a booke that *The Golden Verses*   5650
Is cleped, for the nobilyte
Of the honorable dyte:
'Than, whan thou gost thy body fro,
Free in the heyre thou shalte up go,
And leaven al humanyte,   5655
And purely lyve in deite.'
He is a foole, withouten were,
That troweth have his countrey here:
'In erthe is nat our countre,'
That may these clerkes seyne and se   5660
In Boece *Of Consolation,*
Where it is maked mention
Of our countre playne at the eye,
By techyng of phylosophye,
Where leude men might lere wyt,   5665
Whoso that wolde translaten it.
If he be suche that can wel lyve
After his rent may him yeve,
And not desyreth more to have,
That may fro poverte him save.   5670
A wyse man sayd, as we may sene,
Is no man wretched but he it wene,
Be he kyng, knyght, or rybaude.
And many a rybaude is mery and baude,
That swynketh and bereth, bothe day and
    nyght,   5675
Many a burthen of great myght,
The whiche dothe him lasse offence
For he suffreth in patience.
They laugh and daunce, tryppe and synge,
And lay nought up for her lyvynge,   5680
But in the taverne al dispendeth
The wynnyng that God hem sendeth.
Than gothe he fardels for to bere
With as good chere as he dyd ere.
To swynke and travayle he not fayneth,   5685

5614 mystere, necessity (i.e., fasting is the best cure). **5616 founden,** supported. **5617 berne,** take. **5619 maysondewe,** hospital; Fr. *Otel Dieu.* **5620 caste,** contemplates. **5624 spare,** save. **5625** *mokel* (much): G *mochel.* **5632 importune,** importunate (begging). **5633** *wyght:* G *witte.* **5637 spare,** save. **5638** *frost as hot:* TG *forth as not;* Fr. *froit que le chaut.* **5649–50 Pythagoras ... Golden Verses,** early Greek philosopher whose works are lost. The *Golden Verses* are a fifth-century A.D. summary of his ideas about transmigration of souls. **5652 dyte,** discourse. **5654 heyre,** air. **5658 troweth,** believes. **5663 playne at,** clear to. *Boece* III pr. 5, v pr. 1. **5665 leude ... lere,** ignorant, learn. **5668 After ... rent ... yeve,** i.e., live according to what his income allows. **5672 wene,** believes. **5673–74 rybaude ... baude,** churl (ribald), jolly (bold). **5675 swynketh,** labors. G *wynkith.* **5680 lay ... up,** save. **5683 fardels,** loads. **5685 fayneth,** shirk (pretend). G *feyntith.*

For to robben he disdayneth;
But right anon, after his swynke,
He gothe to taverne for to drinke.
Al these are ryche in habundaunce
That can thus have suffysaunce   5690
Wel more than can an usurere,
As God wel knoweth, without were.
For an usurer, so God me se,
Shal never for rychesse ryche be,
But evermore poore and indygent,   5695
Scarce and gredy in his entent.
   "For sothe it is, whom it displese,
There may no marchaunt lyve at ese,
His herte in suche a were is set,
That it quycke brenneth more to get;   5700
Ne never shal enough have geten;
Though he have golde in garners yeten;
For to be nedy he dredeth sore.
Wherfore to getten more and more
He set his herte and his desyre;   5705
So hote he brenneth in the fyre
Of covetyse that maketh him wood
To purchace other mennes good.
He underfongeth a great payne
That undertaketh to drinke up Sayne,   5710
For the more he drinketh, aye
The more he leaveth, the sothe to saye.
Thus is thurst of false gettyng,
That laste ever in coveyting,
And the anguysshe and distresse   5715
With the fyre of gredynesse.
She fyghteth with hym aye and stryveth
That his herte asonder ryveth.
Suche gredynesse him assayleth
That whan he moste hath, moste he fayleth.   5720
   "Physiciens and advocates
Gone right by the same yates;
They sell her science for wynnyng,
And haunte her crafte for great gettyng.
Her wynnyng is of suche swetnesse   5725

That if a man fall in sicknesse
They are ful glad for her encrese;
For by her wyll, without lese,
Everyche man shulde be seke,
And though they dye, they set not a leke.   5730
After, whan they the golde have take,
Ful lytel care for hem they make.
They wolde that fourty were sicke at ones,
Ye, two hundred, in flesshe and bones,
And yet two thousande, as I gesse,   5735
For to encresen her rychesse.
They wol not worchen, in no wyse,
But for lucre and covetyse.
For physicke gynneth first by *phy*—
The phisycien also sothely;   5740
And sythen it gothe fro *phy* to *sy*—
To truste on hem, it is folye.
For they nyl, in no maner gre,
Do right nought for charyte.
   "Eke in the same secte are sette   5745
Al tho that prechen for to gette
Worshyps, honour, and rychesse.
Her hertes arne in great distresse
That folke lyve not holily.
But aboven al, specially,   5750
Suche as prechen for veynglorie,
And towarde God have no memorie,
But forthe as ypocrites trace,
And to her soules dethe purchace,
And outwarde shewen holynesse,   5755
Though they be ful of cursednesse.
Nat lyche to the apostels twelve,
They disceyve other and hemselve;
Begyled is the gyler than.
For preachyng of a cursed man,   5760
Though it to other maye profyte,
Himselfe aveyleth nat a myte,
For ofte good predicatioun
Cometh of yvel ententioun.
To him nat vayleth his prechyng,   5765

5696 Scarce, niggardly. **5699 were,** distraction (war). TG *where.* **5700 quycke,** eagerly (alive). TG *more* om.; Fr. *plus.* **5701** TG *shal though he hath geten.* **5709 underfongeth,** undertakes. **5710 Sayne,** river Seine, in France. **5721 advocates,** lawyers. **5722 yates,** routes. **5724 haunte,** i.e., pursue. **5727** *her:* G *ther.* **5728 lese,** doubt (loss). **5739–41** The etymologizing is not in *RR.* The "phy" part is found in *La Bible Guiot de Provins,* l. 2582, but the rest is evidently Chaucer's. The point is clear that those who trust in physicians go from "fying" (trusting) to "sying" (sighing). T *fye to fye;* G *phy to sy.* **5743 gre,** pleasure. **5751** TG *for* om.; Fr. *pour.* **5755** *shewen:* TG *shewyng.* **5761** TG *it* om. **5765 vayleth,** avails.

Al helpe he other with his teachyng;
For where they good ensample take,
There is he with vaynglorie shake.

   "But lette us leven these prechours,   MISERS
And speke of hem that in her tours   5770
Heape up her golde, and faste shette,
And sore theron her herte sette.
They neyther love God, ne drede;
They kepe more than it is nede,
And in her bagges sore it bynde,   5775
Out of the sonne and of the wynde;
They putte up more than nede ware,
Whan they sene poore folke forfare,
For hungre dye, and for colde quake—
God can wel vengeaunce therof take.   5780
Thre great mischeves hem assayleth,
And thus in gadring aye travayleth:
With moche payne they wynne rychesse;
And drede hem holdeth in distresse,
To kepe that they gather faste;   5785
With sorowe they leave it at the laste.
With sorowe they bothe dye and lyve
That unto rychesse her hertes yeve;

And in defaute of love it is,
As it sheweth ful wel, ywis.   5790
For if these gredy, the sothe to sayne,
Loveden, and were loved agayne,
And good love reigned over all,
Suche wickednesse ne shulde fall.
But he shulde yeve that moste good
       had   5795
To hem that weren in nede bestad,
And lyve without false usure,
For charyte ful clene and pure.
If they hem yeve to goodnesse,
Defendyng hem from ydelnesse,   5800
In al this worlde than poore none
We shulde fynde, I trowe, not one.
But chaunged in this worlde unstable,
For love is over al vendable;
We se that no man loveth nowe,   5805
But for wynnyng and for prowe;
And love is thralled in servage
Whan it is solde for avauntage;
Yet women wol her bodyes sell;
Suche soules gothe to the dyvel of hell."   5810

FRAGMENT C

   Whan Love had tolde hem his entent,
The baronage to counsayle went.
In many sentences they fyll,
And dyversly they sayde her wyll;
But after discorde they accorded,   5815
And her acorde to Love recorded: LOVE'S
"Sir," sayden they, "we ben at one,   BARONS
By even accorde of everychone,   PLAN THE
Out-take Rychesse al-onely,   ASSAULT
That sworne hath ful hauteynly   5820
That she the castell nyl not assayle,
Ne smyte a stroke in this batayle
With darte ne mace, speare ne knyfe,
For man that speketh or bereth the lyfe,

And blameth your emprise, ywis,   5825
And from our hoste departed is,
At leest way, as in this plyte,
So hath she this man in dispyte.
For she saythe he ne loved her never,
And therfore she wol hate him ever.   5830
For he wol gather no tresore,
He hath her wrathe for evermore.
He agylte her never in other caas;
Lo, here al holy his trepas!
She saythe wel that this other day   5835
He asked her leave to gone the way
That is cleped To-Moche-Yevyng,
And spak ful fayre in his prayeng;

5767 **take,** (should) take. 5778 **forfare,** perish. 5781 *Thre:* TG *The;* Fr. *Treis.* 5782 **gadring . . . travayleth,** accumulating (wealth), distresses. 5789 **in defaute,** instead (default). 5804 **vendable,** for sale. 5806 **prowe,** profit. 5810 Part C picks up at *RR* 10681 (Dunn-Robbins 51). 5819 **Out-take,** except. 5820 **hauteynly,** arrogantly. 5825 **emprise,** undertaking. 5828 **dispyte,** dislike. 5833 **agylte,** offended.

But whan he prayed her, poore was he,
Therfore she warned him the entre. 5840
Ne yet is he not thriven so
That he hath getten a peny or two
That quytely is his owne in holde.
Thus hath Rychese us all tolde;
And whan Rychesse us this recorded, 5845
Withouten her we ben accorded.
   "And we fynde in our accordaunce,
That False-Semblant and Abstynaunce,
With al the folke of her batayle,
Shul at the hynder gate assayle, 5850
That Wicked-Tonge hath in kepyng,
With his Normans, ful of janglyng.
And with hem Curtesy and Largesse,
That shul shewe her hardynesse
To the olde wyfe that kepte so harde 5855
Fayre-Welcomyng within her warde.
Than shal Delyte and Wel-Helyng
Fonde Shame adowne to bring;
With al her hoost, early and late,
They shul assaylen that ylke gate. 5860
Agaynst Drede shal Hardynesse
Assayle, and also Sykernesse,
With al the folke of her leadyng,
That never wyst what was fleyng.
Fraunchise shal fyght, and eke Pyte, 5865
With Daungere, ful of cruelte.
Thus is your hoost ordayned wele;
Downe shal the castel every dele,
If everyche do his entent,
So that Venus be present, 5870
Your mother, ful of vesselage,
That canne ynough of such usage.
Withouten her maye no wight spede
This werke, neither for worde ne dede.
Therfore is good ye for her sende, 5875
For through her maye this worke
    amende."
   "Lordynges, my mother, the goddesse,

That is my lady and my maistresse, NATURE OF
Nys nat at al at my wyllyng, VENUS
Ne dothe nat al my desyringe. 5880
Yet canne she somtyme done labour,
Whan that her luste, in my socour,
Al my nedis for to atcheve,
But nowe I thynke her nat to greve.
My mother is she, and of childehede 5885
I bothe worshippe her and eke drede;
For who that dredeth sire ne dame
Shal it abye in body or name.
And, natheles, yet conne we
Sende after her, if nede be; 5890
And were she nygh, she commen wolde,
I trowe that nothynge myght her holde.
My mother is of great prowesse;
She hath tane many a forteresse,
That coste hath many a pounde er this, 5895
There I nas not present, ywis;
And yet men sayd it was my dede;
But I come never in that stede.
Ne me ne lyketh, so mote I the,
That suche toures ben take withoute me. 5900
For-why me thynketh that in no wyse
It maye be cleped by marchaundyse.
Go bye a courser, blacke or white,
And paye therfore; than arte thou quite.
The marchaunt oweth the right nought, 5905
Ne thou him, whan thou it bought.
I wol nat sellyng clepe yevyng,
For sellyng asketh no guerdonyng;
Here lythe no thanke, ne no meryte,
That one gothe from that other al quyte. 5910
But this sellyng is nat semblable;
For whan his horse is in the stable,
He maye it selle agayne, parde,
And wynnen on it, suche happe maye be;
Al maye the manne nat lese, ywis, 5915
For at the leest the skynne is his.
Or els, if it so betyde

5840 warned, forbade. **5841 thriven**, succeeded. **5843 quytely**, without obligation. **5854 hardynesse**, boldness. **5857 Wel-Helyng**, hide well, Fr. *Bien Celer*. **5858 Fonde**, manage. **5861 Drede**, fear. **5862 Sykernesse**, security. **5864 fleyng**, fleeing. **5865 Fraunchise**, frankness (sincerity). **5866 Daungere**, aloofness. **5870 So that**, i.e., if that. **5872 canne**, knows. **5876 amende**, be helped. **5879 TG *at* om. **5882 luste**, pleases. **5883** *Al my nedis*: TG *As my nede is;* Fr. *A mes besoignes.* **5885 of**, from. **5888 abye**, pay for. **5894 tane**, taken (northern form). **5899 the**, prosper. **5900** *withoute*: T *oute* om. **5902 cleped by marchaundyse**, called buying (love). **5908 guerdonyng**, reward. **5914 wynnen**, make a profit.

That he wol kepe his horse to ryde,
Yet is he lorde aye of his horse.
But thylke chaffare is welle worse 5920
There Venus entremeteth ought;
For whoso suche chaffare hath bought,
He shal not worchyn so wysely
That he ne shal lese al utterly
Bothe his money and his chaffare. 5925
But the seller of the ware
The prise and profyte have shal.
Certayne, the byer shal lese al
For he ne canne so dere it bye
To have lordshippe and ful maistry, 5930
Ne have power to make lettyng
Neyther for yefte ne for preachyng,
That of his chaffare, maugre his,
Another shal have as moche, ywis,
If he wol yeve as moche as he, 5935
Of what countrey so that he be;
Or for right nought, so happe maye,
If he canne flatter her to her paye.
Bene than suche marchauntes wyse?
No, but fooles in every wyse, 5940
Whan they bye suche thynge wylfully,
There as they lese her good fully.
But nathelesse, this dare I saye,
My mother is nat wonte to paye,
For she is neither so foole ne nyce, 5945
To entremete her of suche vyce.
But truste wel, he shal paye al
That repent of his bargayne shal,
Whan Poverte putte him in distresse,
Al were he scholer to Rychesse, 5950
That is for me in great yernyng,
Whan she assenteth to my wyllyng.
  "But by my mother Saynt Venus,
And by her father Saturnus,
That her engendred by his lyfe— 5955
But nat upon his wedded wyfe!—
Yet wol I more unto you swere,
To make this thyng the sikerere.

Nowe by that faithe and that leaute
That I owe to al my bretherne free, 5960
Of whiche there nys wight under hevyn
That canne her fathers names nevyn,
So dyvers and so many there be
That with my mother have be pryvee!
Yet wolde I swere, for sickernesse, 5965
The pole of helle to my wytnesse,
Nowe drynke I nat this yere clarre,
If that I lye, or forsworne be!
(For of the goddes the usage is
That whoso him forswereth amys 5970
Shal that yere drynke no clarre.)
Nowe have I sworne ynough, parde.
If I forswere me, than am I lorne;
But I wol never be forsworne.
Sithe Rychesse hath me fayled here, 5975
She shal abye that trespas ful dere,
Atte leest ways, but she her arme
With swerde, or sparth, or gysarme.
For certes, sythe she loveth nat me,
Fro thylke tyme that she maye se 5980
The castel and the toure toshake,
In sorye tyme she shal awake.
If I maye grype a ryche manne,
I shal so pulle him, if I canne,
That he shal in a fewe stoundes 5985
Lese al his markes and his poundes.
I shal him make his pens outslynge,
But they in his garner sprynge;
Our maydens shal eke plucke him so
That him shel neden fethers mo; 5990
And make him selle his londe to spende,
But he the bette conne him defende.
  "Poore men han made her lorde of me,
Although they nat so mightye be,
That they maye fede me in delyte. 5995
I wol nat have hem in dispyte.
No good man hateth hem, as I gesse,
For chynche and feloun is Richesse,
That so canne chase hem and dispsye,

5920 **chaffare**, bargain. 5921 **entremeteth**, interferes. 5925 **chaffare**, merchandise. 5929 **dere**, expensively. 5931 **lettyng**, hindrance, i.e., power to stop another from getting what he has paid for. 5938 **paye**, satisfaction. 5942 *fully:* TG *folyly;* Fr. *Ou tout.* 5945 **nyce**, foolish. 5946 *vyce:* G *wise.* 5953 TG *by* om. 5958 *sikerere:* TG *suerere.* 5959 *leaute:* TG *beaute;* Fr. *la foi.* 5967 *clarre,* claret wine. 5977 TG *she* om. 5978 **sparth . . . gysarme**, battle-ax, battle scythe. 5984 **pulle**, pluck. 5985 **stoundes**, moments. 5988 **garner sprynge**, i.e., grow voluntarily in his storehouse. 5995 **in delyte**, i.e., with delicacies. 5998 **chynche**, niggard.

And hem defoule in sondrye wyse. 6000
They loven ful bette, so God me spede,
Than dothe the riche, chynchy gnede,
And bene, in good faythe, more stable
And trewer and more servyable.
And therfore it suffyseth me 6005
Her good herte and her leaute.
They han on me sette al her thought,
And therfore I foryet hem nought.
I wol hem bringe in great noblesse,
If that I were god of rychesse, 6010
As I am god of love, sothely,
Suche routhe upon her playnt have I.
Therfore I muste his socour be,
That payneth him to serven me,
For if he deyde for love of this, 6015
Than semeth in me no love there is."
    "Sir," sayde they, "sothe is everydele
That ye reherce, and we wote wele
Thylke othe to holde is resonable;
For it is good and covenable 6020
That ye on riche men han sworne.
For sir, this wote we wel beforne:
If riche men done you homage,
That is as fooles done outrage;
But ye shul nat forsworne be, 6025
Ne lette therfore to drynke clarre,
Or pyment maked fresshe and newe.
Ladyes shul hem suche pepyr brewe
If that they fal into her laas,
That they for wo mowe sayne 'Alas!' 6030
Ladyes shullen ever so curteis be
That they shal quyte your othe al free.
Ne seketh never other vicayre,
For they shal speke with hem so fayre
That ye shal holde ye payde ful wele, 6035
Though ye you medle never a dele.
Lat ladyes worche with her thynges,
They shal hem tel so fele tydinges,

And move hem eke so many requestes
By flatery, that not honest is, 6040
And therto yeve hem suche thankynges,
What with kyssyng, and with talkynges,
That certes, if they trowed be,
Shal never leave hem londe ne fee
That it nyll as the moeble fare, 6045
Of whiche they first delyvered are.
Nowe may ye tell us al your wyll,
And we your hestes shal fulfyll.
    "But False-Semblant dare not, for drede
Of you, sir, medle him of this dede, 6050
For he saythe that ye ben his fo;
He not if ye wol worche him wo. FALSE-
Wherfore we praye you al, beau SEMBLANT
    sire, (HYPOCRISY)
That we forgyve him nowe your ire,
And that he may dwell, as your man, 6055
With Abstynence, his dere lemman;
This our acorde and our wyll nowe."
    "Parfey," sayd Love, "I graunt it you;
I wol wel holde him for my man;
Nowe let him come."—And he forthe
    ran. 6060
"False-Semblant," quod Love, "in this wyse
I take the here to my servyce,
That thou our frendes helpe alway,
And hyndre hem neyther nyght ne day,
But do thy myght hem to releve, 6065
And eke our enemyes that thou greve.
Thyne be this might, I graunt it the:
My kyng of harlotes shalte thou be;
We wol that thou have suche honour.
Certayne, thou arte a false traytour, 6070
And eke a thefe; sythe thou were
    borne,
A thousande tymes thou arte forsworne.
But nathelesse, in our heryng,
To put our folke out of doutyng,

6002 **gnede**, stingy. TG *grede*. 6006 TG *beaute*. 6012 **playnt**, complaint. 6020 **covenable**, suitable. 6027 **pyment**, sweetened wine, (same as *clarre*). 6028 **pepyr**, pepper (slang "mischief"). 6029 **laas**, net (lace). 6032 **quyte . . . free**, fulfill, liberally. 6033 **vicayre**, deputy—i.e., Love need seek no agents but women to subdue rich men. 6037 *worche* (deal): TG *worthe*. 6038 **fele**, many. 6043 **trowed**, believed. 6044 **fee**, property. 6045 **moeble**, movable belongings. 6046 **delyvered**, relieved (defrauded). 6048 **hestes**, orders. 6052 **not**, doesn't know (*ne wot*). 6055 **your man**, your servant. 6056 **lemman**, lover. 6063 *alway*: G *away*. 6068 **kyng of harlotes**, an actual officer in the French royal household (*roi de ribauds*), where he was a sort of bouncer, whose duty it was "to clear out men of bad character who had no business to be there" (Skeat). 6072 **forsworne**, perjured.

I bydde the teche hem, wost thou howe, 6075
By some general signe nowe,
In what place thou shalt founden be,
If that men had myster of the,
And howe men shal the best espye,
For the to knowe is great maistrye; 6080
Tel in what place is thyn hauntyng."
    "Sir, I have ful dyvers wonnyng,
That I kepe not rehersed be,
So that ye wolde respyten me.
For if that I tell you the sothe, 6085
I may have harme and shame bothe;
If that my felowes wysten it,
My tales shulden me be quyt.
For certayne, they wolde hate me
If ever I knewe her cruelte, 6090
For they wolde over al holde hem styll
Of trouthe that is agayne her wyll;
Suche tales kepen they not here.
I myght eftsone bye it ful dere,
If I sayd of hem anythyng 6095
That aught displeaseth to her heryng;
For what worde that hem pricke or byteth,
In that worde none of hem delyteth,
Al were it gospel, the evangyle,
That wolde reprove hem of her gyle, 6100
For they are cruell and hautayne.
And this thyng wote I wel, certayne,
If I speke aught to payre her loos,
Your courte shal not so wel be cloos
That they ne shal wyte it at last. 6105
Of good men am I nought agast,
For they wol taken on hem nothyng
Whan that they knowe al my meanyng:
But he that wol it on him take,
He wol himselfe suspecious make. 6110
That he his lyfe let covertly,
In Gyle and in Ipocrisy,
That me engendred and yave fostryng."
    "They made a ful good engendring,"
Quod Love, "for whoso sothly tell, 6115

They engendred the dyvel of hell.
But nedely, howesoever it be,"
Quod Love, "I wyl and charge the,
To tell anon thy wonnyng places,
Heryng eche wight that in this place is, 6120
And what lyfe that thou lyvest also.
Hyde it no lenger nowe; wherto?
Thou must discover al thy wurchyng,
Howe thou servest, and of what thyng,
Though that thou shuldest for thy sothesawe
Ben al tobeaten and todrawe— 6126
And yet arte thou not wont, parde.
But nathelesse, though thou beten be,
Thou shalt not be the first that so
Hath for soth-sawe suffred wo." 6130
    "Sir, sythe that it may lyken you,
Though that I shulde be slayne right nowe,
I shal done your commaundement,
For therto have I great talent."
    Withouten wordes mo, right than, 6135
False-Semblant his sermon began,
And sayd hem thus in audyence:
"Barons, take hede of my sentence.
That wight that lyste to have knowyng
Of False-Semblant, ful of flateryng, 6140
He must in worldly folke him seke,
And certes in the cloysters eke.
I won nowhere but in hem twey,
But not lyke even, sothe to say.
Shortly, I wol herberowe me 6145
There I hope best to hulstred be;
And certainly, sykerest hydyng
Is underneth humblest clothyng.
Relygious folke ben ful coverte;
Seculer folke ben more apperte. 6150
But nathelesse I wol not blame
Religyous folke, ne hem diffame,
In what habyte that ever they go.
Religyon humble and trewe also
Wol I not blame ne dispyse— 6155
But I nyl loove it in no wyse.

6078 **myster,** need. 6082 **wonnyng,** dwelling. 6083 **kepe not,** care not. 6084 **respyten me,** let me off. 6088 **quyt,** repaid. 6091 **wolde over al,** i.e., would rather. 6094 **eftsone,** soon afterward. 6101 **hautayne,** haughty. 6103 **payre . . . loos,** impair, fame. 6107 **taken on hem,** take personally. 6120 **Heryng,** i.e., in the hearing of. 6124 **of what,** for what. 6125 **sothesawe,** truth telling. 6126 **todrawe,** pulled to pieces. 6127 **not wont,** not accustomed (to be punished). 6144 **lyke even,** equally. 6146 **hulstred,** concealed. 6147 **sykerest,** most secure. 6149 **coverte,** closed (secret). 6150 **apperte,** open.

I meane of false relygious,
That stoute ben, and malycious;
That wollen in an habyte go,
And setten not her herte therto.   6160
    "Relygious folke ben al pytous;
Thou shalt not sene one dispytous;
They loven no pride ne no stryfe,
But humbly they wol lede her lyfe.
With suche folke wol I never be,   6165
And if I dwell, I fayne me.
I may wel in her habyt go;
But me were lever my necke atwo,
Than lette a purpose that I take,
What covenaunt that ever I make.   6170
    "I dwell with hem that proude be,
And ful of wyles and subtelte;
That worshyp of this worlde coveyten,
And great nede connen expleyten,
And gon and gadren great pytaunces,   6175
And purchace hem the acqueyntaunces
Of men that mighty lyfe may leden;
And fayne hem poore, and hemselfe feden
With good morcets delycious,
And drinken good wyne precyous;   6180
And preche us povert and distresse,
And fysshen hemselfe great rychesse
With wyly nettes that they caste.
It wol come foule out at the laste.
They ben fro clene relygion went;   6185
They make the worlde an argument
That hath a foule conclusyon:
'I have a robe of religyon,
Than am I al religyous.'
This argument is al roignous;   6190
It is not worthe a croked brere:
Habyt ne maketh neyther monke ne frere,
But clene lyfe and devocion
Maketh good men of religyon.
Nathelesse, there can none answere,   6195
Howe hygh that ever his heed he shere

With resour whetted never so kene,
That Gyle in braunches cutte thurtene.
There can no wight distyncte it so,
That he dare say a worde therto.   6200
    "But what herberowe that ever I take,
Or what semblant that ever I make,
I meane but gyle, and folowe that;
For right no more than Gybbe our cat
That awayteth myce and rattes to kyllen,   6205
Ne entende I but to begylen.
Ne no wight may, by my clothyng,
Wete with what folke is my dwellyng;
Ne by my wordes yet, parde,
So softe and so plesaunt they be.   6210
Beholde the dedes that I do;
But thou be blynde, thou oughtest so.
For, varye her wordes fro her dede,
They thynke on gyle, without drede,
What maner clothyng that they were,   6215
Or what estate that ever they bere,
Lered or leude, lorde or lady,
Knyght, squyer, burgeys, or bayly."
    Right thus whyle False-Semblant sermoneth,
Eftesones Love him aresoneth,   6220
And brake his tale in his speakyng
As though he had him tolde leasyng,
And sayd, "What, dyvel, is that I here?
What folke haste thou us nempned here?
Maye men fynde relygioun   6225
In wordly habytatioun?"
    "Ye, sir; it foloweth nat that they
Shulde lede a wicked lyfe, parfey,
Ne nat therfore her soules lese
That hem to worldly clothes chese,   6230
For certes it were great pyte.
Menne maye in seculer clothes se
Florisshen hooly relygioun.
Ful many a saynt in felde and towne,
With many a virgyn glorious,   6235
Devoute, and ful relygious,

6158 **stoute**, arrogant. 6162 **dispytous**, scornful. 6165 *suche*: TG *whiche.* 6166 **fayne**, pretend. 6169 **lette**, turn from. 6170 **covenaunt**, vow. 6173 **worshyp**, honor. 6174 **expleyten**, satisfy. 6175 **pytaunces**, contributions. 6177 **mighty**, powerful (high class). 6182 **fysshen**, fish for (accumulate). 6190 **roignous**, ruinous. 6191 **brere**, briar. 6197 *resour*: G *resoun.* 6198 **thurtene**, the usual number in a convent, twelve monks and a prior. 6199 **distyncte**, discern. 6205 Line lacking in G. 6208 **Wete**, know. 6217 **Lered or leude**, learned or ignorant. 6218 **bayly**, bailiff (municipal official). 6220 **aresoneth**, disputes. 6222 **leasyng**, lying. 6233 **Florisshen**, flourish (in).

Han dyed, that commen clothe aye beren,
Yet sayntes neverthelesse they weren.
I coude recken you many a ten.
Ye, wel nygh al these holy women   6240
That menne in churches herry and seke,
Bothe maydens, and these wyves eke
That baren ful many a fayre chylde here,
Weared alwaye clothes seculere,
And in the same dieden they   6245
That sayntes weren, and ben alwaye.
The .xi. thousande maydens dere
That beren in heven her cierges clere,
Of whiche men rede in churche and syng,
Were take in seculer clothyng   6250
Whan they receyved martyrdome,
And wonnen heven unto her home.
Good herte maketh the good thought;
The clothynge yeveth ne reveth nought;
The good thought and the worchyng   6255
That maketh the relygion flouryng—
There lyeth the good relygioun
After the right ententioun.
   "Whoso tooke a wethers skynne,
And wrapped a gredy wolfe therinne,   6260
For he shulde go with lambes white,
Wenest thou nat he wolde hem byte?
Yes, neverthelesse, as he were wode,
He wolde hem wirry and drinke the blode,
And wel the rather hem disceyve;   6265
For sithe they coude nat perceyve
His tregette and his cruelte,
They wolde him folowe, altho he flye.
If there be wolves of suche hewe
Amonges these apostles newe,   6270
Thou, Holy Churche, thou mayste be wayled!
Sythe that thy cyte is assayled
Through knyghtes of thyn owne table,
God wot thy lordshyp is doutable!
If they enforce hem it to wyn   6275

That shulde defende it fro within,
Who myght defence ayenst hem make?
Without stroke it mote be take
Of trepeget or mangonel,
Without displayeng of pensel.   6280
And if God nyl done it socour,
But let hem renne in this colour,
Thou must thy heestes letten be.
Than is there nought, but yelde the,
Or yeve hem trybute, doutles,   6285
And holde it of hem to have pees—
But greater harme betyde the,
That they al maister of it be.
Wel conne they scorne the withall.
By day stuffen they the wall,   6290
And al the nyght they mynen there.
Nay, thou planten muste elsewhere
Thyn ympes, if thou wolt fruite have;
Abyde not there thyselfe to save.
   "But nowe pees! Here I turne agayne;   6295
I wol no more of this thyng sayne
If I may passen me hereby;
I might maken you wery.
But I wol heten you alway
To helpe your frendes what I may,   6300
So they wollen my company;
For they be shent al utterly
But if so fall that I be
Ofte with hem, and they with me.
And eke my lemman mote they serve,   6305
Or they shul not my love deserve.
Forsothe, I am a false traytour;
God juged me for a thefe trechour;
Forsworne I am, but wel nygh none
Wote of my gyle tyl it be done.   6310
   "Through me hath many one deth receyved
That my treget never aperceyved;
And yet receyveth, and shal receyve,
That my falsenesse shal never aperceyve.

6237 **commen,** ordinary. 6241 **herry,** harass. 6245 **dieden,** i.e., died in the same way as saints. T *dyden.* 6248 **cierges,** wax candles. An allusion to the legend of St. Ursula and the 11,000 virgins martyred by the Huns at Cologne. 6254 **reveth,** takes away. 6259 **wethers,** sheep. 6265 **rather,** more quickly. 6267 **tregette,** trickery. 6271 **wayled,** lamented. 6274 **doutable,** in doubt. 6275 **wyn,** conquer. TG *hem* om. 6279 **trepeget . . . mangonel,** two kinds of catapults. 6280 **pensel,** war banner. 6282 **colour,** manner. TG *hem* om. 6283 **heestes,** promises. 6286 **holde it of,** hold as a subject of. 6287 **betyde,** comes to. 6290 **stuffen,** fill with defenders. 6291 **mynen,** undermine (against attack). 6293 **ympes,** seedlings. 6296 *sayne:* TG *fayne;* Fr. *dire.* 6299 **heten,** promise. 6301 **wollen,** will want. 6302 **shent,** destroyed. 6305 **lemman,** lover. 6312 **treget,** trickery.

But whoso dothe, if he wyse be, 6315
Him is ryght good be ware of me.
But so slyghe is the deceyving
That to hard is the aperceyvyng;
For Protheus, that coude him chaunge
In every shappe, homely and straunge, 6320
Coude never suche gyle ne treasoune
As I; for I come never in towne
Ther as I myght knowen be,
Though men me bothe myght here and se.
Ful wel I canne my clothes chaunge, 6325
Take one, and make another straunge.
Nowe am I knyght, nowe chastelayne;
Nowe prelate, and nowe chapelayne;
Nowe preest, nowe clerke, and nowe forstere;
Nowe am I maister, nowe scholere; 6330
Nowe monke, nowe chanon, nowe bayly—
Whatever myster manne am I.
Nowe am I prince, nowe am I page,
And canne by herte every langage.
Somtyme am I hoore and olde; 6335
Nowe am I yonge, stoute, and bolde.
Nowe am I Robert, nowe Robyn;
Nowe frere Mynor, nowe Jacobyn.
And with me foloweth my loteby,
To done me solace and company, 6340
That hight dame Abstynence-Straigned,
In many a queynt arraye fayned.
Ryght as it cometh to her lykyng,
I fulfyl al her desyringe.
Somtyme a wommans clothe take I: 6345
Nowe am I a mayde, nowe lady.
Somtyme I am relygious;
Nowe lyke an anker in an hous.
Somtyme am I prioresse,
And nowe a nonne, and nowe abbesse; 6350

And go through al regiouns,
Sekynge al relygiouns.
But to what order that I am sworne,
I take the strawe and lete the corne.
To gyle folke I enhabyte; 6355
I aske no more but her habite.
What wol ye more? In every wyse,
Ryght as me lyste, I me disgyse.
Wel canne I beare me under wede;
Unlyke is my worde to my dede. 6360
Thus make I into my trappes fal
The people through my privyleges, al
That bene in Christendome alyve.
I may assoyle, and I maye shryve,
That no prelate maye lette me, 6365
Al folke, whereever they founde be;
I not no prelat may done so,
But it the pope be, and no mo,
That made thilke establisshyng.
Nowe is not this a propre thyng? 6370
But were my sleightes aperceyved,
Ne shulde I ben so receyved
As I was wonte; and woste thou why?
For I dyd hem a tregetry.
But thereof yeve I lytel tale; 6375
I have the sylver and the male.
So have I preched and eke shriven,
So have I take, so have me yeven
Through her foly husbonde and wyfe,
That I lede right a joly lyfe, 6380
Through symplesse of the prelacye—
They knowe not al my tregettrye.
"But forasmoche as man and wyfe
Shulde shewe her parisshe preest her lyfe
Ones a yere, as saythe the boke, 6385
Er any wight his housel toke,

6317–18 T *is the aperceyvynge | That al to late cometh knowynge;* Fr. *Mès tant est (griés) la decevance | Que trop est (fort) l'apercevance.* Line 6318 lacking in G; emendation by Kaluza. **6319 Protheus,** Proteus, the shape-shifting Greek sea god. **6320 homely,** familiar. **6321 Coude,** knew. **6329** T *fostere.* **6332 Whatever myster,** of any occupation. **6337 Robert . . . Robyn,** gentleman, farm boy. **6338 Mynor . . . Jacobyn,** Minorite (Franciscan, in reference to their vow of humility), Jacobin (Dominican, after Church of St. Jacques beside which they built their first monastery). **6339 loteby,** sweetheart. **6341 Straigned,** enforced. TG *and raigned.* **6342 fayned,** pretended (affected). **6348 anker,** recluse (hermit). **6354 lete,** leave. TG *be(a)te;* Fr. *lais.* **6355 gyle,** deceive. TG *jolye;* Fr. *enbascler* (deceive). **6359 Wel . . . beare,** appropriately behave. *beare:* G *were.* **6361** G *Thus/I* om. **6362** G *The people* om. **6364 assoyle . . . shryve,** absolve, hear confession. **6365 lette,** prevent. **6369 thilke establisshyng,** that rule. **6372** Line omitted in TG; emendation from Sutherland. **6375 tale,** account. TG *a lytel.* **6376 male,** wallet. **6378 me:** TG *I.* **6385 Ones a yere,** an allusion to the requirement of the Fourth Lateran Council (1215–16) that all Christians must go to confession and take communion at Easter. From this grew a body of penitential literature like that exemplified by Chaucer's Parson's Tale (cf. *CT* x.1027). **6386 housel,** communion.

Than have I privyleges large
That may of moche thyng discharge;
For he may say right thus, parde:
'Sir Preest, in shrifte I tel it the,   6390
That he to whom that I am shriven
Hath me assoyled, and me yeven
Penaunce, sothlye, for my syn,
Whiche that I fonde me gilty in;
Ne I ne have never entencion   6395
To make double confession,
Ne reherce efte my shrift to the.
O shrift is right ynough to me.
This ought the suffyse wele;
Ne be not rebell never a dele.   6400
For certes, though thou haddest it sworne,
I wote no preest ne prelate borne
That may to shrift efte me constrayne.
And if they done, I wol me playne;
For I wote where to playne wele.   6405
Thou shalt not streyne me a dele,
Ne enforce me, ne not me trouble,
To make my confessyon double.
Ne I have none affection
To have double absolution.   6410
The first is right ynough to me;
This latter assoyling quyte I the.
I am unbounde; what mayst thou fynde
More of my synnes me to unbynde?
For he that might hath in his honde   6415
Of al my synnes me unbonde.
And if thou wolte me thus constrayne,
That me mote nedes on the playne.
There shal no juge imperyall,
Ne bysshop, ne offyciall,   6420
Done jugement on me; for I
Shal gone and playne me openly
Unto my shrift-father newe—
That hyght not Frere Wolfe untrewe—
And he shal cheveyse him for me,   6425
For I trowe he can hamper the.

But, lorde, he wolde be wrothe withall
If men him wolde Frere Wolfe call!
For he wolde have no pacience,
But done al cruell vengience.   6430
He wolde his myght done at the leest,
Nothyng spare for Goddes heest.
And, God so wyse be my socour,
But thou yeve me my Savyour
At Easter, whan it lyketh me,   6435
Without preasyng more on the,
I wol forthe, and to him gone,
And he shal housell me anon,
For I am out of thy grutchyng;
I kepe not deale with the nothyng!'   6440
    Thus may he shrive him that forsaketh
His parysshe-preest and to me taketh.
And if the preest wol him refuse,
I am ful redy him to accuse,
And him punisshe and hamper so,   6445
That he his churche shal forgo.
But whoso hath in his felyng
The consequence of suche shrivyng
Shal sene that preest may never have might
To knowe the conscience aright   6450
Of him that is under his cure.
And this is ayenst holy scripture,
That byddeth every heerd honest
Have very knowyng of his beest.
But poore folke that gon by strete,   6455
That have no golde, ne sommes grete,
Hem wolde I let to her prelates,
Or let her preestes knowe her states,
For to me right nought yeve they.
And why? It is for they ne may;   6460
They ben so bare, I take no kepe.
But I wol have the fatte shepe;
Let parisshe preestes have the lene.
I yeve not of her harme a bene!
And if that prelates grutchen it,   6465
That oughten wroth be in her wyt,

6393 G *For penaunce.* **6397 efte,** again. Like Chaucer's Pardoner, False-Semblant sets himself up in competition with the parish priest, taking offerings due the priest and giving lighter penance (cf. *CT* i.221ff., vi.387ff.). **6412 quyte,** reject. **6413 unbounde,** absolved. **6423 shrift-father newe,** new confessor. **6424 hyght not,** irony, since he obviously was called Friar Wolf. T *not* om. **6425 cheveyse,** justify. T *chuse.* **6432 heest,** command. **6434 But . . . Savyour,** unless, communion. **6436 preasyng,** intruding. **6439 grutchyng,** complaining. **6440 kepe,** care. **6446 forgo,** i.e., lose. **6453 heerd,** shepherd. **6454 very,** genuine. **6457 let,** leave. **6465 grutchen,** complain (of). **6466 wroth:** TG *woth.*

To lese her fatte beestes so,
I shal yeve hem a stroke or two,
That they shal lesen with force,
Ye, bothe her mytre and her croce.　6470
Thus jape I hem, and have do longe,
My privileges ben so stronge."
　False-Semblant wolde have stynted here,
But Love ne made him no suche chere
That he was wery of his sawe;　6475
But for to make him glad and fawe,
He said: "Tel on more specially,
Howe that thou servest untruely.
Tel forthe and shame the never a dele,
For as thyn habyt sheweth wele,　6480
Thou semest an holy heremyte."
　"Sothe is, but I am but an ypocryte."
　"Thou gost and prechest poverte?"
　"Ye, sir; but rychesse hath poste."
　"Thou prechest abstynence also?"　6485
　"Sir, I wol fyllen, so mote I go,
My paunche of good meate and wyne,
As shulde a maister of divyne;
For huwe that I me poore fayne,
Yet al poore folke I disdayne.　6490
I love better the acqueyntaunce
Ten tymes of the kyng of Fraunce,
Than of a poore man of mylde mode,
Though that his soule be also good.
For whan I se beggers quakyng　6495
Naked on myxins al stynkyng,
For hongre crye, and eke for care,
I entremet not of her fare.
They ben so poore and ful of pyne,
They might not ones yeve me dyne,　6500
For they have nothyng but her lyfe.
What shulde he yeve that lycketh his
　　knyfe?
It is but folly to entremete,

To seke in houndes nest fatte mete.
Lette beare hem to the spyttle anone,　6505
But for me, comforte gette they none.
But a riche sicke usurere
Wolde I visyte and drawe nere;
Him wol I comforte and rehete,
For I hope of his golde to gete;　6510
And if that wicked dethe him have,
I wol go with him to his grave.
And if there any reprove me,
Why that I lette the poore be,
Wost thou howe I mot ascape?　6515
I saye and swere him ful rape
That riche menne han more tetches
Of synne than han poore wretches,
And hanne of counsayle more myster;
And therfore I wolde drawe hem ner.　6520
　"But as great hurte, it maye so be,
Hath a soule in right great poverte,
As soule in great richesse, forsothe,
Al-be-it that they hurten bothe.
For richesse and mendicitees　6525
Bene cleped two extremytees;
The meane is cleped suffysaunce:
There lyeth of vertue the aboundaunce.
For Salomon, ful wel I wote,
In his Parables us wrote,　6530
As it is knowe of many a wight,
In his thrittene chapiter right,
'God, thou me kepe, for thy poste,
Fro richesse and mendycite;
For if a riche manne him dresse　6535
To thynke to moche on richesse,
His herte on that so ferre is sette
That he his creatour dothe foryette.
And him that begging wol aye greve,
Howe shulde I by his worde him
　　leve?　6540

6469 with force, i.e., with the force of the blow. **6470 croce,** cross; symbols of prelacy. **6471 jape ... have do,** deceive, have done. **6474 no suche chere,** no indication (no such expression). **6475 sawe,** account. **6476 fawe,** happy. **6481 semest:** TG *servest*; Fr. *sembles.* **6482** TG *I am but;* Fr. *mes ie sui.* **6484 poste,** dominion. **6486 so mote,** &c., i.e., whatever happens. **6488 divyne,** divinity. **6489 huwe ... fayne,** however, pretend. **6491** G *that queyntaunce.* **6493 mylde mode,** gentle spirit. **6496 myxins,** dunghills. **6498 entremet,** interfere. **6500 dyne,** food. TG *a dyne.* **6505 Lette ... spyttle,** let them be taken to the hospital. **6509 rehete,** console. **6515 mot ascape,** i.e., must excuse myself. *mot:* TG *not.* **6516 rape,** quickly. **6517 tetches,** blemishes. **6519 myster,** need. **6525 mendicitees,** depending upon alms for a living. **6527 meane,** midpoint (golden mean). **6532** *thrittene,* Fr. *tresime,* although the allusion is to Prov. 30:8–9. **6533 kepe ... poste,** preserve, power. **6535 dresse,** address. **6539** TG *beggeth.* **6540 leve,** believe.

Unneth that he nys a mycher,
Forsworne, or els God is lyer.'
Thus saithe Salomon sawes.
Ne we fynde written in no lawes,
And namely in our Christen laye—   6545
Whoso saithe 'ye', I dare say 'naye'—
That Christ ne his apostels dere,
While that they walked in erthe here,
Were never seen her bred beggyng,
For they nolden beggen for nothyng.   6550
And right thus were men wont to teche;
And in this wyse wolde it preche
The maisters of dyvinyte
Somtyme in Parys the cyte.
And if men wolde theregayne appose   6555
The naked texte, and lette the glose,
It myght soone assoyled be.
For menne maye wel the sothe se,
That, pardie, they myght aske a thynge
Plainly forthe, without beggynge;   6560
For they weren Goddes heerdes dere,
And cure of soules hadden here.
They nolde nothyng begge her foode;
For after Christ was done on rodde,
With their proper hondes they wrought;   6565
And with traveyle, and els nought,
They wonnen al her sustenaunce,
And lyveden forthe in her penaunce;
And the remenaunt yaf awaye
To other poore folkes alwaye.   6570
They neither bylden towre ne halle,
But leye in houses smal withalle.

   "A mighty man, that canne and maye,
Shulde wyth his honde and body alwaye
Wynne him his foode in laboring,   6575
If he ne have rent or suche a thyng,

Although he be relygious,
And God to serven curyous.
Thus mote he done, or do trespas,
But if it be in certayne caas,   6580
That I can reherce, if myster be,
Right wel, whan the tyme I se.
Seke the boke of Saynt Austyne,
Be it in paper or perchmyne,
There-as he writte of these worchynges,   6585
Thou shalt sene that none excusynges
A parfyte man ne shulde seke
By wordes, ne by dedes eke,
Although he be religyous,
And God to serven curyous,   6590
That he ne shal, so mote I go,
With propre hondes and body also,
Get his fode in laboring,
If he ne have proprete of thyng.
Yet shulde he sell al his substaunce,   6595
And with his swynke have sustenaunce,
If he be parfyte in bounte.
Thus han the bookes tolde me.
For he that wol gone ydelly,
And useth it aye besyly   6600
To haunten other mennes table,
He is a trechour, ful of fable;
Ne he ne may, by good reason,
Escuse him by his orison.
For men behoveth, in some gyse,   6605
Somtyme leven Goddes servyse
To gone and purchasen her nede.
Men mote eaten, that is no drede,
And slepe, and eke do other thyng;
So longe may they leave prayeng.   6610
So may they eke her prayer blynne
Whyle that they werke, her meate to wynne.

6541 **Unneth . . . mycher,** scarcely (possible), thief. 6542 *God is:* TG *goddes (is).* 6545 **laye,** law. 6553 **maisters of dyvinyte,** this criticism of the mendicant ideal of the friars, and many of the arguments in the following lines are from the *Tractatus Brevis de Periculis Novissimorum Temporum* by Guillaume de Saint-Amour (cf. l. 6763 below), a professor at the University of Paris. The friars persuaded the pope to condemn the treatise in 1256 and banish Guillaume from France. 6555 **theregayne,** there against. 6556 **naked texte, and lette the glose,** the bare text, and neglect the commentary. 6557 **assoyled,** explained. 6559 **aske,** ask for. 6561 **heerdes,** shepherds. 6562 **cure,** responsibility for (care). 6564 **done . . . rodde,** put, cross. 6565 **proper . . . wrought,** own, worked. 6567 **wonnen,** earned. 6571 **towre . . . halle,** the friars were accused of building elaborate monastic buildings. 6572 *leye:* TG *they.* 6573 **mighty,** strong. 6576 **rent,** income. 6578 **curyous,** zealous. 6580 **caas,** situation. 6581 **myster,** need. 6583 **boke of Saynt Austyne,** St. Augustine, *De Opere Monachorum,* cf. *CT* I.187n. 6594 **proprete,** i.e., independent wealth. 6596 **swynke,** work. 6600 **useth,** is accustomed. *besyly:* G *desily.* 6601 *To:* G *Go.* 6602 **trechour . . . fable,** treacherous person, untruth. 6604 **orison,** prayer. 6606 *Somtyme leven:* TG *Ben somtyme in.* 6607 **purchasen,** i.e., earn for. 6611 **blynne,** leave off.

Seynt Austyn wol therto accorde,
In thilke boke that I recorde.
Justinian eke, that made lawes, 6615
Hath thus forboden, by olde sawes,
'No man, up payne to be deed,
Mighty of body, to begge his breed,
If he may swynke it for to gete;
Men shulde him rather mayme or bete, 6620
Or done of him aperte justyce,
Than suffren him in suche malyce.'
They done not wel, so mote I go,
That taken suche almesse so,
But if they have somme privilege 6625
That of the payne hem wol alege.
But howe that is can I not se,
But if the prince disceyved be,
Ne I ne wene not, sykerly,
That they may have it rightfully. 6630
But I wol not determyne
Of princes power, ne defyne,
Ne by my worde comprehende, iwys,
If it so ferre may stretche in this;
I wol not entremete a dele. 6635
But I trowe that the boke saythe wele,
Who that taketh almesses that be
Dewe to folke that men may se
Lame, feble, wery, and bare,
Poore, or in suche maner care 6640
(That conne wynne hem nevermo,
For they have no power therto),
He eateth his owne dampnyng
But if he lye that made al thyng.
And if ye suche a truaunt fynde, 6645
Chastyse him wel, if ye be kynde.
But they wolde hate you, par caas,
And if ye fyllen in her laas,
They wolde eftsones do you scathe,
If that they might, late or rathe. 6650
For they be not ful pacient,
That han the worlde thus foule blent.

And weteth wel that wher God bad
The good man sell al that he had,
And folowe him, and to poore it yeve, 6655
He wolde not therfore that he lyve
To serven him in mendience,
For it was never his sentence.
But he bad werken whan that nede is,
And folowe him in good dedes. 6660
Saynt Poule, that loved al holy churche,
He bade the apostels for to wurche,
And wynnen her lyvelode in that wyse,
And hem defended truandyse,
And sayd, 'Werketh with your honden.' 6665
Thus shulde the thyng be understonden.
He nolde, iwys, have byd hem beggyng,
Ne sellen gospel, ne prechyng,
Lest they berafte, with her askyng,
Folke of her catel or of her thyng. 6670
For in this worlde is many a man
That yeveth his good, for he ne can
Werne it for shame, or els he
Wolde of the asker delyvered be.
And for he him encombreth so, 6675
He yeveth him good to late him go.
But it can him nothyng profyte;
They lese the yefte and the meryte.
The good folke that Poule to preched
Profred him ofte, whan he hem teched, 6680
Some of her good in charyte;
But therof right nothyng toke he;
But of his hondewerke wolde he gete
Clothes to wryne him, and his mete."

"Tell me than howe a man may lyven 6685
That al his good to poore hath yeven,
And wol but onely bydde his bedes,
And never with hondes labour his nedes.
Maye he do so?" "Ye, sir." "And howe?"

"Sir, I wol gladly tell you: 6690
Seynt Austen saythe, a man may be
In houses that han properte,

6615 Justinian, Emperor of Constantinople who caused the Roman law to be codified. **6621 aperte,** evident. This is from the *Justinian Code,* "De medicantibus validas," xi.25(26). **6626 alege,** exempt. **6634 so ferre,** this far. **6641 wynne,** earn. **6643 eateth . . . dampnyng,** i.e., the able-bodied person who eats solicited food eats his own damnation. **6647 par caas,** perchance. **6648 laas,** net. T *And* om. **6650 rathe,** early. **6652 foule blent,** foully blinded. **6653 TG** *wher* om. **6657 mendience,** begging. **6661 Poule,** I Thess. 4.11. **6669 berafte,** deprived. **6670 catel,** chattels. **6673 Werne,** refuse. **6674 delyvered,** relieved. **6682 TG** *therfore.* **6684 wryne,** cover. **6687 bydde . . . bedes,** pray, prayers. **6688 Line lacking in G.**

As Templers and Hospytelers,
And as these chanons regulers,
Or whyte monkes, or these blake—   6695
I wol no mo ensamples make—
And take therof his susteynyng,
For therin lythe no beggyng.
But otherwayes not, ywys,
If Austyn gabbeth not of this.   6700
And yet ful many a monke laboureth
That God in holy churche honoureth;
For whan her swynkyng is agon,
They rede and synge in churche anon.
    "And for there hath ben great discorde,   6705
As many a wight may beare recorde,
Upon the estate of mendicience,
I wol shortly, in your presence,
Tel howe a man may begge at nede,
That hath not wherwith him to fede,   6710
Maugre his felones jangelynges,
For sothfastnesse wol none hydynges;
And yet, par case, I may abey,
That I to you sothly thus sey.
    "Lo, here the case especial: 6715
If a man be so bestyal
That he of no crafte hath science,
And nought desyreth ignorence,
Than may he go a-beggyng yerne,
Tyl he some maner crafte can lerne,   6720
Through whiche without truandyng,
He may in trouthe have his lyvyng.
Or if he may done no labour,
For elde, or sicknesse, or langour,
Or for his tendre age also,   6725
Than may he yet a-beggyng go.
Or if he have, peraventure,
Through usage of his noriture,
Lyved over delyciously,
Than oughten good folke comenly   6730

Han of his mischefe some pyte,
And suffren him also that he
May gon aboute and begge his breed,
That he be not for honger deed.
Or if he have of crafte connyng,   6735
And strength also, and desyring
To worchen, as he had what,
But he fynde neyther this ne that,
Than may he begge tyl that he
Have geten his necessyte.   6740
Or if his wynnyng be so lyte,
That his labour wol not acquyte
Suffyciantly al his lyvyng,
Yet may he go his breed beggyng;
Fro doore to doore he may go trace,   6745
Tyl he the remenaunt may purchace.
Or if a man wolde undertake
Any emprise for to make,
In the rescous of our lay,
And it defenden as he may,   6750
Be it with armes or lettrure,
Or other covenable cure,
If it be so he poore be,
Than may he begge, tyll that he
May fynde in trouthe for to swynke,   6755
And get him clothes, meate, and drinke.
Swynke he with hondes corporell,
And not with hondes espyrituell.
    "In al this case, and in semblables,
If that there ben mo resonables,   6760
He may begge, as I tell you here,
And els not, in no manere—
As Willyam Seynt Amour wolde preche,
And ofte wolde dispute and teche
Of this mater al openly   6765
At Parys ful solemply.
And also God my soule blesse,
As he had in this stedfastnesse

6693 Templers . . . Hospytelers, military religious orders formed in connection with the Crusades. St. Augustine, of course, wrote 500 years before the foundation of these orders. The military and monastic orders had vast properties, as compared with the mendicants who were supposed to exist on charity. **6694 chanons regulers,** canons living in communities like monks, cf. *CT* VIII.573n. **6695 whyte monkes . . . blake,** Cistercians, Benedictines. **6700 gabbeth,** lies. *If:* TG *Yet.* **6711 felones jangelynges,** evil quarrelings. *felones:* T *felowes.* **6712 wol . . . hydynges,** will (have), hiding places. **6713 abey,** suffer for. **6718 nought desyreth,** i.e., is not to blame. **6721 truandyng,** shirking (truant). **6728 usage . . . noriture,** custom of his rearing. **6729 delyciously,** delicately. **6731 mischefe,** misfortune. **6746 purchace,** secure. **6748 emprise,** enterprise. **6749 rescous of our lay,** i.e., in defending Christianity. **6752 covenable cure,** useful care. **6755 May fynde,** i.e., may find a way. **6756 TG *clothe.* 6759 semblables,** similar cases.

The accorde of the universite,
And of the people, as semeth me. 6770
No good man ought it to refuse,
Ne ought him therof to excuse,
Be wrothe or blythe whoso be;
For I wol speke and tell it the,
Al shulde I dye and be put doun, 6775
As was Seynt Poule, in derke prisoun,
Or be exiled in this caas
With wronge, as mayster William was,
That my mother Hypocrise
Banysshed for her great envye. 6780
My mother flemed him, Seynt Amour:
This noble dyd suche labour
To susteyne ever the loyalte,
That he to moche agylte me.
He made a boke, and let it write, 6785
Wherein his lyfe he dyd al write,
And wolde yche renyed beggyng,
And lyved by my traveylyng,
If I ne had rent ne other good.
What, weneth he that I were wood? 6790
For labour might me never plese;
I have more wyl to ben at ese,
And have wel lever, sothe to say,
Before the people pattre and pray,
And wrie me in my foxerie 6795
Under a cope of papelardie."
    Quod Love, "What, dyvel, is this that I here?
What wordes tellest thou me here?"
    "What, sir?" "Falsnesse, that apert is.
Than dredest thou not God?" "No, certis, 6800
For selde in great thyng shal he spede
In this worlde that God wol drede.
For folke that hem to vertue yeven,
And truely on her owne lyven,
And hem in goodnesse aye contene, 6805

On hem is lytel thrifte ysene.
Suche folke drinken great misese.
That lyfe may me never plese.
But se what golde han usurers,
And sylver eke in her garners, 6810
Taylagiers, and these monyours,
Bayliffes, bedels, provost, countours;
These lyven wel nygh by ravyne;
The smale people hem mote enclyne,
And they as wolves wol hem eten. 6815
Upon the poore folke they geten
Ful moche of that they spende or kepe;
Nys none of hem that he nyl strepe,
And wrine himselfe wel at full;
Without scaldyng they hem pull. 6820
The stronge the feble overgothe;
But I, that weare my symple clothe,
Robbe bothe robbed and robbours,
And gyle gyled and gylours.
    "By my treget I gather and threst 6825
The great tresour into my chest,
That lyeth with me so faste bounde.
Myn hygh paleys do I founde,
And my delytes I fulfyll
With wyne at feestes at my wyll, 6830
And tables ful of entremees;
I wol no lyfe but ease and pees,
And wynne golde to spende also.
For whan the great bagge is go,
It cometh right with my japis. 6835
Make I not wel tomble myn apes?
To wynnen is alway myn entent;
My purchace is better than my rent.
For though I shulde beten be,
Over al I entremet me; 6840
Without me may no wight dure.
I walke soules for to cure—

6769 **accorde,** agreement. 6781 **flemed,** exiled. 6784 **agylte,** offended. 6786 Line lacking in G. 6787 **yche renyed,** I renounced. 6790 **weneth he . . . wood,** does he think, crazy. 6794 **pattre,** recite the Paternoster. 6795 **foxerie,** cleverness; Fr. *renardie.* 6796 **papelardie,** hypocrisy. 6799 **apert,** open. 6806 **thrifte,** success. 6810 TG *her* om.; Fr. *lor.* 6811 **Taylagiers . . . monyours,** tax-gatherers, bankers. 6812 **Bayliffes, bedels, provost, countours,** stewards, municipal officers, overseer, lawyers (accountants). 6813 **ravyne,** plunder. 6816 **Upon,** from. 6818 **hem . . . strepe,** them (i.e., the poor), strip. 6819 **wrine,** cover. TG *hemself.* 6820 **scaldyng . . . pull,** it is customary to scald a fowl before plucking it. 6823–24 *robbed/gyled:* TG *robbyng/gyling.* Fr. *Robe robés/Lobe lobés.* 6825 **treget,** guile. 6831 **entremees,** dainties served between courses. 6834–35 **bagge . . . japis,** i.e., when my treasure bag is empty, I make it full by my tricks. 6836 **Make I . . . tomble,** i.e., don't I make my apes obey (tumble) well? 6837 Cf. *CT* VI.403. 6838 **purchace . . . rent,** i.e., what I buy is more than my income; cf. *CT* I.256. 6840 **entremet,** meddle. 6841 **wight dure,** creature endure. 6842 **cure,** care for (save).

Of al the worlde cure have I
In brede and length. Boldly
I wol bothe preche and eke counsaylen.   6845
With hondes wyl I not travaylen,
For of the pope I have the bull;
I ne holde not my wyttes dull.
I wol not stynten in my lyve
These emperours for to shrive,   6850
Or kynges, dukes, and lordes grete.
But poore folke al quyte I lete;
I love no suche shrivyng, parde,
But it for other cause be.
I recke not of poore men: 6855
Her astate is not worthe an hen.
Where fyndest thou a swynker of labour
Have me unto his confessour?
    "But empresses and duchesses,
These quenes and eke countesses,   6860
These abbesses and eke bygyns,
These great ladyes palasyns,
These jolye knyghtes and baylives,
These nonnes, and these burgeys wyves
That ryche ben and eke plesyng,   6865
And these maydens welfaryng,
Whereso they clad or naked be,
Uncounsayled gothe there none fro me.
And, for her soules savete,
At lorde and lady and her meyne,   6870
I aske, whan they han to me shrive,
The properte of al her lyve,
And make hem trowe, bothe moste and leest,
Her parysshe-preest nys but a beest
Ayens me and my company,   6875
That shrewes ben as great as I.
For whiche I wol not hyde in holde
No pryvite that me is tolde,
That I by worde or signe, ywis,
Ne wol make hem knowe what it is,   6880

And they wollen also tellen me;
They hele fro me no pryvite.
    "And for to make you hem parceyven,
That usen folke thus to disceyven,
I wol you sayne, withouten drede,   6885
What menne maye in the gospel rede
Of Saynt Mathue, the gospelere,
That saythe as I shal you saye here:
'Upon the chayre of Moyses'—
Thus it is glosed, doutlees,   6890
That is the Olde Testament,
For therby is the chayre ment—
'Sytte Scribes and Pharysen'—
That is to sayne, the cursed men
Whiche that we hypocrites call.   6895
'Dothe that they preche, I rede you all,
But dothe nat as they done a dele,
That bene nat wery to saye wele,
But to do wel no wyl have they.
And they wolde bynde on folke
    alwaye,   6900
That bene to be gyled able,
Burdons that ben importable;
On folkes shulders thynges they couchen
That they nyl with her fyngers touchen.' "
    "And why wol they nat touche it?" "Why?
For hem ne lyste nat, sykerly;   6906
For sadde burdons that men taken
Make folkes shulders aken.
And if they do ought that good be,
That is for folke it shulde se.   6910
Her bordurs larger maken they,
And make her hemmes wyde alwaye,
And loven seates at the table
The fyrste and most honorable.
And for to hanne the firste chayris   6915
In synagogges to hem ful dere is;
And wyllen that folke hem loute and grete

6845 Cf. *CT* VI.443ff. 6851 T *Or* om.; G *and* om. 6852 **quyte,** quiet (i.e., unabsolved of their sins). 6857 **swynker,** worker. 6861 **bygyns,** Beguines; lay sisterhoods, largely composed of noblewomen, who devoted themselves to charitable works. 6862 **palasyns,** i.e., connected with palaces (original meaning of "courtesan"). 6863 **baylives,** bailiffs (stewards). 6869 **savete,** safety. 6870 **meyne,** retinue. 6871 **shrive,** confessed. 6872 **properte . . . lyve,** their whole lives as recompense; Fr. *Lor propriétés e lor vies.* 6873 **trowe,** think. 6875 **Ayens,** compared to. 6877 **holde,** safekeeping. 6880 G *Ne* om. 6882 **hele,** hide. 6884 **usen,** are accustomed. 6887 **Mathue,** Matt. 23:1–8, 13–15. 6890 **glosed,** glossed (interpreted). 6896 **Dothe . . . rede,** do what, counsel. 6901 **gyled,** deceived (beguiled). 6906 **ne lyste,** don't want to. 6907 **sadde,** serious. 6911 **bordurs,** borders of their garments, on which were phylacteries (charms). TG *burdons;* Fr. *filatieres* (weavings). 6917 **loute,** bow to.

Whan that they passen through the strete;
And wollen be cleped 'maister' also.
But they ne shulde nat wyllen so— 6920
The gospel is there-agaynst, I gesse.
That sheweth wel her wickednesse.

"Another custome use we
Of hem that wol ayenst us be:
We hate hem deedly everychone, 6925
And we wol werrey hem as one.
Him that one hateth, hate we al,
And conjecte howe to done him fal.
And if we sene him wynne honour,
Rychesse or preyse, through his valour, 6930
Provende, rente, or dignyte,
Ful faste, ywis, compassen we
By what ladder he is clomben so;
And for to maken him downe to go,
With trayson we wol hym defame, 6935
And done him lese his good name.
Thus from his ladder we him take,
And thus his frendes foes we make.
But worde ne wete shal he noon,
Tyl al his frendes bene his foon, 6940
For if we dyd it openly,
We myght have blame redily.
For hadde he wyste of our malyce,
He hadde him kepte, but he were nyce.

"Another is this, that if so fall 6945
That there be one amonge us all
That dothe a good tourne, out of drede,
We sayne it is our alder dede.
Ye, sykerly, though he it fayned,
Or that him lyste, or that him dayned 6950
A manne through him avaunced be,
Therof al parceners be we,
And tellen folke, whereso we go,
That manne through us is sprongen so.
And for to have of menne preysyng, 6955
We purchace, through our flatterynge,
Of riche menne of great poste,

Letters to wytnesse our bounte,
So that manne weneth, that maye us se,
That al vertue in us be. 6960
And alwaye poore we us fayne;
But howe so that we begge or playne,
We bene the folke, without leasyng,
That al thynge have without havyng.
Thus be we dradde of the people, ywis. 6965
And gladly my purpose is this:
I deale with no wight but he
Have golde and treasour great plente.
Her acqueyntaunce wel love I;
This is moche my desyre, shortely. 6970
I entremete me of brocages,
I make peace and mariages,
I am gladly executour,
And many tymes a procuratour;
I am somtyme messagere— 6975
That falleth nat to my mystere.
And many tymes I make enqueste—
For me that offyce is nat honest.
To deale with other mennes thynge,
That is to me a great lykynge. 6980
And if that ye have ought to do
In place that I repeyre to,
I shal it speden through my wyt,
As soone as ye have tolde me it.
So that ye serve me to paye, 6985
My servyce shal be yours alwaye.
But whoso wol chastyce me,
Anone my love loste hath he,
For I love no manne in no gyse
That wol me repreve or chastice. 6990
But I wolde al folke undertake,
And of no wight no teachynge take;
For I, that other folke chastye,
Wol nat be taught fro my folye.

"I love none hermytage more; 6995
Al desertes and holtes hoore,
And great woodes everychone,

6920 **wyllen,** desire. 6925–26 *hem:* TG *him.* 6926 **werrey,** make war against. 6928 **conjecte,** ponder (calculate). 6931 **Provende,** income (prebend). 6932 **compassen,** discover. 6936 **lese,** lose. 6939 **wete,** know (suspect). 6944 **kepte . . . nyce,** protected, foolish. 6948 **alder,** all of (archaic gen.). 6949 **fayned,** pretended. 6952 **parceners,** partners. 6954 **sprongen,** advanced. 6957 **poste,** powers. 6961 **fayne,** pretend. 6971 **entremete me . . . brocages,** involve myself, making deals. 6976 **falleth nat . . . mystere,** is not suitable, occupation (skill). 6977 **enqueste,** inquest (into the validity of other people's transactions). 6978 **honest,** profitable. 6983 **speden,** accomplish (expedite). 6991 **undertake,** rebuke.

I lette hem to the Baptyst John.
I queth him quyte, and him relesse
Of Egipte al the wyldernesse.   7000
To ferre were al my mansyons
Fro al cytees and good towns.
My paleys and myne house make I
There menne maye renne in openly,
And saye that I the worlde forsake.   7005
But al amydde I bylde and make
My house, and swymme and playe therinne
Bette than a fysshe dothe with his fynne.
    "Of Antechristes menne am I,
Of whiche that Christ sayth openly,   7010
They have habyte of holynesse,
And lyven in suche wickednesse.
Outwarde, lamben semen we,
Ful of goodnesse and of pyte,
And inwarde we, withouten fable,   7015
Bene gredy wolves ravysable.
We envyroun bothe londe and see;
With al the worlde werryen we;
We wol ordayne of al thynge,
Of folkes good and her lyvyng.   7020
    "If there be castell or cytee
Wherin that any bougerons be,
Although that they of Myllayne were—
For therof bene they blamed there;
Or if a wyght, out of measure,   7025
Wolde leane his golde and take usure,
For that he is so coveytous,
Or if he be to lecherous,
Or thefe, or haunten simonye,
Or provost ful of trechery,   7030
Or prelate lyveng jolylye,
Or preest that halte his queyn him by,

Or olde hoores hostylers,
Or other baudes or bordellers,
Or els blamed of any vyce,   7035
Of whiche men shulden done justyce:
By al the sayntes that we pray,
But they defende them with lamprey,
With luce, with elys, with samons,
With tendre gees, and with capons,   7040
With tartes, or with chesses fatte,
With deyntie flaunes, brode and flatte,
With caleweys, or with pullayle,
With conynges, or with fyne vitayle,
That we, under our clothes wyde,   7045
Maken through our golet glyde;
Or but he wol do come in haste
Roe-venyson, bake in paste,
Whether so that he loure or groyne,
He shal have of a corde a loygne,   7050
With whiche men shal him bynde and lede,
To brenne him for his synful dede,
That men shul here him crye and rore
A myle-way aboute, and more.
Or els he shal in prison dye,   7055
But if he wol our frendshyp bye,
Or smerten that that he hath do,
More than his gylte amounteth to.
    "But and he couthe through his sleight
Do maken up a toure of heyght,   7060
Nought rought I wheder of stone or tre,
Or erthe, or turves though it be,
Though it were of no vounde stone,
Wrought with squyre and scantilone,
So that the tour were stuffed well   7065
With al rychesse temporell;
And than, that he wolde updresse

6998 Baptyst John, St. John the Baptist retreated, like the monks and hermits, to a retired contemplative life in the desert. **6999 queth him quyte,** declare acquitted to him (i.e., legally transferred). **7000 Of Egipte ... wyldernesse,** Christian monasticism began in the 4th century in the Egyptian desert. **7001 were,** would be. **7012** TG have after this, lines 7109–58, evidently because of a misplaced folio in the exemplar; cf. l. 7159n. **7016 ravysable,** ravishing. **7017 envyroun,** encompass. **7018 werryen,** war upon. **7019 ordayne,** dispose. **7022 bougerons,** sodomites. G *begger.* **7023 Myllayne,** Milan. **7025 Or if:** T *Of.* **7026 leane,** lend. *his:* T *her.* **7029 simonye,** sale of church offices. *thefe, or:* TG *these that;* Fr. *lierres ou.* **7030 provost,** official. **7032 queyn,** mistress. **7033 hoores,** hoary. **7034 bordellers,** brothel keepers. **7037 we:** G *me.* **7038 But ... lamprey,** unless, lamprey fish. **7041 chesses,** cheeses. **7042 flaunes,** tarts with custard fillings (flans). **7043 caleweys ... pullayle,** pears (of Caillous, Burgundy), poultry. **7044 conynges,** rabbits. **7047 wol do,** will make. *he:* G *we.* **7048 paste,** pastry. **7049 loure ... groyne,** scowl, groan. **7050 loygne,** length. **7056 But if,** unless. *our:* TG *his.* **7057 smerten,** smart for. **7060 Do maken,** cause to be made. **7061 rought ... tre,** care, wood. **7062 turves,** sod (turfs). **7063 vounde,** found (southern form), i.e., no known; Fr. *de quelque pierre.* **7064 squyre ... scantilone,** (mason's) square, (architect's) plan. **7065 stuffed,** provided. **7067 updresse,** prepare.

Engyns, bothe more and lesse,
To caste at us, by every syde—
To bere his goode name wyde— 7070
Suche sleightes as I shal you neven,
Barels of wyne, by syxe or seven,
Or golde in sackes great plente,
He shulde soone delyvered be.
And if he have no suche pytences, 7075
Let him study in equipolences,
And lette lyes and fallaces,
If that he wolde deserve our graces;
Or we shal beare him such wytnesse
Of synne, and of his wretchydnesse, 7080
And done his lose so wyde renne,
That al quicke we shulde him brenne,
Or els yeve him such penaunce,
That is wel worse than the pytaunce.

   "For thou shalte never, for nothyng, 7085
Con knowen aright by her clothyng
The traitours ful of trecherye,
But thou her werkes can aspye.
And ne had the good kepyng be
Whylom of the Universyte, 7090
That kepeth the key of Cristendome,
We had ben turmented al and some.
Suche ben the stynkyng prophetis.
Nys none of hem that good prophete is;
For they, through wicked entencion, 7095
The yere of the Incarnacion
A thousande and two hundred yere,
Fyve and fyfty, ferther ne nere,
Broughten a boke, with sory grace,
To yeven ensample in commune place, 7100
That sayd thus, though it were fable:
'This is the Gospel Perdurable,
That fro the Holy Goost is sent.'
Wel were it worthe to ben brent.

Entytled was in suche manere 7105
This boke, of whiche I telle here.
There nas no wight in al Parys,
Beforne Our Lady, at parvys,
That he ne myght bye the book,
To copy, if him talent took. 7110
There myght he se, by great traysoun,
Ful many false comparysoun:
'As moche as through his great myght,
Be it of heate, or of lyght,
The sonne surmounteth the moone, 7115
That troubler is, and chaungeth soone,
And the nutte-kyrnel the shelle—
I skorne nat that I you telle—
Right so, withouten any gyle,
Surmounteth this noble Evangyle 7120
The worde of any evangelyst.'
And to her tytell they token Christ;
And many suche comparysoun,
Of whiche I make no mencioun,
Myght menne in that booke fynde, 7125
Whoso coude of hem have mynde.

   "The Unyversyte, that tho was aslepe,
Gan for to brayde and taken kepe,
And at the noyse the heed upcast,
Ne never sythen slepte it fast; 7130
But up it sterte and armes tooke
Ayenst this false, horryble booke,
Al redy batayle for to make,
And to the juge the booke they take.
But they that broughten the boke there 7135
Hent it anone awaye for fere;
They nolde shewe it no more a dele,
But than it kepte, and kepen wele,
Tyll such a tyme that they maye se
That they so stronge woxen be 7140
That no wight maye hem wel withstonde;

7068 Engyns . . . more, catapults, big. **7071 sleightes,** tricks (i.e., missiles, with which the friar is pelted). **neven,** name. TG *as* om. **7075 pytences,** charity gifts (alms). G *he have* om. **7076 equipolences,** (Skeat) equivocations; (Langlois) equivalencies. **7077 lette,** leave. **7081 done . . . lose,** make, reputation. **7082 quicke,** alive. **7086 Con,** know. **7089 kepyng,** protection. **7090 Universyte,** i.e., Guillaume de Saint-Amour, and his associates, cf. lines 6553ff. **7092** Line lacking in G. **7099 a boke,** in 1254 (not 1255 as here stated), the friars published a "gospel of the Holy Spirit," which was purported to supersede the gospel of the Son in the New Testament. This arrogance brought upon them the condemnation of the pope and contributed to the disrepute into which they fell during the succeeding century. For details see Langlois, 11796n. **7108 parvys,** the porch of the cathedral of Notre Dame—at that time the site of a school. **7109–10** T has four garbled lines; G has one, 7110 only. These two are from the first line in T and the one in G, emended from Fr. **talent,** inclination. **7116 troubler,** more dim. **7122 tytell,** justification. **7128 brayde,** awake. **7130 sythen,** since. **7133** G *for* om. **7134 take,** undertake. **7136 Hent,** took (grabbed). **7138 kepte,** guarded.

For by that boke they durst nat stonde.
Awaye they gonne it for to bere,
For they ne durste nat answere
By exposytioun ne gloose   7145
To that the clerkes wol appose
Ayenst the cursednesse, ywis,
That in that booke written is.
Nowe wotte I nat, ne I can nat se
What maner ende that there shal be   7150
Of al this boke that they hyde.
But yet algate they shal abyde
Tyl that they maye it bette defende;
This trowe I best wol be her ende.
    "Thus Antechrist abyden we,   7155
For we bene al of his meyne;
And what manne that wol nat be so,
Right soone he shal his lyfe forgo.
We wol a people upon him areyse,
And through our gyle done him seise,   7160
And him on sharpe speares ryve,
Or otherways bringe him fro lyve,
But-if that he wol folowe, ywis,
That in our booke written is.
Thus moche wol our booke signifye,   7165
That whyle Peter hath maistrye,
May never Johan shewe wel his might.
    "Nowe have I you declared right
The meanyng of the barke and rynde
That maketh the entencions blynde.   7170
But nowe at erst I wol begyn
To expowne you the pythe within,
And the seculers comprehende,
That Christes lawe wol defende,
And shulde it kepen and mayntenen   7175
Ayenst hem that al sustenen,
And falsly to the people techen.
For Johan betoketh hem to prechen
That there nys lawe covenable
But thilke Gospel pardurable   7180

That fro the Holy Goste was sent
To turne folke that ben miswent.
The strength of Johan they understonde,
The grace in whiche they say they stonde,
That dothe the synful folke converte,   7185
And hem to Jesu Christ reverte.
Ful many another horriblete
May men in that booke se,
That ben commaunded doutelesse
Ayenst the lawe of Rome expresse.   7190
And al with Antechrist they holden,
As men may in the boke beholden.
And then commaunden they to sleen
Al tho that with Peter been;
But they shal never have that myght,   7195
And God toforne, for stryfe to fyght,
That they ne shal ynough fynde
That Peters lawe shal have in mynde,
And ever holde, and so mayntene,
That at the laste it shal be sene   7200
That they shal al come therto,
For aught that they can speke or do.
And thilke lawe shal not stonde
That they by Johan have understonde;
But maugre hem, it shal adoun,   7205
And ben brought to confusyoun.
But I wol stynte of this matere,
For it is wonder longe to here;
But hadde that ylke boke endured,
Of better estate I were ensured;   7210
And frendes have I yet, parde,
That han me set in great degre.
    "Of al this worlde is emperour
Gyle my father, the trechour,
And emperesse my mother is,   7215
Maugre the Holy Goste, iwys.
Our mighty lynage and our route
Reigneth in every reigne aboute.
And wel is worthy we maistres be,

7143 *Awaye*: G *Alway*. **7145 gloose,** commentary (gloss). *ne*: TG *no*. **7151** TG *boke* om. **7156 meyne,** household. **7159–7206** TG have these lines after 7302, evidently because of a misplaced folio in the exemplar, cf. l. 7012n. **7160 done him seise,** have him seized. *seise*: T *reise*. **7161 ryve,** pierce. **7166–67 Peter . . . Johan,** Peter, the pope; John, the friars. **7169 rynde,** skin (i.e., outer covering). **7173 seculers,** the secular clergy, who were locked in conflict with the friars. **comprehende,** consider. **7178 betoketh,** instructs. **7179 covenable,** suitable. **7197 ne shal ynough,** i.e., that enough people will not remain. **7201 they . . . come therto,** i.e., everyone will accept Peter's law (papal authority). **7202 they can speke,** i.e., the friars can say. **7205 adoun,** fall (a-down). **7215 emperesse,** i.e., Hypocrisy. **7217 route,** band. **7219** *maistres*: TG *mynistres*; Fr. *E bien est drois que nous regnons.*

For al this worlde governe we,   7220
And can the folke so wel disceyve
That none our gyle can perceyve.
And though they done, they dare not say;
The sothe dare no wight bewray.
But he in Christes wrathe him ledeth,   7225
That more than Christ my bretherne dredeth.
He nys no ful good champion,
That dredeth suche similacion,
Nor that for payne wol refusen
Us to correcte and accusen.   7230
He wol not entremete by right,
Ne have God in his eyesight,
And therfore God shal him punyce.
But me ne recketh of no vyce,
Sythen men us loven comunably,   7235
And holden us for so worthy
That we may folke repreve echone,
And we nyll have represe of none.
Whom shulden folke worshypen so
But us, that stynten never mo   7240
To patren whyle that folke may us se,
Though it not so behynde hem be?
  "And where is more woode folye,
Than to enhaunce chivalrye,
And love noble men and gay,   7245
That joly clothes weren alway?
If they be suche folke as they semen,
So clene, as men her clothes demen,
And that her wordes folowe her dede,
It is great pyte, out of drede,   7250
For they wol be non hypocritis!
Of hem, me thynketh, great spyte is;
I canne nat love hem on no syde.
But beggers with these hoodes wyde,
With sleighe and pale faces leane,   7255
And graye clothes nat ful cleane,

But fretted ful of tatarwagges,
And highe shoes, knopped with dagges,
That frouncen lyke a quayle pype,
Or bootes ryvelyng as a gype.   7260
To suche folke, as I you devyse,
Shulde princes and these lordes wyse
Take al her londes and her thynges,
Bothe warre and pees in governynges—
To suche folke shulde a prince hym yeve   7265
That wolde his lyfe in honour lyve.
And if they be nat as they seme,
That serven thus the worlde to queme,
There wolde I dwelle, to disceyve
The folke, for they shal nat parceyve.   7270
  "But I ne speke in no suche wyse,
That men shulde humble habytte dispyse,
So that no pride there-under be;
No manne shulde hate, as thynketh me,
The poore man in such a clothynge.   7275
But God ne preyseth him nothynge
That saith he hath the worlde forsake,
And hath to worldly glorie hym take,
And wol of suche delyces use.
Who maye that begger wel excuse?   7280
That papelarde that him yeldeth so,
And wol to worldly ease go,
And saith that he the worlde hath lefte,
And gredily it grypeth efte,
He is the hounde, shame is to sayne,   7285
That to his castynge gothe agayne.
But unto you dare I nat lye.
But myght I felen or espy,
That ye parceyved it nothynge,
Ye shulde have a starke leasynge   7290
Right in your honde thus to begynne;
I nolde it lette for no synne."
   The god loughe at the wonder tho,

7225–26 **But he ... That more**, i.e., but he who dreads my brethren more than Christ subjects himself to Christ's wrath. 7228 **similacion**, dissimulation. 7231 **entremete**, interfere. 7234 **ne recketh**, don't mind. 7235 **comunably**, commonly. 7241 **patren**, say Paternosters. 7252 **spyte**, envy. 7252–53 *hem*: G *hym*. 7254 **beggers**, Beguines, members of lay charitable orders, originally composed of women; but the order degenerated rapidly. In 1261 it was condemned by the Church, and "beggar" took on its present connotation. Skeat sees it here applied to the Franciscan friars. 7257 **tatarwagges**, ragged patches. 7258 **knopped ... dagges**, knobbed, patches. 7259 **frouncen ... quayle pype**, wrinkled, a quail net (this is a guess—the term is not found elsewhere). 7260 **ryvelyng ... gype**, wrinkling, cassock. 7261 **devyse**, describe. 7263 **Take**, entrust. 7268 **queme**, please. 7270 **for**, i.e., so that. *The*: G *To*. 7281 **papelarde**, hypocrite. 7284 **efte**, still. 7286 **castynge**, vomit. II Pet. 2:22, Prov. 26:11. 7289 **parceyved it nothynge**, were not at all aware of it. 7290 **leasynge**, lying. 7292 **lette**, hesitate.

And every wyght gan laughe also,
And sayd, "Lo here a manne aright   7295
For to be trusty to every wight!
False-Semblant," quod Love, "say to me,
Sythe I thus have avaunced the,
That in my courte is thy dwellyng,
And of rybaudes shalt be my kyng,   7300
Wolt thou wel holden my forwardes?"

   "Ye, sir, from hence forwardes.
Had never your father here beforne
Servaunt so trewe, sythe he was borne."

   "That is ayenst al nature."   7305

   "Sir, put you in that aventure;
For though ye borowes take of me,
The sykerer shal ye never be
For hostages, ne sykernesse,
Or chartres, for to beare wytnesse.   7310
I take yourselfe to recorde here,
That men ne may, in no manere,
Teren the wolfe out of his hyde
Tyl he be flayne, backe and syde,
Though men him beate and al defyle.   7315
What? Wene ye that I ne wol begyle,
For I am clothed mekely?
There-under is al my trechery;
Myn herte chaungeth never the mo
For none habyt in whiche I go.   7320
Though I have chere of symplenesse,
I am not wery of shreudnesse.
My lemman, Strayned-Abstenaunce,
Hath myster of my purveyaunce.
She had ful longe ago be dede,   7325
Nere my counsayle and my rede.
Let her alone, and you and me."

   And Love answerde, "I truste the
Without borowe, for I wol none."
And False-Semblant, the thefe, anone,   7330
Right in that ilke same place,

That had of treson al his face,
Right blacke within and whyte without,
Thankyng him gan on his knees loute.   7334

   Than was there nought but, "Every man
Nowe to assaute, that saylen can,"   ASSAULT
Quod Love, "and that ful hardely."   ON THE
Than armed they hem comenly   TOWER
Of suche armour as to hem fell.
Whan they were armed, fiers and fell,   7340
They went hem forthe, al in a route,
And set the castel al aboute;
They wyl not away for no drede
Tyl it so be that they ben dede,
Or tyl they have the castel take.   7345
And four batels they gan make,
And parted hem in four anon,
And toke her way, and forthe they gone
The foure gates for to assayle,
Of whiche the kepers wol not fayle,   7350
For they ben neyther sicke ne dede,
But hardy folke, and stronge in dede.

   Nowe wol I sayne the countenaunce
Of False-Semblant and Abstynaunce,
That ben to Wicked-Tonge went.   7355
But first they helde her parlyment,
Whether it to done were
To maken hem be knowen there,
Or els walken forthe disgysed.
But at the laste they devysed   7360
That they wolde gone in tapynage,
As it were in a pilgrymage,
Lyke good and holy folke unfeyned.
And Dame Abstynence-Streyned
Toke on a robe of camelyne,   7365
And gan her graithe as a bygyne.
A large coverchiefe of threde
She wrapped al aboute her hede,
But she forgate not her psaltere.

7300 rybaudes . . . kyng, the court bouncer; cf. l. 6068n. above. **7301 forwardes,** agreements. **7302** In TG lines 7159–7206 come here because of a misplaced folio in the exemplar; cf. l. 7012n. **7306 put . . . aventure,** "take the chance." **7307 borowes,** securities. **7308 sykerer,** more secure. **7310 chartres,** written agreements. **7311 I take yourselfe,** i.e., I leave it to you. **7314 flayne,** skinned. TG *slayn;* Fr. *escorchiés.* **7315** G *and al to.* **7316** TG *ne* om. **7321 chere,** appearance. **7323 Strayned,** constrained. G *Streyneth.* **7324 myster . . . purveyaunce,** need, solicitude. **7326 Nere,** were it not for. **7329 borowe,** security. **7334 loute,** bend down. G *Thankith.* **7336 saylen,** assail. **7338 comenly,** mutually. **7341 route,** group. **7342 set,** beset. **7346 batels,** separate battalions. **7353 counten-aunce,** behavior. **7356 her parlyment,** their discussion. **7361 tapynage,** secret. **7363 unfeyned,** sincere. **7365 camelyne,** camel's hair. **7366 graithe . . . bygyne,** dress, Beguine (cf. l. 6861n.). *graithe:* TG *gratche.* **7369 psaltere,** Psalter.

A payre of beedes eke she bere 7370
Upon a lace, al of whyte threde,
On whiche that she her beades bede;
But she ne bought hem never a dele,
For they were gyven her, I wote wele,
God wote, of a ful holy frere, 7375
That sayd he was her father dere,
To whom she had ofter went
Than any frere of his covent.
And he visyted her also,
And many a sermon sayd her to. 7380
He nolde let, for man on lyve,
That he ne wolde her ofte shrive.
And with so great devocion
They made her confession
That they had ofte, for the nones, 7385
Two hedes in one hoode at ones.
Of fayre shappe I devyse her the,
But pale of face somtyme was she;
That false traytouresse untrewe
Was lyke that salowe horse of hewe, 7390
That in the Apocalips is shewed,
That signifyeth tho folke beshrewed,
That ben al ful of trecherye,
And pale, through hypocrisye;
For on that horse no colour is, 7395
But onely deed and pale, ywis.
Of suche a colour enlangoured
Was Abstynence, iwys, coloured.
Of her estate she her repented,
As her visage represented. 7400
She had a burdowne al of thefte
That Gyle had yeve her of his yefte;
And a skryppe of faynte distresse
That ful was of elengenesse;
And forthe she walked sobrely. 7405
 And False-Semblant saynt, je vous die,
Had, as it were for suche mistere,
Done on the cope of a frere,
With chere symple and ful pytous;

His lokyng was not disdeynous, 7410
Ne proude, but meke and ful pesyble.
About his necke he bare a Byble,
And squierly forthe gan he gon.
And for to rest his lymmes upon,
He had of Treason a potent; 7415
As he were feble, his way he went.
But in his sleve he gan to thring
A rasour sharpe and wel bytyng,
That was forged in a forge
Whiche that men clepen Coupe-Gorge. 7420
 So longe forthe her waye they nomen,
Tyl they to Wicked-Tonge comen,
That at his gate was syttyng,
And sawe folke in the way passyng.
The pilgrymes sawe he faste by, 7425
That beren hem ful mekely,
And humbly they with him mette.
Dame Abstynence first him grette,
And sythe him False-Semblant salued,
And he hem; but he not remeued, 7430
For he ne dredde hem not a dele.
For whan he sawe her faces wele,
Alway in herte him thought so,
He shulde knowe hem bothe two.
For wel he knewe Dame Abstynaunce, 7435
But he ne knewe not constreynaunce.
He knewe nat that she was constrayned,
Ne of her theves lyfe fayned,
But wende she come of wyl al free.
But she come in another degree; 7440
And if of good wyl she beganne,
That wyl was fayled her thanne.
And False-Semblant had he sayne also,
But he knewe nat that he was false.
Yet false was he, but his falsnesse 7445
Ne coude he nat espye nor gesse;
For semblant was so slye wrought
That falsenesse he ne espyed nought.
But haddest thou knowen hym beforne.

7370 payre of beedes, string of beads (rosary), cf. the Prioress, *CT,* I.159. **7371 lace,** string. **7372 beades bede,** prayers, might pray. **7381 let,** refrain. **7383–7574** Lines lacking in G. **7386 Two hedes, &c.,** slang for sexual intimacy. **7387 devyse,** describe. T *devysed.* **7390 salowe horse,** the pale horse of death, Rev. 6:8. **7392 beshrewed,** accursed. **tho:** T *to.* **7401 burdowne,** staff. **7403 skryppe,** bag (knapsack). **7404 elengenesse,** cheerlessness; Fr. *soussi.* **7406 saynt,** girdle (cinture). **7407 mistere,** need. **Had:** T *And;* Fr. *Ot.* **7413 squierly,** like a squire? Fr. *Après s'en va sans escuier.* **7415 potent,** crutch. **7417 thring,** thrust. **7420 Coupe-Gorge,** i.e., cutthroat. **7429 sythe,** then. **7430 remeued,** i.e., did not move from the gate. **7443 sayne,** seen.

Thou woldest on a boke have sworne, 7405
Whan thou him saugh in thylke araye,
That he that whilome was so gaye
And of the daunce joly Robyn
Was tho become a Jacobyn.
But sothely, what so menne hem cal, 7455
Frere-prechours bene good menne al.
Her order wickedly they beren,
Suche mynstrelles if they weren.
So bene Augustyns and Cordylers,
And Carmes, and eke Sacked Freers, 7460
And al freres, shodde and bare
(Though some of hem ben great and square),
Ful hooly men, as I hem deme;
Everyche of hem wolde good man seme.
But shalte thou never of apparence 7465
Sene conclude good consequence
In none argument, ywis,
If existens al fayled is.
For menne maye fynde alwaye sopheme
The consequence to enveneme, 7470
Whoso that hath the subtelte
The double sentence for to se.
　Whan the pylgrymes commen were
To Wicked-Tonge, that dwelled there,
Her harneys nygh hem was algate. 7475
By Wicked-Tonge adowne they sate,
That badde hem nere him for to come,
And of tidynges telle him some,
And sayd hem, "What case maketh you
To come into this place now?" 7480
　"Sir," sayd Strayned-Abstynaunce,
"We, for to drye our penaunce,
With hertes pytous and devoute,
Are commen, as pylgrimes gon aboute.
Wel nygh on fote alway we go; 7485
Ful dusty ben our heeles two.
And thus bothe we ben sent
Throughout this worlde that is miswent

To yeve ensample, and preche also.
To fysshen synful menne we go, 7490
For other fysshynge ne fysshe we.
And, sir, for that charyte
As we be wonte, herborowe we crave,
Your lyfe to amende; Christ it save!
And, so it shulde you nat displease, 7495
We wolden, if it were your ease,
A shorte sermon unto you sayne."
　And Wicked-Tonge answered agayne,
"The house," quod he, "such as ye se,
Shal nat be warned you for me, 7500
Say what you lyst, and I wol here."
　"Graunt mercy, swete sir, 　ABSTINENCE'S
　　dere!" 　SPEECH TO
Quod alderfirst Dame 　WICKED-TONGE
　　Abstynence,
And thus began she her sentence:
　"Sir, the firste vertue, certayne, 7505
The greatest and moste soverayne
That may be founde in any man,
For havynge or for wytte he can,
That is his tonge to refrayne;
Therto ought every wight him payne. 7510
For it is better styll be
Than for to speken harme, parde!
And he that herkeneth it gladly,
He is no good man, sykerly.
And, sir, aboven al other synne, 7515
In that arte thou moste gilty inne:
Thou spake a jape not longe ago—
And, sir, that was right yvel do—
Of a yonge man that here repayred,
And never yet this place apayred. 7520
Thou saydest he awayted nothyng
But to disceyve Fayre-Welcomyng.
Ye sayd nothyng sothe of that,
But, sir, ye lye, I tel you plat.
He ne cometh no more, ne gothe, parde! 7525

7454 Jacobyn, Dominican friar, cf. l. 6338n. **7455** *hem:* T *hym.* **7457 they beren,** i.e., would they represent. **7459–60 Augustyns,** Austin friars. **Cordylers,** Franciscan friars (from their twisted rope girdles). **Carmes,** Carmelite friars. **Sacked Freers,** Friars De Penitentia, whose robes were intended to suggest sackcloth and ashes. **7068 existens,** i.e., substance (vs. appearance). **7469 sopheme,** sophism (fallacious reasoning). **7470 enveneme,** poison. **7471** T *hath hadde the.* **7472 double sentence,** double meaning. **7475 harneys,** (war) gear. **7482 drye,** endure. **7485** T *nyght.* **7486 dusty:** T *doughty;* Fr. *poudreus.* **7490 fysshen,** fish for; cf. Matt. 4:19. **7493 herborowe,** shelter. **7500 warned,** denied. **7508 havynge . . . wytte,** i.e., experience, wisdom. **7519 here repayred,** came here. **7520 apayred,** harmed. **7521 awayted,** waited for (wanted).

I trowe ye shal him never se.
Fayre-Welcomyng in prison is,
That ofte hath played with you er this,
The fayrest games that he coude,
Without fylthe, styl or loude;   7530
Nowe dare he nat himselfe solace.
Ye han also the manne do chace,
That he dare neyther come ne go.
What meveth you to hate him so
But properly your wicked thought   7535
That many a false leasyng hath thought?
That meveth your foole eloquence
That jangleth ever in audyence,
And on the folke areyseth blame,
And dothe hem dishonour and shame   7540
For thynge that maye have no prevyng,
But lykelynesse and contryvyng.
For I dare sayne that Reason demeth
It is nat al sothe thynge that semeth;
And it is synne to controve   7545
Thynge that is to reprove.
This wote ye wele, and sir, therfore
Ye arne to blame the more.
And nathelesse, he recketh lyte;
He yeveth nat nowe therof a myte.   7550
For if he thought harme, parfaye,
He wolde come and gone al daye;
He coude himselfe nat abstene.
Nowe cometh he nat, and that is sene,
For he ne taketh of it no cure,   7555
But if it be through aventure,
And lasse than other folke, algate.
And thou her watchest at the gate,
With speare in thyne arest alwaye;
There muse, musarde, al the daye.   7560
Thou wakest night and day for thought;
Iwis, thy traveyle is for nought.
And Jelousye, withouten fayle,
Shal never quyte the thy traveyle.
And skathe is that Fayre-Welcomyng,   7565

Without any trespassyng,
Shal wrongfully in prison be,
There wepeth and languyssheth he.
And though thou never yet, ywis,
Agyltest manne no more but this—   7570
Take nat agrefe—it were worthy
To putte the out of this bayly,
And afterwarde in prison lye,
And fettre the tyl that thou dye.
For thou shalte for this synne dwelle   7575
Right in the dyvels arse of helle,
But if that thou repent the."
     "Ma faye, thou lyest falscly!" quod he.
"What, welcome with myschaunce now?
Have I therfore herbered you   7580
To saye me shame, and eke reprove?
With sorye happe, to your behove,
Am I today your herbegere!
Go herber you elswhere than here,
That han a lyer called me!   7585
Two tregetours arte thou and he,
That in myn house do me this shame,
And for my sothesawe ye me blame.
Is this the sermon that ye make?
To al the dyvels I me take,   7590
Or els, God, thou me confounde!
But er men dydden this castel founde,
It passeth not ten dayes or twelve,
But it is tolde right to myselve,
And as they sayd, right so tolde I: 7595
He kyste the rose prively!
Thus sayd I nowe, and have sayd yore;
I not where he dyd any more.
Why shulde men say me suche a thyng,
If it had been gabbyng?   7600
Right so sayd I, and wol saye yet;
I trowe, I lyed not of it;
And with my bemes I wol blowe
To al neyghbours arowe,
Howe he hath bothe comen and gone."   7605

7530 styl, quietly. **7531 T** *she nat herselfe.* **7532 the manne,** i.e., the Lover. **7536 leasyng,** lie. **7538 jangleth . . . audyence,** babbles, public. **7542 lykelynesse,** plausibility. **7543 demeth,** judges. **7545 controve,** invent. **7549 recketh,** cares. **7550 myte,** smallest coin. **7551 thought harme,** thought to do harm. **7553 abstene,** keep himself away. **7555 cure,** care. **7556 But if . . . aventure,** unless chance. **7559 arest,** rest (holder) for the spear. **7560 musarde,** sluggard. **7564 quyte,** repay. **7565 skathe,** too bad. **7566 trespassyng,** wrongdoing. **7570 Agyltest,** sinned against. **7572 bayly,** custody (of the gate). **7582 behove,** need. **7586 tregetours,** deceivers. **7588 sothesawe,** truth telling. **7598 not where,** don't know whether. **7603 bemes,** trumpets.

Tho spake False-Semblant right anone,
"Al is not gospel, out of doute,
That men sayne in the towne aboute;
Lay no deefe eere to my spekyng;
I swere you, sir, it is gabbyng. 7610
I trowe ye wote wel certaynly
That no man loveth him tenderly
That saythe him harme, if he wote it,
Al be he never so poore of wyt.
And sothe is also, sykerly— 7615
This knowe ye, sir, as wel as I—
That lovers gladly wol visyten
The places there her loves habyten.
This man you loveth and eke honoureth,
This man to serve you laboureth, 7620
And clepeth you his frende so dere;
And this man maketh you good chere,
And everywhere that he you meteth,
He you saleweth, and he you greteth.
He preseth nat so ofte that ye 7625
Ought of his comyng encombred be;
There presen other folke on you
Ful ofter than he dothe nowe.
And if his herte him strayned so
Unto the rose for to go, 7630
Ye shulde hym sene so ofte nede,
That ye shulde take him with the dede.
He coude his comynge nat forbeare,
Though men him thrilled with a speare;
It nere nat than as it is now. 7635
But trusteth wel, I swere it you,
That it is clene out of his thought.
Sir, certes, he ne thynketh it nought;
No more ne dothe Fayre-Welcomyng
That sore abyeth al this thyng. 7640
And if they were of one assent,
Ful soone were the rose hent,
The maugre yours wolde be.
And sir, of o thyng herkeneth me:
Sith ye this man that loveth you 7645
Han sayd suche harme and shame now,

Wytteth wel, if he gessed it,
Ye maye wel demen in your wyt
He nolde nothynge love you so,
Ne callen you his frende also, 7650
But nyght and daye he wol wake,
The castel to destroye and take,
If it were sothe as ye devys.
Or some manne in some maner wyse
Might it warne him everydele, 7655
Or by himselfe parceyve wele,
For sithe he myght nat come and gone
As he was whylome wonte to done,
He myght it soone wyte and se.
But nowe al otherwyse doth he. 7660
Than have ye, sir, al utterly
Deserved helle, and jolyly
The dethe of helle, doutlesse,
That thrallen folke so gyltlesse."
False-Semblant so proveth this thyng 7665
That he canne none answeryng,
And seeth alwaye suche apparaunce
That nygh he fel in repentaunce,
And sayd him, "Sir, it maye wel be.
Semblant, a good manne semen ye; 7670
And, Abstynence, ful wyse ye seme;
Of o talent you bothe I deme.
What counsayle wol ye to me yeven?"
"Right here anon thou shalt be
    shriven,
And say thy synne without more; 7675
Of this shalte thou repent sore,
For I am preest and have poste
To shrive folke of most dignyte
That ben, as wyde as worlde may dure.
Of al this worlde I have the cure, 7680
And that had never yet persoun,
Ne vycarie of no maner toun;
And, God wotte, I have of the
A thousande tymes more pyte
Than hath thy preest parochial, 7685
Though he thy frende be special.

7619 **This man,** i.e., the Lover. 7623 TG *he* om. 7625 **preseth,** intrudes. 7634 **thrilled,** pierced. *men:* TG *he him.* 7640 **sore abyeth,** sorely pays for. 7642 **hent,** taken. 7643 **maugre,** blame (fault). 7655 **warne,** inform. 7657 **sithe,** since. 7659 **wyte and se,** Fr. *s'en fust aperceu* (would guess). 7660 **doth:** TG *wote;* Fr. *fet.* 7661 *ye:* T *we;* G om.; Fr. *vous.* 7662 **jolyly,** completely; Fr. *bien.* 7664 **thrallen,** imprison. 7666 **he,** i.e., Wicked-Tongue. 7667 **apparaunce,** evidence. 7672 **o talent,** the same opinion. 7675 **say,** confess. 7677 **poste,** power. 7680 **cure,** (spiritual) care. 7685 **preest parochial,** parish priest.

I have avauntage, in o wyse,
That your prelates ben not so wyse
Ne halfe so lettred as am I.
I am lycensed boldely 7690
In divynite for to rede,

And to confessen, out of drede.
If ye wol you nowe confesse,
And leave your synnes more and lesse,
Without abode, knele downe anon, 7695
And you shal have absolucion."

Here endeth the Romaunt of the Rose.

7689 lettred, educated. **7691** G *To reden in divinite.* **7692 confessen,** hear confession. G ends here; *And long have red. Explicit.* **7695 abode,** delay.

Boece

INTRODUCTION

Boece

N *De Consolatio Philosophiae* Boethius explores the major intellectual dilemma of medieval Christianity: how human freedom of choice can coexist with divine omnipotence. Belief in sin requires that human beings be free to choose right or wrong, and be held responsible for their choice. Yet divine omnipotence requires that God determine every event in the universe. In addition, the *Consolatio* deals with the eternal question of how a just God can permit the righteous to suffer. These questions were of particular interest to rulers who had power and responsibility yet found they could not control either human or natural events. King Alfred made a very personal translation of the *Consolatio* into Anglo-Saxon. Later Queen Elizabeth was to make her own translation. It is possible that Chaucer's translation was made to help with the education of young King Richard.

The *Consolatio* profoundly influenced Chaucer's poetry. In his words to Adam Scryven (short poem 15) he linked it with *Troylus and Criseyde,* which suggests that he was working on the two pieces at about the same time (between 1380 and 1385). One line of interpretation sees *Troylus* as a study of Boethian determinism. The lovers feel that they are responding to voluntary

814

sentiments, but events prove that they are pawns to fortune. Chaucer appears to have increased the Boethian emphasis in revision (*TC* III.1744 note, and IV.957 note). Even more Boethian is the Knight's Tale. Here Theseus, a model ruler, tries to arrange events in a just and reasonable manner only to have the winner die by accident and the loser get the girl. In the Nun's Priest's Tale the reader looks down on the henyard like God upon the universe and sees the fox lying in wait for Chauntecleer, exemplifying the "conditional necessity" (*CT* VII.3250) by which freedom and foreknowledge can coexist. In addition, the "Boethian" short poems (nos. 10-13), and important images and ideas like the Goddess Fortuna and her wheel, the vanity of temporal affairs, and misfortune as a test of character can be traced directly or indirectly to the *Consolatio*. Two books by H.R. Patch treat the influence of Boethius on medieval thought and art, *The Goddess Fortuna in Medieval Literature* (1927) and *The Tradition of Boethius* (1935).

When we compare the elegant rendering of Boethian dicta in Chaucer's verse with their fumbling expression in his prose translation, we can hardly believe that they are by the same person. T.W. Machan, *Techniques of Translation: Boece* (1985), argues that the translation was not intended for circulation but was a learning process through which Chaucer mastered the mean-

ing of the *Consolatio* and transformed his own world view. This explanation is supported by Caroline Eckhardt, "The Medieval *Prosimetrum* Genre from Boethius to *Boece*," *Genre* (1982), who suggests that is why he translated the verse passages into prose. As R.W. Chambers pointed out, *On the Continuity of English Prose* (1932), there was a homiletic tradition that provided Chaucer with a smoother, more idiomatic style for the Parson's Tale. But English had not been used for technical writing since the Norman Conquest. Chaucer's *Boece* and *Astrolabe* and (possibly) *Equatorie of the Planets* are among the first experiments in Modern English scientific writing, but it took another two centuries for English prose to achieve the lucidity of a Hooker or a Bacon.

Recent scholarship suggests that Chaucer was working from a manuscript that contained three kinds of sources, a Latin text of the *Consolatio*, the French prose translation of Jean de Meun, and commentaries by Nicholas Trivet and other authorities. B.L. Jefferson, *Chaucer and the Consolation of Philosophy* (1917) remains the most complete survey of Chaucer's borrowings, and the textual commentary in the *Riverside Chaucer* (1987) the most recent information on the mergings of the sources. The standard edition and translation of the Latin is by H.F. Stewart and E.K. Rand (Loeb Library, rev. ed. 1968).

Boece

BOOK I

Incipit Liber Boecii de Consolacione Philosophie.

Metre I. Carmina qui quondam.

Allas, I, weping, am constreyned to bygynnen vers of sorwful matere, that whilom in floryssinge studie made delitable ditees. For lo, rendinge Muses of poetes enditen to me thinges to ben writen, and drery vers of wrecchednesse 5 weten my face with verray teres.

At the leeste, no drede ne myhte overcomen tho Muses, that they ne weren felawes and foleweden my wey *(that is to seyn, whan I was exiled)*. Thei that weren glorye of my 10 yowthe, whilom weleful and grene, conforten now the sorwful wierdes of me, olde man. For elde is comen unwarly upon me, hasted by the harmes that I have, and sorwe hath comaunded his age to ben in me. Heres 15 hoore arn shad overtymeliche upon myn heved, and the slake skyn trembleth of myn empted body.

Thilke deth of men is weleful that ne cometh not in yeres that ben swete, but 20 cometh to wrecches often ycleped. Allas, allas, with how def an ere deth, cruwel, torneth awey fro wrecches, and nayteth to closen wepinge eyen! Whil Fortune, unfeithful, favorede me with lyghte goodes, the sorwful 25 howre *(that is to seyn, the deth)*, hadde almost dreynt myn heved. But now for Fortune, clowdy, hath chaunged hir deceyvable chere to me-ward, myn unpitous lyf draweth along unagreable dwellinges in me. O ye, my 30 frendes, what or wherto avauntede ye me to ben weleful? For he that hath fallen stood nat in stidefast degree.

Prose I. Hec dum mecum tacitus.

While that I stille recorede thise things with myself, and markede my weply compleynte with office of poyntel, I sawh, ston-

---

Text based on MS Cambridge Ii.3.21 (I), with significant variants from the Caxton ed. (Cx), Cambridge Ii.1.38 (C), and B.M. 10340 (A); see "The Text of This Edition," p. 966.

I METRE I. Carmina qui quondam, the Latin phrases at the beginning of each section are the opening words of the original text that follows; however, vocabulary, idiom, and syntax show that Chaucer very closely followed the French translation; see "The Text of This Edition." **2 whilom ... in floryssinge studie,** formerly, in happy contemplation. **3 delitable ditees,** pleasing poems. **rendinge,** tearing, but Lat. "torn" or "injured." The Latin in the notes follows the edition of E. K. Rand and H. F. Stewart, The Loeb Classical Library (1918). **4 enditen,** dictate. **6 verray,** genuine. **7 overcomen,** i.e., drove them away. **8 tho ... weren felawes,** those, were companions. **9 that is to seyn,** the glosses in italics are often in the French. **10 Cx glorye** om. **11 whilom weleful,** when (I was) fortunate. **12 wierdes,** fate(s). Lat. gloss *fata*. **13 unwarly,** unexpectedly. **14 harmes,** misfortunes. **15–16 Heres hoore ... overtymeliche,** white hairs, prematurely (untimely). **18 empted,** exhausted (empty). A *empty*. **19 Thilke ... weleful,** that, pleasant. **21 wrecches often ycleped,** i.e., when often called, to persons in misfortune (wretches). **22 torneth,** i.e., death turns away. **23 nayteth,** refuses. A *naieth*. **24 unfeithful,** i.e., untrustworthy (Fortune). **25 lyghte goodes,** transitory benefits. **27 dreynt ... heved,** drowned, head (i.e., killed). **for,** because. **28 clowdy,** i.e., covered by clouds. **deceyvable chere,** deceitful face. **29 unpitous,** miserable (pitiless): I *unpietous*. **30 unagreable dwellinges,** trans. for *ingratas moras* (disagreeable periods of time). CxIC *in me* om. **31 avauntede,** encouraged. **32 weleful,** happy. **33 stidefast degree,** (never stood) in secure position. **I PROSE I. 2 weply,** woeful (causing weeping). **3 office of poyntel,** i.e., wrote with a stylus (in wax). **sawh,** saw. The gh (h) palatal sound was obviously silent to the scribe who copied this MS, which resulted in its omission on some words (through—thorw) and its introduction in words where there is no historical justification (sawh).

dinge aboven the heyhte of myn heved
a womman of ful gret reverence by 5
semblaunt, hir eyen brenninge and cleer-
seinge over the comune myht of men; with
a lyfly colour and with swych vigour and
strengthe that it myhte nat ben empted,
alle were it so that she was ful of so 10
gret age that men ne wolden nat trowen
in no manere that she were of owre elde.
The stature of hir was of a dowtows juggement, for somtyme she constreynede
and shronk hirselven lyk to the comune 15
mesure of men, and sumtyme it semede
that she towchede the hevene with the
heyhte of hir heved; and whan she hef
hir heved hyer, she percede the selve
hevene so that the syhte of men looking 20
was in ydel.

Hir clothes weren maked of riht delye
thredes and subtil craft of perdurable matere,
the whiche clothes she hadde woven with
hir owene handes, as I knewh wel after by 25
hirself declaringe and shewinge to me the
beaute. The whiche clothes a dirknesse of a
forleten and despised elde hadde dusked and
derked, as it is wont to dyrken bismokede
ymages. In the nethereste hem or bordure of 30
thise clothes, men redden ywoven in a
Grekyssh P *(that signifyeth the lyf actyf)*, and
aboven that lettre, in the heyeste bordure, a
Grekyssh T *(that signifyeth the lyf contem-
platyf)*. And bytwixen thise two lettres ther 35

weren seyn degrees nobely ywroght in
manere of laddres, by whiche degrees men
myhten clymben fro the netherest lettre to the
uppereste. Natheles, handes of some men
hadden korven that cloth by vyolence and by 40
strengthe, and everyche man of hem hadde
born awey swiche peeces as he myhte geten.
And forsothe, this forseide woman bar smale
bookes in hir ryht hand, and in hir left hand
she baar a ceptre. 45

And whan she say thise poetical Muses
aprochen abowte my bed, and enditinge wordes
to my wepinges, she was a lytel amoved, and
glowede with cruwel eyen. "Who," quod
she, "hath suffred aprochen to this sike man 50
thise comune strompetes of swich a place
that men clepen the theatre? The whiche nat
oonly ne asswagen nat his sorwes with none
remedies, but they wolden feeden and
noryssen hym with swete venym. Forsothe, 55
thise ben tho that with thornes and pryk-
kinges of talentes or affeccyouns, whiche that
ne ben nothing fructefiinge nor profytable,
destroyen the corn plentyuous of fruites
of resoun. For they holden the hertes of 60
men in usage, but they ne delyvere nat
foolkes fro maledye. But yif ye Muses hadden
withdrawen fro me with yowre flateryes any
unkunninge and unprofitable man, as men
ben wont to fynde comunly amonges the 65
poeple, I wolde wene suffre the lasse grevously, for whi in swiche an unprofitable man

---

4 heyhte . . . heved, height, head. This is Lady Philosophy. **5–6 by semblaunt . . . brenninge,** in appearance, burning. **6–7 cleer-
seinge . . . myht,** clear-sighted, power. **8 lyfly,** bright (lively). **9 empted,** exhausted. **11 trowen,** believe. **12 elde,** period in time.
13 stature . . . dowtows juggement, height, uncertain (doubtful to judge). **14 constreynede,** reduced. **18 heved . . . hef,** head,
raised (heaved). **19 selve hevene,** heaven itself. **21 in ydel,** in vain. **22 delye,** delicate. **23 perdurable,** everlasting. **25 after,**
afterward. **27 dirknesse,** darkness. **28 forleten . . . elde . . . dusked,** neglected, oldness, darkened. **29** *bismokede:* I *the* smokede.
30 ymages, statues. **nethereste,** lowest. **31 redden ywoven,** see (read) woven in. **32 Grekyssh P,** pi, for Practical knowledge;
in I glossed *pratik*. **34 Grekyssh T,** theta, for THeoretical knowledge; in I glossed *theorik*. **36 seyn degrees nobely,** seen degrees
handsomely (i.e., degrees marked as on a scale). **38–39 A** *nethermast/overmast.* **40 korven,** cut (carved). **45 ceptre,** scepter. **46 say,**
saw. **47 enditinge,** dictating (providing). **48 lytel amoved,** momentarily upset. **49 glowede,** glared. **50 aprochen,** to approach.
51 strompetes, strumpets (prostitutes). This condemnation was cited by medieval moralists as an argument against poetry. Since
so much of the *Consolation* is itself in verse, it seems clear that Philosophy was not condemning poetry in general, but a certain kind
of poetry (erotic, escapist). *thise:* I *the;* Lat. *has.* **53 asswagen,** heal (assuage). **56 tho,** those. **57 talentes or affeccyouns,** desires
and passions. **58 ben nothing,** are not at all. **59 corn plentyuous,** plentiful grain; having the modifier follow the noun is an influence
of the French translation. **61 usage,** habit (i.e., they reconcile men's hearts to sorrow). I *ne* om. **62 I** *fro* om. **64 unkunninge and
unprofitable,** ignorant and useless (i.e., if you Muses had taken from me an inferior man). **65 wont,** accustomed. **66 wene suffre . . .
lasse,** think to bear, less. **67 for whi,** because.

myn ententes ne weren nothing endamaged.
But ye withdrawen me this man that hath
be norysshed in the studies or schooles of 70
Eliaticis and of Achademicis in Grece. But
goth now rather awey, ye mermaydenes, whiche
that ben swete til it be at the laste, and suffreth
this man to be cured and heeled by myne
Muses" *(that is to seyn, by noteful sciences).* 75

And thus this companye of Muses,
yblamed, casten wrothly the cheere downward
to the erthe, and shewinge by rednesse her
shame, they passeden sorwfully the thresshfold. And I, of whom the syhte, plownged 80
in teres, was dyrked so that I ne myghte not
knowen what that womman was of so imperial
auctorite, I wax al abaysshed and astoned,
and cast my syht down to the erthe, and
bygan stille for to abyde what she wolde 85
don afterward. Tho com she ner, and sette
hir doun upon the uttereste corner of my bed;
and she, byholdinge my cheere that was cast
to the erthe, hevy and grevous of wepinge,
compleynede with thise wordes that I shal 90
seyen the perturbacyoun of my thowht.

Metre II. Heu quam precipiti mersa profundo.

"Allas, how the thowt of man, dreynt in
overthrowinge depnesse, dulleth, and forleteth
his propre cleernesse, myntinge to goon into
foreyne dyrknesses as ofte as his anoyous
bysynesse wexeth withowte mesure, that is 5

dryven to and fro with worldly wyndes!
This man, that whilom was free, to whom the
hevene was open and knowen, and was wont to
goon in hevenelyche paathes, and sawh the
lyhtnesse of the rede sonne, and sawh the 10
sterres of the colde moone, and whiche sterre
in hevene useth wandringe recourses, iflyt by
diverse speeres—this man, overcomer, hadde
comprehended al this by nowmbre of
acountinge in astronomie. And over this, he 15
was wont to seken the causes whennes the
sowninge wyndes moeven and bysien the
smothe water of the see; and what spiryt
torneth the stable hevene; and whi the
sterre aryseth owt of the rede est to fallen in 20
the westrene wawes; and what atempreth
the lusty howres of the fyrst somer sesoun, that
hyhteth and aparaileth the erthe with rosene
flowres; and who maketh the plentyuos
autompne in fulle yeres fleteth with hevy 25
grapes. And ek this man was wont to telle
the diverse cawses of nature that weren ihydde.
Allas, now lieth he empted of lyht of his thowht,
and his nekke is pressed with hevy cheynes,
and bereth his cheere enclyned adown for 30
the grete weyhte, and is constreyned to
looken on the fool erthe.

Prose II. Set medicine inquit tempus est.

"But tyme is now," quod she, "of medicine
moore than of compleynte." Forsothe than
she, entendinge to me-ward with alle the

68 ententes, plans. **71 Eliaticis . . . Achademicis,** Eleatics (the philosophical school of Elia in Italy, founded by Zeno, regarded as the inventor of dialectic), Academics (the Academy was the traditional name for Plato's school of philosophy in Athens). **72 goth . . . rather . . . mermaydenes,** go, quickly, mermaids (Lat. *sirenes,* the misleaders of sailors). **73 at the laste,** i.e., until the victim has been destroyed. **75 *noteful sciences,*** useful knowledge. **77 yblamed . . . wrothly . . . cheere,** scolded, angrily, faces. **78 rednesse,** i.e., blushing. **80 of whom . . . syhte,** whose sight. **81 dyrked,** darkened. **85 stille . . . to abyde,** to await in silence. **86 Tho . . , ner,** then, nearer. **87 uttereste,** farthest (outermost). **88 cheere,** face (expression). **90–91 compleynede . . . perturbacyoun,** i.e., Philosophy lamented Boethius' perturbation. **I METRE II. 1 dreynt,** drowned. CxC *this man.* **2 forleteth,** leaves. **3 his propre cleernesse,** its accustomed clarity. **myntinge,** intending. **4 as ofte as,** i.e., in proportion as. **6 worldly:** I *wordly.* **7 whilom,** formerly. **9 hevenelyche paathes,** celestial path. **12 wandringe recourses, iflyt,** irregular orbits, moved. **13 speeres,** spheres. **overcomer** (Lat. *victor*), i.e., master scholar. **14 nowmbre,** i.e., computation. *comprehended:* I *comprendyd.* **15 over this:** Cx *al this thing.* **17 sowninge . . . bysien,** sounding, ruffle (busy). **20 rede,** red. **21 wawes,** waves. **atempreth,** tempers (warms). **22 lusty,** invigorating. **23 hyhteth,** adorns. **25 fleteth,** overflow. **26 wont,** accustomed. **27 cawses,** i.e., secrets (causes). **28 empted of lyht,** emptied of the light. Cx *how lightly is.* **32 fool,** senseless. A *foule.* **I PROSE II. 3 entendinge,** looking (attending).

lookinge of hir eyen, seyde: "Art nat
thow he," quod she, "that whilom ynoryssed   5
with my mylk and fostered with myne metes,
were escaped and comen to corage of a parfit
man? Certes, I yaf the swiche armures that
yif thow thyself ne haddest fyrst cast hem
awey, they shulden han defended the in   10
sikernesse that may nat ben overcomen.
Knowestow me nat? Why artow stille? Is
it for shame or for astoninge? It were me
lever that it were for shame; but it semeth
me that astoninge hath oppressed the." And   15
whan she say me nat oonly stille, but withowten office of tunge and al dowmb, she leyde
hir hand softely upon my brest and seyde: "Her
nis no peril," quod she. "He is fallen into
a litargie, whiche that is a comune sykenesse   20
to hertes that ben deceyved. He hath a litel
foryeten hymself, but certes he shal lyhtly
remembren hymself yif so be that he hath
knowen me or now. And that he may so
doon, I wol wypen a litel his eyen, that ben   25
derked by the clowde of mortal thinges."
Thise wordes seyde she, and with the lappe
of hir garment, iplited in a frounce, she
dryede myn eyen, that weren fulle of the   30
wawes of my wepinges.

Metre III. Tunc me discussa liquerunt nocte tenebre.

Thus whan that nyht was discussed and
chased awey, dirknesses forleften me, and to
myn eyen repeyrede ayein her fyrste strength.

And ryht by ensaumple as the sonne is hid
whan the sterres ben clustred *(that is to seyn,*   5
whan sterres ben covered with clowdes) by a
swifte wynde that heyhte Chorus, and that
the fyrmament stant dirked by wete plowngy
clowdes, and that the sterres nat apperen
upon hevene, so that the nyht semeth sprad   10
upon erthe, yif thanne the wind that hyhte
Boryas, isent owt of the kaves of the contre of
Trace, beteth this night *(that is to seyn, chaseth*
it awey), and descovereth the closed day,
thanne shyneth Phebus yshaken with sodeyn   15
lyht, and smyteth with his bemes in merveylinge eyen.

Prose III. Haut aliter tristicie.

Riht so and non oother wyse, the clowdes
of sorwe dissolved and don awey, I took
hevene and receivede mynde to knowen the
face of my fysicien, so that I sette myn eyen
on hir and fastnede my lookinge. I be-   5
hoolde my noryse Philosophie, in whos
howses I hadde conversed and haunted fro
my yowthe, and I seide thus: "O thow maystresse of alle vertuus, descended from the
soverein sete, whi artow comen into this   10
solitarie place of myn exil? Artow comen
for thou art maked coupable with me of false
blames?"
"O," quod she, "my norry, sholde
I forsaken the now, and sholde I nat   15
parten with the, by comune travayle,
the charge that thow hast suffred for envye

---

5 whilom, formerly. **7 escaped,** i.e., escaped from weakness. **corage,** spirit. **8 armures,** armor. **11 sikernesse,** safety. **12 Knowestow . . . artow,** knowest thou, art thou. **13 astoninge,** surprise (astonishment). **16 say,** saw. **20 litargie,** lethargy (stupor). **21
deceyved:** I *desseyvyd,* here and elsewhere. **22 foryeten . . . lyhtly,** forgotten, easily (lightly). **24 or now,** ere (before) this time. **25
wypen,** wipe. **26 derked,** darkened (clouded). **28 iplited . . . frounce,** pleated, ruffle. **31 wawes,** waves. **I METRE III. 1 discussed,**
driven away. **2 dirknesses forleften,** darkness (of sight) left. *forleften:* C *forleten.* **3 repeyrede . . . her fyrste,** returned, their former.
I *ayein* om. **7 heyhte,** named. **Chorus,** Corus, the northwest wind. **8 dirked . . . plowngy,** darkened, stormy. **11 hyhte,** is named.
12 Boryas, Boreas, the north wind. **13 Trace,** Thrace (in modern Bulgaria), regarded by Greeks as the northern wasteland. **14
descovereth . . . closed,** reveals, hiding. **15 Phebus . . . sodeyn,** the sun, sudden. **16 merveylinge,** (our) astonished. **I PROSE III.
2–3 took hevene,** i.e., took note of the sky. **3 receivede mynde,** recovered awareness. I *ressevede,* here and elsewhere. **4 fysicien:**
I *fesissien.* **6 noryse,** nurse. **7 conversed and haunted,** i.e., learned and lived. **8 maystresse,** mistress. **10 soverein sete,** i.e.,
heaven. **12 maked coupable,** i.e., compelled to share (made culpable). **13 blames,** accusations. **14 norry,** foster child (pupil).
16 parten, share (take part). **comune travayle,** shared effort. **17 charge,** burden.

of my name? Certes, it nere nat leveful ne sittinge thing to philosophie to leten withowten compaygnye the wey of him that is innocent. Sholde I thanne redowte my blame, and agrysen as thowh ther were byfallen a newe thing? For trowestow that philosophie be now alderfirst assailed in perils by foolk of wikkede manneres? Have I nat striven with ful gret strif, in olde tyme, byfore the age of my Plato, ayenes the foolhardinesse of folie? And ek, the same Plato lyvinge, his mayster Socrates deservede victorie of unryhtful deth in my presence. The heritage of the which Socrates *(the heritage is to seyn, the doctrine of the whiche Socrates in his opinioun of felicite, that I clepe welefulnesse),* whan that the poeple of Epicuriens and Stoyciens and many oothre enforseden hem to gon ravysse everich man for his part *(that is to seyn, that everich of hem wolde drawen to the defence of his opinioun the wordes of Socrates),* they as in partye of hir preye todrowen me, cryinge and debatinge ther-ayeins, and korven and torenten my clothes that I hadde woven with myn handes; and with tho clowtes that they hadden arraced owt of my clothes they wenten awey,

weninge that I hadde gon with hem everydel. In whiche Epicuriens and Stoyciens for as moche as ther semede some traces or steppes of myn habite, the folie of men, weninge tho Epicuriens and Stoiciens my famuleres, perverted some thorwh the errour of the wikkede or unkunninge multitude of hem. *(This is to seyn, that for thei semede philosophres they weren pursued to the deth and slayn.)* So yif thow hast nat knowen the exilinge of Anaxogore, ne the enpoysoninge of Socrates, ne the tormentes of Zeno, for they weren straungeres, yit mightestow han knowen the Senecciens and the Canyos and the Sorans, of whiche foolk the renoun is neyther over-olde ne unsolempne. The whiche men nothing elles ne browhte hem to the deth but oonly for they weren enformed of myne maneres, and semeden most unlyk to the studies of wikkede foolk. And forthi thow owhtest nat to wondren thowh that I, in the bittre see of this lyf, be fordryven with tempestes blowinge abowte, in the whiche tempestes this is my moost purpos, that is to seyn, to displesen to wikkede men. Of whiche shrewes, al be the oost never so greet, it is to despise, for it nis governed with no leder of resoun, but it is ravyssed only by fleetinge

---

18 leveful, lawful. **19 sittinge ... leten,** fitting, leave. **21 redowte,** fear. **22 agrysen,** shudder. **23 trowestow,** do you believe. **24 alderfirst,** i.e., for the first time (first of all, an archaic genitive). *philosophie:* I *filosophie.* **29 the same ... lyvinge,** while he was living. **30 deservede,** enjoyed (triumphed in). **31–32** *heritage:* I *eritage.* **33–34** *doctrine ... of felicite,* Socrates' "theory of the good" (i.e., Platonism). **34** *welefulnesse,* felicity (happiness). **35 Epicuriens ... Stoyciens,** Epicureans (who taught that the good is pleasure), Stoics (who taught that the good is self-control). Platonism represents to Lady Philosophy the totality of true philosophy, of which Epicureanism and Stoicism are only limited fragments. **36 enforseden hem,** i.e., had the audacity (forced themselves). **37 ravysse,** tear out (ravish). **40 as in partye ... todrowen me,** i.e., as if I were their prey, pulled me apart. **42 torenten,** tore apart. **43** *woven:* Cx *wonnen.* **44 tho clowtes,** those pieces. **arraced,** torn. **46 weninge,** believing. **47 everydel,** completely. **48–49 as ther ... steppes ... habite,** as in them, tracks (footsteps), costume. **50 weninge tho,** believing those. **51–53 famuleres,** familiars (intimate friends). **perverted ... multitude,** i.e., the ignorant multitude were perverted through the error of believing that Epicureanism or Stoicism was true philosophy. **54–55** *pursued to the deth,* i.e., persecution (as of Christian martyrs) was evidence of their supposed virtue. **56 Anaxogore,** Anaxagoras, Greek philosopher (c. 450 B.C.), exiled for his theories about astronomy. **57 Socrates,** the execution of Socrates was the classic example of the martyrdom of true philosophy; see Plato's *Phaedo.* **58 Zeno,** classical philosopher (I Pr. 1.71 note), tortured for trying to defend his countrymen. Boethius compares his misfortunes to those of his fellow philosophers. **59 Senecciens,** Seneca, forced by Nero to commit suicide (A.D. 65). **60 Canyos,** Julius Canius, executed by Caligula (A.D. 40). **Sorans,** Soranus, executed by Nero (A.D. 66). **61 over-olde ne unsolempne,** i.e., fresh and celebrated (the litotes are in the Lat. *nec peruetusta nec incelebris*). **64 myne maneres,** my (Philosophy's) learning (behavior). **65 unlyk ... studies,** unfitted for the learning (behavior). **66 forthi ... owhtest,** therefore, ought. **69 moost,** most important. **70 to displesen,** to be displeasing (i.e., the mark of virtue is to be obnoxious to vice). **71 shrewes ... oost,** evil people, host. **72 to despise,** to be despised. **73 fleetinge,** unstable (fleeting).

errour folyly and lyhtly. And yif they somtyme, makinge an oost ayeins us, assayle us 75
as strenger, owr leder draweth togydere his
rychesses into his towr, and they ben ententyf
abowte sarpuleres or sachels unprofitable for
to taken. But we that ben heye aboven, syker
fro alle tumolte and woode noyse, warne- 80
stored and enclosed in swich a palis, whider
as chateringe or anoyinge folye ne may nat
atayne, we scorne swiche ravyneres and
henteres of fowleste thinges.

Metre IV. Quisquis composito.

"Whoso it be that is cleer of vertu, sad,
and wel ordinat of levinge, that hath put under
foot the prowde wierdes, and looketh upriht
upon eyther fortune, he may his cheere
holde undescounfited. The rage ne the 5
manaces of the see, commoevinge or
chasinge upward heete fro the botme, ne shal
nat moeve that man; ne the unstable mountaygne that hihte Vesevus, that writheth
owt thorwh his brokene chymynees smok- 10
inge fyres; ne the wey of thonder-lyht
that is wont to smyten heye towres ne shal
nat moeve that man. Wharto thanne, o
wrechches, drede ye tyrauntes that ben
woode and felonous withowte any strenghe? 15
Hope after nothing, ne drede nat, and
so shaltow desarmen the ire of thilke unmyhty tyraunt. But whoso that, quakinge,

dredeth or desireth thyng that nis nat
stable of his ryht, that man that so doth 20
hath cast awey his sheld, and is remoeved
from his place, and enlaceth him in the cheyne
with the which he may ben drawen.

Prose IV. Sentisne hec inquit.

"Felistow," quod she, "thise thinges, and
entren thei awht in thi corage? Artow lik
an asse to the harpe? Whi wepistow, whi
spillestow teeres? Yif thow abydest after
help of thi leche, the byhoveth discovere 5
thi wownde."

Tho I, that hadde gadered strengthe in
my corage, answerede and seyde: "And
nedeth it yit," quod I, "of rehersinge or
of amonicioun? And sheweth it nat inowh 10
by hymself the sharpnesse of Fortune,
that wexeth wood ayeins me? Ne moeveth
it nat the to sen the face or the manere of
this place? Is this the librarye which
that thou haddest chosen for a ryht 15
certeyn sete to the in myn hows, theras
thow desputedest ofte with me of the sciences
of thinges towchinge devynyte and mankynde? Was thanne myn habite swich as
now? Was my face or my cheere swich as 20
now, whan I sowhte with the the secretes of
nature, whan thou enformedest my maneres
and the resoun of alle my lyf to the ensaumple
of the ordre of hevene? Is nat this the

---

74 folyly . . . lyhtly, foolishly, insubstantially (lightly). **75 oost,** host (combined strength). **76 as strenger,** i.e., with greater force than ours. **77 ben ententyf,** i.e., are (left) to occupy (themselves with). **78 sarpuleres,** canvas sacks. **79 syker,** secure. **80 woode . . . warnestored,** crazy, protected. *warnestored:* A *ben stored.* **83 ravyneres,** thieves. **84 henteres,** robbers. Cx *hunters.* **I METRE IV. 1 cleer of vertu,** of clear virtue (clearly virtuous). **sad,** serious. **2 wel ordinat . . . levinge,** well-ordered (disciplined), living. **3 wierdes,** fates. **upriht,** courageous. **4 eyther,** either (good or bad). **cheere,** expression (spirit). **6 commoevinge,** clashing (moving together). *manaces:* I *manesses.* **7 heete,** heat (of anger). **9 hihte . . . Vesevus,** is named, Vesuvius (Italian volcano). **11 thonder-lyht,** lightning. **13 Wharto,** why. **15 woode and felonous,** insane and menacing. **16 after,** for. **17 unmyhty,** weak. *desarmen:* I *deserven.* **20 stable . . . ryht,** established as his right. **22 enlaceth him,** binds himself. **I PROSE IV. 1 Felistow,** do you feel (understand). **2 awht,** ought (at all). **in . . . corage,** into your apprehension. **3 asse . . . harpe,** i.e., as insensitive as a donkey to music (proverbial), see *TC* I.731. **4–5 abydest . . . leche,** i.e., if you hope for help from your physician, you must reveal your wound. **7 Tho,** then. **9–10 nedeth . . . rehersinge or amonicioun,** i.e., do I need further advice or admonition? **sheweth it nat inowh,** i.e., isn't it evident enough? **12 wexeth wood ayeins me,** i.e., grows increasingly cruel against me. **13 the to sen the face,** i.e., thee to see the appearance. **15–16 for a ryht certeyn sete to the,** i.e., for your secure seat. **theras,** where. *sete:* A *sege,* Lat. *sedem.* **19 habite,** clothing. **20 cheere,** expression (manner). **22 enformedest,** formed (educated). **23 to the ensaumple,** by the example. **24 ordre of hevene,** the order of the heavens.

gerdoun that I referre to the, to whom 25
I have be obeysaunt? Certes, thow con-
fermedest by the mouth of Plato this sentence,
that is to seyn, that comune thinges or comunalitees weren blysful yif they that hadden
studied al fully to wysdom governeden 30
thilke thinges, or elles yif it so byfille that
the governoures of comunalites studieden to
geten wysdom.

"Thow seydest ek by the mowth of the
same Plato that it was a necessarye cause 35
wise men to taken and desire the governaunce of comune thinges, for that the governementes of citees yleft in the handes of felonous
tormentours citesenes ne sholde nat bryngen
in pestelence and destruccioun to goode 40
foolk. And therfor I, folwinge thilke autorite,
desired to putten forth in execucioun and in
acte of comune administracioun thilke thinges
that I hadde lerned of the among my secre
restingwhiles. Thow and God that putte 45
the in the thowhtes of wise foolk ben knowinge with me that nothing ne browhte me to
maystrye or dignyte but the comune studie of
alle goodnesse. And therof comth it that
bytwixen wikked foolkes and me han ben 50
grevous descordes that ne myhten nat ben
relesed by preyeres; for this liberte hath the
freedom of conscience, that the wraththe of
moore myhty foolkes hath alwey ben des-
pysed of me for savacioun of ryht. 55

"How ofte have I resisted and withstonde
thilke man that hyhte Conigaste, that maade
alwey assawtes ayeins the prospre fortunes of
poore feeble foolkes! How ofte ek have I

put of or cast owt him Trygwille, provost 60
of the kynges hows, bothe of the wronges that
he hadde bygunne to don, and ek fully performed! How ofte have I covered and defended
by the autorite of me put ayeins perils *(that
is to seyn, put myn autorite in peril for)* the 65
wrechched poore foolkes that the covetyse
of straungeres, unpunysshed, tormented alwey
with myseyses and grevaunces owt of nowmbre!
Never man ne drowh me yit fro ryht to
wronge. Whan I say the fortunes and the 70
richesses of the poeple of the provinces ben
harmed or amenused owther by pryve raveynes
or by comune tributes or cariages, as sory was
I as they that suffreden the harm. *(Glosa.
Whan that Theodoric, the king of Gothes, in a* 75
*dere yer hadde his gerneres ful of corn, and
comaundede that no man ne sholde byen no corn tyl
his corn were solde, and that at a grevous deere prys,
Boece withstood that ordinaunce and overcom it,
knowinge al this the kyng hymself.)* Textus. 80
Whan it was in the sowre hungry tyme,
ther was establsshed or cryed grevous and
inplitable co-empcioun, that men sayen wel it
sholde gretly turmenten and endamagen al
the province of Campaygne, I took stryf 85
ayeins the provost of the pretorie for comune
profit. And, the kyng knowinge of it, I overcom
it, so that the co-empcioun ne was nat axed
ne tok effect. *(Co-empcioun is to seyn, comune
achat or byinge togidere, that were establyssed* 90
*upon the poeple by swiche a manere imposiscioun,
as who so bowhte a busshel corn, he moste yeve the
kyng the fifte part.)*

"Paulyn, a counseiller of Rome, the

rychesses of the which Paulyn the howndes 95
of the palays *(that is to seyn, the officeres)*
wolden han devowred by hope and covetise,
yit drowh I him owt of the jowwes of hem that
gapeden. And forasmoche as the peyne of
the accusacioun ajuged byforn ne sholde 100
nat sodeynly henten ne punisse wrongfully
Albyn, a conseyler of Rome, I putte me ayeins
the hates and indignaciouns of the accusor
Cyprian. Is it nat thanne inowh isene that
I have purchased grete discordes ayeins 105
myself? But I owhte be the moore assured
ayeins alle oothre foolk, that for the love of
ryhtwisnesse I ne reserved never nothing to
myself to hem-ward of the kynges halle, by
which I were moore siker. But thorwh tho 110
same accusors acusinge I am condempned.
Of the nowmbyr of the whiche acusors, oon
Basilicis, that whilom was chased owt of the
kynges servise, is now compelled in accusinge of my name for nede of foreyne 115
moneye. Also Opylion and Gaudencius han
accused me, al be it so that the justice regal
hadde whilom demed hem bothe to go into
exil for her trecheryes and fraudes withowte
nowmbyr. To whiche jugement they 120
nolden nat obeye, but defendeden hem by
the sikernesse of holy howses *(that is to seyn,*
fledden into sentuarye). And whan this was
aperceyved to the king, he comaundede that
but they voidede the cite of Ravenne by 125
certeyn day assigned, that men sholde merke
hem on the forheved with an hoot yren and
chasen hem owt of the towne. Now what thing,
semeth the, myhte ben lykned to this

crwelte, for certes thilke same day was 130
received the accusinge of my name by
thilke same accusors. What may ben seid her-to?
Hath my studie and my kunninge deserved
thus, or elles the forseyde dampnacioun of
me made that hem ryhtful acusors or no? 135
Was not Fortune asshamed of this? Certes,
alle hadde nat Fortune ben asshamed that
innocens was accused, yit owte she han had
shame of the fylthe of myne accusours.

"But axestow in somme, of what gylt I 140
am accused? Men seyn that I wolde save
the compaygnye of the senatours. And desirest
thow to heren in what manere? I am accused
that I sholde han destorbed the accusor to
beren lettres, by whiche he sholde han 145
maked the senatoures gylty ayeins the
kynges real majeste. O Maysteresse, what
demestow of this? Shal I forsake this blame,
that I ne be no shame to the? Certes, I
have wold it *(that is to seyn, the savacioun of* 150
the senat), ne I shal never leten to wilne it;
and that I confesse and I am aknowe. But the
entente of the accusor to be destorbed shal cese.
For shal I clepe it thanne a felonye or a
synne that I have desired the savacioun of 155
the ordre of the senat? And certes yit hadde
thilke same senat don by me, thorw her decretes
and her jugementes, as thowh it were a synne
or a felonye *(that is to seyn, to wilne the*
savacioun of hem). But folye, that lieth alwey 160
to hymself, may not chaunge the merite of
thinges. Ne I trowe nat, by the jugement of
Socrates, that it were leveful to me to hide
the sothe ne assente to leesinges. But certes,

---

99 forasmoche, so that. **100 ajuged byforn,** prejudged (guilty). **101 henten,** seize. **104 inowh isene,** seen (clearly) enough. **105 discordes,** enmity. **106 moore assured,** more secure (insured). **110 siker,** secure. **thorwh tho,** through (by) those. **113 whilom,** formerly. *Basilicis:* A *Basilius;* Lat. *Basilius.* **114 in accusinge,** to accuse. **115–16 foreyne moneye,** i.e., debts. I *Caudencius.* **118 demed,** condemned (judged). **122 sikernesse of holy howses,** condemned criminals could seek sanctuary in churches and monasteries. **125 but,** unless. **127 forheved,** forehead. **129 lykned,** compared. **132 same accusors,** i.e., on the day they themselves were condemned, Opylion and Gaudentium accused Boethius of treachery. **134–35 dampnacioun . . . made . . . hem ryhtful,** i.e., did my condemnation make them just accusors? **137 alle hadde nat,** i.e., even though Fortune had not been. **140 in somme,** in sum. **142 compaygnye,** i.e., the Senate. **144 destorbed,** hindered. **145 beren lettres,** i.e., producing evidence. **146 maked,** proved. **147 real,** royal. **Maysteresse,** mistress. **148 demestow,** do you judge. **forsake this blame,** deny this accusation. **150 wold,** desired. **151 leten,** cease. **152 am aknowe,** do acknowledge. Chaucer's version here is different from the Lat. **159 or:** I *and.* **160 that lieth,** that deceives (lies). **162 trowe,** believe. **163 leveful,** lawful. **164 sothe . . . leesinges,** truth, lies.

howsoever it be of this, I put it to gessen or 165
preisen to the jugement of the and of wise
foolk. Of whiche thing al the ordinaunce and
the sothe, for as moche as foolk that ben to
comen after owre dayes shullen knowen it,
I have put it in scripture and in remem- 170
braunce. For towching the lettres falsly
maked, by whiche lettres I am accused to han
hoped the fredom of Roome, what aperteneth
me to speke therof? Of whiche lettres the
fraude hadde ben shewed apertly, yif I 175
hadde had liberte for to han used and ben
at the confessioun of myne accusours, the
whiche thing in alle needes hath gret strengthe.
For what other fredom may men hopen?
Certes, I wolde that som other freedom 180
myhte ben hoped. I wolde thanne han
answered by the wordes of a man that hyhte
Canyus; for whan he was accused by Gayus
Cesar, Germeynes sone, that he (Canius)
was knowinge and consentinge of a con- 185
juracioun ymaked ayeins him (Gayus), this
Canyus answerede thus: 'Yif I hadde wist it,
thou haddest nat wist it.' In which thing sorwe
hath nat so dulled my wit that I pleyne
oonly that shrewede folk apareylen felonies 190
ayeins vertu, but I wondre gretly how that
they may parforme thinges that they han
hoped for to don. For-whi, to wilne shrewednesse, that comth peraventure of owre
defaute. But it is lyk a monstre and a 195
mervayle, how that in the present syhte of
God may ben acheved and performed swiche
thinges as every felonous man hath conceyved
in his thowht ayeins innocentes. For which
thing oon of thy famyleres nat unskylfully 200

axed thus: 'Yif God is, whennes comen
wikkede thinges? And yif God ne is, whennes
comen goode thinges?' But al hadde it ben
leveful that felonous folk that now desiren
the blod and the deth of alle goode men, 205
and ek of alle the senat, han willned to
gon and destroyen me, whom they han seyen
alwey bataylen and defenden goode men and
ek al the senat, yit had I nat desserved of
the faderes *(that is to seyn, of the senatoures)* 210
that they sholden willne my destruccioun.

"Thow remembrest wel, as I gesse, that
whan I wolde doon or seyen anything, thow
thyself, alwey present, rewledest me. At
the cite of Verone, whan that the kyng, 215
gredy of comune slawhtre, caste him to
transporten upon al the ordre of the senat the
gylt of his real majeste, of the whiche gylt that
Albyn was accused, with how gret sykernesse of peril to me deffendede I al the senat. 220
Thow woost wel that I seye soth, ne I ne
avauntede me never in preysinge of myself.
For alwey, whan any wyht receyveth precious
renoun in avauntinge himself of his werkes,
he amenuseth the secre of his conscience. 225
But now thou mayst wel seen to what ende I
am comen for myne innocence: I receyve
peyne of fals felonye for guerdon of verray
vertu. And what open confessioun of
felonye hadde ever juges so acordaunt in 230
crwelte *(that is to seyn, as myn accusinge hath)*
that eyther errour of mannes wit or elles
condicioun of fortune, that is uncerteyn to
alle mortal folk, ne submittede some of hem
(that is to seyn, that it ne enclinede som juge to 235
han pite or compassioun)? For althogh I hadde

165–66 gessen or preisen, conjecture or appraise. **167 ordinaunce,** ordered account. **170 scripture,** i.e., I have written it down.
173 aperteneth, concerns (what good is it). **174** *Of—lettres* om. in I. **175 hadde ben . . . apertly,** would have been, openly. **176 used,**
i.e., used the confession. **177–78 the whiche . . . strengthe,** i.e., which would have been most effective. **179 fredom,** opportunity.
183 Gayus Cesar, the Emperor Caligula. **185 conjuracioun,** conspiracy. **189 pleyne,** complain. **190 apareylen,** prepare. *felonies:*
A *folies;* Lat. *scelarata.* **192 may,** can. **193 For-whi, to wilne shrewednesse,** because to desire evil. **195 defaute,** evilness. **monstre,**
monstrous thing. **200 famyleres,** companions (the quotation is attributed to the philosopher Epicurus). **204 leveful,** lawful. **206**
willned, wished. **207 seyen,** seen. **213 seyen,** say. **214 rewledest,** ruled (directed). **216 gredy of,** greedy for. **caste him,** planned.
217 transporten upon, lay upon. **218 real,** royal (i.e., the treason). **219–20 sykernesse of peril,** i.e., assurance of peril. **221 woost,**
know. **222 avauntede,** boasted. **223 wyht,** person (wight). **225 amenuseth the secre,** diminishes the secret (worth). This differs
from the Lat. **228 for guerdon,** as a reward. **230 acordaunt,** unanimous. **234 submittede,** restrain (subdue). **236 althogh,** if.

ben accused that I wolde brenne holy howses and strangle preestes with wykkede swerde, or that I hadde greythed deth to alle goode men, algates the sentence sholde han 240 punysshed me present, confessed or convict. But now I am remewed fro the cite of Roome almost fyve hundred thowsand paas, I am withowte deffence dampned to proscripcioun and to the deth for the studie and 245 bowntes that I have doon to the senat. But O wel ben they worthi of merite *(as who seyth, nay)*; ther myhte never yit non of hem be convict of swich a blame as myne is! Of whiche trespas, myne accusours sayen ful 250 wel the dignite, the whiche dignite, for they wolden dirken it with medlinge of som felonye, they baren me on hand, and lyeden that I hadde polut and defowled my conscience with sacrilege for coveytise of dignete. And 255 certes, thow thyself that are plaunted in me chasedest owt of the sege of my corage alle coveytyse of mortal thinges; ne sacrelege ne hadde no leeve to han a place in me byforn thyne eyen. For thow droppedest every day 260 in myne eres and my thowt thilke comaundement of Pictagoras, that is to seyn, men shal serve to Godde and not to goddes. Ne it was nat convenient ne no nede to taken help of the fowlest spirites—I, that thow 265 has ordeyned and set in swiche excellence that thow makedest me lyk to God. And over this, the ryht clene secre chaumbre of myne hows *(that is to seyn, my wyf)*, and the compaygnye of myn honest freendes, and my 270 wyves fader, as wel holy as worthi to ben reverenced thorwh his owne dedes, deffenden me from alle suspecioun of swich blame. But

O malice, for they that accusen me taken of the, Philosophie, feyth of so gret blame! For 275 they trowen that I have had affinite to malefice or enchauntement, by cause that I am replenysshed and fulfylled with thy techinges and enformed of thy maneres. And thus it suffiseth not oonly that thy reverence ne 280 avayle me nat, but that thow of thy fre wille rather be blemished with myn offencioun. But certes, to the harmes that I have ther bytydeth yit this encres of harm, that the gessinge and the jugement of moche folk ne looken 285 nothing to the desertes of thinges, but oonly to the aventure of fortune, and jugen that oonly swiche thinges ben purveyed of God whiche that temporel welefulnesse commendeth. *(Glose. As thus, that yif a wyht have prosperite,* 290 *he is a good man and worthi to han that prosperite; and who hath adversite, he is a wikked man and God hath forsake him, and he is worthi to han that adversite. This is the opinioun of some folk.)*

"And therof comth that good gessinge 295 fyrst of alle thing forsaketh wrechches. Certes, it greveth me to thinke riht now the diverse sentenses that the poeple seyth of me. And thus moche I seye, that the laste charge of contrarious fortune is this, that, whan that any 300 blame is leyd upon a caytyf, men wenen that he hath desserved that he suffreth. And I that am put awey fro goode men, and despoyled of dignitees, and defowled of my name by gessinge, have suffred torment for my 305 goode dedes. Certes, me semeth that I se the felonous covynes of wikked men habownden in joye and in gladnesse. And I se that every lorel shapeth him to fynde owt newe fraudes for to accuse goode fook. And I se that 310

---

239 greythed, prepared. **240 algates,** nevertheless. **241 punysshed me present,** i.e., convicted me in my presence. *convict:* I commit. **242 remewed,** removed. **244 dampned to proscripcioun,** condemned to be an outlaw. **245–46 studie and bowntes,** effort and contributions. **247** *merite:* A *mercye;* Lat. *meritos.* **252 dirken . . . medlinge,** tarnish (darken), mixing. **253 baren . . . on hand,** accuse. **lyeden,** lied. **257 sege,** seat. **262 Pictagoras,** Pythagoras (Greek philosopher, 550 B.C.). **269 hows,** house. **275** *Philosophie:* I *philosophre.* **feyth . . . blame,** support, accusation. **276 trowen,** believe. **277 malefice,** evil-doing. **281 I** *but yf that.* **282 offencioun,** offense. **283 bytydeth,** suffered. **284 gessinge,** opinion. **286 desertes of thinges,** i.e., what one deserves. **287 aventure,** chance outcome. **288 purveyed,** provided. **289 welefulnesse,** success. **290** *wyht,* person (wight). **295 gessinge,** opinion (reputation). **298 sentenses,** judgments. **301 caytyf . . . wenen,** sufferer, think. **305 gessinge,** supposition (of his guilt). **306 me semeth,** it seems to me. **307 felonous covynes . . . habownden in,** evil bands, abound in (enjoy). **309 lorel shapeth him,** wretched person schemes.

goode men beth overthrowen for drede of my peril. And every luxurious tourmentour dar doon all felonye unpunysshed and ben excited therto by yiftes. And innocentes ne ben not oonly despoyled of sikernesse but of defence. 315 And therfore me lyst to cryen to God in this wyse:

Metre V. O stelliferi conditor orbis.

"O thow makere of the whel that bereth the sterres, which that art yfastned to thy perdurable chayer, and tornest the hevene with a ravessing sweyh, and constreynest the sterres to suffren thi lawe so that 5 the mone somtyme shyning wyth hir ful hornes, meting with alle the beemes of the sonne hir brother, hydeth the sterres that ben lesse, and somtyme whan the moone paale with hir derke hornes aprocheth 10 the sonne, leeseth hir lyhtes; and that the eve sterre Hesperus, which that in the fyrste tyme of the nyht bryngeth forth hir colde arysinges, cometh eft ayein hir used cours, and is paale by the morwe 15 at the rysing of the sonne, and is thanne cleped Lucyfer. Thow restreynest the day by shorter dwelling in the tyme of colde wynter that maketh the leeves falle. Thow dividest the swyft tydes of the nyht whan 20 the hoote somer ys comen. Thy myht atempreth the varyauntes sesons of the yer so that Zephirus the deboneyre wynd brengeth ayein in the first somer sesoun the leeves that the wynd that hihte Borias hath reft 25

away in autumpne *(that is to seyn, in the laste ende of somer)*, and the sedes that the sterre that hihte Arcturus sawgh ben waxen hyye cornes whan the sterre Syryus eschaufeth hem. Ther nis nothing unbownde 30 fram his oolde lawe, ne forleteth the werke of his propre estat.

"O thow governour, governinge alle thinges by certeyn ende, whi refusestow oonly to governe the werkes of men by dewe manere? 35 Whi suffresthow that slydinge fortune torneth so grete entrechaunginges of thynges, so that anoyous peyne that sholde dewelly punysshe felouns, punyssheth innocentes? And foolk of wykkede maneres sytten in 40 heye chayres? And anoyinge foolk treden, and that unryhtfully, on the nekkes of holy men? And vertu, clere shyninge naturely, is hid in dirke derkenesses? And the ryhtful man bereth the blame and the peyne of the 45 feloun. Ne the forsweringe ne the fraude, covered and kembd with a fals colour, ne anoyeth nat to shrewes, the whiche shrewes, whan hem lyst to usen her strengthe, they rejoysen hem to putten under hem the 50 sovereyne kynges, whiche that poeple withowten nowmbre dreden?

"O thow, whatsoever thow be that knyttest alle bondes of thynges, looke on thise wrecchede erthes! We men that ben nat a 55 fowle partye but a fayre partye of so grete werk, we ben tormented in this see of fortune. Thow governour, withdrawh and restreyne the ravessinge floodes, and fastne and ferme thise

---

311 overthrowen ... drede, overcome, fear. **312 luxurious,** evil (lecherous). **313–14 excited ... yiftes,** incited, bribes. **315 sikernesse,** security. **316 me lyst,** I wish to (it pleases me). **I METRE V. 3 perdurable chayer,** eternal throne. **4 ravessing sweyh,** violent (swift) motion. **5 suffren,** obey. **6–7 ful hornes,** full moon (when it reflects *alle the beemes* of the sun). **9–10 moone paale ... derke hornes,** pale moon (Fr. word order), crescent moon. **11 leeseth hir lyhtes,** i.e., the moon's horns lose their brightness. **12 Hesperus,** Venus as evening star. **13 fyrste tyme,** early part. **14–15 cometh eft ... used cours,** comes again to her usual course. **morwe,** morning. **17 Lucyfer,** Venus as morning star. **20 dividest the swyft tydes,** i.e., increase the swift hours. **22 atempreth,** tempers. **23 Zephirus,** west wind, see *CT* I.5 and note. **deboneyre,** gentle. **25 hihte Borias,** is called Boreas (the north wind). **reft,** ripped. **27 sedes,** seeds. **28 Arcturus,** a star conspicuous in spring. **ben waxen,** are grown (to). **29 hyye cornes,** tall (high) grain. **Syryus eschaufeth,** Sirius (the Dog Star of high summer) warms. **31 his oolde lawe,** its ancient law. **forleteth,** avoids. **35 dewe manere,** proper fashion. **36 slydinge,** changeable. **38 dewelly,** properly (duly). **41 heye chayres,** i.e., "the seats of the mighty." **46 forsweringe,** perjury. **47 kembd,** dressed (kempt). **48 shrewes,** wicked people. **56 partye,** part. **57 see,** sea. **59 ravessinge,** destructive. **ferme,** make firm.

erthes stable with thilke bonde by whiche 60
thow governest the hevene that is so large.''

Prose V. Hic ubi continuato dolore delatraui.

Whan I hadde with a continuel sorwe
sobbed or borken owt thise thinges, she with
hir chere pesyble and nothing amoeved with
my compleyntes seyde thus: "Whan I
say the,'' quod she, "soruful and wepinge, 5
I wyste anon that thow were a wrechche
and exiled, but I wyste never how ferre thine
exil was yif thi tale nadde shewed it me.
But certes, al be thow fer fro thy contre,
thow nart nat put owt of it, but thow 10
hast fayled of thi wey and gon amys.
And yif thow hast levere for to wene that
thow be put owt of thi contree, than hast
thow put owt thyself rather than any
other wyht hath. For no wyht but thy- 15
self ne myhte never han don that to the.
For yif thow remenbre of what contre thow
art born, it nis nat governed by emperours,
ne by governement of multitude, as weren
the contres of hem of Athenes; but oo 20
lord and oo kynge *(and that is God that is
lord of thy contre)* whiche that rejoyseth him
of the dwelling of his cytesenes, and nat for
to put hem in exil; of the whiche lord it is
a soverayne fredom to ben governed by 25
the brydel of him and obeye to his justyce.
Hastow foryeten thylke ryht olde lawe of
thi cite, in the whiche cyte it is ordeyned
and establysshed, that for what wyht
that hath lever fownden therein his sete 30
or his hows than elleswher he may nat

be exiled by no ryht from that place? For
whoso that is contened inwith the palys
and the clos of thilke cite, ther nis no drede
that he may deserve to ben exiled. But 35
whoso that leteth the wyl for to enhabyte
there, he forleteth also to deserve to ben
cytesein of thilke cyte. So that I sey that the
face of this place ne moveth me nat so
mochel as thine owne face, ne I axe nat 40
rather the walles of thi lybrarye, aparayled
and wrowht with yvory and with glas, than
after the sete of thy thowht, in whiche I put
nat whilom bookes, but I put that that maketh bokes worthi of prys or precyous, that is 45
to seyn the sentense of my bookes.

"And certeynly of thy desertes, bystowed in
comune good, thow hast seyde soth, but after
the multitude of thi goode dedes, thow hast
seyd fewe. And of the honeste or of the 50
falsnesse of thinges that ben aposed ayeins
the, thow hast remembred thinges that ben
knowen to alle foolk. And of the felonyes and
fraudes of thine acusours, it semeth the
have itowched it forsothe ryhtfully and 55
shortly, al myhten tho same thinges betere
and moore plenteuousely ben cowth in the
mowthe of the poeple that knoweth al this.
Thow hast ek blamed gretly and compleyned of the wrongful dede of the senat, 60
and thow hast sorwed for my blame, and
thow hast wopen for the damage of thi renoun
that is apayred; and thy laste sorwe eschaufede
ayeins fortune and compleynest that gerdouns ne ben evenlyche yolden to the 65
desertes of foolkes. And in the latere ende
of thi woode muse, thow preyedest that thilke
pees that governeth the hevene sholde governe

I PROSE V. 2 **borken,** barked. 3 **chere pesyble,** expression placid. 5 **say the,** saw you. 6 **wyste anon,** knew immediately. 8 **nadde,** had not. 11 **fayled of,** lost. 12 **levere . . . wene,** prefer to believe. 15 **wyht,** person. 20 **oo,** one. 22 **rejoyseth . . . of,** rejoices in. 23 **dwelling,** i.e., remaining at home. 25 **soverayne,** precious. 27 **foryeten,** forgotten. 30 **hath lever fownden . . . sete,** i.e., preferred to live there, seat (homestead). 31 *elleswher:* I *ellys were.* 33–34 **palys . . . clos,** i.e., the walls (palings) of the close. The "city" is, of course, the heavenly city. 36 **leteth,** loses. 39 **face,** appearance. 40 **I axe nat,** I don't ask for. 41 **aparayled,** decorated. 42–43 **than after,** but rather for. 50 **honeste,** truth (honesty). 51 **aposed,** proposed. 55 **itowched,** touched upon. 57 **cowth,** known. 61 **my blame,** i.e., that Philosophy was likewise censured. 63 **eschaufede,** directed (heated). 64–65 **gerdouns . . . yolden,** rewards, granted. 67 **woode muse,** passionate poem (i.e., Metre v).

828

the erthe. But for that manye trybulacyouns
of affeccyouns han assayled the, and sorwe 70
and ire and wepinge to-drawen the diversely, as thow art now feeble of thowht,
myhtier remedies ne shullen nat yit towchen
the, for whiche we wol usen somdel lyhter
medycynes, so that thilke passyouns that 75
ben woxen harde in swellinge, by perturbacyouns flowing into thi thowht, mowen
wexen esy and softe to receyven the strengthe
of a more myhty and moore egre medycene,
by an esyer towchinge. 80

Metre VI. Cum Phebi radiis graue.

"Whan that the hevy sterre of the Cankyr
eschaufeth by the beemes of Phebus *(that is
to seyn, whan that Phebus the sonne is in the sygne
of the Cankyr)*, whoso yeveth thanne largely
his seedes to the feeldes that refusen to 5
receive hem, lat him gon bygyled of trust
that he hadde to his corn to accornes of okes.
Yif thou wolt gadre vyolettes, ne go thow nat
to the purpure wode whan the feeld,
chyrkinge, agryseth of coolde by the 10
felnesse of the wynde that hyghte Aquylon.
Yif thow desyrest or wolt usen grapes, ne
seke thow nat, with a glotonous hond, to
streyne and presse the stalkes of the vyne
in the ferst somer sesoun, for Bachus, 15
the god of wyne, hath rather yeven his
yiftes to autumpne *(the later ende of somer)*.
God tokneth and assygneth the tymes, ablinge
hem to her propres offices, ne he ne suffreth
nat the stowndes whiche that himself hath 20
devyded and constreyned to ben imedled
togydere. And forthy he that forleteth certeyn
ordinaunce of doinge by overthrowinge wey
he ne hath no glade isswe or ende of his
werkes. 25

Prose VI. Primum igitur paterisne me pauculis.

"Fyrst woltow suffre me to towche and
assaye the estat of thi thowht by a fewe
demaundes, so that I may understonde what
be the manere of thi curacioun?"
"Axe me," quod I, "at thi wille what 5
thou wolt, and I shal answere."
Tho seyde she thus: "Wheyther wenestow,"
quod she, "that this world be governed by
foolyssh happes and fortunows or elles
that ther be in it any governement of 10
resoun?"
"Certes," quod I, "I ne trowe nat in no
manere that so certeyn thinges sholden be
moeved by fortunows folie, but I woot
wel that God, maker and mayster, is 15
governour of his werk, ne never nas yit
day that myhte put me owt of the sothnesse
of that sentence."
"So is it," quod she, "for the same
thing songe thow a lytel her-byforn, 20
and byweyledest and byweptest that oonly
men weren put owt of the cure of God. For
of alle oether thinges thou ne dowtedest nat
that they nere governed by resoun. But
owh, I wondre gretly, certes, why that 25
thow art syk, syn that thow art put in
so holsom a sentence. But lat us seken depper:
I conjecte that ther laketh I not nere what.
But sey me this: syn that thow ne dowtest
nat that this world be governed by God, 30
with which governayles takestow heede
that it is governed?"
"Unnethe," quod I, "knowe I the sentense
of thi questioun, so that I ne may yit
answeren to thi demaundes." 35
"I nas nat deceyved," quod she, "that

---

71 **to-drawen**, pull apart. 77 **mowen**, may. I METRE VI. 2 **eschaufeth**, heats. 4 **largely**, generously. 6–7 **bygyled of trust . . . hadde to his corn**, i.e., one who seeds the reluctant ground in summer will be betrayed of his trust and will have to use acorns for grain. 9 **purpure**, purple. 10 **chyrkinge, agryseth**, rustling, trembles. 11 **felnesse . . . Aquylon**, cruelty, winter wind. 18 **tymes, ablinge**, seasons, enabling. 20 **stowndes**, times. 21 **devyded . . . imedled**, determined, mixed. 22 **forleteth**, departs from. 23 **overthrowinge wey**, i.e., not following the path. I PROSE VI. 3 **demaundes**, questions. 7 **Wheyther wenestow**, do you believe. 13 **certeyn thinges**, specific events. 14 *fortunows folie*: MSS *fortunows fortune*; Lat. *fortuita temerita*; Fr. *fortunele folie*. 22 **cure**, care. 28 **not**, don't know. 31 **which governayles**, what kind of government. 33 **Unnethe . . . sentense**, scarcely, meaning.

ther ne fayleth somwhat, by whiche the maladye of thi perturbacyoun is krept into thy thowt, so as the strengthe of the palys chyning is open. But sey me this: remenbrest thow what is the ende of thinges, and whider that the entencioun of alle kynde tendeth?" 40

"I have herd it toold somtyme," quod I, "but drerynesse hath dulled my memorye." 45

"Certes," quod she, "thow woost wel whennes that alle thinges ben comen and procedeth?"

"I woot wel," quod I, and answerede that God is bygynning of alle. 50

"And how may this be," quod she, "that syn thow knowest the bygynninge of thinges, that thow ne knowest nat what is the ende of thinges? But swiche ben the customes of perturbacyouns, and this power they han, 55 that they may moeve a man owt of his place *(that is to seyn, fro the stablenes and perfeccyoun of his knowinge)*. But certes thei may nat al arace him, ne alyene him in al. But I wolde that thow woldest answere to this: 60 remenbrestow that thou art a man?"

"Whi sholde I nat remenbre that?" quod I.

"Maystow nat telle me thanne," quod she, "what thinge is a man?"

"Axestow me nat," quod I, "wheither 65 that I be a resonable mortal beest? I woot wel and I confesse wel that I am it."

"Wystestow never yit that thow were any other thinge?" quod she.

"No," quod I. 70

"Now woot I," quod she, "oother cause of thy maladye, and that ryht grete. Thow hast left for to knowen thiself, what thow art; thorwh whiche I have pleynly fownde the cause of thi maladye, or elles the entre of 75 recoeveringe of thin heele. For-whi for thow art confownded with foryeting of thiself, forthy sorwistow that thow art exiled of thi propre goodes. And for thow ne wost what is the ende of thinges, forthy demestow that fel- 80 onous and wykked men ben myhty and weleful. And for thow hast foryeten by whiche governementes the world is governed, forthy wenestow that thise mutacyouns of fortune fleten withowte governour. Thise ben grete 85 causes nat oonly to maledye, but certes grete causes to deth. But I thanke the auctor and the makere of heele that nature hath nat alle forleten the. I have grete noryssinges of thin heele, and that is the sothe sentense of 90 governaunce of the worlde; that thow bylevest that the governinge of it nis nat subject ne underput to the folie of thise happes aventurous, but to the resoun of God. And therfor dowte the nothinge, for of this lytel 95 sparke thin hete of lyf shal shyne.

"But forasmeche as it is nat tyme yit of fastere remedies, and the nature of thowhtes deceyved is this, that as ofte as they casten awey sothe opiniouns, thei clothen hem in false opyn- 100 youns, of which false opyniouns the dirkenesse of perturbacioun wexeth up that confowndeth the verray insyhte. And that dirkenesse shal I assaye somwhat to maken thinne and wayk by lyhte and menelyche remedyes, so 105 that after that the dirkenesse of deceyvinge desiringes is don awey, thow mowe knowe the shyninge of verray lyht.

Metre VII. Nubibus atris condita.

"The sterres covered with blake clowdes ne mowen yeten adoun no lyht. Yif the trowble wynde that hyht Auster, turning and waluinge the see, medleth the hete *(that is to seyn,*

---

37 ne fayleth somwhat, something is lacking. **40 palys chyning,** gap in the stockade. **41 ende,** purpose. **43 kynde,** nature. **59 arace ... alyene,** root out, alienate. **71 oother,** another. **73 left for,** ceased. **75 entre,** beginning. **76 heele,** health. **For-whi,** because. **77 forthy,** therefore. **82 weleful,** fortunate. **83 I** *governement* (sing.). **85 fleten,** drift (float). **87 I** *thi deth.* **89 forleten,** deserted. **90 sentense,** meaning. **93–94 happes aventurous,** accidental chances. **96 shal shyne,** i.e., shall be rekindled. **98 thowhtes deceyved,** deluded thoughts. **Cx** *the nature is of thoughtes thus deceyved.* **103 verray,** true. **105 menelyche,** moderate. **I METRE VII. 2 yeten,** pour. **3 Auster,** the south wind. **4 medleth,** mixes.

the boylinge up fro the botme), the wawes 5
that whilom weren cleere as glas and
lyk to the faire cleere dayes and brihte withstand anon the syhtes of men by the fylthe
and ordure that is resolved. And the
fletinge strem that royleth down diversly 10
fro hy mountaygnes is arested and resisted
ofte tyme by the encountringe of a stoon
that is departed and fallen fram som roche.

Explicit liber primus.

BOOK II

Incipit liber secundus.

Prose I. Post hec paulisper obticuit.

Aftyr thys she stinte a lytul; and, after
that she hadde gadered by atempre stillenesse
myn atencioun, she seyde thus *(as who myhte*
seyn thus: after thise thinges she stynte a
lytul; and whan she aperceyved by atempre 5
styllenesse that I was ententyf to herkene hir,
she bygan to speke in this wise): "Yif I," quod
she, "have undyrstonden and knowen owtrely
the causes and the habyt of thi maledye,
thow languyssest and art defeted for 10
desire and talent of thi rather fortune.
She—that ilke Fortune—oonly, that is
changed, as thow feynest, to the-ward, hath perverted the clernesse and the estat of thy corage. I understonde the feele-folde colours 15
and deceytes of thilke mervayles monstre
Fortune, and how she useth ful flateringe
famylaryte with hem that she enforseth to
bygyle, so longe tyl that she confounde
with onsufferabele sorwe hem that she 20
hath left in dyspeyre unpurveyed. And
yif thow remenbrest wel the kynde, the
maneres, and the desert of thilke Fortune,
thow shalt wel knowe that, as in hir,
thow nevere ne haddest ne hast ylost any 25
fayr thinge. But, as I trowe, I shal nat
gretly travaylen to do the remenbre on this
thinges. For thow were wont to hurtelen
and despysen hir with manly wordes,
whan she was blawndyssinge and present, 30
and purswedest hir with sentenses that
weren drawen owt of myn entre *(that is to*
sayn, of myn enformacyoun). But no sodeyn
mutacyoun ne bytydeth nat withowte
a manere chaunginge of corages, and 35
so is it byfallen that thow art a lytel departed
fro the pes of thi thowght.

"But now is tyme that thow drynke and

7–8 withstand . . . the syhtes, i.e., the mud churned up prevents people from seeing through the water. **10 fletinge,** flowing. **14 forthy,** therefore. **16 weyve,** avoid. **17 dryf . . . fleme,** run (drive), flee. **19 *blende*,** blind. **21–22 whereas . . . reygnen,** where, rule. **II PROSE I. 1 stinte,** paused. **2 *she*:** I *I*. **11 talent . . . rather,** desire, earlier. A *talent and desir.* **12 ilke,** same. **13 feynest,** believe. **14 corage,** spirit. **15 feele-folde,** many. **18–19 enforseth to bygyle,** undertakes to deceive. **21 unpurveyed,** unprovided for (utter). **24 as in hir,** as far as she is concerned. **27 travaylen to do,** labor to make. **28 hurtelen,** attack. **29 manly,** bold (Lat. *virilibus verbis*). **34 bytydeth,** happens.

ataaste some softe and delitable thinges, so that whan they ben entred within the, it mowe maken wey to strengere drynkes of medicines. Com now forth therfore the suasioun of swetenesse rethoryen, whiche that goth oonly the ryht wey whil she forsaketh nat myne estatutes. And with Rhetorice com forth Musyce, a damysel of owre hows, that syngeth now lyhter moedes or prolacyouns, now hevyere. What eyleth the, man? What is it that hath cast the into morninge and into wepinge? I trowe that thow hast seyn som newe thinge and unkowth. Thow wenest that Fortune be chaunged ayein the; but thow wenest wrong, yif thow that wene. Alwey tho ben hir maneres; she hath rather kept, as to the-ward, hir propre stabylnesse in the chaunginge of hirself. Ryht swich was she whan she flatered the and deceyved the with unleffeful lykinges of fals welfulnesse. Thow hast now knowen and ataynt the dowtous or dowble vysage of thilke blynde goddesse Fortune. She that yit covereth and wympleth hir to oother foolkes hath shewed hir everydel to the. Yif thow aprovest hir and thinkest that she is god, use hir maneres and pleyne the nat. And yif thow agrysest hir false trecherye, despyse and cast awey hir that pleyeth so harmfully. For she that is now cause of so mochel sorwe to the sholde ben cause to the of pes and of joye. She hath forsaken the, forsothe, the whiche that never man may ben syker that she ne shal forsake hym. (*Glose. But natheles, some bookes han the texte thus: Forsothe, she hath forsaken the, ne ther nis no man syker that she ne hath nat forsake.*)

"Holdestow thanne thilke welefulnesse precyous to the, that shal passen? And is present Fortune dereworthe to the, which that nis nat feythfulle for to dwelle; and whan she goth awey, that she bryngeth a wiht in sorwe? For syn she may nat ben withholden at a mannes wille, she maketh him a wrecche whan she departeth fro him. What oother thing is flyttinge Fortune but a maner shewinge of wrecchednesse that is to comen? Ne it ne suffiseth nat oonly to loken on thynge that is present byforn the eyen of a man. But wysdom loeketh and amesureth the ende of thinges; and the same chaunginge fram oon into another (*that is to seyn, from adversite into prosperite*) maketh that the manasses of Fortune ne ben nat for to dreden, ne the flateringes of hir to ben desired. Thus, at the laste, it byhoveth the to suffren with evene wylle in paciense al that is don in-with the floor of Fortune (*that is to seyn, in this world*), syn thow hast ones put thi necke under the yok of hir. For yif thow welt wryten a lawe of wendinge and of dwellinge to Fortune, whiche that thow hast chosen freely to ben thi ladye, artow nat wrongful in that, and makest Fortune wroth and aspere by thine inpacience, and yit thou mayst nat chaunge hir?

"Yif thow commyttest and bytakest thi sayles to the wynde, thow shalt be shoven nat theder that thou woldest, but wheder that the wynde showveth the. Yif thow castest thi sedes into the feeldes, thow sholdest han in mynde that the yeres ben amonges otherwhyle plenteuous and otherwhile barayne. Thow hast bytaken thiself to the governaunce of Fortune, and forthi it bihoveth the to ben obeysaunt to the maneres of thi lady. Enforcest thow the to aresten or withholden the swyftnesse and the sweyh of hir turninge wheel? O thow fool of alle mortal fooles, yif Fortune bygan to dwelle stable, she cesede thanne to ben Fortune!

---

41 **mowe,** may. **42–43 Com now . . . swetenesse rethoryen,** i.e., let the persuasion of sweet rhetoric come forth. **45 estatutes,** statutes. **47 moedes or prolacyouns,** strains of music (moods), poems. I *probasyons.* **51 unkowth,** strange (uncouth). **55 I** *stabylnesse standeth in.* **58 unleffeful lykinges of fals welfulnesse,** illegitimate pleasure of false affluence. **59 ataynt,** perceived (attained). **64 use hir maneres,** get used to her behavior. **65 agrysest,** tremble at. **71 syker,** sure. **76 welefulnesse,** good fortune. **80 wiht,** person. **81 withholden,** held fast. **84–85 a maner shewinge,** a kind of foreshadowing. **91 manasses,** menaces. **99 wendinge,** changing. **109 ben amonges,** are sometimes. **114 Enforcest thow,** do you try.

Metre I. Hec cum superba.

"Whan that Fortune with a prowd ryht
hand hath torned hir chaunginge stowndes,
she fareth lik the maneres of the boylinge
Eurippe. *(Glosa. Eurippe is an arm of the
see that ebbeth and floweth, and somtyme the*   5
strem is on o syde, and somtyme on the other.)
Text. She, crwel Fortune, casteth adown
kynges that whilom weren ydrad; and she,
deceyvable, enhanseth up the umble cheere
of him that is descounfited. Ne she neyther   10
hereth ne rekketh of wrecchede wepinges,
and she is so hard that she laugheth and
scorneth the wepinges of hem the whiche she
hath maked wepe with hir free wille. Thus
she pleyeth, and thus she proeveth hir   15
strengthes, and sheweth a grete wonder
to alle hir servauntes, yif that a wiht is seyn
weleful and overthrowe in an houre.

Prose II. Vellem quidem pauca.

"Certes, I wolde pleten with the a fewe
thynges, usinge the wordes of Fortune. Tak
hede now thyself, yif that she axeth ryht.
'O thow man, wherfore makest thow me
gylty by thyne every dayes playninges?   5
What wronge have I don the? What
goodes have I byreft the that weren thyne?
Stryf or pleten wyth me byforn what juge
that thow wolt of the possessyoun of
rychesses or of dignitees, and yif thow   10
mayst shewen me that evere any mortal
man hath receyved any of tho thinges to
ben his in propre, than wol I graunte frely
that alle thylke thynges weren thyne
whiche that thow axest. Whan that nature   15
browht the forth owt of thi moder wombe,
I receyved the naked and nedy of alle thinges,
and I noryssede the with my rychesses, and

was redy and ententyf throw my favour
to susteyne the—and that maketh the   20
now inpacyent ayeins me; and I envyrounde
the with alle the aboundance and shyninge
of alle goodes that ben in my ryht. Now it
lyketh me to withdrawen myn hand.
Thow hast had grace as he that used of   25
foreyne goodes; thow hast no ryht to
pleyne the as thowh thow haddest outrely
forlorn alle thi thinges. Why pleynesthow
thanne? I have don the no wrong.
Rychesses, honours, and swyche other   30
thinges ben of my ryht. My servauntes
knowen me for her lady; they comen with
me, and departen when I wende. I dar wel
affermen hardyly that yif tho thinges
of whiche thow pleynest that thow hast   35
forlorn hadde ben thyne, thow ne haddest
not lorn hem. Shal I thanne, oonly, ben
deffended to usen my ryht?

'Certes, it is leveful to the hevene to
make cleere dayes, and after that to coeveren   40
tho same dayes with dirke nyghtes. The
yer hath ek leve to apayrelen the visage of the
erthe now with flowres and now with frut, and
to confownden hem somtyme with reynes
and with coldes. The see hath ek his ryht   45
to ben somtyme kalm and blawndyssinge
with smothe water, and somtyme to ben horible
with wawes and tempestes. But the covetyse
of men, that may nat ben stanched, shal it
bynde me to ben stidefast, syn that stide-   50
fastnesse is unkowth to my maneres? Swych
is my strengthe, and this pley I pleye con-
tinuely. I torne the whirlinge wheel with the
torninge cercle. I am glad to chaungen the
lowest to the heyest, and the heyest to the   55
lowest. Worth up, yif thow wolt, so it be by
this lawe, that thow ne holde nat that I do the
wronge thogh thow dessende adoun whan the
resoun of my pley axeth it.

II METRE I. 2 **stowndes,** hours. 4 **Eurippe,** Euripus, a strait between Boeotia (on the Greek mainland) and Euboea (a Greek island). 12 *laugheth:* I *lyssheth.* 16 **sheweth a . . . wonder,** reveals a marvel. II PROSE II. 1 **pleten,** urge (plead). 5 *gylty:* MSS *gyltyf.* 8 **Stryf or pleten,** contend or litigate. 13 **in propre,** in absolute possession. 21 **envyrounde,** surrounded. 25–26 **used of foreyne,** made use of other people's. 28 **forlorn,** lost. 37 I *I shall thanne.* 38 **deffended,** prevented. 39 **leveful,** lawful. 40 *coeveren:* Cx *overcome.* 49 **stanched,** checked (stopped). 56 **Worth,** be.

'Wistestow nat how Cresus, the kyng of 60
Lydyens, of whiche Kyng Cyrus was ful sore
agast a lytel byforn, that this rewlyche Cresus
was kawht of Cyrus and lad to the fyr to ben
brent, but that a rayn dessendede down fro
hevene that rescowede him? And is it owt 65
of thy minde how that Pawlus, consul of
Rome, whan he hadde taken the kyng of
Percyens, weep pitowsly for the kaptivite of
the self kynge? What other thing bywaylen
the cryinges of tragedyes but oonly the dedes 70
of Fortune, that with an unwar stroke over-
torneth realmes of grete noblye? *(Glose. Tragedye
is to seyn, a dite of a prosperite for a tyme that
endeth in wrecchednesse.)*

'Lernedest nat thow in Greke, whan thow 75
were yonge, that in the entre or in the
celere of Jupyter ther ben cowched two tonnes,
that on is ful of good, that oother is ful of harm?
What ryht hastow to pleyne, yif thow hast
taken more plenteously of the goode syde 80
(that is to seyn, of my rychesses and prosperites),
and what ek yif I ne be nat al departed fro the?
What ek yif my mutabylyte yeveth the ryhtful
cause of hope to han yit beter thinges?
Natheles dysmaye the nat in thi thowght; 85
and thow that art put in the comune realme
of alle, ne desire nat to lyven by thin oonly
propre ryht.

Metre II. Si quantas rapidis.

'Thowgh Plentee *(that is goddesse of rychesses)*
hielde adown with ful horn, and withdraweth
nat hir hand, as many richesses as the see
torneth upward sandes whan it is moeved
with ravyssinge blastes, or elles as many 5
rychesses as ther shynen bryhte sterres
on hevene on the sterry nyhtes, yit for al that,
mankynde nolde nat cese to wepe wrecchede
pleyntes. And al be it so that God recey-

veth gladly her preyers, and yeveth them, 10
as fool-large, meche gold, and aparayleth
coveytous men with noble or cleere honours,
yit semeth hem haven ygeten nothinge; but
alwey her crewel ravyne, devowringe al
that thei han geten, sheweth oother 15
gapinges *(that is to seyn, gapen and desyren
yit after mo rychesses).* What brydles myhten
wytholden, to any certeyn ende, the desordene
covetyse of men, whan ever the rather
that it fleteth in large yiftes, the more ay 20
brenneth in hem the thurst of havinge?
Certes he that, quakinge and dredful, weneth
himselven nedy, he ne leveth nevermore ryche.'

Prose III. Hiis igitur verbis si pro se.

"Therfor yif that Fortune spake with the
for hirself in this manere, forsothe thow ne
haddest nat what thow myhtest answere.
And yif thow hast anythinge wherwith
thow mayst ryhtfully defenden thy com- 5
pleynt, it byhoveth the to shewen it, and
I wol yeven thee spase to tellen it."

"Certeinly," quod I thanne, "thise beth
fayre thinges, and enoynted with hony
swetenesse of rethorike and musyke; and 10
oonly whil thei ben herd they ben dylycious,
but to wreches is a depper feelinge of harm
*(this is to seyn, that wrecches feelen the harmes
that they suffren more grevously than the remedies
or the delytes of thise wordes mowen gladen 15
or comforten hem)* so that whan thise thinges
stynten for to sowne in eres, the sorwe that
is inset greveth the thowght."

"Ryht so is it," quod she. "For thise
ne ben yit none remedyes of thi maledye, 20
but they ben a maner noryssinges of
thi sorwes yit rebel ayein thi curacioun.
For whan that tyme is, I shal moeve swych
thinges that percen hemself depe. But

---

62 **rewlyche,** pitiable. 71 **unwar,** unexpected. Recall the monk's definition of tragedy, *CT* vii.1973. 77 **cowched two tonnes,** stored two wine casks. 84 **yit,** i.e., again. 88 **propre ryht,** personal privilege (vs. the common rights of mankind). II METRE II. 2 **hielde,** reached (held). 11 **fool-large,** foolishly lavish. 20 **fleteth,** flows. 23 **leveth,** lives (i.e., who thinks himself poor is poor). II PROSE III. 11 Cx *thei ben herd and sowne in eeres, thei.* 17 **stynten,** cease. 21 **noryssinges,** encouragement (nourishing). 22 **yit rebel,** which still resist. 23 CxC *meve and ajuste.*

natheles, that thow shalt nat wylne to 25
leten thiself a wrecche, hastow foryeten
the nowmber and the manere of thi welefulnesse? I hoolde me stylle how that the soverane
men of the cyte token the in cure and
kepinge, whan thow were orphelin of 30
fader and moder, and were chosen in
affynite of prinses of the cyte. And thow
begunne rather to be leef and deere than
forto ben a neysshebour, the whiche
thing is the moost precyous kynde of any 35
propinquite or alyaunce that may ben.
Who is it that ne seyde tho that thow were
ryht weleful, with so grete a nobleye of thi
fadyres-in-lawe, and with the chastete
of thi wyf, and with the oportunite and 40
noblesse of thi masculyn chyldren *(that
is to seyn, thy sones)*? And over al this—me
lyste to passen the comune thinges—how
thow haddest in thi yowthe dygnites that
weren werned to oolde men. But it delyteth 45
me to comen now to the singuler up-
hepinge of thi welfulnesse. Yif any frute of
mortal thinges may han any weyhte or pris
of welfulnesse, myhtestow ever foryeten,
for any charge of harm that myhte befalle, 50
the remembraunce of thilke day that
thow saye thy two sones maked conseileres,
and ilad togedere fro thin howse under so
greet asemble of senatoures and under
the blythenesse of peeple, and whan 55
thow saye hem set in the court in here
chayeres of dignitees? Thow, rethoryen or
pronouncere of kynges preysinges, desservedest
glorye of wit and of eloquence whan thow,
syttinge bitwyen thy two sones conseyleres, 60
in the place that hihte circo, fulfyldest the
abydinge of the multitude of poeple that was

sprad abowten the with so large preysinge and
laude as men syngen in victories. Tho yave
thow wordes to Fortune, as I trowe *(that is 65
to seyn, tho feffedest thow Fortune with glosinge
wordes and deceyvedest hir)* whan she acoyede
the and noryssede the as hir owne delyces.
Thow bar away of Fortune a yifte *(that is to
seyn, swiche gerdoun)* that she never yaf to 70
pryve man. Wilt thow therfor lye a rekeninge with Fortune? She hath now twyncled
fyrst upon the with wyckede eye. Yif thow
consydere the nowmbre and the manere
of thy blysses and of thy sorwes, thow mayst 75
nat forsaken that thow art yit blysseful. For
yif thow therfor wenest thiself nat weleful,
for thynges that tho semeden joyful ben passed,
ther nis nat whi thow sholdest wene thyself
a wrecche, for things that semen now sorye 80
passen also.

"Art thow now comen fyrst, a sodeyn gest,
into the shadwe or tabernacle of this lyf? Or
trowestow that any stedefastnesse be in
mannes thinges, whan ofte a swyft howre 85
dyssolvede the same man *(that is to seyn,
whan the sowle departeth fro the body)*? For althowgh
that selde is ther any feith that fortunous
thinges wolen dwellen, yit natheles the laste
day of a mannes lyf is a manere deth to 90
Fortune, and also to thilke that hath dwelt.
And therfor what wenestow that recke, yif
thow forlete hir in deyinge, or elles that she
(Fortune) forlete the in fleinge awey?

Metre III. Cum polo Phebus.

"Whan Phebus *(the sonne)* bygynneth to
spreden his cleernesse with rosene charyettes,
thanne the sterre, ydymmed, paleth hir white

25–26 **wylne . . . wrecche,** desire, distressed person. 28 **soverane,** principal. 30 **orphelin,** orphaned. 31 **were,** (you) were. 33 **leef,** beloved. 34 **neysshebour,** neighbor (in Lat. *proximus,* blood relation). 38 **nobleye,** high birth. 42–43 **me lyste to passen,** I wish to pass over. 45 **werned,** denied. 46 **singuler,** especial. 50 **charge,** burden. 52 **saye,** saw. 56 Cx *in hye chayeres.* 57 **rethoryen,** orator. In the Lat., "they sat in their chairs of state while you made a speech in honor of the king." 61–62 **hihte circo,** is called the circus (public meeting place). **fulfyldest . . . abydinge,** i.e., satisfied the expectations. 66 **feffedest,** presented (enfeoffed). *glosinge,* deceiving: A *glories.* 67 **acoyede,** caressed. 68 **delyces,** favorite (delight). 69 **bar away:** A *hast had.* 70 **gerdoun,** reward. 71 **pryve,** private. **lye a reckeninge,** try (lay) to bargain. 72 **twyncled,** winked. 73 **fyrst,** for the first time. 78 **tho,** then (formerly). 81 **passen,** will pass. 82 **sodeyn,** unexpected. 87–88 I *al that thowgh that.* 89 **dwellen,** endure. 92 **recke,** matters. II METRE III. 2 **rosene charyettes,** ruddy chariot(s).

cheeres by the flambes of the sonne that
overcometh the sterre-lyght. *(This is to* 5
seyn, whan the sonne is rysen the day-sterre
wexeth paale, and leseth hir lyht for the grete bryht-
nesse of the sonne.) Whan the wode wexeth rody
of rosen flowres in the fyrst somer sesoun
thorwh the brethe of the wynde Zepherus 10
that wexeth warm, yif the clowdy wynde
Auster blowe fellyche, than goth awey the
fairenesse of thornesse. Ofte the see is cleer
and kalm, withowte moevinge floedes; and
ofte the horyble wynd Aquilon moeveth 15
boylinge tempestes and over-whelveth the
see. Yif the forme of this worlde is so selde
stable, and yif it turneth by so many entrechaunginges, woltow thanne trusten in the
tovmblinge fortunes of men? Woltow 20
trowen on flettinge goodes? It is certeyn
and establyssed by lawe perdurable that
nothinge that is engendred nys stedefast ne
estable."

Prose IV. Tum ego vera inquam.

Thanne seyde I thus: "O norice of alle
vertuus, thow seyst ful soth; ne I may nat
forsake the ryht swyfte cours of my prosperite
(that is to seyn, that prosperite ne be comen to
me wonder swyftly and sone). But this is a thinge 5
that gretely smerteth me whan it remembreth me. For in alle adversyte of fortune, the
moost unsely kynde of contrarious fortune is
to han ben weleful."

"But that thow," quod she, "abyest thus 10
the tormentes of thy false opynioun, that
maystow nat ryhtfully blamen ne aretten to
thinges *(as who seyth, for thow hast yit many*
habundaunce of thinges). Text. For al be it so
that the ydel name of aventurous weleful- 15
nesse moeveth the now, it is leefful that
thow rekne with me of how manye grete
thinges thow hast yit plente. And therfor, yif
that thilke thinge that thow haddest for
moost precyous in al thi rychesse of fortune 20
be kept to the yit, by the grace of God,
unwemmed and undefowled, maystow thanne
pleyne ryhtfully upon the meschef of Fortune,
syn thow hast yit thy beste thinges? Certes,
yit leveth in good poynt thilke precious 25
honour of mankynde, Symacus, thy wyves
fader, which that is a man maked alle of
sapyence and vertu, the whiche man how
woldest byen redely with the pris of thin
owne lyf. He bewayleth the wronges that 30
men don to the, and nat for hymself, for
he leveth in sykernesse of any sentences put
ayeins him. And yit lyveth thy wyf, that is
atempre of wyt, and passinge oother
wymmen in clennesse of chastete; and for I 35
wol closen shortely hir bownte, she is lik to
hir fader. I telle the wel that she lyveth loth
of this lyf, and keepeth to the oonly hir goost,
and is al maat and overkomen by wepinge
and sorwe for desyr of the, in the wheche 40
thing oonly I moot graunten that thi
welefulnesse is amenyssed. What shal I seyn
ek of thi two sones conseylours, of whiche, as
of chyldren of her age, ther shyneth the
lykenesse of the wyt of her fader or of her 45
eldefader? And syn the sovereyn cure of
alle mortel folk is to saven hir owen lyves, O
how weleful art thow yif thow knowe thy

---

10 **Zepherus**, the west wind, see *CT* I.5. 12 **Auster**, the south wind. **fellyche**, fiercely. 13 **fairenesse of thornesse**, i.e., takes away
the blossoms, leaving only the thorns. 15 **Aquilon**, the north wind. 21 **flettinge**, fleeting. 22 **perdurable**, eternal. 23 **engendred**,
born. **II PROSE IV. 3 forsake**, deny. 6 **smerteth**, pains. 8 **unsely**, unpleasant. This is one of the most famous lines in the *Consolation*
of Philosophy, used in Dante's *Inferno* v.121–23, in *TC* III.625–28, and elsewhere. 9 **weleful**, fortunate. 10 **abyest**, suffer. 12 **aretten**,
impute. 13 **thinges**, external things. 14 **al be it**, although. 15 **aventurous welefulnesse**, accidental good fortune. 16 **leefful**,
proper (lawful). 17 **grete**, good (great). 19 **thilke . . . that thow haddest**, i.e., you considered. 22 **unwemmed**, uninjured. 23
pleyne, complain. 25 **good poynt**, good condition. 29 **byen**, buy. 32 **leveth in sykernesse**, lives in safety. 34 **atempre . . . passinge**,
mild, surpassing. 36 **closen . . . bownte**, summarize, goodness. 37 **loth**, i.e., loathing. 38 **keepeth to the . . . goost**, i.e., devotes
her spirit only to you. 39 **maat**, miserable. 42 **amenyssed**, diminished. 46 **eldefader**, grandfather. **sovereyn cure**, principal
concern. 48 A *though thou know;* Cx *yf thou knowe thyself, thy goodes make the more weleful.*

goodes! For yit ben ther thinges dwelled to the-ward that no man dowteth that they ne 50 ben more dereworthe to the than thin owen lyf. And forthy drye thy teeres, for yit nis nat everych fortune al hateful to-the-ward, ne over gret tempest hath nat yit fallen upon the, whan that thyn ancres cleven faste, that 55 neyther wolen suffren the counfort of this tyme present ne the hope of tyme cominge to passen ne to faylen."

"And I preye," quod I, "that faste moten they halden; for whyles that they halden, 60 howsoever that thinges ben, I shal wel fleeten forth and escapen. But thow mayste wel sen how grete aparayles and aray that me lakketh, that ben passed away fro me."

"I have somwhat avaunsed and forthered 65 the," quod she, "yif that thow anoye nat, or forthinke nat of al thi fortune *(as who seyth, I have somwhat conforted the, so that thow tempest the nat thus with al thi fortune, syn thow hast yit thi beste thinges).* But I may nat suffren 70 thi delices, that pleynest so wepinge and angwissous, for that ther lacketh somwhat to thi welefulnesse. For what man is so sad, or of so parfyt welefulnesse, that he ne stryveth and pleyneth on som halve ayen the qualite 75 of his estat? Forwhy ful angwissous thing is the condysyoun of mannes goodes, for eyther it comth nat altogydere to a wyht or elles it last nat perpetuel. For sum man hath grete rychesses, but he is ashamed of his ungentel 80 lynage, and som is renowned of noblesse of kynrede, but he is enclosed in so grete angwysshe of nede of thinges that him were levere that he were unknowe. And som man haboundeth bothe in rychesse and noblesse, but yit 85 he bewayleth his chaste lyf for he ne hath no wyf. And som man is wel and selyly ymaryed, but he hath no chyldren and noriseth his rychesses to the eyres of strange foolkes. And som man is gladed with chyldren, but 90 he weepeth ful sory for the trespace of his sone or of his dowter. And for this ther ne acordeth no wyht lyhtly to the condycioun of his fortune; for alwey to every man ther is in somwhat that, unassaied, he ne wot nat, 95 or elles he dredeth that he hath asayed. And adde this also, that every weleful man hath a ful delycat feelinge so that but yif alle thinges byfalle at his owne wyl, for he is inpacyent or is nat used to han non ad- 100 versyte, anon he is throwen adoun for every litul thinge. And ful litul thinges ben tho that withdrawen the somme or the perfeccyoun of blysfulnesse fro hem that ben moost fortunat. How many men, trowestow, wolden demen 105 hemself to ben almoost in hevene yif they myhten atayne to the leest party of the remnaunt of thi fortune? This same place that thow clepest exil is contre to hem that enhabyten heere, and forthi nothing is 110 wrecched but whan thow wenest hit *(as who seyth, thow thyself, ne no wyht elles, nis a wrechche, but whan he weneth hymself a wrechche by reputacoun of his corage).* And ayeinward, alle fortune is blisful to a man by the egreablete 115 or by the egalyte of him that suffreth hit.

"What man is that that is so weleful that nolde changen his estat whan he hath lost pacience? The swetnesse of mannes welefulnesse is sprayned with many beternesses; 120 the whiche welefulnesse, althowgh it seme swete and joyful to hem that useth hit, yit may it nat ben withholden that it ne goth away whan it woole. Thanne is it wel sene how wrecched is the blysfulnesse of mortal 125 thinges, that neyther it dureth perpetuel

---

49 dwelled, remaining (in your possession). **55 ancres cleven,** anchors hold. **59 moten,** may (must). **62 fleeten,** sail (float). **63 aparayles,** belongings. **66 thow anoye nat,** you are not distressed. **67 forthinke,** regret. **68 *tempest*,** be concerned. **71 delices,** weakness. I *delites.* **87 selyly,** happily. **88–89 noriseth . . . to the eyres,** augments (cares for), for the heirs. **93 acordeth no wyht lyhtly,** no person approves easily (completely). **95 unassaied,** undone (untried). **98 delycat,** sensitive. **109 contre,** i.e., home (native country). **110 *nothing is*:** I A *is* om.; Lat. *nihil est.* **113 *reputacoun*,** i.e., the feelings. I *reputasyn.* **115–16 egreablete . . . egalyte,** agreeableness, equanimity. **120 sprayned,** scattered. Cx *spreint.* **123 withholden,** prevented.

with hem that every fortune receiven agreablely or egaly, ne it delyteth nat in al to hem that ben angwissous. O ye mortal folk, what seke ye thanne blysfulnesse owt of yowrself 130 whiche that is put in yowrself? Erroure and folye confowndeth yow.

"I shal shewe the shortely the poynt of sovereyne blysfulnesse. Is ther anythinge more precyous to the than thiself? Thow 135 wolt answere nay. Thanne yif hit so be that thow art myhty over thiself *(that is to seyn, by tranquillite of thy sowle)*, than hast thow thinge in thi power that thow noldest never leesen, ne Fortune ne may nat beneme it the. And 140 that thow mayst knowe that blyssefulnesse ne may nat standen in things that ben fortunous and temporel, now understonde and gadere it togidere thus: yif blisfulnesse be the sovereyn good of nature that lyveth by 145 resoun, ne thilke thinge nis nat sovereyn good that may be taken awey in any wyse, for more worthi thinge and more digne is thilke thinge that may nat ben take awey—than sheweth it wel, that the unstablenesse of 150 fortune may nat atayne to receyven verray blysfulnesse. And yit moreover, what man that this towmbling welefulnesse ledeth, eyther he woot that it is chaungeable or elles he woot hit nat. And yif he woot it nat, what blys- 155 ful fortune may ther ben in the blyndnesse of ignorance? And yif he wot that it is chaungeable, he moot alwey ben adrad that he ne lese that thinge that he ne dowteth nat but that he may leesen hit *(as who seyth, he mot ben 160 alway agast lest he leese that he wot wel he may leese it)*; for which the continuel drede that he hath ne suffreth him nat to ben weleful, or elles yif he leese it, he weneth to be dyspysed and forleten. Certes ek, that is a ful lytul 165 good that is born with evene herte whan it

is lost *(that is to seyn, that men do no more fors of the lost than of the havinge)*. And for as meche as thow thiself art he to whom it hath ben shewed and proved by ful manye demon- 170 stracyouns, as I wot wel, that the sowles of men ne mowe nat deyen in no wise, and ek syn it is cleer and certeyn that fortunous welefulnesse endeth by the deth of the body, it may nat ben dowted that yif that 175 deth may take awey blysfulnesse, that alle the kynde of mortal thinges ne dessendeth into wrecchednesse by the ende of the deth. And syn we knowen wel that many a man hath sowht the frut of blysfulnesse nat oonly with 180 suffringe of deth but ek with suffringe of peynes and tormentes, how myhte thanne this present lyf maken men blysful, syn that whan thilke selve lyf is ended it ne maketh foolkes no wrecches?   185

Metre IV. Quisquis volet perhennem cautus.

"What maner man, stable and waar, that wole fownden him a perdurable sete, and ne wole nat ben cast down with the lowde blastes of the wynd Eurus, and wole despyse the see manasinge with floodes, lat him eschewen 5 to bylde on the cop of the mountaygne or in the moyste sandes. For the felle wynd Auster tormenteth the cop of the montaygne with alle his strengthes, and the lause sandes refusen to beren the hevy wyhte. And forthy, 10 if thow wolt fleen the perylous aventure *(that is to seyn, of the worlde)*, have mynde certeynly to fychchen thin hows of a merye site in a lowh stoon. For althowgh the wynde, trowblinge the see, thondre with 15 overthrowinges, thow that art put in quiete,

---

129 **what,** i.e., why. 139 **leesen,** lose. 140 **beneme,** take from. 145 **sovereyn,** highest. 153 **ledeth,** controls (leads). 154 **woot,** knows. 165 **forleten,** deserted (left). 167 *that men do no more fors,* i.e., if men don't care more. 172 **mowe,** may. 173–74 **fortunous welefulnesse,** the benefits of fortune. 177–78 **kynde . . . deth,** i.e., that all mankind fall into misery by death. 184–85 **ne maketh . . . wrecches,** i.e., loss of life causes no misery. II METRE IV. 1 **waar,** prudent. 2 **perdurable sete,** i.e., permanent situation. 4 **Eurus,** the southeast wind. 9 **lause,** loose: A *lowe see.* 10 **wyhte,** weight. 13–14 **fychchen,** fix. **merye site,** safe site.

and weleful by strengthe of thi palis, shalt leden a cler age, scorninge the woodnesses and the ires of the eyr.

Prose V. Set quidem racionum in te iam.

"But for as moche as the noryssinges of my resouns dessenden now into the, I trowe it were tyme to usen a lytel strengere medycynes. Now understond heere, al were it so that the yiftes of Fortune ne were nat brutel ne 5 transitorye, what is ther in hem that may be thyn in any tyme, or elles that it nis fowl, yif that it be consydered and loked perfytly? Rychesses, ben they precyous by the nature of hemself, or elles by the nature of the? 10 What is most worth of rychesses? Is it nat gold or myht of moneye assembled? Certes, thilke gold and thilke moneye shyneth and yeveth betere renoun to hem that despenden it thanne to thilke folk that mokeren 15 it; for avarice maketh alwey mokereres to ben hated, and largesse maketh folk cler of renoun. For syn that swich thinge as is transferred fram o man to another ne may nat dwellen with no man, certes thanne is thilke 20 moneye precyous whan it is translated into oother folkes and stenteth to ben had by usage of large yevinge of him that hath yeven it. And also yif al the moneye that is over al in the worlde were gadered toward o man, 25 it sholde maken alle oother men to ben nedy as of that. And certes a voys al hool *(that is to seyn, withowte amenusinge)*, fulfylleth togydere the hering of moche folk. But certes, yowre richesses ne mowen nat passen 30 into moche folke withowte amenusinge, and whan they ben apassed, nedes they maken hem pore that forgon the rychesses. O streyte and nedy clepe I this rychesse syn that many

folk ne may nat han it al, ne al may it nat 35 comen to o man withowten poverte of alle other folk!

"And the shyninge of gemmes *(that I clepe precyous stoones)* draweth it nat the eyen of folk to hem-ward *(that is to seyn, for the* 40 *beautes)*? But certes, yif ther were beaute or bounte in the shyninge of stones, thilke clernesse is of the stones hemself, and nat of men, for whiche I wondre gretely that men mervaylen on swyche thynges. For-why, what 45 thing is it that, yif it wanteth moeving and joynture of sowle and body, that by ryht myhte semen a fayr creature to him that hath a sowle of resoun? For al be it so that gemmes drawen to hemself a lytel of the last beaute 50 of the world thorw the entente of her creatour and thorw the distinccioun of hemself, yit for as mochel as they ben put under yowre excellense, they ne han nat desserved by no wey that ye sholden mervaylen on hem. 55

"And the beaute of feldes, delyteth it nat mochel unto yow?"

Boece. "Why sholde it nat delyten us, syn that it is a ryht fayr porsyoun of the ryht fayre werke *(that is to seyn, of this world)*? 60 And ryht so ben we gladed somtyme of the face of the see whan it is cler; and also merveyllen we on the hevene, and on the sterres, and on the sonne, and on the moone."

Philosophie. "Aperteneth," quod she, 65 "any of thilke thinges to the? Why darstow gloryfyen the in the shyninge of any swyche thinges? Artow distingwed and embelysed be the sprynginge flowres of the fyrst somer sesoun, or swelleth thy plente in the fructes 70 of somer? Whi artow ravyssed with ydel joyes? Whi enbracest thow straunge goedes as they weren thyne? Fortune ne shal never maken that swyche thynges ben thyne, that

---

17 **palis**, enclosure. 18 **cler age**, serene life. 19 **ires of the eyr**, furies of the elements (air). II PROSE V. 2 **resouns**, arguments. 5 **brutel**, brittle. 14 **despenden**, spend. 15 **mokeren**, heard. 17 **largesse**, generosity. 21 **translated into**, passed on to. 22 **stenteth**, ceases. 27 **al hool**, out loud; om. in I. 28 ***amenusinge***, diminishing. 33 **forgon**, surrender. 42 **bounte**, value. **clernesse**, brightness. 46 **wanteth moeving**, lacks movement (life). 53 **ben put under**, i.e., are less valued. 58–64 **Boece.** In the Latin texts this passage is usually a continuation by Philosophy. Identification of the speaker, here and below, is not found in the Latin. 65 **Aperteneth**, belong. 72 **straunge**, i.e., not belonging to you.

nature of things hath maked foreyne fro
the. Soth is that withowten dowte the frutes
of the erthe owen to ben to the noryssinge of
bestes. And yif thou wolt fulfylle thy nede after
that it suffiseth to nature, than is it no nede
that thow seke after the superflwite of
fortune. For with ful fewe things and with
ful lytel things nature halt hir apayed; and
yif thou wolt achoken the fulfyllinge of nature
with superflwites, certes thilke things that
thou wolt thresten or powren into nature
shullen ben unjoyful to the, or elles anoyous.

"Wenest thow ek that it be a fayre thing to
shyne with diverse clothinge? Of which kloth-
inge yif the beaute be agreable to loken
upon, I wol mervaylen on the nature of the
matere of thilke klothes, or elles on the
werkman that wrowht hem. But also a longe
rowte of meyne, maketh that a blysful man?
The whiche servantes, yif they ben vicious
of condiciouns, it is a gret charge and a
distrucsyoun to the hows, and a gret enemy
to the lord himself. And yif they ben goode
men, how shal straunge or foreyne goodnesse
ben put in the nowmbre of thi rychesse? So
that by all thyse forseide things, it is cleerly
ishewed that never oon of thilke things
that thow acountedest for thine goodes nas nat
thi good. In the whyche things, yif ther be no
beaute to ben desyred, why sholdestow ben
sory yif thow leese hem, or why sholdestow
rejoysen the to holden hem? For yif they
ben fayre of her owne kynde, what aperteneth
that to the? For al so wel sholden they han ben
fayre by hemselve, thowgh they weren departed fram alle thyne rychesses. For-why
fayre ne precyous ne weren they nat for
that they comen amonge thy rychesses, but
for they semeden fayre and precyous, therfor
thow haddest lever rekne hem amonges thy
rychesses.

"But what desirest thow of Fortune with
so grete a noyse and with so gret a fare? I
trowe thow seke to dryve awey nede with
habundaunce of thinges; but certes it
torneth to yow al in the contrarye. For-why
certes it nedeth of ful manye helpinges to
kepen the diversite of precyous ostelementes.
And soth it is that of manye things han they
nede that many thinges han; and ayeinward, of lytul nedeth hem that mesuren her
fille after the nede of kynde and nat after
the owtrage of coveytyse. Is it thanne so that
ye men ne han no proper goode iset in yow,
for whiche ye moten seken owtward yowre
goodes in foreyne and subgyt thinges? So is
thanne the condicyoun of thinges torned
up-so-down, that a man, that is a devine beest
by meryte of his resoun, thinketh that himself
nis neyther fayre ne noble but yif it be
thorw possessyoun of ostelmentes that ne
han no sowles. And certes, al oother things
ben apayed of hir owne beautes; but ye men,
that ben semblable to God by yowr resonable
thowght, desyren to apayrelen yowr excellent kynde of the lowest thinges. Ne ye
understonden nat how gret a wrong ye don
to yowre creatour. For he wolde that mankynde
were most worthy and noble of any oothre
worldly thinges, and ye threste adown yowre
dignitees bynethe the lowest thinges. For
yif that al the good of every thing be more
precyous than is thilke thing whos that the
good is, syn ye demen that the fowlest thinges
ben yowre goodes, thanne submitten ye
and putten yowrselven under the fowleste
thinges by yowre estimacioun. And certes,
this tydeth nat withowte yowre desertes, for
certes, swyche is the condysyoun of alle mankynde, that oonly when it hath knowinge of
itselve, than passeth it in noblesse alle
oother thinges; and when it forleteth the
knowinge of itself, than is it browht bynethen
alle beestes. For-why al oother levinge bestes

---

77 owen, ought. **82 apayed,** satisfied. **83 achoken,** stifle (choke). **85 powren,** pour. **93 rowte of meyne,** string of servants. **95 charge,** burden. **107 kynde,** nature. **121 manye helpinges,** much assistance. **122 kepen ... ostelementes,** guard, household goods. **130 subgyt,** misreading of Lat. *sepositis* (separate), as *suppositis* (subject, inferior). **137 apayed,** satisfied. **152 tydeth ... desertes,** happens, deserving (it).

han of kynde to knowe nat hemself; but
whan men leten the knowinge of hemself, 160
it comth hem of vice. But how brode
sheweth the erroure and the folye of yow men,
that wenen that any thinge may ben aparayled
with straunge aparaylementes! But forsothe,
that may nat ben doon. For yif a wyht shy- 165
neth with thinges that ben put to him *(as
thus, if thilke thinges schynen with which a man is
aparayled)*, certes thilke thinges ben comended
and preysed with whych he is aparaled; but
natheles, the thinge that is covered and 170
wrapped under that dwelleth in his felthe.

"And I denye that thilke thinge be good
that anoyeth him that hath it. Gabbe I of
this? Thow wolt seye nay. Certes, rychesses
han anoyed ful ofte hem that han tho rych- 175
esses syn that every wycked shrewe—and
for his wyckednesse the more gredy after oother
folkes rychesses, whersoever it be in any place,
be it gold or precious stones—weneth
him only most worthi that hath hem. Thow 180
thanne, that so bysy dredest now the swerd
and now the spere, yif thow haddest entred
in the path of this lyf a voyde wayferinge man,
than woldest thow synge byforn the thef
(as who seyth, a pore man that berth no rychesse 185
on him by the weye may boldely synge byforn
theves, for he hath nat wherof to ben robbed). O
precyous and ryht cler is the blysfulnesse of
mortal rychesses that whan thou hast geten
it, than hast thow lorn thi sikernesse! 190

Metre V. Felix nimium prior etas.

"Blysful was the fyrst age of men. They
helden hem apayed with the metes that the
trewe feeldes browhten forth. They ne dys-
troyede nor deceivede nat hemself with
owtrage. They weren wont lyhtly to slaken 5
her hunger at even with accornes of okes.
They ne cowde nat medly the yifte of Bachus
to the cleer hony *(that is to seyn, they cowde*
make no pyment nor clarree), ne they cowde nat
medle the bryhte fleeses of the contre of 10
Seryens with the venym of Tyrye *(this is to*
seyn, they cowde nat deyen white fleses of Syryen
contre with the bloode of a manere shyllefyssh that
men fynden in Tyrye, with whiche blood men
deyen purpur). They slepen holsom slepes 15
upon the gras, and dronken of the renninge
wateres, and layen under the shadwes of the
heye pyn trees. Ne no gest ne straungere ne
karf yit the heye see with oores or with
shippes, ne they ne hadde seyn yit none newe 20
strondes to leden marchaundyse into diverse
contres. Tho weren the crwel claryouns ful
hust and ful stylle. Ne blod ishad by egre hate
ne hadde nat deyed yit armures. For wherto
or whych wodnesse of enemys wolde fyrst 25
moeven armes whan they say crwel
woundes, ne none meedes be of blod ishad?

"I wolde that owre tymes sholde torne ayein
to the olde maneres! But the angwissous
love of havinge brenneth in folk moore 30
crwely than the fyr of mowntaigne Ethna
(that ay brenneth). Allas, what was he that fyrst
dalf up the gobetes or the weyhtes of gold
covered under erthe, and the precyous
stoones that wolden han be hydd? He dalf 35
up precyous perils *(that is to seyn, that he that*
hem fyrst up dalf, dalf up a precyous peril, for-whi
for the precyousnesse of swyche thinge hath many man
be in peril).

Prose VI. Quid autem de dignitatibus.

"But what shal I seye of dignites and of
powers the whiche ye men that neyther knowen
verray dignite ne verray power areysen hem

---

160 leten, loses. **173 Gabbe,** lie. **181 bysy,** agitated (busy). **183 voyde,** poor (empty). **190 sikernesse,** safety. **II METRE V. 2 apayed,** satisfied. Chaucer also rendered this metre in verse as "The Former Age" (short poem 13). **5 owtrage,** excess. **7 medly,** mix. **9 pyment . . . clarree,** sweetened wines. **10 fleeses,** wool (fleece). **11 Seryens,** Lat. *Serum* (Chinese), but Fr. *Sirians* suggests Syrians. **venym of Tyrye,** *venym* (poison) is a mistranslation of Lat. *veneno* (dye). **22 claryouns,** war trumpets. **25 wodnesse,** frenzy. **26 say,** saw. **27 meedes,** profit. **31 Ethna,** volcano in Sicily. **33 dalf . . . gobetes,** dug, chunks. **II PROSE VI. 3 areysen,** exalt (hold valuable).

as heye as the hevene? The whiche dignites
and powers, yif they comen to any wycked 5
man, they don as grete damages and
destrucciouns as doth the flawmbe of the
mountaigne Ethna whan the flawmbe walweth
up; ne no deluge ne doth so crwel harmes.
Certes, the remenbreth wel, as I trowe, that 10
thilke dignite that men clepen the imperye
of consulers, the whyche that whilom was
bygynninge of fredom, yowre eldres coveiteden
to han don away that dignitee for the pride
of the consulers. And ryht for the same 15
pride, yowr eldres byforn that tyme hadden
don awey owt of the cyte of Rome the kynges
name *(that is to seyn, they nolde han no lengere
no kynge)*.

"But now, yif so be that dignites and 20
powers ben yeven to goode men—the
which thing is ful selde—what agreable thinges
is ther in tho dignites or powers but oonly the
goodnesse of foolkes that usen hem? And
therfor it is thus that honour ne comth nat 25
to vertu for cause of dignite, but, ayeinward,
honour comth to dignite for cause of vertu. But
whiche is thilke yowre dereworthe power, that
is so cleer and so requerable? O ye erthelyche bestes, considere ye nat over which 30
thinge that it semeth that ye han power?
Now yif thow saye a mous amonges other
muses, that chalenged to himself-ward ryht and
power over alle oother muses, how gret scorn
woldestow han of hit! *(Glosa. So fareth it by* 35
men; the body hath power over the body). For yif
thow looke wel upon the body of a wyht, what
thing shaltow fynde moore freele than is
mankynde—the whiche men wel ofte ben
slayn with bytinge of smale flyes, or elles 40
with the entringe of crepinge wormes into
the privetes of mannes body? But wher shal
man fynden any man that may excercen or
haunten any ryht upon another man, but

oonly on his body, or elles upon thinges 45
that ben lowere than the body, the which
I clepe fortunows possessyouns? Maystow ever
have any comaundement over a fre corage?
Maystow remwen fro the estat of his propre
reste a thowht that is clyvinge togidere in 50
himself by stidefast resoun? As whylom a
tyraunt wende to confownde a freman of
corage, and wende to constreyne him by
torment to maken him discoveren and
acusen folk that wysten of a conjuracioun 55
(which I clepe a confederacie) that was cast
ayeins this tyraunt, but this freman boot of
his owne tonge and cast it in the visage of
thilke woode tyraunt, so that the tormentes
that this tyraunt wende to han maked 60
matere of crwelte, this wise man maked it
matere of vertu.

"But what thing is it that a man may don
to another man, that he ne may receyven
the same thinge of oother folkes in himself 65
(or thus, what may a man don to folk that folkes
ne may don him the same)? I have herd told of
Busirides, that was wont to slen his gestes that
herberweden in his hows, and he was sleyn
himself of Ercules that was his gest. Regulus 70
hadde taken in batayle many men of Affryke
and cast hem into feteres, but sone after he
moste yeve hys handes to ben bounde with
the cheynes of hem that he hadde whylom
overcomen. Wenestow thanne that he be 75
myhty that hath no power to don a thinge,
that oothre ne may don in him that he doth
in oothre? And yit mooreover, yif it so were
that thise dignites or poweres hadden any
propre or natural goodnesse in hemself, 80
never nolden they comen to shrewes. For
contraryous thinges ne ben nat wont to ben
ifelawshiped togidere. Nature refuseth that
contrarious thinges ben ijoigned. And so, as
I am in certein that ryht wycked folk han 85

---

11 **imperye**, authority. 22 **thing . . . selde**, i.e., thing seldom happens. 28 **dereworthe**, beloved. 29 **cleer . . . requerable**, bright, desirable. 33 **chalenged**, claimed. 37 **wyht**, person (wight). 43–44 **excercen or haunten**, exercise or practice. 48 **fre corage**, i.e., a free mind. 50 **clyvinge**, clinging. 54 **discoveren**, reveal. 55 **conjuracioun**, conspiracy. 56 **cast**, planned. 57 **boot**, bit. 68 **Busirides**, King of Egypt, see MkT, *CT* VII.2103. 70 **Regulus**, Roman consul (c. 255 B.C.), who first defeated and then was captured by the Carthaginians. 81 **shrewes**, evil people.

dignites ofte tyme, than sheweth it wel that dignites and powers ne ben nat goode of her owne kinde, syn that they suffren hemself to cleven or joinen hem to shrewes. And certes, the same thing may I moost digneliche jugen and seyn of alle the yiftes of Fortune that moost plenteuously comen to shrewes. Of the which yiftes I trowe that it owhte ben considered that no man dowteth that he nis strong in whom he seth strengthe; and in whom that swyftnesse is, soth it is that he is swift. Also musike maketh musiciens, and phisike maketh phisiciens, and rethoryke rethoryens. For-why the nature of everything maketh his proprete, ne it nis nat entremedled with the effectes of the contraryous thinges; and, as of wil it chaseth owt thinges that to it ben contrarie. But certes, rychesse may not restreyne avarice unstaunched; ne power ne maketh nat a man myhty over himself, whiche that vicyous lustes holden destreyned with cheynes that ne mowen nat be unbownden. And dignites that ben yeven to shrewede folkes nat oonli ne maketh hem nat digne, but it sheweth rather al opynly that they ben unworthi and undigne. And why is it thus? Certes, for ye han joye to clepen thinges with false names that beren hem alle in the contrarye, the which names ben ful ofte reproeved by the effecte of the same thinges. So that thise ilke rychesse ne owhten nat by ryht to ben cleped rychesses; ne swich power ne owhte nat ben cleped power; ne swich dignite ne owhte nat ben cleped dignite. And at the laste, I may conclude the same thing of alle the yiftes of Fortune, in which ther nis nothinge to ben desired, ne that hath in himself naturel bownte, as it is ful wel iseene. For neyther they ne joignen hem nat alwey to goode men, ne maken hem alwey goode to whom that they ben ijoigned.

90
95
100
105
110
115
120
125

Metre VI. Novimus quantas dederit ruinas.

"We han wel knowen how many grete harmes and destruccyouns weren don by the Emperour Nero. He let brennen the cyte of Rome, and made slen the senatoures. And he, crwel, whilom slow his brother. And he was maked moyst with the blood of his moder *(that is to seyn, he let slen and slitten the body of his moder, to sen wher he was conseyved)*, and he looked on every halve upon her colde dede body ne no teere ne wette his face, but he was so hard-herted that he myhte ben domesman or juge of hir dede beaute. And natheles, yit governede this Nero by ceptre alle the poeples that Phebus the sonne may sen, cominge fram his owtereste arysinge til he hide his bemes under the wawes *(that is to seyn, he governed alle the poeples by sceptre inperial that the sonne goth abowte, from est to west)*. And ek this Nero governed by ceptre alle the poeples that ben under the colde sterres that hyhten Sevene Tryones *(this is to seyn, he governede alle the poeples that ben under the party of the north)*. And ek Nero governede alle the poeples that the vyolent wynd Nothus scorkleth, and baketh the brenning sandes by his drye hete *(that is to seyn, alle the poeples in the sowth)*. But yit ne myhte nat al his hye power torne the woodnesse of this wikked Nero. Allas, it is a grevous fortune, it is, as ofte as wykked swerd is joigned to crwel venym" *(that is to seyn, venimous crwelte to lordshippe)*.

5
10
15
20
25
30

Prose VII. Tum ego scis inquam.

Thanne seyde I thus: "Thow wost wel thyself that the coveytise of mortal thinges ne hadden never lordshipe of me; but I have wel desyred matere of thinges to done *(as who*

107 **destreyned,** restrained. 109 **shrewede,** evil. 115 **reproeved,** contradicted. II METRE VI. 21 **Sevene Tryones,** *Septem Triones,* the seven chief stars of Ursa Minor. IC *vii tyryones.* 25 **Nothus,** Notus, the south wind. **scorkleth,** scorches. 28 **torne . . . woodnesse,** turn (heal), insanity. II PROSE VII. 4 **matere . . . to done,** opportunity to do things.

seyth, I desyred to han matere of governaunce over 5
comunalitees) for vertu stille ne sholde nat
elden" (that is to seyn, that lest that, or he wax old
his vertu, that lay now ful stylle, ne sholde nat
perisse unexcercised in governaunce of comune,
for which men myghten speken or wryten of his 10
goode governement).

Philosophie. "For sothe," quod she, "and
that is a thing that may drawen to governaunce
swiche hertes as ben worthi and noble of hir
nature, but natheles hit may nat drawen or 15
tollen swiche hertes as ben ibrowht to the
fulle perfeccyoun of vertu, that is to seyn,
coveytyse of glorye and renoun to han wel
admynystred the comune thinges or don
gode desertes to profyt of the comune. For 20
se now and consydere how lytul and how
voyde of alle prys is thilke glorie. Certein thing
is, as thow hast lerned by the demonstracyoun
of astronomye, that al the envyroninge of
the erthe abowte ne halt but the resoun of a 25
prikke at regard of the gretnesse of hevene;
that is to seyn, that yif ther were maked com
parisoun of the erthe to the gretnesse of hevene,
men wolden jugen in al that the erthe ne
helde no space. Of the whyche litel regioun 30
of this worlde, the ferthe partye is enhabited
with lyvinge bestes that we knowen, as thou hast
thyself ylerned by Tholome that proveth it. And
yif thow haddest withdrawen and abated in
thy thowht fro thilke ferthe partye as 35
moche space as the see and the mareys
contenen and overgoon, and as moche space as
the regioun of drowhte overstrechcheth *(that*
is to seyn, sandes and desertes) wel unnethe
sholde ther dwellen a ryht streyt place to 40
the habitasyoun of men. And ye thanne,
that ben envyroned and closed within the
leste prykke of thilke prykke, thinken ye to
manyfesten yowre renoun and don yowre

name to ben born forth? But youre glorye, 45
that is so narwh and so streyte ithrongen
into so lytul bowndes, how mochel coveyteth
it in largesse and in gret dooinge? And also
sette this therto, that many a nacyoun,
diverse of tonge and of maneres and ek of 50
resoun of her lyvinge, ben enhabyted in the
clos of thilke lytul habytacule. To the whiche
naciouns, what for deficulte of weyes, and what
for dyversite of langages, and what for
defawte of unusage and entrecomuninge of 55
marchaundise, nat only the names of syngler
men ne may nat strecchen, but ek the fame of
cytes ne may nat strecchen. At the laste, certes,
in the tyme of Marchus Tulius, as himself
writ in his book that the renoun of the 60
comune of Rome ne hadde nat passed ne
clowmben over the mountaigne that hyhte
Caucasus, and yit was thilke tyme Roome wel
waxen and gretly redowted of the Parthes,
and ek of other folk enhabytinge abowte. 65
Sestow nat thanne how streyt and how
compressed is thilke glorye that ye travaylen
abowte to shewe and to multiplye? May
thanne the glorye of a singler Romayne
strechchen thyder as the fame of the name 70
of Rome may nat clymben ne passen? And
ek, seystow nat that the maneres of dyverse
folk and ek her lawes ben discordaunt among
hemself, so that thilke thinge that som men
jugen worthy of preysinge, oother folk 75
jugen that it is worthi of torment? And
therof comth it that thogh a man delyte him in
preysinge of his renoun, he may nat in no
wyse bryngen forth ne spreden his name
to many maner poeples. Therefor every 80
manere man owhte to ben apayed of his
glorye that is publyssed among his owne
neighbours. And thilke noble renoun shal ben
restreyned within the bowndes of o manere

6–7 vertu . . . elden, i.e., that my virtue should not grow old (weak). *lest:* IA *list.* **22–23 Certein . . . is,** it is certain. **26 at regard,**
compared to. **33 Tholome,** Ptolemy, the astronomer and geographer. **36 mareys,** marshes. **40 dwellen . . . streyt,** remain, narrow.
44 don, make. **46 ithrongen,** squeezed. **51 resoun,** i.e., mode. **54 I** *deficulte of langages.* **55 defawte of unusage,** i.e., lack of contact.
entrecomuninge, interchange. **59 Tulius,** Cicero, in the *Republic* 6.22. **61 comune,** republic. **64 redowted,** feared. **Parthes,**
Parthians (ancient Persians). **67 travaylen,** labor. **81 apayed,** satisfied.

folk. But how many a man that was ful 85
noble in his tyme hath the wrechched and
nedy foryetinge of wryteres put owt of mynde
and don awey! Al be it so that, certes, thilke
wrytinges profyten lytul, the whyche wrytinges long and derk elde doth awey, bothe 90
hem and ek her autours. But yow men
semeth to geten yow a perdurablete, whan ye
thinken that in tyme tocominge yowre fame
shal lasten. But natheles, yif thow wolt
maken comparysoun to the endeles spaces 95
of eternite, what thing hast thow by whiche
thow mayst rejoysen the of long lastinge of thy
name? For yif ther were maked comparysoun
of the abydinge of a moment to ten thowsand
wynter, for as mochel as bothe the spaces 100
ben ended, for yit hath the moment som
porcyoun of it, althowgh it lytul be. But
natheles, thilke selve nowmbre of yeres, and
ek as many yeres as therto may be multy-
plyed, ne may nat, certes, ben comparysoned 105
to the perdurablyte that is endeles, for of
things that han ende may be maked comparysoun, but of things that ben withowten
ende to things that han ende may be
maked no comparysoun. And forthi is it 110
that althowgh renoun of as longe tyme as
evere the lyst to thinken were thowt to the
regard of eternite, that is unstaunchable and
infynyt, it ne sholde nat oonly semen lytel,
but pleynlyche ryht nawht. But ye men, 115
certes, ne konne don nothinge aryght, but
yif it be for the audience of poeple and for
idil rumours, and ye forsaken the grete worthinesse of conscience and of vertu, and ye
seken your gerdouns of the smale wordes of 120
straunge folkes.

"Have now, her and understonde, in the
lyhtnesse of swych pride and veyne glorye how
a man scornede festyvaly and meryly swych
vanite. Whilom ther was a man that hadde 125

assayed with stryvinge wordes another man,
the whiche nat for usage of verray vertu but
for prowd veyne glorye had taken upon him
falsly the name of a philosophre. This
rather man that I spak of thowhte he wolde 130
assaye wher he thilke were a philosophre or
no—that is to seyn, yif that he wolde han
suffred lyhtly in pacience the wronges that
weren don unto him. This feynede philosophre took pacience a lytel whyle, and 135
whan he hadde receyved wordes of owtrage,
he as in stryvinge ayein and rejoysinge of
himself seyde at the laste ryht thus: 'Understondestow nat that I am a philosophre?'
That oother man answerde ayein ful bytingly 140
and seyde: 'I hadde wel understonden it yif
thow haddest holden thy tonge stille.' But what
is it to thise noble worthi men—for, certes,
of swyche foolke speke I—that seken
glorye with vertu? What is it?" quod 145
she. "What atteyneth fame to swyche foolk,
whan the body is resolved by the deth at the
laste? For yif it so be that men dyen in al *(that
is to seyn, body and sowle)*, the whyche thing
owre resoun deffendeth us to byleven, 150
thanne is ther no glorye in no wyse. For
what sholde thilke glorye ben whan he of whom
thilke glorye is seyd to be nis ryht nawht in no
wyse? And yif the sowle, whyche that hath
in itself science of goode werkes, unbownden 155
fro the prison of the erthe, wendeth frely to
the hevene, despyseth it nat thanne alle erthely
occupacioun, and being in hevene rejoyseth
that it is exempt fro alle erthely thinges?
(As who seith, thanne rekketh the sowle of no 160
glorye of renoun of this world).

Metre VII. Quicunque solam mente.

"Whoso that with overthrowinge thowght
oonly seketh glorye of fame, and weneth that it

87 nedy foryetinge, mistranslation of *scriptorum inops* (want of writers). **92 perdurablete,** perpetuity. **100** *the spaces:* Cx *tho spaces;* C *two spaces.* **112 the lyst,** you wished. **113 unstaunchable,** inexhaustible. **120 gerdouns,** rewards. **130 rather,** former. **131 wher,** whether. **137 stryvinge . . . rejoysinge,** i.e., as if triumphing. **146 What atteyneth fame,** what does fame attain. **150 deffendeth,** prohibits. **155 science,** knowledge. **156** *erthe:* I gloss *corporis.* **157** *it:* I gloss *anima.* **II METRE VII. 1 overthrowinge thowght,** overwhelming desire.

be sovereyn good, lat him looken upon the brode shewinge contreyes of hevene, and upon the streyte site of this erthe, and he shal ben ashamed of the encres of his name that may nat fulfylle the litel compas of the erthe. O what coveyten prowde folk to lyften up her nekkes in ydel in the dedly yok of this worlde? For althowgh that renoun ysprad, passinge to ferne poeples, goth by diverse tonges, and althowgh that grete howses or kynredes shynen with cler titles of honours, yit natheles deth despyseth alle heye glorye of fame, and deth wrappeth togydere the heye hevedes and the lowe, and maketh egal and evene the heyeste to the loweste. Wher wonen now the bones of trewe Fabrycius? What is now Brutus, or stierne Catoun? The thynne fame yit lastinge of hir ydel names is marked with a fewe lettrees; but althowgh that we han knowen the fayre wordes of the fames of hem, it is nat yeven to knowe hem that ben dede and consumpte. Liggeth thanne stille, al owtrely unknowable, ne fame ne maketh yow nat knowe. And yif ye wene to lyven the longere for wynde of yowre mortal name, whan o cruwel day shal ravysshe yow, thanne is the seconde deth dwellinge unto yow." (*Glose. The fyrst deth he clepeth heere departinge of the body and the sowle, and the seconde deth he clepeth as heere the stintinge of the renoun of fame.*)

Prose VIII. Set ne me inexorabile.

"But for as mochel as thow shalt nat wenen," quod she, "that I bere untretable batayle ayeins Fortune, yit somtyme it byfalleth that she, desseyvable, desserveth to han ryht good thank of men; and that is whan she hirself opneth and whan she descovereth hir frownt, and sheweth hir maneres. Peraventure yit understondestow nat that I shal seye. It is a wonder that I desyre to telle, and forthy unnethe may I unpleyten my sentense with wordes—for I deme that contraryous Fortune profiteth more to men than Fortune debonayre. For alwey whan Fortune semeth debonayre, than she lyeth falsly in byhetinge the hope of welefulnesse; but forsothe contraryous Fortune is alwey sothfast whan she sheweth hirself unstable thorw hir chaunginge. The amyable Fortune desseyveth folk; the contrarye Fortune techeth. The amyable Fortune byndeth with the beaute of false goodes the hertes of folk that usen hem; the contrarye Fortune unbyndeth hem by the knowinge of freele welefulnesse. The amyable Fortune maystow sen alwey wyndinge and flowinge, and ever mysknowinge of hirself; the contrarye Fortune is atempre and restreyned, and wys thorw excersyse of hir adversitee. At the laste, amyable Fortune with hir flateringes draweth myswandringe men fro the sovereyne good; the contraryous Fortune ledeth ofte folk ayein to soothfast goodes, and haleth hem ayein as with an hooke. Wenestow thanne that thow owhtest to leten this a lytel thing, that this aspre and horible Fortune hath discovered to the the thowhtes of thy trewe frendes? For-why this ilke Fortune hath departed and uncovered to the bothe the certeyn vysages and ek the dowtous visages of thy felawes. Whan she departed awey fro the, she took awey hir frendes and lafte the thyne frendes. Now whan thow were ryche and weleful, as the semede, with how mochel woldestow han bowht the fulle knowinge of

---

5 *site*: I *cyte*; Lat. *situm*. 9 **in ydel,** in vain. *A folk liften upon hire nekkes in ydel and dedly.* 12 Cx *houses of*. 18 **Fabrycius,** Roman consul (282 B.C.). 19 **Brutus,** Roman consul (509 B.C.). **Catoun,** Cato, Roman consul (195 B.C.). 24 **consumpte,** decayed (consumed). 27 **wynde,** breath. **II PROSE VIII. 2 untretable,** irreconcilable. **4 desseyvable,** one who deceives. **6 hirself opneth,** opens herself. **6–7 descovereth hir frownt,** reveals her face. **9 wonder,** a marvel. **10 unnethe . . . unpleyten,** scarcely, untangle. **15 byhetinge,** promising. **23 freele,** frail. **25 wyndinge,** windy. **26 mysknowinge,** ignorant. **30 myswandringe,** wandering. **33 haleth hem ayein,** i.e., hauls them back. **34 to leten,** to hinder (stop). **36 discovered,** revealed. **39 certeyn . . . dowtous,** trustworthy, untrustworthy.

this *(that is to seyn, the knowinge of thy verray* 45
freendes)? Now pleyne the nat thanne of
rychesse ilorn, syn thow hast fownden the moste
precyous kynde of rychesses, that is to seyn, thy
verray frendes.

Metre VIII. Quod mundus stabili fide.

"That the world with stable feith varieth
acordable chaunginges; that the contraryous
qualite of elementes holden among hemself
aliaunce perdurable; that Phebus the
sonne with his goldene chariet bryngeth 5
forth the rosene day; that the mone hath
commaundement over the nyhtes, whiche
nyhtes Hesperus the eve sterre hath browht;
that the se, gredy to flowen, constreyneth

with a certeyn ende his floodes, so that it is 10
nat leveful to strechche his brode termes or
bowndes upon the erthes *(that is to seyn, to
covere alle the erthe)*—al this acordaunce of
thinges is bownden with Loove, that
governeth erthe and see, and hath also 15
comaundementes to the hevenes. And yif
this Loove slakede the brydeles, alle thinges
that now loven hem togederes wolden maken a
batayle contynuely, and stryven to fordoon
the fasoun of this worlde, the which they 20
now leden in acordable feith by fayre
moevinges. This Loove halt togideres poeples
joigned with an hooly bond, and knytteth
sacrement of maryages of chaste looves; and
Love enditeth lawes to trewe felawes. O 25
weleful were mankynde yif thilke Love that
governeth hevene governed yowre corages!"

Explicit liber secundus.

BOOK III

Incipit liber tercius.

Prose I. Iam cantum illa finierat.

By this she hadde ended hir songe, whan the
sweetnesse of hir ditee hadde thorw-perced me
that was desirous of herkninge, and I astoned
hadde yit streyhte myn eres *(that is to seyn,
to herkne the bet what she wolde seye)*, so that a 5
litel hereafter I seyde thus: "Oh thow that
art sovereyn comfort of angwissous corages, so
thow hast remounted and norysshed me with
the weyhte of thy sentenses and with delit
of thy synginge so that I trowe nat now 10
that I be unparygal to the strokes of

Fortune *(as who seyth, I dar wel now suffren al the
assautes of Fortune, and wel deffende me fro hir)*. And
tho remedies whyche that thow seydest
her-byforn that weren ryht sharpe, nat 15
oonly that I am nat agrysen of hem now,
but I, desirous of heringe, axe gretely to heren
the remedyes."

Than seyde she thus: "That feelede I ful
wel," quod she, "whan that thow, ententyf 20
and stylle, ravysshedest my wordes. And I
abood til that thow haddest swych habyte of thy
thowght as thow hast now, or elles tyl that I
myself had maked to the the same habyt,

---

47 **ilorn**, lost. **II METRE VIII. 1–2 varieth acordable chaunginges**, varies (alternates) with harmonies. This metre is adapted in
TC III.1744–64. **17 slakede**, slacked. **19–20 fordoon the fasoun**, destroy the conduct (fashion). **25 enditeth . . . felawes**, prescribes,
companions. **III PROSE I. 4 streyhte**, stretched. **8 remounted**, strengthened. **11 unparygal**, unequal. **16 agrysen**, afraid. **22
abood**, waited.

which that is a moore verray thing. And 25
certes, the remenaunt of thinges that ben
yit to seye ben swyche that fyrst whan men
tasten hem they ben bytinge, but whan they ben
receyved withinne a whyht, than ben they
swete. But for thow seyst that thow art so 30
desirous to herkne hem, with how gret
brenninge woldesthow glowen yif thou wystest
whyder I wol leden the!"

"Whyder is that?" quod I.

"To thilke verray welefulnesse," quod 35
she, "of whyche thyn herte dremeth. But
for as moche as thy syhte is ocupied and
distorbed by imagynasyoun of erthely thinges,
thow mayst nat yit sen thilke selve welefulnesse." 40

"Do," quod I, "and shewe me what is
thilke verray welefulnesse, I preye thee,
withowte taryinge."

"That wole I gladly don," quod she, "for
the cause of the. But I wol fyrst marken the 45
by wordes, and I wol enforcen me to
enformen the thilke false cause of blisfulnesse
that thow more knowest, so that whan thow
hast fully byholden thilke false goodes and
torned thyne eyen to that oother syde, thow 50
mowe knowe the clernesse of verray
blysfulnesse.

Metre I. Qui serere ingenuum volet agrum.

"Whoso wole sowe a feeld plentiuous, lat him
fyrst delyvere it fro thornes and kerve asunder
with his hook the bushes and the fern so that the
korn may comen hevy of eres and of
greynes. Hony is the more swete yif mowthes 5
han fyrst tasted savoures that ben wyckid.
The sterres shynen more agreablely whan the
wynd Nothus leteth his plowngy blastes; and
after that Lucifere the day sterre hath
chased awey the dirke nyht, the day the 10
fayrere ledeth the rosene hors of the sonne.

And ryht so thow, byholdinge fyrst the false
goodes, bygyn to withdrawen thy nekke fro the
yok of erthely affecciouns; and afterward
the verray goodes shollen entren into thy 15
corage."

Prose II. Tum defixo paululum visu.

Tho fastnede she a lytul the syhte of hir eyen,
and withdrowh hir ryht as it were into the
streyte sete of hir thowht, and bygan to speke
ryht thus: "Alle the cures," quod she, "of
mortal foolk, whiche that travaylen hem in 5
many manere studies, goon certes by
diverse weyes, but natheles they enforsen hem
alle to comen oonly to oon ende of blysfulnesse.
And blysfulnesse is swyche a good that
whoso that hath geten it, he ne may over 10
that nothing moore desyre. And this thing
is forsothe the sovereyn good that conteyneth in
hymself alle manere goodes, to the whyche good
yif ther faylede anything, it myhte nat ben
cleped sovereyn good, for thanne were ther 15
som good, owt of this ilke sovereyn good,
that myhte ben desyred. Now is it clere and
certein thanne, that blysfulnesse is a perfyt
estat by the congregasyoun of alle goodes;
the whyche blysfulnesse, as I have seyd, alle 20
mortal foolk enforsen hem to geten by
dyverse weyes. For-why the coveytise of verray
good is naturelly yplaunted in the hertes of men,
but the myswandringe errour mysledeth
hem into false goodes. Of the whyche men, 25
som of hem wenen that sovereyn good be
to lyven withowte nede of anything, and
travaylen hem to be haboundaunt of rychesses.
And som oother men demen that sovereyn
good be for to ben ryht digne of reverence, 30
and enforcen hem to ben reverenced among
hir neyghbours by the honours that they han
ygeten. And some folk ther ben that holden
that ryht heyh power be sovereyn good, and

---

29 whyht, person (wight). **36** I *whyche thynge*. **38** I *herthely*. **43** I *withhowte*. **45 marken,** declare (indicate). **III METRE I. 3** *bushes*: I
bosses. **8 Nothus leteth his plowngy,** the south wind ceases its stormy. **11 rosene hors,** ruddy horse. **III PROSE II. 3 streyte sete,**
narrow (deep) seat: I *cyte*. **8 blysfulnesse,** felicity (supreme happiness). **12 Cx** *so sovereyn*. **21 enforsen hem,** try. **22 verray:** Cx *every*.
28 travaylen, strive.

enforcen hem for to regnen, or elles to 35
joignen hem to hem that regnen. And it
semeth to some oother foolk that noblesse of
renoun be the sovereyn good, and hasten hem
to geten gloryous name by the arts of werre
and of pees. And many folk mesuren and 40
gessen that sovereyn good be joye and
gladnesse, and wenen that it be ryht blysful
thyng to plowngen hem in voluptuous delit.
And ther ben folk that entrechaungen the
causes and the endes of thyse forseyde 45
goodes, as they that desyren rychesses to han
power and delytes; or elles they desyren power
for to han moneye, or for cause of renoun. In
thise thinges, and in swyche oothre thynges,
is torned alle the entencioun of desyringes 50
and of werkes of men, as thus, noblesse and
favoure of poeple, whyche that yeveth to men,
as it semeth hem, a manere clernesse of renoun;
and wyf and chyldren, that men desyren for
cause of delit and of merynesse. But 55
forsothe, frendes ne sholden nat be rekned
among the godes of fortune, but of vertu, for yt
ys a ful hooly manere thyng. Alle thise oothre
thinges, forsothe, ben taken for cause of
power or elles for cause of delit. Certes, now 60
am I redy to referren the goodes of the body
to thise forseyde thinges aboven. For it semeth
that strengthe and gretnesse of body yeven
power and worthynesse, and that beaute
and sweftnesse yeven noblesses and glorye 65
of renoun, and hele of body semeth yeven
delit. In alle thise thinges it semeth oonly that
blysfulnesse is desired. For-why thilke thing
that every man desyreth most over alle
thinges, he demeth that yt be the sovereyn 70
good. But I have deffyned that blysfulnesse
is the sovereyn good, for whych every whyht
demeth that thilke estat that he desyreth over
alle thinges that it be blysfulnesse.

"Now hast thow thanne byforn thyn eyen 75
almest al the purposed forme of the welefulnesse of mankynde, that is to seyn, rychesses,
honours, power, and glorye, and delits. The
whiche delit oonly consyderede Epicurus,
and juged and establysshed that delit is the 80
sovereyn good; for as moche as alle oothre
thinges, as him thowhte, byrefte awey joye and
myrthe fram the herte. But I retorne ayein to
the studies of men, of whiche men the
corage alwey reherseth and seketh the 85
sovereyn good, al be it so that it be with
a dirked memorye; but he not by whiche
paath, ryht as a dronken man not nat by
whiche paath he may retorne him to his
hows. Semeth it thanne that foolk foleyen 90
and erren that enforcen hem to have nede
of nothing? Certes, ther nis non oother thyng
that may so wel performe blysfulnesse as an
estat plentyous of alle goodes, that ne hath
nede of non oother thing, but that it is 95
suffysaunt of hymself unto hymself. And
foleyen swyche folk, thanne, that wenen that
thilke thing that is ryht good, that it be ek ryht
worthy of honour and of reverence? Certes,
nay. For that thing nys neyther foul ne 100
worthy to ben despised that welneyh alle
the entencyoun of mortal foolk travaylen for to
geten yt. And powere, owhte nat that ek to ben
rekened amonges goodes? What elles? For
it is nat to wene that thilke thyng that is 105
most worthy of alle thinges be feble and
withowte strengthe. And cleernesse of renoun,
owhte that to ben despised? Certes, ther may
no man forsake that alle thyng that is ryht
excellent and noble, that it ne semeth to ben 110
ryht cleer and renomed. For certes, it nedeth
nat to seye that blysfulnesse be nat angwyssous
ne drery, ne subgyd to grevaunces ne to sorwes,
syn that in ryht lytel thynges folk seken to
have and to usen that may delyten hem. 115
Certes, thise ben the thinges that men
wolen and desyren to geten. And for this cause
desyren they rychesses, dignites, regnes, glorye,
and delices. For therby wenen they to han
suffysaunse, honour, power, renoun, and 120

gladnesse. Than is it good that men seken thus by so many diverse studies. In whiche desyr it may lyghtly ben shewed how gret is the strengthe of nature, for how so that men han diverse sentences and discordinge, 125 allgates men acorden alle in lovinge the ende of good.

Metre II. Quantas rerum flectat.

"It lyketh me to shewe by subtil song, with slakke and delitable soun of strenges, how that Nature, myhty, enclyneth and flitteth the governementes of thinges, and by whyche lawes she, purveyable, kepeth the grete 5 world, and how she, byndinge, restreyneth alle thinges by a bonde that may nat ben unbownde. Al be it so that the lyouns of the contre of Pene beren the fayre chaynes, and taken metes of the handes of folk that yeven 10 it hem, and dreden her sturdy maystres of whiche they ben wont to suffren betinges. Yif that her horyble mowthes ben bybled *(that is to seyn, of bestes devowred)*, her corage of tyme passed, that hath ben ydel and rested, 15 repeyreth ayein, and they roren grevously, and remembren on her nature, and slaken her nekkes fram hir chaynes unbownde; and her mayster, fyrst to-torn with blody toth, assayeth the wode wrathes of hem *(this is to 20 seyn, they freten hir mayster)*. And the jangelinge bryd that syngeth on the heye braunches *(that is to seyn, in the wode)* and after is enclosed in a streyht cage althowh that the pleyinge bysynesse of men yeveth hem 25 honyede drynkes and large metes with swete studye, yit natheles yif thylke bryd, skyppinge owt of hir streyte cage, seth the agreables shadewes of the wodes, she defowleth with hir feet hir metes ishad, and 30

seketh mowrninge oonly the wode, and twitereth desyringe the wode with hir swete voys. The yerde of a tre that is haled adown by myhty strengthe boweth redyly the crop adown, but yif that the hand of hym that it 35 bent lat it goon ayein, anon the crop loketh upryht to hevene. The sonne Phebus that falleth at even in the westrene wawes retorneth ayein eftsones his carte by pryve paath thereas it is wont aryse. Alle thinges seken 40 ayein to her propre cours, and alle thinges rejoysen hem of her retorninge ayein to her nature. Ne non ordynaunce nis bytaken to thinges but that that hath joyned the endinge to the bygynninge and hath maked 45 the cours of itself stable *(that it chaungeth nat from his propre kynde)*.

Prose III. Vos quoque o terrena animalia.

"Certes also ye men, that ben erthelyche beestes, dremen alwey yowre bygynninge, althowh it be with a thynne imagynacyoun; and by a maner thowghte, al be it nat clerly ne perfytly, ye loken fram afer to 5 thylke verray fyn of blysfulnesse. And therfore naturel entencyoun ledeth yow to thylke verray good, but many maner errours mystorneth yow therfro. Considere now yif that by thylke thinges by whiche a man 10 weneth to geten him blysfulnesse, yif that he may comen to thylke ende that he weneth to come by nature. For yif that moneye or honours or thyse oother forseyde thinges bryngen to men swych a thyng that no good ne fayle 15 hem ne semeth fayle, certes than wole I graunte that they ben maked blysful by thylke thinges that they han geten. But yif so be that thylke thynges ne mowen nat performen that they byheten, and that ther be defaute 20 of manye goodes, sheweth it nat thanne

125 **sentences,** opinions. **III METRE II. 2 slakke,** soft. **strenges,** strings. **3 flitteth,** changes (shifts). **5 purveyable,** with provident care. **9 Pene,** in North Africa. **13 bybled,** covered with blood. **21** *freten,* eat (cf. German distinction between *essen* and *fressen*). **22 jangelinge,** noisy. **25** *pleyinge:* I *pleynynge;* A *pleiyng;* Lat. *ludens.* **30 ishad,** shed (distributed, artificially cut up?). **33 yerde,** top (sapling). **43 non ordynaunce,** no law. **III PROSE III. 2 dremen alwey,** dream always about. **20 byheten,** promise.

clerly that fals beaute of blysfulnesse is knowen and ataynt in thylke thynges? Fyrst and forward thow thyself, that haddest habundaunces of rychesses nat long agoon, I axe yif that, in the habundaunce of alle thylke richesses, thow were never angwissous or sory in thy corage of any wrong or grevaunce that bytydde the on any syde?"

"Certes," quod I, "it ne remembreth me nat that evere I was so free of my thowht that I ne was alwey in angwyssh of somwhat."

"And was nat that," quod she, "for that the lacked somwhat that thow noldest nat han lacked, or elles thow haddest that thow noldest nat han had?"

"Ryht so is it," quod I.

"Thanne desiredest thow the presence of that oon and the absence of that oother?"

"I graunte wel," quod I.

"Forsothe," quod she, "than nedeth ther somwhat that every man desireth?"

"Ye, ther nedeth," quod I.

"Certes," quod she, "and he that hath lacke or nede of awht nis nat in every wey suffysaunte to hymself?"

"No," quod I.

"And thow," quod she, "in al the plente of thy rychesses haddest thilke lacke of suffisaunse?"

"What elles?" quod I.

"Thanne may nat rychesses maken that a man nis nedy, ne that he be suffisaunt to hymself; and yit that was it that they byhyhten, as it semeth. And ek certes I trowe that thys be gretly to consydere, that moneye ne hath nat in his owne kynde that it ne may ben bynomen of hem that han it, mawgre hem."

"I byknowe it wel," quod I.

"Why sholdesthow nat byknowen it," quod she, "whan every day the strengere folk bynemen it fro the feblere, mawgre hem? For whennes comen elles alle thyse foreyne compleyntes or quereles of pletynges but

for that men axen ayein here moneye that hath ben bynomen hem by force or by gyle, and alwey mawgre hem?"

"Right so is it," quod I.

"Than," quod she, "hath a man nede to seken him foreyne help by whyche he may deffende his moneye?"

"Who may sey nay?" quod I.

"Certes," quod she, "and him nedede non help yif he ne hadde no moneye that he myhte lese."

"That is dowteles," quod I.

"Than is this thing torned into the contrarye," quod she. "For richesses, that men wenen sholde make suffisaunce, they maken a man rather han nede of foreyne help. Whych is the manere or the gyse," quod she, "that rychesse may dryve awey nede? Ryche foolk, may they neyther han hunger ne thurst? Thyse ryche men, may they fele no coold on her lymes on wynter? But thow wolt answeren that ryche men han ynow wherwith they may staunchen her honger, slaken her thurst, and don awey coold. In thys wyse may nede be counforted by rychesses, but certes nede ne may nat al utrely ben don awey. For thowgh this nede, that is alwey gapinge and gredy, be fulfyld with rychesses and axe anything, yit dwelleth thanne a nede that myhte be fulfyld. I holde me stille and telle nat how that lytel thyng suffiseth to nature, but certes to averyce ynowh ne suffiseth nothing. For syn that rychesses ne may nat al doon awey nede, but rychesses maken nede, what may it thanne be that ye wenen that richesses mowen yeven yow suffisaunce?"

Metre III. Quamvis fluente dives auri gurgite.

"Al were it so that a ryche coveytous man hadde a ryver fletinge al of gold, yit sholde it never staunchen his coveytyse; and thow he hadde his nekke ycharged with precyous

---

23 **ataynt,** apprehended (attained). 34 **noldest,** did not wish. 57–58 **kynde . . . bynomen,** i.e., nothing in its nature prevents it from being taken. 63-64 **foreyne compleyntes,** public appeals. 97 *awey:* I *alwey.* III METRE III. 4 **ycharged,** loaded.

stones of the Rede See, and thow he do ere   5
his feeldes plentyuous with an hundred
oxen, never ne shal his bytinge bysynesse
forleten him whyl he leveth, ne the lyhte
rychesses ne shol nat beren him compaignie
whan he is ded.   10

Prose IV. Set dignitates honorabilem.

"But dignitees, to whom they ben comen,
maken they him honorable and reverent? Han
they nat so gret strengthe that they may putte
vertuus in the hertes of foolk that usen the
lordshippes of hem? Or elles may they don   5
awey the vyces? Certes, they ne be nat wont
to don awey wykkednesse, but they ben wont
rather shewen wykkednesse. And therof comth
it that I have ryht gret desdaigne that
dignites ben yeven ofte to wykked men. For   10
which thyng Catullus cleped (*a consul of
Rome, that hyhte*) Nomyus, 'postum' or 'boch'
(*as who seyth, he cleped him a congregasyoun of vyces
in his brest, as a postum is ful of corupsyoun*), al
were this Nomyus set in a chayre of dignite.   15
Sesthow nat thanne how gret vilenye
dignitees don to wykked men? Certes, unworthynesse of wykked men sholde be the lasse
isene yif they nere renomed of none
honours. Certes, thow thyself ne myhtest   20
nat ben browht with as manye perils as
thou myhtest suffren that thow woldest beren
the magestrat with Decorat (*that is to seyn, that
for no peril that myhte befallen the by offense of
the Kyng Theodoryke thow noldest nat be   25
felawe in governaunce with Decorat*) whan
thou saye that he hadde wykked corage of a
lykerous shrewe and of an acusor. Ne I ne may
nat for swyche honours jugen hem worthy

of reverence that I deme and holde   30
unworthy to han thylke same honours. Now
yif thow saye a man that were fulfild of wysdom,
certes thow ne myhtest nat deme that he were
unworthy to the honour or elles to the
wysdom of which he is fulfyld?"   35
"No," quod I.
"Certes, dignites," quod she, "apertienen
proprely to vertu, and vertu transporteth
dignite anon to thilke man to whych she
hirself is conjoigned. And for as moche as   40
honours of poeple ne may nat maken folk
digne of honour, it is wel seyn clerly that they
ne han no propre beaute of dignite. And yit
men owhten taken mor heed in thys. For
yif it so be that a wykked whyht be so   45
mochel the fowlere and the moore owtcast
that he is despised of most folk, so as dignite ne
may nat maken shrewes digne of reverence, the
whych shrewes dignete sheweth to moche
foolk, thanne maketh dignete shrewes rather   50
so moche more despised than preysed; and
forsothe nat unpunisshed (*that is for to seyn, that
shrewes revengen hem ayeinward upon dignetes*), for
they yilden ayein to dignetes as gret
gerdoun, whan they byspotten and defowlen   55
dignetes with hire vylenie. And for as
mochel as thow mowe knowe that thilke verray
reverence ne may nat comen by thyse shadwy
transitorye dignetes, undyrstond now thus:
yif that a man hadde used and had many   60
maner dignitees of consules, and were
comen peraventure amonges straunge nacyouns,
sholde thilke honour maken him worshipful and
redowted of straunge foolk? Certes, yif that
honour of poeple were a naturel yift to   65
dignites, it ne myhte never cesen nowher
amonges no manere foolk to don his offyce,

8 lyhte, unstable (light). **III PROSE IV. 11 Catullus,** Roman poet (1st cent. B.C.), *Carmen* 52. **12 postum . . . boch,** abscess, botch (pustule). **19 renomed,** renowned. **21–22 browht with . . . perils,** etc., i.e., could any threats have persuaded you to share office with Decorat (a Roman official, c. 508 B.C.)? **28 lykerous shrewe,** lecherous villain. **29 swyche honours,** i.e., honors do not make worthy those unworthy of such honors. **32 fulfild,** filled (rich in). **33 deme,** judge. **44–52** A *For if it so be that he that is most outcast that most folk dispisen, or as dignite ne may not maken shrewes worthi of no reverences, than make the dignites shrewes more despised than preised, the whiche shrewes dignite scheweth to moche folk, and forsothe nat unpunised.* . . . **49–50 moche foolk,** many people. **54–55 as gret gerdoun,** as great a reward. **60 many,** i.e., many times the dignity of a Roman consul. **64 redowted,** feared.

ryht as fyre in every contre ne stynteth nat to eschaufen and to ben hoot. But for as mochel as for to ben holden honourable or reverent ne cometh nat to foolk of her propre strengthe of nature, but oonly of the false opynioun of foolk *(that is to seyn, that wenen that dignetes maken foolk digne of honour)*, anon therfore, whan that they comen thereas folk ne knowen nat thylke dignites, her honours vanesshen awey, and that anon. But that is amonges straunge folk, maysthow seyn. Ne amonges hem ther they weren born ne duren nat thylke dignitees alwey? Certes, the dignite of the provostrye of Rome was whylom a gret power; now is it nothing but an idel name, and the rente of the senatorye a gret charge. And yif a whyht whylom hadde the office to taken heede to the vytayles of the poeple, as of corn and oother thynges, he was holden amonges grete. But what thyng is now more owtcast than thylke provostrye? And as I have seyd a lytel her-byforn, that thylke thyng that hath no propre beaute of hymself receyveth somtyme prys and shyninge and somtyme leseth it by the opinioun of usaunces. Now yif that dignitees thanne ne mowen nat maken foolk digne of reverence, and yif that dignites wexen fowle of her wylle by the felthe of shrewes, and yif that dignites lesen her shyninge by chaunginge of tymes, and yif they wexen fowle by estymacyoun of poeple, what is it that they han in hemself of beaute that owhte ben desyred? *(As who seyth, non)*. Thanne ne mowen they yeven no beaute of dignete to non oother.

Metre IV. Quamvis se Tyrio superbus ostro.

"Al be it so that the prowde Nero, with alle his woode luxurie, kembde him and aparaylede him with fayre purpres of Tyrye, and with whyte perles, algates yit throf he hateful to alle foolk *(this is to seyn, that al was he behated of alle folk, yit this wycked Nero hadde gret lordshippe)*, and yaf whylom to the reverents senatours the unworshipful setes of dignitees. *(Unworshipful setes he clepeth here, for that Nero, that was so wykked, yaf tho dignites.)* Whoso wolde thanne resonably wenen that blysfulnesse were in swyche honours as ben yeven by vycyous shrewes?

Prose V. An vero regna.

"But regnes and famyliarites of kynges, may they maken a man to ben myhty? How elles, whan her blysfulnesse dureth perpetualy? But certes, the olde age of tyme passed, and ek of present tyme now, is ful of ensaunpyles how that kynges ben chaunged into wrechchednesse owt of her welefulnesse. O a noble thing and a cleer thing is power, that is nat fownden myhty to kepen itself! And yif that power of reaumes be auctour and makere of blysfulnesse, yif thilke power lacketh on any syde amenuseth it nat thilke blysfulnesse and bryngeth in wrechchednesse? But yit al be it so that the reaumes of mankynde strechchen brode, yit mot ther nede ben moche foolk over whyche that every kyng ne hath no lordshipe ne comaundement. And certes, upon thilke side that power fayleth, whych that maketh foolk blysful, ryht on that same syde none-power entreth undernethe that maketh hem wrechches. In this manere thanne moten kynges han more porcioun of wrechchednesse than of welefulnesse. A tyraunt, that was kyng of Sysile, that hadde assayed the peril of his estat shewede by symylitude the dredes of reaumes by gastnesse of a swerd that heng over

---

81 provostrye, being provost (business manager). **83 rente,** i.e., the cost of the office is a great burden on the Senate. **93 usaunces,** usage (public whim). **III METRE IV. 4 algates,** nevertheless. **III PROSE V. 9 kepen,** protect. **12 amenuseth,** diminish. **20 none-power,** powerlessness. C *noun-power.* **24 Sysile,** Dionysius, King of Sicily, who suspended a sword over the head of his favorite, Damocles. **25 assayed,** recognized. **27 gastnesse,** terror.

the heved of his famylier. What thyng is thanne this power, that may nat doon awey the bytinges of bysynesse ne eschue the prikkes 30 of drede? And certes, yit wolden they lyven in sikernesse, but they may nat; and yit they gloryfye hem in her power. Holdest thow thanne that thylke man be myhty that thow seyst that he wolde don that he may nat 35 doon? And holdest thou thanne him a myhty man that hath envyrownede his sydes with men of armes or serjaunts, and dredeth more hem that he maketh agast than they dreden him, and that is put in the handes 40 of his servaunts for he sholde seme myhty? But of famylieres or servaunts of kynges what sholde I telle the anything, syn that I myself have shewed the that reames hemself ben ful of gret feblesse? The whyche famylieres, 45 certes, the ryal power of kynges in hool estat and in estat abated ful ofte throweth adown. Nero constreynede Senek, his famylier and his mayster, to chesen on what deeth he wolde deyen. Antonius comaundede 50 that knyghtes slowen with her swerdes Papynian his famylier, which Papynian that hadde ben longe tyme ful myghty amonges hem of the court. And yit certes they wolden bothe han renounced her power; of whyche 55 two Senecke enforcede him to yeven to Nero his richesses, and also to han gon into solytarye exil. But whan the grete weyhte *(that is to seyn, of lordes power or of fortune)* draweth hem that sholen falle, neyther of hem ne 60 myhte do that he wolde. What thing is thanne thilke power, that thowh men han it, yit they ben agast, and whanne thow woldest han it, thow nart nat siker; and yif thow woldest forleten it, thow mayst nat eschuen 65 it? But wheyther swyche men ben frendes at nede, as ben conseyled by fortune and nat by vertu? Certes, swyche foolk as weleful fortune maketh freendes, contraryous fortune

maketh hem enemys. And what pestylence 70 is moore myhty for to anoye a wyht than a famylier enemy?

Metre V. Qui se volet esse potentem.

"Whoso wole be myhty, he mot daunten his crwel corage, ne putte nat his nekke, overcomen, under the fowle reynes of lecherye. For al be it so that thy lordshype strechche so fer that the contre of Ynde quaketh at thy 5 comaundements or at thy lawes, and that the last ile in the see that hyhte Tyle be thral to the, yit yif thou mayst nat putten awey thy fowle dyrke desyrs, and dryven owt fro thee wrechched complayntes, certes, it nis no 10 powere that thow hast.

Prose VI. Gloria vero quam fallax.

"But glorye, how deceyvable and how fowl is it ofte! For whych thyng nat unskylfully a tragedyen *(that is to seyn, a makere of ditees that hyhten tragedies)* cryde and seyde: 'O glorye, glorye,' quod he, 'thow nart nothing elles 5 to thowsandes of foolkes but a gret swellere of eres!' For manye han had ful gret renoun by the false opynioun of the poeple, and what thyng may ben thowht fowlere than swyche preysinge? For thylke foolk that ben 10 preysed falsly, they moten nedes han shame of her preysinges. And yif that foolk han geten hem thonk or preysinge by her desertes, what thyng hath thylke prys eched or encresed to the conscience of wyse folk, that 15 mesuren her good nat by the rumour of the poeple but by the sothfastnesse of conscience? And yif it seme a fayr thyng a man to han encresed and spred his name, than folweth it that it is demed to ben a fowl thing yif it 20 ne be isprad and encresed. But, as I seyde a lytul her-biforn, that syn ther mot nedes ben

---

56 **enforcede him,** tried. 58 **weyhte,** weight. 63 **agast,** afraid. 65 **forleten,** surrender. 66 **But wheyther,** i.e., But are. **III METRE V. 1 daunten,** overcome. **2 crwel corage,** unruly spirit. **7 Tyle,** *ultima Thule,* the northernmost place in the world according to ancient geographers (Iceland?). **III PROSE VI. 14 eched,** increased.

many foolk to whyche foolk the renoun of a man ne may nat comen, it befalleth that he that thow wenest be glorious and renomed 25 semeth in the nexte partie of the erthes to ben withowte glorye and withowte renoun.

"And certes, amonges thyse thynges I ne trowe nat that the prys and grace of the poeple nis neyther worthy to ben remen- 30 bred, ne cometh of wyse jugement, ne is ferme perdurably. But now, of thys name of gentellesse, what man is it that ne may wel sen how veyn and how flyttinge a thyng it is? For yif the name of gentellesse be refferred 35 to renoun and clernesse of lynage, thanne is gentyl name but a foreyne thyng *(that is to seyn, to hem that gloryfien hem of her lynage)*. For it semeth that gentellesse be a maner preysinge that comth of the deserte of auncestres. And 40 yif preysinge maketh gentilesse, thanne moten they nedes be gentyl that ben preysed. For which thing it folueth that yif thow ne have no gentellesse of thyself *(that is to seyn, preyse that comth of thy deserte)*, foreyne gentyllesse 45 ne maketh the nat gentyl. But certes, yif ther be any good in gentyllesse, I trowe it be aloonly this, that it semeth as that a maner necessitee be inposed to gentel men for that they ne sholden nat owtrayen or forlyven 50 fro the vertuus of her noble kynrede.

Metre VI. Omne hominum genus in terris.

"Al the lynage of men that ben in erthe ben of semblable byrthe. On allone is fader of thynges. On allone mynystreth alle thinges. He yaf to the sonne his beemes, he yaf to the moene hir hornes, he yaf the men to the 5 erthe, he yaf the sterres to the hevene. He encloseth with menbres the sowles that comen fram his hye sete. Thanne comen alle mortal folk of noble sede. Why noysen ye or bosten of yowre eldres, for yif thow loke yowr 10

bygynninge, and God yowr auctor and yowre makere, thanne nis ther no forlyved wyht, but yif he norysse his corage unto vyces and forlete his propre burthe.

Prose VII. Quid autem de corporis.

"But what shal I seye of delites of body, of whyche delites the desyringes ben ful of angwyssh, and the fulfyllinges of hem ben ful of penaunce? How gret sykenesse and how gret soruwes unsufferable, ryht as a manere 5 frut of wyckednesse, ben thilke delytes wont to bryngen to the bodyes of foolk that usen hem! Of whyche delytes I not what joye may ben had of her moevinge. But thys wot I wel, that whosoever wole remenbren him of his 10 luxures, he shal wel understonde that the yssues of delites ben sorwful and sorye. And yif thylke delites mowen maken folk blysful, than by the same cause moten thyse bestes ben cleped blysful, of whyche bestes al the 15 entencyoun hasteth to fulfylle her bodyly jolite. And the gladnesse of wyf and chyldren were an honest thyng, but it hath ben seyd that it is over mochel ayeins kynde that chyldren han ben fownden tormentours to her 20 fadres—I nat how manye—of whyche chyldren how bytinge is every condycioun it nedeth nat to tellen it the that hast or thus tyme assayed it, and art yit now angwyssous. In this approve I the sentence of my disciple 25 Eurydyppys, that seyde that he that hath no chyldren is weleful by infortune.

Metre VII. Habet hoc voluptas.

"Every delit hath this, that it anguisseth hem with prikkes that usen it. It resembleth to thise flyenge flyes that we clepen ben, that after he hath shad his agreable honyes, he fleth awey and styngeth the hertes of hem that 5 ben ysmyte with bytinge overlonge holdinge.

---

36 **clernesse**, purity. 50 **owtrayen . . . forlyven**, stray from (outrage), dishonor (live down). **III METRE VI. 3 mynystreth**, governs. This metre is echoed in WBT, *CT* iv.1109ff., and "Moral Balade" (short poem 12). 12 **forlyved**, dishonorable. C *forlyved wyght or ongentil*. **III PROSE VII. 1ff.** *delites*: AC *delices*; Cx *delites* (t and c are easily confused in the MSS). 17 **gladnesse of**, pleasure in. 22 **bytinge**, painful. 23 **or thus**, before this. 26 **Eurydyppys**, Euripides; the reference is to *Andromache*, 418–20. **III METRE VII.** 6 **ben ysmyte . . . holdinge**, i.e., are smitten with the pain (sting) of having held too long.

Prose VIII. Nihil igitur dubium.

"Now is it no dowte thanne that thise weyes ne ben a manere mysledinges to blysfulnesse, ne that they ne mowe nat leden folk thyder as they byheten to leden hem. But with how grete harmes thise forseyde weyes ben enlaced I shal shewe the shortly. For-why yif thow enforcest the to asemble moneye, thow most byreven him his moneye that hath it. And yif thow wolt shynen with dignetes, thow most bysechen and supplien hem that yeven tho dignitees. And yif thow coveytest by honour to gon byforn oother folk, thow shal defowle thyself thorw humblesse of axinge. Yif thow desyrest power, thow shalt by awaytes of thy subgits anoyously ben cast under by many peryles. Axestow glorye? Thow shalt ben so destrat by aspre thinges that thou shalt forgoon sykernesse. And yif thow wolt leden thy lyf in delites, every wyht shal despisen the and forleten the, as thow that art thral to thing that is ryht fowl and brotel *(that is to seyn, servaunt to thy body).* Now is it thanne wel seen, how lytel and how brotel possessyoun they coveyten that putten the goodes of the body aboven her owne resoun. For maysthow sormounten thyse olyfaunts in gretnesse or weyht of body? Or maysthow ben strengere than the bole? Maysthow ben swyftere than the tygre? Byhold the spaces and the stablenesse and the swyft cours of the hevene, and stynt somtyme to wondren on fowle thinges. The whych hevene, certes, nis nat rather for thyse thynges to ben wondred upon than for the resoun by whych it is governed. But the shyning of thy forme *(that is to seyn, the beaute of thy body),* how swyftly passinge is it, and how transytorye! Certes, it is more flyttinge than the mutabylytee of flowers of the somer sesoun. For so Arystotle telleth, that yif that men hadden eyen of a beest that hyhte lynx, so that the lokinge of foolk myghte percen thorw the thynges that withstonden it, whoso loked thanne in the entrayles of the body of Alcidiades, that was ful fayre in superfyce withowte, it sholde seme ryht fowl. And forthy, yif thow semest fayr, thy nature maketh nat that, but the desceyvaunce of the feblesse of the eyen that loken. But preyse the goodes of the body as mochel as ever the list, so that thow knowe algates that whatso it be *(that is to seyn, of the godes of thy body)* whych that thow wondrest upon may ben destroyed or dyssolved by the hete of a fevere of thre dayes. Of alle whyche forseyde thinges I may reducen this shortly in somme, that thyse worldly goodes whyche that ne mowen nat yeven that they beheten, ne ben nat perfyt by congregacioun of alle goodes, that they ne ben nat weyes ne pathes that bryngen man to blysfulnesse, ne maken men to ben blysful.

Metre VIII. Eheu! que miseros tramite.

"Allas, whych folye and whych ygnoraunce mysledeth wandringe wrechches fro the paath of verray goode! Certes, ye ne seken no gold in grene trees, ne ye ne gaderen nat precyous stones in the vynes, ne ye ne hyden nat yowre gynnes in the hye mountaygnes to kachche fyssh of whyche ye may maken ryche festes. And yif yow lyketh to honte to rooes, ye ne gon nat to the foordes of the water that hyhte Tyrene. And over this, men knowen wel the crykes and the cavernes of the see yhyd in floodes, and knowen ek whych water is most plentyuous of whyte perles, and knowen whych water habowndeth most of rede purpre *(that is to seyn, of a manere shellefish with whych men dyen purpre),* and knowen

III PROSE VIII. 4 **byheten,** promise. 8 **byreven,** steal from. 10 **supplien,** beg. 14 **awaytes,** snares. 17 **destrat ... aspre,** bothered, unpleasant (sharp). 21 **brotel,** brittle. 26 **olyfaunts,** elephants. 30 **stynt,** stop. 31 **wondren,** admire. **39–44 Arystotle ... Alcidiades,** the allusion has not been found in Aristotle; Alcibiades was a Greek youth notable for his beauty and bad character. 47 **desceyvaunce,** misapprehension (deception). I *deceyvable or the.* III METRE VIII. 6 **gynnes,** traps. 8 **honte to rooes,** hunt deer. 10 **Tyrene,** Tyrrhenian Sea; Virgil, *Aeneid* I.67.

whych strondes habownden most with tendre fysshes, or of sharpe fysshes that hyhten echynnes. But folk suffren hemself to ben so blynde that hem ne rechcheth nat to knowe 20 where thilke godes ben ihydd whyche that they coveyten, but plowngen hem in erthe and seken there thylke good that sormounteth the hevene that bereth the sterres. What preyere may I maken that be digne to the 25 nyce thowhtes of men? But I preye that they coveyten rychesse and honours, so that whan they han geten tho false goodes with gret travayle, that therby they mowe knowen the verray goodes. 30

Prose IX. Hactenus mendacis formam.

"It suffyseth that I have shewed hyderto the forme of false welefulnesse, so that yif thow loke now clerly, the order of myn entencyoun requireth from hennesforth to shewen the the verray welefulnesse." 5

"For sothe," quod I, "I se wel now that suffysaunce may nat comen by rychesses, ne power by reames, ne reverence by dignitees, ne gentylesse by glorye, ne joye by delices."

"And hasthow wel knowen the causes," 10 quod she, "why it is?"

"Certes, me semeth," quod I, "that I se hem ryht as thowgh it were thorw a lytel klyfte. But me were levere knowen hem more opynly of the." 15

"Certes," quod she, "the resoun is al redy. For thylke thing that symply is o thing, withowten any devysyoun, the errour and folye of mankynde departeth and devydeth it, and mysledeth it, and transporteth from 20 verray and parfyt good to goodes that ben false and unparfyt. But sey me this: wenesthow that he that hath nede of power, that him ne lacketh nothing?"

"Nay," quod I. 25

"Certes," quod she, "thow seyst aryht.

For yif so be that ther ys a thing that in any partye be feblere of power, certes, as in that, it mot nedes ben nedy of foreyne help."

"Ryht so is it," quod I. 30

"Suffysaunce and power ben thanne of o kinde?"

"So semeth it," quod I.

"And demesthow," quod she, "that a thing that is of this manere *(that is to seyn,* 35 *suffysaunt and myhty)* owhte ben despyced, or elles that it be ryht digne of reverence aboven alle thinges?"

"Certes," quod I, "it nis no dowte that it is ryht worthy to ben reverenced." 40

"Lat us," quod she, "adden thanne reverence to suffysaunce and to power, so that we demen that thise thre thinges be al o thing."

"Certes," quod I, "lat us adden it, yif we wolen graunten the sothe." 45

"What demesthow thanne?" quod she. "Is that a dyrk thing and nat noble *(that is suffisaunt, reverent, and myhty)* or elles that it is ryht noble and ryht cler by celebryte of renoun? Considere thanne," quod she, "as 50 we han graunted her-byforn, that he that ne hath nede of nothing, and is most myhty and most digne of honour, yif hym nedeth any clernesse of renoun, whych clernesse he mighte nat graunten of hymself, so that, for 55 lacke of thylke clernesse, he myghte seme the febelere on any side or the more owtcast." *(Glose. This is to seyn, nay. For whoso that is suffysaunt, myhty, and reverent, clernesse of renoun folweth of the forseyde thinges; he hath it* 60 *al redy of his suffysaunce.)*

Boece. "I may nat," quod I, "denye it; but I mot graunte as it is, that this thing be ryht celebrable by clernesse of renoun and noblesse." 65

"Thanne folweth it," quod she, "that we adden clernesse of renoun to the thre forseyde thinges, so that ther ne be amonges hem no difference?"

---

19 **echynnes**, sea urchins. 26 **nyce**, foolish. **III PROSE IX. 13 klyfte**, crack (cleft). 60 C *forseyde thynges, so that there ne be amonges hem no difference; he hath....*

"This is a consequens," quod I.   70

"This thing thanne," quod she, "that ne hath nede of no foreyne thing, and that may don alle thinges by his strengthes, and that is noble and honorable, nis nat that a mery thing and a joyful?"   75

Boece. "But whennes," quod I, "that any sorwe myhte comen to this thing that is swyche, certes, I may nat thinke."

Philosophie. "Than moten we graunte," quod she, "that this thing be ful of gladnesse,   80 yif the forseyde thinges ben sothe. And certes, also mote we graunten that suffysaunce, power, noblesse, reverence, and gladnesse ben only diverse by names, but her substaunce hath no diversite."   85

Boece. "It mot nedly ben so," quod I.

Philosophie. "Thilke thing thanne," quod she, "that is oon and symple in his nature, the wykkednesse of men departeth yt and devydeth it; and whan they enforcen hem   90 to geten partye of a thing that ne hath no part, they ne geten hem neyther thilke partye that nis non, ne the thing all hool that they ne desyre nat."

Boece. "In whych manere?" quod I.   95

Philosophie. "Thilke man," quod she, "that secheth richesses to flen povertee, he ne travayleth him nat for to gete power, for he hath levere ben dyrk and vyl and ek withdraweth from hymself many naturel   100 delites for he nolde lese the moneye that he hath assembled. But certes, in this manere he ne geteth him nat suffisaunce, that power forleteth, and that moleste prykketh, and that fylthe maketh owtcast, and that dyrkenesse   105 hydeth. And certes, he that desireth oonly power, he wasteth and scatereth rychesse, and despyseth delits, and ek honour that is withowte power, ne he ne preyseth glorye nothing. Certes, thus seesthow wel that manye   110 thinges faylen to hym, for he hath somtyme defaute of many necessytees, and many ang-

wysses byten him. And whan he ne may nat don tho defautes awey, he forleteth to ben myhty, and that is the thing that he most   115 desyreth. And ryht thus may I maken semblable resouns of honours, and of glorye, and of delits. For so as every of thyse forseyde thinges is the same that thise oother thinges ben *(that is to seyn, al oon thing)*, whoso that   120 ever seketh to geten that oon of thise and nat that oothre, he ne geteth nat that he desireth."

Boece. "What seysthow thanne, yif that a man coveyteth to geten alle thise thinges   125 togydere?"

Philosophie. "Certes," quod she, "I wolde seye that he wolde geten him sovereyn blysfulnesse; but that shal he nat fynde in tho thinges that I have shewed, that ne mowen   130 nat yeven that they beheten."

Boece. "Certes, no," quod I.

"Thanne," quod she, "ne sholden men nat by no wey seken blysfulnesse in swyche thinges as men wene that they ne mowen yeven, but   135 o thing sengtely of alle that men seken."

Boece. "I graunte wel," quod I, "ne no sothere thing ne may ben sayd."

Philosophie. "Now hasthow thanne," quod she, "the forme and the causes of false   140 welefulnesse. Now torne and flitte the eyen of thy thowght, for there shalthow sen anon thilke verray blysfulnesse that I have byhyht the."

Boece. "Certes," quod I, "it is cler and   145 open, thowh it were to a blynde man. And that shewedest thow me ful wel a lytel herebiforn, whan thou enforcedest the to shewe me the causes of the false blysfulnesse. For but yif I be bygyled, thanne is thilke the verray   150 blysfulnesse parfyt that parfytly maketh a man suffisaunt, myhty, honourable, noble, and ful of gladnesse. And for thow shalt wel knowe that I have wel understonden thyse thinges within my herte, I knowe wel that thilke   155

---

104 moleste, vexation (to molest). **131 beheten,** promise. **141 flitte,** move (look over). *the eyen of:* Cx *agayn to.* **148 enforcedest,** took pains.

blysfulnesse that may verrayly yeven oon of
the forseyde thinges, syn they ben al oon, I
knowe, dowteles, that thilke thing is the fulle
blysfulnesse."

Philosophie. "O my norye," quod she,   160
"by this opinioun I seye that thow art
blysful, yif thow putte this therto that I shal
seyn."

"What is that?" quod I.

"Trowesthow that ther be anything in   165
thise erthely mortal towmbling thinges that
may bryngen this estat?"

"Certes," quod I, "I trowe it nawht; and
thow hast shewed me wel that over thilke
good ther nis nothing more to ben desired."   170

Philosophie. "Thise thinges thanne,"
quod she, *(that is to sey, erthely suffisaunce and
power and swyche thinges)* "eyther they semen
lyckenesses of verray good, or elles it
semeth that they yeve to mortal foolk a   175
manere of goodes that ne ben nat parfyt.
But thilke good that is verray and parfyt, that
may they nat yeven."

Boece. "I acorde me wel," quod I.

Philosophie. "Thanne," quod she, "for as   180
mochel as thow hast knowen which is
thilke verray blysfulnesse, and ek whiche
thilke thinges ben that lyen falsly blysfulnesse
*(that is to seyn, that by deceite semen verray
goodes),* now byhoveth the to knowe   185
whennes and where thow mowe seke thilke
verray blysfulnesse."

"Certes," quod I, "that desire I gretly, and
have abyden longe tyme to herknen it."

"But for as moche," quod she, "as it   190
liketh to my dissipule Plato in his book of
in Tymeo, that in ryht lytel thinges men sholden
bysechen the help of God, what jugest thow
that be now to done, so that we may deserve
to fynde the sete of thilke verray good?"   195

Boece. "Certes," quod I, "I deme that
we shollen clepen the fader of alle goodes, for

withowten him nis ther nothing fownden
aryht."

"Thow seyst aryht," quod she, and bygan   200
anon to syngen ryht thus:

Metre IX. O qui perpetua mundum.

"O thow fader, creator of hevene and of
erthes, that governest this world by perdurable
resoun, that comaundest the tymes to gon from
syn that age hadde bygynninge; thow that
dwellest thyself ay stedefast and stable, and   5
yevest alle oothre thinges to ben moeved, ne
foreyne causes necesseden the nevere to compowne werk of floteringe matere, but oonly the
forme of sovereyn good iset within the
withowte envye, that moevede the frely.   10
Thow that art alderfayrest, beringe the
fayre world in thy thowht, formedest this world
to the lyknesse semblable of that fayre world in
thy thowht. Thow drawest al thing of thy
sovereyn ensaumpler, and comaundest that   15
this world, parfytlyche imaked, have freely
and absolut his parfyt partyes. Thow byndest
the elementes by nowmbyres porcionables, that
the colde thinges mowen acorden with the
hote thinges, and the drye thinges with the   20
moyste thinges; that the fyr, that is purest,
ne fle nat over hye, ne that the hevynesse ne
drawen nat adown overlowe the erthes that ben
plownged in the wateres. Thow knyttest
togydere the mene sowle of treble kynde,   25
moevinge alle thinges, and devydest it by
menbres acordinge. And whan it is thus
devyded, and it hath asembled a moevinge into
two rowndes, it goth to torne ayein to
hymself, and envyrowneth a ful deep   30
thowht, and torneth the hevene by
semblable ymage. Thow by evene-lyke causes
enhansest the sowles and the lasse lyves, and,
ablinge hem heye by lyhte cartes, thow
sowest hem into hevene and into erthe. And   35

---

160 **norye,** pupil (nourish). 174 **lyckenesses,** imitations (likenesses). 192 *Tymeo,* Metre IX is an epitome of the first part of Plato's
Timaeus. III METRE IX. 7 **foreyne,** external. **compowne,** create. 8 **floteringe,** mutable (unstable). 17 I *and absolut* om. 18 AC
proporcionables. 25 **mene sowle,** common (world) soul. I gloss *anima mundi.* 29 **two rowndes,** two circles (of movement). 32 **evene-**
lyke, similar. 33 **lasse lyves,** lesser forms of life. 34 **ablinge . . . lyhte cartes,** enabling, light chariots.

whan they ben converted to the by thy
benigne lawe, thow makest hem retorne ayein
to the by ayein-ledinge fyr.

"O fader, yive thow to the thowht to
styen up into the streyte sete, and graunte   40
him to envirowne the welle of good; and
the lyhte yfownde, graunte him to fychen the
clere syhtes of his corage in the. And skatere
thow and to-breke thow the weyhtes and
the clowdes of erthely hevynesse, and shyne   45
thow by thy bryhtnesse. For thow art
clernesse; thou art peysyble reste to debonayre
folkes; thow thyself art bygynninge, berere,
ledere, paath, and terme; to loke on the,
that is owre ende.   50

Prose X. Quoniam igitur que sit.

"For as moche thanne as thow hast seyn
which is the forme of good that nis nat parfyt
and whych is the forme of good that is parfyt,
now trowe I that it were good to shewe in
what this perfeccyoun of blysfulnesse is set.   5
And in this thing, I trowe that we sholden
fyrst enquere for to wyten yif that any swyche
manere good as thilke good that thow hast
dyffynyssed a lytel heere-biforn *(that is to
seyn, sovereyn good)* may ben fownde in the   10
nature of thinges, for that veyn ymagyna-
cyoun of thowght ne deceyve us nat, and putte
us owt of the sothfastnesse of thilke thing that is
summitted to us. But it may nat ben
deneyed that thilke good ne is, and that it   15
nis ryht as a welle of alle goodes. For alle
thing that is cleped inparfyt is proeved inparfyt
by the amenusinge of parfeccioun, or of thing
that is parfyt. And therof comth it that in
everything general, yif that men sen   20
anything that is inparfyt, certes, in thilke
general ther mot ben somthing that is parfyt.
For yif so be that perfeccyoun is don awey, men
may nat thinke ne seye fro whennes thilke
thing is that is cleped inparfyt. For the   25

nature of thinges ne took nat hir begynninge
of thinges amenused and inparfyt, but it
procedeth of thinges that ben al hoole and
absolut, and dessendeth so down into
owtterest thinges, and into thinges empty   30
and withowten frut. But, as I have ishewed
a lytul her-byforn, that yif ther be a blysfulnesse
that be freele and veyn and inparfyt, ther may
no man dowte that ther nis som blysfulnesse
that is sad, stydefast, and parfyt."   35

Boece. "This is concluded," quod I,
"fermely and sothfastly."

Philosophie. "But considere also," quod she,
"in wham this blysfulnesse enhabyteth. The
comune acordaunce and conseite of the   40
corages of men proeveth and graunteth that
God, prynce of alle thinges, is good. For so as
nothing ne may ben thowht bettre than God, it
may nat ben dowted thanne that he that
nothing nis bettre, that he nis good. Certes,   45
resoun sheweth that God is so good that it
proeveth by verray force that parfyt good is in
him. For yif God ne is swych, he ne may nat ben
prinse of alle thinges. For certes somthing
possessing in itself parfyt good sholde be   50
more worthy than God, and it sholde
semen that thilke thing were fyrst and eldere
than God. For we han shewed apertly that alle
thinges that ben parfyt ben fyrst or thinges
that ben unparfyt. And for-thy, for as   55
moche as that my resoun or my processes
ne go nat awey withowte an ende, we owen to
graunten that the sovereyn God is ryht ful of
sovereyn parfyt good. And we han establysshed that the sovereyn good is verray   60
blysfulnesse: thanne mot it nedes be that
verray blysfulnesse is set in sovereyn God."

Boece. "This take I wel," quod I, "ne this ne
may nat ben withseid in no manere."

"But I preye the," quod she, "see now   65
how thou mayst proeven, holyly and withowte corupcioun, this that I have seyd, that the
sovereyn God is ryht ful of sovereyn good."

---

37 *benigne:* I *bygynnynge.* **40 styen,** climb. **41 envirowne,** dwell near. **42 fychen,** fasten (fix). **49 terme,** distinction. **III PROSE X.**
9 dyffynyssed, defined. **14 summitted,** submitted. **18 amenusinge,** diminishing. **35 sad,** serious. **53 apertly,** openly. **54 or,**
before (ere). **66 holyly,** wholly.

"In whych manere?" quod I.

"Wenesthow awht," quod she, "that this prynce of alle thinges have itake thilke sovereyn good anywher owt of himself—of whych sovereyn good men proveth that he is ful—ryht as thow myhtest thinken that God, that hath blysfulnesse in hymself, and thilke blysfulnesse that is in him, weren dyvers in substaunce? For yif thow wene that God have receyved thilke good owt of himself, thow mayst wene that he that yaf thilke good to God be more worthy thanne is God. But I am byknowen and confesse, and that ryht dignely, that God is ryht worthy aboven alle thinges. And yif so be that this good be in him by nature, but that it is dyvers fro him by weninge resoun, syn we speke of God prynce of alle thinges—faigne whoso feigne may—who was he that hath conjoigned thise diverse thinges togider? And ek, at the laste, se wel that a thing that is divers from anything, that thilke thing nis nat that same thing fro whych it is undyrstonden to ben divers. Thanne folweth it that thilke thing that by his nature is divers fro soverein good, that that thing nis nat sovereyn good, but certes, that were a felonous corsednesse to thinken that of him that nothing is more worth. For alwey, of alle thinges, the nature of hem ne may nat ben bettre than his bygynning. For whych I may concluden, by ryht verray resoun, that thilke that is bygynning of alle thinges, thilke same thing is sovereyn good in his substaunce."

Boece. "Thow hast seyd ryhtfully," quod I.

Philosophie. "But we han graunted," quod she, "that the sovereyn good is blysfulnesse."

"And that is soth," quod I.

"Thanne," quod she, "moten we nedes graunten and confessen that thilke same sovereyn good be God."

"Certes," quod I, "I ne may nat denye ne withstonde the resouns purposed, and I se wel that it folweth by strengthe of the premysses."

"Loke now," quod she, "yif this be proved yit more fermely thus: that ther ne mowen nat ben two sovereyn goodes that ben diverse amonge hemself. For certes, the goodes that ben dyverse amonges hemself, that oon nis nat that that othre is; thanne ne mowen neyther of hem ben parfyt, so as eyther of hem lakketh to other. But that that nis nat parfyt, men may sen apertly that it is nat sovereyn. The thinges thanne that ben sovereynly goode ne mowen by no wey ben diverse. But I have wel concluded that blysfulnesse and God ben the sovereyn good, for whyche it mot nedes ben that sovereyn blysfulnesse is sovereyn divynyte."

"Nothing," quod I, "nis more sothfast than this, ne more ferme by resoun; ne a more worthy thing than God may nat ben concluded."

Philosophie. "Upon thise thinges thanne," quod she, "ryht as thyse geometryens, whan they han shewed her proposiciouns, ben wont to bryngen in thinges that they clepen porysmes (or declaraciouns of forseyde thinges), ryht so wole I yeve the heere as a corolarye (or a mede of coroune). For-why for as moche as by the getinge of blysfulnesse men ben maked blysful, and blysfulnesse is divinitee, thanne is it manyfest and open that by the getinge of divynitee men ben maked blysful. Ryht as by the getinge of justice they ben maked just, and by the getinge of sapience they ben maked wyse: ryht so, nedes, by the semblable resoun, whan they han geten devynyte, they ben maked goddes. Thanne is every blysful man god. But certes, by nature ther nis but o God; but by the partycypasioun of devynyte ther ne let ne desturbeth nothing that ther ne ben many goddes."

---

81 byknowen, certain (I assert). **84 dyvers,** different (separated). **86 faigne,** pretend (imagine). **95 corsednesse,** cursedness. **138 porysmes,** deductions (conclusions). **140 *mede of coroune*,** gift of garland ("corollary" comes from Lat. *corolla,* garland; it meant money paid for a garland of flowers, hence a gratuity). **146 *they ben maked just*** not in English text; supplied from Fr.

"This is," quod I, "a fayr thing and a 155
precyous, clepe it as thow wolt, be it
porisme or corellarye" *(or meede of corowne or
declaringes).*

"Certes," quod she, "nothing nis fayrere
than is the thing that by resoun sholde ben 160
added to thyse forseyde thinges."

"What thing?" quod I.

"So," quod she, "as it semeth that blysfulnesse conteneth many thinges, it were for
to whyten wheyther that alle this thinges 165
maken or conjoignen as a manere body of
blysfulnesse, be diversite of partyes or of
menbres, or elles yif any of alle thilke thinges be
swych that it acomplyse by hymself the
substaunce of blysfulnesse, so that alle 170
thise oothre thinges ben refferred and
browht to blysfulnesse" *(that is to seyn, as to the
chef of hem).*

"I wolde," quod I, "that thow makedest
me clerly to understonde what thow seyst, 175
and that thow recordedest me the forseyde
thinges."

"Have I nat juged," quod she, "that
blysfulnesse is good?"

"Yis, forsothe," quod I, "and that 180
sovereyn good."

"Adde thanne," quod she, "thilke good *(that
is maked of blysfulnesse)* to alle the forseyde
thinges. For thilke same blysfulnesse that is
demed to ben sovereyn suffisaunce, thilke 185
selve is sovereyn power, sovereyn reverence,
sovereyn clernesse *(or noblesse)*, and sovereyn
delit. Conclusio. What seyst thow thanne of
alle this thinges, that is to seyn, suffysaunce,
power, and this oothre thinges—ben they 190
thanne as menbres of blysfulnesse, or ben
they referred and browht to sovereyn good,
ryht as alle thinges that ben browht to the chief
of hem?"

Boece. "I undyrstonde wel," quod I, 195
"what thow purposest to seke, but I desire
for to herkne that thow shewe it me."

Philosophie. "Tak now thus the discressioun
of this questyoun," quod she. "Yif alle
thise thinges," quod she, "weren menbres 200
to felicite, than weren they diverse that oon
from that oother. And swych is the nature of
partyes or of menbres that diverse menbres
compownen a body."

"Certes," quod I, "it hath wel ben 205
shewed heere-biforn that alle thise thinges
ben alle o thing."

"Thanne ben they none menbres," quod
she, "for elles it sholde seme that blysfulnesse were conjoigned al of on menbre 210
allone, but that is a thing that may nat be
don."

"This thing," quod I, "nis nat dowtous; but I
abyde to herknen the remnaunt of thy
questyoun." 215

"This is open and cler," quod she, "that
alle oothre thinges ben referred and browht to
good. For therfore is suffisaunce requered, for it
is demed to ben good; and forthy is power
requered, for men trowen also that it be 220
good. And this same thing mowen we
thinken and conjecten of reverence, and of
noblesse, and of delit. Thanne is sovereyn good
the somme and the cause of al that awhte
ben desyred. For-why thilke thing that 225
withholdeth no good in itself, ne semblaunce
of good, it ne may nat wel in no manere be
desired ne required. And the contrarye, for
thogh that thinges by her nature ne ben nat
goode, algates yif men wene that they ben 230
goode, yit ben they desyred as thowgh that
they weren verraylyche goode. And therfor is it
that men owhten to wene by ryht, that bounte
be the sovereyn fyn and the cause of alle the
thinges that ben to requeren. But certes, 235
thilke that is cause for which men requeren
anything, it semeth that thilke same thing be
most desyred. As thus, yif that a wyht wolde
ryden for cause of hele, he ne desyreth nat
so mochel the moevinge to ryden as the 240

---

165 **whyten,** know (wit). 176 **recordedest,** remind. 183 *maked of* supplied from Fr. 198 **discressioun,** discernment. 204 **compownen,**
compose. 213 **dowtous,** doubtful. 233 **bounte,** goodness. 234 **sovereyn fyn,** chief end.

effect of his hele. Now thanne, syn that alle
thinges ben required for the grace of good, they
ne ben nat desyred of alle foolk moore thanne the
same good. But we han graunted that
blysfulnesse is that thing for whyche that 245
alle thyse oothre thinges ben desyred;
thanne is it thus that certes oonly blysfulnesse is
requered and desired. By whyche thing it
sheweth clerly, that of good and of blysfulnesse is al oon and the same substaunce." 250

"I se nat," quod I, "wherfore that men
myhten discorden in this."

"And we han shewed that God and verray
blysfulnesse is al oo thing."

"That is soth," quod I. 255

"Thanne mowen we conclude sikerly that
the substaunce of God is set in thilke same good,
and in non oother place.

Metre X. Huc omnes pariter venite capti.

"O cometh alle togyder now, ye that ben
icawht and ibownde with wyckede cheynes by
the decyvable delyt of erthely thinges enhabytinge in yowre thowht! Her shal ben
the reste of yowre labours; her is the havene 5
stable in peysyble quiete; this allone is the
open refut to wrechches. *(Glosa. This is to seyn,
that ye that ben combred and deceived with worldely
affeccyouns, cometh now to this sovereyn good that
is God, that is refut to hem that wolen comen to 10
him.)* Textus. Alle the thinges that the ryver
Tagus yeveth yow with his goldene gravayles,
or elles alle the thinges that the ryver Herynus
yeveth with his rede brynke, or that Indus
yeveth that is next the hote party of the 15
world, that medleth the grene stones with
the whyte, ne sholde nat cleeren the lookinge of
yowre thowht, but hyden rather yowre blynde
corages within her dyrknesse. Al that
lyketh yow heere, and exciteth and moeveth 20
yowre thowhtes, the erthe hath norysshed it

in his lowe caves. But the shyning by whyche
the hevene is governed and whennes he hath
his strengthe, that eschueth the dyrke
overthrowinge of the sowle, and whoso may 25
knowen thilke lyht of blysfulnesse, he shal
wel seyn that the whyte bemes of the sonne ne
ben nat cleer."

Prose XI. Assencior inquam.

Boece. "I assente me," quod I, "for alle
thise thinges ben strongly bownden with ryht
ferme resouns."

Philosophie. "How mochel wylthow
preysen it," quod she, "yif that thow 5
knowe what thilke good is?"

"I wol preys it," quod I, "by preys withowten
ende yif it shal betidde me to knowe also
togydere God that is good."

"Certes," quod she, "that shal I do the 10
by verray resouns, yif that tho thinges that
I have concluded a litel her-byforn dwellen
oonly in her fyrst graunting."

Boece. "They dwellen graunted to the,"
quod I. *(This is to seyn, as who seyth, I 15
graunte thy forseyde conclusiouns.)*

"Have I nat shewed the," quod she, "that
the thinges that ben requered of many folkes ne
ben nat verray goodes ne parfyte, for they
ben dyverse that oon fro that oothre; and 20
so as ech of hem is lackinge to other, they
ne han no power to bryngen a good that is ful
and absolut? But thanne at erst ben they verray
good, whan they ben gadered togidere alle
in to o forme and into on wyrkinge, so that 25
thilke thinge that is suffisaunce, thilke same
be power, and reverence, and noblesse, and
myrthe. And forsothe, but yif alle thyse thinges
ben alle oon same thing, they ne han nat
wherby that they mowen ben put in the 30
nowmber of thinges that owhten ben
requered or desyred."

---

252 discorden, disagree. **III METRE X. 12 Tagus,** river in Spain. **13 Herynus,** Hermus, river in Lydia (now Turkey). **14 Indus,**
river in India. **16–17 grene stones with the whyte,** emeralds and pearls. **17 cleeren the lookinge,** clear the vision. **III PROSE XI.**
10 do the, make you (know).

Boece. "It is shewed," quod I, "ne herof may no man dowten."

Philosophie. "The thinges thanne," quod 35 she, "that ne ben no goodes whanne they ben diverse, and whan they bygynnen to ben alle oon thing thanne ben they goodes—ne comth it hem nat thanne by the getinge of unite that they ben maked goodes?" 40

Boece. "So it semeth," quod I.

"But alle thing that is good," quod she, "grauntesthow that it be good by the participacioun of good, or no?"

"I graunte it," quod I. 45

"Thanne mosthow graunten," quod she, "by semblable resoun, that oon and good be oo same thing. For of thinges of whyche that the effect nis nat naturely diverse, nedes the substance mot be oo same thinge." 50

"I ne may nat denye that," quod I.

"Hasthow nat knowen wel," quod she, "that alle thing that is hath so longe his dwellinge and his substaunce as longe as it is oon, but whan it forleteth to ben oon yit mot nedes 55 dyen and corumpe togyder?"

"In which manere?" quod I.

"Ryht as in bestes," quod she, "whan the sowle and the body ben conjoigne in oon and dwellen togydyre, it is cleped a beest. 60 And whan her unite is destroyed by the desseveraunce that oon from that oother, thanne sheweth it wel that it is a ded thing, and that it nis no lengere no beest. And the body of a whyht, whil it dwelleth in oo forme by 65 conjunccyoun of menbres, it is wel seyn that it is a figure of mankynde. And yif the partyes of the body ben so devyded and disseverd (*that oon fro that oother*) that they destroyen unite, the body forleteth to ben 70 that it was byforn. And, who wolde renne in the same manere by alle thinges, he sholde seen that withowte dowte everything is in his substaunce as longe as it is oon, and whan it forleteth to ben oon it dieth and periseth." 75

Boece. "Whan I consydere," quod I, "manye thinges, I se non oother."

"Is ther anything thanne," quod she, "that in as moche as it lyveth naturelly, that forleteth the talent or appetyt of his beinge, 80 and desireth to come to deth and to corupcioun?"

"Yif I consydere," quod I, "the beestes that han any manere nature of wylninge and of nyllinge, I ne fynde no beest but yif it ben 85 constreyned fro withowte forth that forleteth or despiseth the entensyoun to lyven and to duren, or that wole his thankes hasten hym to dyen. For every beest travayleth him to deffende and kepe the savacioun of his lyf, 90 and eschueth deth and destrucioun. But certes, I dowte me of herbes and of trees (*that is to seyn, that I am in a dowte of swiche thinges as herbes or trees*) that ne han no feelinge sowles (*ne no naturel wyrkinges servinge to* 95 *appetytes as bestes han*) wheither thei han appetid to dwellen and to duren."

"Certes," quod she, "ne therof thar the nat dowte. Now loke upon thise herbes and thise trees. They wexen first in swyche 100 places as ben covenable to hem, in whyche places they ne mowen nat sone dyen ne dryen, as longe as her nature may deffenden hem. For som of hem waxen in feeldes, and som in mountaignes, and oothre waxen in marys, 105 and oothre cleven on roches, and summe waxen plentyuous in sondes, and yif that any wyht enforce him to beren hem into oothre places, they wexen drye. For nature yeveth to everything that that is convenient to him, 110 and travayleth that they ne dye nat, as longe as they han power to dwellen and to lyven. What woltow seyn of this, that they drawen alle her noryssinges by her rootes, ryht as they hadden her mowthes iplounged 115 within the erthes, and sheden by her maryes her wode and her bark? And what woltow seyn of this, that thilke thing that is ryht

softe, as the marye is, that is alwey hidd in
the sete al withinne, and that is defended 120
fro withowte by the stidefastnesse of wode,
and that the uttereste bark is put ayeins the
destemperaunce of the hevene as a defendowr
myhty to suffren harm? And thus, certes,
maystow wel sen how gret is the diligence 125
of nature. For alle thinges renovelen and
puplisshen hem with seed imultiplyed, ne ther
nis no man that ne wot wel that they ne ben
ryht as a foundement and edyfice for to
duren nat only for a tyme but ryht as for to 130
duren perdurably by generacyoun. And
the thinges ek that men wenen ne haven none
sowles, ne desire they nat ech of hem by
semblable resoun to kepen that is hers *(that
is to seyn, that is acordinge to her nature in* 135
conservacioun of her beinge and enduringe)? For
wherfor elles bereth lyhtnesse the flaumbes up,
and the weyhte presseth the erthe adoun, but
for as moche as thilke places and thilke
moevinges ben covenable to everich of 140
hem? And forsothe everything kepeth thilke
that is acordinge and propre to him, ryht as
thinges that ben contraryes and enemys
corompen hem. And yit the harde thinges,
as stoones, clyven and holden her partyes 145
togyder ryht faste and harde, and deffenden
hem in withstondinge that they ne departe nat
lyhtly atwyne. And the thinges that ben softe
and fletinge, as is water and eyr, they
departen lyhtly and yeven place to hem 150
that breken or devyden hem, but natheles,
they retornen sone ayein into the same thinges
fro whennes they ben arraced. But fyr fleeth and
refuseth alle devysyoun. Ne I ne trete nat
heere now of wilful moevinges of the sowle 155
that is knowinge, but of the naturel
entencioun of thinges, as thus ryht as we
swolwe the mete that we recyven and ne
thinke nat on it, and as we drawen owre
breth in slepinge that we wite it nat whil 160
we slepen. For certes, in the beestes the love
of her lyvynges ne of her beinges ne comth nat

of the wilninges of the sowle, but of the
bygynninges of nature. For certes, thorw
constreyninge causes wil desireth and 165
embraceth ful ofte tyme the deth that
nature dredeth. *(That is to seyn as thus, that a man
may ben constreyned so by som cause that his wil
desireth and taketh the deth which that nature
hateth and dredeth ful sore.)* And somtyme we 170
seeth the contrarye, as thus that the wil of a
wiht destorbeth and constreyneth that that
nature desireth and requereth al-wey, that is to
seyn, the werk of generacioun, by the
whiche generacioun only dwelleth and is 175
sustened the longe durablete of mortal
thinges.

"And thus this charite and this love, that
everything hath to hymself, ne comth nat of
the moevinge of the sowle, but of the 180
entencioun of nature. For the purvyaunce
of God hath yeven to thinges that ben creat of
him this that is a ful gret cause to lyven and to
duren, for which they desiren naturelly her
lyf as longe as ever they mowen. For whych 185
thow maist nat drede by no manere that
alle the thinges that ben anywhere, that they ne
requeren naturelly the ferme stablenesse of
perdurable dwellinge, and ek the eschuinge
of destruccyoun." 190

Boece. "Now confesse I wel," quod I,
"that I see now wel certeynly, withowte
dowtes, the thinges that whylom semeden
uncerteyn to me."

Philosophie. "But," quod she, "thilke 195
thyng that desireth to be and to dwellen
perdurably, he desireth to ben oon, for yif that
that oon were destroied, certes, beinge ne
shulde ther non dwellen to no wiht."

"That is soth," quod I. 200

"Thanne," quod she, "desiren alle
thinges oon."

"I assente," quod I.

"And I have shewed," quod she, "that
thilke same oon is thilke that is good?" 205

Boece. "Ye, for sothe," quod I.

---

122 **uttereste,** outermost. 127 **puplisshen,** propagate. 129 **ryht as,** just as. 153 **arraced,** torn apart. 155 *wilful:* I *weleful;* Lat. *voluntariis.* 163 **wilninges,** conscious desires. 181 **purvyaunce,** provision. 186 **drede,** doubt. 202 **oon,** unity.

"Alle thinges thanne," quod she, "reqyren good, and thilke good thanne maist thow descryven ryht thus: good is thilke thing that every wyht desireth." 210

"Ther ne may be thowht," quod I, "no moore verray thing. For either alle thinges ben referred and browht to nowht, and floteren withowte governour, despoiled of oon as of her propre heved, or elles, yif ther be anything to which that alle thinges tenden and hyen, that thing moste ben the sovereyn good of alle goodes." 215

Philosophie. Thanne seyde she thus: "O my nory," quod she, "I have gret gladnesse 220 of the, for thow hast fichched in thyn herte the myddel sothfastnesse, that is to seyn, the prikke. But this thing hath ben descovered to the in that thow seydest that thow wystest nat a lytel her-byforn." 225

"What was that?" quod I.

"That thow ne wystest nat," quod she, "whych was the ende of thinges. And certes, that is the thing that every wiht desireth. And for as mochel as we han gadered and 230 comprehended that good is thilke thing that is desired of alle, thanne moten we nedes confessen that good is the fyn of alle thinges.

Metre XI. Quisquis profunda mente.

"Whoso that seketh soth by a deep thoght, and coveyteth nat to ben deceyved by no mysweyes, lat him rollen and trenden withinne hymself the lyht of his inward syhte; and lat him gadere ayein, enclyninge into a 5 compas, the longe moevinges of his thowhtes; and lat him techen his corage that he hath enclosed and hyd in his tresors, al that he compaseth or seketh fro withowte. And thanne thilke thing that the blake cloude 10 of errour whilom hadde ycovered shal lyhten more clerly thanne Phebus hymself ne shyneth. (*Glosa. Whoso wole seken the dep grounde*

of soth in his thowht, and wol nat be deceyved by false proposiciouns that goon amys fro the 15 *trouthe, lat him wel examine and rolle withinne hymself the nature and the propretes of the thing; and lat him yit eftsones examine and rollen his thowhtes by good deliberacioun or that he deme; and lat him techen his sowle that it hath, by naturel pryncyples* 20 *kyndeliche yhid within itself, alle the trowthe the whiche he ymagyneth to ben in thinges withowte. And thanne alle the dyrknesse of his mysknowinge shal seme more evydently to syhte of his understondinge thanne the sonne ne semeth to syhte withowteforth.)* 25

"For certes the body, brynginge the weyhte of foryetinge, ne hath nat chased owt of yowre thowhte al the clernesse of yowre knowing, for certeynly the seed of sooth haldeth and clyveth within yowre corage, 30 and it is awaked and excited by the wynde and by the blastes of doctryne. For wherefor elles demen ye of yowre owne wyl the ryhtes whan he ben axed, but yif so were that the noryssinges of resoun ne lyvede iplownged 35 in the depthe of yowre herte? (*This is to seyn, how sholden men demen the sooth of anything that were axed, yif ther nere a roote of sothfastnesse that were yplownged and hyd in the naturel pryncyples, the whiche sothfastnesse lyved within* 40 *the depnesse of the thowght?*) And yif so be that the Muse and the doctryne of Plato syngeth sooth, al that every whyht lerneth, he ne doth nothing elles thanne but recordeth, as men recorden thinges that ben foryeten." 45

Prose XII. Tum ego Platoni inquam.

Thanne seide I thus: "I acorde me gretly to Plato, for thow remenbrest and recordest me thise thinges yit the secounde tyme, that is to seyn, fyrst whan I loste my memorye by the contagyous conjuncsioun of the body with 5 the sowle, and eftsones afterward whan I loste it, confownded by the charge and by the burdene of my sorwe."

---

215 **propre heved,** own head(s). 221 **fichched,** fixed. 233 **fyn,** end. **III METRE XI.** 5–6 **enclyninge into a compas,** gathering into a circle (ball). 19 *deme,* decide. 33 **ryhtes,** truths. 42 **Plato,** *Phaedo* 72E. 44 **recordeth,** recall. **III PROSE XII.** 5 *contagyous:* Cx *contrarious.*

And thanne seide she thus: "Yif thow looke," quod she, "fyrst the thinges that thow hast graunted, it ne shal nat ben ryht fer that thow ne shalt remembren thilke thing that thow seydest that thow nystest nat."

"What thing?" quod I.

"By which governement," quod she, "that this world is governed."

"Me remenbreth it wel," quod I, "and I confesse wel that I ne wiste it nawght. But al be it so that I se now from afer what thow purposest, algates I desire yit to herkene it of the more pleynly."

"Thow ne wendest nat," quod she, "a litel her-byforn that men sholden dowte that this world nis governed by God."

"Certes," quod I, "ne yit ne dowte I it nawht, ne I nel never wene that it were to dowte *(as who seith, but I wot wel that God governeth this world)*. And I shal shortly answeren the by what resouns I am browht to this. This world," quod I, "of so manye diverse and contrarious parties, ne myhte never han ben assembled in o forme but yif ther nere oon that conjoignede so manye diverse thinges. And the same diversite of her natures, that so discorden that oon fro that oother, moste departen and unjoignen the thinges that ben conjoigned yif ther ne were oon that contenede that he hath conjoyned and ibownde. Ne the certeyn ordre of nature ne sholde nat brynge forth so ordene moevinges—by places, by tymes, by dooinges, by spaces, by qualites —yif ther ne were oon that were ay stedefast dwellinge, that ordeynede and disponede thise diversitees of moevinges. And thilke thing, whatsoever it be, by which that alle thinges ben maked and ilad, I clepe him 'god', that is a word that is used to alle foolk."

Thanne seyde she: "Syn thow feelest thus thise thinges," quod she, "I trowe that I have litel moore to done that thow, myhty of welefulnesse, hool and sounde, ne see eftsones thy contre. But lat us loken the thinges that we ha purposed her-byforn. Have I nat nowmbred and seyd," quod she, "that suffisaunce is in blesfulnesse, and we han acorded that God is thilke same blysful-nesse?"

"Yis, forsothe," quod I.

"And that to governe this world," quod she, "ne shal he never han nede of non help fro withowte? For elles, yif he hadde nede of any help, he ne sholde nat have no ful suffisaunce?"

"Yis, thus it mot nedes be," quod I.

"Thanne ordeyneth he by hymself allone alle thinges?" quod she.

"That may nat be deneyed," quod I.

"And I have shewed that God is the same good?"

"It remembreth me wel," quod I.

"Thanne ordeyneth he alle thinges by thilke good," quod she, "syn he, which that we han acorded to be good, governeth alle thinges by hymself; and he is as a keye and a stiere, by which that the edifice of this world is ikept stable and withowte coroumpinge."

"I acorde me gretely," quod I. "And I aperceivede a lytul her-byforn that thow woldest seye thus, al be it so that it were by a thinne suspecyoun."

"I trowe it wel," quod she, "for, as I trowe, thow ledest now moore ententyfly thyne eyen to loken the verray goodes. But natheles the thing that I shal telle thee yit ne sheweth nat lasse to looken."

"What is that?" quod I.

"So as men trowen," quod she, "and that ryhtfully, that God governeth alle thinges by the keye of his goodnesse, and alle thise same thinges, as I have tawht the, hasten hem by naturel entencyoun to comen to good. Ther may no man dowten that they ne

---

10 fyrst the thinges, the earlier things. **13 nystest,** didn't know. **22 wendest nat,** didn't think. **37 contenede,** maintained (contained). **40 ordene,** well-ordered. **52 eftsones,** soon. **74 stiere,** rudder (Lat. *clavus*, helm, has been mistaken for *clavis*, key). **80 thinne suspecyoun,** tentative guess. **85 sheweth . . . looken,** i.e., is no less obvious. **89 keye,** again mistranslation of *clavus* (l. 74 above).

ben governed voluntaryely, and that they ne converten hem of her owne wil to the wil of her ordenour, as they that ben acordinge 95 and enclyninge to her governoure and her kyng."

"It mot nedes be so," quod I, "for the reaume ne sholde nat semen blysful yif ther were a yok of mysdrawinges in diverse 100 partyes, ne the savinge of obedient thinges ne sholde nat be."

"Thanne is ther nothing," quod she, "that kepeth his nature, that enforceth him to goon ayein God?" 105

"No," quod I.

"And yif that anything enforcede him to withstonde God, myhte it avaylen at the laste ayeins him that we han graunted to ben almyghty by the ryht of blysfulnesse?" 110

"Certes," quod I, "al owtrely it ne myhte nat avaylen him."

"Thanne is ther nothing," quod she, "that eyther wole or may withstonden to this sovereyn good?" 115

"I trowe nat," quod I.

"Thanne is thilke the sovereyn good," quod she, "that alle thinges governeth strongly, and ordeyneth hem softely."

Thanne seyde I thus: "I delite me," quod 120 I, "nat oonly in the endes or in the somme of the resouns that thow hast concluded and proeved, but thilke wordes that thow usest deliten me moche moore. So at the laste fooles that sumtyme renden grete thinges 125 owhten ben ashamed of hemself." *(That is to seyn, that we fooles that reprehenden wikkedly the thinges that towchen Goddes governaunce, we owhten ben asshamed of owreself, as I, that seyde that God refuseth oonly the werkes of men, and ne 130 entremeteth nat of it.)*

Philosophie. "Thow hast wel herd," quod she, "the fables of the poetes, how the gyaunts assayleden the hevene with the goddes; but forsothe, the debonayre force of God 135 deposede hem, as it was worthy *(that is to seyn, destroyede the giaunts, as it was worthy).* But wilthow that we joignen togidere thilke same resouns? For peraventure, of swych conjuncioun may sterten up som fair sparkle of 140 soth."

"Do," quod I, "as the liste."

"Wenest thow," quod she, "that God ne be almyhty? No man is in dowte of it."

"Certes," quod I, "no wyht ne dowteth 145 it, yif he be in his mynde."

"But he," quod she, "that is almyhty—ther nis nothing that he ne may?"

"That is soth," quod I.

"May God don yvel?" quod she. 150

"Nay, forsothe," quod I.

"Thanne is yvel nothing," quod she, "syn that he ne may nat don yvel that may don alle thinges."

"Scornest thow me," quod I, *(or elles 155 pleyesthow or deceivesthow me)* "that hast so woven me with thy resouns the hows of Dydalus, so entrelaced that it is unable to be unlaced? Thow that oother whyle entrest ther thou issest, and oother whyle issest ther thow 160 entrest, ne fooldesthow nat togydere *(by replycasioun of wordes)* a manere wonderful cercle or envyroninge of the symplicyte devyne? For certes, a lytel her-byforn, whan thow bygunne at blysfulnesse, thow seydest that 165 it is sovereyn good, and seidest that it is set in sovereyn God, and seydest that God hymself is sovereyn good, and that God is the fulle blysfulnesse. For which thou yave me as a covenable yift, that is to seyn, that no wyht 170 nis blysful but yif he be good also therwith. And seidest ek that the forme of good is the substaunce of God and of blysfulnesse. And seidest that thilke same oon is thilke same good that is requered and desired of alle the 175 kynde of thinges. And thow proevedest in disputinge that God governeth alle the thinges of the world by the governements of bownte,

---

100 mysdrawinges, contention. **125 renden,** tear (?) (Lat. "folly which so much vexed me"). **136** *deposede*: IA *desposede*; Lat. *deposuit*. **157 hows of Dydalus,** the Labyrinth. **161 fooldesthow,** i.e., create (fold together). **178 bownte,** goodness.

and seydest that alle thinges wolen obeyen
to him, and seydest that the nature of yvel 180
nis nothing. And thise thinges ne shewedest
thow nat with none resouns itaken fro withowte,
but by proeves in cercles and hoomlich knowen,
the whiche proeves drawen to hemself her
feith and her acord, everich of hem of 185
oother."

Thanne seyde she thus: "I ne scorne the nat
(*ne pleye, ne deceyve the*), but I have shewed the
the thing that is grettest over alle thinges
by the yift of God that we whilom preyeden. 190
For this is the forme of the devyne substaunce, that is swich that it ne slydeth nat into
owtterest foreyne thinges, ne ne resseiveth no
straunge thinges in him. But ryht as
Parmanydes seide in Grec of thilke devyne 195
substaunce, he seide thus, that thilke
devyne substaunce torneth the world and the
moevable cercle of thinges, whil thilke devyne
substaunce kepeth itself withowte moevinge.
(*That is to seyn, that it ne moeveth nevermo, and* 200
yit it moeveth alle oothre thinges.) But natheles,
yif I have styred resouns that ne ben nat taken
fro withowte the compas of thing of which we
treten, but resouns that ben bystowed
within that compas, ther nis nat why that 205
thow sholdest merveylen, syn thow hast
lerned by the sentense of Plato that nedes the
wordes moten be cosynes to the thinges of
which they speken.

Metre XII. Felix qui potuit boni.

"Blysful is that man that may sen the clere
welle of good; blysful is he that may unbynden
him fro the bondes of the hevy erthe. The poete
of Trace (*Orpheus*), that whilom hadde
ryht gret sorwe for the deth of his wyf, 5
after that he hadde maked by his wepply

songes the wodes moevable to rennen, and
hadde maked the ryveres to stonden stylle, and
hadde maked the hertes and the hyndes to
joignen dredeles her sydes to cruwel lyouns 10
(*for to herknen his songe*), and hadde maked
that the hare was nat agast of the hownde,
which that was plesed by his songe; so whan
the moste ardent love of his wif brende the
entrayles of his brest, ne the songes that 15
hadden overcomen alle thinges ne myhten
nat asswagen hir lord (*Orpheus*), he pleynede
him of the hevene goddes that weren crwel to
him. He wente him to the howses of helle,
and there he temprede his blaundysshinge 20
soonges by resowninge strenges, and spak
and soonge in wepinge al that ever he hadde
receyved, and laved owt of the noble welles of
his moder (*Calyope*), the goddesse. And he
soonge with as mochel as he myhte of 25
wepinge, and with as moche as love that
dowblede his sorwe myhte yeve him and
thechen him; and he commoevede the helle,
and requerede and bysowhte by swete
preyere the lordes of sowles in helle of 30
relesinge (*that is to seyn, to yilden him his wyf*).

"(*Cerberus*) the porter of helle, with his thre
hevedes, was cawht and al abayst for the newe
songe; and the thre goddesses (*Furies*) and
vengeresses of felonies that tormenten and 35
agasten the sowles by anoy woxen soruful
and sory, and wepen teeres for pite. Tho ne was
nat the heved of Yxion itormented by the
overthrowinge wheel; and Tantalus, that
was destroyed by the woodnesse of longe 40
thurst, despiseth the flodes to drynke; the
fowl that hihte voltor, that eteth the stomak or
the gyser of Ticyus, is so fulfyld of his song that
it nil eten ne tyren no more. At the laste
the lord and juge of sowles was moeved to 45
misericordes and cryde, 'We ben overcomen,' quod he. 'Yive we to Orpheus his wyf

---

183 hoomlich knowen, familiarity understood. **195 Parmanydes,** Parmenides, Greek philosopher. I *Apermanides*. **202 styred resouns,** used arguments. **207 Plato,** *Timaeus* 29B; Chaucer quotes this dictum twice, *CT* I.741, IX.207. **III METRE XII. 3** Cx *hevy bondes of therthe.* **6 wepply,** sad. **23 laved owt,** dipped from. **24 Calyope,** Calliope, chief of the Muses. **28 thechen,** teach. A *techen him in his seke herte.* **32 Cerberus,** the three-headed watchdog of hell. **38 Yxion,** Ixion, fastened to the ever-revolving wheel. **39 Tantalus,** tormented by perpetual thirst ("tantalize"). **42–43 voltor . . . Ticyus,** Tityus, tormented by having his liver torn by vultures. **44 tyren,** tear.

to bere him compaignye. He hath wel ibowht
hir by his song and his ditee. But we wol
putte a lawe in this, and covenaunt in the   50
yifte, that is to seyn, that til he be owt of
helle, yif he looke byhynde him, that his wyf
shal comen ayein unto us.'

"But what is he that may yive a lawe to
loveres? Love is a gretter lawe and a   55
strengere to himself *(than any lawe that men
may yeven)*. Allas, whan Orpheus and his wyf
weren almost at the termes of the nyht *(that is
to seyn, at the laste bowndes of helle)*, Orpheus

lookede abakward on Erudice his wyf, and   60
loste hir, and was ded. This fable apar-
tieneth to yow alle, whosoever desireth or
seketh to lede his thowht into the sovereyn day
(that is to seyn, to clernesse of sovereyn god). For
whoso that ever be so overcomen that he   65
fychche his eyen into the putte of helle *(that
is to seyn, whoso sette his thowhtes in erthely things)*,
al that evere he hath drawen of the noble good
celestial, he leseth it whan he loketh the
helles," *(that is to seyn, into lowe thinges of the   70
erthe)*.

Explicit liber tercius.

BOOK IV

Incipit liber quartus.

Prose I. Hec dum Philosophia dignitate vultus.

   When Philosophie hadde songen softely and
delitablely the forseyde thinges, kepinge the
dignite of hir cheere and the weyhte of hir
wordes, I thanne, that ne hadde nat
al owterly foryeten the wepinge and the   5
mowrninge that was set in myn herte,
forbrak the entencyoun of hir that entendede
yit to seyn some oothre thinges. "O," quod I,
"thow that art gyderesse of verrey lyht, the
thinges that thow hast seid me hiderto ben   10
so cleere to me and so shewinge by the
devyne lookinge of hem, and by thy resouns,
that they ne mowen ben overcomen. And
thilke thinges that thou toldest me, al be it
so that I hadde whilom foryeten hem for   15

the sorwe of the wrong that hath ben don
to me, yit natheles thei ne weren nat al owtrely
unknowen to me. But this same is namely a
ryht gret cause of my sorwe, that so as the
governoure of thinges is good, yif that yveles   20
mowen ben by any weyes, or elles yif that
yveles passen withowte punyssinge. The whiche
thing oonly how worthi it is to ben wondred
upon, thow considerest it wel thyself
certeynly. But yit to this thing ther is yit   25
another thing ijoigned more to be wondred
upon. For felonye is imperisse, and flowreth
(ful of rychesses). And vertu nis nat aloonly
withowte meedes, but it is cast under and
fortroden under the feet of felonous foolk,   30
and it abieth the torments instide of
wikkede felounes. Of alle whiche thinges ther
nis no wyht that may merveylen ynowh, ne

54-55 lawe to loveres, quoted in KT, *CT* I.1164. **55** *gretter:* I *gret;* Lat. *maior.* **66 fychche . . . putte,** fix, pit. **IV PROSE I. 6**
mowrninge (mourning): Cx *moevyng* (emotion). **9 gyderesse,** feminine guide. **11 shewinge,** convincing. **19 so as,** because. **27**
imperisse, empress. **31 abieth . . . instide of,** receives, in place of.

compleyne that swiche thinges ben doon in
the regne of God, that alle thinges woot and   35
alle thinges may, and ne wole nat but oonly
good thinges."

Thanne seyde she thus: "Certes," quod she,
"that were a gret mervayle, and an
enbasshinge withowten ende, and wel moore   40
horible than al monstres, yif it were as thow
wenest, that is to seyn, that in the ryht ordenee
hows of so mochel a fader and an ordenoure of
meyne, that the vesseles that ben fowle and
vyl sholden ben honoured and heryed, and   45
the precyous vesseles sholden ben defowled
and vyl. But it nis nat so, for yif tho thinges that
I have concluded a lytel her-byforn ben kept
hoole and unraced, thow shalt wel knowe
by the autoryte of God, of the whos regne I   50
speke, that certes the goode foolk ben alwey
mighty and shrewes ben alwey owtcast and
feble; ne the vices ne ben nevermo withowte
peyne, ne the vertues ne ben nat withowte
mede; and that blysfulnesses comen alwey to   55
goode folk, and infortune comth alwey to
wikked foolk. And thow shalt wel knowe manye
thinges of this kynde that shollen cesen thy
pleyntes, and strengthen the with stidefast
sadnesse. And for thow hast seyn the forme   60
of the verray blysfulnesse by me, that have
whilom shewed it the, and thow hast knowen in
whom blysfulnesse is iset, alle thinges itreted
that I trowe ben necessarye to putten forth,
I shal shewe the the wey that shal bryngen   65
the ayein unto thin hows. And I shal
fycchen fetheres in thi thowht, by whiche it may
areysen in hyhte so that, alle tribulacyoun ydon
awey, thow by my gydinge and by my
paath and by my sledes shalt mowe retorne   70
hool and sownd into thi contree.

Metre I. Sunt etenim penne volucres mihi.

"I have, forsothe, swifte fetheres that sur-
mounten the heyhte of hevene. Whan the
swifte thowht hath clothed itself in tho fetheres,

it despiseth the hateful erthes, and surmounteth the rowndnesse of the grete ayr;   5
and it seth the clowdes byhynde his bak;
and passeth the heyghte of the regyon of the
fyr, that eschaufeth by the swifte moevinge of
the fyrmament, til that he areyseth hym
into the howses that beren the sterres, and   10 ●
joyneth his weyes with the sonne Phebus,
and felawshipeth the wey of the olde colde
Saturnis; and he ymaked a knyht of the clere
sterre *(that is to seyn, that the thowght is maked
goddes knyht by the sekinge of trowthe to comen   15
to the verray knoleche of God)*. And thilke
thoght renneth by the cercle of the sterres, in
alle places ther as the shyninge nyht is painted
*(that is to seyn, the nyht that is clowdeles, for on
nyhtes that ben clowdeles it semeth as the hevene   20
were peynted with diverse ymages of sterres)*.
And whanne he hath idoon ther inowh, he shal
forleten the laste hevene, and he shal pressen
and wynden on the bak of the swifte
firmament, and he shal ben maked parfit of   25
the worshipful lyht of God. Ther halt the
Lord of Kynges the ceptre of his myht, and
atempreth the governementes of the world, and
the shyninge juge of thinges, stable in
hymself, governeth the swifte cart or wayn   30
*(that is to seyn, the circuler moevinge of the
sonne)*. And yif thy wey ledeth the ayein so that
thow be browht thider, thanne wolthow seye
now that that is the contre that thow
requerest, of which thow ne haddest no   35
mynde: 'But now it remembreth me wel,
her was I born, her wol I fastne my degree
(heer wole I dwelle).' But yif the liketh thanne to
loken on the dyrknesse of the erthe that thow
hast forleten, thanne shalthow sen that   40
thise felonous tyraunts that the wrecchede
people dredeth now shollen ben exiled fro
thilke fayre contre."

Prose II. Tum ego pape inquam.

Than seyde I thus: "Owh, I wondre me that
thou bihetest me so grete thinges; ne I ne dowte

---

40 enbasshinge, bewilderment. **42 ordenee,** regulated. **44 meyne,** household. **45 heryed,** praised. **67 fycchen fetheres,** affix wings.
70 sledes, vehicles. **IV METRE I. 9** *he areyseth* : A *she* and feminine following. **14** *thowght* : A *soule*. **IV PROSE II. 2 bihetest,** promise.

nat that thou ne mayst wel performe that thou byhetest. But I preye the oonly this, that thow ne tarye nat to telle me thilke thinges 5 that thow hast moeved."

"Fyrst," quod she, "thow moost nedes knowen that goode folk ben alwey stronge and myhty, and the shrewes ben feeble and desert and naked of alle strengthes. And of 10 thise thinges, certes, everich of hem is declared and shewed by other. For so as good and yvel ben two contraries, yif so be that good be stidefast, than sheweth the feblesse of yvel al openly. And yif thou knowe clerly 15 the frelenesse of yvel, the stidefastnesse of good is knowen. But for as moche as the fey of my sentence shal be the more ferme and haboundaunt, I wil gon by that oo wey and by that other; and I wole conferme the 20 thinges that ben purposed, now on this side and now on that side. Two thinges ther ben in whiche the effect of alle the dedes of mankynde standeth, that is to seyn, wil and power. And yif that oon of thise two fayleth, ther nis 25 nothing that may be don. For yif that wil lakkit, ther nis no wiht that undertaketh to don that he wol nat don; and yif power fayleth, the wil nis but in ydel and stant for nawht. And therof comth it that yif thow see a wiht that 30 wolde geten that he may nat geten, thow mayst nat dowten that power ne fayleth hym to haven that he wolde."

"This is open and cler," quod I; "ne it ne may nat ben deneyed in no manere." 35

"And yif thou see a wyht," quod she, "that hath doon that he wolde doon, thou nylt nat dowten that he ne hath had power to doon it?"

"No," quod I. 40

"And in that that every wyht may, in that men may holden him myhty *(as who seyth, in so moche as man is myhty to doon a thing, in so mochel men halt him myhty)*, and in that that he ne may, in that men demen him to ben 45 feble."

"I confesse it wel," quod I.

"Remenbreth the," quod she, "that I have gaddered and shewed by forseyde resouns that al the entencioun of the wil of man- 50 kynde, which that is lad by diverse studies, hasteth to comen to blisfulnesse."

"It remembreth me wel," quod I, "that it hath ben shewed."

"And recordeth the nat thanne," quod 55 she, "that blisfulnesse is thilke same good that men requeren; so that whan blisfulnesse is requered of alle, that good also is requered and desired of alle?"

"It ne recordeth me nat," quod I, "for I 60 have it gretly alwey fichched in my memorie."

"Alle folk thanne," quod she, "goode and eke badde, enforcen hem withowte defference of entencioun to comen to good." 65

"This is a verray consequence," quod I.

"And certein is," quod she, "that by the getinge of good ben men ymaked goode."

"This is certeyn," quod I.

"Thanne geten goode men that they 70 desiren?"

"So semeth it," quod I.

"But wikkede folk," quod she, "yif they geten the good that they desiren, they ne mowe nat be wikkede." 75

"So is it," quod I.

"Thanne so as that oon and that other," quod she, "desiren good, and the goode foolk geten good, and nat the wikke foolk, thanne nis it no dowte that the goode foolk ne ben myhty 80 and wikkede foolk ben feeble?"

"Whoso that ever," quod I, "dowteth of this, he ne may nat considere the nature of thinges ne the consequence of resouns."

"And over this," quod she, "yif that ther 85 be two thinges that han oo same purpose by kynde, and that oon of hem pursueth and parformeth thilke same thing by naturel office, and that oother ne may nat doon thilke naturel office, but folweth by other manere 90

17 **fey,** truth. 27 **wiht,** person. 51 **studies,** ways (manners). 55 **recordeth,** recall. 61 **fichched,** fixed. 66 **consequence,** conclusion. 87 **kynde,** their nature.

thanne is convenable to nature him that acomplesseth his purpos kyndeli, and yit he ne acomplesseth nat his owne purpos—wheither of thise two demestow for moore myhty?"

"Yif that I conjecte," quod I, "that thou   95 wolt seye, algates yit I desire to herkne it more pleynly of the."

"Thow nylt nat thanne deneye," quod she, "that the moevement of goinge nis in men by kynde?"   100

"No, forsothe," quod I.

"Ne thou ne dowtest nat," quod she, "that thilke naturel office of goinge ne be the office of feet?"

"I ne dowte it nat," quod I.   105

"Thanne," quod she, "yif that a wyht be myhty to moeve and goth upon his feet, and another, to whom thilke naturel office of feet lakketh, enforceth him to goon crepinge upon his handes, which of thise two owhte   110 to ben holden the moore myhty by ryht?"

"Knyt forth the remenaunt," quod I, "for no wyht ne dowteth that he that may gon by naturel office of feet ne be moore myhty than he that ne may nat."   115

"But the soveryn good," quod she, "that is eveneliche purposed to the good foolk and to badde, the goode folk seken it by naturel office of vertuus, and the shrewes enforcen hem to geten it by diverse coveytyse *(of erthely*   120 *things)*, which that nis no naturel office to geten thilke same soveryen good. Trowestow that it be any other wyse?"

"Nay," quod I, "for the consequence is open and shewinge of things that I have   125 graunted—that nedes goode folk moten ben myhty and shrewes feeble and unmyhty."

"Thow rennest aryht biforn me," quod she, "and this is the jugement *(that is to seyn, I juge of the)*, ryht as thise leches ben wont to   130 hopen *(of sike folk)*, whan they aperceyven that nature is redressed and withstondeth to the maledye. But for I se the now al redi to the understondinge, I shal shewe the moore thikke and continuel resouns. For loke now,   135 how gretly sheweth the feblesse and infirmite of wikkede folk, that ne mowen nat comen to that her naturel entencioun ledeth hem, and yit almost thilke naturel entencioun constreineth hem. And what *(were to*   140 *demen thanne of shrewes)* yif thilke naturel help hadde forleten hem, the which *(naturel help of intencioun)* goth alwey biforn hem, and is so gret that unnethe it may ben overcome? Considere thanne how gret deffaute of   145 power and how gret feblesse ther is in wikkede felonous folk. *(As who seyth, the gretter thing that is coveyted and the desire nat acomplised, of the lasse myht is he that coveyteth it and may nat acomplisse. And forthi Philosophie seyth thus by*   150 *sovereyn good:)* Ne shrewes ne requeren nat lyhte meedes ne veyn games, whiche they ne may folwen ne holden. But they faylen of thilke somme and of the heyhte of things *(that is to seyn, sovereyn good)*, ne thise   155 wrechches ne comen nat to the effect *(of sovereyn good)* the which they enforcen hem oonly to geten by nyhtes and by dayes, in the getinge of which good the strengthe of good foolk is ful wel ysene. For ryht so as thow   160 myhtest demen him myhty of goinge that goth on his feet tyl he myhte come to thilke place fro the whiche place ther ne laye no wey forthere to ben gon, ryht so most thow nedes demen him for ryht myhty that geteth   165 and ateyneth to the ende of alle things that ben to desire, byyonde the whiche ende ther nis nothing to desire. Of the which power of good folk men may conclude that the wikked men semen to be bareyne and naked   170 of alle strengthe. For why forleten they vertuus and folwen vices? Nis it nat for that they ne knowen nat the goodes? But what thing is moore feeble and more caytyf thanne is the blyndnesse of ignoraunce? Or elles they   175 knowen ful wel whiche things that they

---

91 convenable, appropriate. **99 goinge,** walking. **107 myhty,** strong enough. **130 leches,** physicians. **135 thikke,** deep. **151 ne requeren,** lack not. **152 lyhte meedes,** spurious rewards. **157 they enforcen,** they try. **174 caytyf,** miserable.

owhten folwe, but lecherie and coveytyse overthroweth hem mystorned, and certes, so doth distemperaunce to feeble men that ne mowen nat wrastlen ayeines the vices. Ne 180 knowen they nat thanne wel that they forleten the good wilfully and tornen hem wilfully to vyces? And in this wyse they ne forleten nat oonly to ben myhty, but they forleten al owtrely in any wyse for to ben. 185 For they that forleten the comune fyn of alle thinges that ben, they forleten also ther-withal for to ben.

"And peraventure it sholde semen to som folk that this were a merveyle to seyen, that 190 shrewes, whiche that contienen the moore partye of men, ne ben nat ne han no beinge. But natheles it is so, and thus stant this thing. For thei that ben shrewes, I deneye nat that they ben shrewes, but I deneye, and seye 195 simpleli and pleynly, that they ne ben nat, ne han no beinge. For ryht as thow myhtest seyen of the carayne of a man that it were a ded man, but thow ne myhtest nat symplely callen it a man, so graunte I wel forsothe 200 that visious folk ben wikked, but I ne may nat graunten absolutly and symplely that they ben. For thilke thing that withholdeth ordre and kepeth nature, thilke thing is, and hath beinge; but what thing that fayleth of that 205 *(that is to seyn, that he forleteth naturel ordre),* he forleteth thilke beinge that is set in his nature. But thow wolt seyn that shrewes mowen. Certes, that ne deneye I nat; but certes, her power ne dessendit nat of strengthe but of 210 feeblesse. For they mowen don wikked-nesses, the whiche they ne myhte nat don yif they myhten dwellen in the forme and in the doinge of good folk. And thilke power sheweth ful evidently that they ne mowen 215 ryht nawht. For so as I have gadered and proeved a litel her-byforn that yvel is nawht, and so as shrewes mowen oonly but shrewed-nesses, this conclusioun is al cleer, that

shrewes ne mowen ryht nawht, ne han no 220 power. And for as moche as thou under-stonde which is the strengthe of this power of shrewes, I have difinissed a litel her-byforn that nothing is so myhty as sovereyn good."

"That is soth," quod I. 225

"And thilke same sovereyn good may don non yvel?"

"Certes no," quod I.

"Is ther any wyht thanne," quod she, "that weneth that men mowen doon alle 230 thinges?"

"No man," quod I, "but he be owt of his witte."

"But, certes, shrewes mowen don yvel?" quod she. 235

"Ye, wolde God," quod I, "that they myhten don non!"

"Thanne," quod she, "so as he that is myhty to doon only but goode thinges may don alle thinges, and they that ben myhty to 240 don yvele thinges ne mowen nat alle thinges, thanne is it open thing and manifest that they that mowen don yvel ben of lasse power. And yit *(to proeve this conclusioun)* ther helpeth me this, that I have ishewed 245 her-byforn, that alle power is to be nowmbred among thinges that men owhten requere. And I have shewed that alle thinges that owhten ben desired ben referred to good, ryht as to a maner heyhte of her 250 nature. But for to mowen don yvel and felonye ne may nat ben referred to good. Thanne nis nat yvel of the nowmbyr of thinges that owhte ben desired. But alle power owhte ben desired and requered. Than is it 255 open and cler that the power ne the mowinge of shrewes nis no power. And of alle thise thinges it sheweth wel that the goode folk ben certeynly myhty, and the shrewes dowteles ben unmyhty. And it is cler and 260 open that thilke sentence of Plato is verray and soth, that seyth that oonly wyse men may

---

182 forleten, abandon. **186 comune fyn,** common end. **198 carayne,** corpse (carrion). **203 withholdeth,** preserves (pursues). **208 mowen,** are able (to do things). **223 difinissed,** explained (defined). **250 heyhte,** height. **251 to mowen,** to be able.

doon that they desiren. And shrewes mowen hawnten that hem liketh, but that they desiren *(that is to seyn, to comen to sovereygn* 265 *good)*, they ne han no power to accomplissen that. For shrewes don that hem lyst whan by the thinges in which they deliten, they wenen to ateyne to thilke good that they desyren, but they ne geten ne ateynen nat therto, for 270 vices ne comen nat to blisfulnesse.

Metre II. Quos vides sedere celsos.

"Whoso that the covertoures of her veyn aparayles myhte strepen of thise prowde kynges, that thou seest sitten on heyh in her chayres, glyteringe in shyninge purpre, envyrowned with sorwful armures, manassinge with 5 crwel mowth, blowinge by woodnesse of herte, he sholde seen thanne that thilke lordes beren withinne her corages ful streyte cheynes. For lecherie tormenteth hem in that oon syde with gredy venyms, and trowblable ire 10 that arayseth in him the floodes of trowblinges tormenteth upon that oother side her thowht, or sorwe halt hem wery and ykawht, or slidinge and deceyvinge hope tormenteth hem. And therfore, syn thow 15 seest oon heed *(that is to seyn, oon tyraunt)* beren so manye tyranyes, thanne ne doth thilke tyraunt nat that he desireth, syn he is cast doun with so manye wikkede lordes *(that is to seyn, with so manye vices that han so* 20 *wikkedly lordshippes over him)*.

Prose III. Videsne igitur quanto.

"Seestow nat thanne in how gret fylthe thise shrewes ben ywrapped, and with which cleernesse thise good foolk shynen? In this sheweth it wel that to goode foolk ne lakketh nevermo her meedes, ne shrewes lakken 5 nevermo torments. For of alle thinges that ben ẏdoon, thilke thing for which anything is

don, it semeth as by ryht that thilke thing be the meede of that—as thus, yif a man renneth in the stadie *(or in the forlong)* for 10 the corone, thanne lyth the meede in the corone for which he renneth. And I have shewed that blysfulnesse is thilke same good for which that alle thinges ben doon. Thanne is thilke same good purposed to the workes 15 of mankinde ryht as a comune meede, which meede ne may ben dessyvered fro good foolk. For no wiht as by ryht fro thennesforth that him lakketh goodnesse ne shal ben cleped good. For which thing, folk of goode 20 maneres, her meedes ne forsaken hem nevermo. For al be it so that shrewes wexen as woode as hem list *(ayenes goode folk)*, yit neverthelesse the corone of wyse men shal nat fallen ne faaden. For foreyne shrewed- 25 nesse ne bynymeth nat fro the corages of goode foolk her propre honour. But yif that any wyht rejoyse him of goodnesse that he hadde taken fro withowte *(as who seyth, yif that any wiht hadde his goodnesse of any oother man than* 30 *of himself)*, certes he that yaf him thilke goodnesse, or elles som oother wyht, myhte benyme it him. But for as moche as to every wyht his owne propre bownte yeveth him his meede, thanne at erst shal he faylen of 35 meede whan he forleteth to ben good. And at the laste so as alle meedes ben requered for men wenen that they ben goode, who is he that nolde deme that he that is ryht myhty of good were partles of meede? And of what 40 meede shal he be gerdoned? Certes, of ryht fayre meede and ryht grete aboven alle meedes. Remembre the of thilke noble corolarye that I yaf the a litel her-byforn, and gadere it togider in this manere: so as good 45 hymself is blisfulnesse, thanne is it cleer and certeyn that alle good folk ben maked blysful for they ben goode. And thilke folk that ben blysful, it acordeth and is covenable to ben goddes. Thanne is the meede of goode folk 50 swich that no day shal enpeyren it, ne no

---

264 **hawnten,** behave (live in). **IV METRE II. 5 sorwful armures,** stern soldiers. **6 blowinge,** panting. **8 streyte,** tight (strait).
IV PROSE III. 10 stadie, stadium. **11 meede,** reward. **25 foreyne shrewednesse,** external evil. **33 benyme,** deprive. **40 partles,**
without a share. **51 enpeyren,** impair.

wikkednesse ne shal derken it, ne power of no wyht ne shal nat amenusen it, that is to seyn, to ben maked goddes.

"And syn it is thus *(that goode men ne faylen nevermo of her meede)*, certes no wys man ne may dowte of undepartable peyne of the shrewes *(that is to seyn, that the peyne of shrewes ne departeth nat from hemself nevermo)*. For so as goode and yvel, and peyne and meedes ben contrarye, it mot nedes ben that ryht as we seen bytyden in gerdoun of goode, that also mot the peyne of yvel answery by contrarye party to shrewes. Now thanne, so as bownte and prowesse ben the meede to goode foolk, also is shrewednesse itself torment to shrewes. Thanne whoso that ever is entechched and defowled with peyne, he ne dowteth nat that he is entechched and defowled with yvel. Yif shrewes thanne wolen preysen hemself, may it semen to hem that they ben withowten party of torment, syn they ben swiche that the uttereste wikked-nesse *(that is to seyn, wikkede thewes, which that is the owttereste and the worste kynde of shrewednesse)* ne defowleth ne entechcheth nat hem oonly, but infecteth and envenymeth hem gretly? And also looke on shrewes, that ben the contrarye party of goode men, how gret peyne felawshippeth and folweth hem! For thou hast lerned a lytel her-byforn that alle thing that is and hath beynge is oon, and thilke same oon is good. Thanne is this the consequence that it semeth wel, that alle that is and hath beynge is good *(this is to seyn, as who seyth that beinge and unite and goodnesse is al oon)*. And in this manere it folweth thanne that alle thing that fayleth to ben good, it stynteth for to be and for to han any beinge; wherfore it is that shrewes stynten for to ben that they weren. But thilke oother forme of mankynde, that is to seyn the forme of the body withowte, sheweth yit that thise shrewes weren whilom men;

wherfor whan they ben perverted and torned into malice, certes than han they forlorn the nature of mankynde. But so as oonly bownte and prowesse may enhawnsen every man oover other men, thanne mot it nedes be that shrewes, which that shrewednesse hath cast owt of the condicioun of man-kynde, ben put under the merite and the desert of men. Thanne bytydeth it that yif thou seest a wyht that be transformed into vices, thow ne mayst nat wene that he be a man. For yif he be ardaunt in averyce, and that he be a ravaynour by vyolence of foreyne richesse, thow shalt seyn that he is lyke to the wolf. And yif he be felonows and withowte reste, and exersise his tonge to chidinges, thou shalt lykkne him to the hownd. And yif he be a prevey awaytour ihidd, and rejoyseth him to ravysse by wiles, thou shalt seyn him lyke to the fox-whelpes. And yif he be distempre and quaketh for ire, men shal wene that he bereth the corage of a lyoun. And yif he be dredful and fleinge, and dredeth thinges that ne owhten nat to ben dredd, men shal holden him lyk to the hert. And yif he be slowh and astoned and lache, he lyveth as an asse. And yif he be liht and unstidefast of corage, and chaungeth ay his studies, he is lykned to bryddes. And yif he be plownged in fowle and unclene luxuris, he is withholden in the fowle delices of the fowle sowe. Thanne folueth it that he that forleteth bownte and prowesse, he forleteth to ben a man; syn he may nat passen into the condicioun of God, he is torned into a best.

Metre III. Vela Naricii ducis.

"Eurus the wynd aryvede the sayles of Ulixes, duc of the contre of Narice, and his wandringe shippes by the see into the ile ther as Circes, the fayre goddesse, dowhter of the sonne, dwelleth, that medleth to hir newe

---

57 **undepartable,** inseparable. 62 **bytyden,** happen. 68 **entechched,** stained. I *peyne—defowled with* om. 72 **withowten party of,** have no part in. 74 *thewes*, habits. 89 **stynteth,** ceases. 112 **awaytour,** one who lies in wait. 120 **astoned . . . lache,** dazed, indolent. **IV METRE III. 1 Eurus,** the southeast wind. **aryvede,** caused to arrive. 2 **Narice,** Neritos, a mountain in Ithaca, of which Ulysses was ruler. 4 **Circes,** Circe. 5 **medleth to,** mixes for.

gestes drynkes that ben towched and
maked with enchauntements. And after that
hir hand, myhty over the herbes, hadde
chaunged hir gestes into diverse maneres,
that oon of hem is covered his face with   10
forme of a boere, that oother is chaunged
into a lyoun of the contre of Marmorike, and
his nayles and his teth wexen, that oother of
hem is neweliche chaunged into a wolf, and
howleth whan he wolde wepe, that oother   15
goth debonayrely in the hows as a tygre of
Inde. But al be it so that the godhed of Mercurie,
that is cleped the bryd of Archadie, hath had
mercy of the duc Ulixes, biseged with
diverse yveles, and hath unbownden him   20
fro the pestelence of his oostesse, algates the
roweres and the maryneres hadden by this
idrawen into her mowthes and dronken the
wikkede drynkes. They that weren wexen
swyn hadden by this ichaunged her mete of   25
bred for to eten akkornes of okes. Non of
her lemes ne dwelleth with hem hool, but they
han lost the voyce and the body; oonly her
thowht dwelleth with hem stable, that
weepeth and byweyleth the monstruous   30
chaunginge that they suffren. O overlyht
hand! *(As who seyth, O feble and lyht is the hand of
Circes the enchaunteresse, that chaungeth the bodies of
folkes into bestes, to regard and to comparisoun of
mutassioun that is maked by vices!)* Ne the   35
herbes of Circes ne ben nat myhty. For al be
it so that they may chaungen the lymes of the
body, algates yit they may nat chaunge the
hertes, for withinne is yhydd the strengthe
and vigor of men, in the secre toure of her   40
hertes *(that is to seyn, the strengthe of resoun).*
But thilke venyms of vices todrawen a man to
hem moore myhtyly than the venym of Circes.
For vices ben so cruel that they percen and
thorwpassen the corage withinne; and, thogh   45
they ne anoye nat the body, yit vices wooden
to destroyen men by wownde of thowht."

Prose IV. Tum ego fateor inquam.

Than seyde I thus: "I confesse and am
aknowe it," quod I, "ne I ne se nat that men
may sayn, as by ryht that shrewes ne ben
chaunged into bestes by the qualyte of her
sowles, al be it so that they kepen yit the   5
forme of the body of mankynde. But I
nolde nat of shrewes, of which the thowht crwel
woodeth alwey into destruccioun of goode men,
that if were leveful to hem to don that."

"Certes," quod she, "ne it nys nat leveful   10
to hem, as I shal wel shewe the in covenabele
place; but natheles, yif so were that thilke that
men wenen be leveful to shrewes were bynomen
hem *(so that they ne myhte nat anoyen or doon
harm to goode men),* certes a gret partye of   15
the peyne to shrewes sholde ben allegged
and releved. For al be it so that this ne seme nat
credible thing, peraventure, to some folk, yit
moot it nedes be that shrewes ben moore
wrecches and unsely whan they may doon   20
and performe that they coveyten than yif
they myhte nat complyssen that they coveyten.
For yif so be that it be wrecchednesse to wylne
to don yvel, than is moore wrecchednesse
to mowen doon yvel, withowte whiche   25
mowinge the wrecched wil sholde languesse
withowte effect. Than, syn that everyche of
thise thinges hath his wrechchednesse *(that is to
seyn, wyl to doon yvel and mowinge to don yvel),*
it mot nedes be that they ben constreyned by   30
three unselynesses, that woolen and mowen
and performen felonyes and shrewednesses."

"I acorde me," quod I; "but I desire gretly
that shrewes losten sone thilke unselynesses,
that is to seyn, that shrewes weren despoyled   35
of mowinge to don yvel."

"So shullen they," quod she, "sonner
peraventure than thow woldest, or sonner than
they hemself wene to lakken mowinge to don
yvel. For ther nis nothing so late, in so short   40

---

12 **Marmorike,** North Africa (Libya). 18 **bryd of Archadie,** Lat. *Numen Arcidis alitis* (the divine winged Arcadian), because Mercury was born in the Arcadian mountains. 20 **unbownden,** i.e.. preserved. 33, 36 *Circes:* I *Cirtes.* 46 **wooden,** rage. IV PROSE IV. 3 **as by ryht,** justly. 7 **nolde nat,** wish that it were not. 9 **leveful,** permitted. 13–14 **bynomen hem,** taken from them. 22 **complyssen,** achieve. 25 **mowen,** be able. 31 **unselynesses,** sorrows. **woolen,** desire. *three:* ICx *the;* Lat. *triplici.* 39–40 ICx *lakken—yvel* om.

bowndes of this lyf, that is long to abyde, namelyche, to a corage inmortel, of whiche shrewes the grete hope and the hye compassinges of shrewednesses is ofte destroyed by a sodeyn ende or they ben war. And that 45 thing estableth to shrewes the ende of her shrewednesse. For yif that shrewednesse maketh wrechches, than mot he nedes ben most wrechched that lengest is a shrewe; the whiche wikked shrewes wolde I demen 50 aldermost unsely and caytyfs, yif that her shrewednesse ne were fynyshed at the leste wey by the owttereste deth. For yif I have concluded soth of the unselynesse of shrewednesse, than sheweth it cleerly that thilke wrechched- 55 nesse is withowten ende, the whiche is certeyn to ben perdurable."

"Certes," quod I, "this conclusioun is hard and wonderful to graunte, but I knowe wel that it acordeth moche to the things that I 60 have graunted her-byforn."

"Thou hast," quod she, "the ryht estimacioun of this. But whosoever wene that it be a hard thing to acorde him to a conclusioun, it is ryht that he shewe that some of the 65 premysses ben false; or elles he moot shewe that the collacions of proposiciouns nis nat spedful to a necessarye conclusioun. And yif it ne be nat so, but that the premysses ben ygraunted, ther nis not why he sholde 70 blame the argument. For this thing that I shal telle thee now ne shal nat seme lasse wonderful, but of the things that ben taken also it is necessarie" *(as who seyth, it folweth of that which that is purposed byforn).* 75

"What is that?" quod I.

"Certes," quod she, "that is that thise wikked shrewes ben moore blysful *(or elles lasse wrechches)* that abyen the torments that they han deserved than yif no peyne of justice ne 80 chastysede hem. Ne this ne seye I nat now for that any man myhte thinke that the maners of shrewes ben coriged and chastised by venyaunce, and that they ben browht to the ryht wey by the drede of the torment, 85

ne for that they yeven to oother folk ensaumple to flen fro vices; but I understande yit in another manere that shrewes ben moore unsely whan they ne ben nat punyssed, al be it so that ther ne be had no resoun or 90 lawe of correcsioun, ne non ensaumple of lookinge."

"And what manere shal that ben," quod I, "oother than hath be told her-byforn?"

"Have we nat thanne graunted," quod 95 she, "that goode folk ben blysful, and shrewes ben wrechches?"

"Yis," quod I.

"Thanne," quod she, "yif that any good were added to the wrechchednesse of any 100 wyht, nis he nat moore weleful than he that he hath no medlinge of good in his solitarye wrechchednesse?"

"So semeth it," quod I.

"And what seystow thanne," quod she, 105 "of thilke wrechche that lakked alle goodes *(so that no good nis medled in his wrechchednesse),* and yit, over al his wykkednesse for which he is a wrechche, that ther be yit another yvel anexed and knytte to him? Shal nat men 110 demen him more unsely than thilke wrechche of whiche the unselynesse is releved by the partycipacioun of som good?"

"Whi sholde he nat?" quod I.

"Thanne, certes," quod she, "han 115 shrewes, whan they ben punysshed, somwhat of good anexed to her wrechchednesse, that is to seyn, the same peyne that they suffren which that is good by the resoun of justyce; and whan thilke same shrewes 120 ascapen withowte torment, than han they somwhat more of yvel yit over the wikkednesse that they han don, that is to seyn, defaute of peyne, which defaute of peyne, thow hast graunted, is yvel for the deserte of felonye." 125

"I ne may nat denye it," quod I.

"Moche moore thanne," quod she, "ben shrewes unsely whan they ben wrongfully delyvered fro peyne than whan they ben punysshed by ryhtful venyaunce. But this is 130

41 **to abyde,** to wait for. 79 **abyen,** receive. 83 **coriged,** corrected. 91-92 **ensaumple of lookinge,** example for consideration.

open thyng and cleer, that it is ryht that
shrewes ben punysshed, and it is wykkednesse
and wrong that they escapen unpunysshed."

"Who myhte deneye that?" quod I.

"But," quod she, "may any man denye 135
that al that is ryht nis good; and also the
contrarye, that al that is wrong is wykke?"

"Certes," quod I, "these thinges ben cleere
inowh, and that we han concluded a lytel
her-byforn. But I preye the that thow telle 140
me yif thou acordest to leten no torment to
sowles after that the body is ended by the
deeth?" (*This is to seyn, understandestow awht that
sowles han any torment after the deth of the body?*)

"Certes," quod she, "yee, and that ryht 145
gret. Of which sowles," quod she, "I trowe
that some ben tormented by asprenesse of
peyne, and some sowles, I trowe, ben exersised
by a purginge mekenesse. But my conseyl
nis nat to determenye of thise peynes. But I 150
have travayled and told yit hiderto for thow
sholdest knowe that the mowinge of shrewes,
which mowinge the semeth to ben unworthy,
nis no mowinge. And ek of shrewes, of
which thou pleynedest that they ne were 155
nat punysshed, that thou woldest seyn that
they ne weren nevermo withowten the torments
of her wykkednesse. And of the licence (*of the
mowinge to don yvel*) that thow preydest that
it myhte sone ben ended, and that thou 160
woldest fayn lernen that it ne sholde nat
longe dure. And that shrewes ben moore unsely
yif they were of lengere duringe, and most
unsely yif they weren perdurable. And after
this, I have shewed the that moore unsely 165
ben shrewes whan they escapen withowte
her ryghtful peyne than whan they ben
punyssed by ryhtful venyaunce. And of this
sentence folweth it that thanne ben shrewes
constreyned at the laste with most grevous 170
torment, whan men wene that they ne be
nat punysshed."

"Whan I considere thy resoun," quod I, "I
ne trowe nat that men seyn anything moore

verayly. And yif I torne ayeyn to the 175
studyes of men, who is he to whom it sholde
seme that he ne sholde nat oonly leven thise
thinges but ek gladly herkne hem?"

"Certes," quod she, "so it is. But men
may nat, for they han her eyen so wont to 180
the derknesse (*of erthely thinges*) that they
ne may nat lyften hem up to the lyht of cleer
sothfastnesse. But they ben lyke to bryddes of
which the nyht lyhtneth her lokinge and
the day blyndeth hem. For whan men 185
looken nat the ordre of thinges, but her
lustes and talents, they wene that eyther the
leve or the mowinge to don wykkednesse, or
elles the scapinge withowte peyne, be
weleful. But considere the jugement of the 190
perdurable lawe. For yif thou conferme thy
corage to the beste thinges, thou ne hast no nede
of no juge to yeven the prys or mede, for thow
hast joyned thyself to the moost excellent
thing. And yif thow have enclyned thy 195
studyes to the wykked thinges, ne sek no
foreyne wrekere owt of thyself. For thow
thyself hast thryst thyself into wikke thinges
ryht as thow myhtest loken by diverse
tymes the fowle erthe and the hevene, and 200
that alle other thinges stynten fro withowte
(*so that thow nere neyther in hevene ne in erthe, ne
saye nothing moore*). Than it sholde semen to
the, as by oonly resoun of lookinge, that
thow were now in the sterres and now in the 205
erthe. But the poeple ne looketh nat on thise
thinges. What thanne? Shal we thanne aprochen
us to hem that I have shewed that they ben lyk
to bestes? And what woltow seyn of this: yif
that a man hadde al forlorn his syhte, and 210
hadde foryeten that he ever sawh, and
wende that nothing ne faylede him of perfeccioun of mankynde—now we that myhten
sen the same thinges, wolde we nat wene
that he were blynde? Ne also ne acordeth 215
nat the poeple to that I shal seyn, the which
thing is sustened by a stronge fowndement of
resouns, that is to seyn, that moore unsely ben

141 **leten,** hinder. 147 **asprenesse,** bitterness. 152 **mowinge,** efficacy (ability). 197 **wrekere,** avenger (punisher). 217 **fowndement,**
foundation.

they that don wrong to oothre folk than
they that the wrong suffren."   220

"I wolde heren thilke same resouns,"
quod I.

"Denyesthow," quod she, "that alle shrewes
ne ben worthy to han torment?"

"Nay," quod I.   225

"But," quod she, "I am certein, by many
resouns, that shrewes ben unsely."

"It acordeth," quod I.

"Thanne ne dowtestow nat," quod she,
"that thilke folk that ben worthi of torment,   230
that they ne ben wrechches?"

"It acordeth wel," quod I.

"Yif thow were thanne yset a juge or a
knower of thinges, whether trowestow that
men sholden tormenten him that hath don   235
the wrong or elles him that hath suffred the
wrong?"

"I ne dowte nat," quod I, "that I nolde don
suffisaunt satisfaccioun to him that hadden
suffred the wrong by the sorwe of him that   240
hadden don the wrong."

"Thanne semeth it," quod she, "that the
doere of wrong is moore wrechche than he that
suffred wrong?"

"That folweth wel," quod I.   245

"Than," quod she, "by thise causes, and
by othre causes that ben enforced by the same
roote, fylthe or synne by the propre nature of it
maketh men wrechches. And it sheweth wel
that the wrong that men don nis nat the   250
wrechchednesse of him that reseyveth the
wrong, but the wrechchednesse of him that doth
the wrong. But certes," quod she, "thise
oratours or advocats don al the contrarye,
for they enforcen hem to commoeve the   255
juges to han pite of hem that han suffred
and resseyved the thinges that ben grevous and
aspre, and yit men sholden moore ryhtfully han
pite of hem that don the grevaunces and the
wronges. The whiche shrewes, it were a   260
moore covenable thing that the accusours or
advocats, nat wroth, but pitous and debonayre,

ledden tho shrewes that han don wrong to the
jugement, ryht as men leden syke folk to
the leche, for that they sholden seken owt   265
the maladies of synne by torment. And by
this covenaunt, ether the entente of deffendours
or advokats sholde faylen and cesen in al, or
elles yif the office of advocats wolde bettre
profyten to men, it sholde ben torned into   270
the habite of accusacioun *(that is to seyn,*
they sholden accuse shrewes, and nat excuse hem). And
ek the shrewes hemself, yif hit were leveful to
hem to sen at any clyfte the vertu that they
han forleten, and sawh that they sholden   275
putten adown the felthes of her vices by the
torments of peynes, they ne owhte nat, ryht for
the recompensacyoun for to geten hem bownte
and prowesse which that they han lost,
demen ne holden that thilke peynes weren   280
torments to hem; and ek they wolden refuse
the attendaunce of her advocats, and taken
hemself to her juges and to her accusors. For
which it bytideth that as to the wyse folk,
ther nis no place ileten to hate *(that is to* 285
seyn, that ne hate hath no place amonges wyse
men). For no wyht nyl haten goode men but yif
he were over-mochel a fool; and for to haten
shrewes, it nis no resoun. For ryht so as
langwissinge is maledye of body, ryht so   290
ben vyces and synne maledye of corage.
And so as we ne deme nat that they that ben
syke of her body ben worthy to ben hated, but
rather worthy of pyte, wel moore worthi
nat to ben hated but for to ben had in pite   295
ben they of whiche the thowhtes ben
constreyned by felonows wykkednesse, that
is moore cruwel than any langwyssinge of
body.

Metre IV. Quid tantos iuvat excitare motus.

"What deliteth yow to exciten so grete
moevinge of hateredes, and to hasten and
bysien the fatal disposicioun of yowr deth with

---

227 **unsely,** unhappy. 251–52 I *but the wrechchednesse—the wrong* om. 255 **enforcen hem . . . commoeve,** try, influence. **IV METRE**
IV. 1 What deliteth yow, why are you pleased.

yowr propre handes? *(That is to seyn, by batayles or by kontek?)* For yif ye axen the 5 deth, it hasteth him of his owne wyl; ne deth ne taryeth nat his swifte hors. And the men that the serpent and the lyown and the tygre and the bere and the boor seken to slen with her teth, yit thilke same men seken to 10 slen everych of hem oother with swerd. Lo, for her maneres ben diverse and descordaunt, they moeven unryhtful oostes and crwel batayles, and wylnen to perise by entre- chaunginges of dartes! But the resoun of 15 crweltee nis nat inowh ryhtful. Wiltow thanne yelden a covenable gerdoun to the desertes of men? Love ryhtfully goode folk, and have pite on shrewes."

Prose V. Hic ego video inquam.

"Thus se I wel," quod I, "eyther what blysfulnesse or elles what unselynesse is estab- lyssed in the desertes of goode men and of shrewes. But in this ilke fortune of poeple I se somwhat of good and somwhat of yvel. 5 For no wyse man hath levere ben exiled poore and nedy and nameles than for to dwellen in his cyte and flowren of rychesses and be redowtable by honour and strong of power. For in this wyse more clerly and 10 more witnessefully is the office of wyse men itreted, whan the blysfulnesse and the powste of governours is, as it were, yshad amonges poeples that be neighebours and subgits, syn that namely prysoun, lawe, and thise oothre 15 torments of laweful peynes ben rather owed to felonous citezeins—for the whiche felonous citezeins tho peynes ben establysshed—than for good folk.

"Thanne I mervayle me gretly," quod I, 20 "why that the thinges ben so mysentre- chaunged that torments of felonyes pressen and confownden goode folk, and shrewes ravysshen medes of vertu *(and ben in honours and in gret estats)*. And I desyre ek for to weten of 25 the what semeth the to ben the resoun of this so wrongful a conclusioun? For I wolde wondre wel the lasse, yif I trowede that al thise thinges weren medled by fortunous happe. But now hepeth and encreseth myn 30 astonyenge God, governour of thinges, that so as God yeveth ofte tymes to goode men goodes and myrthes, and to shrewes yveles and aspre thinges, and yeveth ayeinward to goode folk hardnesses, and to shrewes he 35 graunteth hem her wyl and that they desiren. What defference thanne may ther be bytwixen that that God doth and the happe of fortune, yif men ne knowe nat the cause why that it is?" 40

"Ne it nis no merveyle," quod she, "thowgh that men wenen that ther be somwhat folyssh and confuse, whan the resoun of the ordre is unknowe. But althogh that thou ne knowe nat the cause of so gret a disposi- 45 cioun, natheles for as moche as God, the goode governour, atempreth and governeth the world, ne dowte the nat that alle thinges ben doon aryht.

Metre V. Si quis Arcturi sidera.

"Whoso that ne knowe nat the sterres of Arctour itorned neygh to the sovereyn centre or poynt *(that is to seyn, itorned neyh to the sovereyn pool of the fyrmament)*, and wot nat why the sterre Boetes passeth or gadereth his 5 weynes and drencheth his late flambes in the see, and whi that Boetes the sterre unfoldeth his over swifte arysinges, thanne shal he wondren of the lawe of the heye eyr. And ek yif that he ne knowe nat why that the 10 hornes of the fulle moone wexen paale and infect by the bowndes of the derke nyht, and how the moone, dyrk and confuse, discovereth the sterres that she hadde icovered by hir cleere visage. The comune erroure moeveth 15

---

5 **kontek**, strife. 13 **moeven**, incite. IV PROSE V. 12 **itreted**, described. **powste**, power. IV METRE V. 2 **Arctour . . . centre**, constellation Arcturus (another name for Boötes), north pole. 5 **Boetes**, actually Arcturus is the brightest star in the constellation Boötes. 6 **weynes**, carts. 13 **discovereth**, reveals. 15 **erroure**, superstition. Beating on metal pots and pans to recall the moon from eclipse is still practiced in the Orient.

folk, and maket wery her basyns of bras by thikke strokes. *(That is to seyn, that ther is a manere of poeple that hihte Coribandes that wenen that, whan the moone is in the eclypse, that it be enchaunted, and therfore, for to rescowe the moone,* 20 *they beten her basyns with thikke strokes.)* Ne no man ne wondreth whan the blastes of the wynd Chorus beten the strondes of the see by quakinge floodes; ne no man wondreth whan the weyhte of the snowh, iharded by the colde, 25 is resolved by the brenninge hete of Phebus the sonne, for her sen men redely the causes.

"But the causes ihid *(that is to seyn, in hevene)* trowblen the brestes of men; the moevable poeple is astoned of alle thinges that comen 30 selde and sodeynly in owre age. But yif the trowbly erroure of owre ignoraunce departede fro us *(so that we wysten the causes why that swyche thinges bityden)*, certes they sholden cese to seme wondres." 35

Prose VI. Ita est inquam.

"Thos is it," quod I. "But so as thou hast yeven or byhyht me to unwrappen the hyd causes of thinges, and to discovere me the resouns covered with dyrknesses, I prey the that thou devyse and juge me of this matere, 5 and that thou don me to understonden it; for this meracle or this wonder trowbleth me ryht gretly."

And thanne she, a lytel what smylinge, seyde: "Thou clepest me," quod she, "to 10 telle thing that is grettest of alle thinges that mowen ben axed, and to the whiche questioun unnethes is ther awht inogh to laven it *(as who seyth, unnethes is ther suffisauntly anything to answere parfytly to thy questioun)*. For the 15 matere of it is swych that whan o dowte is determyned and kut awey, ther wexen oother dowtes withowte nowmber, ryht as the hevedes wexen of Ydre *(the serpent that Ercules slowh)*. Ne ther ne were no manere ne non 20 ende but yif that a wyht constreynede tho

dowtes by a ryht lyfly and quyk fyre of thowht *(that is to seyn, by vigour and strengthe of wit)*. For in this matere men weren wont to maken questions of the simplicite of the purvyaunce 25 of God, and of the order of destine, and of sodeyn happe, and of the knowinge and predestinacioun divine, and of the lyberte of fre wille, the whiche thinges thou thyself aperceyvest wel of what weyht they ben. 30 But for as mochel as the knowinge of thise thinges is a manere porcyoun of the medicine of the, al be it so that I have lytel tyme to don it, yit natheles I wol enforcen me to shewe somwhat of it. But althogh the norysinges of 35 dite of musike deliteth the, thou most suffren and forberen a litel of thilke delite whyle that I weve to the resouns yknit by ordre."

"As it lyketh to the," quod I, "so do."

Tho spak she ryht as by another 40 bygynninge, and seyde thus: "The engendringe of alle thinges," quod she, "and alle the progressiouns of muable nature and al that moeveth in any manere taketh his causes, his ordre, and his formes of the stablenesse 45 of the dyvine thowght. And thilke devyne thowht, that is yset and put in the towr *(that is to seyn, in the heyhte)* of the symplicite of God, stablyssheth many manere gyses to thinges that ben to done. The whiche manere, whan 50 that men looken it in thilke pure klennesse of the divyne intelligence, it is ycleped purvyaunce; but whan thilke maner is referred by men to thinges that it moveth and disponeth, thanne of olde men it was 55 cleped destyne. The whiche thinges, yif that any wyht looketh wel in his thowht the strengthe of that oon and of that oother, he shal lyhtly mowen seen that thise two thinges ben diverse. For purvyaunce is thilke devyne 60 reson that is enstablysshed in the sovereyn prynce of thinges, the whiche purvyaunce disponeth alle thinges. But destine is the disposicioun and ordinaunce clyvinge to moevable thinges, by the whiche disposicioun 65

---

27 her sen, here see. **29 moevable,** changeable (fickle). **31 selde,** seldom. **IV PROSE VI. 1 Thos,** thus. **13 laven it,** satisfy it. **19 Ydre,** Hydra. **27 sodeyn happe,** unexpected event. **30 weyht,** importance. **32 porcyoun,** portion. **53 purvyaunce,** providence. **55 disponeth,** arranges. **64 ordinaunce clyvinge,** disposition clinging. **65 moevable,** changeable.

the purvyaunce knitteth alle thinges in her ordres. For purvyaunce embraceth alle thinges to-hepe, althogh that they ben diverse, and althowgh they ben infynyte; but destyne departeth and ordeyneth alle thinges 70 singulerly, and dyvyded in moevinges, in places, in formes, in tymes. As thus: lat the unfoldinge of temporel ordynaunce, assembled and ooned in the lookinge of the dyvyne thowt, be cleped purvyaunce; and thilke 75 same assemblinge and ooninge, devyded and unfolden by tymes, lat that ben called destyne. And al be it so that thise thinges ben diverse, yit natheles hangeth that oon of that oother, for-why the order destynal 80 procedeth of the symplycite of purvyaunce. For ryht as a werkman that aperceyveth in his thoght the forme of the thing that he wol make, and moeveth the effect of the werk, and ledeth that he hadde loked byforn in his 85 thowht symperly and presently, by temporel ordinaunce, certes, ryht so God disponeth in his purvyaunce, syngulerly and stably, the thinges that ben to done, but he amynystreth in many maneres and in 90 dyverse tymes by destine thilke same thynges that he hath desponed.

"Thanne, wheyther that destyne be exer-cysed owther by some dyvyne spyrits, servaunts to the devyne purvyaunce, or 95 elles by som sowle, or elles by alle nature servinge to God, or elles by the celestial moevinges of sterres, or elles by the vertu of angeles, or elles by the diverse subtylyte of develes, or elles by any of hem, or elles by 100 hem alle, the destinal ordynaunce is ywoven and acomplyssed. Certes, it is open thing that the purvyaunce is an unmoevable and simple forme of thinges to done; and the moveable bond and the temporel ordynaunce of 105 thinges, whiche that the devyne symplycite of purvyaunce hath ordeyned to done, that is destine. For which it is that alle thinges that ben

put under destyne ben, certes, subgits to porvyaunce, to whiche purvyaunce destyne 110 itself is subgit and under. But some thinges ben put under purvyaunce that surmownten the ordynaunce of destyne; and tho ben thilke that stablely ben yfechched negh to the fyrste godhed. They surmownten the ordre of 115 destynal moevablete. For ryht as of cercles that tornen abowte a same centre or abowte a poynte, thilke cercle that is innerest or most withinne joyneth to the simplesse of the myddel, and is, as it were, a centre or a 120 poynt to that oother cercles that tornen abowten him. And thilke that is owtterest, compased by larger envyronninge, is unfolden by largere spaces in so moche as it is fertherest fro the myddel simplicite of the 125 poynt. And yif ther be anything that knytteth and felawshippeth himself to thilke myddel poynt, it is constreyned into symplicite *(that is to seyn, into unmoevablete)*, and it ceseth to be shad and to fleten diversely. Ryht so, 130 by semblable resoun, thilke thing that departeth fyrthest fro the fyrst thowht of God, it is unfolden and summytted to grettere bondes of destinye; and in so moche is the thing moore fre and laus fro destine, as it axeth 135 and holdeth him nere to thilke centre of thinges *(that is to seyn, God)*. And yif the thing clyveth to the stydefastnesse of the thoght of God, and be withowte moevinge, certes, it sormownteth the necissite of destyne. 140 Thanne ryht swych comparysoun as it is of skylinge to understondinge, and of thing that is engendred to thing that is, and of tyme to eternite, and of the cerkle to the centre, ryht so is the ordre of moevable destyne to 145 the stable symplycite of purvyaunce.

"Thilke ordynaunce moeveth the hevene and the sterres, and atempreth the elyments togydere amonges hemself, and transformeth hem by entrechaungeable mutasioun. And thilke 150 same ordre neweth ayein alle thinges

---

68 **to-hepe,** together. 70 **departeth,** separates out. 74 **ooned,** united. 85 **ledeth,** executes. 98 **vertu,** power. 102 **open,** evident. 114 **yfechched,** fixed. 116 **moevablete,** mutability. 123 **is unfolden,** is enfolded (surrounded). 130 **shad . . . fleten,** spread, flow. 133 **summytted,** submitted. 135 **laus,** loose. 142 **skylinge,** reason. 145 **moevable,** changeable. 150 **entrechaungeable mutasioun,** in the Lat., "mutual interchange."

growinge and fallinge adown, by semblable progressiouns of sedes and of sexes *(that is to seyn, male and femele).* And this ilke ordre constreyneth the fortunes and the dedes of 155 men by a bond of causes nat able to ben unbownde; the whiche destynal causes, whan they passen owt fro the bygynninges of the unmoevable purvyaunce, it mot nedes be that they ne be nat mutable. And thus ben 160 the thinges ful wel ygoverned, yif that the symplicite dwellinge in the dyvyne thoght sheweth forth the ordre of causes, unable to ben ybowed; and this ordre constreyneth by his propre stablete the moevable thinges or 165 elles they sholden fleten folyly. For which it is that alle thinges semen to ben confus and trowble to us men, for we ne mowen nat considere thilke ordynaunce; natheles, the propre manere of everythinge, dressinge 170 hem to goode, disponeth hem alle. For ther nis nothing don for cause of yvel; ne thilke thing that is don by wykkede folk nis nat don for yvel. The wheche shrewes, as I have shewed ful plentiuously, seken good, but 175 wikked errour mystorneth hem, ne the ordre cominge fro the poynt of sovereyn good ne declyneth nat fro his bygynninge.

But thou mayst seyn, what unreste may ben a worse confusioun than that goode 180 men han somtyme adversite and somtyme prosperite, and shrewes also han now thinges that they desiren, and now thinges that they haten? Wheyther men lyven now in swych hoolnesse of thowht *(as who seyth, ben men 185 now so wyse),* that swyche folk as they demen to ben goode folk or shrewes, that it moste nedes ben that folk ben swyche as they wenen? But in this manere the domes of men discorden, that thilke men that some folk demen 190 worthy of mede, oother folk demen hem worthy of torment. But lat us graunt, I pose, that som man may wel demen or knowen the goode folk and the badde; may he thanne

knowen and sen thilke inneryste atem- 195 praunce of corages, as it hath ben wont to ben seyd of bodies? *(As who seyth, may a man speken and determinen of atempraunces in corages, as men were wont to demen or speken of complexiouns and atempraunces of bodies?)* Ne it ne is nat 200 an unlyk myracle to hem that ne knowen it nat *(as who seyth, but it is lyk a merveyle or a myracle to hem that ne knowen it nat)* why that swete thinges ben covenable to some bodies that ben hoole, and to some bodies bittere 205 thinges ben covenable, and also why that some syke folk ben holpen with lyhte medicynes, and some folk ben holpen with sharppe medicynes. But natheles, the leche that knoweth the manere and the atempraunce 210 of hele and of maledye ne merveyleth of it nothing. But what oother thing semeth hele of corages but bownte and prowesse? And what other thing semeth maledye of corage but vices? Who is elles kepere of good or dryvere 215 awey of yvel but God, governour and lechere of thowhtes? The wheche God, whan he hath byholden from the heye toure of his purveaunce, he knoweth what is covenable to every wyht, and leneth hem that he wot 220 that is covenable to hem. Lo, herof comth and herof is don this noble myracle of the ordre destynal, whan God, that al knoweth, doth swyche thing, of which thing that un-knowinge folk ben astoned. But for to 225 constreine *(as who seyth, but for to comprehende and telle)* a fewe thinges of the devyne depnesse, the whiche that mannes resoun may under-stonde, thilke man that thou wenest to ben ryht juste and ryht kepinge of equite, the 230 contrarye of that semeth to the devyne purveaunce that al wot. And Lukan, my famyler, telleth that the victorious cawse lykede to the goddes, and the cause overcomen lykede to Catoun. Thanne what so ever thou 235 mayst sen that is don in this world unhoped or unwened, certes, it is the ryht ordre of

---

153 sedes, seeds. *sexes,* Lat. *fetuum* (offspring), trans. in Fr. *sexes.* **166 fleten folyly,** float foolishly. **170 dressinge,** disposing. **189 domes . . . discorden,** judgments disagree. **195 atempraunce,** quality. **201 unlyk,** dissimilar. **212 hele,** health. **220 leneth,** gives. **229 thou wenest,** you believe. **232 Lukan,** Lucan, Roman poet (1st cent. A.D.), *Pharsalia* I.128. **233 lykede,** pleased. **236–37 unhoped or unwened,** i.e., unexpected.

thinges, but as to thy wykkede opynyoun, it is a confusioun. But I soppose that som man be so wel ithewed that the devyne jugement 240 and the jugement of mankynde acorden hem togyder of him, but he is so unstidefast of corage that yif any adversite come to hem, he wol forleten, paraventure, to continue innocence, by the whiche he ne may nat 245 withholden fortune. Thanne the wyse dispensacioun of God spareth him, the whiche man adversite myhte enpeyren, for that God wol nat suffren him to travayle, to whom that travaile nis nat covenable. Another 250 man is parfyt in alle vertus, and is an holy man, and negh to God, so that the purvyaunce of God wolde demen that it were a felonye that he were towched with any adversites, so that he wol nat suffre that swych a man be 255 moeved with any bodyly maledye. But so as seyde a phylosophre, the moore excellent by me *(he seyde in Grec)* that 'vertuus han edified the body of the holy man.' And ofte tyme it bytydeth that the somme of thinges that 260 ben to done is taken to governe to goode folk for that the malyce haboundaunt of shrewes sholde ben abated. And God yeveth and departeth to oothre folk prosperites and adversites ymedled tohepe after the qualite 265 of her corages, and remordeth some folk by adversitee, for they ne sholde nat wexen prowde by longe welefulnesse. And oother folk he suffreth to ben travayled with harde thinges for that they sholden confermen the 270 vertus of corages by the usage and exercita-cioun of pacience. And oother folk dreden moore than they owhten the whiche they myhten wel beren; and somme dispyse that they mowe nat beren. And thilke folk God ledeth into 275 experience of hymself by aspre and sorwful thinges. And many oothre folk han bowht honourable renoun of this world by the prys of gloryous deth. And som men that ne

mowen nat ben overcomen by torments han 280 yeven ensaumple to othre folk that vertu may nat ben overcomen by adversites. And of alle thinges ther nis no dowte that they ne ben don ryhtfully and ordenely, to the profyt of hem to whom we sen thise thinges bytyde. 285 For certes, that adversite comth somtyme to shrewes, and somtyme that that they desiren, it comth of thise forseide cawses. And of sorwful thinges that bytyden to shrewes, certes no man ne wondreth, for alle men wenen that 290 they han wel deserved it, and that they ben of wykkede meryte. Of whiche shrewes the torment somtyme agasteth oothre to don felonies, and somtyme it amendeth hem that suffren the torments. And the prosperite 295 that is yeven to shrewes sheweth a gret argument to goode folk, what thing they sholden demen of thilke welefulnesse, the whiche prosperite men sen ofte serven to shrewes. In the which thing I trowe that 300 God dispenseth, for peraventure the nature of som man is so overthrowinge to yvel, and so uncovenable, that the nedy poverte of his howshold myhte rather egren him to don felonyes. And to the maladie of him God 305 putteth remedie, to yeven hym richesses. And som oother man byholdeth his conscience defowled with synnes, and maketh comparisoun of his fortune and of himself, and dredeth peraventure that his blysfulnesse, of which 310 the usage is joyeful to him, that the leesinge of thilke blysfulnesse ne be nat sorwful to him; and therfor he wol chaunge his maneres, and for he dredeth to leese his fortune, he forleteth his wykkednesse. To oothre folk is 315 welefulnesse yyeven unworthyly, the wheche overthroweth hem into distruccioun that they han desserved. And to som oothre folk is yeven power to punyssen, for that it shal be cause of contumacioun and exercysinge to goode 320 folk, and cause of torment to shrewes. For

---

240 **wel ithewed,** i.e., of such good habits. 248 **enpeyren,** injure. 249 **travaile,** suffer. 257 **excellent by me,** Lat. "more excellent than I"; Boethius evidently forgets that Philosophy is the speaker. The quotation has not been identified. 258 **edified,** created, Lat. *aedificaverunt.* 261 **to governe,** to be governed by. 266 **remordeth,** troubles. 270 **confermen,** strengthen. 274–75 ICA *and somme— beren* om; found in Cx. 298 **demen,** judge (value). 304 **egren,** incite. 311 **leesinge,** loss. 320 **contumacioun,** disobedience. C *continuacioun;* Fr. *coutumance.* Lat. has only *exercitium.*

so as ther nis non alyaunce bytwixe goode folk and shrewes, ne shrewes ne mowen nat acorden amonges hemself. And why nat? For shrewes discorden of hemself by her vices, 325 the whiche vices al torenden her consciences, and don ofte tyme thinges, the whiche thinges whan they han don hem, they demen that tho thinges ne sholden nat han ben don. For which thing thilke sovereyn purveaunce 330 hath maked ofte tyme faire myracle, so that shrewes han maked shrewes to ben goode men. For whan that som shrewes sen that they suffren wrongfully felonyes of oothre shrewes, they wexen eschaufet into hate of hem that 335 anoyeden hem, and retornen to the frut of vertu, whan they studien to ben unlyk to hem that they han hated. Certes, oonly this is the devyne myht, to the wheche myht yveles ben thanne goode whan it useth tho yveles 340 covenably and draweth owt the effect of any goode *(as who seyth, that yvel is good oonly to the myht of God, for the myht of God ordeyneth thilke yvel to good).*

"For oon ordre enbraseth alle thinges, so 345 that what wyht that departeth fro the resoun of thilke ordre which that is assygned to him, algates yit he slydeth into another ordre, so that nothing nis leveful to folye in the reame of the devyne purvyaunce *(as* 350 *who seyth, nothing nis withowten ordinaunce in the reame of the devyne purvyaunce)*; syn that the ryht stronge God governeth alle thinges in this world. For it nis nat leveful to man to comprehenden by wit, ne unfolden by word, 355 alle the subtyl ordinaunces and disposisiouns of the devyne entente. For oonly it owhte suffise to han looked that God hymself, makere of alle natures, ordeyneth and dresseth alle thinges to goode. Whyl that he hasteth to 360 withholden the thinges that he hath maked into his semblaunce *(that is to seyn, for to withholden thinges into good, for he hymself is good)*, he chaseth owt al yvel fro the bowndes of his communalyte by the ordre of necessite 365 destynable. For which it folweth that yif thou looke the purvyaunce ordeyninge the thinges that men wenen ben outrageous or habowndant in erthes, thou ne shalt nat sen in no place nothing of yvel. But I se now 370 that thou art charged with the weyhte of the questyoun, and wery with the lengthe of my resoun, and that thow abydest som swetnesse of songe. Tak thanne this drawht; and whan thou art wel refresshed and refect, thow 375 shal be moore stydefast to stye into heyere questyouns.

Metre VI. Si vis celsi iura tonantis.

"If thou, wys, wilt demen in thy pure thowht the ryhtes or the lawes of the heye thonderere *(that is to seyn, of God)*, loke thou and byhold the heyhtes of the sovereyn hevene. There kepen the sterres by ryhtful alliaunce 5 of thinges her olde pees. The sonne, imoeved by his rody fyr, ne distorbeth nat the colde cercle of the moone. Ne the sterre ycleped the Bere, that enclyneth his ravysshinge cours abowten the sovereyn heyhte of the 10 worlde, ne the same sterre Ursa nis nevermo wasshen in the depe westrene see, ne coveyteth nat to deeyn his flaumbes in the se of the occian, althogh he se oothre sterres iplownged in the see. And Hesperus the 15 sterre bodeth and telleth alwey the late nyhtes; and Lucifer the sterre bringeth ayein the cleere day.

"And thus maketh love entrechaunge-able the perdurable courses; and thus is 20 discordable batayle iput owt of the contre of the sterres. This acordaunce atempreth by evenelyk maneres the elyments, that the moyste thinges stryvinge with the drye thinges yeven place by stowndes; and the colde 25 thinges joynen hem by feyth to the hote thinges; and that the lyhte fyr aryseth into

---

335 eschaufet, heated. **366 destynable,** subject to destiny. **369 habowndant,** superfluous. **375 refect,** recreated. **376 stye,** climb. **IV METRE VI. 9–11 Bere . . . Ursa,** Ursa Major, the Big Dipper, which never sets in the northern hemisphere. **13 deeyn,** dye; Lat. *tingere.* **15 Hesperus,** the evening star. **17 Lucifer,** the morning star. **19 love entrechaungeable,** mutual love. **23 evenelyk,** serene. **25 by stowndes,** in season(s).

heyhte; and the hevy erthes avalen by her weyhtes. By thise same causes the flowry yer yildeth swote smelles in the fyrste 30 somer sesoun warminge; and the hoote somer dryeth the cornes; and autumpne comth ayein, hevy of apples; and the fletinge reyn bydeweth the wynter. This atempraunce norisseth and bryngeth forth alle thing that 35 bretheth lyf in this world; and thilke same atempraunce, ravysshinge, hideth and byny-meth, and drencheth under the laste deth, alle thinges iborn.

"Amonges thise thinges sitteth the heye 40 makere, kyng and lord, welle and bygynninge, lawe and wys juge, to don equite; and governeth and enclyneth the brydles of thinges. And tho thinges that he stereth to gon by moevinge he withdraweth and 45 aresteth, and affermeth the moevable or wandringe thinges. For yif that he ne klepede nat ayein the ryht goinge of thinges, and yif that he ne constreynede hem nat eftsones into rowndnesses enclynede, the thinges that 50 ben now continued by stable ordinaunce, they sholden departen from her welle *(that is to seyn, from her bygynninge)*, and faylen *(that is to seyn, torne into nowht)*. This is the comune love to alle thinges. And alle thinges axen 55 to ben holden by the fyn of good, for elles ne myhten they nat lasten, yif they ne come nat eftsones ayein, by love retorned, to the cause that hath yeven hem beinge *(that is to seyn, to God).* 60

Prose VII. Iamne igitur vides.

"Sestow nat thanne what thing folweth alle the thinges that I have seyd?"

"What thing?" quod I.

"Certes," quod she, "al outrely that alle fortune is good." 5

"And how may that be?" quod I.

"Now understand," quod she, "so as alle fortune, wheyther so it be joyeful fortune or aspre fortune, is yeven eyther by cause of gerdoninge or elles of exersysinge of good 10 folk, or elles by cause to punnysshen or elles chastysen shrewes, thanne is alle fortune good, the whiche fortune is certeyn that it be eyther ryhtful or elles profitable."

"Forsothe, this is a ful verray resoun," 15 quod I; "and yif I considere the purvyaunce and the destyne that thou tawhtest me a lytel her-byforn, this sentence is sustened by stydefast resouns. But yif it lyke unto the, lat us nowmbren hem amonges thilke 20 thinges of whiche thou seydest a litel her-byforn that they ne were nat able to ben wened to the poeple."

"Why so?" quod she.

"For that the comune word of men," 25 quod I, "mysuseth this manere speche of fortune, and seyn oftetymes that the fortune of som wyht is wykkede."

"Wyltow thanne," quod she, "that I aproche a lytel to the wordes of the poeple, 30 so that it seme nat to hem that I be over-moche departed as fro the usage of mankynde?"

"As thou wolt," quod I.

"Demestow nat," quod she, "that alle thing that profiteth is good?" 35

"Yis," quod I.

"And certes, thilke thing that exersiseth or coriget, profiteth?"

"I confesse it wel," quod I.

"Thanne is it good?" quod she. 40

"Why nat?" quod I.

"But this is the fortune," quod she, "of hem that eyther ben put in vertu and bataylen ayeins aspre thinges, or elles of hem that eschwen and declynen fro vices and taken 45 the wey of vertu."

"This ne may I nat denye," quod I.

"But what seystow of the myrye fortune that is yeven to good folk in gerdoun? Demeth awht the poeple that it is wykked?" 50

---

28 avalen, fall downward. **34 bydeweth,** moistens (bedews). **44 stereth,** stirs (causes). **46 affermeth,** makes stable (firm). **56 holden,** held (controlled). **IV PROSE VII. 10 gerdoninge,** rewarding. **22 wened,** believed (apprehended). **38 coriget,** corrects. **48 myrye,** pleasant (merry). **49** *Demeth:* A *devinith;* Lat. *decernit.*

"Nay, forsothe," quod I; "but they demen, as it soth is, that it is ryht good."

"And what seystow of that oother fortune," quod she, "that, althogh that it be aspre, and restreyneth the shrewes by ryhtful torment, weneth awht the poeple that it be good?" 55

"Nay," quod I, "but the poeple demeth that it is most wrechched of alle thinges that may ben thoght." 60

"War now and loke wel," quod she, "lest that we, in folwinge the opynyoun of the poeple, have confessed and concluded thing that is unable to ben wened to the poeple."

"What is that?" quod I. 65

"Certes," quod she, "it folweth or comth of thinges that ben graunted, that alle fortune, whatsoever it be, of hem that ben eyther in poscessioun of vertu, or in the encres of vertu, or elles in the purchasinge 70 of vertu, that thilke fortune is good, and that alle fortune is ryht wikkede to hem that dwellen in shrewednesse" *(as who seyth, and thus weneth nat the poeple).*

"That is soth," quod I, "al be it so that 75 no man dar confesse it ne byknowen it."

"Why so?" quod she. "For ryht as the stronge man ne semeth nat to abayssen or disdaignen as ofte tyme as he hereth the noyse of the batayle, ne also it ne semeth 80 nat to the wyse man to beren it grevously, as ofte as he is lad into the stryf of fortune. For bothe to that oon man and ek to that oother, thilke difficulte is the matere: to that oon man of encres of his glorious renoun, and to 85 that other man to confirme his sapience *(that is to seyn, to the aspresnesse of his estat).* For therfore is it called vertu, for that it susteneth and enforseth by his strengthes that it nis nat overcomen by adversites. Ne certes, 90 thou that art put in the encres or in the heyhte of vertu ne hast nat comen to fleten with

delices, and for to welken in bodily luste. Thow sowest or plawntest a ful egre batayle in thy corage ayenes every fortune. For that the 95 sorwful fortune ne confownde the nat, ne that the merye fortune ne corumpe the nat, ocupye the mene by stydefast strengthes. For al that ever is under the mene, or elles al that overpasseth the mene despiseth welefulnesse 100 *(as who seyth, it is vicious),* and ne hath no meede of his travaile. For it is set in yowr hand *(as who seyth, it lyth in yowr powere)* what fortune yow is levest *(that is to seyn, good or yvel).* For alle fortune that semeth sharp or aspre, yif 105 it ne exersyse nat the good folk ne chastiseth the wykked folk, it punysseth.

Metre VII. Bella bis quinis.

"The wrekere Attrides *(that is to seyn, Agamenon)* that wrowhte and continuede the batayles by ten yer, recovered and purgede in wrekinge by the destrucsyoun of Troye the loste chaumbres of maryaage of his brother. 5 *(This is to seyn, that he, Agamenon, wan ayein Eleyne that was Menelaus wyf his brother.)* In the mene while that thilke Agamenon desirede to yeven sayles to the Grekyssh navye, and bowhte ayein the wyndes by blod, he 10 unclothede him of pyte of fader, and the sory preest yeveth in sacryfyinge the wrechched kuttinge of throte of the dowhter. *(That is to seyn, that Agamenon let kutten the throte of his dowhter by the preest to maken allyaunce with his 15 goddes, and for to han wynde with whiche he myhte wenden to Troye.)*

"Ytakus *(that is to seyn, Ulixes)* bywepte his felawes ylorn, the whiche felawes the feerse Poliphemus, ligginge in his grete cave, 20 hadde freten and dreynt in his empty wombe. But natheles Pholiphemus, wood for his blynde visage, yald to Ulixes joye by his sorwful teeres. *(This is to seyn, that Ulixes*

76 **byknowen,** admit. **78 abayssen,** capitulate. **92–93 fleten .... delices ... welken,** float, sensual delights, wither. **98 mene,** middle ground. **102 meede,** reward. **IV METRE VII. 1 wrekere Attrides,** avenger Atrides, i.e., Agamemnon, son of Atreus. **7 *Menelaus wyf his brother,*** his brother Menelaus' wife (the OE split possessive, used until Malory and later). **18 Ytakus,** Lat. *Ithacus.* **21 freten and dreynt,** eaten and drowned.

smot owt the eye of Poliphemus that stood in his   25
forehed, for which Ulixes hadde joye, whan he
say Poliphemus wepinge and blynde.)

Hercules is celebrable for his harde travayles.
He dawntede the prowde Centaures *(half
hors, half man)*, and he birafte the dispoylinge   30
from the crwel lyoun *(that is to seyn, he
slowh the lyoun and rafte him his skyn)*. He smot the
briddes *(that hyhten Arpiis)* with certeyn arwes.
He ravysshede apples fro the wakinge
dragown, and his hand was the moore hevy   35
for the goldene metal. He drowh Cerberus
(the hownd of helle) by his treble cheyne. He,
overcomer, as it is seyd, hath put an unmeke
lord foddre to his crwel hors. *(This is to seyn,
that Hercules slowgh Dyomedes, and make his*   40
hors to freten him.) And he, Ercules, slowh
Idra *(the serpent)* and brende the venym. And
Achelows the flood, defowled in his forhed,
dreynte his shamefast visage in his strondes.
(This is to seyn, that Achelows koude transfigure   45
*himself into diverse lyknesses; and as he fawght
with Ercules, at the laste he tornede him into a bole;*

and Hercules brak of oon of his hornes, and he, for
shame, hidde him in his river.) And he, Ercules,
caste adown Antheus *(the gyaunt)* in the   50
strondes of Lybye; and Kacus apaysede the
wraththes of Evander. *(This is to seyn, that
Hercules slowgh the monstre Kacus, and apaysede
with that deth the wraththe of Evander.)* And
the brystlede boor markede with scomes the   55
shuldres of Herkules, the whiche sholdres
the heye cercle of hevene sholde thriste. And
the laste of his labours was that he sustened the
hevene upon his nekke unbowed; and he
deservede eftsones the hevene to ben the   60
prys of his laste travayle.

"Goth now thanne, ye stronge men, theras
the heye wey of the grete ensaumple ledeth yow.
O nyce men, why nake ye yowre backes?
(As who seyth, O ye slowe and delicat men, why   65
*flee ye adversytes, and ne fyhten nat ayenes hem
by vertu, to wynnen the mede of the hevene?)* For the
erthe, overcomen, yeveth the sterres." *(This is to
seyn, that whan that erthely lust is overcomen, a
man is maked worthy to the hevene.)*   70

Explicit liber quartus.

BOOK V

Incipit liber quintus.

Prose I. Dixerat oracionisque quibus cursum.

She hadde seyd, and torned the cours of hir
resoun to some oothre thinges to ben treted and
to ben ysped. Thanne seyde I, "Certes, ryhtful
is thin amonestinge and ful digne by

autorite. But that thou seydest whilom that   5
the questyoun of the divyne purviaunce is
enlaced with many oother questiouns, I
understonde wel and proeve it by the same
thing. But I axe yif that thou wenest that
hap be anything in any weys; and yif thou   10
wenest that hap be anything, what is it?"

---

27 *say,* saw. **29 dawntede,** tamed. **33** *Arpiis,* Harpies. **certeyn,** sure (accurate). **43 Achelows ... defowled,** the river Achelous, dishonored (by the loss of his horns). **51 Kacus apaysede,** and (by killing Cacus) appeased. **55 scomes,** foam (scum). **57 sholde thriste,** were to carry (thrust). Hercules took Atlas' place in supporting the world. **64 nyce ... nake,** foolish, show (i.e., run away). **V PROSE I. 4 amonestinge,** advising. **6** *the divyne:* I *thy divyne.* **10 hap,** chance.

Thanne quod she, "I haste me to yilden and assoylen to the the dette of my byhest, and to shewen and opnen the wey by which wey thou mayst come ayein to thy contre. But al be it so that the thinges which that thou axest ben ryht profitable to knowe, yit ben they diverse somwhat fro the paath of my purpos. And it is to dowten that thou ne be maked wery by mysweyes so that thou ne mayst nat suffice to mesuren the ryht wey."

"Ne dowte the therof nothing," quod I. "For for to knowen thilke thinges togedere, in the whiche thinges I delite me gretly, that shal ben to me instyde of reste, syn it is nat to dowten of the thinges folwinge, whan every syde of thy disputacioun shal han be stydefast to me by undowtous feith."

"Thanne," seyde she, "that manere wol I don the," and bygan to speken ryht thus: "Certes," quod she, "yif any wyht deffenisshe hap in this manere, that is to seyn, 'hap is bytydinge ibrowht forth by foolissh moevinge and by no knettinge of causes,' I conferme that hap nis ryht nawht in no wyse; and I deme alowtrely that hap nis, ne dwelleth but a voyce *(as who seyth, but an idel word)*, withowten any sygnificacioun of thing submitted to that vois. For what place myhte ben lefte, or dwellinge, to folye and to disordenaunce, syn that God ledeth and constreyneth alle thinges by ordre? For this sentence is verray and soth, that 'nothing ne hath his beinge of nawht'. To the whiche sentence none of thise olde folk ne withseyde never, al be it so that they ne understonden ne meneden it nawht by God prince and bygynnere of werkinge, but they casten as a manere fowndement of subject material, that is to seyn, of the nature of alle resoun. And yif that anything is woxen or comen of no cawses, thanne shal it seme that thilke thing is comen or woxen of nawht. But yif this ne may nat ben don, thanne is it nat possible that hap be any swych thing as I have diffynisshed a lytel her-biforn."

"How shal it thanne be?" quod I. "Nys ther thanne nothing that by ryht may be cleped eyther 'hap' or elles 'aventure of fortune'; or is ther awht, al be it so that it is hidd fro the poeple, to which thise wordes ben convenable?"

"Myn Arystotulis," quod she, "in the book of his *Phisik* diffynyssheth this thing by short resoun and negh to the sothe."

"In which manere?" quod I.

"As ofte," quod she, "as men don anything for grace of any oother thing, and another thing than thilke thing that men entenden to don bytydeth by some causes, it is cleped 'hap.' Ryht as a man dalf the erthe bycause of tylyinge of the feeld, and fownde there a gobet of gold bydolven, thanne wenen folk that it is byfalle by fortunows bytydinge. But for sothe, it nis nat of nawht, for it hath his propre causes, of whiche causes the cours unforeseyn and unwar semeth to han maked hap. For yif the tylyere of the feld ne dolve nat in the erthe, and yif the hyder of the gold ne hadde hidde the gold in thilke place, the gold ne hadde nat ben fownde. Thise ben thanne the causes of the abregginge of fortuit hap, the which abregginge of fortuit hap comth of causes encowntringe and flowinge togydere to hemself, and nat by the entencioun of the doere. For neither the hidere of the gold ne the delvere of the feeld ne understonden nat that the gold sholde han ben fownde; but as I sayde, it bytydde and ran togydere that he dalf theras that oother hadde hyd the gold. Now may I thus dyffynisse 'hap': hap is an unwar bytydinge of causes assembled in thinges that ben don for som oother thing. But thilke ordre, procedinge by an uneschuable byndinge

---

13 **assoylen ... dette ... byhest,** fulfill the obligation of my promise. 20 **mysweyes,** bypaths. 28 **undowtous,** certain. 31 **deffenisshe,** define. 33 **foolissh,** confused. 54 *that hap be:* CxA *that there hath he* (*ben*). 63–64 **Arystotulis ...** *Phisik,* Aristotle, *Physics* II.5. 70 **bytydeth,** results. 82 **abregginge,** diminishing (explaining). 92 **dyffynisse ... unwar,** define, unplanned. 95 **uneschuable,** inescapable.

togydere, which that descendeth fro the
welle of purvyaunce that ordeyneth alle thinges
in her places and in her tymes, maketh that the
causes rennen and assemblen togydere.

Metre I. Rupis Achimenie scopulis.

"Tigris and Eufrates resolven and spryngen of
oo welle in the kragges of the roche of the contre
of Achemenie, ther as the fleynge batayle
fichcheth her dartes retorned in the brestes
of hem that folwen hem. And soone after　5
tho same ryveres, Tigris and Eufrates,
unjoinen and departen her wateres. And yif
they comen togyderes, and ben assembled and
cleped togydere into o cours, thanne moten
thilke thinges fleten togydere which that the　10
water of the entrechaunginge flod bringeth.
The shippes and the stokkes arraced with the
flood moten assemblen, and the wateres
imedled wrappeth or implieth many
fortunel happes or maneres, the whiche　15
wanderinge happes, natheles, thilke de-
clyninge lownesse of the erthe and the flowinge
ordre of the slydinge water governeth. Ryht so
Fortune, that semeth as that it fleteth with
slaked or ungovernede brydles, it suffereth　20
brydles *(that is to seyn, to ben governed)*, and
passeth by thilke lawe" *(that is to seyn, by thilke
devyne ordenaunce)*.

Prose II. Animadverto inquam.

"This undirstonde I wel," quod I, "and I me
acorde wel that it is ryht as thou seyst. But I
axe yif ther be any liberte of fre wil in this ordre
of causes that clyven thus togidere in
hymself; or elles I wolde witen yif that the　5
destynal cheyne constreyneth the movinges
of the corages of men?"

"Yis," quod she, "ther is liberte of fre wil, ne
ther ne was nevere no nature of resoun that
it ne hadde liberte of fre wil. For everything　10
that may natureli usen resoun, it hath doom
by which it decerneth and demeth everything.
Thanne knoweth it by itself thinges that ben to
fleen and thinges that ben to desiren. And
thilke thing that any wyht demeth to ben　15
desired, that axeth or desireth he; and
fleeth thilke thing that he troweth to ben to
fleen. Wherfore in alle thinges that resoun is, in
hem also is liberte of wyllinge and of
nyllinge. But I ne ordeyne nat *(as who seyth,*　20
I ne graunte nat) that this liberte be evene-lyk
in alle thinges. For-why in the sovereynes
dyvynes substaunces *(that is to seyn, in spirits)*
jugement is moore cleere, and wil nat
icoromped, and myht redy to speden　25
thinges that ben desired. But the sowles of
men moten needes be moore free whan they
looken hem in the speculacioun or lookinge of
the devyne thoght, and lasse free whan they
slyden into the bodies, and yit lasse free　30
whan they ben gadered togidere and
comprehended in erthely membres. But the
laste servage is whan that they ben yeven to
vices, and han yfalle from the possessioun
of her propre resoun. For after that they　35
han cast awey her eyen fro the lyht of the
sovereyn sothfastnesse to lowe thinges and
derke, anon they derken by the clowdes of
ignoraunce and ben trowbled by felonous
talents; to whiche talents whan they　40
aprochen and asenten, thei hepen and
encresen the servage which they han joyned to
hemself. And in this manere they ben kaytyſs
fro her propre liberte. The whiche thinges,
nathelesse, the lookinge of the devyne　45
purvyaunce seth, that alle thinges byholdeth
and seth fro eterne, and ordeyneth hem everych

V METRE I. **3 Achemenie,** the Achaemenian rocks are in Armenia where the two rivers originate. **fleynge batayle,** fleeing troops; the Parthians were reputed to shoot arrows at their pursuers while retreating. **4 fichcheth,** fixes. **7 unjoinen,** the sources of the Tigris and Euphrates are close but not identical. **12 arraced,** pulled up. **14 implieth,** enwrap. **20 slaked . . . suffereth,** slack, bears. V PROSE II. **4 clyven,** cleave. **9 nature of resoun that,** reasonable nature if. **11 doom,** judgment. **21 evene-lyk,** equal. **25 icoromped,** corrupted. **28 looken . . . speculacioun,** i.e., when they contemplate the world under the influence. **40 talents,** desires. **41** Cx *they assenten and approchen and encresen.*

in her merites as they ben predestynat. *(And it is seyd in Grek that)* alle thinges he seth and alle thinges he hereth. 50

Metre II. Puro clarum lumine.

"Homer with the hony mowth *(that is to seyn, Homer with the swete dites)* syngeth that the sonne is cleer by pure lyht; natheles yit ne may it nat, by the infirme lyht of his beemes, breken or percen the inwarde entrailes of 5 the erthe or elles of the see. So ne seth nat God, makere of the grete world. To him that looketh alle thinges from an heh ne withstondeth no thinges by hevynesse of erthe, ne the nyht ne withstondeth nat to him by the 10 blake klowdes. Thilke God seeth, in oo strokk of thoght, alle thinges that ben, or weren, or sholle comen, and thilke God, for he loketh and seth alle things alone, thow mayst seyn that he is the verray sonne." 15

Prose III. Tum ego en inquam.

Thanne seyde I, "Now am I confownded by a moore hard dowte than I was."

"What dowte is that?" quod she. "For certes, I conjecte now by whiche thinges thou art trowbled." 5

"It semeth," quod I, "to repugnen and to contraryen gretly that God knoweth byforn alle thinges, and that there is any freedom of liberte. For yif so be that God looketh alle thinges byforn, ne God ne may nat ben 10 deceyved in no manere, than mot it nedes ben that alle thinges bytyden the whiche that the purvyaunce of God hath seyn byforn to comen. For which, yif that God knoweth byforn nat oonly the werkes of men, but also 15 her conseyles and her willes, thanne ne shal ther be no liberte of arbitre. Ne certes ther ne may be noon oother dede, ne no wil, but thilke which that the devyne purvyaunce, that

may nat ben deceyved, hath feeled byforn. 20 For yif that they myhten wrythen awey in oothre manere than they ben purveyed, thanne sholde ther be no stydefast prescience of thing to comen, but rather an uncerteyn opynyoun, the whiche thing to trowen of 25 God, I deme it felonye and unleveful. Ne I ne proeve nat thilke same resoun *(as who seyth, I ne alowe nat, or I ne preyse nat, thilke same resoun)* by which that som men wenen that they mowen assoylen and unknytten the knotte of 30 this questioun. For certes, they seyn that thing nis nat to comen for that the purvyaunce of God hath seyn it byforn that is to comen, but rather the contrarye *(and that is this)*, that for that the thing is to comen, therfore ne 35 may it nat ben hidde fro the purvyaunce of God; and in this manere this necessite slydeth ayein into the contrarye partye. Ne it ne byhoveth nat, nedes, that thinges bytyden that ben purvyed, but it byhoveth, nedes, 40 that thinges that ben to comen ben yporveyed—but as it were ytravayled *(as who seyth, that thilke answere procedeth ryht as thogh men travayleden or weren bysy)* to enqueren the whiche thing is cause of the whiche thing, 45 as wheyther the prescience is cause of the necessite of thinges to comen, or elles that the necessite of thinges to comen is cause of the purvyaunce. But I ne enforce me nat now to shewen it, that the bitydinge of thinges 50 iwist biforn is necessarie, how so or in what manere that the ordre of causes hath itself; althogh that it ne seme nat that the prescience bringe in necessite of bytydinge to thinges to comen. For certes, yif that any wight sitteth, 55 it bihoveth by necessite that the opinioun be soth of him that conjecteth that he sitteth. And ayeinward also is it of the contrarye: yif the opynioun be sooth of any wyht for that he sitteth, it byhoveth by necessite that he 60 sitte. Thanne is heere necessite in that oon and in that oother, for in that oon is necessite

---

V METRE II. **8 an heh,** on high. V PROSE III. **6–7 repugnen . . . contraryen,** be repugnant and wrong. **7 knoweth byforn,** knows things beforehand. **21 wrythen,** twist. **23 prescience,** foreknowledge. **30 assoylen,** solve. **39 byhoveth,** need be. **42 yporveyed,** foreseen. **ytravayled,** necessary. **50 bitydinge,** befalling.

of sittinge, and certes in that oother is necessite of sooth. But therfore ne sitteth nat a wight for that the opynyoun of the sittinge is soth, but the opynioun is rather sooth for that a wyht 65 sitteth byforn. And thus, althogh that the cause of the sooth cometh of that other syde *(as who seith, that althogh the cause of soth comth of the sitting, and nat of the trewe opynyoun)*, algates 70 yit is there comune necessite in that on and in that oother. Thus sheweth it that I may make semblable skyles of the purvyaunce of God and of thinges to comen. For althowh that for that thinges ben to comen, therfore ben 75 they purveyed, nat certes for they ben purveyed, therfore ne bytyde they nat. Yit natheles, byhoveth it by necessite that eyther the thinges to comen ben ypurveyed of God, or elles that the thinges that ben purveyed 80 of God bytyden *(by necessite)*. And this thing only suffiseth ynowh to destroyen the freedom of owre arbitre *(that is to seyn, of owre free wil)*. But now, certes *(sheweth it wel how fer fro the sothe and)* how up-so-down is this thing that 85 we seyn, that the bytydinge of temporel thinges is cause of the eterne prescience. But for to wenen that God purvyeth the thinges to comen for they ben to comen, what oother thing is it but for to wene that thilke thinges 90 that bytydden whilom ben causes of thilke sovereyn purvyaunce *(that is in God)*? And herto *(I adde yit this thing:)* that ryht as whan that I wot that a thing is, it byhoveth by necessite that thilke selve thing be; and ek 95 whan I have knowe that anything shal bytyden, so byhoveth it by necessite that thilke same thing bytyde; so folweth it thanne that the bytydinge of the thing iwist biforn ne may nat ben eschwed. And at the laste, yif that 100 any wyht wene a thing to ben oother weyes thanne it is, it is nat oonly unscience, but it is deceyvable opynyoun ful diverse and fer fro the soothe of science. Wherfore, yif anything be so to comen, so that the bytydinge of hit ne 105

be nat certeyn ne necessarye, who may weten byforn that thilke thing is to comen? For ryht as scyence ne may nat ben medled with falsnesse *(as who seyth, that yif Y wot a thing, it ne may nat be false that I ne wot it)*, ryht 110 so thilke thing that is conceyved by science ne may nat ben non oother weys thanne as it is conceyved. For that is the cause whi that science wanteth lesing *(as who seyth, why that wytinge ne receyveth nat leesinge of that it wot)*. 115 For it byhoveth by necessite that everything be ryht as science comprehendeth it to be. What shal I thanne seyn? In which manere knoweth God byforn the thinges to comen yif they ne be nat certein? For yif that he deme that 120 they ben to comen uneschewably, and so may be that it is possyble that they ne shollen nat comen, God is deceyved. But nat oonly to trowen that God is deceyved, but for to speke it with mowth, it is a felonous synne. 125 But yif that God wot that ryht so as thinges ben to comen, so shullen they comen, so that he wite egaly *(as who seyth, indifferently)* that thinges mowen ben doon or elles nat ydoon, what is thilke prescience that ne 130 comprehendeth no certeyn thing ne staable? Or elles what difference is ther bitwixe the prescience and thilke japeworthy dyvyninge of Tyresye the dyvynour, that seyde, 'Al that I seye,' quod he, 'either it shal be, or elles it 135 ne shal nat be'? Or elles how mochel is worth the dyvyne prescience moore than the opynyoun of mankynde, yif so be that it demeth the thinges uncerteyn, as men doon, of the whiche domes of men the bytydinge 140 nis nat certein? But yif so be that non uncerteyn thing ne may ben in him that is ryht certein welle of alle thinges, thanne is the bytydinge certeyn of thilke thinges whiche he hath wist byforn fermely to comen. For 145 which hit folweth that the freedom of the conseyles and of the werkes of mankynd nis non, syn that the thoght of God, that seth alle

---

68–69 I A *of the sooth—the cause* om. (eyeskip); found in Cx. **73 skyles,** inferences. **114 lesing,** falsehood (lying). **121 uneschewably,** inescapably. **128 egaly,** equally. **134 Tyresye,** Tiresias, the blind prophet of Thebes. **147–48 nis non,** is nothing.

things withowten errowr of falsnesse, byndeth and constreyneth hem to a 150 bitydinge *(by necessite)*. And yif this thing be oones ygraunted and receyved *(that is to seyn, that ther nis no free wille)* than sheweth it wel how gret destruccyoun and how grete damages ther folwen of thinges of mankynde. For in 155 ydel ben ther thanne purposed and byhyht meedes to goode folk and peynes to badde folk, syn that no moevinge of fre corage voluntarye ne hath nat deserved hem *(that is to seyn, neyther meede ne peyne)*. And it sholde seme 160 thanne that thilke thing is alderworst which that is now demed for aldermoost just and most ryhtful, that is to seyn, that shrewes ben punysshed, or elles that goode foolk ben ygerdoned. The whiche foolk, syn that her 165 propre wil ne sent hem nat to that oon ne to that oother *(that is to seyn, neyther to goode ne to harm)*, but constreyneth hem certeyn necessite of thinges to comen, thanne ne shollen ther nevere ben, ne nevere weren, vice ne vertu, 170 but it sholde rather ben confusioun of alle dissertes medled withowten discrecioun. And yit ther folweth anoother inconvenyent, of the whiche ther ne may ben thoght no moore felonous ne moore wykke, and that is this: 175 that so as the ordre of thinges is yled and comth of the purvyaunce of God, ne that nothing nis leveful to the conseyles of mankynde *(as who seyth, that men han no power to doon nothing, ne wilne nothing)*, than folweth it that 180 owre vices ben referred to the makere of alle good *(as who seyth, thanne folweth it that God owhte han the blame of owre vices, syn he constreyneth us by necessite to doon vices)*.

"Thanne is ther no resoun to hopen in 185 God, ne for to preyen to God. For what sholde any wyht hopen to God, or why sholde he preyen to God, syn that the ordenaunce of destyne, which that ne may nat ben inclyned, knytteth and streyneth alle thinges 190 that men may desyren? Thanne sholde ther be doon awey thilke oonly allyaunce bytwixen God and men, that is to seyn, to hopen and to preyen. But by the prys of rihtwessenesse and of verray mekenesse we desserven the 195 gerdoun of the dyvyne grace, which that is inestymable *(that is to seyn, that it is so gret that it ne may nat ben ful ypreysed)*. And this is oonly the manere *(that is to seyn, hope and preyeres)* for which it semeth that men mowen speke with 200 God, and by resoun of supplicacioun be conjoined to thilke cleernesse that nis nat aproched no rather or that men beseken it and impetren it. And yif men wene nat that hope ne preyeres ne han no strengthes by the 205 necessite of thinges to comen yreceyved, what thing is ther thanne by whiche we mowen ben conjoined and clyven to thilke sovereyn prynce of thinges? For which it byhoveth by necessitee that the lynage of mankynde, as 210 thou songe a lytel her-byforn, be departed and unjoined from his welle, and faylen *(of his bygynninge, that is to seyn, God)*.

Metre III. Quenam discors.

"What discordable cause hath to-rent and unjoygned the byndinge or the alliaunce, of thinges *(that is to seyn, the conjunccioun of God and man)*? Whiche God hath establysshed so gret batayle bitwixen thise two soothfast or 5 verray thinges *(that is to seyn, bytwixen the purvyaunce of God and fre wil)* that they ben synguler and devyded, ne that they ne wolen nat ben meddeled ne cowpeled togydere? But ther nis no discord to the verray thinges, 10 but they clyven, certeyn, alwey to hemself. But the thoht of man, confownded and over-thrown by the dirke menbres of the body, ne may nat by fyr of his derked looking *(that is to seyn, by the vigour of his insyhte, whyl the 15 sowle is in the body)*, knowe the thinne subtyl knyttinges of thinges. But wherfore eschaufeth it so, by so gret love, to fynden thilke notes of

---

156 byhyht, promised. **161 alderworst**, worst of all. **165 ygerdoned**, rewarded. **203 no rather or that**, no more quickly than by (no other way than by). **204 impetren**, implore. **V METRE III. 17 eschaufeth**, burns.

soth icovered. *(That is to seyn, wherfore
eschaufeth the thoght of man by so gret desyr to*   20
*knowen thilke notificasions that ben ihyd under the
covertoures of sooth?)* Wot it awht thilke thing
that it, angwyssous, desireth to knowe? *(As who
seyth, nay; for no man travayleth for to witen
things that he wot. And therfore the texte seyth*   25
thus:) But who travayleth to witen thinges
yknowe? And yif that he ne knoweth hem nat,
what seketh thilke blynde thoght? What is he
that desireth anything of which he not ryht
nawht? *(As who seith, whoso desireth anything,*   30
*nedes somwhat he knoweth of it, or elles he ne
kowde nat desire it.)* Or who may folwen thinges
that ne ben nat iwist? And thogh that he seke
tho thinges, wher shal he fynde hem? What
wyht that is al unkunninge and ignoraunt   35
may knowe the forme that is yfownde? But
whan the sowle byholdeth and seth the heye
thoght *(that is to seyn, God)*, thanne knoweth it
togidere the somme and the syngularitees
(that is to seyn, the principules and everych by   40
hymself).

"But now, whil the sowle is hidde in the
clowde and in the derkenesse of the menbres of
the bodi, it ne hath nat al foryeten itself, but
it withholdeth the somme of things and   45
leeseth the syngularites. Thanne whoso that
seketh sothnesse, he nis in neyther nother
habite. For he not nat al, ne he ne hath nat al
foryeten, but yit him remembreth the
somme of things that he withholdeth, and   50
axeth conseyl, and retreteth deepliche
thinges iseyn byforn *(that is to seyn, the grete
somme in his mynde)*, so that he mowe adden the
partyes that he hath foryeten to thilke that
he hath withholden."   55

Prose IV. Tum illa vetus inquit.

Thanne seyde she: "This is," quod she, "the
olde questioun of the purvyaunce of God. And

Marchus Tullius, whan he devyded the dyvyna-
ciouns *(that is to seyn, in his book that he wroot
Of Divinaciouns)*, he moevede gretly this   5
questioun; and thou thyself has isowht it
mochel, and owtrely, and longe. But yit ne hath
it nat ben determyned ne isped fermely and
diligently of any of yow. And the cause of
this dirkenesse and of this dificulte is for   10
that the moevinge of the resoun of mankynde ne may nat moeven to *(that is to seyn,
applien or joynen to)* the symplicite of the dyvyne
prescience; the whiche *(symplicite of the devyne
prescience)* yif that men myhten thinken it in   15
any maner *(that is to seyn, that yif men myhten
thinken and comprehenden the things as God seth
hem)*, thanne ne sholde ther dwellen owtrely no
dowte: the whiche resoun and cause of
difficulte I shal assaye at the laste to shewe   20
and to speden, whan I have fyrst yspended
and answered to the resouns by which thou art
ymoeved. For I axe why thou wenest that
thilke resouns of hem that assoylen this
questioun ne be nat spedful ynowh ne   25
sufficient: the whiche solucioun, or the
whiche resoun, for that it demeth that the
prescience nis nat cause of necessite to things
to comen, than ne weneth it nat that fredom
of wyl be destorbed or ylett by prescience.   30
For ne drawestow nat arguments from elleswhere of the necessite of things tocomen *(as
who seyth, any oother wey than thus)* but that
thilke things that the prescience wot byforn
ne mowen nat unbytyde? *(That is to seyn,*   35
that they moten bytyde.) But thanne, yif that
prescience ne putteth no necessite to things to
comen, as thow thyself hast confessed it and
byknowen a litel her-biforn, what cause or
what is it *(as who seyth, ther may no cause be)*   40
by which that the endes voluntarie of
thinges myhten be constreyned to certeyn
bytydinge? For by grace of positioun, so that
thou mowe the betere understonde this that

---

22 Wot it awht, does it at all realize. **26 witen,** understand. **45 withholdeth,** retains (remembers). **47 in neyther nother,** in neither
the one nor the other. **48 not,** ne wot (doesn't know). **51 retreteth,** reconsiders. **V PROSE IV. 3 Tullius,** Cicero, *De Divinatione*
II.60. *devyded:* I *devynede;* Lat. *distribuit.* **30 ylett,** hindered. **35 unbytyde,** fail to happen. **43** *positioun* (hypothesis): ICA *possessioun;*
Lat. *positionis.*

folweth, I pose *(per impossibile)* that ther ne 45
be no prescience. Thanne axe I," quod she,
"in as mochel as apertieneth to that, sholden
thanne things that comen of fre wyl ben
constreyned to bytyden by necessite?"

Boece. "Nay," quod I. 50

"Thanne ayeinward," quod she, "I
suppose that ther be prescience, but that it ne
putteth no necessite to things; thanne trowe I
that thilke selve fredom of wil shal dwellen
al hool and absolut and unbownden. But 55
thou wolt seyn that, al be it so that
prescience nis nat cause of the necessite of
bytydinge to things to comen, algates yit it is a
syngne that the things ben to bityden by
necessite. By this manere thanne, althogh 60
the prescience ne hadde never iben, yit
algate or at the leeste weye it is certeyn thing
that the endes and bytydinges of things to
comen sholden ben necessarye. For every
signe sheweth and signefieth oonly what the 65
thing is, but it ne maketh nat the thing that
it signefieth. For which it byhoveth fyrst to
shewen that nothing ne bytydeth that it ne
bytydeth by necessite, so that it may appere
that the prescience is syngne of this 70
necessite; or elles yif ther nere no necessite,
certes thilke prescience ne myhte nat be syne
of thing that nis nat. But certes, it is now
certeyn that the proeve of this, ysustened by
stydefast resoun, ne shal nat ben lad ne 75
proeved by syngnes, ne by arguments
itaken fro withowte, but by causes covenable
and necessarye. But thou mayst seyn, how may
it be that the things ne bytyden nat that
ben ypurveyed to comen? But certes, ryht 80
as we trowen that tho things which that
the purvyance wot byforn to comen ne ben nat
to bytyden. But that ne sholden we nat demen,
but rather, althogh that they shal bytyden,
yit ne have they no necessite of her kynde 85
to betyden. And this maystow lihtly
aperceyven by this that I shal seyn. For we sen

many things whan they ben doon byforn owre
eyen, ryht as men sen the kartere worken
in the torninge and atempringe or 90
adressinge of his kartes or charietes. And by
this manere *(as who seyth, maystow undirstonde)* of
alle oother workmen. Is ther thanne any necessite *(as who seyth, in owre lookinge)* that constreyneth or compelleth any of thilke 95
things to ben don so?"

Boece. "Nay," quod I, "for in ydel and in
veyn were all the effect of craft, yif that alle
things weren moeved by constreyninge"
(that is to seyn, by constreyninge of owre eyen or 100
of owre syht).

Philosophie. "The things thanne," quod
she, "that whan men doon hem ne han no
necessite that men doon hem, ek tho same
things fyrst or they ben doon they ben to 105
comen withowte necessite. For-why ther ben
somme things to bytyden, of which the endes
and the bytydinges of hem ben absolute and
qwit of alle necessite. For certes, I ne trowe
nat that any man wolde seyn this, that tho 110
things that men doon now, that they ne
weren to bytyden fyrst or they weren idoon; and
thilke same things, althogh that men hadde
ywist hem byforn, yit they han free
bytydinges. For ryht as science of things 115
present ne bryngeth in no necessite to
things that men doon, ryht so the prescience of
things to comen ne bryngeth in no necessite to
things to betyden. But thou mayst seyn
that of thilke same it is idowted, as wheither 120
that of thilke things that ne han non issues
and bitidinges necessaries, yif therof may ben
any prescience; for certes, they semen to
discorden. For thou wenest that yif that
things ben iseyn byforn, that necessite 125
folweth hem, and yif necessite fayleth hem,
they ne myhten nat ben wyst byforn; and that
nothing ne may ben comprehended by science
but certein, and yif tho things that ne han
no certeyn bytydinges ben purveyed as 130

---

59 **syngne**, sign. 69–71 I *so that—this necessite* om. 85 **kynde**, nature. 90 **atempringe**, guiding. 91 **adressinge**, driving. 105 **or**,
before (ere). 112 **fyrst**, beforehand.

certeyn, it sholde ben dirknesse of opynioun, nat soothfastnesse of science. And thou wenest that it be diverse fro the hoolnesse of science that any man sholde deme a thing to ben ootherweys thanne it is itself. And the cause 135 of this erroure is that of alle the thinges that every wyht hath yknowe, they wenen that tho thinges ben iknowe aloonly by the strengthe and by the nature of the thinges that ben iwist or iknowe; and it is al the contrarye. For al 140 that ever is yknowe, it is rather compre-hended and knowen nat after his strengthe and his nature, but after the faculte *(that is to seyn, the power and the nature)* of hem that knowen. And for this thing shal mowen shewen by a 145 short ensaumple: the same rowndnesse of a body, ootherweys the sihte of the eye knoweth it, and ootherweyes the towchinge. The lookinge, bi castinge of his beemes, waiteth and seth from afer al the body togidere, 150 withowte moevinge of itself; but the towchinge clyveth and conjoigneth to the rownde body, and moeveth abowte the en-vyroninge, and comprehendeth by partyes the rowndnesse. And the man himself, 155 ootherweys wit byholdeth him, and oother-weys ymaginacioun, and oother weys resoun, and other weys intelligense. For the wit comprehendeth withowte-forth the figure of the body of the man that is establyssed in 160 the matere subject, but the ymaginacioun comprehendeth only the figure withowte the matere. Resoun surmounteth ymaginacioun, and comprehendeth by an universal lookinge the comune spece that is in the 165 singuler peces. But the eye of intelligence is heyere, for it surmounteth the envyroninge of the universite, and loketh over that bi pure subtilite of thoght thilke same symple forme *(of man that is perdurably in the dyvyne thoght).* 170 In whiche this owhte gretly to ben con-sidered, that the heyeste strengthe to compre-henden thinges enbraseth and contieneth the lowere strengthe; but the lowere strengthe

ne aryseth nat in no manere to heyere 175 strengthe. For witte ne may nothing comprehende owt of matere, ne the ymagyna-cioun ne looketh nat the universels speces, ne resoun taketh nat the symple forme so as intelligence taketh; but intellygence, that 180 looketh al aboven, whan it hath compre-hended the forme, it knoweth and demeth alle the thinges that ben under that forme. But she knoweth hem in thilke manere in the whiche it comprehendeth thilke same 185 symple forme that ne may never ben knowen to none of that oother *(that is to seyn, to none of tho thre forseyde thinges of the sowle).* For it knoweth the universite of resoun, and the figure of the ymaginacioun, and the 190 sensible material conceyved bi wit. Ne it ne useth nat nor of resoun ne of ymagynacioun ne of wit withowte-forth, but it biholdeth alle thinges, so as I shal seye, bi a strok of thoght formely, withowte discours or colla- 195 cioun. Certes, resoun, whan it looketh anything universel, it ne useth nat of ymagina-cioun, nor of witte, and algates yit it compre-hendeth the thinges ymaginable and sensible. For resoun is she that diffynisseth 200 the universel of hir conseyte ryht thus: man is a resonable two-foted beest. And how so that this knowinge is universel, yet nis ther no wyht that ne woot wel that a man is a thing ymaginable and sensible. And this same 205 considereth wel resoun; but that nis nat by ymagynacioun nor by wit, but it looketh it by a resonable concepcioun. Also ymaginacioun, al be it so that it taketh of wit the bygynninges to seen and to formen the figures, algates 210 althogh that wit ne were nat present, yit it envyrowneth and comprehendeth alle thinges sensible, nat by resoun sensible of deeminge, but bi resoun imaginatif. Sestow nat thanne that alle the thinges in knowinge usen 215 moore of her faculte or of her power thanne they doon of the faculte or power of thinges that ben iknowe? Ne that nis nat wrong; for so

---

147 **ootherweys,** in one way. 195 **collacioun,** comparison. 200 **diffynisseth,** defines. 213 **deeminge,** judging.

as every jugement is the dede or doinge of
him that demeth, it byhoveth that every 220
wyht performe the werk and his entencioun,
nat of foreyne power, but of his propre power.

Metre IV. Quondam porticus attulit.

"The Porche *(that is to seyn, a gate of the town
of Athenes ther as philosophres hadden her congre-
gasioun to desputen)*, thilke Porche browhte
somtyme olde men, ful dirke in her sentenses
(that is to seyn, philosophres that hyhten 5
Stoyciens), that wenden that ymages and
sensibilitees *(that is to seyn, sensible ymaginaciouns,
or elles ymagynaciouns of sensible thinges)* weren
enpreynted into sowles fro bodies withowteforth *(as who seyth, that thilke Stoyciens* 10
*wenden that the sowle hadde ben naked of itself,
as a myroure or a cleene parchemyn, so that alle
fygures mosten fyrst comen fro thinges fro withowteforth into sowles, and ben aprented into sowles)*,
Text, ryht as we ben wont somtyme, by a 15
swyfte poyntel, to ficchen lettres empreinted
in the smothenesse or in the pleynnesse of the
table of wex or in parchemin that ne hath no
figure ne note in it. *(Glose. But now argueth
Boece ayenes that opynyoun, and seyth thus:)* 20
But yif the thryvinge sowle ne unpleyteth
nothing *(that is to seyn, ne dooth nothing)* by his
propre moevinges, but suffreth and lith subgit
to tho figures and to tho notes of bodies
withowteforth, and yildeth ymages ydel and 25
veyn in the manere of a myrour, whennes
thryveth thanne or whennes comth thilke
knowinge in oure sowle that descerneth and
byholdeth alle thinges? And whennes is
thilke strengthe that biholdeth the synguler 30
thinges? Or whennes is the strengthe that
devydeth thinges iknowe; and thilke strengthe
that gadereth togydere the thinges devyded;
and the strengthe that cheseth his entrechawnged wey? For somtyme it heveth up 35
the heved *(that is to seyn, that it heveth up the

entencioun to ryht heye thinges)*, and somtyme it
dessendeth into ryht lowe thinges. And whan it
retorneth into hymself, it reproeveth and
distroyet the false thinges by the trewe 40
thinges. Certes, this strengthe is cause moore
efficient, and mochel moore myhty to sen and
to knowe thinges, thanne thilke cause that
suffreth and receyveth the notes and the
figures inpressed in maner of matere. 45
Algates the passioun *(that is to seyn, the
suffraunce or the wit)* in the qwyke body goth
byforn, excitinge and moevinge the strengthes
of the thoght. Ryht so as whan that
clernesse smyteth the eyen and moeveth 50
hem to sen, or ryht so as voys or sown
hurteleth to the eeres *and commoeveth hem to
herkne*, than is the strengthe of the thoght
imoeved and excited, and clepeth forth to
semblable moevinges the speces that it halt 55
withinne itself; and addeth tho speces to the
notes and to the thinges withowteforth, and
medleth the ymages of thinges withowteforth to
tho formes ihidde withinne hymself.

Prose V. Quod si in corporibus sentiendis.

"But what yif that in bodies to ben feeled
*(that is to seyn, in the takinge of knowelechinge of
bodyly thinges)*, and al be it so that the qualites of
bodies, that ben objecte fro withowteforth
moeven and entalenten the instruments of 5
the wittes; and al be it so that the passioun
of the bodi *(that is to seyn, the witte or the
suffraunce)* goth toforn the strengthe of the
workinge corage, the which passioun or
suffraunce clepeth forth the dede of the 10
thoght in himself, and moeveth and
exiteth in this menewhile the formes that
resten withinneforth; and yif that in sensibele
bodies, as I have seyd, owre corage nis nat
itawht or empreinpted by passioun to 15
knowe thise thinges, but demeth and
knoweth of his owne strengthe the passioun or

V METRE IV 16 **ficchen,** affix. **21 unpleyteth,** unravels. **34 entrechawnged,** various. **52** *hurteleth:* Cx *hurleth;* C *hurteth.* **V PROSE V. 5 entalenten,** stimulate.

suffraunce subject to the body: moche more thanne tho thinges that ben absolut and quite fro alle talents or affecciouns of bodies *(as God or his aungeles)* ne folwen nat in discerninge thinges object fro withowteforth, but they accomplyssen and speden the dede of her thoght. By this resoun thanne ther comen many maner knowinges to diverse and differinge substaunces. For the wit of the body, the whiche wit is naked and despoyled of alle oother knowinges, thilke wit comth to beestes that ne mowe nat moeven hemself her and ther, as *(oystres and muscules and other swiche)* shellefyssh of the see that clyven and ben norysshed to roches. But the ymaginacioun comth to remuable beestes, that semen to han talent to fleen or to desiren anything. But resoun is aloonly to the lynage of mankynde, ryht as intelligence is oonly to the devyne nature. Of which it folweth that thilke knowinge is moore worth thanne thise othre, syn it knoweth by his propre nature nat oonly his subject *(as who seyth, it ne knoweth nat aloonly that apertieneth properly to his knowinge)*, but it knoweth the subjects of alle oother knowinges. But how shal it thanne be yif that wit and ymaginacioun stryven ayein resoninge, and seyn that of thilke universels thinges that resoun weneth to sen, that it nis ryht nawht? For wit and imaginacioun seyn that that, that is sensible or ymaginable, it ne may nat be universel. Thanne is eyther the jugement of resoun soth ne that ther nis nothing sensible; or elles, for that resoun wot wel that many thinges ben subject to wit and to ymaginacioun, thanne is the concepcioun of resoun veyn and false, which that looketh and comprehendeth that that is sensible and synguler as universel. And yif that resoun wolde answeren ayein to thise two *(that is to seyn, to witte and to ymaginacioun)*, and seyn that soothly she hirself *(that is to seyn, resoun)* loketh and comprehendeth, by resoun of universalite,

bothe that that is sensible and that that is ymaginable; and that thilke two *(that is to seyn, wit and ymaginacioun)* ne mowen nat strechchen ne enhansen hemself to the knowinge of universalite, for that the knowinge of hem ne may exceden ne surmounte the bodyly figures: certes, of the knowinge of thinges, men owhten rather yeven credence to the moore stidefast and to the moore parfyt jugement. In this manere stryvinge thanne, we that han strengthe of resoninge and of ymagininge and of wit *(that is to seyn, bi resoun and by ymaginacioun and bi wit)*, we sholde rather preyse the cause of resoun *(as who seyth, than the cause of wit and of ymaginacioun)*.

"Semblable thing is it that the resoun of mankynde ne weneth nat that the devyne intelligence biholdeth or knoweth thinges to comen, but ryht as the resoun of mankynde knoweth hem. For thou arguest and seyst thus: that yif it ne seme nat to men that some thinges han certeyn and necessarye bytydinges, they ne mowen nat ben wyst byforn certeynly to bytyden. And thanne nist ther no prescience of thilke thinges. And yif we trowe that prescience be in thise thinges, thanne is ther nothing that it ne bitydeth by necessite. But certes, yif we myhten han the jugement of the dyvyne thoght, as we ben parsoneres of resoun, ryht so as we han demed that it bihoveth that imaginacioun and wit be bynethe resoun, ryht so wolde we demen that it were ryhtful thing that mannes resoun owhte to submitten itself and to ben bynethe the dyvyne thoght. For which, yif that we mowen *(as who seyth, that yif we mowen, I conseyle that)* we enhanse us into the heihte of thilke sovereyn intelligence; for ther shal resoun wel seen that that it ne may nat biholden in itself. And certes that is this, in what maner the prescience of God seth alle thinges certeins and diffinisshed, althowh they ne han no certeyn issues or bitidinges. Ne this nis non opinioun, but it is rather the simplicite

---

33 **remuable,** i.e., able to move. 90 **parsoneres,** partakers. 103 **diffinisshed,** defined.

of the sovereyn science that nis nat enclosed nor ishet within none bowndes.

Metre V. Quam variis terris animalia.

"The beestes passen bi the erthes bi ful diverse figures. For som of hem han her bodies strawght and crepen in the dust, and drawen after hem a traas or a forwh ikontynued *(that is to seyn, as nadres or snakes)*. And 5 oother beestes, by the wandringe lyhtnesse of her winges, beten the wyndes, and over-swymmen the spaces of the longe eyr by moist fleeinge. And oother bestes gladen hemself to diggen her traas or her steppes in the 10 erthe with her goings or with her feet, and to gon eyther by the greene feeldes, or elles to walken under the woodes. And al be it so that thou seest that they alle discorden bi diverse formes, algates her faces, enclyned, 15 hevyeth her dulle wittes. Oonly the lynage of man heveth heyeste his heye heved, and stondeth lyht with his upryht body, and byhooldeth the erthes under him. And but yif thou, erthely man, wexest yvel owt of 20 thy wit, this figure amonesteth the, that axest the hevene with thy ryhte visage and hast areysed thy foreheved, to beren up aheygh thy corage, so that thy thoght ne be nat ihevyed ne put lower under foote, syn that 25 thy body is so heye areysed.

Prose VI. Quoniam igitur uti paulo ante.

"Therfore thanne, as I have shewed a litel her-byforn, that alle thing that is iwyst nis nat knowen by his nature propre but by the nature of hem that comprehenden it, lat us loke now in as mochel as it is leveful to us *(as who 5 seyth, lat us loke now as we mowen)* which that the estat is of the devyne substaunce, so that we mowen ek knowen what his science is.

The commune jugement of alle creatures resonables thanne is this, that God is eterne. 10 Lat us considere thanne what is eternite; for certes that shal shewen us togidere the devyne nature and the devyne science.

"Eternite, thanne, is parfyt possessioun and altogidere of lyf intermynable. And 15 that sheweth moore cleerly bi the com-parisoun or the collacioun of temporel thinges. For alle thing that lyveth in tyme, it is present, and procedeth fro preterits into futures *(that is to seyn, fro tyme passed into tyme 20 cominge)*; ne ther nys nothing establysshed in tyme that may enbracen togider al the space of his lyf. For certes, yit ne hath it taken the tyme of tomorwe, and it hath lost the tyme of yisterday. And certes, in the lyf of this 25 day ye ne lyven no moore but ryht as in the moevable and transitorye moment. Thanne thilke thing that suffreth temporel condicioun, althogh that it nevere bygan to be, ne thogh it never cese for to be, as Aristotle 30 demed of the world, and althogh that the lyf of it be strechched with infinite of tyme, yit algates nis it no swych thing that men myhten trowen by ryht that it is eterne. For althogh that it comprehende and embrace the 35 space of lyf infynit, yit algates ne embraseth it nat the space of the lyf altogidere, for it ne hath nat the futures that ne ben nat yit *(ne it ne hath no lengere the preterits that ben idoon or ipassed)*. But thilke thing, thanne, that hath 40 and comprehendeth togider al the plente of the lyf intermynable, to whom ther ne fayleth nawht of the future, and to whom ther nis nawht of the preterite escaped nor ipassed, thilke same is iwitnessed and iproeved by 45 ryht to be eterne. And it byhoveth by necessite that thilke thing be alwey present to hymself, and compotent *(as who seyth, alwey present to hymself, and so myhty that al be ryht at his plesaunce)*, and that he have al present 50 the infynyte of the moevable tyme. Wherfore

---

V **METRE V. 3 strawght**, stretched. **4 traas . . . forwh ikontynued**, trace (track), continuous furrow. **5** *snakes*: Cx *snailes*. **8–9 moist fleeinge**, Lat., "liquid (easy) flight." **14 discorden**, are different. **15–16 enclyned . . . hevyeth**, bent (toward the earth), benumb. V **PROSE VI. 22 enbracen togider**, embrace at one time. **48 compotent**, all-powerful.

som men trowen wrongfulli that whan they
heren that it semede to Plato that this world ne
hadde never bygynninge of tyme, ne that
it never shal han faylinge, they wenen in   55
this manere that this world be maked
co-eterne with his makere. *(As who seyth, they
wene that this world and God ben maked togider
eterne, and that is a wrongful weninge.)* For
oother thing is it to ben ilad by lyf in-   60
termynable, as Plato graunted to the
world, and oother thing is it to enbrace togydere
al the present of the lyf intermynable, the
whiche thing it is cleer and manyfest that
it is propre to the devyne thoght.   65

"Ne it ne sholde nat semen to us that
God is eldere thanne things that ben imaked by
quantyte of tyme, but rather by the proprete of
his symple nature. For this ilke infynyt
moevinge of temporel things folweth this   70
presentarye estat of lyf unmoevable; and so
as it ne may nat countrefeten it, ne feynen it, ne
be evenlyke to it for the inmoevablete *(that is to
seyn, that is in the eternite of God)*, it faileth
and falleth into moevinge fro the simplicite   75
of the presence of God, and disencreseth
into the infynit quantite of future and of
preterit. And so as it ne may nat han togider al
the plente of the lyf, algates yit for as moche
as it ne ceseth nevere for to ben in som   80
manere, it semeth somdel to us that it
folweth and resembleth thilke thing that it ne
may nat atayne to ne fulfyllen, and byndeth
itself to som manere presence of this litel
and swyfte moment, the which presence of   85
this lytele and swifte moment, for that it
bereth a manere ymage or lyknesse of the
ay-dwellinge presence of God, it graunteth to
swyche manere things as it bitydeth to
that it semeth hem as thise things han   90
yben and ben.

"And for that the presence of swych lytel
moment ne may nat dwelle, therfor it ravysshed
and took the infynyte wey of tyme *(that is*

to seyn, bi successioun). And bi this manere   95
is it idoon for that it sholde contynue the
lyf in gooinge, of the which lyf it ne myhte nat
enbrace the plente in dwellinge. And for-thy,
yif we wollen putten worthi names to
things, and folwen Plato, lat us seye   100
thanne sothly that God is 'eterne', and the
world is 'perpetuel.' Thanne, syn that every
jugement knoweth and comprehendeth by his
owne nature things that ben subject unto
him, ther is sothly to God alweys an eterne   105
and presentarie estat; and the science of
him, that over-passeth al temporel moevement,
dwelleth in the symplycyte of his presence, and
embraceth and considereth alle the infynyt
spaces of tymes, preterits and futures, and   110
looketh in his symple knowinge alle things
of preterit ryht as they weren idoon presently
ryht now. Yif thou wolt thanne thinken and
avyse the prescience, bi which it knoweth
alle things, thou ne shalt nat demen it as   115
prescience of things to comen, but thou
shalt demen it moore ryhtfully that it is science
of presence, or of instaunce, that never ne
fayleth. For which it nis nat ycleped
'previdence,' but it sholde rather ben   120
cleped 'purviaunce,' that is establysshed
ful fer fro ryht lowe things, and byhooldeth
from afer alle things, ryht as it were fro the
heye heyhte of things.

"Why axestow thanne, or why desputes-   125
tow thanne, that thilke things ben doon
bi necessite whiche that ben yseyn and knowen
bi the devyne syhte, syn that forsothe men ne
maken nat thilke things necessarye which
that they sen ben idoon in her syhte? For   130
addeth thy bihooldinge any necessite to
thilke things that thou bihooldest presente?"

"Nay," quod I.

Philosophie. "Certes, thanne, if men
mighte maken any digne comparisoun or   135
collacioun of the presence divine and of the
presence of mankynde, ryht so as ye sen some

---

65 propre to, i.e., characteristic of. **70 folweth,** imitates. **76 disencreseth,** dwindles. **93 dwelle,** endure. **114 avyse,** consider. **120 previdence,** foreseeing. **121 purviaunce,** providence. **136 presence divine,** the divine present.

thinges in this temporel present, ryht so seth
God alle thinges bi his eterne present.
Wherfore this devyne prescience ne 140
chaungeth nat the nature ne the proprete
of thinges, but bihooldeth swyche thinges
present to hym-ward as they shullen bityde to
yow-ward in tyme to comen. Ne it ne
confowndeth nat the jugement of thinges; 145
but bi o syhte of his thowht, he knoweth the
thinges to comen, as wel necessarye as nat
necessarye. Ryht so as whan ye seen togidere a
man walken on the erthe and the sonne
arysen in the hevene, al be it so that ye sen 150
and biholden that oon and that oother
togider, yit natheles ye demen and discernen
that that oon is voluntarye and that oother
necessarie. Ryht so thanne the devyne
lookinge, byholdinge alle thinges under him, 155
ne trowbleth nat the qualite of thinges that
ben certeynly present to hym-ward; but, as to
the condicioun of tyme, forsothe they ben
future. For which it folweth that this nis
non opinioun, but rather a stidefast 160
knowinge, istrengthed by sothnesse, that
whanne that God knoweth anything to be, he
ne unwot nat that thilke thing wanteth
necessite to be. *(This is to seyn, that whan
that God knoweth anything to bityde, he wot wel* 165
that it ne hath no necessite to bityde.)

"And yif thou seyst heere that thilke thing
that God seth to bityde, it ne may nat unbityde
(as who seith, it mot bityde), and thilke
thing that ne may nat unbityde, it mot 170
bityde bi necessite. And that thou streyne
me by this name of 'necessite', certes I wol wel
confessen and byknowe a thing of ful sad
trowthe, but unnethe shal ther any wyht
mowe sen it or come therto but yif that he 175
be byholder of the devyne thoght. For I
wol answeren the thus: that thilke thing that is
future, whan it is referred to the devyne
knowinge, thanne is it necessarye; but
certes, whan it is understonden in his owne 180

kynde, men sen it is owtrely fre, and
absolut *(fro alle necessite)*.

For certes, ther ben two maneres of necessite.
That oon necessite is symple, as thus: that
it bihoveth bi necessite that alle men be 185
mortal *(or dedly)*. Anoother necessite is
condicionel, as thus: yif thou wost that a man
walketh, it bihoveth by necessite that he walke.
Thilke thing thanne that any wyht hath
iknowe to be, it ne may ben non oother 190
weyes thanne he knoweth it to be. But this
condicioun ne draweth nat with hir thilke
necessite symple. For certes, this necessite
condicionel, the propre nature of it ne
maketh it nat, but the adjeccioun of the 195
condicioun maketh it. For no necessite ne
constreyneth a man to gon that goth bi his
propre wil, al be it so that whan he goth, that
it is necessarie that he goth. Ryht on this
same manere thanne, yif that the pur- 200
vyaunce of God seeth anything present,
than mot thilke thing ben bi necessite, althogh
that it ne have no necessite of his owne nature.
But certes, the futures that bityden bi
freedom of arbitre, God seth hem alle 205
togidere present. Thise thinges thanne, yif
they ben referred to the devyne syhte, thanne
ben they maked necessarye bi the condicioun of
the devyne knowinge. But certes, yif thilke
thinges be considered bi hemself, they ben 210
absolut of necessite, and ne forleten nat ne
cesen nat of the liberte of her owne nature.
Thanne, certes, withowte dowte alle the thinges
shollen ben doon which that God wot
biforn that they ben to comen. But som of 215
hem comen and bityden of free arbitre *(or
of free wille)* that, al be it so that they bytyden,
yit algates ne lese they nat her propre nature in
beynge, by the which fyrst, or that they
weren idoon, they hadden power nat to han 220
bityd."

Boece. "What is this to seyn thanne," quod
I, "that thinges ne ben nat necessarye by her

---

140 **prescience,** foreknowledge. 173 **byknowe . . . sad,** admit, serious. 194 **propre nature,** essential nature. 195 **adjeccioun,**
addition. 211 **absolut,** devoid.

propre nature, so as they comen in alle maneres in the lyknesse of necessite by the 225 condicioun of the devyne science?"

Philosophie. "This is the difference," quod she; "that tho things that I purposede the a lytel her-byforn, that is to seyn the sonne arysinge and the man walkinge, that 230 ther-whiles that thilke thinges ben ydoon, they ne myhte nat ben undoon; natheles, that oon of hem or it was ydoon, it byhoved by necessite that it was idoon, but nat that oother. Ryht so is hit here that the thinges 235 that God hath present, withowte dowte they shollen ben. But som of hem descendeth of the nature of thinges (*as the sonne arysinge*), and som descendeth of the powere of the doeres (*as the man walkinge*). Thanne seyde I no 240 wrong, that yif that these thinges ben referred to the devyne knowinge, thanne ben they necessarye; and yif they ben considered by hemself, thanne ben they absolut fro the bond of necessite. Ryht so as alle thinges 245 that apiereth or sheweth to the wittes, yif thou referre it to resoun, it is universel; and yif thou referre it or loke it to itself, than is it singuler. But now yif thou seyst thus, that yif it be in my power to chaunge my purpos, 250 than shal I voyde the purvyaunce of God whan that peraventure I shal han chaunged the thinges that he knoweth byforn, thanne shal I answere the thus: Certes, thou mayst wel chaungen thy purpos. But for as mochel as 255 the present sothnesse of the devyne purvyaunce biholdeth that thou mayst chaunge thy purpos, and wheyther thou wolt chaunge it or no, and whyderward that thou torne it, thou ne mayst nat eschuen the devyne 260 prescience, ryht as thou ne mayst nat fleen the syhte of the presente eye althowh that thow torne thyself by thi free wyl into diverse accioun. But thou mayst seyn ayein, how shal it thanne be? Shal nat the devyne 265

science be chaunged bi my disposicioun, whan that I wol o thing now, and now anoother? And thilke prescience, ne semeth it nat to entrechaunge stowndes of knowinge?" (*As who seyth, ne shal it nat seme to us that the* 270 *devyne prescience entrechaungeth his diverse stowndes of knowinge, so that it knowe sumtyme o thing and somtyme the contrarie of that thing?*)

"No, forsothe," quod I.

Philosophie. "For the devyne syhte 275 renneth toforn, and seth alle futures, and clepeth hem ayein, and retorneth hem to the presence of his propre knowinge. Ne he ne entrechaungeth nat, so as thou wenest, the stoundes of forknowinge, as now this, now 280 that; but he ay-dwellinge comth byforn, and embraseth at o strook alle thy mutaciouns. And this presence to comprehenden and to sen alle thinges, God ne hath nat taken it of the bitydinge of thinges to come, but of his 285 propre simplicite. And herbi is assoyled thilke thing that thou puttest a litel her-byforn, that is to seyn, that it is unworthy thing to seyn that owr futures yeven cause of the science of God. For certes, this strengthe of the 290 devyne science, which that embraceth alle thinges bi his presentarye knowinge, establyssheth maner to alle thinges, and it ne oweth nawht to latter thinges. And syn that these thinges ben thus (*that is to seyn, syn* 295 *that necessite nis nat in thinges by the devyne prescience*), than is ther freedom of arbitre that dwelleth hool and unwemmed to mortal men. Ne the lawes ne purposen nat wykkedly medes and peynes to the wyllinges of men 300 that ben unbownden and quite of alle necessite. And God, byholder and forwitere of alle thinges, dwelleth above; and the present eternite of his syhte renneth alwey with the diverse qualite of owre dedes, despensinge 305 and ordeyninge meedes to goode men, and tormentes to wykked men. Ne in ydel ne in

---

260 **eschuen,** escape. 269 **entrechaunge stowndes,** confuse occasions. 274 **No . . . quod I.** In the Lat., the "no" is part of Philosophy's speech. Cx *No quod I. No forsothe quod she.* 286 **assoyled,** resolved. 292 **presentarye,** ever-present. 294 **latter,** subsequent. 297 **arbitre,** choice. 298 **unwemmed,** unimpaired. 299 **purposen,** propose (prescribe). 300 **wyllinges,** willful decisions. 302 **forwitere,** foreknower.

veyn ne ben ther nat put in God hope and
preyeres, that ne mowen nat ben unspedful ne withowte effect, whan they ben 310
ryhtful.

"Withstond thanne and eschue thou vices;
worshipe and love thou virtuus; areys thy
corage to ryhtful hopes; yilde thou humble
preyeres aheyh. Gret necessite of prowesse 315
and vertue is encharged and commaunded
to yow, yif ye nyl nat dissimulen, syn that ye
worken and doon *(that is to seyn, yowre dedes
or yowre workes)* byforn the eyen of the juge
that seth *(and demeth)* alle thinges." *(To whom* 320
be glorye and worshipe bi infynyt tymes. Amen.*)*

Explicit Liber Boecii.

309 unspedful, ineffective. **315 aheyh,** on high.

Treatise on the Astrolabe

INTRODUCTION

Treatise on the Astrolabe

N Chaucer's day, as in our own, people lived in time, but they did not calculate time by clocks and watches. The first tower clock in England was installed at Westminster in 1288, but pocket watches were not common until after the seventeenth century. Until then, people told time by the sky. Besides telling time by the sky, people believed—as much of the world's population still believes—that terrestrial events were influenced by the heavenly bodies. We still "know" that two of the bodies, the sun and moon, affect plant growth and the tides. Medieval people extended similar influence to the planets and the constellations. The planets known in the Middle Ages were Sun, Moon, Mercury, Venus, Mars, Jupiter, and Saturn, which were also identified with the classical gods. Each was most influential at certain hours on certain days within the signs of the zodiac. The configurations of the planets within the signs of the zodiac were thought to govern all terrestrial events.

The astrolabe is an instrument to determine the positions of the planets at any time of day or season or, conversely, to determine the date and time of day when the positions of the planets are known. Since it can be made small enough to be portable, it was in effect the medieval pocket watch, but was used less to tell time than to calculate the positions of the stars for purposes of diagnosis or divinition. Although as Chauncey Wood points out, *Chaucer and the Country of the Stars* (1970), Chaucer in the *Astrolabe* (II.4.57ff) specifically repudiates judicial astrology, many of his characters believe in it, and his poems are filled with allusions to it. He is the first English author to make regular use of astronomical and astrological periphrasis, and astrology was important to his plots and characterizations, as elucidated by both Chauncey Wood and W.C. Curry, *Chaucer and the Medieval Science* (2nd ed., 1960). *Treatise on the Astrolabe* shows that Chaucer's interest extended beyond the popular to the scientific. In the first problem in Part II, it is dated 1391.

The treatise was planned to be in five parts (ll.69ff): (1) description of the parts of the astrolabe; (2) forty astronomical problems for the astrolabe; (3) tables of the positions of the planets in relation to the longitude of cities; (4) tables of the positions of the planets in relation to the moon; and (5) rules of astrology. Only Parts I and II are extant, and the disarray of the end of Part II in the manuscripts seems to indicate that Chaucer, as usual, grew bored with his enterprise as he went along and broke off incomplete.

The exposition is enhanced by diagrams that occur in some manuscripts. These have been reproduced and explained by R.T. Gunther, *Chaucer and Mesahalla on the Astrolabe* (1929). Twenty- two of the sixty-two have been reproduced in this edition to show the "user's manual" technique of the exposition. Skeat's *Oxford Chaucer* (III, 1894) has a detailed discussion of the functions of an astrolabe. A make-it-yourself construction kit is sold by the Royal Maritime Museum in Greenwich.

The Prologue to the *Astrolabe* is our only example of Chaucer's free composition in prose, which still falls short of his verse in charm and assurance of expression. "Litell Lowys" for whom it was written is presumed to be Lewis Chaucer, named in a 1403 record along with Chaucer's other son, Thomas. MS Dd asserts that the *Astrolabe* was compiled by Geoffrey Chaucer for his son Lewis, then a scholar at Oxford under the tutelage of "N. Strode." N. Strode is unidentified, but R[alph] Strode was the London lawyer to whom Chaucer dedicated *Troylus*. It is now established that before taking up his London legal career, this Strode had been a fellow of Merton College, Oxford, the fourteenth-century English center of astronomical calculation. Ralph Strode died in 1387, before Part II of *Astrolabe* was written; but perhaps the enigmatic colophon may suggest who it was that introduced Chaucer to the mysteries of astronomy.

Treatise on the Astrolabe

PROLOGUE

Litell Lowys my sone, I have perceived well
by certeyne evidences thine abilite to lerne
sciencez touchinge noumbres and propor-
ciouns; and as wel considere I thy bisi preyere in special to lerne the Tretis of the   5
Astrelabie. Than for as mechel as a
philosofre seith, "He wrappeth him in his
frend that condescendeth to the rihtful preiers
of his frend," therfor have I geven the a
suffisaunt astralabie as for owre orizonte,   10
compowned after the latitude of Oxenford,
upon which by mediacion of this litel tretis
I purpose to teche the a certein nombre of
conclusions apertenyng to the same instrument. I seye a certein of conclusiouns   15
for thre causes. The furste cause is this:
truste wel that alle the conclusiouns that
han ben fownde, or elles possibli myhten
be fownde in so noble an instrument as
an astralabie, ben unknowe perfitly to   20
any mortal man in this regioun, as I
suppose. Another cause is this: that sothly,
in any tretis of the astrelabie that I have
seyn there ben some conclusiouns that
wole nat in alle thinges performen hir   25
byhestes. And some of hem ben to harde
to thy tendre age of x yer to conseyve.

This tretis, divided in 5 parties, wole I
shewe the under ful lihte rewles and
naked wordes in Englissh, for Latyn   30
ne kanstow yit but smal, my litel sone.
But natheles, suffise to the thise trewe conclusiouns in Englissh, as wel as suffisith to
thise noble clerkes Grekes thise same
conclusiouns in Grek, and to Arabiens in   35
Arabik, and to Jewes in Ebrew, and to the
Latyn folk in Latyn; whiche Latyn folk han hem
furst owt of othre diverse langages, and writen in
hir owne tonge, that is to sein, in Latyn.
And God wot that in alle this langages, and   40
in many mo, han thise conclusiouns ben
suffisantly lerned and tawht, and yit by diverse
rewles, ryht as diverse pathes leden diverse folk
the ryhte wey to Roome. Now wol I prey
mekely every discret persone that redith or   45
herith this litel tretis, to have my rewde
endytyng for excused, and my superfluite of
wordes, for two causes. The firste cause is for

Text based on MS Cambridge Dd. 3.53 (D), with corrections and variants from Bodley 619 (B), Bodley Rawlinson D. 913 (R), and Harvard University (Z). B&c have the title *Brede and milke for Children*. The figures are from R. T. Gunther's translation of D; see "The Text of This Edition," p. 966. Skeat, *Oxford Chaucer*, III.175ff, provides a modern English paraphrase at the foot of the page.

1 *Litell:* B *Lyte.* have *perceived:* B *aperceyve.* Z *Certeyne evydences, my lytel sone Lewes, have do me to understande thyne abylte.* **7 philosofre,** the quotation has not been identified. The reference to a "frend" has been interpreted to mean that the audience for the treatise was not really Chaucer's son. **8 condescendeth,** accedes. **10 suffisaunt,** good enough (not a toy). **10–11 owre orizonte, compowned after the latitude of Oxenford,** our horizon, constructed (marked) according to the latitude of Oxford. This instrument was intended for use with the Oxford-based tables of John Somer and Nicholas Lynne (below, l. 89). In contrast, the original tables attached to the *Equatorie of the Planets* are corrected for the latitude of London indicating that if they were by or for Chaucer, he was making progress in his astronomical studies. **14 conclusions,** mathematical propositions. **26 byhestes,** promises. R *harde to understonde and to conceyve to the tendre age of the.* **27 x yer,** Skeat speculates that because this age would mean that little Lewis was born about 1380, near the time when Chaucer was securing his quittance for the rape of Cecily Champain, Lewis might possibly be Chaucer's son by Cecily, but, he adds, this is "mere conjecture"; see "Chaucer in His Time," p. 959. **29 lihte,** easy (light). **38 B** *writen hem.*

908

that curious enditing and hard sentence is
ful hevy at ones for swich a child to lerne. 50
And the seconde cause is this, that sothly
me semeth betre to writen unto a child twies a
good sentence than he forgete it ones.

And Lowis, yif so be that I shewe the in my
lihte Englissh as trewe conclusiouns towch- 55
eng this matere, and nahwt only as trewe but
as many and as subtil conclusiouns as ben
shewed in Lafyn in ani commune tretis of the
astrelabie, kon me the more thank; and
preye God save the King, that is lord of this 60
langage, and alle that him feyth bereth and
obeieth, everech in his degree, the more and the
lasse. But considere wel that I ne usurpe nat to
have fownde this werk of my labour or of
myn engin. I nam but a lewd compilatour of 65
the labour of olde astrologens, and have hit
translated in myn Englissh only for thi doctrine.
And with this swerd shal I slen envie.

The firste partie of this tretis shal reherse
the figures and the membres of thin astro- 70
labie, by cause that thow shalt han the
grettre knowyng of thine owne instrument.

The second partie shal teche the werken the
verrey practic of the forseide conclusiouns,
as ferforth and as narwe as may be shewyd 75
in so smal an instrument portatif aboute.
For wel wot every astrologien that smalest fraccions ne wol nat ben shewid in so smal an instrument, as in subtil tables calkuled for a kawse.

The 3 partie shal contienen diverse tables 80
of longitudes and latitudes of sterres fixe for
the astrolabie, and tables of declinacions of the
sonne, and tables of longitudes of citeez and of
townes—and as wel for the governance
of a clokke as for to finde the altitude me- 85
ridian—and many nother notable conclusioun, after the kalendres of the reverent
clerkes, frere J. Somer and frere N. Lenne.

The 4 partie shal ben a theorik to declare
the moevinge of the celestial bodies with 90
causes. The whiche ferthe partie in special
shal shewen a table of the verray moeving of the
mone from howr to howre, every day and in
every signe, after thyn almenak. Upon which
table ther folwith a canon suffisant to teche 95
as wel the maner of the wyrkyng of that
same conclusioun as to knowe in owre orizonte
with which degree of the zodiak that the mone
arisith in any latitude, and the arising of
any planete after his latitude fro the ecliptik 100
lyne.

The 5 partie shal ben an introductorie after
the statutz of owr doctours, in which thow
maist lerne a gret part of the general rewles
of theorik in astrologie. In which 5 partie 105
shaltow fynde tables of equacions of howses
aftur the latitude of Oxenford, and tables of
dignetes of planetes, and other noteful thinges,
yif God wol vouchesauf, and his Modur the
Mayde, mo than I behete, &c. 110

---

49 curious enditing, complicated composition (structure). **58 commune,** ordinary. **59 kon,** give. **60–61 King, that is lord of this langage,** this is the earliest reference to "the King's English," and reveals Chaucer's awareness of the influence of the royal Chancery in establishing the official form of written English. Z *these langagis.* **64 fownde,** created. **65 engin,** ingenuity. **66 olde astrologens,** Skeat, *Oxford Chaucer* III.lxixff, details Chaucer's indebtedness to the *Composatio et Operatio Astrolabii* of Messahala, 8th century Jewish-Arabian astronomer. Other sources have been suggested. However, no exact source has been found, and it would appear that Chaucer was a "compiler" rather than merely a "translator." **68** Z *swerd only.* **73 the werken,** you to work (perform). **75 narwe,** exactly. **76 portatif,** portable. As with any gauge, the larger the scale, the more accurate the measurement. **77 smalest:** B&c *smale.* **80 3 partie,** the *Treatise on the Astrolabe* contains only the first and second parts. *The Equatorie of the Planets* is composed of the sorts of materials that would have been covered in Parts III–V. **82 declinacions,** the angle of the sun to the equator at different times of year. **84 governance,** regulation. B *and tables as well.* **85 altitude meridian,** height above the horizon of a meridian (a line circling the earth passing through the two poles). **87–88 kalendres . . . J. Somer . . . N. Lenne,** John Somer and Nicholas Lynne, Carmelite friars associated with Oxford, both constructed calendars for the meridian of Oxford. The medieval calendar resembled a modern almanac, with tables indicating the elevations of the sun, phases of the moon, positions of the planets, etc. **100–01 ecliptik line,** line through the middle of the zodiac marking the path of the sun. **103 statutz,** rules (astronomical). The first four parts were to be astronomical, the last astrological. **106 howses,** the twelve equal parts into which the heavens were divided for purposes of astrology. **108 dignetes,** beneficial (influential) positions. **109–10 vouchesauf . . . behete,** i.e., if God will grant more than I promise.

PART I

Here bygynneth the descripcion of the astrelabie.

1. Thyn astrelabie hath a ring to putten on the thoumbe of thy ryht hand in takyng the heyhte of thynges. And tak kep, for from hennesforthward I wol clepe the heyhte of anything that is taken by thy rewle   5 "the altitude" withowte mo wordes.

2. This ring rennyth in a maner turet, fast to the moder of thyn astrelabie, in so rowm a space that hit desturbeth nat the instrument to hangen after his rihte centre.   *[Figure 1]*   4

[Figure 1]

3. The Moder of thin astrelabie is the thik-keste plate, perced with a large hole, that rescevieth in hir wombe the thynne plates compowned for diverse clymatz, and thy riet shapen in manere of a net or of a webbe   5 of a loppe. And for the more declaracioun, lo here the figure.   *[Figure 2]*

4. This moder is devyded on the bak half with a lyne that cometh dessendinge fro the ryng down to the nethereste bordure. The whiche lyne, fro the forseide ryng unto the centre of the large hole amydde, is cleped the   5 Sowth Lyne, or elles the Lyne Meridional. And the remenant of this lyne downe to the bordure is cleped the North Lyne, or elles the Lyne of Midnyht. And for the more declaracioun, lo here the figure.   *[Figure 3]*   10

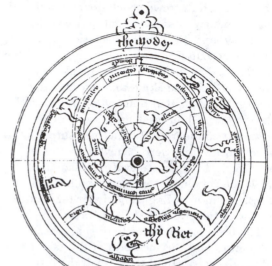

[Figure 2]

5. Over thwart this forseide longe lyne, ther crosseth hym another lyne of the same lengthe from est to west. Of the whiche lyne, from a litel croys + in the bordure unto the centre of the large hole, is cleped the Est Lyne, or   5 elles the Lyne Orientale; and the remenant of this lyne, fro the forseide centre unto the bordure, is cleped the West Lyne, or the Lyne Occidentale. Now hastow her the 4 quarters of thyn astrelabie, devyded after the 4   10 principals plages or quarters of the firma-ment. And for the more declaracioun, lo here thi figure.   *[Figure 4]*

1.3 heyhte, altitude from the horizon. **2.1 turet,** eye. **3.1–2 thikkeste plate,** i.e., the main body of the astrolabe. **3.2 hole,** the hollow space in the front of the astrolabe in which revolve the other plates. **3.4 diverse clymatz,** different latitudes. **3.6 loppe,** spider. **4.1 bak half,** note that the *back* of the astrolabe is being described in articles 4–14. **4.3 nethereste,** lowest. **5.1 Over thwart,** horizontally across. **5.7 *centre*:** D&c+; B hool. **5.11 principals plages,** principal spaces (here and elsewhere note Fr. agreement of adj. with noun).

left side. Forget nat this, lite Lowys. Put the
ring of thyn astralabie upon the thowmbe
of thy ryht hand, and thanne wole his right 5
syde be toward thy left side, and his left
syde wol be toward thy right side. Tak this
rewle general, as wel on the bak as on the
wombe side. Upon the ende of this est lyne,
as I first seide, is marked a litel +, wher as 10
everemo generaly is considered the entring
of the first degree in which the sonne ariseth.
And for the more declaracioun, lo here the
figure. [*Figure 5*]

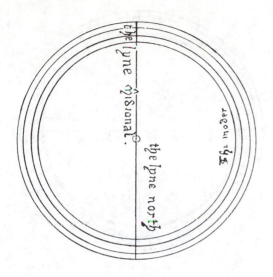

[*Figure 3*]

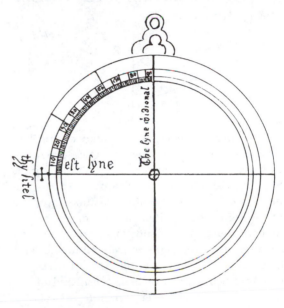

[*Figure 5*]

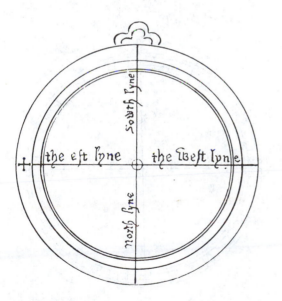

[*Figure 4*]

6. The est side of thin astrelabie is cleped
the riht side, and the west side is cleped the

7. Fro this litel + up to the ende of the
lyne meridional under the ring shaltow fynden
the bordure devyded with 90 degres; and by that
same proporcioun is every quarter of thine
astrolabie devyded. Over the whiche degres 5
ther ben nowmbres of augrym that devyden
thilke same degres fro 5 to 5, as shewith by longe
strykes bytwene. Of whyche longe strykes the
space bytwene contienith a mile wey. And
every degree of the bordure contieneth 4 10

minutes, that is to seyn, minutes of an howre. And for more declaracioun, lo here the figure.

[Figure 6]

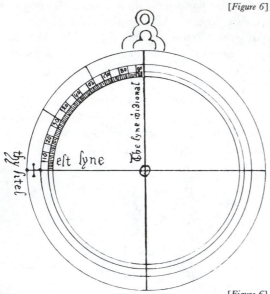

[Figure 6]

8. Under the compas of thilke degres ben writen the names of the 12 signes, as Aries, Taurus, Gemini, Cancer, Leo, Virgo, Libra, Scorpio, Sagittarius, Capricornus, Aquarius, Pisces; and the nombres of the degres 5 of tho signes ben writen in augrim above, and with longe devysiouns, fro 5 to 5, devyded fro tyme that the signe entreth unto the laste ende. But understond wel that thise degrees of signes ben everich of hem considered of 10 60 mynutes, and every minute of 60 seceondes, and so forth into smale fraccions infinit, as seith Alkabucius. And therfor, know wel that a degree of the bordure contieneth 4 mynutes, and a degre of a signe contieneth 15 60 mynutes, and have this in mynde. And for the more declaracioun, lo here thy figure.

[Figure 7]

9. Next this folwyth the Cercle of the Dayes, that ben figured in maner of degrees, that contienen in nowmbre 365, dyvyded also with longe strikes fro 5 to 5, and the nombres in

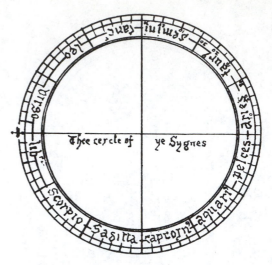

[Figure 7]

augrym writen under that cercle. And for 5 more declaracioun, lo heere thy figure. [Figure 8]

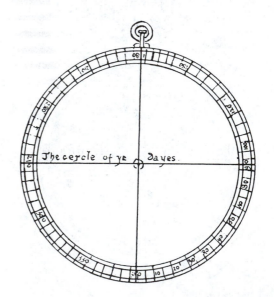

[Figure 8]

10. Next the cercle of the dayes folweth the Cercle of the names of the Monthes; that is

---

8.1 compas, circle. **8.11 60 mynutes,** both minutes of time and of angular measurement. **8.13 Alkabucius,** Al-Qabisi, 10th century Arabic astronomer, *Introductorium ad scientiam judicialem astronomiae.*

to seyen, Januare, Februare, Marcius, April, Mayus, Juyn, Julius, Augustus, Septembre, October, Novembre, Decembre. The names 5 of thise monthes were cleped thus, somme for hir propretes, and some by statutz of lordes Arabyens, some by other lordes of Rome. Ek of thise monthes, as liked to Julius Cesar and to Cesar Augustus, some were compowned of 10 diverse nombres of dayes, as Juyl and August. Thanne hath Januare 31 daies, Februare 28, March 31, Aprill 30, May 31, Junius 30, Julius 31, Augustus 31, September 30, Octobre 31, Novembre 30, December 31. 15 Natheles, althowh that Julius Cesar tok 2 dayes out of Feverer and put hem in his monith of Juyll, and Augustus Cesar cleped the monyth of August after his name and ordeyned it of 31 daies, yit truste wel that the sonne dwel- 20 leth therfor nevere the more ne lesse in on signe than in another.

11. Than folwen the names of the Halidayes in the Kalender, and next hem the lettres of the ABC on which they fallen. And for the more declaracioun, loo here thi figure. [*Figure 9*]

12. Next the forseide Cercle of the ABC under the cros lyne is marked the skale, in maner of 2 squyres, or elles in manere of laddres, that serveth by his 12 poyntes and his devisiouns of ful many a subtil conclusioun. Of this 5 forseide skale, fro the croos lyne unto the verrey angle is cleped *Umbra Recta*, or elles *Umbra Extensa*, and the nether partie is cleped the *Umbra Versa*. And for the more declaracioun, lo here the figure. [*Figure 10*] 10

13. Thanne hastow a brod Rewle that hath on either ende a squar plate perced with a certein holes, some more and some lesse, to resseyven the stremes of the sonne by day, and ek by mediacioun of thyn eye to knowe 5 the altitude of sterres by nyhte. And for the more declaracioun, lo here thi figure. [*Figure 11*]

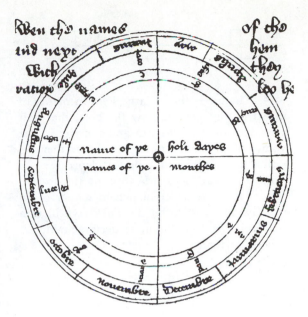

[*Figure 9*]

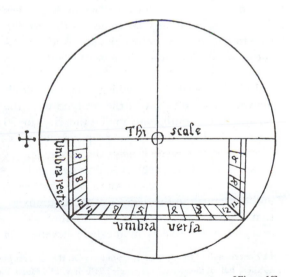

[*Figure 10*]

10.6 thus: D *cleped in Arabyens.* **10.9 Julius Cesar,** as Robinson points out, the historical information is garbled, but the description of the Julian calendar is essentially correct. **10.20–21 sonne dwelleth,** not true, as pointed out by the glosses in some MSS. **11.1 Halidayes,** holy days. **11.3 ABC,** the Sunday or Dominical letters by which the dates of movable feasts were determined from year to year. **12.2 skale,** the shadow scale, for measuring the height of terrestrial objects. **12.7–9** *Umbra Recta* and *Versa* are reversed here as in nearly all the MSS. Eds. often emend. **13.1 Rewle,** a movable hand on the back of the astrolabe. **13.3 more . . . lesse,** large, small.

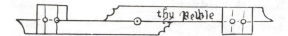

[*Figure 11*]

14. Thanne is ther a large Pyn, in maner of
an extre, that goth thorow the hole, that halt
the tables of the clymates and the riet in the
wombe of the moder, thorw which pyn ther
goth a litel wegge which that is cleped the   5
Hors, that streyneth alle thise parties to-
hepe. This forseide grete pyn in maner of an
extre is ymagynd to be the Pol Artyk in thin
astralabie. And for the more declaracioun,
lo here the figure.   [*Figure 12*]   10

[*Figure 12*]

15. The wombe side of thyne astrelabie is
also devyded with a longe croys in 4 quarters
from est to west, fro sowth to north, fro riht
side to left side, as is the bak side. And for
the more declaracioun, lo here thi figure.   5
[*Figure 13*]

16. The bordure of which wombe side is
devyded fro the poynt of the est lyne unto the
poynt of the south lyne under the ring in 90
degres. And by that same proporcioun is
every quarter devyded, as ys the bak syde.   5
That amonteth 360 degres. And understond
wel that degres of this bordure ben answering
and consentrik to the degrees of the Equinoxial,
that is devyded in the same nombre as
every othere cercle is in the heie hevene.   10

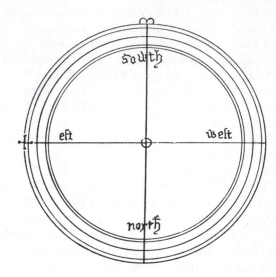

[*Figure 13*]

This same bordure is devyded also with 23
lettres capitals and a smal croys + above the
south lyne, that sheweth the 24 howres equals of
the clokke. And, as I have said, 5 of thise
degrees maken a mile wey, and 3 mile wey   15
maken an howre. And every degree of this
bordure conteneth 4 minutes, and every minut
60 secoundes. Now have I told the twye. And
for the more declaracioun, lo here the figure.
[*Figure 14*]

17. The plate under thi riet is descrived with
3 principal cercles, of whiche the leste is cleped
the Cercle of Cancer, bycause that the heved of
Cancer turneth evermore consentrik upon
the same cercle. In this heved of Cancer is   5
the grettest declinacioun northward of the
sonne. And therfor is he cleped the Solsticioun
of Somer; whiche declinacioun, after Ptholome,
is 23 degrees and 50 minutes as wel in Cancer

14.2 **extre,** axle. 14.3 **clymates,** latitudes. **riet,** the topmost plate on the front side of the astrolabe, showing the fixed stars and the northern half of the zodiac; see article 1.21 below. 14.6 **Hors,** the cotter pin that held the plates and hands onto the central axle was sometimes shaped like a horse, and called a horse in whatever language the astrolabe was being described. **streyneth,** holds. 14.8 **Pol Artyk,** north pole. 15.1 **wombe side,** i.e., the front side, with the movable plates. 16.8 **Equinoxial,** the basic scale of the astrolabe postulates a day of 24 equal hours. 16.11–12 **23 lettres,** including the cross at the top, this indicates 24 divisions, one for each hour. In 14th-century practice, there were only 23 distinctive letters in the alphabet; J, V, and W were merely variant forms. 16.15 **mile wey,** 5 degrees; see above, 7.9 note. 16.18 **twye,** twice. 17.2 B *principal* om.; D&c *tropical.* 17.5 **heved of Cancer,** i.e., the beginning point of the zodiacal sign. 17.8 **Ptholome,** Ptolemy, Alexandrian astronomer, whose collected works were called the "Almagest" (*al,* Arabic "the"; *magest,* Greek "greatest"). This article is not in Messahala.

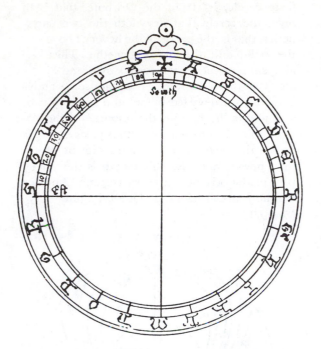

[*Figure 14*]

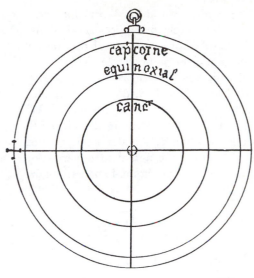

[*Figure 15*]

as in Capricorne. This signe of Cancre is 10
cleped the Tropik of Somer, of *tropos*, that
is to seyn "agaynward", for thanne bygynneth
the sonne to passe fro usward. And for the more
declaracioun, lo here the figure.   [*Figure 15*]

The middel cercle in wydnesse of thise 3   15
is cleped the Cercle Equinoxial, upon
whiche turneth evermo the hedes of Aries and
Libra. And understond wel that evermo this
cercle equinoxial turnyth justly fro verrey
est to verrey west as I have shewed the in   20
the spere solide. This same cercle is cleped
also the Weyere *(equator)* of the day, for whan
the sonne is in the hevedes of Aries and Libra,
than ben the daies and the nyhtes illike of
lengthe in al the world. And therfore ben   25

thise two signes called the Equinoxies. And
alle that moevyth within the hevedes of thise
Aries and Libra, his moeving is cleped northward; and alle that moevyth withoute thise
hevedes, his moevyng is clepid sowthward   30
as fro the equinoxial. Tak keep of thise
latitudes north and sowth, and forget it nat.
By this cercle equinoxial ben considered the
24 howres of the clokke, for everemo the
arisyng of 15 degrees of the equinoxial   35
maketh an howre equal of the clokke. This
equinoxial is cleped the gyrdel of the firste
moevyng, or elles of the *angulus primi motus vel
primi mobilis.* And *nota* that firste moevyng
is cleped moevyng of the firste moevable of   40
the 8 spere, whiche moevyng is fro est to
west, and eft agayn into est. Also it is cleped
gyrdel of the first moeving, for it departeth the

17.12 agaynward, away; Greek "turning." **17.21 spere solide,** M. H. Liddell, in the *Globe Chaucer* (1908), identifies this (and the refs. at I.21.83 and II.26.1) as John de Sacrobosco, *De Sphaera,* which contains parallels to Part I of Chaucer's *Astrolabe.* However, Skeat and Robinson suggest that these may be references to yet another astronomical treatise by Chaucer. **17.22 Weyere,** weigher (Lat. *equator*), because it divides the day and night. **17.23 Aries and Libra,** these are the signs that mark the beginning and end of *CT,* I.8 and X.11. **17.35 arisyng,** i.e., of the sun. **17.39–41 firste moevyng . . . 8 spere,** the *primum mobile* was usually considered the 9th sphere, which gave motion to all the others; see Skeat III.75–77. *firste moevyng:* B *first moevable.*

firste moevable, that is to seyn, the spere, in
2 ilike parties evene distantz fro the poles   45
of this world.

The wydeste of thise 3 principal cerkles is
cleped the Cercle of Capricorne bycause that
the heved of Capricorne turneth evermo consentrik upon the same cercle. In the heved   50
of this forseide Capricorne is the grettest
declinacioun sowthward of the sonne, and
therfor is it cleped the Solsticioun of Wynter.
This signe of Capricorne is also cleped the
Tropik of Wynter, for thanne bygynneth   55
the sonne to come agayn to usward. And
for the more declaracioun, lo here thi figure.

[*Figure 16*]

firste cercle, is clepid the Orisonte, that is to
seyn, the cercle that devydeth the two emysperies, that is, the partie of the hevene above
the erthe and the partie benethe. Thise   10
almykanteras ben compowned by 2 and 2,
albeit so that on divers astrelabies some almykanteras ben devyded by on, and some by two,
and somme by 3, after the quantite of the
astrelabie. This forseide cenyth is ymagened   15
to ben the verrey point over the crowne of
thyn heved; and also this senyth is the verrey
pool of the orisonte in every regioun. And for
the more declaracioun, lo here thi figure.

[*Figure 17*]

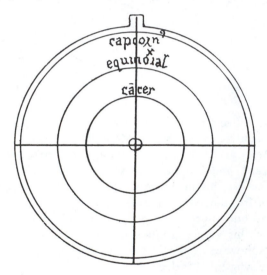

[*Figure 16*]

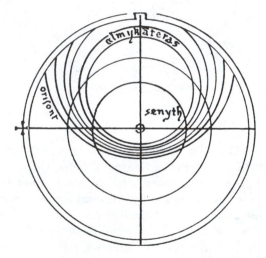

[*Figure 17*]

18. Upon this forseide plate ben compassed
certein cercles that hihten Almicanteras, of
which som of hem semen perfit cercles, and
somme semen inperfit. The centre that
standith amiddes the narwest cercle is cleped   5
the Senith. And the netherest cercle, or the

19. From this senyth, as it semeth, ther come
a maner krokede strykes lyke to the clawes of
a loppe, or elles like to the werk of a womanes
calle, in kervyng overthwart the almykanteras. And thise same strykes or divi-   5
sioun ben cleped Azymuthz. And they
devyden the orisonte of thin astrelabie in 24

18.2 Almicanteras, circles that indicate altitude. **18.6 Senith,** zenith, the point in the celestial sphere directly over the head of the
observer. **18.7 Orisonte,** horizon. **18.8 emysperies,** hemispheres. **18.11 compowned by 2,** on the best astrolabes, an almicantarath
is marked for every degree of latitude; on the one Chaucer is describing, every second degree is marked. **18.17–18 verrey pool,** true
pole. **19.3 loppe,** spider. **19.3–4 womanes calle,** woman's hairnet. **kervyng overthwart,** cutting across. **19.6 Azymuthz,** lines
extending from the zenith to the horizon.

devisiouns. And thise azimutz serven to knowe
the costes of the firmament, and to othre
conclusiouns, as for to knowe the cenyth of 10
the sonne and of every sterre. And for more
declaracioun, lo here thi figure. [*Figure 18*]

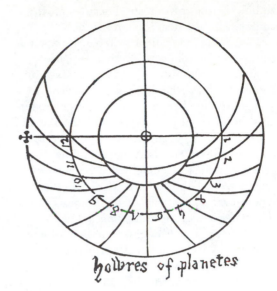

holbres of planetes

[*Figure 19*]

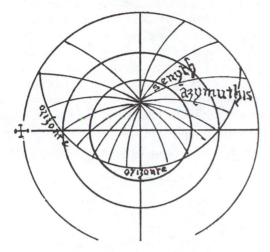

[*Figure 18*]

20. Next thise azymutz, under the cercle of
Cancer, ben ther 12 devysiouns embelif, moche
like to the shap of the azimutes, that shewen
the spaces of the howres of planetes. And
for mor declaracioun, lo here thi figure.   5
[*Figure 19*]

21. The riet of thine astrelabie with thy
zodiak, shapen in maner of a net or of a lop-
webbe aftur the olde descripcioun, which thow
maist tornen up and doun as thyself liketh,
conteneth certein nombre of sterres fixes,   5
with hir longitudes and latitudes deter-
mynat, yif so be that the makere have nat erred.
The names of the sterres ben writen in the margin of the riet ther as they sitte, of whiche
sterres the smale poynt is cleped the Centre.   10

And understond also that alle sterres sittinge wythin the zodiak of thin astrolabie ben
cleped sterres of the north, for they arysen by
northe the est lyne. And alle the remenant
fixed, out of the zodiak, ben cleped sterres   15
of the sowth—but Y sey nat that they
arysen alle by sowthe the est lyne; witnesse on
Aldeberan and Algomeysa. Generally understond this rewle, that thilke sterres that ben
cleped sterres of the north arysen rather than   20
the degree of hir longitude, and alle sterres
of the sowth arisen after the degre of hir longitude—this is to seyn, sterres fixed in thin
astralabie. The mesure of this longitude of
sterres is taken in the lyne eclyptik of hevene,   25
under which lyne, whan that the sonne and
the mone ben lyne-riht, or elles in the superfice
of this lyne, than is the eclips of the sonne or of
the mone, as Y shal declare, and ek the cause
why. But sothly the Ecliptik Lyne of thy   30

19.9 costes, i.e., the parts to be observed. **19.10 cenyth,** not zenith, but the point on the horizon denoting the place of the sun or a
planet in azimuth. **20.2 embelif,** oblique. **20.4 howres of planetes,** see II.12 below. **21.1 riet,** see above I.14.3 note. **21.3 olde
descripcioun,** former description, see I.3 above. **21.4 maist tornen,** i.e., the rete may be revolved on the central axle. **21.5 sterres
fixes,** fixed stars; see Skeat III.78 for a detailed listing. **21.10 smale poynt,** the little point on the tongue of the rete marked the exact
position of the star. **21.18 Aldeberan and Algomeysa,** stars south of the ecliptic but north of the equator. B *Aldeberan Menker Algenze
cor Leonis* with a marginal gloss indicating that these were inscribed on the Merton College astrolabe. **21.20 rather,** earlier. **21.27
lyne-riht ... superfice,** exactly in line, very close to.

zodiak is the owttereste bordure of thy zodiak, ther the degrees ben marked.

Thy Zodiak of thine astralabie is shapen as a compas which that contieneth a large brede, as aftur the quantite of thine astralabie; in ensample that the zodiak in hevene is ymagened to ben a superfice contenyng a latitude of 12 degrees, wheras al the remenant of cercles in the hevene ben ymagined verrey lynes withowte eny latitude. Amiddes this celestial zodiak is ymagined a lyne which that is cleped the Ecliptik Lyne, undur which lyne is evermo the way of the sonne. Thus ben ther 6 degrees of the zodiak on that on side of the lyne, and 6 degrees on that other. This zodiak is devided in 12 principal devisiouns, that departen the 12 signes. And, for the streitnes of thin astrelabie, than is every smal devisioun in a signe departid by two degrees and two—I mene degrees contenyng 60 minutes. And this forseide hevenissh zodiak is cleped the Cercle of the Signes, or the Cercle of the Bestes, for *zodia* in langage of Grek sownyth "bestes" in Latyn tonge. And in the zodiak ben the 12 signes that han names of bestes, or elles for whan the sonne entreth in any of the signes, he taketh the proprete of swich bestes; or elles for that the sterres that ben there fixed ben disposed in signes of bestes, or shape like bestes, or elles whan the planetes ben under thilke signes they causen us by hir influence operaciouns and effectes lik to the operaciouns of bestes.

And understonden also that whan an hot planete comyth into an hot signe, than encresseth his hete; and yif a planete be cold, thanne amenuseth his coldnesse bycause of the hote signe. And by this conclusioun maystow take ensample in alle the signes, be they

moist or drye, or moeble or fix, rekenyng the qualite of the planete as I first seide. And everich of thise 12 signes hath respecte to a certein parcelle of the body of a man and hath it in governance, as Aries hath thin heved, and Taurus thy nekke and thy throte, Gemyni thyn armholes and thin armes, and so forth, as shal be shewed more pleyn in the 5 partie of this tretis. This zodiak, which that is part of the 8 spere, overkerveth the equinoxial. And he overkerveth hym again in evene parties, and that on half declineth sowthward, and that other northward, as pleynly declareth the Tretis of the Spere. And for more declaracioun, lo here thi figure.

[*Figure 20*]

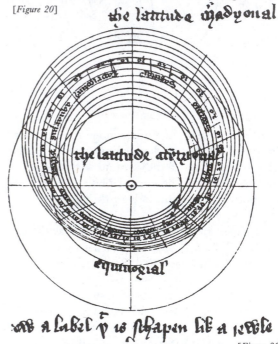

the latitude meridyonal

the latitude circurional

equinoxial

As a Label þ is shapen lik a rewle

[*Figure 20*]

22. Thanne hastow a Label that is schapen lik a rewle, save that it is streit and hath no

21.34 brede, breadth. **21.37 superfice,** surface. **21.40 Amiddes,** in the middle of. **21.47 departen,** divide (is divided into). **21.48 streitnes,** small size (narrowness). **21.55–63 names of bestes,** of the various explanations, the third is the correct one: that the signs are named for their fancied resemblance to creatures. **21.65 hot signe,** Skeat III.77 cites authorities on the properties of the planets and the signs of the zodiac. **21.67 amenuseth,** diminishes. **21.79 overkerveth,** cuts across. **21.81 evene,** equal. **21.83 Tretis of the Spere,** see above 1.17.21 note. The foregoing discussion resembles that in Sacrobosco's *De Sphaera*. **22.2 streit,** narrow. B&c *streight*.

plates on either ende with holes. But with the
smale point of the forseide label shaltow
kalcule thyne equaciouns in the bordure of   5
thine astrolabie, as by thine almury. And
for the more declaracioun, lo here thy figure.

[*Figure 21*]

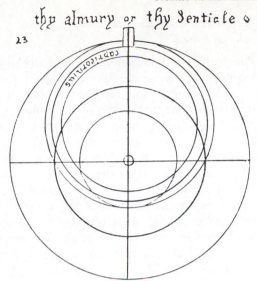

[*Figure 22*]

[*Figure 21*]

23. Thine almury is cleped the Denticle of
Capricorne, or elles the Kalculer. This same
almury sit fix in the hed of Capricorne, and it
serveth of many a necessarie conclusioun
in equaciouns of thynges, as shal be shewed.   5
And for the more declaracioun, lo here thy
figure.   [*Figure 22*]

Her endith the descripcion of the astrelabie.

PART II

Her bygynnen the conclusions of the astrelabie.

*1. To fynde the degree in whych the sonne is
day by day, after hir cours abowte.*

Rekene and knowe which is the day of thi
monthe, and ley thi reule up that same day,
and thanne wol the verray point of thy rewle
sitten in the bordure, upon the degree of thy
sonne.   5

Ensample as thus: the Yer of Oure Lord
1391, the 12 day of March at midday, I wolde
knowe the degree of the sonne. I sowhte in the
bak half of myn astrelabie and fond the
cercle of the daies, the which I knowe by   10
the names of the monthes writen undir
the same cercle. Tho leide I my rewle over

this forseide day, and fond the point of my
rewle in the bordure upon the firste degree
of Aries, a litel within the degree. And   15
thus knowe I this conclusioun.

Another day I wolde knowe the degree of
my sonne, and this was at midday in the 13 day
of Decembre. I fond the day of the monthe
in maner as I seide. Tho leide I my rewle   20
upon this forseide 13 day, and fond the
point of my rewle in the bordure upon the
first degree of Capricorne, a lite within the
degree. And than hadde I of this conclusioun the ful experience. And for the   25
more declaracioun, lo here thy figure.

22.6 almury, the point of the rete near the head of Capricorn. **1.7 1391, the 12 day of March,** this date, which helps to date
the composition of the *Astrolabe*, is "old style" following the Julian calendar; according to the "new style" Gregorian calendar (introduced into Europe in 1582 and into England and the American colonies in 1752), the date would be 20 March.

2. *To knowe the altitude of the sonne, or of othre celestial bodies.*

Put the ring of thine astrelabie upon thy riht thowmbe, and turne thi lift side agayn the light of the sonne, and remeve thi rewle up and down til that the stremes of the sonne shyne thorgh bothe holes of thi rewle.   5
Loke thanne how many degrees thy rewle is areised fro the litel crois upon thine est line, and take ther the altitude of thi sonne. And in this same wyse maistow knowe by nyhte the altitude of the mone   10
or of brihte sterres. This chapitre is so general ever in on that ther nedith no more declaracion, but forget it nat. And for the more declaracioun, lo here the figure.

3. *To knowe every tyme of the day bi liht of the sonne, and every tyme of the nyht by the sterres fixe, and eke to knowe by nyht or by day the degree of any signe that assendeth on the est orisonte, which that is cleped communly the assendent, or elles oruscupum.*

Tak the altitude of the sonne whan the list, as I have said; and set the degree of the sonne, in cas that it be byforn the middel of the day, among thyne almykanteras on the est side of thine astralabie; and   5
yif it be after the middel of the day, set the degree of thy sonne upon the west side —take this manere of settyng for a general rewle, ones for evere. And whan thow hast set the degree of thy sonne up as   10
many almykanteras of heyhte as was the altitude of the sonne taken by thi rewle, ley over thi label upon the degree of the sonne. And thanne wol the point of thi label siten in the bordure upon the verrey   15
tid of the day.

Ensample as thus: the Yer of Oure Lord 1391, the 12 day of March, I wold knowe the tyd of the day. I tok the altitude of my sonne, and fond that it was 25 degrees and 30 of minutes of   20
heyhte in the bordure on the bak syde. Tho turnede I myn astrelabie, and bycause that it was byforn midday, I turnede my riet and sette the degree of the sonne, that is to seyn, the 1 degree of Aries, on the right syde of myn   25
astrolabie, upon that 25 degrees and 30 of minutes of heyhte among myn almikanteras. Tho leide I my label upon the degree of my sonne, and fond the poynte of my label in the bordure upon a capital lettre that is   30
cleped an X. Tho rekened I alle the capital- les lettres fro the lyne of midnyht unto this for- seide lettre X, and fond that it was 9 of the clokke of the day. Tho loked I down upon the est orisonte, and fond ther the 20 degree   35
of Gemynis assending, which that I tok for myn assendent. And in this wyse hadde I the experience for evermo in which maner I sholde knowe the tyde of the day, and ek myn assen- dent.   40

Tho wolde I wyte the same nyht folwyng the howr of the nyht, and wrowhte in this wyse: Among an hep of sterris fixe, it liked me for to take the altitude of the feire white sterre that is cleped Alhabor; and fond hir sitting   45
on the west side of the line of midday, 18 degres of heyhte taken by my rewle on the bak syde. Tho sette I the centre of this Alhabor upon 18 degrees among myn almikanteras upon the west side, bycause that she was fonden   50
on the west side. Tho leide I my label over the degree of the sonne that was descended under the weste orizonte, and rikened alle the lettres capitals fro the lyne of midday unto the point of my label in the bordure; and   55
fond that it was passed 8 of the clokke the

2.2 agayn, towards. **2.12 ever in on,** always the same. **3 cleped,** called. **assendeth,** the point on the ecliptic which, at any given moment, is ascending above the horizon. **oruscupum,** horoscope. This article helps explain the astronomical periphrasis at *CT* II.2ff, and x.2ff. **3.4 almykanteras,** circles marking altitude, see I.18.2. **3.40 assendent,** Skeat III.81 here prints an addition from MS Bodley 619. Other additions to the D text are printed and cited elsewhere by Skeat and Robinson. **3.42 wrowhte,** wrought (worked). **3.45 Alhabor,** Arabic name for Sirius, the Dog Star.

space of 2 degrees. Tho loked I doun upon myn est orisonte, and fond ther 23 degrees of Libra assending, whom I tok for myn assendent. And thus lerned I to knowe ones for ever 60 in which manere I shuld come to the howr of the nyht and to myn assendent, as verreyli as may be taken by so smal an instrument.

But natheles in general wolde I warne the for evere, ne mak the nevere bold to have 65 take a just ascendent by thin astrolabie, or elles to have set justly a clokke, whan any celestial body by which that thow wenest governe thilke thynges ben ney the sowth lyne. For trust wel, whan that the sonne is 70 ney the meridional lyne, the degre of the sonne rennyth so longe consentrik upon the almikanteras that sothly thow shalt erre fro the just assendent. The same conclusioun sey I by the centre of any sterre fix by nyht; and 75 moreover, by experience I wot wel that in owre orisonte, from xi of the clokke unto on of the clokke, in takyng of a just assendent in a portatif astrelabie, hit is to hard to knowe —I mene from xi of the clokke byforn the 80 howre of noon til on of the clok next folwing. And for the more declaracion, lo here thi figure.

4. Special declaracion of the assendent.

The assendent sothly, as well in alle nativitez as in questiouns and elecciouns of tymes, is a thing which that thise astrologiens gretly observen. Wherfore me semeth convenient, sin that I speke of the assendent, to make 5 of it special declaracioun. The assendent sothly, to take it at the largeste, is thilke degree that assendeth at any of thise for-seide tymes upon the est orisonte. And therfor, yif that any planet assende 10 at that same tyme in thilke forseide degree, than hath he no latitude fro the ecliptic lyne, but he is than in the degree of the ecliptic whiche that is the degree of his longitude. Men seyn that thilke 15 planete is *in horoscopo*. But sothly, the hows of the assendent, that is to seyn the firste hous or the est angle, is a thing more brod and large. For after the statutz of astrologiens, what celestial body that 20 is 5 degres above thilk degre that as-sendeth, or within that nowmbre, that is to seyn, ner the degree that assendeth, yit rikne thei thilke planet in the assendent. And what planete that is under thilke degree that 25 assendith the space of 15 degrees, yit sein thei that thilke planete is lyk to him that is in the hows of the assendent. But sothly, yif he passe the bondes of thise forseide spaces, above or bynethe, they seyn that the planete is failling 30 fro the assendent. Yit sein thise astrologiens that the assendent, and eke the lord of the assendent, may be shapen for to be fortunat or infortunat.

As thus: a fortunat assendent clepen they 35 whan that no wykkid planete, as Saturne or Mars, or elles the Tail of the Dragoun, is in the hows of the assendent, ne that no wikked planete have non aspecte of enemyte upon the assen-dent. But they wol caste that thei have a 40 fortunat planete in hir assendent, and yit in his felicite, and than sey they that it is wel. Fortherover, they seyn that the infortunyng of an assendent is the contrarie of thise forseide thinges. The lord of the assendent sey they 45 that he is fortunat whan he is in god place fro the assendent as in angle, or in a succedent whereas he is in his dignite and conforted with frendly aspectes of planetes and wel res-ceyved. And eke that he may sen the assen- 50 dent, and that he be nat retrograd ne com-bust, ne joigned with no shrewe in the same signe, ne that he be nat in his descencioun, ne joigned with no planete in his discencioun,

---

3.62 verreyli, accurately. **4 assendent,** the part of the heaven about to rise. This astrological section is not in Messahala. **4.7 largeste,** most general. **4.12–14** *than hath—is the degree* om. in all MSS except B. **4.32–33 lord of the assendent,** the planet that governs the "house" (zodiacal sign). **4.47 succedent,** i.e., following the most important houses. **4.48 dignite,** influential position. **4.51 retrograd ne combust,** moving in a direction contrary to that of the sun or being so near the sun as to be invisible. **4.52 shrewe,** evil planet. **4.54 discencioun,** descending in the sky (losing influence).

ne have upon him non aspecte infortunat; 55
and than sey they that he is wel.

Natheles, thise ben observauncez of judicial
matiere and rytes of paiens, in which my spirit
ne hath no feith, ne no knowyng of hir *horo-*
scopum. For they seyn that every signe is 60
departed in 3 evene parties by 10 degrees,
and thilke porcioun they clepe a Face. And
althogh that a planete have a latitude fro the
ecliptik, yit sey some folk so that the planete
aryse in that same signe wyth any degree of 65
the forseide face in which his longitude is
rekned, that yit is the planete *in horoscopo,* be it in
nativite or in eleccioun, &c. And for the more
declaracioun, lo here the figure.

5. To knowe the verrey equacioun of the degree of the sonne, yif so be that it falle bytwixe thyn almikanteras.

For as moche as the almykanteras in thine
astrelabie ben compownet by two and two,
whereas some almykanteras in sondry astrelabies ben compowned by on and on,
or elles by 2 and 2, it is necessarie to 5
thy lernyng to teche the first to knowe
and worke with thine owne instrument.
Wherfor whan that the degree of thy sonne
falleth bytwixe two almikanteras, or elles
yif thine almykanteras ben graven with 10
over gret a point of a compas (for bothe
thise thinges may causen errour as wel in
knowyng of the tid of the day as of the
verrey assendent), thow most werken in
this wise: set the degree of thy sonne 15
upon the heyer almykanteras of bothe,
and waite wel wheras thine almury towcheth the bordure, and set ther a prikke of
ynke. Set down agayn the degree of
thy sonne upon the nethere almykan- 20
teras of bothe, and set ther another prikke.

Remewe thanne thine almury in the bordure evene amiddes bothe prikkes, and this
wol lede justly the degree of thi sonne to sitte
bytwixe bothe almykanteras in his riht place. 25
Ley thanne thy label over the degree of thy
sonne, and find in the bordure the verrey tide
of the day or of the nyht. And as verreyly shaltow
finde upon thyn est orisonte thyn assendent.
And for more declaracioun, lo here thy 30
figure.

6. To knowe the spring of the dawing and the ende of the evening, the which ben called the two crepusculis.

Set the nadir of thy sonne upon 18 degrees
of heihte among thyn almykanteras on the
west side, and ley thy label on the degre of
thy sonne, and thanne shal the poynt
of thi label shewe the spryng of day. 5
Also set the nadair of thy sonne upon
18 degres of heyhte among thine almykanteras on the est side, and ley over thy label
upon the degree of the sonne, and with
the point of thy label find in the bordure 10
the ende of the evenyng, that is, verrey
nyht. The nadir of the sonne is thilke degree
that is opposit to the degree of the sonne,
in the 7 signe.

As thus: every degree of Aries bi ordre 15
is nadir to every degree of Libra by ordre;
and Taurus to Scorpion; Gemini to Sagittare; Cancer to Capricorne; Leo to Aquarie;
Virgo to Pisces; and yif any degree in
thi zodiak be dirk, his nadir shal declare 20
him. And for the more declaracioun,
lo here thy figure.

7. To knowe the arch of the day, that some folk kallen the day artificial, from the sonne arysing til hit go to reste.

4.57 judicial, dealing with human destiny. Compare this doubt as to the efficacy of astrology with FrankT, *CT* v.1132ff. **4.58 rytes of paiens,** pagan observances. **5.4 compowned by on,** an astrolabe with almicanteraths marked for each degree would be more accurate than one marked by two degrees. **5.22 Remewe,** more. **6 spring of the dawing,** starting point of dawn. **6.1 nadir,** the point on the ecliptic opposite to the sun. **6.8 est:** D *west.* **7 arch,** arc; the angular distance on the meridian passed over during the day (see II.13 below). This varies with the season and hence is "artificial" in comparison with the "natural" day composed of 24 equal hours.

Set the degree of thy sonne upon thine est orisenonte, and ley thy label on the degree of the sonne, and at the poynt of thy label in the bordure set a prikke. Turn thanne thy riet aboute til the degree of the sonne 5 sit upon the west orisonte, and ley thy label upon the same degree of the sonne, and at the point of thy label set another prikke. Rekne thanne the quantitee of tyme in the bordure bytwixe bothe prikkes, and 10 tak ther thin ark of the day. The remenant of the bordure under the orisonte is the ark of the nyht. Thus maistow rekne bothe arches, or every porcioun, of wheither that the liketh. And by this manere of 15 wyrkyng maistow se how longe that any sterre fix dwelleth above the erthe, fro tyme that he riseth til he go to reste. But the day natural, this is to seyn 24 houres, is the revolucioun of the equinoxial with as 20 moche partie of the zodiak as the sonne of his propre moevinge passeth in the mene whyle. And for the more declaracioun, lo here thi figure.

8. To turn the howres inequales in howres equales.

Knowe the nombre of the degrees in the howres inequales, and departe hem by 15, and tak ther thyn howres equales. And for the more declaracioun, lo here thy figure.

9. To knowe the quantite of the day vulgare, that is to seyen, from spring of the day unto verrey nyht.

Know the quantite of thi crepusculis, as I have tawht in the chapitre byforn, and adde hem to the arch of thy day artificial; and tak ther the space of alle the hole day vulgar, unto verrey nyht. The same 5 manere maistow worke to knowe the quantite of the vulgar nyht. And for the more declaracioun, lo here the figure.

10. To knowe the quantite of howres inequales by day.

Understond wel that thise howres inequales ben cleped howres of planetes, and understond wel that somtyme ben thei lengere by day than by nyht, and somtyme the contrarie. But understond wel that ever- 5 mo generaly the howr inequal of the day with the howre inequal of the nyht contenen 30 degrees of the bordure, whiche bordure is evermo answering to the degrees of the equinoxial. Wherfor departe the arch 10 of the day artificial in 12, and tak ther the quantite of the howre inequal by day. And yif thow abate the quantite of the howre inequal by daye owt of 30, than shal the remenant that leveth performe the howre 15 inequal by nyht. And for the more declaracioun, lo here the figure.

11. To knowe the quantite of howres equales.

The quantite of howres equales, that is to seyn, the howres of the clokke, ben departed by 15 degrees alredy in the bordure of thin astralabie, as wel by nyht as by day, generaly for evere. What nedeth more 5 declaracioun? Wherfor, whan the list to know how manye howres of the clokke ben passed, or any part of any of thise howres that ben passed, or elles how many howres or partie of howres ben to come, fro swich a 10 tyme to swych a tyme, by day or by nyhte, knowe the degree of thy sonne, and ley thy label on it. Turne thy riet abowte joyntly with thy label, and with the point of it rekne in the bordure fro the sonne arise unto the 15 same place ther thow desirest, by day as by nyhte. This conclusioun wol I declare in the laste chapitre of the 4 partie of this tretis so openly that ther shal lakke no worde that nedeth to the declaracioun. And for 20 the more declaracioun, lo here the figure.

12. *Special declaracioun of the houres of planetes.*

Understond wel that everemo fro arysing of
the sonne til it go to reste, the nadir of the sonne
shal shewe the howre of the planete. And fro
that tyme forward al the nyht til the sonne
arise, than shal the verrey degree of the   5
sonne shewe the howre of the planete.

Ensample as thus: the 13 day of March fil
upon a Saterday per aventure, and at the arising
of the sonne I fond the secounde degree of
Aries sitting upon myn est orisonte, al be it   10
that it was but lite. Than fond I the 2 degree
of Libra, nadir of my sonne, dessending on my
west orisonte. Upon which west orisonte every
day generally at the sonne ariste entreth the
howre of any planete, after which planete   15
the day bereth his name, and endeth in the
nexte strik of the plate under the forseide west
orisonte. And evere, as the sonne clymbeth
uppere and uppere, so goth his nadir
downere and downere, techyng by swich   20
strikes the howres of planetes by ordre as
they sitten in the hevene. The first howre inequal of every Satterday is to Saturne; and the
secounde to Jupiter; the 3 to Mars; the 4 to
the Sonne; the 5 to Venus; the 6 to Mer-   25
curius; the 7 to the Mone; and thanne agayn
the 8 is to Saturne; the 9 to Jupiter; the 10 to
Mars; the 11 to the Sonne; the 12 to Venus.
And now is my sonne gon to reste as for that
Setterday. Thanne sheweth the verrey   30
degree of the sonne the howr of Mercurie
entryng under my west orisonte at eve; and next
him succedeth the Mone; and so forth by ordre,
planete after planete, in howre after howre,
al the nyht longe til the sonne arise. Now   35
riseth the sonne that Sonday by the morwe,
and the nadir of the sonne, upon the west
orisonte, sheweth me the entring of the howre
of the forseide sonne. And in this maner
succedeth planete under planete, fro   40
Saturne unto the Mone, and fro the Mone

up agayn to Saturne, howre after howre generaly. And thus know I this conclusioun. And for
the more declaracioun, lo here the figure.

13. *To knowe the altitude of the sonne in middes of the day, that is cleped the altitude meridian.*

Set the degree of the sonne upon the lyne
meridional, and rikene how many degrees of
almikanteras ben bytwixe thyn est orisonte and
the degree of the sonne. And tak ther thyn
altitude meridian, this is to seyne, the heiest   5
of the sonne as for that day. So maistow
knowe in the same lyne, the heiest cours that any
sterre fix clymbeth by nyht; this is to seyn that
whan any sterre fix is passed the lyne meridional, than bygynneth it to descende, and   10
so doth the sonne. And for the more declaracioun, lo here thy figure.

14. *To knowe the degree of the sonne by thy riet, for a maner curiosite, &c.*

Sek bysily with thi rewle the heiest of the sonne
in midde of the day. Turne thanne thyn astrelabie, and with a prikke of ynk marke the
nombre of that same altitude in the lyne
meridional. Turne thanne thy ryet abowte   5
til thow fynde a degree of thi zodiak acord-
ing with the prikke, this is to seyn, sittynge on the
prikke. And in soth, thow shalt fynde but 2
degrees in al the zodiak of that condicioun,
and yit thilke 2 degrees ben in diverse signes.   10
Than maistow lyhtly by the sesoun of the yer
knowe the signe in which that is the sonne.

15. *To know which day is lik to which day as of lengthe, &c.*

Loke whiche degrees ben allik fer fro the
hevedes of Cancer and Capricorn, and lok,
whan the sonne is in any of thilke degrees, than
ben the dayes ilike of lengthe. This is to seyn,
that as long is that day in that monthe as   5

---

12 houres of planetes, this astrological section is not found in Messahala. The idea that the first unequal hour of the day is governed by the planet for which the day is named is adapted for narrative purposes in KT, *CT* i.2217ff. **12.8 Saterday,** 13 March fell on Saturday in 1389 and 1395. **12.29 my sonne,** this familiar idiom (see ii.25.39, ii.39.9) is used also in the *Equatorie,* l. 342, etc. **13** articles 13–18 follow 21 in one MS group.

was swych a day in swich month; ther
varieth but lite. Also, yif yow take 2 daies
naturaly in the yer ilike fer fro eyther pointes of
the equinoxial in the opposit parties, than as
long is the day artificial of that on day as is 10
the nyht of that othere, and the contrarie.
And for the more declaracioun, lo here thi figure.

16. *This chapitre is a maner declaracioun to*
conclusiouns that folwen.

Understond wel that thy zodiak is departid in
2 halfe cercles, as fro the heved of Capricorne
unto the heved of Cancer, and agaynward fro
the heved of Cancer unto the heved of
Capricorne. The heved of Capricorne is the 5
lowest point wheras the sonne goth in winter,
and the heved of Cancer is the heyest point in
whiche the sonne goth in somer. And therfor
understond wel that any two degrees that
ben ilike fer fro any of thise two hevedes, 10
truste wel that thilke two degrees ben of
ilike declinacioun be it sowthward or northward,
and the daies of hem ben ilike of lengthe, and
the nyhtes also, and the shadwes ilike, and
the altitudes ilike at midday for evere. And 15
for more declaracioun, lo here thi figure.

17. *To knowe the verrey degree of any maner sterre*
straunge or unstraunge after his longitude, thow
he be indeterminat in thine astralabie, sothly to
the trowthe, thus he shal be knowe.

Take the altitude of this sterre whan he is on
the est side of the lyne meridional, as ney as
thow maist gesse; and tak an assendent anon
riht by som maner sterre fix which that thow
knowest; and forget nat the altitude of the 5
firste sterre, ne thyn assendent. And whan
that this is don, espie diligently whan this same
firste sterre passeth anything the sowth westward, and cacche him anon riht in the same
nowmbre of altitude on the west side of this 10
lyne meridional as he was kawht on the est
side. And tak a newe assendent anon riht by som

maner sterre fixe which that thow knowest; and
forget nat this secounde assendent. And
whan that this is don, rikne thanne how 15
manye degrees ben bytwixe the firste assendent and the seconde assendent, and rikne wel
the middel degree bytwyne bothe assendentes,
and set thilke middel degree upon thin est
orisonte. And waite thanne what degre that 20
sit upon the lyne meridional, and tak ther
the verrey degre of the ecliptik in which the
sterre stondeth for the tyme. For in the ecliptik
is the longitude of a celestial body rekened,
evene fro the hed of Aries unto the ende of 25
Pisces. And his latitude is rikned after the
quantite of his declinacion, north or sowth
towarde the poles of this world.

As thus: yif it be of the sonne or of any
fix sterre, rekene his latitude or his declina- 30
cioun fro the equinoxial cercle; and yif it be
of a planete, rekne than the quantite of his
latitude fro the ecliptik lyne. Al be it so that fro
the equinoxial may the declinacion or the
latitude of any body celestial be rikned, 35
after the site north or south, and after the
quantite of his declinacion. And riht so may the
latitude or the declinacion of any body celestial
(save only of the sonne, after his site north or
sowth, and after the quantite of his declina- 40
cioun) be rekned fro the ecliptik lyne, fro
which lyne alle planetes som tyme declinen
north or sowth, save only the forseide sonne.
And for the more declaracioun, lo here thi
figure. 45

18. *To knowe the degrees of the longitudes of fixe*
sterres after that they ben determinant in thine
astrolabie, yif so be that they ben trewly set.

Set the centre of the sterre upon the lyne
meridional, and tak kep of thi zodiak, and loke
what degree of any signe that sit on the same
lyne meridional at that same tyme, and tak
the degree in which the sterre standeth; and 5
with that same degree comth that same

---

17 straunge, unfamiliar; not represented on the rete. Robinson paraphrases the procedure. Skeat observes that this article, while not correct in theory, can be made nearly so in practice.

sterre unto that same lyne fro the orisonte. And
for more declaracioun, lo here thi figure.

19. *To knowe with which degree of the zodiak any sterre fixe in thine astrelabie ariseth upon the est orisonte, althey his dwellyng be in another signe.*

Set the centre of the sterre upon the est
orisonte, and loke what degre of any signe that
sit upon the same orisonte at that same tyme.
And understond wel that with that same
degre ariseth that same sterre. And thys   5
merveyllous arising with a strange degree
in another signe is bycause that the latitude of
the sterre fix is either north or sowth fro the
equinoxial. But sothly, the latitudes of
planetes ben comunly rekned fro the   10
ecliptik, bicause that non of hem declineth
but fewe degrees owt fro the brede of the zodiak.
And tak god kep of this chapitre of arising of the
celestial bodies. For truste wel that neyther
mone ne sterre as in owre embelif orisonte   15
ariseth with that same degree of his longitude, save in o cas, and that is whan they have
no latitude fro the ecliptik lyne. But natheles,
som tyme is everiche of thes planetes under
the same lyne. And for more declaracioun,   20
lo here thi figure.

20. *To knowe the declinacioun of any degree in the zodiak fro the equinoxial cercle, &c.*

Set the degree of any signe upon the lyne
meridional, and rikne his altitude in almykanteras fro the est orizonte up to the same
degree set in the forseide lyne, and set ther a
prikke. Turne up thanne thy riet, and set the   5
heved of Aries or Libra in the same meridional lyne, and set ther another prikke. And
whan that this is don, considere the altitudes of
hem bothe; for sothly the difference of thilke
altitudes is the declinacion of thilke degre   10
fro the equinoxial. And yif so be that thilke
degree be northward fro the equinoxial, than is
his declinacion north; yif it be sowthward, than

is it sowth. And for the more declaracioun,
lo here thi figure.   15

21. *To knowe for what latitude in any regioun the almikanteras of any table ben compowned.*

Rikne how manye degrees of almikanteras in
the meridional lyne be fro the cercle equinoxial
unto the senith, or elles fro the pool artik unto
the north orisonte; and for so gret a latitude
or for so smal a latitude is the table com-   5
powned. And for more declaracion, lo here
thi figure.

22. *To knowe in special the latitude of owre country—I mene after the latitude of Oxenford—and the heyhte of owre pol.*

Understond wel that as fer is the heved of
Aries or Libra in the equinoxial from owre
orisonte as is the senyth from the pole artik;
and as hey is the pol artik fro the orisonte as
the equinoxial is fer fro the senyth. I prove   5
it thus by the latitude of Oxenford. Understond wel that the heyhte of owre pool artik fro
owre north orisonte is 51 degrees and 50 minutes;
than is the senyth from owre pool artik 38
degrees and 10 minutes; than is the equin-   10
oxial from owre senyth 51 degrees and 50
minutes; than is owre south orisonte from owre
equinoxial 38 degrees and 10 minutes. Understond wel this reknyng. Also forget nat that
the senyth is 90 degrees of heyhte fro the   15
orisonte, and owre equinoxial is 90 degrees
from owre pool artik. Also this shorte rewle is
soth, that the latitude of any place in a regioun
is the distance fro the senyth unto the
equinoxial. And for more declaracioun, lo   20
here thi figure.

23. *To prove evidently the latitude of any place in a regioun by the preve of the heyhte of the pol artik in that same place.*

In some wynters nyht, whan the firmament is
clere and thikke-sterred, waite a tyme til that any

19.15 **embelif**, oblique. 22–23 Not in Messahala. 22 *owre countray:* other MSS *owre centur.*

sterre fix sit lyne-riht perpendiculer over the pol artik, and clepe that sterre A. And wayte another sterre that sit lyne-riht under A, and under the pol, and clepe that sterre F. And understand wel that F is nat consideret but only to declare that A sit evene overe the pool. Take thanne anon riht the altitude of A from the orisonte, and forget it nat. Lat A and F go farwel til agayns the dawenyng a gret while, and come thanne agayn, and abid til that A is evene under the pol and under F. For sothly, than wole F sitte over the pool, and A wol sit under the pool. Tak than eft sones the altitude of A from the orisonte, and note as wel his secounde altitude as his firste altitude. And whan that this is don, rikne how manye degrees that the firste altitude of A excedeth his seconde altitude, and tak half thilke porcioun that is exceded, and adde it to his seconde altitude. And tak ther the elevacioun of thy pool, and eke the latitude of thy regioun. For thise two ben of a nombre; this is to seyn, as many degrees as thy pool is elevat, so michel is the latitude of the regioun.

Ensample as thus: par aventure, the altitude of A in the evening is 56 degrees of heyhte. Than wol his seconde altitude or the dawing be 48; that is 8 lasse than 56, that was his firste altitude at even. Tak thanne the half of 8 and adde it to 48, that was his seconde altitude, and than hastow 52. Now hastow the heyhte of thy pol, and the latitude of the regioun. But understond wel that to prove this conclusioun and many another fair conclusioun, thow most have a plomet hanging on a lyne heyer than thin heved on a perche, and thilke lyne mot hange evene perpendiculer bytwixe the pool and thine eye. And thanne shaltow sen yif A sitte evene over the pool and over F at evene, and also yif F sitte evene over the pool and over A or day. And for more declaracion, lo here thi figure.

24. *Another conclusioun to prove the heyhte of the pool artik fro the orisonte.*

Tak any sterre fixe that nevere dissendeth under the orisonte in thilke regioun, and considere his heiest altitude and his lowest altitude fro the orisonte; and make a nombre of bothe thise altitudes. Tak thanne and abate half that nombre, and tak ther the elevacioun of the pol artik in that same regioun. And for more declaracioun, lo here thi figure.

25. *Another conclusioun to prove the latitude of the regioun, &c.*

Understond wel that the latitude of any place in a regioun is verreyly the space bytwixe the senyth of hem that dwellen there and the equinoxial cerkle, north or sowthe, takyng the mesure in the meridional lyne, as sheweth in the almykanteras of thine astrelabie. And thilke space is as moche as the pool artik is hey in the same place fro the orisonte. And than is the depressioun of the pol antartik, that is to seyn, than is the pol antartik bynethe the orisonte the same quantite of space, neither more ne lasse. Thanne, yif thow desire to knowe this latitude of the regioun, tak the altitude of the sonne in the middel of the day, whan the sonne is in the hevedes of Aries or of Libra (for thanne moeveth the sonne in the lyne equinoxial), and abate the nombre of that same sonnes altitude owt of 90, and thanne is the remenaunt of the noumbre that leveth the latitude of the regioun.

As thus: I suppose that the sonne is thilke day at noon 38 degrees and 10 minutes of heyhte. Abate thanne thise degrees and minutes owt of 90; so leveth there 51 degrees and 50 minutes, the latitude. I sey nat this but for ensample, for wel I wot the latitude of Oxenforde is certein minutes lasse, as I myhte prove. Now yif so be that the semeth to long a taryinge

---

23.4 **sterre A,** Skeat identifies this as the polestar. 23.8 **evene,** exactly. 23.29 **or the dawing,** before dawn. 24.5 **abate,** subtract. 25.27 **certein minutes lasse,** Skeat points out that the latitude of Oxford is 51°45′, but probably Chaucer originally used 52° as in article II.23.

to abide til that the sonne be in the hevedes of Aries or of Libra, thanne waite whan the 30
sonne is in any other degree of the zodiak, and considere the degree of his declinacion fro the equinoxial lyne. And yif it so be that the sonnes declinacion be northward fro the equinoxial, abate thanne fro the sonnes 35
altitude at noon the nombre of his declina- cion, and thanne hastow the heyhte of the hevedes of Aries and Libra.

As thus: my sonne is par aventure in the firste degre of Leoun 58 degrees and 10 40
minutes of heyhte at noon, and his declina- cion is almost 20 degrees northward fro the equinoxial. Abate thanne thilke 20 degrees of declinacion owt of the altitude at noon; than leveth thee 38 degrees and odde minutes 45
—lo ther the heved of Aries or Libra, and thyn equinoxial in that regioun. Also yif so be that the sonnes declinacioun be sowthward fro the equinoxial, adde thanne thilke declina- cion to the altitude of the sonne at noon; 50
and tak ther the hevedes of Aries and Libra, and thyn equinoxial. Abate thanne the heyhte of the equinoxial owt of 90 degrees, and thanne leveth there the distans of the pole 51 degrees and 50 minutes of that regioun fro 55
the equinoxial. Or elles, yif the lest, take the heiest altitude fro the equinoxial of any sterre fix that thow knowest, and tak his nethere elongacioun lengthing fro the same equin- oxial lyne, and wirke in the maner forseid. 60
And for more declaracion, lo here thi figure.

26. *Declaracioun of the assencioun of signes, &c.*

The excellence of the sper solide, amonges other noble conclusiouns, sheweth manifeste the diverse assenciouns of signes in diverse places, as wel in the rihte cercle as in the embelif cercle. Thise auctours writen that thilke 5
signe is cleped of riht ascensioun with which

more part of the cercle equinoxial and lasse part of the zodiak ascendeth; and thilke signe assen- deth embelif with whiche lasse part of the equinoxial and more part of the zodiak as- 10
sendeth. Fertherover they seyn that in thilke cuntrey where as the senith of hem that dwellen there is in the equinoxial lyne, and her orisonte passing by the poles of this worlde, thilke folke han this riht cercle and the riht ori- 15
sonte.

And everemo the arch of the day and the arch of the niht is ther ylike long, and the sonne twyes every yer passinge thorow the cenyth of her heved; and 2 someres and 2 wynteres 20
in a yer han this forseide poeple. And the almykanteras in her astrolabies ben streyhte as a lyne, so as sheweth in this figure. The utilite to knowe the assenciouns in the rihte cercle is this: truste wel that by mediacioun of thilke 25
assenciouns thise astrologiens by hir tables and hir instrumentz knowen verreyly the assen- cioun of every degree and mynut in al the zodiak, as shal be shewed. And *nota* that this forseid rihte orisonte, that is cleped *orison* 30
rectum, divideth the equinoxial into riht angles; and the embelif orisonte, wheras the pol is enhawsed upon the orisonte, overkerveth the equinoxial in embelif angles, as sheweth in the figure. And for the more declaracioun, lo here the figure.

27. *This is the conclusioun to knowe the assenciouns of signes in the riht cercle, that is, circulus directus, &c.*

Set the heved of what signe the liste to knowe his assending in the riht cercle upon the lyne meridional, and waite wher thine almury towcheth the bordure, and set ther a prikke. Turne thanne thy riet westward til that the 5
ende of the forseide signe sitte upon the meri- dional lyne, and eft sones waite wher thin almury

towcheth the bordure, and set ther another prikke. Rikne thanne the nombre of degrees in the bordure bytwyxe bothe prikkes, and tak the assencioun of the signe in the riht cercle. And thus maystow wyrke with every porcioun of thy zodiak, &c. And for the more declaracioun, lo here thy figure.

28. *To knowe the assencions of signes in the*
    embelif cercle in every regioun, I mene in
    circulo obliquo.

Set the heved of the signe which as the list to knowe his ascensioun upon the est orisonte, and waite wher thyn almury towcheth the bordure, and set ther a prikke. Turne thanne thy riet upward til that the ende of the same signe sitte upon the est orisonte, and waite eft sones wher as thine almury towcheth the bordure, and set ther another prikke. Rikne thanne the nowmbre of degrees in the bordure bytwyxe bothe prikkes, and tak ther the assencioun of the signe in the embelif cercle. And understond wel that alle signes in thy zodiak, fro the heved of Aries unto the ende of Virgo, ben cleped signes of the north fro the equinoxial; and these signes arisen bytwyxe the verrey est and the verrey north in owre orisonte generaly forevere. And alle signes fro the heved of Libra unto the ende of Pisces ben cleped signes of the sowth fro the equinoxial; and thise signes arisen evermo bytwyxe the verrey est and the verrey sowth in owre orisonte. Also every signe bytwixe the heved of Capricorne unto the ende of Geminis ariseth on owre orisonte in lasse than 2 howres equales; and thise same signes, fro the heved of Capricorne unto the ende of Geminis, ben cleped "tortuos signes" or "kroked signes," for they arisen embelif on oure orisonte; and thise krokede signes ben obedient to the signes that ben of riht assencioun. The signes of riht assencioun ben fro the heved of Cancer

to the heed of Sagittare; and thise signes arisen more upriht, and they ben called ek sovereyn signes; and everich of hem ariseth in more space than in to howres. Of which signes, Gemini obeieth to Cancer; and Taurus to Leo; Aries to Virgo; Pisces to Libra; Aquarius to Scorpioun; and Capricorne to Sagittare. And thus evermo 2 signes that ben ilike fer fro the heved of Capricorne obeien everich of hem til other. And for more declaracioun, lo here the figure.

29. *To knowe justly the foure quarters of the*
    world, as est, west, north, and sowth.

Tak the altitude of thy sonne whan the list, and note wel the quarter of the world in which the sonne is for the tyme by the azymutz. Turne the thanne thine astrolabie, and set the degree of the sonne in the almikanteras of his altitude on thilke side that the sonne stant, as is the manere in taking of howres; and ley thy label on the degree of the sonne, and rikene how many degres of the bordure ben bytwixe the lyne meridional and the point of thy label; and note wel that nowmbre. Turne thanne agayn thyn astralabie, and set the poynt of thy gret rewle, ther thow takest thyne altitudes, upon as many degrees in his bordure fro his meridional as was the point of thy label fro the lyne meridional on the wombe side. Tak thanne thyn astrolabie with bothe handes sadly and slely, and lat the sonne shyne thorow bothe holes of thy rewle; and sleyly in thilke shynynge lat thyn astre-labie kowch adown evene upon a smothe grond, and thanne wol the verrey lyne mery-dional of thyn astrolabie lye evene sowth, and the est lyne wole lye est, and the west lyne west, and north lyne north, so that thow werke softly and avisely in the cowching; and thus hastow the 4 quarters of the firmament.

28.31–32 D *Cancer—heed of* inserted in later hand. Only Z and Bodley 68 have correct reading *end of Sagittare*. **29.18 sadly and slely,** i.e., very carefully.

And for the more declaracioun, lo here the figure.

30. *To knowe the altitude of planetes fro the wey of the sonne, whether so they be north or sowth fro the forseide wey.*

Lok whan that a planete is in the lyne meridional, yif that hir altitude be of the same heyhte that is the degree of the sonne for that day, and than is the planete in the verrey wey of the sonne, and hath no latitude. And yif the altitude of the planete be heyere than the degree of the sonne, than is the planete north fro the wey of the sonne swych a quantite of latitude as sheweth by thyn almykanteras. And yif the altitude of the planete be lasse than the degree of the sonne, thanne is the planete sowth fro the wey of the sonne swich a quantite of latitude as sheweth by thine almykanteras —this is to seyn, fro the wey wheras the sonne wente thilke day, but nat from the wey of the sonne in every place of the zodiak. And for the more declaracioun, lo here the figure.

31. *To knowe the senyth of the arysing of the sonne, this is to seyn, the partie of the orisonte in which that the sonne ariseth.*

Thow most first considere that the sonne ariseth nat alwey verrey est, but sometyme by north the est, and somtyme by sowthe the est. Sothly, the sonne ariseth nevermo verrey est in owere orisonte but he be in the heved of Aries or Libra. Now is thine orisonte departed in 24 parties by thy azymutz, in significacioun of 24 partiez of the world (al be it so that shipmen rikne thilke partiez in 32). Thanne is ther no more but waite in which azymutz that thi sonne entreth at his arisyng, and tak ther the senyth of the arysing of the sonne.

The manere of the devisioun of thine astralabie is this—I mene as in this cas: first is it divided in 4 plages principaly with the lyne that goth from est to west, and than with another lyne that goth fro south to north. Than is it divided in smale partiez of azymutz, as est, and est by sowthe, whereas is the firste azimut above the est lyne; and so forth fro partie to partie til that thow come agayn unto the est lyne. Thus maistow understond also the senyth of any sterre, in which partie he riseth, &c. And for the more declaracion, lo here the figure.

32. *To knowe in which partie of the firmament is the conjunccioun.*

Considere the tyme of the conjunccion by thy kalender, as thus: lok how many howres thilke conjunccion is fro the midday of the day precedent, as sheweth by the canoun of thy kalender. Rikne thanne thilke nombre of howres in the bordure of thyn astralabie, as thow art wont to do in knowyng of the howres of the day or of the nyht; and ley thy label over the degree of the sonne; and thanne wol the point of thy label sitte upon the hour of the conjunccion. Loke thanne in which azymut the degree of thy sonne sitteth, and in that partie of the firmament is the conjunccioun. And for the more declaracioun, lo here thy figure.

33. *To knowe the senyth of the altitude of the sonne, &c.*

This is no more to seyn but any tyme of the day tak the altitude of the sonne; and by the azymut in which he stondeth maistow sen in whiche partie of the firmament he is. And the same wyse maistou sen by the nyht of any sterre, whether the sterre sitte est or west or north, or any partie bytwene, after the name of the azimut in which is the sterre. And

---

30. wey of the sonne, not the ecliptic, but the sun's apparent path on any day of the year. When the sun is "low," its "way" will appear to be smaller. **30.17** *zodiak,* other MSS add *for on the morowe wyl the sonne be on another degree.* **31** *senyth,* as used here, not the point directly overhead, but the point of sunrise. **31.9 partiez in 32,** the modern compass is divided into 32 parts for more accurate measurement. Evidently this began with navigation; see Skeat III.214. **32** *conjunccioun,* the close approach of two celestial bodies (here the sun and the moon). **33.3 azymut,** azimuth, an arc extending from the zenith to the horizon.

for the more declaracioun, lo here the figure. 10

34. *To knowe sothly the degree of the longitude of the mone, or of any planete that hath no latitude for the tyme fro the ecliptik lyne.*

Tak the altitude of the mone, and rikne thine altitude up among thyne almykanteras on which side that the mone stande, and set ther a prikke. Tak thanne anon riht upon the mones side the altitude of any sterre fix 5 which that thow knowest, and set his centre upon his altitude among thin almykanteras ther the sterre is fownde. Waite thanne which degree of the zodiak toucheth the prikke of the altitude of the mone, and tak ther the degree 10 in which the mone standeth. This conclusioun is verrey soth yif the sterres in thine astrolabie stonden after the trowthe. Of comune, tretis of astrolabie ne make non excepcioun wheyther the mone have latitude or non, 15 ne on wheither side of the mone the altitude of the sterre fix be taken. And *nota* that yif the mone shewe himself by liht of day, than maistow wyrke this same conclusioun by the sonne, as wel as by the fix sterre. And for the more 20 declaracioun, lo here thy figure.

35. *This is the workinge of the conclusioun to knowe yif that any planete be directe or retrograde.*

Tak the altitude of any sterre that is cleped a planete, and note it wel. And tak ek anon the altitude of any sterre fix that thow knowest, and note it wel also. Come thanne agayn the thridde or the ferthe nyht next folwing, for 5 thanne shaltow aperceyve wel the moeving of a planete, wheither so he moeve forthward or bakward. Awaite wel thanne whan that thy sterre fix is in the same altitude that she was

whan thow toke hir firste altitude; and tak 10 than eftsones the altitude of the forseide planete, and note it wel. For trust wel, yif so be that the planete be on the riht side of the meridional lyne, so that his seconde altitude be lasse than his firste altitude was, thanne is 15 the planete directe. And yif he be on the west side in that condicion, thanne is he retrograd. And yif so be that this planete be upon the est side whan his altitude is taken, so that his secounde altitude be more than his firste 20 altitude, thanne is he retrograde, and yif he be on the west side, than is he directe. But the contrarie of thise parties is of the cours of the moone; for sothly, the moone moeveth the contrarie from other planetes as in hir epi- 25 sicle, but in non other manere. And for the more declaracioun, lo here thy figure.

36. *The conclusiouns of equaciouns of howses, after the astralabie, &c.*

Set the bygynnyng of the degree that assendeth upon the ende of the 8 howr inequal; thanne wol the bygynnyng of the 2 hows sitte upon the lyne of midnyht. Remeve thanne the degree that assendeth and set him on 5 the ende of the 10 howr inequal; and thanne wol the bygynnyng of the 3 hows sitte upon the midnyht lyne. Bryng up agayn the same degree that assendeth first, and set him upon the orisonte; and thanne wol the begynnyng of 10 the hows sitte upon the lyne of midnyht. Tak thanne the nadir of the degree that first assendeth, and set him on the ende of the 2 howr inequal; and thanne wol the bygynnyng of the 5 hows sitte upon the lyn of midnyht; 15 set thanne the nadir of the assendent on the ende of the 4 howre; than wol the bygynnyng of the 6 house sitte on the midnyht lyne. The bygynnyng of the 7 hows is nadir of the

---

34.15 mone have latitude, i.e., since the moon never varies more than $5\frac{1}{4}°$ from the ecliptic, it is considered to follow the ecliptic. **35** *retrograde,* moving in the opposite direction from the sun in the ecliptic. **35.25 episicle,** epicycle, a small circle, the center of which moves along the circumference of a larger circle; hence, at certain stages of their individual orbits, the moon and planets appear to move in retrograde. **36** After this point the MSS vary, some inserting spurious articles. D and B follow to the end of 40. **36.3 hows,** cf. Prol. 107. **36.4 lyne of midnyht,** see 1.4. This article and the next deal with methods of dividing the sphere into its 12 houses.

assendent, and the bygynnyng of the 8 hows 20
is nadir of the 2; and the bygynnyng of the
9 hows is nadir of the 3; and the bygynnyng of
the 10 hows is the nadir of the 4; and the
bygynnyng of the 11 hows is nader of the 5;
and the bygynnyng of the 12 hows is nadir 25
of the 6. And for the mor declaracion, lo
here the figure.

37. Another manere of equaciouns of howses by the astralabie.

Tak thine assendent, and thanne hastow thi
4 angles; for wel thow wost that the opposit of
thin assendent, that is to seyn thy bygynnyng of
the 7 hows, sit upon the west orizonte; and
the bygynnyng of the 10 hows sit upon the 5
lyne meridional; and his opposit upon the
lyne of mydnyht. Thanne ley thi label over the
degree that assendeth, and rekne fro the point
of thy label alle the degrees in the bordure,
til thow come to the meridional lyne; and 10
departe alle thilke degrees in 3 evene parties,
and tak the evene equacion of 3. For ley thy label
over everich of 3 parties, and than maistow se by
thy label in which degree of the zodiak is
the bygynnyng of everich of thise same 15
howses fro the assendent: that is to seyn,
the begynnyng of the 12 hows next above thine
assendent; and thanne the bygynnyng of the 11
hows; and thanne the 10, upon the meridional lyne, as I first seide. The same wyse 20
wyrke thow fro the assendent down to the
lyne of midnyht, and thanne thus hastow other
3 howses: that is to seyn, the bygynnyng of the
2 and the 3 and the 4 howses. Thanne is the
nader of thise 3 howses the bygynnyng of 25
the 3 howses that folwen. And for the more
declaracioun, lo here thi figure.

38. To fynde the lyne merydional to dwelle fix in any certein place.

Tak a rond plate of metal—for werpinge,

the brodere the bettre—and make therupon
a just compas, a lite within the bordure; and
ley this ronde plate upon an evene grond, or
on an evene ston, or on an evene stok fix in 5
the gronde; and ley it even by a level. And
in centre of the compas stike an evene pyn or a
wir upriht, the smaller the betere. Set thy pyn
by a plom-rewle evene upryht; and let this
pyn be no lengere than a quarter of the 10
diametre of thi compas fro the centre. And
waite bisily aboute 10 or 11 of the clokke and
whan the sonne shyneth, whan the shadwe of
the pyn entreth anything within the cercle
of thi plate an her-mele, and mark ther a 15
prikke with inke. Abide thanne stille waityng on the sonne after 1 of the clokke, til that
the schadwe of the wyr or of the pyn passe
onything owt of the cercle of the compas,
be it never so lite; and set ther another 20
prikke of ynke. Tak than a compas and
mesure evene the middel bytwixe bothe prikkes,
and set ther a prikke. Take me thanne a rewle,
and draw a strike evene alyne fro the pyn
unto the middel prikke; and tak ther thy 25
lyne meridional for everemo, as in that same
place. And yif thow drawe a croslyne overthwart
the compas, justly over the lyne meridional,
than hastow est and west and sowth; and
par consequence than the nadir of the sowth 30
lyne is the north lyne. And for more declaracioun, lo here thi figure.

39. Descripcion of the meridional lyne, of longitudes, and latitudes of citees and townes from on to another, and of clymatz.

This lyne meridional ys but a maner descripcioun or lyne ymagined, that passeth upon the
pooles of this world and by the cenyth of owre
heved. And hit is cleped the lyne meridional,
for in what place that any maner man is at 5
any tyme of the yer, whan that the sonne, by
moeving of the firmament, cometh to his verrey

38.1 for werpinge, against warping. **38.14 anything,** at all. **38.15 her-mele,** the breadth of a hair. **39** From this point on B is copied from a text like D, and both are poor. The present text is corrected from R as printed by Skeat III.237. Only a few of the variants are here included as examples. **39.2** D *or the lyne.* **39.3 cenyth of owre heved,** zenith overhead. **39.3** D *this the world.* **39.4** D *hit is the same lyne.* **39.6–7** *by moeving:* D *shyneth onything.*

meridian place, than is hit verrey midday, that we clepen owre noon, as to thilke man; and therfore is it cleped the lyne of midday.   10

And *nota* that for evermo of any 2 citees or of 2 townes, of whiche that o town aprocheth neer the est than doth that other town, truste wel that thylke townes han diverse meridians. *Nota* also that the arch of the equinoxial that is conteyned or bounded bytwixe the 2 meridians ys cleped the longitude of the town. And yif so be that two townes have illike meridian, or on meridian, than is the distance of hem bothe illike fer fro the est; and the contrarie. And in this manere they chaunge nat her meridian, but sothly they chaungen her almikanteras for the enhansing of the pool and the distance of the sonne.   15 ... 20

The longitude of a clymat is a lyne ymagined fro est to west illike distant fro the equinoxial. The latitude of a clymat is a lyne ymagined from north to south the space of the erthe, fro the bygynnyng of the firste clymat unto the verrey ende of the same climat, evene directe agayns the poole artik. Thus seyn some auctours, and somme of hem seyn that yif men clepen the latitude thay mene the arch meridian that is contiened or intercept bytwixe the cenyth and the equinoxial. Thanne sey they that the distaunces fro the equinoxial unto the ende of a clymat, evene agayns the poole artyk, is the latitude of a climat for sothe. And for more declaracioun, lo here thi figure.   25 ... 30 ... 35 ... 40

40. *To knowe with which degree of the zodiak that any planete assendith on the orisonte, wheyther so that his latitude be north or sowth.*

Knowe be thine almenak the degree of the ecliptik of any signe in which that the planete is rekned for to be, and that is cleped the degree of his longitude; and knowe also the degree of his latitude fro the ecliptik north or   5

sowth. And by this samples folwynge in special maistow wyrke for sothe in every signe of the zodiak. The degree of the longitude, par aventure, of Venus or of another planete was 6 of Capricorne, and the latitude of him was northward 2 degrees fro the ecliptik lyne. I tok a subtil compas and cleped that on poynt of my compas A, and that other poynt F. Than tok I the point of A, and set it in the ecliptik line evene in my zodiak, in the degree of the longitude of Venus, that is to seyn, in the 6 degree of Capricorne. And thanne sette I the point of F upward in the same signe, bycause that the latitude was north, upon the latitude of Venus, that is to seyn, in the 6 degree fro the heved of Capricorne. And thus have I 2 degrees bytwixe my two prikkes. Than leide I down softely my compas, and sette the degree of the longitude upon the orisonte. Tho tok I and wexede my label in maner of a peyre tables to resceyve distinctly the prikkes of my compas. Tho tok I this forseide label and leide it fix over the degree of my longitude. Tho tok I up my compas and sette the point of A in the wex on my label, as evene as I kowde gesse over the ecliptik lyne, in the ende of the longitude; and sette the point of F endlang in my label upon the space of the latitude, inwarde and over the zodiak, that is to seyn, northward fro the ecliptik. Than leide I down my compas and lokede wel in the wey upon the prikke of A and of F. Tho turned I my riet til that the prikke of F sat upon the orisonte. Than saw I wel that the body of Venus in hir latitude of 2 degrees septentrionalis assended in the ende of the 6 degree in the heved of Capricorne. And *nota* that in the same maner maistow wyrke with any latitude septentrional in alle signes; but sothly the latitude meridional of a planete in Capricorne may not be take bycause of the litel space bytwixe the ecliptik and the bordure   10 ... 15 ... 20 ... 25 ... 30 ... 35 ... 40 ... 45

39.11 D *evermo any lynes or of 2 townes.* **39.13 neer,** nearer. **39.25 longitude . . . clymat,** length, the zone between two lines of latitude. **39.26 illike,** equally. **39.27 latitude,** breadth. **39.31 evene directe,** in line with. **40.7** *sothe:* D *sonne.* **40.9** D *planete that* inserted. **40.10** *6 of Capricorne:* B has different (impossible) degrees; in R the figures were never filled in. **40.23 softely,** carefully. **40.41 septentrionalis,** northward.

of the astrelabie; but sothly, in alle other signes it may.

Also the degree, par aventure, of Juppiter 50 or of another planete was in the first degree of Pisces in longitude, and his latitude was 3 degrees meridional. Tho tok I the point of A and sette it in the firste degree of Pisces on the ecliptik, and thanne set I the point of F 55 downward in the same signe, bycause that the latitude was sowth 3 degrees, that is to seyn, fro the heved of Pisces. And thus have I 3 degrees bytwixe bothe prikkes. Thanne sette I the degree of the longitude upon the orisonte. 60 Tho tok I my label, and leide it fix upon the degree of the longitude. Tho sette I the point of A on my label, evene over the ecliptik lyne, in the ende evene of the degree of the longitude,

and set the point of F endlang in my label 65 the space of 3 degrees of the latitude fro the zodiak, this is to seyn, sowthward fro the ecliptik, toward the bordure; and turned my riet til the prikke of F sat upon the orisonte. Thanne say I wel that the body of Juppiter in his 70 latitude of 3 degrees meridional ascended with 14 degrees of Pisces *in horoscopo.* And in this maner maistow wyrke with any latitude meridional, as I first seide, save in Capricorne. And yif thow wolt pleie this craft with the 75 arysing of the mone, loke thow rekne wel her cours howre by howre; for she ne dwelleth nat in a degree of his longitude but a litel while, as thow wel knowest. But natheles, yif thow rekne hir verreye moeving by thy tables 80 howre after howre [breaks off].

Explicit tractatus de Conclusionibus Astrolabii, compilatus per Galfridum Chauciers ad filium suum Lodewicum, scolarem tunc temporis Oxonie, ac sub tutela illius nobilissimi philosophi Magistri N. Strode, etc.

40.81 Late MSS finish the sentence *thou shalt do wel ynowe.* In late manuscripts, there follow six more articles; see "The Text of This Edition," p. 966.

Equatorie of the Planets

INTRODUCTION

Equatorie of the Planets

N 1951, MS Peterhouse 75.1, now in the Cambridge University Library, was first studied by D.J. Price. In looking through it, he found on folio 5^v an indication of the number of days in 1392 years and a notation that can be expanded to read "defferentia Christi et Radix Chaucer" or "the difference (in number of days) between (the year of Christ's birth) and the (year of) the radix of Chaucer." Radix in this sense means December 1392, the basic date for the tables and calculations in the *Equatorie*.

The manuscript is composed of seventy-eight folios, ff. 1-70 containing astronomical tables in the hand of a professional scribe, and ff. 71-78, a separate physical unit, containing an essay on the construction and use of the equatorie. The essay is holograph, full of corrections, incomplete, and still in the process of composition when its author laid it aside. Both the essay and tables were on loose quires intended for later recopying. Their present order is the result of binding by a sixteenth-century Peterhouse librarian.

D.J. Price and R.M. Wilson produced a careful edition and study of the text (1955). In his linguistic analysis, Wilson observes that nothing in the language argues against the essay's being by Chaucer, and the style and vocabulary argue for his authorship. Other scholars have concurred, and Margaret Schlauch, in *Chaucer and Chaucerians*, ed. D. S. Brewer (1965), has pointed out that the essay reveals the same literary personality as the *Astrolabe*.

The equatorie is a geometric device for ascertaining the position of the planets in relation to one another. It is composed of a series of concentric circles divided in degrees, with a revolving hand by which to calculate the epicycles of the planets, that is their own orbits as they revolve around the earth according to the Ptolemaic cosmology. This is a more complicated instrument than the astrolabe, and its use requires a higher degree of mathematical sophistication. The style indicates that the essay was based on the Latin translation of an Arabic original, but the author was composing his own problems because he recognized that some of them are incorrect.

In his analysis of the contents, Price points out that the *Equatorie* contains many ingredients of the missing parts of the *Astrolabe* although it can in no sense be considered a continuation. A more logical explanation would be that after Chaucer had written the first two parts of the *Astrolabe*, he began compiling the tables promised in the third and fourth parts, and looking for a suitable discussion of the motions of the planets. As Price observes, an equatorie was regarded as a companion instrument to an astrolabe (the only extant medieval equatorie is engraved on the back of an astrolabe in Merton College). Hence, a treatise on an equatorie might have been considered an appropriate "theorik to declare the moevinge of the celestial bodies and causes" (*Astrolabe* II.89-91). The greater mathematical sophistication of the *Equatorie* problems and the correction of its calculations and tables from Oxford to London would indicate that Chaucer was moving ahead in his astronomical studies.

If the *Equatorie* is by Chaucer, it is further interesting as the only example we have of his handwriting and his working copy (see the illustration, p. 335). The corrections in the text and the added sheets and quires suggest the nature of the "foul papers" in which both *Canterbury Tales* and *Troylus and Criseyde* are now assumed to have been preserved (see John H. Fisher, "Animadversions on the Text of Chaucer, 1988," *Speculum*, 1988). For a study of this aspect, one must turn to the excellent facsimiles in Price's edition. The diagrams in the *Equatorie*, which have been reproduced below, are in the same style as those for the *Astrolabe*. These rough sketches by the author lend support to the possibility that the *Astrolabe* diagrams were also originally by the author.

937

Equatorie of the Planets

In the name of God pitos and merciable.
Seide [Leyk] the largere that thow makest this
instrument, the largere ben thi chef devisiouns.
The largere that ben tho devisiouns, in hem
may ben mo smale fracciouns. And evere 5
the mo of smale fracciouns, the ner the
trowthe of thy conclusiouns.

Tak therfore a plate of metal, or elles a bord
that be smothe shave by level, and evene
polised. Of which, whan it is rownd by 10
compas, the hole diametre shal contene 72
large enches, or elles 6 fote of mesure. The
whiche rownde bord, for it shal nat werpe ne
krooke the egge of the circumference, shal
be bownde with a plate of yren in maner 15
of a karte whel. This bord, yif the likith,
may be vernissed or elles glewed with perchemyn
for honestyte.

Tak thanne a cercle of metal that be
2 enche of brede, and that the hole dyametre 20
within this cercle shal contene 68 enches,
or 5 fote and 8 enches, and subtili lat this cercle
be nayled upon the circumference of this bord
or ellis mak this cercle of glewed perchemyn.
This cercle wole I clepe the Lymbe of myn 25
equatorie, that was compowned the Yer of
Crist 1392 complet, the laste meridie of
Decembre.

This lymbe shaltow devyde in 4 quarters
by 2 diametral lynes in maner of the lymbe 30
of a comune astrelabye, and lok thy croys
be trewe proved by geometrical conclusioun.
Tak thanne a large compas that be trewe,
and set the fyx point over the middel of the
bord on which middel shal be nayled a 35
plate of metal rownd. The hole diametre of
this plate shal contiene 16 enches large, for in
this plate shollen ben perced alle the centris of
this equatorie, and ek in proces of tyme
may this plate be turned abowte after that 40
auges of planetes ben moeved in the 9 spere.
Thus may thin instrument laste perpetuel.

Tak thanne, as I have seid byforn, the fix fot
of thy compas and set it in the middel of
this plate, and with the moevable point of 45
thi compas descrive a cercle in the ferthest
circumference of thy lymbe. And *nota* that the
middel poynt of this plate wher as the fix fot of
thy compas stondith wole I calle Centre
Aryn. 50

Text based on MS Peterhouse 75.1 as edited and translated by D. J. Price, *The Equatorie of the Planetis* (1955); see "The Text of This Edition," p. 966.

1 In the name of, the traditional Arabic opening *bismillah* (in the name of Allah) reveals that this work, like the *Treatise on the Astrolabe,* is based on a source ultimately Arabic in origin. **2 Leyk,** the word has been erased, but can be read under ultraviolet illumination. Price can suggest no satisfactory identification but notes that it might be a mistranslation (read from left to right instead of right to left) of the Arabic word *qīla* (it is said). **3 the largere ben thi . . . devisiouns,** see *Astrolabe* I.18, II.5. Price notes that this was a traditional caution in treatises describing the construction of astronomical instruments. **9 by level,** verified by a level. **12 large enches,** the old Saxon inch, equal to 1.1 modern inches. The modern inch was mandated by Edward I in 1305, but the traditional inch continued to be used, particularly in trade. Chaucer's experience with weights and measures in the Custom House might have made him use the popular measure. **14 egge,** edge. **18 honestyte,** evenness (to have a smooth surface). **22 subtili,** carefully. The author's revision can be followed here under the erasure. Originally he appears to have written *tak thanne a cercle of metal that be 2 enche of brede | & that the hole dyametre contene 72 enches | or 6 fote | & subtili . . . .* The revised wording removes any ambiguity. **26–27 Yer of Crist 1392,** this date translates as 31 December 1392. The other dates in the *Equatorie,* like those in the *Astrolabe,* are in 1391. **complet,** not counting the year current in which the date is taken (i.e., 1392 complete is 1393 incomplete). **laste meridie,** last meridian (moon). **31 comune astrelabye,** see *Astrolabe* I.5. **41 auges,** apogees; farthest points in the orbits of the moon and stars. These move about one inch a century. **50 Aryn,** in medieval geography, the center of the habitable earth; here the hub of the geocentric planetary system, glossed *terre* at l. 346.

Mak thanne a narwer cercle that be descrived upon the same centre aryn but litel quantite fro the forthest forseid cercle in the lymbe, in whiche space shollen ben devyde mynutes of the lymbe. Mak thanne a   55 narwere cercle somwhat ferther distaunt fro the laste seid cercle, in which shal be devyded the degres of the same lymbe. Mak yit a narwere cercle somwhat ferthere distaunt fro this laste seid cercle, in which shal ben   60 writen the nombres of degres. Mak yit a narwere cercle somwhat ferther distaunt fro this laste seid cercle, in which shollen ben writen the names of 12 signes. And *nota* that this laste seid cercle wole I calle the   65 Closere of the Signes.

Now hastow 5 cercles in thy lymbe and alle ben descrived upon centre aryn. And everich of the 4 quarters in thi lymbe shal ben devided in 90 degres, that is to sein, 3 signes.   70 And everi degre shal be devided in 60 minutes. And shortly, thi lymbe is devided in maner of the lymbe in the bak side of an astrelabie.

Devyde thanne thilke lyne that goth fro   75 centre aryn unto the cercle closere of the sygnes in 32 parties equales, whiche parties ben cleped Degres of the Semydiametre. Marke thise parties dymli, and *nota* that this diametral lyne devided in 32 parties shal be cleped   80 Lyne Alhudda.

Set thanne the fix point of thy compas upon the ende of the firste devysioun fro centre aryn in lyne alhudda, and the moevable point upon the ende of the 30 devisioun fro the   85 fix poynt of thi compas in the same lyne. So dwelleth ther but 1 devisioun bytwixe thy moevable point and the closere of the signes,

and 1 devysioun bitwixe thy fix poynt and the centre aryn. And descryve thus a cercle,   90 and tak ther the eccentrik cercle of the sonne. Scrape thanne awey the devysiouns of lyne alhudda.

Devyde yit dymly the same lyne alhudda fro centre aryn unto the closere of the   95 signes in 60 parties equales. Set thanne the fix poynt of thy compas in centre aryn, and the moevable point in 12 degres and 28 minutes of lyne alhudda, and descrive a cercle. And that is the Centre Defferent of the mone.   100

Perce thanne al the circumference of this defferent in 360 subtil holes, equales of space, and thise spaces bytwixe the holes ben devyded owt of the degres of the lymbe. And *nota* that the Yer of Crist 1392 complet, the aux   105 of Saturnus was the last meridie of Decembre at Londone; I seye the aux of Saturne in the 9 spere was 4 dowble signes 12 degres 7 minutes 3.2 etc. The remenaunt of auges sek hem in the table of auges folwynge.   110

Tak thanne a rewle and ley that on ende in centre aryn and that other ende in the lymbe, in the ende of the minut wher as endith the aux of the planete. And draw ther a lyne with a sharp instrument fro centre aryn unto the   115 closere of the signes, and no ferthere for empeiryng of the lymbe. And fasteby this lyne, writ the name of the planete. This rewle is general for alle planetis.

Sek thanne in thi table of centris the   120 distaunce of the centre equant of Saturne fro centre aryn, which is 6 degres 50 minutes. Set thanne the fix point of thy compas in centre arin, and the moevable poynt in 6 degres and 50 minutes in lyne alhudda fro centre   125 aryn. Turne than softely thy compas abowte

---

51 narwer cercle, Price observes that these scales are described loosely and could not contain the minute divisions indicated. **64 12 signes,** signs of the zodiac. **73 bak side,** see *Astrolabe* I.4ff. **77 sygnes,** interlinear gloss *versus finem geminorum* (toward the end of Gemini). **78–79 Marke . . . dymli,** lightly; interlinear *ut postea deleantur* (later to be deleted). **81 Alhudda,** perigee, nadir of the apogee (l. 41 above). The word is from Arabic. **94 dymly,** interlinear *occulte*. **102 360 subtil holes,** drilling 360 holes evenly in a 7-inch circle is an ideal hope. Price suggests that the full number were never drilled (see ll. 168–69, 503, where the author confesses the limitations of his instrument). **105 complet,** 1392 completed years from the birth of Christ (the date would be 1393 incomplete); *complet* is interlinear followed by *ultimo 10.bre in meridie London* erased. **aux,** sing. of auges (above l. 41 note). **110 table of auges,** the table is on f. 6ᵛ of the MS as now bound. **117 empeiryng,** spoiling. **118 *planete*:** interlinear *cuius est aux* (whose aux it is).

til that the moevable poynt towche the lyne of
the aux of Saturne. And stondinge alwey stille
the fix poynt of thy compas in centre aryn,
marke with thy moevable poynt in the lyne   130
of the aux of Saturnus a dep prikke, for in
that prikke shal be perced a smal hole for the
centre equant of Saturnus. And faste by this
hole mak an E in signefyeng of equant.

Thanne tak awey thy compas and loke   135
in thi table of centris the distaunce of the
centre defferent of Saturnus, and that is 3
degres and 25 minutes. Set thanne the fix point
of thy compas in centre aryn, and thy
moevable point in 3 degres and 25 minutes   140
in lyne alhudda, and torne softely thi
compas til that the moevable point towche the
forseide lyne of the aux of Saturne. And stondyng
stille thy fix poynt of thi compas in centre
aryn, marke with the moevable poynt in the   145
lyne of the aux of Saturne a dep prikke, for
therin shal be perced a smal hole for the centre
defferent of Saturnus, and fasteby this hole mak
an D for defferent.

And *nota* that by this ensample of   150
Saturnus shaltow make the centres def-
ferentes, and ek the equantes, of alle the planetis
after hir distaunces fro centre aryn, and prikke
hem in the lynes of hir auges.

Thanne shaltow sette the fix point of thy   155
compas in the lyne of the aux of Mercurie,
evene bytwixe the centre E and centre D of
Mercurius, and strid the moevable poynt til it
wole towche bothe centre E and ek centre
D of Mercurius, and descryve ther a litel   160
cercle. And thanne shaltow se that the lyne
of the aux of Mercurie departith this litel cercle
in 2 arkes equals, this is to seye that the lyne
kerveth this litel cercle evene amidde.

This litel cercle shal be perced ful of   165

smale holes *in circumferencia circuli* by evene
proporcioun, as is the centre defferent of the
mone in 360 holes yif it be possible, or in 180,
or in 90 atte leste. But sothly, the spaces
bytwixe the holes ne shal nat be devided   170
owt of the grete lymbe of the instrument,
as is the centre defferent of the mone, but owt of
the circumference of the same litel cercle it shal
be devided by thy compas.

Scrape thanne awey thilke 60 devysiouns   175
in lyne alhudda, and yit devyde the same
lyne alhudda in 5 parties equales by compas fro
centre aryn unto the cercle that is closere of the
signes. And everych of thilke 5 parties shal
be devided in 60 parties. Thise divisouns   180
ne shal nat ben scraped awey.

Devyde thanne the line that goth fro centre
aryn to the hed of Capricone, which lyne is
cleped in the Tretis of the Astrelabie the
midnyht line. I seye devyde this midnyht   185
lyne in 9 parties equals fro centre aryn unto
the closere of the signes. And everich of thise
devysiouns shal be devided by thy compas in
60 parties equales. Thise devysiouns ne shal
nat be scraped awey.   190

Laus Deo vero. Now hastow the visage of
this precios equatorie. *Nota* that thise last seid
9 divisiouns in the midnyht lyne shollen serven
for equacioun of the 8 spere.

Now for the composicioun of the epicicle   195
for the visage of thyn equatorie, thow shalt
make a cercle of metal of the same brede and
of the same widnesse in circumference, in
diametre, and in alle thinges lik to the
lymbe of thin instrument. And in the same   200
manere shal it be devyded in mynutis, in
degres, in nombres, in names of signes, and in
5 cercles compased as is the firste seid lymbe,
save that the eccentrik of the sonne ne shal

---

136 table of centris, there is no table in the MS as now bound of the distances of equants and deferents from Aryn. **153** *distaunces*: interlinear *in tabulis* (in the table). **158 strid,** extend. **162 departith,** divides. **166** *in circumferencia circuli,* interlinear. **168 360 holes,** see above l. 102 note. **184 Tretis of the Astrelabie,** evidently a reference to Chaucer's *Treatise on the Astrolabe,* the only English version known to have existed at this time. **185–86 midnyht lyne,** see *Astrolabe* I.4. **191 Laus Deo vero,** "praised be the true God," again, translation of an Arabic exhortation. **195 epicicle,** the epicycle part of the equatorie instrument is lower case to distinguish it from the planetary Epicycle (i.e., the orbits of the individual planet along the ecliptic).

nat be in the epicicle, and also that it be nat 205
filed to ney to the closere of his signes list
thow perce the hole of thi commune centre
defferent amys or elles list the hole breke. This
epicicle mot have suffisaunt thikkenesse to
sustene hymself. 210

Tak thanne this epicicle and ley it sadly
and evene upon the visage of thin equatorie so
that Aries of thin epicle lie evene upon the hed
of Aries in the lymbe of thin equatorie, and
Libra upon Libra, and Cancer upon 215
Cancer, and Capricorne upon Capricorne,
and every signe upon signe—this is to seyn,
the hed of every signe upon hed of every signe.

Tak thanne a renspyndle or a boydekyn,
and in direct of the hed of Cancer thow 220
shalt in the cercle that is closere of the signes
make a litel hole thorw the epicicle. And thanne
shaltow se that yif thow have trewely compased
thy cercles, that the poynt of thy renspindle
shal have towched the closere of the signes 225
in direct of the hed of Cancer in thyn
equatorie. This litel hole that is no grettere
than a smal nedle shal be cleped the Comune
Centre Defferent of Planetes.

Tak thanne a barre of metal of the 230
brede of a large enche and of suffisaunt
thyknesse. Of the whiche barre, that on ende
shal be sowded to the closere of the signes in
direct of Aries in this epicicle, and that
other ende shal be sowded to the closere of 235
the signes in direct of Libra in the same
epicicle. Draw thanne by thi rewle a lyne fro
the hed of Aries to the hed of Libra endelong
the barre, and draw swich another lyne
overthwart the barre fro the hed of Cancer 240
to the hed of Capricorne. And in the seccioun of this crois is the centre of the epicicle.

Tak thanne a rewle of latoun that ne be nat
ful thykke, and lat it be the brede of an
enche, and the lengthe shal be as long as al 245
hol the diametre of the epicicle. This rewle
mot be shape in maner of a label on an
astrelabie. The centre of this rewle shal be
nayled to the centre of the forseide barre
in swich a manere that this label may torne 250
abowte as doth the label of an astrelabie.
In middes of this nayl that fastnyth the barre
and the label togidere, ther mot be a smal
prikke that be dep, which prikke is the
centre of thin epicicle. 255

Tak thanne by thy large compas the
distaunce bytwixe centre aryn and the closere
of the signes, which distaunce is the lengthe of
lyne alhudda. And be it on a long rewle or
elles be it on a long percemyn, marke with 260
thy compas the forseide distaunce, and
devyde it in 60 parties equals. And than hastow
a newe lyne alhudda.

Sek thanne in thy table of centres the
semydiametre of the Epicicle of Saturnus, 265
and that is 6 degres and 30 minutes of
swiche degres as ben 60 in line alhudda. Tak
thanne with thy compas the space of 6 degres
and 30 minutes of lyne alhudda, and set the
fix point of thy compas in the centre of thin 270
epicicle that is the poynt in the hed of the
nail. And endelong the label set the moevable
poynt of thi compas, and with that moevable
poynt mak a marke, a strik in the label,
and fasteby the strik writ SA for Saturne. 275
This ensample of Saturne techith how to
maken in the label alle the semydiametres of
Epicicles of alle the planetis. *Nota* that the sonne
ne hath non Epicicle, and *nota* that alwey as
the label turnyth, so shewith it the Epicicle 280
of every planete.

Laus Deo vero. Now hastow complet thyn

204–08 *the eccentrik—hole breke,* these lines are written at the top of the page and marked for insertion. *hole:* interlinear *foramen* (hole).
206 filed, i.e., cut too close to the line called the "closer of signs" (above, l. 66). **list,** lest. **210 sustene hymself,** be rigid. **211–12
sadly and evene,** carefully and evenly. **213** *Aries:* interlinear *capud* (head). **219 renspyndle . . . boydekyn,** pivot-rod, bodkin
(large needle). **220 in direct,** exactly. **233 sowded,** soldered. **238 endelong,** along. **240 overthwart,** across. **243 latoun,** brass.
247 label, see illustration in *Astrolabe* I.22. **254** *prikke:* interlinear *id est punctus* (that is, a puncture). **271** *poynt:* interlinear *punctus*.
282 Laus Deo vero, Price observes that the source probably ended here, and a second section from this or another source begins at
l. 343 below. The intervening summary and illustrations are original. They show similarity to the commentary and illustrations in the
Astrolabe.

equatorie with alle hise membris. And *nota* that eccentrik of the sonne shal nat be compassed in this epicicle. Explicit. 285

The Face of the Equatorie

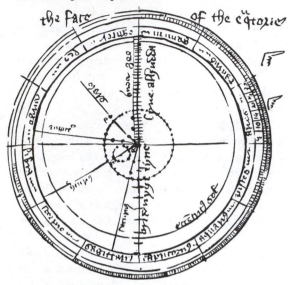

the Face of the eqtorie

The Face of the Equatorie

Nota that every centre mot ben also smal as a nedle, and in every equant mot be a silk thred.

Nota that the eccentrik of the sonne is compaced on the bord of the instrument 290 and nat on the lymbe for sparing of metal.

Nota shortly that but so be that bothe the closeres of the signes ben precisly ilike of widnesse, and but so be that centre aryn stonde precise as fer fro his closere of the signes as 295 the centre of thin epicicle stondith fro the comune centre defferent precise, thyn epicicle is fals. But natheles, yif thow myshappe in this cas I shal teche the a remedie. Knokke thi centre defferent innere or owtre til it stonde 300 precise upon the closere of the signes in the lymbe of thin equatorie. So wole thanne the centre of thin epicicle precise stonde upon centre aryn.

The sixte cercle is the eccentric of the 305 sonne. And the 5 cercle that is red is the closere of the signes. And the seccioun of the crois is centre aryn. And that other centre is the centre of the eccentrik of the sonne. And the lyne devyded in 9 is the midnyht lyne (I 310 wot wel it is figured boistosly). And the cercle abowte centre aryn is the centre defferent of the mone. The litel cercle is the defferent of mercurie. The smale lynes ben lynes of auges. The prikkes in the lynes ben the 315 centris equantis and defferentis. And alle thise centres save the equant of Mars ben bytwixe centre aryn and the centre defferent of the mone. The owterest space is mynutis, and the nexte space is degres, and the 320 thridde space is nombres of degres, and the ferthe space is for names of signes. But natheles, the narwere cercle of the signes is cleped the closere of the signes, and it is compased with red. 325

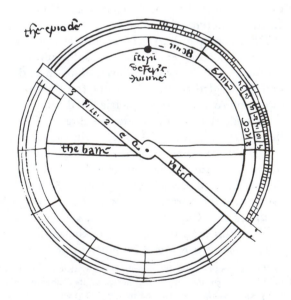

the epicicle

The Epicicle

306 cercle that is red, in both MS. D of the *Astrolabe* and Peterhouse 75 of the *Equatorie*, important lines in the figures are in red.
311 boistosly, crudely. This comment supports the other evidence that MS Peterhouse 75 is the author's original copy. Although not professionally drafted, the diagrams are unusually correct in detail.

The Epicicle

Nota, file nat to ney the rede cercle that is closere of the signes list the commune centre defferent breke. Lat stonde a litel lippe as shewith in direct of the hed of Cancer.

Nota, I conscile the ne write no names of 330 signes til that thow hast proved that thi comune centre defferent is trewli and justli set in direct of the closere of the signes of thin equatorie.

This epicicle is devyded and compased 335 in alle thinges lik to the lymbe of the equatorie, but it hath non eccentrik of the sonne. The prikke that stant in the closere of the signes in direct of the ende of Geminis is the commune centre defferent. 340

But natheless thus lith thin instrument whan thow makest equacioun of thy mone:

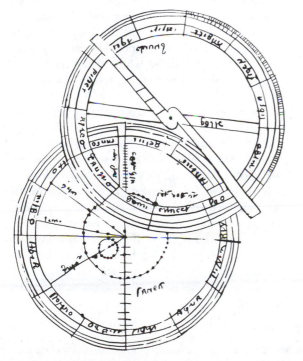

Sek medius motus of Saturnus, Juppiter, Mars, and Venus, and hir mene argumentis in thy tables, and writ hem in thy sklat. Put 345 thanne a blak thred in centre aryn, and a whit thred in centre equant of any planete that the list have of equacion. And put the comune centre defferent of thyn Epicicle upon the centre different in thy plate of thilke planete 350 that thow desirest to have equacioun. I sey that with a nedle thow shalt stike the comune centre defferent of thin epicicle upon the centre defferent that is perced on thy plate for swich a planete as the list to have of 355 equacioun.

Loke thanne fro the hed of Aries wher the mene motus of thy planete endith, in the grete lymbe of thy plate, and ley ther thy blake thred. Ley thanne thy white thred eque- 360 distant by the blake thred in the same lymbe, and proeve by a compas that thy thredes lyen equedistant. Under whiche white thred ley the pool of thyn epicicle, and stondinge thyn epicicle stille in this maner—I seye, 365 stondinge the pool of thin epicicle undir thy white thred stille, and the commune centre different fix with thy nedle to the foreseide centre defferent of the planete desired—tak than thy blake thred and ley it so that it 370 kerve the centre of the epicicle and streche forth up unto upperest part of the same epicicle. And than shal this blake thred shewe bothe the verrey motus of the epicicle in the grete lymbe, and ek the verrey aux of the planete 375 in the epicicle. And thanne the ark bytwixe

326 **ney,** near. 329 **in direct of,** exactly at. 331 *signes:* interlinear *id est in epiciclo* (that is, on the epicycle). 342 **makest equacioun,** find the position. **thy mone,** this familiar phrasing resembles that of the *Astrolabe,* see II.12.29 note. Price, pp. 107–10, explains the technical terms in the text: *mene (medius)* is used to refer to a point moving uniformly or to an angle increasing at a constant rate; *equacion* (equation) is the correction of this uniform motion; the corrected reading is the *verrey* (true) *argument; motus* is motion. 343 Gloss at head of page, *pro argumentis trium superiorum minue eorum med' mot' de med' mot' solis et remanet argumentum* (for the arguments of the three superior planets, take away their medius motus from the medius motus of the sun, and the arguments will remain). 346 *aryn:* interlinear *terre.* 349–50 **defferent . . . different,** these forms are used interchangeably for astronomical "deferent" and the modifier "different". 357 **Loke thanne,** interlinear *pro successione signorum* (by the succession of signs, i.e., anticlockwise).

medios motus of the planete and the verrey
motus of the epicicle is cleped the equacion of
his centre in the lymbe, to whom is lik the
equacion of his argument in his epicicle. 380
That is to sein the ark bytwixe his mene aux
and his verrey aux. For sothly, the mene aux is
shewed in the epicicle, by the white thred under
which thow puttest the pol of the epicicle,
and the verrey aux is shewed in the epicicle 385
by the blake thred.

And stondinge stille thin epicicle in this same
disposicioun, ley the ende of thy label that is
graven fro the white thred as many signes,
degres, and minutes as shewith the mene 390
argument in thy tables for that day of thy
planete desired. And rekne this mene argument
fro the white thred after successioun of signes of
every planete, save only of the mone. And
ligginge the marked ende of thy label upon 395
the ende of this mene argument in the
epicicle, ley thy blake thred upon the marke of
thy planete that is graven in thi label. And
wher as the same blake thred kervyth the
lymbe of thy plate, tak ther the verrey place 400
of the planete in the 9 spere. And the ark
bytwixe the verrey place of the planete and the
verrey place of the epicicle considered in the
lymbe is cleped Equacioun of his Argument.

This maner of equacioun is for Saturnus, 405
Juppiter, Mars, and Venus, but in the
remenaunt of planetes in some thinges it
varieth.

Sol

The mene motus of the sonne ben rekned
fro the hed of Aries after successioun of 410
signes. The sonne hath non Epicicle, ne non

equant, and therfor the pol of the epicicle mot
ben inside of the body of the sonne in the 9
spere. The white thred that thow puttest in
his centre defferent in the plate mot ben 415
inside of the white thred that othre
planetes han in hir centres equantis.

The blake thred that evermo stant in centre
aryn mot be leid at the ende of his mene
motus. Tak thanne his white thred and lei 420
it equedistant in the lymbe by the blake
thred, whiche blake thred shewith the mene
motus of the sonne.

Fixe thanne with thy nedle the commune
centre defferent of thyn epicicle to centre 425
aryn, and remew nat thy nedle. And under
this white thred ley softely the pol of the epicicle,
and wher as the white thred kervyth the grete
lymbe tak ther the verrey place of the sonne
in the 9 spere. 430

The ark of the lymbe bytwixe his aux,
that is now in Cancer, and the blake thred, is
the argument of the sonne. The ark bytwixe
the blake thred and the white in the lymbe
is the equacion of the sonne, which ark nis 435
but litel.

The mene motus of the sonne is the ark in the
lymbe bytwixe the hed of Aries and the blake
thred in the same lymbe. The verrey motus
of the sonne is the ark of the lymbe bytwixe 440
the hed of Aries and the blake thred whan
it is remewed fro the mene motus and crossith
the white thred in the pol of the epicicle.
The same verrey motus was shewed erst by
the white thred of the defferent whan it lay 445
equedistant by the blake thred in the limbe.

And *nota* that the markes in thy label
descriven the Epicicles of planetes as the label
turneth.

---

378 *motus:* interlinear *locum* (place). 379 *lymbe:* interlinear *zodiacus.* 387–88 **stondinge ... disposicioun,** i.e., keeping it in the same
position. 389 **graven,** marked (engraved). 392 **mene argument,** tables of mean arguments are included in the MS. On the page, the
designation is *grene tables,* with the word *grene* cancelled; none of the appropriate tables can be described as green. Price, p. 54, has a
figure illustrating this calculation. 400 *place:* interlinear *locum.* 402 *place:* interlinear *locum. planete:* interlinear *in limbo* (on the limb).
405 **equacioun,** finding the position. 410–11 **successioun of signes,** anticlockwise. 413 **ben instide,** be used in place of. 415 *plate:*
interlinear *lamia* (plate). 441 *whan it:* interlinear *id est filium* (that is, the thread).

Mercurius (this canon is false)

Rekne after succession of signes fro the   450
hed of Aries in the lymbe the mene motus of
Mercurius, and considere ek how mochel in the
same lymbe is bytwixe the hed of Aries, and the
lyne of his aux that yit is in the lattere ende of
Libra. And rekne alwey after successioun   455
of signes.

Withdraw thanne the quantite in the lymbe
bytwix the hed of Aries and the forseid aux owt
of his mene motus and considere how moche
is the remnaunt of his mene motus whan   460
this aux is thus withdrawe owt of al the
hoole mene mot. And so mochel rekne after
succession of signes in his litel cercle, fro the
lyne of his aux that kervyth the same litel
cercle. I seye, rekne after successioun of   465
signes, from lettere D that is graven in his
lytel cercle, and procede in the same litel cercle
toward lettere E opposit to D.

I sey rekne thilke remnaunt of the mene
motus that dwelde whan the quantite of   470
his aux was withdraw owt of his hole mene
motus, as I have seid byforn. And wher as thilk
remnaunt forseid endith in the litel cercle, tak
ther the verrey centre defferent of Mercurie,
as it happith diversely somtyme in on hole   475
and somtyme in an other. For lettere D ne
servyth of nothyng ellis but for to shewe the
wher thow shalt bygynne thy reknyng in thy
litel cercle; ne lettere E ne servyth nat but
for to shewe the which wey that thow shalt   480
procede fro lettere D.

Now hastow founde thy defferent and thin
equant, in which equant put a whit thred and
stike with a nedle the comune centre defferent upon his centre defferent in the plate.   485
And with thin epicicle wirk and with thy
thredes as thow workest with Saturnus, Juppiter,
Mars, and Venus.

Nota that yif the aux of Mercurie be fro
the hed of Aries more than his mene motus   490
fro the same hed, than shaltow adde 12
signes to his mene motus. Than maistow withdraw his aux owt of his mene motus.

And *nota* generaly that thy nedle ne be
nat remewed whan it is stikyd thorw the   495
commune centre defferent into any centre
different on thy plate til thin equacion of the
planete be endid, for yif thy commune centre
different stirte fro the centre on thy plate,
al thin equacion of thy planete desired is   500
lorn.

Hic nota that the centre defferent of Mercurie
hath but 24 holes as in myn instrment, wherfor
I rekne but 2 holes for a signe, as in the
gretter cerkle of Mercurie fro the lyne of   505
his aux.

Luna

Rekne after succession of signes fro the hed of
Aries in the lymbe the mene motus of the mone,
and rekne in the same manere the mene
motus of the sonne as fer as it strechcheth.   510
Withdraw thanne the mene motus of the
sonne owt of the mene motus of the mone, and
considere that difference. And the quantite of
that difference, that I clepe the remenaunt.
Rekne it fro the ende of the mene motus of   515
the sonne in the lymbe bakward agayn successioun of signes, and wheras endith this
remenaunt mak a mark in the lymbe.

Draw thanne thy blake thred to this
forseide mark, and wher as thy blake thred   520
kervyth the cercle defferent of the mone, in
that same hole is the centre defferent of the
mone, as it happith. And in the nadyr of this
hole is the centre equant. Put thanne in
this centre equant a whit thred. Now hastow   525
thy two centres.

Stike thanne thy commune centre defferent
upon the centre defferent of the mone. With

Mercurius, the page containing ll. 450–506 has been marked for excision. **455 successioun,** this is one of the errors; the calculations
here should proceed clockwise. **480 for to shewe,** here are more errors, see Price, p. 71 (1.22). **501 lorn,** lost. **510** *sonne:* interlinear
a capite arietis (from the head of Aries). **512 of the mone,** *and as moche as the mene mot of the mone is more than the mene mot of the sonne*
cancelled. **516 bakward agayn successioun,** i.e., clockwise.

thy nedle yit rekne agayn the mene motus
of the mone fro the hed of Aries after succes- 530
sioun of signes, and ley ther thy blake thred.
And ley thy white thred equedistant by the
blake thred in the lymbe.

Moeve thanne softely the pool of thyn
epicicle under thy blake thred. Tak thanne 535
thy white thred and ley it over the pol of
the epicicle, and wheras thy white thred kervyth
the cercle of the epicicle, tak ther the mene aux
in thyn epicicle, and fro this white thred
rekne in thyn epicicle bakward agayns 540
successioun of signes thy mene argument.

I seye rekne it in the degres of thin epicicle,
and where as endith thy reknynge in the epicicle,
ley ther the marked ende of thy label. And
ley thy blake thred upon the mark of the 545
mone in thy label. And wher as this same
blake thred kervyth the lymbe, tak ther the
verrey place of the mone in the 9 spere.

Nota that the pool of the epicicle ne shal
nat ben leyd under the blake thred of non 550
other planete save only of the mone.

(this canon is fals)

And *nota* that yif the mene motus of the sonne
is more than the mene mot of the mone, than
shaltow adde 12 signes to the mene mot of
the mone, and thanne maistow withdrawe 555
the mene mot of the sonne owt of the mene
motus of the mone.

And shortly for to speken of this theorike, I
sey that the centre of hir *(lune)* epicicle *in
volvella* moevyth equaly aboute the centre 560
of the zodiac, that is to sein, aboute the pol
of the epicicle that is thy riet.

And thy blake thred, whan it first leid thorw
the pol of thyn epicicle, it shewith the verrey

aux of the planete, riht as the white thred 565
shewith the mene aux in the same epicicle.

Item, whan thow hast rekned the argument of
a planete in thin epicicle, thanne is the body of
the planete in thin epicicle at the ende of
thyn argument. And whan thy blak thred 570
is leid thorw the marke of a planete in thi
label, in maner forseid, than shewith thy blake
thred the verre place of the planete at regard of
the 9 spere, as shewith in thy lymbe.

And the ark bytwixe the verrey motus 575
and the mene motus of the mone is the
equacion of his argument in the lymbe. And
the ark bytwixe his mene aux and his verrey
aux is the equacion of his argument in the
epicicle. 580

To knowe the latitude of the mone by
thyn instrument, loke in thyn almenak the
verrey motus of the mone and the verrey motus
of Caput Draconis Lune at the same tyme.
And yif so be that thy verre mot of thy 585
mone be lasse than 6 signes fro Caput
Draconis, withdraw the verrey motus of Caput
owt of the verrey motus of the mone and writ
that difference, for that is hir *(lune)* verrey
argument. 590

And so many signes, degres, and minutes
as thow hast in the verrey argument of hir
latitude, rekne hem fro the hed of Aries after
successioun of signes in thy lymbe, and
wher as endith thy reknyng, ley that on end 595
of thy thred. And the middel of thy thred
shal kerve the meridional lyne and strechche so
forth overthwart al the dyametre of thy plate
unto the lymbe.

As thus, I suppose that on ende of thy 600
thred laye after succession of signes 10

532 equedistant, parallel. **535–37** *Tak thanne—the epicicle*, interlinear addition. **552** Lines 553–80 have been struck through as have
ll. 450–506 above. Price finds no serious error in the calculation. **558 theorike**, a term used to describe the intended treatment in
Part v of the *Astrolabe*, Prol. 106. **559–60** *in volvella*, interlinear (on the rotating portion of the instrument). *lune*, interlinear. **562 riet**, evidently the author thought of the epicycle part of the instrument as similar to the rete of an astrolabe, see *Astrolabe*, I.21. **565** *planete :*
interlinear *in epiciclo*. **567 argument**, corrected motion; see l. 342 note. **575–76 verrey motus . . . mene motus**, corrected motion,
uncorrected motion; see l. 342 note. **577 equacion . . . argument**, correction, movement. **584 Caput Draconis Lune**, head of the
moon dragon; the point where the moon's ascending orbit intersects the ecliptic plane causing an eclipse. The dragon is the legendary
beast which swallows the moon causing the eclipse. **585 mot**, motion *(motus)*. **589** *difference :* interlinear *id est verum argumentum latitudinis lune* (that is, the true argument of the latitude of the moon). *lune*, interlinear. **590** *argument :* interlinear *id est latitudinis*. **600 on ende**,
one end.

degres fro the hed of Aries; in the lymbe that other ende of thy thred shold lye 20 degres of Virgo in the lymbe. Considere thanne how many degres and minutes that the middel 605 of thy thred lith fro centre aryn wher as evermo bygynnith this reknyng—I seye, considere in the seccions of the meridional lyne how many degres and minutes lith the middel of thy thred fro centre aryn, and tak 610 ther the nombre of the latitude septentrional of thy mone fro the ecliptik, which latitude ne passith never 5 degres.

And yif the verrey motus of the mone be more than 6 signes fro the verrey mot of 615 Caput, than shaltow withdraw the verrey motus of Cauda owt of the verrey motus of the mone, and bygynne thy reknynge at the hed of Libra and procede bakward agayns successioun of signes. 620

As thus, that yif that on ende of thy thred laye agayn successioun of signes 10 degres fro the hed of Libra, than sholde that other ende lye in the 10 degres fro the hed of Aries after successioun of signes. 625

Considere thanne in the meridional lyne the quantite meridional of the latitude of thy mone fro the ecliptik, as I have told byforn, that the quantite of degres and minutes that the middel of thy thred in the meridional lyne 630 lith fro centre aryn, the same quantite of degres and minutes is the latitude of the mone fro the ecliptik, be it north, be it sowth.

And *nota* that generaly evermo bothe endes of thy thred shollen lyen equedistant 635 fro thilke diametre that kervyth the hevedes of Aries and Libra.

Yit quykly understond this canon. I sey whan the forseide verrey argument of the mone is precisly 90 degres fro the hed of Aries in the 640

lymbe after succession of signes, tak ther the grettest latitude of the mone septentrional. And yif so be that hir verrey argument passe anything 90 degres fro the hed of Aries, styrt over the meridional lyne into the firste 645 of Cancer, and ley ther that on ende of thy thred and that other ende into the laste of Geminis. And so forth, day by day, shaltow descende in the meridional lyne after that the reknynge of thy verrey argument 650 requerith til thow come agayn to centre aryn, for than hastow mad equacion of latitudes for 6 signes, as I first seide. And everemo lith thy thred equedistant fro the diametre that kervyth the hevedes of Aries and Libra. 655

And evermo as many degres and minutes as the midel of thy thred lith in the meridional lyne fro centre aryn, so many degres and minutes is the latitude of the mone fro the ecliptik. And whan thy verrey argument passith 660 6 signes, wyrk with Cauda as I tawhte the, and ascende upward in the meridional lyne day by day to the laste of Geminis in the lymbe. And fro thennes discende agayn, as I have seid byforn. 665

And *nota* that whan the mone is direct with Caput or Cauda, she hath no latitude, and when she passith Caput til she be 3 signes in distance fro Caput she is septentrional ascendinge, and in hir grettest latitude 670 septentrional. And fro the ende of thilke 3 signes she is septentrional descending til she come to the opposit of Caput, that is to seyn Cauda Draconis, and fro Cauda til she come mid wey bytwix Capud and Cauda. 675 And fro thennes is she meridional assending til she come agayn at Capud.

(1391, 17 Decembris) Ensample: my mone was 12 degres 21 minutes of Virgo, and

---

611 septentrional, northward. **617 Cauda (Draconis)**, the tail of the moon dragon; point of the descending orbital intersection. **642** *septentrional*: interlinear *id est ab ecliptica* (that is, from the ecliptic). **652 mad equacion**, worked out. **666–67 direct with**, exactly at. **669** *in distance*: interlinear *pro successionibus signorum* (by succession of signs). **675 and Cauda**, Price here adds "it is south descending" as necessary to the sense (pp. 59, 72). *mid wey*: interlinear *in medio*. **678 Ensample**, Price observes (p. 72) that these dates and numbers conform to the tables in the MS and hence are probably genuine illustrations (as contrasted with the theoretical examples in the *Astrolabe*). Although there are errors, the calculations are so accurate that they must have been obtained by calculation from the tables rather than by manipulation of the equatorie instrument. **my mone,** see l. 342 note.

Caput was 4 degres 46 minutes of Aries. 680
Tho drow I the verrey motus of Caput, that
is to seyn 0 in signes 4 degres 46 minutes, owt
of the verrey moevyng of the mone, that is to
sein owt of 5 signes 12 degres 21 minutes.
Tho fond I that the verrey argument of the 685
mone dwelde 5 signes 7 degres 35 minutes.

Tho rekned I after successioun of signes fro
the hed of Aries in the lymbe the same 5 signes
7 degres 35 minutes, and ther leide I that
on ende of my thred, and that other ende 690
lay in 22 degres 35 minutes of Aries. Tho
karf the midel of my thred the meridional lyne,
1 degre and 54 minutes fro centre aryn, by
which I knew that the latitude of my mone
was 1 degre and 54 minutes septentrional 695
descending fro the ecliptik.

(1391, 19 Februarii) Another ensample: I
fond my mone in 8 degres 13 minutes of Virgo,
and Caput Draconis in 20 degres and 42
minutes of Aries. Tho drow I the verrey 700
motus of Caput fro the verrey motus of the
mone in this manere. I say wel that I myht nat
drawe 20 degres owt of 8 degres, ne 42 minutis
owt of 13 minutes. Tho added I 30 degres
to the forseide 8 degres of Virgo, and 60 705
minutes to the 13 minutes of the same Virgo.
And tho drow I the verrey motus of Caput owt
of the verrey motus of the mone. Tho dwelde me
the verrey argument of the latitude of the
mone, that is to seyn 4 signes 17 degres 710
31 minutes.

Tho leide I that on ende of my thred 4 signes
17 degres 31 minuta fro the hed of Aries in the
lymbe after successioun of signes, and that
other ende lay equedistant fro the diametre 715
that passith by the hevedes of Aries and
Libra. And tho fond I the middel of my thred
karf the meridional lyne at 3 degres and 22
minutes fro the centre of the erthe that is
centre aryn. Wherfor I knew wel that my 720
mone was 3 degres 22 minutes in latitude

septentrional descendinge fro the ecliptik.

(1391, 23 Februarii) The thridde ensample
is this: I fond in myn almenak the verrey
motus of the mone was 6 degres 24 minutes 725
of Scorpio, and the verrey motus of Caput
was 20 degres 29 minutes of Aries. Tho moste I
wirke with Cauda bycause that verre motus of
my mone passed mor than 6 signes. Tho
drow I the verrey motus of Cauda owt of 730
the verrey motus of the mone in this maner.
I added 30 degres to 6 degres of Scorpio and
60 minutes to 24 minutes of the same Scorpio.
Tho dwelde me the verrey argument of
latitude of the mone, 0 in signes 15 degres 735
55 minutes.

Tho leide I that on ende of my thred 0 in
signes 15 degres 55 minutes fro the hed of Libra
agains succession of signes bycause that I
wirke with Cauda. And that other ende of 740
my thred lay equedistant fro the diametre
that passith by the hevedes of Aries and Libra.
And tho fond I that the middel of my thred
karf the meridional lyne, 1 degre 22
minutes fro centre aryn. Bi which I knew 745
the latitude of my mone was 1 degre 22
minutes fro the ecliptil meridional discendinge.

Thus shaltow procede day by day upward fro
the hed of Libra unto 90 degres agayns
succession of signes, that is to seyn unto the 750
firste of Cancer, and thanne stirt over the
meridional lyne whan thy verrey argument of
thy latitude of the mone passit anything 90
degres, and ley that on ende of thy thred in
Gemini and that other ende in Cancer and 755
so com downward day bi day til thow come
agayn at centre aryn. And thanne wirk with
Caput as I have told byfore.

And *nota* that whan any eclips *(lune)*
fallith in Aries, Taurus, Gemini, Cancer, 760
Leo, Virgo, than is the eclips in Caput, and
the remenant of the eclipses ben in
Cauda.

---

681 Tho, then. **698** *I fond:* interlinear *scilict in almenak* (that is, in the almanac). **713** *31 minuta,* interlinear (Lat.). **759** *lune,* interlinear.

The Place of Chaucer

Chaucer in His Time

Chaucer's Language and Versification

The Text of This Edition

THE PLACE OF CHAUCER

Before assaying the place of Chaucer, one must decide on the place of language and literature in our culture. Only then will it be possible to say something meaningful about Chaucer's place in English poetry. Cultural anthropologists have argued that the identifying characteristic of a "society" is interdependence. This interdependence is achieved through the making and interpreting of signs and signals between members of the society. Human society, in contrast to animal societies, is characterized by the complexity of its communication, particularly the metaphors and metonymies that constitute large areas of language, particularly poetic language.

Although signs and signals can communicate directly sense-impressions like hunger or fear, language requires that these impressions be converted to sense-images. These images can take the visual form of pictures or the oral form of language. In either form they are symbolic. As they grow more abstract, the symbols come to embody clusters of sense-images and relationships; they become concepts. This conceptual system is not created anew by each individual or each generation. It represents the gradually developed consciousness of the culture, indeed of the human race. Much of its material, like that concerning birth, sex, and death, is universal. Some of it, like that concerning the way in which these universals are perceived—kinship systems, social controls, and so on—is peculiar to an individual culture.

The customs of a culture and the rationale by which they are supported are tradition. Artists, priests, and teachers (in the Middle Ages they were the same) have the task of elucidating and memorializing the traditions that hold the culture together. The more successful they are in capturing in art or language the essence of their own cultural tradition, the more they are revered by succeeding generations. Their works become "classics."

The General Prologue to the *Canterbury Tales* of Geoffrey Chaucer stands at the threshold of the Anglo-American literary tradition. This is the earliest piece written in such language and embodying such concepts that later generations in the culture respond instinctively to it, respond with what Edmund Wilson called the "shock of recognition." This does not mean that the language of the Prologue offers no problems or that we understand the full significance of its images and allusions. Chaucer was the most bookish and derivative of artists, himself the end product of a thousand years of European tradition now foreign to us. Much of the study of Chaucer is trying to understand what he is really saying and how what he is saying relates to the aesthetic and intellectual context upon which he drew. But these scholarly activities would not be so important if Chaucer's poetry itself did not generate a spontaneous reaction and if it had not had such a formative influence on succeeding writers.

Chaucer did not create the standard language, as he was formerly credited with doing. Standard Modern English was beginning to be developed by the English civil service—of which he was a member—to carry on the official business of the nation. Yet man does not live by bread alone. As a symbolic system, the essence of language is more the comprehension and expression of concepts than the communication of basic needs. Chaucer's poetry is the earliest effective use of the new medium to express feelings and ideas, rather than for government and business transactions. The Pilgrims in the *Canterbury* Prologue and the action and sentiment in the *Canterbury Tales* and *Troylus* are archetypes for later expression of ideas in English poetry.

Although the General Prologue to the *Canterbury Tales* has emerged as the most enduring influence, Chaucer's other writings display a mastery of expression and a range of interest that have also delighted later generations. The tales that follow the Prologue are nearly as familiar as the Prologue itself, even though some deal with concepts that are now fairly foreign to most people. *Troylus and Criseyde*, considered somewhat lesser in importance now, was, until 1660, referred to more often and praised more highly than the *Canterbury Tales*. Furthermore, because language evokes such intimately personal sense-images, the personalities of creators in language capture our attention much more than the personalities of other equally influential arbiters in a society, such as architects or theologians. The enormous importance of the *Canterbury Tales* and *Troylus* in our literary tradition gives importance to everything that Chaucer wrote, and by extension to Chaucer's own biography, even though there is diminishing objective importance in his minor works and in what is known of his life. Nevertheless, in trying to fathom the reasons for the influence of Chaucer's major works, the breadth of his interest is an important factor. Few authors have ranged so widely. Not only do we have the moral and stylistic span from the humor and bawdry of the Miller's Tale to the formal religiosity of the Parson's Tale, and the span from the lyric and narrative poems to the moral and philosophical prose, but we also have the span from literature and philosophy to the technical writing in the astronomical treatises. Poems like the *Book of the Duchess* and treatises like the *Astrolabe* have not had a continuing direct influence on our culture, but they did influence Chaucer's contemporaries and successors in developing what has become the modern English literary tradition throughout the world. Besides, they cast light on the vitality and intelligence that underlie the major works.

Chaucer was immediately recognized in his own time. In 1386, even before he had written the *Canterbury Tales*, Eustace Deschamps, whose position in the French court paralleled almost exactly Chaucer's position in the English court, sent him the following balade (printed with a translation). It is the first such tribute in English literature. It has biographical implications in that it is the only contemporary linking of Chaucer the man of affairs with Chaucer the poet; Aulus Gellius (1. 2), famous for his *Attic Nights*, was renowned in the Middle Ages as both a writer and a judge. But principally the poem reflects an appreciation of Chaucer's major accomplishment, transmuting into English the elegance of French court poetry.

O Socrates plains de philosophie,
Seneque en meurs, et Auglux en pratique,
Ovides grans en ta poëterie,
Briés en parler, saiges en rethorique,
Aigles treshaulz, qui par ta theorique
Enlumines le regne d'Eneas,
L'isle aux geans (ceuls de Bruth), et qu'i as
Semé les fleurs et planté le rosier
Aux ignorans de la langue pandras—
Grant translateur, noble Geffroy Chaucier.

Tu es d'amours mondains dieux en Albie;
Et *de la Rose*, en la terre Angelique—
Qui, d'Angela saxonne est puis flourie
Angleterre, d'elle ce nom s'applique
Le derrenier en l'ethimologique—
En bon Anglès le *Livre* translatas;

O Socrates full of wisdom,
Seneca in morals, Aulus Gellius in practical affairs,
Ovid great in thy poetics,
Concise in speech, experienced in rhetoric,
Lofty eagle, who by thy science
Dost illumine the kingdom of Aeneas,
The isle of giants (those of Brutus), and who there hast
Sown the flowers and planted the rose-tree;
Thou wilt enlighten those ignorant (of French),
O great translator, noble Geoffrey Chaucer;

Thou art a mundane god of love in Albion;
And *of the Rose* in the Angelic land—
Which from Lady Angela the Saxon has since become
England, for from her this name is taken
As final in the etymology—
Into good English *The Book* thou hast translated;

Et un vergier, où du plant demandas
De ceuls qui font pour eulx auctorisier,
A ja long temps que tu edifias,
Grant translateur, noble Geffroy Chaucier.

A toy pour ce de la fontaine Helye
Requier avoir un buvraige autentique,
Dont la doys est du tout en ta baillie,
Pour rafrener d'elle ma soif ethique,
Qui en Gaule seray paralitique
Jusques a ce que tu m'abuveras.
Eustaces sui, qui de mon plant aras;
Mais pran en gré les euvres d'escolier
Que par Clifford de moy avoir pourras,
Grant translateur, noble Geffroy Chaucier.

L'envoy

Poëte hault, loënge d'escuîrie,
En ta jardin ne seroie qu'ortie,
Considéré ce que j'ay dit premier—
Ton noble plant, ta douce melodie;
Mais, pour sçavoir, de rescripre te prie,
Grant translateur, noble Geffroy Chaucier.

And a garden, for which thou hast asked plants
From those who poetize to win them fame,
Now for a long time thou hast been constructing,
Great translator, noble Geoffrey Chaucer.

Of thee therefore from the Heleian spring
I ask to have an authentic draught,
For the spring is entirely in thy keeping,
To assuage therewith my feverish thirst,
Who in Gaul shall be as one paralyzed
Until thou shalt make me drink.
An Eustache[1] am I, and thou shalt have a plant
  from me;
But treat with favor the writings of a novice
Which by Clifford[2] thou shalt receive from me,
Great translator, Geoffrey Chaucer.

L'envoy

Excellent poet, glory of squiredom,
In thy garden I should be but a nettle,
In comparison to what I have just spoken of—
Thy noble plant, thy sweet melody;
But, for my information, I beg thee an official verdict,
Great translator, noble Geoffrey Chaucer.

Caroline Spurgeon in *Five Hundred Years of Chaucer Allusion* (3 vols., 1925) has gathered other examples of "enthusiastic and reverential" praise by his contemporaries and immediate successors. These compliments were principally for his linguistic achievement in the creation of a new poetic language. He is the "firste fyndere of our faire langage," "the flour of eloquence" (Lydgate); "clere in sentence / in langage excellent," "shewyng the pyked grayn of sentence uttered by crafty and sugred eloquence" (Caxton). As time passed, the linguistic achievement seemed less remarkable, and in the sixteenth century Chaucer came to be praised by the Protestant reformers as a forerunner of their break with Rome because of his exposure of the corruption of medieval religion. John Foxe in the *Book of Martyrs* (1570) observed that Chaucer "saw in Religion as much almost, as even we do now, and uttereth in hys works

no lesse, and seemeth to be a right Wiclevian . . . and that all his workes almost . . . will testifie (albeit it be done in myrth, & covertly)." In the process, Foxe and others attributed to him many anticlerical pieces which are not his.

The seventeenth century is the low point in Chaucer's reputation, when knowledge of his language and prosody had been lost, and he was regarded as antiquated and barbarous. Henry Peacham remarked (1622), "although the stile for the antiquitie, may distaste you, yet under a bitter and rough rinde, there lyeth a delicate kernell of conceit and invention." At the end of the century, Dryden uttered the famous dictum that Chaucer's verse "is not Harmonious to us; . . . They who lived with him, and some time after him thought it Musical. . . . There is the rude Sweetness of a *Scotch* tune in it, which is natural and pleasing, though not perfect." But Dryden voiced the eighteenth century's awaken-

---

[1] *Eustache*, a pruning knife.
[2] *Clifford*, evidently Sir Lewis Clifford, who took the balade to Chaucer. Text and translation from J. M. Manly, ed., *Canterbury Tales* (1928), pp. 23–25, except that for "pandras," l. 9, I follow James Wimsatt, in D. Brewer, ed., *Geoffrey Chaucer* (1974), p. 109.

ing interest in the native tradition which was eventually to dethrone the classics in favor of English literature: "he has taken into the Compass of his *Canterbury Tales*, the various Manners and Humours of the whole *English* nation, in his age." Pope in his *Essay on Criticism* (1709) lamented, "Our sons their father's failing language see, / And such as Chaucer is shall Dryden be"; but he was also reported by Spence as saying, "I read Chaucer still with as much pleasure as almost any of our poets. He is a master of manners, of description, and the first tale-teller in the true and enlivened natural way."

The period between Speght in 1598 and Urry in 1721 is the longest period since the introduction of printing without a new edition of Chaucer (there were two later editions of Speght). But by the middle of the eighteenth century, the emerging popular interest in the languages and literature of the British Isles revived interest in Chaucer as the father of English poetry. Thomas Warton in the first *History of English Poetry* (1774) summed up his evaluation: "In a word, [Chaucer] appeared with all the lustre and dignity of a true poet, in an age which compelled him to struggle with a barbarous language, and a national want of taste; and when to write verses at all, was regarded as a singular qualification." The publication of Tyrwhitt's great edition of 1775 firmly established Chaucer as an English classic author, with explanatory apparatus that made him accessible to every reader (Tyrwhitt employed the syllabic *e* to give rhythm to Chaucer's lines). It is amazing today to see how little critical progress has been made beyond Tyrwhitt's edition, although the factual data have been much refined.

Germanic philological and historical scholarship in the nineteenth century began the collection of this factual information. By the end of that century, historical grammar and the work of the Early English Text Society, the Chaucer Society, and an emerging cadre of professional students of literature—led by F. J. Child in

America and F. J. Furnivall in England—had ironed out most of the problems in Chaucer's pronunciation and grammar, had gone far toward making his English and Continental contemporaries accessible in good texts, and had begun the collection of biographical and historical data which dispelled the myths about Chaucer's life and career. This factual approach to Chaucer was the one current at the advent of American scholarship at the beginning of the twentieth century. Kittredge, Lowes, Manly, Tatlock, and others came to match their English and European colleagues both in their learning and in their enthusiasm for Chaucer. But it was characteristic of the approach of these scholars that they took Chaucer at face value. He was a cheery, dear old man with good-humored wrinkles around his eyes, who told funny stories. The emphasis was on identifying his sources and explaining the historic precedents for the characters and situations in his writings.

This concern for factual explanation was brought to an end by C. S. Lewis's *The Allegory of Love* (1936), which demonstrated that Chaucer and other medieval literature could be read as abstrusely and conceptually as any modern literature. "Chaucer, whatever we may think of him," he says, "was not a 'regular fellow,' *un vrai businessman*, or a rotarian. He was a scholar, a courtier, and a poet, living in a highly subtle and sophisticated civilization." And again, "allegory was in no sense a mere device, or figure of rhetoric or fashion. It was not simply a better or worse way of telling a story. On the contrary, it was originally forced into existence by a profound moral revolution occurring in the latter days of paganism. For reasons of which we know nothing at all—here again comes the 'seminal form' not to be explained by history—men's gaze turned inward."

Lewis's book coincided with the rejection of the factual and historical approach to literature by the "new critics," such as I. A. Richards in England and Cleanth Brooks and Robert Penn Warren in the United States. From that time to the present most Chaucer criticism has been devoted to the many-sidedness of Chaucer's art. Raymond Preston, *Chaucer* (1952), was one of the first to observe that "Chaucer has his own way of examining the sides of a question; he will look at them one by one...It is not merely that Chaucer tells a story with different layers. He tells it...from different points of view" (p.65). Two years later, E. Talbot Donaldson, "Chaucer the Pilgrim," *PMLA* (1954), distinguished between the voice of the poet, the voice of the persona, and the voices of the characters in the stories. This makes possible at least three levels of awareness in any speech or situation. Next came Charles Muscatine, *Chaucer and the French Tradition* (1957), which redefined the high, middle, and low styles of classical rhetoric as the courtly and bourgeois styles of romance and fabliau. The generation of J. M. Manly had envisaged rhetoric as artifice from which the true poet had to struggle to free himself in order to express his own art. Wayne Booth, *The Rhetoric of Fiction* (1961), redefined rhetoric as the inevitable relationship between the sender and receiver of any message. Every message is characterized by "doubleness"—its explicit communication, and its implicit effort to influence the ideas and behavior of the receiver. Chaucer's writings are now being explored for their "doubleness"—for the contrast between their surface meanings and their deep meanings.

Attention to the styles and voices in Chaucer's poems has directed fresh attention to their audiences. The view of Chaucer as a court entertainer is being increasingly called into question. D. W. Robertson, Jr., and his students see his poems (and, indeed, all medieval literature) more as admonition than diversion, devoted either directly or ironically to exploring the tension between charity and cupidity. This "exegetical" interpretation has been followed by the articles of Anne Middleton and Paul Strohm who identify Chaucer and his audience as the "new men"—lawyers, bureaucrats, merchants— who were increasingly taking charge in society. The "public poetry" of Chaucer and his London contemporaries treats the concerns of this sophisticated executive class rather than to those of the agrarian aristocracy. Books and articles by Dieter Mehl, Piero Boitani, John H. Fisher and others argue that Chaucer's poems were not composed to be recited but to be read, that the addresses to his hearers or readers are not evidence of their mode of presentation, but intended to create a "fictional audience" which he manipulates to secure the active participation of the reader.

All of these represent traditional criticism which still focuses on the intentions and achievement of Chaucer as an individual author. But his works are also being subjected to revisionist criticsm by David Aers, Sheila Delany, Mary Carruthers, and others who are interested in them less as the achievements of a remarkable individual than as products of his culture, and are concerned to lay bare the "deep structure" of the economic, sexual, or political power struggle of which the author himself may have been only partially aware—although in the Wife of Bath's Prologue and Tale, Chaucer shows himself more aware than most. Again, this criticism perceives a doubleness in Chaucer's poetry, the explicit story or lyric cry and the implicit illumination of the "alterity" of the medieval world view.

The current hypothesis that Chaucer never completed or arranged his texts presents problems about the unity and structure of his works, particularly the order of the *Canterbury Tales*. Many scholars now view the various orders as scribal and suggest that criticism should focus on the achievement of individual tales rather than on the dramatic structure of the whole compilation, but some, like Robert Jordan, *Chaucer and the Shape of Creation: The Aesthetic Possibilities of Inorganic Structure* (1967), argue for an associative "gothic" sense of structure in the Middle Ages, while others, like Donald Howard, *The Idea of the Canterbury Tales* (1976), have tried to look beneath the surface disarray for the "gestalt" the poet was striving to achieve. Recent critical developments are summarized by Derek Pearsall, *The Canterbury Tales* (1985).

CHAUCER IN HIS TIME

Not one of the 493 records printed and discussed in the *Chaucer Life-Records*, ed. M. M. Crow and C. Olson (1966), identifies Chaucer as an author. They chronicle the distinguished career of a courtier, diplomat, and civil servant. This must have been the character in which Chaucer viewed himself. His poetry he must have regarded as a fortunate talent by which he could advance his career in government. Only this can account for the fact that so many of his pieces were never finished and for the fact that, so far as we can tell, no manuscript of his works dates from before his death. Evidently, like Shakespeare, he gave no thought to the "publication" of his writings. The performance satisfied their intention. But this lack of interest in preserving an official canon contrasts with the hints we have of his desire to be remembered as a poet—in the *House of Fame*, at the conclusion of *Troylus and Criseyde*, in the lists of his titles in the *Legend of Good Women* and the Retraction to the *Canterbury Tales*.

The life-records show Chaucer emerging from the class in society that has produced the most notable writers in England and elsewhere, the prosperous upper middle class that must continue to work for a living, but with cultivation, education, some leisure, and resources to collect and create in the intellectual and aesthetic sphere. Until F. J. Furnivall in 1876 discovered a deed of conveyance of a house on Thames Street in which Chaucer described himself as "me Galfridum Chaucer filium Johannis Chaucer vinetarii Londonie," his specific parentage was not known. But as early as 1598, Thomas Speght, in the biography attached to his edition, had surmised of his parents, "whether they were Merchants, (for in the places where they have dwelled, the Armes of the Merchants of the Staple have been seene in

the glasse windowes), or whether they were of other calling, it is not necessary to search; but wealthy no doubt they were, and of good account in the commonwealth, who brought up their Sonne in such sort, that both he was thought fitte for the Court at home, and to be imployed for matters of State in forraine countreyes." This surmise has been largely confirmed by modern scholarship. Chaucer's father and other relatives were wealthy vintners (wine importers and wholesale merchants), who served in the army, furnished provisions for the court, and occupied official positions both for the king and the city of London.

The nature of the first records reveals how fragmentary and fortuitous our knowledge of Chaucer is. These turned up in 1851 on some scraps used as stuffing in the covers of a manuscript recently bought by the British Library. They are a list of the expenses and gifts from 1356 to 1359 of the household of Elizabeth, Countess of Ulster and wife of Lionel, second son of Edward III. Her two attendants mentioned most frequently are Philippa Pan' and Galfrido Chaucer. Chaucer's function is not indicated; presumably he was a page. Philippa's identity has been much debated. The most attractive theory is that "Pan' " is a contraction of "Panneto," one form of the name of Sir Paon de Roet, father of Philippa Chaucer and Katherine Swynford, who was mistress and eventually (1396) wife of John of Gaunt, Duke of Lancaster, third son of Edward III. If this surmise is correct, Chaucer married the damoiselle with whom he had served as a young boy.

The date of Chaucer's birth is not known. In the Scrope-Grosvenor trial of 1386, he gave his age as "xl ans et plus armeez par xxvii ans" —forty years and more, having borne arms for twenty-seven years. Efforts have failed to make these terms precise, but the first part sets Chaucer's birth before 1346. The customary age for going to war was 16 or 17, which would move the date back to 1342 or earlier. The twenty-seven years is quite accurate, because in 1359–1360 he served in the French war. In 1360 he was captured and ransomed for £16— 13s 4d less than for Sir Robert de Clinton's horse, as has been often remarked. Such military experience for Chaucer, as for his father before him, was clearly expected of one who hoped to be accepted by an aristocracy whose business was still war, even though his own ambitions might run in a totally different direction. Chaucer had no doubt been given a good elementary education before he joined the household of the Countess. Serving in a noble household and joining Prince Lionel on a military expedition must have been regarded as a continuation of his education.

But the period between the 1360 record of his military service and 1366, when he reappears traveling in Spain, is the longest gap in Chaucer's life-records after their commencement in 1357. Indeed, there are records every year from 1366 until the last one in 1400. The best supposition is that during these six years he was continuing his education in the Inns of Chancery and Inns of Court, which prepared him for an administrative career. In the Inns of Chancery, aspiring clerks were taught, first, the Chancery hand in which all official documents had to be written and, second, the forms and language (in Chaucer's time still Latin and French) in which they were enrolled. Without such training, Chaucer could not have been appointed controller of customs in 1374 with the provision that "rotulos suos dicta officia tangentes manu sua propria scribat"—that he write the rolls touching said office in his own hand. After two or three years in an Inn of Chancery, he could proceed to an Inn of Court, where he would hear lectures on law and government. The only evidence for such education comes much too late. Speght, in the 1598

life already referred to, said that "manye yeres since, master Buckley did see a recorde [of the Inner Temple], where Geffrye Chaucer was fined two shillinges for beatinge a Franciscane fryer in fletestreate." No records from the Inns of Court in Chaucer's day have survived, but Edith Rickert discovered that Master Buckley was keeper of the records of the Inner Temple in Speght's time, and so in a position to see such a record, and the offense and penalty are similar to others listed in the earliest records that do survive.

By 1366 this period was over and Chaucer reappears traveling in Spain, probably in connection with the Black Prince's campaign in support of Don Pedro of Castile, to whose fate Chaucer later alluded in the Monk's Tale (*CT* vii.2375ff), but possibly simply on a pilgrimage to the shrine of St. James of Compostella (*CT* i.466). In the same year the King granted Philippa Chaucer a life annuity of 10 marks as a damoiselle in attendance upon Queen Philippa, and in 1367 the King granted Geoffrey his first annuity of 20 marks. Scholars have debated the timing and the wording of these grants. The facts that Philippa was referred to in her own person rather than as the wife of Geoffrey Chaucer and that she received her grant first make it appear that Chaucer had married above himself and that Philippa's connections in court would do his career no harm. Her father, Sir Paon de Roet, had come from Hainault in northern France in Queen Philippa's personal entourage, and he was Guienne King of Arms—that is, he was charged with recording the genealogies of the noble families in England's valuable territories in southern France.

From 1367 to 1374 Chaucer was "vallectus" (yeoman), in 1368 promoted to "armiger" (esquire), in the King's household, but without specific assignment. His status during this period is described in the *Liber Niger* of the household of Edward IV (the household ordinances of Edward III have not survived): "These Esquires of household of old be accustomed, winter and summer, in afternoones and eveninges to drawe to Lordes chambres within court, there to keep honest company after there Cunninge [i.e., skill, knowledge], in talking of Chronicles of Kinges, and of otheres pollicies, or in pipeing or harpeing, songinges, or other actes marcealles, to helpe to occupie the Court, and accompanie estraingers till the time require of departing." We can see how one with a gift for story-telling and poetry would be in demand. ("Chronicles of kings" are specifically referred to in the *Book of the Duchess*, ll. 57–58.) The contacts one made in such a situation would be the foundations for a career.

We see this career developing as Chaucer is assigned to carry messages abroad and serve on diplomatic missions, in 1368 and 1370 to France and in 1372–1373 on a six-month trip to Italy. On this trip he visited Genoa and Florence. Boccaccio was in Florence that winter, lecturing on Dante, and Petrarch was living in Padua, near Venice. There is no evidence that Chaucer met either, but it is hard to believe that one concerned with poetry would have missed the opportunity. Upon his return to England, he began immediately to show the influence of Dante and Boccaccio, and the Clerk (*CT* IV.27) says that he learned his tale from Petrarch in Padua. If Chaucer ever did meet either Boccaccio or Petrarch, it would have had to be at this time, because Petrarch died in 1374 and Boccaccio in 1375, before Chaucer's next trip to Italy in 1378.

Chaucer's extended absence in 1372–1373 involves a domestic situation that has troubled some scholars, notably Russell Krauss in *Three Chaucer Studies* (1932). One of the problems of Chaucer biography is his relation to Thomas Chaucer, one of the wealthiest men in England in the fifteenth century, whose daughter became Duchess of Suffolk, whose grandson married the sister of Edward IV, and whose great-grandson was declared heir apparent to Richard III, only to be killed in battle. Thomas Chaucer is referred to as the son of Geoffrey Chaucer in contem-

porary records, but his birth and early years are shrouded in mystery. After using the Chaucer coat of arms for a few years, he shifted to the de Roet arms of his mother. It has been suggested that the reason for his rapid advancement was that he was the illegitimate son of John of Gaunt by Philippa. From Gaunt's illegitimate children by Philippa's sister Katherine (legitimized by Gaunt's marriage to Katherine in 1396) were descended all of the English kings after Henry VI. If there is any truth in the conjecture that Philippa was also Gaunt's mistress—which is not unimportant in view of Chaucer's treatment of women in his writings and in view of the progress of his own career—it depends on the timing of events in 1373–1374.

When Chaucer departed for Italy in December, 1372, Philippa was one of the damoiselles in waiting upon Gaunt's second wife, Constance of Castile, and Katherine (who that year bore Gaunt John Beaufort) was governess to his children by Blanche of Lancaster. Chaucer returned on May 23, 1373. On July 13 Gaunt went to lead a campaign in France. He returned to England in April, 1374, and within two months Chaucer was made financially independent: on April 23 the King granted him a pitcher of wine daily (perhaps $6000 a year at present values); on May 10 he was given the house over Aldgate rent-free; on June 8 he was appointed controller of customs (another £10—$5000 a year); and on June 13 he and Philippa together were granted another life annuity of £10 by John of Gaunt. All of this, together with previous grants and subsequent gifts and wardships, made Chaucer a prosperous man.

Philippa continued to receive gifts and payments from Gaunt, always in her own name, and the year before her death in 1387 she was admitted, again without her husband, to the fraternity of Lincoln Cathedral in a ceremony honoring the admission of Gaunt's oldest son, the future Henry IV. Although her annuity was usually drawn at the hand of her husband, warrants transferring payments in 1378–1379 to receivers in Lincolnshire indicate that Philippa did not live with Chaucer over Aldgate the entire period after 1374, a circumstance that may throw light on the wry self-portrait in the *House of Fame* (ll.641–660). And while we are setting down these personal details, there is the curious business of the legal release granted in May, 1380, by Cecily Champain to Geoffrey Chaucer for her "raptus." Despite arguments to the contrary, legal opinion holds that the word means what it says—that Chaucer had been sued for rape and had to seek legal quittance. Since the quittance came after the fact, this episode must have occurred around the time that Philippa was living in Lincolnshire. Skeat conjectured that "Litell Lowys," to whom the *Treatise on the Astrolabe* is addressed, might have been the consequence of this episode (*Astrolabe*, l. 27 note).

Chaucer's earliest poetry is related to the household of John of Gaunt. Whether or not the *Prier a Nostre Dame* (short poem 1) was written for Blanche of Lancaster, the *Book of the Duchess* was certainly composed as an elegy on her death in 1368. John Shirley asserted that the *Complaint of Mars* (short poem 3) was likewise composed at the command of John of Gaunt. So both in documented fact and in undocumented tradition and surmise, Chaucer's literary and personal lives were entangled with the house of Lancaster.

But Chaucer's main career continued to be as esquire to the King. In 1376 and 1377, he was sent three times to France to negotiate for peace. This involved discussion of marriage between 10-year-old Richard (who succeeded his grandfather in 1377) and 11-year-old Marie, daughter of the King of France, which appears to be satirized in the *Parliament of Fowls*. In 1378, he went again to Italy, leaving his power of attorney with his friends the poet John Gower and Richard Forester. This trip was to negotiate with Barnabo Visconti, ruler of Milan, whose fate is described in the Monk's Tale (*CT* vii.2399ff). On these occasions, he was allowed to appoint a deputy in the office of controller.

In February, 1385, Chaucer was given license to appoint a permanent deputy in his office. This represents another crux in his career. By October of that year he had been appointed a justice of the peace in Kent. In August, 1386, he was elected a member of parliament from Kent. In October, the Aldgate residence was leased to Richard Forester. That December, Adam Yardley replaced Chaucer as controller of customs. And in 1388, when the "Merciless Parliament" was investigating all of the grants made by Edward III and Richard II, he transferred his royal annuity to John Scalby. These events are all associated with the coup in the English government by which Thomas of Woodstock, youngest son of Edward III, replaced his brother John of Gaunt as the power behind the throne. All of the members of Richard's and Gaunt's households found themselves under suspicion. Richard's ineptitude, which was part of what led to this development, may be criticized in Alceste's speech to the god of love in the *Legend of Good Women* (ll.342ff) and in *Lack of Steadfastnesse* (short poem 14), and Chaucer's own discouragement at the situation may be reflected in *Balade de Bon Conseil* (short poem 11). In any case, it may have been the prospect of freedom from administrative responsibility that led Chaucer to lay plans for an extensive work like the *Canterbury Tales*.

However, this period of comparative retirement did not last long. In 1389 Richard declared himself of age, dismissed Thomas of Woodstock from the Council, and took the rule into his own hands. Chaucer was immediately given the heaviest responsibilities of his career: clerkship of the King's works, overseeing the maintenance of Westminster Palace, the Tower of London, and many of the King's other castles, manors, and properties (such as the wool quay). In this capacity he supervised a large staff and handled great sums of money to pay for materials and labor. In connection with the large sums he had to carry about with him, Chaucer was robbed three times in four days in September, 1390—at the "Fowle Ok" in Kent, at Hatcham in Surrey, and in Westminster. The beating and injuries mentioned in the inquest concerning these robberies may have been a factor in his giving up the clerkship the next June (1391). Meanwhile, he had been appointed sub-forester of Petherton Park, Somersetshire (1390). Probably this was a sinecure that allowed him to live near London, although he may have lived for a while in Somerset. Other than this, after his retirement from the clerkship of the King's works, Chaucer appears not to have held an official position.

In 1394, King Richard granted Chaucer a new annuity of £20, but he evidently had difficulty collecting the money due him. He was sued for debt; he transferred real estate; he borrowed money. Matters appeared to improve when the new king, Henry IV, doubled his annuity in an enrollment dated the day of his coronation, October 13, 1399. But this grant, too, had problems, since it was not actually made until February 1400, and backdated to October. That December, 1399, Chaucer signed a fifty-three-year lease for a dwelling in Westminster Close. This may have been simply because he wanted to live in Westminster, but it has been pointed out that Westminster Abbey was a refuge for debtors, and his move there may have been connected with his financial exigency. (The question as to why he signed such a long lease in the last year of his life is explained by the conventions of English land tenure, where it is customary to buy the unexpired term of a long lease rather than to buy freehold.) A final record indicates that he received his last tun of wine on the royal grant before September 29, 1400. But he died before he could collect the money due him from Henry IV's annuity,

The date of Chaucer's death, inscribed on his sixteenth-century tomb in Westminster Abbey is October 25, 1400. He was buried in the Abbey because, as a resident of the close, he was a member of the parish. However, his burial there

initiated the "poet's corner" in Westminster Abbey.

One gets the impression that Chaucer was most active as a writer when he was busiest as an administrator. Before 1374 he had translated all or part of the *Romaunt of the Rose* and written the *Book of the Duchess* and some other short poems. During his twelve years in the controller's office and in the midst of many trips abroad, he wrote *Parliament of Fowls, House of Fame, Boece, Troylus and Criseyde,* and *Palamon and Arcite* (the Knight's Tale). During his three years out of office he began *Legend of Good Women* and *Canterbury Tales.* During the three years of the clerkship of the King's works he no doubt continued work on *Canterbury Tales* and began one, possibly two, astronomical treatises, *Astrolabe* and *Equatorie.* Except for the revision of the Prologue to *Legend of Good Women,* there is nothing except two "begging" balades that we can assign with assurance to the eight years of his retirement. His *Lenvoy a Scogan* (short poem 17) implies that he may have felt his poetic gift was drying up. The *Complaint to His Purse* (short poem 18) is a final plea to King Henry.

It is impossible to write a biography of Chaucer in the modern sense because the materials (manuscripts, letters, observations by intimate contemporaries) are simply not available before the seventeenth century. Writing materials were too expensive; literacy was not sufficiently widespread. However, two excellent recent attempts are *Chaucer and His World* (1978), a beautifully illustrated volume by Derek S. Brewer which places Chaucer in his fourteenth-century London milieu, and *Chaucer: His Life, His World, His Works* (1987) by Donald Howard, which relates his writings to his life records. The "Chaucer Chronology" in the front endpapers of this edition summarize the important dates connected with Chaucer's life. Yet we go out pretty much as we came in. Little in the biographical records throws light on the personality of the poet or the meaning of the poems. Yet the charisma of the poems makes us endlessly curious about the nature of the man.

CHAUCER'S LANGUAGE AND VERSIFICATION

Chaucer's language is important, not only intrinsically as the language of a great poet, but also as an example of the language from which Modern Standard English developed. Chaucer did not create modern written English. That was evolved in the fifteenth century when the clerks in the English civil service—Chancery, as it was then called—switched government and parliamentary record-keeping from French and Latin to English. Chaucer did his own writing as a civil servant in French and Latin. But the governing classes by his time were *speaking* English, even though they were still *writing* in French and Latin. So Chaucer took the brave step (which his friend John Gower did not, at first) of writing his poems for the entertainment of the court in the vernacular—the spoken language. Like Chancery Standard, when it developed in the next century, the language that Chaucer and his London companions developed for poetry used a vocabulary more than half French, with many French idioms and expressions (*man of law, playn eleccioun, parfay, entrechaunge*). This was because his literary models were French and because he was writing for an audience still essentially bilingual.

The miracle is that the language of Chaucer's poetry is as close to the idiom of Modern English as it is. This is not true of his prose, or of fifteenth-century Chancery prose, even though the grammatical forms were quickly standardized. The greater facility of Chaucer's poetry illustrates what scholars have so often observed —that verse is the earliest mode of artistic expression in any language. It takes centuries to develop a lucid prose style, and this prose tradition must be passed from one generation to the next. When it ceases to be taught, it disappears, as Latin prose did after the fourth century and as Old English prose did after 1066.

Chaucer's spelling and pronunciation were more different from Modern English than his grammar and vocabulary. This is because of two changes in pronunciation that affected the language between Chaucer's time and Shakespeare's: (1) long vowels all underwent what is called "the great vowel shift"; (2) inflectional endings weakened or disappeared. For convenience, the differences in pronunciation have been listed in the back endpapers of this edition. Here we discuss only the principles that underlie the changes.

1. In Chaucer's time, the difference between the vowels of *fat–fate, met–mete, bit–bite, god–good, but–about* was length, not quality. In the century following Chaucer, length ceased to have phonemic value in English, and the long vowels all shifted in quality, as indicated in the diagram on p. 962. Spelling began to be standardized before this shift in sound was completed. This means that the spelling of the shifted vowels in Modern English is different from the spelling of equivalent sounds in other languages using the Latin alphabet: English *ice*—French *ici*, English *demon*—French *démon*. Hence, the generalization is that the long vowels of Middle English should be pronounced as the same spellings would be in Latin or any modern European language.

2. A second process that has gone on throughout the history of English is contraction of the sort that has led to the reduction of Old English *hlaford* to *lord* and is today leading to the reduction of *probably* to *probly*. Since spelling in the fourteenth century was still largely phonetic, the generalization is that there are no silent letters or syllables in Chaucer's English. The most widespread difference this makes in the pronunciation of Chaucer's English is that the inflectional endings *es* and *ed*, which have now

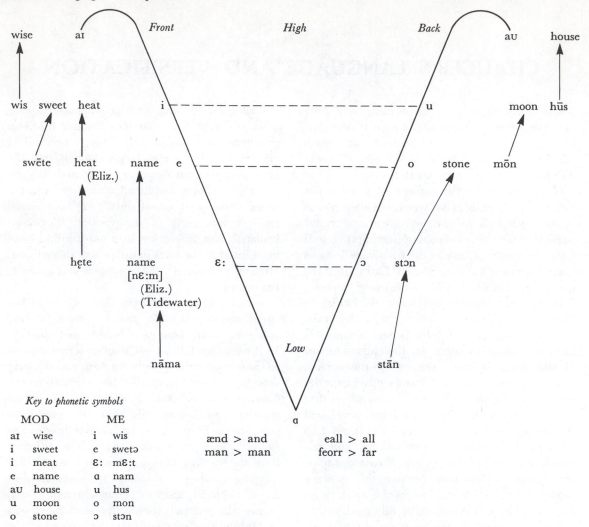

Key to phonetic symbols

MOD		ME	
aɪ	wise	i	wis
i	sweet	e	swetə
i	meat	ɛː	mɛːt
e	name	ɑ	nam
aʊ	house	u	hus
u	moon	o	mon
o	stone	ɔ	stɔn

ænd > and   eall > all
man > man   feorr > far

been contracted, were then pronounced as separate syllables: *walkes, walked, stones*. Thus there were many fewer monosyllabic words in Chaucer's English, which has important implications for rhythm and meter.

Consonants that have since become silent—*gnaw, folk*—were then pronounced. The spelling *gh* (then often spelled *h*) still had the palatal sound it has in Scots and German: *night* (*niht*), *bought* (*bohte*). When this sound occurred finally, it was already changing to *w*, as indicated by spellings like *bow* and *ynowe* (enough).

Also, most important, the many French words being introduced into English in Chaucer's time kept their French accent; *licóur, coráge*.

Pronunciation of all letters, Latinate vowels, alternation of French and English accent, and pronunciation of palatals that have since become vocalized or become silent all mean that Chaucer's poetry has to be read more slowly than modern poetry. If it is hurried over, it loses its music. The fact that the differences in Chaucer's pronunciation were not understood in the seventeenth century resulted in his then being considered a rough and crude prosodist, although his "matter" was thought delightful.

Most of the principles of his exquisite assonance and rhythm were rediscovered by Tyrwhitt and nineteenth-century philologists.

Chaucer's most important contribution to English poetry is the iambic pentameter line, for which he had no model in English. Most poetry after the Norman Conquest was either in relaxed alliterative verse or else in tetrameter couplets modeled on the French and Latin octosyllabics. The four-stress line in couplets or quatrains was the favorite form in English poetry from the *Owl and the Nightingale* to the *Pearl* and Gower's *Confessio Amantis*. Chaucer used it for three of his early poems, the *Romaunt of the Rose* (whatever part of it may be by him), *Book of the Duchess*, and *House of Fame*. Then he turned to the more sophisticated pentameter line. His models for this have frequently been debated. Since he evidently began to use it only after his trip to Italy, and since more than half his lines have feminine endings (thanks to the final *e*), there appears to have been an influence of the hendecasyllabic (eleven syllables), which Dante called the "most famous" line of the Italian poets. On the other hand, the decasyllabic was a line frequently employed in the French poems which served Chaucer as his earliest models. Chaucer's task was to adapt this Continental syllable-counting meter to English stressed rhythm.

Both the French and Italian lines employed the movable caesura, and the movable caesura is a feature of Chaucer's line. However, in native English alliterative verse he found a fixed caesura with two strong stresses and a varying number of weak stresses in each half line. This has led to the assertion by some critics that Chaucer's rhythm—as distinguished from his meter—was really four-beat, two on each side of the caesura, superimposed on a more or less decasyllabic line (since a good many lines run to eleven syllables, and some have only nine). This scansion works well for the opening lines of the *Canterbury Tales: Whān thǎt Aprīll | wǐth hǐs shǒurěs sǒotě || Thē drǒghtě of Mǎrch | hǎth pěrcéd tǒ thē rǒotě.* Most authorities, however, hold that

Chaucer regularly used five stresses in a line: *Whǎn thǎt Aprīll | wǐth hǐs shǒurěs sǒotě || Thē drǒghtě of Mǎrch | hǎth pěrcéd tǒ thē rǒotě.* The different levels of stress that were developing in Middle English made it possible for some stresses to be pronounced more heavily than others, so that while the line employed five stresses from a metrical point of view, the audience heard only the four maximal stresses. The chief mark of Chaucer's facility as a prosodist is the "naturalness" of his verse. The metrical stresses fall on the lexical stresses and reinforce the rhetorical emphasis without strain or distortion. When there are inversions either of stress or syntax, they are pleasurable instead of distracting. This is what is meant by "Chaucer's good ear." Keats said, "if poetry comes not as naturally as the leaves on a tree it had better not come at all." Even though Chaucer had no models for the English iambic pentameter, no subsequent poet has used it with more ease and expressiveness than he. The most recent comprehensive discussions are P. F. Baum, *Chaucer's Verse* (1961), and Ian Robinson, *Chaucer's Prosody* (1971). The principles of Latin, French, and Italian quantitative verse that served as his models are outlined in W. K. Wimsatt, ed., *Versification: Major Language Types* (1972).

Chaucer's grammatical forms and syntax offer less trouble than his pronunciation and prosody. Middle English grammars like Joseph and Elizabeth Wright, *Elementary Middle English Grammar* (1928), give full details concerning Chaucer's and other fourteenth-century dialects. A transformational approach is employed by Charles Jones, *An Introduction to Middle English* (1972). It is sufficient for us here to call attention to the *differences* between Chaucer's grammar and ours.

Nouns. In the case of the noun, Old English dative *e* was preserved in some prepositional phrases: *to ground**e**, in lond**e***. Some words have an uninflected genitive singular form from OE *e*: *sonne, fader, lady* (*his lady grace*). There are more plurals in *en* or *n* than in Modern English:

ashen, bosen, doghtren, foon. Although plurals are usually syllabic *es,* in polysyllabic French words they are sometimes contracted to *s, barouns, conclusions;* when the word ends in *t* this is sometimes represented by *z , advocatz, servantz.*

Nouns appear frequently in apposition to their governing words, *a barrel ale, a manner Latyn corrupt.* The partitive is expressed by *of, Of smale houndes hadde she, Of remedies of love she knew.* Nouns with the possessive ending *es* can be used as modifiers, *lyves creature* (living creature), *shames deth* (shameful death), *I shal nedes have* (I must needs have), *his / hir thankes* (thankfully, willingly). Double possessives continue to be divided as in Old English, *the Seintes Legende of Cupide* (the legend of the saints of Cupid), *the Kyng Priamus sone of Troye* (the son of King Priam of Troy).

Citations for and more examples of these and the following forms can be found by looking up the key words in the Tatlock-Kennedy *Chaucer Concordance.*

Pronouns. The first person pronoun is usually *I;* southern *ich* is used for emphasis and with contractions, *theech* (*thee ich,* may I prosper); northern *ik* is used in the Reeve's Tale. The second person singular is regularly *thou, thyn, thee.* Plural forms *ye, your, you* were already beginning to be used for the singular, generally reflecting formality or respect (e.g., in the Clerk's Tale, *CT* IV.306-50, Walter addresses Janicula with the singular; Janicula addresses Walter with the plural; and Walter addresses Griselda with the plural. Gentles usually address each other with the plural, like the lovers in Franklin's Tale and *Troylus,* but common folk use the singular, as in the Miller's and Reeve's Tales; Pandarus generally uses singular *thou* forms but addresses Criseyde with the plural *ye* forms as they approach Troylus's bed chamber, *TC* II. 1716ff. Such distinctions provide nuances not available in Modern English.) Interrogative *thou* is often elided, *artow, thynkestow.*

The neuter singular was usually *it,* but the possessive continued to be Old English *his,* which should not be mistaken for personifica-tion (as in line 1 of *CT*). The feminine singular forms are *she* and *hir(e) / her(e),* and the third person plural forms, *they, hir(e) / her(e), hem.* There is confusion between feminine singular *her(e)* (her), plural *her(e)* (their), adverb *her* (here), and verb *her / heren* (to hear). In particular, plural *her* (their) should not be mistaken for singular *her* (her). With or without a final *e,* pronouns are always monosyllabic.

Plural of the domonstrative pronoun *that* is *tho. This,* often with a final *e, thise,* is either singular or plural. *Thilke* (*that ilke,* the same) is likewise either singular or plural. Both *that* and *the* are often elided, *th'estate, the tother.*

The relative pronoun may be omitted as a subject, *With hym ther was dwellynge a poure scoler, / **Had** lerned art.* Relative *that* is used as a colloca-tion with pronouns and adverbs, *whom that* (but never *who that*), *if that, whan that;* it should not be mistaken for a demonstrative (as in line 1 of *CT*). Indefinite *man* is frequently used instead of the passive, *she wept if men smoot it.* The "ethical dative" or "dative of advantage" cannot be trans-lated into Modern English, *To seken **hym** a chaun-trie, And to the hors he goth **hym** faire.* The reflexive pronoun is usually the same as the personal, *To be my wyf and reule **hire** after me;* the *self* forms are usually intensive, *Ther walketh now the lymytour **hymself.***

Adjectives. Adjectives that do not already end in *e* frequently take *e* when modifying plural nouns and in "weak" positions, i.e., following articles, demonstratives, or prepositions, or with vocatives: *a fair prelat / yven faire wyves, a young Squier / the yonge sonne, an hard thyng / with harde grace, ye be lief / soothly, leve brother.*

Comparison of adjectives is generally the same as in Modern English except that the Old English mutated vowels of the comparative and superlative are sometimes preserved, *old / elder / eldest, long / lenger / lengest, strong / strenger / strengest.* The French-influenced *more-most* com-parison was usually used with pollysyllabic French words, *Moore delicaat, moore pompous / moost honourable.*

Adverbs. Adverbs are formed by adding *ly* or

liche, but also by by adding *e* unless the adjective already ends in *e, a clene sheepe / caste him clene out of his lady grace, a lyght gypoun / knokkeden ful lighte.* The *s* forms of the adverb occur more frequently than in Modern English, *whiles, eftsones, unnethes,* as do the *en* forms, *abouten, aboven, biforn.* Very is never used as an intensive adverb, but always as an adjective, *He was a varray, parfit, gentil knyght.* The intensive is expressed by special idioms like *for the maistrie, for the nones.* Ther and *ther-as* may be used as relatives, *for over al **ther** he com. As* is sometimes omitted from comparisons, *His nekke* [as] *whit was as;* and omitted when correlative with *so, Ne was so worldly* [as] *for to have office.*

Prepositions. Prepositions may follow the words they govern, *seyde his maister to, rood hym agayns,* but seldom come at the end of the clause, *That men of yelpe, to shorte with oure weye.* An exception is the preposition *in* which can occur at the end spelled *inne: Hire to delivere of wo that she was inne; Doun into helle, where he yet is inne.*

Verbs. The inflections of verbs are second person (with *thou) est (st),* and third person *eth (th)* usually spelled with thorn; *eth* is variously contracted, *rit (rideth), worth (wortheth), halt (holdeth).* Very occasionally (BD 73, 257, HF 426, as confirmed by the rhymes) we find northern third person *es,* which also marks the dialect of the students in the Reeve's Tale.

The mark of the infinitive and the plural indicative and subjunctive is frequently, but not always, *en: they maken, they slepen, He leet the feeste of his nativitee / Doon cryen.* A favorite contraction of *haven* is *han.*

The principle parts of the verbs were much as they are in Modern English, but in Chaucer's English there were more strong verbs (verbs that show tense by change of vowel), *delve / dolf / dolven, crepe / crop / cropen, shouve / shoof / shoven.* The past participles of strong verbs normally end in *en,* but the *n* is often dropped, *founden/ founde.* The preterite of *hoten, highte* has the passive sense "to be named / called." Past participles of both strong and weak verbs may take the prefix *y /i: ydon / I-yeven.*

The impersonal *it* of Modern English is often

lacking, [it] *Bifil that in that seson,* and especially in idioms like *me thynketh* (it seems to me), *me liketh* (it pleases me), *hire lyste nat* (it did not please her).

One of the chief reasons for the different flavor of Chaucer's language is the scarcity of progressive forms, whose sense is expressed by simple verbs, *Ye goon* [are going] *to Canterbury, fowles maken* [were making] *melodye.* The auxiliary verb for the perfect tenses is usually a form of *be* rather than of *have: At nyght were* [had] *come into that hostelrye, That from the tyme of kyng William were* [had] *yfalle.* Auxiliaries that have fallen out of use are *gan* (began), *what that the day gan sprynge, this noble duc gan ryde,* and *doon* (cause to be done), *he dide doon sleen hem* (he had them killed), *If that ye done us bothe dyen* (if you cause us both to die).

Infinitives frequently lack *to. Come soupen* and *if yow liketh knowen* are marked by *en,* but *hym liste ride* and *Bidde hym descende* are unmarked, like the infinitives in Modern English subjunctives (I shall go, I would go). The subjunctive is used more frequently than in Modern English: for condition, *if she telle it;* for wishes, *God yelde yow* (may God reward you); for hypotheses, *I trowe he were a geldyng;* for concessions, *Al were he short.*

Negation. The usual sign of negation is *ne* before the verb, *ne wolde,* frequently elided with the verb, *nolde, nas, nath.* This may be reinforced by a following *nat / nought, it ne seme naught,* which can be reduced by omitting *ne, it availeth noght.* But the more negatives loaded into a clause, the more negative it is, *He nevere yet no vileyne ne sayde / In al his lyf unto no maner wight.*

Syntax. The conversational tone of Chaucer's writing is the result of less formal parallelism and subordination that we find in Modern written English. Among the syntax of oral language, we find Chaucer using **ellipsis**, *And* [we] *made forward erly for to ryse, And by his covenant* [he] *yaf rekenynge,* **parataxis**, *An horn he bar, the bawdryk was of grene; Bad nat every wight he sholde go selle,* **anacoluthon** (shift in grammar), *The reule of seint Maure or seint Beneit, / Bycause that it was old and somdel streit, / This ilke monk leet olde thynges pace.*

THE TEXT OF THIS EDITION

The text of Chaucer in the manuscripts and early editions is good, and so much work has been done on it in the last hundred years that the tools for studying it are excellent. Full collations of the *Canterbury Tales* are to be found in J. M. Manly and Edith Rickert, *The Text of the Canterbury Tales* (8 vols., 1940), of *Troylus and Criseyde* in R. K. Root, *Chaucer's Troilus and Criseyde* (1926), and of nearly all the minor poems in J. Koch, *Chaucers kleinere Dichtungen* (1928). There are discussions of the text in W. W. Skeat, *The Works of Geoffrey Chaucer* (7 vols., 1894–1897; *Oxford Chaucer*), in A. W. Pollard et al., *The Works of Chaucer* (1898; *Globe Chaucer*), and in F. N. Robinson, *The Works of Geoffrey Chaucer* (2nd. ed., 1957). In addition, there are many monographs and articles.

The method of producing the text for this edition has been, on the basis of previous textual discussions, to choose the best manuscript (in the case of the *Romaunt of the Rose* the early edition) and adhere closely to the text and orthography. These have been conservatively emended on the basis of readings in other manuscripts. Although genetic relationships have been observed, the changes have been dictated by logic and aesthetics more than by manuscript families. (A recent discussion of the difficulties with the genetic method of editing is in G. Kane, *Piers Plowman: The A Version*, 1960, Chap. III.) In addition to indicating all the substantive changes in the copy text, the textual notes in italics at the foot of each page give a sampling of the more interesting variants from important manuscripts. These are intended to convey a sense of the texture of the poetry, not to provide the basis for textual criticism.

The following editorial changes have been made silently throughout the edition: (1) Abbreviations have been expanded and the thorn written *th*. (2) Capitalization, punctuation, and some paragraphing have been introduced (although an effort has been made to follow the paragraphing of the copy text). (3) Word division has been regularized. (4) Treatment of the final *e* is conservative. In the manuscripts it is often indicated by a loop flourish, and scribes seem to have been carried away by the flourish. Modern editors have regularized this usage according to current ideas about Chaucer's grammar and meter. The present editor has tried to indulge in as little of this as possible, but some is inevitable. (5) The characters *u* and *v* are given their modern distribution. A special problem is *poure* which developed into *poor*. Both OF and ME had the vowel from Latin *pauper*. In French, the medial *p* becomes *v*. In ME the *u/v* between vowels was a consonant; but Modern *poor* did not develop the *v* sound. As a rhyme-word, three times Chaucer clearly does not pronounce the *v*; within the line *v* seems sometimes called for by the meter. Readers may make their own decision about the pusillanimous transcription *poure*. (6) The character *ff* is changed to *F*. (7) The characters *i* and *j* are given their modern distribution. (8) Obvious miswritings are corrected silently in light of the manuscript tradition and medieval script (as *CT* 1.1337 *sonne* for *somer*). (9) Filler words needed or not needed for scansion are sometimes silently included or omitted in the light of the manuscript tradition—but more often omitted, sometimes causing defective but still rhythmic lines, such as those for which the poet apologized (*HF* 1098).

There is a convention dating from the eighteenth century that Shakespeare should be presented in modern spelling and Chaucer in old spelling. No scholar or publisher today believes that the public would accept an old-spelling Shakespeare or a new-spelling Chaucer. One practical problem with a new-spelling Chaucer is that the higher proportion of obsolete words and forms of words would leave his language strange, even if it were respelled, and would, in any case, often require the invention of modern spellings. Nevertheless, one reason for not presenting the text of Chaucer in modern or in normalized spelling seems to be tradition. Some of the delight we find in Chaucer is the surprise in finding one of the wisest minds and sweetest voices that ever sang in English expressing itself in these strange forms.

Canterbury Tales

The text of the *Canterbury Tales* in this edition is based on the Ellesmere manuscript in the Huntington Library in San Marino, California. Some recent editors have used the Hengwrt manuscript in the National Library of Wales as their copy text because Manly and Rickert came to the conclusion that Hengwrt "represents the earliest attempt after Chaucer's death to arrange in a single MS the tales and links left unarranged by him" (Manly-Rickert, II.477). The Ellesmere was compiled in the same decade as Hengwrt (1400–1410), probably by the same scribe, but under the editorial supervision of "an intelligent person, who was certainly not Chaucer" (Manly-Rickert, I.150). The result is a text more regular in dialect and spelling than Hengwrt and more complete, with the tales in the order which many scholars today regard as nearest to Chaucer's intention. For these reasons, the Ellesmere has been the text on which most editions have been based.

Although Ellesmere and Hengwrt represent the earliest and two of the best texts of the *Canterbury Tales*, the Manly-Rickert collation indicates that they had no common ancestor except the Chaucerian archetype (Manly-Rickert, II.24). Therefore, where these two agree, a reading may usually be taken as authoritative. Where they differ, the evidence of other manuscripts, context, etc., will sometimes help determine the preferable reading. In such instances, the Ellesmere reading (labeled E) is given in the italicized textual notes at the foot of each page. An attempt has been made to list all of the substantive variants from Hengwrt (labeled Hg), and the more interesting variants from other manuscripts (designated simply "other MSS" unless more specific identification appears useful). For example, at *CT* I.148, *oon*: E&c *any* means that the reading *oon* in line 148 of the Prologue is from Hg, and that E and related texts read *any*. At *CT* I.1091, *endure*: Hg&c *endure it* means that what appears in the text is the E reading, but the Hg variant seems interesting. At *CT* I.468, *Gat-tothed*: some MSS *Gap-tothed* means that both E and Hg read *Gat-tothed*, so it is probably authentic, but the scribal change in other MSS is worth observing. At *CT* I.217, E&c *eek* om. means that *eek* is omitted from E and related MSS and has been supplied from Hg. Lack of &c means that a reading is unique to E or Hg; however, these are seldom recorded because an unsupported reading has no great authority, even in these good MSS.

Troylus and Criseyde

The text of *Troylus and Criseyde* is based upon MS. Morgan 817 in the Pierpont Morgan Library in New York. Before it was acquired by the Morgan Library in 1942, and in the transcripts and studies of the Chaucer Society, this was known as the Campsall manuscript. Since it bears on its first page the arms of Henry V when he was Prince of Wales, it must have been written between 1399 and 1413. Most other editions have been based on Corpus Christi College, Cambridge, MS. 61, famous for its frontispiece of Chaucer reciting his poem to members of the court. But the early date of the Morgan, its completeness (e.g., IV.491–532 are lacking from Corpus), and its accessibility have appeared to justify its use as a copy text. The disadvantages have been the tendency of the scribe to omit a good many obvious words, to formalize and modernize the spelling (e.g., conflations like *tencrese* and *atte* are often spelled out *to encrese* and *at the*; *ich*, *swich* and *-lich* often become *I*, *such*, and *-ly*), and to round *a* with *m* and *n* more often than is usual in the London English of the Ellesmere (e.g., *ony*, *thonk*, *no more*). An initial problem was the spelling of the protagonist's name; the *y* has been preserved partly because it reinforces the association between Troylus and Troy.

Arriving at the text of the *Troylus* involves different problems from the *Canterbury Tales* because the manuscripts indicate different stages of authorial revision. R. K. Root in *The Textual Tradition of Chaucer's Troilus* (1916) and in his edition, *Troilus and Criseyde* (1926), concluded that three versions can be discerned: an early version, which he called alpha and we designate A; a revised version, beta, B; and a partially revised version, gamma, G. No manuscript presents either the A or B text throughout, so these readings have to be sifted out by highly sophisticated textual criticism. The G text Professor Root believed was based on an exemplar "derived from Chaucer's own copy at a time when the poet's revision of his work was not yet complete, . . . in the main a very pure copy of the poem, but not that . . . which had undergone Chaucer's personal 'rubbing and scraping'" (*Troilus* ed., lxxv). The earliest and best manuscripts, including both Morgan and Corpus, are the G version, and all editions except Professor Root's own (which sought to recover the B) have presented the G text.

One disappointment is that textual criticism has not been able to discern a controlling purpose or consistent improvement in the variations in the manuscripts. In this edition, no effort has been made to record all A and B variations (which are fully set forth in Root's studies). When they are of interest, A readings are recorded (designated simply A because the corpus of manuscripts upon which they rest changes from section to section: see Root, *Troilus* ed., lxxvi). Occasionally B readings are recorded, but usually non-A variations are simply labelled "other MSS" because so often supposedly B readings are shared by supposedly G manuscripts. An effort has been made to record all substantive variants between the Morgan (M) and Corpus (C), because from these two it is possible to come close to reconstructing an authoritative G text. M&c in the textual notes means that the reading in the text is from Corpus; C&c means that the reading in the text is from Morgan; MC&c means that the G reading has been rejected in favor of an A or B; MA or CA means that Morgan or Corpus shares a reading with A; "other MSS" means non-G and non-A (generally what Root would designate B); &c means that other MSS share a reading, and lack of &c that the reading is unique.

Book of the Duchess

The text of the *Book of the Duchess* is based on MS. Fairfax 16 in the Bodleian Library, copied before 1450 (F in the notes). There are two other manuscripts, Bodley Tanner 346 (Ta) and Bodley 638 (B); and a printed text, Thynne 1532 (T), from a different textual tradition. The text of this poem has undergone a great deal of pruning of the final *e*'s and regularizing of the spelling at the hands of the editors to make it conform to the Ellesmere manuscript. This edition follows F more closely, even though the spelling is not always consistent and produces many hypermetric (though not necessarily unrhythmic) lines. All substantive variants from T have been recorded in the notes. Full textual collations are to be found in Koch, *Chaucers kleinere Dichtungen*.

Parliament of Fowls

The familiar text of the *Parliament of Fowls* shows a good deal of reconstruction. The fifteen manuscripts (including Caxton's edition) fall into two groups. Unfortunately, Fairfax 16 (type B) is in this instance inferior, and the text must be based on Cambridge Gg 4.27 (type A).

However, Cambridge Gg (G in the notes) differs considerably from both Ellesmere and Fairfax in orthography. In keeping with its editorial principle, this edition follows G closely. An effort has been made to record all substantive variations between G and F. Full textual collations are in Koch.

House of Fame

The text of the *House of Fame* is based on MS. Fairfax 16 in the Bodleian (F in the notes). This along with Bodley 638 (B) preserves what has been designated the A text of the poem. Pepys 2006 in Magdalene College, Cambridge, and the Caxton (Cx) and Thynne (Th) editions preserve the B text. This edition follows F and records all substantive variants from Pepys (P). P breaks off at line 1483, and from there on B-text readings are based on Cx-Th. In addition, Cx-Th is used for several omitted and defective lines, as indicated in the notes.

Legend of Good Women

The text of the *Legend of Good Women* is based on MS. Fairfax 16 (F), with substantive variants from the revised version of the poem in MS. Cambridge Gg 4.27 (G). Except for G, which throughout appears to derive independently from Chaucer's original, all eleven manuscripts present the unrevised text. These fall into two groups. F is in the so-called B group (three MSS), and so interesting readings from the A group (eight MSS) have been recorded from MS. Trinity Coll. Camb. R.3.19 (T). Parallel printings of the F and G versions of the Prologue to the *Legend* are found in the Chaucer Society transcriptions, in Skeat's *Oxford Chaucer* (III), and in Robinson's edition. Full textual collations are in Koch.

Short Poems

Discussions of the authenticity of the short poems are in Skeat's *Oxford Chaucer* (I); E. P. Hammond, *Chaucer, A Bibliographical Manual*

(1908); A. Brusendorff, *The Chaucer Tradition* (1925); Robinson's edition; and the articles of G. B. Pace beginning in 1948. Collations of all except 7, 9, and 21 are found in J. Koch, *Chaucers kleinere Dichtungen* (1928). Nearly all the texts have been printed by the Chaucer Society. In this edition, the language and spelling of the announced copy text is followed with a minimum of normalization, and substantive changes and variants are recorded in the notes.

1. *Prier a Nostre Dame:* thirteen MSS and Speght; text from Bodleian Fairfax 16 (F), with variants from Cambridge Ff 5.30 (C).

2. *Anelida and Arcite:* twelve MSS and Caxton; text from Fairfax 16 (F), with corrections and variants from Caxton (C) up to the Complaint, and Pepys 2006 (P) from the Complaint to the end.

3. *Complaint of Mars:* seven MSS, Notary, and Thynne; text from Fairfax 16 (F), with variants from the complete version in Pepys 2006 (P).

4. *Complaint of Venus:* seven MSS, Notary, and Thynne. In all but two MSS, this poem is part of no. 3. Text from Fairfax 16 (F), with variants from Bodleian Ashmole 59 (A), or Trinity Coll. Camb. R.3.2 (T) where A is lacking.

5. *A Complaint unto Pity:* nine MSS and Thynne; text from Fairfax 16 (F), with substantive variants from B. M. Harley 78 (H).

6. *A Balade of Pity:* two MSS and Stowe; text from B. M. Add. 34360 (A), with variants from Harley 78 (H).

7. *Womanly Noblesse:* text found only in B. M. Add. 34360.

8. *To Rosemounde:* text found only in Bodleian Rawl. Poet. 163.

9. *Proverbe of Chaucer:* three MSS and Stowe; text from Fairfax 16 (F), with variants from B. M. Add. 16165 (A).

10. *Fortune:* ten MSS, Caxton, and Thynne; text from Fairfax 16 (F), with corrections and variants from Cambridge Ii 3.21 (I), which is a careful text of Chaucer's *Boece*, and Shirley's Bodleian Ashmole 59 (A).

11. *Balade de Bon Conseil:* twenty-two MSS,

Caxton, and Thynne (the largest number of authorities of any of the short peoms); text from Ellesmere (E), with variants from the first of the two versions in Fairfax 16 (F), and from B. M. Add 10340 (A), which is the only one to include the envoy.

12. *Moral Balade of Gentilesse:* nine MSS, Caxton, and Thynne; text from B. M. Cleopatra D. vii (C), with variants from Ashmole 59 (A).

13. *The Former Age:* two MSS; text from Cambridge Ii 3.21 (I) (see no. 10), with variants from the other version in Cambridge Hh 4.12 (H).

14. *Lack of Steadfastnesse:* fourteen MSS and Thynne; text from B. M. Cleopatra D. vii (C), with variants from B. M. Harley 7333 (H).

15. *To Adam Scryven:* text found only in Trinity Coll. Camb. R.3.20 and Stowe (S).

16. *Lenvoy de Chaucer a Bukton:* text found only in Fairfax 16 (F), Notary (N), and Thynne (T).

17. *Lenvoy de Chaucer a Scogan:* three MSS, Caxton, and Thynne; text from Fairfax 16 (F), with variants from Pepys 2006 (P) and Cambridge Gg 4.27 (G).

18. *Complaint of Chaucer to His Purse:* eleven MSS, Caxton, and Thynne; text from Cambridge Ff.1.6 (Ff), with corrections from Fairfax 16 (F) and variants from B. M. Add. 22139 (A).

19. *Merciless Beauté:* text found only in Pepys 2006, not attributed to Chaucer.

20. *Against Women Unconstant:* three MSS and Stowe; text from Fairfax 16 (F), corrected from B. M. Harley 7578 and Cleopatra D. vii, none of which attribute it to Chaucer.

21. *A Balade of Complaint:* text found only in B. M. Add. 16165, not attributed to Chaucer.

22. *An Amorous Complaint:* three MSS; text from Fairfax 16 (F), with corrections from B. M. Harley 7333. Not attributed to Chaucer in the MSS.

Romaunt of the Rose

There is only one manuscript of the Middle English *Romaunt of the Rose*, Glasgow, Hunterian Museum V.3.7, which dates from the first quarter of the fifteenth century. Its text is not as complete or correct as that printed by Thynne in 1532. Hence Thynne's edition (T) is the copy text for this edition, and the variants from Glasgow (G) are recorded in the notes. When the French is quoted, it is from the text printed by R. Sutherland, *The Romaunt of the Rose and Le Roman de la Rose: A Parallel-Text Edition* (1968). The composite French text which Sutherland has put together from the various manuscripts is closer to the English than those of M. Kaluza (1891), E. Langlois (1914–1924), or F. Lecoy (1966–1970).

Boece

The nine manuscripts of *Boece* are divided into two groups. This edition is based on MS. Cambridge Ii.3.21 (I) of the first group, which Skeat considered closest to Chaucer's original. In that manuscript, Chaucer's translation accompanies a text of the Latin original which includes readings and glosses that also appear in the translation (Skeat, *Oxford Chaucer*, II.xxxvii–xli). Although subsequent research has indicated that the glosses are more widespread than Skeat thought, and therefore less impressive as evidence of a direct connection between this Latin text and Chaucer's translation, their appearance here does lend some weight to the argument that the Latin in I must be rather close to the version that Chaucer worked from. This manuscript also contains the best text of *The Former Age* (short poem 13), appended to the translation of *Boece* II m.5. The Latin phrases at the beginning of each section in this edition are taken from the Latin in I. Four other manuscripts fall into this first group.

Three other manuscripts and Caxton fall into a second group. H. Liddell in the *Globe Chaucer* and Robinson in his edition based their texts on Cambridge Ii.1.38 (C) because it has correct reading where I exhibits errors. However, none of the manuscripts is free from errors. In this edition I has been corrected by C, Cx (the

Caxton edition), and B. M. Add. 10340 (A). The copy text is based on a microfilm of the manuscript, the Chaucer Society transcript, and Skeat's edition; the C readings, on the Globe and Robinson; A and Cx readings on the collations of Skeat, Liddell, and L. Keller, who published collations in *Englische Studien* (1890).

Treatise on the Astrolabe

The twenty-five complete and fragmentary manuscripts of the *Treatise on the Astrolabe* are listed in Robinson's edition (p. 921), following the classifications in Skeat's *Oxford Chaucer* (III.lxiii), and Liddell, *Globe Chaucer* (liv). This edition follows Skeat in adopting Cambridge Dd 3.53 (D) as the copy text because it is one of the oldest manuscripts and because it is one of those containing the most complete set of diagrams that Chaucer evidently intended to illustrate his exposition. *Globe* and Robinson work from Bodleian 619 (B), which, while not illustrated, is somewhat more correct in its readings. (Liddell suggested that it was copied by an astronomer at Merton.) In this edition, D has been corrected by B, and the substantive variations between these two and interesting variants from other manuscripts have been recorded in the notes. Conclusion 39, faulty in

both D and B, has been corrected from Bodleian Rawl. D. 913, as printed by Skeat, III.237.

D has sixty-two figures, an illustration for each proposition. They have all been reproduced by R. T. Gunther, *Chaucer and Mesahalla on the Astrolabe* (1929). From Gunther I have taken only the first twenty-two, which illustrate Part I of the *Treatise*, as these are sufficient to illustrate the way in which Chaucer evidently intended his exposition to blend with the diagrams. (One of the illustrations for Part II is shown in Plate 4.)

The six additional propositions on the *umbra versa* and *umbra recta* (41–43), the mean mote (44–45), and the times of the tides (46), printed by Skeat from St. Johns Coll. Camb. E. 2 (42–43), Digby 72 (44–45), Bodley 619 (46), are not included because they do not occur in D or the other good MSS, and they are not in Chaucer's style; 44 and 45 are dated 1397.

Equatorie of the Planets

The text of the *Equatorie* is based, with permission, on the edition of MS. Peterhouse 75.1 by D. J. Price and R. M. Wilson, *The Equatorie of the Planetis* (Cambridge Univ. Press, 1955). Capitalization and punctuation have been added. The three diagrams are included.

A Note on the Illustrations

The frontispiece is a reproduction of the portrait of Chaucer in Hoccleve's *Regement of Princes*, British Library, MS. Harl. 4866, fol. 88. Neither the text nor the portrait is in Hoccleve's hand, but as the manuscript dates from the first quarter of the fifteenth century, the portrait is by someone who quite possibly had seen the poet. M. H. Spielmann (*Portraits of Geoffrey Chaucer*, Chaucer Society, 1900) points out that nearly all of the other portraits, including the famous equestrian miniature in the Ellesmere manuscript, are derived from this original. Furnivall (*Trial-Forwards*, p. 93) describes the Hoccleve portrait as follows: "The face is wise

and tender, full of sweet and kindly sadness at first sight, but with much bonhommie in it on a further look, with the deepset, farlooking grey eyes. Not the face of a very old man, a totterer, but of one with work in him yet, looking kindly, though seriously, out on the world before him. Unluckily, the parted grey moustache, and the vermillion above and below the lips, render it difficult to catch the expression of the mouth; but the lips seem parted as if to speak. . . . One feels one would like to go to such a man when one was in trouble, and hear his wise and gentle speech."

Plate 1 (p. 5) and the pictures of the pilgrims

at the beginning of each of the *Canterbury Tales* are from the Ellesmere manuscript in the Huntington Library. This is the most elaborately decorated of all the Chaucer manuscripts, executed on commission for a wealthy patron (just possibly Thomas Chaucer; see Manly-Rickert, I.159). The style of its demi-vinet borders has been described by Margaret Rickert (Manly-Rickert, I.565–566) and may be studied in the *Ellesmere Chaucer Reproduced in Facsimile* (Manchester University Press, 1911). The pictures of the pilgrims (described by Margaret Rickert, I.587–593) are from woodcuts of the Ellesmere portraits made by W. H. Hooper for the Chaucer Society transcript of the *Ellesmere Manuscript of the Canterbury Tales*, ed. F. J. Furnivall (Series 1, 1868–1879).

Plate 2 (p. 103) is from the Morgan manuscript of *Troylus*, in the same tradition as the Ellesmere, but made for Henry V while he was still Prince of Wales.

Plate 3 (p. 185) is from MS. Fairfax 16 in the Bodleian Library, a codex of poems evidently made by binding together five booklets bought from a London bookshop (see A. Brusendorff, *The Chaucer Tradition*, p. 186). It is in the hand of a professional scribe, rubricated, but without the elaborate illumination of the specially commissioned manuscripts. As a matter of fact, most of the manuscripts of the *Canterbury Tales* and *Troylus* are of this commercial variety, rather than lavishly commissioned.

Plate 4 (p. 213) is from MS. Cambridge Dd.3.53, again a codex made by binding together works of various kinds. The *Astrolabe*, which comes at the end, is in a neat, professional hand. However, the scribe did not know what he was writing about and made many mistakes. These have been corrected by the hand of someone who clearly did know the subject matter. Skeat (*Oxford Chaucer*, III.lvii) points out that this is exactly the process described by Chaucer in *To Adam Scryven* (short poem 15).

Plate 5 (p. 335), from MS. Peterhouse 75 of the *Equatorie*, is again in a professional hand, but clearly a draft rather than a finished product. If the draft is Chaucer's, we have here a sample of his handwriting. Presumably the figure is also by the author. If so, he may also have provided the originals for the figures in MS. Dd. (Plate 4).

Bibliography

CITATIONS

This second revision of the bibliography suffers from the "explosion of knowledge" about which we hear so much. Between 1974 when the original ended, and 1979 when the first revision was made, 730 books and articles appeared; so 730 of the citations in the original bibliography were removed and replaced with the new citations. However, between 1980 and 1987, there have been 1860 books and articles published on Chaucer. Since our format allows only 1600 citations, it would have been impossible to accommodate all of these entries, besides which it is important to retain citations to important books and articles published before 1980. The compromise has been to choose 1000 citations from among the materials published since 1980, and retain 600 from among the materials published before 1980.

The need for selection is rendered less Draconian because all of the citations appear in the *MLA Annual Bibliography* and the annotated annual bibliography in *Studies in the Age of Chaucer*, and fuller lists in two excellent, recent annotated bibliographies, *Chaucer: A Bibliographical Introduction*, compiled by John Leyerle and Anne Quick (University of Toronto Press, 1986) and *The Essential Chaucer: An Annotated Bibliography of Major Modern Studies*, compiled by Mark Allen and John H. Fisher (G. K. Hall, 1987). The entries in this version of our bibliography have been chosen for their hermeneutic value; omitted are dissertations, collections of essays (important essays from the collections are listed individually), partial editions, works in foreign languages, and most articles of less than five pages in length.

FACSIMILES AND DIPLOMATIC TRANSCRIPTIONS

1. *Bodleian Library, MS Bodley 638: A Facsimile.* Introduction by Pamela Robinson. The Variorum Chaucer Facsimile Series. Norman, OK: Pilgrim Books, 1981.
2. *Bodleian Library, MS Fairfax 16: A Facsimile.* Introduction by John Norton-Smith. London: Scolar, 1979.
3. *Cambridge Library, MS Gg.4.27: A Facsimile.* Introduction by Malcolm Parkes and Richard Beadle. 3 vols. The Variorum Chaucer Facsimile Series. Norman, OK: Pilgrim Books, 1980.
4. *Corpus Christi College, Cambridge, MS 61: A Facsimile.* Introduction by M. B. Parkes and Elizabeth Salter. Cambridge: Brewer, 1978.
5. *The Ellesmere Chaucer.* Reproduced in facsimile. 2 vols. Manchester: Manchester U P, 1911.
6. *The Canterbury Tales: A Facsimile and Transcription of the Hengwrt Manuscript, with Variants from the Ellesmere Manuscript.* Introduction by Donald C. Baker, A. I. Doyle, and M.B. Parkes. *The Variorum Edition of the Works of Geoffrey Chaucer,* Vol. I. Eds. Paul G. Ruggiers and Donald C. Baker. Norman, OK: U of Oklahoma P, 1979.
7. *Magdalene College, Cambridge, MS Pepys 2006: A Facsimile.* Introduction by A.S.G. Edwards. The Variorum Chaucer Facsimile Series. Norman, OK: Pilgrim Books, 1986.
8. *St. John's College, Cambridge, MS L.1: A Facsimile.* Introduction by Richard Beadle and J.J. Griffiths. The Variorum Chaucer Facsimile Series. Norman, OK: Pilgrim Books, 1983.
9. *Bodleian Library, MS Tanner 346: A Facsimile.* Introduction by Pamela Robinson. The Variorum Chaucer Facsimile Series. Norman, OK: Pilgrim Books, 1980.
9a. *Pierpont Morgan Library, MS Morgan M.817.* Introduction by Jeanne Krochalis. The Variorum Chaucer Facsimile Series. Norman, OK: Pilgrim Books, 1986.
10. Chaucer Society Diplomatic Transcriptions, issued in fascicles, 1868-94. For a full listing of Chaucer Society Publications, see Hammond (no. 72 below), pp. 523ff.
11. *A six-text print of the Canterbury Tales.* Ellesmere,

Hengwrt, Cambridge Gg.4.27, Corpus, Petworth, Lansdowne 851. Other single-text prints.

12. *A parallel-text print of Troilus and Criseyde.* Campsell (Morgan M.817), Harleian 2280, Cambridge Gg.4.27. *Three more parallel texts of Troilus and Criseyde.* Corpus Christi 61, Harleian 1239, St. John's College L.1.

13. *A parallel-text edition of the minor poems.*
A Supplementary parallel-text print of the minor poems. Odd texts of the minor poems.
Boece. Add. 10,340, Cambridge Ii.3.21.
Romaunt of the Rose. Thynne, Glasgow MS.
See also 22, 28.

MANUSCRIPTS

14. Doyle, A.I., and M.B. Parkes. "The Production of Copies of the *Canterbury Tales* and the *Confessio Amantis* in the Early Fifteenth Century." In *Essays Presented to N.R. Ker.* Eds. M.B.Parkes and A.G. Watson. London: Scholar, 1979.

15. Ramsey, Vance. "The Hengwrt and Ellesmere Manuscripts of the *Canterbury Tales*: Different Scribes." *SB* 35 (1982), 133-54.

16. ———. "Paleography and Scribes of Shared Training." *SAC* 8 (1986), 107-44.

17. Samuels, M.L. "The Scribe of the Hengwrt and Ellesmere Manuscripts of the *Canterbury Tales*." *SAC* 5 (1983), 49-65.

18. Windeatt, Barry A. "The Scribes as Chaucer's Early Critics." *SAC* 1 (1979), 119-42.

EARLY EDITIONS

19. Caxton, William, ed. and pub. *Canterbury Tales,* c1478 [CX^1]. Text ranks along with the early MSS as an independent authority, see Manly (no. 46 below), I.80.

20. ———. *Troylus,* c1483. Careless edition from a defective MS, see Root (no. 42 below), lxi.

21. ———. *Canterbury Tales,* c1484 [CX^2]. Caxton added an introduction deprecating the text of his previous edition, showing his awareness of textual problems. However, his unsystematic corrections are of no textual value, see Manly I.81. Contains woodcuts of the Pilgrims.

22. ———.*Canterbury Tales, 1484: A Facsimile.* Ed. J.A.W. Bennett. Cambridge: Cornmarket Reprints, 1972.

23. ———. Caxton printed in separate, undated fascicles *PF* (which he called *Temple of Bras*), *HF, Scogan* (short poem 17), *Truth* (short poem 11), *Fortune* (short poem 10), *Mars* (short poem 3), *Anelida* (short poem 2), *Purse* (short poem 18), and *Boece.*

24. Pynson, Richard, print and pub. *Canterbury Tales,* c1492. Reprint of CX^2, including introduction and woodcuts.

25. Wynkyn de Worde, print and pub. *Canterbury Tales,* 1498. Woodcuts from CX^2, but different text, without authority. CT followed by Lydgate (?), *Assembly of Gods,* so here the augmentation begins.

26. Pynson, Richard. *Chaucer's Works,* 1526. In three parts: 1, *TC;* 2, *HF, PF, Truth,* and non-Chaucerian poems; 3, CT. No general title pages. Chaucer texts from Caxton's editions.

27. Thynne, William, ed. *Chaucer's Works,* 1532. Nearly all the canon, including first printings of *BD, LGW, Romaunt,* and other short poems, but also much spurious material—eighteen and a half pieces genuine, twenty-two and a half spurious.

28. ———.*Chaucer's Works, 1532: A Facsimile.* Ed. W.W. Skeat, Oxford: Oxford U P, 1905; ed. D.S. Brewer, London: Scolar, 1969.

29. ———. *Chaucer's Works,* 1542. Contents same as 1532 with addition of "Plowman's Tale" at the end of CT.

30. ———. *Chaucer's Works,* no date. Contents same as 1542 except that Plowman's Tale precedes ParsT.

31. Stowe, John, ed. *Chaucer's Works,* 1561. Two issues, first with Caxton's woodcuts, second without. Adds several poems, mostly from MS Trinity College, Cambridge R.3.19. Only *Adam Scryven* (short poem 15), *Gentilesse* (short poem 12), and *Proverbe* (short poem 9) are genuine.

32. Speght, Thomas, ed. *Chaucer's Works,* 1598. The first edition to add a life, explanatory notes, and a glossary. These called forth "Animaduersions vppon the Annotacions and Corrections of some imperfections of impressiones of Chaucers workes …" by Francis Thynne (son of William), the first piece of Chaucerian—indeed of English literary—scholarship. "Animadversions" reprinted EETS 9, 1865; Chauc. Soc. 2nd ser. 13, 1876.

33. ———. *Chaucer's Works,* 1602. Incorporates some of Thynne's corrections. The first edition to undertake thorough punctuation. Speght's editions added still more apocrypha.

34. ———. *Chaucer's Works,* 1687. Reprint of 1602.

35. Urry, John, ed. *Chaucer's Works,* 1721. Urry finished the text; life and glossary provided by others after his death. The first edition not in black letter (throughout the 17th century, black letter denoted "courtly" literature). Worst text of Chaucer ever produced: Urry "corrected" Chaucer's "unmetrical" lines by adding expletives for syllabic e, es, ed.

36. Morrell, Thomas, ed. *The Canterbury Tales,* 1737. Intended as a variorum edition, including variant readings and translations by Dryden, Pope, et al.

Only one volume appeared, containing GP and KT. Tyrwhitt acknowledged it as a model.

37. Tyrwhitt, Thomas, ed. *The Canterbury Tales of Chaucer. To which are added an Essay on his Language and Versification, and an Introductory Discourse, together with Notes and a Glossary.* 5 vols. 1775-78. The first serious attempt to restore the text by collating 25 MSS. Recognized that the rhythm of Chaucer's verse depended on pronunciation of final e, es, ed (in this he had been anticipated by Thomas Gray and William Mitford). In the final essay he struck out all but five of the spurious works attributed to Chaucer. The annotations and glossary provided the basis for Skeat's edition and modern scholarship.

38. Wright, Thomas, ed. *The Canterbury Tales.* 3 vols. 1847-51. First edition to return to a MS as copy text, except that it chose the faulty Harley 7334 as a base. Important for introducing the "best text" editorial method.

39. Aldine, *The Poetical Works of Geoffrey Chaucer.* 6 vols. 1845. Text from Tyrwhitt, but adds a "Life of Chaucer" by Harris Nicolas, the beginning of sound biographical documentation.

40. Ruggiers, Paul G., ed. *Editing Chaucer: The Great Tradition.* Norman, OK: Pilgrim Books, 1984.

MODERN EDITIONS

41. Skeat, W.W., ed. *The Works of Geoffrey Chaucer.* 7 vols. Oxford:Clarendon, 1894-97. The "Oxford Chaucer." Vol. 6 contains a full glossary; vol. 7 contains the most complete collection of Chaucer apocrypha. Skeat's explanatory notes are still of great value.

42. Root, Robert K.,ed. *The Book of Troilus and Criseyde by Geoffrey Chaucer.* Princeton: Princeton U P, 1926. Fullest collection of textual variants.

43. Koch, John, ed. *Geoffrey Chaucers Kleinere Dichtungen.* Heidelberg: Winter, 1928. Fullest collection of textual variants for the minor poems.

44. Manly, John M., ed. *The Canterbury Tales.* New York: Holt, 1928. Text bowdlerized. Excellent cultural and biographical introduction.

45. Robinson, F. N., ed. *The Works of Geoffrey Chaucer.* Boston: Houghton Mifflin, 1st ed. 1933, 2nd ed. 1957. Now superseded by no. 52 below.

46. Manly, John M., and Edith Rickert, eds. *The Text of the Canterbury Tales, Studied on the Basis of all Known Manuscripts.* 8 vols. Chicago: U of Chicago P, 1940. Full account of the MSS and exhaustive collations of variant readings.

47. Sutherland, Ronald, ed. *The Romaunt of the Rose: A Parallel-Text Edition.* Oxford: Blackwell, 1968. Parallel ME and OF texts.

48. Donaldson, E. T., ed. *Chaucer's Poetry: An Anthology for the Modern Reader.* 2nd ed. New York: Ronald, 1975. Splendid essays of critical interpretation.

49. Blake, N.F., ed. *The Canterbury Tales by Geoffrey Chaucer Edited from the Hengwrt Manuscript.* London: Arnold, 1980.

50. Fisher, John H., ed. *The Complete Poetry and Prose of Geoffrey Chaucer.* 2nd ed. New York: Holt, 1989.

51. Windeatt, B.A., ed. *Geoffrey Chaucer, Troilus & Criseyde.* London:Longman, 1984. Parallel ME and Italian texts.

52. Benson, Larry D., ed. *The Riverside Chaucer. Based on Robinson's Edition.* Boston: Houghton M., 1987.

53. Ruggiers, Paul G., ed. *The Variorum Edition of the Works of Geoffrey Chaucer.* Norman, OK: U of Oklahoma P, 1982—.

54. Ross, Thomas W., ed. *Canterbury Tales: The Miller's Tale.* Variorum vol. 2, pt. 3, 1983.

55. Baker, Donald, ed. *The Canterbury Tales: The Manciple's Tale.* Variorum vol. 2, pt. 10, 1984.

56. Pearsall, Derek, ed. *Canterbury Tales: The Nun's Priest's Tale.* Variorum vol. 2, pt. 9, 1984.

57. Corsa, Helen, ed. *Canterbury Tales: The Physician's Tale.* Variorum vol. 2, pt. 17, 1987.

58. Boyd, Beverly, ed. *The Canterbury Tales: The Prioress's Tale.* Variorum vol. 2, pt. 20, 1987.

59. Pace, George B., and Alfred David, eds. *The Minor Poems, Part One.* Variorum vol. 5, 1982. Includes *Truth, Gentilesse, Lak of Stedfastnesse, Former Age, Fortune, Purse, Adam Scriveyn, Bukton, Scogan, Rosemounde, Merciles Beaute, Against Women Unconstant, Proverbs.*

TRANSLATIONS

60. Beidler, Peter G. "Chaucer and the Trots: What to Do About Those Modern English Translations." *ChauR* 19 (1985), 290-301.

61. Coghill, Neville, trans. *The Canterbury Tales.* Harmondsworth: Penguin, 1951. (verse)

62. ———. *Troilus and Criseyde.* Harmondsworth: Penguin, 1981. (verse)

63. Donohue, James J., trans. *Chaucer's Lesser Poems Complete in Present-Day English.* Dubuque, IA: Loras C P, 1974. (verse)

64. ———. *Chaucer's Troilus and Cressida: Five Books in Present-Day English.* Dubuque, IA: Loras C P, 1975. (verse)

65. ———. *Chaucer's Canterbury Tales Complete in Present-Day English.* Dubuque, IA: Loras C P, 1979. (verse)

66. Dor, Juliette [Caluwé], French trans. *Les Contes de Cantorbéry* I (GP, KT, MilT) Ghent: Éditions Scientifiques, 1977; II (RvT, CkT, MLT, WBT, FrT, SumT) Louvain: Peeters, 1986.

67. Lumiansky, Robert M., trans. *The Canterbury Tales by Geoffrey Chaucer.* New York: Simon, 1948. (prose)

68. ———. *Geoffrey Chaucer's Troilus and Criseyde Rendered into Modern English Prose.* Columbia: U of South Carolina P, 1952.

69. Stanley-Wrench, Margaret, trans. *Troilus and Criseyde.* Arundel, Sussex: Centaur, 1965. (verse)

70. Stone, Brian, trans. *Chaucer's Love Visions: The Book of the Duchess; The House of Fame; The Parliament of Birds; The Legend of Good Women.* Harmondsworth: Penguin, 1983.

71. Wright, David, trans. *The Canterbury Tales.* New York: Random House, 1965. (prose)

BIBLIOGRAPHIES, DICTIONARIES

72. Hammond, Eleanor P. *Chaucer: A Bibliographical Manual* (1908). New York: Peter Smith, 1933.

73. Griffith, Dudley D. *Bibliography of Chaucer 1908-53.* Seattle: U of Washington P, 1955.

74. Crawford, William R. *Bibliography of Chaucer 1954-63.* Seattle: U of Washington P, 1967.

75. Baird [Lange], Lorrayne Y. *Bibliography of Chaucer 1964-73.* Boston: Hall, 1977.

76. Allen, Mark, and John H. Fisher. *The Essential Chaucer: An Annotated Bibliography of Major Modern Studies.* Boston: Hall, 1987. (1900-84)

77. Leyerle, John, and Anne Quick. *Chaucer: A Bibliographical Introduction.* Toronto: U of Toronto P, 1986. (1900-1979)

78. *Studies in the Age of Chaucer.* Annual Annotated Bibliography, 1979—.

79. Peck, Russell A. *Chaucer's Lyrics and Anelida and Arcite: An Annotated Bibliography 1900-1980.* Toronto: U of Toronto P, 1983.

80. Giaccherini, Enrico. "Chaucer and the Italian Trecento: A Bibliography." In *Chaucer and the Italian Trecento.* Ed. Piero Boitani. Cambridge: Cambridge U P, 1983.

81. Dillon, Bert. *A Chaucer Dictionary: Proper Names and Allusions, Excluding Place Names.* Boston: Hall, 1974.

82. Magoun, Francis P. *A Chaucer Gazeteer.* Chicago: U of Chicago P, 1971.

83. Scott, Arthur F. *Who's Who in Chaucer.* London: Elm Tree, 1974.

84. Morris, Lynn King. *Chaucer Source and Analogue Criticism: A Cross-Referenced Guide.* New York: Garland, 1985.

85. Davis, Norman, Douglas Gray, Patricia Ingham, and Anne Wallace-Hadrill. *A Chaucer Glossary.* Oxford: Clarendon, 1979.

86. Tatlock, J.S.P., and A.G. Kennedy. *Concordance to the Complete Works of Chaucer and to the Romaunt of the Rose* (1927). Gloucester, MA: Peter Smith, 1963.

BIOGRAPHY

87. Baugh, Albert C. "Chaucer the Man." In *Companion to Chaucer Studies.* Ed. Beryl Rowland. rev. ed. New York: Oxford U P, 1979.

88. Bland, D.S. "Chaucer and the Inns of Court: A Re-examination." *ES* 33 (1952), 145-55.

89. ———. "When Was Chaucer Born?" *TLS* 26 April 1957, p. 264; Amplifications: Margaret Galway, 10 May 1957, p. 289; C. Warner and C.E. Welch, 17 May 1957, p. 305; G.D.G. Hall, 28 June 1957, p. 397; Margaret Galway, 12 July 1957, p. 427.

90. Braddy, Haldeen. "Chaucer's Philippa, Daughter of Panneto." *MLN* 64 (1949), 342-43.

91. ———. "Chaucer, Alice Perrers, and Cecily Chaumpaigne." *Speculum* 52 (1977), 906-11.

92. Brewer, Derek. *Chaucer and His World.* New York: Dodd, Mead, 1977.

93. Burrow, J.A. "The Poet as Petitioner." *SAC* 3 (1981), 61-75.

94. Crow, Martin M., and Clair C. Olson, eds. *Chaucer Life Records. From materials compiled by John M. Manly and Edith Rickert, with the assistance of Lilian J. Redstone and others.* Oxford: Clarendon, 1966.

95. Galway, Margaret. "Geoffrey Chaucer, J.P. and M.P." *MLR* 36 (1941), 1-36.

96. Gardner, John Champlin. *The Life and Times of Chaucer.* New York: Knopf, 1976.

97. Howard, Donald R. *Chaucer: His Life, His World, His Works.* New York: Dutton, 1987.

98. Hulbert, James R. *Chaucer's Official Life.* Menasha, WI, 1912.

99. Kern, Alfred. *The Ancestry of Chaucer.* Baltimore, MD, 1906.

100. Krauss, Russell. "Chaucer Problems: Especially the Petherton Forestership and the Question of Thomas Chaucer." In *Three Chaucer Studies.* Ed. Carleton Brown, New York: Oxford U P, 1932.

101. Leland, Virginia E. "Chaucer as Commissioner of Dikes and Ditches, 1390." *Michigan Academician* 14 (1981), 71-79.

102. Rudd, Martin B. *Thomas Chaucer.* Research Publications of the U of Minnesota 9, Minneapolis, 1926.

See also 348, 366, 1079, 1448, 1449, 1451, 1463, 1464, 1488, 1523, 1529, 1537, 1546, 1580, 1581, 1582, 1586, 1592, 1603.

THE PERSONA

103. Bethurum [Loomis], Dorothy. "Chaucer's Point of View as Narrator in the Love Poems." *PMLA* 74 (1959), 511-20.

104. Donaldson, E. Talbot. "Chaucer the Pilgrim." *PMLA* 69 (1954), 928-36.

105. Kane, George. *The Autobiographical Fallacy in Chaucer and Langland Studies.* London: H.K. Lewis for U C London, 1965.

107. Knopp, Sherron. "Chaucer and Jean de Meun as Self-Conscious Narrators: The Prologue of the Legend of Good Women and the Roman de la Rose 10307-680." *Comitatus* 1973, pub. 1974, 25-39.

108. Renoir, Alain. "Tradition and Moral Realism: Chaucer's Conception of the Poet." *SN* 35 (1963), 199-210.

109. Wagenknecht, Edward C. *The Personality of Chaucer.* Norman, OK: U of Oklahoma P, 1968.

110. Watts, Ann C. "Chaucerian Selves—Especially Two Serious Ones." *ChauR* 4 (1970), 229-41.

111. Woolf, Rosemary. "Moral Chaucer and Kindly Gower." In *J.R.R. Tolkien: Essays in Memoriam.* Eds. Mary Salu and Robert T. Farrell. Ithaca, NY: Cornell U P, 1979.

See also 157, 545, 602, 1559.

CANON, APOCRYPHA, LOST WORKS

112. Bonner, Frances W. "The Genesis of the Chaucer Apocrypha." *SP* 48 (1951), 461-81.

113. Brusendorff, Aage. *The Chaucer Tradition.* London: Oxford U P, 1925.

114. Moore, Arthur K. "Chaucer's Lost Songs." *JEGP* 48 (1949), 198-208.

115. Skeat, W. W. *The Chaucerian Canon with a Discussion of the Works Associated with the Name of Geoffrey Chaucer.* Oxford: Oxford U P, 1900.

See also 41, 72.

LANGUAGE—GENERAL

116. Davis, Norman. "Chaucer and Fifteenth-Century English." In *Geoffrey Chaucer: Writers and Their Backgrounds.* Ed. D.S. Brewer, London: Bell, 1974.

117. Eliason, Norman E. *The Language of Chaucer's Poetry: An Appraisal of the Verse, Style, and Structure.* Anglistica 17. Copenhagen: Rosenkilde, 1972.

118. Elliott, R. W. V. *Chaucer's English.* London: Deutsch, 1974.

119. Görlach, Manfred. "Chaucer's English: What Remains to Be Done." *ArAA* 4 (1978), 61-79.

120. Hart, Paxton. "Chaucer's Regard for English." *Interpretations* 14 (1982), 1-10.

121. Holley, Linda Tarte. "The Function of Language in Three Canterbury Churchmen." *Parergon* 28 (1980), 36-44.

122. Kerkhof, Jelle. *Studies in the Language of Geoffrey Chaucer.* Leiden U P, 1966.

123. Rex, Richard. "In Search of Chaucer's Bawdy." *MSE* 8 (1982), 20-32.

124. Robbins, Rossell Hope. "Geoffroi Chaucier, poète français, Father of English Poetry." *ChauR* 13 (1978), 93-115.

125. Rogers, William E. "Individualization of Language in the Canterbury Frame Story." *AnM* 15 (1974), 74-108. (Appendix: "Romance and Latinate Loan Words in the Speech of Chaucer's Pilgrims in the Frame Story.")

126. Ross, Thomas W. *Chaucer's Bawdy.* New York: Dutton, 1972.

127. Taylor, Paul B. "Chaucer's Cosyn to the Dede." *Speculum* 57 (1982), 315-27.

See also 185, 483, 612, 711, 1018, 1047, 1054, 1062, 1152, 1508, 1511.

LANGUAGE—PHONOLOGY, SYNTAX

128. Burnley, J.D. *A Guide to Chaucer's Language.* Norman: U of Oklahoma P, 1984.

129. Fisiak, Jacek. *Morphemic Structure of Chaucer's English.* University: U of Alabama P, 1965.

130. Glowka, Arthur W. "Chaucer's Bird Sounds." *LangQ* 21 (1983), 15-17.

131. Kökeritz, Helge. *A Guide to Chaucer's Pronunciation* (1954). New York: Holt, 1962.

132. Roscow, Gregory. *Syntax and Style in Chaucer's Poetry.* Cambridge: Brewer, 1981.

133. Sandved, Arthur O. *Introduction to Chaucerian English.* Cambridge: Brewer, 1985.

See also 168, 682, 1244.

LANGUAGE—LEXICON, DIALECT, PROVERBS

134. Barney, Stephen A. "Suddenness and Process in Chaucer." *ChauR* 16 (1981), 18-37.

135. Baum, Paull F. "Chaucer's Puns." *PMLA* 71 (1956), 225-46. "Chaucer's Puns: A Supplementary List." *PMLA* 73 (1958), 167-70.

136. Benson, Larry D. "The 'Queynte' Punnings of Chaucer's Critics." *SAC,* Proceedings 1 (1985), 23-50.

137. Blake, N. F. "The Northernisms in The Reeve's Tale." *Lore and Language* 3, 1 (1979), 1-8.

138. Blodgett, E. D. "Chaucerian *Pryvetee* and the Opposition to Time." *Speculum* 51 (1976), 477-93.

139. Brosnahan, Leger. "'And don thyn hood' and Other Hoods in Chaucer." *ChauR* 21 (1986), 45-52.

140. Burnley, J. D. "Chaucer's *Termes.*" *YES* 7 (1977), 53-67.

141. ———. *Chaucer's Language and the Philosophers' Tradition.* Cambridge: Brewer, 1979.

142. Costigan, Edward. "'Privetee' in the *Canterbury Tales.*" *SEL* 60 (1983), 217-30.

143. DeWeever, Jacqueline. "Chaucerian Onomastics: The Formation of Personal Names in Chaucer's Works." *Names* 28 (1980), 1-31.

144. Higuchi, Masayuki. "Verbal Exploitation in the Reeve's Tale." *HSELL* 25 (1980), 1-12.

145. Knight, Stephen. *Rymyng Craftily: Meaning in Chaucer's Poetry.* New York: Humanities, 1974.

146. Mersand, Joseph. *Chaucer's Romance Vocabulary* (1937). Port Washington, NY: Kennikat P, 1968.

147. Nakao, Yoshiyuki. "Chaucer's use of proverbs—an aspect of Chaucer's convention and invention." *Phoenix* 15 (1979), 3-20.

148. Robertson, D. W., Jr. "Some Disputed Chaucerian Terminology." *Speculum* 52 (1977), 571-81.

149. Scheps, Walter. "Chaucer's Use of Nonce Words, Primarily in the *Canterbury Tales.*" *NM* 80 (1979), 69-77.

150. Smith, Sarah Stanbury. " 'Game in myn hood': The Traditions of a Comic Proverb." *SIcon* 9 (1983), 1-12.

151. Wentersdorf, Karl P. "The *Termes* of Chaucer's Sergeant of the Law." *SN* 53 (1981), 269-74.

See also 86, 198, 201, 313, 442, 650, 689, 1010, 1017, 1065, 1144, 1290, 1333, 1362.

LANGUAGE—RHETORIC, TRANSLATION

152. Bishop, Ian. "Chaucer and the Rhetoric of Consolation." *MAE* 52 (1983), 38-50.

153. Burnley, J. D. "Chaucer, Usk, and Geoffrey of Vinsauf." *Neophil* 69 (1985), 286-91.

154. Dor [Caluwé], Juliette. "Chaucer's Derivational Morphemes Revisited." In *Linguistic and Stylistic Studies in Medieval English.* Ed. André Crepin. Publications de l'Association des Médiévistes de l'Enseignement Superieur 10. Paris, 1984.

155. ———. "Chaucer's Contribution to the English Vocabulary: A Chronological Survey of French Loan-Words." *Nowele* 2 (1983), 73-91.

156. Jordan, Robert M. "Vision, Pilgrimage, and Rhetorical Composition." *SAC,* Proceedings 1 (1984), 195-200.

157. Payne, Robert O. "Chaucer's Realization of Himself as Rhetor." In *Medieval Eloquence.* Ed. James J. Murphy. Berkeley: U of California P, 1978.

158. ———. "Chaucer and the Art of Rhetoric." In *Companion to Chaucer Studies.* Ed. Beryl Rowland. rev. ed. New York: Oxford P, 1979.

159. Presson, Robert K. "The Aesthetics of Chaucer's Art of Contrast." *English Miscellany* 15 (1964), 9-23.

160. Shoaf, R. A. "Notes Toward Chaucer's Poetics of Translation." *SAC* 1 (1979), 55-66.

161. Weiss, Alexander. "Chaucer's Early Translations from the French: The Art of Creative Transformation." In *Literary and Historical Perspectives of the Middle Ages: Proceedings of the 1981 SEMA Meeting.* Eds. Patricia W. Cummins, Patrick W. Conner, and Charles W. Connell. Morgantown: W V U P, 1982.

See also 181, 199, 200, 205, 206, 251, 715, 821, 922, 929, 1155, 1159, 1167, 1246, 1258, 1351, 1378, 1556, 1598, 1601, 1602.

PROSODY

162. Adams, Percy. "Chaucer's Assonance." *JEGP* 71 (1972), 527-39.

163. Baum, Paull F. *Chaucer's Verse.* Durham, NC: Duke U P, 1961.

164. Biggins, Dennis. "Chaucer's Metrical Lines: Some Internal Evidence." *Parergon* 17 (1977), 17-24.

165. Brewer, Derek. "The Grain of the Text." In *Acts of Interpretation:...Essays in Honor of E. Talbot Donaldson.* Eds. Mary J. Carruthers and Elizabeth D. Kirk. Norman, OK: Pilgrim Books, 1982.

166. Brody, Saul Nathaniel. "Chaucer's Rhyme Royal Tales and the Secularization of the Saint." *ChauR* 10 (1985), 113-31.

167. Fichte, Joerg O. *Chaucer's "Art Poetical": A Study of Chaucerian Poetics.* Tübingen: Narr, 1980.

168. Fifield, Merle. *Theoretical Techniques for the Analysis of Variety in Chaucer's Stress.* Ball State Monograph 23. Muncie, IN: Ball State U, 1973.

169. Gaylord, Alan T. "Scanning the Prosodists: An Essay in Metacriticism." *ChauR* 11 (1976), 22-82.

170. Knight, Stephen. *The Poetry of the Canterbury Tales.* Sydney: Angus, 1973.

171. Lynn, Karen. "Chaucer's Decasyllabic Line: The Myth of the Hundred-Year Hibernation." *ChauR* 13 (1978), 116-27.

172. Mustanoja, Tauno F. "Chaucer's Prosody." In *Companion to Chaucer Studies.* Ed. Beryl Rowland. rev. ed. New York: Oxford U P, 1979.

173. Ogura, Mieko. "Metrics of Chaucer—An Analysis Based on the Kiparsky Theory." *Lexicon* 8 (1978), 1-15.

174. Robinson, Ian. *Chaucer's Prosody: A Study of the Middle English Verse Tradition.* London: Cambridge U P, 1971.

175. Southworth, J. G. *Verses of Cadence: An Introduction to the Prosody of Chaucer.* Oxford: Blackwell, 1954.

176. Stevens, Martin. "The Royal Stanza in Early English Literature." *PMLA* 94 (1979), 67-76.

177. Stokes, Myra. "Recurring Rhymes in *Troilus and Creseyde.*" *SN* 52 (1980), 287-97.

178. Tarlinskaja, Marina G. *English Verse: Theory and History.* The Hague: Mouton, 1976.

179. Woods, Susanne. *Natural Emphasis: English Versification from Chaucer to Dryden.* San Marino: Huntington Library, 1984.

See also 117, 145, 222, 257, 1053.

STYLE, GENRE, COMEDY

180. Ames, Ruth. "Prototype and Parody in Chaucerian Exegesis." *Acta* 4 (1977), 87-105.

181. Andreas, James R. "The Rhetoric of Chaucerian Comedy: The Aristotelian Legacy." *Comparatist* 8 (1984), 56-66.

182. Benson, Robert G. *Medieval Body Language: A Study of Use of Gesture in Chaucer's Poetry.* Copenhagen: Rosenkilde, 1980.

183. Birney, Earle. *Essays on Chaucerian Irony.* Ed. Beryl Rowland. Toronto: U of Toronto P, 1985.

184. Bornstein, Diane. "Chaucer's *Tale of Melibee* as an Example of the *Style clergial.*" *ChauR* 12 (1978), 236-54.

185. Braddy, Haldeen. "Chaucer: Realism or Obscenity?" *ArlQ* 1 (1969), 121-38.

186. Chisnell, Robert E. "Chaucer's Neglected Prose." In *Literary and Historical Perspectives of the Middle Ages.* Eds. Patricia W. Cummins, Patrick W. Conner, and Charles W. Connell. Morgantown: W Virginia U P, 1982.

187. Cosmos, Spencer. "Toward a Visual Stylistics: Assent and Denial in Chaucer." *Visible Language* 12 (1978), 406-27.

188. Diekstra, Frans. "Chaucer's Way with His Sources." *ES* 62 (1981), 215-36.

189. ———. "The Language of Equivocation: Some Chaucerian Techniques." *DQR* 11 (1981), 267-77.

190. Elbow, Peter. *Oppositions in Chaucer.* Middletown, CT: Wesleyan U P, 1975.

192. Finlayson, John. "Definitions of Middle English Romance," Parts I & II. *ChauR* 15 (1980), 44-62, 168-81.

193. Garbáty, Thomas J. "Chaucer and Comedy." In *Versions of Medieval Comedy.* Ed. Paul G. Ruggiers. Norman: U of Oklahoma P, 1977.

194. Green, D. H. *Irony in the Medieval Romance.* New York: Cambridge U P, 1979.

195. Hira, Toshinori. "Chaucer's Laughter." *Bulletin of the Faculty of Liberal Arts, Nagasaki University,* 20 (1979), 27-42.

196. Kern, Edith. *The Absolute Comic.* Bloomington: Indiana U P, 1980.

197. Leonard, Frances McNeely. *Laughter in the Courts of Love: Comedy in Allegory from Chaucer to Spenser.* Norman, OK: Pilgrim Books, 1981.

198. MacDonald, Donald. "Proverbs, *Sententiae,* and Exempla in Chaucer's Comic Tales: The Function of Comic Misapplication." *Speculum,* 41 (1966), 453-65.

199. Manly, John M. "Chaucer and the Rhetoricians" (1926). In *Chaucer Criticism,* Vol. 1 *The Canterbury Tales.* Eds. Richard J. Schoeck and Jerome Taylor. Notre Dame, IN: Notre Dame U P, 1960.

200. Murphy, James J. "A New Look at Chaucer and the Rhetoricians." *RES* 15 (1964), 1-20.

201. ———. *Rhetoric in the Middle Ages.* Berkeley: U of California P, 1974.

202. Muscatine, Charles. *Chaucer and the French Tradition: A Study in Style and Meaning.* Berkeley: U of California P, 1957.

203. Norton-Smith, J. "Chaucer's Epistolary Style." In *Essays on Style and Language.* Ed. R. Fowler. London: Routledge, 1966.

204. Payne, F. Anne. *Chaucer and Menippean Satire.* Madison: U of Wisconsin P, 1981.

205. Payne, Robert O. *The Key of Remembrance: A Study of Chaucer's Poetics.* New Haven: Yale U P, 1963.

206. ———. "Chaucer and the Art of Rhetoric." In *Companion to Chaucer Studies.* Ed. Beryl Rowland. rev. ed. New York: Oxford U P, 1979.

207. Presson, Robert K. "The Aesthetic of Chaucer's Art of Contrast." *EM* 15 (1964), 9-23.

208. Reiss, E. "Medieval Irony." *JHI* 42 (1981), 209-26.

209. Ruggiers, Paul G.. "Toward a Theory of Tragedy in Chaucer." *ChauR* 8 (1973), 89-99.

210. ———. "A Vocabulary for Chaucerian Comedy: A Preliminary Sketch." In *Medieval Studies in Honor of Lillian Herlands Hornstein.* Eds. J. B. Bessinger and R. Raymo. New York: New York U P, 1977.

211. Salmon, Vivian. "The Representation of Colloquial Speech in The Canterbury Tales." In *Style and Text: Studies Presented to Nils Erik Enkvist.* Ed. H. G. Ringbom. Stockholm: Skriptor, 1975.

212. Sarno, Ronald A. "Chaucer and the Satirical Tradition." *CF* 21 (1967), 41-61.

213. Schlauch, Margaret. "Chaucer's Prose Rhythms." *PMLA* 55 (1950), 568-89.

214. ———. "Chaucer's Colloquial English: Its Structural Traits." *PMLA* 67 (1952), 1103-16.

215. ———. "The Art of Chaucer's Prose." In *Chaucer and Chaucerians.* Ed. D. S. Brewer. London: Nelson, 1966.

See also 253, 665, 672, 697, 1062, 1097, 1122, 1172, 1191, 1199, 1351, 1374.

BACKGROUND, GENERAL CRITICISM

216. Aers, David. *Chaucer, Langland and the Creative Imagination.* London: Routledge, 1980.

217. Ames, Ruth M. *God's Plenty: Chaucer's Christian Humanism.* Chicago: Loyola U P, 1984.

218. Bennett, J. A. W. *Chaucer at Oxford and Cambridge.* Oxford: Clarendon, 1974.

219. Bloomfield, Morton W. "Fourteenth-Century England: Realism and Rationalism in Wycliff and Chaucer." *ESA* 16 (1973), 59-70.

220. Bowden, Muriel. *A Reader's Guide to Geoffrey Chaucer.* New York: Ferrar, 1964.

221. Brewer, Derek. *Chaucer in His Time*. London: Nelson, 1963.

222. ———. *Towards a Chaucerian Poetic*. London: Oxford U P, 1974.

223. ———. *English Gothic Literature*. New York: Schocken Books, 1983.

224. ———. *An Introduction to Chaucer*. London: Longman, 1984.

225. ———. *Chaucer the Poet as Storyteller*. London: Macmillan, 1984.

226. Burchfield, Robert. "Realms and Approximations: Sources of Chaucer's Power." *E&S* 35 (1982), 1-13.

227. Chute, Marchette. *Geoffrey Chaucer of England*. New York: Dutton, 1946.

228. Coghill, Nevill. *The Poet Chaucer*. 2nd ed. London: Oxford U P, 1967.

229. Corsa, Helen S. *Chaucer, Poet of Mirth and Morality*. Notre Dame, IN: U of Notre Dame P, 1964.

230. David, Alfred. *The Strumpet Muse: Art and Morals in Chaucer's Poetry*. Bloomington: Indiana U P, 1976.

231. Enkvist, Nils Erik. *Geoffrey Chaucer*. Stockholm: Natur och Kultur, 1964.

232. Gardner, John Champlin. *The Poetry of Chaucer*. Carbondale, IL: Southern Illinois U P, 1977.

233. Gibaldi, Joseph, ed. *Approaches to Teaching Chaucer's Canterbury Tales*. New York: MLA, 1980. Essays by Gibaldi, Florence Ridley, John Fisher, Thomas Garbáty, Donald Howard, Emerson Brown, Mary Carruthers, Robert Jordan, William Provost, Terrie Curran, Thomas Ross, Michael West, Stephen Portch, Susan Schibanoff, D. W. Robertson, Ernest Kaulbach, Julia Holloway.

234. Hieatt, Constance B. " 'to boille the chiknes with the marybones': Hodge's Kitchen Revisited." In *Chaucerian Problems and Perspectives: Essays Presented to Paul E. Beichner, C.S.C.* Eds. Edward Vasta and Zacharias P. Thundy. Notre Dame, IN: U of Notre Dame P, 1979.

235. Hussey, S. S. *Chaucer: An Introduction*. 2nd ed. London: Methuen, 1981.

236. Kane, George. *Chaucer*. New York: Oxford U P, 1984.

237. Kean, P[atricia] M. *Chaucer and the Making of English Poetry*. 2 vols. London: Routledge, 1972.

238. Kelly, Henry Ansgar. "Chaucer's Arts and Our Arts." In *New Perspectives in Chaucer Criticism*. Ed. Donald M. Rose. Norman, OK: Pilgrim Books, 1981.

239. Kittredge, G. L. *Chaucer and His Poetry* (1915). Cambridge, MA: Harvard U P, 1970.

240. Norton-Smith, John. *Geoffrey Chaucer*. London: Routledge, 1974.

241. Olson, Glending. *Literature as Recreation in the Later Middle Ages*. Ithaca, NY: Cornell U P, 1982.

242. Rickert, Edith. *Chaucer's World*. Eds. C.C. Olson and M. M. Crow. New York: Columbia U P, 1948.

243. Robertson, D. W., Jr. *A Preface to Chaucer: Studies in Medieval Perspective*. Princeton: Princeton U P, 1962.

244. ———. "Simple Signs from Everyday Life in Chaucer." In *Signs and Symbols in Chaucer's Poetry*. Eds. John P. Hermann and John J. Burke, Jr. University: U of Alabama P, 1981.

245. Smith, Walter R. "Geoffrey Chaucer, Dramatist." *Interpretations* 1 (1968), 1-10.

245a. Traversi, Derek. *The Literary Imagination: Studies in Dante, Chaucer, and Shakespeare*. Newark: U of Delaware P, 1982.

246. Whitmore, Sister Mary E. *Medieval English Domestic Life and Amusements in the Works of Chaucer*. New York: Cooper Square, 1972.

See also 5, 88, 92, 96, 97, 327.

MODERN CRITICISM

247. Economou, George D. "Introduction: Chaucer the Innovator." In *Geoffrey Chaucer: A Collection of Original Articles*. Ed. George D. Economou. New York: McGraw Hill, 1976.

248. Ferster, Judith. *Chaucer on Interpretation*. Cambridge: Cambridge U P, 1985.

249. Fisher, John H. "Chaucer's Prescience." *SAC* 5 (1983), 3-15.

250. Jordan, Robert M. *Chaucer and the Shape of Creation: The Aesthetic Possibilities of Inorganic Structure*. Cambridge, MA: Harvard U P, 1967.

251. ———. *Chaucer's Poetics and the Modern Reader*. Berkeley: U of California P, 1987.

252. Millns, Tony. "Chaucer's Suspended Judgments." *EIC* 27 (1977), 1-19.

253. Pearsall, Derek. "Epidemic Irony and Modern Approaches to Chaucer's Canterbury Tales." In *Medieval and Pseudo-Medieval Literature*. Eds. Piero Boitani and Anna Torti. Tübingen: Narr, 1984.

254. Stevens, Martin. "Chaucer and Modernism: An Essay in Criticism." In *Chaucer at Albany*. Ed. Rossell Hope Robbins. New York: Franklin, 1975.

255. Tripp, Raymond P., Jr. *Beyond Canterbury: Chaucer, Humanism and Literature*. Church Stretton, Eng.: Soc. for New Lang. Study, 1977.

256. Wetherbee, Winthrop. "Convention and Authority: A Comment on Some Recent Critical Approaches to Chaucer." In *New Perspectives in Chaucer Criticism*. Ed. Donald M. Rose. Norman, OK: Pilgrim Books, 1981.

257. Wood, Chauncey. "Affective Stylistics and the Study of Chaucer." *SAC* 6 (1984), 21-40.

See also 196, 535, 663, 678, 751, 752, 769, 775, 788, 1098, 1111, 1346, 1455, 1513.

NARRATIVE TECHNIQUE

258. Burlin, Robert B. *Chaucerian Fiction.* Princeton: Princeton U P, 1977.

259. Jordan, Robert M. "Chaucerian Narrative." In *Companion to Chaucer Studies.* Ed. Beryl Rowland. rev. ed. New York: Oxford U P, 1979.

260. Long, E. Hudson. "Chaucer as Master of the Short Story." *Delaware Notes*, 16 ser (1943), 11-29.

261. Sklute, Larry. *Virtue of Necessity: Inconclusiveness and Narrative Form in Chaucer's Poetry.* Columbus: Ohio State U P, 1984.

See also 107, 963, 1258, 1259-75, 1281, 1526.

SOURCES AND ANALOGUES

262. Alanus ab Insulis. *Anticlaudianus.* Ed. R. Bossuat, Paris: Textes Philosophiques du Moyen Age, 1955. Trans. W. H. Cornog 1915, James J. Sheridan 1973.

263. ———. *De planctu naturae.* Ed. Nikolaus Haring, *Studi medievali*, 3rd ser. 19 (1979). Trans. *The Plaint of Nature*, Douglas Moffatt 1908, James J. Sheridan 1980. Excerpts in Windeatt, *Chaucer's Dream Poetry.*

264. *Albertanus Brixiensis Liber consolationis et consilii.* Ed. Thor Sundby. London: Chaucer Society, ser. 2, no. 8, 1873.

265. Andreas Capellanus. *De amore libri tres.* Ed. E. Trojel. 2nd ed. 1964. Trans. (abbreviated) *The Art of Courtly Love.* J. J. Parry 1941, P. G. Walsh 1982.

266. Benoit de Sainte-Maure. *Roman de Troie.* Ed. Leopold Constans. 6 vols. Paris: SATF, 1904-12. Trans. (with omissions) in R. K. Gordon, *The Story of Troilus* 1934. Excerpts in Havely, *Chaucer's Boccaccio.*

267. Benson, Larry D., and Theodore Andersson, eds. and trans. *The Literary Context of Chaucer's Fabliaux.* Indianapolis, IN: Bobbs-Merrill, 1971.

268. Boccaccio. *Tutte le opere di Giovanni Boccaccio.* Gen. ed. V. Branca, 1964.

269. ———. *Il Decamerone.* Ed. V. Branca, 1958. Tr. G. H. McWilliam, 1972.

270. ———. *The Filostrato of Giovanni Boccaccio: A Translation with Parallel Text.* Nathaniel E. Griffen and Arthur B. Myrick. Philadelphia: U of Pennsylvania P, 1929. Vol I of *Tutte le opere;* excerpts in Havely, *Boccaccio—Sources of Troilus.*

271. ———. *Teseida.* Ed. S. Battaglia. Florence: Accademia della Crusca, 1938. Vol II of *Tutte le opere.* Trans. Bernadette M. McCoy. *The Book of Theseus.* New York: Medieval Text Association, 1974; excerpts in Havely, *Boccaccio—Sources of Troilus.*

272. Boethius. *De Consolatione Philosophiae.* Ed. and trans. H. F. Stewart and E. K. Rand. London: Loeb Library, rev. ed. 1968.

273. Bryan, W. F., and Germaine Dempster, eds. *Sources and Analogues of Chaucer's Canterbury Tales.* Chicago: U of Chicago P, 1941.

274. Coley, John Smart, trans. *Le Roman de Thebes: The Story of Thebes.* New York: Garland, 1985.

275. Deschamps. *Oeuvres complètes de Eustace Deschamps.* Ed. le Marquis de Saint-Hilaire and G. Raynaud. 11 vols. Paris: SATF, 1878-1903.

276. Gordon, R. K., ed. and trans. *The Story of Troilus as told by Benoit de Sainte-Maure, Giovanni Boccaccio, Geoffrey Chaucer and Robert Henryson.* London: Dent, 1934.

277. Guillaume de Lorris and Jean de Meun. *Le Roman de la Rose.* Ed. Ernest Langlois. 5 vols. Paris: SATF, 1914-24; Felix Lecoy. 3 vols. Paris: Champion, 1965-70. Trans. H. W. Robbins and C. W. Dunn, 1962 (verse), Charles Dahlberg, 1971 (prose).

278. Havely, N. R. *Boccaccio—Sources of Troilus and the Knight's and Franklin's Tales.* Cambridge: Brewer, 1980. Translations of excerpts taken from Bocaccio, *Filostrato, Teseida, Filocolo;* Benoit, *Roman de Troie;* Guido, *Historia Destructionis Troiae.*

279. Machaut. *Poésies lyriques.* Ed. V. Chichmaref. 2 vols. Paris, 1909.

280. ———. *Oeuvres.* Ed. E. Hoepffner. 3 vols. Paris: SATF, 1908-21.

281. Macrobius. *Somnium Scipionis.* In Cicero's *De republica.* Ed. and trans. C. W. Keyes, London: Loeb Library, 1928. Trans. W. H. Stahl, *Commentary on the Dream of Scipio.* New York: Columbia U P, 1952; D. S. Brewer, ed. *Parlement of Fowles,* London: Nelson, 1960; excerpts in Windeatt, *Chaucer's Dream Poetry.*

282. Ovid. *Ars Amatoria.* Ed. and trans. J. H. Mozley. London: Loeb Library, rev. ed. 1957.

283. ———. *Metamorphoses.* Ed. and trans. F. J. Miller; rev. ed. G. P. Gould. London: Loeb Library, 1957.

284. Windeatt, Barry. *Chaucer's Dream Poetry: Sources and Analogues.* Cambridge: Brewer, 1980. Selections translated from Machaut, *Jugement dou Roy de Behaingne;* Froissart, *Paradys d'amours;* Condé, *Messe des Oisiaus;* Cicero, *Somnium Scipionis;* Boccaccio, *Teseide;* Alanus ab Insulis, *Complaint of Nature,* etc.

See also 84, 188, 286, 351, 534, 538, 548, 657, 731, 748, 761, 781, 840, 843, 853, 865, 1073, 1109, 1110, 1131, 1175, 1176, 1212-34, 1424, 1426, 1443, 1444, 1445, 1483, 1487, 1538, 1542, 1600.

CLASSICAL AND CONTINENTAL ASSOCIATIONS

285. apRoberts, Robert P. "Love in *Filostrato*," *ChauR* 7 (1972), 1-26.

286. Bennett, J. A. W. "Chaucer, Dante and Boccaccio." In *Chaucer and the Italian Trecento.* Ed. Piero Boitani. Cambridge: Cambridge U P, 1983.

287. Boitani, Piero. "What Dante Meant to Chaucer." In *Chaucer and the Italian Trecento*. Ed. Piero Boitani. Cambridge: Cambridge U P, 1983.

288. Braddy, Haldeen. "The French Influence on Chaucer." In *Companion to Chaucer Studies*. Ed. Beryl Rowland. rev. ed. New York: Oxford P, 1979.

289. Brewer, Derek. "The Relationship of Chaucer to the English and European Traditions." In *Chaucer and Chaucerians: Critical Studies in Middle English Literature*. London: Nelson, 1966.

290. Brown, Emerson, Jr. "Chaucer and the European Literary Tradition." In *Geoffrey Chaucer: A Collection of Original Articles*. Ed. George D. Economou. New York: McGraw Hill, 1976.

291. Childs, Wendy. "Anglo-Italian Contacts in the Fourteenth Century." In *Chaucer and the Italian Trecento*. Ed. Piero Boitani. Cambridge: Cambridge U P, 1983.

292. Crépin, André. "Chaucer and the French." In *Medieval and Pseudo-Medieval Literature*. Eds. Piero Boitani and Anna Torti. Tübingen: Narr, 1984.

293. Cummings, Hubertis M. *The Indebtedness of Chaucer's Works to the Italian Works of Boccaccio* (1916). New York: Haskell House, 1965.

294. Farnham, Willard. *The Medieval Heritage of Elizabethan Tragedy*. Berkeley: U of California P, 1936.

295. Fisher, John H. "Chaucer and the French Influence." In *New Perspectives on Chaucer Criticism*. Ed. Donald M. Rose. Norman, OK: Pilgrim , 1981.

296. Fyler, John M. *Chaucer and Ovid*. New Haven: Yale U P, 1979.

297. Goodman, Peter. "Chaucer and Boccaccio's Latin Works." In *Chaucer and the Italian Trecento*. Ed. Piero Boitani. Cambridge: Cambridge U P, 1983.

298. Harbert, Bruce. "Chaucer and the Latin Classics." In *Geoffrey Chaucer: Writers and Their Backgrounds*. Ed. D. S. Brewer. London: Bell, 1974.

299. Heffernan, Carol Falvo. "The Use of Simile in Dante's *Divine Comedy* and Chaucer's *Canterbury Tales*." *CJItS* 3 (1980), 72-80.

300. Hoffman, Richard L. *Ovid and the Canterbury Tales*. Philadelphia: U of Pennsylvania P, 1966.

301. ———. "The Influence of the Classics on Chaucer." In *Companion to Chaucer Studies*. Ed. Beryl Rowland. rev. ed. New York: Oxford, 1979.

302. Jefferson, Bernard L. *Chaucer and the Consolation of Philosophy* (1917). New York: Haskell, 1965.

303. Larner, John. "Chaucer's Italy." In *Chaucer and the Italian Trecento*. Ed. Piero Boitani. Cambridge: Cambridge U P, 1983.

304. McCall, John P. *Chaucer Among the Gods: The Poetics of Classical Myth*. University Park: Pennsylvania State U P, 1979.

305. McGrady, Donald. "Chaucer and the *Decameron* Reconsidered." *ChauR* 12 (1977), 1-26.

306. Miller, Robert P., ed. *Chaucer: Sources and Backgrounds*. New York: Oxford U P, 1977.

307. Minnis, A. J. *Chaucer and Pagan Antiquity*. Cambridge: Brewer, 1982.

308. Rogers, William E. "The Raven and the Writing Desk: The Theoretical Limits of Patristic Criticism." *ChauR* 14 (1980), 260- 77.

309. Ruggiers, Paul G. "The Italian Influence on Chaucer." In *Companion to Chaucer Studies*. Ed. Beryl Rowland. rev. ed. NY: Oxford U P, 1979.

310. Schless, Howard. *Chaucer and Dante: A Revaluation*. Norman, OK: Pilgrim Books, 1984.

311. Shannon, Edgar F. *Chaucer and the Roman Poets*. Cambridge, MA: Harvard U P, 1929.

312. Shoaf, R. A. "Dante's Commedia and Chaucer's Theory of Mediation: A Preliminary Sketch." In *New Perspectives on Chaucer Criticism*. Ed. Donald M. Rose. Norman, OK: Pilgrim Books, 1981.

313. ———. *Chaucer and the Currency of the Word: Money, Image, and Reference in Late Medieval Poetry*. Norman, OK: Pilgrim Books, 1983. (Mostly on Chaucer and Dante.)

314. Wallace, David. "Chaucer and the European Rose." *SAC*, Proceedings, 1, 1984, pp. 61-67.

315. ———. *Chaucer and the Early Writings of Boccaccio*. Cambridge: Brewer, 1985.

316. Whitlark, James S. "Chaucer and the Pagan Gods." *AnM* 18 (1977), 63-75.

317. Wimsatt, James I. "Chaucer and French Poetry." In *Geoffrey Chaucer: Writers and Their Backgrounds*. Ed. D. S. Brewer. London: Bell, 1974.

See also 80, 106, 107, 153, 202, 449, 782, 806, 857, 918, 960, 1006, 1019, 1027, 1051, 1080, 1093, 1105, 1114, 1118, 1132, 1134, 1212-34, 1489, 1503, 1504, 1509, 1560.

CONTEMPORARY AND LATER ENGLISH ASSOCIATIONS

318. Alderson, William L., and Arnold C. Henderson. *Chaucer and Augustan Scholarship*. Berkeley: U of California P, 1970.

319. Bennett, H. S. *Chaucer and the Fifteenth Century*. Oxford: Oxford U P, 1947.

320. Boitani, Piero. *English Medieval Narrative in the 13th and 14th Centuries*. Trans. Joan Krakover Hall. Cambridge: Cambridge U P, 1982.

321. Burrow, J. A. *Ricardian Poetry: Chaucer, Gower, Langland and the Pearl Poet*. New Haven, CT: Yale U P, 1971.

322. Crampton, Georgia R. *The Conditions of Creatures: Suffering and Action in Chaucer and Spenser*. New Haven, CT: Yale U P, 1974.

323. Donaldson, E. Talbot. *The Swan at the Well: Shakespeare Reading Chaucer*. New Haven: Yale U P, 1985.

324. Ebin, Lois. "Chaucer, Lydgate, and the 'Myrie Tale.'" *ChauR* 13 (1979), 316-36.

325. Fisher, John H. *John Gower, Moral Philosopher and Friend of Chaucer.* New York: New York U P, 1964.

326. Gallick, Susan. "A Look at Chaucer and His Preachers." *Speculum* 50 (1975), 456-76.

327. Green, Richard Firth. *Poets and Princepleasers: Literature and the English Court in the Late Middle Ages.* Toronto: U of Toronto P, 1980.

328. Hawkins, Harriett. *Poetic Freedom and Poetic Truth: Chaucer, Shakespeare, Marlowe, and Milton.* Oxford: Clarendon, 1976.

329. Hieatt, A. Kent. *Chaucer, Spenser, Milton: Mythopoetic Continuities and Transformations.* Montreal: McGill-Queen's U P, 1975.

330. Kirk, Elizabeth D. "Chaucer and His English Contemporaries." In *Geoffrey Chaucer: A Collection of Original Articles.* Ed. George D. Economou. New York: McGraw Hill, 1976.

331. Miskimin, Alice S. *The Renaissance Chaucer.* New Haven, CT: Yale U P, 1975.

332. Pearsall, Derek. "The English Chaucerians." In *Chaucer and Chaucerians.* Ed. D. S. Brewer. London: Nelson, 1966.

333. Robinson, Ian. *Chaucer and the English Tradition.* Cambridge: Cambridge U P, 1972.

334. Spearing, A. C. "Lydgate's Canterbury Tale: *The Siege of Thebes* and Fifteenth-Century Chaucerianism." In *Fifteenth- Century Studies.* Ed. Robert F. Yeager. Hamden, CT: Archon Books, 1984.

335. ———. "Renaissance Chaucer and Father Chaucer." *English* 34 (1985), 1-38.

336. Spurgeon, Caroline F. E. *Five Hundred Years of Chaucer Criticism and Allusion, 1357-1900* (1914-24), 3 vols. New York: Russell, 1961.

337. Strohm, Paul. "Form and Social Statement in *Confessio Amantis* and *The Canterbury Tales.*" *SAC* 1 (1979), 17-40.

338. Thompson, Ann. *Shakespeare's Chaucer: A Study in Literary Origins.* New York: Barnes & Noble, 1978.

339. Weiss, Alexander. *Chaucer's Native Heritage.* Berne: Peter Lang, 1985.

340. Wenzel, Siegfried. "Chaucer and the Language of Contemporary Preaching." *SP* 73 (1976), 138-61.

See also 19, 289, 484, 588, 591, 796, 829, 834, 1009, 1114, 1170, 1208, 1211, 1218, 1226.

AUDIENCE, AUTHORSHIP, ORAL AND WRITTEN PRESENTATION

341. Christianson, Paul. "Chaucer's Literacy." *ChauR* 11 (1976), 112-27.

342. Coleman, Janet. *Medieval Readers and Writers, 1350-1400.* New York: Columbia U P, 1981.

343. Eade, J. C. "'We Ben to Lewed or to Slowe': Chaucer's Astronomy and Audience Participation." *SAC* 4 (1982), 53-85.

344. Fisher, John H. "Chaucer and the Written Language." In *The Popular Literature of Medieval England.* Ed. Thomas J. Heffernan. Knoxville: U of Tennessee P, 1985.

345. Friedman, John B. "Richard de Thorpe's Astronomical Kalendar and the Luxury Book Trade at York." *SAC* 7 (1985), 137- 60.

346. Gellrich, Jesse M. *The Idea of the Book in the Middle Ages: Language Theory, Mythology, and Fiction.* Ithaca, NY: Cornell U P, 1985.

347. Hanning, R. W. "The Audience as Co-Creator of the First Chivalric Romances." *YES* 2 (1981), 1-28.

348. Lenaghan, R. T. "Chaucer's Circle of Gentlemen and Clerks." *ChauR* 18 (1983), 155-60.

349. Mehl, Dieter. "Chaucer's Audience." *LeedsSE* 10 (1978), 58-74.

350. Middleton, Anne. "Chaucer's 'New Men' and the Good of Literature in the *Canterbury Tales.*" In *Literature and Society.* Ed. Edward W. Said. Baltimore: Johns Hopkins U P, 1980.

351. Millett, Bella. "Chaucer, Lollius, and the Medieval Theory of Authorship." *SAC*, Proceedings 1, 1984, 93-103.

352. Minnis, Alastair. *The Medieval Theory of Authorship.* Cambridge: Brewer, 1982.

353. Neuss, Paula. "Images of Writing and the Book in Chaucer's Poetry." *RES* 32 (1981), 385-97.

354. Olson, Glending. "Making and Poetry in the Age of Chaucer." *CL* 31 (1979), 272-90.

355. Reiss, Edmund. "Chaucer and His Audience." *ChauR* 14 (1980), 390-402.

356. Rosenberg, Bruce A. "The Oral Performance of Chaucer's Poetry." *Forum* 13 (1980), 224-37.

357. Rowland, Beryl. "Pronuntiatio and Its Effect on Chaucer's Audience." *SAC* 4 (1982), 33-51.

358. Strohm, Paul. "Chaucer's Audience." *L&H* 5 (1977), 26- 41.

359. ———. "Chaucer's Fifteenth-Century Audience and the Narrowing of the 'Chaucer Tradition'." *SAC* 4 (1982), 3-32.

360. ———. "Chaucer's Audience(s): Fictional, Implied, Intended, Actual." *ChauR* 18 (1983), 137-45.

361. Walker, Denis. "The Structure of Literary Response in Chaucerian Texts." *Parergon* 3 (1985), 107-14.

See also 982, 1115, 1192, 1269, 1375, 1471, 1506, 1522, 1533.

CHARACTERIZATION

362. Braswell, Mary F. "Poet and Sinner: Literary Characterization and the Mentality of the Late

Middle Ages." *Fifteenth Century Studies* 10 (1984), 39-59.

363. Friedman, John B. "Another Look at Chaucer and the Physiognomists." *SP* 78 (1981), 138-52.

364. Ginsberg, Warren. *The Cast of Character: The Representation of Personality in Ancient and Medieval Literature.* Toronto: U of Toronto P, 1983.

365. Hussey, Stanley S. "Chaucer and Character." In *Medieval Studies Conference, Aachen 1983.* Eds. Wolf-Dietrich Bald and Horst Weinstock. Frankfurt am Main: Verlag Peter Lang, 1984.

366. Manly, John M. *Some New Light on Chaucer* (1926). New York: Peter Smith, 1952.

367. Parr, Roger P. "Chaucer's Art of Portraiture." *SMC* 4 (1974), 428-36.

368. Schroeder, Peter R. "Hidden Depths: Dialogue and Characterization in Chaucer and Malory." *PMLA* 98 (1983), 374-87.

369. Specht, Henrik. "The Beautiful, the Handsome, and the Ugly: Some Aspects of the Art of Character Portrayal in Medieval Literature." *SN* 56 (1984), 129-46.

370. Taitt, Peter S. *Incubus and Ideal: Ecclesiastical Figures in Chaucer and Langland.* Salzburg: Inst. für eng. Sprache & Lit., U of Salzburg, 1975.

See also 445, 546, 821, 1020.

PHILOSOPHY, RELIGION

371. Ackerman, Robert W. "Chaucer, the Church, and Religion." In *Companion to Chaucer Studies.* Ed. Beryl Rowland. rev. ed. New York: Oxford U P, 1979.

372. Alford, John A. "Scriptural Testament in the *Canterbury Tales.*" In *Chaucer and Scriptural Tradition.* Ed. David Lyle Jeffrey. Ottawa: U of Ottawa P, 1984.

373. Ames, Ruth M. "Corn and Shrimps: Chaucer's Mockery of Religious Controversy." In *The Late Middle Ages.* Ed. Peter Cocozella. Binghamton, NY: Center for Medieval and Early Renaissance Studies, 1984 (for 1981).

374. Besserman, Lawrence. "Glosing is a Glorious Thyng: Chaucer's Biblical Exegesis." In *Chaucer and Scriptural Tradition.* Ed. David Lyle Jeffrey. Ottawa: U of Ottawa P, 1984.

375. Boyd, Beverly. *Chaucer and The Liturgy.* Philadelphia: Dorrance, 1967.

376. Braswell, Laurel. "Chaucer and the Legendaries: New Sources for Anti-Mendicant Satire." *ESC* 2 (1976), 373-80.

377. Dunleavy, Gareth W. "Natural Law as Chaucer's Ethical Absolute." *TWA* 52 (1963), 177-87.

378. Fleming, John V. "Gospel Asceticism: Some Chaucerian Images of Perfection." In *Chaucer and Scriptural Tradition.* Ed. David Lyle Jeffrey. Ottawa: U of Ottawa P, 1984.

379. Haskell, Ann. *Essays on Chaucer's Saints.* The Hague: Mouton, 1977.

380. Haas, Renate. "Chaucer's Use of the Lament for the Dead." In *Chaucer in the Eighties.* Eds. Julian N. Wasserman and Robert J. Blanch. Syracuse, NY: Syracuse U P, 1986.

381. Jeffrey, David Lyle. "Chaucer and Wyclif: Biblical Hermeneutic and Literary Theory in XIVth Century." In *Chaucer and Scriptural Tradition.* Ed. David Lyle Jeffrey. Ottawa: U of Ottawa P, 1984.

382. Mogen, Joseph J. Jr. *Chaucer and the Theme of Mutability.* The Hague: Mouton, 1969.

383. Owen, Charles A., Jr. "The Problem of Free Will in Chaucer's Narratives." *PQ* 46 (1967), 433-56.

384. Patch, Howard R. *The Goddess Fortuna in Medieval Literature.* Cambridge, MA: Harvard U P, 1927.

385. ———. *The Tradition of Boethius: A Study of His Importance in Medieval Culture.* New York: Oxford U P, 1935.

386. Peck, Russell A. "Chaucer and the Nominalist Question." *Speculum* 53 (1978), 745-60.

387. Reiss, Edmund. "Biblical Parody: Chaucer's 'Distortions' of Scripture." In *Chaucer and Scriptural Tradition.* Ed. David Lyle Jeffrey. Ottawa: U of Ottawa P, 1984.

388. Robertson, D. W., Jr. "Chaucer and Christian Tradition." In *Chaucer and Scriptural Tradition.* Ed. David Lyle Jeffrey. Ottawa: U of Ottawa P, 1984.

389. Ruggiers, Paul G. "Platonic Forms in Chaucer." *ChauR* 17 (1983), 366-81.

390. Shepherd, Geoffrey. "Religion and Philosophy in Chaucer." In *Geoffrey Chaucer: Writers and Their Backgrounds.* Ed. D. S. Brewer. London: Bell, 1974.

391. Williams, Arnold. "Chaucer and the Friars." *Speculum* 28 (1953), 499-513.

392. Wood, Chauncey. "Artistic Intention and Chaucer's Use of Scriptural Allusion." In *Chaucer and Scriptural Tradition.* Ed. David Lyle Jeffreys. Ottawa: U of Ottawa P, 1984.

See also 141, 217, 326, 340, 370, 494, 497, 503, 504, 507, 510, 585, 641, 730, 799, 815, 855, 867, 1108, 1292-1307, 1597.

ASTROLOGY, SCIENCE

393. Brewer, Derek. "Chaucer and Arithmetic." In *Medieval Studies Conference, Aachen 1983.* Eds. Wolf-Dietrich Bald and Horst Weinstock. Frankfurt am Main: Verlag Peter Lang, 1984.

394. Clark, George. "Chaucer's Third and Fourth of May." *RUO* 52 (1982), 257-65.

395. Curry Walter C. *Chaucer and the Medieval Sciences* (1926). Enlarged ed. NY: Barnes and Noble, 1960.

396. North, J. D. "Kalenderes Enlumyned Ben They: Some Astronomical Terms in Chaucer." *RES* 20 (1969), 129-54, 257-83, 418-44.

397. Rutledge, Sheryl P. "Chaucer's Zodiac of Tales." *Costerus* 9 (1973), 117-43.

398. Smyser, Hamilton M. "A View of Chaucer's Astronomy." *Speculum* 45 (1970), 359-73.

399. Spencer, William. "Are Chaucer's Pilgrims Keyed to the Zodiac?" *ChauR* 4 (1970), 147-70.

400. Wood, Chauncey. *Chaucer and the Country of the Stars: Poetic Uses of Astrological Imagery.* Princeton: Princeton U P, 1970.

401. ———. "Chaucer and Astrology." In *Companion to Chaucer Studies.* Ed. Beryl Rowland. rev. ed. New York: Oxford U P, 1979.

See also 343, 345, 733, 767, 1139, 1141, 1144, 1221, 1288, 1528.

COURTLY LOVE, MARRIAGE, FEMINISM

402. Adams, Henry. *Mont-Saint-Michel and Chartres.* Washington, D. C., 1904.

403. Bosse, Roberta Bux. "Female Sexual Behavior in the Late Middle Ages." *FCS* 10 (1984), 15-37.

404. Davenant, John. "Chaucer's View of the Proper Treatment of Women." *Maledicta* 5 (1981), 153-61.

405. Delany, Sheila. "Slaying Python: Marriage and Misogyny in a Chaucerian Text." In *Writing Woman: Women Writers and Women in Literature Medieval to Modern.* New York: Schocken Books, 1983.

406. Denomy, Alexander J. *The Heresy of Courtly Love.* New York: Macmillan, 1947.

407. Diamond, Arlyn. "Chaucer's Women and Women's Chaucer." In *The Authority of Experience: Essays in Feminist Criticism.* Eds. Arlyn Diamond and Lee R. Edwards. Amherst: U of Massachusetts P, 1977.

408. Green, Donald C. "Chaucer as Nuditarian: The Erotic as a Critical Problem." *PCP* 18 (1983), 59-69.

409. Guerin, Dorothy. "Chaucer's Pathos: Three Variations." *ChauR* 20 (1985), 90-112.

410. Haskell, Ann S. "The Portrayal of Women by Chaucer and His Age." In *What Manner of Woman?* Ed. Marlene Springer. New York: New York U P, 1978.

411. Kane, George. "Chaucer, Love Poetry, and Romantic Love." In *Acts of Interpretation…Essays in Honor of E. Talbot Donaldson.* Eds. Mary Carruthers and Elizabeth D. Kirk. Norman, OK: Pilgrim Books, 1982.

412. Kelly, H. A. *Love and Marriage in the Age of Chaucer.* Ithaca, NY: Cornell U P, 1975.

413. Leach, Eleanor Winsor. "Morwe of May: A Season of Feminine Ambiguity." In *Acts of Interpretation… Essays in Honor of E. Talbot Donaldson.* Eds. Mary Carruthers and Elizabeth D. Kirk. Norman, OK: Pilgrim Books, 1982.

414. Lucas, Angela M. *Women in the Middle Ages.* New York: St. Martin's P, 1983.

415. Murtaugh, Daniel M. "Women and Geoffrey Chaucer." *ELH* 38 (1971), 473-92.

416. O'Donoghue, Bernard. *The Courtly Love Tradition.* Manchester, England: Manchester U P, 1982.

417. Slaughter, Eugene. *Virtue According to Love in Chaucer.* New York: Bookman, 1957.

418. Steadman, John M. "'Courtly Love' as a Problem in Style." In *Chaucer und seine Zeit: Symposium für Walter F. Schirmer.* Tübingen: Niemeyer, 1968.

419. Warner, Marina. *Alone of All Her Sex: The Myth and Cult of the Virgin Mary.* New York: Knopf, 1976.

420. Weissman, Hope Phyllis. "Antifeminism and Chaucer's Characterization of Women." In *Geoffrey Chaucer: A Collection of Originial Articles.* Ed. George D. Edonomou. New York: McGraw Hill, 1976.

See also 572-84, 723, 754, 759, 779, 781, 782, 784, 790, 792, 866, 869, 882, 887, 916, 920, 932, 1123, 1128, 1308-24, 1367, 1541.

GENTILESSE, CHIVALRY, JUSTICE, POLITICS, LAW

420a. Baker, Donald C. "Chaucer's Clerk and the Wife of Bath on the Subject of Gentilesse." *SP* 59 (1962), 631-40.

421. Blamires, Alcuin. "Chaucer's Revaluation of Chivalric Honor." *Mediaevalia* 5 (1979), 245-69.

422. Brewer, Derek. "Class Distinction in Chaucer." *Speculum* 43 (1968), 290-305.

423. ———. "Honour in Chaucer." *E&S* 26 (1973), 1- 19.

424. Coghill, Nevill. *Chaucer's Idea of What is Noble.* Presidential Address, 1971. London: English Association, 1971.

425. Collins, Marie. "Love, Nature, and Law in the Poetry of Gower and Chaucer." In *Court and Poet.* Eds. Glyn S. Burgess, et al. Liverpool: Cairns, 1981.

426. Delasanta, Rodney. "The Theme of Justice in *The Canterbury Tales.*" *MLQ* 31 (1970), 298-307.

427. Dunleavy, Gareth W. "Natural Law and Chaucer's Ethical Absolute." *Transactions of the Wisconsin Academy of Sciences, Arts, and Letters,* 52 (1963), 177-87.

428. Friman, Anne. "Of Bretherhede: The Friendship Motif in Chaucer." *Innisfree* 3 (1976), 24-36.

429. Justman, Stewart. "Medieval Monism and Abuse of Authority in Chaucer." *ChauR* 11 (1976), 95-111.

429a. Kelso, Ruth. *The Doctrine of the English Gentleman in the Sixteenth Century.* Urbana: U of Illinois P, 1929.

430. Knight, Stephen. "Politics and Chaucer's Poetry." In *The Radical Reader*. Eds. Stephen Knight and Michael Wilding. Sydney: Wild and Woolley, 1977.

431. ———. "Chaucer and the Sociology of Literature." *SAC* 2 (1980), 15-51.

432. Loganbill, Dean. "Chaucer as a Social Critic." *PMPA* 3 (1978), 1-9.

433. Mann, Jill. "Now Read On: Medieval Literature." *Encounter* (1980), 60-64.

434. Olson, Paul. *The Canterbury Tales and the Good Society*. Princeton: Princeton U P, 1986.

435. Patch, Howard. "Chaucer and the Common People." *JEGP* 29 (1930), 376-84.

436. Robertson, D. W., Jr. "Chaucer and the 'Commune Profit': The Manor." *Mediaevalia* 6 (1980), 239-59.

437. Silvia, D. S. "Geoffrey Chaucer on the Subject of Men, Women, and Gentilesse." *RLV* 33 (1967), 228-36.

437a. Ullman, Walter. *The Individual and Society in the Middle Ages*. Baltimore, MD: Johns Hopkins U P, 1966.

See also 606, 633, 654, 727, 749, 833, 836, 901, 904, 1069, 1151, 1174, 1349, 1579.

ALLEGORY, IMAGERY, MYTH

438. Baird-Lange, Lorrayne Y. "Symbolic Ambivalence in 'I have a gentil cock.'" *FCS* 11 (1985), 1-5.

439. ———. "Priapus Gallinaceus: The Role of the Cock in Fertility and Eroticism in Classical Antiquity and the Middle Ages." *SIcon* 7-8 (1981-82), 81-111.

440. Barney, Stephen A. *Allegories of History, Allegories of Love*. Hamden, CT: Archon Books, Shoe String P, 1979.

441. Beckman, Sabina. "Color Symbolism in *Troilus and Criseyde*." *CLAJ* 20 (1976), 68-74.

442. Bloomfield, Morton W. "Personification-Metaphors." *ChauR* 14 (1980), 287-97.

443. Boitani, Piero. "Chaucer's Temples of Venus." *Studi Inglesi* 2 (1975), 9-31.

444. ———. "Chaucer and Lists of Trees." *Reading Medieval Studies* (U. of Reading, England), 2 (1976), 28-44.

445. David, Alfred. "An Iconography of Noses: Directions in the History of a Physical Stereotype." In *Mapping the Cosmos*. Eds. Jane Chance and R. S. Wells, Jr. Houston, TX: Rice U P, 1985.

446. Economou, George D. "Chaucer's Use of the Bird in the Cage Image in The *Canterbury Tales*. "*PQ* 54 (1975), 679-84.

447. Fleming, John V. "Chaucer's Ascetical Images." *Christianity and Literature* 28, (1979), 19-26.

448. Gillmeister, Heiner. *Chaucer's Conversion: Allegorical Thought in Medieval Literature*. Aspekt der englischen Geistes- und Kulturgeschichte 2. New York, 1984.

449. Green, Richard H. "Classical Fables and English Poetry in the Fourteenth Century." In *Critical Approaches to Medieval Literature*. Ed. Dorothy Bethurum. New York: Columbia U P, 1960.

450. Gross, Laila. "The Heart: Chaucer's Concretization of Emotions." *McNR* 21 (1974-75), 89-102.

451. Heffernan, Carol Falvo. "Wells and Streams in Three Chaucerian Gardens." *PLL* 15 (1979), 339-57.

452. Hermann, John P, and John J. Burke, Jr., eds. *Signs and Symbols in Chaucer's Poetry*. University: U of Alabama P, 1981.

453. Huppé, Bernard F., and D. W. Robertson, Jr. *Fruyt and Chaf: Studies in Chaucer's Allegories*. Princeton: Princeton U P, 1963.

454. Lewis, C. S. *The Allegory of Love* (1936). Oxford: Galaxy Books, 1958.

455. Madeleva, Sister Mary. *A Lost Language and Other Essays on Chaucer*. New York: Sheed, 1951.

456. Richardson, Janette. *Blameth Nat Me: A Study of the Imagery in Chaucer's Fabliaux*. The Hague: Mouton, 1970.

457. Robertson, D. W., Jr. "The Doctrine of Charity in Medieval Literary Gardens." *Speculum* 26 (1951), 24-49.

458. Rowland, Beryl. *Blind Beasts: Chaucer's Animal World*. Kent, OH: Kent State U P, 1971.

459. ———. "Chaucer's Imagery." In *Companion to Chaucer Studies*. Ed. Beryl Rowland. rev. ed. New York: Oxford U P, 1979.

460. Schuman, Samuel. "The Circle of Nature: Patterns of Imagery in Chaucer's *Troilus and Criseyde*." *ChauR* 10 (1975), 99- 112.

461. Twycross, Meg. *The Medieval Anadyomene: A Study in Chaucer's Mythography*. Oxford: Blackwell, 1972.

462. Windeatt, Barry A. "Gesture in Chaucer." *M&H* 9 (1978), 143-61.

463. Wurtele, Douglas. "Some Uses of Physiognomical Lore in Chaucer's Canterbury Tales." *ChauR* 17 (1982), 130-41.

See also 197, 304, 313, 329, 363, 487, 496, 500, 543, 571, 634, 705, 737, 842, 906, 1057, 1070, 1082, 1084, 1117, 1166, 1274, 1279-91, 1338, 1489, 1519, 1573.

ICONOGRAPHY, ILLUSTRATIONS, MUSIC

464. Chamberlain, David. "Musical Signs and Symbols in *Chaucer: Convention and Originality.* " In *Signs and Symbols in Chaucer's Poetry*. Eds. John P. Hermann and John J. Burke, Jr. U of Alabama Press, 1981.

465. Fisher, John H. "Chaucer's Horses." *SAQ* 60 (1961), 71- 80.

466. ———. "The Intended Illustrations in MS. Corpus Christi 61 of Chaucer's *Troylus and Criseyde*." In *Medieval Studies in Honor of Lillian Herlands Hornstein*. Eds. J. B. Bessinger and R. Raymo. New York: New York U P, 1977.

467. Fleming, John V. "Chaucer and the Visual Arts of His Time." In *New Perspectives on Chaucer Criticism*. Ed. Donald M. Rose. Norman, OK: Pilgrim, 1981.

468. Galway, Margaret. "The *Troilus* Frontispiece." *MLR* 44 (1949), 161-77.

469. Hussey, Maurice, comp. *Chaucer's World: A Pictorial Companion*. Cambridge: Cambridge U P, 1967. (Pictures in the fields of astrology, architecture, medicine, mythology, art and alchemy related to *CT*.)

470. Kendrick, Laura. "The *Troilus* Frontispiece and the Dramatization of Chaucer's *Troilus*." *ChauR* 22 (1987), 81-93.

471. McGregor, James H. "The Iconography of Chaucer in Hoccleve's *De Regimine Principum* and in the *Troilus* Frontispiece." *ChauR* 11 (1977), 338-50.

472. Pearsall, Derek. "The *Troilus* Frontispiece and Chaucer's Audience." *YES* 7 (1977), 68-74.

473. Rowland, Beryl. "The Horse and Rider Figure in Chaucer's Works." *UTQ* 35 (1966), 246-59.

474. Salter, Elizabeth, and Derek Pearsall. "Pictorial Illustration of Late Medieval Poetic Texts: The Role of the Frontispiece or Prefatory Picture." In *Medieval Iconography and Narrative: A Symposium*. Eds. F. G. Anderson, Esther Nyholm, Marianne Powell, and F. T. Stubkjaer. Odense: Odense U P, 1980.

475. Seymour, Michael. "Manuscript Portraits of Chaucer and Hoccleve." *Burlington Magazine* 124 (1982), 618-23.

476. Stevens, Martin. "The Ellesmere Miniatures as Illustrations of Chaucer's *Canterbury Tales*." *SIcon* 7-8 (1981- 82), 113-34.

477. Wilkins, Nigel. *Music in the Age of Chaucer*. Cambridge: Brewer, 1979.

478. ———. *Chaucer Songs*. Cambridge: Brewer, 1980. Performing ed. set to 14th-century French music.
See also 244, 367, 675, 1127, 1543, 1558, 1562.

VARIOUS THEMES

479. Joseph, Gerhard. "Chaucerian 'Game'—'Ernest' and the 'Argument of Herbergage' in the *Canterbury Tales*." *ChauR* 5 (1970), 83-96.

480. Klene, Jean, C.S.C. "Chaucer's Contribution to a Popular Topos: The World Upside-Down." *Viator* 11 (1979), 321-34.

481. Olson, Glending. *Literature as Recreation in the Later Middle Ages*. Ithaca, NY: Cornell U P, 1982.

482. Orme, Nicholas. "Chaucer and Education." *ChauR* 16 (1981), 38-59.
See also 656.

CANTERBURY TALES—General

483. Blake, N. F. "Aspects of Syntax and Lexis in the *Canterbury Tales*." *RCEI* 7 (1983), 1-20.

484. Bowers, John M. "*The Tale of Beryn* and *The Siege of Thebes*: Alternative Ideas of *The Canterbury Tales*." *SAC* 7 (1985), 23-50.

485. Haskell, Ann S. "The Golden Ambiguity of the *Canterbury Tales*." *Erasmus Review* 1 (1979), 1-9.

486. Howard, Donald R. *The Idea of the Canterbury Tales*. Berkeley: U of California P, 1976.

487. Kolve, V. A. *Chaucer and the Imagery of Narrative: The First Five Canterbury Tales*. Stanford, CA: Stanford U P, 1984.

488. Pearsall, Derek. *The Canterbury Tales*. London: Allen and Unwin, 1985.

489. Roney, Lois. "The Theme of Protagonist's Intention Versus Actual Outcome in the *Canterbury Tales*." *ES* 64 (1983), 193-200.

490. Rudat, Wolfgang E. H. "The *Canterbury Tales*: Anxiety Release and Wish Fulfillment." *AI* 35 (1978), 407-18.

491. Ruggiers, Paul G. *The Art of the Canterbury Tales*. Madison: U of Wisconsin P, 1965.

492. Traversi, Derek. *The Canterbury Tales: A Reading*. Newark: U of Delaware P, 1983.

493. Whittock, Trevor. *A Reading of the Canterbury Tales*. Cambridge: Cambridge U P, 1968.
See also 44, 46, 48, 61, 65, 66, 67, 71, 170, 300, 337, 350, 426, 434, 476, 479.

CT—Moral Vision

494. Bartholomew, Barbara. *Fortuna and Natura: A Reading of Three Chaucer Narratives*. The Hague: Mouton, 1966.

495. Deligiorgis, Stavros. "Poetics of Anagogy for Chaucer: *The Canterbury Tales*." In *Geoffrey Chaucer: A Collection of Original Articles*. Ed. George D. Economou. New York: McGraw Hill, 1976.

496. Justman, Stewart. "Literal and Symbolic in the *Canterbury Tales*." *ChauR* 14 (1980), 199-214.

497. Haines, R. Michael. "Fortune, Nature, and Grace in Fragment C." *ChauR* 10 (1976), 220-35.

498. Hanning, Robert W. "The Theme of Art and Life in Chaucer's Poetry." In *Geoffrey Chaucer: A Collection of Original Articles*. Ed. George D. Economou. New York: McGraw Hill, 1976.

499. Harrington, Norman T. "Experience, Art, and

the Framing of the *Canterbury Tales.*" *ChauR* 10 (1976), 187-200.

500. Miller, Robert P. "Allegory in the *Canterbury Tales.*" In *Companion to Chaucer Studies.* Ed. Beryl Rowland. rev. ed. New York: Oxford U P, 1979.

501. Pazdziora, Marian. "The Sapiential Aspect of *The Canterbury Tales.*" *KN* 27 (1980), 413-26.

502. Peck, Russell A. "Biblical Interpretation: St. Paul and the *Canterbury Tales.*" In *Chaucer and Scriptural Tradition.* Ed. David Lyle Jeffrey. Ottawa: U of Ottawa P, 1984.

503. Quinn, Esther C. "Religion in Chaucer's *Canterbury Tales*: A Study in Language and Structure." In *Geoffrey Chaucer: A Collection of Original Articles.* Ed. George D. Economou. New York: McGraw Hill, 1976.

504. Rudat, Wolfgang E. H. "Heresy and Springtime Ritual: Biblical and Classical Allusions in the *Canterbury Tales.*" *RBPH* 54 (1976), 823-36.

505. ———. "Anxiety Release and Wish Fulfillment." *AI* 35 (1978), 407-18.

506. Shaw, Judith. "Wrath in the Canterbury Pilgrims." *ELN* 21:3 (1984), 7-10.

507. Shikii, Kumiko. "A Religious Approach to *The Canterbury Tales.*" *Sella* (March 10, 1980), 28-32.

508. Stugrin, Michael. "Ricardian Poetics and Late Medieval Cultural Pluriformity: The Significance of Pathos in the *Canterbury Tales.*" *ChauR* 15 (1981), 155-67.

509. Thundy, Zacharias. "Chaucer's Quest for Wisdom in *The Canterbury Tales.*" *NM* 77 (1976), 582-98.

510. Woo, Constance, and William Matthews. "The Spiritual Purpose of the Canterbury Tales." *Comitatus* 1 (1970), 85-109.

See also 526.

CT—Evolution, Order

511. Benson, Larry D. "The Order of *The Canterbury Tales.*" *SAC* 3 (1981), 77-120.

512. Blake, N. F. "Critics, Criticism, and the Order to the *Canterbury Tales.*" *Archiv* 218 (1981), 47-58.

513. ———. *The Textual Tradition of the Canterbury Tales.* London: Arnold, 1985.

514. ———. "The Debate on the Order of the Canterbury Tales." *RCEI* 10 (1985), 31-42.

515. Dempster, Germaine. "The Fifteenth-Century Editions of the *Canterbury Tales* and the Problem of Tale Order." *PMLA* 64 (1949), 1123-42.

516. Fisher, John H. "Chaucer's Last Revision of the *Canterbury Tales.*" *MLR* 67 (1972), 241-51.

517. Furnivall, F. J. A. *A Temporary Preface to the Chaucer Society's Six-Text Edition of Chaucer's Canterbury Tales: Part I, Attempting to Show the Right Order of the Tales,*

and the Days and Stages of the Pilgrimage. Chaucer Society, 2nd Series 3, London, 1868.

518. Keiser, George R. "In Defense of the Bradshaw Shift." *ChauR* 12 (1978), 191-201.

519. Lawrence, W. W. *Chaucer and the Canterbury Tales.* New York: Columbia U P, 1950.

520. Owen, Charles A., Jr. *Pilgrimage and Story-Telling in the Canterbury Tales: The Dialectic of "Ernest" and "Game".* Norman: U of Oklahoma P, 1977.

521. ———. "The Alternative Reading of *The Canterbury Tales*: Chaucer's Text and the Early Manuscripts." *PMLA* 97 (1982), 237-50.

522. Pratt, Robert A. "The Order of the *Canterbury Tales.*" *PMLA* 66 (1951), 1141-67.

523. Siegel, Marsha. "What the Debate Is and Why It Founders in Fragment A of the *Canterbury Tales.*" *SP* 82 (1985), 1-24.

524. Tatlock, J. S P. "The *Canterbury Tales* in 1400." *PMLA* 50 (1935), 100-39.

CT—Structure

525. Allen, Judson Boyce, and Theresa Anne Moritz. *A Distinction of Stories: The Medieval Unity of Chaucer's Fair Chain of Narratives for Canterbury.* Columbus: Ohio State U P, 1981.

526. Baldwin, Ralph. *The Unity of the Canterbury Tales.* Anglistica 5. Copenhagen: Rosenkilde & Bagger, 1955.

527. Bloomfield, Morton. "*The Canterbury Tales* as Framed Narratives." *LeedsSE,* n.s. 14 (1983), 44-56.

528. Clawson, W. H. "The Framework of the *Canterbury Tales.*" *UTQ* 20 (1951), 137-54.

529. Cooper, Helen. *The Structure of the Canterbury Tales.* London: Duckworth, 1983.

530. Dean, James. "Dismantling the Canterbury Book." *PMLA* 100 (1984), 746-62.

531. Fisher, John H. "The Three Styles of Fragment I of the *Canterbury Tales.*" *ChauR* 8 (1973), 119-27.

532. Gittes, Katharine Slater. "The *Canterbury Tales* and the Arabic Frame Tradition." *PMLA* 98 (1983), 237-51.

533. Hinton, Norman D. "*The Canterbury Tales* as *Compilatio.*" In *Proceedings of the Illinois Medieval Association* 1. Eds. Roberta Bosse, et al. Macomb, IL: Western Illinois University, 1984.

534. Kirkpatrick, Robin. "The Wake of the *Commedia*: Chaucer's *Canterbury Tales* and Boccaccio's *Decameron*." In *Chaucer and the Italian Trecento.* Ed. Piero Boitani. Cambridge: Cambridge U P, 1983.

535. Lindahl, Carl. "The Festive Form of the *Canterbury Tales.*" *ELH* 52 (1985), 531-74.

536. Lumiansky, Robert M. *Of Sundry Folk: The Dramatic Principle of the Canterbury Tales.* Austin: U of Texas P, 1955.

537. McGerr, Rosemarie Potz. "Retraction and Memory: Retrospective Structure in the *Canterbury Tales*." *CL* 37 (1985), 97-113.

538. Olson, Glending. "Chaucer, Dante, and the Structure of Fragment VIII (G) of the *Canterbury Tales*." *ChauR* 16 (1982), 222- 36.

539. ———. "The Terrain of Chaucer's Sittingbourne." *SAC* 6 (1984), 103-19.

540. Owen, Charles A., Jr. "The Design of the *Canterbury Tales*." In *Companion to Chaucer Studies*. Ed. Beryl Rowland. rev. ed. New York: Oxford U P, 1979.

541. Pison, Thomas. "Liminality in *The Canterbury Tales*." *Genre* 10 (1977), 157-71.

542. Scheps, Walter. "'Up roos oure Hoost, and was oure aller cok': Harry Bailly's Tale-Telling Competition." *ChauR* 10 (1975), 113-28.

543. Thompson, Charlotte. "Cosmic Allegory and Cosmic Error in the Frame of *The Canterbury Tales*." *PCP* 18 (1983), 77-83.

544. Wasserman, J. N. "The Ideal and the Actual: The Philosophical Unity of *Canterbury Tales*. MS. Group III." *Allegorica* 7 (1982), 65-99.

See also 795, 1124, 1185.

CT—Genre, Style

545. Benson, C. David. "Their Telling Difference: Chaucer the Pilgrim and His Two Contrasting Tales." *ChauR* 18 (1983), 61- 76.

546. Boyd, Heather. "Fragment A of the *Canterbury Tales*: Character, Figure, and Trope." *ESA* 26 (1983), 77-97.

547. Davis, R. Evan. "The Pendant in the Chaucer Portraits." *ChauR* 17 (1982), 193-95.

548. Diekstra, F. "Chaucer's Way with His Sources: Accident into Substance and Substance into Accident." *ES* 62 (1981), 215- 36.

549. Freed, E. R. "'Whoso Shal Telle a Tale'—Narrative Voices and Personae in Chaucer's *Canterbury Tales* and *Sir Gawain and the Green Knight*." *UMS* 2 (1985, Pretoria), 80-94.

550. Frost, William. "What is a Canterbury Tale?" *WHR* 27 (1974), 39-59.

551. Hanning, Robert W. "Roasting a Friar, Mis-taking a Wife, and Other Acts of Textual Harassment in Chaucer's *Canterbury Tales*." *SAC* 7 (1985), 3-21.

552. Hoy, Michael, and Michael Stevens. *Chaucer's Major Tales*. London: Norton Bailey, 1970.

553. Knox, Norman. "The Satiric Pattern of the *Canterbury Tales*." In *Six Satirists*. Eds. A. F. Sochatoff, et al. Pittsburgh, PA: Carnegie Institute of Technology, 1966.

554. Lawler, Traugott. *The One and the Many in The Canterbury Tales*. Hamden, CT: Archon, 1980.

555. Leicester, H. Marshall, Jr. "The Art of Impersonation: A General Prologue to the *Canterbury Tales*." *PMLA* 95 (1980), 8-22.

556. Mandel, Jerome. "Other Voices in the *Canterbury Tales*." *Criticism* 19 (1977), 338-49.

557. Olson, Glending. "Rhetorical Circumstances and the Canterbury Storytelling." *SAC*, Proceedings 1 (1984), 211-18.

558. Pison, Thomas. "Liminality in the *Canterbury Tales*." *Genre* 10 (1977), 157-71.

559. Ramsey, Vance. "Modes of Irony in the Canterbury Tales." In *Companion to Chaucer Studies*. Ed. Beryl Rowland. rev. ed. New York: Oxford U P, 1979.

560. Smallwood, T. M. "Chaucer's Distinctive Digressions." *SP* 82 (1985), 437-49.

561. Smith, Walter R. "Geoffrey Chaucer, Dramatist." *Interpretations* 1 (1968), 1-10.

562. Strohm, Paul. "Some Generic Distinctions in the *Canterbury Tales*." *MP* 68 (1971), 321-28.

See also 166, 299, 531, 601, 614, 773.

CT—Fabliaux, Romances

563. Brewer, Derek. "The Fabliaux." In *Companion to Chaucer Studies*. Ed. Beryl Rowland. rev. ed. New York: Oxford U P, 1979.

564. Cooke, Thomas D. *The Old French and Chaucerian Fabliaux: A Study of Their Comic Climax*. Columbia: U of Missouri P, 1978.

565. Jordan, Robert M. "Chaucerian Romance?" *YFS* 51 (1974), 223-34.

566. ———. "The Question of Genre: Five Chaucerian Romances." In *Chaucer at Albany*. Ed. Rossell Hope Robbins. New York: Franklin, 1975.

567. Koretsky, Allen C. "The Heroes of Chaucer's Romances." *AnM* 17 (1976), 22-47.

568. Robbins, Rossell Hope. "The English Fabliaux: Before and After Chaucer." *Moderna Sprak* 64 (1970, Sweden), 231-45.

569. Rowland, Beryl. "What Chaucer Did to the Fabliaux." *SN* 51 (1979), 205-13.

570. Severs, J. Burke. "The Tales of Romance." In *Companion to Chaucer Studies*. Ed. Beryl Rowland. rev. ed. New York: Oxford U P, 1979.

571. Wentersdorf, Karl P. "The Symbolic Significance of *figurae scatologicae* in Gothic Manuscripts." In *Word, Picture, and Spectacle: Papers by Karl P. Wentersdorf, Roger Ellis, Clifford Davidson, and R. W. Hanning*. Ed. Clifford Davidson. Kalamazoo: Western Michigan U Medieval Institute Publications, 1984.

See also 191, 193, 194, 267, 456, 680, 685, 708, 820, 1021, 1022, 1217, 1234.

CT—Marriage Argument, Feminism

572. Berggren, Ruth. "Who *Really* is the Advocate of Equality in the Marriage Group?" *MSE* 6 (1977), 25-36.

573. Cooper, Helen. "The Girl with Two Lovers: Four Canterbury Tales." *Medieval Studies for J. A. W. Bennett.* Ed. P. L. Heyworth. Oxford: Clarendon, 1981.

574. Ginsberg, Warren. "The Lineaments of Desire: Wish- Fulfillment in Chaucer's Marriage Group." *Criticism* 25 (1983), 197-210.

575. Hodge, James L. "The Marriage Group: Precarious Equilibrium." *ES* 46 (1965), 289-300.

576. Kaske, R. E. "Chaucer's Marriage Group." In *Chaucer the Love Poet.* Eds. Jerome Mitchell and William Provost. Athens: U of Georgia P, 1973.

577. Kittredge, G. L. "Chaucer's Discussion of Marriage." *MP* 9 (1912), 435-67.

578. Mandel, Jerome. "Courtly Love in the *Canterbury Tales.*" *ChauR* 19 (1985), 277-89.

579. Middleton, Anne. "War by Other Means: Marriage and Chivalry in Chaucer." *SAC,* Proceedings 1, 1984, 119-33.

580. Olson, Clair C. "The Interlude of the Marriage Group in the *Canterbury Tales.*" In *Chaucer and Middle English Studies in Honour of Rossell Hope Robbins.* Ed. Beryl Rowland. London: Unwin, 1974.

581. Reiss, Edmund. "Chaucer's deerne love and the Medieval View of Secrecy in Love." In *Chaucerian Problems and Perspectives: Essays Presented to Paul E. Beichner, C. S. C.* Eds. Edward Vasta and Zacharias P. Thundy. Notre Dame, IN: U of Notre Dame P, 1979.

582. Richmond, Velma Bourgeois. "'Patience in Adversitee': Chaucer's Presentation of Marriage." *Viator* 10 (1979), 323-54.

583. Surges, Robert S. "*The Canterbury Tales*' Women Narrators: Three Traditions of Female Authority." *MLS* 13 (1983), 41-51.

584. Takimoto, Jiro. "Re-examination of the marriage group in the *Canterbury Tales.*" *Baika Review* 12 (1979), 1-24.

See also 402-420, 446, 938, 939.

CT—Pilgrimage Motif

585. Engelhardt, George J. "The Ecclesiastical Pilgrims of the *Canterbury Tales:* A Study in Ethology." *MS* 37 (1975), 287- 315.

586. Hall, Donald J. *English Medieval Pilgrimage.* London: Routledge, 1965.

587. Henisch, Briget A. *Medieval Armchair Travels.* State College, PA: Carnation P, 1967.

588. Holley, Linda Tarte. "Chaucer, T. S. Eliot, and the Regenerative Pilgrimage." *Studies in Medievalism* 2 (1982), 19-33.

589. Howard, Donald R. *Writers and Pilgrims: Medieval Pilgrimage Narratives and Their Posterity.* Berkeley: U of California P, 1980.

590. Knapp, Daniel. "The Relyk of a Saint: A Gloss on Chaucer's Pilgrimage." *ELH* 39 (1972), 1-26.

591. Kohl, Stephan. "Chaucer's Pilgrims in Fifteenth-Century Literature." *FCS* 7 (1982), 221-36.

592. Littlehales, H. *Some Notes on the Road from London to Canterbury in the Middle Ages.* Chaucer Soc., 2nd series, 30. London, 1898.

593. Reiss, Edmund. "The Pilgrimage Narrative and the *Canterbury Tales.*" *SP* 67 (1970), 295-305.

594. Thundy, Zacharias P. "Significance of Pilgrimage in Chaucer's *Canterbury Tales.*" *LHY* 20 (1979), 64-77.

595. Zacher, Christian. *Curiosity and Pilgrimage.* Baltimore, MD: John's Hopkins U P, 1976.

See also 156.

CT—Number and Names of the Pilgrims

596. Brosnahan, Leger. "The Authenticity of 'And Preestes Thre'." *ChauR* 16 (1982), 293-310.

597. Eckhardt, Caroline D. "The Number of Chaucer's Pilgrims: A Review and Reappraisal." *YES* 5 (1975), 1-18.

598. Eliason, Norman. "Personal Names in the *Canterbury Tales.*" *Names* 21 (1973), 137-52.

599. Rogers, P. Burwell. "The Names of the Canterbury Pilgrims." *Names* 16 (1968), 339-46.

See also 143, 613, 615, 871, 1052.

CT—Harry Bailly

600. Cowgill, Bruce Kent. "'By cor*pus dominus*': Harry Bailey as False Spiritual Guide." *JMRS* 15 (1985), 157-81.

601. Gaylord, Alan T. "*Sentence* and *Solaas* in Fragment VII of the *Canterbury Tales:* Harry Bailly as Horseback Editor." *PMLA* 82 (1967), 226-35.

602. Higgs, Elton D. "'What Man Artow?' Harry Bailly and the 'Elvysh' Chaucer." *MHLS* 2 (1979), 28-43.

603. Keen, William P. "'To Doon Ye Ese': A Study of the Host in the *General Prologue* of the *Canterbury Tales.*" *Topic* 17 (1969), 5-18.

604. Leitch, L. M. "Sentence and Solaas: The Function of the Host in the *Canterbury Tales.*" *ChauR* 17 (1982), 5-20.

605. Page, Barbara. "Concerning the Host." *ChauR* 4 (1970), 1-13.

606. Pichaske, David R., and Laura Sweetland. "Chaucer on the Medieval Monarchy: Harry Bailey in the *Canterbury Tales.*" *ChauR* 11 (1977), 179-200.

607. Richardson, Cynthia C. "The Function of the Host in the *Canterbury Tales*." *TSLL* 12 (1970), 325-44.
See also 542, 973, 977.

CT—General Prologue

608. Badendyck, J. Lawrence. "Chaucer's Portrait Technique and the Dream Vision Tradition." *English Record* 21 (1970), 113- 25.
609. Bowden, Muriel. *A Commentary on the General Prologue to the Canterbury Tales.* New York: Macmillan, 1948.
610. Boyce, Benjamin. *The Theophrastan Character in England to 1642.* Cambridge, MA: Harvard U P, 1947.
611. Cunningham, J. V. "The Literary Form of the Prologue to the *Canterbury Tales*." *MP* 49 (1952), 172-81.
612. Eberle, Patricia J. "Commercial Language and the Commercial Outlook in the *General Prologue*." *ChauR* 18 (1982), 161-74.
613. Garbáty, Thomas. "Chaucer's Guildsmen and Their Fraternity." *JEGP* 59 (1960), 691-709.
614. Gellrich, J. M. "Interpreting the 'Naked Text' in the 'General Prologue' to the *Canterbury Tales*." In *The Idea of the Book in the Middle Ages.* Ithaca, NY: Cornell U P, 1985.
615. Goodall, Peter. "Chaucer's 'Burgesses' and the Aldermen of London." *MAE* 50 (1981), 284-91.
616. Green, Eugene. "The Voices of the Pilgrims in the General Prologue to the *Canterbury Tales*." *Style* 9 (1975), 55-81.
617. Higdon, David L. "The Diverse Melodies in Chaucer's 'General Prologue'." *Criticism* 14 (1972), 97-108.
618. Higgs, Elton D. "The Old Order and the 'Newe World' in the General Prologue to the *Canterbury Tales*." *HLQ* 45 (1982), 155-73.
619. Hoffman, Arthur. "Chaucer's Prologue: Two Voices." *ELH* (1954), 1-16.
620. Kirby, Thomas A. "The General Prologue." In *Companion to Chaucer Studies.* Ed. Beryl Rowland. rev. ed. New York: Oxford U P, 1979.
621. Mann, Jill. *Chaucer and Medieval Estates Satire: The Literature of Social Classes and the General Prologue.* Cambridge: Cambridge U P, 1973.
622. Martin, Loy D. "History and Form in the General Prologue to the *Canterbury Tales*." *ELH* 45 (1978), 1-17.
623. Morgan, Gerald. "The Universality of the Portraits in the *General Prologue* to the *Canterbury Tales*." *ES* 58 (1977), 481- 93.
624. ———. "The Design of the General Prologue to the *Canterbury Tales*." *ES* 59 (1978), 481-98.

625. ———. "Rhetorical Perspectives in the General Prologue to the *Canterbury Tales*." *ES* 62 (1981), 411-22.
626. Nitzche, Jane Chance. "Creation in Genesis and Nature in Chaucer's *General Prologue* 1-18." *PLL* 14 (1978), 459-64.
627. Owen, Charles A., Jr. "Development of the Art of Portraiture in Chaucer's *General Prologue*." *LeedsSE*, n.s. 14 (1983), 116-33.
628. Sklute, Larry. "Catalogue Form and Catalogue Style in the General Prologue of the *Canterbury Tales*." *SN* 52 (1980), 35- 46.
629. Spraycar, Rudy S. "The Prologue to the 'General Prologue': Chaucer's Statement about Nature in the Opening Lines of the *Canterbury Tales*." *NM* 81 (1980), 142-49.
630. Taylor, Paul B. "The Alchemy of Spring in Chaucer's *General Prologue*." *ChauR* 17 (1982), 1-4.
See also 463.

CT—The Knight and His Tale

631. Anderson, David. "Theban Geneology in the Knight's Tale." *ChauR* 21 (1987), 311-20.
632. Andersen, Wallis May. "*Canterbury Tales* 'Rethors': The Knight." *FCS* 10 (1984), 1-14.
633. Blake, Kathleen A. "Order and the Noble Life in Chaucer's *Knight's Tale*." *MLQ* 34 (1973), 3-19.
634. Boheemen, Christel van. "Chaucer's *Knight's Tale* and the Structure of Myth." *DQR* 9 (1979), 1-27.
635. Brooks, Douglas, and Alastair Fowler. "The Meaning of Chaucer's *Knight's Tale*." *MAE* 39 (1970), 123-46.
636. Chaskalson, L. "'What is this world? What asketh men to Have?': Examined Life in *The Knight's Tale*." *UMS* 1 (1983, Pretoria), 90-118.
637. Cowgill, Bruce Kent. "*The Knight's Tale* and the Hundred Years' War." *PQ* 54 (1975), 670-79.
638. Donaldson, E. Talbot. "Arcite's Injury." In *Middle English Studies for Norman Davis.* Eds. Douglas Gray and E. G. Stanley. Oxford: Clarendon P, 1983.
639. Fichte, Joerg O. "Man's Free Will and the Poet's Choice: The Creation of Artistic Order in Chaucer's *Knight's Tale*." *Anglia* 93 (1975), 335-60.
640. Green, Richard Firth. "Arcite at Court." *ELN* 18 (1981), 251-57.
641. Hanning, Robert W. "'The Struggle between Noble Design and Chaos': The Literary Tradition of Chaucer's Knight's Tale." *LittR* 23 (1980), 519-41.
642. Harder, Bernard D. "Fortune's Chain of Love: Chaucer's Irony in Theseus' Marriage Counselling." *UWR* 18 (1984), 47-52.
643. Hatton, Thomas J. "Chaucer's Crusading Knight." *ChauR* 3 (1968), 77-87.

644. Helterman, Jeffrey. "The Dehumanizing Metamorphosis of *The Knight's Tale.*" *ELH* 38 (1971), 493-511.

645. Herzman, Ronald B. "The Paradox of Form: *The Knight's Tale* and Chaucerian Ethics." *PLL* 10 (1974), 339-52.

646. Jones, Terry. *Chaucer's Knight: The Portrait of a Medieval Mercenary.* Baton Rouge: Louisiana State U P, 1980.

647. Justman, Stewart. "'Auctoritee' and the Knight's Tale." *MLQ* 39 (1978), 3-14.

648. Keen, Maurice. "Chaucer's Knight, the English Aristocracy and the Crusade." In *English Court Culture.* Eds. V. J. Scattergood and J. W. Sherborne. New York: St. Martin's P, 1983.

649. Lester, G. A. "Chaucer's Knight and the Medieval Tournament." *Neophil* 46 (1982), 460-68.

650. Luxon, Thomas H. "'Sentence' and 'Solaas': Proverbs and Consolation in the Knight's Tale." *ChauR* 22 (1987), 94-111.

651. McColly, William B. "Chaucer's Yeoman and the Rank of His Knight." *ChauR* 20 (1985), 14-27.

652. Meier, T. K. "Chaucer's Knight as 'Persona': Narration as Control." *English Miscellany* 20 (1969), 11-21.

653. Muscatine, Charles. "Form, Texture, and Meaning in Chaucer's Knight's Tale." *PMLA* 65 (1950), 911-29.

654. Olson, Paul. "Chaucer's Epic Statement and the Political Milieu of the Late Fourteenth Century." *Mediaevalia* 5 (1979), 61-87.

655. Perryman, Judith C. "The 'False Arcite' of Chaucer's Knight's Tale." *Neophil* 68 (1984), 121-33.

656. Reidy, John. "The Education of Chaucer's Duke Theseus." In *The Epic in Medieval Society: Aesthetic and Moral Values.* Ed. Harald Scholler. Tübingen: Niemeyer, 1977.

657. Rudat, Wolfgang H. "Chaucer's Mercury and Arcite: The *Aeneid* and the World of the *Knight's Tale.*" *Neophil* 64 (1980), 307-19.

658. Scheps, Walter. "Chaucer's Duke Theseus and the *Knight's Tale.*" *LeedsSE* n.s. 9 (1976), 19-34.

659. Schweitzer, Edward C. "Fate and Freedom in *The Knight's Tale.*" *SAC* 3 (1981), 13-45.

660. Stroud, Theodore A. "Chaucer's Structural Balancing of *Troilus* and 'Knight's Tale'." *AnM* 21 (1981), 31-45.

661. Tattlebaum, Linda. "Venus' Citole and the Restoration of Harmony in Chaucer's *Knight's Tale.*" *NM* 74 (1973), 649-64.

662. Taylor, Ann M. "Epic Descent in the Knight's Tale." *CF* 30 (1976), 40-56.

663. Turner, Frederick. "A Structuralist Analysis of the *Knight's Tale.*" *ChauR* 8 (1974), 279-96.

664. Van, Thomas. "Theseus and the 'Right Way' of the *Knight's Tale.*" *SLitI* 4 (1971), 83-100.
See also 152, 271, 278, 903.

CT—The Miller and His Tale

665. Ames, Ruth M. "Prototype and Parody in Chaucerian Exegesis." In *The Fourteenth Century* (Acta 4). Eds. P. E. Szarmach and B. S. Levy. Binghamton NY: Center for Medieval and Renaissance Studies, 1977.

666. Beidler, Peter G. "Art and Scatology in the *Miller's Tale.*" *ChauR* 12 (1977), 90-102.

667. Black, Robert. "Chaucer's Allusion to the Sermon on the Mount in the *Miller's Tale.*" *RUO* 55 (1985), 23-32.

668. Boenig, Robert. "The Miller's Bagpipe: A Note on the *Canterbury Tales* A565-566." *ELN* 21 (1983), 1-6.

669. Bowker, Alvin W. "Comic Illusion and Dark Reality in *The Miller's Tale.*" *MLS* 4 (1977), 27-34.

670. Bratcher, James T., and Nicolai A. Von Kreisler. "The Popularity of the *Miller's Tale.*" *SFQ* 35 (1971), 325-35.

671. Cooper, Geoffrey. "'Sely John' in the 'Legende' of the *Miller's Tale.*" *JEGP* 79 (1980), 1-12.

672. Dane, Joseph A. "The Mechanics of Comedy in Chaucer's *Miller's Tale.*" *ChauR* 14 (1980), 215-24.

673. Donaldson, E. Talbot. "Idiom of Popular Poetry in the Miller's Tale." In *Selected Papers from the English Institute* 1941-52. Ed. W. K. Wimsatt, Jr. New York: Columbia U P, 1963.

674. Gallacher, Patrick J. "Perception and Reality in the *Miller's Tale.*" *ChauR* 18 (1983), 38-48.

675. Gellrich, Jesse M. "The Parody of Medieval Music in the *Miller's Tale.*" *JEGP* 73 (1974), 176-88.

676. Goodall, Peter. "*The Reeve's Tale, Le Meunier et les ii Clers* and the *Miller's Tale.*" *Parergon* 27 (1980), 13-16.

677. ———. "The Figure of Absolon in the *Miller's Tale:* Chaucer's most Original Contribution to the Development of a Story." *Parergon* 29 (1981), 33-36.

678. Harwood, Britton J. "The 'Nether Ye' and Its Antithesis: A Structuralist Reading of 'The Miller's Tale'." *AnM* 21 (1981), 5-30.

679. Jennings, Margaret, C.S.J. "Ironic Dancing Absolon in the *Miller's Tale.*" *Florilegium* 5 (1983), 178-88.

680. Jordan, Tracey. "Fairy Tale and Fabliau: Chaucer's *The Miller's Tale.*" *SSF* 21 (1984), 87-93.

681. Hill, Betty. "Chaucer's *The Miller's* and *Reeve's* Tales." *NM* 74 (1973), 665-75.

682. Jambeck, Thomas J. "Characterization and Syntax in the *Miller's Tale.*" *JNT* 5 (1975), 73-85.

683. Jones, George F. "Chaucer and the Medieval Miller." *MLQ* 16 (1955), 3-15.

684. Kiernan, Kevin S. "The Art of the Descending Catalogue, and a Fresh Look at Alisoun." *ChauR* 10 (1975), 1-16.

685. Lewis, Robert E. "The English Fabliau Tradition and Chaucer's 'The Miller's Tale'." *MP* 79 (1982), 241-55.

686. Long, Charles. "The Wife of Bath's Confessions and the Miller's True Story." *Interpretations* 8 (1976), 54-66.

687. Martin, B. K. "The Miller's Tale as Critical Problem and Dirty Joke." In *Studies in Chaucer.* Eds. G.A. Wilkes and A. P. Riemer. U of Sydney, 1981.

688. Miller, Robert P. *The Miller's Tale* as Complaint." *ChauR* 5 (1970), 147-60.

689. Neuss, Paula. "Double Meanings: 1. Double Entendre in *The Miller's Tale.*" *EIC* 24 (1974), 325-40.

690. Revard, Carter. "The Tow on Absalon's Distaff and the Punishment of Lechers in Medieval London." *ELN* 17 (1980), 168-70.

691. Richards, Mary P. "The Miller's Tale: 'By Seinte Note'." *ChauR* 9 (1975), 212-15.

692. Rowland, Beryl. "The Play of the *Miller's Tale:* A Game Within a Game." *ChauR* 5 (1970), 140-46.

693. ———. "Chaucer's Blasphemous Churl: A New Interpretation of the *Miller's Tale.*" In *Chaucer and Middle English Studies in Honour of Rossell Hope Robbins.* Ed. Beryl Rowland. London: Unwin, 1974.

694. Rudat, Wolfgang H. "The Misdirected Kisses in the *Miller's Tale.*" *JEP* 3 (1982), 103-108.

695. Sell, Roger D. "Politeness in Chaucer: Suggestions towards a Methodology for Pragmatic Stylists." *SN* 57 (1985), 175-84.

696. ———. "Tellability and Politeness in T*he Miller's Tale:* First Steps in Literary Pragmatics." *ES* 66 (1985), 446-512.

697. Thro, A. B. "Chaucer's Creative Comedy: A Study of the *Miller's Tale* and the *Shipman's Tale.*" *ChauR* 5 (1970), 97-111.

698. Vaughan, M. F. "Chaucer's Imaginative One-Day Flood." *PQ* 60 (1981), 117-23.

699. Williams, David. "Radical Therapy in the *Miller's Tale.*" *ChauR* 15 (1981), 227-35.

See also 54.

CT—The Reeve and His Tale

700. Brewer, Derek. "The *Reeve's Tale* and the King's Hall, Cambridge." *ChauR* 5 (1970), 311-17.

701. Brown, Peter. "The Confinement of Symkyn: The Function of Space in the *Reeve's Tale.*" *ChauR* 14 (1980), 225-36.

702. Fletcher, Alan J. "Chaucer's Norfolk Reeve." *MAE* 52 (1983), 100-103.

703. Friedman, John B. "A Reading of Chaucer's *Reeve's Tale.*" *ChauR* 2 (1967), 8-19.

704. Grennen, Joseph E. "The Calculating Reeve and His Camera Obscura." *JMRS* 14 (1984), 245-59.

705. Heffernan, Carol Falvo. "A Reconsideration of the Cask Figure in the *Reeve's Prologue.*" *ChauR* 15 (1980), 37-43.

706. Herzman, Ronald B. "The *Reeve's Tale*, Symkyn, and Simon the Magician." *ABR* 33 (1982), 325-33.

707. Lancashire, Ian. "Sexual Innuendo in the *Reeve's Tale.*" *ChauR* 6 (1972), 159-70.

708. Olson, Glending. "The Reeve's Tale as Fabliau." *MLQ* 35 (1974), 219-30.

709. Plummer, John F. "'Hooly Chirches Blood': Simony and Patrimony in Chaucer's Reeve's Tale." *ChauR* 18 (1983), 49-60.

710. Tkacz, Catherine Brown. "Chaucer's Beard-Making." *ChauR* 18 (1983), 127-36.

711. Tolkien, J.R.R. "Chaucer as Philologist: *The Reeve's Tale.*" In *Transactions of the Philological Society,* 1934.

712. Vasta, Edward. "How Chaucer's Reeve Succeeds." *Criticism* 25 (1983), 1-12.

See also 137, 144, 676, 681.

CT—The Cook and His Tale

713. Scattergood, V. J. "Perkyn Revelour and the *Cook's Tale.*" *ChauR* 19 (1984), 14-23.

CT—The Man of Law and His Tale

714. Baugh, Albert C. "Chaucer's Serjeant of the Law and the Year Books." In *Melanges...offerts a Jean Frappier.* Geneva: Droz, 1971.

715. Bestul, Thomas H. "The *Man of Law's Tale* and the Rhetorical Foundations of Chaucerian Pathos." *ChauR* 9 (1975), 216-26.

716. Block, Edward A. "Originality, Controlling Purpose, and Craftsmanship in Chaucer's *Man of Law's Tale.*" *PMLA* 68 (1953), 572-616.

717. Bloomfield, Morton W. "The *Man of Law's Tale:* A Tragedy of Victimization and Christian Comedy." *PMLA* 87 (1972), 384-90.

718. Clark, Susan L., and Julian N. Wasserman. "Exempla in the *Man of Law's Tale:* The Re-Casting of a Romance." *PAPA* 4 (1978), 11-17.

719. ———. "Constance as Romance and Folk Heroine in Chaucer's *Man of Law's Tale.*" *RUS* 64 (1978), 13-24.

720. Clasby, Eugene. "Chaucer's Constance: Womanly Virtue and the Heroic Life." *ChauR* 13 (1979), 221-33.

721. Clogan, Paul M. "The Narrative Style of the *Man of Law's Tale.*" *M&H* 8 (1977), 217-33.

722. Culver, T. D. "The Imposition of Order: A Measure of Art in the *Man of Law's Tale.*" *YES* 2 (1972), 13-20.

723. Delany, Sheila. "Womanliness in the *Man of Law's Tale.*" *ChauR* 9 (1974), 63-72.

724. Delasanta, Rodney. "And of Great Reverence: Chaucer's Man of Law." *ChauR* 5 (1971), 288-310.

725. Farrell, Robert T. "Chaucer's Man of Law and His Tale: the Eccentric Design." In *J. R. R. Tolkien: Essays in Memoriam.* Eds. Mary Salu and Robert T. Farrell. Ithaca, NY: Cornell U P, 1979.

726. Finnegan, Robert Emmett. "The Man of Law, His Tale, and the Pilgrims." *NM* 77 (1976), 227-40.

727. Grennen, Joseph E. "Chaucer's Man of Law and the Constancy of Justice." *JEGP* 84 (1985), 498-514.

728. Hamilton, Marie P. "The Dramatic Suitability of *The Man of Law's Tale.*" In *Studies in Language and Literature in Honour of Margaret Schlauch.* Eds. M. Brahmer et al. Warsaw: Panstwowe, 1966.

729. Harty, Kevin J. "The Tale and Its Teller: The Case of Chaucer's Man of Law." *ABR* 34 (1983), 361-71.

730. Johnson, William C., Jr. "The *Man of Law's Tale:* Aesthetics and Christianity in Chaucer." *ChauR* 16 (1982), 201-21.

731. Lewis, Robert E. "Chaucer's Artistic Use of Pope Innocent III's *De Miseria Humanae Conditionis* in the *Man of Law's Tale.*" *PMLA* 81 (1966), 485-92.

732. ———. "Glosses to the *Man of Law's Tale* from Pope Innocent III's *De Miseria Humanae Conditionis.*" *SP* 64 (1967), 1-16.

733. Loomis, Dorothy Bethurum. "Constance and the Stars." In *Chaucerian Problems and Perspectives: Essays Presented to Paul E. Beichner.* Eds. E. Vasta and Z. P. Thundy. Notre Dame, IN: Notre Dame U P, 1979.

734. McKenna, Isobel. "The Making of a Fourteenth-Century Sergeant of the Law." *RUO* 45 (1975), 244-62.

735. Manning, Stephen. "Chaucer's Constance: Pale and Passive." In *Chaucerian Problems and Perspectives: Essays Presented to Paul E. Beichner.* Ed. E. Vasta and Z. P. Thundy. Notre Dame: Notre Dame U P, 1979.

736. Miller, Robert P. "Constancy Humanized: Trivet's Constance and the Man of Law's Custance." *Costerus* 3 (1975), 49-71.

737. Paull, Michael R. "The Influence of the Saint's Legend Genre in the *Man of Law's Tale.*" *ChauR* 5 (1971), 179-94.

738. Roddy, Kevin. "Mythic Sequence in the Man of Law's Tale." *JMRS* 10 (1980), 1-22.

739. Rowland, Beryl. "The Physician's 'Historial Thyng Notable' and the Man of Law." *ELH* 40 (1973), 165-78.

740. Scheps, Walter. "Chaucer's Man of Law and the Tale of Constance." *PMLA* 89 (1974), 285-95.

741. Schlauch, Margaret. *Constance and Accused Queens.* New York: New York U P, 1927.

742. Theiner, Paul. "The Man of Law Tells His Tale." *SMC* 5 (1975), 173-79.

743. Weissman, Hope Phyllis. "Late Gothic Pathos in the MLT." *JMRS* 9 (1979), 133-53.

744. Wood, Chauncey. "Chaucer's Man of Law as Interpreter." *Traditio* 23 (1967), 149-90.

745. Wurtele, Douglas. "'Proprietas' in Chaucer's Man of Law's Tale." *Neophil* 60 (1976), 577-93.

See also 151, 409.

CT—The Wife of Bath and Her Tale

746. Albertini, Virgil R. "Chaucer's Artistic Accomplishment in Molding the *Wife of Bath's Tale.*" *NwMSCS* 28.4 (1964), 3-16.

747. Axelrod, Steven. "The Wife of Bath and the Clerk." *AnM* 15 (1974), 100-24.

748. Baird-Lange, Lorrayne Y. "Trotula's Fourteenth-Century Reputation, Jankyn's Book and Chaucer's Trot." *SAC* Proceedings 1, (1984), 245-66.

748a. Blake, N.F. "The Wife of Bath and Her Tale." *LeedsSE* 13 (1982), 42-55.

749. Blanch, Robert J. "'Al was this land fulfild of fayerye': The Thematic Employment of Force, Willfulness, and Legal Conventions in Chaucer's *Wife of Bath's Tale.*" *SN* 57 (1985), 41-51.

750. Bolton, W. F. "The Wife of Bath: Narrator as Victim." In *Gender and Literary Voice.* Ed. Janet Todd. New York: Holmes and Meier, 1980.

751. Brown, Eric D. "Transformation and the *Wife of Bath's Tale:* A Jungian Discussion." *ChauR* 10 (1976), 303-16.

752. ———. "Symbols of Transformation: A Specific Archetypal Examination of the *Wife of Bath's Tale.*" *ChauR* 12 (1978), 202-17.

753. Caie, Graham D. "The Significance of the Early Chaucer Manuscript Glosses (with Special Reference to the Wife of Bath's Prologue)." *ChauR* 10 (1976), 350-60.

754. Carruthers, Mary. "The Wife of Bath and the Painting of Lions." *PMLA* 94 (1979), 209-22.

755. ———. "Clerk Jankyn: at hom to bord / With my gossib." *ELN* 23 (1985), 11-20.

756. Cary, Meredith. "Sovereignty and the Old Wife." *PLL* 5 (1969), 375-88.

757. Colmer, Dorothy. "Character and Class in the Wife of Bath's Tale." *JEGP* 72 (1974), 329-39.

758. Cook, James W. "'That She Was Out of Alle Charitee': Point-Counterpoint in the *Wife of Bath's Prologue* and *Tale.*" *ChauR* 13 (1978), 51-65.

759. Delany, Sheila. "Sexual Economics, Chaucer's Wife of Bath and The Book of Margery Kempe." *Minnesota Review,* n.s. 5 (1975), 104-15.

760. Delesanta, Rodney. "Alisoun and the Saved Harlots: A Cozening of Our Expectations." *ChauR* 12 (1978), 218-35.

760a. East, W. G. "By Preeve Which That is Demonstratif." *ChauR* 12 (1977), 78-82.

761. Fischer, Olga C. M. "Gower's *Tale of Florent* and Chaucer's *Wife of Bath's Tale*: A Stylistic Comparison." *ES* 66 (1985), 205-25.

762. Gallacher, Patrick J. "Dame Alice and the Nobility of Pleasure." *Viator* 13 (1982), 275-93.

763. Gerke, Robert S. "Fortitude and Sloth in the *Wife of Bath's Tale* and the *Clerk's Tale*." *PPMRC* 5 (1980), 119-35.

764. Gottfried, Barbara. "Conflict and Relationship, Sovereignty and Survival: Parables of Power in the *Wife of Bath's Prologue*." *ChauR* 19 (1985), 202-24.

765. Hagen, Susan K. "The Wife of Bath, the Lion, and the Critics." In *The Worlds of Medieval Women*. Eds. Constance H. Berman, et al. Morgantown: U of West Virginia P, 1985.

766. Haller, Robert S. "The Wife of Bath and the Three Estates." *AnM* 6 (1965), 47-64.

767. Hamlin, B. F. "Astrology and the Wife of Bath: A Reinterpretation." *ChauR* 9 (1974), 153-65.

768. Harwood, Britton J. "The Wife of Bath and Her Dream of Innocence." *MLQ* 33 (1972), 257-73.

769. Holland, Norman N. "Meaning as Transformation: The Wife of Bath's Tale." *CE* 28 (1967), 279-90.

770. Kernan, Anne. "The Archwife as Eunuch." *ELH* 41 (1974), 1-25.

771. Koban, Charles. "Hearing Chaucer Out: The Art of Persuasion in the *Wife of Bath's Tale*." *ChauR* 5 (1971), 225-39.

772. Levy, Bernard. "The Wife of Bath's Queynte Fantasye." *ChauR* 4 (1970), 106-23.

773. Malvern, Marjorie M. "'Who peyntede the leon, tel me who?': Rhetorical and Didactic Roles Played by an Aesopic Fable in the Wife of Bath's Prologue." *SP* 80 (1983), 238-52.

774. Matthews, William. "The Wife of Bath and All Her Sect." *Viator* 7 (1974), 413-43.

775. Meyer, Robert J. "Chaucer's Tandem Romances: A Generic Approach to the *Wife of Bath's Tale* as Palinode." *ChauR* 18 (1984), 221-38.

776. Miller, Robert P. "The *Wife of Bath's Tale* and Medieval Exempla." *ELH* 32 (1965), 442-56.

777. Murphy, Ann B. "The Process of Personality in Chaucer's *Wife of Bath's Tale*." *CentR* 28 (1984), 204-22.

778. Oberembt, Kenneth J. "Chaucer's Anti-Misogynist Wife of Bath." *ChauR* 10 (1976), 287-302.

779. Palmer, Barbara D. "'To Speke of Wo that Is in Mariage': The Marital Arts in Medieval Literature." In *Human Sexuality in the Middle Ages and Renaissance*. Ed. Douglas Radcliffe-Umstead. Pittsburgh, PA: U of Pittsburgh, Center for Medieval and Renaissance Studies, 1978.

780. Palomo, Dolores, "The Fate of the Wife of Bath's 'Bad Husbands'." *ChauR* 9 (1975), 303-19.

781. Patterson, Lee. "'For the Wyves love of Bathe': Feminine Rhetoric and Poetic Resolution in the *Roman de la Rose* and the *Canterbury Tales*." *Speculum* 58 (1983), 656-95.

782. Pratt, Robert A. "Jankyn's Book of Wikked Wyves: Medieval Antimatrimonial Propaganda in the Universities." *AnM* 3 (1962), 5-27.

783. Quinn, Esther C. "Chaucer's Arthurian Romance." *ChauR* 18 (1984), 211-20.

784. Rhodes, Jewell Parker. "Female Stereotypes in Medieval Literature: Androgyny and the Wife of Bath." *JWSL* 1 (1979), 348-52.

785. Robertson, D. W., Jr., "'And For My Land Thus Hastow Mordred Me?': Land Tenure, the Cloth Industry, and the Wife of Bath." *ChauR* 14 (1980), 403-20.

786. ———. "The Wife of Bath and Midas." *SAC* 6 (1984), 1-20.

787. Sanders, Barry. "Chaucer's Dependence on Sermon Structure in the Wife of Bath's 'Prologue' and 'Tale'." *Studies in Medieval Culture* 4 (1974), 437-45.

788. Sands, Donald B. "The Non-Comic, Non-Tragic Wife: Chaucer's Dame Alys as Sociopath." *ChauR* 12 (1978), 171-82.

789. Schauber, Ellen, and Ellen Spolsky. "The Consolation of Alison: The Speech Acts of the Wife of Bath." *Centrum* 5 (1977), 20-34.

790. Schulenburg, Jane Tibbetts. "Clio's European Daughters: Myopic Modes of Perception.: In *The Prism of Sex: Essays in the Sociology of Knowledge*. Eds. J. A. Sherman and E. T. Beck. U of Wisc. P, 1979.

791. Shapiro, Gloria K. "Dame Alice as Deceptive Narrator." *ChauR* 6 (1971), 130-41.

792. Sheehan, Michael M. "The Wife of Bath and Her Four Sisters: Reflections on a Woman's Life in the Age of Chaucer." *M&H* 13 (1985), 23-42.

793. Shumaker, Wayne. "Alisoun in Wonder-Land: A Study in Chaucer's Mind and Literary Method." *ELH* 18 (1951), 77-89.

794. Singer, Margaret. "The Wife of Bath's Prologue and Tale." In *Studies in Chaucer*. Eds. G. A. Wilkes and A. P. Riemer. Sydney: U of Sydney P, 1981.

795. Szittya, Penn R. "The Green Yeoman as Loathly Lady: The Friar's Parody of the Wife of Bath's Tale." *PMLA* 90 (1975), 386-94.

796. Thundy, Zacharias P. "Matheolus, Chaucer, and the Wife of Bath." In *Chaucerian Problems and Perspectives: Essays Presented to Paul E. Beichner, C.S.C.* Eds. Edward Vasta and Zacharias P. Thundy. Notre Dame IN: U of Notre Dame P, 1979.

797. Verdonk, P. "'Sire Knyght, heer forth ne lith no wey?': A Reading of Chaucer's *The Wife of Bath's Tale*." *Neophil* 60 (1976), 297-308.

798. Weissman, Hope Phyllis. "Why Chaucer's Wife is from Bath." *ChauR* 15 (1980), 11-36.

799. West, Philip. "The Perils of Pauline Theology: The Wife of Bath's Prologue and Tale." *EAS* 8 (1979), 7-16.

800. Williams, Michael E. "Three Metaphors of Criticism and the *Wife of Bath's Tale.*" *ChauR* 20 (1985), 144-57.

801. Wurtele, Douglas. "The Predicament of Chaucer's Wife of Bath: St. Jerome on Virginity." *Florilegium* 5 (1983), 208-36.

See also 152, 420a, 686, 827.

CT—The Friar and His Tale

802. Bloomfield, Morton W. "*The Friar's Tale* as a Liminal Tale." *ChauR* 17 (1983), 286-91.

803. Carruthers, Mary. "Letter and Gloss in the Friar's and Summoner's Tales." *JNT* 2 (1972), 208-14.

804. Hahn, Thomas, and Richard W. Kaeuper. "Text and Context: Chaucer's *Friar's Tale.*" *SAC* 5 (1983), 67-101.

805. Havely, N. R. "Chaucer's Friar and Merchant." *ChauR* 13 (1979), 337-45.

806. ———. "Chaucer, Boccaccio, and the Friars." In *Chaucer and the Italian Trecento.* Ed. Piero Boitani. Cambridge: Cambridge U P, 1983.

807. Hennedy, Hugh L. "The Friar's Summoner's Dilemma." *ChauR* 7 (1971), 213-17.

808. Leicester, H. Marshall, Jr. "'No Vileyns Word': Social Context and Performance in Chaucer's *Friar's Tale.*" *ChauR* 17 (1982), 21-39.

809. Lenaghan, R. T. "The Irony of the *Friar's Tale.*" *ChauR* 7 (1973), 281-94.

810. Richardson, Janette. "Friar and Summoner, The Art of Balance." *ChauR* 9 (1975), 227-36.

See also 121, 822.

CT—The Summoner and His Tale

811. Adams, John F. "The Structure of Irony in the *Summoner's Tale.*" *EIC* 12 (1962), 126-32.

812. Clark, Roy P. "Wit and Witsunday in Chaucer's *Summoner's Tale.*" *AnM* 17 (1976), 48-57.

813. ———. "Doubting Thomas in Chaucer's *Summoner's Tale.*" *ChauR* 11 (1976), 164-78.

814. Haselmayer, L. A. "The Apparitor and Chaucer's Summoner." *Speculum* 12 (1973), 43-57.

815. Fleming, John V. "Anticlerical Satire as Theological Essay: Chaucer's *Summoner's Tale.*" *Thalia* 6 (1983), 5-22.

816. Fleming, Martha H. "'Glosynge is a Glorious Thing, Certyn': A Reconsideration of *The Summoner's Tale.*" In *The Late Middle Ages.* Ed. Peter Cocozzella. Binghamton, NY: Center for Medieval and Renaissance Studies, 1983.

817. Lancashire, Ian. "Moses, Elijah and the Back Parts of God: Satiric Scatology in Chaucer's *Summoner's Tale.*" *Mosaic* 14 (1981), 17-30.

818. Levitan, Alan. "The Parody of Pentecost in Chaucer's *Summoner's Tale.*" *UTQ* 40 (1971), 236-46.

819. McVeigh, Terrence. "Chaucer's Portraits of the Pardoner and Summoner and Wycliff's *Tractatus de Simonia.*" *CF* 29 (1975), 54-58.

820. Pearcy, Roy J. "Structural Models for the Fabliaux and the Summoner's Tale Analogues." *Fabula* 15 (1974), 103-13.

821. Specht, Henrik. "The Beautiful, the Handsome, and the Ugly: Some Aspects of the Art of Character Portrayal in Medieval Literature." *SN* 56 (1984), 129-46.

822. Szittya, Penn R. "The Friar as False Apostle: Antifraternal Exegesis and the *Summoner's Tale.*" *SP* 71 (1974), 19-46.

823. Wentersdorf, Karl P. "The Motif of Exorcism in the *Summoner's Tale.*" *SSF* 17 (1980), 249-54.

824. Zietlow, Paul N. "In Defense of the Summoner." *ChauR* 1 (1966), 4-19.

See also 121, 803, 807, 810, 984.

CT—The Clerk and His Tale

825. Bestul, Thomas H. "True and False Cheere in Chaucer's *Clerk's Tale.*" *JEGP* 82 (1983), 500-14

826. Carruthers, Mary J. "The Lady, the Swineherd, and Chaucer's Clerk." *ChauR* 17 (1983), 221-34.

827. Cherniss, Michael D. "The *Clerk's Tale* and *Envoy,* the Wife of Bath's Purgatory, and the *Merchant's Tale.*" *ChauR* 6 (1972), 235-54.

828. Condren, Edward I. "The Clerk's Tale of Man Tempting God." *Criticism* 26 (1984), 99-114.

829. Dean, James. "Time Past and Time Present in Chaucer's *Clerk's Tale* and Gower's *Confessio Amantis.*" *ELH* 44 (1977), 401-18.

830. Frese, Dolores. "Chaucer's *Clerk's Tale:* The Monsters and the Critics Reconsidered." *ChauR* 8 (1973), 133-46.

831. Gilmartin, Kristine. "Array in the *Clerk's Tale.*" *ChauR* 13 (1979), 234-46.

832. Ginsberg, Warren. "'And Speketh so Pleyn': The *Clerk's Tale* and Its Teller." *Criticism* 20 (1978), 307-23.

833. Hardman, Phillipa. "Chaucer's Tyrants of Lombardy." *RES* 122 (1980), 172-78.

834. Hawkins, Harriett, "The Victim's Side: Chaucer's *Clerk's Tale* and Webster's *Duchess of Malfi.*" *Signs* 1 (1975), 339-61.

835. Grennen, Joseph E. "Science and Sensibility in Chaucer's Clerk," *ChauR* 6 (1971), 81-93.

836. Heffernan, Carol Falvo. "Tyranny and Commune Profit in the *Clerk's Tale.*" *ChauR* 17 (1983), 332-40.

836a. Heninger, S. K. "The Concept of Order in Chaucer's *Clerk's Tale.*" *JEGP* 56 (1957), 282-95.

837. Johnson, Lynn Staley. "The Prince and His People: A Study of the Two Covenants in the *Clerk's Tale.*" *ChauR* 10 (1975), 17-29.

838. Kadish, Emile P., trans. "Petrarch's *Griselda*: An English Translation." *Mediaevalia* 3 (1977), 1-24.

839. Kellogg, Alfred L. "The Evolution of the *Clerk's Tale*. A study in Connotation." In *Chaucer, Langland, Arthur.* Rutgers U P, 1972.

840. Kirkpatrick, Robin. "The Griselda Story in Boccaccio, Petrarch and Chaucer." In *Chaucer and the Italian Trecento.* Ed. Piero Boitani. Cambridge: Cambridge U P, 1983.

841. Knapp, Peggy A. "Knowing the Tropes: Literary Exegesis and Chaucer's Clerk." *Criticism* 27 (1985), 331-45.

842. Krieger, Elliot. "Re-Reading Allegory: *The Clerk's Tale.*" *Paunch* 40-41 (1975), 116-35.

843. Lemos, Brunilda Reichmann. "Some Differences Between Boccaccio's and Chaucer's Tales of Griselda." *Revista Letras* 30 (1981), 7-16.

844. Levy, Bernard S. "*Gentilesse* in Chaucer's *Clerk's* and *Merchant's* Tales." *ChauR* 11 (1977), 306-18.

845. McCall, John P. "The *Clerk's Tale* and the Theme of Obedience." *MLQ* 27 (1966), 260-69.

846. Mann, Jill. "Satisfaction and Payment in Middle English Literature." *SAC* 5 (1983), 17-48.

847. Manning, Stephen. "The Paradox of the Narrator's Styles in Chaucer's *Clerk's Tale.*" *JNT* 15 (1985), 29-42.

848. Middleton, Anne. "The Clerk and His Tale: Some Literary Contexts." *SAC* 2 (1980), 121-50.

849. Morse, Charlotte C. "The Exemplary Griselda." *SAC* 7 (1985), 51-86.

850. Perlman, E. "The Psychological Basis of the *Clerk's Tale.*" *ChauR* 11 (1977), 248-57.

851. Ramsey, Roger. "Clothing Makes a Queen in *The Clerk's Tale.*" *JNT* 7 (1977), 104-15.

852. Rothman, Irving N. "Humility and Obedience in the *Clerk's Tale*, with the Envoy Considered as an Ironic Affirmation." *PLL* 9 (1973), 115-27.

853. Severs, J. Burke. *The Literary Relationships of Chaucer's Clerk's Tale* (1942). Hamden, CT: Archon, 1972.

854. Sledd, James. "The *Clerk's Tale*: The Monsters and the Critics." *MP* 51 (1953), 73-82.

855. Steinmetz, David C. "Late Medieval Nominalism and the *Clerk's Tale.*" ChauR 12 (1977), 38-54.

856. Stepsis, Robert. "*Potentia Absoluta* and the Clerk's Tale." *ChauR* 10 (1975), 129-46.

857. Taylor, Jerome. "Fraunceys Petrak and the Logyk of Chaucer's Clerk." In *Francis Petrarch, Six Centuries Later*: A Symposium. Ed. Aldo Scaglione. Chapel Hill, NC: U of North Carolina P, 1975.

858. Ussery, Huling E. "Fourteenth-Century English Logicians: Possible Models for Chaucer's Clerk." *TSL* 18 (1970), 1-15.

859. Utley, Francis L. "Five Genres in the *Clerk's Tale.*" *ChauR* 6 (1972), 198-228.

860. Wallace, Kristine Gilmartin. "Array as Motif in the *Clerk's Tale.*" *RUS* 62 (1976), 99-110.

861. Wimsatt, James I. "The Blessed Virgin and the Two Coronations of Griselda." *Mediaevalia* 6 (1980), 187-207.

See also 420a, 747, 763.

CT—The Merchant and His Tale

862. Adams, John F. "The Janus Symbolism in the 'Merchant's Tale'." *Studies in Medieval Culture* 4 (1974), 446-51.

863. Annunziata, Anthony. "Tree Paradigms in the *Merchant's Tale.*" *Acta* 4 (1977), 125-35.

864. Beidler, Peter G. "Chaucer's Merchant and the Tale of January." *Costerus* 5 (1972), 1-25.

865. ———. "Chaucer's Merchant's Tale and the *Decameron.*" *Italica* 50 (1973), 266-84.

866. Benson, Donald R. "The Marriage 'Encomium' in the *Merchant's Tale*: A Chaucerian Crux." *ChauR* 14 (1979), 48-60.

867. Besserman, L. L. "Chaucer and the Bible: The Case of the *Merchant's Tale.*" *HUSL* 6 (1978), 10-31.

868. Brown, Emerson, Jr. "The *Merchant's Tale*: Januarie's 'Unlikely Elde'." *NM* 74 (1973), 92-106.

869. ———. "Biblical Women in the Merchant's Tale: Feminism, Antifeminism, and Beyond." *Viator* 5 (1974), 387-412.

870. ———. "Chaucer, the Merchant, and Their Tale: Getting Beyond Old Controversies: Part I." *ChauR* 13 (1978-79), 141-56; Part II, 247-62.

871. ———. "Chaucer and a Proper Name: January in *The Merchant's Tale.*" *Names* 31 (1983), 79-87.

872. Bugge, John. "Damyan's Wanton *Clyket* and an Ironic New *Twiste* to the Merchant's Tale." *AnM* 14 (1973), 53-62.

873. Burger, Douglas A. "Deluding Words in the *Merchant's Tale.*" *ChauR* 12 (1977), 103-10.

874. Burnley, J. D. "The Morality of *The Merchant's Tale.*" *YES* 6 (1976), 16-25.

875. Dolbey, Marcia A. "The Devil in the Garden: Pluto and Proserpine in Chaucer's *Merchant's Tale.*" *NM* 75 (1974), 408-15.

876. Cahn, Kenneth S. "Chaucer's Merchants and the Foreign Exchange: An Introduction to Medieval Finance." *SAC* 2 (1980), 81-119.

877. Frost, Cheryl. "Illusion and Reality: Psychological Truth in Chaucer's Portrait of January." *LiNQ* (James Cook U, No. Queensland), 5 (1976), 37-45.

878. Gates, Barbara T. "'A Temple of False Goddis': Cupidity and Mercantile Values in Chaucer's Fruit Tree Episode." *NM* 77 (1976), 369-75.

879. Grove, Robin. "The *Merchant's Tale*: Seeing, Knowing and Believing." *CR* 18 (1976), 23-38.

880. Kloss, Robert J. "Chaucer's *The Merchant's Tale*: Tender Youth and Stooping Age." *AI* 31 (1974), 65-79.

881. Kossick, S. G. "Geoffrey Chaucer's *The Merchant's Tale*." *Unisa English Studies* 18 (1979), 3-14.

882. Kossick, Shirley. "Love, Sex, and Marriage in the Merchant's and Franklin's Tales." *Communique* 7 (1982), 25-38.

883. Otten, Charlotte F. "Prosperine: *Libratrix Suae Gentis*." *ChauR* 5 (1971), 277-87.

884. Rogers, H. L. "The Tales of the Merchant and the Franklin: Text and Interpretation." In *Studies in Chaucer*. Eds. G. A. Wilkes and A. P. Riemer. Sydney: U of Sydney, 1981.

885. Rudat, W. E. H. "Chaucer's Spring of Comedy: *The Merchant's Tale* and other 'Games' with Augustinian Theology." *AnM* 21 (1981), 111-20.

886. Schleusener, Jay. "The Conduct of the *Merchant's Tale*." *ChauR* 14 (1980), 237-50.

887. Schmidt, Gary D. "The Marriage Irony in the Tales of the Merchant and Franklin." In *Portraits of Marriage in Literature*. Eds. Anne C. Hargrove and Maurine Magliocco. Macomb: Western Illinois U P, 1984.

888. Schroeder, Mary C. "Fantasy in the Merchant's Tale." *Criticism* 12 (1970), 167-79.

889. Schwartz, Robert B. "The Social Character of May Games: A Popular Background for Chaucer's Merchant's Tale." *ZAA* 27 (1979), 43-51.

890. Shores, David L. "The *Merchant's Tale*: Some Lay Observations." *NM* 71 (1970), 119-33.

891. Stevens, Martin. "'And Venus Laugheth': An Interpretation of the *Merchant's Tale*." *ChauR* 7 (1972), 118-31.

892. Tatlock, J. S. P. "Chaucer's *Merchant's Tale*." *MP* 33 (1935), 367-81.

893. Tucker, Edward F. J. "'Parfite Blisses Two': January's Dilemma and the Themes of Temptation and Doublemindedness in MerchT." *ABR* 33 (1982), 172-81.

894. Wentersdorf, Karl P. "Theme and Structure in *The Merchant's Tale*: The Function of the Pluto Episode." *PMLA* 80 (1965), 522-27.

895. Wurtele, Douglas. "Marian Overtones in Chaucer's *Merchant's Tale*." *Proc. of Third Annual Symposium of Ottawa-Carleton Medieval Renaissance Club* 1 (1976), 56-74.

896. ———. "Ironical Resonance in the *Merchant's Tale*." *ChauR* 13 (1978), 66-79.

897. ———. "The Blasphemy of Chaucer's Merchant." *AnN* 21 (1981), 91-110.

See also 805, 827.

CT—The Squire and His Tale

898. Braddy, Haldeen. "The Genre of Chaucer's *Squire's Tale*." *JEGP* 41 (1942), 279-90.

899. DiMarco, Vincent. "Canacee's Magic Ring." *Anglia* 99 (1981), 399-405.

900. Finkelstein (Metlitzki), Dorothee. "The Celestial Origin of Elpheta and Algarsyf in Chaucer's *Squire's Tale*." *EuroAsiatica* 4 (1970), 4-15.

901. Goodman, Jennifer R. "Chaucer's *Squire's Tale* and the Rise of Chivalry." *SAC* 5 (1983), 127-36.

902. Haller, Robert S. "Chaucer's Squire's Tale and the Uses of Rhetoric." *MP* 62 (1965), 285-95.

903. Hatton, Thomas J. "Thematic Relationships between Chaucer's Squire's Portrait and Tale and the Knight's Portrait and Tale." *Studies in Medieval Culture* 4 (1974), 252-58.

904. Kahrl, Stanley J. "Chaucer's *Squire's Tale* and the Decline of Chivalry." *ChauR* 8 (1973), 194-209.

905. Larson, Charles. "*The Squire's Tale*: Chaucer's Evolution from the Dream Vision." *RLV* 43 (1977), 598-607.

906. Meindl, Robert J. "'For Drye as Whit as Chalk': Allegory in Chaucer and Malory." *Studia Mystica* 6 (1983), 45-58.

907. Neville, Marie. "The Function of the *Squire's Tale* in the Canterbury Scheme." *JEGP* 50 (1951), 167-79.

908. Peterson, Joyce E. "The Finished Fragment: A Reassessment of the *Squire's Tale*." *ChauR* 5 (1970), 62-74.

CT - The Franklin and His Tale

909. Bachman, W. Bryant, Jr. "'To Maken Illusioun': The Philosophy of Magic and the Magic of Philosophy in the *Franklin's Tale*." *ChauR* 12 (1977), 55-67.

910. Bleeth, Kenneth A. "The Rocks in the *Franklin's Tale* and Ovid's Medea." *AN&Q* 20 (1982), 130-31.

911. Bloomfield, Morton W. "*The Franklin's Tale*: A Story of Unanswered Questions." In *Acts of Interpretation: Essays . . . in Honor of E. Talbot Donaldson*. Eds. Mary J. Carruthers and Elizabeth D. Kirk. Norman, OK: Pilgrim Books, 1982.

912. Braswell, Mary Flowers. "The Magic of Machinery: A Context for Chaucer's *Franklin's Tale*." *Mosaic* 18 (1985), 101-10.

913. Carruthers, Mary J. "The Gentilesse of Chaucer's Franklin." *Criticism* 23 (1981), 283-300.

914. Clovella, Sister Francis D. "The Speaker of the Wife of Bath Stanza and Envoy." *ChauR* 4 (1970), 267-83.

915. David, Alfred. "Sentimental Comedy in the *Franklin's Tale*." *AnM* 6 (1965), 19-27.

916. Frazier, J. Terry. "The Digression on Marriage in *The Franklin's Tale*." *SAB* 43 (1978), 75-85.

917. Fyler, John M. "Love and Degree in the Franklin's Tale." *ChauR* 21 (1987), 321-37.

918. Hamel, Mary. "The Franklin's Tale and Chrétien de Troyes." *ChauR* 17 (1983), 316-31.

919. Heffernan, Carol Falvo. "The Two Gardens of *The Franklin's Tale*." In *Court and Poet, etc.* Eds. Glyn S. Burgess, et al. Liverpool: Cairns, 1981.

920. Jacobs, Kathryn. "The Marriage Contract of the *Franklin's Tale*: The Remaking of Society." *ChauR* 20 (1985), 132-43.

921. Kee, Kenneth. "Illusion and Reality in Chaucer's *Franklin's Tale*." *ESC* 1 (1975), 1-12.

922. Knight, Stephen. "Rhetoric and Poetry in the *Franklin's Tale*." *ChauR* 4 (1970), 14-30.

923. ———. "Ideology in *The Franklin's Tale*" *Parergon* 28 (1980), 3-31.

924. Lane, Robert. "The *Franklin's Tale*: Of Marriage and Meaning." In *Portraits of Marriage in Literature.* Eds. Anne C. Hargrove and Maurine Magliocco. Macomb: Western Illinois U P, 1984.

925. Lee, Ann Thompson. "'A Woman True and Fair': Chaucer's Portrayal of Dorigen in the *Franklin's Tale*." *ChauR* 19 (1984), 169-78.

926. Luecke, Janemarie. "Dorigen: Marriage Model or Male Fantasy." *JWSL* 1 (1979), 107-21.

927. Luengo, Anthony E. "Magic and Illusion in *The Franklin's Tale*." *JEGP* 77 (1978), 1-16.

928. Magnus, Laury. "The Hem of Philosophy: Free and Bound Motifs in the *Franklin's Tale*." *Assays* 2 (1983), 3-18.

929. Manning, Stephen. "Rhetoric, Game, Morality, and Geoffrey Chaucer." *SAC* 1 (1979), 105-18.

930. Mathewson, Effie Jean. "The Illusion of Morality in *The Franklin's Tale*." *MAE* 52 (1983), 27-37.

931. Miller, Robert P. "Augustinian Wisdom and Eloquence in the F-Fragment of the *Canterbury Tales*." *Mediaevalia* 4 (1978), 245-75.

932. ———. "The Epicurean Homily on Marriage by Chaucer's Franklin." *Mediaevalia* 6 (1980), 151-86.

933. Milosh, Joseph. "Chaucer's Too-Well Told *Franklin's Tale*: A Problem of Characterization." *Wisconsin Studies in Lit.* 5 (1970), 1-11.

934. Morgan, Gerald. "A Defence of Dorigen's Complaint." *MAE* 46 (1977), 77-97.

935. Pearcy, Roy J. "Chaucer's Franklin and the Literary Vavasour." *ChauR* 8 (1973), 33-59.

936. Robertson, D. W., Jr. "Chaucer's Franklin and His Tale." *Costerus* n.s. 1 (1974), 1-26.

937. Rosenberg, Bruce A. "The Bari Widow and the *Franklin's Tale*." *ChauR* 14 (1980), 344-52.

938. Rudat, Wolfgang E. H. "'Aurelius' Quest for Grace: Sexuality and the Marriage Debate in the *Franklin's Tale*." *CEA* 45 (1982), 16-22.

939. ———. "Gentilesse and the Marriage Debate in the *Franklin's Tale*: Chaucer's Squires and the Question of Nobility." *Neophil* 68 (1984), 451-70.

940. Saul, Nigel. "The Social Status of Chaucer's Franklin: A Reconsideration." *MAE* 52 (1983), 10-26.

941. Specht, Henrik. *Chaucer's Franklin in the Canterbury Tales: The Social and Literary Background of a Chaucerian Character.* Publications of the Department of English, U of Copenhagen: Akademisk Forlag, 1981.

942. Storm, Melvin. "Chaucer's Franklin and Distraint of Knighthood." *ChauR* 19 (1984), 162-68.

943. Traversi, Derek. "The Franklin's Tale." In *The Literary Imagination: Studies in Dante, Chaucer, and Shakespeare.* Newark: U of Delaware P, 1982.

944. White, Gertrude M. "The *Franklin's Tale*: Chaucer and the Critics." *PMLA* 89 (1974), 454-62.

See also 152, 278, 882, 884, 887.

CT—The Physician and His Tale

945. Amoils, E. R. "Fruitfulness and Sterility in the *Physician's* and *Pardoner's Tales*." *ESA* 17 (1974), 17-37.

946. Arnold, Richard A. "Chaucer's Physician: The Teller and the Tale." *RUO* 51 (1981), 172-79.

947. Brown, Emerson, Jr. "What is Chaucer Doing with The Physician and His Tale?" *PQ* 60 (1981), 129-49.

948. Crowther, J. D. W. "Chaucer's *Physician's Tale* and Its Saint." *ESC* 8 (1982), 125-37.

949. Delany, Sheila. "Politics and the Paralysis of the Poetic Imagination in the *Physician's Tale*." *SAC* 3 (1981), 47-60.

950. Fichte, Joerg O. "Incident-History-Exemplum-Novella: the Transformation of History in Chaucer's *Physician's Tale*." *Florilegium* 5 (1983), 189-207.

951. Joseph, Gerhard. "The Gifts of Nature, Fortune, and Grace in the *Physician's*, *Pardoner's*, and *Parsons's Tales*." *ChauR* 9 (1975), 237-45.

952. Kempton, Daniel. "The Physician's Tale: The Doctor of Physic's Diplomatic 'Cure'." *ChauR* 19 (1984), 24-38.

953. Kinney, Thomas L. "The Popular Meaning of Chaucer's *Physician's Tale*." *L&P* 28 (1978), 76-84.

954. Mandel, Jerome H. "Governance in the *Physician's Tale*." *ChauR* 10 (1976), 316-25.

955. Middleton, Anne. "The *Physician's Tale* and Love's Martyrs: 'Ensamples Mo Than Ten' as a

Method in the *Canterbury Tales*." *ChauR* 8 (1973), 9-32.

956. Ramsey, Lee C. "'The sentence of it soth is': Chaucer's *Physician's Tale*." *ChauR* 6 (1972), 185-97.

957. Skerpan, Elizabeth P. "Chaucer's Physicians: Their Texts, Contexts, and the *Canterbury Tales*." *JRMRA* 5 (1984), 4-56.

958. Trower, Katherine B. "Spiritual Sickness in the Physician's and Pardoner's Tales: Thematic Unity in Fragment VI of the *Canterbury Tales*." *ABR* 29 (1978), 67-86.

959. Ussery, Huling E. *Chaucer's Physician: Medicine and Literature in the Fourteenth-Century England*. TSE 19. New Orleans, LA: Tulane U Dept. of English, 1971.

960. Waller, Martha S. "The Physician's Tale: Geoffrey Chaucer and Fray Juan Garcia de Castrojeriz." *Speculum* 51 (1976), 292-306.

See also 56, 409.

CT—The Pardoner and His Tale

961. Bauschatz, Paul C. "Chaucer's Pardoner's Beneficent Lie." *Assays* 2 (1983), 19-43.

962. Beidler, Peter G. "The Plague and Chaucer's Pardoner." *ChauR* 16 (1982), 257-69.

963. Bishop, Ian. "The Narrative Art of *The Pardoner's Tale*." *MAE* 36 (1967), 15-24.

964. Bolton, W. F. "Structural Meaning in the Pardoner's Tale and The Nun's Priest's Tale." *L&S* 11 (1978), 201-11.

965. Cespedes, Frank V. "Chaucer's Pardoner and Preaching." *ELH* 44 (1977), 1-18.

966. Collette, Carolyn P. "'Ubi Peccaverant, Ibi Punirentur': The Oak Tree and the *Pardoner's Tale*." *ChauR* 19 (1984), 39-45.

967. Condren, Edward I. "The Pardoner's Bid for Existence." *Viator* 4 (1973), 177-205.

968. Currie, Felicity. "Chaucer's Pardoner Again." *LeedsSE* 4 (for 1972), 11-22.

969. Delasanta, Rodney. "Sacrament and Sacrifice in the *Pardoner's Tale*." *AnM* 14 (1973), 43-52.

970. DeNeef, A. Leigh. "Chaucer's *Pardoner's Tale* and the Irony of Misinterpretation." *JNT* 3 (1974), 85-96.

971. Fritz, Donald W. "Reflections in a Golden Florin: Chaucer's Narcissistic Pardoner." *ChauR* 21 (1987), 321-37.

972. Ginsberg, Warren. "Preaching and Avarice in the *Pardoner's Tale*." *Mediaevalia* 2 (1976), 77-99.

973. Glasser, Marc. "The Pardoner and the Host: Chaucer's Analysis of the Canterbury Game." *CEA* 46 (1983-84), 37-45.

974. Hallissy, Margaret. "Poison Lore and Chaucer's Pardoner." *Massachusetts Studies in English* 9 (1983), 54-63.

975. Halverson, John. "Chaucer's Pardoner and the Progress of Criticism." *ChauR* 4 (1970), 184-202.

976. Hatcher, Elizabeth R. "Life without Death: The Old Man in Chaucer's *Pardoner's Tale*." *ChauR* 9 (1975), 246-52.

977. Jungman, Robert E. "The Pardoner's Quarrel with the Host." *PQ* 55 (1976), 279-81.

978. Kellogg, Alfred, and L. A. Haselmayer. "Chaucer's Satire of the Pardoner." *PMLA* 66 (1951), 251-77.

979. Knight, Stephen. "Chaucer's Pardoner in Performance." *Sydney Studies in English* 9 (1983), 21-36.

980. Lawton, D. A. "The Pardoner's Tale: Morality and Its Context." In *Studies in Chaucer*. Eds. G. A. Wilkes and A. P. Riemer. Sydney: U of Sydney, 1981.

981. Leicester, H. Marshall, Jr. "'Synne Horrible': The Pardoner's Exegesis of His Tale, and Chaucer's." In *Acts of Interpretation:…Essays in Honor of E. Talbot Donaldson*. Eds. Mary J. Carruthers and Elizabeth D. Kirk. Norman, OK: Pilgrim Books, 1982.

982. Luengo, A. "Audience and Exempla in the *Pardoner's Prologue* and *Tale*." *ChauR* 11 (1976), 1-10.

983. McAlpine, Monica E. "The Pardoner's Homosexuality and How it Matters." *PMLA* 95 (1980), 8-22.

984. McVeigh, Terrence A. "Chaucer's Portraits of the Pardoner and Summoner and Wyclif's *Tractatus de Simonia*." *CF* 29 (1975), 54-58.

985. Merrix, Robert P. "Sermon Structure in the *Pardoner's Tale*." *ChauR* 17 (1983), 235-49.

986. Miller, Clarence H., and Roberta A. Bosse. "Chaucer's Pardoner and the Mass." *ChauR* 6 (1972), 171-84.

987. Morgan, Gerald. "The Self-Revealing Tendencies of Chaucer's Pardoner." *MLR* 71 (1976), 241-55.

988. Moore, Bruce. "'I Wol No Lenger Pleye with Thee': Chaucer's Rejection of the Pardoner." *Parergon* 14 (1976), 52-62.

989. Nitecki, Alicia K. "The Convention of the Old Man's Lament in the *Pardoner's Tale*." *ChauR* 16 (1981), 76-84.

990. Olsen, Alexandra Hennessey. "'They shul desiren to dye, and deeth shal flee fro hem': A Reconsideration of the Pardoner's Old Man." *NM* 84 (1983), 367-71.

991. Patterson, Lee W. "Chaucerian Confession: Penitential Literature and the Pardoner." *M&H* 7 (1976), 153-73.

992. Pearsall, Derek. "Chaucer's Pardoner: The Death of a Salesman." *ChauR* 17 (1983), 358-65.

993. Peterson, Joyce E. "With Feigned Flattery: The Pardoner as Vice." *ChauR* 10 (1976), 326-36.

994. Pittock, Malcolm. "The *Pardoner's Tale* and the Quest for Death." *EIC* 24 (1974), 107-23.

995. Rhodes, James F. "Motivation in Chaucer's *Pardoner's Tale*: Winner Take Nothing." *ChauR* 17 (1982), 40-61.

996. ———. "The Pardoner's *Vernycle* and his *Vera Icon*." *MLS* 13 (1983), 34-40.

997. Rowland, Beryl. "Chaucer's Idea of the Pardoner." *ChauR* 14 (1979), 140-54.

998. Rudat, Wolfgang H. "Sexuality and Self-Recognition in *The Pardoner's Tale*." *JEP* 3 (1982), 124-29.

999. Sato, Noriko. "The Old Man in *The Pardoner's Tale*." *Thought Currents in English Literature*, English Literary Society of Aoyama Gakuin University, Tokyo, 54 (1981), 11-36.

1000. Schauber, Ellen, and Ellen Spolsky. "Conversational Noncooperation: The Case of Chaucer's Pardoner." *L&S* 16 (1983), 249-61.

1001. Scheps, Walter. "Chaucer's Numismatic Pardoner and the Personification of Avarice." *Acta* 4 (1977), 107-23.

1002. Sedgewick, G. G. "The Progress of Chaucer's Pardoner, 1880-1940." *MLQ* 1 (1940), 431-58.

1003. Stevens, Martin, and Kathleen Fahey. "Substance, Accident, and Transformations: A Reading of the *Pardoner's Tale*." *ChauR* 17 (1982), 142-58.

1004. Storm, Melvin. "The Pardoner's Invitation: Quaestor's Bag or Becket's Shrine?" *PMLA* 97 (1982), 810-18.

1005. ———. "'A Culpa et a Poena': Christ's Pardon and the Pardoner." *NM* 83 (1982), 439-42.

1006. Taylor, P. B. "Peynted Confessiouns: Boccaccio and Chaucer." *CL* 34 (1982), 116-29.

1007. Tristram, Philippa. "Strange Images of Death." *LeedsSE* n.s. 14 (1983), 196-209.

1008. Yamanaka, Toshio. "Chaucer's Pardoner." *SES* 2 (1977), 1-9.

1009. Yeager, R. F. "Aspects of Gluttony in Chaucer and Gower." *SP* 81 (1984), 42-55.

See also 121, 819, 945, 951, 958.

CT—The Shipman and His Tale

1010. Abraham, David H. "Cosyn and Cosynage: Pun and Structure in the *Shipman's Tale*." *ChauR* 11 (1977), 319-27.

1011. Adams, Robert. "The Concept of Debt in *The Shipman's Tale*." *SAC* 6 (1984), 85-102.

1012. Coletti, Theresa. "The Meeting at the Gate: Hagiography and Symbol in the Shipman's Tale." *SIcon* 3 (1977), 47-56.

1013. ———. "The *Mulier Fortis* and Chaucer's Shipman's Tale." *ChauR* 15 (1981), 236-49.

1014. ———. "Biblical Wisdom: Chaucer's *Shipman's Tale* and the Mulier Fortis." In *Chaucer and Scriptural Tradition*. Ed. David Lyle Jeffrey. Ottawa: U of Ottawa P, 1984.

1015. Gibson, Gail McMurray. "Resurrection as Dramatic Icon in the Shipman's Tale." In *Signs and Symbols in Chaucer's Poetry*. Eds. John P. Hermann and John J. Burke, Jr. University: U of Alabama P, 1981.

1016. Hermann, John P. "Dismemberment, Dissemination, Discourse: Sign and Symbol in the *Shipman's Tale*." *ChauR* 19 (1985), 302-37.

1017. Joseph, Gerhard. "Chaucer's Coinage: Foreign Exchange and the Puns of the *Shipman's Tale*." *ChauR* 17 (1983), 341-47.

1018. Keiser, George R. "Language and Meaning in Chaucer's *Shipman's Tale*." *ChauR* 12 (1977), 147-61.

1019. McClintock, Michael W. "Games and the Players of Games: Old French Fabliaux and the *Shipman's Tale*." *ChauR* 5 (1970), 12-36.

1020. McGalliard, John C. "Characterization in Chaucer's *Shipman's Tale*." *PQ* 54 (1975), 1-18.

1021. Nicholson, Peter. "The Shipman's Tale and the Fabliaux." *ELH* 45 (1978), 583-96.

1022. ———. "The Medieval Tales of the Lover's Gift Regained." *Fabula* 21 (1979), 200-22.

1023. Scattergood, V. J. "The Originality of the *Shipman's Tale*." *ChauR* 11 (1977), 210-31.

1024. Schneider, Paul S. "'Taillynge Ynough': The Function of Money in the *Shipman's Tale*." *ChauR* 11 (1977), 201-09.

1025. Silverman, Albert H. "Sex and Money in Chaucer's *Shipman's Tale*." *PQ* 32 (1953), 329-36.

1026. Stock, Lorraine Kochanske. "The Reenacted Fall in Chaucer's *Shipman's Tale*." *SIcon* 7-8 (1981), 134-45.

1027. ———. "La Vieille and the Merchant's Wife in Chaucer's *Shipman's Tale*." *SHR* 16 (1982), 333-39.

See also 697.

CT—The Prioress and Her Tale

1028. Brennan, John P. "Reflections on a Gloss to the *Prioress's Tale* from Jerome's *Adversus Jovinianum*." *SP* 70 (1974), 243-51.

1029. Burnley, David. "Stylistic Reconstruction and Chaucer's Prioress." *Indian Journal of Applied Linguistics* 10 (1984), 77-90.

1030. Collette, Carolyn P. "Sense and Sensibility in the *Prioress's Tale*." *ChauR* 15 (1981), 138-50.

1031. Davidson, Audrey. "*Alma Redemptoris Mater*: The Little Clergeon's Song." *SMC* 4 (1974), 459-66.

1032. Ferris, Sumner. "The Mariology of the *Prioress's Tale*." *ABR* 32 (1981), 232-54.

1033. ———. "Chaucer at Lincoln (1387): The *Prioress's Tale* as a Political Poem." *ChauR* 15 (1981), 295-321.

1034. Fleissner, Robert E. "That Oath of the Prioress." *NM* 86 (1985), 197-98.

1035. Frank, Hardy Long. "Chaucer's Prioress and the Blessed Virgin." *ChauR* 13 (1979), 346-62.

1036. Frank, Robert Worth, Jr. "Miracles of the Virgin, Medieval Anti-Semitism, and 'Prioress'Tale'." In *The Wisdom of Poetry: Essays …in Honor of Morton W. Bloomfield*. Eds. Larry D. Benson and Siegfried Wenzel. Kalamazoo: Western Michigan U, 1982.

1037. Friedman, Albert B. "The *Prioress's Tale* and Chaucer's Anti-Semitism." *ChauR* 9 (1974), 118-29.

1038. Fritz, Donald W. "The Prioress's Avowal of Ineptitude." *ChauR* 9 (1974), 166-81.

1039. Hamel, Mary. "And now for Something Different: the Relationship between the *Prioress's Tale* and the *Rime of Sir Thopas*." *ChauR* 14 (1980), 251-59.

1040. Hirsh, John C. "Reopening the *Prioress's Tale*." *ChauR* 10 (1975), 30-45.

1041. Jungman, Robert E. "'Amor vincit omnia' and the Prioress's Brooch." *Lore &L* 9 (1983), 1-7.

1042. Langmuir, Gavin I. "The Knight's Tale of Young Hugh of Lincoln." *Speculum* 47 (1972), 459-82.

1043. Moorman, Charles. "The Prioress as Pearly Queen." *ChauR* 13 (1978), 25-33.

1044. Power, Eileen. "Madam Eglentyne: Chaucer's Prioress in Real Life." In *Medieval People*. 10th ed. London: Methuen, 1963.

1045. Rex, Richard. "Chaucer and the Jews." *MLQ* 45 (1984), 107-22.

1046. Ridley, Florence. *The Prioress and the Critics*. U of California English Studies 30. Berkeley: U of California P, 1965.

1047. Rothwell, W. "Stratford atte Bowe and Paris." *MLR* 80 (1985), 39-54.

1048. Witte, Stephen P. "*Muscipula Diaboli* and Chaucer's Portrait of the Prioress." *PLL* 13 (1977), 227-37.

1049. Wood, Chauncey. "Chaucer's Use of Signs in His Portrait of the Prioress." In *Signs and Symbols in Chaucer's Poetry*. Eds. John B. Hermann and John J. Burke, Jr. University: U of Alabama P, 1981.

1050. Wurtele, Douglas. "Prejudice and Chaucer's Prioress." *RUO* 55 (1985), 33-43.

See also 57, 409, 1561.

CT—The Tale of Sir Thopas

1051. Burrow, J. A. "Chaucer's *Sir Thopas* and *La Prise de Neuvile*." In *English Satire and the Satiric Tradition*. Ed. Claude Rawson. Oxford: Blackwell, 1984.

1052. Conley, John. "The Peculiar Name 'Thopas'." *SP* 73 (1976), 42-61.

1053. Gaylord, Alan T. "Chaucer's Dainty 'Dogerel': The 'Elvyssh' Prosody of *Sir Thopas*." *SAC* 1 (1979), 83-104.

1054. ———. "The Moment of Sir Thopas: Towards a New Look at Chaucer's Language." *ChauR* 16 (1982), 311-29.

1055. ———. "The 'Miracle' of *Sir Thopas*." *SAC* 6 (1984), 65-84.

1056. Haskell, Ann S. "Sir Thopas: The Puppet's Puppet." *ChauR* 9 (1975), 253-61.

1057. Kooper, E. S. "Inverted Images in Chaucer's *Tale of Sir Thopas*." *SN* 56 (1984), 147-54.

1058. Olson, Glending. "A Reading of the Thopas-Melibee Link." *ChauR* 10 (1975), 147-53.

1059. Scattergood, V. J. "Chaucer and the French War: *Sir Thopas* and *Melibee*." In *Court and Poet*. Eds. Glyn S. Burgess, et al. Liverpool: Cairns, 1981.

1060. Wood, Chauncey. "Chaucer and 'Sir Thopas': Irony and Concupiscence." *TSLL* 14 (1972), 389-403.

See also 1039.

CT—The Tale of Melibee

1061. Bornstein, Diane. "Chaucer's *Tale of Melibee* as an Example of the *Style clergial*." *ChauR* 12 (1978), 236-54.

1062. Hoffman, Richard L. "Chaucer's Melibee and Tales of Sondry Folk." *C&M* 30 (1969), 552-77.

1063. Lunz, Elisabeth. "Chaucer's Prudence as the Ideal of Virtuous Women." *ELWIU* 4 (1977), 3-10.

1064. Marks, Herbert. "Poetic Purpose in the 'Tale of Melibee'." *MSE* 8 (1982), 50-55.

1065. Oizumi, Akio. "On Collated Words in Chaucer's Translation of *Le livre de Mellibee et Prudence*: A Stylistic Comparison of the English Translation with the French Version." *SELit* 48 (1971), 95-108.

1066. Owen, Charles A., Jr. "The *Tale of Melibee*." *ChauR* 7 (1973), 267-80.

1067. Palomo, Dolores. "What Chaucer Really Did to *Le livre de Melibee*." *PQ* 53 (1974), 304-20.

1068. Ruggiers, Paul G. "Serious Chaucer: *The Tale of Melibeus* and the Parson's Tale." In *Chaucerian Problems and Perspectives: Essays Presented to Paul E. Beichner, C.S.C.* Eds. Edward Vasta and Zacharias P. Thundy. Notre Dame, IN: U of Notre Dame P, 1979.

1069. Stillwell, Gardner. "The Political Meaning of Chaucer's *Tale of Melibee*." *Speculum* 19 (1944), 433-44.

1070. Strohm, Paul. "The Allegory of the *Tale of Melibee*." *ChauR* 2 (1967), 32-42.

See also 184, 1058, 1059.

CT—The Monk and His Tale

1071. Beichner, Paul E. "Daun Piers, Monk and Business Administrator." *Speculum* 34 (1959), 611-19.

1072. Berndt, David E. "Monastic *Acedia* and Chaucer's Characterization of Daun Piers." *SP* 68 (1971), 435-50.

1073. Boitani, Piero. "*The Monk's Tale*: Dante and Boccaccio." *MAE* 45 (1976), 50-69.

1074. Delasanta, Rodney. "'Namore of this': Chaucer's Priest and Monk." *TSL* 13 (1968), 117-32.

1075. Fry, Donald K. "The Ending of the *Monk's Tale*." *JEGP* 71 (1972), 355-68.

1076. Lepley, Douglas L. "The Monk's Boethian Tale." *ChauR* 12 (1977), 162-70.

1077. Olsson, Kurt. "Grammar, Manhood, and Tears: The Curiosity of Chaucer's Monk." *MP* 76 (1978), 1-17.

1078. Shikii, Kumiko. "Chaucer's Anti-clericalism as Seen in the Monk." *The Fleur-de-lis Review* (Dec. 25, 1980), 25-54.

1079. Taggie, Benjamin F. "John of Gaunt, Geoffrey Chaucer and 'O Noble, O Worthy Petro, Glorie of Spayne'." *FCS* 10 (1984), 195-228.

1080. Waller, Martha S. "*The Monk's Tale*: Nero's Nets and Caesar's Father—An Inquiry into the Transformations of Classical Roman History in Medieval Tradition." *Indiana Social Studies Quarterly* 31 (1978), 46-55.

1081. White, Robert B., Jr. "Chaucer's Daun Piers and the Rule of St. Benedict: The Failure of an Ideal." *JEGP* 70 (1971), 13-30.

CT—The Nun's Priest and His Tale

1082. Allen, Judson B. "The Ironic Fruyt: Chauntecleer as Figura." *SP* 66 (1969), 25-35.

1083. Anjum, A. R. "'The Nonnes Preestes Tale': A 'Framework' Story." *Explorations* 5 (1978), 40-48.

1084. Baird, Lorrayne Y. "Christus Gallinaceus: A Chaucerian Enigma; or the Cock as Symbol of Christ." *SIcon* 9 (1983), 19-30.

1085. Bishop, Ian. "*The Nun's Priest's Tale* and the Liberal Arts." *RES* n.s. 30 (1979), 257-67.

1086. Blake, N. F. "Reynard the Fox in England." In *Aspects of the Medieval Animal Epic*. Eds. E. Rombauts and A. Welkenhuysen. The Hague: Nijhoff, 1975.

1087. Bloomfield, Morton W. "The Wisdom of the Nun's Priest's Tale." In *Chaucerian Problems and Perspectives: Essays Presented to Paul E. Beichner, C.S.C.* Eds. Edward Vasta and Zacharias P. Thundy. Notre Dame, IN: U of Notre Dame P, 1979.

1088. Brewer, Derek. "On the *Nun's Priest's Tale*." *BAM* 11 (1977), 115.

1089. Brody, Saul Nathaniel. "Truth and Fiction in the Nun's Priest's Tale." *ChauR* 14 (1979), 33-47.

1090. Broes, Arthur T. "Chaucer's Disgruntled Cleric: The *Nun's Priest's Tale*." *PMLA* 78 (1963), 156-62.

1091. Dean, Nancy. "Chaucerian Attitudes towards Joy with Particular Consideration of the *Nun's Priest's Tale*." *MAE* 44 (1975), 1-13.

1092. Delany, Sheila. "'Mulier est hominis confusio': Chaucer's Anti-popular *Nun's Priest's Tale*." *Mosaic* 17 (1984), 1-8.

1093. DuVal, John. "'Si coume Renart prist Chantecler le coc' and 'The Nonnes Preestes Tale': A Comparison" *PAPA* I, iii (1975), 15-24.

1094. Frese, Delores Warwick. "The Nun's Priest's Tale: Chaucer's Identified Masterpiece?" *ChauR* 16 (1982), 330-43.

1095. Friedman, John B. "The *Nun's Priest's Tale*: The Preacher and the Mermaid's Song." *ChauR* 7 (1973), 250-66.

1096. Gallacher, Patrick. "Food, Laxatives, and the Catharsis in Chaucer's Nun's Priest's Tale." *Speculum* 51 (1976), 49-68.

1097. Gallick, Susan. "Styles of Usage in the *Nun's Priest's Tale*." *ChauR* 11 (1978), 232-47.

1098. Galvan-Reula, J. F. "The Modernity of the 'Nun's Priest's Tale': Narrator, Theme and Ending." *Lore&L* 10 (1984) 63-69.

1099. Hoy, Michael. "The Nun's Priest's Tale." In *Chaucer's Major Tales*. Eds. Michael Hoy and Michael Stevens. London: Bailey, 1969.

1100. Johnson, Lynn Staley. "'To Make in Som Comedye': Chaunticleer, Son of Troy." *ChauR* 19 (1985), 225-44.

1101. Knight, Stephen. "Form, Content and Context in *The Nun's Priest's Tale*." In *Studies in Chaucer*. Eds. G. A. Wilkes and A. P. Riemer. Sydney: U of Sydney, 1981.

1102. Lall, Rama Rani. *Satiric Fables in English: A Critical Study of the Animal Tales of Chaucer, Spenser, Dryden, and Orwell*. New Delhi: New Statesman Publishing Co., 1979.

1103. Lumiansky, Robert M. "The *Nun's Priest's Tale* in the *Canterbury Tales*." *PMLA* 68 (1953), 896-906.

1104. McGinnis, Wayne D. "The Dramatic Fitness of the *Nun's Priest's Tale*." *CEA* 37 (1975), 24-26.

1105. Mann, Jill. "The *Speculum Stultorum* and the Nun's Priest's Tale." *ChauR* 9 (1975), 262-82.

1106. Manning, Stephen. "The Nun's Priest's Morality and the Medieval Attitude Toward Fables." *JEGP* 59 (1960), 403-16.

1107. Meyers, D. E. "Focus and 'Moralite' in the *Nun's Priest's Tale*." *ChauR* 7 (1973), 210-20.

1108. Payne, F. Anne. "Foreknowledge and Free Will: Three Theories in the *Nun's Priest's Tale*." *ChauR* 10 (1976), 201-19.

1109. Pratt, Robert A. "Three Old French Sources of the Nonnes Preestes Tale." *Speculum* 47 (1972), 422-44, 646-68.

1110. ———. "Some Latin Sources of the Nonnes Preest on Dreams." *Speculum* 52 (1977), 538-70.

1111. Schauber, Ellen, and Ellen Spolsky. "Stalking a Generative Poetics." *NLH* 12 (1981), 397-413.

1112. Scheps, Walter. "Chaucer's Anti-Fable: *Reductio ad Absurdum* in the *Nun's Priest's Tale*." *LeedsSE* 4 (1970), 1-10.

1113. Shallers, A. Paul. "The 'Nun's Priest's Tale': An Ironic Exemplum." *ELH* 42 (1975), 319-37.

1114. Simms, Norman. "Nero and Jack Straw in Chaucer's Nun's Priest's Tale." *Parergon* 8 (1974), 2-12.

1115. Thomas, Paul R. "An Ironic Monkish Allusion: Chaucer's Learned Audience in 'The Nun's Priest's Tale'." *Encyclia* 59 (1982), 45-52.

1116. Travis, Peter W. "The Nun's Priest's Tale as Grammar School Primer." *SAC*, Proceedings 1 (1984), 81-91.

1117. Wentersdorf, Karl P. "Symbol and Meaning in Chaucer's *Nun's Priest's Tale*." *NMS* 26 (1982), 29-46.

1118. Yates, Donald. "Chanticleer's Latin Ancestors." *ChauR* 18 (1983), 116-26.

See also 55, 964, 1074.

CT—The Second Nun and Her Tale

1119. Beichner, Paul E. "Confrontation, Contempt of Court, and Chaucer's Cecelia." *ChauR* 8 (1974), 198-204.

1120. Clogan, Paul M. "The Figural Style and Meaning of the *Second Nun's Prologue and Tale*." *M&H* n.s. 3 (1972), 213-40.

1121. Collette, Carolyn P. "A Closer Look at Seinte Cecile's Special Vision." *ChauR* 10 (1976), 337-49.

1122. Eggebroten, Anne. "Laughter in the *Second Nun's Tale*: A Redefinition of the Genre." *ChauR* 19 (1984), 55-61.

1123. Glasser, Narc D. "Marriage and the *Second Nun's Tale*." *TSL* 23 (1978), 1-14.

1124. Grennen, Joseph E. "Saint Cecilia's 'Chemical Wedding': The Unity of the *Canterbury Tales*, Fragment VIII." *JEGP* 65 (1966), 466-81.

1125. Hirsh, John C. "The Politics of Spirituality: The Second Nun and the Manciple." *ChauR* 12 (1977), 129-46.

1126. Johnston, Mark E. "The Resonance of the *Second Nun's Tale*." *MHLS* 3 (1980), 25-38.

1127. Kolve, V. A. "Chaucer's Second Nun's Tale and the Iconography of Saint Cecilia." In *New Perspectives on Chaucer Criticism*. Ed. Donald M. Rose. Norman, OK: Pilgrim Books, 1981.

1128. Landrum, Graham. "The Convent Crowd and the Feminist Nun." *TPB* 13 (1976), 5-12.

1129. Luecke, Janemarie. "Three Faces of Cecilia: Chaucer's Second Nun's Tale." *ABR* 33 (1982), 335-48.

1130. Peck, Russell A. "The Ideas of 'Entente' and Translation in Chaucer's *Second Nun's Tale*." *AnM* 8 (1967), 17-37.

1131. Reames, Sherry L. "The Sources of Chaucer's 'Second Nun's Tale'." *MP* 76 (1978), 111-35.

1132. ———. "The Cecilia Legend as Chaucer Inherited It and Retold It: the Disappearance of an Augustinian Ideal." *Speculum* 55 (1980), 38-57.

1133. Rosenberg, Bruce A. "The Contrary Tales of the Second Nun and the Canon's Yeoman." *ChauR* 2 (1968), 278-91.

1134. Waterhouse, Ruth. "'A Rose by Any Other Name': Two Versions of the Legend of Saint Cecilia." *NM* 79 (1978), 126-36.

CT—The Canon's Yeoman and His Tale

1135. Brown, Dorothy H. "The Unreliable Narrator: The Canon's Yeoman." *New Laurel Review* 12 (1982), 6-16.

1136. Brown, Peter. "Is the 'Canon's Yeoman's Tale' Apocryphal?" *ES* 64 (1983), 481-90.

1137. Campbell, Jackson J. "The Canon's Yeoman as Imperfect Paradigm." *ChauR* 17 (1982), 171-81.

1138. Cook, Robert. "The Canon's Yeoman and His Tale." *ChauR* 22 (1987), 28-40.

1139. Dickson, Donald R. "The 'Slidynge' Yeoman: The Real Drama in the *Canon's Yeoman's Tale*." *SoCR* 2 (1985), 10-22.

1140. Duncan, Edgar H. "The Literature of Alchemy and Chaucer's *Canon's Yeoman's Tale*: Framework, Theme, and Characters." *Speculum* 43, 633-56.

1141. Finkelstein (Metlitzki), Dorothee. "The Code of Chaucer's 'Secree of Secrees': Arabic Alchemical Terminology in *The Canon's Yeoman's Tale*." *Archiv* 207 (1970), 260-76.

1142. Hartung, Albert A. "'Pars Seconda' and the Development of the *Canon's Yeoman's Tale*." *ChauR* 12 (1977), 111-28.

1143. McCracken, Samuel. "Confessional Prologue and the Topography of the Canon's Yeoman." *MP* 68 (1971), 289-91.

1144. Taylor, Paul B. "The Canon's Yeoman's Breath: Emanations of a Metaphor." *ES* 60 (1979), 380-88.

See also 1133.

CT—The Manciple and His Tale

1145. Askins, William. "The Historical Setting of *The Manciple's Tale*." *SAC* 7 (1985), 87-105.

1146. Campbell, Jackson J. "Polonius Among the Pilgrims." *ChauR* 7 (1972), 140-46.

1147. Davidson, Arnold B. "The Logic of Confusion in the *Manciple's Tale.*" *AnM* 19 (1979), 5-13.

1148. Dean, James. "The Ending of the *Canterbury Tales,* 1952-1976." *TSLL* 21 (1979), 17-33.

1149. Diekstra, F.N.M. "Chaucer's Digressive Mode and the Moral of the *Manciple's Tale.*" *Neophil* 67 (1983), 131-48.

1150. Fulk, R.D. "Reinterpreting the Manciple's Tale." *JEGP* 78 (1979), 485-93.

1151. Fradenburg, Louise. "The Manciple's Servant Tongue: Politics and Poetry in the *Canterbury Tales.*" *ELH* 52 (1985), 85- 118.

1152. Harwood, Britton J. "Language and the Real: Chaucer's Manciple." *ChauR* 6 (1972), 268-79.

1153. Hazelton, Richard. "The *Manciple's Tale:* Parody and Critique." *JEGP* 60 (1963), 1-31.

1154. Jones, Donna. "The Manciple's Diplomatic Immunity." *TPB* 21 (1984), 68.

1155. Scattergood, V.J. "The Manciple's Manner of Speaking." *EIC* 24 (1974), 124-46.

1156. Trask, Richard M. "The Manciple's Problem." *SSF* 14 (1977), 109-16.

1157. Traversi, Derek. "The Manciple's Tale." In *The Literary Imagination: Studies in Dante, Chaucer, and Shakespeare.* Newark: U of Delaware P, 1982.

1158. Westervelt, L.A. "The Medieval Notion of Chaucer's *Manciple's Tale.*" *SoRA* 14 (1981), 107-15.

1159. Wood, Chauncey. "Speech, the Principle of Contraries, and Chaucer's Tales of the Manciple and the Parson." *Mediaevalia* 6 (1980), 209-29.

See also 58, 1125.

CT—The Parson and His Tale

1160. Allen, Judson B. "The Old Way and the Parson's Way: An Ironic Reading of the *Parson's Tale.*" *JMRS* 3 (1973), 255-71.

1161. Brown, Emerson, Jr. "The Poet's Last Words: Text and Meaning at the End of the Parson's Prologue." *ChauR* 10 (1976), 236-42.

1162. Delasanta, Rodney. "Penance and Poetry in the *Canterbury Tales.*" *PMLA* 93 (1978), 240-47.

1163. Finke, Laurie A. " 'To Knytte up al this Feeste': The Parson's Rhetoric and the Ending of the *Canterbury Tales.*" *LeedsSE* n.s. 15 (1984), 95-107.

1164. Finlayson, John. "The Satiric Mode and the *Parson's Tale.*" *ChauR* 6 (1971), 94-116.

1165. Glowka, Arthur A. "Chaucer's Parson and the Devil's Other Hand." *Interpretations* 14 (1983), 15-19.

1166. Halissy, Margaret M. "The She-Ape in Chaucer's 'Parson's Tale'." *ELWIU* 9 (1982), 127-31.

1167. Luengo, Anthony B. "Synthesis and Orthodoxy in Chaucer's *Parson's Tale:* An analysis of the concordance of different authoritative *sententiae* according to the principles of the medieval *artes praedicande.*" *Revue de l'Université d'Ottawa* 50 (1980), 223-32.

1168. Olmert, Michael. "The Parson's Ludic Formula for Winning on the Road to Canterbury." *ChauR* 20 (1985), 158-68.

1169. Patterson, Lee W. "The 'Parson's Tale' and the Quitting of the *Canterbury Tales.*" *Traditio* 34 (1978), 331-80.

1170. Pfander, H.G. "Some Medieval Manuals of Religious Instruction in England and Observations on Chaucer's *Parson's Tale.*" *JEGP* 35 (1936), 243-58.

1171. Shaw, Judith. "Corporal and Spiritual Homicide: The Sin of Wrath and the Parson's Tale." *Traditio* 38 (1982), 281- 300.

1172. Shimogasa, Tokujii. "Chaucer's Colloquial Style in *The Parson's Tale.*" *Era* n.s. 2 (Hiroshima, 1981), 41-61.

1173. ———. "Chaucer's Parallelism in *The Parson's Tale.*" *Bulletin of Yamaguchi Women's University* (1982), 11-27.

1174. Taylor, Paul B. "The Parson's Amyable Tongue." *ES* 64 (1983), 401-09.

1175. Wenzel, Siegfried. "The Source of the 'Remedia' in the *Parson's Tale.*" *Traditio* 27 (1971), 433-54.

1176. ———. "The Source of Chaucer's Seven Deadly Sins." *Traditio* 30 (1974), 351-78.

1177. ———. "Chaucer's Parson's Tale, 'Every Tales Strengthe'." In *Europäische Lehrdichtung. Festschrift für Walter Naumann zum 70 Geburtstag.* Eds. H. G. Rötzer and H. Walz. Darmstadt: Wissenschaftliche Buchgesell, 1981.

1178. ———. "Notes on the *Parson's Tale.*" *ChauR* 16 (1982), 237-56.

1179. Wurtele, Douglas. "The Penitance of Geoffrey Chaucer." *Viator* 11 (1980), 355-61.

See also 951, 1068, 1159.

CT—The Retraction

1180. Campbell, A.P. "Chaucer's 'Retraction': Who Retracted What?" *RUO* 35 (1965), 35-53.

1181. Gordon, James D. "Chaucer's Retraction: A Review of Opinion." In *Studies in Medieval Literature in Honor of A. C. Baugh.* Ed. M. Leach. Philadelphia: U of Pennsylvania P, 1961.

1182. Knapp, Robert S. "Penance, Irony, and Chaucer's Retraction." *Assays* 2 (1983), 45-67.

1183. Knighton, Merrell A. "Yeoman, Parson, Poet: A Validation." *PAPA* 8 (1982), 27-32.

1184. Marshall, David. "Unmasking the Last Pilgrim: How and Why Chaucer Used the Retraction to

Close the Tales of Canterbury." *C&L* 31 (1982), 55-74.

1185. McGerr, Rosemarie P. "Retraction and Memory: Retrospective Structure in the *Canterbury Tales.*" *CL* 37 (1985) 97-113.

1186. Reiss, Edmund. "Chaucer and Medieval Irony." *SAC* 1 (1979), 67-82.

1187. Sayce, Olive. "Chaucer's 'Retraction': The Conclusion of the *Canterbury Tales* and Its Place in Literary Tradition." *MAE* 40 (1971), 230-48.

1188. Schricker, Gale C. "On the Relation of Fact and Fiction in Chaucer's Poetic Endings." *PQ* 60 (1981), 13-27.

See also 1179.

TROYLUS AND CRISEYDE

TC— General Criticism, Genre

1189. Bishop, Ian. *Chaucer's Troilus and Criseyde: A Critical Study.* Bristol: U of Bristol Academic Pubs, 1981.

1190. Christmas, Peter. "*Troilus and Criseyde:* The Problems of Love and Necessity." *ChauR* 9 (1975), 285-96.

1191. Clough, Andrea. "Medieval Tragedy and the Genre of *Troilus and Criseyde.*" *M&H* 11 (1982), 211-27.

1192. Clovella, Sister Francis D. "Audience as Determinant of Meaning in the *Troilus.*" *ChauR* 2 (1968), 235-45.

1193. Corsa, Helen S. "Dreams in *Troilus and Criseyde.*" *AI* 27 (1970), 52-65.

1194. Fish, Varda. "The Origin and Original Object of *Troilus and Criseyde.*" *ChauR* 18 (1984), 304-15.

1195. Fyler, John M. "Auctoritee and Allusion in *Troilus and Criseyde.*" *Res Publica Litterarum* 7 (1984), 73-92.

1196. Gordon, Ida L. *The Double Sorrow of Troilus.* Oxford: Oxford U P, 1970.

1197. Kaminsky, Alice R. *Chaucer's Troilus and Criseyde and the Critics.* Athens: Ohio U P, 1980.

1198. Lenta, Margaret. "The Mirror of the Mind: A Study of *Troilus and Criseyde.*" *Theoria* 58 (1982), 33-46.

1199. McAlpine, Monica E. *The Genre of Troilus and Criseyde.* Ithaca: Cornell U P, 1978.

1200. McCall, John P. "*Troylus and Criseyde.*" In *Companion of Chaucer Studies.* Ed. Beryl Rowland. rev. ed. New York: Oxford U P, 1979.

1201. Meech, Sanford B. *Design in Chaucer's Troilus.* Syracuse, NY: Syracuse U P, 1959.

1202. Osberg, Richard H. "Between the Motion and the Act: Intentions and Ends in Chaucer's *Troilus.*" *ELH* 48 (1981), 257-70.

1203. Patterson, Lee W. "Ambiguity and Interpretation: A Fifteenth-Century Reading of *Troilus and Criseyde.*" *Speculum* 54 (1979), 297-330.

1204. Robertson, D. W., Jr. "The Probable Date and Purpose of Chaucer's *Troilus.*" *M&H* 13 (1985), 143-71.

1205. Stiller, Nikki. "Civilization and Its Ambivalence: Chaucer's *Troilus and Criseyde.*" *Journal of Evolutionary Psychology* 6 (1985), 212-23.

1206. Strauss, Jennifer. "*Troilus and Criseyde:* The Idea and the Poem." In *Proceedings of the Thirteenth Congress of the Australasian University Language and Literature Association.* Melbourne: AULLA, 1972.

1207. Wetherbee, Winthrop. *Chaucer and the Poets: An Essay on Troilus and Criseyde.* Ithaca, NY: Cornell U P, 1984.

1208. Whitman, F. H. "*Troilus and Criseyde* and Chaucer's Dedication to Gower." *TSL* 18 (1973), 1-11.

1209. Windeatt, Barry. "The Text of *Troilus.*" In *Essays on Troilus and Criseyde.* Ed. Mary Salu. Cambridge: Brewer, 1979.

1210. Wood, Chauncey. *The Elements of Chaucer's Troilus.* Durham, NC: Duke U P, 1984.

1211. Yeager, Robert E. " 'O Moral Gower': Chaucer's Dedication of *Troilus and Criseyde.*" *ChauR* 19 (1984), 87-99.

See also 42, 51, 62, 64, 68, 69, 152

TC—Literary Relations

1212. Anderson, David. "Theban History in Chaucer's *Troilus.*" *SAC* 4 (1982), 109-33.

1213. Benson, C. David. *The History of Troy in Middle English Literature: Guido delle Colonne's Historia distructionis Troiae in Medieval England.* Cambridge: Brewer, 1980.

1214. Clogan, Paul M. "The Theban Scenes in Chaucer's *Troilus.*" *M&H* n.s. 12 (1984), 167-85.

1215. Dean, James. "Chaucer's *Troilus,* Boccaccio's *Filostrato,* and the Poetics of Closure." *PQ* 64 (1985), 175-84.

1216. Knapp, Peggy Ann. "Boccaccio and Chaucer on Cassandra." *PQ* 56 (1977), 413-17.

1217. Lewis, C. S. "What Chaucer Really Did to *Il Filostrato.*" *E&S* 17 (1932), 56-75.

1218. Longo, Joseph A. "Apropos the Love Plot in Chaucer's *Troilus and Criseyde* and Shakespeare's *Troilus and Cressida.*" *Cahiers* 11 (1977), 1-15.

1219. Mieszkowski, Gretchen. "R.K. Gordon and the *Troilus and Criseyde* Story." *ChauR* 15 (1981), 127-37.

1220. Pratt, Robert A. "Chaucer and *Le Roman de Troyle et de Creseida.*" *SP* 53 (1956), 509-39.

1221. Root, R. K., and H. N. Russell. "A Planetary Date for Chaucer's *Troilus.*" *PMLA* 39 (1924), 48-63.

1222. Sommer, George J. "Chaucer and the Muse of History: A Presumption of Objectivity in *Troilus and Criseyde.*" *Cithara* 23 (1983), 38-47.

1223. Sudo, Jun. "Chaucer's Imitation and Innovation in *Troilus and Criseyde.*" *Poetica* 13 (Tokyo, 1982), 50-74.

1224. Taylor, Karla Terese. "A Text and Its Afterlife: Dante and Chaucer." *CL* 35 (1983), 1-20.

1225. Wheeler, Bonnie. "Dante, Chaucer, and the Ending of *Troilus and Criseyde.*" *PQ* 61 (1982), 105-23.

1227. Wimsatt, James I. "Guillaume de Machaut and Chaucer's *Troilus and Criseyde.*" *MAE* 45 (1976), 277-93.

1228. ———. "Realism in *Troilus and Criseyde* and the *Roman de la Rose.*" In *Essays on Troilus and Criseyde.* Ed. Mary Salu. Cambridge: Brewer, 1979.

1229. ———. "The French Lyric Element in *Troilus and Criseyde.*" *YES* 15 (1985), 18-32.

1230. Windeatt, Barry. "The Text of *Troilus.*" In *Essays on Troilus and Criseyde.* Ed. Mary Salu. Cambridge: Brewer, 1979.

1231. ———. "Chaucer and the *Filostrato.*" In *Chaucer and the Italian Trecento.* Ed. Piero Boitani. Cambridge: Cambridge U P, 1983.

1232. Young, Arthur M. *Troy and Her Legend.* Pittsburgh: U of Pittsburgh P, 1948.

1233. Young, Karl. *The Origin and Development of the Story of Troilus and Criseyde.* London: Chaucer Soc. 2nd Ser. 40, 1908.

1234. ———. "Chaucer's *Troilus and Criseyde* as Romance." *PMLA* 53 (1938), 38-63.

See also 270, 276, 285, 660, 1194, 1356, 1366

TC—Structure

1235. Adamson, Jane. "The Unity of *Troilus and Criseyde.*" *CR* 14 (1971), 17-37.

1236. Colton, Michael E. "The Artistic Integrity of Chaucer's *Troilus and Criseyde.*" *ChauR* 7 (1972), 37-43.

1237. Hansom, Thomas B. "The Center of *Troilus and Criseyde.*" *ChauR* 9 (1975), 297-302.

1238. Hardie, J. Keith. "Structure and Irony in Chaucer's *Troilus and Criseyde.*" *PAPA* 3 (1977), 13-19.

1239. Hart, Thomas Elwood. "Medieval Structuralism: 'Dulcarnoun' and the Five-Book Design of Chaucer's *Troilus.*" *ChauR* 16 (1981), 129-70.

1240. Holley, Linda T. "Medieval Optics and the Framed Narrative in Chaucer's *Troilus and Criseyde.*" *ChauR* 21 (1986), 26-44.

1241. McCall, John P. "The Five-Book Structure in Chaucer's *Troilus.*" *MLQ* 23 (1962), 297-308.

1242. Stevens, Martin. "The Double Structure of Chaucer's *Troilus and Criseyde.*" In *CUNY English Forum 1.* Eds. Saul N. Brody and Harold Schecter. New York: AMS, 1985.

1243. Utley, F. L. "Scene-division in Chaucer's *Troilus and Criseyde.*" In *Studies in Medieval Literature in Honor of A. C. Baugh.* Ed. M. Leach. Philadelphia: U of Pennsylvania P, 1961.

See also 1201.

TC—Style and Rhetoric

1244. Byrd, Forrest M. "Conditional Statements in *Troilus and Criseyde.*" *PAPA* 10 (1984), 29-43.

1245. Crampton, Georgia R. "Action and Passion in Chaucer's *Troilus.*" *MAE* 43 (1974), 22-36.

1246. Frank, Robert W., Jr. "*Troilus and Criseyde:* The Art of Amplification." In *Essays in Honor of Francis Lee Utley.* Eds. J. Mandel and B. A. Rosenberg. New Brunswick, NJ: Rutgers U P, 1970.

1247. Ganim, John M. *Style and Consciousness in Middle English Narrative.* Princeton: Princeton U P, 1983.

1248. Koretsky, Allen C. "Chaucer's Use of the Apostrophe in *Troilus and Criseyde.*" *ChauR* 4 (1970), 242-66.

1249. Lanham, Richard A. "Opaque Style and Its Uses in *Troilus and Criseyde.*" *SMC* 3 (1970), 169-76.

1250. Lawton, David. "Irony and Sympathy in *Troilus and Criseyde:* A Reconsideration." *LeedsSE,* n.s. 14 (1983), 94-115.

1251. Lockhart, Adrienne R. "Semantic, Moral, and Aesthetic Degeneration in *Troilus and Criseyde.*" *ChauR* 8 (1973), 100-18.

1252. Macey, Samuel L. "Dramatic Elements in Chaucer's *Troilus.*" *TSLL* 12 (1970), 301-23.

1253. Manning, Stephen. "*Troilus,* Book V: Invention and the Poem as Process." *ChauR* 18 (1984), 288-303.

1254. Rogers, H. L. "The Beginning (and Ending) of Chaucer's *Troilus and Criseyde.*" In *Festschrift for Ralph Farrell.* Eds. A. Stephens, et al. Bern: Lang. 1977.

1255. Rowe, Donald W. *O Love O Charite! Contraries Harmonized in Chaucer's Troilus.* Carbondale: Southern Illinois U P, 1976.

1256. Schibanoff, Susan. "Prudence and Artificial Memory in Chaucer's *Troilus.*" *ELH* 42 (1975), 507-17.

1257. Wimsatt, James I. "Medieval and Modern in Chaucer's *Troilus and Criseyde.*" *PMLA* 92 (1977), 203-16.

1258. Yeatwood, Stephanie. "The Rhetoric of Narrative Rendering in Chaucer's *Troilus.*" *ChauR* 12 (1977), 27-37.

See also 177.

TC—Narrator, Narrative Technique

1259. Bestul, Thomas H. "Chaucer's *Troilus and Criseyde*: The Passionate Epic and Its Narrator." *ChauR* 14 (1980), 366-78.

1260. Brenner, Gerry. "Narrative Structure in Chaucer's *Troilus and Criseyde*." *AnM* 6 (1965), 5-18.

1261. Dahlberg, Charles. "The Narrator's Frame for *Troilus*." *ChauR* 15 (1980), 85-100.

1262. Falke, Anne. "The Comic Function of the Narrator in *Troilus and Criseyde*." *Neophil* 68 (1984), 134-41.

1263. Frost, Michael H. "Narrative Devices in Chaucer's *Troilus and Criseyde*." *Thoth* 14 (1974), 29-38.

1264. Gaylord, Alan T. "The Lesson of the *Troilus*: Chastisement and Correction." In *Essays on Troilus and Criseyde*. Ed. Mary Salu. Cambridge: Brewer, 1979.

1265. Holly, Linda T. "The Narrative Speculum in *Troilus and Criseyde*." *CLAJ* 25 (1981), 212-24.

1266. Huppé, Bernard F. "The Unlikely Narrator: The Narrative Strategy of the *Troilus*." In *Signs and Symbols in Chaucer's Poetry*. Eds. John P. Hermann and John J. Burke, Jr. University: U of Alabama P, 1981.

1267. McKinnell, John. "Letters as a Type of the Formal Level in *Troilus and Criseyde*. In *Essays on Troilus and Criseyde*. Ed. Mary Salu. Cambridge: Brewer, 1979.

1268. Maybury, James F. "The Character of the Narrator in *Troilus and Criseyde*." *Northern New England Review* 8 (1983), 32-41.

1269. Mehl, Dieter. "The Audience of Chaucer's *Troilus and Criseyde*." In *Chaucer and Middle English Studies in Honour of Rossell Hope Robbins*. Ed. Beryl Rowland. London: Unwin, 1974.

1270. Rudat, Wolfgang E. H. "Chaucer's *Troilus and Criseyde*: Narrator-Reader Complicity." *AI* 40 (1983), 103-13.

1271. ———. "The Character of the Narrator in *Troilus and Criseyde*." *Northern New England Review* 8 (1983), 32-41.

1272. Salter, Elizabeth. "*Troilus and Criseyde*: Poet and Narrator." In *Acts of Interpretation:…Essays in Honor of E. Talbot Donaldson*. Eds. Mary J. Carruthers and Elizabeth D. Kirk. Norman, OK: Pilgrim Books, 1982.

1273. Steadman, John M. *Disembodied Laughter: Troilus and the Apotheosis Tradition: A Reexamination of Narrative and Thematic Contexts*. Berkeley: U of California P, 1972.

1274. Vance, Edward. "Mervelous Signals: Poetics, Sign Theory, and Politics in Chaucer's *Troilus*." *NLH* 10 (1978), 293-337.

1275. Waswo, Richard. "The Narrator of *Troilus and Criseyde*." *ELH* 50 (1983), 1-25.

See also 1360.

TC—Space and Time

1276. Bessent, Benjamin R. "The Puzzling Chronology of Chaucer's *Troilus*." *SN* 41 (1969), 99-111.

1277. Bie, Wendy A. "Dramatic Chronology in *Troilus and Criseyde*." *ELN* 14 (1976), 9-13.

1278. Ganim, John M. "Tone and Time in Chaucer's *Troilus*." *ELH* 43 (1976), 141-53.

TC—Iconography, Imagery, Proverbs

1279. Anderson, David. "Cassandra's Analogy: *Troilus* V. 1450-1521." *HUSL* 13 (1985), 1-17.

1280. Bailey, Susan E. "Controlled Partial Confusion: Concentrated Imagery in *Troilus and Criseyde*." *ChauR* 20 (1985), 83-89.

1281. Boitani, Piero. "Style, Iconography and Narrative: The Lesson of the *Teseida*." In *Chaucer and the Italian Trecento*. Ed. Piero Boitani. Cambridge: Cambridge U P, 1983.

1282. Clark, S. L., and Julian N. Wasserman. "The Heart in *Troilus and Creseyde*: The Eye of the Breast, the Mirror of the Mind, the Jewel and Its Setting." *ChauR* 18 (1984), 316-27.

1283. Gillmeister, Heiner. "Chaucer's *Kan Ke Dort* (*Troilus* II, 1752), and the 'Sleeping Dogs' of the Trouveres." *ES* 59 (1978), 310-23.

1284. Hermann, John P. "Gesture and Seduction in *Troilus and Criseyde*." *SAC* 7 (1985), 107-35.

1285. Houston, Gail Turley. "'White by Black': Chaucer's 'Effect Contraire' in *Troilus and Criseyde*." *Comitatus* 15 (1984), 1-9.

1286. Sadler, Frank. "Storm Imagery in *Troilus and Criseyde*." *WGCR* 10 (1978), 13-18.

1287. Stevens, Martin. "The Winds of Fortune in the *Troilus*." *ChauR* 13 (1979), 285-307.

1288. Stokes, M. "The Moon in Leo in Book V of *Troilus and Criseyde*." *ChauR* 17 (1982), 116-29.

1289. Tavormina, M. Theresa. "The Moon in Leo: What Chaucer Really Did to *Il Filostrato's* Calendar." *BSUF* 22 (1981), 14-19.

1290. Taylor, Karla. "Proverbs and the Authentication of Convention in *Troilus and Criseyde*." In *Chaucer's Troilus: Essays in Criticism*. Ed. Stephen A. Barney. Hamden, CT: Shoestring P, 1980.

1291. Toole, William B., III. "The Imagery of Fortune and Religion in *Troilus and Criseyde*." In *A Fair Day in the Affections: Literary Essays in Honor of Robert B. White, Jr*. Eds. Jack M. Durant and M. Thomas Hester. Raleigh, NC: Winston, 1980.

See also 441, 460, 466, 468, 470, 471, 472, 474.

TC—Philosophical Coloring

1292. apRoberts, Robert P. "The Boethian God and the Audience of the *Troilus*." *JEGP* 69 (1970), 425-36.

1293. Barney, Stephen. "Troilus Bound." *Speculum* 47 (1972), 445-58.

1294. Bloomfield, Morton. "Distance and Predestination in *Troilus and Criseyde*." *PMLA* 72 (1957), 14-26.

1295. Cloete, Nettie. "The Reconsiliation of Superstition and Christian Ideas in *Troilus and Criseyde*." *Communique* 5 (1980), 48-57.

1296. Curry, Walter Clyde. "Destiny in Chaucer's *Troilus*." *PMLA* 45 (1931), 129-68.

1297. Denomy, Alexander J. "The Two Moralities of Chaucer's *Troilus and Criseyde*." In *Proceedings and Transactions of the Royal Society of Canada*. 3rd ser., 44.2 (1950), 35-46. Rptd. *Chaucer Criticism II: Troilus and Criseyde and the Minor Poems*. Eds. R. J. Schoeck and J. Taylor: Notre Dame, IN: Notre Dame U P, 1960.

1298. DiPasquale, Pasquale, Jr. "'Sikerness' and Fortune in *Troilus and Criseyde*." *PQ* 49 (1970), 152-63.

1299. Eldredge, Laurence. "Boethian Epistemology and Chaucer's Troilus in the Light of Fourteenth Century Thought." *Mediaevalia* 2 (1976), 49-75.

1300. Gallagher, Joseph E. "Theology and Intention in Chaucer's *Troilus*." *ChauR* 7 (1972), 44-66.

1301. Howard, Donald R. "The Philosophies in Chaucer's *Troilus*." In *The Wisdom of Poetry: Essays...in Honor of Morton W. Bloomfield*. Eds. Larry D. Benson and Siegfried Wenzel. Kalamazoo, MI: Western Michigan U, 1982.

1302. Morgan, Gerald. "The Freedom of the Lovers in *Troilus and Criseyde*." In *Literature and Learning in Medieval and Renaissance England: Essays Presented to Fitzroy Pyle*. Ed. John Scattergood. Dublin: Irish Academic Press, 1984.

1303. Robertson, D. W., Jr. "Chaucerian Tragedy." *ELH* 19 (1952), 1-37.

1306. VanDyke, Carolynn. "The Errors of Good Men: Hamartia in Two Middle English Poems." In *Hamartia: The Concept of Error in the Western Tradition: Essays in Honor of John M Crossett*. Eds. Donald V. Stumpe et al. New York: Edwin Mellen, 1983.

1307. Zimbardo, Rose A. "Creator and Created: The Generic Perspective of Chaucer's *Troilus and Criseyde*." *ChauR* 11 (1977), 283-98.

See also 1255, 1287.

TC—Love and Marriage

1308. apRoberts, Robert P. "The Central Episode in Chaucer's *Troilus*." *PMLA* 77 (1962), 373-85.

1309. Arn, Mary-Jo. "Three Ovidian Women in Chaucer's *Troilus*: Medea, Helen, Oenone." *ChauR* 15 (1980), 1-10.

1310. Christmas, Peter. "*Troilus and Criseyde*: The Problems of Love and Necessity." *ChauR* 9 (1975), 285-96.

1311. Frankis, John. "Paganism and Pagan Love in *Troilus and Criseyde*." In *Essays on Troilus and Criseyde*. Ed. Mary Salu. Cambridge: Brewer, 1979.

1312. Helterman, Jeffrey. "Masks of Love in *Troilus and Criseyde*." *CL* 26 (1974), 14-31.

1313. Howard, Donald. "Courtly Love and Lust of the Flesh." In *The Three Temptations: Medieval Man in Search of the World*. Princeton U P, 1966.

1314. Hughes, Geoffrey. "The Sovereignty of Venus: The Problem of Courtly Love." *ESA* 25 (1982), 61-77.

1315. Kirk, Elizabeth D. "Paradis Stood Formed in Hire Yen: Courtly Love and Chaucer's Re-Vision of Dante." In *Acts of Interpretation...Essays in Honor of E. Talbot Donaldson*. Eds. Mary J. Carruthers and Elizabeth D. Kirk. Norman, OK: Pilgrim Books, 1982.

1316. Liggins, Elizabeth M. "The Lovers' Swoons in *Troilus and Criseyde*." *Parergon* 3 (1985), 40-60.

1317. Maguire, John B. "The Clandestine Marriage of Troilus and Criseyde." *ChauR* 8 (1974), 262-78.

1318. Morgan, Gerald. "The Significance of the Aubades in *Troilus and Criseyde*." *YES* 9 (1979), 221-35.

1319. Newman, Barbara. "'Feynede Loves', Feigned Love, and Faith in Trouthe." In *Chaucer's Troilus: Essays in Criticism*. Ed. Stephen A. Barney. Hamden, CT: Shoestring P, 1980.

1320. Renoir, Alain. "The Inept Lover and the Reluctant Mistress: Remarks on Sexual Inefficency in Medieval Literature." In *Chaucerian Problems and Perspectives: Essays Presented to Paul E. Beichner, C.S.C.* Eds. Edward Vasta and Zacharias P. Thundy. Notre Dame, IN: Notre Dame U P, 1979.

1321. Taylor, Willene P. "Supposed Antifeminism in Chaucer's *Troilus and Criseyde* and its Retraction in the *Legend of Good Women*." *XUS* 9 (1970), 1-18.

1322. Wack, Mary F. "Lovesickness in *Troilus*." *PCP* 19 (1984), 55-61.

1323. Wentersdorf, Karl P. "Some Observations on the Concept of Clandestine Marriage in *Troilus and Criseyde*." *ChauR* 15 (1980), 101-26.

1324. Windeatt, Barry A. "'Love that oughte ben secree' in Chaucer's *Troilus*." *ChauR* 14 (1979), 116-31.

See also 402-20, 572-584.

TC—Characterization

1325. Brewer, Derek. "The Ages of Troilus, Criseyde, and Pandarus." *SELit* 1 (1972), 3-13.

1326. Bronson, Larry. "The 'Sodeyn Diomede'—Chaucer's Composite Portrait." *BSUF* 25 (1984), 14-19.

1327. Delany, Sheila. "Techniques of Alienation in *Troilus and Criseyde*." In *The Uses of Criticism*. Ed. A. P. Foulkes. Bern: Lang, 1976.

1328. Greenfield, Stanley B. "The Role of Calkas in *Troilus and Criseyde*." *MAE* 36 (1967), 141-51.

1329. Haskell, Ann S. "The Doppelgängers in Chaucer's *Troilus*." *NM* 72 (1971), 723-34.

1330. Johnson, L. Staley. "The Medieval Hector: A Double Tradition." *Mediaevalia* 5 (1979), 165-82.

1331. Milowicki, Edward J. "Characterization in *Troilus and Criseyde*: Some Relationships Centered on Hope." *CRCL* 11 (1984), 12-24.

1332. Schibanoff, Susan. "Argus and Argyve: Etymology and Characterization in Chaucer's *Troilus*." *Speculum* 51 (1976), 647-58.

1333. Stokes, Myra. "'Wordes White': Disingenuity in *Troilus and Criseyde*." *ES* 64 (1983), 18-29.

1334. Tatlock, J. S. P. "The People in Chaucer's *Troilus*." *PMLA* 56 (1941), 85-104.

TC—Troylus

1335. Baron, F. X. "Chaucer's Troilus and Self-Renunciation in Love." *PLL* 10 (1974), 5-14.

1336. Brown, William H., Jr. "A Separate Peace: Chaucer and the Troilus of Tradition." *JEGP* 83 (1984), 492-508.

1337. Drake, Gertrude C. "The Moon and Venus: Troilus' Havens in Eternity." *PLL* 11 (1975), 3-17.

1338. Ebel, Julia. "Troilus and Oedipus: The Geneology of an Image." *ES* 55 (1974), 15-21.

1339. Freiwald, Leah R. "Swych Love of Frendes: Pandarus and Troilus." *ChauR* 6 (1971), 120-29.

1340. Gaylord, Alan T. "The Lesson of the *Troilus*: Chastisement and Correction." In *Essays on Troilus and Criseyde*. Ed. Mary Salu. Cambridge: Brewer, 1979.

1341. Green, Richard T. "Troilus and the Game of Love." In *Essays on Troilus and Criseyde*. Ed. Mary Salu. Cambridge: Brewer, 1979.

1342. Hatcher, Elizabeth R. "Chaucer and the Psychology of Fear: Troilus in Book V." *ELH* 40 (1973), 307-24.

1343. Kiernan, Kevin S. "Hector the Second: The Lost Face of Troilustratus." *AnM* 16 (1975), 52-62.

1344. Mann, Jill. "Troilus' Swoon." *ChauR* 14 (1980), 319-35.

1345. Martin, June Hall. *Love's Fools: Aucassin, Troilus, Calisto and the Parody of the Courtly Lover*. London: Thamesis, 1972.

1346. Masi, Michael. "Troilus: A Medieval Psychoanalysis." *AnM* 11 (1970), 81-88.

1347. Renoir, Alain. "Bayard and Troilus: Chaucerian Non-Paradox in the Reader." *OL* 36 (1981), 116-40.

1348. Rutherford, Charles S. "Troilus' Farewell to Criseyde: The Idealist as Clairvoyant and Rhetorician." *PLL* 17 (1981), 245-54.

1349. Storm, Melvin. "Troilus, Mars, and Late Medieval Chivalry." *JMRS* 12 (1982), 45-65.

1350. Taylor, Ann M. "Troilus' Rhetorical Failure." *PLL* 15 (1979), 357-69.

1351. Taylor, David. "The Terms of Love: A Study of Troilus's Style." *Speculum* 51 (1976), 69-90.

1352. Tkacz, Catherine Brown. "'Troilus the Syke': Boethian Medical Imagery in Chaucer's *Troilus and Criseyde*." *BSUF* 24 (1983), 3-12.

1353. Utley, F. L. "Chaucer's Troilus and St. Paul's Charity." In *Chaucer and Middle English Studies in Honour of Rossell Hope Robbins*. Ed. Beryl Rowland. London: Unwin, 1974.

1354. Vicari, Patricia. "Sparagmos: Orpheus Among the Christians." In *Orpheus: The Metamorphoses of a Myth*. Ed. John Warden. Toronto: U of Toronto P, 1982.

1355. Wenzel, Siegfried. "Chaucer's Troilus of Book IV." *PMLA* 79 (1964), 542-47.

TC—Criseyde

1356. Abshear-Seals, Lisa. "Boccaccio's Criseida and Chaucer's Creseyde." *Spectrum* 27 (1985), 25-32.

1357. Aers, David. "Criseyde: Woman in Medieval Society." *ChauR* 13 (1979), 177-200.

1358. apRoberts, Robert P. "Criseyde's Infidelity and the Moral of the *Troilus*." *Speculum* 44 (1969), 383-402.

1359. ———. "The Growth of Criseyde's Love." In *Medieval Studies Conference Aachen, 1983*. Eds. Wolf-Dietrich Bald and Horst Weinstock. Frankfurt am Main: Lang, 1984.

1360. Asakawa, Junko. "Chaucer's Narrator and Criseyde." *Bulletin of Tsuru University* 21 (1984), 51-57.

1361. Bowers, John M. "How Criseyde Falls in Love." In *The Expansion and Transformation of Courtly Literature*. Eds. N. B. Smith and J. T. Snow. Athens: U of Georgia P, 1980.

1362. Burnley, J. D. "Criseyde's Heart and the Weakness of Women: An Essay in Lexical Interpretation." *SN* 54 (1982), 25-38.

1363. Clogan, Paul M. "Criseyde's Book of the Romance of Thebes." *HUSL* 13 (1985), 18-28.

1364. Collins, David G. "The Story of Diomede and Criseyde: Changing Relationship in an Evolving Legend." *PAPA* 7 (1981), 9-30.

1365. David, Alfred. "Chaucerian Comedy and

Criseyde." In *Essays on Troilus and Criseyde.* Ed. Mary Salu. Cambridge: Brewer, 1979.

1366. Donaldson, E. Talbot. "Briseis, Briseida, Creseyde, Cresseid, Cressid." In *Chaucerian Problems and Perspectives: Essays Presented to Paul E. Beichner, C.S.C.* Eds. Edward Vasta and Zacharias P. Thundy. Notre Dame, IN: U of Notre Dame P, 1979.

1367. Fries, Maureen. "'Slydynge of Corage': Chaucer's Criseyde as Feminist and Victim." In *The Authority of Experience: Essays in Feminist Criticism.* Eds. Arlyn Diamond and Lee R. Edwards. Amherst: U of Massachusetts P, 1977.

1368. Gallagher, Joseph E. "Criseyde's Dream of the Eagle: Love and War in *Troilus and Criseyde.*" *MLQ* 36 (1975), 115-32.

1369. Gross, Laila. "The Two Wooings of Criseyde." *NM* 74 (1972), 113-25.

1370. Knapp, Peggy Ann. "The Nature of Nature: Criseyde's 'Slydyng Corage'." *ChauR* 13 (1978), 133-40.

1371. Lambert, Mark. "*Troilus,* Books I-III: A Criseydan Reading." In *Essays on Troilus and Criseyde.* Ed. Mary Salu. Cambridge: Brewer, 1979.

1372. Maybury, James F. "Pandarus and Criseyde: The Motif of Incest in Chaucer's *Troilus.*" *Xavier Review* 2 (1982), 82-89.

1373. Mieszkowski, Gretchen. *The Reputation of Criseyde: 1155-1500.* Hamden, CT: Archon, 1971.

1374. Pearsall, Derek. "Criseyde's Choices." *SAC,* Proceedings 2 (1986), 17-32.

1375. Rowland, Beryl. "Chaucer's Speaking Voice and Its Effect on His Listeners' Perception of Criseyde." *ESC* 7 (1981), 129-40.

1376. Salemi, Joseph S. "Playful Fortune and Chaucer's Criseyde." *ChauR* 15 (1981), 209-23.

1377. Schibanoff, Susan. "Criseyde's 'Impossible' Aubes." *JEGP* 76 (1977), 326-33.

1378. Woods, Marjorie Curry. "Chaucer the Rhetorician: Criseyde and Her Family." *ChauR* 20 (1985), 28-39.

TC—Pandarus

1379. Braddy, Haldeen. "Chaucer's Playful Pandarus." *SFQ* 34 (1970), 71-81.

1380. Carton, Evan. "Complicity and Responsibility in Pandarus' Bed and Chaucer's Art." *PMLA* 94 (1979), 47-61.

1381. Cook, Richard G. "Chaucer's Pandarus and the Medieval Idea of Friendship." *JEGP* 69 (1970), 407-24.

1382. Cormican, John D. "Motivation of Pandarus in *Troilus and Criseyde.*" *USF Language Quarterly* 18 (1980), 43-48.

1383. Ellis, Deborah. "'Calle It Gentiless': A Compara-tive Study of Two Medieval Go-Betweens." *Comitatus* 8 (1977), 1-13.

1384. Fyler, John M. "The Fabrications of Pandarus." *MLQ* 41 (1980), 115-30.

1385. Robbie, May G. "Three-Faced Pandarus." *CEJ* 31 (1967), 47-54.

1386. Rutherford, Charles S. "Pandarus as a Lover: 'A Joly Wo' or 'Loves Shotes Keene'?" *AnM* 13 (1972), 5-13.

1387. Schibanoff, Susan. "Chaucer and 'Stewart's' Pandarus and the Critics." *SSL* 13 (1978), 92-99.

1388. Slocum, Sally K. "How Old Is Chaucer's Pandarus?" *PQ* 58 (1979), 16-25.

1389. Van, Thomas A. "Chaucer's Pandarus as an Earthly Maker." *SHR* 12 (1978), 89-97.

See also 1339, 1372.

TC—The Ending

1390. Conlee, John W. "The Meaning of Troilus' Ascension to the Eighth Sphere." *ChauR* 7 (1972), 27-36.

1391. Donaldson, E. T. "The Ending of Chaucer's *Troilus.*" In *Early English and Norse Studies Presented to Hugh Smith.* Eds. Arthur Brown and Peter Foote. London: Methuen, 1963.

1392. Dronke, Peter. "The Conclusion of *Troilus and Criseyde.*" *MAE* 33 (1964), 47-52.

1393. Farnham, Anthony E. "Chaucerian Imagery and the Ending of *Troilus.*" *ChauR* 2 (1967), 207-16.

1394. Hussey, S.S. "The Diffcult Fifth Book of *Troilus and Criseyde.*" *MLR* 67 (1972), 721-29.

1395. Kamowski, William. "A Suggestion for Emending the Epilogue of *Troilus and Criseyde.*" *ChauR* 21 (1987), 405-18.

1396. Kean, Patricia M. "Chaucer's Dealings with a Stanza of *Il Filostrato* and the Epilogue of *Troilus and Criseyde.*" *MAE* 33 (1964), 36-46.

1397. Markland, Murry F. "*Troilus and Criseyde:* The Inviolability of Ending." *MLQ* 31 (1970), 147-59.

1398. Medcalf, Stephen. "Epilogue: From *Troilus* to *Troilus.*" In *The Later Middle Ages.* Ed. Stephen Medcalf. New York: Homes and Meier, 1981.

1399. Morgan, Gerald. "The Ending of 'Troilus and Criseyde'." *MLR* 77 (1982), 257-71.

1400. Shigeo, Hisashi. "The 'epilogue' of *Troilus and Criseyde* reconsidered." *The Meiji Gakuin Review* (March, 1979), 137-69. Meiji Gakuin University.

See also 1225, 1254, 1273.

EARLY POEMS, GENERAL

1401. Bridges, Margaret. "The Sense of an Ending: The Case of the Dream Vision." *Dutch Quarterly Review* 14 (1984), 81-96.

1402. Clemen, Wolfgang. *Chaucer's Early Poetry*. Trans. C.A.M. Sym. London: Methuen, 1963.

1403. Hieatt, Constance B. *The Realism of Dream Vision: The Poetic Exploitation of the Dream Experience in Chaucer and His Contemporaries*. The Hague: Mouton, 1967.

1404. Windeatt, Barry A. *Chaucer's Dream Poetry: Sources and Analogues*. Cambridge: Brewer, 1982. Ed. and trans. Machaut, *Roy de Behaingne*, Froissart, *Paradys d'amours*; Condé, *Messe des oisiaus*; 15 other French poems; *Somnium Scipionis;* Boccaccio, *Teseida* [excerpts]; Alanus, *Complaint of Nature* [excerpts].

1405. Winny, James. *Chaucer's Dream Poems*. London: Chatto and Windus, 1973.

See also 63, 70, 103, 284, 608, 1501.

BOOK OF THE DUCHESS

1406. Aers, David R. "Chaucer's *Book of the Duchess*: An Art to Consume Art." *Durham University Journal* 38 (1977), 201-05.

1407. Boardman, Phillip C. "Courtly Language and the Strategy of Consolation in the *Book of the Duchess*." *ELH* 44 (1977), 567-79.

1408. Brown, James N. "Narrative Focus and Function in *The Book of the Duchess*." *MSE* 2 (1970), 71-79.

1409. Dilorenzo, Raymond D. "'Wonder and Words': Paganism, Christianity, and Consolation in Chaucer's *Book of the Duchess*." *UTQ* 52 (1982), 20-39.

1410. Ebi, Hisato. "Light and Darkness in *The Book of the Duchess*—The 'Aesthetics of Light' of Gothic Art." *The Journal of the Liberal Arts Department, Kansai Medical University* (December 1980), 15-126.

1411. Edwards, Robert. "*The Book of the Duchess* and the Beginnings of Chaucer's Narratives." *NLH* 13 (1982), 189-204.

1412. Ferster, Judith. "Intention and Interpretation in the *Book of the Duchess*." *Criticism* 22 (1980), 1-24.

1413. Fichte, Joerg O. "*The Book of the Duchess*—A Consolation?" *SN* 45 (1973), 53-67.

1414. Fyler, John M. "Irony and the Age of Gold in the *Book of the Duchess*." *Speculum* 52 (1977), 314-28.

1415. Johnson, William C., Jr. "Art as Discovery: The Aesthetics of Consolation in Chaucer's *Book of the Duchess*." *SAB* 40 (1975), 53-62.

1416. Jordan, Robert M. "The Compositional Structure of the *Book of the Duchess*." *ChauR* 9 (1974), 99-117.

1417. Kiser, Lisa J. "Sleep, Dreams, and Poetry in Chaucer's *Book of the Duchess*." *PLL* 19 (1983), 92-93.

1418. Kronlins, Ieva. "The Still Point: Artifice in Chaucer's *Book of the Duchess*." *Centerpoint* 1 (1974), 73-81.

1419. Manning, Stephen. "Rhetoric as Therapy: The Man in Black, Dorigen, and Chauntecleer." *KPAB* 5 (1978), 19-25.

1420. Martin, Ellen E. "The Interpretation of Chaucer's Alcyone." *ChauR* 18 (1983), 18-22.

1421. Means, M. H. Th*e Consolatio Genre in Medieval English Literature*. Gainesville: U of Florida P, 1972.

1422. Morse, Ruth. "Understanding the Man in Black." *ChauR* 15 (1981), 204-08.

1423. Neaman, Judith S. "Brain Physiology and Poetics in *The Book of the Duchess*." *Res Publica Litterarium* 3 (1980), 101-13.

1424. Palmer, R. Barton. "The *Book of the Duchess* and *Fonteinne amoureuse*: Chaucer and Machaut Reconsidered." *Canadian Review of Comparative Literature* 7 (1981), 380-93.

1425. Peck, Russell A. "Theme and Number in Chaucer's *Book of the Duchess*." In *Silent Poetry: Essays in Numerological Analysis*. Ed. Alistair Fowler. New York: Barnes & Noble, 1970.

1426. Pelen, Marc M. "Machaut's Court of Love Narratives and Chaucer's *Book of the Duchess*." *ChauR* 11 (1976), 128-55.

1427. Perryman, Judith C. "How They Talk: Speech and Meaning in the 'Book of the Duchess'." *NM* 85 (1984), 227-38.

1428. Philips, Helen. "Structure and Consolation in the *Book of the Duchess*." *ChauR* 16 (1981), 107-18.

1429. Pigott, Margaret B. "The Dialectic of *The Book of the Duchess* and *The Parliament of Fowls*: A Movement Toward the Fifteenth Century." *FCS* 5 (1982), 167-89.

1430. Robertson, D.W., Jr. "The *Book of the Duchess*." In *Companion to Chaucer Studies*. Ed. Beryl Rowland. rev. ed. New York: Oxford U P, 1979.

1431. Ross, Diane M. "The Play of Genres in the *Book of the Duchess*." *ChauR* 19 (1984), 1-13.

1432. Rowland, Beryl. "The Whelp in Chaucer's 'Book of the Duchess'." *NM* 66 (1965), 148-60.

1433. Sadler, Lynn V. "Chaucer's *The Book of the Duchess* and the 'Law of Kinde'." *AnM* 11 (1970), 51-64.

1434. Salter, Elizabeth. "Chaucer and Internationalism." *SAC* 2 (1980), 71-79.

1435. Shoaf, R. A. "Stalking the Sorrowful H(e)art: Penitential Lore and the Hunt Scene in Chaucer's *The Book of the Duchess*." *JEGP* 78 (1979), 313-24.

1436. ———. "'Mutatio Amoris': 'Pententia' and the Form of *The Book of the Duchess*." *Genre* 14 (1981), 163-69.

1437. Spearing, A. C. "Literal and Figurative in *The Book of the Duchess*." *SAC*, Proceedings 1 (1984), 165-71.

1438. Suzuki, Tetsuya. "The Art of Restatement in the *Book of the Duchess*." *Shiron* 23 (1984), 1-21.

1439. Tisdale, Charles P. "Boethian 'Hert-Huntyng':

The Elegaic Pattern of the *Book of the Duchess*." *ABR* 24 (1973), 365-80.

1440. Tripp, Raymond P., Jr. "The Dialectics of Debate and the Continuity of English Poetry." *MSE* 7 (1978), 41-49.

1441. Walker, Denis. "Narrative Inclusiveness and Consolatory Dialectic in the *Book of the Duchess*." *ChauR* 18 (1983), 1-17.

1442. Wimsatt, James I. "The Apotheosis of Blanche in the *Book of the Duchess*." *JEGP* 66 (1967), 26-44.

1443. ———. "The Sources of Chaucer's 'Seys and Alcyone'." *MAE* 36 (1967), 231-41.

1444. ———. *Chaucer and the French Love Poets: The Literary Background of the Book of the Duchess*. Chapel Hill: U of North Carolina P, 1968.

1445. ———. "Chaucer, Fortune, and Machaut's 'Il m'est avis'." In *Chaucerian Problems and Perspectives: Essays Presented to Paul E. Beichner, C.S.C.* Eds. Edward Vasta and Zacharias P. Thundy. Notre Dame, IN: U of Notre Dame P, 1979.

1446. ———. "*The Book of the Duchess*: Secular Elegy or Religious Vision?" In *Signs and Symbols in Chaucer's Poetry*. Eds. John P. Hermann and John J. Burke, Jr. University: U of Alabama P, 1981.

1447. Zimbardo, Rose A. "The *Book of the Duchess* and the Dream of Folly." *ChauR* 18 (1984), 329-46.

See also 152.

BD—History

1448. Condren, Edward I. "The Historical Context of the *Book of the Duchess*: A New Hypothesis." *ChauR* 5 (1971), 195-212.

1449. Hill, John M. "The *Book of the Duchess*, Melancholy, and the Eight-Year Sickness." *ChauR* 9 (1974), 35-50.

1450. Loschiavo, Linda Ann. "The Birth of 'Blanch the Duchesse': 1340 *Versus* 1347." *ChauR* 13 (1978), 128-32.

1451. Palmer, John H. "The Historical Context of the *Book of the Duchess*: A Revision." *ChauR* 8 (1974), 253-61.

1452. Schless, Howard. "A Dating for the *Book of the Duchess*: Line 1314." *ChauR* 19 (1985), 273-76.

1453. Wentersdorf, Karl P. "The Clandestine Marriages of the Fair Maid of Kent." *Journal of Medieval History* 5 (1979), 202-31.

BD—The Persona

1454. Bartlett, Lee A. "Sometimes a Cigar is Just a Cigar: The Dreamer in Chaucer's *Book of the Duchess*." *Thoth* 15 (1974-75), 3-11.

1455. Bronson, Bertrand H. "The *Book of the Duchess* Reopened." *PMLA* 67 (1952), 863-81.

1456. Cherniss, Michael D. "The Narrator Asleep and Awake in Chaucer's *Book of the Duchess*." *PLL* 8 (1972), 115-26.

1457. Lumiansky, Robert M. "The Bereaved Narrator in Chaucer's *Book of the Duchess*." *TSL* 9 (1959), 5-17.

1458. Nolan, Barbara. "The Art of Expropriation: Chaucer's Narrator in *The Book of the Duchess*." In *New Perspectives on Chaucerian Criticism*. Ed. Donald M. Rose. Norman, OK: Pilgrim Books, 1981.

PARLEMENT OF FOULES

1459. Aers, David. "The *Parliament of Fowls*: Authority, the Knower and the Known." *ChauR* 16 (1981), 1-17.

1460. Baker, Donald C. "The *Parliament of Fowls*." In *Companion to Chaucer Studies*. Ed. Beryl Rowland. rev. ed. New York: Oxford U P, 1979.

1461. Bennett, J.A.W. *The Parlement of Foules: An Interpretation*. Oxford: Clarendon, 1957.

1462. ———. "Some Second Thoughts on *The Parlement of Foules*." In *Chaucerian Problems and Perspectives: Essays Presented to Paul E. Beichner, C.S.C.* Eds. Edward Vasta and Zacharias P. Thundy. Notre Dame, IN: U of Notre Dame P, 1979.

1463. Benson, Larry D. "The Occasion of *The Parliament of Fowls*." In *The Wisdom of Poetry: Essays Presented to Morton W. Bloomfield*. Eds. Larry D. Benson and Siegfried Wenzel. Kalamazoo, MI: Medieval Institute Publications, 1982.

1464. Braddy, Haldeen. *Chaucer's Parlement of Foules in Relation to Contemporary Events*. Expanded ed. New York: Octagon P, 1969.

1465. Brown, Emerson, Jr. "Priapus and the *Parlement of Foulys*." *SP* 72 (1975), 258-74.

1466. Cowgill, Bruce Kent. "The *Parlement of Foules* and the Body Politic." *JEGP* 74 (1975), 315-35.

1467. Dean, James. "Artistic Conclusiveness in Chaucer's *Parliament of Fowles*." *ChauR* 21 (1986), 16-25.

1468. Dubbs, Kathleen E., and Stoddard Malarkey. "The Frame of Chaucer's *Parlement*." *ChauR* 13 (1978), 16-24.

1469. Eldredge, Laurence. "Poetry and Philosophy in the *Parlement of Foules*." *RUO* 40 (1970), 441-59.

1470. Entzminger, Robert L. "The Pattern of Time in *The Parlement of Foules*." *JMRS* 5 (1975), 1-11.

1471. Ferster, Judith. "Reading Nature: The Phenomenology of Reading in the *Parliament of Fowls*." *Mediaevalia* 3 (1977), 189-213.

1472. Fowler, David C. "Chaucer's *Parliament of Fowls*, and the Hexameral Tradition." In *The Bible in Middle English Literature*. Ed. David C. Fowler. Seattle: U of Washington P, 1984.

1473. Fujiki, Takayoshi. "Chaucer's 'love' in *The Parlement of Foules*." *Shukugawa Studies in Linguistics and Literature* 4 (1980), 1-13.

1474. Gilbert, A. J. "The Influence of Boethius on *Parlement of Foules*." *MAE* 47 (1978), 292-303.

1475. Hutchinson, Judith. "*The Parliament of Fowls*: A Literary Entertainment. *Neophil* 61 (1977), 143-51.

1476. Jordan, Robert M. "The Question of Unity and the *Parlement of Foules*." *ESC* 3 (1977), 373-85.

1477. Kearney, John A. "The *Parliament of Fowls*: The Narrator, the 'Certeyn Thyng', and the 'Commune Profyt'." *Theoria* 45 (1975), 55-71.

1478. Kelley, Michael R. "Antithesis as the Principle of Design in the *Parlement of Foules*." *ChauR* 14 (1979), 61-73.

1479. Leicester, H. M., Jr. "The Harmony of Chaucer's *Parlement*: A Dissonant Voice." *ChauR* 9 (1974), 15-34.

1480. Loganbill, Dean. "Chaucer as Social Critic." *PMPA* 3 (1978), 1-9.

1481. McCall, John P. "The Harmony of Chaucer's *Parliament*." *ChauR* 5 (1970), 22-31.

1482. McDonald, Charles O. "An Interpretation of Chaucer's *Parlement of Foules*." *Speculum* 30 (1955), 444-57.

1483. Mucchetti, E. A. "The Structural Importance of the Proem and the *Somnium Scipionis* to the Unity of *The Parliament of Fowls*." *PAPA* 4 (1978), 1-10.

1484. Olson, Paul A. "*The Parlement of Foules*: Aristotle's *Politics* and the Foundations of Human Society." *SAC* 2 (1980), 53-69.

1485. Oruch, Jack B. "St. Valentine, Chaucer, and Spring in Feburary." *Speculum* 56 (1981), 534-65.

1486. ———. "Nature's Limitations and the *Demande d'Amour* of Chaucer's *Parlement*." *ChauR* 18 (1983), 23-37.

1487. Pelen, Marc M. "Form and Meaning of the Old French Love Vision: The *Fabliau dou Dieu d'Amors* and Chaucer's *Parliament of Fowls*." *JMRS* 9 (1979), 277-305.

1488. Polzella, Marion L. "'The Craft So Long to Lerne': Poet and Lover in Chaucer's 'Envoy to Scogan' and *Parliament of Fowls*." *ChauR* 10 (1976), 279-86.

1489. Quilligan, Maureen. "Allegory, Allegoresis, and the Deallegorization of Language: The *Roman de la Rose*, the *De Planctu naturae*, and the *Parlement of Foules*." In *Allegory, Myth, and Symbol*. Ed. Morton W. Bloomfield. Cambridge: Harvard U P, 1981.

1490. Reed, Thomas L. "Chaucer's *Parlement of Foules*: The Debate Tradition and the Aesthetics of Irresolution." *RUO* 50 (1980), 215-22.

1491. Rothschild, Victoria. "*The Parliament of Fowls*: Chaucer's Mirror Up to Nature?" *RES* 35 (1984), 164-84.

1492. Sklute, Larry M. "The Inconclusive Form of the *Parliament of Fowls*." *ChauR* 16 (1981), 119-28.

1493. Smith, Frances J. "Mirth and Marriage in *The Parlement of Foules*." *BSUF* 14 (1973), 15-22.

1494. Walker, Denis. "Contentio: The Structural Paradigm of *The Parliament of Fowls*." In *SAC*, Proceedings 1 (1984), 173-80.

1495. Yamamoto, Toshiki. "Chaucer and *The Parliament of Fowls*." *Essays on Classical Studies* (March 1980), 40-50.

See also 281, 1429.

HOUSE OF FAME

1496. Allen, Robert J. "A Recurring Motif in Chaucer's *House of Fame*." *JEGP* 55 (1956), 393-405.

1497. Bennett, J.A.W. *Chaucer's Book of Fame: An Exposition of the House of Fame*. Oxford: Clarendon, 1968.

1498. Boitani, Piero. "Chaucer's Labyrinth: Fourteenth-Century Literature and Language." *ChauR* 17 (1983), 197-220.

1499. ———. *Chaucer and the Imaginary World of Fame*. Cambridge: Brewer, 1984.

1500. Braswell, Mary Flowers. "Architectural Portraiture in Chaucer's *House of Fame*." *JMRS* 11 (1981), 101-12.

1501. Bridges, Margaret. "The Sense of an Ending: The Case of the Dream-Vision." *DQR* 14 (1984), 81-96.

1502. Chiappelli, Carolyn. "Fals Apparences: Satan and Chaucer's *House of Fame*." *PPMRC* 4 (1979), 107-14.

1503. Dean, Nancy. "Ovid's Elegies from Exile and Chaucer's *House of Fame*." *Hunter Coll. Studies* 3 (1966), 75-90.

1504. Delany, Sheila. "Chaucer's *House of Fame* and the *Ovide Moralisé*." *CL* 20 (1968), 254-64.

1505. Dickerson, A. Inskip. "Chaucer's *House of Fame*: A Skeptical Epistemology of Love." *TSLL* 18 (1976), 171-83.

1506. Erzgraber, Willi. "Problems of Oral and Written Transmission as Reflected in Chaucer's *House of Fame*." In *Historical and Editorial Studies in Medieval and Early Modern English*. Eds. Mary-Jo Arn and H. Wirtjes. Groningen: Wolters-Nordhoff, 1985.

1507. Fry, Donald K. "The Ending of the *House of Fame*." In *Chaucer at Albany*. Ed Rossell Hope Robbins. New York: Franklin, 1975.

1508. Gellrich, J. M. "The Origin of Language Reconsidered: Chaucer's *House of Fame*." In *The Idea of the Book in the Middle Ages*. Ed. J. M. Gellrich. Ithaca, NY: Cornell U P, 1985.

1509. Grennen, Joseph E. "Chaucer and Chalcidius: The Platonic Origins of the *House of Fame*." *Viator* 15 (1984), 237-62.

1511. Irvine, Martin. "Medieval Grammatical Theory and Chaucer's *House of Fame.*" *Speculum* 60 (1985), 850-66.

1512. Jeffrey, David Lyle. "Sacred and Secular Scripture: Authority and Interpretation in *The House of Fame.*" In *Chaucer and the Scriptural Tradition.* Ed. David Lyle Jeffrey. Ottawa: U of Ottawa P, 1984.

1513. Jordan, Robert M. "Lost in the Funhouse of Fame: Chaucer and Postmodernism." *ChauR* 18 (1983), 100-15.

1514. Joyner, William. "The Journey Motif in Chaucer's *House of Fame.*" *EngRev* 1 (1973), 28-41.

1515. ———. "Parallel Journeys in Chaucer's *House of Fame.*" *PLL* 12 (1976), 3-19.

1516. Kanno, Masahiko. "The Meaning of *The House of Fame.*" In *Essays in Honour of Professor Hiroshige Yoshida.* Shinozake Shorin P, 1980.

1517. Kelley, Michael R. "Chaucer's *House of Fame:* England's Earliest Science Fiction." *Extrapolation* 16 (1974), 7-16.

1518. Kendrick, Laura. "Chaucer's *House of Fame* and the French Palais de Justice." *SAC* 6 (1984), 121-33.

1519. Koonce, B. G. *Chaucer and the Tradition of Fame: Symbolism in the House of Fame.* Princeton: Princeton U P, 1966.

1520. Leyerle, John. "Chaucer's Windy Eagle." *UTQ* 40 (1971), 247-65.

1521. Meade, Robert. "The Saints and the Problem of Fame in the *House of Fame.*" *NM* 84 (1983), 201-05.

1522. Miller, Jacqueline T. "The Writing on the Wall: Authority and Authorship in Chaucer's *House of Fame.*" *ChauR* 17 (1982), 95-115.

1523. Overbeck, Pat Trefzger. "The 'Man of Gret Auctorite' in Chaucer's *House of Fame.*" *MP* 73 (1975), 157-61.

1524. Rowland, Beryl. "Bishop Bradwardine, the Artificial Memory, and the *House of Fame.*" In *Chaucer at Albany.* Ed. Rossell Hope Robbins. New York: Franklin, 1975.

1525. ———. "The Art of Memory and the Art of Poetry in the *House of Fame.*" *RUO* 51 (1981), 163-71.

1526. Shepherd, Geoffrey T. "Make Believe: Chaucer's Rationale of Story-telling in *The House of Fame.*" In *J. R. R. Tolkien: Essays in Memoriam.* Eds Mary Salu and Robert T. Farrell. Ithaca, NY: Cornell U P, 1979.

1527. Shook, Laurence K. "*The House of Fame.*" In *Companion to Chaucer Studies.* Ed. Beryl Rowland. rev. ed. New York: Oxford U P, 1979.

1528. Stevenson, Kay. "The Endings of Chaucer's *House of Fame.*" *ES* 59 (1978), 10-26.

1529. Teresa, Margaret. "Chaucer's High Rise: Aldgate and the *HF.*" *ABR* 33 (1982), 162-71.

1530. Tisdale, Charles P. "The *House of Fame:* Virgilian Reason and Boethian Wisdom." *CL* 25 (1973), 247-61.

1531. Vance, Eugene. "Chaucer's *House of Fame* and the Poetics of Inflation." *Boundary* 27 (1979), 17-37.

1532. Watts, Ann C. "Amor *gloriae* in Chaucer's *House of Fame.*" *JMRS* 3 (1973), 87-113.

LEGEND OF GOOD WOMEN

1533. Allen, Peter L. "Reading Chaucer's Good Women." *ChauR* 21 (1987), 405-18.

1534. Amy, Ernest F. *The Text of Chaucer's Legend of Good Women* (1918). New York: Haskell, 1965.

1535. Cowen, Janet M. "Chaucer's *Legend of Good Women:* Structure and Tone." *SP* 82 (1985), 416-36.

1536. Fisher, John H. "The *Legend of Good Women.*" In *Companion to Chaucer Studies.* Ed. Beryl Rowland. rev. ed. New York: Oxford U P, 1979.

1537. ———. "The Revision of the Prologue to the *Legend of Good Women*: An Occasional Explanation." *SAB* 43 (1978), 75-84.

1538. Frank, Robert W., Jr. *Chaucer and the Legend of Good Women.* Cambridge: Harvard U P, 1972.

1539. Gaylord, Alan T. "Dido at Hunt, Chaucer at Work." *ChauR* 17 (1983), 300-15.

1540. Gellrich, J. M. "Problems of Misreading: The 'Prologue' to *The Legend of Good Women.*" In *The Idea of the Book in the Middle Ages.* Ed. J. M. Gellrich. Ithaca, NY: Cornell U P, 1985.

1541. Hansen, Elaine. "Irony and the Antifeminist Narrator in Chaucer's *Legend of Good Women.*" *JEGP* 82 (1983), 11-31.

1542. Kiser, Lisa J. *Telling Classical Tales: Chaucer and The Legend of Good Women.* Ithaca, NY: Cornell U P, 1983.

1543. Kolve, V. A. "From Cleopatra to Alceste: An Iconographic Study of *The Legend of Good Women.*" In *Signs and Symbols in Chaucer's Poetry.* Eds. John P. Hermann and John J. Burke, Jr. University: U of Alabama P, 1981.

1544. Lossing, Marian. "The Prologue to the *Legend of Good Women* and the *Lai de Franchise.*" *SP* 39 (1942), 15-35.

1545. Lowes, John L. "The Prologue to the *Legend of Good Women* as Related to the French Marguerite Poems and the *Filostrato.*" *PMLA* 19 (1904), 593-683.

1546. ———. "The Prologue to the *Legend of Good Women* Considered in Its Chronological Relations." *PMLA* 20 (1905), 794-864.

1547. McMillan, Ann. "Heaven, Hell, and *The Legend of Good Women.*" In *The Worlds of Medieval Women.* Eds. Constance H. Berman, et al. Morgantown: U of West Virginia P, 1985.

1548. Payne, Robert O. "Making His Own Myth: The Prologue to Chaucer's *Legend of Good Women.*" *ChauR* 9 (1975), 197-211.

1549. Shigeo, Hisashi. "Chaucer's Idea of 'Love' and 'Goodness' in *The Legend of Good Women.*" *The Meiji Gakuin Review* (October 1980), 37-54.

1550. Smith, Sarah Stanbury. "Cupid's Sight in the Prologue to the *Legend of Good Women.*" *Centerpoint* 4 (1981), 95-102.

1551. Spisak, James W. "Chaucer's Pyramus and Thisbe." *ChauR* 18 (1984), 204-10.

1552. Taylor, Beverly. "The Medieval Cleopatra: The Classical and Medieval Tradition of Chaucer's *Legend of Cleopatra.*" *JMRS* 7 (1977), 249-69.

1553. Thompson, R. Ann. "The Irony of Chaucer's *Legend of Good Women* Perceived in 1576." *Archiv* 213 (1976), 342-43.

1553a. Wimsatt, James I. *The Marguerite Poetry of Guillaume de Machaut.* Chapel Hill: U of North Carolina P, 1970.

See also 409.

SHORT POEMS, GENERAL

1554. Doyle, A. I., and George B. Pace. "Further Texts of Chaucer's Minor Poems." *SB* 28 (1975), 41-61.

1555. Hanning, Robert W. "Chaucer and the Dangers of Poetry." *CEA* 46 (1984), 17-26.

1556. Lampe, David. "The Courtly Rhetoric of Chaucer's Advisory." *RMSt* 9 (1983), 70-83.

1557. Robbins, Rossell Hope. "The Lyrics." In *Companion to Chaucer Studies.* Ed. Beryl Rowland. rev. ed. New York: Oxford U P, 1979.

1558. Stevens, John. "The 'Music' of the Lyric: Machaut, Deschamps, Chaucer." In *Medieval and Pseudo-Medieval Literature.* Eds. Piero Boitani and Anna Torti. Tübingen: Narr, 1984.

1559. ———. "The Uses of Personae and the Art of Obliqueness in Some Chaucer Lyrics." Part I *ChauR* 21 (1987), 360-73; Part II *ChauR* 21 (1987), 459-68; Part III *ChauR* 22 (1987), 41-52.

1560. Wimsatt, James I. "Guillaume de Machaut and Chaucer's Love Lyrics." *MAE* 47 (1978), 66-87.

See also 43, 59, 63, 79, 114.

Prier a Nostre Dame

1561. David, Alfred. "An ABC to the Style of the Prioress." In *Acts of Interpretation...Essays in Honor of E. Talbot Donaldson.* Eds. Mary J. Carruthers and Elizabeth D. Kirk. Norman, OK: Pilgrim Books, 1982.

1562. Pace, George B. "The Adorned Initials of Chaucer's *ABC.*" *Manuscripta* 23 (1979), 88-98.

Anelida and Arcite

1563. Cherniss, Michael D. "Chaucer's *Anelida and Arcite:* Some Conjectures." *ChauR* 5 (1970), 9-21.

1564. David, Alfred. "Recycling *Anelida and Arcite:* Chaucer as a Source for Chaucer." *SAC* Proceedings 1, (1984), 105-15.

1565. Gillam, Doreen M. E. "Lovers and Riders in Chaucer's 'Anelida and Arcite'." *ES* 63 (1982), 394-401.

1566. Norton-Smith, John. "Chaucer's *Anelida and Arcite.*" In *Medieval Studies for J. A. W. Bennett.* Ed. P. L. Heyworth. Oxford: Clarendon, 1981.

1567. Wimsatt, James I. "*Anelida and Arcite:* A Narrative of Complaint and Comfort." *ChauR* 5 (1970), 1-8.

Complaints

1568. Clogan, Paul M. "The Textual Reliability of Chaucer's Lyrics: *A Complaint to His Lady.*" *M&H* 5 (1974), 183-89.

1569. Dean, Nancy, "Chaucer's *Complaint,* a Genre Descended from the *Heroides.*" *CL* 19 (1967), 1-27.

1570. Gray, Douglas. "Chaucer and 'Pite'." In *J. R. R. Tolkien: Essays in Memoriam.* Eds. Mary Salu and Robert T. Farrell. Ithaca, NY: Cornell U P, 1979.

1571. Nolan, Charles J., Jr. "Structural Sophistication in 'The Complaint Unto Pity'." *ChauR* 13 (1979), 363-72.

1572. Parr, Johnstone, and Nancy Ann Holtz. "The Astronomy- Astrology in Chaucer's *The Complaint of Mars.*" *ChauR* 25 (1981), 255-66.

1573. Storm, Melvin. "The Mythological Tradition in Chaucer's *Complaint of Mars. PQ* 57 (1978), 323-35.

To Rosemounde

1574. Fichte, Joerg O. "*Womanly Noblesse* and *To Rosemounde:* Point and Counterpoint of Chaucerian Love Lyrics." *SAC* Proceedings 1 (1984), 181-94.

1575. Rickert, Edith. "A Leaf from a Fourteenth-Century Letter Book." *MP* 25 (1927), 249-55.

1576. Robbins, Rossell Hope. "Chaucer's 'To Rosemounde'." *SLitI* 4 (1971), 73-81.

1577. Vasta, Edward. "*To Rosemounde:* Chaucer's 'Gentil' Dramatic Monologue." In *Chaucerian Problems and Perspectives: Essays Presented to Paul E. Beichner, C.S.C.* Eds. Edward Vasta and Zacharias P. Thundy. U of Notre Dame P, 1979.

Lak of Stedfastnesse

1578. Norton-Smith, John. "Textual Tradition, Monarchy and Chaucer's *Lak of Stedfastnesse.*" *Reading Medieval Studies* 8 (1982), 3-10.

1579. Scattergood, John. "Social and Political Issues in Chaucer: An Approach to *Lak of Stedfastnesse.*" *ChauR* 21 (1987), 469-76.

Complaint to His Purse

1580. Ferris, "The Date of Chaucer's Final Annuity and of the 'Complaint to His Empty Purse'." *MP* 65 (1967), 42-52.

1581. Finnel, Andrew J. "The Poet as Sunday Man: 'The Complaint of Chaucer to His Purse'." *ChauR* 8 (1973), 147-58.

1582. Scott, Florence R. "A New Look at 'The Complaint of Chaucer to His Empty Purse'." *ELN* 2 (1964), 81-87.

Boethian Balades

1583. Chance, Jane. "Chaucerian Irony in the Boethian Short Poems: The Dramatic Tension between Classical and Christian." *ChauR* 20 (1986), 235-54.

1584. Davis, Norman. "Chaucer's *Gentilesse:* A Forgotten Manuscript, with Some Proverbs." *RES* 20 (1969), 43-50.

1585. David, Alfred. "The Truth About 'Vache'." *ChauR* 11 (1977), 334-37.

1586. Galway, Margaret. "Chaucer Among Thieves." *TLS* 20 April 1946, p. 187. (*Fortune*)

1587. Nichols, Robert E., Jr. "Chaucer's *Fortune, Truth,* and *Gentilesse:* The 'Last' Unpublished Manuscript Transcriptions." *Speculum* 44 (1969), 46-50.

1588. Scattergood, V. J. "Chaucer's Curial Satire: the *Balade de bon Conseyl.*" *Hermathena* 133 (1982), 29-45.

1589. Schmidt, A. V. C. "Chaucer and the Golden Age." *EIC* 26 (1976), 99-115.

Envoy to Scogan

1590. Chance, Jane. "Chaucerian Irony in the Verse Epistles 'Words Unto Adam', 'Lenvoy a Scogan', and 'Lenvoy a Bukton'." *PLL* 21 (1985), 115-28.

1591. David, Alfred. "Chaucer's Good Counsel to Scogan." *ChauR* 3 (1969), 265-74.

1592. Hallmundsson, May Newman. "Chaucer's Circle: Henry Scogan and His Friends." *M&H* n.s. 10 (1981), 129-39.

1593. Kaske, R. E. "*Clericus Adam* and Chaucer's *Adam Scriveyn.*" In *Chaucerian Problems and Perspectives:* *Essays Presented to Paul E. Beichner, C.S.C.*. Eds. Edward Vasta and Zacharias P. Thundy. Notre Dame, IN: U of Notre Dame P, 1979.

1594. Lenaghan, R. T. "Chaucer's *Envoy to Scogan:* The Uses of Literary Conventions." *ChauR* 10 (1975), 46-61.

See also 1488.

Proverbs

1595. Pace, George B. "The Chaucerian *Proverbs.*" *SB* 18 (1965), 41-48.

BOECE

1596. Eckhardt, Caroline D. "The Medieval *Prosimetrum* Genre from Boethius to *Boece.*" *Genre* 16 (1983), 21-38.

1597. Fischer, Olga. "A Comparative Study of Philosophical Terms in the Alfridian and Chaucerian *Boethius.*" *Neophil* 63 (1979), 622-39.

1598. Machan, Tim William. *Techniques of Translation: Chaucer's Boece.* Norman, OK: Pilgrim Books, 1985.

1599. Pace, George B., and Linda E. Voigts. "A 'Boece' Fragment." *SAC* 1 (1979), 143-50.

See also 272, 302.

ASTROLABE, PLANETIS

1600. Gunther, R. T. *Chaucer and Messahalla on the Astrolabe.* Oxford: Oxford U P, 1929.

1601. Lipson, Carol. "'I n'am but a lewd compilator': Chaucer's 'Treatise on the Astrolabe' as Translation." *NM* 84 (1983), 192-200.

1602. Masi, Michael. "Chaucer, Messahalla, and Bodleian Selden Supra 78." *Manuscripta* 19 (1975), 36-47.

1603. Owen, Charles A. Jr. "A Certein Nombre of Conclusions: The Nature and Nurture of Children of Chaucer." *ChauR* 16 (1981), 60-75.

1604. Price, D. J. "The *Equatorie of the Planetis.* Peterhouse MS (1). Attributed to Simon Bredon. Now Suggested as an Unknown Work by Chaucer." *TLS* 29 February 1952, p. 164, and 7 March 1952, p. 180.

1605. Price, Derek, ed. *The Equatorie of the Planetis.* With a Linguistic Analysis by R. M. Wilson. Cambridge: Cambridge U P, 1955.

CLASSIFICATIONS

TC—Characterization, 1325-1334
TC—Troylus, 1335-1355
TC—Criseyde, 1356-1378
TC—Pandarus, 1379-1389
TC—The Ending, 1390-1400

Early Poems, General, 1401-1405
Book of the Duchess, 1406-1447
    BD—History, 1448-1453
    BD—The Persona, 1454-1458
The Parlement of Foules, 1459-1495
The House of Fame, 1496-1532
The Legend of Good Women, 1533-1553a

Short Poems, General, 1554-1560
    Prier a Nostre Dame, 1561-1562
    Anelida and Arcite, 1563-1567
    Complaints, 1568-1573
    To Rosemounde, 1574-1577
    Lak of Stedfastnesse, 1578-1579
    Complaint to His Purse, 1580-1582
    Boethian Balades, 1583-1589
    Envoy to Scogan, 1590-1594
    Proverbs, 1595

Boece, 1596-1599
Astrolabe, Planetis, 1600-1605

JOURNAL ABBREVIATIONS

ABR	American Benedictine Review
AI	American Imago: A Psychoanalytic Journal
AN&Q	American Notes and Queries
AnM	Annuale Mediaevale
ArAA	Arbeiten aus Anglistik und Amerikanistik
ArlQ	Arlington Quarterly
BAM	Bulletin des Anglicistes Médiévistes (Paris)
BSUF	Ball State University Forum
C&L	Christianity and Literature
C&M	Classica et Mediaevalia
CE	College English
CEA	CEA Critic: Journal of the College English Association
CEJ	California English Journal
CentR	Centennial Review (Michigan State U)
CF	Classical Folia
ChauR	Chaucer Review
CJItS	Canadian Journal of Italian Studies
CL	Comparative Literature
CLAJ	College Language Association Journal
CR	Critical Review (Canberra)
CRCL	Canadian Review of Comparative Literature
E&S	Essays and Studies
EAS	Essays in Arts and Sciences
ELH	English Literary History
ELN	English Language Notes
EIC	Essays in Criticism (Oxford)
ELWIU	Essays in Literature (Western Illinois U)
EM	English Miscellany
EngRev	English Review (Salem C)
ES	English Studies
ESA	English Studies in Africa (Johannesburg)
ESC	English Studies in Canada
DQR	Dutch Quarterly Review of Anglo-American Letters
FCS	Fifteenth Century Studies

HSELL	Hiroshima Studies in Language and Literature
HLQ	Huntington Library Quarterly
HUSL	Hebrew University Studies in Literature and the Arts
JEGP	Journal of English and Germanic Philology
JEP	Journal of Evolutionary Psychology
JHI	Journal of the History of Ideas
JMRS	Journal of Medieval and Renaissance Studies
JNT	Journal of Narrative Technique
JRMRA	Journal of the Rocky Mountain Medieval and Renaissance Association
JWSL	Journal of Women Studies in Literature
KN	Kwartalnik Neofilologiczny (Warsaw)
KPAB	Kentucky Philological Association Bulletin
L&H	Literature and History
L&P	Literature and Psychology (Teaneck, NJ)
Lang&S	Language and Style
LangQ	The USF Language Quarterly
LeedsSE	Leeds Studies in English
LHY	Literary Half-Yearly
LittR	Literary Review (Madison, NJ)
Lore&L	Lore and Language
M&H	Medievalia et Humanistica
MAE	Medium Aevum
McNR	McNeese Review
MHLS	Mid-Hudson Language Studies
MLQ	Modern Language Quarterly
MLS	Modern Language Studies
MS	Medieval Studies (Toronto)
MSE	Massachusetts Studies in English
Neophil	Neophilologus (Groningen)
NLH	New Literary History
NM	Neuphilologische Mitteilungen
NMS	Nottingham Medieval Studies
NwMSCS	Northwest Missouri State College Studies

OL	*Orbis Litterarum*	SHR	*Southern Humanities Review*
		SIcon	*Studies in Iconography*
PAPA	*Publications of the Arkansas Philological Association*	SLitI	*Studies in Literary Imagination*
		SMC	*Studies in Medieval Culture*
PCP	*Pacific Coast Philology*	SN	*Studia Neophilologica*
PLL	*Papers on Language and Literature*	SoCR	*South Central Review*
PMLA	*Publications of the Modern Language Association of America*	SoRA	*Southern Review* (Adelaide)
		SP	*Studies in Philology*
PMPA	*Publications of the Missouri Philological Association*	SSF	*Studies in Short Fiction*
		SSL	*Studies in Scottish Literature* (Columbia, SC)
PPMRC	*Annual Publication of the International Patristic Mediaeval and Renaissance Conference*		
		TLS	*London Times Literary Supplement*
PQ	*Philological Quarterly*	TPB	*Tennessee Philological Bulletin*
		TSE	*Tulane Studies in English*
RBPH	*Revue Belge de Philologie et d'Histoire*	TSL	*Tennessee Studies in Literature*
RCEI	*Revista Canaria de Estudios Ingleses*	TSLL	*Texas Studies in Language and Literature*
RES	*Review of English Studies*	TWA	*Transactions of the Wisconsin Academy of Sciences, Arts, and Letters*
RLV	*Revue des Langues Vivants*		
RMSt	*Reading Medieval Studies*		
RUO	*Revue de l'Université d'Ottawa / University of Ottawa Quarterly*	UMS	*Unisa Medieval Studies*
		UTQ	*University of Toronto Quarterly*
RUS	*Rice University Studies*	UWR	*University of Windsor Review* (Ontario)
SAB	*South Atlantic Bulletin*	WGCR	*West Georgia College Review*
SAC	*Studies in the Age of Chaucer*	WHR	*Western Humanities Review*
SAQ	*South Atlantic Quarterly*		
SB	*Studies in Bibliography*	XUS	*Xavier University Studies*
SeijoB	*Seijo University Bulletin* (Japan)		
SEL	*Studies in English Literature, 1500-1900*	YES	*Yearbook of English Studies*
SELit	*Studies in English Literature* (Tokyo)	YFS	*Yale French Studies*
SES	*Sophia English Studies*		
SFQ	*Southern Folklore Quarterly*	ZAA	*Zeitschrift für Anglistik und Amerikanistik*

INDEX OF AUTHORS

Davis, R. Evan, 547
Dean, James, 530, 829, 1148, 1215, 1467
Dean, Nancy, 1091, 1503, 1569
Delany, Sheila, 405, 723, 759, 949, 1092, 1327, 1504
Delasanta, Rodney, 426, 724, 760, 969, 1074, 1162
Deligiorgis, Stavrus, 495
Dempster, Germaine, 273, 515
DeNeef, A. Leigh, 970
Denomy, Alexander J., 406, 1297
Deschamps, 275
DeWeever, Jacqueline, 143
Diamond, Arlyn, 407
Dickerson, A. Inskip, 1505
Dickson, Donald R., 1139
Diekstra, Frans, 188, 189, 548, 1149
Dillon, Bert, 81
Dilorenzo, Raymond D., 1409
DiMarco, Vincent, 899
DiPasquale, Pasquale, Jr., 1298
Dolbey, Marcia A., 875
Donaldson, E. T., 48, 104, 323, 638, 673, 1366, 1391
Donohue, James J., 63, 64, 65
Dor [Caluwé], Juliette, 66, 154, 155
Doyle, A. I., 6, 14, 1554
Drake, Gertrude C., 1337
Dronke, Peter, 1392
Dubbs, Kathleen E., 1468
Duncan, Edgar H., 1140
Dunleavy, Gareth W., 377, 427
Dunn, C. W., 277
DuVal, John, 1093

Eade, J. C., 343
East, W. G., 760a
Ebel, Julia, 1338
Eberle, Patricia J., 612
Ebi, Hisato, 1410
Ebin, Lois, 324
Eckhardt, Caroline D., 597, 1596
Economou, George D., 247, 446
Edwards, A. S. G., 7
Edwards, Robert, 1411
Eggebroten, Anne, 1122
Elbow, Peter, 190
Eldredge, Laurence, 1299, 1469
Eliason, Norman E., 117, 598
Elliott, R. W. V., 118
Ellis, Deborah, 1383
Ellis, Roger, 571
Engelhardt, George J., 585
Enkvist, Nils Erik, 231
Entzminger, Robert L., 1470
Erzgraber, Willi, 1506

Fahey, Kathleen, 1003

Falke, Anne, 1262
Farnham, Anthony E., 1393
Farnham, Willard, 294
Farrell, Robert T., 725
Ferris, Sumner, 1032, 1033, 1580
Ferster, Judith, 248, 1412, 1471
Fichte, Joerg O., 167, 639, 950, 1413, 1574
Fifield, Merle, 168
Finke, Laurie A., 1163
Finlayson, John, 192, 1164
Finnegan, Robert Emmett, 726
Finnel, Andrew J., 1581
Fischer, Olga C. M, 761, 1597
Fish, Varda, 1194
Fisher, John H., 50, 76, 249, 295, 325, 344, 465, 466, 516, 531, 1536, 1537
Fisiak, Jacek, 129
Fleissner, Robert E., 1034
Fleming, John V., 378, 447, 467, 815
Fleming, Martha H., 816
Fletcher, Alan J., 702
Fowler, Alistair, 635
Fowler, David C., 1472
Fradenburg, Louise, 1151
Frank, Hardy Long, 1035
Frank, Robert Worth, Jr., 1036, 1246, 1538
Frankis, John, 1311
Frazier, J. Terry, 916
Freed, E. R., 549
Freiwald, Leah R., 1339
Frese, Dolores, 830, 1094
Friedman, Albert B., 1037
Friedman, John B., 345, 363, 703, 1095
Fries, Maureen, 1367
Friman, Anne, 428
Fritz, Donald W., 971, 1038
Frost, Cheryl, 877
Frost, Michael H., 1263
Frost, William, 550
Fry, Donald K., 1075, 1507
Fujiki, Takayoshi, 1473
Fulk, R. D., 1150
Furnivall, F. J. A., 517
Fyler, John M., 296, 917, 1195, 1384, 1414

Gallacher, Patrick J., 674, 762, 1096
Gallagher, Joseph E., 1300, 1368
Gallick, Susan, 326, 1097
Galvan-Reula, J. F., 1098
Galway, Margaret, 89, 95, 468, 1586
Ganim, John M., 1247, 1278
Garbáty, Thomas J., 193, 613
Gardner, John Champlin, 96, 232
Gates, Barbara T., 878
Gaylord, Alan T., 169, 601, 1053, 1054, 1055, 1264, 1340, 1539

Newman, Barbara, 1319
Nicolas, Harris, 39
Nichols, Robert E., Jr., 1587
Nicholson, Peter, 1021, 1022
Nitecki, Alicia, K., 989
Nolan, Barbara, 1458
Nolan, Charles T., Jr., 1571
North, J. D., 396
Norton-Smith, John, 2, 203, 240, 1566, 1578

Oberembt, Kenneth J., 778
O'Donoghue, Bernard, 416
Ogura, Mieko, 173
Oizumi, Akio, 1065
Olmert, Michael, 1168
Olsen, Alexandra Hennessey, 990
Olson, Clair C., 94, 580
Olson, Glending, 241, 354, 481, 538, 539, 557, 708,
    1058
Olson, Paul, 434, 654, 1484
Olsson, Kurt, 1077
Orme, Nicholas, 482
Oruch, Jack B., 1485, 1486
Osberg, Richard H., 1202
Otten, Charlotte F., 883
Overbeck, Pat Trefzger, 1523
Ovid, 282, 283
Owen, Charles A., Jr., 383, 520, 521, 540, 627, 1006,
    1603

Pace, George B, 59, 1554, 1562, 1595, 1599
Page, Barbara, 605
Palmer, Barbara D., 779
Palmer, John H., 1451
Palmer, R. Barton, 1424
Palomo, Dolores, 780, 1067
Parkes, Malcolm, 3, 4, 6
Parr, Johnstone, 1572
Parr, Roger P., 367
Parry, J. J., 265
Patch, Howard R., 384, 385, 435
Patterson, Lee, 781, 991, 1169, 1203
Paull, Michael R., 737
Payne, F. Anne, 204, 1108
Payne, Robert O., 157, 158, 205, 206, 1548
Pazdziora, Marian, 501
Pearcy, Roy J., 820, 935
Pearsall, Derek, 55, 253, 332, 472, 474, 488, 992,
    1374
Peck, Russell A., 79, 386, 502, 1130, 1425
Pelen, Marc M., 1426, 1487
Perlman, E., 850
Perryman, Judith C., 655, 1427
Peterson, Joyce E., 908, 993
Pfander, H. G., 1170

Philips, Helen, 1428
Pichaske, David R., 606
Pigott, Margaret B., 1429
Pison, Thomas, 541, 558
Pittock, Malcolm, 994
Plummer, John F., 709
Polzella, Marion L., 1488
Power, Eileen, 1044
Pratt, Robert A., 522, 782, 1109, 1110, 1220
Presson, Robert K., 159, 207
Price, Derek, 1604, 1605
Pynson, Richard, 24, 26

Quick, Anne, 77
Quilligan, Maureen, 1489
Quinn, Esther C., 503, 783

Ramsey, Lee C., 956
Ramsey, Roger, 851
Ramsey, Roy Vance, 15, 16, 559
Rand, E. K., 272
Raynaud, G., 275
Reames, Sherry L., 1131, 1132
Reed, Thomas L., 1490
Reidy, John, 656
Reiss, Edmund, 208, 355, 387, 581, 593, 1186
Renoir, Alain, 108, 1320, 1347
Revard, Carter, 690
Rex, Richard, 123, 1045
Rhodes, Jewell Parker, 784
Rhodes, James F., 995, 996
Richards, Mary P., 691
Richardson, Cynthia C., 607
Richardson, Janette, 456, 810
Richmond, Velma B., 582
Rickert, Edith, 46, 242, 1575
Ridley, Florence, 1046
Robbie, May G., 1385
Robertson, D. W., Jr., 148, 243, 244, 388, 436, 453,
    457, 785, 786, 936, 1204, 1303, 1430
Robbins, H. W., 277
Robbins, Rossell Hope, 124, 568, 1557, 1576
Robinson, F. N., 45
Robinson, Ian, 174, 333
Robinson, Pamela, 1, 9
Roddy, Kevin, 738
Rogers, H. L., 884, 1254
Rogers, P. Burwell, 599
Rogers, William E., 125, 308
Roney, Lois, 489
Root, Robert K., 42, 1221
Roscow, Gregory, 132
Ross, Diane M., 1431
Ross, Thomas W., 54, 126
Rosenberg, Bruce A., 356, 937, 1133

Strauss, Jennifer, 1206
Strohm, Paul, 337, 358, 359, 360, 562, 1070
Stroud, Theodore A., 660
Stugrin, Michael, 508
Sudo, Jun, 1223
Sundby, Thor, 264
Surges, Robert S., 583
Sutherland, Ronald, 47
Suzuki, Tetsuya, 1438
Sweetland, Laura, 606
Szittya, Penn, 795, 822

Taitt, Peter S., 370
Taggie, Benjamin, F., 1079
Takimoto, Jiro, 584
Tarlinskaja, Marina G., 178
Tattlebaum, Linda, 661
Tatlock, J. S. P., 86, 524, 892, 1334
Tavormina, M. Theresa, 1289
Taylor, Ann M., 662, 1350
Taylor, Beverly, 1552
Taylor, David, 1351
Taylor, Jerome, 857
Taylor, Karla Terese, 1224, 1290
Taylor, Paul B., 127, 630, 1006, 1144, 1174
Taylor, Willene P., 1321
Teresa, Margaret, 1529
Theiner, Paul, 742
Thomas, Paul R., 1115
Thompson, Charlotte, 543
Thompson, R. Ann, 338, 1553
Thro, A. B., 697
Thundy, Zacharias, 509, 594, 796
Thynne, William, 27, 28, 29, 30
Tisdale, Charles P., 1439, 1530
Tkacz, Catherine Brown, 710, 1352
Tolkien, J. R. R., 711
Toole, William B., III, 1291
Trask, Richard M., 1156
Traversi, Derek, 245a, 492, 943, 1157
Travis, Peter W., 1116
Tripp, Raymond P., Jr., 255, 1440
Tristram, Philippa, 1007
Trojel, E., 265
Trower, Katherine B., 958
Tucker, Edward F. J., 893
Turner, Frederick, 663
Twycross, Meg, 461
Tyrwhitt, Thomas, 37

Ullman, Walter, 437a
Urry, John, 35
Ussery, Huling E., 858, 959
Utley, Francis L. 859, 1243, 1353

Van, Thomas, 664, 1389
Vance, Edward, 1274
Vance, Eugene, 1531
VanDyke, Carolynn, 1306
Vasta, Edward, 712, 1577
Vaughan, M. F., 698
Verdonk, P. 797
Vicari, Patricia, 1354
Voigts, Linda, 1599
Von Kreisler, Nicolai A., 670

Wack, Mary F., 1322
Wagenknecht, Edward C., 109
Walker, Denis, 361, 1441, 1494
Wallace, David, 314, 315, 860
Wallace-Hadrill, Anne, 85
Waller, Martha S., 960, 1080
Walsh, P. G., 265
Warner, Marina, 419
Wasserman, J. N., 544, 718, 719
Waswo, Richard, 1275
Waterhouse, Ruth, 1134
Watts, Ann C., 110, 1532
Weiss, Alexander, 161, 339
Weissman, Hope Phyllis, 420, 743, 798
Wentersdorf, Karl P., 151, 571, 823, 894, 1117, 1323, 1453
Wenzel, Siegfried, 340, 1175, 1176, 1177, 1178, 1355
West, Philip, 799
Westervelt, L. A., 1158
Wetherbee, Winthrop, 256, 1207
Wheeler, Bonnie, 1225
White, Robert B., Jr., 1081
White, Gertrude M., 944
Whitlark, James S., 316
Whitman, Frank H., 1208
Whitmore, Sister Mary E., 246
Whittock, Trevor, 493
Williams, Arnold, 391
Williams, David, 699
Williams, Michael E., 800
Wilkins, Nigel, 477, 478
Wimsatt, James I., 317, 861, 1227, 1228, 1229, 1257, 1442, 1443, 1444, 1445, 1446, 1553a, 1560, 1567
Windeatt, Barry A., 18, 51, 284, 462, 1209, 1230, 1231, 1324, 1404
Winny, James, 1405
Witte, Stephen P., 1048
Woo, Constance, 510
Wood, Chauncey, 257, 392, 400, 401, 744, 1049, 1060, 1159, 1210
Woods, Marjorie Curry, 1378
Woods, Susanne, 179

GLOSSARY

The most complete Chaucer glossary, with line citations, is the inexpensive, paperback *Chaucer Glossary* (Oxford: Clarendon, 1979) compiled by Norman Davis, Douglas Gray, Patricia Ingham, and Anne Wallace-Hadrill. Chaucer's vocabulary is displayed, without definitions, in the *Concordance to the Complete Works of Chaucer and to the Romaunt of the Rose* (1927, Gloucester, MA: Peter Smith, 1963). Definitions to all of . Chaucer's words and usages may be found in the *Oxford English Dictionary*, but they must be looked up under their modern spellings. They are listed under their Middle English spellings in the *Middle English Dictionary* now approaching completion.

Since substantive words have been glossed on the pages where they occur, the following glossary is composed chiefly of form words: verb forms, adverbs, prepositions, and variant spellings. The great difficulty with creating a Middle English glossary, as with reading the texts, is that spellings were not standardized. Each scribe spelled as he thought he heard the words in his head, and felt little compunction about spelling the same word differently in contiguous passages. The Chaucer surname was spelled at least six ways in the records: Chaucer, Chaucere, Chaucey, Chauser, Chausier, and Chawceres. The reader should bear in mind the common variations in orthography: *i* and *y* are interchangeable (*ire, yre*); *e* and *i* are interchangeable (*be, bi*); *ee, ie*, and *e* are interchangeable (*leef, lief, lefe*); *o* and *ou* are interchangeable (*conseil, counseil*); vowels and consonants may be doubled (*brode, brood; unethe, unnethe*); metathesis may occur (*thorp, throp*); and there are other variations (see the essay on Chaucer's Language, esp. pp. 964-65). Imagination, context, and association must be called on to interpret both words and forms.

a, a, one, on
abaissen, to be dismayed
abandoune, to devote
abiden, to wait for, to dwell
abit, waited for
abite, habit, clothes
abayst, abashed, shy
aboghte, bought, paid for, endured
abood, waited for, delayed
aboute, about, engaged in
abreyden, to awake, to start up
abyden, to wait for, to endure
accioun, action, accusation
acorsen, to curse
acoyen, to caress
adawen, to awake
adoun, downwards, at the bottom
advertence, attention
afered, afraid
aferen, to frighten
affect, desire (*noun*)
affiance, trust (*noun*)
aforyeyn, opposite
after, after, in accordance with
again, against, towards, compared with

agains, instead of, near to
agilten, to do wrong
agref, in grief, angry
agreggen, to aggravate
agroos, trembled, was terrified
agroted, satiated, surfeited
agrysen, to tremble, to be terrified
acknowen, to acknowledge
alday, continually
alder, of all (*archaic genitive*)
alderbest, best of all
aldernext, nearest of all
algate, always, at any rate, nevertheless
alleggen, to allege, to alleviate
allowen, to approve, to applaud
alosen, to praise
alther, see *alder*
altherfastest, as fast as possible
alyne, in line
amased, to be amazed
amayen, to dismay
amelen, to enamel
amenusen, to lessen, to diminish
ameven, to move, to dismay
among, all the while

amonges, sometimes
amortisen, to kill
anguisshen, to cause pain
anhangen, to hang
anientissen, to annihilate
anlas, dagger
anon, at once
anything, at all
apayen, to satisfy
apeiren, to injure
apert, evident, openly
appetyt, desire
apposen, to question
appreven, to approve, to prove
apyken, to adorn
aquyten, to pay back
aracen, to uproot, to erase, to eradicate
areden, to explain, to reveal
arewe, arowe, in a row
arowe, arrow
arten, to induce
ascaunces, as if
ascry, outcry, alarm (*noun*)
aslaken, to satisfy, to diminish
aspre, sharp, bitter

1035

assoilen, to absolve, to pay, to explain
asterten, to escape
ataken, to overtake
auntren, to risk it
avalen, to fall down
avauncen, to advance, to be profitable
avaunten, to boast
aventure, luck, fortune
avouterye, adultery
avowen, to proclaim
avys, advice
avysen, to consider
await, surveillance
awhapen, to amaze, to frighten
axen, to ask
aydwellinge, everlasting
ayein, ayeins, see *again, agains*

bachelere, aspirant to a profession
bacin, basin
baiten, to feed
bale, sorrow
balke, roof beam
bane, death, cause of death
barbe, veil
barm clooth, apron
batailled, notched with battlements
baude, bawd, pimp
bauderie, mirth, obscenity
baume, balm
baundon, (feudal) power
bebled, covered with blood
beden, to offer, to command
beeth, be (*imperative*)
bekken, to nod
belwen, to bellow
bely, belly, bellows
benden, to bend, to turn
bent, grassy slope
beren, to bear, to carry, to conduct
    oneself
bespreynt, sprinkled
beten, to heal
beten, to beat
bidden, to ask, to command
biheste, promise, command
biheten, to promise
bihighte, promised
bihoten, to promise
bihove, profit (*noun*)
bihoven, to suit, to be necessary
biknowen, to acknowledge
bileve, belief
bileven, to believe, to stay behind
binimen, to take away
bireven, to take away, to deprive
biseyen, to gaze; **wel beseye**, good
    looking
bishenden, to bring to ruin
bishitten, to shut up
bisinesse, work, attention

bistad, in trouble
bitraisen, to betray
bitrent, encircled
bityden, to happen
bitymes, early
biwreyen, to reveal
biwryen, to betray
blenden, to make blind
blent, blinded
blinnen, to cease
boden, to proclaim
boist, box
boistous, crude, plain
bolt-upright, flat on the back
bord, table
borwe, security (*noun*)
bote, benefit, remedy (*noun*)
botelees, without remedy
bour, bedroom
bourde, joke
brede, breadth
breme, furious, furiously
brennen, to burn
bretful, full to the brim
breyden, to awake, to start up
brood, broad, large
brotel, brittle, fickle
brouken, to enjoy, to use
burel, crude, ignorant
buxom, obedient
by, concerning
byden, to wait
byen, to buy, to redeem
byhighte, promised
bynt, (he) binds
byrde, maiden

caas, case, event, chance
caitif, captive, miserable wretch
can, to be able, to know
canstow, do you know
cart, cart, chariot
casten, to throw, to calculate
casuelly, accidentally
catel, chattels, property
ceynt, girdle
chacen, to chase, to hunt
chaffaren, to bargain
chaire, chair, throne
chalangen, to claim
chapman, merchant
char, chariot
charge, load (*noun*)
chaunce, chance, destiny
chep, trade, bargain (*noun*); cheap
    (*adj*)
chere, face, expression, behavior
chesen, to choose
child, child, young man
cleer, clear, bright
clene, clean, pure

clepen, to call, to name
cleren, to grow clear, to grow bright
clippen, to cut, to embrace
clom, be quiet, "clam" up (*imperative*)
clombe, climbed
clos, enclosure
clos, close, secret (*adj*)
clout, rag
commeven, to persuade
con, grant (*imperative*)
conjecten, to conjecture
connen, to be able
conning, skill, knowledge
conseil, council, secret
constreinen, to comprise, to bring
    together
contek, strife
converten, to change
conveyen, to convey, to accompany
corage, courage, heart, spirit,
    disposition
corny, strongly malt
corps, cors, body
cosin, cousin, relative
cote armure, coat of arms
couchen, to lie down, to lay down
coude, could, knew
counten, to calculate accounts
counting-bord, accounting office
couthe, could, knew, known
covenable, fitting, suitable
covert, secret
covyne, deceitfulness
coy, quiet
craft, trade, cunning
creaunce, belief (*noun*)
creauncen, to borrow on credit
crop, new growth
croys, cross
cunnen, to know
cunning, skill

daliaunce, small talk, flirting
dan, daun, lord (title of respect, from
    Lat. *dominus*)
daswen, to be dazed
daunger, aloofness, disdain, control
daunten, to tame, to subdue
debaat, quarrel
debonair, kind, gentle
deedly, deadly, causing death, subject
    to death
deel, part
defaut, fault
delicat, dainty, sensitive
delices, delights, pleasures
demen, to judge, to decide
departen, to separate, to divide
dereworthe, beloved, valuable
despyt, spite, malice, disdain
destreynen, to compel, to distress

devoir, duty
devys, device, discretion
devysen, to devise, to tell
deynte, valuable (*noun*); pleasant, rare (*adj*)
dighten, to prepare, to dress
discoveren, to reveal
discryven, to describe, to discover
disese, discomfort, displeasure
dispenden, to spend
dispitous, spiteful, cruel
disponen, to dispose, to arrange
disporten, to play, to amuse
divynen, to guess
doom, judgment, opinion
doon, to do, to cause to be done
douten, to fear, to frighten
drenchen, to drown
dressen, to dress, to address, to direct, to prepare
dreynte, drowned
dreyen, to suffer, to endure
duren, to endure, to last
durren, to dare
durring, daring, courage
dwellen, to remain, to delay

echen, to increase
echoon, each one
eft, again
eft-sone, immediately, afterwards, once again
egre, bitter, fierce
elde, old age
elden, to grow old
emforth, to the extent of
enchaufen, to burn, to grow hot
enchesoun, reason, occasion
endelong, lengthwise, alongside
endyten, to compose, to write
engyn, contrivance, ingenuity
entecchen, to stain, to infect
entenden, to give attention to, to attend
entremetten, to interfere
enstryken, to ensnare
eren, to plow
ermen, to feel sad
ers, buttocks
eschaufen, to burn, to grow hot
eschewen, to escape, to avoid
esily, easily, slowly
espyen, to observe, to perceive, to inquire
estat, rank, condition
estres, interior (of a building)
ethe, easy
expert, expert, experienced
eyr, air, heir

facultee, disposition, capacity

fallen, to befall, to happen
falsen, to deceive, to be untrue
farcen, to stuff
fare, conduct, behavior, business
faren, to behave, to travel
fawe, glad, anxious
fayn, glad, eager
fee, reward, compensation
feendly, fiendlike
feet, feat, deed, performance
feffen, to enfeoff, to endow, to present
fel, skin
fel, cruel, terrible
felawe, companion
felden, fell (past t. of *fallen*)
fele, many
felonous, fierce, wicked
ferd, fear (*noun*); frightened, feared (past t. *verb*)
fere, mate, companion
feren, to frighten, to be afraid
ferforth, as far as
ferly, strange
ferme, income, rent
fermen, to make firm
fern, long ago
ferne, distant
ferre, distant, farther
feste, feast, pleasure
festen, to feast, to please
fet, fette, fetched
fetis, neat, attractive
fey, faith
feynen, to feign, to pretend
ficchen, to fix
fil, fild, befell, happened
finden, to find, to provide for
fint, finds
flaugh, (has) flown
fleen, to fly, to flee
fleigh, (it) flies
flemen, to banish
flen, (they) fly
fleten, to float, to drift
fley, flew
flitten, to pass away
flokmele, in a group
flough, flew
flyen, to fly; (they) fled
foisoun, abundance
folily, foolishly
fonden, to try
fongen, to receive
for-, intensifying prefix
forbrused, badly bruised
fordon, to destroy
forlesen, to lose
forleten, to forsake
forlorn, lost
fors, force; **no fors**, no matter

forthy, therefore
for-why, for what reason
foryaf, forgave
foryeten, to forget
foryeven, to forgive
fot-hoot, hot-footed, immediately, quickly
foul, fowl, bird; dirty, ugly
foundement, foundation
foynen, to thrust, to stab
foyson, abundance
fraynen, freynen, to ask, to beseech
free, generous, bounteous
fremede, foreign, wild
freten, to eat (like an animal), to devour
fro, from
froten, to rub
frounce, wrinkle
frount, front, face, countenance
furlong, 220 yards
furlong-wey, brief time (time it takes to walk a furlong)
furthren, to help
fyn, end, result (*noun*); refined
fynt, (he) finds

gabbe, boast (*noun*)
galen, to sing, to yell
gamen, to play, to amuse
gan, began
gat, got
gaude, toy, trick
gauden, to decorate
gay, dressed up, decorated
geaunt, giant
geeth, goes
gent, refined
gerdoun, reward
gere, equipment, apparel
gery, changeable
geste, tale, story
gif, if
gin, snare, contrivance
ginne, to begin, to try
girle, young person, girl
glede, live coal
glood, glided
glosen, to gloss, to interpret, to lie
gniden, to rub
gobet, piece
gon, to go, to walk
governaunce, management, rule
grame, anger, harm
gras, grace, favor
graven, to engrave, to dig, to bury
gree, favor; rank
greet, great, principal
greythen, to prepare, to adorn
greven, to harm, to feel unhappy
grint, ground (past t. of *grind*)

grisly, horrible
grobben, to dig
gropen, to grope, to search, to examine
grucchen, to grumble
gruf, grovelling
guerdon, reward
gyen, to guide
gylour, beguiler
gyte, dress (*noun*)

haf, heaved
halen, to pull, to attract
halke, corner
halp, helped
hals, neck
halt, held
halten, to limp
hap, chance, luck
happed, (it) happened
hardely, boldly
harwed, harried, despoiled
hastow, hast thou
hatte, promised, was named
haunten, to engage in, to practice
heef, (he) lifts
heet, was named
hele, health
helen, to conceal
henten, to catch
her, her, here, their
heren, to hear
herien, to praise
herth, (he) hears
heste, command (*noun*)
heten, to promise
hethen, hence
hette, promised, was named
heven, to heave, to lift
heved, head
hevy, heavy, sad
heye, high, aristocratic
hider, hither
highte, promised, was named
hir, her, their
hit, it
holly, wholly
holpe, helped
holt, woodland
holt, (he) holds
honest, creditable, honorable
hongen, to hang
hool, whole
hoten, to command, to promise
housbondrye, domestic management
hoven, to hover, to attend
hy, high
hye, haste
hyen, to hasten

ich, I

ilke, same
in, inne, dwelling
inned, lodged

janglen, to chatter
jape, trick, joke
journee, day's march
juyse, justice

keen, cows
keepen, to care for, to notice
kemben, to comb
kempte, combed, neatly dressed
kene, keen, eager
kinde, nature, lineage, disposition
kindely, naturally
knitten, to join
kythen, to show, to display

lakken, to blame, to disparage
lappe, flap, edge of a garment
lappen, to enfold
large, large, generous
las, lace, net, snare
last, burden
laude, praise, honor
launde, grassy clearing
laus, loose
lay, song; law
leef, lief, dear, agreeable
lees, deceit
leigh, lay (past t. of *lie, remain*)
lemman, sweetheart
lenen, to lend
lere, flesh, skin
leren, to teach
lesen, to lose
lesing, untruth
lest, inclination, pleasure
leten, to permit, to abandon
letten, to prevent, to hinder
leven, to believe, to allow
lever, rather, preferable
lewed, unlearned, ignorant, immoral
liche, like
liggen, to lie
light, light, joyous, fickle
lightly, easily, quickly
likerous, lecherous
lisse, comfort, solace
list, pleasure, desire; (with dative *me list, you list*) it pleases
loos, praise
lufsom, lovable
lust, desire, pleasure
lyflode, means of living
lyst, lystow, you lie

maistrye, skill, professional competence
make, mate

malgre, in spite of
mat, dejected, dead
maugre, in spite of
may, maiden
medlen, to mingle, to mix
meed, reward, bribe
mene, middle, mediator
menen, to say
meten, to dream
meynee, household, followers
misese, trouble, discomfort
mo, more
moeble, moveable property, furniture
moot, mot, mote, must, ought to, shall
moutance, amount
mowen, to be able

n-, negative prefix
nadde, had not (*ne had*)
nam, am not
nas, was not
nayten, to withold
ne, not, nor
nempnen, to name, to say
nere, nearer
nether, lower
nevenen, to name, to say
nexte, nearest
nil, will not
nolde, would not
noot, don't know
nost, don't know
nouthe, now, at present
ny, nigh, near
nyce, foolish

or, ere, before
owen, to own, to be obligated
owher, anywhere

paas, pas, pace, step
pacen, to pass, to go, to proceed
pardee, an exclamation (Fr. *par Dieu*)
parfey, an exclamation (Fr. *par fei*)
parten, to share, to divide
partye, portion
passen, to surpass, to overcome
perdurable, eternal
peyne, pain, torture
pighte, pitched, fell
plat, flat
pleten, to plead, to argue
pleyne, to complain, to lament
plighte, plucked, pulled
plighten, to pledge
port, behavior, carriage
possen, to push
preef, proof, assertion
prees, press, crowd, throng
prest, ready, prompt

preven, to prove, to test
preyen, to beseech
priken, to puncture, to urge, to incite
pris, prize, value
privee, secret, intimate
process, process, argument
propre, one's own, especial, well made
proven, to test
pyne, pain, torture

queynt, strange, curiously contrived
quiken, to revive
quod, said
quyten, to repay, to reward

rage, anger, passion, grief
rathe, soon, quickly
rather, earlier, more willingly
real, royal
recchen, to reck, to care about
reden, to read, to advise
reed, counsel, advice
refut, refuge
regne, realm, dominion over
reckenen, to reckon, to calculate accounts
rekken, to reck, to care about
remuable, capable of motion, changeable
reneyen, to deny, to renounce
rente, income, revenue
repairen, to return, to go home
repreve, reproof, reproach
requeren, to be sought for, to demand
resoun, right, correct, argument
respyt, delay
ret, (he) reads, advises
reven, to rob, to bereave
reward, regard, attention
rewde, rude, plain
rewen, to have pity
rewthe, pity
rihtwis, righteous
rode, cross; complexion
ron, rained
ronne, ran
roof, pierced
ropen, reaped
roser, rose bush
rote, by heart (*by rote*)
rote, root; fiddle
rounen, to whisper
route, band, company
routen, to roar, to snore
routhe, pity
rowe, rough
ryven, to pierce

sad, sober, firm

sans, sauns, without
sauf, save, expect
sawe, speech, saying
science, science, wisdom
scripture, writing
scrit, writing
sechen, to seek
secree, secret, confidential
see, seat
sein, seyn, to say
sekernes, security
sely, holy, good, innocent, pitiable, foolish (an interesting range of meanings)
semblable, similar
semblaunt, appearance
semely, seemly, estimable
sentence, meaning, subject
sermoun, discourse, sermon
servage, servitude
sewen, to follow
sey, saw (past t. of *see*)
shapen, to plan, to contrive, to intend
shenden, to disgrace, to destroy
shene, bright, shining
sheten, to shoot
shetten, to shut
shiften, to provide, to distribute
shonde, shame, disgrace
shrewe, scoundrel, wicked person
shrewednesse, wickedness
siker, sure, secure
sith, sithen, since, afterwards
sithes, times
skile, reason, cause
skilful, reasonable
slee, slay
sleighte, trickery
socour, help
solas, consolation, (sexual) pleasure
sond, sand
sonde, messenger
sort, lot, destiny
soot, sot, sweet
sounen, to sound, to incline towards, to accord with
sours, source, springing upwards
sovereyn, supreme, principal
speden, to succeed, to hasten, to finish
spillen, to spill, to destroy
statut, law
stede, horse; place
stenten, to leave off, to stop
steren, to stir up
sterten, to start, to move quickly
sterven, to die
stevene, voice
stinten, to leave off, to stop
stounde, hour, time, while
streit, narrow

streynen, to compress, to constrain
suffisaunce, sufficiency, wealth
sweven, dream
swich, such
swink, work
swote, sweet
swoune, swoon, faint
swythe, quickly
swyven, have sexual intercourse
syk, sick, sigh
sythe, time

t'-, prefix *to*
t'acord, to accord
talen, to tell a story
talent, wish, appetite
t'anende, to an end
tene, vexation
terme, appointed time
th'-, prefix *the, thee*
th'absence, the absence
th'alight, thee alight
thar, it is necessary
theen, to prosper
theech, theek, I (may) prosper
th'ende, the end
thewes, habits, morals
thilke, that same, that sort
thinken, to seem; **me thinkes**, it seems to me; **how thinketh you**, how does it seem to you
thirlen, to pierce
tho, those
tholen, to suffer
thonke, thank(s)
thorp, village
thral, slave, subject
thresten, to thrust
thridde, third
thrift, welfare, success
thriftily, carefully
thringen, to crowd, to press
throwe, short time
thryven, to thrive, to prosper
to-, intensifying prefix
tobreken, to break to pieces
todriven, to scatter
tohepe, together
tollen, to take a toll; to attract
toracen, to tear to pieces
tough, tough, haughty, troublesome
travaile, labor
tretys, well-fashioned, neat
triste, trust
trouthe, fidelity, promise
trowen, to believe
twinnen, to separate, to sever
tyden, to befall, to happen

uncouth, strange, curious
uncunninge, ignorant, foolish

undern, early morning
undernom, perceived
unethe, scarcely, with difficulty
unkinde, unnatural
unlust, disinclination
unmete, unfit
unstraunge, familiar
unwist, unknown
upright, upright, flat on one's back
usage, usage, custom
usen, to be accustomed
utter, outer

verray, true, genuine
vertu, quickening power
viage, voyage, trip
vileinye, shameful action, disgrace
vouche sauf, affirm, agree (avouch as safe)

waden, to wade, to enter upon
waiten, to attend upon
wanten, to be wanting, to be absent
war, prudent, cautious
warien, to curse
warnen, to reject, to refuse
wayten, to wait, to expect, to observe
welden, to rule over

welken, sky
welle, spring, source
wenden, to go
wenen, to suppose, to imagine
wenestow, do you suppose
wente, turn, path
werche, work
were, doubt
weren, to wear; to defend
werien, to make weary
wernen, to refuse
werreyen, to make war
waxen, to wax, to become
wey, way, path
weyven, to waive, to turn aside, to dodge
whylom, once, formerly
wight, (*noun*) person, living creature; (*adj*) active, nimble
wikke, wicked
wilnen, to desire
wilninge, willing
winnen, to win, to gain
wirchen, to work
wissen, to teach
wiste, knew
witen, to know
witestow, knewest thou

withseyen, to contradict, to renounce
witing, knowledge
wol, (I) will
wolt, woltow, wilt thou
wolde, would
wone, custom, wont
wonen, to dwell, to inhabit
wood, mad, insane
worthen, to be, to become
wot, (I) know, (he) knows
wost, wostow, thou knowest
wraw, angry, fretful
wre, cover
wrecche, wretch, unhappy being
wreche, vengeance
wroghte, worked
wryen, to cover, to hide; to turn aside
wrythen, to twist aside
wyke, week
wyten, to blame, to accuse

yaf, gave
yare, ready
yate, gate
yede, walked
yerne, eager, brisk
yeven, to give
ywis, certainly